The **R&A**

GOLFER'S HANDBOOK 2012

EDITOR RENTON LAIDLAW

The R&A is golf's world rules and development body and organiser of The Open Championship.
It operates with the consent of more than 130 national and international, amateur and
professional organisations, from over 120 countries and on behalf of an estimated
30 million golfers in Europe, Africa, Asia–Pacific and The Americas (outside the
USA and Mexico). The United States Golf Association (USGA) is the
game's governing body in the United States and Mexico.

MACMILLAN

The R&A Golfer's Handbook first published 1899

First published 1984 by Macmillan
This edition published 2012 by Macmillan
an imprint of Pan Macmillan, a division of Macmillan Publishers Limited
Pan Macmillan, 20 New Wharf Road, London N1 9RR
Basingstoke and Oxford
Associated companies throughout the world
www.panmacmillan.com

ISBN: 978-0-230-759763 (Cloth)

ISBN: 978-0-230-75977-0 (Paper laminate case)

Note
Whilst every care has been taken in compiling the information contained in
this book, the Publishers, Editor and Sponsors accept no responsibility for
any errors or omissions.

Correspondence
Letters on editorial matters should be addressed to:
The Editor, The R&A Golfer's Handbook, Pan Macmillan,
20 New Wharf Road, London N1 9RR

> The information on golf courses and clubs contained in
> this Handbook is available for purchase on disk as
> mailing labels. For further information please
> e-mail golfmailing@macmillan.co.uk

9 8 7 6 5 4 3 2 1

A CIP catalogue record for this book is available from the British Library

Designed and typeset by Penrose Typography, Maidstone, Kent

Colour reproduction by Aylesbury Studios Bromley Ltd, Bromley, Kent

Printed and bound in Great Britain by Mackays of Chatham plc, Chatham, Kent

Contents

Alistair Low takes over as Captain of The Royal and Ancient Golf Club

Alistair Low, who has taken over as Captain of the Royal and Ancient Golf Club for 2011–2012, is an accomplished amateur golfer and highly respected administrator.

Winner of the British Youths Championship in 1963, he reached the semi-final of the Scottish Amateur Championship in 1964, 1968 and 1970, represented Scotland in the 1965 European Amateur Team Championship and was a member of 1964 and 1965 sides for the Home Internationals.

A member of the Royal and Ancient Golf Club since 1968, he chaired the Championship Committee from 1985 to 1988 during which time he was responsible for the smooth running of three Opens at Turnberry, Muirfield and Royal Lytham and St Annes. From 1991 to 1994 he was Chairman of the Club's General Committee. Eight years later he took over as Chairman of the Scottish Golf Union – a post he held until 2008.

Educated at Dundee High School and St Andrews University, where he graduated in 1964 with a degree in Mathematics and Applied Mathematics, he qualified as an actuary in 1967 pursuing a career in benefit consulting, before retiring in 2000.

His early golf was played at Downfield Golf Club in Dundee and, after moving to Edinburgh, at Duddington Golf Club. Now a resident of Gullane in East Lothian, he is a member of both Gullane Golf Club and The Honourable Company of Edinburgh Golfers, where he is the immediate Past Captain. Playing to a handicap of 4, he is also a member of the Boat of Garten, Pine Valley and Caves Valley Golf Clubs and an honorary member of Royal Porthcawl and Olympia Fields. A keen hill-walker and skier, he is married to Shona and has three children and four grandchildren.

The game is prospering but no room for complacency

Peter Dawson on a compelling year in golf

Drama, accomplishment and challenge were among the recurring themes in a compelling year for golf. There were the demands of an economic downturn to be faced off the course while on the links there were exhilarating performances from a host of champions which enhanced the reputation of the game around the world.

The identity of the outstanding golfer in 2011 shouldn't provoke much argument. Yani Tseng enjoyed one of the truly memorable seasons, winning 12 times around the world, including two women's Majors. Her performances were phenomenal and merit comparison with Tiger Woods at the peak of his powers. In Europe, the Solheim Cup match also did much to showcase the women's game. The way the European ladies rallied at Killeen Castle to secure victory over the USA was thrilling and it was impressive to see Suzann Pettersen, one of The R&A's Working for Golf Ambassadors, take such a leading role.

If there's an obvious Queen of golf, the identity of the King is less clear now Woods is no longer such a dominant force. Perhaps the most remarkable storyline in the men's game last year was the success of Northern Ireland's golfers. What with Rory McIlroy winning the US Open and Darren Clarke hoisting the Claret Jug – both men following in the footsteps of Graeme McDowell, winner of the US Open in 2010 – it was little wonder Tourism Ireland began promoting Ulster as "The Home of Champions".

The sport has opened up for men and we are seeing far more first time winners. At the time of writing, there have been 13 consecutive different winners of the Majors, a notable figure, though by no means exceptional: the longest streak unfolded between 1983 and 1988 when there were 18 different winners. But this trend is not restricted to the Majors. When you look at the season past on the various Tours, there were fewer multiple winners. On the PGA Tour, no golfer won more than twice in 2011 and on the European Tour only Luke Donald and Thomas Björn won three events. In many ways, this breadth of talent capable of winning is good for the game, but golf also needs its stars.

Luke Donald is on his way to stellar status. He won four events last year and topped the money lists on the PGA and European Tours. He delivered superb performances on both sides of the Atlantic. To go to Florida knowing he needed to win the Disney Classic in order to secure the US money list and then reel off six consecutive birdies in a final round of 64 to clinch victory was evidence of his resolve as well as his quality. I'm sure Luke would have wished to contend more in the Majors but what he accomplished last season will give him added confidence to make his mark in 2012.

When I started working for The R&A in 1999, Luke was a member of the Great Britain and Ireland side which defeated the USA 15–9 in the Walker Cup match at Nairn. I suppose it's natural that top amateurs become top professionals and the Walker Cup has been a wonderful finishing school for so many emerging players. In 2011, GB&I again defeated their American counterparts in Scotland at Royal Aberdeen and one member of that side, Tom Lewis, went on to win the Portugal Masters in only his third event as a professional. That victory surely highlighted the strength of the modern amateur game. Since Woods won the silver medal at Lytham

Yani Tseng

Darren Clarke

Luke Donald

Tom Lewis

in 1996, Justin Rose, McIlroy, Matteo Manassero and Lewis are among the others who have finished as leading amateur at The Open. If it was once the case that golfers making the transition from the unpaid to the paid ranks had to serve a long apprenticeship, now they're ready to win from the off.

Around the world, elite amateurs – essentially full time players in a way that wasn't the case 30 years ago – are more battle hardened to become professionals than past generations. The changes to the amateur status rules that took effect from January were grounded in realism and designed to make sure no young player is financially disadvantaged. Through the work I've been doing for Olympic golf I know that elite athletes in almost every sport – boxing is a rare exception – are professionals because you have to commit full-time to reach the top. That said, amateur status is worth preserving in golf for a number of reasons. Personally, I wouldn't like to see handicap golfers put under the pressure of competing for prize money. Just imagine the arguments that would raise about handicaps! Moreover, at elite amateur level, it creates a division of competition between the codes which allows young men and women to gauge if they are good enough to make a living from the sport.

Incidentally, agreement with the United States Golf Association on a worldwide code for amateur status was just one example of the strength of the relationship between the USGA and The R&A, which has never been closer.

While it's no exaggeration to reflect that the world has experienced a degree of financial difficulty, I believe the professional game has coped resolutely with a period of recession. By and large, the various Tours have continued to stage strong schedules. The lengthy contract extension for network TV rights agreed by the PGA Tour in America will ensure stability in the years ahead. Around the globe, prize money also held up well, which in challenging times financially, was quite an achievement. The popularity, as well as the profitability of the four major championships, remained encouraging.

As far as the economic performance of The Open is concerned, our TV contracts are secure and unchanged in their intrinsic value. At Royal St George's, the number of spectators who attended the championship – in spite of weather which was an obvious deterrent – was just shy of 180,000 and only a fraction down on the total when The Open was previously at Sandwich in 2003.

Although corporate spending at The Open has been down in recent years, the patrons' programme is resilient. We had a vacancy last year but have more than made up for that in 2012 with Mastercard coming on board together with Polo Ralph Lauren. They have joined Doosan, HSBC, Mercedes Benz, Nikon and Rolex as our patrons.

We like to take The Open around the country. While some of the nine venues which currently take turns to stage the oldest major attract higher attendances, there's no prospect of economic circumstances forcing us to favour some clubs over others. For a start, many of the links where we play are private members' clubs: in practical terms, for them, hosting The Open around once every ten years is about right. The point is also worth making that a venue such as Turnberry, where attendances are not as high as elsewhere on the rota, offers other compensations. Few of our great links, for example, look more striking on TV than the Ailsa. What an advert to send around the world encouraging tourists to visit Scotland. Moreover, while transport and accommodation issues can be demanding, we've had some of our most thrilling championships over the years at Turnberry. Let's be clear, though. No one in golf can afford to be complacent about the economic situation and we must continue to strive in order to make the sport exciting and appealing.

Looking at golf purely from the perspective of participation, in what might be described as the more mature markets, it's true the numbers playing the game are under pressure. However, that aspect is more than outweighed by the growth of the game in new territories. Already, notably in eastern Europe and parts of Asia, we are starting to see the benefit of golf being reintroduced to the Olympic Games in 2016.

One of the challenges we face in social golf is pace of play and the length of time it now takes to get round. I have my own theory on this and feel perhaps that people play more fourball golf today than they did 20 years ago. Inevitably, this has an impact on the duration of the round, particularly if there are a lot of fourballs out on the course. It used to be that a game of golf took up half a day before leaving home and getting back and now it can be two-thirds, which is too much in a changing society where demands on time through work and family are so pressing. While there are various versions of shorter forms of golf emerging, a simple solution for those pressed for time is to play nine holes.

On equipment, the most discussed story in 2011 was the proliferation of long and belly putters and the debate surrounding their legitimacy which followed Keegan Bradley's success when he lifted the PGA championship. Ironically, before last season, enthusiasm for these putters appeared to be on the wane. Now a hot issue is back on the radar.

Finally, it would be remiss of me not to mention the passing of Seve Ballesteros, who was one of the brightest lights of our game and an inspiration to millions. In his early years, he brought a youthful enthusiasm to golf which widened its appeal for both golfers and non-golfers alike. His iconic celebration here at St Andrews, on the 18th green in 1984, ranks as one of the greatest and most enduring moments in sport. Seve will be sorely missed.

Walker Cup

Captained by former Cup player Nigel Edwards, the 2011 GB&I Walker Cup team were worthy winners over a star-studded USA team at Royal Aberdeen.

Solheim Cup

Alison Nicholas captained the 2011 European Solheim Cup side to victory at Killeen Castle in Ireland with Norway's Suzann Pettersen leading a dramatic last gasp fight back against the Americans.

Men's Amateur Champions 2011

Bryden Macpherson (AUS)
British Amateur Champion

Manuel Trappel (AUT)
European Amateur Champion

Kelly Kraft (USA)
United States Amateur Champion

Hideki Matsuyama (JPN)
Asian Amateur Champion

Women's Amateur Champions 2011

Lauren Taylor (ENG)
British Amateur Champion

Lisa Maguire (IRL)
European Amateur Champion

Danielle Kang (USA)
United States Amateur Champion

Consistency and style make Luke and Yani my Golfers of the Year

Renton Laidlaw assesses the superb record of them both

There are those – and not least those who have never won one – who suggest that to determine a player's greatness or otherwise by assessing his career on major titles won is hardly ideal. They may well have a point.

Yet the players themselves use victories in golf's four annual Grand Slam events as the ultimate determining factor on whether a golfer has reached that much sought after elite status or not.

The reason is obvious enough. The majors are the most difficult tournaments to win. Some golfers never do manage to get across the line, some that do stumble over it just once. There is a long list of under-achievers when it comes to winning the tournaments that really matter, the events that define a player's special qualities.

Of course, we can all think of golfers who have won a major but whose careers could otherwise have been described as nothing more than ordinary just as there are plenty of golfers – notably Colin Montgomerie and Sergio García – who have never won a major title but have a golfing record of which

© Getty Images

Luke Donald's year was a model of consistency

they can be rightly proud. I suggest, however, that no truly great golfer has failed to win multiple majors.

It is difficult to define greatness, indeed the term is much over-used. A friend who knows a thing or two about the game does not describe a player who has won less than five majors as a true great. Men such as Hogan Nicklaus, Player, Palmer, Faldo, Watson, Bobby Jones and of course Seve Ballesteros, whose death at 54 shocked us all, are just some who come into that category ... and maybe one day Luke Donald and Rory McIlroy will be members of that very élite club.

But to the matter in hand. There is no doubt who the best woman golfer was in 2011 – Yani Tseng who won two majors and ten other titles around the world. There are, however, three candidates as far as the men are concerned.

World No 1 Luke Donald, who made history by finishing top money earner on both the PGA and European Tours, the hugely talented Rory McIlroy who played superbly to become the youngest winner of the US Open since 1923 and his fellow Ulsterman Darren Clarke whose victory in The Open at Royal St George's was, for me, the most emotional major win.

Just when the 42-year-old thought he would never win a major, lo and behold fate dealt him a winning card enabling him to master the wind and rain at Royal St George's last July as effectively as he had being doing for years in similiar weather conditions at Royal Portrush. The rough conditions may have fazed some of the top stars but not Darren. It was his week and we rejoiced for him

Of course I have not forgotten the electrifying birdie, birdie, birdie, birdie finish of Charl Schwartzel which enabled the South African to add a Green Jacket to his wardrobe or the exciting victory of little-known Keegan Bradley wielding a long putter to win the US PGA Championship but few will dispute my putting the three European players on my short list.

A propos my earlier comments about majors, both McIlroy and Clarke have the advantage of a major victory on their CVs which to some might give them the edge over Donald who has not yet won a Grand Slam title. Of the two Northern Irish

Luke Donald's Year – Played 27 Wins 4 Top Tens 19

Tournament	Pos.	Rounds and total	To par	Money
Northern Trust Open	MC	68-79-0-0—147	+5	
WGC–Accenture Match Play	1			$1,400,000
The Honda Classic	T10	73-68-72-66—279	−1	$136,800
WGC–Cadillac Championship	T6	67-72-66-72—277	−11	$271,000
Masters Tournament	T4	72-68-69-69—278	−10	$330,667
Volvo World Match Play	2			€377,770
The Heritage	2*	67-65-70-70—272	−12	$615,600
Zurich Classic of New Orleans	T8	68-71-70-69—278	−10	$172,800
The Players Championship	T4	69-67-71-71—278	−10	$418,000
BMW PGA Championship	1	64-72-72-70—278	−6	€750,000
The Memorial Tournament	T7	70-69-73-68—280	−8	$174,116
US Open	T45	74-72-74-69—289	+5	$31,264
Barclays Scottish Open	1	67-67-63—197	−19	€550,249
The Open Championship	MC	71-75-0-0—146	+6	
RBC Canadian Open[1]	T17	70-73-72-67—282	+2	$78,000
WGC–Bridgestone Invitational	T2	68-69-64-66—267	−13	$665,000
US PGA Championship	T8	70-71-68-68—277	−3	$224,500
The Barclays	T18	70-66-66—202	−11	$100,800
Deutsche Bank Championship	T3	66-70-68-67—271	−13	$416,000
BMW Championship	4	75-66-67-68—276	−8	$384,000
Tour Championship	T3	66-68-70-69—273	−7	$418,666
Alfred Dunhill Links C/ship	9	69-71-63-70—273	−15	€60,961
Bankia Madrid Masters	11	68-70-70-72—280	−8	€17,233
Children's Miracle Network	1	66-71-70-64—271	−17	$846,000
Nedbank Challenge	7	70-71-70-72—283	−5	SAR24,3002
Dubai World Championship	3	70-68-66-66—272	−16	€359,832
JBWere Masters	T12	69-70-69-72—280	−4	AU$14,285

golfers McIlroy has a charisma not dissimiliar but hardly equal to the late Severiano Ballesteros yet things seem to happen when he is around – exciting shots, dramatic bursts of birdies. He has a most pleasing personality but there is a steely determination in his make-up which reminds me of Tony Jacklin in the early days.

Clarke is almost twice his age but when on song Darren, whose career has been affected by personal tragedy, can be a larger-than-life performer just as exciting to watch as Rory without the intensity of the younger man. Donald's personality is so different from the other two. Luke Donald is undemonstrative, a shy quiet achiever … so quiet his performances sometimes slip under the radar.

Yet in 2011 he proved how good a golfer he is with a stunningly consistent performance on both sides of the Atlantic marred only by disappointingly missing the cut at The Open. His record in 2011 stands comparison with most others except Tiger Woods when at his peak. In terms of world ranking points he made more than 500 on the calendar year – only the third player to achieve this after, inevitably, Woods and Vijay Singh who won nine times on the PGA Tour in 2004.

If you are looking for proof that a major victory is a certainty in the future think back to the way in which, knowing he needed to win to finish No 1 on the American money, he moved up a gear on the back nine in the last event of the US season at Disney World and made his dream come true with a victory of truly immense courage, determination and style.

Some may consider he is not a great player because he has not yet won a major – the most difficult of tournaments to win because of the pressure involved. Some may believe that his impact during the season was not as dramatic as that of McIlroy or Clarke in that it did not capture as effectively the public's imagination. Others may point out that for several years the most successful money man in Europe and America in the same season was Tiger but he was not a member and his European Tour winnings were always unofficial. Let's not quibble about that. Quite simply Luke Donald was the "Stand and Deliver" man in 2011. So he didn't win a major. So what.

As for women's golf Yani Tseng is clearly my Golfer of the Year. She won around the world with consummate ease. Elsewhere Lewine Mair reminds

Yani Tseng – looking how to improve this year on her brilliant 2011

victories worldwide. I rather liked the way one American writer began an article about Yani last year. He wrote, "She went to a friend's wedding last weekend giving everyone else on Tour a chance to win." In short she was always the one to beat.

She dominated women's golf with as consistent a performance as Donald and had two more majors to celebrate than him. She has now won five and at 22 could become the youngest golfer to win a Grand Slam if she is successful this year in the US Women's Open – the only major she hasn't yet won.

Four years ago when asked about Tseng's potential Annika Sörenstam, who has been her mentor and has had such a positive influence on her career, predicted that by 2012 she would be the best golfer in the world. Annika's no fool.

Can this competitive dynamo maintain her mix of desire and determination to emerge in time as one of the greatest of all women golfers? We can only wait and see but in my opinion her record in 2011 was as impressive in women's golf as history-making Luke Donald was on the men's scene. This is why they are both my top golfers of the year.

us how the Taiwan star successfully defended the British Open title at Carnoustie just one of her 12

Yani Tseng's Year – Played 26 Wins 12 Top Tens 19

Tournament	Pos.	Rounds and total	To par	Money
Taifong Open	1	77-73-68—218	+2	NT$2,000,000
IPS Handa Australian Ladies' Open	1	70-67-68-71—276	−16	€65,500
ANZ RACV Masters	1	67-67-63-68—264	−25	€62,500
Honda LPGA Thailand	1	66-71-70-66—273	−15	$217,500
HSBC Women's Champions	3	70-72-69-67—278	−13	$96,370
RR Donnelley LPGA Founders Cup	29T	73-73-69—215	+1	$7,400
Kia Classic	5T	71-73-72-67—283	−9	$64,953
Kraft Nabisco Championship	2	70-68-66-74—278	−10	$184,255
Avnet LPGA Classic	MC	77-72-0-0—149	+5	
Sybase Match Play Championship	T5			$37,500
ShopRite LPGA Classic	7	73-68-65—206	−7	$42,747
LPGA State Farm Classic	1	67-66-66-68—267	−21	$255,000
Wegmans LPGA Championship	1	66-70-67-66—269	−19	$375,000
US Women's Open	15T	73-73-71-73—290	−2	$48,658
Evian Masters	12T	69-73-68-69—279	−9	$56,125
Ricoh Women's British Open	1	71-66-66-69—272	−16	$392,133
Safeway Classic	13T	72-69-73—214	+1	$21,694
CN Canadian Women's Open	29T	71-71-69-73—284	−4	$16,716
Walmart NW Arkansas C/ship	1	66-67-68—201	−12	$300,000
Navistar LPGA Classic	25T	68-73-75-69—285	−3	$10,787
LPGA Hana Bank Championship	1	65-70-67—202	−14	$270,000
Suzhou Taihu Ladies Open	1	68-66-60—200	−16	$62,550
Sime Darby LPGA Malaysia	2	69-67-69-65—270	−14	$176,791
Sunrise LPGA Taiwan Championship	1	68-71-67-66—272	−16	$300,000
Lorena Ochoa Invitational	19T	76-69-74-72—291	+3	$13,027
CME Group Titleholders	6T	70-76-66-74—286	−2	$35,057
Swinging Skirts TLPGAS Invitational	1	72-70-68—210	−6	

The magical irresistibility of a true golfing genius

Hugh McIlvanney writes affectionately about Seve

Severiano Ballesteros: the name itself was like a quiet roll of drums, the announcement of a dramatic presence. It suited the bearer so perfectly that for me there was a trace of regret when just about everybody in sport and many in the wider world beyond came to know him simply as Seve. The abbreviation was apparently adopted at the instigation of his first business manager, Ed Barner, and it was readily embraced by a public that swiftly developed an affectionate intimacy with his greatness. My mourning of a syllable or two and their poetic ring was no doubt rather foolish and it certainly wouldn't have been echoed by my newspaper brethren who wrote the headlines Ballesteros repeatedly created. In any case, being called Federico Bloggs couldn't have prevented him from ranking as one of the outstanding wonders in the sporting experience of all who witnessed him in action.

He was the embodiment of the mysterious power of games-playing at its highest levels to move to the marrow those who are merely watching. The emotional commitment with which he prosecuted his genius was irresistibly contagious. Passion in the context of an intensified pastime has never seemed more natural than when he was on a golf course. He tended to encounter so many tests, tribulations and vicissitudes in a round – many of them the result of refusing to let wayward shots temper the boldness of his self-belief – that there was sometimes the feeling he should have had John Bunyan on the bag.

But the miracles of recovery and surges to triumph he produced could not have been quite as compelling as they were if he hadn't looked so wonderful in the process. He was ridiculously handsome and the limitless expressiveness of his dark features combined with the prowling grace of his movements to make him a godsend for the camera. In his prime, there was a spontaneous and magnetic theatricality about everything he did as a competitor, whether he was swinging with violent abandon on the tee or exhibiting the delicacy of a miniaturist around the greens. Even when he was at work in the immediate company of other great golfers, averting the eyes from him took a conscious effort.

By the mid-1970s, professional golf had been given plenty of indications that a prodigy from the fishing village of Pedrena on the Bay of Biscay coast of northern Spain might be capable of becoming a global figure in the game. And none of us in this country harboured any doubts about the scale of potential attached to the 19-year-old Ballesteros after he finished tied with Jack Nicklaus for second place behind Johnny Miller in the Open Championship of 1976. He was already a serial winner of important tournaments, with an especially notable success on the US Tour in 1978, when he made his breakthrough in the majors at 22 in the 1979 Open at a bitingly cold and blustery Royal Lytham.

We felt then that his huge hands, whose size and strength were priceless allies of his imaginative scope as a shot-maker, would be frequently lifting the most coveted trophies of his sport in the years ahead. And it can hardly be said that the omens were let down. Two further victories in the Open (in 1984 at St Andrews and 1988 back at Lytham)

Severiano Ballesteros … loved by millions, mourned by all after his death at 54

The friendship between Severiano Ballesteros and José Maria Olazábal went much deeper than golf and the Ryder Cup

and Masters triumphs at Augusta in 1980 and 1983, along with an unrivalled contribution to Europe's charge to prolonged ascendancy in the Ryder Cup, amount to a catalogue of achievements more than remarkable enough to ensconce him securely in golf's pantheon. Yet there is a lingering conviction that gifts as extraordinary as his should have planted an even more glittering entry in the record books. Perhaps, however, to think in such a way is to miss the point about a career bound to reverberate endlessly through golf history not as a consequence of its statistical impact but because of the sense of a unique player's capacity for drama and beauty and defiance of probability that has been left in what might be called the game's folk memory.

Some people considered it amazing that he accomplished as much as he did, given the severity of the problems, technical and physical, that were always waiting to ambush the divine possibilities of his play. Whatever can be validly claimed for this ultimate "feel" player concerning the premeditation of improbable trajectories and calculated decisions about favourable landing places in the rough (a dominant theme at Lytham in 1979), it should surely be admitted that the unreliability of his driving was a permanently recurring curse. Even an alchemist of Seve's powers could not constantly depend on transmuting the base metal of erratic tee shots into the gold of birdies and eagles.

His physical handicap was, of course, the back trouble that was the ineradicable legacy of an injury suffered while boxing as a 14-year-old. So it was a small fight that put the most combative of golfers into the big fight against an affliction whose assaults fluctuated in their seriousness over the years but inevitably exerted a cumulatively debilitating effect. It was cruelly influential in curtailing his glory years. He was only 31 when he won the last of his five majors, and by the time he recorded his final tournament victory seven years later (bringing his aggregate to an astonishing 87) he was far into a pain-racked downward spiral.

Obviously, irreversible decline tends to be an agony for all great sportsmen but few can have had less aptitude for mellowing acceptance than Seve. Direct confrontation – with the challenges of a golf course, with the governing bodies of the game, with opponents (especially if they were American), indeed with anybody or anything responsible for a real or imagined slight to his sense of himself – was a core element of his behaviour. Resigned succumbing to the savage deterioration of his abilities was beyond him and that ensured the early years of the 21st century saw his career enveloped in a sad twilight, while his private life was devastated by divorce from Carmen, the mother of his three children, a break-up for which hardly anyone believed Carmen was to blame. What is perhaps most striking about those years is that they never diminished the immense warmth felt towards Seve, both by millions who had known him only at a distance and by many who had come through the more exacting experience of personal dealings with him.

In a fine biography published in 2006, Robert Green drew on considerable familiarity with his subject when he wrote: "He is a complex character – charming and manipulative, gregarious and withdrawn, open and suspicious, generous and mean – depending on how the mood takes him." But there is in Green, as in a multitude of us, a vast reservoir of regard for Seve, an emotional connection that has nothing to do with the allegiances generated by the celebrity culture. I think we were, from first exposure to the Spanish genius, aware we were in the presence of a strange, flawed but undeniably magical human being.

There was certainly nothing contrived about the welling up of sorrow in 2008 when the world learned he had undergone surgery for a brain tumour, or the grief that spread with the news that, at 54, he had lost his characteristically spirited battle against the cancer in May of 2011. My feelings then reminded me of what it was, above all, that made Severiano Ballesteros such a thrilling figure on the golf course. It was the raw humanity he brought to his endeavours. No sportsman other than Muhammad Ali ever moved me more.

So many wonderful memories of majestic days on his beloved links

Mike Aitken celebrates Seve Ballesteros at The Open

When Roberto de Vicenzo, the champion at Hoylake in 1967, counselled Severiano Ballesteros on how he might approach The Open, on the eve of the championship at Royal Lytham in 1979, the Argentine could hardly have guessed the Spaniard would channel his advice into a motto for glory. "You have the hands," observed the older man, "now play with your heart."

It was thanks to a cocktail of pure imagination and raw courage Seve was able make the kind of impact in The Open which surpassed the mere accumulation of distinction – his name was inscribed on the Claret Jug three times – and transformed his performances on the British linksland into the stuff of legend. Handsome, fearless and dashing, he became European golf's first matinee idol, a man embraced by the galleries who followed his every move at the oldest major for over 30 years.

Between his first appearance at Carnoustie in 1975 and his farewell in 2006 at Royal Liverpool, there were perhaps four Opens which stood out from the rest. In 1976 at Royal Birkdale when he

caught the attention of the global game when finishing runner up to Johnny Miller, in 1979 and 1988 when he won at Lytham and most memorably when he was hailed as "champion golfer of the year" at St Andrews in 1984.

Seve missed the cut on his debut by ten shots in Angus, blaming a foot injury, and was more determined than ever 12 months later to make an impact at Birkdale. Just 19 years of age, not only did Ballesteros mount a challenge for the title but he also made a connection with the British public which would endure for a lifetime. The spectators at The Open instinctively recognised the appeal of a self-made prodigy from Pedrena, the farmer's son who learned to play the game on the beach with a battered iron.

The week before Birkdale, the teenager preparing to take on the world had been bailing hay at home. Now, with a policeman by the name of Dick Draper carrying his clubs, he was duelling with Americans of the calibre of Miller and Jack Nicklaus. The weather in Southport was hot, the fair-

R&A secretary Keith Mackenzie trying to get a tearful Seve to record his score in 1979 after he was engulfed by his jubiliant brothers at Royal Lytham and St Annes

© Getty Images

ways were baked and Ballesteros opened with a brace of 69s to lead by two strokes at the halfway mark. On the third day, conditions were wet and windy and both Ballesteros and Miller carded 73s. As the final round began, Seve was three strokes in front after the first hole. But double bogeys at the second and fourth and a triple at the 11th surrendered the advantage to the American. Miller led by eight shots after 13 holes and not even a sensational finish from Seve – he was five under par for the closing four holes – could bridge the gap. Nevertheless, a new star had flared across The Open sky.

Three years later at Lytham, Ballesteros became the first Continental golfer to win The Open since Arnaud Massy when he overcame erratic driving with cavalier recovery shots. Dave Musgrove was on the bag for the so-called "car park champion" that week and recalled how, for all his wayward tendencies, the Spaniard knew exactly where he could and couldn't stray off line. "He found loopholes in the rough, if you like," explained the caddie. "There was no fluke to Seve's playing out of the rough in 1979. Seve was not as lucky as people think. It was all well planned."

After opening with 73, Ballesteros regarded his second round of 65 "as a turning point in the tournament and very likely in my life as well." Determined to pursue a strategy which, in the 21st century would become more or less standard practice among the top pros, Ballesteros hit his drives long and hard and then took his chances from the rough. Famously, he drove into a car park to the right of the 16th fairway in the final round. After a free drop, he turned calamity into triumph by finding the green and holing a 30 foot putt. His first major championship was secured through boldness off the tee and exquisite wedge play around the greens. Seve found 15 greenside bunkers that week but saved par no fewer than 14 times.

At the Old Course in 1984, Seve faced perhaps the stiffest test of his Open career when he had to overcome the challenge posed by Tom Watson, arguably the greatest links golfer of the modern era. Watson was seeking his third consecutive Open title that summer and, after three rounds, led the championship on 11 under par. Seve was two strokes behind until birdies at the fifth and eighth holes in the final round propelled him into the lead. The outcome of the championship, however, was settled on the Road Hole.

Having made three bogeys on the 17th in previous rounds, Ballesteros believed par here would earn him victory. He opted to drive left before rifling a 6 iron 200 yards from the rough onto the green. From 50 feet, he made a two putt par. Watson, meanwhile, struck a glorious drive, only to take too much club, a 2 iron, for his second. He carded 5 as Seve was adding another birdie on the 18th. Never a man to hide his feelings, the Spaniard's emotive celebration in St Andrews became an iconic moment in Open history. "It was the happiest single shot of my life," he said of that 12 foot putt.

Seve's second victory at Lytham in 1988 spun a different story from his triumph in Lancashire nine years earlier. Now a seasoned champion, with two Opens and two Masters to his name, he dominated the tournament and in the final round eclipsed both of his closest challengers, Nick Faldo and Nick Price. Ballesteros never played a finer round of golf in The Open than the 65 which took his haul of major titles to five.

For all his natural talent, Seve always honed his gifts through diligent practice. In his pomp, he made the game look easy on the links because he worked so hard. "Funny game is golf," he once remarked after a pro-am. "The professionals practice all the time and the amateurs never practice. Me, I am like a pianist. Even when I'm not playing in a tournament, I practice for six or seven hours a day."

It was because of this rare combination of brilliance and graft that Seve was able to conduct a four movement symphony as romantic as any in the old championship's history. And the sweep of that soaring Spanish flamenco will never be forgotten by anyone fortunate enough to watch Ballesteros strike a chord at The Open.

Seve's career highlights

In a long and successful career, Seve realised many notable achievements.

Major championships: The Open (1979, 1984, 1988) and The Masters (1980, 1983).

European Tour: Fifty victories.   US PGA Tour: Nine victories.

Ryder Cup: 1979, 1983, 1985, 1987, 1989, 1991, 1993 and 1995. Seve captained the 1997 European team who beat the USA 14½ to 13½.

Winner – European Tour Order of Merit: 1976, 1977, 1978, 1986, 1988, 1991.

European Tour Player of the Year: 1986, 1988, 1991.

Seve was inducted into the World Golf Hall of Fame in 1999.

Stylish young champions share top honours with veteran star

Derek Lawrenson sums up the 2011 majors

From an historic finish at the Masters to a runaway success at the United States Open, this was a year in the majors that saw an explosion of youthful promise.

By the time we got to the PGA another young man was showing the indomitability of a Gary Player to make it four of the last five majors won by players aged 26 or less. No, it's not you; major championship winners really are getting younger, and they're blowing a hole in the popular theory that golfers reach their prime in their thirties.

Mind you, there are always exceptions to every rule, and the one winner in this sequence well past the first flush of enthusiasm brought a smile to the faces of golfers wherever the game is played. First he saw one of his proté gé s win the US Open in Rory McIlroy and then, barely a month later, 42 year old Darren Clarke stepped forward to provoke a worldwide feeling of joy by claiming The Open Championship itself.

If there's one thing better than watching a young man fulfil his potential it might be seeing a grizzled veteran who always looked destined to win an Open gaining his due. Peter Dawson, chief executive of The R&A, summed up Clarke's victory perfectly the morning after he had announced him the champion golfer of the year. "I don't think he was on anyone's list to win but as it became an increasing possibility he became the champion we really wanted to have, because of his stature in the game and all he represents," he said.

The organisers of the other three majors will be happy with their stylish winners as well. South African Charl Schwartzel, Ulsterman McIlroy and American Keegan Bradley represent some of the finest young talent to be found on three continents and all three won their titles in a manner which brooked no argument. What happened to twenty-somethings needing to be tested a few times in the firmament of Sunday afternoons at the majors before realising their dream?

That went out of the window owing to the fearless nature of today's competitors. All start out these days armed with much more knowledge than their predecessors. Managers, coaches, sports psychologists, experienced caddies – virtually every player has such a team around him, preparing him for the task ahead.

The four majors in 2011 threw up such an exotic variety of storylines they covered virtually the entire range of human emotion. Only one thing was missing, and that was the glorious sight of Tiger Woods in his pomp.

There was the merest hint of it at Augusta, a fabulous two-hour rewinding to past majors when the game witnessed a combination of talent and will of the rarest potency. Over the front nine at the Masters on Sunday, Woods was young once more, holing putts and pulling off shots that sent cheers

Fellow Ulstermen Rory McIlroy and Darren Clarke, nearly twice Rory's age, played outstanding golf to land the US Open and The Open last summer

echoing through the Georgia pines and telling his fellow competitors their Green Jacket ambitions were in grave danger.

Then came nine holes where all the scars and mental damage inflicted over a barren 18 month period marked by scandal and controversy came back to haunt him. At the 17th came an all too painful reminder of his mortality. Trying to play a difficult shot under a tree, he aggravated two long-standing injuries and wouldn't be a factor in the majors again, missing the next two and being painfully out of sorts in the other.

When Augusta's other hopefuls found they could breathe again that Sunday, what we were left with was a golfing version of a massed sprint finish. Who would break out of the peloton?

Step forward Schwartzel. He might never have been in contention to win a major to that point but he would emphatically prove he was ready, becoming the first Masters champion ever to finish with four birdies in a row.

By his side on the plane to the next tournament was McIlroy who, at just 21, had dominated the tournament from the first to the 63rd hole. In the days and weeks that followed he was bombarded with advice over his fateful last nine holes, all of which ignored one vital thing: no-one learns more from his mistakes than McIlroy.

So it was, in the shadow of the White House and at the course of choice for senators and congressmen, McIlroy was sworn in as a major champion, owning the US Open from first shot to last to win by the Woods-like margin of eight strokes. With a vivid illustration of the prevailing theme of the year in the majors, he had become the youngest champion since Bobby Jones in 1923, and the youngest European major winner since Young Tom Morris collected his fourth Open title at the age of 21 in 1872.

Clarke had shown throughout his career that whenever he was on his game he could beat anybody. He had won two world championship events leaving Woods trailing in his wake on both occasions. But never at an Open had he brought his gifts to bear. How this must have hurt, given he was arguably the finest links golfer of his generation. How he made it tell at Royal St George's.

Was there a better display of ball striking in 2011 than the one Clarke delivered during his Saturday masterclass? If there was, I missed it. Twenty-four hours later it was all about keeping his nerve, and Clarke did that wonderfully as well. In the massive stands and around the globe they applauded this man who has seen more than his fair share of tragedy and come through the other side. His victory was nothing less than a testament to the endurance of the human spirit.

By now the Americans were getting anxious. Question of the year came in Atlanta on the eve of the PGA, when Lee Westwood was asked, by one plaintive US voice: "Do you think, in our lifetime, we will ever see an American win a major again?"

Once more the man who broke the unprecedented sequence of six majors without an American victory was not on anyone's list. Again he showed the stuff of a major champion down the stretch. Not many men run up a triple bogey six four holes from home and bounce back to win, but that was the achievement of 25 year old Bradley, the nephew of Pat Bradley, one of the finest lady golfers of all time.

And so we finished as we started, in Georgia with the next generation becoming the present generation and laying down a statement. In 2012, we await to see if the thirty-somethings can rise to the challenge.

Maybe even Darren Clarke could not quite believe that in the rain and wind at Royal St George's he had finally got his hands on the most coveted trophy in golf – the Claret Jug

How two major wins brought pride and joy back to Ulster

Bill Elliott on good golfers and good men

It is not that Darren Clarke, Graeme McDowell and Rory McIlroy grew up knowing each other, it is just that had they been born around the same time instead of spanning three decades, they could have done.

Because whatever else Northern Ireland is – and here one could insert a great many adjectives, not all of which would be entirely desirable – it is a small country. Indeed it is so small that it is debateable that it is even a country.

The BBC, for example, calls Northern Ireland a province while the European Union prefers region. Some call it Ulster but this is incorrect because Ulster is a province and consists of nine Irish counties, only six of which are within the Northern Irish border and that, in the strictest sense, is not really a border any longer. No wonder so many of us are confused.

I just call it home or, at least, the place where I was born and grew up (nearly anyway, I left when I was twelve for England, wisely taking my parents with me). The years spent in Belfast, however, have left their mark and so I stumble through life secure in the knowledge that nothing is entirely predictable and that nothing is so bad that it cannot be cured for a while by a long drink and an even longer chat with someone who mostly holds the opposite point of view but who also offers some wit while arguing the case.

What, however, is beyond sensible debate is that over the last two years this wee country, this province or region, this hectic collection of six counties and fewer than 1.7 million people has not so much punched above its weight at the playing of the grand, old game but has kicked and scratched and pummelled and sprinted and flown as well.

For McDowell, McIlroy and Clarke to secure victories in the 2010 United States Open, the 2011 United States Open and the 2011 Open Championship beggars many things, the principal one of which is sane belief. What is also true is that these achievements have brought pride and some significant joy back to a land that has not been the happiest place on the planet over the last several decades.

The old problems may still bubble and hiss beneath and cause worry to many but the really bad times are over and, at least for the present, North-ern Ireland is known more for its production of champion golfers than it is for any of the other stuff.

How and why could this happen? It is tempting to believe that something other than potatoes and mutton, carrots and onions, has been parlayed into Irish stew or that somewhere there has been a secret breeding programme designed to produce outstanding golfers but, clearly, there is more to it than this. Or maybe less.

What is certain is that the Golf Union of Ireland offers an efficient template when it comes to embracing and encouraging and improving young golfers. Not yet a breeding programme but impressive enough in its industry and ambition. As with rugby, golf in Ireland is just that, which is to say the sport is run by an organisation representing every inch of the island.

Kevin Stevens is the man who runs the Ulster branch and as general secretary he is currently quite rightly satisfied with how things appear to be going. There are 122 clubs in Ulster of which 90 are in Northern Ireland. There are 42,000 members. It's where the three champions started and where, to an extent, they remain.

What struck me after a long and pleasant conversation with Mr Stevens is that the most crucial thing the GUI does with its young golfers is to throw them as soon as is reasonable into competitive play. "Our coaching is done through the winter, summer

Darren Clarke benfitted from a tough winter regime to get back to full fitness ... and won The Open

© Getty Images

Graeme McDowell started it all off with his victory in the US Open at Pebble Beach

is for playing the game and we have Under-12, Under-14, Under-16 and Elite Boys teams all playing competitive golf. Having Graeme, Rory and Darren achieve what they have naturally helps us. The boys see what can be done and they want to try to do it themselves. The enthusiasm and passion is there."

It is not just about technical improvement or competitive hardening, the GUI also offers a strength and conditioning programme designed by the experts at the University of Ulster. This is no 'how much can you press' regime but a programme designed to add suppleness as well as strength. Ulster boys have an often instinctive desire to play rugby as well as golf and this causes headaches. "The two games don't mix because the physical requirements are so different," he said. "Eventually a boy who is talented at rugby and golf has to make a choice."

This was the choice Clarke made, of course, and though he retains the look of a man who could still scrum down quite effectively it is clear he made the correct turn when he decided to focus on golf. Now 43, his victory in The Open is perhaps the most surprising of the three successes.

It is indeed tempting to suggest that he won at Royal St George's more because he had all but given up on the likelihood of such a thing than because he went into the week more determined than ever. What is true is that a winter spent beating balls into the gales available at his new home in Portrush prepared him perfectly for the squally, bleak weather that attacked him and everyone else on the Kent coast last summer.

Clarke beat those balls not because he wanted to win the championship but because he wanted to claw back some of the form that mostly deserted him following the death of his wife Heather in 2006. His tough winter regime was borne out of a stubborn determination to regain some lost ground. In the event he conquered one of the highest peaks

and everyone, whether Northern Irish or not, was delighted to see his ascent.

McDowell has the abiding pleasure of starting it all off in June last year. His own refusal to buckle under some heavy conditions at the almost incomparable Pebble Beach on America's West Coast was a heady, everlasting achievement. His form this year may have been patchy as he suffered an understandable reaction to all that had gone before but, at 32, there is time hopefully for much more from this intelligent man.

Meanwhile, what is there to say about 22 years old McIlroy's own US Open win, a victory achieved with such distant panache that it mocked his capitulation just two months earlier at Augusta. McIlroy won because occasionally he has the key to a secret place inhabited by only the very finest performers and he has this key partly because he possesses an extraordinary talent but mostly because he believes deeply that he does indeed have this extraordinary talent. From Rory, surely, there are only good times ahead.

How dear Fred Daly, Northern Ireland's only other major champion at the 1947 Open, would have loved these times. Jack Magowan would, if anything, have loved them even more. Jack wrote about golf for the *Belfast Telegraph* for fifty years until his death in 2009. He was a perceptive journalist and a man rarely stuck for a sensible answer.

I suspect his reply to how on earth Northern Ireland produced three major champions in so few months would be direct and to the point and along the lines of 'they are very, very good players and, more importantly, they are very, very good men. It was their time'.

Until someone comes up with a better one, this thought will have to do. You may as well ask how the old place came up with men like Van Morrison, George Best, CS Lewis or Louis MacNeice. I'm just glad it did.

© Phil Sheldon Golf Picture Library

Rory McIlroy thrilled everyone with his victory in the US Open at Congressional – a performance which show-cased all his many golfing talents

Luke Donald has a stellar year but what he wants are majors

John Huggan on a golfer whose stage really is the world

In these ever-bigger, stronger, faster times, the best golfer in the world isn't supposed to look like the five-foot nine-inch, 160-pound Luke Donald. Or play like him. In this "hit it as hard as you can and go find it" era of what is euphemistically known as "bomb and gouge," a man whose average drive expires more than 30-yards behind the longest-hitters should have little or no chance of success at the very highest level.

But, happily for those who increasingly despair that the professional game is nowadays more science than art, it can be done. During 2011, in fact, no one played more good golf than Donald, an unassuming 34 year old from Hemel Hempstead, the first man ever to top the official money lists on both sides of the Atlantic in the same year. The 2001 Art Theory and Practice graduate of North-western University near Chicago displayed a con-sistency of performance seen only rarely on either the PGA or European tours. For all his undoubted steadiness, however, it will be for a spectacular 18-hole performance that Donald's season will be most vividly recalled.

Knowing he almost certainly had to finish first in the last PGA Tour event of the season at Disney World if he was to pip Webb Simpson and be lead-ing money-winner, "mister consistency" went out and did just that, courtesy of a closing round of 64 that contained ten birdies, including six in succes-sion from the turn. Yes, ten and yes, six in a row.

Given the importance of the occasion, it was a prolonged burst of brilliance that represented golf and nerve of the very highest order, one that set off a flurry of awestruck compliments.

"That was pretty close to flawless," said Don-ald's playing partner, Scott Gutschewski, neatly summing up the prevailing mood. "It was fun to watch." The verdict of Simpson who was pipped at the post for the Arnold Palmer Trophy was: "Luke played some great golf this week and he did it at the end, when it really counts."

Even the man himself was impressed. "That was a dream (PGA Tour) year," was Donald's immediate reaction. "I think I answered a lot of critics' ques-tions."

Donald has proved you do not need to be a long hitter to get to the top

© Phil Sheldon Golf Picture Library

There was the disappointment, of course, that after finishing a strong fourth in the Masters Donald failed to contend in any of the other three majors championships with his failure to qualify for the weekend at The Open Championship the most obvious if unexpected fall from grace. Perhaps the only disappointment was that, after finishing a strong fourth in the Masters, Donald failed to con-tend in any of the other three major champi-onships, with his failure to qualify for the weekend at the Open Championship the most obvious fall from grace.

"It's so important to have periods where you can relax and get away from the game for a bit," he says. "It's sometimes difficult to know exactly what to do, but my week-to-week results during 2011 were so good I feel like I came pretty close. Still, there were times when I was dragging a bit and this

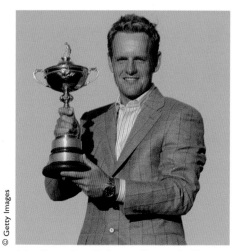

Luke will never give up his European Tour membership because he enjoys playing in the Ryder Cup so much

© Getty Images

year I'm going to be even more careful in the lead-up to the majors. I did feel a bit tired at the US Open last year.

"Majors have always been my ultimate goal. So it's vital to be fresh and ready to play your best when you arrive at all four. Looking at the way I performed during 2011, I'm hopeful that I'm not going to have to 'peak' for the majors. I like to think my game will be good enough to at least compete, no matter what. And coming up with the right schedule is part of that."

Donald is nothing if not methodical, however. As you'd expect from such a studious on-course performer, he is one who learns from the mistakes he tends not to make more than once. Four years ago, for example, he messed with his beautifully rhythmic swing in a misguided attempt to close that 30+yard gap between himself and the game's muscle-bound siege-gunners.

"I did go through a period where I was trying to hit the ball farther in an effort to keep up with the big-hitters," he admits. "That was a mistake and got my swing into a bad place. And it has taken me three or four years to get back to where I'm more comfortable. But most of my success has always come though having a great short game rather than excelling from tee-to-green.

"Which is not to say that I haven't worked hard to improve both the accuracy of my drives and my 'greens in regulation.' Neither was very good maybe three years ago. But they both got better in 2011. I still have a bit to go though and that will be one key to my winning a major or majors. I'll

have to get the ball in the fairway a bit more especially.

"The short game is the thing at majors though. Getting up-and-down is a little bit tougher because the greens tend to be a little more severe. Which, of course, only makes hitting more fairways and greens even more vital, even though I feel like my pitching, chipping and bunker play are pretty sharp."

Donald's expertise from sand is worthy of special mention. Perhaps only South Africa's Ernie Els is his peer when it comes to technique and touch from bunkers.

"I've always thought of myself as a good bunker player," concedes Donald. "But when I got out on tour I discovered I was no better than average. So I've had to work hard in that department and it has improved. There are actually aspects of my bunker play I'd like to adopt in my full swing. But yes, I do feel like I am one of the best in the world from sand."

Another admirable aspect of the Donald character is his willingness to embrace the concept of 'world player.' A member of both the PGA and European Tours, he has long accepted that travel can help broaden not only the mind but a golf game too.

"That I need to be a member of the European Tour to be eligible for the Ryder Cup means I will never resign," he says. "It's an easy decision. I've always said that a global schedule makes you a better player. You have to deal with so many things – the travel, the jetlag, different courses – it makes you stronger and tougher. So I see myself playing both tours for the foreseeable future."

Speaking of the Ryder Cup, further evidence of Donald's prowess can be gleaned from his stellar (eight wins, two losses, one half) record in the biennial contest between Europe and the United States. Throw in the fact that he is the reigning World Match Play champion and his ability in head-to-head contests is even more obvious.

"I'm very proud of my Ryder Cup record," he says with some justification. "That the team wins is most important, but I take pride in my own winning percentage too."

Most ominously for those whose aim is the number one spot on the rankings is Donald's dissatisfaction with the status quo.

"Continuing to improve is always the goal," he says. "Knowing that there are no limits to what I can achieve is most important. If I do that, I can win more tournaments and, hopefully, some majors. Major winners get more headlines, more recognition. And I want some of that."

Five major titles for Taiwan's Yani and surely more to come

Lewine Mair on the Asian star who is re-writing the record books

Rory McIlroy was rightly feted when he won the US Open last June at the age of 22. Yet only a month or so later, Yani Tseng, who is only a couple of months older than the Irishman, was bagging what was the fifth major of her career, the Ricoh Women's British Open at Carnoustie.

It was the Taiwanese golfer's second major of the 2011 season while, by the end of the year, she had amassed seven titles on the American LPGA Tour alone and five more around the world.

Tseng's season started as she meant it to continue. Playing in the Taifong Ladies' Open in her homeland, she won by four shots and promptly handed over her NT 2 million cheque to her mother who had fulfilled a long-time wish in caddying for her daughter over a last 18 holes. Mrs Tseng had not put a foot wrong, having adhered to her daughter's cheerful instruction that she should desist from offering advice of any kind.

In the following fortnight, Tseng won twice in Australia before making it four in a row at the Handa LPGA Open in Thailand.

It was at this point that there were suggestions along the lines that her rush of wins could not go down as an official four-in-a-row streak in that only one among the four tournaments was an LPGA event.

Juli Inkster, who has always had what it takes to see the bigger picture, was quick to put things to rights. This regular member of the US Solheim Cup side said, unequivocally, "A win is a win ... I don't know about the strength of the field in Taiwain but there were good fields for both of the Australian events and again in Thailand. Yani has had to play great to win what she has won so far ..."

Michelle Wie, who played with Tseng in the last round in Thailand, was quick to agree. "Yani played like a rock star out there. She made every putt and zero mistakes."

By the time Tseng came over to Carnoustie for the Ricoh Women's British Open, she had further separated herself from the rest by capturing the LPGA championship, her fourth major, by an astonishing ten-shot margin.

This battling little competitor was ready for the challenge of Carnoustie, the toughest links on the

men's Open Championship rota, but, sadly for those who would have enjoyed seeing the world's greatest woman golfer of the moment being stretched to the full, the course was less demanding that it might have been. The notorious 18th, for example, had been transformed into the mildest of par-fours.

Yet still the links were able to identify the best player.

Tseng was two behind Caroline Masson going into the last round. She did not take long to overtake the relatively inexperienced German but, when she dropped a shot at each of the 12th and 13th, she was uncomfortably aware that Brittany Lang and Scotland's Catriona Matthew were only a couple of shots to her rear.

It was at the 467 yards, par five 14th, The Spectacles, that Tseng produced the kind of mighty shot which has become her trademark. Oliver Fisher, winner of the 2011 Czech Open and a golfer who used to play alongside Tseng in the Faldo Series,

Yani Tseng has already won five majors, including the Ricoh Women's British Open at Carnoustie in 2011

© Getty Images

will tell you how he and the rest of the boys tended to bracket her with them in terms of length and strength. "It's amazing the amount of zip Yani gets through the ball," he said.

That zip was there as she caught that 14th green in two to pave the way for the birdie which allowed for a bit more breathing space.

Tseng arrived on the 18th tee with a three shot lead – something which, for anyone who knows his or her golfing history, was not the best news in the world. Jean Van de Velde had enjoyed precisely that advantage when he played the hole in the 1999 Open before losing out to Paul Lawrie in the play-off.

As Tseng was settling to her tee shot, a fleeting picture crossed her mind of Van de Velde standing, shoeless and sockless, in the Barry Burn en route to his seven. But a small voice inside wasted no time in telling her that she was being ridiculous and, without any further ado, she unleashed a great drive followed by a nine-iron which finished three feet from the hole.

Tseng revelled in the fact she had won at Carnoustie. "So many great players have made history on this course and I feel honoured to be among them," she said. Ben Hogan, Gary Player and Tom Watson were just three of the game's giants who would have been on her list.

The daughter of a scratch handicap man in Taiwan, Tseng played much her junior golf in Korea, the nearest country to offer good competition for Under 18s. While there, she could not but be struck by the influence Se Ri Pak had on Korea's golfing youth and she determined that she would go all out to have the same effect on the juniors in her homeland.

For now, Tseng is based in the States, where the Yani Tseng tale which strikes a chord with all her fans concerns how, in 2009, she moved into Annika Sörenstam's old house and inherited the Swede's old trophy cabinet.

No-one, as it turns out, could have made a better fist of re-stacking its shelves.

Colourful Musselburgh Fishwives on the ball 200 years ago

The 200th anniversary celebrations of the world's first women's golf competition, the Fishwives Tournament, took place last year over the same Musselburgh links which hosted the original event on New Year's Day, 1811. Descendants of the original fishwives, colourfully attired in full fishwives regalia, mingled with the golfers on a day when the victor was Pamela Williamson, a former Scottish Senior champion.

Williamson was rejoicing in being involved in such a historic occasion even before she received a handsome silver salver along with a fishwife doll. The latter's costume, incidentally, had been lovingly dressed – for the most part in original materials – by 90-year-old Jean Wilkie who had been a fishwife herself for a couple of years.

"I love golf's history and I love golfing memorabilia," said Williamson at the prize-giving ceremony. "I felt honoured just to play – and positively overcome to win."

The original fishwives were as tough as they come. They would carry their husbands down to their boats to save them getting their feet wet prematurely. Then, when their menfolk returned, they would load the fish in their baskets – a creel and a skull – and carry them into the streets of Edinburgh. The filled baskets would weigh 100 odd pounds or, to put it another way, three times as much as a Tiger Woods' golf bag. "Sometimes," said one of Jean Wilkie's peers, "Your legs went wobbly as you were helped on with the baskets but you straightened up ..."

Not least because of their crisp and colourful uniforms and their sheer professionalism, the women were held in high regard wherever they went. People would help them on and off the buses and trams while, when it came to Christmas, they would often return to Musselburgh with their baskets as heavily laden as they had been on the outward journey. Every customer would have a present at the ready and it is probably not too fanciful to suggest that there was the odd feathery ball in the mix.

Unfortunately, there is absolutely no indication of how the fishwives scored in their tournament of 1811. All that remains is a list of the prizes which included a replica of a creel and a couple of Barcelona handkerchiefs.

That there is no mention of any further events could be down to the fact that women were discouraged from playing full-scale golf for much of the 1800s on the grounds that it was a less-than-ladylike pursuit.

In which connection, you can only assume that the fishwives had contributed to this state of affairs by becoming too long and strong for their own good ... it would not have needed too many of them to out-hit the men of Musselburgh before the men were suggesting, with feigned concern, that it would be better for their reputations were they to stick to the putting green.

Walker Cup "underdogs" are the stars at Royal Aberdeen

Alistair Tait on an historic win against the Americans

Any national golf union looking to set up a successful national team could do worse than look to Great Britain & Ireland's victory in the 43rd Walker Cup at Royal Aberdeen. Nigel Edwards' ten men delivered the points to win the match for the first time since 2003, but the seeds of success were sown long before Edwards led his team to the north of Scotland.

The United States might lead the biennial series 34–8 with one match tied, but since 1993 the contest has become much closer. Over the last 10 matches the score stands at five victories apiece. Why? Well, GB&I's 14–12 triumph in the Granite City provides ample explanation.

Edwards and his team appeared to have little chance of regaining the cup. Indeed, according to all the predictions, all the USA had to do was turn up and the match was theirs. They were far stronger on paper than the home side.

United States captain Jim Holtgrieve brought a US team to Aberdeen that dominated the World Amateur Golf Ranking. Holtgrieve, who played on three victorious Walker Cup teams, counted the top four players in the world in his team in Patrick Cantlay, Jordan Spieth, Patrick Rodgers and Peter Uihlein. World number six Harris English gave him five of the top six, while Chris Williams at world number ten made it six of the top 10. It is arguably the strongest US Walker Cup team ever assembled.

Andy Sullivan and Tom Lewis at world number five and seven respectively, were the only two world top 10 players in the GB&I line up. No wonder the US were heavy favourites. Yet Edwards turned up in Aberdeen with one clear message to his team. "The match isn't played on paper," he told them.

The message got through. Against all the odds, GB&I won the opening foursomes session 3–1 and never looked back. They halved the first day's singles 4–4, and then nearly whitewashed the US in the second foursomes, wining the session 3½–½ to take a commanding 10½–5½ point lead into the final singles. Needing to win seven and half points out of ten to retain the cup, and eight points to win it, the US had left themselves too much to do. They stormed back

to win the final session 6½–3½ but couldn't stop a GB&I victory, one that Edwards had felt confident of all along.

"Did I expect to be sat here winning?" Edwards said. "Absolutely. I had had a quiet look at the things people had said and written, but I told the boys from the outset that they did not need worry about anyone else. All they needed to do was focus on themselves. They are very special and they proved that this week."

Scotland's Michael Stewart spoke for the team when he confirmed that Edwards had managed to instil belief in his players. "I don't think at any point we were underdogs," he said.

Stewart was one of the senior players in the GB&I team and led by example by winning two and a half points out of four. Northern Ireland's Paul Cutler ended the match as GB&I's highest points

© The R&A

Captain Nigel Edwards reminded his team that the match was not going to be won on paper!

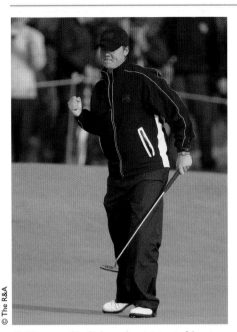

Welsh teenager Rhys Pugh won three points out of three in the GB&I triumph at Royal Aberdeen

© The R&A

they are nothing new to us. That was the idea of asking The R&A if we could come up here twice. It worked out well in the end. The session we had in May I thought was pretty similar to these conditions. The golf course was playing pretty similar. You prepare properly, you get the just rewards."

That last sentence should be framed and placed on the desk of any golf administrator hoping to breed success.

Ironically, GB&I's success in the 43rd Walker Cup can be traced back to the 1993 match, when GB&I was trounced 19–5 at Interlachen, Minnesota. That humbling forced some deep soul searching.

Out of that Minnesota misery came an entirely new approach to the biennial match. A squad system was introduced. Nowadays potential candidates are identified and brought together for training sessions at the match venue so players can familiarise themselves with the course, and the captain can identify possible pairings. Nine members of the victorious GB&I team came from the initial 23-man training squad named in November 2010. England's Steven Brown was the odd man out, although he was a late addition to the squad.

The system paid immediate dividends when GB&I won the 1995 match at Royal Porthcawl against a US team that included Tiger Woods. GB&I brought further parity to the match with three straight victories from 1999. Even though US had won three straight matches heading into Aberdeen, two of those matches (2005, 2007) were separated by just one point.

So GB&I heads to the National Golf Links on Long Island, New York in 2013 as holders of the cup former United States Golf Association President George Herbert Walker bequeathed to golf in 1920. The US will probably enter the match as favourites given that they are on home turf, and potentially could have several members of the side that played at Royal Aberdeen, including possibly Spieth, Rodgers, Cantlay and two time veteran Nathan Smith.

Only Pugh will be available to play for the GB&I side after his nine teammates turned professional. At this point in time it would seem a tall order for GB&I to win the next match, but then the same was said before Royal Aberdeen. Rest assured the visitors will be well prepared. Recent history has made sure of that.

scorer, winning three and a half points out of four. How-ever, Welsh teenager Rhys Pugh, at 17 years old the youngest player on both teams, turned out to be the surprise package. He won three points out of three to help the GB&I cause.

The conditions helped the home team. Strong winds and rain swept across one of the most quintessential links in the British Isles. The US team struggled to cope, but GB&I felt right at home.

"I think the real difference was the conditions," Holtgrieve admitted. "Even though my guys have played in windy conditions, it does take time to get used to those conditions. The conditions were tough for GB&I, but I think just being around these conditions as much as they are might have given them the edge."

The GB&I team might have been more comfortable with the weather, but there was an added advantage. Edwards had made sure his team were ready for whatever Royal Aberdeen threw up.

"We prepared for these conditions," Edwards said. "The boys have played in them all year. So

Walker Cupper Tom Lewis quick to win as a pro

Tom Lewis, who played his part in the Great Britain and Ireland Walker Cup success in 2011, joined the paid ranks immediately after the match and quickly made his mark on the European Tour winning the Castello Masters at Castellon in only his third start as a professional.

Winning is so important to all South African golfers

James Corrigan on the reasons for the Rainbow Nation's successes

First there was Bobby, then followed Gary, soon after arrived Ernie, shadowed by Retief, then Trevor held centre stage with Tim Clark until Charl and Louis stepped up to the podium. South Africa's golfing production line must be the smoothest running piece of equipment in the sports business.

Certainly, in golf it has no equal. No country, other than the United States, has won more majors since the Second World War and no country, other than the United States, can boast more individual major-winners since the Second World War. Of course, America's predominance in those charts needs little extolling, but consider they have an estimated 27 million golfers while in South Africa the figure is believed to be 500,000. If the US had the same golfer-per-major success they wouldn't have hailed 194 since 1945 – but 810.

So what is it about the Rainbow Nation which allows them to keep digging into this pot of golfing gold. After all, they hold no top-flight events as such. Pete Cowen is the coach of Louis Oost-huizen, the 2010 Open champion and also honed the sweet motion of Charl Schwartzel, the 2011 Master champion, when he first travelled across to Britain. "You can't underestimate the effect of the weather in South Africa," said the Yorkshireman who also oversees the likes of Lee Westwood, Darren Clarke and Graeme McDowell. "They can play so much, in great conditions. It may sound daft, but if you are playing in short sleeves all the year round it does make a difference."

Think of any South African great and they all have one attribute in common ... their aggression. Of course, there was the "up and at 'em" mindset of Player countered against the nonchalant "come and get me" style of Els. But when it came to holding a club in their hands their vision was similarly gung ho. "Playing in perfect weather all the time teaches you to be aggressive," said Cowen. "You have no excuse but to be aggressive and, in the heat of the battle, it's the best attitude to have. Far fewer players have won tournaments when trying to not lose them compared to those who have lost tournaments when trying to win them. The South Africans have an innate understanding of this."

Cowen also believes the sunshine helps South African swings blossom. Again, the differences in their swings is often stark. To stay on the Player–Els comparison, the former was 5ft 6in while the latter is 6ft 3in. For reasons of geometry, if nothing else, their swings were bound to be poles apart, yet they were both among the bigger-hitters of their generation. "They learn how to get more out of their bodies, learn how to get more flexibility," said Cowen, "and the heat is great for the body, in avoiding muscle injuries and keeping the back loose, that sort of thing. The facilities over there are great and the year-long sun lets them do for a whole 12 months what Britons can only do for five to six months."

But there is something more; there has to be. "It's a mental thing as well," agreed Cowen. "They are a sporting people who put great emphasis on winning. It's bred into them. South Africans do work hard. There will be another group coming through after this lot ... I guarantee it. Because

Bobby Locke had an unorthodox swing but set high standards for those who followed to emulate

© Getty Images

© The R&A

Former Open champion Louis Oosthuizen benefitted from early coaching and, like Ernie Els and others, is helping to encourage younger players

they have role-models. Player had Locke, Els and Goosen had Player, Charl and Louis had Ernie and Retief and now the young ones will have Charl and Louis. It's self-perpetuating really."

That's bad news for their rivals. Yet they can't say they weren't warned. Back in the early 70s, Player, the winner of nine majors and one of only five golfers to achieve the career "Grand Slam", foresaw the conveyor belt. He had received his inspiration and knew what it meant.

"The last thing in the world you would want to do is copy Bobby Locke's swing," he said. "Everything he did was completely unorthodox. But the thing Bobby Locke did, I think, was set a standard. That was the influence he had on me. I had this great desire to beat him and his record. Which is

what I have done now in South Africa. Now the new young boys at home have a desire to beat me and knock me off the pedestal. That's healthy – a great thing. And it'll go on and on."

Locke was an outsider in America. He was so successful in the Forties in America he was suspended. "He was too good. They had to ban him," said Claude Harmon, the famous professional, whose son, Butch, now teaches Els. Locke thrived on the odds against him defying the US dominance, just as Player did two years later. This belligerence can be traced through to the current crop.

Chubby Chandler is Els' former manager and currently oversees the likes of Oosthuizen, Schwartzel and other South African winners on the European Tour such as Richard Sterne, Anton Haig and James Kingston. He has his own theory for the country's golfing success story.

"They are tough because of what has happened in their country … apartheid and bans on playing," said the Boltonian. "They're like the Northern Irishmen in that sense, with all the Troubles in their history. They've probably been brought up a bit differently to other kids and they're a bit tougher than lads from other countries. It can't be a coincidence that from the 2010 US Open four of the next five majors were won by two South Africans and two Northern Irishmen."

If Chandler's theory is correct then imagine what this could mean if the foundations are successful in reaching out to the whole of the population. "Golf has the chance to become a sport for all South Africans," says Robert Baker, the South African coach who has worked with former world No 1s. "Thanks to Els's school (supported by The R&A) and the likes of Johann Rupert's South African Development Board thousands of South African children like Oosthuizen, who wouldn't be able to afford to play, are learning the game. The days of the country club are over, which means that maybe, just maybe, the next great South African golfer to emerge will have dark skin."

Seven South African winners of major titles since 1949

Gary Player, winner of nine titles, is the most successful South African golfer to have won majors since Bobby Locke started the ball rolling when he won the first of his four Opens in 1949. Since then, seven South Africans including most recently Louis Oosthuizen and Charl Schwartzel have been successful. The list is:

Name	Open	US Open	Masters	US PGA	Total
Gary Player	3	1	3	2	9
Bobby Locke	4	0	0	0	4
Ernie Els	1	2	0	0	3
Retief Goosen	0	2	0	0	2
Trevor Immelman	0	0	1	0	1
Louis Oosthuizen	1	0	0	0	1
Charl Schwartzel	0	0	1	0	0

Four years away but already the talk is of Olympic gold

Mark Garrod on the re-introduction of golf into the Games in 2016

The eyes of the sporting world will be on London this summer when England's capital city hosts the Olympics for the first time since 1948. Come the 2016 Games in Rio de Janeiro, however, a 112-year gap will be bridged, with golfers back chasing gold, silver and bronze alongside the runners, swimmers, boxers and assorted other sportsmen and women.

How different it is all sure to look in comparison to the 1904 competition, when a total of 77 golfers (74 from the United States, three from Canada, all men, all amateurs) participated in St Louis, Missouri. Not that golf stood out from the crowd in that respect. Of the 94 events only 42 included athletes who were not from America and there were some curious goings-on as the near five-month festival – opening ceremony July 1, closing ceremony November 23 – took place as something of a sideshow to the World Fair.

In the marathon, for instance, first to arrive at the finish line was American Frederick Lorz, who actually stopped after nine miles, was given a lift in a car for the next 11 before it broke down then continued to the stadium on foot and was greeted as the winner. He did not confess until after the medal ceremony, was banned, then reinstated and a year later won the Boston Marathon.

One presumes nothing of the kind will take place in Brazil when golf takes its first steps back as an Olympic sport with 60 men and 60 women competing for individual medals and possibly team ones as well. Impossible to predict, of course, how the world rankings will look in four years' time, but based on current positions the spread of nations who will be involved almost covers the globe, perfectly in keeping with the aims set out when the sport made its bid for re-introduction.

Peter Dawson, Chief Executive of The R&A and President of the International Golf Federation, the body overseeing golf's return, said: "I have no doubt that Olympic golf is comfortably the biggest grow-the-game opportunity that exists to help us bring golf to so many countries where it's just starting up."

Equally India's Jeev Milkha Singh is convinced about the impact it could have on his country of more than 1.2 billion people, second only to China and over 17% of the world's total. The United States, out of interest, accounts for less than 5%.

"I think it's going to be huge for golf to come under the IOC (International Olympic Committee) wing," said Singh. "Other sports in India are funded by the government and I'm requesting that with us becoming an Olympic sport again they open up more public driving ranges so that the common man or a child whose family are not members of private clubs can easily try the game out. I think it's our fastest-growing sport, but we have one public course at the moment. Cricket is a religion and hockey is a national sport, but I would rank golf two or three now."

Singh, 40 in December, has personal reasons too for setting the Rio Games in 2016 as a target. In Rome in 1960 his father Milkha Singh, known as "The Flying Sikh" and the Commonwealth Games champion, lost out for the 400 metres bronze medal in a photo finish after leading for much of the race. "I would love to represent my country just as my father did. It would be fantastic for me and for him – it would be a dream come true for the family."

The qualifying format is still being discussed but it could be that the top 15 on the world rankings earn

Jeev Milkha Singh's father was an Olympian in 1960 and he wants to emulate his father in Rio de Janiero 46 years on

© Phil Sheldon Golf Picture Library

© Golf Canada Archives

Canadian George Lyon was the last man to win an Olympic gold in golf ... and that was in 1904

a maximum of two from other countries. At time of writing this would mean 41 different countries represented in the men's and women's competitions with Jeev Milkha Singh qualifying for India.

"Golf truly is an international sport with 60 million playing the game in close to 120 different countries," says Dawson, "and it is continuing to grow with new initiatives to teach the game to both young and old. The time is right for golf to be brought back to the Olympic Games."

Among the facts presented to the IOC during the bid process was that professional golf is televised every week in 216 countries, translated into 35 languages, with a reach of more than 500 million households.

The IOC made it clear to the International Golf Federation that they wanted the game's best players to be involved and every four years therefore the dates of majors affected will be adjusted accordingly. In Rio de Janeiro the Games are scheduled for August 5–21.

A site has now been chosen for the new course, a designer has been chosen and as it takes shape excitement will grow about the sport's return.

Since 1904, Canadian George Lyon has been the last man to have the title "Olympic golf champion" against his name. Soon that will no longer be the case.

spots regardless of how many are from the same country and for the field of 60 to be completed with

George walked on his hands to collect his Olympic gold!

It is unlikely that Luke Donald, assuming he is involved, will walk on his hands to collect a gold medal for winning the golf competition at the Olympics in 2016 ... but that is exactly what the last (and indeed only) Olympic golfing gold medal winner did in 1904!

George Seymour Lyon from Richmond, Ontario, who beat Chandler Egan 3 and 2 in the final to win the Olympic competition at Glen Eco, St Louis in 1904, was an accomplished golfer who won the Canadian Amateur Championship eight times despite only taking up the game at the Rosedale Club at the age of 38. A friend with whom he had been playing cricket suggested he might enjoy golf and eight years later he was Olympic champion.

Lyon, one of 13 children raised on a farm, was a natural at almost every sport he tried. He played baseball, rugby union, and football. He curled, was an accomplished athlete and pole vaulter and played cricket for his country ... but initially did not care for golf. When persuaded to give it a go (and hit his first drive straight down the middle of the fairway) this colourful extrovert character was converted.

In fact he might well have won a second golfing gold in London in 1908, the last time golf was an official Olympic sport, but because of a dispute all the British contestants withdrew and he was left as the only medal challenger. He was offered the medal for turning up but, in the circumstances, he declined.

Lyon, who founded the Canadian Senior's Golf Association and then won 10 of the 15 Senior Championships in which he played, was elected President of the Royal Canadian Golf Association in 1923 and later inducted into the Canadian Golf Hall of Fame although not until 1971 – 33 years after his death.

Golf was included in the 1900 Olympic Games but all the sports including somewhat unusually life saving, cannon shooting, fire fighting, boules. pelota and kite flying in addition to golf, were organised in connection with the 1900 World Fair. There were 95 events in the Paris Olympics which opened in May and were completed in October.

The swimming events were staged on the River Seine and the golf at Compeigne. The first gold medal winner in golf was actually Charles Sands in 1900 but at that time there was no medal. In fact Margaret Ives Abbott, an art student who shot 47 for nine holes to win the women's golfing competition that she thought was just a holiday affair died in 1955 before the event was designated an official Olympic tournament. She never ever knew she was an Olympian!

College golf in America is still the greatest deal of a lifetime

Jaime Diaz admits, however, that for some it's best to turn pro early

One of the best things about being a professional golfer is that it's a long journey. It's often a cruel one, but no other sport offers as many opportunities for resurgence. If the traveller is lucky, the odyssey will end in the sweet anticlimax of one of mankind's great inventions – a senior tour.

What's become interesting, however, is the question of how the journey should begin. Specifically, with or without the foundation of a few years spent in the once vaunted and now oft-maligned American college golf system?

It's a debate that has become more provocative because of the dramatic ascendance of European golf. In the last two seasons, after the stunning fall of Tiger Woods, the first two players to succeed him as world No 1 were Lee Westwood of England and Martin Kaymer of Germany. Now Luke Donald, another Englishman, is No 1. Last year 21 year old Rory McIlroy of Northern Ireland utterly dominated the US Open with an eight stroke victory, while Matteo Manassero of Italy set records by winning two European Tour events before the age of 18. None of these four played golf at an American university.

Of course, that's been more or less the norm for Europeans and most non-American stars for decades. When Europe's Big Six – Seve Ballesteros, Nick Faldo, Sandy Lyle, Bernhard Langer, José Maria Olazábal and Ian Woosnam – walked the earth in the 1980s, only Faldo and Lyle among them had ever tried an American college. Lyle lasted three weeks at the then-powerhouse University of Houston, Faldo just a little longer – 10.

Similarly, Australia's longtime No 1, Greg Norman, never attended college (college golf is little more than a club sport in countries other than America). But Norman's era was still a time a strong majority of the best players in the world were Americans who had done their golf apprenticeships at colleges in the US. The most successful programmes were proudly referred to as "golf factories," and they seemed the most logical way to success for a junior star. A four-year scholarship – the so-called "full ride" – presented its lucky recipient with regular practice among equally gifted teammates, access to good courses, and formidable competition. As a respite, there was pastoral campus life including a generally cushy curriculum.

Arnold Palmer began the parade of Hall of Famers who played college golf when he starred at Wake Forest. He was followed by Jack Nicklaus at Ohio State, Johnny Miller at BYU, Hale Irwin at Colorado, Ben Crenshaw and Tom Kite, University at Texas, Tom Watson at Stanford, Hubert Green at Alabama, Lanny Wadkins and Curtis Strange, Wake Forest. Only a few of them actually graduated, but they all extolled the experience. It seemed that among the American elite, only Lee Trevino, who grew up poor and dropped out of school in the eighth grade, was the exception.

The American tradition has continued. Phil Mickelson, David Duval, and Tiger Woods all starred at major universities. And today's best young Americans, including Dustin Johnson, Rickie Fowler, Matt Kuchar, Nick Watney, Webb Simpson, Bubba Watson and Keegan Bradley, did the same.

Meanwhile, golfers from Europe and the rest of the world have mostly decided to take other routes. An early exception was Colin Montgomerie, who played well at Houston Baptist. Luke Donald

Nick Faldo won six majors and made it to No 1 but lasted only ten weeks at an American university

© Getty Images

© Getty Images

Jack Nicklaus believes a college scoring system that used to be based on match play produces winners

earned a degree in art from Northwestern, becoming only the second college graduate – joining Tom Lehman – to attain world No 1 status. Paul Casey and Graham McDowell both had dominating careers at Arizona State and Alabama Birmingham, respectively, and Scotland's Martin Laird built his game at Colorado State. For the record, Darren Clarke stopped in for a year of fun at Wake Forest.

But as the American grip on golf dominance has loosened, there are discernibly fewer former college golfers at the highest level of the game. Last fall, a count of the Top 50 in the Official World Golf Ranking revealed that fully half did not play college golf. All of the 21 Americans did. But 14 of the 19 Europeans didn't, nor did any of the remaining six players from the rest of the world.

So what is the best path for future professionals? Leading swing instructors David Leadbetter and Hank Haney have each advocated that top talents are better off going pro earlier. Their argument is that, all else being equal, the 18-year-old who works his way through the rigours of the minor professional tours will, at age 23 or so, be farther along mentally, technically and competitively than the player who played at an American college. They point not only to Europeans including Ian Poulter bypassing an American golf scholarship, but young major winners, like South Africans Charl Schwartzel and Louis Oosthuizen and Australian Geoff Ogilvy doing the same.

With the shifting tide has come more criticism of the college system. Some think the players are over coached, and don't learn enough self sufficiency. Others say a scoring format in which the best four scores among five players are taken doesn't force a player having a bad day to keep grinding. Jack Nicklaus and Lanny Wadkins have both bemoaned the

passing of a scoring system based on match play. "College players don't have to beat anyone anymore," says Wadkins. "Consequently, they don't know how to win."

For what it's worth, here's my take.

For the special true prodigy, like a McIlroy or a Manassero, especially if there is economic hardship and a healthy dollop of psychological and physical maturity, it makes more sense to pass on college and turn pro young. That decision will always be more logical for a non-American whose progress could be further slowed by the culture shock of moving to a new country.

On the other hand, the road is strewn with the stalled careers of supposed prodigies who went for the money. In America, the most cited examples are Ty Tryon and Tadd Fujikawa, both of whom now toil in the lower divisions of pro golf. Both, it is widely held, would have been better off going to an American college.

So, I think, would the great majority of promising junior players. That includes those from foreign countries who wouldn't suffer from a disabling language barrier. The college golf system may be under fire, but a full scholarship to an American university to play golf remains for all but the rarest few the deal of a lifetime.

More than anything, it is a place that can provide needed balance in necessarily narrow lives. In women's professional golf, where there have been more teenage winners, and where there are even fewer Americans at the top of the game, college golf seems less vital. However, there have been enough stories of early burnout that the LPGA instituted a rule setting the minimum age for membership at 18. Ironically, former prodigy Michelle Wie seemed to stop the decline in her career by finding sanctuary at Stanford, where she doesn't even play on the golf team.

Tiger Woods has said that his game probably would have progressed faster if he'd passed on college, but that his two years at Stanford were among the best of his life. Perhaps two more years would have given him a stronger defense against the forces ahead. Ballesteros, Faldo and Lyle arguably suffered from their lack of a broader life experience. Faldo wishes he had been better able to interact socially while he was a champion, Lyle lost his game too soon and the tragic Ballesteros often expressed regrets over "lost youth". Among contemporary players, Sergio García began playing in professional events at age 15 and now fights an ennui that has left him ambivalent about his once seemingly destined career. Justin Rose turned pro at 17 and promptly missed his first 21 cuts. He saved himself, but barely. Golfers should endeavor to make the journey as long as possible.

Certainly ground can be lost by going slowly, but it's rushing that is a greater threat to making a career shorter.

Royal Lytham and The Open are so very different 50 years on

Keith Mackie in reflective mood as he heads to Lancashire

When the international golfing circus descends like a swarm of bees on Royal Lytham & St Annes for the 2012 Open it will be the 50th Championship since Bob Charles (now Sir Bob) won the last 36-hole play-off for the title over the same classic links in 1963. The nature of the contest has changed mightily in that time but innovations introduced that year laid the foundations for the massive development of the game's oldest championship over the following half-century.

As golf entered its modern era with the emergence of Arnold Palmer and the soon-to-be dominant Jack Nicklaus, the running of the game's oldest Championship still carried overtones of Victorian amateurism. There was no such thing as the spectacular weekend of sport that will bring the 2012 Open to its climax.

In that year of 1963 the Championship was played over three days, from Wednesday to Friday. Only the two-round play-off between Bob Charles and American Phil Rodgers extended play into a spectator-friendly Saturday. One round was played on Wednesday and one on Thursday, for which there was a charge of 10 shillings a day for spectators, or 50p in today's money. The field was cut after 36 holes and 47 players, all professionals, played two rounds on the Friday with play starting at 9.0am and 1.30pm. The charge for entry on the final day was £1.

But there were encouraging signs that the problems of the chaotic contest at Troon the previous year were being decisively tackled. Fairways were fenced off for the first time to prevent the spectator stampedes that had marred the 1962 event and stands at strategic points around the course were packed throughout the week. There were the rudiments of a tented village and the innovations of mobile scoreboards and caddie bibs gave spectators much more information than in previous years. Golf on television was still in its infancy, but at Lytham in 1963 coverage was expanded with the construction of scaffolding towers to give views of eight holes. Compare that with the 60 or so cameras that give wall-to-wall coverage of today's Championships.

The international nature of the game was evident even in the sixties and home players did not fare well. Although 27 made the cut, only one finished in the top 10 – Christy O'Connor taking a £350 prize for sixth place after yo-yo rounds of 74-68-76-68, nine shots behind the leaders. Jack Nicklaus was one shot shy of the play-off, Kel Nagle and Peter Thomson were in fourth and fifth. Ramon Sota and Gary Player shared seventh place and Jean Garaialde tied with Sebastian Miguel in ninth.

A glance further down the prize list shows that home stalwarts Tom Haliburton and Ken Bousfield were in 30th place with a 19-year-old youngster from England called Anthony Jacklin. They took home a prize of £57 each. Six years later over the same course Jacklin was to become the first home winner for 18 years.

Firm favourite Arnold Palmer, aiming for a hat-trick of victories after winning the Championship in 1961 and 1962, was devastated after failing to make the cut. A series of blocked tee shots into Lytham's lethal rough and a breakdown of his charging

© Phil Sheldon Golf Picture Library

Tony Jacklin's home win in 1969 will always ensure Royal Lytham and St Annes a place in the minds of British golfers

When Bobby Jones went off course for a sandwich at Lytham in 1926, the over-zealous security guard would not let him back in unless he paid. He stood in the queue, paid and went on to win the title!

putting style left him with two rounds of 76. He cut a disconsolate figure as he stood beneath the 18th green stand, looked up at the scaffolding supports and asked: "Is this where you hang yourself?"

If the changes in The Open since 1963 are dramatic, they are matched equally by the early development of Royal Lytham & St Annes from a fateful date in February 1886 when 19 enthusiasts agreed to the formation of the club. It took them just a week to lay out a course through the rough-hewn valleys and dunes before they held their first competition. Four years later, with an enthusiastic membership of 400, they were forced to move to a new location two miles further south, and they started over again, creating the basis of the course that has since staged some of the most exhilarating Open Championships.

Just as in 1963, innovation was very much the theme of the 1926 Open, the first to be held at Lytham. For the first time regional qualifying reduced the initial entry of 293 down to a manageable 117, the Championship was played over three

days rather than two and gate money was introduced to control the number of spectators after players had been swept away by crowds at Prestwick the year before.

The Championship also produced a champion who was soon to capture the imagination of the entire golfing world. Bobby Jones was 24 years old and had twice won the US Amateur when he travelled to Lytham after the Walker Cup match at St Andrews. But his triumph was not to be achieved without drama. In the break between the final two rounds Jones returned to the Majestic Hotel for a sandwich and a brief respite, but failed to take his competitor's badge with him. Notoriously short-tempered on the course in his early days, the nascent champion was refused entry by an officious steward and stood meekly in the queue of spectators to pay his was back to the course.

The winning shot he hit that afternoon was from 175 yards in sandy rough to the left of the 17th hole to a hidden green. A plaque marks the spot to this day. Four years later he re-wrote the record books with victories in the Amateur and Open Championships of Britain and America in the same season.

The victory by South African Bobby Locke at Lytham in 1952 was also marked by an off-course incident and bizarrely he started his final day of the Championship clattering around the back streets of Blackpool on a milk cart. He had rented space in a garage next to his hotel, but on that morning the doors were firmly locked. A passing milkman knew where the owner lived and abandoned his round so that Locke could retrieve the keys. He arrived at the course with just enough time to change his shoes and go straight to the first tee. Locke always projected an air of unhurried calm on the course and he proved that day it was more than skin deep. After a fine tee shot at the short first he rolled in the birdie putt and sailed on to his third Open triumph in four years.

There have been no such bizarre incidents in the eight Opens that have followed, but memorable among them are Tony Jacklin's home win in 1969 with the word "tempo" written on the back of his glove, Gary Player's left-handed jab from the flower bed by the clubhouse wall on his way to victory in 1974 and two swashbuckling triumphs by Seve Ballesteros in 1979 and 1988. Expect more of the same when Lytham becomes the focus of world golfing attention again in 2012.

Lytham winners and total prize money

Year	Winner		Score	Prize	Year	Winner		Score	Prize
1926	Bobby Jones	(USA)	291	£225	1974	Gary Player	(RSA)	282	£50,000
1952	Bobby Locke	(RSA)	287	£1,700	1979	Seve Ballesteros	(ESP)	283	£155,000
1958	Peter Thomson	(AUS)	278	£4,850	1988	Seve Ballesteros	(ESP)	273	£700,000
1963	Bob Charles	(NZL)	277	£8,500	1996	Tom Lehman	(USA)	271	£1,400,000
1969	Tony Jacklin	(ENG)	280	£30,334	2001	David Duval	(USA)	274	£3,300,000

The remarkable history of golf in just ten interesting items

Mike Aitken visits the popular museum at St Andrews

If it's possible to relate a history of the world in 100 objects, as the Director of the British Museum, Neil MacGregor, attempted in a series of superb programmes for BBC Radio 4, then it's surely no disservice to golf to pull off the same narrative trick with ten "things" currently on display in St Andrews at the British Golf Museum.

Thanks to the invaluable aid of Angela Howe, Director of Museum and Heritage for The R&A, we set about choosing ten "prisms" to explore the story of the ancient game. Both of us were keen to include artefacts which illustrate the inclusive nature of the sport. So, of course, the great and the good are represented in this swing through time, but there are also pertinent examples from the brave and the eccentric.

Here, then, are ten examples of the pictures, equipment, trophies, documents and items of clothing on display at the museum which detail the progress of golf from the 18th century to the present day.

1 Articles & Laws in Playing the Golf

This document lists the first known Rules of Golf. Originally, they were drawn up by the Gentlemen Golfers of Edinburgh (later the Honourable Company) for the first organised championship which was staged on Leith Links in the spring of 1744. The 13 rules governing the Silver Club Challenge are still recognised as the principles which underpin golf

today. They include the motto which would become the very essence of the worldwide game – "If a ball be stopped by any person, horse or dog or anything else, the ball so stopp'd must be played where it lyes." Ten years later, in 1754, an almost identical set of rules was drafted by the St Andrews golfers (later the Royal and Ancient) for their own competition. They are illustrated here.

2 The Procession of the Silver Club by David Allan, 1793

Allan was a society painter who has been described as the Lord Lichfield of his day. This little drawing reflects the importance of the first competition as the winner of the Silver Club Challenge was announced by a procession through the city of Edinburgh. The Silver Club itself was donated, in what was the game's first act of sponsorship, by

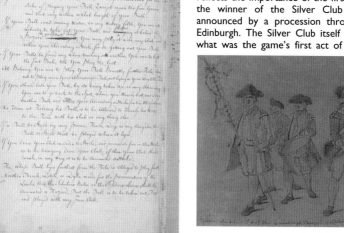

Loaned by The Royal Burgess Golfing Society

Edinburgh Town Council. Each winner had to attach a silver ball to the club, inscribed with the victor's name. John Rattray, an Edinburgh surgeon who signed the 1744 Rules, won the Silver Club three times after fighting in the Jacobite Rebellion for Bonnie Prince Charlie. He might not have lived to tell the tale had he not formed a friendship on the links with the Lord President of the Court of Session, Duncan Forbes, a pillar of the establishment who successfully pleaded for his friend's life.

3 Feather golf balls made by Allan Robertson, c.1840

Allan Robertson was the outstanding golfer of his generation. The first man to break 80 on the Old Course, he took part in a series of epic matches against Musselburgh's Willie Dunn in the 1840s, losing only once. Robertson was considered the outstanding ball and club maker of the age and his equipment was exported around the world. Old Tom Morris worked as an apprentice in his shop. Not only did Robertson earn a living making feather balls but he was also responsible for the creation of the double greens at St Andrews in 1856. His premature death following an attack of jaundice in 1859 at the age of 44 meant he was denied the opportunity of competing in The Open – a championship which was first staged at Prestwick a year later to find his successor as the "champion golfer".

4 Driving putter

Few artefacts link more of the great names in the early days of The Open Championship than this club made by Hugh Philp, a carpenter in St Andrews who became a revolutionary clubmaker. Philp's designs broke the mould and other craftsmen would forge his name into their own clubs in a bid to increase sales. The driving putter was used to keep the ball low under the wind in blustery conditions. It was owned by J O Fairlie, the Ayrshire landowner who was one of the 57 founding members of Prestwick and a key figure in establishing The

Open. Willie Park, who won the red Morocco belt in 1860 and 1863, asked Fairlie if he could borrow the club for the Championship in 1864. However, it was already promised to Old Tom Morris, the winner in 1861 and 1862, who duly used the implement to succeed again. Around 100 Philp originals still exist today.

5 Young Tom Morris' Open Medal, 1872

Young Tom's hat-trick of Open wins between 1868 and 1870 at Prestwick, the links where he learned to play the game, meant he retained the Challenge Belt. When the Championship resumed in 1872, under the co-management of Prestwick, the Honourable Company and The R&A, there was no trophy, so the winner, Morris again, was presented with a gold medal. The tradition continues to this day. The story of Young Tom is one of triumph and tragedy. His untimely death on Christmas Day 1875, aged 24, brought to an end the career of a golfer who won his first Open at 17 – a remarkable feat which still makes him the youngest major champion in history.

6 1904 Olympic trophy

Due to return to the Olympic arena in 2016, golf was part of the summer programme in the games of 1900 and 1904. This is the runner-up trophy that was presented to the American golfer Henry Chandler Egan during the 1904 Games in Missouri. Because of his victory over Walter Travis in the US Amateur, Egan, 26, was favourite for gold. However, he was beaten 3 and 2 by George Lyon, 46, a

Loaned by the LA 84 Foundation

former cricketer from Canada at the Glen Eco Country Club in St. Louis. Remarkably, Lyon first picked up a golf club at the age of 38.

7 Gloria Minoprio outfit

A magician who once traveled to India to raise money for charity by performing conjuring tricks for the maharajahs, Gloria Minoprio was the first female to wear trousers when competing in the 1933 English Ladies Close Chamopionship in which she used only one club – a cleek. She was also a gifted pianist playing one-handed! Her stylish outfit, white makeup and scarlet lipstick cause outraged among the LGU, which decried "this departure from the usual golfing costume". Henry Longhurst observed that "never in the history of women's golf has a competitor caused such a sensation as Miss Gloria Minoprio." The mysterious one club girl died from septicaemia in 1958 at the age of 50.

Loaned by the Women Golfers Museum

8 Golf balls made by prisoners of war

These two rubber golf balls were made by prisoners of war, G A Archer and William Sampson. Rubber from gym shoes was used as a centre for the balls, which was then covered with stitched leather. The cane ball was made by a PoW in Edinburgh. The balls help to illustrate the ingenuity of mankind under the most adverse circumstances and how the game of golf endures in the wider world.

9 Bobby Jones portrait painted by J A A Berrie, 1930

Perhaps America's most revered golfer, particularly in Scotland where he was awarded the Freedom of the City of St Andrews in 1958, Jones sat for this portrait on the Sunday prior to the 1930 Open Championship. It was commissioned by Sir Ernest Roydon, captain of Wallasey Golf Club and painted by fellow member John Berrie, RA. The year this portrait was painted, Jones completed the Grand Slam – all four major championships in one year – a feat which remains unequalled to this day.

Loaned by Wallasey Golf Club

10 Seve Ballesteros' shoes

While Seve's trademark outfit of navy blue and white was celebrated by the game's leading golfers during the second round of the BMW PGA Championship at Wentworth last year, these shoes were donated to the British Golf Museum by the stylish Spaniard after he wore them at the Scottish Open in 1991. The winner of three Open Championships and two Masters titles, Ballesteros was a restless champion. His shoes are a reminder of the tireless search for glory.

The sad day when Seve called time on his fabulous career

Passionate, determined, competitive and the great entertainer

When Severiano Ballesteros decided in 2007 that it was time to call it a day as a competitor he chose Carnoustie to tell us. It was a logical decision because it had been there in 1975 that the farmer's son from Pedrena had played in his first Open which he considered the best of all Championships. In fact he made an inauspicious start. He missed the half-way cut hampered by a foot injury incurred just a few days before the Championship began.

A year later at Royal Birkdale, however it was very different. He finished tied second with Jack Nicklaus behind Johnnie Miller. He had arrived. Suddenly the charismatic young Spaniard who, at the time, spoke little English and could not understand much of what was written about him in the British press was a headline-maker.

It was the start of a fabulous career. As George O'Grady, chief executive of the PGA European Tour, put it: "We have all been blessed to have lived in the Seve era." It's true that when Seve smiled the world smiled with him and when things were going wrong for him we were sad. His great friend and Ryder Cup partner José Maria Olazábal put it this way: "What impressed me most about him was his strength, his fighting spirit and the passion he put into everything he did."

© Getty Images

Seve was philosophical when he announced at Carnoustie that his competitive playing days were over

Seve was a golfing great who really did live up to that over-used and often unwarranted billing ... he was a genuine superstar. "It was his creativity, his imagination, his desire to compete," said Jack Nicklaus, "that made him so popular. His enthusiasm was unmatched. When Seve was around you knew you would be entertained. He was golf's great entertainer."

For over 30 years we had enjoyed his company but now it was over. There would no more of those incredible shots played from impossible lies. That day in Carnoustie he told us: "Golf gave me so much over the years that it is hard to give back even 25 per cent of how much I was given. It gave me not only the pleasure of competing but also [a chance] to enjoy the competition and feel the glory of winning.

"The people from the United Kingdom were really fantastic. There was a good feeling between them and I. There was a good connection, good chemistry. Most of the tournaments I won was thanks to them.

"Obviously thanks to you, the media – you really put my name in headlines and in articles all over the world. Thanks to the sponsors, the referees, the European Tour and the players whom I had the privilege and honour to play with whether it was [against them] in medal play or side-by-side in the Ryder Cup.

"I have so many Open memories. I remember Royal Birkdale in 1976 very well. I caddied for my brother in qualifying and then when I shot 69 on the first day they said 'Manuel, Manuel congratulations, a 69.' and he said 'No its not me. It's my brother.' 'Who is your brother?' 'This guy sitting over here,' he said. 'I thought he was your caddie.' 'Yeah he was but he is also my brother and a really good player!'

"I remember when I won at Royal Lytham my three brothers were there and they all hugged me. It was fantastic. So, too, was the 1984 Open at St Andrews and then there was a great round I played with Nick Price and Nick Faldo at Lytham in 1988. Now that *was* a great round."

And then he was gone, planning for a future in golf but not as a player. Sadly that future was cut short all too quickly in May last year ... but Severiano Ballesteros will never be forgotten. After all, he was the special one.

Championship dates

	The Masters	US Open	The Open	US PGA Championship
2012	**April 5–8** Augusta National, Augusta, GA	**June 14–17** The Olympic Club, San Francisco, CA	**July 19–22** Royal Lytham & St Annes, Lancashire	**August 9–12** Kiawah Island GR (Ocean Course)
2013	**April 11–14** Augusta National, Augusta, GA	**June 13–16** Merion GC (East course), Ardmore, PA	**July 18–21** Muirfield, East Lothian	**August 8–11** Oak Hill CC (East Course), Pittsford, NY
2014	**TBC** Augusta National, Augusta, GA	**June 12–15** Pinehurst Resort (Course No 2), NC	**July 17–20** Royal Liverpool, Hoylake, Cheshire	**TBA** Valhalla GC, Louisville, KY
2015		**June 18–21** Chambers Bay, University Place, WA	**July 16–19** Old course, St Andrews, Fife	**TBA** Whistling Straits GC (Straits Course), Kohler, WI
2016		**June 16–19** Oakmont CC, PA		**TBA** Baltusrol GC (Lower Course), Springfield, NJ
2017		**June 15–18** Erin Hills, Erin, WI		**TBA** Quail Hollow GC, Charlotte, NC

Ryder Cup
2012 Medinah Country Club, IL, USA   Sept 28–30
2014 Gleneagles Hotel, Perthshire, Scotland   Sept 26–28
2016 Hazeltine National GC, Chaska, MN
2018 Le Golf National, Versailles, France
2020 Whistling Straits, Kohler, WI
2022 Venue to be announced

Solheim Cup
2013 Colorado GC, Parker, CO
2015 Venue to be announced

Presidents Cup
(USA v Rest of the World except Europe)
2013 Muirfield Village GC, Ohio – October 2–6
2015 South Korea – venue and date to be announced

Curtis Cup
2012 Nairn GC, Scotland – June 8–10
2014 Venue to be announced – June 6–8

R&A Contacts
Peter Dawson, Chief Executive

Business Affairs
Michael Tate, Executive Director – Business Affairs
Robin Bell, Marketing Director   Malcolm Booth, Communications Director
Angus Farquhar, Commercial Director

Championships
Johnnie Cole-Hamilton, Executive Director – Championships.
Rhodri Price, Director – Championship Operations
Michael Wells, Director – Championship Staging

Finance
John Murray, Executive Director – Finance
Rules and Equipment Standards
David Rickman, Executive Director – Rules and Equipment Standards
Grant Moir, Director – Rules   Steve Otto, Director – Research and Testing

Working for Golf
Duncan Weir, Executive Director – Working for Golf
Angela Howe, Museum and Heritage Director   Steve Isaac, Director Golf Course Management
Peter Lewis, Director – Film Archive

Dominic Wall, Director – Asia/Pacific

Up-to-date news of The R&A and its activities can be found at www.randa.org
The R&A can be contacted on: Tel 01334 460000 Fax 01334 460001

R&A championship dates, 2012–2014

	2012	2013	2014
The Open Championship	**July 19–22** Royal Lytham and St Annes	**July 18–21** Muirfield	**July 17–20** Royal Liverpool
The Open Championship Final Qualifying (local)	**July 3** Hillside Southport and Ainsdale St Anne's Old Links West Lancs	**July 2** Dunbar Gullane Musselburgh North Berwick	**July 1** Glasgow – Gailes Links Hillside Royal Cinque Ports Woburn
The Senior Open Championship	**July 26–29** Turnberry	**July 25–28** Royal Birkdale	TBA
The Amateur Championship	**June 18–23** Royal Troon Glasgow – Gailes Links	**June 17–22** Royal Cinque Ports Prince's	TBA
The Senior Open Amateur Championship	**August 8–10** Machynys Peninsula	**August 7–9** Royal Aberdeen	TBA
The Junior Open Championship	**July 16–18** Fairhaven	—	TBA
The Boys' Amateur Championship	**August 14–19** Notts Coxmoor	**August 13–18** Royal Liverpool Wallasey	TBA
The Boys' Home Internationals	**August 7–9** County Louth	**August 6–8** Forest Pines	TBA
The Jacques Léglise Trophy	**August 31–Sept. 1** Portmarnock	**August 30–31** Royal St Davids	**August 29–30** Sweden
The Walker Cup	—	**September 7–8** National Golf Links of America, Southampton, NY	—
The St Andrews Trophy	**August 31–Sept. 1** Portmarnock	—	**August 29–30** Sweden
The World Amateur Team Championships (Espirito Santo Trophy)	**September 27–30** Antalya, Turkey	—	**September 3–6** Karuizwa, Japan
The World Amateur Team Championships (Eisenhower Trophy)	**October 4–7** Antalya, Turkey	—	**September 11–14** Karuizwa, Japan

Other fixtures and tour schedules can be found on pages 484–491

Abbreviations

ALB	Albania	HKG	Hong Kong	PAN	Panama
ARG	Argentina	HUN	Hungary	PAR	Paraguay
AUS	Australia	INA	Indonesia	PER	Peru
AUT	Austria	IND	India	PHI	Philippines
BAH	Bahamas	IOM	Isle of Man	PNG	Papua New Guinea
BAN	Bangladesh	IRI	Iran	POL	Poland
BAR	Barbados	IRL	Ireland	POR	Portugal
BDI	Burundi	ISL	Iceland	PUR	Puerto Rico
BEL	Belgium	ISR	Israel	QAT	Qatar
BER	Bermuda	ITA	Italy	ROM	Romania
BHU	Bhutan	JAM	Jamaica	RSA	South Africa
BOL	Bolivia	JOR	Jordan	RUS	Russia
BOT	Botswana	JPN	Japan	SAM	Samoa
BRA	Brazil	KAZ	Kazakhstan	SCO	Scotland
BRN	Bahrain	KEN	Kenya	SIN	Singapore
BUL	Bulgaria	KGZ	Kyrgyzstan	SKA	St Kitts & Nevis
CAM	Cambodia	KOR	Korea (South)	SLO	Slovenia
CAN	Canada	KSA	Saudi Arabia	SOL	Solomonn Islands
CAY	Cayman Islands	KUW	Kuwait	SRI	Sri Lanka
CHI	Chile	LAO	Laos	SUI	Switzerland
CHN	China	LAT	Latvia	SVK	Slovakia
CIV	Côte d'Ivoire	LBA	Libya	SWE	Sweden
COK	Cook Islands	LBN	Lebanon	SWZ	Swaziland
COL	Colombia	LCA	Saint Lucia	TCI	Turks and Caicos
CRC	Costa Rica	LTU	Lithuania		Islands
CRO	Croatia	LUX	Luxembourg	THA	Thailand
CYP	Cyprus	MAC	Macau	TPE	Taiwan
CZE	Czech Republic	MAR	Morocco		(Chinese Taipei)
DEN	Denmark	MAS	Malaysia	TRI	Trinidad and
DOM	Dominican Rep.	MEX	Mexico		Tobago
ECU	Ecuador	MGL	Mongolia	TUN	Tunisia
EGY	Egypt	MON	Monaco	TUR	Turkey
ENG	England	MYA	Myanmar	UAE	United Arab
ESA	El Salvador	NAM	Namibia		Emirates
ESP	Spain	NCA	Nicaragua	UGA	Uganda
EST	Estonia	NED	Netherlands	UKR	Ukraine
FIJ	Fiji	NEP	Nepal	URU	Uruguay
FIN	Finland	NIG	Niger	USA	United States
FRA	France	NIR	Northern Ireland	VAN	Vanuatu
GER	Germany	NGR	Nigeria	VEN	Venezuela
GRE	Greece	NOR	Norway	VIE	Vietnam
GUA	Guatemala	NZL	New Zealand	WAL	Wales
GUM	Guam	PAK	Pakistan	ZIM	Zimbabwe

GB&I   Great Britain and Ireland

(am)	Amateur	(M)	Match play	Jr	Junior
(D)	Defending champion	(S)	Stroke play	Sr	Senior

Where available, total course yardage and the par for a course are displayed in square brackets, i.e. [6686–70]

* indicates winner after play-off

Honours for major winners Clarke and McIlroy

Two British golfers from Northern Ireland who won major titles in 2011 were awarded honours in the Queen's New Year's Honour List. Open champion Clarke received an OBE and McIlroy, winner of the US Open, earned an MBE.

Forty-two-year-old Clarke, playing in his 54th major, won The Open at his 20th attempt. His victory in rough weather at Royal St George's last July was his 14th European Tour title success in a 21 year professional career

"I had a fantastic year and this just caps it off," said Clarke. "It is a privilege to be recognised with an OBE – it's a lot to take in.

"I could not have envisaged the year I have had. Winning The Open was obviously a dream come true; I had had chances before and at 42, I thought that maybe it was just not to be.

"But it was a life changing moment really and in many ways my feet have not touched the floor since. And now this. It reflects everything I have achieved in the game which makes me feel very proud."

Clarke became the oldest Open Champion since Roberto de Vicenzo triumphed at Royal Liverpool in 1967 and his victory sparked yet another celebratory party across Northern Ireland just a month after Rory McIlroy became the youngest US Open winner since 1933 and a year after Graeme McDowell's triumph in the same event.

Clarke's success also extended The European Tour's winning streak in the Major Championships to an unprecedented six in a row following McDowell (2010 US Open), Louis Oosthuizen (2010 Open), Martin Kaymer (2010 US PGA), Charl Schwartzel (2011 Masters) and McIlroy (2011 US Open).

Not that Clarke has been a stranger to setting records. In1999 at the European Open he became the first player to shoot 60 for a second time, having achieved it first in the 1992 Monte Carlo Open. In 2001 he became the first Irishman to win on home soil since John O'Leary in 1982, when he captured The European Open at The K Club.

In 2002 he became the first player to win the English Open three times and in 2003 became the first player, apart from Tiger Woods, to capture more than one World Golf Championship title when he won the WGC–NEC Invitational to add to his triumph in the 2000 WGC–Accenture Match Play.

A dedicated worker for charity, he set up the Darren Clarke Foundation, which not only helps further the development of junior golf in Ireland, but now also raises money for Breast Cancer Awareness in memory of his wife Heather who died in 2006.

Twenty two year old McIlroy was recognised six months after producing one of golf's greatest performances when winning the US Open Championship at Congressional Country Club by eight shots with a tournament record score of 16 under par 268.

McIlroy's triumphant win was all the more remarkable coming, as it did, just two months after starting the final round with a four shot lead he shot 80 and finished tied 15th.

"I am delighted to be named in the Queen's New Year Honours list," he said. "It is quite humbling to be included in such a list of worthy recipients. Many people on the Honours list have made huge personal sacrifices and contributed significantly to society during their lives. I feel very fortunate to be in their company."

The US Open triumph was the highlight of a superb 2011 European Tour season for McIlroy who pushed Luke Donald all the way in the Race to Dubai.

The Northern Irishman was in truly stunning form at the end of the year, finishing in the top four in four consecutive tournaments – the Omega European Masters, the KLM Open, the Alfred Dunhill Links Championship and the WGC–HSBC Championship before claiming victory in the season's penultimate event, the UBS Hong Kong Open.

Although his 11th place finish was not enough to stop Donald winning the Race and finishing Number One. It did, however, emphasise McIlroy's position as one of the most exciting golfing talents.

In a glittering amateur career, McIlroy topped the World Amateur Rankings and in 2005 became the youngest winner of the prestigious West of Ireland and Irish Closed Championship.

Like many top golfers, McIlroy is involved in charitable work and this year took up a position as UNICEF Ireland Ambassador, with his first visit being to Haiti to oversee the work being done to help the country after the devastating earthquake in January 2010.

PART I

The Major Championships

The Open Championship

Darren Clarke triumphs at Royal St George's

Forty-year-old is latest Ulsterman to win a major title

Not since Roberto de Vicenzo held the Claret Jug aloft at Hoylake in 1967 at the age of 44 had an older or, perhaps, wiser golfer won The Open Championship. For Darren Clarke, at the age of 42 years, 11 months and three days, victory at Royal St George's provided a fitting validation for a career tempered by both triumph and tragedy. It was a welcome accomplishment for a golfer from Dungannon in Northern Ireland, steeped in the nuances of the linksland, who knew how to ride the wind to victory.

Darren Clarke

In what was his 54th attempt to win a major championship – not only that, it was his 20th start in The Open itself – Clarke finally found the right mixture of desire and serenity required to accommodate the purity of the ball striking skills which have always been part and parcel of his game. Five years on from the death of his wife, Heather, who lost a battle with breast cancer, Clarke paid a moving tribute to his late partner.

As the third golfer from Ulster to win a major championship in the space of just 13 months – he followed in the footsteps of compatriots Graeme McDowell and Rory McIlroy – Clarke's success naturally struck a particular chord at home in Ireland. But as an ordinary guy, who enjoys a pint, smokes and relishes a hearty dinner, Clarke's victory was also a triumph for those who enjoy the good life.

Embraced by the galleries as well as admired by his peers – even the absent Tiger Woods sent a text message of support – the people's champion played superbly from first to last to become the first British winner of The Open since Paul Lawrie in 1999 at Carnoustie. Thanks to a closing round of 70 for the five under par total of 275, Clarke won by three strokes from Phil Mickelson and Dustin Johnson. Thomas Bjørn was a shot further back on one under par. One of the most popular winners of The Open since Seve Ballesteros, Clarke's victory speech was as measured as his golf. "I've been writing this speech for 20 years now and it's been a long bumpy road," he said. "I've had good and bad things happen to me on the way. Sometimes I was good, sometimes I was bad but I have had so much support from everyone."

While Clarke eased into position after the first round with a solid 68, and an Englishman, as expected, shared top billing, the pacesetter wasn't one of the usual suspects. With Luke Donald, the world No 1, and Lee Westwood, the No 2, featuring in the top half of the draw which faced stronger winds, it was left to the amateur, Tom Lewis, 20, to make hay in the more benign conditions which prevailed in the afternoon.

A past winner at Royal St George's, he won the British Boys' title at Sandwich in 2009, as well as at the Old Course, where he lifted the St Andrews Trophy earlier in the summer, Lewis became the first amateur since Sir Michael Bonallack at Carnoustie in 1968 to lead The Open. Moreover, his opening salvo of 65 was the lowest score yet recorded by an amateur in the ancient championship, bettering by a stroke the 66s returned by Frank Stranahan in 1950, Tiger Woods in 1996 and Justin Rose in 1998.

Those who enjoyed the best of the weather on Thursday afternoon were blessed with even finer overhead conditions on Friday morning. In spite of decent weather, a number of the elite failed to live up to expectations as Donald, who dropped four strokes over the closing four holes, Westwood, Padraig Harrington, Matt Kuchar and Graeme McDowell were among the golfers who left Sandwich early on Friday evening. It was the first time since the world rankings began in 1986 that the world No 1 and No 2 had both missed the cut at the same major.

If the first round was a celebration of youth, day two placed the spotlight on age and experience as Lewis fell back with 74. Although the challenge appeared fairly straightforward, a number of awkward pin positions meant the scoring was higher than expected. Clarke added another 68 to lead on four under while Miguel Angel Jiménez, 47, Bjørn, 40, Tom Lehman, 52, and Davis Love III, 47, all featured in the top seven after 36 holes. Patience is usually a virtue on the British linksland and it was mostly the old heads who worked out how to get the job done in the second round. Even Watson, 61, eased into the weekend action on two over par, thanks in part, to a thrilling ace on the 178 yard sixth hole which bounced once before leaping into the hole and prompting a huge ovation from the galleries surrounding the green.

Not always the most even tempered of men, it was to Clarke's credit he didn't allow a double bogey 6 at the fourth to upset his mood. Instead he held firm, fired five birdies, including a fine 3 at the last, thanks to some astute putting. Clarke had consulted Dr Bob Rotella, the American sports psychologist, on the practice putting green on Wednesday night, and felt the great man's words of wisdom were useful.

Sharing top billing with Clarke was Lucas Glover, the former US Open champion, who followed up an opening 66 with a tidy round of level par, offsetting two bogeys with two birdies. The American's facial hair prompted almost as much discussion as his golf when it emerged that no bearded golfer had lifted the Claret Jug since Bob Ferguson in 1882. Meanwhile Mickelson, on one under, said he was looking forward to the forecasted bad weather.

That was just as well, since conditions on Saturday morning were a pungent combination of wind, rain and cold. No one who teed off early made a move up the leaderboard and it took a consummate performance from Tom Watson, arguably the greatest links golfer of modern times, to post 72. At that stage, the notional par was at least 74. The worth of that brilliant round of golf, however, was devalued in late afternoon when the fire from the St George's dragon cooled. The wind eased, the rain departed and the leaders completed their third rounds under blue skies with only the relics of abandoned broken umbrellas left to serve as a reminder of the brutality of the earlier challenge. By the time the day was done, Watson trailed the leader by nine strokes.

Opening with a birdie when those who preceded him were more than relieved to make par, Clarke knew the golfing gods had smiled on him. Even so, he needed to strike the ball beautifully to shoot 69 and might have been more than a stroke in front going into the last day if he'd holed out better. In full command of the links repertoire of fades and draws, low runners and abbreviated follow-throughs, Clarke was masterly.

Hot on his heels were a brace of young Americans who first made their mark on the British linksland as part of the winning US Walker Cup side at Royal County Down in 2007. Johnson, 27, notched six birdies in a fine round of 68 to earn a spot alongside Clarke in Sunday's last group. Even more impressive was Rickie Fowler, who eclipsed McIlroy's performance by six strokes. Showing a sound grasp of technique and imagination, the 22-year-old from California also brought the steely resolve to St George's which made him one of the more impressive members of the 2010 US Ryder Cup side at Celtic Manor.

Sunday's weather remained windy, though drier conditions meant a good score was possible. The silver medal for leading amateur was won by Lewis, beating the American Peter Uihlein by three strokes. His winning margin might have been even more emphatic but for a triple bogey 8 at the 14th.

In pole position, the challenge facing Clarke was to hold steady and avoid mistakes. The rest needed to take a run at the leader and it was pushing a foot on the accelerator which eventually undid the hopes of the eventual runners-up, Mickelson and Johnson. The left hander made a blazing start to his round, reaching the turn in 30 and adding another birdie on the tenth to reach six under par. His thrilling pursuit of Clarke stalled, however, when he missed from a couple of feet on the 11th for par. "Just a stupid mistake," he rued later.

Johnson, who was on a roll after birdies at the tenth and 12th, also made a costly error on the par 5 14th when he carved a 2 iron for his second shot out of bounds. By the time he'd tapped in for a double bogey 7, Johnson, like Mickelson before him, had made life a little easier for Clarke.

Earlier in the round, the champion golfer holed a testing 15 foot putt for par on the first, reined in Mickelson with an eagle putt from 25 feet on the seventh and twice skipped over bunkers. When the American was shedding strokes on the back nine, Clarke was a rock, reeling off nine consecutive pars. His grip on the Claret Jug was so firm he could eventually afford to make bogeys at both the 17th and 18th holes and still win by three shots from the nearest challengers.

Although half-a-dozen of the men who finished in the top ten at Sandwich were American, this was the sixth consecutive major won by a member of the European Tour. Amazingly, three of those champions were from Northern Ireland, two from South Africa and one from Germany. As McIlory mischievously tweeted: "Northern Ireland ... golf capital of the world."

First Round	Second Round	Third Round	Fourth Round
−5 Thomas Bjørn	−4 Darren Clarke	−5 Darren Clarke	−5 Darren Clarke
−5 Tom Lewis	−4 Lucas Glover	−4 Dustin Johnson	−2 Phil Mickelson
−4 Miguel Angel	−3 Chad Campbell	−2 Thomas Bjørn	−2 Dustin Johnson
Jiménez	−3 Martin Kaymer	−2 Rickie Fowler	−1 Thomas Bjørn
−4 Lucas Glover	−3 Thomas Bjørn	−1 Lucas Glover	= Rickie Fowler
−4 Webb Simpson	3 Miguel Angel	−1 Miguel Angel	= Chad Campbell
−2 Simon Dyson	Jiménez	Jiménez	= Anthony Kim
−2 Darren Clarke	−2 Pablo Larrazabal	= Martin Kaymer	+1 Raphael Jacquelin
−2 Graeme McDowell	−2 Charl Schwartzel	= David Love III	+2 Sergio García
−2 Kyle Stanley	−2 Davis Love III	= Anders Hansen	+2 Davis Love III
−2 Martin Kaymer	−2 Tom Lehman	= Phil Mickelson	+2 Simon Dyson

The Open Championship (140th) *Royal St George's*   July 14–17   [7204–70]

Total Prize Money: £5 million. Entries: 1,955. 16 Regional Qualifying Courses: Abridge, Berwick-upon-Tweed (Goswick), Bruntsfield Links, Buckinghamshire, Clitheroe, Coventry, East Sussex National, Enville, Ferndown, Gog Magog, Hankley Common, Lindrick, Mere, Pannal, Royal Dublin and The London.

International Final Qualifying:

Africa (Royal Johannesburg & Kensington)
Jan 19–20

Floris De Vries (NED)	64-68—132
Neil Schietekat (RSA)	70-66—136
Martin Maritz (RSA)	69-67—136

America (Gleneagles, Plano, TX)   May 23
Reduced to one round due to bad weather

Brian Davis (ENG)	64
Chad Campbell (USA)	65
Nathan Green (AUS)	66
Davis Love III (USA)	66
Spencer Levin (USA)	66
Chris Tidland (USA)	66
Bob Estes (USA)	66
Jerry Kelly (USA)	67

Asia (Amata Spring, Thailand)   Feb 24–25

Prom Meesawat (THA)	67-65—132
Tetsuji Hiratsuka (JPN)	70-64—134
Chih-Bing Lam (SIN)	68-67—135
Jason Zon (USA)	69-67—136

Australasia (Kingston Heath)   Jan 11

Matthew Millar (AUS)	66-68—134
Kurt Barnes (AUS)	66-69—135
Rick Kulacz (AUS)	70-66—136

Europe (Sunningdale, England)   June 6

Graeme Storm (ENG)	65-62—127
Alexander Noren (SWE)	66-64—130
Gary Boyd (ENG)	65-66—131
Thomas Levet (FRA)	65-66—131
Peter Whiteford (SCO)	67-64—131
Alejandro Canizares (ESP)	67-65—132
Kenneth Ferrie (ENG)	68-64—132
Gregory Bourdy (FRA)	67-65—132
Richard McEvoy (ENG)	64-68—132
George Coetzee (RSA)	68-65—133

Local Final Qualifying:

Littlestone

Andy Smith (Tudor Park)	70-68—138
Markus Brier (AUT)	69-70—139
Lee Corfield (Burnham & Berrow)	70-69—139

Prince's

Simon Edwards (Windermere)	68-69—137
Thomas Shadbolt (Brocket Hall)	66-73—139
Francis McGuirk (Prince's)	68-71—139

Royal Cinque Ports

Craig Hinton (The Oxfordshire) (am)	69-70—139
Andrew Johnston (North Middlesex)	66-74—140
Simon Lilly (Wellingborough)	70-70—140

Rye

Tom Lewis (Welwyn Garden City) (am)	63-65—128
Adam Wootton (Oxford Golf Centre)	63-68—131
Mark Laskey (The Shire London)	65-68—133

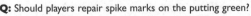

What is the answer?

Q: Should players repair spike marks on the putting green?

A: On completion of the hole by all the players in the group, spike marks should be repaired. The repair of spike marks, hole plugs, ball marks and other damage prior to completion of the hole is not allowed if it might assist in the playing of the hole.

The final field of 156 players included six amateurs. 71 players (including two amateurs) qualified for the last two rounds with scores of 146 or less.

1	Darren Clarke (NIR)	68-68-69-70—275	€999,540
2	Dustin Johnson (USA)	70-68-68-72—278	474,782
	Phil Mickelson (USA)	70-69-71-68—278	474,782
4	Thomas Bjørn (DEN)	65-72-71-71—279	288,756
5	Chad Campbell (USA)	69-68-74-69—280	201,759
	Rickie Fowler (USA)	70-70-68-72—280	201,759
	Anthony Kim (USA)	72-68-70-70—280	201,759
8	Raphaël Jacquelin (FRA)	74-67-71-69—281	144,378
9	Simon Dyson (ENG)	68-72-72-70—282	115,873
	Sergio García (ESP)	70-70-74-68—282	115,873
	Davis Love III (USA)	70-68-72-72—282	115,873
12	Lucas Glover (USA)	66-70-73-74—283	86,997
	Kaymer (GER)	68-69-73-73—283	86,997
	Steve Stricker (USA)	69-71-72-71—283	86,997
15	George Coetzee (RSA)	69-69-72-74—284	75,521
	Richard Green (AUS)	70-71-73-71—285	62,194
	Fredrik Jacobson (SWE)	70-70-73-72—285	62,194
	Zach Johnson (USA)	72-68-71-74—285	62,194
	Charl Schwartzel (RSA)	71-67-75-72—285	62,194
	Webb Simpson (USA)	66-74-72-73—285	62,194
16	Y E Yang (KOR)	71-69-73-72—285	62,194
22	Anders Hansen (DEN)	69-69-72-76—286	49,607
	Tom Lehman (USA)	71-67-73-75—286	49,607
	Tom Watson (USA)	72-70-72-72—286	49,607
25	Miguel Angel Jiménez (ESP)	66-71-72-78—287	43,313
	Rory McIlroy (NIR)	71-69-74-73—287	43,313
	Adam Scott (AUS)	69-70-73-75—287	43,313
28	Charles Howell III (USA)	71-70-73-74—288	39,149
	Ryan Moore (USA)	69-74-76-69—288	39,149
30	Stewart Cink (USA)	70-71-77-71—289	32,445
	Jason Day (AUS)	71-70-76-72—289	32,445
	Pablo Larrazábal (ESP)	68-70-76-75—289	32,445
	Tom Lewis (ENG) (am)	65-74-76-74—289	Silver Medal
	Seung-yul Noh (KOR)	69-72-75-73—289	32,445
	Ryan Palmer (USA)	68-71-72-78—289	32,445
	Bubba Watson (USA)	69-72-74-74—289	32,445
	Gary Woodland (USA)	75-68-74-72—289	32,445
38	Gary Boyd (ENG)	71-70-76-73—290	24,988
	Yuta Ikeda (JPN)	69-71-75-75—290	24,988
	Trevor Immelman (RSA)	70-72-72-76—290	24,988
	Simon Khan (ENG)	71-72-77-70—290	24,988
	Jeff Overton (USA)	68-71-78-73—290	24,988
	Robert Rock (ENG)	69-71-74-76—290	24,988
44	K J Choi (KOR)	71-72-75-73—291	19,644
	Spencer Levin (USA)	72-69-81-69—291	19,644
	Justin Rose (ENG)	72-70-79-70—291	19,644
	Kyle Stanley (USA)	68-72-77-74—291	19,644
48	Robert Allenby (AUS)	69-72-75-76—292	16,215
	Grégory Bourdy (FRA)	73-70-77-72—292	16,215
	Floris De Vries (NED)	70-73-76-73—292	16,215
	Jim Furyk (USA)	72-70-76-74—292	16,215
	Richard McEvoy (ENG)	69-72-75-76—292	16,215
	Peter Uihlein (USA) (am)	71-71-75-75—292	
54	Paul Casey (ENG)	74-69-78-72—293	14,771
	Louis Oosthuizen (RSA)	72-70-747-7—293	14,771
	Rory Sabbatini (RSA)	71-70-77-75—293	14,771
57	Fredrik Andersson Hed (SWE)	68-75-77-74—294	14,160
	Ricky Barnes (USA)	68-74-78-74—294	14,160
	Stephen Gallacher (SCO)	70-71-77-76—294	14,160

139th Open Championship *continued*

57T	Bill Haas (USA)	72-70-79-73—294	14,160
	Grégory Havret (FRA)	72-71-78-73—294	14,160
	Bo Van Pelt (USA)	73-69-73-79—294	14,160
63	Joost Luiten (NED)	73-69-79-75—296	13,660
	Matthew Millar (AUS)	71-72-80-73—296	13,660
	Mark Wilson (USA)	74-68-75-79—296	13,660
66	Paul Lawrie (SCO)	73-70-81-73—297	13,383
67	Edoardo Molinari (ITA)	69-74-76-78—297	13,383
	Henrik Stenson (SWE)	72-71-75-80—298	13,216
69	Harrison Frazar (USA)	72-70-77-80—299	13,105
70	Kenneth Ferrie (ENG)	71-71-76-83—301	12,994
71	Jung-gon Hwang (KOR)	68-74-83-79—304	12,883

The following players missed the cut:

72	Thomas Aiken (RSA)	74-70—144	3,887
	Alejandro Cañizares (ESP)	73-71—144	3,887
	Ben Crane (USA)	71-73—144	3,887
	Ross Fisher (ENG)	71-73—144	3,887
	Peter Hanson (SWE)	73-71—144	3,887
	Padraig Harrington (IRL)	73-71—144	3,887
	J B Holmes (USA)	69-75—144	3,887
	Rick Kulacz (AUS)	74-70—144	3,887
	Justin Leonard (USA)	70-74—144	3,887
	Bryden MacPherson (AUS) (am)	71-73—144	
	Hunter Mahan (USA)	75-69—144	3,887
	Sean O'Hair (USA)	73-71—144	3,887
	Graeme Storn (ENG)	70-74—144	3,887
	Lee Westwood (ENG)	71-73—144	3,887
	Danny Willett (ENG)	69-75—144	3,887
87	Matteo Manassero (ITA)	73-72—145	3,165
	Graeme McDowell (NIR)	68-77—145	3,165
	Alexander Noren (SWE)	69-76—145	3,165
	Brandt Snedeker (USA)	75-70—145	3,165
	Camilo Villegas (COL)	71-74—145	3,165
	Nick Watney (USA)	74-71—145	3,165
	Peter Whiteford (SCO)	70-75—145	3,165
94	Angel Cabrera (ARG)	72-74—146	3,165
	John Daly (USA)	72-74—146	3,165
	Luke Donald (ENG)	71-75—146	3,165
	Jason Dufner (USA)	74-72—146	3,165
	Robert Karlsson (SWE)	72-74—146	3,165
	Neil Chietekat (RSA)	73-73—146	3,165
	Kevin Streelman (USA)	76-70—146	3,165
101	Lee Corfield (ENG)	72-75—147	3,165
	Charley Hoffman (USA)	72-75—147	3,165
	Jason Knutzon (USA)	75-72—147	3,165
	Martin Laird (SCO)	72-75—147	3,165
	Martin Maritz (RSA)	73-74—147	3,165
	Prom Meesawat (THA)	72-75—147	3,165
	Geoff Ogilvy (AUS)	74-73—147	3,165
	Thorbjørn Olesen (DEN)	73-74—147	3,165
	Ian Poulter (ENG)	69-78—147	3,165
110	Sang-moon Bae (KOR)	72-76—148	2,888
	Lucas Bjerregaard (DEN) (am)	73-75—148	
	Mark Calcavecchia (USA)	69-79—148	2,888
	Ernie Els (RSA)	72-76—148	2,888

110T	Robert Garrigus (USA)	74-74—148	2,888
	Tetsuji Hiratsuka (JPN)	75-73—148	2,888
	Bernhard Langer (GER)	75-73—148	2,888
	Francesco Molinari (ITA)	73-75—148	2,888
	Tadahiro Taakayama (JPN)	70-78—148	2,888
119	Kurt Barnes (AUS)	68-81—149	2,888
	Jonathan Byrd (USA)	75-74—149	2,888
	Brad Kennedy (AUS)	77-72—149	2,888
	Mark Laskey (WAL)	73-76—149	2,888
	Sandy Lyle (SCO)	73-76—149	2,888
	Kevin Na (KOR)	74-75—149	2,888
125	Aaron Baddeley (AUS)	77-73—150	2,888
	Nathan Green (AUS)	74-76—150	2,888
	Scott Jamieson (SCO)	75-75—150	2,888
	Simon Lilly (ENG)	74-76—150	2,888
	Steve Marino (USA)	74-76—150	2,888
	Tom Shadbolt (ENG)	74-76—150	2,888
	Chris Tidland (USA)	77-73—150	2,888
132	Ben Curtis (USA)	77-74—151	2,610
	Brian Davis (ENG)	75-76—151	2,610
	Hiroyuki Fujita (JPN)	75-76—151	2,610
	Thongchai Jaidee (THA)	75-76—151	2,610
	Matt Kuchar (USA)	74-77—151	2,610
	Chih-bing Lam (SIN)	76-75—151	2,610
138	Bob Estes (USA)	74-78—152	2,610
	Kyung-tae Kim (KOR)	75-77—152	2,610
	Mark O'Meara (USA)	76-76—152	2,610
141	Rhys Davies (WAL)	75-78—153	2,610
	Andrew Johnston (ENG)	74-79—153	2,610
	Jerry Kelly (USA)	74-79—153	2,610
	Prayad Marksaeng (THA)	76-77—153	2,610
	Francis G McGuirk (ENG)	77-76—153	2,610
	Adam Wootton (ENG)	71-82—153	2,610
147	Ryo Ishikawa (JPN)	74-80—154	2,610
	Alvaro Quiros (ESP)	75-79—154	2,610
	Andy Smith (ENG)	81-73—154	2,610
150	David Duval (USA)	78-77—155	2,610
	Hiroo Kawai (JPN)	75-80—155	2,610
152	Todd Hamilton (USA)	77-79—156	2,610
153	Markus Brier (AUT)	77-80—157	2,610
154	Simon Edwards (WAL)	82-79—161	2,610
155	Craig Hinton (ENG) (am)	82-87—169	
156	Retief Goosen (RSA)	76 RTD	

2010 Open Championship *Old Course, St Andrews* July 15–18 [7305–72]

Total Prize Money: £4.8 million. Entries: 2,500. 16 Regional Qualifying Courses: Abridge, Berwick upon Tweed (Goswick), Clitheroe, County Louth, Coventry, East Sussex National, Effingham, Enville, Ferndown, Gog Magog, Lindrick, Mere, Musselburgh, Old Fold Manor, Pannal, The London. Final field: 156 (7 amateurs) of whom 77 (1 amateur) made the half-way cut with scores of 146 or less.

1	Louis Oosthuizen (RSA)	65-67-69-71—272	£1,011,840	14T	Dustin Johnson (USA)	69-72-69-74—284	68,076
2	Lee Westwood (ENG)	67-71-71-70—279	595,200		Robert Karlsson (SWE)	69-71-72-72—284	68,076
3	Paul Casey (ENG)	69-69-67-75—280	305,536		Tom Lehman (USA)	71-68-75-70—284	68,076
	Rory McIlroy (NIR)	63-80-69-68—280	305,536		Charl Schwartzel (RSA)	71-75-68-70—284	68,076
	Henrik Stenson (SWE)	68-74-67-71—280	305,536	23	Stephen Gallacher (SCO)	71-73-70-71—285	49,996
6	Retief Goosen (RSA)	69-70-72-70—281	208,320		Trevor Immelman (RSA)	68-74-75-68—285	49,996
7	Martin Kaymer (GER)	69-71-68-74—282	144,336		Graeme McDowell (NIR)	71-68-76-70—285	49,996
	Sean O'Hair (USA)	67-72-72-71—282	144,336		Tiger Woods (USA)	67-73-73-72—285	49,996
	Robert Rock (ENG)	68-78-67-69—282	144,336	27	Alejandro Cañizares (ESP)	67-71-71-77—286	37,200
	Nick Watney (USA)	67-73-71-71—282	144,336		Bradley Dredge (WAL)	66-76-74-70—286	37,200
11	Luke Donald (ENG)	73-72-69-69—283	97,216		Ryo Ishikawa (JPN)	68-73-75-70—286	37,200
	Jeff Overton (USA)	73-69-72-69—283	97,216		Miguel Angel Jiménez	72-67-74-73—286	37,200
	Alvaro Quiros (ESP)	72-70-74-67—283	97,216		(ESP)		
14	Rickie Fowler (USA)	79-67-71-67—284	68,076		Matt Kuchar (USA)	72-74-71-69—286	37,200
	Sergio García (ESP)	71-71-70-72—284	68,076		Edoardo Molinari (ITA)	69-76-73-68—286	37,200
	Ignacio Garrido (ESP)	69-71-73-71—284	68,076		Kevin Na (USA)	70-74-70-72—286	37,200
	J B Holmes (USA)	70-72-70-72—284	68,076		Adam Scott (AUS)	72-70-72-72—286	37,200
	Jin Jeong (KOR) (am)	68-70-74-72—284	Silver Medal		Marcel Siem (GER)	67-75-74-70—286	37,200

Other players who made the cut: Ross Fisher (ENG), Peter Hanson (SWE), Søren Kjeldsen (DEN), Shane Lowry (IRL), Hunter Mahan (USA), Colin Moriarty (IRL), Vijay Singh (FIJ) 287; Ricky Barnes (USA), Darren Clarke (NIR), Bo Van Pelt (USA), Camilo Villegas (COL) 288; Stewart Cink (USA), John Daly (USA), Simon Dyson (ENG), Lucas Glover (USA), Kyung-tae Kim (KOR), Phil Mickelson (USA), John Senden (AUS) 289; Danny Chia (MAS); Simon Khan (ENG), Steve Marino (USA), Zane Scotland (ENG), Steve Stricker (USA) 290; Jason Day (AUS), Marc Leishman (AUS), Tom Pernice Jr (USA), Ian Poulter (ENG), Peter Senior (AUS), Heath Slocum (USA), Toru Taniguchi (JPN), Y E Yang (KOR) 291; Fredrik Andersson Hed (SWE), Hirofumi Miyase (JPN), Colin Montgomerie (SCO), Steven Tiley (ENG) 292; Andrew Coltart (SCO) 293; Mark Calcavecchia (USA) 294; Thomas Aiken (RSA), Richard S Johnson (SWE) 295; Zach Johnson (USA). Scott Verplank (USA) 296

2009 Open Championship *Turnberry* July 16–19 [7173–70]

Total Prize Money: £4.26 million. Entries: 2,418. 16 Regional Qualifying Courses: Abridge, Alwoodley, Berwick-upon-Tweed (Goswick), Coventry, Effingham, Enville, Ferndown, Gog Magog, Lindrick, Mere, Musselburgh, Old Fold Manor, Pleasington, Rochester & Cobham Park, Royal Ashdown Forest, Royal Dublin. Final qualifying courses: Glasgow Gailes, Kilmarnock (Barassie), Western Gailes. Final field: 156 (2 amateurs) of whom 73 (1 amateur) made the half-way cut with scores of 144 or less.

1	Stewart Cink (USA)*	66-72-71-69—278	£750,000	13T	Jeff Overton (USA)	70-69-76-67—282	50,900
2	Tom Watson (USA)	65-70-71-72—278	450,000		Andres Romero (ARG)	68-74-73-67—282	50,900
	*Cink won after a four-hole play-off				Justin Rose (ENG)	69-72-71-70—282	50,900
3	Lee Westwood (ENG)	68-70-70-71—279	255,000		Henrik Stenson (SWE)	71-70-71-70—282	50,900
	Chris Wood (ENG)	70-70-72-67—279	255,000		Camilo Villegas (COL)	66-73-73-70—282	50,900
5	Luke Donald (ENG)	71-72-70-67—280	157,000		Boo Weekley (USA)	67-72-71-72—282	50,900
	Mathew Goggin (AUS)	66-72-69-73—280	157,000	24	Angel Cabrera (ARG)	69-70-72-72—283	36,333
	Retief Goosen (RSA)	67-70-71-72—280	157,000		Peter Hanson (SWE)	70-71-72-70—283	36,333
8	Thomas Aiken (RSA)	71-72-69-69—281	90,400		Oliver Wilson (ENG)	72-70-71-70—283	36,333
	Ernie Els (RSA)	69-72-72-68—281	90,400	27	Mark Calcavecchia (USA)	67-69-77-71—284	29,357
	Søren Hansen (DEN)	68-72-74-67—281	90,400		John Daly (USA)	68-72-72-72—284	29,357
	Richard S Johnson (SWE)	70-72-69-70—281	90,400		James Kingston (RSA)	67-71-74-72—284	29,357
	Justin Leonard (USA)	70-70-73-68—281	90,400		Søren Kjeldsen (DEN)	68-76-71-69—284	29,357
13	Ross Fisher (ENG)	69-68-70-75—282	50,900		Kenichi Kuboya (JPN)	65-72-75-72—284	29,357
	Thongchai Jaidee (THA)	72-69-72-69—282	50,900		Davis Love III (USA)	69-73-73-69—284	29,357
	Miguel Angel Jiménez	64-73-76-69—282	50,900		Nick Watney (USA)	71-72-71-70—284	29,357
	(ESP)			34	Jim Furyk (USA)	67-72-70-76—285	23,500
	Matteo Manassero (ITA) (am)	71-70-72-69—282	Silver Medal		Martin Kaymer (GER)	69-70-74-72—285	23,500
					Graeme McDowell (NIR)	68-73-71-73—285	23,500
	Francesco Molinari (ITA)	71-70-71-70—282	50,900		Richard Sterne (RSA)	67-73-75-70—285	23,500

2009 Open Championship *continued*

Other players who made the cut: Nick Dougherty (ENG), Sergio García (ESP), Thomas Levet (FRA), Steve Marino (USA), Vijay Singh (FIJ) 286; Branden Grace (RSA), Paul McGinley (IRL), Bryce Molder (USA), Anthony Wall (ENG) 287; Paul Casey (ENG), Gonzalo Fernandez-Castaño (ESP), Zach Johnson (USA), Paul Lawrie (SCO), Rory McIlroy (NIR) 288; Robert Allenby (AUS), Darren Clarke (NIR), Johan Edfors (SWE), David Howell (ENG), Billy Mayfair (USA), Kenny Perry (USA), Graeme Storm (ENG), Steve Stricker (USA) 289; Paul Broadhurst (ENG), David Drysdale (SCO), Tom Lehman (USA), Kevin Sutherland (USA) 290; Ryuji Imada (JPN) 291; Fredrik Andersson Hed (SWE), Stuart Appleby (AUS), Padraig Harrington (IRL), Sean O'Hair (USA) 292; J B Holmes (USA) 293; Fredrik Jacobson (SWE), Mark O'Meara (USA) 295; Paul Goydos (USA) 303; Daniel Gaunt (AUS) 304

2008 Open Championship *Royal Birkdale* July 17–20   [7173–70]

Total Prize Money: £4.26 million. Entries: 2,418. 16 Regional Qualifying Courses: Abridge, Alwoodley, Berwick-upon-Tweed (Goswick), Coventry, Effingham, Enville, Ferndown, Gog Magog, Lindrick, Mere, Musselburgh, Old Fold Manor, Pleasington, Rochester & Cobham Park, Royal Ashdown Forest, Royal Dublin. Final qualifying courses: Hillside, Southport & Ainsdale, West Lancashire. Final field: 156 (5 amateurs) of whom 83 (2 amateurs) made the half-way cut with scores of 149 or less.

1	Padraig Harrington (IRL)	74-68-72-69—283	£750,000		19T	Grégory Havret (FRA)	71-75-77-71—294	37,770
2	Ian Poulter (ENG)	72-71-75-69—287	450,000			Trevor Immelman (RSA)	74-74-73-73—294	37,770
3	Greg Norman (AUS)	70-70-72-77—289	255,000			Fredrik Jacobson (SWE)	71-72-79-72—294	37,770
	Henrik Stenson (SWE)	76-72-70-71—289	255,000			Davis Love III (USA)	75-74-70-75—294	37,770
5	Jim Furyk (USA)	71-71-77-71—290	180,000			Graeme McDowell (NIR)	69-73-80-72—294	37,770
	Chris Wood (ENG) (am)	75-70-73-72—290	Silver			Rocco Mediate (USA)	69-73-76-76—294	37,770
			Medal			Phil Mickelson (USA)	79-68-76-71—294	37,770
7	Robert Allenby (AUS)	69-73-76-74—292	96,944			Alexander Noren (SWE)	72-70-75-77—294	37,770
	Stephen Ames (CAN)	73-70-78-71—292	96,944			Thomas Sherreard	77-69-76-72—294	
	Paul Casey (ENG)	78-71-73-70—292	96,944			(ENG) (am)		
	Ben Curtis (USA)	78-69-70-75—292	96,944			Jean Van de Velde (FRA)	73-71-80-70—294	37,770
	Ernie Els (RSA)	80-69-74-69—292	96,944			Simon Wakefield (ENG)	71-74-70-79—294	37,770
	David Howell (ENG)	76-71-78-67—292	96,944			Paul Waring (ENG)	73-74-76-71—294	37,770
	Robert Karlsson (SWE)	75-73-75-69—292	96,944		32	Retief Goosen (RSA)	71-75-73-76—295	25,035
	Anthony Kim (USA)	72-74-71-75—292	96,944			Richard Green (AUS)	76-72-76-71—295	25,035
	Steve Stricker (USA)	77-71-71-73—292	96,944			Todd Hamilton (USA)	74-74-72-75—295	25,035
16	K J Choi (KOR)	72-67-75-79—293	53,166			Tom Lehman (USA)	74-73-73-75—295	25,035
	Justin Leonard (USA)	77-70-73-73—293	53,166			Nick O'Hern (AUS)	74-75-74-72—295	25,035
	Adam Scott (AUS)	70-74-77-72—293	53,166			Andres Romero (ARG)	77-72-74-72—295	25,035
19	Anders Hansen (DEN)	78-68-74-74—294	37,770			Heath Slocum (USA)	73-76-74-72—295	25,035

Other players who made the cut: Thomas Aiken (RSA), Woody Austin (USA), Grégory Bourdy (FRA), Bart Bryant (USA), Ariel Canete (ARG), David Duval (USA), Ross Fisher (ENG), Simon Khan (ENG), Graeme Storm (ENG), Camilo Villegas (COL), Mike Weir (CAN), Jay Williamson (USA) 296; Stuart Appleby (AUS), Michael Campbell (NZL), David Frost (RSA), Sergio García (ESP), Zach Johnson (USA), Doug Labelle II (USA), Anthony Wall (ENG) 297; Richard Finch (ENG), Tom Gillis (USA), Peter Hanson (SWE), Colin Montgomerie (SCO), Kevin Stadler (USA), Scott Verplank (USA) 298; Søren Hansen (DEN), Wen Chong Liang (CHN), Jonathan Lomas (ENG) 299; Jean-Baptiste Gonnet (FRA), David Horsey (ENG), Lee Westwood (ENG) 300; Brendan Jones (AUS), Pablo Larrazabal (ESP), Jose-Filipe Lima (POR), Jeff Overton (USA), Craig Parry (AUS), John Rollins (USA), Justin Rose (ENG), Martin Wiegele (AUT) 301; Nick Dougherty (ENG), Lucas Glover (USA) 302; Martin Kaymer (GER) 303; Philip Archer (ENG) 304; Sean O'Hair (USA) 306; Chih Bing Lam (SIN) 311

At Royal St George's Tom Lewis impressed the man he was named after!

If the events at Royal St George's during the 140th Open Championship hadn't delivered enough of a fairytale story, it soon emerged that amateur and Silver Medal winner Tom Lewis, who was playing with Tom Watson, was named by his father, a teaching professional who idolised the veteran American, after the five time winner of the championship. "And my brother is Jack, so you can imagine who that was after," Tom smiled.

Watson, who played with and was full of praise for teenager Matteo Manassero during the 2009 Open at Turnberry, was just as impressed in Kent by Lewis whose coach Peter Cowen also works with Thomas Björn. Watson would have been even more impressed later in the year when Lewis was in the winning Walker Cup side against America and, in only his third European event as a professional, won the Portugal Masters.

2007 Open Championship Carnoustie July 19–22 [7421–71]

Total Prize Money: £4.2 million. Entries: 2,443. 16 Regional Qualifying Courses: Ashridge, Effingham, Enville, Gog Magog, Minchinhampton, Musselburgh, Notts, Old Fold Manor, Pannal, Pleasington, Prestbury, Rochester & Cobham Park, Royal Ashdown Forest, Royal Dublin, Silloth-on-Solway, Trentham. Final qualifying courses: Downfield, Monifieth, Montrose, Panmure. Final field: 156 (6 amateurs) of whom 70 (1 amateur) made the half-way cut with scores of 146 or less.

| 1 | Padraig Harrington (IRL)* | 69-73-68-67—277 | £750,000 |
| 2 | Sergio García (ESP) | 65-71-68-73—277 | 450,000 |

Four-hole play-off – Harrington 3-3-4-5; García 5-3-4-4

3	Andres Romero (ARG)	71-70-70-67—278	290,000
4	Ernie Els (RSA)	72-70-68-69—279	200,000
	Richard Green (AUS)	72-73-70-64—279	200,000
6	Stewart Cink (USA)	69-73-68-70—280	145,500
	Hunter Mahan (USA)	73-73-69-65—280	145,500
8	K J Choi (KOR)	69-69-72-71—281	94,750
	Ben Curtis (USA)	72-74-70-65—281	94,750
	Steve Stricker (USA)	71-72-64-74—281	94,750
	Mike Weir (CAN)	71-68-72-70—281	94,750
12	Markus Brier (AUT)	68-75-70-69—282	58,571
	Paul Broadhurst ENG)	71-71-68-72—282	58,571
	Telle Edberg (SWE)	72-73-67-70—282	58,571
	Jim Furyk (USA)	70-70-71-71—282	58,571
	Miguel Angel Jiménez (ESP)	69-70-72-71—282	58,571
	Justin Rose (ENG)	75-70-67-70—282	58,571
	Tiger Woods (USA)	69-74-69-70—282	58,571
19	Paul McGinley (IRL)	67-75-68-73—283	46,000
20	Rich Beem (USA)	70-73-69-72—284	42,000

20T	Zach Johnson (USA)	73-73-68-70—284	42,000
	Pat Perez (USA)	73-70-71-70—284	42,000
23	Jonathan Byrd (USA)	73-72-70-70—285	35,562
	Mark Calcavecchia (USA)	74-70-72-69—285	35,562
	Chris DiMarco (USA)	74-70-66-75—285	35,562
	Retief Goosen (RSA)	70-71-73-71—285	35,562
27	Paul Casey (ENG)	72-73-69-72—286	28,178
	Lucas Glover (USA)	71-72-70-73—286	28,178
	J J Henry (USA)	70-71-71-74—286	28,178
	Rodney Pampling (AUS)	70-72-72-72—286	28,178
	Ian Poulter (ENG)	73-73-70-70—286	28,178
	Adam Scott (AUS)	73-70-72-71—286	28,178
	Vijay Singh (FIJ)	72-71-68-75—286	28,178
34	Angel Cabrera (ARG)	68-73-72-74—287	24,000
35	Niclas Fasth (SWE)	75-69-73-71—288	20,107
	Mark Foster (ENG)	76-70-73-69—288	20,107
	Charley Hoffman (USA)	75-69-72-72—288	20,107
	Shaun Micheel (USA)	70-76-70-72—288	20,107
	Nick Watney (USA)	72-71-70-75—288	20,107
	Boo Weekley (USA)	68-72-75-73—288	20,107
	Lee Westwood (ENG)	71-70-73-74—288	20,107

Other players who made the cut: Nick Dougherty (ENG), Rory McIlroy (NIR) (am) (Silver Medal), Ryan Moore (USA) 289; Ross Bain (SCO), Arron Oberholser (USA), Carl Pettersson (SWE), John Senden (AUS) 290; Jerry Kelly (USA), Won Joon Lee (KOR) 291; Tom Lehman (USA), Kevin Stadler (USA) 293; Thomas Bjørn (DEN), Grégory Bourdy (FRA), Brian Davis (ENG), David Howell (ENG) 294; Michael Campbell (NZL), Anders Hansen (DEN), Scott Verplank (USA) 295; Trevor Immelman (RSA), Mark O'Meara (USA), Toru Taniguchi (JPN) 296; John Bevan (ENG), Luke Donald (ENG) 297; Raphaël Jacquelin (FRA), Sandy Lyle (SCO) 298; Alastair Forsyth (SCO), Sean O'Hair (USA) 299; Fredrik Andersson Hed (SWE), Peter Hanson (SWE) 300

2011 Open Championship – rulings of the day – Thursday

A total of 96 rulings were given during the first round of the 2011 Open Championship at Royal St George's. Many of these involved relief from the grandstands and television structures which are temporarily situated on the links to facilitate the Championship.

One of the more unusual situations of the day arose on the 18th hole when Phil Mickelson's ball came to rest against a chocolate bar wrapper as he was finishing his first round. Anything artificial, such as the wrapper, is by definition an obstruction. If the item may be moved without unreasonable effort, without undue delay and without causing any damage, it is considered to be a movable obstruction and it may be removed.

Mickelson was therefore entitled to remove the wrapper. The complication was that in moving the wrapper it was likely that his ball would move. Rule 24-1 states that if the ball moves when removing a movable obstruction, the ball must be replaced and there is no penalty provided the movement of the ball was directly attributable to the removal of the obstruction.

Anticipating that the ball might move, the referee asked Mickelson to mark the position of the ball. Rule 24-1a does not require the player to mark the position of the ball but it is considered good practice to do so because if the ball does move, the player can be certain that the ball is returned to its original position. The ball did in fact roll away when the wrapper was removed, so Mickelson was required to replace his ball without penalty.

Mickelson attempted to replace the ball on the spot from which it moved, but was unsuccessful as the ball would not come to rest on that spot. Rule 20-3d covers the situation when a ball that is to be replaced will not come to rest: there is no penalty and the ball must be replaced again. If the ball still fails to come to rest, then if the ball was not in a hazard (i.e. a bunker or water hazard) the player must place it at the nearest spot where it will come to rest, that is not nearer the hole and not in a hazard.

Mickelson tried to replace the ball for a second time but again the ball moved. He was therefore required to place the ball at the nearest spot where it would come to rest. Mickelson went on to chip over the greenside bunker and sink his putt for a par 4 and a level par round of 70.

2006 Open Championship Royal Liverpool, Hoylake July 20–23   [7528–72]

Total Prize Money: £3,898,000. Entries: 2,434. 16 Regional Qualifying Courses: Ashridge, County Louth, Effingham, Little Aston, Minchinhampton, Musselburgh, Notts, Old Fold Manor, Orsett, Pannal, Pleasington, Prestbury, Rochester & Cobham Park, Royal Ashdown Forest, Silloth-on-Solway, Trentham. Final qualifying courses: Conwy, Formby, Wallasey, West Lancashire. Final field: 156 (4 amateurs) of whom 71 (2 amateurs) made the half-way cut on 143 or less.

1	Tiger Woods (USA)	67-65-71-67—270	£720,000	16T	Brett Rumford (AUS)	68-71-72-71—282	45,000
2	Chris DiMarco (USA)	70-65-69-68—272	430,000	22	Mark Hensby (AUS)	68-72-74-69—283	35,375
3	Ernie Els (RSA)	68-65-71-71—275	275,000		Phil Mickelson (USA)	69-71-73-70—283	35,375
4	Jim Furyk (USA)	68-71-66-71—276	210,000		Greg Owen (ENG)	67-73-68-75—283	35,375
5	Sergio García (ESP)	68-71-65-73—277	159,500		Charl Schwartzel (RSA)	74-66-72-71—283	35,375
	Hideto Tanihara (JPN)	72-68-66-71—277	159,500	26	Paul Broadhurst (ENG)	71-71-73-69—284	29,100
7	Angel Cabrera (ARG)	71-68-66-73—278	128,000		Jerry Kelly (USA)	72-67-69-76—284	29,100
8	Carl Pettersson (SWE)	68-72-70-69—279	95,333		Hunter Mahan (USA)	73-70-68-73—284	29,100
	Andres Romero (ARG)	70-70-68-71—279	95,333		Rory Sabbatini (RSA)	69-70-73-72—284	29,100
	Adam Scott (AUS)	68-69-70-72—279	95,333		Lee Slattery (ENG)	69-72-71-72—284	29,100
11	Ben Crane (USA)	68-71-71-70—280	69,333	31	Simon Khan (ENG)	70-72-68-75—285	24,500
	S K Ho (KOR)	68-73-69-70—280	69,333		Scott Verplank (USA)	70-73-67-75—285	24,500
	Anthony Wall (ENG)	67-73-71-69—280	69,333		Lee Westwood (ENG)	69-72-75-69—285	24,500
14	Retief Goosen (RSA)	70-66-72-73—281	56,500		Thaworn Wiratchant (THA)	71-68-74-72—285	35,591
	Sean O'Hair (USA)	69-73-72-67—281	56,500	35	Michael Campbell (NZL)	70-71-75-70—286	19,625
16	Robert Allenby (AUS)	69-70-69-74—282	45,000		Luke Donald (ENG)	74-68-73-71—286	19,625
	Mikko Ilonen (FIN)	68-69-73-72—282	45,000		Marcus Fraser (AUS)	68-71-72-75—286	19,625
	Peter Lonard (AUS)	71-69-68-74—282	45,000		Robert Karlsson (SWE)	70-71-71-74—286	19,625
	Geoff Ogilvy (AUS)	71-69-70-72—282	45,000		Rod Pampling (AUS)	69-71-74-72—286	19,625
	Robert Rock (ENG)	69-69-73-71—282	45,000		John Senden (AUS)	70-73-73-70—286	19,625

Other players who made the cut: Stephen Ames (CAN), Thomas Bjørn (DEN), Mark Calcavecchia (USA), Miguel Angel Jiménez (ESP), Brandt Jobe (USA), Søren Kjeldsen (DEN), Jeff Sluman (USA) 287; John Bickerton (ENG), Simon Dyson (ENG), Gonzalo Fernandez Castano (ESP), Andrew Marshall (ENG), Henrik Stenson (SWE), Marius Thorp (NOR) (am) (Silver Medal), Tom Watson (USA), Simon Wakefield (ENG) 288; Tim Clark (RSA), David Duval (USA), Keiichiro Fukabori (JPN), José-María Olazábal (ESP), Mike Weir (CAN) 289; Andrew Buckle (AUS), Graeme McDowell (NIR) 290; Mark O'Meara (USA), Marco Ruiz (PAR) 291; Chad Campbell (USA) 292; Fred Funk (USA), Vaughn Taylor (USA) 294; Todd Hamilton (USA), Edoardo Molinari (ITA) (am) 295; Bart Bryant (USA) 296; Paul Casey (ENG) 298

2005 Open Championship St Andrews (Old Course) June 14–17   [7279–72]

Total Prize Money: £3,854,900. Entries: 2,499 (record). 16 Regional Qualifying Courses: Alwoodley, Ashridge, Hadley Wood, Hindhead, The Island, Little Aston, Minchinhampton, Notts, Orsett, Pleasington, Prestbury, Renfrew, Rochester & Final qualifying courses: Ladybank, Leven, Lundin, Scotscraig. Cobham Park, Royal Ashdown Forest, Silloth-on-Solway, Trentham. Final Field: 156 (7 amateurs), of whom 80 (4 amateurs) made the half-way cut on 145 or less.

1	Tiger Woods (USA)	66-67-71-70—274	£720,000	15T	Lloyd Saltman (SCO) (am)	73-71-68-71—283	Silver
2	Colin Montgomerie (SCO)	71-66-70-72—279	430,000				Medal
3	Fred Couples (USA)	68-71-73-68—280	242,500	23	Bart Bryant (USA)	69-70-71-74—284	32,500
	José-María Olazábal (ESP)	68-70-68-74—280	242,500		Tim Clark (RSA)	71-69-70-74—284	32,500
5	Michael Campbell (NZL)	69-72-68-72—281	122,167		Scott Drummond (SCO)	74-71-69-70—284	32,500
	Sergio García (ESP)	70-69-69-73—281	122,167		Brad Faxon (USA)	72-66-70-76—284	32,500
	Retief Goosen (RSA)	68-73-66-74—281	122,167		Nicholas Flanagan (AUS)	73-71-69-71—284	32,500
	Bernhard Langer (GER)	71-69-70-71—281	122,167		Tom Lehman (USA)	75-69-70-70—284	32,500
	Geoff Ogilvy (AUS)	71-74-67-69—281	122,167		Eric Ramsay (SCO) (am)	68-74-74-68—284	
	Vijay Singh (FIJ)	69-69-71-72—281	122,167		Tadahiro Takayama (JPN)	72-72-70-70—284	32,500
11	Nick Faldo (ENG)	74-69-70-69—282	66,750		Scott Verplank (USA)	68-70-72-74—284	32,500
	Graeme McDowell (NIR)	69-72-74-67—282	66,750	32	Richard Green (AUS)	72-68-72-73—285	26,500
	Kenny Perry (USA)	71-71-68-72—282	66,750		Sandy Lyle (SCO)	74-67-69-75—285	26,500
	Ian Poulter (ENG)	70-72-71-69—282	66,750	34	Simon Dyson (ENG)	70-71-75-70—286	22,000
15	Darren Clarke (NIR)	73-70-67-73—283	46,286		Ernie Els (RSA)	74-67-75-70—286	22,000
	John Daly (USA)	71-69-70-73—283	46,286		Peter Hanson (SWE)	72-72-71-71—286	22,000
	David Frost (RSA)	77-65-72-69—283	46,286		Thomas Levet (FRA)	69-71-75-71—286	22,000
	Mark Hensby (AUS)	67-77-69-70—283	46,286		Joe Ogilvie (USA)	74-70-73-69—286	22,000
	Trevor Immelman (RSA)	68-70-73-72—283	46,286		Adam Scott (AUS)	70-71-70-75—286	22,000
	Sean O'Hair (USA)	73-67-70-73—283	46,286		Henrik Stenson (SWE)	74-67-73-72—286	22,000
	Nick O'Hern (AUS)	73-69-71-70—283	46,286				

Other players who made the cut: Stuart Appleby (AUS), K J Choi (KOR), Hiroyuki Fujita (JPN), Søren Hansen (DEN), Tim Herron (USA), Simon Khan (ENG), Maarten Lafeber (NED), Paul McGinley (IRL), Bob Tway (USA), Tom Watson (USA), Steve Webster (ENG) 287; Robert Allenby (AUS), Luke Donald (ENG), Fredrik Jacobson (SWE), Thongchai Jaidee (THA), Miguel Angel Jiménez (ESP), Paul Lawrie (SCO), Justin Leonard (USA), Bo Van Pelt (USA) 288; John Bickerton (ENG), Mark Calcavecchia (USA), Phil Mickelson (USA), Edoardo Molinari (ITA) (am), Greg Norman (AUS), Tino Schuster (GER) 289; Peter Lonard (AUS) 290; Chris DiMarco (USA), Pat Perez (USA), Chris Riley (USA), Robert Rock (ENG), David Smail (NZL), Duffy Waldorf (USA) 291; Patrik Sjöland (SWE) 292; Scott Gutschewski (USA), S K Ho (KOR), Ted Purdy (USA) 293; Steve Flesch (USA), 294; Rodney Pampling (AUS), Graeme Storm (ENG) 296; Matthew Richardson (ENG) (am) 297

2004 Open Championship Royal Troon July 15–18   [7175–71]

Total Prize Money: £4,064,000. Entries: 2221 Regional Qualifying Courses: Alwoodley, Ashridge, Co.Louth, Hadley Wood, Hindhead, Little Aston, Minchinhampton, Notts, Orsett, Pleasington, Prestbury, Renfrew, Rochester & Cobham Park, Royal Ashdown Forest, Silloth-on-Solway, Trentham. Final qualifying courses: Glasgow (Gailes), Irvine, Turnberry Kintyre, Western Gailes. Final Field: 156 (5 amateurs), of whom 73 (1 amateur) made the half-way cut on 145 or less.

1	Todd Hamilton (USA)*	71-67-67-69—274	£720,000	
2	Ernie Els (RSA)	69-69-68-68—274	430,000	
Four-hole play-off: Hamilton 4-4-3-4; Els 4-4-4-4				
3	Phil Mickelson (USA)	73-66-68-68—275	275,000	
4	Lee Westwood (ENG)	72-71-68-67—278	210,000	
5	Thomas Levet (FRA)	66-70-71-72—279	159,500	
	Davis Love III (USA)	72-69-71-67—279	159,500	
7	Retief Goosen (RSA)	69-70-68-73—280	117,500	
	Scott Verplank (USA)	69-70-70-71—280	117,500	
9	Mike Weir (CAN)	71-68-71-71—281	89,500	
	Tiger Woods (USA)	70-71-68-72—281	89,500	
11	Mark Calcavecchia (USA)	72-73-69-68—282	69,333	
	Darren Clarke (NIR)	69-72-73-68—282	69,333	
	Skip Kendall (USA)	69-66-75-72—282	69,333	
14	Stewart Fink (USA)	72-71-71-69—283	56,500	
	Barry Lane (ENG)	69-68-71-75—283	56,500	
16	K J Choi (KOR)	68-69-74-73—284	47,000	
	Joakim Haeggman (SWE)	69-73-72-70—284	47,000	
	Justin Leonard (USA)	70-72-71-71—284	47,000	
	Kenny Perry (USA)	69-70-73-72—284	47,000	
20	Michael Campbell (NZL)	67-71-74-73—285	38,100	
20T	Paul Casey (ENG)	66-77-70-72—285	38,100	
	Bob Estes (USA)	73-72-69-71—285	38,100	
	Gary Evans (ENG)	68-73-73-71—285	38,100	
	Vijay Singh (FIJ)	68-70-76-71—285	38,100	
25	Colin Montgomerie (SCO)	69-69-72-76—286	32,250	
	Ian Poulter (ENG)	71-72-71-72—286	32,250	
27	Takashi Kamiyama (JPN)	70-73-71-73—287	29,000	
	Rodney Pampling (AUS)	72-68-74-73—287	29,000	
	Jyoti Randhawa (IND)	73-72-70-72—287	29,000	
30	Kelichiro Fukabori (JPN)	73-71-70-74—288	24,500	
	Shigeki Maruyama (JPN)	71-72-74-71—288	24,500	
	Mark O'Meara (USA)	71-74-68-75—288	24,500	
	Nick Price (ZIM)	71-71-69-77—288	24,500	
	David Toms (USA)	71-71-74-72—288	24,500	
	Bo Van Pelt (USA)	72-71-71-74—288	24,500	
36	Stuart Appleby (AUS)	71-70-73-75—289	18,750	
	Kim Felton (AUS)	73-67-72-77—289	18,750	
	Tetsuji Hiratsuka (JPN)	70-74-70-75—289	18,750	
	Steve Lowery (USA)	69-73-75-72—289	18,750	
	Hunter Mahan (USA)	74-69-71-75—289	18,750	
	Tjaart Van Der Walt (RSA)	70-73-72-74—289	18,750	

Other players who made the cut: Kenneth Ferrie (ENG), Charles Howell III (USA), Trevor Immelman (RSA), Andrew Oldcorn (SCO), Adam Scott (AUS) 290; Paul Bradshaw (ENG), Alastair Forsyth (SCO), Mathias Grönberg (SWE), Migel Angel Jiménez (ESP), Jerry Kelly (USA), Shaun Micheel (USA), Sean Whiffin (USA) 291; Steve Flesch (USA), Ignacio Garrido (ESP), Rafaël Jacquelin (FRA) 292; James Kingston (RSA), Paul McGinley (IRL), Carl Pettersson (SWE) 293; Paul Broadhurst (ENG), Gary Emerson (ENG), Brad Faxon (USA) 294; Chris DiMarco (USA), Mark Foster (ENG), Stuart Wilson (SCO) (am) (Silver Medal) 296; Mårten Olander (SWE), Rory Sabbatini (RSA) 297; Martin Erlandsson (SWE), Paul Wesselingh (ENG) 298; Bob Tway (USA) 299; Rich Beem (USA), Christian Cévaër (FRA) 300; Sandy Lyle (SCO) 303

2011 Open Championship – rulings of the day – Friday

David Duval incurred a penalty of one stroke whilst playing the 3rd hole during the 2nd round of The Open Championship at Royal St George's when he accidentally dropped his club which landed on his ball, causing it to move.

When a player's ball is in play, if the player, his partner or either of their caddies lifts or moves it, touches the ball purposely or causes the ball to move, the player incurs a penalty of one stroke and the ball must be replaced (Rule 18-2a).

While Duval had no intention to move his ball, the reality was that when he let the club slip from his hand and it unfortunately fell onto his ball, he had caused his ball in play to move. Duval consulted with the referee walking with his game who confirmed that he would incur a one stroke penalty and that the ball had to be replaced.

Duval correctly replaced the ball and finished up with a bogey four at the par-3 3rd hole. Despite birdies on the 7th and 13th, the former Open Champion missed the cut.

2003 Open Championship *Royal St George's* July 17–20   [7034–71]

Prize Money £3.9 million. Entries: 2152. Regional qualifying courses: Alwoodley, Ashridge, Blackmoor, Co.Louth, Hadley Wood, Hindhead, Little Aston, Minchinhampton, Notts, Ormskirk, Orsett, Renfrew, Silloth-on-Solway, Stockport, Trentham, Wildernesse. Final qualifying courses: Littlestone, North Foreland, Prince's, Royal Cinque Ports. Final Field: 156 (3 amateurs), of whom 75 (no amateurs) made the half-way cut on 150 or less.

1	Ben Curtis (USA)	72-72-70-69—283	£700,000	22T	Peter Fowler (AUS)	77-73-70-71—291	32,917
2	Thomas Bjørn (DEN)	73-70-69-72—284	345,000		Padraig Harrington (IRL)	75-73-74-69—297	32,917
	Vijay Singh (FIJ)	75-70-69-70—284	345,000		Thomas Levet (FRA)	71-73-74-73—291	32,917
4	Davis Love III (USA)	69-72-72-72—285	185,000		JL Lewis (USA)	78-70-72-71—291	32,917
	Tiger Woods (USA)	73-72-69-71—285	185,000	28	Mark Foster (ENG)	73-73-72-74—292	26,000
6	Brian Davis (ENG)	77-73-68-68—286	134,500		SK Ho (KOR)	70-73-72-77—292	26,000
	Fredrik Jacobson (SWE)	70-76-70-70—286	134,500		Paul McGinley (IRL)	77-73-69-73—292	26,000
8	Nick Faldo (ENG)	76-74-67-70—287	97,750		Andrew Oldcorn (SCO)	72-74-73-73—292	26,000
	Kenny Perry (USA)	74-70-70-73—287	97,750		Nick Price (ZIM)	74-72-72-74—292	26,000
10	Gary Evans (ENG)	71-75-70-72—288	68,000		Mike Weir (CAN)	74-76-71-71—292	26,000
	Sergio García (ESP)	73-71-70-74—288	68,000	34	Stewart Cink (USA)	75-75-75-68—293	18,778
	Retief Goosen (RSA)	73-75-71-69—288	68,000		José Coceres (ARG)	77-70-72-74—293	18,778
	Hennie Otto (RSA)	68-76-75-69—288	68,000		Bob Estes (USA)	77-71-76-69—293	18,778
	Phillip Price (WAL)	74-72-69-73—288	68,000		Shingo Katayama (JPN)	76-73-73-71—293	18,778
15	Stuart Appleby (AUS)	75-71-71-72—289	49,333		Scott McCarron (USA)	71-74-73-75—293	18,778
	Chad Campbell (USA)	74-71-72-72—289	49,333		Adam Mednick (SWE)	76-72-76-69—293	18,778
	Pierre Fulke (SWE)	77-72-67-73—289	49,333		Gary Murphy (IRL)	73-74-73-73—293	18,778
18	Ernie Els (RSA)	78-68-72-72—290	42,000		Marco Ruiz (PAR)	73-71-75-74—293	18,778
	Mathias Grönberg (SWE)	71-74-73-72—290	42,000		Duffy Waldorf (USA)	76-73-71-73—293	18,778
	Greg Norman (AUS)	69-79-74-68—290	42,000	43	Robert Allenby (AUS)	73-75-74-72—294	14,250
	Tom Watson (USA)	71-77-73-69—290	42,000		Rich Beem (USA)	76-74-75-69—294	14,250
22	Angel Cabrera (ARG)	75-73-70-73—291	32,917		Tom Byrum (USA)	77-72-71-74—294	14,250
	K J Choi (KOR)	77-72-72-70—291	32,917				

Other players who made the cut: Markus Brier (AUT), Fred Couples (USA), Brad Faxon (USA), Mathew Goggin (AUS), Tom Lehman (USA), Ian Poulter (ENG), Anthony Wall (ENG) 295; Michael Campbell (NZL), Trevor Immelman (RSA), Raphaèl Jacquelin (FRA), David Lynn (ENG), Mark McNulty (ZIM), Rory Sabbatini (RSA) 296; Darren Clarke (NIR), Alastair Forsyth (SCO), Skip Kendall (USA), Peter Lonard (AUS), Phil Mickelson (USA), Craig Parry (AUS) 297; Charles Howell III (USA), Stephen Leaney (AUS), Len Mattiace (USA), Mark O'Meara (USA) 298; Katsuyoshi Tomori (JPN) 300; John Rollins (USA) 301; Chris Smith (USA) 302; John Daly (USA), Ian Woosnam (WAL) 303; Jesper Parnevik (SWE), Mark Roe (ENG) DQ

2011 Open Championship – rulings of the day – Saturday

Playing the par-3 11th hole on the third day of the 2011 Open Championship, Gary Boyd played his second stroke from a bunker onto the green. Due to the wet conditions, a considerable amount of sand was extracted from the bunker when he made the stroke, which landed on and around Robert Allenby's ball that was at rest on the fringe of the green.

As Allenby's ball was not on the putting green, he was not entitled to mark, lift or clean his ball (Rule 16-1). Moreover, whilst sand is a natural substance, sand is only a loose impediment when it lies on the putting green. Thus when the ball lies through the green, sand must not be removed (see Definition of Loose Impediments).

Normally if the sand had been on the fringe of the green before Allenby's ball had come to rest, he would not have been entitled to relief without penalty. However, as Allenby's ball had originally been lying in a position where the ball and his line of play had not been affected by the sand, the referee confirmed that he was in fact entitled to remove the sand.

Decision 13-2/8.5 clarifies that a player is entitled to the lie and line of play he had when his ball came to rest. Accordingly, in equity (Rule 1-4), Allenby was entitled to remove the sand deposited by Boyd's stroke and lift and clean his ball, without penalty.

Allenby chipped onto the green and took two putts for a bogey four on route to shooting a five-over-par round, in testing conditions at Royal St George's.

2002 Open Championship Muirfield July 18–21 [7034–71]

Prize Money £3.885 million. Entries: 2260. Regional qualifying courses: Alwoodley, Blackmoor, Co.Louth, Hadley Wood, Hindhead, Little Aston, Minchinhampton, Northamptonshire County, Notts, Ormskirk, Orsett, Renfrew, Silloth-on-Solway, Stockport, Trentham, Wildernesse. Final qualifying courses: Dunbar, Gullane No.1, Luffness New, North Berwick. Final Field: 156 (3 amateurs), of whom 83 (no amateurs) made the half-way cut on 144 or less.

1	Ernie Els (RSA)*	70-66-72-70—278	£700,000
2	Stuart Appleby (AUS)	73-70-70-65—278	286,667
	Steve Elkington (AUS)	71-73-68-66—278	286,667
	Thomas Levet (FRA)	72-66-74-66—278	286,667

Four-hole play-off: Appleby, Elkington, Els and Levet. Sudden death: Els and Levet

5	Gary Evans (ENG)	72-68-74-65—279	140,000
	Padraig Harrington (IRL)	69-67-76-67—279	140,000
	Shigeki Maruyama (JPN)	68-68-75-68—279	140,000
8	Thomas Bjørn (DEN)	68-70-73-69—280	77,500
	Sergio García (ESP)	71-69-71-69—280	77,500
	Retief Goosen (RSA)	71-68-74-67—280	77,500
	Søren Hansen (DEN)	68-69-73-70—280	77,500
	Scott Hoch (USA)	74-69-71-66—280	77,500
	Peter O'Malley (AUS)	72-68-75-65—280	77,500
14	Justin Leonard (USA)	71-72-68-70—281	49,750
	Peter Lonard (AUS)	72-72-68-69—281	49,750
	Davis Love III (USA)	71-72-71-67—281	49,750
	Nick Price (ZIM)	68-70-75-68—281	49,750
18	Bob Estes (USA)	71-70-73-68—282	41,000
	Scott McCarron (USA)	71-68-72-71—282	41,000
	Greg Norman (AUS)	71-72-71-68—282	41,000
	Duffy Waldorf (USA)	67-69-77-69—282	41,000
22	David Duval (USA)	72-71-70-70—283	32,000
	Toshimitsu Izawa (JPN)	76-68-72-67—283	32,000
	Mark O'Meara (USA)	69-69-77-68—283	32,000
	Corey Pavin (USA)	69-70-75-69—283	32,000
	Chris Riley (USA)	70-71-76-66—283	32,000
	Justin Rose (ENG)	68-75-68-72—283	32,000

28	Bradley Dredge (WAL)	70-72-74-68—284	24,000
	Niclas Fasth (SWE)	70-73-71-70—284	24,000
	Pierre Fulke (SWE)	72-69-78-65—284	24,000
	Jerry Kelly (USA)	73-71-70-70—284	24,000
	Bernhard Langer (GER)	72-72-71-69—284	24,000
	Jesper Parnevik (SWE)	72-72-70-70—284	24,000
	Loren Roberts (USA)	74-69-70-71—284	24,000
	Des Smyth (IRL)	68-69-74-73—284	24,000
	Tiger Woods (USA)	70-68-81-65—284	24,000
37	Darren Clarke (NIR)	72-67-77-69—285	16,917
	Andrew Coltart (SCO)	71-69-74-71—285	16,917
	Neal Lancaster (USA)	71-71-76-67—285	16,917
	Stephen Leaney (AUS)	71-70-75-69—285	16,917
	Scott Verplank (USA)	72-68-74-71—285	16,917
	Ian Woosnam (WAL)	72-72-73-68—285	16,917
43	Trevor Immelman (RSA)	72-72-71-71—286	13,750
	Steve Jones (USA)	68-75-73-70—286	13,750
	Carl Pettersson (SWE)	67-70-76-73—286	13,750
	Esteban Toledo (MEX)	73-70-75-68—286	13,750
47	Paul Eales (ENG)	73-71-76-67—287	12,000
	Jeff Maggert (USA)	71-68-80-68—287	12,000
	Rocco Mediate (USA)	71-72-74-70—287	12,000
50	Fredrik Andersson (SWE)	74-70-74-70—288	10,267
	Warren Bennett (ENG)	71-68-82-67—288	10,267
	Ian Garbutt (ENG)	69-70-74-75—288	10,267
	Mikko Ilonen (FIN)	71-70-77-70—288	10,267
	Shingo Katayama (JPN)	72-68-74-74—288	10,267
	Barry Lane (ENG)	74-68-72-74—288	10,267
	Ian Poulter (ENG)	69-69-78-72—288	10,267
	Bob Tway (USA)	70-66-78-74—288	10,267

Other players who made the cut: Stewart Cink (USA), Joe Durant (USA), Nick Faldo (ENG), Richard Green (AUS), Kuboya Kenichi (JPN), Paul Lawrie (SCO), Steve Stricker (USA) 289; Chris DiMarco (USA), Phil Mickelson (USA), Jarrod Moseley (AUS) 290; Stephen Ames (TRI), Jim Carter (USA), Matthew Cort (ENG), Len Mattiace (USA), Toru Taniguchi (JPN), Mike Weir (CAN) 291; Sandy Lyle (SCO), Chris Smith (USA) 292; Anders Hansen (DEN), Roger Wessels (RSA) 293; David Park (WAL) 294; Mark Calcavecchia (USA), Lee Janzen (USA) 295; Colin Montgomerie (SCO) 297; David Toms (USA) 298

2011 Open Championship – rulings of the day – Sunday

As a result of the gusting 30mph winds that swept over Royal St George's on Sunday morning, in the more exposed areas, balls were oscillating on the putting greens and on some occasions, actually moving in the wind.

On the 10th green, before Ryan Moore replaced his ball on the putting green, he asked the referee for clarification of when his ball would be considered back "in play". Moore was concerned that his ball may move due to the wind once he had replaced it and asked when it would be considered replaced and if by leaving his ball-marker in position, this would make a difference.

Decision 20-4/1 provides the guidance and answer to Moore's question. Under Rule 20-4, a ball is in play when it is replaced, whether or not the object used to mark its position has been removed. If the wind then subsequently moves the ball, the ball must be played from its new position regardless of the fact the ball-marker is still on the ground.

In Moore's case, when he replaced the ball on the 10th green, the ball remained at rest when replaced and he was able to putt out for his par. Finishing with a birdie 3 on 18, Moore completed his 2011 Open Championship tied for 28th place.

Open Championship History

The Belt

Date		Winner	Score	Venue	Entrants	Prize money £
1860	Oct 17	W Park, Musselburgh	174	Prestwick	8	—
1861	Sept 26	T Morris Sr, Prestwick	163	Prestwick	12	—
1862	Sept 11	T Morris Sr, Prestwick	163	Prestwick	6	—
1863	Sept 18	W Park, Musselburgh	168	Prestwick	14	10
1864	Sept 16	T Morris Sr, Prestwick	167	Prestwick	6	15
1865	Sept 14	A Strath, St Andrews	162	Prestwick	10	20
1866	Sept 13	W Park, Musselburgh	169	Prestwick	12	11
1867	Sept 26	T Morris Sr, St Andrews	170	Prestwick	10	16
1868	Sept 23	T Morris Jr, St Andrews	154	Prestwick	12	12
1869	Sept 16	T Morris Jr, St Andrews	157	Prestwick	14	12
1870	Sept 15	T Morris Jr, St Andrews	149	Prestwick	17	12

Having won it three times in succession, the Belt became the property of Young Tom Morris and the Championship was held in abeyance for a year. In 1872 the Claret Jug was, and still is, offered for annual competition but it was not available to present at the time to Tom Morris Jr in 1872.

The Claret Jug

Date		Winner	Score	Venue	Entrants	Prize money £
1872	Sept 13	T Morris Jr, St Andrews	166	Prestwick	8	20
1873	Oct 4	T Kidd, St Andrews	179	St Andrews	26	20
1874	April 10	M Park, Musselburgh	159	Musselburgh	32	29
1875	Sept 10	W Park, Musselburgh	166	Prestwick	18	20
1876	Sept 30	B Martin, St Andrews	176	St Andrews	34	27
(D Strath tied but refused to play off)						
1877	April 6	J Anderson, St Andrews	160	Musselburgh	24	20
1878	Oct 4	J Anderson, St Andrews	157	Prestwick	26	20
1879	Sept 27	J Anderson, St Andrews	169	St Andrews	46	45
1880	April 9	B Ferguson, Musselburgh	162	Musselburgh	30	†
1881	Oct 14	B Ferguson, Musselburgh	170	Prestwick	22	21
1882	Sept 30	B Ferguson, Musselburgh	171	St Andrews	40	45
1883	Nov 16	W Fernie*, Dumfries	158	Musselburgh	41	20
After a play-off with B Ferguson, Musselburgh: Fernie 158; Ferguson 159						
1884	Oct 3	J Simpson, Carnoustie	160	Prestwick	30	23
1885	Oct 3	B Martin, St Andrews	171	St Andrews	51	34
1886	Nov 5	D Brown, Musselburgh	157	Musselburgh	46	20
1887	Sept 16	W Park Jr, Musselburgh	161	Prestwick	36	20
1888	Oct 6	J Burns, Warwick	171	St Andrews	53	24
1889	Nov 8	W Park Jr*, Musselburgh	155	Musselburgh	42	22
After a play-off with A Kirkaldy: Park Jr 158; Kirkaldy 163						
1890	Sept 11	J Ball, Royal Liverpool (am)	164	Prestwick	40	29.50
1891	Oct 6	H Kirkaldy, St Andrews	166	St Andrews	82	30.50

After 1891 the competition was extended to 72 holes and for the first time entry money was imposed

Date		Winner	Score	Venue	Entrants	Prize money £
1892	Sept 22–23	H Hilton, Royal Liverpool (am)	305	Muirfield	66	100
1893	Aug 31–Sept 1	W Auchterlonie, St Andrews	322	Prestwick	72	100
1894	June 11–12	J Taylor, Winchester	326	Royal St George's	94	100
1895	June 12–13	J Taylor, Winchester	322	St Andrews	73	100
1896	June 10–11	H Vardon*, Ganton	316	Muirfield	64	100
After a 36-hole play-off with JH Taylor: Vardon 157; Taylor 161						
1897	May 19–20	H Hilton, Royal Liverpool (am)	314	Royal Liverpool	86	100
1898	June 8–9	H Vardon, Ganton	307	Prestwick	78	100
1899	June 7–8	H Vardon, Ganton	310	Royal St George's	98	100
1900	June 6–7	J Taylor, Mid-Surrey	309	St Andrews	81	125
1901	June 5–6	J Braid, Romford	309	Muirfield	101	125
1902	June 4–5	A Herd, Huddersfield	307	Royal Liverpool	112	125
1903	June 10–11	H Vardon, Totteridge	300	Prestwick	127	125

† prize money not known

Date	Winner	Score	Venue	Entrants	Qualifiers	Prize-money £
1904 June 8–10	J White, Sunningdale	296	Royal St George's	144		125
1905 June 7–9	J Braid, Walton Heath	318	St Andrews	152		125
1906 June 13–15	J Braid, Walton Heath	300	Muirfield	183		125
1907 June 20–21	A Massy, La Boulie	312	Royal Liverpool	193		125
1908 June 18–19	J Braid, Walton Heath	291	Prestwick	180		125
1909 June 10–11	J Taylor, Mid-Surrey	295	Royal Cinque Ports	204		125
1910 June 22–24	J Braid, Walton Heath	299	St Andrews	210		135
1911 June 26–29	H Vardon*, Totteridge	303	Royal St George's	226		135

*After a play-off with A Massy. The play-off was over 36 holes, but Massy picked up at the 35th before holing out. He had taken 148 for 34 holes, and when Vardon holed out at the 35th hole his score was 143

Date	Winner	Score	Venue	Entrants	Qualifiers	Prize-money £
1912 June 24–25	E Ray, Oxhey	295	Muirfield	215		135
1913 June 23–24	J Taylor, Mid-Surrey	304	Royal Liverpool	269		135
1914 June 18–19	H Vardon, Totteridge	306	Prestwick	194		135
1915–19 No Championship						
1920 June 30–July 1	G Duncan, Hanger Hill	303	Royal Cinque Ports	190	81	225
1921 June 23–25	J Hutchison*, Glenview, Chicago	296	St Andrews	158	85	225

*After a play-off with R Wethered (am): Hutchison 150; Wethered 159

Date	Winner	Score	Venue	Entrants	Qualifiers	Prize-money £
1922 June 22–23	W Hagen, Detroit, USA	300	Royal St George's	225	80	225
1923 June 14–15	A Havers, Coombe Hill	295	Troon	222	88	225
1924 June 26–27	W Hagen, Detroit, USA	301	Royal Liverpool	277	86	225
1925 June 25–26	J Barnes, USA	300	Prestwick	200	83	225
1926 June 23–25	R Jones, USA (am)	291	Royal Lytham & St Annes	293	117	225
1927 July 13–15	R Jones, USA (am)	285	St Andrews	207	108	275
1928 May 9–11	W Hagen, USA	292	Royal St George's	271	113	275
1929 May 8–10	W Hagen, USA	292	Muirfield	242	109	275
1930 June 18–20	R Jones, USA (am)	291	Royal Liverpool	296	112	400
1931 June 3–5	T Armour, USA	296	Carnoustie	215	109	500
1932 June 8–10	G Sarazen, USA	283	Sandwich, Prince's	224	110	500
1933 July 5–7	D Shute*, USA	292	St Andrews	287	117	500

*After a play-off with C Wood, USA: Shute 149; Wood 154

Date	Winner	Score	Venue	Entrants	Qualifiers	Prize-money £
1934 June 27–29	T Cotton, Waterloo, Belgium	283	Royal St George's	312	101	500
1935 June 26–28	A Perry, Leatherhead	283	Muirfield	264	109	500
1936 June 25–27	A Padgham, Sundridge Park	287	Royal Liverpool	286	107	500
1937 July 7–9	T Cotton, Ashridge	290	Carnoustie	258	141	500
1938 July 6–8	R Whitcombe, Parkstone	295	Royal St George's	268	120	500
1939 July 5–7	R Burton, Sale	290	St Andrews	254	129	500
1940–45 No Championship						
1946 July 3–5	S Snead, USA	290	St Andrews	225	100	1,000
1947 July 2–4	F Daly, Balmoral	293	Royal Liverpool	263	100	1,000
1948 June 30–July 2	T Cotton, Royal Mid-Surrey	284	Muirfield	272	97	1,000
1949 July 6–8	A Locke*, RSA	283	Royal St George's	224	96	1,500

*After a play-off with H Bradshaw: Locke 135; Bradshaw 147

Date	Winner	Score	Venue	Entrants	Qualifiers	Prize-money £
1950 July 5–7	A Locke, RSA	279	Troon	262	93	1,500
1951 July 4–6	M Faulkner, England	285	Royal Portrush	180	98	1,700
1952 July 9–11	A Locke, RSA	287	Royal Lytham & St Annes	275	96	1,700
1953 July 8–10	B Hogan, USA	282	Carnoustie	196	91	2,500
1954 July 7–9	P Thomson, Australia	283	Royal Birkdale	349	97	3,500
1955 July 6–8	P Thomson, Australia	281	St Andrews	301	94	3,750
1956 July 4–6	P Thomson, Australia	286	Royal Liverpool	360	96	3,750
1957 July 3–5	A Locke, RSA	279	St Andrews	282	96	3,750
1958 July 2–4	P Thomson*, Australia	278	Royal Lytham & St Annes	362	96	4,850

*After a play-off with D Thomas: Thomson 139; Thomas 143

Date	Winner	Score	Venue	Entrants	Qualifiers	Prize-money £
1959 July 1–3	G Player, RSA	284	Muirfield	285	90	5,000
1960 July 6–8	K Nagle, Australia	278	St Andrews	410	74	7,000
1961 July 12–14	A Palmer, USA	284	Royal Birkdale	364	101	8,500
1962 July 11–13	A Palmer, USA	276	Troon	379	119	8,500
1963 July 10–12	R Charles*, New Zealand	277	Royal Lytham & St Annes	261	119	8,500

*After a play-off with P Rodgers, USA: Charles 140; Rodgers 148

Date	Winner	Score	Venue	Entrants	Qualifiers	Prize-money £
1964 July 8–10	T Lema, USA	279	St Andrews	327	119	8,500
1965 July 7–9	P Thomson, Australia	285	Royal Birkdale	372	130	10,000
1966 July 6–9	J Nicklaus, USA	282	Muirfield	310	130	15,000
1967 July 12–15	R De Vicenzo, Argentina	278	Royal Liverpool	326	130	15,000
1968 July 10–13	G Player, RSA	289	Carnoustie	309	130	20,000
1969 July 9–12	A Jacklin, England	280	Royal Lytham & St Annes	424	129	30,334
1970 July 8–11	J Nicklaus*, USA	283	St Andrews	468	134	40,000

*After a play-off with Doug Sanders, USA: Nicklaus 72; Sanders 73

Date	Winner	Score	Venue	Entrants	Qualifiers	Prize-money £
1971 July 7–10	L Trevino, USA	278	Royal Birkdale	528	150	45,000
1972 July 12–15	L Trevino, USA	278	Muirfield	570	150	50,000
1973 July 11–14	T Weiskopf, USA	276	Troon	569	150	50,000

Open Championship Claret Jug winners history *continued*

Date	Winner	Score	Venue	Entrants	Qualifiers	Prize-money £
1974 July 10–13	G Player, RSA	282	Royal Lytham & St Annes	679	150	50,000
1975 July 9–12	T Watson*, USA	279	Carnoustie	629	150	50,000

After a play-off with J Newton (AUS): Watson 71; Newton 72

Date	Winner	Score	Venue	Entrants	Qualifiers	Prize-money £
1976 July 7–10	J Miller, USA	279	Royal Birkdale	719	150	75,000
1977 July 6–9	T Watson, USA	268	Turnberry	730	150	100,000
1978 July 12–15	J Nicklaus, USA	281	St Andrews	788	150	125,000
1979 July 18–21	S Ballesteros, Spain	283	Royal Lytham & St Annes	885	150	155,000
1980 July 17–20	T Watson, USA	271	Muirfield	994	151	200,000
1981 July 16–19	B Rogers, USA	276	Royal St George's	971	153	200,000
1982 July 15–18	T Watson, USA	284	Royal Troon	1,121	150	250,000
1983 July 14–17	T Watson, USA	275	Royal Birkdale	1,107	151	310,000
1984 July 19–22	S Ballesteros, Spain	276	St Andrews	1,413	156	445,000
1985 July 18–21	A Lyle, Scotland	282	Royal St George's	1,361	149	530,000
1986 July 17–20	G Norman, Australia	280	Turnberry	1,347	152	634,000
1987 July 16–19	N Faldo, England	279	Muirfield	1,407	153	650,000
1988 July 14–18	S Ballesteros, Spain	273	Royal Lytham & St Annes	1,393	153	700,000
1989 July 20–23	M Calcavecchia*, USA	275	Royal Troon	1,481	156	750,000

Four-hole play-off (1st, 2nd, 17th and 18th): Calcavecchia 4-3-3-3, W Grady (AUS) 4-4-4-4, G Norman (AUS) 3-4-4-X

Date	Winner	Score	Venue	Entrants	Qualifiers	Prize-money £
1990 July 19–22	N Faldo, England	270	St Andrews	1,707	152	825,000
1991 July 18–21	I Baker-Finch, Australia	272	Royal Birkdale	1,496	156	900,000
1992 July 16–19	N Faldo, England	272	Muirfield	1,666	156	950,000
1993 July 15–18	G Norman, Australia	267	Royal St George's	1,827	156	1,000,000
1994 July 14–17	N Price, Zimbabwe	268	Turnberry	1,701	156	1,100,000
1995 July 20–23	J Daly*, USA	282	St Andrews	1,836	159	1,250,000

Four-hole play-off (1st, 2nd, 17th and 18th): Daly 4-3-4-4, C Rocca (ITA) 5-4-7-3

Date	Winner	Score	Venue	Entrants	Qualifiers	Prize-money £
1996 July 18–21	T Lehman, USA	271	Royal Lytham & St Annes	1,918	156	1,400,000
1997 July 17–20	J Leonard, USA	272	Royal Troon	2,133	156	1,586,300
1998 July 16–19	M O'Meara*, USA	280	Royal Birkdale	2,336	152	1,800,000

Four-hole play-off (15th–18th): O'Meara 4-4-5-4, B Watts (AUS) 5-4-5-5

Date	Winner	Score	Venue	Entrants	Qualifiers	Prize-money £
1999 July 15–18	P Lawrie*, Scotland	290	Carnoustie	2,222	156	2,000,000

Four-hole play-off: Lawrie 5-4-3-3, J Leonard (USA), J Van de Velde (FRA) 5-4-4-5

Date	Winner	Score	Venue	Entrants	Qualifiers	Prize-money £
2000 July 20–23	T Woods, USA	269	St Andrews	2,477	156	2,750,000
2001 July 19–22	D Duval, USA	274	Royal Lytham & St Annes	2,255	156	3,300,000
2002 July 18–21	E Els*, RSA	278	Muirfield	2,260	156	3,800,000

Four hole play-off: Els 4-3-5-4–16, T Levet (FRA) 4-2-5-5, S Appleby (AUS) 4-4-4-5, S Elkington (AUS) 5-3-4-5. Sudden death: Els 4, Levet 5

Date	Winner	Score	Venue	Entrants	Qualifiers	Prize-money £
2003 July 17–20	B Curtis, USA	283	Royal St George's	2,152	156	3,898,000
2004 July 15–18	T Hamilton*, USA	274	Royal Troon	2,221	156	4,064,000

Four-hole play-off: Hamilton 4-4-3-4, Els (RSA) 4-4-4-4

Date	Winner	Score	Venue	Entrants	Qualifiers	Prize-money £
2005 July 14–17	T Woods, USA	274	St Andrews	2,499	156	4,000,000
2006 July 20–23	T Woods, USA	270	Royal Liverpool	2,434	156	4,000,000
2007 July 19–22	P Harrington, Ireland*	277	Carnoustie	2,443	156	4,200,000

Four-hole play-off: Harrington 3-3-4-5, S García (ESP) 5-3-4-4

Date	Winner	Score	Venue	Entrants	Qualifiers	Prize-money £
2008 July 17–20	P Harrington, Ireland	283	Royal Birkdale	2,418	156	4,260,000
2009 July 16–19	S Cink*, USA	278	Turnberry	2,418	156	4,260,000

Four-hole play-off: Cink 4-3-4-3, T Watson (USA) 5-3-7-5

Date	Winner	Score	Venue	Entrants	Qualifiers	Prize-money £
2010 July 15–18	L Oosthuizen, RSA	272	St Andrews	2,500	156	4,800,000
2011 July 14–17	D Clarke, Northern Ireland	275	Royal St George's	1,995	156	5,000,000

Major championships 2011

Of the 11 players who made the half-way cut and played all four rounds in the majors, South African Charl Schwartzel earned the most with a total of $1,765,747 edging out Rory Mcilroy, the only other player to make more than a million. by just under $200,000. Schwartzel, at 14-under-par for the majors, was ten shots better than Sergio García and Steve Stricker, his nearest rivals under par. Schwartzel had the best last round average in the majors with 68.75. Fastest starter in the majors was McIlroy whose average totals for the first two rounds were 67.75 and 69.25.

The Open Silver Medal winners 1949–2011

The Open Championship's Silver Medal was first presented to the leading amateur who plays all four rounds in 1949. In the early years, American Frank Stranahan was top amateur five out seven years from 1947 but won only four silver medals because he was leading amateur in 1947 before the medals were awarded.

Among those who had or still have silver medals in their trophy cabinets are Ireland's Joe Carr who was twice lowest amateur, England's Michael Bonallack, who took the medal on three occasions, Scotland's Ronnie Shade, England's Peter McEvoy, another double winner, Spain's José María Olazábal and American Tiger Woods.

Today, in addition to the leading amateur receiving the silver medal, any amateur who makes all four rounds of the Championship earns a bronze medal. No medals have been awarded on 16 occasions since 1949 when no amateurs managed to complete 72 holes. Since 1946 the four leading amateurs who missed out on medals were:

    1946   K Bell (ENG), St Andrews
    1947   Frank Stranahan (USA), Royal Liverpool
    1948   Mario Gonzalez (BRA), E Kingsley (USA), Muirfield

Year	Name	Venue	Final Position	Final Score
1949	Frank Stranahan (USA)	Royal St George's	13	290
1950	Frank Stranahan (USA)	Troon	9	286
1951	Frank Stranahan (USA)	Royal Portrush	12	295
1952	J.W. Jones (ENG)	Royal Lytham & St Annes	27	304
1953	Frank Stranahan (USA)	Carnoustie	2	286
1954	Peter Toogood (AUS)	Royal Birkdale	15	291
1955	Joe Conrad (USA)	St Andrews	22	293
1956	Joe Carr (IRL)	Hoylake	36	306
1957	W.D. Smith (SCO)	St Andrews	5	286
1958	Joe Carr (IRL)	Royal Lytham & St Annes	37	298
1959	Reid Jack (SCO)	Muirfield	5	288
1960	Guy Wolstenholme (ENG)	St Andrews	6	283
1961	Ronald White (ENG)	Royal Birkdale	38	306
1962	Charles Green (SCO)	Troon	37	308
1965	Michael Burgess (ENG)	Royal Birkdale	29	299
1966	Ronnie Shade (SCO)	Muirfield	16	293
1968	Michael Bonallack (ENG)	Carnoustie	21	300
1969	Peter Tupling (ENG)	Royal Lytham & St Annes	28	294
1970	Steve Melnyk (USA)	St Andrews	41	298
1971	Michael Bonallack (ENG)	Royal Birkdale	22	291
1973	Danny Edwards (USA)	Troon	39	296
1978	Peter McEvoy (ENG)	Carnoustie	39	293
1979	Peter McEvoy (ENG)	Royal Lytham & St Annes	17	294
1980	Jay Sigel (USA)	Muirfield	38	291
1981	Hal Sutton (USA)	Royal St George's	47	295
1982	Malcolm Lewis (ENG)	Royal Troon	42	300
1985	José-María Olazábal (ESP)	Royal St George's	24	289
1987	Paul Mayo (IRL)	Muirfield	57	297
1988	Paul Broadhurst (ENG)	Royal Lytham & St Annes	57	296
1989	Russell Claydon (ENG)	Royal Troon	69	293
1991	Jim Payne (ENG)	Royal Birkdale	38	284
1992	Daren Lee (ENG)	Muirfield	68	293
1993	Iain Pyman (ENG)	Royal St George's	27	281
1994	Warren Bennett (ENG)	Turnberry	70	286
1995	Steve Webster (ENG)	St Andrews	24	289
1996	Tiger Woods (USA)	Royal Lytham & St Annes	21	281
1997	Barclay Howard (SCO)	Royal Troon	59	293
1998	Justin Rose (ENG)	Royal Birkdale	4	282
2001	David Dixon (ENG)	Royal Lytham & St Annes	30	285
2004	Stuart Wilson (SCO)	Royal Troon	63	296
2005	Lloyd Saltman (SCO)	St Andrews	15	283
2006	Marius Thorp (NOR)	Hoylake	48	288
2007	Rory McIlroy (NIR)	Carnoustie	42	289
2008	Chris Wood (ENG)	Royal Birkdale	5	290
2009	Matteo Manassero (ITA)	Turnberry	13	282
2010	Jin Jeong (KOR)	St Andrews	14	284
2011	Tom Lewis (ENG)	Royal St George's	30	289

US Open Championship

McIlroy rewrites the record book at US Open

Superb performance to become the youngest winner since 1923

He became the youngest winner of the US Open since Bobby Jones in 1923. His 16 under par total of 268, eight shots clear of the field, was the lowest score in the championship's history as well as the lowest number in relation to par. And, thanks to his extraordinary ball striking, which located 62 out of 72 greens in regulation figures, he bettered or matched a dozen records kept by the United States Golf Association.

Yet for all Rory McIlroy's blizzard of accomplishments at Congressional – surely the most impressive performance by any first time major winner since Tiger Woods broke through to win the Masters in 1997

Rory McIlroy

© Getty Images

by a dozen shots – it was the scale of the empathy between the golfer and the galleries in Maryland which truly stood out. It was typical, for example, of the common touch shown by the 22-year-old from Holywood in Northern Ireland as he walked off the fourth green during Sunday's final round that he made an effort to throw his ball to a youngster behind the ropes.

Hailing from a working class background in Ulster – his father, Gerry, worked three jobs to fund his son's career – McIlroy is a grounded young man with no airs and graces. And the overwhelming show of affection from the American crowds was clearly a reward not only for his brilliance in victory but also for the dignity shown by the golfer in defeat after he lost a four shot lead and ran up 80 in the closing round of the Masters.

Following in the footsteps of his compatriot Graeme McDowell as US Open champion – a feat not achieved in consecutive years by golfers from the UK since Cyril Walker and Willie MacFarlane in 1924 and 1925 – McIlroy performed so magnificently that even the world's No 1 tennis player, Rafael Nadal, was moved to describe the golfer as an inspirational sportsman.

Finishing eight shots clear of Australia's Jason Day, who reeled off his third consecutive top ten finish in just three appearances at the majors, and ten shots ahead of England's Lee Westwood, Korea's Y E Yang and America's Robert Garrigus and Kevin Chappell, McIlroy delivered a bewitching combination of skill and charisma. "I felt like this golf course was well suited to me," he explained. "The conditions helped, as well, because it was soft. With my high ball flight, I was able to stop it on the greens. When you hit the fairways like I was able to do this week, you're going to give yourself a lot of opportunities for birdies. It's a great feeling to get my first major championship out of the way quite early on in my career."

Bearing in mind that the previous ten US Open champions had collectively posted a total of 14 under par, McIlroy's 16 under mark was every bit as remarkable as Bob Beamon's record leap in the long jump at the 1968 Olympics. Indeed, the best adjective to describe the golfer's performance in Bethesda was probably 'astonishing'.

America's national championship is supposed to be the hardest annual test of all the majors and the USGA always pride themselves on setting a tough exam. Although, because of damp weather, Congressional would become a softer touch as the 111th staging of the Championship progressed, the demanding nature of a course which punished anyone who got out of position in the first round meant that many of the world's finest struggled.

By the time the afternoon's stellar three-ball of Phil Mickelson, Dustin Johnson and McIlroy got underway in front of a vast gallery lining the par 3 tenth, Mickelson marked his 41st birthday with a double bogey 5 while Johnson was in the water twice on the 11th and ran up 7. The left hander later confided he struck the ball so poorly he could easily have scored in the 80s. Instead, he returned 74 while Johnson signed for 75. Overall, the stroke average on day one was over 74.

Amidst all this carnage, McIlroy was a picture of absolute serenity as he wiped clean any lingering regrets left on the slate about that final round of 80 at Augusta in April. His opening score of 65, six under, was good enough to forge a three shot advantage over two major winners, Yang and Charl Schwartzel. Moreover, it was the biggest lead held after 18 holes by any golfer at the US Open since Mike Reid was four shots clear in 1976.

Matching peerless ball striking with a smooth putting stroke which had been refined with the help of Dave Stockton since the Masters, McIlroy was sanguine about his ability to operate in the moment and locate 17 out of 18 greens in regulation as well as keep a bogey off his card. "I don't know if it says that I've just got a very short memory," he smiled. "I took the experience from Augusta, and I learned a lot from it."

Of course, the 22-year-old came into the US Open with a track record of setting the heather on fire in the first round of majors. He opened up with 63 in the first round of The Open at St Andrews in 2010 as well as carding 65 in the first round of the 2011 Masters. Where he'd gone astray in previous majors was by following bright starts with calamity. Over the Old Course, for example, he ran up 80 on the second day.

There was no chance of history repeating itself in the second round at Congressional, though, as the Ulsterman kept up the good work with 66 for an 11 under par total which established a six stroke lead over Yang, a record equalling mark which matched Tiger Woods' six stroke advantage over Thomas Bjørn and Miguel Angel Jiménez after 36 holes at Pebble Beach in 2000. McIlroy's derring-do ensured the statisticians who monitor the record books at America's national championship were kept busy working overtime.

When his wedge shot from 113 yards spun back into the cup on the eighth hole for an eagle 2 – the key shot in this championship – no one in the US Open had ever reached ten under par in fewer holes. His halfway total of 131 was also one shot better than Ricky Barnes in 2009 while 13 under was the lowest in the Championship's history, bettering Woods in 2000 and Gil Morgan in 1992 by a stroke. McIlroy was now the only story in town.

While McDowell, the champion at Pebble Beach in 2010, highlighted the critical intervention of Mother Nature in Maryland – Congressional was a much softer test than the USGA would have liked – it said a great deal about the organisers' relaxed attitude to low scoring that the tees on some of the par 5s were moved up during the tournament. This prompted a spate of scores in the mid-60s on Saturday with Day and Westwood both carding 65 and Webb Simpson signing for 66. McIlroy, however, kept the competition at bay with 68, thereby establishing a new 54 hole benchmark total of 199.

Eight strokes clear of the field going into the closing round, McIlroy acknowledged how nerves had affected him a little at the start of the third round and why he'd located fewer fairways and greens in regulation than in the previous rounds. "I knew that I was going to feel a little bit of pressure and a little bit of nerves, and it took me a few holes to get into the round," he explained. A crafty par save from the rough at the third hole, however, seemed to lift his spirits and birdies at the ninth and 14th helped him to better 70 for the third day running. Holing out well, McIlroy's putting stroke was sound enough to complete another day's work without a three-putt. In fact, he would have only one all week at the 21st hole.

Any notion, though, that the championship was now a done deal met with a raised eyebrow from Westwood, who remembered his friend had scored 80 or more in two of the previous three majors. "You don't know how Rory is going to do," cautioned the Englishman. McIlroy himself, of course, also knew exactly what was required. "You can't get complacent," he reasoned. "No lead is big enough."

With the final round taking place on Father's Day, Rory was glad to have his Dad, Gerry, around. "It's always nice to hear his re-assuring words," he said. "Growing up, my Mum and Dad made huge sacrifices for me." Whether Gerry's words of re-assurance made a difference or not, there was never any chance of Rory falling into the same trap which cost him a Green Jacket. Playing conservatively on a course with soft greens and receptive fairways, the scope for disaster was limited in the final round and McIlroy was able to calm his nerves and control his own destiny.

Starting with a soothing birdie 3 courtesy of a smart 3 wood off the tee, a well judged approach to the green and a solid putt, McIlroy immediately served notice that he wasn't about to give the competition much encouragement. His closing 69 was just about as stress-free as it's possible to get in the final round of a major, with the highlight a thrilling tee shot which set up a birdie on the tenth.

While McIlroy talked afterwards of striving to emulate Woods, it was another legendary figure, Jack Nicklaus, who played a part in erasing the painful memory of what happened to the 22-year-old at Augusta National. "I didn't think he would make the same mistakes again after talking to him and he certainly hasn't," said Nicklaus. "I like everything about Rory. He's humble when he needs to be humble and cocky when he needs to be cocky. I have no doubts he is going to have a great career."

First Round	Second Round	Third Round	Fourth Round
−6 Rory McIlroy	−11 Rory McIlroy	−14 Rory McIlroy	−16 Rory McIlroy
−3 Y E Yang	−5 Y E Yang	−6 Y E Yang	−8 Jason Day
−3 Charl Schwartzel	−2 Sergio García	−5 Lee Westwood	−6 Lee Westwood
−2 Sergio García	−2 Robert Garrigus	−5 Jason Day	−6 Kevin Chappell
−2 Ryan Palmer	−2 Zach Johnson	−5 Robert Garrigus	−6 Robert Garrigus
−2 Kyung-tae Kim	−2 Brandt Snedeker	−4 Sergio García	−6 Y E Yang
−2 Louis Oosthuizen	−2 Matt Kuchar	−4 Matt Kuchar	−5 Sergio García
−2 Scott Hend	−1 Robert Rock	−4 Fredrik Jacobson	−5 Peter Hanson
−2 Alexandre Rocha	−1 Davis Love III	−3 Kyung-tae Kim	−4 Charl Schwartzel
	−1 Alvaro Quiros		−4 Louis Oosthuizen

US Open Championship (111th)   *Congressional CC, Bethesda, MD*   [7574–71]

Prize Money: $7.5 million. Entries 8,300   June 16–19

Players are of American nationality unless stated

Final Qualifying

Walton Heath, Surrey, UK

Nicolas Colsaerts (BEL)	64-71—135
Shane Lowry (IRL)	69-67—136
Maarten Lafeber (NED)	73-63—136
Thomas Levet (FRA)	66-71—137
Robert Rock (ENG)	70-68—138
David Howell (ENG)	72-66—138
Alexander Noren (SWE)	67-72—139
Stephen Gallacher (SCO)	70-69—139
Robert Dinwiddie (ENG)	69-70—139
Marcel Siem (GER)	67-72—139
Johan Edfors (SWE)	70-70—140

Ibaraki, Japan

Scott Barr (AUS)	72-63—135
Do-Hoon Kim (KOR)	70-65—135
Kenichi Kuboya (JPN)	66-69—135
Sang-Moon Bae (KOR)	70-66—136

Glendale, CA

Scott Pinckney (am)	67-70—137
Matthew Edwards	67-70—137
Beau Hossler Jr (am)	67-71—138
Steven Irwin (am)	67-71—138
Brian Locke	69-70—139

St Charles, IL

Bennett Blakeman	68-67—135
Brad Benjamin	67-69—136
Christopher Deforest	71-65—136

Ball Ground, GA

Brett Patterson (am)	70-62—132
Ryan Nelson	66-66—132
Russell Henley (am)	68-65—133

Tunica, MS

Scott Pinckney (am)	67-70—137
Matthew Edwards	67-70—137
Beau Hossler Jr (am)	67-71—138
Steven Irwin (am)	67-71—138
Brian Locke	69-70—139

Gold Mountain, WA

Chris Williams	70-68—138
Wes Heffernan (CAN)	69-70—139
Adam Hadwin (CAN)	68-71—139
John Ellis	67-73—140

Vero Beach, FL

Joey Lamielle	68-72—140
Michael Barbosa	68-73—141
Sam Saunders	69-72—141

Rockville, MD

Kirk Triplett	69-64—133
Jon Mills (CAN)	70-64—134
Fred Funk	67-68—135
Elliot Gealy	70-65—135
Michael Tobiason Jr	69-66—135
Ty Tryon	71-64—135
Bubba Dickerson	72-64—136
Christo Greyling	67-69—136
David May	68-68—136
Will Wilcox	67-69—136

Dallas, TX

Michael Smith	69-64—133
Todd Hamilton	67-68—135
Harrison Frazar	72-64—136
Greg Chalmers	66-70—136

Springfield, OH

Seung Yul Noh (KOR)	66-66—132
Jesse Hutchins	71-64—135

Columbus, OH

Chez Reavie	69-63—132
Brandt Jobe	62-70—132
Robert Garrigus	67-66—133
Adam Long	70-65—135
Justin Hicks	69-66—135
Nick O'Hern (AUS)	68-67—135
Patrick Cantlay (am)	65-70—135
Chris Wilson	70-66—136
Marc Turnesa	69-67—136
John Senden	68-68—136
D A Points	68-68—136
Marc Leishman	68-68—136
Kevin Chappell	68-68—136
Kyle Stanley	70-67—137
Tim Petrovic	69-68—137
Webb Simpson	68-69—137
J J Henry	68-69—137
Brett Wetterich	67-70—137
Scott Hend	64-73—137

Summit, NJ

Geoffrey Sisk	67-70—137
Cheng-tsung Pan (TPE) (am)	72-66—138
Alexander Rocha	71-67—138
Matt Richardson (ENG)	69-69—138

Final Field: 156 (12 amateurs), of whom 83 (including 3 amateurs) made the cut on 146 or less.

1	Rory McIlroy (NIR)	65-66-68-69—268	$1,440,000
2	Jason Day (AUS)	71-72-65-68—276	865,000
3	Kevin Chappell	76-67-69-66—278	364,241
	Robert Garrigus	70-70-68-70—278	364,241
	Lee Westwood (ENG)	75-68-65-70—278	364,241
	Y E Yang (KOR)	68-69-70-71—278	364,241
7	Peter Hanson (SWE)	72-71-69-67—279	228,416
	Sergio García (ESP)	69-71-69-70—279	228,416
9	Charl Schwartzel (RSA)	68-74-72-66—280	192,962
	Louis Oosthuizen (RSA)	69-73-71-67—280	192,962
11	Brandt Snedeker	70-70-72-69—281	163,083
	Davis Love III	70-71-70-70—281	163,083
	Heath Slocum	71-70-70-70—281	163,083
14	Graeme McDowell (NIR)	70-74-69-69—282	129,517
	Webb Simpson	75-71-66-70—282	129,517
	Matt Kuchar	72-68-69-73—282	129,517
	Fredrik Jacobson (SWE)	74-69-66-73—282	129,517
	Bo Van Pelt	76-67-68-71—282	129,517
19	Johan Edfors (SWE)	70-72-74-67—283	105,905
	Steve Stricker	75-69-69-70—283	105,905
21	Ryan Palmer	69-72-73-70—284	97,242
	Patrick Cantlay (am)	75-67-70-72—284	
23	Robert Rock (ENG)	70-71-76-68—285	76,455
	Gary Woodland	73-71-73-68—285	76,455
	Retief Goosen (RSA)	73-73-71-68—285	76,455
	Dustin Johnson	75-71-69-70—285	76,455
	Bill Haas	73-73-68-71—285	76,455
	Brandt Jobe	71-70-70-74—285	76,455
	Henrik Stenson (SWE)	70-72-69-74—285	76,455
30	Ryo Ishikawa (JPN)	74-70-74-68—286	50,436
	Gregory Havret (FRA)	77-69-71-69—286	50,436
	Seung-yul Noh (KOR)	72-70-73-71—286	50,436
	Rory Sabbatini (RSA)	72-73-70-71—286	50,436
	John Senden (AUS)	70-72-72-72—286	50,436
	Do-Hoon Kim (KOR)	73-71-70-72—286	50,436
	Harrison Frazar	72-73-68-73—286	50,436
	Zach Johnson	71-69-72-74—286	50,436
	Kyung-tae Kim (KOR)	69-72-69-76—286	50,436
39	Adam Hadwin (CAN)	75-71-73-68—287	41,154
	Martin Kaymer (GER)	74-70-72-71—287	41,154
	Sunghoon Kang (KOR)	74-72-70-71—287	41,154
42	Sang-Moon Bae (KOR)	75-71-75-67—288	37,351
	Lucas Glover	76-69-73-70—288	37,351
	Russell Henley (am)	73-69-71-75—288	
45	Charley Hoffman	71-74-75-69—289	31,264
	Luke Donald (ENG)	74-72-74-69—289	31,264
	Michael Putnam	74-71-73-71—289	31,264
	Chez Reavie	70-75-72-72—289	31,264
	Robert Karlsson (SWE)	79-67-71-72—289	31,264
	Padraig Harrington (IRL)	71-73-72-73—289	31,264
51	Scott Piercy	73-71-76-70—290	24,708
	Alexander Noren (SWE)	75-67-74-74—290	24,708
	Marc Leishman (AUS)	73-69-72-76—290	24,708
54	J J Henry	72-73-76-70—291	21,792
	Anthony Kim (KOR)	74-72-75-70—291	21,792
	Phil Mickelson	74-69-77-71—291	21,792
	Matteo Manassero (ITA)	74-72-73-72—291	21,792
	Edoardo Molinari (ITA)	74-70-74-73—291	21,792
	Alvaro Quiros (ESP)	70-71-72-78—291	21,792
60	Todd Hamilton	73-72-77-70—292	19,763

US Open Championship *continued*

60T	Justin Hicks	74-71-76-71—292	19,763
	Marcel Siem (GER)	79-66-74-73—292	19,763
63	Bubba Watson	71-75-74-73—293	18,620
	Brian Gay	73-71-74-75—293	18,620
	Jeff Overton	72-72-74-75—293	18,620
	William Cauley	71-72-74-76—293	18,620
67	Kevin Streelman	73-73-74-75—295	17,819
68	Alexandre Rocha (BRA)	69-76-76-76—297	17,178
	Christo Greyling (RSA)	72-74-75-76—297	17,178
	Kenichi Kuboya (JPN)	73-73-74-77—297	17,178
71	Wes Heffernan (CAN)	75-71-79-78—303	16,539
72	Brad Benjamin (am)	72-73-80-80—305	

The following players missed the half-way cut:

73	Chad Campbell	76-71—147	96T	Andres Gonzales	79-70—149	128T	Robert Dinwiddie	78-74—152
	Paul Casey (ENG)	73-74—147		Trevor Immelman	75-74—149		(ENG)	
	Stewart Cink	70-77—147		(RSA)			Hiroyuki Fujita (JPN)	79-73—152
	Christopher	71-76—147		Jon Mills (CAN)	76-73—149		David Howell (ENG)	78-74—152
	DeForest			Francesco Molinari	75-74—149		Cheng-Tsung Pan	74-78—152
	John Ellis	74-73—147		(ITA)			(TPE) (am)	
	Rickie Fowler	74-73—147		D A Points	74-75—149		Michael Smith	76-76—152
	Stephen Gallacher	73-74—147		Sam Saunders	74-75—149		Michael Whitehead	77-75—152
	(SCO)			Michael Tobiason Jr	75-74—149		Chris Wilson	74-78—152
	Scott Hend (AUS)	69-78—147		David Toms	74-75—149	138	Brad Adamonis	77-76—153
	Jesse Hutchins	76-71—147		Marc Turnesa	76-73—149		Beau Hossler (am)	76-77—153
	Martin Laird (SCO)	73-74—147		Camilo Villegas (COL)	77-72—149		Dae-Hyun Kim (KOR)	79-74—153
	Hunter Mahan	74-73—147		Chris Williams (am)	76-73—149		Maarten Lafeber	79-74—153
	David May	71-76—147	113	Scott Barr (AUS)	75-75—150		(NED)	
	Nick O'Hern (AUS)	77-70—147		Angel Cabrera (ARG)	71-79—150		Brian Locke	75-78—153
	Justin Rose (ENG)	74-73—147		K J Choi (KOR)	77-73—150		Adam Long	76-77—153
	Adam Scott (AUS)	74-73—147		Nicholas Colsaerts	76-74—150		Ryan Nelson	75-78—153
88	Aaron Baddeley	71-77—148		(BEL)		145	Andreas Harto	78-76—154
	(AUS)			Matthew Edwards	75-75—150		(DEN)	
	Ben Crane	77-71—148		Fred Funk	75-75—150		Scott Pinckney (am)	79-75—154
	Ernie Els (RSA)	73-75—148		Miguel Angel Jiménez	77-73—150		Will Wilcox	79-75—154
	Elliot Gealy	77-71—148		(ESP)		148	Steve Irwin (am)	78-77—155
	Shane Lowry (IRL)	72-76—148		Ryan Moore	73-77—150		Kevin Na	80-75—155
	Ian Poulter (ENG)	75-73—148		Peter Uihlein (am)	72-78—150		Brett Patterson (am)	77-78—155
	Nick Watney	75-73—148	122	Robert Allenby (AUS)	73-78—151		Geoffery Sisk	77-78—155
	Mark Wilson	78-70—148		Bubba Dickerson	70-81—151	152	David Chung (am)	82-75—157
96	Briny Baird	75-74—149		Joey Lamielle	76-75—151		Ty Tryon	84-73—157
	Bennett Blakeman	76-73—149		Thomas Levet (FRA)	75-76—151	154	Matthew Richardson	77-81—158
	(am)			Geoff Ogilvy (AUS)	75-76—151		(ENG)	
	Alex Cejka (GER)	75-74—149		Kirk Triplett	76-75—151	155	Michael Barbosa	83-83—166
	Greg Chalmers	76-73—149	128	Jonathan Byrd	75-77—152		(am)	
	(AUS)			Zach Byrd	77-75—152			
	Jason Dufner	75-74—149		Michael Campbell	75-77—152	WD	Tim Petrovic	
	Jim Furyk	74-75—149		(NZL)				

What is the answer?

Q: I placed my ball on a tee on the teeing ground and, in taking a practice swing, I accidentally caused it to fall off the tee peg. Do I incur a penalty?

A: As the ball was not yet in play when you moved it – you moved it when practice swinging – there is no penalty. Just retrieve the ball, or put another on the tee, and carry on.

2010 US Open Pebble Beach, CA June 17–20 [7260–71]

Prize money: $7.5 million. Entries: 9,052

1	Graeme McDowell (NIR)	71-68-71-74—284	$1,350,000
2	Grégory Havret (FRA)	73-71-69-72—285	810,000
3	Ernie Els (RSA)	73-68-72-73—286	480,687
4	Phil Mickelson	75-66-73-73—287	303,119
	Tiger Woods	74-72-66-75—287	303,119
6	Matt Kuchar	74-72-74-68—288	228,255
	Davis Love III	75-74-68-71—288	228,255
8	Alex Cejka (GER)	70-72-74-73—289	177,534
	Dustin Johnson	71-70-66-82—289	177,534
	Martin Kaymer (GER)	74-71-72-72—289	177,534
	Brandt Snedeker	75-74-69-71—289	177,534
12	Tim Clark (RSA)	72-72-72-74—290	143,714
	Sean O'Hair	76-71-70-73—290	143,714
14	Ben Curtis	78-70-75-68—291	127,779
	Justin Leonard	72-73-73-73—291	127,779
16	Jim Furyk	72-75-74-71—292	108,458
	Peter Hanson (SWE)	73-76-74-69—292	108,458
	Russell Henley (am)	73-74-72-73—292	
	Scott Langley (am)	75-69-77-71—292	
	Charl Schwartzel (RSA)	74-71-74-73—292	108,458
	Lee Westwood (ENG)	74-71-76-71—292	108,458
22	Angel Cabrera (ARG)	75-72-74-72—293	83,634
	Sergio García (ESP)	73-76-73-71—293	83,634
	Padraig Harrington (IRL)	73-73-74-73—293	83,634

22T	John Malinger	77-72-70-74—293	83,634
	Shaun Micheel	69-77-75-72—293	83,634
27	Ricky Barnes	72-76-74-72—294	67,195
	Robert Karlsson (SWE)	75-72-74-73—294	67,195
29	Robert Allenby (AUS)	74-74-73-74—295	54,871
	Stuart Appleby (AUS)	73-76-76-70—295	54,871
	Henrik Stenson (SWE)	77-70-74-74—295	54,871
	Tom Watson	78-71-70-76—295	54,871
33	Brendon De Jonge (ZIM)	69-73-77-77—296	44,472
	Jason Dufner	72-73-79-72—296	44,472
	Ryo Ishikawa (JPN)	70-71-75-80—296	44,472
	Søren Kjeldsen (DEN)	72-71-75-78—296	44,472
	Ryan Moore	75-73-75-73—296	44,472
	Kenny Perry	72-77-73-74—296	44,472
	David Toms	71-75-76-74—296	44,472
40	Paul Casey (ENG)	69-73-77-78—297	34,722
	Stewart Cink	76-73-71-77—297	34,722
	Bobby Gates	75-74-71-77—297	34,722
	Ross McGowan (ENG)	72-73-78-74—297	34,722
	Noh Seung-yul (KOR)	74-72-76-75—297	34,722
	Vijay Singh (FIJ)	74-72-75-76—297	34,722
	Bo Van Pelt	72-75-82-68—297	34,722

Other players who made the cut: Jason Allred, Rafael Cabrera Bello (ESP), K J Choi (KOR), Luke Donald (ENG), Jason Gore, Jim Herman, Thongchai Jaidee (THA), Edoardo Molinari (ITA), Ian Poulter (ENG), Chris Stroud, Scott Verplank 298; Hiroyuki Fujita (JPN), Lucas Glover, Retief Goosen (RSA), Yuta Ikeda (JPN), Steve Stricker 299; Eric Axley, Jerry Kelly, Steve Marino, Gareth Maybin (NIR), Toru Taniguchi (JPN), Steve Wheatcroft 300; Erick Justesen 301; Matt Bettencourt, David Duval, Fred Funk, Camilo Villegas (COL) 302; Rhys Davies (WAL), Kent Jones 303; Nick Watney 305; Craig Barlow, Zach Johnson, Matthew Richardson (ENG) 306; Ty Tryon, Mike Weir (CAN) 307; Pablo Martin (ESP), Jason Preeo 311

2009 US Open Bethpage, Farmingdale, NY June 18–21 [7426–70]

Prize money: $7.5 million. Entries: 9,086

1	Lucas Glover	69-64-70-73—276	$1,350,000
2	Ricky Barnes	67-65-70-76—278	559,830
	David Duval	67-70-70-71—278	559,830
	Phil Mickelson	69-70-69-70—278	559,830
5	Ross Fisher (ENG)	70-68-69-72—279	289,146
6	Søren Hansen (DEN)	70-71-70-69—280	233,350
	Hunter Mahan	72-68-68-72—280	233,350
	Tiger Woods	74-69-68-69—280	233,350
9	Henrik Stenson (SWE)	73-70-70-68—281	194,794
10	Stephen Ames (CAN)	74-66-70-72—282	154,600
	Matt Bettencourt	75-67-71-69—282	154,600
	Sergio García (ESP)	70-70-72-70—282	154,600
	Rory McIlroy (NIR)	72-70-72-68—282	154,600
	Ryan Moore	70-69-72-71—282	154,600
	Mike Weir (CAN)	64-70-74-74—282	154,600
16	Retief Goosen (RSA)	73-68-68-74—283	122,128
	Anthony Kim	71-71-71-70—283	122,128
18	Peter Hanson (SWE)	66-71-73-74—284	100,308
	Graeme McDowell (NIR)	69-72-69-74—284	100,308
	Ian Poulter (ENG)	70-74-73-67—284	100,308
	Michael Sim (AUS)	71-70-71-72—284	100,308
	Bubba Watson	72-70-67-75—284	100,308

23	Sean O'Hair	69-69-71-76—285	76,422
	Steve Stricker	73-66-72-74—285	76,422
	Lee Westwood (ENG)	72-66-74-73—285	76,422
	Oliver Wilson (ENG)	70-70-71-74—285	76,422
27	Stewart Cink	73-69-70-74—286	56,041
	Johan Edfors (SWE)	70-74-68-74—286	56,041
	J B Holmes	73-67-73-73—286	56,041
	Francesco Molinari (ITA)	71-70-74-71—286	56,041
	Vijay Singh (FIJ)	72-72-73-69—286	56,041
	Azuma Yano (JPN)	72-65-77-72—286	56,041
33	Jim Furyk	72-69-74-72—287	47,404
	Kevin Sutherland	71-73-73-70—287	47,404
	Camilo Villegas (COL)	71-71-72-73—287	47,404
36	Todd Hamilton	67-71-71-79—288	42,935
	Carl Pettersson (SWE)	75-68-73-72—288	42,395
	Adam Scott (AUS)	69-71-73-75—288	42,395
	Nick Taylor (am)	73-65-75-75—288	
40	Tim Clark (RSA)	73-71-74-71—289	38,492
	Dustin Johnson	72-69-76-72—289	38,492
	Billy Mayfair	73-70-72-74—289	38,492
	Drew Weaver (am)	69-72-74-74—289	
44	Kenny Perry	71-72-75-72—290	35,536

Other players who made the cut: Thomas Levet (FRA), John Mallinger 291; K J Choi (KOR), Tom Lehman, Rocco Mediate, Geoff Ogilvy (AUS), Andres Romero (ARG), Gary Woodland 292; Kyle Stanley (am) 293; Angel Cabrera (ARG), Jean-François Lucquin (FRA), Andrew McLardy (RSA) 294; Ben Curtis, 296; Jeff Brehaut 297, Trevor Murphy 297; Fred Funk 301

2008 US Open *Torrey Pines, La Jolla, CA* June 12–15   [7643–71]

Prize money: $7.5 million. Entries: 8,390

1	Tiger Woods*	72-68-70-73—283	$1,350,000	18T	Mike Weir (CAN)	73-74-69-74—290	87,230
2	Rocco Mediate	69-71-72-71—283	810,000	26	Anthony Kim	74-75-70-72—291	61,252
Tiger Woods won at the 19th hole of the extra round					Adam Scott (AUS)	73-73-75-70—291	61,252
3	Lee Westwood (ENG)	70-71-70-73—284	491,995		Boo Weekley	73-76-70-72—291	61,252
4	Robert Karlsson (SWE)	70-70-75-71—286	307,303	29	Aaron Baddeley (AUS)	74-73-71-74—292	48,482
	D J Trahan	72-69-73-72--286	307,303		Bart Bryant	75-70-78-69—292	48,482
6	Miguel Angel Jiménez	75-66-74-72—287	220,686		Jeff Quinney	79-70-70-73—292	48,482
	(ESP)				Patrick Sheehan	71-74-74-73—292	48,482
	John Merrick	73-72-71-71—287	220,686		Steve Stricker	73-76-71-72—292	48,482
	Carl Pettersson (SWE)	71-71-77-68—287	220,686		Michael Thompson	74-73-73-72—292	
9	Eric Axley	69-79-71-69—288	160,769		(am)		
	Geoff Ogilvy (AUS)	69-73-72-74—288	160,769		Scott Verplank	72-72-74-74—292	48,482
	Heath Slocum	75-74-74-65—288	160,769	36	Stuart Appleby (AUS)	69-70-79-75—293	35,709
	Brandt Snedeker	76-73-68-71—288	160,769		Daniel Chopra (SWE)	73-75-75-70—293	35,709
	Camilo Villegas (COL)	73-71-71-73—288	160,769		Robert Dinwiddie	73-71-75-74—293	35,709
14	Stewart Cink	72-73-77-67—289	122,159		(ENG)		
	Ernie Els (RSA)	70-72-74-73—289	122,159		Jim Furyk	74-71-73-75—293	35,709
	Retief Goosen (RSA)	76-69-77-67—289	122,159		Todd Hamilton	74-74-73-72—293	35,709
	Rod Pampling (AUS)	74-70-75-70—289	122,159		Padraig Harrington (IRL)	78-67-77-71—293	35,709
18	Robert Allenby (AUS)	70-72-73-75—290	87,230		Justin Leonard	75-72-75-71—293	35,709
	Chad Campbell	77-72-71-70—290	87,230		Jonathan Mills	72-75-75-71—293	35,709
	Sergio García (ESP)	76-70-70-74—290	87,230		Joe Ogilvie	71-76-73-73—293	35,709
	Ryuji Imada (JPN)	74-75-70-71—290	87,230		Pat Perez	75-73-75-70—293	35,709
	Brandt Jobe	73-75-69-73—290	87,230		Andres Romero (ARG)	71-73-77-72—293	35,709
	Hunter Mahan	72-74-69-75—290	87,230		Oliver Wilson (ENG)	72-71-74-76—293	35,709
	Phil Mickelson	71-75-76-68—290	87,230				

Other players who made the cut: Tim Clark (RSA), Dustin Johnson, Matt Kuchar, Jarrod Lyle (AUS), John Rollins 294; Ben Crane, Søren Hansen (DEN), Martin Kaymer (GER), Davis Love III, Kevin Streelman 295; Stephen Ames (CAN), Rory Sabbatini (RSA) 296; Alastair Forsyth (SCO), Rickie Fowler (am), Brett Quigley, David Toms, Nick Watney 297; Paul Casey (ENG), Trevor Immelman (RSA), John Malinger, Vijay Singh (FIJ) 298; Derek Fathauer (am), D A Points 299; Woody Austin, Andrew Dresser, Andrew Svoboda 300; Justin Hicks, Ian Leggatt (CAN), Jesper Parnevik (SWE) 301; Ross McGowan (ENG) 303; Rich Beem, Chris Kirk 304, Luke Donald (ENG) WD

2007 US Open *Oakmont, PA* June 14–17   [7230–70]

Prize money: $6.8 million. Entries: 8,544

1	Angel Cabrera (ARG)	69-71-76-69—285	$1,260,000	20T	Mike Weir (CAN)	74-72-73-75—294	86,200
2	Jim Furyk	71-75-70-70—286	611,336	23	Ken Duke	74-75-73-73—295	71,905
	Tiger Woods	71-74-69-72—286	611,336		Nick O'Hern (AUS)	76-74-71-74—295	71,905
4	Niclas Fasth (SWE)	71-71-75-70—287	325,923		Brandt Snedeker	71-73-77-74—295	71,905
5	David Toms	72-72-73-72—289	248,948	26	Stuart Appleby (AUS)	74-72-71-79—296	57,026
	Bubba Watson	70-71-74-74—289	248,948		J J Henry	71-78-75-72—296	57,026
7	Nick Dougherty (ENG)	68-77-74-71—290	194,245		Camilo Villegas (COL)	73-77-75-71—296	57,026
	Jerry Kelly	74-71-73-72—290	194,245		Boo Weekley	72-75-77-72—296	57,026
	Scott Verplank	73-71-74-72—290	194,245	30	D J Brigman	74-74-74-75—297	45,313
10	Stephen Ames (CAN)	73-69-73-76—291	154,093		Fred Funk	71-78-74-74—297	45,313
	Paul Casey (ENG)	77-66-72-76—291	154,093		Peter Hanson (SWE)	71-74-78-74—297	45,313
	Justin Rose (ENG)	71-71-73-76—291	154,093		Pablo Martin (ESP)	71-76-77-73—297	45,313
13	Aaron Baddeley (AUS)	72-70-70-80—292	124,706		Graeme McDowell	73-72-75-77—297	45,313
	Lee Janzen	73-73-73-73—292	124,706		(NIR)		
	Hunter Mahan	73-74-72-73—292	124,706		Charl Schwartzel (RSA)	75-73-73-76—297	45,313
	Steve Stricker	75-73-68-76—292	124,706	36	Mathew Goggin (AUS)	77-73-74-74—298	37,159
17	Jeff Brehaut	73-75-70-75—293	102,536		Shingo Katayama (JPN)	72-74-79-73—298	37,159
	Jim Clark (RSA)	72-76-71-74—293	102,536		Jeev Milkha Singh (IND)	75-75-73-75—298	37,159
	Carl Pettersson (SWE)	72-72-75-74—293	102,536		Tom Pernice	72-72-75-79—298	37,159
20	Anthony Kim	74-73-80-67—294	86,200		Ian Poulter (ENG)	72-77-72-77—298	37,159
	Vijay Singh (FIJ)	71-77-70-76—294	86,200		Lee Westwood (ENG)	72-75-79-72—298	37,159

Other players who made the cut: Kenneth Ferrie (ENG), Geoff Ogilvy (AUS), John Rollins 299; Olin Browne, Ben Curtis, Chris DiMarco, Marcus Fraser (AUS), Zach Johnson, José-María Olazábal (ESP) 300; Ernie Els (RSA), Charles Howell III, Rory Sabbatini (RSA), Dean Wilson 301; Anders Hansen (DEN), Michael Putnam 302; Chad Campbell 303; Michael Campbell (NZL), Bob Estes, Harrison Frazar, Kevin Sutherland 304; Jason Dufner 305; George McNeill 306

2006 US Open Winged Foot, Mamaroneck, NY June 15–18 [7264–70]

Prize money: $6.25 million. Entries: 8,584

1	Geoff Ogilvy (AUS)	71-70-72-72—285	$,1225,000	16T	Arron Oberholser	75-68-74-74—291	99,417
2	Jim Furyk	70-72-74-70—286	501,249	21	Peter Hedblom (SWE)	72-74-71-75—292	74,252
	Phil Mickelson	70-73-69-74—286	501,249		Trevor Immelman (RSA)	76-71-70-75—292	74,252
	Colin Montgomerie (SCO)	69-71-75-71—286	501,249		José-María Olazábal (ESP)	75-73-73-71—292	74,252
5	Padraig Harrington (IRL)	73-69-74-71—287	255,642		Tom Pernice Jr	79-70-72-71—292	74,252
					Adam Scott (AUS)	72-76-70-74—292	74,252
6	Kenneth Ferrie (ENG)	71-70-71-76—288	183,255	26	Craig Barlow	72-75-72-74—293	52,314
	Nick O'Hern (AUS)	75-70-74-69—288	183,255		Angel Cabrera (ARG)	74-73-74-72—293	52,314
	Vijay Singh (FIJ)	71-74-70-73—288	183,255		Ernie Els (RSA)	74-73-74-72—293	52,314
	Jeff Sluman	74-73-72-69—288	183,255		Sean O'Hair	76-72-74-71—293	52,314
	Steve Stricker	70-69-76-73—288	183,255		Ted Purdy	78-71-71-73—293	52,314
	Mike Weir (CAN)	71-71-72-72—288	183,255		Henrik Stenson (SWE)	75-71-73-74—293	52,314
12	Luke Donald (ENG)	78-69-70-72—289	131,670	32	Woody Austin	72-76-72-74—294	41,912
	Ryuji Imada (JPN)	76-73-69-71—289	131,670		Bart Bryant	72-72-73-77—294	41,912
	Ian Poulter (ENG)	74-71-70-74—289	131,670		Scott Hend (AUS)	72-72-75-75—294	41,912
15	Paul Casey (ENG)	77-72-72-69—290	116,735		Steve Jones	74-74-71-75—294	41,912
16	Robert Allenby (AUS)	73-74-72-72—291	99,417		Rodney Pampling (AUS)	73-75-75-71—294	41,912
	David Duval	77-68-75-71—291	99,417	37	Stewart Cink	75-71-77-72—295	36,647
	David Howell (ENG)	70-78-74-69—291	99,417		Jay Haas	75-72-74-74—295	36,647
	Miguel Angel Jiménez (ESP)	70-75-74-72—291	99,417		Charles Howell III	77-71-73-74—295	36,647

Other players who made the cut: Tommy Armour III, Chad Collins, John Cook, Jason Dufner, Fred Funk, Stephen Gangluff (CAN), Bo Van Pelt, Lee Williams 296; Phillip Archer (ENG), Thomas Bjørn (DEN), Fred Couples, Charley Hoffman, J B Holmes, Kent Jones, Graeme McDowell (NIR), Charl Schwartzel (RSA) 297; Darren Clarke (NIR) 298; Ben Curtis 299; Kenny Perry 301; Skip Kendal, Jeev Milkha Singh (IND), Camilo Villegas (COL) 302; Ben Crane 303; Tim Herron 305

2005 US Open Pinehurst No.2, NC June 16–19 [7214–70]

Prize money: $6.25 million. Entries: 9,048

1	Michael Campbell (NZL)	71-69-71-69—280	$1,170,000	15T	Peter Jacobsen	72-73-69-75—289	88.120
					David Toms	70-72-70-77—289	88.120
2	Tiger Woods	70-71-72-69—282	700,000	23	Olin Browne	67-71-72-80—290	59.633
3	Tim Clark (RSA)	76-69-70-70—285	320,039		Paul Claxton	72-72-72-74—290	59.633
	Sergio García (ESP)	71-69-75-70—285	320,039		Fred Funk	73-71-76-70—290	59.633
	Mark Hensby (AUS)	71-68-72-74—285	320,039		Justin Leonard	76-71-70-73—290	59.633
6	Davis Love III	77-70-70-69—286	187,813		Kenny Perry	75-70-71-74—290	59.633
	Rocco Mediate	67-74-74-71—286	187,813	28	Stephen Allan (AUS)	72-69-73-77—291	44.486
	Vijay Singh (FIJ)	70-70-74-72—286	187,813		Matt Every (am)	75-73-73-70—291	44.486
9	Arron Oberholser	76-67-71-73—287	150,834		Jim Furyk	71-70-75-75—291	44.486
	Nick Price (ZIM)	72-71-72-72—287	150,834		Geoff Ogilvy (AUS)	72-74-71-74—291	44.486
11	Bob Estes	70-73-75-70—288	123,857		Adam Scott (AUS)	70-71-74-76—291	44.486
	Retief Goosen (RSA)	68-70-69-81—288	123,857	33	Angel Cabrera (ARG)	71-73-73-75—292	35.759
	Peter Hedblom (SWE)	77-66-70-75—288	123,857		Steve Elkington (AUS)	74-69-79-70—292	35.759
	Corey Pavin	73-72-70-73—288	123,857		Tim Herron	72-72-75-75—292	35.759
15	K J Choi (KOR)	69-70-74-76—289	88,120		Brandt Jobe	68-73-79-72—292	35.759
	Stewart Cink	73-74-73-69—289	88.120		Bernhard Langer (GER)	74-73-71-74—292	35.759
	John Cook	71-76-70-72—289	88.120		Shigeki Maruyama (JPN)	71-74-72-75—292	35.759
	Fred Couples	71-74-74-70—289	88.120		Phil Mickelson	69-77-72-74—292	35.759
	Ernie Els (RSA)	71-76-72-70—289	88.120		Ted Purdy	73-71-73-75—292	35.759
	Ryuji Imada (JPN)	77-68-73-71—289	88.120		Lee Westwood (ENG)	68-72-73-79—292	35.759

Other players who made the cut: Chad Campbell, Peter Lonard (AUS), Paul McGinley (IRL), Colin Montgomerie (SCO), Tom Pernice, Rob Rashell, Mike Weir (CAN) 293; Jason Gore, J L Lewis, Nick O'Hern (AUS) 294; Thomas Bjørn (DEN), Nick Dougherty (ENG), Richard Green (AUS), Søren Kjeldsen (DEN), Thomas Levet (FRA) 295; Tommy Armour III, Luke Donald (ENG), Keiichiro Fukabori (JPN), J J Henry, Lee Janzen, Steve Jones, Frank Lickliter, Jonathan Lomas (ENG), Ryan Moore (am), Ian Poulter (ENG) 296; Michael Allen, Steve Flesch, Bill Glasson, John Mallinger 297; Stephen Ames (TRI), D J Brigman, J Hayes, Rory Sabbatini (RSA) 298; John Daly, Charles Howell III, Omar Uresti, 299; Jeff Maggert, Bob Tway 300; Graeme McDowell (NIR), Chris Nallen 301; Craig Barlow 303; Jerry Kelly 305

2004 US Open Shinnecock Hills, Southampton, NY June 17–20   [6996–70]

Prize money: $6.25 million. Entries: 8,726

1	Retief Goosen (RSA)	70-66-69-71—276	$1,125,000
2	Phil Mickelson	68-66-73-71—278	675,000
3	Jeff Maggert	68-67-74-72—281	424,604
4	Shigeki Maruyama (JPN)	66-68-74-76—284	267,756
	Mike Weir (CAN)	69-70-71-74—284	267,756
6	Fred Funk	70-66-72-77—285	212,444
7	Robert Allenby (AUS)	70-72-74-70—286	183,828
	Steve Flesch	68-74-70-74—286	183,828
9	Stephen Ames (TRI)	74-66-73-74—287	145,282
	Ernie Els (RSA)	70-67-70-80—287	145,282
	Chris DiMarco	71-71-70-75—287	145,282
	Jay Haas	66-74-76-71—287	145,282
13	Tim Clark (RSA)	73-70-66-79—288	119,770
	Tim Herron	75-66-73-74—288	119,770
	Spencer Levin (am)	69-73-71-75—288	
16	Angel Cabrera (ARG)	66-71-77-75—289	109,410
17	Skip Kendall	68-75-74-73—290	98,477
	Corey Pavin	67-71-73-79—290	98,477
	Tiger Woods	72-69-73-76—290	98,477
20	Mark Calcavecchia	71-71-74-75—291	80,644
	Sergio García (ESP)	72-68-71-80—291	80,644
20T	David Toms	73-72-70-76—291	80,644
	Kirk Triplett	71-70-73-77—291	80,644
24	Daniel Chopra (SWE)	73-68-76-75—292	63,328
	Lee Janzen	72-70-71-79—292	63,328
	Tim Petrovic	69-75-72-76—292	63,328
	Nick Price (ZIM)	73-70-72-77—292	63,328
28	Shaun Micheel	71-72-70-80—293	51,774
	Vijay Singh (FIJ)	68-70-77-78—293	51,774
30	Ben Curtis	68-75-72-79—294	46,089
31	K J Choi (KOR)	76-68-76-75—295	41,759
	Padraig Harrington (IRL)	73-71-76-75—295	41,759
	Peter Lonard (AUS)	71-73-77-74—295	41,759
	David Roesch	68-73-74-80—295	41,759
	Bo Van Pelt	69-73-73-80—295	41,759
36	Charles Howell III	75-70-68-83—296	36,813
	Hidemichi Tanaka (JPN)	70-74-73-79—296	36,813
	Lee Westwood (ENG)	73-71-73-79—296	36,813
	Casey Wittenberg (am)	71-71-75-79—296	

Other players who made the cut: Bill Haas (am), Jerry Kelly, Stephen Leaney (AUS), Spike McRoy, Joe Ogilvie, Pat Perez, Geoffrey Sisk, Scott Verplank 297; Kristopher Cox, Jim Furyk, Zachary Johnson, Chris Riley, John Rollins 298; Dudley Hart, Scott Hoch 299; Tom Carter, Trevor Immelman (RSA) 300; Joakim Haeggman (SWE), Tom Kite, Phillip Price (WAL) 302; Alex Cejka (GER), Craig Parry (AUS) 303; Cliff Kresge, Chez Reavie (am) 304; J J Henry 306; Kevin Stadler 307; Billy Mayfair 310

2003 US Open Olympia Fields CC (North Course), IL June 12–15   [7190–70]

Prize money: $6 million. Entries: 7,820

1	Jim Furyk	67-66-67-72—272	$108,0000
2	Stephen Leaney (AUS)	67-68-68-72—275	650,000
3	Kenny Perry	72-71-69-67—279	341,367
	Mike Weir (CAN)	73-67-68-71—279	341,367
5	Ernie Els (RSA)	69-70-69-72—280	185,934
	Fredrik Jacobson (SWE)	69-67-73-71—280	185,934
	Nick Price (ZIM)	71-65-69-75—280	185,934
	Justin Rose (ENG)	70-71-70-69—280	185,934
	David Toms	72-67-70-71—280	185,934
10	Padraig Harrington (IRL)	69-72-72-68—281	124,936
	Jonathan Kaye	70-70-72-69—281	124,936
	Cliff Kresge	69-70-72-70—281	124,936
	Billy Mayfair	69-71-67-74—281	124,936
	Scott Verplank	76-67-68-70—281	124,936
15	Jonathan Byrd	69-66-71-76—282	93,359
	Tom Byrum	69-69-71-73—282	93,359
	Tim Petrovic	69-70-70-73—282	93,359
	Eduardo Romero (ARG)	70-66-70-76—282	93,359
	Higemichi Tamaka (JPN)	69-71-71-71—282	93,359
20	Mark Calcavecchia	68-72-67-76—283	64,170
	Robert Damron	69-68-73-73—283	64,170
	Ian Leggatt (RSA)	68-70-68-77—283	64,170
	Justin Leonard	66-70-72-75—283	64,170
	Peter Lonard (AUS)	72-69-74-68—283	64,170
	Vijay Singh (FIJ)	70-63-72-78—283	64,170
	Jay Williamson	72-69-69-73—283	64,170
	Tiger Woods	70-66-75-72—283	64,170
28	Stewart Cink	70-68-72-74—284	41,254
	John Maginnes	72-70-72-70—284	4,1254
	Dicky Pride	71-69-66-78—284	41,254
	Brett Quigley	65-74-71-74—284	41,254
	Kevin Sutherland	71-71-72-70—284	41,254
	Kirk Triplett	71-68-73-72—284	41,254
	Tom Watson	65-72-75-72—284	41,254
35	Angel Cabrera (ARG)	72-68-73-72—285	32,552
	Chad Campbell	70-70-69-76—285	32,552
	Chris DiMarco	72-71-71-71—285	32,552
	Fred Funk	70-73-71-71—285	32,552
	Sergio García (ESP)	69-74-71-71—285	32,552
	Brandt Jobe	70-68-76-71—285	32,552
	Mark O'Meara	72-68-67-78—285	32,552

Other players who made the cut: Darren Clarke (NIR), Retief Goosen (RSA), Bernhard Langer (GER), Steve Lowery, Colin Montgomerie (SCO), Loren Roberts 286; Woody Austin, Marco Dawson, Niclas Fasth (SWE), Dan Forsman, Darron Stiles 287; Charles Howell III, John Rollins 288; Lee Janzen, Phil Mickelson 289; Trip Kuehne (am), Len Mattiace 290; Ricky Barnes (am), Olin Browne 291; Chris Anderson, Alexander Cejka (GER), Brian Davis (ENG) 292; Jay Don Blake, JP Hayes 293; Fred Couples, Brian Henninger 295; Ryan Dillon 301

2002 US Open Bethpage State Park, Black Course, Farmingdale, NY August 13–16 [7214–70]

Prize money: $5.5 million. Entries: 8,468

1	Tiger Woods	67-68-70-72—277	$1,000,000	24	Jim Carter	77-73-70-71—291	47,439
2	Phil Mickelson	70-73-67-70—280	585,000		Darren Clarke (NIR)	74-74-72-71—291	47,439
3	Jeff Maggert	69-73-68-72—282	362,356		Chris DiMarco	74-74-72-71—291	47,439
4	Sergio García (ESP)	68-74-67-74—283	252,546		Ernie Els (RSA)	73-74-70-74—291	47,439
5	Nick Faldo (ENG)	70-76-66-73—285	182,882		Davis Love III	71-71-72-77—291	47,439
	Scott Hoch	71-75-70-69—285	182,882		Jeff Sluman	73-73-72-73—291	47,439
	Billy Mayfair	69-74-68-74—285	182,882	30	Jason Caron	75-72-72-73—292	35,639
8	Tom Byrum	72-72-70-72—286	138,669		K J Choi (KOR)	69-73-73-77—292	35,639
	Padraig Harrington (IRL)	70-68-73-75—286	138,669		Paul Lawrie (SCO)	73-73-73-73—292	35,639
	Nick Price (ZIM)	72-75-69-70—286	138,669		Scott McCarron	72-72-70-78—292	35,639
11	Peter Lonard (AUS)	73-74-73-67—287	119,357		Vijay Singh (FIJ)	75-75-67-75—292	35,639
12	Robert Allenby (AUS)	74-70-67-77—288	102,338	35	Shingo Katayama (JPN)	74-72-74-73—293	31,945
	Jay Haas	73-73-70-72—288	102,338		Bernhard Langer (GER)	72-76-70-75—293	31,945
	Dudley Hart	69-76-70-73—288	102,338				
	Justin Leonard	73-71-68-76—288	102,338	37	Stuart Appleby (AUS)	77-73-75-69—294	26,783
16	Shigeki Maruyama (JPN)	76-67-73-73—289	86,372		Thomas Bjørn (DEN)	71-79-73-71—294	26,783
					Niclas Fasth (SWE)	72-72-74-76—294	26,783
	Steve Stricker	72-77-69-71—289	86,372		Donnie Hammond	73-77-71-73—294	26,783
18	Luke Donald (ENG)	76-72-70-72—290	68,995		Franklin Langham	70-76-74-74—294	26,783
	Charles Howell III	71-74-70-75—290	68,995		Rocco Mediate	72-72-74-76—294	26,783
	Steve Flesch	72-72-75-71—290	68,995		Kevin Sutherland	74-75-70-75—294	26,783
	Thomas Levet (FRA)	71-77-70-72—290	68,995		Hidemichi Tanaka (JPN)	73-73-72-76—294	26,783
	Mark O'Meara	76-70-69-75—290	68,995				
	Craig Stadler	74-72-70-74—290	68,995				

Other players who made the cut: Tom Lehman, Frank Lickliter, Kenny Perry, David Toms, Jean Van de Velde (FRA) 295; Craig Bowden, Tim Herron, Robert Karlsson (SWE), José María Olazábal (ESP) 296; Harrison Frazar, Ian Leggatt (CAN), Jesper Parnevik (SWE), Corey Pavin 297; Brad Lardon 298; John Maginnes, Greg Norman (AUS), Bob Tway 299; Andy Miller, Jeev Milkha Singh (IND), Paul Stankowski 300; Spike McRoy 301; Angel Cabrera (ARG), Brad Faxon 302; Kent Jones, Len Mattiace 303; John Daly, Tom Gillis 304; Kevin Warrick (am) 307

US Open Championship History

Year	Winner	Runner-up	Venue	Score
1894	W Dunn	W Campbell	St Andrews, NY	2 holes

After 1894 decided by stroke-play. From 1895–1897. 36-holes From 1898 72-holes

Year	Winner	Venue	Score	Year	Winner	Venue	Score
1895	HJ Rawlins	Newport	173	1913	F Ouimet* (am)	Brookline, MA	304
1896	J Foulis	Southampton	152	*After a play-off: Ouimet 72, H Vardon 77, T Ray 78			
1897	J Lloyd	Wheaton, IL	162	1914	W Hagen	Midlothian	297
1898	F Herd	South Hamilton, MA	328	1915	J Travers (am)	Baltusrol	290
1899	W Smith	Baltimore	315	1916	C Evans (am)	Minneapolis	286
1900	H Vardon (ENG)	Wheaton, IL	313	1917-18	No Championship		
1901	W Anderson*	Myopia, MA	315	1919	W Hagen*	Braeburn	301
*After a play-off: Anderson 85, A Smith 86				*After a play-off: Hagen 77, M Brady 78			
1902	L Auchterlonie	Garden City	305	1920	E Ray (ENG)	Inverness	295
1903	W Anderson*	Baltusrol	307	1921	J Barnes	Washington	289
*After a play-off: Anderson 82, D Brown 84				1922	G Sarazen	Glencoe	288
1904	W Anderson	Glenview	304	1923	R Jones Jr* (am)	Inwood, NY	295
1905	W Anderson	Myopia, MA	335	*After a play-off: Jones 76, R Cruikshank 78			
1906	A Smith	Onwentsia	291	1924	C Walker	Oakland Hills	297
1907	A Ross	Chestnut Hill, PA	302	1925	W MacFarlane*	Worcester	291
1908	F McLeod*	Myopia, MA	322	*After a play-off: MacFarlane 147, R Jones Jr 148			
*After a play-off: McLeod 77, W Smith 83				1926	R Jones Jr (am)	Scioto	293
1909	G Sargent	Englewood, NJ	290	1927	T Armour*	Oakmont	301
1910	A Smith*	Philadelphia	289	*After a play-off: Armour 76, H Cooper 79			
*After a play-off: Smith 71, J McDermott 75, M Smith 77				1928	J Farrell*	Olympia Fields	294
1911	J McDermott*	Wheaton, IL	307	*After a play-off: Farrell 143, R Jones Jr (am) 144			
*After a play-off with M Brady and G Simpson: McDermott 80, Brady 82, Simpson 85				1929	R Jones Jr* (am)	Winged Foot, NY	294
				*After a play-off: Jones 141, A Espinosa 164			
1912	J McDermott	Buffalo, NY	294	1930	R Jones Jr (am)	Interlachen	287

Year	Winner	Venue	Score
1931	B Burke*	Inverness	292
*After a play-off: Burke 149-148, G von Elm 149-149			
1932	G Sarazen	Fresh Meadow	286
1933	J Goodman (am)	North Shore	287
1934	O Dutra	Merion	293
1935	S Parks	Oakmont	299
1936	T Manero	Springfield	282
1937	R Guldahl	Oakland Hills	281
1938	R Guldahl	Cherry Hills	284
1939	B Nelson*	Philadelphia	284
*After a play-off: Nelson 138, C Wood 141, D Shute 76			
1940	W Lawson Little*	Canterbury, OH	287
*After a play-off: Little 70, G Sarazen 73			
1941	C Wood	Fort Worth, TX	284
1942–45	No Championship		
1946	L Mangrum*	Canterbury	284
*After a play-off: Mangrum 144, B Nelson 145, V Ghezzi 145			
1947	L Worsham*	St Louis	282
*After a play-off: Worsham 69, S Snead 70			
1948	B Hogan	Los Angeles	276
1949	Dr C Middlecoff	Medinah, IL	286
1950	B Hogan*	Merion, PA	287
*After a play-off: Hogan 69, L Mangrum 73, D Fazio 75			
1951	B Hogan	Oakland Hills, MI	287
1952	J Boros	Dallas, TX	281
1953	B Hogan	Oakmont	283
1954	E Furgol	Baltusrol	284
1955	J Fleck*	San Francisco	287
*After a play-off: Fleck 69, B Hogan 72			
1956	Dr C Middlecoff	Rochester, NY	281
1957	D Mayer*	Inverness	282
*After a play-off: Mayer 72, C Middlecoff 79			
1958	T Bolt	Tulsa, OK	283
1959	W Casper	Winged Foot, NY	282
1960	A Palmer	Denver, CO	280
1961	G Littler	Birmingham, MI	281
1962	J Nicklaus*	Oakmont	283
*After a play-off: Nicklaus 71, A Palmer 74			
1963	J Boros*	Brookline, MA	293
*After a play-off: Boros 70, J Cupit 73, A Palmer 76			
1964	K Venturi	Washington	278
1965	G Player* (RSA)	St Louis, MO	282
*After a play-off: Player 71, K Nagle 74			
1966	W Casper*	San Francisco	278
*After a play-off: Casper 69, A Palmer 73			
1967	J Nicklaus	Baltusrol	275
1968	L Trevino	Rochester, NY	275
1969	O Moody	Houston, TX	281
1970	A Jacklin (ENG)	Hazeltine, MN	281
1971	L Trevino*	Merion, PA	280
*After a play-off: Trevino 68, J Nicklaus 71			

Year	Winner	Venue	Score
1972	J Nicklaus	Pebble Beach	290
1973	J Miller	Oakmont, PA	279
1974	H Irwin	Winged Foot, NY	287
1975	L Graham*	Medinah, IL	287
*After a play-off: Graham 71, J Mahaffey 73			
1976	J Pate	Atlanta, GA	277
1977	H Green	Southern Hills, Tulsa	278
1978	A North	Cherry Hills	285
1979	H Irwin	Inverness, OH	284
1980	J Nicklaus	Baltusrol	272
1981	D Graham (AUS)	Merion, PA	273
1982	T Watson	Pebble Beach	282
1983	L Nelson	Oakmont, PA	280
1984	F Zoeller*	Winged Foot	276
*After a play-off: Zoeller 67, G Norman 75			
1985	A North	Oakland Hills, MI	279
1986	R Floyd	Shinnecock Hills, NY	279
1987	S Simpson	Olympic, San Francisco	277
1988	C Strange*	Brookline, MA	278
*After a play-off: Strange 71, N Faldo 75			
1989	C Strange	Rochester, NY	278
1990	H Irwin*	Medinah	280
*After a play-off: Irwin 74, M Donald 74 (Irwin won sudden death play-off 3 to 4 at first extra hole)			
1991	P Stewart*	Hazeltine, MN	282
*After a play-off: Stewart 75, S Simpson 77			
1992	T Kite	Pebble Beach, FL	285
1993	L Janzen	Baltusrol	272
1994	E Els* (RSA)	Oakmont, PA	279
*After a play-off: Els 74, L Roberts 74, C Montgomerie 78 (Els won sudden death playoff: Els 4,4, Roberts 4,5)			
1995	C Pavin	Shinnecock Hills, NY	280
1996	S Jones	Oakland Hills, MI	278
1997	E Els (RSA)	Congressional, Bethesda	276
1998	L Janzen	Olympic, San Francisco	280
1999	P Stewart	Pinehurst No. 2, NC	279
2000	T Woods	Pebble Beach, CA	272
2001	R Goosen* (RSA)	Southern Hills CC, OK	276
*After a play-off: Goosen 70, M Brooks 72			
2002	T Woods	Farmingdale, NY	277
2003	J Furyk	Olympia Fields, IL	272
2004	R Goosen (RSA)	Shinnecock Hills, NY	276
2005	M Campbell (NZL)	Pinehurst No.2, NC	280
2006	G Ogilvy (AUS)	Winged Foot, NY	285
2007	A Cabrera (ARG)	Oakmont, PA	285
2008	T Woods*	Torrey Pines, CA	283
*Beat R Mediate at 19th hole of extra round			
2009	L Glover	Farmingdale, NY	276
2010	G McDowell (NIR)	Pebble Beach, CA	284
2011	R McIlroy (NIR)	Congressional, Bethesda, MD	268

Rory's amazing début

Rory McIlroy's victory at the Bethesda Country Club was noteworthy not just for the fact that it was his first major victory but for the number of records he smashed. Not quite the youngest-ever victor in the US Open Championship – that distinction goes to Johnny McDermott who was 19 years, 10 months and 12 days old when he won at Chicago in 1911 – McIlroy made the record books with the lowest winning aggregate of 268, lowest score in relation to par (16 under), lowest first 36 holes (131), lowest first 54 holes (199) and lowest final 54 holes (203). Not only that but he joined an illustrious list of outright leaders after every round – Craig Wood, 1941; Arnold Palmer, 1960; Jack Nicklaus, 1972; Raymond Floyd, 1976.

The Masters Tournament

April 7–10

Charl Schwartzel collects the Green Jacket
South African's explosive late birdie burst is decisive at Augusta

Half a century after compatriot Gary Player became the first international golfer to win the Masters, South Africa's Charl Schwartzel made a piece of history of his own when he birdied all four of the closing holes at Augusta National to slip into a Green Jacket. It was a golfing feat never previously accomplished at the Masters and enabled the 26-year-old to eclipse the mark set by Adam Scott and Jason Day, two players who strove manfully to become the first Australian ever to win the season's first major.

Following in the footsteps of his friend, Louis Oosthuizen, who won the The Open Championship at St Andrews in 2010 thanks to a peerless display of ball-striking, Schwartzel was the second South African in nine months to win a major title and the seventh since Bobby Locke first won The Open in 1949. Schwartzel emulated Locke, Player, Els, Goosen, Immelman and Oosthuizen by coming home in 32 blows at Augusta for a closing score of 66 and the 14 under par total of 274. Day and Scott finished two strokes adrift on 276 while Tiger Woods, Geoff Ogilvy and Luke Donald were on 278.

© Getty Images

Charl Schwartzel

Back in 15th spot was Rory McIlroy, the young golfer from Northern Ireland who carried a four stroke lead after 54 holes. Only Greg Norman in 1996, Ed Sneed in 1979 and Ken Venturi in 1956 had previously failed to win after holding leads of four shots or more going into the last round at Augusta.

Tormented by poor putting and a destructive pull-hook off the tee, however, McIlroy ran up an ugly 80 and lost the tournament, though not his dignity. He blamed the tee shot on the tenth for his woes and admitted unravelling thereafter. His back nine of 43 was sore to watch and at the end was a far more damaging flaw.

But for McIlroy's meltdown, Schwartzel might have only been a footnote in Masters' folklore rather than the main event. As it was, he swatted away challenges from Woods, who went to the turn in 31 questioning suggestions he might be a spent force, as well as the eight other players from all corners of the globe who reached ten under par at one stage or another during one of the most thrilling afternoons in major championship history.

While rarely have so many enjoyed so great an opportunity to secure major success, it was Schwartzel who made the decisive move on Augusta's back nine in spite of never previously finishing in the top ten at a major. Before his electrifying finish, he chipped in at the first for birdie and holed his approach for eagle at the third. "It's always nice when things start in the right direction," he said. "I don't think I've ever heard a roar that loud around me. It was just a great way to start. But it was always going to come down to the back nine and to who made the birdies coming in."

One of the reasons Schwartzel putted so well at Augusta was because of advice he'd been given by the former Open champion Nick Price. "Previously, I'd never hit putts so softly from 40 feet and I struggled with that," he acknowledged. "Nick told me when he came over, he used to find the fastest putt on every green and work on that and that's what I did for the last three weeks. Every tournament I went to, I just practised the fastest putt I could find, even though they were only five feet, to learn to hit the putts that softly."

Although he didn't truly command the spotlight until Sunday afternoon, Schwartzel began the week aggressively, reeling off birdies in the first round at the second, sixth and 16th holes as well as eagling the par 5 eighth. His opening salvo of 69 would have been even more impressive but for dropped shots at the tenth and 18th.

Making only his second appearance at Augusta National, Schwartzel was able to call on Jack Nicklaus' unsurpassed knowledge of the course when he was introduced to the six times champion by Johan Rupert, the South African businessman, before his debut in 2010. Another player who heeded Nicklaus' advice about minimising mistakes on the first day was McIlroy. As it turned out, during the opening round, McIlroy not only kept a bogey off his card but also carded four birdies on the front nine and three on the back. His opening 65 was effortless and sparked comparisons with the 63 he posted at St Andrews in 2010 during The Open Championship. Although Spain's Alvaro Quiros, who was playing in the last group, birdied the closing 17th and 18th holes to join McIlroy on seven under par, the Irishman's share of the first round lead meant he became the youngest ever golfer to show the rest the way at Augusta. Seve Ballesteros, then 23, was the previous youngest first round leader in 1980. Playing with America's Rickie Fowler, 22, who shot 70, and Australia's Day, 23, who posted 73, McIlroy was part of a young guns grouping which brought out the best in him. "We talked about cars, boats — anything but golf, really," he grinned.

The story of the second round concentrated on the continuing exploits of McIlroy, Day and Fowler. This three-ball fed off each other's exploits and played better golf than any other group on Thursday and Friday. At the halfway mark, the youthful trio were collectively 23 under par for 36 holes. Between them, they made 34 birdies.

McIlroy again led the way, adding 69 to his opening 65 for ten under par. For 29 holes, the Irishman was the only player in the field yet to drop a stroke to par. On the short 12th, however, McIlroy's tee shot came up short in the front trap and his recovery shot from the bunker never threatened the hole. Because it was a day when McIlroy's putting from ten feet and under was largely indifferent, he made a two putt bogey and offset some of the good work he had accomplished with birdies at the second, fifth, ninth and 13th holes.

Still, the 21-year-old struck the ball well — his shot from the fairway bunker on the 18th was particularly exquisite — and took a two shot lead over the field into the third round. The Irishman, though, had to play second fiddle to Day on Friday as the Australian signed for an exhilarating 64 which included eight birdies. Holing the kind of putts which McIlroy mostly missed in the second round, Day covered the back nine in just 31 blows. His endeavours matched the record low second round score set at Augusta by Miller Barber in 1979 and Jay Haas in 1995. With both McIlroy and Fowler enjoying higher profiles in the game, Day quipped to his contemporaries as they walked down the first hole that he was going to have to pay people to shout his name. By the time he'd recorded birdies on the 14th, 16th and 18th holes, however, all the patrons at Augusta were familiar with Jason Day.

The second round was also notable for the moves made by more experienced players, most notably Woods and Ogilvy. Seeking his fifth Green Jacket, Woods recovered from a shaky start to card 66, twice reeling off runs of three consecutive birdies. As for Schwartzel, he largely kept his head below the parapet on Friday, carding 71 and offsetting two bogeys with three birdies. With the course set up over the opening 36 holes in a manner designed to restore excitement at Augusta, perhaps it was no surprise the cut should fall at the one over par mark of 145, thereby matching the lowest number in 75 years.

On Saturday, the pin positions were tougher, the atmosphere more subdued, though the course remained more open to attack than in recent years. McIlroy, if anything, holed fewer putts from ten feet or longer than in the previous rounds — the double breaking 30 footer for a birdie 3 on the 17th which produced the loudest roar of the day was an exception rather the rule — but his play from tee to green remained demonstrably better than that of anyone else in the field. For 54 holes, no one shaped more accurate iron shots to find 80 per cent of greens in regulation. Consequently, the Irishman's 70 for 12 under par increased his lead to four strokes going into the final day.

One of the peculiarities of the third day's play was how, for the first time in the tournament's 75 year history, no American played well enough to feature in the top five. Schwartzel, who carded 68, Choi of Korea, 71, and Day of Australia, 72, were the closest challengers to McIlroy on the same mark as Angel Cabrera. Schwartzel putted beautifully on Saturday as he posted six birdies and dropped just two strokes. His average of 1.56 putts per hole for the week was bettered only by Luke Donald who posted a 1.42 average. On the final day, though, the South African also enjoyed the measure of good fortune every champion needs from off the green chipping in from 75 feet for a birdie at the first before holing out from the middle of the fairway on the third for an eagle 2. In the blink of an eye, McIlroy, who made such a nervous start, had lost his lead.

True, the South African dropped a gear in the middle of the round, giving back a stroke to par on the fourth hole and then reeling off four birdies in a row from the 15th he holed successive putts. If the advantage during that period seemed to lie with others, it was Schwartzel's extraordinary finish which crowned him champion. Reeling off four consecutive birdies between the 15th and the 18th, he holed successive putts from eight, 15, 12 and 15 feet respectively. While plenty of his rivals gave themselves a chance of victory, only the South African embraced destiny.

First Round	Second Round	Third Round	Fourth Round
−7 Rory McIlroy	−10 Rory McIlroy	−12 Rory McIlroy	−14 Charl Schwartzel
−7 Alvaro Quiros	−8 Jason Day	−8 Jason Day	−12 Jason Day
−5 K J Choi	−7 Tiger Woods	−8 Angel Cabrera	−12 Adam Scott
−5 Y E Yang	−7 K J Choi	−8 K J Choi	−10 Luke Donald
−4 Matt Kuchar	−6 Geoff Ogilvy	−8 Charl Schwartzel	−10 Tiger Woods
−4 Ricky Barnes	−6 Alvaro Quiros	−7 Luke Donald	−10 Geoff Ogilvy
−3 Ross Fisher	−5 Lee Westwood	−7 Adam Scott	−9 Angel Cabrera
−3 Sergio García	−5 Fred Couples	−6 Bo Van Pelt	−8 Bo Van Pelt
−3 Brandt Snedeker	−5 Rickie Fowler	−5 Tiger Woods	−8 K J Choi
−3 Charl Schwartzel	−5 Y E Yang	−5 Fred Couples	−6 Ryan Palmer

The Masters (75th) *Augusta National GC, GA*   April 7–10   [7435–72]

Prize money: $7.5m. Final field of 93 players (six amateurs) of whom 49 (including one amateur) made the final half-way cut on 145 or less.

Players are of American nationality unless stated.

1	Charl Schwartzel (RSA)	69-71-68-66—274	$1,444,000
2	Jason Day (AUS)	72-64-72-68—276	704,000
	Adam Scott (AUS)	72-70-67-67—276	704,000
4	Luke Donald (ENG)	72-68-69-69—278	330,667
	Geoff Ogilvy (AUS)	69-69-73-67—278	330,667
	Tiger Woods	71-66-74-67—278	330,667
7	Angel Cabrera (ARG)	71-70-67-71—279	268,000
8	K J Choi (KOR)	67-70-71-72—280	240,000
	Bo Van Pelt	73-69-68-70—280	240,000
10	Ryan Palmer	71-72-69-70—282	216,000
11	Edoardo Molinari (ITA)	74-70-69-70—283	176,000
	Justin Rose (ENG)	73-71-71-68—283	176,000
	Steve Stricker	72-70-71-70—283	176,000
	Lee Westwood (ENG)	72-67-74-70—283	176,000
15	Fred Couples	71-68-72-73—284	128,000
	Ross Fisher (ENG)	69-71-71-73—284	128,000
	Trevor Immelman (RSA)	69-73-73-69—284	128,000
	Rory McIlroy (NIR)	65-69-70-80—284	128,000
	Brandt Snedeker	69-71-74-70—284	128,000
20	Ricky Barnes	68-71-75-71—285	93,200
	Ryo Ishikawa (JPN)	71-71-73-70—285	93,200
	Martin Laird (SCO)	74-69-69-73—285	93,200
	Y E Yang (KOR)	67-72-73-73—285	93,200
24	Jim Furyk	72-68-74-72—286	70,400
	David Toms	72-69-73-72—286	70,400
	Gary Woodland	69-73-74-70—286	70,400
27	Charley Hoffman	74-69-72-72—287	54,400
	Miguel Angel Jiménez (ESP)	71-73-70-73—287	54,400
	Robert Karlsson (SWE)	72-70-74-71—287	54,400
	Matt Kuchar	68-75-69-75—287	54,400
	Hideki Matsuyama (JPN) (am)	72-73-68-74—287	
	Phil Mickelson	70-72-71-74—287	54,400
	Ian Poulter (ENG)	74-69-71-73—287	54,400
	Alvaro Quiros (ESP)	65-73-75-74—287	54,400
35	Alex Cejka (GER)	72-71-75-70—288	43,200
	Sergio García (ESP)	69-71-75-73—288	43,200
	Ryan Moore	70-73-72-73—288	43,200
38	Paul Casey (ENG)	70-72-76-71—289	36,600
	Rickie Fowler	70-69-76-74—289	36,600
	Dustin Johnson	74-68-73-74—289	36,600
	Bubba Watson	73-71-67-78—289	36,600
42	Bill Haas	74-70-74-72—290	32,000
	Steve Marino	74-71-72-73—290	32,000
44	Kyung-tae Kim (KOR)	70-75-78-68—291	28,800
	Jeff Overton	73-72-72-74—291	28,800
46	Nick Watney	72-72-75-73—292	26,400
47	Aaron Baddeley (AUS)	75-70-74-74—293	24,000
	Ernie Els (RSA)	75-70-76-72—293	24,000
49	Camilo Villegas (COL)	70-75-73-76—294	21,920

The following players missed the half-way cut. Each professional player received $10,000:

50	Robert Allenby (AUS)	75-71—146	64T	Peter Hanson (SWE)	72-76—148	82T	Martin Kaymer (GER)	78-72—150
	Stewart Cink	71-75—146		Yuta Ikeda (JPN)	74-74—148		Larry Mize	73-77—150
	Tim Clark (RSA)	73-73—146		Lion Kim (am)	76-72—148		José Maria Olazábal	73-77—150
	Lucas Glover	75-71—146		Carl Pettersson	75-73—148		(ESP)	
	Zach Johnson	73-73—146		(SWE)			Mark O'Meara	77-73—150
	Anthony Kim	73-73—146		D A Points	72-76—148		Rory Sabbatini (RSA)	74-76—150
	Hunter Mahan	75-71—146		Heath Slocum	72-76—148	88	Arjun Atwal (IND)	80-71—151
	Francesco Molinari	75-71—146		Jhonattan Vegas (VEN)	72-76—148		Jonathan Byrd	73-78—151
	(ITA)		75	Hiroyuki Fujita (JPN)	70-79—149		Craig Stadler	80-71—151
	Sean O'Hair	70-76—146		Anders Hansen	72-77—149		Tom Watson	79-72—151
59	Stuart Appleby (AUS)	75-72—147		(DEN)		92	Davis Love III	75-77—152
	Jerry Kelly	74-73—147		Padraig Harrington	77-72—149		Nathan Smith (am)	75-77—152
	Graeme McDowell	74-73—147		(IRL)		94	Sandy Lyle (SCO)	73-80—153
	(NIR)			Grégory Havret	70-79—149	95	Vijay Singh (FIJ)	76-78—154
	Kevin Na (KOR)	73-74—147		(FRA)		96	Ben Crenshaw	78-77—155
	Mark Wilson	76-71—147		Louis Oosthuizen	75-74—149		Mike Weir (CAN)	76-79—155
64	Jason Bohn	73-75—148		(RSA)			Ian Woosnam (WAL)	78-77—155
	David Chung (am)	72-76—148		Kevin Streelman	75-74—149	99	Henrik Stenson	83-74—157
	Ben Crane	73-75—148		Peter Uihlein (am)	72-77—149		(SWE)	
	Retief Goosen (RSA)	70-78—148	82	Jin Jeong (KOR) (am)	73-77—150			

2010 Masters April 8–11   [7435–72]

Prize money: $7.5 million. Field of 96 players (six amateurs) of whom 48 (including one amateur) made the half-way cut.

1	Phil Mickelson	67-71-67-67—272	$1,350,000	24T	Matt Kuchar	70-73-74-71—288	69,000
2	Lee Westwood (ENG)	67-69-68-71—275	810,000	26	Bill Haas)	72-70-71-76—289	57,750
3	Anthony Kim	68-70-73-65—276	510,000		Geoff Ogilvy (AUS)	74-72-69-74—289	57,750
4	K J Choi (KOR)	67-71-70-69—277	330,000		Kenny Perry	72-71-72-74—289	57,750
	Tiger Woods	68-70-70-69—277	330,000	29	Yuta Ikeda (JPN)	70-77-72-71—290	53,250
6	Fred Couples	66-75-68-70—279	270,000	30	Jason Dufner	75-72-75-69—291	45,563
7	Nick Watney	68-76-71-65—280	251,250		Søren Kjeldsen (DEN)	70-71-75-75—291	45,563
8	Hunter Mahan	71-71-68-71—281	225,000		Francesco Molinari (ITA)	70-74-75-72—291	45,563
	Y E Yang (KOR)	67-72-72-70—281	225,000		Sean O'Hair	72-71-72-76—291	45,563
10	Ricky Barnes	68-70-72-73—283	195,000		Charl Schwartzel (RSA)	69-76-72-74—291	45,563
	Ian Poulter (ENG)	68-68-74-73—283	195,000		Steve Stricker	73-73-74-71—291	45,563
12	Miguel Angel Jiménez	72-75-72-66—285	165,000	36	Lucas Glover	76-71-71-74—292	38,625
	(ESP)				Matteo Manassero (ITA)	71-76-73-72—292	
	Jerry Kelly	72-74-67-72—285	165,000		(am)		
14	Trevor Immelman (RSA)	69-73-72-72—286	131,250	38	Steve Flesch	75-71-70-78—294	34,500
	Steve Marino	71-73-69-73—286	131,250		Retief Goosen (RSA)	74-71-76-73—294	34,500
	Ryan Moore	72-73-73-68—286	131,250		Dustin Johnson	71-72-76-75—294	34,500
	David Toms	69-75-71-71—286	131,250		Camilo Villegas (COL)	74-72-71-77—294	34,500
18	Angel Cabrera (ARG)	73-74-69-71—287	94,500	42	Zach Johnson	70-74-76-75—295	30,750
	Ernie Els (RSA)	71-73-75-68—287	94,500	43	Robert Karlsson (SWE)	71-72-77-76—296	28,500
	Adam Scott (AUS)	69-75-72-71—287	94,500		Mike Weir (CAN)	71-72-76-77—296	28,500
	Heath Slocum	72-73-70-72—287	94,500		Robert Allenby (AUS)	72-75-78-73—298	24,750
	Scott Verplank	73-73-73-68—287	94,500		Chad Campbell	79-68-80-71—298	24,750
	Tom Watson	67-74-73-73—287	94,500		Sergio García (ESP)	74-70-76-78—298	24,750
24	Ben Crane	71-75-74-68—288	69,000	48	Nathan Green (AUS)	72-75-80-75—302	21,750

Month by month in 2011

To nobody's surprise José Maria Olazábal succeeds Colin Montgomerie as Ryder Cup captain. South Africans Louis Oosthuizen and Charl Schwartzel win home events, while Martin Kaymer romps to his third victory in Abu Dhabi in four years, this time by eight shots over Rory McIlroy. Jhonattan Vegas becomes the first Venezuelan winner on the PGA Tour.

2009 Masters April 9–12 [7445–72]

Prize money: $7 million. Field of 96 players (FIVE amateurs) of whom 50 (no amateurs) made the half-way cut.

1	Angel Cabrera (ARG)*	68-68-69-71—276	$1,350,000		Rory McIlroy (NIR)	72-73-71-70—286	71,400
2	Kenny Perry	68-67-70-71—276	660,000		Ian Poulter (ENG)	71-73-68-74—286	71,400
	Chad Campbell	65-70-72-69—276	660,000		Justin Rose (ENG)	74-70-71-71—286	71,400
*Cabrera won at the second extra hole					Rory Sabbatini (RSA)	73-67-70-76—286	71,400
4	Shingo Katayama (JPN)	67-73-70-68—278	360,000	30	Stuart Appleby (AUS)	72-73-71-71—287	46,575
5	Phil Mickelson	73-68-71-67—279	300,000		Ross Fisher (ENG)	69-76-73-69—287	46,575
6	Steve Flesch	71-74-68-67—280	242,813		Dustin Johnson	72-70-72-73—287	46,575
	John Merrick	68-74-72-66—280	242,813		Larry Mize	67-76-72-72—287	46,575
	Steve Stricker	72-69-68-71—280	242,813		Vijay Singh (FIJ)	71-70-72-74—287	46,575
	Tiger Woods	70-72-70-68—280	242,813	35	Ben Curtis	73-71-74-70—288	38,625
10	Jim Furyk	66-74-68-73—281	187,500		Ken Duke	71-72-73-72—288	38,625
	Hunter Mahan	66-75-71-69—281	187,500		Padraig Harrington (IRL)	69-73-73-73—288	38,625
	Sean O'Hair	68-76-68-69—281	187,500	38	Robert Allenby (AUS)	73-72-72-72—289	33,000
13	Tim Clark (RSA)	68-71-72-71—282	150,000		Luke Donald (ENG)	73-71-72-73—289	33,000
	Camilo Villegas (COL)	73-69-71-69—282	150,000		Sergio García (ESP)	73-67-75-74—289	33,000
15	Todd Hamilton	68-70-72-73—283	131,250		Henrik Stenson (SWE)	71-70-75-73—289	33,000
	Geoff Ogilvy (AUS)	71-70-73-69—283	131,250	42	Bubba Watson	72-72-73-73—290	29,250
17	Aaron Baddeley (AUS)	68-74-73-69—284	116,250	43	Lee Westwood (ENG)	70-72-70-79—291	27,250
	Graeme Mcdowell (NIR)	69-73-73-69—284	116,250	44	Dudley Hart	72-72-73-75—292	27,250
19	Nick Watney	70-71-71-73—285	105,000	45	D J Trahan	72-73-72-76—293	27,250
20	Stephen Ames (CAN)	73-68-71-74—286	71,400	46	Miguel Angel Jiménez (ESP)	70-73-78-73—294	21,850
	Paul Casey (ENG)	72-72-73-69—286	71,400		Kevin Sutherland	69-76-77-72—294	21,850
	Ryuji Imada (JPN)	73-72-72-69—286	71,400		Mike Weir (CAN)	68-75-79-72—294	21,850
	Trevor Immelman (RSA)	71-74-72-69—286	71,400	49	Andres Romero (ARG)	69-75-77-76—297	19,200
	Anthony Kim	75-65-72-74—286	71,400	50	Rocco Mediate	73-70-78-77—298	19,200
	Sandy Lyle (SCO)	72-70-73-71—286	71,400				

2008 Masters April 10–13 [7445–72]

Prize money: $7.4 million. Field of 93 players (three amateurs) of whom 45 (no amateurs) made the half-way cut.

1	Trevor Immelman (RSA)	68-68-69-75—280	$1,350,000	20T	Bubba Watson	74-71-73-73—291	84,300
2	Tiger Woods	72-71-68-72—283	810,000		Boo Weekley	72-74-68-77—291	84,300
3	Stewart Cink	72-69-71-72—284	435,000	25	Stephen Ames (CAN)	70-70-77-75—292	54,844
	Brandt Snedeker	69-68-70-77—284	435,000		Angel Cabrera (ARG)	73-72-73-74—292	54,844
5	Steve Flesch	72-67-69-78—286	273,750		J B Holmes	73-70-73-76—292	54,844
	Padraig Harrington (IRL)	74-71-69-72—286	273,750		Arron Oberholser	71-70-74-77—292	54,844
	Phil Mickelson	71-68-75-72—286	273,750		Ian Poulter (ENG)	70-69-75-78—292	54,844
8	Miguel Angel Jiménez (ESP)	77-70-72-68—287	217,500		Adam Scott (AUS)	75-71-70-76—292	54,844
					Jeev Milkha Singh (IND)	71-74-72-75—292	54,844
	Robert Karlsson (SWE)	70-73-71-73—287	217,500		Richard Sterne (RSA)	73-72-73-74—292	54,844
	Andres Romero (ARG)	72-72-70-73—287	217,500	33	Nick Dougherty (ENG)	74-69-74-76—293	42,375
11	Paul Casey (ENG)	71-69-69-79—288	172,500		Jim Furyk	70-73-73-77—293	42,375
	Nick Watney	75-70-72-71—288	172,500		Heath Slocum	71-76-77-69—293	42,375
	Lee Westwood (ENG)	69-73-73-73—288	172,500	36	Todd Hamilton	74-73-75-73—295	36,875
14	Stuart Appleby (AUS)	76-70-72-71—289	135,000		Justin Rose (ENG)	68-78-73-76—295	36,875
	Sean O'Hair	72-71-71-75—289	135,000		Johnson Wagner	72-74-74-75—295	36,875
	Vijay Singh (FIJ)	72-71-72-74—289	135,000	39	Niclas Fasth (SWE)	75-70-76-75—296	33,000
17	Retief Goosen (RSA)	71-71-72-76—290	112,500		Geoff Ogilvy (AUS)	75-71-76-74—296	33,000
	Henrik Stenson (SWE)	74-72-72-72—290	112,500	41	K J Choi (KOR)	72-75-78-73—298	30,750
	Mike Weir (CAN)	73-68-75-74—290	112,500	42	Robert Allenby (AUS)	72-74-72-81—299	28,500
20	Brian Bateman	69-76-72-74—291	84,300		David Toms	73-74-72-80—299	28,500
	Zach Johnson	70-76-68-77—291	84,300	44	Ian Woonam (WAL)	75-71-76-78—300	26,250
	Justin Leonard	72-74-72-73—291	84,300	45	Sandy Lyle (SCO)	72-75-78-77—302	24,750

2007 Masters April 5–8 [7445–72]

Prize money: $7.4 million. Field of 96 players, of whom 60 (no amateurs) made the half-way cut.

1	Zach Johnson	71-73-76-69—289	$1,305,000
2	Retief Goosen (RSA)	76-76-70-69—291	541,333
	Rory Sabbatini (RSA)	73-76-73-69—291	541,333
	Tiger Woods	73-74-72-72—291	541,333
5	Jerry Kelly	75-69-78-70—292	275,500
	Justin Rose (ENG)	69-75-75-73—292	275,500
7	Stuart Appleby (AUS)	75-70-73-75—293	233,812
	Padraig Harrington (IRL)	77-68-75-73—293	233,812
9	David Toms	70-78-74-72—294	210,250
10	Paul Casey (ENG)	79-68-77-71—295	181,250
	Luke Donald (ENG)	73-74-75-73—295	181,250
	Vaughn Taylor	71-72-77-75—295	181,250
13	Tim Clark (RSA)	71-71-80-74—296	135,937
	Jim Furyk	75-71-76-74—296	135,937
	Ian Poulter (ENG)	75-75-76-70—296	135,937
	Vijay Singh (FIJ)	73-71-79-73—296	135,937
17	Stewart Cink	77-75-75-70—297	108,750
	Tom Pernice Jr	75-72-79-71—297	108,750
	Henrik Stenson (SWE)	72-76-77-72—297	108,750
20	Mark Calcavecchia	76-71-78-73—298	84,462
	Lucas Glover	74-71-79-74—298	84,462
	John Rollins	77-74-76-71—298	84,462
	Mike Weir (CAN)	75-72-80-71—298	84,462
24	Stephen Ames (CAN)	76-74-77-72—299	63,000
	Phil Mickelson	76-73-73-77—299	63,000
	Geoff Ogilvy (AUS)	75-70-81-73—299	63,000
27	K J Choi (KOR)	75-75-74-76—300	53,650
	Davis Love III	72-77-77-74—300	53,650
	Adam Scott (AUS)	74-78-76-72—300	53,650
30	Fred Couples	75-74-78-74—301	43,085
	Charles Howell III	75-77-75-74—301	43,085
30T	Robert Karlsson (SWE)	77-73-79-72—301	43,085
	Scott Verplank	73-77-76-75—301	43,085
	Lee Westwood (ENG)	79-73-72-77—301	43,085
	Dean Wilson	75-72-76-78—301	43,085
	Yong-Eun Yang (KOR)	75-74-78-74—301	43,085
37	Angel Cabrera (ARG)	77-75-79-71—302	31,900
	J J Henry	71-78-77-76—302	31,900
	Tim Herron	72-75-83-72—302	31,900
	Rod Pampling (AUS)	77-75-74-76—302	31,900
	Jeev Milkha Singh (IND)	72-75-76-79—302	31,900
	Brett Wetterich	69-73-83-77—302	31,900
43	Sandy Lyle (SCO)	79-73-80-71—303	26,825
44	Bradley Dredge (WAL)	75-70-76-83—304	22,533
	David Howell (ENG)	70-75-82-77—304	22,533
	Miguel Angel Jiménez (ESP)	79-73-76-76—304	22,533
	Shingo Katayama (JPN)	79-72-80-73—304	22,533
	José-María Olazábal (ESP)	74-75-78-77—304	22,533
49	Jeff Sluman	76-75-79-75—305	18,560
	Craig Stadler	74-73-79-79—305	18,560
51	Brett Quigley	76-76-79-75—306	17,835
52	Aaron Baddeley (AUS)	79-72-76-80—307	17,255
	Carl Pettersson (SWE)	76-76-79-76—307	17,255
54	Rich Beem	71-81-75-81—308	16,820
55	Ben Crenshaw	76-74-84-75—309	16,530
	Niclas Fasth (SWE)	77-75-77-80—309	16,530
	Trevor Immelman (RSA)	74-77-81-77—309	16,530
58	Arron Oberholser	74-76-84-76—310	16,240
59	Billy Mayfair	76-75-83-77—311	16,095
60	Fuzzy Zoeller	74-78-79-82—313	15,950

2006 Masters April 6–9 [7445–72]

Prize money: $7 million. Field of 90 players, of whom 47 (no amateurs) made the half-way cut.

1	Phil Mickelson	70-72-70-69—281	$1,260,000
2	Tim Clark (RSA)	70-72-72-69—283	758,000
3	Chad Campbell	71-67-75-71—284	315,700
	Fred Couples	71-70-72-71—284	315,700
	Retief Goosen (RSA)	70-73-72-69—284	315,700
	José-María Olazábal (ESP)	76-71-71-66—284	315,700
	Tiger Woods	72-71-71-70—284	315,700
8	Angel Cabrera (ARG)	73-74-70-68—285	210,000
	Vijay Singh (FIJ)	67-74-73-71—285	210,000
10	Stewart Cink	72-73-71-70—286	189,000
11	Stephen Ames (CAN)	74-70-70-73—287	161,000
	Miguel Angel Jiménez (ESP)	72-74-69-72—287	161,000
	Mike Weir (CAN)	71-73-73-70—287	161,000
14	Billy Mayfair	71-72-73-72—288	129,500
	Arron Oberholser	69-75-73-71—288	129,500
16	Geoff Ogilvy (AUS)	70-75-73-71—289	112,000
	Rod Pampling (AUS)	72-73-72-72—289	112,000
	Scott Verplank	74-70-74-71—289	112,000
19	Stuart Appleby (AUS)	71-75-73-71—290	91,000
	David Howell (ENG)	71-71-76-72—290	91,000
	Nick O'Hern (AUS)	71-72-76-71—290	91,000
22	Robert Allenby (AUS)	73-73-74-71—291	67,200
	Darren Clarke (NIR)	72-70-72-77—291	67,200
22T	Jim Furyk	73-75-68-75—291	67,200
	Mark Hensby (AUS)	80-67-70-74—291	67,200
	Davis Love III	74-71-74-72—291	67,200
27	Ernie Els (RSA)	71-71-74-76—292	49,700
	Padraig Harrington (IRL)	73-70-75-74—292	49,700
	Shingo Katayama (JPN)	75-70-73-74—292	49,700
	Carl Pettersson (SWE)	72-74-73-73—292	49,700
	Adam Scott (AUS)	72-74-75-71—292	49,700
32	Thomas Bjørn (DEN)	73-75-76-69—293	40,512
	Brandt Jobe	72-76-77-68—293	40,512
	Zach Johnson	74-72-77-70—293	40,512
	Ted Purdy	72-76-74-71—293	40,512
36	Tim Herron	76-71-71-76—294	34,416
	Rocco Mediate	68-73-73-80—294	34,416
	Rory Sabbatini (RSA)	76-70-74-74—294	34,416
39	Jason Bohn	73-71-77-74—295	30,100
	Ben Curtis	71-74-77-73—295	30,100
	Justin Leonard	75-70-79-71—295	30,100
42	Rich Beem	71-73-73-79—296	25,900
	Luke Donald (ENG)	74-72-76-74—296	25,900
	Larry Mize	75-72-77-72—296	25,900
45	Olin Browne	74-69-80-74—297	23,100
46	Sergio García (ESP)	72-74-79-73—298	21,700
47	Ben Crenshaw	71-72-78-79—300	20,300

2005 Masters April 7–10 [7290–72]

Prize money: $7 million. Field of 93 players, of whom 50 (including two amateurs) made the half-way cut.

1	Tiger Woods*	74-66-65-71—276	$1,260,000	25T	Joe Ogilvie	74-73-73-70—290	61,600
2	Chris DiMarco	67-67-74-68—276	756,000		Craig Parry (AUS)	72-75-69-74—290	61,600
*Play-off: Woods 3, DiMarco 4				28	Jim Furyk	76-67-74-74—291	53,900
3	Luke Donald (ENG)	68-77-69-69—283	406,000	29	Steve Flesch	76-70-70-76—292	50,750
	Retief Goosen (RSA)	71-75-70-67—283	406,000		Kenny Perry	76-68-71-77—292	50,750
5	Mark Hensby (AUS)	69-73-70-72—284	237,300	31	Miguel Angel Jiménez	74-74-73-72—293	46,550
	Trevor Immelman	73-73-65-73—284	237,300		(ESP)		
	(RSA)				Mark O'Meara	72-74-72-75—293	46,550
	Rodney Pampling (AUS)	73-71-70-70—284	237,300	33	K J Choi (KOR)	73-72-76-73—294	39,620
	Vijay Singh (FIJ)	68-73-71-72—284	237,300		Shingo Katayama (JPN)	72-74-73-75—294	39,620
	Mike Weir (CAN)	74-71-68-71—284	237,300		Luke List (am)	77-69-78-70—294	
10	Phil Mickelson	70-72-69-74—285	189,000		Ian Poulter (ENG)	72-74-72-76—294	39,620
11	Tim Herron	76-68-70-72—286	168,000		Adam Scott (AUS)	71-76-72-75—294	39,620
	David Howell (ENG)	72-69-76-69—286	168,000		Casey Wittenberg	72-72-74-76—294	39,620
13	Tom Lehman	74-74-70-69—287	135,333	39	Tim Clark (RSA)	74-74-72-75—295	32,200
	Justin Leonard	75-71-70-71—287	135,333		Fred Couples	75-71-77-72—295	32,200
	Thomas Levet (FRA)	71-75-68-73—287	135,333		Todd Hamilton	77-70-71-77—295	32,200
	Ryan Moore (am)	71-71-75-70—287			Ryan Palmer	74-74-74-77—295	32,200
17	Chad Campbell	73-73-67-75—288	112,000	43	Stuart Appleby (AUS)	69-76-72-79—296	28,000
	Darren Clarke (NIR)	72-76-69-71—288	112,000		Jonathan Kaye	72-74-76-74—296	28,000
	Kirk Triplett	75-68-72-73—288	112,000	45	Stephen Ames (CAN)	73-74-75-75—297	25,200
20	Stewart Cink	72-72-74-71—289	84,840		Nick O'Hern (AUS)	72-72-76-77—297	25,200
	Jerry Kelly	75-70-73-71—289	84,840	47	Ernie Els (RSA)	75-73-78-72—298	23,100
	Bernhard Langer (GER)	74-74-70-71—289	84,840	48	Jay Haas	76-71-76-78—301	21,700
	Jeff Maggert	74-74-72-69—289	84,840	49	Chris Riley	71-77-78-78—304	20,300
	Scott Verplank	72-75-69-73—289	84,840	50	Craig Stadler	75-73-79-79—306	19,180
25	Thomas Bjørn (DEN)	71-67-71-81—290	61,600				

2004 Masters April 8–11 [7290–72]

Prize money: $6 million. Field of 93, of whom 44 (including two amateurs) made the half-way cut.

1	Phil Mickelson	72-69-69-69—279	$1,170,000	22T	Shaun Micheel	72-76-72-70—290	70,200
2	Ernie Els (RSA)	70-72-71-67—280	702,000		Justin Rose (ENG)	67-71-81-71—290	70,200
3	K J Choi (KOR)	71-70-72-69—282	442,000		Tiger Woods	75-69-75-71—290	70,200
4	Sergio García (ESP)	72-72-75-66—285	286,000	26	Alex Cejka (GER)	70-70-78-73—291	57,200
	Bernhard Langer (GER)	71-73-69-72—285	286,000	27	Mark O'Meara	73-70-75-74—292	51,025
6	Paul Casey (ENG)	75-69-68-74—286	189,893		Bob Tway	75-71-74-72—292	51,025
	Fred Couples	73-69-74-70—286	189,893	29	Scott Verplank	74-71-76-72—293	48,100
	Chris DiMarco	69-73-68-76—286	189,893	30	José María Olazábal	71-69-79-75—294	46,150
	Davis Love III	75-67-74-70—286	189,893		(ESP)		
	Nick Price (ZIM)	72-73-71-70—286	189,893	31	Bob Estes	76-72-73-74—295	41,275
	Vijay Singh (FIJ)	75-73-69-69—286	189,893		Brad Faxon	72-76-76-71—295	41,275
	Kirk Triplett	71-74-69-72—286	189,893		Jerry Kelly	74-72-73-76—295	41,275
13	Retief Goosen (RSA)	75-73-70-70—288	125,667		Ian Poulter (ENG)	75-73-74-73—295	41,275
	Padraig Harrington	74-74-68-72—288	125,667	35	Justin Leonard	76-72-72-76—296	35,913
	(IRL)				Phillip Price (WAL)	71-76-73-76—296	35,913
	Charles Howell III	71-71-76-70—288	125,667	37	Paul Lawrie (SCO)	77-70-73-77—297	32,663
	Casey Wittenberg (am)	76-72-71-69—288			Sandy Lyle (SCO)	72-74-75-76—297	32,663
17	Stewart Cink	74-73-69-73—289	97,500	39	Eduardo Romero (ARG)	74-73-74-77—298	30,550
	Steve Flesch	76-67-77-69—289	97,500	40	Todd Hamilton	77-71-76-75—299	29,250
	Jay Haas	69-75-72-73—289	97,500	41	Tim Petrovic	72-75-75-78—300	27,950
	Fredrik Jacobson (SWE)	74-74-67-74—289	97,500		Brandt Snedeker (am)	73-75-75-77—300	
	Stephen Leaney (AUS)	76-71-73-69—289	97,500	43	Jeff Sluman	73-70-82-77—302	26,650
22	Stuart Appleby (AUS)	73-74-73-70—290	70,200	44	Chris Riley	70-78-78-78—304	25,350

2003 Masters April 10–13   [7290–72]

Prize money: $6 million. Field of 93, of whom 49 (including three amateurs) made the half-way cut.

1	Mike Weir (CAN)*	70-68-75-68—281	$1,080,000
2	Len Mattiace	73-74-69-65—281	648,000
Play-off: Weir 4, Mattiace 6			
3	Phil Mickelson	73-70-72-68—283	408,000
4	Jim Furyk	73-72-71-68—284	288,000
5	Jeff Maggert	72-73-66-75—286	240,000
6	Ernie Els (RSA)	79-66-72-70—287	208,500
	Vijay Singh (FIJ)	73-71-70-73—287	208,500
8	Jonathan Byrd	74-71-71-72—288	162,000
	José María Olazábal (ESP)	73-71-71-73—288	162,000
	Mark O'Meara	76-71-70-71—288	162,000
	David Toms	71-73-70-74—288	162,000
	Scott Verplank	76-73-70-69—288	162,000
13	Tim Clark (RSA)	72-75-71-71—289	120,000
	Retief Goosen (RSA)	73-74-72-70—289	120,000
15	Rich Beem	74-72-71-73—290	93,000
	Angel Cabrera (ARG)	76-71-71-72—290	93,000
	K J Choi (KOR)	76-69-72-73—290	93,000
	Paul Lawrie (SCO)	72-72-73-73—290	93,000
	Davis Love III	77-71-71-71—290	93,000
	Tiger Woods	76-73-66-75—290	93,000
21	Ricky Barnes (am)	69-74-75-73—291	
22	Bob Estes	76-71-74-71—292	72,000
23	Brad Faxon	73-71-79-70—293	57,600
	Scott McCarron	77-71-72-73—293	57,600
23T	Nick Price (ZIM)	70-75-72-76—293	57,600
	Chris Riley	76-72-70-75—293	57,600
	Adam Scott (AUS)	77-72-74-70—293	57,600
28	Darren Clarke (NIR)	66-76-78-74—294	43,500
	Fred Couples	73-75-69-77—294	43,500
	Sergio García (ESP)	69-78-74-73—294	43,500
	Charles Howell III	73-72-76-73—294	43,500
	Hunter Mahan (am)	73-72-73-76—294	
33	Nick Faldo (ENG)	74-73-75-73—295	36,375
	Rocco Mediate	73-74-73-75—295	36,375
	Loren Roberts	74-72-76-73—295	36,375
	Kevin Sutherland	77-72-76-70—295	36,375
37	Shingo Katayama (JPN)	74-72-76-74—296	31,650
	Billy Mayfair	75-70-77-74—296	31,650
39	Robert Allenby (AUS)	76-73-74-74—297	27,000
	Craig Parry (AUS)	74-73-75-75—297	27,000
	Kenny Perry	76-72-78-71—297	27,000
	Justin Rose (ENG)	73-76-71-77—297	27,000
	Philip Tataurangi (NZL)	75-70-74-78—297	27,000
44	Jeff Sluman	75-72-76-75—298	23,400
45	Ryan Moore (am)	73-74-75-79—301	
	Pat Perez	74-73-79-75—301	22,200
47	John Rollins	74-71-80-77—302	21,000
48	Jerry Kelly	72-76-77-79—304	19,800
49	Craig Stadler	76-73-79-77—305	18,600

2002 Masters April 10–13   [7270–72]

Prize money: $5.6 million. Field of 89, of whom two withdrew and 45 (with no amateurs) made the half-way cut.

1	Tiger Woods	70-69-66-71—276	$1,008,000
2	Retief Goosen (RSA)	69-67-69-74—279	604,800
3	Phil Mickelson	69-72-68-71—280	380,800
4	José María Olazábal (ESP)	70-69-71-71—281	268,800
5	Ernie Els (RSA)	70-67-72-73—282	212,800
	Padraig Harrington (IRL)	69-70-72-71—282	212,800
7	Vijay Singh (FIJ)	70-65-72-76—283	187,600
8	Sergio García (ESP)	68-71-70-75—284	173,600
9	Angel Cabrera (ARG)	68-71-73-73—285	151,200
	Miguel Angel Jiménez (ESP)	70-71-74-70—285	151,200
	Adam Scott (AUS)	71-72-72-70—285	151,200
12	Chris DiMarco	70-71-72-73—286	123,200
	Brad Faxon	71-75-69-71—286	123,200
14	Nick Faldo (ENG)	75-67-73-72—287	98,000
	Davis Love III	67-75-74-71—287	98,000
	Shigeki Maruyama (JPN)	75-72-73-67—287	98,000
	Colin Montgomerie (SCO)	75-71-70-71—287	98,000
18	Thomas Bjørn (DEN)	74-67-70-77—288	81,200
	Paul McGinley (IRL)	72-74-71-71—288	81,200
20	Darren Clarke (NIR)	70-74-73-72—289	65,240
	Jerry Kelly	72-74-71-72—289	65,240
20T	Justin Leonard	70-75-74-70—289	65,240
	Nick Price (ZIM)	70-76-70-73—289	65,240
24	Mark Brooks	74-72-71-73—290	46,480
	Stewart Cink	74-70-72-74—290	46,480
	Tom Pernice	74-72-71-73—290	46,480
	Jeff Sluman	73-72-71-74—290	46,480
	Mike Weir (CAN)	72-71-71-76—290	46,480
29	Robert Allenby (AUS)	73-70-76-72—291	38,080
	Charles Howell III	74-73-71-73—291	38,080
	Jesper Parnevik (SWE)	70-72-77-72—291	38,080
32	John Daly	74-73-70-75—292	32,410
	Bernhard Langer (GER)	73-72-73-74—292	32,410
	Billy Mayfair	74-71-72-75—292	32,410
	Craig Stadler	73-72-76-71—292	32,410
36	Fred Couples	73-73-76-72—294	26,950
	Rocco Mediate	75-68-77-74—294	26,950
	Greg Norman (AUS)	71-76-72-75—294	26,950
	David Toms	73-74-76-71—294	26,950
40	Steve Lowery	75-71-76-73—295	22,960
	Kirk Triplett	74-70-74-77—295	22,960
	Tom Watson	71-76-76-72—295	22,960
43	Scott Verplank	70-75-76-75—296	20,720
44	Lee Westwood (ENG)	75-72-74-76—297	19,600
45	Bob Estes	73-72-75-78—298	18,480

The Masters History (players are American unless stated)

Date	Winner	Score	Date	Winner	Score
1934 Mar 22–25	H Smith	284	1976 Apr 8–11	R Floyd	271
1935 Apr 4–8	G Sarazen*	282	1977 Apr 7–10	T Watson	276
After a play-off: Sarazen 144, C Wood 149			1978 Apr 6–9	G Player (RSA)	277
1936 Apr 2–6	H Smith	285	1979 Apr 12–15	F Zoeller*	280
1937 Apr 1–4	B Nelson	283	*After a play-off: Zoeller 4,3; T Watson 4,4;*		
1938 Apr 1–4	H Picard	285	*E Sneed 4,4*		
1939 Mar 30–Apr 2	R Guldahl	279	1980 Apr 10–13	S Ballesteros (ESP)	275
1940 Apr 4–7	J Demaret	280	1981 Apr 9–12	T Watson	280
1941 Apr 3–6	C Wood	280	1982 Apr 8–11	C Stadler*	284
1942 Apr 9–12	B Nelson*	280	*After a play-off with Dan Pohl: Stadler 4, Pohl 5*		
After a play-off: Nelson 69, B Hogan 70			1983 Apr 7–11	S Ballesteros (ESP)	280
1946 Apr 4–7	H Keiser	282	1984 Apr 12–15	B Crenshaw	277
1947 Apr 3–6	J Demaret	281	1985 Apr 11–14	B Langer (GER)	282
1948 Apr 8–11	C Harmon	279	1986 Apr 10–13	J Nicklaus	279
1949 Apr 7–10	S Snead	283	1987 Apr 9–12	L Mize*	285
1950 Apr 6–9	J Demaret	282	*After a play-off ; Mize 4,3, G Norman 4,4,*		
1951 Apr 5–8	B Hogan	280	*S Ballesteros 5*		
1952 Apr 3–6	S Snead	286	1988 Apr 7–10	A Lyle (SCO)	281
1953 Apr 9–12	B Hogan	274	1989 Apr 6–9	N Faldo (ENG)*	283
1954 Apr 8–12	S Snead*	289	*After a play-off: Faldo 5,3, S Hoch 5,4*		
After a play-off: Snead 69, B Hogan 70			1990 Apr 5–8	N Faldo (ENG)*	278
1955 Apr 7–10	C Middlecoff	279	*After a play-off: Faldo 4,4; R Floyd 4,5*		
1956 Apr 5–8	J Burke	289	1991 Apr 11–14	I Woosnam (WAL)	277
1957 Apr 4–7	D Ford	283	1992 Apr 9–12	F Couples	275
1958 Apr 3–6	A Palmer	284	1993 Apr 8–11	B Langer (GER)	277
1959 Apr 2–5	A Wall	284	1994 Apr 7–10	JM Olazábal (ESP)	279
1960 Apr 7–10	A Palmer	282	1995 Apr 6–9	B Crenshaw	274
1961 Apr 6–10	G Player (RSA)	280	1996 Apr 11–14	N Faldo (ENG)	276
1962 Apr 5–9	A Palmer*	280	1997 Apr 10–13	T Woods	270
After a play-off: Palmer 68, G Player 71,			1998 Apr 9–12	M O'Meara	279
D Finsterwald 77			1999 Apr 8–11	JM Olazábal (ESP)	280
1963 Apr 4–10	J Nicklaus	286	2000 Apr 6–9	V Singh (FIJ)	278
1964 Apr 9–12	A Palmer	276	2001 Apr 5–8	T Woods	272
1965 Apr 8–11	J Nicklaus	271	2002 Apr 11–14	T Woods	276
1966 Apr 7–11	J Nicklaus*	288	2003 Apr 10–13	M Weir (CAN)*	281
After a play-off: Nicklaus 70, T Jacobs 72,			*After a play-off: Weir 4, L Mattiace 6*		
G Brewer Jr 78			2004 Apr 8–11	P Mickelson	279
1967 Apr 6–9	G Brewer	280	2005 Apr 7–10	T Woods*	276
1968 Apr 11–14	R Goalby	277	*After a play-off: Woods 3, C DiMarco 4*		
1969 Apr 10–13	G Archer	281	2006 Apr 6–9	P Mickelson	281
1970 Apr 9–13	W Casper*	279	2007 Apr 5–8	Z Johnson	289
After a play-off: Casper 69, G Littler 74			2008 Apr 10–13	T Immelman (RSA)	280
1971 Apr 8–11	C Coody	279	2009 Apr 9–12	A Cabrera (ARG)	276
1972 Apr 6–9	J Nicklaus	286	*After a play-off with Kenny Perry and Chad*		
1973 Apr 5–9	T Aaron	283	*Campbell*		
1974 Apr 11–14	G Player (RSA)	278	2010 Apr 8–11	P Mickelson	272
1975 Apr 10–13	J Nicklaus	276	2011 Apr 7–10	C Schwartzel (RSA)	274

US PGA Championship

August 11–14

Keegan Bradley earns US PGA title in Atlanta

Play-off victory for yet another first time major winner

Only the third player in nearly a century to win a major championship at the first attempt – he followed in the footsteps of Ben Curtis at The Open in 2003 and Francis Ouimet at the US Open in 1913 – Keegan Bradley overcame fellow American Jason Dufner in a three hole play-off at Atlanta Athletic Club to secure the US PGA title.

Only 25-years-old and ranked outside the world's top 100 before the championship began, Bradley was the first golfer to win one of the game's most coveted tournaments wielding a long putter. The seventh consecutive first time major winner, Bradley followed in the footsteps of Graeme McDowell, Louis

© Getty Images

Keegan Bradley

Oosthuizen, Martin Kaymer, Charl Schwartzel, Rory McIlroy and Darren Clarke. He also ended an American drought in the majors which unfolded after Phil Mickelson's victory at Augusta in 2010.

A fresh faced rookie from Woodstock, Vermont, Bradley played with a smile on his face and produced one of the biggest upsets in golf since Paul Lawrie won The Open at Carnoustie. When he chipped into the water at the par 15th in the closing round and carded a triple bogey 6, Bradley was written off by the bookmakers who offered odds of 270-1 against him winning the title.

No one, though, told Bradley he had no chance. Birdies at the 16th and 17th holes as well as par at the last helped him to make up ground on the faltering Dufner before winning a three hole play-off by a stroke. Little known before this victory, Bradley said: "Ever since I was ten years old, I've kind of flown under the radar, I guess you could say. I had what I thought was a pretty good college career. I never really got noticed. Same in junior golf and kind of the same out here."

Safe to say he'll be noticed now, particularly after heeding advice from Phil Mickelson not to over-react in the face of either triumph or adversity. "He told me to stay more patient out there. And the major thing I tried to do this week was under-react to everything whether it was a good thing or a terrible thing. I under-reacted to the triple but I overreacted a little to making the 40 foot on the 17th. But that was something which just came out of me."

Two and a half years after grinding to make a living on the Hooters Tour, Bradley began life in the majors quietly with 71 in his first round while all the attention was focused on Steve Stricker's 63 and Rory McIlroy's injured wrist. During a compelling first day of action which saw pre-tournament favourite McIlroy play through the pain barrier, it turned out to be a rewarding experience for the more seasoned competitors in the field with Stricker, Jerry Kelly, Shaun Micheel and Scott Verplank – all golfers over 40 – showing their younger brethren the way.

Stricker, 44, gave himself an opportunity with a 15 foot putt on his closing hole to record the lowest score in major championship history. He made a good stroke but the ball shaved the right side of the cup and the Wisconsin veteran had to settle for becoming only the 23rd player to shoot 63 in golf's most important championships. Bearing in mind Tiger Woods carded 77 and Ryo Ishikawa ran up 85, however, Stricker didn't have any cause for complaint.

The highest rated American going into the final major of the season – he was fifth in the world rankings before the event – Stricker's strengths of accuracy off the tee and smooth putting largely neutralised the threat posed by the Atlanta Athletic Club. He made seven birdies, including an exceptional brace on the 15th and 18th, to post 63. Although the performance of the veterans was noteworthy, much attention also centred on the US Open champion who found the trees on the third hole and injured his wrist by hitting a risky full blown iron shot which struck a tree root and mangled the club. In obvious discomfort, McIlroy received medical attention and had his arm and wrist strapped. Many other golfers would have erred on the side of caution and withdrawn, but McIlroy showed great fortitude to play on. While Woods made a tidy start with three birdies in his first five holes, the former world No 1 made countless mistakes. He rattled up three double bogeys and signed for his worst score in the majors since shooting 81 in high winds at Muirfield. His opening 77 was no fewer than 14 strokes off the lead held by Stricker.

Few golfers who shoot exceptionally low in the first round of a major, however, succeed in repeating the feat. That was Sticker's fate as he took 11 strokes more on Friday than Thursday to navigate Atlanta Athletic Club. After keeping a bogey off his card in the first round, Stricker ran up six in the second as he posted 74 and fell back to three under. Dufner, 65 for 135, and Bradley, 64 for the same five under mark, were the men who made waves in the second round with Jim Furyk, the former US Open champion, also in the mix after carding 65 for 136. A PGA Tour rookie playing in his first major, Bradley was barely a household name in his own house before this tournament. "The worst one is when you sign an autograph and the kid looks at you and asks you what your name is," he confessed. After winning the PGA, it's not an experience he should encounter too often in 2012.

The son of a PGA professional and the nephew of Pat Bradley, winner of six women's majors, he hails from a pedigree golf background. Dufner, 34, didn't have anything like the same connections, but shared Bradley's low profile. After six years as a Tour player, he was still looking for his first win. Woods, meanwhile, was also unrecognisable from the unstoppable force of old as he added 73 to his opening 77 to finish on ten over par and miss the cut. Five double bogeys provided evidence of the golfer's continuing struggle after being sidelined for three months through injury. The man who once won The Open by avoiding a single bunker over four days in St Andrews found 22 in two rounds. Martin Kaymer, the defending champion, and Darren Clarke, The Open champion, also went home early.

Saturday is regarded as moving day in the big championships and the first golfer to clamber up the leaderboard in the third round was the winner of this event ten years earlier at the same course in Georgia. Toms turned back the clock with a thrilling 65 sparked by an eagle on the par 5 12th. The former champion, who also holed a bunker shot on the 14th, played the closing seven holes in five under to make a step forward where most of the field took a step back. His 65 for 210, left Toms, who started the day in 59th spot, in a tie for eighth.

After a run of majors without an American winner, no fewer than seven of the top 12 after 54 holes hailed from the USA. Mark you, even in their homeland, Dufner, Bradley and Steele cut anonymous figures. Their rise to prominence on an unyielding lay-out was partly down to their own efforts and partly because of stumbling performances from the game's leading lights. Donald, the world No 1, dropped three strokes over the closing four holes while Westwood, the No 2, was bedevilled by indifferent putting. His 70 could easily have been 65. Asked what he might do in future to hole out more effectively, the Englishman rued: "I could change my religion. I have tried everything else in the last year."

Steele, in his first major, showed true grit by bouncing back from a double bogey on the seventh. He made four birdies over the next seven holes and pieced together a tidy 66 to earn a share of the lead. He was on the same mark as Dufner, who compensated for a brace of three-putt bogeys on the back nine with consecutive birdies, missed only one green and signed for 68. Bradley, playing in the final group, opened with a double bogey, but also fought back, played error free golf on the back nine and posted 69.

On Sunday, the expectation was this inexperienced trio would wilt under pressure. In the end, only Steele collapsed with 77 and fell back to 19th place while Bradley and Dufner duelled for the title. True, there were final round surges from a brace of Scandinavians as Anders Hansen shot 66 for 273 and Robert Karlsson 67 for 275, the same mark as Toms, who clambered into the top four with 67. Westwood and Donald, meantime, both promised more than they eventually delivered on 277.

The story of the final round was all about Bradley and Dufner. At one stage, on the 15th, the older man led by five strokes and looked a sure bet to succeed. However, a combination of his own errors – bogeys at the 15th, 16th and 17th holes – and Bradley's refusal to concede (he made birdies at the 16th and 17th) led to a three-hole play-off. By this stage Dufner looked frazzled as Bradley seized the initiative at the first extra hole with a birdie. Dunfner then three-putted the next to enhance Bradley's advantage. Although Dufner holed from 15 feet for birdie at the last, Bradley kept his nerve to make a two putt par and win the Wannamaker Trophy at the first attempt.

First round	Second round	Third round	Fourth round
−7 Steve Stricker	−5 Jason Dufner	−7 Jason Dufner	−8 Keegan Bradley
−5 Jerry Kelly	−5 Keegan Bradley	−7 Brendan Steele	−8 Jason Dufner
−4 Shaun Micheel	−4 D A Points	−6 Keegan Bradley	−5 Robert Karlsson
−3 Scott Verplank	−4 Scott Verplank	−5 Scott Verplank	−5 David Toms
−2 Brendon de Jonge	−4 Scott Verplank	−4 Steve Stricker	−5 Scott Verplank
−2 Matteo Manassero	−4 im Furyk	−3 Anders Hansen	−4 Adam Scott
−2 Davis Love III	−3 Steve Stricker	−3 D A Points	−3 Luke Donald
−2 Simon Dyson	−3 Anders Hansen	−2 David Toms	−2 Kevin Na
−2 Anders Hansen	−3 Brendan Steele	−2 Charl Schwartzel	
−2 Bill Haas	−3 Brandt Jobe	−2 Robert Karlsson	

US PGA Championship (93rd)   *Atlanta Athletic Club, Johns Creek, GA*   August 12–15
[7467–70]

Prize money: $8 million. Final field of 156 players, of whom 75 made the half-way cut on 144 or less.

Players are of American nationality unless stated

1	Keegan Bradley*	71-64-69-68—272	$1,445,000
2	Jason Dufner	70-65-68-69—272	865,000

*Bradley beat Dufner in three hole play-off

3	Anders Hansen (DEN)	68-69-70-66—273	545,000
4	Robert Karlsson (SWE)	70-71-67-67—275	331,000
	David Toms	72-71-65-67—275	331,000
	Scott Verplank	67-69-69-70—275	331,000
7	Adam Scott (AUS)	69-69-70-68—276	259,000
8	Lee Westwood (ENG)	71-68-70-68—277	224,500
	Luke Donald (ENG)	70-71-68-68—277	224,500
10	Kevin Na	72-69-70-67—278	188,000
	D A Points	69-67-71-71—278	188,000
12	Trevor Immelman (RSA)	69-71-71-68—279	132,786
	Gary Woodland	70-70-71-68—279	132,786
	Sergio García (ESP)	72-69-69-69—279	132,786
	Bill Haas	68-73-69-69—279	132,786
	Nick Watney (AUS)	70-71-68-70—279	132,786
	Charl Schwartzel (RSA)	71-71-66-71—279	132,786
	Steve Stricker	63-74-69-73—279	132,786
19	Brian Davis (ENG)	69-73-69-69—280	81,214
	Phil Mickelson	71-70-69-70—280	81,214
	Ryan Palmer	71-70-69-70—280	81,214
	Matt Kuchar	71-71-68-70—280	81,214
	Hunter Mahan	72-72-66-70—280	81,214
	John Senden (AUS)	68-68-72-72—280	81,214
	Brendan Steele	69-68-66-77—280	81,214
26	Charles Howell III	72-68-73-68—281	51,062
	Robert Allenby (AUS)	72-70-71-68—281	51,062
	Jerry Kelly	65-73-74-69—281	51,062
	Bubba Watson	74-68-70-69—281	51,062
	Mark Wilson	69-71-71-70—281	51,062
	Scott Piercy	71-68-71-71—281	51,062
	Brendon de Jonge (RSA)	68-72-69-72—281	51,062
	Spencer Levin	71-70-68-72—281	51,062
34	Chris Kirk	72-72-69-69—282	40,000
	Francesco Molinari (ITA)	72-71-67-72—282	40,000
	Alexander Noren (SWE)	70-72-68-72—282	40,000
37	Matteo Manassero (ITA)	68-74-71-70—283	36,250
	Ben Crane	71-72-66-74—283	36,250
39	Johan Edfors (SWE)	71-70-73-70—284	30,250
	Harrison Frazar	72-69-72-71—284	30,250
	Ian Poulter (ENG)	74-68-70-72—284	30,250
	K J Choi (KOR)	70-73-69-72—284	30,250
	Bill Lunde	71-71-69-73—284	30,250
	Jim Furyk	71-65-73-75—284	30,250
45	Pablo Larrazabal (ESP)	70-73-76-66—285	21,500
	Ross Fisher (ENG)	71-69-76-69—285	21,500
	Seung-yul Noh (KOR)	71-70-75-69—285	21,500
	Andres Romero (ARG)	72-70-74-69—285	21,500
	Yuta Ikeda (JPN)	73-68-72-72—285	21,500
	Brandt Jobe	68-69-73-75—285	21,500
51	Rickie Fowler	74-69-75-68—286	17,500
	John Rollins	72-72-70-72—286	17,500
	Jhonattan Vegas (COL)	70-68-74-74—286	17,500
	Johnson Wagner	71-69-72-74—286	17,500

51T	Simon Dyson (ENG)	68-72-71-75—286	17,500
56	Ryan Moore	75-69-76-67—287	16,600
	Ricky Barnes	69-75-71-72—287	16,600
	Bryce Molder	74-69-70-74—287	16,600
59	Michael Bradley	70-74-74-70—288	16,033
	Zach Johnson	71-72-73-72—288	16,033
	K T Kim (KOR)	73-71-70-74—288	16,033
62	Robert Garrigus	70-70-74-76—290	15,750
	Kevin Streelman	73-71-71-75—290	15,750
64	Sean O'Hair	71-73-77-70—291	15,400
	Peter Hanson (SWE)	71-71-76-73—291	15,400
	Padraig Harrington (IRL)	73-69-75-74—291	15,400
	Rory McIlroy (NIR)	70-73-74-74—291	15,400
	Miguel Angel Jiménez (ESP)	69-73-72-77—291	15,400
69	Edoardo Molinari (ITA)	75-69-76-72—292	15,000
	Y E Yang (KOR)	71-73-74-74—292	15,000
	Mike Small	73-71-70-78—292	15,000
72	Paul Casey (ENG)	72-72-78-72—294	14,750
	Davis Love III	68-71-76-79—294	14,750
74	Shaun Micheel	66-78-77-74—295	14,550
	Rory Sabbatini (RSA)	73-69-73-80—295	14,550

The following players missed the half-way cut:

76	Aaron Baddeley (AUS)	77-68—145
	Thomas Bjørn (DEN)	74-71—145
	Jonathan Byrd	71-74—145
	Angel Cabrera (ARG)	72-73—145
	Jason Day (AUS)	71-74—145
	Brian Gay	72-73—145
	Tetsuji Hiratsuka (JPN)	72-73—145
	Martin Kaymer (GER)	72-73—145
	Anthony Kim	74-71—145
	Justin Rose (ENG)	71-74—145
	Bob Sowards	69-76—145
	Bo Van Pelt	73-72—145
88	Ernie Els (RSA)	74-72—146
	Geoff Ogilvy (AUS)	75-71—146
	Jeff Overton	75-71—146
	Alvaro Quiros (ESP)	73-73—146
	Cameron Tringale	74-72—146
	Camilo Villegas (COL)	70-76—146
94	Stewart Cink	69-78—147
	Hiroyuki Fujita (JPN)	73-74—147
	J J Henry	74-73—147
	Dustin Johnson	75-72—147
	Martin Laird (SCO)	73-74—147
	Steve Marino	71-76—147
	Heath Slocum	80-67—147
	Brandt Snedeker	74-73—147
	Scott Stallings	73-74—147
103	Gregory Bourdy (FRA)	76-72—148
	Sean Dougherty	74-74—148
	Steve Elkington (AUS)	73-75—148

103T	Tom Gillis	76-72—148
	Charley Hoffman	75-73—148
	Steve Schneiter	72-76—148
109	Thomas Aiken (RSA)	76-73—149
	Mark Brooks	73-76—149
	Jeff Coston	76-73—149
	Richard Green (AUS)	79-70—149
	David Horsey (ENG)	72-77—149
	Fredrik Jacobson (SWE)	76-73—149
	Webb Simpson	75-74—149
116	Jamie Donaldson (WAL)	77-73—150
	Raphael Jacquelin (FRA)	76-74—150
	Wenchong Liang (CHN)	77-73—150
	Robert McClellan	78-72—150
	Louis Oosthuizen (RSA)	76-74—150
	Vijay Singh (FIJ)	76-74—150
	Charlie Wi (KOR)	73-77—150
	Tiger Woods	77-73—150
124	Arjun Atwal (IND)	78-73—151
	Stephen Gallacher (SCO)	74-77—151
	Mike Northern	77-74—151
127	Ryuji Imada (JPN)	75-77—152
	Graeme McDowell (NIR)	74-78—152
129	John Daly	77-76—153

129T	Larry Nelson	78-75—153
	Stuart Smith	72-81—153
	Craig Stevens	76-77—153
	D J Trahan	77-76—153
134	Darren Clarke (NIR)	78-76—154
	Brendan Jones (AUS)	78-76—154
	Rob Moss	78-76—154
137	Fredrik Andersson Hed (SWE)	74-81—155
	Rich Beem	74-81—155
	Tommy Gainey	81-74—155
	Lucas Glover	80-75—155
	Faber Jamerson	77-78—155
	Dan Olsen	78-77—155
143	David Hutsell	76-80—156
	Brad Lardon	73-83—156
	José Maria Olazábal (ESP)	78-78—156
	Jerry Pate	77-79—156
147	Ryo Ishikawa (JPN)	85-72—157
148	Jeff Sorenson	75-83—158
149	Marty Jertson	75-84—159
150	Daniel Balin	81-79—160
151	Todd Camplin	82-79—161
	Scott Erdmann	80-81—161
153	Brian Cairns	85-79—164
	Retief Goosen (RSA)	WD
	Rocco Mediate	WD
	J B Holmes	WD

2010 US PGA Championship Whistling Straits, Kohler, WI   August 12–15   [7507–72]

Prize money: $7.5 million. Field of 156, of whom 72 made the half-way cut.

1	Martin Kaymer (GER)*	72-68-67-70—277	$1,350,000
2	Bubba Watson	68-71-70-68—277	810,000

Kaymer won after a 3-hole play-off: Kaymer 4-2-5; Watson 3-3-6

3	Zach Johnson	69-70-69-70—278	435,000
	Rory McIlroy (NIR)	71-68-67-72—278	435,000
5	Dustin Johnson	71-68-67-73—279	206,410
	Jason Dufner	73-66-69-71—279	206,410
	Steve Elkington (AUS)	71-70-67-71—279	206,410
8	Liang Wen-chong (CHN)	72-71-64-73—280	210,000
	Camilo Villegas (COL)	71-71-70-68—280	210,000
10	Jason Day (AUS)	69-72-66-74—281	175,800
	Matt Kuchar	67-69-73-72—281	175,800
12	Paul Casey (ENG)	72-71-70-69—282	138,050
	Simon Dyson (ENG)	71-71-68-72—282	138,050
	Phil Mickelson	73-69-73-67—282	138,050
	Bryce Molder	72-67-70-73—282	138,050
16	Robert Karlsson (SWE)	71-71-71-70—283	110,050
	D A Points	70-72-70-71—283	110,050
18	Stewart Cink	77-68-66-73—284	84,733
	Ernie Els (RSA)	68-74-69-73—284	84,733
	Stephen Gallacher (SCO)	71-69-72-72—284	84,733
	Charl Schwartzel (RSA)	73-69-72-70—284	84,733
	Steve Stricker	72-72-68-72—284	84,733
	Nick Watney	69-68-66-81—284	84,733
24	Jim Furyk	70-68-70-77—285	58,600
	J B Holmes	72-66-77-70—285	58,600
	Simon Khan (ENG)	69-70-71-75—285	58,600
	Carl Pettersson (SWE)	71-70-71-73—285	58,600
28	David Horsey (ENG)	71-70-72-73—286	46,700
	Troy Matteson	72-72-70-72—286	46,700
	Noh Seung-yui (KOR)	68-71-72-75—286	46,700
	Bo Van Pelt	73-67-72-74—286	46,700
	Tiger Woods	71-70-72-73—286	46,700
33	Gonzalo Fernandez-Castaño (ESP)	70-73-73-71—287	37,133
	Edoardo Molinari (ITA)	71-72-70-74—287	37,133
	Francesco Molinari (ITA)	68-73-71-75—287	37,133
	Ryan Palmer	71-68-75-73—287	37,133
	Heath Slocum	73-72-68-74—287	37,133
	David Toms	74-71-67-75—287	37,133
39	K J Choi (KOR)	74-69-71-74—288	25,933
	Tim Clark (RSA)	72-71-70-75—288	25,933
	Ben Crane	73-68-73-74—288	25,933
	Brian Davis (ENG)	71-72-69-76—288	25,933
	Justin Leonard	73-69-73-73—288	25,933
	Hunter Mahan	74-71-68-75—288	25,933
	Adam Scott (AUS)	72-73-71-72—288	25,933
	Vijay Singh (FIJ)	73-66-73-76—288	25,933
	Brandt Snedeker	75-70-67-76—288	25,933

Other players who made the cut: Darren Clarke (NIR), Brendon de Jonge (ZIM), Charles Howell III, Kim Kyung-tae (KOR), Martin Laird (SCO), Marc Leishman (AUS), Shaun Micheel 289; Retief Goosen (RSA), Tom Lehman, Davis Love III 290; Grégory Bourdy (FRA), Rickie Fowler, Peter Hanson (SWE), Kevin Na (KOR) 291; Fredrik Andersson Hed (SWE), Chad Campbell, Rhys Davies (WAL) 292; Brian Gay, Ryan Moore 293; D J Trahan 294; Stuart Appleby (AUS), Rob Labritz 295; Ross McGowan (ENG) 297; Jeff Overton 298; Ian Poulter (ENG) WD

2009 US PGA Championship Hazeltine, Chaska, MN   August 13–16   [7674–72]

Prize money: $7.5 million. Field of 156, of whom 80 made the half-way cut.

1	Yong-Eun Yang (KOR)	73-70-67-70—280	$1,350,000
2	Tiger Woods	67-70-71-75—283	810,000
3	Rory McIlroy (NIR)	71-73-71-70—285	435,000
	Lee Westwood (ENG)	70-72-73-70—285	435,000
5	Lucas Glover	71-70-71-74—286	300,000
6	Ernie Els (RSA)	75-68-70-74—287	233,125
	Martin Kaymer (GER)	73-70-71-73—287	233,125
	Søren Kjeldsen (DEN)	70-73-70-74—287	233,125
	Henrik Stenson (SWE)	73-71-68-75—287	233,125
10	Padraig Harrington (IRL)	68-73-69-78—288	150,633
	Dustin Johnson	72-73-73-70—288	150,633
	Zach Johnson	74-73-70-71—288	150,633
	Graeme McDowell (NIR)	70-75-71-72—288	150,633
	John Merrick	72-72-74-70—288	150,633
	Francesco Molinari (ITA)	74-73-69-72—288	150,633
16	Tim Clark (RSA)	76-68-71-74—289	106,566
	Hunter Mahan	69-75-74-71—289	106,566
	Vijay Singh (FIJ)	69-72-75-73—289	106,566
19	Michael Allen	74-71-72-73—290	81,760
	Ross Fisher (ENG)	73-68-73-76—290	81,760
	Corey Pavin	73-71-71-75—290	81,760
	Ian Poulter (ENG)	72-70-76-72—290	81,760
	Oliver Wilson (ENG)	74-72-72-72—290	81,760
24	Robert Allenby (AUS)	69-75-75-72—291	53,112
	Stephen Ames (CAN)	74-71-70-76—291	53,112
	K J Choi (KOR)	73-72-73-73—291	53,112
24T	Ben Curtis	73-72-73-73—291	53,112
	Brendan Jones (AUS)	71-70-73-77—291	53,112
	Scott McCarron	75-72-71-73—291	53,112
	Alvaro Quiros (ESP)	69-76-69-77—291	53,112
	John Rollins	73-73-68-77—291	53,112
32	Gonzalo Fernandez-Castaño (ESP)	70-77-73-72—292	40,387
	Steve Flesch	74-73-69-76—292	40,387
	Jeff Overton	72-74-75-71—292	40,387
	Kevin Sutherland	73-72-74-73—292	40,387
36	Woody Austin	73-73-73-74—293	31,735
	Fred Couples	74-74-73-72—293	31,735
	Søren Hansen (DEN)	72-76-74-71—293	31,735
	Thongchai Jaidee (THA)	70-76-73-74—293	31,735
	Miguel Angel Jiménez (ESP)	75-73-71-74—293	31,735
	David Toms	69-75-72-77—293	31,735
	Boo Weekley	74-74-71-74—293	31,735
43	Rich Beem	71-76-75-72—294	21,112
	Chad Campbell	74-73-73-74—294	21,112
	Ben Crane	70-75-72-77—294	21,112
	Luke Donald (ENG)	71-77-73-73—294	21,112
	Kevin Na	73-75-71-75—294	21,112
	Geoff Ogilvy (AUS)	71-73-78-72—294	21,112
	Kenny Perry	74-70-78-72—294	21,112
	Charl Schwartzel (RSA)	76-70-72-76—294	

Other players who made the cut: Retief Goosen (RSA), Anthony Kim, Thomas Levet (FRA), Michael Sim (AUS), Camilo Villegas (COL), 295; Hiroyuki Fujita (JPN), Ryo Ishikawa (JPN), Bob Tway, Charlie Wi (KOR) 296; Richard Green (AUS), Tom Lehman, John Mallinger 297; Angel Cabrera (ARG), Jim Furyk, Nathan Green (AUS), J J Henry 298; Stewart Cink, Paul Goydos, Justin Leonard, Rory Sabbatini (RSA), Jeev Milkha Singh (IND), David Smail (NZL) 299; Phil Mickelson 300; Greg Bisconti 301; Sean O'Hair 302; Bob Estes, Grant Sturgeon, Chris Wood (ENG) 303; Alastair Forsyth (SCO) 305; Richard Sterne (RSA) Rtd

2008 US PGA Championship Oakland Hills (South Course), Bloomfield, MI August 7–10 [7131–70]

Prize money: $7.5 million. Field of 156, of whom 73 made the half-way cut.

1	Padraig Harrington (IRL)	71-74-66-66—277	$1,350,000	20T	Boo Weekley	72-71-79-66—288	78.900
				24	Mark Brown (NZL)	77-69-74-69—289	57,000
2	Ben Curtis	73-67-68-71—279	660.000		Retief Goosen (RSA)	72-74-69-74—289	57,000
	Sergio García (ESP)	69-73-69-68—279	660.000		Fredrik Jacobson (SWE)	75-71-70-73—289	57,000
4	Henrik Stenson (SWE)	71-70-68-72—281	330.000		Brandt Snedeker	71-71-74-73—289	57,000
	Camilo Villegas (COL)	74-72-67-68—281	330.000		Nicholas Thompson	71-72-73-73—289	57,000
6	Steve Flesch	73-70-70-69—282	270.000	29	Jim Furyk	71-77-70-72—290	47.550
7	Phil Mickelson	70-73-71-70—284	231,250		J B Holmes	71-68-70-81—290	47.550
	Andres Romero (ARG)	69-78-65-72—284	231,250	31	Robert Allenby (AUS)	76-72-72-71—291	38.825
9	Alastair Forsyth (SCO)	73-72-70-70—285	176.725		Chris DiMarco	75-72-72-72—291	38.825
	Justin Rose (ENG)	73-67-74-71—285	176.725		Ernie Els (RSA)	71-75-70-75—291	38.825
	Jeev Milkha Singh (IND)	68-74-70-73—285	176.725		Paul Goydos	74-69-73-75—291	38.825
	Charlie Wi	70-70-71-74—285	176.725		Geoff Ogilvy (AUS)	73-74-74-70—291	38.825
13	Aaron Baddeley (AUS)	71-71-71-73—286	137,250		Sean O'Hair	69-73-76-73—291	38.825
	Ken Duke	69-73-73-71—286	137,250		Ian Poulter (ENG)	74-71-73-73—291	38.825
15	Stuart Appleby (AUS)	76-70-69-72—287	107.060		D J Trahan	72-71-76-72—291	38.825
	Paul Casey (ENG)	72-74-72-69—287	107.060	39	Steve Elkington (AUS)	71-73-73-75—292	30.200
	Graeme McDowell (NIR)	74-72-68-73—287	107.060		Rory Sabbatini (RSA)	72-73-73-74—292	30.200
					Steve Stricker	71-75-77-69—292	30.200
	Prayad Marksaeng (THA)	76-70-68-73—287	107.060	42	Briny Baird	71-72-73-77—293	24,500
	David Toms	72-69-72-74—287	107.060		Michael Campbell (NZL)	73-71-75-74—293	24,500
20	Angel Cabrera (ARG)	70-72-72-74—288	78.900		Tom Lehman	74-70-75-74—293	24,500
	Brian Gay	70-74-72-72—288	78.900		John Senden (AUS)	76-72-72-73—293	24,500
	Robert Karlsson (SWE)	68-77-71-72—288	78.900		Mike Weir (CAN)	73-75-71-74—293	24,500

Other players who made the cut: Michael Allen, Charles Howell III, Billy Mayfair, Carl Petterson (SWE), Dean Wilson 294; Peter Hanson (SWE), John Merrick, Charl Schwartzel (RSA) 295; Tim Clark (RSA), Anthony Kim, James Kingston (RSA) 296; Justin Leonard, Pat Perez 297; John Malinger, Steve Marino, Chez Reavie 298; Paul Azinger, Mark Calcavecchia, Niclas Fasth (SWE), Corey Pavin, Kevin Sutherland 299; Hiroyuki Fujita (JPN), Peter Lonard (AUS) 300; Bubba Watson 301; Richard Green (AUS), 303; Rocco Mediate 304; Louis Oosthuizen (RSA) 306

Only eleven made the half-way cut in all four majors

Six Americans, three Europeans, a South African and a Korean were the only players to make the half-way cut in all four majors in 2011. Charl Schwartzel, who won The Masters at Augusta, had the most consistent record finishing in the top 15 in the remaining three majors – ninth in the US Open at Congressional, 15th. in The Open at Royal St George's and tied 12th in the US PGA Championship at the Atlanta Atheltic Club.

Name	The Masters	US Open	The Open	US PGA
Sergio Garcia (ESP)	T35	T7	T9	T12
Bill Haas (USA)	T42	T23	T57	T12
Rory McIlroy (NIR)	T15	1	T25	T64
Phil Mickelson (USA)	T27	T54	T2	T19
Edoardo Molinari (ITA)	T11	T54	T67	T69
Ryan Palmer (USA)	10	T21	T30	T19
Charl Schwartzel (RSA)	1	T9	T15	T12
Steve Stricker (USA)	T11	T19	T12	T12
Bubba Watson (USA)	T38	T63	T30	T26
Gary Woodland (USA)	T24	T23	T30	T12
Y E Yang (KOR)	T20	T3	T16	T69

2007 US PGA Championship *Southern Hills, Tulsa, OK* August 9–12   [7131–70]

Prize money: $7 million. Field of 156, of whom 72 made the half-way cut.

1	Tiger Woods	71-63-69-69—272	$1,260,000		23T	Peter Hanson (SWE)	72-71-69-73—285	51,000
2	Woody Austin	68-70-69-67—274	756,000			Kenny Perry	72-72-71-70—285	51,000
3	Ernie Els (RSA)	72-68-69-66—275	476,000			Ian Poulter (ENG)	71-73-70-71—285	51,000
4	Arron Oberholser	68-72-70-69—279	308,000			Heath Slocum	72-70-72-71—285	51,000
	John Senden (AUS)	69-70-69-71—279	308,000			Steve Stricker	77-68-69-71—285	51,000
6	Simon Dyson (ENG)	73-71-72-64—280	227,500			Camilo Villegas (COL)	69-71-74-71—285	51,000
	Trevor Immelman (RSA)	75-70-66-69—280	227,500		32	Brad Bryant	74-70-72-70—286	34,750
	Geoff Ogilvy (AUS)	69-68-74-69—280	227,500			Stewart Cink	72-70-72-72—286	34,750
9	Kevin Sutherland	73-69-68-71—281	170,333			John Daly	67-73-73-73—286	34,750
	Scott Verplank	70-66-74-71—281	170,333			Luke Donald (ENG)	72-71-70-73—286	34,750
	Boo Weekley	76-69-65-71—281	170,333			Shaun Micheel	73-71-70-72—286	34,750
12	Stephen Ames (CAN)	68-69-69-76—282	119,833			Phil Mickelson	73-69-75-69—286	34,750
	Stuart Appleby (AUS)	73-68-72-69—282	119,833			Lee Westwood (ENG)	69-74-75-68—286	34,750
	K J Choi (KOR)	71-71-68-72—282	119,833			Brett Wetterich	74-71-70-71—286	34,750
	Anders Hansen (DEN)	71-71-71-69—282	119,833		40	Paul Casey (ENG)	72-70-74-71—287	27,350
	Justin Rose (ENG)	70-73-70-69—282	119,833			Richard Green (AUS)	72-73-70-72—287	27,350
	Adam Scott (AUS)	72-68-70-72—282	119,833		42	Darren Clarke (NIR)	77-66-71-74—288	20,850
18	Ken Duke	73-71-69-71—284	81,600			Niclas Fasth (SWE)	71-68-79-70—288	20,850
	Joe Durant	71-73-70-70—284	81,600			Padraig Harrington (IRL)	69-73-72-74—288	20,850
	Hunter Mahan	71-73-72-68—284	81,600			Charles Howell III	75-70-72-71—288	20,850
	Pat Perez	70-69-77-68—284	81,600			Colin Montgomerie (SCO)	72-73-73-70—288	20,850
	Brandt Snedeker	74-71-69-70—284	81,600			Sean O'Hair	70-72-70-76—288	20,850
23	Steve Flesch	72-73-68-72—285	51,000			Rod Pampling (AUS)	70-74-72-72—288	20,850
	Retief Goosen (RSA)	70-71-74-70—285	51,000			David Toms	71-74-71-72—288	20,850
	Nathan Green (AUS)	75-68-67-75—285	51,000					

Other players who made the cut: Brian Bateman, Lucas Glover, Frank Lickliter II, Shingo Katayama (JPN), Anthony Kim, Nick O'Hern, Bob Tway 289; Chad Campbell, Robert Karlsson (SWE), Will MacKenzie 290; Billy Mayfair, Paul McGinley (IRL) 291; Thomas Bjørn (DEN), Corey Pavin, Brett Quigley, Graeme Storm (ENG) 293; Todd Hamilton, Tim Herron, Troy Matteson 294; Tom Lehman, Mike Small 296; Ryan Benzel 297; Sergio García (ESP) DQ

2006 US PGA Championship *Medinah, Il* August 16–20   [7561–72]

Prize money: $6.5 million. Field of 156, of whom 70 made the half-way cut.

1	Tiger Woods	69-68-65-68—270	$1,224,000		24	Chad Campbell	71-72-75-66—284	53,100
2	Shaun Micheel	69-70-67-69—275	734,400			Stewart Cink	68-74-73-69—284	53,100
3	Luke Donald (ENG)	68-68-66-74—276	353,600			Tim Clark (RSA)	70-69-75-70—284	53,100
	Sergio García (ESP)	69-70-67-70—276	353,600			Steve Flesch	72-71-69-72—284	53,100
	Adam Scott (AUS)	71-69-69-67—276	353,600			Anders Hansen (DEN)	72-71-70-71—284	53,100
6	Mike Weir (CAN)	72-67-65-73—277	244,800		29	Jim Furyk	70-72-69-74—285	41,100
7	K J Choi (KOR)	73-67-67-71—278	207,787			Robert Karlsson (SWE)	71-73-69-72—285	41,100
	Steve Stricker	72-67-70-69—278	207,787			Heath Slocum	73-70-72-70—285	41,100
9	Ryan Moore	71-72-67-69—279	165,000			Lee Westwood (ENG)	69-72-71-73—285	41,100
	Geoff Ogilvy (AUS)	69-68-68-74—279	165,000			Dean Wilson	74-70-74-67—285	41,100
	Ian Poulter (ENG)	70-70-68-71—279	165,000		34	Retief Goosen (RSA)	70-73-68-75—286	34,500
12	Chris DiMarco	71-70-67-72—280	134,500			Trevor Immelman (RSA)	73-71-70-72—286	34,500
	Sean O'Hair	72-70-70-68—280	134,500			Davis Love III	68-69-73-76—286	34,500
14	Tim Herron	69-67-72-73—281	115,000		37	Richard Green (AUS)	73-69-73-72—287	29,250
	Henrik Stenson (SWE)	68-68-73-72—281	115,000			J B Holmes	71-70-68-78—287	29,250
16	Woody Austin	71-69-69-73—282	94,000			Graeme McDowell (NIR)	75-68-72-72—287	29,250
	Ernie Els (RSA)	71-70-72-69—282	94,000			Billy Mayfair	69-69-73-76—287	29,250
	Phil Mickelson	69-71-68-74—282	94,000		41	Billy Andrade	67-69-78-74—288	23,080
	David Toms	71-67-71-73—282	94,000			Daniel Chopra (SWE)	72-67-76-73—288	23,080
20	Robert Allenby (AUS)	68-74-71-70—283	71,250			J J Henry	68-73-73-74—288	23,080
	Jonathan Byrd	69-72-74-68—283	71,250			Chris Riley	66-72-73-77—288	23,080
	Harrison Fraser	69-72-69-73—283	71,250			Justin Rose (ENG)	73-70-70-75—288	23,080
	Fred Funk	69-69-74-71—283	71,250					

Other players who made the cut: Olin Browne, Lucas Glover 289; Jerry Kelly 290; Rich Beem, Nathan Green (AUS), Ryan Palmer, Corey Pavin, Kenny Perry, Joey Sindelar 291; Stephen Ames (CAN), Stuart Appleby (AUS), Aaron Baddeley (AUS), José-María Olazábal (ESP), Hideto Tanihara (JPN) 292; Ben Curtis, Steve Lowery 293; Jason Gore, Jeff Maggert, Charles Warren 295; Miguel Angel Jiménez (ESP), Bob Tway 296; David Howell (ENG) 297; Jay Haas, Don Yrene 300; Jim Kane 301

2005 US PGA Championship Baltusrol, NJ August 11–15 [7392–70]

Prize money: $6.25 million. Field of 156, of whom 79 made the half-way cut.

1	Phil Mickelson	67-65-72-72—276	$1,1700,00	23T	Shingo Katayama (JPN)	71-66-74-72—283	56,400
2	Thomas Bjørn (DEN)	71-71-63-72—277	572,000		Paul McGinley (IRL)	72-70-72-69—283	564,00
	Steve Elkington (AUS)	68-70-68-71—277	572,000		Tom Pernice Jr	69-73-69-72—283	56,400
4	Davis Love III	68-68-68-74—278	286,000		Kenny Perry	69-70-70-74—283	56,400
	Tiger Woods	75-69-66-68—278	286,000	28	Chad Campbell	71-71-70-72—284	41,500
6	Michael Campbell	73-68-69-69—279	201,500		Stewart Cink	71-72-66-75—284	41,500
	(NZL)				Bob Estes	71-72-73-68—284	41,500
	Retief Goosen (RSA)	68-70-69-72—279	201,500		Arron Oberholser	74-68-69-73—284	41,500
	Geoff Ogilvy (AUS)	69-69-72-69—279	201,500		Jesper Parnevik (SWE)	68-69-72-75—284	41,500
	Pat Perez	68-71-67-73—279	201,500		Vaughn Taylor	75-69-71-69—284	41,500
10	Steve Flesch	70-71-69-70—280	131,800	34	Jason Bohn	71-68-68-78—285	31,917
	Dudley Hart	70-73-66-71—280	131,800		Ben Curtis	67-73-67-78—285	31,917
	Ted Purdy	69-75-70-66—280	131,800		Jim Furyk	72-71-69-73—285	31,917
	Vijay Singh (FIJ)	70-67-69-74—280	131,800		Fredrik Jacobson (SWE)	72-69-73-71—285	31,917
	David Toms	71-72-69-68—280	131,800		Jerry Kelly	70-65-74-76—285	31,917
15	Stuart Appleby (AUS)	67-70-69-75—281	102,500		Scott Verplank	71-72-71-71—285	31,917
	Charles Howell III	70-71-68-72—281	102,500	40	K J Choi (KOR)	71-70-73-72—286	22,300
17	Tim Clark (RSA)	71-73-70-68—282	82,500		Ben Crane	68-76-72-70—286	22,300
	Trevor Immelman (RSA)	67-72-72-71—282	82,500		Miguel Angel Jiménez	72-72-69-73—286	22,300
	Jack Johnson	70-70-73-69—282	82,500		(ESP)		
	Joe Ogilvie	74-68-69-71—282	82,500		John Rollins	68-71-73-74—286	22,300
	Bo Van Pelt	70-70-68-74—282	82,500		Steve Schneiter (CAN)	72-72-72-70—286	22,300
	Lee Westwood (ENG)	68-68-71-75—282	82,500		Adam Scott (AUS)	74-69-72-71—286	22,300
23	Sergio García (ESP)	72-70-71-70—283	56,400		Patrick Sheehan	73-71-71-71—286	22,300

Other players who made the cut: Fred Funk, Todd Hamilton, Bernhard Langer (GER), JL Lewis, José María Olazábal (ESP), Greg Owen (ENG), Ryan Palmer, Ian Poulter (ENG), Heath Slocum, Henrik Stenson (SWE). Mike Wier (CAN), Yong-Eun Yang (KOR) 287; Paul Casey (ENG), Carlos Franco (PAR), Peter Hanson (SWE), Mark Hensby (AUS), Scott McCarron, Sean O'Hair, Steve Webster (ENG) 288; Woody Austin, Luke Donald (ENG), Ron Philo Jr, Chris Riley 289; Mark Calcavecchia, Fred Couples 290; Stephen Ames (CAN), Joe Durant 291; John Daly, Rory Sabbatini (RSA) 292; Mike Small 295; Kevin Sutherland 296; Darrell Kestner 299; Hal Sutton 300

2004 US PGA Championship Whistling Straits, Kohler, WI August 12–15 [7514–72]

Prize money: $6.25 million. Field of 155, of whom 73 made the half-way cut.

1	Vijay Singh (FIJ)*	67-68-69-76—280	$1,125,000	17T	David Toms	72-72-69-72—285	76,857
2	Justin Leonard	66-69-70-75—280	550,000	24	Tom Byrum	72-73-71-70—286	46,714
	Chris DiMarco	68-70-71-71—280	550,000		Chad Campbell	73-70-71-72—286	46,714
	*Three hole play-off: Singh 3-3-4; Leonard 4-3-4; DiMarco 4-3-4				Luke Donald (ENG)	67-73-71-75—286	46,714
4	Ernie Els (RSA)	66-70-72-73—281	267,500		JL Lewis	73-69-72-72—286	46,714
	Chris Riley	69-70-69-73—281	267,500		Shaun Micheel	77-68-70-71—286	46,714
6	K J Choi (KOR)	68-71-73-70—282	196,000		Geoff Ogilvy (AUS)	68-73-71-74—286	46,714
	Paul McGinley (IRL)	69-74-70-69—282	196,000		Tiger Woods	75-69-69-73—286	46,714
	Phil Mickelson	69-72-67-74—282	196,000	31	Carlos Daniel Franco	69-75-72-71—287	34,250
9	Robert Allenby (AUS)	71-70-72-70—283	152,000		(PAR)		
	Stephen Ames (CAN)	68-71-69-75—283	152,000		Charles Howell III	70-71-72-74—287	34,250
	Ben Crane	70-74-69-70—283	152,000		Miguel Angel Jiménez	76-65-75-71—287	34,250
	Adam Scott (AUS)	71-71-69-72—283	152,000		(ESP)		
13	Darren Clarke (NIR)	65-71-72-76—284	110,250		Nick O'Hern (AUS)	73-71-68-75—287	34,250
	Brian Davis (ENG)	70-71-69-74—284	110,250		Chip Sullivan	72-71-73-71—287	34,250
	Brad Faxon	71-71-72-70—284	110,250		Bo Van Pelt	74-71-70-72—287	34,250
	Arron Oberholser	73-71-70-70—284	110,250	37	Briny Baird	67-69-75-77—288	24,687
17	Stuart Appleby (AUS)	68-75-72-70—285	76,857		Steve Flesch	73-72-67-76—288	24,687
	Stewart Cink	73-70-70-72—285	76,857		Jay Haas	68-72-71-77—288	24,687
	Matt Gogel	71-71-69-74—285	76,857		Todd Hamilton	72-73-75-68—288	24,687
	Fredrik Jacobson (SWE)	72-70-70-73—285	76,857		Trevor Immelman (RSA)	75-69-72-72—288	24,687
	Jean-François Remesy	72-71-70-72—285	76,857		Zach Johnson	75-70-69-74—288	24,687
	(FRA)				Ian Poulter (ENG)	73-72-70-73—288	24,687
	Loren Roberts	68-72-70-75—285	76,857		Brett Quigley	74-69-73-72—288	24,687

Other players who made the cut: Tommy Armour III, Niclas Fasth (SWE), Padraig Harrington (IRL), David Howell (ENG) 289; Michael Campbell (NZL), Nick Faldo (ENG), Joe Ogilvie, Patrick Sheehan, Duffy Waldorf 290; Carl Pettersson (SWE) 291; Paul Azinger, S K Ho (KOR), Rod Pampling (AUS), Craig Parry (AUS), Eduardo Romero (ARG), Hidemichi Tanaka (JPN), Bob Tway 292; Woody Austin, Shingo Katayama (JPN), Jeff Sluman, Scott Verplank 293; Scott Drummond (SCO), Bernhard Langer (GER) 294; Robert Gamez, Mark Hensby (AUS) 296; Colin Montgomerie (SCO) 297; Roy Biancalana 299; Jeff Coston 301; Skip Kendall 304

2003 US PGA Championship Oak Hill CC, Rochester, NY August 14–17   [7134–70]

Prize money: $6 million. Field of 156, of whom 70 made the half-way cut.

1	Shaun Micheel	69-68-69-70—276	$1,080,000	23T	Luke Donald (ENG)	73-72-71-72—288	52,000
2	Chad Campbell	69-72-65-72—278	648,000		Phil Mickelson	66-75-72-75—288	52,000
3	Tim Clark (RSA)	72-70-68-69—279	408,000		Adam Scott (AUS)	72-69-72-75—288	52,000
4	Alex Cejka (GER)	74-69-68-69—280	288,000	27	Woody Austin	72-73-69-75—289	43,000
5	Ernie Els (RSA)	71-70-70-71—282	214,000		Geoff Ogilvy (AUS)	71-71-77-70—289	43,000
	Jay Haas	70-74-69-69—282	214,000	29	Todd Hamilton	70-74-73-73—290	36.600
7	Fred Funk	69-73-70-72—284	175.667		Padraig Harrington		
	Loren Roberts	70-73-70-71—284	175.667		(IRL)	72-76-69-73—290	36.600
	Mike Weir (CAN)	68-71-70-75—284	175.667		Frank Lickliter II	71-72-71-76—290	36.600
10	Billy Andrade	67-72-72-74—285	135,500		Peter Lonard (AUS)	74-74-69-73—290	36.600
	Niclas Fasth (SWE)	76-70-71-68—285	135,500		David Toms	75-72-71-72—290	36.600
	Charles Howell III	70-72-70-73—285	135,500	34	Fred Couples	74-71-72-74—291	29,000
	Kenny Perry	75-72-70-68—285	135,500		Lee Janzen	68-74-72-77—291	29,000
14	Robert Gamez	70-73-70-73—286	98,250		JL Lewis	71-75-71-74—291	29,000
	Tim Herron	69-72-74-71—286	98,250		Jesper Parnevik (SWE)	73-72-72-74—291	29,000
	Scott McCarron	74-70-71-71—286	98,250		Vijay Singh (FIJ)	69-73-70-79—291	29,000
	Rod Pampling (AUS)	66-74-73-73—286	98,250	39	Robert Allenby (AUS)	70-77-73-72—292	22,000
18	Carlos Franco (PAR)	73-73-69-72—287	73,000		Briny Baird	73-71-67-81—292	22,000
	Jim Furyk	72-74-69-72—287	73,000		Mark Calcavecchia	73-71-76-72—292	22,000
	Toshimitsu Izawa (JPN)	71-72-71-73—287	73,000		Joe Durant	71-76-75-70—292	22,000
	Rocco Mediate	72-74-71-70—287	73,000		Hal Sutton	75-71-67-79—292	22,000
	Kevin Sutherland	69-74-71-73—287	73,000		Tiger Woods	74-72-73-73—292	22,000
23	Stuart Appleby (AUS)	74-73-71-70—288	52,000				

Other players who made the cut: Angel Cabrera (ARG), Tom Pernice Jr, Duffy Waldorf 293; Ben Crane, Trevor Immelman (RSA), Shigeki Maruyama (JPN) 294; José Coceres (ARG), Gary Evans (ENG), Brian Gay, Len Mattiace, José María Olazábal (ESP) 295; Chris DiMarco 296; Aaron Baddeley (AUS), Bob Estes, Scott Hoch, Bernhard Langer (GER) 297; Jonathan Kaye, Billy Mayfair, Ian Poulter (ENG), Eduardo Romero (ARG), Philip Tataurangi (NZL) 298; Paul Casey (ENG) 299; Bob Burns 300; Rory Sabbatini (RSA) 302; Michael Campbell (NZL), K J Choi (KOR) 304

2002 US PGA Championship Hazeltine National, Chaska, MN August 15–18   [7360–72]

Prize money: $5.5 million. Field of 156 (one amateur), of whom 72 made the half-way cut.

1	Rich Beem	72-66-72-68—278	$990,000	22	Heath Slocum	73-74-75-69—291	57,000
2	Tiger Woods	71-69-72-67—279	594,000	23	Michael Campbell (NZL)	73-70-77-72—292	44,250
3	Chris Riley	71-70-72-70—283	374,000		Retief Goosen (RSA)	69-69-79-75—292	44,250
4	Fred Funk	68-70-73-73—284	235,000		Bernhard Langer (GER)	70-72-77-73—292	44,250
	Justin Leonard	72-66-69-77—284	235,000		Justin Rose (ENG)	69-73-76-74—292	44,250
6	Rocco Mediate	72-73-70-70—285	185,000		Adam Scott (AUS)	71-71-76-74—292	44,250
7	Mark Calcavecchia	70-68-74-74—286	172,000		Jeff Sluman	70-75-74-73—292	44,250
8	Vijay Singh (FIJ)	71-74-74-68—287	159,000	29	Brad Faxon	74-72-75-72—293	33,500
9	Jim Furyk	68-73-76-71—288	149,000		Tom Lehman	71-72-77-73—293	33,500
10	Robert Allenby (AUS)	76-66-77-70—289	110,714		Craig Perks (NZL)	72-76-74-71—293	33,500
	Stewart Cink	74-74-72-69—289	110,714		Kenny Perry	73-68-78-74—293	33,500
	José Coceres (ARG)	72-71-72-74—289	110,714		Kirk Triplett	75-69-79-70—293	33,500
	Pierre Fulke (SWE)	72-68-78-71—289	110,714	34	David Duval	71-77-76-70—294	26,300
	Sergio García (ESP)	75-73-73-68—289	110,714		Ernie Els (RSA)	72-71-75-76—294	26,300
	Ricardo Gonzalez (ARG)	74-73-71-71—289	110,714		Neal Lancaster	72-73-75-74—294	26,300
	Steve Lowery	71-71-73-74—289	110,714		Phil Mickelson	76-72-78-68—294	26,300
17	Stuart Appleby (AUS)	73-74-74-69—290	72,000		Mike Weir (CAN)	73-74-77-70—294	26,300
	Steve Flesch	72-74-73-71—290	72,000	39	Chris DiMarco	76-69-77-73—295	21,500
	Padraig Harrington (IRL)	71-73-74-72—290	72,000		Joel Edwards	73-74-77-71—295	21,500
	Charles Howell III	72-69-80-69—290	72,000		John Huston	74-74-75-72—295	21,500
	Peter Lonard (AUS)	69-73-75-73—290	72,000		Scott McCarron	73-71-79-72—295	21,500

Other players who made the cut: Briny Baird, Søren Hansen (DEN), Shigeki Maruyama (JPN), Loren Roberts, Kevin Sutherland 296; Angel Cabrera (ARG), Steve Elkington (AUS), Davis Love III, Len Mattiace, Tom Watson 297; Cameron Beckman, Tim Clark (RSA), Brian Gay, Toshimitsu Izawa (JPN), Lee Janzen, Greg Norman (AUS), Chris Smith 298; Joe Durant, Nick Faldo (ENG), Hal Sutton 299, JJ Henry 301; Don Berry, Matt Gogel, JP Hayes, Joey Sindelar 302; Dave Tentis 304; José María Olazábal (ESP) 305; Pat Perez 309; Thomas Levet (FRA) 310; Stephen Ames (TRI) W/D

US PGA Championship History

Date	Winner	Runner-up	Venue	By
1916 Oct 8–14	J Barnes	J Hutchison	Siwanoy, NY	1 hole
1919 Sept 15–20	J Barnes	F McLeod	Engineers' Club, NY	6 and 5
1920 Aug 17–21	J Hutchison	D Edgar	Flossmoor, IL	1 hole
1921 Sept 26–Oct 1	W Hagen	J Barnes	Inwood Club, NY	3 and 2
1922 Aug 12–18	G Sarazen	E French	Oakmont, PA	4 and 3
1923 Sept 23–29	G Sarazen	W Hagen	Pelham, NY	38th hole
1924 Sept 15–20	W Hagen	J Barnes	French Lick, IN	2 holes
1925 Sept 21–26	W Hagen	W Mehlhorn	Olympic Fields, IL	6 and 4
1926 Sept 20–25	W Hagen	L Diegel	Salisbury, NY	4 and 3
1927 Oct 31–Nov 5	W Hagen	J Turnesa	Dallas, TX	1 hole
1928 Oct 1–6	L Diegel	A Espinosa	Five Farms, MD	6 and 5
1929 Dec 2–7	L Diegel	J Farrell	Hill Crest, CA	6 and 4
1930 Sept 8–13	T Armour	G Sarazen	Fresh Meadows, NY	1 hole
1931 Sept 7–14	T Creavy	D Shute	Wannamoisett, RI	2 and 1
1932 Aug 31–Sept 4	O Dutra	F Walsh	St Paul, MN	4 and 3
1933 Aug 8–13	G Sarazen	W Goggin	Milwaukee, WI	5 and 4
1934 July 24–29	P Runyan	C Wood	Buffalo, NY	38th hole
1935 Oct 18–23	J Revolta	T Armour	Oklahoma, OK	5 and 4
1936 Nov 17–22	D Shute	J Thomson	Pinehurst, NC	3 and 2
1937 May 26–30	D Shute	H McSpaden	Pittsburgh, PA	37th hole
1938 July 10–16	P Runyan	S Snead	Shawnee, PA	8 and 7
1939 July 9–15	H Picard	B Nelson	Pomonok, NY	37th hole
1940 Aug 26–Sept 2	B Nelson	S Snead	Hershey, PA	1 hole
1941 July 7–13	V Ghezzie	B Nelson	Denver, CO	38th hole
1942 May 23–31	S Snead	J Turnesa	Atlantic City, NJ	2 and 1
1943 No Championship				
1944 Aug 14–20	B Hamilton	B Nelson	Spokane, WA	1 hole
1945 July 9–15	B Nelson	S Byrd	Dayton, OH	4 and 3
1946 Aug 19–25	B Hogan	E Oliver	Portland, OR	6 and 4
1947 June 18–24	J Ferrier	C Harbert	Detroit, MI	2 and 1
1948 May 19–25	B Hogan	M Turnesa	Norwood Hills, MO	7 and 6
1949 May 25–31	S Snead	J Palmer	Richmond, VA	3 and 2
1950 June 21–27	C Harper	H Williams	Scioto, OH	4 and 3
1951 June 27–July 3	S Snead	W Burkemo	Oakmont, PA	7 and 6
1952 June 18–25	J Turnesa	C Harbert	Louisville, KY	1 hole
1953 July 1–7	W Burkemo	F Lorza	Birmingham, MI	2 and 1
1954 July 21–27	C Harbert	W Burkemo	St Paul, MN	4 and 3
1955 July 20–26	D Ford	C Middlecoff	Meadowbrook, MI	4 and 3
1956 July 20–24	J Burke	T Kroll	Canton, MA	3 and 2
1957 July 17–21	L Hebert	D Finsterwald	Dayton, OH	3 and 1

Changed to stroke play in 1958

Date	Winner	Venue	Score
1958 July 17–20	D Finsterwald	Llanerch, PA	276
1959 July 30–Aug 2	B Rosburg	Minneapolis, MN	277
1960 July 21–24	J Hebert	Firestone, Akron, OH	281
1961 July 27–31	J Barber*	Olympia Fields, IL	277
After a play-off: Barber 67, D January 68			
1962 July 19–22	G Player (RSA)	Aronimink, PA	278
1963 July 18–21	J Nicklaus	Dallas, TX	279
1964 July 16–19	B Nichols	Columbus, OH	271
1965 Aug 12–15	D Marr	Laurel Valley, PA	280
1966 July 21–24	A Geiberger	Firestone, Akron, OH	280
1967 July 20–24	D January*	Columbine, CO	281
After a play-off: January 69, D Massengale 71			
1968 July 18–21	J Boros	Pecan Valley, TX	281
1969 Aug 14–17	R Floyd	Dayton, OH	276
1970 Aug 13–16	D Stockton	Southern Hills, OK	279
1971 Feb 25–28	J Nicklaus	PGA national, FL	281
1972 Aug 3–6	G Player (RSA)	Oakland Hills, MI	281
1973 Aug 9–12	J Nicklaus	Canterbury, OH	277
1974 Aug 8–11	L Trevino	Tanglewood, NC	276
1975 Aug 7–10	J Nicklaus	Firestone, Akron, OH	276
1976 Aug 12–16	D Stockton	Congressional, MD	281
1977 Aug 11–14	L Wadkins*	Pebble Beach, CA	287
After a play-off: Wadkins 4-4-3; G Littler 4-4-4			
1978 Aug 3–6	J Mahaffey*	Oakmont, PA	276
After a play-off: Mahaffey 4-3; J Pate 4,4; T Watson 4-4			
1979 Aug 2–5	D Graham (AUS)	Oakland Hills, MI	272
After a play-off: Graham 4-4-2; B Crenshaw 4-4-4			
1980 Aug 7–10	J Nicklaus	Oak Hill, NY	274
1981 Aug 6–9	L Nelson	Atlanta, GA	273
1982 Aug 5–8	R Floyd	Southern Hills, OK	272
1983 Aug 4–7	H Sutton	Pacific Palisades, CA	274
1984 Aug 16–19	L Trevino	Shoal Creek, AL	273
1985 Aug 8–11	H Green	Cherry Hills, Denver, CO	278
1986 Aug 7–10	R Tway	Inverness, Toledo, OH	276
1987 Aug 6–9	L Nelson*	PGA National, FL	287
After a play-off: Nelson 4, L Wadkins 5			
1988 Aug 11–14	J Sluman	Oaktree, OK	272
1989 Aug 10–13	P Stewart	Kemper Lakes, IL	276
1990 Aug 9–12	W Grady (AUS)	Shoal Creek, AL	282
1991 Aug 8–11	J Daly	Crooked Stick, IN	276
1992 Aug 13–16	N Price (ZIM)	Bellerive, MS	278

US PGA Championship History *continued*

Date	Winner	Venue	Score	Date	Winner	Venue	Score
1993 Aug 12–15	P Azinger*	Inverness, Toledo, OH	272	2003 Aug 14–17	S Micheel	Oak Hill, NY	276
After a play-off: Azinger 4-4, G Norman 4-5				2004 Aug 12–15	V Singh (FIJ)*	Whistling Straits, WI	280
1994 Aug 11–14	N Price (ZIM)	Southern Hills, OK	269	*After a play-off: Singh 3,3,4, C DiMarco 4,3,4, J Leonard 4,3,4*			
1995 Aug 10–13	S Elkington (AUS)*	Riviera, LA	267	2005 Aug 11–15	P Mickelson	Baltusrol, NJ	276
				2006 Aug 16–20	T Woods	Medinah, IL	270
After a play-off: Elkington 3, C Montgomerie 4				2007 Aug 9–12	T Woods	Southern Hills, OK	272
1996 Aug 8–11	M Brooks*	Valhalla, Kentucky	277	2008 Aug 7–10	P Harrington	Oakland Hills, MI	277
After a play-off against Kenny Perry: Brooks 4, Perry 5				2009 Aug 14–16	Y E Yang	Hazeltine, Chaska, MN	280
1997 Aug 14–17	D Love III	Winged Foot, NY	269				
1998 Aug 13–16	V Singh (FIJ)	Sahalee, Seattle, WA	271	2010 Aug 12–15	M Kaymer*	Whistling Straits, WI	277
1999 Aug 12–15	T Woods	Medinah, IL	277	*After a play-off: Kaymer 4,2,5, B Watson 3,3,6*			
2000 Aug 17–20	T Woods*	Valhalla, Louisville KY	270	2011 Aug 11–14	K Bradley*	Atlanta Athletic Club, GA	272
After a play-off: Woods 3,4,5, B May 4,4,5							
2001 Aug 16–19	D Toms	Atlanta Athletic Club, GA	265	*After a play-off: Bradley 3,3,4, J Dufner 4,4,3*			
2002 Aug 15–18	R Beem	Hazeltine National, MN	278				

How the courses played in the 2011 Grand Slam events

THE MASTERS – National Golf Club, Augusta, GA
Course: 7,435 yards Par 72 – Average score 74.4257
Eagles scored during the week 33; Birdies 1,028.
Toughest Hole: The 11th – 505 yards Par 4 – Average score 4.3311
Easiest Hole: The13th – 510 yards Par 5 – Average score 4.5912
Winner: Charl Schwartzel (RSA) 274 (–14)

THE US OPEN CHAMPIONSHIP – Congressional GC, Washington DC
Course: 7,574 yards Par 71 – Average score 73.0054
Eagles scored during the week 16; Birdies 1,218
Toughest Hole: The 11th – 494 yards Par 4 – Average score 4.449
Easiest Hole: The 6th – 555 yards Par 5 – Average score 4.7873
Winner: Rory McIlroy (NIR) 268 (–16)

THE OPEN CHAMPIONSHIP – Royal St George's Golf Club, Sandwich
Course: 7,211 yards Par 70 – Average score 73.018
Eagles scored during the week 23; Birdies 994
Toughest Hole: The 4th – 495 yards Par 4 – Average score 4.52*
(*only 16 birdies all week)
Easiest Hole: The 7th – 564 yards Par 5 – Average score 4.563
Winner: Darren Clarke (NIR) 275 (–5)

US PGA CHAMPIONSHIP – Atlanta Athletic Club, Johns Creek, GA
Course: 7,467 yards Par 70 – Average score 72.377
Eagles scored during the week 24; Birdies 1225
Toughest Hole: The 18th – 507 yards Par 4 – Average score 4.584
Easiest Hole: The 5th – 565 yards Par 5 – Average score 4.66
Winner: Keegan Bradley (USA) 272 (–8)

Men's Grand Slam Titles

Jack Nicklaus

Tiger Woods

Walter Hagen

The modern Grand Slam comprises four events – the British and US Open Championships, the US PGA Championship and The Masters Tournament at Augusta.

	Open	US Open	Masters	US PGA	Total Titles
Jack Nicklaus (USA)	3	4	6	5	18
Tiger Woods (USA)	3	3	4	4	14
Walter Hagen (USA)	4	2	0	5	11
Ben Hogan (USA)	1	4	2	2	9
Gary Player (RSA)	3	1	3	2	9
Tom Watson (USA)	5	1	2	0	8
Arnold Palmer (USA)	2	1	4	0	7
Gene Sarazen (USA)	1	2	1	3	7
Sam Snead (USA)	1	0	3	3	7
Lee Trevino (USA)	2	2	0	2	6
Nick Faldo (ENG)	3	0	3	0	6

The original Grand Slam comprised the British and US Open Championships and the British and US Amateur Championships.

	Open	US Open	Amateur	US Amateur	Total Titles
Bobby Jones (USA)	3	4	1	5	13
John Ball (ENG)	1	0	8	0	9
Harold Hilton (ENG)	2	0	4	1	7
Harry Vardon (ENG)	6	1	0	0	7

Note: Tiger Woods won three consecutive US Amateur Championships in 1994, 1995 and 1996. Only Bobby Jones has won all four recognised Grand Slam events in the same year – 1930.

Ricoh Women's British Open Championship

July 28–31

Unstoppable Tseng wins her fifth major title

Impressive four-stroke victory at a gentler Carnoustie

Just as she enjoyed the distinction of becoming the youngest golfer in LPGA history to win four major titles, Yani Tseng savoured the distinction of becoming the most fresh faced player in the modern era to win five of the most coveted titles in golf after she mounted a successful defence of the Ricoh Women's British Open at Carnoustie.

© Getty Images

Yani Tseng

Thanks to a four stroke victory over Brittany Lang – she signed off with 69 for a 16-under-par total of 272 – the Taiwanese golfer moved past Tiger Woods, who won his fifth major at 24 years and seven months, as the youngest multiple major winner. At the age of just 22 years and six months, Tseng has won four of the last eight women's majors.

Blessed with mental strength, physical power and an athletic swing, Tseng began the last round at Carnoustie trailing the little known German golfer, Caroline Masson, by two strokes. The margin was up to three when she carded a bogey at the first. However, Tseng's reslience and Masson's nerves saw the defending champion take the lead with a birdie on the sixth hole. It was an advantage she never let slip thereafter.

Although still to to win the US Women's Open, Tseng is a force of nature in the UK. She finished second on her début at Sunningdale in 2008, 20th at Lytham in 2009 and took home the trophy in 2010 as well as 2011. "It's wonderful [to win five majors]," she said. "I mean, especially winning on this golf course, Carnoustie, in the home of golf. There's just so many great players making history on this golf course. It's my honour to be part of this. I just feel very special to win on a links golf course and the British Open. It's not like you're playing lousy and you can win a tournament; you have to play good, and there's so many challenges for this whole week. I just was really patient, and felt I did a good job."

Hosting the Women's British Open for the first time, Carnoustie was more of a tiger during this Championship and Tseng, for one, felt the set-up should have been tougher. "They could have set it up longer," she said. On Thursday, 30 golfers bettered the par of 72 and 48 players matched it. While Tseng was six shots off the pace on day one after opening with 71, Meena Lee took control with an impressive opening seven under par 65 to lead by two shots from America's Brittany Lincicome and three from a group of players on 68, including Masson, who was the leading European after 18 holes.

If Lee was unfortunate to get the worst of the weather in the afternoon when the rain arrived, Lady Luck smiled on her as she played the closing hole. Famous for undermining the major ambitions of Jean Van de Velde and Sergio García, Carnoustie's shortened 18th gave Lee a helping hand. When she landed the ball short of the hazard, it took a fortunate bounce over the Barry Burn and rolled close to the hole. While she missed the putt for birdie, par was good enough to keep a bogey off her card.

Scottish summers are rarely reliable,but there is usually enough respite from the wind and rain to confuse visitors. Lincicome seemed to be preparing for a game in the Arctic when she stepped onto the tee at 7.36am. "Of course I have 3 layers of pants and jackets anticipating snow, but this morning it was beautiful," she recalled. "You could have had on shorts and a short-sleeved shirt and been perfectly fine ... It was unlike the British Open actually. It was really pretty."

For all the bouquets and brickbats Carnoustie has earned over the years, it's doubtful if this stern links has been described as "really pretty" too often. Still, Lincicome took advantage of the gentle conditions on a shortened lay-out by delivering four birdies, two bogeys and an eagle on the 14th hole. Also off to a positive start was Angela Stanford, who hails from the same club in Texas – Shady Oaks – which produced Ben Hogan, the American maestro who won at Carnoustie on his only visit to Scotland in 1953.

On Friday, Carnoustie continued to accommodate rather than intimidate as conditions remained calm. When Masson signed for 65 and the 11 under total of 133, it was the lowest ever score recorded at the halfway mark in Women's British Open history. The German reeled off seven birdies, gave nothing away to par, and led the way into the weekend action.

The 22-year-old golfer from Gladbeck, near Dusseldorf, is the daughter of a tennis coach and played both sports as a child. She's been tutored by Guenter Kessler, Martin Kaymer's swing coach, for ten years and came to Carnoustie looking for her first win as a professional. "I saw him [Kessler] for two weeks before I came here, and we worked on these things like keeping the ball low. What was probably most important, he told me what Martin told him about his [British Open experiences], his attitude and all that. You really have to like links golf and accept whatever comes along, whatever conditions you have, and I think that helped me quite a lot."

There was also a significant move from Se Ri Pak, the Korean woman who did more than any other to inspire a new generation of her compatriots. After shooting an impressive 64, the five time major winner also had some words of advice for the obsessive young Koreans who devote their lives to the game. "They work so hard, 24/7, each day, every single second, every moment," she said. "They never have any relax or light time. That's basically the most difficult thing to do. So now I tell them if you're focused on your game, make sure 100 per cent you're trying to get release, and you can really play better." Tseng, meanwhile, was stalking her prey like a big cat as she forced her way up the leaderboard with 66.

Masson set another record for 54 holes in the championship by signing for 68 on Saturday and posting the 15 under mark of 201. While there was no doubt she'd played splendidly, many felt the course set-up erred on the side of generous and one of the fiercest tests in golf was toothless. In the third round, the pin positions were trickier than on the first two days and only 20 players bettered par compared to the 46 golfers who were in red figures over 36 holes.

Playing in only her second major, it seemed as if nerves might get the better of Masson when she struck a wayward drive on the first tee and three-putted for bogey. To her credit, however, the German went on to make six birdies before a dropped shot on the closing hole reduced her lead to two shots after 54 holes. While Masson was rated a lowly 141st in the Rolex Rankings before Carnoustie, her nearest challenger, Tseng, had long since annexed the No 1 position and was generally regarded as the best female golfer on the planet.

The defending champion got off to a quiet start on Saturday when she covered the front nine on even par. Over the inward half, however, she came home in 30 blows, with the highlight a 70 foot putt for eagle on the 14th. "I played awesome," said Tseng of her second consecutive 66. "There were some tough pins out there but I played real smart. On this golf course two shots is nothing ..."

Although she was six shots off the lead Catriona was hoping the wind would stir on Sunday and give the Scot an opportunity to emulate the success of her countryman, Paul Lawrie, who came from ten strokes behind to win The Open in 1999. The champion at Royal Lytham forced her way into contention with a tidy 68 for nine under, a score entirely befitting her role as an ambassador for Carnoustie Country.

The pressure eventually told on Masson during the final round as her putting touch deserted her. Playing with the world No 1, she dropped shots at the second and third holes and was out of the running when she made bogey on the seventh. Three more bogeys after the turn as well as a double at the 12th swept the young German down the field before closing birdies at the 17th and 18th holes enabled her to sign for 78 – ten more strokes than she'd required on Saturday.

Tseng, meanwhile, was impressively resilient. After giving the rest hope by dropping a shot at the first, the Taiwanese golfer was back on course with birdies at the third and sixth holes. True, there was a wobble in the middle of the round when she made bogeys at the 12th and 13th, but Tseng came roaring back with three birdies over the closing five holes.

Leading by three strokes standing on the last, the champion admitted the memory of Van de Velde's misfortune re-inforced her levels of concentration. "When you come on this golf course you're going to think about him," she admitted after relishing an entirely different outcome by wafting a 9 iron close to the pin and holing the putt which earned another major victory.

First Round	Second Round	Third Round	Fourth Round
−7 Meena Lee	−11 Caroline Masson	−15 Caroline Masson	−16 Yani Tseng
−5 Brittany Lincicome	−10 In-Bee Park	−13 Yani Tseng	−12 Brittany Lang
−4 Angela Stanford	−10 Meena Lee	−9 Catriona Matthew	−11 Sophie Gustafson
−4 Amy Yang	−8 Si Ri Pak	−9 In-Bee Park	−10 Amy Yang
−4 Caroline Masson	−8 Dewi Clare	−8 Na Yeon Choi	−9 Catriona Matthew
−4 Sophie Gustafson	−8 Na Yeon Choi	−7 Brittany Lang	−9 Caroline Masson
	−7 Yani Tseng	−7 Sophie Gustafson	−8 Sun Young Yoo
		−7 Si Ri Pak	−8 Anna Nordqvist
			−8 Na Yeon Choi
			−8 In-Bee Park

Ricoh Women's British Open Championship

Carnoustie Links [6490–72]

Prize money: €1,875,000. Final field of 144 (7 amateurs), of whom 68 (2 amateurs) made the half-way cut on 145 or under.

Final Qualifying at Panmure:

68 Kym Larratt (ENG)	69 Dewi Claire Schreefel (NED)	70 Joanna Klatten (FRA)
Lynnette Brooky (NZL)	70 Frances Noelle Bondad (AUS)	71 Beth Allen (USA)
69 Jessica Korda (USA)	Holly Aitchison (ENG)	Stephanie Meadow (IRL) (am)
Jenny Shin (KOR)	Sophie Sandolo (ITA)	Kylie Walker (SCO)
Veronica Zorzi (ITA)	Anna Rossi (ITA)	Jacyln Sweeney (USA)
Nikki Foster (ENG) (am)	Felicity Johnson (ENG)	Rebecca Codd (IRL)

1	Yani Tseng (TPE)	71-66-66-69—272	€272,365
2	Brittany Lang (USA)	70-70-69-67—276	170,736
3	Sophie Gustafson (SWE)	68-71-70-68—277	119,515
4	Amy Yang (KOR)	68-70-73-67—278	93,498
5	Catriona Matthew (SCO)	70-69-68-72—279	71,546
	Caroline Masson (GER)	68-65-68-78—279	71,546
7	Sun Young Yoo (KOR)	71-70-69-70—280	52,236
	Anna Nordqvist (SWE)	70-71-69-70—280	52,236
	Na Yeon Choi (KOR)	69-67-72-72—280	52,236
	In-Bee Park (KOR)	70-64-73-73—280	52,236
11	Stacy Lewis (USA)	74-68-71-68—281	39,025
	Dewi Claire Schreefel (NED)	70-66-74-71—281	39,025
13	Maria Hjörth (SWE)	72-69-73-68—282	34,147
14	Katie Futcher (USA)	71-74-74-64—283	25,964
	Cristie Kerr (USA)	72-69-74-68—283	25,964
	Candie Kung (TPE)	72-73-69-69—283	25,964
	Song-Hee Kim (KOR)	69-72-71-71—283	25,964
	Sun Ju Ahn (KOR)	71-71-70-71—283	25,964
	Mika Miyazato (JPN)	69-69-72-73—283	25,964
	Se Ri Pak (KOR)	72-64-73-74—283	25,964
21	Jiyai Shin (KOR)	75-66-72-71—284	21,138
22	Karen Stupples (ENG)	74-68-72-71—285	18,394
	Hee-Kyung Seo (KOR)	72-71-71-71—285	18,394
	Karrie Webb (AUS)	70-71-72-72—285	18,394
	Rachel Jennings (ENG)	71-73-69-72—285	18,394
	Momoko Ueda (JPN)	69-71-72-73—285	18,394
	Angela Stanford (USA)	68-72-72-73—285	18,394
28	Michelle Wie (USA)	74-68-72-72—286	15,752
	Vicky Hurst (USA)	70-71-71-74—286	15,752
30	Amy Hung (TPE)	69-72-78-68—287	13,444
	Haeji Kang (KOR)	75-70-73-69—287	13,444
	Beth Allen (USA)	71-70-75-71—287	13,444
	Tiffany Joh (USA)	71-69-75-72—287	13,444
	Caroline Hedwall (SWE)	69-69-76-73—287	13,444
	Brittany Lincicome (USA)	67-71-76-73—287	13,444
	Shanshan Feng (CHN)	70-75-67-75—287	13,444
37	Melissa Reid (ENG)	75-70-73-70—288	10,772
	Eun Hee Ji (KOR)	70-71-75-72—288	10,772
	Suzann Pettersen (NOR)	76-66-73-73—288	10,772
	Meena Lee (KOR)	65-69-80-74—288	10,772
	Linda Wessberg (SWE)	73-66-75-74—288	10,772
	In Kyung Kim (KOR)	71-72-71-74—288	10,772
43	Hiromi Mogi (JPN)	72-72-74-71—289	8,333
	Hee Won Han (KOR)	73-71-74-71—289	8,333
	Lorie Kane (CAN)	69-76-73-71—289	8,333
	Hee Young Park (KOR)	70-70-76-73—289	8,333
	Kristy McPherson (USA)	71-71-74-73—289	8,333

43T	Paula Creamer (USA)	69-70-71-79—289	8,333
49	Azahara Muñoz Guijarro (ESP)	73-71-73-73—290	6,301
	Danielle Kang (USA) (am)	72-69-75-74—290	
	Morgan Pressel (USA)	70-71-75-74—290	6,301
	Pat Hurst (USA)	70-69-74-77—290	6,301
	Cindy LaCrosse (USA)	72-69-72-77—290	6,301
54	Christel Boeljon (NED)	76-69-73-73—291	4,593
	Janice Moodie (SCO)	75-67-75-74—291	4,593
	Sandra Gal (GER)	71-70-74-76—291	4,593
	Chella Choi (KOR)	74-70-71-76—291	4,593
	Amanda Blumenherst (USA)	73-71-70-77—291	4,593
59	Miki Saiki (JPN)	72-72-76-72—292	3,504
	Kylie Walker (SCO)	72-72-74-74—292	3,504
	Holly Aitchison (ENG)	71-74-72-75—292	3,504
	Julieta Granada (PAR)	71-74-70-77—292	3,504
	Sophie Giquel-Bettan (FRA)	71-68-72-81—292	3,504
64	Virginie Lagoutte-Clement (FRA)	75-70-73-77—295	2,927
	Jaclyn Sweeney (USA)	74-71-72-78—295	2,927
66	Georgina Simpson (ENG)	71-73-79-74—297	2,683
67	Sophie Popov (GER) (am)	70-75-77-77—299	
68	Jimin Kang (KOR)	74-70-72-RTD	1,139

The following players missed the cut:

69	Kristie Smith (AUS)	70-76—146		94T	Mina Harigae (USA)	74-74—148
	Becky Morgan (WAL)	73-73—146			Grace Park (KOR)	76-72—148
	Rebecca Codd (IRL)	71-75—146		109	Beatriz Recari (ESP)	79-70—149
	Heather Bowie Young (USA)	72-74—146			Reilley Rankin (USA)	71-78—149
	Jin Young Pak (KOR)	73-73—146			Alena Sharp (CAN)	77-72—149
	M J Hur (KOR)	73-73—146			Jee Young Lee (KOR)	74-75—149
	Pamela Pretswell (SCO) (am)	72-74—146			Minea Blomqvist (FIN)	75-74—149
76	Diana Luna (ITA)	75-72—147			Caroline Afonso (FRA)	77-72—149
	Juli Inkster (USA)	73-74—147			Mindy Kim (SKO)	72-77—149
	Natalie Gulbis (USA)	71-76—147			Sarah Kemp (AUS)	76-73—149
	Belen Mozo (ESP)	76-71—147		117	Stacy Prammanasudh (USA)	77-73—150
	Kym Larratt (ENG)	77-70—147			Lynnette Brooky (NZL)	75-75—150
	Frances Bondad (AUS)	72-75—147			Stephanie Sherlock (CAN)	77-73—150
	Ashleigh Simon (RSA)	74-73—147			Nikki Foster (ENG)	78-72—150
	Moira Dunn (USA)	74-73—147			Laura Davies (ENG)	73-77—150
	Felicity Johnson (ENG)	74-73—147			Stefania Croce (ITA)	75-75—150
	Silvia Cavalleri (ITA)	78-69—147			Zuzana Kamasova (SVK)	79-71—150
	Ai Miyazato (JPN)	76-71—147		124	Sakura Yokomine (JPN)	81-70—151
	Yuri Fudoh (JPN)	73-74—147			Stephanie Meadow (IRL) (am)	75-76—151
	Becky Brewerton (WAL)	70-77—147			Sherri Steinhauer (USA)	78-73—151
	Danah Bordner (USA)	76-71—147			Kiran Matharu (ENG)	75-76—151
	Meaghan Francella (USA)	75-72—147			Yoo Kyeong Kim (KOR)	73-78—151
	Seon Hwa Lee (KOR)	76-71—147		129	Anja Monke (GER)	76-76—152
	Malene Jorgensen (DEN)	73-74—147			Karen Lunn (AUS)	81-71—152
	Jennifer Johnson (USA)	77-70—147			Nicole Hage (USA)	77-75—152
94	Gwladys Nocera (FRA)	78-70—148			Anne-Lise Caudal (FRA)	76-76—152
	Pornanong Phatlum (THA)	75-73—148			Paige Mackenzie (USA)	76-76—152
	Gerina Piller (USA)	75-73—148			Mi Hyun Kim (KOR)	76-76—152
	Jenny Shin (KOR)	75-73—148			Kyeong Bae (KOR)	75-77—152
	Jessica Korda (USA) (am)	76-72—148			Lindsey Wright (AUS)	77-75—152
	Aree Song (KOR)	73-75—148		137	Joanna Klatten (FRA)	74-79—153
	Veronica Zorzi (ITA)	74-74—148			Sophie Sandolo (ITA)	78-75—153
	Lee-Anne Pace (RSA)	71-77—148			Connie Chen (RSA)	75-78—153
	Wendy Ward (USA)	74-74—148		140	Christina Kim (USA)	79-75—154
	Jennifer Song (USA)	75-73—148			Florentyna Parker (ENG)	79-75—154
	Sarah-Jane Smith (AUS)	77-71—148		142	Carin Koch (SWE)	76-81—157
	Jane Park (USA)	76-72—148			Stacey Keating (AUS)	79-78—157
	Lauren Taylor (ENG) (am)	74-74—148		144	Anna Rossi (ITA)	82-78—160

2010 Ricoh Women's British Open   Royal Birkdale   [6463–72]

Prize money: €2.5 million

1	Yani Tseng (TPE)	68-68-68-73—277	€313,530
2	Katherine Hull (AUS)	68-74-66-70—278	196,541
3	Na Yeon Choi (KOR)	74-70-69-68—281	122,604
	In-Kyung Kim (KOR)	70-72-68-71—281	122,604
5	Cristie Kerr (USA)	73-67-72-70—282	77,992
	Hee-Kyung Seo (KOR)	73-69-70-70—282	77,992
	Amy Yang (KOR)	69-71-74-68—282	77,992
8	Morgan Pressel (USA)	77-71-65-71—284	62,707
9	Christina Kim (USA)	74-68-70-74—286	47,544
	Brittany Lincicome (USA)	69-71-71-75—286	47,544
	Ai Miyazato (JPN)	76-70-73-67—286	47,544
	In-Bee Park (KOR)	72-71-77-66—286	47,544
	Momoko Ueda (JPN)	72-70-70-74—286	47,544
14	Maria Hernandez (ESP)	73-70-73-71—287	33,224
	Suzann Pettersen (NOR)	73-68-71-75—287	33,224
	Jiyai Shin (KOR)	71-71-72-73—287	33,224
17	Gwladys Nocera (FRA)	71-75-72-70—288	28,779
	Michelle Wie (USA)	70-76-71-71—288	28,779
19	Song-Hee Kim (KOR)	75-73-71-70—289	25,971
	Azahara Muñoz (ESP)	74-71-72-72—289	25,971
21	Chie Arimura (JPN)	77-68-70-75—290	22,032
	Becky Brewerton (WAL)	73-73-71-73—290	22,032

21T	Paula Creamer (USA)	74-74-70-72—290	22,032
	Juli Inkster (USA)	71-70-76-73—290	22,032
	Jeong Jang (KOR)	74-73-74-69—290	22,032
	Lee-Anne Pace (RSA)	74-72-71-73—290	22,032
27	Caroline Hedwall (SWE) (am)	74-75-72-70—291	
	Karine Icher (FRA)	74-72-70-75—291	18,484
	Jimin Kang (KOR)	74-73-74-70—291	18,484
	Mindy Kim (KOR)	72-75-73-71—291	18,484
31	Anne-Lise Caudal (FRA)	69-73-75-75—292	14,292
	Katie Futcher (USA)	74-74-72-72—292	14,292
	M J Hur (KOR)	74-68-75-75—292	14,292
	Vicky Hurst (USA)	77-71-74-70—292	14,292
	Haeji Kang (KOR)	75-74-72-71—292	14,292
	Mi Hyun Kim (KOR)	72-77-73-70—292	14,292
	Stacy Lewis (USA)	71-74-75-72—292	14,292
	Ji Young Oh (KOR)	79-69-75-69—292	14,292
	Melissa Reid (ENG)	77-71-74-70—292	14,292
	Sakura Yokomine (JPN)	74-71-75-72—292	14,292
	Sun Young Yoo (KOR)	69-72-78-73—292	14,292
	Henrietta Zuel (ENG)	74-73-73-72—292	14,292

Other players who made the cut: Sophie Gustafson (SWE), Amy Hung (TPE), Brittany Lang (USA), Meena Lee (KOR), Stacy Prammanasudh (USA), Ashleigh Simon (RSA), Karrie Webb (AUS) 293; Irene Cho (KOR), Moira Dunn (USA), Angela Stanford (USA), Sherri Steinhauer (USA), Kristin Tamulis (USA) 294; Carin Koch (SWE), Janice Moodie (SCO), Hee Young Park (KOR), Florentyna Parker (ENG), Sarah-Jane Smith (AUS), Iben Tinning (DEN), Wendy Ward (USA) 295; Seon Hwa Lee (KOR), Jee Young Lee (KOR) 296; Sarah Lee (KOR), Anja Monke (GER), Alena Sharp (CAN) 297; Stacy Bregman (RSA), Eunjang Yi (KOR) 298; Laura Davies (ENG), Meaghan Francella (USA), Anna Nordqvist (SWE), Mariajo Uribe (COL) 299; Shanshan Feng (CHN), Giulia Sergas (ITA) 300; Jennifer Rosales (PHI) 302

2009 Ricoh Women's British Open   Royal Lytham & St Annes   [6492–72]

Prize money: €1.5 million

1	Catriona Matthew (SCO)	74-67-71-73—285	€235,036
2	Karrie Webb (AUS)	77-71-72-68—288	147,336
3	Paula Creamer (USA)	74-74-70-71—289	76,825
	Hee-Won Han (KOR)	77-73-69-70—289	76,825
	Christina Kim (USA)	73-71-71-74—289	76,825
	Ai Miyazato (JPN)	75-71-70-73—289	76,825
7	Kristy McPherson (USA)	74-74-72-70—290	51,918
8	Na Yeon Choi (KOR)	80-71-70-70—291	42,797
	Cristie Kerr (USA)	76-71-75-69—291	42,797
	Ji-Yai Shin (KOR)	77-71-68-75—291	42,797
11	Maria Hjörth (SWE)	72-76-73-71—292	28,590
	Song-ee Kim (KOR)	70-73-74-75—292	28,590
	Mika Miyazato (JPN)	76-72-69-75—292	28,590
	Hee Young Park (KOR)	71-75-73-73—292	28,590
	Giulia Sergas (ITA)	74-67-78-73—292	28,590
	Michelle Wie (USA)	73-76-74-69—292	28,590
17	Kyeong Bae (KOR)	73-71-74-75—293	21,048
	Jane Park (USA)	74-72-72-75—293	21,048
	Michelle Redman (USA)	75-75-73-70—293	21,048
20	In-Kyung Kim (KOR)	81-71-70-73—294	17,890
	Se-Ri Pak (KOR)	76-71-73-74—294	17,890

20T	Angela Stanford (USA)	70-76-74-74—294	17,890
	Yani Tseng (TPE)	74-70-78-72—294	17,890
24	In-Bee Park (KOR)	76-72-76-71—295	16,137
25	Jeong Jang (KOR)	79-73-72-72—296	15,172
	Shinobu Moromizato (JPN)	74-73-71-78—296	15,172
27	Jade Schaeffer (FRA)	79-71-75-72—297	14,383
28	Katie Futcher (USA)	75-77-70-76—298	12,839
	Vicky Hurst (USA)	74-75-77-72—298	12,839
	Brittany Lincicome (USA)	77-73-79-69—298	12,839
	Teresa Lu (TPE)	75-76-77-70—298	12,839
	Lorena Ochoa (MEX)	75-77-72-74—298	12,839
33	Yuri Fudoh (JPN)	80-73-70-76—299	10,524
	Sandra Gal (GER)	69-80-75-75—299	10,524
	Sophie Gustafson (SWE)	74-71-82-72—299	10,524
	Brittany Lang (USA)	81-70-71-77—299	10,524
	Yuko Mitsuka (JPN)	71-71-79-78—299	10,524
	Becky Morgan (WAL)	80-71-72-76—299	10,524
	Sun-Young Yoo (KOR)	79-73-75-72—299	10,524
40	Allison Hanna (USA)	76-76-73-75—300	8,945
	Katherine Hull (AUS)	75-77-77-71—300	8,945

Other players who made the cut: Martina Eberl (GER), Meena Lee (KOR), Morgan Pressel (USA), Marianne Skarpnord (NOR) 301; Carmen Alonso (ESP), Il Mi Chung (KOR), Laura Davies (ENG), Mi-Jung Hur (JPN), Ursula Wikstrom (FIN) 302; Irene Cho (KOR), Samantha Head (ENG), Sarah Lee (KOR), Anna Nordqvist (SWE) 303; Jin Young Pak (KOR), Louise Stahle (SWE), Momoko Ueda (JPN) 304; Christel Boeljom (NED), Eunjang Yi (KOR) 305; Anne-Lise Caudal (FRA), Young Kim (KOR), Emma Zackrisson (SWE) 306; Lee-Anne Pace (RSA), Reilley Rankin (USA) 307; Kristin Tamulis (USA) 308; Vikki Laing (SCO) 309; Laura Diaz (USA), Shanshan Feng (CHN), Stacy Prammanasudh (USA) 310; Karin Sjodin (SWE) Rtd; Eun Hee Ji (KOR) DQ

2008 Ricoh Women's British Open   *Sunningdale*   [6408–72]

Prize money: £1.55 million

1	Ji-Yai Shin (KOR)	66-68-70-66—270	€202,336	21T	Kristy McPherson (USA)	67-75-74-65—281	15,175
2	Ya-Ni Tseng (TPE)	70-69-68-66—273	126.460	24	Meredith Duncan (USA)	71-73-71-67—282	11,786
3	Eun Hee Ji (KOR)	68-70-69-67—274	79.037		Sophie Gustafson (SWE)	69-69-74-70—282	11,786
	Yuri Fudoh (JPN)	66-68-69-71—274	79.037		Mi Hyun Kim (KOR)	70-70-67-75—282	11,786
5	Ai Miyazato (JPN)	68-69-68-70—275	56.907		Eun-A Lin (KOR)	74-71-72-65—282	11,786
6	Cristie Kerr (USA)	71-65-70-70—276	49.319		Jane Park (USA)	69-70-73-70—282	11,786
7	Lorena Ochoa (MEX)	69-68-71-69—277	42.464		Suzann Pettersen (NOR)	70-70-71-71—282	11,786
	Momoko Ueda (JPN)	66-72-70-69—277	42.464		Stacy Prammanasudh	66-74-72-70—282	11,786
9	Paula Creamer (USA)	72-69-70-67—278	30.603		(USA)		
	Natalie Gulbis (USA)	69-68-70-71—278	30.603		Annika Sörenstam (SWE)	72-72-70-68—282	11,786
	Hee Won Han (KOR)	71-69-71-67—278	30.603		Karen Stupples (ENG)	67-73-72-70—282	11,786
	In-Kyung Kim (KOR)	71-68-72-67—278	30.603		Sakura Yokomine (JPN)	71-72-69-70—282	11,786
	Karrie Webb (AUS)	72-69-69-68—278	30.603	34	Laura Diaz (USA)	66-72-75-70—283	9,010
14	Juli Inkster (USA)	65-70-71-73—279	21.709		Anja Monke (GER)	73-67-70-73—283	9,010
	Seon Hwa Lee (KOR)	71-68-70-70—279	21.709		Angela Park (BRA)	71-74-71-37—283	9,010
	Hee Young Park (KOR)	69-71-69-70—279	21.709		Bo Bae Song (KOR)	68-68-74-73—283	9,010
17	Shi Hyun Ahn (KOR)	68-72-71-69—280	17.625	38	Ji-Hee Lee (KOR)	68-75-68-73—284	7,745
	Minea Blomqvist (FIN)	68-73-72-67—280	17.625		Leta Lindley (USA)	71-71-72-70—284	7,745
	Jee Yound Lee (KOR)	71-72-71-66—280	17.625		Paula Marti (ESP)	68-72-72-72—284	7,745
	Ji Young Oh (KOR)	66-73-71-70—280	17.625		Catriona Matthew	68-75-72-69—284	7,745
21	Nicole Castrale (USA)	69-72-72-68—281	15,175		(SCO)		
	Na Yeon Choi (KOR)	69-71-68-73—281	15,175				

Other players who made the cut: Candie Kung (TPE), Anna Nordqvist (SWE) (am), Reilley Rankin (USA) 285; Lora Fairclough (ENG), Janice Moodie (SCO), Sun Young Yoo (KOR) 286; Hye Jung Choi (KOR), Jin Joo Hong (KOR), Katherine Hull (AUS), Jill McGill (USA), Joanne Mills (AUS), Gloria Park (KOR), Karin Sjodin (SWE), Lotta Wahlin (SWE) 287; Helen Alfredsson (SWE), Il-Mi Chung (KOR), Rebecca Hudson (ENG) 288; Jimin Kang (KOR), Teresa Lu (TPE), Becky Morgan (WAL), Kris Camulis (USA), Wendy Ward (USA) 289; Erica Blasberg (USA), Christina Kim (USA), Gwladys Nocera (FRA), Marianne Skarpnord (NOR), Sherri Steinhauer (USA) 290; Tania Elosegui (ESP), Johanna Head (ENG), Rachel Hetherington (AUS), Maria Hjörth (SWE), Trish Johnson (ENG) 291; Becky Brewerton (WAL) 292; Moira Dunn (USA), Maria Jose Uribe (COL) (am) 294; Laura Davies (ENG) 295; Mhairi McKay (SCO) 296

2007 Ricoh Women's British Open   *St Andrews Old Course*   [6638–73]

Prize money: £2.5 million

1	Lorena Ochoa (MEX)	67-73-73-74—287	£160.000	16T	Melissa Reid (ENG) (am)	73-75-76-72—296	
2	Maria Hjörth (SWE)	75-73-72-71—291	85,000		Annika Sörenstam (SWE)	72-71-77-76—296	14.041
	Jee Young Lee (KOR)	72-73-75-71—291	85,000	23	Beth Bader (USA)	73-77-75-72—297	11.060
4	Reilley Rankin (USA)	73-74-74-71—292	55,000		Natalia Gulbis (USA)	73-76-76-72—297	11.060
5	Eun Hee Ji (KOR)	73-71-77-72—293	42,000		Alena Sharp (CAN)	77-70-79-71—297	11.060
	Se Ri Pak (KOR)	73-73-75-72—293	42,000		Sherri Steinhauer (USA)	72-71-80-74—297	11.060
7	Paula Creamer (USA)	73-75-74-72—294	30,500		Wendy Ward (USA)	71-70-80-76—297	11.060
	Catriona Matthew (SCO)	73-68-80-73—294	30,500	28	Jimin Kang (KOR)	77-72-75-75—299	9,100
	Miki Saiki (JPN)	76-70-81-67—294	30,500		Sarah Lee (KOR)	72-76-79-72—299	9,100
	Linda Wessberg (SWE)	74-73-72-75—294	30,500		Suzann Pettersen (NOR)	74-76-78-71—299	9,100
11	Yuri Fudoh (JPN)	74-69-81-71—295	20,300		Ji-Yai Shin (KOR)	76-74-77-72—299	9,100
	Brittany Lincicome (USA)	71-76-75-73—295	20,300		Karrie Webb (AUS)	77-73-74-75—299	9,100
	Mhairi McKay (SCO)	75-74-79-67—295	20,300	33	Louise Friberg (SWE)	69-76-80-75—300	7,062
	Na On Min (KOR)	72-75-75-73—295	20,300		Sophie Gustafson (SWE)	73-72-81-74—300	7,062
	In-Bee Park (KOR)	69-79-76-71—295	20,300		Kim Hall (USA)	74-74-79-73—300	7,062
16	Becky Brewerton (WAL)	74-75-74-73—296	14.041		Juli Inkster (USA)	79-68-82-71—300	7,062
	Karine Icher (FRA)	72-71-77-76—296	14.041		Trish Johnson (ENG)	75-75-77-73—300	7,062
	Virginie Lagoutte-	72-73-78-73—296	14.041		Cristie Kerr (USA)	77-71-79-73—300	7,062
	Clement (FRA)				Candie Kung (TPE)	77-75-75-73—300	7,062
	Gloria Park (KOR)	74-75-76-71—296	14.041		Meena Lee (KOR)	71-76-79-74—300	7,062
	Stacy Prammanasudh	74-76-72-74—296	14.041		Gwladys Nocera (FRA)	78-72-75-75—300	7,062
	(USA)						

Other players who made the cut: Rebecca Hudson (ENG), In-Kyung Kim (KOR), Michele Redman (USA), Kerry Smith (ENG) (am), Karen Stupples (ENG), Lotta Wahlin (SWE) 301; Hye Yong Choi (KOR) (am), Catrin Nilsmark (SWE) 303; Dina Ammaccapane (USA), Rachel Bell (ENG), Beth Daniel (USA), Grace Park (KOR), Sally Watson (SCO) (am) 304; Rachel Hetherington (AUS), Bélen Mozo (ESP) (am), Momoko Ueda (JPN) 305; Lisa Hall (ENG), Jin Joo Hong (KOR), Christina Kim (USA), Ai Miyazato (JPN), Anna Nordquist (SWE) (am), Iben Tinning (DEN) 306; Joanne Mills (AUS) 308; Diana D'Alessio (USA), Martina Eberl (GER) 309; Nicole Castrale (USA) 310; Meg Mallon (USA) 311; Naomi Edwards (ENG) (am) 312

2006 Weetabix Women's British Open   Royal Lytham & St Annes   [6308–72]

Prize money: £1.05 million

1	Sherri Steinhauer (USA)	73-70-66-72—281	£160,000	22T	Jee Young Lee (KOR)	72-77-69-74—292	11,500
2	Sophie Gustafson (SWE)	76-67-69-72—284	85,000	25	Shi Hyun Ahn (KOR)	75-73-69-76—293	10,600
	Cristie Kerr (USA)	71-76-66-71—284	85,000	26	Jackie Gallagher-Smith	77-74-71-72—294	9,460
4	Juli Inkster (USA)	66-72-74-73—285	50,000		(USA)		
	Lorena Ochoa (MEX)	74-73-65-73—285	50,000		Tracy Hanson (USA)	74-77-70-73—294	9,460
6	Beth Daniel (USA)	73-70-71-72—286	37,000		Jeong Jang (KOR)	78-73-68-75—294	9,460
	Lorie Kane (CAN)	73-69-74-70—286	37,000		Michelle Wie (USA)	74-74-72-74—294	9,460
8	Julieta Granada (PAR)	71-73-70-73—287	32,000		Young-A Yang (KOR)	72-75-68-79—294	9,460
9	Ai Miyazato (JPN)	71-75-75-67—288	29,000	31	Nicole Castrale (USA)	73-75-71-76—295	7,810
10	Hee Won Han (KOR)	80-71-69-70—290	21,250		Anja Monke (GER)	75-76-70-74—295	7,810
	Karine Icher (FRA)	72-73-71-74—290	21,250		Liselotte Neumann	76-72-70-77—295	7,810
	Joo Mi Kim (KOR)	73-73-73-71—290	21,250		(SWE)		
	Candie Kung (TPE)	72-70-71-77—290	21,250		Annika Sörenstam	72-71-73-79—295	7,810
	Nina Reis (SWE)	70-76-69-75—290	21,250		(SWE)		
	Karen Stupples (ENG)	73-69-70-78—290	21,250		Lindsey Wright (USA)	71-71-74-79—295	7,810
16	Il-Mi Chung (KOR)	72-71-75-73—291	14,041	36	Becky Brewerton (WAL)	76-73-73-74—296	6,375
	Laura Davies (ENG)	72-72-73-74—291	14,041		Vicki Goetze-Ackerman	75-72-71-78—296	6,375
	Natalie Gulbis (USA)	72-74-67-78—291	14,041		(USA)		
	Gwladys Nocera (FRA)	70-73-71-77—291	14,041		Young Jo (KOR)	80-70-74-72—296	6,375
	Sukura Yokomine (JPN)	72-73-75-71—291	14,041		Angela Stanford (USA)	76-69-80-71—296	6,375
	Heather Young (USA)	72-74-70-75—291	14,041		Sun Young Yoo (KOR)	76-74-71-75—296	6,375
22	Kyeong Bae (KOR)	73-73-75-71—292	11,500		Veronica Zorzi (ITA)	74-76-78-68—296	6,375
	Paula Creamer (USA)	72-71-73-76—292	11,500				

Other players who made the cut: Yuri Fudoh (JPN), Nikki Garrett (AUS), Patricia Meunier-Lebouc (FRA) 297; Chieko Amanuma (JPN), Silvia Cavalleri (ITA), Maria Hjörth (SWE), Christina Kim (USA), Sarah Lee (KOR) 298; Marisa Baena (COL), Rita Hakkarainen (FIN), Allison Hanna (USA), Teresa Lu (TPE), Joanne Morley (ENG), Lee Ann Walker-Cooper (USA) 299; Brittany Lincicome (USA), Becky Morgan (WAL), Morgan Pressel (USA), Kris Tamulis (USA) 300; Amy Yang (KOR) (am) 301; Lynnette Brooky (NZL), Seon Hwa Lee (KOR), Elisa Serramia (ESP), Ursula Wikstrom (FIN) 302; Laura Diaz (USA) 303; Marta Prieto (ESP) 304; Helena Alterby (SWE), Wendy Ward (USA) 305; Rachel Hetherington (AUS) 306; Bélen Mozo (ESP) (am) 307; Iben Tinning (DEN) 311

2005 Weetabix Women's British Open   Royal Birkdale, Southport, Lancashire   [6463–72]

Prize money: £1.05 million

1	Jeong Jang (KOR)	68-66-69-69—272	£160.000	21	Catriona Matthew (SCO)	73-72-72-67—284	13,500
2	Sophie Gustafson (SWE)	69-73-67-67—276	100,000	22	Brandie Burton (USA)	74-75-71-65—285	117,67
3	Young Kim (KOR)	74-68-67-69—278	70,000		Cecilia Ekelundh (SWE)	77-69-71-68—285	11,767
	Michelle Wie (USA) (am)	75-67-67-69—278			Candie Kung (TAI)	76-71-67-71—285	11,767
5	Cristie Kerr (USA)	73-66-69-71—279	46,333		Nicole Perrot (CHI)	70-72-69-74—285	11,767
	Liselotte Neumann	71-70-68-70—279	46,333		Sophie Sandolo (ITA)	71-73-73-68—285	11,767
	(SWE)				Linda Wessberg (SWE)	72-71-73-69—285	11,767
	Annika Sörenstam (SWE)	73-69-66-71—279	46,333	28	Shi Hyun Ahn (KOR)	78-68-67-73—286	9,283
8	Natalie Gulbis (USA)	76-70-68-66—280	33,500		Becky Brewerton (WAL)	75-71-65-75—286	9,283
	Grace Park (KOR)	77-68-67-68—280	33,500		Laura Davies (ENG)	76-70-66-74—286	9,283
	Louise Stahle (SWE) (am)	73-65-73-69—280			Christina Kim (USA)	79-70-71-66—286	9,283
11	Ai Miyazato (JPN)	72-73-69-67—281	25,250		Anja Monke (GER)	73-73-70-70—286	9,283
	Michele Redman (USA)	75-71-67-68—281	25,250		Miriam Nagl (GER)	74-75-69-68—286	9,283
	Karen Stupples (ENG)	74-71-65-71—281	25,250	34	Heather Bowie (USA)	74-69-72-72—287	7,530
	Karrie Webb (AUS)	75-66-69-71—281	25,250		Marty Hart (USA)	79-70-71-67—287	7,530
15	Paula Creamer (USA)	75-69-65-73—282	17,300		Rebecca Hudson (ENG)	78-70-71-68—287	7,530
	Yuri Fudoh (JPN)	75-69-69-70—282	17,300		Emilee Klein (USA)	71-73-70-73—287	7,530
	Juli Inkster (USA)	74-68-68-72—282	17,300		Jill McGill (USA)	76-70-72-69—287	7,530
	Carin Koch (SWE)	76-68-66-72—282	17,300	39	Minea Blomquist (SWE)	78-68-72-70—288	6,500
	Becky Morgan (WAL)	79-66-67-70—282	17,300		Wendy Doolan (AUS)	77-72-67-72—288	6,500
20	Pat Hurst (USA)	75-65-70-73—283	14,250		Sherri Steinhauer (USA)	74-73-70-71—288	6,500

Other players who made the cut: Helen Alfredsson (SWE), Michelle Ellis (AUS), Riikka Hakkarainen (FIN), Rachel Hetherington (AUS), Riko Higashio (JPN), Amanda Moltke-Leth (DEN), Gwladys Nocera (FRA), Kim Saiki (USA), Iben Tinning (DEN), Kris Tschetter (USA) 289; Carlota Ciganda (ESP) (am), Moira Dunn (USA), Kris Lindstrom (USA), Kimberley Williams (USA) 290; Catherine Cartwright (USA), Beth Daniel (USA) 291; Young Jo (KOR), Lorie Kane (CAN), Aree Song (KOR), Bo Bae Song (KOR) 292; Judith Van Hagen (NED), Shani Waugh (AUS) 293; Laura Diaz (USA), Sung Ah Yim (KOR) 294; Amy Hung (TAI), Paula Marti (ESP) 295; Siew-Ai Lim (MAS), Yu Ping Lin (TAI) 296; Karen Lunn (AUS) 301

2004 Weetabix Women's British Open Sunningdale (Old Course) [6392–72]

Prize money: £1.05 million

1	Karen Stupples (ENG)	65-70-70-64—269	£160,000	21T	Se Ri Pak (KOR)	73-70-69-69—281	12,250
2	Rachel Teske (AUS)	70-69-65-70—274	100,000	23	Jeong Jang (KOR)	70-68-73-71—282	11,250
3	Heather Bowie (USA)	70-69-65-71—275	70,000		Aree Song (KOR)	72-70-70-70—282	11,250
4	Lorena Ochoa (MEX)	69-71-66-70—276	55,000	25	Juli Inkster (USA)	71-75-69-68—283	10,200
5	Beth Daniel (USA)	69-69-71-68—277	39,667		Seol-An Jeon (KOR)	69-69-70-75—283	10,200
	Michele Redman (USA)	70-71-70-66—277	39,667		Toshimi Kimura (JPN)	70-75-68-70—283	10,200
	Guilia Sergas (ITA)	72-71-67-67—277	39,667	28	Alison Nicholas (ENG)	75-71-70-69—285	9,450
8	Minea Blomqvist (FIN)	68-78-62-70—278	29,000	29	Candie Kung (TPE)	73-69-71-73—286	8,925
	Laura Davies (ENG)	70-69-69-70—278	29,000		Catriona Matthew (SCO)	68-74-68-76—286	8,925
	Jung Yeon Lee (KOR)	67-72-70-69—278	29,000	31	Wendy Doolan (AUS)	71-72-74-70—287	7,950
11	Pat Hurst (USA)	72-72-66-69—279	23,000		Natascha Fink (AUT)	74-70-70-73—287	7,950
	Cristie Kerr (USA)	69-73-63-74—279	23,000		Gloria Park (KOR)	72-73-75-67—287	7,950
13	Laura Diaz (USA)	70-69-70-71—280	15,906		Kirsty Taylor (ENG)	72-74-72-69—287	7,950
	Natalie Gulbis (USA)	68-71-70-71—280	15,906	35	Soo-Yun Kang (KOR)	71-74-74-69—288	7,000
	Hee Won Han (KOR)	72-68-70-70—280	15,906		Becky Morgan (WAL)	74-72-69-73—288	7,000
	Christina Kim (USA)	73-68-68-71—280	15,906		Jennifer Rosales (PHI)	75-70-70-73—288	7,000
	Carin Koch (SWE)	70-70-70-70—280	15,906	38	Denise Killeen (USA)	72-72-70-75—289	6,125
	Paula Marti (ESP)	73-66-68-73—280	15,906		Jill McGill (USA)	71-72-71-75—289	6,125
	Grace Park (KOR)	71-70-69-70—280	15,906		Patricia Meunier-Lebouc (FRA)	70-75-71-73—289	6,125
	Annika Sörenstam (SWE)	68-71-70-71—280	15,906		Nadina Taylor (AUS)	69-74-72-74—289	6,125
21	Michelle Estill (USA)	70-72-68-71—281	12,250				

Other players who made the cut: Hiromi Mogi (JPN), Shiho Ohyama (JPN), Ana B Sanchez (ESP), Louise Stahle (SWE) (am); Sherri Steinhauer (USA) 290; Bettina Hauert (GER), Angela Jerman (USA), Pamela Kerrigan 291; Ashli Bunch (USA), Audra Burks (USA), Johanna Head (ENG), Katherine Hull (AUS), Kelli Kuehne (USA), Gwladys Nocera (FRA) 292; Lynnette Brooky (NZL), A J Eathorne (CAN), Wendy Ward (USA) 293; Emilee Klein (USA) 294; Helen Alfredsson (SWE), Hsiao Chuan Lu (CHN), Betsy King (USA), Janice Moodie (SCO) 295; Raquel Carriedo (ESP), Ana Larraneta (ESP) 296; Vicki Goetze-Ackerman (USA), Laurette Maritz (RSA) 297; Samantha Head (ENG) 298; Maria Hjörth (SWE) 305

2003 Weetabix Women's British Open Royal Lytham and St Annes, Lancashire [6308–72]

Prize money: £1.05 million

1	Annika Sörenstam (SWE)	68-72-68-70—278	£160,000	19T	Laura Davies (ENG)	75-70-70-74—289	12,500
2	Se Ri Pak (KOR)	69-69-69-72—279	100,000		Hee Won Han (KOR)	75-71-70-73—289	12,500
3	Grace Park (KOR)	74-65-71-70—280	62,500		Lorie Kane (CAN)	69-75-70-75—289	12,500
	Karrie Webb (AUS)	67-72-70-71—280	62,500		Becky Morgan (WAL)	72-70-71-76—289	12,500
5	Patricia Meunier-Lebouc (FRA)	70-69-67-76—282	45,000	24	Brandie Burton (USA)	76-69-69-76—290	8,996
6	Vicki Goetze-Ackerman (USA)	73-71-68-71—283	37,000		Moira Dunn (USA)	70-74-74-72—290	8,996
	Wendy Ward (USA)	67-71-69-76—283	37,000		Michiko Hattori (JPN)	78-69-71-72—290	8,996
8	Sophie Gustafson (SWE)	73-69-71-71—284	32,000		Pat Hurst (USA)	73-71-74-72—290	8,996
9	Young Kim (KOR)	73-70-72-70—285	29,000		Soo-Yun Kang (KOR)	70-75-72-73—290	8,996
10	Candie Kung (TPE)	73-71-69-73—286	25,000		Emilee Klein (USA)	72-70-74-74—290	8,996
	Gloria Park (KOR)	70-75-69-72—286	25,000		Lorena Ochoa (MEX)	74-65-77-74—290	8,996
12	Paula Marti (ESP)	71-70-70-76—287	21,000		Dottie Pepper (USA)	71-75-71-73—290	8,996
	Karen Stupples (ENG)	69-74-70-74—287	21,000		Jennifer Rosales (PHI)	69-72-76-73—290	8,996
14	Lynnette Brooky (NZL)	70-74-75-69—288	16,150		Iben Tinning (DEN)	71-73-73-73—290	8,996
	Beth Daniel (USA)	74-71-67-76—288	16,150		Hiroko Yamaguchi (JPN)	72-71-75-72—290	8,996
	Laura Diaz (USA)	73-74-71-70—288	16,150		Young-A Yang (KOR)	71-75-71-73—290	8,996
	Jeong Jang (KOR)	76-69-72-71—288	16,150	36	Georgina Simpson (ENG)	69-73-74-75—291	7,000
	Cristie Kerr (USA)	74-71-71-72—288	16,150	37	Christine Kuld (DEN)	69-76-75-72—292	6,375
19	Heather Bowie (USA)	70-66-74-79—289	12,500		Meg Mallon (USA)	71-72-71-78—292	6,375
					Michele Redman (USA)	71-69-76-76—292	6,375
					Nadina Taylor (AUS)	71-74-72-75—292	6,375

Other players who made the cut: Elisabeth Esterl (GER), Akiko Fukushima (JPN), Johanna Head (ENG), Juli Inkster (USA), Catrin Nilsmark (SWE) 293; Kelli Kuehne (USA), Elisa Serramia (ESP) (am), Rachel Teske (AUS), Karen Weiss (USA) 294; Kasumi Fujii (JPN), Angela Jerman (USA), Carin Koch (SWE), Kelly Robbins (USA) 295; Cherie Byrnes (AUS), Michelle Ellis (AUS), Woo-Soon Ko (KOR), Shani Waugh (AUS) 296; Heather Daly-Donofrio (USA), Susan Parry (USA), Kirsty Taylor (ENG) 297; Helen Alfredsson (SWE), Alison Nicholas (ENG) 298; Beth Bauer (USA) 299; Silvia Cavalleri (ITA), Sophie Sandolo (ITA), Angela Stanford (USA) 300; Suzanne Strudwick (ENG) 303; Marnie McGuire (NZL) 308

2002 Weetabix Women's British Open   Turnberry, Ayrshire   [6407–72]

Prize money: £1,000,000

1	Karrie Webb (AUS)	66-71-70-66—273	£154,982	24	Patricia Meunier	69-71-69-76—285	10,249
2	Michelle Ellis (AUS)	69-70-68-68—275	84,990		Lebouc (FRA)		
	Paula Marti (ESP)	69-68-69-69—275	84,990		Suzann Pettersen (NOR)	72-71-72-70—285	10,249
4	Jeong Jang (KOR)	73-69-66-69—277	42,308	26	Dorothy Delasin (PHI)	70-71-70-75—286	9,366
	Candie Kung (TPE)	65-71-71-70—277	42,308		Elisabeth Esterl (GER)	67-71-72-76—286	9,366
	Catrin Nilsmark (SWE)	70-69-69-69—277	42,308		Emilee Klein (USA)	68-71-72-75—286	9,366
	Jennifer Rosales (PHI)	69-70-65-73—277	42,308	29	Brandie Burton (USA)	71-70-71-75—287	7,949
8	Beth Bauer (USA)	70-67-70-71—278	25,164		Cristie Kerr (USA)	72-71-69-75—287	7,949
	Carin Koch (SWE)	68-68-68-74—278	25,164		Kelli Kuehne (USA)	75-67-71-74—287	7,949
	Meg Mallon (USA)	69-71-68-70—278	25,164		Yu Ping Lin (TPE)	73-69-74-71—287	7,949
11	Sophie Gustafson (SWE)	69-73-69-68—279	19,748		Iben Tinning (DEN)	71-69-71-76—287	7,949
	Se Ri Pak (KOR)	67-72-69-71—279	19,748	34	Toshimi Kimura (JPN)	74-70-70-74—288	7,249
13	Natalie Gulbis (USA)	69-70-67-74—280	16,581	35	Kathryn Marshall (SCO)	70-71-76-72—289	6,499
	Pat Hurst (USA)	69-70-69-72—280	16,581		Catriona Matthew (SCO)	73-71-70-75—289	6,499
	Angela Stanford (USA)	69-70-69-72—280	16,581		Liselotte Neumann	70-71-71-77—289	6,499
16	Tina Barrett (USA)	67-70-70-76—283	14,348		(SWE)		
	Beth Daniel (USA)	73-68-68-74—283	14,348		Kelly Robbins (USA)	70-75-68-76—289	6,499
18	Jean Bartholomew	71-72-72-69—284	12,099		Shani Waugh (AUS)	70-73-74-72—289	6,499
	(USA)			40	Helen Alfredsson (SWE)	70-75-71-74—290	5,249
	Wendy Doolan (AUS)	70-69-71-74—284	12,099		Lora Fairclough (ENG)	71-69-73-77—290	5,249
	Jane Geddes (USA)	71-69-70-74—284	12,099		Becky Iverson (USA)	69-76-72-73—290	5,249
	Marine Monnet (FRA)	71-70-70-73—284	12,099		Karen Lunn (AUS)	73-71-72-74—290	5,249
	Fiona Pike (AUS)	72-73-67-72—284	12,099		Sophie Sandolo (ITA)	71-74-68-77—290	5,249
	Rachel Teske (AUS)	67-74-68-75—284	12,099				

Other players who made the cut: Asa Gottmo (SWE), Mhairi McKay (SCO) 291; Heather Daly-Donofrio (USA), Federica Dassu (ITA), Tracy Hanson (USA), Johanna Head (ENG), Becky Morgan (WAL), Giulia Sergas (ITA) 292; Heather Bowie (USA), Grace Park (KOR), Suzanne Strudwick (ENG) 293; Raquel Carriedo (ESP), Karen Stupples (ENG), Wendy Ward (USA) 294; Betsy King (USA) 295; Vicki Goetze-Ackerman (USA) 296; Mi Hyun Kim (KOR), Charlotta Sörenstam (SWE) 297; Tonya Gill (USA) 298; Riikka Hakkarainen (FIN) 299; Marina Arruti (ESP) 301; Ana Larraneta (ESP) 302

Women's British Open History

Year	Winner	Country	Venue	Score
1976	J Lee Smith	England	Fulford	299
1977	V Saunders	England	Lindrick	306
1978	J Melville	England	Foxhills	310
1979	A Sheard	South Africa	Southport and Ainsdale	301
1980	D Massey	USA	Wentworth (East)	294
1981	D Massey	USA	Northumberland	295
1982	M Figueras-Dotti	Spain	Royal Birkdale	296
1983	*Not played*			
1984	A Okamoto	Japan	Woburn	289
1985	B King	USA	Moor Park	300
1986	L Davies	England	Royal Birkdale	283
1987	A Nicholas	England	St Mellion	296
1988	C Dibnah*	Australia	Lindrick	296
Won play-off after a tie with S Little				
1989	J Geddes	USA	Ferndown	274
1990	H Alfredsson*	Sweden	Woburn	288
Beat J Hill at the fourth exyta hole				
1991	P Grice-Whittaker	England	Woburn	284
1992	P Sheehan	USA	Woburn	207
Reduced to 54 holes by rain				
1993	K Lunn	Australia	Woburn	275
1994	L Neumann	Sweden	Woburn	280
1995	K Webb	Australia	Woburn	278
1996	E Klein	USA	Woburn	277
1997	K Webb	Australia	Sunningdale	269
1998	S Steinhauer	USA	Royal Lytham & St Annes	292
1999	S Steinhauer	USA	Woburn	283
2000	S Gustafson	Sweden	Royal Birkdale	282

Year	Winner	Country	Venue	Score
2001	S R Pak	Korea	Sunningdale	277
2002	K Webb	Australia	Turnberry	273
2003	A Sörenstam	Sweden	Royal Lytham & St Annes	278
2004	Karen Stupples	England	Sunningdale (Old Course)	269
2005	Jeong Jang	Korea	Royal Birkdale	272
2006	Sherri Steinhauer	USA	Royal Lytham & St Annes	281
2007	Lorena Ochoa	Mexico	St Andrews Old Course	287
2008	Ji-Yai Shin	Korea	Sunningdale	270
2009	Catriona Matthew	Scotland	Royal Lytham & St Annes	285
2010	Yani Tseng	Chinese Tapei	Royal Birkdale	277
2011	Yani Tseng	Chinese Tapei	Carnoustie Links	272

Yani Tseng wants to be the youngest to win a Grand Slam

World No 1 Yani Tseng has the opportunity this year at Blackwolf Run golf course in Kohler, Wisconsin, to become the youngest golfer in history (male or female) to complete a career Grand Slam. All that's currently lacking in Tseng's impressive resumé in major championships is victory in a US Women's Open Championship.

Tseng, who became the youngest golfer in LPGA history to win four majors with her victory at the 2011 Wegmans LPGA Championship and the youngest to win five when she successfully defended her British title at Carnoustie later in the year, is keener than ever to complete her career Grand Slam.

Last year before the US Women's Open at The Broadmoor where she finished 15th, Tseng posted a photo on her Facebook page of the empty space in her trophy room that is reserved specifically for the US. Women's Open trophy.

Tseng lives in Annika Sörenstam's former house at Lake Nona in Florida and Sörenstam, who won three US Women's Open titles, had created a special spot for the tournament's sizeable trophy.

"I always feel so much pressure on a US Open course," said Tseng. "It's always such a tough, tough golf course but after I see Rory McIlroy win the US Open at Congressional last year I feel much more relaxed. I mean you can still beat a course but at a major you have to have fun and enjoy the pressure and the big crowds."

Tseng is already on track to put herself in Sörenstam's company when it comes to major championships. Five of Tseng's 11 career victories on the LPGA Tour have come in majors. When the long-hitter from Taiwan was asked what it was about majors that makes her step up her game she said:

"I think I just focus more on a major, and I love a tough course. I love a challenge. I know at a major you're not going to be shooting lots of low scores. You just need to be patient. Lots of people are going to make bogeys. So if you make a bogey it's no worries."

Tseng and Sörenstam have developed a special bond in recent years. Tseng looks to Sörenstam as her mentor, both in terms of the success that she had on the golf course and also the numerous things the LPGA and World Golf Halls of Fame member has done to help the game of golf as well.

When the pair met up and talked about what the 22-year-old will face in trying to complete a career Grand Slam it was interesting.

"She tell me shes really enjoying to watch me play, and that made me feel lots of confidence," said Tseng. "Then she told me: 'Always smile and have good body language, and then be aggressive.'"

US Women's Open Championship

July 7–10

So Yeon Ryu triumphs in all-Korean play-off

Becomes third youngest winner of the US Women's Open

At 21, South Korea's So Yeon Ryu became the third youngest winner of the $3.25 million US Women's Open after Inbee Park and Se Ri Pak, as well as the fifth Korean to lift the title, thanks to an impressive play-off victory over compatriot Hee Kyung Seo at the Broadmoor's East Course in Colorado Springs.

© Getty Images

So Yeon Ryu

In a championship which didn't finish until Monday because of a succession of severe weather delays – there were five separate suspensions of play over 72 holes – Ryu, who plays most of her golf in Korea, proved her game travels exceptionally well when she marked her first success on the LPGA by winning a major title.

About to graduate from Yonsei University, Ryu had planned to attend qualifying school in America and attempt to win her LPGA Tour card in 2012. One of the perks of winning the Open was that she automatically became an LPGA member. Taking home the first prize of $585,000 after signing for the three under total of 281 wasn't exactly a penance either.

A talented musician, as a child Ryu played golf for fun and hoped to become a violinist. Inspired by Pak's success, she changed tack and opted to try and follow in the footsteps of the renowned golfer – partly because in sport the art of winning is less subjective. In music, there can often be varying opinions on the same performance. In professional golf, the lowest score always wins.

The victory became even more special for Ryu when Pak, a Korean golf legend, was among the players showering her with champagne following the win. "When I finished, Se Ri told me: 'It's really great play. You're a really great person'," Ryu said. "Last year I play with Se Ri in Korea, and she told me, you have a lot of talent, so keep going. Keep practising hard. But I finished the play-off and Se Ri told me congratulations. That's really special for me."

Even though Seo lost the playoff, she said it was still a special occasion for two Koreans to face each other in a play-off for a major. "Lots of Korean fans were waiting for one of us to win this year, " Seo revealed. "So I think they were cheering both of us. I feel very happy a South Korea player won this great tournament."

Due to the threat of lightning and the arrival of inclement weather in Colorado, the first round of the championship was curtailed before lunchtime on Thursday and didn't resume until Friday. With many of the game's best players unable to complete their rounds – Ryu was down the field on 74 – the spotlight fell on a teenage amateur who experienced a sense of shock when she glanced at the leaderboard and saw her name on top.

Amy Anderson, 18, who enlisted her brother Nathan to carry her bag and help read the putts, acknowl-edged the moment was as surprising as it was special. "That was surreal," smiled the teenager. "My brother and I joked: 'Well, somebody better get a picture of that. Because it's not going to be up there for very long.' But it's going to be up there all night, so I'm excited. I was pretty nervous on the first tee this morning and then settled down. I hit my first drive really good, and that helped me."

Anderson, who already holds one United States Golf Association title – the 2009 US Girls Junior – is a student at North Dakota State University in Fargo where she majors in accounting with a minor in fraud investigation. A native of Oxbow, Anderson hails from a curiosity of a small town with a population of 300 which has a golf course but neither shops nor a petrol station. "Basically, it's a golf course with houses," she explained. Unsurprisingly, she played a lot of golf growing up.

Having slept on a score of two under par after 12 holes, Anderson resumed her round on Friday morn-ing on the 13th green. She wanted to continue her run of form and duly made pars on the 13th and 14th holes before spilling a stroke at the 15th. To the youngster's credit, however, she subsequently birdied the par 4 17th and signed for 69.

It was a solid performance based on accurate work off the tee – she located 13 out of 14 fairways – as well as a smooth putting stroke. Anderson used her blade just 28 times on slow paced greens and kept all but one bogey off her card. "I like being the underdog," she added, "It's a position I'm really comfortable with. I mean, I don't expect to go out and win this or continue playing like this. This is an awesome experience that's once in a lifetime."

By the time the first round was eventually completed, Anderson was tucked in behind Stacy Lewis, who had grabbed the lead thanks to an impressive 68. The winner of the 2011 Kraft Nabisco, starting on the 10th, matched par on the inward half before carding back-to-back birdies at the first and second holes. "That just kind of got me back into what I was doing and I kind of cruised in from there," she said.

Although it took three days to complete 36 holes, the tournament limped into Sunday with not one but two Miyazatos leading the way. In spite of the coincidence of sharing the same name and hailing from the same place – Okinawa in Japan – Mika and Ai are not related. However, the golfers are friends who have known each other since they were little girls. "Everybody thinks we're sisters," said Mika. "I think that way everybody remembers me, because Ai is playing great. In a way it's good for me. But we're not related."

Mika was the frontrunner on five under par thanks to a second round of 67. Having finished in the top ten at both the LPGA and the Kraft Nabisco, she came into America's national championship with a positive showing in the majors. Ai was also in fine form, shooting 68, to claim a spot alongside her namesake over the closing rounds.

For Lewis, who showed the rest the way in the first round, it took over 14 hours to complete her second round as she faded over the closing stretch and dropped back to one under par. Paula Creamer, the defending champion, who was in the group on level par, explained the sense of frustration in the face of so much disruption. "You either are above it, move on and you just kind of accept that this is what it is, or you dwell on it and let it get to your and let it affect your game out there," she said.

Anderson's spell in contention, incidentally, was as shortlived as the amateur herself expected. She signed for 77 in the second round, carding four bogeys and a double, before tumbling down the leaderboard and eventually finishing in 63rd place.

Play did start in the third round on Saturday but only 19 of the 72 golfers who made the cut were on the course before more bad weather stopped play. It meant an early start of 6.45am for the players on Sunday morning as Mika Miyazato fell back with 76 while Ryu and Cristie Kerr carded 69 to join Stanford as the leaders going into the afternoon's final round.

A member of the Korean LPGA Tour, Ryu was playing in only her second US Women's Open after finishing 25th on her debut in 2010. It was also only her second appearance on the LPGA Tour in 2011, having previously finished in the top 50 at the 2011 Kraft Nabisco Championship. Compared to Kerr, the champion at Pine Needles in 2007 and a 14 time winner in America, the Korean was a novice.

Not that she looked like one as she eventually posted 68 in the final round to join the lead on three under par after play was again suspended and spilled over into a Monday finish. With three holes left to play, Ryu birdied the 18th to remain in contention and participate in a three hole play-off after matching the overnight target set by Seo of 281.

Perhaps it was to Ryu's advantage that she'd just played the three holes selected for the play-off in what was the first showdown between international golfers in a US Women's Open. "Same pin position and same teeing ground, so it was really good for me," she recalled. "A really huge benefit, yeah."

Both women selected 7 irons to find the green on the 163 yard 16th hole. Seo and Ryu each missed birdie putts of around 15 feet and settled for pars. On the 600 yard 17th, Seo hit a poor drive and found a bunker off the tee while Ryu was on the fairway. With only 129 yards left to the green for her third shot, Ryu hit a wedge to eight feet. When Seo made bogey, Ryu holed her birdie putt to take a two-shot advantage onto the final hole. Again, Ryu stuck her approach close before making a four footer to win the play-off by three strokes and secure the biggest prize in women's golf.

First Round	Second Round	Third Round	Fourth Round
−3 Stacy Lewis	−5 Mika Miyazato	−1 So Yeon Ryu	−3 So Yeon Ryu
−2 Amy Anderson	−4 Ai Miyazato	−1 Cristie Kerr	−3 Hee Kyung So
−2 Lizette Salas	−3 I K Kim	−1 Angela Stanford	−1 Cristie Kerr
−2 Ryann O'Toole	−1 Stacy Lewis	= Hee Kyung Seo	= Angela Stanford
−1 I K Kim	−1 Ryann O'Toole	= Mika Miyazato	+1 Mika Miyazato
−1 Lindy Duncan	= Paula Creamer	+1 Inbee Park	+2 Karrie Webb
−1 Ai Miyazato	= Lizette Salas	+1 Ai Miyazato	+2 Ai Miyazato
−1 Karrie Webb	= Angela Stanford	+2 Karrie Webb	+2 Inbee Park
−1 Maria Hjörth	= Wendy Ward	+2 Paula Creamer	+3 Ryann O'Toole
−1 Mika Miyazato	= Sun Young Yoo	+2 Lizette Salas	+4 Jiyai Shin

US Women's Open Championship (66th)

The Broadmoor (East Course), Colorado Springs, CO   [7047–71]

Prize Money: $3,250,000. Entries 1,295. Field 158 (21 amateurs) of whom 71 (including five amateurs) made the cut on 149 or less

Players are of American nationality unless stated

1	So Yeon Ryu (KOR)*	74-69-69-69—281	$585,000
2	Hee Kyung Seo (KOR)	72-73-68-68—281	350,000
	So Yeon Ryu won at the third extra hole		
3	Cristie Kerr	71-72-69-71—283	215,493
4	Angela Stanford	72-70-70-72—284	150,166
5	Mika Miyazato (JPN)	70-67-76-72—285	121,591
6	Karrie Webb (AUS)	70-73-72-71—286	98,128
	Ai Miyazato (JPN)	70-68-76-72—286	98,128
	Inbee Park (KOR)	71-73-70-72—286	98,128
9	Ryann O'Toole	69-72-75-71—287	81,915
10	Jiyai Shin (KOR)	73-72-73-70—288	70,996
	Amy Yang (KOR)	75-69-73-71—288	70,996
	I K Kim (KOR)	70-69-76-73—288	70,996
13	Chella Choi (KOR)	71-76-70-72—289	60,780
	Candie Kung (TPE)	76-69-71-73—289	60,780
15	Karen Stupples (ENG)	72-77-73-68—290	48,658
	Suzann Pettersen (NOR)	71-75-72-72—290	48,658
	Junthima Gulyanamitta (THA)	73-76-68-73—290	48,658
	Yani Tseng (TPE)	73-73-71-73—290	48,658
	Lizette Salas	69-73-73-75—290	48,658
	Paula Creamer	72-70-73-75—290	48,658
21	Catriona Matthew (SCO)	76-70-74-71—291	36,374
	Meena Lee (KOR)	75-71-72-73—291	36,374
	Morgan Pressel	75-72-71-73—291	36,374
	Leta Lindley	73-71-72-75—291	36,374
25	Mi-Jeong Jeon (KOR)	72-73-76-71—292	30,122
	Sun Young Yoo (KOR)	74-68-77-73—292	30,122
27	Brittany Lincicome	75-74-74-70—293	24,042
	Sakura Yokomine (JPN)	72-74-77-70—293	24,042
	Beatriz Recari (ESP)	76-72-72-73—293	24,042
	Alison Walshe	74-73-73-73—293	24,042
	Eun-Hee Ji (KOR)	73-69-74-77—293	24,042
32	Natalie Gulbis	73-75-74-72—294	21,189
	Moriya Jutanugarn (THA) (am)	76-69-76-73—294	
34	Shinobu Moromizato (JPN)	76-72-74-73—295	18,370
	Mina Harigae	75-74-72-74—295	18,370
	Sandra Gal (GER)	77-72-72-74—295	18,370
	Maria Hjörth (SWE)	70-78-73-74—295	18,370
	Stacy Lewis	68-73-79-75—295	18,370
	Jessica Korda	73-75-72-75—295	18,370
	Song-Hee Kim (KOR)	73-73-74-75—295	18,370
	Wendy Ward	73-69-74-79—295	18,370
42	Shanshan Feng (CHN)	76-72-77-71—296	14,943
	Karin Sjodin (SWE)	74-73-75-74—296	14,943
	Meaghan Francella	76-73-72-75—296	14,943
45	Vicky Hurst	76-72-76-73—297	12,458
	Hee Young Park (KOR)	73-71-80-73—297	12,458
	Azahara Muñoz (ESP)	74-71-79-73—297	12,458
	Jennifer Johnson	75-74-74-74—297	12,458
	Se Ri Pak(KOR)	74-70-77-76—297	12,458
50	Brittany Lang	72-74-81-71—298	9,790
	Jin Young Pak (KOR)	77-72-76-73—298	9,790
	Soo-Jin Yang (KOR)	75-74-75-74—298	9,790
	Sue Kim (CAN)	73-74-77-74—298	9,790
	Lindsey Wright (AUS)	76-71-75-76—298	9,790

55	Michelle Wie	78-71-78-72—299	8,680
	Danah Bordner	73-74-79-73—299	8,680
	Lee-Anne Pace (RSA)	75-72-77-75—299	8,680
	Mariajo Uribe (COL)	75-69-79-76—299	8,680
59	Yoo Kyeong Kim	74-74-77-75—300	8,141
	Lindy Duncan (am)	70-78-76-76—300	
	Victoria Tanco (ARG) (am)	78-69-77-76—300	
	Jean Chua (MAS)	77-69-77-77—300	8,141
63	Amy Anderson (am)	69-77-81-74—301	
64	Anya Sarai Alvarez	73-76-82-71—302	7,735
	Shin-Ae Ahn (KOR)	74-75-78-75—302	7,735
	Haru Nomura (JPN)	77-70-79-76—302	7,735
	Becky Morgan (WAL)	75-72-78-77—302	7,735
68	Danielle Kang (am)	72-77-75-79—303	
69	Paola Moreno (COL)	73-76-77-78—304	7,408
70	Sherri Steinhauer	72-76-78-79—305	7,277
71	Gwladys Nocera (FRA)	78-71-76-82—307	7,146
	Bo-Mee Lee (KOR)	77-72-76—225 WD	7,014

The following players missed the cut:

72	Amanda Blumenherst	76-74—150
	Sophie Gustafson (SWE)	74-76—150
	M J Hur (KOR)	74-76—150
	Juli Inkster	74-76—150
	Jimin Kang (KOR)	75-75—150
	Mi Hyun Kim (KOR)	74-76—150
	Teresa Lu (TPE)	73-77—150
	Anna Nordqvist (SWE)	74-76—150
	Christine Proteau (CAN) (am)	77-73—150
	Jennifer Rosales (PHI)	76-74—150
	Kelly Shon (am)	74-76—150
	Momoko Ueda (JPN)	78-72—150
84	Hee-Won Han (KOR)	74-77—151
	Cindy Lacrosse	71-80—151
	Sarah Jane Smith (AUS)	74-77—151
	Jaclyn Sweeney	80-71—151
88	Sun-Ju Ahn (KOR)	76-76—152
	Silvia Cavalleri (ITA)	79-73—152
	Na Yeon Choi (KOR)	78-74—152
	Christina Kim	74-78—152
	Stephanie Kono (am)	78-74—152
	Jee Young Lee (KOR)	75-77—152
	Reilley Rankin	80-72—152
	Sae-Hee Son (KOR)	76-76—152
	Aree Song	74-78—152
	Emma Talley (am)	75-77—152
98	Laura Davies (ENG)	78-75—153
	Julieta Granada (PAR)	75-78—153
	Anna Grzebien	77-76—153
	Katherine Hull (AUS)	74-79—153
	Amy Hung (TPE)	77-76—153

98T	Haeji Kang (KOR)	78-75—153
	Hye-Youn Kim (KOR)	76-77—153
	Xiyu Lin (CHN) (am)	72-81—153
	Kristy McPherson	73-80—153
	Belen Mozo (ESP)	75-78—153
	Stacy Prammanasudh	75-78—153
	Melissa Reid (ENG)	77-76—153
	Rachel Rohanna (am)	73-80—153
	Alena Sharp (CAN)	74-79—153
	Alexis Thompson	77-76—153
113	Yukari Baba (JPN)	75-79—154
	Heather Bowie Young	76-78—154
	Katie Futcher	78-76—154
	Nicole Hage	76-78—154
	Pat Hurst	75-79—154
	Ariya Jutanugarn (THA) (am)	75-79—154
	Jennifer Kirby (CAN) (am)	77-77—154
	Erynne Lee (am)	80-74—154
	Michele Redman	75-79—154
	Jennifer Song	78-76—154
	Young-A Yang	75-79—154
124	Shi Hyun Ahn (KOR)	81-74—155
	Kyeong Bae (KOR)	78-77—155
	Mallory Blackwelder	77-78—155
	Laura Diaz	75-80—155
	Katy Harris	78-77—155
	Sarah Kemp (AUS)	77-78—155
	Kyung Kim (am)	75-80—155
	Seon Hwa Lee (KOR)	74-81—155

132	Emily Collins (am)	78-78—156
	Brittany Marchand (CAN) (am)	81-75—156
	Lisa McCloskey (am)	76-80—156
	Na On Min (KOR)	77-79—156
	Dewi Claire Schreefel (NED)	77-79—156
139	Joanna Coe	80-77—157
	Birdie Kim (KOR)	83-74—157
141	Whitney Wade	80-78—158
	Chelsia Mochia (am)	81-78—159
143	Doris Chen (TPE) (am)	80-80—160
	Betsy King	83-77—160
	Whitney Neuhauser	80-80—160
146	Lauren Doughtie	80-81—161
	Brittany Johnston	81-80—161
	Jane Park	76-85—161
	Garrett Phillips	79-82—161
	Christine Wolf (AUT) (am)	77-84—161
151	Sofie Andersson (SWE)	79-83—162
152	Ashley Prange	79-84—163
	Mariah Stackhouse (am)	79-84—163
154	Jessi Gebhardt	82-82—164
	Margarita Ramos (am)	85-79—164
156	Gabriella Then (am)	80-85—165
157	Mariel Galdiano (am)	85-85—170

Month by month in 2011

February

Luke Donald beats Martin Kaymer to take the WGC–Accenture Match Play title – he never trailed all week – but reaching the final is enough to take the German to World No 1 ahead of Lee Westwood. Alvaro Quiros holes-in-one en route to winning the Dubai Desert Classic, while Mark Wilson is the unlikely first double winner of the season in America.

2010 US Women's Open Championship *Oakmont, PA*   [6613–71]

Prize money: $3.25 million

1	Paula Creamer	72-70-70-69—281	$585,000	19T	Jeong Jang (KOR)	73-72-74-75—294	39,285
2	Na Yeon Choi (KOR)	75-72-72-66—285	284,468		Kristy McPherson	72-78-74-70—294	39,285
	Suzann Pettersn (NOR)	73-71-72-69—285	284,468		Azahara Muñoz (ESP)	75-74-71-74—294	39,285
4	In-Kyung Kim (KOR)	74-71-73-68—286	152,565		Angela Sanford	73-72-74-75—294	39,285
5	Jiyai Shin	76-71-72-68—287	110,481	25	Jee Young Lee (KOR)	72-76-76-71—295	29,625
	Brittany Lang	69-74-75-69—287	110,481		Brittany Lincicome	73-78-71-73—295	29,625
	Amy Yang (KOR)	70-75-71-71—287	110,481		So Yeon Ryu (KOR)	74-74-76-71—295	29,625
8	Inbee Park (KOR)	70-78-73-68—289	87,202	28	Chie Arimura (JPN)	74-72-76-74—296	24,096
	Christine Kim	72-72-72-73—289	87,202		Maria Hjörth (SWE)	73-72-75-76—296	24,096
10	Alexis Thompson	73-74-70-73—290	72,131		Candie Kung (TPE)	76-72-79-69—296	24,096
	Saura Yokomine (JPN)	71-71-76-72—290	72,131	31	Ashli Bunch	78-74-75-70—297	21,529
	Yani Tseng (TPE)	73-76-73-68—290	72,131		M J Hur (KOR)	70-81-74-72—297	21,529
13	Song-Hee Kim (KOR)	72-76-78-65—291	63,524		Ai Miyazato (JPN)	73-74-80-70—297	21,529
14	Natalie Gulbis	73-73-72-74—292	56,659	34	Meaghan Francella	75-72-77-74—298	18,980
	Stacy Lewis	75-70-75-72—292	56,659		Jeong Eun Lee (KOR)	72-78-73-75—298	18,980
	Wendy Ward	72-73-70-77—292	56,659		Mhairi McKay (SCO)	71-78-76-73—298	18,980
17	Cristie Kerr	72-71-75-75—293	49,365		Shinobu Moromizato (JPN)	72-77-77-72—298	18,980
	Karrie Webb (AUS)	74-72-73-74—293	49,365		Morgan Pressel	74-75-75-74—298	18,980
19	Shi Hyun Ahn (KOR)	72-77-73-72—294	39,285				
	Sophie Gustafson (SWE)	72-72-74-76—294	39,285				

Other players who made the cut: Eun-Hee Ji (KOR). Karen Stupples (ENG) 299; Maria Hernandez (ESP), Katherine Hull (AUS), Vicky Hurst, Jennifer Johnson (am), Hee Young Park (KOR), Jennifer Rosales (PHI), Heather Young 300; Alena Sharp (CAN), Louise Stahle (SWE), Lindsay Wright (AUS) 301; Sandra Gal (GER) 302; Naon Min (KOR), Sherri Steinhauer 303; Allison Fouch 304; Paige Mackenzie, Anna Rawson (AUS), Christine Wong (CAN) (am) 305; Tamie Durdin (AUS), Libby Smith, Jennifer Song 307; Chella Choi (KOR) 308; Lisa McCloskey (am), Heekyung Seo (KOR) 309; Danielle Kang (am) 310; Meredith Duncan, Kelli Shean (RSA) (am) 312; Sarah Kemp (AUS) 313; Tiffany Lim (am) 320

2009 US Women's Open Championship *Interlachen CC, Edina, MN*   [6789–73]

Prize money: $3.1 million

1	Eun-Hee Ji (KOR)	71-72-70-71—284	$585,000	17T	Akiko Fukushima (JPN)	76-72-72-72—292	42,724
2	Candie Kung (TPE)	71-77-68-69—285	350,000		Anna Grzebien	73-77-69-73—292	42,724
3	Cristie Kerr	69-70-72-75—286	183,568		Jimin Kang (KOR)	76-71-74-71—292	42,724
	In-Kyung Kim (KOR)	72-72-72-70—286	183,568		Teresa Lu (TPE)	76-69-70-77—292	42,724
5	Brittany Lincicome	72-72-73-70—287	122,415		Jean Reynolds	69-72-74-77—292	42,724
6	Paula Creamer	72-68-79-69—288	99,126		Lindsay Wright (AUS)	74-70-77-71—292	42,724
	Ai Miyazato (JPN)	74-74-71-69—288	99,126	26	He Yong Choi (KOR)	77-74-74-68—293	27,420
	Suzann Pettersen (NOR)	74-71-72-71—288	99,126		Juli Inkster	78-73-72-70—293	27,420
					Jessica Korda (am)	72-77-75-69—293	
9	Kyeong Bae (KOR)	75-73-69-72—289	76,711		Alison Lee (am)	75-72-76-70—293	
	Na Yeon Choi (KOR)	68-74-76-71—289	76,711		Anna Nordqvist (SWE)	71-75-75-72—293	27,420
	Hee Young Park (KOR)	70-74-72-73—289	76,711		Lorena Ochoa (MEX)	69-79-73-72—293	27,420
12	Song-Hee Kim (KOR)	74-69-75-72—290	66,769		Inbee Park (KOR)	75-71-77-70—293	27,420
13	Sun Ju Ahn (KOR)	75-71-72-73—291	59,428	33	Sun Young Yoo (KOR)	72-74-72-76—294	22,603
	Morgan Pressel	74-75-69-73—291	59,428	34	Louise Friberg (SWE)	75-72-73-75—295	20,702
	Ji-Yai Shin (KOR)	72-75-76-68—291	59,428		Maria Hernandez (ESP)	74-72-77-72—295	20,702
	Jennifer Song (am)	72-74-73-72—291			Kristy McPherson	71-74-77-73—295	20,702
17	Nicole Castrale	74-71-74-73—292	42,724		Alexis Thompson (am)	71-73-78-73—295	
	Laura Davies (ENG)	72-75-73-72—292	42,724		Karrie Webb (AUS)	75-72-74-74—295	20,702
	Meaghan Francella	73-72-74-73—292	42,724		Amy Yang (KOR)	75-71-75-74—295	20,702

Other players who made the cut: Misun Cho (KOR), Sandra Gal (GER), Young Kim (KOR), Brittany Lang, Azahara Muñoz (ESP) (am), Ji Young Oh (KOR), Michele Redman, Momoko Ueda (JPN) 296; Shanshan Feng (CHN), Stacy Lewis, Hee-Kyung Seo (KOR), Maria Jose Uribe (COL) 297; Amanda Blumenherst, Hye Jung Choi (KOR), Christina Kim, Giulia Sergas (ITA), Karen Stupples (ENG) 298; Yuri Fudoh (JPN), Haeji Kang (KOR), Mika Miyazato (JPN), Stacy Prammanasudh 299; Cindy Lacrosse, Ji Hee Lee (KOR), Meena Lee (KOR), Becky Morgan (WAL) 300; Allison Fouch, Allie White (am) 301; Karine Icher (FRA), Mina Harigae, Jennie Lee 304; Candace Schepperle (am) 306; Carolina Llano (COL) 307; Lisa Ferrero 312

2008 US Women's Open Championship Interlachen CC, Edina, MN [6789–73]

Prize money: $3.1 million

I	Inbee Park (KOR)	72-69-71-71—283	$585,000	19T	Jessica Korda (CZE) (am)	72-78-75-69—294		
2	Helen Alfredsson (SWE)	70-71-71-75—287	350,000		Candy Kung (TPE)	72-70-79-73—294	43,376	
3	In-Kyung Kim (KOR)	71-73-69-75—288	162,487		Ji-Yai Shin (KOR)	69-74-79-72—294	43,376	
	Stacy Lewis	73-70-67-78—288	162,487	24	Pat Hurst	67-78-77-73—295	35,276	
	Angela Park (BRA)	73-67-75-73—288	162,487		Song-Hee Kim (KOR)	68-76-75-76—295	35,276	
6	Nicole Castrale	74-70-74-71—289	94,117		Annika Sörenstam (SWE)	75-70-72-78—295	35,276	
	Paula Creamer	70-72-69-78—289	94,117	27	Minea Blomqvist (FIN)	72-69-76-79—296	28,210	
	Mi Hyun Kim (KOR)	72-72-70-75—289	94,117		Laura Diaz	77-70-73-76—296	28,210	
	Giulia Sergas (ITA)	73-74-72-70—289	94,117		Seon Hwa Lee (KOR)	75-70-73-78—296	28,210	
10	Teresa Lu (TPE)	71-72-73-74—290	75,734		Ai Miyazato (JPN)	71-72-76-77—296	28,210	
	Maria Jose Uribe (COL) (am)	69-74-72-75—290		31	Sun-Ju Ahn (KOR)	76-71-78-72—297	21,567	
12	Stacy Prammanasudh	75-72-71-73—291	71,002		Young Kim (KOR)	74-71-71-81—297	21,567	
13	Cristie Kerr	72-70-75-75—292	60,878		Brittany Lang	71-75-74-77—297	21,567	
	Jee Young Lee (KOR)	71-75-74-72—292	60,878		Lorena Ochoa (MEX)	73-74-76-74—297	21,567	
	Suzann Pettersen (NOR)	77-71-73-71—292	60,878		Ji Young Oh (KOR)	67-76-76-78—297	21,567	
					Karen Stupples (ENG)	74-73-75-75—297	21,567	
	Momoko Ueda (JPN)	72-71-73-76—292	60,878		Alison Walshe (am)	73-74-73-77—297		
17	Catriona Matthew (SCO)	70-77-73-73—293	51,380	38	Amanda Blumenherst (am)	72-78-71-77—298		
	Morgan Pressel	74-74-72-73—293	51,380		Jennifer Rosales (PHI)	74-72-77-75—298	18,690	
19	Na Yeon Choi (KOR)	76-71-71-76—294	43,376		Sherri Steinhauer	75-75-71-77—298	18,690	
	Jeong Jang (KOR)	73-69-74-78—294	43,376		Karrie Webb (AUS)	75-75-72-76—298	18,690	

Other players who made the cut: Rachel Hetherington (AUS), Katherine Hull (AUS), Eun-Hee Ji (KOR), Ma On Min (KOR), Paola Moreno (COL) (am), Jane Park, Reilley Rankin, Yani Tseng (TPE), Lindsey Wright (AUS) 299; Maria Hjörth (SWE), Sakura Yokamine (JPN) 300; Louise Friberg (SWE), Christina Kim, Leta Lindley, Sherri Turner 301; Linda Wessberg (SWE) 302; Marcy Hart, Brittany Lincicome, Meg Mallon, Karin Sjodin (SWE), Angela Stanford, Whitney Wade 303; Shi Hyun Ahn (KOR), Na Ri Kim (KOR), Sydnee Michaels (am), Janice Moodie (SCO) 304; Jimin Kang (KOR) 305; Kim Hall 306; Michele Redman 307; Il Mi Chung (KOR), Hee-Won Han (KOR), Tiffany Lua (am) 308; Meena Lee (KOR) 311

2007 US Women's Open Championship Southern Pines, SC [6664–71]

Prize money: $3.1 million

I	Cristie Kerr	71-72-66-70—279	$560,000	25T	Il Mi Chung (KOR)	73-72-74-72—291	24,767	
2	Lorena Ochoa (MEX)	71-71-68-71—281	271,022		Katherine Hull (AUS)	72-74-71-74—291	24,767	
	Angela Park (BRA)	68-69-74-70—281	271,022		Mi-Jeong Jeon (KOR)	76-72-73-70—291	24,767	
4	Se Ri Pak (KOR)	74-72-68-68—282	130,549		Young Kim (KOR)	75-71-72-73—291	24,767	
	In-Bee Park (KOR)	69-73-71-69—282	130,549		Seon Hwa Lee (KOR)	72-73-71-75—291	24,767	
6	Ji-Yai Shin (KOR)	70-69-71-74—284	103,581		Sherri Steinhauer	75-72-72-72—291	24,767	
7	Jee Young Lee (KOR)	72-71-71-71—285	93,031	32	Laura Davies (ENG)	72-75-72-73—292	19,754	
8	Jeong Jang (KOR)	72-71-70-73—286	82,464		Moire Dunn	73-71-74-74—292	19,754	
	Mi Hyun Kim (KOR)	71-75-70-70—286	82,464		Annika Sörenstam (SWE)	70-77-72-73—292	19,754	
10	Kyeong Bae (KOR)	74-71-72-70—287	66,177	35	Nicole Castrale	75-73-70-75—293	17,648	
	Julieta Granada (PAR)	70-69-75-73—287	66,177		Natalie Gulbis	74-72-74-73—293	17,648	
	Ai Miyazato (JPN)	73-73-72-69—287	66,177		Charlotte Mayorkas	70-73-78-72—293	17,648	
	Morgan Pressel	71-70-69-77—287	66,177		Kris Tamulis	72-71-74-76—293	17,648	
14	Joo Mi Kim (KOR)	70-73-70-75—288	55,032	39	Shi Hyun Ahn (KOR)	70-72-76-76—294	14,954	
	Brittany Lincicome	71-74-71-72—288	55,032		Erica Blasberg	74-69-75-76—294	14,954	
16	Paula Creamer	72-74-71-72—289	44,219		Laura Diaz	74-72-73-75—294	14,954	
	Amy Hung (TPE)	70-69-75-75—289	44,219		Jennie Lee (am)	71-74-75-74—294		
	Jimin Kang (KOR)	73-73-73-70—289	44,219		Janice Moodie (SCO)	71-76-74-73—294	14,954	
	Birdie Kim (KOR)	73-70-71-75—289	44,219		Becky Morgan (WAL)	75-72-73-74—294	14,954	
	Catriona Matthew (SCO)	75-67-74-73—289	44,219		Jennifer Song (KOR) (am)	72-73-73-76—294		
	Angela Stanford	72-71-73-73—289	44,219	46	Diana D'Alessio	73-70-77-75—295	12,268	
22	Dina Ammaccapane	75-72-70-73—290	33,878		Wendy Doolan (AUS)	73-70-75-77—295	12,268	
	Shiho Ohyama (JPN)	69-73-73-75—290	33,878		Meena Lee (KOR)	71-75-74-75—295	12,268	
	Sakura Yokomine (JPN)	72-71-74-73—290	33,878		Sherri Turner	73-74-73-75—295	12,268	
25	Hye Jung Choi (KOR)	77-68-70-76—291	24,767					

Other players who made the cut: Amanda Blumenherst (am), Jimin Jeong (KOR), Song-Hee Kim (KOR), Su A Kim (KOR), Leta Lindley, Teresa Lu (TPE), Amy Yang (KOR), Sung Ah Yim (KOR) 296; Katie Futcher, Candie Kung (TPE), Jane Park 297; Pat Hurst, In-Kyung Kim (KOR) 298; Allison Fouch, Karin Sjodin (SWE) 300; Aree Song (KOR) 301; Mina Harigae (am), Karine Icher (FRA) 305

2006 US Women's Open Championship Newport CC, Newport, RI   [6564–71]

Prize money: $3.1 million

1	Annika Sörenstam (SWE)*	69-71-73-71—284	$560,000	20T	Kristina Tucker (SWE)	72-74-74-76—296	41,654
2	Pat Hurst	69-71-75-69—284	335,000	24	Amy Hung (TPE)	76-72-77-72—297	32,873
*Play off: 18 holes: Sörenstam 70, Hurst 74					Lorie Kane (CAN)	73-72-75-77—297	32,873
3	Se Ri Pak (KOR)	69-74-74-69—286	156,038		Sherri Steinhauer	72-75-72-78—297	32,873
	Stacy Prammanasudh	72-71-71-72—286	156,038		Shani Waugh (AUS)	77-72-73-75—297	32,873
	Michelle Wie	70-72-71-73—286	156,038	28	Tracy Hanson	75-71-78-74—298	22,529
6	Juli Inkster	73-70-71-73—287	103,575		Jeong Jang (KOR)	72-71-75-80—298	22,529
7	Brittany Lincicome	72-72-69-78—291	93,026		Cristie Kerr	73-74-75-76—298	22,529
10	Amanda Blumenherst (am)	70-77-73-73—293			Carin Koch (SWE)	74-73-73-78—298	22,529
	Sophie Gustafson (SWE)	72-72-71-78—293	66,174		Candie Kung (TPE)	74-70-77-77—298	22,529
	Young Kim (KOR)	75-69-75-74—293	66,174		Ai Miyazato (JPN)	74-75-70-79—298	22,529
	Jee Young Lee (KOR)	71-75-70-77—293	66,174		Becky Morgan (WAL)	70-74-77-77—298	22,529
	Patricia Meunier-Lebouc (FRA)	72-73-73-75—293	66,174		Suzann Pettersen (NOR)	73-74-75-76—298	22,529
	Jane Park (am)	69-73-75-76—293			Morgan Pressel	76-74-75-73—298	22,529
16	Paula Creamer	71-72-76-75—294	53,577	37	Dawn Coe-Jones (CAN)	74-75-73-77—299	17,647
	Natalie Gulbis	76-71-74-73—294	53,577		Karrie Webb (AUS)	73-76-74-76—299	17,647
	Sherri Turner	72-74-76-72—294	53,577		Lindsey Wright (AUS)	74-73-76-76—299	17,647
19	Catriona Matthew (SCO)	74-76-72-73—295	48,007		Heather Young	76-71-77-75—299	17,647
20	Lorena Ochoa (MEX)	71-73-77-75—296	41,654	41	Maria Hjörth (SWE)	74-75-73-78—300	14,954
	Gloria Park (KOR)	70-78-76-72—296	41,654		Mi Hyun Kim (KOR)	75-72-75-78—300	14,954
	Karen Stupples (ENG)	78-72-70-76—296	41,654		Yu Ping Lin (TPE)	76-74-75-75—300	14,954
					Aree Song (KOR)	77-72-79-72—300	14,954
					Wendy Ward	77-73-77-73—300	14,954

Other players who made the cut: Yuri Fudoh (JPN), Julieta Granada (PAR), Nancy Scranton 301; Dana Dormann, Seon Hwa Lee (KOR), Siew-Ai Lin (MAS), Alena Sharp (CAN), Karin Sjodin (SWE), Angela Stanford 302; Moira Dunn, Karine Icher (FRA) 303; Nicole Castrale, Silvia Cavalleri (ITA), Rosie Jones, Ashley Knoll (am), Diana Luna (MON) 304; Beth Bader 305; Dana Ammaccapane 306; Denise Munzlinger, Sung Ah Yin (KOR) 307; Kimberly Kim (am), Kim Saiki 309; Lynnette Brooky (NZL) 311

2005 US Women's Open Championship Cherry Hill, CO   [6749–71]

Prize money: $1.5 million

1	Birdie Kim (KOR)	74-72-69-72—287	$560,000	23T	Sarah Huarte	74-76-73-73—296	34,556
2	Brittany Lang (am)	69-77-72-71—289			Gloria Park (KOR)	74-75-74-73—296	34,556
	Morgan Pressel (am)	71-73-70-75—289			Nicole Perrot (CHI)	70-70-78-78—296	34,556
4	Natalie Gulbis	70-75-74-71—290	272,723		Jennifer Rosales (PHI)	72-76-73-75—296	34,556
	Lorie Kane (CAN)	74-71-76-69—290	272,723		Annika Sörenstam (SWE)	71-75-73-77—296	34,556
6	Karine Icher (FRA)	69-75-75-72—291	116,310		Michelle Wie (am)	69-73-72-82—296	
	Young Jo (KOR)	74-71-70-76—291	116,310	31	Rachel Hetherington (AUS)	74-69-76-78—297	23,479
	Candie Kung (TPE)	73-73-71-74—291	116,310		Mi Hyun Kim (KOR)	72-73-76-76—297	23,479
	Lorena Ochoa (MEX)	74-68-77-72—291	116,310		Brittany Lincicome	74-74-78-71—297	23,479
10	Cristie Kerr	74-71-72-75—292	80,523		Catriona Matthew (SCO)	73-72-75-77—297	23,479
	Angela Stanford	69-74-73-76—292	80,523		Karrie Webb (AUS)	76-73-73-75—297	23,479
	Karen Stupples (ENG)	75-70-69-78—292	80,523	36	Kim Saiki	74-73-74-77—298	20,386
13	Tina Barrett	73-74-71-75—293	61,402		Wendy Ward	74-74-75-75—298	20,386
	Heather Bowie	77-73-69-74—293	61,402	38	Il Mi Chung (KOR)	75-71-76-77—299	17,939
	Jamie Hullett	75-72-70-76—293	61,402		Johanna Head (ENG)	74-73-74-78—299	17,939
	Soo Yun Kang (KOR)	74-74-74-71—293	61,402		Juli Inkster	77-71-75-76—299	17,939
	Paige MacKenzie (am)	75-75-69-74—293			Young Kim (KOR)	73-73-70-83—299	17,939
	Meg Mallon	71-74-75-73—293	61,402		Sarah Lee (KOR)	79-70-75-75—299	17,939
19	Paula Creamer	74-69-72-79—294	47,480		Amanda McCurdy (am)	75-75-71-78—299	17,939
	Rosie Jones	73-72-74-75—294	47,480		Aree Song (KOR)	77-70-72-80—299	17,939
	Leta Lindley	73-76-73-72—294	47,480				
	Liselotte Neumann (SWE)	70-75-73-76—294	47,480				
23	Helen Alfredsson (SWE)	72-73-74-77—296	34,556				
	Laura Diaz	75-73-72-76—296	34,556				

Other players who made the cut: Se Ri Pak (KOR), Nancy Scranton 300; Beth Bader, Dorothy Delasin (PHI), Hee Won Han (KOR), 301; Arnie Cochran (am), Jeong Janh (KOR) 302; Katie Allison, Eva Dahllof (SWE), Stephanie Louden, Grace Park (KOR), Suzann Pettersen (NOR), Kris Tschetter 303; Katie Futcher, Sophie Gustafson (SWE), Kaori Higo (JPN), Carri Wood 304; Candy Hannemann (BRA) 307; Jean Bartholomew 309.

2004 US Women's Open Championship The Orchards, South Hadley, MA   [6473–71]

Prize money: $3.1 million

1	Meg Mallon	73-69-67-65—274	$560,000	20T	Kate Golden	74-71-72-71—288	38,660
2	Annika Sörenstam (SWE)	71-68-70-67—276	335,000		Johanna Head (ENG)	76-69-70-73—288	38,660
					Rosie Jones	74-72-72-70—288	38,660
3	Kelly Robbins	74-67-68-69—278	208,863		Young Kim (KOR)	71-73-76-68—288	38,660
4	Jennifer Rosales (PHI)	70-67-69-75—281	145,547		Kim Saiki	70-68-74-76—288	38,660
5	Candie Kung (TPE)	70-68-74-70—282	111,173		Liselotte Neumann (SWE)	72-72-72-72—288	38,660
	Michele Redman	70-72-73-67—282	111,173				
7	Moira Dunn	73-67-72-71—283	86,744	27	Beth Daniel	69-74-71-75—289	29,195
	Pat Hurst	70-71-71-71—283	86,744		Cristie Kerr	73-71-74-71—289	29,195
	Jeong Jang (KOR)	72-74-71-66—283	86,744	29	Shi Hyun Ahn (KOR)	73-71-72-74—290	24,533
10	Michelle Ellis (Aus)	70-69-72-73—284	68,813		Lorie Kane (CAN)	75-70-72-73—290	24,533
	Carin Koch (SWE)	72-67-75-70—284	68,813		Deb Richard	71-73-72-74—290	24,533
	Rachel Teske (AUS)	71-69-70-74—284	68,813	32	Allison Hanna	71-75-74-71—291	20,539
13	Paula Creamer (am)	72-69-72-72—285			Becky Morgan (WAL)	71-74-73-73—291	20,539
	Patricia Meunier–Labouc (FRA)	67-75-74-69—285	60,602		Se Ri Pak (KOR)	70-76-71-74—291	20,539
					Sherri Steinhauer	74-71-73-73—291	20,539
	Michelle Wie (am)	71-70-71-73—285			Karen Stupples (ENG)	71-72-77-71—291	20,539
16	Mi Hyun Kim (KOR)	76-68-71-71—286	54,052	37	Jenna Daniels	76-71-72-73—292	16,897
	Suzann Pettersen (NOR)	74-72-71-69—286	54,052		AJ Easthorne (CAN)	73-72-75-72—292	16,897
	Karrie Webb (AUS)	72-71-71-72—286	54,052		Natalie Gulbis	73-71-75-73—292	16,897
19	Catriona Matthew (SCO)	73-71-72-71—287	48,432		Jamie Hullett	72-74-74-72—292	16,897
					Christina Kim	74-71-76-71—292	16,897
20	Dawn Coe-Jones (CAN)	71-73-72-72—288	38,660		Jill McGill	71-75-71-75—292	16,897
					Gloria Park (KOR)	76-71-73-72—292	16,897

Other players who made the cut: Donna Andrews, Laura Diaz, Jennifer Greggain, Ji-Hee Lee, Mhairi McKay (SCO), Lorena Ochoa (MEX) 293; Jennie Lee (am) 294; Katherine Hull 295; Tina Barrett, Catherine Cartwright, Hee-Won Han (KOR) 296; Brittany Lincicome (am) 297; Loraine Lambert, Aree Song (KOR) 298; Liz Earley, Allison Finney, Juli Inkster 299; Mee Lee (KOR), Seol-An Jeon (KOR), Courtney Swaim 300; Hilary Lunke, Grace Park (KOR) 301; Li Ying Ye (CHN) 304.

2003 US Women's Open Championship Pumpkin Ridge GC, North Plains, OR   [6509–71]

Prize money: $3.1 million

1	Hilary Lunke*	71-69-68-75—283	$560,000	20	Beth Daniel	73-69-77-74—293	43,491
2	Kelly Robbins	74-69-71-69—283	272,004		Yuri Fudoh (JPN)	74-72-75-72—293	43,491
	Angela Stanford	70-70-69-74—283	272,004	22	Lorie Kane (CAN)	73-75-73-73—294	36,575
*Play-off rounds: Hilary Lunke 70, Angela Stanford 71, Kelly Robbins 73					Christina Kim	74-74-72-74—294	36,575
					Leta Lindley	73-69-77-75—294	36,575
4	Annika Sörenstam (SWE)	72-72-67-73—284	150,994		Catriona Matthew (SCO)	74-70-76-74—294	36,575
5	Aree Song (am)	70-73-68-74—285		26	Danielle Ammaccapane	74-74-73-74—295	28,354
6	Jeong Jang (KOR)	73-69-69-75—286	115,333		Dorothy Delasin (PHI)	79-70-76-70—295	2,8354
	Mhairi McKay (SCO)	66-70-75-75—286	115,333		Kelli Kuehne	72-74-75-74—295	28,354
8	Juli Inkster	69-71-74-73—287	97,363		Paula Marti (ESP)	71-76-76-72—295	28,354
9	Rosie Jones	70-72-73-73—288	90,241	30	Ashli Bunch	71-73-77-75—296	22,678
10	Grace Park (KOR)	72-76-73-68—289	79,243		Annette DeLuca	71-73-78-74—296	22,678
	Suzann Pettersen (NOR)	76-69-69-75—289	79,243		Elizabeth Janangelo (am)	75-73-73-75—296	
12	Donna Andrews	69-72-72-77—290	71,362		Mi-Hyun Kim (KOR)	73-73-73-77—296	22,678
13	Laura Diaz	71-71-74-76—292	56,500		Jane Park (am)	76-73-74-73—296	
	Natalie Gulbis	73-69-72-78—292	56,500	35	Candy Hannemann (BRA)	75-69-73-80—297	20,360
	Cristie Kerr	72-73-73-74—292	56,500		Stephanie Louden	71-74-77-75—297	20,360
	Patricia Meunier-Labouc (FRA)	73-69-74-76—292	56,500		Guilia Sergas (ITA)	70-74-79-74—297	20,360
	Lorena Ochoa (MEX)	71-75-72-74—292	56,500		Kirsty Taylor (ENG)	71-75-73-78—297	20,360
	Jennifer Rosales (PHI)	74-69-76-73—292	56,500	39	Michele Redman	71-74-74-79—298	18,783
	Rachel Teske (AUS)	71-73-72-76—292	56,500				

Other players who made the cut: Heather Bowie, Karen Stupples (ENG) 299; Beth Bauer, Hee-Won Han (KOR), Jamie Hullett, Emilee Klein, Becky Morgan (WAL), Karen Weiss 300; Sherri Turner 301; Se Ri Pak (KOR) 302; Leigh Ann Hardin (am) 303; Morgan Pressel (am) 304; Alison Nicholas (ENG), Suzanne Strudwick (ENG), Michelle Vinieratos 305; Yu Ping Lin (TPE) 306; Mollie Fankhauser (am) 307; Irene Cho (am) 308; Mardi Lunn (AUS) 309

2002 US Women's Open Championship Prairie Dunes, Hutchinson, KS　　　[6253–70]

Prize money: $3 million.

I	Juli Inkster	67-72-71-66—276	$535,000	22T	Susan Ginter-Brooker	74-72-70-74—290	26.894
2	Annika Sörenstam	70-69-69-70—278	315,000		Jeong Jang (KOR)	73-73-74-70—290	26.894
	(SWE)				Rosie Jones	71-77-69-73—290	26.894
3	Shani Waugh (AUS)	67-73-71-72—283	202.568		Mi Hyun Kim (KOR)	74-72-70-74—290	26.894
4	Raquel Carriedo (ESP)	75-71-72-66—284	141.219		Meg Mallon	73-75-73-69—290	26.894
5	Se Ri Pak (KOR)	74-75-68-68—285	114.370		Catriona Matthew		
6	Mhairi McKay (SCO)	70-75-71-70—286	101.421		(SCO)	69-80-72-69—290	26.894
7	Beth Daniel	71-76-71-69—287	78.016		Stacy Prammanasudh	75-74-72-69—290	26.894
	Laura Diaz	67-72-77-71—287	78.016		Michele Redman	71-69-73-77—290	26.894
	Kelli Kuehne	70-76-72-69—287	78.016	32	Brandie Burton	70-74-76-71—291	18.730
	Janice Moodie (SCO)	71-72-71-73—287	78.016		Laura Davies (ENG)	75-73-68-75—291	18.730
	Jennifer Rosales (PHI)	73-72-74-68—287	78.016		Hee-Won Han (KOR)	72-77-70-72—291	18.730
12	Lynnette Brooky (NZL)	73-73-69-73—288	54.201		Cristie Kerr	74-71-72-74—291	18.730
	Stephanie Keever	72-71-73-72—288	54.201		Charlotta Sörenstam	73-70-77-71—291	18.730
	Jill McGill	71-70-69-78—288	54.201		(SWE)		
	Joanne Morley (ENG)	78-68-73-69—288	54.201	37	Jenna Daniels	72-70-77-73—292	15.209
	Kelly Robbins	71-74-74-69—288	54.201		Wendy Doolan (AUS)	73-76-75-68—292	15.209
	Rachel Teske (AUS)	75-71-72-70—288	54.201		Jackie Gallagher-Smith	70-76-73-73—292	15.209
18	Donna Andrews	74-74-70-71—289	40.738		Carin Koch (SWE)	73-72-70-77—292	15.209
	Beth Bauer	74-72-71-72—289	40.738		Liselotte Neumann	72-74-70-76—292	15.209
	Lorie Kane (CAN)	69-77-69-74—289	40.738		(SWE)		
	Grace Park (KOR)	71-77-71-70—289	40.738		Karen Stupples (ENG)	80-68-72-72—292	15.209
22	Danielle Ammaccapane	74-71-73-72—290	26.894		Kris Tschetter	72-77-72-71—292	15.209
	Michelle Ellis (AUS)	71-71-75-73—290	26.894				

Other players who made the cut: Jean Bartholomew, Audra Burke, Mitzi Edge, Jung Yeon Lee (KOR), Gloria Park (KOR), Cindy Schreyer, Leslie Spalding 293; Alicia Dibos (PER), Vicki Goetze-Ackerman, Angela Jerman (am), Ara Koh (KOR), Sherri Steinhauer, Karen Weiss, Aree Song Wongluekiet (THA) 294; Amy Fruhwirth, Kim Saiki; Sherri Turner 295; Heather Bowie, Soo Young Moon (KOR) 296; Patricia Meunier-Lebouc (FRA) 297; Dawn Coe-Jones (CAN), Dorothy Delasin (PHI), Pearl Sin (KOR) 298; Allison Finney 299; Tracy Hanson 300; Michele Vinieratos 301.

US Women's Open History

Year	Winner	Runner-up		Venue	Score
1946	P Berg	B Jamieson		Spokane	5 and 4

Changed to strokeplay

Year	Winner	Venue	Score
1947	B Jamieson	Greensboro	300
1948	B Zaharias	Atlantic City	300
1949	L Suggs	Maryland	291
1950	B Zaharias	Wichita	291
1951	B Rawls	Atlanta	294
1952	L Suggs	Bala, PA	284
1953	B Rawls*	Rochester, NY	302

After a play-off with J Pung 71-77

1954	B Zaharias	Peabody, MA	291
1955	F Crocker	Wichita	299
1956	K Cornelius*	Duluth	302

After a play-off with B McIntire (am) 75-82

1957	B Rawls	Mamaroneck	299
1958	M Wright	Bloomfield Hills, MI	290
1959	M Wright	Pittsburgh, PA	287
1960	B Rawls	Worchester, MA	292
1961	M Wright	Springfield, NJ	293
1962	M Lindstrom	Myrtle Beach	301
1963	M Mills	Kenwood	289
1964	M Wright*	San Diego	290

After a play-off with R Jessen 70-72

Year	Winner	Venue	Score
1965	C Mann	Northfield, NJ	290
1966	S Spuzich	Hazeltine National, MN	297
1967	C Lacoste (FRA) (am)	Hot Springs, VA	294
1968	S Berning	Moselem Springs, PA	289
1969	D Caponi	Scenic-Hills	294
1970	D Caponi	Muskogee, OK	287
1971	J Gunderson-Carner	Erie, PA	288
1972	S Berning	Mamaroneck, NY	299
1973	S Berning	Rochester, NY	290
1974	S Haynie	La Grange, IL	295
1975	S Palmer	Northfield, NJ	295
1976	J Carner*	Springfield, PA	292
*After a play-off: Carner 76, S Palmer 78			
1977	H Stacy	Hazeltine, MN	292
1978	H Stacy	Indianapolis	299
1979	J Britz	Brooklawn, CN	284
1980	A Alcott	Richland, TN	280
1981	P Bradley	La Grange, IL	279
1982	J Alex	Del Paso, Sacramento, CA	283
1983	J Stephenson (AUS)	Broken Arrow, OK	290
1984	H Stacy	Salem, MA	290
1985	K Baker	Baltusrol, NJ	280
1986	J Geddes*	NCR	287
*After a play-off with Sally Little			
1987	L Davies (ENG)*	Plainfield	285
*After a play-off: Davies 71, A Okamoto 73, J Carner 74			
1988	L Neumann (SWE)	Baltimore	277
1989	B King	Indianwood, MI	278
1990	B King	Atlanta Athletic Club, GA	284
1991	M Mallon	Colonial, TX	283
1992	P Sheehan*	Oakmont, PA	280
*After a play-off: Sheehan 72, J Inkster 74			
1993	L Merton	Crooked Stick	280
1994	P Sheehan	Indianwood, MI	277
1995	A Sörenstam (SWE)	The Broadmore, CO	278
1996	A Sörenstam (SWE)	Pine Needles Lodge, NC	272
1997	A Nicholas (ENG)	Pumpkin Ridge, OR	274
1998	SR Pak (KOR)*	Blackwolf Run, WI	290
*After a play-off: Pak 5,3; J Chausiriporn (am) 5,4			
1999	J Inkster	Old Waverley, West Point, MS	272
2000	K Webb (AUS)	Merit Club, Libertyville, IL	282
2001	K Webb (AUS)	Pine Needles Lodge & GC, NC	273
2002	J Inkster	Prairie Dunes, KS	276
2003	H Lunke*	Pumpkin Ridge GC, OR	283
*After a play-off: Lunke 70, A Stanford 71, K Robins 73			
2004	M Mallon	The Orchards, S Hadley, MA	274
2005	B Kim (KOR)	Cherry Hills CC, CO	287
2006	A Sörenstam (SWE)*	Newport CC, RI	284
*After a play-off: Sörenstam 70, P Hurst 74			
2007	C Kerr	Southern Pines, NC	279
2008	I Park (KOR)	Interlachen, MN	283
2009	E-H Ji (KOR)	Saucon Valley, PA	284
2010	P Creamer	Oakmont, PA	281
2011	S Y Ryu (KOR)*	Colorado Springs, CO	281
*Beat H K Seo (KOR) at the third extra hole			

LPGA Championship

presented by Wegmans

June 23–26

Yani Tseng leads from start to finish in LPGA

Brilliant Taiwanese sweeps to an inspired 10 shot victory

While not even Rory McIlroy in 2011 could boast a winning margin of ten shots in a major championship, that was the emphatic margin of victory relished at Locust Hill country club by Yani Tseng as her closing 66 for the 19 under par total of 269 in the Wegmans LPGA secured the fourth major triumph of her career.

Yani Tseng

© Getty Images

Playing almost flawless golf – she found 38 of 56 fairways, 57 of 72 greens in regulation and took only 111 putts – the 22-year-old Taiwanese golfer became the youngest ever player to win four major titles. Patty Berg was previously the best woman at the youngest age, winning her fourth major at 23 in 1941.

Remarkably, of the eight tournaments won so far by Tseng on the LPGA as a professional, half are majors. Her three previous major successes were the 2008 LPGA Championship, the 2010 Kraft Nabisco Championship and the 2010 Ricoh Women's British Open.

The dominant figure in women's golf, Tseng enjoyed her third victory in the past six majors and knew it should have been the fourth. Like McIlroy, she'd squandered a third round advantage in her previous major appearance, squandering a five stroke lead at the Kraft Nabisco in April.

This time, though, Tseng, who led the championship from first to last, simply ran away from the field, winning by ten from Morgan Pressel and by 11 from Cristie Kerr and Suzann Pettersen. Hailed by Annika Sörenstam as the new face of women's golf, Tseng was grateful for the backing of the galleries in New York. "I just feel like I'm all the way from Taiwan, a little country, but the people here are really supportive," she said. "I really appreciate that and I almost cried at the end because it was so emotional."

Boosted by victory two weeks previously at the State Farm Classic, Tseng showed the rest the way from the start in Rochester with an opening score of 66 which made light of narrow fairways lined by testing rough. Tseng dropped a couple of shots on the first day at Locust Hill but also prised eight birdies from the tight lay-out. She'd been transfixed by McIlroy's performance at the US Open. Both 22-year-olds were part of the Faldo Junior Series as amateurs and she took inspiration from the young Irishman's victory.

As is often the case in major championship golf, the leader reaped a reward from sticking to the straight and narrow off the tee. "I think I just hit it on the fairway more," Tseng reflected. "I missed some but I still hit lots [of tee shots] on the fairway. This course is so tight, so narrow. I just hit it on the fairway and that gave me more chances for birdie. I think that will be my strategy for the week. I hit the approaches very good, very close to the pins. So I kind of swung very consistently. My aim is to try to hit it on the fairway and be patient."

But for a three-putt on the 17th, Creamer would have matched Tseng's first round mark. But she bounced back with a birdie on the closing hole after hitting a sweet 7 iron inside two feet and was content to post 67. "Normally I kind of shoot myself in the foot after the first day by putting pressure on myself wanting to do so well," she said. "This time I hit 15 greens [in regulation]. So I gave myself a lot of opportunities. But overall I never really had any big problems out there, I guess you could say that I hit it really solid and made a lot of good putts."

Angela Stanford on 68 also took advantage of a lay-out softened by rain while easily the largest gallery of the first day in New York followed the stellar grouping of world No 2 and defending champion Kerr, No 10 Michelle Wie and No 14 Brittany Lincicome. In spite of the understandable enthusiasm of the home crowd for this all American pairing, the trio never engaged top gear. Kerr, who felt under the weather with flu, posted 72; Wie also matched par and it was a measure of Lincicome's putting woes that she found 15 greens in regulation yet still shot 74.

Tseng held on to the lead at the halfway mark on eight under after signing for 70 though not before making a mess of the 18th – her ninth – by driving into the trees and missing a short putt from 18 inches. That double bogey undid some of the good work of three consecutive birdies crafted between the 13th and 15th holes. The world No 1, though, is a fighter and she responded like a champion to her 18th hole set-back with another birdie on the first.

"I felt a little bit disappointed about that round," she recalled. "I hung in there, tried my best every shot but I missed two very short putts, which is disappointing. Like I said, I missed that two footer [on the eighth], and another one of 18 inches ... putts I should not miss. I probably try too hard and think too much. I'm over-thinking."

While Tseng struggled on the greens, Pat Hurst putted well – she holed from 40 feet on the eighth – and forced her way up the leaderboard in the second round thanks to a tidy 67. At 42, Hurst has been a regular on the LPGA for 18 seasons and can reflect on six victories as well as $7 million in earnings. Her most recent success, though, was back in 2009 and life as a wife, mother and member of the LPGA advisory board all took a toll on her golf. "A lot of little things took up a lot of time," she confessed. "But I love to play."

While Hurst fell back on Saturday with 75, Tseng used moving day to put space between herself and the rest of the field. Signing for the low score, 67, of the third round, Tseng completed 54 holes in 203 shots and led by five strokes from Pressel and Cindy LaCrosse. Dropping only one shot to par, Tseng fired six birdies – a notable feat bearing in mind that only eight golfers shot in the 60s during the third round.

Remembering how well she'd driven during the first round, Tseng had gone to the range to work on rhythm and tempo off the tee. Once she'd found the pace of her swing, the leader was again able to hit fairways – she only missed two on Saturday – and that meant she could create birdie opportunities. Able to work the ball both ways, Tseng had no doubt that accurate driving was the key for her. "I can shape the ball, a little fade, a little draw," she explained. "On these narrow fairways, I feel like I'm driving pretty good."

Playing in only her second major, LaCrosse was among those close to Tseng. The daughter of Doug LaCrosse, Cindy had caddied for her father when the 2008 Senior PGA Championship was also held in Rochester at Oak Hill. The leading player on the Futures Tour in 2010, LaCrosse earned her card on the LPGA without undergoing the trial of Qualifying school. After carding 69, the 24-year-old admitted a little surprise as well as delight at briefly finding herself in contention.

It was more predictable to find Pressel, Creamer and Kerr spearheading the American challenge in an event which brought the cream to the top. Five players – Tseng, Pressel, Stacy Lewis, Creamer and Kerr – could count eight major titles between them.

The defending champion had recovered from a slow start in the tournament to jump 38 places to a share of fifth thanks to a third round of 67. No one, though, was more surprised than the world No 2 Kerr to match the low score of the day. "To be quite honest, I made ridiculous par saves on the fifth, sixth, seventh and ninth holes," reported Cristie. "So the fact I somehow shot under par on the front was a miracle."

If there seemed to be a glimmer of hope for the others when Tseng dropped a shot on the first hole of Sunday's final round, the leader responded with a blistering run of form. She made five birdies on the front nine and was ten strokes clear as she stepped onto the tenth tee. By that stage, she was grappling with history rather than the competition as further birdies on the 14th and 17th holes helped her match the 19 under par tally previously set by Dottie Pepper at the 1999 Kraft Nabisco Championship, Karen Stupples at the 2004 Weetabix Women's British Open and Kerr in the same event last year.

Pettersen, who made a notable move herself on the last day with 67, was full of admiration for Tseng's performance. "Yani is a phenomenal golfer," said the Norwegian. " She has enough experience now and is never going to choke. She is the new No 1 and she pushes the edges like Annika used to do and Lorena [Ochoa] used to do. Now Yani is gaining an edge on us."

First Round	Second Round	Third Round	Fourth Round
−6 Yani Tseng	−8 Yani Tseng	−13 Yani Tseng	−19 Yani Tseng
−5 Paula Creamer	−7 Pat Hurst	−8 Morgan Pressel	−9 Morgan Pressel
−4 Stacy Prammanasudh	−6 Hee Young Park	−8 Cindy LaCrosse	−8 Cristie Kerr
−4 Diana D'Alessio	−6 Morgan Pressel	−6 Hee Young Park	−8 Suzann Pettersen
−4 Meena Lee	−6 Minea Blomqvist	−5 Cristie Kerr	−8 Paula Creamer
−3 Morgan Pressel	−5 Amy Yang	−5 Stacy Lewis	−6 Stacy Lewis
−3 Stacy Lewis	−5 Paula Creamer	−5 Paula Creamer	−6 Meena Lee
−3 Minea Blomqvist	−5 Cindy LaCrosse	−5 Meena Lee	−5 Mika Miyazato
−3 Amy Hung	−4 Angela Stanford	−4 Maria Hjörth	−5 Maria Hjörth
−3 Hee Young Park		−4 Mika Miyazato	−5 Pat Hurst
			−5 Azahara Muñoz

LPGA Championship   *Locust Hill, Pittsford, NY*   [6534–72]

Prize Money: $2.5 million. Field of 150 players, of whom 78 made the half-way cut on 146 or less.

Players are of American nationality unless stated

1	Yani Tseng (TPE)	66-70-67-66—269	$375,000
2	Morgan Pressel	69-69-70-71—279	228,695
3	Suzann Pettersen (NOR)	72-72-69-67—280	132,512
	Paula Creamer	67-72-72-69—280	132,512
	Cristie Kerr	72-72-67-69—280	132,512
6	Meena Lee (KOR)	68-73-70-71—282	77,630
	Stacy Lewis	69-72-70-71—282	77,630
8	Maria Hjörth (SWE)	71-71-70-71—283	53,840
	Pat Hurst	70-67-75-71—283	53,840
	Mika Miyazato (JPN)	72-72-68-71—283	53,840
	Azahara Muñoz (ESP)	70-71-71-71—283	53,840
12	Amy Yang (KOR)	70-69-74-71—284	42,445
	I K Kim (KOR)	73-70-69-72—284	42,445
14	Amy Hung (TPE)	69-73-73-70—285	33,765
	Heather Bowie Young	72-70-73-70—285	33,765
	Inbee Park (KOR)	73-69-71-72—285	33,765
	Katie Futcher	75-68-69-73—285	33,765
	Hee Young Park (KOR)	69-69-72-75—285	33,765
	Cindy LaCrosse	70-69-69-77—285	33,765
20	Brittany Lincicome	74-72-71-69—286	26,795
	Sun Young Yoo (KOR)	73-72-72-69—286	26,795
	Paige Mackenzie	72-73-70-71—286	26,795
	Karrie Webb (AUS)	74-69-71-72—286	26,795
	Candie Kung (TPE)	71-71-71-73—286	26,795
25	Hee-Won Han (KOR)	71-72-74-70—287	22,162
	Anna Nordqvist (SWE)	73-70-74-70—287	22,162
	Jimin Kang (KOR)	71-70-73-73—287	22,162
	Pornanong Phatlum (THA)	71-72-71-73—287	22,162
	Tiffany Joh	71-70-72-74—287	22,162
30	Jennifer Song (KOR)	72-72-72-72—288	18,531
	Reilley Rankin	73-68-74-73—288	18,531
	Angela Stanford	68-72-74-74—288	18,531
	Momoko Ueda (JPN)	72-69-71-76—288	18,531
34	Karen Stupples (ENG)	72-74-78-65—289	14,232
	M J Hur (KOR)	70-75-76-68—289	14,232
	Jiyai Shin (KOR)	75-71-73-70—289	14,232
	Se Ri Pak (KOR)	78-68-72-71—289	14,232
	Juli Inkster	74-70-73-72—289	14,232
	Catriona Matthew (SCO)	73-69-75-72—289	14,232
	Michele Redman	73-70-73-73—289	14,232
	Yoo Kyeong Kim (KOR)	72-72-71-74—289	14,232
	Hee Kyung Seo (KOR)	71-73-71-74—289	14,232
43	Taylor Leon	75-70-75-70—290	10,285
	Eun-Hee Ji (KOR)	70-76-73-71—290	10,285
	Mindy Kim (KOR)	70-75-74-71—290	10,285
	Mi Hyun Kim (KOR)	75-67-76-72—290	10,285
	Na Yeon Choi (KOR)	73-70-74-73—290	10,285
	Jennifer Johnson	69-76-72-73—290	10,285
	Karin Sjodin (SWE)	72-70-73-75—290	10,285
50	Shanshan Feng (CHN)	75-66-80-70—291	8,138
	Kristy McPherson	72-74-74-71—291	8,138
	Sarah Jane Smith	73-72-75-71—291	8,138
	Julieta Granada (PAR)	73-73-73-72—291	8,138
	Sarah Kemp (AUS)	74-71-74-72—291	8,138
	Beatriz Recari (ESP)	71-74-73-73—291	8,138
	Danielle Kang (am)	74-70-72-75—291	
57	Becky Morgan (WAL)	75-71-78-68—292	6,249

57T	Christel Boeljon (NED)	73-72-77-70—292	6,249
	Sophie Gustafson (SWE)	73-72-76-71—292	6,249
	Ryann O'Toole	69-76-76-71—292	6,249
	Leta Lindley	72-72-75-73—292	6,249
	Dewi Claire Schreefel (NED)	73-72-74-73—292	6,249
	Lorie Kane (CAN)	73-72-73-74—292	6,249
	Laura Davies (ENG)	75-71-70-76—292	6,249
	Jeehae Lee (KOR)	74-72-69-77—292	6,249
	Stacy Prammanasudh	68-73-74-77—292	6,249
	Katherine Hull (AUS)	70-72-72-78—292	6,249
68	Jennie Lee	72-71-78-72—293	5,196
	Jenny Shin (KOR)	72-70-79-72—293	5,196
	Natalie Gulbis	71-73-72-77—293	5,196
	Minea Blomqvist (FIN)	69-69-77-78—293	5,196
72	Kyeong Bae (KOR)	72-74-75-73—294	4,883
	Michelle Wie	72-72-75-75—294	4,883
	Haeji Kang (KOR)	74-72-71-77—294	4,883
75	Sherri Steinhauer	73-73-76-73—295	4,729
	Silvia Cavalleri (ITA)	75-69-77-74—295	4,729
77	Grace Park (KOR)	73-73-73-77—296	4,641
78	Diana D'Alessio	68-77-80-76—301	4,582

The following players missed the cut:

79	Chie Arimura (JPN)	78-69—147	92T	Stephanie Sherlock	74-74—148	129	Danah Bordner	74-78—152
	Beth Bader	77-70—147		(CAN)			Annette DeLuca	75-77—152
	Chella Choi (KOR)	74-73—147		Mariajo Uribe (COL)	78-70—148		Brittany Lang	74-78—152
	Moira Dunn	72-75—147	108	Dina Ammaccapane	74-75—149		Lexi Thompson	74-78—152
	Mollie Fankhauser	72-75—147		Ashli Bunch	75-74—149	133	Karen Davies	75-78—153
	Meaghan Francella	74-73—147		Sandra Gal (GER)	75-74—149		Sarah Lee (KOR)	76-77—153
	Christina Kim	72-75—147		Marcy Hart	74-75—149		Janice Moodie (SCO)	77-76—153
	Song-Hee Kim	75-72—147		Jimin Jeong (KOR)	72-77—149	136	Mhairi McKay (SCO)	80-74—154
	(KOR)			Aree Song (KOR)	73-76—149		Belen Mozo (ESP)	77-77—154
	Jessica Korda	73-74—147		Jenny Suh	73-76—149		Jean Reynolds	77-77—154
	Haru Nomura (JPN)	74-73—147	115	Amanda	76-74—150		Lindsey Wright	78-76—154
	Jin Young Pak (KOR)	74-73—147		Blumenherst			(AUS)	
	Alena Sharp (CAN)	74-73—147		Pernilla Lindberg	75-75—150	140	Sara Brown	78-77—155
	Kris Tamulis	73-74—147		(SWE)			Louise Friberg	81-74—155
92	Shi Hyun Ahn (KOR)	77-71—148		Gwladys Nocera	80-70—150		(SWE)	
	Allison Fouch	76-72—148		(FRA)			Sue Ginter	77-78—155
	Nicole Hage	78-70—148		Gerina Piller	74-76—150		Christine Song	78-77—155
	Julie Hennessy	76-72—148	119	Dori Carter	76-75—151	144	Lisa DePaulo	81-75—156
	Vicky Hurst	71-77—148		Laura Diaz	75-76—151		Birdie Kim (KOR)	78-78—156
	Ilhee Lee (KOR)	74-74—148		Mina Harigae	77-74—151		Louise Stahle (SWE)	77-79—156
	Jee Young Lee (KOR)	72-76—148		Stephanie Louden	76-75—151	147	Na On Min (KOR)	79-78—157
	Seon Hwa Lee	76-72—148		Lisa Meldrum (CAN)	74-77—151	148	Debbi Koyama (JPN)	81-79—160
	(KOR)			Jane Park	75-76—151			
	Amelia Lewis	72-76—148		Samantha Richdale	75-76—151		Anna Grzebien	79 WD
	Ai Miyazato (JPN)	75-73—148		(CAN)			Allison Hanna	81 WD
	Angela Oh	75-73—148		Jennifer Rosales	76-75—151			
	Ji Young Oh (KOR)	74-74—148		(PHI)				
	Giulia Sergas (ITA)	75-73—148		Alison Walshe	77-74—151			
	Jessica Shepley	76-72—148		Wendy Ward	73-78—151			
	(CAN)							

Who is known as "The Boss of the Moss"?

The answer can be found on page 905

2010 McDonald's LPGA Championship Locust Hill, Pitsford, NY   [6506–72]

Prize money: $2.25 million

1	Cristie Kerr	68-66-69-66—269	$337,500	19T	Michelle Wie	72-74-73-70—289	24,800
2	Song-Hee Kim (KOR)	72-71-69-69—281	207,790	25	Natalie Gulbis	72-75-71-72—290	18,669
3	Ai Miyazato (JPN)	76-71-70-66—283	133,672		Sophie Gustafson (SWE)	73-75-72-70—290	18,669
	Jiyai Shin (KOR)	72-70-70-71—283	133,672		Jeong Jang (KOR)	71-73-75-71—290	18,669
5	In-Kyung Kim (KOR)	72-70-72-70—284	85,323		Christina Kim	70-76-70-74—290	18,669
	Karrie Webb (AUS)	72-72-69-71—284	85,323		Anna Nordqvist (SWE)	73-72-73-72—290	18,669
7	Meaghann Francella	73-71-70-71—285	54,323		Angela Stanford	74-74-74-68—290	18,669
	Jimin Kang (KOR)	74-67-70-74—285	54,323		Sakura Yokomine (JPN)	71-72-73-74—290	18,669
	Inbee Park (KOR)	69-70-75-71—285	54,323		Sun Young Yoo (KOR)	72-75-71-72—290	18,669
	Morgan Pressel	72-76-68-69—285	54,323		Heather Bowie Young	70-77-74-69—290	18,669
11	Azahara Muñoz (ESP)	72-69-70-75—286	41,238	34	Shi Hyun Ahn (KOR)	74-71-72-74—291	13,182
	Suzann Pettersen (NOR)	74-72-69-71—286	41,238		Chie Arimura (JPN)	73-72-73-73—291	13,182
13	Mika Miyazato (JPN)	69-70-72-76—287	37,314		Katherine Hull (AUS)	74-73-76-68—291	13,182
14	Stacy Lewis	68-74-73-73—288	31,398		Amy Hung (TPE)	72-76-73-70—291	13,182
	Brittany Lincicome	71-69-75-73—288	31,398		M J Hur (KOR)	72-73-73-73—291	13,182
	Sarah Jane Smith	74-71-69-74—288	31,398		Haeji Kang (KOR)	73-73-72-73—291	13,182
	Lindsey Wright (AUS)	69-74-72-73—288	31,398		Catriona Matthew (SCO)	74-71-69-77—291	13,182
	Amy Yang (KOR)	73-67-76-72—288	31,398		Jennifer Rosales (PHI)	73-74-72-72—291	13,182
19	Meena Lee (KOR)	71-76-74-68—289	24,800	42	Helen Alfredsson (SWE)	75-73-69-75—292	10,079
	Seon Hwa Lee (KOR)	68-74-73-74—289	24,800		Paula Creamer	71-72-74-75—292	10,079
	Na On Min (KOR)	74-67-74-74—289	24,800		Mi Hyun Kim (KOR)	75-73-75-69—292	10,079
	Karin Sjodin (SWE)	74-73-74-68—289	24,800		Brittany Lang	75-71-71-75—292	10,079
	Yani Tseng (TPE)	75-71-70-73—289	24,800		Michele Redman	74-67-79-72—292	10,079

Other players who made the cut: Chelia Choi (KOR), Laura Davies (ENG), Hee-Won Han (KOR), Yoo Kyeong Kim (KOR), Janice Moodie (SCO), Paola Moreno (COL), Alena Sharp (CAN) 293; Shanshan Feng (CHN), Vicky Hurst, Soo-Yun Kang (KOR), Sherri Steinhauer, Gloria Park (KOR) 294; Irene Cho, Mina Harigae, Teresa Lu (TPE) 295; Silvia Cavalleri (ITA), Juli Inkster 296; Louise Friberg (SWE), Lorie Kane (CAN), Stacy Prammanasudh 297; Louise Stahle (SWE), Mariajo Uribe (COL), Wendy Ward, Leah Wigger 298; Amanda Blumenherst 299; Candie Kung (TPE) 301; Giulia Sergas (ITA) 306

2009 McDonald's LPGA Championship Bulle Rock, Havre de Grace, MD   [6641–72]

Prize money: $2 million

1	Anna Nordqvist (SWE)	66-70-69-68—273	$300,000	23T	Eun-Hee Ji (KOR)	74-69-73-71—287	18,105
2	Lindsey Wright (AUS)	70-68-69-70—277	182,950		Mindy Kim	74-69-72-72—287	18,105
3	Ji-Yai Shin (KOR)	73-68-69-68—278	132,717		Paige Mackenzie	68-77-69-73—287	18,105
4	Kyeong Bae (KOR)	70-69-72-68—279	102,668		Lorena Ochoa (MEX)	72-69-73-73—287	18,105
5	Nicole Castrale	65-72-74-69—280	68,947		Yani Tseng (TPE)	73-71-69-74—287	18,105
	Kirsty McPherson	70-70-70-70—280	68,947		Michelle Wie	70-74-73-70—287	18,105
	Angela Stanford	70-71-70-69—280	68,947	31	Beth Bader	73-73-74-68—288	13,146
8	Na Yeon Choi (KOR)	68-71-70-72—281	49,582		Heather Bowie Young	75-70-70-73—288	13,146
9	Song Hee Kim (KOR)	73-72-68-69—282	39,440		Soo-Yun Kang (KOR)	73-71-72-72—288	13,146
	Stacy Lewis	68-72-71-71—282	39,440		Cristie Kerr	76-70-70-72—288	13,146
	Jin Young Pak	69-71-69-73—282	39,440		Na Ri Kim (KOR)	71-73-72-72—288	13,146
	Amy Yang (KOR)	68-74-70-70—282	39,440		Young Kim (KOR)	72-74-71-71—288	13,146
13	Brandie Burton	73-71-72-67—283	32,853		Michele Redman	72-73-72-71—288	13,146
14	Irene Cho (KOR)	72-75-65-72—284	29,949		Ashleigh Simon (RSA)	68-74-74-72—288	13,146
	Inbee Park (KOR)	70-72-73-69—284	29,949	39	Brittany Lang	72-72-72-73—289	10,016
16	Shi Hyun Ahn (KOR)	73-70-72-70—285	25,041		Seon Hwa Lee (KOR)	74-71-76-68—289	10,016
	Paula Creamer	74-70-71-70—285	25,041		Mika Miyazato (JPN)	74-73-70-72—289	10,016
	Sophie Gustafsson (SWE)	69-74-70-72—285	25,041		Janice Moodie (SCO)	74-73-70-72—289	10,016
	Katherine Hull (AUS)	69-69-76-71—285	25,041		Ji Young Oh (KOR)	73-74-71-71—289	10,016
	In-Kyung Kim (KOR)	72-74-68-71—285	25,041	44	Minea Blomqvist (FIN)	73-69-70-78—290	8,213
21	Natalie Gulbis	72-75-69-70—286	21,836		Anna Grzebien	74-73-69-74—290	8,213
	Hee-Won Han (KOR)	70-69-73-74—286	21,836		M J Hur (KOR)	71-72-74-73—290	8,213
23	Allison Hanna-Williams	72-74-69-72—287	18,105		Juli Inkster	73-71-73-73—290	8,213
	Maria Hjörth (SWE)	71-75-72-69—287	18,105		Kris Tschetter	70-72-73-75—290	8,213

Other players who made the cut: Sandra Gal (GER), Stacy Prammanasudh, Karrie Webb (AUS), Sun Young Yoo (KOR) 291; Chella Choi (KOR), Moira Dunn, Johanna Mundy (ENG), Eunjung Yi (KOR) 292; Helen Alfredsson (SWE), Il Mi Chung (KOR), Wendy Doolan (AUS), Candie Kung (TPE), Taylor Leon, Karin Sjodin (SWE), Aree Song (KOR), Monoko Ueda (JPN) 293; Marty Hart, Jee Young Lee (KOR), Becky Morgan (WAL), Se Ri Pak (KOR) 294; Katie Futcher, Carin Koch (SWE) 295; Meaghan Francella, Jamie Hullett, Teresa Lu (TPE) 296; Karine Icher (FRA) 297; Julieta Granada (PAR) 298; Marisa Baena (COL) 299; Jackie Gallagher-Smith 303

2008 McDonald's LPGA Championship Bulle Rock, Havre de Grace, MD   [6596–72]

Prize money: $2 million

1	Yani Tseng (TPE)*	73-70-65-68—276	$300000	18T	Lindsey Wright (AUS)	67-68-73-74—282	21,929
2	Maria Hjörth (SWE)	68-72-65-71—276	180180	25	Jimin Kang (KOR)	72-68-70-73—283	17,806
*Tseng won at the fourth extra hole					Kristy McPherson	73-70-72-68—283	17,806
3	Lorena Ochoa (MEX)	69-65-72-71—277	115911		Angela Stanford	72-71-67-73—283	17,806
	Annika Sörenstam (SWE)	70-68-68-71—277	115911		Momoko Ueda (JPN)	72-67-71-73—283	17,806
5	Laura Diaz	71-68-69-70—278	81,385	29	H J Choi (KOR)	69-74-71-70—284	14,896
6	Shi Hyun Ahn (KOR)	73-69-69-69—280	53,763		Eun-Hee Ji (KOR)	72-70-72-70—284	14,896
	Irene Cho (KOR)	72-68-69-71—280	53,763		Liselotte Neumann	70-72-71-71—284	14,896
	Kelli Kuehne	69-70-71-70—280	53,763		(SWE)		
	Morgan Pressel	73-69-70-68—280	53,673		Ji Young Oh (KOR)	69-68-72-75—284	14,896
10	Nicole Castrale	68-72-71-70—281	31,938		Karrie Webb (AUS)	71-71-69-73—284	14,896
	Paula Creamer	71-70-71-69—281	31,938	34	Louise Friberg (SWE)	70-73-73-69—285	11,887
	Jimin Jeong (KOR)	73-68-69-71—281	31,938		Sophie Gituel (FRA)	70-72-72-71—285	11,887
	Cristie Kerr	71-70-71-69—281	31,938		Young Kim (KOR)	69-73-69-74—285	11,887
	Mi Hyun Kim (KOR)	72-70-71-68—281	31,938		Brittany Lincicome	75-68-70-72—285	11,887
	Candie Kung (TPE)	70-72-70-69—281	31,938		Jane Park	72-69-70-74—285	11,887
	Seon Hwa Lee (KOR)	73-71-70-67—281	31,938		Suzann Pettersen (NOR)	71-68-74-72—285	11,887
	Giulia Sergas (ITA)	71-71-69-70—281	31,938	40	Il Mi Chung (KOR)	71-71-72-72—286	9,289
18	Marisa Baena (COL)	68-70-71-73—282	21,929		Michelle Ellis (AUS)	71-67-76-72—286	9,289
	Na Yeon Choi (KOR)	75-67-71-71—282	21,929		Hee-Won Han (KOR)	69-71-73-73—286	9,289
	Jeong Jang (KOR)	72-72-68-70—282	21,929		Amy Hung (TPE)	71-71-75-69—286	9,289
	Brittany Lang	70-67-71-74—282	21,929		Lorie Kane (CAN)	66-70-76-74—286	9,289
	Jee Young Lee (KOR)	70-69-65-78—282	21,929		Gloria Park (KOR)	70-69-71-76—286	9,289
	Jill McGill	72-70-72-68—282	21,929				

Other players who made the cut: Kyeong Bae (KOR), Karine Icher (FRA), Rachel Hetherington (AUS), Su A Kim (KOR), Carolina Llano (COL), Se Ri Pak (KOR), Inbee Park (KOR), Stacy Prammanasudh, Jennifer Rosales (PHI), Sherri Steinhauer 287; Wendy Doolan (AUS), Sandra Gal (GER) 288; Silvia Cavelleri (ITA), Shanshan Feng (CHN), Candy Hannemann (BRA), Jin Joo Hong (KOR), Michele Redman, Nancy Scranton, Karen Stupples (ENG) 289; Julieta Granada (PAR), Leta Lindley, Becky Lucidi, Mhairi McKay (SCO), Linda Wessberg (SWE) 290; Angela Park (BRA), 291; Charlotte Mayorkas, Young-A Yang (KOR) 292; Moira Dunn, Tracy Hanson, Soo-Yun Kang (KOR), Alena Sharp (CAN) 293; Meaghan Francella, Sun Young Yoo (KOR) 294; Danielle Downey 295; Jamie Hullett 297; Allison Fouch 299

Multiple winners

Since its inauguration in 1955, there have been 13 multiple winners of the LPGA Championship:

Mickey Wright (USA)	1958, 1960, 1961, 1963
Kathy Whitworth (USA)	1967, 1971, 1975
Nancy Lopez (USA)	1978, 1985, 1989
Patty Sheehan (USA)	1983, 1984, 1993
Annika Sörenstam (SWE)	2003, 2004, 2005
Se Ri Pak (KOR)	1998, 2002, 2006
Betsy Rawls (USA)	1959, 1969
Mary Mills (USA)	1964, 1973
Sandra Haynie (USA)	1965, 1974
Donna Caponi (USA)	1979, 1981
Laura Davies (ENG)	1994, 1996
Juli Inkster (USA)	1999, 2000
Yani Tseng (TPE)	2008, 2011

For the first decade of the championship, players from the USA won every title. They almost achieved a perfect ten for the next decade with only Canadian Sandra Post spoiling their record in 1968. US players maintained their dominance for the next two decades with seven and nine victories with England's Laura Davies spoiling their perfect ten in 1994, the first of her two LPGA victories.

During the following decade (1995–2004), the US victory tally fell to four with Europe coming a close second with Laura Davies' second title in 1996 and Swede Annika Sörenstam's two victories in 2003 and 2004 on her way to a record-breaking three in a row.

Thus far, in the first seven years of the current decade, honours are divided equally between Europe and Asia with three victories apiece with the US taking the remaining slot.

2007 McDonald's LPGA Championship Bulle Rock, Havre de Grace, MD   [6596–72]

Prize money: $2 million

1	Suzann Pettersen (NOR)	69-67-71-67—274	$300,000	21T	In-Kyung Kim (KOR)	73-70-71-71—285	20,585
2	Karrie Webb (AUS)	68-69-71-67—275	179,038	25	Wendy Doolan (AUS)	76-70-70-70—286	17,350
3	Ma On Min (KOR)	71-70-65-70—276	129,880		Pat Hurst	69-75-76-66—286	17,350
4	Lindsey Wright (AUS)	71-70-71-66—278	100,473		Jeong Jang (KOR)	73-71-71-71—286	17,350
5	Angela Park (BRA)	67-73-68-71—279	80,869		Birdie Kim (KOR)	67-71-73-75—286	17,350
6	Paula Creamer	71-68-73-68—280	53,422		Kim Saiki-Maloney	67-73-70-76—286	17,350
	Sophie Gustafson (SWE)	70-71-71-68—280	53,422	30	Laura Davies (ENG)	68-75-71-73—287	14,801
	Brittany Lincicome	69-69-73-69—280	53,422		Leta Lindley	76-69-72-70—287	14,801
	Lorena Ochoa (MEX)	71-71-69-69—280	53,422		Teresa Lu (TPE)	70-72-72-73—287	14,801
10	Nicole Castrale	70-73-68-70—281	35,730	33	Maria Hjörth (SWE)	69-75-74-70—288	13,069
	Jee Young Lee (KOR)	71-72-68-70—281	35,730		Se Ri Pak (KOR)	73-70-74-71—288	13,069
	Sarah Lee (KOR)	71-69-72-69—281	35,730		Angela Stanford	73-71-72-72—288	13,069
	Catriona Matthew (SCO)	71-69-74-67—281	35,730	36	Kate Golden	74-73-74-68—289	11,096
14	Morgan Pressel	68-71-70-73—282	30,192		Jimin Kang (KOR)	73-72-74-70—289	11,096
15	Mi Hyun Kim (KOR)	70-73-71-69—283	26,925		Seon Hwa Lee (KOR)	71-74-71-73—289	11,096
	Stacy Prammanasudh (AUS)	68-74-71-70—283	26,925		Nancy Scranton	73-73-74-69—289	11,096
	Annika Sörenstam (SWE)	70-69-73-71—283	26,925		Giulia Sergas (ITA)	69-74-74-72—289	11,096
18	Cristie Kerr	75-70-73-66—284	23,396	41	Irene Cho	72-72-76-70—290	9,037
	Siew-Ai Lim (MAS)	72-69-70-73—284	23,396		Johanna Head (ENG)	75-72-75-68—290	9,037
	Mhairi McKay (SCO)	71-69-74-70—284	23,396		Becky Morgan (WAL)	73-72-75-70—290	9,037
21	Shi Hyun Ahn (KOR)	71-73-71-70—285	20,585		Reilley Rankin	71-71-74-74—290	9,037
	Meaghan Francella	72-75-68-70—285	20,585		Sherri Turner	71-73-74-72—290	9,037
	Juli Inkster	73-73-73-66—285	20,585				

Other players who made the cut: Kyeong Bae (KOR), Dorothy Delasin, Kimberly Hall, Marcy Hart, Joo Mi Kim (KOR), Mena Lee (KOR), Ji-Young Oh (KOR), Gloria Park (KOR), Michele Redman, Linda Wessberg (SWE) 291; Christina Kim, Charlotte Mayorkas, Sherri Steinhauer 292; Rachel Hetherington (AUS), Karin Sjodin (SWE), Heather Young 293; Silvia Cavalleri (ITA), Katherine Hull (AUS), Lorie Kane (CAN), Yu Ping Lin (TPE), In-Bee Park (KOE), Young-A Yang (KOR) 294; Liselotte Neumann (SWE) 295; Maria Baena (COL), Il Mi Chung (KOR), Moira Dunn, Jackie Gallagher-Smith, Brittany Lang 296; Virada Nirapathpongporn (THA), Jane Park 297; Erica Blasberg, Eva Dahllof (SWE), Karen Davies, Vicki Goetze-Ackerman, Sung Ah Yim (KOR) 298; Laura Diaz 299; Meredith Duncan, Patricia Meunier-Lebouc (FRA) 299; Michelle Wie 309

2006 McDonald's LPGA Championship Bulle Rock, Havre de Grace, MD   [6596–72]

Prize money: $1.8 million

1	Se Ri Pak (KOR)*	71-69-71-69—280	$270,000	25T	Hee-Won Han (KOR)	68-73-75-71—287	16,207
2	Karrie Webb (AUS)	70-70-72-68—280	163,998		Heather Young	71-75-70-71—287	16,207
*Play-off: 1st extra hole: Pak 3, Webb 4				29	Il-Ne Chung (KOR)	71-72-75-70—288	13,558
3	Mi Hyun Kim (KOR)	68-71-71-71—281	105,501		Liselotte Neumann (SWE)	69-74-75-70—288	13,558
	Ai Miyazato (JPN)	68-72-69-72—281	105,501		Nancy Scranton	73-73-73-69—288	13,558
5	Shi Hyun Ahn (KOR)	69-70-71-72—282	57,464		Angela Stanford	70-76-72-70—288	13,558
9	Young Kim (KOR)	69-72-73-69—283	34,174		Kris Tamulis	73-71-75-69—288	13,558
	Lorena Ochoa (MEX)	68-72-71-72—283	34,174	34	Marisa Baena (COL)	72-72-74-71—289	11,044
	Reilley Rankin	68-73-74-68—283	34,174		Nicole Castrale	64-75-74-76—289	11,044
	Annika Sörenstam (SWE)	71-69-75-68—283	34,174		Rachel Hetherington (AUS)	70-72-74-73—289	11,044
	Sung Ah Yim (KOR)	72-68-74-69—283	34,174		Juli Inkster	70-74-73-72—289	11,044
14	Jee Young Lee (KOR)	70-71-70-73—284	26,847		Nina Reis (SWE)	70-73-73-73—289	11,044
	Meena Lee (KOR)	71-72-69-72—284	26,847	39	Beth Daniel	71-71-73-75—290	8,979
16	Silvia Cavalleri (ITA)	69-71-72-73—285	22,896		Allison Hanna	74-69-78-69—290	8,979
	Seon Hwa Lee (KOR)	67-74-75-69—285	22,896		Maria Hjörth (SWE)	68-77-73-72—290	89,79
	Sherri Steinhauer	70-71-71-73—285	22,896		Nicole Perrot (CHI)	70-71-76-73—290	8,979
	Wendy Ward	69-74-70-72—285	22,896		Michele Redman	73-72-73-72—290	8,979
20	Yuri Fudoh (JPN)	69-74-71-72—286	19,215	44	Julieta Grenada (PAR)	71-73-71-76—291	7,363
	Natalie Gulbis	72-73-72-69—286	19,215		Sophie Gustafson (SWE)	72-72-75-72—291	7,363
	Young Jo (KOR)	72-72-70-72—286	19,215		Candie Kung (TPE)	68-78-71-74—291	7,363
	Suzann Pettersen (NOR)	70-72-74-70—286	19,215		Yu Ping Lin (TPE)	74-72-72-73—291	7,363
	Lindsey Wright (AUS)	72-73-68-73—286	19,215		Jessica Reese-Quayle	73-73-72-73—291	7,363
25	Minea Blomqvist (FIN)	71-71-70-75—287	16,207				
	Laura Diaz	71-74-72-70—287	16,207				

Other players who made the cut: Paula Creamer, Rosie Jones, Carin Koch (SWE), Brittany Lincicome, Kim Saiki 292; Michelle Ellis (AUS), Jill McGill, Miriam Nagl (GER), Mikaela Parmlid (SWE), Jackie Gallagher-Smith, Jeong Jang (KOR), Teresa Lu (TPE) 294; Christina Kim, Siew-Ai Lim (MAS), Gloria Park (KOR), Karin Sjodin (SWE) 295; Laura Davies (ENG), Wendy Doolan (AUS), Birdie Kim (KOR), Sarah Lee (KOR) 296; Ashli Bunch, Dorothy Delasin, Morgan Pressel, Karen Stupples (ENG) 297; Kristi Albers 299; Moira Dunn 300; Jamie Fischer, Becky Iverson 302

2005 McDonald's LPGA Championship Bulle Rock, Havre de Grace, MD [6486–72]

Prize money: $1.8 million

1	Annika Sörenstam (SWE)	68-67-69-73—277	$270,000	20T	Laura Diaz	67-72-76-73—288	19,797
2	Michelle Wie (am)	69-71-71-69—280			Meena Lee (KOR)	70-71-72-75—288	19,797
3	Paula Creamer	68-73-74-67—282	140,517		Karrie Webb (AUS)	74-75-72-67—288	19,797
	Laura Davies (ENG)	67-70-74-71—282	140,517	25	Shi Hyun Ahn (KOR)	78-71-72-68—289	16,096
5	Natalie Gulbis	67-71-73-73—284	82,486		Kirsti Albers	70-72-73-74—289	16,096
	Lorena Ochoa (MEX)	72-72-68-72—284	82,486		Il Mi Chung (KOR)	71-68-79-71—289	16,096
7	Moira Dunn	71-68-72-74—285	43,993		Hee-Won Han (KOR)	73-74-72-70—289	16,096
	Pat Hurst	72-73-71-69—285	43,993		Leta Lindley	72-72-75-70—289	16,096
	Mi Hyun Kim (KOR)	69-75-74-67—285	43,993		Karen Stupples (ENG)	72-71-71-75—289	16,096
	Young Kim (KOR)	73-68-68-76—285	43,993	31	Rosie Jones	72-69-74-75—290	13,733
	Carin Koch (SWE)	74-70-69-72—285	43,993		Liselotte Neumann		
	Gloria Park (KOR)	71-71-72-71—285	43,993		(SWE)	70-71-74-75—290	13,733
13	Juli Inkster	75-71-71-69—286	29,309	33	Jamie Hullett	70-75-71-75—291	11,225
	Jeong Jang (KOR)	71-71-69-75—286	29,309		Jimin Kang (KOR)	73-74-72-72—291	11,225
	Candie Kung (TAI)	72-73-73-68—286	29,309		Cristie Kerr	74-72-67-78—291	11,225
16	Marisa Baena (COL)	70-69-73-75—287	23,899		Christina Kim	73-72-78-68—291	11,225
	Jennifer Rosales (PHI)	71-73-69-74—287	23,899		Brittany Lincicome	72-72-75-72—291	11,225
	Angela Stanford	69-73-73-72—287	23,899		Meg Mallon	74-69-76-72—291	11,225
	Lindsey Wright (AUS)	71-72-72-72—287	23,899		Janice Moodie (SCO)	73-72-74-72—291	11,225
20	Beth Bader	72-72-72-72—288	19,797		Stacy Prammanasudh	72-76-72-71—291	11,225
	Heather Bowie	72-71-71-74—288	19,797				

Other players who made the cut: Birdie Kim (KOR) 292; Rachel Hetherington (AUS), Hilary Lunke, Paula Marti (ESP), Joanne Morley (ENG) 293; Johanna Head (ENG), Lorie Kane (CAN), Aree Song (KOR) 294; Heather Daly-Donofrio, Catriona Matthew (SCO), Suzann Pettersen (NOR), Michele Redman, Kim Saiki 295; Dawn Coe-Jones (CAN), Beth Daniel, Wendy Doolan (AUS), Yu Ping Lin (TAI), Stephanie Louden, Jill McGill, Nicole Perrot (CHI), Nancy Scranton, Sung Ah Yim (KOR) 296; Tina Barrett, Patricia Baxter-Johnson, Tina Fischer (GER), Laurel Kean, Emilee Klein, Bernadette Luse, Sae-Hee Son (KOR), Kris Tschetter 297; Maria Hjörth (SWE) 298; Katie Allison, Catherine Cartwright, A J Eathorne (CAN), Katherine Hull (AUS), Reilley Rankin 299; Laurie Rinker, Nadina Taylor (AUS) 300; Candy Hannemann (BRA) 302; Barb Mucha 305.

2004 McDonald's LPGA Championship Du Pont CC, DE [6408–71]

Prize money: $1.6 million

1	Annika Sörenstam	68-67-64-72—271	$240,000	17T	Betsy King	76-70-70-68—284	18,654
	(SWE)				Se Ri Pak (KOR)	69-73-70-72—284	18,654
2	Shi Hyun Ahn (KOR)	69-70-69-66—274	144,780	23	Tina Barrett	75-71-68-71—285	14,596
3	Grace Park (KOR)	68-70-70-68—276	105,028		Jeong Jang (KOR)	71-71-71-72—285	14,596
4	Gloria Park (KOR)	67-72-68-71—278	73,322		Siew-Ai Lim (MAS)	72-70-71-72—285	14,596
	Angela Stanford	69-71-67-71—278	73,322		Stacy Prammanasudh	73-71-69-72—285	14,596
6	Juli Inkster	70-66-70-73—279	49,145		Kim Saiki	69-72-72-72—285	14,596
	Christina Kim	74-69-64-72—279	49,145		Sherri Steinhauer	69-72-74-70—285	14,596
8	Wendy Doolan (AUS)	73-70-65-72—280	35,538		Chiharu Yamaguchi	67-73-70-75—285	
	Soo-Yun Kang	69-68-71-72—280	35,538		(JPN)		14,596
	Lorena Ochoa (MEX)	71-67-67-75—280	35,538	30	Moira Dunn	68-74-72-72—286	10,631
11	Carin Koch (SWE)	69-71-68-73—281	28,734		Mi-Hyun Kim (KOR)	72-70-74-70—286	10,631
	Reilley Rankin	70-67-71-73—281	28,734		Young Kim (KOR)	70-73-74-69—286	10,631
13	Pat Hurst	69-69-75-69—282	24,466		Patricia Meunier-	71-70-76-69—286	
	Mhairi McKay (SCO)	72-69-69-72—282	24,466		Labouc (FRA)		10,631
	Jennifer Rosales (PHI)	66-70-74-72—282	24,466		Janice Moodie (SCO)	72-71-73-70—286	10,631
16	Meg Mallon	69-73-70-71—283	21,718		Aree Song (KOR)	71-72-69-74—286	10,631
17	Kristi Albers	70-74-69-71—284	18,654		Charlotta Sörenstam	74-70-70-72—286	
	Dawn Coe-Jones (CAN)	72-72-70-70—284	18,654		(SWE)		10,631
	Michelle Ellis (AUS)	72-70-69-73—284	18,654		Karen Stupples (ENG)	67-73-73-73—286	10,631
	Cristie Kerr	69-73-71-71—284	18,654		Wendy Ward	72-72-71-71—286	10,631

Other players who made the cut: Beth Daniel, Stephanie Louden (AUS), Karrie Webb (AUS) 287; Jean Bartholomew, Ashli Bunch, Laura Davies (ENG), Becky Iverson, Becky Morgan (WAL), Deb Richard, Karen Pearce (AUS) 289; Heather Daly-Donofrio, Hee-Won Han (KOR), Lorie Kane (CAN), Yu Ping Lin (TPE), Kelly Robbins, Giulia Sergas (ITA), Rachel Teske (AUS) 290; Pat Bradley, Diana D'Alessio, Kate Golden, Jamie Hullett, Emilee Klein 291; Helen Alfredsson (SWE), Natalie Gulbis, Catriona Matthew (SCO) 292; Amy Fruhwirth, Tammy Green, Seol-An Jeon (KOR), Angela Jerman, Candie Kung (TPE), Soo Young Moon (KOR) 293; Isabelle Beisiegel (CAN), Vicki Goetz-Ackerman, Jill McGill, Dotty Pepper 294; Jenna Daniels, Sophie Gustafson (SWE), Kim Williams 295; Candy Hannemann (BRA) 296; Jackie Gallagher-Smith 297; Heather Bowie 299.

2003 McDonald's LPGA Championship Du Pont CC, DE   [6408–71]

Prize money: $1.6 million

1	Annika Sörenstam (SWE)*	70-64-72-72—278	$240,000	20	Donna Andrews	73-70-70-74—287	16,719
					Tina Barrett	76-69-71-71—287	16,719
2	Grace Park (KOR)	69-72-70-67—278	147,934		Michelle Ellis (AUS)	73-70-71-73—287	16,719
*Sörenstam won at the first extra hole					Natalie Gulbis	71-69-78-69—287	16,719
3	Beth Daniel	71-71-70-72—284	85718		Kelli Kuehne	73-73-65-76—287	16,719
	Rosie Jones	73-68-72-71—284	85,718		Lorena Ochoa (MEX)	72-72-71-72—287	16,719
	Rachel Teske (AUS)	69-70-74-71—284	85,718		Karen Stupples (ENG)	73-73-71-70—287	16,719
6	Kate Golden	72-70-68-75—285	41,873	27	Danielle Ammaccapane	74-72-74-68—288	13,769
	Young Kim (KOR)	70-73-72-70—285	41,873		Meg Mallon	74-69-70-75—288	13,769
	JoAnne Mills (AUS)	68-73-75-69—285	41,873		Angela Stanford	72-73-71-72—288	13,769
	Becky Morgan (WAL)	73-70-70-72—285	41,873	30	Laura Diaz	73-70-75-71—289	11,987
	Young-A Yang (KOR)	73-74-69-69—285	41,873		Tracy Hanson	71-77-70-71—289	11,987
11	Akiko Fukushima (JPN)	72-68-74-72—286	24,037		Mi-Hyun Kim (KOR)	72-72-71-74—289	11,987
	Hee-Wan Han (KOR)	67-69-74-76—286	24,037		Deb Richard	75-71-74-69—289	11,987
	Jeong Jang (KOR)	72-73-69-72—286	24,037	34	Moira Dunn	78-70-72-70—290	10,367
	Angela Jerman	73-72-69-72—286	24,037		Lorie Kane (CAN)	72-75-70-73—290	10,367
	Patricia Meunier-Lebouc (FRA)	75-69-72-70—286	24,037		Cristie Kerr	74-69-75-72—290	10,367
	Suzann Pettersen (NOR)	70-71-75-70—286	24,037	37	Juli Inkster	71-72-71-77—291	8,970
	Michele Redman	74-70-69-73—286	24,037		Hilary Lunke	72-70-75-74—291	8,970
	Jennifer Rosales (PHI)	74-68-74-70—286	24,037		Catriona Matthew (SCO)	72-73-75-71—291	8,970
	Wendy Ward	68-69-75-74—286	24,037		Jan Stephenson (AUS)	74-72-69-76—291	8,970

Other players who made the cut: Jill McGill, Terry-Jo Myers 292; Vicki Goetze-Ackerman, Pat Hurst, Giulia Sergas (ITA) 293; Marisa Baena (COL), Brandie Burton, Jung Yeon Lee (KOR), Se Ri Pak (KOR), Leslie Spalding 294; Yu Ping Lin (TPE), Kathryn Marshall (SCO), Joanne Morley (ENG) 295; Dorothy Delasin (PHI), Kim Saiki 296; Dawn Coe-Jones (CAN), Jane Crafter (AUS), Wendy Doolan (AUS), Jackie Gallagher-Smith, Karrie Webb (AUS) 297; Fiona Pike (AUS) 298; Heather Bowie 299; Marnie McGuire (NZL) 300; Mitzi Edge, Marcy Hart, Michelle McGann 301; Marilyn Lovander, Liselotte Neumann (SWE), Dottie Pepper 304; Kim Williams 306

2002 McDonald's LPGA Championship Du Pont CC, DE   [6408–71]

Prize money: $1.4 million

1	Se Ri Pak (KOR)	71-70-68-70—279	$225,000	20T	Barb Mucha	70-73-75-75—293	16.950
2	Beth Daniel	67-70-68-77—282	136.987	22	Silvia Cavalleri (ITA)	72-73-73-76—294	15.450
3	Annika Sörenstam (SWE)	70-76-73-65—284	99.375		Maria Hjörth (SWE)	78-70-75-71—294	15.450
					Kelly Robbins	70-75-74-75—294	15.450
4	Juli Inkster	69-75-70-71—285	69.375	25	Danielle Ammaccapane	73-76-73-73—295	12.543
	Karrie Webb (AUS)	68-71-72-74—285	69.375		Brandie Burton	74-76-74-71—295	12.543
6	Carin Koch (SWE)	68-73-73-72—286	46,500		Vicki Goetze-Ackerman	72-72-74-77—295	12.543
	Michele Redman	74-69-70-73—286	46,500		Tammie Green	70-78-73-74—295	12.543
8	Catriona Matthew (SCO)	70-73-75-70—288	37.125		Leta Lindley	72-77-71-75—295	12.543
					Kathryn Marshall (SCO)	73-73-72-77—295	12.543
9	Kristi Albers	74-73-73-70—290	30.625		Gloria Park (KOR)	75-72-73-75—295	12.543
	Michelle McGann	71-72-72-75—290	30.625		Kris Tschetter	74-75-75-71—295	12.543
	Karen Stupples (ENG)	75-70-70-75—290	30.625	33	Eva Dahllof (SWE)	75-73-75-73—296	9.056
12	Meg Mallon	73-72-76-70—291	24.650		Dorothy Delasin (PHI)	79-68-73-76—296	9.056
	Kim Saiki	71-71-69-80—291	24.650		Moira Dunn	74-75-75-72—296	9.056
	Karen Weiss	70-74-75-72—291	24.650		Michelle Ellis (AUS)	72-77-74-73—296	9.056
15	Akiki Fukushima (JPN)	71-71-76-74—292	19.650		Lorie Kane (CAN)	70-74-76-76—296	9.056
	Natalie Gulbis	72-72-75-73—292	19.650		Mi Hyun Kim (KOR)	77-71-72-76—296	90,56
	Kelli Kuehne	71-75-74-72—292	19.650		Charlotta Sörenstam (SWE)	75-73-74-74—296	90,56
	Grace Park (KOR)	72-73-73-74—292	19.650		Sherri Turner	74-73-76-73—296	90,56
	Rachel Teske (AUS)	72-71-77-72—292	19.650				
20	Laura Diaz	73-71-71-78—293	16.950				

Other players who made the cut: Jane Crafter (AUS), Heather Daly-Donofrio, Tracy Hanson, Pat Hurst, Cristie Kerr, Mhairi McKay (SCO) 297; Angela Buzminski, Jackie Gallagher-Smith, Betsy King, Joanne Morley (ENG), Jennifer Rosales (PHI) 298; Beth Bauer, Jenna Daniels, Michelle Estill, Liselotte Neumann (SWE), Susie Parry 299; Hee-Won Han (KOR), Jeong Jang (KOR) 300; Stephanie Keever, Angela Stanford 301; Denise Killeen, Marnie McGuire (NZL), Patricia Meunier-Lebouc 302; Emilee Klein 303; Becky Iverson, Val Skinner 304; Chris Johnson 305; A J Eathorne (CAN) 307; Karen Pearce 308; Alicia Dibos (PER), Shiho Katano (JPN) 309

LPGA Championship History

The Championship was known simply as the LPGA Championship from its inauguration in 1955 until 1987. It was sponsored by Mazda from 1988 until 1993 when the sponsorship was taken over by McDonald's. Only in the first year was it decided by match-play when Beverly Hanson beat Louise Suggs in the final.

1955	B Hanson	Orchard Ridge	4 and 3
1956	M Hagge*	Forest Lake	291
*After a play-off with P Berg			
1957	L Suggs	Churchill Valley	285
1958	M Wright	Churchill CC	288
1959	B Rawls	Churchill CC	288
1960	M Wright	French Lick	292
1961	M Wright	Stardust	287
1962	J Kimball	Stardust	282
1963	M Wright	Stardust	294
1964	M Mills	Stardust	278
1965	S Haynie	Stardust	279
1966	G Ehret	Stardust	282
1967	K Whitworth	Pleasant Valley	284
1968	S Post*	Pleasant Valley	294
*After a play-off with K Whitworth			
1969	B Rawls	Concord	293
1970	S Englehorn*	Pleasant Valley	285
*After a play-off with K Whitworth			
1971	K Whitworth	Pleasant Valley	288
1972	K Ahern	Pleasant Valley	293
1973	M Mills	Pleasant Valley	288
1974	S Haynie	Pleasant Valley	288
1975	K Whitworth	Pine Ridge	288
1976	B Burfeindt	Pine Ridge	287
1977	C Higuchi (JPN)	Bay Tree	279
1978	N Lopez	Kings Island	275
1979	D Caponi	Kings Island	279
1980	S Little (SA)	Kings Island	285
1981	D Caponi	Kings Island	280
1982	J Stephenson (AUS)	Kings Island	279
1983	P Sheehan	Kings Island	279
1984	P Sheehan	Kings Island	272
1985	N Lopez	Kings Island	273
1986	P Bradley	Kings Island	277

1987	J Geddes	Kings Island	275
1988	S Turner	Kings Island	281
1989	N Lopez	Kings Island	274
1990	B Daniel	Bethesda	280
1991	M Mallon	Bethesda	274
1992	B King	Bethesda	267
1993	P Sheehan	Bethesda	275
1994	L Davies (ENG)	Wilmington, Delaware	275
1995	K Robbins	Wilmington, Delaware	274
1996	L Davies (ENG)	Wilmington, Delaware	213
Reduced to 54 holes – bad weather			
1997	C Johnson	Wilmington, Delaware	281
1998	Se Ri Pak (KOR)	Wilmington, Delaware	273
1999	J Inkster	Wilmington, Delaware	268
2000	J Inkster*	Wilmington, Delaware	281
Beat S Croce (ITA) at the second extra hole			
2001	K Webb (AUS)	Wilmington, Delaware	270
2002	Se Ri Pak (KOR)	Wilmington, Delaware	279
2003	A Sörenstam (SWE)*	Wilmington, Delaware	271
Beat G Park (KOR) at the first extra hole			
2004	A Sörenstam (SWE)	Wilmington, Delaware	271
2005	A Sörenstam (SWE)	Bulle Rock, MD	277
2006	Se Ri Pak (KOR)*	Bulle Rock, MD	280
Beat K Webb (AUS) at first extra hole			
2007	S Pettersen (NOR)	Bulle Rock, MD	274
2008	Y Tseng (TPE)*	Bulle Rock, MD	278
Beat M Hjörth (SWE) at the fourth extra hole			
2009	A Nordqvist (SWE)	Bulle Rock, MD	273
2010	C Kerr	Locust Hill, Pitsford, NY	269
2011	Y Tseng (TPE)	Locust Hill, Pitsford, NY	269

What is the answer?

Q: My ball was lying on the fairway, and, in taking a practice swing, I accidentally moved it. Do I incur a penalty?

A: Although you did not have the intention of making a stroke, you caused your ball to move so you incur a one stroke penalty and must replace the ball to its original spot before playing on.

Kraft Nabisco Championship

formerly known as the Nabisco Dinah Shore   March 31–April 3

Deserved major victory for courageous Stacy

Overhauls Yani Tseng on dramatic last day at Kraft Nabisco

Having already overcome long-standing back problems caused by scoliosis, perhaps it was no surprise Stacy Lewis demonstrated exactly the brand of patience and fortitude needed to win a major championship when she held off a challenge from Yani Tseng, the world No 1, to earn her first victory as a professional at the Kraft Nabisco.

Stacy Lewis

The 26-year-old American followed in the footsteps at Mission Hills of Helen Alfredsson in 1993 and Morgan Pressel in 2007 by mounting the winner's podium for the first time in a major. In what turned out to be a morale boosting tournament for women's golf in America – five of the first six were from the USA – Lewis carded four consecutive sub-par rounds to post the winning total of 13-under-par 275, and collect the winner's cheque for $300,000.

A member of the US Curtis Cup side which won the trophy at St Andrews in 2008, she turned professional later that year and immediately made an impact in the paid ranks by finishing third in the US Women's Open. A hugely successful amateur golfer, she made her way in the game in spite of wearing a back brace for 18 hours a day to correct the curvature in her spine.

Eventually she underwent surgery which placed a titanium rod and screws in her back. A devout Christian, she found her faith a comfort when her grandfather died on the eve of the championship. "Other players had told me, you'll win when it's your time and you'll win when it's the right time," she reflected. "I had a good feeling coming into the week because I love this golf course and I've played well here before. Even when my grandfather died, I felt there was a reason that happened this week and there's a reason my parents were here. It all worked out the way it should, I think."

The obvious exception to that positive spin for the Lewis family came when her mother Carol joined Stacy in the traditional Kraft Nabisco celebration by jumping into the lake beside the 18th. Unfortunately for Carol, the leap broke her left leg when she struck the bottom of the pond.

Her daughter, meanwhile, rose to the top of the leaderboard on the first day of play by carding a pace-setting 66. While women's golf wanted a hot start to the majors, soaring temperatures in the California desert made life tricky. As the thermometer tipped 100 degrees and the course at Mission Hills turned fast and furious – caddies were allowed to remove their overalls in the sweltering heat – it was a source of surprise to most onlookers that the best scores of the first round were recorded in the afternoon when the greens were even firmer than they had been in the morning.

Lewis and Brittany Lincicome, two friends who had gone for dinner together on the eve of the championship, were again side by side at the top of the leaderboard after mastering the challenging conditions and posting six under par scores. Having responded to her only bogey of the day on the 12th by reeling off three consecutive birdies, Lewis felt the lack of wind was probably a help to the afternoon starters. She'd made swing changes over the winter which had added 25 yards or so to her drives. Fitter and stronger, the eventual champion was drawing the benefits from a more efficient action.

Lincicome reckoned the trick in Rancho Mirage was to allow for plenty of release when the ball landed, even when hitting wedges into the greens. "They were super firm," said the American. "They were already firm when we got here [earlier in the week]. You just have to allow the ball to release and know it's going to release, even with a lob wedge or sand wedge. I'm someone who can normally can spin the ball pretty good, but I was allowing for a lot of release with the wedges."

A stroke behind the joint leaders on 67 was the 25-year-old German golfer, Sandra Gal, who played junior golf with world No.1 Martin Kaymer. She kept up the good form she'd shown in nearby Los Angeles the week before when she defeated Jiyai Shin and won for the first time on the LPGA Tour at the Kia Classic. Although she has an Irish caddie, Royston Clarke on the bag, the daughter of Czech parents has spent her career in America and has never been a member of the Ladies European Tour. When asked about the Solheim Cup, she smiled: "There is always a way if you show exceptional qualities ..."

Playing with Tseng, the defending champion, Gal has started to believe she can now compete with the world's best players, though she wasn't able to sustain a bright start and eventually fell back to finish 15th with scores of 74, 75 and 73. Japan's Mika Miyazato, meanwhile, also posted 67 in the first round thanks to five birdies and no dropped shots. Along with two other Japanese players, Ai Miyazato and Momoka Ueda, she had been active in setting up a website to raise funds for the victims of the tsunami in Japan.

On Friday, Lewis continued to press forward, totting up birdies at the first, second, 13th and 14th holes before carding a single bogey at the 12th. Her 69 for nine under par at the halfway mark was sufficient to establish a three stroke lead over Lincicome, the joint first round leader. For all she posted a good number, Lewis felt some way short of her best form and had to rely on her short game to save par when she struggled for a run of holes between the sixth and ninth. "I was all over the place, but I made some really good up and downs and stayed really patient on the back nine," she said. "I was fortunate to get away with a couple of pars that I probably shouldn't have and posted a good number."

Lincicome was not so fortunate and undid the good work of four birdies with four bogeys to match the par of 72. She didn't fare any better on the week-end and eventually finished in a share of 13th.

The key move in the second round was made by the World No 1 and defending champion who took advantage of the firm fairways by thrashing a 320 yard drive on the third hole, Even her 3 wood was running out to 270 yards. Tseng's 68 included seven birdies and left the three time major champion feeling like she could win a fourth. At halfway she was tied with Lincicombe and Jane Park.

Having finished the first round in a tie for 54th place, Michelle Wie was also on the move in the second round, carding a blistering outward half of 32 in an impressive 67 which included half-a-dozen birdies and just one bogey. Although she thought the weather was more humid than the previous day and the conditions every bit as testing, Wie was able to move up a gear or two and push into contention. This was in spite of an unsettling start when she struck a child with an off line tee shot. "I never felt so horrible about a shot ever," she lamented. "I felt so bad about hitting that poor little girl."

All told, 75 players made the cut which fell on the five-over-par mark of 149. One notable who missed out was Cristie Kerr. The winner of two major titles had made 36 consecutive cuts in major championships before the Kraft Nabisco.

Tseng's standing early in 2011 as the best player in women's golf became more apparent on Saturday when she erased the three shot lead enjoyed by Lewis and established a two shot advantage of her own. The Taiwanese golfer's six under round of 66 took her to 12 under for the championship as she sought to become only the eighth woman to win the Kraft Nabisco more than once.

Thrilled to card six birdies and keep a card clear of dropped shots, Tseng, who had already won four times in 2011, spoke of a growing sense of faith in her own ability. Hitting more fairways, finding more greens in regulation and setting up more birdie opportunities, it was little wonder the Taiwanese golfer found it easy to keep smiling at the week-end. Remembering how she won the Ricoh British Women's Open in 2010 as the leader after 54 holes, the 22-year-old planned to rely on that experience to see her through in Rancho Mirage. Although she didn't sleep well and felt nervous at Birkdale, Tseng kept telling herself: "I can do this". It was a mantra she was unable to to heed at Mission Hills the following day, however, when she dropped four strokes to par.

Although she'd lost the 54 hole lead, Lewis, who carded 71, was closest to Tseng after three consecutive sub-par rounds. She'd had to scramble to save par on many holes because of a wayward day with the driver. "It's really frustrating to have to make those putts hole after hole, and to be hacking out of the rough," recalled the American. "I mean I just made it really hard on myself, but I was lucky to get away with shooting under par."

Lewis knows the importance of resolve in the majors and was able to capitalise on her fortitude in the final round when she duelled with Tseng for supremacy. Both golfers birdied the second hole and, after Lewis birdied the third by holing a 30 foot putt, there was never more than a shot between them until the ninth hole. On this pivotal par 5, Lewis made an eight foot putt for birdie to punish Tseng's bogey. The impact of this two shot swing helped Lewis to take charge on the back nine.

On what was a cooler, blustery afternoon, Lewis did spill a shot on the 15th but held her nerve and holed an improbable 20 footer with a lot of break for par on the 17th. It was the stroke which effectively sealed her first professional victory. Lewis' 69 matched the low score of the last day – and with Tseng recording a 74 the young American's three year wait for glory was over.

First Round	Second Round	Third Round	Fourth Round
−6 Stacy Lewis	−9 Stacy Lewis	−12 Yani Tseng	−13 Stacy Lewis
−6 Brittany Lincicome	−6 Yani Tseng	−10 Stacy Lewis	−10 Yani Tseng
−5 Sandra Gal	−6 Brittany Lincicome	−8 Morgan Pressel	−4 Morgan Pressel
−5 Mika Miyazato	−6 Jane Park	−6 Michelle Wie	−4 Angela Stanford
−4 Chie Arimura	−5 Amy Yang	−5 Angela Stanford	−4 Katie Futcher
−4 Jane Park	−5 Morgan Pressel	−4 Mika Miyazato	−3 Michelle Wie
−3 Karrie Webb	−4 Sophie Gustafson	−4 Chie Arimura	−2 Julieta Granada
−2 Yani Tseng	−3 Michelle Wie	−4 Brittany Lincicome	−2 Chie Arimura
−2 Morgan Pressel	−3 Jimin Kang		−2 Mika Miyazato

Kraft Nabisco Championship   *Mission Hills CC, Rancho Mirage, CA*   [6238–72]

Prize money: $2m. Final field of 113 players (including six amateurs), of whom 75 (including one amateur) made the final half-way cut on 149 or less.   *(Players are of American nationality unless stated)*

1	Stacy Lewis	66-69-71-69—275	$300,000
2	Yani Tseng (TPE)	70-68-66-74—278	184,255
3	Katie Futcher	70-71-74-69—284	106,763
	Angela Stanford	72-72-67-73—284	106,763
	Morgan Pressel	70-69-69-76—284	106,763
6	Michelle Wie	74-67-69-75—285	68,093
7	Julieta Granada (PAR)	72-70-75-69—286	50,608
	Chie Arimura (JPN)	68-73-71-74—286	50,608
	Mika Miyazato (JPN)	67-75-70-74—286	50,608
10	In-Kyung Kim (KOR)	75-67-75-70—287	37,997
	Anna Nordqvist (SWE)	69-74-73-71—287	37,997
	Se Ri Pak (KOR)	73-71-71-72—287	37,997
13	Karrie Webb (AUS)	69-74-74-71—288	32,079
	Brittany Lincicome	66-72-74-76—288	32,079
15	Christel Boeljon (NED)	74-73-71-71—289	27,035
	Juli Inkster	73-73-71-72—289	27,035
	Sandra Gal (GER)	67-74-75-73—289	27,035
	Sophie Gustafson (SWE)	72-68-74-75—289	27,035
19	Stacy Prammanasudh	71-75-73-71—290	21,992
	Suzann Pettersen (NOR)	75-71-72-72—290	21,992
	Paula Creamer	73-74-70-73—290	21,992
	Maria Hjorth (SWE)	75-70-72-73—290	21,992
	Amy Yang (KOR)	70-69-76-75—290	21,992
	Jimin Kang (KOR)	72-69-72-77—290	21,992
25	Meaghan Francella	75-71-73-72—291	18,562
	Ariya Jutanugarn (THA) (am)	74-73-71-73—291	
	Alena Sharp (CAN)	71-73-73-74—291	18,562
	Eun-Hee Ji (KOR)	75-71-69-76—291	18,562
29	Inbee Park (KOR)	76-72-71-73—292	16,166
	Jiyai Shin (KOR)	73-72-74-73—292	16,166
	Leta Lindley	72-71-75-74—292	16,166
	Karen Stupples (ENG)	71-72-71-78—292	16,166
33	Song-Hee Kim (KOR)	71-74-76-72—293	12,698
	Ai Miyazato (JPN)	71-75-73-74—293	12,698
	Melissa Reid (ENG)	71-75-73-74—293	12,698
	Hee Kyung Seo (KOR)	76-71-72-74—293	12,698
	Momoko Ueda (JPN)	70-76-73-74—293	12,698
	Becky Morgan (WAL)	72-73-73-75—293	12,698
	Wendy Ward	70-71-77-75—293	12,698
	Mi Hyun Kim (KOR)	70-75-69-79—293	12,698
41	Karine Icher (FRA)	74-72-76-72—294	9,499
	Amanda Blumenherst	74-73-73-74—294	9,499
	Kristy McPherson	74-74-72-74—294	9,499
	So Yeon Ryu (KOR)	75-72-73-74—294	9,499
	Vicky Hurst	72-77-69-76—294	9,499
	Jane Park	68-70-76-80—294	9,499
47	Laura Diaz	74-73-77-71—295	7,666
	Mariajo Uribe (COL)	70-75-75-75—295	7,666
	Na Yeon Choi (KOR)	73-74-72-76—295	7,666
	Natalie Gulbis	73-73-73-76—295	7,666
	Seon Hwa Lee (KOR)	72-70-75-78—295	7,666
52	Azahara Munoz (ESP)	76-73-76-71—296	6,658
	Lindsey Wright (AUS)	76-73-72-75—296	6,658
	Maria Hernandez (ESP)	73-74-72-77—296	6,658
55	Shanshan Feng (CHN)	72-77-73-75—297	6,154
	Reilley Rankin	69-75-75-78—297	6,154
57	Shi Hyun Ahn (KOR)	73-75-76-74—298	5,447

57T	Laura Davies (ENG)	73-74-75-76—298	5,447
	Paige Mackenzie	72-75-75-76—298	5,447
	Brittany Lang	75-73-72-78—298	5,447
	Gwładys Nocera (FRA)	72-72-76-78—298	5,447
62	Candie Kung (TPE)	78-70-77-74—299	4,792
	Kyeong Bae (KOR)	73-72-77-77—299	4,792
	Stephanie Sherlock (CAN)	73-75-73-78—299	4,792
	Sun Young Yoo (KOR)	74-68-77-80—299	4,792
66	Nicole Castrale	76-71-79-74—300	4,439
	Mindy Kim (KOR)	71-75-80-74—300	4,439
	Shiho Oyama (JPN)	71-77-76-76—300	4,439
69	Katherine Hull (AUS)	76-73-74-78—301	4,236
70	Hee Young Park (KOR)	72-76-80-74—302	4,086
	Lee-Anne Pace (RSA)	76-72-70-84—302	4,086
72	Pornanong Phatlum (THA)	75-74-81-74—304	3,986
73	Sarah Jane Smith	72-72-85-76—305	3,933
74	Yukari Baba (JPN)	74-75-79-79—307	3,883
75	Eunjung Yi (KOR)	74-75-80-80—309	3,833

The following players missed the cut.

76	Hee-Won Han (KOR)	74-76—150		95	Cydney Clanton (am)	77-76—153
	Cristie Kerr	78-72—150			Louise Friberg (SWE)	79-74—153
	Christina Kim	76-74—150			Mina Harigae	78-75—153
	Jee Young Lee (KOR)	77-73—150			Marcy Hart	71-82—153
	Meena Lee (KOR)	74-76—150			Pernilla Lindberg (SWE)	74-79—153
	Teresa Lu (TPE)	75-75—150			Jennifer Rosales (PHI)	77-76—153
	Grace Park (KOR)	76-74—150			Heather Bowie Young	74-79—153
83	Anna Grzebien	77-74—151		102	Yuri Fudoh (JPN)	77-77—154
	M J Hur (KOR)	77-74—151			Amy Hung (TPE)	77-77—154
	Mi-Jeong Jeon (KOR)	80-71—151			Danielle Kang (am)	77-77—154
	Haeji Kang (KOR)	73-78—151			Ji Young Oh (KOR)	78-76—154
	Na On Min (KOR)	72-79—151		106	Chella Choi (KOR)	74-81—155
	Beatriz Recari (ESP)	74-77—151			Karin Sjodin (SWE)	78-77—155
	Michele Redman	73-78—151		108	Lisa McCloskey (am)	76-81—157
	Kris Tamulis	77-74—151			Sherri Steinhauer	81-76—157
91	Shin-Ae Ahn (KOR)	80-72—152		110	Meghan Stasi (am)	79-83—162
	Helen Alfredsson (SWE)	76-76—152		111	Silvia Cavalleri (ITA)	78-85—163
	Pat Hurst	74-78—152			Giulia Sergas (ITA)	75 WD
	Catriona Matthew (SCO)	79-73—152			Kristen Park (am)	0 DQ

Multiple winners

Since its classification as a major in 1983, there have been six multiple winners of the Kraft Nabisco Championship:

Amy Alcott (USA)	1983, 1988, 1991
Betsy King (USA)	1987, 1990, 1997
Annika Sörenstam (SWE)	2001, 2002, 2005
Juli Inkster (USA)	1984, 1989
Dottie Pepper (USA)	1992, 1999
Karrie Webb (AUS)	2000, 2006

From 1983 to the present the victory tallies by nationality are: USA 19, Sweden four, Australia two, France, Korea, Mexico and Taiwan one apiece.

2010 Kraft Nabisco Championship   [6702–72]
Prize money: $2 million

1	Yani Tseng (TPE)	69-71-67-68—275	$300,000	21	Brittany Lincicome	70-74-72-73—289	21,939
2	Suzann Pettersen (NOR)	67-73-67-69—276	183,814		Hee Kyung Seo (KOR)	72-73-76-68—289	21,939
3	Song-Hee Kim (KOR)	69-68-72-70—279	133,344		Jennifer Song (KOR) (am)	71-71-76-71—289	
4	Lorena Ochoa (MEX)	68-70-71-73—282	103,152	24	Katherine Hull (AUS)	72-71-72-75—290	20,329
5	Cristie Kerr	71-67-74-72—284	64,408		Gwladys Nocera (FRA)	75-70-71-74—290	20,329
	Jiyai Shin (KOR)	72-72-69-71—284	64,408		Alexis Thompson (am)	74-72-73-71—290	
	Karen Stupples (ENG)	69-69-68-78—284	64,408	27	Na Yeon Choi (KOR)	74-73-72-72—291	17,151
	Karrie Webb (AUS)	69-70-72-73—284	64,408		Jimin Kang (KOR)	72-74-72-73—291	17,151
9	Chie Arimura (JPN)	73-72-68-72—285	44,784		Na On Min (KOR)	69-75-71-76—291	17,151
10	Sophie Gusatafson (SWE)	70-73-70-73—286	35,544		Momoko Ueda (JPN)	72-78-68-73—291	17,151
	Brittany Lang	72-71-69-74—286	35,544		Michelle Wie	71-71-71-78—291	17,151
	Anna Nordqvist (SWE)	74-72-69-71—286	35,544		Amy Yang (KOR)	75-73-72-71—291	17,151
	Grace Park (KOR)	71-74-68-73—286	35,544		Sakura Yokomina (JPN)	70-71-72-78—291	17,151
	Inbee Park (KOR)	73-74-70-69—286	35,544	34	Heather Bowie Young	76-74-72-70—292	13,183
15	Catriona Matthew (SCO)	73-74-67-73—287	26,971		Sandra Gal (GER)	72-70-80-70—292	13,183
	Se Ri Pak (KOR)	79-71-67-70—287	26,971		Hee-Won Han (KOR)	71-76-72-73—292	13,183
	Hee Young Park (KOR)	73-71-70-73—287	26,971		Paige Mackenzie	75-74-70-73—292	13,183
	Angela Stanford	78-68-69-72—287	26,971		Kirsty McPherson	72-72-78-70—292	13,183
19	Stacy Lewis	71-68-75-74—288	23,549		Melissa Reid (ENG)	73-75-71-73—292	13,183
	Morgan Pressel	71-72-72-73—288	23,549				

Other players who made the cut: Mi-Jeong Jeon (KOR), Jee Young Lee (KOR), Mika Miyazato (JPN), Shinobu Moromizato (JPN) 293; Vicky Hurst, In-Kyung Ki, (KOR), Teresa Lu (TPE), Jane Park 294; Laura Davies (ENG), Katie Futcher, Pat Hurst, Jeong Jang (KOR), Haeji Kang (KOR), Sarah Lee (KOR), Stacy Prammanasudh, Michele Redman 295; Shi Hyun Ahn (KOR), Hye Jung Choi (KOR), Karine Icher (FRA), Mi Hyun Kim (KOR), Meena Lee (KOR), Seon Hwa Lee (KOR), Giulia Sergas (ITA), Alena Sharp (CAN) 296; Louise Friberg (SWE), Carin Koch (SWE), So Yeon Ryu (KOR) 297; Jessica Korda (am), Sherri Steinhauer 298; Candie Kung (TPE), Yuko Mitsuka (JPN), Eunjung Yi (KOR) 299; Becky Brewerton (WAL), Allison Fouch, Jennifer Rosales (PHI) 300; Julieta Granada (PAR), Eun-Hee Ji (KOR) 301; Ilmi Chung (KOR), Becky Morgan (WAL) 303; Jennifer Johnson (am) 305

2009 Kraft Nabisco Championship   [6673–72]
Prize money: $2 million

1	Brittany Lincicome	66-74-70-69—279	$300,000	21	Tiffany Joh (am)	71-75-73-71—290	
2	Cristie Kerr	71-68-70-71—280	161,853		Song-Hee Kim (KOR)	69-78-72-71—290	22,392
	Kristy McPherson	68-70-70-72—280	161,853		Ji-Yai Shin (KOR)	72-76-71-71—290	22,392
4	Lindsey Wright (AUS)	70-71-71-70—282	105,281		Alexis Thompson (am)	72-72-77-69—290	
5	Meaghan Francella	72-73-69-69—283	77,036	25	Nicole Castrale	71-75-73-72—291	20,372
	Suzann Pettersen (NOR)	71-72-74-66—283	77,036		Allison Fouch	76-73-69-73—291	20,372
7	Christina Kim	69-69-75-72—285	58,034		Sakura Yokomine (JPN)	72-73-74-72—291	20,372
8	Katherine Hull (AUS)	69-74-71-72—286	44,167	28	Hee-Won Han (KOR)	75-73-72-72—292	18,540
	Pat Hurst	71-71-73-71—286	44,167		In-Kyung Kim (KOR)	70-73-75-74—292	18,540
	Jimin Kang (KOR)	71-70-71-74—286	44,167	30	Young Kim (KOR)	76-71-75-71—293	15,835
	Karrie Webb (AUS)	73-72-72-69—286	44,167		Candie Kung (TPE)	72-73-74-74—293	15,835
12	Helen Alfredsson (SWE)	72-70-72-73—287	31,841		Seon Hwa Lee (KOR)	74-77-69-73—293	15,835
	Lorena Ochoa (MEX)	73-73-72-69—287	31,841		Janice Moodie (SCO)	75-73-74-71—293	15,835
	Michele Redman	72-73-72-70—287	31,841		Jane Park	74-76-68-75—293	15,835
	Angela Stanford	67-75-74-71—287	31,841		Momoko Ueda (JPN)	76-72-75-70—293	15,835
	Sun Young Yoo (KOR)	70-78-73-66—287	31,841	36	Yuri Fudoh (JPN)	71-76-76-74—294	12,891
17	Paula Creamer	70-72-77-69—288	25,542		Eun-Hee Ji (KOR)	75-72-76-71—294	12,891
	Brittany Lang	67-80-71-70—288	25,542		Ji Young Oh (KOR)	67-78-78-71—294	12,891
	Yani Tseng (TPE)	69-75-75-69—288	25,542		Wendy Ward	75-73-72-74—294	12,891
20	Jee Young Lee (KOR)	69-80-72-68—289	23,624				

Other players who made the cut: Na Yeon Choi (KOR), Joo Mi Kim (KOR), Azahara Muñoz (ESP) (am), Se Ri Pak (KOR), Morgan Pressel, Alena Sharp (CAN) 295; Hye Jung Choi (KOR), Natalie Gulbis 296; Mi Hyun Kim (KOR), Gwladys Nocera (FRA), Angela Park (BRA), Jennifer Rosales (PHI), Giulia Sergas (ITA) 297; Soo-Yun Kang (KOR), Teresa Lu (TPE), Hee Young Park (KOR) 298; Shi Hyun Ahn (KOR), Moira Dunn, Rachel Hetherington (AUS), Inbee Park (KOR) 299; Laura Diaz, Ji-Hee Lee (KOR), Becky Morgan (WAL) 301; Il Mi Chung (KOR) 302; Sophie Gustafson (SWE), Stacy Lewis, Heather Young 303; Diana D'Alessio, Michelle Wie 304; Ai Miyazato (JPN) 305; Silvia Cavalleri (ITA) 306

2008 Kraft Nabisco Championship [6673–72]

Prize money: $2 million

1	Lorena Ochoa (MEX)	68-71-71-67—277	$300,000	21T	Paula Creamer	71-74-73-74—292	19,506
2	Suzann Pettersen (NOR)	74-75-65-68—282	160,369		Cristie Kerr	74-72-66-80—292	19,506
	Annika Sörenstam (SWE)	71-70-73-68—282	160,369		Candie Kung (TPE)	73-74-75-70—292	19,506
4	Maria Hjörth (SWE)	70-70-72-71—283	104,317		Brittany Lang	75-70-72-75—292	19,506
5	Seon Hwa Lee (KOR)	73-71-68-72—284	83,963		Jee Young Lee (KOR)	73-71-75-73—292	19,506
6	Na Yeon Choi (KOR)	74-72-69-70—285	58,859		Angela Park (BRA)	77-71-73-71—292	19,506
	Hee-Won Han (KOR)	72-69-70-74—285	58,859		Michele Redman	71-72-76-73—292	19,506
	Mi Hyun Kim (KOR)	70-70-76-69—285	58,859		Yani Tseng (TPE)	72-71-75-74—292	19,506
9	Inbee Park (KOR)	73-70-70-73—286	45,289	30	Amanda Blumenhurst (am)	73-73-73-74—293	
10	Se Ri Pak (KOR)	72-70-73-72—287	39,692	31	Heather Daly-Donofrio	75-71-73-75—294	14,190
	Heather Young	69-70-74-74—287	39,692		Rachel Hetherington (AUS)	76-69-74-75—294	14,190
12	Karen Stupples (ENG)	67-75-74-72—288	35,621		Jeong Jang (KOR)	73-73-74-74—294	14,190
13	Natalie Gulbis	69-74-73-73—289	32,364		Ai Miyazato (JPN)	68-74-77-75—294	14,190
	Karrie Webb (AUS)	76-70-69-74—289	32,364		Ji-Young Oh (KOR)	77-72-71-74—294	14,190
15	Diana D'Alessio	74-69-72-75—290	27,275		Shiho Oyama (JPN)	72-72-76-74—294	14,190
	Meg Mallon	73-73-72-72—290	27,275		Ji-Yai Shin (KOR)	73-71-76-74—294	14,190
	Liselotte Neumann (SWE)	70-72-71-77—290	27,275	38	Katherine Hull (AUS)	76-70-74-75—295	11,271
	Angela Stanford	75-73-71-71—290	27,275		Hee Young Park (KOR)	75-72-74-74—295	11,271
19	Janice Moodie (SCO)	73-73-74-71—291	23,815		Morgan Pressel	71-74-75-75—295	11,271
	Sakura Yokomini (JPN)	76-73-72-70—291	23,815		Giulia Sergas (ITA)	74-75-77-69—295	11,271
21	Helen Alfredsson (SWE)	75-72-73-72—292	19,506				

Other players who made the cut: Shi Hyun Ahn (KOR), H J Choi (KOR), Sophie Gustafson (SWE), Mhairi McKay (SCO), Lindsey Wright (AUS), 296; Beth Bader, Marisa Baena (COL), Minea Blomqvist (FIN), Momoko Ueda (JPN), 297; Silvia Cavalleri (ITA), Russy Gulyanamitta (THA), Soo-Yun Kang (KOR), Becky Morgan (WAL), 298; Laura Davies (ENG), Pat Hurst, Reilley Rankin, 299; Il Mi Chung (KOR), Juli Inkster, Teresa Lu (TPE), Maria Jose Uribe (am), Wendy Ward, 300; Moira Dunn, Julieta Granada (PAR), Carin Koch (SWE), Meena Lee (KOR), Sarah Lee (KOR), 301; Mallory Blackwelder (am), Alena Sharp (CAN), 302; Meaghan Francella, 303; Sung Ah Yim (KOR), 312

2007 Kraft Nabisco Championship [6673–72]

Prize money: $1.8 million

1	Morgan Pressel	74-72-70-69—285	$300,000	20T	Karrie Webb (AUS)	70-77-73-73—293	22,881
2	Brittany Lincicome	72-71-71-72—286	140,945	24	Juli Inkster	75-75-72-72—294	20,451
	Catriona Matthew (SCO)	70-73-72-71—286	140,945		Christina Kim	72-77-71-74—294	20,451
	Suzann Pettersen (NOR)	72-69-71-74—286	140,945	26	Jimin Kang (KOR)	76-73-73-73—295	19,337
5	Shi Hyun Ahn (KOR)	68-73-74-72—287	69,688	27	Nicole Castrale	76-71-74-75—296	17,565
	Meaghan Francella	72-72-69-74—287	69,688		Julieta Granada (PAR)	74-77-72-73—296	17,565
	Stacy Lewis (am)	71-73-73-70—287			Angela Park (BRA)	73-74-75-74—296	17,565
	Stacy Prammanasudh	76-70-70-71—287	69,688		Lindsey Wright (AUS)	74-69-77-76—296	17,565
9	Maria Hjörth (SWE)	70-73-72-73—288	50,114	31	Laura Diaz	73-79-71-74—297	14,116
10	Lorena Ochoa (MEX)	69-71-77-72—289	41,340		Young Jo (KOR)	74-76-72-75—297	14,116
	Se Ri Pak (KOR)	72-70-70-77—289	41,340		Mi Hyun Kim (KOR)	74-72-74-77—297	14,116
	Angela Stanford	72-75-73-69—289	41,340		Leta Lindley	73-75-73-76—297	14,116
13	Jee Young Lee (KOR)	70-77-71-72—290	34,321		Hee-Young Park (KOR)	73-74-77-73—297	14,116
	Sarah Lee (KOR)	72-74-70-74—290	34,321		Annika Sörenstam (SWE)	75-76-71-75—297	14,116
15	Paula Creamer	73-67-73-78—291	28,651		Heather Young	74-75-76-72—297	14,116
	Brittany Lang	71-73-75-72—291	28,651	38	Helen Alfredsson (SWE)	78-69-74-77—298	10,782
	Ai Miyazato (JPN)	76-73-69-73—291	28,651		Marisa Baena (COL)	73-75-73-77—298	10,782
	Ji-Yai Shin (KOR)	76-72-71-72—291	28,651		Dorothy Delasin	73-76-74-75—298	10,782
19	Moira Dunn	76-73-72-71—292	25,108		Yuri Fudoh (JPN)	73-76-75-74—298	10,782
20	Laura Davies (ENG)	74-73-73-73—293	22,881		Pat Hurst	71-76-74-77—298	10,782
	Cristie Kerr	75-73-72-73—293	22,881		Gwladys Nocera (FRA)	72-77-72-77—298	10,782
	Sherri Steinhauer	71-78-70-74—293	22,881				

Other players who made the cut: Sophie Gustafson (SWE), Kim Saiki-Maloney, Sakura Yokomine (JPN) 299; Wendy Doolan, Shiho Oyama (JPN), Gloria Park (KOR) 300; Tina Barrett, Hee-Won Han (KOR), Young Kim (KOR), Becky Morgan (WAL) 301; Karine Icher (FRA), Jeong Jang (KOR), Reilley Rankin, Veronica Zorzi (ITA) 302; Diana D'Alessio, Soo-Yun Kang (KOR), Aree Song (KOR) 303; Carin Koch (SWE). Candie Kung (TPE), Liselotte Neumann (SWE), Nicole Perrot (CHI) 304; Mi-Jeong Jeon (KOR) 305; Tracy Hanson, Taylor Leon (am), Michele Redman 306; Esther Choe (am); Joo Mi Kim (KOR), Grace Park (KOR) 307; Jin Joo Hong (KOR) 310; Meg Mallon 311

2006 Kraft Nabisco Championship

Prize money: $1.8 million

[6569–72]

1	Karrie Webb* (AUS)	70-68-76-65—279	$270,000
2	Lorena Ochoa (MEX)	62-71-74-72—279	168,226

*Webb won sudden death play-off:: Webb 5, Ochoa 6

3	Natalie Gulbis	73-71-68-68—280	108,222
	Michelle Wie	66-71-73-70—280	108,222
5	Juli Inkster	69-73-74-68—284	75,985
6	Hee-Won Han (KOR)	75-72-68-71—286	57,104
	Annika Sörenstam (SWE)	71-72-73-70—286	57,104
8	Shi Hyun Ahn (KOR)	70-71-71-75—287	41,293
	Helen Alfredsson (SWE)	70-72-72-73—287	41,293
	Brittany Lang	70-74-72-71—287	41,293
11	Stacy Prammanasudh	67-73-76-72—288	33,388
	Michele Redman	72-72-72-72—288	33,388
13	Beth Daniel	72-72-72-73—289	29,289
	Morgan Pressel	69-76-70-74—289	29,289
15	Yuri Fudoh (JPN)	75-73-69-73—290	26,710
	Angela Park (am)	68-73-75-74—290	
17	Pat Hurst	73-73-73-72—291	24,592
	Karen Stupples (ENG)	69-74-72-76—291	24,592
19	Tina Barrett	72-75-74-71—292	21,221
	Jeong Jang (KOR)	71-75-76-70—292	21,221
	Young Kim (KOR)	74-73-70-75—292	21,221
	Seon Hwa Lee (KOR)	69-69-74-80—292	21,221

19T	Veronica Zorzi (ITA)	74-72-75-71—292	21,221
24	Paula Creamer	69-71-79-74—293	1,7610
	Dorothy Delasin	72-72-74-75—293	17,610
	Karine Icher (FRA)	73-73-77-70—293	17,610
	Carin Koch (SWE)	70-72-76-75—293	17,610
	Candie King (TAI)	72-75-72-74—293	17,610
29	Young Jo (KOR)	72-73-75-74—294	14,199
	Meena Lee (KOR)	72-76-72-74—294	14,199
	Patricia Meunier-Lebouc (FRA)	77-67-77-73—294	14,199
	Ai Miyazato (JPN)	70-77-72-75—294	14,199
	Becky Morgan (WAL)	76-70-75-73—294	14,199
	Jennifer Rosales (PHI)	72-76-73-73—294	14,199
35	Il Mi Chung (KOR)	72-77-73-73—295	11,329
	Cristie Kerr	71-76-75-73—295	11,329
	Grace Park (KOR)	74-72-78-71—295	11,329
	Sherri Steinhauer	72-77-75-71—295	11,329
	Wendy Ward	71-75-76-73—295	11,329
40	Suzann Pettersen (NOR)	75-72-75-74—296	9,763
	Aree Song (KOR)	74-76-72-74—296	9,763
42	Marisa Baena (COL)	75-72-71-79—297	8,842
	Mi Hyun Kim (KOR)	75-74-75-73—297	8,842
	Rachel Hetherington (AUS)	74-75-76-72—297	8,842

Other players who made the cut: Kyeong Bae (KOR), Jimin Kang (KOR), Birdie Kim (KOR), Sarah Lee (KOR), Janice Moodie (SCO), Liselotte Neumann (SWE), Se Ri Pak (KOR) 298; Johanna Head (ENG), Christine Kim, Gwladys Nocera (FRA), Kim Saiki 299; Jee Young Lee (KOR), Sung Ah Yim (KOR) 300; Lorie Kane (CAN), Soo Young Moon (KOR), Reilley Rankin 301; Brandie Burton 302; Maru Martinez (am), In-Bee Park (am) 304; Joo Mi Kim (KOR) 305; Nicole Perrot (CHI) 306; Katherine Hull (AUS), Meg Mallon 307; Kate Golden, Sydnee Michaels (am) 308; A J Eathorne (CAN) 314

2005 Kraft Nabisco Championship

Prize money: $1.8 million

[6460–72]

1	Annika Sörenstam (SWE)	70-69-66-68—273	$270,000
2	Rosie Jones	69-70-71-71—281	166,003
3	Laura Diaz	75-69-71-68—283	106,791
	Cristie Kerr	72-70-70-71—283	1067,91
5	Mi Hyun Kim (KOR)	69-71-72-72—284	68,165
	Grace Park (KOR)	73-68-76-67—284	68,165
7	Juli Inkster	70-74-72-69—285	51,350
8	Lorie Kane (CAN)	71-76-69-70—286	44,988
9	Beth Daniel	74-72-69-72—287	34,591
	Dorothy Delasin (PHI)	71-72-73-71—287	34,591
	Wendy Doolan (AUS)	74-69-73-71—287	34,591
	Candie Kung (TPE)	72-73-71-71—287	34,591
	Reilley Rankin	73-68-74-72—287	34,591
14	Brandie Burton	72-71-72-73—288	27,175
	Kim Saiki	74-71-70-73—288	27,175
	Michelle Wie (am)	70-74-73-71—288	
17	Natalie Gulbis	73-71-72-73—289	24,267
	Hee-Won Han (KOR)	76-71-69-73—289	24,267
19	Shi Hyun Ahn (KOR)	77-76-71-66—290	2,1692
	Paula Creamer	74-72-72-72—290	21,692
	Young Kim (KOR)	76-70-70-74—290	21,692
	Morgan Pressel (am)	70-73-72-75—290	

23	Laura Davies (ENG)	73-71-71-77—292	19,086
	Pat Hurst	71-74-74-73—292	19,086
	Sherri Steinhauer	71-72-75-74—292	19,086
	Karen Stupples (ENG)	69-80-70-73—292	19,086
27	Dawn Coe-Jones (CAN)	74-73-74-72—293	16,723
	Jeong Jang (KOR)	77-74-71-71—293	16,723
	Se Ri Pak (KOR)	77-70-70-76—293	16,723
30	Michelle Estill	71-79-71-73—294	14,565
	Julieta Granada (PAR) (am)	75-71-70-78—294	
	Carin Koch (SWE)	70-73-75-76—294	14,565
	Jill McGill	73-72-77-72—294	14,565
	Stacy Prammanasudh	75-74-74-71—294	14,565
35	Helen Alfredsson (SWE)	76-72-74-73—295	12,383
	Leta Lindley	74-77-73-71—295	12,383
	Lorena Ochoa (MEX)	76-75-73-71—295	12,383
	Jennifer Rosales (PHI)	71-79-74-71—295	12,383
39	Tina Barrett	73-77-71-75—296	10,288
	Yuri Fudoh (JPN)	75-75-75-71—296	10,288
	Rachel Hetherington (AUS)	77-73-72-74—296	10,288
	Christina Kim	76-71-73-76—296	10,288
	Janice Moodie (SCO)	74-77-74-71—296	10,288

Other players who made the cut: Joo Mi Kim (KOR), Catriona Matthew (SCO), Ai Miyazato (JPN), Gloria Park (KOR), Charlotta Sörenstam (SWE), Karrie Webb (AUS) 297; Heather Bowie, Tina Fischer (GER), Meg Mallon, Jane Park (am), Wendy Ward 298; Liselotte Neumann (SWE), Giulia Sergas (ITA), Bo Bae Song (KOR) 299; Katherine Hull (AUS), Kelli Kuehne, Michele Redman, Angela Stanford 300; Donna Andrews, Betsy King 301; Trish Johnson (ENG), Aree Song (KOR) 302; Sophie Gustafson (SWE), Emilee Klein 303; Stephanie Arricau (FRA), Hilary Lunke 304; Heather Daly-Donofrio, Candy Hannemann (BRA) 305; Nancy Scranton 306; Catrin Nilsmark (SWE) 310; Jamie Hullett 311; Laurel Kean 316

2004 Nabisco Dinah Shore [6673–72]

Prize money: $1.6 million

1	Grace Park (KOR)	72-69-67-69—277	$240,000	23	Jeong Jang (KOR)	76-71-70-72—289	17,203
2	Aree Song (KOR)	66-73-69-70—278	146,826	24	Brandie Burton	70-76-71-73—290	15,944
3	Karrie Webb (AUS)	68-71-71-69—279	106,512		Tammie Green	71-78-71-70—290	15,944
4	Michelle Wie (am)	69-72-69-71—281			Jane Park (am)	71-74-73-72—290	
5	Cristie Kerr	71-71-71-69—282	74,358		Dottie Pepper	68-70-74-78—290	15,944
	Catriona Matthew (SCO)	67-75-70-70—282	74,358	28	Danielle Ammaccapane	75-77-73-66—291	13,682
7	Mi-Hyun Kim (KOR)	71-70-71-71—283	54,261		Donna Andrews	70-74-73-74—291	13,682
8	Rosie Jones	67-73-71-73—284	36,737		Tina Barrett	75-70-73-73—291	13,682
	Christina Kim	72-72-70-70—284	36,737		Juli Inkster	74-74-73-70—291	13,682
	Candie Kung (TPE)	69-75-71-69—284	36,737		Wendy Ward	72-74-70-75—291	13,682
	Jung Yeon Lee (KOR)	69-69-71-75—284	36,737	33	Vicki Goetze-Ackerman	73-79-71-69—292	11,897
	Lorena Ochoa (MEX)	67-76-74-67—284	36,737		Kelly Robbins	69-74-78-71—292	11,897
13	Hee-Won Han (KOR)	72-71-71-71—285	26,420	35	Dorothy Delasin (PHI)	76-71-71-75—293	10,306
	Stacy Prammanasudh	71-71-69-74—285	26,420		Pat Hurst	72-76-69-76—293	10,306
	Annika Sörenstam (SWE)	71-76-69-69—285	26,420		Lorie Kane (CAN)	72-74-76-71—293	10,306
16	Laura Davies (ENG)	71-77-70-68—286	20,633		Rachel Teske (AUS)	75-71-71-76—293	10,306
	Wendy Doolan (AUS)	70-69-72-75—286	20,633		Iben Tinning (DEN)	70-75-77-71—293	10,306
	Young Kim (KOR)	74-72-67-73—286	20,633	40	Helen Alfredsson (SWE)	75-72-71-76—294	8,541
	Carin Koch (SWE)	70-72-71-73—286	20,633		Beth Daniel	72-74-74-74—294	8,541
	Se Ri Pak (KOR)	72-73-72-69—286	20,633		Kate Golden	73-78-74-69—294	85,41
	Karen Stupples (ENG)	70-76-68-72—286	20,633		Elizabeth Janangelo (am)	71-78-70-75—294	
22	Michele Redman	73-73-70-71—287	17,846		Emilee Klein	71-73-76-74—294	8,541

Other players who made the cut: Beth Bauer, Paula Creamer (am), Jill McGill 295; Sophie Gustafson (SWE), Stephanie Louden, Meg Mallon, Sherri Steinhauer 296; Michelle Ellis (AUS), Laurel Kean, Becky Morgan (WAL) 297; Jackie Gallagher-Smith, Ji-Hee Lee (KOR), Charlotta Sörenstam (SWE) 298; Moira Dunn, Natalie Gulbis, Betsy King, Jennifer Rosales (PHI) 300; Marisa Baena (COL), Heather Bowie, Heather Daly-Donofrio, Soo-Yun Kang (KOR), Miho Koga (JPN), Yu Ping Lin (TPE), Janice Moodie (SCO) 301; Hilary Lunke 302; JoAnne Carner, Dawn Coe-Jones, Joanne Mills (AUS) 303; Mhairi McKay (SCO), Shani Waugh (AUS) 304; Mardi Lunn (AUS) 305; Kelli Kuehne 306; Amy Alcott 308; Nancy Lopez WD

2003 Nabisco Dinah Shore [6520–72]

Prize money: $1.6 million

1	Patricia Meunier Lebouc (FRA)	70-68-70-73—281	$240,000	21T	Jeong Jang (KOR)	75-73-76-69—293	17,440
					Virada Nirapathpongporn (am)	76-72-72-73—293	
2	Annika Sörenstam (SWE)	68-72-71-71—282	146,120		Michele Redman	70-72-76-75—293	17,440
3	Lorena Ochoa (MEX)	71-70-74-68—283	106,000		Aree Song (am)	72-77-73-71—293	
4	Laura Davies (ENG)	70-75-69-70—284	82,000		Karrie Webb (AUS)	70-79-71-73—293	17,440
5	Beth Daniel	75-74-68-70—287	51,200	27	Leta Lindley	76-70-75-73—294	15,840
	Laura Diaz	76-71-69-71—287	51,200	28	Tammie Green	77-71-73-74—295	14,160
	Maria Hjörth (SWE)	72-72-73-70—287	51,200		Christina Kim	72-76-71-76—295	14,160
	Catriona Matthew (SCO)	71-74-72-70—287	51,200		Betsy King	75-74-70-76—295	14,160
9	Jennifer Rosales (PHI)	74-70-72-72—288	35,600		Candie Kung (TPE)	74-75-74-72—295	14,160
	Michelle Wie (am)	72-74-66-76—288			Charlotta Sörenstam (SWE)	73-74-71-77—295	14,160
11	Juli Inkster	75-74-66-75—290	29,160	33	Heather Bowie	72-78-72-74—296	11,373
	Cristie Kerr	74-71-74-71—290	29,160		Heather Daly-Donofrio	74-77-72-73—296	11,373
	Woo-Soon Ko (KOR)	74-73-70-73—290	29,160		Moira Dunn	74-80-73-69—296	11,373
	Rosie Jones	71-75-72-72—290	29,160		Amy Fruhwirth	73-75-75-73—296	11,373
15	Dawn Coe-Jones (CAN)	72-74-72-73—291	22,080		Vicki Goetze-Ackerman	75-74-74-73—296	11,373
	Dorothy Delasin (PHI)	71-71-76-73—291	22,080		Meg Mallon	72-76-73-75—296	11,373
	Catrin Nilsmark (SWE)	71-78-73-69—291	22,080	39	Beth Bauer	74-76-70-77—297	9,440
	Se Ri Pak (KOR)	71-72-71-77—291	22,080		Jackie Gallagher-Smith	75-74-74-74—297	9,440
	Karen Stupples (ENG)	71-71-76-73—291	22,080		Lorie Kane (CAN)	72-72-78-75—297	9,440
20	Hee-Won Han (KOR)	73-74-75-70—292	19,040				
21	Danielle Ammaccapane	75-68-78-72—293	17,440				

Other players who made the cut: Brandie Burton, Raquel Carriedo (ESP), Michelle Ellis (AUS), Liselotte Neumann (SWE), Gloria Park (KOR), Kelly Robbins 298; Natalie Gulbis, Rachel Teske (AUS), Wendy Ward 299; Sophie Gustafson (SWE), Pat Hurst, Kelli Kuehne, Barb Mucha, Dottie Pepper, Angela Stanford 300; Nanci Bowen, Akiko Fukushima (JPN), Laurel Kean, Mi-Hyun Kim (KOR), Joanne Morley (ENG), Kim Saiki, Lindsey Wright (AUS) (am) 301; Helen Alfredsson (SWE), Donna Andrews, Emilee Klein, Stephanie Louden, Janice Moodie (SCO), Shani Waugh (AUS) 302; Mhairi McKay (SCO), Patty Sheehan 303; Suzanne Strudwick (ENG) 304; Tina Fischer (GER) 305; Tracy Hanson 306; Kasumi Fujii (JPN), Yu Ping Lin (TPE) 307; Pat Bradley 308; Dale Eggeling 310; Mardi Lunn (AUS) 311

2002 Nabisco Dinah Shore

Prize money: $1.5 million

[6460–72]

1	Annika Sörenstam (SWE)	70-71-71-68—280	$225,000	21T	Janice Moodie (SCO)	73-73-73-70—289	16,350
2	Liselotte Neuman (SWE)	69-70-73-69—281	136,987	25	Sophie Gustafson (SWE)	77-69-71-73—290	13,800
3	Rosie Jones	72-69-72-69—282	88,125		Hee-Won Han (KOR)	74-74-73-69—290	13,800
	Cristie Kerr	74-70-70-68—282	88,125		Laurel Kean	79-74-71-66—290	13,800
5	Akiko Fukushima (JPN)	73-76-68-66—283	56,250		Suzann Pettersen (NOR)	74-71-73-72—290	13,800
	Carin Koch (SWE)	73-73-71-66—283	56,250		Michele Redman	75-70-72-73—290	13,800
7	Karrie Webb (AUS)	75-70-67-72—284	42,375	30	Laura Diaz	74-73-73-71—291	12,225
8	Lorena Ochoa (am)	75-69-71-70—285			Aree Song Wongluekiet	71-74-73-73—291	
9	Becky Iverson	71-74-68-73—286	31,050		(am)		
	Lorie Kane (CAN)	73-72-70-71—286	31,050	32	Heather Daly-Donofrio	74-73-72-73—292	11,100
	Leta Lindley	72-72-72-70—286	31,050		Kathryn Marshall (SCO)	75-72-73-72—292	11,100
	Se Ri Pak (KOR)	74-71-71-70—286	31,050		Alison Nicholas (ENG)	76-71-70-75—292	11,100
	Grace Park (KOR)	75-73-70-68—286	31,050		Gloria Park (KOR)	70-76-75-71—292	11,100
14	Vicki Goetze-Ackerman	74-73-68-72—287	21,900	36	Marisa Baena (COL)	79-74-68-72—293	8,524
	Heather Bowie	75-71-72-69—287	21,900		Maria Hjörth (SWE)	76-73-69-75—293	8,524
	Beth Daniel	71-70-75-71—287	21,900		Pat Hurst	78-72-71-72—293	8,524
	Dorothy Delasin (PHI)	72-73-69-73—287	21,900		Chris Johnson	75-71-76-71—293	8,524
	Kris Tschetter	74-69-73-71—287	21,900		Betsy King	71-75-73-74—293	8,524
19	Juli Inkster	73-76-71-68—288	18,225		Kelli Kuehne	74-73-73-73—293	8,524
	Mhairi McKay (SCO)	73-72-73-70—288	18,225		Meg Mallon	75-73-74-71—293	8,524
21	Laura Davies (ENG)	75-75-69-70—289	16,350		Sherri Steinhauer	73-78-70-72—293	8,524
	Wendy Doolan (AUS)	78-70-72-69—289	16,350		Wendy Ward	77-74-73-69—293	8,524
	Mi Hyun Kim (KOR)	74-75-69-71—289	16,350				

Other players who made the cut: Helen Alfredsson (SWE), Yuri Fudoh (JPN), Jeong Jang (KOR), Yu Ping Lin (TPE) 294; Donna Andrews, Barb Mucha 295; Penny Hammel, Karin Icher (FRA), Catriona Matthew (SCO), Deb Richard 296; Tina Barrett, Amy Fruhwirth, Jill McGill 298; Moira Dunn, Kelly Robbins, Pearl Sinn (KOR), Naree Song Wongluekiet (am) 299; Brandie Burton, Charlotta Sörenstam (SWE), Sherri Turner 300; Dina Ammaccapane, Rachel Teske (AUS), Karen Weiss 301; Amy Alcott, Kate Golden 302; Emilee Klein 303; Patty Sheehan 305; Tammie Green 306; Meredith Duncan (am) 307; Hiromi Kobayashi (JPN) 312

Kraft Nabisco History

This event was inaugurated in 1972 as the Colgate Dinah Shore and continued to be sponsored by Colgate until 1981. Nabisco took over the sponsorship in 1982; and the Nabisco Dinah Shore was designated a Major Championship in 1983. The Championship became the Kraft Nabisco in 2005. Mission Hills CC, Rancho Mirage, California, is the event's permanent venue.

Year	Winner	Score		Year	Winner	Score
1972	J Blalock	213		1991	A Alcott	273
1973	M Wright	284		1992	D Mochrie*	279
1974	J Prentice*	289		*After a play-off with J Inkster		
*After a play-off with J Blalock and S Haynie				1993	H Alfredsson (SWE)	284
1975	S Palmer	283		1994	D Andrews	276
1976	J Rankin	285		1995	N Bowen	285
1977	K Whitworth	289		1996	P Sheehan	281
1978	S Post*	283		1997	B King	276
*After a play-off with P Pulz				1998	P Hurst	281
1979	S Post*	276		1999	D Pepper	269
*After a play-off with N Lopez				2000	K Webb (AUS)	274
1980	D Caponi	275		2001	A Sörenstam (SWE)	281
1981	N Lopez	277		2002	A Sörenstam (SWE)	280
1982	S Little	278		2003	P Meunier-Lebouc (FRA)	281
1983	A Alcott	282		2004	G Park (KOR)	277
1984	J Inkster*	280		2005	A Sörenstam (SWE)	273
*After a play-off with P Bradley				2006	K Webb (AUS)*	279
1985	A Miller	278		*After a play-off with L Ochoa		
1986	P Bradley	280		2007	M Pressel	285
1987	B King*	283		2008	L Ochoa (MEX)	277
*After a play-off with P Sheehan				2009	B Lincicombe	279
1988	A Alcott	274		2010	Y Tseng (TPE)	275
1989	J Inkster	279		2011	S Lewis	275
1990	B King	283				

du Maurier Classic History

The du Maurier Classic was inaugurated in 1973 and designated a Major Championship in 1979.
It was discontinued after 2000 and was replaced as a major on the US LPGA schedule by the Weetabix Women's British Open.

Players are of American nationality unless stated

1973	J Bourassa*	Montreal GC, Montreal	214
After a play-off with S Haynie and J Rankin			
1974	CJ Callison	Candiac GC, Montreal	208
1975	J Carner*	St George's CC, Toronto	214
After a play-off with C Mann			
1976	D Caponi*	Cedar Brae G&CC, Toronto	212
After a play-off with J Rankin			
1977	J Rankin	Lachute G&CC, Montreal	214
1978	J Carner	St George's CC, Toronto	278
1979	A Alcott	Richelieu Valley CC, Montreal	285
1980	P Bradley	St George's CC, Toronto	277
1981	J Stephenson (AUS)	Summerlea CC, Dorian, Quebec	278
1982	S Haynie	St George's CC, Toronto	280
1983	H Stacy	Beaconsfield CC, Montreal	277
1984	J Inkster	St George's CC, Toronto	279
1985	P Bradley	Beaconsfield CC, Montreal	278
1986	P Bradley*	Board of Trade CC, Toronto	276
After a play-off with A Okamoto			
1987	J Rosenthal	Islesmere GC, Laval, Quebec	272
1988	S Little (RSA)	Vancouver GC, Coquitlam, BC	279
1989	T Green	Beaconsfield CC, Montreal	279
1990	C Johnston	Westmount G&CC, Kitchener, Ontario	276
1991	N Scranton	Vancouver GC, Coquitlam, BC	279
1992	S Steinhauer	St Charles CC, Winnipeg, Manitoba	277
1993	B Burton*	London H&CC, Ontario	277
After a play-off with B King			
1994	M Nause	Ottawa Hunt Club, Ontario	279
1995	J Lidback	Beaconsfield CC, Montreal	280
1996	L Davies (ENG)	Edmonton CC, Edmonton, Alberta	277
1997	C Walker	Glen Abbey GC, Toronto	278
1998	B Burton	Essex G&CC, Ontario	270
1999	K Webb (AUS)	Priddis Greens G&CC, Calgary, Alberta	277
2000	M Mallon	Royal Ottawa GC, Aylmer, Quebec	282

Month by month in 2011

Nick Watney captures the second of the year's World Golf Championships, beating Dustin Johnson by two with Tiger Woods securing his first top 10 finish of the season, and there are two Scottish winners on the same day. Paul Lawrie triumphs in Spain and a few hours later Martin Laird takes the Arnold Palmer Invitational.

Women's Grand Slam Titles

Patty Berg   Mickey Wright   Louise Suggs

Photographs © Phil Sheldon and Empics

	British Open[1]	US Open[2]	McDonald's LPGA[3]	Kraft Nabisco[4]	du Maurier[5]	Title-holders[6]	Western[7]	Total Titles
Patty Berg (USA)	0	1	0	—	—	7	7	15
Mickey Wright (USA)	0	4	4	—	—	2	3	13
Louise Suggs (USA)	0	2	1	—	—	4	4	11
Annika Sörenstam (SWE)	1	3	3	3	0	—	—	10
'Babe' Zaharias (USA)	0	3	—	—	—	3	4	10
Karrie Webb (AUS)	3	2	1	2	1	—	—	9
Betsy Rawls (USA)	0	4	2	—	—	0	2	8
Juli Inkster (USA)	0	2	2	2	1	—	—	7

[1] The Weetabix Women's British Open was designated a major on the LPGA Tour in 2001
[2] The US Open became an LPGA major in 1950
[3] The McDonald's LPGA Championship was designated a major in 1955
[4] The Kraft Nabisco event was designated a major in 1983
[5] The du Maurier event was designated a major in 1979 but discontinued after 2000
[6] The Titleholders Championship was a major from 1937–1966 and in 1972
[7] The Western event was a major from 1937 to 1967

Super Career Grand Slam: Only Karrie Webb has won five of the qualifying majors – the Women's British Open, the US Open, the LPGA Championship, the Kraft Nabisco and du Maurier. She completed her Super Grand Slam in 2002.

Career Grand Slam: Only Louise Suggs (1957), Mickey Wright (1962), Pat Bradley (1986), Julie Inkster (1999), Karrie Webb (2001) and Annika Sörenstam (2003) have won all the designated majors at the time they were playing.

Grand Slam: Only Babe Zaharias in 1950 (three majors) and Sandra Haynie (USA) in 1964 (two majors) have won all the majors available that season.

Note: Glenna Collett Vare (USA) won six US Amateurs between 1922 and 1935 including three in a row in 1928, 1929 and 1930. Jo Anne Carner (USA) won five US Amateurs between 1957 and 1968. Julie Inkster won three US Amateurs in 1980, 1981 and 1982.

PART II

Men's Professional Tournaments

World Golf Rankings 2011

Notable gains in the 2011 World Rankings included Aaron Baddeley, Webb Simpson, Bae sang-moon, Fredrik Jacobsen, Thomas Björn and Darren Clarke plus Keegan Bradley who earned a place in the top 50 in his first listing in the rankings.

Ranking		Name	Country	Points Average	Total Points	No. of Events	2009/2010 Pts Lost	2011 Pts Gained
1	(9)	Luke Donald	ENG	10.03	541.46	54	−302.60	+533.49
2	(1)	Lee Westwood	ENG	8.06	362.83	45	−361.00	+298.87
3	(10)	Rory McIlroy	NIR	7.77	388.59	50	−279.45	+360.27
4	(3)	Martin Kaymer	GER	6.55	334.07	51	−309.08	+287.35
5	(20)	Adam Scott	AUS	5.50	258.31	47	−160.30	+232.63
6	(5)	Steve Stricker	USA	5.33	218.48	41	−255.83	+211.52
7	(14)	Dustin Johnson	USA	5.27	268.92	51	−208.27	+251.10
8	(35)	Jason Day	AUS	5.07	243.41	48	−129.11	+244.98
9	(38)	Charl Schwartzel	RSA	5.06	273.21	54	−196.68	+288.47
10	(208)	Webb Simpson	USA	5.03	271.49	54	−72.42	+297.62
11	(12)	Matt Kuchar	USA	4.71	254.39	54	−223.73	+231.05
12	(32)	Nick Watney	USA	4.69	239.43	51	−179.23	+252.97
13	(11)	Graeme McDowel	NIR	4.55	245.68	54	−246.24	+158.88
14	(4)	Phil Mickelson	USA	4.47	210.32	47	−280.55	+202.69
15	(47)	K J Choi	KOR	4.31	232.96	54	−145.44	+238.88
16	(8)	Ian Poulter	ENG	3.88	194.19	50	−226.21	+147.60
17	(78)	Sergio García	ESP	3.87	185.80	48	−96.15	+194.03
18	(28)	Justin Rose	ENG	3.84	207.61	54	−158.83	+185.50
19	(18)	Hunter Mahan	USA	3.76	203.00	54	−192.01	+180.75
20	(7)	Paul Casey	ENG	3.73	186.28	50	−214.22	+135.17
21	(27)	Bubba Watson	USA	3.69	184.30	50	−155.73	+182.79
22	(46)	Alvaro Quiros	ESP	3.68	187.44	51	−146.89	+193.57
23	(2)	Tiger Woods	USA	3.59	143.68	40	−277.79	+106.22
24	(16)	Robert Karlsson	SWE	3.55	184.34	52	−145.03	+142.54
25	(30)	Kim Kyung-Tae	KOR	3.52	190.31	54	−135.30	+145.62
26	(80)	David Toms	USA	3.50	175.01	50	−104.61	+187.78
27	(61)	Bill Haas	USA	3.43	185.30	54	−117.20	+180.32
28	(63)	Simon Dyson	ENG	3.38	182.45	54	−107.50	+171.94
29	(45)	Bo Van Pelt	USA	3.37	182.11	54	−132.64	+157.10
30	(150)	Bae Sang-moon	KOR	3.28	140.90	43	−42.93	+138.19
31	(—)	Keegan Bradley	USA	3.26	176.10	54	−35.91	+190.18
32	(25)	Rickie Fowler	USA	3.24	175.22	54	−121.55	+158.78
33	(93)	Jason Dufner	USA	3.21	160.64	50	−95.53	+172.34
34	(70)	Anders Hansen	DEN	3.17	161.92	51	−109.65	+165.34
35	(127)	Thomas Björn	DEN	3.16	161.39	51	−73.92	+170.89
36	(43)	Geoff Ogilvy	AUS	3.13	153.14	49	−148.54	+121.01
37	(21)	Zach Johnson,	USA	3.09	154.68	50	−160.46	+123.99
38	(87)	Brandt Snedeker	USA	3.09	166.97	54	−100.94	+182.01
39	(132)	Fredrik Jacobson	SWE	3.08	157.09	51	−69.09	+163.94
40	(23)	Louis Oosthuizen	RSA	3.07	165.69	54	−155.04	+123.14
41	(15)	Francesco Molinari	ITA	3.05	164.69	54	−182.61	+105.71
42	(40)	Peter Hanson	SWE	2.97	154.66	52	−121.48	+137.42
43	(83)	John Senden	AUS	2.91	156.96	54	−87.10	+148.03
44	(29)	Miguel Angel Jiménez	ESP	2.88	155.61	54	−168.43	+125.44
45	(39)	Y E Yang	KOR	2.84	153.12	54	−160.27	+153.98
46	(278)	Aaron Baddeley	AUS	2.79	147.92	53	−66.97	+180.03
47	(49)	Martin Laird	SCO	2.76	149.30	54	−135.95	+143.12
48	(100)	Darren Clarke	NIR	2.74	142.62	52	−80.20	+144.73
49	(92)	Gonzalo Fdez-Castano	ESP	2.73	117.33	43	−60.81	+94.07
50	(6)	Jim Furyk	USA	2.73	136.39	50	−237.46	+87.82

Ranking in brackets indicates position at end of 2010 season

European Tour Race to Dubai 2011

(at end of 2011 season) www.europeantour.com

Final Order of Merit (Top 117 keep their cards for the 2012 season)

1	Luke Donald (ENG)	€4,216,226	61	Stephen Gallacher (SCO)	499,387
2	Rory McIlroy (NIR)	3,171,787	62	Steve Webster (ENG)	480,689
3	Martin Kaymer (GER)	2,935,446	63	Peter Whiteford (SCO)	478,674
4	Charl Schwartzel (RSA)	2,486,959	64	Bernd Wiesberger (AUT)	469,499
5	Lee Westwood (ENG)	2,052,090	65	Richard Green (AUS)	461,580
6	Alvaro Quiros (ESP)	1,927,090	66	Tom Lewis (ENG)	459,266
7	Anders Hansen (DEN)	1,769,893	67	Padraig Harrington (IRL)	457,389
8	Sergio García (ESP)	1,685,930	68	Marcus Fraser (AUS)	457,248
9	Thomas Björn (DEN)	1,565,001	69	Søren Kjeldsen (DEN)	452,147
10	Simon Dyson (ENG)	1,473,344	70	Anthony Wall (ENG)	449,266
11	Darren Clarke (NIR)	1,396,659	71	Robert Coles (ENG)	437,586
12	Miguel Angel Jiménez (ESP)	1,390,539	72	Pablo Martin (ESP)	437,132
13	Peter Hanson (SWE)	1,334,514	73	Ryan Moore (USA)	433,000
14	Alexander Noren (SWE)	1,275,407	74	Richard Finch (ENG)	425,529
15	Louis Oosthuizen (RSA)	1,270,730	75	James Kingston (RSA)	405,962
16	Graeme McDowell (NIR)	1,230,461	76	Kenneth Ferrie (ENG)	405,149
17	Pablo Larrazábal (ESP)	1,183,040	77	José Manuel Lara (ESP)	403,370
18	Paul Lawrie (SCO)	1,142,013	78	Gary Boyd (ENG)	395,924
19	Gonzalo Fernandez-Castaño (ESP)	1,114,060	79	Robert-Jan Derksen (NED)	395,504
20	Nicolas Colsaerts (BEL)	1,091,504	80	S S P Chowrasia (IND)	392,702
21	Francesco Molinari (ITA)	1,087,852	81	George Murray (SCO)	386,710
22	Thomas Aiken (RSA)	1,055,894	82	Lee Slattery (ENG)	380,087
23	Ian Poulter (ENG)	1,015,671	83	Martin Wiegele (AUT)	372,253
24	Joost Luiten (NED)	976,540	84	Danny Lee (NZL)	358,477
25	Michael Hoey (NIR)	967,668	85	Thongchai Jaidee (THA)	357,602
26	George Coetzee (RSA)	913,128	86	Seung-Yul Noh (KOR)	348,140
27	Grégory Havret (FRA)	906,859	87	Marcel Siem (GER)	343,654
28	Richie Ramsay (SCO)	904,002	88	Alejandro Cañizares (ESP)	342,928
29	Paul Casey (ENG)	879,088	89	Chris Wood (ENG)	339,534
30	Rafael Cabrera-Bello (ESP)	862,685	90	Romain Wattel (FRA)	337,476
31	Matteo Manassero (ITA)	859,461	91	Danny Willett (ENG)	333,727
32	Mark Foster (ENG)	853,840	92	Jbe Kruger (RSA)	332,289
33	Y E Yang (KOR)	846,230	93	Jean-Baptiste Gonnet (FRA)	330,408
34	Robert Rock (ENG)	818,014	94	Jeev Milkha Singh (IND)	329,262
35	David Lynn (ENG)	788,413	95	Oliver Fisher (ENG)	328,222
36	Raphaël Jacquelin (FRA)	783,817	96	Bradley Dredge (WAL)	324,853
37	Robert Karlsson (SWE)	773,347	97	Ignacio Garrido (ESP)	323,795
38	Jamie Donaldson (WAL)	771,563	98	Tano Goya (ARG)	315,165
39	Fredrik Andersson Hed (SWE)	769,849	99	Ricardo Gonzalez (ARG)	314,713
40	Johan Edfors (SWE)	764,807	100	Fabrizio Zanotti (PAR)	314,124
41	Shane Lowry (IRL)	764,778	101	Graeme Storm (ENG)	311,308
42	Retief Goosen (RSA)	752,573	102	Colin Montgomerie (SCO)	300,287
43	David Horsey (ENG)	718,444	103	David Howell (ENG)	294,081
44	Fredrik Jacobson (SWE)	709,445	104	David Drysdale (SCO)	292,750
45	Thomas Levet (FRA)	695,397	105	Michael Jonzon (SWE)	285,714
46	Edoardo Molinari (ITA)	686,391	106	Victor Dubuisson (FRA)	285,401
47	Grégory Bourdy (FRA)	650,863	107	Joel Sjöholm (SWE)	280,311
48	Thorbjørn Olesen (DEN)	637,703	108	Richard McEvoy (ENG)	277,098
49	Lorenzo Gagli (ITA)	622,846	109	Søren Hansen (DEN)	272,637
50	Jaco Van Zyl (RSA)	611,280	110	Brett Rumford (AUS)	271,782
51	Ernie Els (RSA)	591,508	111	Oscar Floren (SWE)	264,783
52	Ross Fisher (ENG)	583,569	112	Carlos Del Moral (ESP)	262,965
53	Hennie Otto (RSA)	583,296	113	Keith Horne (RSA)	261,804
54	Felipe Aguilar (CHI)	573,086	114	Marc Warren (SCO)	258,971
55	Justin Rose (ENG)	571,283	115	Damien McGrane (IRL)	258,939
56	Rhys Davies (WAL)	571,088	116	Markus Brier (AUT)	258,513
57	James Morrison (ENG)	556,549	117	Gareth Maybin (NIR)	254,807
58	Peter Lawrie (IRL)	546,660	118	Phillip Price (WAL)	252,083
59	Scott Jamieson (SCO)	523,754	119	Mark Tullo (CHI)	250,806
60	Christian Nilsson (SWE)	521,587	120	Simon Khan (ENG)	250,132

Career Money List (at end of 2011 season)

Lee Westwood is top career earner

Lee Westwood moves up two places to displace Ernie Els at the top of the table. English players occupied 22 places in the top 100 followed by Sweden with 16, Scotland with nine places and South Africa and Spain with seven apiece.

1	Lee Westwood (ENG)	€26,346,678	51	Nick Dougherty (ENG)		6,034,704
2	Ernie Els (RSA)	26,222,911	52	Louis Oosthuizen (RSA)		5,944,855
3	Colin Montgomerie (SCO)	24,360,237	53	Gary Orr (SCO)		5,814,607
4	Padraig Harrington (IRL)	22,486,192	54	Andrew Coltart (SCO)		5,733,959
5	Retief Goosen (RSA)	21,109,519	55	Oliver Wilson (ENG)		5,684,034
6	Darren Clarke (NIR)	19,713,018	56	Grégory Havret (FRA)		5,678,913
7	Miguel Angel Jiménez (ESP)	18,982,599	57	Gonzalo Fernandez-Castaño (ESP)		5,652,934
8	Sergio Garcia (ESP)	16,453,873	58	Stephen Gallacher (SCO)		5,616,738
9	Ian Poulter (ENG)	15,428,326	59	Sam Torrance (SCO)		5,491,084
10	Thomas Björn (DEN)	15,374,448	60	Mark McNulty (IRL)		5,366,794
11	Robert Karlsson (SWE)	14,318,177	61	Ricardo Gonzalez (ARG)		5,348,140
12	Paul Casey (ENG)	14,289,413	62	John Bickerton (ENG)		5,334,989
13	Vijay Singh (FIJ)	13,938,274	63	Simon Khan (ENG)		5,067,558
14	Angel Cabrera (ARG)	13,845,993	64	Thongchai Jaidee (THA)		5,032,851
15	Martin Kaymer (GER)	13,363,577	65	Peter Hedblom (SWE)		5,002,433
16	Luke Donald (ENG)	13,137,835	66	Alastair Forsyth (SCO)		4,935,185
17	Bernhard Langer (GER)	12,653,862	67	Fredrik Jacobson (SWE)		4,861,585
18	Graeme McDowell (NIR)	11,934,489	68	Johan Edfors (SWE)		4,804,943
19	José María Olazábal (ESP)	11,796,843	69	Jeev Milkha Singh (IND)		4,751,393
20	Michael Campbell (NZL)	11,495,679	70	Robert-Jan Derksen (NED)		4,666,010
21	Henrik Stenson (SWE)	10,761,126	71	Jarmo Sandelin (SWE)		4,660,632
22	Paul McGinley (IRL)	10,700,086	72	Maarten Lafeber (NED)		4,571,959
23	David Howell (ENG)	10,657,679	73	Graeme Storm (ENG)		4,483,269
24	Anders Hansen (DEN)	10,566,955	74	Joakim Haeggman (SWE)		4,481,351
25	Rory McIlroy (NIR)	10,406,829	75	Costantino Rocca (ITA)		4,369,211
26	Niclas Fasth (SWE)	9,892,928	76	Jean Van De Velde (FRA)		4,354,592
27	Charl Schwartzel (RSA)	9,833,081	77	Brian Davis (ENG)		4,338,561
28	Ian Woosnam (WAL)	9,592,582	78	José Manuel Lara (ESP)		4,317,822
29	Paul Lawrie (SCO)	9,495,440	79	Pierre Fulke (SWE)		4,310,837
30	Søren Kjeldsen (DEN)	8,910,020	80	Brett Rumford (AUS)		4,306,200
31	Søren Hansen (DEN)	8,607,437	81	Peter Lawrie (IRL)		4,249,726
32	Simon Dyson (ENG)	8,554,360	82	Stephen Dodd (WAL)		4,243,262
33	Richard Green (AUS)	8,372,595	83	Gordon Brand Jr (SCO)		4,084,502
34	Peter Hanson (SWE)	8,356,216	84	Peter Baker (ENG)		4,030,726
35	Sir Nick Faldo (ENG)	8,001,656	85	Alexander Noren (SWE)		4,029,489
36	Raphaël Jacquelin (FRA)	7,957,362	86	Richard Sterne (RSA)		4,020,901
37	Francesco Molinari (ITA)	7,739,953	87	Jean-François Remesy (FRA)		3,961,735
38	Ross Fisher (ENG)	7,493,158	88	Markus Brier (AUT)		3,929,399
39	Thomas Levet (FRA)	7,486,841	89	Damien McGrane (IRL)		3,814,753
40	Bradley Dredge (WAL)	7,327,692	90	Jamie Spence (ENG)		3,811,210
41	Trevor Immelman (RSA)	7,284,928	91	Sandy Lyle (SCO)		3,802,301
42	Phillip Price (WAL)	6,983,883	92	Grégory Bourdy (FRA)		3,794,843
43	Barry Lane (ENG)	6,970,284	93	Fredrik Andersson Hed (SWE)		3,792,943
44	Paul Broadhurst (ENG)	6,831,802	94	Y E Yang (KOR)		3,787,139
45	Peter O'Malley (AUS)	6,788,752	95	Patrik Sjöland (SWE)		3,779,217
46	Anthony Wall (ENG)	6,567,251	96	Mathias Grönberg (SWE)		3,770,894
47	Steve Webster (ENG)	6,374,556	97	David Gilford (ENG)		3,756,909
48	Ignacio Garrido (ESP)	6,357,792	98	Per-Ulrik Johansson (SWE)		3,619,023
49	David Lynn (ENG)	6,304,204	99	Jesper Parnevik (SWE)		3,571,845
50	Alvaro Quiros (ESP)	6,235,047	100	James Kingston (RSA)		3,550,015

Tour Statistics (Genworth Financial Statistics)

Stroke Average

Pos	Name	Total Rounds	Stroke Avg,
I	Luke Donald (ENG)	41	69.12
2	Rory McIlroy (NIR)	68	69.16
3	Charl Schwartzel (RSA)	62	69.44
4	Sergio García (ESP)	52	69.56
5	Lee Westwood (ENG)	63	69.79
6	Fredrik Jacobson (SWE)	18	69.94
7	Martin Kaymer (GER)	74	70.11

Driving accuracy

Pos	Name	Rounds	%
I	Luke Donald (ENG)	19	75.6
2	Richie Ramsay (SCO)	100	75.1
3	Peter Lawrie (IRL)	89	74.4
4	Francesco Molinari (ITA)	53	72.8
5	Michael Campbell (NZL)	52	72.0
6	Anders Hansen (DEN)	54	71.7
7	Matteo Manassero (ITA)	64	70.6

Luke Donald headed four categories in the European Tour statistics including a stroke average of 69.12

Driving distance

Pos	Name	Rounds	Avg. yards
I	Alvaro Quiros (ESP)	54	312.7
2	Pelle Edberg (SWE)	20	308.6
3	Daniel Vancsik (ARG)	22	308.5
4	Lloyd Saltman (SCO)	73	306.9
5	Seung-Yul Noh (KOR)	34	304.8
6	Elliot Saltman (SCO)	36	304.7
7	Nicolas Colsaerts (BEL)	73	303.8

Average putts per round

Pos	Name	Rounds	Putts per round
I	Retief Goosen (RSA)	38	28.3
2	Tetsuji Hiratsuka (JPN)	29	28.4
3	Brett Rumford (AUS)	81	28.5
4	Thaworn Wiratchant (THA)	22	28.6
5	David Howell (ENG)	81	28.7
6	Marcus Fraser (AUS)	62	28.7
7	George Coetzee (RSA)	79	28.8

Greens in regulation

Pos	Name	Rounds	%
I	Luke Donald (ENG)	19	77.5
2	Justin Rose (ENG)	18	77.2
3	Lorenzo Gagli (ITA)	88	77.1
4	Rory McIlroy (NIR)	44	76.4
5	Chapchai Nirat (THA)	20	76.4
6	Louis Oosthuizen (RSA)	45	76.3
7	Richie Ramsay (sco)	100	75.9

Sand saves

Pos	Name	Rounds	%
I	Peter Karmis (RSA)	22	100
2	Jbe Kruger (RSA)	41	80
3	Luke Donald (ENG)	19	78.6
4	Ian Poulter (ENG)	28	69.4
5	Tetsuji Hiratsuka (JPN)	29	68.4
6	Miguel Angel Jiménez (ESP)	70	68.1
7	Marcus Fraser (AUS)	62	67.6

Putts per greens in regulation

Pos	Name	Rounds	Putts per GIR
I	Luke Donald (ENG)	19	1,694
2	Thaworn Wiratchant (THA)	22	1.696
3	Retief Goosen (RSA)	38	1.719
4	Charl Schwartzel (RSA)	34	1.727
5	Brett Rumford (AUS)	81	1.736
6	Graeme McDowell (NIR)	36	1.739
7	Martin Kaymer (GER)	54	1,742

Scrambles (where player makes par after missing GIR)

Pos	Name	Rounds	%
I	Prayad Marksaeng (THA)	15	66.3
2	Sergio García (ESP)	31	65.2
3	Marcus Fraser (AUS)	62	64.1
4	Retief Goosen (RSA)	38	63.1
5	Francesco Molinari (ITA)	53	62.8
6	Rory McIlroy (NIR)	44	62.0
7	Miguel Angel Jiménez (ESP)	70	61.9

PGA European Tour statistics 2011

Thirty-four holes-in-one

Richard Bland – South African Open
Charl Schwartzel – South African Open
Soren Kjeldsen – HSBC Golf Championship
Ricardo Gonzalez – HSBC Golf Championship
Paul Casey – HSBC Golf Championship
Keith Horne – Omega Dubai Desert Classic
David Howell– Omega Dubai Desert Classic
Raphael Jacquelin – Omega Dubai Desert Classic
Alavro Quiros – Omega Dubai Desert Classic
Maarten Lafeber – Avantha Masters
Julio Zapata – Open de Andalucia
David Horsey – Trophée Hassan II
Niccolo Quintarelli – Open de España
Mark Brown – Iberdrola Open
Eirik Tage Johansen – Iberdrola Open
Elliot Saltman – Saab Wales Open
George Murray – Saab Wales Open

Elliot Saltman – Saab Wales Open
Rafa Echenique – BMW Italian Open
Marcus Fraser – BMW Italian Open
David Dixon – Saint-Omer Open
Alexander Knappe – BMW International Open
Phillip Price – Barclays Scottish Open
Steve Webster – Barclays Scottish Open
Dustin Johnson – 140th Open Championship
Tom Watson – 140th Open Championship
Jim Furyk – WGC–Bridgestone Invitational
Gareth Maybin – KLM Open
James Byrne – Alfred Dunhill Links C/ship
Elliot Saltman – Bankia Madrid Masters
Oliver Wilson – Andalucia Masters
Rick Kulacz – Barclays Singapore Open
Gareth Maybin – UBS Hong Kong Open
Anirban Lahiri – UBS Hong Kong Open

Thirty-two course records

63 (–9)	Volvo Golf Champions – Soren Kjeldsen, Richard Finch
65 (–6)[†]	Sicilian Open – Stephen Dodd, Jose Manuel Lara, Alastair Forsyth
60 (–10)	Open de Andalucia – Kenneth Ferrie
62 (–10)	Trophée Hassan II – Thomas Björn (Palais Royal)
66 (–5)	Trophée Hassan II (Golf de L'Ocean) – John Bickerton
63 (–9)	Volvo China Open – Pablo Martin
65 (–7)	Open de España – Robert–Jan Derksen
63 (–7)	Iberdrola Open – Grégory Bourdy, Shane Lowry
63 (–9)	Madeira Islands Open – Simon Wakefield
64 (–8)	Barclays Scottish Open – Graeme McDowell, Angel Cabrera, Paul Lawrie
65 (–5)	140th Open Championship – Thomas Björn, Tom Lewis
63 (–9)	Nordea Masters – Alex Noren
63 (–7)[†]	US PGA Championship – Steve Stricker
65 (–7)	Austrian GolfOpen – Robert Coles
63 (–9)[†]	Alfred Dunhill Links Championship (St Andrews) – Simon Dyson, Luke Donald
63 (–9)[†]	WGC–HSBC Champions – Martin Kaymer
65 (–7)	South African Open Championship (Nov 2011) – Jaco Ahlers, Hennie Otto
64 (–6)	UBS Hong Kong Open – Rory McIlroy, Alvaro Quiros, David Horsey
64 (–8)[†]	Dubai World Championship – Peter Hanson, Alvaro Quiros, Martin Kaymer

[†] equals existing record

Eleven multiple winners

Charl Schwartzel – Joburg Open, Masters Tournament
Luke Donald – WGC–Accenture Match Play Championship, BMW PGA Championship, Barclays Scottish Open
Darren Clarke – Iberdrola Open, 140th Open Championship
Alex Noren – Saab Wales Open, Nordea Masters
Thomas Björn – Commercialbank Qatar Masters, Johnnie Walker Championship, Omega European Masters

Simon Dyson – Irish Open, KLM Open
Michael Hoey – Madeira Islands Open, Alfred Dunhill Links Championship
Sergio García – Castello Masters, Andalucia Masters
Martin Kaymer – Abu Dhabi HSBC Golf Championship, WGC–HSBC Champions
Rory McIlroy – US Open Championship, UBS Hong Kong Open
Alvaro Quiros – Omega Dubai Desert Classic, Dubai World Championship

PGA European Tour statistics 2011

Eleven first-time winners

Nick Watney – WGC–Cadillac Championship
Nicolas Colsaerts – Volvo China Open
Thomas Aiken – Open de España
Robert Rock – BMW Italian Open
Matthew Zions – Saint-Omer Open
Keegan Bradley – US PGA Championship

Oliver Fisher – Czech Open
Lee Slattery – Bankia Madrid Masters
Tom Lewis – Portugal Masters
Joost Luiten – Iskandar Johor Open
Garth Mulroy – Alfred Dunhill Championship

Most top ten finishes

12: Rory McIlroy	Jamie Donaldson	Lorenzo Ggali
10: Charl Schwartzel	Martin Kaymer	David Lynn
9: Luke Donald	George Coetzee	Sergio Garcia
Thomas Aiken	7: Alex Noren	Francesco Molinari
Peter Hanson	Louis Oosthuizen	Gregory Havret
8: Lee Westwood	Joost Luiten	Richie Ramsay
Simon Dyson	6: Pablo Larrazabal	

Dates fixed for 40th Ryder Cup at Gleneagles Hotel

The 2014 Ryder Cup being played at Gleneagles Hotel will be staged from Friday September 26 to Sunday September 28. Although there has been talk of the event being extended from three to four days no change has been made by the Ryder Cup committee.

Europe are the current holders of the Cup having won 14½–13½ at Celtic Manor in Wales two years ago but America will be hoping to win it back when Davis Love III's side take on a European team captained by José Maria Olazábal at Medinah Country Club near Chicago from September 28 to 30 this year.

The Cup match is being played in Scotland for only the second time in its history. In 1973 the Americans were successful against Great Britain and Ireland at the Muirfield course of the Honourable Company of Edinburgh Golfers. Six years later Continental European players were included in the side to meet America.

Since 1979 the European side have won eight times, the Americans seven and one match has been drawn. More details of the match and ticketing is available on the European Tour website – www.europeantour.com

Seve's son Javier plans a professional career after university

It is a tough call but Javier Ballesteros plans to follow in the footsteps of his famous father by turning professional after he has completed his university education.

Ballesteros, whose father passed away last year at the age of 54, will relinquish his amateur status on completion of his law degree at the George Washington University in America.

The 21-year-old from Santander, who is a member of the Spanish National Team, told reporters in Madrid during the Bankia Madrid Masters: "As soon as I finish my studies, I would like to give pro golf a shot.

"At the moment I manage to hit around 200 balls every day, but only play once a week. Playing is when you really learn. My father was always my coach but now that that is not possible Angel Matallana at Golf Santander is helping me make changes to my swing."

World Number One Luke Donald, who played alongside Ballesteros Jr in the Madrid Pro-Am, praised the young Spaniard's game.

"I was very impressed with Javier, he is so like his late father. I guess the genes have been passed down."

After watching the young Ballesteros split the fairway with an opening drive one journalist said, tongue in cheek, "and he's a lot straighter off the tee than his dad used to be!"

European Tour top 20

MC Missed cut

2010 2011

	Alfred Dunhill C/ship	South African Open	Africa Open	Joburg Open	Abu Dhabi Championship	Volvo Golf Champions	Qatar Masters	Dubai Desert Classic	Avantha Masters	WGC-Accenture MP	WGC-Cadillac C/ship	Sicilian Open	Open de Andalucia	Trophée Hassan II	The Masters	Maybank Malaysian	Volvo China Open	Ballantine's C/ship	Open de España	Iberdrola Open
1 Luke Donald (ENG)	—	—	—	—	—	—	—	—	—	1	T6	—	—	—	T4	—	—	—	—	—
2 Rory McIlroy (NIR)	—	—	—	—	2	—	—	T10	—	T17	T10	—	—	—	T15	3	—	—	—	—
3 Martin Kaymer (GER)	—	—	—	—	1	—	T28	T31	—	2	T24	—	—	—	MC	T9	—	—	—	—
4 Charl Schwartzel (RSA)	T2	4	T4	1	T8	—	—	—	—	T17	T24	—	—	—	1	T11	—	—	—	—
5 Lee Westwood (ENG)	—	—	—	—	—	—	MC	T15	—	T17	T18	—	—	—	T11	—	—	1	—	—
6 Alvaro Quiros (ESP)	—	—	—	T23	T8	2	1	—	T33	T64	—	T51	—	T27	—	—	—	—	MC	—
7 Anders Hansen (DEN)	—	—	—	T18	T13	MC	2	—	T33	T3	—	—	—	MC	—	—	—	—	2	—
8 Sergio García (ESP)	—	—	—	—	T30	T9	T20	—	—	—	—	—	—	—	—	T35	—	T22	—	—
9 Thomas Björn (DEN)	—	—	—	MC	T44	1	MC	—	T17	T28	—	T15	—	—	—	—	—	—	—	—
10 Simon Dyson (ENG)	—	—	—	MC	MC	—	73	T28	—	—	—	T5	MC	T29	—	7	T52	T35	T5	—
11 Darren Clarke (NIR)	—	T26	20	MC	T8	T12	T48	—	—	—	MC	77	—	—	—	—	—	—	—	1
12 Miguel Angel Jiménez (ESP)	—	—	—	T11	T2	T74	T40	—	T5	T55	—	MC	—	T27	—	—	2	T46	—	—
13 Peter Hanson (SWE)	—	—	—	MC	T2	T70	9	—	T33	T55	—	—	—	MC	—	—	—	—	—	—
14 Alexander Noren (SWE)	—	—	—	T31	T8	MC	—	—	—	—	MC	T23	—	—	—	T4	MC	T5	T11	—
15 Louis Oosthuizen (RSA)	—	3	1*	—	MC	—	T37	—	—	T33	T18	—	—	—	MC	T72	—	—	—	—
16 Graeme McDowell (NIR)	—	—	—	—	T3	—	—	—	—	T9	T42	—	—	—	MC	—	—	—	—	—
17 Pablo Larrazábal (ESP)	—	—	—	T11	T24	MC	MC	T5	—	—	MC	T18	T44	—	—	T29	T10	—	T3	T49
18 Paul Lawrie (SCO)	—	—	—	MC	T30	T19	MC	—	—	—	T45	1	—	—	—	—	—	—	—	—
19 Gonzalo Fernández-Castaño (ESP)	—	—	—	MC	MC	MC	—	—	—	—	—	—	—	—	—	—	—	—	—	—
20 Nicolas Colsaerts (BEL)	—	—	—	T11	—	MC	T28	—	—	—	T5	T57	MC	—	T17	—	1	—	T22	—

2011 performances at a glance

— Did not play   * Involved in play-off

Volvo World MP	Madeira Islands Open	BMW PGA Championship	Italian Open	Saab Wales Open	US Open	St Omer Open	BMW International Open	Open de France	Barclays Scottish Open	140th Open Championship	Nordea Masters	Irish Open	WGC–Bridgestone Inv.	US PGA Championship	Czech Open	Johnnie Walker C/ship	Omega European Masters	KLM Open	Austrian GolfOpen	Dunhill Links C/ship	Madrid Masters	Portugal Masters	Castelló Masters	Andalucia Masters	WGC–HSBC Champions	Barclay's Singapore	Iskandar Johor Open	South African Open	Hong Kong Open	Dubai World Championship
—	—	1*	—	—	T45	—	—	—	1	MC	—	—	2	T8	—	—	—	—	T9	T11	—	—	—	—	—	—	—	—	—	3
T9	—	T24	—	1	—	—	—	T25	—	T34	T6	T64	—	T3	3	—	2	—	—	—	T4	—	—	—	—	—	—	1	—	T4
T3	—	T31	—	T39	—	T18	4	—	T12	—	—	T29	MC	—	2	MC	—	T30	—	T8	—	T23	1	—	—	—	—	—	—	T11
T5	—	MC	—	T9	—	—	—	T16	—	—	T53	T12	—	—	—	—	T9	—	—	—	T4	—	—	—	—	—	—	—	—	5
T9	—	2*	—	—	T3	—	—	—	T14	MC	—	—	T9	T8	—	—	T6	5	—	T30	—	—	—	T13	—	—	—	—	—	T29
T5	—	T8	—	T54	—	—	MC	—	MC	—	—	T53	MC	—	—	—	—	T68	T37	T16	—	MC	T49	—	—	—	—	—	T7	1
T17	—	T18	T2	—	—	—	T30	T66	T22	—	T29	3	—	T31	—	T25	—	—	—	—	—	—	T23	T11	—	—	—	—	—	T44
—	—	—	—	T7	—	2*	—	—	T9	—	T53	T12	—	—	—	—	—	—	—	I	I	—	—	—	—	—	—	—	—	T11
—	—	T66	—	—	MC	T57	—	4	—	T68	MC	—	I*	I	—	MC	—	T8	—	T15	T42	MC	—	—	—	—	—	—	—	T29
—	—	3	T20	—	—	MC	MC	T25	T9	—	I	T33	T51	—	T15	T16	I	—	T9	—	MC	—	T16	T33	—	MC	—	—	—	T46
—	—	T45	63	T46	—	—	MC	T66	I	—	MC	T68	MC	—	T35	—	MC	—	—	—	T38	—	—	—	—	—	—	—	—	57
T17	—	MC	T66	—	MC	—	T39	MC	—	T25	—	72	T64	MC	—	T9	—	T14	MC	—	MC	—	2	T38	T19	—	—	—	T11	T44
—	—	T18	T4	—	T7	—	MC	T10	MC	—	T21	T64	—	T25	MC	—	T9	T6	T11	—	T10	T33	—	—	—	—	—	—	3	4
—	—	MC	I	—	MC	—	T37	MC	I	—	T34	—	T9	—	T39	—	T29	T3	35	T49	T46	—	—	—	—	—	—	—	—	T37
T17	—	MC	—	T9	—	—	T54	—	T37	MC	—	T35	MC	—	T5	—	—	T7	T3	T8	—	—	—	—	—	—	—	—	—	6
T5	—	MC	T30	—	T14	—	T42	MC	—	T25	65	MC	—	—	—	T3	—	T43	3	T13	—	—	—	—	—	—	—	—	—	T11
—	—	T4	T11	—	18	MC	MC	T30	—	74	T45	—	28	T48	MC	—	T58	—	T11	MC	T38	T20	MC	—	—	—	—	—	MC	10
T17	—	MC	—	—	T54	—	T25	T66	—	—	—	T59	T35	T16	—	T45	T59	T11	—	T49	MC	—	—	—	—	—	—	—	T46	2
—	—	—	—	—	—	—	—	—	—	—	—	—	—	MC	—	T23	—	T18	MC	T21	—	TC	MC	2	T12	—	I*	—	—	T29
T3	—	MC	—	MC	—	T11	T3	—	—	—	—	—	—	—	—	—	—	T61	—	T9	T14	T44	—	T28	T20	MC	—	—	T35	T19

2011 European Tour
(in chronological order)

For past results see earlier editions of *The R&A Golfer's Handbook*

2010

Alfred Dunhill Championship *Leopard Creek, Mpumalanga, RSA* [7249–72]

1	Pablo Martin (ESP)	69-70-68-70—277	€158,500
2	Thorbjørn Oleson (DEN)	71-68-74-66—279	77,767
	Anthony Michael (RSA)	66-69-71-73—279	77,767
	Charl Schwartzel (RSA)	70-70-69-70—279	77,767

100th South African Open Championship *Pearl Valley Golf Estates* [7309–72]

1	Richie Ramsay (SCO)*	67-75-68-65—275	€158,500
2	Shiv Kapur (IND)	71-68-69-67—275	115,000

*Ramsay won at the first extra hole

3	Anders Hansen (DEN)	66-69-72-69—276	69,200

2011

Africa Open *East London, Eastern Cape, RSA* [6770–73]

1	Louis Oosthuizen (RSA)	70-67-69-70—276	€158,500
2	Manuel Quiros (ESP)	71-68-68-69—276	92,100
	Chris Wood (ENG)	72-69-67-68—276	92,100

Joburg Open *Royal Johannesburg and Kensington, RSA* [East 7592–71, West 7237–71]

1	Charl Schwartzel (RSA)	68-61-69-67—265	€206,050
2	Garth Multoy (RSA)	65-64-69-71—269	149,500
3	Thomas Aiken (RSA)	64-66-68-72—270	89,960

Abu Dhabi HSBC Golf Championship *Abu Dhabi, UAE* [7590–72]

1	Martin Kaymer (GER)	67-65-66-66—264	€334,398
2	Rory McIlroy (NIR)	71-67-65-69—272	222,932
3	Retief Goosen (RSA)	70-71-69-64—274	112,960
	Graeme McDowell (NIR)	66-70-71-67—274	112,960

Volvo Golf Champions *The Royal Golf Club, Bahrain* [7224–72]

1	Paul Casey (ENG)	67-67-66-68—268	€283,330
2	Peter Hanson (SWE)	66-67-67-69—269	147,590
	Miguel Angel Jiménez (ESP)	68-65-69-67—269	147,590

Commercialbank Qatar Masters *Doha* [7388–72]

1	Thomas Bjørn (DEN)	74-65-66-69—274	€303,114
2	Alvaro Quiros (ESP)	75-69-66-68—278	202,073
3	Markus Brier (AUT)	71-66-69-73—279	102,393
3	Rafael Cabrera-Bello (ESP)	77-68-66-68—279	102,393

Omega Dubai Desert Classic *Emirates, Dubai, UAE* [7301–72]

1	Alvaro Quiros (ESP)	73-68-68-68—277	€301,353
2	Anders Hansen (DEN)	69-68-71-70—278	157,045
	James Kingston (RSA)	72-72-67-67—278	157,045

Avantha Masters DLF G&CC, New Delhi, India   [7156–72]

1	SSP Chowrasia (IND)	70-69-67-67—273	€300,000
2	Robert Coles (ENG)	70-67-67-70—274	200,000
3	Grégory Havret (FRA)	72-67-68-68—275	112,680

WGC – Accenture Match Play Championship Ritz-Carlton, Dove Mountain, AZ, USA
[7791–72]

Winner:	Luke Donald (ENG)	€1,027,923
Runner-up:	Martin Kaymer (GER)	624,096
Third place:	Matt Kuchar (USA)	440,538

Full details of this event can be found on page 189

WGC – Cadillac Championship Doral, Orlando, FL, USA   [7334–72]

1	Nick Watney (USA)	67-70-68-67—272	€999,572
2	Dustin Johnson (USA)	69-69-65-71—274	606,883
3	Anders Hansen (DEN)	71-69-68-67—275	332,001
	Francesco Molinari (ITA)	68-68-70-69—275	332,001

Full details of this event can be found on page 190

Sicilian Open Donnafugata Golf Resort & Spa, Sicily   [7158–71]

1	Raphaël Jacquelin (FRA)	66-69-69-68—272	€166,660
2	Anthony Wall (ENG)	66-67-72-68—273	111,110
3	José Manuel Lara (ESP)	65-75-68-69—277	56,300
	Joel Sjöholm (SWE)	70-68-70-69—277	56,300

Open de Andalucía Parador de Málaga Golf, Málaga, Spain   [6817–70]

1	Paul Lawrie (SCO)	66-67-65-70—268	€166,660
2	Johan Edfors (SWE)	65-71-65-68—269	111,110
3	Felipe Aguilar (CHI)	67-69-66-68—270	62,600

Trophée Hassan II Golf du Palais Royal and Golf de L'Océan, Agadir, Morocco [6844–72, 6799–71]

1	David Horsey (ENG)	67-71-67-69—274	€250,000
2	Rhys Davies (WAL)	67-70-68-69—274	130,280
	Jaco Van Zyl (RSA)	68-73-65-68—274	130,280

The MASTERS TOURNAMENT Augusta National, GA, USA   [7435–72]

1	Charl Schwartzel (RSA)	69-71-6-866—274	€1,011,691
2	Jason Day (AUS)	72-64-72-68—276	494,604
	Adam Scott (AUS)	72-70-67-67—276	494,604

Full details of this event can be found on page 73

Maybank Malaysian Open Kuala Lumpur, Malaysia   [7000–72]

1	Matteo Manassero (ITA)	66-71-67-68—272	€288,466
2	Grégory Bourdy (FRA)	71-69-66-67—273	192,308
3	Rory McIlroy (NIR)	69-64-72-69—274	108,349

Volvo China Open Luxehills International Country Club, Chengdu, China   [7335–72]

1	Nicolas Colsaerts (BEL)	65-67-66-66—264	€350,946
2	Søren Kjeldsen (DEN)	65-71-66-66—268	140,086
	Peter Lawrie (IRL)	68-64-68-68—268	140,086
	Danny Lee (NZL)	66-68-69-65—268	140,086
	Pablo Martín (ESP)	70-68-67-63—268	140,086

Ballantine's Championship   *Blackstone GC, Incheon, South Korea*   [7275–72]

1	Lee Westwood (ENG)	72-68-69-67—276	€367,500
2	Miguel Angel Jiménez (ESP)	70-67-69-71—277	245,000
3	Sang-hyun Park (KOR)	67-72-70-69—278	138,033

Open de España   *Real Club de Golf El Prat*   [7298–72]

1	Thomas Aiken (RSA)	68-68-72-70—278	€333,330
2	Anders Hansen (DEN)	69-72-69-70—280	222,220
3	Scott Jamieson (SCO)	66-72-72-71—281	112,600
	Pablo Larrazábal (ESP)	67-70-73-71—281	112,600

Iberdrola Open   *Pula GC, San Servera, Mallorca, Spain*   [6915–70]

1	Darren Clarke (NIR)	65-70-70-69—274	€166,660
2	David Lynn (ENG)	68-68-71-70—277	86,855
	Chris Wood (ENG)	67-65-69-76—277	86,855

Volvo World Match Play Championship   *Finca Cortesin GC. Malaga, Spain*   [7380–72]

Quarter Finals:
Martin Kaymer (GER) beat Alvaro Quiros (ESP) 2 holes
Luke Donald (ENG) beat Charl Schwartzel (RSA) 2 holes
Nicolas Colsaerts (BEL) beat Graeme McDowell (NIR) 2 and 1
Ian Poulter (ENG) beat Francesco Molinari (ITA) 2 Holes

Semi-Finals:
Luke Donald beat Martin Kaymer 5 and 3
Ian Poulter beat Nicolas Colsaerts at 19th

Final:
Ian Poulter beat Luke Donald 2 and 1

Winner: €566,660
Runner-up: €377,770
3rd: €191,4001

Madeira Islands Open   *Porto Santo, Madeira, Portugal*   [7047–72]

1	Michael Hoey (NIR)	72-68-67-71—278	€116,660
2	Jamie Elson (ENG)	71-68-68-73—280	60,795
	Chris Gane (ENG)	67-72-70-71—280	60,795

BMW PGA Championship   *Wentworth Club, Surrey, England*   [7251–71]

1	Luke Donald (ENG)*	64-72-72-70—278	€750,000
2	Lee Westwood (ENG)	72-69-69-68—278	500,000

Donald won at the first extra hole

3	Simon Dyson (ENG)	71-68-72-69—280	281,700
4	Marcus Fraser (AUS)	70-72-73-67—282	191,100
	Raphaël Jacquelin (FRA)	72-70-69-71—282	191,100
	Shane Lowry (IRL)	74-72-69-67—282	191,100
7	Jamie Donaldson (WAL)	71-71-72-69—283	99,750
	Johan Edfords (SWE)	66-75-71-71—283	99,750
	David Horsey (ENG)	70-68-74-71—283	99,750
	Matteo Manassero (ITA)	66-70-72-75—283	99,750
	Colin Montgomerie (SCO)	69-75-71-68—283	99,750
	Peter Whiteford (SCO)	71-69-73-70—283	99,750
13	Felipe Aguilar (CHI)	70-70-73-71—284	69,150
	Ricardo Gonzales (ARG)	74-70-73-67—284	69,150
	Tano Goya (ARG)	77-69-72-66—284	69,150
16	Ernie Els (RSA)	75-68-72-70—285	62,100
	Thomas Levet (FRA)	69-71-74-71—285	62,100
18	Rhys Davies (WAL)	74-70-71-71—286	53,400
	Retief Goosen (RSA)	74-71-70-71—286	53,400
	Anders Hansen (DEN)	69-72-72-73—286	53,400
	Peter Hanson (SWE)	70-73-69-74—286	53,400

18T	Ian Poulter (ENG)	68-74-73-71—286	53,400
	Alvaro Quiros (ESP)	69-67-76-74—286	53,400
24	Paul Casey (ENG)	72-71-72-72—287	44,100
	Ignacio Garrido (ESP)	75-71-70-71—287	44,100
	Thongcha Jaidee (THA)	74-69-75-69—287	44,100
	José Manuel Lara (ESP)	68-70-74-75—287	44,100
	Rory McIlroy (NIR)	76-70-68-73—287	44,100
	Y E Yang (KOR)	71-70-72-74—287	44,100
	Fabrizio Zanotti (PAR)	71-70-69-77—287	44,100
31	S S P Chowrasia (IND)	71-71-75-71—288	34,538
	Kenneth Ferrie (ENG)	69-75-74-70—288	34,538
	Oscar Floren (SWE)	67-77-72-72—288	34,538
	Michael Hoey (NIR)	71-74-74-69—288	34,538
	Shiv Kapur (IND)	74-71-70-73—288	34,538
	Martin Kaymer (GER)	74-71-72-71—288	34,538
	Matt Morris (ENG)	75-71-70-72—288	34,538
	Martin Wiegele (AUT)	77-65-72-74—288	34,538
39	Thomas Aiken (RSA)	71-67-77-74—289	27,900
	Bradley Dredge (WAL)	68-74-69-78—289	27,900
	Ross Fisher (ENG)	75-68-70-76—289	27,900
	David Howell (ENG)	71-71-72-75—289	27,900
	Edoardo Molinari (ITA)	74-72-69-74—289	27,900
	Jaco van Zyle (RSA)	76-68-75-70—289	27,900
45	Darren Clarke (NIR)	69-72-74-75—290	24,300
	Robert Rock (ENG)	73-71-72-74—290	24,300
47	Carlos del Moral (ESP)	75-71-72-73—291	22,050
	Mark Foster (ENG)	71-75-75-70—291	22,050
	Hennie Otto (RSA)	70-71-78-72—291	22,050
50	Jason Levermore (ENG)	74-72-76-70—292	19,350
	Francesco Molinari (ITA)	75-71-73-73—292	19,350
	Graeme Storm (ENG)	74-71-75-72—292	19,350
53	Andrew Dodt (AUS)	71-73-75-74—293	16,650
	Ross McGowan (ENG)	68-74-75-76—293	16,650
	Marcel Siem (GER)	77-69-71-76—293	16,650
	Seve Benson (ENG)	74-72-75-73—294	13,838
	Jamie Elson (ENG)	72-71-73-78—294	13,838
	Steven O'Hara (SCO)	74-71-71-78—294	13,838
	John Parry (ENG)	71-71-77-75—294	13,838
60	Alvaro Velasco (ESP)	71-70-77-77—295	12,600
61	Fredrik Andersson Hed (SWE)	73-73-74-78—298	12,150
62	Paul Broadhurst (ENG)	76-69-74-81—300	11,250
	Grieg Hutcheon (SCO)	74-71-79-76—300	11,250
62	Gareth Maybin (NIR)	74-70-83-73—300	11,250
65	Scott Jamieson (SCO)	71-69-85-78—303	10,350
66	Scott Strange (AUS)	72-71-84-78—305	9,900

Saab Wales Open   *Celtic Manor, Newport*   [7378–71]

1	Alexander Noren (SWE)	67-67-71-70—275	€344,358
2	Grégory Bourdy (FRA)	67-73-70-67—277	179,456
	Anders Hansen (DEN)	70-70-66-71—277	179,456

BMW Italian Open   *Royal Park G&CC, Turin*   [7282–72]

1	Robert Rock (ENG)	64-68-68-67—267	€250,000
2	Gary Boyd (ENG)	69-65-68-66—268	130,280
	Thorbjørn Olesen (DEN)	65-71-70-62—268	130,280

111th US OPEN CHAMPIONSHIP   Pebble Beach, CA, USA   [7574–71]

1	Rory McIlroy (NIR)	65-66-68-69—268	€1,003,414
2	Jason Day (AUS)	71-72-65-68—276	602,745
3	Kevin Chappell (USA)	76-67-69-66—278	253,809
	Robert Garrigus (USA)	70-70-68-70—278	253,809
	Lee Westwood (ENG)	75-68-65-70—278	253,809
	Y E Yang (KOR)	68-69-70-71—278	253,809

Full details of this event can be found on page 62

St Omer Open   St Omer, Lumbres, France   [6846–71]

1	Matthew Zions (AUS)	68-72-67-69—276	€100,000
2	Daniel Denison (ENG)	69-74-67-73—283	44,740
	Peter Gustafsson (SWE)	73-71-70-69—283	44,740
	Craig Lee (SCO)	69-68-74-72—283	44,740

BMW International Open   München Eichenried, Germany   [7073–72]

1	Pablo Larrazábal (ESP)	68-67-69-68—272	€333,330
2	Sergio García (ESP)	69-71-64-68—272	222,220

* Larrazábal won at the fifth extra hole

3	George Coetzee (RSA)	67-67-70-70—274	88,000
	Mark Foster (ENG)	68-68-66-72—274	88,000
	Retief Goosen (RSA)	68-69-67-70—274	88,000
	Scott Jamieson (SCO)	69-69-72-64—274	88,000
	Joost Luiten (NED)	70-69-68-67—274	88,000

Alstom Open de France   Le Golf National, Paris, France   [7347–71]

1	Thomas Levet (FRA)	70-70-67-70—277	€500,000
2	Mark Foster (ENG)	68-68-68-74—278	260,565
	Thorbjørn Olesen (DEN)	66-71-71-70—278	260,565

The Barclay's Scottish Open   Castle Stuart, Inverness, Scotland   [7050–72]

1	Luke Donald (ENG)	67-67-63—197	€550,250
2	Fredrik Andersson Hed (SWE)	73-66-62—201	366,830
3	Angel Cabrera (ARG)	71-64-67—202	126,117
	George Coetzee (RSA)	66-69-67—202	126,117
	Nicolas Colsaerts (BEL)	69-66-67—202	126,117
	Lorenzo Gagli (ITA)	68-68-66—202	126,117
	Scott Jamieson (SCO)	67-66-69—202	126,117
	Mark Tullo (CHI)	65-71-66—202	126,117
	Martin Wiegele (AUT)	69-68-65—202	126,117

Event reduced to 54 holes due to bad weather

The 140th OPEN CHAMPIONSHIP   Royal St George's, Sandwich, England   [7204–70]

1	Darren Clarke (NIR)	68-68-69-70—275	€999,540
2	Dustin Johnson (USA)	70-68-68-72—278	474,782
	Phil Mickelson (USA)	70-69-71-68—278	474,782

Full details of this events can be found on page 46

Nordea Masters   (formerly SAS Masters)   Bro Hof Slott, Stockholm, Sweden   [7607–72]

1	Alexander Noren (SWE)	67-66-63-77—273	€250,000
2	Richard Finch (ENG)	69-72-70-69—280	166,660
3	Niklas Lemke (SWE)	68-72-70-73—283	93,900

Irish Open Killarney, Co. Kerry, R.o.l. [7161–71]

1	Simon Dyson (ENG)	70-65-67-67—269	€250,000
2	Richard Green (AUS)	67-68-67-68—270	166,660
3	Stephen Gallacher (SCO)	71-66-67-68—272	93,900

WGC – Bridgestone Invitational Firestone CC, Akron, OH, USA [7400–70]

1	Adam Scott (AUS)	62-70-66-65—263	€972,148
2	Luke Donald (ENG)	68-69-64-66—267	461,770
	Rickie Fowler (USA)	68-64-69-66—267	461,770

Full details of this event can be found on page 191

US PGA CHAMPIONSHIP Atlanta Athletic Club, Johns Creek, GA, USA [7467–70]

1	Keegan Bradley (USA)*	71-64-69-68—272	€1,028,126
2	Jason Dufner (USA)	70-65-68-69—272	615,452

*Bradley won at the third extra hole

3	Anders Hansen (DEN)	68-69-70-66—273	387,771

Full details of this event can be found on page 82

Czech Open (formerly Moravia Silesia Open) Prosper, Čeladná, Czech Republic [7452–72]

1	Oliver Fisher (ENG)	71-67-68-69—275	€250,000
2	Mikael Lundberg (SWE)	68-68-72-69—277	166,660
3	Fabrizio Zanotti (PAR)	71-71-71-66—279	93,900

Johnnie Walker Championship Gleneagles, Scotland [7316–72]

1	Thomas Bjørn (DEN)	68-69-71-69—277	€266,629
2	George Coetzee (RSA)	77-66-67-67—277	106,429
	Mark Foster (ENG)	66-71-68-72—277	106,429
	Pablo Larrazábal (ESP)	70-68-70-69—277	106,429
	Bernd Wiesberger (AUT)	69-71-68-69—277	106,429

* Bjørn won at the fifth extra hole

Omega European Masters Crans-sur-Sierre, Switzerland since 1939 [6822–71]

1	Thomas Bjørn (DEN)	68-68-66-62—264	€333,330
2	Martin Kaymer (GER)	65-70-68-65—268	222,220
3	Jamie Donaldson (WAL)	68-66-65-70—269	103,333
	Rory McIlroy (NIR)	65-69-67-68—269	103,333
	Jaco Van Zyl (RSA)	67-68-70-64—269	103,333

The KLM Open (formerly Dutch Open) Hilversum, The Netherlands [6906–70]

1	Simon Dyson (ENG)	65-66-71-66—268	€300,000
2	David Lynn (ENG)	67-66-68-68—269	200,000
3	Rory McIlroy (NIR)	70-65-68-67—270	112,680

The Vivendi Seve Trophy Saint-Nom-la-Breteche, France [6983–71]

Great Britain & Ireland 15½, Continent of Europe 12½
Full details of this event can be found on page 210

Austrian GolfOpen Atzenbrugg, Austria   [7386–72]

1	Kenneth Ferrie (ENG)*	72-70-67-67—276	€166,660
2	Simon Wakefield (ENG)	73-66-70-67—276	111,110

*Ferrie won at the first extra hole

3	Joost Luiten (NED)	67-70-72-68—277	62,600

Alfred Dunhill Links Championship St Andrews (Old course) [7279–72]
Kingsbarns [7150–72]
Carnoustie [7412–72]

1	Michael Hoey (NIR)	66-66-66-68—266	€588,149
2	Rory McIlroy (NIR)	70-67-66-65—268	392,097
3	Graeme McDowell (NIR)	67-67-67-69—270	198,677
	George Murray (SCO)	70-66-67-67—270	198,677

Bankia Madrid Masters Alcalá de Henares, Spain   [7561–72]

1	Lee Slattery (ENG)	67-66-69-71—273	€166,660
2	Lorenzo Gagli (ITA)	65-70-69-70—274	111,110
3	Eduardo de la Riva (ESP)	67-67-72-70—276	56,300
	Cesar Monasterio (ARG)	68-70-67-71—276	56,300

Portugal Masters Oceânico Victoria, Vilamoura, Portugal   [7231–72]

1	Tom Lewis (ENG)	70-64-68-65—267	€416,660
2	Rafael Cabrera-Bello (ESP)	69-65-64-71—269	277,770
3	Felipe Aguilar (CHI)	66-66-67-71—270	110,000
	George Coetzee (RSA)	70-69-66-65—270	110,000
	Grégory Havret (FRA)	66-69-71-64—270	110,000
	David Lynn (ENG)	70-68-68-64—270	110,000
	Christian Nilsson (SWE)	69-64-66-71—270	110,000

Castelló Masters Club de Campo del Mediterráneo, Castellón, Spain   [7073–71]

1	Sergio García (ESP)	67-63-64-63—257	€333,330
2	Gonzalo Fernandez-Castaño (ESP)	69-66-69-64—268	222,220
3	Alexander Noren (SWE)	69-63-73-64—269	112,600
	Richie Ramsay (SCO)	72-64-68-65—269	112,600

Andalucia Masters (formerly Volvo Masters) Club de Golf Valderrama, Cadiz, Spain   [6988–71]

1	Sergio García (ESP)	70-70-67-71—278	€500,000
2	Miguel Angel Jiménez (ESP)	71-70-68-70—279	333,330
3	Richie Ramsay (SCO)	65-72-73-70—280	187,800

WGC – HSBC Champions Tournament Sheshan GC, Shanghai, China   [7266–72]

1	Martin Kaymer (GER)	69-68-68-63—268	€842,218
2	Fredrik Jacobson (SWE)	67-66-67-71—271	473,747
3	Graeme McDowell (NIR)	69-69-67-67—272	301,795

Full details of this event can be found on page 193

Barclay's Singapore Open Sentosa GC   [7357–71]

1	Gonzalo Fernandez-Castaño (ESP)*	66-61-72—199	€720,877
2	Juvic Pagunsan (PHI)	66-66-67—199	480,580

*Fernandez-Castaño won at the second extra hole

3	Anthony Kim (USA)	70-66-64—200	243,512
	Louis Oosthuizen (RSA)	72-63-65—200	243,512

Reduced to 54 holes due to bad weather

Alfred Dunhill Championship *Leopard Creek, Mpumalanga, RSA* [7326–72]

1	Garth Mulroy (RSA)	69-68-64-68—269	€158,500
2	George Murray (SCO)	66-69-69-67—271	115,000
3	Felipe Aguilar (CHI)	71-64-68-72—275	48,750
	George Coetzee (RSA)	66-71-69-69—275	48,750
	Jaco Van Zyl (RSA)	68-68-72-67—275	48,750
	Peter Whiteford (SCO)	73-67-64-71—275	48,750

Iskandar Johor Open *Johor, Malaysia* [6782–71]

1	Joost Luiten (NED)	63-70-65—198	€242,581
2	Daniel Chopra (SWE)	64-65-70—199	161,720
3	Rhys Davies (WAL)	70-65-65—200	75,201
	Padraig Harrington (IRL)	64-67-69—200	75,201
	James Morrison (ENG)	66-65-69—200	75,201

Tournament reduced to 54 holes

South African Open *Ekurhuleni, South Africa* [7761–72]

1	Hennie Otto (RSA)	70-67-65-72—274	€158,500
2	Bernd Wiesberger (AUT)	69-68-70-68—275	115,000
3	Thomas Aiken (RSA)	68-69-68-72—277	53,200
	Richard McEvoy (ENG)	70-70-69-68—277	53,200
	Ockie Strydom (RSA)	69-72-67-69—277	53,200

56th World Cup of Golf *Mission Hills GC, China* [7441–72]

1	USA (Matt Kuchar and Gary Woodland)	64-70-63-67—264	€1,814,196
2	England (Ian Poulter and Justin Rose)	66-69-68-63—266	982,689
	Germany (Martin Kaymer and Alex Cejka)	65-71-61-69—266	982,689

Full details of this event can be found in International Team Events, page 214

UBS Hong Kong Open *Hong Kong GC, Fanling* [6730–70]

1	Rory McIlroy (NIR)	64-69-70-65—268	€341,724
2	Grégory Havret (FRA)	70-69-66-65—270	227,813
3	Peter Hanson (SWE)	68-68-65-70—271	128,352

Dubai World Championship *Earth Course, Jumeirah Golf Estates, Dubai, UAE* [7675–72]

1	Alvaro Quiros (ESP)	68-64-70-67—269	€922,645
2	Paul Lawrie (SCO)	65-73-66-67—271	615,094
3	Luke Donald (ENG)	72-68-66-66—272	359,832

4 Peter Hanson (SWE) 274; 5 Charl Schwartzel (RSA) 275; 6 Francesco Molinari (ITA), Louis Oosthuizen (RSA) 276; 8 Robert Rock (ENG), Shane Lowry (IRL) 277; 10 Pablo Larrazábal (ESP) 278; 11 Graeme McDowell (NIR), Robert Karlsson (SWE), Rory McIlroy (NIR), Sergio García (ESP), Martin Kaymer (GER) 279; 16 Johan Edfors (SWE), David Lynn (ENG), Paul Casey (ENG) 280; 19 Fredrik Andersson Hed (SWE), Thorbjørn Olesen (DEN), Nicolas Colsaerts (BEL) 282; 22 Hennie Otto (RSA), George Coetzee (RSA), Jaco Van Zyl (RSA), Ian Poulter (ENG) 283; 26 Thomas Aiken (RSA), Rafael Cabrera-Bello (ESP), Jamie Donaldson (WAL) 284; 29 Thomas Björn (DEN), Grégory Bourdy (FRA), Gonzalo Fernandez-Castaño (ESP), Edoardo Molinari (ITA), Lee Westwood (ENG) 285; 34 Mark Foster (ENG), Ernie Els (RSA), Matteo Manassero, (ITA) 286; 37 Retief Goosen (RSA), Lorenzo Gagli (ITA), Felipe Aguilar (CHI), David Horsey (ENG), Alexander Noren (SWE) 287; 42 Thomas Levet (FRA), Richie Ramsay (SCO), Miguel Angel Jiménez (ESP), Anders Hansen (DEN) 290; 46 Simon Dyson (ENG), Ross Fisher (ENG) 291; 48 Grégory Havret (FRA), Raphaël Jacquelin (FRA), Rhys Davies (WAL) 292; 51 Joost Luiten (NED), Peter Lawrie (IRL) 293; 53 James Morrison (ENG) 294; 54 Scott Jamieson (ENG), Michael Hoey (NIR), 296; 56 Christian Nilsson (SWE) 297; Darren Clarke (NIR)299; Y E Yang (KOR) retd.

Top money earners on the European Tour 1972–2011
(European Tour members only)

1972	Bob Charles (NZL)	€25,953		2000	Lee Westwood (ENG)	€3,125,147
1975	Dale Hayes (RSA)	€28,710		2005	Colin Montgomerie (SCO)	€2,794,223
1980	Greg Norman (AUS)	€104,761		2009	Lee Westwood (ENG)	€4,237,762
1985	Sandy Lyle (SCO)	€356,595		2010	Martin Kaymer (GER)	€4,461,011
1990	Ian Woosnam (WAL)	€1,033,169		2011	Luke Donald (ENG)	€4,216,226
1995	Colin Montgomerie (SCO)	€1,454,205				

Continentals fight back but to no avail at St Nom

For several hours on the final day it looked as if the Continental side captained by Hong Kong–based Frenchman Jean Van de Velde were poised to record one of the greatest fight-backs in team golf history in the Vivendi Seve Trophy.

Going into the singles at St Nom La Bretche, remembered as the venue for many years of the Trophée Lancome, the Great Britain and Ireland team captained by Paul McGinley, who had led them to success at the same venue two years earlier, were all but home and dry. They needed only three of the ten points on offer on the last day to win. The Continentals needed to win eight of the 10. Game over!

Yet what was expected to be a stroll to victory by the visitors turned into a tense nightmare before GBI finally secured the winning point. Started as a match-play work-out in alternate years to the Ryder cup by the late Severiano Ballesteros, the 2011 fixture did not lack excitement.

Although World No 2 Lee Westwood won three of the first five holes with birdies against three-time 2011 European title winner Thomas Björn, it was the Dane who won on the 17th green and although Darren Clarke as reigning Open champion was expected to have the edge on Miguel Angel Jiménez, the Ulsterman lost on the 16th green and with Anders Hansen, Francesco Molinari and Alexander Noren all winning in the top half of the singles draw the match was suddenly tied. It was game on.

Yet on a topsy-turvy final day when play had been started early in order to avoid early afternoon storms, the Continentals were unable to win any more points.

David Horsey halved with Nicholas Colsaerts and Peter Hanson and Ross Fisher in the last match called it a half too because by then the Trophy had been won and lost but the other points, much to McGinley's relief, were won by his team.

Two were scored by rookies to the Great Britain and Ireland v Continntal Europe match – Glasgow's Scott Jamieson and Worksop's Mark Foster – and a third point was won by experienced Ryder Cupper Ian Poulter who put in a true bravura performance to record a string of birdies at the end including one at the last to disappoint Italian teenager Matteo Manassero who had had the edge most of the way round. In the end the indomitable Poulter, who had not been at his most brilliant best but still oozed confidence, ended up the top points scorer for the team with five out of five.

So their hopes had been dashed. The Continentals had lost 15½–12½. It was their sixth defeat in a row. Their only victory came in the first match in 2000 when the then playing captains Severiano Ballesteros and Colin Montgomerie battled for the crucial winning point and, in the circumstances, it was probably fair that Seve, the man who thought up the fixture, scored the winning point.

Who was known as "The von"?

The answer can be found on page 905

European Senior Tour 2011

www.europeantour.com

Final Ranking (Top 30 earn full Tour card for 2012)

1	Peter Fowler (AUS)	€302,327		51	Noel Ratcliffe (AUS)	35,847
2	Barry Lane (ENG)	271,173		52	Domingo Hospital (ESP)	34,820
3	Andrew Oldcorn (SCO)	188,981		53	Doug Johnson (USA)	34,812
4	Gary Wolstenholme (ENG)	181,637		54	Glenn Ralph (ENG)	33,089
5	Ian Woosnam (WAL)	179,160		55	Anders Forsbrand (SWE)	29,270
6	Boonchu Ruangkit (THA)	148,387		56	Steve Van Vuuren (RSA)	27,813
7	David Frost (RSA)	147,986		57	Massy Kuramoto (JPN)	27,560
8	Mike Harwood (AUS)	143,789		58	Delroy Cambridge (JAM)	25,805
9	Juan Quiros (ESP)	140,511		59	Horacio Carbonetti (ARG)	24,632
10	Carl Mason (ENG)	136,162		60	Mike Clayton (AUS)	23,300
11	Roger Chapman (ENG)	129,816		61	Jeb Stuart (USA)	23,002
12	Des Smyth (IRL)	122,653		62	Jean Pierre Sallat (FRA)	20,741
13	Gordon Brand Jr (SCO)	121,429		63	Manuel Moreno (ESP)	20,701
14	Mark Mouland (WAL)	117,768		64	Wayne Grady (AUS)	19,651
15	Sandy Lyle (SCO)	113,203		65	Fraser Mann (SCO)	19,452
16	Chris Williams (RSA)	113,175		66	Denis Durnian (ENG)	19,061
17	Angel Franco (PAR)	105,375		67	Peter Dahlberg (SWE)	19,002
18	Marc Farry (FRA)	103,429		68	Andrew Murray (ENG)	18,495
19	Ross Drummond (SCO)	98,771		69	Giuseppe Cali (ITA)	18,225
20	Sam Torrance (SCO)	95,801		70	John Chillas (SCO)	17,294
21	Mark James (ENG)	83,485		71	Steve Cipa (ENG)	15,858
22	Bob Cameron (ENG)	82,926		72	Paul Curry (ENG)	15,391
23	Bill Longmuir (SCO)	81,911		73	Claude Grenier (AUT)	14,140
24	Tim Thelen (USA)	80,110		74	Eamonn Darcy (IRL)	13,104
25	David Merriman (AUS)	79,021		75	Jim Rhodes (ENG)	12,019
26	Angel Fernandez (CHI)	75,964		76	Manuel Piñero (ESP)	11,384
27	Nick Job (ENG)	73,077		77	François Illouz (FRA)	11,151
28	Bobby Lincoln (RSA)	68,410		78	Stephen Bennett (ENG)	9,122
29	Mike Cunning (USA)	67,283		79	Jimmy Heggarty (NIR)	8,536
30	David J Russell (ENG)	64,788		80	Joe Stansberry (USA)	8,291
31	George Ryall (ENG)	63,706		81	Hiroshi Ueda (JPN)	7,952
32	John Harrison (ENG)	61,694		82	Matt Briggs (ENG)	7,377
33	Gordon J Brand (ENG)	60,526		83	Peter A Smith (SCO)	6,729
34	Gordon Manson (AUT)	60,425		84	Lyndsay Stephen (AUS)	6,521
35	Graham Banister (AUS)	58,978		85	Tony Charnley (ENG)	6,474
36	Kevin Spurgeon (ENG)	56,026		86	Antonio Garrido (ESP)	5,700
37	Katsuyoshi Tomori (JPN)	54,550		87	Maurice Bembridge (ENG)	5,256
38	Bertus Smit (RSA)	52,718		88	James Murphy (ENG)	4,838
39	Mark Belsham (ENG)	52,401		89	Jeff Hall (ENG)	3,499
40	Adan Sowa (ARG)	48,796		90	Emilio Rodriguez (ESP)	3,254
41	José Rivero (ESP)	48,007		91	Mike Miller (SCO)	2,882
42	Costantino Rocca (ITA)	47,264		92	Martin Gray (SCO)	2,789
43	Andrew Sherborne (ENG)	47,126		93	Eddie Polland (NIR)	2,626
44	Tony Johnstone (ZIM)	45,259		94	Glyn Davies (WAL)	2,547
45	Jerry Bruner (USA)	45,234		95	Victor Garcia (ESP)	2,481
46	Denis O'Sullivan (IRL)	42,099		96	Mitch Kierstenson (ENG)	2,382
47	Peter Mitchell (ENG)	41,691		97	Bill Hardwick (CAN)	2,369
48	Rodger Davis (AUS)	40,183		98	Mike Williams (ZIM)	1,847
49	Luis Carbonetti (ARG)	38,138		99	Terry Burgoyne (SCO)	1,769
50	John Gould (ENG)	37,311		100	Ken Tarling (CAN)	1,717

Career Money List

1	Carl Mason (ENG)		€2,283,462	51	Pete Oakley (USA)	527,204
2	Tommy Horton (ENG)		1,527,506	52	Martin Gray (SCO)	526,986
3	Nick Job (ENG)		1,477,881	53	David Huish (SCO)	512,325
4	Sam Torrance (SCO)		1,467,152	54	Ray Carrasco (USA)	505,330
5	Noel Ratcliffe (AUS)		1,356,875	55	Bobby Verwey (RSA)	496,778
6	Bill Longmuir (SCO)		1,268,452	56	Jay Haas (USA)	484,013
7	Jerry Bruner (USA)		1,256,866	57	Brian Waites (ENG)	482,280
8	Tom Watson (USA)		1,251,116	58	David Merriman (AUS)	473,232
9	Denis O'Sullivan (IRL)		1,237,342	59	Alberto Croce (ITA)	469,904
10	Jim Rhodes (ENG)		1,194,766	60	Liam Higgins (IRL)	469,088
11	John Chillas (SCO)		1,106,444	61	Peter Mitchell (ENG)	467,080
12	Bob Cameron (ENG)		1,092,063	62	Boonchu Ruangkit (THA)	463,722
13	Seiji Ebihara (JPN)		1,055,381	63	Bob Lendzion (USA)	462,937
14	Terry Gale (AUS)		1,026,697	64	Bob Shearer (AUS)	459,657
15	Delroy Cambridge (JAM)		1,007,558	65	Gordon Brand Jr (SCO)	458,050
16	Denis Durnian (ENG)		955,976	66	Kevin Spurgeon (ENG)	455,793
17	David Good (AUS)		945,648	67	Mike Miller (SCO)	455,395
18	Gordon J Brand (ENG)		931,360	68	Ian Mosey (ENG)	443,469
19	Neil Coles (ENG)		928,968	69	Glenn Ralph (ENG)	427,314
20	Luis Carbonetti (ARG)		926,919	70	Katsuyoshi Tomori (JPN)	425,666
21	Des Smyth (IRL)		917,525	71	Christy O'Connor Jr (IRL)	423,516
22	Juan Quiros (ESP)		895,548	72	Chris Williams (RSA)	423,025
23	Eduardo Romero (ARG)		879,607	73	Tom Lehman (USA)	422,754
24	Giuseppe Cali (ITA)		848,568	74	Gery Watine (FRA)	416,791
25	Malcolm Gregson (ENG)		833,972	75	Bill Hardwick (CAN)	416,305
26	Maurice Bembridge (ENG)		783,929	76	Paul Leonard (NIR)	414,918
27	David J Russell (ENG)		783,650	77	Mark James (ENG)	412,406
28	José Rivero (ESP)		754,923	78	Tom Kite (USA)	394,814
29	Ian Woosnam (WAL)		752,021	79	Peter Fowler (AUS)	394,128
30	Simon Owen (NZL)		747,697	80	Bernard Gallacher (SCO)	390,919
31	Horacio Carbonetti (ARG)		737,603	81	Priscillo Diniz (BRA)	388,580
32	Bob Charles (NZL)		719,968	82	Gary Player (RSA)	386,206
33	Loren Roberts (USA)		688,651	83	Bertus Smit (RSA)	385,647
34	Eamonn Darcy (IRL)		687,299	84	Barry Lane (ENG)	382,068
35	Guillermo Encina (CHI)		682,238	85	Michael Allen (USA)	375,161
36	Bernhard Langer (GER)		680,628	86	David Jones (NIR)	374,369
37	John Bland (RSA)		669,879	87	John Fourie (RSA)	371,197
38	David Creamer (ENG)		664,121	88	Roger Chapman (ENG)	354,907
39	Eddie Polland (NIR)		651,591	89	Bruce Heuchan (CAN)	353,380
40	Brian Huggett (WAL)		638,783	90	Andrew Oldcorn (SCO)	352,095
41	Antonio Garrido (ESP)		609,245	91	Denis Watson (ZIM)	345,234
42	Ian Stanley (AUS)		607,584	92	Mike Harwood (AUS)	332,381
43	Ross Drummond (SCO)		597,049	93	Craig Defoy (WAL)	326,196
44	Alan Tapie (USA)		590,860	94	Russ Cochran (USA)	326,126
45	Angel Franco (PAR)		580,402	95	Adan Sowa (ARG)	326,046
46	Tony Johnstone (ZIM)		577,614	96	David Frost (RSA)	320,835
47	Stewart Ginn (AUS)		572,687	97	Peter Senior (AUS)	311,874
48	Costantino Rocca (ITA)		559,654	98	Angel Fernandez (CHI)	310,326
49	John Grace (USA)		539,694	99	Manuel Piñero (ESP)	306,333
50	Bobby Lincoln (RSA)		537,134	100	Emilio Rodriguez (ESP)	304,655

Tour Results

Handa Australian Senior Open	Royal Perth GC, WA	Peter Senior (AUS)	207 (–9)
Handa Cup Senior Masters	Ohmurasaki GC, Saitama, Japan	Massy Kuramoto (JPN)	206 (–17)
Mauritius Commercial Bank Open	Constance Belle Mare Plage, Mauritius	David Frost (RSA)	203 (–13)
Aberdeen Brunei Senior Masters	The Empire, Brunei	Chris Williams (RSA)	201 (–12)
ISPS Handa Senior World Championship	Mission Hills, China	Sandy Lyle (SCO)	204 (–12)
OKI Open de España Senior	El Valle, Murcia, Spain	Carl Mason (ENG)	200 (–13)

US Senior PGA Championship — Louisville, KY, USA

1	Tom Watson (USA)*	70-70-68-70—278
2	David Eger (USA)	74-68-69-67—278

Watson won at the first extra hole

3	Kiyoshi Murota (JPN)	66-67-74-72—279

IPS Handa Senior Masters	Stapleford Park, England	Peter Fowler (AUS)	209 (–10)
De Vere PGA Seniors Championship	Slaley Hall, England	Andrew Oldcorn (SCO)	277 (–11)
Berenberg Bank Masters	Cologne, Germany	Ian Woosnam (WAL)	207 (–9)
Van Lanschot Senior Open	The Hague, Netherlands	Des Smyth (IRL)	210 (–6)
Bad Ragaz PGA Seniors Open	Bad Ragaz, Switzerland	Peter Fowler (AUS)	196 (–14)

The Senior Open — Walton Heath, England

1	Russ Cochran (USA)	72-70-67-67—276
2	Mark Calcavecchia (USA)	68-69-72-69—278
3	Corey Pavin (USA)	72-69-69-69—279
	Tom Watson (USA)	75-68-69-67—279

US Senior Open — Toledo. OH. USA

1	Olin Browne (USA)	64-69-65-71—269
2	Mark OMeara (USA)	66-68-66-72—272
3	Mark Calcavecchia (USA)	68-67-69-69—273

Cleveland Golf/Srixon Scottish Senior Open	Fairmont St. Andrews, Scotland	Barry Lane (ENG)	202 (–14)
Travis Perkins plc Senior Masters	Duke's Course, Woburn GC, Woburn, England	Boonchu Ruangkit (THA)	207 (–9)
Casa Serena Open	Kutná Hora, Czech Republic	Barry Lane (ENG)	198 (–15)
Cannes Mougins Masters	Cannes, France	Juan Quiros (ESP)*	206 (–10)

Quiros beat Des Smyth (IRL) at the second extra hole

Belas Clube de Campo Senior Open de Portugal	Lisbon, Portugal	Mark Mouland (WAL)	207 (–9)
Benahavis Senior Masters	La Quinta G&CC, Benahavis, Spain	Carl Mason (ENG)	204 (–9)
Fubon Senior Open	Miramar G&CC, Taipei	Chien Soon Lu (TPE)	204 (–12)
MCB Tour Championship	Constance Belle Mare Plage, Mauritius	Tom Lehman (USA)	204 (–12)

Senior Tour Records 2011

Low 9 holes	28 (–7)	Angel Fernandez	Bad Ragaz PGA Seniors Open
	28 (–7)	Des Smyth	Bad Ragaz PGA Seniors Open
Low 18 holes	61 (–9)	Angel Fernandez	Bad Ragaz PGA Seniors Open
Largest Winning Margin	9 shots	Andrew Oldcorn	De Vere Club PGA Seniors Championship
Largest 18 Hole Lead	3 shots	Angel Fernandez	Bad Ragaz PGA Seniors Open
	3 shots	Lu Chien Soon	Fubon Senior Open

Senior Tour Records 2011

First time winners

Peter Senior	Handa Australian Senior Open
Massy Kuramoto	Handa Cup Senior Masters
David Frost	Mauritius Commercial Bank Open
Chris Williams	Aberdeen Brunei Senior Masters
Sandy Lyle	ISPS Handa Senior World Championship
Peter Fowler	ISPS Handa Senior Masters
Andrew Oldcorn	De Vere Club PGA Seniors Championship
Russ Cochran	Senior Open Championship
Olin Browne	US Senior Open
Mark Mouland	Belas Club de Campo Senior Open de Portugal
Lu Chien Soon	Fubon Senior Open

Course records

Peter Senior Open	65 (–7) (equal)	Australian Senior Open
Ian Woosnam	63 (–9)	Handa Cup Senior Masters
Bobby Lincoln	64 (–7)	OKI Open de Espana Senior
Angel Fernandez	61 (–9) (equal)	Bad Ragaz PGA Seniors Open
Peter Fowler	65 (–7)	Cleveland Golf/Srixon Scottish Senior Open
Denis O'Sullivan	65 (–7) (equal)	Cleveland Golf/Srixon Scottish Senior Open
Barry Lane	62 (–9)	Casa Serena Open

Multiple winners

Peter Fowler	ISPS Handa Senior Masters, Bad Ragaz PGA Seniors Open
Barry Lane	Cleveland Golf/Srixon Scottish Senior Open, Casa Serena Open

Fowler is third Australian to top Senior Tour Money list

Australian Peter Fowler beat former Ryder Cup player Barry Lane to win the 2011 European Senior Tour Order of Merit and the John Jacobs Trophy following a dramatic final day of the season at the MCB Tour Championship in Mauritius.

Fowler, who succeeds Thailand's Boonchu Ruangkit, is the third Australian to finish No 1, following Noel Ratcliffe in 2000 and Ian Stanley in 2001.

The 52-year-old finished the year with earnings of €302,327 finishing €32,154 clear of runner-up Lane in the Order of Merit.

After struggling for two years with a disc problem in his back which happened in practice before his Senior Tour début, Fowler won twice in 2011 capturing his maiden Senior Tour title in the ISPS Handa Senior World Championship in June before coming from seven shots back on the final day to win the Bad Ragaz PGA Seniors Open in Switzerland the following month.

He was also runner-up in the ISPS Handa Senior World Championship presented by Mission Hills China and the Casa Serena Open and tied second in the Van Lanschot Senior Open.

In total he finished inside the top ten in 13 of his 18 appearances in 2011, with nine of those inside the top five.

"I've played pretty solidly and consistently last year," said Fowler. who played 519 events on the European Tour in a career spanning 25 years, winning once in the 1993 BMW International Open when he held off Ian Woosnam and Bernhard Langer.

Former Walker Cup player Gary Wolstenholme moved past former Masters Champion Ian Woosnam into fourth position with earnings of €181,636 to be the Tour's Rookie of the Year. In his first full season on the European Tour he had nine top ten finishes.

European Challenge Tour 2011

www.europeantour.com

Final Order of Merit (top 20 earn card for PGA European Tour)

1	Tommy Fleetwood (ENG)	€148,913	51	Benn Barham (ENG)	33,034
2	Andrea Pavan (ITA)	133,052	52	Joaquin Estevez (ARG)	32,911
3	Sam Little (ENG)	130,798	53	Bjorn Åkesson (SWE)	32,623
4	Ricardo Santos (POR)	97,516	54	Christophe Brazillier (FRA)	32,006
5	Benjamin Hebert (FRA)	91,293	55	Colm Moriarty (IRL)	31,140
6	Daniel Denison (ENG)	86,898	56	Daniel Vancsik (ARG)	30,688
7	Federico Colombo (ITA)	81,834	57	Maximilian Kieffer (GER)	29,950
8	Jamie Moul (ENG)	80,771	58	Pierre Relecom (BEL)	29,605
9	Jorge Campillo (ESP)	80,041	59	Adrien Bernadet (FRA)	29,545
10	Matthew Baldwin (ENG)	76,972	60	Gary Lockerbie (ENG)	29,112
11	Edouard Dubois (FRA)	75,623	61	James Heath (ENG)	27,818
12	Simon Thornton (IRL)	74,712	62	Anders Schmidt Hansen (DEN)	26,787
13	Julien Quesne (FRA)	74,027	63	Roland Steiner (AUT)	26,457
14	Craig Lee (SCO)	73,792	64	Sion E Bebb (WAL)	26,080
15	Andrew Johnston (ENG)	70,987	65	Alastair Forsyth (SCO)	25,685
16	Sam Walker (ENG)	67,584	66	Garry Houston (WAL)	25,477
17	Charles-Edouard Russo (FRA)	67,192	67	Charlie Ford (ENG)	25,035
18	Pelle Edberg (SWE)	66,282	68	Chris Paisley (ENG)	24,926
19	Chris Gane (ENG)	64,488	69	Olly Whiteley (ENG)	24,646
20	Alessandro Tadini (ITA)	62,630	70	Andreas Hartø (DEN)	24,076
21	Anthony Snobeck (FRA)	61,829	71	Jordi Garcia (ESP)	23,768
22	Florian Praegant (AUT)	61,725	72	Andrea Perrino (ITA)	22,724
23	José-Filipe Lima (POR)	61,292	73	Mikael Lundberg (SWE)	22,310
24	Branden Grace (RSA)	60,242	74	Andrew McArthur (SCO)	21,872
25	Andrew Marshall (ENG)	59,698	75	Matthew Cryer (ENG)	21,626
26	Matthew Southgate (ENG)	58,561	76	Michael Lorenzo-Vera (FRA)	21,336
27	Jamie Elson (ENG)	55,931	77	Baptiste Chapellan (FRA)	20,665
28	Chris Lloyd (ENG)	55,184	78	Ben Evans (ENG)	20,280
29	Peter Gustafsson (SWE)	54,830	79	Jack Doherty (SCO)	20,276
30	Knut Borsheim (NOR)	53,159	80	André Bossert (SUI)	19,963
31	Julien Guerrier (FRA)	52,390	81	Agustin Domingo (ESP)	19,724
32	Steven Tiley (ENG)	51,221	82	Andrea Maestroni (ITA)	19,643
33	Victor Riu (FRA)	50,505	83	Gavin Dear (SCO)	19,458
34	Bernd Ritthammer (GER)	48,891	84	Jamie McLeary (SCO)	18,786
35	Espen Kofstad (NOR)	47,996	85	Matteo Delpodio (ITA)	17,447
36	Chris Doak (SCO)	47,896	86	Joakim Lagergren (SWE)	16,937
37	Phillip Archer (ENG)	47,483	87	Jason Palmer (ENG)	15,826
38	Nicolas Meitinger (GER)	46,835	88	Pablo Del Grosso (ARG)	15,412
39	Andrew Tampion (AUS)	46,180	89	Carl Suneson (ESP)	15,203
40	Martin Erlandsson (SWE)	43,708	90	Mads Vibe-Hastrup (DEN)	15,019
41	François Delamontagne (FRA)	41,472	91	James Hepworth (ENG)	14,449
42	Tyrone Ferreira (RSA)	41,234	92	Jurrian Van Der Vaart (NED)	14,314
43	Lasse Jensen (DEN)	40,688	93	Leif Westerberg (SWE)	14,151
44	Lloyd Kennedy (ENG)	39,142	94	Tom Whitehouse (ENG)	13,283
45	Michiel Bothma (RSA)	39,111	95	Stuart Davis (ENG)	13,134
46	Klas Eriksson (SWE)	36,389	96	Sebi Garcia (ESP)	12,632
47	Daniel Brooks (ENG)	36,317	97	Wil Besseling (NED)	12,578
48	Sam Hutsby (ENG)	36,163	98	Francis Valera (ESP)	12,431
49	Callum Macaulay (SCO)	34,209	99	Julien Grillon (FRA)	12,283
50	Matt Ford (ENG)	33,995	100	Julien Clément (SUI)	12,141

Results

Tournament	Venue	Winner	Score
Gujarat Kensville Challenge	Ahmedabad, India	Gaganjeet Bhullar (IND)	283 (–5)
Abierto International Copa Antioquia	Club Campestre, La Macarena, Colombia	Joaquin Estevez (ARG)*	274 (–10)

Estevez beat Charles-Edouard Russo (FRA) at the first extra hole

Tournament	Venue	Winner	Score
Barclays Kenya Open	Muthaiga GC, Nairobi, Kenya	Michiel Bothma (RSA)	270 (–14)
ALLIANZ Challenge de France	Golf Disneyland, Paris	Nicolas Meitinger (GER)*	269 (–15)

Meitinger beat Maximilian Kieffer (GER) at the second extra hole

Tournament	Venue	Winner	Score
Mugello-Tuscany Open	Scarperia, Florence, Italy	Anthony Snobeck (FRA)	272 (–12)
Madeira Island Open	Porto Santo, Portugal	Michael Hoey (NIR)	278 (–10)
Telenet Trophy	Lasne, Belgium	Andrew Tampion (AUS)	280 (–8)
Kärnten Open	Klagenfurt-Seltenheim, Austria	Edouard Dubois (FRA)	265 (–23)
ALLIANZ Open Cotes d'Armor – Bretagne	Le Val André, France	Phillip Archer (ENG)	273 (–7)
St Omer Open	St Omer, Lumbres, France	Matthew Zions (AUS)	276 (–8)
Scottish Hydro Challenge	Aviemore, Scotland	Edouard Dubois (FRA)	271 (–13)
The Princess	Bara, Sweden	Ricardo Santos (POR)	272 (–16)
Acaya Open	Puglia, Italy	Jamie Moul (ENG)	272 (–8)
Credit Suisse Challenge	Lucerne, Switzerland	Benjamin Hebert (FRA)	272 (–12)
English Challenge	Stoke by Nayland, Colchester, England	Benjamin Hebert (FRA)	276 (–12)
Norwegian Challenge	Slattum, Norway	Andrea Pavan (ITA)	276 (–9)
ECCO Tour Championship	Nimtofte, Denmark	Daniel Denison (ENG)	208 (–8)
Rolex Trophy	Geneva, Switzerland	Herbert Benjamin (FRA)	269 (–19)
Kazakhstan Open	Almaty, Kazakhstan	Tommy Fleetwood (ENG)	273 (–15)
M2M Russian Challenge Cup	Moscow, Russia	Sam Little (ENG)	277 (–11)
ALLIANZ Golf Open du Grand Toulouse	Seilh, France	Sam Little (ENG)	268 (–16)
Fred Olsen Challenge de España	La Gomera, Canary Is., Spain	Matthew Baldwin (ENG)	263 (–21)
ALLIANZ Golf Open de Lyon	Monthieux, France	Julien Quesne (FRA)	268 (–16)
Roma Golf Open	Olgiata GC, Rome, Italy	Sam Little (ENG)*	273 (–11)

Little beat Pelle Edberg (SWE) at the fourth extra hole

Tournament	Venue	Winner	Score
Apulia San Domenico Grand Final	Puglia, Italy	Andrea Pavan (ITA)	267 (–17)

Challenge Tour Records 2011

Low 9 holes	29 (–7)	Andrew Johnston (ENG)	Fred Olsen Challenge de España
	29 (–6)	Phillip Archer (ENG)	ALLIANZ Open Cotes d'Armor Bretagne
Low 18 holes	61 (–9)	Phillip Archer (ENG)	ALLIANZ Open Cotes d'Armor Bretagne
Largest winning margin	7 shots	Matthew Zions (AUS)	Saint Omer Open

Multiple winners

Edouard Dubois (FRA)	Kärnten Open; Scottish Hydro Challenge
Benjamin Hebert (FRA)	Credit Suisse Challenge; English Challenge; Rolex Trophy
Sam Little (ENG)	M2M Russian Challenge Cup; ALLIANZ Golf Open du Grand Toulouse; Roma Golf Open
Andrea Pavan (ITA)	Norwegian Challenge; Apulia San Domenico Grand Final

Most top 5 finishes
4 Matthew Baldwin (ENG)
   Sam Little (ENG)
   Jamie Moul (ENG)
   Julien Quesne (FRA)

Most top 5 finishes
8 Federico Colombo (ITA)
   Ricardo Santo (POR)
   Julien Quesne (FRA)

Low finish by a winner
63 (–9) Edouard Dubois (FRA)   Kärnten Golf Open

Largest 18 hole lead
3 shots Jamie Moul (ENG)   Acaya Open
         Daniel Vancsik (ARG)   M2M Russian Challenge Cup

Largest 36 hole lead
7 shots Andrea Pavan (ITA)   Kärnten Golf Open

The 2012 season just got tougher – Tiger's back

For the cream of the crop in 2011 – Luke Donald, Rory McIlroy, Martin Kaymer, Lee Westwood, Webb Simpson, Nick Watney and Dustin Johnson – the 2012 season may just have become a lot tougher. Tiger's back.

Okay, it was not the strongest of limited fields, it was an unofficial, relaxed end-of-season get-together for which Tiger had to be given an invitation to play because he was outside the top 50 in the world rankings on which the field is based. So what? He won the exotically named Chevron World Championship – his own event – dramatically enough by finishing birdie, birdie to beat former Masters champion Zach Johnson. Tiger's 83rd career win was mightily significant.

Golf has done well enough without Tiger for the past two years but it will always do better when he's around. After all, it is extra special for any golfer to win an event in which Tiger has played well. If what he did at Chevron really is a true indication of a return to his best form then Woods' goal of beating Jack Nicklaus' 18 major titles – he has not won a major since taking the US Open in 2008 – and re-establishing himself as World No 1 is realistic enough.

You can bet that the rest of the professionals will be looking forward, too, to his return if only to underline how good they are themselves. The prospect of Rory McIlroy going head to head with Woods, or of Luke Donald trading birdies with Tiger as the British golfer tries to hold on to the World No 1 spot just adds an extra dimension to the 2012 season.

With all his personal problems behind him Tiger is free again to concentrate on what he does best – play golf. He will hope he remains injury free and that his new swing continues to work well. If he does and it does he may once again emerge as the intimidating opponent he was in the 90's and the earlier part of this century but the competition he will face will be a lot tougher than it was at Thousand Oaks last December.

The Chevron win gave him a massive boost in the long haul to get to No 1 again. Despite the fact that the Chevron event is not included on any official Tour it still – some might say controversially – offered world ranking points and, incredibly, with one giant leap Woods moved up from 52nd to 21st.

It was an exciting enough 2011 season but what will the world rankings look like at the end of this year? It's an intriguing thought.

Scot Russell Knox joins Martin Laird on PGA Tour

Scotland will have two representatives on the PGA Tour this year after 26-year-old Russell Knox from Inverness earned his Tour card by finishing 12th on the American Nationwide money list.

Knox will join Glasgow-born Martin Laird who won over $1 million for winning the Arnold Palmer Invitational at Bay Hill last year. No doubt he received a letter of congratulation from Arnie as did Knox when he won the Chiquita Classic at the TPC River Bend course – designed by Palmer.

Although born to an American father and a Scottish mum, Knox feels "100 per cent Scottish". He has worked hard for his success realising after playing in the Scottish Youths team in the European Championship that if he was to make his career in professional golf he would need to work at it.

He went to America, studied at the University of Jacksonville and gained All-American status in 2006. Then he played the Third Division Hooters Tour before gaining playing rights on the Nationwide Tour.

He hopes this year to make it to The Open and the Scottish Open at Castle Stuart. With his local connections – his home was just 10 minutes from the course – he wrote (more in hope than expectation) for an invitation to play in the Scottish event last year but not only didn't get one, he did not even get a reply!

Among others who have made it through to the PGA Tour by their performance on last year's Nationwide Tour are 21-year-old Korean-born New Zealander Danny Lee, a former World No 1 who as an amateur won the Johnnie Walker Asian Classic at The Vines in Perth, and England's Gary Christian, who won the Mylan Classic and finished ninth on the Nationwide money list. Daniel Chopra and Jonas Blixt from Sweden, 43-year-old Gavin Coles from Australia and courageous American Erik Compton who has survived not one but two heart transplants are others who have made it through to the PGA Tour this year.

US PGA Tour 2011

Players are of US nationality unless stated   www.pgatour.com

Final Ranking

The top 125 on the money list retained their cards for the 2012 season. The top 40 earned a spot at The Masters.

1	Luke Donald (ENG)	$6,683,214	50	Ben Crane	1,679,595	98	Michael Thompson	935,265
2	Webb Simpson	6,347,353	51	Brandt Jobe	1,629,764	99	Chris Couch	922,496
3	Nick Watney	5,290,673	52	Carl Pettersson	1,540,723	100	Marc Leishman (AUS)	916,330
4	K J Choi (KOR)	4,434,691		(SWE)		101	Stewart Cink	909,162
5	Dustin Johnson	4,309,961	53	Jim Furyk	1,529,690	102	Tim Herron	909,135
6	Matt Kuchar	4,233,920	54	Sergio García (ESP)	1,524,091	103	J J Henry	873,377
7	Bill Haas	4,088,637	55	Kyle Stanley	1,523,657	104	David Hearn (CAN)	869,072
8	Steve Stricker	3,992,785	56	Robert Garrigus	1,503,923	105	Greg Chalmers (AUS)	832,191
9	Jason Day (AUS)	3,962,647	57	Sean O'Hair	1,483,948	106	Tom Gillis	814,147
10	David Toms	3,858,090	58	Charley Hoffman	1,462,591	107	Padraig Harrington	802,839
11	Adam Scott (AUS)	3,764,797	59	George McNeill	1,458,110		(IRL)	
12	Phil Mickelson	3,763,488	60	Robert Allenby (AUS)	1,452,567	108	Retief Goosen (RSA)	796,360
13	Keegan Bradley	3,758,600	61	Jerry Kelly	1,451,797	109	Billy Mayfair	780,578
14	Brandt Snedeker	3,587,206	62	J B Holmes	1,398,583	110	Josh Teater	769,324
15	Hunter Mahan	3,503,540	63	Paul Goydos	1,385,328	111	Kevin Stadler	768,172
16	Bubba Watson	3,477,811	64	John Rollins	1,370,566	112	Heath Slocum	767,216
17	Gary Woodland	3,448,591	65	Kris Blanks	1,350,010	113	Chris DiMarco	761,932
18	Justin Rose (ENG)	3,401,420	66	Kevin Chappell	1,339,640	114	James Driscoll	741,010
19	Mark Wilson	3,158,477	67	Jimmy Walker	1,336,556	115	Ian Poulter (ENG)	739,926
20	Aaron Baddeley (AUS)	3,094,693	68	Cameron Tringale	1,327,807	116	Joe Ogilvie	726,866
21	Jason Dufner	3,057,860	69	Harrison Frazar	1,322,267	117	Louis Oosthuizen	717,965
22	Jonathan Byrd	2,938,920	70	Andres Romero	1,313,133		(RSA)	
23	Martin Laird (SCO)	2,676,509		(ARG)		118	David Mathis	715,404
24	Charl Schwartzel	2,604,558	71	Brian Davis (ENG)	1,308,009	119	John Merrick	704,789
	(RSA)		72	Kevin Streelman	1,300,006	120	Sunghoon Kang (KOR)	702,382
25	Charles Howell III	2,509,223	73	Pat Perez	1,295,253	121	Tom Pernice Jr	694,981
26	Fredrik Jacobson	2,488,325	74	Jeff Overton	1,290,962	122	Matt Bettencourt	692,545
	(SWE)		75	Scott Piercy	1,250,957	123	Arjun Atwal (IND)	690,237
27	Rory Sabbatini (RSA)	2,420,655	76	Brendon de Jonge	1,241,326	124	Rod Pampling (AUS)	668,768
28	Vijay Singh (FIJ)	2,371,050		(ZIM)		125	D J Trahan	668,166
29	Bo Van Pelt	2,344,546	77	Camilo Villegas (VEN)	1,231,918			
30	Kevin Na	2,336,965	78	Johnson Wagner	1,224,556	126	Bobby Gates	666,735
31	Spencer Levin	2,320,038	79	Scott Verplank	1,194,178	127	Roland Thatcher	666,371
32	Y E Yang (KOR)	2,314,865	80	Charlie Wi (KOR)	1,188,494	128	Tiger Woods	660,238
33	John Senden (AUS)	2,294,811	81	Trevor Immelman	1,165,604	129	Stuart Appleby (AUS)	657,150
34	Chez Reavie	2,285,067		(RSA)		130	Bill Lunde	639,548
35	Tommy Gainey	2,174,191	82	Brian Gay	1,157,525	131	Angel Cabrera (ARG)	628,079
36	Rickie Fowler	2,084,681	83	Chad Campbell	1,104,024	132	Steven Bowditch	621,378
37	D A Points	2,034,156	84	Blake Adams	1,100,558		(AUS)	
38	Brendan Steele	1,976,310	85	Chris Stroud	1,096,499	133	Matt Jones	602,392
39	Steve Marino	1,975,076	86	Graeme McDowell	1,088,898	134	Steve Flesch	594,622
40	Bryce Molder	1,957,944		(NIR)		135	Bob Estes	594,104
			87	Anthony Kim	1,085,846	136	Paul Casey (ENG)	590,386
41	Scott Stallings	1,957,162	88	Davis Love III	1,056,300	137	Matt McQuillan (CAN)	582,933
42	Ryan Moore	1,942,906	89	Hunter Haas	1,039,987	138	Tim Clark (RSA)	571,000
43	Geoff Ogilvy (AUS)	1,916,994	90	Ryuji Imada (JPN)	990,319	139	Stephen Ames (CAN)	547,589
44	Zach Johnson	1,880,406	91	Justin Leonard	952,962	140	Billy Horschel	533,024
45	Chris Kirk	1,877,627	92	Ricky Barnes	951,587	141	William McGirt	532,933
46	Jhonattan Vegas (COL)	1,854,414	93	Ernie Els (RSA)	948,872	142	Garrett Willis	526,390
47	Ryan Palmer	1,850,530	94	Troy Matteson	946,989	143	Shane Bertsch	488,584
48	Lucas Glover	1,823,327	95	Briny Baird	942,286	144	Cameron Beckman	455,085
49	Robert Karlsson	1,779,815	96	Nick O'Hern (AUS)	940,224	145	Scott McCarron	436,270
	(SWE)	1,779,815	97	Michael Bradley	935,934	146	Tim Petrovic	428,011

Career Money List (at end of 2011 season)

1	Tiger Woods	$94,817,542	51	Nick Watney	15,688,051
2	Vijay Singh (FIJ)	65,691,439	52	Lee Janzen	15,649,122
3	Phil Mickelson	63,440,877	53	Carl Pettersson (SWE)	15,601,866
4	Jim Furyk	49,095,654	54	Woody Austin	15,568,262
5	Ernie Els (RSA)	41,318,291	55	Sean O'Hair	15,543,433
6	Davis Love III	41,218,723	56	Steve Elkington	15,505,418
7	David Toms	37,207,350	57	Kevin Sutherland	15,412,187
8	Kenny Perry	31,720,992	58	Ben Crane	15,278,462
9	Steve Stricker	31,659,540	59	Hal Sutton	15,267,685
10	Justin Leonard	31,321,245	60	Jesper Parnevik (SWE)	15,254,801
11	Stewart Cink	30,359,822	61	John Rollins	15,155,080
12	Sergio García (ESP)	28,072,459	62	Loren Roberts	15,154,767
13	Scott Verplank	27,369,774	63	Steve Lowery	15,114,746
14	Retief Goosen (RSA)	26,954,468	64	John Huston	14,967,146
15	Mike Weir (CAN)	26,821,949	65	Lucas Glover	14,907,873
16	K J Choi (KOR)	26,404,797	66	Jonathan Byrd	14,868,549
17	Stuart Appleby (AUS)	26,380,298	67	Bo Van Pelt	14,848,528
18	Robert Allenby (AUS)	25,599,894	68	Brian Gay	14,803,323
19	Adam Scott (AUS)	25,406,897	69	Tom Pernice Jr	14,760,687
20	Luke Donald (ENG)	25,348,410	70	Heath Slocum	14,606,562
21	Geoff Ogilvy (AUS)	24,482,934	71	Greg Norman (AUS)	14,484,458
22	Rory Sabbatini (RSA)	24,336,018	72	Paul Azinger	14,467,496
23	Mark Calcavecchia	24,023,484	73	Jay Haas	14,440,317
24	Jerry Kelly	23,199,462	74	Camilo Villegas (COL)	14,358,419
25	Charles Howell III	22,464,003	75	Mark O'Meara	14,169,805
26	Fred Couples	22,087,938	76	Aaron Baddeley (AUS)	14,098,158
27	Chris DiMarco	22,006,220	77	Kirk Triplett	14,089,515
28	Zach Johnson	21,773,048	78	Shigeki Maruyama (JPN)	13,809,170
29	Tom Lehman	21,428,810	79	Dustin Johnson	13,550,879
30	Fred Funk	21,052,458	80	John Senden (AUS)	13,427,486
31	Nick Price (ZIM)	20,576,104	81	Joe Durant	13,352,458
32	Chad Campbell	20,386,018	82	Rod Pampling	12,979,418
33	Padraig Harrington (IRL)	20,099,542	83	John Cook	12,685,199
34	Bob Estes	19,600,692	84	Paul Goydos	12,681,439
35	Billy Mayfair	19,468,273	85	Scott McCarron	12,611,793
36	Stephen Ames (CAN)	19,186,730	86	Dudley Hart	12,566,495
37	David Duval	18,813,237	87	Briny Baird	12,480,752
38	Scott Hoch	18,530,156	88	Billy Andrade	12,380,805
39	Jeff Sluman	18,165,266	89	Bubba Watson	12,314,646
40	Steve Flesch	18,030,350	90	José Maria Olazábal (ESP)	12,248,553
41	Tim Clark (RSA)	17,974,497	91	Anthony Kim	12,172,449
42	Brad Faxon	17,769,249	92	Pat Perez	12,128,721
43	Hunter Mahan	17,703,700	93	Fredrik Jacobson (SWE)	12,123,609
44	Tim Herron	17,605,861	94	Bill Haas	11,749,443
45	Jeff Maggert	17,299,336	95	Payne Stewart	11,737,008
46	Matt Kuchar	16,896,154	96	Duffy Waldorf	11,699,508
47	Justin Rose (ENG)	16,840,687	97	Frank Lickliter II	11,681,116
48	Rocco Mediate	16,550,263	98	J J Henry	11,494,113
49	Corey Pavin	15,962,250	99	Chris Riley	11,315,882
50	Bob Tway	15,785,815	100	Ryan Palmer	11,233,706

Top ten finishes on the 2011 PGA Tour

No less than seven players won two events apiece in 2011. They were: Keegan Bradley – HP Byron Nelson, US PGA Championship; Luke Donald (ENG) – WGC–Accenture, Children's Miracle N/work; Webb Simpson – Wyndham Championship, Deutsch Bank Championship; Steve Stricker – Memorial Tourn., John Deere Classic; Nick Watney – WGC–Cadillac, AT&T National; Bubba Watson – Farmers Ins. Open, Zurich Classic; Mark Wilson – Sony Open, Waste Management Phoenix Open.

2011 Tour Statistics

Driving accuracy
(Percentage of fairways hit in regulation)

Pos	Name	Rds	%
1	Joe Durant	71	75.65
2	Heath Slocum	89	74.92
3	Jerry Kelly	85	73.30
4	Brian Gay	90	72.77
5	Ben Curtis	66	71.91
6	David Toms	78	71.82
7	Nick O'Hern (AUS)	89	71.67
8	Zach Johnson	79	71.06
9	Billy Mayfair	94	70.41
10	Brian Davis (ENG)	105	70.33

Greens in regulation

Pos	Name	Rds	%
1	Boo Weekley	66	71.68
2	Heath Slocum	89	71.40
3	Joe Durant	71	71.26
4	Chad Campbell	99	71.13
5	John Senden (AUS)	94	70.86
6	David Toms	78	70.20
7	Ernie Els (RSA)	71	69.89
8	Webb Simpson	98	69.84
9	Bubba Watson	85	69.83
10	Justin Rose (ENG)	79	69.48

Driving distance (Average yards per drive)

Pos	Name	Rds	Yds
1	J B Holmes	57	318.4
2	Bubba Watson	85	314.9
3	Dustin Johnson	72	314.2
4	Robert Garrigus	83	313.4
5	Gary Woodland	93	310.5
6	Steven Bowditch (AUS)	86	308.3
7	Scott Piercy	78	305.4
8	Jhonattan Vegas (VEN)	84	304.9
9	Kyle Stanley	98	304.6
10	Will Strickler	51	304.1

Putting averages (Average per round)

Pos	Name	Rds	Avg
1	Andres Gonzales	60	1.411
2	Joe Ogilvie	75	1.421
	Jim Renner	65	1.421
4	D J Brigman	67	1.425
5	George McNeill	69	1.426
6	Fredrik Jacobson (SWE)	92	1.430
7	Rod Pampling (AUS)	72	1.431
8	Shane Bertsch	62	1.445
9	Scott Gutschewski	67	1.447
10	Woody Austin	59	1.448

Sand saves

Pos	Name	Rds	%	Pos	Name	Rds	%
1	Brian Gay	90	63.40	6	Matt Kuchar	94	58.86
2	Greg Chalmers (AUS)	88	61.68	7	Retief Goosen (RSA)	50	58.75
3	Paul Stankowski	78	61.17	8	Chris Riley	76	58.18
4	Jason Day (AUS)	76	60.96	9	Justin Rose (ENG)	79	58.16
5	Luke Donald (ENG)	73	59.09	10	Woody Austin	59	58.11

Scoring averages

Pos	Name	Rds	Avg	Pos	Name	Rds	Avg
1	Luke Donald (ENG)	73	68.86	11	Fredrik Jacobson (SWE)	92	69.85
2	Webb Simpson	98	69.25		Spencer Levin	113	69.85
3	Steve Stricker	70	69.36	13	Brandt Snedeker	85	69.86
4	Matt Kuchar	94	69.51	14	Adam Scott (AUS)	60	69.87
5	Nick Watney	80	69.52		Gary Woodland	93	69.87
6	Sergio García (ESP)	61	69.56	16	Phil Mickelson	79	69.89
7	Charl Schwartzel (RSA)	58	69.62	17	Hunter Mahan	92	69.90
8	Charles Howell III	108	69.66	18	Zach Johnson	79	69.97
9	Jason Day (AUS)	76	69.71	19	K J Choi (KOR)	77	69.99
	David Toms	78	69.71	20	Rickie Fowler	84	70.01

Top ten finishes on the 2011 PGA Tour

Four players achieved top ten finishes in double figures in 2011. They were:

	Top ten	Events played
Luke Donald (ENG)	14	19
Webb Simpson	12	26
Jason Day (AUS)	10	21
Nick Watney	10	22

Multiple winners

There were seven players with two victories apiece in 2011. They were:

Keegan Bradley – HP Byron Nelson Championship; US PGA Championship
Luke Donald (ENG) – WGC–Accenture Match Play Championship;
                    Children's Miracle Network Classic
Webb Simpson – Wyndham Championship; Deutsche Bank Championship
Steve Stricker – Memorial Tournament; John Deere Classic
Nick Watney – WGC–Cadillac Championship; AT&T National
Bubba Watson – Farmers Insurance Open; Zurich Classic
Mark Wilson – Sony Open; Waste Management Phoenix Open

Luke Donald is Race to Dubai Golfer of the Year

Thirty-four-year-old Luke Donald, who made history by topping the 2011 money lists in both the PGA Tour and the European Tour, was the unanimous winner of the European Tour's Race to Dubai Golfer of the Year.

"To achieve the accolade of European Tour Golfer of the Year means a lot to me," said World No 1 Donald when told of the award. "It is always nice to be appreciated especially by the people in the sport who know the game inside out. I will certainly look back on the year with fond memories.

"As a professional golfer you are always trying to do your best and it was good to see all the hard work I have put in coming to fruition. It is rewarding that consistency does pay off. Everyone dreams of having a year like this and I am very excited and feel fortunate it happened to me."

Donald, who proved that you do not need to be a big-hitter to make golf history, earned a record €5,323,400 in prize and bonus money in 2011 and, when taking his PGA Tour prize-money into account, his total earnings for the year was just €33,564 short of €10 million.

Seven international players win US PGA Tour cards

Three Korean golfers, two Australians, a Brazilian and an Englishman all won their cards at the 2011 Qualifying School for the right to play on the this year's US Tour.

Twenty-year-old Noh Seung-yul, twice a winner on the Asian circuit and a former Asian No 1, made it along with the 2011 leading money winner on the Japanese circuit, Bae Sang-Moon, and John Huh who finished strongly with rounds of 68 and 69.

Jarrod Lyle, who scored in the 60's in three of his last four rounds, and former New Zealand Open champion and European Tour member Nathan Green were the two Australians who made it.

England's Greg Owen and Brazilian Alexandre Rocha who has played on the European Tour were the only other international players among the 29 who were successful.

Former Ryder Cup golfers Jeff Maggert and Vaughn Taylor were successful in the six round competition headed by 26-year-old American Brandon Todd. Maggert was one of four golfers in the upper 40's who survived the difficult examination. Bob Estes, a four time winner on Tour, is 45, Maggert 47 and Marco Dawson and Scott Dunlap are both 48.

One golfer who breathed a sigh of relief was former World Amateur No 1 Colt Knost who thought he had missed out when he double-bogeyed his final hole but he made it in the end on the button.

US PGA Tour top 20

MC Missed cut   — Did not play

Players are of US nationality unless stated otherwise

Player	Hyundai Tournament	Sony Open	Humana Challenge	Farmers Insurance Open	Phoenix Open	AT&T Pebble Beach	Northern Trust Open	WGC–CA Accenture	Mayakoba Classic	The Honda Classic	Puerto Rico Open	WGC–Cadillac C/ship	Transitions Championship	Arnold Palmer Invitational	Shell Houston Open	The Masters	Valero Texas Open	Verizon Heritage	Zurich Classic
1 Luke Donald (ENG)	—	—	—	—	—	—	MC	1	—	T10	—	T6	—	—	—	T4	—	2*	T8
2 Webb Simpson	—	T46	T13	MC	T8	—	—	—	T24	—	2	MC	T16	—	—	—	T14	—	2*
3 Nick Watney	—	—	—	T6	T5	T6	—	T9	—	—	—	1	T13	—	46	—	—	—	T20
4 K J Choi (KOR)	—	MC	—	T29	—	T39	T7	T17	—	—	—	T39	MC	T6	—	T8	—	—	T3
5 Dustin Johnson	T9	—	—	T3	T29	T55	MC	T33	—	—	—	2	—	MC	—	T38	—	—	—
6 Matt Kuchar	T6	T5	T7	—	—	—	T35	3	—	T17	—	5	—	—	T8	T27	—	T21	—
7 Bill Haas	8	—	2*	T9	T29	—	T12	T3	—	—	—	T31	MC	MC	—	T42	—	T30	—
8 Steve Stricker	T4	T9	—	—	—	—	T29	T33	—	—	—	T18	—	T4	T11	—	—	—	T13
9 Jason Day (AUS)	T9	T20	—	—	—	—	MC	T9	—	—	—	T45	T51	—	MC	T2	—	T9	—
10 David Toms	—	—	T33	—	MC	MC	—	—	T5	—	—	T37	T3	—	T24	T8	—	—	T18
11 Adam Scott (AUS)	T21	MC	—	—	—	—	T33	—	—	MC	—	T6	—	—	—	T2	T23	—	—
12 Phil Mickelson	—	—	—	2	T29	T9	T35	T17	—	—	—	T55	—	T24	1	T27	—	—	—
13 Keegan Bradley	—	T68	T7	T25	—	T15	MC	—	—	MC	T18	—	MC	MC	T51	—	T9	MC	T26
14 Brandt Snedeker	—	MC	T9	T8	MC	MC	—	—	—	WD	—	4	MC	—	—	T15	4	1*	MC
15 Hunter Mahan	T25	—	—	T6	T29	2	T55	T9	—	—	—	9	—	T38	T8	MC	—	—	—
16 Bubba Watson	T25	—	MC	1	T29	—	WD	4	—	—	—	DNS	T28	T4	—	T38	—	—	1*
17 Gary Woodland	—	MC	2*	T58	T5	MC	—	—	—	T6	—	—	1	MC	T13	—	T24	—	—
18 Justin Rose (ENG)	T12	T13	—	T25	—	—	T9	T17	—	—	—	T42	T5	T3	—	T11	—	—	MC
19 Mark Wilson	—	1	T61	—	1*	MC	T74	T17	—	—	—	T49	T57	T9	—	MC	—	T21	—
20 Aaron Baddeley (AUS)	—	T34	—	MC	T37	T6	1	—	MC	—	—	T28	—	T12	T4	T47	—	T6	—

2011 performances at a glance

* Involved in play-off   WD Withdrew   DNS Did not start

Wells Fargo C/ship	The Players C/ship	Crowne Plaza Invitational	Byron Nelson C/ship	Memorial Tournament	Fedex St Jude Classic	US Open Championship	Travelers Championship	AT&T National	John Deere Classic	The Open Championship	Viking Classic	RBC Canadian Open	Greenbrier Classic	Reno-Tahoe Open	WGC-CA Bridgestone	US PGA Championship	Wyndham Championship	The Barclays	Deutsche Bank C/ship	BMW Championship	Tour Championship	Justin Timberlake Open	Frys.com Open	The McGladrey Classic	Children's Miracle N/work	WGC-HSBC Champions
—	T4	—	—	T7	—	T45	—	—	—	MC	—	T17	—	—	T2	T8	—	T18	T3	4	T3	—	—	—	1	—
T21	T69	—	—	T7	—	T14	T13	T8	—	T16	—	—	T9	—	—	MC	1	T10	1*	5	22	—	—	2*	T6	—
MC	T4	—	T8	—	MC	T13	1	—	MC	—	—	—	T23	T12	—	T10	T61	T22	T26	2	—	—	—	—	—	T33
—	1*	—	T40	T22	—	MC	—	2	—	T44	—	—	T59	T39	—	T32	MC	T10	T3	—	—	—	—	—	—	T16
MC	T57	—	T20	4	—	T23	—	—	—	T2	—	—	T48	MC	—	1	T42	T65	T23	—	—	—	—	—	—	—
—	T54	T16	T6	T2	—	T14	—	—	—	MC	—	MC	—	T19	T19	—	2	—	T22	T20	—	T20	—	—	—	—
4	MC	T8	—	T45	—	T23	—	T34	—	T57	—	2*	T63	T12	MC	T24	T61	T16	1*	—	—	—	—	—	—	T42
—	T12	—	—	1	—	T19	—	—	1	T12	—	—	14	T12	—	T24	T42	WD	15	—	—	—	—	—	—	—
—	T6	T31	5	—	2	—	T68	T30	—	—	—	—	T4	MC	—	T13	T3	T49	T6	—	—	—	—	—	—	—
T24	2*	1	—	MC	MC	T17	—	WD	—	—	—	—	T9	T4	T17	MC	T59	T10	T16	—	—	—	—	MC	—	T59
—	MC	T65	—	—	—	MC	—	T3	—	T25	—	—	1	7	—	T67	T8	T37	T6	—	—	—	—	—	—	T11
T9	T33	—	T13	—	T54	—	—	—	T2	—	MC	—	T48	T19	—	T43	T10	T56	10	—	—	—	—	—	—	—
MC	72	—	1*	MC	T25	—	T63	MC	—	—	—	T22	T43	—	T15	1*	—	MC	MC	T16	T11	—	—	—	—	T16
—	MC	T16	—	T15	T11	T24	—	MC	—	—	—	T33	MC	MC	T3	T3	T22	T16	—	—	—	T32	—	—	—	—
T16	T6	T10	—	T13	—	MC	T43	T30	—	MC	—	T34	—	T37	T19	—	T43	T8	T42	2*	—	—	—	—	—	T7
T48	T45	—	T42	—	T63	T38	—	T30	—	—	—	—	T21	T26	—	MC	T16	T53	T23	—	—	—	—	—	—	—
T68	MC	—	T49	6	—	T23	—	T47	—	T30	—	T4	T45	T12	—	T13	T25	T16	T13	—	—	—	—	T12	—	—
T28	T45	—	MC	—	MC	—	T15	—	T44	—	—	—	T33	MC	—	T6	T68	1	T20	—	—	—	—	MC	—	T7
MC	MC	T31	—	T7	—	MC	—	MC	T30	T63	—	—	T17	T26	—	T24	T56	T22	T6	—	—	—	—	MC	—	T56
—	T6	—	—	T45	—	MC	T24	—	—	MC	—	—	T11	MC	—	T13	T77	T22	T3	—	—	—	—	—	—	T23

Tour Results 2011 (in chronological order)

Players are of US nationality unless stated

Hyundai Tournament of Champions *Plantation Course, Kapalua, HI*
[7411–73]

1	Jonathan Byrd*	66-68-67-67—268	$1,120,000
2	Robert Garrigus	69-63-69-67—268	635,000

Byrd won at the second extra hole

3	Graeme McDowell (NIR)	71-68-68-62—269	412,000

Sony Open *Waialae CC, Honolulu, HI*
[7068–70]

1	Mark Wilson	65-67-65-67—264	$990,000
2	Tim Clark (RSA)	68-68-66-64—266	485,000
	Steve Marino	65-67-66-68—266	485,000

Humana Challenge *La Quinta, Bermuda Dunes, CA*
[6930–72]

1	Jhonattan Vegas (VEN)*	64-67-67-66-69—333	$900,000
2	Bill Haas	69-68-68-62-66—333	440,000
	Gary Woodland	65-69-64-66-69—333	440,000

Vegas won as the second extra hole

Farmers Insurance Open *Torrey Pines, San Diego, CA*
[6874–72]

1	Bubba Watson	71-65-69-67—272	$1,044,000
2	Phil Mickelson	67-69-68-69—273	626,400
3	Dustin Johnson	69-69-71-66—275	336,400
	Jhonattan Vegas (VEN)	69-69-69-68—275	336,400

Waste Management Phoenix Open *TPC Scottsdale, AZ*
[7216–71]

1	Mark Wilson*	65-64-68-69—266	$1,098,000
2	Jason Dufner	65-68-67-66—266	658,000

Wilson won at the second extra hole

3	Vijay Singh (FIJ)	69-65-68-66—268	353,800
	Martin Laird (SCO)	68-71-64-65—268	353,800

AT&T Pebble Beach National Pro-Am *Pebble Beach, CA*
[6816–72]

1	D A Points	63-70-71-67—271	$1,134,000
2	Hunter Mahan	70-67-70-66—273	680,400
3	Tom Gillis	67-68-70-70—275	428,400

Northern Trust Open (formerly the Nissan Open)
Riviera CC, Pacific Palisades, CA
[7298–71]

1	Aaron Baddeley (AUS)	67-69-67-69—272	$1,170,000
2	Vijay Singh (FIJ)	68-70-67-69—274	702,200
3	Kevin Na	71-66-67-71—275	442,200

WGC – Accenture Match Play Championship
Ritz-Carlton, Dove Mountain, AZ
[7791–72]

Winner:	Luke Donald (ENG)	$1,441,970
Runner-up:	Martin Kaymer (GER)	875,481
Third place:	Matt Kuchar	617,986

Donald beat Kaymer 3 and 2 in the final

Full details of this event can be found on page 189

Mayakoba Classic *El Camaleon, Riviera-Cancun Maya, Mexico* [6923–71]

1	Johnson Wagner*	69-66-65-67—267	$666,000
2	Spencer Levin	68-67-67-65—267	399,600

Wagner won at the first extra hole

3	John Cook	70-68-66-66—270	351,600

Honda Classic *Palm Beach Gardens, FL* [7158–70]

1	Rory Sabbatini (RSA)	71-64-66-70—271	$1,026,000
2	Y E Yang (KOR)	68-71-67-66—272	615,600
3	Jerry Kelly	71-67-68-67—273	387,600

Puerto Rico Open *Rio Grande, Puerto Rico* [7569–72]

1	Michael Bradley*	68-68-68-68—272	$630,000
2	Troy Matteson	67-67-66-72—272	378,000

Bradley won at the first extra hole

3	Stephen Ames (CAN)	69-66-73-66—274	203,000
	Hunter Haas	67-68-68-71—274	203,000

WGC – Cadillac Championship *Doral, Orlando, FL* [7266–72]

1	Nick Watney	67-70-68-67—272	$1,400,000
2	Dustin Johnson	69-69-65-71—274	850,000
3	Anders Hansen (DEN)	71-69-68-67—275	465,000
	Francesco Molinari (ITA)	68-68-70-69—275	465,000

Full details of this event can be found on page 190

Transitions Championship *Innisbrook, Copperhead, Palm Harbor, FL*

[7340-71]

1	Gary Woodland	67-68-67-67—269	$990,000
2	Webb Simpson	67-67-67-69—270	594,000
3	Scott Stallings	66-70-66-70—272	374,000

Arnold Palmer Invitational *Bay Hill, Orlando, FL* [7381–72]

1	Martin Laird (SCO)	70-65-70-75—280	$1,080,000
2	Steve Marino	71-67-71-72—281	648,000
3	Justin Rose (ENG)	72-72-70-68—282	312,000
	Marc Leishman (AUS)	73-72-66-71—282	312,000
	David Toms	74-67-69-72—282	312,000

Shell Houston Open *Redstone, Humble, TX* [7457–72]

1	Phil Mickelson	70-70-63-65—268	$1,062,000
2	Chris Kirk	66-69-69-67—271	519,200
	Scott Verplank	73-65-65-68—271	519,200

THE MASTERS *Augusta National, GA* [7435–72]

1	Charl Schwartzel (RSA)	69-71-6-866—274	$1,444,000
2	Jason Day (AUS)	72-64-72-68—276	704,000
	Adam Scott (AUS)	72-70-67-67—276	704,000

Full details of this event can be found on page 73

Valero Texas Open *San Antonio, TX* [7522–72]

1	Brendan Steele	69-72-68-71—280	$1,116,000
2	Charley Hoffman	68-73-72-68—281	545,600
	Kevin Chappell	68-73-70-70—281	545,600

The Heritage *Harbour Town, Hilton Head Island, SC* [6973–71]

1	Brandt Snedeker*	69-67-72-64—272*	$1,026,000
2	Luke Donald (ENG)	67-65-70-70—272	615,600
Snedeker won at the third extra hole			
3	Tommy Gainey	71-67-67-68—273	387,600

Zurich Classic of New Orleans *TPC Louisiana, Avondale, LA* [7341–72]

1	Bubba Watson*	66-68-70-69—273	$1,152,000
2	Webb Simpson	68-69-67-69—273	691,200
Watson won at the second extra hole			
3	Jason Dufner	68-69-72-66—275	332,800
	Tommy Gainey	67-71-68-69—275	332,800
	K J Choi (KOR)	68-71-67-69—275	332,800

Wells Fargo Championship *Quail Hollow, Charlotte, NC* [7442–72]

1	Lucas Glover*	67-68-69-69—273	$1,170,000
2	Jonathan Byrd	66-68-67-72—273	702,000
Glover won at the first extra hole			
3	Rory Sabbatini (RSA)	72-71-66-65—274	442,000

The Players Championship *TPC, Sawgrass, Ponte Vedra Beach, FL*
[7215-72]

1	K J Choi (KOR)*	70-68-67-70—275	$1,710,000
2	David Toms	66-68-71-70—275	1,026,000
Choi won at the first extra hole			
3	Paul Goydos	69-70-69-69—277	646,000
4	Luke Donald (ENG)	69-67-71-71—278	418,000
	Nick Watney	64-71-72-71—278	418,000
6	Jason Day (AUS)	69-70-72-68—279	287,375
	Hunter Mahan	70-67-73-69—279	287,375
	J B Holmes	68-69-73-69—279	287,375
	Alvaro Quiros (ESP)	67-73-68-71—279	287,375
	Jason Dufner	69-70-68-72—279	287,375
	Aaron Baddeley (AUS)	70-67-70-72—279	287,375
12	Chris Stroud	71-67-74-68—280	175,071
	Zach Johnson	74-70-70-66—280	175,071
	Brian Gay	71-69-71-69—280	175,071
	Sergio García (ESP)	74-68-73-65—280	175,071
	Spencer Levin	72-69-68-71—280	175,071
	Steve Stricker	69-67-71-73—280	175,071
	Davis Love III	68-69-70-73—280	175,071
19	Matt Jones (AUS)	72-72-69-68—281	107,214
	Steve Marino	70-72-69-70—281	107,214
	Kevin Streelman	70-69-75-67—281	107,214
	Stewart Cink	70-72-69-70—281	107,214
	Peter Hanson (SWE)	72-72-66-71—281	107,214
	Martin Kaymer (GER)	67-72-70-72—281	107,214
	Sean O'Hair	71-71-67-72—281	107,214
26	Chad Campbell	73-71-69-69—282	67,450
	Jeff Overton	69-71-73-69—282	67,450
	Brian Davis (ENG)	69-69-73-71—282	67,450
	Charl Schwartzel (RSA)	72-71-71-68—282	67,450
	Charley Hoffman	72-71-68-71—282	67,450

26T	Robert Karlsson (SWE)	71-67-72-72—282	67,450
	Rory Sabbatini (RSA)	67-71-71-73—282	67,450
33	Trevor Immelman (RSA)	70-73-70-70—283	50,191
	Ryan Moore	71-69-71-72—283	50,191
	Phil Mickelson	71-71-69-72—283	50,191
	Carl Pettersson (SWE)	73-71-71-68—283	50,191
	Bryce Molder	70-73-67-73—283	50,191
	Graeme McDowell (NIR)	67-69-68-79—283	50,191
39	Kenny Perry	72-71-68-73—284	41,800
	Andres Romero (ARG)	72-69-69-74—284	41,800
41	Angel Cabrera (ARG)	70-74-68-73—285	36,100
	Greg Chalmers (AUS)	73-65-74-73—285	36,100
	Jonathan Byrd	71-73-72-69—285	36,100
	Charlie Wi (KOR)	70-72-68-75—285	36,100
45	Garrett Willis	70-74-69-73—286	27,816
	Justin Rose (ENG)	70-69-74-73—286	27,816
	Ben Crane	68-76-71-71—286	27,816
	Corey Pavin	72-69-74-71—286	27,816
	Bubba Watson	76-66-76-68—286	27,816
50	Ben Curtis	71-73-70-73—287	23,132
	Chris Couch	71-72-71-73—287	23,132
	Lucas Glover	65-71-74-77—287	23,132
	Robert Allenby (AUS)	69-74-68-76—287	23,132
54	Rocco Mediate	72-69-71-76—288	21,850
	Matt Kuchar	69-72-73-74—288	21,850
	Scott Verplank	73-71-71-73—288	21,850
57	Justin Leonard	70-73-72-74—289	21,185
	Dustin Johnson	72-70-73-74—289	21,185
	Ian Poulter (ENG)	70-72-74-73—289	21,185
	Arjun Atwal (IND)	73-70-77-69—289	21,185
61	Retief Goosen (RSA)	73-69-72-76—290	20,520
	Jason Bohn	71-73-72-74—290	20,520
	Troy Merritt	69-75-73-73—290	20,520
64	Fredrik Jacobson (SWE)	67-75-73-76—291	19,760
	Matteo Manassero (ITA)	72-70-73-76—291	19,760
	Jerry Kelly	73-70-73-75—291	19,760
	Hunter Haas	72-71-75-73—291	19,760
	Kris Blanks	69-72-81-69—291	19,760
69	Webb Simpson	70-73-74-75—292	19,000
	Martin Laird (SCO)	72-70-76-74—292	19,000
	Kevin Chappell	71-73-80-68—292	19,000
72	Keegan Bradley	75-69-72-77—293	18,620
73	Robert Garrigus	74-69-76-75—294	18,430
74	Mark O'Meara	66-74-79-77—296	18,240

71 players missed the cut

Crowne Plaza Invitational Colonial, Forth Worth, TX [7240–70]

1	David Toms	62-62-74-67—265	$1,116,000
2	Charlie Wi (KOR)	64-67-66-69—266	669,600
3	Bo Van Pelt	68-69-68-65—270	421,600

HP Byron Nelson Championship TPC Four Seasons, Irving, TX
[7166–70]

| 1 | Keegan Bradley* | 66-71-72-68—277 | $1,170,000 |
| 2 | Ryan Palmer | 65-67-73-72—277 | 702,000 |

*Bradley won at the first extra hole

| 3 | Joe Ogilvie | 66-70-72-70—278 | 442,000 |
| | Ryuji Imada (JPN) | 69-68-70-71—278 | 442,000 |

Memorial Tournament *Muirfield Village, Dublin, OH*   [7265–72]

1	Steve Stricker	68-67-69-68—272	$1,116,000
2	Matt Kuchar	69-71-68-65—273	545,600
	Brandt Jobe	71-68-69-65—273	545,600

Fedex St Jude Classic *TPC Southwind, Memphis, TN*   [7244–70]

1	Harrison Frazar*	71-65-64-67—267	$1,008,000
2	Robert Karlsson (SWE)	66-65-68-68—267	604,800

Frazar won at the third extra hole

3	Camilo Villegas (COL)	69-69-70-64—272	252,560
	Tim Herron	73-65-69-65—272	252,560
	Ryuji Imada (JPN)	70-68-68-66—272	252,560
	Charles Howell III	72-67-67-66—272	252,560
	Retief Goosen (RSA)	68-71-64-69—272	252,560

111th US OPEN Championship *Congressional CC, Bethesda, MD*
                                                                       [7574–71]

1	Rory McIlroy (NIR)	65-66-68-69—268	$1,440,000
2	Jason Day (AUS)	71-72-65-68—276	865,000
3	Kevin Chappell	76-67-69-66—278	364,241
	Robert Garrigus	70-70-68-70—278	364,241
	Lee Westwood (ENG)	75-68-65-70—278	364,241
	Y E Yang (KOR)	68-69-70-71—278	364,241

Full details of this event can be found on page 62

Travelers Championship *River Highlands, Cromwell, CT*   [6844–70]

1	Fredrik Jacobson (SWE)	65-66-63-66—260	$1,080,000
2	John Rollins	65-68-65-63—261	528,000
	Ryan Moore	64-70-64-63—261	528,000

AT&T National *Aronimink, Newtown, PA*   [7178–70]

1	Nick Watney	70-69-62-66—267	$1,116,000
2	K J Choi (KOR)	69-64-69-67—269	669,600
3	Charles Howell III	68-68-69-66—271	322,400
	Jeff Overton	71-65-68-67—271	322,400
	Adam Scott (AUS)	66-71-66-68—271	322,400

John Deere Classic *TPC Deere Run, Silvis, IL*   [7257–71]

1	Steve Stricker	66-64-63-69—262	$792,000
2	Kyle Stanley	65-67-65-66—263	486,000
3	Matt McQuillan (CAN)	64-69-70-64—267	299,200
	Zach Johnson	66-69-67-65—267	299,200

140th OPEN CHAMPIONSHIP *R St George's, England*   [7204–70]

1	Darren Clarke (NIR)	68-68-69-70—275	$1,452,078
2	Dustin Johnson	70-68-68-72—278	687,057
	Phil Mickelson	70-69-71-68—278	687,057

Full details of this event can be found on page 46

Viking Classic *Annandale, Madison MS*   [7199–72]

1	Chris Kirk	67-67-64-68—266	$648,000
2	Tom Pernice Jr	66-67-67-67—267	316,800
	George McNeill	67-65-67-68—267	316,800

RBC Canadian Open Vancouver, British Columbia, Canada [7010–70]

1	Sean O'Hair*	69-73-66-68—276	$936,000
2	Kris Blanks	67-71-69-69—276	561,600

*O'Hair won at the first extra hole

3	Andres Romero (ARG)	72-68-67-70—277	353,600

The Greenbrier Classic White Sulphur Springs, WV [7020–70]

1	Scott Stallings	70-65-66-69—270	$1,080,000
2	Bill Haas	71-67-65-67—270	528,000
	Bob Estes	69-72-65-64—270	528,000

Reno-Tahoe Open Montreux G&CC, Reno, NV [7472–72]

1	Scott Piercy	72-70-61-70—273	$540,000
2	Pat Perez	73-68-65-68—274	324,000
3	Steve Flesch	68-69-70-68—275	174,000
	Blake Adams	67-72-67-69—275	174,000

WGC – Bridgestone Invitational Firestone CC, Akron, OH [7400–70]

1	Adam Scott (AUS)	62-70-66-65—263	$1,400,000
2	Luke Donald (ENG)	68-69-64-66—267	665,000
	Rickie Fowler	68-64-69-66—267	665,000

Full details of this event can be found on page 191

US PGA CHAMPIONSHIP Atlanta Athletic Club, Johns Creek, GA

[7467–70]

1	Keegan Bradley (USA)*	71-64-69-68—272	$1,445,000
2	Jason Dufner (USA)	70-65-68-69—272	865,000

*Bradley won at the third extra hole

3	Anders Hansen (DEN)	68-69-70-66—273	545,000

Full details of this event can be found on page 82

Wyndham Championship Sedgefield, Greensboro, NC [7130–70]

1	Webb Simpson	66-65-64-67—262	$936,000
2	George McNeill	65-70-66-64—265	561,600
3	Tommy Gainey	63-65-69-69—266	353,600

The Barclays Plainfield CC, Edison, NJ [6964–71]

1	Dustin Johnson	66-63-65—194	$1,440,000
2	Matt Kuchar	63-65-68—196	864,000
3	Brandt Snedeker	70-66-61—197	464,000
	Vijay Singh (FIJ)	65-64-68—197	464,000

Event shortened to 54 holes due to impending hurricane

Deutsche Bank Championship TPC Boston, Norton, MA [7214–71]

1	Webb Simpson*	69-68-67-65—269	$1,440,000
2	Chez Reavie	67-68-68-66—269	864,000

*Simpson won at the second extra hole

3	Brandt Snedeker	69-64-72-66—271	416,000
	Luke Donald (ENG)	66-70-68-67—271	416,000
	Jason Day (AUS)	67-69-67-68—271	416,000

BMW Championship *Cog Hill, Lemont, Il*   [7386–71]

1	Justin Rose (ENG)	63-68-69-71—271	$1,440,000
2	John Senden (AUS)	68-66-70-69—273	864,000
3	Geoff Ogilvy (AUS)	69-68-68-69—274	544,000

Tour Championship *East Lake GC, Atlanta, GA*   [7154–70]

1	Bill Haas*	68-67-69-68—272	$1,440,000
2	Hunter Mahan	67-68-66-71—272	864,000

*Haas won at the third extra hole

3	Luke Donald (ENG)	66-68-70-69—273	418,666
	KJ Choi (KOR)	68-65-70-70—273	418,666
	Aaron Baddeley (AUS)	68-69-64-72—273	418,666

JTS Hospitals for Children Open *TPC Summerlin. Las Vegas, NV*
[7223–71]

1	Kevin Na	67-63-66-65—261	$792,000
2	Nick Watney	65-67-64-67—263	475,200
3	Tommy Gainey	67-67-64-68—266	225,200
	Paul Goydos	66-66-66-68—266	225,200

Frys.com Open *CordeValle GC, San Martin, CA*   [7368–71]

1	Bryce Molder*	71-67-65-64—267	$900,000
2	Briny Baird	67-69-64-67—267	540,000

*Molder won at the sixth extra hole

3	Bud Cauley	69-66-68-66—269	340,000

The McGladrey Classic *Sea Island, GA*   [7055–70]

1	Ben Crane*	65-70-67-63—265	$720,000
2	Webb Simpson	63-67-69-66—265	432,000

*Crane won at the second extra hole

3	Michael Thompson	65-65-67-69—266	272,000

PGA Grand Slam of Golf[1] *Port Royal Golf Course, Bermuda*   [6845–71]

1	Keegan Bradley	67-71—138	
2	Charl Schwartzel (RSA)	74-65—139	
3	Rory McIlroy (NIR)	67-75—142	
4	Darren Clarke (NIR)	77-74—151	

Children's Miracle Network Classic
Magnolia and Palm Courses, Lake Buena Vista, FL   [7516–72, 6957–72]

1	Luke Donald (ENG)	66-71-70-64—271	$846,000
2	Justin Leonard	69-63-70-71—273	507,600
3	Tom Pernice Jr	68-69-68-69—274	244,400
	Sunghoon Kang (KOR)	68-71-67-68—274	244,400
	Kevin Chappell	70-66-66-72—274	244,400

CIMB Asia Pacific Classic Malaysia[1] *Mines Resort & GC, Selangor,*
Malaysia   [6966–71]

1	Bo Van Pelt	66-64-67-64—261	$1,300,000
2	Jeff Overton	67-62-69-69—267	550,000
3	Fredrik Jacobson (SWE)	65-64-71-68—268	420,000

[1]Event not co-sponsored by the PGA Tour

WGC – HSBC Champions Tournament *Sheshan GC, Shanghai, China*

[7266-72]

1	Martin Kaymer (GER)	69-68-68-63—268	$1,200,000
2	Fredrik Jacobson (SWE)	67-66-67-71—271	675,000
3	Graeme McDowell (NIR)	69-69-67-67—272	430,000

Full details of this event can be found on page 193

ADT Skills Challenge[1] *The Breakers, Palm Beach, FL*

1	Zach Johnson and Jerry Kelly	$286,000
2	Mark O'Meara and Nick Price (ZIM)	185,000
3	Rocco Mediate and Nick Faldo (ENG)	168,000
4	Annika Sörenstam (SWE) and Morgan Pressel*	161,000

*This is the first time female players have participated in this event

Wendy's 3-Tour Challenge[1] *Rio Secco GC, NV*

See page 234

The Presidents Cup *Royal Melbourne Golf Club, Victoria, Australia*

International Team 15, USA 19

Full details of this event can be found in International Team Events, page 212

56th World Cup of Golf[1] *Mission Hills GC, China*

[7441-72]

1	USA (Matt Kuchar and Gary Woodland)	64-70-63-67—264	
			$2,400,000
2	England (Ian Poulter and Justin Rose)	66-69-68-63—266	
			1,300,000
	Germany (Martin Kaymer and Alex Cejka)	65-71-61-69—266	
			1,300,000

Full details of this event can be found in International Team Events, page 214

Chevron World Challenge[1] *Sherwood CC, Thousand Oaks, CA* [7027-72]

1	Tiger Woods	69-67-73-69—278	$120,000
2	Zach Johnson	73-67-68-71—279	650,000
3	Paul Casey (ENG)	79-68-67-69—283	400,000

Franklin Templeton Shoot-out[1] *Tiburon GC, Naples, FL* [7288-72]

1	Keegan Bradley and Brendan Steele	63-62-59—184	$375,000 each
2	Rory Sabbatini nd Jhonattan Vegas	67-60-60—187	$187,500 each
	Mark Calcavecchia and Nick Price	63-63-61—187	$187,500 each

[1]Event not co-sponsored by the PGA Tour

Who is known as "The Wild Thing"?

The answer can be found on page 905

US Champions Tour 2011

www.pgatour.com

Final Ranking *Players are of American nationality unless stated*

1	Tom Lehman	$2,081,526	26	Chip Beck	636,833
2	Mark Calcavecchia	1,867,991	27	Hale Irwin	624,811
3	John Cook	1,747,075	28	Tommy Armour III	614,392
4	Jay Don Blake	1,531,877	29	Tom Pernice Jr	611,724
5	Russ Cochran	1,503,090	30	Brad Bryant	590,087
6	Jeff Sluman	1,493,672	31	Bob Gilder	534,146
7	Peter Senior (AUS)	1,434,119	32	Mark McNulty (IRL)	510,307
8	Nick Price (ZIM)	1,300,443	33	Fred Funk	494,758
9	Olin Browne	1,251,473	34	Mike Goodes	493,703
10	Mark O'Meara	1,237,797	35	Joe Ozaki (JPN)	493,242
11	Michael Allen	1,161,306	36	Hal Sutton	457,062
12	Jay Haas	1,067,467	37	Larry Mize	455,014
13	Fred Couples	1,042,953	38	Mark Brooks	422,884
14	David Eger	982,904	39	Ted Schulz	405,516
15	Kenny Perry	964,851	40	Eduardo Romero (ARG)	394,123
16	Mark Wiebe	931,652	41	Bob Tway	389,787
17	John Huston	866,290	42	Steve Lowery	380,691
18	Corey Pavin	848,252	43	Tom Kite	357,838
19	Tom Watson	815,675	44	Bill Glasson	354,406
20	David Frost (RSA)	802,019	45	Dan Forsman	346,822
21	Loren Roberts	762,265	46	Keith Fergus	343,574
22	Rod Spittle (CAN)	731,144	47	Brad Faxon	331,711
23	Joey Sindelar	708,337	48	Gary Hallberg	329,550
24	Chien Soon Lu (TPE)	702,597	49	David Peoples	328,197
25	Bernhard Langer (GER)	678,769	50	Steve Pate	310,593

Career Money List

1	Hale Irwin	$26,195,615	26	Mike Hill	8,383,104
2	Gil Morgan	20,010,748	27	Tom Wargo	7,996,775
3	Tom Kite	14,883,500	28	D A Weibring	7,982,894
4	Dana Quigley	14,782,223	29	Morris Hatalsky	7,903,236
5	Bruce Fleisher	14,721,417	30	Bernhard Langer (GER)	7,901,831
6	Larry Nelson	14,035,192	31	Craig Stadler	7,873,390
7	Jim Thorpe	13,524,329	32	Doug Tewell	7,728,223
8	Tom Watson	13,400,115	33	Mark McNulty (IRL)	7,601,857
9	Tom Jenkins	13,370,249	34	Tom Purtzer	7,553,487
10	Allen Doyle	13,333,865	35	Mike McCullough	7,548,481
11	Jay Haas	12,117,422	36	John Bland	7,511,059
12	Jim Colbert	11,734,237	37	Brad Bryant	7,505,690
13	Dave Stockton	11,211,471	38	John Cook	7,440,466
14	Loren Roberts	11,089,136	39	Bruce Lietzke	7,416,223
15	Bob Gilder	10,750,174	40	J C Snead	7,406,161
16	Lee Trevino	9,869,613	41	Bob Murphy	7,221,956
17	Jay Sigel	9,483,744	42	Jose Maria Canizares (ESP)	7,184,131
18	Raymond Floyd	9,474,009	43	Dale Douglass	7,019,089
19	Isao Aoki (JPN)	9,367,507	44	Walter Hall	7,003,528
20	Graham Marsh (AUS)	9,223,851	45	Bobby Wadkins	6,819,078
21	Bruce Summerhays	9,046,957	46	David Eger	6,667,811
22	Bob Charles (NZL)	9,044,003	47	Fred Funk	6,646,345
23	Jim Dent	9,022,981	48	Chi Chi Rodriguez	6,642,834
24	Vicente Fernandez (ARG)	8,867,174	49	Andy Bean	6,551,174
25	John Jacobs	8,690,800	50	Dave Eichelberger	6,429,037

Tour Results

Mitsubishi Electric Championship	Hualalai, Ka'upulehu-Kona, HI	John Cook	194 (−8)
Champions Skins Game	Royal Kaanapaii, Lahaina, HI	Jack Nicklaus and Tom Watson	
Allianz Championship	Broken Sound, Boca Raton, FL	Tom Lehman	203 (−13)
The ACE Group Classic	The Quarry, Naples, FL	Bernhard Langer (GER)	196 (−20)
Toshiba Classic	Newport Beach, CA	Nick Price (RSA)	196 (−17)
Mississippi GR Classic	Fallen Oak, Biloxi, MI	Tom Lehman	200 (−16)
Outback Steakhouse Pro-Am	TPC Tampa Bay, Lutz, FL	John Cook	204 (−9)
Liberty Mutual Legends of Golf	Savannah Harbor, GA	David Eger and Mark McNulty (IRL)*	

Eger and McNulty beat Scott Hoch and Kenny Perry at the second extra hole

Regions Tradition	Shoal Creek, AL	Tom Lehman*	275 (−13)

Lehman beat Peter Senior (AUS) at the second extra hole

US Senior PGA Championship — Valhalla GC, Louisville, KY

1	Tom Watson*	70-70-68-70—278
2	David Eger	74-68-69-67—278

Watson won at the first extra hole

3	Kiyoshi Murota (JPN)	66-67-74-72—279

Principal Charity Classic	Glen Oaks, West Des Moines, IA	Bob Gilder	199 (−14)
Greater Hickory Classic	Rock Barn Golf & Spa, Conover, NC	Mark Wiebe*	197 (−19)

Weibe beat James Mason at the third extra hole

Dick's Sporting Goods Open	En-Joie GC, Endicott, NY	John Huston	200 (−7)
Montreal Championship	Montreal, Quebec, Canada	John Cook	195 (−21)
Nature Valley First Tee Open	Pebble Beach, CA	Jeff Sluman	206 (−10)

The Senior Open — Walton Heath, England

1	Russ Cochran	72-70-67-67—276
2	Mark Calcavecchia	68-69-72-69—278
3	Corey Pavin	72-69-69-69—279
	Tom Watson	75-68-69-67—279

US Senior Open — Toledo, OH

1	Olin Browne	64-69-65-71—269
2	Mark OMeara	66-68-66-72—272
3	Mark Calcavecchia	68-67-69-69—273

3M Championship	TPC Twin Cities, Blaine, MN	Jay Haas	201 (−15)
Constellation Energy Senior Players Championship	Harrison, NY	Fred Couples	273 (−11)
Boeing Classic	Snoqualmie, WA	Mark Calcavecchia*	202 (−14)

Calcavecchia beat Russ Cochran at the first extra hole

Songdo IBD Championship	Jack Nicklaus GC, Songdo City, Korea	Jay Don Blake*	203 (−13)

Beat Mark O'Meara, John Cook and Peter Senior (AUS) at the fifth extra hole

SAS Championship	Prestonwood CC, Cary, NC	Kenny Perry	205 (−11)
Insperity Championship	The Woodlands, TX	Brad Faxon	134 (−10)

Round three was cancelled due to bad weather

AT&T Championship	San Antonio, TX	Fred Couples	193 (−23)
Charles Schwab Cup Championship	San Francisco, CA	Jay Don Blake	276 (−8)
Wendy's 3-Tour Challenge	Rio Secco GC, NV	See page 234	

Golf's Big Three together again at Augusta

Gary Player, a three times winner of the Green Jacket, joins Arnold Palmer and Jack Nicklaus as an honorary starter at The Masters this year.

Between them the "Big Three" won 13 Masters titles – six of them by Jack, four by Arnie and three in 1961, 1974 and 1978 by Gary. Player, the first international player to win at Augusta in 1961, competed in the event a record 52 times between 1957 and 2010 making two more appearances than Palmer. The South African missed only the 1973 tournament when he was injured.

Tour Statistics

Driving accuracy

Pos	Name	Rounds	%
1	Corey Pavin	59	82.11
2	John Morse	38	81.27
3	Hale Irwin	67	80.51
4	Fred Funk	46	80.41
5	Olin Browne	74	80.07
6	Larry Mize	60	79.77
7	Lee Rinker	47	79.57
8	Bruce Fleisher	54	79.55
9	Wayne Levi	58	79.34
10	Mark Wiebe	63	78.63

Sand saves

Pos	Name	Rounds	%
1	Dan Forsman	63	68.57
2	Olin Browne	74	63.22
3	Larry Mize	60	61.67
4	Jay Don Blake	62	61.33
5	Corey Pavin	59	57.75
6	John Huston	45	56.14
7	Loren Roberts	61	55.56
8	Chip Beck	67	55.42
9	David Eger	70	54.88
10	Mark O'Meara	65	54.55

Driving distance

(Average yards per drive)

Pos	Name	Rounds	Yds
1	Steve Lowery	61	293.3
2	John Huston	45	292.0
3	Michael Allen	62	288.5
4	Jim Rutledge (CAN)	51	287.6
5	Eduardo Romero (ARG)	47	287.4
	Hal Sutton	66	287.4
7	Mark Calcavecchia	71	287.0
8	Tom Lehman	68	286.7
9	Keith Fergus	67	286.2
10	Lonnie Nielsen	51	286.1

Scrambling

(Made par after missing greens in regulation)

Pos	Name	Rounds	%
1	Peter Senior (AUS)	71	69.13
2	Russ Cochran	57	69.03
3	Corey Pavin	59	66.92
4	Larry Mize	60	65.99
5	Tom Pernice Jr	51	65.60
6	Jay Don Blake	62	65.56
7	Mark Calcavecchia	71	65.46
8	Nick Price (ZIM)	67	65.20
9	Olin Browne	74	65.03
10	Morris Hatalsky	62	65.00

Greens in regulation

Pos	Name	Rounds	%
1	Tom Lehman	68	77.68
2	Joey Sindelar	57	74.21
3	Tom Watson	41	74.01
4	Jeff Sluman	77	73.88
5	Hal Sutton	66	73.61
6	John Huston	45	73.31
	Tom Purtzer	57	73.31
8	Russ Cochran	57	73.29
9	John Cook	70	73.12
10	Steve Lowery	61	73.08

Putts per round

Pos	Name	Rounds	%
1	Chien Soon Lu (TPE)	72	28.47
	Corey Pavin	59	28.47
3	Michael Allen	62	28.56
4	Gary Hallberg	70	28.58
5	Nick Price (ZIM)	67	28.62
6	Tom Pernice Jr	51	28.64
7	Mark Calcavecchia	71	28.67
8	Olin Browne	74	28.80
9	Mark Wiebe	63	28.81
10	Mark O'Meara	65	28.82

US Champions Tour Records 2011

Multiple winners

John Cook	Mitsubishi Electric Championship; Outback Steakhouse Pro-Am; Montreal Championship
Tom Lehman	Allianz Championship; Mississippi GR Classic; Regions Tradition
Jay Don Blake	Songdo IBD Championship; Charles Schwab Cup Championship
Fred Couples	Constellation Energy Senior Players Championship; AT&T Championship

Top Ten Finishes

Mark Calcavecchia	15	Russ Cochran	11	Jeff Sluman	10
Tom Lehman	12	Michael Allen	10		
Peter Senior (AUS)	12	Nick Price (ZIM)	10		

US Nationwide Tour 2011

www.pgatour.com

Players are of American nationality unless stated

Final Ranking (Top 25 earned US Tour Card)

1	J J Killeen	$414,273		51	Steve Friesen	122,926
2	Ted Potter Jr	402,470		52	Greg Owen (ENG)	121,259
3	Mathew Goggin (AUS)	378,492		53	Kirk Triplett	117,168
4	Jason Kokrak	338,092		54	Ryan Armour	115,706
5	Jonas Blixt (SWE)	327,020		55	Andrew Svoboda	108,213
6	Danny Lee (NZL)	326,100		56	Roger Tambellini	107,707
7	Ken Duke	313,241		57	Justin Bolli	106,717
8	Scott Brown	282,502		58	Craig Bowden	105,027
9	Gary Christian (ENG)	260,054		59	John Kimbell	104,392
10	Miguel Angel Carballo (ARG)	258,833		60	Travis Hampshire	101,690
11	Troy Kelly	248,064		61	Nicholas Thompson	93,893
12	Russell Knox (SCO)	242,821		62	Charles Warren	92,809
13	Erik Compton	239,737		63	Tim Wilkinson (NZL)	92,747
14	John Mallinger	237,779		64	Andrew Buckle (AUS)	92,388
15	Kyle Thompson	233,949		65	Harris English	90,488
16	Kyle Reifers	233,677		66	Brian Stuard	89,859
17	Gavin Coles (AUS)	229,991		67	James Hahn	88,186
18	Matt Every	229,066		68	Tyrone Van Aswegen	85,891
19	Daniel Chopra (SWE)	225,637		69	Chris Nallen	85,686
20	Steve Wheatcroft	225,054		70	Brice Garnett	85,006
21	Garth Mulroy (RSA)	201,732		71	Jon Mills (CAN)	83,948
22	Mark Anderson	188,550		72	James Sacheck	82,427
23	Roberto Castro	186,563		73	Doug LaBelle II	81,717
24	Martin Flores	182,612		74	Josh Geary (NZL)	79,586
25	Billy Hurley III	180,191		75	Sunghoon Kang (KOR)	76,981
26	James Nitties	174,850		76	Scott Sterling	72,594
27	David Lingmerth (SWE)	170,980		77	Won Joon Lee (AUS)	72,464
28	Josh Broadaway	169,293		78	Scott Gardiner (AUS)	72,429
29	Brett Wetterich	167,300		79	Andres Gonzales	67,925
30	Jeff Gove	166,440		80	Brad Elder	66,564
31	Tommy Biershenk	160,513		81	Nick Flanagan (AUS)	64,417
32	Marco Dawson	156,067		82	Brian Vranesh	62,884
33	Darron Stiles	155,436		83	Jin Park (KOR)	62,434
34	Matt Davidson	153,309		84	Brendon Todd	60,035
35	Camilo Benedetti (COL)	151,654		85	Rahil Gangjee (IND)	59,645
36	Will Wilcox	149,123		86	Brent Delahoussaye	58,631
37	Richard H Lee (CAN)	143,243		87	Matt Weibring	56,761
38	Luke List	142,600		88	Jason Schultz	55,726
39	Cliff Kresge	142,132		89	Peter Lonard (AUS)	53,831
40	Paul Claxton	140,544		90	Dicky Pride	51,484
41	Brenden Pappas (RSA)	137,918		91	Elliot Gealy	50,024
42	Brian Smock	136,037		92	Clayton Rask	49,953
43	Aaron Watkins	130,950		93	Matthew Giles (AUS)	49,152
44	Rob Oppenheim	129,594		94	Bob Heintz	48,747
45	Matt Hendrix	129,427		95	Ron Whittaker	48,531
46	Bubba Dickerson	127,806		96	Jeff Brehaut	47,083
47	Casey Wittenberg	127,772		97	Rich Barcelo	46,650
48	B J Staten	127,010		98	Diego Velasquez (COL)	43,835
49	Alistair Presnell (AUS)	125,525		99	David Vanegas (COL)	43,310
50	Aaron Goldberg	125,223		100	Dawie van der Walt (RSA)	43,293

Tour Results

Panama Claro Championship	Panama City	Matthew Coggin (AUS)	269 (–11)
Pacific Rubiates Bogotá Open	Bogotá	Brendan Pappas (RSA)	133 (–9)
Chitimacha Louisiana Open	Le Triomphe, Broussard, LA	Brett Wetterich	271 (–13)
Fresh Express Classic	Stonebrae, Hayward, CA	Daniel Chopra (SWE)	198 (–12)
South Georgia Classic	Kinderlou Forest, Valdosta, GA	Ted Potter Jr	272 (–16)
Stadion Classic	Univ. of GA	Russell Henley	272 (–12)
BMW Charity Pro-Am	Greer, SC; Mill Spring, NC; Spartanburg, SC	Garth Mulroy (RSA)	268 (–18)
Melwood Prince George's County Open	College Park, MD	Tommy Gainey	255 (–20)
Rex Hospital Open	Wakefield Plantation, Raleigh, NC	Kyle Thompson	270 (–14)
Preferred Health Systems Wichita Open	Wichita, KS	Matthew Coggin (AUS)	266 (–18)
Mexico Open	El Bosque Golf Club, Leon, Guanajuato, Mexico	Erik Compton	271 (–17)
Chiquita Classic	River's Bend, Maineville, OH	Russell Knox (SCO)	263 (–25)
Nationwide Children's Hospital Invitational	Scarlet, Columbus, OH	Harris English (am)	270 (–14)
Utah Championship	Willow Creek CC, Sandy, UT	J J Killeen	262 (–22)
Cox Classic	Champions Run, Omaha, NE	J J Killeen	262 (–22)
Price Cutter Charity C/ship	Springfield, MO	Steve Friesen	262 (–26)
Midwest Classic	Overland Park, KS	James Nitties	258 (–26)
News Sentinel Open	Knoxville, TN	Kirk Triplett	267 (–21)
Mylan Classic	Canonsburg, PA	Gary Christian (ENG)	267 (–17)
Albertsons Boise Open	Boise, ID	Jason Kokrak	266 (–18)
Soboba Golf Classic	San Jacinto, CA	Ted Potter Jr*	270 (–14)

Beat Andres Gonzales and Miguel Carballo (ARG) at the second extra hole

WNB Golf Classic	Midland, TX	Danny Lee (NZL)*	270 (–18)

Beat Harris English at the first extra hole

Children's Hospital Classic	Chattanooga, TN	Miguel Carballo (ARG)	264 (–24)
Miccosukee Championship	Miami, FL	Jason Kokrak	264 (–20)
Winn-Dixie Jacksonville Open	Ponte Vedra, FL	Gavin Coles (AUS)	274 (–6)
Nationwide Tour Championship	Charleston, SC	Ken Duke	278 (–10)

US Nationwide Tour statistics leaders 2011

Driving distance – Jason Kokrak (54 rounds), 318.6 yards average

Driving accuracy – Geoffrey Sisk (68 rounds), 77.20%

Greens in regulation – Brock Mackenzie (35 rounds), 76.44%

Putts per round – J J Killeen (90 rounds), 28.24 average

Sand saves – Jin Park (KOR) (69 rounds), 67.39%

Scrambling – Tim Wilkinson (NZL), (75 rounds), 67%

Top Ten finishes – Danny Lee (NZL), (9)

Longest drive – Cody Slover, 444 yards

Putting average – J J Killeen (90 rounds), 1.703

US Nationwide Tour records 2011

Multiple winners

Matthew Coggin (AUS) – Panama Claro Championship; Preferred Health Systems Wichita Open

J J Killeen – Utah Championship; Cox Classic

Jason Kokrak – Albertsons Boise Open; Miccosukee Championship

Ted Potter Jr – South Georgia Classic; Soboba Golf Classic

Asian Tour 2011

www.asiantour.com

Avantha Masters	DKLF G&CC, New Delhi	S S P Chowrasia (IND)	273 (–15)
WGC – Accenture Match Play Championship	Ritz Carlton GC, AZ	Final: Luke Donald (ENG) beat MartinKaymer (GER) 3 and 2	
WGC – Cadillac Championship	TPC Blue Monster at Doral, FL	Nick Watney (USA)	272 (–16)
SAIL Open	Delhi GC, New Delhi	Kiradech Aphibarnrat (THA)	272 (–16)
Panasonic Open (India)	Delhi GC, New Delhi	Anirban Lahiri (IND)*	275 (–13)

Beat Mardan Mamat (SIN) and Manav Jalni (IND) at first extra hole

Masters Tournament	Augusta National GC, GA	Charl Schwartzel (RSA)	274 (–14)
Maybank Malaysian Open	Kuala Lumpur G&CC	Matteo Manassero (ITA)	272 (–16)
Indonesian Masters	Royale Jakarta GC	Lee Westwood (ENG)	269 (–19)
Ballantines Championship	Blackstone Resort, Seoul South Korea	Lee Westwood (ENG)	276 (–12)
ITCSI Philippine Open	Wack Wack G&CC, Manila	Berry Henson (USA)	283 (–5)
US Open	Congressional CC, MD	Rory McIlroy (NIR)	268 (–16)
Queen's Cup	Santibui Samui CC, Koh Samul, Thailand	Chawalit Plaphol (THA)	273 (–11)
The Open Championship	Royal St George's, Kent, England	Darren Clarke (NIR)	275 (–5)
Worldwide Holdings Selengor Masters	Kota Permai G&CC, Shah Alam, Malaysia	Joonas Granberg (FIN)	273 (–15)
WGC Bridgestone Invitational	Firestone CC, Ohio, USA	Adam Scott (AUS)	263 (–17)
US PGA Championship	Atlanta AC, Georgia, USA	Keegan Bradley (USA)*	272 (–8)

Beat Jason Dufner (USA) at the third extra hole

| Omega European Masters | Crans-sur-Sierre, Switzerland | Thomas Bjorn (DEN) | 264 (–20) |
| IPS Handa Singapore Classic | Orchid CC, Singapore | Himmat Rai (IND)* | 271 (–9) |

Beat Elmer Salvador (PHI), Guido Van Der Valk (NED), Tjart Van Der Walt (RSA) and Adilson Da Silva (BRA) at the sixth extra hole

Macau Open	Macau G&CC	Chan Yih-Shin (TPE)	270 (–14)
Asia Pacific Panasonic Open	Biwako CC, Shiga, Japan	Tetsuji Hiratsuke (JPN)	276 (–8)
Yeangder Tournament Players Championship	Linkou International GC, Taipei	Lu Wei-chih (TPE)	283 (–5)
Hero Indian Open	Delhi GC, New Delhi	David Gleeson (AUS)	268 (–20)
CJ Invitational hosted by KJ Choi	Haesley Nine Bridges Club, Korea	KJ Choi (KOR)	271 (–17)
CIMB Asia Pacific Classic	The Mines Resort and GC, Kuala Lumpur, Malaysia	Bo Van Pelt (USA)	261 (–23)
Mercuries Taiwan Masters	Taiwan G&CC, Taipei	Lu Wei-chih (TPE)	278 (–10)
WGC – HSBC Champions	Sheshan GC, Shanghai	Martin Kaymer (ger)	268 (–20)
Barclays Singapore Open	Sentosa GC ((Tanjong and Serapong courses), Singapore	Gonzalo Fernadez-Castaño (ESP)*	199 (–14)

Beat Juvic Pagunsan (PHI) at second extra hole – tournament reduced to 54 holes because of bad weather

| Iskandar Johor Open | Horizon Hills G&CC, Johor Bahru, Malaysia | Joost Luiten (NED) | 198 (–15) |

Tournament reduced to 54 holes because of bad weather

Omega Mission Hills World Cup	Mission Hills Resort, Hainan Island	USA (Matt Kuchar and Gary Woodland	264 (–24)
UBS Hong Kong Open	Hong Kong Golf Club, Fanling	Rory McIlroy (NIR)	268 (–12)
Thailand Golf Championship	Amata Spring CC, Bangkok	Lee Westwood (ENG)	266 (–22)

Final Ranking (events played in brackets)

1	Juvic Pagunsan (PHI)	(14)	US$788,298	6	David Gleeson (AUS)	(15)	292,880
2	Tetsuji Hiratsuka (JPN)	(8)	456,667	7	Kiradech Aphibarnrat (THA)	(11)	291,967
3	SSP Chowrasia (IND)	(12)	444,528	8	Mohammad Siddikur (BAN)	(17)	291,653
4	Jbe Kruger (RSA)	(16)	362,233	9	Lu Wei-Chih (TPE)	(10)	269,230
5	Thaworn Wiratchant (THA)	(19)	340,942	10	Thongchai Jaidee (THA)	(10)	266,245

PGA Tour of Australasia 2011

www.pgatour.com.au

Players are of Australian nationality unless stated

Victorian Open	Spring Valley GC	Paul Sheehan	276 (–8)
Cellarbrations Victorian PGA	Sandhurst North	James Nitties	198 (–18)
South Pacific Golf Open	Tina GC	Matt Griffin*	273 (–15)
Beat Terry Pilkadaris at the second extra hole			
Brunei WA PGA Championship	Novotel Vines Resort & CC, Perth	Michael Wright	273 (–15)
Surf Coast Knock Out	The Sands GC, Torquay	Peter O'Malley	200 (–16)
Cellarbrations Queensland PGA	City GC	Gareth Paddison (NZL)	202 (–18)
John Hughes Geely WA Championship	The Vines Resort, Perth	Rohan Blizzard	278 (–10)
NSW PGA Championship	Woollongong GC	Matthew Guyatt	197 (–13)
Emirates Australian Open	The Lakes GC, Sydney	Greg Chalmers	275 (–13)

1904	Hon Michael Scott (am)	1933	M Kelly	1964	Jack Nicklaus (USA)	1989	Peter Senior
1905	Dan Soutar	1934	Bill Bolger	1965	Gary Player (RSA)	1990	John Morse (USA)
1906	Carnegie Clark (am)	1935	F McMahon	1966	Arnold Palmer (USA)	1991	Wayne Riley
1907	Hon Michael Scott (am)	1936	Gene Sarazen (USA)	1967	Peter Thomson	1992	Steve Elkington
		1937	George Naismith	1968	Jack Nicklaus (USA)	1993	Brad Faxon (USA)
1908	Clyde Pearce (am)	1938	Jim Ferrier (am)	1969	Gary Player (RSA)	1994	Robert Allenby
1909	C Felstead (am)	1939	Jim Ferrier (am)	1970	Gary Player (RSA)	1995	Greg Norman
1910	Carnegie Clark (am)	1940–1945	*not played*	1971	Jack Nicklaus (USA)	1996	Greg Norman
1911	Carnegie Clark (am)	1946	Ossie Pickworth	1972	Peter Thomson	1997	Lee Westwood (ENG)
1912	Ivo Whitton (am)	1947	Ossie Pickworth	1973	J C Snead (USA)	1998	Greg Chalmers
1913	Ivo Whitton (am)	1948	Ossie Pickworth	1974	Gary Player (RSA)	1999	Aaron Baddeley (am)
1914–1919	*not played*	1949	Eric Cremin	1975	Jack Nicklaus (USA)		
1920	Joe Kirkwood	1950	Norman Von Nida	1976	Jack Nicklaus (USA)	2000	Aaron Baddeley
1921	A Le Fevre	1951	Peter Thomson	1977	David Graham	2001	Stuart Appleby
1922	C Campbell	1952	Norman Von Nida	1978	Jack Nicklaus (USA)	2002	Steve Allan
1923	T Howard	1953	Norman Von Nida	1979	Jack Newton	2003	Peter Lonard
1924	A Russell (am)	1954	Ossie Pickworth	1980	Greg Norman	2004	Peter Lonard
1925	Fred Popplewell	1955	Bobby Locke (RSA)	1981	Bill Rogers (USA)	2005	Robert Allenby
1926	Ivo Whitton (am)	1956	Bruce Crampton	1982	Bob Shearer	2006	John Senden
1927	R Stewart	1957	Frank Phillips	1983	Peter Fowler	2007	Peter Lonard
1928	Fred Popplewell	1958	Gary Player (RSA)	1984	Tom Watson (USA)	2008	Tim Clark*
1929	Ivo Whitton (am)	1959	Kel Nagle	1985	Greg Norman		*Beat Matthew Coggin at 1st extra hole*
1930	F Eyre	1960	Bruce Devlin (am)	1986	Rodger Davis		
1931	Ivo Whitton (am)	1961	Frank Phillips	1987	Greg Norman	2009	Adam Scott
1932	Mick Ryan (am)	1962	Gary Player (RSA)	1988	Mark Calcavecchia (USA)	2010	Geoff Ogilvy
		1963	Gary Player (RSA)				

NSW Open	Newcastle GC	Adam Crawford	282 (–6)
Australian PGA Championship	Coolum Resort	Greg Chalmers*	276 (–12)
Beat Robert Allenby and Marcus Fraser at the first extra hole			
BMW New Zealand Open	Clearwater Resort, Christchurch	Brad Kennedy*	281 (–7)
Beat Craig Parry at the first extra hole			
JBWere Masters	Victoria GC	Ian Poulter (ENG)	269 (–15)

Final Ranking

1	Greg Chalmers	Aus$554,285	6	Geoff Ogilvy		126,030
2	Marcus Fraser	229,125	7	Adam Scott		121,500
3	John Senden	204,285	8	Aaron Baddeley		105,000
4	Robert Allenby	141,410	9	Nick O'Hern		104,000
5	Brad Kennedy	134,833	10	Adam Crawford		92,401

Canadian Tour 2011

www.cantour.com

Players are of Canadian nationality unless stated

Pacific Colombia Tour Barranquilla Open	Barranquilla CC	Cody Slover (USA)	287 (–1)
Pacific Colombia Tour Championship	Club Campestre, Guaymaral, Bogota	Adam Hadwin	263 (–25)
Mexican PGA Championship	Estrella del Mar	José de Jesus Rodriguez (MEX)*	274

*Beat Roger Sloan at first extra hole of play off

Spring Qualifying	Morningstar GC, Parksville, BC	Andrew Kelly (AUS)	287 (–1)
Times Colonist Island Savings Open	Uplands GC, BC	Roger Sloan	265 (–23)
The Western Open	Rivershore Golf Links, Kamloops, BC	Roger Sloan	265 (–23)
Syncrude Boreal Open	Fort McMurray GC, AB	Danny Sahl	272 (–16)
ATB Financial Classic	Bearspaw GC, Calgary, AB	Hugo Leon (CHI)	271 (–13)
Dakota Dunes Casino Open	Dakota Dunes, Saskatoon, SK	Joe Pazeri (USA)	273 (–15)
Canadian Tour Players Championship	Pine Ridge GC, Winnipeg, MA	Tom Hage (USA)	268 (–16)
RBC Canadian Open	Shaughnessy G&CC, Vancouver, BC	Sean O'Hair (USA)*	276 (–4)

*Beat Kris Blanks (USA) at the first extra hole

1904 J H Oke	1934 T Armour	1961 J Cupit (USA)	1988 K Green (USA)
1905 G Cumming	1935 G Kunes	1962 T Kroll (USA)	1989 S Jones (USA)
1906 C Murray	1936 L Little	1963 D Ford (USA)	1990 W Levi (USA)
1907 P Barrett	1937 H Cooper	1964 KDG Nagle (AUS)	1991 N Price (ZIM)
1908 A Murray	1938 S Snead (USA)	1965 G Littler (USA)	1992 G Norman (AUS)
1909 K Keffer	1939 H McSpaden (USA)	1966 D Massengale (USA)	1993 D Frost (RSA)
1910 D Kenny	1940 S Snead (USA)	1967 W Casper (USA)	1994 N Price (ZIM)
1911 C Murray	1941 S Snead (USA)	1968 RJ Charles (NZL)	1995 M O'Meara (USA)
1912 G Sargent	1942 C Wood (USA)	1969 T Aaron (USA)	1996 D Hart (USA)
1913 A Murray	1943–1944 *not played*	1970 D Zarley (USA)	1997 S Jones (USA)
1914 K Kesser	1945 B Nelson (USA)	1971 L Trevino (USA)	1998 B Andrade (USA)
1915–1918 *not played*	1946 G Fazio (USA)	1972 G Brewer Jr (USA)	1999 H Sutton (USA)
1919 J D Edgar	1947 AD Locke (RSA)	1973 T Weiskopf (USA)	2000 T Woods (USA)
1920 J D Edgar	1948 CW Congdon	1974 B Nichols (USA)	2001 S Verplank (USA)
1921 W H Trovinger	1949 E J Harrison	1975 T Weiskopf (USA)	2002 J Rollins (USA)
1922 A Watrous	1950 J Ferrier	1976 J Pate (USA)	2003 R Tway (USA)
1923 C W Hackney	1951 J Ferrier	1977 L Trevino (USA)	2004 V Singh (FIJ)
1924 L Diegel	1952 J Palmer (USA)	1978 B Lietzke (USA)	2005 M Calcavecchia
1925 L Diegel	1953 D Douglas (USA)	1979 L Trevino (USA)	(USA)
1926 M Smith	1954 P Fletcher	1980 B Gilder (USA)	2006 J Furyk (USA)
1927 T Armour	1955 A Palmer (USA)	1981 P Oosterhuis (ENG)	2007 J Furyk (USA)
1928 L Diegel	1956 D Sanders (am)	1982 B Lietzke (USA)	2008 C Reavie (USA)
1929 L Diegel	(USA)	1983 J Cook (USA)	2009 N Green (AUS)*
1930 T Armour	1957 G Bayer (USA)	1984 G Norman (AUS)	**Beat R Goosen (RSA) at*
1931 W Hagen	1958 W Ellis Jr (USA)	1985 C Strange (USA)	*the 2nd extra hole*
1932 H Cooper	1959 D Ford (USA)	1986 B Murphy (USA)	2010 C Petterssen (SWE)
1933 J Kirkwood	1960 A Wall Jr (USA)	1987 C Strange (USA)	

Seaforth Country Open	Seaforth GC, ON	Brian Unk (USA)	260 (–20)
Canadian Tour Championship	Ambassador GC, Windsor, ON	Stuart Anderson*	263 (–21)

*Beat Richard Scott at the second extra hole

Sovereign Insurance International Team Matches	Scarboro G&CC, Toronto, ON	Canada	562 (–14)
Desert Dunes Classic	Desert Hot Springs GC, California, USA	Byron Smith (USA)	272 (–16)

Final Ranking (Figure in brackets indicates number of tournaments played)

1	José de Jesus Rodriguez (MEX)	(10)	$80,227	6	Dustin Risdon	(8)	45,645
2	Hugo Leon (CHI)	(11)	66,994	7	Adam Hadwin	(11)	43,627
3	Benjamin Alvarado (CHI)	(8)	57,691	8	Garrett Sapp (USA)	(8)	39,574
4	Stuart Anderson	(8)	54,469	9	Danny Sahl	(9)	38,450
5	Roger Sloan	(9)	49,788	10	Joe Panzeri (USA)	(10)	37,304

Japan PGA Tour 2011

Players are of Japanese nationality unless stated   www.jgto.org/jgto/WG01000000Init.do

Masters Tournament	Augusta Nagtional GC	Charl Schwartzel (RSA)	274 (−14)
Token Homemate Cup	Token Rado CC, Nagoya	Tadahiro Takayama	276 (−8)
Tsuruya Open	Yamanohara G , Hyogo	Tomohiro Kondo	265 (−19)
The Crowns 2011	Nagoya GC (Wago course), Aichi	Brendan Jones (AUS)*	271 (−15)
Beat I J Jank (KOR) at the first extra hole			
PGA Championship Nissin Cupnoodle Cup	Ono Toyo GC, Hyogo	Hiroo Kawai	275 (−9)
Totoumi Hamamatsu Open	Grandee Hamanako GC, Shizuoka	Masanori Kobayashi*	268 (−20)
Beat Ryo Ishikawa at the second extra hole			
Diamond Cup Golf	Chiba CC (Umesato course), Chiba	Koumei Oda	272 (−16)
Japan Golf Tour Championship Citibank Cup	Shishido Hills CC, Ibaraki	J B Park (KOR)	278 (−6)
US Open Championship	Congressional CC, WA	Rory McIlroy (NIR)	268 (−16)
Gate Way to The Open Mizuno Open	JFE Setonaikai GC, Okayama	Jung-Gon Hwang (KOR)	275 (−13)
KB Financial Million Yard Cup	Gimhae	Korea 11½, Japan 8½	
The Open Championship	Royal St George's GC, Kent, England	Darren Clarke (NIR)	275 (−5)
Nagashima Shigeo Invitational (SEGA Sammy Cup)	The North Country GC, Hokkaido	Kyung-Tae Kim (KOR)	273 (−15)
Sun Chlorella Classic	Otaru CC, Hokkaido	Yuta Ikeda	274 (−4)
Kansai Open Golf Championship	Ono GC, Hyogo	Min-Gyu Cho (KOR)	270 (−14)
Vana H Cup KBC Augusta	Keya GC, Fukuoka	Sang-Moon Bae (KOR)	266 (−22)
Japan PGA Fujisankei Classic	Fujizakara CC Yamanashi	Masatsuga Morofuji	136 (−6)
Toshin Golf Tournament	Toshin Lake Wood GC, Mie	Dong-Huan Lee (KOR)	268 (−20)
ANA Open	Sapporo GC (Wattsu course), Hokkaido	Kurt Barnes (AUS)	275 (−13)
Asia Pacific Panasonic Open	Biwako CC, Shiga, Japan	Tetsuji Hiratsuke	276 (−8)
42nd. Coca Cola Tokai Classic	Miyoshi CC (West course), Aichi	Bae Sang Moon (KOR)	282 (−7)
Canon Open	Totsuka CC, Kanagawa	Kenichi Kuboya	274 (−14)
Japan Open	Takanodai CC	Bae Sang Moon (KOR)*	282 (−2)
Beat Kenichi Kuboya at the first extra hole			
Bridgestone Open	Sodegaura CC (Sodegaura course), Chiba	Toru Taniguchi	269 (−15)
Mynavi ABC Championship	ABC GC, Hyogo	Koichira Kawana*	273 (−15)
Beat Bae Sang Moon (KOR) at the sixth extra hole			
Mitsui Sumitomo VISA Taiheiyo Masters	Taiheiyo Club (Gotemba course), Shizuoka	Hideki Matsuyama (am)	203 −13)
Tournament reduced to 54 holes because of bad weather			
Dunlop Phoenix	Phoenix Seagaia Resort, Miyazaki	Toshinori Muto	201 (−12)
Tournament reduced to 54 holes because of bad weather			
Casio World Open	Kochi Kuroshio CC	Tadahiro Takayama	273 (−15)
Omega Mission Hills World Cup	Mission Hills Resort, Hainan	USA (Gary Woodland and Matt Kuchar)	264 (−24)
Golf Nippon Series JT Cup	Tokyo Yomiuri CC	Hiroyuki Fujita*	200 (−6)
beat Toro Taniguchi at the second extra hole – Reduced to 54 holes because of bad weather			

Final Ranking (Japanese Tour events only)

1	Sang-Moon Bae (KOR)	¥147,942,969	6	Koumei Oda	92,046,659
2	Tadahiro Takayama	98.718,202	7	Tomohiro Kondo	78,374,189
3	Ryo Ishikawa	86,222,295	8	Toshinori Muto	77,694,778
4	Toru Taniguchi	96,888,944	9	Tetsuji Hiratsuka	73,482.234
5	Hiroyuki Fujita	94,355,200	10	Kenichi Kuboya	73,482.234

SBS Korean PGA Tour 2011

Players are of Korean nationality unless stated   http://eng.kgt.co.kr/main/english.aspx

Twayair Open	Ora CC	Andrew Tschudin (AUS)	277 (–11)
Ballantines Championship	Blackstone Resort, Seoul, South Korea	Lee Westwood (ENG)	276 (–12)
30th GS Caltex Maekyung Open	NamSeoul G&CC	Kin Kyung-tae	267 –21)
Volvik Gunsan CC Open	GunSan CC	Lee Seoong-ho	^????
SK Telecom Open	Pinx GC	Kurt Barnes (AUS)	202 (–14)
Event reduced to three rounds because of fog on last day			
Lake Hills Open	Lake Hills Gyeongh Nam CC	Choi Ho-sung	280 (–8)
Suburu Classic	Jisan CC	Hong Soon-sang	276 (–8)
Dongbu Promi Open	Ostar GC	Kang Kyun-Nam	280 (–8)
KB Financial Million Yard Cup	Gimhae	Korea 11½, Japan 8½	
The Charity High 1 Open	High 1 CC	*Cancelled because of bad weather*	
Johnnie Walker Open	Ora CC	Park Do Kyu	204 (–12)
54th Daishin Securities KPGA Championship	Asiana GC	Kim Byung Jun	273 (–15)
27th Shinhan Donghae Open	Kaya G&CC, Busan	Paul Casey (ENG)	288 (E)
Munsingwear Match Play Championship	Castle Pine GC	Final: Hang Soon-sang beat Park Do Gyu 4 and 3	
54th Kolon Korean Open	Woo Jeong Hills	Rickie Fowler (USA)	266 (–16)
6th Meritz Solomoro Open	Solomoro CC	Kang Kyung Nam	277 (–7)
CJ Invitational hosted by KJ Choi	Haesley Nine Bridges CC	K J Choi	271 (–17)
NH Open	Sky Valley CC	Lee Sang Hee	272 (–12)

Final Ranking (Figure in brackets indicates number of tournaments played)

1	Kim Kyung Tae	(6)	₩451,773,549	6	Lee Seong Ho	(14)	192,793,670
2	Park Sang Hyun	(18)	398,473,067	7	K J Choi	(3)	185,442,917
3	Hong Soon Sang	(18)	392,266,942	8	Kim Dae Hyun	(13)	184,128,549
4	Kang Kyung Nam	(18)	267,197,921	9	Noh Seung Yul	(4)	175,581,250
5	Choi Ho Sung	(18)	198,798,333	10	Park Do Kyu	(17)	170,431,458

Kim Kyung Tae tops 2011 Korean Order of Merit

Twenty-five-year-old Kim Kyung Tae headed the 2011 Korean PGA Tour Order of Merit despite playing in only six of the season's events. Despite his slim schedule on his home tour he did win the GS Caltex Maekyung Open and came second in the SK Telecom event and was runner-up to Paul Casey in the 27th Shinhan Donghae Open.

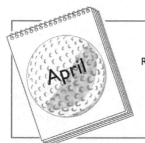

Month by month in 2011

Rory McIlroy, four ahead with a round to go in The Masters, crashes to an 80 and the winner instead is Charl Schwartzel after he birdies the final four holes to beat Australians Adam Scott and Jason Day by two. Lee Westwood regains the world No 1 spot by winning in Indonesia and American Stacy Lewis takes the first of the women's majors.

Tour de las Americas 2011

www.tourdelasamericas.com

85th Abierto de Chile	Prince of Wales CC, Santiago	Benjamin Alvarado (CHI)	266 (–22)
Pacific Colombia Tour Championship	Club Campestre, Guaymaral, Bogota	Adam Hadwin (CAN)	263 (–25)
Pacific Colombia Tour Baranquilla	CC de Baranquilla	Cody Slover (USA)	287 (–1)
III Abierto Internacional de Golf Copa Antioqua	Club Campestre El Rode, Medallin, Colombia	Joaquin Estevez (ARG)*	274 (–10)

Beat Charles Russo (Fr Guy) at the first extra hole

85th Abierto de Chile	Prince of Wales CC, Santiago	Benjamin Alvarado (CHI)	266 (–22)
Campeonato Abierto del Centro	Villa Allende, Cordoba, Argentina	Hector Cespedes (PAR)*	279 (–5)

Beat Joaquin Estevez (ARG) at the first extra hole

TLA Televisa Players Championship	Acapulco Princess, Mexico	Julian Etulain (ARG)	189 (–21)
Toyota Peru Open	Los Inkas CC, Lima, Peru	Benjamin Alvarado	266 (–22)
53rd Abierto de Golf Ciudad de Bucaramanga	CC de Bucaramanga	Alvaro Jose Arizabaleta (COL)*	274 (–12)

Beat José Manuel Garrido (COL) at the first extra hole

51st Abierto Internacional de Golf Copa Sura	Club Deportivo El Rodeo, Medellin	Cesar Augustin Costilla (ARG)*	277 (–11)

Beat Rafael Romero (COL) at the second extra hole

Pacific Colombia Tour Cali	Club Campestre Farralones	*Not played*	
Omega Mission Hills World Cup Qualifying (Copa Renaissance) (Full details available on page 214)	Caracas CC, Venezuela	Brazil (Adilson de Silva and Lucas Lee)	253 (–31)
58th Aberto de Brasil	São Fernando GC, São Paulo	Oscar Alvarez (COL)	275 (–9)
VI Abierto Internacional de Golf (Hacienda Chicureo Copa Claro)	Hacienda GC, Chicureo, Santiago, Chile	Paulo Pinto (ARG)	273 (–15)
Abierto de Nordeste	Resistencia, Chaco, Argentina	Emilio Dominguez (ARG)	274 (–14)
Carlos Franco Invitational	Carlos Franco G&CC	Fabrizio Zanotti (CHI)	270 (–14)
Roberto de Vicenzo Classic	San Eliseo G&CC, San Vicente, Argentina	Nelson Ledesma (ARG)*	280 (–8)

Beat Fernando Zacarias (ARG) and Rafael Gomez (ARG) at the first extra hole

Torneo de Maestros 2011 (Copa Personal)	Olivos GC, Buenos Aries, Argentina	José Coceres (ARG)	276 (–8)
106th Visa Open de Argentina	Pilar GC, Buenos Aries	Maximiliano Goddy (ARG)	278 (–6)
52nd Abierto Sport Frances Copa	Sport France GC, Santiago, Chile	Francisco Cerda (CHI)*	279 (–9)

Beat Federico Damus (ARG) at the first extra hole

Final Ranking

1	Joaquin Estevez (ARG)	51,970 pts	6	Oscar Alvarez (COL)	36,590
2	Benjamin Alvarado (CHI)	48,800	7	Maximiliano Goddy (ARG)	30,336
3	Cesar Augustin Costilla (ARG)	45,006	8	Paulo Pinto (ARG)	28,838
4	Diego Vanegas (COL)	42,883	9	Rafael Gomez (ARG)	28,036
5	Julian Etulain (ARG)	39,233	10	Sebastian Fernandez (ARG)	25,992

Brazilian junior golf receives funding boost

The most extensive junior programme in the history of Brazilian golf is being launched this year. The scheme, organized by the Brazilian Golf Confederation with the help of a grant from The R&A, will introduce thousands of youngsters aged between seven and 14 to the game.

The first stage of the country-wide programme will take golf into schools in the capital Brasilia and Curitaba by providing training and funding for more than 600 youngsters to receive golf lessons from trained PE teachers during sports classes. Those who show interest and ability will then go onto more advanced coaching sessions at local clubs with golf professionals.

PGTI Tour 2011

www.pgtindia.org

Players are of Indian nationality unless stated

Gugurat Kennsville Challenge	Kensville G&CC, Ahmedabad	Gaganjeet Bhullar	283 (−5)
Bangladesh Open	Kurmitola GC, Dhaka	Gaganjeet Bhullar	274 (−14)
PGTI Players Championship	Royal Calcutta GC	Raju Ali Mollah	242 (−18)
PGTI Players Championship	Royal Calcutta GC	Gaganjeet Bhullar	275 (−13)
Aircel PGTI Players Championship	Tollygunge GC, Kolkata	Anirban Lahiri	262 (−18)
Avantha Masters	DLF G&CC, Gurgaon	SSP Chowrasia	273 (−15)
PGTI Players Championship	Rambagh GC, Jaipur	Sanjay Kumar	264 (−16)
Aircel PGTI Players Championship	Chandigrh GC	Gaganjeet Bhullar	277 (−11)
SAIL Open	Delji GC, New Delhi, India	Kiradech Aphibarnrat (THA)	272 (−16)
Aircel PGTI Players Championship	Panchkula GC, Haryana	Anirban Lahiri	274 (−14)
Panasonic Open	Delhi GC, New Delhi	Anirban Lahiri*	275 (−13)
*Beat Mardan Mamat (SIN) and Manav Jaini at the first extra hole			
Surya Nepal Masters	Gokama GR, Kathmandu	Rashid Khan	268 (−20)
SRF All India Match Play	Delhi GC, Delhi	Final: Manav Jaini beat Ashok Kumar 5 and 4	
PGTI Players Championship	Poona GC	Shankar Das*	271 (−13)
*Beat R Murthy at first extra hole			
PGTI Players Championship	Oxford G&CC, Poona	Sujjan Singh	277 (−11)
PGTI Players Championship	Classic GR, Mewat, Haryana	Jyoti Randhawa	277 (−11)
IPS Handa Singapore Classic	Orchid CC, Singapore	Himmat Rai (IND)*	271 (−9)
*Beat Elmer Salvador (PHI), Guido Van Der Valk (NED), Tjart Van Der Walt (RSA) and Adilson Da Silva (BRA) at the sixth extra hole			
The Global Green Bangalore Open	Kamataka GA	Anura Rohana (SRI)	276 (−12)
Aircel PGTI Players' Championship	Willingdon Sports Club	Feroz Ali Mollah*	244 (−16)
*Beat Chiragh Kumar at the third extra hole			
DLF Masters	DLF G&CC, Gurgeon	Himmat Singh Rai	284 (−4)
Haryana Open	Panchula GC, Haryana	Mithun Perera	270 (−180)
Hero Indian Open	Delhi GC, New Delhi	David Gleeson (AUS)	268 (−20)
10th Tata Open	Beldih & Golmuri GC	Jamshedpur Vinod Kumar	276 (−8)
IndianOil Xtra Premium Masters	Digboi Golf Links, Assam	Shankar Das*	277 (−11)
*Beat Shamim Khan at the second extra hole			
CG Open	Bombay Presidency GC, Mumbai	Jyoti Randhawa	262 (−18)

Final Ranking (tournaments played in brackets)

1	Chiragh Kumar	(17)	₹3,706,821	6	Shamim Kahn	(18)		2,512,000
2	Jyoti Randhawa	(6)	3,360,817	7	Himmat Sigh Rai	(8)		2,416,675
3	Mukesh Kumar	(17)	2,842,592	8	Mithun Perera (SRI)	(18)		2,401,799
4	Rashid Kahn	(16)	2,713,800	9	Gaganjeet Bhullar	(10)		2,378,863
5	Anirban Lahiri	(6)	2,705,325	10	Vikrant Chopra.	(17)		2,288,942

What is the answer?

Q: Can I apply lead tape to a clubhead or shaft before the start of a round?

A: The use of lead tape is allowable providing that it is firmly fixed and there is no reasonable likelihood of the tape working loose during the round. please note that you cannot add, remove or alter lead tape during a round although any lead tape that has become detached in the normal course of play may be replaced.

OneAsia Tour 2011

www.oneasia.asia

Indonesian PGA Championship	Imperial Klub Golf	Andre Stolz (AUS)	274 (−14)
Volvo China Open	Luxehills International CC	Nicolas Colsaerts (BEL)	264 (−24)
Maekyung Open	Namseoul G&CC	Kim Kyung-tae (KOR)	267 (−21)
SK Telecom Open	Pinx GC	Kurt Barnes (AUS)	202 (−14)

Final round cancelled because of fog

Nanshan China Masters	Nashan International GC, China	Kim Bi-o (KOR)*	278 (−10)

*Beat Craig Hancock (AUS), Michael Long (NZL) and Scott Laycock (AUS) at third extra hole

The Charity High I Open	High I GC Gangwon-Do, South Korea	*Cancelled because of persistent bad weather*	
Enjoy Jakarta Indonesian Open	Damai Indah GC, PIK	Thaworn Wirachant (THA)	275 (−13)
Thailand Open	Suwan G&CC	Andre Stolz (AUS)	266 (−22)
54th Kolon Korean Open	Woo Jeong Hills	Rickie Fowler (USA)	266 (−16)
Emirates Australian Open	The Lakes GC, Sydney	Greg Chalmers (AUS)	275 (−13)
Australian PGA Championship	Coolum Resort	Greg Chalmers (AUS)*	276 (−12)

*Beat Robert Allenby (AUS) and Marcus Fraser (AUS) at the first extra hole

Final Ranking

1	Andre Stolz (AUS)	US$464,811	6	Michael Hendry (NZL)	136,741
2	Kim Kyung Tae (KOR)	327,178	7	Han Chang-won (KOR)	135,078
3	Thaworn Wirichant (THA)	235,812	8	Kim Men-whee (KOR)	106,830
4	Kurt Barnes (AUS)	210,830	9	Gareth Paddison (NZL)	104,314
5	Choi Jin-ho (KOR)	169,790	10	Tony Pilkdaris (AUS)	100,402

OneAsia moves headquarters to Hong Kong

Hong Kong is to become the focal point of both administrative and operational affairs for OneAsia. The move from Singapore will allow OneAsia to shift resources closer to key growth markets in North Asia, including China and South Korea.

Sang Y Chun, the Tour's Commissioner and Chairman, has been based in Hong Kong for the past year and will be joined there by Chief Business Officer Rob Neal, Director of Tour Operations David Parkin and Director of Business Affairs Tina Lee but Ben Sellenger, the Chief Executive Officer since 2008, has decided to pursue some personal business interests outside of OneAsia.

Commissioner Chun said: "We fully understand Ben Sellenger's wish to pursue other challenges at this time. He has done an outstanding job for us and we wish him the very best in his future endeavours."

In reply Sellenger said: "I would like to thank everyone at OneAsia for a wonderful three years when we achieved so much. It has been an incredibly satisfying experience watching OneAsia grow from strength to strength − from a blank page in 2009 to a schedule this year boasting prize money of over US$11 million and five national Opens."

Prior to his tenure at OneAsia, Sellenger was also the Commissioner of the PGA of Australasia from 2006 to 2009.

South African Sunshine Tour

Players are of South African nationality unless stated   www.sunshinetour.com

Africa Open	East London GC	Louis Oosthuizen	276 (−16)
Joburg Open	Royal Johannesburg and Kensington GC	Charl Schwartzel	265 (−19)
Africom Zimbabwe Open	Royal Harare GC	Theunis Spangenberg	201 (−15)
Dimension Data Pro-am	Fancourt, George	Hennie Otto	273 (−16)
Telkom PGA Championship	Country Club, Johannesburg	George Coetzee	261 (−27)
MTC Namibia PGA Championship	Windhoek CC	JG Claassen	268 (−16)
Investec Royal Swazi Open	Royal Swazi Sun CC	Justin Walters	45 pts
Nashua Golf Challenge	Gary Player CC, Sun City	Adilson da Silva (BRA)	202 (−14)
Vodacom Origins of Golf	Pretoria CC	Jean Hugo	205 (−11)
Lombard Insaurance Classic	Royal Swazi Sun CC	Justin Harding	202 (−14)
Vodacom Origins if Golf	Arabelle GC, Western Cape	Chris Swanepoel	205 (−11)
¹Klipdrift Gold Sun International Touring Pro-Am	Gary Player CC	Jacques Blaauw	213 (−3)
Vodacom Origins of Golf	Simola Golf Estate, Eastern Cape	Jean Hugo*	201 (−15)
*Beat Peter Karmi at the first extra hole			
Vodacom Origins of Golf	Wild Coast CC, Kwazulu-Natal	Darren Fichardt	204 (−6)
Vodacom Origins of Golf	Sishen GC	Adilson de Silva (BRA)	206 (−10)
Telcom PGA Pro-am	Centurion CC, Gauteng	Jaco Van Zyl	197 (−19)
Vodacom Origins of Golf Final	Legend Golf and Safari Resort, Limpopo	Jean Hugo	208 (−8)
Platinum Classic	Mooinooi GC North West	Hennie Otto	199 (−17)
KCM Zambia Open	Nchanga GC, Chingola	Doug McGuigan (SCO)*	272 (−16)
*Beat Jean Hugo at the fifth extra hole			
Suncoast Classic	Durban CC	Darren Fichardt	203 (−13)
BMG Classic	Glendower GC, Johannesburg	James Kamte*	207 (−9)
*Beat Dawie Van der Walt at first the extra hole			
Nashua Masters	Wild Coast CC, Kwazulu-Natal	Shaun Norris	271 (−9)
Nedbank Affinity Cup	Lost City GC	Warren Abery	205 (−11)
Alfred Dunhill Championship	Leopard Creek CC, Malelane	Garth Mulroy	269 (−19)
South African Open Championship	Serengeti GC, Ekurhuleni	Hennie Otto	274 (−14)

1903 Laurie Waters	1934 Sid Brews	1964 No tournament (two played in 1963)	1989 Fred Wadsworth
1904 Laurie Waters	1935 Bobby Locke		1990 Trevor Dodds
1905 AG Gray	1936 Clarence Olander	1965 Gary Player	1990–91 Wayne Westner
1906 AG Gray	1937 Bobby Locke	1966 Gary Player	1991–92 Ernie Els
1907 Laurie Waters	1938 Bobby Locke	1967 Gary Player	1992–93 Clinton Whitelaw
1908 George Fotheringham	1939 Bobby Locke	1968 Gary Player	1993–94 Tony Johnstone
1909 John Fotheringham	1940 Bobby Locke	1969 Gary Player	1994–95 Retief Goosen
1910 George Fotheringham	1941–1945 Not played	1970 Tommy Horton	1995–96 Ernie Els
1911 George Fotheringham	1946 Bobby Locke	1971 Simon Hobday	1996–97 Vijay Singh (FIJ)
1912 George Fotheringham	1947 Ronnie Glennie (am)	1972 Gary Player	1997–98 Ernie Els
1913 James Prentice	1948 Mickey Janks	1973 Bob Charles (NZL)	1998–99 David Frost
1914 George Fotheringham	1949 Sid Brews	1974 Bobby Cole	1999–2000 Matthias Grönberg (SWE)
1915–1918 Not played	1950 Bobby Locke	1975 Gary Player	
1919 WH Horne	1951 Bobby Locke	1976 Dale Hayes	2000–01 Mark McNulty (IRL)
1920 Laurie Waters	1952 Sid Brews	1976 Gary Player	2001–02 Tim Clark
1921 Jock Brews	1953 Jimmy Boyd	1977 Gary Player	2002–03 Trevor Immelman
1922 F Jangle	1954 Reg Taylor (am)	1978 Hugh Baiocchi	2003–04 Trevor Immelman
1923 Jock Brews	1955 Bobby Locke	1979 Gary Player	2004–05 Tim Clark
1924 Bertie Elkin	1956 Gary Player	1980 Bobby Cole	2005–06 Retief Goosen
1925 Sid Brews	1957 Harold Henning	1981 Gary Player	2006–07 Ernie Els
1926 Jock Brews	1958 Arthur Stewart (am)	1982 No tournament (two played in 1976)	2007 James Kingston
1927 Sid Brews	1959 Denis Hutchinson (am)		2008 Richard Sterne*
1928 Jock Brews	1960 Gary Player	1983 Charlie Bolling	*Beat Gareth Maybin (NIR) at 1st extra hole
1929 Archie Tosh	1961 Retief Waltman	1984 Tony Johnstone	
1930 Sid Brews	1962 Harold Henning	1985 Gavin Levenson	2009 Richie Ramsay (SCO)*
1931 Sid Brews	1963 Retief Waltman	1986 David Frost	*Beat Shiv Kapur (IND) at 1st extra hole
1932 Charles McIlveny	1963 Allan Henning	1987 Mark McNulty (IRL)	
1933 Sid Brews		1988 Wayne Westner	2010 Ernie Els

South African Sunshine Tour *continued*

[1]Gary Player Invitational	Zimbali Lodge G&CC	George Coetzee and Mark James (ENG)	125 (−19)
Nedbank Challenge	Gary Player CC, Sun City	Lee Westwood (ENG)	273 (−15)

[1]Indicates the event is not an official tournament

Final Ranking (tournaments played in brackets)

1	Garth Mulroy	(6)	SAR3,464,463	6	Louis Oosthuizen	(1)	1,394,800
2	Hennie Otto	(7)	2,806,214	7	Bernd Wiesberger (AUT)	(4)	1,325,510
3	Charl Schwartzel	(3)	2,211,553	8	George Murray (SCO)	(4)	1,277,508
4	George Coetzee	(9)	1,586,586	9	Jaco Van Zyl	(8)	1,231,134
5	Thomas Aiken	(6)	1,569,896	10	Jean Hugo	(24)	961,347

Other Tours

Results from the following Tours can be found on the following websites:

Adams Tour	www.adamsgolfprotourseries.com
Allianz Tour	www.allianzgolftour.fr
Alps Tour	www.alpstourgolf.com
Asean Tour	www.aseanpgatour.com
Asian Development Tour	www.asiantour.com
Charles Tour	www.golf.co.nz
Dakotas Tour	www.dakotastour.com
Ecco Tour	www.ecco.com
e-golf Tour	www.egolf.org.uk
EPD Tour	www.epdtour.de
Europro Tour	www.europrotour.com
France Tour	www.franceprogolftour.com
Gateway Tour	www.gatewaytour.com
Golden State Tour	www.gstour.com
Hi5 Tour	www.hi5protour.com
Hooters Tour	www.ngatour.com
Iberian Tour	www.igtour.net
Italian Tour	www.italianprotour.com
Jamega Tour	ww.jamegatour.co.uk
Japan Challenge Tour	www.jgto.org
Nordic Tour	www.nordicgolftour.com
PGTI Feeder Tour	www.pgtofindia.com
PGA New Zealand	www.pga.org.nz
Singha Tour	www.pgtofindia.com
Suncoast Tour	www.suncoastseries.com
TPGA Argentina	www.pgargentina.org.ar

Two new Canadian Golf Hall-of-Famers in 2011

Long-time Royal Canadian Golf Association executive director Stephen Ross and professional Richard Zokol, who played the PGA Tour for 20 years, have both been inducted into the Canadian Golf Hall of Fame.

Mexican José de Jesus Rodriguez is No 1 on Canadian Tour

Thirty-year-old José de Jesus Rodriguez from Mexico topped the Canadian Tour Order of Merit in 2011. The golfer from Irapuato, Guanajuato, took top spot helped by victory in the Mexican PGA Championship and the Times Colonial Island Savings Open. He came second in the ATB Financial Classic as well. Chilean players filled the next two spots on the rankings with Hugo Leon coming second and 26 year-old Benjamin Alvarado, who won the 2011 Chile Open on the Tour de las Americas, filling third spot. Twenty-seven-year-old Leon did not win during the season but never missed a cut while Alvarado, a two-time All American attending Arizona State University, had three seconds and three other top 10 finishes in his eight starts. Leading Canadian was Stuart Anderson in fourth spot.

World Championship Events

WGC – Accenture Match Play Championship

Ritz-Carlton, Dove Mountain, AZ, USA   [7791–72]

First Round:
Lee Westwood (ENG) beat Henrik Stenson (SWE) 2 and 1
Nick Watney (USA) beat Anthony Kim (USA) 5 and 4
K J Choi (KOR) beat Retief Goosen (RSA) 1 up
Ryan Moore (USA) beat Francesco Molinari (ITA) 3 and 1
Matteo Manassero (ITA) beat Steve Stricker (USA) 2 and 1
Charl Schwartzel (RSA) beat Ryo Ishikawa (JPN) at 20th
Luke Donald (ENG) beat Charley Hoffman (USA) 6 and 5
Edoardo Molinari (ITA) beat Martin Laird (SCO) 3 and 2

Martin Kaymer (GER) beat Seung-Yul Noh (KOR) 7 and 6
Justin Rose (ENG) beat Zach Johnson (USA) 2 and 1
Robert Karlsson (SWE) beat Hiroyuki Fujita (JPN) 5 and 3
Hunter Mahan (USA) beat Sean O'Hair (USA) 4 and 3
Rory McIlroy (NIR) beat Jonathan Byrd (USA) 4 and 2
Ben Crane (USA) beat Adam Scott (AUS) 4 and 2
Ryan Palmer (USA) beat Jim Furyk (USA) 2 up
Miguel Angel Jiménez (ESP) beat Yuta Ikeda (JPN) 2 and 1

Phil Mickelson (USA) beat Brendan Jones (AUS) 6 and 5
Rickie Fowler (USA) beat Peter Hanson (SWE) 1 up
Matt Kuchar (USA) beat Anders Hansen (DEN) at 22nd
Bo Van Pelt (USA) beat Louis Oosthuizen (RSA) 2 up
Graeme McDowell (NIR) beat Heath Slocum (USA) 4 and 3
Robert Allenby (AUS) beat Ross Fisher (ENG) 4 and 3
Stewart Cink (USA) beat Ian Poulter (ENG) at 19th
Y E Yang (KOR) beat Alvaro Quiros (ESP) at 20th

Thomas Bjorn (DEN) beat Tiger Woods (USA) at 19th
Geoff Ogilvy (AUS) beat Padraig Harrington (IRL) 4 and 3
Mark Wilson (USA) beat Dustin Johnson (USA) at 19th
Bubba Watson (USA) beat Bill Haas (USA) 3 and 2
Paul Casey (ENG) beat Richard Green (AUS) at 19th
Jason Day (AUS) beat Kyung-Tae Kim (KOR) 3 and 2
Ernie Els (RSA) beat Jeff Overton (USA) at 19th
J B Holmes (USA) Camilo Villegas (COL) 4 and 2

Second Round:
Watney beat Westwood 1 up
Moore beat Choi 5 and 4
Manassero beat Schwartzel 1 up
Donald beat E Molinari 2 and 1
Kaymer beat Rose at 20th
Mahan beat Karlsson 2 up
Crane beat McIlroy 6 and 7
Jiménez beat Palmer 4 and 2

Fowler beat Mickelson 6 and 5
Kuchar beat Van Pelt 3 and 2
McDowell beat Fisher 4 and 2
Yang beat Cink 4 and 3
Ogilvy beat Bjorn 1 up
Watson beat Wilson 6 and 5
Day beat Casey 4 and 2
Holmes beat Els 1 up

Third Round:
Moore beat Watney at 19th
Donald beat Manassero 3 and 2
Kaymer beat Mahan 2 and 1
Jiménez beat Crane 7 and 6

Kuchar beat Fowler 2 and 1
Yang beat McDowell 3 and 2
Watson beat Ogilvy 6 and 4
Holmes beat Day 1 up

Quarter-finals:
Donald beat Moore 5 and 4
Kaymer beat Jiménez 1 up

Kuchar beat Yang 2 and 1
Watson beat Holmes at 19th

WGC – Accenture Match Play Championship   *continued*

Semi-finals:
Donald beat Kuchar 6 and 5
Kaymer beat Watson 1 up

Third Place Match:
Kuchar beat Watson 2 and 1

Final:
Luke Donald beat Martin Kaymer 3 and 2

Winner:	$1,400,000	€1,027,923	Quarter Finals:	$278,000	€198,242
Runner-up:	$875,000	€624,096	3rd Round:	$144,000	€102,792
3rd Place:	$617,000	€440,538	2nd Round:	$98,000	€69,752
4th Place:	$504,000	€359,773	1st Round:	$46,000	€33,040

2000	Darren Clarke (NIR) beat Tiger Woods (USA) 4 and 3 at La Costa, Carlsbad, CA, USA
2001	Steve Stricker (USA) beat Pierre Fulke (SWE) 4 and 3 at Metropolitan GC, Melbourne, Australia
2002	Kevin Sutherland (USA) beat Scott McCarron (USA) 1 hole at La Costa, Carlsbad, CA, USA
2003	Tiger Woods (USA) beat David Toms (USA) 2 and 1 at La Costa, Carlsbad, CA, USA
2004	Tiger Woods (USA) beat Davis Love III (USA) 3 and 2 at La Costa, Carlsbad, CA, USA
2005	David Toms (USA) beat Chris DiMarco (USA) 6 and 5 at La Costa, Carlsbad, CA, USA
2006	Geoff Ogilvy (AUS) beat Davis Love III (USA) 3 and 2 at La Costa, Carlsbad, CA, USA
2007	Henrik Stenson (SWE) beat Geoff Ogilvy (AUS) 2 and 1 at Gallery, Tucson, AZ, USA
2008	Tiger Woods (USA) beat Stewart Cink (USA) 8 and 7 at Gallery, Tucson, AZ, USA
2009	Geoff Ogilvy (AUS) beat Paul Casey (ENG) 4 and 3 at Dove Mountain, AZ, USA
2010	Ian Poulter (ENG) beat Paul Casey (ENG) 4 and 3 at Dove Mountain, AZ, USA

WGC – Cadillac Championship   (formerly WGC – CA Championship)
Doral, Orlando, FL, USA   [7266–72]

1	Nick Watney (USA)	67-70-68-67—272	$1,400,000
2	Dustin Johnson (USA)	69-69-65-71—274	850,000
3	Anders Hansen (DEN)	71-69-68-67—275	465,000
	Francesco Molinari (ITA)	68-68-70-69—275	465,000
5	Matt Kuchar (USA)	68-69-68-71—276	350,000
6	Adam Scott (AUS)	68-70-68-71—277	271,000
	Luke Donald (ENG)	67-72-66-72—277	271,000
8	Rickie Fowler (USA)	71-73-68-66—278	200,000
9	Hunter Mahan (USA)	64-71-71-73—279	175,000
10	Tiger Woods (USA)	70-74-70-66—280	129,000
	Jonathan Byrd (USA)	70-74-68-68—280	129,000
	Padraig Harrington (IRL)	68-71-68-73—280	129,000
	Martin Laird (SCO)	67-70-70-73—280	129,000
	Rory McIlroy (NIR)	68-69-69-74—280	129,000
15	Robert Allenby (AUS)	72-72-69-68—281	100,000
	Ernie Els (RSA)	69-70-73-69—281	100,000
	Kevin Streelman (USA)	68-72-72-69—281	100,000
18	Lee Westwood (ENG)	70-74-70-68—282	89,000
	Louis Oosthuizen (RSA)	71-73-67-71—282	89,000
	Steve Stricker (USA)	68-71-69-74—282	89,000
	Paul Casey (ENG)	70-71-69-72—282	89,000
22	Ryan Moore (USA)	70-74-70-69—283	83,000
	Vijay Singh (FIJ)	68-72-68-75—283	83,000
24	Charl Schwartzel (RSA)	71-71-75-67—284	77,250
	Charley Hoffman (USA)	67-75-73-69—284	77,250
	Zach Johnson (USA)	72-75-68-69—284	77,250
	Martin Kaymer (GER)	66-70-74-74—284	77,250
28	Rory Sabbatini (RSA)	74-74-67-70—285	73,000
	Thomas Bjorn (DEN)	71-73-70-71—285	73,000
	Aaron Baddeley (AUS)	72-66-73-74—285	73,000
31	Bill Haas (USA)	74-68-71-73—286	69,500
	Robert Karlsson (SWE)	69-73-71-73—286	69,500
	Retief Goosen (RSA)	69-76-68-73—286	69,500
	Jhonattan Vegas (VEN)	69-74-69-74—286	69,500
35	Kevin Na (USA)	74-75-69-69—287	65,000
	Thomas Aiken (RSA)	68-75-74-70—287	65,000

35T	Camilo Villegas (COL)	71-71-73-72—287	65,000
	Bo Van Pelt (USA)	71-74-66-76—287	65,000
39	Y E Yang (KOR)	73-72-72-71—288	52,000
	K J Choi (KOR)	73-69-72-74—288	52,000
	Edoardo Molinari (ITA)	71-73-70-74—288	62,000
42	Justin Rose (ENG)	77-71-70-71—289	59.000
	Graeme McDowell (NIR)	70-73-71-75—289	59,000
	Ryo Ishikawa (JPN)	65-76-70-78—289	59,000
45	Marcus Fraser (AUS)	69-78-71-72—290	55,500
	Jason Day (AUS)	71-76-71-72—290	55,500
	Ian Poulter (ENG)	73-70-74-73—290	55,500
	D A Points (USA)	68-72-71-79—290	55,500
49	Geoff Ogilvy (AUS)	76-73-72-70—291	50,500
	S S P Chowrasia (IND)	74-72-72-73—291	50,500
	Mark Wilson (USA)	72-75-71-73—291	50,500
	Kyung-tae Kim (KOR)	73-70-73-75—291	50,500
	Jim Furyk (USA)	74-71-71-75—291	50,500
	Ryan Palmer (USA)	73-73-68-77—291	50,500
55	Yuta Ikeda (JPN)	74-73-74-71—292	45,500
	Peter Hanson (SWE)	73-73-73-73—292	45,500
	Miguel Angel Jiménez (ESP)	71-72-73-76—292	45,500
	Phil Mickelson (USA)	73-71-72-76—292	45,500
59	Seung-yul Noh (KOR)	72-70-79-72—293	43,000
60	Anthony Kim (USA)	80-74-68-72—294	42,500
61	Ross Fisher (ENG)	69-76-76-74—295	41,500
	Rhys Davies (WAL)	73-76-72-74—295	41,500
	Hiroyuki Fujita (JPN)	71-73-74-77—295	41,500
64	Alvaro Quiros (ESP)	70-77-74-75—296	40,250
	Peter Senior (AUS)	75-73-73-75—296	40,250
66	Jeff Overton (USA)	75-77-73-73—298	39,750

1999	Tiger Woods* (USA)	71-69-70-68—278	at Valderrama GC, Cadiz, Spain
*Woods beat Miguel Angel Jiménez (ESP) at the first extra hole			
2000	Mike Weir (CAN)	68-75-65-69—277	at Valderrama GC, Cadiz, Spain
2001	Cancelled		
2002	Tiger Woods (USA)	65-65-67-66—263	at Mount Juliet, Kilkenny, Ireland
2003	Tiger Woods (USA)	67-66-69-72—274	at Capital City, Atlanta, GA
2004	Ernie Els (RSA)	69-64-68-69—270	at Mount Juliet, Kilkenny, Ireland
2005	Tiger Woods* (USA)	67-68-68-67—270	at Harding Park, San Francisco, CA
*Woods beat John Daly at the second extra hole			
2006	Tiger Woods (USA)	63-64-67-67—261	at The Grove, Chandlers Cross, Herts
2007	Tiger Woods (USA)	71-66-68-73—278	at Doral, Orlando, FL, USA
2008	Geoff Ogilvy (AUS)	65-67-68-71—271	at Doral, Orlando, FL, USA
2009	Phil Mickelson (AUS)	65-66-69-69—269	at Doral, Orlando, FL, USA
2010	Ernie Els (RSA)	68-66-70-66—270	at Doral, Orlando, FL, USA

WGC – Bridgestone Invitational *Firestone CC, Akron, OH* [7400–70]

1	Adam Scott (AUS)	62-70-66-65—263	$1,400,000
2	Luke Donald (ENG)	68-69-64-66—267	665,000
	Rickie Fowler (USA)	68-64-69-66—267	665,000
4	Jason Day (AUS)	63-70-66-69—268	332,500
	Ryo Ishikawa (JPN)	67-68-64-69—268	332,500
6	Zach Johnson (USA)	70-68-64-68—270	215,000
	Kyung-tae Kim (KOR)	66-72-66-66—270	215,000
	Rory McIlroy (NIR)	68-68-67-67—270	215,000
9	David Toms (USA)	68-68-68-67—271	152,500
	Lee Westwood (ENG)	67-71-68-65—271	152,500
11	Aaron Baddeley (AUS)	68-70-69-65—272	117,333
	Fredrik Jacobson (SWE)	68-66-67-71—272	117,333
	Martin Laird (SCO)	66-67-67-72—272	117,333
14	Steve Stricker (USA)	71-65-67-70—273	100,000
15	Keegan Bradley (USA)	67-65-68-74—274	95,500
	Francesco Molinari (ITA)	73-64-68-69—274	95,500
17	Robert Karlsson (SWE)	68-65-72-70—275	89,500

WGC – Bridgestone Invitational   *continued*

17T	Mark Wilson (USA)	69-69-71-66—275	89,500
19	Matt Kuchar (USA)	71-69-65-71—276	85,000
	D A Points (USA)	66-70-72-68—276	85,000
21	Peter Hanson (SWE)	70-67-70-70—277	81,250
	Bubba Watson (USA)	69-70-68-70—277	81,250
23	Jim Furyk (USA)	73-69-67-69—278	75,250
	Lucas Glover (USA)	68-68-72-70—278	75,250
	Retief Goosen (RSA)	72-68-68-70—278	75,250
	Ryan Moore (USA)	66-66-74-72—278	75,250
	Bo Van Pelt (USA)	68-70-71-69—278	75,250
	Nick Watney (USA)	65-70-70-73—278	75,250
29	Anders Hansen (DEN)	72-70-67-70—279	68,500
	Martin Kaymer (GER)	69-70-73-67—279	68,500
	Hennie Otto (RSA)	69-66-75-69—279	68,500
	Scott Stallings (USA)	69-68-72-70—279	68,500
33	Simon Dyson (ENG)	77-66-69-68—280	64,500
	Edoardo Molinari (ITA)	72-66-70-72—280	64,500
	Justin Rose (ENG)	71-70-72-67—280	64,500
	Brandt Snedeker (USA)	66-68-74-72—280	64,500
37	Ernie Els (RSA)	71-71-71-68—281	58,500
	Richard Green (AUS)	69-68-74-70—281	58,500
	Charley Hoffman (USA)	68-69-70-74—281	58,500
	Hunter Mahan (USA)	71-69-72-69—281	58,500
	Matteo Manassero (ITA)	70-72-67-72—281	58,500
	Geoff Ogilvy (AUS)	68-70-76-67—281	58,500
	Louis Oosthuizen (RSA)	71-71-70-69—281	58,500
	Tiger Woods (USA)	68-71-72-70—281	58,500
45	Paul Casey (ENG)	73-71-71-67—282	53,000
	Stewart Cink (USA)	66-70-71-75—282	53,000
	Gary Woodland (USA)	70-66-73-73—282	53,000
48	Robert Allenby (AUS)	70-73-70-70—283	49,300
	Dustin Johnson (USA)	73-69-70-71—283	49,300
	Phil Mickelson (USA)	67-73-71-72—283	49,300
	Rory Sabbatini (RSA)	66-77-71-69—283	49,300
	Brendan Steele (USA)	69-74-74-66—283	49,300
53	Sergio García (ESP)	68-72-72-72—284	46,500
	Alexander Noren (SWE)	69-73-70-72—284	46,500
	Alvaro Quiros (ESP)	73-74-67-70—284	46,500
	Charl Schwartzel (RSA)	74-71-68-71—284	46,500
	Y E Yang (KOR)	72-71-69-72—284	46,500
58	Heath Slocum (USA)	71-65-75-74—285	45,000
59	Jonathan Byrd (USA)	67-74-75-70—286	43,750
	K J Choi (KOR)	74-71-70-71—286	43,750
	Padraig Harrington (IRL)	71-70-73-72—286	43,750
	Sean O'Hair (USA)	72-72-69-73—286	43,750
63	Arjun Atwal (IND)	68-73-71-76—288	42,250
	Bill Haas (USA)	72-72-70-74—288	42,250
65	Graeme McDowell (NIR)	71-72-75-71—289	41,500
66	Harrison Frazar (USA)	72-72-77-70—291	40,750
	Jhonattan Vegas (VEN)	73-70-74-74—291	40,750
68	Thomas Björn (DEN)	66-72-75-79—292	39,250
	Darren Clarke (NIR)	77-74-69-72—292	39,250
	Jeff Overton (USA)	72-73-73-74—292	39,250
	Ian Poulter (ENG)	71-69-80-72—292	39,250
72	Miguel Angel Jiménez (ESP)	73-73-74-73—293	38,000
73	Jae-bum Park (KOR)	73-72-77-72—294	37,500
74	Pablo Larrazábal (ESP)	66-76-74-79—295	37,000
75	Yuta Ikeda (JPN)	74-72-77-74—297	36,500
76	Stuart Appleby (AUS)	73-76-78-72—299	36,000

1999	T Woods (USA)	66-71-62-71—270	at Firestone CC, Akron, OH
2000	T Woods (USA)	64-61-67-67—259	at Firestone CC, Akron, OH
2001	T Woods (USA)	66-67-66-69—268	at Firestone CC, Akron, OH
2002	C Parry (AUS)	72-65-66-65—268	at Sahalee, Redmond, WA
2003	D Clarke (NIR)	65-70-66-67—268	at Firestone CC, Akron, OH
2004	S Cink (USA)	63-68-68-70—269	at Firestone CC, Akron, OH
2005	T Woods (USA)	66-70-67-71—274	at Firestone CC, Akron, OH
2006	T Woods (USA)	67-64-71-68—270	at Firestone CC, Akron, OH
2007	V Singh (FIJ)	67-66-69-68—270	at Firestone CC, Akron, OH
2008	V Singh (FIJ)	67-66-69-68—270	at Firestone CC, Akron, OH
2009	T Woods (USA)	68-70-65-65—268	at Firestone CC, Akron, OH
2010	H Mahan (USA)	71-67-66-64—268	at Firestone CC, Akron, OH

WGC – HSBC Champions Tournament   *Sheshan GC, Shanghai*   [7266-72]

1	Martin Kaymer (GER)	69-68-68-63—268	€842,218
2	Fredrik Jacobson (SWE)	67-66-67-71—271	473,747
3	Graeme McDowell (NIR)	69-69-67-67—272	301,795
4	Paul Casey (ENG)	70-66-70-67—273	181,311
	Rory McIlroy (NIR)	70-69-65-69—273	181,311
	Charl Schwartzel (RSA)	70-69-69-65—273	181,311
7	Hunter Mahan (USA)	71-67-69-67—274	108,786
	Louis Oosthuizen (RSA)	71-63-68-72—274	108,786
	Justin Rose (ENG)	68-70-70-66—274	108,786
10	Jhonattan Vegas (VEN)	69-73-65-68—275	87,731
11	Adam Scott (AUS)	69-65-69-73—276	77,203
11	Bo van Pelt (USA)	67-69-70-70—276	77,203
13	Ian Poulter (ENG)	70-68-69-71—278	63,166
13	Lee Westwood (ENG)	69-68-67-74—278	63,166
	Xin-Jun Zhang (CHN)	74-68-64-72—278	63,166
16	Keegan Bradley (USA)	65-70-72-72—279	55,680
	K J Choi (KOR)	68-70-72-69—279	55,680
	Simon Dyson (ENG)	69-69-70-71—279	55,680
19	John Senden (AUS)	72-68-70-70—280	52,639
20	Nicolas Colsaerts (BEL)	74-69-68-70—281	49,831
	Lucas Glover (USA)	76-68-71-66—281	49,831
	Pablo Larrazábal (ESP)	70-69-70-72—281	49,831
23	Aaron Baddeley (AUS)	69-68-73-72—282	43,865
	Jonathan Byrd (USA)	71-68-70-73—282	43,865
	Anders Hansen (DEN)	71-69-70-72—282	43,865
	Jbe Kruger (RSA)	70-70-68-74—282	43,865
	Francesco Molinari (ITA)	70-70-71-71—282	43,865
	Jeev Milkha Singh (IND)	72-73-69-68—282	43,865
29	Harrison Frazar (USA)	70-75-64-74—283	39,654
	Yuta Ikeda (JPN)	70-71-68-74—283	39,654
	Thongchai Jaidee (THA)	68-69-72-74—283	39,654
	Rory Sabbatini (RSA)	69-71-71-72—283	39,654
33	Ernie Els (RSA)	75-69-72-68—284	36,496
	Peters Hanson (SWE)	69-73-71-71—284	36,496
	Robert Rock (ENG)	70-70-71-73—284	36,496
	Lee Slattery (ENG)	76-71-68-69—284	36,496
	Nick Watney (USA)	71-75-71-67—284	36,496
38	Darren Clarke (NIR)	73-76-67-69—285	33,338
	Jim Herman (USA)	74-70-73-68—285	33,338
	Miguel Angel Jiménez (ESP)	72-68-68-77—285	33,338
	Chinnarat Phadungsil (THA)	71-69-74-71—285	33,338
42	Stuart Appleby (AUS)	77-70-71-69—287	30,530
	Thomas Björn (DEN)	72-71-71-73—287	30,530
	Bill Haas (USA)	74-69-68-76—287	30,530
	Scott Stallings (USA)	70-74-72-71—287	30,530
46	Ben Crane (USA)	75-71-74-68—288	28,425
	Hiroyuki Fujita (JPN)	74-71-70-73—288	28,425
	Keith Horne (RSA)	71-70-73-74—288	28,425
49	Jung-Gon Hwang (KOR)	72-72-70-75—289	26,670

WGC – HSBC Champions Tournament *continued*

49T	Kyung-Tae Kim (KOR)	73-77-71-68—289	26,670
	Paul Lawrie (SCO)	72-71-72-74—289	26,670
	Alexander Noren (SWE)	67-75-70-77—289	26,670
	Alvaro Quiros (ESP)	72-67-71-79—289	26,670
	Mohd Siddikur (BAN)	75-73-67-74—289	26,670
	Ashun Wu (CHN)	72-69-70-78—289	26,670
56	Robert Karlsson (SWE)	74-75-68-73—290	24,916
	Geoff Ogilvy (AUS)	75-69-69-77—290	24,916
	Mark Wilson (USA)	71-73-77-69—290	24,916
59	Tetsuji Hiratsuka (JPN)	72-70-72-77—291	23,863
	Michio Matsumura (JPN)	74-71-71-75—291	23,863
	David Toms (USA)	68-76-71-76—291	23,863
62	Jim Furyk (USA)	78-68-73-73—292	22,810
	Michael Hoey (NIR)	76-70-74-72—292	22,810
	Wen-Chong Liang (CHN)	72-73-71-76—292	22,810
65	S S P Chowrasia (IND)	73-74-73-73—293	22,108
66	Kiradech Aphibarnrat (THA)	79-72-71-72—294	21,582
	D A Points (USA)	73-71-73-77—294	21,582
68	Chez Reavie (USA)	70-75-68-82—295	21,055
69	Matteo Manassero (ITA)	82-71-70-73—296	20,705
70	Thomas Aiken (RSA)	76-75-69-77—297	20,354
71	David Gleeson (AUS)	71-70-76-81—298	20,003
72	Yih-Shin Chan (TPE)	75-74-76-74—299	19,476
	Alistair Presnell (AUS)	75-75-73-76—299	19,476
74	Hao Yuan (CHN)	72-78-74-76—300	18,950
75	Pablo Martin (ESP)	76-71-74-80—301	18,599
76	Tom Lewis (ENG)	78-71-72-83—304	18,248
77	Adam Bland (AUS)	75-76-81-80—312	17,897
	Bobby Gates (USA)	75-68-69-WD—212	

2006 David Howell (ENG)	2008 (2009 season)	2010 F Molinari (ITA)
2007 Yang-Eun Yang (KOR)	Sergio García (ESP)*	
2008 Phil Mickelson (USA)*	*Beat O Wilson (ENG) at 2nd extra hole	
*Beat Ross Fisher (ENG) at 2nd extra hole	2009 Phil Mickelson (USA)	

Dubai World Championship   *Earth Course, Jumeirah Golf Estates, Dubai, UAE*

Full results can be found on page 151

Month by month in 2011

Severiano Ballesteros dies of brain cancer at the age of 54. Luke Donald is the new world No 1 after he beats Lee Westwood in a play-off for the BMW PGA Championship a week after losing the final of the Volvo World Match Play to Ian Poulter. Korean K J Choi wins the Players Championship after a play-off with David Toms, who wins a week later in Texas.

International Team Events 2011

Ryder Cup – inaugurated 1927

2010 *Celtic Manor, Wales* Oct 1–4
Result: Europe 14½, USA 13½
Captains: Colin Montgomerie (Eur), Corey Pavin (USA)
Non-playing captains: Europe: Colin
Montgomerie (SCO); USA: Corey Pavin
*Heavy rain delayed play from the first day forcing a departure
from the customary format, requiring an extra day to complete
all the matches*

First Session – Fourballs
Westwood & Kaymer beat Mickelson & Johnson 3 and 2
McIlroy & McDowell halved with Cink & Kuchar
Poulter & Fisher lost to Stricker & Woods 2 holes
Donald & Harrington lost to Watson & Overton 3 and 2

Second Session – Foursomes
E Molinari & F Molinari lost to Johnson & Mahan 2 holes
Westwood & Kaymer halved with Furyk & Fowler
Harrington & Fisher beat Mickelson & Johnson 3 and 2
Jiménez & Hanson lost to Stricker & Woods 4 and 3
Poulter & Donald Bubba Watson & Overton 2 and 1
McIlroy & McDowell lost to Cink & Kuchar 1 hole

Third Session – Foursomes
Donald & Westwood beat Stricker & Woods 6 and 5
McIlroy & McDowell beat Johnson & Mahan 3 and 1

Fourballs
Harrington & Fisher beat Furyk & Johnson 2 and 1
Jiménez & Hanson beat Watson & Overton 2 holes
E Molinari & F Molinari halved with Cink & Kuchar
Poulter & Kaymer beat Mickelson & Fowler 2 and 1

Fourth Session – Singles
Lee Westwood (ENG) lost to Steve Stricker 2 and 1
Rory McIlroy (NIR) halved with Stewart Cink
Luke Donald (ENG) beat Jim Furyk 1 hole
Martin Kaymer (GER) lost to Dustin Johnson 6 and 4
Ian Poulter (ENG) beat Matt Kuchar 5 and 4
Ross Fisher (ENG) lost to Jeff Overton 3 and 2
Miguel Angel Jiménez (ESP) beat Bubba Watson 4 and 3
Francesco Molinari (ITA) lost to Tiger Woods 4 and 3
Edoardo Molinari (ITA) halved with Rikki Fowler
Peter Hanson (SWE) lost to Phil Mickelson 4 and 2
Padraig Harrington (IRL) lost to Zach Johnson 3 and 2
Graeme McDowell (NIR) beat Hunter Mahan 2 and 1

2008 *Valhalla, Louisville, KY* Sept 18–20
Result: USA 16½, Europe 11½
Captains: Paul Azinger (USA), Nick Faldo (Eur)
First Day, Morning – Foursomes
Mickelson & Kim halved with Harrington & Karlsson
Leonard & Mahan beat Stenson & Casey 3 and 2
Cink & Campbell beat Poulter & Rose 1 hole
Perry & Furyk halved with Westwood & García
Afternoon – Fourballs
Mickelson & Kim beat Harrington & McDowell 2 holes
Stricker & Curtis lost to Poulter & Rose 4 and 2
Leonard & Mahan beat García & Jiménez 4 and 3
Holmes & Weekley halved with Westwood & Hansen

Second Day, Morning – Foursomes
Cink & Campbell lost to Poulter & Rose 4 and 3
Leonard & Mahan halved with Jiménez & McDowell
Mickelson & Kim lost to Stenson & Wilson 2 and 1
Perry & Furyk beat Harrington & Karlsson 3 and 1
Afternoon – Fourballs
Holmes & Weekley beat Westwood & Hansen 2 and 1
Stricker & Curtis halved with García & Casey
Perry & Furyk lost to Poulter & McDowell 1 hole
Mickelson & Mahan halved with Stenson & Karlsson
Third Day – Singles
Anthony Kim beat Sergio García (ESP) 5 and 4
Hunter Mahan halved with Paul Casey (ENG)
Justin Leonard lost to Robert Karlsson (SWE) 5 and 3
Phil Mickelson lost to Justin Rose (ENG) 3 and 2
Kenny Perry beat Henrik Stenson (SWE) 3 and 2
Boo Weekley beat Oliver Wilson (ENG) 4 and 2
J B Holmes beat Søren Hansen (DEN) 2 and 1
Jim Furyk beat Miguel Angel Jiménez (ESP) 2 and 1
Stewart Cink lost to Graeme McDowell (NIR) 2 and 1
Steve Stricker lost to Ian Poulter (ENG) 3 and 2
Ben Curtis beat Lee Westwood (ENG) 2 and 1
Chad Campbell beat Padraig Harrington (IRL) 2 and 1

2006 *K Club, Straffan, Ireland* Sept 22–24
Result: Europe 18½, USA 9½
Captains: Ian Woosnam (Eur), Tom Lehman (USA)
First Day, Morning – Fourballs
Harrington & Montgomerie lost to Woods & Furyk 1 hole
Casey & Karlsson halved with Cink & Henry
García & Olazábal beat Toms & Wetterich 3 and 2
Clarke & Westwood beat Mickelson & DiMarco 1 hole
Afternoon – Foursomes
Harrington & McGinley halved with Campbell & Johnson
Howell & Stenson halved with Cink & Toms
Westwood & Montgomerie halved with Mickelson &
DiMarco
Donald & García beat Woods & Furyk 2 holes
Second Day, Morning – Fourballs
Casey & Karlsson halved with Cink & Henry
García & Olazábal beat Mickelson & DiMarco 3 and 2
Clarke & Westwood beat Woods & Furyk 3 and 2
Stenson & Harrington lost to Verplank & Johnson 2 and 1
Afternoon – Foursomes
García & Donald beat Mickelson & Toms 2 and 1
Montgomerie & Westwood halved with Campbell & Taylor
Casey & Howell beat Cink & Johnson 5 and 4
Harrington & McGinley lost to Woods & Furyk 3 and 2
Third Day – Singles
Colin Montgomerie (SCO) beat David Toms 1 hole
Sergio García (ESP) lost to Stewart Cink 4 and 3
Paul Casey (ENG) beat Jim Furyk 2 and 1
Robert Karlsson (SWE) lost to Tiger Woods 3 and 2
Luke Donald (ENG) beat Chad Campbell 2 and 1
Paul McGinley (IRL) halved with JJ Henry
Darren Clarke (NIR) beat Zach Johnson 3 and 2
Henrik Stenson (SWE) beat Vaughn Taylor 4 and 3
David Howell (ENG) beat Brett Wetterich 5 and 4
José María Olazábal (ESP) beat Phil Mickelson 2 and 1
Lee Westwood (ENG) beat Chris DiMarco 2 holes
Padraig Harrington (IRL) lost to Scott Verplank 4 and 3

2004 *Oakland Hills Country Club, Bloomfield,*
Detroit, MI, USA Sept 17–19
Result: USA 9½, Europe 18½
Captains: Hal Sutton (USA),
Bernhard Langer (Eur)
First Day, Morning – Fourball
Woods & Mickelson lost to Montgomerie & Harrington
2 and 1
Love & Campbell lost to Clarke & Jiménez 5 and 4
Riley & Cink halved with McGinley & Donald
Toms & Furyk lost to García & Westwood 5 and 3
Afternoon – Foursomes
DiMarco & Haas beat Jiménez & Levet 3 and 2
Love & Funk lost to Montgomerie & Harrington 4 and 2
Mickelson & Woods lost to Clarke & Westwood 1 hole
Perry & Cink lost to García & Donald 2 and 1
Second Day, Morning – Fourball
Haas & DiMarco halved with García & Westwood
Woods & Riley beat Clarke & Poulter 4 and 3
Furyk & Campbell lost to Casey & Howell 1 hole
Cink & Love beat Montgomerie & Harrington 3 and 2
Afternoon – Foursomes
DiMarco & Haas lost to Clarke & Westwood 5 and 4
Mickelson & Toms beat Jiménez & Levet 4 and 3
Funk & Furyk lost to Donald & García 1 hole
Love & Woods lost to Harrington & McGinley 4 and 3
Third Day – Singles
Tiger Woods beat Paul Casey (ENG) 3 and 2
Phil Mickelson lost to Sergio García (ESP) 3 and 2
Davis Love III halved with Darren Clarke (NIR)
Jim Furyk beat David Howell (ENG) 6 and 4
Kenny Perry lost to Lee Westwood (ENG) 1 hole
David Toms lost to Colin Montgomerie (SCO) 1 hole
Chad Campbell beat Luke Donald (ENG) 5 and 3
Chris DiMarco beat Miguel Angel Jiménez (ESP)
1 hole
Fred Funk lost to Thomas Levet (FRA) 1 hole
Chris Riley lost to Ian Poulter (ENG) 3 and 2
Jay Haas lost to Padraig Harrington (IRL) 1 hole
Stewart Cink lost to Paul McGinley (IRL) 3 and 2

2002 *The Brabazon Course, The De Vere Belfry,*
Sutton Coldfield, West Midlands, England
September
Result: Europe 13½, USA 12½
Captains: Sam Torrance (Eur), Curtis Strange (USA)
First Day, Morning – Fourball
Bjørn & Clarke beat Azinger & Woods 1 hole
García & Westwood beat Duval & Love 4 and 3
Langer & Montgomerie beat Furyk & Hoch 4 and 3
Fasth & Harrington lost to Mickelson & Toms 1 hole
Afternoon – Foursomes
Bjørn & Clarke lost to Sutton & Verplank 2 and 1
García & Westwood beat Calcavecchia & Woods
2 and 1
Langer & Montgomerie halved with Mickelson & Toms
Harrington & McGinley lost to Cink & Furyk 3 and 2
Second Day, Morning – Foursomes
Fulke & Price lost to Mickelson & Toms 2 and 1
García & Westwood beat Cink & Furyk 2 and 1
Langer & Montgomerie beat Hoch & Verplank 1 hole
Bjørn & Clarke lost to Love & Woods 4 and 3
Afternoon – Fourball
Fasth & Parnevik lost to Calcavecchia & Duval 1 hole
García & Westwood lost to Love & Woods 1 hole
Harrington & Montgomerie beat Mickelson & Toms 2 and 1
Clarke & McGinley halved with Furyk & Hoch

Third Day – Singles
Colin Montgomerie (SCO) beat Scott Hoch 5 and 4
Sergio García (ESP) lost to David Toms 1 hole
Darren Clarke (NIR) halved with David Duval
Bernhard Langer (GER) beat Hal Sutton 4 and 3
Padraig Harrington (IRL) beat Mark Calcavecchia 5 and 4
Thomas Bjørn (DEN) beat Stewart Cink 2 and 1
Lee Westwood (ENG) lost to Scott Verplank 2 and 1
Niclas Fasth (Swe) halved with Paul Azinger
Paul McGinley (IRL) halved with Jim Furyk
Pierre Fulke (SWE) halved with Davis Love III
Phillip Price (WAL) beat Phil Mickelson 3 and 2
Jesper Parnevik (SWE) halved with Tiger Woods

1999 *The Country Club, Brookline, MA., USA*
Sept 24–26
Result: USA 14½, Europe 13½
Captains: Ben Crenshaw (USA), Mark James (Eur)
First Day: Morning – Foursomes
Duval & Mickelson lost to Montgomerie & Lawrie
3 and 2
Lehman & Woods lost to Parnevik & García 2 and 1
Love & Stewart halved with Jiménez & Harrington
Sutton & Maggert beat Clarke & Westwood 3 and 2
Afternoon – Fourball
Love & Leonard halved with Montgomerie & Lawrie
Mickelson & Furyk lost to Parnevik & García 1 hole
Sutton & Maggert lost to Jiménez & Olazábal 2 and 1
Duval & Woods lost to Clarke & Westwood 1 hole
Second Day: Morning – Foursomes
Sutton & Maggert beat Montgomerie & Lawrie 1 hole
Furyk & O'Meara beat to Clarke & Westwood 3 and 2
Pate & Woods beat Jiménez & Harrington 1 hole
Stewart & Leonard lost to Parnevik & García 3 and 2
Afternoon – Fourball
Mickelson & Lehman beat Clarke & Westwood 2 and 1
Love & Duval halved with Parnevik & García
Leonard & Sutton halved with Jiménez & Olazábal
Pate & Woods lost to Montgomerie & Lawrie 2 and 1
Third Day – Singles
Tom Lehman beat Lee Westwood 3 and 2
Hal Sutton beat Darren Clarke 4 and 2
Phil Mickelson beat Jarmo Sandelin 4 and 3
Davis Love III beat Jean Van de Velde 6 and 5
Tiger Woods beat Andrew Coltart 3 and 2
David Duval beat Jesper Parnevik 5 and 4
Mark O'Meara lost to Padraig Harrington 1 hole
Steve Pate beat Miguel Angel Jiménez 2 and 1
Justin Leonard halved with José Maria Olazábal
Payne Stewart lost to Colin Montgomerie 1 hole
Jim Furyk beat Sergio García 4 and 3
Jeff Maggert lost to Paul Lawrie 4 and 3

1997 *Valderrama Golf Club, Sotogrande, Cadiz,*
Spain Sept 26–28
Result: Europe 14½, USA 13½
Captains: Seve Ballesteros (Eur), Tom Kite (USA)
First Day: Morning – Fourball
Olazábal & Rocca beat Love & Mickelson 1 hole
Faldo & Westwood lost to Couples & Faxon 1 hole
Parnevik & Johansson beat Lehman & Furyk 1 hole
Montgomerie & Langer lost to Woods & O'Meara 3 and 2
Afternoon – Foursomes
Rocca & Olazábal lost to Hoch & Janzen 1 hole
Langer & Montgomerie beat O'Meara & Woods 5 and 3
Faldo & Westwood beat Leonard & Maggert 3 and 2
Parnevik & Garrido halved with Lehman & Mickelson

Second Day: Morning – Fourball
Montgomerie & Clarke beat Couples & Love 1 hole
Woosnam & Bjørn beat Leonard & Faxon 2 and 1
Faldo & Westwood beat Woods & O'Meara 2 and 1
Olazábal & Garrido halved with Mickelson & Lehman

Afternoon – Foursomes
Montgomerie & Langer beat Janzen & Furyk 1 hole
Faldo & Westwood lost to Hoch & Maggert 2 and 1
Parnevik & Garrido halved with Leonard & Woods
Olazábal & Rocca beat Love & Couples 5 and 4

Third Day – Singles
Ian Woosnam lost to Fred Couples 8 and 7
Per-Ulrik Johansson beat Davis Love III 3 and 2
Costantino Rocca beat Tiger Woods 4 and 2
Thomas Bjørn halved with Justin Leonard
Darren Clarke lost to Phil Mickelson 2 and 1
Jesper Parnevik lost to Mark O'Meara 5 and 4
José Maria Olazábal lost to Lee Janzen 1 hole
Bernhard Langer beat Brad Faxon 2 and 1
Lee Westwood lost to Jeff Maggert 3 and 2
Colin Montgomerie halved with Scott Hoch
Nick Faldo lost to Jim Furyk 3 and 2
Ignacio Garrido lost to Tom Lehman 7 and 6

1995 *Oak Hill Country Club, Rochester, NY, USA*
    Sept 22–24
Result: USA 13½, Europe 14½
Captains: Lanny Wadkins (USA),
    Bernard Gallacher (Eur)
First Day: Morning – Foursomes
Pavin & Lehman beat Faldo & Montgomerie 1 hole
Haas & Couples lost to Torrance & Rocca 3 and 2
Love & Maggert beat Clark & James 4 and 3
Crenshaw & Strange lost to Langer & Johansson 1 hole

Afternoon – Fourball
Faxon & Jacobsen lost to Gilford & Ballesteros
    4 and 3
Maggert & Roberts beat Torrance & Rocca 6 and 5
Couples & Love beat Faldo & Montgomerie 3 and 2
Pavin & Mickelson beat Langer & Johansson 6 and 4

Second Day: Morning – Foursomes
Haas & Strange lost to Faldo & Montgomerie
    4 and 2
Love & Maggert lost to Torrance & Rocca 6 and 5
Roberts & Jacobsen beat Woosnam & Walton 1 hole
Pavin & Lehman lost to Langer & Gilford 4 and 3

Afternoon – Fourball
Faxon & Couples beat Torrance & Montgomerie
    4 and 2
Love & Crenshaw lost to Woosnam & Rocca 3 and 2
Haas & Mickelson beat Ballesteros & Gilford
    3 and 2
Pavin & Roberts beat Faldo & Langer 1 hole

Third Day – Singles
Tom Lehman beat Seve Ballesteros 4 and 3
Peter Jacobsen lost to Howard Clark 1 hole
Jeff Maggert lost to Mark James 4 and 3
Fred Couples halved with Ian Woosnam
Davis Love III beat Costantino Rocca 3 and 2
Brad Faxon lost to David Gilford 1 hole
Ben Crenshaw lost to Colin Montgomerie 3 and 1
Nick Faldo beat Curtis Strange 1 hole
Loren Roberts lost to Sam Torrance 2 and 1
Corey Pavin beat Bernhard Langer 3 and 2
Jay Haas lost to Philip Walton 1 hole
Phil Mickelson beat Per-Ulrik Johansson 2 and 1

1993 *The Brabazon Course, The De Vere Belfry,*
    Sutton Coldfield, West Midlands, England
    Sept 24–26
Result: Europe 13, USA 15
Captains: Bernard Gallacher (Eur), Tom Watson
    (USA)
First Day: Morning – Foursomes
Torrance & James lost to Wadkins & Pavin 4 and 3
Woosnam & Langer beat Azinger & Stewart 7 and 5
Ballesteros & Olazábal lost to Kite & Love 2 and 1
Faldo & Montgomerie beat Floyd & Couples 4 and 3

Afternoon – Fourball
Woosnam & Baker beat Gallagher & Janzen 1 hole
Lane & Langer lost to Wadkins & Pavin 4 and 2
Faldo & Montgomerie halved with Azinger & Couples
Ballesteros & Olazábal beat Kite & Love 4 and 3

Second Day: Morning – Foursomes
Faldo & Montgomerie beat Wadkins & Pavin 3 and 2
Langer & Woosnam beat Couples & Azinger 2 and 1
Baker & Lane lost to Floyd & Stewart 3 and 2
Ballesteros & Olazábal beat Kite & Love 2 and 1

Afternoon – Fourball
Faldo & Montgomerie lost to Beck & Cook 2 holes
James & Rocca lost to Pavin & Gallagher 5 and 4
Woosnam & Baker beat Couples & Azinger 6 and 5
Olazábal & Haeggman lost to Floyd & Stewart 2 and 1

Third Day – Singles
Ian Woosnam halved with Fred Couples
Barry Lane lost to Chip Beck 1 hole
Colin Montgomerie beat Lee Janzen 1 hole
Peter Baker beat Corey Pavin 2 holes
Joakim Haeggman beat J Cook 1 hole
Sam Torrance (withdrawn at start of day) halved with
    Lanny Wadkins (withdrawn at start of day)
Mark James lost to Payne Stewart 3 and 2
Constantino Rocca lost to Davis Love III 1 hole
Seve Ballesteros lost to Jim Gallagher Jr 3 and 2
José Maria Olazábal lost to Ray Floyd 2 holes
Bernhard Langer lost to Tom Kite 5 and 3
Nick Faldo halved with Paul Azinger

1991 *The Ocean Course, Kiawah Island, SC, USA*
    Sept 26–29
Result: USA 14½, Europe 13½
Captains: Dave Stockton (USA),
    Bernard Gallacher (Eur)
First Day: Morning – Foursomes
Azinger & Beck lost to Ballesteros & Olazábal 2 and 1
Floyd & Couples beat Langer & James 2 and 1
Wadkins & Irwin beat Gilford & Montgomerie 4 and 2
Stewart & Calcavecchia beat Faldo & Woosnam 1 hole

Afternoon – Fourball
Wadkins & O'Meara halved with Torrance & Feherty
Azinger & Beck lost to Ballesteros & Olazábal 2 and 1
Pavin & Calcavecchia lost to Richardson & James 5 and 4
Floyd & Couples beat Faldo & Woosnam 5 and 3

Second Day: Morning – Foursomes
Irwin & Wadkins beat Torrance & Feherty 4 and 2
Calcavecchia & Stewart beat James & Richardson 1 hole
Azinger & O'Meara beat Faldo & Gilford 7 and 6
Couples & Floyd lost to Ballesteros & Olazábal 3 and 2

Afternoon – Fourball
Azinger & Irwin lost to Woosnam & Broadhurst 2 and 1
Pate & Pavin lost to Langer & Montgomerie 2 and 1
Wadkins & Levi lost to James & Richardson 3 and 1
Couples & Stewart halved with Ballesteros & Olazábal

1991 *continued*

Third Day – Singles
Ray Floyd lost to Nick Faldo   2 holes
Payne Stewart lost to David Feherty   2 and 1
Mark Calcavecchia halved with Colin Montgomerie
Paul Azinger beat José Maria Olazábal   2 holes
Corey Pavin beat Steven Richardson   2 and 1
Wayne Levi lost to Seve Ballesteros   3 and 2
Chip Beck beat Ian Woosnam   3 and 1
Mark O'Meara lost to Paul Broadhurst   3 and 1
Fred Couples beat Sam Torrance   3 and 2
Lanny Wadkins beat Mark James   3 and 2
Hale Irwin halved with Bernhard Langer
Steve Pate (withdrawn – injured) halved with David Gilford
  (withdrawn)

1989 *The Brabazon Course, The De Vere Belfry,*
  Sutton Coldfield, West Midlands, England
  Sept 22–24

Result: Europe 14, USA 14
Captains: Tony Jacklin (Eur), Ray Floyd (USA)

First Day: Foursomes – Morning
Faldo & Woosnam halved with Kite & Strange
Clark & James lost to Stewart & Wadkins   1 hole
Ballesteros & Olazábal halved with Beck & Watson
Langer & Rafferty lost to Calcavecchia & Green   2 and 1

Fourball – Afternoon
Brand & Torrance beat Azinger & Strange   1 hole
Clark & James beat Couples & Wadkins   3 and 2
Faldo & Woosnam beat Calcavecchia & McCumber   1 hole
Ballesteros & Olazábal beat O'Meara & Watson   6 and 5

Second Day: Foursomes – Morning
Faldo & Woosnam beat Stewart & Wadkins   3 and 2
Brand & Torrance lost to Azinger & Beck   4 and 3
O'Connor & Rafferty lost to Calcavecchia & Green   3 and 2
Ballesteros & Olazábal beat Kite & Strange   1 hole

Fourball – Afternoon
Faldo & Woosnam lost to Azinger & Beck   2 and 1
Canizares & Langer lost to Kite & McCumber   2 and 1
Clark & James beat Stewart & Strange   1 hole
Ballesteros & Olazábal beat Calcavecchia & Green   4 and 2

Third Day: Singles
Seve Ballesteros lost to Paul Azinger   1 hole
Bernhard Langer lost to Chip Beck   3 and 1
José Maria Olazábal beat Payne Stewart   1 hole
Ronan Rafferty beat Mark Calvecchia   1 hole
Howard Clark lost to Tom Kite   8 and 7
Mark James beat Mark O'Meara   3 and 2
Christy O'Connor Jr beat Fred Couples   1 hole
José Maria Canizares beat Ken Green   1 hole
Gordon Brand Jr lost to Mark McCumber   1 hole
Sam Torrance lost to Tom Watson   3 and 1
Nick Faldo lost to Lanny Wadkins   1 hole
Ian Woosnam lost to Curtis Strange   1 hole

1987 *Muirfield Village Golf Club, Dublin, OH, USA*
  Sept 25–27

Result: Europe 15, USA 13
Captains: Jack Nicklaus (USA), Tony Jacklin (Eur)

First Day: Foursomes – Morning
Kite & Strange beat Clark & Torrance   4 and 2
Pohl & Sutton beat Brown & Langer   2 and 1
Mize & Wadkins lost to Faldo & Woosnam   2 holes
Nelson & Stewart lost to Ballesteros & Olazábal   1 hole

Fourball – Afternoon
Crenshaw & Simpson lost to Brand & Rivero   3 and 2
Bean & Calcavecchia lost to Langer & Lyle   1 hole

Pohl & Sutton lost to Faldo & Woosnam   2 and 1
Kite & Strange lost to Ballesteros & Olazábal   2 and 1

Second Day: Foursomes – Morning
Kite & Strange beat Brand & Rivero   3 and 1
Mize & Sutton halved with Faldo & Woosnam
Nelson & Wadkins lost to Langer & Lyle   2 and 1
Crenshaw & Stewart lost to Ballesteros & Olazábal
  1 hole

Fourball – Afternoon
Kite & Strange lost to Faldo & Woosnam   5 and 4
Bean & Stewart beat Brand & Darcy   3 and 2
Mize & Sutton beat Ballesteros & Olazábal   2 and 1
Nelson & Wadkins lost to Langer & Lyle   1 hole

Third Day: Singles
Andy Bean beat Ian Woosnam   1 hole
Dan Pohl lost to Howard Clark   1 hole
Larry Mize halved with Sam Torrance
Mark Calcavecchia beat Nick Faldo   1 hole
Payne Stewart beat José Maria Olazábal   2 holes
Scott Simpson beat José Rivero   2 and 1
Tom Kite beat Sandy Lyle   3 and 2
Ben Crenshaw lost to Eamonn Darcy   1 hole
Larry Nelson halved with Bernhard Langer
Curtis Strange lost to Seve Ballesteros   2 and 1
Lanny Wadkins beat Ken Brown   3 and 2
Hal Sutton halved with Gordon Brand Jr

1985 *The Brabazon Course, The De Vere Belfry,*
  Sutton Coldfield, West Midlands, England
  Sept 13–15

Result: Europe 16½, USA 11½
Captains: Tony Jacklin (Eur), Lee Trevino (USA)

First Day: Foursomes – Morning
Ballesteros & Pinero beat Strange & O'Meara   2 and 1
Faldo & Langer lost to Kite & Peete   3 and 2
Brown & Lyle lost to Floyd & Wadkins   4 and 3
Clark & Torrance lost to Stadler & Sutton   3 and 2

Fourball – Afternoon
Way & Woosnam beat Green & Zoeller   1 hole
Ballesteros & Pinero beat Jacobsen & North   2 and 1
Canizares & Langer halved with Stadler & Sutton
Clark & Torrance lost to Floyd & Wadkins   1 hole

Second Day: Fourball – Morning
Clark & Torrance beat Kite & North   2 and 1
Way & Woosnam beat Green & Zoeller   4 and 3
Ballesteros & Pinero lost to O'Meara & Wadkins
  3 and 2
Langer & Lyle halved with Stadler & Strange

Foursomes – Afternoon
Canizares & Rivero beat Kite & Peete   7 and 5
Ballesteros & Pinero beat Stadler & Sutton   5 and 4
Way & Woosnam lost to Jacobsen & Strange   4 and 3
Brown & Langer beat Floyd & Wadkins   3 and 2

Third Day: Singles
Manuel Pinero beat Lanny Wadkins   3 and 1
Ian Woosnam lost to Craig Stadler   2 and 1
Paul Way beat Ray Floyd   2 holes
Seve Ballesteros halved with Tom Kite
Sandy Lyle beat Peter Jacobsen   3 and 2
Bernhard Langer beat Hal Sutton   5 and 4
Sam Torrance beat Andy North   1 hole
Howard Clark beat Mark O'Meara   1 hole
Nick Faldo lost to Hubert Green   3 and 1
José Rivero lost to Calvin Peete   1 hole
José Maria Canizares beat Fuzzy Zoeller   2 holes
Ken Brown lost to Curtis Strange   4 and 2

1983 *PGA National Golf Club, Palm Beach Gardens, FL, USA* Oct 14–16

Result: USA 14½, Europe 13½
Captains: Jack Nicklaus (USA), Tony Jacklin (Eur)

First Day: Foursomes – Morning
Watson & Crenshaw beat Gallacher & Lyle 5 and 4
Wadkins & Stadler lost to Faldo & Langer 4 and 2
Floyd & Gilder lost to Canizares & Torrance 4 and 3
Kite & Peete beat Ballesteros & Way 2 and 1

Fourball – Afternoon
Morgan & Zoeller lost to Waites & Brown 2 and 1
Watson & Haas beat Faldo & Langer 2 and 1
Floyd & Strange lost to Ballesteros & Way 1 hole
Crenshaw & Peete halved with Torrance & Woosnam

Second Day: Foursomes – Morning
Floyd & Kite lost to Faldo & Langer 3 and 2
Wadkins & Morgan beat Canizares & Torrance 7 and 5
Gilder & Watson lost to Ballesteros & Way 2 and 1
Haas & Strange beat Waites & Brown 3 and 2

Fourball – Afternoon
Wadkins & Stadler beat Waites & Brown 1 hole
Crenshaw & Peete lost to Faldo & Langer 2 and 1
Haas & Morgan halved with Ballesteros & Way
Gilder & Watson beat Torrance & Woosnam 5 and 4

Third Day: Singles
Fuzzy Zoeller halved with Seve Ballesteros
Jay Haas lost to Nick Faldo 2 and 1
Gil Morgan lost to Bernhard Langer 2 holes
Bob Gilder beat Gordon J Brand 2 holes
Ben Crenshaw beat Sandy Lyle 3 and 1
Calvin Peete beat Brian Waites 1 hole
Curtis Strange lost to Paul Way 2 and 1
Tom Kite halved with Sam Torrance
Craig Stadler beat Ian Woosnam 3 and 2
Lanny Wadkins halved with José Maria Canizares
Ray Floyd lost to Ken Brown 4 and 3
Tom Watson beat Bernard Gallacher 2 and 1

1981 *Walton Heath GC, Tadworth, Surrey, England* Sept 18–20

Result: USA 18½, Europe 9½
Captains: John Jacobs (Eur), Dave Marr (USA)

First Day: Foursomes – Morning
Langer & Pinero lost to Trevino & Nelson 1 hole
Lyle & James beat Rogers & Lietzke 2 and 1
Gallacher & Smyth beat Irwin & Floyd 3 and 2
Oosterhuis & Faldo lost to Watson & Nicklaus 4 and 3

Fourball – Afternoon
Torrance & Clark halved with Kite & Miller
Lyle & James beat Crenshaw & Pate 3 and 2
Smyth & Canizares beat Rogers & Lietzke 6 and 5
Gallacher & Darcy lost to Irwin & Floyd 2 and 1

Second Day: Fourball – Morning
Faldo & Torrance lost to Trevino & Pate 7 and 5
Lyle & James lost to Nelson & Kite 1 hole
Langer & Pinero beat Irwin & Floyd 2 and 1
Smyth & Canizares lost to Watson & Nicklaus 3 and 2

Foursomes – Afternoon
Oosterhuis & Torrance lost to Trevino & Pate 2 and 1
Langer & Pinero lost to Watson & Nicklaus 3 and 2
Lyle & James lost to Rogers & Floyd 3 and 2
Gallacher & Smyth lost to Nelson & Kite 3 and 2

Third Day: Singles
Sam Torrance lost to Lee Trevino 5 and 3
Sandy Lyle lost to Tom Kite 3 and 2
Bernard Gallacher halved with Bill Rogers
Mark James lost to Larry Nelson 2 holes
Des Smyth lost to Ben Crenshaw 6 and 4
Bernhard Langer halved with Bruce Lietzke
Manuel Pinero beat Jerry Pate 4 and 2
José Maria Canizares lost to Hale Irwin 1 hole
Nick Faldo beat Johnny Miller 2 and 1
Howard Clark beat Tom Watson 4 and 3
Peter Oosterhuis lost to Ray Floyd 2 holes
Eamonn Darcy lost to Jack Nicklaus 5 and 3

From 1979 GB&I became a European team

1979 *The Greenbrier, White Sulphur Springs, WV, USA* Sept 14–16

Result: USA 17, Europe 11
Captains: Billy Casper (USA), John Jacobs (Eur)
First Day: Fourball – Morning
Wadkins & Nelson beat Garrido & Ballesteros 2 and 1
Trevino & Zoeller beat Brown & James 3 and 2
Bean & Elder beat Oosterhuis & Faldo 2 and 1
Irwin & Mahaffey lost to Gallacher & Barnes 2 and 1
Foursomes – Afternoon
Irwin & Kite beat Brown & Smyth 7 and 6
Zoeller & Green lost to Garrido & Ballesteros 3 and 2
Trevino & Morgan halved with Lyle & Jacklin
Wadkins & Nelson beat Gallacher & Barnes 4 and 3
Second Day: Foursomes – Morning
Elder & Mahaffey lost to Lyle & Jacklin 5 and 4
Bean & Kite lost to Oosterhuis & Faldo 6 and 5
Zoeller & Hayes halved with Gallacher & Barnes
Wadkins & Nelson beat Garrido & Ballesteros 3 and 2
Fourball – Afternoon
Wadkins & Nelson beat Garrido & Ballesteros 5 and 4
Irwin & Kite beat Lyle & Jacklin 1 hole
Trevino & Zoeller lost to Gallacher & Barnes 3 and 2
Elder & Hayes lost to Oosterhuis & Faldo 1 hole
Third Day: Singles
Lanny Wadkins lost to Bernard Gallacher 3 and 2
Larry Nelson beat Seve Ballesteros 3 and 2
Tom Kite beat Tony Jacklin 1 hole
Mark Hayes beat Antonio Garrido 1 hole
Andy Bean beat Michael King 4 and 3
John Mahaffey beat Brian Barnes 1 hole
Lee Elder lost to Nick Faldo 3 and 2
Hale Irwin beat Des Smyth 5 and 3
Hubert Green beat Peter Oosterhuis 2 holes
Fuzzy Zoeller lost to Ken Brown 1 hole
Lee Trevino beat Sandy Lyle 2 and 1
Gil Morgan, Mark James: injury; match a half

1977 *Royal Lytham & St Annes GC, St Annes, Lancs, England* Sept 15–17

Result: USA 12½, GB&I 7½
Captains: Brian Huggett (GB&I), Dow Finsterwald (USA)

First Day: Foursomes
Gallacher & Barnes lost to Wadkins & Irwin 3 and 1
Coles & Dawson lost to Stockton & McGee 1 hole
Faldo & Oosterhuis beat Floyd & Graham 2 and 1
Darcy & Jacklin halved with Sneed & January
Horton & James lost to Nicklaus & Watson 5 and 4

1977 *continued*
Second Day: Fourball
Barnes & Horton lost to Watson & Green 5 and 4
Coles & Dawson lost to Sneed & Wadkins 5 and 3
Faldo & Oosterhuis beat Nicklaus & Floyd 3 and 1
Darcy & Jacklin lost to Hill & Stockton 5 and 3
James & Brown lost to Irwin & Graham 1 hole

Third Day: Singles
Howard Clark lost to Lanny Wadkins 4 and 3
Neil Coles lost to Lou Graham 5 and 3
Peter Dawson beat Don January 5 and 4
Brian Barnes beat Hale Irwin 1 hole
Tommy Horton lost to Dave Hill 5 and 4
Bernard Gallacher beat Jack Nicklaus 1 hole
Eamonn Darcy lost to Hubert Green 1 hole
Mark James lost to Ray Floyd 2 and 1
Nick Faldo beat Tom Watson 1 hole
Peter Oosterhuis beat Jerry McGee 2 holes

1975 *Laurel Valley Golf Club, Ligonier, PA, USA*
    Sept 19–21
Result: USA 21, GB&I 11
Captains: Arnold Palmer (USA),
    Bernard Hunt (GB&I)
First Day: Foursomes – Morning
Nicklaus & Weiskopf beat Barnes & Gallacher
    5 and 4
Littler & Irwin beat Wood & Bembridge 4 and 3
Geiberger & Miller beat Jacklin & Oosterhuis
    3 and 1
Trevino & Snead beat Horton & O'Leary 2 and 1

Fourball – Afternoon
Casper & Floyd lost to Jacklin & Oosterhuis 2 and 1
Weiskopf & Graham beat Darcy & Christy O'Connor Jr
    3 and 2
Nicklaus & Murphy halved with Barnes & Gallacher
Trevino & Irwin beat Horton & O'Leary 2 and 1

Second Day: Fourball – Morning
Casper & Miller halved with Jacklin & Oosterhuis
Nicklaus & Snead beat Horton & Wood 4 and 2
Littler & Graham beat Barnes & Gallacher 5 and 3
Geiberger & Floyd halved with Darcy & Hunt

Foursomes – Afternoon
Trevino & Murphy lost to Jacklin & Barnes 3 and 2
Weiskopf & Miller beat O'Connor & O'Leary
    5 and 3
Irwin & Casper beat Oosterhuis & Bembridge
    3 and 2
Geiberger & Graham beat Darcy & Hunt 3 and 2

Third Day: Singles – Morning
Bob Murphy beat Tony Jacklin 2 and 1
Johnny Miller lost to Peter Oosterhuis 2 holes
Lee Trevino halved with Bernard Gallacher
Hale Irwin halved with Tommy Horton
Gene Littler beat Brian Huggett 4 and 2
Billy Casper beat Eamonn Darcy 3 and 2
Tom Weiskopf beat Guy Hunt 5 and 3
Jack Nicklaus lost to Brian Barnes 4 and 2

Singles – Afternoon
Ray Floyd beat Jacklin 1 hole
JC Snead lost to Oosterhuis 3 and 2
Al Geiberger halved with Gallacher
Lou Graham lost to Horton 2 and 1
Irwin beat John O'Leary 2 and 1
Murphy beat Maurice Bembridge 2 and 1
Trevino lost to Norman Wood 2 and 1
Nicklaus lost to Barnes 2 and 1

1973 *Honourable Company of Edinburgh Golfers,*
    Muirfield, Gullane, East Lothian, Scotland
    Sept 20–22
Result: USA 19, GB&I 13
Captains: Bernard Hunt (GB&I), Jack Burke (USA)
First Day: Foursomes – Morning
Barnes & Gallacher beat Trevino & Casper 1 hole
O'Connor & Coles beat Weiskopf & Snead 3 and 2
Jacklin & Oosterhuis halved with Rodriguez & Graham
Bembridge & Polland lost to Nicklaus & Palmer 6 and 5

Fourball – Afternoon
Barnes & Gallacher beat Aaron & Brewer 5 and 4
Bembridge & Huggett beat Nicklaus & Palmer 3 and 1
Jacklin & Oosterhuis beat Weiskopf & Casper 3 and 1
O'Connor & Coles lost to Trevino & Blancas 2 and 1

Second Day: Foursomes – Morning
Barnes & Butler lost to Nicklaus & Weiskopf 1 hole
Jacklin & Oosterhuis beat Palmer & Hill 2 holes
Bembridge & Huggett beat Rodriguez & Graham 5 and 4
O'Connor & Coles lost to Trevino & Casper 2 and 1

Fourball – Afternoon
Barnes & Butler lost to Snead & Palmer 2 holes
Jacklin & Oosterhuis lost to Brewer & Casper 3 and 2
Clark & Polland lost to Nicklaus & Weiskopf 3 and 2
Bembridge & Huggett halved with Trevino & Blancas

Third Day: Singles – Morning
Brian Barnes lost to Billy Casper 2 and 1
Bernard Gallacher lost to Tom Weiskopf 3 and 1
Peter Butler lost to Homero Blancas 5 and 4
Tony Jacklin beat Tommy Aaron 3 and 1
Neil Coles halved with Gay Brewer
Christy O'Connor lost to JC Snead 1 hole
Maurice Bembridge halved with Jack Nicklaus
Peter Oosterhuis halved with Lee Trevino

Singles – Afternoon
Brian Huggett beat Blancas 4 and 2
Barnes lost to Snead 3 and 1
Gallacher lost to Brewer 6 and 5
Jacklin lost to Casper 2 and 1
Coles lost to Trevino 6 and 5
O'Connor halved with Weiskopf
Bembridge lost to Nicklaus 2 holes
Oosterhuis beat Arnold Palmer 4 and 2

1971 *Old Warson Country Club, St Louis, MO, USA*
    Sept 16–18
Result: USA 18½, GB&I 13½
Captains: Jay Hebert (USA), Eric Brown (GB&I)
First Day: Foursomes – Morning
Casper & Barber lost to Coles & O'Connor 2 and 1
Palmer & Dickinson beat Townsend & Oosterhuis
    2 holes
Nicklaus & Stockton lost to Huggett & Jacklin 3 and 2
Coody & Beard lost to Bembridge & Butler 1 hole

Foursomes – Afternoon
Casper & Barber lost to Bannerman & Gallacher 2 and 1
Palmer & Dickinson beat Townsend & Oosterhuis
    1 hole
Trevino & Rudolph halved with Huggett and Jacklin
Nicklaus & Snead beat Bembridge & Butler 5 and 3

Second Day: Fourball – Morning
Trevino & Rudolph beat O'Connor & Barnes 2 and 1
Beard & Snead beat Coles & John Garner 2 and 1
Palmer & Dickinson beat Oosterhuis & Gallacher
    5 and 4
Nicklaus & Littler beat Townsend & Bannerman 2 and 1

Fourball – Afternoon
Trevino & Casper lost to Oosterhuis & Gallacher 1 hole
Littler & Snead beat Huggett & Jacklin 2 and 1
Palmer & Nicklaus beat Townsend & Bannerman 1 hole
Coody & Beard halved with Coles & O'Connor

Third Day: Singles – Morning
Lee Trevino beat Tony Jacklin 1 hole
Dave Stockton halved with Bernard Gallacher
Mason Rudolph lost to Brian Barnes 1 hole
Gene Littler lost to Peter Oosterhuis 4 and 3
Jack Nicklaus beat Peter Townsend 3 and 2
Gardner Dickinson beat Christy O'Connor 5 and 4
Arnold Palmer halved with Harry Bannerman
Frank Beard halved with Neil Coles

Singles – Afternoon
Trevino beat Brian Huggett 7 and 6
JC Snead beat Jacklin 1 hole
Miller Barber lost to Barnes 2 and 1
Stockton beat Townsend 1 hole
Charles Coody lost to Gallacher 2 and 1
Nicklaus beat Coles 5 and 3
Palmer lost to Oosterhuis 3 and 2
Dickinson lost to Bannerman 2 and 1

1969 *Royal Birkdale Golf Club, Southport, Lancs,*
England Sept 18–20
Result: USA 16, GB&I 16
Captains: Eric Brown (GB&I), Sam Snead (USA)
First Day: Foursomes – Morning
Coles & Huggett beat Barber & Floyd 3 and 2
Gallacher & Bembridge beat Trevino & Still 2 and 1
Jacklin & Townsend beat Hill & Aaron 3 and 1
O'Connor & Alliss halved with Casper & Beard

Foursomes – Afternoon
Coles & Huggett lost to Hill & Aaron 1 hole
Gallacher & Bembridge lost to Trevino & Littler 2 holes
Jacklin & Townsend beat Casper & Beard 1 hole
Hunt & Butler lost to Nicklaus & Sikes

Second Day: Fourball – Morning
O'Connor & Townsend beat Hill & Douglass 1 hole
Huggett & Alex Caygill halved with Floyd & Barber
Barnes & Alliss lost to Trevino & Littler 1 hole
Jacklin & Coles beat Nicklaus & Sikes 1 hole

Fourball – Afternoon
Townsend & Butler lost to Casper & Beard 2 holes
Huggett & Gallacher lost to Hill & Still 2 and 1
Bembridge & Hunt halved with Aaron & Floyd
Jacklin & Coles halved with Trevino & Barber

Third Day: Singles – Morning
Peter Alliss lost to Lee Trevino 2 and 1
Peter Townsend lost to Dave Hill 5 and 4
Neil Coles beat Tommy Aaron 1 hole
Brian Barnes lost to Billy Casper 1 hole
Christy O'Connor beat Frank Beard 5 and 4
Maurice Bembridge beat Ken Still 1 hole
Peter Butler beat Ray Floyd 1 hole
Tony Jacklin beat Jack Nicklaus 4 and 3

Singles – Afternoon
Barnes lost to Hill 4 and 2
Bernard Gallacher beat Trevino 4 and 3
Bembridge lost to Miller Barber 7 and 6
Butler beat Dale Douglass 3 and 2
O'Connor lost to Gene Littler 2 and 1
Brian Huggett halved with Casper
Coles lost to Dan Sikes 4 and 3
Jacklin halved with Nicklaus

1967 *Champions Golf Club, Houston, TX, USA*
Oct 20-22
Result: USA 23½, GB&I 8½
Captains: Ben Hogan (USA), Dai Rees (GB&I)
First Day: Foursomes – Morning
Casper & Boros halved with Huggett & Will
Palmer & Dickinson beat Alliss & O'Connor 2 and 1
Sanders & Brewer lost to Jacklin & Thomas 4 and 3
Nichols & Pott beat Hunt & Coles 6 and 5

Foursomes – Afternoon
Boros & Casper beat Huggett & Will 1 hole
Dickinson & Palmer beat Gregson & Boyle 5 and 4
Littler & Geiberger lost to Jacklin & Thomas 3 and 2
Nichols & Pott beat Alliss & O'Connor 2 and 1

Second Day: Fourball – Morning
Casper & Brewer beat Alliss & O'Connor 3 and 2
Nichols & Pott beat Hunt & Coles 1 hole
Littler & Geiberger beat Jacklin & Thomas 1 hole
Dickinson & Sanders beat Huggett & Will 3 and 2

Fourball – Afternoon
Casper & Brewer beat Hunt & Coles 5 and 3
Dickinson & Sanders beat Alliss & Gregson 4 and 3
Palmer & Boros beat Will & Boyle 1 hole
Littler & Geiberger halved with Jacklin & Thomas

Third Day: Singles – Morning
Gay Brewer beat Hugh Boyle 4 and 3
Billy Casper beat Peter Alliss 2 and 1
Arnold Palmer beat Tony Jacklin 3 and 2
Julius Boros lost to Brian Huggett 1 hole
Doug Sanders lost to Neil Coles 2 and 1
Al Geiberger beat Malcolm Gregson 4 and 2
Gene Littler halved with Dave Thomas
Bobby Nichols halved with Bernard Hunt

Singles – Afternoon
Palmer beat Huggett 5 and 3
Brewer lost to Alliss 2 and 1
Gardner Dickinson beat Jacklin 3 and 2
Nichols beat Christy O'Connor 3 and 2
Johnny Pott beat George Will 3 and 1
Geiberger beat Gregson 2 and 1
Boros halved with Hunt
Sanders lost to Coles 2 and 1

1965 *Royal Birkdale Golf Club, Southport, Lancs,*
England Oct 7–9
Result: GB&I 12½, USA 19½
Captains: Harry Weetman (GB&I),
Byron Nelson (USA)
First Day: Foursomes – Morning
Thomas & Will beat Marr & Palmer 6 and 5
O'Connor & Alliss beat Venturi & January 5 and 4
Platts & Butler lost to Boros & Lema 1 hole
Hunt & Coles lost to Casper & Littler 2 and 1

Foursomes – Afternoon
Thomas & Will lost to Marr & Palmer 6 and 5
Martin & Hitchcock lost to Boros & Lema 5 and 4
O'Connor & Alliss beat Casper & Littler 2 and 1
Hunt & Coles beat Venturi & January 3 and 2

Second Day: Fourball – Morning
Thomas & Will lost to January & Jacobs 1 hole
Platts & Butler halved with Casper & Littler
Alliss & O'Connor lost to Marr & Palmer 5 and 4
Coles & Hunt beat Boros & Lema 1 hole

Fourball – Afternoon
Alliss & O'Connor beat Marr & Palmer 1 hole
Thomas & Will lost to January & Jacobs 1 hole
Platts & Butler halved with Casper & Littler
Coles & Hunt lost to Lema & Venturi 1 hole

1965 *continued*
Third Day: Singles – Morning
Jimmy Hitchcock lost to Arnold Palmer
   3 and 2
Lionel Platts lost to Julius Boros 4 and 2
Peter Butler lost to Tony Lema 1 hole
Neil Coles lost to Dave Marr 2 holes
Bernard Hunt beat Gene Littler 2 holes
Peter Alliss beat Billy Casper 1 hole
Dave Thomas lost to Tommy Jacobs 2 and 1
George Will halved with Don January
Singles – Afternoon
Butler lost to Palmer 2 holes
Hitchcock lost to Boros 2 and 1
Christy O'Connor lost to Lema 6 and 4
Alliss beat Ken Venturi 3 and 1
Hunt lost to Marr 1 hole
Coles beat Casper 3 and 2
Will lost to Littler 2 and 1
Platts beat Jacobs 1 hole

1963 *East Lake CC, Atlanta, GA, USA*
   Oct 11–13
Result: USA 23, GB&I 9
Captains: Arnold Palmer (USA),
   John Fallon (GB&I)
First Day: Foursomes – Morning
Palmer & Pott lost to Huggett & Will 3 and 2
Casper & Ragan beat Alliss & O'Connor 1 hole
Boros & Lema halved with Coles & B Hunt
Littler & Finsterwald halved with Thomas &
   Weetman
Foursomes – Afternoon
Maxwell & Goalby beat Thomas & Weetman
   4 and 3
Palmer & Casper beat Huggett & Will 5 and 4
Littler & Finsterwald beat Coles & G Hunt 2 and 1
Boros & Lema beat Haliburton & B Hunt 1 hole
Second Day: Fourball – Morning
Palmer & Finsterwald beat Huggett & Thomas 5 and 4
Littler & Boros halved with Alliss & B Hunt
Casper & Maxwell beat Weetman & Will 3 and 2
Goalby & Ragan lost to Coles & O'Connor 1 hole
1963 *continued*
Fourball – Afternoon
Palmer & Finsterwald beat Coles & O'Connor
   3 and 2
Lema & Pott beat Alliss & B Hunt 1 hole
Casper & Maxwell beat Haliburton & G Hunt 2 and 1
Goalby & Ragan halved with Huggett & Thomas
Third Day: Singles – Morning
Tony Lema beat Geoffrey Hunt 5 and 3
Johnny Pott lost to Brian Huggett 3 and 1
Arnold Palmer lost to Peter Alliss 1 hole
Billy Casper halved with Neil Coles
Bob Goalby beat Dave Thomas 3 and 2
Gene Littler lost to Tom Haliburton 6 and 5
Julius Boros lost to Harry Weetman 1 hole
Dow Finsterwald lost to Bernard Hunt 2 holes
Singles – Afternoon
Arnold Palmer beat George Will 3 and 2
Dave Ragan beat Neil Coles 2 and 1
Tony Lema halved with Peter Alliss
Gene Littler beat Tom Haliburton 6 and 5
Julius Boros beat Harry Weetman 2 and 1
Billy Maxwell beat Christy O'Connor 2 and 1
Dow Finsterwald beat Dave Thomas 4 and 3
Bob Goalby beat Bernard Hunt 2 and 1

1961 *Royal Lytham & St Annes GC, St Annes,*
   Lancs, England Oct 13–14
Result: USA 14½, GB&I 9½
Captains: Jerry Barber (USA), Dai Rees (GB&I)
First Day: Foursomes – Morning
O'Connor & Alliss beat Littler & Ford 4 and 3
Panton & Hunt lost to Wall & Hebert 4 and 3
Rees & Bousfield lost to Casper & Palmer 2 and 1
Haliburton & Coles lost to Souchak & Collins
   1 hole
Foursomes – Afternoon
O'Connor & Alliss lost to Wall & Hebert 1 hole
Panton & Hunt lost to Casper & Palmer 5 and 4
Rees & Bousfield beat Souchak & Collins 4 and 2
Haliburton & Coles lost to Barber & Finsterwald
   1 hole
Second Day: Singles – Morning
Harry Weetman lost to Doug Ford 1 hole
Ralph Moffitt lost to Mike Souchak 5 and 4
Peter Alliss halved with Arnold Palmer
Ken Bousfield lost to Billy Casper 5 and 3
Dai Rees beat Jay Hebert 2 and 1
Neil Coles halved with Gene Littler
Bernard Hunt beat Jerry Barber 5 and 4
Christy O'Connor lost to Dow Finsterwald
   2 and 1
Singles – Afternoon
Weetman lost to Wall 1 hole
Alliss beat Bill Collins 3 and 2
Hunt lost to Souchak 2 and 1
Tom Haliburton lost to Palmer 2 and 1
Rees beat Ford 4 and 3
Bousfield beat Barber 1 hole
Coles beat Finsterwald 1 hole
O'Connor halved with Littler

1959 *Eldorado Country Club, Palm Desert, CA, USA*
   Nov 6–7
Result: USA 8½, GB&I 3½
Captains: Sam Snead (USA), Dai Rees (GB&I)
Foursomes
Rosburg & Souchak beat Hunt & Brown 5 and 4
Ford & Wall lost to O'Connor & Alliss 3 and 2
Boros & Finsterwald beat Rees & Bousfield 2 holes
Snead & Middlecoff halved with Weetman & Thomas
Singles
Doug Ford halved with Norman Drew
Mike Souchak beat Ken Bousfield 3 and 2
Bob Rosburg beat Harry Weetman 6 and 5
Sam Snead beat Dave Thomas 6 and 5
Dow Finsterwald beat Dai Rees 1 hole
Jay Hebert halved with Peter Alliss
Art Wall Jr beat Christy O'Connor 7 and 6
Cary Middlecoff lost to Eric Brown 4 and 3

1957 *Lindrick Golf Club, Sheffield, Yorks, England*
   Oct 4–5
Result: GB&I 7½, USA 4½
Captains: Dai Rees (GB&I),
   Jack Burke (USA)
Foursomes
Alliss & Hunt lost to Ford & Finsterwald 2 and 1
Bousfield & Rees beat Art Wall Jr & Hawkins 3 and 2
Faulkner & Weetman lost to Kroll & Burke 4 and 3
O'Connor & Brown lost to Mayer & Bolt 7 and 5

Singles
Eric Brown beat Tommy Bolt 4 and 3
Peter Mills beat Jack Burke 5 and 3
Peter Alliss lost to Fred Hawkins 2 and 1
Ken Bousfield beat Lionel Hebert 4 and 3
Dai Rees beat Ed Furgol 7 and 6
Bernard Hunt beat Doug Ford 6 and 5
Christy O'Connor beat Dow Finsterwald 7 and 6
Harry Bradshaw halved with Dick Mayer

1955 *Thunderbird G and C Club, Palm Springs,*
    CA, USA Nov 5–6
Result: USA 8, GB&I 4
Captains: Chick Harbert (USA), Dai Rees (GB&I)
Foursomes
Harper & Barber lost to Fallon & Jacobs 1 hole
Ford & Kroll beat Brown & Scott 5 and 4
Burke & Bolt beat Lees & Weetman 1 hole
Snead & Middlecoff beat Rees & Bradshaw
  3 and 2
Singles
Tommy Bolt beat Christy O'Connor 4 and 2
Chick Harbert beat Syd Scott 3 and 2
Cary Middlecoff lost to John Jacobs 1 hole
Sam Snead beat Dai Rees 3 and 1
Marty Furgol lost to Arthur Lees 3 and 1
Jerry Barber lost to Eric Brown 3 and 2
Jack Burke beat Harry Bradshaw 3 and 2
Doug Ford beat Harry Weetman 3 and 2

1953 *West Course, Wentworth GC, Surrey,*
    England Oct 2–3
Result: USA 6½, GB 5½
Captains: Henry Cotton (GB),
  Lloyd Mangrum (USA)
Foursomes
Weetman & Alliss lost to Douglas & Oliver 2 and 1
Brown & Panton lost to Mangrum & Snead 8 and 7
Adams & Hunt lost to Kroll & Burke 7 and 5
Daly & Bradshaw beat Burkemo & Middlecoff 1 hole
Singles
Dai Rees lost to Jack Burke 2 and 1
Fred Daly beat Ted Kroll 9 and 7
Eric Brown beat Lloyd Mangrum 2 holes
Harry Weetman beat Sam Snead 1 hole
Max Faulkner lost to Cary Middlecoff 3 and 1
Peter Alliss lost to Jim Turnesa 1 hole
Bernard Hunt halved with Dave Douglas
Harry Bradshaw beat Fred Haas Jr 3 and 2

1951 *Pinehurst No.2, Pinehurst, NC, USA*
    Nov 2–4
Result: USA 9½, GB 2½
Captains: Sam Snead (USA), Arthur Lacey (GB)
Foursomes
Heafner & Burke beat Faulkner & Rees 5 and 3
Oliver & Henry Ransom lost to Ward & Lees 2 and 1
Mangrum & Snead beat Adams & Panton 5 and 4
Hogan & Demaret beat Daly & Bousfield 5 and 4
Singles
Jack Burke beat Jimmy Adams 4 and 3
Jimmy Demaret beat Dai Rees 2 holes
Clayton Heafner halved with Fred Daly
Lloyd Mangrum beat Harry Weetman 6 and 5
Ed Oliver lost to Arthur Lees 2 and 1
Ben Hogan beat Charlie Ward 3 and 2
Skip Alexander beat John Panton 8 and 7
Sam Snead beat Max Faulkner 4 and 3

1949 *Ganton Golf Club, Scarborough, Yorks, England*
    Sept 16–17
Result: USA 7, GB 5
Captains: Charles Whitcombe (GB), Ben Hogan (USA)
Foursomes
Faulkner & Adams beat Harrison & Palmer 2 and 1
Daly & Ken Bousfield beat Hamilton & Alexander 4 and 2
Ward & King lost to Demaret & Heafner 4 and 3
Burton & Lees beat Snead & Mangrum 1 hole
Singles
Max Faulkner lost to Dutch Harrison 8 and 7
Jimmy Adams beat Johnny Palmer 2 and 1
Charlie Ward lost to Sam Snead 6 and 5
Dai Rees beat Bob Hamilton 6 and 4
Dick Burton lost to Clayton Heafner 3 and 2
Sam King lost to Chick Harbert 4 and 3
Arthur Lees lost to Jimmy Demaret 7 and 6
Fred Daly lost to Lloyd Mangrum 1 hole

1947 *Portland Golf Club, Portland, OR, USA* Nov 1–2
Result: USA 11, GB 1
Captains: Ben Hogan (USA), Henry Cotton (GB)
Foursomes
Oliver & Worsham beat Cotton & Lees 10 and 9
Snead & Mangrum beat Daly & Ward 6 and 5
Hogan & Demaret beat Adams & Faulkner 2 holes
Nelson & Herman Barron beat Rees & King 2 and 1
Singles
Dutch Harrison beat Fred Daly 5 and 4
Lew Worsham beat Jimmy Adams 3 and 2
Lloyd Mangrum beat Max Faulkner 6 and 5
Ed Oliver beat Charlie Ward 4 and 3

Although no matches were played between 1939 and 1945, Great Britain selected a side in 1939 and the Americans chose sides in 1939 to 1943. No alternative fixture was played in 1939 but the Americans played matches amongst themselves in the other four years. They resulted in:

1940	Cup Team 7, Gene Sarazen's Challengers 5
1941	Cup Team 6½, Bobby Jones' Challengers 8½
1942	Cup Team 10, Walter Hagen's Challengers 5
1943	Cup Team 8½, Walter Hagen's Challengers 3½

1949 *continued*

Singles *continued*
Byron Nelson beat Arthur Lees 2 and 1
Sam Snead beat Henry Cotton 5 and 4
Jimmy Demaret beat Dai Rees 3 and 2
Herman Keiser lost to Sam King 4 and 3

1937 *Southport & Ainsdale GC, Southport, Lancs,*
England June 29–30

Result: USA 8, GB 4
Captains: Charles Whitcombe (GB),
Walter Hagen (USA)

Foursomes
Padgham & Cotton lost to Dudley & Nelson 4 and 2
Lacey & Bill Cox lost to Guldahl & Manero 2 and 1
Whitcombe & Rees halved with Sarazen & Shute
Alliss & Burton beat Picard & Johnny Revolta 2 and 1

Singles
Alf Padgham lost to Ralph Guldahl 8 and 7
Sam King halved with Densmore Shute
Dai Rees beat Byron Nelson 3 and 1
Henry Cotton beat Tony Manero 5 and 3
Percy Alliss lost to Gene Sarazen 1 hole
Dick Burton lost to Sam Snead 5 and 4
Alf Perry lost to Ed Dudley 2 and 1
Arthur Lacey lost to Henry Picard 2 and 1

1935 *Ridgewood Country Club, Paramus, NJ, USA*
Sept 28–29

Result: USA 9, GB 3
Captains: Walter Hagen (USA),
Charles Whitcombe (GB)

Foursomes
Sarazen & Hagen beat Perry & Busson 7 and 6
Picard & Revolta beat Padgham & Alliss 6 and 5
Runyan & Smith beat Cox & Jarman 9 and 8
Dutra & Laffoon lost to C Whitcombe & E Whitcombe
   1 hole

Singles
Gene Sarazen beat Jack Busson 3 and 2
Paul Runyon beat Dick Burton 5 and 3
Johnny Revolta beat Charles Whitcombe 2 and 1
Olin Dutra beat Alf Padgham 4 and 2
Craig Wood lost to Percy Alliss 1 hole
Horton Smith halved with Bill Cox
Henry Picard beat Ernest Whitcombe 3 and 2
Sam Parks halved with Alf Perry

1933 *Southport & Ainsdale GC, Southport, Lancs,*
England June 26–27

Result: GB 6½, USA 5½
Captains: JH Taylor (GB), Walter Hagen (USA)

Foursomes
Alliss & Whitcombe halved with Sarazen & Hagen
Mitchell & Havers beat Dutra & Shute 3 and 2
Davies & Easterbrook beat Wood & Runyan 1 hole
Padgham & Perry lost to Dudley & Burke 1 hole

Singles
Alf Padgham lost to Gene Sarazen 6 and 4
Abe Mitchell beat Olin Dutra 9 and 8
Arthur Lacey lost to Walter Hagen 2 and 1
William H Davies lost to Craig Wood 4 and 3
Percy Alliss beat Paul Runyan 2 and 1
Arthur Havers beat Leo Diegel 4 and 3
Syd Easterbrook beat Densmore Shute 1 hole
Charles Whitcombe lost to Horton Smith 2 and 1

1931 *Scioto Country Club, Columbus, OH, USA*
June 26–27

Result: USA 9, GB 3
Captains: Walter Hagen (USA),
Charles Whitcombe (GB)

Foursomes
Sarazen & Farrell beat Compston & Davies 8 and 7
Hagen & Shute beat Duncan & Havers 10 and 9
Diegel & Espinosa lost to Mitchell & Robson 3 and 1
Burke & Cox beat Easterbrook & E Whitcombe
   3 and 2

Singles
Billy Burke beat Archie Compston 7 and 6
Gene Sarazen beat Fred Robson 7 and 6
Johnny Farrell lost to William H Davies 4 and 3
Wilfred Cox beat Abe Mitchell 3 and 1
Walter Hagen beat Charles Whitcombe 4 and 3
Densmore Shute beat Bert Hodson 8 and 6
Al Espinosa beat Ernest Whitcombe 2 and 1
Craig Wood lost to Arthur Havers 4 and 3

1929 *Moortown Golf Club, Leeds, Yorkshire,*
England May 26–27

Result: GB 7, USA 5
Captains: George Duncan (GB),
Walter Hagen (USA)

Foursomes
C Whitcombe & Compston halved with Farrell &
   Turnesa
Boomer & Duncan lost to Diegel & Espinosa
   7 and 5
Mitchell & Robson beat Sarazen & Dudley 2 and 1
E Whitcombe & Cotton lost to Golden & Hagen
   2 holes

Singles
Charles Whitcombe beat Johnny Farrell 8 and 6
George Duncan beat Walter Hagen 10 and 8
Abe Mitchell lost to Leo Diegel 9 and 8
Archie Compston beat Gene Sarazen 6 and 4
Aubrey Boomer beat Joe Turnesa 4 and 3
Fred Robson lost to Horton Smith 4 and 2
Henry Cotton beat Al Watrous 4 and 3
Ernest Whitcombe halved with Al Espinosa

1927 *Worcester Country Club, Worcester, MA, USA*
June 3–4

Result: USA 9½, GB 2½
Captains: W Hagen (USA), E Ray (GB)

Foursomes
Hagen & Golden beat Ray & Robson 2 and 1
Farrell & Turnesa beat Duncan & Compston
   8 and 6
Sarazen & Watrous beat Havers & Jolly 3 and 2
Diegel & Mehlhorn lost to Boomer & Whitcombe
   7 and 5

Singles
Bill Mehlhorn beat Archie Compston 1 hole
Johnny Farrell beat Aubrey Boomer 5 and 4
Johnny Golden beat Herbert Jolly 8 and 7
Leo Diegel beat Ted Ray 7 and 5
Gene Sarazen halved with Charles Whitcombe
Walter Hagen beat Arthur Havers 2 and 1
Al Watrous beat Fred Robson 3 and 2
Joe Turnesa lost to George Duncan 1 hole

Unofficial Ryder Cups

Great Britain v USA

1926 West Course, Wentworth GC, Surrey, England June 4–5

Result: GB 13½, USA 1½

Singles
Abe Mitchell beat Jim Barnes 8 and 7
George Duncan beat Walter Hagen 6 and 5
Aubrey Boomer beat Tommy Armour 2 and 1
Archie Compston lost to Bill Mehlhorn 1 hole
George Gadd beat Joe Kirkwood 8 and 7
Ted Ray beat Al Watrous 6 and 5
Fred Robson beat Cyril Walker 5 and 4
Arthur Havers beat Fred McLeod 10 and 9
Ernest Whitcombe halved with Emmett French
Herbert Jolly beat Joe Stein 3 and 2

Foursomes
Mitchell & Duncan beat Barnes & Hagen 9 and 8
Boomer & Compston beat Armour & Kirkwood 3 and 2
Gadd & Havers beat Mehlhorn & Watrous 3 and 2
Ray & Robson beat Walker & McLeod 3 and 2
Whitcombe & Jolly beat French & Stein 3 and 2

1921 King's Course, Gleneagles Hotel, Perthshire, Scotland June 6

Result: GB 9 USA 3
(no half points were awarded)

Singles
George Duncan beat Jock Hutchison 2 and 1
Abe Mitchell halved with Walter Hagen
Ted Ray lost to Emmet French 2 and 1
JH Taylor lost to Fred McLeod 1 hole
Harry Vardon beat Tom Kerrigan 3 and 1
James Braid beat Charles Hoffner 5 and 4
AG Havers lost to WE Reid 2 and 1
J Ockenden beat G McLean 5 and 4
J Sherlock beat Clarence Hackney 3 and 2
Joshua Taylor beat Bill Melhorn 3&2

Foursomes
George Duncan & Abe Mitchell halved with Jock Hutchison & Walter Hagen
Ted Ray & Harry Vardon beat Emmet French & Tom Kerrigan 5 and 4
James Braid & JH Taylor halved with Charles Hoffner & Fred McLeod
AG Havers & J Ockenden beat WE Reid & G McLean 6 and 5
J Sherlock & Joshua Taylor beat Clarence Hackney & W Melhorn 1 hole

Three matches were halved

INDIVIDUAL RECORDS

Matches were contested as Great Britain v USA from 1927 to 1953; as Great Britain & Ireland v USA from 1955 to 1977 and as Europe v USA from 1979. Non-playing captains are shown in brackets.

GB/GB&I/Europe

Name	Year	Played	Won	Lost	Halved
Jimmy Adams	*1939-47-49-51-53	7	2	5	0
Percy Alliss	1929-33-35-37	6	3	2	1
Peter Alliss	1953-57-59-61-63-65-67-69	30	10	15	5
Laurie Ayton	1949	0	0	0	0
Peter Baker	1993	4	3	1	0
Severiano Ballesteros (ESP)	1979-83-85-87-89-91-93-95-(97)	37	20	12	5
Harry Bannerman	1971	5	2	2	1
Brian Barnes	1969-71-73-75-77-79	25	10	14	1
Maurice Bembridge	1969-71-73-75	16	5	8	3
Thomas Bjørn (DEN)	1997-2002	6	3	2	1
Aubrey Boomer	1927-29	4	2	2	0
Ken Bousfield	1949-51-55-57-59-61	10	5	5	0
Hugh Boyle	1967	3	0	3	0
Harry Bradshaw	1953-55-57	5	2	2	1
Gordon J Brand	1983	1	0	1	0
Gordon Brand Jr	1987-89	7	2	4	1
Paul Broadhurst	1991	2	2	0	0
Eric Brown	1953-55-57-59-(69)-(71)	8	4	4	0
Ken Brown	1977-79-83-85-87	13	4	9	0
Stewart Burns	1929	0	0	0	0
Dick Burton	1935-37-*39-49	5	2	3	0
Jack Busson	1935	2	0	2	0
Peter Butler	1965-69-71-73	14	3	9	2
José Maria Canizares (ESP)	1981-83-85-89	11	5	4	2
Paul Casey	2004-06-08	9	3	2	4
Alex Caygill	1969	1	0	0	1
Clive Clark	1973	1	0	1	0
Howard Clark	1977-81-85-87-89-95	15	10	7	3
Darren Clarke	1997-99-2002-04-06	20	7	7	3
Neil Coles	1961-63-65-67-69-71-73-77	40	12	21	7

In 1939 a GB team was named but the match was not played because of the Second World War

Name	Year	Played	Won	Lost	Halved
Andrew Coltart	1999	1	0	1	0
Archie Compston	1927-29-31	6	1	4	1
Henry Cotton	1929-37-*39-47-(53)	6	2	4	0
Bill Cox	1935-37	3	0	2	1
Allan Dailey	1933	0	0	0	0
Fred Daly	1947-49-51-53	8	3	4	1
Eamonn Darcy	1975-77-81-87	11	1	8	2
William Davies	1931-33	4	2	2	0
Peter Dawson	1977	3	1	2	0
Luke Donald	2004-06-10	11	8	2	1
Norman Drew	1959	1	0	0	1
George Duncan	1927-29-31	5	2	3	0
Syd Easterbrook	1931-33	3	2	1	0
Nick Faldo	1977-79-81-83-85-87-89-91-93-95-97-(08)	46	23	19	4
John Fallon	1955-(63)	1	1	0	0
Niclas Fasth (SWE)	2002	3	0	2	1
Max Faulkner	1947-49-51-53-57	8	1	7	0
David Feherty	1991	3	1	1	1
Ross Fisher	2010	4	2	2	0
Pierre Fulke (SWE)	2002	2	0	1	1
George Gadd	1927	0	0	0	0
Bernard Gallacher	1969-71-73-75-77-79-81-83-(91)-(93)-(95)	31	13	13	5
Sergio García (ESP)	1999-2002-04-06-08	24	14	6	4
John Garner	1971-73	1	0	1	0
Antonio Garrido (ESP)	1979	5	1	4	0
Ignacio Garrido (ESP)	1997	4	0	1	3
David Gilford	1991-95	6	3	3	0
Eric Green	1947	0	0	0	0
Malcolm Gregson	1967	4	0	4	0
Joakim Haeggman (SWE)	1993	2	1	1	0
Tom Haliburton	1961-63	6	0	6	0
Søren Hansen (DEN)	2008	3	0	2	1
Peter Hanson (SWE)	2010	3	1	2	0
Jack Hargreaves	1951	0	0	0	0
Padraig Harrington	1999-2002-04-06-08-10	25	9	13	3
Arthur Havers	1927-31-33	6	3	3	0
Jimmy Hitchcock	1965	3	0	3	0
Bert Hodson	1931	1	0	1	0
Reg Horne	1947	0	0	0	0
Tommy Horton	1975-77	8	1	6	1
David Howell	2004-06	5	3	1	1
Brian Huggett	1963-67-69-71-73-75-(77)	25	9	10	6
Bernard Hunt	1953-57-59-61-63-65-67-69-(73)-(75)	28	6	16	6
Geoffrey Hunt	1963	3	0	3	0
Guy Hunt	1975	3	0	2	1
Tony Jacklin	1967-69-71-73-75-77-79-(83)-(85)-(87)-(89)	35	13	14	8
John Jacobs	1955-(79)-(81)	2	2	0	0
Mark James	1977-79-81-89-91-93-95-(99)	24	8	15	1
Edward Jarman	1935	1	0	1	0
Miguel Angel Jiménez (ESP)	1999-2004-08-10	15	4	8	3
Per-Ulrik Johansson (SWE)	1995-97	5	3	2	0
Herbert Jolly	1927	2	0	2	0
Robert Karlsson (SWE)	2006-08	7	1	2	4
Martin Kaymer (GER)	2010	4	2	1	0
Michael King	1979	1	0	1	0
Sam King	1937-*39-47-49	5	1	3	1
Arthur Lacey	1933-37-(51)	3	0	3	0
Barry Lane	1993	3	0	3	0
Bernhard Langer (GER)	1981-83-85-87-89-91-93-95-97-2002-(04)	42	21	15	6
Paul Lawrie	1999	5	3	1	1
Arthur Lees	1947-49-51-55	8	4	4	0
Thomas Levet (FRA)	2004	3	1	2	0
Sandy Lyle	1979-81-83-85-87	18	7	9	2
Graeme McDowell	2008-10	8	4	2	2
Paul McGinley	2002-04-06	9	2	2	5
Rory McIlroy (NIR)	2010	4	1	1	2
Jimmy Martin	1965	1	0	1	0
Peter Mills	1957-59	1	1	0	0
Abe Mitchell	1929-31-33	6	4	2	0
Ralph Moffitt	1961	1	0	1	0
Edoardo Molinari (ITA)	2010	3	0	1	2
Francesco Molinari (ITA)	2010	3	0	2	1
Colin Montgomerie	1991-93-95-97-99-2002-04-06-(10)	36	20	9	7

Name	Year	Played	Won	Lost	Halved
Christy O'Connor Jr	1975-89	4	1	3	0
Christy O'Connor Sr	1955-57-59-61-63-65-67-69-71-73	36	11	21	4
José María Olazábal (ESP)	1987-89-91-93-97-99-2006	31	18	8	5
John O'Leary	1975	4	0	4	0
Peter Oosterhuis	1971-73-75-77-79-81	28	14	11	3
Alf Padgham	1933-35-37-*39	6	0	6	0
John Panton	1951-53-61	5	0	5	0
Jesper Parnevik (SWE)	1997-99-2002	11	4	3	4
Alf Perry	1933-35-37	4	0	3	1
Manuel Pinero (ESP)	1981-85	9	6	3	0
Lionel Platts	1965	5	1	2	2
Eddie Polland	1973	2	0	2	0
Ian Poulter	2004-08-10	11	8	3	0
Phillip Price	2002	2	1	1	0
Ronan Rafferty	1989	3	1	2	0
Ted Ray	1927	2	0	2	0
Dai Rees	1937-*39-47-49-51-53-55-57-59-61-(67)	18	7	10	1
Steven Richardson	1991	4	2	2	0
José Rivero (ESP)	1985-87	5	2	3	0
Fred Robson	1927-29-31	6	2	4	0
Costantino Rocca (ITA)	1993-95-97	11	6	5	0
Justin Rose	2008	4	3	1	0
Jarmo Sandelin (SWE)	1999	1	0	1	0
Syd Scott	1955	2	0	2	0
Des Smyth	1979-81	7	2	5	0
Henrik Stenson (SWE)	2006-08	7	2	3	2
Dave Thomas	1959-63-65-67	18	3	10	5
Sam Torrance	1981-83-85-87-89-91-93-95-(2002)	27	7	15	5
Peter Townsend	1969-71	11	3	8	0
Jean Van de Velde (FRA)	1999	1	0	1	0
Brian Waites	1983	4	1	3	0
Philip Walton	1995	2	1	1	0
Charlie Ward	1947-49-51	6	1	5	0
Paul Way	1983-85	9	6	2	1
Harry Weetman	1951-53-55-57-59-61-63-(65)	15	2	11	2
Norman Wood	1975	3	1	2	0
Ian Woosnam	1983-85-87-89-91-93-95-97-(2006)	31	14	12	5
Lee Westwood	1997-99-2002-04-06-08-10	28	14	8	6
Charles Whitcombe	1927-29-31-33-35-37-*39-(49)	9	3	2	4
Ernest Whitcombe	1929-31-35	6	1	4	1
Reg Whitcombe	1935-*39	1	0	1	0
George Will	1963-65-67	15	2	11	2
Oliver Wilson	2008	2	1	1	0

United States of America

Name	Year	Played	Won	Lost	Halved
Tommy Aaron	1969-73	6	1	4	1
Skip Alexander	1949-51	2	1	1	0
Paul Azinger	1989-91-93-2002-(08)	16	5	8	3
Jerry Barber	1955-61	5	1	4	0
Miller Barber	1969-71	7	1	4	2
Herman Barron	1947	1	1	0	0
Andy Bean	1979-87	6	4	2	0
Frank Beard	1969-71	8	2	3	3
Chip Beck	1989-91-93	9	6	2	1
Homero Blancas	1973	4	2	1	1
Tommy Bolt	1955-57	4	3	1	0
Julius Boros	1959-63-65-67	16	9	3	4
Gay Brewer	1967-73	9	5	3	1
Billy Burke	1931-33	3	3	0	0
Jack Burke	1951-53-55-57-59-(73)	8	7	1	0
Walter Burkemo	1953	1	0	1	0
Mark Calcavecchia	1987-89-91-2002	14	6	7	1
Chad Campbell	2004-06-08	9	3	4	2
Billy Casper	1961-63-65-67-69-71-73-75-(79)	37	20	10	7
Stewart Cink	2002-04-06-08-10	19	5	7	7
Bill Collins	1961	3	1	2	0
Charles Coody	1971	3	0	2	1
John Cook	1993	2	1	1	0
Fred Couples	1989-91-93-95-97	20	7	9	4
Wilfred Cox	1931	2	2	0	0

* In 1939 a GB team was named but the match was not played because of the Second World War

Name	Year	Played	Won	Lost	Halved
Ben Crenshaw	1981-83-87-95-(99)	12	3	8	1
Ben Curtis	2008	3	1	1	1
Jimmy Demaret	*1941-47-49-51	6	6	0	0
Gardner Dickinson	1967-71	10	9	1	0
Leo Diegel	1927-29-31-33	6	3	3	0
Chris DiMarco	2004-06	8	2	4	2
Dale Douglass	1969	2	0	2	0
Dave Douglas	1953	2	1	0	1
Ed Dudley	1929-33-37	4	3	1	0
Olin Dutra	1933-35	4	1	3	0
David Duval	1999-2002	7	2	3	2
Lee Elder	1979	4	1	3	0
Al Espinosa	1927-29-31	4	2	1	1
Johnny Farrell	1927-29-31	6	3	2	1
Brad Faxon	1995-97	6	2	4	0
Dow Finsterwald	1957-59-61-63-(77)	13	9	3	1
Ray Floyd	1969-75-77-81-83-85-(89)-91-93	31	12	16	3
Doug Ford	1955-57-59-61	9	4	4	1
Rikki Fowler	2010	3	0	1	2
Fred Funk	2004	3	0	3	0
Ed Furgol	1957	1	0	1	0
Marty Furgol	1955	1	0	1	0
Jim Furyk	1997-99-2002-04-06-08-10	27	8	15	4
Jim Gallagher Jr	1993	3	2	1	0
Al Geiberger	1967-75	9	5	1	3
Vic Ghezzi	*1939-*41	0	0	0	0
Bob Gilder	1983	4	2	2	0
Bob Goalby	1963	5	3	1	1
Johnny Golden	1927-29	3	3	0	0
Lou Graham	1973-75-77	9	5	3	1
Hubert Green	1977-79-85	7	4	3	0
Ken Green	1989	4	2	2	0
Ralph Guldahl	1937-*39	2	2	0	0
Fred Haas Jr	1953	1	0	1	0
Jay Haas	1983-95-2004	12	4	6	2
Walter Hagen	1927-29-31-33-35-(37)	9	7	1	1
Bob Hamilton	1949	2	0	2	0
Chick Harbert	1949-55	2	2	0	0
Chandler Harper	1955	1	0	1	0
EJ (Dutch) Harrison	1947-49-51	3	2	1	0
Fred Hawkins	1957	2	1	1	0
Mark Hayes	1979	3	1	2	0
Clayton Heafner	1949-51	4	3	0	1
Jay Hebert	1959-61-(71)	4	2	1	1
Lionel Hebert	1957	1	0	1	0
J J Henry	2006	3	0	0	3
Dave Hill	1969-73-77	9	6	3	0
Jimmy Hines	*1939	0	0	0	0
Scott Hoch	1997-2002	7	2	3	2
Ben Hogan	*1941-47-(49)-51-(67)	3	3	0	0
J B Holmes	2008	3	2	0	1
Hale Irwin	1975-77-79-81-91	20	13	5	2
Tommy Jacobs	1965	4	3	1	0
Peter Jacobsen	1985-95	6	2	4	0
Don January	1965-77	7	2	3	2
Lee Janzen	1993-97	5	2	3	0
Dustin Johnson	2010	4	1	3	0
Zach Johnson	2006–10	7	3	3	1
Herman Keiser	1947	1	0	1	0
Anthony Kim	2008	4	2	1	1
Tom Kite	1979-81-83-85-87-89-93-(97)	28	15	9	4
Ted Kroll	1953-55-57	4	3	1	0
Matt Kuchar	2010	4	1	3	0
Ky Laffoon	1935	1	0	1	0
Tom Lehman	1995-97-99-(2006)	10	5	3	2
Tony Lema	1963-65	11	8	1	2
Justin Leonard	1997-99-08	12	2	4	6
Wayne Levi	1991	2	0	2	0
Bruce Lietzke	1981	3	0	2	1
Gene Littler	1961-63-65-67-69-71-75	27	14	5	8
Davis Love III	1993-95-97-99-2002-04	26	9	12	5
Jeff Maggert	1995-97-99	11	6	5	0
John Mahaffey	1979	3	1	2	0

* US teams were selected in 1939 and 1941, but did not play because of the Second World War

Name	Year	Played	Won	Lost	Halved
Hunter Mahan	2008–10	8	3	2	3
Mark McCumber	1989	3	2	1	0
Jerry McGee	1977	2	1	1	0
Harold McSpaden	*1939-*41	0	0	0	0
Tony Manero	1937	2	1	1	0
Lloyd Mangrum	*1941-47-49-51-53	8	6	2	0
Dave Marr	1965-(81)	6	4	2	0
Billy Maxwell	1963	4	4	0	0
Dick Mayer	1957	2	1	0	1
Bill Mehlhorn	1927	2	1	1	0
Dick Metz	*1939	0	0	0	0
Phil Mickelson	1995-97-99-2002-04-06-08–10	34	11	17	6
Cary Middlecoff	1953-55-59	6	2	3	1
Johnny Miller	1975-81	6	2	2	2
Larry Mize	1987	4	1	1	2
Gil Morgan	1979-83	6	1	2	3
Bob Murphy	1975	4	2	1	1
Byron Nelson	1937-*39-*41-47-(65)	4	3	1	0
Larry Nelson	1979-81-87	13	9	3	1
Bobby Nichols	1967	5	4	0	1
Jack Nicklaus	1969-71-73-75-77-81-(83)-(87)	28	17	8	3
Andy North	1985	3	0	3	0
Ed Oliver	1947-51-53	5	3	2	0
Mark O'Meara	1985-89-91-97-99	14	4	9	1
Jeff Overton	2010	4	2	2	0
Arnold Palmer	1961-63-65-67-71-73-(75)	32	22	8	2
Johnny Palmer	1949	2	0	2	0
Sam Parks	1935	1	0	0	1
Jerry Pate	1981	4	2	2	0
Steve Pate	1991-99	4	2	2	0
Corey Pavin	1991-93-95-(2010)	8	5	3	0
Calvin Peete	1983-85	7	4	2	1
Kenny Perry	2004-08	6	2	3	1
Henry Picard	1935-37-*39	4	3	1	0
Dan Pohl	1987	3	1	2	0
Johnny Pott	1963-65-67	7	5	2	0
Dave Ragan	1963	4	2	1	1
Henry Ransom	1951	1	0	1	0
Johnny Revolta	1935-37	3	2	1	0
Chris Riley	2004	3	1	1	1
Loren Roberts	1995	4	3	1	0
Chi Chi Rodriguez	1973	2	0	1	1
Bill Rogers	1981	4	1	2	1
Bob Rosburg	1959	2	2	0	0
Mason Rudolph	1971	3	1	1	1
Paul Runyan	1933-35-*39	4	2	2	0
Doug Sanders	1967	5	2	3	0
Gene Sarazen	1927-29-31-33-35-37-*41	12	7	2	3
Densmore Shute	1931-33-37	6	2	2	2
Dan Sikes	1969	3	2	1	0
Scott Simpson	1987	2	1	1	0
Horton Smith	1929-31-33-35-37-*39-*41	4	3	0	1
C Snead	1971-73-75	11	9	2	0
Sam Snead	1937-*39-*41-47-49-51-53-55-59-(69)	13	10	2	1
Ed Sneed	1977	2	1	0	1
Mike Souchak	1959-61	6	5	1	0
Craig Stadler	1983-85	8	4	2	2
Payne Stewart	1987-89-91-93-99	19	7	10	2
Ken Still	1969	3	1	2	0
Dave Stockton	1971-77-(91)	5	3	1	1
Curtis Strange	1983-85-87-89-95-2002	20	6	12	2
Steve Stricker	2008-10	7	3	3	1
Hal Sutton	1985-87-99-2002-(04)	16	7	5	4
Vaughn Taylor	2006	2	0	1	1
David Toms	2002-04-06	12	4	6	2
Lee Trevino	1969-71-73-75-79-81-(85)	30	17	7	6
Jim Turnesa	1953	1	1	0	0
Joe Turnesa	1927-29	4	1	2	1
Ken Venturi	1965	4	1	3	0
Scott Verplank	2002-06	5	4	1	0
Lanny Wadkins	1977-79-83-85-87-89-91-93-(95)	33	20	11	2
Art Wall Jr	1957-59-61	6	4	2	0
Al Watrous	1927-29	3	2	1	0

* US teams were selected in 1939 and 1941, but did not play because of the Second World War

Name	Year	Played	Won	Lost	Halved
Bubba Watson	2010	4	1	3	0
Tom Watson	1977-81-83-89-(93)	15	10	4	1
Boo Weekley	2008	3	2	0	1
Tom Weiskopf	1973-75	10	7	2	1
Brett Wetterich	2006	2	0	2	0
Craig Wood	1931-33-35-*41	4	1	3	0
Tiger Woods	1997-99-2002-04-06-10	29	13	14	2
Lew Worsham	1947	2	2	0	0
Fuzzy Zoeller	1979-83-85	10	1	8	1

The Vivendi Seve Trophy (inaugurated 2000) *St Nom La Bretche, France*

Captains: Continental Europe – Jean Van de Velde (FRA); GB&I – Paul McGinley (IRL)

First Day – Four balls
Miguel Angel Jiménez and Pablo Larrazabal lost to Symon Dyson and Jamie Donaldson 2 and 1
Peter Hanson and Raphael Jacquelin lost to Ross Fisher and Scott Jamieson 6 and 4
Anders Hansen and Francesco Molinari beat Lee Westwood and Mark Foster 1 hole
Matteo Manassero and Nicolas Colsaerts lost to Darren Clarke and David Horsey 2 and 1
Thomas Björn and Alex Noren lost to Ian Poulter and Robert Rock 5 and 3

Match position: Continental Europe 1, GB&I 4

Second Day – Four balls
Thomas Björn and Raphael Jacquelin halved with Simon Dyson and Jamie Donaldson
Peter Hanson and Alex Noren beat Robert Rock and Ian Poulter 5 and 3
Nicolas Colsaerts and Matteo Manassero beat Scott Jamieson and Ross Fisher 1 hole
Anders Hansen and Matteo Molinari lost to Mark Foster and Lee Westwood 5 and 3
Pablo Larrazabal and Miguel Angel Jiménez beat Darren Clarke and David Horsey 2 and 1

Match position: Continental Europe 4½, GB&I 5½

Third Day – Morning: Greensomes
Nicolas Colsaerts and Matteo Manassero lost to Symon Dyson and Jamie Donaldson 2 and 1
Peter Hanson and Alex Noren halved with David Horsey and Darren Clarke
Thomas Björn and Raphael Jacquelin lost to Ian Poulter and Ross Fisher 2 and 1
Miguel Angel Jiménez and Pablo Larrazabal lost to Lee Westwood and Scott Jamieson 4 and 3

Afternoon: Foursomes
Francesco Molinari and Matteo Manassero halved with Jamie Donaldson and Robert Rock
Ross Fisher and Mark Foster lost to Thomas Björn and Anders Hansen 3 and 2
Symon Dyson and Ian Poulter beat Alex Noren and Pablo Larrazabal 3 and 1
Lee Westwood and David Horsey beat Nicolas Colsaerts and Raphael Jacquelin 4 and 3

Match position: Continental Europe 6½, GB&I 11½

Fourth Day – Singles
Thomas Björn (DEN) beat Lee Westwood (ENG) 2 and 1
Anders Hansen (DEN) beat Symon Dyson (ENG) 1 hole
Francesco Molinari (ITA) beat Jamie Donaldson (WAL) 4 and 3
Alex Noren (SWE) beat Robert Rock (ENG) 4 and 3
Miguel Angel Jiménez (ESP) beat Darren Clarke (NIR) 4 and 2
Nicolas Colsaerts (BEL) halved with David Horsey (ENG)
Pablo Larrazabal (ESP) lost to Scott Jamieson (SCO) 1 hole
Matteo Manassero (ITA) lost to Ian Poulter (ENG) 1 hole
Raphael Jacquelin (FRA) lost to Mark Foster (ENG) 1 hole
Peter Hanson (SWE) halved with Ross Fisher (ENG)

Result: Continental Europe 12½, GB&I 15½

2000	Sunningdale, England	GB&I 12½, Europe 13½	
2002	Druid's Glen, Ireland	Europe 12½, GB&I 14½	
2003	El Saler, Spain	Europe 13, GB&I 15	
2005	The Wynyard, England	GB&I 16½, Europe, 11½	
2007	The Heritage, Ireland	GB&I 16½, Europe 11½	
2009	Golf de Saint-Nom-la-Bretèche, France	GB&I 16½, Europe 11½	

25th PGA Cup (Llandudno Trophy) (Instituted 1973) *CordeValle, San Martin, California*
Great Britain and Ireland Club Professionals v United States Club Professionals

Captains: USA – Jim Remy (Ludlow, Vermont); GB&I – Russell Weir (Dunoon)

First Day – Morning: Fourballs
David Hutsell (The Elkridge Club, MD) and Mark Sheftic (Merion, PA) beat Simon Edwards (Windermere) and David Shacklady (Mossock Hall) 3 and 2

Mike Small (University of Illinois) and Faber Jamerson (Falling River, VA) halved with Stuart Little (Minchinhampton) and Chris Gill (Exeter)

Danny Balin (Burning Tree, CT) and Scott Erdmann (Oswego Lake, OR) lost to John Wells (Cherry Burton) and Gary Brown (Malton) 1 hole.

Rob McClellan (Butler, PA) and Marty Jertson (Ping, AZ) beat Craig Goodfellow (Carlisle DR) and Rob Giles (Greenore, Co Louth) 1 hole

First Day – Afternoon: Foursomes
Sonny Skinner (River Pointe, GA) and Brad Lardon (Miramont. TX) halved with Simon Edwards and David Shacklady

David Hutsell and Mark Sheftic beat David Mortimer (Galway) and John Kennedy (Wexham Park) 6 and 5

Danny Balin and Scott Erdmann beat Chris Gill and Stuart Little 6 and 5

Rob McClellan and Marty Jertson beat Craig Goodfellow and Rob Giles 6 and 5

Match position: USA 6, GB&I 2

Second Day – Morning: Fourballs
David Hutsell and Mark Sheftic lost to David Shacklady and Simon Edwards 2 and 1

Mike Small and Faber Jamerson beat John Wells and Gary Brown 3 and 2

Danny Balin and Scott Erdmann lost to Chris Gill and Stuart Little 5 ad 4

Sonny Skinner and Brad Lardon halved with David Mortimer and Craig Goodfellow

Second Day – Afternoon: Foursomes
Rob McClellan and Marty Jertson beat Simon Edwards and David Shacklady 2 and 1

David Hutsell and Mark Sheftic lost to John Wells and Gary Brown 2 holes

Mike Small and Faber Jamerson beat John Kennedy and Chris Gill 4 and 3

Sonny Skinner and Brad Lardon beat Stuart Little and David Mortimer 2 holes

Match position: USA 10½, GB&I 5½

Third Day: Singles
Marty Jertson beat Craig Goodfellow 5 and 4

Danny Balin beat Chris Gill 1 hole

Sonny Skinner halved with Stuart Little

Mike Small lost to Rob Giles 1 hole

David Hutsell lost to David Shacklady 3 and 2

Mark Sheftic beat John Wells 1 hole

Rob McClellan halved with Simon Edwards

Faber Jamerson beat Gary Brown 3 and 2

Brad Lardon beat David Mortimer 6 and 4

Scott Erdmann beat John Kennedy 6 and 5

Result: 17½, GB&I 8½

Year	Result	Venue	Score	Year	Result	Venue	Score
1973	USA	Pinehurst, NC	13–3	1988	USA	The Belfry, England	15½–10½
1974	USA	Pinehurst, NC	11½–4½	1990	USA	Turtle Point, Kiawah Island, SC	19–7
1975	USA	Hillside, Southport, England	9½–6½	1992	USA	K Club, Ireland	15–11
1976	USA	Moortown, Leeds, England	9½–6½	1994	USA	Palm Beach, Florida	15–11
1977	Halved	Mission Hills, Palm Springs	8½–8½	1996	Halved	Gleneagles, Scotland	13–13
1978	GB&I	St Mellion, Cornwall	10½–6½	1998	USA	The Broadmoor, Colorado Springs, CO	11½–4½
1979	GB&I	Castletown, Isle of Man	12½–4½				
1980	USA	Oak Tree, Edmond, OK	15–6	2000	USA	Celtic Manor, Newport, Wales	13½–12½
1981	Halved	Turnberry Isle, Miami, FL	10½–10½	2002	Cancelled		
1982	USA	Holston Hills, Knoxville, TN	13–7	2003	USA	Port St Lucie, FL	19–7
1983	GB&I	Muirfield, Scotland	14½–6½	2005	GB&I	K Club, Dublin, R.o.I.	15–11
1984	GB&I	Turnberry, Scotland	12½–8½	2007	USA	Reynolds Plantation, GA	13½–12½
Played alternate years from 1984				2009	USA	The Carrick, Loch Lomond, Scotland	17½–8½
1986	USA	Knollwood, Lake Fore, IL	16–9				

Sovereign Insurance International Team Matches *Scarboro G&CC, Toronto, Canada*
1 Canada 562; 2 USA 567; 3 International 572

Winning team: Canada (eight scores to count) – Stuart Anderson 70, Brad Fritsch 71, Richard Scott 70, Adam Hadwin 69, Mike Mezei 73, Dustin Risdon 69, Devin Carrey 68, Roger Sloan 76, Danny Sahl 72, Robbie Greenwell 77

PGAs of Europe International Team Championship   *Vale Do Lobo, Portugal*

1	France (Bernard Cornut, Stephane Lahary and Benjamin Nicolay)	140-140-138-139—557
2	Scotland (Jim McKinnon, Alan Lockhart and Chris Currie)	145-137-141-143—566
	Spain (Francisco Cea, Ismael del Castillo and Fernando Roca)	142-138-145-141—566

Other scores: 4 Italy 567; 5 England 568; 6 Ireland, Denmark 569; 8 Austria 575; 9 Sweden 578; 10 Poland 582; 11 The Netherlands 583; 12 South Africa, Portugal, Germany 584; 15 Wales 585; 16 Switzerland 587; 17 Czech Republic 593; 18 UAE 603; 19 Norway, Belgium 608; 21 Finland 615; 22 Croatia 616; 23 Iceland 620; 24 Slovenia, Russia 624; 26 Hungary 626

1990	Scotland	1995	Spain	2000	Wales	2005	France	2008	Ireland
1991	Netherlands	1996	Scotland	2001	Spain	2006	Scotland	2009	Wales
1992	Scotland	1997	Scotland	2002	Spain	2007	Austria*	2010	England
1993	Scotland	1998	Ireland	2003	Spain	*Beat Wales at 2nd		
1994	*Not played*	1999	England	2004	England	extra hole		

The Royal Trophy   (Asia v Europe)   *Black Mountain GC, Hua Hin, Thailand*   [7420–72]

Captains: Asia: Naomichi (Joe) Osaki (JPN); Europe: Colin Montgomerie (SCO)

Asia names first

First Day – Foursomes
Liang & Noh beat Stenson & Edfors 3 and 2
Ikeda & Kim lost to Montgomerie & Davies 2 and 1
Ishikawa & Sonoda beat Manassero & Martin 3 and 2
Jaidee & Singh lost to Hanson & Andersson Hed 7 and 5

Second Day – Fourball
Liang & Noh beat Montgomerie & Davies 5 and 4
Ishikawa & Sonoda beat Manassero & Martin 3 and 2
Kim & Singh beat Stenson & Edfors 1 up
Ikeda & Jaidee beat Hanson & Andersson Hed 1 up

Third Day – Singles
Liang Wen-chong (CHN) lost to Peter Hanson (SWE) 7 and 6
Noh Seung-yul (KOR) halved with Henrik Stenson (SWE)
Yuta Ikeda (JPN) lost to Fredrik Andersson Hed (SWE) 2 and 1
Ryo Ishikawa (JPN) lost to Rhys Davies (WAL) 5 and 2

Shunsuke Sonoda (JPN) lost to Matteo Manassero (ITA) 1 up
Kim Kyung-tae (KOR) lost to Colin Montgomerie (SCO) 3 and 1
Jeev Milkha Singh (IND) lost to Pablo Martin (ESP) 1 up
Thongchai Jaidee (THA) halved with Johan Edfors (SWE) 5 and 4

Result: Asia 7, Europe 9

2006	Europe 9, Asia 7	Amata Spring CC, Chonburi, Thailand	2009	Asia 10, Europe 6	Amata Spring CC, Chonburi, Thailand
2007	Europe 12½, Asia 3½	Amata Spring CC, Chonburi, Thailand	2010	Europe 8½, Asia 7½	Amata Spring CC, Chonburi, Thailand
2008	*Cancelled*				

9th Presidents Cup   (Instituted 1994)   *Royal Melbourne Golf Club, Victoria, Australia*

Captains: Fred Couples (USA), Greg Norman (International)   *International names first*

First Day – Foursomes
Ernie Els (RSA) and Ryo Ishikawa (JPN) lost to Bubba Watson and Webb Simpson 4 and 2
Geoff Ogilvy (AUS) and Charl Schwartzel (RSA) halved with Jay Haas and Nick Watney
Aaron Baddeley (AUS) and Jason Day (AUS) halved with Dustin Johnson and Matt Kuchar
Retief Goosen (RSA) and Robert Allenby (AUS) lost to Phil Mickelson and Jim Furyk 4 and 3
K T Kim (KOR) and Y E Yang (KOR) lost to Hunter Mahan and David Toms 6 and 5
Adam Scott (AUS) and K J Choi (KOR) beat Tiger Woods and Steve Stricker 7 and 6

Match position: International 2, USA 4

Second Day – Fourballs

Els and ishikawa lost to Watson and Simpson
3 and 1

Baddeley and Day beat Johnson and Woods 1 hole

Scott and Kim lost to Mickelson and Furyk
2 and 1

Match position: International 5, USA 7

Ogilvy and Choi beat Haas and Watney 1 hole

Yang and Allenby lost to Kuchar and Stricker
4 and 3

Goosen and Schwartzel beat Mahan and Toms
2 and 1

Third Day – Foursomes

Allenby and Ogilvy lost to Simpson and Watson
3 and 2

Els and Ishikawa beat Haas and Kuchar 1 hole

Goosen and Schwartzel lost to Mahan and Toms
5 and 4

Scott and Choi lost to Woods and Johnson 3 and 2

Baddeley and Day lost to Mickelson and Furyk
2 and 1

Match position: International 9, USA 13

Third Day – Fourballs

Goosen and Schwartzel beat Simpson and Watson
2 and 1

Kim and Yang beat Woods and Johnson 1 hole

Ogilvy and Choi beat Stricker and Kuchar 1 hole

Baddeley and Day lost to Mahan and Haas
2 and 1

Scott and Els lost to Furyk and Watney 1 hole

Fourth Day – Singles

K T Kim beat Webb Simpson 1 hole

Charl Schwartzel beat Dustin Johnson 2 and 1

Ryo Ishikawa beat Bubba Watson 3 and 2

Geoff Ogilvy beat Jay Haas 2 holes

Jason Day lost to Hunter Mahan 5 and 3

K J Choi lost to Nick Watney 3 and 2

Adam Scott beat Phil Mickelson 2 and 1

Retief Goosen beat Matt Kuchar 1 hole

Ernie Els lost to Jim Furyk 4 and 3

Robert Allenby lost to David Toms 7 and 5

Aaron Baddeley lost to Tiger Woods 4 and 3

Y E Yang lost to Steve Stricker 2 and 1

Result: International 15, USA 19

1994 United States 20 International Team 12
 Captains: USA Hale Irwin; International David Graham
 Robert Trent Jones GC, Prince William County, Virginia
1996 United States 18½, International 15½
 Captains: USA Arnold Palmer; International Peter Thomson
 Robert Trent Jones GC, Prince William County, Virginia
1998 Interntational 20½, USA 12½
 Captains: USA Jack Nicklaus; Internationals Peter Thomson
 Royal Melbourne GC, Victoria , Australia
2000 United States 21½, Interntational 10½
 Captains: USA Ken Venturi; International Peter Thomson
 Robert Trent Jones GC, Prince William County, Virginia

2003 United States 17, Interntaional Team 17
 Captains: USA Jack Nicklaus; International Gary Player
 The Links at Fancourt Hotel and CC Estate, South Africa
2005 United States 18½, International 15½
 Captains: USA Jack Nicklaus; International Gary Player
 Robert Trent Jones GC, Prince William County, Virginia
2007 United States 19½, International 14½
 Captains: USA Jack Nicklaus; International Gary Player
 The Royal Montreal GC, Quebec, Canada
2009 United States 19½, Interntational 14½
 Captains: USA Fred Couples; International Greg Norman
 Harding Park Golf Course, San Francisco, California

Hyundai Capital Invitational (KB Financial Million Yard Cup – Korea v Japan)   *Gimhae, Korea*

Korean names first

First Day – Foursomes:

Soon Sang Hong and Dae Hyun Kim 71, Komei Oda and Hiroo Kawai 68

Ho Sung Choi and Do Hoon Kim 71, Michio Matsumura and Fujita Hiroyuki 66

Sang Hyun Park and Seong Ho Lee 75, Tadahiro Takayama and Tomohiro Kondo 71

Kyung Nam Kang and Sang Moon Bae 71, Ryo Ishikawa and Shunsuke Sonoda 72

Y E Yang and Kyung Tae Kim 70, Shingo Katayama and Yuta Ikeda 73

Match position: Korea 2 Japan 3

Second Day – Fourballs:

Do Hoon Kim and Ho Sung Choi 63, Tadahiro Takayama and Tomohiro Kondo 63

Seong Ho Lee and Soon Sang Hong 62, Komei Oda and Hiroo Kawai 64

Dae Hyun Kim and Sang Hyun Park 65, Michio Matsumura and Fujita Hiroyuki 65

Sang Moon Bae and Kyung Nam Kang 64, Shingo Katayama and Yuta Ikeda 62

Y E Yang and Kyung Tae Kim 62, Ryo Ishikawa and Shunsuke Sonoda 66

Match position: Korea 5, Japan 5

Hyundai Capital Invitational *continued*

Third Day – Singles:
Ho Sung Choi 69, Komei Oda 76
Sang Hyun Park 68, Shunsuke Sonoda 71
Do Hoon Kim 70, Matsumura Michio 74
Seong Ho Lee 72, Hiroo Kawai 71
Soon Sang Hong 67, Tadahiro Takayama 66

Kyung Nam Kang 70, Ryo Ishikawa 68
Dae Hyun Kim 67, Tomohiro Kondo 69
Sang Moon Bae 68, Yuta Ikeda 77
Kyung Tae Kim 70, Hiroyuki Fujita 70
Y E Yang 68, Shingo Katayama 72

Result: Korea 11½, Japan 8½▵221

2010   Korea 9½, Japan 10½   Haechivi Jeju CC, Korea

Mission Hills World Cup Qualifiers
(Format: Fourballs 1st and 3rd rounds, foursomes 2nd and 4th)

Asia Qualifier   *Seri Selangor GC, Petaling Jaya, Malaysia*   [Par 71]
New Zealand* (Michael Hendry and Gareth Paddison)   65-75-64-67—271
Singapore (Mardan Mamat and Lam Chih-Bing)   63-70-66-72—271
Singapore conceded victory to New Zealand)
South Korea (Kim Hyung-Sung) and Park Sung-Joon)   70-69-67-69—275

Philippines, Malaysia 278; 6 India 280; 7 Myanmar, Pakistan 283; 9 Sri Lanka 284; 10 Chinese Tapiei 292; 11 Indonesia 298; 12 Hong Kong 299; 13 Ghana 301; 14 Vietnam 302; 15 Senegal 317; 16 Brunei Disq.

Europe Qualifier   *Estonia G and CC*   [6462–72]
Austria (Roland Steiner and Florian Pragant)   63-73-61-67—264
Netherlands (Joost Luiten and Robert Jan Derksen)   62-74-63-68—267
Portugal (Ricardo and Hugo Santos)   69-71-61-72—273

Greece 274; 5 Switzerland 275; 6 Chile 276; 7 Finland, Estonia, Poland, 286; 10 Slovenia 290, 11 Croatia 303

South America Qualifier   *Caracas, Venezuela.*
Brazil (Adilson de Silva and Lucas Lee)   63-65-60-65—253
Mexico (José de Jesus Rodriguez and Oscar Serna)   62-70-59-68—259
Guatemala (José Toledo and Pablo Acuna)   62-67-64-67—260

4 Argentina 262; 5 Canada 263; 6 Venezuela, Dominican Republic 270; 8 Paraguay 271; 9 Puerto Rico 274; 10 Peru 279; 11 Bolivia, Bermuda 283; 13 Uruguay 286; 14 Costa Rica 291

56th World Cup of Golf   *Mission Hills, Shenzhen, China*   [7441–72]

(formerly known as the Canada Cup but now run separately by the various world golf tours. In 2010, it was announced that the event would change from annual to biennial, held in odd-numbered years, to accommodate the 2016 inclusion of golf in the Olympics)

				$ per team
1	United States	Matt Kuchar and Gary Woodland	64-70-63-67—264	2,400,000
2	England	Ian Poulter and Justin Rose	66-69-68-63—266	1,300,000
	Germany	Alex Cejka and Martin Kaymer	65-71-61-69—266	1,300,000
4	Australia	Richard Green and Brendon Jones	61-70-67-69—267	430,000
	Netherlands	Robert-Jan Derksen and Joost Luiten	64-71-64-68—267	430,000
	Ireland	Graeme McDowell and Rory McIlroy	63-68-64-72—267	430,000
	Scotland	Stephen Gallacher and Martin Laird	63-69-69-66—267	430,000
8	Wales	Rhys Davies and Jamie Donaldson	67-69-65-67—268	200,000
9	Spain	Miguel Angel Jiménez and Alvaro Quiros	65-69-68-67—269	150,000
	Korea	Kim Hyung-Sung and Park Sung-Joon	66-71-64-68—269	150,000
11	Zimbabwe	Brendon de Jonge and Bruce McDonald	66-70-67-67—270	105,000
12	South Africa	Louis Oosthuizen and Charl Schwartzel	68-68-61-74—271	96,000
13	Denmark	Thorbjørn Olesen and Anders Hansen	65-72-68-67—272	87,000
	France	Grégory Bourdy and Raphaël Jacquelin	66-70-68-68—272	87,000
	Mexico	José de Jesus Rodríguez and Óscar Serna	66-69-65-72—272	87,000
16	New Zealand	Michael Hendry and Gareth Paddison	66-68-68-71—273	74,000
17	Italy	Edoardo Molinari and Francesco Molinari	67-69-64-74—274	72,000
18	China	Liang Wen-Chong and Zhang Xin-Jun	68-68-68-71—275	70,000

18T	Thailand	Kiradech Aphibarnrat and Thongchai Jaidee	66-70-68-71—275	70,000
20	Austria	Florian Praegant and Roland Steiner	69-72-65-70—276	66,000
	Japan	Tetsuji Hiratsuka and Yuta Ikeda	66-70-66-74—276	66,000
	Portugal	Hugo Santos and Ricardo Santos	70-68-66-72—276	66,000
23	Brazil	Lucas Lee and Adilson da Silva	68-71-67-72—278	60,000
	Colombia	Camilo Villegas and Manuel Villegas	65-76-64-73—278	60,000
25	Sweden	Robert Karlsson and Alexander Noren	66-74-66-73—279	56,000
26	Singapore	Lam Chih Bing and Mardan Mamat	68-75-65-74—282	54,000
27	Guatemala	Pablo Acuna and José Toledo	75-74-66-70—285	52,000
28	Belgium	Nicolas Colsaerts and Jérôme Theunis	67-77-68-84—296	50,000

1953 I Argentina (A Cerda and R de Vicenzo); 2 Canada (S Leonard and B Kerr) 287 Montreal
(Individual: A Cerda, Argentina, 140)

1954 I Australia (P Thomson and K Nagle); 2 Argentina (A Cerda and R de Vicenzo) 556 Laval-Sur-Lac
(Individual: S Leonard, Canada, 275)

1955 I United States (C Harbert and E Furgol); 2 Australia (P Thomson and K Nagle) 560 Washington
(Individual: E Furgol*, USA (*after a play-off with P Thomson and F van Donck, 279))

1956 I United States (B Hogan and S Snead); 2 South Africa (A Locke and G Player) 567 Wentworth
(Individual: B Hogan, USA, 277)

1957 I Japan (T Nakamura and K Ono); 2 United States (S Snead and J Demaret) 557 Tokyo
(Individual: T Nakamura, Japan, 274)

1958 I Ireland (H Bradshaw and C O'Connor); 2 Spain (A Miguel and S Miguel) 579 Mexico City
(Individual: A Miguel*, Spain (*after a play-off with H Bradshaw, 286))

1959 I Australia (P Thomson and K Nagle); 2 United States (S Snead and C Middlecoff) 563 Melbourne
(Individual: S Leonard*, Canada, 275 (*after a tie with P Thomson, Australia))

1960 I United States (S Snead and A Palmer); 2 England (H Weetman and B Hunt) 565 Portmarnock
(Individual: F van Donck, Belgium, 279)

1961 I United States (S Snead and J Demaret); 2 Australia (P Thomson and K Nagle) 560 Puerto Rico
(Individual: S Snead, USA, 272)

1962 I United States (S Snead and A Palmer); 2 Argentina (F de Luca and R De Vicenzo) 557 Buenos Aires
(Individual: R De Vicenzo, Argentina, 276)

1963 I United States (A Palmer and J Nicklaus); 2 Spain (S Miguel and R Sota) 482 St Nom-La-
(Individual: J Nicklaus, USA, 237 – tournament reduced to 36 holes because of fog) Breteche

1964 I United States (A Palmer and J Nicklaus); 2 Argentina (R De Vicenzo and L Ruiz) 554 Maui, Hawaii
(Individual: J Nicklaus, USA, 276)

1965 I South Africa (G Player and H Henning); 2 Spain (A Miguel and R Sota) 571 Madrid
(Individual: G Player, South Africa, 281)

1966 I United States (J Nicklaus and A Palmer); 2 South Africa (G Player and H Henning) 548 Tokyo
(Individual: G Knudson* Canada, 272 (*after a play-off with H Sugimoto, Japan))

1967 I United States (J Nicklaus and A Palmer); 2 New Zealand (R Charles and W Godfrey) 557 Mexico City
(Individual: A Palmer, USA, 276)

1968 I Canada (A Balding and G Knudson); 2 United States (J Boros and L Trevino) 569 Olgiata, Rome
(Individual: A Balding, Canada, 274)

1969 I United States (O Moody and L Trevino); 2 Japan (T Kono and H Yasuda) 552 Singapore
(Individual: L Trevino, USA, 275)

1970 I Australia (B Devlin and D Graham); 2 Argentina (R De Vicenzo and V Fernandez) 545 Buenos Aires
(Individual: R De Vicenzo, Argentina, 269)

1971 I United States (J Nicklaus and L Trevino); 2 South Africa (H Henning and G Player) 555 Palm Beach, Florida
(Individual: J Nicklaus, USA, 271)

1972 I Taiwan (H Min-Nan and LL Huan); 2 Japan (T Kono and T Murakami) 438 Melbourne
(Three rounds only – Individual: H Min-Nan, Taiwan, 217)

1973 I United States (J Nicklaus and J Miller); 2 South Africa (G Player and H Baiocchi) 558 Marbella, Spain
(Individual: J Miller, USA, 277)

1974 I South Africa (R Cole and D Hayes); 2 Japan (I Aoki and M Ozaki) 554 Caracas
(Individual: R Cole, South Africa, 271)

1975 I United States (J Miller and L Graham); 2 Taiwan (H Min-Nan and KC Hsiung) 554 Bangkok
(Individual: J Miller, USA, 275)

1976 I Spain (S Ballesteros and M Pinero); 2 United States (J Pate and D Stockton) 574 Palm Springs
(Individual: EP Acosta, Mexico, 282)

1977 I Spain (S Ballesteros and A Garrido); 2 Philippines (R Lavares and B Arda) 591 Manilla, Philippines
(Individual: G Player, South Africa, 289)

1978 I United States (J Mahaffey and A North); 2 Australia (G Norman and W Grady) 564 Hawaii
(Individual: J Mahaffey, USA, 281)

1979 I United States (J Mahaffey and H Irwin); 2 Scotland (A Lyle and K Brown) 575 Glyfada, Greece
(Individual: H Irwin, USA, 285)

1980 I Canada (D Halldorson and J Nelford); 2 Scotland (A Lyle and S Martin) 572 Bogota
(Individual: A Lyle, Scotland, 282)

1981 *Not played*

World Cup of Golf continued

1982   1 Spain (M Pinero and JM Canizares); 2 United States (B Gilder and B Clampett)   563   Acapulco
(Individual: M Pinero, Spain, 281)
1983   1 United States (R Caldwell and J Cook); 2 Canada (D Barr and J Anderson)   565   Pondok Inah,
(Individual: D Barr, Canada, 276)   Jakarta
1984   1 Spain (JM Canizares and J Rivero); 2 Scotland (S Torrance and G Brand Jr)   414   Olgiata, Rome
(Played over 54 holes because of storms – Individual: JM Canizares, Spain, 205)
1985   1 Canada (D Halidorson and D Barr); 2 England (H Clark and P Way)   559   La Quinta, Calif.
(Individual: H Clark, England, 272)
1986   Not played
1987   1 Wales* (I Woosnam and D Llewelyn); 2 Scotland (S Torrance and A Lyle)   574   Kapalua, Hawaii
(*Wales won play-off – Individual: I Woosnam, Wales, 274)
1988   1 United States (B Crenshaw and M McCumber); 2 Japan (T Ozaki and M Ozaki)   560   Royal Melbourne,
(Individual: B Crenshaw, USA, 275)   Australia
1989   1 Australia (P Fowler and W Grady); 2 Spain (JM Olazábal and JM Canizares)   278   Las Brisas, Spain
(Played over 36 holes because of storms – Individual: P Fowler)
1990   1 Germany (B Langer and T Giedeon); 2 England (M James and R Boxall)   tied   556   Grand Cypress
Ireland (R Rafferty and D Feherty)   Resort, Orlando,
(Individual: P Stewart, USA, 271)   Florida
1991   1 Sweden (A Forsbrand and P-U Johansson); 2 Wales (I Woosnam and P Price)   563   La Querce, Rome
(Individual: I Woosnam, Wales, 273)
1992   1 USA (F Couples and D Love III); 2 Sweden (A Forsbrand and P-U Johansson)   548   La Moraleja II,
(Individual: B Ogle*, Australia, 270 (*after a tie with Ian Woosnam, Wales))   Madrid, Spain
1993   1 USA (F Couples and D Love III); 2 Zimbabwe (N Price and M McNulty)   556   Lake Nona, Orlando,
(Individual: B Langer, Germany, 272)   Forida
1994   1 USA (F Couples and D Love III); 2 Zimbabwe (M McNulty and T Johnstone)   536   Dorado Beach,
(Individual: F Couples, USA, 265)   Puerto Rico
1995   1 USA (F Couples and D Love III); 2 Australia (B Ogle and R Allenby)   543   Mission Hills,
(Individual: D Love III, USA, 267)   Shenzhen, China
1996   1 South Africa (E Els and W Westner); 2 USA (T Lehman and S Jones)   547   Erinvale, Cape Town
(Individual: E Els, S. Africa, 272)   South Africa
1997   1 Ireland (P Harrington and P McGinley); 2 Scotland (C Montgomerie and R Russell)   545   Kiawah Island, SC
(Individual: C Montgomerie, Scotland, 266)
1998   1 England (N Faldo and D Carter); 2 Italy (C Rocca and M Florioli)   568   Auckland,
(Individual: Scott Verplank, USA, 279)   New Zealand
1999   1 USA (T Woods and M O'Meara); 2 Spain (S Luna and MA Martin)   545   The Mines Resort,
(Individual: Tiger Woods, USA, 263)   K Lumpur, Malaysia
2000   1 USA (T Woods and D Duval); 2 Argentina (A Cabrera & E Romero)   254   Buenos Aires GC
Argentina
2001   1 South Africa* (E Els and R Goosen); 2 New Zealand (M Campbell and D Smail)   The Taiheiyo Club,
USA (D Duval and T Woods)   tied   254   Japan
Denmark (T Bjørn and S Hansen)
*South Africa won at the second extra hole
2002   1 Japan (S Maruyama and T Izawa); 2 USA (P Mickelson and D Toms)   252   Puerto Vallarta,
Mexico
2003   1 South Africa (T Immelman and R Sabbatini); 2 England (J Rose and P Casey)   275   Kiawah Island, SC
2004   1 England (L Donald and P Casey); 2 Spain (MA Jiménez and S García)   257   Real Club de Sevilla,
Reduced to 54 holes because of rain   Spain
2005   1 Wales (B Dredge and S Dodd); 2 Sweden (N Fasth and H Stenson)   189   Vilamoura, Portugal
Reduced to 54 holes because of bad weather
2006   1 Germany* (B Langer and M Siem); 2 Scotland (C Montgomerie and M Warren)   268   Sandy Lane Resort,
*Germany beat Scotland at the first extra hole   Barbados
2007   1 Scotland* (C Montgomerie and M Warren); 2 Germany (B Weekley and H Slocum)   263   Shenzhen, China
*Scotland beat USA at the third extra hole
2008   1 Sweden (R Karlsson and H Stenson); 2 Spain (MA Jiménez and P Larrazabal)   261   Shenzhen, China
2009   1 Italy (E Molinari and F Molinari); 2T Ireland (G McDowell and R McIlroy)/   259   Shenzhen, China
Sweden (R Karlsson and H Stenson)
2010   Not played – this event will now be held bienially in odd-numbered years

National Championships 2011

Glenmuir PGA Club Professionals' Championship *The Belfry (PGA National)*

1	Craig Goodfellow (Carlisle DR)	70-71-69-71—281
2	Robert Giles (Greenore)	68-72-72-72—284
3	Gary Brown (Ganton)	72-70-70-73—285

De Vere Club PGA Seniors Championship *De Vere Slaley Hall (Hunting)*

1	Andrew Oldcorn (Kings Acre)	73-66-68-70—277
2	Gordon Brand Jr (Players)	72-71-69-74—286
3	Peter Fowler (Ping)	77-68-74-69—288
	Mike Harwood (AUS)	72-70-74-72—288

Senior PGA Professional Championship *Northamptonshire County*

1	Peter Smith (Deeside)	67-70-74—211
2	Robin Mann (Southwold)	72-74-69—215
	Iain Parker (Royal North Devon)	73-70-72—215
	Richard Green (Bramhall)	73-70-72—215

Powerade PGA Assistants Championship *East Sussex National*

1	Matthew Cort (Rothley Park)	73-74-64—211
2	Kevin Harper (Sidmouth)	76-70-71—217
3	Paul Newman (East Berkshire)	71-71-76—218
	Steve Fawcitt (Morpeth)	75-71-72—218

Virgin Atlantic Southern Open *The Drift*

1	Richard Wallis (Walmer and Kingsdown)	66-68-67—205
2	Michael McLean (Limpsfield Chart)	70-70-67—207
3	Michael Ahluwalia (Gravesend)	69-71-70—210

English PGA Championship

Not played. This event will next be held in 2012

101st Irish PGA Championship *Seapoint GC*

1	Simon Thornton	66-66-71-66—269
2	Gary Murphy	70-72-64-69—275
3	Desmond Smyth	67-68-71-70—276
	Seamus McMonagle	70-66-73-67—276

Irish Club Professionals Tournament *Dundalk GC*

1	Michael Collins (Mallow GR)	68-67—135
2	David Higgins (Waterville)	68-69—137
3	Neil O'Briain	70-68—138

Scottish PGA Championship *King's Course, Gleneagles*

1	Alan Lockhart (Ladybank)	71-68-68-68—275
2	Greig Hutcheon (Banchory)	70-70-68-68—276
	Christopher Currie (Caldwell)	70-67-69-70—276

Scottish Young Professionals Championship   *West Lothian*

1	David Patrick (Elie Sports Centre)*	74-70-69-66—279
2	Neil Fenwick (Dunbar)	73-70-69-67—279

Patrick won at the first extra hole

3	Gareth Wright (West Linton)	74-71-68-70—283

Paul Lawrie Young Professionals Matchplay Championship

Not played

Aberdeen Asset Management Northern Open   *Meldrum House Hotel*

1	David Law (Hazlehead) (am)	67-69-62-68—266
2	Stephen Gray (Hayston GC)	69-65-67-67—268
3	Neil Fenwick (Dunbar GC)	67-67-68-68—270

Reduced to 36-holes because of relentless rain

David Law also won the Bookless Cup as the leading amateur

Welsh National PGA Championship   *Southerndown*

1	Stephen Dodd (unattached)	69-67—136
2	Matthew Tottey (North Wales)	71-68—139
3	Liam Bond (Marriott St Pierre)	70-73—143

Farmfoods British Par-3 Championship   *Nailcote Hall Hotel*

1	Andrew Sherborne	55-50—105
2	Simon Wakefield	54-53—107
3	Mark Smith	57-51—108
	Seve Benson	54-54—108

PGAs of Europe Fourball Championship   *Antalya (Sultan and Pasha courses), Turkey*

1	Jurgen Maurer and Michael Moser (AUT)	66-59-71—196
2	Daniel and Andrej Kaljic (SLO)	67-65-69—201
	Grant Hamerton and David Smith (NED)	64-65-72—201

Unicredit PGA Professional Championship of Europe   *Pravets GR and Spa, Bulgaria*

1	Hugo Santos (POR)*	67-69-69-72—277
2	Ben Collier (NED)	67-67-73-70—277

Santos won at the first extra hole

3	Ralph Miller (NED)	72-65-71-72—280

Month by month in 2011

Rory McIlroy hits back from The Masters with an eight-shot victory at the United States Open, finishing a record 16 under par and becoming the event's youngest winner since Bobby Jones in 1933. He succeeds fellow Ulsterman Graeme McDowell as champion. Not to be outdone, Taiwan's Yani Tseng, also 22, wins her fourth major at the LPGA Championship by 10 strokes.

County, District and other Regional Championships

Bedford & Cambridge PGA
Not played

Berks, Bucks & Oxon
Adam Wootton

Cheshire & North Wales Open
Jonathan Cheetham

Cornish Festival
Chris Gill

Cumbria Masters
Chris Gill

Derbyshire PGA
not available

Derbyshire Open
not available

Devon Open
Billy Hemstock

Dorset Open
Lee James

Dorset PGA
Michael Watson and Lee Thompson (shared)

East Anglian Open
Jack Clarke

East Region PGA
Stuart Brown

Essex Open
Matt King

Essex PGA
James Levermore

Gloucestershire & Somerset
Ian Brown

Hampshire PGA
James Ablett

Hampshire Match Play
Kevin Saunders

Hampshire, Isle of Wight and Channel Islands Open
Nick Redfern

Hertfordshire County PGA
Rob Leonard (MP)   P Hetherington (SP)

Kent Open
Francis McGuirk

Kent PGA
Andrew Butterfield

Lancashire Open
John Wells

Lancashire PGA
David Smith

Leeds Cup
David Smith

Leicestershire & Rutland Open
Craig Shave

Lincolnshire Open
Paul Streeter

Lincolnshire PGA
Stephen Bennett

Lincolnshire Match Play
Neil Evans

Manchester Open
Aran Wainwright

Midland Open
James Whatley

Midland Professionals
Matt Cort

Middlesex Open
Kieron Dardis (am

Norfolk Open
Ian Ellis (MP & SP)

Northamptonshire PGA
not available

North East/North West
Vincent Guest (SP)   Graeme Bell (MP)

North Region PGA
Ryan O'Neill

Northumberland & Durham Open
Graeme Bell

Nottinghamshire PGA
John Vaughan

Shropshire & Hereford Open
Justin Griffiths

Shropshire & Hereford PGA
Phil Hinton

Southern Assistants
David Callaway

Southern Masters
Not played

Southern Professionals
Guy Woodman

Staffordshire Open
Freddie Sheridan-Mills (am)

Staffordshire PGA
Peter Baker

South Wales Festival
James Maxwell

Suffolk Open
Patrick Spraggs (am)

Suffolk PGA
Chris Smith (MP)   Robert Pritchard (SP)

Surrey Open
Nick Redfern

Surrey PGA
Neil Reilly

Sussex Open
Ryan Fenwick

Sussex Professionals
Darren Mustchin

Ulster PGA
James Quinlivan

Warwickshire Open
not available

Warwickshire PGA
Paul Broadhurst

Warwickshire Masters
Ben Challis

West Region PGA
Jon Bevan

Wiltshire Professionals
Andy Beal

Worcestershire Open
Chris Nugent (am)

Worcestershire PGA
Dean Lake

Yorkshire Open
Christopher Hanson

Yorkshire Professionals
Neil Cheetham

PART III

Women's Professional Tournaments

Rolex Women's World Golf Rankings at the end of the European, American and Japanese Tour seasons

Rank	Name	Country	Events	Total points	Average points
1	Yani Tseng	TPE	49	876.66	17.89
2	Suzann Pettersen	NOR	41	427.67	10.43
3	Cristie Kerr	USA	43	432.29	10.05
4	Na Yeon Choi	KOR	52	521.28	10.02
5	Paula Creamer	USA	37	301.79	8.16
6	Sun Ju Ahn	KOR	53	425.25	8.02
7	Jiyai Shin	KOR	53	408.51	7.71
8	I K Kim	KOR	44	306.09	6.96
9	Ai Miyazato	JPN	50	342.23	6.84
10	Stacy Lewis	USA	52	351.81	6.77
11	Brittany Lincicome	USA	46	310.21	6.74
12	Amy Yang	KOR	46	279.78	6.08
13	Shanshan Feng	CHN	46	262.61	5.71
14	Chie Arimura	JPN	63	357.03	5.67
15	Morgan Pressel	USA	47	258.27	5.50
16	Ji-Hee Lee	KOR	54	296.09	5.48
17	Michelle Wie	USA	41	214.61	5.23
18	Karrie Webb	AUS	43	224.86	5.23
19	Angela Stanford	USA	45	234.43	5.21
20	Sakura Yokomine	JPN	64	317.71	4.96
21	Catriona Matthew	SCO	40	193.33	4.83
22	Maria Hjörth	SWE	44	209.93	4.77
23	Inbee Park	KOR	62	293.94	4.74
24	Mika Miyazato	JPN	55	247.28	4.50
25	Yuri Fudoh	JPN	48	214.54	4.47
26	Yukari Baba	JPN	65	285.17	4.39
27	So-Yeon Ryu	KOR	48	204.28	4.26
28	Mi-Jeong Jeon	KOR	59	250.34	4.24
29	Miki Saiki	JPN	63	263.37	4.18
30	Song-Hee Kim	KOR	47	195.56	4.16
31	Anna Nordqvist	SWE	47	186.52	3.97
32	Brittany Lang	USA	45	175.66	3.90
33	Hee Kyung Seo	KOR	47	179.77	3.82
34	Shiho Oyama	JPN	38	138.75	3.65
35	Se-Ri Pak	KOR	36	130.95	3.64
36	Ha Neul Kim	KOR	38	137.12	3.61
37	Caroline Hedwall	SWE	28	121.42	3.47
38	Lexi Thompson	USA	23	120.87	3.45
39	Hee Young Park	KOR	52	179.26	3.45
40	Azahara Muñoz	ESP	50	167.88	3.36
41	Sandra Gal	GER	49	163.00	3.33
42	Soo-Jin Yang	KOR	42	136.91	3.26
43	Bo Bae Song	KOR	47	152.91	3.25
44	Sun Young Yoo	KOR	46	144.92	3.15
45	Melissa Reid	ENG	45	137.75	3.06
46	Saiki Fujita	JPN	59	169.18	2.87
47	Na Ri Kim	KOR	60	170.29	2.84
48	Sophie Gustafson	SWE	52	146.97	2.83
49	Katherine Hull	AUS	51	141.48	2.77
50	Mayu Hattori	JPN	65	179.44	2.76

Ladies European Tour

www.ladieseuropeantour.com

Final Henderson Money List

(figures in brackets show number of tournaments played)

1	Ai Miyazato (JPN)	(2)	€363,079	51	Georgina Simpson (ENG)	(18)	48,224
2	Melissa Reid (ENG)	(19)	286,577	52	Alison Walshe (USA)	(9)	47,443
3	Caroline Hedwall (SWE)	(20)	278,528	53	Jade Schaeffer (FRA)	(13)	46,683
4	Diana Luna (ITA)	(18)	223,405	54	Kaisa Ruuttila (FIN)	(17)	46,023
5	Lee-Anne Pace (RSA)	(21)	209,444	55	Veronica Zorzi (ITA)	(19)	45,515
6	Sophie Gustafson (SWE)	(7)	188,889	56	Malene Jorgensen (DEN)	(19)	44,640
7	Caroline Masson (GER)	(16)	167,187	57	Cassandra Kirkland (FRA)	(20)	42,392
8	Christel Boeljon (NED)	(10)	161,171	58	Anja Monke (GER)	(20)	41,591
9	Suzann Pettersen (NOR)	(2)	142,087	59	Vikki Laing (SCO)	(22)	41,159
10	In Kyung Kim (KOR)	(2)	141,275	60	Nontaya Srisawang (THA)	(13)	40,381
11	Amy Yang (KOR)	(2)	129,340	61	Elizabeth Bennett (ENG)	(19)	39,738
12	Catriona Matthew (SCO)	(4)	128,562	62	Julieta Granada (PAR)	(6)	38,944
13	Becky Brewerton (WAL)	(24)	124,008	63	Sarah Kemp (AUS)	(9)	38,308
14	Linda Wessberg (SWE)	(20)	109,763	64	Louise Stahle (SWE)	(13)	38,260
15	Ashleigh Simon (RSA)	(20)	98,472	65	Louise Larsson (SWE)	(18)	35,433
16	Maria Hjörth (SWE)	(3)	95,090	66	Holly Aitchison (ENG)	(18)	34,110
17	Anna Nordqvist (SWE)	(4)	95,069	67	Lucie Andre (FRA)	(14)	33,264
18	Pernilla Lindberg (SWE)	(13)	91,054	68	Rebecca Codd (IRL)	(23)	31,722
19	Beth Allen (USA)	(21)	91,054	69	Kym Larratt (ENG)	(14)	31,343
20	Kristie Smith (AUS)	(16)	90,449	70	Rebecca Flood (AUS)	(19)	31,163
21	Giulia Sergas (ITA)	(12)	90,224	71	Trish Johnson (ENG)	(18)	30,838
22	Sophie Giquel-Bettan (FRA)	(21)	88,673	72	Julie Greciet (FRA)	(12)	30,551
23	Jiyai Shin (KOR)	(3)	87,726	73	Klara Spilkova (CZE)	(14)	27,549
24	Becky Morgan (WAL)	(14)	86,896	74	Sandra Gal (GER)	(5)	26,051
25	Minea Blomqvist (FIN)	(13)	83,386	75	Lydia Hall (WAL)	(13)	25,797
26	Virginie Lagoutte-Clement (FRA)	(21)	83,288	76	Margherita Rigon (ITA)	(18)	25,725
27	Caroline Afonso (FRA)	(22)	81,591	77	Danielle Montgomery (ENG)	(16)	25,722
28	Florentyna Parker (ENG)	(24)	81,403	78	Marianne Skarpnord (NOR)	(13)	25,577
29	Anne-Lise Caudal (FRA)	(24)	71,607	79	Tara Davies (WAL)	(13)	25,415
30	Rachel Jennings (ENG)	(16)	71,167	80	Lisa Holm Sorensen (DEN)	(19)	25,346
31	Karen Lunn (AUS)	(22)	68,813	81	Bree Arthur (AUS)	(16)	25,327
32	Felicity Johnson (ENG)	(23)	67,130	82	Joanna Klatten (FRA)	(17)	24,741
33	Tania Elosegui (ESP)	(19)	64,775	83	Jaclyn Sweeney (USA)	(16)	24,583
34	Nikki Garrett (AUS)	(20)	63,599	84	Lynnette Brooky (NZL)	(14)	24,539
35	Christina Kim (USA)	(10)	63,412	85	Rebecca Hudson (ENG)	(19)	24,030
36	Frances Bondad (AUS)	(19)	61,820	86	Sara Brown (USA)	(11)	23,568
37	Stefania Croce (ITA)	(17)	58,916	87	Titiya Plucksataporn (THA)	(19)	23,375
38	Dewi Claire Schreefel (NED)	(10)	56,288	88	Lotta Wahlin (SWE)	(15)	23,339
39	Ursula Wikstrom (FIN)	(20)	54,340	89	Stefanie Michl (AUT)	(19)	23,329
40	Hannah Jun (USA)	(15)	54,337	90	Pornanong Phatlum (THA)	(2)	22,837
41	Zuzana Kamasova (SVK)	(17)	53,863	91	Diana D'Alessio (USA)	(9)	22,770
42	Azahara Muñoz Guijarro (ESP)	(3)	53,457	92	Sophie Walker (ENG)	(22)	22,306
43	Karen Stupples (ENG)	(5)	53,190	93	Connie Chen (RSA)	(13)	21,800
44	Carin Koch (SWE)	(12)	53,057	94	Line Vedel (DEN)	(17)	21,536
45	Stacey Keating (AUS)	(21)	52,704	95	Julie Maisongrosse (FRA)	(20)	21,266
46	Gwladys Nocera (FRA)	(13)	51,285	96	Carmen Alonso (ESP)	(14)	20,559
47	Kylie Walker (SCO)	(23)	50,626	97	Belen Mozo (ESP)	(8)	20,452
48	Laura Davies (ENG)	(18)	50,363	98	Caroline Rominger (SWI)	(18)	19,212
49	Stacy Lee Bregman (RSA)	(19)	50,107	99	Jenni Kuosa (FIN)	(20)	18,397
50	Kiran Matharu (ENG)	(16)	48,285	100	Caroline Westrup (SWE)	(10)	18,045

2011 Tour Statistics

Stroke average

		Rnds.	Pts Av.				Rnds.	Pts Av.
1	Suzann Pettersen (NOR)	11	69.36	6	Florence Luscher (SWI)		3	70.33
2	Catriona Matthew (SCO)	14	69.57	7	Anna Nordqvist (SWE)		15	70.40
3	Amy Yang (KOR)	8	69.75	8	In Kyung Kim (KOR)		8	70.50
4	Maria Hjörth (SWE)	11	69.82	9	Jiyai Shin (KOR)		12	70.67
5	Ai Miyazato (JPN)	6	70.00	10	Pornanong Phatlum (THA)		5	70.80

Driving accuracy

		Holes	%			Holes	%
1	Stefania Croce (ITA)	657	84.02	6	Hannah Jun (USA)	611	80.85
2	Georgina Simpson (ENG)	717	83.82	7	Sophie Sandolo (ITA)	649	79.51
3	Rebecca Hudson (ENG)	730	83.42	8	Mariana Macias Capuzzi (ESP)	110	79.09
4	Titiya Plucksataporn (THA)	627	83.25	9	Nontaya Srisawang (THA)	511	78.86
5	Barbara Genuini (FRA)	282	81.21	10	Becky Morgan (WAL)	641	78.78

Driving distance

		Holes	Av.			Holes	Av.
1	Carmen Alonso (ESP)	13	288.92	6	Emma Cabrera-Bello (ESP)	30	270.77
2	Maria Hjörth (SWE)	6	276.83	7	Morgana Robbertze (RSA)	35	270.74
3	Marjet van der Graaff (NED)	32	273.28	8	Helen Alfredsson (SWE)	3	266.00
4	Jade Schaeffer (FRA)	34	272.38	9	Laura Davies (ENG)	50	265.66
5	Carly Booth (SCO)	22	271.77	10	Kaisa Ruuttila (FIN)	45	264.84

Greens in regulation

		Holes	%			Holes	%
1	In Kyung Kim (KOR)	18	88.89	6	Caroline Hedwall (SWE)	80	82.69
2	Ai Miyazato (JPN)	36	86.11	7	Anna Nordqvist (SWE)	162	82.10
3	Jiyai Shin (KOR)	90	84.44	8	Suzann Pettersen (NOR)	54	81.48
4	Smriti Mehra (IND)	36	83.33	9	Catriona Matthew (SCO)	144	81.25
	Isabella Ramsay (SWE)	18	83.33	10	Maria Hjörth (SWE)	90	81.11

Sand saves

		Holes	%			Holes	%
1	Kirsty J Fisher (ENG)	4	100.00	6	Becky Morgan (WAL)	63	66.67
	Ai Miyazato (JPN)	2	100.00		Jo Clingan (ENG)	9	66.67
3	Marina Arruti (ESP)	12	91.67		Jiyai Shin (KOR)	9	66.67
4	Audrey Riguelle (FRA)	21	80.95		Benedicte Toumpsin (BEL)	6	66.67
5	Jessica Ji (KOR)	5	80.00		Amy Yang (KOR)	3	66.67
					Denise-Charlotte Becker (GER)	3	66.67

2011 Tour Results (in chronological order)

For past results see earlier editions of The R&A Golfer's Handbook

ISPS Handa Women's Australian Open Commonwealth GC, Melbourne, Australia [6644–73]

1	Yani Tseng (TPE)	70-67-68-71—276	€65,500
2	Melissa Reid (ENG)	70-73-72-68—283	32,847
	Eun Hee Ji (KOR)	69-70-70-74—283	32,847
	Jiyai Shin (KOR)	67-72-69-75—283	32,847

ANZ RACV Ladies' Masters Royal Pines, Gold Coast, Queensland, Australia [6410–72]

1	Yani Tseng (TPE)	67-66-63-68—264	€62,500
2	Nikki Campbell (AUS)	68-67-69-64—268	35,208
	Stacy Lewis (USA)	67-65-67-69—268	35,208

Pegasus New Zealand Women's Open Pegasus, Christchurch, New Zealand [6365–72]

1	Kristie Smith (AUS)	71-64-73-68—276	€33,333
2	Tiffany Joh (USA)	74-67-68-70—279	18,888
	Giulia Sergas (ITA)	64-69-70-76—279	18,888

Lalla Meryem Cup Soleil Golf Course, Agadir, Morocco [6102–72]

1	Zuzana Kamasova (SVK)	71-68-71-76—286	€48,750
2	Alexandra Bonetti (FRA) (am)	75-76-71-66—288	
	Caroline Masson (GER)	69-73-75-71—288	27,868
	Kiran Matharu (ENG)	74-70-70-74—288	27,868

European Nations Cup La Sella, Alicante, Spain [6283–72]

1	Sophie Gustafson & Anna Nordqvist (SWE)	68-63-68-68—267	€42,000
2	Anja Monke & Caroline Masson (GER)	71-64-70-65—270	18,550
	Laura Davies & Melissa Reid (ENG)	67-70--67-66—270	18,550

4 Wales 271; 5 Australia 272; 6 France 275; 7 USA, Spain 276; 9 Scotland, Netherlands 277
18 teams took part

Turkish Airlines Ladies Open National GC, Antalya, Turkey [6211–73]

1	Christel Boeljon (NED)	73-71-70-73—287	€37,500
2	Florentyna Parker (ENG)	72-73-70-75—290	21,437
	Becky Brewerton (WAL)	74-73-68-75—290	21,437

ISPS Handa Portugal Ladies Open Campo Real, Portugal [5905-72]

1	Ashleigh Simon (RSA)	66-67-67—200	€30,000
2	Gwladys Nocera (FRA)	64-68-71—203	20,300
3	Christel Boeljon (NED)	68-67-72—207	14,000

UniCredit Ladies German Open (formerly Hypo Vereinsbank Ladies German Open)
Gut Häusern, Munich [6204–72]

1	Diana Luna (ITA)	67-67-65-65—264	€52,500
2	Minea Blomqvist (FIN)	67-67-67-70—271	35,525
3	Becky Morgan (WAL)	65-69-69-69—272	24,500

Allianz Ladies Slovak Open Gray Bear, Slovakia [6296–72]

1	Caroline Hedwall (SWE)	71-67-67—205	€52,500
2	Christel Boeljon (NED)	68-75-64—207	35,525
3	Rachel Jennings (ENG)	67-68-74—209	24,500

Deloitte Ladies Open Broekpolder, Rotterdam, Netherlands [6386–72]

1	Melissa Reid (ENG)	71-72-70—213	€37,500
2	Caroline Afonso (FRA)	76-71-67—214	18,791
	Caroline Hedwall (SWE)	75-69-70—214	18,791
	Holly Aitchison (ENG)	67-71-76—214	18,791

Tenerife Ladies Match Play Golf Las Americas, Tenerife [6237–72]

Final day – stroke play:

1	Becky Brewerton (WAL)	68	€40,000
2	Carlota Ciganda (ESP)	69	17,500
	Nikki Garrett (AUS)	69	17,000

Deutsche Bank Ladies Swiss Open Golf Gerre Losone, Ticino, Switzerland [6266–72]

1	Diana Luna (ITA)	69-67-67—203	€78,750
2	Lee-Anne Pace (RSA)	70-66-68—204	39,462
	Kristie Smith (AUS)	70-66-68—204	39,462
	Sophie Giquel-Bettan (FRA)	68-68-68—204	39,462

Finnair Masters Helsinki, Finland [5916–71]

1	Caroline Hedwall (SWE)	69-65-68—202	€30,000
2	Christel Boeljon (NED)	68-69-67—204	20,300
3	Carin Koch (SWE)	69-68-68—205	14,000

Evian Masters Evian Masters GC, France [6347–72]

1	Ai Miyazato (JPN)	68-68-67-70—273	€363,079
2	Stacy Lewis (USA)	69-67-69-70—275	225,225
3	Miki Saiki (JPN)	68-67-70-71—276	130,502
	In Kyung Kim (KOR)	74-68-64-70—276	130,502
	Angela Stanford (USA)	70-66-69-71—276	130,502

RICOH WOMEN'S BRITISH OPEN Carnoustie Links [6490–72]

1	Yani Tseng (TPE)	71-66-66-69—272	€272,365
2	Brittany Lang (USA)	70-70-69-67—276	170,736
3	Sophie Gustafson (SWE)	68-71-70-68—277	119,515

Full details of this event can be found on page 94

AIB Ladies Irish Open Killeen Castle, Co Meath, R.o.I. [6418–72]

1	Suzann Pettersen (NOR)	71-63-64—198	€60,000
2	Azahara Muñoz Guijarro (ESP)	67-68-69—204	40,600
3	Melissa Reid (ENG)	70-66-69—205	24,800
	Alison Walshe (USA)	66-70-69—205	24,800

Aberdeen Ladies Scottish Open Archerfield Links, East Lothian, Scotland [6354–72]

1	Catriona Matthew (SCO)	70-65-66—201	€33,000
2	Hannah Jun (USA)	66-73-72—211	22,330
3	Caroline Afonso (FRA)	70-71-71—212	15,400

UNIQA Ladies Open Föhrenwald, Wiener Neustadt, Austria   [6179–72]

1	Caroline Hedwall (SWE)	73-67-64—204	€30,000
2	Caroline Afonso (FRA)	67-67-74—208	20,300
3	Melissa Reid (ENG)	67-71-71—209	10,070
	Linda Wessberg (SWE)	69-69-71—209	10,070
	Giulia Sergas (ITA)	67-69-73—209	10,070
	Kaisa Ruuttila (FIN)	67-66-76—209	10,070

Raiffeisenbank Prague Golf Masters Prague, Czech Republic   [6354–72]

1	Jade Schaeffer (FRA)	69-64-70—203	€30,000
2	Julie Greciet (FRA)	69-71-65—205	21,100
3	Linda Wessberg (SWE)	69-69-68—206	15,500

Open de España Femenino La Quinta G&CC, Spain   [6182–72]

1	Melissa Reid (ENG)	71-69-70-70—280	€52,500
2	Tania Elosegui (ESP)	68-65-79-69—281	26,308
	Lee-Anne Pace (RSA)	68-69-73-71—281	26,308
	Beth Allen (USA)	69-68-72-72—281	26,308

Solheim Cup Killeen Castle, Ireland   [7700–72]

Result: Europe 15, USA 13

Full details of this event can be found on page 241

Lacoste Ladies Open de France Paris International GC, France   [6143–72]

1	Felicity Johnson (ENG)*	68-70-69-67—274	€37,500
2	Diana Luna (ITA)	69-68-67-70—274	25,375

*Johnson won at the first extra hole

3	Minea Blomqvist (FIN)	68-69-71-67—275	17,500

Sicilian Ladies Italian Open Il Picciolo GC, Sicily   [5815–72]

1	Christina Kim (USA)	70-69-70—209	€30,000
2	Giulia Sergas (ITA)	71-69-73—213	20,300
3	Stefania Croce (ITA)	68-73-73—214	12,400
	Gwladys Nocera (FRA)	72-66-76—214	12,400

Sanya Ladies Open Yalong Bay GC, China   [6433–72]

1	Frances Bondad (AUS)	68-70-67—205	€30,000
2	Vikki Laing (SCO)	69-69-68—206	20,300
3	Ashleigh Simon (RSA)	69-70-69—208	12,400
	Pan Yan Hong (CHN)	67-69-72—208	12,400

Suzhou Taihu Ladies Open Suzhou Taihu, China   [6320–72]

1	Yani Tseng (TPE)	68-66-66—200	€45,000
2	Pernilla Lindberg (SWE)	72-65-70—207	30,450
3	Melissa Reid (ENG)	71-69-68—208	18,600
	Lee-Anne Pace (RSA)	68-70-70—208	18,600

Hero Honda Women's Indian Open DLF G&CC, New Delhi, India   [5878–72]

1	Caroline Hedwall (SWE)	67-68-69—204	€33,750
2	Pornanong Phatlum (THA)	67-69-70—206	22,837
3	Becky Morgan (WAL)	70-69-69—208	15,750

Omega Dubai Ladies Masters   *Emirates GC, Dubai, UAE*   [6437–72]

1	Alexis Thompson (USA)	70-66-70-67—273	€75,000
2	Lee-Anne Pace (RSA)	69-72-67-69—277	50,750
3	Sophie Gustafson (SWE)	71-67-69-71—278	35,000

Women's World Cup
Not played
For list of past winners, see page 248

LET Access Series

www.letaccess.com

Terre Blanche Ladies Open	Terre Blanche, Nice, France	Henrietta Zuel (ENG)	140 (–6)
La Nivelle Ladies Open	La Nivelle, Biarritz, France	Anne-Lise Caudal (FRA)	204 (–6)
LETAS Ladies Open	Hazlemere, Bucks, England	Henrietta Zuel (ENG)	206 (–4)
Dinard Ladies Open	Dinard Golf, Saint Briac Sur Mer, France	Julie Maisongrosse (FRA)	197 (–13)
Trophée Preven's	Golf de Bussy Guermante, Paris, France	Marieke Nivard (NED)	208 (–8)
Murcia Ladies Open	La Manga, Cartagena, Spain	Carlota Ciganda (ESP)	214 (–5)
Azores Ladies Open	São Miguel Island, Portugal	Marieke Nivard (NED)	216 par

Final Ranking

1	Marieke Nivard (NED)	15,106 pts	6	Joanna Klatten (FRA)	7,482
2	Henrietta Zuel (ENG)	13,616	7	Camille Fallay (FRA)	7,475
3	Marjet van der Graaff (NED)	12,035	8	Maria Beautell (ESP)	7,340
4	Julie Tvede (DEN)	9,645	9	Anna Rossi (ITA)	6,815
5	Julie Maisongrosse (FRA)	8,700	10	Margherita Rigon (ITA)	6,008

If you are good enough age does not matter – Laura

Laura Davies may be 48 but she remains adamant that age is irrelevant when it comes to winning golf tournaments.

As a winner of 79 titles worldwide over a 26 year career, she should know. She collected five trophies last season and was part of the European team that won The Solheim Cup in Ireland last September.

"If you're good enough, you're good enough. It doesn't matter how old you are. Tom Watson nearly won the The Open at Turnberry in 2009 at the age of 60. I've got 11 years on that.

"These days I just play where I like the golf courses. If I play a tournament one year and don't like the course, I don't go back, but on the whole, the courses I like, I play and will keep playing. What's to slow down for? I'm still good enough. This year I've not won but I have played well, I've just not holed any putts. The scoring could have been very different this year."

Davies' season-best finish is a share of seventh at the New Zealand Ladies Open on the Ladies European Tour, where she is currently ranked 42nd on the Henderson Money List, compared with second in 2010.

Since turning professional in 1985 she has won at least one tournament every year bar 2005 and 2011. Last year she played in the final four events of the 2011 Ladies European Tour season in an attempt to keep up her exemplary record. Sadly it did not happen but you can be sure that the talented Laura, still waiting to be inducted into the World Golf Hall of Fame, will be playing this year as enthusiastic about her chances as ever.

European Tour honour for Louise Solheim

Louise Solheim who, with her late husband Karsten founded the Solheim Cup in 1990, has become the first honorary member of the Ladies European Tour.

The Cup match, which is the women's equivalent of the men's Ryder Cup, is played in alternate years in Europe and America.

Alison Nicholas, captain of the 2011 European side, announced the award on the eve of the match, staged at Killeen Castle in County Meath, Ireland.

"During the past 22 years, Louise Solheim has been one of the greatest supporters of women's professional golf," said Nicholas. Alexandra Armas, the executive director the Ladies European Tour added: "We would like to thank Louise for her role in developing the game and providing such wonderful opportunities for women and girls across Europe."

Louise Solheim has attended all 12 Solheim Cups which have been staged in America, Scotland (twice), Sweden (twice), Wales and Ireland. The USA have won the event nine times. Mrs Solheim's late husband, who founded the Arizona-based PING golf manufacturing company, is the only manufacturer to have earned a place in the World Golf Hall of Fame.

Lexi Thompson is youngest winner on the LPGA Tour at 16!

Lexi Thompson was just 16 years, 7 months and 8 days old when she won the 2011 Navistar LPGA Classic over the Senator course at the RTJ Golf Trail, Capitol Hill in Prattville, Alabama.

Thompson shot rounds of 66, 68, 67 and 70 for a 17-under-par total of 271 to beat Tiffany Joh by five shots and set a new youngest-ever record on the LPGA Tour by over two years.

Marlene Hagge had been the previous youngest winner on Tour when she won the 18-hole Sarasota Open in 1952 at the age of 18 years and 14 days. The youngest winner previously of a 72-hole event on Tour had been Paula Creamer who was 18 years, 9 months and 17 days old when she took the 2005 Sybase Classic title.

Lexi is no stranger to making golfing history. In 2007 at the age of 12 she became the youngest qualifier to play in the US Women's Open.

With her father Scott on the bag at the Navistar, she told reporters: "I just loved the walk up at the 18th with my dad. It was the best experience."

The teenager won $195,000 and gave $20,000 of her winnings to the tournament's charity – The Wounded Warrior Project.

Teenage winner Alexis writes more golfing history in Dubai

Three months after winning the 2011 Navistar LPGA Classic on the LPGA Tour, 16 year old Alexis Thompson from Coral Springs, Florida, swept to victory in the 2011 Dubai Ladies Championship last year. Her victories, just three months apart, both made history.

With her Navistar success she became the youngest ever winner of an LPGA title and with it persuaded the powers that be to bend their rules and allow her to play full time on the Tour instead of making her wait until she was 18.

In Dubai, the attractive six footer became the youngest professional winner on the Ladies European Tour at 16 years, 10 months and 8 days. She was, however, only the second youngest winner on the European circuit as Amy Yang was 16 years, 6 months and 8 days when, as an amateur, she won the ANZ Ladies Masters in Australia.

Inspired by her brothers whom she plays against regularly and with her dad on the bag – he has caddied for her from her junior days – Alexis (Lexi) is no stranger to writing golfing history. As a 12-year-old she became the youngest qualifier for the US Women's Open.

Now that she is a transatlantic winner does she feel pressure to perform? "There's not really any pressure," she told reporters in Dubai. "I'm just playing my game and doing what I love."

The first American winner of the Dubai event in its six year history, Alexis delighted locals when she announced she would be back to defend in 2012 … and in the final round will certainly be wearing a blue shirt. "I am superstitious and that will always be the colour on the final day," she said.

LPGA Tour

www.lpga.com

Players are American unless stated

Money List

1	Yani Tseng (TPE)	$2,921,713	35	Chella Choi (KOR)	325,273	69	Becky Morgan (WAL)	98,485
2	Cristie Kerr	1,470,979	36	Juli Inkster	298,123	70	Heather Bowie Young	97,612
3	Na Yeon Choi (KOR)	1,357,382	37	Candie Kung (TPE)	287,580	71	Seon Hwa Lee (KOR)	93,889
4	Stacy Lewis	1,356,211	38	Mindy Kim	262,055	72	Leta Lindley	90,291
5	Suzann Pettersen (NOR)	1,322,770	39	Jimin Kang (KOR)	255,901	73	Alison Walshe	90,088
6	Brittany Lincicome	1,154,234	40	Hee-Won Han (KOR)	245,264	74	M J Hur (KOR)	87,221
7	Angela Stanford	1,017,196	41	Tiffany Joh	237,365	75	Kris Tamulis	85,156
8	Ai Miyazato (JPN)	1,007,633	42	Amy Hung (TPE)	226,623	76	Lindsey Wright (AUS)	84,767
9	Paula Creamer	926,338	43	Beatriz Recari (ESP)	223,053	77	Haeji Kang (KOR)	81,691
10	Amy Yang (KOR)	912,160	44	Wendy Ward	204,165	78	Alena Sharp (CAN)	77,982
11	I K Kim (KOR)	885,952	45	Vicky Hurst	201,425	79	Jennifer Song	77,421
12	Hee Young Park (KOR)	851,781	46	Ryann O'Toole	192,748	80	Reilley Rankin	75,301
13	Morgan Pressel	845,466	47	Paige Mackenzie	184,384	81	Grace Park (KOR)	71,625
14	Karrie Webb (AUS)	757,671	48	Eun-Hee Ji (KOR)	181,743	82	Jin Young Pak (KOR)	71,158
15	Jiyai Shin (KOR)	720,735	49	Mina Harigae	178,683	83	Marcy Hart	68,369
16	Catriona Matthew (SCO)	692,340	50	Pat Hurst	177,349	84	Meaghan Francella	66,813
17	Maria Hjörth (SWE)	630,320	51	Natalie Gulbis	176,337	85	Sarah Kemp (AUS)	58,503
18	Michelle Wie	627,936	52	Christel Boeljon (NED)	170,553	86	Gwladys Nocera (FRA)	57,626
19	Brittany Lang	627,691	53	Mi Hyun Kim (KOR)	165,304	87	Karine Icher (FRA)	55,398
20	Sandra Gal (GER)	623,526	54	Amanda Blumenherst	164,930	88	Lorie Kane (CAN)	55,309
21	Hee Kyung Seo (KOR)	619,429	55	Jenny Shin (KOR)	160,571	89	Sarah Jane Smith (AUS)	54,478
22	Mika Miyazato (JPN)	591,688	56	Kristy McPherson	157,025	90	Pernilla Lindberg (SWE)	53,353
23	Anna Nordqvist (SWE)	589,774	57	Pornanong Phatlum (THA)	149,657	91	Ilhee Lee (KOR)	52,900
24	Azahara Muñoz (ESP)	520,269	58	Christina Kim	149,275	92	Jessica Korda	52,275
25	Sun Young Yoo (KOR)	476,672	59	Stacy Prammanasudh	143,916	93	Karin Sjodin (SWE)	50,993
26	Sophie Gustafson (SWE)	427,586	60	Katherine Hull (AUS)	137,884	94	Haru Nomura (JPN)	50,106
27	Se Ri Pak (KOR)	415,447	61	Julieta Granada (PAR)	137,221	95	Giulia Sergas (ITA)	50,090
28	Meena Lee (KOR)	408,114	62	Dewi Claire Schreefel (NED)	136,140	96	Silvia Cavalleri (ITA)	49,320
29	Karen Stupples (ENG)	397,081	63	Jennifer Johnson	128,974	97	Shi Hyun Ahn (KOR)	43,600
30	Katie Futcher	373,630	64	Caroline Hedwall (SWE)	126,801	98	Jane Park	42,261
31	Inbee Park (KOR)	365,231	65	Cindy LaCrosse	114,800	99	Na On Min (KOR)	41,556
32	Shanshan Feng (CHN)	362,097	66	Kyeong Bae (KOR)	109,142	100	Taylor Leon	40,633
33	Song-Hee Kim (KOR)	350,376	67	Belen Mozo (ESP)	104,323			
34	Momoko Ueda (JPN)	333,494	68	Gerina Piller	103,322			

Thai Junthima Gulyanamitta heads LPGA school

Thailand's Junthima Gulyanamitta, whose often-used nickname is Numa, headed the list of 20 players who made it on to the 2012 LPGA Tour from the Qualifying School last year.

Three European golfers were successful – Spain's Elisa Serramia, Finland's Minea Blomqvist and 23-year-old English golfer Jodi Ewart who attended the University of New Mexico. Before heading to America Jodi had won the English Amateur Championship twice and also played in the 2008 Curtis Cup.

Two Canadians were successful in earning their cards – Maude-Aimee LeBlanc and Rebecca Lee-Bentham as was Mexican golfer Tanya Dergal.

2011 Tour Results (in chronological order)

Honda LPGA Thailand Chonburi, Thailand   [6469–72]

1	Yani Tseng (TPE)	66-71-70-66—273	$217,500
2	Michelle Wie	69-68-71-70—278	140,360
3	Karrie Webb (AUS)	74-68-68-69—279	90,294
	In Kyung Kim (KOR)	63-73-72-71—279	90,294

HSBC Women's Champions Tanah Merah, Singapore   [6547–72]

1	Karrie Webb (AUS)	70-66-70-69—275	$210,000
2	Chie Arimura (JPN)	68-66-71-71—276	132,846
3	Yani Tseng (TPE)	70-72-69-67—278	96,370

RR Donnelley LPGA Founders Cup La Costa, Carlsbad, CA
    [6613–72]

1	Karrie Webb (AUS)	71-67-66—204	$150,000
2	Paula Creamer	69-70-66—205	85,110
	Brittany Lincicome	67-68-70—205	85,110

KIA Classic Pacific Palms Resort, CA   [6716–73]

1	Sandra Gal (GER)	67-68-70-71—276	$255,000
2	Jiyai Shin (KOR)	70-64-70-73—277	158,182
3	Cristie Kerr	74-70-71-66—281	101,759
	In Kyung Kim (KOR)	70-69-72-70—281	101,759

KRAFT NABISCO CHAMPIONSHIP
Mission Hills CC, Rancho Mirage, CA   [6738–72]

1	Stacy Lewis	66-69-71-69—275	$300,000
2	Yani Tseng (TPE)	70-68-66-74—278	184,255
3	Katie Futcher	70-71-74-69—284	106,763
	Angela Stanford	72-72-67-73—284	106,763
	Morgan Pressel	70-69-69-76—284	106,763

Full details of this event can be found on page 124

Avnet LPGA Classic RJT Golf Trail, Mobile, AL   [6502–72]

1	Maria Hjörth (SWE)	70-74-67-67—278	$195,000
2	Song-Hee Kim (KOR)	67-72-70-71—280	118,921
3	Na Yeon Choi (KOR)	69-72-71-69—281	76,502
	Suzann Pettersen (NOR)	72-68-71-70—281	76,502

Sybase Match-Play Championship
Hamilton Farm, Gladstone, NJ   [6585–72]

Final: Suzann Pettersen (NOR) ($375,000) beat Cristie Kerr ($225,000
1 up

HSBC Brasil Cup Itanhanga, Rio de Janeiro, Brazil   [6339–73]

1	Mariajo Uribe (COL)	69-66—135	$108,000
2	Lindsey Wright (AUS)	68-68—136	83,990
3	Maria Hjorth (SWE)	70-67—137	60,929

ShopRite LPGA Classic *Dolce Seaview Resort, Galloway, NJ* [6150–71]

1	Brittany Lincicome	72-64-66—202	$225,000
2	Jiyai Shin (KOR)	66-71-66—203	119,219
	Cristie Kerr	69-65-69—203	119,219

LPGA State Farm Classic *Panther Creek, Springfield, IL* [6746–72]

1	Yani Tseng (TPE)	67-66-66-68—267	$255,000
2	Cristie Kerr	70-67-66-67—270	155,512
3	Paula Creamer	68-68-69-67—272	100,041
	Brittany Lincicome	67-69-66-70—272	100,041

Wegmans LPGA Championship *Locust Hill, Pittsford, NY*

[6534–72]

1	Yani Tseng (TPE)	66-70-67-66—269	$375,000
2	Morgan Pressel	69-69-70-71—279	228,695
3	Suzann Pettersen (NOR)	72-72-69-67—280	132,512
	Paula Creamer	67-72-72-69—280	132,512
	Cristie Kerr	72-72-67-69—280	132,512

Full details of this event can be found on page 114

66th US WOMEN'S OPEN CHAMPIONSHIP
Colorado Springs, CO [7047–71]

1	So Yeon Ryu (KOR)*	74-69-69-69—281	$585,000
2	Hee Kyung Seo (KOR)	72-73-68-68—281	350,000

*So Yeon Ryu won at the third extra hole

3	Cristie Kerr	71-72-69-71—283	215,493

Full details of this event can be found on page 104

Evian Masters *Evian Masters GC, France* [6347–72]

1	Ai Miyazato (JPN)	68-68-67-70—273	$487,500
2	Stacy Lewis	69-67-69-70—275	302,406
3	Miki Saiki (JPN)	68-67-70-71—276	175,223
	In Kyung Kim (KOR)	74-68-64-70—276	175,223
	Angela Stanford	70-66-69-71—276	175,223

RICOH WOMEN'S BRITISH OPEN
Carnoustie Links [6490–72]

1	Yani Tseng (TPE)	71-66-66-69—272	$392,133
2	Brittany Lang	70-70-69-67—276	231,065
3	Sophie Gustafson (SWE)	68-71-70-68—277	161,746

Full details of this event can be found on page 94

Safeway Classic *North Plains, OR* [6552–72]

1	Suzann Pettersen (NOR)*	69-74-64—207	$225,000
2	Na Yeon Choi (KOR)	65-69-73—207	135,702

*Pettersen won at the first extra hole

3	Hee Young Park (KOR)	71-70-67—208	98,442

CN Canadian Women's Open *Mirabel, Quebec, Canada* [6604–72]

1	Brittany Lincicome	68-68-69-70—275	$337,500
2	Stacy Lewis	69-71-69-67—276	177,981
	Michelle Wie	67-69-68-72—276	177,981

Walmart NW Arkansas Championship Rogers, AR [6284–71]

1	Yani Tseng (TPE)	66-67-68—201	$300,000
2	Amy Yang (KOR)	69-64-68—201	182,127
3	Ai Miyazato (JPN)	69-67-66—202	132,120

Navistar LPGA Classic Prattville, AL [6460–72]

1	Lexi Thompson	66-68-67-70—271	$195,000
2	Tiffany Joh	68-75-65-68—276	120,057
3	Angela Stanford	73-69-69-66—277	87,093

Solheim Cup Killeen Castle, Ireland [7700–72]

Result: USA 16, Europe 15, USA 13

Full details of this event can be found on page 241

LPGA Hana Bank Championship Incheon, S. Korea [6364–72]

1	Yani Tseng (TPE)	65-70-67—202	$270,000
2	Na Yeon Choi (KOR)	67-68-68—203	168,366
3	Brittany Lincicome	71-68-66—205	97,556
	Jimin Kang (KOR)	68-69-68—205	97,556
	Soo-Jin Yang (KOR)	69-65-71—205	97,556

Sime Darby LPGA Malaysia Kuala Lumpur, Malaysia [6208–71]

1	Na Yeon Choi (KOR)	66-68-67-68—269	$285,000
2	Yani Tseng (TPE)	69-67-69-65—270	176,791
3	Azahara Muñoz (ESP)	67-68-68-69—272	128,250

LPGA Taiwan Championship Yang Mei, Taoyuan, Taiwan [6390–72]

1	Yani Tseng (TPE)	68-71-67-66—272	$300,000
2	Amy Yang (KOR)	72-68-70-67—277	154,498
2	Azahara Muñoz (ESP)	71-66-72-68—277	154,498

Mizuno Classic Shima-Shi Mie, Japan [6506–72]

1	Momoko Ueda (JPN)*	67-64-69—200	$180,000
2	Shanshan Feng (CHN)	68-67-65—200	109,523

*Ueda won at the third extra hole

3	Na Yeon Choi (KOR)	69-68-64—201	79,451

Lorena Ochoa Invitational Guadalajara CC, Jalisco, Mexico [6644–72]

1	Catriona Matthew (SCO)	69-68-68-71—276	$200,000
2	In Kyung Kim (KOR)	72-67-70-71—280	89,247
	Anna Nordqvist (SWE)	71-65-73-71—280	89,247

Titleholders Grand Cypress GC, Orlando, FL [6518–72]

1	Hee Young Park (KOR)	71-69-69-70—279	$500,000
2	Paula Creamer	69-71-71-70—281	95,516
	Sandra Gal (GER)	69-69-71-72—281	95,516

Wendy's 3-Tour Challenge   *Rio Secco GC, NV*

1	Champions Tour – Kenny Perry, Jay Haas and Mark Calcavecchia	$500,000
2	LPGA Tour – Paula Creamer, Cristie Kerr and Natalie Gulbis	270,000
3	PGA Tour – Boo Weekley, Gary Woodland and Jonathan Byrd	230,000

LPGA Tour statistics

Scoring average

		Total Rounds	Average
1	Yani Tseng (TPE)	77	69.66
2	Na Yeon Choi (KOR)	73	70.53
3	Cristie Kerr	77	70.71
4	Jiyai Shin (KOR)	63	70.81
5	Paula Creamer	75	70.84
6	Suzann Pettersen (NOR)	73	70.97
7	Stacy Lewis	81	70.98
8	I K Kim (KOR)	72	71.01
9	Brittany Lincicome	75	71.03
10	Amy Yang (KOR)	76	71.12

Driving average

		Average
1	Yani Tseng (TPE)	269.2
2	Maria Hjörth (SWE)	267.8
3	Brittany Lincicome	267.0
4	Michelle Wie	266.9
5	Gerina Piller	265.1
6	Jessica Korda	264.8
7	Ryann O'Toole	264.0
8	Nicole Hage	264.0
9	Brittany Lang	263.5
10	Vicky Hurst	263.1

Driving accuracy

		Possible Fairways	Fairways	%
1	Paola Moreno (COL)	269	321	0.838
2	Christine Song	275	334	0.823
3	Leta Lindley	405	492	0.823
4	Paula Creamer	679	845	0.804
5	Jenny Suh	245	306	0.801
6	Lindsey Wright (AUS)	438	548	0.799
7	Mika Miyazato (JPN)	572	716	0.799
8	Cindy LaCrosse	417	522	0.799
9	Becky Morgan (WAL)	437	551	0.793
10	Jiyai Shin (KOR)	461	582	0.792

Greens in Regulation

		%
1	Suzann Pettersen (NOR)	0.745
2	Yani Tseng (TPE)	0.743
3	Paula Creamer	0.743
4	Shanshan Feng (CHN)	0.738
5	Brittany Lincicome	0.717
6	Cristie Kerr	0.712
7	Maria Hjörth (SWE)	0.711
8	Catriona Matthew (SCO)	0.711
9	Jiyai Shin (KOR)	0.709
10	Momoko Ueda (JPN)	0.708

Top money earners on the LPGA Tour 1950–2011

1950	Babe Zaharias	$14,800
1960	Louise Suggs	$16,892
1970	Kathy Whitworth	$30,235
1980	Beth Daniel	$231,000
1990	Beth Daniel	$863,578
2000	Karrie Webb (AUS)	$1,876,853
2005	Annika Sörenstam (SWE)	$2,588,240

2006	Lorena Ochoa (MEX)	$2,592,872
2007	Lorena Ochoa (MEX)	$4,364,994
2008	Lorena Ochoa (MEX)	$2,763,193
2009	Ji Yai Shin (KOR)	$1,807,334
2010	Na Yeon Choi (KOR)	$1,871,166
2011	Yani Tseng (TPE)	$2,921,713

Holes in one

Ten players achieved an ace on the 2011 Tour:

Heather Bowie Young	Sarah Kemp (AUS)	Jenny Suh
Na Yeon Choi (KOR)	Pernilla Lindberg (SWE)	Jaclyn Sweeney
Vicky Hurst	Jessica Shepley (CAN)	
Juli Inkster	Jiyai Shin (KOR)	

Asian players on top again

Of the 24 events on the 2011 LPGA Tour, no less than 19 were won by non-American players. Asian golfers dominated the list once again with Taipei's Yani Tseng capturing seven titles. Karrie Webb (AUS), Suzann Pettersen (NOR) and Brittany Lincicome won two apiece.

Top ten finishes

Seven players achieved top ten finishes in double figures in 2011. They were:

		Top ten	Events played
1	Yani Tseng (TPE)	14	22
2	Na Yeon Choi (KOR)	12	21
	Cristie Kerr	12	22
	Stacy Lewis	12	23
5	Suzann Pettersen (NOR)	11	20
6	Paula Creamer	10	21
	I K Kim	10	21

German golfer Gal one of four first time winners

Germany's Sandra Gal was one of only four Rolex first time winners on the LPGA Tour in 2011. Gal shot 16-under-par 276 to beat Jiyai Shin by a shot in the Kia Classic.

The other first time winners were American Stacey Lewis whose 13-under par 275 total was good enough for her to beat Yani Tseng in the first major of 2011 – the Kraft Nabisco Championship.

Japan's Momoka Ueda needed a play-off in the Mizuno Classis to beat Shanshan Feng after both had tied on 16-under-par 200 while Hee Young Park from South Korea beat Sandra Gal and Paula Creamer by two shots in the CME Group Titleholders event.

In 2010 there were only two first-timers but in 2009 there were seven and in 2008 eight including Taiwan's Yani Tseng, now the No 1 on the LPGA Tour.

Multiple winners dominate the LPGA money list

Since its inception in 1950, there have been 15 multiple winners of the annual LPGA Tour money list. Kathy Whitworth and Annika Sörenstam tie for the lead with eight years apiece with Mickey Wright on four and Patty Berg, JoAnne Carner, Beth Daniel, Nancy Lopez, Betsy King, Lorena Ochoa and Karrie Webb with three each. Two-time winners are Pat Bradley, Judy Rankin, Louise Suggs and Babe Zaharias who topped the list for the first two years. In the 62 year history of the Tour, the lowest annual tally was $12,639 by Beverly Hanson in 1958 and the highest was $4,364,994 won by Lorena Ochoa in 2007. The full list is:

Patty Berg 1954, 1955, 1957
Pat Bradley 1986, 1991
JoAnne Carner 1974, 1982, 1983
Na Yeon Choi (KOR) 2010
Beth Daniel 1980, 1981, 1990
Laura Davies (ENG) 1994
Marlene Hagge 1956
Beverly Hanson 1958
Nancy Lopez 1978, 1979, 1985
Betsy King 1984, 1989, 1993

Carol Mann 1969
Dottie (Pepper) Mochrie 1992
Lorena Ochoa (MEX), 2006, 2007, 2008
Ayako Okamoto (JPN) 1987
Sandra Palmer 1975
Judy Rankin 1976, 1977
Betsy Rawls 1952, 1959
Annika Sörenstam (SWE) 1995, 1997, 1998, 2001, 2002, 2003, 2004, 2005

Louise Suggs 1953, 1960
Yani Tseng (TPE) 2011
Sherri Turner 1988
Ji-Yai Shin (KOR) 2009
Karrie Webb (AUS) 1996, 1999, 2000
Kathy Whitworth 1965, 1966, 1967, 1968, 1970, 1971, 1972, 1973
Mickey Wright 1961, 1962, 1963, 1964
Babe Zaharias 1950, 1951

Ladies Asian Golf Tour 2011

www.lagt.org

Royal Open	Hsinchu, Taiwan	Lee Mi Rim (KOR)	213 (−3)
Taifong Open	Chang Hua, Taiwan	Yani Tseng (TPE)	218 (+2)
Hitachi Classic	Taoyan, Taiwan	Phatlum Pornanong (THA)	211 (−5)
Thailand Ladies Open	Lakewood CC, Bangkok	Tanaporn Kongkiatkrai (THA)*	208 (−8)

Beat Cho A-ram (KOR) at ninth extra hole

Yumeya Championship	Hirao CC, Nagoya, Japan	Yokomine Sakura (JPN)	208 (−8)
Swinging Skirt TLPGA Open	Miramar Lin-Kou G&CC, Taiwan	Hsieh Yu Ling (TPE)	215 (−1)
Sanya Ladies Open	Yalong Bay CC, Hainan, China	Frances Bondad (AUS)	205 (−11)
Suzhou Ladies Open	Suzhou Taihu International GC, Jiang-su, China	Yani Tseng (TPE)	200 (−16)
Hero Honda Women's Indian Open	DLF G&CC New Delhi	Caroline Hedwall (SWE)	204 (−12)

Final Ranking (tournaments played in brackets)

1	1 Yani Tseng (TPE)	(1)	US$62,550	6	Vikki Laing (SCO)	(3)		35,602
2	Caroline Hedwall (SWE)	(2)	53,132	7	Pornanong Phatlum (THA)	(2)		34,028
3	Pernilla Lindberg (SWE)	(2)	52,076	8	Melissa Reid (ENG)	(2)		27,685
4	Frances Bondad (AUS)	(3)	47,150	9	Nontaya Srosawang (THA)	(5)		26,911
5	Lee-Anne Pace (RSA)	(3)	43,817	10	Becky Morgan (WAL)	(2)		24,245

Australian LPG Tour 2010–2011

Players are of Australian nationality unless stated

www.alpg.com.au

St George's Basin Pro-am	St George's Basin GC	Joanne Mills	43 (−1)
Xstrata Coal Branxton Pro-am	Branxton GC	Rachel L Bailey	139 (−5)
NRE Gujurat Russell Vale Challenge Cup	Russell Vale GC	Ryann O'Toole (USA)	57 (−3)
Moss Vale Ladies Classic	Moss Vale GC	Katherine Hull	131 (−11)
Mount Broughton Classic	Mount Broughton G&CC	Katherine Hull	134 (−10)
Bing Lee Samsung NSW Ladies Open	Oaklands GC	Caroline Hedwall (SWE)	205 (−11)
Actew AGL Royal Canberra Classic	Royal Canberra GC	Ashley Ona (am)	207 (−12)
ISPS Handa Australian Ladies Open	Commonwealth GC, Melbourne	Yani Tseng (TPE)	276 (−16)
ANZ RACV Masters	RACV Royal Pines Resort	Yani Tseng (TPE)	264 (−24)
Pegasus New Zealand Women's Open	Pegasus G and SC	Kristie Smith	276 (−12)
Lady Anne Funerals Ryde Paramatta Pro-am	Ryde Paramatta GC	Sara Kemp*	69 (°4)

Kemp beat Sarah Oh at the second hole

Final Ranking 2010–2011 (tournaments played in brackets)

1	Kristie Smith	(8)	A$60,333	6	Frances Bonded	(8)		27,436
2	Nikkin Campbel	(3)	56,320	7	Stephanie Na	(8)		27,156
3	Katherine Hull	(4)	39.895	8	Karrie Webb	(2)		25,412
4	Sarah-Jane Smith	(19)	31,752	9	Rachel L Bailey	(8)		17.173
5	Sarah Kemp	(10)	27,727	10	Sarah Oh	(10)		13,879

China LPGA Tour

www.clpga.org

Players are of Chinese nationality unless stated

Event	Venue	Winner	Score
Shanghai Classic	Shanghai Orient GC	Ye Liying	271 (+1)
Yangzhou Challenge	Yangzhou Orient GC	Porani Chutichai (THA)	210 (−6)
Beijing Renji Challenge	Beijing Renji GC	Porani Chutichai (THA)	215 (−1)
Beijing Pearl Challenge	Orient Pearl GC	Patcharajutar Kongkraphan (THA)	208 (−8)
Yantai Yangmadao Challenge	Yantai Orient GC, Shandong	Tian Hong	220 (+4)
Caofeidian Challenge	Caofeidian Wetlands International GC	Patcharajutar Kongkraphan (THA)	212 (−4)
Wenzhou Yangyi	Wenshau Orient GC	Pan Yong Hong	207 (−9)
Wuhan Challenge	Wuhan Orient GC	Porani Chutichai (THA)	214 (−2)
Sanya Ladies Open	Sanya Yalong Bay GC	Frances Bondad (AUS)	205 (−11)
Suzhou Ladies Open	Suzhou Taihu International GC, Jiang-su	Yani Tseng (TPE)	200 (−16)
Hyundai China Ladies Open	Orient Xiamen GC	Kim Hye-youn (KOR)	210 (−6)

Final Ranking

1	Porani Chutichai (THA)	BMG 239,415		6	Tian Hong	191,980
2	Pan Yan Hong	220,356		7	Guo Cai Zhu	134,571
3	Lia Jia Yun	212,931		8	Huang Ping	127,227
4	Patcharajutar K (THA)	204,498		9	Zhan Yuyang	126,695
5	Thidipa Suwannapura (THA)	199,279		10	Yan Pan Pan	114,325

Miyazato is first Japanese to be European No 1

Ai Miyazato has become the first Japanese player to win the Ladies European Tour's Henderson Money List title.

The 26-year-old from Okinawa was the top earner in 2011 with €363,079.68 from just two tournaments played. She earned all of her prize money with her bumper first prize cheque at the Evian Masters presented by Societe Generale in France, which she won for the second time in July, later donating a substantial part of her winnings, ¥20,000,000 (around €197,000), to tsunami relief efforts in Japan.

"To be honest I have mixed feelings because I'm receiving the award from just winning one event on the LET. However I've never won the money title on any tour so I'm really happy," Miyazato said.

"I don't just play for results or awards but professionals are in a way judged by accomplishments and I will be proud of this award when I look back at my career."

In March, the Japanese trio of Ai Miyazato, Momoko Ueda and Mika Miyazato set up a fundraising website with the slogan "Makeruna Nippon – Never Give Up Japan" to help Japan in its recovery from the tragic earthquake and tsunami. In Japan alone they raised over $100,000.

Alexandra Armas, Executive Director of the Ladies European Tour, praised Miyazato's on and off-course achievements. "We would like to congratulate Ai on winning the 2011 Henderson Money List, but also on the way in which she has conducted herself this year, through a devastating period when she challenged herself to bring as many smiles as possible back to the faces of the disaster victims in Japan. She is a tremendous ambassador for women's golf and an inspiration to all."

Duramed Futures Tour 2011

www.duramedfuturestour.com

Players are of American nationality unless stated

Ekey pips Ferrero for Futures No 1 spot

Kathleen Ekey from Ohio edged out Lisa Ferrero from California for Player of the Year honours in the 2011 Futures Tour. Despite missing the cut in the second last tournament and finishing just inside the top 50 in the final event of the season Ekey, who has a degree in sports communications from the University of Alabama, amassed $66,412 and headed the list of 10 golfers who gained full LPGA Tour cards at the end of the Futures season.

Ekey, Ferrero and Sydnee Michaels from California, who took the Gaelle Truet Rookie of the Year honours, all had two wins during the season with Michaels moving up dramatically in the last two weeks .

In contrast to Ekey, 23-year-old Michaels, who has a degree in history from the University of California LA, won the final two events of the season shooting 17-under par for her last six rounds and picking up $32,200 to finish fourth in the rankings with $56,232.

Players from 39 States in America and from 36 countries around the world took part in the 2011 Futures season in which American players won 11 of the 16 tournaments and overseas players five. There were 10 first-time winners.

Michaels, who with her fast finish beat French golfer Valentine Derrey to Rookie honours, had five top 10 finishes and was one of 38 Californian players competing on the Futures Tour last year .

Tournament	Venue	Winner	Score
Florida's Natural Charity Classic	Lake Region Y&CC, Winter Haven	Tzu-Chi Lin (TPE)	206 (−10)
Daytona Beach Invitational	LPGA Interntional	Haru Nomura (JPN)	207 (−9)
Santorini Riviera Najarit Classic	El Tigre G and CC, Najarit, Mexico	Ryan O'Toole	211 (−8)
Symatra Classic	The Dominion CC, San Antonio, TX	Lisa Ferrero	210 (−6)
Ladies Titan Tire Challenge	Hunters Ridge GC, Marion, IA	Kathleen Ekay	215 (−1)
Teva Championship	The Golf Centre at King's Island, Mason, OH	Lisa Ferrero	207 (−6)
Tate and Lyle Players Championship	Hickory Point GC, Decatur, IL	Valetine Derrey (FRA)	272 (−6)
Island Resort Championship	Sweetgrass GC, Harris, MI	Stephanie Kim	209 (−7)
South Shore Championship	White Hawk CC, IN	Tiffany Joh	138 (−6)
Event shortened due to rain			
ING New England Golf Classic	Wintonbury Hills GC, Bloomfield, CT	Brittany Johnson	199 (−11)
The International at Concord	Beaver Meadow GC, Concord, NH	Jessica Shepley (CAN)	203 (−13)
Alliance Bank Golf Classic	Drumlins CC (East Course), Syracuse, NY	Kathleen Ekay	205 (−8)
Pennsylvania Classic	Felicity Mountain Resort and Spa, Harrisburg, PA	Cathryn Bristow (NZL)	135 (−9)
(Event reduced to 36 holes because of bad weather)			
Eagle Classic	Richmond CC, Richmond, VA	Mo Martin	203 (−13)
Vidalia Championship	Hawk's Point GC, Vidalia, GA	Sydnee Michaels	207 (−9)
Price Chopper Tour Championship	Capital Hills at Albany, Albany, NY	Sydnee Michaels	202 (−8)

Final Ranking

Top ten win cards for the LPGA Tour in 2012 and the next five gain entry into the LPGA final qualifying competition. Figures in brackets indicate tournaments played.

1	Kathleen Ekey	(16)	$66,412	9	Jenny Gleason	(15)	30,331
2	Lisa Ferrero	(16)	58,808	10	Tzu-Chi Lin (TPE)	(14)	29,861
3	Mo Martin	(16)	58,218	11	Sophia Sheridan (MEX)	(16)	28,724
4	Sydnee Michaels	(15)	56,232	12	Jackie Barenborg	(15)	27,433
5	Jan Rah	(15)	46,669	13	Dawn Shockley	(16)	27,332
6	Tiffany Joh	(7)	37.566	14	Ayaka Kaneko (JPN)	(16)	26,882
7	Valentine Derrey (FRA)	(15)	34,572	15	Ashley Prange	(16)	25,925
8	Hanna Kang (KOR)	(15)	32,992				

Japan LPGA Tour 2011

Players are of Japanese nationality unless stated

http://en.wikipedia.org/wiki/LPGA_of_Japan_Tour

Daikin Orchid Ladies	Ryukyu GC, Okinawa	Park In Bee (KOR)	205 (–11)
Yokohama Tire PRGR Ladies Cup	Kochi	Cancelled	
T Point Ladies	Kagoshima	Cancelled	
Yamaha Ladies Open	Shizuoka	Cancelled	
Studio Alice Open	Hyago	Cancelled	
Nashijin Ladies Classic	Kumamoto	Yuri Fudoh*	211 (–5)
*Beat Yukari Baba at the first extra hole			
Fujisankei Ladies Classic	Shizuoka	Kumiko Kaneda	211 (–5)
Cyber Agent Ladies	Chiba	Yuri Fudoh	201 (–10)
World Ladies Championship (Salonpas Cup)	Ibaraki	Ahn Sun-ju (KOR)	278 (–10)
Fundokin Ladies	Fukuoka	Miki Saiki	208 (–8)
Chukyo TV Bridgestone Ladies Open	Aichi	Harukyo Nomura	203 (–13)
Yonex Ladies	Niigata	Hiromi Mogi	211 (–5)
Resort Trust Ladies	Grand Karuizawa GC, Miyota, Nagano	Sakura Yokomine	206 (–10)
Suntory Ladies Open	Hyago	Ahn Sun-ju (KOR)	204 (–14)
Nicherei Ladies	Sauguardo, Chiba	Lee Ji-hee (KOR)	204 (–12)
Nichi-Iko Ladies Open	Yatsuo CC, Toyama	Ayako Uehara	200 (–16)
Stanley Ladies	Tomei CC, Shiuzuoka	Chie Arimura	201 (–15)
Meiji Cup	Sappora International CC, Hokkaido	Shanshan Feng (CHN)	202 (–14)
NEC Karuizawa 72	Nogano	Ahn Sun Ju (KOR)	200 (–16)
CAT Ladies	Dai Hakone CC, Hakone	Chie Arimura	281 (–11)
Nitori Ladies	Hokkaido	Ritsuko Ryo	209 (–7)
Golf 5 Ladies	Gifu	Ye Liying (KOR)	136 (–6)
Japan LPGA Championship (Konica Minolta Cup)	Grandage GC, Nara	Yuko Mitsuka	282 (–6)
Munsingwear Ladies Tokai Classic	Aichi	Mayu Hattori	206 (–10)
Dunlop Women's Open (Cup Miyagiterebi)	Rifu GC	Shanshan Feng (CHN)	208 (–8)
44th Japan Women's Open	Nagoya GC (Wago course), Aichi	Yukari Baba	292 (+12)
Fujitsu Ladies	Tokyu 700 Club, Chiba	Saiki Fujita	209 (–7)
Sankyo Ladies Open	Gunma	Ahn Sun-ju (KOR)	207 (–9)
Masters GC Ladies	Hyogo	Shiho Oyhama*	209 (–7)
*Beat Paula Creamer (USA) at the third extra hole			
Hisako Higuchi-Morinaga Weider Ladies	Chiba	Chie Arimura*	209 (–7)
*Beat Yukari Baba at the third extra hole			
Mizuno Classic	Kintetsu Kashikojima CC, Shima-shi, Mie	Momoka Ueda*	200 (–16)
*Beat Shanshan Feng (CHN) at the third extra hole			
Ito En Ladies	Chiba	Asako Fujimoto	206 (–10)
Daio Paper Elleair Ladies Open	Kagawa	Lee Ji-Hee (KOR)*	207 (–9)
*Beat Bo-Bae Song (KOR) at the first extra hole			
Japan LPGA Tour Championship (Ricoh Cup)	Miyazaki CC	Jeon Mi-Jeong (KOR)	280 (–8)

Final Ranking

1	Ahn Sun-ju (KOR)	¥127.93m	6	Jeon Mi-jeong (KOR)	67.78m
2	Lee Ji-Hee (KOR)	102.32m	7	Shanshan Feng (CHN)	67.14m
3	Chie Arimura	88.69m	8	Miki Saiki	62.73m
4	Sakura Yokomine	87.30m	9	Yuri Fudoh	60.52m
5	Yukari Baba	76.29m	10	Ritsuko Ryu	57.56m

Korean LPGA Tour 2011

Players are of Korean nationality unless stated   http://wapedia.mobi/en/LPGA_of_Korea_Tour

Hyundai China Ladies Open	Orient CC, Xiamin	Kim Hye-youn	212 (−4)
Lotte Mart Ladies Open	Sky Hill, Seogwipo	Shim Hyun-hwa	276 (−12)
Hyundai E&C Seokyung Ladies Open	Suwon	Kim Ha-neul*	210 (−6)
*Beat Lee Hyun-Joo at second extra hole			
Taeyoung Cup Korea Women's Open	Gyeongju	Jeong Yeon-joo	285 (−3)
Rush and Cash Charity Classic	Jeju	Lee Seung-hyun*	209 (−7)
*Beat Jang Ji-hye and Lee Bo-mee at the fourth extra hole			
Doosan Match Play Championship	Chuncheon	Final: Yang Soo-jun beat Shin Hyun-hwa 4 and 3	
Woori Investment and Securities Ladies Championship	Pocheon	Yoon Seul-ah	209 (−7)
SBS Tour Lottee Cantata Ladies Open	Seogwipo	Ryu So-Yeon	202 (−14)
S-Oil Champions Invitational	Jeju City	Lee Mi-Rim	200 (−16)
Hidden Valley Ladies Open	Jincheon	Hyun Min Pyun*	208
*Beat Bo A Kim at the first extra hole			
Nefs Masterpiece	Echo Land GR	Lee Jeong-eun	202 (−14)
LIG Classic	Pocheon	Hyun Hee (Honey) Moon*	211 (−5)
*Beat Lee Min-young at the third extra hole			
Hanwha Finance Network Open	Taean	Choi Na-yeon	287 (−1)
MetLife Hankyung KLPGA Championship	Pyeongchang	Choi Hye-jung (HJ)	282 (−6)
Golden Age Cup Daewoo Securities Classic	Jisan CC, Yogen, Icheon	Yu Na Park	211 (−5)
LPGA Hana Bank Championship	Sky 72 GC (Ocean course), Incheon	Yani Tseng (TPE)	202 (−14)
LPGA Malaysia	Kuala Lumpur G&CC	Choi Na-yeon	269 (−15)
Hite Cup Championship	Yeoju	Kim Ha-neul	285 (−3)
KB Star Tour	Incheon	Amy Yang	274 (−14)
eDaily-KYJ Golf Ladies Open	Seogwipo	Kim Ha-Neul	205 (−11)
ADT CAPS Championship	Seogwipo	Ji Won Yoon	213 (−3)
2012 season			
Hyundai Chin Ladies Open	Orient Xiamin GC	Kim Hye-youn	210 (−6)

Final Ranking   (events played in brackets)

1	Kim Ha-neul	(19)	₩524,297,417	6	Kim Hye-yoon	(19)	256,523,125
2	Shim Hyun-hwa	(19)	342,113,958	7	Lee Seung-hyun	(19)	243,324,833
3	Ryu So-hyun	(19)	332,097,626	8	Choi Hye-yong	(19)	234,355,375
4	Yang Soo-jin	(18)	312,855,546	9	Choi Hye-jung	(18)	223,805,000
5	Jeong Yeon-joo	(19)	280,313,667	10	Yoon Seul-ah	(18)	215,802,223

Stunning 62 earns Choi Hye-jung a Korean major

There was nothing to suggest earlier in the week that Choi Hye-jung – always referred to as "HJ" – was poised to win a major on the 2011 Korean Tour. She had shot what many would have considered a title-shattering second round 76 at the MetLife Hankyung KLPGA Championship at Pyeongchang yet she produced one of the most electrifying finishes to any tournament far less one on the Korean LPGA circuit.

Hye-jung trimmed 14 shots off her score of the previous day for a career low 62 to win by one on six under par 282 from Yang Soo-jin. What makes HJ's score all the more remarkable is that only one player was under par after 54 holes and nobody else other than HJ on the final day shot better than 67!

After rounds of 71, 73 and 76 Choi came alive on Sunday making 10 birdies for her 62.

International Team Events

Europe stage dramatic fight back to win the Solheim Cup

Just when it looked as if the Americans were going to win the Solheim Cup for a ninth time Europe, captained by the indomitable Alison Nicholas, rallied at Killeen Castle in County Meath to record a dramatic last gasp success.

With Europe still requiring two points to reach the magical 14½ pts total which would guarantee success they were down in two of the three games left on the course and square in the other. After a day in which flooded greens, a waterlogged course and thunder and lightening caused three momentum-stopping delays it looked good for captain Rosie Jones and her American side.

With Cristie Kerr unable to play because of a wrist injury and, under the captain's agreement, conceding a point to Karen Stupples, it meant that Europe led 9–8 with 11 singles to come. The task they faced was to win five and a half points for only their fourth victory. since the fixture was first played at Lake Nona in 1990

Scotland's rock-solid Catriona Matthew and Sweden's Sophie Gustafson,who ended the week with four wins out of four, gave the Europeans a perfect start with respective victories over Paula Creamer by 6 and 5 and Stacey Lewis on the last green.

Then it became decidedly uneasy for Europe. After being one up with one to play Laura Davies, the 47-year-old who has played in all 12 games and is top Cup points scorer with 24½ points, halved with 51-year-old Julie Inkster, the oldest player to compete in the Cup, and then with Anna Nordqvist losing to Morgan Pressel, Sandra Gal going down to Brittany Lang, Melissa Reid losing out to Vicky Hurst and Maria Hjorth to Christina Kim the pendulum had swung very much America's way.

Hope of a European victory was rekindled when rookie Christel Boeljon from the Netherlands kept her cool to score a last green win over long-hitting Brittany Lincicome. The overall score was now 12½–12½ but America were still in a strong position.

On the course Suzanne Pettersen, the World No 2 was two down with three to play against Michelle Wie but the 30-year-old Norwegian began the fight back by making birdies at the last three holes to win them all and a point. It was an inspirational performance.

Then Swede Caroline Hedwall, a double winner on the Ladies European Tour in her first season and with her twin on the bag, came back from two down with two to play against American rookie Ryann O'Toole to gain a half point and to cap it all Spain's Azahara Muñoz finished strongly to edge out Angela Stanford on the last green. Job done. Europe 15, USA 13.

For the team and captain Nicholas, who in 1997 held off the determine challenge of Nancy Lopez to win the US Women's Open, it was a day to remember and savour. Even allowing for her major successes in America and in Britain in 1987 Nicholas insisted: "This is the best day ever. It was agony watching out there but my team played with heart and passion. The rookies were fantastic but this was a great team effort. " Her controversial decision to rest some of her most experienced and strongest players on day two to leave them fresh for the crucial last day singles had paid off.

From the start, Europe had played with courage, belief and determination against the stronger American side. The first series of foursomes were shared 2–2 and the home side edged in front at the end of the first day by winning the first series of fourballs 2½–1½ . On that first afternoon only Davies and Reid were losers against Pressel and Creamer.

On the second day, Swedes Gustafson and Hedwall and Nordqvist and Hjorth picked up foursomes points against Lewis and Stanford and Lang and Inkster and with Matthew and Muñoz finishing all square with Kerr and Creamer Europe led 7–5 and then went 8–5 up when Davies and Reid beat Lang and Wie in the first of the second series of fourballs.

The remaining three points in the afternoon games went, however, to the Americans leaving the overall score 8–8 with 12 singles to come. The rest is history.

The Solheim Cup   *Killeen Castle, County Meath, Ireland*

Captains: Europe: Alison Nicholas; USA: Rosie Jones

First Day, Foursomes
Maria Hjorth (SWE) and Anna Nordqvist (SWE) lost to Michell Wie and Cristie Kerr 2 and 1
Karen Stupples (ENG) and Melissa Reid (ENG) lost to Paula Creamer and Brittany Lincicome 1 hole
Catriona Matthew (SCO) and Azahara Muñoz (ESP) beat Stacey Lewis and Angela Stanford 3 and 2
Suzann Pettersen (NOR) and Sophie Gustafson (SWE) beat Brittany Lang and Julie Inkster 1 up

First Day, Fourballs
Laura Davies (ENG) and Reid lost to Morgan Pressell and Creamer 1 hole
Matthew and Sandra Gal (GER) halved with Kim and Ryanne O'Toole
Gustafson and Caroline Hedwall (SWE) beat Hurst and Lincicome 5 and 4
Pettersen and Nordqvist beat Kerr and Wie 2 holes
Match position: Europe 4½ USA 3½

Second Day, Foursomes
Hedwall and Gustafson beat Stanford and Lewis 6 and 5
Stupples and Christel Boeljon (NED) lost to Pressel and O'Toole 3 and 2
Hjorth and Nordqvist beat Lang and Inkster 3 and 2
Matthew and Muñoz halved with Kerr and Creamer

Second Day, Fourballs
Davies and Reid beat Lang and Wie 4 and 3
Pettersen and Hedwall lost to Pressel and Kerr 1 hole
Gal and Boeljon lost to Lewis and O'Toole 2 and 1
Hjorth and Muñoz lost to Creamer and Lincicome 3 and 2
Match position: Europe 8, USA 8

Third Day – Singles
Matthew beat Creamer 6 and 5
Gustafson beat Lewis 2 holes
Norqvist lost to Pressel 2 and 1
Davies halved with Inkster
Reid lost to Hurst 2 holes
Boeljon beat Lincicome 2 holes
Gal lost to Lang 6 and 5
Hjorth lost to Kim 4 and 2
Pettersen beat Wie 1 hole
Hedwall halved with O'Toole
Munoz beat Stanford 1 hole
Stupples beat Kerr (withdrew, wrist injury)

Final result: Europe 15, USA 13

	Previous results		
1990	USA 11½	Europe 4½	Lake Nona, Florida
1992	Europe 11½	USA 6½	Dalmahoy, Scotland
1994	USA 13	Europe 7	The Greenbrier, West Virginia
1996	USA 17	Europe 11	St Pierre, Wales
1998	USA 16	Europe 12	Muirfield Village, Ohio
2000	Europe 14½	USA 11½	Loch Lomond, Scotland
2002	USA 15½	Europe 12½	Interachen, Minnesota
2003	Europe 17½	USA 10½	Barseback, Sweden
2005	USA 15½	Europe 12½	Crooked Stick Indiana
2007	USA 16	Europe 12	Halmstad, Sweden
2009	USA 16	Europe 12	Rich Harvest Farms, Illinois

2009 *Rich Harvest Farms, IL, USA* Aug 17–23

Result: USA 16, Europe 12

Captains: Beth Daniel (USA), Alison Nicholas (Europe)

First Day – Fourball
Creamer and Kerr beat Pettersen and Gustafson 1 hole
Stanford and Inkster lost to Alfredsson and Elosegui
1 hole
Lang and Lincicome beat Davies and Brewerton 5 and 4
Pressel and Wie halved with Matthew and Hjörth

Foursomes
Kim and Gulbis beat Pettersen and Gustafson 4 and 2
Stanford and Castrale lost to Brewerton and Nocera
3 and 1
McPherson and Lincicome lost to Hjörth and Nordqvist
3 and 2
Creamer and Inkster beat Matthew and Moodie 2 and 1

Second Day – Fourball
Kim and Wie beat Alfredsson and Elosegui 5 and 4
Lang and Stanford halved with Luna and Matthew
Castrale and Kerr lost to Nordqvist and Pettersen
1 hole
Lincicome and McPherson lost to Hjörth and Nocera
1 hole

Foursomes
Creamer and Inkster lost to Gustafson and Moodie
4 and 3
McPherson and Pressel beat Alfredsson and Pettersen
2 holes
Gulbis and Kim lost to Brewerton and Nocera 5 and 4
Kerr and Wie beat Hjörth and Nordqvist 1 hole

Third Day – Singles
Paula Creamer beat Suzann Pettersen (NOR) 3 and 2
Angela Stanford beat Becky Brewerton (WAL) 5 and 4
Michelle Wie beat Helen Alfredsson (SWE) 1 hole
Brittany Lang halved with Laura Davies (ENG)
Juli Inkster halved with Gwladys Nocera (FRA)
Kristy McPherson lost to Catriona Matthew (SCO)
3 and 2
Brittany Lincicome beat Sophie Gustafson (SWE) 3 and 2
Nicole Castrale lost to Diana Luna (ITA) 3 and 2
Christina Kim beat Tania Elosegui (ESP) 2 holes
Cristie Kerr halved with Maria Hjörth (SWE)
Morgan Pressel beat Anna Nordqvist (SWE) 3 and 2
Natalie Gulbis halved with Janice Moodie (SCO)

2007 *Halmstad, Tylosand, Sweden* Sept 14–16

Result: USA 16, Europe 12

*Captains: Helen Alfredsson (Europe),
Betsy King (USA)*

First Day – Foursomes
Pettersen & Gustafson halved with Hurst & Kerr
Sörenstam & Matthew lost to Steinhauer & Diaz
4 and 2
Davies & Brewerton lost to Inkster & Creamer 2 and 1
Nocera & Hjörth beat Gulbis & Pressel 3 and 2

Fourballs
Matthew & Iben Tinning beat Hurst & Lincicome 4 and 2
Sörenstam & Hjörth halved with Stanford &
Prammanasudh
Gustafson & Nocera lost to Castrale & Kerr 3 and 2
Johnson & Davies halved with Creamer & Pressel

Second Day – Foursomes
Hjörth & Nocera halved with Steinhauer & Diaz
Gustafson & Pettersen halved with Inkster & Creamer
Tinning & Hauert lost to Hurst & Stanford 4 and 2
Sörenstam & Matthew beat Castrale & Kerr 1 hole

Fourballs
Wessberg & Hjörth halved with Creamer & Lincicome
Johnson & Tinning halved with Inkster & Prammanasudh
Brewerton & Davies beat Gulbis & Castrale 1 hole
Sörenstam & Pettersen beat Kerr & Pressel 3 and 2

Third Day – Singles
Catriona Matthew (SCO) beat Laura Diaz 3 and 2
Sophie Gustafson (SWE) lost to Pat Hurst 2 and 1
Suzann Pettersen (NOR) lost to Stacy Prammanasudh
2 holes
Iben Tinning (DEN) lost to Juli Inkster 4 and 3
Becky Brewerton (WAL) halved with Sherri Steinhauer
Trish Johnson (ENG) lost to Angela Stanford 3 and 2
Annika Sörenstam (SWE) lost to Morgan Pressel 2 and 1
Laura Davies (ENG) beat Brittany Lincicome 4 and 3
Bettina Hauert (GER) lost to Nicole Castrale 3 and 2
Maria Hjörth (SWE) lost to Paula Creamer 2 and 1
Linda Wessberg (SWE) beat Cristie Kerr 1 hole
Gwladys Nocera (FRA) lost to Natalie Gulbis 4 and 3

2005 *Crooked Stick GC, Carmel, IN, USA* Sept 9–11

Result: USA 15½, Europe 12½

*Captains: Nancy Lopez (USA),
Catrin Nilsmark (Europe)*

First Day – Foursomes
Daniel & Creamer halved with Koch & Matthew
Kerr & Gulbis lost to Davies & Hjörth 2 and 1
Kim & Hurst halved with Gustafson & Johnson
Redman & Diaz lost to Sörenstam & Pettersen 1 hole

Fourballs
Jones & Mallon beat Hjörth & Tinning 3 and 2
Hurst & Ward beat Sörenstam & Matthew 2 and 1
Kerr & Gulbis lost to Gustafson & Stupples 2 and 1
Creamer & Inkster lost to Davies & Pettersen 4 and 3

Second Day – Foursomes
Kim & Gulbis beat Nocera & Kreutz 4 and 2
Creamer & Inkster beat Davies & Hjörth 3 and 2
Diaz & Ward lost to Gustafson & Koch 5 and 3
Redman & Hurst beat Sörenstam & Matthew 2 holes

Fourballs
Hurst & Kim lost to Davies & Sörenstam 4 and 2
Daniel & Inkster halved with Tinning & Johnson
Kerr & Creamer beat Koch & Matthew 1 hole
Jones & Mallon halved with Gustafson & Pettersen

Third Day – Singles
Juli Inkster beat Sophie Gustafson (SWE) 2 and 1
Paula Creamer beat Laura Davies (ENG) 7 and 5
Pat Hurst beat Trish Johnson (ENG) 2 and 1
Laura Diaz beat Iben Tinning (DEN) 6 and 5
Christina Kim beat Ludivine Kreutz (FRA) 5 and 4
Beth Daniel lost to Annika Sörenstam (SWE) 4 and 3
Natalie Gulbis beat Maria Hjörth (SWE) 2 and 1
Wendy Ward lost to Catriona Matthew (SCO) 3 and 2
Michele Redman lost to Carin Koch (SWE) 2 and 1
Cristie Kerr lost to Gwladys Nocera (FRA) 2 and 1
Meg Mallon beat Karen Stupples (ENG) 3 and 1
Rosie Jones halved with Suzann Pettersen (NOR)

2003 *Barsebäck, Sweden* Sept 12–14

Result: Europe 17½, USA 10½

*Captains: Catrin Nilsmark (Europe),
Patty Sheehan (USA)*

First Day – Foursomes
Koch & Davies halved with Daniel & Robbins
Moodie & Matthew beat Inkster & Ward 5 and 3
Sörenstam & Pettersen beat Diaz & Bowie 4 and 3
Gustafson & Esterl beat Mallon & Jones 3 and 2

2003 *continued*

Fourball
Davies & Matthew lost to Kuehne & Kerr 2 and 1
Sörenstam & Koch lost to Inkster & Daniel 1 hole
Pettersen & Meunier-Labouc beat Stanford & Mallon 3 and 2
Tinning & Gustafson lost to Redman & Jones 2 holes

Second Day – Foursomes
Gustafson & Pettersen beat Kuehne & Kerr 3 and 1
Esterl & Tinning halved with Stanford & Redman
Sörenstam & Koch beat Ward and Bowie 3 and 4
Moodie & Matthew halved with Mallon & Robbins

Fourball
Sanchez & McKay lost to Daniel & Inkster 5 and 4
Gustafson & Davies lost to Kerr & Kuehne 2 and 1
Matthew & Moodie beat Ward & Jones 4 and 3
Sörenstam & Pettersen beat Robbins & Diaz 1 hole

Third Day – Singles
Janice Moodie (SCO) beat Kelli Kuehne 3 and 2
Carin Koch (SWE) lost to Juli Inkster 5 and 4
Sophie Gustafson (SWE) beat Heather Bowie 5 and 4
Iben Tinning (DEN) beat Wendy Ward 2 and 1
Ana Belen Sanchez (ESP) lost to Michele Redman 3 and 1
Catriona Matthew (SCO) beat Rosie Jones 2 and 1
Annika Sörenstam (SWE) beat Angela Stanford 3 and 2
Suzann Pettersen (NOR) lost to Cristie Kerr conceded
Laura Davies (ENG) beat Meg Mallon conceded
Elisabeth Esterl (GER) lost to Laura Diaz 5 and 4
Mhairi McKay (SCO) beat Beth Daniel conceded
Patricia Meunier-Labouc (FRA) beat Kelly Robbins conceded

2002 *Interlachen CC, Madina, MN* Sept 20–22

Result: USA 15½, Europe 12½
Captains: Patty Sheehan (USA),
*   Dale Reid (Europe)*

First Day – Foursomes
Inkster & Diaz lost to Davies & Marti 2 holes
Daniel & Ward beat Carriedo & Tinning 1 hole
Hurst & Robbins lost to Alfredsson & Pettersen 4 and 2
Kuehne & Mallon lost to Koch & Sörenstam 3 and 2

Fourball
Jones & Kerr beat Davies & Marti 1 hole
Diaz & Klein beat Gustafson & Icher 4 and 3
Mallon & Redman beat Hjörth & Sörenstam 3 and 1
Inkster & Kuehne lost to Koch & McKay 3 and 2

Second Day – Foursomes
Kerr & Redman lost to Koch & Sörenstam 4 and 3
Klein & Ward beat McKay & Tinning 3 and 2
Inkster & Mallon beat Davies & Marti 2 and 1
Diaz & Robbins beat Alfredsson & Pettersen 3 and 1

Fourball
Daniel & Ward lost to Koch & Sörenstam 4 and 3
Hurst & Kuehne lost to Hjörth & Tinning 1 hole
Jones & Kerr lost to Carriedo & Icher 1 hole
Klein & Robbins lost to Davies & Gustafson 1 hole

Third Day – Singles
Juli Inkster beat Raquel Carriedo (ESP) 4 and 3
Laura Diaz beat Paula Marti (ESP) 5 and 3
Emilee Klein beat Helen Alfredsson (SWE) 2 and 1
Kelli Kuehne lost to Iben Tinning (DEN) 4 and 3
Michele Redman halved with Suzann Pettersen (NOR)
Wendy Ward halved with Annika Sörenstam (SWE)
Kelly Robbins beat Maria Hjörth (SWE) 5 and 3
Cristie Kerr lost to Sophie Gustafson (SWE) 3 and 2

Meg Mallon beat Laura Davies (ENG) 3 and 2
Pat Hurst beat Mhairi McKay (SCO) 4 and 2
Beth Daniel halved with Carin Koch (SWE)
Rosie Jones beat Karine Icher (FRA) 3 and 2

2000 *Loch Lomond* Oct 6–8

Result: Europe 14½, USA 11½
Captains: Dale Reid (Europe), Pat Bradley (USA)

First Day – Foursomes
Davies & Nicholas beat Pepper & Inkster 4 and 3
Johnson & Gustafson beat Robbins & Hurst 3 and 2
Nilsmark & Koch beat Burton & Iverson 2 and 1
Sörenstam & Moodie beat Mallon & Daniel 1 hole

First Day – Foursomes
Davies & Nicholas lost to Iverson & Jones 6 and 5
Johnson & Gustafson halved with Inkster & Steinhauer
Neumann & Alfredsson lost to Robbins & Hurst 2 holes
Moodie & Sörenstam beat Mallon & Daniel 1 hole

Second Day – Fourball
Nilsmark & Koch beat Scranton & Redman 2 and 1
Neumann & Meunier Labouc halved with Pepper & Burton
Davies & Carriedo halved with Mallon & Daniel
Sörenstam & Moodie lost to Hurst & Robbins 2 and 1
Johnson & Gustafson beat Jones & Iverson 3 and 2
Nicholas & Alfredsson beat Inkster & Steinhauer 3 and 2

Third Day – Singles
Annika Sörenstam lost to Juli Inkster 5 and 4
Sophie Gustafson lost to Brandie Burton 4 and 3
Helen Alfredsson beat Beth Daniel 4 and 3
Trish Johnson lost to Dottie Pepper 2 and 1
Laura Davies lost to Kelly Robbins 3 and 2
Liselotte Neumann halved with Pat Hurst
Alison Nicholas halved with Sherri Steinhauer
Patricia Meunier Labouc lost to Meg Mallon 1 hole
Catrin Nilsmark beat Rosie Jones 1 hole
Raquel Carriedo lost to Becky Iverson 3 and 2
Carin Koch beat Michele Redman 2 and 1
Janice Moodie beat Nancy Scranton 1 hole

1998 *Muirfield Village, Dublin, OH* Sept 18–20

Result: USA 16, Europe 12
Captains: Judy Rankin (USA), Pia Nilsson (Europe)

First Day – Foursomes
Pepper & Inkster beat Davies & Johnson 3 and 1
Mallon & Burton beat Alfredsson & Nicholas 3 and 1
Robbins & Hurst beat Hackney & Neumann 1 hole
Andrews & Green beat A Sörenstam & Matthew 3 and 2

Fourball
King & Johnson halved with Davies & C Sörenstam
Hurst & Jones beat Hackney & Gustafson 7 and 5
Robbins & Steinhauer lost to Alfredsson & de Lorenzi 2 and 1
Pepper & Burton beat A Sörenstam & Nilsmark 2 holes

Second Day – Foursomes
Andrews & Steinhauer beat A Sörenstam & Matthew 3 and 2
Mallon & Burton lost to Davies & C Sörenstam 3 and 2
Pepper & Inkster beat Alfredsson & de Lorenzi 1 hole
Robbins & Hurst beat Neumann & Nilsmark 1 hole

Fourball
King & Jones lost to A Sörenstam & Nilsmark 5 and 3
Johnson & Green lost to Davies & Hackney 2 holes
Andrews & Steinhauer beat Alfredsson & de Lorenzi 4 and 3
Mallon & Inkster beat Neumann & C Sörenstam 2 and 1

Third Day – Singles

Pat Hurst lost to Laura Davies 1 hole
Juli Inkster lost to Helen Alfredsson 2 and 1
Donna Andrews lost to Annika Sörenstam 2 and 1
Brandie Burton lost to Liselotte Neumann 1 hole
Dottie Pepper beat Trish Johnson 3 and 2
Kelly Robbins beat Charlotta Sörenstam 2 and 1
Chris Johnson lost to Marie Laure de Lorenzi 1 hole
Rosie Jones beat Catrin Nilsmark 6 and 4
Tammie Green beat Alison Nicholas 1 hole
Sherri Steinhauer beat Catriona Matthew 3 and 2
Betsy King lost to Lisa Hackney 6 and 5
Meg Mallon halved with Sophie Gustafson

1996 St Pierre, Chepstow Sept 20–22
Result: USA 17, Europe 11
Captains: Judy Rankin (USA), Mickey Walker (Europe)

First Day – Foursomes
Sörenstam & Nilsmark halved with Robbins & McGann
Davies & Nicholas lost to Sheehan & Jones 1 hole
de Lorenzi & Reid lost to Daniel & Skinner 1 hole
Alfredsson & Neumann lost to Pepper & Burton 2 and 1

Fourball
Davies & Johnson beat Robbins & Bradley 6 and 5
Sörenstam & Marshall beat Skinner & Geddes 1 hole
Neumann & Nilsmark lost to Pepper & King 1 hole
Alfredsson & Nicholas halved with Mallon & Daniel

Second Day – Foursomes
Davies & Johnson beat Daniel & Skinner 4 and 3
Sörenstam & Nilsmark beat Pepper & Burton 1 hole
Neumann & Marshall halved with Mallon & Geddes
de Lorenzi & Alfredsson beat Robbins & McGann 4 and 3

Fourball
Davies & Hackney beat Daniel & Skinner 6 and 5
Sörenstam & Johnson halved with McGann & Mallon
de Lorenzi & Morley lost to Robbins & King 2 and 1
Nilsmark & Neumann beat Sheehan & Geddes 2 and 1

Third Day – Singles
Annika Sörenstam beat Pat Bradley 2 and 1
Kathryn Marshall lost to Val Skinner 2 and 1
Laura Davies lost to Michelle McGann 3 and 2
Liselotte Neumann halved with Beth Daniel
Lisa Hackney lost to Brandie Burton 1 hole
Trish Johnson lost to Dottie Pepper 3 and 2
Alison Nicholas halved with Kelly Robbins
Marie Laure de Lorenzi lost to Betsy King 6 and 4
Joanne Morley lost to Rosie Jones 5 and 4
Dale Reid lost to Jane Geddes 2 holes
Catrin Nilsmark lost to Patty Sheehan 2 and 1
Helen Alfredsson lost to Meg Mallon 4 and 2

1994 The Greenbrier, WA Oct 21–23
Result: USA 13, Europe 7
Captains: JoAnne Carner (USA),
Mickey Walker (Europe)

First Day – Foursomes
Burton & Mochrie beat Alfredsson & Neuman 3 and 2
Daniel & Mallon lost to Nilsmark & Sörenstam 1 hole
Green & Robbins lost to Fairclough & Reid 2 and 1
Andrews & King lost to Davies & Nicholas 2 holes
Sheehan & Steinhauer beat Johnson & Wright 2 holes

Second Day – Fourball
Burton & Mochrie beat Davies & Nicholas 2 and 1
Daniel & Mallon beat Nilsmark & Sörenstam 6 and 5
Green & Robbins lost to Fairclough & Reid 4 and 3

Andrews & King beat Johnson & Wright 3 and 2
Sheehan & Steinhauer lost to Alfredsson & Neumann
1 hole

Third Day – Singles

Betsy King lost to Helen Alfredsson 2 and 1
Dottie Pepper Mochrie beat Catrin Nilsmark 6 and 5
Beth Daniel beat Trish Johnson 1 hole
Kelly Robbins beat Lora Fairclough 4 and 2
Meg Mallon beat Pam Wright 1 hole
Patty Sheehan lost to Alison Nicholas 3 and 2
Brandie Burton beat Laura Davies 1 hole
Tammie Green beat Annika Sörenstam 3 and 2
Sherri Steinhauer beat Dale Reid 2 holes
Donna Andrews beat Liselotte Neumann 3 and 2

1992 Dalmahoy, Edinburgh Oct 2–4
Result: Europe 11½, USA 6½
Captains: Mickey Walker (Europe),
Kathy Whitworth (USA)

First Day – Foursomes
Davies & Nicholas beat King & Daniel 1 hole
Neumann & Alfredsson beat Bradley & Mochrie 2 and 1
Descampe & Johnson lost to Ammaccapane & Mallon
1 hole
Reid & Wright halved with Sheehan & Inkster

Second Day – Fourball
Davies & Nicholas beat Sheehan & Inkster 1 hole
Johnson & Descampe halved with Burton & Richard
Wright & Reid lost to Mallon & King 1 hole
Alfredsson & Neumann halved with Bradley & Mochrie

Third Day – Singles
Laura Davies beat Brandie Burton 4 and 2
Helen Alfredsson beat Danielle Ammaccapane 4 and 3
Trish Johnson beat Patty Sheehan 2 and 1
Alison Nicholas lost to Juli Inkster 3 and 2
Florence Descampe lost to Beth Daniel 2 and 1
Pam Wright beat Pat Bradley 4 and 3
Catrin Nilsmark beat Meg Mallon 3 and 2
Kitrina Douglas lost to Deb Richard 7 and 6
Liselotte Neumann beat Betsy King 2 and 1
Dale Reid beat Dottie Pepper Mochrie 3 and 2

1990 Lake Nona, FL Nov 16–18
Result: USA 11½, Europe 4½
Captains: Kathy Whitworth (USA),
Mickey Walker (Europe)

First Day – Foursomes
Bradley & Lopez lost to Davies & Nicholas 2 and 1
Gerring & Mochrie beat Wright & Neumann 6 and 5
Sheehan & Jones beat Reid & Alfredsson 6 and 5
Daniel & King beat Johnson & de Lorenzi 5 and 4

Second Day – Fourball
Sheehan & Jones beat Johnson & de Lorenzi 2 and 1
Bradley & Lopez beat Reid & Alfredsson 2 and 1
King & Daniel beat Davies & Nicholas 4 and 3
Gerring & Mochrie lost to Neumann & Wright
4 and 2

Third Day – Singles
Cathy Gerring beat Helen Alfredsson 4 and 3
Rosie Jones lost to Laura Davies 3 and 2
Nancy Lopez beat Alison Nicholas 6 and 4
Betsy King halved with Pam Wright
Beth Daniel beat Liselotte Neumann 7 and 6
Patty Sheehan lost to Dale Reid 2 and 1
Dottie Mochrie beat Marie Laure de Lorenzi 4 and 2
Pat Bradley beat Trish Johnson 8 and 7

Solheim Cup – Individual Records   Brackets indicate non-playing captain
Europe

Name		Year	Played	Won	Lost	Halved
Helen Alfredsson	SWE	1990-92-94-96-98-2000-02-(07)-09	28	11	15	2
Becky Brewerton	WAL	2007-09	7	3	3	1
Raquel Carriedo	ESP	2000-02	5	1	3	1
Laura Davies	ENG	1990-92-94-96-98-2000-02-03-05-07-09	43	21	17	5
Florence Descampe	BEL	1992	3	0	2	1
Kitrina Douglas	ENG	1992	1	0	1	0
Tania Elosegui	ESP	2009	3	1	2	0
Elisabeth Esterl	GER	2003	3	1	1	1
Lora Fairclough	ENG	1994	3	2	1	0
Sophie Gustafson	SWE	1998-2000-02-03-05-07-09	27	10	11	6
Lisa Hackney	ENG	1996-98	6	3	3	0
Bettina Hauert	GER	2007	2	0	2	0
Maria Hjörth	SWE	2000-04-05-07-09	17	5	7	5
Karine Icher	FRA	2002	3	1	2	0
Trish Johnson	ENG	1990-92-94-96-98-2000-05-07	25	5	13	7
Carin Koch	SWE	2000-02-03-05	16	10	3	3
Ludivine Kreutz	FRA	2005	2	0	2	0
Laure de Lorenzi	FRA	1990-96-98	11	3	8	0
Diana Luna	ITA	2009	2	1	0	1
Mhairi McKay	SCO	2002-03	5	2	3	0
Kathryn Marshall	SCO	1996	3	1	1	1
Paula Marti	ESP	2002	4	1	3	0
Catriona Matthew	SCO	1998-03-05-07-09	21	9	8	4
Patricia Meunier Labouc	FRA	2000-03	4	2	1	1
Janice Moodie	SCO	2000-03-09	11	7	2	2
Joanne Morley	ENG	1996	2	0	2	0
Liselotte Neumann	SWE	1990-92-94-96-98-2000	21	6	10	5
Alison Nicholas	ENG	1990-92-94-96-98-2000-(09)	18	7	8	3
Catrin Nilsmark	SWE	1992-94-96-98-2000-(03)-(05)	16	8	7	1
Pia Nilsson	SWE	(1998)	0	0	0	0
Gwladys Nocera	FRA	2005-07-09	10	5	3	2
Anna Nordqvist	SWE	2009	4	2	2	0
Suzann Pettersen	NOR	2002-03-05-07-09	21	9	7	5
Dale Reid	SCO	1990-92-94-96-(2000-02)	11	4	6	1
Ana Belen Sanchez	ESP	2003	2	0	2	0
Annika Sörenstam	SWE	1994-96-98-2000-02-03-05-07	37	21	12	4
Charlotta Sörenstam	SWE	1998	4	1	2	1
Karen Stupples	ENG	2005	2	1	1	0
Iben Tinning	DEN	2002-03-05-07	14	4	7	3
Mickey Walker	ENG	(1990)-(92)-(94)-(96)	0	0	0	0
Linda Wessberg	SWE	2007	2	1	0	1
Pam Wright	SCO	1990-92-94	6	1	4	1

United States

Name	Year	Played	Won	Lost	Halved
Danielle Ammaccapane	1992	2	1	1	0
Donna Andrews	1994-98	7	4	3	0
Heather Bowie	2003	3	0	3	0
Pat Bradley	1990-92-96-(2000)	8	2	5	1
Brandie Burton	1992-94-96-98-2000	14	8	4	2
Jo Anne Carner	(1994)	0	0	0	0
Nicole Castrale	2007-09	7	2	5	0
Paula Creamer	2005-07-09	14	8	5	1
Beth Daniel	1990-92-94-96-2000-02-03-05-(09)	29	10	9	7
Laura Diaz	2002-03-05-07	13	6	6	1
Jane Geddes	1996	4	1	2	1
Cathy Gerring	1990	3	2	1	0
Tammie Green	1994-98	6	2	4	0
Natalie Gulbis	2005-07-09	10	4	5	1
Pat Hurst	1998-2000-02-05-07	20	11	6	3
Juli Inkster	1992-98-2000-02-03-05-07-09	31	15	12	4
Becky Iverson	2000	4	2	2	0
Chris Johnson	1998	3	0	2	1
Rosie Jones	1990-96-98-2000-02-03-05	22	11	9	2
Cristie Kerr	2002-03-05-07-09	21	8	11	2

Name	Year	Played	Won	Lost	Halved
Christina Kim	2005-09	8	5	2	1
Betsy King	1990-92-94-96-98-(07)	15	7	6	2
Emilee Klein	2002	4	3	1	0
Kelli Kuehne	2002-03	8	2	6	0
Brittany Lang	2009	3	1	0	2
Brittany Lincicombe	2007-09	7	3	4	0
Nancy Lopez	1990-(2005)	3	2	1	0
Michelle McGann	1996	4	1	1	2
Kristy McPherson	2009	4	1	3	0
Meg Mallon	1992-94-96-98-2000-02-03-05	29	13	9	7
Alice Miller	(1992)*	0	0	0	0
Dottie Pepper	1990-92-94-96-98-2000	20	13	5	2
Stacy Prammanasudh	2007	3	1	1	1
Morgan Pressel	2007-09	7	3	2	2
Judy Rankin	(1996)-(98)	0	0	0	0
Michele Redman	2000-02-03-05	11	4	5	2
Deb Richard	1992	2	1	0	1
Kelly Robbins	1994-96-98-2000-02-03	24	10	10	4
Nancy Scranton	2000	2	0	2	0
Patty Sheehan	1990-92-94-96-(2002)-(03)	13	5	7	1
Val Skinner	1996	4	2	2	0
Angela Stanford	2003-07-09	7	1	4	2
Sherri Steinhauer	1994-98-2000-07	13	6	5	2
Wendy Ward	2002-03-05	11	3	7	1
Kathy Whitworth	(1990)-(92)*	0	0	0	0
Michelle Wie	2009	4	3	0	1

Solheim Cup statistics

Largest margin of victory (individual matches):
In the 1990 Singles, Pat Bradley (USA) beat Trish Johnson by 8 and 7. Also in 1990, Cathy Gerring and Dottie Mochrie (USA) beat Pam Wright and Liselotte Neumann by 6 and 5 and Patty Sheehan and Rosie Jones (USA) beat Dale Reid and Helen Alfredsson by the same margin, both in Foursomes matches.

This margin was repeated in the 2000 Foursomes when Becky Iverson and Rosie Jones (USA) beat Laura Davies and Alison Nicholas.

In the 1998 Fourballs, Pat Hurst and Rosie Jones (USA) beat Lisa Hackney and Sophie Gustafson by 7 and 5.

Largest margin of victory (overall competition):
In 1990, the USA defeated Europe by a score of 11½ to 4½, a margin of seven points. This margin was repeated in 2003 when Europe were the victors with a score of 17½ to 10½.

Most events played (from 12 contests):
12 Laura Davies (EUR); 9 Juli Inkster (USA); 8 Beth Daniel (USA), Trish Johnson (EUR), Meg Mallon (USA); Annika Sörenstam (EUR), Helen Alfredsson (EUR), Sophie Gustafson (EUR); 7 Rosie Jones (USA) 6 Liselotte Neumann (EUR), Alison Nicholas (EUR), Dottie Pepper (USA), Kelly Robbins (USA).

Most matches won:
22 Annika Sörenstam (EUR), Laura Davies (EUR); 15 Juli Inkster (USA).

Most points earned:
25 Laura Davies (EUR); 24 Annika Sörenstam (EUR); 18½ Juli Inkster (USA); 16½ Meg Mallon (USA).

Teams' won and lost record (*denotes a home win):
USA 8–4 (1990*; 1994*; 1996; 1998*; 2002*; 2005*; 2007; 2009*).
Europe 4–8 (1992*; 2000*; 2003*; 2011*).

Most times as captain:
4 Mickey Walker (EUR), 1990, 1992, 1994, 1996.

LPGA Legends Handa Cup   *Wentworth-by-the-sea CC, Rye*

Christa Johnson and Beth Daniel beat Dawn Coe-Jones and Nancy Harvey   1 hole
Nancy Scranton and Cindy Rarick beat Jenny Lidback and Gail Graham   6 and 5
Patty Sheahan and Pat Bradley lost to Alicia Dobbs and Liselotte Neumann   4 and 2
Michelle Redman and Joanne Carner beat Lorie Kane and Alison Nicholas   1 hole
Meg Mallon and Nancy Lopez beat Tina Tombs and Annie Marie Palli   3 and 1
Sherrie Steinhauer and Rosie Jones beat Sally Little and Mieko Nomura   4 and 2

Singles:

Rarick lost to Nicholas   3 and 2
Daniel beat Kane   2 holes
Johnson beat Harvey   6 and 5
Mallon beat Graham   5 and 4
Carner beat Palli   5 and 3
Lopez lost to Lidback   6 and 5

Sheehan lost to Nomura   3 and 2
Redman beat Neumann   4 and 3
Bradley lost to Dibos   4 and 3
Steinhauer beat Little   8 and 7
Jones beat Tombs   4 and 3
Scranton lost to Coe-Jones   1 hole

Result: USA 34, The World 14

Women's World Cup

2000	Sweden (K Koch and S Gustafson)	425
2001–2004	*Not played*	
2005	Japan (A Miyazato and R Kitada)	289
2006	Sweden (A Sörenstam and L Neumann)	281
2007	Paraguay (J Granada and C Troche)	279
2008	Philippines (J Rosales and D Deelasin)	198
2009	*Not played*	
2010	*Not played*	
2011	*Not played*	

Lexus Cup   (Team Asia v Team International)   (inaugurated 2005)

2005	Asia 8, International 16	Tanah Merah GC, Singapore
2006	Asia 12½, International 11½	Tanah Merah GC, Singapore
2007	Asia 15, International 9	The Vines, Perth, Australia
2008	Asia 11½, International 12½	Singapore Island GC
2009	*Not played*	
2010	*Not played*	
2011	*Not played*	

Lorie Kane honoured by Canadian Red Cross

Professional golfer and Edward Island native Lorie Kane received the 2011 Humanitarian Award for Prince Edward Island for her work with children's charities and for accessing sport.

"Lorie Kane's success as a professional golfer has inspired many Islanders, but it is her generous contribution to her community through KidSport and other organizations that will have a lasting impact on the Island," said John L Byrne, director general of the Canadian Red Cross in Atlantic Canada.

Kane has been involved with KidSport, an organization that aims to eliminate financial barriers to allow children to participate in sport, in Prince Edward Island since 1997. She has served as honourary spokesperson, promoter and ambassador of the programme and is also its most generous contributor. More than 400 young people receive support from this programme annually.

She's also helped raise more than $850,000 over the years through the annual Lorie Kane Charity Golf Classic, to support several charities including KidSport, Ronald MacDonald Children's Charities, the ALS Society and the QEH Foundation.

Month by month in 2011

Northern Ireland's remarkable run continues when 42-year-old Darren Clarke wins The Open at the 20th attempt at Royal St George's. He is the oldest winner since Roberto de Vicenzo in 1967. Thomas Levet wins his home French Open, jumps in the lake to celebrate and fractures his shin. Yani Tseng retains the Ricoh Women's British Open for her fifth major.

PART IV

Men's Amateur Tournaments

World Amateur Golf Ranking

Cantlay deservedly wins McCormack Medal

Californian's special summer helps him to World No 1 spot

After the outstanding summer he had enjoyed on the golf course it was no surprise that Patrick Cantlay became the latest winner of the Mark McCormack Medal presented to the golfer who tops the Men's World Amateur Golf Rankings at the end of a 12-month period culminating in 2011 with the US Amateur Championship.

© The R&A

The presentation of the McCormack Medal. From left to right: Peter Dawson (Chief Executive of The R&A), Patrick Cantlay, Leslie McCormack Gathy and Mike Davis (Executive Director, USGA)

"This is special," Cantlay said. "Any time you are recognised as the best in your respective sport it means a lot. I am very honoured to win the award."

It would have been appropriate had Cantlay won the American title at Erin Hills in Wisconsin but having reached the final in the last points-counting event of the 2010–2011 season he was beaten on the last green of the 36-hole final by Kelly Kraft, winner earlier in the season of the Texas Amateur.

For Cantlay it was disappointing. He had come back from four down to lead with four holes to play only to lose the 33rd and 34th holes and eventually the title because of mental errors he admitted. Yet throughout the summer he had produced some devastating golf to overhaul Peter Uihlein, the 2009–2010 No 1.

It had been Uihlein who had beaten him in the semi-final of the 2010 US Amateur after Cantlay had qualified in second spot

Cantlay, a 19-year-old student at UCLA, had a sterling collegiate season. He was named the NCAA Division I Player and Freshman of the Year and was the PAC-10 Player and Freshman of the Year as well.

He did well against the professionals as well. Having qualified for the US Open he made the cut and finished 21st – the best finish in that event by an amateur in 40 years. It earned him top amateur spot at Congressional where he averaged a driving distance of 304.3 yards.

Winner of the Jack Nicklaus Award as college golf's Player of the Year, Cantlay next moved on to The Travelers event on the PGA Tour where he had been awarded a sponsor's exemption. Maintaining his excellent form, he finished 24th behind winner Freddie Jacobsen and in the process made his own bit of golfing history. After opening with a 67 he fired a second round 10-under-par 60 – the lowest round ever recorded by an amateur in a PGA Tour event. He went on to finish 20th. at the AT&T Championship and ninth in the Canadian Open.

During his busy summer the Los Alamitos resident also won the Southern Californian Golf Association Championship and finished runner up in the Western Amateur.

Talking of his year he said: "I have played well and it has been a lot of fun. It has been my first summer of playing high profile tournaments so it means a lot that I have been able to play and compete."

Cantlay is the third American to win the McCormack Medal since 2007. Colt Knost was the winner that first year and Peter Uihlein was top man in 2010. Canadian Nick Taylor took the Medal honours in 2009 and New Zealander Danny Lee ended the year top amateur in 2008.

Cantlay, who enjoys playing table-tennis and watching films, first played golf at age three and as a young man could be found at the Virginia Country Club in Long Beach, California. As a junior he won the 2008 Hogan Cup.

He will not be turning professional immediately. He plans to remain an amateur until he has completed his University degree. Perhaps his father Steve summed up his son's 12-month rise to No 1 amateur in the world best when he commented: "It's been quite a whirlwind." It certainly has.

Cantlay was presented with the McCormack Medal at a ceremony during the Walker Cup at Royal Aberdeen last September.

R&A World Amateur Golf Ranking 2010–2011 – Top 100

Players from the USA occupy most places in the Top 100 with 56 entries, six in the top ten. England takes second place with nine entries, two in the top ten. Swedish players account for four entries with Australia, France, Scotland and South Africa on three apiece. Although there are only two Japanese entries on the list, both are in the top ten. By region the totals are: Americas 57, Europe 29, Asia six, Australasia five and Africa three.

			Divisor	Points					Divisor	Points
1	Patrick Cantlay	USA	73	1678.08		51	John Hahn	USA	73	1024.66
2	Jordan Spieth	USA	44	1490.91		52	Cody Proveaux	USA	47	1023.40
3	Patrick Rodgers	USA	49	1414.29		53	Ben Campbell	NZL	66	1022.73
4	Peter Uihlein	USA	78	1333.33		54	Matthew Stieger	AUS	104	1021.15
5	Andrew Sullivan	ENG	75	1294.67		55	Blayne Barber	USA	62	1020.97
6	Harris English	USA	67	1274.63		56	Martin Trainer	USA	47	1017.02
7	John Peterson	USA	65	1263.08		57	Pontus Widegren	SWE	44	1013.64
8	Tom Lewis	ENG	69	1234.78		58	Chris Brant	USA	51	1009.80
9	Yoshinori Fujimoto	JPN	38	1234.21		59	Vince India	USA	57	1007.02
10	Hideki Matsuyama	JPN	54	1207.41		60	Zac Blair	USA	76	1006.58
11	Chris Williams	USA	72	1195.83		61	Abraham Ancer	USA	47	1006.38
12	Jack Senior	ENG	75	1185.33		62	Scott Harvey	USA	39	1005.13
13	Kelly Kraft	USA	79	1183.54		63	Ethan Tracy	USA	66	1004.55
14	Andrew Yun	USA	61	1168.85		64	Cory Whitsett	USA	59	1000.00
15	Michael Stewart	SCO	61	1163.93		65	Michael Hollick	RSA	33	1000.00
16	Sebastian Cappelen	DEN	44	1163.64		66	Ben Kohles	USA	60	998.33
17	Corbin Mills	USA	70	1148.57		67	Shun Yat Hak	HKG	30	996.67
18	Jordan Russell	USA	71	1142.25		68	Thomas Pieters	BEL	59	994.92
19	Steven Brown	ENG	57	1133.33		69	Alex Moore	USA	52	990.38
20	Manuel Trappel	AUT	33	1127.27		70	Jonathan Randolph	USA	69	989.86
21	Arnond Vongvanij	USA	63	1123.81		71	Alex Ching	USA	59	981.36
22	Andrew Putnam	USA	66	1121.21		72	Brad Hopfinger	USA	48	979.17
23	Luke Guthrie	USA	54	1120.37		73	James Byrne	SCO	52	976.92
24	Russell Henley	USA	62	1119.35		74	Pedro Figueiredo	POR	39	976.92
25	Derek Ernst	USA	68	1110.29		75	Joakim Mikkelsen	NOR	54	975.93
26	John Spaun	USA	53	1105.66		76	Tyrrell Hatton	ENG	48	975.00
27	Paul Cutler	IRL	57	1092.98		77	Dylan Frittelli	RSA	59	974.58
28	Cheng-tsung Pan	TPE	38	1092.11		78	Garrick Porteous	ENG	47	974.47
29	James White	USA	55	1087.27		79	David Coupland	ENG	43	974.42
30	Timothy Madigan	USA	56	1082.14		80	Rhys Pugh	WAL	64	973.44
31	Jeff Karlsson	SWE	42	1080.95		81	Paul Haley	USA	55	972.73
32	Daniel Miernicki	USA	56	1078.57		82	Bobby Wyatt	USA	50	972.00
33	Jared Harvey	RSA	55	1076.36		83	Tarquin MacManus	AUS	67	971.64
34	Gary Stal	FRA	63	1069.84		84	Jeffrey Kang	USA	67	968.66
35	Harold Varner	USA	63	1068.25		85	Billy Kennerly	USA	38	968.42
36	Stiggy Hodgson	ENG	52	1061.54		86	Bhavik Patel	USA	58	965.52
37	Julien Brun	FRA	52	1055.77		87	Beau Hossler	USA	46	965.22
	Jack Fields	USA	52	1055.77		88	Will Collins	USA	59	964.41
39	Ryan Fox	NZL	74	1054.05		89	Andrew Vijarro	USA	49	963.27
40	Jason Millard	USA	53	1049.06		90	David Law	SCO	75	961.33
41	Todd Baek	KOR	47	1048.94		91	Mark Hubbard	USA	57	952.63
42	Robert Karlsson	SWE	46	1043.48		92	Niclas Carlsson	SWE	39	951.28
43	Anton Arboleda	USA	38	1042.11			Manav Shah	USA	39	951.28
44	Daan Huizing	NED	58	1041.38		94	Nick Delio	USA	46	950.00
45	Philipp Fendt	AUT	56	1035.71		95	Kevin Penner	USA	39	948.72
46	Jake Higginbottom	AUS	72	1031.94		96	Evan Beck	USA	67	947.76
47	Jace Long	USA	65	1030.77		97	Gregor Main	USA	59	945.76
48	Lee Bedford	USA	68	1027.94		98	Khalin Joshi	IND	51	945.10
49	Albin Choi	CAN	61	1027.87		99	Gregory Eason	ENG	40	945.00
50	Edouard Espana	FRA	48	1027.08		100	Ben Westgate	WAL	30	943.33

The European Amateur Ranking Top 100 can be found on page 355

World Amateur Golf Ranking 2010–2011

The World Amateur Golf Ranking, compiled by The R&A as a service to golf, comprises a men's ranking which was launched in January 2007 and a women's ranking which began in January 2011. The week's rankings are announced every Wednesday at 12.00 pm

Statistics are compiled each week for over 8,000 players in over 2,000 events around the world. The ranking is based on counting every stroke reported to The R&A in stroke play events and matches won in counting match play events. The men's ranking runs throughout a rolling period of 52 weeks culminating at the end of either the European or US Amateur Championship which ever is later on the calendar. The leading player at the end of the ranking period wins the Mark McCormack Medal. The women's ranking also runs through a rolling period of 52 weeks.

Counting events are divided into seven categories:
The elite events: For men: The Amateur Championship, the US Amateur, the European Amateur and the Asian Amateur; and for women: The Ladies British Amateur, the NCAA Championship, the US Women's Amateur and the European Women's Amateur.
Category A: Counting events ranked 1-30 in the World Ranking Event Rating
Category B: Counting events ranked 31-100
Category C: Counting events ranked 101-200
Category D: Counting events ranked 201-300
Category E: Counting events ranked 301-400
Category F: Counting events ranked from 401

Counting events are stroke play competitions over a minimum of three rounds or two rounds if it is a match play qualifying competition.

Full details of how a ranking is earned and information on how the ranking works can be found on The R&A website – www.randa.org

The rankings are displayed by month and are subdivided into the following regions:
Africa
The Americas (North, South and Central America and the Caribbean)
Asia (incorporating the Middle East)
Australasia (incorporating the Pacific Islands)
Europe

Winners are from the country hosting the event unless otherwise stated.
An asterisk indicates a newly ranked player.
(P) indicates player has turned professional and is no longer included in the world rankings.
A list of country abbreviations can be found on Page 43; WWAGR can be found on pages 360–384.

Elite and Category "A" Events

Elite

2010 Asian Amateur Championship   *Kasumagaseki GC, Japan*   (RSS 75-75-75-72)

			SP	Bonus	Pts	Div
1	Hideki Matsuyama (JPN)	68-69-65-67 - 269	60	36	96	4
2	Tarquin MacManus (AUS)	71-67-67-69 -274	55	24	79	4
3	Yosuke Asaji (JPN)	67-69-72-67 -275	54	12	66	4

2011 Amateur Championship   *Hillside and Hesketh GCs, England*   (RSS 78-76-75-73)

			SP	MP	Pts	Div
1	Bryden Macpherson (AUS)	75-71—145	22	180	202	8
2	Michael Stewart (SCO)	72-72—144	23	140	163	7
3	Greg Paterson (SCO)	72-70—142	25	104	129	6
	Sebastian Gros (GER)	73-74—147	20	104	124	6

Full details can be found on page 290

2011 European Amateur Championship   Halmstad GK, Sweden   (RSS 73-75-71-73)

			SP	Bonus	Pts	Div
1	Manuel Trappel (AUT)	68-69-71-70—278	46	48	94	4
2	Steven Brown (ENG)	65-71-74-68—278	46	36	83	4
3	Julien Brun (FRA)	69-68-73-69—279	45	24	69	4

Full details can be found on page 296

2011 US Amateur Championship   Erin Hills and Wauwatosa (Blue Mount) GCs, Wisconsin

(RSS 74-71-74-70)

			SP	MP	Pts	Div
Winner	Kelly Kraft	71-70—141	19	180	199	8
Runner-up	Patrick Cantlay	71-69—140	20	140	160	7
Semi-finalists	Jordan Russell	72-68—140	21	104	125	6
	Jack Senior (ENG)	73-67—140	21	104	125	6

Full details can be found on page 298

Category "A"

Scratch Players Championship   Gig Harbor, Washington, USA   (RSS 74-75-73-75)

			SP	Bonus	Pts	Div
1	Romain Wattel (FRA)	71-72-68-72—283	45	18	63	4
2	Cheng-tsung Pan (TPE)	70-69-75-70—284	42	6	48	4
3	Chan Kim (P)	72-72-72-69—285				

OFCC/Fighting Illini Invite   Oly Fields, Illinois, USA   (RSS 73-72-73)

1	Peter Uihlein	69-65-70—204	38	36	74	3
2	Arnond Vongvanij (P)	70-67-70—207				
3	Patrick Reed (P)	72-70-67—209				

Ping–Golfweek Preview   Stillwater, Oklahoma, USA   (RSS 78-75-76)

1	Pontus Widegren (SWE)	75-70-69—214	39	36	75	3
2	Hudson Swafford (P)	75-68-73—216				
	Peter Uihlein	72-74-70—216	37	18	55	3

Isleworth Collegiate Invitational   Windermere, Florida, USA   (RSS 76-76-77)

1	Arnond Vongvanij (P)	74-70-68—212
2	Robin Wingardh (SWE) (P)	71-68-75—214
3	Morgan Hoffman (P)	71-71-74—216

World Amateur Team Championship (individual)   Buenos Aires, Argentina (RSS 75-76-77)

1	Joachim Branat Hansen (DEN) (P)	67-69-73—209				
2	Alexander Levy (FRA)	68-72-72—212	40	18	58	3
3	Romain Wattel (FRA) (P)	69-70-74—213				

Fourth round cancelled because of bad weather

The Gifford Collegiate Championship   San Martin, California, USA   (RSS 76-73-75)

1	Patrick Cantlay	67-69-71—207	41	36	77	3
2	Daniel Miernicki	72-70-69—211	37	18	55	3
	Henrik Norlander (SWE) (P)	68-73-70—211				

Western Refining College All-American   *El Paso, Texas, USA*   (RSS 71-71-70)

			SP	Bonus	Pts	Div
1	Alex Ching	67-67-67—201	35	36	71	3
2	John-Tyler Griffin (P)	71-65-68—204				
	Tain Lee	64-69-71—204	32	18	50	3

Jones Cup Invitational   *Sea Island, Georgia, USA*   (RSS 79-75-77)

1	John Peterson	76-73-68—217	38	36	74	3
2	Jordan Spieth	73-70-74—217	38	18	56	3
3	Patrick Rodgers	73-71-74—218	37	12	49	3

The Amer Ari Invitational   *Kohala Coast, Hawaii, USA*   (RSS 71-72-72)

1	Daniel Miernicki	62-69-72—203	36	36	72	3
2	Patrick Cantlay	74-64-65—203	36	18	54	3
	Bobby Hudson	69-67-67—203	36	18	54	3

Southern Highlands Collegiate Masters   *Las Vegas, Nevada, USA*   (RSS 76-75-75)

1	Morgan Hoffman (P)	69-68-69—206				
2	Jordan Russell	64-71-73—208	42	18	60	3
3	Patrick Cantlay	75-67-71—213	37	12	49	3

USC Collegiate Invitational   *Westlake Village, California, USA*   (RSS 73-74-73)

1	Patrick Cantlay	67-72-68—207	27	36	73	3
2	Scott Pinckney (P)	71-71-67—209				
3	Johan Carlsson (SWE) (P)	68-69-73—210				
	Tyler Raber	70-73-67—210	34	12	46	3

Western Intercollegiate   *Santa Cruz, California, USA*   (RSS 73-74-74)

1	Timothy Madigan	69-68-70—207	38	36	74	3
2	Mark Hubbard	69-69-71—209	36	18	54	3
	Patrick Reed (P)	66-75-68—209				
	Andrew Yun	68-70-71—209	36	18	54	3

NCAA South Central-Colorado Region   *Erie, Colorado, USA*   (RSS 73-72-73)

1	Kevin Tway (P)	72-65-69—206				
2	Scott Pinckney (P)	69-70-68—207				
3	Talor Gooch	70-71-68—209	33	12	45	3

PAC-10 Championship   *Stanford, California, USA*   (RSS 73-72-73-72)

1	Martin Trainer	68-68-69-70—275	47	36	83	4
2	Alex Moore	71-65-69-70—276	47	18	65	4
3	Alex Shi Yup Kim (KOR)	68-71-70-68—277	45	12	57	4

NCAA Division I Stroke Play Championship   *Stillwater Oklahoma, USA*   (RSS 76-75-76)

1	John Peterson	74-65-72—211	40	36	76	3
2	Patrick Cantlay	72-69-71—212	39	18	57	3
3	Lion Kim (P)	72-70-73—215				
	Cameron Peck	68-74-73—215	36	12	48	3
	Patrick Reed (P)	69-75-71—215				
	John Spaun	69-75-71-215	36	12	48	3
	Peter Uilein	73-69-73—215	36	12	48	3

Full details can be found on page 301

NCAA Division 1 Match Play Championship *Stillwater, Oklahoma, USA*

		MP	Div
1	Russell Henley	72	3
	Bryden Macpherson (AUS)	72	3
	Patrick Reed (P)		

Northeast Amateur *Rumford, Rhode Island, USA* (RSS 70-70-70-69)

			SP	Bonus	Pts	Div
1	Peter Uihlein	66-68-62-65—261	50	36	86	4
2	James White	70-67-63-64—264	47	18	65	4
3-	Blayne Barber	70-66-65-64—265	46	12	58	4

Palmer Cup *The Stanwich Club, Greenwich, Connecticut, USA*

		MP	Div
1	Sebastian Cappelen (DEN)	44	2
	Andrew Yun	44	2
3	Blayne Barber	20	1
	Patrick Cantlay	20	1
	Jeff Karlsson (SWE)	20	1
	Daniel Miernicki	20	1
	Arnond Vongvanij (P)		
	Pontus Widegren (SWE)	20	1
	Chris Williams	20	1

Full details can be found on page 351

Sunnehanna Amateur *Johnstown, Pennsylvania, USA* (RSS 72-70-70-72)

			SP	Bonus	Pts	Div
1	Nathan Smith	68-68-70-66—272	44	36	80	4
2	Lee Bedford	68-64-69-71—272	44	18	62	4
2	Zac Blair	71-67-66-68—272	44	18	62	4

Pacific Coast Amateur *Truckee, California, USA* (RSS 75-75-74-73)

			SP	Bonus	Pts	Div
1	Chris Williams	73-72-66-66—277	52	36	88	4
2	Anton Arboleda (PHI)	71-72-69-67—279	50	18	68	4
	Taylor Travis	69-70-69-71—279	50	18	68	4

Players Amateur *Bluffton, South Carolina, USA* (RSS 73-72-71-72)

			SP	Bonus	Pts	Div
1	Corbin Mills	67-69-68-72—276	44	36	80	4
2	Patrick Rodgers	72-69-69-67—277	43	18	61	4
	Curtis Thompson	71-72-68-66—277	43	18	61	4

Porter Cup *Niagara Falls CC, New York State, USA* (RSS 70-70-70-70)

			SP	Bonus	Pts	Div
1	Patrick Rodgers	68-63-69-68—208	44	36	80	4
2	Wesley Bryan	69-70-63-66—208	44	18	62	4
3	Dylan Frittelli (RSA)	68-68-68-65—209	43	12	55	4
	Paul Haley	64-66-69-70—209	43	12	55	4

Southern Amateur *Innisbrook Resort, Florida, USA* (RSS 73-74-72-72)

			SP	Bonus	Pts	Div
1	Harris English	69-68-73-65—275	48	36	84	4
2	Tarquin MacManus (AUS)	73-74-66-72—278	45	18	63	4
	Richard Werenski	68-71-68-71—278	45	18	63	4
	Bobby Wyatt	70-72-70-66—278	45	18	63	4

US Amateur Public Links   *Bandon Dunes, Oregon, USA*   (RSS 76-74)

			SP	MP	Pts	Div
Winner	Corbin Mills	71-67—138	28	180	208	8
Runner-up	Derek Ernst	70-75—145	21	140	161	7
Semi-finalists	Jonathan Randolph	70-71—141	25	104	129	6
	Harris English	73-70—143	23	104	127	6

Western Amateur   *North Shore CC, Illinois, USA*   (RSS 73-73-71-72)

			SP	MP	Pts	Div
Winner	Ethan Tracy	74-68-70-69—281	40	120	160	8
Runner-up	Patrick Cantlay	73-67-72-70—282	39	84	123	7
Semi-finalists	Cheng-Tsung Pan (TPE)	71-71-69-68—279	42	52	94	6
	Jeffrey Tang	72-71-67-71—281	40	52	92	6

St Andrews Links Trophy   *Old and New courses, St Andrews, Scotland*   (RSS 75-75-73-73)

			SP	MP	Pts	Div
1	Tom Lewis (ENG)	68-74-70-67—279	48	36	84	4
2	Rhys Enoch (WAL)	66-74-71-72—283	44	18	62	4
	Daan Huizing (NED)	71-68-74-70—283	44	18	62	4
	Sebastian MacLean (BOL)	71-71-67-74—283	44	18	62	4

European Team Championship Individual   *Oceanico Victoria, Portugal*   (RSS 72-73)

			SP	MP	Pts	Div
1	Alexander Levy (FRA)	66-73—139	22	72	94	5
2	Pedro Figueiredo (POR)	70-71—141	20	72	92	5
	Ricardo Gouveia (POR)	69-72—141	20	72	92	5

How a player makes it onto the World Amateur Rankings is a question often asked. The system is easy to understand if, by necessity, somewhat complex. It is best to look at the criteria in three different ways – by doing well in a Stroke Play event, with a good performance in a Match Play tournament or in an event in which both Stroke and Match Play elements are involved. Just taking part does not necessarily mean a place on the ranking. There are certain criteria to becoming one of now over 3,000 ranked players around the world.

In Stroke Play a player will have to:
Made the cut in an Elite event
Finished in the top 40 and ties in an "A" event
Finished in the top 32 and ties in a "B" event
Finished in the top 16 and ties in a "C" event

Finished in the top 8 and ties in a "D" event
Finished in the top 4 and ties in an "E" event
Finished in the top 2 and ties in an "F" event

Or, for male players, participation in The Open, Masters or US Open Championship, an event on the European or US PGA Tours, the Australasian or Japan Tours, the Asian. Nationwide or Sunshine Tours the Canadian, Challenge, Korean or OneAsia Tours or the Tour de las Americas.

Finish in a position to gain bonus points in any other professional event recognised by the committee.

In Match Play a player will make the ranking if they:
Make the last 32 in a Category "A" event
Make the last 16 in a Category "B:" event
Make the last 8 in a Category "C" event
Win a match against ranked player in an Elite team Match Play event

Make the last 8 in a Category "D" event
Make the last 4 in a Category "E" event
Make the last 4 in a Category "F" event

If the event is a combination of Stroke Play and Match Play what a player needs to become ranked is:
Qualify for the Match Play stage or finish on the qualifying score in an Elite Stroke Play event
Finish in the top 32 and ties in a Category "A" Stroke Play event
Make the last 32 of a Category "A" event
Finish in the top 16 and ties in the Stroke Play stage of a Category "B" event
Make the last 16 of a Category "B" event
Finish in the top 8 and ties in the Stroke Play stage of a Category "C" event
Make the last 8 in a Category "C" event
Finish in the top 4 and ties in the Stroke Play stage of a Category "D" event
Make the last 8 in a Category "D" event
Finish in the top 2 and ties in the Stroke Play stage of a Category "E" event
Make the last 4 in a Category "E" event
Lead the qualifiers in the Stroke Play section of a Category "F" event
Make the last 4 of a Category "F" event.

Ranking Scratch Score

The RSS is the calculated standard used to convert a player's Counting Scores to Stroke Play Ranking Points.

The RSS for a Counting Round is calculated by use of the formula (a) / (b), where (a) is the sum total of the gross scores of the leading (X) players in the round, with (X) representing the total number of Ranked Players in the round and (b) is the total number of gross scores in (a) above.

Fractions from the RSS calculation will be rounded to the nearest whole number.

If less than three Ranked Players play a Counting Round, the RSS for that round will be the average of the lowest three scores by amateur golfers.

If fewer than three Amateurs play a Counting Round, the RSS will equate to par.

In any official event from other professional tours, the RSS will equate to par.

September

Africa

C	Mpumalanga Open	Nelspruit	Daniel van Tonder	RSA

Americas

A	OFCC/Fighting Illini Invite	Oly Fields, IL	Peter Uihlein	USA
A	Ping-Golfweek Preview	Stillwater, OK	Pontus Widegren (SWE)	USA
B	Carpet Capital Collegiate	Rock Face, GA	Lee Bedford	USA
B	Kikkor Golf Husky Invitational	Auburn, WA	Josh Anderson	USA
B	Wolf Run Intercollegiate	Zionsville, IN	Connor Arendell	USA
C	Fighting Irish Gridiron Classic	South Bend, IN	Ji Hwan Park/Taylor Travis	USA
C	Gene Miranda Falcon Invite	USAF Academy, CO	Ryan Peterson	USA
C	Golfweek Conference Challenge	Burlington, IA	Chris Brant/Vince India	USA
C	Mark Simpson Colorado Invite	Erie, CO	Mark Hubbard	USA
C	The Gopher Invitational	Wazata, MN	John Hahn	USA
C	The Junior Players Championship	Ponte Vedra Beach, FL	Michael Johnson	USA
C	VCU Shootout	Manakin Sabot, VA	Nate McCoy	USA
C	Windon Memorial	Glenview, IL	Lion Kim	USA
D	California State Fair Amateur	Sacramento, CA	Grant Rappleye	USA
D	Cardinal Intercollegiate	Simpsonville, KY	Aaron Boggs*	USA
D	Mason Rudolph Championship	Franklin, TN	Jack Belote	USA
D	The Sam Hall Intercollegiate	Hattiesburg, MS	Jeff Karlsson (SWE)	USA
D	US Mid-Amateur	Atlantic GC	Nathan Smith	USA
D	USGA State Championship	Santa Rosa, CA	Bryan Norton	USA
D	UTA/Waterchase Invitational	Arlington, TX	Curtis Donahoe/Derek Plucienski	USA
D	Abierto Jockey Club de Rosario	Jockey Club de Rosario	Tomas Cocha	ARG
E	Adams Cup of Newport	Newport, RI	Gregory Eason (ENG)	USA
E	Marshall Invitational	Huntington, WV	Sebastian MacLean (BOL)	USA
E	Turning Stone Tiger Intercollegiate	Turning Stone Resort	Jakob Ziegler (GER)	USA
F	Atlantic Region Invitational	River Greens GC, OH	Brad Boyle (CAN)*	USA
F	BGSU John Piper Intercollegiate	Bowling Green, OH	Drew Preston	USA
F	Bob Hurley Auto ORU Shootout	Tulsa, OK	Gustaf Kocken (SWE)	USA
F	Bucknell Fall Invite	Lewisburg, PA	CG Mercatoris	USA
F	Canadian International Junior Challenge	Oslerbrook G&CC	Juan Sebastian Munoz (COL)	CAN
F	Cavalier Classic	Prineville, OR	Sam Holland	USA
F	Colorado Mid-Amateur	Fort Collins, CO	Keith Humerickhouse*	USA
F	Cornell Invitational	Ithaca, NY	Jake Katz	USA
F	Crump Cup	Pine Valley, NJ	Mike McCoy	USA
F	Erv Kaiser Invitational	Oxbow, ND	Sam Weber*	USA
F	Evangel Fall Invitational	Springfield, MO	Greg MacAulay (CAN)*	USA
F	Fairway Club Invitational	Ne City, NE	Mike Coatman	USA
F	Flagler Collegiate Jennison Memorial	St Augustine, FL	John Pannone	USA
F	Fort Worth City Championship	Fort Worth, TX	Clarke Kincaid*	USA
F	Golfweek Fall Invitational D3	Haines City, FL	Michael Elder*	USA
F	Green Bay Invitational	Green Bay, WI	Brandon White*	USA
F	Grizzly Invitational	Alamosa, CO	Brandon Bingaman	USA
F	Hartford Hawk Invitational	South Kent, CT	D.J. Lantz*	USA
F	High Country Shootout	Sierra Blanca Ruidoso, NM	Jordan McColl (SCO)	USA
F	International Junior Tour – Hershey	Hershey CC – East Course	Alex Daubert*	USA

Americas (continued)

F	Jim Colbert Intercollegiate	Manhattan, KS	Gideon Pienaar (RSA)	USA
F	Jim Redgate Invitational	Meridian, MS	Paul Harriss*	USA
F	John Bohmann Memorial Invitational	Seguin, TX	Ryan Kiel	USA
F	John Dallio Memorial	Lemont, IL	Ben Engle*	USA
F	Junior At The Greenbrier	White Sulphur Springs, WV	Brendan Connolly*	USA
F	Kansas Invitational	Lawrence, KS	Gustaf Kocken (SWE)*	USA
F	Labor Day Invitational	Mobile, AL	Chris Piumelli	USA
F	Laker Collegiate Invitational	Hampton, GA	Jake Greer	USA
F	LCU Fall Invitational	Lubbock, TX	Johan Andersson (SWE)	USA
F	MacRae Invitational	Linville, NC	Bill Argabrite*	USA
F	Manor Intercollegiate	Farmville, VA	Ross Sumner*	USA
F	Maryland Intercollegiate	Cambridge, MD	Mike Miller	USA
F	Massachusetts Mid-Amateur	Dedham, MA	Daniel Falcucci*	USA
F	Minnesota Mid-Amateur	Minneapolis GC/Burl Oaks GC	Troy Johnson	USA
F	New York Mid-Amateur	East Aurora, NY	Tim Hume	USA
F	North Carolina Mid-Amateur	Raleigh, NC	Uly Grisette	USA
F	NSIC/RMAC Regional Crossover	Gothenburg, NE	Gordy Diekman*	USA
F	Oldfield Labor Day Classic	Oldfield CC	Dak Spivey*	USA
F	Outlaw Cup	Riverbend GC	Danny Paniccia	USA
F	Pacific Amateur Classic	Sunriver, OP	Michael Dominick*	USA
F	Pacific Northwest Mid-Amateur	Redmond, OR	Dan Whitaker	USA
F	Palouse Collegiate	Pullman, WA	Damian Telles	USA
F	Peaks Classic	LaVeta, CO	Brian Morfeld*	USA
F	Prairie Club Invitational	Valentine, NE	Kyle Schock*	USA
F	Rutgers Invitation	Piscataway, NJ	John Dawson Neufeld (CAN)*	USA
F	Sandestin Collegiate Championship	Destin, FL	Chase Smith	USA
F	Sea Trail Intercollegiate	Sunset Beach, NC	Chase Wilson	USA
F	Sonoma State Invite	Santa Rosa, CA	Ryan Sheffer*	USA
F	Spring Hill Suites Intercollegiate	Florence, SC	Chris Robb (SCO)	USA
F	St Martins Invitational	Olympia, WA	Xavier Dailly	USA
F	Tennessee Mid-Amateur	Spring Creek Ranch CC	Tim Jackson	USA
F	Texas Mid-Amateur	Fredericksburg, TX	Mike Minicucci*	USA
F	The Fossum	East Lansing, MI	James Ross (SCO)	USA
F	The Invitational at Kiawah	Kiawah Island, SC	John Duke Hudson	USA
F	The McLaughlin	Farmingdale, NY	Brendan Kelly/Joshua Briere	USA
F	The Oklahoma Collegiate	Lawton, OK	Alex Carpenter/Joshua Creel	USA
F	The Vandersluis Memorial	Bemidji, MN	Chris Curb*	USA
F	UC Ferguson Classic	Oklahoma City, OK	Clark Collier	USA
F	University of Great Falls Invite	Great Falls, MT	Connor Rakowski	USA
F	Wallace State Fall Invite	Cullman, AL	Brandt Garon	USA
F	Wasioto Winds Fall Kick-off	Pineville, KY	Patrick Newcomb*	USA
F	Webber Intercollegiate	Lake Wales, FL	Jon Pannone	USA
F	Westminster Invitational	SLC, UT	Connor McCracken	USA
F	WWU Invitational	Bellingham, WA	Brian Barhanovich/Patrick Bauer	USA
F	Abierto de Farallones	Farallones, Cali	Daniel Zuluaga	COL
F	Abierto El Nogal	Guaymaral	Juan Felipe Ruiz	COL
F	Abierto Guayaquil	Guayaquil CC	Alex Falquez	ECU
F	Campeonato Argentino Mid Amateur	GC Argentino	Manuel Vidal Aleman*	ARG
F	Campeonato Juvenil de Venezuela	Caracas	David Arismendy*	VEN
F	Campeonato Nacional Infantil	San Andres, Bogota	Felipe Vallejo*	COL
F	Colombian Mid-Amateur 4th Stage	Manizales	Juan Fernando Mejia	COL
F	Copa Johnnie Walker	Lima	Patricio Alzamora	PER
F	Nacional De Menores	Los Andes, Cali	Daniel Zuluaga	COL
F	Sudamericano Pre-Juvenil Individual	Montevideo	Manuel Arzuaga (ARG)*	URU

Asia

C	Topy Cup of Japan	Tanakura CC	Yoshinori Fujimoto	JPN
D	Northern India Amateur	Delhi	Abhinav Lohan	IND
F	Asian Games Test Event	Dragon Lake GC, Guangzhou	Joshua Shou (SIN)	CHN
F	China-Korea Friendly Event	Dragon Lake GC, Guangzhou	Wenyi Huang	CHN

F	Guam National Tryout	Guam International CC	Louie Sunga	GUM
F	Hokkaido Mid Amateur	Ana Diamond GC	Keita Sato*	JPN
F	Hokkaido Open Championship	Hokkaido	Naruhito Ueda*	JPN
F	Hong Kong Open and Mid Amateur	Clearwater Bay G&CC	Lok Tin Liu	HKG
F	Ilsong Cup	Lakehills Jeju	Kwan-hee Nam*	KOR
F	JC Kau Sai Chau Amateur Open	Jockey Club Sai Chau Golf Course, North Course	Lip Shien Chong*	HKG
F	Kanto Mid-Amateur	Hamamatsu Seaside GC	Nobuhiro Sawada*	JPN
F	Karambunai Amateur Open	Nexus Golf Resport, Sabah	Lam Yu Shuen	MAS
F	Korean Amateur	Namseoul CC	Sang-yeop Lee	KOR
F	KSGA Div 1 Collegiate In Fall	Ibaraki	Yoshinori Fujimoto	JPN
F	KSGA Div 2 Collegiate In Fall	Ibaraki	Katsuyuki Sakurai	JPN
F	KSGA Div 3 Collegiate In Fall	Ibaraki	Shimpei Okumura*/Ugiru Cho*	JPN
F	KSGA Div 4 Collegiate In Fall	Ibaraki	Noriaki Takeuchi*	JPN
F	KSGA Div 5 Collegiate In Fall	Ibaraki	Tomonori Ino*	JPN
F	KSGA Div 6 Collegiate In Fall	Ibaraki	Kazuki Kawai*	JPN
F	Malaysian Junior Open	Karambunai	Miguel Luis Tabuena (PHI)	MAS
F	National Ranking 4th Game	Sentosa/Keppel	Jonathan Woo	SIN
F	Pahang Amateur Open	Bukit Tinggi	Mohd Iyia Jamil	MAS

Australasia

F	New South Wales Junior Boys	Sydney	Jordan Zunic	AUS
F	New Zealand Under 19 Championship	Otago GC, Otago	Simon Brownlee	NZL
F	South Australian Senior Amateur	Grange GC, SA	Greg Corben*	AUS

Europe

C	Turkish Open	Gloria GC, Antalya	Miro Veijalainen (FIN)	TUR
D	Duke of York Young Champions Trophy	Royal St Georges GC	Gudmundur Kristjansson (ISL)*	ENG
D	Eisenhower Invitational	Blairgowrie, Rosemount	Ross Kellett	SCO
E	Italian International Amateur	Villa d'Este	Lionel Weber (FRA)	ITA
E	Team Championship Qualifying 2	Golfclub Houthalen	Robin Kind (NED)	BEL
F	Austrian Mid-Amateur	Klagenfurt-Seltenheim	Helmut Konrad*	AUT
F	Bulgarian Amateur	Blacksearama	Koray Varli (TUR)	BUL
F	Campeonato Internacional Junior	Campo De Golf De Talayuela	Javier Sainz	ESP
F	Estonian Match Play	Saaremaa GC	Torel Neider*	EST
F	Faldo Series Grand Final	Lough Erne	Masamichi Ito (JPN)	IRL
F	German Stroke Play	GC Gleidingen	Sebastian Schwind	GER
F	International Collegiate	Fairmont, St Andrews	Alexander Culverwell	SCO
F	International de France Mid-Amateur	Omaha Beach	Soares Rodrigo Lacerda (BRA)	FRA
F	Israel Boys	Caesarea/Gaash	Asaf Cohen	ISR
F	Italian Under 16 Championship	Biella	Matthias Schwab (AUT)	ITA
F	Junior Masters Invitational	Norrkopings GC	Viktor Edin	SWE
F	Munster Mid-Amateur Open	Limerick GC	Pat Murray	IRL
F	National Championship Medal	Torino	Mattia Miloro	ITA
F	Netherlands National Match Play	Hooge Graven	Daan Huizing	NED
F	Netherlands National Match Play U21	Domburgsche GC	Teemu Bakker	NED
F	Panellinio Stroke Play	Glyfada GC	Lefteris Perros*	GRE
F	Polish Amateur	Toya G&CC	Adrian Meronk	POL
F	Skandia Tour elit 6	Kalmar GC	Bjorn Hellgren	SWE
F	Skandia Tour riks 6 Hudiksvalls	Hudiksvalls GK	Jonas Bederoff Eriksson*	SWE
F	Skandia Tour riks 6 Linkopings	Linkopings GK	Tobias Eden*	SWE
F	Skandia Tour riks 6 Mariestads	Mariestads GK	Robert Fredriksson	SWE
F	Suisse Romande Championship	Les Bois	Nicolas D'Incau	SUI
F	Titleist Tour Skjeberg	Skjeberg GC	Mikkel Bjerch-Andresen	NOR
F	Trofeo Glauco Lolli Ghetti	Margara	Jacopo Jori	ITA

October

Africa

C	Ekurhuleni Open	Benoni CC	Tyrone Ryan	RSA
D	Egyptian Amateur Open	Katameya Heights	Jack Senior (ENG)	EGY
F	West Africa Team Championship-Individual	Royal Valley, Offa	Y Abdullah (NGR)*	NIG

Americas

A	Isleworth Collegiate Invititational	Windermere, FL	Arnond Vongvanij	USA
A	World Amateur Team Championship – Individual	Buenos Aires	Joachim Brandt Hansen (DEN)	ARG
B	Bank of Tennessee @ The Ridges	Jonesborough, TN	Mackenzie Hughes (CAN)	USA
B	Brickyard Collegiate Championship	Macon, GA	Russell Henley	USA
B	Jack Nicklaus Invitational	Columbus, OH	Luke Guthrie	USA
B	Jerry Pate National Intercollegiate	Birmingham, AL	Niclas Carlsson (SWE)	USA
B	The Prestige at PGA WEST	La Quinta, CA	Andrew Yun	USA
B	US Collegiate Championship	Alpharetta, GA	James (USA) White	USA
C	Alister MacKenzie Invitational	Fairfax, CA	Alex Kang	USA
C	DA Weibring Intercollegiate	Normal, IL	Chris DeForest	USA
C	David Toms Intercollegiate	Baton Rouge, LA	Austin Gutgsell	USA
C	Gary Koch Invitational	Tampa, FL	Ben Kohles	USA
C	Kauai Collegiate Invite	Lihue, HI	Gunner Wiebe	USA
C	Rod Myers Invitational	Durham, NC	Albin Choi (CAN)	USA
C	Santa Clara Cabo Collegiate	Cabo, Mexico	Jamie Marshall (YSA)	MEX
C	The Ping Invitational	Stillwater, OK	Jordan Spieth	USA
C	UNCG Bridgestone Collegiate	Greensboro, NC	Blayne Barber/David Lipsky	USA
C	William H Tucker	Albuquerque, NM	Andrew Putnam/Carlos Ortiz (MEX)/ Joon Heui Lee	USA
C	Wolf Pack Classic	Stateline, NV	Alex Ching	USA
C	Wolfpack Intercollegiate	Raleigh, NC	Albin Choi (CAN)	USA
D	Herb Wimberly Intercollegiate	Las Cruces, NM	Matt Rawitzer/Timothy Madigan	USA
D	LA Tech Squire Creek Classic	Choudrant, LA	Horacio Leon (CHI)	USA
D	Memphis Intercollegiate	Memphis, TN	Jack Hiluta (ENG)	USA
D	Rees Jones Intercollegiate	Daufuskie Is, SC	Matt Nagy	USA
E	Bill Cullum Invitational	Simi Valley, CA	Nick Delio	USA
E	Lone Star Invite @ Briggs Ranch	San Antonio, TX	Carlos Ortiz (MEX)	USA
E	Old Dominion / OBX Collegiate	Powell's Point, NC	Harold Varner	USA
E	Saint Mary's Invitational	Seaside, CA	Tom Usher (ENG)	USA
E	The Firestone Invitational	Akron, OH	David Erdy/John Popeck	USA
E	Campeonato Argentino de Menores	Estudiantes de Olavarria	Julian Lerda	ARG
F	Alabama State Mid-Amateur	Wynlakes G&CC	Steven Hudson	USA
F	Bearcat Invitational	Traditions GC	Jeff Dick	USA
F	Bill Ross Intercollegiate	Kansas City, MO	Nate Barbee	USA
F	Brook Hollow Invitational	Dallas, TX	Robby McWilliams	USA
F	Bruce Williams Memorial Invitational	San Antonio, TX	Alex Carpenter/Colby Shrum	USA
F	Burbank City Amateur	DeBell GC	Brennan Amirkhizi*	USA
F	Butler Fall Invitational	Indianapolis, IN	Michael Sainz	USA
F	Cactus Thaw/RMAC #3	Silver City, NM	Ross Prachar*	USA
F	CMS Invitational	Rancho Cocamonga	Tain Lee	USA
F	Colorado Mines Fall Invitational	Westminster, CO	Jim Knous	USA
F	Davidson College Invitational	Davidson, NC	Brent Whitehead*	USA
F	F&M Bank APSU Intercollegiate	Clarksville, TN	Charlie Olson*	USA
F	Firestone Grill Cal Poly Invite	Nipomo, CA	Mario Clemens	USA
F	Florida Mid-Am	Jacksonville, FL	Stephen Anderson*	USA
F	Georgetown Intercollegiate	Members Club @ Four StreamsBeallsville, MD	Austin Kelly (CAN)	USA
F	GLIAC Golf Championship	Grosse Ile, MI	Kyle Wittenbach*	USA
F	Golfweek National Championship	Hilton Head, SC	Chase Wilson	USA
F	Grand Canyon Fall Invitational	Goodyear, AZ	Dylan Goodwin*	USA
F	Greater Houston Amateur	Memorial Park GC	Kip Guidry*	USA
F	Gustavus Twin Cities Classic	Elk River, MN	Justin Johnson*	USA
F	Harvey Penick Invitational	Austin, TX	Nicholas Cristea	USA
F	HBU Intercollegiate	Missouri City, TX	Kristjan Einarsson (ISL)*	USA
F	HNU Fall Invitational	North Alameda, CA	Tyler Kato*	USA
F	InterWest Wildcat Classic	Chico, CA	John Jackson	USA
F	Lindenwood Fall Invitational	St Charles, MO	Derrick Meier	USA
F	MGA Regional Preview	Jefferson City	Laurence Noott (ENG)*	USA
F	MIAC Championship	Coon Rapids, MN	Andrew Whitchurch*	USA
F	Middle Atlantic Amateur	Columbia CC	Will Bowman	USA

F	Mission Inn Fall Intercollegiate	Howey-In-The-Hills, FL	Evan Beirne	USA
F	Mizuno Savannah Intercollegiate	Savannah, GA	Richard Fountain*	USA
F	Montverde Academy Junior All-Star	Howey-in-the-Hills, FL	Hayden Shieh*	USA
F	Murray State Invitational	Murray, KY	William Hunt	USA
F	NCCAA Championship	Panama City, FL	Kevin Anderson	USA
F	New Hampshire Mid-Amateur	Rochester, NH	Jeff Sullivan*	USA
F	NJCAA DI National Preview	Odessa, TX	Jordan McColl (SCO)	USA
F	NSU Shark Invitational	Palm Beach Garden	Jose Maria Joia (POR)	USA
F	Purple and Red Invitational	Layton, UT	Jake Johnson	USA
F	Renaissance Invitational	Fort Myers, FL	Sebastian MacLean (BOL)	USA
F	Richmond Intercollegiate	Midlothian, VA	Ian McConnell	USA
F	Rollins College Invitational	Ocoee, FL	Ricardo Melo Gouveia (POR)	USA
F	Ryan Palmer Foundation Invite	Amarillo, TX	Matt Charlson	USA
F	SeeMore Putters NAIA Intercollegiate	Savannah, GA	Esteban Aristizabal (COL)	USA
F	Service Academy Golf Classic	Andrews AFB, MD	Anthony Kim*	USA
F	SHSU Harold Funston Invite	Huntsville, TX	Axel Ochoa (ARG)	USA
F	SIUE Intercolligiate	Edwardsville, IL	Will Hogan	USA
F	Skyhawk Classic	Buchanan, TN	Josh Thomas*	USA
F	South Carolina Mid-Am	Spartanburg, SC	Steven Liebler	USA
F	St Augustine Amateur	St Augustine, FL	Chris Bray	USA
F	Stocker Cup Invitational	Carmel, CA	Kevin Marsh	USA
F	Telich/Sunlife Financial	Chardon, OH	Justin Lower	USA
F	Texoma Championship	Kingston, OK	Axel Ochoa (ARG)	USA
F	The Connecticut Cup	Ellington, CT	Justin Deitz	USA
F	The Macdonald Cup	New Haven, CT	Kevin Josephson	USA
F	UMAC Golf Championships	Alexandria, MN	Ty Liljander*	USA
F	US Senior Amateur	Lake Nona	Paul Simson	USA
F	Virginia Mid-Am	Newport News, VA	Scott Shingler	USA
F	Vulcan Invitational	Belle Vernon, PA	Paul Tighe*	USA
F	Will Wilson SE Preview	Clemmons, NC	Daniel Stanley	USA
F	WVIAC Championship	Daniels, WV	Emmanuel Charmat (FRA)	USA
F	Aberto De Golf Do Estado Do RS	Belem Novo GC	Ivan Tsukazan	BRA
F	Aberto de Golfe da FPCG	Curitibano	Ivo Leao	BRA
F	Abierto Hacienda Chicureo	Hacienda De Chicureo GC	Patricio Salem (PER)	CHI
F	Abierto Opita de Golf	Neiva	Jose Adan Rodriguez*	COL
F	Copa Claro	Los Inkas GC	Patricio Alzamora	PER
F	Copa Eduardo Herrera	El Rincon, Bogota	Daniel Zuluaga	COL
F	Copa Enrique Santos	Guayaquil CC	Juan Eduardo Cerda (CHI)	ECU

Asia

D	Putra Cup	Selangor GC	Poom Saksansin (THA)	MAS
F	All India Mid Amateur	Royal Calcutta GC, Kolkata	Sudeep Chitlangia*	IND
F	Johor Amateur Open	Legends G&CC	Benedict Ho (SIN)	MAS
F	Lion City Cup	Selangor GC	Edgar Oh (SIN)	MAS
F	Melaka Amateur Open	A'Famosa Resort	Kenneth De Silva	MAS
F	National Sports Festival	Changwon CC	Youn-Ho Bae	KOR
F	Rajasthan Open	Jaipur	Karan Vasudeva	IND
F	Shaikh Rashid Trophy	Jebel Ali Resort & Spa, UAE	Michael Harradine (SUI)	UAE
F	TGA-CAT Junior Ranking	Blue Sapphire Island Golf & Resort	Chaiwat Poolsombut*	THA

Australasia

F	Australian Senior Amateur Match Play	Thirteenth Beach, VIC	Chris Coats*	AUS
F	Fiji Premium Open	Vatuwaqa, Suva	Anuresh Chandra	FIJ
F	Gary Player Classic	Pacific, QLD	Cameron Smith	AUS
F	Jack Newton Srixon Classic	Maitland GC	Ryan Smith*	AUS
F	Victorian Senior Amateur	The Sands, Torquay	Stefan Albinski	AUS

Europe

E	Championnat de France Amateur	Domangere	Antoine Schwartz	FRA
E	Trophee des Regions	Massane	Antoine Schwartz	FRA
F	Austrian Match Play	Diamond CC	Tobias Nemecz	AUT
F	Championatt de France Cadets	Saint-Cyprien	Thomas Elissalde	FRA
F	European Club Trophy	Estela GC, Portugal	Jerome Lando Casanova (FRA)	POR
F	Grand Prix d'Arcachon	d'Arcachon	Thomas Elissalde	FRA
F	Grand Prix de Fontcaude	Fontcaude	Robin Martinazzo*	FRA
F	Israel Amateur Open	Caesarea GC	Asaf Cohen	ISR
F	Italian National Mid-Amateur	Castle Tolcin	Franz Pfoestl	ITA
F	La Quercia d'Oro	Querce	Alessandro Catto	ITA
F	Portuguese Federation Cup	Oporto GC	Manuel Violas	POR
F	SUS Order of Merit Event 2	Fairmont, St Andrews	Graeme Robertson	SCO

November

Africa

C	Central Gauteng Open	Royal Johannesburg & Kensington	Daniel van Tonder	RSA
C	Eastern Province Stroke Play	Humewood GC	Daniel van Tonder	RSA
C	Harry Oppenheimer Trophy	Maccauvlei	Herman Minnie	RSA
C	International Teams Stroke Play	Maccauvlei, RSA	Daniel van Tonder	RSA

Americas

A	The Gifford Collegiate Championship	San Martin, CA	Patrick Cantlay	USA
A	Western Refining College All America	El Paso, TX	Alex Ching	USA
B	Royal Oaks Intercollegiate	Dallas, TX	Vince India	USA
C	Campeonato Argentino de Aficionados	Highland Park CC	Julian Lerda	ARG
C	Copa Juan Carlos Tailhade	Los Lagartos	Andrew Sullivan (ENG)	ARG
D	Polo Junior Classic	Palm Beach Gardens, FL	Cody Proveaux	USA
D	Stockton Sports Com Pacific Invite	Stockton, CA	T J Bordeaux	USA
E	Kiawah Island Intercollegiate	Kiawah, SC	Michael Young (CAN)	USA
F	Dade Amateur	Miami, Florida	Marcus Segerstrom (SWE)	USA
F	Dennis Rose Invitational	Waikaloa, HI	Oskar Nystrom (SWE)	USA
F	IJGT TPC Sawgrass	TPC Sawgrass	Matthew Rushton (RSA)*	USA
F	Mustang Invitational	St Clarita, CA	Stephen Edman	USA
F	Preview at the Point	Alexander City, AL	Brandt Garon	USA
F	Queens Invitational	TPC, Sawgrass	Alex Carpenter	USA
F	Southeastern Fire Invitational	Lakeland, FL	Esteban Aristizabal (COL)	USA
F	Stetson/CFSC Invitational	DeLand, FL	Daniel Mazziotta	USA
F	UC San Diego Triton Invitation	San Diego, CA	Kenny Pigman	USA
F	Abierto Cuenca	Cuenca GC	Alejandro Larriva*	ECU
F	Abierto de Golf	Tennis Golf, Cucuta	Pablo Vasquez*	COL
F	Abierto del Polo	Club de Polo	Anibal Reinoso	CHI
F	Abierto Las Palmas	Las Palmas	Alvaro Flano*	CHI
F	Abierto Los Leones	Club de Golf Los Leones	Nicolas Norambuena	CHI
F	Abierto PWCC	Prince of Wales CC	Juan Eduardo Cerda	CHI
F	Colombian Mid-Amateur-Quinta Parada	Armenia	Mark Clayton Sperling	COL
F	Copa Luis Enrique Rueda Otero	Jaraguay GC	Jose Mario Vega	COL
F	Copa Swissotel	La Planicie	Patricio Alzamora	PER
F	Parada Nacional de Menores III	CC Pereira	Esteban Castro	COL

Asia

B	Asian Games Individual	Guangzhou	Meen-whee Kim (KOR)	CHN
E	Aaron Baddeley IJC	Lion Lake CC, Guangdong	Byron Meth (USA)	CHN
F	Abu Dhabi Junior Championship	Abu Dhabi GC	Ben Taylor (ENG)	UAE
F	Eastern India Junior/Sub Junior	Tollygunge Club, Kolkata	Rahul Ravi*	IND
F	Japan Mid-Amateur	Hanno, Saitama	Naoyuki Tamura	JPN
F	Maharashtra Open Amateur	Poona Club, Pune	Khalin Joshi	IND
F	National Middle School-Junior	Taichung GC	Sung-I Yu	TPE
F	National Middle School-Senior	Taichung GC	Teng Kao/Chieh-Po Lee	TPE

F	Sarawak Chief Minister's Cup	Kelab Golf Sarawak	Thiraphat Phuanglamyai (THA)*/	MAS
			Malcolm Adam Tay Ak Kunjin*	
F	Singha Thailand Junior World	Royal Hua Hin GC	Chanachoke Dejpiratanamongkol*	THA
F	Western India Junior/Sub Junior	Bombay Presidency GC, Mumbai	Rohan Sharma*	IND

Australasia

F	Australian Mid-Amateur	The National GC, Victoria	Jason Perry	AUS

Europe

F	Coppa D'Oro Citta di Castelgandolfo	Castelgandolfo, Italy	Enrico Di Nitto	ITA
F	Grand Prix Ligue PACA	Golf de Servanes	Lionel Weber	FRA

December

Americas

B	Dixie Amateur	Coral Springs, FL	Peter Uihlein	USA
E	Junior Orange Bowl International	Coral Gables, FL	Maximilian Rottluff (GER)	USA
F	Doral Publix Junior Classic 14-15	Miami, FL	Franco Romero (ARG)	USA
F	Doral Publix Junior Classic 16-18	Miami, FL	Pierre Tillement (FRA)	USA
F	Florida International Junior	Port St Lucie, FL	William Brueckner*	USA
F	Holiday Classic	Barton Creek	Brenden Redfern	USA
F	Jones Cup Junior Invitational	Sea Island GC	Motin Yeung	USA
F	United States Junior Masters	Ponte Vedra Beach, FL	Maximilian Rottluff (GER)	USA
F	World Junior Challenge	Innisbrook Golf Resort	Timothy Colanta	USA
F	Abierto Brisas De Chicureo	Las Brisas de Chicureo	Nicolas Flanagan*	CHI
F	Campeonato Juvenil Do Estado De Sao Paulo	Sao Paulo, Brazil	Ivan Tsukazan	BRA
F	Costa Rica National Amateur	Valle de Sol	Alvaro Ortiz	CRC

Asia

D	Acer National Elites Match play	Sunrise G&CC	Chien-Yao Hung	TPE
D	Acer National Fall Ranking	Nan Pao G&CC	Chien-Yao Hung	TPE
E	China Amateur Open	Guangdong Province, China	Jake Higginbottom (AUS)	CHN
F	All India Junior	Eagleton-The Golf Resort, Bangalore	Senapaa Chikkarangappa	IND
F	Bhutan Amateur	Royal Thimphu GC	Ugyen Dorji*	BHU
F	East India Amateur	Royal Calcutta GC	Karan Vasudeva	IND
F	Interstate Amateur	Kolkata	Karan Vasudeva	IND
F	National Ranking 5th Game	Tanah Merah, SIN	Joshua Shou	SIN
F	Penang Amateur Open	Penang Golf Resort	Abel Tam	MAS
F	Perak Amateur Open	Meru Valley G&CC	Chan Tuck Soon	MAS
F	Sabah International Junior Masters	Sabah G&CC	Gavin Kyle Green	MAS
F	SICC JIGC	Singapore Island	Miguel Luis Tabuena (PHI)	SIN
F	Western India Amateur	Oxford G&CC	Angad Cheema	IND

Australasia

E	Port Phillip Amateur	Victoria	Kalem Richardson	AUS
E	The Dunes Medal	The Dunes, VIC	Deyen Lawson*	AUS
E	Victorian Amateur Match Play	Woodlands GC, Victoria	Jack Wilson*	AUS

Europe

F	Copa Nacional Puerta De Hierro	Real Club Pineda de Sevilla	Antonio Hortal	ESP

January

Africa

B	Gauteng North Open	Pecanwood CC	Jaco Mouton	RSA
C	KwaZulu-Natal Open	San Lameer CC	Coenie Bester	RSA
C	Prince's Grant Invitational	Prince's Grant	Brandon Stone	RSA

Americas

D	New Year's Invitational	St Petersburg, FL	Brandon Hagy	USA
E	Abierto de Granadilla	Club de Campo, Granadilla	Gustavo Silva	CHI
E	Abierto Rocas de Santo Domingo	Rocas de Santo Domingo	Juan Carlos Cortes	CHI
E	Puerto Rico Junior Open	Rio Grande	Jason Roets (RSA)*	PUR
F	Golfweek Senior Championship	Doral Resort, FL	Chip Lutz	USA
F	Abierto Cachagua	Club de Golf de Cachagua	Juan Leon O	CHI
F	Abierto Marbella	Marbella CC	Juan Carlos Cortes/Gustavo Silva/	CHI
			Claudio Corrrea*	
F	Brazilian Junior Championship	Belem Novo GC	Gustavo Chuang	BRA
F	Campeonato Nacional de Menores	CC Ibague	Esteban Castro	COL
F	Copa Jose G Artigas–Individual	Cantegril CC	Nicolas Palazzo (ARG)	URU
F	Copa La Prensa	Mar del Plata GC	Franco Romero	ARG
F	Internacional de Menores Individual	Lima GC	Juan Alvarez (URU)	PER
F	Torneo I De Menores	Granja Azul Country Club de Golf	Miguel Tola	PER
F	Torneo II de Menores	Granja Azul Country Club de Golf	Enrique Grau	PER
F	Torneo III de Menores	Country Club de Planicie	Miguel Tola	PER
F	Central American Junior	Mayan Golf Club	Jose Mendez	CRC

Asia

F	Asia Junior Team Individual	Damai Laut, Perak	Ratanon Wannasrichan (THA)	MAS
F	HSBC China Junior Open	Zheng Zhong GC, Shenzhen	Li Haotong	CHN
F	Mission Hills Junior Tour Grand Final	Mission Hills, Shenzhen	Zheng Kai Bai*	CHN
F	National Juniors Challenge Classic	Zhuhai Lakewood GC	Xu Guozhen*	CHN
F	Philippine International Junior Championship	Greenfields G&CC	Jobim Carlos	PHI
F	Selangor Amateur Open	Perangsang Templer GC	Kenneth De Silva	MAS

Australasia

B	Australian Master of the Amateurs	Royal Melbourne GC	Tarquin MacManus	AUS
B	Lake Macquarie Amateur	Belmont GC, NSW	Brady Watt	AUS
E	Harvey Norman Junior	Sydney, NSW	Jarrod Freeman	AUS
F	Auckland Anniversary Tournament	Akarana GC	Fraser Wilkin	NZL
F	Avondale Amateur Medal	Sydney, NSW	Allan Haughie	AUS
F	Boroondara Cup	Green Acres & Kew GC, VIC	Matthew Dowling	AUS
F	Hastings Stroke Play	Hastings GC, Bridge Pa	Joshua Munn	NZL
F	Morcom Cup	Devonport GC	Nathan Gatehouse	AUS
F	North Island U19	Hamilton	Owen Burgess	NZL
F	Otago Stroke Play	Balmacewen GC, Dunedin	Jeremy Hall	NZL
F	South Australia Boys Amateur	The Vines of Reynella GC	Sam Earl*	AUS
F	South Australia Junior Masters	Royal Adelaide GC	Will Somerfield*	AUS
F	Tamar Valley Junior Cup	Greens Beach GC, TAS	Lucas Herbert*	AUS
F	Tasmanian Junior Masters	Ulverstone GC, TAS	Sam Daley*	AUS
F	Tasmanian U24 Championship	Ulverstone GC	Cameron Allen*	AUS
F	Victorian Junior Masters	Waverley GC	Cameron Smith	AUS

Europe

F	TGF Golf League 1st Leg	AGK-Sultan	Hamza Sayin	TUR
F	TGF Golf League 2nd Leg	AGK-Sultan	Hamza Sayin	TUR

February

Africa

B	South African Stroke Play	Mount Edgecom	Jared Harvey	RSA
C	Free State & Northern Cape Amateur	Bloemfontein GC	Daniel Hammond	RSA

Americas

A	Jones Cup Invitational	Sea Island, GA	John Peterson	USA
A	The Amer Ari Invitational	Kohala Coast, HI	Daniel Miernicki	USA
B	Arizona Intercollegiate	Tucson, AZ	Andrew Putnam	USA

B	Battle at the Beach	NewportCoast, CA	Kenneth McCready	USA
B	John Burns Intercollegiate	Wahiawa, HI	Ben Kohles	USA
B	Sun Trust Gator Invitational	Gainesville, FL	Andres Echavarria (COL)	USA
B	Wyoming Desert Intercollegiate	Palm Desert, CA	Kevin Penner/Scott Travers	USA
B	Puerto Rico Classic	Rio Grande, PR	James White (USA)	PUR
C	Anteater Invitational	Newport Beach, CA	Bryan Harris	USA
C	HP Boys at Carlton Woods	The Woodlands, TX	Jordan Spieth	USA
C	JU Invitational	Ponte Vedra, FL	Arnond Vongvanij	USA
C	Seahawk Intercollegiate	Wilmington, NC	Thomas Bass	USA
C	UTSA / Oak Hills Invitational	San Antonio, TX	Nils Floren (SWE)	USA
D	Mobile Bay Intercollegiate	Mobile, AL	Jason Millard	USA
E	Rice Intercollegiate	Houston, TX	Gaston De La Torre	USA
E	Wexford Plantation Intercollegiate	Hilton Head, SC	Brant Peaper	USA
E	WSU Snowman Getaway	Chandler, AZ	Emilio Cuartero (ESP)	USA
F	AASU Pirate Invitational	Dooler, GA	Joel Dahlenburg*	USA
F	BCU Spring Invitational	Daytona Beach, FL	Willie Mack	USA
F	Bronco Invitational	Roswell, NM	Roberto Sebastian (ESP)	USA
F	CSU San Marcos Invitational	Bonsall, CA	Ryan Indovina	USA
F	CSUB Invitational	Bakersfield, CA	Ryan Indovina	USA
F	Jack Brown Memorial Invite	Laredo, TX	John Paul Taylor*	USA
F	Matlock Collegiate Classic	Lakeland, FL	Billy Shida	USA
F	NJCAA District 5 Preview	Abiline, TX	Neil Gowan (ENG)	USA
F	Ponte Vedra Invitational	Ponte Vedra, FL	Michael Furci	USA
F	Start 2 Finish Webber Classic	Lake Wales, FL	Preston Knox*	USA
F	Titan Winter Invitational	Melbourne, FL	Zach Potter	USA
F	William Jessup Spring Classic	Auburn, CA	Daniel Covrig	USA
F	Aberto do Estado do Rio Grande do Sul	Belem Novo GC	Felipe Lessa	BRA
F	Abierto Brisas de Santo Domingo	Brisas de Santo Domingo	Matias Calderon	CHI
F	Abierto De Los Chillos	Los Chillos Club Campestre	Jose Andres Miranda	ECU
F	Abierto La Serena	La Serena	Jose Luis Larrain*	CHI
F	Abierto Santa Augusta	Santa Augusta	Gustavo Silva	CHI
F	Campeonato Nacional Juvenil	Club De Golf Del Cerro	Juan Alvarez	URU
F	Campeonato Nacional por Golpes	Martindale CC	Franco Romero	ARG
F	Parada Nacional Mid Amateur	CC Pereira	Juan Fernando Mejia	COL
F	Torneo de Golf Aficionado	La Pradera de Postosi	Marcelo Toro*	COL
F	Torneo Internacional Infantil y Juvenil	Club Militar de Golf	Esteban Castro	COL
F	Torneo Selectivo Suramericano Juvenil	Club Campestre La Sabana	Esteban Castro/Javier Franco*	COL
F	Torneo V de Menores	Los Andes GC	Nicolas Nunez	PER
F	Torneo VI de Menores	Country Club La Planicie	Eithel McGowen	PER
F	Torneo XXVIII Nacional de Aficionados	Club Deportivo el Rodeo – La Macarena	Santiago Tobon	COL
F	Trujillo Open	G&CC de Trujillo	Eithel McGowen*	PER
F	Central American Amateur	Cariari CC	Roberto Moore (ESA)*	CRC

Asia

E	Acer National Winter Ranking	Nantou GC	Jack Tsai*	TPE
E	All India Amateur	KGA, Bangalore	Senapaa Chikkarangappa	IND
E	DHL-WWW Philippine Amateur	Canlubang G&CC	Jeung Hun Wang (KOR)*	PHI
F	Emirates Amateur Open	Emirates GC, Faldo & Majlis	Joel Neale (ENG)*	UAE
F	February Grand Prix	Royal Colombo GC	N Thangaraja	SRI
F	GCC Championship	Royal GC	Ahmed Almusharekh (UAE)	BRN
F	Haryana Open	Golden Greens, Gurgaon	Arshad Ali*	IND
F	Hong Kong Close Amateur	The Hong Kong GC	Shinichi Mizuno	HKG
F	Kuala Lumpur Amateur	Bukit Jalil G&CC	Gavin Kyle Green	MAS
F	SGA 1st National Ranking Game	Laguna National & Tanah Merah GC	Lam Zhiqun	SIN
F	The Delhi NCR Cup	Delhi GC	Kanishk Madan	IND
F	Tryouts for Pacific Games	Guam International GC	Louie Sunga	GUM

		Australasia		
B	New South Wales Medal & Amateur	Cumberland, Liverpool & NSW Golf Clubs	Andrew Sullivan (ENG)/ Jack Senior (ENG)	AUS
C	Tasmanian Open	Kingston Beach GC	Matthew Stieger	AUS
F	Canterbury Stroke Play	Windsor GC	Sujin Ji (KOR)*	NZL
F	Dunedin Stroke Play	St ClairG C, Otago	Brent McEwan	NZL
F	GNW Championship	Devonport GC	John Cassidy	AUS
F	Grant Clements Memorial	Mt Maunganui, NZL	Ryan Fox	NZL
F	LawnMaster Classic	Manawatu	Joshua Munn	NZL
F	New Zealand Men's Seniors	New Plymouth GC	Murray Martin*	NZL
F	South Island Stroke Play	Timaru GC	Vaughan McCall	NZL
F	Tasmanian Senior Amateur	Mowbray GC	Ross Percy*	AUS

		Europe		
B	Portuguese Amateur	Golf do Montado	Eddie Pepperell (ENG)	POR
F	Copa Baleares	CG Son Antem	Jon Rahm-Rodriguez	ESP
F	TGF Golf League 3rd Leg	Tat	Hamza Sayin	TUR
F	TGF Golf League 4th Leg	Tat	Fahrettin Kok	TUR

March

		Africa		
C	North West Open	Potchefstroom	Brandon Stone	RSA
C	Northern Amateur Open	Randpark	David Law (SCO)	RSA
C	South African Amateur	Vaal de Grace	Michael Stewart (SCO)	RSA
F	EP/Border Championship	Fish River	Phillip Kruse*	RSA
F	Northern Cape Open	Kimberley GC	Theuns Pieters	RSA
F	South African Junior Masters	George, South Africa	Armandt Scholtz	RSA

		Americas		
A	Southern Highlands Collegiate Masters	Las Vegas, NV	Morgan Hoffmann	USA
A	USC Collegiate Invitational	Westlake Village, CA	Patrick Cantlay	USA
B	Annual Louisiana Classics	Lafayette, LA	John Hahn	USA
B	Bandon Dunes Championship	Bandon, OR	Charlie Hughes (CAN)	USA
B	Barona Collegiate Cup	Lakeside, CA	Glen Scher	USA
B	Cleveland Palmetto Invitational	Aiken, SC	Bud Cauley	USA
B	General Hackler Championship	Murrells Inlet, SC	Henrik Norlander (SWE)	USA
B	Hootie @ Bulls Bay Intercollegiate	Awendaw, SC	Mitch Sutton (CAN)	USA
B	John Hayt Collegiate Invitational	Ponte Vedra, FL	Philip Choi	USA
B	Linger Longer Invitational	Greensboro, GA	Cory Whitsett	USA
B	San Diego Intercollegiate	Chula Vista, CA	Paul McConnell	USA
B	Schenkel Invitational	Statesboro, GA	Arnond Vongvanij	USA
B	The Azalea Invitational	Country Club of Charleston, SC	Cheng-tsung Pan (TPE)	USA
B	The Duck Invitational	Eugene, OR	Chris Williams	USA
C	Annual Del Walker	Long Beach, CA	Gregor Main	USA
C	Border Olympics	Laredo, TX	Michael Whitehead	USA
C	Desert Shootout	Goodyear, AZ	Abraham Ancer	USA
C	Fresno State Lexus Classic	Fresno, CA	Alex Johnson	USA
C	Furman Intercollegiate	Greenville, SC	William Sjaichudin (INA)	USA
C	LA Tech Bulldog Classic	Choudrant, LA	Hunter Green	USA
C	National Invitational Tournament	Tuscon, AZ	Jonathan Khan	USA
C	OGIO Santa Barbara Invite	Goleta, CA	Daniel Miernicki/Jack Dukeminier	USA
C	Rio Pinar Invitational	Orlando, FL	Daniel Mazziotta	USA
C	Seminole Intercollegiate	Tallahassee, FL	Drew Kittleson/Jeff Karlsson (SWE)/ Sebastian Cappelen (DEN)	USA
C	UALR/First Tee Classic	Little Rock, AR	Jace Long	USA
C	USF Invitational	Dade City, FL	Hunter Green	USA
D	FAU Spring Break Championship	DelRay Beach, FL	Brad Smith	USA
D	Fireline Towson Invitational	Grasonville, MD	John Hahn	USA
D	Folino Invitational	Irvine, CA	Geoff Gonzalez	USA

	Tournament	Location	Winner	Country
D	Pinehurst Intercollegiate by Gatorade	Pinehurst, NC	Josh Brock	USA
E	Barefoot at the Beach	Myrtle Beach, SC	Matt Nagy	USA
E	Jackrabbit Invitational	Primm, NV	Jace Long	USA
E	San Francisco City Championship	San Francisco, CA	Brandon Hagy	USA
E	St Edward's Invitational	Austin, TX	Alex Carpenter	USA
E	Triumph at Pauma Valley	San Diego, CA	Ji Hwan Park	USA
F	Annual Eagle Invitational	Daytona Beach, FL	Casey Flenniken*	USA
F	Argonaut Invitational	Pensacola, FL	Jace Windom*	USA
F	Arizona Publinks	Randolph North GC	Philip Bagdade	USA
F	Beu/Mussatto Invitational	Macomb, IL	Andrew Godfrey*	USA
F	Bobcat Invitational	Eatonton, GA	Otto Bonning (SWE)	USA
F	Camp LeJeune Gold	Camp LeJeune, NC	Omar Tejeira (PAN)	USA
F	Camp LeJeune Scarlet Consolation	Camp LeJeune, NC	Michael Dowd*	USA
F	Caribbean Intercollegiate	Puerto Rico	Adam Goins*	USA
F	CBU Spring Break	Primm, NV	Greg Richards (SCO)	USA
F	Charleston Shootout	Charleston, SC	Jacobo Pastor (ESP)	USA
F	CLU Kingsmen Invitational	Lompoc, CA	Tain Lee	USA
F	College of Idaho Invitational	Wilder, ID	Tyler Falk	USA
F	Concord U Invitational	Daniels, WV	Ryan Terdik (CAN)/Sean Burke(CAN)*	USA
F	Coyote Classic	San Bernadino, CA	Eric Frazzetta	USA
F	Crawford-Wade Invite	Pottsboro, TX	Christopher Leasor*/Travis Chrietzberg*	USA
F	DBU Patriot Invitational	Dallas, TX	Alex Carpenter	USA
F	Docuteam Invitational	Adairsville, GA	Erwan Vieilledent (FRA)	USA
F	Florida Azalea	Palatka, FL	JD Tomlinson	USA
F	George Washington Invitational	Bethany Beach, DE	Andres Pumariega	USA
F	Golfweek Spring Invitatational-Div II	Orlando, FL	Alex Carpenter	USA
F	Goosepond Fling	Scottsboro, AL	Jake Worthington*	USA
F	Grand Canyon Thunderbird Invitational	Goodyear, AZ	Matt Pridey*	USA
F	Grub Mart-Young Oil Intercollegiate	Jacksonville, AL	Kristjan Einarsson (ISL)/Seth Reeves/ Tom Robson (ENG)	USA
F	Hal Sutton Intercollegiate	Bossier City, LA	Gregory Berthelot*	USA
F	Hawaii State Amateur	Pearl Country Club	Lorens Chan	USA
F	Jekyll Island Collegiate Invitational	Jekyll Island, GA	Chris Morris	USA
F	Jekyll Island Indvidual Invite	Jekyll Island, GA	Clay Hinton*	USA
F	Lamkin Grip Cal Poly Challenge	Arroya Grande, CA	Jake Johnson	USA
F	Midwestern State Invitational	Wichita Falls, TX	Ed Herzog*	USA
F	Mission Inn Spring Fling	Howey In The Hills	Sam Ryder	USA
F	Mustang Intercollegiate	Albaquerque, NM	John Jackson	USA
F	NDNU Argonaut Invitational	Livermore, CA	Dylan Jackson*	USA
F	North Alabama Spring Classic	Muscle Shoals, AL	Jake Greer	USA
F	North Texas Mid-Amateur	Trophy Club, TX	Aaron Hickman	USA
F	Omega Chemical/Midland College	Midland, TX	Roberto Sebastian (ESP)	USA
F	OMNI Financial Intercollegiate	Savannah, GA	Nate Fridley*	USA
F	Pioneer Shootout	Vallejo, CA	Kenny Pigman	USA
F	Point Loma/Smee Builders Invitational	Jamul, CA	Aaron Flores	USA
F	Quintero Invitational	Peoria, AZ	Ben Freeman	USA
F	Ronnie Black Collegiate Invitational	Lovington/Hobbs, NM	Chance Nichols*	USA
F	Salinas City Match Play	Salinas, CA	Ricky Stockton	USA
F	Samford Intercollegiate	Oneonta, AL	Steven Lecuyer (CAN)	USA
F	SCGA Public Links Championship	Pasadena, CA	Tim Hogarth	USA
F	Senior Florida Azalea Amateur	Palatka, FL	Chip Lutz	USA
F	SoCal Intercollegiate D2	Mission Viejo, CA	Colby Shrum	USA
F	South Texas Mid-Amateur	Sugar Land, TX	Mike Mccaffrey*	USA
F	Southeastern Collegiate	Valdosta, GA	Patrick Garrett*	USA
F	St. Paddy's Day Classic	Beaumont, CA	Jeremy Sanders*	USA
F	The Grover Page Classic	Jackson, TN	Cameron Carrico	USA
F	UTD Spring Classic	Richardson, TX	Enrique Livas	USA
F	Warner Pacific Invitational	Vancouver, WA	Taylor Schmidt*	USA
F	Abierto De Arrayanes	Arrayanes CC	Jose Andres Miranda	ECU
F	Abierto de Chile	Santiago	Gustavo Silva	CHI
F	Abierto de Verano	Asia GC	Miguel Tola	PER

Americas (continued)

F	Abierto La Posada	Club De Golf La Posada	Hugo Leon*	CHI
F	Abierto Las Araucarias	Las Araucarias	Martin Cancino	CHI
F	Abierto Los Lirios	Club De Golf Los Lirios	Gustavo Silva	CHI
F	Campeonato Aberto Bandeirantes De Golfe	Aruja Golf Club	Pedro Costa Lima	BRA
F	Campeonato Nacional de Mayores	Club Campestre Bucaramanga	Santiago Gomez	COL
F	Master Infantil Y Juvenil de Golf	Club Campestre Farallones	Mateo Gomez Villegas	COL
F	National Mid Amateur 2nd Stage	Ruitoque GCC	Delgado Felipe Harker	COL
F	Bermuda Match Play	Mid Ocean Club	Jarryd Dillas	BER
F	Costa Rica Junior	Cariari CC	Jose Mendez Vargas	CRC
F	Costa Rica National Match Play	Valle del Sol Golf Course	Jose Mendez	CRC
F	Trinidad & Tobago Open Amateur	St Andrews GC, Moka	James Johnson (BAR)	TRI

Asia

D	Faldo Series Asia Grand Final	Mission Hills GC, Shenzhen	Abhijit Chadha (IND)	CHN
D	Montecillo Junior Team Championship	Mount Malarayat G&CC	Jobim Carlos	PHI
F	Asia Pacific Junior Qalifier	Royal Hills Golf Course	Smithti Teeratrakul	THA
F	China Amateur Tour I	Dongguan	Jin Daxing*	CHN
F	HSBC Youth Challenge 1st Leg	Warren G&CC	Joshua Ho	SIN
F	Mindanao Regional Tournament	Del Monte GC	Art Arbole	PHI
F	Perlis Amateur Open	Putra GC	Ng Choo Teck	MAS
F	Qatar Open Amateur	Doha GC	Max Williams (ENG)	QAT
F	Sri Lanka Grand Prix	Royal Colombo GC	Vijitha Bandara*	SRI
F	TGA-CAT Junior Ranking Stage 5	Evergreen Hills GC	Shang Choomchuay*	THA
F	Visayas Regional Tournament	Negros Occidental G&CC	Chepe Dulay*	PHI

Australasia

B	Australian Stroke Play & Amateur	Victoria and Woodlands GC's	Cameron Smith/Matthew Stieger	AUS
B	Riversdale Cup	Melbourne, VIC	Nathan Holman	AUS
E	Federal Amateur	Federal GC, Canberra	Tim Hart	AUS
F	NSW Senior Championship	Bermagui GC	Peter King	AUS
F	Rotorua Open	Rotorua, BOP	Landyn Edwards/Ho Jun Sung*	NZL
F	SBS Invitational-Individual	Invercargill GC	Ryan Fox	NZL
F	WA State Senior Championship	Mandurah, WA	Stefan Albinski	AUS

Europe

B	Spanish International Amateur	Real Club de Golf el Prat	Laurie Canter (ENG)	ESP
D	Copa And lucia	Club de Campo de Sanlucar	Juan Sarasti	ESP
E	Darwin Salver	Rye GC	Tyrrell Hatton	ENG
E	Grand Prix Du Cap D'Agde	Golf Du Cap D'Agde	Julien Brun	FRA
F	Campeonato de Catalunya Junior	CG Emporda	Carlos Pigem	ESP
F	Grand Prix Carcassonne	Golf Club De Carassonne	Clement Batut	FRA
F	Grand Prix Du Lys	As Club Du Lys Chantilly	Franck Daux/Berre Thomas Le*	FRA
F	Grand Prix Federal De Toulouse	Golf De Toulouse	Xavier Diana*	FRA
F	Leone Di San Marco	Circolo Golf Venezia	Gabrielle Heinrich	ITA
F	Scottish Universities 3rd Order of Merit	Ayrshire, Scotland	Daniel Sommerville	SCO
F	SGU Junior Tour I	Arbroath Links, Scotland	Ewan Scott	SCO
F	SUS Championship	Moray Old and New, Scotland	James White	SCO

April

Africa

C	Cape Province Open	Kingswood & George	Riekus Nortje	RSA
C	Western Province Amateur Championship	Westlake	Jared Harvey/Graham van der Merwe	RSA

Americas

A	Western Intercollegiate	Santa Cruz, CA	Timothy Madigan	USA
B	ASU Thunderbird Invitational	Tempe, AZ	John Spaun	USA

B	Atlantic Coast Conference	New London, NC	Paul Haley	USA
B	Big 12 Championship	Hutchinson, KS	Morgan Hoffmann	USA
B	Illini Spring Classic	Urbana, IL	William Sjaichudin (INA)	USA
B	Insperity ASU Invitational	Augusta, GA	Kevin Tway	USA
B	Morris Williams Intercollegiate	Austin, TX	Tom Hoge	USA
B	Robert Kepler Intercollegiate	Columbus, OH	John Hahn/Luke Guthrie	USA
B	SEC Championship	Sea Island, GA	Andres Echavarria (COL)	USA
B	Terra Cotta Invitational	Naples, FL	Emiliano Grillo (ARG)	USA
B	The Aggie Invitational	Bryan, TX	Peter Uihlein	USA
C	Atlantic Sun Championship	Braselton, GA	Jeff Karlsson (SWE)	USA
C	BancorpSouth Intercollegiate	Madison, MS	Philipp Westermann (GER)	USA
C	C-USA Championship	Texarkana, TX	Jonathan Fly	USA
C	ECU/UNCW River Landing Intercollegiate	Wallace, NC	Josh Brock	USA
C	Hawkeye TaylorMade Invite	Iowa City, IA	Andy Sajevic/Vince India	USA
C	Irish Creek Collegiate	Kannapolis, NC	Lee Bedford	USA
C	Junior Invitational	Sage Valley GC	Nicholas Reach	USA
C	LSU Invitational	Baton Rouge, LA	Stephan Jaeger (GER)	USA
C	Ping Golf Cougar Classic	Provo, UT	Zac Blair	USA
C	Southland Conference	Ft Worth, TX	MJ Daffue (RSA)	USA
C	West Coast Conference Championship	Hollister, CA	Taylor Travis	USA
C	Wyoming Cowboy Classic	Scottsdale, AZ	Tarquin MacManus (AUS)	USA
D	Big South Championship	Ninety-Six, SC	Preston Dembowiak	USA
D	COG Mizzou Intercollegiate	Columbia, MO	Jace Long	USA
D	Coleman Invitational	Seminole GC	Michael McCoy	USA
D	Jim West Intercollegiate	Victoria, TX	Philipp Westermann (GER)	USA
E	Adidas Hoosier Invitational	Bloomington, IN	Tyler Merkel*	USA
E	Boilermaker Invitational	W Lafayette, IN	Adam Schenk	USA
E	Coca-Cola Wofford Invitational	Spartanburg, SC	Jacobo Pastor (ESP)	USA
E	Southern Conference Championship	Florence, SC	Richard Fountain	USA
E	Campeonato Sudamericano Juvenil	CC de Ville	Thomas Baik (ARG)	PER
E	Internacional de Aficionados	Lima GC	James Burnett (ENG)*	PER
F	AAC Direct Qualifier	Winchester, TN	Michael Alread*	USA
F	AJGA Junior at Innsbrook	Palm Harbor, FLA	Shun Yat Hak (HKG)	USA
F	Alameda Commuters Championship	Alameda, CA	Rick Reinsberg	USA
F	American Southwest Conference Championship	Horseshoe Bay, TX	Jacob Walsh	USA
F	Arizona Stroke Play	Scottsdale, AZ	Peter Kyo Won Koo*	USA
F	ASU Red Wolf Intercollegiate	Jonesboro, AR	Brandt Garon	USA
F	Baker University Spring Invite	Lawrence, KS	Matt Mickelson*	USA
F	Big East Championship	Innisbrook, FL	Max Scodro	USA
F	Bobby Krig Invitational	LeSueur, MN	Peyton Olson*	USA
F	Bobcat Spring Invitational	Miami Lakes, FL	Nicholas Soglanich (RSA)/Omar Tejeira (PAN)	USA
F	Branson Creek Invitational	Hollister, MO	Neal McCarty	USA
F	Braveheart Classic	Beaumont, CA	Jake Sarnoff	USA
F	Bucanner Presented by Carrabba's	Miami Beach, FL	Jack Bartlett (ENG)	USA
F	CAA Conference Championship	Pinehurst, NC	Josh Brock	USA
F	Carolinas Mid Amateur	Charlotte, NC	Paul Tucker	USA
F	CCAA Championship	Paso Robles, CA	Scott Yeakel	USA
F	CCC Championship	Monroe, OR	Jed Dalton	USA
F	Conference Carolina's Championship	Vass, NC	CJ DeBerg	USA
F	Detroit Titans Invitational	Highland, MI	Mark Hicks (CAN)*	USA
F	Earl Yestingsmeier Invitational	Muncie, IN	Eric Steger	USA
F	Frontier Conference	Opportunity, MT	Connor McCracken	USA
F	GLVC Championship	Springfield, IL	Andrew Troyanek*	USA
F	GNAC Championship	Coeur D Alene Resort GC	Nick Varelia	USA
F	Golfweek Senior Amateur	Classic Club	Bob Wernick*	USA
F	Gulf South Conference	Hot Springs, AR	Carlos Rodriguez (COL)	USA
F	Hanny Stanislaus Invitational	Turlock, CA	Scott Yeakel	USA
F	Heart of America Invitational	Warrensburg, MO	Joe Migdal*	USA
F	Heartland Conference	Round Rock, TX	Noah Smithson	USA
F	Horizon League Championship	HowieInTheHills	Michael Klaric/Andrew Bailey*	USA

Americas (continued)

F	IIAC Championship	Storm Lake, IA	Jason Harvey*	USA
F	Intercollegiate at Cog Hill	Lemont, IL	Casey Pyne	USA
F	Ivy League Championship	Galloway, NJ	Peter Williamson	USA
F	Junior All Star at Chateau Elan	Braselton, GA	Corey Carlson*	USA
F	Junior at Traditions	Bryan, TX	Ty Dunlap	USA
F	Kelly Cup Invitational	Burbank, CA	Michael Hyland	USA
F	KJCCC Region VI Championship	Nweton, KS	Chien Hau Tan (MAS)	USA
F	LeTourneau Spring Classic	Longview, TX	Justin Weant*	USA
F	Lone Star Championships	San Antonio, TX	Colby Shrum	USA
F	Los Angeles City Junior	Los Angeles, CA	Yi Keun Chang	USA
F	Lou Hart Invitational	Meridian, MS	Blaise Wilson	USA
F	MEAC Showcase	Savannah, GA	Ryan Lassiter*	USA
F	MIAA Championship	Kansas City, MO	Matt Miller	USA
F	Mid South Conference	Bardstown, KY	Pierre Carlsson (SWE)	USA
F	Mount St. Mary's Spring Invitational	Littlestown, PA	CG Mercatoris	USA
F	MWC Championship	Rockford, IL	Eric Busalacchi*	USA
F	NAIA All Conference	Victoria, TX	Darren Hupfer (CAN)	USA
F	NAIA SSAC Championship	Columbus, GA	Matt Youmans/Arvid Bengtsson* (SWE)	USA
F	NJCAA DI Region XXII Championship	Willow Point CC	Brandt Garon	USA
F	NJCAA DI Region 17	Jekyll Island, GA	Joe Sakulpolphaisan (THA)/Shad Tuten*	USA
F	NJCAA DII Region 17	Jekyll Island, GA	Terry English*	USA
F	NJCAA District 2 Championship	Seminole, OK	Nathan Anderson*	USA
F	Northwood Spring Invitational	De Soto, TX	Nick Chacon*	USA
F	NSIC Spring Championship	Lake City, MN	Adam Fields	USA
F	OAC Spring Invitational	Pataskala, OH	Ricky Jaskolski*	USA
F	ODAC Championship	Cape Charles, VA	Mike Redwood	USA
F	Ohio Valley Conference Championship	Dickson, TN	Andres Schonbaum (ARG)/Johan Eriksson (SWE)/Matt Wallace (ENG)	USA
F	Oklahoma City Spring Classic	Ardmore, OK	Bradley Sinnitt (RSA)	USA
F	Pac West Conference Championship	St George, UT	Blake Snyder*	USA
F	Peach Belt Conference Championship	Pooler, GA	Joel Dahlenburg	USA
F	Phoenix City Amateur Championship	Phoenix, AZ	Michael Wog	USA
F	Princeton Invitational	Princeton, NJ	Sam Bernstein	USA
F	RMAC DQ Wolf Pack Invitational	Pueblo, CO	Scott Wyers*	USA
F	RMAC Spring Championship	Goodyear, AZ	Chad Novak/Gavin Lyons*	USA
F	RRAC Championship	Laguna Vista, TX	Armando Villarreal (MEX)	USA
F	Rutherford Intercollegiate	State College, PA	Travis Howe	USA
F	SAC Championship	Conover, NC	Daniel Stanley	USA
F	Sacramento Valley Match Play	Roseville, CA	Jeff Hoffman	USA
F	SCAC Conference Championship	Horseshoe Bay, TX	Chris Morris	USA
F	SCGA Mid-Amateur	Costa Mesa, CA	Scott Almquist	USA
F	Seniors Masters Championship	Indian Wells, CA	Douglas Pool*	USA
F	SLIAC Championship	St Louis, MO	Kaleb Kessler*	USA
F	Sooner Athletic Conference	Catoosa, OK	Preston Wilkins	USA
F	SSC Tournament	Boca Raton, FL	Daniel Stapff (BRA)	USA
F	St Johns Spring Invitational	Monticello CC	Alex Kolquist/Andy Stahlman*/ Casey Vangsness*	USA
F	State Farm MVC Championship	Lake/Ozarks, MO	Cody Schweinefus	USA
F	Summit League Championship	Primm, NV	Michael Powell	USA
F	Sun Conference	Port St Lucie, FL	Esteban Aristizabal (COL)	USA
F	SWAC Championship	Alexandria, LA	Bradley Story*	USA
F	Texas Junior College Championships	Granbury, TX	Greyden Blevins*	USA
F	TSU Big Blue Intercollegiate	Spring Hill, TN	Cameron Carrico	USA
F	Tucson City Amateur	Tucson, AZ	Justin Stacy*	USA
F	UCO/Kickingbird Classic	Edmond, OK	Colby Shrum/Jason Timmis (ENG)	USA
F	UK Bluegrass Invitational	Lexington, KY	Chris Woeste	USA
F	Under Armour Hunter Mahan Championship	Plano, TX	Branson Davis	USA
F	Union University Spring Invitational	Union City, TN	Joey Bradley	USA

F	West Region Invitational	Round Rock, TX	Eddie Diaz de Leon	USA
F	Winn Grips Heather Farr Classic	Mesa, AR	Zachary Wright	USA
F	Abierto De Brasilia	Clube de Golfe de Braslilia	Felipe Lessa	BRA
F	Campeonato de Chile Match Play	Club De Golf Los Leones	Matias Dominguez	CHI
F	Copa Camilo Villegas	Club Manzales	Mauricio Cuartas	COL
F	Copa Manuel J de la Rosa	Barrabquilla CC	Edgardo Arrazola	COL
F	Rio de Janeiro Open	Buzios Golf Club	Leonardo Conrado	BRA
F	Torneo Club Campestre de Popayan	Club Campestre de Popayan	Santiago Gomez	COL
F	Caribbean Junior Open Championship	St Andrews GC	Andrei Collins*	TRI

Asia

E	Bangladesh Amateur	Kurmitola GC	Khalin Joshi (IND)	1	BAN
F	China Amateur Tour Leg 2	Jiangsu	Huang Yong Le*		CHN
F	China Futures Tour 1	Golden Gulf GC, Zhuhai	Guan Tianlang*		CHN
F	Malaysian Amateur Closed	Seri Selangor GC	Gavin Kyle Green		MAS
F	Northern India Amateur	Chandigarh GC	Abhijit Chadha		IND
F	Pakistan Amateur	Islamabad GC	Hamza Amin		PAK
F	Philippine Amateur	Riviera GC, Silang Cavite	Jeung Hun Wang (KOR)		PHI
F	Presidents Gold Medal	Islamabad GC	Waseem Rana		PAK
F	Royal Palm Championship	Royal Palm G&CC	Taimur Hassan Amin		PAK
F	Sabah Amateur Open	Tawau GC	Jobim Carlos (PHI)		MAS
F	SGA 2nd National Ranking Game	Singapore Island CC/Changi GC	Lam Zhiqun		SIN
F	SICC Open Invitation	Singapore Island CC	Lam Zhiqun		SIN
F	TGA-CAT Junior Ranking Stage 6	Royal Hill GC	Nonthapat Hattakanont*		THA

Australasia

C	Mandurah Easter Amateur	Mandurah CC	Michael Dennis	AUS
C	New Zealand Amateur	Russley, GC	Ryan Fox/Mathew Perry	NZL
D	Australian Boys Amateur	Sydney, NSW	Cameron Smith	AUS
D	Western Australian State Amateur	Perth, WA	Matthew Stieger/Ben Seward*	AUS
E	North Island Stroke Play	Whitford Park GC, Auckland	Ryan Fox	NZL
F	Fiji Amateur	Fiji GC, Suva	Vikrant Chandra	FIJ
F	South Australian Amateur Championship	Various, SA	Tom Bond/Brad Moules	AUS
F	South Island Under 19 Championship	Timaru GC, Aorangi	Tim Leonard (NZL)	AUS
F	Tasmanian Amateur	CC Tasmania, TAS	Kalem Richardson	AUS

Europe

B	European Nations	Real CG Sotogrande	Julien Brun (FRA)	ESP
B	Hampshire Salver	North Hants GC	Andrew Sullivan	ENG
C	Coupe Frayssineau-Mouchy	Golf de Fontainebleu	Gary Stal	FRA
C	Craigmillar Park Open	Craigmillar Park GC	Greg Paterson	SCO
C	The Duncan Putter	Southerndown GC	James Frazer	WAL
D	Battle Trophy	Grail Golfing Society	Alexander Culverwell	SCO
D	West of Ireland Open Championship	County Sligo GC	Paul Cutler	IRL
E	DGV Match Play	Frankfurter GC	Hinrich Arkenau	GER
E	Peter McEvoy Trophy	Copt Heath GC	Nathan Kimsey	ENG
E	Scottish Champion of Champions	Leven Golfing Society, Scotland	Brian Soutar	SCO
E	Trubshaw Cup	Tenby/Ashburnham GCs	Oliver Farr	WAL
E	West of England Open Amateur	Saunton East, England	Alex Christie	ENG
F	BUCS Stroke Play Finals	West Lancashire GC	Chris O'Neill (WAL)*	ENG
F	Campeonato de Barcelona	RCG El Prat	Xavi Puig	ESP
F	Campeonato de Espana Boys	CG Larrabea	Scott Fernandez	ESP
F	Campeonato de Espana Universitario	C G Leon	Jose Bondia	ESP
F	Campeonato Nacional Absoluto	Oporto GC	Goncalo Pinto	POR
F	Campeonato Nazionale Ragazzi Match Play	Golf Club Poggio Dei Medici	Gianmaria Trinchero	ITA
F	Citta di Roma Coppa d'Oro	Circolo Del Golf Di Roma	Mattia Miloro	ITA
F	Grand Prix AFG	Golf de Rigenee	Thomas Detry	BEL
F	Grand Prix D'Albi	Golf Albi Lasbordes	Benjamin Forges	FRA
F	Grand Prix de Bordeaux Lac	Golf de Bordeaux-Lac	Brice Chanfreau	FRA
F	Grand Prix De Haute Savoie	Golf Club Esery	Arthur Gabella-Wenne (SUI)	FRA
F	Grand Prix de Limere	Golf de Limere	Mervin Rocchi/Franck Daux	FRA

Europe (continued)

F	Grand Prix de Nimes Campagne	Golf Club de Nimes Campagne	Bastien Melani	FRA
F	Grand Prix De Saint Cyprien	Golf De Saint Cyprien	Etlin Joris*	FRA
F	Italian National Match Play	Golf Club Castello di Tolcinasco	Federico Zucchetti	ITA
F	Leinster Youths Championship	Knightsbrook GC	Brian Casey	IRL
F	Munster Youths Open	Killarney GC	Steffan O'Hara*	IRL
F	Open D'Arcachon	Golf International D'Arcachon	Flohic Thomas Le*	FRA
F	Open International Amateurs	Golf Du Bassin Bleu	Benjamin Kedochim*	FRA
F	R&A Foundation Scholars Tournament	Eden & Old Course, St Andrews	Nick Macandrew*	SCO
F	Scottish Boys Championship	Dunbar GC	David Wilson*	SCO
F	South Wales Boys Championship	Wenvoe Castle GC	Jack Bush	WAL
F	TGF Golf League 5th Leg	Kemer	Koray Varli	TUR
F	TGF League 6th Leg	Kemer	Hamza Sayin	TUR
F	Ticino Championship	Ascona	Richard Heath (AUS)	SUI
F	Trofeo Vecchio Monastero	Varese GC	Nicolas Thommen (SUI)	ITA
F	Trophee Carlhian	Golf De Belle Dune	Kristoffer Ventura (NOR)	FRA
F	Trophee Thomas de Kristoffy	Golf Stade Français Courson	Sebastien Gros	FRA

May

Africa

C	Boland Open	Arabella GC	Haydn Porteous	RSA
C	Kwazulu Natal Amateur	Beachwood	Michael Hollick	RSA
F	Botswana Open	Phakalane Golf Estate	Charlton Makoko*	BOT
F	South Africa Mid Amateur Stroke Play	East London GC	Denis Jones*	RSA

Americas

A	NCAA South Central-Colorado Region	Erie, CO	Kevin Tway	USA
A	Pac-10 Championship	Stanford, CA	Martin Trainer	USA
B	Big Ten Championship	W. Lafayette, IN	Luke Guthrie	USA
B	NCAA Central-Indiana Regional	Zionsville, IN	Lion Kim/Luke Guthrie	USA
B	NCAA East-VA Tech Regional	Blacksburg, VA	Abraham Ancer	USA
B	NCAA Southeast-Florida Region	Ocala, FL	Jace Long/Mitch Sutton (CAN)/ Patrick Reed	USA
B	NCAA Southwest-Arizona Region	Tucson, AZ	Matt Hansen	USA
B	NCAA West-San Diego Regional	Rancho Santa fe	Patrick Cantlay	USA
C	Mid-American Conference	Miami, OH	Mackenzie Hughes (CAN)	USA
C	Mountain West Conference	Tucson, AZ	Derek Ernst	USA
C	WAC Championship	Henderson, NV	Mark Hubbard	USA
D	Big West Championship	Mission Viejo, CA	Austin Graham	USA
D	Thunderbird International Junior	Scottsdale, AZ	Brad Dalke	USA
E	Carlton Woods Invitational	The Woodlands, TX	David Bartman	USA
E	Fresno City Championship	Fresno, CA	Danny Paniccia	USA
E	Lupton Invitational	Ooltewah, TN	Kris Mikkelsen	USA
E	Memorial Amateur	Carmichael, CA	John Catlin	USA
E	Metropolitan Match Play	Saint Louis, MO	Justin Bryant	USA
E	NCAA Division II Championship	Florence, AL	Kyle Souza	USA
E	Scott Robertson Memorial	Roanoke, VI	James Yoon (PAR)	USA
E	Signal Mountain Invitational	Signal Mountain, TN	Stephan Jaeger (GER)	USA
E	Abierto del Norte	Jockey Club de Tucuman	Franco Romero	ARG
F	AMC Championship	Howard, OH	Justin Lower	USA

Uihlein still on top

2010 U.S Amateur Golf Champion and McCormack Medal winner Peter Uihlein leads the May World Amateur Golf Ranking (WAGR) issued by The R&A. American players dominate the top 10 with the exception being Andres Echavarria of Colombia in third position.

In the top 20 the leading European golfer is Andrew Sullivan of England in 14th position with Jared Harvey of South Africa in 16th place, Australian Matthew Stieger in 17th and Ben Campbell of New Zealand occupying the 18th slot.

F	America Sky Conference	Scottsdale, AZ	Nick Despain	USA
F	Arkansas Match Play	Bryant, AR	Juan Gonzalez*	USA
F	Atlantic 10 Championship	Howie-In-The-Hills	Herbert Day (ESA)	USA
F	Bridgestone Tournament of Champions 15-19	Grand Cypress Resort	Kazuki Higa (JPN)*	USA
F	Bridgestone Tournament of Champions U 14	Grand Cypress Resort	Anthony Perrino*	USA
F	Centennial Conference Championship	Elverson, PA	Peter Ruymann*	USA
F	Charleston City Amateur	Charleston, SC	Tom Bullock*	USA
F	CN Future Links Pacific Championship	Arbutus Ridge G&CC	Wilson Bateman	CAN
F	FCWT 11-13 National Championship	PGA National GC	Jackson Lang*	USA
F	FCWT 13-15 National Championship	PGA National GC	Matt Williams (CAN)	USA
F	FCWT 16-18 National Championship	PGA National GC	Zach Foushee*	USA
F	Florida Mid-Amateur	Gainesville, FL	Don Bell*	USA
F	Fox-Puss Invitational	Lynchburg, VA	Ben Lasso	USA
F	Georgia State Mid Amateur	Kinderlou Forest GC	Mark Strickland	USA
F	Glen Oaks MCCAA Invite	Centerville, MI	Andrew Jared*	USA
F	Havemeyer Invitational	Southward Ho CC, NY	Michael Blum*	USA
F	Heart of America Conference	Hamilton, IL	Greg MacAulay (CAN)	USA
F	Horton Smith Invitational	Detroit, MI	Marty Jeppesen	USA
F	Illinois State Mid-Amateur	Flossmoor, IL	Todd Mitchell	USA
F	Investors Group Junior Spring Classic	Uxbridge, ON	Matthew Scobie*	CAN
F	KCAC Conference Championship	Garden City, KS	Tim Jasper*	USA
F	MAAC Championship	Lake Buena Vista	Don Denyse*	USA
F	Mid Central Conference	Winona Lake, IN	Jordan Dawes*	USA
F	Nacional-Internacional Juvenil	El Tigre GC	David Faraudo Godinez*	MEX
F	NAIA Championship	Silvis, IL	Oscar Stark (SWE)	USA
F	NCAA D2 Cent/West Region	Albuquerque, NM	John Jackson	USA
F	NCAA D2 East/Atl. Region	Hershey, PA	Jared Schmader	USA
F	NCAA D2 MW/South Cen Region	Gorgetown, KY	Cyril Bouniol (FRA)	USA
F	NCAA D2 South/SE Region	Deland, FL	Ricardo Gouveia (POR)/ Michael Marshburn*	USA
F	NCAA Division III Championship	Greensboro, NC	Chris Morris	USA
F	NCAC Championship	Chesterland, OH	Craig Osterbrock*	USA
F	NCAC Championship Event #2	Fowlers Mill GC	Craig Osterbrock	USA
F	NEC Championship	Celebration, FL	CG Mercatoris	USA
F	New Jersey Mid-Amateur	Deal G&CC NJ	Kevin McSorley*	USA
F	NJCAA DI Region I Championship	Phoenix, AZ	Robert Perrott III*	USA
F	NJCAA Div 11 Championship	Scottsboro, AL	Filip Timmerman (CHI)	USA
F	NJCAA Division I District 3 Championship	Lawrence, KS	Steven Ihm	USA
F	NJCAA National Championship DI	Odessa, TX	William Anderson	USA
F	NJCAA Region 12	Battle Creek, MI	Mark Foster	USA
F	NJCAA Region 24 Championship	Fairview Heights, IL	Filip Timmerman (CHI)	USA
F	NJCAA Region I DII Championship	Goodyear, AZ	Eddie DeLashmutt*	USA
F	Norman Bryant Colonial Invitational	Jackson, MS	Scott Rhodes	USA
F	OAC Championship	W. Lafayette, OH	Scott Miller*	USA
F	Palm Springs Desert Amateur	La Quinta, CA	Paul Misko	USA
F	Pasadena City Golf Championship	Pasadena, CA	Jake Sarnoff	USA
F	Patriot League Championship	Annapolis, MD	Matt Krembel	USA
F	PGA Minority Championship DI	Port St Lucie, FL	Matthew McKnight (IRL)*	USA
F	PGA Minority Championship DII	Port St Lucie, FL	John M Cole	USA
F	PGA Minority Championship Individual	Port St Lucie, FL	Christian Heavens	USA
F	R Jay Sigel Match Play	Export, PA	Nathan Smith	USA
F	Richardson Memorial Invitational	Hewlett, NY	Joe Saladino	USA
F	Russell C Palmer Cup	Simsbury, CT	Branden Chicorka	USA
F	Santa Barbara City Championship	Santa Barbara, CA	Andrew Perez	USA
F	TranSouth Championship	Blytheville, AR	Dustin Thomas*	USA
F	Tyrell Garth Invitational	Beaumont, TX	Kelsey Clime*	USA
F	Walter J Travis Invitational	Garden City, NY	Nick Gilliam	USA
F	West Virginia Match Play	Parkersberg CC	Woody Woodward*	USA
F	Abierto Del Quito	Quito GC	Sergio Roman*	ECU
F	Abierto Del Quito	Quito GC	Juan Miguel Heredia	ECU
F	Campeonato Aberto Sul-Brasileiro	Porto Alegre CC	Eduardo Vasconcellos*	BRA
F	Campeonato Nacional Mid Amateur	Hotel Melia Varadero, Cuba	Juan Fernando Mejia	COL

Americas (continued)

F	Copa Komatsu-Mitsui	Lima GC	Wolfgang Pedal Baertl	PER
F	Torneo Final Del Ranking	Golf Club Argentino	Franco Romero	ARG
F	Garry Sobers Championships	Barbados	James Johnson	BAR

Asia

D	Acer National Spring Ranking Tournament	Nan Fong GC	Tao Huang	TPE
D	Malaysian Amateur Open	Melaka	Daniel Bringolf (AUS)	MAS
E	Kurnia Saujana Championship	Saujana G&CC	Gavin Kyle Green	MAS
F	China Amateur Tour Leg 3	Chang Sha	Liu Yu Xiang*	CHN
F	China Futures Tour Leg 2	Zhejiang	Guan Tianlang	CHN
F	Faldo Series – Philippines	TAT Filipinas GC, San Pedro	Alexes Nallos*	PHI
F	Grand Prix	Royal Colombo GC	N Thangaraja	SRI
F	Jack Nicklaus Junior Championship	Shenzhen	Tian Lang Guan*	CHN
F	Johor Open	Royal Johor CC	Joshua Shou (SIN)	MAS
F	Junior World Championship Qualifier	Blue Sapphire Golf Course	Chanachoke Dejpiratanamongkol	THA
F	Negeri Sembilan Amateur Open	SIGC	Jerome Ng (SIN)	MAS
F	Philippine Junior Amateur	Alabang CC	Rupert Zaragosa*	PHI
F	Rolex Junior Championship	Sanko 72 CC	Hirotaka Ashizawa*	JPN
F	Sarawak Amateur Open	Sarawak Club Golf Resort	Hirotaka Ashizawa (JPN)*	MAS

Australasia

C	Keperra Bowl	Keperra GC, QLD	Jake Higginbottom	AUS
C	SA Amateur Classic	Glenelg GC	Brett Drewitt	AUS
D	Handa Junior Masters	The Vines Resort CC	Jake Higginbottom	AUS
E	Queensland Amateur Championship	Arundel Hills GC	Daniel McGraw/Jake Higginbottom	AUS
E	Wairarapa 72 Hole Open	Masterton GC, Wellington	Richard Squire*	NZL
F	Arafura Games	Darwin GC, NT	Ian Walker*	AUS
F	Australian Senior	Tanunda Pines GC, SA	Stefan Albinski	AUS
F	City of Perth Championship	Perth, WA	Cruze Strange*	AUS
F	Waikato Seniors	Waikare, Narrows & Hamilton GCs	Arthur Parkin*	NZL

Europe

B	Irish Amateur Open	Royal Dublin GC	Rhys Pugh (WAL)	IRL
B	Lytham Trophy	Royal Lytham & St Annes	Jack Senior	ENG
B	Scottish Open Stroke Play	Lansdowne, Blairgowrie	Andrew Sullivan (ENG)	SCO
B	Welsh Open Stroke Play	St Pierre	Darren Wright (ENG)	WAL
C	Campeonato de Espana Absoluto	RCG La Coruna	Adrian Otaegui	ESP
C	Coupe Murat	Chantilly	Gary Stal	FRA
D	Irish Amateur Close	Shannon GC	Paul Cutler	IRL
D	National Stroke Play	De Gelpenberg	Daan Huizing	NED
E	Italian International Match Play	Villa d'Este GC	Nicolas D'Incau (SUI)	ITA
E	Lagonda Trophy	Gog Magog GC	Philip Ridden	ENG
F	Amateur Tour Event 1	Kuneticka Hora	Simon Zach*	CZE
F	Amateur Tour Event 2	Mnich	Ondrej Lieser	CZE
F	Basel Championship	GC Basel	Lionel Weber (FRA)	SUI
F	Campeonato de Espana Cadetes	RCG La Coruna	Javier Elejabeitia Cortezo*	ESP
F	Campeonato de Madrid Absoluto	CG Bco Santander	Jon Rahm-Rodriguez	ESP
F	Clwyd Open	Wrexham & Prestatyn GCs	Joe Vickery	WAL
F	Cornwall Amateur Championship	St Austell GC	Tom Fox*	ENG
F	Coupe Didier Illouz	Racing Club de France	Mathieu Decottignies-Lafon	FRA
F	Coupe Yves Caillol	Golf D'Aix Marseille	Gary Colinet*	FRA
F	Cto Absoluto de Castilla la Mancha	CG Cabanillas	Carlos Lucendo Diaz*	ESP
F	Cyprus Amateur Open	Aphrodite Hills GC	Mathew Daley (ENG)*	CYP
F	Czech International Mid-Amateur	Ypsilon Golf Resort	Marcel Grass (SUI)*	CZE
F	Dorset County Championship	Ferndown GC	Tom Leech*	ENG
F	Fairhaven Trophy	Fairhaven	Tom Harris (IOM)*	ENG
F	Gloucestershire County Championship	Stinchcombe Hill GC	Thomas Workman*	ENG
F	Grand Prix De BoulouParis	Golf Club De La Ouenghi	Kevin Bosio*	FRA

F	Italian Team Championship A2	Castelgandolfo	Domenico Geminiani	ITA
F	Italian Team Championship A3	Cus Ferrara – Le Fonti	Filippo Zucchetti	ITA
F	King's Prize	Millenium GC	Thomas Detry	BEL
F	Lancashire Links Trophy	Southport & Ainsdale/Formby GCs	John Carroll*	ENG
F	Mattone d'Oro	Bergamo GCb	Marco Bo*	ITA
F	Midland Scratch Cup	Carlow GC	Jack Pierse*	IRL
F	Munster Stroke Play Championship	Cork GC	Niall Gorey	IRL
F	North Wales Boys Open	Abergele & Rhuddlan GCs	Otto Johan Mand	WAL
F	Palla d'Oro Memorial G Silva	Torino La Mandria GC	Luca Saccarello	ITA
F	Scottish Youths Open	Paisley	Lyle McAlpine*	SCO
F	SGU Junior Tour Event 2	Rowallan Castle	Bob MacIntyre*	SCO
F	Skandia Junior Open	Falkensbergs GK	Oscar Lengden	SWE
F	Skandia Tour Elit # 1	St Arilds GK	Olle Almèn	SWE
F	Skandia Tour Riks # 2 Ronneback	Ronnebacks GK	Filip Brattse*	SWE
F	Skandia Tour Riks #1 Blekinge	Trummenas GK	Robin Dahlstedt	SWE
F	Skandia Tour Riks #1 Halland	Haverdals GK	Alexander Frykler*	SWE
F	Skandia Tour Riks #1 Skane	Allerum GK	Oskar Lundgren*	SWE
F	Skandia Tour Riks #2	Bro-Balsta GK	Axel Rannar*	SWE
F	Skandia Tour Riks #2 Smaland	Lagans GK	Marcus Gran	SWE
F	Slovenian Amateur	Bled	Jakob Ziegler (GER)	SLO
F	South East of England Links	Royal Cinque Ports & Royal St George's GCs	Sam Robertshawe	ENG
F	Staffordshire Stag Trophy	Beau Desert/Trentham GCs	Mark Gayes*	ENG
F	Suisse Orientale Championship	Waldkirch	Andrea Gurini	SUI
F	Swiss National Championship	Rheinblick	Victor Doka	SUI
F	Titleist Tour 1	Fana GC	Vetle Maroy	NOR
F	Trofeo Umberto Agnelli	Royal Park G&CC	Filippo Zucchetti	ITA
F	Welsh Open Youths	Clyne GC	Ben Stow (ENG)	WAL
F	Wiltshire County Championship	West Wilts & Hampton	Ben Stow	ENG

June

Africa

F	Kenya Amateur Match Play	Limuru CC	James Karanja*	KEN

Americas

A	NCAA Division 1 Match Play	Stillwater, OK	Francois Censier (FRA)*/ Thomas Gambier (FRA)*	USA
A	NCAA Division 1 Stroke Play	Stillwater, OK	John Peterson	USA
A	Northeast Amateur	Rumford, RI	Peter Uihlein	USA
A	Palmer Cup	The Stanwich Club	Peter Uihlein	USA
A	Sunnehanna Amateur	Johnstown, PA	Nathan Smith	USA
B	Monroe Invitational	Pittsford, NY	Albin Choi (CAN)	USA
C	California State Amateur	Daily City, CA	Bhavik Patel	USA
C	North Carolina Amateur	Greensboro, NC	Harold Varner	USA
C	Southeastern Amateur	Columbus, GA	Seth Reeves	USA
C	Texas State Amateur	Austin, TX	Kelly Kraft	USA
D	Florida Amateur	Doral Golf Resort and Spa	Tyler McCumber	USA
D	Footjoy Invitational	Sedgefield CC	Billy Kennerly	USA
D	Ike Championship	Bernardsville, NJ	Tommy McDonagh	USA
D	Indiana Amateur	Otter Creek GC	Tyler Duncan	USA
D	Missouri Amateur	Augusta, MO	Richard Berkmeyer	USA
D	Rice Planters Amateur	Mount Pleasant, SC	Austin Cody	USA
D	Southwestern Amateur	El Paso, TX	Stephen Carney	USA
E	Alabama State Amateur	Sylacauga, AL	Smylie Kaufman	USA
E	Campeonato Nacional de Aficionados	Club Campestre Monterrey	Sebastian Vazquez	MEX
E	Greystone Invitational	Greystone G&CC	Bo Andrews	USA
E	Kenridge Invitational	Charlottesville, VA	Will Collins	USA
E	Mexican International Amateur	San Pedro Garza, NL	Sebastian Vazquez	MEX
E	Minnesota Players Championship	Pequot Lakes, MN	Ryan Peterson	USA
E	Oregon Amateur	Portland, OR	Jack Dukeminier	USA

Americas (continued)

E	Royal Oaks Invitational	Vancouver, WA	Kevin Pomerleau	USA
E	South Carolina Match Play	Spartanburg, SC	Mark Joye	USA
F	AJGA Junior at Quad Cities	East Moline	Max Donohue*	USA
F	AJGA Junior at Steelwood	Loxley, AL	Jake McBride	USA
F	Alberta Mid Amateur	Priddis Greens G&CC	Frank Van Dornick*	CAN
F	Arkansas Junior Match Play	Little Rock, AR	Austin Eoff*	USA
F	Arkansas Stroke Play	Rogers, AR	Joey Nichols	USA
F	Aspen Junior Golf Classic	Aspen, CO	Cole Nygren*	USA
F	Birmingham National Invitational	Birmingham, AL	Greg Kennedy	USA
F	Blue Top Ridge at Riverside	Riverside, IA	Brian Bullington*	USA
F	Bluegrass Junior	Ashland, KY	Nick Duffield*	USA
F	British Columbia Mid Amateur	Storey Creek GC	Cory Renfrew	CAN
F	Burgett H Mooney Junior	Coosa CC	Andy Shim	USA
F	Canadian Universities/College Championship	Ashburn, ON	Mark Hoffman	CAN
F	Chicago Cook County Amateur	Columbus Park Golf Course	Michael Fastert*	USA
F	Cleveland Junior Open	Avon, OH	Beau Titsworth	USA
F	Clubcorp Mission Hills Desert Junior	Rancho Mirage, CA	John Lee*	USA
F	CN Future Links Ontario Championship	Deerhurst Highlands	Wilson Bateman	CAN
F	CN Future Links Prairie Championship	The Willows G&CC	Lucas Kim	CAN
F	Collegiate Players Tour - Empire Lakes GC	Rancho Cucamonga, CA	Tyler Torano	USA
F	Collegiate Players Tour - Heatherwoode GC	Springboro, OH	Logan Jones*	USA
F	Collegiate Players Tour - Laurel Springs GC	Suwanee, GA	Winston Gibbs*	USA
F	Collegiate Players Tour - Spring TX	Gleannloch Pines GC	Cash Wilkerson*	USA
F	Collegiate Players Tour - The University Club	Lexington, KY	Korey Ward*	USA
F	Colorado Junior Match Play	Kings Deer GC, Monument	John Ahern*	USA
F	Colorado Public Links	Buffalo Run Golf Course	CJ Kim*	USA
F	Connecticut State Amateur	Wilton, CT	Tommy McDonagh	USA
F	Elbit Systems Junior	Fort Worth, TX	Eric Ricard*	USA
F	Evitt Foundation RTC Junior All-Star	Ringgold, GA	Tyler McDaniel*	USA
F	Florida Junior Championship	Weston, FL	Edward Figueroa*	USA
F	Florida Public Links	Orlando, FL	William (USA) Anderson	USA
F	Franklin Junior	Franklin, TN	Zack Jaworski*	USA
F	Future Masters 11-12 Group	Dothan, AL	Wilson Furr*	USA
F	Future Masters 13-14 Group	Dothan, AL	Braden Thornberry*	USA
F	Georgia Junior Championship	Augusta CC	Greyson Sigg*	USA
F	Glencoe Invitational	Calgary, Alberta	Mackenzie Hughes	CAN
F	Greater Cincinnati Met Amateur	Hebron, KY	Brad Wilder	USA
F	Greater San Antonio Amateur	The Republic GC	J J Wall*	USA
F	GST Amateur Match Play	Temecula	Sejun Yoon	USA
F	Hawaii State Match Play - Manoa Cup	Honolulu, HI	David Fink	USA
F	Hilton Head Junior	Bluffton, SC	Austin (TX) Connelley*	USA
F	Hudson Junior Invitational	Hudson, OH	David Faraudo Godinez (MEX)	USA
F	Idaho Match Play	Hailey, ID	Jordan Hamblin	USA
F	Junior All Star at Penn State	State College, PA	Austin (TX) Connelley	USA
F	Junior All-Star at Eagle Ridge	Galena, IL	Philip Barbaree*	USA
F	Kansas Junior Amateur	Salinas, KS	Michael Gellerman*	USA
F	Kansas Stroke Play	Sand Creek, Newton	Hunter Sparks	USA
F	Kentucky State Amateur	Richmond, KY	Patrick Newcomb	USA
F	Las Vegas Junior Open	Henderson, NV	Taylor Montgomery*	USA
F	Long Beach Match Play Championship	Long Beach, CA	Stephen Edman	USA
F	Los Angeles City Championship	Los Angeles, CA	Tyler Weworski	USA
F	Louisiana Amateur	Lafayette, LA	Gregory Berthelot	USA
F	Maryland Amateur	Phoenix, MD	Mark Cusic*	USA
F	Mesquite Amateur	Mesquite, NV	Jay Lappen*	USA
F	Michigan Amateur	Harbor Springs, MI	Willie Mack	USA
F	Minnesota Mid Championship	Eden Prarie, MN	Erik Christopherson	USA
F	Mississippi State Amateur	West Point, MS	Clay Homan	USA
F	Missouri Junior Match Play	Hartsburg, MO	Mitch Rutledge*	USA
F	Nebraska Junior Match Play	Oakland, NE	Alex Totusek*	USA
F	Nebraska Match Play	Gothenburg, NE	Kevin Stanek	USA
F	New Hampshire Junior Championship	Salen, NH	Joe Leavitt*	USA

	Event	Location	Winner	Country
F	New Jersey Amateur	Bedminster, NJ	David Sanders	USA
F	New Mexico State University Golf Club	Las Cruces, NM	Christian De La Cruz*	USA
F	North Carolina Junior Championship	Charlotte, NC	Stanhope Johnson Jr	USA
F	Nova Scotia Mid Amateur	Osprey Ridge GC	Leon Carter*	CAN
F	Oklahoma Boys Championship	Kickingbird GC	Quade Cummins*/ Brady Richardson*	USA
F	Ontario Match Play	The Lake Joseph Club, ON	Zak Kempa*	CAN
F	Ontario Mid-Amateur	Wildfire GC	Graham Hill	CAN
F	Philadelphia Amateur	Glenside, PA	Michael Hyland	USA
F	Ping Phoenix Junior	Phoenix, AZ	Taylor Zoller*	USA
F	Quebec Mid-Amateur	Whitlock, Quebec	Adelard Collin*	CAN
F	Santa Clara County Championship	San Jose, CA	Jay Myers	USA
F	SCPGA Junior Match Play Championship	Los Serranos CC	Jack Chung*	USA
F	Signsational Signs Junior	The Woodlands, TX	Vincent Martino*	USA
F	South Carolina Junior Championship	Oldfield GC	Austin Langdale*	USA
F	Southern Junior Championship 13-14	Mesquite, TX	William Gordon*	USA
F	Southern Junior Championship 15-18	Mesquite, TX	Peyton Vitter*	USA
F	Sun Country Match Play	Sandia Park, NM	Greg Condon	USA
F	Texas Oklahoma Junior	Wichita Falls, TX	Jacob Oaks*	USA
F	Texas Public Links	San Antonio, TX	Michael Smith	USA
F	The Walker Course at Clemson University	Clemson, SC	Victor Wiggins	USA
F	Troy Invitational	Troy, NY	Don Denyse	USA
F	Virginia Junior Match Play	Haymarket, VA	Adam Ball	USA
F	Washington Amateur	Port Orchard, WA	Jarred Bossio	USA
F	Western Junior Championship	Chicago, IL	Connor Black	USA
F	Western Pennsylvania Amateur	Oakmont, PA	David Brown	USA
F	Wisconsin Match Play	Lake Geneva, WI	Jack Schultz	USA
F	Wyoming Match Play	Douglas, WY	John Hornbeck*	USA
F	Aberto do Estado do Parana	Alphaville	Rodrigo Luiz Diniz*	BRA
F	Aberto do Estado do Rio de Janeiro	Itanhanga GC	Tomaz Pimenta Pinheiro*	BRA
F	Abierto Cafetero	CC Armenia	Santiago Gomez	COL
F	Abierto Ciudad de Ibague	Ibague	Santiago Mejia	COL
F	Campeonato Nacional de Aficionados	Club de golf Haciendo Chicureo	Marcelo Rozo	CHI
F	Campeonato Nacional De Aficionados	Asia GC	Patricio Alzamora	PER
F	Campeonato Nacional Match Play	Club De Golf Del Uruguay	Juan Alvarez	URU
F	Clasificacion al Sudamericano Pre-Juvenil	Caracas CC	Gustavo Morantes*	VEN
F	Peru Cup	CC De Villa	Patricio Alzamora	PER
F	Torneo Aficionada Cartagena de Indias	Club Campestre de Cartagena	Ricardo Jose Celia	COL
F	Torneo Transgas de Occidente	Club Manizales	Carlos Rodriguez	COL
F	Barbados Open	Royal Westmoreland, St James	James Johnson	BAR
F	Bermuda Open Stroke Play	Port Royal GC	Scott Clark (USA)	BER

Asia

	Event	Location	Winner	Country
D	Neighbors Trophy Team Championship	Sunrise G&CC	Chi-Hsien Hsieh/Chien-Yao Hung	TPE
D	Southern India Amateur	Karnataka, Bengaluru	Senapaa Chikkarangappa	IND
E	Indonesia Amateur Open	Finna G&CC	Natipong Srithong (THA)	INA
E	Inter State Amateur	Coimbatore GC	Senapaa Chikkarangappa	IND
E	Kanto Amateur Championship	Nagaoka, Niigata	Yosuke Asaji	JPN
F	China Amateur Tour leg 4	Kunming	Liu Yuxiang	CHN
F	China Futures Tour Leg 3	Beijing, China	Huang Youngle	CHN
F	Chubu Amateur	Katayamazu GC	Ren Takeuchi	JPN
F	Chugoku Amateur Championship	Tojigaoka Marinehills, Okayama	Toshiki Ishitoku	JPN
F	Hokkaido Amateur	Tukisappu GC	Yuki Imamura*	JPN
F	Ho-Sim Cup	Club 900 CC	Dae Hoan Kim*	KOR
F	HSBC Youth Golf Challenge 2nd Leg	NSRCC	Melvin Chew	SIN
F	Jakarta World Junior Championship	Damai Indah Golf	Jordan Surya Irawan*	INA
F	Korea Mid Amateur	Montvert CC	Bong-Sub Kang*	KOR
F	Kyushu Amateur Championship	Fukuoka	Genzo Tokimatsu	JPN
F	Perak Amateur Open	Meru Valley Golf Course	Mohd Azry Aryaf Mohd Azam*	MAS
F	Philippine Match Play	Wack Wack G&CC	Rupert Zaragosa	PHI
F	Philippine Seniors Amateur	Silang Cavite, Philippines	Pepot Inigo	PHI
F	Selangor International Junior Masters	Seri Selangor GC	Tan Wei Chean*	MAS

Asia (continued)

F	Seletar Junior Open	Seletar CC	Melvin Chew	SIN
F	SGA 3rd National Ranking	Tampines Course	Lam Zhiqun	SIN
F	Shikoku Amateur Championship	Greenfeel GC	Satoshi Hara	JPN
F	Singapore Junior Championship	Keppel Club	Gregory Foo	SIN
F	Sutera Harbour Amateur Open	Sutera Harbour Marina G&CC	Alexander Lau*	MAS
F	Vietnam Open	Danang Golf Club	Chanachoke Dejpiratanamongkol (THA)	VIE

Australasia

D	Northern Territory Open	Darwin, NT	Tim Hart	AUS
F	Fiji Open	Pacific Harbour Golf Course	Vikrant Chandra	FIJ
F	Nadi Open	Nadi	Olaf Allen	FIJ
F	Starwood Classic	Natadola Bay & Denarau GCs	Anuresh Chandra	FIJ

Europe

A	St Andrews Links Trophy	St Andrews Old & New	Tom Lewis (ENG)	SCO
A	The Amateur Championship	Hillside & Hesketh GCs	Bryden Macpherson (AUS)	ENG
B	Brabazon Trophy	Burnham & Berrow GC	Neil Raymond	ENG
C	Berkshire Trophy	The Berkshire	Joshua White	ENG
D	Austrian Stroke Play	Alpe Adria Golf Schloss Finkenstein	Manuel Trappel	AUT
E	Belgian National Stroke Play	Royal Golf Club du Hainaut	Thomas Pieters	BEL
E	East of Ireland Open Championship	Co Louth GC	Richard O'Donovan	IRL
E	Grand Prix International De Lyon	Golf Club De Lyon	Gary Stal	FRA
E	Sir Henry Cooper Junior Masters	Nizels G&CC	Toby Tree	ENG
E	Tennant Cup	Glasgow Gailes	James White	SCO
F	Aberconwy Trophy	Conwy & Llandudno GCs	Jason Shufflebotham	WAL
F	Amateur Tour Event 3	Berovice	Ondrej Lieser	CZE
F	Cambridgeshire County Amateur	Gog Magog GC	Jody Greenall*	ENG
F	Czech International Academic Championship	Ypsilon Golf Resort	Tomasz Kadlec*	CZE
F	Czech National Match Play	Sokolov	David Prochazka	CZE
F	East of Scotland Amateur	Lundin Links GC	Paul Ferrier	SCO
F	Eimskipsmotarodin	Vestmannaeyjavollur	Guojon Henning Hilmarsson*	ISL
F	Estonian Amateur Open	Saaremaa GC	Roger Roper (ENG)	EST
F	European Mid-Amateur	Sola GC	Marco Willberg (FIN)*	NOR
F	European Seniors	Golf and Landclub Achensee, Austria	Tomas Persson (SWE)*	AUT
F	Fioranello D'Oro	Fioranello GC	Federico Ranelletti	ITA
F	German Boys Open	GC St Leon-Rot	Alexander Matlari	GER
F	Gran Premio Monticello	Golf Club Monticello	Matteo Collini*	ITA
F	Grand Prix De Palmola	Golf De Palmola	Thomas Le Flohic	FRA
F	Grand Prix de Valescure	Golf De Valescure	Jerome Lando Casanova	FRA
F	Hertfordshire County Championship	Moor Park	Jamie Rutherford	ENG
F	Isle of Wight & Channel Islands Championship	Army GC	Martin Young	ENG
F	Italian Boys Under 18 Stroke Play	Monticello GC	Edoardo Torrieri	ITA
F	JSM Match Play	Granna GK	Filip Brattse	SWE
F	Kent Amateur Championship	Chart Hills GC	Michael Saunders	ENG
F	Lancashire Amateur Championship	Manchester GC	John Carroll	ENG
F	Leman Championship	Montreux/Lausanne/Domaine Imperial/Geneve	Marco Iten	SUI
F	Middlesex Amateur Championship	West Middlesex GC	Tommy King	ENG
F	National U21 Stroke Play	Noord-Nederlandse	Robbie van West	NED
F	Polish Mid Amateur Championship	Postolowo GC	William Carey (USA)	POL
F	Rudersdal Open	Fureso Golfklub	Nicolai Tinning*	DEN
F	Russian Amateur	Pestovo	Vladimir Osipov*	RUS
F	SGU Junior Tour Event 3	Cardrona	Greg Marchbank*	SCO
F	Skandia Tour Riks #3 – Goteborg	Delsjo GK	Felix Kvarnstrom*	SWE
F	Skandia Tour Riks #3 – Ostergotland	Bravikens GK	Axel Ostensson*	SWE

F	Skandia Tour Riks #3 – Uppland	Soderby GK	Johan Emilsson	SWE
F	Suisse Centrale Championship	Ennetsee GC	Roberto Francioni	SUI
F	Surrey County Championship	Croham Hurst & Addington Palace GCs	Joshua White	ENG
F	Sussex Amateur Championship	Seaford GC	Joe Doherty*	ENG
F	Titleist Tour 2	Notteroy GC	Kristoffer Ventura	NOR
F	TitleistTour 3	Moss & Rykke GK	Kristian Johannessen*	NOR
F	Toya Polish Junior	Wroclaw	Mateusz Gradecki	POL
F	Trofeo Gianni Albertini	Milano	Luca Saccarello	ITA
F	Turkish Amateur	Klassis	Koray Varli	TUR
F	Ulster Boys Amateur Open	Malone GC	John-Ross Galbraith*	IRL
F	Wallaert Devilder	Golf Du Sart	Francois Censier*/ Thomas Gambier*	FRA

July

Africa

C	Limpopo Open	Polokwane, Limpopo	Brandon Stone	RSA
F	Red Sea Amateur	Soma Bay Egypt	Amr Abu El Ela*	EGY

Americas

A	Pacific Coast Amateur	Truckee, CA	Chris Williams	USA
A	Players Amateur	Bluffton, SC	Corbin Mills	USA
A	Porter Cup	Niagara Falls CC	Patrick Rodgers	USA
A	Southern Amateur	Innisbrook Resort	Harris English	USA
A	US Amateur Public Links	Brandon Dunes Golf Resort	Corbin Mills	USA
B	Dogwood Invitational	Atlanta, GA	Nate McCoy	USA
B	Palmetto Amateur	Palmetto Golf Club	Will McCurdy	USA
B	Sahalee Players Championship	Samammish, WA	Chris Williams	USA
B	SCGA Amateur	San Gabriel CC, San Gabriel	Patrick Cantlay	USA
B	Trans-Mississippi Championship	Mission Hills, KS	Kelly Kraft	USA
C	Carolinas Amateur	Myrtle Beach, SC	Scott Harvey	USA
C	Eastern Amateur	Elizabeth Manor G&CC	Steven Liebler	USA
C	North and South Amateur	Pinehurst, NC	Jack Fields	USA
C	Northern Amateur	Sand Creek Country Club	Barrett Kelpin	USA
C	Ontario Amateur	Brampton Golf Club	Mark Hoffman	CAN
C	Pacific Northwest Amateur	Bend, OR	Zac Blair	USA
C	Rolex Tournament Of Champions	Sunriver, OR	Shun Yat Hak (HKG)	USA
C	US Junior Amateur	Bremerton, WA	Jordan Spieth	USA
D	Callaway Junior World Championship 15-17	Torrey Pines Golf Course	Beau Hossler	USA
D	Minnesota Amateur	White Bear Lake, MN	Donald Constable	USA
D	Missouri Stroke Play Amateur	Springfield, MO	Brian Haskell*	USA
D	Virginia Amateur Championship	Bristol, VA	Scott Shingler	USA
D	WE Cole Cotton States Invitational	Bayou DeSiard CC	Riley Pumphrey	USA
D	West Virginia Amateur	The Greenbrier Resort	Christian Brand	USA
D	Brazilian Amateur	Gavea G&CC	Rafael Becker	BRA
E	British Columbia Amateur	The Dunes at Kamloops	David Rose	CAN
E	New England Amateur	East Providence, RI	Jeff Hedden	USA
E	New York State Amateur	Rochester, NY	Dominic Bozzelli	USA
E	Ohio Amateur	NCR CC	Korey Ward	USA
E	Pennsylvania Amateur	Lancaster, PA	Andrew Mason	USA
E	South Carolina Junior Match Play	Sumter, SC	Carson Young*	USA
E	Washington Metropolitan Amateur	The Golf Club at Lansdowne	Scott Shingler	USA
E	Copa Joaquin y Tomas Samper Brush	Club Campestre de Cali	Carlos Rodriguez	COL
F	Aaron's/Bob Estes Abilene Junior	Abilene, TX	Vincent Whaley*	USA
F	AJGA at Centennial	Medford, OR	Skyler Finnell*	USA
F	AJGA Huntsville Junior	Huntsville, AL	Michael Pisciotta*	USA
F	AJGA Lubbock Junior	Lubbock, TX	Tad Darland*	USA
F	Alabama State Junior	Huntsville, AL	Stewart Jolly	USA
F	Alaska State Match Play	Elmendorf AFB, Alaska	Adam Baxter	USA
F	Alaska Stroke Play	Palmer & Anchorage GCs	David Hamilton*	USA

Americas (continued)

F	Alberta Amateur	Stony Plain G&CC	Scott Stiles	CAN
F	Alberta Junior Championship	Drayton Valley GC	Wilson Bateman	CAN
F	Arkansas Junior Stroke Play	Texarkana CC, Arkansas	Wesley Harris*	USA
F	Barbers Point Invitational	Pearl Harbour, HI	Rudy Cabalar*	USA
F	BC Junior Championship	Rossland-Trail CC	Adam Svensson	CAN
F	Bubba Conlee National Junior	Bartlett, TN	Robert Geibel	USA
F	C R Miller Match Play Invitational	Pittsburgh, PA	Brett Rinker*	USA
F	Callaway Junior World Championship 13-14	Riverwalk GC	Zecheng Dou	USA
F	Carolinas Junior Championship	Gastonia, NC	Will Long*	USA
F	Chicago District Amateur	Medinah CC	Kyle English*	USA
F	Cleveland Healthcare Foundation Junior	Shelby, NC	Zachary Bauchou*	USA
F	CN Future Links Atlantic	Sussex Golf & Curling Club	Chad MacMillan*	CAN
F	Coca-Cola Junior	Harbor Springs, MI	Doug Ghim	USA
F	Collegiate Player Tour-Jimmie Austin/ OU Golf Club	Norman, OK	Thomas Birdsey	USA
F	Collegiate Players Tour–Bear Trace at Harrison Bay	Harrison, TN	Taylor Hall	USA
F	Collegiate Players Tour–Myrtlewood GC	Myrtle Beach, SC	Nate Barnard*	USA
F	Collegiate Players Tour–Radley Run CC	West Chester, PA	Johno Hendrickson*	USA
F	Collegiate Players Tour–Santa Maria Golf Course	Baton Rouge, LA	Cody Gonzalez*	USA
F	Colorado Junior Stroke Play	Greeley, CO	Steven Kupcho*	USA
F	Colorado Match Play	Denver, CO	Michael Lee	USA
F	Columbus Junior	Columbus, OH	Tee-k Kelly*	USA
F	Connecticut Junior Amateur	Watertown, CT	John Flaherty*	USA
F	Delaware Amateur	Middletown, DE	Dan Ott*	USA
F	Deutsche Bank Junior Shoot Out	Plymouth, MA	Nick Rodriguez*	USA
F	Emerson Junior Classic	Poway, CA	Dylan Wu*	USA
F	E-Z-GO Vaughn Taylor Championship	Augusta, GA	Austin Padova*	USA
F	Firecracker Open	Austin, TX	Alex Ellis	USA
F	Florida Junior Championship 13-15	Vero Beach, FL	Sam Horsfield*	USA
F	Florida Junior Championship 16-18	Vero Beach, FL	Hunter†O'Mahony*	USA
F	Florida Junior Match Play	Dade City, FL	Dustin Dingus*	USA
F	Francis Ouimet Memorial	Various, MA	John Gilmartin	USA
F	Future Links Western Championship	Panoka, Aberta	Austin Cruickshank*	CAN
F	Future Masters 15-18 Group	Dothan, AL	Michael Hines*	USA
F	Georgia Amateur	Atlanta, GA	David Noll	USA
F	Golf Pride Junior Classic	Pinehurst, NC	Anthony Alex*	USA
F	Idaho State Amateur	Victor, ID	Tanner Higham*	USA
F	Indiana Match Play	Westfield, IN	Bob Stephens	USA
F	Indiana State Junior	West Lafayette, IN	Adam Wood	USA
F	Industry Hills City Championship	City of Industry, CA	Arnold Yoon*	USA
F	International Junior Masters	East Aurora, NY	Rhyne Jones	USA
F	Iowa Amateur	West Des Moines, IA	Gene Elliott	USA
F	Iowa Match Play	Burlington, IA	Jon Olson*	USA
F	Jack Kramer Memorial	Los Serranos Golf Course	Kyle Nelius*	USA
F	Junior All-Star at The Ritz	Sarasota, FL	Ryan Celano	USA
F	Junior Americas Cup	Hiwan GC	Jonah Texeira	USA
F	Kansas Amateur Match Play	Leawood, KA	Kyle Smell	USA
F	Kansas City Amateur	Raymore, MO	Jon Troutman	USA
F	Kansas City Junior	Kansas City, MO	Jared Carver*	USA
F	Kansas Junior Match Play	Dodge City, KA	Myles Miller	USA
F	Kearney Hill Golf Links	Lexington, KY	Billy Tom Sargent*	USA
F	Killington Junior Championship	Killington, VT	Jake Shuman*	USA
F	Lessing's Classic	Sparta, NJ	Peter Kim*	USA
F	Long Beach City Championship	Long Beach, CA	Derek Zellmer	USA
F	Long Island Amateur	Brookville, NY	Joe Saladino	USA
F	Louisiana Junior Amateur	Beaver Creek GC	Chuck Spears	USA
F	Maine Amateur	Falmouth, ME	Ryan Gay	USA
F	Manitoba Amateur	Portage Golf Club	Jesse Skelton	CAN

F	Manitoba Junior Championship	Winnipeg, Manitoba	Myles Sullivan*	CAN
F	Manitoba Mid-Amateur	Selkirk G&CC	Ben Bandura*	CAN
F	Massachusetts Amateur	Wyantenuck CC	Ryan Riley	USA
F	McArthur Towel & Sports Future Legends	Hartland, WIS	Doug Ghim	USA
F	Metropolitan Junior Championship	Chatham, NJ	Charles Edler	USA
F	Midwest Junior Players	Spring Green, WI	Landon Kowalski*	USA
F	Mississippi Greenwood Invitational	Greenwood MS	Chad Ramey	USA
F	Mississippi Junior Amateur	Madison, MS	Jacob Ross*	USA
F	Mississippi Mid-Amateur	Philadelphia, MS	Clay Homan	USA
F	Montana State Amateur	Canyon River GC	Nathan Bailey	USA
F	Monterey City Championship	Monterey, CA	Cory McElyea	USA
F	Nebraska Amateur	Omaha, NB	Andy Sajevic	USA
F	Nebraska Junior Amateur	The Country Club of Lincoln	Drew Taylor*	USA
F	Nevada State Match Play	Cascata GC	Steven Fink*	USA
F	New Brunswick Amateur Championship	Royal Oaks Golf Course	Mathieu Gingras	CAN
F	New Brunswick Junior Championship	Gowan Brae GC	Todd Eckstein*	CAN
F	New Hampshire State Amateur	Nashua, NH	Jim Cilley*	USA
F	New Mexico-West Texas Amateur	Albuquerque, NM	Greg Condon	USA
F	NLGA Amateur & Mid Amateur	St John's, Newfoundland	Jeff Sharpe*	CAN
F	NLGA Junior Championship	Salmonier River, Newfoundland	Blair Bursey*	CAN
F	North & South Junior Championship	Pinehurst, NC	Chad Cox	USA
F	North Dakota Match Play	Grand Forks CC	Tim Skarperud	USA
F	Northern California Junior Championship	Pebble Beach, CA	Michael Grenz*	USA
F	Northern California Stroke Play	Peeble Beach, CA	Scott Hardy	USA
F	Nova Scotia Amateur	Truro GC	Eric Banks	CAN
F	Nova Scotia Junior Championship	Highland GC	Eric Banks	CAN
F	Oglethorpe Invitational	Savannah, GA	Taylor Floyd	USA
F	Oklahoma State Amateur	Tulsa, OK	Cameron Meyers*	USA
F	Ontario Boys Championship	Bay of Quinte G&CC	Lucas Kim	CAN
F	Ontario Boys Match Play	Waterloo, Ontario	David French*	CAN
F	Optimist International Junior 16-18	Palm Beach Garden, FL	Will Davenport	USA
F	Optimist Junior 14-15	Palm Beach Gardens, FL	Evan Deroche*	USA
F	Oregon Coast Invitational	Warrenton, OR	Chris Shepard*	USA
F	Oregon Junior Amateur	Klamath Falls, OR	Alistair Docherty*	USA
F	Oregon Junior Stroke Play	OGA Golf Course	Nicholas Huff*	USA
F	Palm Beach County Amateur	Boynton Beach, FL	Daniel Eggertsson*	USA
F	Penn State University	State College, PA	Ryan Celano*	USA
F	Philadelphia Junior Championship	Elmer, NJ	Brandon Matthews*	USA
F	Premier Elans CN du Quebec	Sherbrooke, Quebec	Truman Tai*	CAN
F	Purdue University	Kampen Course	Michael Bernard	USA
F	Quebec Amateur	Alpin GC	Nicolas Fortin*	CAN
F	Quebec Junior	Outaouais GC	Joey Savoie*	CAN
F	Rhode Island Amateur	Potowomut GC	Brad Valois	USA
F	Rhode Island Stroke Play	Warwick, RI	Charlie Blanchard	USA
F	San Diego City Amateur	Torrey Pines Golf Course	Bucky Coe*	USA
F	Saskatchewan Amateur	The Legends	Troy Bulmer*	CAN
F	Saskatchewan Junior Championship	Chinook Players Club	Jerry Christiansen*	CAN
F	Saskatchewan Mid-Amateur	Lloydminster G&CC	Cadmus Delorme	CAN
F	South Dakota Match Play	Dakota Dunes, SD	Tyler Rachetto*	USA
F	Spirit of America Championship	Decatur, AL	Hunter Hawkins/Will McCurdy	USA
F	Tennessee Amateur	Loudon, TN	Steven Fox	USA
F	Tennessee Junior Amateur	Nashville, TN	Grant Daugherty*	USA
F	Texas Collegiate Tour @ Redstone	Redstone GC	Sang Yi (KOR)	USA
F	Texas Mid-Amateur Match Play	Horseshoe Bay, TX	Jess Bonneau*	USA
F	Texas State Junior	Horseshoe Bay, TX	Stratton Nolen	USA
F	The Birchmont	Bemidji, MI	Johnny Larson	USA
F	The Birchmont Junior	Bemidji, MI	Trey Dale*	USA
F	Tippecanoe City Championship	West Lafayette, IN	Jacob Yocum*	USA
F	Toronto Star Amateur	Toronto, Ontario	Garrett Rank	CAN
F	Toyota Tour Santa Ana	Santa Ana CC	Jake Knapp/Jonathan Sanders	USA
F	Trader Joe's Junior	Pleasanton, CA	Ryan Han*	USA
F	Utah State Amateur	Midway, UT	Jeff Evans	USA

Americas (continued)

F	Valero Texas Open Junior Shootout	Fair Oaks Ranch, TX	Matt Gilchrest*	USA
F	Vermont Amateur	Brandon, VT	Devin Komline	USA
F	Vermont Junior Match Play	Essex Junction, VT	Ben Hayes	USA
F	Virginia Junior Amateur	Suffolk, VA	Jake Mondy	USA
F	W Duncan MacMillan Classic	Maple Grove, MN	Juan Yumar*	USA
F	Washington State Junior	Walla Walla, WA	Tyler Salsbury*	USA
F	West Texas Amateur	Abilene, TX	Beau Davis*	USA
F	Westbrook Country Club	Mansfield, OH	Grant Weaver*	USA
F	Wisconsin State Amateur	Madison, WI	Mike McDonald	USA
F	Wyoming Amateur	The Golf Club at Devils Tower	Edward Stewart	USA
F	Caribbean Junior Championship 14–15	Barbados GC	Daniel Caban* (PUR)	BAR
F	Caribbean Junior Championship 16–17	Barbados GC	Jose O Rodriguez (PUR)	BAR
F	Abierto de Golf Ciudad De Bucaramanga	CC Bucaramanaga	Marcelo Rozo	COL
F	Abierto Internacional de Golf Copa Sura	Club Deportivo el Rodeo Sede Medelin	Santiago Mejia	COL
F	Abierto International del Eje Cafatero	Club Campestre de Pereira	Carlos Rodriguez	COL
F	Abierto Los Cerros	Los Cerros GC	Juan Miguel Heredia	ECU
F	Faldo Series Brazil	Damha GC	Juan Alvarez (URU)	BRA
F	Venezuelan Amateur	Caracas CC	Felipe Velazquez	VEN

Asia

C	Japan Amateur	Rifu GC, Miyagi	Katsuyuki Sakurai	JPN
F	Asean School Games	Seletar CC	Chan Tuck Soon (MAS)	SIN
F	China Futures Tour Leg 4	Yiyang Hunan	Yao Xuefeng*	CHN
F	China National Junior Championship	Yantai City, Shandong Province	Chen Zihao	CHN
F	China Team Selection	Beijing, China	Jin Daxing	CHN
F	Delhi Junior Open	Jaypee Greens Golf Resort	Honey Basoya	IND
F	Faldo Series Pakistan	Karachi GC	Mubariz Ahmed*	PAK
F	Guam Amateur	Guam International CC	Louie Sunga	GUM
F	Hanwha Finance Network Amateur C/ship	Plaza CC Seorak	Dae Hoan Kim	KOR
F	Indian Mid-Amateur	KGA, Bangaluru	Sanjay Lakra	IND
F	July Grand Prix	Victoria G&CC	Vijitha Bandara	SRI
F	Kelantan Amateur Open	Kelantan G&CC	Mohd Shafiq Norzi*	MAS
F	Sindh Open	Karachi	Sajid Khan*	PAK
F	Usha Chandigarh Junior Championship	Chandigarh GC	Yashas Chandra*	IND
F	Warren Amateur Open	Warren G&CCb	Koh Dengshan	SIN

Australasia

D	Subaru State Age Championships	Lakes, Terry Hills, Concord & Australian GCs	Jake Higginbottom	AUS
F	Bay Of Plenty Open	Whakatane Golf Course	Blair Riordan	NZL
F	Darwin Open	Darwin GC	Ian Walker	AUS
F	Graham Marsh Junior	Busselton, Dunsborough Lakes & Capel GCs	Lukas Michel*	AUS
F	Queensland Boys Aamteur	Bargara GC	Viraat Badhwar*	AUS
F	Queensland Senior Amateur	Gold Coast, QLD	Greg Corben	AUS
F	Victoria Junior Amateur	Melbourne, VIC	Lucas Herbert	AUS
F	Waikato Winter Stroke Play	Lochiel GC	Keelan Kilpatrick	NZL

Europe

A	European Team Championship	Oceanico Victoria	Jose O Rodriguez (PUR)	POR
C	Austrian Amateur	GC Adamstal	Joel Stalter (FRA)	AUT
C	Biarritz Cup	Golf de Biarritz	Teremoana Beaucousin*	FRA
C	English Amateur	Woburn	Steven Brown	ENG
C	German International Amateur	Golf Club Neuhof	Daan Huizing (NED)	GER
C	Scottish Amateur	Western Gales	David Law	SCO
D	BrabantsOpen/Zomerwedstrijid	Eindhovensche Golfclub	Daan Huizing	NED
D	Riverwoods Junior Open	Glofclub Toxandria	Robin Kind	NED
D	Tillman Trophy	Hunstanton	Henry Smart	ENG

E	Cameron Corbett Vase	Haggs Castle GC	Scott Crichton	SCO
E	Carris Trophy	Broadstone GC	Harry Casey	ENG
E	Essex County Championship	Crondon Park GC	Ross Dee	ENG
E	Grand Prix D'Anglet Chiberta	Golf De Chiberta	Thomas Elissalde	FRA
E	Grand Prix des Landes-Hossegor	Golf d'Hossegor	Victor Perez	FRA
E	National Youth Championship U18	Ribagolfe II	Goncalo Pinto	POR
E	Newlands Trophy	Lanark GC	Allyn Dick	SCO
E	St David's Gold Cross	Royal St David's GC	Oliver Farr	WAL
E	Welsh Amateur Championship	Aberdovey GC	Jason Shufflebotham	WAL
F	Arionbank Junior Match Play 15-16	Borgarnes	Kristinn Sigurdsson*	ISL
F	Arionbank Junior Match Play 17-18	Borgarnes	Bjarki Petursson*	ISL
F	Austrian Stroke Play U16	Colony Club Gutenhof	Jakob van de Flierdt*	AUT
F	Austrian Stroke Play U18	Colony Club Gutenhof	Markus Maukner	AUT
F	Austrian Stroke Play U21	Colony Club Gutenhof	Markus Habeler	AUT
F	Belgium National Match Play	Royal Waterloo GC	Thomas Detry	BEL
F	Boyd Quaich	St Andrews	Benjamin Wescoe (USA)	SCO
F	Campeonato Ayuntamiento de Llanes	C G Llanes	Victor Pastor Rufian	ESP
F	Campeonato De La Comunidad Valenciana	CG Escorpion	Salvador Paya*	ESP
F	Campeonato de Madrid Junior	RACE	Jorge Simon	ESP
F	Cheshire Strokeplay Championship	Caldy GC	Fraser Macleod*	ENG
F	Classic Du Prieure Peter Fleming	Golf Du Prieure	Benjamin Maupas	FRA
F	Connacht Boys Open	Loughrea GC	Jack Leacy*	IRL
F	Copa Siero	CG La Barganiza	Alvarez Postigo Gutierrez*	ESP
F	Czech International Junior U18	Austerlitz	Mateusz Gradecki (POL)	CZE
F	Czech International Junior U21	Austerlitz	Jiri Korda	CZE
F	Czech National Youth Championship	Mlada Boleslav	David Mrazek*	CZE
F	Danish Amateur	Silkeborg GC	Kasper Estrup	DEN
F	Danish International Youths	Smorun GC	Edoardo Torrieri (ITA)	DEN
F	Danish Stroke Play	Aarhus Aadal GC	Thomas Sorensen	DEN
F	English Mid Amateur	Purdis Heath, Ipswich	Neill Williams*	ENG
F	European Young Masters	Royal Balaton Golf & Yacht Club	Kenny Subregis (FRA)	HUN
F	Faldo Russian Championship	Agalarov G&CC	Nikolay Kovalevskiy*	RUS
F	Faldo Series Netherlands	Goyer G&CC	Michael Kraaij	NED
F	Finnish Stroke Play	Helsinki	Tapio Pulkkanen	FIN
F	Gran Premio Citta di Cervia	Cervia GC	Riccardo Palumbo*	ITA
F	Gran Premio Padova	Padova GC	Valentino Dall'Arche	ITA
F	Grand Prix de la Baule	Golf International de La Baule	Thibaut Carmignano*/ Yohann Desrousseaux*	FRA
F	Grand Prix de Saint Nom La Breteche	Golf de Saint Nom la Breteche	Kevin Turlan	FRA
F	Grand Prix Des Volcans	Golf Des Volcans	Jonathan Armstrong (ENG)	FRA
F	International Trophy	Oslo GC	Tor Erik Knudsen	NOR
F	Irish Youths Amateur Close	Tramore	Brian Casey	IRL
F	Italian Boys Under 14 Chamionship	Le Fronde GC	Guido Migliozzi*	ITA
F	Italian Under 16 Championship	Asolo GC	Giacomo Garbin	ITA
F	JSM Slag	Frosaker GK	Oscar Lengden	SWE
F	Latvian Amateur	Ozo GC	Davis Puksts	LAT
F	Latvian Junior Championship	Riga, Latvia	Roberts Eihmanis*	LAT
F	Leinster Boys Open	Bray GC	Ryan McKinstry*	IRL
F	Luxembourg Amateur	Golf de Luxembourg	Robbie van West (NED)	LUX
F	McGregor Trophy	South Moor GC	Jack Hermeston	ENG
F	Munster Boys Open	Monkstown	Gary Hurley	IRL
F	National Youth Championship U16	Ribagolfe II	Joao Magalhaes*	POR
F	Niitvalja Karikas	Niitvalja	Jonathan Nylen* (FIN)	EST
F	North of Ireland Open	Royal Portrush GC	Patrick McCrudden*	IRL
F	Oceanico World Junior	Amendoeira Golf Resort	Bandit Chaisuk* (THA)	POR
F	Polish Junior Championship	Binowo Park GC	Adrian Meronk	POL
F	Scottish Boys Open Stroke Play	Nairn Dunbar	Joshua Jamieson*	SCO
F	Scottish Under 16 Open Stroke Play	Forfar GC	Benjamin Kinsley	SCO
F	Skandia Tour Riks #4 A6	A6 GK	David Hagenblad*	SWE
F	Skandia Tour Riks #4 Agesta	Agesta GK	Johan Cavallin*	SWE
F	Skandia Tour Riks #4 Hammaro	Hammaro GK	Emil Adamsson*	SWE
F	Slovak Amateur Open	Velka Lomnica, Slovakia	Juraj Zvarik	SVK

Europe (continued)

F	Slovak Junior Open	Gray Bear, Tale	Pavol Bielik	SVK
F	South of Ireland	Lahinch GC	Stephen Walsh	IRL
F	Sutherland Chalice	Dumfries & Galloway GC	Fraser McKenna	SCO
F	Swiss Junior Championship	Lausanne	Joel Girrbach	SUI
F	Targa D'Oro	Villa D'Este GC	Gianmarco Libardi	ITA
F	Tirol International Junior	GC Mieminger Plateau	Markus Habeler	AUT
F	Titleist Junior Tour 5	Miklagard GC	Mathias Schjolberg	NOR
F	Tucker Trophy	Whitchurch & Newport GCs	Mike Hearne	WAL
F	Waterford Senior Scratch Cup	Waterford City	James Fox	IRL
F	Welsh Boys' Championship	Cradoc GC	David Boote	WAL
F	Yorkshire Amateur Championship	Ganton GC	Daniel Wasteney	ENG

August

Africa

C	Southern Cape Amateur	Knysna	CJ du Plessis	RSA
F	JGF Trophy	Sigona GC	Kush Mediratta*	KEN
F	Kenya Boys Championship	Muthaiga GC	Daniel Nduva*	KEN
F	R&A Trophy	Sigona GC	Gael Ntore	KEN
F	Sigona Junior Strokeplay	Sigona GC	Amin Hasham*	KEN
F	Windsor Trophy	Sigona GC	John Mburu*	KEN

Americas

A	US Amateur	Erin and Wauwatosa, WI	Kelly Kraft	USA
A	Western Amateur	North Shore CC	Ethan Tracy/Chris Williams	USA
B	Canadian Amateur	Winnipeg, Manitoba	Mackenzie Hughes	CAN
B	Cardinal Amateur	Greensboro, NC	Olafur Loftsson (ISL)	USA
C	Southern California Match Play	Goleta, CA	Anton Arboleda	USA
C	Tennessee Amateur	Cordova, TN	Bobby Hudson	USA
D	Arizona Amateur	Scottsdale, AZ	Bowen Osborn*	USA
D	Illinois State Amateur	Glen Ellyn, IL	Brad Hopfinger	USA
D	Junior PGA Championship	Sycamore Hills GC	Cody Proveaux	USA
D	North Carolina Match Play	Salisbury, NC	Harold Varner	USA
D	Northern California Match Play	Pebble Beach, CA	John Catlin	USA
D	Oregon Stroke Play	Creswell, OR	Nick Chianello	USA
D	Valentine Invitational	Hermitage CC	Scott Vincent (ZIM)	USA
E	South Carolina Amateur	Bluffton, SC	Austin Reeves	USA
E	Campeonato Sudamericano Amateur	Club Campestre de Bucaramanga	Franco Romero (ARG)	COL
F	AJGA Junior at Oxmoor Valley	Birmingham, AL	Juan Gonzalez	USA
F	AJGA Junior Challenge	Beaumont, CA	Luke Park*	USA
F	AJGA Nebraska Junior at Quarry Oaks	Ashland, NE	Dominic Kieffer*	USA
F	AJGA Northern Virginia Junior	Haymarket, VA	Harrison Shih*	USA
F	AJGA Philadelphia Open	Huntingdon Valley, PA	Cody Cox*	USA
F	AJGA Stonehenge Junior Open	Winona Lake, IN	Adam Wood	USA
F	Alabama State Match Play	Opelika, AL	McLain Leberte	USA
F	Arizona Mid-Amateur	Lone Tree Golf Club	Grant Cesarek*	USA
F	Austin City Championship	Austin, TX	Kody King	USA
F	Bluebonnet Cup	Austin, TX	Joe Bendetti*	USA
F	California State Junior	The Country Club at Soboba Springs	Austin Smotherman	USA
F	Canadian Junior Championship	Morgan Creek Golf Course	Kevin Kwon	CAN
F	CJGA National Championship 15-19	Grey Silo Golf Course	Colton Kalkanis*	CAN
F	CJGA National Championship U 14	Grey Silo	Jonathan MacDonald*	CAN
F	Collegiate Players Tour–Flintrock Falls GC	Lakeway, TX	Paul McConnell	USA
F	Collegiate Players Tour–National Championship	Euless, TX	Paul McConnell	USA
F	Colorado Stroke Play	Aurora, CO	Zahkai Brown	USA
F	CorseMax/Philadelphia Runner Junior	Malvern, PA	Nick McLaughlin	USA
F	Dogwood State Junior	Snow Hill, NC	Daniel Brantley*	USA

F	Florida Match Play	Brooksville, FL	Don Bell	USA
F	Florida Mid-Senior Championship	Bear Lakes CC, West Palm Beach, FL	Michael Weeks*	USA
F	Frederica Junior Open	St Simons Island, GA	Joe Lewis	USA
F	Genesis Junior at White Beeches	Haworth, NJ	Kristian Caparros*	USA
F	Genesis Junior Championship	El Cajon, CA	Corey Shaun	USA
F	Greater San Antonio Match Play	San Antonio, TX	Michael Carnes	USA
F	Greens & Dreams Junior Invitational	Shelburne G&CC	Owen Bates*	CAN
F	Harvey Penick Junior All-Star	Austin, TX	Osama Khan* (BAR)	USA
F	Humboldt Amateur	Beau Pre, Baywood, Redwood Empire, Eureka, CA	Bridger Cotton*	USA
F	Junior All-Star at Robinson Ranch	Santa Clarita, CA	Sahith Theegala	USA
F	Los Angeles City Match Play	Los Angeles	Jeff Wibawa	USA
F	Louisiana Mid-Amateur	English Turn G&CC	Patrick Christovich	USA
F	Louisiana Senior Amateur	The University Club, LA	Rod Baronet*	USA
F	Maine State Match Play	Augusta CC, ME	Ryan Gay	USA
F	Manitoba Seniors Championship	Transcona GC	Tom Humniski*	CAN
F	Massachusetts Junior Amateur	Haverhill, MA	Nick McLaughlin*	USA
F	Met Amateur Championship	Locust Valley, NY	Mike Miller	USA
F	Metropolitan Amateur	St Louis CC, MO	Ryan Penfield*	USA
F	MGA/MetLife Boys Championship	Rumson CC	Theo Humphrey	USA
F	Michigan Junior Amateur	Marshall, MI	Henry Do	USA
F	Michigan Stroke Play	Barton Hills CC, MI	Marty Jeppesen	USA
F	Montana State Mid-Amateur	Meadow Lark CC	Ben Leestma*	USA
F	Nevada State Amateur	Hidden Valley CC	Jonathan Cockerill	USA
F	New England Junior	Brattleboro CC, VT	Peter French*	USA
F	New Hampshire Stroke Play	Hudson, NH	Nick MacDonald*	USA
F	North Texas Amateur	Gleaneagles CC	Danny Lovell*	USA
F	Nova Scotia Senior	Lingan CC	Gerry MacMillan*	CAN
F	Oklahoma GA Stroke Play	Muskogee CC, OK	Hunter Sparks	USA
F	Pacific Northwest Junior	Sunriver, OR	Kevin Murphy	USA
F	Pacific Northwest Master-40	East Wenatchee, WA	Kevin PomArleau	USA
F	Palm Beach Mid Amateur Match Play	The Ritz Carlton	Frank Babusik*	USA
F	Payne Stewart Junior	Springfield, MO	Alvaro Ortiz* (MEX)	USA
F	Pine to Palm Championship	Detroit Lakes, MN	Connor Holland*	USA
F	Pine to Palm Mid-Am	Detroit Lakes, MN	Jay Olafson	USA
F	Quebec Boys Match Play	Val des Lacs GC	Jean-Sebastien Bonin*	CAN
F	Quebec Match Play	Val des Lacs GC	Max Gilbert*	CAN
F	Randy Wise Junior Open	Grand Blanc, MI	Henry Do	USA
F	Rochester Open	Victor, NY	David Pompey*	USA
F	Show Me Summer Shootout	Fulton, MO	Chris Reinert*/Julian Taylor* (ENG)	USA
F	South Dakota Amateur	Brookings CC	Tom Carlson	USA
F	South Texas Amateur	Missouri City, TX	Mike Booker*	USA
F	Stockton Junior Open	Stockton, CA	Andrew Buchanan*	USA
F	Texas Amateur Collegiate Tour 16-18	Gleneagles CC	Ryan Evans*	USA
F	Texas Amateur Collegiate Tour Boys	Gleneagles CC, TX	Brian Boaz	USA
F	Texas Collegiate Boys	TPC San Antonio	Adam Wennerstrom	USA
F	Texas Collegiate Boys 16-18	TPC San Antonio	Kirby Gorzell	USA
F	TPC San Antonio Major Championship	San Antonio, TX	Valentin Almendarez*	USA
F	Trusted Choice Big 1 National C/ship	Madison, MS	JT Poston*	USA
F	Vermont Mid-Amateur	CC of Vermont	Kim Perry*	USA
F	Virginia Public Links	Independence GC	Tom Batthany*	USA
F	Webb Simpson Junior Championship	Clemmons, NC	Dylan Harris	USA
F	West Virginia Mid-Amateur	The Raven at Snowshoe Mountain	Sam O'Dell	USA
F	Western Canada Summer Games	Kamloops, BC	Mark Valliere*	CAN
F	Wisconsin Junior Championship	La Crosse CC	Jack McKinney*	USA
F	Wyoming Mid-Amateur	Gillette, WY	John Hornbeck	USA
F	Caribbean Team Championship	Millenium Lakes GC	Erick Morales (PUR)	TRI
F	Abierto de Lacosta	Lacosta G&CC	Jose Andres Miranda/ Andres Felipe Arango	ECU
F	Abierto Juvenil de Chile	Club de Golf Brisas de Chicureo	Juan Eduardo Cerda	CHI
F	Abierto Petrolero	Club Internacional	Santiago Jaimes*	COL

Americas (continued)

F	Abierto Pre Juvenil de Chile	Club de Golf Brisas de Chicureo	Lucas Rosso*	CHI
F	Campeonato Aberto do Estado de Sao Paulo	Sao Fernando GC	Pedro Costa Lima	BRA
F	Campeonato Auspiciador	Los Inkas Golf Club	Daniel Antunez De Mayolo*	PER
F	Campeonato Federacion Chilena de Golf	Santiago	Matias Dominguez	CHI
F	Campeonato Internacional Juvenil e Infantil	San Andres, Bogota	Juan F Londono	COL
F	Campeonato Suramericano Prejuvenil	Ruitoque G&CC	Juan Ignacio Gaitan*	COL
F	Copa Coomeva	Club Campestre Los Andes	Mateo Gomez Villegas	COL
F	Nacional Mid-Amateur Parada 3	El Rodeo	Juan Fernando Mejia	COL
F	Torneo de Golf	Club Campestre los Arrayanes	Santiago Mejia	COL

Asia

B	World Universiade Championship	Mission Hills GC	Hideki Matsuyama (JPN)	CHN
C	Japan Collegiate Championship	Three Lakes	Hideki Matsuyama	JPN
D	Acer National Summer Ranking Tournament	Royal Kuan Hsi GC	Chi-Hsien Hsieh	TPE
E	Iksung Cup-Maekyung Amateur	Lake Side, Seoul	Chang-woo Lee	KOR
E	Japan Junior Championship 15-17	Kasumigaseki, Saitama	Masahiro Kawamura	JPN
E	Singapore Open Amateur	Seletar CC	Hao-Sheng Hsu (TPE)	SIN
F	Asia Pacific Junior Championship	Royal Hills Golf Resort & Spa	Smithti Teeratrakul	THA
F	China Amateur Tour leg 5	Shenyang Liaoning	Liu Yuxiang	CHN
F	China Futures Tour Leg 5	Shandong	Lv Hao Yuan*	CHN
F	China-Korea Junior Invitational	Anhui	Ouyang Zheng*	CHN
F	Grand Prix	Victoria G&CC, Kandy	N Thangaraja	SRI
F	HSBC National Junior Team Championship	Jinnan CC	Wang Yichen*	CHN
F	Japan Junior Championship 12-14	Kasumigaseki, Saitama	Fumiaki Saito*	JPN
F	Kansai Regional Collegiate	Hashimoto CC, Wakayama	Yuki Mori	JPN
F	Kanto Regional Collegiate	Takanodia CC Chiba	Tomohiko Ogata	JPN
F	Singapore National Amateur	Raffles CC	Lam Zhiqun	SIN
F	Song Am Cup	DaeGu	Youn-Ho Bae	KOR

Australasia

C	Nomura Cup Individual	Denarau and Natadola Bay	Cameron Smith (AUS)	FIJ
F	Cambridge Classic	Cambridge	Compton Pikari*	NZL
F	Cobram Barooga Open	Cobram Barooga, VIC	Geoffrey Drakeford	AUS
F	Kapi Tareha	Napier GC	Brad Hayward	NZL
F	New Zealand Under 19 Championship	Omokoroa GC, BPO	Sam An	NZL
F	North Harbour	Muriwai GC	Sam Davis	NZL
F	Northern Territory Country Championship	Humpty Doo, NT	Don Jordan*	AUS
F	Port Augusta Classic	Port Augusta, SA	Michael Warren*	AUS
F	Portsea Open	Portsea, VIC	Nathan Holman	AUS
F	Tusker Vanuatu Open	Mele, Port Vila	Josepho Matuatu	VAN

Europe

A	European Amateur	Halmstad GK	Manuel Trappel (AUT)	SWE
B	Home Internationals	County Sligo	England	IRL
C	Coupe Ganay	Grenoble	Jerome Lando Casanova	FRA
C	Swiss International Amateur	Ascon	Andrea Gurini	SUI
D	Lee Westwood Trophy	Rotherham GC	Ashley Chesters	ENG
D	Mullingar Scratch Trophy	Mullingar GC	Nick Grant	IRL
E	Belgian International Youths	RGC of Belgium Ravenstein	Nicolai von Dellingshausen (GER)	BEL
E	Boys Amateur Championship	Burnham & Berrow/Enmore Park	Harrison Greenberry*	ENG
E	Finnish Amateur	Helsinki GC	Albert Eckhardt	FIN
E	Harder German Junior Masters	Heddesheim	Victor Gebhard Osterby (DEN)	GER
F	Amateur Tour Event 5	Ropice	Ondrej Lieser	CZE
F	Arionbank Junior Championship	Grafarholt	Bjarki Petursson	ISL
F	Berks Bucks & Oxon County Championship	Sonning	John Kemp	ENG
F	Campeonato Absoluto de Asturias	GC La Llorea	Alberto Fernandez	ESP

For further information, visit www.randa.org/wagr

F	Campeonato Absoluto Pais Vasco	Basozabal GC	Juan Sarasti	ESP
F	Copa Vasca De Golf	CC Laukariz	Daniel Berna	ESP
F	Czech International Amateur	Kuneticka Hora	David Prochazka	CZE
F	Czech International Senior	Karlovy Vary	Kai Flint* (GER)	CZE
F	Estonian National Stroke Play	Joelahtme	Eero Sikka*	EST
F	Faldo Series Slovakia	Black Stork Golf Resort, Velka Lomnica	Vitek Novak* (CZE)	SVK
F	Finnish Tour 4	Reikapelimstruus	Ville Lagerblom	FIN
F	Grand Prix de la Nivelle	Golf de la Nivelle	Thomas Elissalde	FRA
F	Grand Prix de Savoie	Golf D'Aix Les Bains	Jonathan Armstrong (ENG)	FRA
F	Grand Prix de Valcros	Golf De Valcros	Maxime Laute	FRA
F	Grand Prix du Medoc	Les Vignes, Golf du Medoc	Florent Ales	FRA
F	Grand Prix du Pau	Pau GC 1856	Florent Ales*	FRA
F	Grand Prix Valgarde	Golf de Valgarde	Timothee Guin*	FRA
F	Hungarian Amateur Open	Pannonia G&CC	Claas-Eric Borges (GER)	HUN
F	Hungarian Junior Open	Magyar GC	Daniel Kovari	HUN
F	Icelandic Match Play	Hella	Arnor Ingi Finnbjornsson	ISL
F	Irish Boys Amateur Close	Ardee	Jordan Hood*	IRL
F	Italian Under 18 A1 Team C/ship (Indiv)	ASD Golf Club Margara	Domenico Geminiani	ITA
F	Italian Under 18 A2 Team C/ship (Indiv)	Golf Colline Del Gavi	Bellani Giorgio Orvid*	ITA
F	Latvian Amateur Match Play	Riga	Karlis Broders	LAT
F	Latvian Amateur Open	Ozo GC	Mathias Boesmans* (BEL)	LAT
F	Leinster Mid-Amateur	The Grange GC	Jim Carvill	IRL
F	Leven Gold Medal	Leven GC	Ross Bell	SCO
F	Lithuanian Amateur	Capitals GC	Kornelijus Baliukonis*	LTU
F	Midland Open Championship	Holme Hall & Forest Pines	Nick Watson*	ENG
F	National Juniors	Fontaines, Brussels	Bertrand Mommaerts	BEL
F	North East Open	Inchmarlo	Jordan Findlay	SCO
F	North of England Open Youths	Middlesbrough GC	Jamie Bower	ENG
F	North of England Under 16	Pannal	Mario Galiano Aguilar (ESP)	ENG
F	North of Ireland Stroke Play	Galgorm Castle GC	Ciaran Molloy	IRL
F	North of Scotland Amateur	Nairn Dunbar GC	James White	SCO
F	Reid Trophy	Porters Park	Bradley Moore*	ENG
F	Senior Open Amateur	Royal Portrush	Chip Lutz (USA)	IRL
F	Skandia Tour Elit # 5 Arninge	Arninge GK	Mikael Lindberg	SWE
F	Skandia Tour Riks #5 Forsgardens	Forsgardens GK	Hannes Ronneblad*	SWE
F	Skandia Tour Riks #5 Hofors	Hofors GK	Markus Kjellin*	SWE
F	Skandia Tour Riks #5 Katrineholms	Katrineholms GK	John Abrahamsson*	SWE
F	Slovenian Boys Open	Bled G&CC	Enej Sarkanj*	SLO
F	South East District Open Championship	Musselburgh GC	Graeme Robertson	SCO
F	South of England Boys	Yeovil/Sherborne GCs	Matthew Pearson*	ENG
F	The Solvent Salver	Stoneham/Brockenhurst Manor	Martin Young	ENG
F	Ukranian Open Club Cup Trophy	Kiev GC	Dmitry Vakhnenko	UKR
F	Ulster Youths Open	Royal Portrush	Ryan McKinstry	IRL
F	Waterford Trophy	Sundridge Park	Max Orrin	ENG
F	Zurich Championship	Breitenloo/Schoenenberg/Hittnau	Fabrizio Santamato*	SUII

Season 2011–2012

The R&A Men's World Amateur Golf Ranking season runs from September until the following August when the Mark McCormack Medal is presented following the US Men's Amateur Championship. Results for the remainder of the calendar year will be included in the following year's edition of The R&A Golfer's Handbook.

Major Amateur Championships 2011

3rd Asian Amateur Championship (Inaugurated 2009)   *Singapore Island Country Club*

Matsuyama retains his Asian Amateur title

Hideki Matsuyama successfully defended the Asian Amateur Championship title at the Singapore Island Club. The 19-year-old student at Tohoku University finished one stroke ahead of 17-year-old Korean Lee Soo-min and two in front of 20-year-old Ben Campbell from New Zealand to once again earn an invitation to play in the 2012 Masters at Augusta and gain automatic entry into final qualifying for The Open at Royal Lytham and St Annes.

Matsuyama clinched his victory with two excellent closing rounds – a record equalling 65 and a closing 66. Over the last two days he did not drop a shot to par. Lee had led after the first day by two shots while Campbell, playing just five weeks after a foot operation, had been the pace-setter at half-way and after three rounds.

One hundred and twenty golfers from 35 of the 36 member nations of the Asia Pacific Golf Federation took part in the third staging of the Championship which in 2012 will be played at Amata Springs near Bangkok in Thailand during the first week in November.

Matsuyama, aware that victory would earn him a chance again to play in the Masters where in 2011 he finished joint 27th with Phil Mickelson and earned the Silver Cup as low amateur, admitted he felt considerable extra pressure compared to the previous year when he won the title in Japan.

In an event which was disrupted regularly throughout by thunder and lightening and heavy rain, it was Lee who took the lead on the first day with a record-equalling 65. Admitting the tight course suited his game Lee, who came home in 30, finished two in front of Matsuyama, Kenneth da Silva from Malaysia and Campbell.

The reigning Australian Boys champion Cameron Smith from Brisbane was well placed after he added a 69 to his opening 67. Although he shot two more rounds in the 60's – the only player to have four sub-70 rounds during the week – he ended up in fourth spot.

Campbell took over on the second day adding a 66 for an 11 under par total of 133 but Matsuyama, the World No 5 and top ranked amateur in the field, could only manage a 71 and on 138 trailed the leader by five. Sixty-one of the original 120 made the halfway cut.

Although Matsuyama equalled the course record with a seven birdie 65 on the third day it was not enough to overhaul Campbell who birdied the last for 69 to retain a one shot lead going into the final day. Ironically when winning the title the previous year Matsuyama had shot a 65 and it proved a good omen as he went on to win the title for the second successive year.

Although firing a closing record 64 for 17 under Lee was unable to force a play-off coming up one shot behind Matsuyama but he did ease into second spot ahead of Campbell who closed with a 70

1	Hideki Matsuyama (JPN)	67-71-65-67—270
2	Soo-min Lee (KOR)	65-72-70-64—271
3	Ben Campbell (NZL)	67-66-69-70—272
4	Cameron Smith (AUS)	68-69-69-67—273
5	Masamichi Ito (JPN)	70-70-68-68—276
6	Jake Higginbottom (AUS)	68-72-72-65—277
7	Masahiro Kawamura (JPN)	70-75-69-66—280
	Tae Wan Lee (KOR)	72-67-73-68—280
9	Mathew Perry (NZL)	71-69-72-69—281
	Tze Huang Choo (SIN)	68-72-72-69—281
	Vaughan McCall (NZL)	69-72-67-73—281
12	Shinji Tomimura (JPN)	72-69-73-68—282
	Low Khai Jel (MAS)	73-69-71-69—282
14	Matthew Stieger (AUS)	70-72-69-72—283
	Eric Chun (KOR)	73-69-70-71—283
16	Chang-Woo Lee (KOR)	73-77-67-67—284

17	George Gandranata (INA)	71-70-77-67—285
	Natipong Srithong (THA)	75-69-70-71—285
	Kenneth Christian John de Silva (MAS)	67-69-73-76—285
	Ryan Fox (NZL)	69-70-70-76—285
21	Sam An (NZL)	74-73-70-69—286
	Zhiqun Lam (SIN)	74-66-74-72—286
23	Luke Humphries (AUS)	75-69-73-70—287
24	Clyde Mondilla (PHI)	73-73-71-71—288
	Ahmed Al Musharrekh (UAE)	75-70-72-71—288
	Alex Shi Yup Kim (KOR)	73-70-72-73—288
	George Foo (SIN)	73-72-71-72—288
28	Teng Kao (TPE)	73-71-73-72—289
	Chien-Yao Hung (TPE)	71-74-72-72—289
	Olaf Allen (FIJ)	77-71-69-72—289
	Yosuke Asaji (JPN)	69-74-67-79—289
32	Rupert Zaragosa (PHI)	70-69-77-74—290
	Philip Matsson (THA)	72-75-71-72—290
	Art Markhael Arbole (PHI)	68-72-72-78—290
	Chieh-Po Lee (TPE)	72-71-69-78—290
36	Wei-Hou Liu (TPE)	71-77-73-71—292
	Thangaraja Nadaraja (SRI)	75-75-72-70—292
38	Hamza Amin (PAK)	72-69-75-77—293
	Gregory Foo (SIN)	74-71-73-75—293
	Hao-Sheng Hsu (TPE)	75-72-74-72—293
	Ian Andrew (INA)	67-77-78-71—293
	Kenta Konishi (JPN)	75-75-72-71—293
43	Matthew Smith (AUS)	73-76-73-72—294
	Terrence Ng (HKG)	73-73-77-71—294
	Jerome Ng (SIN)	74-74-75-71—294
46	Rinaldi Adiyandono (INA)	70-73-75-77—295
	Marc Ong (SIN)	72-78-68-77—295
	Si-woo Kim (KOR)	73-73-74-75—295
	Honey Honey (IND)	76-72-73-74—295
	Chikkarangappa Senapaa (IND)	72-74-76-73—295
51	Ratanon Wannasrichan (THA)	72-75-76-73—296
	Maung Maung Oo (MYA)	74-74-77-71—296
53	Trishul Chinnappa Ajjikuttira (IND)	74-72-78-73—297
54	Mohd Ali Hai (PAK)	70-76-74-78—298
	Melvin Chew (SIN)	71-76-73-78—298
	Paul San Weng Yau (MAS)	76-74-73-75—298
	Angad Cheema (IND)	71-79-74-74—298
58	Khalin Hitesh Joshi (IND)	76-74-73-76—299
59	Joshua Shou (SIN)	75-74-79-72—300
60	Juan Miguel Yee (PHI)	71-74-80-77—302
61	Abhijit Singh Chadha (IND)	74-75-78-76—303

The following players missed the cut:

62	Yan Myo Aye (MYA)	78-73—151
	Taimur Amin (PAK)	71-80—151
	Joshua Munn (NZL)	76-75—151
	Joshua Ho (SIN)	72-79—151
66	Zanie Boy Gialon (PHI)	72-81—153
	Lip Shien Chong (HKG)	78-75—153
68	Vikrant Chandra (FIJ)	82-72—154
	Sung-I Yu (TPE)	75-79—154
	Jeremiah Leun Kwang (MAS)	79-75—154
	Abel Tam Kwang Yuan (MAS)	73-81—154
	Chirat Jirasuwan (THA)	77-77—154
	Khalid Al Jasmi (UAE)	79-75—154
	Md Nazim (BAN)	73-81—154
	Nasser Yacoob Saleh (BRN)	78-76—154
	Brad Moules (AUS)	78-76—154

68T	Mohamad Hisyam Abdul Majid (MAS)	77-77—154
	Chanachok Dejpiratanamongkol (THA)	79-75—154
79	John Abdon (PHI)	79-76—155
	Soti Dinki (PNG)	77-78—155
	Vijitha Bamdara (SRI)	77-78—155
82	Vic Borja (GUM)	78-78—156
	Niko Vui (SAM)	78-78—156
	Muhammad Waseem Rana (PAK)	78-78—156
	Naveenda Ranga Gamage (SRI)	76-80—156
	Atthachai Jaichalad (THA)	81-75—156
87	Johnson Poh (SIN)	74-83—157
88	Robin James (PNG)	78-80—158

88T	Ziwang Gurung (BHU)	77-81—158
	Ned Howard (COK)	83-75—158
91	Md Jakiruzzaman (BAN)	81-78—159
92	Anuresh Chandra (FIJ)	80-80—160
	Hamad Mubarak Afnan (BRN)	82-78—160
95	Thammasack Bouahom (LAO)	80-81—161
	George Rukabo (SOL)	81-80—161
	Rachid Akl (LBN)	81-80—161
	Md Dulal Hossain (BAN)	76-85—161
99	Thuy Vo Ta (VIE)	81-81—162
	Patrick Tom (CAM)	83-79—162

Asian Amateur Championship *continued*

101	Lon Lindsey (GUM)	86-77—163	108	Royle Brogan (COK)	83-86—169	115	Delegermaa	89-86—175
	Hassan Karimian	81-81—163		Vasin Manibanseng	86-83—169		Ulziidelger (MGL)	
	Noshahr (IRI)			(LAO)		116	Ebrahim Nouri (IRI)	88-88—176
	Jieyu Xiao (MAC)	79-84—163	110	Tashi Ghale (NEP)	86-84—170		Tho Van Trinh (VIE)	86-90—176
104	Patrick Fepuleai	83-81—164		Ben Felani (SOL)	86-84—170	118	Altynbek Imanaliev	86-98—184
	(SAM)		112	Matt Moucharafieh	83-89—172		(KGZ)	
105	Saleh Ali M K Al	86-79—165		(LBN)			Aidar Asanov (KGZ)	102-97—120
	Kaabi (QAT)		113	Tashi Tsering (NEP)	90-83—173		Palden Togbye	WD
106	Vanseilha Seng (CAM)	84-82—166			+29		Thinley (BHU)	
107	Muhammad Rehman	83-85—168		Ali Abdullah A M	79-94—173		Gangaa	Rtd
	(PAK)			Al Bishi (QAT)			Mendsaikhan (MGL)	

2009   Chang-Won Han (KOR)   2010   Hideki Matsuyama (JPN)

116th British Amateur Championship (Inaugurated 1885)   *Hillside and Hesketh*

Australian Bryden Macpherson wins Amateur title at Hillside

When Bryden Macpherson won the 116th Amateur Championship at Hillside he was only the second Australian to capture the title. Only Doug Bachli in 1954 had it Down Under previously.

Twenty-year-old Macpherson, who is studying in America at the University of Georgia, achieved a life-time dream with his 3 and 2 victory over Scotland's Michael Stewart in the final. His win earned him a place in the 2011 Open Championship at Royal St George's and a start in the 2012 Masters at Augusta.

Although he sadly missed the half-cut on his Open début at Sandwich, he was happy to have competed in what he calls his dream event. "If I could choose to win just one title in my life I would choose The Open," he had admitted before the Amateur final.

The keys to Macpherson's success in Lancashire were his remarkable judgement of speed, his patience and his ability to stay in the moment. "It's hard to believe but I had complete confidence it was going to happen for me this week," said Macpherson, adding:" It feels pretty good to bridge that 57-year gap."

Although he lost the first hole the Victorian, helped by winning the sixth and the ninth holes, had edged ahead by the turn in the morning and was always in front in the 36-hole final after that.

For 21-year-old Stewart from Troon in Ayrshire it was disappointing.

"I just did not play well in the final. I cannot explain it. I just did not feel comfortable over the ball." He missed several shortish putts and his long game was not up to his usual standard in the morning round. "It wasn't that he was winning holes in the morning rather than I was giving them to him. It was a better game in the afternoon. I played better and when I holed a putt to win the 11th (the 29th) I thought I still had a chance to take the title".

It was not to be, however, as Macpherson, putting superbly, held on for the most important victory of his amateur career.

Stroke Play Qualifying:

Gregory Eason (Kirby Muxloe)	71-68—139	Adrien Saddler (FRA)	74-70—144
Alastair Jones (Radyr)	72-68—140	Hamza Sayin (TUR)	76-68—144
Steven Brown (Wentworth)	72-69—141	Mike Bedford (Prestbury)	76-68—144
Adrian Otaegui (ESP)	68-74—142	Michael Stewart (Troon Welbeck)	72-72—144
Victor Flatau (SWE)	73-69—142	Maximilian Rottluff (GER)	77-67—144
Garrick Porteous (Bamburgh Castle)	70-72—142	David Booth (Rotherham)	72-73—145
Jason Timmis (Newcastle-under-Lyme)	72-70—142	Bryden Macpherson (AUS)	75-70—145
		Thomas Detry (BEL)	73-72—145
Greg Paterson (New, St Andrews)	72-70—142	Marc Dobias (SUI)	74-71—145
Ben Campbell (NZL)	73-69—142	Garth McGee (Malone)	74-71—145
Andy Sullivan (Nuneaton)	72-71—143	Antonio Hortal (ESP)	74-71—145
Neil Raymond (Corhampton)	70-73—143	Dylan Boshart (NED)	72-73—145
Landyn Edwards (NZL)	68-75—143	Victor Perez (FRA)	78-67—145
Ross Dee (Woolston Manor)	73-70—143	Joshua White (Chipstead)	74-71—145
Reikus Nortje (RSA)	73-70—143	Oskar Arvidsson (SWE)	77-68—145
Josh Loughrey (Wrag Barn)	75-69—144	Moritz Lampert (GER)	73-72—145
George Thacker (Kedleston Park)	72-72—144	Ben Stow (Rushmore)	74-72—146
Phillip Westermann (GER)	73-71—144	Tom Lewis (Welwyn Garden City)	76-70—146
Mark Bookless (Sandyhills)	73-71—144	Gary Stal (FRA)	76-70—146
Le Riche Ehlers (RSA)	73-71—144	David Coupland (Boston)	71-75—146

Jack Bartlett (Worthing)	78-68—146	Steven Rennie (Drumpellier)	78-71—149
Toni Hakula (FIN)	74-72—146	Todd Adcock (Nevill)	78-71—149
Philipp Fendt (AUT)	76-70—146	Warren Harmiston (Wentworth)	73-77—150
Patrick Sprags (Stowmarket)	79-67—146	Graeme Robertson (Glenbervie)	74-76—150
Kris Nicol (Fraserburgh)	76-70—146	Jack Senior (Heysham)	76-74—150
James Fox (Portmarnock)	76-70—146	Mikkel Bjerch Andresen (NOR)	75-75—150
Tim Gornik (SLO)	77-69—146	Nils Floren (SWE)	78-72—150
Ashley Chester (Hawkstone Park)	73-73—146	Tiago Rodrigues (POR)	73-77—150
Alex Johnson (USA)	77-69—146	Jack Hiluta (Chelmsford)	76-74—150
Matthew Wallace (Moor Park)	75-71—146	Tommy King (Sudbury)	75-75—150
Kenny Subregis (FRA)	75-71—146	Gordon Stevenson (Whitecraigs)	74-76—150
Conor O'Neil (Pollok)	75-72—147	Chris Selfridge (Moyola Park)	74-76—150
Paul Cutler (Portstewart)	72-75—147	Benjamin Rusch (SUI)	73-77—150
Mark Young (Longridge)	73-74—147	Arthur Gabella (SUI)	79-71—150
Henry Smart (Banstead Downs)	75-72—147	James White (Lundin)	77-73—150
Olafur Loftsson (ISL)	74-73—147	Stefan Engell Andersen (KEN)	80-70—150
Paul Lockwood (Hessle)	76-71—147	Richard Smith (Notts)	76-74—150
José Maria Joia (POR)	74-73—147	François Rouilleaux (FRA)	78-72—150
Stuart Phillips (Royston)	79-68—147	Ben Taylor (Walton Heath)	77-73—150
Joakim Mikkelsen (NOR)	75-72—147	Pontus Gad (SWE)	78-72—150
Oliver Farr (Ludlow)	75-72—147	Graham Roberts (Eaton)	77-73—150
Daniel Stapff (BRA)	77-70—147	Jared Harvey (RSA)	79-71—150
Simon Richardson (Boston)	75-72—147	Arnaud Abbas (FRA)	75-76—151
Tapio Pulkkanen (FIN)	75-72—147	Brian Soutar (Leven GS)	75-76—151
Sebastien Gros (FRA)	73-74—147	Jorge Fernandez Valdes (ARG)	78-73—151
Richard Bentham (St Pierre)	75-72—147	Florian Loutre (FRA)	76-75—151
Stiggy Hodgson (Sunningdale)	75-73—148	Marcos Pastor (ESP)	77-74—151
Sebastian Maclean (BOL)	74-74—148	Kristoffer Ventura (NOR)	75-76—151
Philip McLean (Peterhead)	70-78—148	Tao Huang (TPE)	75-76—151
Lionel Weber (FRA)	74-74—148	Jack Brooks (Pleasington)	75-76—151
Teemu Bakker (NED)	76-72—148	Stefano Pitoni (ITA)	77-74—151
Jason Shufflebotham (Prestatyn)	72-76—148	David Gregory (Burnham & Berrow)	75-76—151
Brandon Stone (RSA)	74-74—148	Lucas Bjerregaard (DEN)	75-76—151
Chi-Hsien Hsieh (TPE)	77-71—148	Mackenzie Hughes (CAN)	76-75—151
Kevin Hesbois (BEL)	74-74—148	Bobby Rushford (Grangemouth)	77-74—151
Jonathan Hurst (Pleasinton)	71-77—148	Matt Kippen (Enmore Park)	74-77—151
Reeve Whitson (Mourne)	75-73—148	Alex Christie (Tyrrells Wood)	79-72—151
James Byrne (Banchory)	78-70—148	Alexander Levy (FRA)	81-70—151
Peter Tarver-Jones (Worthing)	77-71—148	Thomas Usher (Warren)	78-73—151
Victor Henum (DEN)	76-72—148	Luke Lennox (Moyola Park)	76-75—151
Tyrrell Hatton (Harleyford)	78-70—148	Julien Brun (FRA)	76-75—151
Paul Howard (Southport & Ainsdale)	77-71—148	Rhys Pugh (Vale of Glamorgan)	77-74—151
Thomas Elissalde (FRA)	78-70—148	Scott Campbell (Hallowes)	80-71—151
Daan Huizing (NED)	78-70—148	John Greene (Carlow)	75-76—151
Ben Loughrey (Wrag Barn)	74-74—148	Paul Barjon (FRA)	80-71—151
Victor Doka (SUI)	79-69—148	Chieh-Po Lee (TPE)	77-74—151
Matthias Schwab (AUT)	77-71—148	Horacio Leon (CHI)	78-73—151
Mads Soegaard (DEN)	78-70—148	Ricardo Melo Gouveia (POR)	78-73—151
Cyril Bouniol (FRA)	74-75—149	Matthew Stieger (AUS)	77-74—151
Ross Kellett (Colville Park)	75-74—149	Thomas Pieters (BEL)	80-71—151
Toby Tree (Worthing)	78-71—149	Michael Saunders (Dartford)	78-73—151
Juan Sarastri (ESP)	79-70—149	Adam Dunton (McDonald)	73-79—151
Sam Claridge (Harpenden Common)	78-71—149	James Ross (Royal Burgess)	79-73—152
Tyler Lock (NZL)	76-73—149	Stephan Jaeger (GER)	75-77—152
Marcel Schneider (GER)	73-76—149	Martijn Vermel (NED)	73-79—152
Robin Kind (NED)	75-74—149	Clement Batut (FRA)	80-72—152
Harry Casey (Enfield)	73-76—149	Maxwell Scodro (USA)	75-77—152
Haydn Porteous (RSA)	75-74—149	Miro Veijalainen (FIN)	80-72—152
Robin Goger (AUT)	76-73—149	Thabo Maseko (RSA)	75-77—152
Francesco Laporta (ITA)	79-70—149	Kelan McDonagh (Athlone)	78-74—152
Andrew Palmer (Chorley)	73-76—149	Jacobo Pastor (ESP)	78-74—152
Domenico Geminiani (ITA)	80-69—149	Manuel Trappel (AUT)	76-76—152
Richard Prophet (Sandwell Park)	77-72—149	Craig Martin (Kilkenny)	77-75—152
Daniel Hammond (RSA)	79-70—149	Jules Bordonado (FRA)	75-77—152
Rory McNamara (Headfort)	78-71—149	Rafael Becker (BRA)	75-77—152

British Amateur Championship *continued*

Pierre Henri Leclerc (FRA)	75-78—153	Billy Downing (Truro)	80-75—155
David Law (Hazlehead)	78-75—153	Emilio Cuartero (ESP)	76-79—155
Fraser McKenna (Balmore)	78-75—153	Sebastian Heisele (GER)	74-82—156
Gavin Samuels (Leighton Buzzard)	79-74—153	Pierre Tillement (FRA)	82-74—156
Jordan Findlay (Fraserburgh)	76-77—153	Daniel Pearce (NZL)	79-77—156
Edouard Espana (FRA)	77-76—153	Antoine Schwartz (FRA)	79-77—156
Peter Latimer (New, St Andrews)	77-76—153	Jacopo Jori (ITA)	77-79—156
Neil Henderson (Glen)	73-80—153	Craig Hinton (The Oxfordshire)	80-76—156
Alexander Culverwell (Dunbar)	74-79—153	Roberto Sebastian (ESP)	81-75—156
Brett Drewitt (AUS)	72-81—153	Michael Hollick (RSA)	77-79—156
Paul Shields (Kirkhill)	78-75—153	Alberto Fernandez (ESP)	81-75—156
Jonathan Bale (Royal Porthcawl)	77-76—153	Kenny Goosen (RSA)	84-72—156
Cedric Van Wassenhove (BEL)	76-77—153	Luke Cornford (East Sussex National)	78-78—156
Bell Ross (Downfield)	77-76—153		
Seb Crookall-Nixon (Workington)	76-77—153	Xavier Feyaerts (BEL)	82-74—156
Michael Hearn (Bolton)	80-73—153	Benedict Staben (GER)	85-72—157
James Frazer (Pennard)	80-73—153	Steve Jones (Hanbury Manor)	81-76—157
Jonathan Corke (Rowany)	77-76—153	Ignacio Elvira (ESP)	79-78—157
Oliver Mena (ESP)	79-74—153	Lorenzo Scotto (ITA)	81-76—157
Samuel Echikson (BEL)	79-74—153	Goncalo Pinto (POR)	82-75—157
Clement Sordet (FRA)	83-70—153	Craig Hamilton (Omanu)	82-75—157
Alan Dunbar (Rathmore)	80-73—153	Stanislas Gautier (FRA)	82-75—157
Rae Mackie (RSA)	78-75—153	Nicolas D'Incau (SUI)	81-76—157
Rhodri Fieldhouse (Wrexham)	73-80—153	Xavi Puig (ESP)	80-77—157
Kevin Turlan (FRA)	83-70—153	John Duff (Newmachar)	85-73—158
Jack Hesman (West Essex)	81-72—153	Pedro Figueiredo (POR)	79-79—158
Ryan McCarthy (AUS)	80-73—153	Fraser Wilkin (NZL)	81-77—158
Tom Wilde (Castle Royle)	81-72—153	Stephen Neilson (Dunbar)	77-81—158
Tom Berry (Wentworth)	80-73—153	David Blick (East Devon)	83-75—158
Kalem Richardson (AUS)	77-76—153	Anders Engell (NOR)	82-76—158
Steven Walther (SUI)	80-73—153	Sam Binning (Ranfurly Castle)	84-74—158
Freddie Sheridan-Mills (Walsall)	79-75—154	Stephen Speirs (Portpatrick)	78-80—158
Hugo Dobson (Fynn Valley)	74-80—154	Mervin Rocchi (FRA)	82-77—159
Felipe Navarro (BRA)	78-76—154	Mads Kristensen (DEN)	81-78—159
Daniel Keddie (Belton Park)	77-77—154	Koray Varll (TUR)	84-75—159
Graham Van Der Merwe (RSA)	79-75—154	Grant Forrest (Craigielaw)	83-76—159
Richard O'Donovan (Lucan)	77-77—154	Sean Ryan (Royal Dublin)	84-75—159
Nathan Kimsey (Woodhall Spa)	74-80—154	Jordan McColl (Scotscraig)	82-78—160
Fernand Osther (NED)	78-76—154	Tyler Hogarty (Rodway Hill)	86-74—160
Chris Robb (Inchmarlo)	79-75—154	Max Eichmeier (GER)	84-77—161
Gerard Piris (ESP)	77-77—154	Chris J. Wood (AUS)	79-82—161
Scott Crichton (Aberdour)	79-75—154	Paul Ferrier (Baberton)	78-83—161
Charlie Wilson (Littlestone)	79-75—154	Jeff Hopkins (Skerries)	83-78—161
Franco Romero (ARG)	78-76—154	Olivier Rozner (FRA)	83-78—161
Michael Daily (Erskine)	77-77—154	Lee Heaton (Tandridge)	86-75—161
Chien-Yao Hung (TPE)	79-75—154	Miguel Gaspar (POR)	84-77—161
Jack McDonald (Kilmarnock [Barassie])	79-75—154	Valentino Dall'Arche (ITA)	78-84—162
		Sebastian Schwind (GER)	79-83—162
Scott Fernandez (ESP)	83-71—154	James Hendrick (Pollok)	80-82—162
Callum Shinkwin (Moor Park)	83-71—154	Steven Maxwell (Windyhill)	84-79—163
Sam Forgan (Stowmarket)	77-78—155	Andrew Wallace (Glenbervie)	87-77—164
Darren Wright (Rowlands Castle)	79-76—155	Matthew Moseley (Carmarthen)	82-82—164
James Doswell (Highwoods)	78-77—155	Gonzalo Berlin (ESP)	81-84—165
Andrew Hogan (Newlands)	75-80—155	Gareth Blease (Burhill)	86-79—165
Joe Vickery (Newport)	75-80—155	Christopher Piumelli (USA)	81-85—166
Rhys Enoch (Truro)	76-79—155	Fred Jewsbury (Ladbrook Park)	82-85—167
Edouard Amacher (SUI)	77-78—155	Andrew Cooley (Chobham)	82-86—168
Fraser Moore (Glenbervie)	82-73—155	Kasper Sorensen (DEN)	92-82—174
Jonathan Bell (Royal Blackheath)	82-73—155	Max Smith (Newbury Racecourse)	84 scr

Round One:
Richard Bentham (St Pierre) beat Tapio Pulkkanen (FIN) 2 and 1

Round Two:
Matthew Wallace (Moor Park) beat Gregory Eason (Kirby Muxloe) 2 and 1
Ashley Chesters (Hawkstone Park) beat Thomas Detry (BEL) at 19th
Simon Richardson (Boston) beat Maximilian Rottluff (GER) 4 and 2
Sebastian Gros (FRA) beat Mark Bookless (Sandyhills) 1 hole

Ben Campbell (NZL) beat Conor O'Neil (Pollok) 1 hole
Joakim Mikkelsen (NOR) beat Garth McGee (Malone) at 19th
Jason Timmis (Newcastle-under-Lyme) beat Gary Stal (FRA) 2 and 1
Stuart Phillips (Royston) beat Mike Bedford (Prestbury) 2 holes
Philipp Fendt (AUT) beat Victor Flatau (SWE) 2 and 1
Paul Cutler (Portstewart) beat Vicor Perez (FRA) 5 and 4
Daniel Stapff (BRA) beat Reikus Nortje (RSA) 4 and 3
Michael Stewart (Troon Welbeck) beat Mark Young (Longridge) 5 and 4
Tom Lewis (Welwyn Garden City) beat Garrick Porteous (Bamburgh Castle) 2 holes
David Booth (Rotherham) beat Moritz Lampert (GER) 3 and 2
Andy Sullivan (Nuneaton) beat Olafur Loftsson (ISL) at 20th
Kenny Subregis (FRA) beat Josh Loughrey (Wrag Barn) 1 hole
Oskar Arvidsson (SWE) beat Phillipp Westermann (GER) 5 and 4
Oliver Farr (Ludlow) beat Ross Dee (Woolston Manor) 1 hole
Antonio Hortal (ESP) beat Tim Gornik (SLV) 3 and 2
David Coupland (Boston) beat Adrian Otaegui (ESP) 4 and 3
Marc Dobias (SUI) beat George Thacker (Kedleston Park) at 19th
Landyn Edwards (NZL) beat James Fox (Portmarnock) 4 and 2
Bryden Macpherson (AUS) beat Henry Smart (Banstead Downs) at 21st
Patrick Spraggs (Stowmarket) beat Steven Brown (Wentworth) 3 and 2

Le Riche Ehlers (RSA) beat Paul Lockwood (Hessle) 3 and 1
Jack Bartlett (Worthing) beat Neil Raymond (Corhampton) 1 hole
Ben Stow (Rushmore)) beat Joshua White (Chipstead) at 22nd
Greg Paterson (New, St Andrews) beat Jose Maria Joia (POR) 2 and 1
Alex Johnson (USA) beat Hamza Sayin (TUR) 2 and 1
Adrien Saddler (FRA) beat Kris Nicol (Fraserburgh) 1 hole
Toni Hakula (FIN) beat Dylan Boshart (NED) 2 and 1
Alastair Jones (Radyr) beat Richard Bentham (St Pierre) 1 hole

Round Three:
Chesters beat Wallace 1 hole
Gros beat Richardson 6 and 5
Mikkelsen beat Campbell 2 holes
Timmis beat Phillips 6 and 4
Fendt beat Cutler 2 and 1
Stewart beat Stapff 4 and 3
Lewis beat Booth 1 hole
Sullivan beat Subregis 5 and 4
Farr beat Arvidsson 5 and 4
Hortal beat Coupland 6 and 5
Dobias beat Edwards at 19th
Macpherson beat Spraggs 4 and 2
Bartlett beat Ehlers 3 and 1
Paterson beat Stow 5 and 4
Johnson beat Saddler 3 and 1
Jones beat Hakula at 24th

Round Four:
Gros beat Chesters at 19th
Mikkelsen beat Timmis 4 and 2
Stewart beat Fendt 2 holes
Lewis beat Sullivan 6 and 4
Hortal beat Farr 2 and 1
Macpherson beat Dobias 2 and 1
Paterson beat Bartlett 7 and 6
Jones beat Johnson 2 holes

Quarter Finals:
Gros beat Mikkelsen at 19th
Stewart beat Lewis 4 and 3
Macpherson beat Hortal 2 and 1
Paterson beat Jones 1 hole

Semi-Finals:
Stewart beat Gros 5 and 4
Macpherson beat Paterson 4 and 2

Final: Bryden Macpherson (AUS) beat Michael Stewart (Troon Welbeck) 3 and 2

British Amateur Championship *continued*

1885	A MacFie beat H Hutchinson	7 and 6	Hoylake, Royal Liverpool	entrants 44
1886	H Hutchinson beat H Lamb	7 and 6	St Andrews	42
1887	H Hutchinson beat J Ball	I hole	Hoylake, Royal Liverpool	33
1888	J Ball beat J Laidlay	5 and 4	Prestwick	38
1889	J Laidlay beat L Melville	2 and I	St Andrews	40
1890	J Ball beat J Laidlay	4 and 3	Hoylake, Royal Liverpool	44
1891	J Laidlay beat H Hilton	at 20th	St Andrews	50
1892	J Ball beat H Hilton	3 and I	Sandwich, Royal St George's	45
1893	P Anderson beat J Laidlay	I hole	Prestwick	44
1894	J Ball beat S Fergusson	I hole	Hoylake, Royal Liverpool	64
1895	L Melville beat J Ball	at 19th	St Andrews	68
From 1896 final played over 36 holes				
1896	F Tait beat H Hilton	8 and 7	Sandwich, Royal St George's	64
1897	A Allan beat J Robb	4 and 2	Muirfield	74
1898	F Tait beat S Fergusson	7 and 5	Hoylake, Royal Liverpool	77
1899	J Ball beat F Tait	at 37th	Prestwick	101
1900	H Hilton beat J Robb	8 and 7	Sandwich, Royal St George's	68
1901	H Hilton beat J Low	I hole	St Andrews	116
1902	C Hutchings beat S Fry	I hole	Hoylake, Royal Liverpool	114
1903	R Maxwell beat H Hutchinson	7 and 5	Muirfield	142
1904	W Travis (USA) beat E Blackwell	4 and 3	Sandwich, Royal St George's	104
1905	A Barry beat Hon O Scott	3 and 2	Prestwick	148
1906	J Robb beat C Lingen	4 and 3	Hoylake, Royal Liverpool	166
1907	J Ball beat C Palmer	6 and 4	St Andrews	200
1908	E Lassen beat H Taylor	7 and 6	Sandwich, Royal St George's	197
1909	R Maxwell beat Capt C Hutchison	I hole	Muirfield	170
1910	J Ball beat C Aylmer	10 and 9	Hoylake, Royal Liverpool	160
1911	H Hilton beat E Lassen	4 and 3	Prestwick	146
1912	J Ball beat A Mitchell	at 38th	Westward Ho!, Royal North Devon	134
1913	H Hilton beat R Harris	6 and 5	St Andrews	198
1914	J Jenkins beat C Hezlet	3 and 2	Sandwich, Royal St George's	232
1915–19	*Not played*			
1920	C Tolley beat R Gardner (USA)	37th hole	Muirfield	165
1921	W Hunter beat A Graham	12 and 11	Hoylake, Royal Liverpool	223
1922	E Holderness beat J Caven	I hole	Prestwick	252
1923	R Wethered beat R Harris	7 and 6	Deal, Royal Cinque Ports	209
1924	E Holderness beat E Storey	3 and 2	St Andrews	201
1925	R Harris beat K Fradgley	13 and 12	Westward Ho!, Royal North Devon	151
1926	J Sweetser (USA) beat A Simpson	6 and 5	Muirfield	216
1927	Dr W Tweddell beat D Landale	7 and 6	Hoylake, Royal Liverpool	197
1928	T Perkins beat R Wethered	6 and 4	Prestwick	220
1929	C Tolley beat J Smith	4 and 3	Sandwich, Royal St George's	253
1930	R Jones (USA) beat R Wethered	7 and 6	St Andrews	271
1931	E Smith beat J De Forest	I hole	Westward Ho!, Royal North Devon	171
1932	J De Forest beat E Fiddian	3 and I	Muirfield	235
1933	Hon M Scott beat T Bourn	4 and 3	Hoylake, Royal Liverpool	269
1934	W Lawson Little (USA) beat J Wallace	14 and 13	Prestwick	225
1935	W Lawson Little (USA) beat Dr W Tweddell	I hole	Royal Lytham and St Annes	232
1936	H Thomson beat J Ferrier (AUS)	2 holes	St Andrews	283
1937	R Sweeney Jr (USA) beat L Munn	3 and 2	Sandwich, Royal St George's	223
1938	C Yates (USA) beat R Ewing	3 and 2	Troon	241
1939	A Kyle beat A Duncan	2 and I	Hoylake, Royal Liverpool	167
1940–45	*Not played*			
1946	J Bruen beat R Sweeny (USA)	4 and 3	Birkdale	263
1947	W Turnesa (USA) beat R Chapman (USA)	3 and 2	Carnoustie	200
1948	F Stranahan (USA) beat C Stowe	5 and 4	Sandwich, Royal St George's	168
1949	S McCready beat W Turnesa (USA)	2 and I	Portmarnock	204
1950	F Stranahan (USA) beat R Chapman (USA)	8 and 6	St Andrews	324
1951	R Chapman (USA) beat C Coe (USA)	5 and 4	Royal Porthcawl	192
1952	E Ward (USA) beat F Stranahan (USA)	6 and 5	Prestwick	286
1953	J Carr beat E Harvie Ward (USA)	2 holes	Hoylake, Royal Liverpool	279
1954	D Bachli (AUS) beat W Campbell (USA)	2 and I	Muirfield	286
1955	J Conrad (USA) beat A Slater	3 and 2	Royal Lytham and St Annes	240
1956	J Beharrell beat L Taylor	5 and 4	Troon	200
1957	R Reid Jack beat H Ridgley (USA)	2 and I	Formby	200
In 1956 and 1957 the Quarter Finals, Semi-Finals and Final were played over 36 holes				
1958	J Carr beat A Thirlwell	3 and 2	St Andrews	488
In 1958, Semi-Finals and Final only were played over 36 holes				
1959	D Beman (USA) beat W Hyndman (USA)	3 and 2	Sandwich, Royal St George's	362
1960	J Carr beat R Cochran (USA)	8 and 7	Royal Portrush	183
1961	MF Bonallack beat J Walker	6 and 4	Turnberry	250
1962	R Davies (USA) beat J Povall	I hole	Hoylake, Royal Liverpool	256
1963	M Lunt beat J Blackwell	2 and I	St Andrews	256

Year	Result	Margin	Venue	Score
1964	G Clark beat M Lunt	at 39th	Ganton	220
1965	MF Bonallack beat C Clark	2 and 1	Royal Porthcawl	176
1966	R Cole (RSA) beat R Shade	3 and 2	Carnoustie (18 holes)	206

Final played over 18 holes because of sea mist

1967	R Dickson (USA) beat R Cerrudo (USA)	2 and 1	Formby	
1968	MF Bonallack beat J Carr	7 and 6	Royal Troon	249
1969	MF Bonallack beat W Hyndman (USA)	3 and 2	Hoylake, Royal Liverpool	245
1970	MF Bonallack beat W Hyndman (USA)	8 and 7	Newcastle, Royal Co Down	256
1971	S Melnyk (USA) beat J Simons (USA)	3 and 2	Carnoustie	256
1972	T Homer beat A Thirlwell	4 and 3	Sandwich, Royal St George's	253
1973	R Siderowf (USA) beat P Moody	5 and 3	Royal Porthcawl	222
1974	T Homer beat J Gabrielsen (USA)	2 holes	Muirfield	330
1975	M Giles (USA) beat M James	8 and 7	Hoylake, Royal Liverpool	206
1976	R Siderowf (USA) beat J Davies	at 37th	St Andrews	289
1977	P McEvoy beat H Campbell	5 and 4	Ganton	235
1978	P McEvoy beat P McKellar	4 and 3	Royal Troon	353
1979	J Sigel (USA) beat S Hoch (USA)	3 and 2	Hillside	285
1980	D Evans beat D Suddards (RSA)	4 and 3	Royal Porthcawl	265
1981	P Ploujoux (FRA) beat J Hirsch (USA)	4 and 2	St Andrews	256
1982	M Thompson beat A Stubbs	4 and 3	Deal, Royal Cinque Ports	245

Qualifying round introduced

1983	P Parkin beat J Holtgrieve (USA)	5 and 4	Turnberry	288
1984	JM Olazábal (ESP) beat C Montgomerie	5 and 4	Formby	291
1985	G McGimpsey beat G Homewood	8 and 7	Royal Dornoch	457
1986	D Curry beat G Birtwell	11 and 9	Royal Lytham and St Annes	427
1987	P Mayo beat P McEvoy	3 and 1	Prestwick	373
1988	C Hardin (SWE) beat B Fouchee (RSA)	1 hole	Royal Porthcawl	391
1989	S Dodd beat C Cassells	5 and 3	Royal Birkdale	378
1990	R Muntz (NED) beat A Macara	7 and 6	Muirfield	510
1991	G Wolstenholme beat B May (USA)	8 and 6	Ganton	345
1992	S Dundas beat B Dredge	7 and 6	Carnoustie	364
1993	I Pyman beat P Page	at 37th	Royal Portrush	279
1994	L James beat G Sherry	2 and 1	Nairn	288
1995	G Sherry beat M Reynard	7 and 6	Hoylake, Royal Liverpool	288
1996	W Bladon beat R Beames	1 hole	Turnberry	288
1997	C Watson beat T Immelman (RSA)	3 and 2	Royal St Georges, Royal Cinque Ports	369
1998	S García (ESP) beat C Williams	7 and 6	Muirfield	537
1999	G Storm beat A Wainwright	7 and 6	Royal County Down, Kilkeel	433
2000	M Ilonen (FIN) beat C Reimbold	2 and 1	Royal Liverpool and Wallasey	376
2001	M Hoey beat I Campbell	1 hole	Prestwick & Kilmarnock	288
2002	A Larrazábal (ESP) beat M Sell	1 hole	Royal Porthcawl and Pyle & Kenfig	286
2003	G Wolstenholme beat R De Sousa (SUI)	6 and 5	Royal Troon and Irvine	289
2004	S Wilson beat L Corfield	4 and 3	St Andrews, Old and Jubilee Courses	288
2005	B McElhinney beat J Gallagher	5 and 4	Royal Birkdale and Southport & Ainsdale	406
2006	J Guerrier (FRA) beat A Gee	4 and 3	Royal St George's and Prince's	284
2007	D Weaver (USA) beat T Stewart (AUS)	2 and 1	Royal Lytham & St Annes and St Annes Old Links	284
2008	R Saxton (NED) beat T Fleetwood (ENG)	3 and 2	Turnberry	288
2009	M Manassero (ITA) beat S Hutsby (ENG)	4 and 3	Formby and West Lancashire	284
2010	Jin Jeong (KOR) beat J Byrne (Banchory)	5 and 4	Muirfield and North Berwick	288

The 2012 Amateur Championship is being played from June 18–23 at Royal Troon Golf Club in Ayrshire.

Ireland hosting 2012 European Amateur Championship

For the first time in the 25 year history of the event Ireland is hosting the European Amateur Championship this year. The Montgomerie Course at Carton House has been chosen as the venue of the event from August 8–11.

Previously the championship has been held in Denmark, France, Sweden, Germany, Italy, Finland, Scotland, Belgium, Portugal, Wales, Austria, Switzerland, Spain, England and The Netherlands.

Additionally, the championship is one of only four on the World Amateur Golf Rankings points system with "elite" status – the other three being the Asian Amateur, British Amateur and US Amateur Championships.

Some of the biggest names in the world of professional golf have won the European title in previous years including current US Open Champion Rory McIlroy.

Prominent past winners in addition to McIlroy include five-time Ryder Cup star Sergio García, France's Grégory Havret – who finished runner-up at the US Open in 2010 – and Sweden's Carl Pettersson who has won four times on the PGA Tour in America.

23rd European Amateur Championship (inaugurated 1986)   *Halmstad, Sweden*

In form Austrian Manuel Trappel wins European title play-off

Manuel Trappel became European Amateur champion after a three hole play-off with England's Steven Brown at Halmsted in Sweden. The two golfers had completed 72 holes tied on ten-under-par 278. Trappel then completed the extra holes in one shot better than the Englishman.

Twenty-four countries were represented in the Championship which has been won in the past by Rory McIlroy, Sergio García, Lee Westwood, Paul Casey and Graeme McDowell.

On the first day 64 in the field of 144 matched or beat par with Brown shooting a record 65. In a stronger wind on the second day scoring was higher with Dutchman Daan Huizing shooting a best-of-the-day 67 which included a double bogey.

Brown with a 71 stayed in front on eight-under-par 136 by a shot from fout players including Trappel who move into the lead on the third with a 71. Brown shot 74 and on 210 was tied third with Frenchman Julien Brun both of whom were passed by England's Stiggy Hodgson who fired a 68. Sixty one players made the third round cut.

On the last day Brown's closing 68 tied him with Trappel necessitating the three hole play-off which decided the winner.

1	Manuel Trappel (AUT)*	68-69-71-70—278
2	Steven Brown (ENG)	65-71-74-68—278

*Trappel won after a 3-hole play-off

3	Julien Brun (FRA)	69-68-73-69—279
4	Thomas Pieters (BEL)	68-72-71-70—281
	Gary Stal (FRA)	66-71-73-71—281
	Stiggy Hodgson (ENG)	71-70-68-72—281
7	Andrew Cooley (ENG)	69-71-73-71—284
	George Thacker (ENG)	68-69-75-72—284
9	Thomas Detry (BEL)	70-76-70-69—285
	James Byrne (SCO)	68-74-74-69—285
	Richard O'Donovan (IRL)	70-75-70-70—285
	Emilio Cuartero (ESP)	72-70-72-71—285
	Rhys Pugh (WAL)	71-70-72-72—285
	Paul Cutler (IRL)	69-75-68-73—285
	Robert Karlsson (SWE)	70-73-69-73—285
	Kevin Phelan (IRL)	73-69-70-73—285
	Garrick Porteous (ENG)	68-72-70-75—285
18	Antoine Schwartz (FRA)	71-74-71-70—286
	Tim Gornik (SLO)	70-73-71-72—286
	Kris Nicol (SCO)	72-70-71-73—286
	Niclas Carlsson (SWE)	69-74-69-74—286
	Daan Huizing (NED)	71-67-72-76—286
23	Craig Hinton (ENG)	75-70-73-69—287
	Rhys Enoch (WAL)	71-76-69-71—287
	Jacobo Pastor (ESP)	69-75-69-74—287
	Edouard Espana (FRA)	73-73-67-74—287
27	Darren Wright (ENG)	70-73-75-70—288
	Paul Barjon (FRA)	71-77-70-70—288
29	Ondrej Lieser (CZE)	74-77-69-69—289
	Oliver Farr (WAL)	70-75-73-71—289
	Kenny Subregis (FRA)	71-72-75-71—289
	Philipp Westermann (GER)	75-71-71-72—289
	Alan Dunbar (IRL)	68-75-73-73—289
	Greg Paterson (SCO)	71-74-70-74—289
	Xavi Puig (ESP)	72-72-71-74—289
	Miro Veijalainen (FIN)	72-71-72-74—289
37	Thomas Sørensen (DEN)	75-73-72-70—290
	Goncalo Pinto (POR)	73-76-69-72—290
	Lorenzo Scotto (ITA)	70-77-71-72—290
	Edouard Amacher (SUI)	71-76-70-73—290
	Arthur Gabelia-Wenne (SUI)	75-72-70-73—290
	Hugo Rouillon (FRA)	73-72-70-75—290

37T	David Law (SCO)	68-75-72-75—290
	Benedict Staben (GER)	69-73-71-77—290
45	Ignacio Elvira (ESP)	75-74-71-71—291
	Carlos Pigem (ESP)	69-74-75-73—291
	Tapio Pulkkanen (FIN)	72-71-69-79—291
	Leonardo Motta (ITA)	71-72-68-80—291
49	Sébastien Gros (FRA)	72-76-72-72—292
	Saddier Adrien (FRA)	72-77-69-74—292
51	Kristofer Ventura (NOR)	73-70-76-74—293
	Warren Harmston (ENG)	72-74-72-75—293
	Filippo Bergamaschi (ITA)	72-70-75-76—293
	Stefano Pitoni (ITA)	73-71-73-76—293
55	Lionel Weber (FRA)	69-77-74-74—294
	Benjamin Rusch (SUI)	75-68-73-78—294
57	Dylan Boshart (NED)	70-75-75-75—295
	Sebastian Söderberg (SWE)	71-78-71-75—295
	Oscar Lengdén (SWE)	73-76-70-76—295
60	Niccoló Quintarelli (ITA)	70-72-77-77—296
	Michael Stewart (SCO)	72-73-74-77—296

The following players missed the cut after three rounds:

62 (221)		
Cyril Bouniol (FRA)	75-74-72	
Ross Kellett (SCO)	75-74-72	
Victor Flatau (SWE)	73-76-72	
Philipp Fendt (AUT)	75-73-73	
Marcel Schneider (GER)	73-74-74	
Mathieu Decottignies Lafon (FRA)	70-77-74	
Dermot McElroy (IRL)	69-78-74	
Niclas Månsson (SWE)	73-72-76	
Sean Einhaus (GER)	72-73-76	
71 (222)		
Pontus Widegren (SWE)	70-83-69	
Niclas Hellberg (FIN)	75-77-70	
Joakim Mikkelsen (NOR)	77-74-71	
Mattia Miloro (ITA)	77-74-71	
Maximilian Roehrig (GER)	76-75-71	
James White (SCO)	73-75-74	
Moritz Lampert (GER)	74-73-75	
Franck Daux (FRA)	73-74-75	
Lukas Nemecz (AUT)	71-74-77	
80 (223)		
Mikkel Bjerch-Andresen (NOR)	76-77-70	
Ólafur Björn Loftsson (ISL)	77-76-70	
Nils Florén (SWE)	75-76-72	
Anders Engell (NOR)	73-77-73	
Daniel Jennevret (SWE)	73-75-75	
Olivier Rozner (FRA)	74-74-75	
Francesco Laporta (ITA)	72-76-75	
Jean-Pierre Verselin (FRA)	71-75-77	
Robin Kind (NED)	72-74-77	
Victor Henum (DEN)	72-69-82	
90 (224)		
Paul Shields (SCO)	74-81-69	
Jordan Findlay (SCO)	73-80-71	
Maximilian Rottluff (GER)	78-74-72	

Filippo Zuchetti (ITA)	77-74-73	
Antonio Hortal (ESP)	71-79-74	
Clèment Berardo (FRA)	74-76-74	
Domenico Geminiani (ITA)	71-77-76	
Juan Francisco Sarasti (ESP)	72-74-78	
98 (225)		
Luca Saccarello (ITA)	75-77-73	
Marc Dobias (SUI)	74-77-74	
José Maria Jóia (POR)	75-76-74	
Alfred Kerstis (SWE)	76-74-75	
Oskar Arvidsson (SWE)	74-75-76	
Albert Eckhardt (FIN)	74-74-77	
104 (226)		
Ben Loughrey (ENG)	77-76-73	
Mads Søgaard (DEN)	72-80-74	
Ricardo Melo Gouveia (POR)	73-79-74	
Fernand Osher (NED)	71-79-76	
108 (227)		
Cedric van Wassenhove (BEL)	78-75-74	
Gerhard Piris (ESP)	74-78-75	
Paul Dunne (IRL)	76-75-76	
Rowin Caron (NED)	79-72-76	
Oliver Mena (ESP)	76-75-76	
Matthias Schwab (AUT)	68-79-80	
114 (228)		
Nicolas D'Incau (SUI)	77-79-72	
Andrea Bolognesi (ITA)	72-82-74	
Martijn Vermei (NED)	78-76-74	
Scott William Fernandez (ESP)	73-80-75	
Anton Kirstein (GER)	78-73-77	
119 (229)		
Mads Kristensen (DEN)	80-73-76	
120 (230)		
Tom Berry (ENG)	77-82-71	
Joshua White (ENG)	78-74-78	

122 (231)		
Jerome Lando Casanova (FRA)	73-82-76	
Stanislas Gautier (FRA)	73-78-80	
Juraj Zvarik (SVK)	73-73-85	
125 (232)		
Christoffer Arvidsson (SWE)	75-77-80	
Victor Doka (SUI)	73-76-83	
FINLEY EWING (usa)	80-76-76	
Gudmundur Agust Kristjansson (ISL)	73-78-81	
Vetie Maroy (NOR)	81-79-72	
Alfredo Pazzeschi (ITA)	73-79-80	
Oscar Stark (SWE)	79-76-77	
132 (234)		
Vaita Guillaume (FRA)	72-88-74	
Kevin Turlan (FRA)	75-80-79	
134 (235)		
Tuomas Salminen (FIN)	73-83-79	
135 (236)		
Hamza Sayin (TUR)	76-81-79	
Andrea Gurini (SUI)	78-79-79	
Nikita Ponomarev (RUS)	77-78-81	
Arnaud Abbas (FRA)	76-78-82	
139 (237)		
Martin Stanic (SLO)	78-83-76	
Pontus Gad (SWE)	80-81-76	
141 (239)		
Hugo Dobson (ENG)	82-74-83	
W/D		
Max Smith (ENG)	81-81-98	
Lucas Justra Bjerregaard (DEN)	73-78-98	

1986	Anders Haglund (SWE)	Eindhoven GC, Netherlands
1988	David Ecob (AUS)	Falkenstein GC, Germany
1990	Klas Erikson (SWE)	Aalborg GC, Denmark
1991	Jim Payne (ENG)	Hillside GC, England
1992	Massimo Scarpa (ITA)	La Querce GC, Italy
1993	Morten Backhausen (DEN)*	Dalmahoy GC, Scotland
	*after play-off with Lee Westwood (ENG)	
1994	Stephen Gallacher (SCO)	Aura GC, Finland
1995	Sergio Garcia (ESP)	El Prat GC, Spain
1997	Didier de Voogt (BEL)	Domaine Imperial, Switzerland

1998	Gregory Havret (FRA)	Celtic Manor Resort, Wales
1999	Paddy Gribben (IRL)	Golf du Medoc, France
2000	Carl Pettersen (SWE)	Syrian GC, Austria
2001	Stephen Browne (IRL)	Odense Eventyr GC, Denmark
2002	Ralph Peliciolli (FRA)	Troia GC, Portugal
2003	Brian McElhinney (IRL)	Nairn GC, Scotland
2004	Matthew Richardson (ENG)	Skovde GC, Sweden
2005	Marius Thorp (NOR)	Antwerp International GC, Belgium
2006	Rory McIlroy (NIR)	Biella GC, Italy

European Amateur Championship *continued*

2007	Benjamin Hebert (FRA)*	Sporting Club, Berlin, Germany	

*after play-off with Joel Sjoholm (SWE)

2008	Stephan Gross (GER)	Esberg GC, Denmark
2009	Victor Dubuisson (FRA)	Golf de Chantilly, France
2010	Lucas Bjerregaard (DEN)	Vanajanlinna, Finland

111th United States Amateur Championship   *Erin Hills CC*   [7760–72]
(US unless stated)

Kelly Kraft surprises World No 1 Cantlay in US final

Kelly Kraft, a 22-year-old from Denton, Texas, may not have been one of the pre-Championship favourites but he produced excellent golf at Erin Hills to beat World Amateur No 1 Patrick Cantlay by two holes in the 36-hole final of the US Amateur Championship.

One down with four to play Kelly, who had earlier in the season won the Trans Mississippi and Texas State Championships, won three of the last four holes when Cantlay admitted he made mental errors at the 33rd and 34th holes to let a one hole advantage slip. "I was not able to recover from those mistakes," said Cantlay, who had been four down earlier in the final. "I feel like I threw away the the tournament. I played well all week but you don't come to a golf tournament to finish second!"

Cantlay had been favourite to end the 12-month qualifying period for the McCormack Medal that goes to the world's most successful amateur with victory at Erin Hills. Earlier in the year he had not only qualified for the US Open won by Rory McIlroy at Congressional but had finished a hugely creditable 21st. He had tied ninth in the Canadian Open and shot an amateur record 60 in the PGA Tour's Travelers Championship at TPC River Highlands. He was enjoying a remarkable year.

Victory in the US Amateur would have been the perfect way for Cantlay to end a remarkable summer of consistent play but on the day of the final Kelly, who has still to complete his sociology degree at the Southern Methodist University, proved the steadier over the closing stretch.

"It's awesome," said Kelly, grasping the Havemeyer Trophy. "It is such an honour to win this Championship." He was the third MSU student to win the title, the others being Hank Kuehne in 1998 and former Amateur No 1 Colt Knost in 2007.

Kelly's victory qualified him for the 2012 Open and US Open and an invitation to The Masters at Augusta. Immediately after the final, captain Jim Holtgrieve told him he had a place on the 2011 Walker Cup team.

Stroke Play Qualifying:

Gregor Main (Danville, CA)	65-67—132	Jim Markovitz (Bridgeville, PA)	69-70—139
Blake Biddle (St Charles, IL)	67-67—134	Jonathan Garrick (Atherton, CA)	66-73—139
Beau Hossler (Mission Viejo, CA)	69-66—135	Chase Wright (Muncie, IN)	68-71—139
Blayne Barber (Lake City, FL)	68-67—135	Max Scodro (Chicago, IL)	67-72—139
Russell Henley (Macon, GA)	66-69—135	John Peterson (Fort Worth, TX)	68-71—139
Ben Geyer (Arbuckle, CA)	69-66—135	John Hahn (Las Vegas, NV)	65-74—139
Patrick Rodgers (Avon, IN)	66-70—136	Mackenzie Hughes (CAN)	73-67—140
Peter Uihlein (Orlando, FL)	68-69—137	Harris English (Thomasville, GA)	73-67—140
Scott Langley (St. Louis, MO)	74-63—137	Andrew Yun (Chandler, AZ)	72-68—140
Sunil Jung (KOR)	72-65—137	Peter Williamson (Hanover, NH)	72-68—140
Jordan Spieth (Dallas, TX)	68-69—137	Hunter Hamrick (Montgomery, AL)	74-66—140
Cory Whitsett (Houston, TX)	69-68—137	Todd Baek (KOR)	69-71—140
Patrick Christovich (New Orleans, LA)	69-69—138	Patrick Cantlay (Los Alamitos, CA)	71-69—140
Justin Thomas (Goshen, KY)	68-70—138	Jonathan Randolph (Brandon, MS)	70-70—140
Cameron Wilson (Rowayton, CT)	72-66—138	Charlie Hughes (CAN)	73-67—140
Will McCurdy (Fort Payne, AL)	69-69—138	Dylan Frittell (RSA)	74-66—140
Zahkai Brown (Arvada, CO)	69-69—138	Mitch Sutton (CAN)	71-69—140
Andrew Putnam (University Place, WA)	70-68—138	Tim Madigan (Rio Rancho, NM)	72-68—140
Corbin Mills (Easley, SC)	75-64—139	Lee Bedford (Cary, NC)	69-71—140
Chris Williams (Moscow, ID)	73-66—139	Kevin Penner (Sammamish, WA)	69-71—140
Tom Lewis (ENG)	71-68—139	David Lee (Houston, TX)	70-70—140
Will Collins (Salisbury, NC)	72-67—139	Jack Senior (ENG)	67-73—140
Denny McCarthy (Rockville, MD)	73-66—139	Juan Salcedo (The Woodlands, TX)	68-72—140
Daniel Nisbet (AUS)	70-69—139	Jordan Russell (College Station, TX)	68-72—140

Bryson Dechambeau (Clovis, CA)	73-68—141	Eugene Wong (CAN)	73-68—141
Kelly Kraft (Denton, TX)	71-70—141	Jack Fields (Southern Pines, NC)	68-73—141
Michael Stewart (SCO)	71-70—141	Ryan Peterson (Eagan, MN)	68-73—141
Max Buckley (Rye, NY)	71-70—141	Kevin Dougherty (Murrieta, CA)	68-73—141
David Kim (Redondo Beach, CA)	71-70—141	Marty Jeppesen II (Ypsilanti, MI)	73-69—142
Jade Scott (Daingerfield, TX)	74-67—141	Stephan Jaeger (GER)	70-72—142
Matt Ewald (Topeka, KS)	72-69—141	David Denlinger (Lancaster, PA)	69-73—142
Donald Constable (Deephaven, MN)	74-67—141	Bobby Leopold (Cranston, RI)	72-70—142

First Round:
Bobby Leopold beat Gregor Main 2 and 1
Harris English beat Andrew Yun 3 and 1
Bryson Dechambeau beat Will McCurdy 3 and 2
Jordan Russell beat Zahkai Brown 1 hole
Peter Uihlein beat Eugene Wong (CAN) 3 and 1
Dylan Frittelli (RSA) beat Jim Markovitz 5 and 4
Scott Langley beat Donald Constable 3 and 2
Mitch Sutton (CAN) beat Daniel Nisbet (AUS)
  2 and 1
Stephan Jaeger (GER) beat Blayne Barber 3 and 2
John Peterson beat Todd Baek (KOR) at 22nd.
Max Buckley beat Patrick Christovich 2 holes
Chris Williams beat David Lee 2 and 1
Russell Henley beat Kevin Dougherty 3 and 1
Patrick Cantlay beat Max Scodro 5 and 4
Cory Whitsett beat David Kim 5 and 3
Tom Lewis (ENG) beat Kevin Penner 1 hole
Blake Biddle beat Marty Jeppesen II 5 and 3
Peter Williamson beat Mackenzie Hughes (CAN)
  1 hole
Kelly Kraft beat Cameron Wilson 3 and 2
Andrew Putnam beat Juan Salcedo 6 and 5
Patrick Rodgers beat Jack Fields 2 and 1
Jonathan Garrick beat Charlie Hughes (CAN)
  2 holes
Sunil Jung (KOR) beat Matt Ewald 2 and 1
Tim Madigan beat Denny McCarthy 3 and 2
Beau Hossler beat David Denlinger 2 and 1
John Hahn beat Hunter Hamrick 2 and 1
Justin Thomas beat Michael Stewart (SCO) 5 and 3
Jack Senior (ENG) beat Corbin Mills 6 and 4
Ben Geyer beat Ryan Peterson 3 and 2
Chase Wright beat Jonathan Randolph 3 and 2
Jordan Spieth beat Jade Scott 2 and 1
Lee Bedford beat Will Collins 6 and 5

Second Round:
Bobby Leopold beat Harris English 4 and 3
Jordan Russell beat Bryson Dechambeau 5 and 3
Peter Uihlein beat Dylan Frittelli 5 and 4
Scott Langley beat Mitch Sutton 4 and 3
John Peterson beat Stephan Jaeger 1 hole
Max Buckley beat Chris Williams 1 hole
Patrick Cantlay beat Russell Henley at 21st
Tom Lewis beat Cory Whitsett at 19th
Blake Biddle beat Peter Williamson 2 holes
Kelly Kraft beat Andrew Putnam 3 and 2
Patrick Rodgers beat Jonathan Garrick 6 and 4
Sunil Jung beat Tim Madigan 5 and 4
John Hahn beat Beau Hossler 2 holes
Jack Senior beat Justin Thomas 4 and 3
Ben Geyer beat Chase Wright 4 and 3
Jordan Spieth beat Lee Bedford 2 and 1

Third Round:
Jordan Russell beat Bobby Leopold at 19th
Peter Uihlein beat Scott Langley 2 and 1
Max Buckley beat John Petersen at 19th
Patrick Cantlay beat Tom Lewis 3 and 1
Kelly Kraft beat Blake Biddle at 23rd
Patrick Rodgers beat Sunil Jung 4 and 3
Jack Senior beat John Hahn 3 and 2
Jordan Speith beat Ben Geyer 7 and 5

Quarter Finals:
Jordan Russell beat Peter Uihlein 2 and 1
Patrick Cantlay beat Max Buckley at 19th
Kelly Kraft beat Patrick Rodgers 6 and 4
Jack Senior beat Jordan Speith 1 hole

Semi-Finals:
Patrick Cantlay beat Jordan Russell 4 and 3
Kelly Kraft beat Jack Senior 3 and 2

Final: Kelly Kraft (Denton, Texas) beat Patrick Cantlay (Los Alamitos, California) 2 holes

1895	CB Macdonald beat C Sands	12 & 11	Newport GC, RI	Entrants 32
1896	HJ Whigham beat JG Thorp	8 & 7	Shinnecock Hills GC, NY	58
1897	HJ Whigham beat WR Betts	8 & 6	Chicago GC, IL	58
1898	FS Douglas beat WB Smith	5 & 3	Morris County GC, NJ	120
1899	HM Harriman beat FS Douglas	3 & 2	Onwentsia Club, IL	112
1900	WJ Travis beat FS Douglas	2 up	Garden City, GC NY	120
1901	WJ Travis beat WE Egan	5 & 4	CC of Atlantic City, NJ	142
1902	LN James beat EM Byers	4 & 2	Glenview Club, IL	157
1903	WJ Travis beat EM Byers	5 & 4	Nassau CC, NY	140
1904	HC Egan beat F Herreshof	8 & 6	Baltusrol GC, NJ	142
1905	HC Egan beat DE Sawyer	6 & 5	Chicago GC, IL	146
1906	EM Byers beat GS Lyon	2 up	Englewood GC, NJ	141
1907	JD Travers beat A Graham	6 & 5	Euclid Club, OH	118
1908	JD Travers beat MH Behr	8 & 7	Garden City GC, NY	145
1909	RA Gardner beat HC Egan	4 & 3	Chicago GC, IL	120
1910	WC Fownes Jr beat WK Wood	4 & 3	The Country Club, Brookline, MA	217
1911	HH Hilton (ENG) beat F Herreshof	1 up	Apawamis Club, Rye, NY	186

US Amateur Championship *continued*

1912	JD Travers beat C Evans Jr	7 & 6	Chicago GC, IL	86
1913	JD Travers beat JG Anderson	5 & 4	Garden City, NY	149
1914	F Ouimet beat JD Travers	6 & 5	Ekwanok CC, VT	115
1915	RA Gardner beat JG Anderson	5 & 4	CC of Detroit, MI	152
1916	C Evans Jr beat RA Gardner	4 & 3	Merion Cricket Club (East), PA	163
1917–18 *Not played*				
1919	SD Herron beat RT Jones Jr	5 & 4	Oakmont CC, PA	150
1920	C Evans Jr beat F Ouimet	7 & 6	Engineers CC, NY	235
1921	JP Guildford beat RA Gardner	7 & 6	St Louis CC, MO	159
1922	JW Sweetser beat C Evans Jr	3 & 2	The Country Club, Brookline, MA	161
1923	MR Marston beat JW Sweetser	1 up	Flossmoor CC, IL	143
1924	RT Jones Jr beat G Von Elm	9 & 8	Merion Cricket Club (East), PA	142
1925	RT Jones Jr beat W Gunn	8 & 7	Oakmont CC, PA	141
1926	G Von Elm beat RT Jones Jr	2 & 1	Baltusrol CC (Lower), NJ	157
1927	RT Jones Jr beat C Evans Jr	8 & 7	Minikahda Club, MN	174
1928	RT Jones Jr beat TP Perkins	10 & 9	Brae Burn CC, MA	158
1929	HR Johnston beat OF Willing	4 & 3	Del Monte G&CC, CA	162
1930	RT Jones Jr beat EV Homans	8 & 7	Merion Cricket Club (East), PA	175
1931	F Ouimet beat J Westland	6 & 5	Beverly CC, IL	583
1932	CR Somerville beat J Goodman	2 & 1	Five Farms CC (East), MD	600
1933	GT Dunlap Jr beat MR Marston	6 & 5	Kenwood CC, OH	601
1934	W Lawson Little Jr beat D Goldman	8 & 7	The Country Club, Brookline, MA	758
1935	W Lawson Little Jr beat W Emery	4 & 2	The Country Club, Cleveland, OH	945
1936	JW Fischer beat J McLean	37 holes	Garden City GC, NY	1,118
1937	J Goodman beat RE Billows	2 up	Alderwood CC, OR	619
1938	WP Turnesa beat BP Abbott	8 & 7	Oakmont CC, PA	871
1939	MH Ward beat RE Billows	7 & 5	North Shore CC, IL	826
1940	RD Chapman beat WB McCullough	11 & 9	Winged Foot GC (West), NY	755
1941	MH Ward beat BP Abbott	4 & 3	Omaha Field Club, NE	637
1942–45 *Not played*				
1946	SE Bishop beat S Quick	1 up	Baltusrol CC (Lower), NJ	899
1947	RH Riegel beat JW Dawson	2 & 1	Del Monte G&CC, CA	1,048
1948	WP Turnesa beat RE Billows	2 & 1	Memphis CC, TN	1,220
1949	CR Coe beat R King	11 & 10	Oak Hill CC (East), NY	1,060
1950	S Urzetta beat FR Stranahan	1 up	Minneapolis GC, MN	1,025
1951	WJ Maxwell beat J Gagliardi	4 & 3	Saucon Valley GC (Old), PA	1,416
1952	J Westland beat A Mengert	3 & 2	Seattle GC, WA	1,029
1953	G Littler beat D Morey	1 up	Oklahoma City GC, OK	1,284
1954	A Palmer beat R Sweeney	1 up	CC Of Detroit, MI	1,278
1955	E Harvie Ward beat W Hyndman	9 & 8	CC of Virginia (James River Course), VA	1,493
1956	E Harvie Ward beat C Kocsis	5 & 4	Knollwood Club, IL	1,600
1957	H Robbins beat FM Taylor	5 & 4	The Country Club (Anniversary Course), Brookline, MA	1,578
1958	CR Coe beat TD Aaron	5 & 4	The Olympic Club (Lake Course), CA	1,472
1959	JW Nicklaus beat CR Coe	1 up	Broadmoor GC (East), CO	1,696
1960	DR Beman beat RW Gardner	6 & 4	St Louis CC, MO	1,737
1961	JW Nicklaus beat HD Wysong	8 & 6	Pebble Beach GC, CA	1,995
1962	LE Harris Jr beat D Gray	1 up	Pinehurst CC (No.2 Course), NC	2,044
1963	DR Beman beat RH Sikes	2 & 1	Wakonda Club, IA	1,768
1964	WC Campbell beat EM Tutweiler	1 up	Canterbury GC, OH	1,562

Changed to stroke play

1965	Robert J Murphy Jr	291	Southern Hill CC, OK	1.476
1966	Gary Cowan (CAN)*	285	Merion GC (East), PA	1,902

Cowan beat Deane Beman 75-76 in 18-hole play-off

1967	RB Dickson	285	Broadmoor GC (WEst), CO	1,784
1968	B Fleisher	284	Scioto GC, OH	2,057
1969	S Melnyk	286	Oakmont CC, PA	2,142
1970	L Wadkins*	279	Waverley GC, OR	1,853
1971	G Cowan (CAN)	280	Wilmington CC (South), DE	2,327
1972	Marvin Giles III	285	Charlotte CC, NC	2,295

Reverted to match play

1973	C Stadler beat D Strawn	6 & 5	Inverness Club OH	2,110
1974	J Pate beat J Grace	2 & 1	Ridgewood CC, NJ	2,420
1975	F Ridley beat K Fergus	2 up	CC of Virginia (James River Course), VA	2,528
1976	B Sander beat CP Moore	8 & 6	Bel Air CC, CA	2,681
1977	J Fought beat D Fischesser	9 & 8	Aromink CC, PA	2,950
1978	J Cook beat S Hoch	5 & 4	Plainfield GC, NJ	3,035
1979	M O'Meara beat J Cook	8 & 7	Canterbury GC, OH	3,916
1980	H Sutton beat B Lewis	9 & 8	CC of North Carolina, NC	4,008

1981	N Crosby beat B Lindley	1 up	The Olympic Club (Lake Course), CA	3,525
1982	J Sigel beat D Tolley	8 & 7	The Country Club, Brookline, MA	3,685
1983	J Sigel beat C Perry	8 & 7	North Shore CC, IL	3,553
1984	S Verplank beat S Randolph	4 & 3	Oak Tree GC, OK	3,679
1985	S Randolph beat P Persons	1 up	Montclair GC, NJ	3,816
1986	S Alexander beat C Kite	5 & 3	Shoal Creek GC, AL	4,069
1987	W Mayfair beat E Rebmann	4 & 3	Jupiter Hills Club (Hills Course), FL	4,085
1988	E Meeks beat D Yates	7 & 6	Hot Springs CC (Cascades Course), VA	4,320
1989	C Patton beat D Green	3 & 1	Merion GC (East), PA	4,603
1990	P Mickelson beat M Zerman	5 & 4	Cherry Hills CC, CO	4,763
1991	M Voges beat M Zerman	7 & 6	The Honors Course, TN	4,985
1992	J Leonard beat T Scherrer	8 & 7	Muirfield Village GC, OH	5,758
1993	J Harris beat D Ellis	5 & 3	Champions GC (Cypress Creek Course), TX	5,614
1994	T Woods beat T Kuehne	2 up	TPC at Sawgrass (Stadium Course), FL	5,128
1995	T Woods beat G Marucci	2 up	Newport CC, RI	5,248
1996	T Woods beat S Scott	38 holes	Pumpkin Ridge GC, OR	5,538
1997	M Kuchar beat J Kribel	2 & 1	Cog Hill G&CC (No.4 Course), IL	6,666
1998	H Kuehne beat T McKnight	2 and 1	Oak Hill CC (East), NY	6,627
1999	D Gossett beat Sung Yoon Kim	9 and 8	Pebble Beach GC, CA	7,920
2000	J Quinney beat J Driscoll	39 holes	Baltusrol GC, NJ	7,124
2001	B Dickerson beat R Hamilton	1 up	Eastlake GC, GA	7,762
2002	R Barnes beat H Mahon	2 and 1	Oakland Hills CC (South Course), MI	7,597
2003	N Flanagan (AUS) beat C Wittenberg	37 holes	Oakmont CC, PA	7,541
2004	R Moore beat L List	2 up	Winged Foot GC (West Course), NY	7,356
2005	E Molinari (ITA) beat D Dougherty	4 and 3	Merion GC (East Course), PA	7,320
2006	R Ramsay (SCO) beat J Kelly	4 and 2	Hazeltine National GC, MN	7,182
2007	C Knost beat M Thompson	2 and 1	The Olympic Club (Lake Course), CA	7,398
2008	D Lee (NZL) beat D Kittleson	5 and 4	Pinehurst Resort and CC, NC	7,298
2009	B An (KOR) beat B Martin	7 and 5	Southern Hills CC, Tulsa, OK	9,086
2010	P Uihlein beat D Chung	4 and 3	Chambers Bay, WA	6,485

NCAA Championships (Men) *Karsten Creek GC, Stillwater, Oklahoma*

Augusta State make it back-to-back in Oklahoma

Augusta State, who had finished seventh behind UCLA in the NCAA Stroke Play Championship, swept to a 3–2 success over Georgia in the Match Play event recording the first back-to-back success since Houston achieved the feat in 1984 and 1985.

In the quarter-finals, Augusta State beat Georgia Tech and in the semi-finals Oklahoma, whom they had beaten in the 2010 final. In this year's final, Augusta-born Patrick Reed scored a 2 and 1 success against Harris English in the deciding game on a sweltering day at Karsten Creek Golf Club in Stillwater, Oklahoma.

Reed, who had beaten Peter Uihlein in the semi-final, made the winning point after Carter Newman had overwhelmed T J Mitchell by 7 and 5 and Mitchell Krywulycz had taken care of Hudson Swafford 2 and 1. Earlier, Augusta State's Olle Bengtsson, a former Swedish Junior champion, had lost to Bryden MacPherson 6 and 4 and another Swede, Henrik Norlander, had been beaten 3 and 2 by Georgia's Russell Henley who was one of three players who did not lose any games over the three days. The others were Bryden MacPherson, who would go on to win the Amateur Championship in Britain, and Patrick Read.

It was the last time the winning team will play together but their delighted coach Josh Gregory said: "What a way to end. This week has been incredible. Now they are all going their separate ways but they leave having accomplished something special."

Only Reed, who moved from Georgia to Augusta State to play in Gregory's side, is turning profession-al.   He finished joint third in the individual Championship which was won by LSU's John Peterson from Fort Worth. Peterson fired a record 65 on the second day but after going to the turn in four-over-par 40 on the final day steadied for an inward 32 and a one shot victory over Patrick Cantlay from UCLA.

"I knew the course well because have played on it through High School, College and Regionals," said Peterson." but I am always happiest on the back nine." In the end birdies at the 11th, 14th and the last two holes earned Peterson what was an historic victory.

His victory and that of LSU's Austin Ernst in the Women's NCAA Championship earlier in the year meant that for the first time the winners of both the men's and women's competitions came from the same school.

NCAA Championships *continued*

Stroke Play Championship – Team event:

1	UCLA	286-288-290—872
2	Georgia Tech	283-290-302—875
3	Oklahoma State	292-293-294—879
	Illinois	291-287-301—879
5	Georgia	291-288-305—884

6 Ohio State 887; 7 Augusta State 888; 8 Duke 889; 9 Texas A&M 890; 10 Iowa, Michigan 892;
12 Southern California, Texas 895; 14 Alabama 896; 16 Arkansas 897; 16 San Diego, San Diego State 898;
18 Arizona State 899; 19 California, Kent State 902; 21 LSU 905; 22 Northwestern 906; 23 Florida 908;
24 Tennessee 910; 25 Pepperdine 919; 26 Kennesaw State 921; 27 North Carolina State 922;
28 Oklahoma 930; 29 Arizona 933; 30 Colorado State 937

Winning team: UCLA 872 – Patrick Cantlay 72-69-71—212; Gregor Main 72-70-78—220; Alex Kim 71-76-75—222; Pedro Figueiredo 71-74-79—224; Pontus Widegren 79-75-74—228

Individual Championship:

1	John Peterson (LSU)	74-65-72—211
2	Patrick Cantlay (UCLA)	72-69-71—212
3	Lion Kim (Michigan)	72-70-73—215
	Cameron Peck (Texas A&M)	68-74-73—215
	Patrick Reed (Augusta State)	69-75-71—215
	J J Spaun (San Diego State)	69-75-71—215
	Peter Uihlein (Oklahoma State)	73-69-73—215
8	Michael Weaver (California)	71-71-74—216
	James White (Georgia Tech)	67-73-76—216
10	Todd Baek (San Diego State)	72-72-73—217
	Austin Cook (Arkansas)	70-74-73—217
	Harris English (Georgia)	70-71-76—217
13	Chris DeForest (Illinois)	72-72-74—218
	Luke Guthrie (Illinois)	72-69-77—218
	Brinson Paolini (Duke)	72-72-74—218
	Bank Vongvanij (Florida)	74-73-71—218
17	J T Griffin (Georgia Tech)	73-72-74—219
	Max Homa (California)	73-74-72—219
	Brad Smith (Ohio State)	72-74-73—219
20	Chris Brant (Iowa)	76-70-74—220
	Dylan Frittelli (Texas)	75-73-72—220
	Paul Haley (Georgia Tech)	71-72-77—220
	Jeffrey Kang (S. California)	72-73-75—220
	Jeff Karlsson (Kennesaw State)	72-73-75—220
	Gregor Main (UCLA)	72-70-78—220
	Thomas Pieters (Illinois)	76-74-70—220
	Ryan Sirman (Oklahoma)	71-72-77—220
	Matt Thompson (Michigan)	74-76-70—220
29	Tim Gornik (Duke)	75-72-74—221
	Hunter Hamrick (Alabama)	71-74-76—221
	Kyle Scott (Georgia Tech)	72-74-75—221
32	Lee Bedford (Wake Forest)	74-73-75—222
	Ignacio Elvira (Texas A&M)	72-77-73—222
	Phil Francis (Arizona State)	78-72-72—222
	Alex Kim (UCLA)	71-76-75—222
	Jason Millard (Middle Tennessee State)	76-71-75—222
	Alex Redfield (Ohio State)	74-75-73—222
38	Eric Chun (Northwestern)	77-70-76—223
	Bo Hoag (Ohio State)	71-75-77—223
	Morgan Hoffmann (Oklahoma State)	75-73-75—223

38T	Brad Hopfinger (Iowa)	74-72-77—223
	David Lipsky (Northwestern)	74-74-75—223
	Kevin Miller (Kent State)	81-69-73—223
	Ben Murray (San Diego)	72-75-76—223
	Garrick Porteous (Tennessee)	77-73-73—223
	Andrew Putnam (Pepperdine)	77-75-71—223
	Mitchell Sutton (North Carolina State)	76-76-71—223
	Hudson Swafford (Georgia)	71-74-78—223
	Kevin Tway (Oklahoma State)	77-74-72—223
50	James Byrne (Arizona State)	74-73-77—224
	Bud Cauley (Alabama)	70-73-81—224
	Michael Cress (Ohio State)	74-75-75—224
	Pedro Figueiredo (UCLA)	71-74-79—224
	Talor Gooch (Oklahoma State)	72-77-75—224
	Carter Newman (Augusta State)	74-75-75—224
56	Joey Garber (Michigan)	77-72-76—225
	Cody Gribble (Texas)	75-77-73—225
	Toni Hakula (Texas)	73-73-79—225
	Barrett Kelpin (Iowa)	81-73-71—225
	Steve Lim (S. California)	78-72-75—225
	Jace Long (Missouri)	70-77-78—225
	Henrik Norlander (Augusta State)	80-69-76—225
	Jordan Russell (Texas A&M)	73-77-75—225
	Manav Shah (San Diego)	71-74-80—225
	Cory Whitsett (Alabama)	73-71-81—225
66	Sebastian Cappelen (Arkansas)	76-72-78—226
	Austin Cody (Duke)	77-77-72—226
	Sean Einhaus (Oklahoma State)	72-80-74—226
	Mason Jacobs (Illinois)	74-72-80—226
	Matt Nagy (Kennesaw State)	73-80-73—226
	Scott Pinckney (Arizona State)	73-80-73—226
	Martin Trainer (S, California)	75-75-76—226
	Bobby Wyatt (Alabama)	74-74-78—226
74	Phillip Choi (Florida)	77-71-79—227

74T	John Hahn (Kent State)	74-75-78—227
	Russell Henley (Georgia)	76-72-79—227
	Tarquin MacManus (Arizona)	73-77-77—227
	Jamie Marshall (Arkansas)	75-75-77—227
	Ethan Tracy (Arkansas)	75-75-75—227
	Robin Wingardh (Tennessee)	77-75-75—227
81	Abraham Ancer (Oklahoma)	77-76-75—228
	Mackenzie Hughes (Kent State)	76-80-72—228
	Vince India (Iowa)	77-77-74—228
	Kenneth McCready (San Diego)	79-78-71—228
	Sebastian Soderberg (Coastal Carolina)	77-79-72—228
	Julian Suri (Duke)	81-74-73—228
	Pontus Widegren (UCLA)	79-75-74—228
88	Zahkai Brown (Colorado State)	78-77-74—229
	Albin Choi (N. Carolina State)	78-74-77—229
	Bryden MacPherson (Georgia)	82-71-76—229
	Conrad Shindler (Texas A&M)	77-73-79—229
	Julio Vegas (Texas)	76-78-75—229
	Sang Yi (LSU)	76-83-70—229
94	Bobby Hudson (Texas)	77-78-75—230
	Jesper Kennegard (Arizona State)	78-68-84—230
	Mitchell Krywulycz (Augusta State)	71-81-78—230
	T J Mitchell (Georgia)	74-81-75—230
	Taylor Pendrith (Kent State)	76-78-76—230
	Jack Perry (Northwestern)	74-77-79—230
	Andrew Widmar (Pepperdine)	80-75-75—230
	Gunner Wiebe (San Diego)	78-77-75—230
102	Brandon Detweiler (N. Carolina State)	77-78-76—231
	Stephen Hale (California)	75-80-76—231
	Darren Renwick (Tennessee)	78-79-74—231
	Richy Werenski (Georgia Tech)	76-73-82—231
106	Josh Anderson (Pepperdine)	74-80-78—232
	Alex Ching (San Diego)	80-80-72—232
	Josh Dupont (Northwestern)	81-75-76—232
	Jonathan Khan (Arizona)	73-79-80—232
	Ryan Peterson (Colorado State)	77-81-74—232
	Jack Schultz (Michigan)	84-74-74—232
	Jay Vandeventer (Tennessee)	78-73-81—232
113	Johan Carlsson (San Diego State)	76-77-80—233
	Andres Echavarria (Florida)	74-76-83—233
	Alex Kang (San Diego State)	78-77-78—233
	Tyler McCumber (Florida)	75-79-79—233

113T	T J Vogel (S. California)	78-73-82—233
118	Corey Conners (Kent State)	78-81-75—234
119	Parker Page (Pepperdine)	78-81-76—235
	Will Pearson (Arkansas)	77-78-80—235
121	Jed Dirksen (Iowa)	77-81-78—236
	Danny Keddie (Tennessee)	76-78-82—236
	Jonathan Klotz (Kennesaw State)	75-78-83—236
	Riley Pumphrey (Oklahoma)	80-75-81—236
125	Kory Harrell (Colorado State)	73-82-82—237
	Ken Looper (LSU)	79-77-81—237
	Wes Roach (Duke)	79-75-83—237
128	Austin Gutgsell (LSU)	81-75-82—238
129	Stefan Cox (Arizona)	82-72-85—239
	Scott Langley (Illinois)	73-86-80—239
	Tommy Mou (Florida)	78-81-80—239
132	Chad Day (N. Carolina State)	80-80-80—240
	Nicholas Losole (Northwestern)	81-82-77—240
	Chad Wilson (Kennesaw State)	75-82-83—240
135	John Hurley (Texas A&M)	76-81-84—241
	Eric Mina (California)	84-76-81—241
	Erik Oja (Arizona)	80-82-79—241
138	Kirby Pettitt (Colorado State)	79-83-80—242
139	Olle Bengtsson (Augusta State)	86-75-82—243
	Oscar Zetterwall (Arizona State)	79-83-81—243
141	Andrew Loupe (LSU)	77-77-90—244
	Mike Sorenson (Colorado State)	82-82-80—244
143	Colin Featherstone (San Diego State)	86-78-81—245
	Juan Pablo Hernandez (Arizona)	76-82-87—245
145	Michael Schoolcraft (Oklahoma)	85-81-80—246
146	Graham Baillargeon (N. Carolina State)	79-85-83—247
	Geoff Gonzalez (Cal Poly)	81-81-85—247
148	Dan Charen (Ohio State)	90-82-76—248
	John MacArthur (Pepperdine)	81-80-87—248
	Trey Mullinax (Alabama)	84-80-84—248
151	Rahul Bakshi (Michigan)	86-87-76—249
	Ben Greene (Kennesaw State)	84-81-84—249
153	Ben Klaus (Oklahoma)	90-84-86—260
	Matt Hansen (UC Davis)	73 W W
	Sam Smith (S. California)	D 71-77
	Ben An (California)	81-78 W

NCAA Championships *continued*

Match Play Championship:

Quarter-finals: Duke 3½, UCLA 1½
Georgia 3½, Illinois 1½
Augusta State 3 Georgia Tech 2
Oklahoma State 3½, Ohio State 3½

Semi-finals: Georgia 3, Duke 2
Augusta State 3, Oklahoma 2

Final: Augusta State 3, Georgia 2

Olle Bengtsson lost to Bryden MacPherson 6 and 4
Carter Newman beat T J Mitchell 7 and 5
Mitchell Krywulycz beat Hudson Swafford 2 and 1
Henrik Norlander lost to Russell Henley 3 and 2
Patrick Reed beat Harris English 2 and 1

Callaway Handicapping

It frequently occurs in social competitions such as office or business association outings that many of the competitors do not have official handicaps. In such cases the best solution is to use the Callaway handicapping system, so called after the name of its inventor, as it is simple to use yet has proved equitable.

Competitors complete their round marking in their gross figures at every hole and their handicaps are awarded and deducted at the end of the 18 holes using the following table:

Competitor's Gross Score	Handicap Deduction
par or less	none
one over par – 75	½ worst hole
76–80	worst hole
81–85	worst hole plus ½ next worse
86–90	two worst holes
91–95	two worst holes plus ½ next
96–100	three worst holes
101–105	three worst holes plus ½ next
106–110	four worst holes
111–115	four worst holes plus ½ next
116–120	five worst holes
121–125	five worst holes plus ½ next
126–130	six worst holes

Note 1: Worst hole equals highest score at any hole regardless of the par of the hole except that the maximum score allowed for any one hole is twice the par of the hole.

Note 2: The 17th and 18th holes are not allowed to be deducted.

Example: Competitor scores 104. From the table he should deduct as his handicap the total of his three worst (i.e. highest) individual hole scores plus half of his fourth worst hole. If he scored one 9, one 8 and several 7's he would therefore deduct a total of 27½ from his gross score of 104 to give a net score of 76½.

National Championships 2011

For past winners not listed here, please see earlier editions of *The R&A Golfer's Handbook*

Players are from the host nation unless stated

Africa

Sanlam South African Amateur Championship (inaugurated 1892)

Val de Grace Golf Estate

Semi-finals:
Paul Shields beat Jaques Kruysevik 3 and 2
Michael Stewart (SCO) beat Jordan Findlay at 19th

Final:
Michael Stewart (SCO) beat Paul Shields 5 and 4

1892 D Walker	1924 AL Forster	1956 RC Taylor	1984 M Wiltshire
1893 DG Proudfoot	1925 TG McLelland	1957 A Stewart	1985 N Clarke
1894 DG Proudfoot	1926 WS Bryant	1958 JR Boyd	1986 E Els
1895 DG Proudfoot	1927 GJ Chantler	1959 A Walker	1987 B Fouche
1896 DG Proudfoot	1928 B Wynne	1960 WM Grinrod	1988 N Clarke
1897 DG Proudfoot	1929 C Hunter	1961 JG Le Roux	1989 C Rivett
1898 DG Proudfoot	1930 B Wynne	1962 J Hayes	1990 R Goosen
1899 DG Proudfoot	1931 C Coetzer	1963 D Symons	1991 D Botes
1900–01 Not played	1932 CE Olander	1964 JR Langridge	1992 B Davidson
1902 DG Proudfoot	1933 B Wynne	1965 P Vorster	1993 L Chitengwa (ZIM)
1903 R Law	1934 CE Olander	1966 Comrie du Toit	1994 B Vaughan
1904 JR Southey	1935 AD Locke	1967 Derek Kemp	1995 W Abery
1905 HCV Nicholson	1936 CE Olander	1968 R Williams	1996 T Moore
1906 Lt. HM Ballinghall	1937 AD Locke	1969 D Thornton	1997 T Immelman
1907 Lt. HM Ballinghall	1938 B Wynne	1970 H Baiocchi	1998 J Hugo
1908 JAW Prentice	1939 O Hayes	1971 C Dreyer	1999 R Sterne
1909 JAW Prentice	1940 HEP Watermeyer	1972 N Dundelson	2000 J Van Zyl
1910 Dr EL Steyn	1941–45 Not played	1973 A. Oosthuizen	2001 D Dixon (ENG)
1911 JAW Prentice	1946 JR Boyd	1974 T Lagerwey	2002 R Loubser
1912 HG Stewart	1947 C de G Watermeyer	1975 P Vorster	2003 A Haig
1913 JAW Prentice	1948 RR Ryan	1976 R Kotzen	2004 H Rootman
1914 SM McPherson	1949 RW Glennie	1977 EA Webber (ZIM)	2005 G Coetzee
1915–18 Not played	1950 EA Dalton	1978 EA Webber (ZIM)	2006 N Edwards (WAL)
1919 HG Stewart	1951 ES Irwin	1979 L Norval	2007 L de Jager
1920 HG Stewart	1952 M Janks	1980 E Grienewald	2008 J Blaauw
1921 AL Forster	1953 R Brews	1981 D Suddards	2009 R Dreyer
1922 WCE Stent	1954 A Jackson	1982 N James	2010 L Canter
1923 WCE Stent	1955 B Keyter	1983 C-C Yuan (CHN)	

South African Amateur Stroke Play Championship (inaugurated 1969)

Mount Edgecombe GC

1	Jared Harvey*	69-65-69-71—274
2	David Law (SCO)	64-67-71-72—274

Harvey won play-off at first extra hole

3	Ryan Dreyer	69-69-67-71—276

Red Sea Amateur Tournament *Soma Bay, Egypt*

1	Amr Abu El Ela	74-75-76—225
2	Nasser Yacoub Saleh (BRN)	74-77-79—230
3	Abdelmonem El Shafie	79-79-77—235

Seniors: Abdulla Sultan Al Hakam (BRN) 81-73—154

Americas

Argentine Amateur Championship   *San Isidro GC*

Semi-finals: Patricio Tolosa beat Jarred Harvey (RSA) 2 holes
Daniel Huizing (NED) beat Joaquin Bonjour 5 and 4

Final: Daniel Huizing beat Patricio Tolosa 9 and 7

Barbados Open Amateur Championship   *Royal Westmoreland GC, Barbados*

1	James Johnson	70-67-71—208
2	Carlson Leacock	74-73-74—221
3	Ansari Muhajiri	78-75-72—225

Canadian Amateur Championship (inaugurated 1895)   *Niakwa CC and Elmhurst G&CC, Winnipeg, Manitoba*

1	Mackenzie Hughes (Duncla)	68-72-64-70—274
2	Albin Choi (Toronto)	69-67-70-70—276
3	Jacob Patte (Oshawa)	69-68-74-66—277
	Wilson Bateman (Spruce Grove)	68-67-72-70—277
	Cory Renfrew (Victoria)	67-68-72-70—277
	Corey Conners (Listowel)	71-72-63-71—277

1895	TH Harley	1926	CR Somerville	1958	B Castator	1985	B Franklin (USA)
1896	JS Gillespie	1927	DD Carrick	1959	J Johnston	1986	B Franklin (USA)
1897	WAH Kerr	1928	CR Somerville	1960	RK Alexander	1987	B Franklin (USA)
1898	GS Lyon	1929	E Held	1961	G Cowan	1988	D Roxburgh
1899	Vere C Brown	1930	CR Somerville	1962	R Taylor	1989	P Major
1900	GS Lyon	1931	CR Somerville	1963	N Weslock	1990	W Sye
1901	WAH Kerr	1932	GB Taylor	1964	N Weslock	1991	J Kraemer
1902	FR Martin	1933	A Campbell	1965	G Henry	1992	D Ritchie
1903	GS Lyon	1934	A Campbell	1966	N Weslock	1993	G Simpson
1904	J Percy Taylor	1935	CR Somerville	1967	S Jones	1994	W Sye
1905	GS Lyon	1936	F Haas Jr	1968	J Doyle	1995	G Willis (USA)
1906	GS Lyon	1937	CR Somerville	1969	Wayne McDonald	1996	R McMillan
1907	GS Lyon	1938	T Adams	1970	A Miller	1997	D Goehring
1908	Alex Wilson	1939	K Black	1971	R Siderowf (USA)	1998	C Matthew
1909	E Legge	1940–44	Not played	1972	D Roxburgh	1999	Han Lee (USA)
1910	F Martin	1946	H Martell	1973	G Burns (USA)	2000	Han Lee (USA)
1911	GH Hutton	1947	FR Stranahan (USA)	1974	D Roxburgh	2001	G Paddison (NZL)
1912	George S Lyon	1948	FR Stranahan (USA)	1975	J Nelford	2002	D Pruitt (USA)
1913	GH Turpin	1949	RD Chapman (USA)	1976	J Nelford	2003	R Scott
1914	George S Lyon	1950	W Mawhinney	1977	R Spittle	2004	D Wallace
1915–19	Not played	1951	W McElroy	1978	R Spittle	2005	R Scott
1920	CB Grier	1952	L Bouchey	1979	R Alarcon (MEX)	2006	R Scott
1921	F Thompson	1953	D Cherry	1980	G Olson	2007	N Taylor
1922	CC Fraser	1954	E Harvie Ward (USA)	1981	R Zokol	2008	C Burke
1923	WJ Thompson	1955	M Norman	1982	D Roxburgh	2009	C Burke
1924	F Thompson	1956	M Norman	1983	D Milovic	2010	A Choi
1925	DD Carrick	1957	N Weslock	1984	W Swartz		

Canadian Men's Senior Championship   *Twin Rivers GC, Newfoundland*

1	Chip Lutz (USA)	67-70-72-68—277
2	Paul Simson (USA)	68-71-71-76—286
3	Gudmund Lindbjerg	70-73-76-74—293

Caribbean Amateur Championship (Hoerman Cup)   *Millenium Lakes GC, Trinidad*

1 Puerto Rico 1,170; 2 Dominican Republic 1,198; 3 Trinidad and Tobago 1,203; 4 Barbados 1,203; 5 Jamaica 1,217; 6 Bahamas 1,257; 7 OECS 1,267; 8 Cayman Islands 1,314; 9 Turks and Caicos Islands 1,416

Winning team: Erick Morales, Robert Calvesbert, Alfred Colon, Christian Rivera and Andrew Baez

Mexican Amateur Championship *Campestre Monterey, San Pedro Garza Garcia*

1	Sebastian Vazquez	69-69-69-67—274
2	Eugenio Parrodi Weichers	69-70-66-71—276
3	Cristobal del Solar (CHI)	76-69-67-67—279

111th North and South Men's Amateur Championship *Pinehurst Resort*

Semi-finals: David Erdy (Boonville) beat Brad Benjamin (Rockford) 2 and 1
Jack Fields (Southern Pines) beat Brad Schneider (Valrico) 3 and 2
Final: Jack Fields beat David Erdy 5 and 4

South American Amateur Championship *Buenos Aries CC, Bella Vista, Argentina*

1	Franco Romero (ARG)	72-72-71-68—283
2	Juan Cerda (CHI)	69-69-73-73—285
3	Cristobal Del Solar (CHI)	68-75-72-71—286
	Marcelo Rozo (COL)	69-75-70-72—286
	Mateo Gomez (COL)	68-73-69-76—286

US Amateur Championship *see page 298*

US Mid-Amateur Championship *Shadow Hawk GC, Richmond, Texas*

Semi-finals: Randal Lewis (Alma, MI) beat Nathan Smith (Pittsburgh, PA) at 19th
Kenny Cook (Noblesville, IN) beat John Engler (Augusta, GA) 6 and 5
Final: Randal Lewis beat Kenny Cook 3 and 2
Medallist: Mike McCaffrey (League City, TX) 68-68—136

US Amateur Seniors Championship *Kinloch GC, Manikin-Saboy, Virginia*

Semi-finals: Philip Pleat (Nashua) beat Chip Lutz (Reading) 1 hole
Louis Lee (Heber Springs) beat William Thomas Doughtie (Amarillo) 5 and 4
Final: Louis Lee beat Philip Pleat 1 hole

US Amateur Public Links Championship *Old Macdonald, Bandon Dunes, Oregon*

Semi-finals: Corbin Mills (Easley) beat Harris English (Thomasville) 5 and 3
Jonathan Randolph beat Derek Ernst (Clovis) 3 and 2
Final: Corbin Mills beat Jonathan Randolph at 37th

Asia

Hong Kong Close Amateur Championship *Fanling*

1	Shinichi Mizuno	74-68-74-71—287
2	Max Wong	74-71-72-72—289
3	Terrence Ng	73-74-74-69—290

110th All-India Amateur Championship *Karnkata, Bangalore*

Semi-finals: Pritim Haridas beat Udayan Mane 3 and 2
Senappa Chikkarangappa beat N Thangaraja 1 hole
Final: Senappa Chikkarangappa beat Pritim Haridas 3 and 2

50th Japanese Amateur Championship *Myoshi CC (West Course)*

Semi-finals: Katsuyuki Sakurai beat Koki Furuta 2 and 1
Yoshinori Fujimoto beat Yosuke Asaji 2 and 1
Final: Katsuki Sakurai beat Yoshinori Fujimoto 1 hole

109th Malaysian Open Amateur Championship *A'Famosa GR*

1	Daniel Bringolf (AUS)	67-69-67-71—276
2	Chieh Po Lee (TPE)	65-67-71-77—280
3	Abhijit Chadha (IND)	69-70-71-71—281

Malaysian Close Amateur Championship *Seri Selangor GC*

1	Gavin Kyle Green	73-71-72—216
2	Ng Choo Teck	70-76-75—221
3	Abel Tam	82-71-71—224

Pakistan Amateur Championship *Islamabad GC*

1	Hamza Taimur Amiri (Islamabad)	71-72-78-71—292
2	Muhammad Ali Hai (Karachi)	76-72-73-75—296
3	Taimur Hassan Amin (Islamabad)	77-72-78-73—300

Singapore National Amateur Championship *Raffles CC*

Semi-finals: Jerome Ng beat Gregory Foo 2 and 1
Lam Zhiqun beat Marc Ong 3 and 1

Final: Lam Zhiqun beat Jerome Ng 4 and 2

3rd place play-off: Ong beat Foo at 21st.

Medallist: Gregory Foo 71-70—141

Taiwan Amateur Championship *Sunrise G&CC*

1	Taihei Sato (JPN)	72-72-68-64—276
2	Fei-Hao Yang (TPE)	71-71-75-67—284
2	Wei-Lun Wang (TPE)	74-69-69-72—284

Australasia

Srixon Australian Amateur Championship (inaugurated 1894) *Victoria GC, Melbourne*

Semi-finals: Matthew Steiger (NSW) beat Bryden Macpherson (VIC) 5 and 4
Ben Campbell (NZL) beat Ryan Fox (NZL) at 21st

Final: Matthew Steiger beat Ben Campbell 1 hole

1894	LA Whyte	1922	Ivo Witton	1950	H Berwick	1974	TR Gale
1895	RAA Balfour	1923	Ivo Witton	1951	Peter Heard	1975	C Bonython
	Melville	1924	H Sinclair	1952	R Stevens	1976	P Sweeney
1896	HA Howden	1925	H Sinclair	1953	Peter Heard	1977	AY Gresham
1897	HA Howden	1926	Len Nettlefold	1954	P Toogood	1978	MA Clayton
1898	HA Howden	1927	WS Nankivell	1955	J Rayner	1979	J Kelly
1899	CES Gillies	1928	Len Nettlefold	1956	H Berwick	1980	R Mackay
1900	LA Whyte	1929	MJ Ryan	1957	BH Warren	1981	O Moore
1901	HA Howden	1930	HW Hattersley	1958	K Hartley	1982	EM Couper
1902	H Macneil	1931	HL William	1959	BW Devlin	1983	WJ Smith
1903	DG Soutar	1932	Dr RH Bettington	1960	Ted Ball	1984	BP King
1904	JD Howden	1933	WL Hope	1961	T Crow	1985	B Ruangkit (THA)
1905	Hon. Michael Scott	1934	TS McKay	1962	D Bachli	1986	DJ Ecob
1906	EA Gill	1935	J Ferrier	1963	J Hayes (RSA)	1987	B Johns
1907	Hon. Michael Scott	1936	J Ferrier	1964	B Baker	1988	S Bouvier
1908	Clyde Pearce	1937	HL Williams	1965	K Donohoe	1989	SJ Conran
1909	Hon. Michael Scott	1938	J Ferrier	1966	W Britten	1990	CD Gray
1910	Hon. Michael Scott	1939	J Ferrier	1967	J Muller	1991	LKJ Parsons
1911	JD Howden	1940–45	*Not played*	1968	R Stott	1992	MS Campbell (NZL)
1912	Hector Morrison	1946	AN Waterson	1969	RA Shearer	1993	GJ Chalmers
1913	AR Lempriere	1947	HW Hattersley	1970	PA Bennett	1994	W Bennett (ENG)
1914–19	*Not played*	1948	D Bachli	1971	GR Hicks	1995	MC Goggin
1920	EL Apperley	1949	WD Ackland-	1972	CR Kaye	1996	DC Gleeson
1921	CL Winser		Horman	1973	RJ Jenner	1997	K Felton

1998	B Rumford	2002	K Barnes	2006	T Stewart	2010	M Jager
1999	BM Jones	2003	J Doherty (SCO)	2007	R Blizard		
2000	BP Lamb	2004	A Martin	2008	A Kristiansen (NOR)		
2001	S Bowditch	2005	E Ramsay (SCO)	2009	S Arnold		

Srixon Australian Stroke Play Championship (inaugurated 1958)
Victoria GC and Woodlands GC

1	Cameron Smith (QLD)*	66-71-70-68—275
2	David Coupland (ENG)	72-71-67-65—275

Smith won at first extra hole

3	Ben Campbell (NZL)	71-69-70-69—279

Australian Men's Mid-Amateur Championship *The National GC (Ocean course)*

1	Jason Perry (VIC)	73-68-74—215
2	Warwick Oxenford (QLD)	77-72-75—224
3	Matthew McKenna (VIC)	75-72-78—225
	Guy Wall (NSW)	80-73-72—225

Lion Foundation New Zealand Amateur Championship (inaugurated 1893)
Russley GC, Christchurch

Semi-finals: Steven Heyes beat Joshua Munn at 19th
Matthew Perry beat Blair Riordan at 20th

Final: Matthew Perry (Hamilton) beat Steven Heyes (Russley) 4 and 2

1893	JA Somerville	1924	L Quin	1957	EJ McDougall	1985	G Power
1894	H Macneil	1925	TH Horton	1958	WJ Godfrey	1986	P O'Malley (AUS)
1895	G Gosset	1926	ADS Duncan	1959	SG Jones	1987	O. Kendall
1896	MS Todd	1927	S Morpeth	1960	R Newdick	1988	B Hughes (AUS)
1897	D Pryde	1928	TH Horton	1961	SG Jones	1989	L Peterson
1898	W Pryde	1929	S Morpeth	1962	SG Jones	1990	M Long
1899	ADS Duncan	1930	HA Black	1963	J Durry	1991	L Parsons (AUS)
1900	ADS Duncan	1931	R Wagg	1964	SG Jones	1992	R Lee
1901	ADS Duncan	1932	R Wagg	1965	J Durry	1993	P Tatamaugi
1902	SH Gollan	1933	BV Wright	1966	SG Jones	1994	P Fitzgibbon
1903	K Tareha	1934	BM Silk	1967	J Durry	1995	S Bittle
1904	AH Fisher	1935	JP Hornabrook	1968	BA Stevens	1996	D Somerville
1905	ADS Duncan	1936	JP Hornabrook	1969	G Stevenson	1997	C Johns
1906	SH Gollan	1937	BM Silk	1970	EJ McDougall	1998	B MacDonald
1907	ADS Duncan	1938	PGF Smith	1971	SG Jones	1999	A Duffin
1908	HC Smith	1939	JP Hornabrook	1972	RC Murray	2000	E Burgess
1909	ADS Duncan	1940–45	*Not played*	1973	MN Nicholson	2001	B Gallie
1910	HB Lusk	1946	WG Horne	1974	RM Barltrop	2002	M Fraser (AUS)
1911	ADS Duncan	1947	BM Silk	1975	SF Reese	2003	J Nitties (AUS)
1912	BB Wood	1948	A Gibbs	1976	TR Pulman	2004	G Flint (AUS)
1913	BB Wood	1949	J Holden	1977	TR Pulman	2005	MI Brown (AUS)
1914	ADS Duncan	1950	DL Woon	1978	F Nobilo	2006	A Green
1915–18	*Not played*	1951	DL Woon	1979	J Durry	2007	D Lee
1919	H Crosse	1952	H Berwick	1980	PE Hartstone	2008	T Spearman-Burn
1920	S Morpeth	1953	DL Woon	1981	T Cochrane	2009	M Jager (AUS)
1921	AG Syme	1954	DL Woon	1982	J Peters	2010	M Jager (AUS)
1922	ADS Duncan	1955	SG Jones	1983	C Taylor		
1923	J Goss Jr	1956	PA Toogood	1984	J Wagner		

Lion Foundation New Zealand Stroke Play Championship (inaugurated 1969)
Russley GC, Christchurch

1	Ryan Fox (Royal Auckland)	68-69-73-73—283
2	Shaun Jones (Russley)	68-69-76-75—288
3	Blake McGrory (AUS)	73-72-72-72—289

Fiji Amateur Championship   *Fiji GC, Suva*

1	Vikrant Chandra	70-69-69—208
2	Olaf Allen	72-71-78—221
3	Anuresh Chandra	72-77-74—223

Europe

Austrian Amateur Championship   *GC Adamstal*

1	Joel Stalter*	63-72-72-73—280
2	Manuel Trappel	70-71-69-70—280
2	Steven Walther	72-65-72-72—281

Stalter beat Trappel in the play-off

Belgian Amateur Omnium Classic   *Limburg GC*

1	Pierre Alexis Rolland	71-71-71-69—282
2	Steven De Wispelaere	76-70-67-74—287
3	Cedric Van Wassenhove	70-70-74-74—288

British Amateur Championship   *see page 290*

British Seniors Open Amateur Championship   (inaugurated 1969)   *Walton Heath GC*

1	Chip Lutz (USA)	72-71-71—214
2	Arthur Pierse (Tipperary)	73-72-70—215
3	Frank Ford III (USA)	69-70-77—216

Bulgarian State National Amateur Championship   *Pirin G&CC*

1	Peter Kaloyanov	79-79—158
2	Emil Markov	80-81—161
3	Radoslav Rashev	81-81—162

Danish Amateur Championship   *Silkeborg GC*

1	Kasper Estrup	76-70-72-73—291
2	Morten Findsen Schou	74-73-77-70—294
3	Mads Sogaard	71-80-72-72—295

English Open Amateur Stroke Play Championship (Brabazon Trophy)
Burnham & Berrow   (inaugurated 1947)

1	Neil Raymond (Corhampton)	70-68-74-75—287
2	Alan Dunbar (Rathmore)	72-68-79-69—288
	Andy Sullivan (Nuneaton)	75-72-70-71—288

English Amateur Championship   (inaugurated 1925)   *Woburn*

Leading Qualifier: Sam Whitehead (Woburn) 68-71—139

Semi-Finals: Steven Brown (Wentworth) beat Tyrrell Hatton (Harleyford) 3 and 2
Jamie Clare (Burnham & Berrow) beat Callum Shinkwin (Moor Park) 2 and 1

Final: Steven Brown beat Jamie Clare 7 and 5

English Seniors' Amateur Championship   *Northamptonshire County and Northampton*

1	Alan Squires (Oldham)	69-73-79—221
2	Chris Reynolds (Littlestone)	78-70-78—226
3	Graham Meddings (Hever Castle)	73-72-82—227

English Open Mid-Amateur Championship (Logan Trophy) *Ipswich (Purdis Heath)*

1	Neill Williams (Walton Heath)	68-70-68—206
2	Steven Graham (Littlehampton)	76-69-64—209
3	Richard Latham (Woodhall Spa)	67-74-72—213

English County Champions Tournament *Woodhall Spa*

1	Jamie Rutherford (Hertfordshire)	70-66—136
2	Ben Stow (Wiltshire)	71-68—139
3	William Bowe (Cumbria)	69-74—143

Estonian Amateur Championship *Saare Golf*

1	Davis Puksts (LAT)	81-79-75—235
2	Egeti Liiv	81-81-78—240
3	Jani Hietanen (FIN)	87-81-77—245

European Amateur Championship *see page 295*

European Seniors' Championship (inaugurated 1999) *Achensee, Austria*

1	Tomas Persson (SWE)*	72-71-69—212
2	Hans-Günter Retter (GER)	71-70-71—212

Persson won at the third extra hole

3	Knut Skabo (NOR)	76-73-70—219
	Mats Andersson (SWE)	73-74-72—219

Super Seniors (over 65): David Lane (ENG)   224

European Mid-Amateur Championship (inaugurated 1999) *Solta. Norway*

1	Marco Willberg (FIN)	75-75-71—221
2	Jacobo Cestino (ESP)	71-71-80—222
3	Niklas Rosenqvist (SWE)	77-73-73—223
	Jani Michelsson (FIN)	72-74-77—223

Finnish Open Amateur Championship *Tali GC*

1	Albert Eckhardt	72-67-68—207
2	Atte Rauhala	70-69-69—208
	Miki Kuronen	66-68-74—208

French Amateur Championship *Chantilly GC*

1	Gary Stal	72-66-71-71—280
2	Eduardo Espana	71-68-76-73—288
3	Benedict Staben (GER)	72-72-69-76—289

German Amateur Championship *G&CC Seddiner See, Berlin*

1	Daan Huizing (NED)	71-68-71-71—281
2	Sebastian Kannler	72-69-72-69—282
3	Daniel Schmieding	69-67-71-77—284

Irish Amateur Open Championship *Royal Dublin*

(inaugurated 1892 but not contested between 1960 and 1994)

1	Rhys Pugh (Vale of Glamorgan) (WAL)*	72-70-74-78—294
2	Gordon Stevenson (Whitecraigs)	74-69-76-75—294

Pugh won at the third extra hole

3	Daan Huizing (NED)	77-70-74-74—295
	Paul Dunne (Greystones)	73-71-79-72—295

Irish Amateur Close Championship (inaugurated 1893)   *Shannon*

1	Paul Cutler (Portstewart)	69-73-77-71—290
2	Aaron Kearney (Castlerock)	76-71-72-73—292
	Pat Murray (Limerick)	75-74-70-73—292

Irish Seniors' Amateur Open Championship   *Rosslare*

1	Hugh Smyth (Mourne)	78-75-75—228
2	Adrian Morrow (Portmarnock)	84-73-72—229
3	Anthony Smith (The Island)	81-74-76—231

Irish Seniors' Amateur Close Championship   *Thurles*

1	Garth McGimpsey (Bangor)	74-69-72—215
2	Maurice Kelly (Killeen)	75-74-72—221
3	Adrian Morrow (Portmarnock)	74-76-72—222

Italian International Open   *Villa d'Este GC*

Final: Nicolas D'incau (SUI) beat Adrien Saddier

Medallist: Florian Loutre (FRA)   66-67—133

Latvian Amateur Championship   *Ozo GC*

1	Mathias Boesmans (BEL)	67-77-75—219
2	Michele Cea (ITA)	74-74-75—223
3	Jani Hietanen (FIN)	73-75-76—224

Lithuanian Amateur Championship   *Capitals GC*

1	Kornelijus Baliukonis	74-78-70—222
2	Andrius Belkus (AUS)	76-73-79—228
3	Davis Puksts (LAT)	84-71-75—230

Luxembourg Amateur Championship   *Golf Club Grand-Ducal*

1	Robbie Van West (NED)	65-69-67—201
2	Rutger Buschow (NED)	67-68-69—204
3	Joel Stalter (AUT)	62-75-70—207

61st Portuguese Amateur Championship   *Campo Montado*

1	Eddie Pepperell (ENG)	68-69-72—209
2	Jean Pierre Verselin (FRA)	70-73-67—210
3	Daan Avizing (NED)	72-70-69—211
	Domenico Geminiani (ITA)	71-73-67—211
	Edouardo Espara (FRA)	74-73-64—211

Russian Amateur Championship   *Pestovo G and YC*

1	Steve Uzzell (ENG)	67-69-71-73—280
2	Jamie Abbott (ENG)	70-71-74-75—290
	Peter Svajlen (SVK)	72-72-71-75—290

Scottish Amateur Championship (inaugurated 1922)   *Western Gailes*

Semi-Finals: David Law (Hazlehead) beat James Ross (Royal Burgess) 4 and 3
Daniel Kay (Dunbar) beat James Byrne (Banchory) at 19th

Final: David Law beat Daniel Kay 6 and 5

Scottish Open Amateur Stroke Play Championship (inaugurated 1967)

Blairgowrie Lansdowne

1	Andy Sullivan (Nuneaton) (ENG)	65-71-77-69—282
2	Steven Brown (Wentworth) (ENG)	73-67-73-70—283
3	Paul Shields (Kirkhill)	69-73-72-72—286

Scottish Seniors Open Amateur Stroke Play Championship *Irvine (Bogside)*

1	Charles Banks (Stanton on the Wolds)	73-74-73—220
2	John Fraser (Royal Burgess)	75-71-76—222
3	Ian Hutcheon (Monifieth)	74-77-73—224
	John Baldwin (Sunningdale)	76-76-72—224

Scottish Seniors Match Play Championship *Monifieth*

Semi-Finals: Ian Brotherston (Dumfries & County) beat Scott MacDonald (Dunfermline) 3 and 1
Gordon MacDonald (Callander) beat Fraser McCluskey (Royal Burgess) 1 hole
Final: Ian Brotherston beat Gordon MacDonald 3 and 2

Scottish Champion of Champions *Leven*

1	Brian Soutar (Leven)	69-75-68-67—279
2	Kyle McClung (Wigtownshire)	72-71-72-68—283
3	Jordan Findlay (Fraserburgh)	69-69-76-70—284

UniCredit Slovakia Amateur Championship *Golf Resort Black Stork, Velka Lomnica*

1	Juraj Zvarik	77-71-70—218
2	Kasper Estrup (DEN)	72-70-76—218
3	David Strouf (CZE)	74-77-71—222
	Lukas Lipold (AUT)	81-69-72—222

Slovenian International Amateur Championship *Bled GC*

1	Jacob Ziegler (GER)*	73-71-71-69—284
	Simon Zach (CZE)	71-73-73-67—284

*Ziegler beat Zach in the play-off

3	Teemu Toivonen (FIN)	71-72-71-71—285

78th Spanish Amateur Championship *Real Club de Golf El Prat, Barcelona*

1	Goncalo Pinto (Villamoura)	73-68-65-73—279
2	Bernardo Frere (Estoril)	75-67-72-70—284
3	Miquel Valdrez (Estella)	74-75-66-73—288

Swiss International Amateur Championship *Ascona*

1	Andrea Gorini	68-69-67-63—267
2	Yannick Bludau (GER)	68-65-70-66—269
3	Filippo Bergamaschi (ITA)	71-68-68-65—272
	Mattia Milaro (ITA)	67-69-66-70—272

Turkish Amateur Championship *Atalya Sultan course, Turkey*

1	Daan Huizing (NED)	75-66-67-68—276
2	Marcel Schneider (GER)	68-68-71-72—279
	Mathieu Decottignies-Lafon (FRA)	72-71-66-70—279
	Moritz Lambert (GER)	73-65-75-66—279

Team event: 1 Germany 412; 2 Netherlands 417; 3 Switzerland 427; 4 Scotland, Denmark 429; 6 Italy, England 434; 8 Turkey 436; 9 Czech Republic 437; 10 Finland 438; 11 Russia 460; 12 Slovenia 471

Winning team: Benedict Staben, Marcel Schneider and Moritz Lambert

Welsh Amateur Championship (inaugurated 1895) *Aberdovey*

Semi-Finals: Jason Shufflebotham (Prestatyn) beat Lee Jones (Conwy) 3 and 2
Rhys Pugh (Vale of Glamorgan) beat Richard Hooper (Neath) at 21st

Final: Jason Shufflebotham beat Rhys Pugh 1 hole

Welsh Open Amateur Stroke Play Championship (inaugurated 1967) *St Pierre*

1	Darren Wright (Rowlands Castle)	71-72-70-71—284
2	Ben Stow (Rushmore)	72-75-70-71—288
3	Ben Loughrey (Wrag Barn)	70-74-70-76—290

Welsh Seniors' Close Amateur Championship (inaugurated 1975) *always at Aberdovey*

1	Glyn Rees (Fleetwood)	75-71-73—219
2	Paul Bloomfield (Chippenham)	74-80-72—226
3	Basil Griffths (Llanymynach)	74-79-77—230
	Peter Middleton (Churston)	77-74-79—230

Welsh Seniors' Open Championship *Rhuddlan*

1	Glyn Rees (Fleetwood)	69-73-76—218
2	Andrew Stracey (Littlestone)	75-74-73—222
3	Christopher Reynolds (Littlestone)	76-73-74—223
	Adrian Donkersley (Gerrards Cross)	74-75-74—223

Welsh Tournament of Champions *always at Cradoc*

1	James Frazer (Pennard)	74-66—140
2	Jonathan Davison (Llanwern)	71-73—144
3	Joe Vickery (Newport)	74-72—146

Asian amateur champion Matsuyama wins Japanese pro event

Two birdies on the back nine and a glorious eagle at the last hole enabled 19-year-old Hideki Matsuyama, who a few weeks earlier had successfully defended his Asian Amateur title in Singapore, to win the Mitsui-Sumitomo Taiheiyo Masters on the Japanese circuit.

His closing 68 on the Gotemba course for a winning 13-under-par 203 in the rain-shortened 54 hole event gave him a two shot victory over Toro Taniguchi.

"I did not expect to win. I was only wanting to be low amateur," said Matsuyama who played all four rounds in his first appearance at the Masters last April and finished low amateur.

The talented Japanese golfer was only the third amateur ever to win a professional event in his home country. Twenty-five-year-old amateur Masahiro Kuramoto won the Chugoku-Shikoku Open in 1980 and Ryo Ishikawa won the 2007 Munsingwear Open KSB Cup when only 15 years of age.

Fifteen years on "Old Man" Lewis can think about The Masters

When Randal Lewis from Alma, Michigan, was in the final of the US Mid-Amateur Championship in 1996 and lost over 18-holes to John "Spider" Miller he admitted that what upset his focus on that occasion was thinking that victory could earn him a place in the Masters.

This time at Shadow Creek in Richmond, Texas, in a final now played over 36-holes he did not give Augusta a thought as he beat Kenny Cook from Noblesville, Indiana, 3 and 2. Well, not until he had won because this time he is likely to make it to the first major of the year.

Lewis at 54 is the oldest winner of the Robert T Jones Memorial Trophy and the Championship gold medal. In fact he is almost 20 years older than the average age of the previous 30 winners of the title – 34.8 yrs!

En route to victory he beat the Championship Medallist Mike McCaffrey and the defending champion Nathan Smith yet only just scraped through to the knock out section on 148 – 12 behind leader McCaffrey. Nick-named "Old Man Lewis" the champion is married with two sons the youngest of whom has the Christian name Nicklaus!

Walker Cup named Scottish Sports Event of the Year

The Walker Cup was voted Scottish Sports Event of the Year at the 2011 Scottish Sports Awards.

Royal Aberdeen hosted the two-day biennial men's team competition last September which attracted thousands of spectators to watch the 10 best amateurs from Great Britain & Ireland take on their counterparts from the United States.

GB&I went into the contest as underdogs against a US team that included six of the world's top 10 amateurs but brilliant performances, from among others Welsh teenager Rhys Pugh and Open Championship Silver Medallist Tom Lewis, saw the team win for the first time since 2003.

Captained by Nigel Edwards, the victory means that GB&I has now claimed four of the last five Walker Cups played on home soil, dating back to 1995 at Royal Porthcawl in Wales.

R&A Championship Operations Director Rhodri Price, who was GB&I Team Manager at Royal Aberdeen, said: "The Club staged a wonderful Walker Cup that will live long in the memories of all those involved. Despite having to deal with some pretty severe wind and rain, the big crowds witnessed thrilling golf and were able to toast a home victory. This award recognises the hard work put in by all those involved in staging what was a truly world class sporting event."

Amateur winners of professional events – a rare breed

When Asian Amateur champion Hideki Matsuyama beat the professionals to win the Mitsui Sumitomo Visa Taiheiyo Masters in the shadow of Mount Fuji, he was only the third amateur to have done so on the Japanaese Tour.

The other two? – Masahiro Kuramoto who won the Chushikoku Open in 1980 and Ryo Ishukawa who took the Munsingwear Open KSB Cup in 2007 at the age of just 15 years and eight months.

Amateur wins are rare on other Tours as well although on the European Tour Shane Lowry at the 3Irish Open at Drogheda and Danny Lee at the Johnnie Walker Asian Classic at The Vines did so in the same year – 2009. The only other amateur winner on the Tour since it started in 1972 has been Pablo Martin who won the Estoril Open de Portugal in 2007.

On the Asian Tour there have also been three amateur winners of pro events – Korean Kim Dae-sub who took the Korean Open in 1998, New Zealander Eddie Lee who won the 2002 Maekyung Open in Korea and Chinnerat Phadungsil from Thailand who was successful in the 2005 Double A International in his own country.

Since 1945 there have been six amateur victories on the PGA Tour in America. That year Fred Haas won the Memphis Invitational and Cary Middlecoff the North and South Open. In 1954 Gene Littler took the San Diego Open and in 1956 Doug Sanders was successful in the Canadian Open which is to date the only amateur victory on the Canadian Tour.

More recently, Scott Verplank surprised the professionals when he won the prestigious Western Open and left-hander Phil Mickelson was the winner of the 1991 Northern Telecom Open before he turned professional.

In 1904 in Australia the amateur golfer The Hon. Michael Scott was the first winner of the Australian Open and won again in 1907. Between 1904 and 1932 there were 13 wins by amateurs including three by Carnegie Clark and five by Ivo Whitton.

Jim Ferrier was an amateur when he won in 1938 and successfully defended a year later but in more recent times only Bruce Devlin in 1960 and Aaron Baddeley and Brett Rumford in 1999 have taken titles as amateurs. Baddeley won the Australian Open in 1999 and successfully defended the following year as a pro! One week after Baddeley's 1999 success, Rumford won the ANZ Tour Players' Championship in Queensland.

In the last 65 years there have been only three amateur winners of the South African Open – Ronnie Glennie in1947, Arthur Stewart in 1958 and Denis Hutchinson in 1959. No statistics are available for the Sunshine Tour.

USA State Championships 2011

US unless stated

Alabama	Smylie Kaufman (SP)	Farm Links
	McLaine Leberte (MP)	Limestone Springs
Alaska	David Hamilton	Palmer and Anchorage
Arizona	Bowen Osborn	DC Ranch
Arkansas	Joey Nichols (SP)	Shadow Valley
	Juan Gonzalez (MP)	Hurricane
California	Bharak Patel	Olympic Club
Colorado	Zakhai Brown	Common Ground
Connecticut	Tommy McDonagh	Rolling Hills
Delaware	Dan Ott (SP)	Back Creek
	Greg Wolfe (MP)	Back Creek
Florida	Tyler McCumber (SP)	Doral
	Don Bell (MP)	Southern Hills Plantation
Georgia	David Noll Jr	Cherokee
Hawaii	Lorens Chan (SP)	Pearl
	David Fink (MP)	Ohau
Idaho	Tanner Higham (SP)	Teton Springs
	Jordan Hamblin (MP)	The Valley Club
Illinois	Brad Hopfinger	Glen Oak
Indiana	Tyler Duncan (SP)	Otter Creek
	Bob Stephens (MP)	Wood Wind
Iowa	Gene Elliott (SP)	Glen Oaks
	Jon Olson (MP)	Burlington
Kansas	Hunter Sparks	Hallbrook
Kentucky	Patrick Newcomb	Kearney Hill
Louisiana	Greg Berthelot	Oakbourne
Maine	Ryan Gay	Portland
Maryland	Mark Cusic	Hillendale
Massachussets	Ryan Riley	Wyantenuckj
Michigan	Marty Jeppeson (SP)	Barton Hills
	Willie Mack III (MP)	Boyne Resorts

Minnesota	Donald Constable	White Bear
Mississippi	Clay Homan	Old Waverley
Missouri	Richard Berkmeyer	Boone Valley
Montana	Nathan Bailey	Canyon River
Nebraska	Andy Sajevic	Shadow Ridge
Nevada	Jonathan Cockerill	Hidden Valley
New Hampshire	Nicholas MacDonald	Hudson
New Jersey	David Sanders	Trump National
New Mexico	Greg Condon	Albuquerque
New York	Dominic Bozzelli	Oak Hill
N. Carolina	Harold Varner	Salisbury
N. Dakota	Tim Skarperud	Grand Forks
Ohio	Korey Ward	NCR
Oklahoma	Cameron Myers	Meadowbrook
Oregon	Nick Chianello (SP)	Cresswell
	Jack Dukeminier (MP)	Waverley
Pennsylvania	Andrew J Mason	Lancaster
Rhode Island	Charlie Blanchard	Warwick
S. Carolina	Austin Reeves	Colleton River Plantation
S. Dakota	Tom Carlson	Brookings
Tennessee	Bobby Hudson	Colonial
Texas	Kelly Kraft	Austin
Utah	Jeff Evans	Soldier Hollow
Vermont	Devin Komline	Neshobe
Virginia	Scott Shingler	Virginian
Washington	Jarred Bossio	McCormick Woods
W. Virginia	Christian Brand	The Greenbrier Resort
Wisconsin	Mike McDonald	Maple Bluff
Wyoming	Edward Stewart	GC at Devil's Tower

Canadian Provincial Championships 2011

Canadian unless stated

Alberta	Scott Stiles	Stoney Plain
British Columbia	David Rose	The Dunes
Manitoba	Jesse Skelton	Portage
New Brunswick	Mathieu Gingras	Royal Oaks
Newfoundland and Labrador	Adam Stanley	Bally Holy

Nova Scotia	Eric Banks	Truro
Ontario	Mark Hoffman	Brampton
Prince Edward Island	Chris Welton	Belvedere
Quebec	Nicolas Fortin	Alpin
Saskatchewan	Troy Bulmer	The Legends

Australian State Championships 2011

Australian unless stated

New South Wales   Cumberland, Liverpool and
                NSW GCs
Final: Jack Senior (Haysham, England) beat Andy
  Sullivan (Nuneaton, England) 3 and 2
Medallist: Andy Sullivan
Queensland   Pacific Harbour and Arundel
                Hills GCs
Final: Jake Higginbottom (The Australian) beat Tim
  Hart (Indooroopilly) 2 and 1
Medallist: Daniel McGraw
South Australia   Mount Osmond, Blackwood and
                Glenelg GCs
Final: Brad Moules (Royal Adelaide) beat Chris
  Austin (Tee Tree Gully) 1 hole

Tasmania   CC Tasmania
Final: Kalem Richardson (Riverside) beat Nathan
  Gatehouse (Tasmania) at 37th
Victoria (Match Play)
Final: Nathan Holmes beat Troy Moses
Victoria (Stroke Play)
  Cruze Strange (Royal Perth) 284
Western Australia Melville Glades GC
Final: Matt Stieger (NSW) beat Ray Chow
  (Gosnells, WA) at 37th
Medallist: Ben Seward

South African Provincial Championships 2011

South African nationality unless stated

Cape Province	Rickus Nortje	George and Kingswood	Gauteng North	Jaco Mouton	Pecanwood
Central Gauteng	Daniel Hammond	Royal Johannesburg	KwaZulu-Natal	Michael Hollick	Beachwood
			Limpopo	Brandon Stone	Polokwane
Eastern Province and Border	Philip Kruse	Fish River Sun	Mpumalanga	Hendre Celliers	Middleburg
			Northern Cape	Theunis Pieters	Kimberley
Eastern Province Open	Ray Taverner	Port Elizabeth	North West	Brandon Stone	Potchefstroom
			Southern Cape	C J Du Plessis	Knysna
Free State & Northern Cape	Daniel Hammond	Bloemfontein	Western	Jarred Harvey (SP)	Westlake
				Graham Van der Merwe (MP)	

New Zealand Provincial Championships 2011

New Zealand nationality unless stated

Otago SP	Jeremy Hall	Balmacewen GC, Dunedin
South Island SP	Vaughan McCall	Timaru
North Island SP	Ryan Fox	Whitford Park

Month by month in 2011

For only the second time since 1913 a major is won by a player appearing in his very first one. After Ben Curtis at the 2003 Open it is Keegan Bradley in the USPGA Championship. Five behind with three to go he birdies the next two and wins a play-off after Jason Dufner had three-bogeys in a row. It is also the first major victory by someone using a long putter.

National Orders of Merit 2011

England – PING Order of Merit

1	Tom Lewis (Welwyn Garden City)	1201	6	Ben Stow (Rushmore)	655
2	Andrew Sullivan (Nuneaton)	1023	7	Stiggy Hodgson (Sunningdale)	644
3	Steven Brown (Wentworth)	976	8	Neil Raymond (Corhampton)	517
4	Tyrrell Hatton (Harleyford)	818	9	Craig Hinton (The Oxfordshire)	508
5	Jack Senior (Heysham)	693	10	Ben Loughrey (Wrag Barn)	427

Ireland – Willie Gill Award

1	Paul Cutler (Portstewart)	800	6	Pat Murray (Limerick)	250
2	Alan Dunbar (Rathmore)	504	7	Aaron Kearney (Castlerock)	235
3	Richard O'Donovan (Lucan)	314	8	Patrick McCrudden (Royal Portrush)	200
4	Stephen Walsh (Baltinglass/UCD)	310	9	Nick Grant (Knock)	190
5	Andrew Hogan (Newlands)	278	10	Harry Diamond (Belvoir Park)	186

Scotland – Order of Merit

1	James White (Lundin)	879	6	David Law (Hazlehead)	382
2	Graeme Robertson (Glenbervie)	768	7	Peter Latimer (St Andrews New)	370
3	Scott Crichton (Aberdour)	448	8	Adam Dunton (McDonald)	365
4	Paul Shields (Kirkhill)	414	9	Fraser McKenna (Balmore)	345
5	Greg Paterson (St Andrews New)	384		Philip McLean (Peterhead)	345

Wales – Pinnacle Order of Merit

1	Rhys Pugh (Vale of Glamorgan)	623	6	Rhys Enoch (Truro)	311
2	Oliver Farr (Ludlow)	601	7	Richard Bentham (St Pierre)	272
3	Jason Shufflebotham (Prestatyn)	400	8	Ben Westgate (Trevose)	240
4	James Frazer (Pennard)	348	9	Joe Vickery (Newport)	235
5	Alastair Jones (Radyr)	330	10	Richard Hooper (Neath)	221

New Zealand Order of Merit

(events played in brackets)

1	Ryan Fox	(20)	256.04	6	Joshua Munn	(13)	78.14
2	Benjamin Campbell	(18)	214.68	7	Keelan Kilpatrick	(16)	77.85
3	Vaughan McCall	(16)	139.51	8	Blair Riordan	(11)	74.99
4	Matthew Perry	(19)	109.80	9	Cameron Jones	(21)	63.89
5	Sam An	(21)	82.46	10	Brad Hayward	(15)	57.32

Australian Order of Merit

(events played in brackets)

1	Matt Steiger (NSW)	(18)	101.0	6	Ryan Fox (NZL)	(7)	70.08
2	Jake Higginbotham (NSW)	(10)	91.23	7	Daniel Bringolf (NSW)	(12)	67.76
3	Brett Drewitt (NSW)	(11)	89.77	8	Brad Moules (SA)	(11)	66.19
4	Ben Campbell (NZL)	(9)	88.42	9	Nathan Holman (VIC)	(13)	65.85
5	Cameron Smith (QLD)	(9)	73.58	10	Luke Humphries (NSW)	(10)	55.57

South African Order of Merit

1	Brandon Stone (GN)	51.2	6	Jared Harvey (KN)		34.2
2	Haydn Porteous (CG)	42.6	7	Shaun Smith (SC)		26.4
3	Ruan de Smidt (CG)	41.9	8	Daniel Hammond (CG)		25.7
4	Graham Van Der Merwe (CG)	38.0	9	Riekus Nortje (SC)		25.4
5	CJ du Plessis (LP)	35.8	10	Hendre Celliers (GN)		23.6

Austrian Order of Merit
(events played in brackets)

1	Manuel Trappel	(9)	303.00	6	John Steiner	(11)	72.84
2	Luke Nemecz	(13)	153.68	7	Markus Habeler	(5)	67.94
3	Matthias Schwab	(8)	84.44	8	Amin Hanza	(10)	60.40
4	Philipp Fendt	(4)	84.00	9	Robin Goger	(7)	48.24
5	Tano Kromer	(6)	73.91	10	Patrick Oswald	(7)	47.94

German Order of Merit
(events played in brackets)

1	Marcel Schneider	(14)	1957	6	Julian Kunzenbacker	(7)	1214
2	Benedict Staben	(16)	1830	7	Maximilian Rotluff	(10)	1206
3	Sebastian Kannler	(11)	1380	8	Maximilian Mehles	(10)	1192
4	Philip Westermann	(11)	1273	9	Moritz Lambert	(7)	1072
5	Stephen Jager	(8)	1254	10	Yannick Bludau	(7)	1036

French Order of Merit

1	Gary Stal	2308.66	6	Antoine Schwarz	1362.42
2	Julien Brun	2286.17	7	Adrien Saddier	1272.57
3	Edouardo Espana	1653,08	8	Kenny Subregis	1025.75
4	Adrian Otegui Jauregui	1582.17	9	Clement Sordet	1025.16
5	Sebastian Gros	1427.83	10	Lionel Weber	913.92

Canadian Order of Merit
(events played in brackets)

1	Mackenzie Hughes (ON)	(8)	950	6	Garrett Rank (ON)	(8)	518
2	Mitch Sutton (ON)	(7)	785	7	Mark Hoffman (ON)	(2)	450
3	Albin Choi (ON)	(5)	770	8	Wilson Bateman (AB)	(2)	440
4	Richard Jung (ON)	(4)	558	9	Eric Banks (NS)	(3)	411
5	Cory Renfrew (BC)	(4)	520	10	Jacob Patte (ON)	(2)	400

Award winning reporter Jim Huber dies at 67

Emmy Award-winning essayist Jim Huber has died of acute leukemia. He was 67. Among many achievements in his career, Huber was the signature host in support of PGA of America pro-grammes. For eight consecutive years, Huber hosted The PGA of America Awards, conducted annually during the PGA Merchandise Show in Orlando, Florida. Since the mid-1990s he alternated between commentator/reporter and master of ceremonies at the season-ending PGA Grand Slam of Golf.

"Anyone who knew Jim Huber beyond his wonderful words in front of a camera or in print understood that he had a special gift. Jim made us all pause and feel a bit better about ourselves," said PGA of America President Allen Wronowski.

Team Events

For past winners not listed here, please see earlier editions of *The R&A Golfer's Handbook*

Dramatic Walker Cup victory
for Great Britain and Ireland

They arrived at the Balgownie Links of the Royal Aberdeen Golf Club as under-dogs but the Great Britain and Ireland team inspired by their captain Cup stalwart Nigel Edwards left as champions ending a run of three successive defeats by beating a strong American side fielding six of the top 10 amateurs in the world rankings 14–12.

An elated Edwards said of his team: "They are a very special bunch of guys." Although they had won six and a half points from the eight foursomes and halved the first series of singles 4–4, the GB&I side knew the final session of 10 singles would be tough. Captain Edwards, a veteran of four Walker Cups as a player, reminded his side, however, that despite the obvious strength of the opposition the game is not played on paper.

GB&I, winning the event for only the eighth time, did not , however, lack confidence. Having built up a 10½–5½ lead after the first three sessions they needed to win only three more points for victory. Indeed they might have been even further ahead had American teenager Jordan Speith and Patrick Rodgers not come four down with six to play on the second morning to halve with Michael Stewart and Open Championship silver medallist Tom Lewis!

The Americans Russell Henley and Speith took the first two singles on Sunday afternoon and looked like taking the third until Jack Senior, semi-finalist in the 2011 US Amateur Championship, rolled in a 35 footer on the last for a half with Nathan Smith. Then Stewart gave GB&I another point with victory over Rodgers.

Just one and a half points needed now for victory and they were achieved when Steven Brown halved with Blayne Barber and 17-year-old Rhys Pugh, the youngest man on the team, maintained his unbeaten record by following up a first day victory over World Amateur No 3 Rodgers with a stunning 2 and 1 success over the US Amateur champion Kelly Kraft.

Only Rhys and Paul Cutler who had built up a four-up lead with four to play against McCormack Medal winner Patrick Cantlay had 100 per cent records for the home side. Although Cutler lost the last four and finished all square by then the match had been won.

In the match which was first played officially in 1923, victories by GB&I have been rare. The triumph at Royal Aberdeen was only their eighth in nearly 80 years. They had to wait until 1938 at St Andrews for a first success. The 1965 match at Five Farms in Maryland was drawn but there was a home win again at St Andrews in 1971. When Jim Milligan got a half against Jay Sigel in the final single on the second day at Peachtree in 1989, GB&I scored their first victory on US soil.

The match has been a much closer affair since 1995 when GB&I won at Royal Porthcawl. There followed successes at Nairn in 1999, Sea Island in 2001 and Ganton in 2003 when the 2011 captain Edwards played his part on the course.

Alistair Tait writes about the match on page 27.

A close shave

The Great Britain and Ireland team almost fell foul of the Rules when it emerged that Jack Senior had employed the services of his brother Joe, a professional golfer, as his caddie. This constituted a breach of the official conditions of competition and if the error been discovered during the match Senior and his partner Andy Sullivan would have been penalised by up to two holes.

However, the breach was not confirmed by the authorities until after the pair's 2 and 1 victory over Russell Henley and Kelly Kraft had been completed. The decision taken was that the error had not been made intentionally and therefore the result was allowed to stand.

International

Walker Cup (Instituted 1922)
Great Britain & Ireland v USA *(home team names first)*

2011 *Royal Aberdeen Golf Club, Scotland*   [6900–71]

Captains: GB&I: Nigel Edwards (Whitchurch); USA: Jim Holtgrieve (St Louis, MO)

First Day – Foursomes
Tom Lewis & Michael Stewart beat Peter Uihlein & Harris English 2 and 1
Jack Senior & Andy Sullivan beat Russell Henley & Kelly Kraft 2 and 1
Paul Cutler & Alan Dunbar beat Nathan Smith & Blayne Barber 5 and 4
Steven Brown & Stiggy Hodgson lost to Patrick Cantlay & Chris Williams 5 and 4

Match position: GB&I 3, USA 1

Singles
Tom Lewis lost to Peter Uihlein 2 and 1
Jack Senior lost to Jordan Spieth 3 and 2
Andy Sullivan lost to Harris English 2 and 1
Rhys Pugh beat Patrick Rodgers 2 and 1
Steven Brown beat Russell Henley 1 hole
James Byrne beat Nathan Smith 2 and 1
Paul Cutler beat Kelly Kraft 2 and 1
Michael Stewart lost to Patrick Cantlay 2 and 1

Match position: GB&I 7, USA 5

Second Day – Foursomes
Tom Lewis & Michael Stewart halved with Jordan Spieth & Patrick Rodgers
Jack Senior & Andy Sullivan beat Peter Uihlein & Harris English 3 and 2
Paul Cutler & Alan Dunbar beat Kelly Kraft & Blayne Barber 2 and 1
James Byrne & Rhys Pugh beat Patrick Cantlay & Chris Williams 5 and 3

Match position: GB&I 10½, USA 5½

Singles
Tom Lewis (Welwyn Garden City) lost to Russell Henley (Macon, GA) 4 and 2
Andy Sullivan (Nuneaton) lost to Jordan Spieth (Dallas, TX) 3 and 2
Jack Senior (Heysham) halved with Nathan Smith (Pittsburgh, PA)
Michael Stewart (Troon Welbeck) beat Patrick Rodgers (Avon, IN) 3 and 2
Stiggy Hodgson (Sunningdale) lost to Peter Uihlein (Orlando, FL) 2 and 1
Steven Brown (Wentworth) halved with Blayne Barber (Lake City, FL) 1 hole
Rhys Pugh (Vale of Glamorgan) beat Kelly Kraft (Dallas, TX) 2 and 1
Alan Dunbar (Rathmore) lost to Chris Williams (Moscow. ID) 1 hole
James Byrne (Banchory) lost to Harris English (Thomasville, GA) 2 and 1
Paul Cutler (Portstewart) halved with Patrick Cantlay (Los Alamitos, CA)

Result: GB&I 14, USA 12

Walker Cup Captains return in 2013

The United States Golf Association has appointed Jim Holtgrieve to captain the US Walker Cup team in 2013 at the National Golf Links of America on Long Island, New York. The Walker Cup veteran, who played in three winning American Cup sides, captained the team that lost narrowly at Royal Aberdeen last year so earns a quick opportunity to win the Cup back.

Meanwhile, The R&A have re-appointed Welshman Nigel Edwards who captained the winning Great Britain and Ireland side to victory last September to be in charge again at the 44th Cup match in 2013. The Cup holders will be bidding to hold on to the Cup and score what would be only their third victory on American soil. They won at Peachtree in Atlanta in 1989 and again at Ocean Forest, Sea Island, in 2001.

America have won 34 and lost eight matches and one match was drawn at Five Farms in 1965. The competition comprises 18 singles and eight foursomes.

2009 Merion GC, Ardmore, PA　Sept 12–13

Result: USA 16½, GB&I 9½

Captains: George Marucci (USA), Colin Dalgleish (GB&I)

First Day – Foursomes

B Harman & M Hoffmann beat W Booth & S Hutsby
　2 and 1
P Uihlein & N Smith beat G Dear & M Haines　1 hole
R Fowler & B Cauley beat L Goddard & D Whitnell
　6 and 5
C Tringale & A Mitchell lost to S Hodgson & N Kearney
　3 and 1

Singles

B Harman halved with G Dear
R Fowler beat S Hutsby　7 and 6
C Tringale halved with W Booth
M Hoffmann halved with M Haines
P Uihlein beat T Fleetwood　2 and 1
D Weaver halved with C Paisley
B Cauley beat N Kearney　2 and 1
B Gielow lost to S Hodgson　2 and 1

Second Day – Foursomes

B Harman & A Mitchell beat G Dear & M Haines　3 and 2
R Fowler & B Caley beat S Hodgson & N Kearney　1 hole
D Weaver & B Gielow lost to W Booth & S Hutsby
　3 and 2
N Smith & P Uihlein beat C Paisley & D Whitnell　5 and 4

Singles

Brian Harman lost to Gavin Dear (SCO)　3 and 2
Ricki Fowler beat Matt Haines (ENG)　2 and 1
Peter Uihlein beat Stiggy Hodgson (ENG)　3 and 1
Morgan Hoffmann beat Wallace Booth (SCO)　1 hole
Bud Cauley halved with Chris Paisley (ENG)
Adam Mitchell lost to Sam Hutsby (ENG)　1 hole
Drew Weaver lost to Tommy Fleetwood (ENG)　1 hole
Cameron Tringale beat Luke Goddard (ENG)　8 and 6
Nathan Smith lost to Niall Kearney (IRL)　3 and 2
Brendan Gielow beat Dale Whitnell (ENG)　4 and 3

2007 Royal County Down GC, Co Down　Sept 8–9

Result: USA 12½, GB&I 11½

Captains: Colin Dalgliesh (GB&I), Buddy Marucci (USA)

First Day – Foursomes

L Saltman & R Davies lost to B Horschel & R Fowler
　4 and 3
R McIlroy & J Caldwell halved with C Knost &
　D Johnson
J Parry & D Horsey beat T Kuehne & K Stanley　2 and 1
J Moul & D Willett halved with W Simpson & J Moore

Singles

R McIlroy lost to B Horschel　1 hole
L Saltman lost to　R Fowler　5 and 4
R Davies beat D Johnson　5 and 4
D Willett lost to C Knost　2 holes
L Matthews lost to J Lovemark　5 and 4
N Edwards beat K Stanley　1 hole
J Moul beat C Kirk　1 hole
D Horsey beat W Simpson　1 hole

Second Day – Foursomes

Caldwell & McIlroy lost to Horschel & Fowler　2 and 1
Davies & Edwards lost to Knost & Johnson　1 hole
Moul & Willett lost to Kuehne & Moore　4 and 2
Horsey & Parry lost to　Kirk & Lovemark　1 hole

Singles

McIlroy beat Horschel　4 and 2
Davies beat Fowler　3 and 2
Willett halved with Knost

Saltman beat Kuehne 2 and 1
Caldwell beat Stanley　2 holes
Edwards lost to　Moore　1 hole
Moul lost to Lovemark　4 and 3
Horsey beat Simpson　1 hole

2005 Chicago GC, Wheaton, IL　Aug 13–14

Result: USA 12½, GB&I 11½

*Captains: Bob Lewis (USA),
　Garth McGimpsey (GB&I)*

First Day – Foursomes

A Kim & B Harman halved with NB Edwards &
　R Davies
L Williams & M Every beat G Lockerbie & R Dinwiddie
　1 hole
J Overton & M Putnam beat O Fisher & M Richardson
　2 and 1
K Reifers & B Hurley lost to R Ramsay & L Saltman
　4 and 3

Singles

M Every lost to R Davies　4 and 3
A Kim beat G Lockerbie　6 and 5
L Overton beat NB Edwards　5 and 4
M Putnam lost to O Fisher　2 holes
N Thompson lost to M Richardson　5 and 4
B Hurley lost to L Saltman　1 hole
J Holmes beat G Wolstenholme　1 hole
L Williams beat B McElhinney　2 and 1

Second Day – Foursomes

Kim & Harman beat Ramsay & Saltman　4 and 2
Every & Williams lost to Davies & Edwards　2 and 1
Thompson & Holmes beat Fisher & Richardson　2 and 1
Putnam & Overton lost to Lockerbie & Dinwiddie
　5 and 3

Singles

Kim lost to Wolstenholme　1 hole
Harman beat Davies　6 and 5
Putnam halved with Fisher
Every halved with Dinwiddie
Holmes lost to Richardson　5 and 4
Reifers lost to Saltman　1 hole
Overton beat Edwards　1 hole
Williams beat Lockerbie　4 and 3

2003 Ganton GC, North Yorkshire　Sept 6–7

Result: GB&I 12½, USA 11½

*Captains: Garth McGimpsey (GB&I),
　Bob Lewis (USA)*

First Day – Foursomes

GP Wolstenholme & M Skelton lost to W Haas
　& T Kuehne　2 and 1
S Wilson & D Inglis beat L Williams & G Zahringer
　2 holes
NB Edwards & S Manley beat C Nallen & R Moore
　3 and 2
N Fox & C Moriarty beat A Rubinson & C Wittenberg
　4 and 2

Singles

GP Wolstenholme lost to W Haas　1 hole
O Wilson halved with T Kuehne
D Inglis lost to B Mackenzie　3 and 2
S Wilson halved with M Hendrix
NB Edwards beat G Zahringer　3 and 2
C Moriarty lost to C Nallen　1 hole
N Fox lost to A Rubinson　3 and 2
G Gordon lost to C Wittenberg　5 and 4

Second Day – Foursomes
GP Wolstenholme & O Wilson beat W Haas & T Kuehne
 5 and 4
N Fox & C Moriarty lost to B Mackenzie & M Hendrix
 6 and 5
S Wilson & D Inglis halved with C Wittenberg &
 A Rubinson
NB Edwards & S Manley halved with L Williams &
 G Zahringer

Singles
O Wilson beat W Haas 1 hole
GP Wolstenholme beat C Wittenberg 3 and 2
M Skelton beat A Rubinson 3 and 2
C Moriarty lost to B Mackenzie 3 and 1
S Wilson lost to M Hendrix 5 and 4
D Inglis beat R Moore 4 and 3
NB Edwards halved with L Williams
S Manley beat T Kuehne 3 and 2

2001 *Ocean Forest, Sea Island, GA* Aug 11–12
Result: GB&I 15, USA 9
Captains: D Yates Jr (USA), P McEvoy (GB&I)
First Day – Foursomes
D Green & DJ Trahan lost to S O'Hara &
 GP Wolstenholme 5 and 3
N Cassini & L Glover beat L Donald & N Dougherty
 4 and 3
D Eger & B Molder halved with J Elson & R McEvoy
J Driscoll & J Quinney lost to G McDowell & M Hoey
 3 and 1

Singles
E Compton beat G Wolstenholme 3 and 2
DJ Trahan beat S O'Hara 2 and 1
J Driscoll lost to N Dougherty 2 and 1
N Cassini beat N Edwards 5 and 4
J Harris lost to M Warren 5 and 4
J Quinney lost to L Donald 3 and 2
B Molder beat G McDowell 2 and 1
L Glover beat M Hoey 1 hole

Second Day – Foursomes
E Compton & J Harris lost to L Donald & N Dougherty
 3 and 2
N Cassini & L Glover lost to G McDowell & M Hoey
 2 and 1
D Eger & B Molder beat S O'Hara & M Warren 7 and 6
D Green & DJ Trahan lost to J Elson & R McEvoy 1 hole

Singles
L Glover lost to L Donald 3 and 2
J Harris lost to S O'Hara 4 and 3
DJ Trahan lost to N Dougherty 1 hole
J Driscoll lost to M Warren 2 and 1
B Molder beat G McDowell 1 hole
D Green lost to M Hoey 1 hole
E Compton halved with J Elson
N Cassini lost to GP Wolstenholme 4 and 3

1999 *Nairn GC, Nairnshire, Scotland* Sept 11–12
Result: GB&I 15, USA 9
Captains: P McEvoy (GB&I), D Yates Jr (USA)
First Day – Foursomes
Rankin & Storm lost to Haas & Miller 1 hole
Casey & Donald beat Byrd & Scott 5 and 3
Gribben & Kelly lost to Gossett & Jackson 3 and 1
Rowe & Wolstenholme beat Kuchar & Molder 1 hole

Singles
G Rankin lost to E Loar 4 and 3
L Donald beat T McKnight 4 and 3
G Storm lost to H Haas 4 and 3
P Casey beat S Scott 4 and 3

D Patrick lost to J Byrd 6 and 5
S Dyson halved with D Gossett
P Gribben halved with B Molder
L Kelly lost to T Jackson 3 and 1
Second Day – Foursomes
Rankin & Storm beat Loar & McKnight 4 and 3
Dyson & Gribben lost to Haas & Miller 1 hole
Casey & Donald beat Gossett & Jackson 1 hole
Rowe & Wolstenholme beat Kuchar & Molder 4 and 3
Singles
Rankin beat Scott 1 hole
Dyson lost to Loar 5 and 4
Casey beat Miller 3 and 2
Storm beat Byrd 1 hole
Donald beat Molder 3 and 2
Rowe beat Kuchar 1 hole
Gribben beat Haas 3 and 2
Wolstenholme beat Gossett 1 hole

1997 *Quaker Ridge GC, NY* Aug 9–10
Result: USA 18, GB&I 6
Captains: AD Gray Jr (USA), C Brown (GB&I)
First Day – Foursomes
Elder & Kribel beat Howard & Young 4 and 3
Courville & Marucci beat Rose & Brooks 5 and 4
Gore & Harris beat Wolstenholme & Nolan 6 and 4
Leen & Wollman beat Coughlan & Park 1 hole

Singles
D Delcher lost to S Young 5 and 4
S Scott lost to C Watson 1 hole
B Elder beat B Howard 5 and 4
J Kribel lost to J Rose 1 hole
R Leen beat K Nolan 3 and 2
J Gore beat G Rankin 3 and 2
C Wollman halved with R Coughlan
J Harris beat GP Wolstenholme 1 hole

Second Day – Foursomes
Harris & Elder beat Young & Watson 3 and 2
Courville & Marucci beat Howard & Rankin 5 and 4
Delcher & Scott beat Coughlan & Park 1 hole
Leen & Wollman lost to Wolstenholme & Rose 2 and 1

Singles
Kribel lost to Young 2 and 1
Gore halved with Watson
J Courville beat Rose 3 and 2
Elder beat Nolan 2 and 1
Harris beat M Brooks 6 and 5
G Marucci beat D Park 4 and 3
D Delcher beat Wolstenholme 2 and 1
Scott beat Coughlan 2 and 1

1995 *Royal Porthcawl GC, Mid Glamorgan, Wales*
Sept 9–10
Result: GB&I 14, USA 10
Captains: C Brown (GB&I), AD Gray Jr (USA)
First Day – Foursomes
Sherry & Gallacher lost to Harris & Woods 4 and 3
Foster & Howell halved with Bratton & Riley
Rankin & Howard lost to Begay & Jackson 4 and 3
Harrington & Fanagan beat Cox & Kuehne 5 and 3

Singles
G Sherry beat N Begay 3 and 2
L James lost to K Cox 1 hole
M Foster beat B Marucci 4 and 3
S Gallacher beat T Jackson 4 and 3
P Harrington beat J Courville Jr 2 holes
B Howard halved with A Bratton
G Rankin lost to J Harris 1 hole
GP Wolstenholme beat T Woods 1 hole

1995 continued

Second Day – Foursomes
Sherry & Gallacher lost to Bratton & Riley 4 and 2
Howell & Foster beat Cox & Kuehne 3 and 2
Wolstenholme & James lost to Marucci & Courville 6 and 5
Harrington & Fanagan beat Harris & Woods 2 and 1

Singles
Sherry beat Riley 2 holes
Howell beat Begay 2 and 1
Gallacher beat Kuehne 3 and 2
Fanagan beat Courville 3 and 2
Howard halved with Jackson
Foster halved with Marucci
Harrington lost to Harris 3 and 2
Wolstenholme lost to Woods 4 and 3

1993 Interlachen GC, Edina, MN Aug 18–19
Result: USA 19, GB&I 5
Captains: M Giles III (USA), G Macgregor (GB&I)
First Day – Foursomes
Abandoned – rain & flooding
Singles
A Doyle beat I Pyman 1 hole
D Berganio lost to M Stanford 3 and 2
J Sigel lost to D Robertson 3 and 2
K Mitchum halved with S Cage
T Herron beat P Harrington 1 hole
D Yates beat P Page 2 and 1
T Demsey beat R Russell 2 and 1
J Leonard beat R Burns 4 and 3
B Gay lost to V Phillips 2 and 1
J Harris beat B Dredge 4 and 3
Second Day – Foursomes
Doyle & Leonard beat Pyman & Cage 4 and 3
Berganio & Demsey beat Stanford & Harrington 3 and 2
Sigel & Mitchum beat Dredge & Phillips 3 and 2
Harris & Herron beat Russell & Robertson 1 hole
Singles
Doyle beat Robertson 4 and 3
Harris beat Pyman 3 and 2
Yates beat Cage 2 and 1
Gay halved with Harrington
Sigel beat Page 5 and 4
Herron beat Phillips 3 and 2
Mitchum beat Russell 4 and 2
Berganio lost to Burns 1 hole
Demsey beat Dredge 3 and 2
Leonard beat Stanford 5 and 4

1991 Portmarnock GC, Co Dublin, Ireland Sept 5–6
Result: USA 14, GB&I 10
Captains: G Macgregor (GB&I),
  JR Gabrielsen (USA)
First Day – Foursomes
Milligan & Hay lost to Mickelson & May 5 and 3
Payne & Evans lost to Duval & Sposa 1 hole
McGimpsey & Willison lost to Voges & Eger 1 hole
McGinley & Harrington lost to Sigel & Doyle 2 and 1
Singles
A Coltart lost to P Mickelson 4 and 3
J Payne beat F Langham 2 and 1
G Evans beat D Duval 2 and 1
R Willison lost to B May 2 and 1
G McGimpsey beat M Sposa 1 hole
P McGinley lost to A Doyle 6 and 4
G Hay beat T Scherrer 1 hole
L White lost to J Sigel 4 and 3

Second Day – Foursomes
Milligan & McGimpsey beat Voges & Eger 2 and 1
Payne & Willison lost to Duval & Sposa 1 hole
Evans & Coltart beat Langham & Scherrer 4 and 3
White & McGinley beat Mickelson & May 1 hole
Singles
Milligan lost to Mickelson 1 hole
Payne beat Doyle 3 and 1
Evans lost to Langham 4 and 2
Coltart beat Sigel 1 hole
Willison beat Scherrer 3 and 2
Harrington lost to Eger 3 and 2
McGimpsey lost to May 4 and 3
Hay lost to Voges 3 and 1

1989 Peachtree GC, GA Aug 16–17
Result: GB&I 12½, USA 11½
Captains: F Ridley (USA), GC Marks (GB&I)
First Day – Foursomes
Gamez & Martin beat Claydon & Prosser 3 and 2
Yates & Mickelson halved with Dodd & McGimpsey
Lesher & Sigel lost to McEvoy & O'Connell 6 and 5
Eger & Johnson lost to Milligan & Hare 2 and 1
Singles
R Gamez beat JW Milligan 7 and 6
D Martin lost to R Claydon 5 and 4
E Meeks halved with SC Dodd
R Howe lost to E O'Connell 5 and 4
D Yates lost to P McEvoy 2 and 1
P Mickelson beat G McGimpsey 4 and 2
G Lesher lost to C Cassells 1 hole
J Sigel halved with RN Roderick
Second Day – Foursomes
Gamez & Martin halved with McEvoy & O'Connell
Sigel & Lesher lost to Claydon & Cassells 3 and 2
Eger & Johnson lost to Milligan & Hare 2 and 1
Mickelson & Yates lost to McGimpsey & Dodd 2 and 1
Singles
Gamez beat Dodd 1 hole
Martin halved with Hare
Lesher beat Claydon 3 and 2
Yates beat McEvoy 4 and 3
Mickelson halved with O'Connell
Eger beat Roderick 4 and 2
Johnson beat Cassells 4 and 2
Sigel halved with Milligan

1987 Sunningdale GC, Berkshire, England May 27–28
Result: USA 16½, GB&I 7½
Captains: GC Marks (GB&I), F Ridley (USA)
First Day – Foursomes
Montgomerie & Shaw lost to Alexander & Mayfair 5 and 4
Currey & Mayo lost to Kite & Mattice 2 and 1
Macgregor & Robinson lost to Lewis & Loeffler 2 and 1
McHenry & Girvan lost to Sigel & Andrade 3 and 2
Singles
D Currey beat B Alexander 2 holes
J Robinson lost to B Andrade 7 and 5
CS Montgomerie beat J Sorenson 3 and 2
R Eggo lost to J Sigel 3 and 2
J McHenry lost to B Montgomery 1 hole
P Girvan lost to B Lewis 3 and 2
DG Carrick lost to B Mayfair 2 holes
G Shaw beat C Kite 1 hole

Second Day – Foursomes
Currey & Carrick lost to Lewis & Loeffler 4 and 3
Montgomerie & Shaw lost to Kite & Mattice 5 and 3
Mayo & Macgregor lost to Sorenson & Montgomery
    4 and 3
McHenry & Robinson beat Sigel & Andrade 4 and 2

Singles
Currey lost to Alexander 5 and 4
Montgomerie beat Andrade 4 and 2
McHenry beat Loeffler 3 and 2
Shaw halved with Sorenson
Robinson beat Mattice 1 hole
Carrick lost to Lewis 3 and 2
Eggo lost to Mayfair 1 hole
Girvan lost to Sigel 6 and 5

1985 *Pine Valley GC, NJ* Aug 21–22
Result: USA 13, GB&I 11
Captains: J Sigel (USA), CW Green (GB&I)

First Day – Foursomes
Verplank & Sigel beat Montgomerie & Macgregor 1 hole
Waldorf & Randolph lost to Hawksworth & McGimpsey
    4 and 3
Sonnier & Haas lost to Baker & McEvoy 6 and 5
Podolak & Love halved with Bloice & Stephen

Singles
S Verplank beat G McGimpsey 2 and 1
S Randolph beat P Mayo 5 and 4
R Sonnier halved with J Hawksworth
J Sigel beat CS Montgomerie 5 and 4
B Lewis lost to P McEvoy 2 and 1
C Burroughs lost to G Macgregor 2 holes
D Waldorf beat D Gilford 4 and 2
J Haas lost to AR Stephen 2 and 1

Second Day – Foursomes
Verplank & Sigel halved with Mayo & Montgomerie
Randolph & Haas beat Hawksworth & McGimpsey 3 and 2
Lewis & Burroughs beat Baker & McEvoy 2 and 1
Podolak & Love beat Bloice & Stephen 3 and 2

Singles
Randolph halved with McGimpsey
Verplank beat Montgomerie 1 hole
Sigel lost to Hawksworth 4 and 3
Love beat McEvoy 5 and 3
Sonnier lost to Baker 5 and 4
Burroughs lost to Macgregor 3 and 2
Lewis beat Bloice 4 and 3
Waldorf lost to Stephen 2 and 1

1983 *Royal Liverpool GC, Merseyside, England*
May 25–26
Result: USA 13½, GB&I 10½
Captains: CW Green (GB&I), J Sigel (USA)

First Day – Foursomes
Macgregor & Walton beat Sigel & Fehr 3 and 2
Keppler & Pierse lost to Wood & Faxon 3 and 1
Lewis & Thompson lost to Lewis & Holtgrieve 7 and 6
Mann & Oldcorn beat Hoffer & Tentis 5 and 4

Singles
P Walton beat J Sigel 1 hole
SD Keppler lost to R Fehr 1 hole
G Macgregor halved with W Wood
DG Carrick lost to B Faxon 3 and 1
A Oldcorn beat B Tuten 4 and 3
P Parkin beat N Crosby 5 and 4
AD Pierse lost to B Lewis Jr 3 and 1
LS Mann lost to J Holtgrieve 6 and 5

Second Day – Foursomes
Macgregor & Walton lost to Crosby & Hoffer 2 holes
Parkin & Thompson beat Faxon & Wood 1 hole
Mann & Oldcorn beat Lewis & Holtgrieve 1 hole
Keppler & Pierse halved with Sigel & Fehr

Singles
Walton beat Wood 2 and 1
Parkin lost to Faxon 3 and 2
Macgregor lost to Fehr 2 and 1
Thompson lost to Tuten 3 and 2
Mann halved with Tentis
Keppler lost to Lewis 6 and 5
Oldcorn beat Holtgrieve 3 and 2
Carrick lost to Sigel 3 and 2

1981 *Cypress Point Club, CA* Aug 28–29
Result: USA 15, GB&I 9
Captains: J Gabrielsen (USA), R Foster (GB&I)

First Day – Foursomes
Sutton & Sigel lost to Walton & Rafferty 4 and 2
Holtgrieve & Fuhrer beat Chapman & McEvoy 1 hole
Lewis & von Tacky beat Deeble & Hutcheon 2 and 1
Commans & Pavin beat Evans & Way 5 and 4

Singles
H Sutton beat R Rafferty 3 and 1
J Rassett beat CR Dalgleish 1 hole
R Commans lost to P Walton 1 hole
B Lewis lost to R Chapman 2 and 1
J Mudd beat G Godwin 1 hole
C Pavin beat IC Hutcheon 4 and 3
D von Tacky lost to P Way 3 and 1
J Sigel beat P McEvoy 4 and 2

Second Day – Foursomes
Sutton & Sigel lost to Chapman & Way 1 hole
Holtgrieve & Fuhrer lost to Walton & Rafferty
    6 and 4
Lewis & von Tacky lost to Evans & Dalgleish
    3 and 2
Rassett & Mudd beat Hutcheon & Godwin 5 and 4

Singles
Sutton lost to Chapman 1 hole
Holtgrieve beat Rafferty 2 and 1
Fuhrer beat Walton 4 and 3
Sigel beat Way 6 and 5
Mudd beat Dalgleish 7 and 5
Commans halved with Godwin
Rassett beat Deeble 4 and 3
Pavin halved with Evans

1979 *Muirfield, East Lothian, Scotland* May 30–31
Result: USA 15½, GB&I 8½
Captains: R Foster (GB&I), RL Siderowf (USA)

First Day – Foursomes
McEvoy & Marchbank lost to Hoch & Sigel 1 hole
Godwin & Hutcheon beat West & Sutton 2 holes
Brand Jr & Kelley lost to Fischesser & Holtgrieve
    1 hole
Brodie & Carslaw beat Moody & Gove 2 and 1

Singles
P McEvoy halved with J Sigel
JC Davies lost to D Clarke 8 and 7
J Buckley lost to S Hoch 9 and 7
IC Hutcheon lost to J Holtgrieve 6 and 4
B Marchbank beat M Peck 1 hole
G Godwin beat G Moody 3 and 2
MJ Kelley beat D Fischesser 3 and 2
A Brodie lost to M Gove 3 and 2

1979 *continued*

Second Day – Foursomes
Godwin & Brand lost to Hoch & Sigel 4 and 3
McEvoy & Marchbank beat Fischesser & Holtgrieve 2 and 1
Kelley & Hutcheon halved with West & Sutton
Carslaw & Brodie halved with Clarke & Peck

Singles
McEvoy lost to Hoch 3 and 1
Brand lost to Clarke 2 and 1
Godwin lost to Gove 3 and 2
Hutcheon lost to Peck 2 and 1
Brodie beat West 3 and 2
Kelley lost to Moody 3 and 2
Marchbank lost to Sutton 3 and 1
Carslaw lost to Sigel 2 and 1

1977 *Shinnecock Hills GC, NY* Aug 26–27
Result: USA 16, GB&I 8
Captains: LW Oehmig(USA),
AC Saddler (GB&I)

First Day – Foursomes
Fought & Heafner beat Lyle & McEvoy 4 and 3
Simpson & Miller beat Davies & Kelley 5 and 4
Siderowf & Hallberg lost to Hutcheon & Deeble 1 hole
Sigel & Brannan beat Brodie & Martin 1 hole

Singles
L Miller beat P McEvoy 2 holes
J Fought beat IC Hutcheon 4 and 3
S Simpson beat GH Murray 7 and 6
V Heafner beat JC Davies 4 and 3
B Sander lost to A Brodie 4 and 3
G Hallberg lost to S Martin 3 and 2
F Ridley beat AWB Lyle 2 holes
J Sigel beat P McKellar 5 and 3

Second Day – Foursomes
Fought & Heafner beat Hutcheon & Deeble 4 and 3
Miller & Simpson beat McEvoy & Davies 2 holes
Siderowf & Sander lost to Brodie & Martin 6 and 4
Ridley & Brannan lost to Murray & Kelley 4 and 3

Singles
Miller beat Martin 1 hole
Fought beat Davies 2 and 1
Sander lost to Brodie 2 and 1
Hallberg beat McEvoy 4 and 3
Siderowf lost to Kelley 2 and 1
Brannan lost to Hutcheon 2 holes
Ridley beat Lyle 5 and 3
Sigel beat Deeble 1 hole

1975 *St Andrews, Fife, Scotland* May 28–29
Result: USA 15½, GB&I 8½
Captains: DM Marsh (GB&I), ER Updegraff (USA)

First Day – Foursomes
James & Eyles beat Pate & Siderowf 1 hole
Davies & Poxon lost to Burns & Stadler 5 and 4
Green & Stuart lost to Haas & Strange 2 and 1
Macgregor & Hutcheon lost to Giles & Koch
5 and 4

Singles
M James beat J Pate 2 and 1
JC Davies halved with C Strange
P Mulcare beat RL Siderowf 1 hole
HB Stuart lost to G Koch 3 and 2
MA Poxon lost to J Grace 3 and 1
IC Hutcheon halved with WC Campbell
GRD Eyles lost to J Haas 2 and 1
G Macgregor lost to M Giles III 5 and 4

Second Day – Foursomes
Mulcare & Hutcheon beat Pate & Siderowf 1 hole
Green & Stuart lost to Burns & Stadler 1 hole
James & Eyles beat Campbell & Grace 5 and 3
Hedges & Davies lost to Haas & Strange 3 and 2

Singles
Hutcheon beat Pate 3 and 2
Mulcare lost to Strange 4 and 3
James lost to Koch 5 and 4
Davies beat Burns 2 and 1
Green lost to Grace 2 and 1
Macgregor lost to Stadler 3 and 2
Eyles lost to Campbell 2 and 1
Hedges halved with Giles

1973 *The Country Club, Brookline, MA* Aug 24–25
Result: USA 14, GB&I 10
Captains: JW Sweetser (USA), DM Marsh (GB&I)

First Day – Foursomes
Giles & Koch halved with King & Hedges
Siderowf & Pfeil beat Stuart & Davies 5 and 4
Edwards & Ellis beat Green & Milne 2 and 1
West & Ballenger beat Foster & Homer 2 and 1

Singles
M Giles III beat HB Stuart 5 and 4
RL Siderowf beat MF Bonallack 4 and 2
G Koch lost to JC Davies 1 hole
M West lost to HK Clark 2 and 1
D Edwards beat R Foster 2 holes
M Killian lost to MG King 1 hole
W Rodgers lost to CW Green 1 hole
M Pfeil lost to WT Milne 4 and 3

Second Day – Foursomes
Giles & Koch & Homer & Foster 7 and 5
Siderowf & Pfeil halved with Clark & Davies
Edwards & Ellis beat Hedges & King 2 and 1
Rodgers & Killian beat Stuart & Milne 1 hole

Singles
Ellis lost to Stuart 5 and 4
Siderowf lost to Davies 3 and 2
Edwards beat Homer 2 and 1
Giles halved with Green
West beat King 1 hole
Killian lost to Milne 2 and 1
Koch halved with Hedges
Pfeil beat Clark 1 hole

1971 *St Andrews, Fife, Scotland* May 26–27
Result: GB&I 13, USA 11
Captains: MF Bonallack (GB&I),
JM Winters Jr (USA)

First Day – Foursomes
Bonallack & Humphreys beat Wadkins & Simons
1 hole
Green & Carr beat Melnyk & Giles 1 hole
Marsh & Macgregor beat Miller & Farquhar 2 and 1
Macdonald & Foster beat Campbell & Kite 2 and 1

Singles
CW Green lost to L Wadkins 1 hole
MF Bonallack lost to M Giles III 1 hole
GC Marks lost to AL Miller III 1 hole
JS Macdonald lost to S Melnyk 3 and 2
RJ Carr halved with W Hyndman III
W Humphreys lost to JR Gabrielsen 1 hole
HB Stuart beat J Farquhar 3 and 2
R Foster lost to T Kite 3 and 2

Second Day – Foursomes
Marks & Green lost to Melnyk & Giles I hole
Stuart & Carr beat Wadkins & Gabrielsen I hole
Marsh & Bonallack lost to Miller & Farquhar 5 and 4
Macdonald & Foster halved with Campbell & Kite

Singles
Bonallack lost to Wadkins 3 and I
Stuart beat Giles 2 and I
Humphreys beat Melnyk 2 and I
Green beat Miller I hole
Carr beat Simons 2 holes
Macgregor beat Gabrielsen I hole
Marsh beat Hyndman I hole
Marks lost to Kite 3 and 2

1969 *Milwaukee GC, WI* Aug 22–23
Result: USA 10, GB&I 8[†]
Captains: WJ Patton (USA), MF Bonallack (GB&I)

First Day – Foursomes
Giles & Melnyk beat Bonallack & Craddock 3 and 2
Fleisher & Miller halved with Benka & Critchley
Wadkins & Siderowf lost to Green & A Brooks
W Hyndman III & Inman Jr beat Foster & Marks 2 and I

Singles
B Fleisher halved with MF Bonallack
M Giles III beat CW Green I hole
AL Miller III beat B Critchley I hole
RL Siderowf beat LP Tupling 6 and 5
S Melnyk lost to PJ Benka 3 and I
L Wadkins lost to GC Marks I hole
J Bohmann beat MG King 2 and I
ER Updegraff beat R Foster 6 and 5

Second Day – Foursomes
Giles & Melnyk halved with Green & Brooks
Fleisher & Miller lost to Benka & Critchley 2 and I
Siderowf & Wadkins beat Foster & King 6 and 5
Updegraff & Bohmann lost to Bonallack & Tupling 4 and 3

Singles
Fleisher lost to Bonallack 5 and 4
Siderowf halved with Critchley
Miller beat King I hole
Giles halved with Craddock
Inman beat Benka 2 and I
Bohmann lost to Brooks 4 and 3
Hyndman halved with Green
Updegraff lost to Marks 3 and 2

1967 *Royal St George's GC, Kent, England* May 19–20
Result: USA 13, GB&I 7[†]
Captains: JB Carr (GB&I), JW Sweetser (USA)

First Day – Foursomes
Shade & Oosterhuis halved with Murphy & Cerrudo
Foster & Saddler lost to Campbell & Lewis I hole
Bonallack & Attenborough lost to Gray & Tutwiler 4 and 2
Carr & Craddock lost to Dickson & Grant 3 and I

Singles
RDBM Shade lost to WC Campbell 2 and I
R Foster lost to RJ Murphy Jr 2 and I
MF Bonallack halved with AD Gray Jr
MF Attenborough lost to RJ Cerrudo 4 and 3
P Oosterhuis lost to RB Dickson 6 and 4
T Craddock lost to JW Lewis Jr 2 and I
AK Pirie halved with DC Allen
AC Saddler beat MA Fleckman 3 and 2

Second Day – Foursomes
Bonallack & Craddock beat Murphy & Cerrudo 2 holes
Saddler & Pirie lost to Campbell & Lewis I hole
Shade & Oosterhuis beat Gray & Tutwiler 3 and I
Foster & Millensted beat Allen & Fleckman 2 and I

Singles
Shade lost to Campbell 3 and 2
Bonallack beat Murphy 4 and 2
Saddler beat Gray 3 and 2
Foster halved with Cerrudo
Pirie lost to Dickson 4 and 3
Craddock beat Lewis 5 and 4
Oosterhuis lost to Grant I hole
Millensted lost to Tutwiler 3 and I

1965 *Baltimore GC, MD* Sept 3–4
Result: USA 11, GB&I 11[†]
Captains: JW Fischer (USA), JB Carr (GB&I)

First Day – Foursomes
Campbell & Gray lost to Lunt & Cosh I hole
Beman & Allen halved with Bonallack & Clark
Patton & Tutwiler beat Foster & Clark 5 and 4
Hopkins & Eichelberger lost to Townsend & Shade 2 and I

Singles
WC Campbell beat MF Bonallack 6 and 5
DR Beman beat R Foster 2 holes
AD Gray Jr lost to RDBM Shade 3 and I
JM Hopkins lost to CA Clark 5 and 3
WJ Patton lost to P Townsend 3 and 2
D Morey lost to AC Saddler 2 and I
DC Allen lost to GB Cosh 2 holes
ER Updegraff lost to MSR Lunt 2 and I

Second Day – Foursomes
Campbell & Gray beat Saddler & Foster 4 and 3
Beman & Eichelberger lost to Townsend & Shade 2 and I
Tutwiler & Patton beat Cosh & Lunt 2 and I
Allen & Morey lost to CA Clark & Bonallack 2 and I

Singles
Campbell beat Foster 3 and 2
Beman beat Saddler I hole
Tutwiler beat Shade 5 and 3
Allen lost to Cosh 4 and 3
Gray beat Townsend I hole
Hopkins halved with CA Clark
Eichelberger beat Bonallack 5 and 3
Patton beat Lunt 4 and 2

1963 *Turnberry, Ayrshire, Scotland* May 24–25
Result: USA 12, GB&I 8[†]
Captains: CD Lawrie (GB&I), RS Tufts (USA)

First Day – Foursomes
Bonallack & Murray beat Patton & Sikes 4 and 3
Carr & Green lost to Gray & Harris 2 holes
Lunt & Sheahan lost to Beman & Coe 5 and 3
Madeley & Shade halved with Gardner & Updegraff

Singles
SWT Murray beat DR Beman 3 and I
MJ Christmas lost to WJ Patton 3 and 2
JB Carr beat RH Sikes 7 and 5
DB Sheahan beat LE Harris I hole
MF Bonallack beat RD Davies I hole
AC Saddler halved with CR Coe
RDBM Shade beat AD Gray Jr 4 and 3
MSR Lunt halved with CB Smith

[†] *No points were given for halved matches between 1922 and 1969. There was a total of 12 points 1922–61 and 24 points 1963–69.*

1963 *continued*

Second Day – Foursomes
Bonallack & Murray lost to Patton & Sikes 1 hole
Lunt & Sheahan lost to Gray & Harris 3 and 2
Green & Saddler lost to Gardner & Updegraff 3 and 1
Madeley & Shade lost to Beman & Coe 3 and 2

Singles
Murray lost to Patton 3 and 2
Sheahan beat Davies 1 hole
Carr lost to Updegraff 4 and 3
Bonallack lost to Harris 3 and 2
Lunt lost to Gardner 3 and 2
Saddler halved with Beman
Shade beat Gray 2 and 1
Green lost to Coe 4 and 3

1961 *Seattle GC, WA* Sept 1–2
Result: USA 11, GB&I 1
Captains: J Westland (USA), CD Lawrie (GB&I)

Foursomes
Beman & Nicklaus beat Walker & Chapman 6 and 5
Coe & Cherry beat Blair & Christmas 1 hole
Hyndman & Gardner beat Carr & G Huddy 4 and 3
Cochran & Andrews beat Bonallack & Shade 4 and 3

Singles
DR Beman beat MF Bonallack 3 and 2
CR Coe beat MSR Lunt 5 and 4
FM Taylor Jr beat J Walker 3 and 2
W Hyndman III beat DW Frame 7 and 6
JW Nicklaus beat JB Carr 6 and 4
CB Smith lost to MJ Christmas 3 and 2
RW Gardner beat RDBM Shade 1 hole
DR Cherry beat DA Blair 5 and 4

1959 *Muirfield, East Lothian, Scotland* May 15–16
Result: USA 9, GB&I 3
Captains: GH Micklem (GB&I), CR Coe (USA)

Foursomes
Jack & Sewell lost to Ward & Taylor 1 hole
Carr & Wolstenholme lost to Hyndman & Aaron 1 hole
Bonallack & Perowne lost to Patton & Coe 9 and 8
Lunt & Shepperson lost to Wettlander & Nicklaus 2 and 1

Singles
JB Carr beat CR Coe 3 and 1
GB Wolstenholme lost to EH Ward Jr 9 and 8
RR Jack beat WJ Patton 5 and 3
DN Sewell lost to W Hyndman III 4 and 3
AE Shepperson beat TD Aaron 2 and 1
MF Bonallack lost to DR Beman 2 holes
MSR Lunt lost to HW Wettlander 6 and 5
WD Smith lost to JW Nicklaus 5 and 4

1957 *The Minikahda Club, MN* Aug 30–31
Result: USA 8, GB&I 3†
Captains: CR Coe (USA), GH Micklem (GB&I)

Foursomes
Baxter & Patton beat Carr & Deighton 2 and 1
Campbell & Taylor beat Bussell & Scrutton 4 and 3
Blum & Kocsis lost to Jack & Sewell 1 hole
Robbins & Rudolph halved with Shepperson & Wolstenholme

Singles
WJ Patton beat RR Jack 1 hole
WC Campbell beat JB Carr 3 and 2
R Baxter Jr beat A Thirlwell 4 and 3
W Hyndman III beat FWG Deighton 7 and 6

JE Campbell lost to AF Bussell 2 and 1
FM Taylor Jr beat D Sewell 1 hole
EM Rudolph beat PF Scrutton 3 and 2
H Robbins Jr lost to GB Wolstenholme 2 and 1

1955 *St Andrews, Fife, Scotland* May 20–21
Result: USA 10, GB&I 2
Captains: GA Hill (GB&I), WC Campbell (USA)

Foursomes
Carr & White lost to Ward & Cherry 1 hole
Micklem & Morgan lost to Patton & Yost 2 and 1
Caldwell & Millward lost to Conrad & Morey 3 and 2
Blair & Cater lost to Cudd & Jackson 5 and 4

Singles
RJ White lost to EH Ward Jr 6 and 5
PF Scrutton lost to WJ Patton 2 and 1
I Caldwell beat D Morey 1 hole
JB Carr lost to DR Cherry 5 and 4
DA Blair beat JW Conrad 1 hole
EB Millward lost to BH Cudd 2 holes
RC Ewing lost to JG Jackson 6 and 4
JL Morgan lost to RL Yost 8 and 7

1953 *The Kittansett, MA* Sept 4–5
Result: USA 9, GB&I 3
Captains: CR Yates (USA), AA Duncan (GB&I)

Foursomes
Urzetta & Venturi beat Carr & White 6 and 4
Ward & Westland beat Langley & AH Perowne 9 and 8
Jackson & Littler beat Wilson & MacGregor 3 and 2
Campbell & Coe lost to Micklem & Morgan 4 and 3

Singles
EH Ward Jr beat JB Carr 4 and 3
RD Chapman lost to RJ White 1 hole
GA Littler beat GH Micklem 5 and 3
J Westland beat RC MacGregor 7 and 5
DR Cherry beat NV Drew 9 and 7
K Venturi beat JC Wilson 9 and 8
CR Coe lost to JL Morgan 3 and 2
S Urzetta beat JDA Langley 3 and 2

1951 *Birkdale GC, Lancashire, England* May 11–12
Result: USA 6, GB&I 3†
Captains: RH Oppenheimer (GB&I),
WP Turnesa (USA)

Foursomes
White & Carr halved with Stranahan & Campbell
Ewing & Langley halved with Coe & McHale
Kyle & Caldwell lost to Chapman & Knowles Jr 1 hole
Bruen Jr & Morgan lost to Turnesa & Urzetta 5 and 4

Singles
SM McCready lost to S Urzetta 4 and 3
JB Carr beat FR Stranahan 2 and 1
RJ White beat CR Coe 2 and 1
JDA Langley lost to JB McHale Jr 2 holes
RC Ewing lost to WC Campbell 5 and 4
AT Kyle beat WP Turnesa 2 holes
I Caldwell halved with HD Paddock Jr
JL Morgan lost to RD Chapman 7 and 6

1949 *Winged Foot GC. NY* Aug 19–20
Result: USA 10, GB&I 2
Captains: FD Ouimet (USA), PB Lucas (GB&I)

Foursomes
Billows & Turnesa lost to Carr & White 3 and 2
Kocsis & Stranahan beat Bruen & McCready 2 and 1

---

† *No points were given for halved matches between 1922 and 1969. There was a total of 12 points 1922–61 and 24 points 1963–69*

Bishop & Riegel beat Ewing & Micklem 9 and 7
Dawson & McCormick beat Thom & Perowne 8 and 7
Singles
WP Turnesa lost to RJ White 4 and 3
FR Stranahan beat SM McCready 6 and 5
RH Riegel beat J Bruen Jr 5 and 4
JW Dawson beat JB Carr 5 and 3
CR Coe beat RC Ewing 1 hole
RE Billows beat KG Thom 2 and 1
CR Kocsis beat AH Perowne 4 and 2
JB McHale Jr beat GH Micklem 5 and 4

1947 St Andrews, Fife, Scotland May 16–17
Result: USA 8, GB&I 4
Captains: JB Beck (GB&I), FD Ouimet (USA)
Foursomes
Carr & Ewing lost to Bishop & Riegel 3 and 2
Crawley & Lucas beat Ward & Quick 5 and 4
Kyle & Wilson lost to Turnesa & Kammer 5 and 4
White & Stowe beat Stranahan & Chapman 4 and 3
Singles
LG Crawley lost to MH Ward 5 and 3
JB Carr beat SE Bishop 5 and 3
GH Micklem lost to RH Riegel 6 and 5
RC Ewing lost to WP Turnesa 6 and 5
C Stowe lost to FR Stranahan 2 and 1
RJ White beat AF Kammer Jr 4 and 3
JC Wilson lost to SL Quick 8 and 6
PB Lucas lost to RD Chapman 4 and 3

1938 St Andrews, Fife, Scotland June 3–4
Result: GB&I 7, USA 4[†]
Captains: JB Beck (GB&I), FD Ouimet (USA)
Foursomes
Bentley & Bruen halved with Fischer & Kocsis
Peters & Thomson beat Goodman & Ward 4 and 2
Kyle & Stowe lost to Yates & Billows 3 and 2
Pennink & Crawley beat Smith & Haas 3 and 1
Singles
J Bruen Jr lost to CR Yates 2 and 1
H Thomson beat JG Goodman 6 and 4
LG Crawley lost to JW Fischer 3 and 2
C Stowe beat CR Kocsis 2 and 1
JJF Pennink lost to MH Ward 12 and 11
RC Ewing beat RE Billows 1 hole
GB Peters beat R Smith 9 and 8
AT Kyle beat F Haas Jr 5 and 4

1936 Pine Valley GC, NJ Sept 2–3
Result: USA 9, GB&I 0[†]
Captains: FD Ouimet (USA), W Tweddell (GB&I)
Foursomes
Goodman & Campbell beat Thomson & Bentley
  7 and 5
Smith & White beat McLean & Langley 8 and 7
Yates & Emery halved with Peters & Dykes
Givan & Voigt halved with Hill & Ewing
Singles
JG Goodman beat H Thomson 3 and 2
AE Campbell beat J McLean 5 and 4
JW Fischer beat RC Ewing 8 and 7
R Smith beat GA Hill 11 and 9
W Emery beat GB Peters 1 hole
CR Yates beat JM Dykes 8 and 7
GT Dunlap Jr halved with HG Bentley
E White beat JDA Langley 6 and 5

1934 St Andrews, Fife, Scotland May 11–12
Result: USA 9, GB&I 2[†]
Captains: Hon M Scott (GB&I), FD Ouimet (USA)
Foursomes
Wethered & Tolley lost to Goodman & Little 8 and 6
Bentley & Fiddian lost to Moreland & Westland
  6 and 5
Scott & McKinlay lost to Egan & Marston 3 and 2
McRuvie & McLean beat Ouimet & Dunlap 4 and 2
Singles
Hon M Scott lost to JG Goodman 7 and 6
CJH Tolley lost to WL Little Jr 6 and 5
LG Crawley lost to FD Ouimet 5 and 4
J McLean lost to GT Dunlap Jr 4 and 3
EW Fiddian lost to JW Fischer 5 and 4
SL McKinlay lost to GT Moreland 3 and 1
EA McRuvie halved with J Westland
TA Torrance beat MR Marston 4 and 3

1932 The Country Club, Brookline, MA Sept 1–2
Result: USA 8, GB&I 1[†]
Captains: FD Ouimet (USA), TA Torrance (GB&I)
Foursomes
Sweetser & Voigt beat Hartley & Hartley 7 and 6
Seaver & Moreland beat Torrance & de Forest 6 and 5
Ouimet & Dunlap beat Stout & Burke 7 and 6
Moe & Howell beat Fiddian & McRuvie 5 and 4
Singles
FD Ouimet halved with TA Torrance
JW Sweetser halved with JA Stout
GT Moreland beat RW Hartley 2 and 1
J Westland halved with J Burke
GJ Voigt lost to LG Crawley 1 hole
MJ McCarthy Jr beat WL Hartley 3 and 2
CH Seaver beat EW Fiddian 7 and 6
GT Dunlap Jr beat EA McRuvie 10 and 9

1930 Royal St George's GC, Sandwich, Kent
  May 15–16
Result: USA 10, GB&I 2
Captains: RH Wethered (GB&I), RT Jones Jr (USA)
Foursomes
Tolley & Wethered beat Von Elm & Voigt 2 holes
Hartley & Torrance lost to Jones & Willing 8 and 7
Holderness & Stout lost to MacKenzie & Moe
  2 and 1
Campbell & Smith lost to Johnston & Ouimet 2 and 1
Singles
CJH Tolley lost to HR Johnston 5 and 4
RH Wethered lost to RT Jones Jr 9 and 8
RW Hartley lost to G Von Elm 3 and 2
EWE Holderness lost to GJ Voigt 10 and 8
JN Smith lost to OF Willing 2 and 1
TA Torrance beat FD Ouimet 7 and 6
JA Stout lost to DK Moe 1 hole
W Campbell lost to RR MacKenzie 6 and 5

1928 Chicago GC, IL Aug 30–31
Result: USA 11, GB&I 1
Captains: RT Jones Jr (USA), W Tweddell (GB&I)
Foursomes
Sweetser & Von Elm beat Perkins & Tweddell 7 and 6
Jones & Evans beat Hezlet & Hope 5 and 3
Ouimet & Johnston beat Torrance & Storey 4 and 2
Gunn & MacKenzie beat Beck & Martin 7 and 5

† *No points were given for halved matches between 1922 and 1969. There was a total of 12 points 1922–61 and 24 points 1963–69.*

1928 *continued*

Singles
RT Jones Jr beat TP Perkins 13 and 12
G Von Elm beat W Tweddell 3 and 2
FD Ouimet beat CO Hezlet 8 and 7
JW Sweetser beat WL Hope 5 and 4
HR Johnston beat EF Storey 4 and 2
C Evans Jr lost to TA Torrance 1 hole
W Gunn beat RH Hardman 11 and 10
RR MacKenzie beat GNC Martin 2 and 1

1926 *St Andrews, Fife, Scotland* June 2–3

Result: USA 6, GB&I 5[†]

Captains: R Harris (GB&I), RA Gardner (USA)

Foursomes
Wethered & Holderness beat Ouimet & Guilford 5 and 4
Tolley & Jamieson lost to Jones & Gunn 4 and 3
Harris & Hezlet lost to Von Elm & Sweetser 8 and 7
Storey & Brownlow lost to Gardner & MacKenzie 1 hole

Singles
CJH Tolley lost to RT Jones Jr 12 and 11
EWE Holderness lost to JW Sweetser 4 and 3
RH Wethered beat FD Ouimet 5 and 4
CO Hezlet halved with G Von Elm
R Harris beat JP Guilford 2 and 1
Hon WGE Brownlow lost to W Gunn 9 and 8
EF Storey beat RR MacKenzie 2 and 1
A Jamieson Jr beat RA Gardner 5 and 4

1924 *Garden City GC, NY* Sept 12–13

Result: USA 9, GB&I 3

Captains: RA Gardner (USA), CJH Tolley (GB&I)

Foursomes
Marston & Gardner beat Storey & Murray 3 and 1
Guilford & Ouimet beat Tolley & Hezlet 2 and 1
Jones & Fownes Jr lost to Scott & Scott Jr 1 hole
Sweetser & Johnston beat Torrance & Bristowe 4 and 3

Singles
MR Marston lost to CJH Tolley 1 hole
RT Jones Jr beat CO Hezlet 4 and 3
C Evans Jr beat WA Murray 2 and 1
FD Ouimet beat EF Storey 1 hole
JW Sweetser lost to Hon M Scott 7 and 6
RA Gardner beat WL Hope 3 and 2
JP Guilford beat TA Torrance 2 and 1
OF Willing beat DH Kyle 3 and 2

1923 *St Andrews, Fife, Scotland* May 18–19

Result: USA 6, GB&I 5[†]

Captains: R Harris (GB&I), RA Gardner (USA)

Foursomes
Tolley & Wethered beat Ouimet & Sweetser 6 and 5
Harris & Hooman lost to Gardner & Marston
7 and 6
Holderness & Hope beat Rotan & Herron 1 hole
Wilson & Murray beat Johnston & Neville 4 and 3

Singles
RH Wethered halved with FD Ouimet
CJH Tolley beat JW Sweetser 4 and 3
R Harris lost to RA Gardner 1 hole
WW Mackenzie lost to GV Rotan 5 and 4
WL Hope lost to MR Marston 6 and 5
EWE Holderness lost to FJ Wright Jr 1 hole
J Wilson beat SD Herron 1 hole
WA Murray lost to OF Willing 2 and 1

1922 *National Golf Links, NY* Aug 28–29

Result: USA 8, GB&I 4

Captains: WC Fownes (USA), R Harris (GB&I)

Foursomes
Guilford & Ouimet beat Tolley & Darwin 8 and 7
Evans & Gardner lost to Wethered & Aylmer 5 and 4
Jones & Sweetser beat Torrance & Hooman 3 and 2
Marston & Fownes beat Caven & Mackenzie 2 and 1

Singles
JP Guilford beat CJH Tolley 2 and 1
RT Jones Jr beat RH Wethered 3 and 2
C Evans Jr beat J Caven 5 and 4
FD Ouimet beat CC Aylmer 8 and 7
RA Gardner beat WB Torrance 7 and 5
MR Marston lost to WW Mackenzie 6 and 5
WC Fownes Jr lost to B Darwin 3 and 1
JW Sweetser lost to CVL Hooman at 37th

Unofficial match
1921 *Hoylake* 21 May

Result: USA 9, GB&I 3

Foursomes
Simpson & Jenkins lost to Evans & Jones 5 and 3
Tolley & Holderness lost to Ouimet & Guilford 3 and 2
de Montmorency & Wethered lost to Hunter & Platt
1 hole
Aylmer & Armour lost to Wright & Fownes 4 and 2

Singles
CJH Tolley beat C Evans Jr 4 and 3
JLC Jenkins lost to FD Ouimet 6 and 5
RH de Montmorency lost to RT Jones Jr 4 and 3
JG Simpson lost to JP Guilford 2 and 1
CC Aylmer beat P Hunter 2 and 1
TD Armour beat JW Platt 2 and 1
EWE Holderness lost to F Wright 2 holes
RH Wethered lost to WC Fownes Jr 3 and 1

† *No points were given for halved matches between 1922 and 1969. There was a total of 12 points 1922–61 and 24 points 1963–69*

Walker Cup – INDIVIDUAL RECORDS

Notes: Bold type indicates captain; in brackets, did not play
      † indicates players who have also played in the Ryder Cup

Great Britain and Ireland

Name		Year	Played	Won	Lost	Halved
MF Attenborough	ENG	1967	2	0	2	0
CC Aylmer	ENG	1922	2	1	1	0
†P Baker	ENG	1985	3	2	1	0
JB Beck	ENG	1928-(38)-(47)	1	0	1	0
PJ Benka	ENG	1969	4	2	1	1
HG Bentley	ENG	1934-36-38	4	0	2	2
DA Blair	SCO	1955-61	4	1	3	0
C Bloice	SCO	1985	3	0	2	1
MF Bonallack	ENG	1957-59-61-63-65-67-**69-71**-73	25	8	14	3
JT Bookless	SCO	(1932)	0	0	0	0
W Booth	SCO	2009	4	1	2	1
†G Brand Jr	SCO	1979	3	0	3	0
OC Bristowe	ENG	(1923)-24	1	0	1	0
A Brodie	SCO	1977-79	8	5	2	1
A Brooks	SCO	1969	3	2	0	1
M Brooks	SCO	1997	2	0	2	0
C Brown	WAL	**(1995-97)**	0	0	0	0
S Brown	ENG	2011	3	1	1	1
Hon WGE Brownlow	IRL	1926	2	0	2	0
J Bruen	IRL	1938-49-51	5	0	4	1
JA Buckley	WAL	1979	1	0	1	0
J Burke	IRL	1932	2	0	1	1
R Burns	IRL	1993	2	1	1	0
AF Bussell	SCO	1957	2	1	1	0
J Byrne	SCO	2011	3	2	1	0
S Cage	ENG	1993	3	0	2	1
I Caldwell	ENG	1951-55	4	1	2	1
J Caldwell	IRL	2007	3	1	1	1
W Campbell	SCO	1930	2	0	2	0
JB Carr	IRL	1947-49-51-53-55-57-59-61-63-**(65)-67**	20	5	14	1
RJ Carr	IRL	1971	4	3	0	1
DG Carrick	SCO	1983-87	5	0	5	0
IA Carslaw	SCO	1979	3	1	1	1
†P Casey	ENG	1999	4	4	0	0
C Cassells	ENG	1989	3	2	1	0
JR Cater	SCO	1955	1	0	1	0
J Caven	SCO	1922-(23)	2	0	2	0
BHG Chapman	ENG	1961	1	0	1	0
R Chapman	ENG	1981	4	3	1	0
MJ Christmas	ENG	1961-63	3	1	2	0
†CA Clark	ENG	1965	4	2	0	2
GJ Clark	ENG	1965	1	0	1	0
†HK Clark	ENG	1973	3	1	1	1
R Claydon	ENG	1989	4	2	2	0
†A Coltart	SCO	1991	3	2	1	0
GB Cosh	SCO	1965	4	3	1	0
R Coughlan	IRL	1997	4	0	3	1
T Craddock	IRL	1967-69	6	2	3	1
LG Crawley	ENG	1932-34-38-47	6	3	3	0
B Critchley	ENG	1969	4	1	1	2
D Curry	ENG	1987	4	1	3	0
P Cutler	IRL	2011	4	3	0	1
CR Dalgleish	SCO	1981-**(07)**-**(09)**	3	1	2	0
B Darwin	ENG	1922	2	1	1	0
JC Davies	ENG	1973-75-77-79	13	3	8	2
R Davies	WAL	2005-07	8	4	3	1
G Dear	SCO	2009	4	1	2	1
P Deeble	ENG	1977-81	5	1	4	0
FWG Deighton	SCO	(1951)-57	2	0	2	0
R Dinwiddie	ENG	2005	3	1	1	3
SC Dodd	WAL	1989	4	1	1	2
†L Donald	ENG	1999-01	8	7	1	0
N Dougherty	ENG	2001	4	3	1	0

Walker Cup Individual Records *continued*

Name		Year	Played	Won	Lost	Halved
B Dredge	WAL	1993	3	0	3	0
†NV Drew	IRL	1953	1	0	1	0
A Dunbar	IRL	2011	3	2	1	0
AA Duncan	WAL	(1953)	0	0	0	0
JM Dykes	SCO	1936	2	0	1	1
S Dyson	ENG	1999	3	0	2	1
NB Edwards	WAL	2001-03-05-07-(2011)	12	4	5	3
R Eggo	ENG	1987	2	0	2	0
J Elson	ENG	2001	3	1	0	2
D Evans	WAL	1981	3	1	1	1
G Evans	ENG	1991	4	2	2	0
RC Ewing	IRL	1936-38-47-49-51-55	10	1	7	2
GRD Eyles	ENG	1975	4	2	2	0
J Fanagan	IRL	1995	3	3	0	0
EW Fiddian	ENG	1932-34	4	0	4	0
O Fisher	ENG	2005	4	1	2	1
T Fleetwood	ENG	2009	2	1	1	0
J de Forest	ENG	1932	1	0	1	0
M Foster	ENG	1995	4	2	0	2
R Foster	ENG	1965-67-69-71-73-(79)-(81)	17	2	13	2
N Fox	IRL	2003	3	1	2	0
DW Frame	ENG	1961	1	0	1	0
S Gallacher	SCO	1995	4	2	2	0
†D Gilford	ENG	1985	1	0	1	0
P Girvan	SCO	1987	3	0	3	0
L Goddard	ENG	2009	2	0	2	0
G Godwin	ENG	1979-81	7	2	4	1
G Gordon	SCO	2003	1	0	1	0
CW Green	SCO	1963-69-71-73-75-(83)-(85)	17	4	10	3
P Gribben	IRL	1999	4	1	2	1
M Haines	ENG	2009	4	1	3	0
RH Hardman	ENG	1928	1	0	1	0
A Hare	ENG	1989	3	2	0	1
†P Harrington	IRL	1991-93-95	9	3	5	1
R Harris	SCO	(1922)-23-26	4	1	3	0
RW Hartley	ENG	1930-32	4	0	4	0
WL Hartley	ENG	1932	2	0	2	0
J Hawksworth	ENG	1985	4	2	1	1
G Hay	SCO	1991	3	1	2	0
P Hedges	ENG	1973-75	5	0	2	3
CO Hezlet	IRL	1924-26-28	6	0	5	1
GA Hill	ENG	1936-(55)	2	0	1	1
S Hodgson	ENG	2009-11	6	2	4	0
M Hoey	IRL	2001	4	3	1	0
Sir EWE Holderness	ENG	1923-26-30	6	2	4	0
TWB Homer	ENG	1973	3	0	3	0
‡CVL Hooman	ENG	1922-23	3	†1	2	†0
WL Hope	SCO	1923-24-28	5	1	4	0
D Horsey	ENG	2007	4	3	1	0
DB Howard	SCO	1995-97	6	0	4	2
†D Howell	ENG	1995	3	2	0	1
G Huddy	ENG	1961	1	0	1	0
W Humphreys	ENG	1971	3	2	1	0
IC Hutcheon	SCO	1975-77-79-81	15	5	8	2
S Hutsby	ENG	2009	4	2	2	0
D Inglis	SCO	2003	4	2	1	1
RR Jack	SCO	1957-59	4	2	2	0
L James	ENG	1995	2	0	2	0
†M James	ENG	1975	4	3	1	0
A Jamieson Jr	SCO	1926	2	1	1	0
N Kearney	IRL	2009	4	2	2	0
MJ Kelley	ENG	1977-79	7	3	3	1
L Kelly	SCO	1999	2	0	2	0
SD Keppler	ENG	1983	4	0	3	1
†MG King	ENG	1969-73	7	1	5	1
AT Kyle	SCO	1938-47-51	5	2	3	0
DH Kyle	SCO	1924	1	0	1	0
JA Lang	SCO	(1930)	0	0	0	0

‡In 1922 Hooman beat Sweetser at the 37th – on all other occasions halved matches have counted as such.

Name		Year	Played	Won	Lost	Halved
JDA Langley	ENG	1936-51-53	6	0	5	1
CD Lawrie	SCO	(**1961**)-(**63**)	0	0	0	0
ME Lewis	ENG	1983	1	0	1	0
T Lewis	ENG	2011	4	1	2	1
G Lockerbie	ENG	2005	4	1	3	0
PB Lucas	ENG	(1936)-47-(**49**)	2	1	1	0
MSR Lunt	ENG	1959-61-63-65	11	2	8	1
†AWB Lyle	SCO	1977	3	0	3	0
AR McCallum	SCO	1928	1	0	1	0
SM McCready	IRL	1949-51	3	0	3	0
JS Macdonald	SCO	1971	3	1	1	1
†G McDowell	IRL	2001	4	2	2	0
B McElhinney	IRL	2005	1	0	1	0
P McEvoy	ENG	1977-79-81-85-89-(**99**)-(**01**)	18	5	11	2
R McEvoy	ENG	2001	2	1	0	1
G McGimpsey	IRL	1985-89-91-(**03**)-(**05**)	11	4	5	2
†P McGinley	IRL	1991	3	1	2	0
G Macgregor	SCO	1971-75-83-85-87-(**91**)-(**93**)	14	5	8	1
RC MacGregor	SCO	1953	2	0	2	0
J McHenry	IRL	1987	4	2	2	0
†R McIlroy	IRL	2007	4	1	2	1
P McKellar	SCO	1977	1	0	1	0
WW Mackenzie	SCO	1922-23	3	1	2	0
SL McKinlay	SCO	1934	2	0	2	0
J McLean	SCO	1934-36	4	1	3	0
EA McRuvie	SCO	1932-34	4	1	2	1
JFD Madeley	IRL	1963	2	0	1	1
S Manley	WAL	2003	3	2	0	1
LS Mann	SCO	1983	4	2	1	1
B Marchbank	SCO	1979	4	2	2	0
GC Marks	ENG	1969-71-(**87**)-(**89**)	6	2	4	0
DM Marsh	ENG	(1959)-71-(**73**)-(**75**)	3	2	1	0
GNC Martin	IRL	1928	1	0	1	0
S Martin	SCO	1977	4	2	2	0
L Matthews	WAL	2007	1	0	1	0
P Mayo	WAL	1985-87	4	0	3	1
GH Micklem	ENG	1947-49-53-55-(**57**)-(**59**)	6	1	5	0
DJ Millensted	ENG	1967	2	1	1	0
JW Milligan	SCO	1989-91	7	3	3	1
EB Millward	ENG	(1949)-55	2	0	2	0
WTG Milne	SCO	1973	4	2	2	0
†CS Montgomerie	SCO	1985-87	8	2	5	1
JL Morgan	WAL	1951-53-55	6	2	4	0
C Moriarty	IRL	2003	4	1	3	0
J Moul	ENG	2007	4	2	1	1
P Mulcare	IRL	1975	3	2	1	0
GH Murray	SCO	1977	2	1	1	0
SWT Murray	SCO	1963	4	2	2	0
WA Murray	SCO	1923-24-(26)	4	1	3	0
K Nolan	IRL	1997	3	0	3	0
E O'Connell	IRL	1989	4	2	0	2
S O'Hara	SCO	2001	4	2	2	0
A Oldcorn	ENG	1983	4	4	0	0
†PA Oosterhuis	ENG	1967	4	1	2	1
R Oppenheimer	ENG	(**1951**)	0	0	0	0
P Page	ENG	1993	2	0	2	0
C Paisley	ENG	2009	3	0	1	2
D Park	WAL	1997	3	0	3	0
P Parkin	WAL	1983	3	2	1	0
J Parry	ENG	2007	2	1	1	0
D Patrick	SCO	1999	1	0	1	0
J Payne	ENG	1991	4	2	2	0
JJF Pennink	ENG	1938	2	1	1	0
TP Perkins	ENG	1928	2	0	2	0
GB Peters	SCO	1936-38	4	2	1	1
V Phillips	ENG	1993	3	1	2	0
AD Pierse	IRL	1983	3	0	2	1
AH Perowne	ENG	1949-53-59	4	0	4	0
AK Pirie	SCO	1967	3	0	2	1
MA Poxon	ENG	1975	2	0	2	0

Walker Cup Individual Records *continued*

Name		Year	Played	Won	Lost	Halved
D Prosser	ENG	1989	1	0	1	0
R Pugh	WAL	2011	3	3	0	0
I Pyman	ENG	1993	3	0	3	0
†R Rafferty	IRL	1981	4	2	2	0
R Ramsay	SCO	2005	2	1	1	0
G Rankin	SCO	1995-97-99	8	2	6	0
M Richardson	ENG	2005	4	2	2	0
D Robertson	SCO	1993	3	1	2	0
J Robinson	ENG	1987	4	2	2	0
RN Roderick	WAL	1989	2	0	1	1
J Rose	ENG	1997	4	2	2	0
P Rowe	ENG	1999	3	3	0	0
R Russell	SCO	1993	3	0	3	0
AC Saddler	SCO	1963-65-67-(77)	10	3	5	2
L Saltman	SCO	2005-07	7	4	3	0
Hon M Scott	ENG	1924-34	4	2	2	0
R Scott, Jr	SCO	1924	1	1	0	0
PF Scrutton	ENG	1955-57	3	0	3	0
J Senior	ENG	2011	4	2	1	1
DN Sewell	ENG	1957-59	4	1	3	0
RDBM Shade	SCO	1961-63-65-67	14	6	6	2
G Shaw	SCO	1987	4	1	2	1
DB Sheahan	IRL	1963	4	2	2	0
AE Shepperson	ENG	1957-59	3	1	1	1
G Sherry	SCO	1995	4	2	2	0
AF Simpson	SCO	(1926)	0	0	0	0
M Skelton	ENG	2003	2	1	1	0
JN Smith	SCO	1930	2	0	2	0
WD Smith	SCO	1959	1	0	1	0
M Stanford	ENG	1993	3	1	2	0
AR Stephen	SCO	1985	4	2	1	1
M Stewart	SCO	2011	4	2	1	1
EF Storey	ENG	1924-26-28	6	1	5	0
G Storm	ENG	1999	4	2	2	0
JA Stout	ENG	1930-32	4	0	3	1
C Stowe	ENG	1938-47	4	2	2	0
HB Stuart	SCO	1971-73-75	10	4	6	0
A Sullivan	ENG	2011	4	2	2	0
A Thirlwell	ENG	1957	1	0	1	0
KG Thom	ENG	1949	2	0	2	0
MS Thompson	ENG	1983	3	1	2	0
H Thomson	SCO	1936-38	4	2	2	0
CJH Tolley	ENG	1922-23-24-26-30-34	12	4	8	0
TA Torrance	SCO	1924-28-30-32-34	9	3	5	1
WB Torrance	SCO	1922	2	0	2	0
†PM Townsend	ENG	1965	4	3	1	0
LP Tupling	ENG	1969	2	1	1	0
W Tweddell	ENG	1928-(36)	2	0	2	0
J Walker	SCO	1961	2	0	2	0
†P Walton	IRL	1981-83	8	6	2	0
M Warren	SCO	2001	3	2	1	0
C Watson	SCO	1997	3	1	1	1
†P Way	ENG	1981	4	2	2	0
RH Wethered	ENG	1922-23-26-30-34	9	5	3	1
L White	ENG	1991	2	1	1	0
RJ White	ENG	1947-49-51-53-55	10	6	3	1
D Whitnell	ENG	2009	3	0	3	0
D Willett	ENG	2007	4	0	2	2
R Willison	ENG	1991	4	1	3	0
J Wilson	SCO	1923	2	2	0	0
JC Wilson	SCO	1947-53	4	0	4	0
O Wilson	ENG	2003	3	2	0	1
S Wilson	SCO	2003	4	1	1	2
GB Wolstenholme	ENG	1957-59	4	1	2	1
GP Wolstenholme	ENG	1995-97-99-01-03-05	19	10	9	0
S Young	SCO	1997	4	2	2	0

United States of America

Name	Year	Played	Won	Lost	Halved
†TD Aaron	1959	2	1	1	0
B Alexander	1987	3	2	1	0
DC Allen	1965-67	6	0	4	2
B Andrade	1987	4	2	2	0
ES Andrews	1961	1	1	0	0
D Ballenger	1973	1	1	0	0
B Barber	2011	3	0	2	1
R Baxter, Jr	1957	2	2	0	0
N Begay III	1995	3	1	2	0
DR Beman	1959-61-63-65	11	7	2	2
D Berganio	1993	3	1	2	0
RE Billows	1938-49	4	2	2	0
SE Bishop	1947-49	3	2	1	0
AS Blum	1957	1	0	1	0
J Bohmann	1969	3	1	2	0
M Brannan	1977	3	1	2	0
A Bratton	1995	3	1	0	2
GF Burns III	1975	3	2	1	0
C Burroughs	1985	3	1	2	0
J Byrd	1999	3	1	2	0
AE Campbell	1936	2	2	0	0
JE Campbell	1957	1	0	1	0
WC Campbell	1951-53-(**55**)-57-65-67-71-75	18	11	4	3
P Cantlay	2011	4	2	1	1
N Cassini	2001	4	2	2	0
B Cauley	2009	4	3	0	1
RJ Cerrudo	1967	4	1	1	2
RD Chapman	1947-51-53	5	3	2	0
D Cherry	1953-55-61	5	5	0	0
D Clarke	1979	3	2	0	1
RE Cochran	1961	1	1	0	0
CR Coe	1949-51-53-(**57**)-**59**-61-63	13	7	4	2
R Commans	1981	3	1	1	1
E Compton	2001	3	1	1	1
JW Conrad	1955	2	1	1	0
J Courville Jr	1995-97	6	4	2	0
K Cox	1995	3	1	2	0
N Crosby	1983	2	1	1	0
BH Cudd	1955	2	2	0	0
RD Davies	1963	2	0	2	0
JW Dawson	1949	2	2	0	0
D Delcher	1997	3	2	1	0
T Demsey	1993	3	3	0	0
RB Dickson	1967	3	3	0	0
A Doyle	1991-93	6	5	1	0
J Driscoll	2001	3	0	3	0
GT Dunlap Jr	1932-34-36	5	3	1	1
†D Duval	1991	3	2	1	0
D Edwards	1973	4	4	0	0
HC Egan	1934	1	1	0	0
D Eger	1989-91-01	8	4	3	1
D Eichelberger	1965	3	1	2	0
B Elder	1997	4	4	0	0
J Ellis	1973	3	2	1	0
W Emery	1936	2	1	0	1
H English	2011	4	2	2	0
C Evans Jr	1922-24-28	5	3	2	0
M Every	2005	4	1	2	1
J Farquhar	1971	3	1	2	0
†B Faxon	1983	4	3	1	0
R Fehr	1983	4	2	1	1
JW Fischer	1934-36-38-(**65**)	4	3	0	1
D Fischesser	1979	3	1	2	0
MA Fleckman	1967	2	0	2	0
B Fleisher	1969	4	0	2	2
J Fought	1977	4	4	0	0
†R Fowler	2007-09	8	7	1	0
WC Fownes Jr	**1922-24**	3	1	2	0

Walker Cup Individual Records *continued*

Name	Year	Played	Won	Lost	Halved
F Fuhrer III	1981	3	2	1	0
JR Gabrielsen	1977-(**81**)-(**91**)	3	1	2	0
R Gamez	1989	4	3	0	1
RA Gardner	1922-**23-24-26**	8	6	2	0
RW Gardner	1961-63	5	4	0	1
B Gay	1993	2	0	1	1
B Gielow	2009	3	1	2	0
M Giles III	1969-71-73-75-(**93**)	15	8	2	5
HL Givan	1936	1	0	0	1
L Glover	2001	4	2	2	0
JG Goodman	1934-36-38	6	4	2	0
J Gore	1997	3	2	0	1
D Gossett	1999	4	1	2	1
M Gove	1979	3	2	1	0
J Grace	1975	3	2	1	0
JA Grant	1967	2	2	0	0
AD Gray Jr	1963-65-67-(**95**)-(**97**)	12	5	6	1
D Green	2001	3	0	3	0
JP Guilford	1922-24-26	6	4	2	0
W Gunn	1926-28	4	4	0	0
B Haas	2003	4	2	2	0
†F Haas Jr	1938	2	0	2	0
H Haas	1999	4	3	1	0
†JD Haas	1975	3	3	0	0
J Haas	1985	3	1	2	0
G Hallberg	1977	3	1	2	0
GS Hamer Jr	(1947)	0	0	0	0
B Harman	2005-09	7	4	1	2
J Harris	1993-95-97-01	14	10	4	0
LE Harris Jr	1963	4	3	1	0
V Heafner	1977	3	3	0	0
M Hendrix	2003	3	2	0	1
R Henley	2011	3	1	2	0
SD Herron	1923	2	0	2	0
T Herron	1993	3	3	0	0
†S Hoch	1979	4	4	0	0
W Hoffer	1983	2	1	1	0
M Hoffmann	2009	3	2	0	1
J Holmes	2005	3	2	1	0
J Holtgrieve	1979-81-83-(**2011**)	10	6	4	0
JM Hopkins	1965	3	0	2	1
B Horschel	2007	4	3	1	0
R Howe	1989	1	0	1	0
W Howell	1932	1	1	0	0
B Hurley	2005	2	0	2	0
W Hyndman III	1957-59-61-69-71	9	6	1	2
J Inman Jr	1969	2	2	0	0
JG Jackson	1953-55	3	3	0	0
T Jackson	1995-99	6	3	2	1
†D Johnson	2007	3	1	1	1
GK Johnson	1989	3	1	2	0
HR Johnston	1923-24-28-30	6	5	1	0
RT Jones Jr	1922-24-26-**28-30**	10	9	1	0
AF Kammer Jr	1947	2	1	1	0
M Killian	1973	3	1	2	0
A Kim	2005	4	2	1	1
C Kirk	2007	2	1	1	0
C Kite	1987	3	2	1	0
†TO Kite Jr	1971	4	2	1	1
RE Knepper	(1922)	0	0	0	0
C Knost	2007	4	2	0	2
RW Knowles Jr	1951	1	1	0	0
G Koch	1973-75	7	4	1	2
CR Kocsis	1938-49-57	5	2	2	1
K Kraft	2011	4	0	4	0
J Kribel	1997	3	1	2	0
†M Kuchar	1999	3	0	3	0
T Kuehne	1995-03-07	10	2	7	1

Name	Year	Played	Won	Lost	Halved
F Langham	1991	3	1	2	0
R Leen	1997	3	2	1	0
†J Leonard	1993	3	3	0	0
G Lesher	1989	4	1	3	0
B Lewis Jr	1981-83-85-87-(03)-(05)	14	10	4	0
JW Lewis	1967	4	3	1	0
WL Little Jr	1934	2	2	0	0
†GA Littler	1953	2	2	0	0
E Loar	1999	3	2	1	0
B Loeffler	1987	3	2	1	0
†D Love III	1985	3	2	0	1
J Lovemark	2007	3	2	1	0
B Mackenzie	2003	3	3	0	0
RR Mackenzie	1926-28-30	6	5	1	0
MJ McCarthy Jr	(1928)-32	1	1	0	0
BN McCormick	1949	1	1	0	0
T McKnight	1999	2	0	2	0
JB McHale	1949-51	3	2	0	1
MR Marston	1922-23-24-34	8	5	3	0
D Martin	1989	4	1	1	2
G Marucci	1995-97-(07)-(09)	6	4	1	1
L Mattiace	1987	3	2	1	0
R May	1991	4	3	1	0
B Mayfair	1987	3	3	0	0
E Meeks	1989	1	0	0	1
SN Melnyk	1969-71	7	3	3	1
†P Mickelson	1989-91	8	4	2	2
AL Miller III	1969-71	8	4	3	1
J Miller	1999	3	2	1	0
L Miller	1977	4	4	0	0
A Mitchell	2009	3	1	2	0
K Mitchum	1993	3	2	0	1
DK Moe	1930-32	3	3	0	0
B Molder	1999-01	8	3	3	2
B Montgomery	1987	2	2	0	0
G Moody III	1979	3	1	2	0
J Moore	2007	3	2	0	1
R Moore	2003	2	0	2	0
GT Moreland	1932-34	4	4	0	0
D Morey	1955-65	4	1	3	0
J Mudd	1981	3	3	0	0
†RJ Murphy Jr	1967	4	1	2	1
C Nallen	2003	2	1	1	0
JF Neville	1923	1	0	1	0
†JW Nicklaus	1959-61	4	4	0	0
LW Oehmig	(1977)	0	0	0	0
FD Ouimet	1922-23-24-26-28-30-**32**-**34**-(**36**)-(**38**)-(**47**)-(**49**)	16	9	5	2
†J Overton	2005	4	3	1	0
HD Paddock Jr	1951	1	0	0	1
†J Pate	1975	4	0	4	0
WJ Patton	1955-57-59-63-65-(69)	14	11	3	0
†C Pavin	1981	3	2	0	1
M Pfeil	1973	4	2	1	1
M Podolak	1985	2	1	0	1
M Putnam	2005	4	1	2	1
M Peck	1979	3	1	1	1
SL Quick	1947	2	1	1	0
J Quinney	2001	2	0	2	0
S Randolph	1985	4	2	1	1
J Rassett	1981	3	3	0	0
K Reifers	2005	2	0	2	0
F Ridley	1977-(**87**)-(**89**)	3	2	1	0
RH Riegel	1947-49	4	4	0	0
C Riley	1995	3	1	1	1
H Robbins Jr	1957	2	0	1	1
P Rodgers	2011	3	0	2	1
†W Rogers	1973	2	1	1	0
GV Rotan	1923	2	1	1	0
A Rubinson	2003	4	1	2	1

Walker Cup Individual Records *continued*

Name	Year	Played	Won	Lost	Halved
†EM Rudolph	1957	2	1	0	1
B Sander	1977	3	0	3	0
T Scherrer	1991	3	0	3	0
S Scott	1997-99	6	2	4	0
CH Seaver	1932	2	2	0	0
RL Siderowf	1969-73-75-77-(**79**)	14	4	8	2
J Sigel	1977-79-81-**83-85**-87-89-91-93	33	18	10	5
RH Sikes	1963	3	1	2	0
JB Simons	1971	2	0	2	0
†S Simpson	1977	3	3	0	0
W Simpson	2007	3	0	2	1
CB Smith	1961-63	2	0	1	1
N Smith	2009-11	6	2	3	1
R Smith	1936-38	4	2	2	0
R Sonnier	1985	3	0	2	1
J Sorensen	1987	3	1	1	1
J Speith	2011	3	2	0	1
M Sposa	1991	3	2	1	0
†C Stadler	1975	3	3	0	0
K Stanley	2007	3	0	3	0
FR Stranahan	1947-49-51	6	3	2	1
†C Strange	1975	4	3	0	1
†H Sutton	1979-81	7	2	4	1
‡JW Sweetser	1922-23-24-26-28-32-(**67**)-(73)	12	7	†4	1
FM Taylor	1957-59-61	4	4	0	0
D Tentis	1983	2	0	1	1
N Thompson	2005	2	1	1	0
DJ Trahan	2001	4	1	3	0
C Tringale	2009	3	1	1	1
RS Tufts	(**1963**)	0	0	0	0
WP Turnesa	1947-49-**51**	6	3	3	0
B Tuten	1983	2	1	1	0
EM Tutweiler Jr	1965-67	6	5	1	0
ER Updegraff	1963-65-69-(**75**)	7	3	3	1
S Urzetta	1951-53	4	4	0	0
P Uihlein	2009	8	6	2	0
†K Venturi	1953	2	2	0	0
†S Verplank	1985	4	3	0	1
M Voges	1991	3	2	1	0
GJ Voigt	1930-32-36	5	2	2	1
G Von Elm	1926-28-30	6	4	1	1
D von Tacky	1981	3	1	2	0
†JL Wadkins	1969-71	7	3	4	0
D Waldorf	1985	3	1	2	0
EH Ward Jr	1953-55-59	6	6	0	0
MH Ward	1938-47	4	2	2	0
D Weaver	2009	3	0	2	1
M West III	1973-79	6	2	3	1
J Westland	1932-34-53-(**61**)	5	3	0	2
HW Wettlaufer	1959	2	2	0	0
E White	1936	2	2	0	0
C Williams	2011	3	2	1	0
L Williams	2003-05	7	3	2	2
OF Willing	1923-24-30	4	4	0	0
JM Winters Jr	(**1971**)	0	0	0	0
C Wittenberg	2003	4	1	2	1
C Wollman	1997	3	1	1	1
W Wood	1983	4	1	2	1
†T Woods	1995	4	2	2	0
FJ Wright Jr	1923	1	1	0	0
CR Yates	1936-38-(**53**)	4	3	0	1
D Yates III	1989-93-(**99**)-01	6	3	2	1
RL Yost	1955	2	2	0	0
G Zahringer	2003	3	0	2	1

‡*In 1922 Hooman beat Sweetser at the 37th – on all other occasions halved matches have counted as such.*

World Amateur Team Championship (Eisenhower Trophy)   (inaugurated 1958)

History: From 1958 to 2004, Great Britain & Ireland competed as a team. Now each Home country is represented, hence Scotland's win in 2008.

1958	1 Australia* 918; 2 United States 918	Old Course, St Andrews, Fife, Scotland
	Play-off: Australia 222; United States 224	
1960	1 United States 834; 2 Australia 836	Merion GC East, Ardmore, PA, USA
1962	1 United States 854; 2 Canada 862	Fuji GC, Kawana, Japan
1964	1 Great Britain & Ireland 895; 2 Canada 897	Olgiata GC, Rome, Italy
1966	1 Australia 877; 2 United States 879	Club de Golf, Mexico City, Mexico
1968	1 United States 868; 2 Great Britain & Ireland 869	Royal Melbourne GC, Australia
1970	1 United States 854; 2 New Zealand 869	Real Club de Puerta Hierro, Madrid, Spain
1972	1 United States 865; 2 Australia 870	Olivos GC 1980, Buenos Aires, Argentina
1974	1 United States 888; 2 Japan 898	Campo de Golf Cajules, Dominican Republic
1976	1 Great Britain & Ireland 892; 2 Japan 894	Penina GC, Portimão, Algarve, Portugal
1978	1 United States 873; 2 Canada 886	Pacific Harbour GC, Fiji
1980	1 United States 848; 2 South Africa 875	Pinehurst No.2, NC, USA
1982	1 United States 859; 2 Sweden 866	Lausanne GC, Switzerland
1984	1 Japan 870; 2 United States 877	Royal Hong Kong GC, Fanling, Hong Kong
1986	1 Canada 838; 2 United States 841	Lagunita CC, Caracas, Venezuela
1988	1 Great Britain & Ireland 882; 2 United States 887	Ullna GC, Stockholm, Sweden
1990	1 Sweden 879; 2 New Zealand 892	Christchurch GC, New Zealand
1992	1 New Zealand 823; 2 United States 830	Capilano G&CC and Marine Drive GC, Vancouver, BC, Canada
1994	1 United States 838; 2 Great Britain & Ireland 849	La Boulie GC and Le Golf National, Versailles, France
1996	1 Australia 838; 2 Sweden 849	Manila Southwoods (Masters and Legends) GC, Philippines
1998	1 Great Britain and Ireland 852; 2 Australia 856	Club de Golf los Leones and Club de Golf La Dehesa, Santiago, Chile
2000	1 United States 841; 2 Great Britain & Ireland 857	Berlin Sporting Club and Club de Golf Bad Saaron, Germany
2002	1 United States 568; 2 France 571	Sanyana G&CC (Palm and Bunga Raya Courses), Malaysia
2004	1 United States 407; 2 Spain 416	Rio Mar GC (Ocean and River Courses), Puerto Rico
2006	1 Netherlands 554; 2 Canada 556	De Zalse GC and Stellenbosch GC, South Africa
2008	1 Scotland 560; 2 USA 569	The Grange GC (West Course) and Royal Adelaide GC, Australia
2010	1 France 423; 2 Denmark 427	Buenos Aires GC and Olivos GC, Argentina

Europe v Asia–Pacific (Sir Michael Bonallack Trophy)   (inaugurated 1998)

This event will next be held in 2012

St Andrews Trophy (Great Britain & Ireland v Continent of Europe)

Match inaugurated 1956, trophy presented 1964

History: Since 1956, Great Britain & Ireland have won 24 times, Continent of Europe on four occasions. This event will next be held in 2012

Four Nations Cup (inaugurated 1987)   *Hills GC, New Zealand*

1	Australia	216-222-203-210—851
2	New Zealand	223-216-216-207—862
3	Argentina	220-230-219-216—885
4	South Africa	225-222-221-221—889

Winning team: Brett Drewitt, Todd Sinnott, Ryan Peake and Maverick Antcliffe.

Individual:

1	Brett Drewitt (AUS)	72-76-69-68—281
2	Ben Campbell (NZL)	75-70-72-69—286
	Todd Sinnott (AUS)	76-72-66-72—286

Asia–Pacific Amateur Team Championship (Nomura Cup) *Denarau G&RC and Natadola Bay GC. Fiji*
(Rounds 1 and 4 at Denarau and 2 and 3 at Natadola)

1	Australia	207-212-220-201—840
2	New Zealand	211-224-217-209—861
3	India	208-226-220-211—865
4	Korea	218-213-232-207—870
5	Japan	215-233-233-206—887
6	Philippines	213-228-236-214—891
7	Chinese Taipei	214-229-233-221—897
8	China	213-234-234-217—898
9	Hong Kong	221-235-229-214—899
10	Thailand	216-236-240-209—901
11	Fiji	221-232-240-217—910
12	Singapore	217-231-249-214—911
13	Guam	232-237-245-224—938
14	United Arab Emirates	218-249-254-224—945
15	Samoa	225-247-255-224—951
16	Papua New Guinea	238-260-258-236—992
17	Iran	244-263-265-240—1,012
18	Kyrgyzstan	279-329-335-281—1,224

Winning team: Australia: Cameron Smith, Jake Higginbottom, Daniel Bringolf and Marika Batibasaga

Individual:

1	Cameron Smith (AUS)	67-71-73-68—279
2	Jake Higginbottom (AUS)	69-70-76-66—281
3	Daniel Bringolf (AUS)	71-76-71-67—285
	Ryan Fox (NZL)	70-73-71-71—285
	Khalin H Joshi (IND)	70-75-72-68—285

History: Australia has won nine times, Japan eight times, Chinese Taipei five times, India, South Korea and New Zealand once.

Africa

African Amateur Team Championship *The Club Benoi*

1	South Africa	212-202-211-210—835
2	Namibia	227-231-219-215—892
3	Kenya	236-222-221-221—900
4	Swaziland	231-234-234-219—918
5	Botswana	234-223-243-223—923
6	Zimbabwe	233-231-236-226—926
7	Zambia	248-240-244-225—957
	Mauritius	241-242-237-237—957

Australia retains Nomura Cup in Fiji

Australia led from start to finish to win the Nomura Cup at the Asia-Pacific Teams Championship played over the Denarau and Natadola golf clubs in Fiji. Cameron Smith, Jake Higginbottom and Daniel Bringolf, three members of the four-man Australian squad, finished in the gold, silver and bronze positions in the individual competition.

The Australians finished with a team total of 840 beating New Zealand into second place by 21 shots. The Indian quartet were third 25 shots behind the winners.

Defending champions Korea finished fourth but team member Jae Hyeok Lee set a course record at Natadola with 68 and Sang Yeop Lee also set a new record with his 65 at Denarau.

It was the first time the event had been staged in Fiji and it was only the second international team event to be held there. In 1978 the World Amateur Team Championship was won by the Amerians at Pacific Harbour Golf and Country Club.

Samoa and Kyrgyzstan were in the field for the first time bringing the number of contesting countries to 18.

9	Reunion Island	246-250-240-228—964
10	Uganda	247-242-237-239—965
11	Ivory Coast	257-243-242-235—977

Winning team: Graham Van der Merwe, Riekus Nortje, Daniel Hammond and C J du Plessis

Individual Championship:

1	Riekus Nortje (RSA)	68-65-70-70—273
2	Stuart Smith (BOT)	74-68-72-69—283
	Daniel Hammond (RSA)	70-66-75-72—283
	Stefan Anderson (KEN)	72-70-68-73—283

South African Men's Inter-Provincial Championship *Bloemfontein GC*

Day 1: Western Province 6, Gauteng North 6; KwaZulu Natal 8, Southern Cape 4; Central Gauteng 6½, Boland 5½

Day 2: Central Gauteng 9½, Southern Cape 2½; Gauteng North 8½, KwaZulu Natal 3½; Boland 8, Western Province 4

Day 3: KwaZulu Natal 6, Central Gauteng 6; Gauteng North 9½, Boland 2½; Western Province 11, Southern Cape 1

Day 4: Western Province 6, Central Gauteng 6; Southern Cape 6½, Gauteng North 5½; KwaZulu Natal 9, Boland 3

Day 5: Boland 11, Southern Cape 1; Central Gauteng 6½, Gauteng North 5½; Western Province 6½, KwaZulu Natal 5½

Final table:	Pld	W	D	L	Games	Pts
1 Central Gauteng	5	3	2	0	34½	8
2 Western Province	5	2	2	1	33½	6
3 Gauteng North	5	2	1	2	35	5
4 KwaZulu Natal	5	2	1	2	32	5
5 Boland	5	2	0	3	30	4
6 Southern Cape	5	1	0	4	15	2

Winning team: Ruan de Smidt, Michael Dixon, Daniel Hammond, Callum Mowat, Damien Naicker, Muzi Nethunzwi, Haydn Porteous and Graham Van de Merwe

"B" section: 1 Limpopo; 2 Ekurhuleni; 3 Free State and North Cape; 4 Mpumalanga; 5 Eastern Province; 6 North West; 7 Border

South African Mid-Amateur Provincial Tournament *Humewood*

Day 1: Ekurhuleni 5, Mpumalanga 7; Kwazulu-Natal 8, Western Province 4; Central Gauteng 8.5, Boland 3.5

Day 2: Western Province 4.5, Central Gauteng 7.5; Mpumalanga 4, Kwazulu-Natal 8; Boland 5.5, Ekurheleni 6.5

Day 3: Kwazulu-Natal 6, Central Gauteng 6; Mpumalanga 2.5, Boland 9.5; Ekurheleni 6.5, Western Province 5.5

Day 4: Ekurheleni 7.5, Central Gauteng 4.5; Western Province, 9 Mpumalanga 3; Kwazulu-Natal 6, Boland 6

Day 5: Boland 4.5, Western Province 7.5; Central Gauteng 8.5, Mpumalanga 3.5; Kwazulu-Natal 7, Ekurheleni 5

Final table:	W	D	L	Pts	Games
1 Kwazulu-Natal	3	2	0	8	35
2 Central Gauteng	3	1	1	7	35
3 Ekurheleni	3	0	2	6	30½
4 Western Province	2	0	3	4	30½
5 Boland	1	1	3	3	29
6 Mpumalanga	1	0	4	2	20

Winning team: David Brown, Garry Coetzee, Sean Fenger, Murray Gilson, Elton James, Barry McGhee, Lyall McNeill and Simon Taylor

Zone VI African Team Championship *Nyali Golf Club, Mombasa, Kenya*

1 South Africa 20 pts; 2 Kenya 19; 3 Tanzania, Zimbabwe 13

Third Regional All-Africa Championship *Royal Harare GHC, Zimbabwe*

1	South Africa	456
2	Zimbabwe	458
3	Namibia	467
4	Botswana	557
5	Angola	680

South African Senior Women's Team Championship *Woodhill and Wingate Park*

1 Mpumalanga A 476; 2 Gauteng B 484; 3 Eastern Province A 490; 4 East Rand A 492; 5 Gauteng A 493; Gauteng North A 494; 7 Western Province 497; 8 Boland A 499; 9 Western Province A 502; 10 Gauteng C 506; 11 Mpumalanga B, Gauteng D. Gauteng North B 507; 14 KwaZulu Natal A 510; 15 KwaZulu Natal B 511; Border A 4 514; Mpumalanga C 517

Winning Team: Mpumalanga A   Allison Edwards, Lynn Levy, Pippa Griffiths, Kathy Cruikshanks

Americas

USGA Men's State Team Championship

This event will next be held in 2012

Juan Carlos Tailhade Cup *Los Lagartos G&CC, Buenos Aires, Argentina*

1	Holland	145-139-145-144—573
2	Australia	144-143-143-145—575
3	South Africa	151-140-143-145—579

4 Argentina 585; 5 Spain 588; 6 New Zealand 591; 7 Finland 593; 8 Canada 594; 9 Mexico 598; 10 England 599; 11 Switzerland 602; 12 Colombia 616; 13 Italy 618; 14 Peru 619

Winning team: Daniel Huizing and Robin Kind

Asia

Etiqa ASEAN Cup *Kuala Lumpur G and CC*

First and third rounds fourball better ball; second and fourth foursomes

1	Singapore (Jerome Ng and Marc Ong)	69-77-69-75—290
2	Myanmar (Myo Win Aung and Maung Maung Oo)	68-78-72-76—294
3	Malaysia (Kenneth de Silva and Tan Wei Chean)	73-79-69-78—299

4 Thailand 303; 5 Philippines 307; 6 Cambodia 324

What is the answer?

Q: May partners share clubs?

A: Partners may share clubs provided the total number of clubs selected for play between the two players does not exceed 14. For example, if Player A has six clubs and her partner Player B has eight clubs, they may share as the total does not exceed 14 (Rule 4-4b).

Australian Men's Interstate Team Championships   *Royal Perth GC*

Day 1 – S. Australia 5½, Tasmania 1½; W. Australia 4, Victoria 3; New South Wales 1, Queensland 6
Day 2 – Queensland 4½, W. Australia 2½; New South Wales 3½, W. Australia 3½; Tasmania 2, Victoria 5
Day 3 – Queensland 3½, W. Australia 3½; Victoria 5, S. Australia 2; New South Wales 3, Tasmania 4
Day 4 – W. Australia 4½, Tasmania 2½; S. Australia 2, New South Wales 5; Victoria 6, Queensland 1
Day 5 – Victoria 6, New South Wales 1; Tasmania 2, Queensland 5; W. Australia 3½, S. Australia 3½

Final table: Victoria – games won 25, matches won 4; 2 Queensland 20–3½; 3 Western Australia 19–3½; South Australia 15½–1½; 5 New South Wales 13½–1½; Tasmania 12–1

Final: Queensland 7½. Victoria 4½; 3rd place play-off: Western Australia 6½, South Australia 5½; 5th place play-off: New South Wales 8. Tasmania 4

Winning team: Queensland – Nathan Holman, Geoff Drakeford, Rory Bourke, Todd Sinnott, Lachlan Cain, Anthony Houston, Terry Vogel and James Gibellini.

Australian Mid-Amateur Team Championship

1	Queensland	233-241-228—702
2	Victoria	241-228-234—703
	New South Wales	235-224-244—703

Winning team: Warwick Oxenford, Steve Thompson and Katrina Jones

112th *Edinburgh Evening News Dispatch* Trophy   (inaugurated 1890)   *always at Braid Hills*

Semi-finals: Silverknowes beat Carrickvale 1 hole
          Barnton Hotel beat Temple Seniors 5 and 3
Final: Silverknowes beat Barnton Hotel 8 and 7
Winning team: Tam Caldwell, Keith Reilly, Graham Robertson and Paul Heggie

European Men's Challenge Trophy   (inaugurated 2002)

This is now a biennial event and will next be held in Iceland in 2012

European Amateur Team Championship   (inaugurated 1959)   *Vilamoura, Portugal*

Strokeplay Qualification: 1 Spain 696; 2 Germany 700; 3 France 702

Individual:
1	Scott Fernandez (ESP)	66-69—135
2	Thomas Pieters (BEL)	70-67—137
	Adrian Otaegui (ESP)	67-70—137

Final Team placings: 1 France; 2 Switzerland; 3 Sweden; 4 Germany; 5 Spain; 6 Scotland; 7 Finland; 8 Ireland; 9 Wales; 10 Austria; 11 Denmark; 12 Norway; 13 Italy; 14 Netherlands; 15 England; 16 Iceland; 17 Portugal; 18 Belgium; 19 Slovakia; 20 Russia

Winning team: Edouard Espana, Gary Stal, Alexander Levy, Cyril Bouniol, Julien Brun, Sebastien Gros

Team Results:
"A Flight" – Day One: Germany 4, Scotland 3; France 4½, Ireland 2½; Switzerland 5, Finland 2; Sweden 5½, Spain 1½. *Day Two:* France 4½, Germany 2½; Switzerland 4½, Sweden 2½; Scotland 3½, Ireland 1½; Spain 5, Finland 0. *Day Three – Final:* France 4½, Switzerland 2½; Sweden 4, Germany 3; Spain 3½, Scotland 1½; Finland 3, Ireland 2

"B Flight" – Day One: Norway 4, Iceland 1; Austria 4, Italy 1; Denmark 3½. Netherlands 1½; Wales 4, England 1. *Day Two:* Austria 3, Norway 2; Wales 3½, Denmark 1½; Italy 4, Iceland 1; Netherlands 3, England 2. *Day Three:* Wales 3½, Austria 1½; Denmark 4, Norway 1; Italy 3½, Netherlands 1½; England 4, Iceland 1

"C Flight" – Day One: Belgium 3½, Slovakia 1½; Portugal 5, Russia 0. *Day Two:* Belgium 4, Russia 1; Portugal 5, Slovakia 0. *Day Three:* Slovakia 4, Russia 1; Portugal 4½, Belgium ½

European Senior Men's Team Championship (inaugurated 2006)   Troia, Portugal

Stroke Play: I Sweden 765; 2 Germany 794; 3 Netherlands 802; 4 Italy 808; 5 Spain, France 815; 7 Finland 831; 8 Portugal 834; 9 Belgium 835; 10 Switzerland 846; 11 Austria 865; 12 Denmark 869; 13 Norway 875; 14 Poland 892; 15 Luxembourg 897

Individual: I Hans Gunter-Reiter (GER) 74-74—148; Stefan Lindberg (SWE) 74-74—148; Tomas Persson (SWE) 78-70—148

Match Play:

Quarter-finals: Finland 3½, Germany 1½; Netherlands 3, France 2; Spain 4, Italy 1; Sweden 4, Portugal 1

Semi-finals: Netherlands 3, Finland 2; Sweden 3, Spain 2

Third place play-off: Spain 3. Finland 2

Final: Sweden 3½, Netherlands 1½

Final ranking: I Sweden; 2 Netherlands; 3 Spain; 4 Finland; 5 Germany; 6 Italy; 7 Portugal; 8 France; 9 Belgium; 10 Switzerland; 11 Austria; 12 Norway; 13 Denmark; 14 Poland; 15 Luxembourg

Winning team: Sweden – Bob Backstedt, Goran Thenfors, Mats Anderson, Stefan Lindberg, Tomas Persson and Ulf Sundberg

---

European Club Cup (Albacom Trophy)   (inaugurated 1975)   Antalya, Turkey

I	Golf Club de Lyon (FRA)	138-147-135—420
2	Ormesson (FRA)	144-142-139—425
3	Kymen Golf (FIN)	145-143-143—431

4 Klassis G&CC (TUR) 440; 5 Toya GC (POL) 441; 6 Real Club De Golf Basozabal (ESP) 444; 7 GC Houtrak (NED) 445; 8 GC La Margherita (ITA) 447; 9 GC Lausanne (SUI) 449; 10 Portmarnock (IRL) 450; 11 GC Ta`le (SVK) 451; 12 Odense Eventyr GC (DEN) 452; 13 Stavanger GC (NOR) 453; 14 Formby (ENG), GC Reykjavik (ISL) 460; 16 Neath GC (WAL) 461; 17 The Moscow City GC (RUS), GC Cechie (CZE) 463; 19 GC Hubbelrath (GER) 467; 20 GC Schloss Schönborn (AUT) 471; 21 Club de Golf de Troia (POR) 472; 22 GC Velenje (SLO) 477; 23 Balloshmyle (SCO) 481; 24 GC Grand Ducal (LUX) 495; 25 Superior GC (UKR) 506; 26 Estonian G&CC 517; 27 GC Qercus (CRO) 533; 28 Paul Tomita GC (ROM) 566; 29 Royal GC of Belgium DNF

Winning team: Pierre Mainvaud Arnaud, Adrien Saddler, Gary Stal

Individual: Adrien Saddler (GC de Lyon) 68-72-68—208

Home Internationals (Raymond Trophy) (inaugurated 1932)   County Sligo

Day One: England 7, Ireland 8; Scotland 9, Wales 6
Day Two: Ireland 11, Wales 4; Scotland 4½, England 10½
Day Three: England 9½, Wales 5½; Ireland 6½, Scotland 8½

Result: I England 2 pts, 27; 2 Ireland 2 pts, 25½; 3 Scotland 2 pts, 22; 4 Wales 0 pts, 15½

Winning team: Steven Brown (Wentworth), Dave Coupland (Boston), Tyrrell Hatton (Harleyford), Craig Hinton (The Oxfordshire), Ben Loughrey (Wrag Barn), Garrick Porteous (Bamburgh Castle). Neil Raymond (Corhampton), Jack Senior (Heysham), Ben Stow (Rushmore), Andrew Sullivan (Nuneaton), Ben Taylor (Walton Heath), Todd Aitken (Nevill) withdrew, ill

History: England 36 wins, Scotland 20, Ireland 8, Wales 1. England, Ireland and Scotland have tied on four occasions, Ireland and Scotland once, England and Ireland once and Scotland and England once.

Senior Home Internationals (inaugurated 2002)   Woodhall Spa

Day One: Scotland 7½, Wales 1½; Ireland 7, England 2
Day Two: Ireland 7, Wales 2; Scotland 3, England 6
Day Three: Ireland 5, Scotland 4; England 5, Wale 4

Result: I Ireland 3 pts, 19; 2 England 2 pts, 13; 3 Scotland 1 pt, 4½; 4 Wales 0 pts, 7½

Winning team: Michael Coote (Tralee), Maurice Kelly (Killeen), Garth McGimpsey (Bangor). Seamus McParland (Greenore), Adrian Morrow (Portmarnock), Arthur Pierse (Tipperary), Hugh Smyth (Mourne)

English County Championship (inaugurated 1928) *Ganton*

Day One:
Wiltshire 8, Warwickshire 1
Lancashire 3, Surrey 6

Day Two:
Wiltshire4, Lancashire 5
Surrey 6½, Warwickshire 2½

Day Three:
Lancashire 5, Warwickshire 4
Surrey 3, Wiltshire 6

Result: 1 Wiltshire 2 (18); 2 Surrey 2 (15½); 3 Lancashire 2 (13); 4 Warwickshire 0 (7½)

Winning team: Tom Burley, Ali James, Ben Loughrey, Josh Loughrey, Jordan Smith, Ben Stow

History: Since 1928, the following countries have won: Yorkshire 19 times, Surrey and Lancashire 10, Staffordshire 6, Warwickshire 5, Northumberland 4, Berkshire, Buckinghamshire, Oxfordshire, Middlesex, Worcestershire 3, Gloucestershire 2, Cheshire, Devon, Dorset, Essex, Hampshire, Hertfordshire, Kent, Lincolnshire, Wiltshire 1. In 1985, Hertfordshire and Devon tied.

English Champion Club Tournament (inaugurated 1984) *Scarcroft*

1	Formby	214-210—424* (James Bolton, Mark Duncalf, Jack Kelly)
2	Dartford	212-212—424
3	Wike Ridge	209-215—424

*best 2nd round score

Irish Inter-Provincial Championship *Co Sligo*

Day One   Ulster 5½, Connaught 5½   Day Three   Ulster 8, Munster 3
           Leinster 4½, Munster 6 ½   Connaught 5½, Leinster 5½
Day Two   Ulster 5, Leinster 6
           Munster 5, Connaught 6

Final Table	W	D	L
Connaught	1	2	0
Ulster	1	1	1
Leinster	1	1	1
Munster	1	0	2

Winning team: Barry Anderson (Co Sligo), Eddie McCormack (Galway), Steffan O'Hara (Co Sligo), Sean Cannon (Loughrea), Gary McDermott (Co Sligo), Kelan McDonagh (Athlon/NUIM), Michael Duncan (Co Sligo), Joe Lyons (Birr). Captain: Adrian Wynn (Strandhill)

Scottish Area Team Championship (inaugurated 1990) *Prestwick and Prestwick St Nicholas*

Stroke Play Qualifying: North East 718, Lothians 735, Fife 746, Ayrshire 747, Lanarkshire 748, Renfrewshire 782, Angus 757, Glasgow 762, Clackmannanshire 762, North 762, South 764, Stirlingshire 766, Perth & Kinross 767, Dunbartonshore 771, Borders 798, Argyll & Bute 808

Individual: Myles Cunningham (Lothians)   74-68—142
                   Kris Nicol (North East)   72-70—142

Match-play – Semi-finals:
North East beat Ayrshire 4½–½
Fife beat Lothians 4–1

Final:
Fife beat North East 3½–1½

Winning team: Kevin Blyth, Scott Crichton, Peter Latimer, Brian Soutar, Scott Stewart-Caton, James White

Scottish Club Handicap Championship *Fairmont, St Andrews*

1	63	Bathgate (Colin McGarry, Alan Aitken)	
2	65	Balbirnie Park	
3	65	Strathaven	Result decided on countback
4	65	Edinburgh Western	
5	65	Balfron	

Scottish Club Championship   (inaugurated 1985)   *Falkirk Tryst*

I	Ballochmyle:	279	(Craig Hamilton, Graeme Rowan, William Fleming)
2	Blairgowrie	283	
3	Edzell	285	

Sotogrande Cup   *Sotogrande GC, Spain*

I	England	216-208-209-219—852
2	France	211-220-209-214—854
3	Spain	212-213-217-213—855

4 Scotland 864; 5 Ireland, Denmark 870; 7 Italy 871; 8 Wales 874; 9 Germany 881; 10 Holland 883; 11 Austria 884; 12 Portugal 899; Gallin Belgica 901; 14 Sweden 905.

Winning team: Laurie Canter, Tom Lewis, Jack Senior and Andy Sullivan

Welsh Inter-Counties Championship   *Borth & Ynyslas*
Abandoned due to bad weather

Welsh Team Championship   *Monmouthshire*

Semi-Finals: Newport 3, Whitchurch 2
                   Neath 3, Langland Bay 2

Final: Neath beat Newport

Winning team: Richard Williams (captain), Matthew Arbourne, Daniel Davies, Damion Gee, Richard Hooper, Craig Melding

---

Richard Heath is new EGA General Secretary

Richard Heath, who for the last six years has been the European Golf Association's Championships Manager, has taken over as General Secretary following the retirement in 2011 after 25 years in the post of John Storjohann.

Mr Storjohann, best known in golfing circles as "Johnny", was responsible for the current structure of the EGA with its executive, its championship golf course management and handicapping committee and the course rating committee serving 40 national authorities

European golf is on a steady footing insists the retiring General Secretary pointing out that most if not all the European players who have taken part in the more recent Solheim and Ryder Cup matches have gone through the national development programme guided and motivated by the annual European Championships.

Over the past six years the new General Secretary Richard Heath has revamped many of the championship procedures, developed the European Amateur Ranking and re-organised selection methods for the various European and Continent of Europe teams. He is on The R&A and USGA World Amateur Golf Ranking committee.

The 40-year-old Swiss administrator is a formally qualified sports manager with a Master of Advanced Studies in Sports Administration and Technology, a Bachelor of Science degree with honours and a Bachelor of Applied Science degree as well. He plays off plus 1 at the Lausanne Club.

The 40 members of the EGA are: GB&I Zone – England, Scotland, Ireland and Wales; North Zone – Denmark, Estonia, Finland, Iceland, Latvia, Lithuania, Norway, Poland, Russia, Sweden and Ukraine; Central Zone – Austria, Belgium, Bulgaria, Czech Republic, Germany, Hungary Liechtenstein, Netherlands, Romania, Slovakia and Switzerland; South Zone – Croatia, Cyprus, France, Greece, Israel, Italy, Kazakhstan, Malta, Portugal, Serbia, Slovenia, Spain and Turkey.

Other Tournaments 2011

For past results see earlier editions of *The R&A Golfer's Handbook*

Aberconwy Trophy (inaugurated 1976) *always at Conwy and Llandudno (Maesdu), Gwynedd*
Jason Shufflebotham (Prestatyn)   70-72-76-74—292

The Antlers (inaugurated 1933) *always at Royal Mid-Surrey*
Not played

The Battle Trophy (inaugurated 2011) *Crail, Craighead*
Alexander Culverwell (Dunbar)   70-74-68-74—288

Berkhamsted Trophy (inaugurated 1960) *always at Berkhamsted*
Sam Claridge (Harpenden Common)   65-73—138

Berkshire Trophy (inaugurated 1946) *always at The Berkshire*
Josh White (Chipstead)   71-70-70-66—277

Burhill Family Foursomes (inaugurated 1937) *always at Burhill, Surrey*
Final: Gerrard and Laura O'Connor (Worplesdon) beat Sally and Tom Parrish (Burhill) 3 and 2

Cameron Corbett Vase (inaugurated 1897) *always at Haggs Castle, Glasgow*
Scott Crichton (Aberdour)*   67-70-68-68—273
Beat Philip McLean (Peterhead) at the first extra hole

Clwyd Open (inaugurated 1991) *always at Prestatyn and Wrexham*
Joe Vickery {Newport)   70-66-70-73—279

Craigmillar Park Open (inaugurated 1961) *always at Craigmillar Park, Edinburgh*
Greg Paterson (St Andrews New)   67-64-64-62—257

Duncan Putter (inaugurated 1959) *always at Southerndown, Bridgend, Glamorgan*
James Frazer (Pennard)   70-72-65-65—272

East of Ireland Open Amateur (inaugurated 1989) *Co. Louth*
Richard O'Donovan (Lucan)   71-78-71-66—286

East of Scotland Open Amateur Stroke Play (inaugurated 1989) *Lundin*
Paul Ferrier (Baberton)   73-66-66-68—273

Edward Trophy (inaugurated 1892) *always at Glasgow GC*
Graham Robertson (Silverknowes)   72-71-71-67—281

Fathers and Sons Foursomes   *always at West Hill, Surrey*
Final: Alan Barker (Sandiway) and Ian Barker (Burhill) beat Michael Dawson (Cotswolds) and Mark Dawson (Gatton Manor) 3 and 1

Frame Trophy   (inaugurated 1986 for players aged 50+)   *always at Worplesdon, Surrey*
John Harridge   78-70-73—221

Golf Illustrated Gold Vase   (inaugurated 1909, discontinued 2003)
For results see 2007 edition of The R&A Golfer's Handbook

Hampshire Hog   (inaugurated 1957)   *always at North Hants*
Jack Senior (Heysham)   68-68—136

Hampshire Salver   (inaugurated 1979)   *always at North Hants/Blackmoor*
Andy Sullivan (Nuneaton)   71-70-60-69—270

John Cross Bowl   (inaugurated 1957)   *always at Worplesdon, Surrey*
Andrew Devonport (Windlesham)*   71-67—138
Beat David Corben (Hindhead) after play-off

King George V Coronation Cup   *always at Porters Park, Herts*
Robert Sutton (Dunstable Downs)   68-71—139

Lagonda Trophy   *1975–1989 at Camberley and from 1990 at The Gog Magog*
Philip Ridden (City of Newcastle)   69-67-69-70—275

Lake Macquarie Tournament   (inaugurated 1958)   *always at Belmont GC, NSW, Australia*
(Australian unless stated)
Brady Watt (WA)   68-69—69-70—276

Lytham Trophy   (inaugurated 1965)   *always at Royal Lytham & St Annes and Fairhaven*
Jack Senior (Heysham)   71-82-72-74—299

Midland Open   (inaugurated 1976)   *Holme Hall and Forest Pines*
Nick Watson (Stoke Rochford)   69-68-67-72—276

Mullingar Grant Thornton Scratch Trophy   *Mullingar*
Nick Grant (Knock)   73-71-69-69—282

Newlands Trophy   *Lanark*
Allyn Dick (Kingsknowe)   68-66-71-70—275

North of Ireland Open Amateur   (inaugurated 1989)   *always at Royal Portrush*
Final: Patrick McCrudden (Royal Portrush) beat Harry Diamond (Belvoir Park) at 19th

North of Scotland Open Amateur Stroke Play (David Blair Trophy)
Nairn Dunbar
James White (Lundin)   69-70-70-69—278

North-East Scotland District Championship *Inchmarlo*
Jordan Findlay (Fraserburgh)   72-69-69-68—278

Prince of Wales Challenge Cup (inaugurated 1928) *always at Royal Cinque Ports*
Steve Mitchell   77-74—151

Rosebery Challenge Cup (inaugurated 1933) *always at Ashridge*
Matt Wallace (Moor Park)   70-73—143

St Andrews Links Trophy (inaugurated 1989) *always at St Andrews (Old, New and Jubilee)*
Tom Lewis (Welwyn Garden City)   68-74-70-67—279

St David's Gold Cross (inaugurated 1930) *always at Royal St David's, Gwynedd*
Oliver Farr (Ludlow)   71-69-79-73—292

Selborne Salver (inaugurated 1976) *always at Blackmoor*
Andy Sullivan (Nuneaton)   60-69—129

Sutherland Chalice (inaugurated 2000) *Dumfries & Galloway*
Fraser McKenna (Balmore)*   69-67-68-68—272
Beat Graeme Robertson (Glenbervie) at the second extra hole

South of England Open Amateur (inaugurated 2005) *Walton Heath*
Will Shucksmith (Alwoodley)   68-70-71-74—283
Shucksmith beat Robin Kins (NED) at the first extra hole

South East England Links Championship (inaugurated 2010)
Royal Cinque Ports and Royal St George's
Sam Robertshawe (Army)   71-73-69-71—284

South of Ireland Open Amateur *Lahinch*
Final: Stephen Welsh (Baltinglass) beat Andrew Hogan (Newlands) 3 and 2

South-East Scotland District Championship *Musselburgh*
Graeme Robertson (Glenbervie)   72-69—141

Standard Life Leven Gold Medal (inaugurated 1870) *always at Leven Links, Fife*
Ross Bell (Downfield)   64-69-71-74—278

Sunningdale Foursomes (inaugurated 1934) *always at Sunningdale*
Final: Seb Crookhall-Nixon (Workington) and James Atkinson (Kendal) beat Hayley Davis (Ferndown) and Scott Goldfrey (Ferndown) 1 hole

Tennant Cup (inaugurated 1880)   *always at Glasgow GC (Glasgow Gailes and Killermont)*
James White (Lundin)   69-68-71-68—276

Tillman Trophy (inaugurated 1980)   *Hunstanton*
Henry Smart (Banstead Downs)   72-69-74-67—282

Trubshaw Cup (inaugurated 1989)   *always at Ashburnham and Tenby*
Oliver Farr (Ludlow)   69-66-69-66—270

Tucker Trophy (inaugurated 1991)   *Whitchurch and Newport*
Mark Hearne (Southerndown)   70-70-71-67—278

West of England Open Amateur Match Play (inaugurated 1912)
always at Burnham & Berrow
Final (36 holes): David Gregory (Burnham & Berrow) beat Matt Sheehan (Cobtree Manor) 3 and 2

West of England Open Amateur Stroke Play (inaugurated 1968)   *Saunton*
Alex Christie (Tyrrells Wood)   71-67-71-70—279

West of Ireland Open Amateur   (inaugurated 1989)   *Co. Sligo (Rosses Point)*
Final: Paul Cutler (Portstewart) beat Alan Dunbar (Rathmore) 2 holes

West of Scotland Open Amateur
Not played

Worplesdon Mixed Foursomes (inaugurated 1921)   *always at Worplesdon, Surrey*
Final: Laura Webb and David Cowap (East Berkshire) beat Harriett & Giles Legg (Ferndown)

Month by month in 2011
Not a good month for American teams. They lose the Walker Cup to Great Britain and Ireland by 14–12 at Royal Aberdeen, then the Solheim Cup to Europe by 15–13 at Killeen Castle in Ireland. Justin Rose captures the third leg of the FedEx Cup play-offs, but victory in the concluding Tour Championship gives Bill Haas the $10 million bonus.

University and School Events 2011

For past results see earlier editions of *The R&A Golfer's Handbook*

Palmer Cup (USA university students v European university students) *Stanwich Club, Greenwich, CT*

Round One – Fourballs (American names first):
Arnond Vongvanij and Andrew Yun beat Sebastian Cappelen (DEN) and Ignacio Elvira (ESP) 2 and 1
Patrick Cantlay and Alex Carpenter lost to Nils Floren (SWE) and Jeff Karlsson (SWE) 4 and 2
Daniel Miernicki and Chris Williams beat Robert Karlsson (SWE) and Nick MacAndrew (SCO) 4 and 3
Blayne Barber and Russell Henley beat Henrik Norlander (SWE) and Pontus Widegren (SWE) 3 and 2

Round Two – Foursomes:
Vongvanij and Yun beat Floren and MacAndrew 5 and 4
Barber and Carpenter lost to Cappelen and Elvira 5 and 3
Miernicki and Williams halved with R Karlsson and J Karlsson
Cantlay and Henley lost to Norlander and Widegren 5 and 4

Round Three – Singles:
Vongvanij lost to Widegren 6 and 4
Yun beat MacAndrew 7 and 6
Miernicki lost to Floren 3 and 2
Carpenter lost to J Karlsson 2 and 1
Cantlay halved with R Karlsson
Henley lost to Cappelen 1 hole
Williams halved with Elvira
Barber beat Norlander 2 and 1

Round Four – Singles:
Cantlay beat MacAndrew 3 and 1
Carpenter lost to Floren 4 and 2
Vongvanij beat J Karlsson 6 and 5
Miernicki beat R Karlsson 5 and 3
Henley lost to Cappelen 1 hole
Barber halved with Elvira
Williams beat Norlander 3 and 2
Yun beat Widegren 1 hole

Result: USA 5½, Europe 2½

History: The United States of America have won the event eight times, Europe on six occasions and Great Britain and Ireland once with one match drawn.

1997	USA 19, Great Britain and Ireland 5	Bay Hill GC
1998	USA 12, Great Britain and Ireland 12	Old Course, St Andrews
1999	USA 17½, Great Britain and Ireland 6½	Honors GC Chattanooga
2000	Great Britain and Ireland 12½, USA 11½	Royal Liverpool GC
2001	USA 18, Great Britain and Ireland 6	Baltusrol (Lower) GC
2002	USA 15½, Great Britain and Ireland 8½	Doonbeg GC
2003	Europe 14, USA 10	Cassique GC Kiawah
2004	Europe 14½, USA 9½	Ballybunion GC.
2005	USA 14, Europe 10	Whistling Straits GC
2006	Europe 19½, USA 4½	Prestwick GC
2007	USA 18, Europe 6	Caves Valley GC
2008	Europe 14, USA 10	Glasgow Gailes GC
2008	Europe 14, USA 10	Glasgow Gailes GC
2009	Europe 13, USA 11	Cherry Hills CC, CO
2010	USA 13, Europe 11	Royal Portrush

Halford-Hewitt Cup (inaugurated 1924)
always at Royal Cinque Ports, Deal, and Royal St George's

Final: Watsonians beat Malvern 3½–1½

Winning team: Andrew Weir (Craigielaw), non-playing Captain; Jamie Kennedy, Andrew Hogg, Scott James, Greg Nicolson (Mortonhall), David Crummey, Martin Hopley (Gullane), Brian Tait (Royal Burgess), Brian Bingham (Royal Troon), Andrew Helm (Merchants), Richard Johnston (Glenbervie)

Senior Halford-Hewitt Competitions (inaugurated 2000)

Bernard Darwin Trophy (Original 16) *always at Woking GC:* Marlborough beat Charterhouse 2–1
GL Mellin Salver (Second 16) *always at West Hill GC* Haileybury beat Oundle 2–1
Cyril Gray Trophy (Remaining 32) *always at Worplesdon:* Wrekin beat Fettes 2½–½

Grafton Morrish Trophy (inaugurated 1963)   *Hunstanton GC and Royal West Norfolk GC*

Final: Birkenhead beat Merchant Taylors 2½–½

Winning team: Marcus Stam (Captain), Carl Adams, Kristopher Archer, John Hargreaves, Anthony Shields, Phil Whitehurst

122nd Oxford v Cambridge University Match (inaugurated 1878)   *Royal Cinque Ports*

Result: Oxford beat Cambridge by 8 matches to 7

History: Cambridge have won the match on 64 occasions, Oxford on 51. Seven matches were halved

Oxford and Cambridge Golfing Society for the President's Putter

(inaugurated 1920)   *Littlestone and Rye*

Final: Mark Benka (Lady Margaret Hall) beat Richard Marett (St Anne's)   at 19th

63rd Boyd Quaich (University Championship)   *always at St Andrews (Old and New)*

1	Benjamin Wescoe (Cambridge)	73-70-67-71—281
2	Sean Fotheringhame (St Andrews)	70-71-70-71—282
3	Steven Smith (Heriot Watt)	75-74-71-70—290
	Ian O'Rourke (Cork)	74-70-72-74—290

57th Queen Elizabeth Coronation Schools Trophy   (inaugurated 1953)

always at Royal Burgess, Barnton

Final: Lenzie Academicals beat Stewart's Melville FP 2–1

Winning Team: J Paton (non-playing captain); C Peddie, G Minnes, D Wiley, G Stewart, R Law, S Penman

History: Winning teams: 11 Watsonians; 10 Glasgow HSFP; 6 Merchistonians; 4 Daniel Stewart's FP; 3 Old Lorettonians, George Heriot's FP; 2 Dollar Academicals, Hillhead HSFP, Levinside Academy, Old Carthusians, Perth Academy FP, Breadalbane Academicals; 1 Glasgow Academicals, Fettesians, Morrisonians, Hutcheson GSFP, Old Uppinghamians, Ayr Academy FP, Gordonians, Madras College FP, Lenzie Academicals

British Universities Championship   *West Lancashire*

1	Chris O'Neil (UW-Newport)	77-69-74-70—290
2	Ben Stow (Plymouth)	78-76-68-71—293
3	David Booth (Stirling)	75-73-76-71—295

Scottish Universities Championship   *Moray GC, Lossiemouth*

1	James White (Stirling)	70-71-68-68—277
2	Bobby Rushford (Stirling)	69-68-71-74—280
3	Colin Thomson (Stirling)	71-71-69-70—281

Canadian University and Colleges Championship *Royal Ashburn CC, Ontario*

1	Humber College	293-307-291-299—1,190
2	University of British Columbia	296-318-292-302—1,208
3	Université Laval Rouge et Bleu	307-318-302-299—1,226

Winning team: Mark Hoffman, Gregory Belsito. Adrian Cord, David Lang and Alex Dumais

Individual:

1	Mark Hoffman (Humber)	73-74-71-69—287
2	Garrett Rank (Waterloo)	70-79-72-72—293
3	Andrew Robb (British Columbia)	72-74-73-76—295

13th World Universities Golf Championship *Antiquera Golf, Malaga, Spain*

1	Korea	227-213-211-218—869
2	Japan	223-222-209-218—872
3	Spain	216-212-232-213—873

4 Chinese Taipei 874; 5 Canada 881; 6 Italy 889; 7 Switzerland 892; 8 Great Britain 894; 9 USA 900; 10 South Africa 902; 11 Thailand 906; 12 France 913; 13 Ireland 915; 14 China 942; 15 Poland 980

Winning team: Byun Jin-Jae, Lee Kyoung-Hoon, Park Jong-Dae and Park Sung-Heak

Individual winner: Gerard Piris Mateu (ESP) 72-69-72-68—281

British Universities Golf Championship *West Lancashire GC*

1	Chris O'Neill (UW, Newport)	77-69-74-70—290
2	Ben Stow (Plymouth)	78-76-68-71—293
3	David Booth (Stirling)	75-73-76-71—295

British Universities Match Play Championship *Ganton*

Final: Stirling University 6½, Bournemouth 2½

Stirling University golfers are three-time winners

Stirling University golfers coached by former Tour professionals Dean Robertson and Lesley Mackay did well in 2011. At Moray Golf Club in Lossiemouth the men retained the Charles McNeil Trophy in the Scottish Universitites Championship with a 12½–2½ victory over Aberdeen.

They also held on to the Wallace Crimson Cup with a 6½–2½ victory in a repeat final over Bournemouth at Ganton while Kelsey MacDonald won the British Universities women's individual title at West Lancs by 17 shots over former winner Jane Turner from Robert Gordon's.

Then they won both the European Universities Men's and Women's Championships in Slovenia with Graeme Robertson and Harriett Beasley taking the individual titles ahead of their Stirling team mates David Booth and Hannah McCook.

County and other Regional Championships 2011

England

Bedfordshire: Miguel Moitas

Berks, Bucks & Oxon:
John Kemp

Cambridgeshire: Jody Greenall

Cheshire: Mark Geddes (M),
Fraser MacLeod (S)

Cornwall: Tom Fox

Cumbria: William Bowe

Derbyshire: Sam Claypole

Devon: Leon Fricker

Dorset: Tom Leech

Durham: Martin McCririck

Essex: Ross Dee

Gloucestershire:
Thomas Workman

Hampshire, Isle of Wight and
Channel Islands:
Martin Young

Hertfordshire: Jamie Rutherford

Isle of Man: David Jones

Kent: Michael Saunders

Lancashire: John Carroll

Leicestershire and Rutland:
David Gibson

Lincolnshire: Jordan Wrisdale

Middlesex: T P King

Norfolk: Luke Johnson

Northamptonshire: Mark Davis

Northumberland:
Nicholas Maddison

Nottinghamshire: Alex Hull

Shropshire and Herefordshire:
Tom Young

Somerset: Sam Day

Staffordshire: Dave Walley

Suffolk: Nathan Overton

Surrey: Josh White

Sussex: Joe Doherty

Warwickshire: Tom Ibbertson

Wiltshire: Ben Stow

Worcestershire: George Palmer

Yorkshire: Daniel Wasteney

Ireland

East of Ireland (Leinster):
Liam MacNamara

North of Ireland (Ulster):
Garth McGimpsey

South of Ireland (Munster):
Michael Coote

West of Ireland (Connacht):
Nigel Duke

Munster Stroke Play:
Niall Gorey

Scotland

Angus: Graeme Bell (M),
Raymond Perry (S)

Argyll and Bute:
George MacMillan (M).
Alan McKie (S)

Ayrshire: Michael Smyth (M),
Jamie Mackay (S)

Borders: Brian Graham (M),
Jamie Morris (S)

Clackmannanshire:
S Moffat (M),
Lawrence Allan (S)

Dunbartonshire
Richard Docherty (M),
Andrew Campbell (S)

Fife: Gary Sharp (M),
Scott Stewart-Cation (S)

Glasgow Stephen Machin (M),
Gordon Miller (S)

Lanarkshire: Mark O'Donnell
(M), James Steven (S)

Lothians: Alan Anderson (M),
Stephen Simants (S)

North: Bryan Fotheringham

North-East: Jordan Findlay

Perth and Kinross:
Glenn Campbell (M),
Thomas White (S)

Renfrewshire:
Christopher Mooney (M),
Lee Jenkins (S)

South: Kyle McClung (M + S)

Stirlingshire: Hugh Nelson (M),
Tommy Morrison (S)

Wales

Anglesey: Mark Perdue

Brecon and Radnor:
Gareth Powell

Caernarfon and District:
Geraint Jones

Denbigh: Rhodri Fieldhouse

Dyfed: Cancelled – bad weather

Flintshire: Adam Tuft

Glamorgan: Ryan Thomas

Gwent: Neil Oakley (M),
Richard Tayler (S)

European Amateur Ranking 2010–2011

English players dominated the European Amateur Ranking in 2010–2011 with 18 entries in the top 100. Scotland was second with 12 places and France third with nine. Germany, Spain and Wales each had seven players in the top 100 with Ireland and Sweden finishing the season with six apiece. The European Rankings are extracted from WAGR and are finalised at the same time.

		Points			Points			Points
1	Andrew Sullivan (ENG)	1,294.67	36	Philipp Westermann (GER)	912.96	68	Josh Loughrey (ENG)	815.28
2	Tom Lewis (ENG)	1,234.78				69	Sebastian Kannler (GER)	814.71
3	Jack Senior (ENG)	1,185.33	37	Goncalo Pinto (POR)	912.24			
4	Michael Stewart (SCO)	1,180.00	38	Dylan Boshart (NED)	900.00	70	Mattia Miloro (ITA)	813.33
5	Sebastian Cappelen (DEN)	1,163.64	39	Sebastien Gros (FRA)	896.83	71	Oliver Farr (WAL)	810.61
			40	Ricardo Gouveia (POR)	896.30	72	Philip McLean (SCO)	807.14
6	Manuel Trappel (AUT)	1,127.27	41	Sean Einhaus (GER)	885.71	73	Gary McDermott (IRL)	807.14
7	Steven Brown (ENG)	1,105.17	42	Ben Taylor (ENG)	885.71	74	Paul Lockwood (ENG)	805.88
8	Paul Cutler (IRL)	1,101.72	43	Benedict Staben (GER)	884.00	75	Jacobo Pastor (ESP)	805.66
9	Daan Huizing (NED)	1,078.95	44	Olafur Loftsson (ISL)	880.00	76	Neil Raymond (ENG)	803.45
10	Julien Brun (FRA)	1,076.36	45	Tim Gornik (SLO)	877.08	77	Maximilian Rottluff (GER)	803.23
11	Jeff Karlsson (SWE)	1,064.44	46	Marcel Schneider (GER)	868.89			
12	Gary Stal (FRA)	1,063.77	47	James Frazer (WAL)	865.31	78	Emilio Cuartero (ESP)	802.50
13	Stiggy Hodgson (ENG)	1,056.25	48	Jon Rahm-Rodriguez (ESP)	861.29	79	Brian Soutar (SCO)	802.38
14	Robert Karlsson (SWE)	1,043.48				80	Christoph Weninger (AUT)	802.13
15	Philipp Fendt (AUT)	1,035.71	49	Kristoffer Ventura (NOR)	854.76			
16	Edouard Espana (FRA)	1,025.00	50	Kevin Hesbois (BEL)	852.94	81	Linus Gillgren (SWE)	800.00
17	Garrick Porteous (ENG)	1,023.40	51	Benjamin Rusch (SUI)	851.72	82	Nuno Henriques (POR)	800.00
18	Pontus Widegren (SWE)	1,013.64	52	Sebastian Soderberg (SWE)	850.00	83	David Prochazka (CZE)	796.88
						84	Marc Dobias (SUI)	796.55
19	Thomas Pieters (BEL)	1,008.47	53	Ben Stow (ENG)	849.21	85	Matt Wallace (ENG)	796.55
20	James Byrne (SCO)	1,000.00	54	Miro Veijalainen (FIN)	845.90	86	Paul Shields (SCO)	795.24
21	Rhys Pugh (WAL)	998.48	55	Cedric Scotto (FRA)	843.75	87	Jason Timmis (ENG)	794.44
22	Robin Kind (NED)	987.88	56	Alan Dunbar (IRL)	843.40	88	Carlos Pigem (ESP)	793.33
23	David Law (SCO)	979.76	57	Jack Hiluta (ENG)	842.59	89	Darren Wright (ENG)	792.86
24	David Coupland (ENG)	967.44	58	Kris Nicol (SCO)	839.06	90	Giulio Castagnara (ITA)	791.30
25	Joakim Mikkelsen (NOR)	966.67	59	Jason Shufflebotham (WAL)	838.89	91	Kevin Phelan (IRL)	790.38
26	Stuart Ballingall (SCO)	957.58				92	Domenico Geminiani (ITA)	788.06
27	Pedro Figueiredo (POR)	957.14	60	Dermot McElroy (IRL)	837.50			
28	Gregory Eason (ENG)	952.50	61	Ross Kellett (SCO)	834.85	93	Hugo Rouillon (FRA)	787.76
29	Niclas Carlsson (SWE)	950.00	62	Graeme Robertson (SCO)	832.47	94	Andrea Gurini (SUI)	786.49
30	Ben Westgate (NED)	943.33				95	Pat Murray (IRL)	785.71
31	Rhys Enoch (WAL)	931.43	63	Kenny Subregis (FRA)	831.82	96	David Booth (ENG)	784.78
32	Toni Hakula (FIN)	921.95	64	Thomas Detry (BEL)	829.82	97	James White (SCO)	784.62
33	Stephan Jaeger (GER)	916.13	65	Adrien Saddier (FRA)	826.15	98	Scott Fernandez (ESP)	783.33
34	Antonio Hortal (ESP)	915.52	66	Alastair Jones (WAL)	815.62	99	Rowin Caron (NED)	779.63
35	Clement Sordet (FRA)	913.46	67	Greg Paterson (SCO)	815.62	100	Juan Sarasti (ESP)	778.26

For the full European Amateur Rankings, visit www.ega-golf.ch

Uihlein too good for Jeong in the pre-Masters Georgia Cup

American champion Peter Uihlein beat British title-holder Jin Jeong by 4 and 2 in the 14th annual Georgia Cup match on the Lakeside course at the The Golf Club of Georgia. With his victory Uihlein, a former World No 1, gave America an 8–6 lead in the traditional match staged just before The Masters at Augusta.

Although Uihlein, a junior at Oklahoma State, had built up a four-up lead by the turn in the 18-hole match, Jeong, the first Korean to win the Amateur title in Britain, kept the game alive with putting on the back nine that was reminiscent of the way he played when winning at Muirfield in 2010.

His challenge ended on the 16th, however, when he missed from 12 feet and then conceded Uihlein's three-footer. "Jin did not play his best golf today and I was able to capitalise on some of mistakes early on," said the American.

Traditionally, the players play the remaining holes and ironically Jeong came close to holing his tee shot at the short 17th and then was inches away from making a double eagle (albatross) at the 18th.

"I'm glad it was over when it was," said Uihlein. "I doubt I would have won the last two holes we played."

Former World Amateur No 1 joins Chandler Stable

Peter Uihlein, who spent a year ranked as the world's best amateur and won last year's US Amateur Championship, has joined Chubby Chandler's management stable.

Uihlein, whose father Wally Uihlein is the CEO of Titleist, is a former No 1 in the World Amateur Rankings and it is thought he will spend some of his first year as professional playing the European Tour.

The American golfer is allowed seven tournament invitations and has to make enough money from them to be in the top 150 in the Race to Dubai before accepting any more.

Royal Portrush a happy hunting ground for American Chip Lutz

Chip Lutz from Pennsylvania, who was runner-up in the 2010 Seniors Open Amateur Championship, took the title 12 months later at Royal Portrush.

In a tight finish Lutz, who plays off +4 at the Ledge Rock Golf Club, edged out former winner Arthur Pierse from Ireland and another American, Frank Ford III. His closing 71 was enough to give him victory by a shot on two-under-par 214.

"This I so emotional. I'm overwhelmed to have won," said the delighted Lutz, on winning his first national Championship title.

On the final day, Lutz made a fast start eagling the the par 5 second hole and making a birdie at the third to put the pressure on Ford who had held the lead after two days but then stumbled to a third round 77 for third place behind Pierse.

It came down to the wire, however, with Lutz delighted that he managed to keep his composure at the end. Ford, despite his early problems, had a birdie putt on the last which could have forced a play-off but he missed and then lost out on the runner-up spot by missing his putt for par as well.

Pierse, from Tipperary, kept the pressure on Lutz when he holed a lengthy putt for par at the last forcing Lutz to make par to win. The Irishman, who took the title in 2007 at Nairn in Scotland, had cause to regret his slow start on the first day when he was five-over-par for the first nine.

Another American, Patrick Tallent, fired the low round of the week – a seven birdie closing 65 – to finish fourth. Defending champion Paul Simson, who won the British, American and Canadian Seniors titles in 2010, finished tied 24th.

The Over-65 category was won by the 1993 American Walker Cup captain Vinny Giles with a total of 229. "This was a wonderful week and we got a break with the weather. Royal Portrush is such a wonderful course. I simply enjoyed playing it," said Giles.

The 2012 Seniors Open Amateur Championship will be played from August 8–10 in Wales at Machynys Peninsula.

PART V

Women's Amateur Tournaments

World Amateur Golf Ranking

New Zealand teenager Lydia Ko is first McCormack Medal winner

Lydia Ko, the Korean-born golfer who moved to New Zealand with her parents when she was five, has written another chapter of golfing history into her so far remarkable career. As No 1 golfer in the newly instituted Women's World Amateur Golf Rankings following the US Women's Amateur Championship, 14-year-old Lydia is the first recipient of the Mark H McCormack Medal which will be presented annually to the most successful woman golfer of the year.

Lydia Ko won the New Zealand Amateur Championship on her way to topping the Women's Rankings and the award of the McCormack Medal

© Getty Images

The new award matches the McCormack Medal presented to the most successful male golfer over a period of 12 months won in 2011 by American Patrick Cantlay.

Although the men's ranking has been operational since 2007 the women's version organised by The R&A with the support of the USGA only began officially in February 2011.

It is the first time the women's game has been able to compare amateur player performance in elite competition and it currently includes a calendar of 1,750 counting events with around 3,500 ranked players representing 82 countries.

Ko arrived on the game's international stage at the age of 12 when she finished leading amateur in the 2010 Pegasus New Zealand Women's Open. She tied for seventh, and in the process became the youngest woman to make the cut in a Ladies European Tour event. She then narrowly missed becoming the youngest player to win a pro event after missing a putt to make it into a play-off at the 2011 New South Wales Open.

The 14-year-old has continued to break records, becoming the first player to win both the Australian and New Zealand Ladies' Stroke Play Championships in the same year.

Ko was also co-Medalist at the US Women's Amateur Championship before being knocked out in the second round of match play.

A delighted Ko said: "My goal when I started playing golf was to become the best in the world, and this is a tick in the box for sure.

"It is great to follow fellow Kiwi Danny Lee's footsteps. This is a great reward for all the countless hours I and my team put in, and to become the first female, even better. It's been a huge year for me, one of many firsts, and this is just the cherry on the top. Thank you so much to The R&A and USGA."

The women's ranking is quickly catching up with the men's which now encompasses more than 2,500 counting events and, almost 6,000 players representing 100 countries worldwide.

USGA Executive Director Mike Davis said: "As the first female recipient of the McCormack medal, Lydia Ko has achieved an historic honour in women's amateur golf. With her boundless talent and dedication to the game, many more are sure to follow."

R&A Director Michael Tate said: "Lydia Ko has consistently proved throughout the season that she is a golfer of incredible promise and is a worthy winner of the first Mark H McCormack medal."

R&A World Amateur Golf Ranking 2011 – Top 100

Players from the USA occupy most places in the Top 100 with 28 entries. Australia and South Africa share takes second place with eight entries apiece. French players account for seven entries with England on six. Although there are only two New Zealand entries on the list, both are in the top ten occupying first and second places. South Africa has the most top ten places with three entries. By region the totals are: Americas 34, Europe 34, Asia 13, Australasia 10 and Africa nine.

			Divisor	Points
1	Lydia Ko	NZL	53	1818.87
2	Cecilia Cho	NZL	53	1745.28
3	Kim Williams	RSA	64	1667.19
4	Stephanie Meadow	IRL	53	1588.68
5	Austin Ernst	USA	40	1545.00
6	Iliska Verwey	RSA	59	1532.20
7	Leona Maguire	IRL	51	1531.37
8	Ariya Jutanugarn	THA	57	1512.28
9	Erica Popson	USA	42	1483.33
10	Bertine Strauss	RSA	56	1439.29
11	Charley Hull	ENG	49	1428.57
12	Marta Silva	ESP	47	1421.28
13	Tiffany Lua	USA	45	1391.96
14	Victoria Tanco	ARG	60	1390.00
15	Madelene Sagstrom	SWE	38	1384.21
16	Lindy Duncan	USA	39	1382.05
17	Jaye Marie Green	USA	43	1369.77
18	Kayla Mortellaro	USA	36	1369.44
19	Ashlee Dewhurst	AUS	45	1364.44
20	Sophia Popov	GER	52	1346.15
21	Minjee Lee	AUS	68	1336.76
22	Holly Clyburn	ENG	41	1334.15
23	Hyo-Joo Kim	KOR	49	1316.33
24	Lauren Taylor	ENG	40	1315.00
25	Amy Anderson	USA	38	1311.84
26	Julie Yang	KOR	36	1308.33
27	Amy Boulden	WAL	45	1306.67
28	Cheyenne Woods	USA	46	1302.17
29	Henriette Frylinck	RSA	50	1298.00
30	Emily Tubert	USA	46	1297.83
31	Brooke Pancake	USA	43	1297.67
32	Stephanie Kono	USA	53	1296.70
33	Pamela Pretswell	SCO	39	1294.87
34	Kelsey Vines	USA	41	1289.02
35	Lisa Maguire	IRL	48	1285.42
36	Jessica Speechley	AUS	54	1283.33
37	Madison Pressel	USA	42	1278.57
38	Katerina Ruzickova	CZE	48	1268.75
39	Manon Gidali	FRA	38	1268.42
40	Dottie Ardina	PHI	73	1267.12
41	Laura Gonzalez-Escallon	BEL	38	1265.79
42	Celine Boutier	FRA	56	1257.14
43	Lee Lopez	USA	48	1253.12
44	Caroline Powers	USA	42	1250.00
45	Hayley Davis	ENG	33	1240.91
46	Alexandra Bonetti	FRA	48	1225.00
47	Whitney Hillier	AUS	35	1222.86
48	Monique Smit	RSA	25	1221.43
49	Maria Salinas	PER	36	1219.44
50	Perrine Delacour	FRA	61	1218.03

			Divisor	Points
51	Breanna Elliott	AUS	50	1214.00
52	Natalia Forero	COL	44	1211.36
53	Brittany Altomare	USA	50	1210.00
54	Annie Park	USA	45	1195.56
55	Moriya Jutanugarn	THA	54	1194.44
56	Manuela Carbajo Re	ARG	65	1187.69
57	Yi-Chen Liu	TPE	43	1186.05
58	Antonia Scherer	GER	46	1184.78
59	Alex Stewart	USA	41	1180.49
60	Nobuhle Dlamini	SWZ	23	1178.57
61	Grace Na	USA	37	1177.03
62	Emma de Groot	AUS	32	1171.88
63	Brianna Do	VIE	33	1169.70
64	Nicole Becker	RSA	44	1168.18
65	Kelly Tidy	ENG	36	1161.11
66	Chihiro Ikeda	PHI	71	1156.34
67	Kyle Roig	PUR	47	1155.32
68	Ashley Ona	AUS	44	1154.55
69	Marina Alex	USA	46	1152.17
70	Grace Lennon	AUS	45	1148.89
71	Nicole Broch Larsen	DEN	41	1148.78
72	Karolin Lampert	GER	38	1147.37
73	Annie Choi	KOR	29	1141.38
74	Charlotte Kring Lorentzen	DEN	49	1140.82
75	Margaux Vanmol	BEL	47	1140.43
76	Ha Rang Lee	ESP	31	1138.71
77	Camilla Hedberg	ESP	47	1136.17
78	Calle Nielson	USA	42	1133.33
79	Cyna Rodriguez	PHI	39	1130.77
80	Ashleigh Albrecht	USA	49	1126.53
81	Isabelle Boineau	FRA	42	1119.05
82	Jayvie Agojo	PHI	55	1118.18
83	Karen Chung	USA	29	1117.24
84	Pia Halbig	GER	36	1113.89
85	Kelsey MacDonald	SCO	52	1107.69
86	Soo-Bin Kim	CAN	33	1106.06
87	Emilie Alonso	FRA	57	1105.93
88	Marissa Steen	USA	36	1105.56
89	Lovelyn Guioguio	PHI	52	1103.85
90	Casey Kennedy	USA	27	1103.57
91	Marta Sanz	ESP	38	1102.63
92	Doris Chen	USA	39	1097.44
93	Bronte Law	ENG	29	1096.55
94	Sally Watson	SCO	45	1095.56
95	Ji-Hee Kim	KOR	38	1094.74
96	Alana Van Greuning	RSA	35	1088.57
97	Demi Runas	USA	56	1083.93
98	Joanne Lee	USA	37	1083.78
99	Justine Dreher	FRA	30	1080.00
100	Paula Reto	RSA	39	1079.49

World Amateur Golf Ranking 2011

The World Amateur Golf Ranking, compiled by The R&A as a service to golf, comprises a men's ranking which was launched in January 2007 and a women's ranking which began in January 2010. The week's rankings are announced every Wednesday at 12.00 pm.

Statistics are compiled each week for over 8,000 players in over 2,000 events around the world. The ranking is based on counting every stroke reported to The R&A in stroke play events and matches won in counting match play events. The women's ranking also runs through a rolling period of 52 weeks.

Counting events are divided into seven categories:

The elite events: For men: The Amateur Championship, the US Amateur, the European Amateur and the Asian Amateur; and for women: The Ladies British Amateur, the NCAA Championship, the US Women's Amateur and the European Ladies Amateur.

Category A: Counting events ranked 1-30 in the World Ranking Event Rating
Category B: Counting events ranked 31-100
Category C: Counting events ranked 101-200
Category D: Counting events ranked 201-300
Category E: Counting events ranked 301-400
Category F: Counting events ranked from 401

Counting events are stroke play competitions over a minimum of three rounds or two rounds if it is a match play qualifying competition.

Full details of how a ranking is earned and information on how the ranking works can be found on The R&A website – www.randa.org

The rankings are displayed by month and are subdivided into the following regions:

Africa
The Americas (North, South and Central America and the Caribbean)
Asia (incorporating the Middle East)
Australasia (incorporating the Pacific Islands)
Europe

Winners are from the country hosting the event unless otherwise stated.
An asterisk indicates a newly ranked player.
(P) indicates player has turned professional and is no longer included in the world rankings.
A list of country abbreviations can be found on Page 43; MWAGR can be found on pages 250–287.

Elite and Category "A" Events

Elite

Ladies British Amateur Championship   *Royal Portrush*   (RSS 78-78)

			SP	MP	Pts	Div
1	Lauren Taylor (ENG)	73-79—152	20	180	200	8
2	Alexandra Bonetti (FRA)	77-77—154	18	140	158	7
3	Amy Boulden (WAL)	74-72—146	26	104	130	6
	Kelly Tidy (ENG)	77-72—149	23	104	127	6

Full details can be found on page 386

European Ladies Amateur Championship   *Noordwijkse GC, Netherlands*   (RSS 78-80-81-81)

			SP	Bonus	Pts	Div
1	Lisa Maguire (IRL)	73-68-73-79—293	59	48	107	4
2	Stephanie Meadow (IRL)	78-71-75-73—297	55	36	91	4
3	Charlotte Kring Lorentzen (DEN)	74-70-75-79—298	34	18	72	4

Full details can be found on page 389

US Women's Championship   *Rhode Island CC*   (RSS 75-75)

			SP	MP	Pts	Div
1	Danielle Kang	71-73—144	22	180	202	8
2	Moriya Jutanugarn (THA)	70-67—137	29	140	169	7
3	Austin Ernst	71-71—142	26	104	128	6
	Brooke Pancake	71-73—144	23	104	127	6

Full details can be found on page 390

Harder Hall Invitational *Sebring, Florida, USA* (RSS 74-75-76-76)

			SP	Bonus	Pts	Div
1	Ashleigh Albrecht	63-74-69-72—278	55	36	91	4
2	Cheyenne Woods	67-69-70-73—279	54	18	72	4
3	Kyle Roig (PUR)	67-73-68-73—281	52	12	64	4

SALLY *Ormond Beach, Florida, USA* (RSS 78-79-77-76)

1	Jaye Marie Green	69-73-74-67—283	59	36	95	4
2	Charley Hull (ENG)	74-75-69-69—287	55	18	73	4
3	Ashlan Ramsey	74-75-73-73—295	47	12	59	4
	Ericka Schneider	78-72-76-69—295	47	12	59	4

Central District Invitational *Parrish, Florida, USA* (RSS 75-76-74)

1	Austin Ernst	72-69-72—213	36	36	72	3
2	Brooke Beeler	65-73-76—214	35	18	53	3
3	Laurence Herman (BEL)	76-71-69—216	33	12	45	3
	Megan McChrystal (P)	71-72-73—216				

Northrop Grumman Reg Challenge *Palos Verdes, California, USA* (RSS 77-75-77)

1	Carlota Ciganda (ESP) (P)	73-70-72—215				
2	Natalie Sheary (P)	76-67-74—217				
3	Ani Gulugian	76-68-76—220	33	12	45	3
	Danielle Kang	77-70-73—220	33	12	45	3
	Tiffany Lua	70-74-76—220	33	12	45	3
	Cheyenne Woods	76-71-73—220	33	12	45	3

Lady Puerto Rico Classic *San Juan, Puerto Rico* (RSS 77-77-76)

1	Stephanie Meadow (IRL)	73-70-69—212	42	36	78	3
2	Maria Salinas (PER)	71-73-69—213	41	18	59	3
3	Marta Silva (ESP)	76-68-70—214	40	12	52	3

Allstate Sugar Bowl Invitational *New Orleans, Louisiana, USA* (RSS 76-75-74)

1	Stephanie Meadow (IRL)	72-66-73—211	38	38	74	3
2	Megan McChrystal (P)	69-70-73—212				
3	Laetitia Beck (ISR)	66-76-71—213	36	12	48	3
3	Lindy Duncan	73-72-68—213	36	12	48	3

Battle at Rancho Bernardo *San Diego, California, USA* (RSS 77-78-76)

1	Laura Gonzalez-Escallon (BEL)	70-71-68—209	46	36	82	3
2	Lizette Salas (P)	73-71-71—215				
2	Therese Koelbaek (DEN) (P)	72-70-73—215				

Bryan National Collegiate *Brown Summit., North Carolina, USA* (RSS 76-77-80)

1	Erica Popson	70-77-73—220	37	36	73	3
2	Michelle Shin (P)	70-75-76—221				
3	Kim Donovan	74-73-75—222	35	12	47	3
	Portland Rosen	74-74-75—222	35	12	47	3

LSU Golf Classic *Baton Rouge, Louisiana, USA* (RSS 78-78-76)

1	Lindy Duncan	72-75-71—218	38	36	74	3
2	Anna Karin Ljungstrom (SWE)	75-74-69—218	38	18	56	3
3	Emily Tubert	78-70-71—219	37	12	49	3

Liz Murphey Collegiate Classic *Athens, Georgia, USA* (RSS 78-78-75)

				SP	Bonus	Pts	Div
I	Marta Silva (ESP)		74-71-67—212	43	36	79	3
2	Emily Tubert		72-73-69—214	41	18	59	3
3	Laetitia Beck (ISR)		74-74-69—217	38	12	50	3
	Stepanie Meadow (IRL)		73-73-71—217	38	12	50	3

PAC-10 Championship *Tempe, Arizona, USA* (RSS 75-75-75)

				SP	Bonus	Pts	Div
I	Sophia Popov (GER)		69-71-70—210	39	36	75	3
2	Tiffany Lua		68-72-70—210	39	18	57	3
3	Carlota Ciganda (ESP) (P)		74-69-70—213				

PING/ASU Invitational *Tempe, Arizona, USA* (RSS 74-75-77)

				SP	Bonus	Pts	Div
I	Sophia Popov (GER)		69-71-71—211	39	36	75	3
2	Tiffany Lua		67-74-72—213	37	18	55	3
3	Stephanie Kono		70-69-75—214	36	12	48	3

SEC Women's Championship *Auburn, Alabama, USA* (RSS 75-77-75)

				SP	Bonus	Pts	Div
I	Erica Popson		66-74-70—210	41	36	77	3
2	Marta Silva (ESP)		70-74-67—211	40	18	58	3
3	Cydney Clanton (P)		69-72-73—214				

NCAA Division I Central *Notre Dame, Indiana, USA* (RSS 78-78-77)

				SP	Bonus	Pts	Div
I	Stephanie Kono		74-76-68—218	39	36	75	3
	Megan McChrystal (P)		72-75-71—218				
3	Austin Ernst		74-72-73—219	38	12	50	3

NCAA Division I East *Daytona Beach, Florida, USA* (RSS 76-75-76)

				SP	Bonus	Pts	Div
I	Stephanie Meadow (IRL)		71-67-69—207	44	36	80	3
2	Pia Halbig (GER)		73-70-70—213	38	18	56	3
3	Jessica Alexander		69-78-69—216	35	12	47	3
	Jessica Negron		69-73-74—216	35	12	47	3
	Daniela Ordonez (COL)		76-70-70—216	35	12	47	3

NCAA Division I West *Auburn, Washington, USA* (RSS 77-77-78)

				SP	Bonus	Pts	Div
I	Erica Popson		68-69-71—208	48	36	84	3
2	Lizette Salas (P)		73-67-73—213				
3	Sophia Popov (GER)		69-73-73—215	41	12	53	3

Women's Western Amateur *Sawgrass, Florida, USA* (RSS 78-77)

			SP Pts	Pts	Pts	Div
Winner	Victoria Tanco	66-73—139	32	156	188	8
Runner-up	Emma Lavy	74-71—145	26	120	146	7
Semi-finalists	Madison Pressel	72-66—138	33	88	121	6
	Jackie Chang	73-76—139	22	88	110	6

North & South Match Play *Pinehurst, North Carolina, USA*

		MP	Div
Winner	Daniella Kang	156	6
Runner-up	Doris Chan	120	5
Semi-finalists	Marina Alex	88	4
	Lisa McCloskey (COL)	88	4

US Women's Public Links   *Bandon, Oregon, USA*   (RSS 80-77)

			SP	MP	Pts	Div
1	Brianna Do (VIE)	82-73—155	18	156	174	8
2	Marisa Dodd	76-78—154	19	120	139	7
3	Tiffany Lua	81-72—154	19	88	107	6
	Annie Park	75-83—158	15	88	103	6

Queen Sirikit Cup   *Delhi, India*   (RSS 77-75-75)

			SP	MP	Pts	Div
1	Dottie Ardina (PHI)	71-70-70—211	40	36	70	3
2	Hyo Joo Kim (KOR)	69-69-74—212	39	18	57	3
3	Ji Hee Kim (KOR)	78-66-79—213	38	12	50	3
	Gauri Monga (IND)	73-70-70—213	38	12	50	3

Full details can be found on page 421

Australian Women's Amateur Championship   *Victoria GC*

		MP	Div
Winner	Ashlee Dewhurst	140	5
Runner-up	Minjee Lee	104	4
Semi-finalists	Cecilia Cho (NZL)	72	3
	Jessica Speechley	72	3

Full details can be found on page 398

Australian Women's Stroke Play Championship   *Huntingdale, Victoria*   (RSS 78-77-77-78)

			SP	Bonus	Pts	Div
1	Lydia Ko (NZL)	70-73-71-72—286	56	36	92	4
2	Cecilia Cho (NZL)	70-77-69-70—286	56	18	74	4
3	Minjee Lee	77-67-74-75—293	49	12	61	4

Full details can be found on page 398

Riversdale Cup   *Melbourne, Victoria, Australia*   (RSS 77-76-78-75)

1	Cecilia Cho (NZL)	73-65-73-70—281	57	6	93	4
2	Lydia Ko (NZL)	73-68-75-69—285	53	18	71	4
3	Su-Hyun Oh (KOR)	72-72-73-70—287	51	12	63	4

Astor Trophy   *Fairhaven GC, England*

		MP	Div
1	Pamela Pretswell (SCO)	88	4
2	Kim Williams (RSA)	88	4
3	Julianne Alvarez (NZL)	60	3
	Holly Clyburn (ENG)	60	3
	Lydia Ko (NZL)	60	3
	Kelsey MacDonald (SCO)	60	3
	Jessica Wallace (CAN) (P)		

Vagliano Trophy   *Royal Porthcawl GC, Wales*

		MP	Div
1	Alexandra Bonetti (FRA)	36	2
	Therese Koelbaek (DEN) (P)		
	Leona Maguire (IRL)	36	2
	Sophia Popov (GER)	36	2
	Marta Silva (ESP)	36	2

Full details can be found on page 420

European Ladies Team Stroke-play Championship   *Murhof, Austria*   (RSS 74-74)

			SP	Div
1	Leona Maguire (IRL)	72-64—136	28	2
2	Stephanie Kirchmayr (GER)	72-65—137	27	2
	Daisy Nielsen (DEN)	68-69—137	27	2
	Marta Silva (ESP)	68-69—137	27	2

European Ladies Team Championship "A" Flight   *Murhof, Austria*   (RSS 74-74)

		MP	Div
1	Daniela Holmquist (SWE)	72	72
	Sophia Popov (GER)	72	72
	Marta Silva (ESP)	72	72

Ladies British Open Stroke-play Championship   *Royal Ashdown Forest, England*

(RSS 79-78-77-75)

			SP	Bonus	Pts	Div
1	Leona Maguire (IRL)	75-75-69-69—288	53	36	89	4
2	Laurence Herman (BEL)	73-78-74-69—294	47	18	65	4
3	Meghan McLaren	73-77-74-72—296	45	12	57	4

Cougar Classic   *Charleston, North Carolina, USA*   (RSS 75-75-73)

1	Austin Ernst	67-69-67—203	44	36	80	3
2	Erica Poopson	66-69-72—207	40	18	58	3
3	Camilla Hedberg (SWE)	71-67-70—208	39	12	51	3
	Tessa Teachman	67-72-69—208	39	12	51	3

Mason Rudolph Fall Preview   *Nashville, Tennessee, USA*   (RSS 76-75-76)

1	Lindy Duncan	75-69-68—212	39	36	75	3
2	Jennifer Kirby (CAN)	72-66-74—212	39	18	57	3
	Brittany Altomare	75-70-69—214	37	12	51	3
	Lauren Stratton	72-71-71—214	37	12	51	3

Junior Solheim Cup   *Knightsbrook Hotel, Trim, County Meath, Ireland*

		MP Pts	Div
1	Amy Boulden (WAL)	16	1
	Jaye Marie Green (USA)	16	1
	Alison Lee (USA)	16	1
	Esther Lee (USA)	16	1
	Leona Maguire (IRL)	16	1
	Summar Roachell (USA)	16	1
	Antonia Scherer (GER)	16	1
	Gabriella Then (USA)	16	1
	Margaux Vanmol (BEL)	16	1
	Lindsey Weaver (USA)	16	1

Mercedes-Benz SEC/PAC 12 Challenge   *Knoxville, Tennessee, USA*   (RSS 76-75-75)

			SP	Bonus	Pts	Div
1	Stephanie Meadow (IRL)	68-71-72—211	39	36	75	3
2	Lauren Stratton	68-72-73—213	37	18	55	3
3	Kaitlyn Rohrback	71-72-71—214	36	12	48	3
	Marta Sanz (ESP)	74-71-69—214	36	12	48	3

Stanford Intercollegiate   *Stanford, California, USA*   (RSS 72-72-73)

1	Soo-Bin Kim (CAN)	66-68-66—200	41	36	77	3
2	Stephanie Kono	67-69-66—202	39	18	57	3
3	Cassy Isagawa	67-67-70—204	37	12	49	3

Tar Heel Invitational   *Chapel Hill, North Carolina, USA*   (RSS 74-74-74)

			SP	Bonus	Pts	Div
1	Marta Sanz (ESP)	69-70-68—207	39	36	75	3
2	Augusta James (CAN)	70-69-69—208	38	18	56	3
	Brooke Pancake	69-70-69—208	38	18	56	3
	Caroline Powers	69-68-71—208	38	18	56	3

How a player makes it onto the World Amateur Rankings is a question often asked. The system is easy to understand if, by necessity, somewhat complex. It is best to look at the criteria in three different ways – by doing well in a Stroke Play event, with a good performance in a Match Play tournament or in an event in which both Stroke and Match Play elements are involved. Just taking part does not necessarily mean a place on the ranking. There are certain criteria to becoming one of now over 3,000 ranked players around the world.

In Stroke Play a player will have to have:
Made the cut in an Elite event
Finished in the top 40 and ties in an "A" event   Finished in the top 8 and ties in a "D" event
Finished in the top 32 and ties in a "B" event   Finished in the top 4 and ties in an "E" event
Finished in the top 16 and ties in a "C" event   Finished in the top 2 and ties in an "F" event

Or, for female players, participation in The Ladies British Amateur, the NCAAA Championships, the US Women's Amateur and the European Women's Amateur.

Finish in a position to gain bonus points in any other professional event recognised by the committee.

In Match Play a player will make the ranking if they:
Make the last 32 in a Category "A" event   Make the last 8 in a Category "D" event
Make the last 16 in a Category "B:" event   Make the last 4 in a Category "E" event
Make the last 8 in a Category "C" event   Make the last 4 in a Category "F" event
Win a match against ranked player in an Elite team Match Play event

If the event is a combination of Stroke Play and Match Play what a player needs to become ranked is:
Qualify for the Match Play stage or finish on the qualifying score in an Elite Stroke Play event
Finish in the top 32 and ties in a Category "A" Stroke Play event
Make the last 32 of a Category "A" event
Finish in the top 16 and ties in the Stroke Play stage of a Category "B" event
Make the last 16 of a Category "B" event
Finish in the top 8 and ties in the Stroke Play stage of a Category "C" event
Make the last 8 in a Category "C" event
Finish in the top 4 and ties in the Stroke Play stage of a Category "D" event
Make the last 8 in a Category "D" event.
Finish in the top 2 and ties in the Stroke Play stage of a Category "E" event
Make the last 4 in a Category "E" event
Lead the qualifiers in the Stroke Play section of a Category "F" event
Make the last 4 of a Category "F" event.

Ranking Scratch Score
The RSS is the calculated standard used to convert a player's Counting Scores to Stroke Play Ranking Points.
   The RSS for a Counting Round is calculated by use of the formula (a) / (b), where (a) is the sum total of the gross scores of the leading (X) players in the round, with (X) representing the total number of Ranked Players in the round and (b) is the total number of gross scores in (a) above.
   Fractions from the RSS calculation will be rounded to the nearest whole number.
   If less than three Ranked Players play a Counting Round, the RSS for that round will be the average of the lowest three scores by amateur golfers.
   If fewer than three Amateurs play a Counting Round, the RSS will equate to par.
   In any official event from other professional tours, the RSS will equate to par.

January

Americas

A	Harder Hall Invitational	Sebring, FL	Ashleigh Albrecht	USA
A	SALLY	Ormond Beach, FL	Jaye Marie Green	USA
B	Dixie Amateur	Coral Springs, FL	Paula Reto (RSA)	USA
C	Ione D Jones/Doherty Championship	Fort Lauderdale, FL	Charley Hull (ENG)	USA
C	Mexican Open Amateur	Vallescondido	Margarita Ramos	MEX
C	Copa De Oro Eugenio Blanco	Los Acantilados	Manuela Carbajo Re	ARG
D	Copa Rio de la Plata	Punta del Este	Sun La Jun (PAR)*	URU
E	Abierto Rocas de Santo Domingo	Rocas de Santo Domingo	Paz Echeverria	CHI

Americas (continued)

E	Copa David Leadbetter	Obague	Ana Maria Rengifo	COL
E	Marbella Open	Marbella	Daniela Vial	CHI
E	Torneo de Menores de Peru	Lima	Natalia Forero (COL)	PER
E	Puerto Rico Junior Open	Trump International, Rio Grande	Monifa Sealy (TRI)	PUR
F	Abierto de Granadilla	Granadilla	Francisca Vargas	CHI
F	Torneo de Menores 1	Granya Azul	Lucia Gutierrez	PER
F	Torneo de Menores 2	Granja Azul	Lucia Gutierrez	PER
F	Torneo de Menores 3	La Planicie	Anneke Strobach*	PER
F	Central America Junior Team	Guatemala City	Lucia Polo Galvez	GUA

Asia

C	Philippine Ladies Open	Canlubang	Chihiro Ikeda	PHI
D	Selangor Amateur Open	Perangsang Templer	Kelly Tan	MAS
E	HSBC China Junior Open	Shen	Chi Yi Wang*	CHN
E	Tollygunge Club Amateur	Kolkata	Gauri Monga	IND
F	BPGC Open	Bombay Presidency, Mumbai	Nikita Arjun*	IND
F	Mission Hills Junior Tour Final	Shenzhen, China	Rui Xin Liu	CHN
F	Philippine International Junior	Calamba	Andrea Unson	PHI

Australasia

B	Lake Macquarie Women's Amateur	Newcastle, NSW	Breanna Elliott	AUS
E	Judy Elphinstone Tournament	Ulverstone, TAS	Ashlee Dewhurst	AUS
F	Golf SA Girls Championship	Vines of Reynella	Jenny Lee	AUS
F	Golf SA Junior Masters	Royal Adelaide	Jenny Lee*	AUS
F	North Island U19	Hamilton	Hanna Seifert/Chantelle Cassidy	NZL
F	Tamar Valley Junior Cup	Greens Beach	Jaimee Dougan*	AUS
F	Tasmanian Junior Masters	Ulverstone, TAS	Emily McLennan	AUS

Europe

B	Portuguese International Amateur	Aroeira	Leona Maguire (IRL)	POR
C	I Puntuable Nacional Feminino	El Valle	Camilla Hedberg	ESP
E	Andalucia Junior European Open	Finka Cortesin	Samantha Giles (ENG)/Poppy Finlay (ENG)*	ESP
F	TGF League 1	Ayak Bayanlar	Tugce Erden	TUR
F	TGF League 2	Ayak Bayanlar	Beyhan Goldman*	TUR

February

Africa

C	Eastern Cape Championship	Humewood	Iliska Verwey	RSA

Americas

A	Central District Invitational	Parrish, FL	Austin Ernst	USA
A	Northrop Grumman Reg Challenge	Palos Verdes, CA	Carlota Ciganda (ESP)	USA
A	Lady Puerto Rico Classic	San Juan	Stephanie Meadow (IRL)	PUR
B	ANNIKA Invitational	Reunion, FL	Celine Boutier (FRA)	USA
B	Arizona Wildcat Invitational	Tucson, AZ	Isabelle Boineau (FRA)	USA
B	Kiawah Island Intercollegiate	Kiawah, SC	Mitsuki Katahira (JPN)/Sarah Bejgrowicz	USA
B	UCF Challenge	Sorrento, FL	Ashleigh Albrecht/Teresa Puga (ESP)	USA
C	Claud Jacobs Intercollegiate	Victoria, TX	Kamryn Ruffin/Krista Puisite (LAT)	USA
C	JU Women's Classic	Jacksonville, FL	Mitsuki Katahira (JPN)	USA
C	Lady Moc Golf Classic	Lakeland, FL	Taylor Collins	USA
D	Challenge at Fleming Island	Orange Park, FL	Nicole Ferre (VEN)	USA
D	Gold Rush by Golfsmith	Seal Beach, CA	Simone Hoey	USA
D	Campeonato Nacional por Golpes	Martindale CC	Maria Olivero*	ARG
D	Selectivo Suramericano Juvenil	La Sabana, Bogota	Natalia Forero	COL
F	BCU Spring Invitational	Daytona Beach, FL	Kimberly Wong	USA

F	JAGS President's Junior Cup	Beaumont, CA	Savannah Vilaubi*	USA
F	Jim McLean Doral Event	Doral. FL	Anna Young (CAN)	USA
F	Western States Junior Players Cup	Menifee, CA	Casie Cathrea	USA
F	Abierto de Los Chillos	Los Chillos	Coralia Arias	ECU
F	Abierto Santa Augusta	Santa Augusta	Isidora San Martin	CHI
F	Campeonato Nacional de Menores	Villa	Lucia Gutierrez	PER
F	Campeonato Nacional Juvenil	Cerro	Pilar Bologna (URU)*	ECU
F	Clasificacion Campeonato Sudamericano Juvenil	Caracas	Maria Andreina Merchan	VEN
F	Torneo de Golf Aficionados	La Pradera de Potosi	Maria Alejandra Villalobos	COL
F	Torneo de Menores 5	Los Andes	Lucia Gutierrez	PER
F	Torneo de Menores 6	La Planicie	Lucia Gutierrez	PER
F	Torneo Nacional de Aficionados	El Rodeo	Maria Llano*	COL
F	Trujillo Open	Trujillo	Maria Veronica Noriega	PER
F	Campeonato de Golf Interclubes	San Jose	Laura Restrepo (COL)	CRC

Asia

D	Acer National Winter Ranking	Nantou	Chieh Peng	TPE
D	Southern Ladies	Bacolod	Chihiro Ikeda	PHI
D	WWWExpress-DHL National Amateur	Canlubang	Love Lynn Guioguio	PHI
E	All-India Women's Championship	Begaluru	Gauri Monga	IND
F	Hong Kong Close Amateur	Discovery Bay	Tiffany Chan	HKG
F	KL Ladies Amateur	Bukit Jalil	Iman Ahmed Nordin	MAS
F	National Ranking Game I	Tampines	Sock Hwee Koh	SIN
F	Pacific Games Tryout I	Yona	Tessie Blair	GUM

Australasia

C	Victorian Women's Stroke Play	Melbourne	Courtney Massey	AUS
F	Canterbury Stroke Play	Windsor, Canterbury	Sumin Jo (KOR)	NZL
F	Grant Clements Memorial	Mt Maunganui, BOP	Jesse Hamilton	NZL
F	Press Invitational Tournament	Waitikiri	Sumin Jo (KOR)*	NZL
F	South Island Stroke Play	Timaru, Aorangi	Jesse Hamilton	NZL

Europe

C	Spanish International Lady Junior	F Montecastrove	Emilie Alonso (FRA)	ESP
F	Hacienda Del Alamo Open	Murcia	Amber Ratcliffe (ENG)	ESP
F	TGF League 3	Ayak Bayanlar	Beyhan Goldman	TUR
F	TGF League 4	Ayak Bayanlar	Sena Ersoy*	TUR

March

Africa

C	Border Championships	East London	Bertine Strauss	RSA
C	KeNako SA Junior Masters	Kingswood, George	Claudia Lim (AUS)	RSA
C	KZNLGA Championships	Durban	Iliska Verwey	RSA
C	Western Province Championship	Clovelly	Iliska Verwey	RSA

Americas

A	Allstate Sugar Bowl Intercollegiate	New Orleans, LA	Stephanie Meadow (IRL)	USA
A	Battle at Rancho Bernardo	Rancho Bernardo	Laura Gonzalez-Escallon (BEL)	USA
A	Bryan National Collegiate	Brown Summit, NC	Erica Popson	USA
A	LSU Golf Classic	Baton Rouge, LA	Lindy Duncan	USA
B	Bruin Wave Invitational	Santa Clarita, CA	Lee Lopez	USA
B	Dr Donnis Thompson Invitational	Honolulu, HI	Carlota Ciganda (ESP)	USA
B	JMU Eagle Landing Invite	Orange Park, FL	Christine Wolf (AUT)	USA
B	John Kirk/Panther Intercollegiate	Stockbridge, GA	Mitsuki Katahira (JPN)	USA
B	Juli Inkster Spartan Invite	San Jose, CA	Emily Childs	USA
B	Kinderlou Forest Challenge	Valdosta, GA	Casey Kennedy	USA
B	Mountain View Collegiate	Tucson, AZ	Emily Tubert	USA
B	Peggy Kirk Bell Invitational	West Springs, FL	Melanie Audette	USA

Americas (continued)

B	SunTrust Gator Invite	Gainesville, FL	Hannah Thomson (AUS)	USA
B	UNLV Spring Rebel Invitational	Boulder City, NV	Kelsey Vines	USA
C	Administaff Lady Jaguar Intercollegiate	Augusta, GA	Casey Kennedy	USA
C	Anteater Invitational	Dove Canyon, CA	Lauren Taylor (CAN)	USA
C	Sir Pizza Cards Challenge	Weston, FL	Shena Yang	USA
C	UALR Women's Golf Classic	Hot Springs, AR	Laura Stempfle (GER)	USA
C	Univ of Cincinnati Spring Invitational	Crystal River, FL	Briana Carlson	USA
C	Tortugas CC Event	Tortugas CC	Victoria Tanco	ARG
D	Barefoot at the Beach Invitational	Myrtle Beach, SC	Fanny Wolte (AUT)	USA
D	BYU at Entrada Classic	St George, UT	Demi Mak (HKG)	USA
D	Fresno State Lexus Classic	Fresno, CA	Katrina Hegge	USA
D	Islander Classic	Corpus Christi, TX	Crystal Reeves	USA
D	Jackrabbit Invitational	Primm, NV	Amy Anderson	USA
D	Rio Verde Invitational	Rio Verde, AZ	Catherine Dolan	USA
E	Lumberjack Shootout at Wigwam	Park, AZ	Bethany Leclair/Carla Cooper	USA
E	Campeonato Nacional De Mayores	Bucaramanga	Isabella Loza	COL
F	Audible Closed Championship	Dallas, TX	Elcin Ulu (TUR)	USA
F	College of Idaho Invitational	Wilder, ID	Sara Molyneux	USA
F	EKU El Diablo Intercollegiate	Citrus Springs, FL	Harin Lee	USA
F	Hal Sutton Intercollegiate	Bossier City, IA	Landa Stewart	USA
F	Jekyll Island Women's Collegiate	Jekyll Island, GA	Kelsie Carralero	USA
F	Lamkin Grip Cal Poly Challenge	Arroyo Grande, CA	Samantha Safford	USA
F	Samford U Intercollegiate	Oneonta, AL	Liz Balkcom	USA
F	San Francisco City Championship	San Francisco, CA	Hannah Suh	USA
F	Spring Fling at Mission Inn	Howie in the Hills, FL	Kimberly Wong	USA
F	Tina Barrett Longwood Invite	Farmville VA	Amanda Steinhagen	USA
F	USA Lady Jaguar Invitational	Mobile, AL	Kristen Golightly*	USA
F	Warner Pacific Invitational	Vancouver, WA	Sara Taylor	USA
F	Abierto De Arrayanes	Arrayanes	Coralia Arias	ECU
F	Abierto de Chile	PWCC	Paz Echeverria	CHI
F	Abierto de Verano	Asia	Lucia Gutierrez	PER
F	Abierto Las Araucarias	Las Araucarias	Anita Ojeda	CHI
F	Master Infantil y Juvenil	Farallones	Valentina Romero	COL
F	Bermuda Ladies Match Play	Mid Ocean	Tariqah Walikraam*	BER
F	Costa Rica National Match Play	Valle del Sol	Aideen Kellaghan*	CRC

Asia

A	Queen Sirikit Cup	Delhi	Dottie Ardina (PHI)	IND
D	Faldo Series Grand Final	Mission Hills	Yi-Chen Liu (TPE)	CHN
D	Thailand Ladies Amateur Open	Bangkok	Chihiro Ikeda (PHI)	THA
D	Thailand National Team 2	Royal Hills	Chonlada Chayanan	THA
E	Montecillo Championship	Mount Malarayat, Lipa	Andrea Unson	PHI
E	National Team Qualifying Event 1	Blue Sapphire	Ornnicha Konsunthea/Panitta Yusabai	THA
F	China Amateur Tour 1	Dongguan	Yang Jiaxin	CHN
F	HSBC Youth Challenge 1	Warren	Jo Ee Kok	SIN
F	Mindanao Tournament	Del Monte	Sarah Jane Smith	PHI
F	TGA-CAT CG Junior Championship	Nakornnayok	Virunpat O-Lankitkunchai*	THA
F	TGA-CAT Junior Championship	Royal Hill	Budsabakorn Sukapan	THA
F	TGA-CAT Junior Ranking 5	Evergreen Hill	Parinda Phokan*	THA

Australasia

A	Australian Women's Amateur	Victoria, VIC	Ashlee Dewhurst	AUS
A	Australian Women's Stroke Play	Huntingdale, VIC	Lydia Ko (NZL)	AUS
A	Riversdale Cup	Melbourne, VIC	Cecilia Cho (NZL)	AUS
E	Sunshine Coast Open Amateur	Headland, QLD	Lauren Mason	AUS

For further information, visit www.randa.org/wagr

Europe

B	Spanish Ladies Amateur	Jerez	Lisa Maguire (IRL)	ESP
D	Abierto de Madrid	Santander	Luna Sobron	ESP
D	SUS Order of Merit - Dundonald	Dundonald Links	Jane Turner	SCO
E	Leone di San Marco	Venezia	Laura Sedda	ITA
F	Catalonia Community U18	Emporda	Ivon Reijers	ESP
F	Coupe De France Dames	Pont Royal	Laure Castelain	FRA
F	Grand Prix Carcassone	Carcassone	Marion Veysseyre*	FRA
F	Grand Prix du Cap d'Agde	Golf du Cap d'Agde	Alice Dubois*	FRA
F	Grand Prix du Lys Chantilly	Les Chenes	Carole Danten-Azfi	FRA
F	Grand Prix Federal de Toulouse	Vieille Toulouse	Beatrice Soubiron	FRA
F	SUS Golf Ladies Championship	Moray	Susan Jackson	SCO

April

Africa

B	South African Amateur	Rustenburg	Kim Williams	RSA
B	South African Match Play	Rustenburg	Iliska Verwey	RSA
E	South Africa Girls Rosebowl	Clovelly	Kim Daniels	RSA

Americas

A	Liz Murphey Collegiate Classic	Athens, GA	Marta Silva (ESP)	USA
A	PAC-10 Championship	Tempe, AZ	Sophia Popov (GER)	USA
A	PING/ASU Invitational	Tempe, AZ	Sophia Popov (GER)	USA
A	SEC Women's Championship	Auburn, AL	Erica Popson	USA
B	ACC Women's Championship	Greensboro, NC	Cheyenne Woods	USA
B	Big 12 Women's Championship	Columbia, MO	Madison Pressel	USA
B	Big Ten Championship	Glencoe, IL	Numa Gulyanamitta (THA)	USA
B	Lady Buckeye Spring Invite	Columbus, OH	Caroline Powers	USA
B	Pacific Coast Intercollegiate	Half Moon Bay, CA	Katerina Ruzickova (CZE)	USA
B	Rebel Intercollegiate	Oxford, MS	Nathalie Mansson (SWE)	USA
B	World Golf Village Intercollegiate	St Augustine, FL	Mitsuki Katahira (JPN)	USA
C	Atlantic Sun Championship	Deland, FL	Alex Buelow	USA
C	Baylor Spring Invitational	Waco, TX	Alexandra Gibson (PER)	USA
C	Big East Women's Championship	Innisbrook, FL	Harin Lee	USA
C	C-USA Women's Championship	Gulf Shores, AL	Teresa Nogues (ESP)	USA
C	Indiana Invitational	Columbus, IN	Maria Castellanos	USA
C	Junior All-Star at Innisbrook	Palm Harbor, FL	Christina Foster (CAN)	USA
C	MAC Championship	Nashport, OH	Sarah Johnson	USA
C	Mountain West Conference Championship	Phoenix, AZ	Therese Koelbaek (DEN)	USA
C	WAC Women's Championship	Mesa, AZ	Kayla Mortellaro	USA
C	West Coast Conference Championship	Hollister, CA	Grace Na	USA
C	Winn Grips Heather Farr Classic	Mesa, AZ	Moriya Jutanugarn (THA)	USA
C	Campeonato Sudamericano Juvenil	Villa	Natalia Forero (COL)	PER
D	CAA Women's Championship	Pinehurst, NC	Charlotte Guilleux (FRA)	USA
D	Hoya Invitational	Beallsville, MD	Sandra Changkija	USA
D	Los Angeles City Junior Girls	Los Angeles, CA	Alison Lee	USA
D	Pinehurst Challenge	Pinehurst, SC	Leigh Whittaker (GER)	USA
D	Southern Conference Championship	Hilton Head, SC	Emma de Groot (AUS)	USA
D	Southland Conference Women	Corpus Christi	Stine Pedersen (DEN)	USA
D	SSC Championship	Boca Raton, FL	Sandra Changkija	USA
D	Summit League Championship	Primm, NV	Amy Anderson	USA

New Zealand teen takes top place

Thirteen-year-old New Zealander Lydia Ko took over top spot from Japan's Mitsuki Katahira in the Women's World Amateur Golf Ranking issued by The R&A. Ko achieved a remarkable double in being first player to win both the Australian and New Zealand stroke play championships in the same year.

Americas (continued)

D	Sun Belt Conference Tournament	Muscle Shoals, AL	Anna Carling (WAL)	USA
D	Campeonato Cordoba de Menores	Cordoba	Manuela Carbajo Re	ARG
E	Big Sky Women's Championship	Chander, AZ	Britney Yada	USA
E	Big South Women's Championship	Ninety-Six, SC	Jessica Alexander	USA
E	Big West Women's Championships	Sab Luis Obispo, CA	Alice Kim	USA
E	EKU Lady Colonel Classic	Richmond, KY	Emma Jonsson (SWE)	USA
E	Houston Baptist Intercollegiate	Missouri City, TX	Shelby Hardy	USA
E	Ivy League Women's Championship	Northfield, NY	Michelle Piyapattra	USA
E	Laredo Energy Junior	Bryan, TX	Taylor Coleman	USA
E	Ohio Valley Conference Championship	Dickson, TN	Emma Jonsson (SWE)	USA
E	State Farm MVC Championship	Normal, IL	Brianna Cooper (CAN)	USA
E	Wyoming Cowgirl Classic	Chandler, AZ	Britney Yada	USA
E	Abierto de Verano	Asia	Lucia Gutierrez	PER
F	CCC Championship/NAIA Qualifier	Diamond Woods	Nathalie Silva (BRA)	USA
F	Conference Carolina's Championship	Vass, NC	Melissa Siviter (ENG)	USA
F	Detroit Titans Invitational	Redford, MI	Alainna Stefan	USA
F	GLIAC Championship	Ashland, OH	Erin Misheff	USA
F	Great West Conference Championship	Traditions	Kelsey Lou-Hing (TRI)*	USA
F	Horizon League Championship	Howie in the Hills, FL	Michele Nash	USA
F	Innisbrook Easter Junior	Innisbrook, FL	Isabella DiLisio*	USA
F	Junior All-Star at Chateau Elan	Braselton, GA	Sierra Brooks*	USA
F	Lone Star Championships	San Antonio, TX	Carla Cooper	USA
F	NEC Women's Championship	Daytona, FL	Anna Palsson (SWE)*	USA
F	NJCAA Region 17 Championship	Jekyll Island, GA	Christain Liggin*	USA
F	SAC Women's Championship	Conover, NC	Brenna Martens*	USA
F	SCAC Championship	Horseshoe Bay, TX	Paige Gooch*	USA
F	Troy University Invite	Troy, AL	Sofia Bjorkman (SWE)	USA
F	Under Armour/Hunter Mahan Championship	Plano, TX	Kaitlin Park	USA
F	Campeonato do Rio de Janeiro	Buzios	Larissa Rocha Pombo*	BRA
F	Copa Camilo Villegas	Manizales	Ana Maria Rengifo	COL
F	Caribbean Junior Open	St Andrews	Brittany Marquez	TRI

Asia

C	Philippine Amateur	Silang Cavite	Andrea Unson	PHI
D	Truevisions International Junior	Ban Chang	Dottie Ardina (PHI)/Benyapa Niphatsophon	THA
E	National Team Qualifying 3	Lam Luk Ka	Panitta Yusabai	THA
E	National Team Qualifying Event 4	Narai Hill	Pinrath Loomboonruang	THA
F	China Amateur Tour 2	Wuxi, Jiangsu	Zhang Jian*	CHN
F	China Futures Tour 1	Zhuhai	Yin Zijun	CHN
F	Malaysian Amateur Close	Seri Selangor	Isza Fariza	MAS
F	Sabah Amateur Open	Tawau	Nur Durriyah Damian	MAS
F	SGA National Ranking 2	Changi	Jo Ee Kok	SIN
F	TGA-CAT Ranking 6	Royal Hills	Arpasiree Chulya*	THA
F	TrueVisions-Singha Junior 2	The Pine	Chanatcha Kunsuthi*	THA

Australasia

B	New Zealand Amateur	Christchurch	Lydia Ko	NZL
B	New Zealand Women's Stroke Play	Christchurch	Lydia Ko	NZL
B	North Island Stroke Play	Auckland	Lydia Ko	NZL
B	Western Australia Stroke Play	Lake Karrinyup	Jessica Speechley	AUS
C	Australian Girls Amateur	Fern Bay, NSW	Cathleen Santoso	AUS
C	Queensland Women's Stroke Play	Sanctuary Cove	Saki Suzuki (JPN)	AUS
D	Tasmania Women's Amateur	CC Tasmania	Tammy Hall	AUS
E	South Australian Amateur	Adelaide	Sarah King	AUS
F	Alice Springs Open	Alice Springs	Sarah Shacklady*	AUS
F	South Island U19 Championship	Timaru, Aorangi	Sarah Jane Ababa (PHI)	NZL

For further information, visit www.randa.org/wagr

Europe

B	Copa RCG Sotogrande	Sotogrande	Camilla Hedberg	ESP
B	Helen Holm Scottish Stroke Play	Troon	Charlotte Ellis (ENG)	SCO
B	Internationaux de France Juniors Filles	Saint Cloud	Madelene Sagstrom (SWE)	FRA
C	DGV Match Play Trophy	Frankfurter	Quirine Eijkenboom	GER
C	R&A Foundation Scholars	St Andrews Eden & Old	Jane Turner	SCO
D	British Universities Stroke Play	West Lancashire	Kelsey MacDonald (SCO)	ENG
D	French Lady Juniors - Cartier Trophy	Saint Cloud	Karolin Lampert (GER)	FRA
D	Spanish Team Championship	Basozabal	Ane Urchegui	ESP
E	Grand Prix AFG	Rigenee	Camille Richelle	BEL
E	Italian National Match Play	Castello di Tolcinasco	Chiara Bandini*	ITA
E	Ticino Championship	Ascona	Sarah Baumann*	SUI
F	Campeonato Barcelona	El Prat	Andrea Vilarasau	ESP
F	Citta di Roma Coppa d'Oro	Rome	Alessandra Averna	ITA
F	Grand Prix d'Albi	Albi Lasbordes	Beatrice Soubiron	FRA
F	Grand Prix de Haute Savoie	Esery	Lorellen Gros	FRA
F	Grand Prix de Limere	Limere	Celia Mansour	FRA
F	Grand Prix de Nimes Campagne	Nimes Campagne	Emilie Simmons*	FRA
F	Grand Prix de Saint Cyprien	Saint Cyprien	Anais Meysonnier*	FRA
F	Grand Prix Stade Francais	Racing Club de France	Justine Dreher	FRA
F	Italian National Match Play	Poggio dei Medi	Laura Lonardi	ITA
F	Munster Championship	Ballykisteen	Tara Gribben	IRL
F	Munster Junior Championship	Ballykisteen	Nora O'Connor*	IRL
F	Open Amateur BBCC	Bassin Bleu, Reunion	Cecile Ah Fe*	FRA
F	Open d'Arcachon	Arcachon	Eleonore Chambrin*	FRA
F	Portuguese National Stroke Play	Oporto	Magda Carrilho	POR
F	Spanish University Championship	Leon	Ana Fernandez de Mesa	ESP
F	TGF League 5	Ayak Bayaniar	Sena Ersoy	TUR
F	TGF League 6	Ayak Bayanlar	Sena Ersoy	TUR
F	Trofeo Vecchio Monastero	Varese	Tullia Calzavara	ITA

May

Africa

B	Gauteng Amateur Championship	Randpark Windsor	Monique Smit	RSA
B	South Africa 72 Hole Teams Championship	Langebaan	Henriette Frylinck	RSA
C	Free State Ladies Open	Sandrivier	Bertine Strauss	RSA

Americas

A	NCAA D1 Women's Central Region	Notre Dame, IN	Megan McChrystal/Stephanie Kono	USA
A	NCAA D1 Women's East Regional	Daytona Beach, FL	Stephanie Meadow (IRL)	USA
A	NCAA D1 Women's West Regional	Auburn, WA	Erica Popson	USA
B	NJCAA Women's National Championship	Daytona Beach, FL	Mitsuki Katahira (JPN)	USA
B	Thunderbird International Junior	Scottsdale, AZ	Karen Chung	USA
C	NCAA Division II Championship	Allendale, MI	Taylor Collins	USA
C	Scott Robertson Memorial	Roanoke, VA	Moriya Jutanugarn (YHA)	USA
C	Copa AAG – Pinguinos	Pinguinos	Manuela Carbajo Re	ARG
D	Florida State Match Play	Sarasota, FL	Page Halpin*	USA
D	NCAA D2 Women's Super Region 2	Lakeland, FL	Sandra Changkija	USA
D	Copa Komatsu-Mitsui	Lima	Maria Salinas (PER)	PER
D	Torneo Final del Ranking	GC Argentino	Liliana Cammisa	ARG
E	Bridgestone Tournament of Champions	Grand Cypress	Laura Restrepo (PAN)*	USA
F	Arizona Match Play	Phoenix, AZ	Kylee Duede*	USA
F	Campeonato Nacional Infantil/Juvenil	Riviera Nayarit	Gabriela Lopez	MEX
F	Canadian University/College Championship	Royal Ashburn	Kylie Barros	CAN
F	City of Charleston Amateur	Charleston	Kory Thompson*	USA
F	CN Future Links Pacific	Arbutus Ridge	Jisoo Keel	CAN
F	FCWT National Championship	PGA National, FL	Monifa Sealy (TRI)	USA
F	FJT Mission Inn Major	Howey in the Hills, FL	Madison Lellyo	USA
F	Jennie K Wilson Invitational	Mid-Pacific, HI	Eri Joma (JPN)	USA
F	MAAC Championship	Lake Buena Vista, FL	Katelynn Mannix*	USA

Americas (continued)

F	NAIA Women's Championships	Greenville, TN	Kylie Barros (CAN)	USA
F	NCAA D2 Women's Super Region 1	California, PA	Erin Misheff	USA
F	NCAA D2 Women's Super Region 3	St Paul, MN	Allie Ostrander*	USA
F	NCAA D2 Women's Super Region 4	Amarillo, TX	Carla Cooper	USA
F	NCAA Division III Championship	Howey in the Hills, FL	Paige Caldwell	USA
F	Ontario Junior Spring Classic	Weston, ONT	Elizabeth Tong	CAN
F	PGA Minority Championship	Port St Lucie, FL	Kimberly Wong	USA
F	PGA Minority Championship-Ind.	Port St Lucie, FL	Airielle Dawson	USA
F	Women's Carolinas Amateur Championship	Cornelius, NC	Courtney Gunter	USA
F	Abierto del Quito	Quito	Maria Jose Ferro	ECU

Asia

C	Malaysian Amateur Open	Melaka	Aretha Pan	MAS
D	Acer National Spring Ranking	Nan Fong	Yi-Chen Liu	TPE
D	Johor Amateur Open	Royal Johor	Chihiro Ikeda (PHI)	MAS
D	Sarawak Open Ladies	Sarawak	Lovelyn Guioguio (PHI)	MAS
E	National Team Qualifying 5	Springfield Village	Pavarisa Yoktuan	THA
E	TGA-CAT Junior Championship	Blue Sapphire	Wad Phaewchimplee	THA
F	China Amateur Futures Tour 1	Haining Zhejiang	Zhang Weiwei	CHN
F	China Amateur Tour 3	Chang Sha, Hunan	Zhang Weiwei	CHN
F	Faldo Series – Philippines Championship	TAT Filipinas	Regina De Guzman*	PHI
F	Mission Hills Jack Nicklaus Junior	Shenzhen	Liu Ruixin	CHN
F	Negeri Sembilan Amateur	Singapore Island	Isza Fariza	MAS
F	Philippines Junior Match Play	Alabang	Mia Legaspi*	PHI
F	Rolex Junior Championship	Takasaki City, Gunma	Akiho Sato*	JPN

Australasia

B	NSW Stroke Play Championship	The Lakes	Ashley Ona/Jessica Speechley	AUS
C	Arafura Games	Darwin	Ashlee Dewhurst	AUS
C	Handa Junior Masters	The Vines, WA	Minjee Lee	AUS
C	North Shore Classic	North Shore, Harbour	Lydia Ko	NZL
C	NSW Amateur Championship	The Australian	Grace Lennon	AUS
D	Queensland Amateur	Arundel Hills	Saki Suzuki (JPN)	AUS
D	South Australian Stroke Play	Glenelg	Ebony Heard	AUS
F	Northern Territory Amateur	Alice Springs	Cali Heap	AUS

Europe

B	Italian International Stroke Play	Castelconturbia	Justine Dreher (FRA)	ITA
B	St Rule Trophy	St Andrews	Ashley Ona (AUS)	SCO
C	Campeonato Nacional Individual	Pedrena	Camilla Hedberg	ESP
C	English Close Amateur	West Sussex	Lucy Williams	ENG
C	German International Ladies	Dusseldorfer	Fanny Cnops (BEL)	GER
C	Skandia Tour Elit 1	St Arild	Linn Andersson	SWE
C	Valencian Community Amateur	Panoramica	Camilla Hedberg	ESP
C	Welsh Open Stroke Play	Tenby	Charley Hull (ENG)	WAL
D	Scottish Ladies Amateur Championship	Machrihanish	Louise Kenney	SCO
E	Championnat de Basle	Geissberg	Fanny Vuignier	SUI
E	Championnat de Suisse Orientale	Waldkirch	Fanny Vuignier	SUI
E	Dutch National Stroke Play	De Gelpenberg	Krista Bakker	NED
E	Memorial Giuseppe Silva	Torino	Alessandra Averna	ITA
E	Royal Tour Damer 1	Logstor	Daisy Nielsen	DEN
E	Skandia Junior Open	Falkenbergs	Isabella Deilert	SWE
E	Welsh Close Championship	Royal St David's	Becky Harries	WAL
F	Coupe Didier Illouz	Racing Club de France	Claudia Chemin	FRA
F	Coupe Yves Caillol	Golf d'Aix-Marseille	Marion Duvernay	FRA
F	Czech Amateur Tour 1	Kuneticka Hora	Karolina Vlckova	CZE
F	Czech Amateur Tour 2	Mnich	Karolina Vlckova	CZE
F	Fairhaven Trophies	Fairhaven	Amber Ratcliffe	ENG
F	Faxe Kondi Tour Piger 1	Logstor	Malene Krolboll	DEN

F	Federal Tour 2	Royal Belgian Golf Federation	Stephanie Fransolet	BEL
F	Irish Women's Close Championship	Carlow	Danielle McVeigh	IRL
F	Mattone d'Oro	Bergamo	Camilla Acquarone	ITA
F	Skandia Tour Riks I Allerum	Allerum	Sofie Nilsson Heiskanen*	SWE
F	Skandia Tour Riks I Haverdals	Haverdals	Elina Bergvall*	SWE
F	Skandia Tour Riks I Trummenas	Trummenas	Mila Pulliainen (FIN)*	SWE
F	Skandia Tour Riks 2 – Skane	Ronnebacks	Martina Edberg	SWE
F	Skandia Tour Riks 2– Smaland	Lagans	Cajsa Persson	SWE
F	Skandia Tour Riks 2 – Stockholm	Bro-Baksta	Ebba Simonsson	SWE
F	Slovenian International Ladies Amateur	Bled	Anja Purgauer (AUT)	SLO
F	Spanish National Under 16	La Coruna	Ha Rang Lee	ESP
F	Titleist Tour I	Fana	Annette Lucia Lyche	NOR
F	Trofeo Umberto Agnelli	Royal Park	Alessandra Averna	ITA

June

Africa

E	South African Girls Championship	Orkney	Bianca Theron	RSA

Americas

A	Western Amateur	Sawgrass	Victoria Tanco (ARG)	USA
B	Rolex Junior Championship	Byron	Ariya Jutanugarn (THA)	USA
C	Eastern Amateur	Charleston, SC	Katie Burnett	USA
D	AJGA Florida Junior	Weston, FL	Natalia Forero (COL)	USA
D	Oregon Amateur	Portland, OR	Jillian Carlile*	USA
D	Ping Phoenix Junior	Phoenix, AZ	Jennifer Hahn	USA
D	Southern Amateur	Atlanta, GA	Calle Nielson	USA
D	Tennessee Amateur	Blackthorn, TN	Kendall Martindale	USA
E	Bluegrass Junior	Ashland, KY	Emma Talley	USA
E	Collegiate Players Tour 5	Lexington, KY	Ashleigh Albrecht	USA
E	Delaware Amateur	Shawnee, DE	Christina Vosters	USA
E	Greater Cincinnati Amateur	Miamitown, OH	Marissa Steen	USA
E	Washington State Amateur	DuPont, WA	Erynne Lee	USA
F	AJGA Franklin Junior	Franklin, TN	Emma Talley	USA
F	AJGA Junior at Quad Cities	East Moline, IL	Emma Talley	USA
F	AJGA Junior at Steelwood	Loxley, AL	Mariah Stackhouse	USA
F	Alabama State Amateur	Mobile, AL	Kathy Hartwiger	USA
F	Alabama State Junior	Birmingham, AL	Alex Harrell*	USA
F	Arkansas Match Play	Pine Bluff	C J Bobbitt	USA
F	Aspen Junior Classic	Aspen, CO	Alexandra Wong*	USA
F	BC Women's Amateur	Port Alberni	Christina Proteau	CAN
F	Burgett H Mooney Rome Classic	Rome GA	Marissa Kay	USA
F	California Girls	Monterey, CA	Carly Childs	USA
F	Canadian University/College Championship	Royal Ashburn	Kylie Barros	CAN
F	Cleveland Junior Open	Avon, OH	Jessica Porvasnik	USA
F	Clubcorp Mission Hills Desert Junior	Rancho Mirage, CA	Kaitlin Park	USA
F	CN Future Links Ontario	Deerhurst Highlands	MacKenzie Brooke Henderson	CAN
F	CN Future Links Prairie	Saskatoo, SAS	Anna Young	CAN
F	Collegiate Players Tour I	Spring, TX	Katie Petrino*	USA
F	Collegiate Players Tour 2	Ranch Cucamonga, CA	Maddie Sheils	USA
F	Collegiate Players Tour 3A	Suwanee, GA	Morgan Jackson	USA
F	Collegiate Players Tour 3B	Springboro, OH	Alex Carl	USA
F	Colorado Stroke Play	Cherry Creek, CO	Brooke Collins	USA
F	Connecticut Championship	Wethersfield, CT	Nicole Yatsenick*	USA
F	Elbit Systems Junior	Fort Worth, TX	Alexandra Rossi	USA
F	Evitt Foundation Junior All-Star	Ringgold, GA	Janet Mao*	USA
F	Georgia Girls Championship	Atlanta, GA	Rachel Dai	USA
F	Georgia Match Play	Carrollton, GA	Margaret Shirley	USA
F	Greater San Antonio Championship	San Antonio, TX	Jessica Borth	USA
F	Idaho Amateur	Boise, ID	Trish Gibbens	USA
F	Idaho Women's Match Play	Hailey, ID	Kareen Markle*	USA
F	Illinois Amateur	Kishwaukee, IL	Nora Lucas	USA

Americas (continued)

F	Indiana Match Play	Prairie View	Kristtini Cain	USA
F	Junior All-Star at Eagle Ridge	Galena, IL	Shawn Rennegarbe*	USA
F	Junior All-Star at Hilton Head	Bluffton, SC	Isabella Skinner*	USA
F	Junior All-Star at Penn State	State College, PA	Isabella DiLisio	USA
F	Kentucky Amateur	Murray, KY	April Emerson	USA
F	Las Vegas Junior Open	Henderson, NV	Jennifer Hahn	USA
F	Nebraska Stroke Play	Beatrice, NB	Kayla Knopik	USA
F	North Carolina Amateur	Wallace, NC	Katherine Perry	USA
F	Ohio State Amateur	Concord, OH	Erin Misheff	USA
F	Oklahoma Match Play	Muskogee, OK	Whitney McAteer	USA
F	Ontario Match Play	Hawk Ridge	Brianna Cooper	CAN
F	PGA Junior 4	New Mexico State	Jordan Lippetz	USA
F	PGA Junior 5	Colorado Springs, CO	Shelby Martinek	USA
F	Signsational Signs Junior	The Woodlands, TX	Maddie Szeryk	USA
F	South Carolina Junior	Sumter, SC	Kelsey Badmauv*	USA
F	Texas Oklahoma Junior	Wichita Falls, TX	Megan Blonien*	USA
F	Toronto Star Women's Amateur	Toronto	Brittany Henderson	CAN
F	Virginias Stroke Play	Richmond, VA	Lauren Greenlief	USA
F	Walker Course at Clemson	Clemson, SC	Sarah Harris	USA
F	Wisconsin Match Play	Racine, WI	Jaclyn Shepherd	USA
D	Campeonato Nacional Peru	Asia	Maria Salinas	PER
E	Golf Cup Peru	Villa	Anneke Strobach	PER
F	Abierto Cuidad de Ibague	Ibague	Laura Munoz	COL
F	Campeonato Nacional Match Play	Golf del Uruguay	Manuela Barros	URU
F	Clasificacion Sudamericano Pre-Juvenil	Caracas	Maria Andreina Merchan	VEN
F	Parana Open	Brazil	Larissa Souza*	BRA
F	Torneo Cartagena de Indias	Cartagena	Marcela Coronel*	COL
F	PRGA Championship	Palmas Athletic Club	Paola Robles	PUR

Asia

C	Hosim Cup	Club 900	Hyo-Joo Kim	KOR
C	Korean Amateur	Yoosung	Kyu-jung Baek	KOR
C	Neighbors Trophy	Taoyuan County	Yi-Chen Liu	TPE
C	Philippine Closed Match Play	Wack Wack	Dottie Ardina	PHI
D	Japan Women's Amateur	Hyogo	Mamiko Higa	JPN
D	Perak Amateur	Jelapang	Vivienne Chin	MAS
E	Enjoy Jakarta World Junior Class A	Jakarta	Kok Jo Ee (SIN)	INA
F	China Challenge Tour 1	Zhengzhou City	Yunyan Bai*	CHN
F	China Futures Tour 2	Beijing	Zhangjie Nalin*	CHN
F	Enjoy Jakarta World Junior Class B	Jakarta	Benyapa Niphatsophon (THA)	INA
F	Hokkaido Amateur	Sapporo	Hikari Fujita	JPN
F	HSBC Youth Challenge 2	Kranji Sanctuary	Kok Jo Ee	SIN
F	KGNS Mazda Amateur Open	Negara Subang	Isza Fariza	MAS
F	Seletar Junior Open	Seletar	Saraswati Oka*	SIN
F	SGA Ranking Game 3	Tampines	Goh Jen	SIN
F	Singapore Junior Championship	Keppel	Kok Jo Ee	SIN
F	Sutera Harbour Amateur	Kota Kinabalu	Aretha Herng Pan	MAS
F	Vietnam Amateur	Vietnam	Bao Nghi Ngo	VIE

Europe

B	Irish Open Stroke Play	Elm Park	Leona Maguire	IRL
C	German Girls Open	St Leon-Rot	Karolin Lampert	GER
D	Belgian National Stroke Play	Hainaut	Joelle Van Baarle	BEL
E	Austrian Stroke Play	Schloss Finkenstein	Sarah Schober	AUT
E	Classic de Joyenval	Joyenval	Emilie Alonso	FRA
E	Danish Match Play	Holstebro	Nicole Broch Larsen	DEN
E	JSM Match	Granna	Sofie Nilsson Heiskanen	SWE
E	Netherlands National Stroke Play	Noord-Nederlandse	Karlijn Zaanen	NED
E	Royal Tour 2	Dragor	Caroline Nistrup	DEN
E	Rudersdal Open	Fureso	Daisy Nielsen	DEN

E	Trofeo Gianni Albertini	Milan	Bianca Fabrizio	ITA
F	Connaught Championship	Ballinrobe	Sarah Faller	IRL
F	Czech Amateur Tour 3	Berovice	Petra Kvidova	CZE
F	Czech National Match Play	Sokolov	Karolina Vlckova	CZE
F	Estonian Amateur	Saaremaa	Mara Puisite (LAT)	EST
F	Faxe Kondi Tour 2	Dragor	Malene Krolboll	DEN
F	FFSportU	Bordeaux Lac	Clemence Abrahamian	FRA
F	Finnish Tour 3	Kytaja	Sanna Nuutinen	FIN
F	Finnish Tour Opening	Peuramaa	Annika Nykanen	FIN
F	Fioranello d'Oro	Fioranello	Benedetta Manfredi*	ITA
F	Gran Premio Monticello	Milan	Laura Lonardi	ITA
F	Grand Prix de Lyon	Lyon	Mathilde Revilliod*	FRA
F	Grand Prix de Palmola	Palmola	Celia Mansour	FRA
F	Italian Girls Stroke Play	Monticello	Roberta Liti	ITA
F	Leman Championship	Various	Natalie Karcher	SUI
F	Memorial Oliver Barras	Crans-sur-Sierre	Fanny Vuignier	SUI
F	Polish Amateur	Mazury	Martyna Mierzwa	POL
F	Skandia Tour Riks 3 Goteborg	Delsjo	Anna Svenstrup	SWE
F	Skandia Tour Riks 3 Ostergotland	Bravikens	Marta Mansson*	SWE
F	Skandia Tour Riks 3 Uppland	Soderby	Sofie Kvarnstrom	SWE
F	Spanish Mid-Amateur	Platja de Pals	Maria Orueta	ESP
F	Suisse Centrale Championship	Ennetsee	Fabia Rothenfluh	SUI
F	Titleist Tour 2	Notteroy	Olivia Hullert	NOR
F	Titleist Tour 5	Moss & Rygge	Katerina Jaeger*	NOR
F	Trophee Jean Louis Jurion	Valescure	Julie Aime	FRA
F	Turkish National Stroke Play	Klassis	Elcin Ulu	TUR
F	Ulster Girls	Farnham Estate	Chloe Ryan	IRL
F	US Kids Golf European	Gullane	Aimee Wilson (ENG)*	SCO

July

Africa

B	Gauteng North Championship	Centurion	Kim Williams	RSA

Americas

A	North & South Match Play	Pinehurst, NC	Danielle Kang	USA
A	US Women's Public Links	Bandon, OR	Brianna Do (VIE)	USA
B	Callaway Junior World 15-17	San Diego, CA	Hyo-Joo Kim (KOR)	USA
B	Canadian Women's Amateur	Duncan, BC	Rebecca Lee-Bentham	CAN
B	Rolex Tournament of Champions	Sunriver, OR	Gabriella Then	USA
B	Trans-National Championship	Sheridan, WY	Julie (Ja-Ryung) Yang (KOR)	USA
B	US Girls Championship	Olympia Fields	Ariya Jutanugarn (THA)	USA
C	Florida Stroke Play	Ormond Beach, FL	Mitsuki Katahira (JPN)	USA
C	Optimist Junior 15-18	Palm Beach Gardens, FL	Panitta Yusabai (THA)	USA
C	Pacific Northwest Amateur	Port Ludlow, WA	Aaren Ziegler*	USA
D	Alberta Championship	Cottonwood	Nicole Zhang	CAN
D	Emerson Junior Classic	Poway, CA	Minjia Luo	USA
D	Western Junior Girls	Flossmoor, IL	Ashley Armstrong	USA
D	Abierto de Colombia	Club Militar, Bogota	Natalia Forero	COL
E	Collegiate Players Tour 9B	Norman, OK	Crystal Reeves	USA
E	Lessing's AJGA Classic	Sparta, NJ	Annie Park	USA
E	Missouri Amateur	St Louis, MO	Catherine Dolan	USA
E	Ontario Women's Amateur	Cutten Fields	Augusta James	CAN
E	Steve Marino Junior All-Star	Sarasota, FL	Katharine Patrick*	USA
E	Texas Amateur	Montgomery, TX	Maggie Noel*	USA
E	Virginia Amateur	Alexandria, VA	Amanda Steinhagen	USA
E	Abierto de Pereira	Pereira	Daniela Ordonez	COL
E	Copa Sura	El Rodeo	Paula Hurtado	COL
F	Abilene Junior	Abilene, TX	Alexandra White	USA
F	AJGA Huntsville Junior	Huntsville, AL	Thanya Pattamakijsakul (THA)	USA
F	AJGA Junior at Centennial	Medford, OR	Catherina Li	USA

Americas (continued)

F	AJGA Lubbock Junior	Lubbock, TX	Allie Johnston*	USA
F	Alabama Stroke Play	Grayson Valley, AL	Haley Lawrence	USA
F	Alaska State Match Play	Eagleglen	Rynae Baca*	USA
F	Alberta Junior Girls	Canmore	Jennifer Ha	CAN
F	Arkansas Stroke Play	Little Rock, AR	Megan Vaughn	USA
F	BC Junior Girls	Kamloops	Jennifer Yang	CAN
F	Bubba Conlee National Junior	Bartlett, TN	Summar Roachell	USA
F	California State Championship	Temecula, CA	Stephanie Arcala	USA
F	Callaway Junior World 11-12	San Diego, CA	Xiang Sui* (CHN)	USA
F	Callaway Junior World 13-14	San Diego, CA	Lilia Vu	USA
F	Carolinas Match Play	Stanley, NC	Dawn Woodard	USA
F	Cleveland Healthcare Junior	Shelby, NC	Giovana Maymon (MEX)	USA
F	CN Future Links Atlantic	Sussex, New Brunswick	Younjin Kim	CAN
F	CN Future Links Quebec	Milby	Younjin Kim*	CAN
F	CN Future Links Western	Panoka, AL	Jennifer Ha	CAN
F	Coca Cola Junior Championship	Harbor Springs, MI	Ashley Armstrong	USA
F	Collegiate Players Tour 6A	Harrison, TN	Patricia Holt*	USA
F	Collegiate Players Tour 6B	West Chester, PA	Christina Vosters	USA
F	Collegiate Players Tour 8	Baton Rouge, LA	Brooke Stephens*	USA
F	Collegiate Players Tour 9A	Myrtlewood, SC	Stani Schiavone	USA
F	Colorado Match Play	Common Ground, CO	Somin Lee	USA
F	Columbus Junior	Columbus, OH	Kendall Prince	USA
F	Deutsche Bank Partners Junior	Plymouth, MA	Samantha Marks	USA
F	Duncan MacMillan Classic	Maple Grove, MN	Casey Danielson	USA
F	E-Z-GO Vaughn Taylor Championship	Augusta, GA	Jessica Hoang	USA
F	Genesis Shootout	Fair Oaks Ranch, TX	Kayli Quinton	USA
F	Georgia Amateur	Eatonton, GA	Sara Butts	USA
F	Golf Pride Junior Classic	Pinehurst, NC	Allison Emrey	USA
F	Indiana Amateur	Indianapolis, IN	Kristi O'Brien	USA
F	Iowa Amateur	Sunnyside, IA	Kristin Paulson	USA
F	Junior North & South	Pinehurst, NC	Kari Bellville	USA
F	Kansas Amateur	McPherson, KS	Gianna Misenhelter	USA
F	Killington Junior	Killington, VT	Isabel Southard	USA
F	Lockton Kansas City Junior	Kansas City, KS	Sammi Lee*	USA
F	Manitoba Amateur	Teulon	Jessie Choi*	CAN
F	Manitoba Women's Junior	Winnipeg, MB	Winnie Hyun*	CAN
F	McArthur Future Legends	Hartland, WS	Lindsey Weaver	USA
F	Michigan Amateur	Harbor Springs, MI	Christine Meier	USA
F	Michigan Girls Amateur	Forest Akers	Kelly Hartigan	USA
F	Midwest Junior Players Championship	Spring Green, WI	Kelly Grassel	USA
F	Montana Amateur	Helena, MT	Maggie Crippen*	USA
F	Nebraska Match Play	Omaha, NE	Mary Narzisi	USA
F	New Brunswick Championship	Aroostook Valley	Margo McLeod	CAN
F	New Brunswick Junior Girls	Bathhurst	Morgan Matchett*	CAN
F	New England Championship	Kensington, CT	Pam Kuong	USA
F	New Hampshire State Amateur	Stratham, NH	Tara Watt*	USA
F	New York Amateur	Rome, NY	Victoria DeGroodt*	USA
F	NIVO Championship	Blainvillier	Anne-Catherine Tanguay	CAN
F	Nova Scotia Amateur	Kingston, NS	Anne Balser	CAN
F	Nova Scotia Junior	Ingonish Beach, NS	Bernadette Little*	CAN
F	Ontario Girls Championship	Goderich Sunset	Brooke Henderson	CAN
F	Optimist Junior 10-12	Palm Beach Gardens, FL	Clare Legaspi (PHI)	USA
F	Optimist Junior 13-14	Palm Beach Gardens, FL	Brooke Henderson (CAN)	USA
F	Oregon Junior Amateur	North Plains, OR	Gigi Stoll	USA
F	Oregon Junior Stroke Play	Woodburn, OR	Monica Vaughn	USA
F	Pennsylvania Junior	Bethlehem, PA	Erica Herr	USA
F	PGA Junior Kearney Hill	Lexington, KY	Emily Joers	USA
F	PGA Junior Penn State	State College, PA	Aurora Kan	USA
F	PGA Junior Purdue University	West Lafayette, IN	Katherine Hepler	USA
F	PGA Junior Westbrook	Mansfield, OH	Jessica Porvasnik	USA
F	Philadelphia Championship	Plymouth Meeting, PA	Lauren Bernard	USA

F	Quebec Junior Championship	Outaouais	Josee Doyon	CAN
F	Redstone Tournament	Humble, TX	Susannah Grunden	USA
F	Rhode Island Amateur	Pawtucket, RI	Samantha Morrell	USA
F	San Diego City Amateur	San Diego, CA	Kaitlin Drolson	USA
F	Saskatchewan Amateur	Lloydminster, SK	Anna Young	CAN
F	SGI Canada Junior	Swift Current, SK	Thea Hedemann*	CAN
F	South Carolina Junior Match Play	Sumter, SC	McKenzie Talbert	USA
F	South Dakota Amateur	Sioux Falls, SD	Kimberly Kaufman	USA
F	South Dakota Match Play	Pierre, SD	Shannon Johnson*	USA
F	Teen World Championship	Pinehurst, NC	Yuanru Yin* (CHN)	USA
F	Tennessee Girls Amateur	Gallatin, TN	Blakesly Warren*	USA
F	Trader Joe's Junior	Pleasanton, CA	Hannah Suh	USA
F	Utah State Amateur	Layton, UT	Julie McMullin*	USA
F	Wyoming Amateur	Caspar, WY	Emily Podlesny*	USA
F	Caribbean Junior	Christv Church	Paola Robles (PUR)	BAR
F	Campeonato Amador do Brasil	Gavea	Mariana de Biase	BRA
F	Faldo Series South America	Sao Paulo	Daniela Murray	BRA

Asia

C	KB Financial Group Cup	Wonjoo-si	Jung-Su Kim*	KOR
E	Malaysian Ladies Amateur	Mines	Kelly Tan	MAS
F	3rd Asean Schools Games	Seletar	Kelly Tan (MAS)	SIN
F	China Futures Tour 4	Chengdu	Xiao QiFeng*	CHN
F	China National Junior	Yantai City	Shi Yuting	CHN
F	China Team Selection Event	Beijing Huihuang	Zhang Weiwei	CHN
F	Guam Amateur	Dededo	Nalathai Vongjalorn*	GUM
F	Usha Delhi Junior	Greater Noida	Gurbani Singh	IND
F	Warren Amateur Open	Warren	Koh Sock Hwee	SIN

Australasia

B	BOP Open	Whakatane, BOP	Chantelle Cassidy	NZL
D	Western Australia Amateur	Perth, WA	Minjee Lee	AUS
F	Bangara Junior Classic	Bangara, QLD	Lauren Mason	AUS
F	Darwin Open	Darwin, NT	Chantelle Hughes*	AUS
F	Fiji Amateur Women	Fiji	Gye Oh	FIJ
F	Northern Territory Country Championship	Humpty Doo	Chantelle Shaw*	AUS
F	NSW Girls Championship	Sydney, NSW	Cathleen Santoso	AUS
F	Ruth Middleton Classic	Matamata	Zoe Brake	NZL

Europe

A	European Ladies Team Stroke Play	Murhof	Leona Maguire (IRL)	AUT
B	European Girls Team Stroke Play	IS Molas	Emily Taylor (ENG)	ITA
C	Danish International Ladies Amateur	Silkeborg	Nicole Broch Larsen	DEN
C	DM Slagspil Damer	Aarhus Aadal	Charlotte Kring Lorentzen	DEN
C	JSM Slag Flickor	Frosaker	Frida Gustafsson-Spang	SWE
C	Riverwoods (Dutch) Junior Open	Riverwoods	Lauren Taylor (ENG)	NED
D	Austrian International Amateur	St Florian	Leigh Whittaker (GER)	AUT
D	European Young Masters	Royal Balaton	Ha Rang Lee (ESP)	HUN
D	Grand Prix Des Landes – Hossegor	Hossegor	Andrea Vilarasau (ESP)	FRA
D	Omnium Swiss	Geneva	Anais Maggetti	SUI
E	Belgian National Ladies Match Play	Royal Waterloo	Margaux Vanmol	BEL
E	Brabants Open	Valkenswaard	Karlijn Zaanen	NED
E	East Leinster Championship	Milltown	Paula Grant	IRL
E	English Girls Close	Ellesborough	Hayley Davis	ENG
E	Scottish Junior Open Stroke Play	Cardross	Kelsey MacDonald	SCO
F	Arionbank Junior Matchplay	Borgarnes	Guorun Bjorgvinsdottir*[1]	ISL
F	Austrian Junior Championship	Gutenhof	Marina Stuetz	AUT
F	Biarritz Cup	Biarritz	Laure Castelain	FRA
F	Campeonato de Madrid Junior	Madrid	Maria Elena Villamil	ESP
F	Campeonato Nacional de Jovens	Ribagolfe	Sofia Camara	POR
F	Campionato Nazionale Pulcine	Fronde	Camilla Mortigliengo	ITA

Europe (continued)

F	Championnat National Girls	Lausanne	Cylia Damerau	SUI
F	Classic du Prieure Peter Fleming	Prieure	Raphaelle Vilatte	FRA
F	Cup Caroline	Trelleborgs	Jessica Tamen*	SWE
F	Czech International Junior	Austerlitz	Franziska Friedrich* (GER)	CZE
F	Czech National Youth	Mlada Boleslav	Marie Lunackova*	CZE
F	English Girls Under 13	Mentmore	Samantha Fuller*	ENG
F	English Girls Under 15	Mentmore	Gabriella Cowley	ENG
F	English Open Mid-Amateur	Collingtree Park	Claire Smith*	ENG
F	Faldo Series Netherlands	Goyer, Amsterdam	Michelle Naafs	NED
F	Faldo Series Russia Championship	Agalarov	Zhanna Tarasko*	RUS
F	Gran Premio Citta di Cervia	Cervia	Stefania Avanzo	ITA
F	Gran Premio Padova	Padova	Tullia Calzavara	ITA
F	Grand Prix de Chiberta	Chiberta	Celia Barquin (ESP)	FRA
F	Grand Prix de La Baule	La Baule	Lise Peigne*	FRA
F	Grand Prix de Saint-Nom	Nom La Breteche	Louise Gateau-Chovelon	FRA
F	Grand Prix des Volcans	Volcans	Charlotte Le Provost*	FRA
F	Icelandic Championship	Reykjanesbaer	Olafia Kristinsdottir	ISL
F	Irish Girls Close	Donegal	Paula Grant	IRL
F	Italian National Girls U-16	Asolo	Camilla Mazzola	ITA
F	Latvian National Amateur	Ozo	Krista Puisite	LAT
F	Leinster Girls Championship	Black Bush	Mary Doyle*	IRL
F	Luxembourg Amateur	Grand-Ducal	Olivia Cowan* (ENG)	LUX
F	North of Scotland Championship	Nairn	Laura Murray	SCO
F	Omnium Classic of Belgium	Limburg	Manon De Roey	BEL
F	Rosenpokalen	Holbaek	Johanne Svendsen	DEN
F	Scottish Girls Close Amateur	Glenisla	Eilidh Briggs	SCO
F	Skandia Tour Riks 4 Smaland	A6 GK	Elina Bergvall	SWE
F	Skandia Tour Riks 4 Stockholm	Agesta	Emilie Alpe*	SWE
F	Skandia Tour Riks 4 Varmland	Hammaro	Johanna Christiansson*	SWE
F	Slovak Amateur	Black Stork, Velka Lomnica	Katerina Prorokova (CZE)	SVK
F	Slovak Junior Championship	Tale	Dominika Czudkova	SVK
F	SM-Lyontipeli	Vuosaari	Oona Vartiainen	FIN
F	Targa d'Oro	Villa d'Este	Elisabetta Bertini	ITA
F	Tirol International Junior	Mieminger Plateau	Anna Fuld	AUT
F	Titleist Tour NM Junior	Miklagard	Nicoline Skaug	NOR
F	Welsh Girls Match Play	Clays	Kate Bradbury	WAL

August

Africa

F	Kenya Junior Stroke Play	Nairobi	Pooja Patel*	KEN

Americas

B	Junior PGA Championship	Fort Wayne, IN	Ariya Jutanugarn (THA)	USA
C	Campeonato Sudamericano Amateur	Bucaramanga	Manuela Carbajo Re (ARG)	COL
D	Webb Simpson Junior	Clemmons, NC	Kacie Komoto	USA
E	Arizona State Stroke Play	San Tan Valley, AZ	Saki Iida	USA
E	Genesis Junior Championship	El Cajon, CA	Alexandra Kaui	USA
E	Chile Junior Open	Brisas de Chicureo	Delfina Acosta (ARG)	CHI
F	AJGA Junior at Oxmoor Valley	Birmingham, AL	Rinko Mitsunaga	USA
F	AJGA Junior Challenge	Beaumont, CA	Esther Lee	USA
F	AJGA Nebraska Junior	Quarry Oaks, NB	Xiaoyu Zhu* (CHN)	USA
F	AJGA Northern Virginia Junior	Haymarket, VA	Alexandra White	USA
F	AJGA Philadelphia Open	Huntingdon Valley, PA	Anna Kim	USA
F	AJGA Stonehenge Open	Winona Lake, IN	Lindsey Weaver	USA
F	Big I National	Madison, MS	Ally McDonald*	USA
F	Canadian Junior Girls	Richmond, BC	Jennifer Yang	CAN
F	CJGA Mizuno National	Waterloo, ON	Kiersten Klekner-Alt*	CAN
F	Collegiate Players Tour 11	Lakeway, TX	Megan Rosenfeld	USA
F	Collegiate Players Tour National	Euless, TX	Katie Petrino	USA

F	CorseMax/Philadelphia Runner Junior	Malvern, PA	Anne Cheng	USA
F	Dogwood State Junior	Snow Hill, NC	Evelyn Dole*	USA
F	Frederica Junior Open	St Simons Island, GA	Anna Kim	USA
F	Genesis Junior	Haworth, NJ	Brooke Henderson (CAN)	USA
F	Greens & Dreams Junior Girls	Shelburne, ON	Stephanie Tucker	CAN
F	Harvey Penick Junior	Austin, TX	Taylor Coleman	USA
F	Junior All-Star at Robinson Ranch	Santa Clarita, CA	Sarah Cho*	USA
F	Maine State Championship	Penobscot Valley	Emily Bouchard*	USA
F	Massachusetts Amateur	Weston, MA	Katie Nelson*	USA
F	Minnesota Amateur	Hastings, MN	Celia Kuenster*	USA
F	New Jersey Amateur	Oradell, NJ	Scotland Preston*	USA
F	Northern California Match Play	Novato, CA	Lynne Cowan	USA
F	Ontario Girls Match Play	Barcovan	Olivia Richards*	CAN
F	Pacific Northwest Girls	Molalla, OR	Morgan Thompson	USA
F	Payne Stewart Junior	Springfield, MO	Sarah Schmelzel	USA
F	Pennsylvania Amateur	York, PA	Kelli Pry	USA
F	Quebec Match Play - Girls	Val des Lacs	Valerie Tanguay*	CAN
F	Quebec Match Play - Women	Val des Lacs	Marie-Therese Torti	CAN
F	Randy Wise Junior Open	Grand Blanc, MI	Talia Campbell	USA
F	Rochester Open	Victor, NY	Courtney Hooton	USA
F	Stockton Convention Junior Open	Stockton, CA	Amy Lee	USA
F	Texas Collegiate Tour - Collegiate	Gleneagles, TX	Sarah Zwartynski	USA
F	Texas Collegiate Tour - Girls 16-18	Gleneagles, TX	Stephanie Carlozza*	USA
F	Texas Collegiate Tour 1	TPC San Antonio	Shannon Jungman	USA
F	TPC San Antonio Major	San Antonio, TX	Courtney Dow*	USA
F	Vermont State Amateur	Rutland, VT	Kimberly Wong	USA
F	West Virginia Amateur	Parkersburg, WV	Samantha DiDomenico*	USA
F	Western Canada Summer Games	Kamloops, BC	Taylor Kim	CAN
F	Caribbean Women's Championship	Millenium Lakes	Monifa Sealy	TRI
F	Abierto Estado de Sao Paulo	Sao Paulo	Ruriko Nakamura	BRA
F	Abierto de Golf Scotiabank	Los Inkas	Lucia Gutierrez	PER
F	Campeonato Chilena	San Cristobal	Carla Jane (ESP)	CHI
F	Campeonato Club St Andres	San Andres	Maria Camila Serrano	COL
F	Copa Coomeva	Campestre Los Andes	Valentina Romero	COL
F	Torneo Arrayanes	Bogota	Laura Blanco	COL
F	Torneo Manuel de la Rosa	Barranquilla	Maria Alejandra Villalobos	COL

Asia

B	World Universiade	Shenzhen	Katerina Ruzickova (CZE)/ Min-Jung Ko (KOR)	CHN
C	Iksung Cup-Maekyung Amateur	Lake Side, Seoul	Min-Sun Kim	KOR
C	Song Am Cup	DaeGu	Hyo-Joo Kim	KOR
D	SLGA Amateur Open	Singapore Island	Minjee Lee (AUS)	SIN
E	HSBC National Junior Team	Mission Hills	Shi Yuting	CHN
E	Japan Girls Championship 15-17	Kasumagaseki	Eri Joma	JPN
F	Acer Summer Ranking	Royal Kuan His	Chi Wang	TPE
F	ANNIKA Invitational 12-15	Mission Hills	Ru Qing Guan*	CHN
F	ANNIKA Invitational 16-18	Mission Hills	Charlotte Thomas (ENG)	CHN
F	Asia-Pacific Junior Championship Group A	Royal Hills	Supamas Sangchan*	THA
F	Asia-Pacific Junior Championship Group B	Royal Hills	Pinyada Kuvanun	THA
F	China Futures Tour 5	Qingdao Shandong	Wu Sha	CHN
F	China-Korea Junior Girls A	Huangshan	Shi Yuting	CHN
F	China-Korea Junior Girls B	Huangshan	Han-Sol Ji* (KOR)	CHN
F	Chinese Amateur Tour 5	Shenyang	Wu Sha	CHN
F	Japan Girls Championship 12-14	Kasumagaseki	Shoko Sasaki*	JPN
F	Japan Women's Collegiate	Mie	Misae Yanagisawa	JPN
F	Kansai Collegiate	Wakayama	Ayumi Takeuchi*	JPN
F	Kanto Regional Collegiate	Saitama	Mikoto Seino*	JPN
F	Singapore National Amateur	Raffles	Amelia Yong	SIN

Australasia

| C | New Zealand Under 19 | Omokoroa, BOP | Cecilia Cho | NZL |
| F | Kapi Tareha | Napier, Hawkes Bay | Wenyung Keh | NZL |

Europe

A	Ladies British Open Stroke Play	Royal Ashdown Forest	Leona Maguire (IRL)	ENG
B	British Girls Open	Gullane No 1	Margaux Vanmol (BEEL)	SCO
C	English Open Stroke Play	Alwoodley	Charley Hull	ENG
C	Total International Juniors of Belgium	RGC of Belgium	Caroline Nistrup (DEN)	BEL
D	Finnish Amateur	Tali, Helsinki	Karlijn Zaanen (NED)	FIN
D	German Girls Under 16	Main Taunus	Karolin Lampert	GER
D	Harder German Junior Masters	Gut Neuzenhof	Lynn Carlsson (SWE)	GER
D	Royal Tour III	Hilleroed	Daisy Nielsen	DEN
D	Swiss International Championship	Ascona	Franziska Blum (GER)	SUI
E	Championnat de France Dames	Chantilly	Fiona Puyo	FRA
E	Czech International Amateur	Kuneticka Hora	Karolina Vlckova	CZE
E	Finnish Tour 7	Naiset	Annika Nykanen	FIN
E	German Girls Under 18	Main Taunus	Antonia Scherer	GER
E	Norgesmesterskapet	Kristiansand	Solveig Helgesen	NOR
E	Skandia Tour Riks 5 Goteborg	Forsgardens	Anna Svenstrup	SWE
F	Arionbank Junior Championship	Reykjavik	Gudrun Bjorgvinsdottir	ISL
F	Belgian National Junior	7 Fontaines	Margaux Vanmol	BEL
F	Campeonato Absoluto Pais Vasco	Basozabal	Irene Rollan*	ESP
F	Connaught Girls	Athenry	Jessica Carty	IRL
F	Copa Federacion Vasca	Laukariz	Adriana Martinez*	ESP
F	Czech Amateur Tour 5	Ropice	Radka Vlasinova*	CZE
F	DM for Piger Hulspil	Struer	Puk Lyng Thomsen*	DEN
F	Estonian National Stroke Play	Joelahtme	Merlin Palm	EST
F	Faldo Series – Slovakia	Black Stork	Natalia Heckova	SVK
F	Faxe Kondi Tour III	Hilleroed	Malene Krolboll	DEN
F	German Girls Under 14	Main Taunus	Finnja Kietzke*/Antonia-Leonie Eberhard*	GER
F	Grand Prix de la Nivelle	Golf de la Nivelle	Fiona Puyo	FRA
F	Grand Prix de Savoie	Aix les Bains	Lorellen Gros	FRA
F	Grand Prix de Valcros	Valcros	Emie Peronnin	FRA
F	Grand Prix du Medoc	Medoc	Louise Labaigt	FRA
F	Grand Prix du Pau	Pau	Louise Latorre	FRA
F	Grand Prix Valgarde	Golf de Valgarde	Lea Cherel/Emie Peronnin*	FRA
F	Hungarian Amateur Open	Pannonia	Marlene Krejcy (AUT)	HUN
F	Hungarian Junior Amateur	Old Lake	Rozsa Csilla*	HUN
F	Icelandic Match Play	Hella	Olafia Kristinsdottir	ISL
F	Italian Girls Team	Villa Carolina	Bianca Fabrizio	ITA
F	Latvian Amateur Match Play	Riga	Anna Diana Svanka*	LAT
F	Latvian Amateur Open	Riga	Krista Puisite	LAT
F	Lithuanian Open	V GC	Linda Dobele (LAT)	LTU
F	Mid-Leinster Women's Championship	Mount Wolseley	Emma Murphy*	IRL
F	North of England Under 16	Pannal	Bethan Popel	ENG
F	Siljan Open	Rattviks	Rebecca Hellbom	SWE
F	Skandia Tour Elit Flickor 5	Arninge	Isabella Deilert	SWE
F	Skandia Tour Riks 5 Gastrike/Halsinge	Hofors	Ebba Gustafsson*	SWE
F	Skandia Tour Riks 5 Sodermanland	Katrineholms	Ellinor Haag	SWE
F	Slovenian International Girls	Bled	Ursa Orehek	SLO
F	St Andrews Junior Ladies	St Andrews	Jessica Meek	SCO
F	Strathtyrum Trophy	St Andrews	Karen Marshall	SCO
F	Ukrainian Club Cup	Kiev	Valerie Sapronova*	UKR
F	Ulster Amateur	City of Derry	Louise Coffey	IRL
F	Zurich Championship	Breitenloo/Hittnau	Sheila Gut-Lee*	SUI

For further information, visit www.randa.org/wagr

September

Americas

A	Cougar Classic	Charleston, NC	Austin Ernst	USA
A	Mason Rudolph Fall Preview	Nashville, TN	Lindy Duncan	USA
B	Branch Law Firm/Dick McGuire	Albuquerque, NM	Sofia Hoglund (FIN)*	USA
B	Golfweek Conference Challenge	Vail, CO	Chirapat Jao-Javanil (THA)	USA
B	Ptarmigan Ram Fall Classic	Fort Collins, CO	Demi Runas	USA
B	Texas A & M Mo'morial	Bryan, TX	Carlie Yadloczky	USA
C	AJGA Girls Championship	Greenville, SC	Emma Talley	USA
C	Chip-N Club Invitational	Lincoln, NE	Felicia Espericueta	USA
C	Dale McNamara Invitational	Owasso, OK	Guilia Molinaro (ITA)	USA
C	WSU Cougar Cup	Pullman, WA	Sally Watson (SCO)	USA
C	Abierto Jockey Club de Rosario	Rosario	Victoria Tanco	ARG
D	Badger Invitational	Madison, WI	Felicia Espericueta	USA
D	Chris Banister Gamecock Classic	Huntsville, AL	Marissa Steen	USA
D	Circling Raven Collegiate Invitational	Worley, IN	Caitlin McCleary	USA
D	Golfweek Program Challenge	Myrtle Beach, SC	Christina Miller	USA
D	Marilynn Smith Sunflower Invitational	Manhattan, KS	Malin Lundberg (SWE)	USA
D	Mary Fossum Invitational	E Lansing, MI	Caroline Powers	USA
D	Campeonato de Menores y Menores de 15	Jockey Club Venado Tuerto	Manuela Carbajo Re	ARG
D	Campeonato National Infantil 14-15	Baranquilla	Laura Sojo	COL
E	Princeton Women's Invitational	Princeton, NJ	Tiffany Lim	USA
E	US Women's Mid-Amateur	Virginia Beach, VA	Ellen Port	USA
E	Yale Fall Intercollegiate	New Haven, CT	Seo Hee Moon	USA
F	Bucknell Women's Invitational	Lewisburg, PA	Kortnie Maxoutopoulis	USA
F	Carroll College Invitational	Helena, MT	Mari Hutsi (EST)*	USA
F	Copa Laguna	Cuernavaca, Morelos	Giovana Maymon	MEX
F	Murray State Drake Creek Invitational	Ledbetter, KY	Marisa Kamelgarn	USA
F	Redbird Invitational	Normal, IL	Bailey Arnold*	USA
F	Rocky Mountain Invitational	Billings, MO	Kalli Stanhope	USA
F	Rose City Collegiate	Wilsonville, OR	Rochelle Chan	USA
F	South Carolina Stroke Play	Charleston, SC	Cecilia Fournil*	USA
F	ULM Fred Marx Invitational	Monroe, LA	Whitney McAteer	USA
F	USGA Senior Women's Amateur	Chattanooga, TN	Terri Frohnmayer*	USA
F	Warner Pacific Invitational	Vancouver, WA	Trish Gibbens	USA
F	Woodward Video Junior at The Greenbrier	White Sulphur Springs, WV	Lauren Salazar	USA
F	Abierto de Farallones	Farallones	Anna Bohmer	COL
F	Abierto del Guayaquil	Guayaquil	Coralia Arias	ECU
F	Campeonato Juvenil de Venezuela	Valle Arrba	Ana Raga	VEN
F	Campeonato Nacional de Menores 11	Armenia	Maria Andrea Donado*	COL
F	Campeonato National Infantil 12-13	Baraquilla	Maria Vesga	COL
F	Copa BBVA	Medellin	Manuela Uribe	COL

Asia

C	Hong Kong Ladies Open	Hong Kong GC	Jayvie Agojo (PHI)	HKG
C	Santi Cup	Clearwater Bay	Pinrath Loomboonruang (THA)	HKG
D	Korea Junior Championship Women (High)	Lakehills Jeju	Hyo-Joo Kim	KOR
D	Malaysian Junior Open	Saujana, Subang	Dottie Ardina (PHI)	MAS
E	National Middle School Senior High	Taichung	Chi Wang	TPE
F	China Amateur Championship	Yantai, Shandong	Xiao Yi	CHN
F	Faldo Series Asia – India	Poona	Aditi Ashok	IND
F	Korea Junior Championship Women (Middle)	Lakehills Jeju	Su-Min Park*	KOR
F	National Middle School - Junior High	Taichung	Ssu-Chia Cheng	TPE
F	National Ranking Game 4	Changi	Amelia Yong	SIN
F	Southern India Ladies	Bangalore	Mehar Atwal	IND
F	Taiwan Amateur Championship	Sunrise	Saki Nagamine (JPN)*	TPE
F	Terengganu Amateur Open	Kuala Terengganu	Nur Durriyah Damian	MAS
F	TGA-CAT Junior Ranking 3	Evergreen Hills	Suthavee Chanachai*	THA

Australasia

B	Australia Interstate Teams	Western Australian	Suthavee Chanachai (THA)*	AUS
E	Carrus Open	Tauranga	Emily Perry	NZL
E	Katherine Hull Classic – Open	Maroochydore, QLD	Lauren Mason	AUS
E	Victorian Amateur Girls	Melbourne, VIC	Rio Watanabe*	AUS
F	Katherine Hull Classic – U15	Maroochydore, QLD	Jessica Park	AUS
F	Victorian Amateur Girls U16	Melbourne, VIC	Sian Zigomanis*	AUS
F	Wellington Stroke Play	Shandon	Julianne Alvarez	NZL

Europe

A	Junior Solheim Cup	Knightsbrook	Julianne Alvarez (NZL)	IRL
B	Duke of York Young Champions	Royal Liverpool	Ha Rang Lee (ESP)	ENG
B	Home Internationals Women	Hillside	Ha Rang Lee (ESP)	ENG
C	German National Championship	Gleidingen	Antonia Scherer	GER
C	Turkish Amateur	Gloria, Antalya	Nicole Broch Larsen (DEN)	TUR
D	European Ladies Club Trophy	Corfu	Ane Urchegui (ESP)	GRE
D	Stirling Invitational	Gleneagles	Eilidh Briggs	SCO
E	Faldo Series Grand Final	Lough Erne	Brogan Townend (ENG)	IRL
E	Finnish Tour 9	Vuosaari	Anne Hakula	FIN
E	Italian National Stroke Play	Bogogno	Bianca Fabrizio	ITA
E	Mandatum Life Final	Nordcenter	Noora Tamminen	FIN
E	Netherlands National Match Play	Beesterswaag	Lianne Jansen	NED
E	Skandia Tour Elit 6	Oijared	Emma Henrikson	SWE
E	Suisse Romande	Neuchatel	Anais Maggetti	SUI
F	Bulgarian Amateur	Thracian Cliffs & BlackSeaRama	Damla Bilgic (TUR)	BUL
F	Cancello D'Oro	Villa Condulmer	Tullia Calzavara	ITA
F	Chevrolet Open	Gardabae	Sunna Vidisdottir	ISL
F	European Universities Championship	Otocec	Harriet Beasley (ENG)	SLO
F	Finnish Tour Karsinta	Karsinta	Kati Nieminen*	FIN
F	Fiorino D'Oro	Firenze	Martina Flori*	ITA
F	French Mid-Amateur Women	Saint Laurent	Jenny Bjerling (SWE)*	FRA
F	Grand Prix de Massane	Montpellier	Claire Ulmann	FRA
F	Junior Masters Invitational	Haninge	Jenny Haglund	SWE
F	National Match Play U21	Domburgsche	Giulia van den Berg	NED
F	Norgescup Finale	Drobak	Mariell Bruun*	NOR
F	Titleist Tour 6	Sarpsborg	Marthe Wold	NOR
F	Titleist Tour Finale	Kragero	Marthe Wold	NOR

October

Africa

B	Boland Championship	Strand GC	Kim Williams	RSA
B	Gus Ackerman Championship	Westlake GC	Cara Gorlei	RSA

Americas

A	Mercedes-Benz SEC/PAC 12 Challenge	Knoxville, TN	Stephanie Meadow (IRL)	USA
A	Stanford Intercollegiate	Stanford, CA	Soo-Bin Kim (CAN)	USA
A	Tar Heel Invitational	Chapel Hill, NC	Marta Sanz (ESP)	USA
B	Landfall Tradition	Wilmington, NC	Paula Reto (RSA)	USA
B	Ping Invitational	Stillwater, OK	Jaye Marie Green	USA
B	Windy City Collegiate	Golf, IL	Isabelle Boineau (FRA)/Kelsey Vines	USA
C	Edean Ihlanfeldt Invitational	Sammamish, WA	Madeleine Sheils	USA
C	Lady Northern Intercollegiate	French Lick, IN	Meagan Bauer	USA
C	Lady Paladin Invitational	Greenville, SC	Charlotte Kring Lorentzen (DEN)	USA
C	Lady Pirate Intercollegiate	Greenville, NC	Samantha Morrell	USA
C	Las Vegas Collegiate Showdown	Boulder City, NV	Grace Na	USA
C	Price's Give Em Five Intercollegiate	Las Cruces, NM	Jaclyn Jansen/Kayla Mortellaro	USA
C	Susie Maxwell Berning Classic	Norman, OK	Anne-Catherine Tanguay (CAN)	USA
C	USGA State Team Championship Individual	Savannah, GA	Rachel Dai	USA
D	Bettie Lou Evans Fall Invitational	Lexington, KY	Ashleigh Albrecht	USA

D	Bob Hurley Auto ORU Shootout	Tulsa, OK	Jessica Schiele (ENG)	USA
D	Hoosier Fall Invitational	Carmel, IN	Becca Huffer	USA
D	Johnie Imes Invitational	The Club at Old Hawthorne, Columbia, MO	Lejan Lewthwaite (RSA)	USA
D	LPGA Xavier International	Daytona Beach, FL	Amy Anderson	USA
D	Memphis Invitational	Germantown, TN	Marissa Steen	USA
D	Nittany Lion Women's Invitational	State College, PA	Ariel Witmer	USA
D	Palmetto Intercollegiate	Kiawah Island, SC	Fanny Cnops (BEL)	USA
D	UNCG Starmount Fall Classic	Greensboro, NC	Charlotte Kring Lorentzen (DEN)	USA
D	Copa Eduardo Herrera	Club Los Andes	Laura Estefenn	COL
D	Sudamericano Pre-Juvenil	Cuidad del Este	Sofia Goicoechea (ARG)	PAR
E	Copa Enrique Santos	Guayaquil Country Club	Lucia Gutierrez (PER)	ECU
E	Blue Raider Invitational	Murfreeboro, TN	Karisa Akin	USA
E	FIU Pat Bradley Invitational	Fort Myers, FL	Shelby Coyle	USA
E	MSU/Payne Stewart Memorial	Springfield, MO	Hermine Greyling	USA
E	Spider Invitational	Midlothian, VA	Stephanie Hsieh	USA
E	USF-Waterlefe Invitational	Bradenton, FL	Christina Miller	USA
E	Wyoming Cowgirl Desert Invite	Palm Desert, CA	Christine Wong (CAN)	USA
F	CCIW Championship	Davenport, IA	Katie Klosterman	USA
F	Corban Invitational	Salem, OR	Trish Gibbens	USA
F	Embry Riddle AZ Invitational	Prescott, AZ	Lisa Copeland*	USA
F	Firestone Grill College Invitational	Nipomo, CA	Caitlin McCleary	USA
F	IIAC Championship	Storm Lake, IA	Sarah Paulson*	USA
F	Lady Red Wolf Classic	Jonesboro, AR	Jennifer Loiacano	USA
F	MIAC Championship	Coon Rapids, MN	Vanessa Kleckner*	USA
F	Midwest Conference Championship	Springfield, IL	Angelina Parrinello*	USA
F	Montverde Academy Junior All-Star Inv.	Montverde, FL	Sierra Brooks	USA
F	NAC Championships	West Chicago, IL	Muriel Mcintyre* (CAN)	USA
F	Nevada State Stroke Play	Silverstone, Las Vegas	Laurie Johnson*	USA
F	WIAC Championships	Wisconsin Rapids, WI	Mary Welsh	USA
F	Wolf Pack Classic	Dayton, NV	Alex Buelow	USA
F	Abierto de Golf Serrezuela	Serrezuela CC	Ana Maria Morales*	COL
F	Abierto Internacional Copa Claro	Golf Hacienda Chicureo	Valentina Haupt	CHI
F	Abierto San Cristobal	Club San Cristobal	Maria Jose Vial	CHI
F	Colombian Mid Amateur	Caujaral Club	Julie Pauline Saenz Starnes*	COL

Asia

C	National Sports Festival	Dongyeoju CC	Ji-Hee Kim	KOR
C	Singha Thailand Open	Panya Indra Golf Course	Dottie Ardina (PHI)	THA
E	Fangshan Changyang Amateur	California County GC	Andrea Unson (PHI)	CHN
E	Pune Open Amateur	Pune G&CC, Pune	Mehar Atwal	IND
E	Western India Amateur	BPGC, Mumbai	Vani Kapoor	IND
F	China Junior Championship 11-14	Stone Bay Golf & Resort	Wu Sha	CHN
F	China Junior Championship 15-17	Stone Bay Golf & Resort	Wang Xi Yue*	CHN
F	Faldo Series Malaysia	The Royal Selangor GC	Aretha Herng Pan	MAS
F	HSBC National Junior Championship Final	Shanghai	Guan Ruqing*	CHN
F	TGA-CAT Junior Championship	Royal Hills Golf Resort & Spa	Jinjuta Thongtan	THA

Australasia

C	Grange Classic	The Grange GC, Auckland	Cecilia Cho	NZL
C	Srixon International Junior Classic	Maitland GC, NSW	Minjee Lee	AUS
E	Port Taranaki Open	Port Taranaki	Emily Perry	NZL
F	Australian Senior Championship	Toowoomba, QLD	Sylvia Donohoe*	AUS
F	BOP Classic	Whangamata GC, Coromandel	Emily Perry	NZL
F	Shirley Open	Christchurch GC	Emily Perry	NZL
F	Wanganui Open	Manawatu	Stephanie McKillop*	NZL

Europe

B	Cecile De Rothchild Trophy	Monfontaine GC	Perrine Delacour	FRA
D	Championnat de France Cadet	St Cyprien	Manon Gidali	FRA
F	Austrian Match Play	Diamond CC	Marina Stuetz	AUT

Europe (continued)

F	Campionato Nazionale Mid-Amateur	Argentario	Giuliana Colavito*	ITA
F	Coppa d'Oro Castelli	Roma	Virginia Paglialunga*	ITA
F	Grifo d'Oro	Perugia	Anna Dalessio*	ITA
F	Israel Open	Caesarea GC	Hadas Libman	ISR
F	La Quercia D'Oro Girls	Le Querce	Alice Di Piero	ITA
F	Taca de FPG	Aroeira 11	Susana Ribeiro	POR
F	Trofeo Glauco Lolli Ghetti	GC Margara	Elisabetta Bertini	ITA

November

Africa

F	South African Mid-Amateur	Kingswood Golf Estate	Sandra Winter	RSA

Americas

B	Betsy Rawls Longhorn Invite	Austin, TX	Nicole Vandermade (CAN)	USA
B	Polo Junior Classic	Palm Beach Gardens, FL	Nicole Morales	USA
B	Rainbow Wahine Invitational	Kapolei, HI	Lee Lopez	USA
C	Alamo Invitational	San Antonio, TX	Fabiola Arriaga (MEX)	USA
C	Challenge at Onion Creek	Austin, TX	Gabriella Dominguez	USA
D	Fighting Camel Fall Classic	Buies Creek, NC	Amy Anderson	USA
D	Argentine Amateur	San Isidro Golf Club	Manuela Carbajo Re	ARG
E	Tourneo Shalom	Shalom	Natalia Forero	COL
F	California Amateur	Carmel, CA	Jenni Jenq	USA
F	Champions Gate (13-18)	Champions Gate Resort	Kari Bellville	USA
F	Dennis Rose Invitational	Waikaloa, HI	Courtney Soekland	USA
F	Holiday Inn Express/ Hatter	DeLand, FL	Alex Buelow	USA
F	IJGT Major at TPC Sawgrass	TPC Sawgrass	Ana Ruiz (MEX)	USA
F	Omni Tucson National 13-18	Omni Tucson National Resort	Haley Moore*	USA
F	Guatemala Amateur	Guatemala CC	Lucia Polo	GUA
F	Abierto Las Palmas	Las Palmas GC	Macarena Haupt	CHI
F	Abierto Los Leones	Los Leones	Carla Jane	CHI
F	Abierto Prince of Wales CC	Prince of Wales CC	Valentina Haupt	CHI
F	Abierto Valle Escondido	Valle Escondido	Florencia Vinagre*	CHI
F	Copa Ciudad de Barranquilla	CC Barranquilla	Laura Sojo	COL
F	Federacao de Baiana de Golfe	Iberostar Praia do Forte GC	Lucia Maria Guilger	BRA
F	Internacional Infantil y Juvenil Caribe	Lagos de Caujaral	Laura Estefenn	COL
F	Master Infantil y Juvenil - 12-13	Farallones	Maria Alejandra Hoyos	COL
F	Tercera Parada Nacional Menores	Bucaramanga	Maria Vesga	COL
F	Torneo Ciudad de Cucuta	Tennis GC, Cucuta	Maria Camila Serrano	COL
F	Torneo Nacional La Paz	La Paz GC	Natalia Soria*	BOL
F	V Parada Mid-Amateur	Armenia CC	Diana Rueda Jaramillo*	COL

Asia

C	Abu Dhabi Junior	Abu Dhabi GC	Hayley Davis (ENG)	UAE
C	SEA Games (Individual)	Jagorawi G&CC	Tatiana W*	INA
E	Acer National Fall Ranking Tournament	Chia Nan GC	Szu-Han Chen TPE	
F	Albatross International Junior	Classic Golf Resort, Gurgaon	Moyu Sasaki (JPN)*	IND
F	Army Ladies Amateur	Army GC	Gurbani Singh	IND
F	China Amateur Tour Match Play	Sanya, Hainan Province	Chen Cuixia	CHN
F	Melaka Amateur Open	Ayer Keroh CC	Loy Hee Ying	MAS
F	Northern India Amateur	Noida	Vani Kapoor	IND
F	Rajasthan Junior	Rambagh GC, Jaipur	Millie Saroha	IND
F	Selangor Amateur Open	Rawang	Aretha Herng Pan	MAS
F	SGA 5th National Ranking Game	Jurong CC	Lim Jia Yi	SIN
F	Singha Junior World Championship	Royal Hua Hin Golf Course	Pannarat Thanapolboonyaras	THA

Australasia

B	Tasmanian Stroke Play	Launceston GC, TAS	Minjee Lee	AUS
F	Australian Mid-Amateur	Mornington Peninsula, VIC	Katrina Jones	AUS

| F | Bream Bay Classic | Waipu GC, Northland | Samantha Dangen*/Kylie Jacoby* | NZL |
| F | Omanu Classic | Omanu GC, BOP | Emily Perry | NZL |

Europe

| F | Championnat de Nouvelle Caledonie | Ouengi, New Caledonia | Ophelie Rague* | FRA |

December

Africa

| F | JGF Stroke Play | Royal Nairobi GC | Naomi Wafula* | KEN |
| F | KwaZulu Natal Nomads | Selbourne Country Club | Cara Gorlei | RSA |

Americas

C	Doral Publix Junior Classic 16–18	Miami, FL	Matilda Castren (FIN)	USA
D	Gate American Junior	Ponte Vedra Beach, FL	Marina Stuetz (AUT)	USA
E	Doral Publix Junior Classic 14–15	Miami, FL	Emily Pedersen (DEN)	USA
E	Campeonato Abierto Ciudad de Montevideo	Club de Golf del Uruguay	Paloma Vaccaro (PAR)	URU
F	Barton Creek Collegiate	Barton Creek	Minami Levonowich	USA
F	Ka'anapali Hawaiian Junior	Maui, FL	Lisa Kang	USA
F	Toyota Junior Tour Cup Series	SilverRock Resort	Avery French*	USA
F	TPC Craig Ranch Collegiate	TPC Craig Ranch	Taylor Schmidt (CAN)	USA
F	Costa Rica National Stroke Play	Hacienda los Reyes	Hilda Von Saalfeld*/Silvia Perez*	CRC
F	Torneo Nacional Vuelta Bolivia	Las Palmas CC, Santa Cruz	Michelle Ledermann*	BOL

Asia

C	Aaron Baddeley International Junior	Lion Lake CC, Guangzhou	Su-Hyun Oh (KOR)	CHN
E	All India Championship	Chandigarh GC	Aditi Ashok	IND
E	East India Tolly Ladies	Kolkata	Aditi Ashok	IND
F	Arab Games Individual	Doha	Feriel Chahed (TUN)*	QAT
F	China Amateur Open	Guangdong	Saya Aono (JPN)	CHN
F	HSBC Youth Challenge 3rd Leg	Laguna National G&CC	Phoebe Nicole Tan	SIN
F	Sabah International Junior Masters	Kota Kinabalu	Diana Tham	MAS
F	SICC Junior Invitational	SICC Island Course	Benyapa Niphatsophon (THA)	SIN

Australasia

B	Dunes Medal	The Dunes GC, VIC	Lee Park	AUS
B	New Zealand Interprovincial	Whakatane GC	Lee Park (AUS)	NZL
C	Victorian Amateur	Melbourne, VIC	Charlotte Thomas (ENG)	AUS
D	GNJGF Junior Masters	Coolangatta Tweed Heads GC	Su-Hyun Oh (KOR)	AUS
F	2XU Champions Trophy	Moss ValeGC & Mount Broughton G&CC	Shelly Shin (KOR)	AUS
F	Queensland Schoolgirls	Nudgee GC	Lauren Mason	AUS

Europe

| F | TGF Ligi 1 Ayak | Gloria Old/Gloria New | Tugce Erden/Yasemin Sari (GER) | TUR |
| F | TGF Ligi 2 | Gloria GC | Sena Ersoy/Tugce Erden | TUR |

At the time of going to Press, the results for December were incomplete. These will be reproduced in full in the next edition of *The R&A Golfer's Handbook*.

Major Amateur Championships 2011

Ladies British Open Amateur Championship (inaugurated 1893)

Royal Portrush [6401–71]

British Champion Lauren Taylor rewrites the record book

Sixteen-year-old Lauren Taylor, who plays her golf at Woburn, became the youngest winner of the Ladies British Open Amateur Championship when she beat French teenager Alexandra Bonetti 6 and 5 in the 18-hole final at Royal Portrush in Northern Ireland.

In doing so, Lauren beat the 112-year-old record previously held by May Hezlett who took the title in 1899 when aged 17.

England girl international Lauren who had her father on the bag, had qualified for the match play section in 42nd spot but then played brilliantly for the rest of the week. On her way to the final she beat World No 2 Cecilia Cho from New Zealand and in the final against Bonetti, the first French player to reach the final since Marine Monnet beat Rebecca Hudson in 1999 at Royal Birkdale, had built up a five hole lead by the turn.

"I told me dad that we were both going to relax this week. I usually try too hard in the big Championships and let myself down. I play best when I am stress free and dad was more laid back than he has ever been as my caddie," said the delighted Lauren.

Lauren, who plans to study at Baylor University in Texas, got off to a fast start in the final winning the first two holes, the fourth where her opponent lost a ball, the fifth and the sixth to be quickly five up. Bonetti, a former British Girls' champion who also plans to study in America at the Texas Christian University, did not produce the form that enabled her to beat Maesdu's Amy Boulden in her semi-final.

Taylor, who had beaten the defending champion Kelly Tidy at the 20th in the semi-final, ended the final in style by chipping in for a birdie – her sixth of the round – at the 13th.

Stroke Play Qualifying:

Camilla Hedberg (ESP)	71-69—140	Rachael Watton (Mortonhall)	79-70—149
Louise Kristersson (SWE)	73-69—142	Thea Hoffmeister (GER)	77-72—149
Nathalie Manson (SWE)	76-67—143	Kelly Tidy (Royal Birkdale)	77-72—149
Christine Wong (CAN)	73-71—144	Lara Katzy (GER)	75-74—149
Sophia Popov (GER)	71-73—144	Pia Halbig (GER)	75-74—149
Lydia Ko (NZL)	71-73—144	Giulia Molinaro (ITA)	72-77—149
Holly Clyburn (Woodhall Spa)	75-70—145	Justine Dreher (FRA)	74-76—150
Charley Hull (Woburn)	74-72—146	Stephanie Meadow (Royal Portrush)	74-76—150
Amy Boulden (Maesdu)	74-72—146	Laure Castelain (FRA)	79-72—151
Cecilia Cho (NZL)	73-73—146	Stephanie Kirchmayr (GER)	78-73—151
Marita Engzelius (NOR)	71-75—146	Marta Silva (ESP)	75-76—151
Therese Koelbaek (DEN)	76-71—147	Marta Sanz Barrio (ESP)	75-76—151
Lauren Blease (Burhill)	76-71—147	Rebecca Lee-Bentham (CAN)	75-76—151
Lisa Maguire (Slieve Russell)	75-72—147	Kelsey MacDonald (Nairn Dunbar)	78-74—152
Sally Watson (Elie & Earlsferry)	73-74—147	Fanny Vuignier (SUI)	77-75—152
Valerie Sternebeck (GER)	73-74—147	Kyle Rolg (USA)	75-77—152
Nicole Vandermade (CAN)	71-76—147	Louise Kenney (Pitreavie)	74-78—152
Leona Maguire (Slieve Russell)	78-70—148	Lauren Taylor (Woburn)	73-70—152
Celine Boutier (FRA)	76-72—148	Sara Monberg (DEN)	73-79—152
Anne-Catherine Tanguay (CAN)	75-73—148	Patricia Sanz Barrios (ESP)	82-71—153
Iliska Verway (RSA)	75-73—148	Charlene Reid (Royal Portrush)	76-77—153
Charlotte Kring Lorentzen (DEN)	74-74—148	Charlotte Wild (Mere)	76-77—153
Danielle McVeigh (Royal Co Down)	72-76—148	Perrine Delacour (FRA)	73-80—153
Minjee Lee (AUS)	68-80—148		

First Round:
Camilla Hedberg (ESP) beat Emma O'Driscoll (Ballybunion) 4 and 3
Stephanie Meadow (Royal Portrush) beat Laura Castelain (FRA) 2 holes
Myrte Eikenaar (NED) beat Nicole Vandermade (CAN) 2 holes
Kim Williams (RSA) beat Valerie Sternebeck (GER) 4 and 3
Amy Boulden (Maesdu) beat Jess Wilcox (Blankney) 1 hole
Minjee Lee (AUS) beat Louise Kenney (Pireavie) 4 and 2
Kyle Roig (USA) beat Rachael Watton (Mortonhall) 4 and 2
Anais Maggetti (SUI) beat Charley Hull (Woburn) 2 holes

Sophia Popov (GER) beat Emma Broze (FRA) 3 and 2
Rebecca Lee-Bentham (CAN) beat Lara Katzy (GER) 1 hole
Iliska Verwey (RSA) beat Patricia Sanz Barrios (ESP) 3 and 2
Therese Koelbaek (DEN) beat Breanna Elliott (AUS) 4 and 3
Alexandra Bonetti (FRA) beat Lauren Blease (Burhill) 1 hole
Anne-Catherine Tanguay (CAN) beat Charlene Reid (Royal Portrush) 5 and 3
Marta Sanz Barrio (ESP) beat Pia Halbig (GER) 5 and 4
Alexandra Vilatte (FRA) beat Christine Wong (CAN) 7 and 6

Pamela Pretswell (Bothwell Castle) beat Nathalie Mansson (SWE) 2 and 1
Marta Silva (ESP) beat Giulia Molinaro (ITA) 3 and 2
Charlotte Wild (Mere) beat Celine Boulier (FRA) 2 holes
Deirdre Smith (Co Louth) beat Lisa Maguire (Slieve Russell) 1 hole
Marita Engzelius (NOR) beat Johanna Tilström (SWE) 4 and 2
Sara Monberg (DEN) beat Charlotte Kring Lorentzen (DEN) 3 and 2
Kelly Tidy (Royal Birkdale) beat Kelsey MacDonald (Nairn Dunbar) 2 and 1
Lydia Ko (NZL) beat Ailsa Summers (Carnoustie Ladies) 3 and 2

Victoria Bradshaw (Bangor) beat Holly Clyburn (Woodhall Spa) 3 and 2
Thea Hoffmeister (GER) beat Fanny Vuignier (SUI) 7 and 5
Lauren Taylor (Woburn) beat Danelle McVeigh (Royal Co Down Ladies) 2 and 1
Cecilia Cho (NZL) beat Bertine Strauss (RSA) 4 and 3
Sally Watson (Elie & Earlsferry Ladies) beat Jessica Wallace (CAN) 4 and 2
Perrine Delacour (FRA) beat Leona Maguire (Slieve Russell) at 20th
Stephanie Kirchmayr (GER) beat Justine Dreher (FRA) 3 and 2
Louise Kristersson (SWE) beat Alexandra Peters (Notts Ladies) 1 hole

Second Round:
Meadow beat Hedberg at 19th
Williams beat Eikenaar 7 and 5
Boulden beat Lee 4 and 3
Roig beat Maggetti 4 and 3
Popov beat Lee-Bentham 4 and 3
Verway beat Koelbaek 3 and 2
Bonetti beat Tanguay 3 and 2
Sanz Barrio beat Vilatte 1 hole
Silva beat Pretswell 3 and 1
Wild beat Smith 4 and 3
Engzelius beat Monberg 3 and 2
Tidy beat Ko 2 and 1
Hoffmeister beat Bradshaw 2 and 1
Taylor beat Cho 3 and 2
Delacour beat Watson 2 and 1
Kristersson beat Kirchmayr at 19th

Third Round:
Williams beat Meadeow 4 and 3
Boulden beat Roig 1 hole
Verwey beat Popov 1 hole
Bonetti beat Sanz Barrio 2 and 1
Wild beat Silva 1 hole
Tidy beat Engzelius 5 and 4
Taylor beat Hoffmeister 1 hole
Delacour beat Kristersson 4 and 3

Quarter Finals:
Boulden beat Williams 5 and 3
Bonetti beat Verwey at 19th
Tidy beat Wild 4 and 3
Taylor beat Delacour 4 and 3

Semi-Finals:
Bonetti beat Boulden 4 and 3
Lauren Taylor beat Kelly Tidy 3 and 2

Final: Lauren Taylor (Woburn) beat Alexandra Bonetti (ITA) 6 and 5

Ladies British Amateur Championship *continued*

1893	M Scott beat I Pearson 7 and 5		1956	M Smith (USA) beat M Janssen (USA) 8 and 7
1894	M Scott beat I Pearson 2 and 2		1957	P Garvey beat J Valentine 4 and 3
1895	M Scott beat E Lythgoe 5 and 4		1958	J Valentine beat E Price 1 hole
1896	Miss Pascoe beat L Thomson 2 and 2		1959	E Price beat B McCorkindale at 37th
1897	EC Orr beat Miss Orr 4 and 2		1960	B McIntyre (USA) beat P Garvey 4 and 2
1898	L Thomson beat EC Neville 7 and 5		1961	M Spearman beat DJ Robb 7 and 6
1899	M Hezlet beat Magill 2 and 1		1962	M Spearman beat A Bonallack 1 hole
1900	Adair beat Neville 6 and 5		1963	B Varangot (FRA) beat P Garvey 2 and 1
1901	Graham beat Adair 2 and 1		1964	C Sorenson (USA) beat BAB Jackson at 37th
1902	M Hezlet beat E Neville at 19th		1965	B Varangot (FRA) beat IC Robertson 4 and 3
1903	Adair beat F Walker-Leigh 4 and 3		1966	E Chadwick beat V Saunders 2 and 2
1904	L Dod beat M Hezlet 1 hole		1967	E Chadwick beat M Everard 1 hole
1905	B Thompson beat ME Stuart 2 and 2		1968	B Varangot (FRA) beat C Rubin (FRA) at 20th
1906	Kennon beat B Thompson 4 and 3		1969	C Lacoste (FRA) beat A Irvin 1 hole
1907	M Hezlet beat F Hezlet 2 and 1		1970	D Oxley beat IC Robertson 1 hole
1908	M Titterton beat D Campbell at 19th		1971	M Walker beat B Huke 2 and 1
1909	D Campbell beat F Hezlet 4 and 3		1972	M Walker beat C Rubin (FRA) 2 holes
1910	Miss Grant Suttie beat L Moore 6 and 4		1973	A Irvin beat M Walker 2 and 2
1911	D Campbell beat V Hezlet 2 and 2		1974	C Semple (USA) beat A Bonallack 2 and 1
1912	G Ravenscroft beat S Temple 2 and 2		1975	N Syms (USA) beat S Cadden 2 and 2
1913	M Dodd beat Miss Chubb 8 and 6		1976	C Panton beat A Sheard 1 hole
1914	C Leitch beat G Ravenscroft 2 and 1		1977	A Uzielli beat V Marvin 6 and 5
1915–18	*Not played*		1978	E Kennedy (AUS) beat J Greenhalgh 1 hole
1919	*Abandoned because of railway strike*		1979	M Madill beat J Lock (AUS) 2 and 1
1920	C Leitch beat M Griffiths 7 and 6		1980	A Quast (USA) beat L Wollin (SWE) 2 and 1
1921	C Leitch beat J Wethered 4 and 3		1981	IC Robertson beat W Aitken at 20th
1922	J Wethered beat C Leitch 9 and 7		1982	K Douglas beat G Stewart 4 and 2
1923	D Chambers beat A Macbeth 2 holes		1983	J Thornhill beat R Lautens (SUI) 4 and 2
1924	J Wethered beat Mrs Cautley 7 and 6		1984	J Rosenthal (USA) beat J Brown 4 and 3
1925	J Wethered beat C Leitch at 37th		1985	L Beman (IRL) beat C Waite 1 hole
1926	C Leitch beat Mrs Garon 8 and 7		1986	M McGuire (NZL) beat L Briars (AUS) 2 and 1
1927	T de la Chaume (FRA) beat Miss Pearson 5 and 4		1987	J Collingham beat S Shapcott at 19th
1928	N Le Blan (FRA) beat S Marshall 2 and 2		1988	J Furby beat J Wade 4 and 3
1929	J Wethered beat G Collett (USA) 2 and 1		1989	H Dobson beat E Farquharson 6 and 5
1930	D Fishwick beat G Collett (USA) 4 and 3		1990	J Hall beat H Wadsworth 2 and 2
1931	E Wilson beat W Morgan 7 and 6		1991	V Michaud (FRA) beat W Doolan (AUS) 2 and 2
1932	E Wilson beat CPR Montgomery 7 and 6		1992	P Pedersen (DEN) beat J Morley 1 hole
1933	E Wilson beat D Plumpton 5 and 4		1993	C Lambert beat K Speak 2 and 2
1934	AM Holm beat P Barton 6 and 5		1994	E Duggleby beat C Mourgue d'Algue 2 and 1
1935	W Morgan beat P Barton 2 and 2		1995	J Hall beat K Mourgue d'Algue 2 and 2
1936	P Barton beat B Newell 5 and 3		1996	K Kuehne (USA) beat B Morgan 5 and 3
1937	J Anderson beat D Park 6 and 4		1997	A Rose beat M McKay 4 and 3
1938	AM Holm beat E Corlett 4 and 3		1998	K Rostron beat G Nocera (FRA) 2 and 2
1939	P Barton beat T Marks 2 and 1		1999	M Monnet (FRA) beat R Hudson 1 hole
1940–45	*Not played*		2000	R Hudson beat E Duggleby 5 and 4
1946	GW Hetherington beat P Garvey 1 hole		2001	M Prieto (ESP) beat E Duggleby 4 and 3
1947	B Zaharias (USA) beat J Gordon 5 and 4		2002	R Hudson beat L Wright 5 and 4
1948	L Suggs (USA) beat J Donald 1 hole		2003	E Serramia (ESP) beat P Odefey (GER) 2 holes
1949	F Stephens beat V Reddan 5 and 4		2004	L Stahle (SWE) beat A Highgate 4 and 2
1950	Vicomtesse de St Sauveur (FRA) beat J Valentine 3 and 2		2005	L Stahle (SWE) beat C Coughlan 2 and 2
			2006	B Mozo (ESP) beat A Nordqvist (SWE) 2 and 1
1951	PJ MacCann beat F Stephens 4 and 3		2007	C Ciganda (ESP) beat A Nordqvist (SWE) 4 and 3
1952	M Paterson beat F Stephens at 39th		2008	A Nordqvist (SWE) beat C Hedwall (SWE) 3 and 2
1953	M Stewart (CAN) beat P Garvey 7 and 6		2009	A Muñoz (ESP) beat C Ciganda (ESP) 2 and 1
1954	F Stephens beat E Price 4 and 3		2010	K Tidy beat K MacDonald 2 and 1
1955	J Valentine beat B Romack (USA) 7 and 6			

Who is known as "Spaceman"?

The answer can be found on page 905

Ladies European Open Amateur Championship (inaugurated 1986)

Noordwijkse, Netherlands [5589m–72]

Lisa Maguire battles the wind to give Ireland a first European title

Irish golfers did well in the International European Ladies Championship at windswept Noorwijkse Golf Club in the Netherlands. Not only did Lisa Mguiure win the title but her twin Leona finish fourth and Stephanie Meadow, another of the Irish contingent, finished second just ahead of Charlotte Kring Lorentzen of Denmark who finished third.

"Leona has won twice this year in Portugal and Ireland I had won in Spain but now we are even," said Lisa adding "This was the title I really wanted to win."

Sixteen-year-old Lisa from Ballyconnel in County Cavan opened with a 73 to be two behind first round leader Marta Silva Zamora, the only player to break par on the first day, but moved in front with a second round record 68 for 141 which put her three ahead of Perrine Delacour from France.

After a third round 73 Lisa held a four shot lead over Delacour and Kring Lorentzen and by the turn on the final day had turned that into a commanding seven shot advantage on a difficult scoring day with a cruel wind lashing the course. Then on the back nine the Irish teenager dropped three shots, quickly and Kring Lorentzen made a birdie.

Now with only three shots in it Kring Lorentzen found the rough at long 14th, moved a bramble that was still attached to the ground and incurred a two shot penalty. "I really did not know it was attached," she said. Nineteen years earlier in the Dutch Open at Noordwijkse, Michael Mclean had incurred the same penalty by improving his lie in similar fashion – a mistake which cost him the title.

Seventeen-year-old Kring Lorentzen's mistake made it easier for Maguire whose five-over-par 293 total after a closing 79 gave her a well-deserved title success.

1	Lisa Maguire (IRL)	73-68-73-79—293
2	Stephanie Meadow (IRL)	78-71-75-73—297
3	Charlotte Kring Lorentzen (DEN)	74-70-75-79—298
4	Leona Maguire (IRL)	73-75-72-80—300
	Noora Tamminen (FIN)	72-77-78-75—302
	Thea Hoffmeister (GER)	73-80-78-72—303
	Charlotte Ellis (ENG)	75-79-76-74—304
	Manon Gidali (FRA)	78-73-76-77—304
	Noemi Jiménez (ESP)	73-73-80-78—304
10	Tessa De Bruijn (NED)	78-76-74-77—305
	Laetitia Beck (ISL)	73-75-75-82—305
12	Isabella Deilert (SWE)	76-78-72-80—306
	Anne Hakula (FIN)	74-72-80-80—306
	Perrine Delacour (FRA)	75-69-74-88—306
15	Sophia Popov (GER)	73-78-77-79—307
	Céline Boutier (FRA)	74-74-74-85—307
17	Laure Castelain (FRA)	81-77-76-74—308
	Amy Boulden (WAL)	76-76-79-77—308
19	Danielle McVeigh (IRL)	80-74-77-78—309
	Antonia Scherer (GER)	74-80-81-74—309
	Sally Watson (SCO)	73-81-75-80—309
	Rocio Sanchez (ESP)	72-78-75-84—309
23	Giulia Molinaro (ITA)	76-79-75-80—310
	Isabelle Boineau (FRA)	79-73-82-76—310
	Emelie Ferlin (SWE)	76-76-75-83—310
	Caroline Nistrup (DEN)	73-78-80-79—310
	Nicoline Skaug (NOR)	75-73-78-84—310
28	Belen Buendia (ESP)	80-78-78-75—311
	Quirine Eijkenboom (GER)	78-77-77-79—311
	Camilia Hedberg (ESP)	73-79-79-80—311
	Anne Van Dam (NED)	73-77-81-80—311
	Fanny Cnops (BEL)	74-76-80-81—311
33	Mirele Prat (ESP)	80-77-75-80—312
	Natalie Wille (SWE)	73-79-81-79—312
35	Malin Jansson (SWE)	82-77-76-78—313
	Emily Pedersen (DEN)	75-82-78-78—313
	Jeanne Metivier (FRA)	74-82-77-80—313

Ladies European Open Amateur Championship *continued*

35T	Joelie Van Baarle (BEL)	74-78-79-82—313
	Julie Finne-Ipsen (DEN)	78-73-75-87—313
40	Manon Mollé (FRA)	72-77-81-84—314
41	Emelie Lundström (SWE)	78-80-76-81—315
	Karolin Lampert (GER)	77-80-74-84—315
	Karolina Vlckova (CZE)	79-78-73-85—315
	Nina Mühl (AUT)	76-79-78-82—315
	Sanna Nuutinen (FIN)	76-78-76-85—315
46	Nicola Rössler (GER)	79-77-79-81—316
	Marta Silva (ESP)	71-80-79-86—316
48	Shannon Aubert (FRA)	78-77-81-81—317
	Daniela Holmqvist (SWE)	78-75-78-86—317
	Kelsey MacDonald (SCO)	79-71-84-83—317
51	Becky Harries (WAL)	79-78-80-81—318
	Anjelika Hammar (SWE)	78-78-78-84—318
	Ane Urchegui (ESP)	75-77-83-83—318
54	Cylia Damerau (SUI)	76-80-80-83—319
55	Myrte Eikenaar (NED)	76-73-81-90—320
56	Roberta Roeller (GER)	80-83-73-85—321
	Teresa Puga (ESP)	76-78-82-85—321
58	Pia Halbig (GER)	81-80-76-85—322
59	Emily Penttilä (FIN)	75-80-82-86—323
60	Eugenia Ferrero (ITA)	78-77-81-89—325
61	Jana Niedballa (GER)	81-75-81-93—330

The remaining 83 players missed the cut on 237

1986	Martina Koch (GER)	Morfontaine GC, France
1988	Florence Descampe (BEL)*	Pedrena GC, Spain
after a play-off with Delphine Bourson (FRA)		
1990	Matina Koch (GER)	Zumikon GC, Switzerland
1991	Delphine Bourson (FRA)	Schonborn GC, Austria
1992	Joanne Morton (ENG)	Estoril GC, Portugal
1993	Vibeke Stensrud (NOR)	Torino GC, Italy
1994	Martina Fischer (GER)	Bastadt GC, Sweden
1995	Maria Hjorth (SWE)	Berlin GC, Germany
1996	Silvia Cavalerri (ITA)	Furesoe GC, Denmark
1997	Silvia Cavalerri (ITA)	Formby GC, England
1998	Guilia Sergas (ITA)	Noordwijke GC, Netherlands
1999	Sofia Sandolo (ITA)	Karlovy Vary GC, Czech Rep.

2000	Emma Duggelby (ENG)	Amber Baltic GC, Poland
2001	Martina Eberl (GER)	Biella GC, Italy
2002	Becky Brewerton (WAL)	Kristianstad GC, Sweden
2003	Virginie Beauchet (FRA)	Shannon GC, Ireland
2004	Carlota Ciganda (ESP)	Ulzama GC, Spain
2005	Jade Schaeffer (FRA)	Santo da Serra GC, Madeira
2006	Belen Mozo (ESP)	Falkenstein GC, Germany
2007	Caroline Hedwall (SWE)*	Golf National, France
after play-off with Carlota Ciganda (ESP)		
2008	Carlota Ciganda (ESP)*	GC Schloss Schonborn, Austria
after play-off with Maria Hernandez (ESP)		
2009	Caroline Hedwall (SWE)	Falsterbo GC, Sweden
2010	Sophia Popov (GER)	Kunetickà Hora, Czech Rep.

111th United States Women's Amateur Championship (inaugurated 1895)

Rhode Island CC (Players are of US nationality unless stated) [SP 6399–71; MP 6350–71]

Kang successfully defends US Women's title in style

Eighteen-year-old Danielle Kang from Westlake Village in California became the first golfer to successfully defend the US Women's Amateur title since Kelli Kuehne in 1996 and only the fourth since the end of the Second World War to win the ttle back-to-back. In addition to Kuehne, Kim Cockrill in 1987 and Juli Inkster who held on to the title in 1981 and1982 have achieved the feat. Since the start of the Championship in 1896 only 11 players have done so.

At the Rhode Island Country Club, Kang produced some of the best golf of her career in the 36-hole final against the 17-year-old Moiya Jutanugarn from Thailand racking up 11 birdies. She had swept into a six-up led by the 13th, was four up at lunch and ended up winner by 6 and 5.

Kang's victory ended her amateur career. "I know I shall miss the Curtis Cup but I did play in the World Amateur Team Championship in Argentina in 2010. All amateurs ask themselves when they decide to turn professional whether or not they are ready to do so. I know I am."

The former Pepperdine University student, who earlier in the season won the North and South Women's Amateur at Pinehurst No 2 and made the cut in the US LPGA Championship and the US Women's Open, was also low amateur in the Ricoh Women's British Open at Carnoustie.

Kang had been focussing on her short game after having 17 three-putts and a four-putt at the US Women' Open. "I don't know why I had such difficulty with my putting at that event and the LPGA as well but my coach Brad Riggs had the answer. He took away the putter I had been using and put me back on a mallet putter. He told me to trust it and told me to keep telling myself I was a good putter anyway," said Kang.

Stroke Play Qualifying:

Jihee Kim (KOR)	66-70—136	Breanna Elliott (AUS)	74-70—144
Lydia Ko (NZL)	70-66—136	Stephanie Kono (Honolulu, HI)	71-73—144
Moriya Jutanugarn (THA)	70-67—137	Cyna Rodriguez (PHI)	70-74—144
Emma Talley (Princeton, KY)	70-68—138	Talia Campbell (Dallas, TX)	74-71—145
Casey Gric (College Station, TX)	72-67—139	Manuela Carbajo Re (ARG)	74-71—145
Doris Chen (Bradenton, FL)	69-71—140	Casey Danielson (Osceola, WI)	75-70—145
Pamela Pretswell (SCO)	69-72—141	Kristina Merkle (Honolulu, HI)	72-73—145
Xi Yu Lin (CHN)	68-73—141	Erynne Lee (Silverdale, WA)	72-73—145
Annie Park (Levittown, NY)	71-70—141	Jennifer Kirby (CAN)	75-70—145
Austin Ernst (Seneca, SC)	71-71—142	Kristen Park (Buena Park, CA)	72-73—145
Ariya Jutanugarn (THA)	70-72—142	Lindy Duncan (Fort Lauderdale, FL)	72-73—145
Lisa McCloskey (Montgomery, TX)	71-71—142	Julie Yang (Mesa, AZ)	75-70—145
Jaye Marie Green (Boca Raton, FL)	71-71—142	Cindy Ha (Demarest, NJ)	73-73—146
Victoria Tanco (Bradenton, FL)	72-70—142	Sarah Ababa (PHI)	73-73—146
Tiffany Lua (Rowland Heights, CA)	73-69—142	Mackenzie Brooke Henderson (CAN)	74-72—146
Courtney Gunter (Matthews, NC)	70-72—142	Emma De Groot (AUS)	73-73—146
Nicole Morales (South Salem, NY)	72-70—142	Christine Wong (CAN)	73-73—146
Gabriella Then (Rancho Cucamonga, CA)	74-69—143	Kelly Shon (Port Washington, NY)	72-74—146
Chihiro Ikeda (PHI)	72-71—143	Jessica Wallace (CAN)	72-74—146
Marina Alex (Wayne, NJ)	71-72—143	Chelsea Mocio (Fort Worth, TX)	71-75—146
Andrea Unson (PHI)	70-73—143	Holly Clyburn (ENG)	72-74—146
Lauren Stratton (Spring Hill, TN)	70-73—143	Sophia Popov (GER)	74-72—146
Michelle Piyapattra (Corona, CA)	73-70—143	Sally Watson (SCO)	72-75—147
Amy Meier (Rochester Hills, MI)	72-71—143	Calle Nielson (Nashville, TN)	74-73—147
Mariel Galdiano (Pearl City, HI)	68-75—143	Tiffany Lim (San Jose, CA)	72-75—147
Lee Lopez (Whittier, CA)	71-72—143	Stephanie Kim (Tempe, AZ)	71-76—147
Brianna Cooper (CAN)	71-73—144	Gabriela Lopez (MEX)	73-75—148
Demi Frances Runas (Torrance, CA)	72-72—144	Ket Preamchuen (Kennesaw, GA)	76-72—148
Danielle Kang (Westlake Village, CA)	71-73—144	Shu-Yin Liu (TPE)	75-73—148
Amy Anderson (Oxbow, ND)	73-71—144	Crystal Reeves (Broken Arrow, OK)	74-74—148
Madeleine Sheils (Boise, ID)	71-73—144	Lauren Dobashi (Gold River, CA)	72-76—148
Brooke Pancake (Chattanooga, TN)	71-73—144	Elyse Smidinger (Crofton, MD)	76-73—149

First Round:

Elyse Smidinger beat Jihee Kim (KOR) 2 and 1
Brooke Pancake beat Breanna Elliott (AUS) 1 hole
Christine Wong (CAN) beat Courtney Gunter 4 and 3
Nicole Morales beat Emma De Groot (AUS) at 19th
Tiffany Lim beat Xi Yu Lin (CHN) 1 hole
Erynne Lee beat Mariel Galdiano 6 and 4
Annie Park beat Calle Nielson at 24th
Amy Meier beat Jennifer Kirby (CAN) 2 holes
Emma Talley beat Shu-Yin Liu (TPE) 5 and 3
Danielle Kang beat Talia Campbell 3 and 2
Jaye Marie Green beat Chelsea Mocio 1 hole
Cindy Ha beat Marina Alex 1 hole
Kate Preamchuen beat Casey Grice 3 and 2
Demi Frances Runas beat Manuela Carbajo Re (ARG) 6 and 4
Lisa McCloskey beat Holly Clyburn (ENG) 1 hole
Julie Yang beat Andrea Unson (PHI) 1 hole
Lydia Ko (NZL) beat Lauren Dobashi 4 and 3

Stephanie Kono beat Madeleine Sheils at 19th
Tiffany Lua beat Kelly Shon at 20th
Mackenzie Brooke Henderson (CAN) beat Gabriella Then at 19th
Stephanie Kim beat Pamela Pretswell (SCO) at 19th
Lee Lopez beat Kristina Merkle 4 and 2
Austin Ernst beat Sally Watson (SCO) 1 hole
Michelle Piyapattra beat Kristen Park 3 and 2
Moriya Jutanugarn (THA) beat Crystal Reeves 1 hole
Amy Anderson beat Cyna Rodriguez (PHI) 1 hole
Victoria Tanco beat Jessica Wallace (CAN) 3 and 2
Sarah Ababa (PHI) beat Chihiro Ikeda (PHI) 1 hole
Gabriel Lopez (MEX) beat Doris Chen at 20th
Casey Danielson beat Brianna Cooper (CAN) 5 and 4
Ariya Jutanugarn (THA) beat Sophie Popov (GER) at 19th
Lindy Duncan beat Lauren Stratton 2 and 1

US Women's Amateur Championship *continued*

Second Round:
Brooke Pancake beat Elyse Smidinger 2 and 1
Nicole Morales beat Christie Wong 3 and 1
Erynee Lee beat Tiffany Lim 4 and 2
Annie Park beat Amy Meier 1 hole
Danielle Kang beat Emma Tally 6 and 4
Cindy Ha beat Jaye Marie Green 4 and 2
Demi Frances Runas beat Ket Preamchuen 3 and 2
Lisa McCloskey beat Julie Yang 1 hole
Stephanie Kono beat Lydia Ko 3 and 2
Tiffany Lua beat Mackenzie Brooke Henderson 3 and 2
Lee Lopez beat Stephanie Kim 2 and 1
Austin Ernst beat Michelle Piyapattra 1 hole
Moriya Juanugarn beat Amy Anderson 1 hole
Victoria Tanco beat Sarah Ababa 3 and 1
Casey Danielson beat Gabriela Lopez 3 and 2
Lindy Duncan beat Ariya Jutanugarn 2 and 1

Third Round:
Brooke Pancake beat Nicole Morales 4 and 3
Erynne Lee beat Annie Park at 19th
Danielle Kang beat Cindy Ha 2 and 1
Demi Frances Runas beat Lisa McCloskey at 19th
Stephanie Kono beat Tiffany Lua 3 and 2
Austin Ernst beat Lee Lopez 3 and 2
Moriya Jutanugarn beat Victoria Tanco 1 hole
Casey Danielson beat Lindy Duncan at 19th

Quarter Finals:
Brooke Pancake beat Erynne Lee at 21st
Danielle Kang beat Demi Frances Runas 4 and 3
Austin Ernst beat Stephanie Kono 5 and 4
Moriya Jutanugarn beat Casey Danielson 2 and 1

Semi-Finals:
Danielle Kang beat Brooke Pancake 1 hole
Moriya Jutanugarn beat Austin Ernst 1 hole

Final: Danielle Kang (Westlake Village, California) beat Moriya Jutanugarn (THA) 6 and 5

1895	LB Brown (132) beat N Sargent 134	Meadowbrook GC, NY		

Changed to match play

1896	B Hoyt beat A Tunure 2 and 1	Morris County GC, NJ	*Entrants*	29
1897	B Hoyt beat N Sargent 5 and 4	Essex CC, MA		29
1898	B Hoyt beat M Wetmore 5 and 3	Ardsley Club, NY		61
1899	R Underhill beat M Fox 2 and 1	Philadelphia CC (Bala Course)		78
1900	FC Griscom beat M Curtis 6 and 5	Shinnecock Hills GC, NY		62
1901	G Hecker beat L Herron 5 and 3	Baltusrol GC, NJ		89
1902	G Hecker beat LA Wells 4 and 3	The Country Club, Brookline, MA		96
1903	B Anthony beat JA Carpenter 7 and 6	Chicago GC, IL		64
1904	GM Bishop beat EF Sanford 5 and 3	Merion Cricket Club, PA		86
1905	P Mackay beat M Curtis 1 hole	Morris City GC, NJ		69
1906	HS Curtis beat MB Adams 2 and 1	Brae Burn CC, MA		75
1907	M Curtis beat HS Curtis 7 and 6	Midlothian CC (Blue Island Course), IL		87
1908	KC Harley beat TH Polhemus 6 and 5	Chevy Chase GC, MD		41
1909	D Campbell beat N Barlow 3 and 2	Merion Cricket Club, PA		86
1910	D Campbell beat GM Martin 2 and 1	Homewood CC, IL		57
1911	M Curtis beat LB Hyde 5 and 4	Baltusrol GC, NJ		67
1912	M Curtis beat N Barlow 3 and 2	Essex CC, MA		62
1913	G Ravenscroft beat M Hollins 2 holes	Wilmington CC, DE		88
1914	KC Harley beat EV Rosenthal 1 hole	Nassau CC, NY		93
1915	F Vanderbeck beat M Gavin (ENG) 3 and 2	Onwentsia Club, IL		119
1916	A Stirling beat M Caverly 2 and 1	Belmont Springs CC, MA		63
1917–1918	*Not played*			
1919	A Stirling beat M Gavin (ENG) 6 and 5	Shawnee CC, De		114
1920	A Stirling beat D Campbell Hurd 5 and 4	Mayfield CC, OH		114
1921	M Hollins beat A Stirling 5 and 4	Hollywood GC, NJ		181
1922	G Collett beat M Gavin (ENG) 5 and 4	Glenbrier GC, WV		196
1923	E Cummings beat A Stirling 3 and 2	Westchester GC, NY		196
1924	D Campbell Hurd beat MK Browne 7 and 6	Rhode Island CC, RI		98
1925	G Collett beat A Stirling Fraser 9 and 8	St Louis CC, MO		85
1926	H Stetson beat E Goss 2 and 1	Merion Cricket Club (East), PA		134
1927	MB Horn beat M Orcutt 5 and 4	Cherry Valley Club, NY		150
1928	G Collett beat V Van Wie 13 and 12	Hot Springs CC (Cascades Course), VA		123
1929	G Collett beat L Pressler 4 and 3	Oakland Hills CC (South Course), MI		98
1930	G Collett beat V Van Wie 6 and 5	Los Angeles CC (North Course), CA		102
1931	H Hicks beat G Collett Vare 2 and 1	CC of Buffalo, NY		102
1932	V Van Wie beat G Collett Vare 10 and 8	Salem CC, MA		90
1933	V Van Wie beat H Hicks 4 and 3	Exmoor CC, IL		120
1934	V Van Wie beat D Traung 2 and 1	Whitemarsh Valley CCm PA		157
1935	G Collett Vare beat P Berg 3 and 2	Interlachen CC, MN		94
1936	P Barton (ENG) beat M Orcutt 4 and 3	Canoe Brook CC (South Course), NJ		188
1937	EL Page beat P Berg 7 and 6	Memphis CC, TN		136
1938	P Berg beat EL Page 6 and 5	Westmoreland CC, IL		118
1939	B Jameson beat D Kirby 3 and 2	Wee Burn CC, CT		201

1940	B Jameson beat J Cochran 6 and 5	Del Monte G&CC, CA	163
1941	E Hicks Newell beat H Sigel 5 and 3	The Country Club, Brookline, MA	124
1942–1945	Not played		
1946	B Zaharias beat C Sherman 11 and 9	Southern Hills CC, OK	69
1947	L Suggs beat D Kirby 2 holes	Franklin Hills CC, MI	83
1948	G Lenczyk beat H Sigel 4 and 3	Del Monte G&CC, CA	116
1949	D Porter beat D Kielty 3 and 2	Merion Cricket Club (East), PA	171
1950	B Hanson beat M Murray 6 and 4	Atlanta Athletic Club, GA	110
1951	D Kirby beat C Doran 2 and 1	Town and CC, MN	79
1952	J Pung beat S McFedters 2 and 1	Waverley CC, OR	159
1953	ML Faulk beat P Riley 3 and 2	Rhode Island CC, RI	158
1954	B Romack beat M Wright 4 and 2	Allegheny CC, PA	151
1955	P Lesser beat J Nelson 7 and 6	Myers Park CC, NC	112
1956	M Stewart beat J Gunderson 2 and 1	Meridian Hills CC, IN	116
1957	J Gunderson beat AC Johnstone 8 and 6	Del Paso CC, CA	100
1958	A Quast beat B Romack 3 and 2	Wee Burn CC, CT	195
1959	B McIntyre beat J Goodwin 4 and 3	Congressional CC, Washington, DC	128
1960	J Gunderson beat J Ashley 6 and 5	Tulsa CC, OK	109
1961	A Quast beat P Preuss 14 and 13	Tacoma G&CC, WA	107
1962	J Gunderson beat A Baker 9 and 8	CC of Rochester, NY	128
1963	A Quast beat P Conley 2 and 1	Taconic CC, MA	128
1964	B McIntyre beat J Gunderson 3 and 2	Prairie Dunes CC, KS	93
1965	J Ashley beat A Quast 5 and 4	Lakewood CC, CO	88
1966	J Gunderson Carner beat JD Stewart Streit at 41st	Sewickley Heights GC, PA	115
1967	ML Dill beat J Ashley 5 and 4	Annandale GC, CA	119
1968	J Gunderson Carner beat A Quast 5 and 4	Birmingham CC, MA	110
1969	C Lacoste (FRA) beat S Hamlin 3 and 2	Las Colinas CC, TX	103
1970	M Wilkinson beat C Hill 3 and 2	Wee Burn CC, CT	139
1971	L Baugh beat B Barry 1 hole	Atlanta CC, GA	102
1972	M Budke beat C Hill 5 and 4	St Louis CC, MO	134
1973	C Semple beat A Quast 1 hole	Montclair GC, NJ	142
1974	C Hill beat C Semple 5 and 4	Broadmoor GC, WA	121
1975	B Daniel beat D Horton 3 and 2	Brae Burn CC, MA	154
1976	D Horton beat M Bretton 2 and 1	Del Paso CC, CA	157
1977	B Daniel beat C Sherk 3 and 1	Cincinnati CC, OH	162
1978	C Sherk beat J Oliver 4 and 3	Sunnybrook GC, PA	207
1979	C Hill beat P Sheehan 7 and 6	Memphis CC, TN	273
1980	J Inkster beat P Rizzo 2 holes	Prairie Dunes CC, KS	281
1981	J Inkster beat L Goggin (AUS) 1 hole	Waverley CC, OR	240
1982	J Inkster beat C Hanlon 4 and 3	Broadmoor GC (South Course), CO	262
1983	J Pacillo beat S Quinlan 2 and 1	Canoe Brook CC (North Course), NJ	259
1984	D Richard beat K Williams at 37th	Broadmoor GC, WA	290
1985	M Hattori (JPN) beat C Stacy 5 and 4	Fox Chapel CC, PA	329
1986	K Cockerill beat K McCarthy 9 and 7	Pasatiempo GC, CA	387
1987	K Cockerill beat T Kerdyk 3 and 2	Rhode Island CC, RI	359
1988	P Sinn beat K Noble 6 and 5	Minikahda Club, MN	384
1989	V Goetze beat B Burton 4 and 3	Pinehurst CC (No.2), NC	376
1990	P Hurst beat S Davis at 37th	Canoe Brook CC (North Course), NJ	384
1991	A Fruhwirth beat H Voorhees 5 and 4	Prairie Dunes CC, KS	391
1992	V Goetze beat A Sörenstam (SWE) 1 hole	Kemper Lakes GC, IL	441
1993	J McGill beat S Ingram 1 hole	San Diego CC, CA	442
1994	W Ward beat J McGill 2 and 1	The Homestead (Cascades Course), VA	451
1995	K Kuehne beat A-M Knight 4 and 2	The Country Club, Brookline, MA	452
1996	K Kuehne beat M Baena 2 and 1	Firethorn GC, NE	495
1997	S Cavalleri (ITA) beat R Burke 5 and 4	Brae Burn CC, MA	557
1998	G Park (KOR) beat J Chuasiriporn 7 and 6	Barton Hills CC, MI	620
1999	D Delasin beat J Kang 4 and 3	Biltmore Forest CC, NC	676
2000	N Newton beat L Myerscough 8 and 7	Waverley CC, OR	682
2001	M Duncan beat N Perrot at 37th	Flint Hills National GC, KS	768
2002	B Lucidi beat B Jackson 3 and 2	Sleepy Hollow CC, NY	793
2003	V Nirapathpongporn beat J Park 2 and 1	Philadelphia CC, PA	814
2004	J Park beat A McCurdy 2 holes	The Kahkwa Club, PA	868
2005	M Pressel beat M Martinez 9 and 8	Ansley GC (Settingdown Creek Course)	873
2006	K Kim* beat K Schallenberg	Pumpkin Ridge GC (Witch Hollow Course)	969

*at 14, the youngest-ever winner

2007	MJ Uribe beat A Blumenherst 1 hole	Crooked Stick GC, IN	935
2008	A Blumenhurst beat A Muñoz (ESP) 2 and 1	Eugene CC, OR	920
2009	J Song beat J Johnson 3 and 1	St Louis, MO	1,278
2010	Danielle Kang beat Jessica Korda 2 and 1	Charlotte CC, NC	1,296

1896–1952	18-hole stroke play qualifying before match play
1953–1963	All match play
1964–1972	36-hole stroke play qualifying before match play
1973–1979	18-hole stroke play qualifying before match play
1980–	36-hole stroke play qualifying before match play

NCAA Championships (Women) *Traditions GC, Bryan Texas*

Two 66's help Austin Ernst to victory for LSU

Austin Ernst from LSU became the first freshman to win the NCAA Division I women's title when she beat Arkansas golfer Kelli Shean by three shots with a four round total of 281 which included two rounds of 66. The last freshman to be successful in the competition was USC's Jennifer Rosales back in 1998.

The first of Ernst's 66's came on the second day at the Traditions Club in Bryan Texas and the second on the final day when her round included a hole-in-one at the 165 yards second – the fifth ace of the week.

Taking advice from her father "to have fun" Ernst's feat for LSU was matched a few weeks later when another LSU player, John Peterson, won the men's equivalent at the Karsten Creek Club in Stillwater, Oklahoma. It was the first time that golfers from the same school had won the individual titles in the same season.

The LSU head coach Karen Bahnren described Ernst as a tremendous ball striker. Despite Ernst's individual performance, LSU did not win the team event. They finished third behind the winners UCLA who beat defending champions Purdue into second spot by four shots.

Carrie Forsyth, the UCLA coach, described the last day as "pretty intense". Seven shots clear of Purdue with a round to go UCLA had lost their lead by the 13th before rallying over the closing stretch with Stephanie Kono and Glory Yang making birdies at the last. UCLA's top scorer was Tiffany Lua whose 287 total gave her a share of fourth place in the individual event. It was UCLA's third national team title success.

Team event

| 1 | UCLA | 289-295-294-295—1173 | | 3 | LSU | 292-296-303-290—1181 |
| 2 | Purdue | 292-295-298-292—1177 | | 4 | Virginia | 291-300-299-296—1186 |

5 S. California, Arkansas 1190; 7 Texas A&M 1191; 8 N. Carolina, Alabama 1193; 10 Vanderbilt, Florida 1196; 12 California 1197; 13 Tennessee 1200; 14 Wake Forest 1202; 15 Arizona 1205; 16 Washington 1209; 10 Arizona State 1210; 18 S.Carolina 1211; 19 Minnesota 1213; 14 UC Davis 1219; 21 Ohio State 1221; 22 Notre Dame 1224; 23 Stanford 1225; 24 Coastal Carolina 1232

Winning team: UCLA 1173 – Tiffany Lua 71-71-70-75—287; Lee Lopez 73-78-72-74—297; 3 Stephanie Kono 75-71-78-74—298; Glory Yang 70-75-79-76—300; Ami Gulugian 78-81-74-72—305

Individual Championship

1	Austin Ernst (LSU)	72-66-77-66—281
2	Kelli Shean (Arkansas)	75-70-71-68—284
3	Laura Gonzalez (Purdue)	74-71-70-71—286
4	Tiffany Lua (UCLA)	71-71-70-75—287
	Marta Zamora (Georgia)	71-71-72-73—287
6	Caroline Powers (Michigan State)	70-76-69-73—288
	Katerina Ruzickova (Texas A&M)	73-72-73-70—288
8	Lindy Duncan (Duke)	72-74-70-73—289
	Numa Gulyanamitta (Purdue)	71-70-77-71—289
	Joanne Lee (California)	73-71-76-69—289
	Natalie Sheary (Wake Forest)	72-74-71-72—289
12	Brittany Altomare (Virginia)	69-75-72-74—290
	Amy Anderson (N. Dakota State)	74-72-70-74—290
14	Erica Popson (Tennessee)	76-73-72-71—292
15	Anna Leigh Keith (Vanderbilt)	72-72-74-75—293
	Teresa Puga (Minnesota)	77-72-70-74—293
	Amy Simanton (UC Davis)	73-76-71-73—293

15T	Andrea Watts (Florida)	72-74-76-71—293
19	Brooke Pancake (Alabama)	78-75-72-69—294
	Mia Piccio (Florida)	72-70-76-76—294
	Emily Tubert (Arkansas)	76-73-71-74—294
22	Marina Alex (Vanderbilt)	72-76-74-73—295
	Lizette Salas (S. California)	75-73-74-73—295
24	Becca Huffer (Not. Dame)	80-71-73-72—296
	Katherine Perry (N. Carolina)	76-70-75-75—296
26	Kelli Bowers (Washington)	78-74-73-72—297
	Casey Grice (N. Carolina)	75-75-73-74—297
	Jacqueline Hedwall (LSU)	72-76-73-76—297
	Lee Lopez (UCLA)	73-78-72-74—297
	Calle Nielson (Virginia)	71-73-76-77—297
	Sophia Popov (S. California)	78-76-73-70—297
32	Anya Alvarez (Washington)	74-76-72-76—298
	Stephanie Kono (UCLA)	75-71-78-74—298
	Camilla Lennarth (Alabama)	72-79-73-74—298
	Stephanie Meadow (Alabama)	75-74-77-72—298
	Vicky Villanueva (Ohio State)	74-82-70-72—298

37	Nicole Agnello (Virginia)	76-76-74-73—299
	Jessica Alexander (Coastal Carolina)	79-72-73-75—299
	Katie Burnett (S. Carolina)	71-80-70-78—299
	Carlota Ciganda (Arizona State)	72-73-78-76—299
	Alejandra Llaneza (Arizona)	77-72-74-76—299
	Michelle Shin (Wake For.)	70-75-77-77—299
43	Megan McChrystal (LSU)	72-77-76-75—300
	Glory Yang (UCLA)	70-75-79-76—300
45	Evan Jensen (Florida)	76-74-78-73—301
	Sara Monberg (Tennessee)	73-74-77-77—301
	Rachel Morris (S. Calif.)	75-76-75-75—301
	Jessica Negron (Florida State)	72-79-77-73—301
	Inah Park (S. California)	76-78-71-76—301
	Margarita Ramos (Arizona)	74-77-77-73—301
	Paula Reto (Purdue)	73-78-77-73—301
	Sally Watson (Stanford)	73-78-71-79—301
53	Jackie Chang (N. Carolina)	76-73-77-76—302
	Lauren Stratton (Vanderbilt)	76-74-76-76—302
55	Laura Blanco (Arizona State)	75-73-76-79—303
	Pia Halbig (California)	77-74-74-78—303
	Maude-Aimee LeBlanc (Purdue)	74-76-76-77—303
	Cyna Rodriguez (S Calif.).	76-77-74-76—303
	Samantha Sommers (Minnesota)	77-72-75-79—303
	Samantha Swinehart (S. Carolina	78-77-77-71—303
	Cheyenne Woods (Wake Forest)	78-83-72-70—303
	Sarah Zwartynski (Texas A&M)	75-74-76-78—303
63	Karinn Dickinson (Wash.)	80-77-76-71—304
	Susy Grunden (Texas A&M)	74-71-82-77—304
65	Ani Gulugian (UCLA)	78-81-74-72—305
	Daniela Holmqvist (Calif.)	79-72-74-80—305
	Maribel Lopez Porras (Tulane)	78-77-76-74—305
	Amanda Strang (S. Carolina)	75-79-75-76—305
69	Isabelle Boineau (Arizona)	80-72-77-77—306
	Jennifer Kirby (Alabama)	76-75-78-77—306
	Emma Lavy (Arkansas)	80-74-78-74—306
	Catherine O'Donnell (N. Carolina)	78-75-78-75—306
	Daniela Ordonez (Arizona State)	75-81-75-75—306
74	Katie Conway (Not. Dame)	75-78-80-74—307
	Rebecca Durham (Stanford)	79-78-75-75—307
	Michele Edlin (Minnesota)	72-75-80-80—307
	In-Hong Lim (Ohio State)	76-77-78-76—307
	Marissa Mar (Stanford)	79-75-74-79—307
	Demi Runas (UC Davis)	78-74-80-75—307
80	Kyndall Ardoin (Arizona)	78-78-77-75—308
	Susana Benavides (Ohio State)	74-80-74-80—308

80T	Nikki Koller (Arizona)	75-74-82-77—308
	Suzie Lee (S. Carolina)	78-83-76-71—308
	Tessa Teachman (LSU)	81-77-77-73—308
	Allie White (N. Carolina)	84-78-72-74—308
86	Emily Childs (California)	79-76-81-73—309
	Giulia Molinaro (Arizona State)	74-80-80-75—309
88	Sarah Beth Davis (Texas A&M)	78-80-77-75—310
	Brittany Henderson (Coastal Carolina)	81-71-81-77—310
	Alice Kim (UC Davis)	79-79-77-75—310
	Nathalie Mansson (Tenn.)	75-74-79-82—310
	Sadena Parks (Wash.)	80-80-76-74—310
	Rene Sobolewski (Vanderbilt)	77-72-80-81—310
	Victoria Vela (Arkansas)	77-79-77-77—310
95	Joy Kim (Virginia)	75-76-81-79—311
	Justine Lee (Ariz. State)	78-77-79-77—311
	Natalie Reeves (Texas A&M)	73-77-76-85—311
	Kaitlyn Rohrback (Tenn.)	75-78-78-80—311
	Chelsea Stelzmiller (UC Davis)	83-78-79-71—311
	Kristina Wong (Stanford)	78-74-83-76—311
101	Courtney Boe (Coastal Carolina)	80-81-69-82—312
102	Portland Rosen (Virginia)	80-84-77-72—313
	Chessey Thomas (Tenn.)	80-81-84-68—313
	Amalie Valle (LSU)	76-77-80-80—313
105	Hannah Collier (Alabama)	79-80-75-80—314
106	Mary Narzisi (Minnesota)	79-75-82-79—315
	Nicole Zhang (Not. Dame)	77-79-74-85—315
108	Megan Grehan (Vanderbilt)	80-76-83-77—316
	Jessica Yadloczky (Florida)	81-80-80-75—316
110	Isabelle Lendl (Florida)	74-83-79-81—317
111	Kaitlin Higginbotham (Coastal Carolina)	82-78-78-80—318
	So-Hyun Park (Not. Dame)	81-82-80-75—318
113	Amy Meier (Ohio State)	79-81-76-83—319
	Corinna Rees (Arkansas)	77-79-77-86—319
115	Alexandra Bodemann (Wake Forest)	78-86-81-77—322
	Katie Rose Higgins (South Carolina)	84-79-79-80—322
	Kristina Nhim (Not. Dame)	76-85-83-78—322
	Rachel Rohanna (Ohio State)	86-77-82-77—322
	Jackie Shepherd (Minn.)	84-80-83-75—322
120	Alicia Grier (Coastal Carolina)	82-85-78-78—323
121	Jessica Chulya (UC Davis)	84-77-83-83—327
	Olafia Kristinsdottir (Wake Forest)	80-75-89-83—327
123	Lila Barton (Stanford)	78-85-83-83—329
	A Ram Choi (Wash.)	87-81-79-82—329
	Nicola Roessler (Calif.)	77-75 W
	Thea Hoffmeister (Purdue)	74-81-75 D

National Championships 2011

For past winners not listed here see earlier editions of The R&A Golfer's Handbook

Players are from the host nation unless stated

Africa

Sanlam South African Amateur Match-Play Championship *Rustenburg GC*
Leading qualifier: Kim Williams (Gauteng North) 70-74-68—212
Semi-finals: Iliska Verwey (Southern Cape) beat Kim Williams (Gauteng North) 3 and 1
Nobuhle Dlamini (Gauteng North) beat Bertine Strauss (North West) 3 and 2
Final: Iliska Verwey beat Nobuhle Dlamini 3 and 2

Red Sea Amateur Tournament *Soma Bay, Egypt*
1	Sabine Repond (SUI)	83-86—169
2	Maha El Senousy	98-95—193
3	Nagwa Kamy	98-96—194

Zimbabwe Ladies Championship *Royal Harare GC*
1	Claire Minter (Chapman)	75-75-74—224
2	Bonita Bredenhann (NAM)	74-78-74—226
3	Alana Van Gruening (RSA)	78-76-76—230

Americas

Argentine Women's Amateur Championship *San Isidro GC*
Final: Manuela Carbajo beat Maria Oliviera 1 hole

Canadian Women's Amateur Championship *Duncan Meadows G&CC, British Columbia*
1	Rebecca Lee-Bentham*	77-71-74-72—294
2	Lee Lopez (USA)	74-74-73-73—294
*Lee-Bentham won at the first extra hole		
3	Erynne Lee (USA)	78-73-70-74—295
	Jennifer Kirby	73-74-72-76—295
	Alex Stewart (USA)	73-73-74-75—295

Royale Cup Canadian Women's Senior Championship *Whitevale GC, Ontario*
1	Mary Ann Hayward	77-77-72—226
2	Jackie Little	77-78-74—229
3	Terrill Samuel	78-75-78—231

Caribbean Amateur Championship (George Teale Trophy)
Millenium Lakes GC, Trinidad

1 Trinidad and Tobago 593; 2 Puerto Rico 604; 3 Cayman Islands 634; 4 Barbados 660; 5 OECS 663;
6 Jamaica 683; 7 Dominican Republic 699
Winning team: Monifa Sealy, Tracey Clarke, Martine De Gannes

109th North and South Women's Championship *Pinehurst Resort*
Semi-Finals: Danielle Kang (Thousand Oaks) beat Lisa McCloskey (Houston) 4 and 2
Doris Chen (Bradenton) beat Marina Alex (Wayne) 3 and 2
Final: Danielle Kang beat Doris Chen 2 and 1

US Women's Mid-Amateur Championship *Bayville GC, Virginia Beach, Virginia*
Semi-Finals: Ellen Port (St Louis, MO) beat beat Helene Beat (Sylvania, OH) 4 and 3
Martha Leach (Hebron, KY) beat Tara Joy-Connelly (Pembroke, MA) at 19th
Final: Ellen Port beat Martha Leach 2 and 1
Medallist: Brenda Pictor (Marietta, GA) 72-74,146

US Amateur Women's Senior Championship *The Honors Course, Chattanooga, Tennessee*
Semi-Finals: Terri Frohnmayer (Salem) beat Lisa Schlesinger (Laytonsville) at 20th
Mina Hardin (Fort Worth) beat Anna Schultz (Rockwall) 4 and 3
Final: Terri Frohnmayer beat Mina Hardin 2 and 1

US Amateur Public Links Championship *Old Macdonald, Bandon Dunes, Oregon*
Semi-Finals: Brianna Do (VIE) beat Annie Park (Levittown) 2 and 1
Marissa Dodd (Allen) beat Tiffany Lua 2 and 1
Final: Brianna Do beat Marissa Dodd 1 hole

US Women's Amateur Championship *see page 390*

Asia

Hong Kong Ladies Close Amateur Championship *Discovery Bay GC*
1	Tiffany Chan	76-73-70—219
2	Mimi Ho	76-71-78—225
3	Kitty Tam	78-76-73—227

All-India Women's Amateur Championship
Final: Gauri Monga beat Shreya Ghei 2 and 1

53rd Japanese Amateur Championship *Takarazuka GC (New Course)*
Semi-finals: Mamiko Higa beat Natsuka Hori 5 and 3
Chihiro Ikeda beat Akane Saeki 3 and 2
Final: Mamiko Higa beat Chihiro Ikeda 6 and 5

Malaysian Ladies Open Amateur Championship *A'Famosa GC*
1	Aretha Pan Heng	68-69-73—210
2	Dottie Ardina (PHI)	71-72-69—212
3	Jayvie Agojo (PHI)	69-73-71—213

Malayasian Ladies Close Amateur Championship *Seri Selangor GC*
1	Isza Fariza Ismail	73-75-77—225
2	Iman Ahmad Nordin	79-71-76—226
	Nur Durriyah Damian	74-76-76—226

Pakistan Women's Amateur Championship *Islamabad GC*

1	Ghazala Yasmin (Lahore Garrison)	84-84-81—249
2	Ami Qin (Islamabad)	88-80-86—254
3	Tahiri Nazir (Rawalpindi)	86-88-84—258

Singapore National Women's Amateur Championship *Raffles CC*

Semi-finals: Amelia Yong beat Koh Sock Hwee 2 and 1
Joey Poh beat Low Si Xuan 4 and 3

Final: Amelia Yong beat Joey Poh 1 hole

3rd Place play-off: Hwee beat Xuan at 19th

Medallist: Koh Sock Hwee 84-76—160

Srixon Australian Women's Amateur Championship (inaugurated 1894)

Victoria GC, Melbourne

Semi-finals: Ashlee Dewhurst (TAS) beat Jessica Speechley (WA) 2 and 1
Minjee Lee (WA) beat Cecilia Cho (NZL) 6 and 5

Final: Ashlee Dewhurst beat Minjee Lee at 38th

2000	Sandy Grimshaw	2003	Katy Jarochowicz	2006	Helen Oh	2009	Justine Lee
2001	Helen Beatty	2004	Marousa Poalis	2007	Sunny Park	2010	S Keating
2002	Nikki Campbell	2005	Sarah Oh	2008	Kristie Smith		

Srixon Australian Women's Amateur Stroke-play Championship

(inaugurated 1992) *Huntingdale GC and Victoria GC*

1	Lydia Ko (NZL)*	70-73-71-72—286
2	Cecilia Cho (NZL)	70-77-69-70—286
*Ko won at second extra hole		
3	Minjee Lee (WA)	77-67-74-75—293

Australian Women's Mid-Amateur Championship *The National GC (Ocean course*

1	Katrina Jones (QLD)	83-85-76—244
2	Sue Wooster (VIC)	86-79-80—245
3	Angela Jane Thorn (WA)	83-84-82—249

Lion Foundation New Zealand Amateur Championship (inaugurated 1893)

Russley GC, Christchurch

Semi-finals: Lydia Ko beat Chihiro Ikeda 7 and 6
Cecilia Cho beat Caryn Khoo 5 and 4

Final: Lydia Ko (North Shore) beat Cecilia Cho (Paakuranga) 4 and 3

2000	Miss C Butler (AUS)	2003	Miss S McKevitt	2006	Miss L Eruera	2010	Celia Cho
2001	Miss W Hawkes		(ENG)	2007	*Not played*		
2002	Miss M Holmes-	2004	Miss S Nicholson	2008	Miss D Kim		
	Smith (AUS)	2005	Miss A Yang	2009	Miss C Cho		

Lion Foundation New Zealand Stroke Play Championship (inaugurated 1911)

Russley GC, Christchurch

1	Lydia Ko	289
2	Cecilia Cho	298
3	Julianne Alvarez	312

Europe

Belgian Women's Amateur Omnium Classic *Limburg GC*

1	Manon de Roey	74-66-74-71—285
2	Leslie Cloots	74-73-74-72—294
3	Alicia Good	75-72-72-81—300

Ladies British Amateur Championship *see page 386*

Ladies' British Open Amateur Stroke Play Championship (inaugurated 1969)

Royal Ashdown Forest

1	Leona Maguire (Slieve Russell)	75-75-69-69—288
2	Laurence Herman (BEL)	73-78-74-69—294
3	Meghan Maclaren (Wellingborough)	73-77-74-72—296

Senior Ladies' British Open Amateur Championship *Belvoir Park* [5635–72]

1	Felicity Christine (Woking)	78-77-75—230
2	Pat Doran (Donabate)	77-79-75—231
3	Vicki Thomas (Carmarthen)	79-77-76—232
	Maria De Orueta (ESP)	78-74-80—232

Danish Women's Championship *Silkeborg GC*

1	Nicole Broch Larsen	74-73-72-71—290
2	Therese Koelbaek	79-71-71-76—297
3	Nanna Koerstz Madsen	77-74-74-75—300

English Women's Close Amateur Championship (inaugurated 1912) *West Sussex*

Leading Qualifier: Georgia Hall (Remedy Oak) 75-66—141

Semi-Finals: Charley Hull (Woburn) beat Charlotte Wild (Mere) 2 and 1
Lucy Williams (Mid-Herts) beat Charlotte Ellis (Minchinhampton) 5 and 3

Final: Lucy Williams beat Charley Hull at 19th

English Women's Open Amateur Stroke Play Championship (inaugurated 1984)

Alwoodley

1	Charley Hull (Woburn)	70-69-73-67—279
2	Charlotte Wild (Mere)	67-71-72-73—283
3	Kelly Tidy (Royal Birkdale)	75-70-73-71—289

English Women's Open Mid-Amateur Championship (inaugurated 1982)

Collingtree Park

Leading Qualifier: Kimberley Bradbury (Cavendish) 74-70—144

Semi-Finals: Claire Smith (Silsden) beat Emma Sheffield (Newark) 3 and 2
Jessica Bradley (Tiverton) beat Ellie Robinson (Middlesbrough) 3 and 2

Final: Claire Smith beat Jessica Bradley 1 hole

Senior Women's English Close Stroke Play Championship *Saltford*

1	Christine Quinn (Hockley)	76-71-75—222
2	Caroline Marron (Bromborough)	78-75-76—229
3	Beverley New (Lansdown)	79-78-75—232

Senior Women's English Close Match Play Championship *York*
Leading Qualifier: Christine Quinn (Hockley) 73-72—145
Semi-Finals: Janet Melville (Sherwood Forest) beat Barbara Laird (Sandiway) at 20th
Sue Dye (Delamere Forest) beat Roz Adams (Addington Court) 2 and 1
Final: Sue Dye beat Janet Melville 4 and 2

Ladies European Open Amateur Championship *see page 389*

European Senior Ladies Championship (inaugurated 2000) *Achensee, Austria*
1	Cecilia Mourgue D'Algue (FRA)	74-73-70—217
2	Virginie Burrus (FRA)	73-71-79—223
3	Catalina Castillejo (ESP)	73-75-76—224

Super Seniors (over 65): Cecilia Mourgue D'Algue (FRA) 217

Finnish Amateur Championship *Tali, Helsinki*
1	Karlijn Zaanen (NED)	71-73-72—216
2	Emma Henriksson (SWE)	73-73-71—217
	Jinijira Rasmussen (DEN)	69-76-72—217

German International Ladies Championship *GC Mettmann*
1	Fanny Cnoops (BEL)	77-78-70-73—298
2	Perrine Delacour (FRA)	80-77-73-70—300
	Charley Hull (ENG)	80-76-72-72—300
	Noora Tamminen (FIN)	69-73-76-82—300

Irish Women's Close Amateur Championship (inaugurated 1894) *Carlow*
Leading Qualifier: Karen Delaney (Carlow) 78-73--151
Semi-Finals: Karen Delaney (Carlow) beat Patrice Delaney (Birr) 3 and 2
Danielle McVeigh (RCDL) beat Eileen Rose Power (Kilkenny) 5 and 4
Final: Danielle McVeigh beat Karen Delaney at 19th

Irish Women's Open Amateur Stroke Play Championship (inaugurated 1993) *Elm Park*
1	Leona Maguire (Slieve Russell)	64-70-72—206
2	Stephanie Meadow (Royal Portrush)	73-71-70—214
3	Lisa Maguire (Slieve Russell)	68-71-77—216

Irish Senior Women's Close Amateur Championship *Adare Manor*
Leading Qualifiers: Sheena McElroy 78-73—151; Helen Jones 77-74—151
Semi-Finals: Sheena McElroy (Grange) beat Pat Doran (Donabate) 2 and 1
Pauline Walsh (Headfort) beat Helen Jones (Strabane) 7 and 5
Final: Sheena McElroy beat Pauline Walsh 7 and 6

Irish Senior Women's' Open Stroke Play Championship *Greenore*
1	Minna Kaamalahti (FIN)	78-83-77—238
2	Pauline Walsh (Headfort)	87-79-73—239
	Alison Bartlett (SCO)	84-77-78—239
	Helen Jones (Strabane)	79-78-82—239

Latvian Ladies Championship *Ozo GC*

I	Linda Dobele	81-78-78—237
2	Migle Rusteikaite (LIT	83-83-80—246
3	Anna Diana Svanka	92-85-80—257

Luxembourg Women's Amateur Championhip *Golf Club Grand-Ducal*

I	Olivia Cowan (GER)	67-74-77—218
2	Maria Palacios (GER)	74-70-75—219
	Nina Holleder (ESP)	69-74-76—219

Portuguese Women's Championship *Aroeira*

I	Leona Maguire (IRL)	66-70-70-68—274
2	Karolin Lampert (GER)	70-74-72-73—289
	Karlijn Zaanen (NED)	68-73-73-75—289

Scottish Ladies' Close Amateur Championship (inaugurated 1903) *Machrihanish*

Leading Qualifier: Martine Pow (Selkirk) 74-70—144

Semi-Finals: Eilidh Briggs (Kilmacolm) beat Megan Briggs (Kilmacolm) 2 and I
Louise Kenney (Pitreavie) beat Jane Turner (Craigielaw) 4 and 3

Final: Louise Kenney beat Eilidh Briggs 5 and 4

Scottish Ladies' Open Stroke Play Championship (Helen Holm Trophy)
(inaugurated 1973) *Troon Portland & Royal Troon*

I	Charlotte Ellis (Minchinhampton) (ENG)	73-69-71—213
2	Leona Maguire (Slieve Russell)) (IRL)	69-72-73—214
3	Holly Clyburn (Woodhall Spa) (ENG)	74-73-70—217

Scottish Senior Ladies' (Close) Amateur Championship *Portpatrick Dunskey*

Semi-Finals: Heather Anderson (Blairgowrie) beat Alex Glennie (Kilmarnock [Barassie]) 5 and 4
Noreen Fenton (Dunbar) beat Janice Paterson (Drumpeller) I hole

Final: Noreen Fenton beat Heather Anderson I hole

Scottish Champion of Champions *Glasgow Gailes*

I	Pamela Pretswell (Bothwell Castle) [British Stroke Play Champion]	75
2	Lesley Atkins (Gullane) [Scottish Girls Champion]	81
3	Alison Davidson (Stirling) [East of Scotland Champion]	82

Scottish Veteran Ladies Championship *Blairgowrie*

Semi-Finals: Linda Urquhart (North) beat Linda Dyball (Midland) 5 and 3
Noreen Fenton (East) beat Val McKean (Borders) 4 and 2

Final: Noreen Fenton beat Linda Urquhart 2 and I

UniCredit Slovakia Women's Amateur Championship *Black Stork, Velka Lomnica*

I	Katerina Prorokova (CZE)	81-71-71—223
2	Lujza Bubanov	81-73-76—230
3	Lucie Hinnerova (CZE)	81-76-75—232
	Katerina Slukova	80-77-75—232

Slovenian Women's International Championship   *Bled GC*

1	Anja Purgauer (AUT)	74-71-69-76—290
2	Ursa Orehek	74-74-73-77—298
3	Katja Pogocar	70-78-75-78—301

78th Spanish Women's Championship   *Oporto*

1	Magda Carrilho (Quinta do Peru)	85-77-74-73—309
2	Marta Vasconcelos (Oporto)	79-78-80-81—318
3	Mariana Martins (Estella)	79-85-78-79—321

Swiss Women's Amateur Championship   *Ascona*

1	Franziska Blum (GER)	69-68-68-65—270
2	Anais Magetti	69-70-69-64—272
3	Ann-Kathrin Lindner (GER)	70-70-69-70—279

Turkish Women's Amateur Championship   *Gloria GC (New course) Antalya. Turkey*

1	Nicole Broch Larsen (DEN)	68-70-71-74—283
2	Anais Magetti (SUI)	76-69-71-69—285
3	Ileen Domela Nieuwenhuis (NED)	73-76-68-71—288

Team event: 1 Netherlands 428; 2 Switzerland 432; 3 Denmark 433; 4 Finland 442; 5 Italy 451; 6 Germany 454; 7 Turkey 461

Winning team: Charlotte Puts, Ileen Domela Nieuwenhuis and Karlijn Zaanen

Ukranian Ladies Amateur Open Championship   *Kiev GC*

1	Jamila Jaxqliyeva	66-69—135
2	Olena Movchan	85-82—167
3	Tamara Antimonova	81-90—171

Welsh Ladies' Close Amateur Championship   (inaugurated 1905)   *Royal St David's*

Leading Qualifier: Becky Harries (Haverfordwest) 74-74—148

Semi-Finals: Becky Harries (Haverfordwest) beat Jo Nicolson (Wrexham) 5 and 4
Amy Boulden (Maesdu) beat Rachel Lewis (Llanishen) 4 and 3

Final: Becky Harries beat Amy Boulden 1 hole

Welsh Ladies' Open Amateur Stroke Play Championship   (inaugurated 1976)   *Tenby*

1	Charley Hull (Woburn) (ENG)	74-72-79—225
2	Lucy Gould (Bargoed)	77-74-75—226
3	Amy Boulden (Maesdu)	76-75-77—228

Welsh Senior Ladies' Championship   *Radyr*

1	Christine Harries (Llanwern)	76-78—154
2	Jane Rees (Hendon)	76-79—155
3	Ann Lewis (Royal St David's)	76-81—157

What is the answer?

Q: If a player runs out of golf balls during a round, may he or she borrow a ball from another player?

A: There is nothing in the Rules of Golf that prohibits a player from borrowing a golf ball from an opponent or fellow-competitor.

USA State Championships 2011

US unless stated

Alabama	Haley Lawrence (SP)	Grayson Valley		Mississippi	Ally McDonald	Dancing Rabbit
	Kathy Hartwiger (MP)	Mobile		Missouri	Catherine Dola	St Louis
Alaska	Rynae Baca	Eagleglen		Montana	Maggie Crippen	Bill Roberts
Arizona	Saki Iida (SP)	San Tan Valley		Nebraska	Kayla Knopik (SP)	Beatrice
	Kylie Duede (MP)	Papago			Mary Narzisi (MP)	Omaha
Arkansas	Taylor Fisher (SP)	Hot Springs		Nevada	Laurie Johnson	Las Vegas
	Taylor Fisher (MP)	Chenal		New		
California	Stephanie Arcala	Temecula Creek Inn		Hampshire	Tara Watt	Stratham
				New Jersey	Scotland Preston	Hackensack
Carolinas	Courtney Gunter (SP)	Cornelius		New York	Victoria DeGroodt	Rome (NY)
	Dawn Woodward (MP)	Stanley		N. Carolina	Katherine Perry	River Landing
Colorado	Brooke Collins (SP)	Cherry Creek		Ohio	Erin Misheff	Concord
	Somin Lee (MP)	Common Ground		Oklahoma	Ellen Mueller (SP)	Gaillardia
Connecticut	Nicole Yatsanik	Weathersfield			Whitney McAteer (MP)	Muskogee
Delaware	Christina Vosters	Shawnee		Oregon	Jillian Ferrante Carlile	Waverley
Florida	Mitsuki Katahira (JPN) (SP)	Oceanside		Pennsylvania	Kelli Pry	York
	Page Halpin (MP)	The Oaks Club, Osprey		Rhode Island	Samantha Morrell	Pawrtucket
				S. Dakota	Kimberley Kaufman (SP)	Sioux Falls
Georgia	Sara Butts (SP)	Eatonton			Shannon Johnson (MP)	Pierre
	Margaret Shirley (MP)	Carrolton		Tennessee	Kendall Martindale	Blackthorn Club (The Ridges)
Hawaii	Nicole Sakamoto (SP)	Mid-Pacific		Texas	Maggie Noel	Walden on Lake Congro
	Nicole Sakamoto (MP)	Oahu		Utah	Julie McMullin	Valley View
Idaho	Trish Gibbens (SP)	Shadow Valley		Vermont	Kimberley Wong	Montpelier
	Kareen Markle (MP)	Hailey		Virginia	Lauren Greenlief (SP)	Willow Oaks
Illinois	Nora Lucas	Kishwaukee			Amanda Steinhagen (MP)	Belle Haven
Indiana	Kristi O'Brien (SP)	Indianapolis		Washington	Erynne Lee	The Home Course, Dupont
	Kristini Cain (MP)	Prairie View		West Virginia	Samantha DiDomenico	Parkersburg
Iowa	Kristin Paulson	Sunnyside		Wisconsin	Jessie Gerry (SP)	Whispering Springs GC
Kansas	Gianna Misenhellter	McPherson			Jaclyn Shepherd (MP)	Racine
Kentucky	April Emerson	Miller Memorial		Wyoming	Emily Podlesny	Casper
Maine	Emily Bouchard	Penobscot Valley				
Maryland	Kaitlyn Rohrback	Lake Presidential				
Massachusetts	Katie Nelson	Weston				
Michigan	Christine Meier	Prestwick Village				
Minnesota	Celia Kuenster (SP)	Hastings				
	Cassie Deg (MP)	Jewel				

Australian State Championships 2011

Australian unless stated

New South Wales: Cumberland, Liverpool and
NSW GCs
Final: Grace Lennon (Kingston Heath) beat Jessica
Speechley (Lake Karrinyup) at 38th
Queensland: Pacific Harbour and Arundel
Hills GCs
Final: Saki Suzuki (Lakelands) beat Ali Orchard
(Surfer's Paradise)   2 and 1
Medallist: Saki Suzuki
South Australia: Mount Osmond, Blackwood and
Glenelg GCs
Final Sarah King (Royal Adelaide) beat Jenny Lee
(Glenelg) 8 and 6

Tasmania: CC Tasmania
Final: Tammy Hall (Launceston) beat Sarah
Johnstone (Ulverstone) 4 and 3
Victoria:
Final: Charlotte Thomas (SIN) beat Whitney Hillier
4 and 3
Western Australia: Waneroo GC
Final: MinJee Lee (Royal Fremantle) beat Grace
Lennon (Metropolitan Melbourne) 4 and 2.
Medallist : MinJee Lee 71-73—144 (won by 10
shots)

New Zealand Provincial Championships 2011

New Zealand unless stated

South Island Stroke Play – Timaru: Jesse Hamilton
279

North Island Stroke Play– Whitford Park: Lydia Ko
278

Record win for Port in US Mid-Amateur Championship

Ellen Port, from St Louis, Missouri, celebrated her 50th birthday during the US Mid-Amateur Championship by winning the Mildred Prunaret Trophy for a record fourth time.

Mrs Port, married with two children, was never down at the Bayville Club in Virginia Beach when beating 2009 champion Martha Leach from Hebron, Kentucky 2 and 1 in a final which was delayed for a time by a mid-round thunderstorm. In fact, Mrs Port was down only once during the week.

A winner formerly in 1995, 1996 and 2000, Mrs Port earned a 10-year exemption into the Mid-Amateur Championship and a two-year exemption into the US Women's Amateur, the US Women's Senior Amateur and, if eligible, the US Women's Public Links Championship.

The high school golf coach and physical education teacher who said her win was the culmination of a great deal of hard work, broke another record with her win 11 years after her third success. Carole Semple had previously held the record for the number of years elapsed between wins – seven.

Who is known as "Walrus"?

The answer can be found on page 905

National Orders of Merit 2011

EWGA Order of Merit

1	Charley Hull (Woburn)	1,642	6	Charlotte Wild (Mere)		667
2	Holly Clyburn (Woodhall Spa)	1,259	7	Megan MacLaren (Wellingborough)		567
3	Lauren Taylor (Woburn)	1,173	8	Lucy Williams (Mid-Herts)		513
4	Charlotte Ellis (Minchinhampton)	1,055	9	Rachel Goodall (Heswall)		510
5	Kelly Tidy (Royal Birkdale)	912	10	Ellie Robinson (Middlesbrough)		480

ILGU Order of Merit

1	Leona Maguire (Slieve Russell)	1573	6	Gillian O'Leary (Cork)		664
2	Lisa Maguire (Slieve Russell)	1306	7	Emma O'Driscoll (Ballybunion)		528
3	Danielle McVeigh (RCDL)	913	8	Karen Delaney (Carlow)		493
4	Stephanie Meadow (Royal Portrush)	904	9	Louise Coffey (Malone)		455
5	Charlener Reid (Royal Portrush)	759	10	Deirdre Smith (Co. Louth)		439

SLGA Order of Merit

1	Louise Kenney (Pitreavie)	2,375	6	Jane Turner (Craigielaw)		1,290
2	Pamela Pretswell (Bothwell Castle)	1,800	7	Sally Watson (Elie and Earlsferry)		1,073
3	Eilidh Briggs (Kilmacolm)	1,647	8	Kelsey MacDonald (Nairn Dunbar)		1,053
4	Alyson McKechin (Elderslie)	1,476	9	Rachael Watton (Mortonhall)		1,050
5	Megan Briggs (Kilmacolm)	1,459	10	Rachael Taylor (Hartl Golf Resort)		895

WGU Order of Merit

1	Amy Boulden (Maesdu)	799	7	Chloe Williams (Wrexham)		116
2	Becky Harries (Haverfordwest)	523	8	Gemma Bradbury (Cottrell Park)		78
3	Katherine O'Connor (Tadmarton Heath)	446	9	Jo Nicholson (Wrexham)		70
4	Lucy Gould (Bargoed)	291	10	Kirsty O'Connor (Nelson)		50
5	Sam Birks (Wolstanton)	161		Sara Rees Evans (Penrhos)		50
6	Rachel Lewis (Llanishen)	150		Anna Carling (Vale of Glamorgan)		50

Australian Order of Merit
(events played in brackets)

1	Jessica Speechley (WA)	(12)	103.78	6	Lydia Ko (NZL)	(5)	89.22
2	Ashlee Dewhurst (TAS)	(9)	96.36	7	Minjee Lee (WA)	(8)	83.60
3	Ashley Ona (QLD)	(12)	95.91	8	Grace Lennon (VIC)	(16)	77.06
4	Breanna Elliott (VIC)	(13)	95.06	9	Ebony Heard (SA)	(8)	74.44
5	Courtney Massey (QLD)	(13)	91.94	10	Allyce Watkinson	(10)	72.87

Month by month in 2011

Luke Donald grabs the PGA Tour money list title from Webb Simpson with a brilliant closing 64 in the final counting event. Tom Lewis wins the Portugal Masters, only his third event as a professional, Sergio García wins twice in a row in Spain and there is a Northern Irish 1-2-3 at the Dunhill Links with Michael Hoey, Rory McIlroy and Graeme McDowell.

Canadian Order of Merit
(events played in brackets)

1	Rebecca Lee-Bentham (ON)	(6)	1382	6	Jessica Wallace (BC)	(4)	618
2	Jennifer Kirby (ON)	(4)	1085	7	Taylor Kim (BC)	(2)	607
3	Augusta James (ON)	(4)	953	8	Jisoo Keel (BC)	(2)	591
4	Nicole Zhang (AB)	(3)	658	9	Brittany Henderson (ON)	(4)	570
5	Nicole Vandermade (ON)	(3)	630	10	Christine Wong (BC)	(3)	561

French Order of Merit

1	Celine Boutier	2491.63	6	Manon Gidali	1526.30
2	Perrine Delacour	2480.00	7	Isabelle Boineau	1045.17
3	Alexandra Bonetti	2363.04	8	Fiona Puyo	991.33
4	Emilia Alonso	1697.50	9	Laura Castelain	975.58
5	Shannon Aubert	1688.33	10	Justine Dreher	836.08

South African Order of Merit
(events played in brackets)

1	Kim Williams (GN)	(16)	186.0	6	Alana van Greuning (MP)	(16)	72.0
2	Bertine Strauss (NW)	(10)	104.5	7	Nobuhle Diamini (GN)	(7)	59.5
3	Henriette Frylinck (GN)	(14)	100.5	8	Monique Smit (SC)	(7)	54.0
4	Iliska Verwey (SC)	(9)	90.5	9	Tiffany Avern-Taplin (KN)	(8)	44.5
5	Nicole Becker (NW)	(16)	75.0	10	Nicole Garcia (CG)	(13)	43.0

Austrian Order of Merit
(events played in brackets)

1	Sarah Schober	(3)	85.00	6	Nina Muehl	(5)	66,40
2	Marlene Krejcy	(6)	83.21	7	Nadine Dreher	(6)	58.04
3	Martina Hochwimmer	(4)	78.00	8	Marina Supporting	(4)	50.48
4	Christine Wolf	(7)	67.93	9	Fanny Wolte	(9)	46.88
5	Anja Purgau	(5)	67.60	10	Felicitas Witt Dorring	(3)	39.90

German Order of Merit

1	Sophia Popov	2313	6	Vicki Troeltsch	1606
2	Leigh Whittaker	1985	7	Karolin Lampert	1596
3	Antonia Scherer	1984	8	Thea Hoffmeister	1572
4	Stephanie Kirchmayr	1983	9	Quirine-Louise Eijkenboom	1552
5	Lara Katzy	1721	10	Pia Halbig	1519

Brazilian Order of Merit
(after 4th Abierto de Golfe da Bahia)

1	Lucia Maria Guilger	88.70	6	Andrea Ferraz Arruda	41.00
2	Ruriko Nakamura	87.60	7	Clara Teixeira	40.25
3	Larissa Pomba	75.45	8	Mariana de Biase	33.75
4	Carla Ziliotto	64.50	9	Adriana Gianello Oliviera	33.10
5	Maria Elisa Filizola	41.05	10	Vivian Golombek	32.55

Argentinian Order of Merit

1	Manuela Carbajo Re	107.5	6	Victoria Tanco	34.67
2	Delfina Acosta	41.25	7	Maria Laura Raffo	34.50
3	Maria Olivera	40.67	8	Sofia Giocoechea	25.33
4	Valeria Otoya	36.88	9	Belen Giocoechea	20.00
5	Fabiana Yu	36.50	10	Angie Varona	18.17

Team Events

For past winners not listed here see earlier editions of *The R&A Golfer's Handbook*

International

Curtis Cup (Instituted 1932)
USA v Great Britain & Ireland

2010 *Essex CC, Manchester-by-the-Sea, MA*
June 11–13
Result: USA 12½, GB&I 7½
*Captains: Noreen Mohler (USA),
  Mary McKenna (GB&I)*
First Day – Foursomes:
Jennifer Song & Jennifer Johnson halved with Sally Watson
  & Rachel Jennings
Alexis Thompson & Jessica Korda halved with Hannah Barwood & Holly Clyburn
Cydnet Clanton & Stephanie Kono halved with Danielle McVeigh & Leona Maguire
First Day – Fourball:
Song & Kimberly Kim lost to McVeigh & Pamela Pretswell
  4 and 3
Thompson & Johnson beat Jennings & Leona Maguire
  3 and 2
Korda & Tiffany Lua lost to Watson & Lisa Maguire
  1 hole
Second Day – Fourball:
Thompson & Korda beat McVeigh & Pretswell
  2 and 1
Song & Clanton beat Maguire & Maguire 3 and 2
Kono & Kim beat Watson & Jennings 2 holes
Second Day – Foursomes:
Thompson & Korda beat McVeigh & Leona Maguire
  3 and 1
Song & Kono beat Barwood & Clyburn 3 and 1
Lua & Johnson beat Watson & Jennings 3 and 2
Third Day – Singles:
Jennifer Song lost to Danielle McVeigh (IRL) 3 and 2
Alexis Thompson beat Sally Watson (SCO) 6 and 5
Jennifer Johnson beat Rachel Jennings (ENG) 5 and 4
Kimberly Kim lost to Lisa Maguire (IRL) 1 hole
Cydney Clanton beat Hannah Barwood (ENG) 4 and 3
Tiffany Lua lost to Leona Maguire (IRL) 2 and 1
Jessica Korda beat Pamela Pretswell (SCO) 4 and 3
Stephanie Kono lost to Holly Clyburn (ENG) 2 and 1

2008 *Old Course, St Andrews* May 30–June 1
Result: GB&I 7, USA 13
*Captains: Mary McKenna (GB&I),
  Carol Semple Thompson (USA)*
First Day – Foursomes
E Bennett & J Ewart lost to S Lewis & A Walshe
  3 and 1
S Watson &M Thomson beat M Harigae & J Lee 1 hole
B Loucks & F Parker lost to A Blumenherst & T Joh
  1 hole

First Day – Fourballs
C Booth & M Thomson lost to K Kim & M Harigae
  3 and 2
S Watson & K Caithness beat T Joh & M Bolger 3 and 2
F Parker & E Bennett lost to A Blumenherst & S Lewis
  3 and 1
Second Day – Foursomes
C Booth & B Loucks beat K Kim & J Lee 3 and 2
S Watson & M Thomson lost to A Walshe & S Lewis
  5 and 4
E Bennett & J Ewart halved with A Blumenherst & T Joh
Second Day – Fourballs
C Booth & B Loucks lost to K Kim & M Harigae
  2 and 1
S Watson & K Caithness beat A Blumenherst & M Bolger
  3 and 2
E Bennett & F Parker lost to A Walshe & S Lewis 1 hole
Third Day – Singles
Breanne Loucks (WAL) lost to Kimberly Kim 3 and 1
Jodi Ewart (ENG) lost to Amanda Blumenherst 2 and 1
Elizabeth Bennett (ENG) lost to Stacy Lewis 3 and 2
Carly Booth (SCO) lost to Tiffany Joh 6 and 5
Michele Thomson (SCO) halved with Jennie Lee
Florentyna Parker (ENG) beat Meghan Bolger 6 and 4
Krystle Caithness (SCO) beat Mina Harigae 2 and 1
Sally Watson (SCO) lost to Alison Walshe 1 hole

2006 *Bandon Dunes, OR* July 29–30
Result: USA 11½, GB&I 6½
*Captains: Carol Semple Thompson (USA),
  Ada O'Sullivan (Monkstown) (GB&I)*
First Day: Foursomes
P Mackenzie & A Blumenherst beat T Mangan &
  K Matharu 5 and 4
D Grimes & A McCurdy beat M Gillen & N Edwards
  2 holes
J Park & T Leon beat C Coughlan & M Reid 1 hole
Singles
Jenny Suh lost to Kiran Matharu (Cookridge Park)
  2 and 1
Jennie Lee beat Martina Gillen (Beaverstown) 4 and 3
Amanda Blumenherst lost to Breanne Loucks (Wrexham)
  5 and 4
Paige Mackenzie beat Melissa Reid (Chevin) 5 and 4
Jane Park beat Tara Delaney (Carlow) 3 and 2
Taylor Leon beat Claire Coughlan (Cork) 5 and 4
Second Day: Foursomes
J Park & T Leon halved with T Mangan & T Delaney
J Lee & J Suh lost to M Reid & B Loucks 7 and 5
P Mackenzie & A Blumenherst lost to M Gillen &
  N Edwards 1 hole

2006 continued

Singles
Virginia Grimes lost to M Gillen 3 and 2
Amanda McCurdy lost to B Loucks 3 and 2
P Mackenzie beat Tricia Mangan (Ennis) 1 hole
T Leon beat Naomi Edwards (Ganton) 5 and 4
J Lee beat M Reid 3 and 2
J Park beat T Delaney 3 and 2

2004 Formby June 12–13
Result: GB&I 8, USA 10

Captains: Ada O'Sullivan (Monkstown) (GB&I),
Martha Kironac (USA)

First Day: Foursomes
S McKevitt & E Duggleby beat P Creamer & J Park
  3 and 2
N Timmins & D Masters beat S Huarte & A Thurman
  1 hole
A Laing & C Coughlan beat B Lang & M Wie 1 hole

Singles
Emma Duggleby beat Elizabeth Janangelo 3 and 2
Danielle Masters lost to Erica Blasberg 1 hole
Fame More lost to Paula Creamer 5 and 3
Anna Highgate lost to Michelle Wie 5 and 4
Shelley McKevitt lost to Jane Park 4 and 3
Anne Laing lost to Anne Thurman 4 and 3

Second Day: Foursomes
E Duggleby & S McKevitt beat E Blasberg & Sarah Huarte
  2 and 1
A Laing & C Coughlan beat E Janangelo & M Wie 3 and 2
N Timmins & D Masters lost to B Lang & A Thurman
  5 and 4

Singles
E Duggleby lost to P Creamer 3 and 2
A Laing beat J Park 3 and 1
S McKevitt lost to E Janangelo 1 hole
Nicola Timmins lost to M Wie 6 and 5
Claire Coughlan beat Brittany Lang 2 holes
D Masters lost to A Thurman 1 hole

2002 Fox Chapel, PA Aug 3–4
Result: USA 11, GB&I 7

Captains: Mary Budke (USA), Pam Benka (GB&I)
First Day: Foursomes
Duncan & Jerman beat Duggleby & Hudson 4 and 3
Fankhauser & Semple Thompson beat Laing & Stirling
  1 hole
Myerscough & Swaim beat Coffey & Smith 3 and 2

Singles
Emily Bastel lost to Rebecca Hudson 2 holes
Leigh Anne Hardin beat Emma Duggleby 2 and 1
Meredith Duncan beat Fame More 5 and 4
Angela Jerman beat Sarah Jones 6 and 5
Courtney Swaim beat Heather Stirling 4 and 2
Mollie Fankhauser lost to Vikki Laing 1 hole

Second Day: Foursomes
Hardin & Bastel lost to Laing & Stirling 3 and 1
Myerscough & Swaim beat Hudson & Smith 4 and 2
Duncan & Jerman lost to Coffey & Dugglesby 4 and 2

Singles
Mollie Fankhauser beat Rebecca Hudson 3 and 1
Carol Semple Thompson Beat Vikki Laing 1 hole
Leigh Anne Hardin lost to Emma Duggleby 4 and 3
Laura Myerscough beat Heather Stirling 2 holes
Meredith Duncan beat Akison Coffey 3 and 1
Courtney Swaim lost to Sarah Jones 5 and 3

2000 Ganton June 24–25
Result: USA 10, GB&I 8

Captains: Claire Hourihane Dowling (GB&I),
Jane Bastanchury Booth (USA)

First Day: Foursomes
Andrew & Morgan lost to Bauer & Carol Semple
  Thompson 1 hole
Brewerton & Hudson lost to Keever & Stanford 1 hole
Duggleby & O'Brien halved with Derby Grimes &
  Homeyer

Singles
Kim Rostron Andrew lost to Beth Bauer 3 and 2
Fiona Brown lost to Robin Weiss 1 hole
Rebecca Hudson lost to Stephanie Keever 4 and 2
Lesley Nicholson halved with Angela Stanford
Suzanne O'Brien beat Leland Beckel 3 and 1
Emma Duggleby lost to Hilary Homeyer 1 hole

Second Day: Foursomes
Brewerton & Hudson beat Bauer & Thompson 2 and 1
Duggleby & O'Brien beat Keever & Stanford 7 and 6
Andrew & Morgan lost to Derby Grimes & Homeyer
  3 and 1

Singles
Hudson lost to Bauer 1 hole
O'Brien beat Weiss 3 and 2
Duggleby beat Keever 4 and 2
Becky Brewerton lost to Homeyer 3 and 2
Becky Morgan beat Stanford 5 and 4
Andrew beat Virginia Derby Grimes 6 and 5

1998 Minikahda, Minneapolis, MN Aug 1–2
Result: USA 10, GB&I 8

Captains: Barbara McIntire (USA),
Ita Burke Butler (GB&I)

First Day: Foursomes
Bauer & Chuasiriporn lost to Ratcliffe & Rostron 1 hole
Booth & Corrie Kuehn beat Brown & Stupples 2 and 1
Burke & Derby Grimes beat Morgan & Rose 3 and 2

Singles
Kellee Booth beat Kim Rostron 2 and 1
Brenda Corrie Kuehn beat Alison Rose 3 and 2
Jenny Chuasiriporn halved with Rebecca Hudson
Beth Bauer beat Hilary Monaghan 5 and 3
Jo Jo Robertson lost to Becky Morgan 2 and 1
Carol Semple Thompson lost to Elaine Ratcliffe 3 and 2

Second Day: Foursomes
Booth & Corrie Kuehn beat Morgan & Rose 6 and 5
Bauer & Chuasiriporn lost to Brown & Hudson 2 holes
Burke & Derby Grimes beat Ratcliffe & Rostron 2 and 1

Singles
Booth beat Rostron 2 and 1
Corrie Kuehn beat Morgan 2 and 1
Thompson lost to Karen Stupples 1 hole
Robin Burke lost to Hudson 2 and 1
Robertson lost to Fiona Brown 1 hole
Virginia Derby Grimes halved with Ratcliffe

1996 Killarney June 21–22
Result: GB&I 11½, USA 6½

Captains: Ita Burke Butler (GB&I),
Martha Lang (USA)
First Day: Foursomes
Lisa Walton Educate & Wade lost to K Kuehne & Port
  2 and 1
Lisa Dermott & Rose beat B Corrie Kuehn & Jemsek
  3 and 1
McKay & Moodie halved with Kerr & Thompson

Singles
Julie Wade lost to Sarah LeBrun Ingram 4 and 2
Karen Stupples beat Kellee Booth 3 and 2
Alison Rose beat Brenda Corrie Kuehn 5 and 4
Elaine Ratcliffe halved with Marla Jemsek
Mhairi McKay beat Cristie Kerr I hole
Janice Moodie beat Carol Semple Thompson 3 and I

Second Day: Foursomes
McKay & Moodie beat Booth & Ingram 3 and 2
Dermott & Rose beat B Corrie Kuehn & Jemsek
  2 and I
Educate & Wade lost to K Kuehne & Port I hole

Singles
Wade lost to Kerr I hole
Ratcliffe beat Ingram 3 and I
Stupples lost to Booth 3 and 2
Rose beat Ellen Port 6 and 5
McKay halved with Thompson
Moodie beat Kelli Kuehne 2 and I

1994 *Chattanooga, TN* July 30–31
Result: GB&I 9, USA 9
Captains: Lancy Smith (USA),
  Elizabeth Boatman (GB&I)

First Day: Foursomes
Sarah LeBrun Ingram & McGill halved with Matthew
  & Moodie
Klein & Thompson beat McKay & Kirsty Speak
  7 and 5
Kaupp & Port lost to Wade & Walton 6 and 5

Singles
Jill McGill halved with Julie Wade
Emilee Klein beat Janice Moodie 3 and 2
Wendy Ward lost to Lisa Walton I hole
Carol Semple Thompson beat Myra McKinlay 2 and I
Ellen Port beat Mhairi McKay 2 and I
Stephanie Sparks lost to Catriona Lambert Matthew
  I hole

Second Day: Foursomes
Ingram & McGill lost to Wade & Walton 2 and I
Klein & Thompson beat McKinlay & Eileen Rose
  Power 4 and 2
Sparks & Ward lost to Matthew & Moodie 3 and 2

Singles
McGill beat Wade 4 and 3
Klein lost to Matthew 2 and I
Port beat McKay 7 and 5
Wendy Kaupp lost to McKinlay 3 and 2
Ward beat Walton 4 and 3
Thompson lost to Moodie 2 holes

1992 *Hoylake* June 5–6
Result: GB&I 10, USA 8
Captains: Elizabeth Boatman (GB&I),
  Judy Oliver (USA)

First Day: Foursomes
Hall & Wade halved with Fruhwirth & Goetze
Lambert & Thomas beat Ingram & Shannon 2 and I
Hourihane & Morley beat Hanson & Thompson
  2 and I

Singles
Joanne Morley halved with Amy Fruhwirth
Julie Wade lost to Vicki Goetze 3 and 2
Elaine Farquharson beat Robin Weiss 2 and I
Nicola Buxton lost to Martha Lang 2 holes
Catriona Lambert beat Carol Semple Thompson
  3 and 2
Caroline Hall beat Leslie Shannon 6 and 5

Second Day: Foursomes
Hall & Wade halved with Fruhwirth & Goetze
Hourihane & Morley halved with Lang & Weiss
Lambert & Thomas lost to Hanson & Thompson 3 and 2

Singles
Morley beat Fruhwirth 2 and I
Lambert beat Tracy Hanson 6 and 5
Farquharson lost to Sarah LeBrun Ingram 2 and I
Vicki Thomas lost to Shannon 2 and I
Claire Hourihane lost to Lang 2 and I
Hall beat Goetze I hole

1990 *Somerset Hills, NJ* July 28–29
Result: USA 14, GB&I 4
Captains: Leslie Shannon (USA), Jill Thornhill (GB&I)

First Day: Foursomes
Goetze & Anne Quast Sander beat Dobson & Lambert
  4 and 3
Noble & Margaret Platt lost to Wade & Imrie 2 and I
Thompson & Weiss beat Farquharson & Helen
  Wadsworth 3 and I

Singles
Vicki Goetze lost to Julie Wade 2 and I
Katie Peterson beat Kathryn Imrie 3 and 2
Brandie Burton beat Linzi Fletcher 3 and I
Robin Weiss beat Elaine Farquharson 4 and 3
Karen Noble beat Catriona Lambert I hole
Carol Semple Thompson lost to Vicki Thomas I hole

Second Day: Foursomes
Goetze & Sander beat Wade & Imrie 3 and I
Noble & Platt lost to Dobson & Lambert I hole
Burton & Peterson beat Farquharson & Wadsworth
  5 and 4

Singles
Goetze beat Helen Dobson 4 and 3
Burton beat Lambert 4 and 3
Peterson beat Imrie I hole
Noble beat Wade 2 holes
Weiss beat Farquharson 2 and I
Thompson beat Thomas 3 and I

1988 *Royal St George's* June 10–11
Result: GB&I 11, USA 7
Captains: Diane Robb Bailey (GB&I), Judy Bell (USA)

First Day: Foursomes
Bayman & Wade beat Kerdyk & Scrivner 2 and I
Davies & Shapcott beat Scholefield & Thompson 5 and 4
Thomas & Thornhill halved with Keggi & Shannon

Singles
Linda Bayman halved with Tracy Kerdyk
Julie Wade beat Cindy Scholefield 2 holes
Susan Shapcott lost to Carol Semple Thompson I hole
Karen Davies lost to Pearl Sinn 4 and 3
Shirley Lawson beat Pat Cornett-Iker I hole
Jill Thornhill beat Leslie Shannon 3 and 2

Second Day: Foursomes
Bayman & Wade lost to Kerdyk & Scrivner I hole
Davies & Shapcott beat Keggi & Shannon 2 holes
Thomas & Thornhill beat Scholefield & Thompson
  6 and 5

Singles
Wade lost to Kerdyk 2 and I
Shapcott beat Caroline Keggi 3 and 2
Lawson lost to Kathleen McCarthy Scrivner 4 and 3
Vicki Thomas beat Cornett-Iker 5 and 3
Bayman beat Sinn I hole
Thornhill lost to Thompson 3 and 2

1986 *Prairie Dunes, KS* Aug 1–2
Result: GB&I 13, USA 5
Captains: Judy Bell (USA),
*   Diane Robb Bailey (GB&I)*
First Day: Foursomes
Kessler & Schreyer lost to Behan & Thornhill   7 and 6
Ammaccapane & Mochrie lost to Davies & Johnson
  2 and 1
Gardner & Scrivner lost to McKenna & Robertson 1 hole
Singles
Leslie Shannon lost to Patricia (Trish) Johnson 1 hole
Kim Williams lost to Jill Thornhill 4 and 3
Danielle Ammaccapane lost to Lillian Behan 4 and 3
Kandi Kessler beat Vicki Thomas 3 and 2
Dottie Pepper Mochrie halved with Karen Davies
Cindy Schreyer beat Claire Hourihane 2 and 1
Second Day: Foursomes
Ammaccapane & Mochrie lost to Davies & Johnson
  1 hole
Shannon & Williams lost to Behan & Thornhill 5 and 3
Gardner & Scrivner halved with McKenna & Belle
  McCorkindale Robertson
Singles
Shannon halved with Thornhill
Kathleen McCarthy Scrivner lost to Trish Johnson
  5 and 3
Kim Gardner beat Behan 1 hole
Williams lost to Thomas 4 and 3
Kessler halved with Davies
Schreyer lost to Hourihane 5 and 4

1984 *Muirfield* June 8–9
Result: USA 9½, GB&I 8½
Captains: Diane Robb Bailey (GB&I),
*   Phyllis Preuss (USA)*
First Day: Foursomes
New & Waite beat Pacillo & Sander 2 holes
Grice & Thornhill halved with Rosenthal & Smith
Davies & McKenna lost to Farr & Widman 1 hole
Singles
Jill Thornhill halved with Joanne Pacillo
Claire Waite lost to Penny Hammel 4 and 2
Claire Hourihane lost to Jody Rosenthal 3 and 1
Vicki Thomas beat Dana Howe 2 and 1
Penny Grice beat Anne Quast Sander 2 holes
Beverley New lost to Mary Anne Widman 4 and 3
Second Day: Foursomes
New & Waite lost to Rosenthal & Smith 3 and 1
Grice & Thornhill beat Farr & Widman 2 and 1
Hourihane & Thomas halved with Hammel & Howe
Singles
Thornhill lost to Pacillo 3 and 2
Laura Davies beat Sander 1 hole
Waite beat Lancy Smith 5 and 4
Grice lost to Howe 2 holes
New lost to Heather Farr 6 and 5
Hourihane beat Hammel 2 and 1

1982 *Denver, CO* Aug 5–6
Result: USA 14½, GB&I 3½
Captains: Betty Probasco (USA),
*   Maire O'Donnell (GB&I)*
First Day: Foursomes
Inkster & Semple beat McKenna & Robertson 5 and 4
Baker & Smith halved with Douglas & Soulsby
Benz & Hanlon beat Connachan & Stewart 2 and 1

Singles
Amy Benz beat Mary McKenna 2 and 1
Cathy Hanlon beat Jane Connachan 5 and 4
Mari McDougall beat Wilma Aitken 2 holes
Kathy Baker beat Belle McCorkindale Robertson 7 and 6
Judy Oliver lost to Janet Soulsby 2 holes
Juli Inkster beat Kitrina Douglas 7 and 6
Second Day: Foursomes
Inkster & Semple beat Aitken & Connachan 3 and 2
Baker & Smith beat Douglas & Soulsby 1 hole
Benz & Hanlon lost to McKenna & Robertson 1 hole
Singles
Inkster beat Douglas 7 and 6
Baker beat Gillian Stewart 4 and 3
Oliver beat Vicki Thomas 5 and 4
McDougall beat Soulsby 2 and 1
Carol Semple beat McKenna 1 hole
Lancy Smith lost to Robertson 5 and 4

1980 *St Pierre, Chepstow* June 6–7
Result: USA 13, GB&I 5
Captains: Carol Comboy (GB&I),
*   Nancy Roth Syms (USA)*
First Day: Foursomes
McKenna & Nesbitt halved with Terri Moody & Smith
Stewart & Thomas lost to Castillo & Sheehan 5 and 3
Caldwell & Madill halved with Oliver & Semple
Singles
Mary McKenna lost to Patty Sheehan 3 and 2
Claire Nesbitt halved with Lancy Smith
Jane Connachan lost to Brenda Goldsmith 2 holes
Maureen Madill lost to Carol Semple 4 and 3
Linda Moore halved with Mary Hafeman
Carole Caldwell lost to Judy Oliver 1 hole
Second Day: Foursomes
Caldwell & Madill lost to Castillo & Sheehan 3 and 2
McKenna & Nesbitt lost to Moody & Smith 6 and 5
Moore & Thomas lost to Oliver & Semple 1 hole
Singles
Madill lost to Sheehan 5 and 4
McKenna beat Lori Castillo 5 and 4
Connachan lost to Hafeman 6 and 5
Gillian Stewart beat Smith 5 and 4
Moore beat Goldsmith 1 hole
Tegwen Perkins Thomas lost to Semple 4 and 3

1978 *Apawamis, NY* Aug 4–5
Result: USA 12, GB&I 6
Captains: Helen Wilson (USA), Carol Comboy (GB&I)
First Day: Foursomes
Daniel & Brenda Goldsmith lost to Greenhalgh &
  Marvin 3 and 2
Cindy Hill & Smith lost to Everard & Thomson
  2 and 1
Cornett & Carolyn Hill halved with McKenna &
  Perkins
Singles
Beth Daniel beat Vanessa Marvin 5 and 4
Noreen Uihlein lost to Mary Everard 7 and 6
Lancy Smith beat Angela Uzielli 4 and 3
Cindy Hill beat Julia Greenhalgh 2 and 1
Carolyn Hill halved with Carole Caldwell
Judy Oliver beat Tegwen Perkins 2 and 1
Second Day: Foursomes
Cindy Hill & Smith beat Everard & Thomson 1 hole
Daniel & Goldsmith beat McKenna & Perkins 1 hole
Oliver & Uihlein beat Greenhalgh & Marvin 4 and 3

Singles

Daniel beat Mary McKenna 2 and 1
Patricia Cornett beat Caldwell 3 and 2
Cindy Hill lost to Muriel Thomson 2 and 1
Lancy Smith beat Perkins 2 holes
Oliver halved with Greenhalgh
Uihlein halved with Everard

1976 Royal Lytham & St Annes June 11–12

Result: USA 11½, GB&I 6½
Captains: Belle McCorkindale Robertson (GB&I),
  Barbara McIntyre (USA)

First Day: Foursomes
Greenhalgh & McKenna lost to Daniel & Hill
  3 and 2
Cadden & Henson lost to Horton & Massey
  6 and 5
Irvin & Perkins beat Semple & Syms 3 and 2

Singles

Ann Irvin lost to Beth Daniel 4 and 3
Dinah Oxley Henson beat Cindy Hill 1 hole
Suzanne Cadden lost to Nancy Lopez 3 and 1
Mary McKenna lost to Nancy Roth Syms 1 hole
Tegwen Perkins lost to Debbie Massey 1 hole
Julia Greenhalgh halved with Barbara Barrow

Second Day: Foursomes
Cadden & Irvin lost to Daniel & Hill 4 and 3
Henson & Perkins beat Semple & Syms 2 and 1
McKenna & Anne Stant lost to Barrow & Lopez
  4 and 3

Singles

Henson lost to Daniel 3 and 2
Greenhalgh beat Syms 2 and 1
Cadden lost to Donna Horton 6 and 5
Jennie Lee-Smith lost to Massey 3 and 2
Perkins beat Hill 1 hole
McKenna beat Carol Semple 1 hole

1974 San Francisco, CA Aug 2–3

Result: USA 13, GB&I 5
Captains: Sis Choate (USA),
  Belle McCorkindale Robertson (GB&I)

First Day: Foursomes
Hill & Semple halved with Greenhalgh & McKenna
Booth & Sander beat Lee-Smith & LeFeuvre 6 and 5
Budke & Lauer lost to Everard & Walker 5 and 4

Singles

Carol Semple lost to Mickey Walker 2 and 1
Jane Bastanchury Booth beat Mary McKenna
  5 and 3
Debbie Massey beat Mary Everard 1 hole
Bonnie Lauer beat Jennie Lee-Smith 6 and 5
Beth Barry beat Julia Greenhalgh 1 hole
Cindy Hill halved with Tegwen Perkins

Second Day: Foursomes
Booth & Sander beat McKenna & Walker 5 and 4
Budke & Lauer beat Everard & LeFeuvre 5 and 3
Hill & Semple lost to Greenhalgh & Perkins 3 and 2

Singles

Anne Quast Sander beat Everard 4 and 3
Booth beat Greenhalgh 7 and 5
Massey beat Carol LeFeuvre 6 and 5
Semple beat Walker 2 and 1
Mary Budke beat Perkins 5 and 4
Lauer lost to McKenna 2 and 1

1972 Western Gailes June 9–10

Result: USA 10, GB&I 8
Captains: Frances Stephens Smith (GB&I),
  Jean Ashley Crawford (USA)

First Day: Foursomes
Everard & Beverly Huke lost to Baugh & Kirouac
  2 and 1
Frearson & Robertson beat Booth & McIntyre
  2 and 1
McKenna & Walker beat Barry & Hollis Stacy 1 hole

Singles

Mickey Walker halved with Laura Baugh
Belle McCorkindale Robertson lost to Jane Bastanchury
  Booth 3 and 1
Mary Everard lost to Martha Wilkinson Kirouac
  4 and 3
Dinah Oxley lost to Barbara McIntire 4 and 3
Kathryn Phillips beat Lancy Smith 2 holes
Mary McKenna lost to Beth Barry 2 and 1

Second Day: Foursomes
McKenna & Walker beat Baugh & Kirouac 3 and 2
Everard & Huke lost to Booth & McIntyre 5 and 4
Frearson & Robertson halved with Barry & Stacy

Singles

Robertson lost to Baugh 6 and 5
Everard beat McIntyre 6 and 5
Walker beat Booth 1 hole
McKenna beat Kirouac 3 and 1
Diane Frearson lost to Smith 3 and 1
Phillips lost to Barry 3 and 1

1970 Brae Burn, MA Aug 7–8

Result: USA 11½, GB&I 6½
Captains: Carolyn Cudone (USA),
  Jeanne Bisgood (GB&I)

First Day: Foursomes
Bastanchury & Hamlin lost to McKenna & Oxley 4 and 3
Preuss & Wilkinson beat Irvin & Robertson 4 and 3
Jane Fassinger & Hill lost to Everard & Greenhalgh 5 and 3

Singles

Jane Bastanchury beat Dinah Oxley 5 and 3
Martha Wilkinson beat Ann Irvin 1 hole
Shelley Hamlin halved with Belle McCorkindale
  Robertson
Phyllis Preuss lost to Mary McKenna 4 and 2
Nancy Hager beat Margaret Pickard 5 and 4
Alice Dye beat Julia Greenhalgh 1 hole

Second Day: Foursomes
Preuss & Wilkinson beat McKenna & Oxley 6 and 4
Dye & Hill halved with Everard & Greenhalgh
Bastanchury & Hamlin beat Irvin & Robertson 1 hole

Singles

Bastanchury beat Irvin 4 and 3
Hamlin halved with Oxley
Preuss beat Robertson 1 hole
Wilkinson lost to Greenhalgh 6 and 4
Hager lost to Mary Everard 4 and 3
Cindy Hill beat McKenna 2 and 1

1968 Newcastle, Co Down June 14–15

Result: USA 10½, GB&I 7½
Captains: Zara Bolton (GB&I), Evelyn Monsted (USA)

First Day: Foursomes
Irvin & Robertson beat Hamlin & Welts 6 and 5
Pickard & Saunders beat Conley & Dill 3 and 2
Howard & Pam Tredinnick lost to Ashley & Preuss 1 hole

1968 *continued*

Singles

Ann Irvin beat Anne Quast Welts 3 and 2
Vivien Saunders lost to Shelley Hamlin 1 hole
Belle McCorkindale Robertson lost to Roberta Albers
  1 hole
Bridget Jackson halved with Peggy Conley
Dinah Oxley halved with Phyllis Preuss
Margaret Pickard beat Jean Ashley 2 holes

Second Day: Foursomes

Oxley & Tredinnick lost to Ashley & Preuss 5 and 4
Irvin & Robertson halved with Conley & Dill
Pickard & Saunders lost to Hamlin & Welts 2 and 1

Singles

Irvin beat Hamlin 3 and 2
Robertson halved with Welts
Saunders halved with Albers
Ann Howard lost to Mary Lou Dill 4 and 2
Pickard lost to Conley 1 hole
Jackson lost to Preuss 2 and 1

1966 *Hot Springs, VA* July 29–30

Result: USA 13, GB&I 5

Captains: Dorothy Germain Porter (USA),
  Zara Bolton (GB&I)

First Day: Foursomes

Ashley & Preuss beat Armitage & Bonallack 1 hole
Barbara McIntire & Welts halved with Joan Hastings &
  Robertson
Boddie & Flenniken beat Chadwick & Tredinnick 1 hole

Singles

Jean Ashley beat Belle McCorkindale Robertson 1 hole
Anne Quast Welts halved with Susan Armitage
Barbara White Boddie beat Angela Ward Bonallack
  3 and 2
Nancy Roth Syms beat Elizabeth Chadwick 2 holes
Helen Wilson lost to Ita Burke 3 and 1
Carol Sorenson Flenniken beat Marjory Fowler 3 and 1

Second Day: Foursomes

Ashley & Preuss beat Armitage & Bonallack 2 and 1
McIntire & Welts lost to Burke & Chadwick 1 hole
Boddie & Flenniken beat Hastings & Robertson 2 and 1

Singles

Ashley lost to Bonallack 2 and 1
Welts halved with Robertson
Boddie beat Armitage 3 and 2
Syms halved with Pam Tredinnick
Phyllis Preuss beat Chadwick 3 and 2
Flenniken beat Burke 2 and 1

1964 *Porthcawl* Sept 11–12

Result: USA 10½, GB&I 1½

Captains: Elsie Corlett (GB&I), Helen Hawes (USA)

First Day: Foursomes

Spearman & Bonallack beat McIntyre & Preuss 2 and 1
Sheila Vaughan & Porter beat Gunderson & Roth
  3 and 2
Jackson & Susan Armitage lost to Sorenson & White
  8 and 6

Singles

Angela Ward Bonallack lost to JoAnne Gunderson
  6 and 5
Marley Spearman halved with Barbara McIntire
Julia Greenhalgh lost to Barbara White 3 and 2
Bridget Jackson beat Carol Sorenson 4 and 3
Joan Lawrence lost to Peggy Conley 1 hole
Ruth Porter beat Nancy Roth 1 hole

Second Day: Foursomes

Spearman & Bonallack beat McIntyre & Preuss 6 and 5
Armitage & Jackson lost to Gunderson & Roth 2 holes
Porter & Vaughan halved with Sorenson & White

Singles

Spearman halved with Gunderson
Lawrence lost to McIntyre 4 and 2
Greenhalgh beat Phyllis Preuss 5 and 3
Bonallack lost to White 3 and 2
Porter lost to Sorenson 3 and 2
Jackson lost to Conley 1 hole

1962 *Broadmoor, CO* Aug 17–18

Result: USA 8, GB&I 1

Captains: Polly Riley (USA),
  Frances Stephens Smith (GB&I)

Foursomes

Decker & McIntyre beat Spearman & Bonallack
  7 and 5
Jean Ashley & Anna Johnstone beat Ruth Porter &
  Frearson 8 and 7
Creed & Gunderson beat Vaughan & Ann Irvin 4 and 3

Singles

Judy Bell lost to Diane Frearson 8 and 7
JoAnne Gunderson beat Angela Ward Bonallack
  2 and 1
Clifford Ann Creed beat Sally Bonallack 6 and 5
Anne Quast Decker beat Marley Spearman 7 and 5
Phyllis Preuss beat Jean Roberts 1 hole
Barbara McIntyre beat Sheila Vaughan 5 and 4

1960 *Lindrick* May 20–21

Result: USA 6½, GB&I 2½

Captains: Maureen Garrett (GB&I),
  Mildred Prunaret (USA)

Foursomes

Price & Bonallack beat Gunderson & McIntyre 1 hole
Robertson & McCorkindale lost to Eller & Quast
  4 and 2
Frances Smith & Porter lost to Goodwin & Anna
  Johnstone 3 and 2

Singles

Elizabeth Price halved with Barbara McIntyre
Angela Ward Bonallack lost to JoAnne Gunderson
  2 and 1
Janette Robertson lost to Anne Quast 2 holes
Philomena Garvey lost to Judy Eller 4 and 3
Belle McCorkindale lost to Judy Bell 8 and 7
Ruth Porter beat Joanne Goodwin 1 hole

1958 *Brae Burn, MA* Aug 8–9

Result: GB&I 4½, USA 4½

Captains: Virginia Dennehy (USA),
  Daisy Ferguson (GB&I)

Foursomes

Riley & Romack lost to Bonallack & Price 2 and 1
Gunderson & Quast lost to Robertson & Smith 3 and 2
Johnstone & McIntire beat Jackson & Valentine 6 and 5

Singles

JoAnne Gunderson beat Jessie Anderson Valentine
  2 holes
Barbara McIntire halved with Angela Ward Bonallack
Anne Quast beat Elizabeth Price 4 and 2
Anna Johnstone lost to Janette Robertson 3 and 2
Barbara Romack beat Bridget Jackson 3 and 2
Polly Riley lost to Frances Stephens Smith 2 holes

1956 *Prince's, Sandwich* June 8–9
Result: GB&I 5, USA 4
Captains: Zara Davis Bolton (GB&I), Edith Flippin (USA)
Foursomes
Valentine & Garvey lost to Lesser & Smith 2 and 1
Smith & Price beat Riley & Romack 5 and 3
Robertson & Veronica Anstey lost to Downey &
  Carolyn Cudone 6 and 4
Singles
Jessie Anderson Valentine beat Patricia Lesser
  6 and 4
Philomena Garvey lost to Margaret Smith 9 and 8
Frances Stephens Smith beat Polly Riley 1 hole
Janette Robertson lost to Barbara Romack 6 and 4
Angela Ward beat Mary Ann Downey 6 and 4
Elizabeth Price beat Jane Nelson 7 and 6

1954 *Merion, PA* Sept 2–3
Result: USA 6, GB&I 3
Captains: Edith Flippin (USA), Mrs JB Beck (GB&I)
Foursomes
Faulk & Riley beat Stephens & Price 6 and 4
Doran & Patricia Lesser beat Garvey & Valentine 6 and 5
Kirby & Barbara Romack beat Marjorie Peel &
  Robertson 6 and 5
Singles
Mary Lena Faulk lost to Frances Stephens 1 hole
Claire Doran beat Jeanne Bisgood 4 and 3
Polly Riley beat Elizabeth Price 9 and 8
Dorothy Kirby lost to Philomena Garvey 3 and 1
Grace DeMoss Smith beat Jessie Anderson Valentine
  4 and 3
Joyce Ziske lost to Janette Robertson 3 and 1

1952 *Muirfield* June 6–7
Result: GB&I 5, USA 4
*Captains: Lady Katherine Cairns (GB&I),
  Aniela Goldthwaite (USA)*
Foursomes
Donald & Price beat Kirby & DeMoss 3 and 2
Stephens & JA Valentine lost to Doran & Lindsay 6 and 4
Paterson & Garvey beat Riley & Patricia O'Sullivan 2 and 1
Singles
Jean Donald lost to Dorothy Kirby 1 hole
Frances Stephens beat Marjorie Lindsay 2 and 1
Moira Paterson lost to Polly Riley 6 and 4
Jeanne Bisgood beat Mae Murray 6 and 5
Philomena Garvey lost to Claire Doran 3 and 2
Elizabeth Price beat Grace DeMoss 3 and 2

1950 *Buffalo, NY* Sept 4–5
Result: USA 7½, GB&I 1½
*Captains: Glenna Collett Vare (USA),
  Diana Fishwick Critchley (GB&I)*
Foursomes
Hanson & Porter beat Valentine & Donald 3 and 2
Helen Sigel & Kirk lost to Stephens & Price 1 hole
Dorothy Kirby & Kielty beat Garvey & Bisgood 6 and 5
Singles
Dorothy Porter halved with Frances Stephens
Polly Riley beat Jessie Anderson Valentine 7 and 6
Beverly Hanson beat Jean Donald 6 and 5
Dorothy Kielty beat Philomena Garvey 2 and 1
Peggy Kirk beat Jeanne Bisgood 1 hole
Grace Lenczyk beat Elizabeth Price 5 and 4

1948 *Birkdale* May 21–22
Result: USA 6½, GB&I 2½
*Captains: Doris Chambers (GB&I),
  Glenna Collett Vare (USA)*
Foursomes
Donald & Gordon beat Suggs & Lenczyk 3 and 2
Garvey & Bolton lost to Kirby & Vare 4 and 3
Ruttle & Val Reddan lost to Page & Kielty 5 and 4
Singles
Philomena Garvey halved with Louise Suggs
Jean Donald beat Dorothy Kirby 2 holes
Jacqueline Gordon lost to Grace Lenczyk 5 and 3
Helen Holm lost to Estelle Lawson Page 3 and 2
Maureen Ruttle lost to Polly Riley 3 and 2
Zara Bolton lost to Dorothy Kielty 2 and 1

1938 *Essex, MA* Sept 7–8
Result: USA 5½, GB&I 3½
*Captains: Frances Stebbins (USA),
  Mrs RH Wallace-Williamson (GB&I)*
Foursomes
Page & Orcutt lost to Holm & Tiernan 2 holes
Vare & Berg lost to Anderson & Corlett 1 hole
Miley & Kathryn Hemphill halved with Walker &
  Phyllis Wade
Singles
Estelle Lawson Page beat Helen Holm 6 and 5
Patty Berg beat Jessie Anderson 1 hole
Marion Miley beat Elsie Corlett 2 and 1
Glenna Collett Vare beat Charlotte Walker 2 and 1
Maureen Orcutt lost to Clarrie Tiernan 2 and 1
Charlotte Glutting beat Nan Baird 1 hole

1936 *Gleneagles* May 6
Result: USA 4½, GB&I 4½
*Captains: Doris Chambers (GB&I),
  Glenna Collett Vare (USA)*
Foursomes
Morgan & Garon halved with Vare & Berg
Barton & Walker lost to Orcutt & Cheney 2 and 1
Anderson & Holm beat Hill & Glutting 3 and 2
Singles
Wanda Morgan lost to Glenna Collett Vare 3 and 2
Helen Holm beat Patty Berg 4 and 3
Pamela Barton lost to Charlotte Glutting 1 hole
Charlotte Walker lost to Maureen Orcutt 1 hole
Jessie Anderson beat Leona Pressley Cheney 1 hole
Marjorie Garon beat Opal Hill 7 and 5

1934 *Chevy Chase, MD* Sept 27–28
Result: USA 6½, GB&I 2½
*Captains: Glenna Collett Vare (USA),
  Doris Chambers (GB&I)*
Foursomes
Van Wie & Glutting halved with Gourlay & Barton
Orcutt & Cheney beat Fishwick & Morgan 2 holes
Hill & Lucille Robinson lost to Plumpton & Walker
  2 and 1
Singles
Virginia Van Wie beat Diana Fishwick 2 and 1
Maureen Orcutt beat Molly Gourlay 4 and 2
Leona Pressley Cheney beat Pamela Barton 7 and 5
Charlotte Glutting beat Wanda Morgan
Opal Hill beat Diana Plumpton 3 and 2
Aniela Goldthwaite lost to Charlotte Walker 3 and 2

1932 *Wentworth* May 21
Result: USA 5½, GB&I 3½
Captains: J Wethered (GB&I), M Hollins (USA)

Foursomes
Wethered & Morgan lost to Vare & Hill 1 hole
Wilson & JB Watson lost to Van Wie & Hicks 2 and 1
Gourlay & Doris Park lost to Orcutt & Cheney
  1 hole

Singles
Joyce Wethered beat Glenna Collett Vare 6 and 4
Enid Wilson beat Helen Hicks 2 and 1
Wanda Morgan lost to Virginia Van Wie 2 and 1
Diana Fishwick beat Maureen Orcutt 4 and 3
Molly Gourlay halved with Opal Hill
Elsie Corlett lost to Leona Pressley Cheney 4 and 3

Curtis Cup INDIVIDUAL RECORDS

Bold print: captain; bold print in brackets: non-playing captain
Maiden name in parentheses, former surname in square brackets

Great Britain and Ireland

Name		Year	Played	Won	Lost	Halved
Jean Anderson (Donald)	SCO	1948	6	3	3	0
Kim Andrew (Rostron)	ENG	1998-2000	8	2	6	0
Diane Bailey [Frearson] (Robb)	ENG	1962-72-**(84)**-**(86)**-**(88)**	5	2	2	1
Sally Barber (Bonallack)	ENG	1962	1	0	1	0
Pam Barton	ENG	1934-36	4	0	3	1
Hannah Barwood	ENG	2010	3	0	2	1
Linda Bayman	ENG	1988	4	2	1	1
Baba Beck (Pym)	IRL	**(1954)**	0	0	0	0
Charlotte Beddows [Watson] (Stevenson)	SCO	1932	1	0	1	0
Lilian Behan	IRL	1986	4	3	1	0
Veronica Beharrell (Anstey)	ENG	1956	1	0	1	0
Pam Benka (Tredinnick)	ENG	1966-68 **(2002)**	4	0	3	1
Elizabeth Bennett	ENG	2008	5	0	4	1
Jeanne Bisgood	ENG	1950-52-54-**(70)**	4	1	3	0
Elizabeth Boatman (Collis)	ENG	**(1992)**-**(94)**	0	0	0	0
Zara Bolton (Davis)	ENG	1948-**(56)**-**(66)**-**(68)**	2	0	2	0
Angela Bonallack (Ward)	ENG	1956-58-60-62-64-66	15	6	8	1
Carly Booth	SCO	2008	4	1	3	0
Becky Brewerton	WAL	2000	3	1	2	0
Fiona Brown	ENG	1998-2000	4	2	2	0
Ita Butler (Burke)	IRL	1966-**(96)**	3	2	1	0
Lady Katherine Cairns	ENG	**(1952)**	0	0	0	0
Krystle Caithness	SCO	2008	3	3	0	0
Carole Caldwell (Redford)	ENG	1978-80	5	0	3	2
Doris Chambers	ENG	**(1934)**-**(36)**-**(48)**	0	0	0	0
Holly Clyburn	ENG	2010	3	1	1	1
Alison Coffey	IRL	2002	3	1	2	0
Carol Comboy (Grott)	ENG	**(1978)**-**(80)**	0	0	0	0
Jane Connachan	SCO	1980-82	5	0	5	0
Elsie Corlett	ENG	1932-38-**(64)**	3	1	2	0
Claire Coughlan	IRL	2004-06	5	3	2	0
Diana Critchley (Fishwick)	ENG	1932-34-**(50)**	3	1	2	0
Alison Davidson (Rose)	SCO	1996-98	7	4	3	0
Karen Davies	WAL	1986-88	7	4	1	2
Laura Davies	ENG	1984	2	1	1	0
Tara Delanbey	ENG	2006	3	0	2	1
Lisa Dermott	WAL	1996	2	2	0	0
Helen Dobson	ENG	1990	3	1	2	0
Kitrina Douglas	ENG	1982	4	0	3	1
Claire Dowling (Hourihane)	IRL	1984-86-88-90-92-**(2000)**	8	3	3	2
Marjorie Draper [Peel] (Thomas)	SCO	1954	1	0	1	0
Emma Duggleby	ENG	2000-04	8	5	2	1
Lisa Educate (Walton)	ENG	1994-96	6	3	3	0
Naomi Edwards	ENG	2006	3	1	2	0
Mary Everard	ENG	1970-72-74-78	15	6	7	2
Jodi Ewart	ENG	2008	3	0	2	1
Elaine Farquharson	SCO	1990-92	6	1	5	0
Daisy Ferguson	IRL	**(1958)**	0	0	0	0
Marjory Ferguson (Fowler)	SCO	1966	1	0	1	0
Elizabeth Price Fisher (Price)	ENG	1950-52-54-56-58-60	12	7	4	1
Linzi Fletcher	ENG	1990	1	0	1	0
Maureen Garner (Madill)	IRL	1980	4	0	3	1

Name		Year	Played	Won	Lost	Halved
Marjorie Ross Garon	ENG	1936	2	1	0	1
Maureen Garrett (Ruttle)	ENG	1948-(60)	2	0	2	0
Philomena Garvey	IRL	1948-50-52-54-56-60	11	2	8	1
Carol Gibbs (Le Feuvre)	ENG	1974	3	0	3	0
Martine Gillen	IRL	2006	4	2	2	0
Jacqueline Gordon	ENG	1948	2	1	1	0
Molly Gourlay	ENG	1932-34	4	0	2	2
Julia Greenhalgh	ENG	1964-70-74-76-78	17	6	7	4
Penny Grice-Whittaker (Grice)	ENG	1984	4	2	1	1
Caroline Hall	ENG	1992	4	2	0	2
Marley Harris [Spearman] (Baker)	ENG	1962-64	6	2	2	2
Dorothea Hastings (Sommerville)	SCO	1958	0	0	0	0
Lady Heathcoat-Amory (Joyce Wethered)	ENG	**1932**	2	1	1	0
Dinah Henson (Oxley)	ENG	1968-70-72-76	11	3	6	2
Anna Highgate	WAL	2004	1	0	1	0
Helen Holm (Gray)	SCO	1936-38-48	5	3	2	0
Ann Howard (Phillips)	ENG	1956-68	2	0	2	0
Rebecca Hudson	ENG	1998-2000-02	11	5	5	1
Shirley Huggan (Lawson)	SCO	1988	2	1	1	0
Beverley Huke	ENG	1972	2	0	2	0
Ann Irvin	ENG	1962-68-70-76	12	4	7	1
Bridget Jackson	ENG	1958-64-68	8	1	6	1
Rachel Jennings	ENG	2010	5	0	4	1
Patricia Johnson	ENG	1986	4	4	0	0
Sarah Jones	WAL	2002	2	1	1	0
Anne Laing	SCO	2004	4	3	1	0
Vikki Laing	SCO	2002	4	2	2	0
Susan Langridge (Armitage)	ENG	1964-66	6	0	5	1
Joan Lawrence	SCO	1964	2	0	2	0
Wilma Leburn (Aitken)	SCO	1982	2	0	2	0
Jenny Lee Smith	ENG	1974-76	3	0	3	0
Breanne Loucks	WAL	2006-08	7	4	3	0
Kathryn Lumb (Phillips)	ENG	1970-72	2	1	1	0
Leona Maquire	IRL	2010	5	1	3	1
Lisa Maquire	IRL	2010	3	2	1	0
Mhairi McKay	SCO	1994-96	7	2	3	2
Mary McKenna	IRL	1970-72-74-76-78-80-82-84-86-(2008-10)	30	10	16	4
Shelley McKevitt	ENG	2004	4	2	2	0
Myra McKinlay	SCO	1994	3	1	2	0
Suzanne McMahon (Cadden)	SCO	1976	4	0	4	0
Danielle McVeigh	IRL	2010	5	2	2	1
Sheila Maher (Vaughan)	ENG	1962-64	4	1	2	1
Tricia Mangan	IRL	2006	3	0	2	1
Kathryn Marshall (Imrie)	SCO	1990	4	1	3	0
Vanessa Marvin	ENG	1978	4	1	3	0
Danielle Masters	ENG	2004	3	1	2	0
Kiran Matharu	ENG	2006	2	1	1	0
Catriona Matthew (Lambert)	SCO	1990-92-94	12	7	4	1
Tegwen Matthews [Thomas] (Perkins)	WAL	1974-76-78-80	14	4	8	2
Moira Milton (Paterson)	SCO	1952	2	1	1	0
Hilary Monaghan	SCO	1998	1	0	1	0
Janice Moodie	SCO	1994-96	8	5	1	2
Fame More	ENG	2002-04	2	0	2	0
Becky Morgan	WAL	1998-2000	7	2	5	0
Wanda Morgan	ENG	1932-34-36	6	0	5	1
Joanne Morley	ENG	1992	4	2	0	2
Nicola Murray (Buxton)	ENG	1992	1	0	1	0
Beverley New	ENG	1984	4	1	3	0
Lesley Nicholson	SCO	2000	1	0	0	1
Suzanne O'Brien	IRL	2000	4	3	0	1
Maire O'Donnell	IRL	(1982)	0	0	0	0
Ada O'Sullivan	IRL	(2004-06)	0	0	0	0
Florentyna Parker	ENG	2008	4	1	3	0
Margaret Pickard (Nichol)	ENG	1968-70	5	2	3	0
Diana Plumpton	ENG	1934	2	1	1	0
Elizabeth Pook (Chadwick)	ENG	1966	4	1	3	0
Doris Porter (Park)	SCO	1932	1	0	1	0
Pamela Pretswell	SCO	2010	3	1	2	0

Curtis Cup Individual Records *continued*

Name		Year	Played	Won	Lost	Halved
Eileen Rose Power (McDaid)	IRL	1994	1	0	1	0
Elaine Ratcliffe	ENG	1996-98	6	3	1	2
Clarrie Reddan (Tiernan)	IRL	1938-48	3	2	1	0
Joan Rennie (Hastings)	SCO	1966	2	0	1	1
Melissa Reid	ENG	2006	4	1	3	0
Maureen Richmond (Walker)	SCO	1974	4	2	2	0
Jean Roberts	ENG	1962	1	0	1	0
Belle Robertson (McCorkindale)	SCO	1960-66-68-70-72-(**74**)-(**76**)-82-86	24	5	12	7
Claire Robinson (Nesbitt)	IRL	1980	3	0	1	2
Vivien Saunders	ENG	1968	4	1	2	1
Susan Shapcott	ENG	1988	4	3	1	0
Linda Simpson (Moore)	ENG	1980	3	1	1	1
Ruth Slark (Porter)	ENG	1960-62-64	7	3	3	1
Anne Smith [Stant] (Willard)	ENG	1976	1	0	1	0
Frances Smith (Stephens)	ENG	1950-52-54-56-58-60-(**62**)-(**72**)	11	7	3	1
Kerry Smith	ENG	2002	2	0	2	0
Janet Soulsby	ENG	1982	4	1	2	1
Kirsty Speak	ENG	1994	1	0	1	0
Gillian Stewart	SCO	1980-82	4	1	3	0
Heather Stirling	SCO	2002	4	1	3	0
Karen Stupples	ENG	1996-98	4	2	2	0
Vicki Thomas (Rawlings)	WAL	1982-84-86-88-90-92	13	6	5	2
Michele Thomson	SCO	2008	4	1	2	1
Muriel Thomson	SCO	1978	3	2	1	0
Jill Thornhill	ENG	1984-86-88	12	6	2	4
Nicola Timmins	ENG	2004	3	1	2	0
Angela Uzielli (Carrick)	ENG	1978	1	0	1	0
Jessie Valentine (Anderson)	SCO	1936-38-50-52-54-56-58	13	4	9	0
Julie Wade	ENG	1988-90-92-94-96	19	6	10	3
Helen Wadsworth	WAL	1990	2	0	2	0
Claire Waite	ENG	1984	4	2	2	0
Mickey Walker	ENG	1972-74	4	3	0	1
Pat Walker	IRL	1934-36-38	6	2	3	1
Verona Wallace-Williamson	SCO	(**1938**)	0	0	0	0
Nan Wardlaw (Baird)	SCO	1938	1	0	1	0
Sally Watson	SCO	2008-10	10	4	5	1
Enid Wilson	ENG	1932	2	1	1	0
Janette Wright (Robertson)	SCO	1954-56-58-60	8	3	5	0
Phyllis Wylie (Wade)	ENG	1938	1	0	0	1

United States of America

Name	Year	Played	Won	Lost	Halved
Roberta Albers	1968	2	1	0	1
Danielle Ammaccapane	1986	3	0	3	0
Kathy Baker	1982	4	3	0	1
Barbara Barrow	1976	2	1	0	1
Beth Barry	1972-74	5	3	1	1
Emily Bastel	2002	2	0	2	0
Beth Bauer	1998-2000	7	4	3	0
Laura Baugh	1972	4	2	1	1
Leland Beckel	2000	1	0	1	0
Judy Bell	1960-62-(**86**)-(**88**)	2	1	1	0
Peggy Kirk Bell (Kirk)	1950	2	1	1	0
Amy Benz	1982	3	2	1	0
Patty Berg	1936-38	4	1	2	1
Erica Blasberg	2004	2	1	2	1
Amanda Blumenherst	2006-08	8	4	3	1
Barbara Fay Boddie (White)	1964-66	8	7	0	1
Meghan Bolger	2008	3	0	3	0
Jane Booth (Bastanchury)	1970-72-74-(**2000**)	12	9	3	0
Kellee Booth	1996-98	7	5	2	0
Mary Budke	1974-(**2002**)	3	2	1	0
Robin Burke	1998	3	2	1	0
Brandie Burton	1990	3	3	0	0
Jo Anne Carner (Gunderson)	1958-60-62-64	10	6	3	1
Lori Castillo	1980	3	2	1	0
Leona Cheney (Pressler)	1932-34-36	6	5	1	0

Name	Year	Played	Won	Lost	Halved
Sis Choate	(1974)	0	0	0	0
Jenny Chuasiriporn	1998	3	0	2	1
Cydney Clanton	2010	3	2	0	1
Peggy Conley	1964-68	6	3	1	2
Mary Ann Cook (Downey)	1956	2	1	1	0
Patricia Cornett	1978-88	4	1	2	1
Brenda Corrie Kuehn	1996-98	7	4	3	0
Jean Crawford (Ashley)	1962-66-68-(72)	8	6	2	0
Paula Creamer	2004	3	2	1	0
Clifford Ann Creed	1962	2	2	0	0
Grace Cronin (Lenczyk)	1948-50	3	2	1	0
Carolyn Cudone	1956-(70)	1	1	0	0
Beth Daniel	1976-78	8	7	1	0
Virginia Dennehy	(1958)	0	0	0	0
Virginia Derby Grimes	1998-2000	6	3	1	2
Mary Lou Dill	1968	3	1	1	1
Meredith Duncan	2002	4	3	1	0
Alice Dye	1970	2	1	0	1
Mollie Fankhauser	2002	3	1	2	0
Heather Farr	1984	3	2	1	0
Jane Fassinger	1970	1	0	1	0
Mary Lena Faulk	1954	2	1	1	0
Carol Sorensen Flenniken (Sorensen)	1964-66	8	6	1	1
Edith Flippin (Quier)	(1954)-(56)	0	0	0	0
Amy Fruhwirth	1992	4	0	1	3
Kim Gardner	1986	3	1	1	1
Charlotte Glutting	1934-36-38	5	3	1	1
Vicki Goetze	1990-92	8	4	2	2
Brenda Goldsmith	1978-80	4	2	2	0
Aniela Goldthwaite	1934-(52)	1	0	1	0
Joanne Goodwin	1960	2	1	1	0
Virginia Grimes	2006	2	1	1	0
Mary Hafeman	1980	2	1	0	1
Shelley Hamkin	1968-70	8	3	3	2
Penny Hammel	1984	3	1	1	1
Nancy Hammer (Hager)	1970	2	1	1	0
Cathy Hanlon	1982	3	2	1	0
Beverley Hanson	1950	2	2	0	0
Tracy Hanson	1992	3	1	2	0
Patricia Harbottle (Lesser)	1954-56	3	2	1	0
Leigh Anne Hardin	2002	3	1	2	0
Mina Harigae	2008	4	2	2	0
Helen Hawes	(1964)	0	0	0	0
Kathryn Hemphill	1938	1	0	0	1
Helen Hicks	1932	2	1	1	0
Carolyn Hill	1978	2	0	0	2
Cindy Hill	1970-74-76-78	14	5	6	3
Opel Hill	1932-34-36	6	2	3	1
Marion Hollins	(1932)	0	0	0	0
Hilary Homeyer	2000	4	3	0	1
Dana Howe	1984	3	1	1	1
Sarah Huarte	2004	2	0	2	0
Juli Inkster	1982	4	4	0	0
Elizabeth Janangelo	2004	3	1	2	0
Maria Jemsek	1996	3	0	2	1
Angela Jerman	2002	3	2	1	0
Tiffany Joh	2008	4	2	1	1
Jennifer Johnson	2010	4	3	0	1
Ann Casey Johnstone	1958-60-62	4	3	1	0
Mae Murray Jones (Murray)	1952	1	0	1	0
Wendy Kaupp	1994	2	0	2	0
Stephanie Keever	2000	4	2	2	0
Caroline Keggi	1988	3	0	2	1
Tracy Kerdyk	1988	4	2	1	1
Cristie Kerr	1996	3	1	1	1
Kandi Kessler	1986	3	1	1	1
Dorothy Kielty	1948-50	4	4	0	0
Kimberly Kim	2008-10	7	4	3	0
Dorothy Kirby	1948-50-52-54	7	4	3	0
Martha Kirouac (Wilkinson)	1970-72-(2004)	8	5	3	0

Curtis Cup Individual Records *continued*

Name	Year	Played	Won	Lost	Halved
Emilee Klein	1994	4	3	1	0
Nancy Knight (Lopez)	1976	2	2	0	0
Stephanie Kono	2010	4	2	1	1
Jessica Korda	2010	5	3	1	1
Kelli Kuehne	1996	3	2	1	0
Brittany Lang	2004	3	1	2	0
Martha Lang	1992-(**96**)	3	2	0	1
Bonnie Lauer	1974	4	2	2	0
Sarah Le Brun Ingram	1992-94-96	7	2	4	1
Jennie Lee	2006-08	6	2	3	1
Taylor Leon	2006	4	3	0	1
Tiffany Lua	2010	3	1	2	0
Stacy Lewis	2008	5	5	0	0
Marjorie Lindsay	1952	2	1	1	0
Patricia Lucey (O'Sullivan)	1952	1	0	1	0
Paige Mackenzie	2006	4	3	1	0
Amanda McCurdy	2006	2	1	1	0
Mari McDougall	1982	2	2	0	0
Jill McGill	1994	4	1	1	2
Barbara McIntire	1958-60-62-64-66-72-(**76**)	16	6	6	4
Lucile Mann (Robinson)	1934	1	0	1	0
Debbie Massey	1974-76	5	5	0	0
Marion Miley	1938	2	1	0	1
Dottie Mochrie (Pepper)	1986	3	0	2	1
Noreen Mohler (Uihlein)	1978-(**2010**)	3	1	1	1
Evelyn Monsted	(**1968**)	0	0	0	0
Terri Moody	1980	2	1	0	1
Laura Myerscough	2002	3	3	0	0
Karen Noble	1990	4	2	2	0
Judith Oliver	1978-80-82-(**92**)	8	5	1	2
Maureen Orcutt	1932-34-36-38	8	5	3	0
Joanne Pacillo	1984	3	1	1	1
Estelle Page (Lawson)	1938-48	4	3	1	0
Jane Park	2004-06	7	4	2	1
Katie Peterson	1990	3	3	0	0
Margaret Platt	1990	2	0	2	0
Frances Pond (Stebbins)	(**1938**)	0	0	0	0
Ellen Port	1994-96	6	4	2	0
Dorothy Germain Porter	1950-(**66**)	2	1	0	1
Phyllis Preuss	1962-64-66-68-70-(**84**)	15	10	4	1
Betty Probasco	(**1982**)	0	0	0	0
Mildred Prunaret	(**1960**)	0	0	0	0
Polly Riley	1948-50-52-54-56-58-(**62**)	10	5	5	0
Jo Jo Robertson	1998	2	0	2	0
Barbara Romack	1954-56-58	5	3	2	0
Jody Rosenthal	1984	3	2	0	1
Anne Sander [Welts] [Decker] (Quast)	1958-60-62-66-68-74-84-90	22	11	7	4
Cindy Scholefield	1988	3	0	3	0
Cindy Schreyer	1986	3	1	2	0
Kathleen McCarthy Scrivner (McCarthy)	1986-88	6	2	3	1
Carol Semple Thompson	1974-76-80-82-90-92-94-96-(**98**)-2000-02-(**06**)-(**08**)	33	16	13	4
Leslie Shannon	1986-88-90-92	9	1	6	2
Patty Sheehan	1980	4	4	0	0
Pearl Sinn	1988	2	1	1	0
Grace De Moss Smith (De Moss)	1952-54	3	1	2	0
Lancy Smith	1972-78-80-82-84-(**94**)	16	7	5	4
Margaret Smith	1956	2	2	0	0
Jennifer Song	2010	5	2	2	1
Stephanie Sparks	1994	2	0	2	0
Hollis Stacy	1972	2	0	1	1
Claire Stancik (Doran)	1952-54	4	4	0	0
Angela Stanford	2000	4	1	2	1
Judy Street (Eller)	1960	2	2	0	0
Louise Suggs	1948	2	0	1	1
Jenny Suh	2006	2	0	2	0
Courtney Swaim	2002	4	3	1	0
Nancy Roth Syms (Roth)	1964-66-76-(**80**)	9	3	5	1

Name	Year	Played	Won	Lost	Halved
Alexis Thompson	2010	5	4	0	I
Anne Thurman	2004	4	3	I	0
Virginia Van Wie	1932-34	4	3	0	I
Glenna Collett Vare (Collett)	1932-(**34**)-**36**-38-**48**-(**50**)	7	4	2	I
Alison Walshe	2008	4	4	0	0
Wendy Ward	1994	3	I	2	0
Jane Weiss (Nelson)	1956	I	0	I	0
Robin Weiss	1990-92-2000	7	4	2	I
Donna White (Horton)	1976	2	2	0	0
Mary Anne Widman	1984	3	2	I	0
Michelle Wie	2004	4	2	2	0
Kimberley Williams	1986	3	0	3	0
Helen Sigel Wilson (Sigel)	1950-66-(**78**)	2	0	2	0
Joyce Ziske	1954	I	0	I	0

Women's World Amateur Team Championship for the Espirito Santo Trophy
(Inaugurated 1964)

This event will next be held in 2012

1964	I France 588; 2 USA 589	St Germain GC, Paris, France
1966	I USA 580; 2 Canada 589	Mexico City GC, Mexico
1968	I USA 626; 2 Australia 622	Victoria GC, Melbourne, Australia
1970	I USA 598; 2 France 599	RSHE Club de Campo, Madrid, Spain
1972	I USA 583; 2 France 587	The Hindu GC, Argentina
1974	I USA 620; 2 GB and I, Spain 636	Campo de Golf Cajuiles Dominican Republic
1976	I USA 605; 2 France 622	Vilamoura GC, Portugal
1978	I Australia 596; 2 Canada 597	Pacific Harbour GC, Fiji
1980	I USA 588; 2 Australia 595	Pinehurst No.2, NC, USA
1982	I USA 579; 2 New Zealand 596	Geneva GC, Switzerland
1984	I USA 585; 2 France 597	Royal Hong Kong GC
1986	I Spain 580; 2 France 583	Lagunita CC, Colombia
1988	I USA 587; 2 Sweden 588	Drottningholm GC, Sweden
1990	I USA 585; 2 New Zealand 597	Russley GC, Christchurch, New Zealand
1992	I Spain 588; 2 GB&I 599	Marine Drive GC Vancouver, Canada
1994	I USA 569; 2 South Korea 573	Golf National, Versailles, France
1996	I South Korea 438; 2 Italy 440	St Elena GC, Philippines
1998	I USA 558; 2 Italy, Germany 573	Prince of Wales GC, Santiago, Chile
2000	I France 580; 2 South Korea 587	Sporting Club, Berlin (Faldo Course) and Bad Sarrow, GC, Germany
2002	I Australia* 578; 2 Thailand 578	Saujana G&CC (Palm and Bunga Raya Courses), Malaysia
*Australia won play-off		
2004	I Sweden 567; 2 USA, Canada 570	Rio Mar GC (River and Ocean Courses), Puerto Rico
2006	I South Africa* 566; 2 Sweden 566	De Zalze GC and Stellenbosch GC South Africa
*South Africa won play-off		
2008	I Sweden 561; 2 Spain 573	The Grange GC (East and West Courses), Adelaide, Australia
2010	I Korea 546; 2 USA 563	Olivos Golf Club and Buenos Aires GC, Argentina

History: The United States have won the event on 13 occasions, France, Australia, Sweden and South Korea twice and South Africa once.

Astor Trophy (Formerly the Commonwealth Trophy) (Inaugurated 1959)   *Fairhaven GC*
(Each match two foursomes and five singles)

South Africa 2½, New Zealand 4½
Australia 2, GB&I 5
GB&I 6, South Africa I
Canada 2, New Zealand 5
New Zealand 4, Australia 3
Canada 1½, South Africa 5½
Australia 4, Canada 3
New Zealand 2½, GB&I 4½
GB&I 4, Canada 3
South Africa 4, Australia 3

Final table

	Won	Halved	Lost	Pts
GB&I	18	3	7	19½
New Zealand	14	4	10	16
South Africa	13	2	14	14
Australia	12	10	4	14
Canada	9	I	18	9½

Winning team: Amy Boulden (Maesdu), Holly Clyburn (Woodhall Spa), Kelsey MacDonald (Nairn Dunbar), Pamela Pretswell (Bothwell Castle), Kelly Tidy (Royal Birkdale). Captain Tegwen Matthew

Vagliano Trophy – Great Britain & Ireland v Continent of Europe

(Inaugurated 1959)   *Royal Porthcawl GC, Porthcawl, Glamorgan, Wales*

Continentals win Vagliano Trophy with biggest-ever margin.

The Continent of Europe team won the Vagliano Trophy for the third successive year when they beat Great Britain and Ireland 15½—8½ at Royal Porthcawl. It was the biggest winning margin by the Continentals since the event was first staged in 1959.

Captains: GB&I: Tegwen Matthews; Europe: Anne Lanzerac

First Day: *Foursomes (GB&I names first)*

Kelly Tidy (ENG) and Amy Boulden (WAL) beat Sophia Popov (GER) and Lara Katzy (GER) 2 and 1

Holly Clyburn (ENG) and Danielle McVeigh (IRL) lost to Alexandra Bonetti (FRA) and Marion Gidali (FRA) 4 and 3

Kelsey MacDonald (SCO) and Louise Kenney (SCO) beat Marta Silva (ESP) and Camilla Hedberg (ESP) 1 hole

Pamela Pretswell (SCO) and Stephanie Meadow (IRL) lost to Therese Koelbaek (DEN) and Madalene Sagstrom (SWE) 1 hole

Singles

Tidy lost to Bonetti q hole

Boulden lost to Silva 4 and 2

MacDonald beat Celine Boutier (FRA 1 hole

Clyburn lost to Koelbaek 3 and 2

Leona Maguire (IRL beat Gidali 3 and 2

Meadow lost to Sagstrom 1 hole

McVeigh halved with Hedberg

Kenney lost to Popov 1 hole

Second Day: *Foursomes*

Tidy and Boulden beat Bonetti and Gidali 3 and 1

MacDonald and Kenney lost to Silva and Hedberg 2 and 1

Pretswell and Meadow lost to Popov and Katzy 1 hole

Maguire and McVeigh beat Sagstrom and Koelbaek 6 and 4

Singles

Clyburn lost to Silva 1 hole

Maguire beat Boutier 3 and 1

MacDonald lost to Bonetti 3 and 2

Meadow lost to Koelbaek 1 hole

Tidy lost to Katzy 5 and 4

Bouldon lost to Hedberg 2 and 1

Pretswell beat Sagstrom 2 holes

McVeigh lost to Popov 3 and 1

Result: GB&I 8½, Continent of Europe 15½

History: Great Britain & Ireland have won the event 15 times, the Continent of Europe 11 and in 1979 the match was drawn.

1973	Great Britain and Ireland 20, Continent of Europe 10	Eindhoven GC, Netherlands
1975	Great Britain and Ireland 13½, Continent of Europe 10½	Muirfield, Scotland
1977	Great Britain and Ireland 15½, Continent of Europe 8½	Llunghusen GC, Sweden
1979	Great Britain and Ireland 12, Continent of Europe 12	Royal Porthcawl GC, Wales
1981	Continent of Europe 14, Great Britain and Ireland 10	RC de Puerto de Hierro, Madrid, Spain
1983	Great Britain and Ireland 14, Continent of Europe 10	Woodhall Spa GC, England
1985	Great Britain and Ireland 14, Continent of Europe 10	Hamburg GC, Germany
1987	Great Britain and Ireland 15, Continent of Europe 9	The Berkshire GC, England
1989	Great Britain and Ireland 14½, Continent of Europe 9½	Venezia GC, Italy
1991	Great Britain and Ireland 13½, Continent of Europe 10½	Nairn GC, Scotland
1993	Great Britain and Ireland13 ½, Continent of Europe 10½	Morfontaine GC, France
1995	Continent of Europe 14, Great Britain and Ireland 10	Ganton GC, England
1997	Continent of Europe 14, Great Britain and Ireland 10	Halmstad GC, Sweden
1999	Continent of Europe 13, Great Britain and Ireland 11	North Berwick GC, Scotland
2001	Continent of Europe 13 Great Britain and Ireland 11	Circolo GC, Italy
2003	Great Britain and Ireland 12½, Continent of Europe 11½	Co. Louth GC, Ireland
2005	Great Britain and Ireland 13, Continent of Europe 11	Chantilly GC, France
2007	Continent of Europe 15, Great Britain and Ireland 9	Fairmont Hotel, Scotland.
2009	Continent of Europe 13, Great Britain and Ireland 11	Hamburg GC, Germany.

Asia-Pacific Women's Team Championship: Queen Sirikit Cup (inaugurated 1979)
Delhi GC, India

1	Korea	145-137-143—425	Ji Hee Kim, In Gee Chun, Hyo Joo Kim
2	Philippines	147-141-141—429	Chihero Ikeda, Dottie Ardina, Jayvie Maria Agojo
3	China	152-145-144—441	Lin Xiyu, Yaan Jing, Feng Simin

Other placings: 4 India 442; 5 New Zealand 443; 6 Japan 448; 7 Chinese Taipei 452; 8 Malaysia 453; 9 Thailand, Australia, Indonesia 455; 12 Singapore 456; 13 Hong Kong 467; 14 Sri Lanka 542

Individual:

1	Dottie Ardina (PHI)	71-70-70—211
2	Hyo Joo Kim (KOR)	69-69-74—212
3	Ji Hee Kim (KOR)	78-66-79—213
	Gauri Monga (IND)	73-70-70—213

History: South Korea have won 12 times, Australia 8, Japan 6, New Zealand 3, Chinese Taipei 2.

Africa

All-Africa Challenge (inaugurated 1992)
This event will next be held in 2012

Pick n Pay South African Women's Inter-Provincial Championship   *George GC*
Qualifying: 1 Gauteng North A 540; 2 Gauteng A 552; 3 Western Province 553; Boland 557; 5 KwaZulu Natal 558; North West 562; Free State and North Cape 590; 8 Gauteng B 591

Match Play – Section "A"
Day One: Gauteng A 6½, Western Province A 2½; Gauteng North A 7½, Boland 1½
Day Two: Gauteng North A 8, Western Province 1; Gauteng A7½, Bland A 1½
Day Three: Western Province 5, Bland 4; Gauteng North A, 5 Gauteng A 4

Final Table:	Pld	W	D.	L	Games	Pts
1 Gauteng North A	3	3	0	0	20½	6
2 Gauteng A	3	2	0	1	18	4
3 Western Province	3	1	0	2	8½	2
4 Boland A	3	0	0	3	7	0

Winning team: Biance Barnard, Nobuhle Diamini. Emma-Jo de Bruyn, Henriette Frylinck, Carrie Park and Kim Williams.

Match Play – Section "B"
Day One: North West 7, Free State and North Cape 2; KwaZulu Natal 7, Gauteng B 2
Day Two: KwaZulu Natal 9, Free State and North Cape 0; Gauteng B 5, North West 4
Day Three: Free State and North Cape 4½, Gauteng B 4½; North West 5, KwaZulu Natal 4

Final Table:	Pld	W	D.	L	Games	Pts
1 KwaZulu Natal	3	2	0	1	20	4
2 North West	3	2	0	1	16	4
3 Free State and N. Cape	3	1	1	1	11½	3
4 Gauteng B	3	0	1	2	6½	1

South Africa Senior Women's Championship   *Wingate Park and Woodhill*

1	Carina Theron (FS and NC)	79-84—163
2	Melrise Unquerer (Mpumalanga)	83-90—173

Americas

US Women's State Team Championship *The Landings Club, Savannah, Georgia*

1	Georgia (Amira Alexander, Rachel Dai and Laura Coble)	153-146-149—448
2	Tennessee (Maggie Scott, Jennifer Lucas and Calle Nielson)	149-149-152—450
	Texas (Robin Burke, Anna Schultz and Mina Hardin)	146-151-153—450

US Women's State Team Championship *continued*

4 Maryland 451; 5 Mississippi 456; 6 Florida 458; 7 New Jersey 461; 8 Hawaii 466; 9 Minnesota, New York 467; 11 South Carolina, California 468; 13 Arizona 470; 14 North Carolina, Connecticut 471; 16 Oregon 472; 17 Oklahoma 473; 18 Pennsylvania, Kansas 474; 20 Puerto Rico 475; 21 Alabama 477; 22 South Dakota 478; 23 Massachussetts 480; 24 Wisconsin 481; 25 Indiana 484; 26 Michigan, Washington 485; 28 Kentucky 487; 29 Colorado 489; 30 Utah, Louisiana 492; 32 Iowa 496; 33 Nebraska 499; 34 Ohio 501; 35 New Mexico 502; 36 Illinois 503; 37 Idaho 506; 38 Virginia 507; 39 Nevada 513; 40 Maine 516; 41 Arkansas 517; 42 Wyoming, West Virginia 518; 44 District of Columbia 519; 45 Delaware 429; 46 Rhode Island 540; 47 Missouri, Vermont 541; 49 Montana 550; 50 Alaska 555; 51 North Dakota 590

Australasia

Australian Women's Interstate Team Championship
for the Gladys Hay Memorial Cup   *The Western Australian GC, Yokine*

Day 1 – S. Australia 2½, Tasmania 2½; W. Australia 3½, Victoria 1½; New South Wales 4, Queensland 1
Day 2 – Queensland 1½. S. Australia 3½; New South Wales 3, W. Australia 2; Tasmania 0, Victoria 5
Day 3 – Queensland 0, W. Australia 5; Victoria 4, S. Australia 1; New South Wales 4½, Tasmania ½
Day 4 – W. Australia 3, Tasmania 2; S. Australia 0, New South Wales 5; Victoria 2, Queensland 3
Day 5 – Victoria ½, New South Wales 4½; Tasmania 2, Queensland 3; W. Australia 4½, S. Australia ½

Final table: 1 New South Wales – games won 21, matches won 5; 2 Western Australia 18–4; 3 Victoria 13–2; 4 Queensland 8½–2; South Australia 7½–1½; 6 Tasmania 7–½

Final: Western Australia 6. New South Wales 3; 3rd place play-off: Victoria 6, Queensland 3; 5th place play-off: South Australia 7, Tasmania 2

Winning team: Jessica Speechley, Whitney Harvey, Whitney Hiller, Rhianna Davies, MinJee Lee, Hayley Bettancourt

Europe

England Women's County Finals   *Thorndon Park*
Day 1:   Sussex (South) 2½, Lancashire (North) 6½
          Northamptonshire (Midlands South) 3, Gloucestershire (South West) 6
          Lincolnshire (Midlands North) 8, Hertfordshire (East) 1

Day 2:   Lincolnshire 9, Northamptonshire 0   Day 3:   Lincolnshire 6, Lancashire 3
          Lancashire 4½, Hertfordshire 4½   Sussex 8, Northamptonshire 1
          Gloucestershire 5, Sussex 4   Hertfordshire 3½, Gloucestershire 5½

Day 4:   Northamptonshire 4, Hertfordshire 5   Day 5:   Hertfordshire 3, Sussex 6
          Lancashire 6, Gloucestershire 3   Gloucestershire 3, Lincolnshire 6
          Sussex 4, Lincolnshire 5   Northamptonshire 1, Lancashire 8

Result: 1 Lincolnshire (5–34), 2 Lancashire (3½–28), 3 Gloucestershire (3–22½), 4 Sussex (2–24½), 5 Hertfordshire (1½–17), 6 Northamptonshire (0–9)

Winning team: Sophie Beardsall, Holly Clyburn, Helen Hewlett, Helen McDougall, Emily Slater, Emilee Taylor, Emma Tipping, Jess Wilcox

European Ladies Club Trophy   *Corfu GC, Greece*
1	Golf Club St Leon Rot (GER)	139-143-138—420
2	GC Basozabal (ESP)	146-145-143—434
3	GC Royal Park (ITA)	145-145-147—437

4 GC Noordwykse, GC Chechie 438; 6 Racing Club de France 440; 7 GC Rigenee 454; 8 GC Moscow City 459; 9 GC Reykjavik 467; 10 GC Zell am See 468; 11 GC Zurich 471; 12 GC Christnach 473; 13 GC Glyfada 478; 14 GC Tallinn 481; 15 GC Newport 490

Winning team: Karolin Lampert, Ann-Kathrin Lindner, Nicole Lingelbach
Individual: Ane Garcia Urchegui (Basazabal) 69-71-66—206

Women's GB&I Internationals *Hillside*

Day 1:   Scotland 4, Ireland 5; England 6, Wales 3
Day 2:   Wales 6, Ireland 3; England 6, Scotland 3
Day 3:   Ireland 1, England 8; Scotland 4, Wales 5

Result: 1 England 20; 2 Wales 14; 3 Scotland 11; 4 Ireland 7

Winning Team: Holly Clyburn (Woodhall Spa), Charlotte Ellis (Minchinhampton), Georgia Hall (Remedy Oak), Charley Hull (Woburn), Bronte Law (Bramhall), Kelly Tidy (Royal Birkdale), Lauren Taylor (Woburn), Charlotte Wild (Mere)

History: England have been champions 40 times, Scotland 15, Ireland 4 and Wales twice. There have been three ties, once between England and Scotland, once between England, Scotland and Ireland and once between Scotland and Ireland.

European Ladies Team Championship (Inaugurated 1959) *Murhof, Frohnleiten, Austria*

Strokeplay Qualification: 1 Germany 705; 2 Denmark 707; 3 Spain 722

Individual: 1 Leona Maguire (IRL)   72-64—136
　　　　　　 2 Marta Silva (ESP)   68-69—137
　　　　　　 Daisy Nielsen (DEN)   68-69—137
　　　　　　 Stephanie Kirchmayr (GER) 72-65—137

Final Team Placings: 1 Sweden; 2 Spain; 3 Germany; 4 Belgium; 5 England; 6 France; 7 Denmark; 8 Ireland; 9 Scotland; 10 Finland; 11 Austria; 12 Netherlands; 13 Italy; 14 Switzerland; 15 Czech Rep.; 16 Iceland; 19 Wales; 18 Slovenia; 19 Norway; 20 Russia

Winning team: Daniela Holmqvist, Josephine Janson, Nathalie Månsson, Madelene Sagström, Amanda Sträng, Johanna Tillström

Team Results:

"A Flight" – Day One: Germany 4, France 3; Sweden 5, Ireland 2; Spain 5, England 2; Belgium 4, Denmark 3. *Day Two:* Sweden 4, Germany 3; Spain 4½, Belgium 2½; France 3, Ireland 2; England 3, Denmark 2. *Day Three – Final:* Sweden 5, Spain 2; Germany 4, Belgium 3; England 3½, France 1½; Denmark 3, Ireland 2

"B Flight" – Day One: Netherlands 3, Czech Rep. 2; Scotland 4, Switzerland 1; Finland 4½, Iceland ½; Austria 3, Italy 2. *Day Two:* Scotland 4, Netherlands 1; Finland 3, Austria 2; Switzerland 4, Czech Rep. 1; Italy 3, Iceland 2. *Day Three:* Scotland 3, Finland 2; Austria 3, Netherlands 2; Italy 3, Switzerland 2; Czech Rep. 3½, Iceland 1½

"C Flight": Wales 4, Slovenia 1; Norway 4, Russia 1; Slovenia 5, Russia 0; Wales 4, Norway 1; Wales 3, Russia 2; Slovenia 3, Norway 2

History: England have won the event eight times, France on six occasions, Sweden six times. Spain four times, Ireland and Germany twice and Belgium has been successful on one occasion.

European Senior Women's Team Championship *Blacksearama, Bulgaria*

Stroke Play: 1 France 787; 2 Germany 788; 3 Spain 798; 4 Sweden 800; 5 Belgium 806; 6 Italy 808; 7 Switzerland 822; 8 Austria 823; 9 Netherlands 831; 10 Finland 875

Individual: 1 Virginie Burrus (FRA) 74-74—148; 2 Maria Orueta (ESP) 74-78—152, Isabelle Dumont (BEL) 72-80—152

Match Play:

Semi-finals: France 3½, Sweden 1½; Spain 3½, Germany 1½

Third place play-off: Germany 3. Sweden 2.

Final: France 3. Spain 2

Final ranking: 1 France; 2 Spain, 3 Germany; 4 Sweden; 5 Italy; 6 Belgium; 7 Switzerland; 8 Austria; 9 Finland; 10 Netherlands

Winning team: Helene Dutertre, Khadija Boutahehicht, Carine Bourdy, Cecilia Mourgue D'Algue, Laurence Rozner and Virginie Burrus

Jamboree (Ladies Veterans) *Wellingborough*

Day One: North 3½, South 5½
Scotland 6, Midlands 1
Day Two: North 4½, Scotland 4½
South 3½, Midlands 5½
Day Three: Midlands 5½, North 3½
Scotland ½, South 8½

Result: 1 South 2 pts; 2 Midlands 2 pts; 3 Scotland 1½ pts; 4 North ½ pt

Winning team: Cathy Armstrong, Irene Brien, Carole Caldwell, Rosie Hockey, Lulu Housman, Jennie O'Keeffe, Chris Quinn, Carole Weir

11th Ladies Veterans Match (for the Mary McKenna Trophy) *Craigielaw, Scotland*

Scotland 5½, Ireland 6½

Winning team: Pat Doran, Niamh Giblin, Valerie Hassett, Helen Jones, Mairead MacNamara, Violet McBride, Sheena McElroy, Phil O'Gorman

Senior Home Internationals (Sue Johnson Cup) *Tramore*

Day 1: Wales 0, England 8
Ireland 5, Scotland 3
Day 2: Scotland 1, England 7
Ireland 5, Wales 3
Day 3: England 4, Ireland 3
Wales 2½, Scotland 4½

Result: 1 England 19; 2 Ireland 13; 3 Scotland 8½; 4 Wales 5½

Winning team: Rozalyn Adams (Addington Court), Felicity Christine (Woking), Susan Dye (Delamere Forest), Caroline Marron (Bromborough), Janet Melville (Sherwood Forest), Bev New (Lansdown), Christine Quinn (Hockley)

Scottish Ladies County Championship (inaugurated 1992) *Dumfries & County*

Day 1: Midlothian 6, Ayrshire 3
Perth & Kinross 2½, Dumfriesshire 6½
Day 2: Perth & Kinross 2½, Midlothian 6½
Dumfriesshire 2½, Ayrshire 6½
Day 3: Ayrshire 3½, Perth & Kinross 2½
Dumfriesshire 4, Midlothian 2

Result: 1 Midlothian 2 (14½); 2 Dumfriesshire 2 (13); 3 Ayrshire 2 (13); 4 Perth & Kinross 0 (7½)

Heavy rain; singles only on third day.

Winning team: Linda Bain, Kirsten Blackwood, Gabrielle Macdonald, Kate McIntosh, Karen Marshall, Wendy Nicholson, Sally Shepherd, Jane Turner

History: East Lothian have won 5 times, Northern Counties 3, Fife and Midlothian 2, Dunbartonshire & Ayrshire, Stirlingshire & Clackmannanshire and Renfrewshire 1

Welsh Ladies County Championship *Aberdovey*

Final: Mid Wales beat Monmouthshire 7½–1½

Winning team: Sharon Roberts (captain); Judith Davies, Sherrie Edwards, Jill Evans, Julie McAloon, Sara Rees-Evans, Sally Wilkinson

Welsh Ladies Team Championship (inaugurated 1992) *Monmouthshire*

Semi-Finals: Haverfordwest beat Whitchurch 4-1
Newport beat Tenby 3-2
Final: Newport beat Haverfordwest 4-1
Winning team: Ceri Waite (non-playing captain); Mallory Armstrong, Jessica Evans, Lauren Hillier, Jean O'Connor, Christine Rossiter, Judith Wenman

Women's GB&I Internationals *Hillside*

Day 1: Scotland 4, Ireland 5
England 6, Wales 3
Day 2: Wales 6, Ireland 3
England 6, Scotland 3
Day 3: Ireland 1, England 8
Scotland 4, Wales 5

Result: 1 England 20; 2 Wales 14; 3 Scotland 11; 4 Ireland 7

Winning Team: Holly Clyburn (Woodhall Spa), Charlotte Ellis (Minchinhampton), Georgia Hall (Remedy Oak), Charley Hull (Woburn), Bronte Law (Bramhall), Kelly Tidy (Royal Birkdale), Lauren Taylor (Woburn), Charlotte Wild (Mere)

History: England have been champions 40 times, Scotland 15, Ireland 4 and Wales twice. There have been three ties, once between England and Scotland, once between England, Scotland and Ireland and once between Scotland and Ireland.

Five named for US Curtis Cup side at Nairn in June

Five of the eight players to represent the USA in the 2012 Curtis Cup at Nairn Golf club from June 8–10 have been named.

They are: Amy Anderson (19), of Oxbow, North Dakota; Lindy Duncan (20), of Fort Lauderdale, Florida; Austin Ernst (19), of Seneca, South Carolina; Tiffany Lua (20), of Rowland Heights, California; and Brooke Pancake (21), of Chattanooga, Tennessee.

The USA, who won the 2010 Match at Essex County Club in Manchester-by-the-Sea, Massachusetts 12½–7½, will be captained this year by Dr Patricia Cornett who said:

"I am thrilled that these five outstanding young women are on the team. I have had the great pleasure of watching these players over the past year and am confident they will represent the USA in exemplary fashion. I congratulate each on this wonderful and well-deserved honour."

Anderson, a junior at North Dakota State University, won the 2009 US Girls' Junior Championship and was among the first-round leaders at the 2011 US Women's Open Championship, where she finished as the fourth-lowest amateur.

Duncan, a junior at Duke University, was a semi-finalist in the 2006 US Women's Amateur at the age of 15. She also finished as second-lowest amateur at the 2011 Women's Open, and is a two-time National Golf Coaches Association All-American and two-time Atlantic Coast Conference Player of the Year.

Ernst, a sophomore at Louisiana State University, took the individual title at the 2011 NCAA Division I Championship, becoming the first freshman to win in 13 years. She also advanced to the semi-finals at the 2011 US Women's Amateur Championship.

Lua, a junior at UCLA, compiled a 1-2-0 record in the 2010 Curtis Cup Match. She also helped UCLA capture the 2011 NCAA Division I Women's Golf Championship, and was a semi-finalist at the 2011 US Women's Amateur Public Links Championship.

Pancake, a senior at the University of Alabama, advanced to the semi-finals of the 2011 US Women's Amateur and is a three-time NGCA All-American Scholar.

All five players named to the USA Curtis Cup Team finished within the top 20 at the 2011 NCAA Division I Championship. Duncan, Ernst and Pancake were named to the 2011 NGCA All-American first team, while Anderson and Lua received second-team honours.

The USA team has won the last seven matches and leads the series, 27–6 with three drawn games.

Other Tournaments 2011

For past winners see earlier editions of *The R&A Golfer's Handbook*

Astor Salver (inaugurated 1951)   *always at The Berkshire*
Charlotte Ellis (Minchinhampton)   73-68—141   tie
Rachel Lewis (Llanishen)   70-71—141

Bridget Jackson Bowl (inaugurated 1982)   *always at Handsworth*
Katherine O'Connor (Tadmarton Heath)   68-70—138

British Universities Championship   *West Lancashire*
Kelsey MacDonald (Stirling)   75-70-70-74—289

Critchley Salver (inaugurated 1982)   *always at Sunningdale*
Rachel Goodall (Heswall)   77-73—150   countback

Hampshire Rose (inaugurated 1973)   *always at North Hants*
Ashleigh Greenham (West Essex)   73-72—145

Greater Building Society Ladies Lake Macquarie Championship   *Belmont*
Breanna Elliott (VIC)   75-73-74-74—296

The Leveret (inaugurated 1986)   *always at Formby*
Brogan Townend   68-68—136

Liphook Scratch Cup (inaugurated 1992)   *always at Liphook*
Charlotte Thompson (Channels)   73-71—144

London Ladies Foursomes   *The Berkshire*
Final: The Berkshire (Alex Peters, Heidi Baek) beat Sundridge Park 3 and 1

Mackie Bowl (inaugurated 1974)   *always at Gullane No 1*
Rebecca Wilson (Grange)*   75-68—143
Beat Connie Jaffrey (Troon Ladies) with a better second round

Mothers and Daughters Foursomes   27-hole event   *Royal Mid-Surrey*
Elaine and Charlotte Barrow (Brokenhurst Manor)   114

Munross Trophy (inaugurated 1986)   *always at Montrose Links*
Rebecca Wilson (Grange)   70-73—143

Peugeot LGU Coronation Foursomes   *St Andrews (Eden)*
Cath Arter and Alison Mason (Rothley Park, Leicester) 36 pts

Pleasington Putter (inaugurated 1995)   *always at Pleasington*
Katherine O'Connor (Tadmarton Heath)   74-71—145

Riccarton Rose Bowl (inaugurated 1970)   *always at Hamilton*
Cancelled

Roehampton Gold Cup (inaugurated 1926)   *always at Roehampton*
(This event has included women professionals since 1982 and has been an open event since 1987)
Rachel Drummond (Beaconmsfield)   72-71—143

Royal Birkdale Scratch Trophy (inaugurated 1984)   *always at Royal Birkdale*
Charlotte Wild (Mere)   73-68—141

St Rule Trophy (inaugurated 1984)   *always at St Andrews (Old and New)*
Very strong winds caused the two rounds on the Old Course to be abandoned. The result was declared by countback of the Saturday's round on the New Course
Ashley Ona (AUS)   73

The International Trophy was won by Australia (A Ona, B Elliott, and Whitney Hillier)

Scottish Ladies Foursomes   *Glenbervie*
Stroke Play
Elaine Allison (Stirling) and Jill Meldrum (Dullatur)   77

Match Play
Final: Crichton (Rachel Walker and Amy Little) beat Direleton Castle (Hazel Saunders and Terry Reekie) 6 and 3

Scottish Universities Championship   *Moray GC, Lossiemouth*
Susan Jackson (Edinburgh)   78-72-79-68—297

SLGA Commonwealth Spoons   *Forres GC*
Mhairi Hall & Margaret McFarlane (Stirling & Clackmannan)   73

SLGA Silver and Bronze Medals   *Crieff GC*
Silver: **Bronze:**
Marsha Hull (Strathaven)   69   Leanne Wilson (Kelso)   78

Tenby Ladies Open (inaugurated 1994)   *always at Tenby*
Katherine O'Connor (Tadmarton Heath)   69-76—145

Worplesdon Mixed Foursomes (inaugurated 1921)   *always at Worplesdon, Surrey*
Final: Laura Webb and David Cowap (East Berkshire) beat Harriett & Giles Legg (Ferndown)

What is the answer?

Q: After I replaced my ball and removed my ball-marker, but before I addressed the ball, the ball moved. What is the Ruling?

A: As wind is not an outside agency, there is no requirement to replace the ball and the ball must be played from its new position. However, there must be strong evidence that you did not cause the ball to move yourself.

University and School Events 2011

Canadian University and Colleges Championship *Royal Ashburn CC, Ontario*

1	University of British Colombia	314-331-319-320—1,284
2	University of Victoria	324-319-321-321—1,285
3	University of Waterloo	343-349-339-340—1,371

Winning team: Kylie Barras, Janelle Samoluk, Haley Cameron, Vanessa Leon and Lindsay Manion

Individual:

1	Kylie Barras (British Colombia)	77-79-76-74—306
2	Anne Balser (Victoria)	79-75-79-82—315
3	Megan Woodland (Victoria)	82-81-80-77—320
	Alyssa Herkel (Victoria)	81-78-81-80—320

13th World Universities Golf Championship *Antiquera Golf, Malaga, Spain*

1	France	146-150-150-152—598
2	Chinese Taipei	145-158-152-149—604
3	USA	150-156-145-154—605

4 Spain 611; 5 Italy 614; 6 Great Britain 620; 7 Japan 622; 8 Canada 626; 9 South Africa 628; 10 Czech Republic 633; 11 China 641; 12 Ireland 646; 13 Australia 656; 14 Thailand 659

Winning team: Morgane Bazin de Jessay, Margot Coulaud Ivanoff and Manon Ricordeau

Individual winner: Catherine O'Donnell (USA) 75-70-71-74—290

British Universities Golf Championship *West Lancashire GC*

1	Kelsey MacDonald (Stirling)	75-70-70-74—289
2	Jane Turner (Robert Gordon's)	80-78-76-72—306
3	Gemma Bradbury (St Andrews)	76-74-82-78—310

Month by month in 2011

A good month for the United States after their defeats in the Walker and Solheim Cups in September. They retain the Presidents Cup at Royal Melbourne with a 19-15 win, then Matt Kuchar and Gary Woodland come from behind Irish duo Rory McIlroy and Graeme McDowell to capture the World Cup in China. Victory in the WGC–HSBC Champions in Shanghai, though, goes to Martin Kaymer after a back nine 29.

County and other Regional Championships 2011

England

Bedfordshire: Sally Shayler
Berkshire: Elspeth Cooper
Buckinghamshire:
 Jessica Burrows
Cambridgeshire &
 Huntingdonshire: Amy Rae
Cheshire: Natalie Lowe
Cornwall: Sarah-Jane Boyd
Cumbria: Melanie Temple
Derbyshire: Catrin Russell
Devon: Jessica Bradley
Dorset: Sophie Keech
Durham: Rebecca Horner
East Region: Amber Ratcliffe
Essex: Daisy Dyer
Gloucestershire: Bethan Popel
Hampshire: Becky Scott

Hertfordshire: Ella Ofstedahl
Kent: Jessica Gregory
Lancashire: Emma Harris
Leicestershire & Rutland:
 Tracy Bourne
Lincolnshire: Emilee Taylor
Middlesex: Tara Watters
Midlands North Region:
 Lorraine Howd
Midlands South Region:
 Yvonne Sutcliffe
Norfolk: Amber Ratclliffe
Northamptonshire:
 Alison Knowles
Northern Region:
 Alison Knowles
Northumberland: Ami Storey

Nottinghamshire: Emma Howie
Oxfordshire:
 Katherine O'Connor
Shropshire: Anna Smith
Somerset: Amanda Mayne
South Region: Chris Foran
South West Region:
 Bunty Purbrick
Staffordshire: Julie Brown
Suffolk: Blaize Esmond
Surrey: Lisa McGowan
Sussex: Stacey Rodger
Warwickshire: Lisa Burton
Wiltshire: Sarah Gee
Worcestershire &
 Herefordshire:
 Karen Greenfield

Ireland

Connacht: Sarah Faller
East Leinster: Paula Grant

Mid Leinster: Emma Murphy
Munster: Tara Gribben

Ulster: Louise Coffey

Scotland

Yorkshire: Rebecca Wood
Aberdeenshire: Donna Pocock
Angus: Ailsa Summers
Ayrshire: Rachael McQueen
Border Counties: Ailsa Bain
Dumfriesshire: Jordana Graham
Dunbartonshire and Argyll:
 Nichola Ferguson
East Lothian: Clara Young
Eastern Division: Midlothian
 (team); Louise Kenny (ind)

Fife: Louise Kenney
Galloway: Gillian Monteith
Lanarkshire: Rachael Taylor
Midlothian: Karen Marshall
Northern Counties: Jenny Milne
Northern Division: Perth and
 Kinross (team); Laura Murray
 (ind)
Perth and Kinross:
 Nicola Robertson

North of Scotland:
 Laura Murray
Renfrewshire: Eilidh Briggs
Southern Division:
 Dumfriesshire (team);
 Jordana Graham (ind)
Stirling and Clackmannan:
 Louise MacGregor
Western Division: Ayrshire
 (team); Eilidh Briggs (ind)
County winners: Midlothian

Wales

Brecon and Radnor: *not available*
Caernarfonshire & Anglesey: Amy Boulden
Denbighshire & Flintshire: Jo Nicolson

Glamorgan County: Georgia Lewis
Mid-Wales: Sara Rees-Evans
Monmouthshire: Sara Rees-Evans

Dan Jenkins to be inducted into World Golf Hall of Fame

Journalist Dan Jenkins, a legendary golf writer, humorist, commentator and critic from time to time is to be inducted into the World Golf Hall of Fame later this year in the life-time achievement category.

PGA Tour commissioner Tim Finchem making the announcement said "Dan started writing professionally right out of high school. A former columnist for *Sports Illustrated* and *Golf Digest* he also wrote a number of books, three novels that have been made into motion pictures – *Semi Tough* (a number one bestseller), *Dead Perfect* and *Baja Oklahoma*.

"He has covered more than 200 major championships in golf, including over 60 Masters and has been a recipient of the PGA of America's Lifetime Achievement Award in Journalism. In 2005, the Golf Writers Association of America bestowed upon him the William Richardson Award for outstanding contributions to golf.

"Dan has had a spectacular career, and I think I should note that over the years the World Golf Hall of Fame has been very sparse in their recognition of people from Dan's craft, only recognizing the very, very best. I think it's appropriate that Dan take his place on that list".

In response Jenkins said: "I'm delighted and flattered and overwhelmed to take a spot in there with my old friends Herbert Warren Wind and Herb Graffis and people like that who actually covered the sport. I wish I had known Bernard Darwin, but I came along too late for him.

"What can I say? It sounds like I retired, but I haven't. I'm going to stay at it as long as they'll have me or until I'm carried out. I'll be carried out with the typewriter.

"I have gone through the age of faxing, and now I'm in the computer age, and the tweeting age. Even though I was making a stab at humour, I don't think I ever wrote a line I didn't believe. I tried not to draw too much blood. I tried to rave about all the heroes of the game who deserved and earned it."

Asked about the great tournaments he has reported on Jenkins recalled: "The most talked about and the most electrifying at its time was Arnold Palmer at Cherry Hills in the US Open of 1960, when I think I was the first to notice that there was a confluence of three eras of golf coming together – the then current king, Arnold Palmer, the past king Ben Hogan, and the future king, Jack Nicklaus who was yet an amateur. The three of them battled it out over the last 18.

"I'd never experienced, even as a good old, cynical writer, as much excitement with Arnold Palmer winning the title with a six under par 65 in the last round, passing 14 players and coming from seven strokes back, it was unbelievable.

"There have been so many great moments in golf that you even forget some of them. But that one still stands out. When people say, 'What was the greatest day?' I had a lot of great days with Ben Hogan. My first Open that I covered was the 1951 Open at Oakland Hills and Ben shot that 67 in the last round, which was about as good a round of golf on the most difficult golf course in the world.

"Oakland Hills was set up for that Open more like a penitentiary than a golf course. The joke was you had to walk sideways down the fairways to keep the rough from snagging your trousers. In addition Trent Jones put in so many bunkers in the middle of the fairways and the greens were so fast. It was tough.

"Those two days are right in there … and I think Jack Nicklaus winning his sixth Masters in 1986. It's awful hard to avoid that. But there have been so many great tournaments that I've been privileged to see and people paid me to go watch, that I'm awfully grateful for it, and I'm so happy that I chose the profession I did."

PART VI

Mixed Men's and Women's Amateur Tournaments

For past results see earlier editions of *The R&A Golfer's Handbook*

European Nations Cup (formerly the Sherry Cup) *Sotogrande, Spain*

Men:

1	Julien Brun (FRA)	281
2	Lukas Nemecz (AUT)	284
3	Laurie Canter (ENG)	285
	Dermot McElroy (IRL)	285

Team event:

1 England 852; 2 France 854; 3 Spain 855: 4 Scotland 864; 5 Denmark, Ireland 870; 7 Italy 871; 8 Wales 874; 9 Germany 881; 10 Netherlands 883 11 Austria 884; 12 Portugal 899; 13 Belgium 901; 14 Finland 903; 15 Sweden 906; 16 Norway 915; 17 Switzerland 917; 18 Turkey 927; 19 Slovenia 941

Winning Team: Laurie Canter, Tom Lewis, Jack Senior, Andy Sullivan

Women:

1	Camilla Hedberg (ESP)	291
2	Lara Katzy (GER)	297
3	Mireia Prat (ESP)	298

Team event:

1 Spain 590; 2 Belgium 599; 3 Germany 600; 4 Sweden 608; 5 France 611; 6 Italy 613; 7 Wales 619; 8 Netherlands 623; 9 Finland 625; 10 Slovenia 639

Winning Team: Noemi Jiménez, Camilla Hedberg, Mireia Prat

Spirit International

Whispering Pines, Houston, TX

Team competition:

1	USA	133-144-135-133—545 (Kelly Kraft, Nathan Smith, Austin Ernst and Emily Tubart)
2	Mexico	139-145-137-134—555 (Carlos Ortiz, Sebastian Vazquez, Alejandra Lianeza and Gabriela Lopez)
	Argentina	139-142-135-139—555 (Franco Romero, Jorge Valdes, Manuela Carbajo Re and Victoria Tanco)

4 Korea 556; 5 Japan, South Africa, Germany 562; 8 Denmark 564; 9 Canada, Sweden 565; 11 France 567; 12 Italy, England 569; 14 Australia, Colombia 571; 16 Belgium 573; 17 Ireland 575; 18 Switzerland 580; 19 Norway 592; 20 China 666

Men's competition:

1	USA	64-73-69-64—270 (Kelly Kraft and Nathan Smith)
2	Canada	64-68-69-71—272 (Mackenzie Hughes and Garrett Rank)
	Mexico	69-71-67-65—272 (Carlos Ortiz and Sebastian Vasquez)

4 Japan 273; 5 South Africa 274; 6 Australia 275; 7 Germany 278; 8 Denmark, Ireland, Italy, Sweden 280; 12 Argentina, France 281; 14 Korea 283; 15 Belgium 285; 16 England 286.; 17 Switzerland 287; 18 Colombia 290; 19 Norway 295; 20 China 355

Women's competition:

1	Korea	68-70-67-68—273 (Kim Hya-Joo and Baek Kyu-Jung)
2	Argentina	69-68-67-70—274 (Manuela Carbajo Re and Victoria Tanco)
3	USA	69-71-66-69—275 (Austin Ernst and Emily Tubert)

4 Colombia 281; 5 England, Mexico 283; 7 Denmark, Germany 284; 9 Sweden 285; 10 France 286; 11 Belgium, South Africa 288; 13 Italy, Japan 289; 15 Canada, Switzerland 293; 17 Ireland 295; 18 Australia 296; 19 Norway 297; 20 China 311

22nd Grand Prix Chiberta *Chiberta, Biarritz* [6690–70]

Men:

1	Thomas Elissalde (Biarritz) (FRA)	69-65-75-68—277
2	Brice Chanfreau (Hossegor) (FRA)	69-64-73-72—278
3	Victor Perez (Biarritz) (FRA)	70-71-71-67—279

Women:

1	Celia Barquin Arozmena (ESP)	72-71-72-70—285
2	Teresa Caballer (ESP)	74-72-71-69—286
	Ana Arrese (ESP)	71-70-73-72—286

Challenge International de la Ville d'Anglet *Golf de Chiberta, Anglet*

Men:

1	France 2*	139-135—274	(Thomas Elissalde, Hugo Rouillon, Pierre-Henri Leclerc)
2	France 1	139-135—274	
3	England 2	138-140—278	

Women:

1	Spain 1	146-140—286	(Belen Buendia, Ane Urchegui, Elia Folch)
2	France 1	143-144—287	
3	Spain 2	146-144—290	

Copa Los Andes *Gavea GC, Rio de Janiero, Brazil*

Men's competition

1 Brazil 7 pts; 2 Colombia, Argentina, Venezuela, Chile 6 pts; 6 Peru, Equador 2 pts; 8 Bolivia 1 pt; 9 Uruguay 0 pts

Winning team: Rafael Becker, Daniel Staff, Felipe Navarro, Guy Bragance and Pedro Costa Lima

Women's competition

1 Colombia 14pts; 2 Peru 13 pts; 3 Argentina 12 pts; 4 Brazil 10 pts; 5 Paraguay, Equador 7pts; 7 Venezuela 4 pts; 8 Uruguay 3 pts; 9 Chile 2 pts

Winning team: Luz Alejandra Cangrejo, Maribel Lopez, Laura Blanco, Daniela Ordonez, Natalia Nicholls

South-East Asia Amateur Team Championships *Clearwater Bay, Hong Kong*

51st Putra Cup (men)

1	Singapore	215-214-201-216—846
2	Hong Kong	217-207-208-219—851
3	Indonesia	210-215-216-219—860

4 Malaysia 862; 5 Thailand 880; 6 Philippines 883; 7 Myanmar 885

Winning team: Singapore – Choo Tze Huang, Gregory Foo, Jerome Ng and Marc Ong

Indvidual: 1 Choo Tze Huang (SIN) 72-71-67-71—281

5th Lion City Cup (boys under 18)

1	Thailand	215-214-220-220—869
2	Malaysia	226-213-214-220—873
3	Indonesia	220-219-223-226—888

4 Philippines 901; 5 Singapore 904; 6 Hong Kong 937

Winning team: Chanchok Deipiratanamongkol, Pariwat Pinsawat, Somprad Rattanasuwan and Aussarassakorn Voramate

Individual: 1 Khai Jei Low (MAS) 73-71-70-72—286

3rd Santi Cup (women)

1	Thailand	210-208-214-220—852
2	Philippines	207-209-213-224—853
3	Malaysia	221-221-212-223—877

4 Hong Kong 880; 5 Singapore 883; 6 Indonesia 916

Winning team: Pinrath Loomboonruang, Panitta Yusabai, Pavarisa Yoktuan and Wad Phaewchimple

Individual: Pinrath Loomboonruang (THA) 67-69-68-72—276

Who is known as "Boom Boom"?

The answer can be found on page 905

Asian Games

The next staging of this event (the 17th) will be held between September 18 to October 4, 2014 in Incheon, South Korea

Pan Arab Championship *Dar Es-Salam GC, Rabat, Morocco*

Men's competition:

Gold	Mohammad Belaroussia (MAR)	301
Silver	El-Mehedy El Sayessy (MAR)	303
Bronze	Hamad Mubarak (BRN)	304

Ladies' competition:

Gold	Houria Al-Habadi (MAR)
Silver	Nadia Al-Tabba (MAR)
Bronze	Firial Shaheed (TUN)

Youths' competition:

Gold	Hassan Almusharrekh (UAE)	214
Silver	Ayoub Elguirati (MAR)	219
Bronze	Amin Elmalke (MAR)	220

Twelve-year-old golfer Julia wins gold for Kuwait

Julia Al-Humoud may only be 12-years-old but she has already won the 2011 Kuwait Women's Championship and at the 31st Pan Arab Golf Championship playing on the demanding Dar Es-Salam course in Rabat, Morocco, she walked away with a gold medal.

Up against golfers much older than herself she had rounds of 90, 86 and 83 for 259 to finish fifth in the Ladies gross scores section behind Houria Al Abadi but in the nett competition Julia emerged triumphant giving Kuwait a first-ever golfing gold medal.

Kuwaiti Golf Federation treasurer Abdulaziz Al-Mulla, who headed the Kuwaiti team, praised the youngster's performance which, he said, was a result of all the hard work she had put in not least her daily practice sessions and her work with the Kuwaiti Golf Youth programme.

Another 12-year-old Kuwaiti, Ali Al-Anasari who is also benefitting from the Youth scheme, competed in the Youths competition as a member of Kuwait's eight strong team.

The next Pan Arab event, which last year involved 14 teams from Algeria, Bahrain, Egypt, Kuwait, Lebanon, Libya, Oman, Palestine, Qatar, Saudi Arabia, Syria, Tunisia, the United Arab Emirates and hosts Morocco, will be staged in Beirut, Lebanon.

PART VII

Amateur Golf
Around the World

Amateur Golf Around the World

Results from organisations affiliated to The R&A and the USGA

For results marked [1], [2], [3] or [4], further details can be found on pages 305–314, 396–402, 450–453 and 457–458

Players are from the host nation unless stated

Africa

Botswana
Population: 1.98m   Golf Courses: 10
Men's Champion: Charlton Makoko

Egypt
Population: 84.47m   Golf Courses: 14
Egyptian Closed Championship: Mohamed Farouk
Egyptian Men's Open Championship: Amr Abou El
Ela, Ramy Taher
Women's Champion: Sophie Issa
Junior Champion (Boys): Saif Tarraff (12+); Anas Amin
(11 and under)
Junior Champion: Naomi Roos (11 and under)

Kenya
Population: 40.86m
Men's Stroke Play Champion: David Opati
Men's Match Play Champion: James Karanja
Junior Champion (Boys): Daniel Nduva

South Africa
Population: 50.49m
Golfers: 500,000   Golf Courses: 451
Men's Match Play Champion: Michael Stewart (SCO)
beat Paul Shields 5 and 4[1]
Men's Stroke Play Champion: Jared Harvey[1]
Women's Stroke Play Champion: Kim Williams
Women's Match Play: Final – Iliska Verwey beat
Nobuhle Diamini 3 and 2
Mid-Amateur Champion (Men) – East London GC:
Denis Jones 239
Mid-Amateur Champion (Women): Sandra Winter
Mid-Amateur Test Match: Windhoek, Namibia –
Namibia 4, South Africa 14 (Winning team: South
Africa: Jose Fourie (capt), Gerry Coetzee, Lyall
McNeil, Neil Homann, Rowan du Preez and Hugo
Delport)
Senior Champion (Women): Carina Theron[2]
Junior Champion (Girls): Bianca Theron (Boland)
293
Provincial Championships:
Boland Open – Arabella GC: Haydn Porteous 207
Boland Junior Championship – Pearl GC: Bianca
Theron 138
Border Open – East London: Shaun Smith

43rd Border Stroke Play Championship – East
London GC: Kim Williams 145
43rd Border Match Play Championship: Bertine
Strauss beat Michaela Fletcher 4 and 2
Cape Province Open – George and Kingswood:
Rickus Nortje
Country District Championship – Deveronvale
GC: 1 Free State and North Cape; 2 Boland; 3
KwaZulu Natal
Winning team: Riaan Coetzee, Pieter Cronje, Rudi
du Plessis, Heinrich Eraasmus, Kobus Moolman,
Marius Nel, Abrie Swanepoel, Desne Van de Berg
Eastern Cape Stroke Play Championship –
Humewood: Kim Williams 143
Eastern Province and Border Open – Fish River
Sun: Philip Kruse 214
Eastern Province Open – Port Elizabeth: Ray
Taverner
Free State and Northern Cape Open –
Bloemfontein: Daniel Hammond 273
Free State and Northern Cape Championship –
Sand River GC: Bertine Strauss 211
Free State and Northern Cape Junior
Championship – Sand River GC: Bianca Theron
224
Gauteng North Open – Pecanwood GC: Jaco
Mouton 274
Gauteng Stroke Play Championship – Randpark GC
(Windsor course): Kim Williams 142
Gauteng Match Play Championship – Randpark GC:
Monique Smit beat Bertine Strauss 4 and 3
Gauteng North Junior Championship – Wingate
Park GC: Olivia Le Roux 71
Indwe South African Interprovincial Championship
– Parys GC: 1 Western Province 1,777; 2 Central
Gauteng 1,799; 3 Gauteng North A 1,805
Winning team: Francois Le Roux, Andrew
Cleophas, Hennan September, Mark Hair, Joseph
Skebotha, Jannie Strydom, Tony Bailey, Brian
Mampies
Individual champion: David Stratton 286
Kingswood Mid Amateur (Women): Sandra Winter
KwaZulu Natal Mid-Amateur Championship:
Barry McGhee
KwaZulu Natal Open – San Lameer GC: Coenie
Bester 279

KwaZulu Natal Stroke Play – Beachwood: Shaun Smith
KwaZulu Natal Match Play – Beachwood: Michael Hollick
Limpopo Open: Brandon Stone
Lowveld Mid-Amateur Championship: Clifton Stanley
Limpopo Noom: Haydn Porteous
Mpumalanga Open – Middleburg: Hendre Celliers
Nedbank Eastern Cape Stroke Play Championship – Hume Wood GC: Kim Williams 143
Nomads SA Under-16 Stroke Play Championship: Zander Lombard
Nomads SA Under-19 Stroke Play Championship: Stefan Cronje
Nomads SA Under-19 Match Play Championship: Victor Lange
Northern Amateur Stroke Play Championship – Windsor and Randpark: David Law (SCO) 202
Northern Amateur Match Play Championship – Windsor GC: David Law (SCO) beat Graham Van der Merwe 3 and 2
Northern Cape – Kimberley: Theunis Pieters
North West Mid-Amateur Championship: Hendrik Burger
North West Open – Potchefstroom CC: Brandon Stone 273
North West Championship – Rustenburg GC: 1 Alana van Greuning 144; 2 Nicole Becker 144
Prince's Grant– Prince's Grant: Brandon Stone
SA Boys Under-14 Championship: Tristan Strydom
South African Challenge Interprovincial Championship – Metropolitan: 1 Central Gauteng; 2 SA Juniors; 3 Gauteng North
Winning team: Sipho Bujela, Michael Dixon, Victor Lange, Thomas Lovett, Callum Mowat, Muzi Nethunzwi, Steohen Pienaar and Jonathan Raphunga
South African Men's Interprovincial Championship – Bloemfontein: 1 Central Gauteng; 2 Western Province; 3 Gauteng North
Winning team: Ruan de Smidt, Michael Dixon, Daniel Hammond, Callum Mowat, Damien Naicker, Muzi Nethunzwi, Haydn Porteous and Graham Van de Merwe[1]

South African Mid-Amateur Provincial Tournament – Humewood: 1 Kwazulu-Natal; 2 Central Gauteng; 3 Ekurheleni
Winning team: David Brown, Garry Coetzee, Sean Fenger, Murray Gilson, Elton James, Barry McGhee, Lyall McNeill and Simon Taylor
South African Under 23 Inter Provincial Championship – Goose Valley GC: 1 Central Gauteng; 2 Western Province; 3 KwaZulu Natal
Winning team: Jonathan Boas, Muziwalo Eleweni, Victor Lange, Jaco Mouton, Damian Naiker, Muziwalo Nethunzwi, Stephen Pienaar, Haydn Porteous and Graham Van de Merwe[1]
Southern Cape Open: CJ Du Plessis
Western Province Mid-Amateur Championship: Hugo Delport
Western Province Stroke Play Championship (Men) – Westlake GC: Jared Harvey 280
Western Province Stroke Play Championship (Women) – Clovelly CC: Iliska Verwey 142
Western Province Match Play Championship – Westlake GC: Graham Van der Merwe beat Jared Harvey 1 hole
Western Province Match Play Championship (Women) – Iliska Verwey beat Tiffany Avern-Taplin 4 and 3
Western Province Junior Championship – Durbanville GC: Lara Weinstein 144
WGSA Teams Championship (Swiss Team Trophy) – Langebaan GE: 1 Gauteng North "A" 581; 2 North West "A" 607; 3 Southern Cape "A", Mpumalanga 612
Winning team: Henriette Frylinck, Nobuhle Diamini, Kim Williams
Individual winner: Henriette Frylinck 77-68-71-72—288

Tanzania
Population: 45.04m   Golf Courses: 8
Men's Champion: David Opati (KEN)

Zimbabwe
Population: 12.64m
Women's Champion: Claire Minter[2]

Americas

Argentina
Population: 40.67m
Golfers: 100,000   Golf Courses: 310
Men's Match Play Champion: Daan Huizing (NED) beat Patricio Tolosa 9 and 7[1]
Men's Stroke Play Champion: Franco Romero
Women's Match Play Champion: Manuela Carbajo Re
Women's Stroke Play Champion: Maria Olivero
Mid-Amateur Champion (Men): Jose Manuel Alvarez Castro
Junior Champion (Boys): Alejandro Tosti
Junior Champion (Girls): Manuela Carbajo Re

Barbados
Population: 276,000   Golf Courses: 5
Men's Champion: James Johnson[1]

Bermuda
Population: 65,000
Golfers: 2,960   Golf Courses: 7
Men's Match Play Champion: Jarryd Dillas
Men's Open Stroke Play Champion: Scott Clark (USA)
Women's Match Play Champion: Tariqah Walikraam

Americas (continued)

Brazil
Population: 195.42m
Men's Champion: Rafael Becker
Women's Champion: Mariana de Biase
Junior Champion (Boys): Gustavo Chuang
Junior Champion (Girls): Paloma Vaccaro (PAR)
Regional championships:
Rio Grande: Felipe Lessa
Brasilia: Felipe Lessa
Parana (Men): Rodrigo Luiz Diniz
Parana (Women): Rodrigo Larissa Souza
Rio de Janeiro (Men): Tomaz Pimenta Pinheiro
Rio de Janeiro (Women): Tomaz Larissa Rocha
  Pombo
Rio de Janeiro Open: Leonardo Conrado
São Paulo (Men): Pedro Costa Lima
São Paulo (Women): Ruriko Nakamura
South: Eduardo Vasconcellos

Canada
Population: 33.89m
Golfers: 5.95m   Golf Courses: 2,400
Men's Champion: Mackenzie Hughes[1]
Women's Champion: Rebecca Lee-Bentham[2]
Mid-Amateur Champion (Men): Rob Couture (USA)
Senior Champion (Men): Chip Lutz (USA)[1]
Senior Champion (Women): Mary Ann Hayward[2]
Junior Champion (Boys): Kevin Kwan[3]
Junior Champion (Girls): Jennifer Yang
Canadian Universities/College Championship (Men):
  Mark Hoffman
Canadian Universities/College Championship
  (Women): Kylie Barros
Provincial Championships:
Alberta (Men) – Stoney Plain G&CC: Scott Stiles
  (Bearspaw) 277 (–11)
Alberta (Women) – Cottonwood G&CC: Nicole
  Zhang (Silver Springs) 277 (–7)
Alberta Junior Girls: Jennifer Ha
British Columbia (Men) – The Dunes, Kamloops:
  David Rose (West Vancouver) 275 (–13)
British Columbia (Women) – Alberni GC:
  Christina Proteau (Port Alberni) 290 (+6)
British Columbia Junior Girls: Jennifer Yang
Manitoba (Men) – Portage GC: Jesse Skelton
  (Breezy Bend CC) 270 (–10)
Manitoba (Women) – Tuelon G&CC: Jessie Choi
  (Southwood G&CC) 226 (+7)
Manitoba Women's Junior: Winnie Hyun
Newfoundland and Labrador (Men) – Bally Haly
  GC: Adam Stanley 149
Newfoundland and Labrador (Women) – Bally
  Haly GC: Allison Crawford 169
Ontario (Men) – Brampton GC: Mark Hoffman
  (Thornhill) 275 (–9)
New Brunswick (Men) – Royal Oaks GC: Mathieu
  Gingras (Moncton) 284 (–4)
New Brunswick (Women) – Aroostook Valley CC:
  Margo McLeod (Woodstock Golf and Curling)
  232 (+16)

New Brunswick Junior Girls: Morgan Matchett
Nova Scotia (Men) – Truro GC: Eric Banks (Truro)
  282 (–2)
Nova Scotia (Women) – Paragon G&CC: Ann
  Balser 228 (+12)
Nova Scotia Junior: Bernadette Little
Ontario (Women) – Cutten Fields GC: Augusta
  James (Loyalist CC) 213 (E)
Ontario Girls Championship: Brooke Henderson
Ontario Girls Match Play: Olivia Richards
Ontario Junior Spring Classic: Elizabeth Tong
Prince Edward Island (Men) – Belvedere GC: Chris
  Welton 137 (–7)
Quebec (Men) – Alpin GC: Nicolas Fortin (Levis)
  280 (E)
Quebec (Women) – Blainvillier CC: Anne-
  Catherine Tanquay (Royal Quebec) 229 (+13)
Quebec Junior Championship: Josee Doyon
Saskatchewan (Men) – The Legends GC:: Troy
  Bulmer (Saskatoon) 291 (+3)
Saskatchewan (Women) – Lloydminster GC: Anna
  Young (Saskatoon 297 (+4)

Chile
Population: 17.14m
Men's Match Play Champion: Matias Dominguez
Women's Champion: Paz Echeverria
Junior Champion (Boys): Juan Eduardo Cerda
Junior Champion (Girls): Delfina Acosta (ARG)

Colombia
Population: 46.30m
Men's Champion: Santiago Gomez
Women's Champion: Isabella Loza
Mid-Amateur Champion (Men): Juan Fernando Mejia
Mid-Amateur Champion (Women): Julie Pauline
  Saenz Starnes
Junior Champion (Boys): Ivan Camilo Ramirez
  (13–14); Matias Molina Tellez (15–17)
Junior Champion (Girls): Valentina Romero

Costa Rica
Population: 4.64m
Golfers: 3,500   Golf Courses: 11
Men's Match Play Champion: Jose Mendez
Women's Match Play Champion: Aideen Kellaghan
Junior Champion (Boys): Jose Mendez Vargas

Mexico
Population: 110.65m   Golf Courses: 150+
Men's Champion: Sebastian Vazquez[1]
Women's Champion: Margarita Ramos
Junior Champion (Boys): David Faraudo Godinez
Junior Champion (Girls): Gabriela Lopez

Peru
Population: 29.50m
Women's Champion: Maria Salinas
Junior Champion (Boys): Juan Alvarez (URU)
Junior Champion (Girls): Lucia Gutierrez

Puerto Rico
Population: 3.9m
Men's Champion: James White (USA)
Women's Champion: Stephanie Meadow (IRL)
Junior Champion (Boys): Jason Roets (RSA)
Junior Champion (Girls): Monifa Sealy (TRI)

Trinidad and Tobago
Population: 1.34m
Men's Champion: James Johnson (BAR)

Uruguay
Population: 3.37m
Men's Champion: Julien Duxin
Women's Champion: Manuela Barros
Boy's Champion: Juan Alvarez

USA
Population: 317.64m
Golfers: 26.2m   Golf Courses: 16,547
111th US Amateur Championship: Kelly Kraft beat
  Patrick Cantlay 2 holes[1]
111th US Women's Amateur Championship:
  Danielle Kang beat Moriya Jutanugarn (THA)
  6 and 5[2]
North and South Championships (Men): Jack Fields
  beat David Erdy 5 and 4
North and South Championships (Women):
  Danielle Kang beat Doris Chen 2 and 1

Mid-Amateur Champion (Men): Randal Lewis beat
  Kenny Cook 3 and 2[1]
Mid-Amateur Champion (Women): Ellen Port beat
  Martha Leach 2 and 1[2]
Senior Champion (Men): Louis Lee beat Philip Pleat
  1 hole[1]
Senior Champion (Women): Terri Frohnmayer beat
  Mina Hardin 2 and 1[2]
Junior Champion (Boys): Jordan Speith beat Chelso
  Barrett 6 and 5[3]
North and South Junior Championships (Boys):
  Chad Cox (Charlotte) 72-69-70—211
Junior Champion (Girls): Ariya Jutanugarn (THA)
  beat Dottie Ardina (PHI) 2 and 1
North and South Junior Championships (Girls):
  Kari Bellville (Granger) 64-73-73—210
US Amateur Public Links Championship (Men):
  Corbin Mills beat Jonathan Randolph at 37th[1]
US Amateur Public Links Championship (Women):
  Brianna Do beat Marissa Dodd 1 hole[2]
For US State championships see pages 316 and 403

Venezuela
Population: 29.04m
Men's Champion: Felipe Velazquez
Junior Champion (Boys): Manuel Torres
Junior Champion (Girls): Ana Raga

Asia

Bangladesh
Population: 164.43m
Men's Champion: Khalin Joshi (IND)

China
Population: 1,354.15m
Golf Courses: 200+
Men's Champion: Xiao Jun Zhang
Women's Champion: Xiao Yi
China Amateur Open (Women): Sata Aono (JPN)
Junior Champion (Boys): Jiang Zhi Jie (11–14); Shan
  Chuan ChenZe (15–17)
Junior Champion (Girls): Chi Yi Wang

Chinese Taipei (Taiwan)
Population: 25m
Men's Champion: Taikei Sato (JPN)[1]
Women's Champion: Saki Nagamine (JPN)
Junior Champion (Boys): Chieh-Po Lee
Junior Champion (Girls): Wei-Ling Hsu
National Middle School–Junior Boys: Yung-Hua Liu
National Middle School–Senior Boys: Day-Wei
Shen

Hong Kong
Population: 7.07m
Golfers: 200,000   Golf Courses: 6 (18), 4 (9)
Men's Champion: Shinichi Mizuno[1]
Women's Champion: Tiffany Chan[2]

Mid-Amateur Champion (Men): Huang Yongle (CHN)
Senior Champion (Men): Chu Koon Ching
Junior Champion (Boys – Close): Shinichi Mizuno[3]
Junior Champion (Boys – Open): Tsai Tsung Yu (TPE)[3]
Junior Champion (Girls – Close): Tiffany Chan[4]
Junior Champion (Girls – Open): Sathika Ruenreong
  (THA)[4]

India
Population: 1,214.46m
Men's Champion: Senapaa Chikkarangappa beat
  Pritim Haridas 3 and 2[1]
Women's Champion: Gauri Monga beat Shreya Ghei
  2 and 1
Mid-Amateur Champion (Men): Sanjay Lakra
All India Championship (Women): Aditi Ashok
40th Seniors Championship (Men): Laksham Singh
7th Mid-Seniors Championship (Men) Col S K Lakra
Toyota IGU Juniors Championship (Boys): Vashistha
  Pawar
Toyota IGU Juniors Championship (Girls): Aditi Ashok
Provincial Championships:
  The Delhi NCR Cup: Kanishk Madan
  Delhi Junior Open: Honey Basoya
  Eastern India Junior: Syed Saqib Ahmed
  Haryana Open: Arshad Ali
  Northern India Amateur (Men): Abhijit Chadha
  Northern India Amateur (Women): Vani Kapoor
  Southern India Amateur: Senapaa Chikkarangappa
  Southern India Ladies: Mehar Atwal

Asia (continued)

Western India Amateur (Men): Senapaa
  Chikkarangappa
Western India Amateur (Women): Vani Kapoor
Inter-State Amateur: Senapaa Chikkarangappa

Japan
Population: 127m   Golf Courses: 2,442
Men's Champion: Katsuyuki Sakurai beat Yoshinori
  Fujimoto 1 hole[1]
Women's Champion: Mamiko Higa beat Chihiro
  Ikeda 6 and 5[2]
Mid-Amateur Champion (Men): Masayoshi Tanaka
Mid-Amateur Champion (Women): Sayaka Kawakita
Senior Champion (Men): Toshio Shirai
Senior Champion (Women): Itsuko Miki
Mid-Senior Championship (Men): Shigenobu Okawa
Grand-Senior Golf Championship: Toshio Kondo
Junior Champion (Boys): Fumiaki Saito (12–14);
  Masahiro Kawamura (15–17)
Junior Champion (Girls): Shoko Sasaki (12–14);
  Eri Joma (15–17)
Japan Collegiate Championship: Hideki Matsuyama
Japan Women's Collegiate: Misae Yanagisawa
J-sys JGA Cup (Men): Satoshi Arai
J-sys JGA Cup (Women): Mamiko Tanikawa

Korea
Population: 48.50m
Men's Champion: Lei Hyeon hu
Mid-Amateur Champion (Men): Bong-Sub Kang
Women's Champion: Kyu-jung Baek
Junior Championship Women (High): Kim Si-Woo
Junior Championship Women (Middle): Seoyoseop

Malaysia
Population: 27.91m
Golfers: 376,000   Golf Courses: 219
Men's Champion: Gavin Kyle Green[1]
Women's Champion (Open): Aretha Pan Heng[2]
Women's Champion (Closed): Isza Fariza Ismail[2]
Junior Champion (Boys): Muhammad Azry Asyraf
  Noor Azam
Junior Champion (Girls): Dottie Ardina (PHI)
Malaysia Cup – Kuala Lumpur CC: Kenneth de Silva
  and Tan Wei Chean

Pakistan
Population: 184.75m
Golfers: 5,528   Golf Courses: 8 (18), 11 (9)
Men's Champion: Hamza Taimur Amiri[1]
Women's Champion: Ghazala Yasmin[2]

Philippines
Population: 93.62m
Men's Champion: Jeung Hun Wang (KOR)
Women's Champion: Andrea Unson
Junior Champion (Boys): Rupert Zaragosa
Junior Champion (Girls): Mia Legaspi

Qatar
Population: 1.51m
Men's Champion: Max Williams (ENG)

Singapore
Population: 4.84m
Men's Champion: Lam Zhiqun beat Jerome Ng
  4 and 2[1]
Women's Champion: Amelia Yong beat Joey Poh
  1 hole[2]
Junior Champion (Boys): Gregory Foo
Senior Champion (Men): Lakshman Singh (IND)
Junior Champion (Girls): Kok Jo Ee

United Arab Emirates
Population: 4.71m
Men's Champion: Joel Neale (ENG)

Thailand
Population: 68.14m
Men's Champion: Netipong Srithong
Women's Champion: Chihiro Ikeda (PHI)
Junior Champion (Boys): Tawan Phongphun

Vietnam
Population: 90.85m
Men's Champion: Chanachoke Dejpiratanamongkol
  (THA)
Women's Champion: Bao Nghi Ngo

Australasia

Australia
Population: 21.51m
Golfers: 450,000   Golf Courses: 1,511
Men's Match Play Champion: Matthew Steiger beat
  Ben Campbell (NZL) 1 hole[1]
Men's Stroke Play Champion: Cameron Smith 275
Men's Foursomes – Riversdale GC, Melbourne: 1
  Dimi Papadopolus and Kevin Marques (NSW) 136;
  2 Matt Stieger and Brad Drewitt (NSW); Gregory
  Foo and Jerome Ng (SIN) 140

Australian Master of Amateurs – Royal Melbourne
  GC: 1 Tarquin McManus (QLD) 74-67-70-65—276;
  2 Ryan McCarthy (TAS) 65-73-72-69—279;
  Ryan Fox (NZL) 64-74-75-66—279; Andy Sullivan
  (ENG) 68-71-71-69—279
Riversdale Cup – Riversdale GC, Melbourne: Men
  – 1 Nathan Holman (VIC) 280; 2 Matthew
  Stieger (NSW) 280; 3 Brett Drewitt (NSW) 287
  Women – 1 Cecilia Cho (NZL); 2 Lydia Ko (NZL);
  3 Su Hyun Oh (KOR)
Federal Amateur Open: Tim Hart

Women's Match Play Champion: Ashlee Dewhurst beat Minjee Lee at 38th[2]
Women's Stroke Play Champion: Lydia Ko (NZL) 286
Women's Foursomes – Riversdale GC, Melbourne: 1 (tie) Cecilia Cho and Lydia Ko (NZL), Su-Hyun Oh and Lee Park (KOR) 139; 3 Ashle Ona and Courtney Massey 141
Men's Mid-Amateur Championship – The National GC (Ocean course): Jason Perry (VIC)[1]
Women's Mid-Amateur Championship – The National GC (Ocean course): Katrina Jones (QLD)[2]
Mid-Amateur Team Championship: Queensland[1]
Senior Champion (Men): Stefan Albinski[1]
Senior Match Play Champion (Men): Stefan Albinski
Senior Champion (Women): Sylvia Donohoe
Junior Champion (Boys) – Carnarvon GC, Sydney: Cameron Smith (QLD) 73-67-71-68—279
Junior Champion (Girls) – Newcastle GC: Cathleen Santoso (NSW) 73-72 -75—220
Lake MacQuarie Cup– Belmont GC, Newcastle: Men – 1 Brady Watt; 2 Anthony Murcada; 3 Cameron Smith; Women – 1 Breanna Elliott (VIC) 296; 2 Julia Boland (NSW) 297; 3 Courtney Massey (QLD) 298
State Championships:
NSW Senior Amateur (Women) – Cromer GC, Sydney: Final – Jaqui Morgan (Monash CC) beat Sylvia Donohoe (Narooma) 1 hole
NSW Medal: Andy Sullivan (ENG)
NSW Junior Championship: Peter Stojanovski
Queensland Amateur Stroke-play Championship (Men) – Pacific Harbour G&CC, Bribie Island: Daniel McGraw (QLD) 290
Queensland Amateur Stroke-play Championship (Women) – Sanctuary Cove GC (The Pines): Saki Suzuki (JPN) 74-73-68—215
Queensland Mid-Amateur: Lee Manning
Queensland Schoolgirls: Lauren Marsh
South Australian Senior Amateur: Stefan Albinski
Tasmanian Open – Kingston Beach GC: 1 Matt Stieger (NSW) 65-67-69-70–271; 2 Brad Drewitt (NSW) 278; 3 Daniel Bringolf (NSW), David Coupland (ENG) 280;
Tasmanian Senior Amateur – Mowbray GC: Ross Percy (VIC) 73-71-71–215
Tasmanian Amateur Championship (Men) – Country Club GC: Kalem Richardson beat Nathan Gatehouse at 37th
Tasmanian Amateur Championship (Women) – Country Club GC: Final – Tammy Hall (Lauceston) beat Sarah Johnstone (Ulverstone) 4 and 3
Victorian Women's Stroke-play – Heidelberg GC, Melbourne: Courtney Massey (QLD)
Victorian Veteran Women – Ballarat GC: Final – Heather Harley (Kooringal) beat Judy Kruger 2 holes
WA Seniors – Manduraah GC: Stefan Albanski (NSW) 215
WA Amateur Championship (Men) – Blackwood GC and Glenelg GC: Brad Moules (Royal Adelaide) beat Chris Austin (Tea Tree Gully GC) 1 hole

WA Amateur Championship (Women) – Osmond GC, Blackwood GC and Glenelg GC: Sarah King (Royal Adelaide) beat Jenny Lee (Glenelg) 8 and 6
WA Amateur Stroke-play Championship (Men) – Melville Glades GC: 1 Ben Seward 287; 2 Michael Dennis, Matt Steiger 288
WA Stroke-play Championship (Women) – Lake Karrinyup CC, Perth: 1 Jessica Speechley 292; 2 Whitney Hillier 300; Breanna Elliott (VIC) 300
Boys' Interstate Championship – Cabramatta GC: 1 New South Wales; 2 Queensland; 3 South Australia, West Australia, Victoria; 6 Tasmania; 7 ACT; 8 Northern Territory
Winning team: New South Wales – Jake Higginbottom, Jarrod Freeman, Ricky Kato, Nathan Waters and Brayden Petersen
Girls' Interstate Championship: 1 Queensland; 2 Western Australia; New South Wales; 4 Victoria; 5 South Australia
Winning team: Emily McLennan, Jaimee Dougan, Christina Mew, Lauren Mason and Zoe Field

Fiji
Population: 854,000
Men's Champion: Vikrant Chandra
Women's Champion: Gye Oh

New Zealand
Population: 4.30m
Golfers: 482,000   Golf Courses: 400+
Men's Match Play Champion – Russley GC, Matthew Perry beat Steven Heyes 4 and 2[1]
Men's Stroke Play Champion – Russley GC, Ryan Fox[1]
Lion Foundation New Zealand Foursomes (Men) – Russley GC: 1 Sam An and Fraser Wilken 72-71—143; 2 Owen Burges and Mark O'Malley 71-73—144; 3 Keeland Kilpatrick and Cameron Jones 74-70—144
Danny Lee Springfield Open – Springfield GC: Kieran Muir 206
The Press Invitational – Waitikiri GC: Sumin Jo 224
Lawnmaster Classic – Manawatu GC: Men: Joshua Mann 274; Women: Kate Chadwick 291
Grant Clements Memorial – Mt Maungani: Men: Ryan Fox 276; Women: Jesse Hamilton 309
Women's Match Play Champion: Lydia Ko (North Shore) beat Cecilia Cho (Paakuranga) 4 and 3[2]
Women's Stroke Play Champion: Lydia Ko[2]
Mid-Amateur Champion (Men) – Bay of Islands GC: Michael Perrin (Bay of Islands) beat Michael Leeper (Warkworth) 1 hole
New Zealand Under-19 Championship – Omokoroa: Sam An 213
New Zealand Under-19 Women – Omokoroa: Cecilia Cho 212
Senior Champion (Men) – New Plymouth GC: Murray Martin 73-70-72—215
Lion Foundation New Zealand Foursomes (Women): 1 Sarah Jane Ababa and Jayvie Agojo 76-73—153; 2 Julianne Alvarez and Barbara Perreno 79-75—154; 3 Emily Perry and Chantelle Cassidy 78-77—155

Australasia (continued)

Women's Senior Handicap Foursomes: Judy Godfrey and Marge Simpson
Junior Champion (Boys): Sam An (U19)
Junior Champion (Girls): Celia Cho (U19)
New Zealand Autumn Foursomes: H McKimmie and J Pangborn beat S Anderson and S Lepine
Danny Lee Springfield Open – Springfield: Kieran Muir (Men); Chantelle Cassidy (Women)
Grant Clements Memorial: Ryan Fox (Men); Jesse Hamilton (Women)
Lawnmaster Classic: Joshua Mann (Men); Kate Chadwick (Women)
The Press invitational – Waitikiri: Sumin Jo
SBS Invitational: Ryan Fox
Provincial Championships:
  Auckland Anniversary – Akarana GC: Fraser Wilken 210
  Canterbury (Men) – Windsor GC: Ji Sujin 280
  Canterbury (Women) – Windsor GC: Sumin Jo 218
  Dunedin – St Clair GC: Brent McEwan 279
  Hastings – Hastings GC: Joshua Munn 284
  Lochiel – Lochiel GC: Emily Perry and Tidavadee Tongdethsic 146
  Matamata Open (Ruth Middleton Cup): Zoe-Beth Brake
  North Island Under-19 Championship (Boys) – Hamilton GC: Owen Burgess (Russley) 217
  North Island Under-19 Championship (Girls) – Hamilton GC: Chantelle Cassidy (Tokoroa) beat Hanna Siefert (Lochiel)

North Island Stroke play Championship (Women) – Whitford Park: 1 Lydia Ko 278; 2 Cecilia Cho 279; 3 Hanee Song 288
North Shore Classic: Lydia Ko
Otago – Otago GC: Jeremy Hall 288
Rotorua – Rotorua GC: Ho Jun Sung and Landyn Edwards 277
South Island Under-19 Championship (Boys) – Timaru GC: Tim Leonard 72-73-68—213
South Island Under-19 Championship (Girls) – Timaru: Jesse Hamilton (Maungakiekie) 236
South Island Stroke-play Championship (Men) – Timaru GC: 1 Vaughan McCall (Gore) 74-69-67-71—281; 2 Sam An (Titirangi) 68-69-72-73—282; Tim Leonard (Timaru) 70-71-75-65—282
South Island Stroke play Championship (Women) – Timaru GC: 1 Jesse Hamilton (Maungakiekie) 76-70-81-70—297; 2 Catherine Bell (Ashburton) 75-73-76-77—301; 3 Emily Eng (Remuera) 75-73-78-78—304
Waikato Classic: Keelan Kilpatrick
Waikato Winter Stroke Play: Keelan Kilpatrick
Wairapara Stroke Play: Richard Squire
Wellington Stroke Play: Marc Jennings
Women's Inter-Provincial (Individual): Lee Park (AUS)
Women's Inter-Provincial (Team) – Final: Auckland beat North Harbour 4–1

Europe

Austria
Population: 8.39m
Golfers: 104,490   Golf Courses: 149
Men's Stroke Play Champion: Joel Stalter (FRA)
Men's Match Play Champion: Lukas Nemecz
Women's Stroke Play Champion: Sarah Schober
International Amateur Championship (Women): Leigh Whittaker
Mid-Amateur Champion (Men): Johann Quickner
Senior Champion (Men): Herbert Plenk (GER)
Stroke Play U16: Jakob van de Flierdt
Stroke Play U18: Markus Maukner
Stroke Play U21: Markus Habele
Junior Champion (Girls): Marina Stutz

Belgium
Population: 10.70m
Golfers: 55,206   Golf Courses: 79
Men's Champion: Pierre Alexis Rolland[1]
National Stroke Play (Men): Thomas Pieters
National Match Play (Men): Thomas Detry
Women's Champion: Manon de Roey[2]
National Stroke Play (Women): Joelle Van Baarle
National Match Play (Women): Margaux Vanmol

Belgian International Youths: Nicolai von Dellingshausen (GER)
International Juniors (Girls): Caroline Nistrup (DEN)
Junior Champion (Boys): Bertrand Mommaerts
Junior Champion (Girls): Margaux Vanmol

Bulgaria
Population: 7.50m
Golfers: 535   Golf Courses: 6
Men's Champion: Peter Kaloyanov[1]
Women's Champion: Damla Bilgic (TUR)

Croatia
Population: 4.43m
Golfers: 550   Golf Courses: 3
Croatia currently holds no amateur championships

Cyprus
Population: 880,000
Golfers: 1,351   Golf Courses: 9
Cypress Men's Open: Matthew Daley (ENG)
Cypress Men's Senior Open: Patrick O'Flynn
Cypress Women's Senior Open: Sofia Gerardi (GRE)
CGF Cup (Stableford): Paphos Golfers' Assn 185 pts

Czech Republic
Popkulation: 10.41m
Golfers: 49,849   Golf Courses: 89
Men's Champion: David Prochazka
Women's Champion: Karolina Vlckova
Mid-Amateur Champion (Men): Marcel Grass (SUI)
Czech International Senior Champion: Kai Flint (GER)
Junior Champion (Boys): Mateusz Gradecki (POL)
  (U18); Jiri Korda (U21)
National Youth Championship (Boys): David Mrazek
National Youth C/ship (Girls): Marie Lunackova
Junior Champion (Girls): Franziska Friedrich (GER)
Czech International Academic Championship:
  Tomasz Kadlec

Denmark
Population: 5.48m
Golfers: 151,185   Golf Courses: 181
Men's Champion: Kasper Estrup[1]
Danish Stroke Play Champion: Thomas Sorensen
Women's Champion: Nicole Broch Larsen[2]
Junior Champion (Boys): Edoardo Torrieri (ITA)
Rudersdal Open: Nicolai Tinning

England
Population: 49.13m
Golfers: 688,195 affiliated to the EGU; 115,456
  affiliated to the EWGA
Golf Courses: 1,954 affiliated to the EGU; 1,774
  affiliated to the EWGA
English Open Amateur Stroke Play Championship
  (Brabazon Trophy) – Burnham & Berrow: Neil
  Raymond (Corhampton)[1]
English Amateur Championship – Woburn: Steven
  Brown beat Jamie Clare 7 and 5[1]
English Women's Close Amateur Championship –
  West Sussex: Lucy Williams beat Charley Hull
  at 19th[2]
English Women's Open Amater Stroke Play
  Championship – Alwoodley: Charley Hull[2]
English Open Mid-Amateur Championship (Logan
  Trophy) – Ipswich (Purdis Heath): Neill Williams
  (Walton Heath)[1]
English Women's Open Mid-Amateur
  Championship – Collingtree Park: Claire Smith
  (Silsden) beat Jessica Bradley (Tiverton) 1 hole[2]
English Seniors' Amateur Championship –
  Northamptonshire County and Northampton:
  Alan Squires (Oldham)[1]
Senior Women's English Close Stroke Play
  Championship – Saltford: Christine Quinn
  (Hockley)[2]
Senior Women's English Close Match Play
  Championship – York: Sue Dye (Delamere Forest)
  beat Janet Melville (Sherwood Forest) 4 and 2[2]
English County Champions Tournament – Woodhall
  Spa: Jamie Rutherford[1]
English Boys' Stroke Play Championship (Carris
  Trophy) – Broadstone: Harry Casey[3]
English Boys' Under-16 Championship (McGregor
  Trophy) – South Moor: Jack Hermeston[3]
English Girls' Close Championship – Ellesborough:
  Hayley Davis[4]

Estonia
Population: 1.34m
Golfers: 2,088   Golf Courses: 8
Men's Stroke Play Champion: Davis Puksts (LAT)[1]
Men's Match Play Champion: Martin Unn
Women's Stroke Play Champion: Merlin Palm
Women's Match Play Champion: Mara Puisite (LAT)

Finland
Population: 5,35m
Golfers: 142,184   Golf Courses: 126
Men's Champion: Albert Eckhardt[1]
Finnish Stroke Play Champion: Tapio Pulkkanen
Women's Champion: Karlijn Zaanen (NED)[2]

France
Population: 62.64m
Golfers: 407,530   Golf Courses: 578
Men's Champion: Gary Stal[1]
Women's Champion: Fiona Puyo
Mid-Amateur Champion (Men): Thomas Ansersson
  (SWE)
Mid-Amateur Champion (Women): Perrine Delacour
Junior Champion (Boys): Robin Sciot-Siegrist (U18);
  Thomas Le Berre (U16)
Junior Champion (Girls): Manon Gidali (U18); Emma
  Broze (U16)
Regional Championships:
  Grand Prix Du Cap D'Agde (Men): Julien Brun
  Grand Prix Du Cap D'Agde (Women): Alice Dubois
  Grand Prix Carcassonne (Men): Clement Batut
  Grand Prix Carcassonne (Women): Marion
    Veysseyre
  Grand Prix Federal De Toulouse (Men): Xavier
    Diana
  Grand Prix Federal De Toulouse (Women): Beatrice
    Soubiron
  Grand Prix D'Albi (Men): Benjamin Forges
  Grand Prix D'Albi (Women): Beatrice Soubiron
  Grand Prix de Bordeaux Lac: Brice Chanfreau
  Grand Prix De Haute Savoie (Men): Arthur
    Gabella-Wenne (SUI)
  Grand Prix De Haute Savoie (Women): Lorellen
    Gros
  Grand Prix de Limere (Men): Mervin Rocchi/Franck
    Daux
  Grand Prix de Limere (Women): Celia Mansour
  Grand Prix Du Lys (Men): Franck Daux/Berre
    Thomas Le
  Grand Prix Du Lys (Women): Carole Danten-Azfi
  Grand Prix de Nîmes Campagne (Men): Bastien
    Melani
  Grand Prix de Nîmes Campagne (Women): Emilie
    Simmons
  Grand Prix De Saint Cyprien (Men): Etlin Joris
  Grand Prix De Saint Cyprien (Women): Anais
    Meysonnier
  Grand Prix International De Lyon: Gary Stal
  Grand Prix des Landes-Hossegor (Men): Victor
    Perez
  Grand Prix des Landes-Hossegor (Women): Andrea
    Vilarasau (ESP)
  Grand Prix des Volcans (Men): Jonathan Armstrong
    (ENG)

Grand Prix des Volcans (Women): Charlotte Le Provost
Grand Prix de la Nivelle (Men): Thomas Elissalde
Grand Prix de la Nivelle (Women): Fiona Puyo
Grand Prix de Savoie (Men): Jonathan Armstrong (ENG)
Grand Prix de Savoie (Women): Lorellen Gros
Grand Prix de Valcros (Men): Maxime Laute
Grand Prix de Valcros (Women): Emie Peronnin
Grand Prix du Medoc (Men): Florent Ales
Grand Prix du Medoc (Women): Louise Labaigt
Grand Prix du Pau (Men): Florent Ales
Grand Prix du Pau (Women): Louise Latorre
Grand Prix Valgarde (Men): Timothee Guin
Grand Prix Valgarde (Women): Lea Cherel/Emie Peronnin
Grand Prix De BoulouParis (Men): Kevin Bosio
Grand Prix De Palmola (Men): Thomas Le Flohic
Grand Prix De Palmola (Women): Celia Mansour
Grand Prix de Valescure (Men): Jerome Lando Casanova
Grand Prix D'Anglet Chiberta (Men): Thomas Elissalde
Grand Prix de la Baule (Men): Thibaut Carmignano/ Yohann Desrousseaux
Grand Prix de la Baule (Women): Lise Peigne
Grand Prix de Saint Nom La Breteche (Men): Kevin Turlan
Grand Prix de Saint Nom La Breteche (Women): Louise Gateau-Chovelon

Germany
Population: 82.06m
Golfers: 610,104   Golf Courses: 708
Men's Champion: Daan Huizing (NED)[1]
Women's Champion: Fanny Cnoops (BEL)[2]
International Ladies Amateur Championship: Fanny Cnops (BEL)
Junior Champion (Boys): Alexander Matlari
Junior Champion (Girls): Antonia Scherer (U18); Karolin Lampert (U16); Finnja Kietzke/Antonia-Leonie Eberhard (U14)
Junior Masters (Boys): Victor Gebhard Osterby (DEN)
Junior Masters (Girls): Lynn Carlsson (SWE)

Hungary
Population: 9.97m
Golfers: 2,509   Golf Courses: 13
Men's Champion: Claas-Eric Borges (GER)
Women's Champion: Marlene Krejcy (AUT)
Junior Champion (Boys): Daniel Kovari
Junior Champion (Girls): Rozsa Csilla

Iceland
Population: 329,000
Golfers: 15,529   Golf Courses: 66
Men's Champion: Arnor Ingi Finnbjornsson
Women's Champion: Olafia Kristinsdottir
Junior Champion (Boys): Bjarki Petursson
Junior Masters (Boys): Kristinn Sigurdsson (15–16); Bjarki Petursson (17–18)

Ireland (Northern Ireland and Rep. of Ireland)
Population: 6.2m
Golfers: 201,838   Golf Courses: 430
Irish Amateur Open Championship – Royal Dublin: Rhys Pugh (Vale of Glamorgan) (WAL)[1]
Irish Amateur Close Championship – Shannon: Paul Cutler (Portstewart)[1]
Irish Women's Close Amateur Championship – Carlow: Danielle McVeigh (RCDL) beat Karen Delaney (Carlow) at 19th[2]
Irish Women's Open Amateur Stroke Play Championship – Elm Park: Leona Maguire (Slieve Russell)[2]
Irish Seniors' Amateur Open Championship – Rosslare: Hugh Smyth (Mourne)[1]
Irish Seniors' Amateur Close Championship – Thurles: Garth McGimpsey (Bangor)[1]
Irish Senior Women's Close Amateur Championship – Adare Manor: Sheena McElroy (Grange) beat Pauline Walsh (Headfort) 7 and 6[2]
Irish Senior Women's Open Stroke Play Championship – Grenore: Minna Kaamalahti (FIN)[2]
Irish Boys' Close Championshp – Ardee: Jordan Hood[3]
Irish Youths' Amateur Close Championship: Brian Casey[3]
Irish Boys' Under-15 Open Championship – Galway: Marc Boucher[3]
Irish Girls' Close Championship (Blake Cup) – Donegal: Paula Grant beat Jessica Ross 3 and 2[4]
Irish Girls' 54 Hole Open – Knightsbrook: Perrine Delacour (FRA)[4]

Israel
Population: 7.29m
Golfers: 1,300   Golf Courses: 2
Men's Champion: Assaf Cohen
Women's Champion: Hadas Libman
Super Seniors Champion (Men): Mati Geri
Senior Champion (Women): Ruth Oren
Junior Champion (Boys): Assaf Cohen
Junior Champion (Mixed): Assaf Cohen

Italy
Population: 60.10m
Golfers: 100,317   Golf Courses: 269
Men's Stroke Play Champion: Mattia Miloro
Men's Match Play Champion: Nicolas D'Incau (SUI) beat Adrien Saddier[1]
Women's Stroke Play Champion: Chiara Bandini
Women's Match Play Champion: Laura Lonardi
Mid-Amateur Champion (Men): Marcello Grabau
International Amateur Championship: Justine Dreher
Junior Champion (Boys): Edoardo Torrieri (U18); Giacomo Garbin (U16); Guido Migliozzi (U14)
Junior Champion (Girls): Roberta Liti

Kazakhstan
Population: 15.75m
Golfers: 400   Golf Courses: 6
Kazakhstan currently holds no amateur
championships

Latvia
Population: 2.24m
Golfers: 775   Golf Courses: 3
Men's Stroke Play Champion: Davis Puksts
Men's Match Play Champion: Karlis Broders
Men's Champion (Open): Mathias Boesmans (BEL)[1]
Women's Champion: Linda Dobele[2]
Junior Champion (Boys): Roberts Eihmanis

Lithuania
Population: 3.26m
Golfers: 430   Golf Courses: 5
Men's Champion: Kornelijus Baliukonis[1]
Women's Champion: Linda Dobele (LAT)

Luxembourg
Population: 492,000
Golfers: 4,023   Golf Courses: 6
Men's Champion: Robbie Van West (NED)[1]
Women's Champion: Olivia Cowan (GER)[2]

Malta
Population: 410,000
Golfers: 650   Golf Courses: 1
Malta currently holds no amateur championships

The Netherlands
Population: 16.65m
Golfers: 367,659   Golf Courses: 201
Men's Stroke Play Champion: Daan Huizing
Men's Match Play Champion: Fernand Osther
Women's Champion: Krista Bakker
Junior Champion (Boys): Robbie van West (U21);
Rowin Caron
Junior Champion (Girls): Lauren Taylor (ENG)
National Match Play (Girls U21): Giulia van den Berg
Riverwoods (Dutch) Junior Open: Lauren Taylor
(ENG)
National Match Play U21 (Girls): Giulia van den Berg

Poland
Population: 38.04m
Golfers: 2,750   Golf Courses: 29
Men's Champion: Mateusz Gradecki
Women's Champion: Martyna Mierzwa
Mid-Amateur Champion (Men): William Carey (USA)
Junior Champion (Boys): Adrian Meronk

Portugal
Population: 10.73m
Golfers: 14,556   Golf Courses: 88
Men's Champion – Campo Montado: Eddie Pepperell
(ENG)[1]
Women's Champion – Aroeira GC: Leona Maguire
(IRL)[2]
Senior Champion (Men) – Hacienda Riquelme GR:
Angel Macias Romero 223 (–7)

Senior Doubles (Men) – Hacienda Riquelme GR:
Scratch – John Whitcutt and Basil Griffiths (WAL)
75-70—145; Handicap – Bob Backsted and Per
Hildebrand (SWE) 69-73—142
Senior Champion (Women) – Oceanico GC: Sheena
McElroy (IRL) 78-82—160
Senior Doubles Championship (Women): Caslida
and Catalina Castillejo (Oriol, Spain)
Interntional Seniors Championship: David Lane
Junior Champion (Boys): Goncalo Pinto (U18); Joao
Magalhaes (U16)
Junior Champion (Girls): Emilie Alonso (FRA)
70-71—141 (third round cancelled)

Russia
Population: 140.37m
Golfers: 500   Golf Courses: 17
Men's Champion: Steve Uzzell (ENG)

Scotland
Population: 5.16m
Golfers: 183,758   Golf Courses: 541
Scottish Amateur Championship – Western Gailes:
David Law beat Daniel Kay 6 and 5[1]
Scottish Open Amateur Stroke Play Championship –
Blairgowrie Lansdowne: Andy Sullivan (Nuneaton)
(ENG)[1]
Scottish Ladies' Close Amateur Championship –
Machrihanish: Louise Kenney (Pitreavie) beat Eilidh
Briggs (Kilmacolm) 5 and 4[2]
Scottish Ladies' Open Stroke Play Championship
(Helen Holm Trophy) – Troon Portland & Royal
Troon: 1 Charlotte Ellis (Minchinhampton) (ENG)[2]
Scottish Seniors Open Amateur Stroke Play
Championship – Irvine (Bogside): Charles Banks
(Stanton on the Wold)[1]
Scottish Seniors Match Play Championship –
Monifieth: Ian Brotherston (Dumfries & County)
beat Gordon MacDonald (Callander) 3 and 2[1]
Scottish Senior Ladies' (Close) Amateur
Championship – Portpatrick Dunskey: Noreen
Fenton (Dunbar) beat Heather Anderson
(Blairgowrie) 1 hole[2]
Scottish Champion of Champions (Men) – Leven:
Brian Soutar (Leven)[1]
Scottish Champion of Champions (Women) –
Glasgow Gailes: Pamela Pretswell[2]
Scottish Veteran Ladies – Blairgowroe: Noreen
Fenton beat Linda Urquhart 2 and 1[2]
Scottish Boys Championship – Dunbar: David
Wilson beat Liam Johnston at 38th[3]
Scottish Boys' Stroke Play Championship – Nairn
Dunbar: Joshua Jamieson[3]
Scottish Boys Under-16 Open Stroke Play
Championship – Forfar: Ben Kinsley (St Andrews)[3]
Scottish Youths' Open Amateur Stroke Play
Championship – Paisley: Lyle McAlpine (Royal
Dornoch)[3]
Scottish Ladies' Junior Open Stroke Play
Championship – Cardross: Kelsey MacDonald
(Nairn Dunbar)[4]
Scottish Boys' Area Team Championship – Hayston:
Lothians[3]
Scottish Girls' Close Championship – Glenisla:
Eilidh Briggs beat Gemma Dryburgh 1 hole[4]

Europe (continued)

SLGA Under-16 Stroke Play Championship – Strathmore: Bronte Law[4]

Slovakia
Population: 5.41m
Golfers: 6,732   Golf Courses: 13
Men's Champion: Juraj Zvarik[1]
Women's Champion: Katerina Prorokova (CZE)[2]
Junior Champion (Boys): Pavol Bielik
Junior Champion (Girls): Dominika Czudkova

Slovenia
Population: 2.03m
Golfers: 7,900   Golf Courses: 12
Men's Champion: Jakob Ziegler (GER)[1]
Women's Champion: Anja Purgauer (AUT)[2]
Junior Champion (Boys): Enej Sarkanj
Junior Champion (Girls): Ursa Orehek

Spain
Population: 45.32m
Golfers: 338,160   Golf Courses: 345
Men's Champion: Goncalo Pinto[1]
Men's Pairs Championship – Troia: Joao and Tomas Carlota
Women's Champion: Magda Carrilho[2]
Women's Pairs Championship – Troia: Magda Carrillo and Sara Passao
Mid-Amateur Champion (Men) – Campo Belas: Ricardo Oliviera (Troia) 76-75–151
Mid-Amateur Champion (Women) – Campo Belas: Marta Lampreia (Quinta do Peru) 82-80—162
Mid-Amateur Men's Club Championship – Santo Estevo: 1 Troia (Ricardo Oliviera, Sean Conte-Real, Jorge Abreu, Mario Nuno Coello, Antonio Sa and Antonio Castello) 391; 2 Verdegolf 1 394, 3 Oitavos 405
Mid-Amateur Men's Foursomes Championship: 1 Troia 152; 2 Bermen 159; 3 Verdegolf 162
Senior Champion (Men): Leonel Neto (Barmen) 73-71—144
Senior Champion (Women): Deborah Fiuza de Mello (Oitavos) 78-77—155
Junior Champion (Boys): Mario Galiano Aguilar
Junior Champion (Girls): Ha Rang Lee

Switzerland
Population: 8m
Golfers: 79,843   Golf Courses: 94
Men's Champion: Andrea Gorini[1]
Women's Champion: Franziska Blum (GER)[2]
Mid-Amateur Champion (Men): Paul Burkhard
Mid-Amateur Champion (Women): Janou Kamman
Senior Open Championship: Francois Barras
Senior Centrale Championship (Men): Roland Niederberger
Senior Centrale Championship (Women): Colette Crittin

Swiss Foursomes Championship (Men): Rafael Aregger and Louis Muller
Swiss Foursomes Championship (Women): Anne-Laure Simonet and Joanne Wildhaber
Swiss Open Amateur Championship (Men): Michael Thannhauser
Swiss Open Amateur Championship (Women): Anais Maggetti
Junior Champion (Boys): Joel Girrbach (U18); Stefan Sorg (U16); Stefano Gabriel Butti (U14)
Junior Champion (Girls): Cylia Damerau (U18); Celia Gimblett (U16); Yara Berger (U14)

Turkey
Population: 72m
Golfers: 5,538   Golf Courses: 18
Men's Champion: Daan Huizing (NED)[1]
Women's Champion: Nicole Broch Larsen (DEN)[2]

Ukraine
Population: 45.43m
Golfers: 515   Golf Courses: 4
Women's Champion: Jamila Jaxqliyeva[2]

Wales
Population: 2.94m
Golfers: 56,69   Golf Courses: 157
Welsh Amateur Championship – Aberdovey: Jason Shufflebotham (Prestatyn) beat Rhys Pugh (Vale of Glamorgan) 1 hole[1]
Welsh Open Amateur Stroke Play Championship – St Pierre: Darren Wright (Rowlands Castle)[1]
Welsh Ladies' Close Amateur Championship – Royal St David's: Becky Harries (Haverfordwest) beat Amy Boulden (Maesdu) 1 hole[2]
Welsh Ladies' Open Amateur Stroke Play Championship – Tenby: Charley Hull (Woburn) (ENG)[2]
Welsh Seniors' Close Amateur Championship – Aberdovey: Glyn Rees (Fleetwood)[1]
Welsh Seniors' Open Championship – Rhuddlan: Glyn Rees (Fleetwood)[1]
Welsh Senior Ladies' Championship – Radyr: Christine Harries[2]
Welsh Tournament of Champions: James Frazer[1]
Welsh Boys' Championship – Cradoc: David Boote beat Oliver Dickson 4 and 2[3]
Welsh Boys' Under-15 Championship – St Mellons: Robert Evans (Cradoc)[3]
Welsh Boys' Under-13 Championship – St Mellons: Matthew Harris (St Mellons)[3]
Welsh Open Youths' Championship – Clyne: Ben Stow (Rushmore)[3]
Welsh Girls' Championship – Clays: Katie Bradbury beat Sara Rees-Evans 1 hole[4]

Sandy Lyle and Peter Alliss in World Hall of Fame

Former Open and Masters champion Sandy Lyle, who won 29 tournaments around the world and was the first international winner of The Player's Championship on the PGA Tour, will be enshrined later this year in the World Golf Hall of Fame in St Augustine, Florida.

He and BBC commentator Peter Alliss will be joining Phil Mickelson, Hollis Stacey and Dan Jenkins as the inductees in the class of 2012. Lyle was elected through the international ballot while Peter Alliss was selected in the Lifetime Achievement category.

George O'Grady, Chief Executive of the European Tour, said: "This is very special for the European Tour. Both Sandy and Peter are very worthy candidates for the Hall of Fame. Sandy played a pivotal role in raising the image of British and European golf while Peter followed a highly acclaimed playing career by becoming a hugely admired and wonderfully entertaining commentator."

Luke Donald wins 2011 Golf Writers Trophy

Luke Donald is only the second player after Padraig Harrington in 2008 to win the triple crown of golf awards. Having already been named the European Tour Golfer of the Year and PGA Tour Player of the Year he was named winner of the Golf Writers' Trophy voted by members of the Association of Golf Writers.

Darren Clarke, the Open champion, and Rory McIlroy, the US Open champion, tied for second place in the poll, while the European Solheim Cup team, captained by Alison Nicholas, took fourth place.

"Any award you win gives you a great amount of pleasure and for the Golf Writers to consider me as their player of the year means a lot," Donald said. "These are the people who really understand golf and appreciate all that I have achieved this year.

"All the people in the running for the AGW award – Rory, Darren, the Solheim Cup team and the Walker Cup team – would have been worthy winners and therefore it is very gratifying to get the vote ahead of them."

Clarke, who won the Open at his 20th attempt at Sandwich, said: "What Luke Donald has achieved this year is unbelievable. I'm full of admiration for him. And for Rory to win the US Open like he did and so young shows what a fantastic talent he is."

Nicholas, whose team produced an amazing comeback in the late stages to pip the Americans at Killeen Castle, said: "I would like to congratulate the guys for their outstanding performances during 2011 and am delighted the European Solheim Cup team was judged alongside them. "

Donald wins American writers award as well

Luke Donald became the third European Tour golfer in the last four years to win the Golf Writers Association of America (GWAA) Player of the Year Award.

Donald follows earlier European winners of the American award – Graeme McDowell in 2010 and Padraig Harrington in 2008.

Donald, who topped the money lists on both sides of the Atlantic, had already been named The 2011 European Tour Race to Dubai Golfer of the Year, the PGA Tour Player of the Year and the Association of Golf Writers' Player of the Year – proof of the widespread recognition of his remarkable accomplishments.

The 3- year-old will be honoured at the GWAA's Annual Awards Dinner during the 2011 Masters Tournament in Augusta. He was the overwhelming choice of the American journalists, capturing 88 per cent of the votes to finish ahead of Americans Keegan Bradley and Webb Simpson and of Ryder Cup teammate Rory McIlroy.

The GWAA, founded in 1946, takes an active role in protecting the interests of all golf journalists, works closely with all of golf's major governing bodies and the World Golf Hall of Fame.

The British Golf Museum

at the Heart of the Home of Golf

The collections of the British Golf Museum have become Scotland's 38th Recognised Collection of National Significance. The museum received the major award in November 2011. Minister for Commonwealth Games and Sport, Shona Robison, who presented the award, said, "Achieving Recognised status demonstrates the quality and significance of the British Golf Museum collections which tells a fantastic story of our love for the great game."

The British Golf Museum is a five star museum, situated just yards from the 1st tee of the famous Old Course at St Andrews. Containing the largest collection of golf memorabilia in Europe, the museum offers a wealth of sporting heritage spanning more than three centuries. High quality displays bring to life the people and events that have shaped the game's history and influenced its growing popularity, not just in the UK, but worldwide.

The museum is home to star attractions such as the oldest known set of golf clubs in the world, the first Open Championship medal, which was presented to Tom Morris Jr following his 1872 win, and the oldest known footage of a golf match, dating back to 1898. Imaginative exhibitions and stunning displays set the museum apart as the world's premier heritage centre for golf.

At the end of your visit you have the chance to sink a putt to win The Open and have your picture taken with the Claret Jug in The R&A Gallery. This exciting interactive space explores the global work of The R&A, from running international championships to protecting wildlife on the course.

The museum is open 7 days a week throughout the year

Every museum visitor is given a complimentary guidebook as a memento

We look forward to welcoming you in 2012

---

www.britishgolfmuseum.co.uk

PART VIII

Junior Tournaments and Events

Boys' and Youths' Tournaments

For past results see earlier editions of *The R&A Golfer's Handbook*

British Boys Amateur Championship   *Burnham & Berrow and Enmore Park*

Leading Qualifier: Kenny Subregis (FRA) 71-68—139

Quarter Finals:
Jeremy Paul (GER) beat Steffen Harm (GER) 1 hole
Harrison Greenberry (Exeter) beat Oliver Carr (Heswall)
3 and 2
Patrick Kelly (Boston West) beat John-Ross Galbraith
(Whitehead) at 23rd
Thomas Detry (BEL) beat Matthew Fitzpatrick (Hallamshire)
2 and 1

Semi-Finals:
Greenberry beat Paul 2 and 1
Kelly beat Detry 4 and 3

Final:
Harrison Greenberry beat Patrick Kelly
at 37th

British Youths Amateur Championship

This championship bridged the gap between the Boys and the Men's tournaments from 1954 until 1994, when it was discontinued because it was no longer needed. The date on the schedule was used to introduce the Mid Amateur Championship for players over 25 but this event was discontinued after 2007.

For results see the R&A website – www.randa.org

English Boys' Stroke Play Championship (Carris Trophy)   *Broadstone*

1	Harry Casey (Enfield)	70-71-64-69—274
2	Matthew Fitzpatrick (Hallamshire)	70-69-64-72—275
3	Corrado De Stefani (ITA)	67-68-70-72—277

English Boys' Under-16 Championship (McGregor Trophy)   *South Moor*

1	Jack Hermeston (City of Newcastle)	71-68-72-70—281
2	Bradley Neil (Blairgowrie)	71-73-71-70—285
3	Jarand Ekeland Arnqy (NOR)	71-78-73-65—287
	Pierre Mazier (FRA)	72-73-72-70—278

Irish Boys' Close Championship (inaugurated 1983)   *Ardee*

1	Jordan Hood (Galgorm Castle)	70-76-68-72—286
2	William Russell (Clandeboye)	72-71-73-71—287
	Dermot McElroy (Ballymena)	67-73-73-74—287

Irish Youths' Amateur Close Championship (inaugurated 1969)   *Tramore GC*

1	Brian Casey (Headfort)	73-75-69-66—283
2	Stephen Barry (Laytown & Bettystown)	69-69-74-73—285
3	Conor O'Rourke (Naas)	74-69-71-73—287

Irish Boys' Under-15 Open Championship   *Galway*

1	Marc Boucher (Carton House)	73-72—145
2	Rowan Lester (Hermitage)	74-72—146
	Charlie McMicken (Athlone)	73-73—146

Scottish Boys' Championship *Dunbar*

Quarter Finals:
David Wilson (Troon Welbeck) beat Connor Marsland (Kilmacolm) 2 holes
Benjamin Kinsley (St Andrews) beat Craig Oram (Nairn Dunbar) 2 and 1
Liam Johnston (Dumfries & County) beat John Scott (East Renfrewshire) 2 and 1
Calum Hill (Tantallon) beat Greig Marchbank (Dumfries & Galloway) 4 and 3

Semi-Finals:
Wilson beat Kinsley 3 and 2
Johnston beat Hill 6 and 5

Final:
David Wilson beat Liam Johnston at 38th

Scottish Boys' Stroke Play Championship (inaugurated 1970) *Nairn Dunbar*

1	Joshua Jamieson (St Andrews New)	72-69-70-72—283
2	Mikko Lehtovuori (FIN)	73-74-69-69—285
	Liam Johnston (Dumfries & County)	74-69-69-73—285

Scottish Boys Under-16 Open Stroke Play Championship (inaugurated 1990) *Forfar*

1	Ben Kinsley (St Andrews)	70-68-65—203
2	Jack Hermeston (City of Newcastle)	68-69-67—204
3	Euan Walker (Kilmarnock [Barassie])	73-68-64—205

First round abandoned – flooding

Scottish Youths' Open Amateur Stroke Play Championship (inaugurated 1979)

Paisley (reduced to 54 holes due to bad weather)

1	Lyle McAlpine (Royal Dornoch)	71-71-68—210
2	Simon Fairburn (Torwoodlee)	69-74-70—213
	Greig Marchbank (Dumfires & County)	70-72-71—213

Welsh Boys' Championship (inaugurated 1954) *Cradoc*

Leading Qualifier: Ryan Thomas (Vale of Glamorgan) 67-69—136

Quarter Finals:
David Boote (Walton Heath) beat Patrick Mullins (Whitchurch) 4 and 3
Oliver Baker (Cardiff) beat Ryan Haskell (Celtic Manor) 1 hole
Oliver Dickson (Pennard) beat Toby Hunt (St Mellons) at 19th
Evan Griffith (North Wales) beat Sam Lichfield (Oswestry) 6 and 5

Semi-Finals:
Boote beat Baker 2 holes
Dickson beat Griffith 2 and 1

Final:
David Boote beat Oliver Dickson 4 and 2

Welsh Boys Under-13 Championship *St Mellons*

1	Matthew Harris (St Mellons)	77
2	Joseph Blunden (Horsehay Village)	79
3	Sebastian Jones (Castle Royle)	81
	Hari Pachu (Gower)	81

Welsh Boys' Under-15 Championship (inaugurated 1985) *St Mellons*

1	Robert Evans (Cradoc)	80-66—146 (better second round)
2	Thomas Williams (Wrexham)	72-74—146
3	Ioan Jones (Abersoch)	72-78—150

Welsh Open Youths' Championship (inaugurated 1993) *Clyne*

1	Ben Stow (Rushmore)	70-71-70—211
2	Will Jones (Oswestry)	77-68-68—213
3	Chrs Nugent (Fulford Heath)	71-76-74—218

Peter McEvoy Trophy (inaugurated 1988)   *always at Copt Heath*

1	Nathan Kimsey (Woodhall Spa)	69-67-69-67—272
2	Greg Payne (Chobham)	73-68-69-68—278
3	Rhys Pugh (Vale of Glamorgan)	71-71-69-68—279

Midland Boys' Amateur Championship   *Mickleover*

1	Robert Aldred (Stourbridge)*	72-68—140
2	Lee Shepherd (Sherwood Forest)	74-66—140
	Bradley Moore (Kedleston Park)	71-69—140
	Cameron Long (Drayton Park)	70-70—140
	Michael Amos (Beau Desert)	69-71—140

Aldred won after a play-off

Midland Youths' Championship   *Stoke Rochford*

1	Patrick Kelly (Boston West)*	73-66-67-68—274
2	Danny Keddie (Belton Park)	68-67-70-69—274

Kelly won at the first extra hole

3	Jordan Wrisdale (Boston)	71-72-66-67—276

Sir Henry Cooper Junior Masters   *Nizels GC. Kent*

1	Toby Tree (Worthing)	70-72-68-68—278
2	Haydn Porteous (RSA)	72-70-67-70—279
	Gavin Moynihan (Donabate)	70-69-70-70—279

US Junior Amateur Championship   *Gold Mountain GC (Olympic Course)*

Semi-finals: Jordan Speith (Dallas) beat Adam Ball (Richmond) 7 and 5
Chelso Barrett (Keene) beat Nicolas Echavarria (COL) at 19th

Finals: Jordan Speith beat Chelso Barrett 6 and 5

Canadian Junior Boys Championship   *Morgan Creek GC, British Columbia*

1	Kevin Kwan	71-65-67-69—272
2	Richard Jung	71-69-71-72—283
3	Adam Svensson	71-73-69-71—284

Hong Kong Boys Junior Close Championship   *Hong Kong GC (New)*

1	Sunichi Mizuno	69-73—142
2	Terence Ng	76-66—142
3	Lok Tin Lui	68-78—146

Hong Kong Junior Open Championship   *Clearwater Bay GC*

1	Tsai Tsung Yu (TPE)	69-70—139
2	Jonathan Lai (USA)	75-67—142
3	nSmithti Teeratrakul (THA)	72-74—146

Faldo Series expansion as build-up to Olympics

Sir Nick Faldo has revealed plans to help develop golf in South America ahead of the sport's return to the Olympics at Rio 2016.

The six-time Major winner – who admitted he would have "absolutely loved" to have competed for a gold medal – is currently expanding his Faldo Series for golf's return to the Olympic programme after an absence of 112 years.

Apart from Argentina, golf is still very much a minority sport throughout South America but with the Rio Olympics less than five years away work is under way to increase participation.

Already established in Europe and Asia, the Faldo Series recently announced that with the help of The R&A its South America Championship, which began in 2008, will remain in Brazil until at least 2016.

"Our expectation is that the Series will contribute at developmental levels to Brazil's now historic connection to the sport. We are committed to maximising Brazil's rightful place leading up to and beyond golf's return to Rio 2016."

With backing from the Brazilian Golf Confederation it is hoped participation will increase even further in the coming years.

He added: "Worldwide we have 17 events in 13 countries. For example, China has five events to get to their grand final, so that is what I hope will happen in Brazil.

"We have doubled in size. We reach 5,000 golfers and with our Faldo South America Series we have nearly gone global. We want to keep expanding. The more help we can get the bigger we can make it."

Faldo – who won the Open Championship in 1987, 90 and 92 – has taken an active interest since it was announced that golf would return to the Olympic programme. In August, he submitted plans to the International Golf Federation (IGF) for the proposed Olympic course that would see each of the 18 holes designed by a different Major winner in a project overseen by golf architect Tom Fazio.

But it is as a player that he would have liked to have made his mark. "I think the Olympics is a fabulous event. I would absolutely have loved the opportunity to go and win a gold medal. That would have been something special."

Kohei Kinoshita retains Faldo Japan title

Defending champion Kohei Kinoshita successfully retained his title at the fourth Faldo Series Japan Championship.

Sixteen year old Kinoshita beat Tokyo's Ryotaro Ogawa at the first hole of a sudden-death playoff after both had tied at two under par 142 at Shizu Hills Country Club in Ibaraki.

With the tournament played over two venues to accommodate the record field, Mai Arai from Fukuoka and Ibaraki's Yu Okamura shared the girls' championship on seven over par 151 at nearby Shishido Hills Country Club.

All 148 participants – a record field for a Faldo Series event – came together for the prize presentation and a talk from Japanese golfing legend Tsuneyuki Nakajima.

Kinoshita, from Kumamoto, will now return to Mission Hills Golf Club in China later this year for the sixth Faldo Series Asia Grand Final on March 14-16. He will be joined by boys' age-group winners, 19-year-old Mikumu Horikawa from Kanagawa (Under-21) and 17-year-old Taiki Sakurai of Yamanashi (Under-18).

Kanagawa's Masamichi Ito, 16, who has an exemption to Mission Hills as the only player to win Faldo Series Grand Finals in Asia and Europe, finished third in the Boys' Under-16 division, four shots behind Kinoshita and 15-year-old Ogawa.

As winners of the Girls' Under-21 and Under-16 divisions respectively, 19-year-old Arai and Okamura, 14, also qualify for the Grand Final in Shenzhen, a World Amateur Golf Ranking event hosted by six-time Major winner Sir Nick Faldo.

Team Events

European Boys Team Championship Prague City (Zbraslov), Czech Republic

Stroke-play Qualification: 1 Germany 705; 2 Spain, Finland 712

Individual:

1 Robin Goger (AUT)	67-67—134	
2 Richard Broadhurst (ITA)	66-69—135	
3 Frederik Hammer (DEN)	71-66—137	
Florian Loutre (FRA)	65-72—137	

Final Team Placings: 1 Spain; 2 Austria; 3 France; 4 Denmark; 5 Germany; 6 Ireland; 7 Italy; 8 Finland; 9 Sweden; 10 Switzerland; 11 England; 12 Norway; 13 Scotland,; 14 Czech Rep.; 15 Wales,; 16 Netherlands; 17 Belgium; 18 Turkey; 19 Portugal,; 20 Iceland

Winning Team: Pep Angles, Adria Arnaus, Mario Galiano, David Marago, Jon Rahm, Javier Sainz

Team Results:

"A Flight" – *Day One:* France 4, Germany 3; Austria 4½, Italy 2½; Denmark 4, Finland 3; Spain 4, Ireland 3. *Day Two:* Austria 4½, France 2½; Spain 4, Denmark 3; Germany 3½, Italy 1½; Ireland 4, Finland 1. *Day Three – Final:* Spain 5, Austria 2; France 5½, Denmark 1½; Germany 3, Ireland 2; Italy, 3 Finland 2

"B Flight" – *Day One:* Switzerland 4, Czech Rep. 1; Norway 3, Wales 2; Sweden 3, Netherlands 2; England 3, Scotland 2. *Day Two:* Switzerland 4, Norway 1; Sweden 3, England 2; Czech Rep. 3, Wales 2; Scotland 3, Netherlands 2. *Day Three:* Sweden 4, Switzerland 1; England 5, Norway 0; Scotland 4, Czech Rep. 1; Wales 3, Netherlands 2

"C Flight" – *Day One:* Turkey 4, Portugal 1; Belgium 5, Iceland 0. *Day Two:* Turkey 3, Iceland 2; Belgium 3, Portugal 2. *Day Three:* Portugal 5, Iceland 0; Belgium 3½, Turkey 1½

Great Britain & Ireland v Continent of Europe (Jacques Léglise Trophy)

Neguri GC, Spain

Captains: Europe: Gary Strangl (AUT); GB&I: David Boote (WAL)

Continent of Europe names first:

First Day – Foursomes

Jon Rahm (ESP) and Javier Sainz (ESP) lost to Toby Tree (ENG) and Callum Shinkwin (ENG) 6 and 4

Thomas Detry (BEL) and Kenny Subregis (FRA) halved with Gavin Moynihan (IRL) and Gary Hurley (IRL)

Maximilian Rottluff (GER) and Robin Goger (AUT) beat Dermot McElroy (IRL) and David Boote (WAL) 3 and 2

Kristoffer Ventura (NOR) and Goncalo Pinto (POR) lost to Nathan Kimsey (ENG) and Harrison Greenberry (ENG) 2 and 1

Singles

Subregis lost to Shinkwin 5 and 3
Rahm lost to Tree 2 holes
Detry beat Paul Kinnear (ENG) 2 holes
Goger beat Moynihan 2 and 1
Sainz beat Hurley 1 hole
Florian Loutre (FRA) lost to McElroy 4 and 2
Rottluff beat Boote 4 and 3
Ventura lost to Greenberry 1 hole

Second Day – Foursomes

Detry and Subregis lost to Tree and Shinkwin 2 holes

Rahm and Ventura lost to Moynihan and Hurley 4 and 3

Pinto and Sainz halved with McElroy and Boote

Rottluff and Goger lost to Kimsey and Greenberry 1 hole

Singles

Detry lost to Tree 4 and 3
Ventura beat Shinkwin 4 and 3
Sainz lost to Moynihan 3 and 2
Pinto beat Hurley 4 and 3
Loutre halved with Kinnear
Rahm beat Kimsey 5 and 4
Rottluff lost to McElroy 2 and 1
Goger lost to Greenberry 4 and 2

Match result: Europe 9½. GB&I 14½

European Boys Challenge Trophy *Welton GC, Slovakia*

1	Simon Zach (CZE)	70-67-66—203
2	Max Albertus (NED)	70-68-66—204
3	Martijn Broeren (NED)	68-69-68—205

Team competition – Five scores from six to count each day:

1	Netherlands	354-350-337—1,041
2	Czech Republic	355-352-343—1,050
3	Wales	353-348-350—1,051

4 Belgium 1,081; 5 Poland 1,090; 6 Turkey 1,104; 7 Slovakia 1,128; 8 Hungary 1,138; 9 Estonia 1,145; 10 Russia 1,149

Winning Team: Rowin Caron, Max Albertus, Martijn Broeren, Philip Bootsma, Lars Van Meijel and Aaron Van Den Dungen

Boys' Home Internationals (R&A Trophy) (inaugurated 1985) *Royal St David's*

Day One:	Ireland 8½, Wales 6½; Scotland 6, England 9
Day Two:	Ireland 5½, Scotland 9½; England 8½, Wales 6½
Day Three:	Scotland 5½, Wales 9½; England 11, Ireland 4

Result: 1 England 28½; 2 Wales 22½; 3 Scotland 21; 4 Ireland 18

Winning Team: Derek Hughes (non-playing captain); Oliver Carr (Heswall), Harry Casey (Enfield), Matthew Fitzpatrick (Hallamshire), Curtis Griffiths (Wentworth), Patrick Kelly (Boston West), Nathan Kimsey (Woodhall Spa), Paul Kinnear (Formby), Max Orrin (North Foreland), Gregory Payne (Chobham), Callum Shinkwin (Moor Park), Toby Tree (Worthing)

English Boys County Championships *Luffenham Heath*

1 Lincolnshire; 2 Surrey; 3 Yorkshire; 4 Devon

Winning Team: Geoff Smith (Team Manager), Patrick Kelly, Jordan Wrisdale, Ben Anderson, Billy Spooner, Rob Mackay, Chris Pearson, Ashton Turner

Irish Boys Inter-Provisional Championship *Co Sligo*

Day One	Leinster 7½, Connaught 2½
	Ulster 4½, Munster 5½
Day Two	Leinster 6, Ulster 4
	Munster 5, Connaught 5
Day Three	Ulster 6, Connaught 4
	Leinster 3½, Munster 6½

Final Table

	W	D	L
Munster	2	1	0
Leinster	2	0	1
Ulster	1	0	2
Connaught	0	1	2

Winning team: Gary Hurley (West Waterford), Eoin Douglas (Harris), Kieran Lynch (Skibbereen), Colin O'Sullivan (Fota Island), Jack Leacy (Dungarvan), Robin Dawson (Faithlegg), Jack Ryan (Charleville). Captain: Jim Long

Scottish Boys Area Team Championship *Hayston*

1 Lothians 360; 2 Ayrshire 362; 3 Fife 364; 5 South 370; 6 Lanarkshire 371; 7 Glasgow 372; 8 Borders 375; 9 Renfrewshire 378; 10 North 381; 11 Argyll & Bute 382; 12 Clackmannanshire 383; 13 Perth & Kinross 385; 14 Angus 390; 15 North East 392; 16 Stirlingshire, Dumbartonshire 393

Winning Team: Anthony Blaney, Grant Forrest, Calum Hill, Lee Morgan
Individual (Niagara Cup): Jamie Savage (Glasgow) 68

Toyota Junior World Cup
Cancelled

All-Africa Junior Golf Challenge *Windhoek Golf and Country Club, Namibia*

1	South Africa	209-212-212-214—847
2	Namibia	212-215-214-222—863
3	Zimbabwe	225-230-221-221—897
4	Kenya	243-237-232-242—954

Individual:

1	Haydn Porteous (RSA)	67-69-67-67—270
2	Christiaan Bezuidenhout (RSA)	70-71-68-72—281
3	Glen de Waal (NAM)	71-70-70-73—284

Sport in Japan affected by earthquake

The devastation and aftermath of the earthquake and tsunami which hit Japan in March, 2011, played havoc with the country's busy sporting calendar. Among many affected events including those from football, baseball, ice skating, tennis, cycling and athletics were several from the world of golf including the Yokohama Tire PRGR Ladies Cup, T Point Ladies, Yamaha Ladies Open, and Studio Alice Open.

Even when local and national conditions did not prevent the staging of an event, many sportsmen and women expressed their wish not to participate when so many people in Japan were facing difficulties.

Another important golfing event to be cancelled was the Toyota Junior World Cup at Chukyo which, in 2010, saw the Japanese team of Daijiro Izamida, Genzo Tokimazu, Yosuke Asaji and Taihei Sato victorious over the team from the USA with Canada, Denmark and Thailand jointly sharing third place.

Who is known as "Slow Motion"?

The answer can be found on page 905

I AM YOUR BEST SHOT

I AM THE NIKON D3100. I am innovative and simple to use. Featuring Guide Mode and Live View with Scene Auto Selector to help you create great pictures the easy way. With Full HD Movie, 14.2 megapixels, 11-point Autofocus and EXPEED 2 image processing. I am built to help. **www.nikon.co.uk**

At the heart of the image

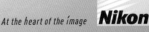

Sustaining

WALKING IN THE FOOTSTEPS OF THE GREATS: PRICELESS®

Designed to give you the perfect drive.

Ditto.

RLX
RALPH LAUREN

GOLF

LUXURY TECHNOLOGY PERFORMANCE
TOP WORLD-RANKED PROFESSIONAL GOLFER
LUKE DONALD

Who helps you get more from your game?

With HSBC Premier, you will enjoy free membership to our HSBC Premier Golf Network. This exclusive service provides players of all abilities with preferential access to some of the best courses in Britain.

Our fantastic green fees, exclusive offers and bespoke lesson packages with PGA Pros will help you get the most out of this great game.

To discover more about HSBC Premier, visit hsbc.co.uk/premier or your local branch.

Or call us on 0800 432 0576.

To find out about our Premier Golf Network, visit www.hsbc.co.uk/premier-golf-network.

Girls' and Junior Ladies' Tournaments

For past results see earlier editions of *The R&A Golfer's Handbook*

British Girls Open Amateur Championship *Gullane No 1*

Leading Qualifier: Noemí Jiménez (ESP) 71-70—141

Quarter-Finals:
Georgie Hall (ENG) beat Emilie Alonso (FRA) 5 and 3
Margaux Vanmol (BEL) beat Sophie Godley (ENG) 7 and 6
Emma Nilsson (SWE) beat Luna Sobrón (ESP) 5 and 4
Celine Boutier (FRA) beat Antonia Scherer (GER) 1 hole

Semi-Finals:
Vanmol beat Hall 3 and 2
Boutier beat Nilsson 3 and 1

Final: Margaux Vanmol beat Celine Boutier 1 hole

English Girls' Close Championship *Ellesborough*

1	Hayley Davis (Ferndown)	70-74-75-66—285
2	Sophie Godley (Lindrick)	75-76-72-70—293
3	Bronte Law (Bramhall)	74-74-72-75—295
	Georgia Hall (Remedy Oak)	77-73-70-75—295

Irish Girls' Close Championship (Blake Cup) (inaugurated 1951) *Donegal*

Leading Qualifier: Paula Grant (Lisburn) 77-74—151

Semi-Finals:
Paula Grant (Lisburn) beat Jean O'Driscoll (Muskerry) 1 hole
Jessica Ross (Clandeboye) beat Eadaoin Cronin (Bantry Bay) at 19th

Final:
Paula Grant beat Jessica Ross 3 and 2

Irish Girls' 54 Hole Open *Knightsbrook*

1	Perrine Delacour (FRA)	71-72-64—207
2	Manon Gidali (FRA)	71-70-70—211
3	Leona Maguire (Slieve Russell)	70-74-68—212

Scottish Ladies' Junior Open Stroke Play Championship (inaugurated 1955)

(formerly Scottish Under-21 Girls Open Stroke Play Championship) *Cardross*

1	Kelsey MacDonald (Nairn Dunbar)	75-70-70—215
2	Nichola Ferguson (Clober)	75-73-73—221
3	Rachel Walker (Dumfries & County)	75-74-73—222

Scottish Girls' Close Championship (inaugurated 1960) *Glenisla*

Semi-Finals:
Eilidh Briggs (Kilmacolm) beat Rachel Walker (Dumfries & County) 3 and 2
Gemma Dryburgh (Beaconsfield) beat Lauren Whyte (St Regulus) 2 and 1

Final: Eilidh Briggs beat Gemma Dryburgh 1 hole

SLGA Under-16 Stroke Play Championship   *Strathmore*
1	Bronte Law (Bramhall) (ENG)	72-70—142	[bsr]
2	Chloe Williams (Wrexham) (ENG)	70-72—142	
3	Amber Ratcliffe (Royal Cromer) (ENG)	74-69—143	

Welsh Girls' Championship (inaugurated 1957)   *Clays*
Leading Qualifier: Katie Bradbury (Cottrell Park) 71-74—145
Semi-Finals:
Katie Bradbury (Cottrell Park) beat Jessica Evans (Newport) 2 and 1
Sara Rees-Evans (Penrhos) beat Myriam Hassan (Southerndown) 2 and 1
Final: Katie Bradbury beat Sara Rees-Evans 1 hole

Welsh Girls' Under-16   *Royal St David's*
1	Nia Greville (Ashburnham)	85
2	Fauve Birch (Pontardawe)	86
	Angharad Basnett (Borth & Ynyslas)	86

St Andrews Junior Ladies   *St Andrews (Strathtyrum and Old Courses)*
Golf Monthly Trophy:
Semi-Finals: Emma Greenlees (Dumfries and Galloway) beat Nicola Haynes (Gosforth Park Ladies)
    1 up
    Jessica Meek (Carnoustie Ladies) beat Eleanor Tunn (Reay) 3 and 2
Final: Jessica Meek beat Emma Greenlees 4 and 2
Girls' Open Quaich:
Semi-Finals: Kara Yule (Goswick) beat Chloé Goadby (St Regulus) 2 up
    Samantha Taylor (Parklands) beat Alexandra Tait (St Regulus) 1 up
Final: Kara Yule beat Samatha Taylor 4 and 2

US Girls' Junior Amateur Championship   *Olympia Fields, Illinois (South Course)*
Semi-finals: Ariya Jutanugarn (THA) beat Amy Lee (USA) 8 and 6
    Dottie Ardina (PHI) beat Yu Liu (CHN) 2 and 1
Finals: Ariya Jutanugarn beat Dottie Ardina 2 and 1

Royale Cup Canadian Junior Girls Championship   *Quilchena G&CC, British Columbia*
1	Jennifer Yang	71-70-74-70—285
2	Anica Yoo	75-71-72-70—288
	Soo Bin Kim	72-72-69-75—288
	Jisoo Keel	70-72-72-74—288

Hong Kong Junior Close Championship   *Hong Kong GC (New)*
1	Tiffany Chan	72-70—142
2	Isabella Leung	79-73—152
3	Mimi Ho	76-77—153

Hong Kong Junior Open Championship   *Clearwater Bay GC*
1	Sathika Ruenreong (THA)	78-68—146
2	Yin Zi Jun (CHN)	75-73—148
3	Isabella Leung	75-74—149

Team Events

European Lady Juniors Team Championship

Discontinued – for past results see the 2008 edition of The R&A Golfer's Handbook

European Girls Team Championship   Is Molas, Italy

Stroke-play Qualification: I England 723; 2 Spain 726; 3 France 736

Individual:
I	Emily Taylor (ENG)	70-67—137
2	Stefania Avanzo (ITA)	70-71—141
3	Georgia Hall (ENG)	70-73—143

Final Ranking: I France; 2 England; 3 Spain; 4 Germany; 5 Sweden; 6 Finland; 7 Belgium; 8 Italy; 9 Denmark; 10 Netherlands; 11 Norway; 12 Switzerland; 13 Austria; 14 Ireland; 15 Turkey; 16 Scotland; 17 Russia; 18 Wales; 19 Slovakia

Winning team: Emilie Alonso, Shannon Aubert, Céline Boutier, Laure Castelain, Perrine Delacour, Marion Gidali

Team Results:

"A Flight" – Day One: England 5½ ,Italy 1½; Germany 4, Finland 3; France 5, Belgium 2; Spain 4½, Sweden 2½. Day Two: England 5, Germany 2; France 4, Spain 3; Finland 3½, Italy 1½; Sweden 4, Belgium 1. Day Three – Final: France 4, England 3; Spain 5½, Germany 1½; Sweden 3, Finland 2; Belgium 3½, Italy 1½

"B Flight" – Day One: Netherlands 4, Ireland 1; Switzerland 3, Turkey 2; Norway 3½, Scotland 1½; Denmark 3, Austria 2. Day Two: Netherlands 4, Switzerland 1; Denmark 3, Norway 2; Ireland 3, Turkey 2; Scotland 3, Austria 2. Day Three: Denmark 3½, Netherlands 1½; Norway 3, Switzerland 2; Austria 3½, Ireland 1½; Turkey 3, Scotland 2

"C Flight": Russia 4, Slovakia 1; Russia 3, Wales 2; Wales 3, Slovakia 2

Girls GB&I Internationals (Stroyan Cup)   Gullane No 2

Day I: Foursomes – Scotland 1, Ireland 2; England 2½, Wales ½
Singles – Scotland 2, Ireland 4; England 2, Wales 4

Day 2: Foursomes – Wales 1½, Ireland 1½; England 3, Scotland 0
Singles – Wales 2½, Ireland 3½; England 2, Scotland 4

Day 3: Foursomes – Ireland 0, England 3; Scotland 2½, Wales ½
Singles – Ireland 1½, England 4½; Scotland 3½, Wales 2½

Final Table: I England (17 pts); 2 Scotland (13 pts); 3 Ireland (12½ pts); 4 Wales (11½ pts)

Winning team: Bronte Law, Emily Taylor, Elizabeth Mallett, Brogan Townend, Hayley Davis, Georgia Hall, Alexandra Peters, Meghan Maclaren

---

Junior Solheim Cup   Jack Nicklaus course, Knightsbrook Hotel, Trim, County Meath, Ireland

Captains: Europe: Liselotte Newmann; USA: Meg Mallon

First day, Foursomes
Lauren Taylor (ENG) and Charley Hull (ENG) lost to Mariah Stackhouse and Jaye Marie Green 2 and 1
Lisa and Leona Maguire (IRL) beat Emma Talley and McKenzie Talbert 1 hole
Amy Boulden (WAL) and Emma Nilsson (SWE) beat Kyung Kim and Summar Roachell 4 and 3
Marian Gidali (FRA) and Celine Boutier (FRA) beat Esther Lee and Gabriella Then 1 hole
Emilie Alonso (FRA) and Luna Sobron (ESP) beat Lindsay Weaver and Ashlan Ramsay 2 holes
Antonia Scherer (GER) and Margaux Vanmol (BEL) beat Karen Clung and Alison Lee 4 and 3

First day, Fourballs
Lisa Maguire and Hull lost to Weaver and Stackhouse 1 hole
Boulden and Nilsson halved with Green and Ramsay
Leona Maguire and Taylor beat Kim and Chung 3 and 2
Alonso and Scherer lost to Talbert and Roachell 2 and 1
Gidali and Boutier halved with Alison Lee ands Esther Lee
Vanmol and Sobron lost to Then and Talley 3 and 1

Match position: Europe 7, USA 5

Junior Solheim Cup *continued*

Second day: Singles

Nilsson lost to Green   3 and 2

Leona Maguire beat Stackhouse   5 and 4

Taylor lost to Then   1 hole

Boulden beat Talley   4 and 2

Gidali halved with Ramsay

Sobron lost to Roachell   1 hole

Lisa Maguire lost to Alison Lee   3 and 2

Scherer beat Talbert   4 and 2

Vanmol beat Kim   3 and 2

Alonso lost to Esther Lee   1 hole

Hull lost to Weaver   1 hole

Boutier halved with Chung

Result: Europe 12, USA 12 (USA retain trophy)

GB&I Under 16 v Continent of Europe Under 16   *Royal Porthcawl, Wales*

Captains: Sue Turner (GB&I), Kirstin Gunhildrud (Europe)

First Day – Foursomes:

Charley Hull (ENG) and Georgia Hall (ENG) beat Karolin Lampert (GER) and Quirine Eijkenboom (GER)   1 hole

Amber Ratcliffe (ENG) and Clara Young (SCO) lost to Clara Baena (ESP) and Ha Rang Lee (ESP)   1 hole

Chloe Williams (WAL) and Bronte Law (ENG) halved with Emily Pedersen (DEN) and Shannon Aubert (FRA)

Singles:

Hull lost to Lampert   4 and 2

Williams lost to Aubert   6 and 5

Ratcliffe lost to Baena   4 and 3

Hall beat Lee   3 and 2

Young lost to Pedersen 7 and 5

Law lost Eijkenboom   3 and 2

Second Day – Foursomes:

Hull and Hall lost to Lampert and Eijkenboom   3 and 2

Ratcliffe and Young lost to Lee and Baena   4 and 3

Williams and Law beat Pedersen and Aubert   6 and 5

Singles:

Law lost to Lampert   1 hole

Hall halved with Baena

Williams beat Lee   2 and 1

Ratcliffe lost to Aubert   4 and 3

Hull lost to Pedersen   2 holes

Young lost to Eijkenboom   4 and 2

Result: GB&I 5, Continent of Europe 3

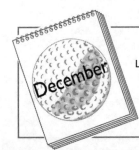

Month by month in 2011

Luke Donald completes unprecedented same season double of money list titles in America and Europe. Rory McIlroy, Alvaro Quiros, Ian Poulter and Lee Westwood (twice) taste success, Tiger Woods finally wins again after more than two years at the Chevron World Challenge and Alexis Thompson, only 16, takes the Dubai Ladies Masters.

Mixed Boys' and Girls' Events

For past results see earlier editions of *The R&A Golfer's Handbook*

R&A Junior Open Championships

This event will next be held in 2012

European Young Masters Nations Cup *Royal Balaton GC, Hungary*

1	657	Spain (Harang Lee, Clara Baena, Mario Galiano, Iván Cantero)
2	670	Italy
3	675	Norway

4 Finland; 5 Sweden; 6 France; 7 Czech Rep.; 8 England; 9 Scotland; 10 Belgium; 11 Netherlands; 12 Switzerland; 13 Germany; 14 Wales; 15 Ireland; 16 Poland, Turkey; 18 Slovenia; 19 Austria; 20 Portugal, Slovakia; 22 Iceland; 23 Russia; 24 Hungary, Latvia

Boys Individual

1	Kenny Subregis (FRA)	72-74-70—216
2	Kai Kürschner (GER)	74-75-74—223
	Kristoffer Ventura (NOR)	76-72-75—223
	Kristian Johannessen (NOR)	71-75-77—223

Girls Individual

1	Harang Lee (ESP)	72-71-68—211
2	Charlotte De Corte (BEL)	73-74-73—220
3	Clara Baena (ESP)	75-75-72—222
	Virginia Elena Carta (ITA)	76-72-74—222

Faldo Series

Established by Sir Nick Faldo in 1996, there are now 35 Faldo Series in 25 countries worldwide. Over 5,000 young golfers take part each year with two major finals – one in Europe and the other in Asia. Among those who have benefitted in the past from the competition have been Taiwanese golfer Yani Tseng, winner of three majors on the LPGA Tour in 2011, and Northern Ireland's Rory McIlroy, the 2011 US Open champion.

Great Britain and Ireland:

Boys:			Girls:		
Moortown	Daniel Wasteney (ENG)	144	Sophie Powell (ENG)	151	
West Lancs	Oliver Carr (ENG)	140	Brogan Townend (ENG)	142	
Walton Heath	Bradley Thomas (ENG)	144	Shannon Flynn (ENG)	155	
Lough Erne	Gavin Moynihan (IRL)	146	—		
R Ashdown Forest	Tom Aspital (ENG)	144	Chelsea Masters (ENG)	150	
Trentham	David Boote (WAL)	148	Natasha Fear (ENG)	161	
Roxburghe	Richard Pickard (ENG)	136	Jordana Graham (SCO)	149	
Pyle & Kenfig	Jordan Smith (ENG)	143	Elizabeth Sweetman (ENG)	157	
The Grove	Ben Stow (ENG)	139	Sophie Madden (ENG)	135	
Hollinwell	Jamie Bower (ENG)	140	Amber Ratcliffe (ENG)	143	

Europe:

Czech Rep.	Ondrej Lieser (CZE)	135	Telc GC
Russia	Nikolay Kovalevsky (RUS)	223	Agalarov G&CC
Greece	Vasili Kartos (USA)	152	Costa Navarino
Netherlands	Michael Kraaij (NED)	217	Goyer G&CC
Germany	Warayu Melzer (GER)	146	Sporting Club, Berlin
Slovakia	Vitek Novak (CXZE)	214	Black Stork

Faldo Series *continued*

South America:

Brazil	Juan Alvarez (URU)	214	Damha, São Paulo

Final *Lough Erne*

1	Gavin Samuels (ENG)	76-78-68—222
2	Cameron Long (ENG)	79-78-70—227
	Adam Andrews (ENG)	76-77-74—227

Asia:

2009–2010	Masamichi Ito (JPN)	75-70-69—214	Mission Hills
2010–2011	Abhijit Chada (IND)	73-69-74—216	Mission Hills

2011–2012 Series:

Philippines	Alexes Nallos (PHI)	223	Filipinas
Shanghai	Tianyi Wu (CHN)	145	Silport
China	Zihao Chen (CHN)	137	Mission Hills
Chinese Taipei	Wei-Lun Wang (TPE)	139	National , Miaoli
Pakistan	Mubariz Ahmed (PAK)	234	Karachi
Vietnam	Truong Chi Quan (VIE)	152	Ocean Dunes
India	Vashishta Pawar (IND)	295	Boona
India (Girls)	Asok Aditi (IND)	221	Boona
Singapore	Joshua Ho Sheng Liang (SIN)	136	Tanah Merah
Malaysia	Hisyam Majid (MAS)	211	Royal Sengalor
Hong Kong	Terrence Ng (HKG)	152	Kau Sai Chau (North)
Brunei	Kumaresan Shanmugam	144.	Empire Hotel

6th Faldo Series Asian Final: Mission Hills (Faldo Course), Shenzhen, China (March 2012)

The Junior Ryder Cup

This event will next be held in 2012

Duke of York Young Champions Trophy   *Royal Liverpool GC, Hoylake*

1	Harry Casey (ENG)*	80-75-71—226
2	Harang Lee (ESP)	78-77-71—226

Casey won at first extra hole

3	Haydn Porteous (RSA)	79-75-73—227
4	Antonia Scherer (GER)	78-75-75—228

Boys:

1	Harry Casey (ENG)	80-75-71—226
2	Haydn Porteous (RSA)	79-75-73—227
3	Cody Proveaux (USA)	79-79-71—229

Girls:

1	Harang Lee (ESP)	78-77-71—226
2	Antonia Scherer (GER)	78-75-75—228
3	Perrine Delacour (FRA)	77-80-74—231
	Amy Boulden (WAL)	78-78-75—231

What is the answer?

Q: Why do golfers shout "fore"?

A: There really is no definite answer. The term "fore", which has been in use since 1881, has some relation to the forecaddie, a person employed to go ahead of players to indicate where their shots finish.

Paul Lawrie Foundation Junior Open Deeside GC

Boys (Scratch):	1 Chris Lamb (Newmacher)	68
	2 Sam Kiloh (Portlethen)	71
	3 Christopher Kelman (Deeside)	75
Boys (Nett):	Greg Morrison (Northern 6)	67
Girls (Scratch):	Kirsten Pryde (Deeside 11)	74

Paul Lawrie Foundation Match-play Championship Newmachar

Boys:

3rd/4th place play-off:
Ben Murray (Portlethan) beat Ray Gordon (Alford) 4 and 3

Final: Chris Lamb (Newmachar) beat Lewis Mutch (Duff House) 2 and 1

Girls:

3rd/4th place play-off:
Tegwen Seivwright (Deeside) beat Kirsten Pryde (Deeside) 2 holes

Final: Kimberley Beveridge (Aboyne) beat Sophie Alexander (Deeside) 5 and 4

Junior Orange Bowl Biltmore GC, Florida

Boys:

| 1 | Juan Cerda (CHI)* | 68-70-70-70—278 |
| 2 | Thomas Detry (BEL) | 72-69-68-69—278 |

*Cerda won at the third extra hole

| 3 | Markus Maukner (AUT) | 68-68-73-70—279 |

Girls:

1	Hyo-Joo Kim (KOR)	68-70-69-74—281
2	Perrina Delacour (FRA)	72-73-70-67—282
3	Brooke Henderson (CAN)	73-71-69-71—284

Callaway Junior Golf Championship California, USA

Boys:			**Girls:**	
15–17	Beau Hossler (USA)	285	Hyo-Joo Kim (KOR)	281
13–14	Zechenq Dou (CHN)	208	Lilia Khatu Uu (USA)	211
11–12	Tian Lang Guan (CHN)	198	Xiang Sui (CHN)	207
9–10	Ricky Castillo (USA)	211	Brooke Seay (USA)	171
7–8	Kota Marukami (JPN)	169	Unamanee Wongaroon (THA)	171
6 and under	Ken Shibata (JPN)	162	Saori Tijima (JPN)	170

Team event:

| 15–17 | 1 Korea; 2 Japan; 3 USA | 1 Japan; 2 Canada; 3 Colombia |

Juan Cerda and Hyo Joo Kim win Orange Bowl

Juan Cerda from Chile eagled the third hole of his sudden death play-off with Belgium's Thomas Detry to win the 2011 Junior Orange Bowl Championship at The Biltmore Golf Club, Coral Gables, Florida. Cerda and Detry completed 72 holes in six under par 278 and played the 18th hole three times both making par and birdie at their first two attempts. On the third occasion, however, Cerda eagled and Detry could only birdie.

Markus Maukner of Austria on 279 and Emil Sogaard of Denmark on 280 finished third and fourth, respectively. Jim Liu, the 2010 US Junior Amateur champion, was part of a three-way tie with France's Kenny Subregis and American Austin Smotherman for fifth at 282.

In the Girls' competition, South Korean Hyo Joo Kim took the title finishing on three under par 281 one shot ahead of France's Perrina Delacour. Canadian Brooke Henderson was third on even par 284 at even par with another French girl Celine Boutier, a shot further back in fourth.

Lewis emulates Sir Nick as Cotton Rookie

Tom Lewis, who made history in October by winning on only his third professional start on The European Tour, was the Sir Henry Cotton Rookie of the Year for 2011.

The 20 year old Englishman from Welwyn Garden City – where Sir Nick Faldo first started to play golf – claimed the prestigious award 34 years after six-time Major Champion Faldo received the rookie award before going on to become the most successful English golfer of all time.

"I appreciate this honour very much. It certainly tops off what has been an amazing year," said Lewis. "I think my dad is more excited about me winning this award than my first Tour victory in October! I am very proud to be named The Sir Henry Cotton Rookie of the Year and I feel very fortunate as there were some strong contenders for this title who played consistently well all season."

Lewis, who shot to prominence with his opening 65 in this year's Open Championship at Royal St. George's – the lowest round by an amateur in The Open's history and one which gave him a share of the lead – produced the same score in the final round of the Portugal Masters three months later to win on his third professional outing, the quickest victory by an Affiliate Member in Tour history.

In between those historic rounds, Lewis played his part of the Great Britain & Ireland Walker Cup side's victory over the United States at Royal Aberdeen before joining the professional ranks and producing a top-ten finish in his first event in Austria.

He then finished 70th in the Alfred Dunhill Links Championship before going on to record his maiden success in Portugal which set up the platform for a final placing of 66th in The Race to Dubai with earnings of €459,266.

To put the achievement in perspective, Tiger Woods required five tournaments to land his first professional title, while Rory McIlroy did not taste success until his 38th European Tour event.

Lewis paid tribute to his father and coach, Brian, a former Tour professional, who has been an influential presence during his son's rise through the amateur game into the professional ranks.

"I might not even have been a golfer if it wasn't for dad, but he has definitely made me into the golfer I've become. He is really the person who made this possible.

"It's been a rollercoaster year. I didn't perform very well in the first half then had the honour of playing with Tom Watson in the first two rounds of The Open, managing to share the first round lead. It was wonderful to win the Silver Medal and shoot 65 in the first round, but I think people will remember the 65 in Portugal because it secured my first professional win."

Lewis was the choice of a panel comprising The R&A, The European Tour and the Association of Golf Writers, ahead of several strong candidates from the 2010 Challenge Tour including Denmark's Thorbjørn Olesen and Scott Jamieson of Scotland, who both finished ahead of Lewis in The Race to Dubai having qualified for the season-ending Dubai World Championship presented by DP World.

Olesen enjoyed three joint second place finishes in accumulating €637,703 to finish 48th in The Race to Dubai, while Jamieson shared third place on three occasions to finish the year with earnings of €523,754 and 59th place in The Race to Dubai.

Lewis is the 47th recipient of The Sir Henry Cotton Rookie of the Year Award, stretching back to 1960, and the 22nd Englishman, following several illustrious fellow countrymen including Faldo, Tony Jacklin, Peter Oosterhuis, Mark James, Ian Poulter and Paul Casey. Chris Wood was the last English winner in 2009 while Lewis succeeds 2010 winner, Italian teenager Matteo Manassero.

PART IX

Tournaments for the Disabled

Tournaments for the Disabled

For past results see earlier editions of *The R&A Golfer's Handbook*

British Blind Open *Hilton Hotel and Golf Resort, Templepatrick, Northern Ireland*
Men:
Overall Champion: John Eakin (ENG) B3 73-69—142
Best B1: Andrea Calcaterra (ITA) 81-81—162   **Best B3:** John Eakin (ENG) 73-69—142
Best B2: Garrett Slattery (RSA) 78-75—153

Women:
Best B1: C Giacossa (ITA) 73-87—160   **Best B2:** Jan Dinsdale (NIR) 82-74—156

British Blind Masters *Tewkesbury Park Hotel. Gloucestershire*
I	Ron Tomlinson B1	72-66-70-67—275

English Match Play Championships (for blind golfers) *Patshull Park GC, Shropshire*
I	Steve Beevers beat Billy McAllister 3 and 2

English Stroke Play Championships (for blind golfers) *Guadet Luce GC, Worcestershire*
I	Bill McAllister B1	58-57—115

Scottish Match Play Championships (for blind golfers) *Gleddoch GC, Port Glasgow*
Alistair Reid beat Gerry Kelly I up

Scottish Stroke Play Championships (for blind golfers) *Drumoig GC*
I	Myles Clark	74-72—146

Scotland v England Blind Golf Competition for the Auld Enemy Cup
Westerwood GCC
Scotland 4, England 2
Torrential rain washed out days two and three and the two Captains agreed that the results from day one should determine the outcome of the match

The Celtic Cup (for blind golfers) Ireland v Scotland   *Royal Dublin GC*
Scotland 6, Ireland 4

World Blind Golf Championships
This event will next be held in 2012

Blind Golf Categories: B1 Totally blind; B2 From the ability to recognise the shape of a hand up to visual acuity of 20/600; B3 From visual acuity above 20/600 up to visual acuity of less than 20/200

Donations to special needs groups

The R&A supports several organisations which run golf events for players with special needs. In 2011, £50,000 was set aside for this purpose and a similar amount will be allocated this year. In addition, The R&A does, on occasion, send referees and other representatives to events run for disabled golfers.

74th One-Armed Golf Society World Championships (inaugurated 1932)
Co Meath GC, Trim, Ireland
Match Play Final: Alex Hjallmarson (Haverdals GC, Sweden) beat Robert Paul (Walmer & Kingsdown GC, England) 1 up
Strokeplay Champion: Darren Grey (Darlington GC, England) Gross 164 for 2 qualifying rounds
Best Nett: John Condie (Antrim GC, Northern Ireland) 144 for 2 qualifying rounds
Bob Hughes Cup: Terry Adnams (Barkston GC, England) 38 points
Cattanach Cup: Mary Fahey (Lucan GC, Ireland) 39 points
Presidents Prize: John Condie (Antrim GC, Northern Ireland) 34 points

Disabled British Open (inaugurated 2009) *East Sussex National*
Overall Gross Champion: Duncan Hamilton-Martin (St George's Hill) 145
Nett Champion Category 1 (Handicap 0–13.4): Andy Gardiner (Banbury) 138
Nett Champion Category 2 (Handicap 13.5–20.4): Alan Jackson (Romford) 130
Nett Champion Category 3 (Stableford – H/cap 20.5+): David Walker (Westgate & Birchington) 73 points
Junior Stableford Winner: Frankie Jones (Welshpool) 83 points

BALASA National Championship *Broome Manor Golf Complex, Swindon*
Gross Champion: Duncan Hamilton-Martin 152

Category 1 Nett:		Category 2 Nett:		Category 3 Stableford:	
1 S Bakker	142	1 M Jelley	145	1 K Cook	69 pts
2 S Lewis	144	2 A Elliot	145	2 M Dalby	64 pts
3 C Foster	146	3 A Gardiner	147	3 K Wallace	61 pts

Cup of Nations *Le Torre GC Murcia, Spain*

1	United Kingdom	447	(D Hamilton-Martin, K Harmison, A Gardiner, M Smith)
2	Denmark	464	(S Morkholt, M Lykke Nielsen, K Schmager)
3	France	468	(C Henri-Quelin, M Cauneau, P Frison, O Lecocq)

College Park Cup (formerly the Robinson Cup) *Rio Verde CC, Rio Verde, AZ*
USA v International (USA names first)
Morning – foursomes:
Brent Bleyenberg and Kimberly Moore beat Jesse Florkowski and Reinhard Friske 2 and 1
John Brough and Scott Fickenscher beat Dan Hewitt and Don Young 6 and 5
Brandon Rowland and Mike Carver beat Bob MacDermott and Dallas Smith 4 and 3
John Novak and Cory Crowell beat Woody Walker and Mike Wraight 2 and 1
Curtis Baker and Dan Cox halved with Caroline Larsson and Vic McClelland
Roe Skidmore and Kenny Bontz beat Josh Williams and Ed Krayewski 4 and 3
Lucian Newman III and Chad Pfeifer beat Johannes Grames and Bernard Ouellet 5 and 4
Kellie Valentine and Bill Harding beat Jennie Frost and Steve Herndon, 6 and 5

Afternoon – singles

Newman beat Hewitt 6 and 4
Brough halved with Young
Crowell beat Krayewski 1 up
Valentine beat Ouellet 4 and 2
Fickenscher lost to Florkowski 7 and 5
Skidmore lost to Wraight 5 and 4

Novak halved with Smith
Bleyenberg lost to Frost 3 and 1
Carver lost to Friske 1 up
Cox lost to Hernden 3 and 2
Baker lost to Walker 1 up
Moore lost to Davies 4 and 2

Pfeifer lost to MacDermott 2 and 1
Bontz halved with Williams
Rowland beat McClelland 4 and 3
Vincent lost to Grames 3 and 2

Result: USA 11½, International 12½

SDGP Competitions

The Dukes: Bob Drysdale
Swanston New: Paul Cunningham
Charleton: Ruairidh Deans
Pumpherston: Jim Gales
Alloa Schawpark: Winning Team
– Steve Bramwell, Steve Cooke,
Mark Cooke
Niddry Castle: Ian White
Bonnyton: Ian White

Balmorral: Steven Cunningham
St Michaels: Colin Brock
Elmwood: Colin Brock
Scottish C/ship – Gross: Alasdair
Berry; Stableford: Colin Brock
World Team Cup: England
Dalmahoy East Course:
Malcolm Gerdes-Hanson

Kittocks Fairmount St Andrews:
Ruairidh Deans
Craigentinny: William McEwan
Carluke: Steven Cunningham
Balburnie Park: Steven
Cunningham
Tulliallan: Peter Osborne
Order of Merit winner: Colin
Brock

Other Events (winners from host nation unless stated)

Australian Amputee Open
Open Champion: Shane Luke; Ladies Champion: Trudy Tassone; Senior Champion: Ray Piper

Australian Blind Golf Open
Overall Champion: Jeff Ellis (Victoria) B3

Australian Stableford Championship
Jeff Ellis (Victoria) B3

Canadian Amputee National Open
Men's Overall Champion: Josh Williams; Senior Champion: Laurent Hurtbise; Super Senior Champion:
Ken Nichols; Ladies' Overall Champion: Gwen Davies

Men's Team World Handigolf Championship
1 Sweden; 2 Denmark; 3 Japan

Nedbank SA Disabled Golf Open
Daniel Slabbert

Norwegian Open
Cat. A: Manuel de los Santos (DOM); Cat. B: Andy Gardiner (ENG)

Swedish Invitational
Stefan Mörkholt (DEN)

USBGA National Championship
B1: David Meador; B2: Jeremy Poincenot; B3: Mike McKone

64th USA National Amputee Championship
National Champion (Men): Chad Pfeifer; (Women): Kimberly Moore

22nd USA National Senior Amputee Championship
National Champion (Men): Bob McDermott; (Women): Judi Brush

Victorian Blind Open
Graham Coulton (NSW) B2

Blind Golf Categories: B1 Totally blind; B2 From the ability to recognise the shape of a hand up to visual acuity of
20/600; B3 From visual acuity above 20/600 up to visual acuity of less than 20/200

Golf organisations for the disabled

International Blind Golf Association
English Blind Golf Association
Scottish Blind Golf Association
BALASA
British Amputee Golf Association
The Society of One Armed Golfers
European Disabled Golf Association
Deaf Golf Association
Disabled British Open

www.internationalblindgolf.org
www.blindgolf.co.uk
www.scottishblindgolf.com
01773 715984
www.baga.org.uk
www.onearmgolf.org
www.edgagolf.com
www.deafgolf.com
www.disabledbritishopen.org

PART X

Record Scoring

Record Scoring

In the Major Championships nobody has shot lower than 63. There have been eight 63s in the Open, four 63s in the US Open, two 63s in The Masters and 11 63s in the USPGA Championship. The lowest first 36 holes is 130 by Nick Faldo in the 1992 Open at Muirfield and the lowest 72 hole total is 265 by David Toms in the 2001 USPGA Championship at the Atlanta Athletic Club.

The Open Championship

Most times champions
6 Harry Vardon, 1896–98–99–1903–11–14
5 James Braid, 1901–05–06–08–10; JH Taylor, 1894–95–1900–09–13; Peter Thomson, 1954–55–56–58–65; Tom Watson, 1975–77–80–82–83

Most times runner-up
7 Jack Nicklaus, 1964–67–68–72–76–77–79
6 JH Taylor, 1896–1904–05–06–07–14

Oldest winner
Old Tom Morris, 46 years 99 days, 1867
Roberto De Vicenzo, 44 years 93 days, 1967

Youngest winner
Young Tom Morris, 17 years 5 months 8 days, 1868
Willie Auchterlonie, 21 years 24 days, 1893
Severiano Ballesteros, 22 years 3 months 12 days, 1979

Youngest and oldest competitor
Young Tom Morris, 15 years, 4 months, 29 days, 1866
Gene Sarazen, 71 years 4 months 13 days, 1973

Widest margin of victory
13 strokes Old Tom Morris, 1862
12 strokes Young Tom Morris, 1870
8 strokes JH Taylor, 1900 and 1913; James Braid, 1908; Tiger Woods, 2000
7 strokes Louis Oosthuizen, 2010

Lowest winning aggregates
267 Greg Norman, 66-68-69-64, Sandwich, 1993
268 Tom Watson, 68-70-65-65, Turnberry, 1977; Nick Price, 69-66-67-66, Turnberry, 1994
269 Tiger Woods, 67-66-67-69, St Andrews, 2000
270 Nick Faldo, 67-65-67-71, St Andrews, 1990; Tiger Woods 67-65-71-67, Hoylake, 2006

Lowest in relation to par
19 under Tiger Woods, St Andrews, 2000
18 under Nick Faldo, St Andrews, 1990; Tiger Woods, Hoylake, 2006

Lowest aggregate by runner-up
269 (68-70-65-66), Jack Nicklaus, Turnberry, 1977; (69-63-70-67), Nick Faldo, Sandwich, 1993; (68-66-68-67), Jesper Parnevik, Turnberry, 1994

Lowest aggregate by an amateur
281 (68-72-70-71), Iain Pyman, Sandwich, 1993; (75-66-70-70), Tiger Woods, Royal Lytham, 1996

Lowest round
63 Mark Hayes, second round, Turnberry, 1977; Isao Aoki, third round, Muirfield, 1980; Greg Norman, second round, Turnberry, 1986; Paul Broadhurst, third round, St Andrews, 1990; Jodie Mudd, fourth round, Royal Birkdale, 1991; Nick Faldo, second round, Payne

Stewart, fourth round, Sandwich, 1993; Rory McIlroy, first round, St Andrews, 2010

Lowest round by an amateur
65 Tom Lewis, first round, Sandwich, 2011

Lowest first round
63 Rory McIlroy, St Andrews, 2010

Lowest second round
63 Mark Hayes, Turnberry, 1977; Greg Norman, Turnberry, 1986; Nick Faldo, Sandwich, 1993

Lowest third round
63 Isao Aoki, Muirfield, 1980; Paul Broadhurst, St Andrews, 1990

Lowest fourth round
63 Jodie Mudd, Royal Birkdale, 1991; Payne Stewart, Sandwich, 1993

Lowest first 36 holes
130 (66-64), Nick Faldo, Muirfield, 1992
132 (67-65), Henry Cotton, Sandwich, 1934; Nick Faldo (67-65) and Greg Norman (66-66), St Andrews, 1990; Nick Faldo (69-63), Sandwich, 1993; Tiger Woods (67-65), Hoylake, 2006; Louis Oosthuizen (65-67), St Andrews, 2010

Lowest second 36 holes
130 (65-65), Tom Watson, Turnberry, 1977; (64-66) Ian Baker-Finch, Royal Birkdale, 1991; (66-64) Anders Forsbrand, Turnberry, 1994

Lowest first 54 holes
198 (67-67-64), Tom Lehman, Royal Lytham, 1996
199 (67-65-67), Nick Faldo, St Andrews, 1990; (66-64-69), Nick Faldo, Muirfield, 1992

Lowest final 54 holes
199 (66-67-66), Nick Price, Turnberry, 1994
200 (70-65-65), Tom Watson, Turnberry, 1977; (63-70-67), Nick Faldo, Sandwich, 1993; (66-64-70), Fuzzy Zoeller, Turnberry, 1994; (66-70-64), Nick Faldo, Turnberry 1994

Lowest 9 holes
28 Denis Durnian, first 9, Royal Birkdale, 1983

Champions in three decades
Harry Vardon, 1986, 1903, 1911; JH Taylor, 1894, 1900, 1913; Gary Player, 1959, 1968, 1974

Biggest span between first and last victories
19 years – JH Taylor, 1894–1913
18 years – Harry Vardon, 1896–1914
15 years – Willie Park, 1860–75
15 years – Gary Player, 1959–74
14 years – Henry Cotton, 1934–48

Successive victories
4 Young Tom Morris, 1868–72 (no championship 1871)
3 Jamie Anderson, 1877–79; Bob Ferguson, 1880–82, Peter Thomson, 1954–56
2 Old Tom Morris, 1861–62; JH Taylor, 1894–95; Harry Vardon, 1898–99; James Braid, 1905–06; Bobby Jones, 1926–27; Walter Hagen, 1928–29; Bobby Locke, 1949–50; Arnold Palmer, 1961–62; Lee Trevino, 1971–72; Tom Watson, 1982–83; Tiger Woods, 2005–06; Padraig Harrington, 2007–08

Amateur champions
John Ball, 1890, Prestwick; Harold Hilton, 1892, Muirfield and 1897, Royal Liverpool; Bobby Jones, 1926, Royal Lytham; 1927, St Andrews; 1930 Royal Liverpool

Highest number of top five finishes
16 JH Taylor and Jack Nicklaus
15 Harry Vardon and James Braid

Players with four rounds under 70
Ernie Els (68-69-69-68), Sandwich, 1993; Greg Norman (66-68-69-64), Sandwich, 1993; Jesper Parnevik (68-66-68-67), Turnberry, 1994; Nick Price (69-66-67-66), Turnberry, 1994; Tiger Woods (67-66-67-69), St Andrews, 2000; Ernie Els (69-69-68-68), Royal Troon, 2004

Highest number of rounds under 70
37 Nick Faldo	**29** Tom Watson
36 Ernie Els	**26** Greg Norman
33 Jack Nicklaus	**25** Nick Price

Outright leader after every round (since Championship became 72 holes in 1892)
James Braid, 1908; Ted Ray, 1912; Bobby Jones, 1927; Gene Sarazen, 1932; Henry Cotton, 1934; Tom Weiskopf, 1973; Tiger Woods, 2005

Record leads (since 1892)
After 18 holes: 4 strokes – Bobby Jones, 1927; Henry Cotton, 1934; Christy O'Connor jr, 1985
After 36 holes: 9 strokes – Henry Cotton, 1934
After 54 holes: 10 strokes – Henry Cotton, 1934. 7 strokes – Tony Lema, 1964. 6 strokes – James Braid, 1908; Tom Lehman, 1996; Tiger Woods, 2000

Champions with each round lower than previous one
Jack White, 1904, Sandwich, 80-75-72-69; James Braid, 1906, Muirfield, 77-76-74-73; Ben Hogan, 1953, Carnoustie, 73-71-70-68; Gary Player, 1959, Muirfield, 75-71-70-68

Champion with four rounds the same
Densmore Shute, 1933, St Andrews, 73-73-73-73 (excluding the play-off)

Biggest variation between rounds of a champion
14 strokes – Henry Cotton, 1934, second round 65, fourth round 79. 11 strokes – Jack White, 1904, first round 80, fourth round 69; Greg Norman, 1986, first round 74, second round 63, third round 74

Biggest variation between two rounds
20 strokes: RG French, 1938, second round 71, third round 91; Colin Montgomerie, 2002, second round 64, third round 84. 18 strokes: A Tingey Jr, 1923, first round 94, second round 76. 17 strokes – Jack Nicklaus, 1981, first round 83, second round 66; Ian Baker-Finch, 1986, first round 86, second round 69; Rory McIlroy, 2010, first round 63, second round 80

Best comeback by champions
After 18 holes: Harry Vardon, 1896, 11 strokes behind the leader
After 36 holes: George Duncan, 1920, 13 strokes behind leader
After 54 holes: Paul Lawrie, 1999, 10 strokes behind the leader (won four-hole play-off)

Best comeback by non-champions
Of non-champions, Greg Norman, 1989, seven strokes behind the leader and lost in a play-off

Best finishing round by a champion
64 Greg Norman, Sandwich, 1993
65 Tom Watson, Turnberry, 1977; Severiano Ballesteros, Royal Lytham, 1988; Justin Leonard, Royal Troon, 1997

Worst finishing round by a champion since 1920
79 Henry Cotton, Sandwich, 1934
78 Reg Whitcombe, Sandwich, 1938
77 Walter Hagen, Hoylake, 1924

Best opening round by a champion
65 Louis Oosthuizen, St Andrews, 2010

Worst opening round by a champion since 1919
80 George Duncan, Deal, 1920 (he also had a second round of 80)
77 Walter Hagen, Hoylake, 1924

Biggest recovery in 18 holes by a champion
George Duncan, Deal, 1920, was 13 strokes behind the leader, Abe Mitchell, after 36 holes and level after 54

Most consecutive appearances
47 Gary Player, 1955–2001

Championship since 1946 with the fewest rounds under 70
St Andrews, 1946; Hoylake, 1947; Portrush, 1951; Hoylake, 1956; Carnoustie, 1968. All had only two rounds under 70

Longest course
Carnoustie, 2007, 7,421 yards (par 71)

Largest entries
2,499 in 2005, St Andrews

Courses most often used
St Andrews 28; Prestwick 24 (but not since 1925); Muirfield 15; Sandwich 13; Hoylake 11; Royal Lytham and St Annes 10; Royal Birkdale 8; Royal Troon 8; Carnoustie 7; Musselburgh 6; Turnberry 4; Deal 2; Royal Portrush and Prince's 1

Albatrosses
Both Jeff Maggert (6th hole, 2nd round) and Greg Owen (11th hole, 3rd round) made albatrosses during the 2001 Open Championship at Royal Lytham and St Annes. No complete record of albatrosses in the history of the event is available but since 1979 there have been only five others – by Johnny Miller (Muirfield 5th hole) in 1980, Bill Rogers (Royal Birkdale 17th) 1983, Manny Zerman (St Andrews 5th hole) 2000, Gary Evans (Royal Troon 4th) 2004 and Paul Lawrie (Turnberry 7th) 2009

Prize Money

Year	Total	First Prize £	Year	Total	First Prize £	Year	Total	First Prize £
1860	nil	nil	1963	8500	1,500	1991	900,000	90,000
1863	10	nil	1965	10,000	1,750	1992	950,000	95,000
1864	16	6	1966	15,000	2,100	1993	1,000,000	100,000
1876	20	20	1968	20,000	3,000	1994	1,100,000	110,000
1889	22	8	1969	30,000	4,250	1995	1,250,000	125,000
1891	28.50	10	1970	40,000	5,250	1996	1,400,000	200,000
1892	110	(am)	1971	45,000	5,500	1997	1,586,300	250,000
1893	100	30	1972	50,000	5,500	1998	1,774,150	300,000
1910	125	50	1975	75,000	7,500	1999	2,029,950	350,000
1920	225	75	1977	100,000	10,000	2000	2,722,150	500,000
1927	275	100	1978	125,000	12,500	2001	3,229,748	600,000
1930	400	100	1979	155,000	15,500	2002	3,880,998	700,000
1931	500	100	1980	200,000	25,000	2003	3,931,000	700,000
1946	1000	150	1982	250,000	32,000	2004	4,006,950	720,000
1949	1700	300	1983	300,000	40,000	2005	3,854,900	720,000
1953	2450	500	1984	451,000	55,000	2006	3,990,916	720,000
1954	3500	750	1985	530,000	65,000	2007	4,185,400	750,000
1955	3750	1,000	1986	600,000	70,000	2008	4,260,000	750,000
1958	4850	1,000	1987	650,000	75,000	2009	4,206,354	750,000
1959	5000	1,000	1988	700,000	80,000	2010	4,546,305	850,000
1960	7000	1,250	1989	750,000	80,000	2011	5,000,000	900,000
1961	8500	1,400	1990	815,000	85,000			

US Open

Most times champion
4 Willie Anderson, 1901–03–04–05; Bobby Jones, 1923–26–29–30; Ben Hogan, 1948–50–51–53; Jack Nicklaus, 1962–67–72–80

Most times runner-up
5 Phil Mickelson 1999–2002–04–06–09

Oldest winner
Hale Irwin, 45 years, 15 days, Medinah, 1990

Youngest winner
Johnny McDermott, 19 years, 10 months, 12 days, Chicago, 1911

Biggest winning margin
15 strokes Tiger Woods, Pebble Beach, 2000

Lowest winning aggregate
268 Rory McIlroy, Congressional, 2011

Lowest in relation to par
16 under Rory McIlroy, Congressional, 2011

Lowest round
63 Johnny Miller, fourth round, Oakmont, 1973; Jack Nicklaus, first round, Baltusrol, 1980; Tom Weiskopf, first round, Baltusrol, 1980; Vijay Singh, second round, Olympia Fields, 2003

Lowest 9 holes
29 Neal Lancaster, Shinnecock Hills, 1995, and Oakland Hills, 1996

Lowest first 36 holes
131 Rory McIlroy, Congressional, 2011

Lowest final 36 holes
132 Larry Nelson, Oakmont, 1983

Lowest first 54 holes
199 Rory McIlroy, Congressional, 2011

Lowest final 54 holes
203 Rory McIlroy, Congressional, 2011

Most consecutive appearances
44 Jack Nicklaus 1957 to 2000

Open attendances

Year	Attendance	Year	Attendance	Year	Attendance	Year	Attendance
1962	37,098	1975	85,258	1988	191,334	2001	178,000
1963	24,585	1976	92,021	1989	160,639	2002	161,000
1964	35,954	1977	87,615	1990	207,000	2003	182,585
1965	32,927	1978	125,271	1991	192,154	2004	176,000
1966	40,182	1979	134,501	1992	150,100	2005	223,000
1967	29,880	1980	131,610	1993	140,100	2006	230,000
1968	51,819	1981	111,987	1994	128,000	2007	153,000
1969	46,001	1982	133,299	1995	180,000	2008	201,500
1970	82,593	1983	142,892	1996	170,000	2009	123,000
1971	70,076	1984	193,126	1997	176,797	2010	201,000
1972	84,746	1985	141,619	1998	180,000	2011	179,700
1973	78,810	1986	134,261	1999	158,000		
1974	92,796	1987	139,189	2000	230,000		

Successive victories
3 Willie Anderson, 1903–04–05

Players with four rounds under 70
Lee Trevino, 69-68-69-69, Oak Hill, 1968; Lee Janzen, 67-67-69-69, Baltusrol, 1993; Rory McIlroy, 65-66-68-69, Congressional, 2011

Outright leader after every round
Walter Hagen, Midlothian, 1914; Jim Barnes, Columbia, 1921; Ben Hogan, Oakmont, 1953; Tony Jacklin, Hazeltine, 1970; Tiger Woods, Pebble Beach, 2000; Tiger Woods, Bethpage, 2002

Best opening round by a champion
63 Jack Nicklaus, Baltusrol, 1980

Worst opening round by a champion
91 Horace Rawlins, Newport, RI, 1895
Since World War II: 76 Ben Hogan, Oakland Hills, 1951; Jack Fleck, Olympic, 1955

Amateur champions
Francis Ouimet, Brookline, 1913; Jerome Travers, Baltusrol, 1915; Chick Evans, Minikahda, 1916; Bobby Jones, Inwood, 1923, Scioto, 1926, Winged Foot, 1929, Interlachen, 1930; Johnny Goodman, North Shore, 1933

The Masters

Most times champion
6 Jack Nicklaus, 1963–65–66–72–75–86
4 Arnold Palmer, 1958–60–62–64; Tiger Woods, 1997–2001–02–05

Most times runner-up
4 Ben Hogan, 1942–46–54–55; Jack Nicklaus, 1964–71–77–81

Oldest winner
Jack Nicklaus, 46 years, 2 months, 23 days, 1986

Youngest winner
Tiger Woods, 21 years, 3 months, 15 days, 1997

Biggest winning margin
12 strokes Tiger Woods, 1997

Lowest winning aggregate
270 Tiger Woods, 1997

Lowest in relation to par
18 under Tiger Woods, Augusta, 1997

Lowest aggregate by an amateur
281 Charles Coe, 1961 (joint second)

Lowest round
63 Nick Price, 1986; Greg Norman, 1996

Lowest 9 holes
29 Mark Calcavecchia, 1992; David Toms, 1998

Lowest first 36 holes
131 Raymond Floyd, 1976

Lowest final 36 holes
131 Johnny Miller, 1975

Lowest first 54 holes
201 Raymond Floyd, 1976; Tiger Woods, 1997

Lowest final 54 holes
200 Tiger Woods, 1997

Most appearances
52 Gary Player 1957–2009
50 Arnold Palmer 1955–2004

Successive victories
2 Jack Nicklaus, 1965–66; Nick Faldo, 1989–90; Tiger Woods, 2001–02

Players with four rounds under 70
None

Outright leader after every round
Craig Wood, 1941; Arnold Palmer, 1960; Jack Nicklaus, 1972; Raymond Floyd, 1976; Rory McIlroy, Congressional, 2011

Best opening round by a champion
65 Raymond Floyd, 1976

Worst opening round by a champion
75 Craig Stadler, 1982

Worst closing round by a champion
75 Trevor Immelman, 2008

Albatrosses
There have been three albatross twos in the Masters at Augusta National: by Gene Sarazen at the 15th, 1935; by Bruce Devlin at the eighth, 1967; and by Jeff Maggert at the 13th, 1994.

USPGA Championship

Most times champion
5 Walter Hagen, 1921–24–25–26–27; Jack Nicklaus 1963–71–73–75–80

Most times runner-up
4 Jack Nicklaus, 1964–65–74–83

Oldest winner
Julius Boros, 48 years 4 months 18 days, Pecan Valley, 1968

Youngest winner
Gene Sarazen, 20 years 5 months 22 days, Oakmont, 1922

Biggest winning margin
7 strokes Jack Nicklaus, Oak Hill, 1980

Lowest winning aggregate
265 −15: David Toms, Atlanta Athletic Club, 2001
267 −17: Steve Elkington and Colin Montgomerie, Riviera, 1995 (beat Colin Montgomerie in sudden death play-off)

Lowest aggregate by runner-up
266 −14: Phil Michelson, Atlanta Athletic Club, 2001
267 −17: Colin Montgomerie, Riviera, 1995 (lost sudden death play-off to Steve Elkington)

Lowest in relation to par
18 under Tiger Woods and Bob May, Valhalla, 2000 (May lost three-hole play-off); Tiger Woods, Medinah, 2006

Lowest round
63 Bruce Crampton, Firestone, 1975; Raymond Floyd, Southern Hills, 1982; Gary Player, Shoal Creek, 1984; Vijay Singh, Inverness, 1993; Michael Bradley and Brad Faxon, Riviera, 1995; José Maria Olazábal, Valhalla, 2000; Mark O'Meara, Atlanta Athletic Club, 2001; Thomas Bjørn, Baltusrol, 2005; Tiger Woods, Southern Hills, 2007; Steve Stricker, Atlanta Athletic Club, 2011

Most successive victories
4 Walter Hagen, 1924–25–26–27

Lowest 9 holes
28 Brad Faxon, Riviera, 1995

Lowest first 36 holes
131 Hal Sutton, Riviera, 1983; Vijay Singh, Inverness, 1993; Ernie Els and Mark O'Meara, Riviera, 1995; Shingo Katayama and David Toms, Atlanta Athletic Club, 2001

Lowest final 36 holes
131 Mark Calcavecchia, Atlanta Athletic Club, 2001
132 Miller Barber, Dayton, 1969; Steve Elkington and Colin Montgomerie, Riviera, 1995; Padraig Harrington, Oakland Hills, 2008

Lowest first 54 holes
196 David Toms, Atlanta Athletic Club, 2001

Lowest final 54 holes
199 Steve Elkington, Colin Montgomerie, Riviera, 1995; Mark Calcavecchia, David Toms, Atlanta Athletic Club, 2001; David Toms, Atlanta Athletic Club, 2011

Most appearances
37 Arnold Palmer; Jack Nicklaus

Outright leader after every round
Bobby Nichols, Columbus, 1964; Jack Nicklaus, PGA National, 1971; Raymond Floyd, Southern Hills, 1982; Hal Sutton, Riviera, 1983

Best opening round by a champion
63 Raymond Floyd, Southern Hills, 1982

Worst opening round by a champion
75 John Mahaffey, Oakmont, 1978

Worst closing round by a champion
76 Vijay Singh, Whistling Straits, 2004 (worst in any major since Reg Whitcombe's 78 in 1938 Open)

Albatrosses
Joey Sindelar had an albatross at the fifth hole at Medinah Country Club during the third round of the 2006 PGA Championship

PGA European Tour

Lowest 72-hole aggregate
258 –14: David Llewellyn, AGF Biarritz Open, 1988. –18: Ian Woosnam, Monte Carlo Open, 1990.
259 –29: Ernie Els, Johnnie Walker Classic, Lake Karrinyup, 2003. –25: Mark McNulty, German Open, Frankfurt, 1987. –21: Tiger Woods, NEC Invitational, 2000 (Note: Sergio Garcia scored 257, 27 under par, at the 2011 Castello Masters, but preferred lies were in operation)

Lowest 9 holes
27 –9: José María Canizares, Swiss Open, Crans-sur-Sierre, 1978; Joakim Haeggman, Alfred Dunhill Cup, St Andrews, 1997; Simon Khan, Wales Open, Celtic Manor, 2004; –7: Andrew Coltart, KLM Open, Kennemer, 2007; Robert Lee, Johnnie Walker Monte Carlo Open, Mont Agel, 1985. –6: Robert Lee, Portuguese Open, Estoril, 1987. (Note: Rafa Echenique, BMW International Open, 2009, also scored 27 (–9), but preferred lies were in operation)

Lowest 18 holes
60 –12: Jamie Spence, Canon European Masters, Crans-sur-Sierre, 1992; Bernhard Langer, Linde German Masters, Motzener See, 1997; Darren Clarke, Smurfit European Open, K Club, 1999; Fredrik Jacobson, Linde

German Masters, Gut Larchenhof, 2003; Ernie Els, Heineken Classic, Royal Melbourne, 2004; –11: Baldovino Dassu, Swiss Open, Crans-sur-Sierre, 1971; Rafael Cabrera-Bello, Austrian Open, Fontana GC, Vienna, 2009; –10: Paul Curry, Bell's Scottish Open, Gleneagles, 1992; Tobias Dier, TNT Open, Hilversum, 2002; –9: Ian Woosnam, Torras Monte Carlo Open, Mont Agel, 1990; Darren Clarke and Johan Rystrom, Monte Carlo Open, Mont Agel, 1992; Phillip Archer, Celtic Manor Wales Open, Celtic Manor, 2006; –8: David Llewellyn, AGF Biarritz Open, Biarritz GC, 1988 (Note: Bradley Dredge, Madeira Island Open, 2003, Colin Montgomerie, Indonesia Open, 2005, Ross McGowan, Madrid Masters, 2009 and Ian Poulter, Hong Kong Open 2010, also scored 60, but preferred lies were in operation)

Lowest 36 holes
124 –18: Colin Montgomerie, Canon European Masters, Crans-sur-Sierre, 1996 (3rd and 4th rounds). –14: Robert Karlsson, Celtic Manor Wales Open, Celtic Manor, 2006 (1st and 2nd rounds). (Note: Ian Poulter also scored 124 (–16, 60-64) in the 2nd and 3rd rounds of the 2010 UBS Hong Kong Open, but preferred lies were in operation)

Lowest 54 holes
189 –18 Robert Karlsson, Celtic Manor Wales Open, 2006 (rounds 1-2-3). (Note: Sergio García scored 190, 23 under par, in rounds 2-3-4 at the 2011 Castello Masters, butpreferred lies were in operation

Lowest 54 holes under par
192 –24 Anders Forsbrand, Ebel European Masters Swiss Open, Crans-Sur-Sierre, 1987 (rounds 2-3-4). (Note: Ross McGowan, Madrid Masters 2009, rounds 1-2-3, and Mikko Ilonen, Madrid Masters 2009, rounds 2-3-4, also scored 192, 24 under par, but preferred lies were in operation)

Lowest round by amateur
62 –10 Shane Lowry, 3 Irish Open, County Louth, 2009; –9 Sven Struver, German Open, Frankfurt GC, 1989; –8 David Palm, SAS Masters, Arlandastad 2008 (Note: Adam Scott's 63 at the 2000 Greg Norman Holden International at The Lakes was 10 under par)

Lowest first 36 holes
125 –17: Frankie Minoza, Caltex Singapore Masters, Singapore Island, 2001. –15: Tiger Woods, NEC Invitational World Championship, Firestone, Akron, Ohio, 2000

Largest winning margin
15 strokes Tiger Woods, United States Open, Pebble Beach, 2000. (Note: Bernhard Langer's 17-stroke victory in 1979 at Cacharel Under-25's Championship in Nîmes is not considered a full European Tour event)

Highest winning score
306 Peter Butler, Schweppes PGA Close Championship, Royal Birkdale, 1963

Youngest winner
Matteo Manassero, 17 years 188 days, Castello Masters, 2010

Youngest to make cut
Jason Hak (amateur), 14 years 304 days, Hong Kong Open, 2008

Oldest to make cut
Bob Charles 71 years 8 months, 2007 Michael Hill New Zealand Open, The Hills Golf Club, Queenstown

Oldest winner
Des Smyth, 48 years 34 days, Madeira Island Open, 2001

Most wins in one season
7 Norman von Nida, 1947

Amateur winners
Pablo Martin, Estoril Portuguese Open, 2007; Danny Lee, Johnnie Walker Classic, 2009; Shane Lowry, 3 Irish Open, 2009

US PGA Tour

Lowest 72-hole aggregate
254 −26: Tommy Armour III, Valero Texas Open, 2003. (*Note:* Steve Stricker's 255 at the 2009 Bob Hope Classic was a record 33 under par)

Lowest 54 holes
188 −25: Steve Stricker, John Deere Classic, 2010 (rounds 1-3). (*Note:* Tim Herron's 190 at the 2003 Bob Hope Chrysler Classic (rounds 2-4) was a record 26 under par)

Lowest 36 holes
122 −18: Troy Matteson, 2009 Frys.com Open (2nd and 3rd rounds). (*Note:* record under par was 123 (−21) Steve Stricker, 2009 Bob Hope Classic (3rd and 4th rounds)

Lowest first 36 holes
124 −20: Pat Perez, 2009 Bob Hope Classic; −16 David Toms, 2001 Crowne Plaza Invitational at Colonial

Lowest 18 holes
59 −13: Al Geiberger, 2nd round, Memphis Classic Colonial CC, 1977 (preferred lies in operation); Chip Beck, 3rd round, Las Vegas Invitational, Sunrise, 1991; David Duval, final round, Bob Hope Chrysler Classic, PGA West Palmer Course, 1999 (won tournament with last hole eagle); −12: Paul Goydos, 1st round, John Deere Classic, TPC Deere Run, 2010 (preferred lies); −11: Stuart Appleby, final round, Greenbrier Classic, Old White course, The Greenbrier, 2010 (won by one with three closing birdies)

Lowest 9 holes
26 −8: Corey Pavin, US Bank Championship, 2006
27 −9: Billy Mayfair, Buick Open, 2001; Robert Gamez, Bob Hope Chrysler Classic, 2004; Brandt Snedeker, Buick Invitational, 2007. −8: Mike Souchak, Texas Open, 1955. −7: Nick Watney, AT&T National, 2011; Andy North, BC Open, 1975

Lowest round by amateur
60 −10 Patrick Cantlay, Travelers Championship, TPC River Highlands, 2011

Largest winning margin
16 strokes J Douglas Edgar, Canadian Open Championship, 1919; Joe Kirkwood, Corpus Christi Open 1924; Bobby Locke, Chicago Victory National Championship, 1948

Youngest winner
Johnny McDermott, 19 years 10 months, US Open, 1911

Youngest to make cut
Bob Panasik, 15 years 8 months 20 days, Canadian Open, 1957

Oldest winner
Sam Snead, 52 years 10 months, Greater Greensboro Open, 1965

Most wins in one season
18 Byron Nelson, 1945

New course records (2011 season)
60 −10 Patrick Cantlay (amateur), Travelers Championship, TPC River Highlands
61 −11 Scott Piercy, Reno-Tahoe Open, Montreux; −10 Brandt Snedeker, The Barclays, Painfield
62 −9 Will MacKenzie, Frys.com Open, Cordevalle; −8 Jeff Maggert, AT&T Pebble Beach Pro-Am, Monterey Peninsular; Nick Watney, AT&T National, Aronimink
63 −7 Steve Stricker, PGA Championship, Atlanta Athletic Club

Albatrosses (2011 season)
Alex Cejka, AT&T Pebble Beach Pro-Am, Monterey Peninsular; J B Holmes, Wells Fargo Championship, Quail Hollow; Fabian Gomez, Wyndham Championship, Sedgefield

Holes in one (2011 season)
Shaun Micheel, Sony Open; Lee Janzen, Humana Challenge; Jarrod Lyle and Brendan Steele, Waste Management Phoenix Open; Nick O'Hern and Sunghoon Kang, AT&T Pebble Beach National Pro-Am; George McNeill, Mayakoba Classic; Cameron Tringale and Scott Stallings, Transitions Championship; Brandt Jobe, Shell Houston Open; Daniel Summerhays, The Heritage; Jim Furyk, Crowne Plaza Invitational at Colonial; Steve Stricker, Memorial Tournament; D J Brigman, Nate Smith and J B Holmes, Travelers Championship; Robert Allenby, AT&T National; Dustin Johnson and Tom Watson, Open Championship; Jim Furyk, WGC–Bridgestone Invitational; Derek Lamely, Wyndham Championship; Greg Chalmers and Brandt Snedeker, Deutsche Bank Championship

National Opens – excluding Europe and USA

Lowest 72-hole aggregate
255 Peter Tupling, Nigerian Open, Lagos, 1981

Lowest 36-hole aggregate
124 −18: Sandy Lyle, Nigerian Open, Ikoyi GC, Lagos, 1978 (his first year as a professional)

Lowest 18 holes
59 Gary Player, second round, Brazilian Open, Gavea GC (6,185 yards), Rio de Janeiro, 1974

Professional events – excluding Europe and US PGA Tour

Lowest 72-hole aggregate
260 Bob Charles, Spalding Masters at Tauranga, New Zealand, 1969; Jason Bohn, Bayer Classic, Huron Oaks, Canada, 2001; Brian Kontak, Alberta Open, Canada, 1998.

Lowest 18-hole aggregate

58 −13: Jason Bohn, Bayer Classic, Huron Oaks, Canada, 2001; −12: Ryo Ishikawa, The Crowns, Japan, 2010
59 Sam Snead, Greenbrier Open, The Greenbrier 1959; Miguel Angel Martin, South Argentine Open, 1987

Lowest 9-hole aggregate

27 Bill Brask at Tauranga in the New Zealand PGA in 1976

Amateur winners

Charles Evans, 1910 Western Open, Beverly, Illinois; John Dawson, 1942 Bing Crosby, Rancho Santa Fe, California; Gene Littler, 1954 San Diego Open, Rancho Santa Fe, California; Doug Sanders, 1956 Canadian Open, Beaconsfield, Quebec; Scott Verplank 1985 Western Open, Butler National, Illinois; Phil Mickelson 1991 Northern Telecom Open, Tucson, Arizona; Brett Rumford, 1999 ANZ Players Championship, Royal Queensland; Aaron Baddeley, 1999 Australian Open, Royal Sydney

Asian PGA Tour

Lowest 72 holes

256 −32: Chapchai Nirat, 2009 SAIL Open, India
259 −29: Ernie Els, 2003 Johnnie Walker Classic.
(Note: Thaworn Wiratchant achieved a 25 under par total of 255 in the 2005 Enjoy Jakarta Standard Chartered Indonesian Open, but preferred lies were in use)

Highest winning score

293 +5: Boonchu Ruangkit, 1996 Myanmar Open

Lowest 54 holes

189 −27: Chapchai Nirat, 2009 SAIL Open, India
193 −23: Ernie Els, 2003 Johnnie Walker Classic; David Howell, 2006 TCL Classic. (Note: Thaworn Wiratchant achieved an 18 under par total of 192 in the 2005 Enjoy Jakarta Standard Chartered Indonesia Open, but preferred lies were in use)

Lowest 36 holes

124 −20 Chapchai Nirat, 2009 SAIL Open, India; Lee Westwood, 2011 Thailand Championship
125 −17 Frankie Minoza, 2001 Caltex Singapore Masters (Note: Peter Karmis has an 18 under par 126 in the 2010 Handa Singapore Classic, but preferred lies were in operation)

Lowest 18 holes

60 −12: Liang Wen-chong, 2008 Hero Honda Indian Open. (Note: Kim Felton and Colin Montgomerie had rounds of 60 in the 2000 Omega Hong Kong Open and 2005 Enjoy Jakarta Standard Chartered Indonesian Open respectively, but preferred lies were in operation. Felton's round was 11 under par, Montgomerie's 10 under). (Note: Kim Felton had an 11 under par 60 in the 2000 Omega Hong Kong Open, Colin Montgomerie a 10 under par 60 in the 2005 enjohy Jakarta Standard Chartered Indonesian Open and Ian Poulter a 10 under par 60 in the 2010 UBS Hong Kong Open, but preferred lies were in operation on all three occasions)

Lowest 9 holes

28 −8: Chung Chun-hsing, 2001 Maekyung LG Fashion Open; Liang Wen-chong, 2008 Hero Honda

Indian Open. −7: Chinnarat Phadungsil, 2007 Midea China Classic; Henrik Bjornstad, 2001 Omega Hong Kong Open; Maarten Lafeber, 2005 UBS Hong Kong Open; Mardan Mamat, 2009 Singha Thailand Open; Brett Rumford, 2009 Omega European Masters

Biggest margin of victory

13 strokes Ernie Els, 2005 BMW Asian Open
12 strokes Bradley Hughes, 1996 Players Championship

Youngest winners

Chinarat Phadungsil (am), 17 years 5 days, 2005 Double A International Open; Kim Dae-sub (am), 17 years 83 days, 1998 Korean Open; Noh Seung-yul, 17 years 143 days, 2008 Midea China Classic

Youngest to play in an Asian event

Ye Jian-fe, 13 years and 20 days, 2004 Sanya Open

Oldest winner

Choi Sang-ho, 50 years and 145 days, 2005 Maekyung Open; Boonchu Ruangkit, 47 years and 258 days, 2004 Thailand Open

Most wins in a season

4 Thaworn Wiratchant, 2005

Most wins on Tour

13 Thongchai Jaidee

First par 6 hole

878-yard fourth, St Andrews Hill, Rayong, Thailand, 2005 Double A International Open

Youngest player to make the cut

Atiwit Janewattananond, 14 years 71 days, 2010 Asian Tour International

Oldest player to make the cut

Hsieh Min-nan, 70 years 53 days, 2010 Mercuries Taiwan Masters

Holes in one at same hole

Chen Chung-cheng, 2004 Thailand Open, fourth hole, days 1 and 3

First woman to make halfway cut

Michelle Wie, 2006 SK Telecom Open, Korea (finished tied 35th)

Japan Golf Tour

Lowest 72 holes

260 −20: Masashi 'Jumbo' Ozaki, 1995 Chunichi Crowns, Nagoya Wago
262 −26: Masashi Ozaki, 1996 Japan Series, Tokyo Yomiuri
263 −17: Tetsuji Hiratsuka, 2009 The Crowns, Nagoya

Lowest 54 holes

193 −23: Masahiro Kuramoto, 1987 Maruman Open, Higashi Matsuyama. −17: Masashi Ozaki, 1995 Chunichi Crowns, Nagoya Wago

Lowest 36 holes

126 −18: Masahiro Kuramoto, 1987 Maruman Open, Higashi Matsuyama

Lowest 18 holes

58 −12: Ryo Ishikawa, 2010 The Crowns (this is the lowest round on a major tour. He came from six behind to win by five, aged 18 at the time)

Lowest 9 holes
28 –8: Isao Aoki, 1972 Kanto Pro, Isogo; Takashi Murakami, 1972 Kanto Pro, Isogo; Yoshinori Kaneko, 1994 Nikkei Cup, Mitsui-kanko Tomakomai; Masayuki Kawamura, 1995 Gene Sarazen Jun Classic; Tsuyoshi Yoneyama, 1998 Sapporo Tokyu, Sapporo Kokusai; Toshimitsu Izawa, 2000 TPC Iiyama Cup, Horai

Largest winning margin
15 Masashi Ozaki, 1994 Daiwa International Hatoyama (pre-1973 tour formation: 19 Akira Muraki, 1930 Japan PGA Championship, Takarazuka)

Youngest winner
Ryo Ishikawa (amateur), 15 years 8 months, 2007 Munsingwear Open KBS Cup

Oldest winner
Masashi Ozaki, 55 years 8 months, 2002 ANA Open, Sapporo Wattsu

Most wins in a season
9 Tsuneyuki 'Tommy' Nakajima, 1983; Masashi 'Jumbo' Ozaki, 1972

Amateur winners
Masahiro Kuramoto, 1980 Chugoku-Shikoku Open; Ryo Ishikawa, 2007 Munsingwear Open KBS Cup; Hideki Matsuyama, 2011 Taiheiyo Masters

South African Sunshine Tour

Lowest 9-hole score
28 Simon Hobday, 2nd round of the 1987 Royal Swazi Sun Pro Am at Royal Swazi Sun Country Club; Mark McNulty, 2nd round of 1996 Zimbabwe Open at Chapman Golf Club; David Frost, 2nd round of the 1997 Alfred Dunhill PGA Championship at Houghton Golf Club; Tertius Claassens, 1st round of the 1982 SAB Masters at Milnerton; Brenden Pappas, 2nd round of the 1996 Dimension Data Pro-Am at Gary Player Country Club; Murray Urquhart, 2nd round of the 2001 Royal Swazi Sun Open at Royal Swazi Sun CC

Lowest 18-hole score
60 Shane Pringle 30-30, 2002 Botswana Open, Gabarone Golf Club

Lowest first 36 holes
127 Barry Painting 62-65, 2004 FNB Botswana Open, Gabarone Golf Club

Lowest last 36 holes
126 Mark McNulty 64-62, 1987 Royal Swazi Sun Pro-Am, Royal Swazi Sun Country Club

Lowest 54 holes
195 Nick Price 61-69-65, 1994 ICL International; Barry Painting 62-65-68, 2004 FNB Botswana Open, Gaberone GC

Lowest 72-hole score
259 Mark McNulty 68-65-64-62, 1987 Royal Swazi Sun Pro-Am, Royal Swazi Sun Country Club; David Frost 64-67-65-63, 1994 Lexington PGA, Wanderers Golf Club

Largest winning margin
12 strokes Nick Price, 1993 Nedbank Million Dollar, Sun City (non-Order of Merit event)
11 strokes Nico van Rensburg, 2000 Vodacom Series Gauteng, Silver Lakes

Most wins in a season
Seven wins in 11 tournaments by Mark McNulty, 1986-87 season – Southern Suns SA Open, AECI Charity Classic, Royal Swazi Sun Pro-Am, Trust Bank Tournament of Champions, Germiston Centenary Golf Tournament, Safmarine Masters, Helix Wild Coast Sun Classic

Most wins in succession
Four Gary Player, 1979-80 – Lexington PGA, Krönenbrau SA Masters, B.A. / Yellow Pages SA Open, Sun City Classic; Mark McNulty, 1986-87 – Southern Suns SA Open, AECI Charity Classic, Royal Swazi Sun Pro-Am, Trust Bank Tournament of Champions

Most birdies in one round
11 Allan Henning, 1st round of the 1975 Rolux Toro Classic, Glendower Golf Club; John Bland, 1st round of the 1993 SA Open Championship, Durban Country Club; Mark McNulty, 2nd round of the 1996 Zimbabwe Open, Royal Harare Golf Club; Alan McLean, 3rd round of the 2005 Telkom PGA Championship at Woodhill Country Club. (Note: Shane Pringle had 10 birdies and an eagle in the 2nd round of the 2002 FNB Botswana Open at Gaborone Golf Club; Marc Cayeux had nine birdies and an eagle in the final round of the 2004 Vodacom Players Championship at Country Club Johannesburg)

Most birdies in a row
9 Alan McLean, from the seventh to the 15th in the 3rd round of the 2005 Telkom PGA Championship at Woodhill Country Club
8 Bobby Lincoln, from the eighth to the 15th in the final round of the AECI Classic, Randpark Golf Club; Mark McNulty, from the ninth to the 16th in the 2nd round of the 1996 Zimbabwe Open, Royal Harare Golf Club

Lowest finish by a winner
62 Gavan Levenson, last round of the 1983 Vaal Reefs Open, Orkney Golf Club; Mark McNulty, 1987 Royal Swazi Sun Pro-Am, Royal Swazi Sun Country Club

Most Order of Merit victories
Eight Mark McNulty, 1981, 82, 85, 86, 87, 93, 98

Youngest winners
Anton Haig, 19 years 4 months, 2005 Seekers Travel Pro-Am, Dainfern; Dale Hayes, 19 years 5 months, Bert Hagerman Invitational, Zwartkops, Dec 1971; Charl Schwartzel, 20 years 3 months, 2004 dunhill championship at Leopard Creek. (Note: Dale Hayes was 18 years 6 months when he won the unofficial Newcastle Open at Newcastle Golf Club in 1971); Mark Murless, 20 years 5 months, 1996 Platinum Classic, Mooinooi Golf Club; Adam Scott, 20 years 6 months, 2001 Alfred Dunhill Championship, Houghton Golf Club; Marc Cayeux, 20 years 9 months, 1998 Zambia Open, Lusaka Golf Club; Trevor Immelman, 20 years 11 months, Vodacom Players Championship, Royal Cape Golf Club

Oldest winner
Mark McNulty, 49 years 44 days, 2003 Vodacom Players Championship, Royal Cape Golf Club

Australasian Tour

Most wins
31 Greg Norman

Youngest winner
A Baddeley (19 years), 1999 Australian Open

Oldest winner
Kel Nagle (54 years), 1975 Clearwater Classic (now the New Zealand PGA Championship

Lowest round
60 –12: Paul Gow, 2001 Canon Challenge, Castle Hill; Ernie Els, 2004 Heineken Classic, Royal Melbourne

Canadian Tour

Lowest 72 holes
256 –28: Brian Unk, 2009 Seaforth Country Classic

Lowest 54 holes
192 –21: Brian Unk, 2009 Seaforth Country Classic

Lowest 36 holes
126 –18: Matt Cole, 1988 Windsor Charity Classic. –16: James Hahn, 2009 Seaforth Country Classic

Lowest 18 holes
58 –13: Jason Bohn, 2001 Bayer Championship

Lowest 9 holes
26 –9: Jason Bohn, 2001 Bayer Championship

Largest winning margin
11 Arron Oberholser, 1999 Ontario Open Heritage Classic

Most wins
13 Moe Norman

Most wins in a season
4 Trevor Dodds (1996 Alberta Open, ED TEL Planet Open, Infiniti Championship, Canadian Masters); Moe Norman (1966 Manitoba Open, Canadian PGA Championship, Quebec Open, Alberta Open)

Oldest winner
Moe Norman, 46 years 11 months, 1976 Alberta Open

Youngest winner
James Lepp, 19 years 7 months, 2003 Greater Vancouver Charity Classic

Youngest to play
Michelle Wie, 13 years 10 months, 2003 Bay Mills Championship

Oldest to make cut
Jim Rutledge, 51 years 2 months, 2010 Players Cup

Tour de las Americas

Lowest 72 holes
265 –23: Jamie Donaldson, Telefonica de Guatemala Open, 2007; Felipe Aguilar, Chile Open, 2008

Largest winning margin
11 Felipe Aguilar, Chile Open, 2008

Youngest winner
Luciano Giometti, 18 years 9 months, Open del Sur Personal, Argentina, 2006

Oldest winner
Vicente Fernandez 54 years 7 months, Argentina Open, Jockey Club, Buenos Aires, 2002

Highest winning aggregate
289 +5: Rafael Gomez and Marco Ruiz, Costa Rica Open, 2002 (Gomez won play-off)

Most wins in a season
3 Jesus Amaya 2001-02; Rafael Gomez, 2008

Most wins
8 Rafael Gomez

Lowest round
59 –11: Cipriano Castro, Siemens Venezuela Open, Valle Arribe, Caracas, 2006

Biggest comeback to win
9 strokes Venezuela, Copa de Naciones, El Tigre, Nueva Vallarta, Mexico 2004; Rafael Ponce, Acapulco Fest, Fairmont Princess, Acapulco, Mexico, 2004 LPGA Tour

LPGA Tour

Lowest 72 holes
258 –22: Karen Stupples, Welch's/Fry's Championship, Dell Urich, Arizona, 2004. (Note: Annika Sörenstam's 261 at 2001 Standard Register Ping, Moon Valley, Arizona, was a record 27 under par)

Lowest 54 holes
192 –24: Annika Sörenstam, Mizuno Classic, Shiga, Japan, 2003

Lowest 36 holes
124 –20: Annika Sörenstam, Standard Register Ping, Moon Valley, Arizona, 2001. –16: Meg Mallon, Welch's/Fry Championship, Dell Urich, Arizona, 2003

Lowest 18 holes
59 –13: Annika Sörenstam, Standard Register Ping, Moon Valley, Arizona, 2001

Lowest 9 holes
27 –8: Jimin Kang, ShopRite Classic, Seaview, New Jersey, 2005. –7: In-kyung Kim, Jamie Farr Owens Corning Classic, Highland Meadows, Ohio, 2007; Paula Creamer, Jamie Farr Corning Classic, Highland Meadows, Ohio, 2008 (Note: the 28s by Mary Beth Zimmerman, Rail Charity Classic, Springfield, Illinois, 1984, Annika Sörenstam, Standard Register Ping, Moon Valley, Arizona, 2001; Candie Kung, Wendy's Championship, Tartan Field, Ohio, 2006; Sarah Lee, Corona Championship, Tres Marias, Mexico, 2007 and Yani Tseng, Corning Classic, Corning CC, New York, 2009 were also 8 under par, as were the 29s by Nicky Le Roux, Rochester International, Locust Hill, New York, 1990, and Kris Tschetter, Weetabix Women's British Open, Royal Birkdale, England, 2005)

Most birdies in a round
13 Annika Sorenstam, Standard Register Ping, Moon Valley, Arizona, 2004

Most consecutive birdies
9 Beth Daniel, Philips Invitational, Onion Creek, Texas, 1999

Largest winning margin
14 strokes Cindy Mackey, MasterCard International Pro-am, Knollwood, New York, 1986

Youngest winner
Alexis Thompson, 16 years 7 months 8 days, 2011 Navistar Classic, Capitol Hill, Prattville, Alabama

Oldest winner
Beth Daniel, 46 years 8 months 29 days, Canadian Open, 2003

Most wins in a season
13 Mickey Wright, 1963

Most wins
88 Kathy Whitworth

Most majors
15 Patty Berg

Youngest major winner
Morgan Pressel, 18 years 10 months 9 days, Kraft Nabisco Championship, 2007

Oldest major winner
Fay Crocker, 45 years 7 months 11 days, Titleholders Championship, 1960

Youngest player
Beverly Klass, 10 years 6 months 3 days, Dallas Civitan Open, 1967

Oldest player
JoAnne Carner, 65 years 11 months 21 days, Kraft Nabisco Championship, 2005

Youngest to make cut
Michelle Wie 13 years 5 months 17 days, Kraft Nabisco Championship, 2003

Oldest to make cut
JoAnne Carner, 64 years 26 days, Chick-fil-A Charity Championship, 2004

Amateur winners
Polly Riley, 1950 Tampa Open; Pat O'Sullivan, 1951 Titleholders Championship; Catherine LaCoste, 1967 US Women's Open; JoAnne Carner, 1969 Burdine's Invitational

Lowest major round
62 −10: Minea Blomqvist, 2004 Weetabix Women's British Open, Sunningdale; −10: Lorena Ochoa, 2006 Kraft Nabisco Championship, Rancho Mirage

Most birdies in a round
13 Annika Sörenstam, Moon Valley Country Club, Phoenix, 2001 Standard Register Ping

Most consecutive birdies
9 Beth Daniel, Onion Creek Club, Austin, 1999 Philips Invitational

Ladies European Tour

Lowest 72 holes
249 −11: Dale Reid and Trish Johnson, 1991 Bloor Homes Eastleigh Classic, Fleming Park

Lowest 72 holes in relation to par
259 −29: Gwladys Nocera, 2008 Goteborg Masters, Lycke, Sweden

Lowest 54 holes
193 −23: Gwladys Nocera, 2008 Goteborg Masters, Lycke, Sweden

Lowest 36 holes
128 −16: Gwladys Nocera, 2008 Goteborg Masters, Lycke, Sweden. (Note: Sophie Gustafson's 129 at the 2003 Ladies Irish Open, Killarney, was a record 17 under)

Lowest 18 holes
58 −7: Dale Reid and Trish Johnson, 1991 Bloor Homes Eastleigh Classic, Fleming Park; Jane Connachan, 1991 Bloor Homes Eastleigh Classic, Fleming Park

Lowest 18 holes in relation to par
61 −11: Kirsty Taylor, 2005 Wales Ladies Championship, Machynys Peninsula; Nina Reis, 2008 Goteborg Masters, Lycke, Sweden; Karrie Webb, 2010 ANZ Ladies Masters, Royal Pines
62 −11: Trish Johnson, 1996 Ladies French Open, Golf D'Arras; Lisa Holm Sorensen, 2009 SAS Masters, Larvik, Norway

Lowest 9 holes
28 −7: Tamie Durdin, 2010 ANZ Ladies Masters, Royal Pines

Highest winning score
292 +4: Raquel Carriedo, 2002 Tenerife Ladies Open, Golf del Sur; Sherri Steinhauer, 1998 Weetabix Women's British Open, Royal Lytham and St Annes

Largest winning margin
16 strokes Laura Davies, 1995 Guardian Irish Holidays Open, St Margaret's

Youngest winner
Amy Yang (amateur), 16 years 191 days, 2006 ANZ Ladies Masters, Royal Pines

Youngest to play
Leona and Lisa Maguire, 12 years 6 months, 2007 BT Northern Ireland Ladies Open

Youngest to make cut
Ariya Jutanugarn, 12 years 9 months, 2008 Finnair Masters, Helsinki Golf Club

Oldest winner
Laura Davies, 47 years 1 month 8 days, 2010 Hero Honda Women's Indian Open

Most wins
44 Laura Davies

Most wins in a year
7 Marie-Laure de Lorenzi, 1988 (French Open, Volmac Open, Hennessy Cup, Gothenburg Open, Laing Charity Classic, Woolmark Matchplay, Qualitair Spanish Open)

Most birdies in a round
12 Kristie Smith, 2009 ANZ Masters, Royal Pines, Australia

Miscellaneous British

72-hole aggregate
Andrew Brooks recorded a 72-hole aggregate of 259 in winning the Skol (Scotland) tournament at Williamwood in 1974.

Lowest rounds
Playing on the ladies' course (4,020 yards) at Sunningdale on 26th September, 1961, Arthur Lees, the professional there, went round in 52, 10 under par. He went out in 26 (2, 3, 3, 4, 3, 3, 3, 3, 2) and came back in 26 (2, 3, 3, 3, 2, 3, 4, 3, 3).

On 1st January, 1936, AE Smith, Woolacombe Bay professional, recorded a score of 55 in a game there with a club member. The course measured 4,248 yards. Smith went out in 29 and came back in 26 finishing with a hole-in-one at the 18th.

Other low scores recorded in Britain are by CC Aylmer, an English International who went round Ranelagh in 56; George Duncan, Axenfels in 56; Harry

Bannerman, Banchory in 56 in 1971; Ian Connelly, Welwyn Garden City in 56 in 1972; James Braid, Hedderwick near Dunbar in 57; H. Hardman, Wirral in 58; Norman Quigley, Windermere in 58 in 1937; Robert Webster, Eaglescliffe in 58, in 1970. Harry Weetman scored 58 in a round at the 6171 yards Croham Hurst on 30th January, 1956.

D Sewell had a round of 60 in an Alliance Meeting at Ferndown, Bournemouth, a full-size course. He scored 30 for each half and had a total of 26 putts. In September 1986, Jeffrey Burn, handicap 1, of Shrewsbury GC, scored 60 in a club competition, made up of 8 birdies, an eagle and 9 pars. He was 30 out and 30 home and no. 5 on his card. Andrew Sherborne, as a 20-year-old amateur, went round Cirencester in 60 strokes. Dennis Gray completed a round at Broome Manor (6906 yards, SSS 73) in the summer of 1976 in 60 (28 out, 32 in).

Playing over Aberdour on 13th June, 1936, Hector Thomson, British Amateur champion, 1936, and Jack McLean, former Scottish Amateur champion, each did 61 in the second round of an exhibition. McLean in his first round had a 63, which gave him an aggregate 124 for 36 holes.

Steve Tredinnick in a friendly match against business tycoon Joe Hyman scored a 61 over West Sussex (6211 yards) in 1970. It included a hole-in-one at the 12th (198 yards) and a 2 at the 17th (445 yards).

Another round of 61 on a full-size course was achieved by 18-year-old Michael Jones on his home course, Worthing GC (6274 yards), in the first round of the President's Cup in May, 1974.

In the Second City Pro-Am tournament in 1970, at Handsworth, Simon Fogarty did the second 9 holes in 27 against the par of 36.

Miscellaneous USA

Lowest rounds

The lowest known scores recorded for 18 holes in America are 55 by E F Staugaard in 1935 over the 6419 yards Montebello Park, California, and 55 by Homero Blancas in 1962 over the 5002 yards Premier course in Longview, Texas. Staugaard in his round had 2 eagles, 13 birdies and 3 pars.

In July 2010 Bobby Wyatt had a 14 under par 57 at the 6,628-yard Country Club of Mobile in the Alabama Boys State Junior Championship. He was 17 at the time. The round contained an eagle and 12 birdies and beat the course record by six.

Equally outstanding is a round of 58 (13 under par) achieved by a 13-year-old boy, Douglas Beecher, on 6th July, 1976, at Pitman CC, New Jersey. The course measured 6180 yards from the back tees, and the middle tees, off which Douglas played, were estimated by the club professional to reduce the yardage by under 180 yards.

In 1941 at a 6100 yards course in Portsmouth, Virginia, Chandler Harper scored 58.

Jack Nicklaus in an exhibition match at Breakers Club, Palm Beach, California, in 1973 scored 59 over the 6200-yard course.

The lowest 9-hole score in America is 25, held jointly by Bill Burke over the second half of the 6384 yards Normandie CC, St Louis in May, 1970 at the age of 29; by Daniel Cavin, who had seven 3s and two 2s on the par 36 Bill Brewer Course, Texas, in September, 1959;

and by Douglas Beecher over the second half of Pitman CC, New Jersey, on 6th July, 1976, at the amazingly young age of 13. The back 9 holes of the Pitman course measured 3150 yards (par 35) from the back tees, but even though Douglas played off the middle tees, the yardage was still over 3000 yards for the 9 holes. He scored 8 birdies and 1 eagle.

Horton Smith scored 119 for two consecutive rounds in winning the Catalina Open in California in December, 1928. The course, however, measured only 4700 yards.

Miscellaneous – excluding GB and USA

Tony Jacklin won the 1973 Los Lagartos Open with an aggregate of 261, 27 under par.

Henry Cotton in 1950 had a round of 56 at Monte Carlo (29 out, 27 in).

In a Pro-Am tournament prior to the 1973 Nigerian Open, British professional David Jagger went round in 59.

Max Banbury recorded a 9-hole score of 26 at Woodstock, Ontario, playing in a competition in 1952.

Women

The lowest score recorded on a full-size course by a woman is 59 by Sweden's Annika Sörenstam on the 6459 yards, par 72 Moon Valley course in Phoenix, Arizona. It broke by two the previous record of 61 by South Korean Se Ri Pak. Sörenstam had begun the tournament with a 65 and by adding rounds of 69 and 68 she equalled the LPGA record of 261 set by Pak (71-61-63-66) at Highland Meadows in Ohio in 1998. Sörenstam's score represents 27 under par, Pak's 23 under.

The lowest 9-hole score on the US Ladies' PGA circuit is 28, first achieved by Mary Beth Zimmerman in the 1984 Rail Charity Classic and since equalled by Pat Bradley, Muffin Spencer-Devlin, Peggy Kirsch, Renee Heiken, Anika Sörenstam and Danielle Ammaccapane.

The Lowest 36-hole score is the 124 (20 under par) by Sörenstam at Moon Valley and the lowest 54-hole score 193 (23 under par) by Karrie Webb at Walnut Hills, Michigan, in the 2000 Oldsmobile Classic and equalled by Sörenstam at Moon Valley.

Patty Berg holds the record for the most number of women's majors with 15; Kathy Whitworth achieved a record number of tournament wins with 88; Mickey Wright's 13 wins in 1963 was the most in one season and the youngest and oldest winners of LPGA events were Marlene Hagge, 18 years and 14 days when she won the 1952 Sarasota Open and JoAnne Carner, 46 years 5 months 11 days when she won the 1985 Safeco Classic.

The lowest round on the European LPGA is 62 (11 under par) by Trish Johnson in the 1996 French Open. A 62 was also achieved by New Zealand's Janice Arnold at Coventry in 1990 during a Women's Professional Golfers' Association tournament.

The lowest 9-hole score on the European LPGA circuit is 29 by Kitrina Douglas, Regine Lautens, Laura Davies, Anne Jones and Trish Johnson.

In the Women's World Team Championship in Mexico in 1966, Mrs Belle Robertson, playing for the

British team, was the only player to break 70. She scored 69 in the third round.

At Westgate-on-Sea GC (measuring 5002 yards), Wanda Morgan scored 60 in an open tournament in 1929.

Since scores cannot properly be taken in matchplay no stroke records can be made in matchplay events. Nevertheless we record here two outstanding examples of low scoring in the finals of national championships. Mrs Catherine Lacoste de Prado is credited with a score of 62 in the first round of the 36-hole final of the 1972 French Ladies' Open Championship at Morfontaine. She went out in 29 and came back in 33 on a course measuring 5933 yards. In the final of the English Ladies' Championship at Woodhall Spa in 1954, Frances Stephens (later Mrs Smith) did the first nine holes against Elizabeth Price (later Mrs Fisher) in 30. It included a hole-in-one at the 5th. The nine holes measured 3280 yards.

Amateurs

National championships

The following examples of low scoring cannot be regarded as genuine stroke play records since they took place in match play. Nevertheless they are recorded here as being worthy of note.

Michael Bonallack in beating David Kelley in the final of the English championship in 1968 at Ganton did the first 16 holes in 61 with only one putt under two feet conceded. He was out in 32 and home in 29. The par of the course was 71.

Charles McFarlane, playing in the fourth round of the Amateur Championship at Sandwich in 1914 against Charles Evans did the first nine holes in 31, winning by 6 and 5.

This score of 31 at Sandwich was equalled on several occasions in later years there. Then, in 1948, Richard Chapman of America went out in 29 in the fourth round eventually beating Hamilton McInally, Scottish Champion in 1937, 1939 and 1947, by 9 and 7.

Francis Ouimet in the first round of the American Amateur Championship in 1932 against George Voigt did the first nine holes in 30. Ouimet won by 6 and 5.

Open competitions

The 1970 South African Dunlop Masters Tournament was won by an amateur, John Fourie, with a score of 266, 14 under par. He led from start to finish with rounds of 65, 68, 65, 68, finally winning by six shots from Gary Player.

Jim Ferrier, Manly, won the New South Wales championship at Sydney in 1935 with 266. His rounds were: 67, 65, 70, 64, giving an aggregate 16 strokes better than that of the runner-up. At the time he did this amazing score Ferrier was 20 years old and an amateur.

Aaron Baddeley became the first amateur to win the Australian Open since Bruce Devlin in 1960 when he took the title at Royal Sydney in 1999. After turning pro he successfully defended the title the following year at Kingston Heath.

On the European Tou,r Spaniard Pablo Martin won the Estoril Open de Portugal as an amateur in 2000 and both Danny Lee (AUS) and Shane Lowry (IRL) were amateur winners in 2009. Lee won the now defunct Johnnie Walker Classic at The Vines in Perth Australia and Lowry the 3 Irish Open at Baltray.

Holes below par

Most holes below par

E.F. Staugaard in a round of 55 over the 6419 yards Montbello Park, California, in 1935, had two eagles, 13 birdies and three pars.

American Jim Clouette scored 14 birdies in a round at Longhills GC, Arkansas, in 1974. The course measured 6257 yards.

Jimmy Martin in his round of 63 in the Swallow-Penfold at Stoneham in 1961 had one eagle and 11 birdies.

In the Ricarton Rose Bowl in Scotland, in August, 1981, Wilma Aitken, a women's amateur internationalist, had 11 birdies in a round of 64, including nine consecutive birdies from the 3rd to the 11th.

Mrs Donna Young scored nine birdies and one eagle in one round in the 1973 Colgate European Women's Open.

Jason Bohn had two eagles and 10 birdies in his closing 58 at the 2001 Bayer Classic on the Canadian Tour at the par 71 Huron Oaks.

Consecutive holes below par

Lionel Platts had ten consecutive birdies from the 8th to 17th holes at Blairgowrie GC during a practice round for the 1973 Sumrie Better-Ball tournament.

Roberto De Vicenzo in the Argentine Centre of the Republic Championship in April, 1974 at the Cordoba GC, Villa Allende, broke par at each of the first nine holes. (By starting his round at the 10th he was in fact the second nine holes played by Vicenzo.) He had one eagle (at the 7th hole) and eight birdies. The par for the 3,602 yards half was 37, completed by Vicenzo in 27.

Nine consecutive holes under par have been recorded by Claude Harmon in a friendly match over Winged Foot GC, Mamaroneck, NY, in 1931; by Les Hardie at Eastern GC, Melbourne, in April, 1934; by Jimmy Smith at McCabe GC, Nashville, Tenn, in 1969; by 13-year-old Douglas Beecher in 1976, at Pitman CC, New Jersey; by Rick Sigda at Greenfield CC, Mass, in 1979; and by Ian Jelley at Brookman Park in 1994.

TW Egan in winning the East of Ireland Championship in 1962 at Baltray had eight consecutive birdies (2nd to 9th) in the third round.

On the United States PGA tour, eight consecutive holes below par have been achieved by six players – Bob Goalby (1961 St Petersburg Open), Fuzzy Zoeller (1976 Quad Cities Open), Dewey Arnette (1987 Buick Open), Edward Fryatt (2000 Doral-Ryder Open), JP Hayes (2002 Bob Hope Chrysler Classic) and Jerry Kelly (2003 Las Vegas Invitational).

Fred Couples set a PGA European Tour record with 12 birdies in a round of 61 during the 1991 Scandinavian Masters on the 72-par Drottningholm course. This has since been equalled by Ernie Els (1994 Dubai Desert Classic), Russell Claydon (1995 German Masters) and Darren Clarke (1999 European Open). Ian Woosnam, Tony Johnstone, Severiano Ballesteros, John Bickerton, Mark O'Meara, Raymond Russell, Darren Clarke, Marcello Santi, Mårten Olander and Craig Spence share another record with eight successive birdies.

The United States Ladies' PGA record is seven consecutive holes below par achieved by Carol Mann in the Borden Classic at Columbus, Ohio in 1975.

Miss Wilma Aitken recorded nine successive birdies (from the 3rd to the 11th) in the 1981 Ricarton Rose Bowl.

This has since been equalled by Ernie Els (1994 Dubai Desert Classic), Russell Claydon and Fredrik Lindgren (1995 Mercedes German Masters) and Darreb Clarke (1999 Smurfit European Open). Ian Woosnam, Tony Johnstone, Severiano Ballesteros, John Bickerton, Mark O'Meara, Raymond Russell, Darren Clarke and Marcello Santi and Marten Olander share another record with eight successive birdies.

Low scoring rarities

At Standerton GC, South Africa, in May 1937, F F Bennett, playing for Standerton against Witwatersrand University, did the 2nd hole, 110 yards, in three 2s and a 1 Standerton is a 9-hole course, and in the match Bennett had to play four rounds.

In 1957 a fourball comprising HJ Marr, E Stevenson, C Bennett and WS May completed the 2nd hole (160 yards) in the grand total of six strokes. Marr and Stevenson both holed in one while Bennett and May both made 2.

The old Meadow Brook Club of Long Island, USA, had five par 3 holes and George Low in a round there in the 1950s scored two at each of them.

In a friendly match on a course near Chicago in 1971, assistant professional Tom Doty (23 years) had a remarkable low run over four consecutive holes: 4th (500 yards) 2; 5th (360 yards, dogleg) 1; 6th (175 yards) 1; 7th (375 yards) 2.

R W Bishop, playing in the Oxley Park, July medal competition in 1966, scored three consecutive 2s. They occurred at the 12th, 13th and 14th holes which measured 151, 500 and 136 yards respectively.

In the 1959 PGA Close Championship at Ashburnham, Bob Boobyer scored five 2s in one of the rounds. American Art Wall scored three consecutive 2s in the first round of the US Masters in 1974. They were at the 4th, 5th and 6th holes, the par of which was 3, 4 and 3.

Nine consecutive 3s have been recorded by RH Corbett in 1916 in the semi-final of the Tangye Cup; by Dr James Stothers of Ralston GC over the 2056 yards 9-hole course at Carradale, Argyll, during the summer of 1971; by Irish internationalist Brian Kissock in the Homebright Open at Carnalea GC, Bangor, in June, 1975; and by American club professional Ben Toski.

The most consecutive 3s in a British PGA event is seven by Eric Brown in the Dunlop at Gleneagles (Queen's Course) in 1960.

Hubert Green scored eight consecutive 3s in a round in the 1980 US Open.

The greatest number of 3s in one round in a British PGA event is 11 by Brian Barnes in the 1977 Skol Lager tournament at Gleneagles.

Fewest putts

The lowest known number of putts in one round is 14, achieved by Colin Collen-Smith in a round at Betchworth Park, Dorking, in June, 1947. He single-putted 14 greens and chipped into the hole on four occasions.

Professional Richard Stanwood in a round at Riverside GC, Pocatello, Idaho on 17th May, 1976 took 15 putts, chipping into the hole on five occasions.

Several instances of 16 putts in one round have been recorded in friendly games.

For 9 holes, the fewest putts is five by Ron Stutesman for the first 9 holes at Orchard Hills G&CC, Washington, USA in 1978.

Walter Hagen in nine consecutive holes on one occasion took only seven putts. He holed long putts on seven greens and chips at the other two holes.

In competitive stroke rounds in Britain and Ireland, the lowest known number of putts in one round is 19, in a medal round at Portpatrick Dunskey GC, Wilmslow GC professional Fred Taggart is reported to have taken 20 putts in one round of the 1934 Open Championship. Padraigh Hogan (Elm Park), when competing in the Junior Scratch Cup at Carlow in 1976, took only 20 putts in a round of 67.

The fewest putts in a British PGA event is believed to be 22 by Bill Large in a qualifying round over Moor Park High Course for the 1972 Benson and Hedges Match Play.

Overseas, outside the United States of America, the fewest putts is 19 achieved by Robert Wynn in a round in the 1973 Nigerian Open and by Mary Bohen in the final round of the 1977 South Australian Open at Adelaide.

The USPGA record for fewest putts in one round is 18, achieved by Andy North (1990); Kenny Knox (1989); Mike McGee (1987) and Sam Trehan (1979). For 9 holes the record is eight putts by Kenny Knox (1989), Jim Colbert (1987) and Sam Trehan (1979).

The fewest putts recorded for a 72-hole US PGA Tour event is 93 by Kenny Knox in the 1989 Heritage Classic at Harbour Town Golf Links.

The fewest putts recorded by a woman is 17, by Joan Joyce in the Lady Michelob tournament, Georgia, in May, 1982.

What is the answer?

Q: During a round, may I enter the clubhouse to purchase a drink or collect an item of clothing I have left behind?

A: Yes. A player may enter the clubhouse, or a half-way house, without penalty but must not unduly delay either his own play, that of his opponent or any other competitor.

PART XI

Fixtures 2012

European Tour Race to Dubai   www.europeantour.com

Jan 5–8	Africa Open, East London GC, Eastern Cape, South Africa
Jan 12–15	Joburg Open, Royal Johannesburg and Kensington Golf Club, Johannesburg, South Africa
Jan 19–22	Volvo Golf Champions, The Links at Fancourt, George, South Africa
Jan 26–29	Abu Dhabi HSBC Golf Championship, Abu Dhabi Golf Club, Abu Dhabi, UAR
Feb 2–5	Commercialbank Qatar Masters presented by Dolphin Energy, Doha GC, Doha, Qatar
Feb 9–12	Omega Dubai Desert Classic, Emirates GC, Dubai, UAR
Feb 16–19	Avantha Masters, DLF Golf and Country Club, New Delhi, India
Feb 22–25	WGC–Accenture Match Play Championship, Ritz-Carlton GC, Marana, USA
Mar 8–11	WGC–Cadillac Championship, Doral Golf Resort & Spa, Florida, USA
Mar 15–18	Open de Andalucia de Golf, Spain (venue to be announced)
Mar 22–25	Trophée Hassan II, Golf du Palais Royal and Golf de L'Océan, Agadir, Morocco
Mar 29–Apr 1	Sicilian Open, Verdura Golf & Spa Resort, Sciacca, Italy
Apr 5–8	**Masters Tournament**, Augusta National, Georgia, USA
Apr 12–15	Maybank Malaysian Open, Kuala Lumpur Golf & Country Club, Kuala Lumpur, Malaysia
Apr 19–22	Volvo China Open,China, Binhai Lake GC, Tianjin, China
Apr 26–29	Ballantine's Championship, Blackstone GC, Icheon, Seoul, South Korea
May 3–6	Open de España, Spain, Real Club de Golf de Sevilla, Seville, Spain
May 10–13	Event and venue to be announced
May 17–20	Volvo World Match Play Championship, Finca Cortesin GC, Casares, Andalucia, Spain
May 17–20	Madeira Islands Open, Madeira, Portugal, Santo da Serra, Madeira, Portugal
May 24–27	BMW PGA Championship, Wentworth Club, Surrey, England
May 31–3	ISPS Handa Wales Open, The Celtic Manor Resort, City of Newport, Wales
Jun 6–9	Nordea Masters, Bro Hof Slott GC, Stockholm, Sweden
Jun 14–17	**US Open Championship**, Olympic Club, San Francisco, USA
Jun 14–17	Saint-Omer Open presented by Neuflize OBC, Aa Saint Omer GC, Lumbres, France
Jun 21–24	BMW International Open, Golf Club Gut Lärchenhof, Cologne, Germany
Jun 28–Jul 1	The Irish Open Presented by Discover Ireland, Republic of Ireland (venue to be announced)
Jul 5–8	Alstom Open de France, Le Golf National, Paris, France
Jul 12–15	The Scottish Open, Castle Stuart Golf Links, Inverness, Scotland
Jul 19–22	**The 141st Open Championship**, Royal Lytham & St Annes Golf Club, Lytham St Annes, England
Jul 26–29	Austrian Golf Open, Diamond Country Club, Atzenbrugg, Austria
Aug 2–5	WGC–Bridgestone Invitational, Firestone CC, Akron, Ohio, USA
Aug 9–12	**US PGA Championship**, Kiawah Island Golf Resort, South Carolina, USA
Aug 16–19	Czech Open, Prosper Golf Resort, Čeladná, Czech Republic
Aug 23–26	Johnnie Walker Championship at Gleneagles, Gleneagles Hotel, Perthshire, Scotland
Aug 30–Sep 2	Omega European Masters, Crans-sur-Sierre, Crans Montana, Switzerland
Sep 6–9	KLM Open, Hilversumsche GC, Hilversum, Netherlands
Sep 13–16	Italian Open, Royal Park I Roveri,Turin, Italy
Sep 20–23	Bankia Madrid Masters, Spain (venue to be announced)
Sep 27–30	**The Ryder Cup**, Medinah Country Club, Illinois, USA
Oct 4–7	Alfred Dunhill Links Championship, Malaysia (venue to be announced)
Oct 11–14	Portugal Masters, Oceânico Victoria Golf Course, Vilamoura, Portugal
Oct 18–21	Andalucia Masters, Spain (venue to be announced)
Oct 18–21	Perth International Golf Championship, Lake Karrinyup CC, Perth, Western Australia
Oct 25–28	BMW China Event, China (venue to be announced)
Oct 25–28	Castello Masters Costa Azahar, Club de Campo del Mediterráneo, Castellón, Valencia, Spain
Nov 1–4	WGC–HSBC Champions, Mission Hills GC, Shenzhen, China
Nov 8–11	Barclays Singapore Open, Sentosa GC, Singapore
Nov 15–18	Hong Kong Open, Hong Kong GC, Fanling,Hong Kong
Nov 22–25	**DP World – Tour Championship**, Jumeirah Golf Estates, Dubai, United Arab Emirates
Dec 6–9	Alfred Dunhill Championship, Leopard Creek CC, Malelane, South Africa – date to be confirmed
Dec 13–16	South African Open Championship, Serengeti Golf Club, Ekurhuleni, South Africa – date to be confirmed

Dixon headed the qualifiers at the European Tour School

England's David Dixon, a former Silver Medallist in The Open, topped the leaderboard at the PGA Catalunya Resort in Girona when 37 players secured their Tour cards for 2012 at the Qualifying School Final Stage.

A closing round of 69 gave Dixon a 21 under par aggregate total and a one shot victory over his compatriot Sam Hutsby, with two more Englishmen, Andy Sullivan and Richard Bland, rounding out the top four on 19 under and 18 under par respectively.

But, as has become traditional, it was further down the leaderboard that the drama really unfolded, none more so than when American Scott Pinckney, who started the day in a tie for 66th place on one under par, fired a best-of-the-day round of 65 to take the 24th card available.

The magic number was seven under par, a mark achieved in dramatic fashion by England's Jamie Elson after he holed a 40 foot birdie putt on the ninth hole – his last.

Similarly, Spaniard Agustin Domingo, whose uncle is Senior Tour champion Domingo Hospital, picked up four shots in his final five holes to claim one of the golden tickets on offer.

Scots Gary Orr and Steven O'Hara retained their cards with top 10 finishes and there was delight for the Dutch when all five of their players who made the cut – Wil Besseling, Reinier Saxton, Maarten Lafeber, Taco Remkes and Tim Sluiter, finished inside the all-important top 30.

A total of 957 players took part in the Qualifying School, with six players successfully coming through all three Stages – Hans Peter Bacher, Besseling, Emiliano Grillo, Adrian Otaegui, Pinckney and Remkes. Of the qualifiers, 17 will be making their débuts on The European Tour next year, with Spaniard Adrian Otaegui the youngest rookie at 19 years and 24 days old.

1	David Dixon (ENG)	−21	€16,000	20	Agustin Domingo (ESP)	−10	2,203
2	Sam Hutsby (ENG)	−20	11,500		Mikael Lundberg (SWE)	−10	2,203
3	Andy Sullivan (ENG)	−19	9,000		Julien Guerrier (FRA)	−10	2,203
4	Richard Bland (ENG)	−18	7,200	23	Adrian Otaegui (ESP)	−9	2,010
5	Steven O'Hara (SCO)	−17	5,490	24	Scott Pinckney (USA)	−8	1,788
	Jordi Garcia (ESP)	−17	5,490		Alex Haindl (RSA)	−8	1,788
7	Knut Borsheim (NOR)	−16	4,740		Wil Besseling (NED)	−8	1,788
8	Gary Orr (SCO)	−15	4,315		Matthew Southgate (ENG)	−8	1,788
9	Emiliano Grillo (ARG)	−15	4,315		Peter Gustafsson (SWE)	−8	1,788
10	Guillaume Cambis (FRA)	−14	3,855		Reinier Saxton (NED)	−8	1,788
	Branden Grace (RSA)	−14	3,855	30	Taco Remkes (NED)	−7	1,660
12	Joakim Lagergren (SWE)	−13	3,455		H P Bacher (AUT)	−7	1,660
	Thomas Nørret (DEN)	−13	3,455		Jamie Elson (ENG)	−7	1,660
14	Matthew Nixon (ENG)	−12	3,095		Tjaart van der Walt (RSA)	−7	1,660
	Bernd Ritthammer (GER)	−12	3,095		Tim Sluiter (NED)	−7	1,660
16	Warren Abery (RSA)	−11	2,635		Andrew Marshall (ENG)	−7	1,660
	Lloyd Kennedy (ENG)	−11	2,635		Maarten Lafeber (NED)	−7	1,660
	Darren Fichardt (RSA)	−11	2,635		Victor Riu (FRA)	−7	1,660
	Adrien Bernadet (FRA)	−11	2,635				

US PGA Tour

www.pgatour.com

Jan 6–9	Hyundai Tournament of Champions, Plantation Course, Kapalua, Hawaii
Jan 12–15	Sony Open, Waialae CC, Honolulu
Jan 19–22	Humana Challenge, PGA West, La Quinta CC, La Quinta, California
Jan 22–29	Farmers Insurance Open, Torrey Pines GC,, San Diego, California
Feb 2–5	Waste Management Phoenix Open, TPC Scottsdale, Scottsdale, Arizona
Feb 9–12	AT&T Pebble Beach National Pro-Am, Pebble Beach, Pebble Beach, California
Feb 16–19	Northern Trust Open, Riviera CC, Los Angeles, California
Feb 22–26	**WGC–Accenture Match Play Championship**, Ritz-Carlton GC, Marana, Arizona
Feb 23–26	Mayakoba Golf Classic, El Camaleon GC, Maya, Mexico
Mar 1–4	Honda Classic, PGA National GC, Palm Beach Gardens, Florida
Mar 8–11	**WGC–Cadillac Championship**, TPC Blue Monster at Doral, Doral, Florida
Mar 8–11	Puerto Rico Open, Trump International GC, Rio Grande, Puerto Rico
Mar 15–18	Transitions Championship, Innisbrook Resort, Palm Harbor, Florida

US PGA Tour *continued*

Mar 22–25	Arnold Palmer Invitational, Bay Hill Club & Lodge, Orlando, Florida
Mar 29–Apr 1	Shell Houston Open, Redstone GC (Tournament Course), Houston, Texas
Apr 5–8	**Masters Tournament**, Augusta National GC, Augusta, Georgia
Apr 12–15	RBC Heritage, Harbourtown GL, Hilton Head Island, South Carolina
Apr 19–22	Valero Texas Open, TPC San Antonio (AT&T Oaks Course), San Antonio, Texas
Apr 26–29	Zurich Classic, TPC Louisiana, New Orleans, Louisiana
May 3–6	Wells Fargo Championship, Quail Hollow Club, Charlotte, North Carolina
May 10–13	The Players Championship, TPC Sawgrass, Ponte Vedra Beach, Florida
May 17–20	HP Byron Nelson Championship, TPC Four Seasons Resort, Las Colinas, Texas
May 24–27	Crowne Plaza Invitational at Colonial, Colonial CC, Fort Worth, Texas
May 31–Jun 3	Memorial Tournament, Muirfield Village GC, Dublin, Ohio
Jun 7–10	FedEx St Jude Classic, TPC Southwind, Memphis, Tennessee
Jun 14–17	**US Open**, The Olympic Club (Lake Course), San Francisco, California
Jun 21–24	Travelers Championship, TPC River Highlands, Hartford, Connecticut
Jun 28–Jul 1	AT&T National, Congressional CC (Blue Course), Bethesda, Maryland
Jul 5–8	The Greenbrier Classic, The Greenbrier, White Sulphur Springs, West Virginia
Jul 12–15	John Deere Classic, TPC Deere Run, Silvis, Illinois
Jul 19–22	**British Open**, Royal Lytham & St Annes, Lytham, England
Jul 19–22	True South Classic, Annandale GC, Madison, Mississippi
Jul 26–29	RBC Canadian Open, Hamilton G&CC, Ancaster, Ontario, Canada
Aug 2–5	**WGC–Bridgestone Invitational**, Firestone CC (South Course), Akron, Ohio
Aug 2–5	Reno-Tahoe Open, Montreaux G&CC, Reno, Nevada
Aug 9–12	**PGA Championship**, Kiawah Island (Ocean Course), Kiawah Island, South Carolina
Aug 16–19	Wyndham Championship, Sedgefield CC, Greensboro, North Carolina
Aug 23–26	The Barclays, Bethpage State Park (Black Course), Farmingdale, New York
Aug 31–Sep 3	Deutsche Bank Championship, TPC Boston, Norton, Massachusetts
Sep 6–9	BMW Championship, Crooked Stick GC, Carmel, Indiana
Sep 20–23	**Tour Championship**, East Lake GC, Atlanta, Georgia
Sep 28–30	**The Ryder Cup**, Medinah CC (No 3), Medinah, Illinois
Oct 4–7	Justin Timberlake Shriners Hospital for Children Open, TPC Summerlin, Las Vegas, Nevada
Oct 11–14	Frys.com Open, CordeValle GC, San Martin, California
Oct 18–21	The McGladrey Classic, Sea Island Resort (Seaside Course), St Simons Island, Georgia
Oct 25–28	CIMB Asia Pacific Classic, The Mines Resort & GC, Selangor, Malaysia
Nov 1–4	WGC–HSBC Champions, China, venue to be announced
Nov 8–11	Children's Miracle Network Classic, Walt Disney World Resort (Magnolia, Palm), Lake Buena Vista, Florida

Three new events on OneAsia 2012 schedule

OneAsia offers an expanded schedule in 2012, featuring at least 14 events, three of them new tournaments, and overall prize money of nearly US$16 million. The schedule includes five national Opens starting with the US$1 million Indonesia Open in March.

The three new tournaments are the China Classic, the PGA Championship of Malaysia and the Guangzhou Open which will be the final tournament of the season from December 13–16. The schedule also includes Korea's three leading events, the Kolon Korea Open, the GS Caltex Maekyung Open and the SK Telecom Open.

The Nanshan China Masters, the Thailand Open and the Volvo China Open, the last mentioned jointly sanctioned by The European Tour, will also be back in 2012 as will the Emirates Australian Open and the Australian PGA Championship presented by Coca-Cola.

The High 1 Resort Open in Korea, which had to be cancelled last year due to inclement weather, is back on the 2012 season schedule as is the Dongfeng Nissan Cup, a team event between Asia Pacific and China. In the inaugural event last year Asia Pacific beat China by a single point at the Tycoon Golf Club in Shenzhen.

Australian Andre Stolz claimed the 2011 OneAsia Order of Merit title. He earned US$464,811 in nine events, including victories in the Indonesia PGA Championship and Thailand Open. Korean Kim Kyung-tae took second place after banking US$327,178.

European Golf Association Championships

www.ega-golf.ch

Jan 9–11	Spanish International Ladies' Stroke Play Championship, Alicante Golf
Jan 26–29	Portuguese International Ladies' Amateur Championship, Montado Golf Resort
Feb 15–18	Portuguese International Amateur Championship, Montado Golf Resort
Feb 29–Mar 4	Spanish International Ladies Amateur Championship, El Valle (Murcia)
Feb 29–Mar 4	Spanish International Amateur Championship, Alcanada GC
Apr 20–22	Cyprus Amateur Men's Open, Minthis Hills GC
Apr 5–9	French International Lady Juniors Championship (Esmond Trophy), Saint Cloud
Apr 5–9	French International Boys Championship (Michel Carlhian Trophy), Belle-Dune
Apr 27–29	Scottish Ladies' Open Stroke Play Championship (Helen Holm), Portland & Old Course, Troon
May 4–6	Lytham Trophy, Royal Lytham & St Annes
May 5–6	Welsh Ladies' Open Stroke Play Championship, Ashburnham GC
May 11–13	Scottish Youths Open Amateur Stroke Play Championship, Ladybank
May 11–13	French International Senior Men's Championship, Omaha Beach
May 11–13	Irish Amateur Open Championship, Royal Dublin
May 15	English Men's Open Amateur Stroke Play Championship (Southern Pre-qualifier Brabazon Trophy), Rochester & Cobham Park GC
May 12–16	Italian International Ladies Match-Play Championship, Castelgandolfo GC
May 12–16	Italian International Amateur Match-Play Championship, Villa d'Este GC
May 17–20	German International Ladies Amateur Championship, Stuttgarter GC Solitude
May 22	English Men's Open Amateur Stroke Play Championship (Northern Pre-qualifier Brabazon Trophy), Worksop GC
May 23–26	Slovenian International Ladies Amateur Championship, G&CC Diners
May 23–26	Slovenian International Amateur Championship, G&CC Bled
May 25–27	Welsh Amateur Open Stroke Play Championship, Prestatyn GC
May 25–27	French Men's Amateur Stroke Play Championship (Murat Cup), Chantilly
May 25–27	Skandia Lady Junior Open (Youth), Varbergs GC (West)
May 25–27	Skandia Junior Open (Youth), Varbergs GC (West)
May 26–27	Irish Women's Open Stroke Play Championship, The Island
Jun 1–3	German Girls Open, GC St Leon-Rot
Jun 1–3	German Boys Open, GC St Leon-Rot
Jun 1–3	Scottish Open Stroke Play Championship, Kilmarnock (Barassie)
Jun 1–3	HENKEL@ Transilvanian Amateur Championship, venue to be announced
Jun 2–3	Welsh Open Youths Championship, Bull Bay
Jun 28–30	Estonian Open Ladies Amateur Championship, Estonian G&CC
Jun 28–30	Estonian Open Amateur Championship, Estonian G&CC
Jun 14–16	Polish Ladies Open Amateur Championship, venue to be announced
Jun 18–23	The Amateur Championship, Royal Troon/Glasgow
Jun 26–30	Ladies' British Open Amateur Championship, Carnoustie
Jun 27–Jul 1	Russian Ladies Amateur Open Championship, venue to be announced
Jun 27–Jul 1	Russian Amateur Open Championship, venue to be announced
Jun 28–Jul 1	English Men's Open Amateur Stroke Play Championship (Brabazon Trophy), Walton Heath GC
Jul 4–6	Scottish Seniors (over 55's) Open Stroke Play Championship, Luffness New GC
Jul 4–6	Slovak Ladies Amateur Championship, venue to be announced
Jul 4–6	Slovak Amateur Championship, venue to be announced
Jul 5–7	Balkan Challenge Trophy, Sofia Golf & Spa
Jul 5–8	English Women's Open Mid Amateur Championship, Wetherby GC
Jul 6–8	Ukrainian Open Amateur Championship, Kiev GC (GolfStream)
Jul 6–8	Ukrainian Ladies Open Amateur Championship, Kiev GC (GolfStream)
Jul 9–11	Polish Junior Championship, venue to be announced
Jul 12–14	Luxembourg Ladies Amateur Championship, GC Grand-Ducal
Jul 12–14	Luxembourg Men Amateur Championship, GC Grand-Ducal
Jul 17–19	Czech International Ladies' Junior Championship, venue to be announced
Jul 17–19	Czech International Junior Championship, venue to be announced
Jul 18–21	Dutch Lady Junior International, GC Toxandria
Jul 18–21	Dutch Junior International, GC Toxandria

JEuropean Golf Association Championships *continued*

ul 19–22	German International Amateur Championship, Golfanlage Green Eagle
Jul 20–22	Lithuanian Amateur Open Championship, venue to be announced
Jul 20–22	Danish International Ladies Amateur Championship, Silkeborg GC
Jul 20–22	Danish International Amateur Championship, Silkeborg GC
Jul 24–27	English Boys (under 18) Open Amateur Stroke Play Championship (Carris Trophy), Royal Cinque Ports GC
Jul 24–26	Scottish Boys (under 18's) Open Stroke Play Championship, Cardross GC
Jul 24–26	Danish International Lady Junior Championship, Smörum GC
Jul 24–26	Danish International Youth Championship, Smörum GC
Jul 25-27	Scottish Ladies' Junior Open Stroke Play Championship, Blairgowrie (Lansdowne)
Aug 1–4	Czech International Ladies Amateur Championship, GC Brno (Kaskada)
Aug 1–4	Czech International Amateur Championship, GC Brno (Kaskada)
Aug 3–5	Swiss Ladies Amateur Championship, GC Schönenberg
Aug 3–5	Swiss Amateur Championship, GC Schönenberg
Aug 7–9	English Women's Open Amateur Stroke Play Championship, Little Aston GC
Aug 8–10	British Senior Open Amateur Championship, Machynys Peninsula
Aug 10–12	Latvian Ladies Amateur Open Championship, Ozo GC
Aug 10–12	Latvian Amateur Open Championship, Ozo GC
Aug 10–12	Hungarian Junior Amateur Open Championship, venue to be announced
Aug 13–17	Girls' British Open Amateur Championship, Tenby GC
Aug 14–19	British Boys Amateur Championship, Notts & Coxmoor
Aug 16–18	Finnish Ladies Amateur Championship, Helsinki GC
Aug 16–18	Finnish Amateur Championship, Helsinki GC
Aug 23–26	Belgian International Ladies Amateur Championship, Royal Antwerp GC
Aug 23–26	Belgian International Amateur Amateur Championship, Royal Antwerp GC
Aug 22–24	Ladies' British Open Amateur Stroke Play Championship, Shandon Park GC
Aug 23–25	Hungarian Open Ladies' Amateur Championship, venue to be announced
Aug 23–25	Hungarian Open Amateur Championship, venue to be announced
Aug 28–30	Italian International Individual (Under 16) Championship, Biella GC
Aug 29–Sep 1	Belgian International Girls (U18) Championship, Royal GC Belgium
Aug 29–Sep 1	Belgian International Boys (U18) Championship, Royal GC Belgium
Sep 12–14	Irish Senior Women's Open Stroke Play Championship, venue to be announced
Sep 12–15	Hellenic Ladies Amateur Championship, venue to be announced
Sep 12–15	Hellenic Amateur Championship, venue to be announced
Sep 13–15	Bulgarian Open Amateur Championship, St Sofia Golf and Spa
Sep 13–15	Bulgarian Open Ladies' Amateur Championship, St Sofia Golf and Spa
Sep 13–16	Austrian International Ladies Amateur Championship, venue to be announced
Sep 13–16	Austrian International Men's Amateur Championship, venue to be announced
Sep 14–16	Polish Open Amateur Championship, venue to be announced
Sep 15–16	Liechtenstein Open Ladies' Amateur Championship, GC Gams-Werdenberg
Sep 15–16	Liechtenstein Open Amateur Championship, GC Gams-Werdenberg
Sep 19–21	Senior Ladies' British Open Amateur Championship, Hunstanton GC

European Golf Association Championships *continued*

Sep 20–23	Spanish International Junior Stroke Play Championship, Layos GC
Sep 27–30	Turkish Open Amateur Championship (Ladies), venue to be announced
Sep 27–30	Turkish Open Amateur Championship (Men), venue to be announced
Oct 12–14	French International Ladies' Amateur Stroke Play Championship (Cécile De Rothschild Trophy), venue to be announced
Oct 21–23	Israel Juniors Boys and Girls Championship, venue to be announced
Oct 29–Nov 1	Israel Amateur Open Championship, venue to be announced
Oct 29–Nov 1	Israel Ladies Amateur Open Championship, venue to be announced

European Team Championships

Jul 12–14	Men's Challenge Trophy, Iceland, venue to be announced
Jul 10–14	Girls, GC St Leon-Rot, Germany
Jul 10–14	Boys, Lidingö GC, Sweden
Sep 4–8	Senior Men's, Estoril GC, Portugal
Sep 4–8	Senior Ladies', Lugano GC, Switzerland
Sep 20–22	Boys' Challenge Trophy, St Sofia GC & Spa, Bulgaria, venue to be announced

International European Championships

Jun 7–9	Mid-Amateur, Estonian G&CC, Estonia
Jun 14–16	Seniors, Golf & Landclub Achensee, Austria
Jul 25–28	Ladies, Slovenia, venue to be announced
Jul 26–28	European Young Masters, Royal Balaton GC, Hungary
Aug 8–11	Men, Ireland, venue to be announced
Sep 27–29	European Ladies' Club Trophy, Corfu GC, Greece
Oct 25–27	European Men's Club Trophy, Cyprus, venue to be announced

International Matches

Apr 25–27	Sir Michael Bonallack Trophy, Monte Rei G&CC, Portugal
Aug 31–Sept 1	St Andrews Trophy, Portmarnock GC, Ireland
Aug 31–Sept 1	Jacques Léglise Trophy, Portmarnock GC, Ireland
Sep 24–25	Junior Ryder Cup, Medinah, Illinois, USA

World Amateur Team Championship

Sep 27–30	Espirito Santo Trophy, Gloria GC, Turkey
Oct 4–7	Eisenhower Trophy, Antalya GC, Turkey

United States Golf Association Championships

www.usga.org

Jun 8–10	**Curtis Cup**, The Nairn Golf Club, Nairn, Scotland
Jun 14–17	**US Open**, The Olympic Club, San Francisco, California
Jun 18–3	US Women's Am Public Links, Neshanic Valley Golf Course, Neshanic, New Jersey
Jul 5–8	**US Women's Open**, Blackwolf Run Golf Course, Kohler, Wisconsin
Jul 9–14	US Amateur Public Links, Soldier Hollow Golf Course, Midway, Utah
Jul 12–15	US Senior Open, Indianwood G&CC, Lake Orion, Michigan
Jul 16–21	US Girls' Junior, Lake Merced GC, Daly City, California
Jul 16–21	US Junior Amateur, Golf Club of New England, Stratham, New Hampshire
Aug 6–12	US Women's Amateur, The Country Club (Ohio), Cleveland, Ohio
Aug 13–19	US Amateur, Cherry Hills CC, Cherry Hills Village, Colorado
Sep 8–13	US Mid-Amateur, Conway Farms GC, Lake Forest, Illinois
Sep 8–13	USGA Senior Women's Amateur, Hershey CC, Hershey, Pennsylvania
Sep 19–21	USGA Men's State Team, Galloway National GC, Galloway, New Jersey
Sep 26–29	Women's World Amateur Team, Gloria Golf Club (Old and New Courses), Antalya, Turkey
Sep 29–Oct 4	USGA Senior Amateur, Mountain Ridge CC, West Caldwell, New Jersey
Oct 4–7	World Amateur Team, Antalya Golf Club (PGA Sultan Course) / Cornelia Golf Club (Faldo Course), Antalya, Turkey
Oct 6–11	US Women's Mid-Amateur, Briggs Ranch GC, San Antonio, Texas

Who was known as "The Hawk"?

The answer can be found on page 905

Japan PGA Tour
www.jgto.org/jgto/WG01000000Init.do

Feb 22–26	**WGC–Accenture Match Play Championship**, The Ritz-Carlton GC, Dove Mountain, Marana Arizona, USA
Mar 8–11	**WGC–Cadillac Championship**, TPC Blue Monster at Doral, Florida, USA
Apr 5–8	**Masters Tournament**, Augusta National GC, Augusta, Georgia, USA
Apr 12–15	Token Homemate Cup, Token Tado Country Club Nagoya, Mie
Apr 19–22	Tsuruya Open, Yamanohara Golf Club, Yamanohara Course, Hyogo
Apr 26–29	The Crowns, Nagoya Golf Club, Wago Course, Aichi
May 10–13	PGA Championship Nissin Cupnoodles Cup, Karasuyamajo Country Club, Tochigi
May17–20	Totoumi Hamamatsu Open, Grandee Hamanako Golf Club, Shizuoka
May 24–27	Diamond Cup Golf, The Country Club Japan, Chiba
May 31–Jun 6	Japan Golf Tour Championship Citibank Cup, Shishido Hills Country Club, West Course, Ibaraki
Jun 14–17	**US Open Championship**, Olympic Club (Lake Course), San Francisco, California, USA
Jun 21–24	Gate Way To The Open Mizuno Open, JFE Setonaikai Golf Club, Okayama
Jun 29–Jul 1	Million Yard Cup, Passage Kinkai Island GC, Nagasaki
Jul 5–8	Nagashima Shigeo Invitational Sega Sammy Cup, The North Country Golf Club, Hokkaido
Jul 19–22	**British Open**, Royal Lytham & St. Annes GC, Lytham, England
Jul 26–29	Sun Chlorella Classic, Otaru Country Club, Hokkaido
Aug 2–5	**WGC–Bridgestone Invitational**, Firestone CC (South Course), Akron, Ohio, USA
Aug 9–12	**US PGA Championship**, Kiawah Island Golf Resort, South Carolina, USA
Aug 16–19	Kansai Open Golf Championship, Izumigaoka Country Club, Osaka
Aug 23–26	Vana H Cup KBC Augusta, Keya Golf Club, Fukuoka
Aug 30–Sep 2	Fujisankei Classic, Fujizakura Country Club, Yamanashi
Sep 6–9	Toshin Golf Tournament In Ryosen, Ryosen Golf Club, Mie
Sep 13–.16	ANA Open, Sapporo Golf Club Wattsu Course, Hokkaido
Sep 20–23	Asia-Pacific Panasonic Open, Higashi Hirono Golf Club, Hyogo
Sep 27–30	Coca-Cola Tokai Classic, Miyoshi Country Club West Course, Aichi
Oct 4–7	Canon Open, Totsuka Country Club, Kanagawa
Oct 11–14	Japan Open, Naha Golf Club, Okinawa
Oct 18–21	Bridgestone Open, Sodegaura Country Club Sodegaura Course, Chiba
Oct 25–28	Mynavi ABC Championship, ABC Golf Club, Hyogo
Nov 1–4	WGC–HSBC Champions, venue to be announced
Nov 8–11	Mitsui Sumitomo VISA Taiheiyo Masters, Taiheiyo Club, Gotemba Course, Shizuoka
Nov 15–18	Dunlop Phoenix, Phoenix Country Club, Miyazaki
Nov 22–25	Casio World Open, Kochi Kuroshio Country Club, Kochi
Nov 29–Dec 2	Golf Nippon Series JT Cup, Tokyo Yomiuri Country Club, Tokyo
Dec 9	Hitachi 3tours Championship, venue to be announced
Dec 14–16	The Royal Trophy, Empire Hotel & CC, Brunei

Ladies European Tour
www.ladieseuropeantour.com

Feb 2–5	RACV Australian Ladies Masters, RACV Royal Pines Resort, Queensland, Australia
Feb 9–12	ISPS Handa Women's Australian Open, Royal Melbourne Golf Club, Melbourne, Australia
Feb 17–19	ISPS Handa New Zealand Women's Open, Pegasus Golf Club, Christchurch, New Zealand
Mar 1–4	Event and venue to be announced
Mar 22–25	Lalla Meryem Cup, Golf de l'Ocean, Agadir, Morocco
May 3–5	Aberdeen Asset Management Ladies Scottish Open, Archerfield Links, East Lothian, Scotland
May 10–13	Turkish Ladies Open, National Golf Club, Belek, Antalya, Turkey
May 24–27	UniCredit Ladies German Open, Golfpark Gut Häusern, near Munich, Germany
Jun 1–3	Deloitte Ladies Open, Golfclub Broekpolder, Rotterdam, The Netherlands
Jun 8–10	Ladies Slovak Open, Golf Resort Tale, Bresno, Tále, Slovakia
Jun 14–17	Deutsche Bank Ladies Swiss Open, Golf Gerre Losone, Ticino, Switzerland
Jun 22–24	Raiffeisenbank Prague Golf Masters, Albatross Golf Resort, Prague, Czech Republic
Jul 26–29	**Evian Masters**, Evian Masters GC, Evian-Les-Bains, France

Aug 3–5	Ladies Irish Open, Killeen Castle, County Meath, Ireland
Aug 16–18	ISPS Handa Ladies British Masters, Buckinghamshire Golf Club, Denham, Buckinghamshire, England
Aug 30–Sep 2	UNIQA Ladies Golf Open, Golfclub Fohrenwald, Wiener Neustadt, Austria
Sep 6–9	Helsingborg Open, Vasatorp Golf Club, Helsingborg, Skane, Sweden
Sep 13–16	**Ricoh Women's British Open**, Royal Liverpool Golf Club, Hoylake, England
Sep 20–23	Open de España Femenino, Spain – venue to be announced
Sep 27–30	Ladies Open of Portugal, Portugal – venue to be announced
Oct 4–7	Lacoste Ladies Open de France, Chantaco Golf Club, Saint-Jean-de-Luz, Aquitaine, France
Oct 10–14	Event and venue to be announced
Oct	Sanya Ladies Open, Yalong Bay Golf Club, Sanya, China – date to be announced
Oct 26–28	China Suzhou Taihu Open, Suzhou International Golf Club, Suzhou, China
Nov 30–Dec 2	Hero Women's Indian Open, DLF Golf & Country Club, New Delhi, India
Dec 5–8	**Omega Dubai Ladies Masters**, Emirates Golf Course, Dubai, United Arab Emirates

Champions Tour

www.pgatour.com

Jan 20–22	Mitsubishi Electric Championship, Hualalai Golf Course, Ka'upulehu-Kona, Hawaii
Feb 10–12	Allianz Championship, The Old Course at Broken Sound, Boca Raton, Florida
Feb 17–19	ACE Group Classic, TwinEagles GC (Talon Course), Naples, Florida
Mar 16–18	Toshiba Classic, Newport Beach CC, Newport Beach, California
Mar 23–25	Mississippi Gulf Resort Classic, Fallen Oak, Biloxi, Mississippi
Apr 13–15	Tampa Bay Pro-Am, TPC Tampa Bay, Lutz, Florida
Apr 20–22	Liberty Mutual Insurance Legends of Golf, Savannah Harbor Golf Resort, Savannah, Georgia
May 4–6	Insperity Championship, The Woodlands CC, The Woodlands, Texas
May 24–27	Senior PGA Championship, The Golf Club at Harbor Shores, Benton Harbor, Michigan
Jun 1–3	Principal Charity Classic, Glen Oaks CC, West Des Moines, Iowa
Jun 7–10	Regions Tradition, Shoal Creek, Shoal Creek, Alabama
Jun 22–24	Montreal Championship, Vallée du Richelieu Vercheres, Sainte-Julie, Quebec, Canada
Jun 28–Jul 1	Constellation Senior Players Championship, Fox Chapel Golf Club, Pittsburgh, Pennsylvania
Jul 6–8	Nature Valley First Tee Open at Pebble Beach, Pebble Beach Golf Links, Monterey Peninsula, California/Del Monte Golf Course, Monterey, California
Jul 12–15	**US Senior Open Championship**, Indianwood G&CC, Lake Orion, Michigan
Jul 26–29	**Senior Open Championship**, Turnberry (Ailsa Course), Turnberry, Scotland
Aug 3–5	3M Championship, TPC Twin Cities, Blaine, Minnesota
Aug 17–19	Dick's Sporting Goods Open, En-Joie GC, Endicott, New York
Aug 24–26	Boeing Classic, TPC Snoqualmie Ridge, Snoqualmie, Washington
Oct 5–7	SAS Championship, Prestonwood CC, Cary, North Carolina
Oct 12–14	Greater Hickory Classic at Rock Barn, Rock Barn G&S, Conover, North Carolina
Oct 26–28	AT&T Championship, TPC San Antonio – ATT Canyons, San Antonio, Texas
Nov 1–4	Charles Schwab Cup Championship, Desert Mountain (Cochise), Scottsdale, Arizona

Annika awarded the 2012 Bob Jones Award

Swedish golfer Annika Sörenstam, one of the most dominant players in the history of women's golf, has been selected as the recipient of the United States Golf Association's 2012 Bob Jones Award.

The USGA's highest honour has been presented annually since 1955 in recognition of distinguished sportsmanship in golf. The Award seeks to recognize a person who emulates Jones' spirit, his personal qualities and his attitude toward the game and its players.

"Annika has consistently exhibited distinguished sportsmanship which the Bob Jones Award was established to recognize, and has done so while achieving a level of success that few have equalled," said USGA President Jim Hyler.

"It is not only the number of tournaments that she won during her incredible career, but the way she conducted herself, always gracious in victory and defeat, always respectful of her opponents and of the game itself."

In 2008, Sörenstam was named an Ambassador of the United States Golf Association, a role in which she helps the USGA make the game more accessible to players of all skill levels. She has helped the USGA educate golfers through a series of "Play by the Rules" video vignettes and served as the honorary chairman for the 2011 US Women's Open at The Broadmoor in Colorado Springs, Colorado.

In 2009, she was named a Global Ambassador by the International Golf Federation, and she supported the successful effort to have golf added to the 2016 Olympic Games in Rio de Janeiro.

She dedicates much of her time to the ANNIKA Foundation, which she started in 2007 as a way to teach children the importance of embracing a healthy, active lifestyle through fitness and nutrition, and offer aspiring junior golfers opportunities to pursue their dreams.

"It is truly an honour to receive the prestigious Bob Jones Award from the USGA, as the past recipients are some of the greatest names in the history of the game," said Sörenstam. "He is known for his character and I have always tried to pride myself on being respectful to others both on and off the course. Though I am no longer competing, I appreciate the USGA recognizing our hard work and I will continue to try to grow and promote the game through many foundation initiatives."

Sörenstam, who began playing golf at the age of 12, enjoyed a successful amateur career that included the 1991 NCAA Division I individual title and a runner-up finish at the 1992 US.Women's Amateur. She was a member of the Swedish team that won the 1992 Women's World Amateur Team Championship shortly before she turned professional.

During her 15-year career, Sörenstam scored 90 professional worldwide victories, including 72 on the LPGA Tour, 10 of which were major championships, including the 1995, 1996 and 2006 US Women's Open titles. She earned a record eight Rolex LPGA Player-of-the-Year awards, a record-tying eight money list titles and six Vare Trophies for the lowest scoring average. She played on eight European Solheim Cup Teams and served as an assistant captain for the victorious European Solheim Cup Team in 2011.

At the LPGA's 2001 Standard Register PING tournament, she became the first woman to shoot 59 in a professional round, and in 2003 became the first woman to compete in a PGA Tour event since 1945 when she played in the Bank of America Colonial at Fort Worth, Texas.

Sörenstam was inducted into the LPGA and World Golf Halls of Fame in 2003.

She stepped away from professional golf after the 2008 season to focus on her family and the ANNIKA brand of businesses, which include a Golf Academy, a Financial Group, a Course Design company, the ANNIKA Collection of apparel with Cutter & Buck, signature high-end wines with Wente Vineyards and an online retail shop. Sörenstam and her husband, Mike McGee, live in Florida with their two young children, Ava and Will.

What is the answer?

Q: Is the person who lifted the player's ball the only person who may replace it?

A: No. Up to a maximum of three different people may replace a ball, depending on the circumstances i.e. the player, his partner or the person who lifted it. For example, in a four-ball match, if a player were to authorise his caddie to lift his ball, the caddie, his partner or the player could replace it. However, if the player lifts the ball himself, only he or his partner may replace it.

PART XII

Annual Awards

Annual Awards

European

European Tour Player of the Year

1985 Bernhard Langer (GER)	1995 Colin Montgomerie (SCO)	2005 Michael Campbell (NZL)
1986 Severiano Ballesteros (ESP)	1996 Colin Montgomerie (SCO)	2006 Paul Casey (ENG)
1987 Ian Woosnam (WAL)	1997 Colin Montgomerie (SCO)	2007 Padraig Harrington (IRL)
1988 Severiano Ballesteros (ESP)	1998 Lee Westwood (ENG)	2008 Padraig Harrington (IRL)
1989 Nick Faldo (ENG)	1999 Colin Montgomerie (SCO)	2009 Lee Westwood (ENG)
1990 Nick Faldo (ENG)	2000 Lee Westwood (ENG)	2010 Martin Kaymer (GER) and
1991 Severiano Ballesteros (ESP)	2001 Retief Goosen (RSA)	Graeme McDowell (NIR)
1992 Nick Faldo (ENG)	2002 Ernie Els (RSA)	2011 Luke Donald (ENG)
1993 Bernhard Langer (GER)	2003 Ernie Els (RSA)	
1994 Ernie Els (RSA)	2004 Vijay Singh (FIJ)	

Association of Golf Writers' Trophy   (Awarded to the man or woman who, in the opinion of golf writers, has done most for European golf during the year)

1951 Max Faulkner (ENG)	1972 Miss Michelle Walker (ENG)	1992 European Solheim Cup Team
1952 Miss Elizabeth Price (ENG)	1973 Peter Oosterhuis (ENG)	(Mickey Walker capt.)
1953 Joe Carr (IRL)	1974 Peter Oosterhuis (ENG)	1993 Bernhard Langer (GER)
1954 Mrs Roy Smith (Miss Frances	1975 Golf Foundation	1994 Laura Davies (ENG)
Stephens) (ENG)	1976 GB&I Eisenhower Trophy Team	1995 European Ryder Cup Team
1955 LGU's Touring Team	(Sandy Saddler capt.)	(Bernard Gallacher capt.)
(Mrs BR Bostock capt.)	1977 Christy O'Connor (IRL)	1996 Colin Montgomerie (SCO)
1956 John Beharrell (ENG)	1978 Peter McEvoy (ENG)	1997 Alison Nicholas (ENG)
1957 Dai Rees (WAL)	1979 Severiano Ballesteros (ESP)	1998 Lee Westwood (ENG)
1958 Harry Bradshaw (IRL)	1980 Sandy Lyle (SCO)	1999 Sergio García (ESP)
1959 Eric Brown (SCO)	1981 Bernhard Langer (GER)	2000 Lee Westwood (ENG)
1960 Sir Stuart Goodwin	1982 Gordon Brand Jr (SCO)	2001 GB&I WalkerCup Team
1961 Commander Charles Roe	1983 Nick Faldo (ENG)	(Peter McEvoy capt.)
1962 Marley Spearman (ENG)	1984 Severiano Ballesteros (ESP)	2002 Ernie Els (RSA)
1963 Michael Lunt (ENG)	1985 European Ryder Cup Team	2003 Annika Sörenstam (SWE)
1964 GB&I Eisenhower Trophy Team	(Tony Jacklin capt.)	2004 European Ryder Cup team
(Joe Carr capt.)	1986 GB&I Curtis Cup Team	(Bernhard Langer capt.)
1965 Gerald Micklem (ENG)	(Diane Bailey capt.)	2005 Annika Sörenstam (SWE)
1966 Ronnie Shade (SCO)	1987 European Ryder Cup Team	2006 European Ryder Cup team
1967 John Panton (SCO)	(Tony Jacklin capt.)	(Ian Woosnam capt.)
1968 Michael Bonallack (ENG)	1988 Sandy Lyle (SCO)	2007 Padraig Harrington (IRL)
1969 Tony Jacklin (ENG)	1989 GB&I Walker Cup Team	2008 Padraig Harrington (IRL)
1970 Tony Jacklin (ENG)	(Peter McEvoy capt.)	2009 Lee Westwood (ENG)
1971 GB&I Walker Cup Team	1990 Nick Faldo (ENG)	2010 Graeme McDowell (NIR)
(Michael Bonallack capt.)	1991 Severiano Ballesteros (ESP)	2011 Luke Donald (ENG)

Award for British Golf Museum at St Andrews

The British Golf Museum, located beside the Royal and Ancient Clubhouse, has been recognized as a Collection of National Significance by Museums Galleries, Scotland.

Angela Howe, Director of the Museum which tells the story of amateur and professional golf from medieval times to the present day, is delighted because it is testament to the important part golf has played for centuries in Scottish society and culture.

The British Golf Museum is the 38th collection of national significance which give great value to the people of Scotland and to the millions of visitors from around the world each year.

(See Mike Aitken's article on the Museum on page 37).

European Tour Harry Vardon Trophy

(Awarded to the PGA member heading the Order of Merit at the end of the season)

1937 Charles Whitcombe	1960 Bernard Hunt	1978 Severiano Ballesteros	1996 Colin Montgomerie
1938 Henry Cotton	1961 Christy O'Connor	1979 Sandy Lyle	1997 Colin Montgomerie
1939 Roger Whitcombe	1962 Christy O'Connor	1980 Sandy Lyle	1998 Colin Montgomerie
1940–45 In abeyance	1963 Neil Coles	1981 Bernhard Langer	1999 Colin Montgomerie
1946 Bobby Locke	1964 Peter Alliss	1982 Greg Norman	2000 Lee Westwood
1947 Norman Von Nida	1965 Bernard Hunt	1983 Nick Faldo	2001 Retief Goosen
1948 Charlie Ward	1966 Peter Alliss	1984 Bernhard Langer	2002 Retief Goosen
1949 Charlie Ward	1967 Malcolm Gregson	1985 Sandy Lyle	2003 Ernie Els
1950 Bobby Locke	1968 Brian Huggett	1986 Severiano Ballesteros	2004 Ernie Els
1951 John Panton	1969 Bernard Gallacher	1987 Ian Woosnam	2005 Colin Montgomerie
1952 Harry Weetman	1970 Neil Coles	1988 Severiano Ballesteros	2006 Padraig Harrington
1953 Flory van Donck	1971 Peter Oosterhuis	1989 Ronan Rafferty	2007 Justin Rose
1954 Bobby Locke	1972 Peter Oosterhuis	1990 Ian Woosnam	2008 Robert Karlsson
1955 Dai Rees	1973 Peter Oosterhuis	1991 Severiano Ballesteros	2009 Lee Westwood
1956 Harry Weetman	1974 Peter Oosterhuis	1992 Nick Faldo	2010 Martin Kaymer
1957 Eric Brown	1975 Dale Hayes	1993 Colin Montgomerie	2011 Luke Donald
1958 Bernard Hunt	1976 Severiano Ballesteros	1994 Colin Montgomerie	
1959 Dai Rees	1977 Severiano Ballesteros	1995 Colin Montgomerie	

Sir Henry Cotton European Rookie of the Year

1960 Tommy Goodwin	1976 Mark James (ENG)	1989 Paul Broadhurst (ENG)	2003 Peter Lawrie (IRL)
1961 Alex Caygill (ENG)	1977 Nick Faldo (ENG)	1990 Russell Claydon (ENG)	2004 Scott Drummond
1962 No Award	1978 Sandy Lyle (SCO)	1991 Per-Ulrik Johansson	(SCO)
1963 Tony Jacklin (ENG)	1979 Mike Miller (SCO)	(SWE)	2005 Gonzolo Fernandez-
1964 No Award	1980 Paul Hoad (ENG)	1992 Jim Payne (ENG)	Castano (ESP)
1966 Robin Liddle (SCO)	1981 Jeremy Bennett (ENG)	1993 Gary Orr (SCO)	2006 Marc Warren (SCO)
1967 No Award	1982 Gordon Brand Jr (SCO)	1994 Jonathan Lomas (ENG)	2007 Martin Kaymer (GER)
1968 Bernard Gallacher (SCO)	1983 Grant Turner (NZL)	1995 Jarmo Sandelin (SWE)	2008 Pablo Larrazabal (ESP)
1969 Peter Oosterhuis (ENG)	1984 Philip Parkin (WAL)	1996 Thomas Bjørn (DEN)	2009 Chris Wood (ENG)
1970 Stuart Brown (ENG)	1985 Paul Thomas (WAL)	1997 Scott Henderson (SCO)	2010 Matteo Manassero
1971 David Llewellyn (WAL)	1986 José Maria Olazàbal	1998 Olivier Edmond (FRA)	(ITA)
1972 Sam Torrance (SCO)	(ESP)	1999 Sergio García (ESP)	2011 Tom Lewis (ENG)
1973 Philip Elson (ENG)	1987 Peter Baker (ENG)	2000 Ian Poulter (ENG)	
1974 Carl Mason (ENG)	1988 Colin Montgomerie	2001 Paul Casey (ENG)	
1975 No Award	(SCO)	2002 Nick Dougherty (ENG)	

Luke Donald first English winner of Jack Nicklaus Trophy

After his remarkable year in America it was no surprise that Luke Donald was named 2011 PGA Tour Golfer of the Year by his fellow Tour members. He is the first English golfer to receive the Jack Nicklaus Trophy.

Keegan Bradley, winner of the US PGA Championship, was voted the Rookie of the Year.

PGA Tour Commissioner Tim Finchem said: "Both players had significant and impressive performances throughout the year, and the member vote reflects the respect their peers have for them. Donald was clearly the best player of the year."

On hearing the announcement, Donald said: "That's a great honour to cap off what has obviously been an amazing year for me."

Donald's win in his final start of the year at the Children's Miracle Network Classic clinched the money title with $6,683,214, earning him the Arnold Palmer Award. He also wrapped up the Byron Nelson Trophy and Vardon Award for lowest adjusted scoring average of 68.86.

Twenty-five year old Bradley earned play-off victories at the HP Byron Nelson Championship and the PGA Championship, becoming the first rookie since Todd Hamilton in 2004 to win twice. With his PGA Championship playoff victory over Jason Dufner at Atlanta Athletic Club, Bradley became the first player since Ben Curtis in 2003 to win a major championship in his first major start.

Ladies European Tour Henderson Money List

1979 Catherine Panton-Lewis (SCO)	1990 Trish Johnson (ENG)	2001 Raquel Carriedo (ESP)
1980 Muriel Thomson (SCO)	1991 Corinne Dibnah (AUS)	2002 Paula Marti (ESP)
1981 Jenny Lee-Smith (ENG)	1992 Laura Davies (ENG)	2003 Sophie Gustafson (SWE)
1982 Jenny Lee-Smith (ENG)	1993 Karen Lunn (AUS)	2004 Laura Davies (ENG)
1983 Muriel Thomson (SCO)	1994 Liselotte Neumann (SWE)	2005 Iben Tinning (DEN)
1984 Dale Reid (SCO)	1995 Annika Sörenstam (SWE)	2006 Laura Davies (ENG)
1985 Laura Davies (ENG)	1996 Laura Davies (ENG)	2007 Sophie Gustafson (SWE)
1986 Laura Davies (ENG)	1997 Alison Nicholas (ENG)	2008 Gwladys Nocera (FRA)
1987 Dale Reid (SCO)	1998 Helen Alfredsson (SWE)	2009 Sophie Gustafson (SWE)
1988 Marie-Laure Taud (FRA)	1999 Laura Davies (ENG)	2010 Lee-Anne Pace (RSA)
1989 Marie-Laure de Laurenzi (FRA)	2000 Sophie Gustafson (SWE)	2011 Ai Miyazato (JPN)

Ladies European Tour Players' Player of the Year

1995 Annika Sörenstam (SWE)	2001 Raquel Carriedo (ESP)	2007 Sophie Gustafson (SWE)
1996 Laura Davies (ENG)	2002 Annika Sörenstam (SWE)	2008 Gwladys Nocera (FRA)
1997 Alison Nicholas (ENG)	2003 Sophie Gustafson (SWE)	2009 Catriona Matthew (SCO)
1998 Sophie Gustafson (SWE)	2004 Stephanie Arricau (FRA)	2010 Lee-Anne Pace (RSA)
1999 Laura Davies (ENG)	2005 Iben Tinning (DEN)	2011 Caroline Hedwall (SWE)
2000 Sophie Gustafson (SWE)	2006 Gwladys Nocera (FRA)	

Ladies European Tour Ryder Cup Wales Rookie of the Year

1984 Katrina Douglas (ENG)	1994 Tracy Hansen (USA)	2004 Minea Blomqvist (FIN)
1985 Laura Davies (ENG)	1995 Karrie Webb (AUS)	2005 Elisa Serramia (ESP)
1986 Patricia Gonzales (COL)	1996 Anne-Marie Knight (AUS)	2006 Nikki Garrett (AUS)
1987 Trish Johnson (ENG)	1997 Anna Berg (SWE)	2007 Louise Stahle (SWE)
1988 Laurette Maritz (USA)	1998 Laura Philo (USA)	2008 Melissa Reid (ENG)
1989 Helen Alfredsson (SWE)	1999 Elaine Ratcliffe (ENG)	2009 Anna Norqvist (SWE)
1990 Pearl Sinn (KOR)	2000 Guila Sergas (ITA)	2010 Kim In-Kyung (KOR)
1991 Helen Wadsworth (WAL)	2001 Suzann Pettersen (NOR)	2011 Anna Nordqvist (SWE)
1992 Sandrine Mendiburu (FRA)	2002 Kirsty S Taylor (ENG)	
1993 Annika Sörenstam (SWE)	2003 Rebecca Stevenson (AUS)	

Daily Telegraph Amateur Woman Golfer of the Year

1982 Jane Connachan (SCO)	1992 GBI Curtis Cup Team (Liz Boatman capt.)	1999 Welsh International Team (Olwen Davies capt.)
1983 Jill Thornhill (ENG)	1993 Catriona Lambert and Julie Hall	2000 Rebecca Hudson (ENG)
1984 Gillian Stewart and Claire Waite (ENG)	1994 GBI Curtis Cup Team (Liz Boatman capt.)	2001 Rebecca Hudson (ENG)
1985 Belle Robertson (SCO)	1995 Julie Hall (ENG)	2002 Becky Brewerton (WAL)
1986 GBI Curtis Cup Team (Diane Bailey capt.)	1996 GBI Curtis Cup Team (Ita Butler capt.)	2003 Becky Brewerton (WAL)
1987 Linda Bayman (ENG)	1997 Alison Rose (ENG)	2004 Emma Duggleby (ENG)
1988 GBI Curtis Cup Team	1998 Kim Andrew	2005 Felicity Johnson (ENG)
1989 Helen Dobson (ENG)		2006 *Not awarded*
1990 Angela Uzielli (ENG)		2007 Melissa Reid (ENG)
1991 Joanne Morley (ENG)		2008 *Discontinued*

Joyce Wethered Trophy (Awarded to the outstanding amateur under 25)

1994 Janice Moodie (SCO)	1998 Liza Walters (ENG)	2003 Sophie Walker (ENG)	2007 Henrietta Brockway (ENG)
1995 Rebecca Hudson (ENG)	1999 Becky Brewerton (WAL)	2004 Melissa Reid (ENG)	2008 *Discontinued*
1996 Mhairi McKay (SCO)	2000 Sophie Walker (ENG)	2005 Becky Harries (ENG)	
1997 Rebecca Hudson (ENG)	2001 Clare Queen (ENG)	2006 Sally Little (SCO) and Carly Booth (SCO)	
	2002 Sarah Jones (ENG)		

American

Winners American unless stated

Arnold Palmer Award (Awarded to the Tour's leading money winner)

1981 Tom Kite	1989 Tom Kite	1997 Tiger Woods	2005 Tiger Woods
1982 Craig Stadler	1990 Greg Norman (AUS)	1998 David Duval	2006 Tiger Woods
1983 Hal Sutton	1991 Corey Pavin	1999 Tiger Woods	2007 Tiger Woods
1984 Tom Watson	1992 Fred Couples	2000 Tiger Woods	2008 Vijay Singh (FIJ)
1985 Curtis Strange	1993 Nick Price (ZIM)	2001 Tiger Woods	2009 Tiger Woods
1986 Greg Norman (AUS)	1994 Nick Price (ZIM)	2002 Tiger Woods	2010 Matt Kuchar
1987 Paul Azinger	1995 Greg Norman (AUS)	2003 Tiger Woods	2011 Luke Donald (ENG)
1988 Curtis Strange	1996 Tom Lehman	2004 Vijay Singh (FIJ)	

Jack Nicklaus Award (Player of the Year decided by player ballot)

1990 Wayne Levi	1996 Tom Lehman	2002 Tiger Woods	2008 Padraig Harrington
1991 Fred Couples	1997 Tiger Woods	2003 Tiger Woods	(IRL)
1992 Fred Couples	1998 Mark O'Meara	2004 Vijay Singh (FIJ)	2009 Tiger Woods
1993 Nick Price (ZIM)	1999 Tiger Woods	2005 Tiger Woods	2010 Jim Furyk
1994 Nick Price (ZIM)	2000 Tiger Woods	2006 Tiger Woods	2011 Luke Donald (ENG)
1995 Greg Norman (AUS)	2001 Tiger Woods	2007 Tiger Woods	

PGA Tour Rookie of the Year (Decided by player ballot)

1990 Robert Gamez	1996 Tiger Woods	2002 Jonathan Byrd	2007 Brandt Snedeker
1991 John Daly	1997 Stewart Cink	2003 Ben Curtis	2008 Andres Romero
1992 Mark Carnevale	1998 Steve Flesch	2004 Todd Hamilton	(ARG)
1993 Vijay Singh (FIJ)	1999 Carlos Franco (PAR)	2005 Sean O'Hair	2009 Marc Leishman (AUS)
1994 Ernie Els (RSA)	2000 Michael Clark II	2006 Trevor Immelman	2010 Rickie Fowler
1995 Woody Austin	2001 Charles Howell III	(RSA)	2011 Keegan Bradley

PGA of America Player of the Year (Decided on merit points)

1948 Ben Hogan	1965 Dave Marr	1982 Tom Watson	1999 Tiger Woods
1949 Sam Snead	1966 Billy Casper	1983 Hal Sutton	2000 Tiger Woods
1950 Ben Hogan	1967 Jack Nicklaus	1984 Tom Watson	2001 Tiger Woods
1951 Ben Hogan	1968 *not awarded*	1985 Lanny Wadkins	2002 Tiger Woods
1952 Julius Boros	1969 Orville Moody	1986 Bob Tway	2003 Tiger Woods
1953 Ben Hogan	1970 Billy Casper	1987 Paul Azinger	2004 Vijay Singh (FIJ)
1954 Ed Furgol	1971 Lee Trevino	1988 Curtis Strange	2005 Tiger Woods
1955 Doug Ford	1972 Jack Nicklaus	1989 Tom Kite	2006 Tiger Woods
1956 Jack Burke	1973 Jack Nicklaus	1990 Nick Faldo (ENG)	2007 Tiger Woods
1957 Dick Mayer	1974 Johnny Miller	1991 Corey Pavin	2008 Padraig Harrington
1958 Dow Finsterwald	1975 Jack Nicklaus	1992 Fred Couples	(IRL)
1959 Art Wall	1976 Jack Nicklaus	1993 Nick Price (ZIM)	2009 Tiger Woods
1960 Arnold Palmer	1977 Tom Watson	1994 Nick Price (ZIM)	2010 Jim Furyk
1961 Jerry Barber	1978 Tom Watson	1995 Greg Norman (AUS)	2011 Luke Donald (ENG)
1962 Arnold Palmer	1979 Tom Watson	1996 Tom Lehman	
1963 Julius Boros	1980 Tom Watson	1997 Tiger Woods	
1964 Ken Venturi	1981 Bill Rogers	1998 Mark O'Meara	

Spirit of Sport Award for Solheim captain Alison

Alison Nicholas MBE, captain of the victorious European Solheim Cup team, received the Sports Journalists' Association of Great Britain's 2011 Spirit of Sport Award, which recognises fair play and those who inspire.

The award was presented in recognition of her incredible achievements as a professional golfer and as an inspirational leader, captaining The 2011 European Solheim Cup team to victory over the United States by a score of 15–13 at Killeen Castle in County Meath, Ireland, last September which the former US Open and British Open winner rates as her career best achievement.

PGA of America Vardon Trophy (For lowest scoring average over 60 PGA Tour rounds or more)

Year	Player	Avg	Year	Player	Avg	Year	Player	Avg
1937	Harry Cooper		1965	Billy Casper	70.85	1989	Greg Norman (AUS)	69.49
1938	Sam Snead		1966	Billy Casper	70.27	1990	Greg Norman (AUS)	69.10
1939	Byron Nelson		1967	Arnold Palmer	70.18	1991	Fred Couples	69.59
1940	Ben Hogan		1968	Billy Casper	69.82	1992	Fred Couples	69.38
1941	Ben Hogan		1969	Dave Hill	70.34	1993	Nick Price (ZIM)	69.11
1942–46	No Awards		1970	Lee Trevino	70.64	1994	Greg Norman (AUS)	69.81
1947	Jimmy Demaret	69.90	1971	Lee Trevino	70.27	1995	Steve Elkington (AUS)	69.82
1948	Ben Hogan	69.30	1972	Lee Trevino	70.89	1996	Tom Lehman	69.32
1949	Sam Snead	69.37	1973	Bruce Crampton (AUS)	70.57	1997	Nick Price (ZIM)	68.98
1950	Sam Snead	69.23	1974	Lee Trevino	70.53	1998	David Duval	69.13
1951	Lloyd Mangrum	70.05	1975	Bruce Crampton (AUS)	70.51	1999	Tiger Woods	68.43
1952	Jack Burke	70.54	1976	Don January	70.56	2000	Tiger Woods	67.79
1953	Lloyd Mangrum	70.22	1977	Tom Watson	70.32	2001	Tiger Woods	68.81
1954	Ed Harrison	70.41	1978	Tom Watson	70.16	2002	Tiger Woods	68.56
1955	Sam Snead	69.86	1979	Tom Watson	70.27	2003	Tiger Woods	68.41
1956	Cary Middlecoff	70.35	1980	Lee Trevino	69.73	2004	Vijay Singh (FIJ)	68.84
1957	Dow Finsterwald	70.30	1981	Tom Kite	69.80	2005	Tiger Woods	68.66
1958	Bob Rosburg	70.11	1982	Tom Kite	70.21	2006	Jim Furyk	68.66
1959	Art Wall	70.35	1983	Ray Floyd	70.61	2007	Tiger Woods	67.79
1960	Billy Casper	69.95	1984	Calvin Peete	70.56	2008	Phil Mickelson	69.17
1961	Arnold Palmer	69.85	1985	Don Pooley	70.36	2009	Tiger Woods	68.05
1962	Arnold Palmer	70.27	1986	Scott Hoch	70.08	2010	Matt Kuchar	69.61
1963	Billy Casper	70.58	1987	Dan Pohl	70.25	2011	Luke Donald (ENG)	68.86
1964	Arnold Palmer	70.01	1988	Chip Beck	69.46			

Payne Stewart Award (Presented for respecting and upholding the traditions of the game)

Year	Recipient	Year	Recipient	Year	Recipient	Year	Recipient
2000	Byron Nelson, Jack Nicklaus, Arnold Palmer	2002	Nick Price	2006	Gary Player (RSA)	2010	Tom Lehman
		2003	Tom Watson	2007	Hal Sutton	2011	David Toms
		2004	Jay Haas	2008	Davis Love III		
2001	Ben Crenshaw	2005	Brad Faxon	2009	Kenny Perry		

Peter Dawson honoured for helping develop golf in China

Peter Dawson, Chief Executive of The R&A and President of the International Golf Federation, was the recipient of the 2011 David Chu Award at a ceremony held during the Omega Mission Hills World Cup in Haikou, China. The award, named after Dr David Chu who passed away earlier this year, recognizes those who have been instrumental in developing golf in China.

As Chief Executive, Dawson leads The R&A's efforts to encourage the playing of golf globally by distributing through grass roots organisions funds to support coaching programs and junior golf and by providing finance to help build and develop golf facilities. The R&A's aim is to encourage more people to play golf in more places, more often.

"Dr Chu's impact on the game of golf in China is unparalleled," Dawson said. "It is an honour to accept an award bearing his name. I hope The R&A's worldwide efforts along with the International Golf Federation can mirror the positive impact that Dr Chu achieved in China."

Dawson played an integral role in having golf named as an Olympic sport beginning with the 2016 Games. This ensures the Olympics will help to bring funds and attention to golf in countries that otherwise have paid little attention to the game.

"Peter has been a major supporter for the growth of golf in China for many years," said Tenniel Chu, Vice Chairman of Mission Hills Golf Club. "As someone who shared my father's vision for the game's bright future in China, we're so pleased to see his contributions formally recognized."

"Peter Dawson personifies everything the David Chu Award stands for," said PGA Tour Commissioner Tim Finchem. "It is fitting that Peter is being honored as the first person other than Dr Chu to receive the award that carries Dr Chu's name. Peter and The R&A have brought golf to many who would not otherwise have had the opportunity to learn from the positive life lessons that our sport teaches."

PGA of America Distinguished Service Award

1988 Herb Graffis	1994 Arnold Palmer	2000 Jack Nicklaus	2006 Fred Ridley
1989 Bob Hope	1995 Patty Berg	2001 Mark McCormack	2007 Jack Burke Jr
1990 No award	1996 Frank Chirkinian	2002 Tim Finchem	2008 Dennis Walters
1991 Gerald Ford	1997 George Bush	2003 Vince Gill	2009 William J Powell
1992 Gene Sarazen	1998 Paul Runyan	2004 Pete Dye	2010 Billy Casper
1993 Byron Nelson	1999 Bill Dickey	2005 Wally Uihlein	2011 Larry Nelson

Bob Jones Award   (Awarded by USGA for distinguished sportsmanship in golf)

1955 Francis Ouimet	1971 Arnold Palmer	1986 Jess W Sweetser	2002 Judy Rankin
1956 Bill Campbell	1972 Michael Bonallack	1987 Tom Watson	2003 Carol Semple
1957 Babe Zaharias	(ENG)	1988 Isaac B Grainger	Thompson
1958 Margaret Curtis	1973 Gene Littler	1989 Chi-Chi Rodriquez	2004 Jackie Burke
1959 Findlay Douglas	1974 Byron Nelson	(PUR)	2005 Nick Price (ZIM)
1960 Charles Evans Jr	1975 Jack Nicklaus	1990 Peggy Kirk Bell	2006 Jay Haas
1961 Joe Carr (IRL)	1976 Ben Hogan	1991 Ben Crenshaw	2007 Louise Suggs
1962 Horton-Smith	1977 Joseph C Dey	1992 Gene Sarazen	2008 Gordon Brewer
1963 Patty Berg	1978 Bob Hope and	1993 P J Boatwright Jr	2009 Mickey Wright
1964 Charles Coe	Bing Crosby	1994 Lewis Oehmig	2010 Lorena Ochoa (MEX)
1965 Mrs Edwin Vare	1979 Tom Kite	1995 Herbert Warren	2011 George H W Bush
1966 Gary Player (RSA)	1980 Charles Yates	Wind	2012 Annika Sörenstam
1967 Richard Tufts	1981 JoAnne Carner	1996 Betsy Rawls	(SWE)
1968 Robert Dickson	1982 Billy Joe Patton	1997 Fred Brand	
1969 Gerald Micklem	1983 Maureen Garrett	1998 Nancy Lopez	
(ENG)	(ENG)	1999 Ed Updegraff	
1970 Roberto De Vicenzo	1984 Jay Sigel	2000 Barbara McIntyre	
(ARG)	1985 Fuzzy Zoeller	2001 Thomas Cousins	

US LPGA Rolex Player of the Year

1966 Kathy Whitworth	1978 Nancy Lopez	1990 Beth Daniel	2002 Annika Sörenstam (SWE)
1967 Kathy Whitworth	1979 Nancy Lopez	1991 Pat Bradley	2003 Annika Sörenstam (SWE)
1968 Kathy Whitworth	1980 Beth Daniel	1992 Dottie Mochrie	2004 Annika Sörenstam (SWE)
1969 Kathy Whitworth	1981 Jo Anne Carner	1993 Betsy King	2005 Annika Sörenstam (SWE)
1970 Sandra Haynie	1982 Jo Anne Carner	1994 Beth Daniel	2006 Lorena Ochoa (MEX)
1971 Kathy Whitworth	1983 Patty Sheehan	1995 Annika Sörenstam (SWE)	2007 Lorena Ochoa (MEX)
1972 Kathy Whitworth	1984 Betsy King	1996 Laura Davies (ENG)	2008 Lorena Ochoa (MEX)
1973 Kathy Whitworth	1985 Nancy Lopez	1997 Annika Sörenstam (SWE)	2009 Lorena Ochoa (MEX)
1974 JoAnne Carner	1986 Pat Bradley	1998 Annika Sörenstam (SWE)	2010 Yani Tseng (TPE)
1975 Sandra Palmer	1987 Ayako Okamoto (JPN)	1999 Karrie Webb (AUS)	2011 Yani Tseng (TPE)
1976 Judy Rankin	1988 Nancy Lopez	2000 Karrie Webb (AUS)	
1977 Judy Rankin	1989 Betsy King	2001 Annika Sörenstam (SWE)	

Louise Suggs Rolex Rookie of the Year

1962 Mary Mills	1976 Bonnie Lauer	1989 Pamela Wright (SCO)	1999 Mi Hyun Kim (KOR)
1963 Clifford Ann Creed	1977 Debbie Massey	1990 Hiromi Kobayashi	2000 Dorothy Delasin
1964 Susie Berning	1978 Nancy Lopez	(JPN)	(PHI)
1965 Margie Masters	1979 Beth Daniel	1991 Brandie Burton	2001 Hee Won Han (KOR)
1966 Jan Ferraris	1980 Myra Van Hoose	1992 Helen Alfredsson	2002 Beth Bauer
1967 Sharron Moran	1981 Patty Sheehan	(SWE)	2003 Lorena Ochoa (MEX)
1968 Sandra Post	1982 Patti Rizzo	1993 Suzanne Strudwick	2004 Shi Hyun Ahn (KOR)
1969 Jane Blalock	1983 Stephanie Farwig	(ENG)	2005 Paula Creamer
1970 JoAnne Carner	1984 Juli Inkster	1994 Annika Sörenstam	2006 Seon-Hua Lee (KOR)
1971 Sally Little (RSA)	1985 Penny Hammel	(SWE)	2007 Angela Park (KOR)
1972 Jocelyne Bourassa	1986 Jody Rosenthal	1995 Pat Hurst	2008 Yani Tseng (KOR)
1973 Laura Baugh	1987 Tammi Green	1996 Karrie Webb (AUS)	2009 Ji-Yai Shin (KOR)
1974 Jan Stephenson	1988 Liselotte Neumann	1997 Lisa Hackney (ENG)	2010 Azahara Muños (ESP)
1975 Amy Alcott	(SWE)	1998 Se Ri Pak (KOR)	2011 Hee Kyung Seo (KOR)

LPGA Vare Trophy

	Scoring av.			Scoring av.			Scoring av.
1953 Patty Berg	75.00	1975 JoAnne Carner	72.40	1996 Annika Sörenstam	70.47
1954 Babe Zaharias	75.48	1976 Judy Rankin	72.25	(SWE)	
1955 Patty Berg	74.47	1977 Judy Rankin	72.16	1997 Karrie Webb (AUS)	70.01
1956 Patty Berg	74.57	1978 Nancy Lopez	71.76	1998 Annika Sörenstam	69.99
1957 Louise Suggs	74.64	1979 Nancy Lopez	71.20	(SWE)	
1958 Beverly Hanson	74.92	1980 Amy Alcott	71.51	1999 Karrie Webb (AUS)	69.43
1959 Betsy Rawls	74.03	1981 Jo Anne Carner	71.75	2000 Karrie Webb (AUS)	70.05
1960 Mickey Wright	73.25	1982 Jo Anne Carner	71.49	2001 Annika Sörenstam	69.42
1961 Mickey Wright	73.55	1983 Jo Anne Carner	71.41	(SWE)	
1962 Mickey Wright	73.67	1984 Patty Sheehan	71.40	2002 Annika Sörenstam	68.70
1963 Mickey Wright	72.81	1985 Nancy Lopez	70.73	(SWE)	
1964 Mickey Wright	72.46	1986 Pat Bradley	71.10	2003 Se Ri Pak (KOR)	70.03
1965 Kathy Whitworth	72.61	1987 Betsy King	71.14	2004 Grace Park (KOR)	69.99
1966 Kathy Whitworth	72.60	1988 Colleen Walker	71.26	2005 Annika Sörenstam	69.25
1967 Kathy Whitworth	72.74	1989 Beth Daniel	70.38	(SWE)	
1968 Carol Mann	72.04	1990 Beth Daniel	70.54	2006 Lorena Ochoa (MEX)	69.23
1969 Kathy Whitworth	72.38	1991 Pat Bradley	70.66	2007 Lorena Ochoa (MEX)	69.68
1970 Kathy Whitworth	72.26	1992 Dottie Mochrie	70.80	2008 Lorena Ochoa (MEX)	69.58
1971 Kathy Whitworth	72.88	1993 Nancy Lopez	70.83	2009 Lorena Ochoa (MEX)	70.16
1972 Kathy Whitworth	72.38	1994 Beth Daniel	70.90	2010 Choi Na Yeon (KOR)	69.96
1973 Judy Rankin	73.08	1995 Annika Sörenstam	71.00	2011 Yani Tseng (TPE)	69.66
1974 JoAnne Carner	72.87	(SWE)			

First Lady of Golf Award

(PGA of America award for women who have made a significant contribution to the game)

From 2009 this award was presented every second year

1998 Barbara Nicklaus	2003 Renee Powell	2008 Carol Mann
1999 Judy Rankin	2004 Alice Dye	2009 Donna Caponi-Byrnes
2000 No award given	2005 Carole Semple-Thompson	2011 Mary Bea Porter-King
2001 Judy Bell	2006 Kathy Whitworth	
2002 Nancy Lopez	2007 Peggy Kirk Bell	

Former President George H W Bush is Bob Jones Award winner

Former US President George H W Bush is the recipient of the 53rd Bob Jones Award. The honour, the USGA's highest, is given in recognition of distinguished sportsmanship in golf. It seeks to recognize a person who emulates Jones' spirit, his personal qualities, his attitude toward the game and its players.

The 83-year-old avid golfer, slowed by recent back surgery, kept the masses laughing throughout his 11-minute acceptance speech.

"As for golf talent, truth be told, my father and grandfather were far more blessed with talent," he said. "Somehow when it came to me there was a genetic power outage."

Bush comes from a lineage of golf blood. His father, Prescott Bush, served as the USGA president in 1935 and his grandfather, Herbert Walker, was instrumental in starting the Walker Cup and he donated the trophy.

A fast player, Bush is known in close circles as a man on the move. It wasn't uncommon for him to play a round in two hours, 15 minutes.

He told the story of how his grandfather once chastised Bob Jones for losing his temper during a USGA event, promising him he'd never play in another one if it happened again. That was before his grandfather told Jones he had the chance to become one of the greatest players ever.

"I'm honoured to receive this award because of a man everyone in the game of golf holds in the highest regard," said Bush.

"Bob Jones remains the golf standard by which every other mortal who tries their luck down the fairway is measured."

PART XIII

Who's Who
in Golf

Who's Who in Golf – Men

Aaron, Tommy (USA)

Born Gainesville, Georgia, 22 February 1937
Turned professional 1961

The 1973 Masters champion who, five years earlier inadvertently marked down a 4 on Roberto de Vicenzo's card for the 17th hole when the Argentinian had taken 3. De Vicenzo signed for the 4 and lost out by one shot on a play-off with Bob Goalby for the Green Jacket.

Allenby, Robert (AUS)

Born Melbourne, 12 July 1971
Turned professional 1992

Pipped by a shot from winning the Australian Open as an amateur in 1991 by Wayne Riley's birdie, birdie, birdie finish at Royal Melbourne, he won the title three years later as a professional and won it again in 1955. After competing on the European Tour and winning four times, he now plays on the US Tour.

Alliss, Peter (ENG)

Born Berlin, 28 February 1931
Turned professional 1946

Following a distinguished career as a tournament golfer in which he won 18 titles between 1954 and 1966 and played eight times in the Ryder Cup between 1953 and 1969, he turned to golf commentating. In Britain he works for the BBC and for the American network ABC at The Open. Twice captain of the PGA in 1962 and 1987 he won the Spanish, Italian and Portuguese Opens in 1958. Author or co-author of several golf books and a novel with a golfing background, he has also designed several courses including the Brabazon course at The Belfry in association with Dave Thomas. In 2003 he was awarded Life Membership of the PGA in honour of his lifelong contribution and commitment to the game. In 2005 he received an honorary degree from St Andrews University and in 2010 a PGA distinguished service award. He was selected through the international ballot to be inducted into the World Golf Hall of Fame in 2012.

An, Byeong-Hun (Ben) (KOR)

Born Korea, 17 September 1991

When just 18 years old he became the youngest winner in the 109-year history of the US Amateur Championship when he beat Ben Martin 7 and 5 in the 2009 final at Southern Hills in Oklahoma. He was the 13th. Korean-born golfer to win a USGA title. An All-American at the University of California he was introduced to the game at the age of seven by his parents both of who were table tennis medallists in the 1988 Olympics in Seoul.

Aoki, Isao (JPN)

Born Abiko, Chiba, 31 August 1942
Turned professional 1964

Successful international performer whose only victory on the PGA Tour came dramatically in Hawaii in 1983

when he holed a 128 yards pitch for an eagle 3 at the last at Waialae to beat Jack Renner. Only Japanese golfer to win on the European Tour taking the European Open in 1983. He also won the World Match Play in 1978 beating Simon Owen and was runner up the following year. He holed in one at Wentworth in that event to win a condominium at Gleneagles. He was top earner five times in his own country and is the Japanese golfer who has come closest to winning a major title finishing runner-up two shots behind Jack Nicklaus in the 1980 US Open at Baltusrol. Inducted into the World Golf Hall of Fame in 2004.

Atwal, Arjun (IND)

Born Asansol, India, 20 March 1973
Turned professional 1995

The first Indian golfer to win on the PGA Tour. In 2010 he triumphed at the Wyndham Championship and in the process became the first Monday qualifier for 24 years to win. When he won the 2002 Caltex Malaysian Open he became only the second Indian to earn a European To The first was Jeev Milkha Singh. He learned the game at Royal Calcutta.

Azinger, Paul (USA)

Born Holyoke, Massachusetts, 6 January 1960
Turned professional 1981

Winner of the 1993 USPGA Championship at the Inverness CC by beating Greg Norman at the second le of a play-off. He had finished joint runner-up with Rodger Davis to Nick Faldo in the 1987 Open at Muirfield. In 1994 he was diagnosed with lymphoma in his right shoulder blade but happily made a good recovery. He played in four Ryder Cup matches between 1989 and 2001 when he holed a bunker shot at the last to halve with Niclas Fasth. He successfully captained the US Ryder Cup side at Valhalla in 2008.

Baddeley, Aaron (AUS)

Born New Hampshire, USA, 17 March 1981
Turned professional 2000

Became the first amateur to win the Australian Open since Bruce Devlin in 1969 and the youngest when he took the title at Royal Sydney in 2000. Then, having turned professional he successfully defended it at Kingston Heath. He had shown considerable promise when at age 15, he qualified for the Victorian Open. Represented Australia in the Eisenhower Trophy and holds both Australian and American passports. He led going into the last round at the US Open at Oakmont in 2007 but finished joint 13th. Now plays on the PGA Tour but returned to Australia to beat Swede Daniel Chopra in a play-off for the 2007 MasterCard Australian Masters at Huntingdale.

Baiocchi, Hugh (RSA)

Born Johannesburg, 17 August 1946
Turned professional 1971

A scratch golfer when he was 15, he joined the Champions Tour after playing with distinction for 23 years on the European Tour. He has played in 31 different countries around the world winning in many of them. He gained an extra special delight at winning the 1978 South African Open emulating his long-time golfing hero Gary Player.

Baker, Peter (ENG)
Born Shifnal, Shropshire, 7 October 1967
Turned professional 1986

Rookie of the year in 1987, Peter was hailed as the best young newcomer by Nick Faldo when he beat Faldo in a play-off for the Benson and Hedges International in 1988. Several times a winner since then he played in the 1993 Ryder Cup scoring three points out of four and in the singles beat former US Open champion Corey Pavin. He was a vice-captain to Ian Woosnam at the 2006 match.

Baker-Finch, Ian (AUS)
Born Namour, Queensland, 24 October 1960
Turned professional 1979

Impressive winner of The Open Championship in 1991 at Royal Birkdale he lost his game completely when teeing up in Tour events and was forced, after an agonising spell, to retire prematurely. He commentated originally for Channel Seven in Australia then for ABC and now for CBS in America.

Barnes, Brian (SCO)
Born Addington, Surrey, 3 June 1945
Turned professional 1964

Extrovert Scottish professional whose father-in-law was the late former Open champion Max Faulkner. He was a ten times winner on the European Tour between 1972 and 1981 and was twice British Seniors champion successfully defending the title in 1996. He played in six Ryder Cup matches most notably at Laurel Valley in 1975 when, having beaten Jack Nicklaus in the morning, he beat him again in the afternoon. Although he retired early because of ill-health caused by rheumatoid arthritis he has started to play and fish again after his rheumatic problem was re-diagnosed as caused by eating meat. He often commentates for Sky Television.

Beem, Rich (USA)
Born Phoenix Arizona, 24 August 1974
Turned professional 1994

Playing in only his fourth major championship he hit the headlines in 2002 when he held off the spirited challenge of Tiger Woods to win the USPGA Championship at Hazeltine preventing Woods from winning three majors in one year for a second time. Rich, a winner of two previous Tour titles, admitted he was "flabbergasted to have won" having arrived with no expectations.. On the final day at Hazeltine, Beem hit a fairway wood to to seven feet for an eagle at the at the 587 yards 11th and a holed a 40 foot putt for a birdie at the 16th to hold off Woods who finished with four birdies in a row. Just a year after turning professional Beem had given up the game to

sell car stereos and mobile phones. After becoming an assistant club professional he returned once again to tournament play in 1999.

Bjørn, Thomas (DEN)
Born Silkeborg, 18 February 1971
Turned professional 1993

A former Danish Amateur champion in 1990 and 1991, he became the first Dane to play in the Ryder Cup when he made the team in 1997. Four down after four holes against Justin Leonard in the last day singles at Valderrama he fought back to halve the match and gain a valuable half-point in the European victory. He missed out because of injury on the 1999 match but was back in the team in 2002 and 2004 and was a vice-captain at Celtic Manor in 2010. He has come close four times to winning major titles. He was third to runaway winner Tiger Woods at Pebble Beach in the 2000 US Open and second to him at St Andrews in The Open a few weeks later. He looked set to win the 2003 Open at Royal St George's when three clear with four to play but dropped a shot at the 15th. and 17th and two shots after taking three to recover from a bunker at the short 16th. losing out eventually to Ben Curtis. In 2005 at Baltusrol he equalled the low round in a major with a 63 at the US PGA Championship but finished third to Phil Mickelson. In 2007 he became chairman of the European Tour Players' committee and in 2011 rediscovered his best form to win on the European Tour in Qatar, at Gleneagles and in Switzerland.

Bonallack KT, OBE, Sir Michael (ENG)
Born Chigwell, Essex, 31 December 1934

One of only four golfing knights (the others are the late Sir Henry Cotton, Sir Bob Charles and Sir Nick Faldo) he won the Amateur Championship five times between 1961 and 1970 and was five times English champion between 1962 and 1968. He also won the English stroke play Championship (the Brabazon Trophy) four times and was twice leading amateur in The Open in 1968 and 1971. In his hugely impressive career he played in nine Walker Cup matches captaining the side on two occasions. He participated in five Eisenhower Trophy matches and five Commonwealth team competitions. He scored his first national title win in the 1952 British Boys' Championship and took his Essex County title 11 times between 1954 and 1972. After serving as secretary of The R&A from 1983 to 1999 he was elected captain for 1999/2000. Twice winner of the Association of Golf Writers' award in 1968 and 1999, he also received the Bobby Jones award for sportsmanship in 1972, the Donald Ross and Gerald Micklem awards in 1991 and the Ambassador of Golf award in 1995. In 2000 he was inducted into the World Hall Golf of Fame. A former chairman of The R&A selection committee, he served as chairman of the PGA from 1976 to 1981 and is now a non-executive director of the PGA European Tour. He served for a time as chairman of the Golf Foundation and was president of the English Golf Union in 1982. His wife is the former English champion Angela Ward.

Bradley, Keegan (USA)

Born Woodstock, Vermont, 1986
Turned professional 2008

Winner of the US PGA Championship in 2011 after savouring a breakthrough success in the Byron Nelson, Bradley enjoyed a notable rookie season on the PGA Tour, earning $3.8 million in his first year among the elite. A graduate from the Nationwide Tour, he was the first golfer since Shaun Micheel in 2003 to win the PGA in his first appearance as well as the first player since Ben Curtis to win any major at the first attempt. He hails from a golfing family and is the nephew of former LPGA player Pat Bradley.

Brooks, Mark (USA)

Born Fort Worth, Texas, 25 March 1961
Turned professional 1983

Winner of the USPGA Championship title in 1996 after a play-off with Kenny Perry at Valhalla. On that occasion he birdied the 72nd hole and the first extra hole to win but lost b two shots to South African Retief Goosen in the 18-hole play-off for the 2000 US Open at Southern Hills in Tulsa.

Brown, Ken (SCO)

Born Harpenden, Hertfordshire, 9 January 1957
Turned professional 1974

Renowned as a great short game exponent, especially with his hickory-shafted putter, he won four times in Europe between 1978 and 85, and took the Southern Open on the US tour in 1987. He played in five Ryder Cups and was on the winning side in 1985 and 1987. After retiring from professional tournament play he became an accomplished and highly respected television commentator working closely for the BBC (with Peter Alliss) and for The Golf Channel.

Cabrera, Angel (ARG)

Born Córdoba, Argentina, September 12, 1969
Turned professional 1989

Big hitting Argentinian winner of two major titles who learned much from former Open champion Roberto de Vicenzo. He won his first major when he held off a strong challenge from Jim Furyk and Tiger Woods to win the 2007 US Open and two years later won The Masters in a play-off at Augusta with Chad Campbell and Kenny Perry.

Cabrera Bello, Rafael (ESP)

Born Las Palmas, Gran Canaria, Spain, May 25, 1984
Turned professional 2005

Young Spanish golfer who won his first event on the European Tour in 2009 by firing a closing record 12-under-par 60 to win the Austrian Open at the Fontana Club in Vienna. Cabrera Bello, who started the final day eight off the lead, missed his eagle putt on the last for what would have been an historic 59. He

was the 14th first-time winner of the season and the 13th person to shoot a 60 on the European Tour. His sister is a professional on the Ladies European Tour.

Calcavecchia, Mark (USA)

Born Laurel, Nebraska, 12 June 1960
Turned professional 1981

Winner of the 1989 Open Championship at Royal Troon after the first four-hole play-off against Australians Greg Norman and Wayne Grady. He was runner-up in the 1987 Masters at Augusta to Sandy Lyle and came second to Jodie Mudd in the 1990 Players' Championship. He played in the 1987, 1989, 1991 and 2002 Ryder Cup sides.

Campbell, Bill (USA)

Born West Virginia, 5 May 1923

One of America's most distinguished amateur players and administrators. He won the US Amateur Championship in 1964 ten years after finishing runner-up in the Amateur Championship at Muirfield to Australian Doug Bachli. One of a select group who have been both President of the United States Golf Association (in 1983) and captain of the Royal and Ancient Golf Club of St Andrews (in 1987/88). He played in eight Walker Cup matches between 1951 and 1975 and was captain in 1955.

Canizares, Alejandro (ESP)

Born Manilva, Malaga, 9 January 1983
Turned professional 2006

A four-time All-American golfer when studying at Arizona State University, he is the son of José Maria Canizares. When he turned professional in July 2006 he won his third event – the Imperial Collection Russian Open in Moscow.

Canizares, José Maria (ESP)

Born Madrid, 18 February 1947
Turned professional 1967

A popular seven-time winner on the European Tour between 1972 and 1992 the popular Spaniard retired after playing on the European Senior and US Champions Tours for a number of years. A former caddie, he played in four Ryder Cup matches in the 1980's winning five and halving two of his 11 games.

Cantlay, Patrick (USA)

Born Long Beach, California, March 17, 1992

Winner of the Mark H McCormack medal for the world's top ranked amateur male golfer at the end of 2011, Cantlay will make his début at The Open in the summer of 2012. His first appearance at the US Open in 2011 was auspicious since he finished 21st and during one round at Congressional covered the back nine in just 30 blows. He also signed for 60 in the Travelers Championship on the US PGA Tour, eventually finishing in 24th place. All told, he registered four top 25s in the four professional events he entered. He first broke 70 at the age of 12.

Sir Bob Charles (NZL)

Born Auckland, 14 March 1936
Turned professional 1960

The first left-handed golfer to win a major championship, Sir Bob became the only New Zealander so far to lift the Claret Jug in 1963 when, three years after turning professional, he defeated Phil Rodgers in a 36-hole play-off for the title at Royal Lytham. He carded 140 to the American's 148. Until the emergence of Mike Weir and Phil Mickelson, Charles was the game's pre-eminent left-hander – an ironic distinction since he does pretty much everything else right-handed apart from games which require the use of both hands.

While 40 years would elapse before another lefty won a major, Charles himself was a runner-up in The Open to Gary Player in 1968 at Carnoustie and to Tony Jacklin in 1969 at Lytham as well as to Julius Boros, the oldest major winner, at the PGA Championship in 1968 at Pecan Valley. He was also a contender at the US Open in 1964 and 1970 when he finished third both times. One of the reasons for his success was that he putted beautifully. When Charles won The Open, he averaged 30 putts per round over the course of 72 holes and just 26 putts during the first round of the play-off.

Blessed with a sure touch from long range on the greens, he was also nerveless from close range. He rarely missed from inside five feet and also holed the majority of ten footers. During the 1972 season, the former bank worker completed 11 successive rounds without a three-putt. That same season he received the OBE from Her Majesty the Queen before being awarded the CBE in 1992. He was knighted in 1999 for his services to golf.

The winner of more than 60 events around the world, Charles enjoyed a new lease of life after turning 50. He won 23 tournaments on the Champions Tour and posted the low scoring average three times in 1988, 1989 and 1993. He was the first left-hander to be inducted into the Hall of Fame and, at 71, he became the oldest player to make the cut on any of the world's Tours when he shot a second round 68 in the Michael Hill New Zealand Open in 2007.

Casey, Paul (ENG)

Born Cheltenham, 21 July 1977 Turned professional 2001

After successfully defending the English Amateur Championship in 2000, he attended Arizona State University where he was a three time All-American and broke records set by Phil Mickelson and Tiger Woods. In the 1999 Walker Cup match, which Great Britain and Ireland won at Nairn, he won all of his four games. After turning professional he earned his European Tour card after just five events an became a winner in only his 11th event when taking the Scottish PGA title at Gleneagles. Coached by Peter Kostis, he played with distinction in the 2004 Ryder Cup at Oakland Hills, Detroit, teaming up with David Howell for a vital foursomes point on the second morning. He played again in the Ryder Cup in 2006 and 2008 but missed out in 2010 despite finish third to Louis Oosthuizen in The Open at St Andrews. In 2006 he won a million pounds by beating Shaun Micheel in the final of the HSBC World Match-play Championship at at Wentworth but was pipped to the No 1 spot in Europe that year by Padraig Harrington. Twice a winner of the Abu Dhabi Championship he won the Shell Houston Open in 2009, the year he also won the BMW PGA Championship in Britain.

Casper, Billy (USA)

Born San Diego, California, 24 June 1931
Turned professional 1954

A three-time major title winner he took the US Open in 1959 and 1966 and the US Masters in 1970. In 1966 he came back from seven strokes behind Arnold Palmer with nine to play to force a play-off which he then won. Between 1956 and 1975 he picked up 51 first prize cheques on the US Tour. His European victories were the 1974 Trophée Lancôme and Lancia D'Oro and the 1975 Italian Open. As a senior golfer he won nine times between 1982 and 1989 including the US Senior Open in 1983. Played in eight Ryder Cups and captained the American side in 1979 at The Greenbrier. He and wife Shirley have 11 children several of them adopted. He was named Father of the Year in 1966. Started playing golf aged 5 and rates Ben Hogan, Byron Nelson and Sam Snead as his heroes. Five times Vardon Trophy winner (for low season stroke-average) and twice top money earner he was USPGA Player of the Year in 1966 and 1970. He was inducted into the World Golf Hall of Fame in 1978 and the USPGA Hall of Fame in 1982. Encouraged by his family to play in The Masters for one last time in 2005 he shot 106 but was disqualified for not handing in his card.

Cévéär, Christian (FRA)

Born New Caledonia, 10 April 1970
Turned professional 1993

A former world junior champion and Stanford graduate he won the Canarias Open de España in 2005 and the 2009 European Open at the London Club.

Chapman, Roger (ENG)

Born Nakuru, Kenya, 1 May 1959
Turned professional 1981

After playing on the European Tour for 18 years without success, he lost his card and returned to the

Clarke, Darren OBE (NIR)

Born Dungannon, Northern Ireland, 14 August 1968
Turned professional 1990

Darren became the fourth golfer from Northern Ireland to win a major when he beat Dustin Johnson and Phil Mickelson in the 2011 Open at Royal St George's. The rough weather did not phase Clarke who learned his golf at Royal Portrush. His victory came weeks after another Ulsterman, Rory McIlroy, had been successful at the US Open and a year after Northern Ireland's Graeme McDowell had won the American title at Pebble Beach. The other Ulster winner of a major was Fred Daly who won The Open in 1947. Darren became the first European Tour player to shoot 60 twice when he returned a record equalling low score at the European Open at the K Club in 1999. Seven years earlier he had shot a nine under par 60 at Mont Angel in the Monte Carlo Open. His 60 in Dublin was 12 under. Tied second in the 1997 Open behind Justin Leonard at Royal Troon he was third behind David Duval at the 2001 Open at Royal Lytham and St Annes before winning the title at Sandwich in 2011. Cigar smoking Clarke became the first European to win a World Golf Championship event when he beat Tiger Woods 4 and 3 in the final of the 2000 Accenture Match Play Championship picking up a $1 million first prize.

He took a second World Championship event in 2003 when he was an impressive winner of the NEC Invitational at Firestone. He played in the 1997, 1999, 2002 and 2004 Ryder Cup matches and again in 2006, bravely competing just a few months after his wife Heather lost her battle with cancer. In that match he won twice with good friend Lee Westwood and gained a single point against Zach Johnson. In 2010 he was a vice captain at Celtic Manor but it was in 2011 that he scored his greatest success with victory at Royal St George's. He received the OBE in the 2011 Queen's New Year Honours list.

qualifying school in 1999. Regaining his playing privileges with a 12th place finish in the six round competition, he made his breakthrough win by beating Padraig Harrington at the second hole of a play-off in the Brazil Rio de Janeiro Five Hundred Years Open. A former English Amateur Champion in 1981 he played in the Walker Cup the same year beating Hal Sutton twice in a day at Cypress Point. In 2010 he earned his card to play the Champions Tour in America.

Choi, K-J (KOR)

Born Wando, South Korea, 19 May 1970
Turned professional 1994

When his high school teacher suggested he take up golf, he studied all Jack Nicklaus' videos. Son of a rice farmer he was the first Korean to earn a PGA Tour card and in 2003 became the first Korean to win on the European Tour when he was successful in the Linde German Masters. Better known as KJ he finished fifth behind Tiger Woods on the 2007 American money list having earned over $4.5 million but failed to become the first Korean to win a major when YE Yang beat Woods in the 2009 US PGA Championship at Hazeltine.

Cink, Stewart (USA)

Born Huntsville, Alabama, 21 May 1973
Turned professional 1995

In a dramatic play-off at Turnberry in 2009 he won his first major by beating Tom Watson by six shots in their four hole play-off after both had tied at the end of 72-holes. This win by the former PGA Tour Rookie of the Year made up for the two-foot putt he

missed which would have earned him a play-off for the 2002 US Open won by Retief Goosen. He has played in every Ryder Cup since 2002. In the 2006 Cup match at the K Club, he beat Sergio García in the singles to prevent the Spaniard winning five points out of five.

Clark, Clive (ENG)

Born Winchester, 27 June 1945
Turned professional 1965

In the 1965 Walker Cup at Five Farms East in Maryland, he holed a 35-foot putt to earn a half point against Mark Hopkins and ensure a first ever drawn match against the Americans on their home soil. After turning professional he played in the 1973 Ryder Cup. Following a career as commentator with the BBC he continued his golf course architecture work in America, and has received awards for his innovative designs.

Clark, Howard (ENG)

Born Leeds, 26 August 1954
Turned professional 1973

A scratch player by the age of 16, he turned professional after playing in the 1973 Walker Cup. An eleven-time winner on the European tour he played in six Ryder Cups and was in the winning team three times – in 1985 at The Belfry, 1987 at Muirfield Village, when the Europeans won for the first time on American soil, and in 1995 when he gained a vital point helped by a hole in one in the last day singles against Peter Jacobsen. In the 1985 World Cup played at La Quinta in Palm Springs he was the individual champion. He played 494 tournaments before giving up full-time competition to concentrate on his job as a highly respected golf analyst for Sky television.

Coles MBE, Neil (ENG)

Born 26 September 1934   Turned professional 1950

An Honorary Life Member of the European Tour he won golf tournaments in six decades. In 2003 he did not win but in the Travis Perkins event over Wentworth's Edinburgh Course (which he helped design) he shot a 64 – outstanding golf by a man who had been a pro at that time for 54 years. He scored his first victory at the Gor-Ray tournament in 1956 when 22 and won the Lawrence Batley Seniors Open at Huddersfield in 2002 when 67 years and 276 days. From 1973 to 1979 he played in 56 events on the main European Tour without missing a half-way cut and became the then oldest winner when he won the Sanyo Open in Barcelona in 1982 at the age of 48 years and 14 days (Des Smyth has since become an even older winner). A member of eight Ryder Cup teams, he has represented his country 19 times since turning professional at the age of 16 with a handicap of 14. He has been chairman of the PGA European Tour's Board of Directors since its inception in 1971 and in 2000 was inducted into the World Golf Hall of Fame. Internationally respected he might well have won more in America but for an aversion to flying caused by a bad experience on an internal flight from Edinburgh to London.

Coltart, Andrew (SCO)

Born Dumfries, 12 May 1970
Turned professional 1991

Twice Australian PGA champion in 1994 and 1997 he was the Australasian circuit's top money earner for the 1997/98 season. He made his Ryder Cup début at Brookline in 1999 as a captain's pick and, having not been used in the foursomes and fourballs he lost in the singles on the final day to Tiger Woods. A former Walker Cup and Eisenhower Trophy player he was a member of the only Scottish team to win the Alfred Dunhill Cup at St Andrews in 1995. His sister Laurae is married to fellow professional Lee Westwood.

Couples, Fred (USA)

Born Seattle, Washington, 3 October 1959
Turned professional 1980

Troubled continually with a back problem he has managed to win only one major – the 1992 US Masters but remains one of the most popular of all American players. He has always been willing to travel and his overseas victories include two Johnnie Walker World Championships, the Johnnie Walker Classic, the Dubai Desert Classic and the Tournoi Perrier de Paris. On the US Tour he won 14 times between 1983 and 1998 and later won the Shell Houston Open. He played in five Ryder Cup matches and has teed up four times for the US in the Presidents Cup in which he acted as captain in 2009 and again in 2011. He will lead the side again in 2011. Couples kept up

his winning ways on the Champions Tour in 2010 with a victory in only his second senior start at the Ace Group Classic. He also won the Toshiba Classic and the Cap Cana Championship to become the first 50-year-old to win three of the first four senior events in which he played. In 2011 he captained the US side in the President's Cup at Royal Melbourne.

Crenshaw, Ben (USA)

Born Austin, Texas, 11 January 1952
Turned professional 1973

One of golf's great putters who followed up his victory in the 1984 Masters with an emotional repeat success in 1995 just a short time after the death of his long-time coach and mentor Harvey Pennick. He played in four Ryder Cup matches between 1981 and 1995 before captaining the side in 1999 when the Americans came from four points back to win with a scintillating last day singles performance. Winner of the Byron Nelson award in 1976 he was also named Bobby Jones award winner in 1991. Now combines playing with an equally successful career as a golf course designer and is an acknowledged authority on every aspect of the history of the game. In 2002 he won the Payne Stewart Award which recognises a player's respect for and upholding of the traditions of the game.

Curtis, Ben (USA)

Born Columbus, Ohio, 26 May 1977
Turned professional 2000

Shock 750–1 outsider who played superbly at Royal St George's to get his name engraved with all the other golfing greats on the famous Claret Jug. His victory in the 2003 Open, while well deserved, was one of golf's biggest shocks in years. It was his first major appearance. He only qualified for the Championship with a 14th place finish in the Western Open in Chicago – a designated qualifying event. He had never played in Britain nor had he any experience of links golf but he outplayed Tiger Woods, Thomas Bjørn, David Love III and Vijay Singh to take the title with a score of 283. He learned the game in Ohio at the golf course his grandfather built at Ostrander. In 2008 he chased Padraig Harrington home to finish second behind the Irishman in the USPGA Championship at Oakland Hill. That year he made his début in captain Paul Azinger's Ryder Cup side which won the trophy back at Valhalla.

Daly, John (USA)

Born Sacramento, California, 28 April 1966
Turned professional 1987

Winner of two majors – the 1991 USPGA Championship and the 1995 Open Championship at St Andrews after a play-off with Costantino Rocca, his career has not been without its ups and downs. He admits he has battled alcoholism and, on occasions, has been his own worst enemy when having run-ins with officialdom but he remains popular because of his long hitting. His average drive is over 300 yards. When he won the USPGA Championship at Crooked Stick he got in as ninth alternate, drove through the night to tee it up without a practice round and shot 69, 67, 69, 71 to beat Bruce Lietzke by three. Given invaluable help by Fuzzy Zoeller he writes his own songs and is a mean performer on the guitar. Despite winning two majors he has never played in the Ryder Cup and now no longer holds a PGA Tour card. He had a stomach band inserted in 2009 in a successful bid to lose weight.

Darcy, Eamonn (IRL)
Born Dalgeny, 7 August 1952
Turned professional 1969

One of Ireland's best known players who played more than 600 tournaments on the European Tour despite suffering for many years with back trouble. First played when he was 10 years old and is renowned for his very distinctive swing incorporating a flying right elbow. He played in four Ryder Cups including the memorable one at Muirfield Village in 1987 when Europe won for the first time in America. He scored a vital point in the last day singles holing a tricky left to right downhill seven footer for a valuable point against Ben Crenshaw. Now plays on the European Senior Tour.

Davis, Rodger (AUS)
Born Sydney, 18 May 1951   Turned professional 1974

Experienced Australian who came joint second with Paul Azinger in the 1987 Open Championship behind Nick Faldo at Muirfield. A regular on the European Tour and for a time on the US Champions Tour he has won 27 titles – 19 of them on the Australasian circuit where, in 1988, he picked up an Aus $1 million first prize in the bicentennial event at Royal Melbourne. Usually played in trademark 'plus twos' but has now retired from all but Australian golf.

Day, Jason (AUS)
Born Beaudesert, Queensland, 1987
Turned professional 2006

Already the winner of more than $9million in prize money after just four seasons on the PGA Tour, Day was runner-up in both the Masters and the US Open in 2011. These excellent performances in the majors followed on from a top ten finish at the US PGA in 2010. He also won the Byron Nelson in 2010. A successful amateur when he was growing up in Queensland, he won the 2006 Australian Amateur Stroke-Play Championship as well as the Australian Junior Championship and the World Junior Championship.

De Vicenzo, Roberto (ARG)
Born Buenos Aires, 14 April 1923
Turned professional 1938

Although he won The Open in 1967 at Royal Liverpool the impressive South American gentleman of the game is perhaps best known for the Major title he might have won. In 1968 he finished tied with Bob Goalby at Augusta or he thought he had. He had finished birdie, bogey to do so but sadly signed for the par 4 that had been inadvertently and carelessly put down for the 17th by Tommy Aaron who was marking his card. Although everyone watching on television and at the course saw the Argentinian make 3 the fact that he signed for 4 was indisputable and he had to accept that there would be no play-off. It remains one of the saddest incidents in golf with the emotion heightened by the fact that that Sunday was de Vicenzo's 45th birthday. The gracious manner in which he accepted the disappointment was remarkable. What a contrast to the scenes at Hoylake nine months earlier when, after years of trying, he finally won The Open beating Jack Nicklaus and Clive Clark in the process thanks to a pressure-packed brilliant last round 70. It was well deserved. He had been runner-up in 1950 and had finished third six times. The father of South American golf he was a magnificent driver and won over 200 titles in his extraordinary career including nine Argentinian Opens between 1944 and 1974 plus the 1957 Jamaican, 1950 Belgian, 1950 Dutch, 1950, 1960 and 1964 French, 1964 German Open and 1966 Spanish Open titles. He played 15 times for Argentina in the World Cup and four times for Mexico. Inducted into the World Golf Hall of Fame in 1989 he is an honorary member of the Royal and Ancient Golf Club of St Andrews. Although he was unable to return to Britain for the 2006 Open Championship at Hoylake were he won in 1967 he made it to the 150th. Anniversary celebrations of The Open at St Andrews in 2010. He was pleased when fellow Argentinian Angel Cabrera won the 2007 US Open but even more elated when Cabrera, inspired by him, became the first Argentinian winner of a Masters Green Jacket.

Dickson, Bob (USA)
Born McAlester, Oklahoma, 25 January 1944
Turned professional 1968

Best remembered for being one of only four players to complete a Transatlantic amateur double. In 1967 he won the US Amateur Championship at Broadmoor with a total of 285 (the Championship was played over 72 holes from 1965 to 1972) and the British Amateur title with a 2 and 1 win over fellow American Ron Cerrudo at Formby.

Donald, Luke (ENG)
Born Hemel Hempstead, Herts., 7 December 1977
Turned professional 2001

The game's outstanding golfer in 2011, Donald made history when he became the first ever player to top the money list on both the European and US PGA Tours. He was also named the PGA Tour's player of the year and enjoyed the same honour in Europe, where he was also celebrated by the Association of Golf Writers. Donald won four times last year, twice in America

Ernie Els (RSA)

Born Johannesburg, 17 October 1969
Turned professional 1989

Blessed with a powerful, smooth swing which laid the foundation for more than 65 tournament wins around the world, the big South African has lifted three major championships – two US Opens and The Open at Muirfield – and built a reputation as a formidable matchplay golfer, winning the World Matchplay on a record seven occasions. Although his nickname "the Big Easy" reflected an engaging personality as well as that rhythmic golf swing, it didn't tell the whole story. From his first victory at the Amatola Sun Classic in 1991 to the 2011 South African Open, Els was able to call upon the ruthless instincts of a serial winner.

As a youngster, he was a budding athlete and won a regional tennis tournament in South Africa at the age of 13. At 14, however, his career path was set after he won the world junior golf championship in California. After joining the professional ranks and following up wins on the Sunshine Tour with victories around the world, he first made his mark in the majors at the 1994 US Open. He came out on top at Oakmont after winning a play-off against Loren Roberts and Colin Montgomerie. The Scot was to regard Els as a nemesis in the majors since he also lost out to the South African in the 1997 US Open at Congressional. Long tipped by his compatriot, Gary Player, to lift the Claret Jug, Els realised his dream of glory in 2002 at The Open by defeating Thomas Levet in a sudden-death play-off. His triumph came at the first extra hole after a four hole play-off had eliminated the Australians Stuart Appleby and Steve Elkington. All four golfers had finished on the six-under-par total of 268. Els executed a brilliant recovery shot from an awkward lie in a greenside trap at the 18th to make the four foot putt for par which earned him his third major title.

His career was disrupted by an anterior cruciate ligament knee injury sustained during a sailing holiday with his family. It took time for Els to recover, though he was back in full cry at Doral and Bay Hill in 2010 when he won the World Golf Championship and the Arnold Palmer Invitational in the space of a couple of weeks. In recent seasons, Els has broadened his horizons beyond the golf course. He became involved in charity work through the Els for Autism Foundation which helps young people like his son, Ben, who is autistic. He's active in course design and was involved in the re-design of Wentworth. He's also been in the wine business for ten years.

where he claimed the Accenture Match Play and the Childrens Miracle Network Hospital Classic; and twice in Europe at the BMW PGA and the Scottish Open. All told, he racked up 20 top ten finishes and missed only two cuts. His short game was second to none and he was the best putter on both sides of the Atlantic. A formidable amateur as well as a successful professional, he was a member of the winning Great Britain and Ireland team against the Americans in the 1999 Walker Cup at Nairn and again in 2001 before joining the paid ranks. In 1999 while attending the North-Western University in Chicago he won the NCAA Championship and was named NCAA Player of the Year. He was twice Big Ten Individual Championship winner and is a former Jack Nicklaus Trophy winner. Prior to 2011, he won three times on the European Tour in Sweden, Switzerland and Spain but went on to play more of his golf in America where he won the rain-shortened Southern Farms Bureau event in 2002 and the Honda tournament in 2006. He was one of five rookies in the winning 2004 European Ryder Cup team in Detroit having been a captain's pick and played again in 2006 and 2010 missing the chance of a place in the 2008 team because of a wrist injury that required surgery. He played an important part in the 2010 European Ryder Cup victory at Celtic Manor and in 2010 finished 15th in the Race to Dubai and 7th on the PGA Tour money list before moving from 28th to 9th in the world rankings.

Made history with his consistency in 2011 when he finished the year as World No 1.

Dougherty, Nick (ENG)

Born Liverpool, 24 May 1982
Turned professional 2001

He played off plus 4 and won the Australian Amateur Championship before turning professional. Started golf at age four and won his first event at six. Sir Henry Cotton Rookie of the Year in 2002, Dougherty's career was hindered by a bout of glandular fever in 2003 but has had victories in Singapore, at St Andrews and in Munich since then. He is married to Sky television presenter Di Stewart. In 2011 his loss of form caused him to lose his Tour card.

Dredge, Bradley (WAL)

Born Tredegar, Wales, 6 July 1973
Turned professional 1996

Winner of the Madeira Island Open in 2003, he had his biggest win when sharing the $1,400,000 first prize with Stephen Dodd in the 2005 World Cup of Golf played over 54 holes because of storms at Vilamoura in Portugal. The Welsh pair shot 61 twice in better-ball play and 67 in foursomes for a winning 27-under-par total. In 2007 he won a place in the GB&I side for the Seve Trophy match.

Drew, Norman (NIR)

Born Belfast, 25 May 1932
Turned professional 1958

Twice Irish Open Amateur champion in 1952 and 1953 he played in the 1953 Walker Cup and six years later represented Great Britain and Ireland in the Ryder Cup.

Dubuisson, Victor (FRA)

Born Cannes, 22 April 1990

Leading French amateur golfer in 2008 and 2009 he won the European Amateur Championship in 2009 at Chantilly. When aged 15 he qualified for the French Open – the youngest golfer ever to do so. He turned professional in 2010.

Duval, David (USA)

Born Jacksonville, Florida, 19 November 1971
Turned professional 1993

A regular winner on the US Tour who wears dark glasses because of an eye stigmatism which is sensitive to light, he won his first major at Royal Lytham and St Annes in 2001 when he became only the second American professional to win The Open over that course. In 1998 and 2001 he was runner-up in The Masters and was third at Augusta in 2003. Although illness and injury affected his career he did finish second to Lucas Glover in the US Open at Bethpage Park black but failed to keep his US Tour card that year. He won the US Tour Championship in 1997 and the Players' Championship in 1999. As an amateur he played in the 1991 Walker Cup and was a member of the winning Ryder Cup side on his début in 1999 but on a losing side in 2002.

Dyson, Simon (ENG)

Born York, 21 December 1977
Turned professional 1999

A three-time winner on the Asian Tour where he was top earner in 2000, he scored his first European Tour success in the joint Asian–European venture in Indonesia in 2006 and later in the season he beat Australian Richard Green in a play-off for the KLM Open at Zandvoort. He won that title again in 2009 and later in that season was successful in the Dunhill Links Championship played over the Old course, St Andrews, Carnoustie and Kingsbarns. In 2007 he shot 64 in the final round of the USPGA Championship to finish in joint sixth place – his best performance in a major. In 2011 he won the KLM Open for the second time and was also successful in the Irish Open. He was a member of the GB&I side in the Vivendi Seve Trophy.

Edfors, Johan (SWE)

Born Varberg, Sweden, 10 October 1975
Turned professional 1997

The number one player on the 2003 Challenge Tour he had a brilliant year on the main Tour in 2006, winning three events – the TCL Classic in China, the Quinn Direct British Masters and the Barclays Scottish Open at Loch Lomond. Since then he has won on the Asian Tour but has not had any more success on the European Tour.

Edwards, Nigel (WAL)

Born Caerphilly, 9 August 1968

Top scoring member of the winning Walker Cup sides in 2001 and again in 2003 at Ganton, he captained the side that won the cup at Royal Aberdeen in 2011. In 2003 he had holed from off the green with the putter at the 17th to ensure a half point with Lee Williams and overall victory for the team. He was again involved in a dramatic finish to the 2005 Walker Cup but one down with one to play and needing to win the last against Jeff Overton his putt narrowly missed. Welshman Edwards also played in the match in 2007, inspired his side to a surprise victory over a talented US side in 2011 reminding his team that although on paper the Americans were the stronger side the game was not played on paper.

Elkington, Steve (AUS)

Born Inverell, 8 December 1962
Turned professional 1985

A former Australian and New Zealand champion he was a regular winner on the PGA Tour despite an allergy to grass. Helped by a closing string of birdies at the Riviera CC in Los Angeles in 1995 he beat Colin Montgomerie in a play-off for the USPGA Championship. He has one of the finest swings in golf and is also an accomplished artist in his spare time. He played four times in the Presidents Cup. In 2002 after pre-qualifying for The Open at Dunbar he played off for the title at Muirfield with Thomas Levet, Stuart Appleby and eventual winner Ernie Els. He nearly won the USPGA Championship in 2005 finishing second with Thomas Bjørn behind Phil Mickelson at Baltusrol and was again in contention in the 2010 Championship at Whistling Straits.

Fasth, Niclas (SWE)

Born Gothenburg, Sweden, 29 April 1972
Turned professional 1989

The studious-looking Swede made the headlines in 2001 when finishing second to David Duval in The Open. He played in the 2002 Ryder Cup and in 2007 he came a creditable fourth in the US Open at Oakmont. In 2008 he split with his long-time coach Graham Crisp who was working with him revamping his swing. The changes took time to settle and he missed out on a Ryder Cup place that year.

Faxon, Brad (USA)

Born Oceanport, New Jersey, 1 August 1961
Turned professional 1983

A former Walker Cup player in 1983 match he has played in two Ryder Cup matches (1995 and 1997). A successful winner on the US Tour he also putted superbly to win the Australian Open at Metropolitan in 1993. In 2005 was named recipient of the Payne

Sir Nicholas A. Faldo (ENG)

Born Welwyn Garden City, 18 July 1957
Turned professional 1976

By a wide margin the most successful British golfer of the modern era – he spent 92 weeks in all as the world number one – his achievements were recognised in style when he became the first professional golfer since Sir Henry Cotton to receive a knighthood for his services to the game. Always single minded in his approach to winning tournaments, few would dispute Peter McEvoy's observation that Faldo sets the gold standard against which everyone else of recent vintage in English golf must be measured.

From the moment a careers officer at school warned him that only one in 10,000 made it as a professional – the Englishman insisted if that was the case then he would prove to be that solitary success – the golfer was as dedicated in his pursuit of glory as he was ambitious. At 14 he had never picked up a club, yet by 17 he was a top rank amateur. He won the British Youths and the English Amateur in 1975 before joining the paid ranks a year later. It was a measure of his rapid progress in the sport that by 20 he was playing in the Ryder Cup. He had only decided to take up the game after watching the Masters on his parents' new colour television when he followed the performance of Jack Nicklaus. "I was just absolutely mesmerised," he recalls.

He is Europe's most successful Major title winner having won three Open Championships in 1987 and 1992 at Muirfield and in 1990 at St Andrews along with three Masters titles in 1989, 1990 and 1996. Of contemporary players only Tiger Woods with 14 majors and Tom Watson with eight have won more majors. When he successfully defended the Masters in 1990 he became only the second golfer (after Nicklaus) to win in successive years. One of the most memorable moments of his career came when he staged a dramatic last day revival to win the 1996 Masters having started the last round six strokes behind Greg Norman.

Unkindly dubbed 'Nick Foldo' when he missed out on opportunities to win both The Open and The Masters in the early Eighties, Faldo nevertheless appreciated his swing was not good enough to win majors and completely revamped his action with the help of coach David Leadbetter. His revised swing and remarkable sense of poise under pressure duly helped him win more major titles than any other player between 1987 and 1996.

His 31 European Tour victories include a record three consecutive Irish Open victories. In 1992 he became the first player to win over £1 million in prize-money during a season. He also played with distinction in 11 Ryder Cup matches including the winning European teams in 1985, 1987, 1995 and 1997. He holds the record for most games played in the Cup, 46, and most points won, 25. In 1995 at Oak Hill he came from behind to score a vital last day point against Curtis Strange, the American who had beaten him in a play-off for the US Open title in 1988 at The Country Club in Boston. He also captained the Ryder Cup side at Valhalla in 2008 when Europe were disappointing and missed out on winning four in a row. His assistant, José Maria Olazábal, blamed Faldo's "poor communication" for the team's failure.

He became the first international player to be named USPGA Player of the Year in 1990 and led the official World Golf Rankings for 81 weeks in 1993–1994. After teaming up with Swedish caddie Fanny Sunesson for ten years, they split, only to be reunited as one of golf's most formidable partnerships in 2001 before parting company a second time.

His Faldo Junior Series, designed to encourage the best young players to improve, continues to expand. It organises more than 30 tournaments in 25 countries for boys and girls aged between 12 and 21. His company, Faldo Enterprises, runs a successful international golf course design business.

In 2006, he embarked on a TV commentating career with the Golf Channel and CBS. He signed an $8m eight-year contract with the American broadcaster and covers many PGA Tour events. He is an insightful analyst who sees his role as stimulating the interest of a broad audience. In 2009 he was knighted by Her Majesty the Queen for his services to golf.

Stewart award for respecting and upholding the traditions of the game. He is a member of the PGA Tour Committee.

Feherty, David (NIR)

Born Bangor, Northern Ireland, 13 August 1958
Turned professional 1976

Quick-witted Ulsterman who gave up his competitive golfing career to become a successful commentator for CBS in America where his one-liners are legendary. He had five European title wins and three victories on the South African circuit before switching his golf clubs for a much more lucrative career behind the microphone.

Fernandez, Vicente (ARG)

Born Corrientes, 5 May 1946
Turned professional 1964

After playing on the European Tour where "Chino" won five times between 1975 and 1992 he joined the US Champions Tour competing with considerable success. Born with one leg shorter than the other he is remembered in Europe for the 87 foot putt he holed up three tiers on the final green at The Belfry in 1992 to win the Murphy's English Open.

Fernandez-Castano, Gonzalo (ESP)

Born Madrid, 13 October 1980
Turned professional 2004

Twice Spanish amateur champion he began playing golf as a five-year-old and turned professional in 2004 when he was playing off plus 4. He represented Spain in the 2002 Eisenhower Trophy and played for the Continent of Europe against Great Britain and Ireland in 2004. He played twice in the Palmer Cup leading the European students to success against the Americans at Ballybunion in 2004. He won for the first time when he took the 2005 KLM Dutch Open title at Hilversum and was named Sir Henry Cotton Rookie of the Year. Although a regular winner he had no successes in 2009 when he came second four times twice losing play-offs. He has a second role in golf as a tournament promoter of the Madrid Masters.

Finsterwald, Dow (USA)

Born Athens, Ohio, 6 September 1929
Turned professional 1951

Winner of the 1958 USPGA Championship he won 11 other competitions between 1955 and 1963. He played in four Ryder Cup matches in a row from 1957 and captained the side in 1977. He was USPGA Player of the Year in 1958.

Fisher, Oliver (ENG)

Born Chingford, Essex, 19 August 1988
Turned professional 2006

Became the youngest ever Walker Cup player when he made the 2005 Great Britain and Ireland side at the age of 17. In 2006 he played in the Eisenhower and Bonallack Trophy matches and when he turned professional he was playing off plus 4.

Fisher, Ross (ENG)

Born Ascot, Berkshire, 22 November 1980
Turned professional 2004

Attached to the Wentworh Club, he has been playing since he was three. In 2007 he won his first European Tour title at the KLM Open and started his 2008 European Tour campaign by finishing joint second to Phil Mickelson after a play-off at the HSBC Champions event in Shanghai. Later in the season he won the European Open at the London Club leading from start to finish and ending up six clear of his nearest rival. He drove into the Swilcan Burn and lost a play-off to Robert Karlsson when he, Martin Kaymer and the Swede played off for the Alfred Dunhill Links Championship at St Andrews in 2008 Fisher drove into the Swilcan Burn at the first extra hole. In 2009 he reached the semi-finals of the Accenture World Match-play Championship and at one point had the lead in all four majors. On the final day he was ahead in The Open at Turnberry only to run up a 7. He did finish in the top 10 in a Championship he had promised to walk out of if there was a chance of his wife giving birth to their first child. In the end he did not need to! He became the proud father of a daughter after the Championship had ended. Late in the year he won the Volvo Match Play Championship beating Anthony Kim at Finca Cortesin in Spain. In 2010, helped by victory in the 3-Irish Open, he made his début in the Ryder Cup at Celtic Manor.

Floyd, Raymond (USA)

Born Fort Bragg, North Carolina, 4 September 1942
Turned professional 1961

A four time major winner whose failure to win an Open Championship title prevented his completing a Slam of Majors. He won the US Open in 1986, the Masters in 1976 when he matched the then 72-hole record set by Jack Nicklaus to win by eight strokes and took the USPGA title in 1969 and 1982. In addition to coming second and third in The Open he was also runner-up three times in the Masters and in the USPGA once. After scoring 22 victories on the main US Tour he has continued to win as a senior. Inducted into the World Golf Hall of Fame in 1989 he is an avid Chicago Cubs baseball fan. Played in eight Ryder Cup matches between 1969 and 1993 making history with his last appearance by being the oldest player to take part in the match. He was 49. He was non-playing captain in 1989 when the match was drawn at The Belfry and was an assistant to Paul Azinger at the 2008 match at Valhalla.

Ford, Doug (USA)

Born West Haven, Connecticut, 6 August 1922
Turned professional 1949

His 25 wins on the PGA Tour between 1955 and 1963 included the 1975 Masters. USPGA Player of the Year in 1955, he competed in four Ryder Cup matches in succession from 1955.

Franco, Carlos (PAR)

Born Asunción, 24 May 1965
Turned professional 1986

Emerged on to the international stage from humble beginnings. He was one of a family of nine who shared a one-room home at the course where his father was greens superintendent and caddie. All five of his brothers play golf and he was appointed Paraguayan Minister of Sport in 1999. Won twice in his rookie year on the US Tour and became the first player to make more than $1 million in each of his first two seasons. Has scored three wins on the US circuit, five times in Japan where he had 11 top 10 finishes in 1997, once in the Philippines and 19 times in South America. First made headlines at St Andrews when he beat Sam Torrance in the Alfred Dunhill Cup. Now plays on the PGA Tour.

Frost, David (RSA)

Born Cape Town, 11 September 1959
Turned professional 1981

He has won as many titles overseas as on the US Tour and played regularly on the European Tour until 2009. The 1993 season was his best in America when he made over $1 million and finished fifth on the money list. He has established a vineyard in South Africa growing 100 acres of vines on the 300-acre estate and has very quickly earned a reputation for producing quality wines. He now plays on the Champions Tour in America and on Europe's Senior Tour.

Funk, Fred (USA)

Born Tacoma Park, Missouri, 14 June 1956
Turned professional 1981

One of five rookies in the 2004 US Ryder Cup side, he scored his sixth US Tour success a few weeks later when he won the Southern Farm Bureau Classic. In 2005 he won the Tournament Players' Championship at Sawgrass and now plays on the Champions Tour. In 2009 he and Mark McNulty lost a play-off to Loren Roberts in the Senior Open at Sunningdale and then won the US Senior Open the following week at Crooked Stick.

Furyk, Jim (USA)

Born West Chester, Pennsylvania, 12 May 1970
Turned professional 1992

Considered one of the best players not to have won a major, Furyk put that right when he won the US Open at Olympia Fields, Chicago. He was one of four first-time major winners in 2003. He clearly enjoys playing in Las Vegas where he has won three Invitational events in 1995, 1999 and 1998. He has teed it up in five Presidents Cups and seven Ryder Cups beating Nick Faldo in the singles at Valderrama in 1997. He has one of the most easily recognisable if idiosyncratic swings in top line golf. His father Mike has been his only coach. In 2006 he came second to Tiger Woods in the US Tour money list earning $7,213,316 but won the Harry Vardon Trophy for the best scoring average of 68.66 for golfers who played 60 rounds or more. In 2010 he won three times on the PGA Tour, won the Fedex Cup $10 million bonus and was named Player of the Year.

Gallacher CBE, Bernard (SCO)

Born Bathgate, Scotland, 9 February 1949
Turned professional 1967

For many years he combined tournament golf with the club professional's post at Wentworth where he was honoured in 2000 by being appointed captain. He took up golf at the age of 11 and nine years later was European No 1. He has scored 30 victories world-wide. Gallacher was the youngest Ryder Cup player when he made his début in the 1969 match in which he beat Lee Trevino in the singles. He played in eight Cup matches and captained the side three times losing narrowly in 1991 at Kiawah Island and 1993 at The Belfry before leading the team to success at Oak Hill in 1995. A former member of the European Tour's Board of Directors, he was afforded honorary membership of the European Tour in 2003.

García, Sergio (ESP)

Born Castellon, 9 January 1980
Turned professional 1999

The Spaniard, who was runner-up to Tiger Woods in the 1999 US PGA Championship, lost his best chance of winning a first major when he missed a putt on the final green at Carnoustie in 2007 and was beaten by Ireland's Padraig Harrington in the subsequent four-hole play-off. He had led for most of the four days. He was again pipped by Harrington in the 2008 USPGA Championship at Oakland Hills. Having won the British Boys' Championship in 1997, he took the Spanish and British Amateur titles in 1998 and in both years was the European Amateur Masters champion. Son of a greenkeeper/professional who now plays on the European Senior Tour, Sergio waited until after the 1999 Master before joining the paid ranks at the Spanish Open. Although only just starting to collect Ryder Cup points he easily made the 1999 team and formed an invaluable partnership with Jesper Parnevik at Brookline scoring three and a half points out of four on the first two days. The 1999 Sir Henry Cotton Rookie of the Year in Europe he again formed a useful partnership this time with Lee Westwood in the 2002 Cup match. Together they won three points out of four. They teamed up again in the winning 2004 side at Oakland Hills. He himself was unbeaten, winning 4½ out of five points including victory over Phil Mickelson in the singles. In the 2006 Ryder Cup at the K Club he again played well with José María Olazábal in the fourballs and Luke Donald in the foursomes. He scored four out of five points, losing only his single to Stewart Cink. His form dipped in the 2008 match at Valhalla but that year he did become the first European-born player since 1937 to win the Vardon Trophy on the PGA Tour with a low score average of 69.12. He ended the year as No. 2 in the World Rankings. Loss of confidence saw him take a break from the game and miss out on the 2010 Ryder Cup. By the end of 2010 he had slipped to 78th in the world rankings but improved to 18th in 2011 when he returned to winning ways with victories in successive weeks at his own event –the Castello Masters – and the Andalucia Masters.

Garrido, Antonio (ESP)

Born Madrid 2 February 1944
Turned professional 1961

Along With Severiano Ballesteros was a member of the first European side to play against the Americans for the Ryder Cup in 1979. Teamed up with Seve two years earlier to win the World Cup of Golf for Spain in the Pbilippines his brother German was also a golf professional and his son Ignacio, a former PGA Champion in 2003 also played in the Ryder Cup in 1997. They are only the second father and son to have played in the match, the others being Percy and Peter Alliss.

Garrido, Ignacio (ESP)

Born Madrid 2 February 1944
Turned professional 1961

Eldest son of Antonio Garrido who played in the 1979 Ryder Cup, Ignacio emulated his father when he made the team at the 1997 match at Valderrama having earlier that year won the Volvo German Open. A former English Amateur Stroke-play title-holder in 1992 his most impressive win on the European Tour was beating Trevor Immelman in a play-off for the 2003 Volvo PGA Championship at Wentworth. In the 80s used to caddie for his father who has since caddied for him on occasion.

Goosen, Retief (RSA)

Born Pietersburg, 3 February 1969
Turned professional 1990

Introduced to golf at the age of 11 the former South African amateur champion scored his first major professional success when leading from start to finish at the 2001 US Open at Tulsa and then beating Mark Brooks in the 18-hole play-off by two shots. Although he suffered health problems after being hit by lightning as a teenager he has enjoyed a friendly rivalry with fellow South African Ernie Els whom he beat in the 2005 South African Airways Open at Fancourt. In 2004 he again won the US Open, this time at Shinnecock Hills GC on Long Island producing, in the process, not only superb control through the green but inspirational form on the lightning fast putting surfaces to prevent Phil Mickelson winning what would have been his second major of the year. Goosen single-putted 11 of the first 17 holes of his final round of 71. In 2005 after finishing tied third at The Masters, he was leading going into the last round of the US Open at Pinehurst No 2 but shot a closing 81 to miss out on a successful defence of his title. He finished 11th behind Michael Campbell but was fifth at The Open and sixth at the USPGA that same year.

When he played again in the Presidents Cup later in the year he beat Tiger Woods in the singles at Lake Mannassas. He continues to play well around the world.

Grady, Wayne (AUS)

Born Brisbane, 26 July 1957
Turned professional 1973 and again in 1978

In 1990 he won the USPGA Championship at Shoal Creek by three shots from Fred Couples. A year earlier he had tied with Greg Norman and eventual winner Mark Calcavecchia for The Open Championship losing out in the first ever four-hole play-off for the title. He is a former chairman of the Australasian Tour and with a reduced schedule on the Champions Tour in America he manages to commentate occasionally for the BBC.

Graham, David (AUS)

Born Windsor, Tasmania, 23 May 1946
Turned professional 1962

Played superbly for a closing 67 round Merion to win the 1981 US Open Championship from George Burns and Bill Rogers. That day he hit every green in regulation. Two years earlier he had beaten Ben Crenshaw at the third extra hole at Oakland Hills to win the USPGA Championship. When he took up the game at age 14 he played with left-handed clubs before making the switch to a right-handed set. Awarded the Order of Australia for his services to golf he is a member of the Cup and Tee committee that sets up Augusta each year for the Masters. A regular winner around the world in the 70s and 80s he won eight times on the US Tour between 1972 and 1983 and has built up a considerable reputation as a course designer.

Green OBE, Charlie (SCO)

Born Dumbarton, 2 August 1932

One of Scotland's most successful amateur golfers who was leading amateur in the 1962 Open Championship. A prolific winner he took the Scottish Amateur title three times in 1970, 1982 and 1983. He played in five and was non-playing captain in two more Walker Cups and was awarded the Frank Moran Trophy for his services to Scottish sport in 1974.

Green, Hubert (USA)

Born Birmingham, Alabama, 18 December 1946
Turned professional 1970

In 1977 he beat Lou Graham at the 1977 US Open at Southern Hills despite being told with four holes to play that he had received a death threat. Three times a Ryder Cup player he also won the 1985 USPGA Championship. Best known for his unorthodox swing and distinctive crouching putting style. he has successfully beaten throat cancer – an illness that has prevented his competing on the US Champions Tour. He was inducted into the World Golf Hall of Fame in 2007.

Padraig Harrington (IRL)

Born Dublin, Ireland, 31 August 1971
Turned professional 1995

The winner of three major championships, Harrington is Ireland's most successful golfer thanks to his triumphs at The Open in 2007 and 2008 and the US PGA in 2007. He became only the second Irishman ever to hoist the Claret Jug when he overcame Sergio García in a four-hole play-off at Carnoustie, 60 years after Belfast's Fred Daly had won the title at Hoylake in 1947.

He savoured the season of his life in 2008 when he became the first European to win both The Open and US PGA titles in the same year and the first European to win the US PGA since Tommy Armour in 1930. At Royal Birkdale he defended the crown by holding off the challenge posed by Ian Poulter and Greg Norman with a closing 66. The highlight of the championship was the 5-wood he struck to two feet on the par 5 17th for a glorious eagle 3 which closed the door on his rivals. It was the first time since James Braid in 1906 that a European had retained the title. At Oakland Hills three weeks later his main challengers were García and Ben Curtis. Again a closing 66 did the trick for the talented Irishman. At the end of his extraordinary year, Harrington was named the European Tour, PGA Tour and PGA of America's Player of the Year. He was only the second European to be given this honour since it was first awarded in 1948.

A qualified accountant, Harrington played three times as an amateur in the Walker Cup before turning professional. He won the Spanish Open in 2006 and has gone on to lift 30 titles, including 14 on the European Tour. His career has been heavily influenced by input from both coach Bob Torrance and sports psychologist Bob Rotella. He won the European Order of Merit in 2006 and has featured on six Ryder Cup teams, four times as a winner. He has gone into the design business with his first course, The Marlbrook, in Co. Tipperary. In 2011, he was named as The R&A's first Working for Golf Ambassador, promoting the work of the game's governing body around the world.

Haas, Bill (USA)

Born Charlotte, North Carolina, 1982
Turned professional 2004

Winner of three events on the PGA Tour, including the Tour Championship by Coca-Cola in 2011, Haas' victory in Atlanta was sufficient not only to collect the first prize of $1.44 million but also the FedEx Cup jackpot of $10m. The son of Jay Haas, who won nine times on the PGA Tour, Bill received a captain's pick from Fred Couples to play in the Presidents Cup at Royal Melbourne.

Haas, Jay (USA)

Born St Louis, Missouri, 2 December 1953
Turned professional 1976

Winner of nine events on the USPGA Tour, he played in his third Ryder Cup as an invitee of the US captain Hal Sutton. He had played in 1983 and 1995. He had played in three Presidents Cups and was a Walker Cup player in 1975. His uncle is former Masters champion Bob Goalby. In 2004 he was named recipient of the Payne Stewart award for respecting and upholding the traditions of the game and received the Bob Jones award for outstanding sportsmanship in 2005. In 2006 and 2007 he edged out Loren Roberts for the No 1 spot on the US Champions Tour winning five times in 2006 and a further four times in 2007.

Haeggman, Joakim (SWE)

Born Kalmar, 28 August 1969
Turned professional 1989

Became the first Swedish player to play in the Ryder Cup when he made the side which lost to the Americans at The Belfry in 1993. He received one of team captain Bernard Gallacher's 'wild cards' and beat John Cook in his last day singles. Gave up ice hockey after dislocating his shoulder and breaking ribs in 1994. Realised then that ice hockey and golf do not mix but has become an enthusiastic angler when not on the links. Equalled the world record of 27 for the first nine holes in the Alfred Dunhill Cup over the Old course at St Andrews in 1997. Occasionally acts as commentator for Swedish TV and was a member of Sam Torrance's Ryder Cup backroom team at The Belfry in 2002 and Bernhard Langer's vice-captain at Oakland Hills in 2004. Returned to the winner's circle in 2004 at Qatar. It was only his second win on the European Tour and his first since 1993.

Hamilton, Todd (USA)

Born Galesburg, Illinois, 18 October 1965
Turned professional 1997

Winner of the 2004 Open Championship at Royal Troon beating Ernie Els in a four-hole play-off after both had tied on ten-under-par 274. Having learned his craft on the Asian Tour and Japanese circuit where he won four times in 2003, he earned his US Tour card in 2004 and won the Honda Classic. His performance in The Open was flawless as he kept his nerve to win against Els, Phil Mickelson and World No 1 Tiger Woods among others. He was American Rookie of the Year in 2004 but has since lost his card to play there and has been a member of the European Tour.

Han, Chang Won (KOR)

Born Jeju Island

The 17-year-old winner of the first Asian Amateur Championship played at Mission Hills in China, he shot a 12-under par score to earn a place in the 2010 Masters at Augusta joining two other foreign teenagers, US Amateur Champion Byeong-Hu An and British Champion Matteo Manassero there.

Hansen, Anders (DEN)
Born Sonderborg, 16 September 1970
Turned professional 1995
Made up eight shots over the last 36 holes to win the BMW PGA Championship for a second time at Wentworth in 2007. He had also won the event in 2002. He ended top money winner on the South African Sunshine Tour in 2009. He won in 2011.

Hansen, Søren (DEN)
Copenhagen, 21 March 1974
Turned professional 1997
Winner of the Murphy's Irish Open in 2002 and the Mercedes-Benz Championship in 2007, he made his début successfully in the 2008 Ryder Cup at Valhalla.

Hanson, Peter (SWE)
Born Svedala, 4 October 1977
Turned professional 1998
In 1998 he won the English Amateur Stroke-play Championship (the Brabazon Trophy) and was also a member of the winning Swedish Eisenhower Trophy team. In 2005 he partnered Robert Karlsson for Sweden in the 2007 Mission Hills World Cup of Golf and in 2008 he ended a ten year wait for a home winner when he won the SAS Scandinavian Masters in poor weather at Arlandastat outside Stockholm. He won twice – at Majorca and the Czech Republic – in 2010 which helped him make his début in the Ryder Cup.

Hayes, Dale (RSA)
Born Pretoria, 1 July 1952
Turned professional 1970
Former South African amateur stroke play champion who was a regular winner in South Africa and Europe after turning professional. He was Europe's top money earner in 1975 but retired from competitive golf to move into business. He is now a successful television commentator in South Africa with a weekly programme of his own often working as a double act with veteran Denis Hutchinson.

Hoch, Scott (USA)
Born Raleigh, North Carolina, 24 November 1955
Turned professional 1979
Ryder Cup, Presidents Cup, Walker Cup and Eisenhower Trophy player who was a regular winner on the US Tour soring 10 wins between 1980 and 2001 with six more victories worldwide. In 1989 he donated $100,000 of his Las Vegas Invitational winnings to the Arnold Palmer Children's Hospital in Orlando where his son Cameron had been successfully treated for a rare bone infection in his right knee. Also remembered for missing a short putt at the first extra hole of a play-off that would have won him a Masters Green Jacket and a first major.

Horton MBE, Tommy (ENG)
Born St Helens, Lancashire, 16 June 1941
Turned professional 1957
A former Ryder Cup player who was No 1 earner on the European Seniors Tour in 1993 and for four successive seasons between 1996 and 1999. Awarded an MBE by Her Majesty the Queen for his services to golf, Tommy is a member of the European Tour Board and is chairman of the European Seniors Tour committee. A distinguished coach, broadcaster, author and golf course architect, Tommy retired as club professional at Royal Jersey in 1999 after 25 years in the post. He continues to play occasionally on the Senior Tour.

Howell, David (ENG)
Born Swindon, 23 June 1975 Turned professional 1995
Winner of the 1999 Dubai Desert Classic, he made his Ryder Cup début in 2004 at Oakland Hills where he teamed up with Paul Casey to gain a valuable foursomes point on the second day. He finished seventh in the 2005 European Tour money list making over £1.2 million and a year later despite his schedule being curtailed by injury, he made over £1.5 million and finished third. Although injury has severely restricted his play he remains an enthusiastic competitor and is often used as an expert analyst by Sky television.

Huggett MBE, Brian (WAL)
Born Porthcawl, Wales, 18 November 1936
Turned professional 1951
Brian won the first of his 16 European Tour titles in Holland in 1962 and was still winning in 2000 when he landed the Beko Seniors Classic in Turkey after a play-off. A dogged competitor he played in six Ryder Cup matches before being given the honour of captaining the side in 1977 – the last year the Americans took on players from only Great Britain and Ireland. A respected golf course designer, Huggett was awarded the MBE for his services to golf and in particular Welsh golf.

Hunt MBE, Bernard (ENG)
Born Atherstone, Warwickshire, 2 February 1930
Turned professional 1946
One of Britain's most accomplished professionals he won 22 times between 1953 and 1973. He was third in the 1960 Open at the Old Course behind Kel Nagle and fourth in 1964 when Tony Lema took the title at St Andrews. Among his other victories were successes in Egypt and Brazil. Having made eight appearances in the Ryder Cup he captained the side in 1973 and again in 1975. He was PGA captain in 1966 and won the Harry Vardon Trophy as leading player in the Order of Merit on three occasions.

Tony Jacklin CBE (ENG)

Born Scunthorpe, 7 July 1944
Turned professional 1962

A long and straight driver as well as a formidable ball striker at his peak, Jacklin was a significant force in the game between 1968 and 1974. It could even be argued that there were spells during his ascendancy when the Englishman was as good as anyone in the sport. In 1969 he won The Open Championship at Royal Lytham and St Annes, in the process becoming a national hero as the first British holder of the title since Max Faulkner in 1951. A year later he led from start to finish to win the US Open at Hazeltine by a seven shot margin – again underscoring his national standing as the first British player to win that event since Ted Ray had been successful in 1920. He was also the first Englishman since Harry Vardon to hold The Open and US Open titles simultaneously. He might well have won further Open championships but a thunderstorm thwarted his bid for the title at St Andrews in 1970, he came third in 1971 and in 1972 Lee Trevino chipped in at the 17th at Muirfield to win a title Jacklin had seemed destined to grasp.

The son of a Scunthorpe lorry driver who travelled by bus to play in assistants' events, he was rookie of the year on the European Tour in 1962 and went on to win 14 times on his home circuit. He was a driving force in the Ryder Cup as a player, taking part in seven consecutive matches from 1967. As a four-time captain of Europe, he twice led the Continent to victory including the first ever win on American soil in 1987. He also played an important and often under-rated role in the growth of the PGA European Tour after it became a self-supporting organisation in 1971. Although playing most of his golf in America he was encouraged by John Jacobs, the then executive director of the European Tour, to return to Europe to help build up the circuit.

He is an honorary member of the Royal and Ancient Golf Club of St Andrews having been elected in 2003 along with Lee Trevino. Played in his last Open in 2005. He has built in Florida with Jack Nicklaus a course known as The Concession, so named because of the putt Jack conceded him in the 1969 Ryder Cup to ensure the overall match was halved. He was awarded the OBE in 1970 and a CBE in 1990 in recognition of his influential Ryder Cup captaincy, which helped revive the standing of the match.

Ilonen, Mikko (FIN)

Born Lahti, 18 December 1979
Turned professional 2001

Became the first Finnish golfer to win the Amateur Championship when he beat Christian Reimbold from Germany 2 and 1 in the 2000 final at Royal Liverpool. He has won both the Finnish amateur match play and stroke play titles. He represented Finland in the 1998 and 2000 Eisenhower Trophy events. Now plays professionally on the European Tour and in 2007 won the Enjoy Jakarta Astro Indonesian Open, a joint venture with the Asian Tour and the Scandinavian Masters at Arlandastad. In 2008 he won the Indonesian Open title again.

Immelman, Trevor (RSA)

Born Cape Town, South Africa, 16 December 1979
Turned professional 1999

The 2008 Masters champion is son of Johan Immelman, former executive director of the South African Sunshine Tour. A former South African Amateur Match Play and Stroke-play champion and twice South African Open champion Trevor played his early professional golf in Europe before moving to the United States where he scored a first major victory leading from start to finish in the 2008 Masters at Augusta. won his first PGA title when he held off a strong field at the Cialis Western Open at Cog Hill. He has played in two Presidents Cups but his career has been dogged by injury and illness causing him to miss three of the four 2009 majors.

Irwin, Hale (USA)

Born Joplin, Montana, 3 June 1945
Turned professional 1968

A three time winner of the US Open (1974, 1979 and 1990) he has been a prolific winner on the main US Tour and, since turning 50, on the US Champions Tour. He had 20 wins on the main Tour including the 1990 US Open triumph where he holed a 45-foot putt on the final green at Medinah to force a play-off with Mike Donald then after both were still tied following a further 18 holes became the oldest winner of the Championship at 45 when he sank a 10-foot birdie putt at the first extra hole of sudden death. Joint runner-up to Tom Watson in the 1983 Open at Royal Birkdale where he stubbed the ground and missed a tap-in putt on the final day – a slip that cost him the chance of a play-off. Three times top earner on the Champions Tour where, prior to the start of the 2001 season, he had averaged $90,573 per start in

130 events coming in the top three in 63 of those events and finishing over par in only nine of them, he was inducted into the World Golf Hall of Fame in 2008.

Ishikawa, Ryo (JPN)

Born Saitama, 17 September 1991
Turned professional 2008

Already established as one of the most exciting young players in world golf – he's nicknamed the "bashful prince" in Japan – the teenager captured headlines around the globe during 2010 when he carded 58 in the final round to win the Crowns tournament at Nagoya on the Japanese Tour. It was the lowest score ever recorded on a sanctioned Tour and included 12 birdies and six pars. The previous record of 59 was shared on the PGA Tour by the Americans Al Geiberger, Chip Beck, David Duval, Paul Goydos and Stuart Appleby. The Crowns tournament was Ishikawa's seventh victory of his career and followed on from an electrifying start to the final round when he birdied nine of the first 11 holes. He first won on the Japan Tour as an amateur at the 2007 Muningswear Open in Okayama. At just 15 years and 245 days he became the youngest man ever to win a professional event. He then went on to become the youngest player to compete in the US PGA Championship at Hazeltine in 2009 as well as the youngest ever to reach the top 50 of the World Golf Rankings.

Jacobs OBE, John (ENG)

Born Lindrick, Yorkshire, 14 March 1925

The first Executive Director of the independently run PGA European Tour, John Jacobs was awarded the OBE in 2000 for his services to golf as a player, administrator and coach. Known as "Dr Golf" Jacobs has built up an awesome reputation as a teacher around the world and is held in high esteem by the golfing fraternity. Top American coach Butch Harmon summed up John's contribution when he said: "There is not one teacher who does not owe something to John. He wrote the book on coaching." With 75 per cent of the votes he was inducted into the World Golf Teachers' Hall of Fame and was described at that ceremony as 'the English genius'. Last year he was also welcomed into the World Golf Hall of Fame in America. Having played in the 1955 Ryder Cup match he captained the side in 1979 when Continental players were included for the first time and again in 1981. Ken Schofield who succeeded him as European Tour supremo believes that John changed the face of golf sponsorship. In 2002 he received the Association of Golf Writers' award for outstanding services to golf.

Jacquelin, Rafaël (FRA)

Born Lyons, 8 May 1974   Turned professional 1995

Ten years after turning professional and in his 238th event Rafaël Jacquelin a former French amateur champion, won his first event as a professional – the 2005 Madrid Open at Club de Campo. The Frenchman with a most graceful swing, who originlly wanted to be a soccer player but a knee injury thwarted his plans and he turned instead to tennis and later to golf. In 2007 he led wire-to-wire when winning the BMW Asian Open. He and Gregory Havret finished third behind Scotland and the USA in the 2007 World Cup of Golf at Mission Hills in China. In 2011 he won the Sicilian Open and took over from the injured Alvaro Quiros in the Continental side captained by Jan Van de Velde against Great Britain and Ireland at St Nom la Breteche.

Jaidee, Thongchai (THA)

Born Lop Buri, Thailand, 8 November 1969
Turned professional 1999

The first Thai golfer to win a title on the European Tour when he won the Carlsberg Malaysian Open in 2004. Learned his golf using a bamboo pole with an old 5-iron head and did not play his first nine holes until he was 16. An ex-paratrooper, Jaidee qualified and played all four rounds in the 2001 US Open. An impressive regular on the Asian Tour, he also competes on the European International schedule where in 2009 he won the Ballantines event in Korea and the Indonesian Open in Bali. Finished top money earner on the Asian Tour for the third time in 2009. He is still top career money earner on the Asian Tour with over $2 million.

James, Mark (ENG)

Born Manchester, 28 October 1953
Turned professional 1976

Veteran of over 500 European tournaments he was for a time chairman of the European Tour's Tournament committee. A seven-time Ryder Cup player including the 1995 match at Oak Hill when he scored a vital early last day point against Jeff Maggert, he captained the side at Brookline in 1999. Four times a top five finisher in The Open Championship he has won 18 European Tour events and four elsewhere but caused some raised eyebrows with his comments in his book reviewing the 1999 Ryder Cup entitled *Into the Bear Pit*. Affectionately known as Jesse to his friends. he qualified for the US Champions Tour in 2004 and won one of that Tour's five majors – the Ford Senior Players Championship. Through 2008 continued to play on the US Champions Tour with only infrequent visits back to play in European Senior events or to join Ken Brown and Peter Alliss on the BBC golf commentating team. In his spare time he is an enthusiastic gardener.

January, Don (USA)

Born Plainview, Texas, 20 November 1929
Turned professional 1955

Winner of the US Open in 1967 he followed up his successful main Tour career in which he had 11 wins between 1956 and 1976 with double that success as a Senior. Much admired for his easy rhythmical style.

Janzen, Lee (USA)

Born Austin, Minnesota, 28 August 1964
Turned professional 1986

Twice a winner of the US Open in 1993 and in 1998 when he staged the best final round comeback since Johnny Miller rallied from six back to win the title 25 years earlier. Five strokes behind the late Payne Stewart after 54 holes at Baltusrol he closed with a 67 to beat Stewart with whom he had also battled for the title in 1993.

Jiménez, Miguel Angel (ESP)

Born Malaga, 4 January 1964
Turned professional 1982

Talented Spaniard with a pony-tail haircut who was runner-up to Tiger Woods in the 2000 US Open. This was a year after making his successful début in the Ryder Cup. One of seven brothers he did not take up golf until his mid-teens. He loves cars, drives a Ferrari and has been nicknamed 'The Mechanic' by his friends. His best-remembered shot was the 3-wood he hit into the hole for an albatross 2 at the infamous 17th hole at Valderrama in the Volvo Masters but he was credited with having played the Canon Shot of the Year when he chipped in at the last to win 1998 Trophée Lancôme. In 2000 lost in a play-off at Valderrama in a World Championship event to Tiger Woods. He played in the 2002, 2004, 2008 and 2010 European Ryder Cup sides gaining a vital point in the last day singles at Celtic Manor. He won four times during the 2004 European season, taking the Johnnie Walker Classic title in Bangkok, the Algarve Portuguese Open at Penina, the BMW Asian Open in Shanghai and the BMW German Open in Munich. and was a three time winner during the 2010 season succeeding in Dubai, Paris and at Crans. He was the 2008 BMW PGA champion beating Oliver Wilson in a play-off at Wentworth. He loves his rioja and is often seen smoking a cigar.

Johansson, Per-Ulrik (SWE)

Born Uppsala, 6 December 1966
Turned professional 1990

A former amateur international at both junior and senior level he became the first Swede to play in two Ryder Cups when he made the 1995 and 1997 teams. In the 1995 match he lost to Phil Mickelson with whom he had studied at Arizona State University. In 1991 he was winner of the Sir Henry Cotton Rookie of the Year award in Europe. For a time, he played in America but returned to Europe, regaining his main Tour card with victory in the Russian Open in Moscow.

Johnson, Dustin (USA)

Born Columbia, South Carolina, 22 June 1984
Turned professional 2007

Winner of the AT&T Pebble Beach Pro-am in both 2009 and 2010, he also led the US Open at Pebble Beach by three strokes after 54 holes but dropped back into a share of eighth place after carding 82 in the final round. Johnson also had a chance to win the US PGA in 2010 after making birdies in the final round at Whistling Straits on the 16th and 17th holes. Standing at 12 under par on the 72nd hole, he hit his tee shot right and landed in a sandy area. Unaware he was in a bunker he grounded his club in the dirt and thought he'd made a bogey to join Martin Kaymer and Bubba Watson in a play-off but he was penalised two strokes for grounding his club and finished in a share of fifth. His victory later in the season over Paul Casey in the BMW Championship, his fourth US PGA Tour win, proved his resilience. He was a member of the 2007 US Walker Cup side and made his début in the Ryder Cup at Celtic Manor in 2010. A year later he was runner-up to Darren Clarke in The Open losing his chance of possible victory by hitting his second shot out of bounds at the par 5 14th at Royal St George's.

Johnson, Zach (USA)

Born Iowa City, 24 February 1976
Turned professional 1998

The winner of the 2004 BellSouth Classic, he made his début in the Ryder Cup at the K Club in 2006 and won The Masters at Augusta in 2007. Later, he won first prize in the AT&T Classic at TPC Sugarloaf and earned a Presidents Cup spot. Surprisingly missed out on Ryder Cup honours in 2008 but mde the team two years later.

Jones, Steve (USA)

Born Artesia, New Mexico, 27 December 1958
Turned professional 1981

First player since Jerry Pate in 1976 to win the US Open after having had to qualify. His 1996 victory was the result of inspiration he received from reading a Ben Hogan book given to him the week before the Championship at Oakland Hills. Uses a reverse overlapping grip as a result of injury. Indeed his career was put on hold for three years after injury to his left index finger following a dirt-bike accident. He dominated the 1997 Phoenix Open shooting 62, 64, 65 and 67 for an 11 shot victory over Jesper Parnevik That week his 258 winning total was just one outside the low US Tour record set by Mike Souchak in 1955. Played in the 1999 Ryder Cup.

Karlsson, Robert (SWE)

Born St Malm, Sweden, 3 September 1969
Turned professional 1989

The tall son of a greenkeeper is the most successful Swede on the European Tour having won 11 times by the end of 2010. He was a member of the winning 2006 Ryder Cup side and the losing 2008 team. He played with Peter Hanson in the 2007 Mission Hills World Cup of Golf in Shenzhen and in 2008 teamed up with Henrik Stenson to win the trophy for Sweden for a second time. It was a fitting finale to a year in which he made the cut in all four majors and towards the end of the season won the Mercedes-Benz German Masters and the Alfred

Dunhill Links Championship to clinch the No 1 spot on the European Tour's Order of Merit. At one point during the summer of 2008 he was never out of the top four in five consecutive events finishing 3,3,3,2,4. An eye problem caused him to miss many tournaments in 2009. A year later, when back to full fitness he won the Dubai World Championship in 2010 and in 2011 played most of his golf in America.

Kaymer, Martin (GER)

Born Dusseldorf, Germany, 26 December 1984

The 2010 US PGA champion produced an outstanding performance at Whistling Straits to secure his first Major title. Coached by Fanny Sunesson, who is better known as Nick Faldo's former caddie and bag carrier for Henrik Stenson, Kaymer was an outstanding amateur golfer who made an immediate impact as a professional. On a satellite circuit he made a name for himself by carding 59 before winning twice on the Challenge Tour in 2006. When he joined the European Tour the following year he ended up with five top ten finishes and won the Sir Henry Cotton Rookie of the Year award. He also won twice in 2008 at Abu Dhabi and Munich and just failed to make the Ryder Cup side, though he was invited to Valhalla as an observer by Faldo. In 2009 he won back to back titles at the French and Scottish Opens before an ankle injury sustained when go-karting in Arizona sidelined him for a spell. Victory in 2010 at the Abu Dhabi championship propelled Kaymer into the world's top ten. And when he defeated Bubba Watson in a play-off at Whistling Straits, Kaymer became only the second German after Bernhard Langer to become a major champion. He also won his next tournament, the KLM Open, before making his Ryder Cup début at Celtic Manor then adding the Dunhill Links Championship to his list of successes. He went on to win the Race to Dubai and was jointly named European Golfer of the Year with Graeme McDowell. In 2011 he began with a third victory in four years at Abu Dhabi and moved to No 2 in the world but then his form deserted him for a while.

Kim, Anthony (USA)

Born Los Angeles, California 19 June 1985
Turned professional: 2006

He spent three years at the University of Oklahoma but turned professional after making $338,067 in just two starts on Tour. A three-time All-American he was a member of the successful 2005 US Walker Cup side and made a winning début in the Ryder Cup at Valhalla in 2008 beating Sergio García in the singles. In the Volvo World Match Play in 2009 he lost in the final to Ross Fisher.

Kim Kyung-Tae (KOR)

Born Seoul, South Korea, 2 September 1986
Turned professional: 2006

It was no surprise that the 24-year-old South Korean topped the Japanese money list in 2010 with total earnings of over 181 million yen. He made it to the top with the help of three victories – the Diamond Cup, the Mynavi ABC Championship and the Japanese Open. His scoring average for the season was 69.41 and he hit more than three greens out of four in regulation during the season. As an amateur he had swept all before him earning a government exemption from National Service for his performance at the 2006 Asian Games where he won the individual honours and helped South Korea to victory in the team event. He won two events on the Korean professional Tour as an amateur and by the end of 2010 had moved from outdo the top 100 in the World Rankings to 30th.

Kite, Tom (USA)

Born Austin, Texas, 9 December 1949
Turned professional 1972

He won the US Open at Pebble Beach in 1992 in difficult conditions when aged 42 to lose the 'best player around never to have won a Major' tag. With 19 wins on the main Tour he was the first to top $6million, $7 million, $8 million and $9 million dollars in prize money. Has been playing since he was 11 and after a lifetime wearing glasses had laser surgery to correct acute near-sightedness. He played in seven Ryder Cups and was captain at Valderrama in 1997. He now plays the US Champions Tour and was inducted into the World Golf Hall of Fame in 2004.

Laird, Martin (SCO)

Born Glasgow, Scotland, 1982
Turned professional 2004

The Arizona based Scot enjoyed his best year so far on the PGA Tour in 2011, winning the Arnold Palmer Invitational at Bay Hill, the first European golfer ever to do so. He produced six top ten finishes and won $2.7 million. A graduate of the Nationwide Tour, his first PGA Tour win came at the Justin Timberlake Shriners Hospitals for Children Open. Laird's journey from junior captain and champion at Hilton Park in Glasgow to winner on the PGA Tour began in 2003. That was the summer he came from behind to clinch a three stroke victory in the Scottish Youths' Open Amateur Strokeplay Championship. He went to college at Colorado State and hasn't left America since, becoming first Scot in 20 years to play full-time on the PGA Tour.

Lane, Barry (ENG)

Born Hayes, Middlesex, 21 June 1960
Turned professional 1976

After winning his way into the 1993 Ryder Cup he hit the headlines when he won the first prize of $1 million in the Andersen Consulting World Championship beating David Frost in the final at Greyhawk in Arizona. He has played over 500 European events, winning five times between 1988 and 2008. In 2004, aged 44, he won the British Masters at Marriott Forest of Arden.

Bernhard Langer (GER)

Born Anhausen, 27 August 1957
Turned professional 1972

While there have been many notable achievements during his enduring career, including collecting two Masters titles at Augusta, winning 40 titles on the European Tour and proving a mainstay of the European Ryder Cup side as both a player and a captain, the German's remarkable accomplishment in winning senior major titles in successive weeks during the summer of 2010 rivalled anything the veteran had accomplished in his prime. The first senior golfer to win back-to-back majors since Tom Watson in 2003, Langer's triumphs were all the more remarkable bearing in mind that his first success came in The Senior British Open at Carnoustie in Scotland and his second was in The US Senior Open in Seattle, Washington State, venues separated by thousands of miles as well as an eight hour time difference. Langer's success on the Champions' circuit, winning more than $2 million in each of his first three years on Tour, however, came as no surprise to those familiar with the track record of this determined champion.

His success at Carnoustie in The Senior British was particularly rewarding since he had come twice and finished third on three occasions in The Open without lifting the Claret Jug. A prolific winner throughout his career, Langer is the second most prolific champion, after Seve Ballesteros, in European Tour history. His most memorable victories, though, came in America where he won the Masters in 1985 and 1993. The latter triumph is best remembered for the eagle 3 he made at the 13th in the final round to set up a four stroke win over Chip Beck. Perhaps there was an element of irony attached to these triumphs at Augusta since Langer has frequently faced putting problems during his career and the Masters is widely regarded as the most demanding test of putting in championship golf. His most successful year as a pro came in 1985 when he won seven tournaments on five continents and was ranked No 1 in the world. Though far from the longest hitter, the consistency of Langer's game also made him a formidable match play golfer. He played in ten Ryder Cup matches and was an outstanding European captain at Oakland Hills in 2004. A member of the World Golf Hall of Fame, he was awarded an honorary OBE for his services to the game.

Lawrie MBE, Paul (SCO)

Born Aberdeen, 1 January 1969
Turned professional 1986

Made golfing history when he came from 10 shots back on the final day to win the 1999 Open Championship at Carnoustie after a play-off against former winner Justin Leonard and Frenchman Jean Van de Velde. With his win he became the first home-based Scot since Willie Auchterlonie in 1893 to take the title. Still based in Aberdeen he hit the opening tee shot in the 1999 Ryder Cup and played well in partnership with Colin Montgomerie in foursomes and four balls and in the singles earned a point against Jeff Maggert. Originally an assistant at Banchory Golf Club on Royal Deeside Lawrie has had a hole named after him at the club. Coached off and on by former Tour player Adam Hunter and Scottish Rugby Union psychologist Dr Richard Cox, Lawrie has been awarded an MBE for his achievements in golf and is a prominent supporter of junior golf in Scotland. In 2011 he won the Andalucian Masters in Malaga, his first victory in nine years. He was also runner-up in the season ending Dubai World Championship.

Lee, Danny (NZL)

Born 24 July 1990

Helped by his victory in the US Amateur Championship in 2008 he moved to the top of the Royal and Ancient Golf Club of St Andrews amateur rankings and won the McCormack Trophy. Although Korean by birth he has been brought up in New Zealand and America. Late in 2008 he became a naturalised New Zealander and led his country in the Eisenhower Trophy competition won by Scotland in Adelaide. He is one of three amateurs to have won titles on the PGA European Tour. Pablo Martin won the Estoril Open de Portugal in 2007 as an amateur, Lee won the last Johnnie Walker Classic title at The Vines in Perth in 2009 and later that season Irish amateur Shane Lowry won the 3-Irish Open at Baltray.

Lehman, Tom (USA)

Born Austin, Minnesota, 7 March 1959
Turned professional 1982

Winner of The Open Championship at Royal Lytham and St Annes in 1996 he was runner-up in the US Open that year and third in 1997. He was runner-up in the 1994 Masters having come third the previous year. He played in four Ryder Cup matches and led the US team in the 2006 Ryder Cup match at the K Club when the Americans lost 18½–9½ to the Europeans led by Ian Woosnam. In 2011 he was the Champions Tour player of the year, winning three times and earning over $2 milllion on the senior circuit.

Leonard, Justin (USA)

Born Dallas, Texas, 15 June 1972
Turned professional 1994

Winner of the 1997 Open at Royal Troon when he beat Jesper Parnevik and Darren Clarke into second

Sandy Lyle MBE (SCO)

Born Shrewsbury, 9 February 1958
Turned professional 1977

With his win in the 1985 Open Championship at Royal St George's he became the first British player to take the title since Tony Jacklin in 1969. He was also the first British player to win a Green Jacket in the Masters at Augusta in 1988 helped by a majestic 7-iron second shot out of sand at the last for a rare winning birdie 3. Although he represented England as an amateur at boys', youths' and senior level he became Scottish when he turned professional, something he was entitled to do at the time because his late father, the professional at Hawkstone Park, was a Scot. This is no longer allowed. He made his international début at age 14 and, two years later, qualified for and played 54 holes in the 1974 Open at Royal Lytham. A tremendously talented natural golfer who won 17 events on the European Tour, he fell a victim later in his career to becoming over-technical. Now lives in Perthshire and Florida. He was part of captain Ian Woosnam's backroom team for the 2006 Ryder Cup at the K Club in 2006. On the European Senior Tour, Sandy ended a 19 year wait for a tournament victory by winning the inaugural ISPS Handa Senior World Championship presented by Mission Hills China in 2011. He will be inducted into the World Golf Hall of Fame in 2012 after being selected through the international ballot.

place with a closing 65 and nearly won the title again in 1999 when he lost to Paul Lawrie in a four-hole play-off with the Scotsman and Jean Van de Velde at Carnoustie. In 1998 came from five back to beat Lee Janzen in the Players Championship and is remembered for his fight back against José Maria Olazábal on the final day of the 1999 Ryder Cup at Brookline. Four down after 11 holes he managed to share a half-point with the Spaniard to help America win the Cup. He was again a member of a winning Ryder Cup side when he played in the 2008 team captained by Paul Azinger at Valhalla but was in the losing side at Celtic Manor in 2010.

Lewis, Tom (ENG)

Born, Welwyn Garden City, Hertfordshire, 5 January 1991   Turned professional 2011

After a season in which he led The Open as an amateur and went on to surpass that feat in the paid ranks by winning in only his third start as a professional, it was fitting Lewis should be named as the European Tour's rookie of the year in 2011. It was a 65 in the first round at Royal St George's – the lowest score ever recorded by an amateur at The Open – which first brought the young Englishman, who won the Boys' Championship in 2009, to the attention of the wider golfing public. Just three months later in the final round of the Portugal Masters he uncorked another 65 to pull off the quickest victory by an affiliate member in Tour history. The son of Brian, a former Tour professional, Lewis' last act as an amateur was to help Great Britain and Ireland defeat the USA in the Walker Cup match at Royal Aberdeen

Levet, Thomas (FRA)

Born Paris, 9 September 1968
Turned professional 1988

Although he was the first Frenchman to play full time on the US Tour and still has a home in Florida, he lost his card and only regained his European Tour card

when he was invited, because of his French national ranking, to play in the 1998 Cannes Open – and won it. Sixth in the 1997 Open at Royal Troon he lost in a play-off to Ernie Els in the 2002 Open at Muirfield. Thomas made his Ryder Cup début at Oakland Hills in 2004, winning his singles game against Fred Funk. He is a gifted linguist speaking seven languages including Japanese. Has also turned his hand very successfully to commentating for French television. In 2011 he won the French Open but injured a food jumping into the lake at the 18th and had to withdraw from The Open at Royal St George's for which he had qualified earlier.

Liang, Wen-Chong (CHN)

Born Zhongshan, China, 2 August 1978
Turned professional 1999

Became the second Chinese winner on the European Tour when he won the Clariden Leu Singapore Open in 2007. His friend and mentor has been Zhang Lian-wei. Introduced to the game while still at school he plays with a most unorthodox swing but it works for him. Finished second to Ian Poulter in the Barclays Singapore Open in 2009 he finished second to Thongchai Jaidee on the Asian Tour's Order of Merit and in 2010 was No 1 on the rival OneAsia Tour's final ranking.

Littler, Gene (USA)

Born San Diego, California, 21 July 1930
Turned professional 1954

Winner of the 1953 US Amateur Championship he had a distinguished professional career scoring 26 victories on the US Tour between 1955 and 1977. He scored his only major triumph at Pebble Beach in 1971 when he beat Bob Goalby and Doug Sanders at Oakland Hills. He had been runner-up in the US Open in 1954 and was runner-up in the 1977 USPGA Championship and the 1970 US Masters. A seven-time Ryder Cup player between 1961 and 1977 he is a former winner of the Ben Hogan, Bobby Jones and Byron Nelson awards. He won the Hogan award after successfully beating cancer.

Love III, Davis (USA)

Born Charlotte, North Carolina, 13 April 1964
Turned professional 1985

Son of one of America's most highly rated teachers who died in a plane crash in 1988, Love has won only one major – the 1997 USPGA Championship at Winged Foot where he beat Justin Leonard by five shots. He has been runner-up in the US Open (1996) and the US Masters (1999). In the World Cup of Golf he won the title in partnership with Fred Couples four years in a row from 1992. He has played in five Ryder Cups and will captain the US Ryder Cup side at Medinah in 2012 and has not given up hope that he might even play in the match as well.

Lowry, Shane (IRL)

Born Clara, County Offaly, Ireland, 2 April 1987.
Turned professional 2009

The former Irish Amateur Close champion shot a 62 at County Louth GC in the Irish Open in 2009 and led from the second day. In the end in driving rain and a strong wind he held his nerve to beat Robert Rock in a play-off for the title becoming only the third amateur to win on the European Tour. Pablo Martin won as an amateur in 2007 and earlier in 2009 Danny Lee had won the Johnnie Walker Classic. Urged by some to remain amateur until after the Walker Cup he chose to turn professional immediately.

McDowell MBE, Graeme (NIR)

Born Ballymoney, Northern Ireland, 30 July 1979
Turned professional 2002

The first European golfer to win the US Open since Tony Jacklin 40 years earlier, he joined an elite group of golfers which includes Tiger Woods, Tom Watson and Jack Nicklaus who have won America's oldest title at Pebble Beach. McDowell enjoyed the most successful season of his career to date in 2010. Two weeks before his triumph in the US Open he also won the Celtic Manor Wales Open thanks to a thrilling performance over the weekend when he shot 63 and 64. The Ulsterman won the Andalucian Masters before the end of the season and finished the year No. 2 in the Race to Dubai. He was named Golfer of the Year by both the European and American Golf Writers. Late in the year he beat Tiger Woods in a play-off at Woods own tournament in California. A member of the winning Great Britain and Ireland Walker Cup team in 2001, he earned his European Tour card in just his fourth event as a professional. McDowell, who had been signed up to represent the Kungsangen Golf Club in Sweden just two weeks earlier, received a last minute sponsor's invitation to play there in the Volvo Scandinavian Masters ... and not only won the event but also broke the course record with an opening round of 64. He beat Trevor Immelman into second place with former USPGA champion Jeff Sluman third. McDowell's winning score of 270 – 14-under-par – earned him a first prize of over £200,000 and a place in the World Golf Championship NEC event at Sahalee in Washington. He was

the European Tour's 12th first-time winner of the season and at 23 the youngest winner of the title. In 2008, helped by victories in the Ballantine's Championship in Korea and the Barclays Scottish Open at Loch Lomond, he qualified automatically for the Ryder Cup at Valhalla and was one of the team's most successful performers. He also represented Europe at Celtic Manor in 2010 when on a tense last day he scored the vital winning point with victory over Hunter Mahan. Crucially he holed tricky downhill putt for a winning birdie at the 16th. In his amateur days he attended the University of Alabama where he was rated No 1 Collegiate golfer winning six of 12 starts with a stroke average of 69.6. In 2004, scored his second European success when he won the Telecom Italia Open. At the end of the year he was voted Irish Sport Personality of the Year and was honoured with an MBE for his services to golf in the 2011 New Year's Honours List by Her Majesty the Queen.

McEvoy OBE, Peter (ENG)

Born London, 22 March 1953

The most capped player for England who has had further success as a captain of Great Britain and Ireland's Eisenhower Trophy and Walker Cup sides. The Eisenhower win came in 1998 and the Walker Cup triumphs at Nairn in 1999 and at Ocean Forest, Sea Island, Georgia in 2001. On both occasions his team won 15–9. A regular winner of amateur events McEvoy was amateur champion in 1977 and 1978 and won the English stroke play title in 1980. He reached the final of the English Amateur the same year. In 1978 he played all four rounds in the Masters at Augusta and that year received the Association of Golf Writers' Trophy for his contribution to European golf. He was leading amateur in two Open Championships – 1978 and 1979. In 2003 he was awarded the OBE by Her Majesty the Queen for his services to golf. He received the Association of Golf Writers' Award in 2009 for his outstanding services to the game.

McGimpsey, Garth (IRL)

Born Bangor, 17 July 1955

A long hitter who was Irish long-driving champion in 1977 and UK long-driving title holder two years later. He was amateur champion in 1985 and Irish champion the same year and again in 1988. He played in three Walker Cup matches and competed in the home internationals for Ireland in 1978 and from 1980 to 1998. He captained the winning Great Britain and Ireland Walker Cup side that beat American 12½–11½ at Ganton in 2003 and again two years later in Chicago when the Americans won by a point.

McGinley, Paul (IRL)

Born Dublin, 16 December 1966
Turned professional 1991

Popular Irish golfer who turned to the game after breaking his left kneecap playing Gaelic football. With Padraig Harrington won the 1977 World Cup at

Kiawah and made his Ryder Cup début when the postponed 2001 match was played in 2002. In a tense finish to his match with Jim Furyk he holed from nine feet to get the half point the Europeans needed for victory. He made the side again in 2004 and was unbeaten as Europe beat the USA 18½–9½ and was one of three Irishmen who helped Europe win by the same margin in 2006. Europe might have won 19–9 had he not conceded a half to J.J. Henry at the last when a streaker ran over the line of the American's 20 foot downhill putt. In 2005 he finished third behind Colin Montgomerie and Michael Campbell in the European Tour Order of Merit making over £1.5 million. During the year he finished third behind Tiger Woods in the WGC–NEC Invitational at Firestone, lost the HSBC World Match-Play at Wentworth to Michael Campbell but ended the season on a high note with victory in the Volvo Masters of Andalucia. In 2007 he was appointed by Nick Faldo to be one of his vice-captains at the 2008 Ryder Cup but later declined in order to try and play himself into the side. He failed to do so. He was a surprise omission from the Great Britain and Ireland side against the Continent of Europe for the Seve Trophy when it was played in Ireland in 2007 but led the Great Britain and Ireland side to victory at St Nom La Breteche in 2009. In 2010 he accepted a vice-captain's role from Colin Montgomerie at the Ryder Cup at Celtic Manor and led Great Britain and Ireland to victory in the Vivendi Seve Trophy for a second time in 2011.

Macgregor, George (SCO)

Born Edinburgh, 19 August 1944

After playing in five Walker Cup matches he captained the side in 1991 and later served as chairman of The R&A Selection committee. He won the Scottish Stroke Play title in 1982 after having been runner up three times.

McIlroy MBE, Rory (NIR)

Born Holywood, May 4 1989
Turned professional 2007

Produced arguably the most exciting performance of 2011 when he led from the start to finish and won the US Open at Congressional. It was the highlight of an outstanding season in which he also won the Hong Kong Open by two shots and finished second behind Luke Donald in the Race to Dubai. In 2010 he shot a spectacular ten under par closing round of 62 to defeat Phil Mickelson by four shots in the Wells Fargo Championship. His eagle-birdie-par-birdie finish at Quail Hollow was electrifying. Twice winner of the Irish and European Amateur titles – he was the youngest winner of the Irish event in 2005 – Rory won the silver medal as leading amateur in the 2007 Open at Carnoustie. After turning professional he won his European Tour card when finishing third in the Alfred Dunhill Links Championship – only his second event as a pro. In 2008 he missed a 15 in. putt to lose a play-off to Jean-François Lucquin at the Omega European

Masters at Crans-sur-Sierre. In 2009 he won his first title – the Dubai Desert Classic – and finshed joint 3rd in the USPGA Championship behind winner Yong-Eun Yang. He finished third in the Race to Dubai after a season in which he had 12 top five finishes. In 2010 he had a first round 63 in The Open at St Andrews before an 80 on the second day meant he had to settle for a share of third place. He was also third in the US PGA and made his début in the Ryder Cup at Celtic Manor. Was surprisingly overlooked for the Rookie of the Year award on the US Tour in 2010. He received the MBE in the 2011 Queen's New Year Honours List.

McNulty, Mark (IRL)

Born Zimbabwe, 25 October 1953
Turned professional 1977

Recognised as one of the best putters in golf he was runner-up with the late Payne Stewart to Nick Faldo in the 1990 Open at St Andrews. Although hampered throughout his career by a series of injuries and illness he has scored 16 wins on the European Tour and 33 around the world including 23 on the South African Sunshine circuit. He won the South African Open in 1987 and again in 2001 holing an 18-foot putt on the last green at East London to beat Justin Rose. Qualified in 2004 to join the US Champions Tour and although originally from Zimbabwe he now plays out of Ireland. He lost a play-off at Sunningdale in the 2009 Senior Open to Loren Roberts. Injury prevented his playing much in 2010.

Mahan, Hunter (USA)

Born Orange, California, 17 May 1982
Turned professional 2003

Although born in California, Mahan was raised in Texas where he went on to win the USGA Junior Championship. An outstanding amateur, he attended Oklahoma State and finished 28th on his début in the Masters before joining the professional ranks. In 2007 he finished sixth in the Open and played on the Presidents Cup. A year later he represented the US in the Ryder Cup and was their top scorer with 3½ points. In 2010 he enjoyed his most successful year to date, winning the Phoenix Open before shooting 64 in the final round to win the WGC–Bridgestone Invitational. He was second in the US Ryder Cup standings for Celtic Manor, earning one of the eight automatic qualifying spots but lost a crucial last day singles to Graeme McDowell.

Mamat, Mardan (SIN)

Born Singapore, 31 October 1967
Turned professional 1994

Became the first Singaporean to win an Asian/ European joint venture in his home country when he took the Osim Singapore Masters in 2006.

Manassero, Matteo (ITA)

Born Verona, 19 April 1993

Made history when he became not only the youngest but the first Italian to win the Amateur Championship

Phil Mickelson (USA)

Born San Diego, California, 16 June 1970
Turned professional 1992

The winner of four major championships, Mickelson is the game's most successful left-handed golfer. He has won more than 50 events and has career earnings on the PGA Tour of $60 million. He has been particularly successful at Augusta where he's won the Masters three times in 2004, 2006 and 2010. He also won the PGA Championship in 2005 at Baltusrol. A hugely gifted amateur golfer, the left-hander won his first PGA Tour event when he was still a student at Arizona State University. When he was nine he watched on TV as Seve Ballesteros won the Masters and told his mother he would be a Masters' champion one day too. He was proved right 22 years later when he pulled off his first major success thanks to a run of five birdies over the closing seven holes, including an 18 foot putt on the last to thwart Ernie Els.

Right-handed in everything else, Mickelson played golf left-handed after watching his father swing a club and mirroring the action. The first left-hander to win the US Amateur, he was only the sixth amateur ever to win a PGA Tour event when he came out on top at the Northern Telecom Open in 1991. He turned professional a year later and broke into the world's top ten in 1996 where he has remained ever since.

His brilliant short game helped set up a second major triumph on the final hole at the PGA when he pitched from greenside rough to a couple of feet and finish a stroke in front of Thomas Bjorn. The following spring he won his second successive major and third in all thanks to another expert performance at Augusta. In 2010, he won the Masters for the third time by carding a final round of 67 to defeat Lee Westwood by three strokes. His total of 16 under par was the lowest score at Augusta since Tiger Woods in 2001. Perhaps the highlight of his fourth major victory came in Saturday's third round when he made back to back eagles on the 13th and 14th holes. Both his wife Amy and mother Mary have been recovering from breast cancer while Phil himself was diagnosed with arthritis.

with a 3 and 1 victory over Sam Hutsby in the final at Formby in 2009. He was only the third golfer in the 124-year history of the event to win after leading the qualifying. Later in the year earned the Silver Medal as leading amateur in The Open at Turnberry where he finished joint 13th. After playing all four rounds in The Masters he turned professional and made his début in the BMW Italian Open. He quickly secured his Tour card and when he won the Castello Masters he became the youngest title winner in European Tour history. In 2011 he won again in Malaysia.

Marsh MBE, Dr David (ENG)

Born Southport, Lancashire, 29 April 1934

Twice winner of the English Amateur Championship in 1964 and 1970, he was captain of The R&A in 1990/1991. He played in the 1971 Walker Cup match at St Andrews and helped the home side win by scoring a vital one hole victory in the singles against Bill Hyndman. He captained the team in 1973 and 1975 and had a distinguished career as a player and then captain for England between 1956 and 1972. He was chairman of The R&A selection committee from 1979 to 1983 and in 1987 was president of the English Golf Union. He was appointed an MBE in the 2011 New Year's Honours List for his voluntary services to amateur golf.

Marsh, Graham (AUS)

Born Kalgoorlie, Western Australia, 14 January 1944
Turned professional 1968

A notable Australian who followed up his international playing career by gaining a reputation for designing fine courses. Although he played in Europe, America and Australasia he spent most of his time on the Japanese circuit where he had 17 wins between 1971 and 1982 . He won 11 times in Europe and scored victories also in the United States, India, Thailand and Malaysia.

Martin, Pablo (ESP)

Born Malaga, 20 April 1986
Turned professional 2007

Became the first amateur to win on the PGA European Tour when he edged out Raphaël Jacquelin of France by a shot in the Estoril Open de Portugal in 2007. A former British Boys' champion in 2001, he played in two Eisenhower Trophy competitions and two Palmer Cups. Winner of the Jack Nicklaus award for top national amateur in 2006 when at Oklahoma State University he gave up his studies to join the professional rank. Curiously another Oklahoma "cowboy", Scott Verplank, has also won as an amateur in his case on the PGA Tour. Martin won the Alfred Dunhill Championship at the start of the 2010 and 2011 European seasons.

Mason, Carl (ENG)

Born Buxton, Derbyshire, 25 June 1953
Turned professional 1973

Carl won twice on the main European Tour in 1994 but has played his best golf on the European Seniors Tour. He finished second on the money list in his first two years and first for the next three years. In

Johnny Miller (USA)

Born San Francisco, California, 29 April 1947
Turned professional 1969

Now perhaps best known as an often insightful and invariably acerbic TV commentator for NBC in America, Miller won two major titles, The Open and the US Open, during the early Seventies when he was one of the leading players in world golf. Like a comet, Miller's game burned brightly for a short period of time. During 1974, when he won five of the first 11 events on the PGA Tour, and 1975 he won 12 tournaments in total and was the most successful player in the game, earning a clothing sponsorship deal worth $1 million. He recalls that period of grace as a "sort of golfing Nirvana."

The high point of his career came at Royal Birkdale in 1976 when he followed in the footsteps of Tony Lema, a fellow member of the Olympic Club in San Francisco, and lifted the Claret Jug. He thwarted both Seve Ballesteros and Jack Nicklaus by the judicious use of a 1 iron off the tee which helped the American card a closing round of 66 and win the championship by six shots. He was also second behind Tom Weiskopf at Royal Troon in 1973. That was the season he secured victory in the US Open in spite of trailing the leader by six shots after 54 holes. He started the final round at Oakmont with four consecutive birdies and eventually posted 63 – the lowest closing score ever recorded in America's national championship. He found all 18 greens in regulation and racked up nine birdies after firing ten of his approach shots inside 15 feet.

After his success at Birkdale, however, Miller wouldn't win another tournament until 1980. He lost the burning desire to win which spurs on the greatest players and became a victim of the yips. Putting with his eyes closed for much of the time, Miller was a grandfather when he won his last PGA Tour event, the AT&T Pebble Beach Pro-Am in 1994. All told, he won 32 events as a professional around the world after first making a name for himself as an amateur in the Sixties by winning the US Junior Amateur title. A member of the World Golf Hall of Fame, he owns a golf design company.

2004 and again in 2007 he won five events in a season.

Matsuyama, Hideki (JPN)

Born Japan, 25 February 1992

Yet to join the paid ranks at the close of 2011, Matsuyama won his first professional event last year after beating an impressive field which included defending champion Ryo Ishikawa and the Masters champion Charl Schwartzel to win the Taiheiyo Masters in Japan. He was only the third amateur to win on the Japanese Tour and had to eagle the final hole to secure victory. The 19-year-old first caught the eye of the golfing world beyond Japan when he finished 27th on his début at the Masters and earned the accolade of low amateur at Augusta. Ranked fourth in the World Amateur Golf Ranking, he's won the Asian Amateur twice as well as the Japan Collegiate Championship and the World University Games.

Micheel, Shaun (USA)

Born Orlando, Florida, 5 January 1969
Turned professional 1962

Surprise winner of the USPGA Championship at Oak Hill in 2003. He fired rounds of 69, 68, 69 and 70 for a winning total of 276. He completed his victory with one of the most brilliant approach irons from the rough to just one foot of the hole at the last. In 2006 at Medinah, he finished second to Tiger Woods again in the USPGA Championship. Later he beat Woods en route to the final of the HSBC World Match Play at Wentworth but lost in the final to Paul Casey.

Milligan, Jim (SCO)

Born Irvine, Ayrshire, 15 June 1963

The 1988 Scottish Amateur champion had his moment of international glory in the 1989 Walker Cup which was won by the Great Britain and Ireland side for only the third time in the history of the event and for the first time on American soil. With GB&I leading by a point at Peachtree in Atlanta only Milligan and his experienced opponent Jay Sigel were left on the course. The American looked favourite to gain the final point and force a draw when two up with three to play but Milligan hit his approach from 100 yards to a few inches to win the 16th with a birdie then chipped in after both had fluffed chips to square at the 17th. The last was halved leaving the Great Britain and Ireland side historic winners by a poin.

Mize, Larry (USA)

Born Augusta, Georgia, 23 September 1958
Turned professional 1980

Only local player ever to win the Masters and he did it in dramatic style holing a 140-foot pitch and run at the second extra hole to edge out Greg Norman and Seve Ballesteros. He had made the play-off by holing a 10-foot birdie on the final green. In 1993 he beat an international field to take the Johnnie Walker World Championship title at Tryall in Jamaica. His middle name is Hogan.

Molinari, Edoardo (ITA)

Born Turin, 11 February 1981
Turned professional 2006

Became the first Italian to win the US Amateur Championship when he beat Dillon Dougherty 4 and 3 in the 2005 final at Merion, Pennsylvania. The 24-year-old, who has earned an engineering degree in his home country, joined his brother Francesco on the European Tour in 2006. He and his brother represented Italy in the 2007 and 2009 World Cup of Golf at Mission Hills in Shenzhen, China and were successful the second time. In 2009 he won three times and topped the Challenge Tour and then, a few weeks later, won the Dunlop Phoenix Tournament in Japan beating Robert Karlsson in a play-off. In 2010 he won twice in Scotland at Loch Lomond and Gleneagles where he finished with three birdies to join his brother in the 2010 Ryder Cup team.

Molinari, Francesco (ITA)

Born Turin, 8 November 1982
Turned professional 2004

Brother of Eduardo Molinari, winner of the US Amateur in 2005, he won his first European Tour title when he took the Italian Open at Castello di Tolcinasco in 2006. Partnering his brother Eduardo he gave Italy a first win in the World Cup of Golf in 2009. A year later he made his Ryder Cup début with his brother at Celtic Manor in 2010 and a few weeks later duelled with and beat the then World No 1 Lee Westwood in the WGC–HSBC Champions event in Shanghai. Played for the Continent in the Vivendi Seve Trophy in 2011.

Montgomerie OBE, Colin (SCO)

Born Glasgow, 23 June 1963
Turned professional 1987

Europe's most consistent golfer who topped the Order of Merit an unprecedented seven years in a row between 1993 and 1999 and again in 2004. He never won a major but came close several times particularly in the US Open. He lost a play-off for the US title to Ernie Els in 1994, was pipped by the South African again in 1997 and was joint second behind Geoff Ogilvy in 2006. In 1992 he was third to Tom Kite. He has come close in The Open and the US PGA Championship as well. He was Open runner-up to Tiger Woods in 2005 at St Andrews and in 1995 he was beaten in a play-off for the USPGA Championship at the Riviera CC in Los Angeles by Australian Steve Elkington who birdied the last three holes to force a play-off and the first extra hole to beat him.. He has had 31 victories around the world and has played with distinction in seven Ryder Cups matches. In 2010 he captained the side to victory at Celtic Manor. He has twice won the Association of Golf Writers' Golfer of the Year award and has been three times Golfer of the Year in Europe. He was honoured by

Her Majesty the Queen for his record-breaking golfing exploits with an MBE which was later upgraded to OBE. In 2007 he teamed up with Marc Warren to win the World Cup of Golf at Mission Hills in China. It was Scotland's first win in the 54-year history of the event. For one reason or another he has found it difficult to hit his best form in the past two years but, free of his Ryder Cup duties, he is determined to move back up the world rankings after dropping from inside the top 50 to outside the top 400. As an amateur he played in the 1985 and 1987 matches and is a former Scottish amateur champion.

Nagle, Kel (AUS)

Born North Sydney, 21 December 1920
Turned professional 1946

In the dramatic Centenary Open at St Andrews in 1960 he edged out Arnold Palmer, winner already that year of the Masters and US Open, to become champion. It was the finest moment in the illustrious career of a golfer who has been a wonderful ambassador for his country. Along with Peter Thomson he competed nine times in the World Cup winning the event in 1954. He is an honorary member of the Royal and Ancient Golf Club of St Andrews and was inducted into the World Golf Hall of Fame in 2007.

Nelson, Larry (USA)

Born Fort Payne, Alabama, 10 September 1947
Turned professional 1971

Often underrated he learned to play by reading Ben Hogan's The Five Fundamentals of Golf and broke 100 first time out and 70 after just nine months. Active as well these days on course design he has won the Jack Nicklaus award. He has been successful in the US Open (1983 at Oakmont) and two USPGA Championships (in 1981 at the Atlanta Athletic Club and in 1987 after a play-off with Lanny Wadkins at PGA National). Three times a Ryder Cup player he has competed equally successfully as a Senior having won 15 titles. He did not play as a youngster but visited a driving range after completing his military service and was hooked. He was named Senior PGA Tour Player of the Year for finishing top earner and winning six times in 2000. At the end of his third full season on the Senior Tour and after 87 events he had won just short of $10 million.

Newton, Jack (AUS)

Born Sydney, 30 January 1950
Turned professional 1969

Runner-up to Tom Watson after a play-off in the 1975 Open at Carnoustie and runner-up to Seve Ballesteros in the 1980 Masters at Augusta, he was a popular personality on both sides of the Atlantic and in his native Australia only to have his playing career ended prematurely when he walked into the

Jack Nicklaus (USA)

Born Columbus, Ohio, 21 January 1940
Turned professional 1961

In the course of a phenomenal playing career which spanned five decades and included 18 victories as a professional in the majors as well as 118 tournament wins around the world, the Golden Bear has been hailed as the outstanding golfer of the 20th century and perhaps the greatest player who ever lived. His career in golf was so illustrious that the magazine, *Sports Illustrated*, chose Nicklaus as the outstanding individual male athlete of the previous century in any sport.

As a fair haired bear of a boy with broad shoulders, a crew cut and the seeds of a revolutionary power game, Jack William Nicklaus from Ohio, in his autobiography, remembers his teenage self as junior version of "the ugly American". If that judgement from the elder statesman seems blunt, he developed the habits of an unrelenting serial winner as an amateur which served him well throughout his professional career. He won his first US national title at 17, made the cut in the US Open at 18 and, as a 19-year-old, won the US Amateur, played in a winning US Walker Cup side at Muirfield and reached the quarter-finals of The Amateur at Royal St George's.

Billed by the American media as "the kid who can beat the pros", in 1960 he was 13th at the Masters as well as runner-up to Arnold Palmer in the US Open at Cherry Hills, where he set a record score for an amateur. Before joining the paid ranks, he won the US Amateur again, was part of a winning US Walker Cup side on home turf and recorded another top four finish at the 1961 US Open.

If the success of his amateur career placed an onerous burden on Nicklaus when he joined the paid ranks in 1962, his first season as a pro made light of that load. From the moment he made his first start in the Los Angeles Open, Nicklaus set the bench mark for a rookie season in golf. He finished in the top ten 16 times and won three tournaments – notably the US Open at Oakmont, only his 17th event as a pro – where he defeated Arnold Palmer in a play-off. In a sign of what was to come in the championships which matter most, he also finished 15th at the Masters, 32nd at the Open and third at the US PGA.

By the time he crossed the Swilken Bridge for the last time in his final major appearance in The Open at St Andrews in 2005, he'd completed an astonishing record of achievment. He won The Open in 1966, 1970 and 1978, the last two at St Andrews. He was runner-up in the oldest major seven times and third on two further occasions. He followed up that US Open win in 1962 with more victories in 1967, 1972 and 1980 and came second four times. He won five US PGA titles in 1963, 1971, 1973, 1975 and 1980 and was runner-up four times and third on two further occasions. He won six Masters in 1963, 1965, 1966, 1972, 1975 and 1986 when, at the age of 46, he became the oldest champion to slip into a Green Jacket. In addition he was runner-up four times and twice third at Augusta. In 1966 he became the first player to successfully defend the Masters. When he retired from competition, Nicklaus had become the only golfer in history to win each of the majors at least three times.

Outisde the majors, he won the Players Championship three times, no fewer than six Australian Opens and played in six Ryder Cups, winning on five occasions, captaining two more in 1983 at Palm Beach Gardens when America won narrowly and in 1987 at Muirfield Village where his side were losers for the first time on home soil.

A shrewd thinker about the game, it was his idea Continental golfers should be included alongside British and Irish players in a European side from 1979. The change transformed the Ryder Cup. Ten years earlier, in a memorable act of sportsmanship, he conceded the 18-inch putt that Tony Jacklin needed to hole for a half at the last when the overall result of the match depended on the result of that game. "I don't think you would have missed," he told the Englishman, "but in the circumstances I would never give you the opportunity".

After winning 73 times on the PGA Tour, he won a further ten times on the US Champions Tour between 1990 and 1996. He has garnered every honour in golf including the Byron Nelson, Ben Hogan and Walter Hagen awards. He was the US top money earner in 1964, 1965, 1967, 1971, 1972, 1973, 1975 and 1976 and is an honorary member of the Royal and Ancient Golf Club of St Andrews. Bobby Jones once said of Nicklaus that 'he played a game with which I am not familiar'. With the constant support of his wife Barbara, Nicklaus has been the personification of all that is good about the game. He joined Arnold Palmer as an honorary starter at the Masters in 2010.

Nicklaus is also a renowned golf course architect who was instrumental in forging the signature design business. So far, he's designed 280 courses world-wide and his company, Nicklaus Design, has 350 courses open for play. He's captained the US Presidents Cup side against the Rest of the World on four occasions so far and when the match is held at his beloved Muirfield Village in 2013 it will mark " my last involvement in anything significant in the game of golf."

Greg Norman (AUS)

Born Mount Isa, Queensland, 10 February 1955
Turned professional 1976

Three times the leading money winner on the PGA Tour, the Australian spent 331 weeks as world No 1 during a career in which he won 91 professional tournaments around the globe. The undoubted highlights of a successful career were his triumphs in 1986 and 1993 at The Open. The fact that he finished in the top ten at the four professional majors on no fewer than 29 occasions – more than 38 per cent of the championships he entered – stands as testimony to his consistency of performance.

If there's a debate that he lost majors he should have won, Norman's most noteworthy achievements came at Turnberry, where he carded a remarkable score of 63 as part of a five shot victory, and at Royal St George's, where his closing 64 set a low winning aggregate of 264 and overcame Nick Faldo by two strokes.

Fair and handsome as well as long off the tee, Norman was handed the moniker of "Great White Shark" during a staging of the Masters in 1981. The nickname was apt and today Norman's various business interests are named Great White Shark Enterprises. Perhaps an even more successful entrepreneur than he was a golfer, Norman didn't take up the sport until he was 15. He'd caddied for his mother and asked to borrow her clubs. Two years later he was a scratch player. He won for the first time as a pro in Australia at the West Lakes Classic in 1976, won the Martini in Europe a year later and first made his mark in the US at the Kemper in 1984. All told he won 20 times on the PGA Tour as well as 71 other events around the world.

For all his success, he also gained a reputation for coming up short in the biggest championships. He lost out in three different types of major play-offs – the 1987 Masters to Larry Mize and the 1993 US PGA to Paul Azinger in sudden death, The Open to Mark Calcavecchia at Royal Troon in a four-hole play-off in 1989 and the US Open over 18 holes to Fuzzy Zoeller at Winged Foot in 1984. In 1986 he led going into the final round of all four majors and won once. Perhaps his most painful loss was at the Masters in 1996 when he led by six strokes going into the final round and lost to Faldo by five shots.

Norman turned the clock back in 2008 at Birkdale to finish third behind Padraig Harrington in The Open after leading with nine holes to play. In 2011 and 2009 he captained the Rest of the World against America in the Presidents Cup. Due to business interests and back issues, he now only plays a handful of events each year.

---

whirling propeller of a plane at Sydney airport. He lost an eye, an arm and had considerable internal injuries but the quick action of a surgeon who happened to be around saved his life. Learned to play one-handed and still competes in pro-ams successfully. Until his retirement in 2000 he was chairman of the Australasian Tour and for many years was Australia's most respected golf commentator in the days when Channel Seven organised the coverage.

Nirat, Chapchai (THA)

Born Pitsanulok, Thailand, 5 June 1983
Turned professional 1998

Scored his first European Tour International circuit victory when he led from start to finish in the TCL Classic. He was the 13th Asian to win and was the ninth first-time winner of the 2007 season. He covered the first 36 holes in 127 (61, 66).

Nobilo, Frank (NZL)

Born Auckland, 14 May 1960
Turned professional 1979

Injury affected his playing career but he remains one of his country's most popular commentators with the Golf Channel. After winning regularly in Europe he moved to America where in 1997 he won the Greater

Greensboro Classic. He has represented New Zealand in nine World Cup matches between 1982 and 1999, played in 11 Alfred Dunhill Cups and three Presidents Cup sides. In 2009 he was deputy captain to Greg Norman for the Rest of the World team.

Noh Seung-Yul (KOR)

Born Seoul 29 May 1991
Turned professional 2007

Korean Junior Amateur and Amateur champion in 2005 Noh won his first professional event in 2008 at the Midea China Classic. He did even better in 2010 when he played a superb pitch at the last to beat KJ Choi in the Maybank Malaysian Masters which qualified him for a European Tour card. In his first season he finished 34th in the Race to Dubai and topped the Asian Tour's Order of Merit.

North, Andy (USA)

Born Thorp, Wisconsin, 9 March 1950
Turned professional 1972

Although this tall American found it difficult to win Tour events he did pick up two US Open titles. His first Championship success came at Cherry Hills in Denver in 1986 when he edged out Dave Stockton and J.C. Snead and the second at Oakland Hills in 1985 when he finished just a shot ahead of Dave Barr,

T.C. Chen and Denis Watson who had been penalised a shot during the Championship for waiting longer than the regulation 10 seconds at one hole to see if his ball would drop into the cup. North is now a golf commentator.

O'Connor Sr, Christy (IRL)
Born Galway, 21 December 1924
Turned professional 1946

Never managed to win The Open but came close on three occasions finishing runner-up to Peter Thomson in 1965 and being third on two other occasions. Played in ten Ryder Cup matches between 1955 and 1973 and scored 24 wins in tournament play between 1955 and 1972. Known affectionately as 'Himself' by Irish golfing fans who have long admired his talent with his clubs. He is a brilliant shot maker. He is an Honorary Member of the PGA European Tour. In 2006 a special dinner was staged in his honour in Dublin by the Irish Food Board on the eve of the Ryder Cup. In 2009 he was inducted into the World Golf Hall of Fame.

O'Connor Jr, Christy (IRL)
Born Galway, 19 August 1948
Turned professional 1965

Nephew of Christy Sr, he finished third in the 1985 Open Championship. A winner on the European and Safari circuits he won the 1999 and 2000 Senior British Open – only the second man to successfully defend. Played in two Ryder Cup matches hitting a career best 2-iron to the last green at The Belfry in 1989 to beat Fred Couples and ensure a drawn match enabling Europe to keep the trophy. His US Champions Tour career was interrupted when he broke a leg in a motorcycle accident.

Ogilvy, Geoff (AUS)
Born Adelaide, South Australia
Turned professional 1998

He became the first Australian to win a major since Steve Elkington's success in the USPGA Championship in 1992 when he won the US Open at Winged Foot beating Colin Montgomerie, Jim Furyk and Phil Mickelson into second place. In 2007 he was beaten by Henrik Stenson in the final of the Accenture Match Play Championship and finished 14th on the US money list. In 2009 he won the Accenture Match-play Championship beating Paul Casey in the final and in 2010 won the Australian Open for the first time.

Olazábal, José María (ESP)
Born Fuenterrabia, 5 February 1966
Turned professional 1985

Twice a winner of the Masters, his second triumph was particularly emotional. He had won in 1994 but had to withdraw from the 1995 Ryder Cup with a foot problem eventually diagnosed as rheumatoid polyarthritis in three joints of the right foot and two

of the left. He was out of golf for 18 months but treatment from Munich doctor Hans-Wilhelm Muller-Wohlfahrt helped him back to full fitness after a period when he was house bound and unable to walk. At that point it seemed as if his career was over, but he came back in 1999 to beat Davis Love III by two shots at Augusta. With over 20 victories in Europe and a further seven abroad, the son of a Real Sebastian greenkeeper who took up the game at the age of four has been one of the most popular players in the game. He competed in seven Ryder Cups between 1987 and 2006 frequently forming the most successful Cup partnership with Severiano Ballesteros winning 11 and losing only two of their 15 games together. He was Nick Faldo's backroom assistant at Valhalla in 2008 and will captain the side at some time in the future. Although he was sidelined again through rheumatic injury in 2008 he still believes he can make the side in 2010. He is a former British Boys', Youths' and Amateur champion. His best performances in The Open have been third behind Nick Faldo in the 1992 Championship at Muirfield and behind Tiger Woods in the 2005 event at St Andrews. Olazábal, who played on both sides of the Atlantic in 2005, finished 10th on the European Money list finishing strongly with a 2nd place finish in the Linde German Masters, victory in the Open de Mallorca and a third place behind Paul McGinley in the Volvo Masters of Andalucia. In 2006 he regained his place in the Ryder Cup team and played well with Sergio García in the fourballs, winning twice. He beat Phil Mickelson in the singles. He is now an irregular competitor on the European and PGA Tours as a result of his continuing rheumatic problems. In 2009 Olazabal, one of the most courageous of competitors, was inducted into the World Golf Hall of Fame. He asked close friend Severiano Ballesteros to do the oration. He has been selected to captain the European Ryder Cup side in America this year.

O'Leary, John (IRL)
Born Dublin, 19 August 1949
Turned professional 1979

After a successful career as a player including victory in the Carrolls Irish Open in 1982 he retired because of injury and now is director of golf at the Buckinghamshire Club. He is a member of the PGA European Tour Board of Directors.

O'Meara, Mark (USA)
Born Goldsboro, North Carolina, 13 January 1957
Turned professional 1980

A former US Amateur Champion in 1979 Mark was 41 when he won his first Major – the US Masters at Augusta. That week in 1998 he did not three putt once on Augusta's glassy greens. Three months later he won The Open at Royal Birkdale battling with, among others, Tiger Woods with whom he has had a particular friendship. He is the oldest player to win two Majors in the same year and was chosen as PGA Player of the Year that season. When he closed birdie, birdie to win the Masters he joined Arnold Palmer and Art Wall as the only players to do that and became only the fifth player in Masters history to win without leading in the first three rounds. He won his Open championship title in a four hole play-off against Brian Watts. O'Meara played in five Ryder Cups between 1985 and 1999.

Oosterhuis, Peter (ENG)

Born London, 3 May 1948
Turned professional 1968

Twice runner up in The Open Championship in 1974 and 1982, he was also the leading British player in 1975 and 1978. He finished third in the US Masters in 1973, had multiple wins on the European Tour and in Africa and won the Canadian Open on the US Tour in 1981. He played in six Ryder Cups partnering Nick Faldo at Royal Lytham and St Annes in 1977 when Faldo made his début. He was top earner in Europe four years in a row from 1971. Following his retirement from top-line golf he turned to commentary work for the Golf Channel CBS and SKY. His contribution to European professional golf is frequently underrated.

Oosthuizen, Louis (RSA)

Born Mossel Bay, 19 October 1982
Turned professional 2003

One of the chosen few who have won The Open at St Andrews – he has Bobby Jones, Jack Nicklaus, Nick Faldo and Tiger Woods for company. His victory in the 150th anniversary staging of the game's oldest championship was as comprehensive as it was unexpected. Oosthuizen won by seven strokes from Lee Westwood in what was only his ninth appearance in a majors. He joined Bobby Locke, Gary Player and Ernie Els in the small band of South Africans who have their names on the Claret Jug. A graduate of the Ernie Els Foundation, Oosthuizen won the Irish Amateur and together with Charl Schwartzel won the World Junior Team Championship for South Africa before turning professional. He once shot 57 over his home course at Mossel Bay and had to persuade his family, who have strong connections with tennis, that he wanted to be a golfer. He enjoyed his breakthrough win on the European Tour in 2010 at the Open de Andalucia.

Ozaki, 'Jumbo' Masashi (JPN)

Born Kaiman Town, Tokushima, 24 January 1947
Turned professional 1980

Along with Isao Aoki is Japan's best known player, but unlike Aoki has maintained his base in Japan where he has scored over 80 victories. His only overseas win was the New Zealand Open early in his career. He is a golfing icon in his native country. His two brothers Joe (Naomichi) and Jet also play professionally. In 2005 he was declared bankrupt. In 2011 he was elected into the World Golf Hall of Fame.

Pagunsan, Juvic (PHI)

Born Manila, 11 May 1978
Turned professional 2006

Winner of the Asian Tour of Merit in 2011, he was the first golfer from the Phillipines to achieve that status. Although he didn't win in 2011, his second place finish after a play-off at the Barclays Singapore Open, where he won $666,660, propelled him to the top spot on the money list. Taught by his father, Juanito, Juvic took up the game at 13 and was a successful amateur, winning the Phillipine, Thailand and Malaysian championships in 2005. He joined the paid ranks a year later and his first win on the Asian Tour was the Pertamina Indonesia President Invitational in 2007.

Parnevik, Jesper (SWE)

Born Danderyd, Stockholm, 7 March 1965
Turned professional 1986

Son of a well-known Swedish entertainer he is one of the most extrovert of golfers best known for his habit of wearing a baseball cap with the brim turned up and brightly coloured drain-pipe style trousers. Winner of events on both sides of the Atlantic he plays most of his golf these days in America. He made history in 1995 when he became the first Swede to win in Sweden when he took the Scandinavian Masters at Barsebäck in Malmo. Has twice finished runner-up in The Open. At Turnberry in 1994 he was two ahead but made a bogey at the last and was passed by Nick Price who finished with an eagle and a birdie in the last three holes. He led by two with a round to go in 1998 but shot 73 and finished tied second with Darren Clarke behind Justin Leonard at Royal Troon. Played in the 1997 and 1999 Ryder Cup teaming up successfully with Sergio García to win three and a half points in 1999. Was also in the 2002 team and halved with Tiger Woods in the singles. He has had two hip operations and at one stage began eating volcanic dust to cleanse his system.

Parry Craig (AUS)

Born Sunshine, Victoria, Australia, 12 January 1966
Turned professional 1985

Australian Parry, winner of 18 titles internationally including the 2002 World Golf Championship NEC Invitational at Sahalee in Washington where he picked up his largest career cheque – $1 million. After 15 years of trying to win in America the chances of him being successful at Salahee seemed slim having missed the four previous cuts. However, the 300–1 long-shot played and putted beautifully covering the last 48 holes without making a bogey to win by four from another Australian Robert Allenby and American Fred Funk. Tiger Woods, trying to win the event for a record fourth-successive year was fourth. Only Gene Sarazen and Walter Hagen have ever won the same four titles in successive years. It was Parry's 236th tournament in the United States and moved him from 118th in the world to 45th. In 2004 he eagled the

Arnold Palmer (USA)

Born Latrobe, Pennsylvania, 10 September 1929
Turned professional 1954

It is a measure of the charismatic appeal of Arnold Palmer that when GQ magazine listed the 25 "coolest" athletes of all time in 2011, the golfer from Latrobe should figure in the countdown some 38 years after his last PGA Tour win. For all the considerable success he enjoyed in the late Fifties and early Sixties, winning seven major titles between 1958 and 1964, it was the manner in which Palmer played the game rather than the championships he won which sealed his reputation. A handsome man with a thrillingly aggressive approach to the game, Palmer was hugely popular with the global audience for golf and when his competitive days were behind him he was able to build a lifelong career as a businessman and course designer because he connected so effectively with the public.

Palmer's high profile coincided with the expansion of televised golf. Unlike the more consistent power play produced by his rival and friend Jack Nicklaus, Palmer's risk-taking generated excitement for TV viewers. His flamboyant style duly helped to grow interest in the game as a spectator sport, both in America and around the world. At Augusta, "Arnie's Army" tracked his every move at The Masters while in Britain his decision to play in the oldest major is credited with helping Keith Mackenzie, then the secretary of the Royal and Ancient Golf Club of St Andrews, revive the fortunes of The Open. Palmer is now a distinguished honorary member of The R&A as well as Augusta National.

Born in Pennsylvania, he was taught by his father, Deacon, the professional and greenkeeper at Latrobe, before attending Wake Forest University on a golf scholarship. His amateur career between 1946 and 1954 delivered 26 victories, including the US Amateur title. After the death of his friend Bud Worsham, he spent three years with the US coastguard. Palmer then decided to try his luck as a professional. He recalls the season of 1954 as the turning point in his life, that victory in the US Amateur coinciding with the moment when the golf press first noticed his go-for-broke style, the habit of hitching up his pants as he walked the fairway and the open manner in which he shared his emotions and engaged with spectators. It was the summer when lightning struck.

In the early years of his career as a pro, Palmer was an irresistible force. His most dominant period was between 1960 and 1963 when he won 29 PGA Tour events in four seasons. In 1960 having already won The Masters and US Open he came to St Andrews for the Centenary Open, hoping to become the first golfer since Ben Hogan in 1953 to win three majors in a season. Although he lost out to Kel Nagle, Palmer would return to the British linksland and win consecutive stagings of The Open in 1961 and 1962. It was those victories which turned Palmer into an international sporting icon rather than just an American celebrity.

Along with Nicklaus and Gary Player he was a member of the Big Three – a concept developed by his manager, the late Mark McCormack – who signed Palmer as IMG's first client. It was the Big Three who effectively created the commercial environment which has made golf such a lucrative sport around the world. All told, Palmer won 61 tournaments in America and 92 around the world, including The Masters of 1958, 1960,1962 and 1964; the US Open of 1960 and the brace of Claret Jugs. He was second in the US PGA three times and narrowly missed out on the career Grand Slam. He played in six Ryder Cups and was US captain twice. He also captained the US in the 1996 Presidents Cup. He was the leading money winner on the PGA Tour four times. Palmer retired from competitive golf in October 2006.

At 81, he still features among the highest earners in the game. Palmer helped to launch the now hugely successful Golf Channel in the United States and presents the Palmer Cup for annual competition between the best young college golfers in America and Europe. He is an honorary starter at The Masters. The owner of Latrobe Country Club as well as Bay Hill in Orlando, he is arguably the most successfully marketed sportsman of all time.

---

hardest hole on the US Tour in a play-off with Scott Verplank to win the Ford Championship in Florida.

Pate, Jerry (USA)

Born Macon, Georgia, 16 September 1953
Turned professional 1975

Winner of the 1976 US Open when he hit a 5-iron across water to three feet at the 72nd hole at the Atlanta Athletic Club. He was a member of what is regarded as the strongest ever Ryder Cup side that

beat the Europeans at Walton Heath in 1981. Has now retired from golf and commentates occasionally on American television.

Pavin, Corey (USA)

Born Oxnard, California, 26 May 1961
Turned professional 1983

Although not one of golf's longer hitters he battled with powerful Greg Norman to take the 1995 US Open title at Shinnecock Hills. A runner-up

Gary Player (RSA)

Born Johannesburg, 1 November 1935
Turned professional 1953

South Africa's pre-eminent sportsman of the 20th century, he celebrated his 50th anniversary as a professional in 2003 and continues to enjoy international admiration for a glorious career which saw the golfer win 176 titles around the world. The highlights of his playing days came in the majors where he won nine championships between 1959 and 1978 as well as nine senior major titles between 1986 and 1997. As the world's most travelled sportsman, clocking up over 14 million air miles, he won at least one tournament in 27 consecutive seasons.

Tipping 5ft 7ins and weighing 11 stone, he was often said to have done more with less than any other player. As well as introducing a revolutionary fitness programme to increase distance, Player's strength of mind was his most enduring asset. His craving for success was insatiable.

Although his swing was flat, Player was one of the most accomplished bunker players the game has ever seen. This prolific winner claimed the Claret Jug on three occasions, in 1959 at Muirfield, 1968 at Carnoustie and 1974 at Royal Lytham and St Annes. He's the only 20th century golfer who succeeded in winning The Open in three different decades.

He also won The Masters three times in 1961, 1974 and 1978, the US PGA championship in 1962 and 1972, and completed the Grand Slam of major titles when he succeeded at the US Open in 1965. His victory that summer at Bellrive at the age of 29, after a play-off against Kel Nagle, was the first by an international player since Ted Ray in 1920. Tiger Woods, Jack Nicklaus, Ben Hogan and Gene Sarazen are the only other players to win all four professional majors.

After taking up the sport at 14, Player spent much of his time during his teenage years on the golf course where all those diligent hours of practice made him a solid judge of distance and a perceptive reader of greens. Perhaps his greatest gift, though, was his indomitability. Player simply never gave up. When he won his first Open at Muirfield – this was in the era when the competitors played 36 holes on the last day – he started the third round eight strokes behind the leader. "Gary has that thing inside him, as much as anyone I ever saw, that champions have," observed Nicklaus.

Player's knack of winning tournaments from situations which many of his peers would have regarded as hopeless was perhaps best illustrated at The Masters in 1974 when, at 42, he went into the last round trailing Hubert Green by seven strokes. However, the South African came home in 30 and equalled the then record score of 64. He birdied seven of the last ten holes at Augusta to win by a stroke.

He was also once seven down to Tony Lema after 19 holes in the semi-final of the World Match Play in 1965 before securing safe passage into the final, where he defeated Peter Thomson, at the first extra hole. "My opponents knew I was like a bull terrier," he said. "I never gave up." One of the exceptional match-play golfers, Player won the World Match Play five times.

The son of a miner and a mother who died when he was eight, Player became a pro at 18 and won his first title, the Egyptian Match Play, in 1955. He liked to wear all black outfits and was one of the first golfers to rely on an exercise programme and a high fibre diet to improve his physique and hit the ball further. It was a regime which helped him to win the Australian Open seven times, the South African Open 13 times and sign for 59 in the 1974 Brazilian Open.

In 2006, he received the Payne Stewart award for his services to golf and charity work, especially in Africa. He has been a captain of the Rest of the World team in the Presidents Cup on three occasions. One of the game's 'Big Three' in the Sixties along with Nicklaus and Arnold Palmer, Player today has widespread global business interests through his company Black Knight International.

in the 1994 USPGA Championship and third in the 1992 US Masters he won 14 times between 1984 and 2006. His only victory in Europe came when he took the German Open title in 1983 while on honeymoon. In 2006, he ended a ten-year winning drought by taking the US Bank Championship in Milwaukee and was one of Tom Lehman's vice-captains at the Ryder Cup at the K Club. He was selected to captain the US Ryder Cup side which lost by a point at Celtic Manor in 2010.

Perry, Kenny (USA)

Born Elizabethtown, Kentucky, 10 August 1960
Turned professional 1982

After winning for times between 1991 and 2001, he had a marvellous 2003 winning the Bank of America Colonial, the Memorial Tournament and the Greater Milwaukee Open between May 25 and July 13. He made his Ryder Cup début at Detroit in 2004 having played in the 1996, 2003 and 2005 Presidents Cups. In 2008 he deliberately by-passed two major Championships in order to ensure he had a place in Paul Azinger's Ryder Cup side for the match against Europe at Valhalla in his home state of Kentucky. He achieved his goal and played with considerable success. He tied with Angel Cabrera and Chad Campbell after 72 holes of the 2009 Masters Tournament but lost the play-off. Campbell went out at the first extra hole and Cabrera won The Green Jacket at the second extra hole.

Phadungsil, Chinarat (THA)
Born Bangkok, Thailand
Turned professional 2005

He became the youngest winner on the Asian Tour when he beat Shiv Kapur at the second hole of their play-off for the Double A International title at the St Andrews Hill (2000) GC in Rayong, Thailand. The reigning World Junior champion, he was only 17 years and 5 days when he won that title and immediately turned professional.

Poulter, Ian (ENG)
Born Hitchen, England, 10 January 1976
Turned professional 1994

One of golf's most extrovert personalities who insists he wants to be noticed for his golfing talent rather than his hairstyles and colourful clothing. Runner-up to Padraig Harrington in The Open at Royal Birkdale in 2008 he was a captain's pick on Nick Faldo's Ryder Cup side later that year at Valhalla. Europe lost but he was top scorer from either side. He also played in the 2004 and 2010 teams. In 2007 he was successful in Japan winning the Dunlop Phoenix event and in 2010 won for the first time on the PGA Tour in America when he beat Paul Casey in the final of the WGC Accenture Match-play Championship in Arizona. Now based in Lake Nona, Florida he was in a play-off for the Dubai World Championship in 2010 and incurred a penalty when he inadvertently dropped his ball on his marker causing it to move.

Price, Nick (ZIM)
Born Durban, South Africa, 28 January 1957
Turned professional 1977

One of the game's most popular players his greatest season was 1994 when he took six titles including The Open at Turnberry when he beat Jesper Parnevik and the USPGA at Southern Hills when Corey Pavin was second. He had scored his first Major triumph two years earlier when he edged out John Cook, Nick Faldo, Jim Gallagher Jr and Gene Sauers at the USPGA at Bellerive, St Louis. Along with Tiger Woods his record of 15 wins in the 90s was the most by any player. One of only eight players to win consecutive Majors, the others being Ben Hogan, Jack Nicklaus, Arnold Palmer, Lee Trevino, Tom Watson, Tiger Woods and Padraig Harrington. Four times a Presidents Cup player he jointly holds the Augusta National record of 63 with Greg Norman. One of only two players in the 90s to win

two Majors in a year, the others being Nick Faldo in 1990 and Mark O'Meara in 1998, Born of English parents but brought up in Zimbabwe he played his early golf with Mark McNulty and Tony Johnstone. He was named recipient in 2002 of the Payne Stewart Award which goes to the player who respects the traditions of the game and works to uphold them. In 2003, ten years after being named PGA Tour Player of the Year, he was inducted into the World Golf Hall of Fame.

Price, Phillip (WAL)
Born Pontypridd, 21 October 1966
Turned professional 1989

He made his Ryder Cup début in 2002 and produced a sterling last day performance when he beat the world No.2 Phil Mickelson 3 and 2 for a vital point. He played on the PGA Tour in 2005 with limited success and, back in Europe, has found it difficult to rediscover his old magic.

Quigley, Dana (USA)
Born Lynnfield Centre, Massachussetts, 14 April 1947
Turned professional 1971

Iron man of the US Champions Tour who played in 278 consecutive events for which he was qualified before missing the 2005 Senior British Open at Royal Aberdeen. He had passed the million dollars mark in prize-money by early June that year and with official money of $2,170,258 he topped the Champions Tour money list at the end of the season.

Quiros, Alvaro (ESP)
Born Cadiz, Spain, 21 January 1983
Turned professional 2004

The Spaniard became the first player in European Tour history to win on his first appearance when he won the 2007 dunhill championship at Leopard Creek in South Africa. He has won five times since then in Portugal, Qatar, Spain and Dubai twice. His victory at the Dubai World Championship in 2011 was the biggest of his career and earned him a cheque for more than €922,000. He has the reputation of being one of Europe's longest hitters averaging over 314 yards.

Rafferty, Ronan (NIR)
Born Newry, Northern Ireland, 13 January 1964
Turned professional 1981

He won the Irish Amateur Championship as a 16 year old in 1980 when he also won the English Amateur Open Stroke Play title, competed in the Eisenhower Trophy and played against Europe in the home internationals. Winner of the British Boys', Irish Youths' and Ulster Youths' titles in 1979, he also played in the senior Irish side against Wales that year. A regular winner on the European tour between 1988 and 1993 he was also victorious in tournaments played in South America, Australia and New Zealand. A wrist injury curtailed his career but he is active on the corporate golf front and has an impressive wine collection.

Ramsay, Richie (SCO)

Born Aberdeen, 15 June 1983
Turned professional 2007

A student at Stirling University he became the first Scot since 1898 and the first British golfer since 1911 to win the US Amateur Championship when he beat John Kelly from St Louis 4 and 2 in the final A member of the 2005 Great Britain and Ireland Walker Cup team, he has played in the Palmer Cup and was the winner of the 2004 Scottish Open Amateur Stroke-play title and the 2005 Irish Open Amateur Stroke-play event. He has shot a 62 at Murcar in Aberdeenshire. Ramsay turned professional after the 2007 Open, missing the chance to play again in the Walker Cup. He failed to survive the first stage of the European Tour School and competed on the 2008 Challenge Tour winning twice and earning his card for the main Tour in 2009 winning the 2010 South African Open at Pearl Valley.

Randhawa, Jyoti (IND)

Born New Delhi, 4 May 1972
Turned professional 1994

First Indian winner on the Japanese Tour when he triumphed in the 2003 Suntory Open. Son of an Indian general, he was top earner on the Asian PGA Tour in 2002 despite missing several events after breaking his collarbone in a motorcycle accident. Practices yoga and now plays on both the European and Asian Tours.

Remesy, Jean-François (FRA)

Born Nimes, 5 June 1964   Turned professional 1987

In 2004 he became the first Frenchman since Jean Garaialde in 1969 to win the Open de France then successfully defended the title the following year at Golf National, Versailles beating Jean Van de Velde in a play-off. Now lives in the Seychelles.

Rivero, José (ESP)

Born Madrid, 20 September 1955
Turned professional 1973

One of only eight Spaniards who have played in the Ryder Cup he was a member of the winning 1985 and 1987 sides. Worked as a caddie but received a grant from the Spanish Federation to pursue his golf career. With José Maria Canizares won the World Cup in 1984 at Olgiata in Italy.

Roberts, Loren (USA)

Born San Luis Obispo, California, 24 June 1955
Turned professional 1975

An eight times winner on the PGA Tour, he earned the nickname "Boss of the Moss" because of his exceptional putting. He played in two Presidents Cup matches and the 1995 Ryder Cup before joining the Champions Tour. He had chalked up seven wins by the end of 2007 and for the second year running had the low average score on that Tour – an impressive

69.31. In a play-off for the 2009 Senior Open at Sunningdale he beat Mark McNulty and Fred Funk to win the title for a second time.

Rocca, Costantino (ITA)

Born Bergamo, 4 December 1956
Turned professional 1981

The first and to date only Italian to play in the Ryder Cup. In the 1999 match at Valderrama he beat Tiger Woods 4 and 2 in a vital singles. Left his job in a polystyrene box making factory to become a club professional and graduated to the tournament scene through Europe's Challenge Tour. In 1995 he fluffed a chip at the final hole in The Open at St Andrews only to hole from 60 feet out of the Valley of Sin to force a play-off against John Daly which he then lost. Now plays on the European Senior Tour.

Rogers, Bill (USA)

Born Waco, Texas, 10 September 1951
Turned professional 1974

USPGA Player of the Year in 1981 when he won The Open at Royal St George's and was runner-up in the US Open. That year he also won the Australian Open but retired from top line competitive golf not long after because he did not enjoy all the travelling. A former Walker Cup player in 1973 he only entered The Open in 1981 at the insistence of Ben Crenshaw. Now a successful club professional and sometime television commentator.

Romero, Eduardo (ARG)

Born Cordoba, Argentina, 12 July 1954
Turned professional 1982

Son of the Cordoba club professional he learned much from former Open champion Roberto de Vicenzo and has inherited his grace and elegance as a competitor. A wonderful ambassador for Argentina he briefly held a US Tour card in 1994 but preferred to play his golf on the European Tour where he won seven times including the 1999 Canon European Masters. He improved his concentration after studying Indian yoga techniques. Used his own money to sponsor Angel Cabrera with whom he finished second in the 2000 World Cup in Buenos Aries behind Tiger Woods and David Duval. Joined the Senior ranks in July 2004 but still plays from time to time on the main European Tour. In 2008 he won the US Senior Open on the Champions Tour.

Rose, Justin (ENG)

Born Johannesburg, South Africa, 30 July 1980
Turned professional 1998

Walker Cup player who shot to attention in the 1998 Open Championship at Royal Birkdale when he finished top amateur and third behind winner Mark O'Meara after holing his third shot at the last on the final day for a closing birdie. Immediately after that Open he turned professional and missed his first 21 half-way cuts before finding his feet. In 2002 was a multiple winner in Europe and also won in Japan and South Africa. Delighted his father who watched him win the Victor Chandler British Masters just a few weeks before he died of leukaemia. He has played most of his golf in America in recent years shooting 60 at the Funai Classic at Walt Disney World in 2006. Although he played only the minimum 12 events on the European Tour in 2007, he won the end of season Volvo Masters at Valderrama to finish No 1 on the money list and became the highest ranked British golfer in the world ranking, moving into seventh place. Later in the year he partnered Ian Poulter into fourth place in the Mission Hills World Cup of Golf in China. He made his début in the Ryder Cup in the 2008 match at Valhalla but failed to make the 2010 side despite winning two titles on the PGA Tour including the prestigious Memorial event at Muirfield Village. In 2011 he won the BMW Championship.

Sandelin, Jarmo (SWE)

Born Imatra, Finland, 10 May 1967
Turned professional 1987

Extrovert Swede who made his début in the Ryder Cup at Brookline in 1999 although he did not play until the singles. Has always been a snazzy dresser on course where he is one of the game's longest hitters often using, in the early days, a 54-inch shafted driver. Five time winner on Tour he met his partner Linda when she asked to caddie for him at a Stockholm pro-am.

Schwartzel, Charl (RSA)

Born Johannesburg, 31 August 1984
Turned professional 2002

The first Masters champion ever to birdie all four of the closing holes at Augusta, Schwartzel savoured one of the most thrilling finishes seen at the majors when he posted a closing round of 66 to earn a two stroke victory over Australians Jason Day and Adam Scott. After claiming a Green Jacket, he was also ninth at the US Open, 16th at The Open and 12th at the US PGA in 2011. Since finishing 16th at the US Open in 2010 he's reeled off seven consecutive top 20 placings in the majors. Charl was playing off plus 4 when he turned professional after an amateur career that had seen him represent South Africa in the Eisenhower Trophy. In only his third event as a pro he finished joint third in the South African Airways Open and became a winner in his 56th event when he won the dunhill championship in a play-off at Leopard Creek. He was South African No 1 in season 2004–5 and was again No 1 in the 2005–6 season. In the 2007 European Tour season he won the Spanish Open but was winless in 2008 until he again played well in Spain to take the Madrid Masters title. He won the Joburg Open in 2010 and 2011 as well as the Africa Open in 2010.

Scott, Adam (AUS)

Born Adelaide, 16 July 1980 Turned professional 2000

Highly regarded young Australian who was ranked World No 2 amateur when he turned professional

in 2000. Coached in the early days by his father Phil, himself a golf professional, Scott now uses Butch Harmon whom he met while attending the University of Las Vegas. Swings very much like another Harmon client Tiger Woods. He made headlines as an amateur when he fired a 10-under-par 63 at the Lakes in the Greg Norman Holden International in 2000 but has shot 62 in the US Junior Championship at Los Coyotes CC. Made his European Tour card in just eight starts and secured his first Tour win when beating Justin Rose in the 2001 Alfred Dunhill Championship at Houghton in Johannesburg. In 2002 he won at Qatar and at Gleneagles Hotel when he won the Diageo Scottish PGA Championship by ten shots with a 26 under par total. He was 22 under par that week for the par 5 holes. In 2003 he was an impressive winner of the Scandinavian Masters at Barsebäck in Sweden and the Deutsche Bank Championship on the US Tour. In 2005 when he again played in the Presidents Cup, his victories included the Johnnie Walker Classic on the European and Asian Tours, the Singapore Open on the Asian Tour and the Nissan Open on the US Tour. In 2006, he won the Players Championship and Tour Championship in America moving to third in the World rankings in mid November. He also won the Singapore Open again. He continued to play well throughout 2008 but was less successful in 2009. In 2010 he won the Valero Texas Open and in 2011, after switching to the belly putter, won the Bridgestone and finished runner-up at the Masters.

Senior, Peter (AUS)

Born Singapore, 31 July 1959
Turned professional 1978

One of Australia's most likeable and underrated performers who has been a regular winner over the years on the Australian, Japanese and European circuits. Converted to the broomstick putter by Sam Torrance – a move that saved his playing career. A former winner of the Australian Open, Australian PGA and Australian Masters titles he had considerable success off the course when he bought a share in a pawn-broking business. Senior now plays irregularly outside Australia where he has taken over as chairman of the Autralasian Tour from Wayne Grady. In 2010 he won the Handa Australian Seniors title and Australian PGA title for a third time.

Sigel, Jay (USA)

Born Narbeth, Pennsylvania, 13 November 1943
Turned professional 1993

Winner of the Amateur Championship in 1979 when he beat Scott Hoch 3 and 2 at Hillside, he also won the US Amateur in 1982 and 1983. He was leading amateur in the US Open in 1984 and leading amateur in the US Masters in 1981, 1982 and 1988. He played in nine Walker Cup matches between 1977 and 1993 and has a record 18 points to his credit. Turned professional in order to join the US Senior Tour where he has had several successes.

Simpson, Scott (USA)

Born San Diego, California, 17 September 1955
Turned professional 1977

Winner of the US Open in 1987 at San Francisco's Olympic Club, he was beaten in a play-off for the title four years later at Hazeltine when the late Payne Stewart won the 18-hole play-off.

Simpson, Webb (USA)

Born Raleigh, North Carolina, 1985
Turned professional 2008

Earned nearly $5.8 million in 2011 on the PGA Tour thanks to two wins in the space of just three weeks at the Wyndham and Deutche Bank championships. A talented amateur golfer, he was a member of the American Walker Cup team in 2007 which defeated Great Britain and Ireland at Royal County Down.

Singh, Jeev Milkha (IND)

Born Chandigarh, India, 15 December 1971
Turned professional 1993

Stylish swinger, he won his first European event when he took the Volvo China Open in Beijing in 2006 but he scored an even greater triumph when he picked up the first prize at the Volvo Masters at Valderrama later in the year. He is the son of the former Olympian Milkha Singh who won a medal in the 1980 games. His victory in the 2007 Barclays Singapore Open enabled him to became the first player to make US $1 million in one season on the Asian Tour and helped him top the money list for the second time. His Singapore win also moved him into the top 50 in the world rankings for the second time. More recently injury has hampered his career.

Singh, Vijay (FIJ)

Born Lautoka, 22 February 1963
Turned professional 1982

An international player who began his career in Australasia, he became the first Fijian to win a major when he won the 1998 USPGA Championship at Sahalee but may well be remembered more for his victory in the 2000 US Masters which effectively prevented Tiger Woods winning all four Majors in a year. Tiger went on to win the US Open, Open and USPGA Championship that year and won the Masters the following year to hold all four Major titles at the one time. Introduced to golf by his father, an aeroplane technician, Vijay modelled his swing on that of Tom Weiskopf. Before making the grade on the European Tour where he won the 1992 Volvo German Open by 11 shots he was a club professional in Borneo. He has won tournaments in South Africa, Malaysia, the Ivory Coast, Nigeria, France, Zimbabwe, Morocco, Spain, England, Germany, Sweden, Taiwan and the United States. He ended Ernie Els' run of victories in the World

Match Play Championship when he beat him in the final by one hole in 1997 when the South African was going for a fourth successive title. One of the game's most dedicated practisers. In 2003 he won the Phoenix Open, the EDS Byron Nelson Championship, the John Deere Classic and the Funai Classic. On the PGA Tour in 2003 Singh ended Woods' run as top money earner when he finished with prize-money totalling $7,753,907 – the second largest total in Tour history – but he was not named Player of the Year. Woods was again the players' choice. In 2004 he had his best ever season and by mid-October was approaching $10 million in year-long winnings on the US Tour, having won eight times, matching Johnnie Miller's eight wins in 1974. Although finally edged out by Woods for the No 1 spot he earned his third major and second USPGA Championship title with a play-off victory at Whistling Straits.

Smyth, Des (IRL)

Born Drogheda, Ireland, 12 February 1953
Turned professional 1973

Became the oldest winner on the PGA European Tour when he won the Madeira Island Open in 2001. Smyth was 48 years and 34 days – 20 days older than Neil Coles had been when he won the Sanyo Open in Barcelona in 1982. One of the Tour's most consistent performers – he played 592 events before switching to the European Seniors Tour and qualifying for the US Champions Tour where he has been a winner. Five times Irish National champion he was a member of the winning Irish side in the 1988 Alfred Dunhill Cup. Won twice on US Champions Tour in 2005 and In Abu Dhabi on the European Senior Tour. He was a vice-captain for the European team in the 2006 Ryder Cup.

Stadler, Craig (USA)

Born San Diego, California, 2 June 1953
Turned professional 1975

Nicknamed "The Walrus" because of his moustache and stocky build, he won the 1982 Masters at Augusta. Winner of 12 titles on the US Tour between 1980 and 1996 he played in two Ryder Cups (1983 and 1985). As an amateur he played in the 1975 Walker Cup two years after winning the US Amateur. He won his first senior major title when he took the Ford Senior Players' Championship just a few weeks after turning 50 then went back to the main tour the following week and won the BC Open against many players half his age. In 2004 he was top earner on the US Champions Tour with over $2 million. His son Kevin, who is also a professional golfer, won the Johnnie Walker Classic at The Vines in 2006.

Stenson, Henrik (SWE)

Born Gothenburg, 5 April 1976
Turned professional 1998

A member of the Swedish Eisenhower Trophy side in 1998 he made his Ryder Cup début In 2006 helping

Europe beat the Americans at The K Club in Ireland. He played for Sweden in the 1998 Eisenhower Trophy and made the 2006 Ryder Cup side helping Europe beat America 18½–9½ at the K Club. In the singles he beat Vaughn Taylor. He again played in the 2008 match at Valhalla. Stenson had played the first part of 2007 in America and was quickly a winner of the Accenture Match-Play Championship after having picked up first prize in the Dubai Desert Classic. Stenson rounded off his 2008 season in style by winning the World Cup at Mission Hills in China with Robert Karlsson. In 2009 he won the Players' Championship at Sawgrass to further underline his international reputation.

Sterne, Richard (RSA)

Born Pretoria, 27 August 1981
Turned professional 2001

Former world junior champion he made history as an amateur in South Africa when becoming the first player to win the junior and senior stroke and match-play titles. He scored his first European Tour success when he won the Open de Madrid in 2004Injury seriously affected his playing schedule in 2010.

Stranahan, Frank R (USA)

Born Toledo, Ohio, 5 August 1922
Turned professional 1954

One of America's most successful amateurs he won the Amateur championship at Royal St George's in 1948 and in 1950 the British and US Amateur titles. He won the Mexican Amateur in 1946, 1948 and 1951 and the Canadian title in 1947 and 1948. He was also leading amateur in The Open in 1947, 1949, 1950, 1951 and 1953. He played in three Walker Cups in 1947, 1949 and 1951.

Strange, Curtis (USA)

Born Norfolk, Virginia, 20 January 1955
Turned professional 1976

Winner of successive US Opens in 1988 and in 1989 when he beat Nick Faldo in an 18-hole play-off at The Country Club Brookline after getting up and down from a bunker at the last to tie on 278. Winner of 17 US Tour titles he won at least one event for seven successive years from 1983. Having played in five Ryder Cup matches he captained the US side when the 2001 match was played at The Belfry in 2002. In 2007 he was inducted into the World Golf Hall of Fame.

Stricker, Steve (USA)

Born Egerton, Wisconsin, 23 February 1967
Turned professional 1990

Started 2001 by winning the $1 million first prize in the Accenture Match Play Championship, one of the World Golf Championship series. In the final he beat Pierre Fulke. Was a member of the winning American Alfred Dunhill Cup side in 1996. In 2007 he won the Barclays Championship ... one of the four end of season Fedex Cup events. In 2008 he was a captain's pick in the US Ryder Cup side at Valhalla. When he started on Tour his wife Nikki caddied for him. Her father Dennis Tiziani was his coach.

Sutton, Hal (USA)

Born Shreveport, Louisiana, 28 April 1958
Turned professional 1981

Winner of the 1983 USPGA Championship at the Riviera CC in Los Angeles beating Jack Nicklaus into second place. Played in the 1985, 1987, 1999 and 2002 Ryder Cup matches. He captained the American team which lost to the Europeans at Oakland Hills in 2004 and in 2007 was given the Payne Stewart award for respecting and upholding the traditions of the game.

Thomas, Dave (WAL)

Born Newcastle-upon-Tyne, 16 August 1934
Turned professional 1949

Twice runner-up in The Open Championship, Welshman Thomas lost a play-off to Peter Thomson in 1958. And was runner-up to Jack Nicklaus in 1966. He played 11 times in the World Cup for Wales and four times in the Ryder Cup. In all he won 10 tournaments between 1961 and 1969 before retiring to concentrate on golf course design. Along with Peter Alliss he designed the Ryder Cup course at The Belfry and was captain of the Professional Golfers' Association in 2001 – their Centenary year – and 2002.

Toms, David (USA)

Born Monroe, LA, 4 January 1967
Turned professional 1989

Highlight of his career was beating Phil Mickelson into second place in the 2001 USPGA Championship at the Atlanta Athletic Club with rounds of 66, 65, 65 and 69 for 265 a record winning Championship aggregate and the lowest aggregate in any Major. Made his Ryder Cup début in 2002, when he was the American side's top points scorer with 3½ points, and played again in 2004. In 2005 Toms won the WGC Accenture Match-play title beating Chris DiMarco 6 and 5 in the final.

Torrance OBE, Sam (SCO)

Born Largs, Ayrshire, 24 August 1953
Turned professional 1970

Between 1976 and 1998 he won 21 times on the European Tour in which he has played over 700 events hitting that mark at the Barclays Scottish Open at Loch Lomond in 2010. Captain of the 2002 European Ryder Cup side having previously played in eight matches notably holing the winning putt in 1985 to end a 28-year run of American domination. He was an inspired captain when the 2001 match was played in September 2002. Tied 8 points each, Torrance's men won the singles for only the third time since 1979 to win 15½–12½. His father Bob, who has been his only coach, looks after the swings these days of several others on the European Tour including Paul

Peter Thomson CBE (AUS)

Born Melbourne, 23 August 1929
Turned professional 1949

The first golfer who was ever shown live on television winning The Open – the occasion was his triumph at St Andrews in 1955 – Peter Thomson enjoys a deserved reputation as one of the most astute links golfer to emerge since young Tom Morris won four consecutive Open titles. One of only four champions to capture five Opens – his other triumphs were at Birkdale twice, in 1954 and 1965, Hoylake in 1956 and Lytham in 1958 – Thomson was placed in the spotlight when the BBC used just three cameras for their first live broadcast from the Old Course.

The Australian found the incentive to win three consecutive Open titles lay in financial necessity. Prize money was relatively modest in the Fifties and sponsorship deals were scarce. Luckily, this largely self-taught golfer with a fluent swing and a knack of eliminating mistakes produced the kind of low ball flight which reaps dividends on the linksland. He made his début in the oldest major at Portrush in 1951 and between 1952 and 1958 never finished outside the first two. His run of extraordinary results during that seven year stretch was second, second, first, first, first, second and first. During that spell he also became the only golfer in the modern era to win three consecutive championships on three different links. (Jamie Anderson in the 1870s and Bob Ferguson in the 1880s are the other Open champions with this distinction.)

One of only four players to win five Opens – Harry Vardon, with six, has the most victories – he matched the feats of J.H. Taylor and James Braid while Tom Watson also won five in eight years from 1975. Thomson's fifth victory, arguably his most impressive, came at Royal Birkdale in 1965 when more Americans, including Jack Nicklaus, Arnold Palmer and Tony Lema, were in the field. He says that the reason for his success in The Open was simple – he built his career around the championship. In the American majors, he played only three times in the US Open, finishing fourth in 1956. He played at Augusta in five Masters with fifth his best finish in 1957. He also won three Australian Opens and in Europe savoured 24 victories between 1954 and 1972. His first victory in 1950 was at the New Zealand Open, a tournament he would win nine times. All told, he won over 100 tournaments around the world.

Raised in the Brunswick suburb of Melbourne, Thomson took up golf as a 12-year-old and was club champion at 15. He studied to become an industrial chemist and first worked for Spalding before becoming a professional in 1949. With one of the most fluent and reliable swings, gripping the club lightly, he made the links game look deceptively easy. Perhaps the greatest Australian player, he was instrumental in developing golf throughout Asia. Thomson placed a premium on accuracy rather than power and, like his rival Bobby Locke, often used a 3 wood from the tee.

When Thomson was ready to retire from competitive golf, he thought about pursuing a career in Australian politics but narrowly missed out on a seat in a state election. He turned instead to the US Senior Tour where he won 11 titles, including a remarkable nine victories in 1985, a record matched only by Hale Irwin. Thomson was also president of the Australian PGA between 1962 and 1994.

He was elected to the World Golf Hall of Fame in 1988, the year he won the Seniors British PGA, his last title, and is an honorary member of the Royal and Ancient Golf Club of St Andrews. His fondness for the Auld Toun persuaded the Australian to keep a house in St Andrews as well as a place in his heart for the Old Course. After his retirement from golf he concentrated on journalism and a successful golf course design business which built more than 100 courses. He's captained the Rest of the World side at the Presidents Cup, including a notable win over the US at Royal Melbourne in 1998. A member of Victoria golf club since 1949, the club celebrated his 80th birthday in 2009 by unveiling a bronze statue of him. He continues to regard the values of common sense, planning and clear thinking among the most useful golfing assets.

McGinley who holed the nine foot putt that brought the Ryder Cup back to Europe in 2002. He was awarded the MBE in 1996. European Tour officials worked out that in his first 28 years Torrance walked an estimated 14,000 miles and played 15,000 shots earning at the rate of £22 per stroke. In 2003 he retired from full-time competition on the European Tour to play on the European Senior Tour and in 2005, 2006 and 2009 was top earner. He is often a member of the BBC commentary team working with Peter Alliss and Ken Brown.

Townsend, Peter (ENG)

Born Cambridge, 16 September 1946
Turned professional 1966

An outstanding amateur golfer regarded as one of the best prospects of the post war era who won the British Boys twice, the British Youths, the Lytham

Lee Trevino, (USA)

Born Dallas, Texas, 1 December 1939
Turned professional 1961

The winner of six major championships and an enduring success over nearly half a century of competition, "Supermex" won as many tournaments on the senior circuit, 29, as he did on the PGA Tour. Using a distinctive swing with an open stance and a strong grip, Trevino was a golfer with a hook who faded the ball. His action was once described as five wrongs which make an immaculate right. If his style of play was unusual, it was his personality which struck a chord with the public. He was a charismatic figure with a sense of humour who played a huge role in the emergence of the Champions Tour. He once quipped that "you can talk to a fade but a hook won't listen."

Born in Texas to a family of Mexican ancestry, he left school at 14 and worked as a caddy. He spent four years with the US Marines before becoming an assistant pro in El Paso. Although he joined the paid ranks in 1960, it wasn't until 1967 that he joined the PGA Tour and was named rookie of the year. The following season he made his name with an outstanding performance in the US Open at Oak Hill. He won by four shots from Jack Nicklaus and his total of 275 – made up of scores of 69, 68, 69 and 69 – was the first in America's national championship to break 70 in each round.

The consistency of Trevino's game was never more evident than in the summer of 1971 when, between May 30 and July 10, he won four events, including The Open and the US Open. At Merion he defeated Nicklaus in a play-off while at Royal Birkdale he thwarted Mr Lu and Tony Jacklin. The following year at Muirfield, Trevino again crossed swords with Jacklin. This time the Englishman and the American were paired together over the closing 36 holes and Trevino's chip-in on the penultimate hole proved decisive. He would enjoy further major success in the PGA Championships of 1974 and 1984. His last major win came at the age of 44 over Shoal Creek in Alabama when once more he shot four rounds below 70.

Trevino never finished higher than tenth in the Masters where he felt a course with so many dog-legs did not suit his game. He was a low fader and believed Augusta required a high draw. He was an outstanding Ryder Cup player, playing six times as well as captaining the US in 1985. He won the Vardon Trophy for low scoring average five times in his career and recovered from being struck by lightning while playing in the Western Open in Chicago. He had to undergo back surgery before returning to competition. He was involved in one of the low scoring matches in the World Match Play Championship with Jacklin in 1972 when again he came out on top. In 2003 he was made an honorary member of the Royal and Ancient Golf Club of St Andrews. Trevino was a blue collar hero with a splash of showmanship who broadened the appeal of the game.

Trophy and the English Amateur titles. He was selected to play for GB&I in the 1965 Walker Cup match, partnering Ronnie Shade in foursomes, contributing three points, and emerging as one of the heroes of a drawn match against the USA. He turned professional the following season, initially struggled with swing changes, but went on to win 14 times, including the Swiss and Dutch Opens on the European Tour. He also won the Western Australian Open as well as recording numerous victories in South America and Africa. Keen to play around the globe, he qualified for the PGA Tour in America where he finished in the top ten three times. Once regarded as a rival to Tony Jacklin, he finished in the top 20 at The Open four times and played in the Ryder Cup matches of 1969 and 1971. A former captain of the PGA he now lives in Sweden.

Van de Velde, Jean (FRA)

Born Mont de Marsan, 29 May 1966
Turned professional 1987

Who ever remembers who came second? Few do but almost everyone recalls Frenchman Jean Van de Velde finishing runner-up after a play-off with eventual winner Paul Lawrie and American Justin Leonard when The Open returned to a somewhat tricked-up Carnoustie in 1999. Playing the last hole he led by three but refused to play safe and paid a severe penalty. He ran up a triple bogey 7 after seeing his approach ricochet off a stand into the rough and hitting his next into the Barry Burn. He appeared to contemplate playing the half-submerged ball when taking off his shoes and socks and wading in but that was never a possibility. Sadly, he was an absentee at the 2007 Open played at the same venue. Took up the game as a youngster when holidaying with his parents in Biarritz. Has scored only one win in Europe (the Roma Masters in 1993) and has returned to the European Tour after a spell in America. Made his Ryder Cup début at Brookline in 1999. Injury prevented him competing regularly in 2003 and 2004 during which time he was part of the BBC Golf Commentary team with, among others, Peter Alliss, Sam Torrance, Mark James and Ken Brown. Came close to winning his national title but lost out in a play-off to fellow Frenchman Jean-François Remesy at Golf National in 2005. Created headlines later in the year when he said that if it was to be made easier for

Tom Watson (USA)

Born Kansas City, Missouri, 4 September 1949
Turned professional 1971

For all the victories he's savoured during an enduringly brilliant career, it was Tom Watson's narrow loss in The Open at Turnberry in 2009, when he was nearing his 60th birthday, which will be discussed and remembered as long as the game of golf is played. A year after undergoing hip replacement surgery, he came within eight feet of relishing a record-equalling sixth championship success. Remarkably, a quarter of a century had elapsed since he'd won his fifth Open. While he missed the putt for glory on the 72nd hole and lost the subsequent play-off for the Claret Jug to Stewart Cink, Watson's performance on the Ailsa, nevertheless, struck a chord with the public and breathed new life into a career already notable for 39 PGA Tour wins, including no fewer than eight major titles.

Born in Missouri, Watson today remains true to his roots and still lives in the midwest of America on a farm near Kansas City. He was introduced to the game by his father, Ray, a scratch golfer, at the age of six. By the time he was 19, he was the state amateur champion, a feat he repeated on three more occasions. After studying psychology at Stanford University, where he graduated in 1971, Watson joined the PGA Tour and earned his first winner's cheque as a pro in 1974 at the Western Open.

When he came up short and twice failed to win the US Open in 1974 and 1975, he was branded as a choker in America. Whether that reputation was deserved or not is moot. But Watson produced the perfect response later in the summer of 1975 when he travelled to Scotland and won The Open on his début at Carnoustie after a play-off with Jack Newton. It was the beginning of the American's life-long affair with the home of golf in which he matched the success rate of J H Taylor, James Braid and Peter Thomson by winning the oldest major five times. He also missed out on an opportunity to collect a sixth Open title by a whisker at St Andrews in 1984 when he struck his second shot close to the wall through the green at the Road Hole and was thwarted by Seve Ballesteros.

Of all his Open triumphs, surely none was more memorable than the "Duel in the Sun" at Turnberry in 1977. At an event many regarded as the greatest championship of modern times, Watson edged out Jack Nicklaus by shooting closing rounds of 65,65 to Nicklaus' 65,66. His other successes on the linksland came in 1980 at Muirfield where he defeated Lee Trevino, in 1982 at Royal Troon where Peter Oosterhuis and Nick Price came second and in 1983 when Andy Bean and Hale Irwin were runners-up.

If his story at The Open provides the legendary narrative for Watson's career, he also produced a spectacular performance in the 1982 US Open at Pebble Beach. Watson's chip shot for birdie from the rough on the short 17th has been immortalised as the most memorable of his life. As at Turnberry, Nicklaus was the man he defeated. He also secured two Green Jackets at Augusta in 1977 and 1981 where Nicklaus finished second on both occasions. It was this talent for defeating arguably the game's greatest player in the tournaments which mattered most that separated Watson from his peers.

However, since he was never better than a runner-up at the US PGA Championship, Watson was unable to join Gene Sarazen, Ben Hogan, Gary Player, Nicklaus and Tiger Woods in the elite club of Grand Slam golfers who have won all four professional majors. Perhaps it's the only accolade missing from his career. He became the oldest winner on the PGA Tour when he won the Mastercard Colonial in 1998, almost 24 years after his first win. And he was the PGA Tour's player of the Year six times and the leading money winner five times.

Watson played in four Ryder Cups in 1977, 1981, 1983 and 1989 before captaining the US side to victory in 1993 at The Belfry. He was inducted into the World Golf Hall of Fame in 1988 and is an honorary member of the Royal and Ancient Golf Club of St Andrews. He also succeeded Sam Snead as the golf professional emeritus at the Greenbrier.

After turning 50, he joined the Champions Tour. He has won 13 events since 1999 in the company of his senior peers, most recently in Hawaii in 2010. Perhaps his finest moment as a senior came at his beloved Turnberry in 2003 when he lifted the Senior British Open title 26 years after the Duel in the Sun.

As a direct consequence of his performance over the Ailsa in 2009, The R&A changed the entry rules and introduced a five year exemption for former champions who finish in the top ten. When the BBC conducted a poll to identify the greatest ever Open champion, it was entirely fitting that Watson was chosen by the British public as the recipient.

women to play in The Open he thought it only fair that he should be allowed to enter the British Women's Open but never followed through on his threat. Captained the Continental side which lost to Great Britain and Ireland in the 2011 Vivendi Seve Trophy.

Verplank, Scott (USA)

Born Dallas, Texas, 9 July 1964
Turned professional 1986

When he won the Western Open as an amateur in 1985 he was the first to do so since Doug Sanders took the 1956 Canadian Open. Missed most of the 1991 and 1992 seasons because of an elbow injury and the injury also affected his 1996 season. He has diabetes and wears an insulin pump while playing to regulate his medication. Curtis Strange chose him as one of his two picks for the 2002 US Ryder Cup side. In the singles on the final day he beat Lee Westwood 2 and 1. He was again a captain's pick in Tom Lehman's side in 2006 and again won his singles, this time against Padraig Harrington. Surprisingly he failed to make the 2008 US side.

Wadkins, Lanny (USA)

Born Richmond, Virginia, 5 December 1949
Turned professional 1971

His 21 victories on the US Tour between 1972 and 1992 include the 1977 USPGA Championship, his only Major. He won that after a play-off with Gene Littler at Pebble Beach but lost a play-off for the same title in 1987 to Larry Nelson at Palm Beach Gardens. He was second on two other occasions to Ray Floyd in 1982 and to Lee Trevino in 1984. In other Majors his best finish was third three times in the US Masters (1990, 1991 and 1993), tied second in the US Open (1986) and tied fourth in the 1984 Open at St Andrews. One of the fiercest of competitors he played eight Ryder Cups between 1977 and 1993 winning 20 of his 33 games, but was a losing captain at Oak Hill in 1995. In 2009 he was inducted into the World Golf Hall of Fame.

Walton, Philip (IRL)

Born Dublin, 28 March 1962
Turned professional 1983

Turned professional 1983

Twice a Walker Cup player he is best remembered for two-putting the last to beat Jay Haas by one hole and clinch victory in the 1995 Ryder Cup at Oak Hill. He played in five Alfred Dunhill Cup competitions at St Andrews and was in the winning side in 1990.

Watney, Nick (USA)

Born Sacramento, California, 1981
Turned professional 2003

Enjoyed the best season of his five year career on the PGA Tour in 2011, winning nearly $5.3 million and relishing victories at the AT&T National and the Cadillac Championship. His record of ten top ten finishes was a model of consistency. Also won the Zurich Classic in 2007 and the Buick Invitational in 2009. Made his Presidents Cup début in 2011.

Warren, Marc (SCO)

Born Rutherglen, near Glasgow, 1 April 1981
Turned professional 2002

Marc, who holed the winning putt in Great Britain and Ireland's Walker Cup victory over America in 2001, had two play-off victories on the European Challenge Tour in 2005 and finished top money earner– in the Ireland Ryder Cup Challenge and the Rolex Trophy. In 2006 Warren scored his first victory on the main Tour when he beat Robert Karlsson in a play-off for the Eurocard Masters at Barsebäck. At the start of the 2007 season he finished fifth behind winner Yang Yong-eun, Tiger Woods, Michael Campbell and Retief Goosen in the HSBC Champions event in Shanghai. He scored his second win in the Johnnie Walker Championship at Gleneagles Hotel by beating Simon Wakefield in a play-off. He was a wild card pick for the GB&I team in the Seve Trophy match and partnered Colin Montgomerie to a first-ever success for Scotland in the 2007 World Cup of Golf at Mission Hills in China. He lost his Tour card in 2010 bt won back in 2011.

Weekley, Boo (USA)

Born Milton, Florida, 23 July 1973
Turned professional 1997

One of six players who made their débuts in the 2008 Ryder Cup at Valhalla. He played well and enjoyed every minute of the American success. Nicknamed Boo after Yogi Bear's sidekick, he made $500,000 on the Nationwide Tour before joining the main Tour. Studied at the Abraham Baldwin Agricultural College and won the Verizon Open in 2007 and 2008.

Weir, Mike (CAN)

Born Sarnia, Ontario, 12 May 1970
Turned professional 1992

A left-hander, he was the first Canadian to play in the Presidents Cup when he made the side in 2000 and the first from his country to win a World Golf Championship event when he took the American Express Championship at Valderrama in 2000. Wrote to Jack Nicklaus as a 13-year-old to enquire whether or not he should switch from playing golf left-handed to right-handed and was told not to switch. In 1997 he led the averages on the Canadian Tour with a score of 69.29 but his greatest triumph came when he became only the third left-hander to win a major when he played beautifully and putted outstandingly to beat Len Mattiace for a Masters Green Jacket in 2003. He had had to hole from 15 feet at the last to take the tournament into extra holes and won at the first when Mattiace failed to

Eldrick 'Tiger' Woods (USA)

Born Cypress, California, 30 December 1975
Turned professional 1996

By a wide margin the dominant golfer of the early 21st century, Woods has been the player to beat around the world ever since he became a professional in the late summer of 1996. His 95 tournament victories include no fewer than 14 major titles – the 1997, 2001, 2002 and 2005 Masters, 1999, 2000, 2006 and 2007 US PGA Championships, 2000, 2002, and 2008 US Open Championships, and The Open Championships of 2000, 2005 and 2006. When he won the Masters for the second time in 2001, Woods became the first golfer in the game's history to hold all four majors at the same time. If the "Tiger Slam" was the highlight to date of a spectacular career, Woods can reflect on many other significant accomplishments. His haul of 71 victories on the US PGA Tour is surpassed only by Sam Snead with 82 and Jack Nicklaus with 73. His career earnings from prize money in America are in excess of $94 million while his global winnings are more than $113m. According to Forbes magazine, he became the first golfer to earn more than a billion dollars from a combination of prize money, sponsorship, appearance fees and golf course design.

From the moment he appeared as a two-year-old child prodigy on the Mike Douglas Show with Bob Hope, Woods carried a gilded reputation. He aced his first hole-in-one at the age of 15 and was a scratch golfer by 13. He won the US Junior Amateur three times between the ages of 15 and 17 and the US Amateur in three consecutive stagings between 1994 and 1996, the only golfer ever to record 18 consecutive match play wins at that event.

When he left university at Stanford and joined the professional ranks as a 20-year-old in 1996, Woods won twice at Las Vegas and Disney World as well as reeling off five consecutive top five finishes and rocketing up the World Golf Ranking. In 1997, his first full season as a pro, Woods won five of the first 16 events he entered, including his first appearance as a pro at Augusta. The youngest Masters champion at the age of 21 years, three months and 14 days, he won the tournament by 12 strokes and set a record 72 hole score of 270 thanks to rounds of 70,66,65 and 69.

It was a demolition of Augusta National which took the breath away and eventually led to the lengthening and toughening of the course as well as introducing the concept of "Tiger proofing" to the golfing lexicon. He became world No 1 in just 42 weeks as a pro. While this was a frightening pace to set, Woods had no qualms about continuing to floor the accelerator. In 1999 his scoring average of 68.43 was low enough to win eight times on the PGA Tour and 11 times around the globe. There was no let-up in 2000 when he won nine times, including three majors, thereby matching Ben Hogan's feat in 1953. His 15 stroke victory at Pebble Beach was the greatest margin of victory in US Open history. When Woods won The Open at St Andrews in 2000, he became the youngest to complete the career Grand Slam of professional majors and only the fifth golfer ever to do so.

Today, Woods holds or shares the record for the low score in relation to par in each of the four major championships. His records are 270 in the Masters, 272 in the US Open, 269 in The Open, and he shares the record of 270 with Bob May in the 2000 PGA Championship. The US Open and Masters victories came by record margins, 15 strokes and 12 strokes respectively, and the US Open triumph swept aside the 13-stroke major championship standard which had stood for 138 years, established by Old Tom Morris in the 1862 Open. The record margin for the US Open had been 11 strokes by Willie Smith in 1899. In the Masters, Woods broke the record margin of nine strokes set by Nicklaus in 1965. Tiger also won The Open by eight strokes, the largest margin since J.H. Taylor in 1913.

Perhaps his most remarkable win of all came at the 2008 US Open at Torrey Pines when he defeated Rocco Mediate in a play-off in spite of suffering from a knee injury and a double stress fracture of his left tibia. When the championship was over, he underwent surgery on his anterior cruciate ligament and missed the rest of the season. All of those extraordinary accomplishments were the work of the son of the late Earl Woods, a retired lieutenant-colonel in the US Army, and Kultida, a native of Thailand. Woods was nicknamed Tiger after a Vietnamese soldier and friend of his father, Vuong Dang Phong, to whom he had also given that nickname.

When Tiger married Elin and the couple had two children, Sam and Charlie, Woods' life seemed blessed. However, controversy surrounding infidelity in his private life led to a divorce from Elin, as well as the loss of numerous sponsorship deals with Gatorade, AT&T, Accenture, Gillette and *Golf Digest*. For the first time in 15 years he failed to win during 2010 and was dethroned as world No 1 after a total of 623 weeks by Lee Westwood before falling out of the world's top 5 golfers after an injury-blighted season. In 2011 he split with long time caddie Steve Williams and fell as low as 58th in the world rankings. However, he ended a winless streak of 107 weeks when he captured the Chevron World Challenge and rose to 23rd in the world.

make par. He has now assumed hero status in Canada and has been inducted into the Canadian Golf Hall of Fame.

Weiskopf, Tom (USA)

Born Massillon, Ohio, 9 November 1942
Turned professional 1964

Winner of only one Major – the 1973 Open Championship at Royal Troon, he lived in the shadow of Jack Nicklaus throughout his competitive career. He was runner-up in the 1976 US Open to Jerry Pate and was twice third in 1973 and 1977. His best finish in the USPGA Championship was third in 1975 – the year he had to be content for the fourth time with second place at the US Masters. He had been runner-up for a Green Jacket in 1969, 1972 and 1974 but played perhaps his best golf ever in 1975 only to be pipped at the post by Nicklaus. With 22 wins to his name he now plays the US Senior Tour with a curtailed schedule because of his course design work for which he and his original partner Jay Morrish have received much praise. One of their designs is Loch Lomond, venue for several years of the revived Scottish Open. Played in just two Ryder Cup matches giving up a place in the team one year in order to go Bighorn sheep hunting in Alaska.

Westwood, Lee (ENG)

Born Worksop, Nottinghamshire, 24 April 1973
Turned professional 1993

The year 2010 was very special for Lee Westwood. The consistent Englishman was the man who finally prised Tiger Woods out of the No 1 spot in the World Rankings he had held for five years. He beat Phil Mickelson and Martin Kaymer to top spot following Tiger Woods dramatic loss of form following an off the course scandal. It was just reward for one of the most consistent of golfers who battled back and made it to the top after having very nearly quit the game a few years earlier. His own loss of form had seen him slump from No,. 4 in the world rankings to a position outside the top 250. He credits David Leadbetter for sorting out his game A former British Youths' champion who missed out on Walker Cup honours, he quickly made the grade in the professional ranks and, in 2000 ended the seven-year reign of Colin Montgomerie by taking the top spot in the Volvo Order of Merit. He was six-time winner that year in Europe and beat Montgomerie at the second extra hole of the Cisco World Match Play final at Wentworth. He has won titles on every major circuit in the world including most notably three victories at the Taiheiyo Masters in Japan, the Australian Open in 1997 when he beat Greg Norman in a play-off and the Freeport McDermott Classic and the New Orleans and St Jude Fedex titles on the US PGATour. He has been a member of the last seven Ryder Cup teams including the 2010 match at Celtic Manor where he played well despite suffering from a painful calf injury. When he

made the 2008 side at Valhalla he equalled Arnold Palmer's record of 12 successive games unbeaten. He has not won a major yet but has come close several times He was third in the 2008 US Open and came close in the 2009 Open at Turnberry where only a last hole bogey prevented his being involved in the play-off for the title with Stewart Cink and Tom Watson. Later that year he finish joint third with Rory McIlroy behind YE Yang and Tiger Woods in the US PGA Championship. In 2009 he ended a two-year winning drought with victory in the Portugal Masters and the Dubai World Championship which helped him finish No 1 in the first Race to Dubai. In 2010 he finished second in two majors – to Phil Mickelson at The Masters and to Louis Oosthuizen at The Open. Early in 2011 he was made an honorary member of the PGA European Tour. . He is married to Laurae Coltart, sister of fellow professional Andrew Coltart.

Wilson, Oliver (ENG)

Born Mansfield, 14 September 1980
Turned professional 2003

He played his way into the 2008 Ryder Cup side at Valhalla and impressed as a rookie, Having attended Augusta College he now lives much of the time in America. He was a member of the winning Great Britain and Ireland Walker Cup side in 2003. Like Padraig Harrington who had so many runner-up finishes before becoming a regular winner, Wilson is still awaiting his first victory.

Wirachant, Thawarn (THA)

Born Bangkok, Thailand, 28 December 1966
Turned professional 1987

He earned a full year's exemption on the European Tour when he won the Enjoy Jakarta Standard Chartered Indonesian Open – a joint venture between the Asian and European Tours. It was his sixth win on the Asian Tour which he joined 10 years earlier. Wirachant is best known for his unorthodox swing which works effectively for him. He is a former Thai Amateur champion.

Wolstenholme, Gary (ENG)

Born Egham, Surrey, 21 August 1960
Turned professional 2008

Nobody has played more often for England. Between 1988 and 2008 when he turned professional to prepare for the European Senior Tour – he represented England an incredible 218 times. Although he can remember swinging a club at the age of 4½ he was off 23 when he started playing seriously at the age of 17. Within six years he was scratch and by the age of 23 he had started representing England. During his amateur career he played in seven St Andrews Trophy matches against the Continent of Europe between 1992 and 2004 during which time he amassed a P19 W10 L9 H0 points record. In six Walker Cups between 1995 and 2005 he had the most individual and team wins.

Awarded the MBE for his services to golf in the 2007 New Year's honours list and the recipient of an honorary MA degree from Northampton University, he represented Leicestershire and Rutland from 1981 to 2007 and Cumbria in 2008. He was playing off plus 4 when he turned professional but at one point was a plus 5 golfer. He has honorary membership of 13 clubs and Associations. Amateur champion at Ganton in 1991 and Royal Troon in 2003 he has also won titles in China. the UAE, Finland, Luxembourg Australia and Spain. He has had 13 holes in one, five of them in competition. Highlights of his outstanding career were beating Tiger Woods at Porthcawl in the 1995 Walker Cup and, more importantly, helping Luke Donald, Paddy Gribben and Lorn Kelly win the World Amateur Team Championship in Chile in 1998. He is now doing well as a professional on the European Senior Tour.

Wood, Chris (ENG)

Born Bristol, 26 November 1987
Turned professional 2008

First made the national newspaper headlines when he finished fifth behind Padraig Harrington at the 2008 Open at Royal Birkdale. He turned professional immediately and earned his Tour card at the 2009 European Qualifying School. In 2009 he went even better in The Open when he finished joint third behind Stewart Cink. A bogey at his final hole prevented his being included in the play-off for the title between Cink and Tom Watson. He ended the season being named the Sir Henry Cotton Rookie of the Year.

Woosnam MBE, Ian (WAL)

Born Oswestry, Shropshire, 2 March 1958
Turned professional 1976

Highlight of his career was winning the Green Jacket at the Masters in 1991 after a last day battle with Spaniard José Maria Olazábal who went on to win in 1994 and again in 1999. Teamed up very successfully with Nick Faldo in Ryder Cup golf and was in four winning teams in 1985, 1987, 1995 and 1997 and was vice-captain in 2001 to Sam Torrance at The K Club before captaining the side to victory in 2006 at the K Club. He scored 28 European Tour victories and twice won the World Match Play Championship in 1987 when he beat Sandy Lyle, with whom he used to play boys' golf in Shropshire, in 1990 when his opponent was Mark McNulty and in 2001 when he beat Retief Goosen, then US Open Champion, Colin Montgomerie, Lee Westwood and then Padraig Harrington in the final. In 1989 he lost a low-scoring final to Nick Faldo on the last green. His lowest round was a 60 he returned in the 1990 Monte Carlo Open at Mont Agel. Partnered by David Llewellyn he won the World Cup of Golf in 1987 beating Scotland's Sam Torrance and Sandy Lyle in a play-off. Honoured with an MBE from Her Majesty the Queen he now lives with his family in Jersey. Finished joint third in the 2001 Open at Lytham after having been penalised two shots for discovering on the

second tee he had 15 clubs (one over the limit) in his bag. He now plays on the European Senior Tour and when he topped the money list in 2008 he became the first player to make it to No 1 on the European Tour and the European Seniors Tour.

Yang, Yong-Eun (KOR)

Born Seoul, Korea, 15 January 1972
Turned professional 1996

Winner of events on his home circuit in Korea and also in Japan, he shot to prominence first when beating Tiger Woods into second place in the 2006 HSBC Champions event in Shanghai – a win that earned him his European Tour card. These days he plays mostly in the United States where he followed up his victory in the 2009 Honda Classic with a first major triumph at Hazeltine in the USPGA Championship. Playing with favourite Tiger Woods on the final day he outscored him and outputted the World No 1 to become the first Asian to win a major. It earned him $1.35 million and he moved from 110th in the world rankings to 34th.

Yeh, Wei-tze (TPE)

Born Taiwan, 20 February 1973
Turned professional 1994

Fisherman's son who became the third Asia golfer after "Mr Lu" and Isao Aoki to win on the European Tour when he won the 2000 Benson and Hedges Malaysian Open. In 2003 he won the ANA Open on the Japanese Tour.

Zhang, Lian-Wei (CHN)

Born Shenzhen, 2 May 1965
Turned professional 1994

Leading Chinese player whose victory in the 2003 Caltex Singapore Open when he edged out Ernie Els was the first by a Chinese golfer on Tour. Initially he trained as a javelin thrower before turning to golf. Self-taught he was also the first Asian golfer to win on the Canadian Tour but remains a stalwart on the Asian circuit. In 2009 he was pipped by Ian Poulter for the Barclays Singapore Open and finished the year in second spot on the Asian Tour Order of Merit to Thongchai Jaidee.

Zoeller, Fuzzy (USA)

Born New Albany, Indiana, 11 November 1951
Turned professional 1973

Winner of the US Masters in 1979 after a play-off with Ed Sneed (who had dropped shots at the last three holes in regulation play) and Tom Watson and was victorious US Open in 1984 at Winged Foot after an 18-hole play-off with Greg Norman. A regular winner on the US Tour between 1979 and 1980, he played on three Ryder Cups in 1979, 1983 and 1985. He announced that the 2008 Masters would be his final appearance at the event.

Who's Who in Golf – Women

Ahn, S-J.	Higuchi, H.	Lewis, S.	Ochoa, L.	Shin, J.-Y.
Alfredsson, H.	Hjörth, M.	Lincicome, B.	Okamoto, A.	Sörenstam, A.
Andrew, K.	Hudson, R.	Lopez, N.	Otto, J.	Steinhauer, S.
Bailey, D.	Inkster, J.	De Lorenzi, M.-L.	Pace, L-A.	Stephenson, J.
Bisgood, J.	Irvin, A.	Lunn, K.	Pak, S.R.	Streit, M.S.
Bonallack, A.	Jackson, B.	McIntire, B.	Panton-Lewis, C.	Stupples, K.
Bradley, P.	Jang, J.	McKay, M.	Park, G.	Suggs, L.
Butler, I.	Ji, E.-H.	McKenna, M.	Park, I.	Thomas, V.
Caponi, D.	Johnson, T.	Mallon, M.	Pepper, D.	Thompson, A.
Carner, J.A.	Kerr, C.	Mann, C.	Pettersen, S.	Tseng, Y.
Cavalleri, S.	Kim, B.	Massey, D.	Prado, C.	Varangot, B.
Creamer, P.	Kim, C.	Matthew, C.	Rawls, B.	Walker, M.
Daniel. B.	King, B.	Meunier-Lebouc, P.	Reid, D.	Webb, K.
Davies, L.	Ko, L.	Miyazato, A.	Robertson, B.	Whitworth, K.
Dibnah, C.	Klein, E.	Moodie, J.	Sander, A.	Wie, M.
Dowling, C.	Koch, K.	Muñoz, A.	Saunders, V.	Wright, J.
Duggleby, E.	Kuehne, K.	Neumann, L.	Segard, P.	Wright, M.
Fudoh, Y.	Laing, A.	Nicholas, A.	Semple Thompson,	Yokomine, S.
Gustafson, S.	Lawrence, J.	Nilsmark, C.	C.	
Haynie, S.	Lee-Smith, J.	Nordqvist, A.	Sheehan, P.	

Ahn, Sun-Ju (KOR)

Born South Korea, 31 August 1987
Turned professional 2006

The first Korean golfer to top the Japan LPGA Tour money list and be Japanese Rookie of the Year as well in 2010. Only other non-Japanese golfer to finish No.1 in Japan has been Chinese Taipei's Ai Yu Tu. In 2010, Ahn won four events and earned 145,07 million Yen.

Alfredsson, Helen (SWE)

Born Gothenburg, 9 April 1965
Turned professional 1989

After earning Rookie of the Year on the 1989 European Tour she won the 1992 Ladies' British Open. Two years later she was Gatorade Rookie of the Year on the American LPGA Tour. She has competed in seven Solheim Cup matches and captained the 2007 Cup side. She has won titles in Europe, America, Japan and Australia.

Andrew, Kim (née Rostron) (ENG)

Born 12 February 1974

After taking the English and Scottish Ladies' stroke play titles in 1997 she won the Ladies' British Open Amateur a year later. She played in the 1998 and 2000 Curtis Cup matches.

Bailey MBE, Mrs Diane (Frearson née Robb) (ENG)

Born Wolverhampton, 31 August 1943

After playing in the 1962 and 1972 Curtis Cup matches she captained the side in 1984, 1986 and

1988. In 1984 at Muirfield the Great Britain and Ireland side lost narrowly to the Americans but she led the side to a first ever victory on American soil at Prairie Dunes in Kansas two years later. The result was a convincing 13–5. She was in charge again when the GB&I side held on to the Cup two years later this time by 11–7 at Royal St George's.

Bisgood CBE, Jeanne (ENG)

Born Richmond, Surrey, 11 August 1923

Three times English Ladies champion in 1951, 1953 and 1957. Having played in three Curtis Cups she captained the side in 1970. Between 1952 and 1955 she won the Swedish, Italian, German, Portuguese and Norwegian Ladies titles.

Bonallack, Lady (née Angela Ward) (ENG)

Born Birchington, Kent, 7 April 1937

Wife of Sir Michael Bonallack OBE, she played in six Curtis Cup matches. She was leading amateur in the 1975 and 1976 Colgate European Opens, won two English Ladies' titles and had victories, too, in the Swedish, German, Scandinavian and Portuguese Championships.

Bradley, Pat (USA)

Born Westford, Massachusetts, 24 March 1951
Turned professional 1974

Winner of four US LPGA majors – the Nabisco Championship, the US Women's Open, the LPGA Championship and the du Maurier Classic, she won 31 times on the American circuit. An outstanding skier and ski instructor as well, she started playing golf when she was 11. Every time she won her mother would ring a bell on the porch of the family home whatever the time of day. The bell is now in the World Golf Hall of Fame. She played in four Solheim Cup sides and captained the team in 2000 at Loch Lomond. Inducted into the LPGA Hall of Fame in 1991 she was Rolex Player of the Year in 1986 and 1991. In 2011 her nephew Keegan Bradley won the USPGA Championship.

Butler, Ita (née Burke) (IRL)

Born Nenagh, County Tipperary

Having played in the Curtis Cup in 1966, she captained the side that beat the Americans by 5 points at Killarney thirty years later.

Caponi, Donna (USA)

Born Detroit, Michigan, 29 January 1945
Turned professional 1965

Twice winner of the US Women's Open in 1969 and 1970 she collected 24 titles on the LPGA Tour between 1969 and 1981. Winner of the 1975 Colgate European Open at Sunningdale, she is now a respected commentator/analyst for The Golf Channel in Orlando.

Carner, Jo Anne (née Gunderson) (USA)

Born Kirkland, Washington, 4 April 1939
Turned professional 1970

Had five victories in the US Ladies' Amateur Championship (1957, 1960, 1962, 1966 and 1968) before turning professional and winning the 1971 and 1976 US Women's Open. She remains the last amateur to win on the LPGA Tour after having taken the 1969 Burdine's Invitational. Between 1970 and 1985 scored 42 victories on the LPGA Tour and was Rolex Player of the Year in 1974, 1981 and 1982. She was inducted into the LPGA Hall of Fame in 1982 and the World Golf Hall of Fame in 1985. She won the Bobby Jones award in 1981 and the Mickey Wright award in 1974 and 1982.

Cavalleri, Silvia (ITA)

Born Milan, 10 October 1972
Turned professional 1997

Became the first Italian to win the US Amateur when she beat Robin Burke 5 and 4 at Brae Burn in the 1997 final. She was five times Italian National Junior champion and won the British Girls' title in 1990 with a 5 and 4 success over E. Valera at Penrith.

Creamer, Paula (USA)

Born Pleasanton, California, 5 August 1986
Turned professional 2005

The youngest and first amateur to win the LPGA qualifying school in 2004. As an amateur she was top ranked American junior in 2003 and 2004 winning 19 national titles. After turning professional she became a winner on the LPGA Tour in her ninth start when she won the Sybase Classic. She began playing golf at the age of 10. Despite being sidelined with a hand injury and undergoing surgery on a thumb in 2010, she won her first major with a victory at the US Women's Open. She has played in four Solheim Cup matches.

Daniel, Beth (USA)

Born Charleston, South Carolina, 14 October 1956
Turned professional 1978

A member of the LPGA Hall of Fame, she won 32 times between 1979 and 1995 including the 1990 US LPGA Championship. She was Rolex Player of the Year in 1980, 1990 and 1994. Before turning professional she won the US Women's Amateur title in 1975 and 1977 and played in the 1976 and 1978 Curtis Cup teams. She has played in eight Solheim Cup competitions since 1990 and was named as vice-captain to Betsy King at the 2007 match in Sweden. She captained of the US side in 2009 at Rich Harvest Farm in Sugar Grove, Illinois. During her career she has won 33 LPGA events and has won $8.7m in prize money. She works as an analyst on the Golf Channel.

Dibnah, Corinne (AUS)

Born Brisbane, 29 July 1962
Turned professional 1984

A former Australian and New Zealand amateur champion, she joined the European Tour after turning professional and won 13 times between 1986 and 1994. A pupil of Greg Norman's first coach Charlie Earp, she was Europe's top earner in 1991.

Dowling, Clare (née Hourihane) (IRL)

Born 18 February 1958

Won three Irish Ladies' Championships in a row – 1983, 1984 and 1985 and won the title again in 1987 and 1991. She won the 1986 British Ladies' Stroke play amateur title. Two years earlier she had made the first of five playing appearances in the Curtis Cup before acting as non-playing captain in 2000.

Duggelby, Emma (ENG)

Born Fulford, York, 5 October 1971

Talented English golfer who won the British Ladies' Open Amateur Championship in 1994 and the English Ladies in 2000 when she made her Curtis Cup début. She also played in the 2004 match winning three points out of four.

Fudoh, Yuri (JPN)

Born Kumamoto, 14 October 1976
Turned professional 1996

A multiple winner on the Japanese Tour who won her first Japanese event in 2003 when she took the Japan LPGA Championship title. She has won 20 events on the Japanese Tour and her winnings in 2000 of ¥120,443,924 was a record. By the end of

Laura Davies CBE (ENG)

Born 10 October 1963
Turned professional 1985

Record-breaking performer who has won 77 events worldwide including the US and British Women's Opens. For six days in 1987 she held both titles having won the American event before joining the US Tour. She was a founder member of the Women's Tour in Europe.. She still holds the record for the number of birdies in a round – 11 which she scored in the 1987 Open de France Feminin. Her 16-shot victory, by a margin of five shots, in the 1995 Guardian Irish Holidays Open at St Margaret's remains the biggest in European Tour history. Her 267 totals in the 1988 Biarritz Ladies' Open and the 1995 Guardian Irish Holidays Open are the lowest on Tour and have been matched only by Julie Inkster in the 2002 Evian Masters. Other major victories include the LPGA Championship twice and the du Maurier Championship. In 1999 she became the first European Tour player to pass through the £1 million in prize-money earnings and finished European No. 1 that year for a record fifth time. She was No.1 again in 2004. The 1996 Rolex Player of the Year in America, she has won almost $5.5 million in US prize-money. Originally honoured with an MBE by Her Majesty the Queen in 1988, she became a CBE in 2000. Enjoys all sports including soccer (she supports Liverpool FC). Among other awards she has received during her career have been the Association of Golf Writers' Trophy for her contribution to European golf in 1994 and the American version in 1994 and 1996 for her performances on the US Tour.

In 1994 she became the first golfer to score victories on five different Tours – European, American, Australasian, Japanese and Asian in one calendar year. As an amateur she played for Surrey and was a Curtis Cup player in 1984. She has competed in all 11 Solheim Cup matches. In 2000 was recognised by the LPGA in their top 50 players' and teachers' honours list. Laura proved how strong a competitor she still is when she took the No.1 spot on the women's tour in Europe for a seventh time in 2006. Although she only won once she had six second-place finishes and ended the year with a total of €471,727 from the 11 events she played. By the end of 2006 she had stretched her winning record to 67 titles and in 2007 made it 68 with victory in the Austrian Open a week after missing the cut in the Scottish Open, the first time she had missed in 23 years competing in events organised solely by the Ladies European Tour. She has failed only once – in 2005 – to win an event. When she successfully defended the Uniqua Ladies' Golf Open in 2008 she took her victory tally to 69.

Her 2010 season was better than average because she won five titles in as many different lands – Australia, Germany, Austria, Spain and India – taking her tally of victories to 77. In amongst her haul of titles there are four majors, starting with the US Women's Open of 1987. Since then, she has bagged a couple of US LPGA championships and a du Maurier, while she also captured the British Women's Open in the days before the event was given major status. She is the oldest player on the Ladies European Tour.

2010 she had become a yen billionaire in prize-money.

Gustafson, Sophie (SWE)

Born Saro, 27 December 1973
Turned professional 1992

Winner of the 2000 Weetabix Women's British Open she had studied marketing, economics and law before turning to professional golf. Credits Seve Ballesteros and Laura Davies as the two players most influencing her career. Her first European victory was the 1996 Swiss Open and her first on the LPGA Tour was the Chick-fil-A Charity Cup in 2000. She has played in every Solheim Cup match since 1998. Previously married to administrator Ty Votaw, the couple later divorced.

Haynie, Sandra (USA)

Born Fort Worth, Texas, 4 June 1943
Turned professional 1961

Twice a winner of the US Women's Open (1965 and 1974) she won 42 times between 1962 and 1982 on the US LPGA Tour. She was elected to the LPGA Hall of Fame in 1977.

Higuchi, Hisako "Chako" (JPN)

Born Saitama Prefecture, Japan, 13 October 1945
Turned professional 1967

A charter member and star of the Japan LPGA Tour, she won 72 victories worldwide during her career. In 2003 she was elected to the World Golf Hall of Fame.

Hjörth, Maria (SWE)

Born Falun, 10 October 1973
Turned professional 1996

After an excellent amateur career when she won titles in Finland, Norway and Spain, she attended Stirling University in Scotland on a golf bursary and graduated with a BA honours degree in English before turning professional. She has played in the Solheim Cup, most notably in 2011. In 2008 she was beaten in a play-off for the McDonald's LPGA Championship by Yani Tseng.

Hudson, Rebecca (ENG)

Born Doncaster, Yorkshire, 13 June 1979
Turned professional 2002

A member of the 1998, 2000 and 2002 Curtis Cup teams she won both the British Match Play and Stroke Play titles, the Scottish and English Stroke play Championships and the Spanish Women's Open in 2000. In addition she made the birdie that ensured Great Britain and Ireland won a medal in the World Team Championship for the Espirito Santo Trophy in Berlin in 2000.

Inkster, Juli (USA)

Born Santa Cruz, California, 24 June 1960
Turned professional 1983

Winner of two majors in 1984 (the Nabisco Championship and the du Maurier) she also had a double Major year in 1999 when she won the US Women's Open and the LPGA Championship which she won for a second time in 2000. In 2002 she won the US Women's Open for a second time. In all she has won seven major titles. In her amateur career she became the first player since 1934 to win the US Women's amateur title three years in a row (1980, 81, 82). Only four other women and one man (Tiger Woods) have successfully defended their national titles twice in a row. Coached for a time by the late London-based Leslie King at Harrods Store. She is a regular in the Solheim Cup competition having played nine times between between 1992 and 2011. By 2010 her career earnings had gone through the $13 million mark and she had collected 31 titles.

Irvin, Ann (ENG)

Born 11 April 1943

Winner of the British Ladies' title in 1973, she played in four Curtis Cup matches between 1962 and 1976. She was Daks Woman Golfer of the Year in 1968 and 1969 and has been active in administration at junior and county level.

Jackson, Bridget (ENG)

Born Birmingham, 10 July 1936

A former President of the Ladies' Golf Union she played in three Curtis Cup matches and captained the Vagliano Trophy side twice after having played four times. Although the best she managed in the British Championship was runner-up in 1964 she did win the English, German and Canadian titles.

Jang, Jeong (KOR)

Born Daejeon, Korea, 11 June 1980
Turned professional 1999

She scored her breakthrough win on the LPGA Tour when winning the Weetabix Women's British Open at Royal Birkdale. She led from start to finish. As an amateur she won the Korean Women's Open in 1997 and the following year was Korean Women's Amateur champion. Just 5ft tall, she started playing

golf at age 13 and has been influenced throughout her career by her father.

Ji, Eun-Hee (KOR)

Born Gapyeong, South Korea, 13 May 1986
Turned professional 2004

A former Korean and Japanese Ladies Tour member she won her first major in 2009 when she was successful in the US Women's Open. She holed a 20-foot putt for a winning birdie at the last to collect a first prize of $580,000.

Johnson, Trish (ENG)

Born Bristol, 17 January 1966
Turned professional 1987

Another stalwart of the Women's Tour in Europe who learned the game at windy Westward Ho. Regular winner on Tour both in Europe and America, she scored two and a half points out of four in Europe's dramatic Solheim Cup win over the Americans at Loch Lomond in 2000. She has played in eight Solheim Cup matches. She was European No.1 earner in 1990. A loyal supporter of Arsenal FC she regularly attends games at The Emirates Stadium.

Kerr, Cristie (USA)

Born Florida, 1977 Turned professional 1997

She relished the second major success of her career in 2010 when she ran away with the LPGA Championship, defeating Song-Hee Kim by a record breaking margin of 12 shots. The first American to hold the No.1 spot in the world rankings, she finished in the top 20 at all four majors in 2010. Her previous major title victory came in the 2007 US Women's Open at Pine Needles, her favourite course. Kerr's official career earnings on the LPGA Tour amount to nearly $12m. In 2006 she had 19 top 10 finishes. In 1996 she played in the Curtis Cup and was low amateur in the US Women's Open. Since turning professional, she's won 14 events and played six times for the USA in the Solheim Cup. Unfortunately, she had to withdraw from the singles in 2011 because of injury, fofeiting a crucial point in the match won by Europe.

Kim, Birdie (KOR)

Born Ik-San, Korea, 26 August 1981
Turned professional 2000

She became the 14th player in the history of the LPGA Tour to score her first win at the US Women's Open and she did it dramatically holing a bunker shot at the last to beat amateurs Brittany Lang and Morgan Pressel by two shots at Cherry Hills, Colorado. A silver medallist at the 1998 Asian Games she won 19 events as an amateur before joining the US Futures Tour in 2001.

Kim, Christina (USA)

Born California, 1984 Turned professional 2002

One of the LPGA's most flamboyant and popular players, the American has won nearly $4m since becoming a regular Tour player in 2003. She's won twice and was a member of the US Solheim Cup teams on three occasions. In 2010 she recorded top ten finishes at both the US Women's Open and the Women's British Open.

King, Betsy (USA)
Born Reading, Pennsylvania, 13 August 1955
Turned professional 1977

Another stalwart of the LPGA Tour in America she won 34 times between 1984 and 2001. Winner of the British Open in 1985 she has also won the US Women's Open in 1989 and 1990, the Nabisco Championship three times in 1987, 1990 and 1997 and the LPGA Championship in 1990. She never managed to win the du Maurier event although finishing in the top six on nine occasions. Three times Rolex Player of the Year in 1984, 1989 and 1993 she was elected to the LPGA Hall of Fame in 1995.

Klein, Emilee (USA)
Born Santa Monica, California, 11 June 1974
Turned professional 1994

The former Curtis Cup player who played in the 1994 match scored her biggest triumph as a professional when winning the Weetabix British Women's Open at Woburn in 1996.

Ko, Lydia (NZL)
Born Korea, April 24 1997

The inaugural recipient in 2011 of the Mark H McCormack medal for the top ranked female amateur golfer, the 14-year-old Kiwi (she was born in Korea but is a New Zealand citizen) was also the first golfer to win both the Australian and New Zealand women's strokeplay championships in the same year. She won four other amateur tournaments in New Zealand last year. In the three professional tournaments she entered, Ko was second in the NSW Open, 4th in the Pegasus NZ Women's Open and 12th in the Handa Australian Open. She was the youngest player ever to make a cut in a Ladies European Tour event after finishing seventh as a 12-year-old at the NZ Women's Open in 2010.

Koch, Carin (SWE)
Born Kungalv, Sweden, 2 February 1971
Turned professional 1992

She has been playing golf since she was nine and in the 2000 and 2002 Solheim Cup matches was unbeaten. In 2000 she won three points out of three and in 2002 she won 2½ points out of three. She also played in the 2003 and 2005 matches.

Kuehne, Kelli (USA)
Born Dallas, Texas, 11 May 1977
Turned professional 1998

Having won the US Women's Amateur Championship in 1995 she successfully defended the title

the following year when she also won the British Women's title – the first player to win both in the same year. She was also the first player to follow up her win in the US Junior Girls' Championship in 1994 with victory in the US Women's event the following year. Her brother Hank is also a professional.

Laing, Anne (SCO)
Born Alexandria, Dunbartonshire, 14 March 1975

Winner of three Scottish Championships in 1996, 2003 and 2004. She made her début in the Curtis Cup in 2004 having played in the Vagliano Trophy in 2003.

Lawrence, Joan (SCO)
Born Kinghorn, Fife, 20 April 1930

After a competitive career in which she three times won the Scottish championship and played in the 1964 Curtis Cup, she has played her part in golf administration. She had two four-year spells as an LGU selector, is treasurer of the Scottish Ladies' Golf Association and has also served on the LGU executive.

Lee-Smith, Jennifer (ENG)
Born Newcastle-upon-Tyne, 2 December 1948
Turned professional 1977

After winning the Ladies' British Open as an amateur in 1976 was named Daks Woman Golfer of the Year. She played twice in the Curtis Cup before turning professional and winning nine times in a six year run from 1979. For a time she ran her own driving range in southern England and is back living in Kent again after having spent time in Florida.

Lewis, Stacy (USA)
Born Toledo, Ohio, 1985   Turned professional 2008

She enjoyed her first LPGA win in the majors by lifting the Kraft Nabisco Championship in 2011. After trailing Yani Tseng by two strokes going into the final round, she rallied behind to overtake the world No 1 and win by three shots. A formidable amateur golfer who became the first player in the history of the Curtis Cup to win all five of her matches over the Old Course in St Andrews, Lewis suffered from scoliosis and spent nearly eight years in a back brace before undergoing spinal surgery which left her unsure if she would be able to walk again.

Lincicome, Britanny (USA)
Born St Petersburg, Florida, 19 September 1985
Turned professional 2004

She won the first 2009 major in spectaular fashion when eagling the final hole at Mission Hills to edge clear of Cristie Kerr and Kristie McPherson. Later in the year played in the Solheim Cup match. As an amateur she won the American Junior Golf Association Championship twice and first hit the

Nancy Lopez, (née Knight) (USA)

Born Torrance, California, 6 January 1957
Turned professional 1977

One of the game's bubbliest personalities and impressive performers who took her first title – the New Mexico Women's Amateur title at age 12. Between 1978 and 1995 she won 48 times on the LPGA Tour and was Rolex Player of the Year on four occasions (1978, 79, 85 and 88). In 1978, her rookie year, she won nine titles including a record five in a row. That year she also lost two play-offs and remains the only player to have won the Rookie of the Year, Player of the Year and Vare Trophy (scoring average) in the same season. A year later she won eight tournaments. Three times a winner of the LPGA Championship in 1978, 1985 and 1989 she has never managed to win the US Women's Open although she was runner-up in 1975 as an amateur, in 1977, 1989 and most recently 1997 when she lost out to Britain's Alison Nicholas. She retired from competitive golf and in 2002 was awarded the PGA's First Lady in Golf award for the contribution she has made to the game. In 2005 she captained the winning American Solheim Cup side at Crooked Stick. She started playing competitively again on a limited basis in 2007.

headlines as a professional when she won the HSBC Women's World Match-play Championship beating Michelle Wie and Lorena Ochoa on the way to the final where she triumphed over Juli Inkster. She was a member of the 2007, 2009 and 2011 US Solheim Cup sides.

De Lorenzi, Marie-Laure (FRA)

Born Biarritz, 21 January 1961
Turned professional 1986
The stylish French golfer won 20 titles in Europe between 1987 and 1997 setting a record in 1988 when she won eight times but for family reasons never spent time on the US Tour.

Lunn, Karen (AUS)

Born Sydney, 21 March 1966
Turned professional 1985
A former top amateur she won the British Women's Open in 1993 at Woburn following the success in the European Ladies' Open earlier in the year by her younger sister Mardi.She is a former chairman of the LET.

McIntire, Barbara (USA)

Born Toledo, Ohio, 1935
One of America's best amateurs who finished runner-up in the 1956 US Women's Open to Kathy Cornelius at Northland Duluth. Winner of the US Women's Amateur title in 1959 and 1964 she also won the British Amateur title in 1960. She played in six Curtis Cups between 1958 and 1962.

McKay, Mhairi (SCO)

Born Glasgow, 18 April 1975
Turned professional 1997
Former British Girls' Champion (1992 and 1993) she has played in the Vagliano Trophy and Curtis Cup.

She was an All-American when studying at Stanford University, where she was a contemporary of Tiger Woods, and made her first appearance in the Solheim Cup at Barsebäck, Sweden, in 2003.

McKenna, Mary (IRL)

Born Dublin, 29 April 1949
Winner of the British Ladies' Amateur Stroke play title in 1979 and eight times Irish champion between 1969 and 1989. One of Ireland's most successful golfers she played in nine Curtis Cup matches and nine Vagliano Trophy matches between 1969 and 1987. She captained the Vagliano team in 1995 and 2009. Three times a member of the Great Britain and Ireland Espirito Santo Trophy side she went on to captain the team in 1986. She was Daks Woman Golfer of the Year in 1979. She captained the Cutis Cup team beaten by the Americans at St Andrews in 2008 and was re-appointed captain for that event in 2010.

Mallon, Meg (USA)

Born Natwick, Maryland, 14 April 1963
Turned professional 1986
Winner of the 1991 US Women's Open, 1991 Mazda LPGA Championship, the 2000 du Maurier Classic and 11 other events between 1991 and 2002. In 2004 she won the US Women's Open for the second time. She holed the winning putt in the 2005 Solheim Cup.

Mann, Carole (USA)

Born Buffalo, New York, 3 February 1940
Turned professional 1960
Winner of 38 events on the LPGA Tour in her 22 years on Tour. A former president of the LPGA she was a key figure in the founding of the Tour and received the prestigious Babe Zaharias award. In 1964 she won the Western Open, then a Major, and in 1965 the US Women's Open but in 1968 she had a

then record 23 rounds in the 60s, won 11 times and won the scoring averages prize with a score of 72.04. Enjoys a hugely successful corporate career within golf. In 2008 she was awarded the prestigious First Lady of Golf award from the PGA of America.

Massey, Debbie (USA)

Born Grosse Pointe, Michigan, 5 November 1950
Turned professional 1977

Best known for winning the British Women's Open in 1980 and 1981.

Matthew, Catriona (SCO)

Born Edinburgh, 25 August 1969
Turned professional 1995

Former Scottish Girls Under-21 and Scottish Amateur champion, Catriona also won the British Amateur in 1993. She played in the 1990, 1992 and 1994 Curtis Cup matches and made her début in the Solheim Cup at Barsebäck in 2003 and had the honour of holing the winning putt. She performed impressively throughout, showing considerable coolness under pressure. She was also a member of the 2005, 2007, 2009 and 2011 European teams. Now plays on both sides of the Atlantic. With Janice Moodie came second to Sweden's Annika Sörenstam and Liselotte Neumann in the 2006 Women's World Cup of Golf. In 2007 made the cut in all four women's majors and finished tied second in the Kraft Nabisco Championship. Sixteen years after she had won the Amateur Championship at Royal Lytham and St Annes she won her first major at that course when she won the Ricoh Women's British Open in 2009. Her victory came just two months after giving birth to her second daughter and a week after escaping with her husband who caddies for her, from a fire in the building they were staying in during the Evian Masters. In 2011 she returned to winning ways in the Aberdeen Scottish Open at Archerfield. The Scot also savoured an end of season victory in 2011 when she won the Lorena Ochoa Invitational in Mexico, her fourth career success on the LPGA Tour.

Meunier-Lebouc, Patricia (FRA)

Born Dijon, 16 November 1972
Turned professional 1993

French amateur champion in 1992, she has been a regular winner in Europe. She played in the 2000 and 2002 Solheim Cup matches and won her first major when she took first prize in the Kraft-Nabisco Championship at Mission Hills in California

Miyazato, Ai (JPN)

Born Okinawa, Japan, 19 June, 1985
Turned professional 2004

Miyazato became the first Japanese golfer ever to top the Order of Merit on the Ladies European Tour when she earned more than 363,000 euros from just two appearances in 2011. She earned all of her prize money from winning the Evian Masters for the second time. She donated a substantial portion of her earnings to the tsunami relief efforts in Japan. She topped the Rolex world rankings for 11 weeks in 2010 and has won six times on the LPGA

Moodie, Janice (SCO)

Born Glasgow, 31 May 1973
Turned professional 1997

The 1992 Scottish Women's Stroke play champion played in two winning Curtis Cup teams and earned All American honours at San José State University where she graduated with a degree in psychology. She has won twice on the LPGA, is married to an American and has a young son, Craig. Started playing at age 11 and was helped considerably by Cawder professional Ken Stevely. In the 2000 Solheim Cup she won three out of four points but was controversially left out of the 2002 team. She was reinstated by captain Catrin Nilsmark for the 2003 match at Barsebäck in Sweden where she teamed up with fellow Scot Catriona Matthew and won her singles. She was a wild card pick for the 2009 Solheim Cup but only had one top ten finish in 2010.

Muñoz, Azahara (ESP)

Born Malaga, 19 November 1987
Turned professional 2009

After winning the British Girls Championship at Lanark in 2004, 21-year-old Muñoz won the British Women's Amateur title with a 2 and 1 victory in an all-Spanish final against Carlota Ciganda. She immediately turned professional and in her rookie year won the Madrid Ladies Masters. Later she qualified to play on the LPGA Tour and ended the 2010 season winning the leading rookie award.

Neumann, Liselotte (SWE)

Born Finspang, 20 May 1966
Turned professional 1985

Having won the US Women's Open in 1988 she won the Weetabix British Women's Open title in 1990 to become one of six players to complete the Transatlantic double. The others are Laura Davies, Alison Nicholas, Jane Geddes, Betsy King and Patty Sheehan. The 1988 Rookie of the Year on the LPGA Tour she played in the first six Solheim Cup matches but was a surprising omission from the team in 2005 when she had one of her best years on the US Tour. With Annika Sörenstam won the 2006 World Cup of Golf in South Africa.

Nicholas MBE, Alison (ENG)

Born Gibraltar, 6 February 1978

In Solheim Cup golf had a successful partnership with Laura Davies. In addition they have both won the British and US Open Championships. Alison's first win on the European Tour came in the 1987 Weetabix British Open and she added the US Open ten years later after battling with Nancy Lopez who was trying

Lorena Ochoa (MEX)

Born Guadalajara, 15 November 1981
Turned professional 2003

Announced her retirement from the LPGA as world No 1 in the spring of 2010 and finished sixth in her last event. She was thrillingly consistent throughout her career, finishing in the top ten at 109 of the 173 events she entered in America. Ochoa won her first major when she took the Ricoh British Women's Open when it was held for the first time over the Old Course at St Andrews. She was the fastest player to reach $3million in prize-money on the LPGA Tour in 2006, although she did not win a major that season, losing the Kraft Nabisco to Karrie Webb in a play-off at Palm Springs. However, she topped the money list and was Player of the Year. In 2006 she had six victories, five second place finishes, two thirds, two fourths and a fifth earning more than $2.5million. She fared even better in 2007 when she won eight times and pocketed $4.36 million in prize-money. In 2008 she won another major – the Kraft Nabisco. From the beginning of March to April 20 she won five times and enjoyed two more late season victories by the end of September. In 2009, she edged Ji Yai Shin for the Rolex Player of the Year Award by a single point. All told she won 27 times between 2004 and 2010 and earned nearly $15m. She chose to step down at the tender age of 29 because she had achieved her professional goals and wanted to start a family

to win her national title for the first time. Alison is a former winner of the Association of Golf Writers' Golfer of the Year award and has been honoured with an MBE. She announced her retirement from top-line competition in 2004. She captained the European Solheim Cup side in America in 2009. Europe lost but it was much closer than most people imagined it would be. Two year later, however, she led Europe to a famous victory at Killeen Castle.

Nilsmark, Catrin (SWE)

Born Gothenburg, Sweden, 28 Aug 1967
Turned professional 1987

Holed the winning putt in Europe's Solheim Cup victory in 1992. Her early career was affected by whiplash injury after a car crash. Used to hold a private pilot's licence but now rides Harley Davidson motorcycles. She captained the European team to victory in the 2003 Solheim Cup matches at Barsebäck in Sweden and captained the team again at Crooked Stick when America regained the trophy.

Nordqvist, Anna (SWE)

Born Esilstuna, Sweden, 10 June 1987
Turned professional 2008

Swedish Junior Player of the Year in 2004 and 2005 and Swedish Player of the Year in 2005 she won the British Girls' Championship in 2005 and the British Women's title in 2008 the year she was a member of the winning Swedish side in the World Amateur Team Championship for the Espirito Santo Trophy at Adelaide. After a hugely successful amateur career while attending Arizona State University, she turned professional and in only her fifth event on the LPGA Tour she won her first major – the McDonald's LPGA Championship. She credited Annika Sörenstam for the advice that helped her win a major so quickly in her professional career. She was a member of the 2009 European Solheim Cup side.

Okamoto, Ayako (JPN)

Born Hiroshima, 12 April 1951
Turned professional 1976

Although she won the British Women's Open in 1984 she managed only a runner-up spot in the US Women's Open and US LPGA Championships despite finishing in the top 20 28 times and missing the cut only four times. In the LPGA Championships she finished second or third five times in six years from 1986. She scored 17 victories in the USA between 1982 and 1992, won the 1990 German Open and was Japanese Women's champion in 1993 and 1997. The LPGA Tour's Player of the Year 1987, she was inducted into the World Golf Hall of Fame in 2005.

Otto, Julie (née Wade) (ENG)

Born Ipswich, Suffolk, 10 March 1967

Secretary of the Ladies' Golf Union from 1996 to 2000 she was one of the most successful competitors in both individual and team golf. Among the many titles she won were the English Stroke Play in 1987 and 1993, the British Ladies' Stroke Play in 1993 and the Scottish Stroke Play in 1991 and 1993. She shared Britain's Golfer of the Year award in 1993 and won it again in 1995 on her own. She played in five Curtis Cup matches including the victories at Royal Liverpool in 1992 and Killarney in 1996 and the drawn match in 1994 at Chattanooga.

Pace, Lee-Anne (RSA)

Born 15 February 1981, Mosel Bay, South Africa
Turned professional 2005

Became the first South African to top the Ladies European Tour money list when she earned €339,517 from 25 events in 2010 and was named Players' Player of the Year. She won five times in 2010 in Switzerland, Wales, Finland, China and South

Korea. She studied at the University of Tulsa and has a degree in Psychology.

Pak, Se Ri (KOR)

Born Daejeon, 28 September 1977
Turned professional 1996

In 1998 she was awarded the Order of Merit by the South Korean government – the highest honour given to an athlete – for having won two Majors in her rookie year on the US Tour. She won the McDonald's LPGA Championship matching Liselotte Neumann in making a major her first tour success. When she won the US Women's Open later that year after an 18-hole play-off followed by two extra holes of sudden death against amateur Jenny Chuasiriporn, she became the youngest golfer to take that title. By the middle of 2001 she had won 12 events on the US tour including the Weetabix Women's British Open at Sunningdale – an event included on the US Tour as well as the European Circuit for the first time. In 2002 she was again a multiple winner on the US Tour adding to her majors by winning the McDonald's LPGA Championship. As an amateur in Korea she won 30 titles and became the first lady professional to make the cut in a men's professional event for 58 years when she played four rounds in a Korean Tour event. In 2006 she returned to the major winner's circle when she beat Karrie Webb in a play off for the McDonald's LPGA Championship. It was her fifth major victory but her first since 2002. In 2007 she was inducted into the World Golf Hall of Fame.

Panton-Lewis, Cathy (SCO)

Born Bridge of Allan, Stirlingshire, 14 June 1955
Turned professional 1978

A former Ladies' British Open Amateur Champion in 1976 when she was named Scottish Sportswoman of the year. She notched up 13 victories as a professional on the European tour between 1979 and 1988. Daughter of the late John Panton, MBE, former honorary professional to the Royal and Ancient Golf Club of St Andrews.

Park, Grace (KOR)

Born Seoul, Korea, 6 March 1979
Turned professional 1999

After having lost a sudden-death play-off to Annika Sörenstam at the McDonald's LPGA Championship in 2003 she did win her first major in 2004 when she was successful in the Nabisco Dinah Shore at Mission Hills in Palm Springs. She was a graduate of the Futures Tour where in 1999 she won five of the ten events. Before turning professional she attended Arizona State University and in 1998 became the first player since Patty Berg in 1931 to win the US Amateur, Western Amateur and Trans-Amateur titles in the same year. She won 55 national junior, college and amateur titles and tied

eighth as an amateur in the 1999 US Women's Open.

Park, Inbee (KOR)

Born South Korea, 1988
Turned professional 2006

Started playing golf at the age of 10 and won nine events on the American Junior Golf Association circuit. She earned her LPGA card in 2006 and won her first major – the 2008 US Women's Open at Interlachen by four shots from Sweden's Helen Alfredsson.

Pepper (Mochrie, Scarinzi), Dottie (USA)

Born Saratoga Springs, Florida, 17 August 1965
Turned professional 1987

Winner of 17 events on the LPGA Tour including two majors. She ranks 13th on the all-time money list with earnings of nearly $7 million. A fierce competitor she won the Nabisco Dinah Shore title in 1992 and again in 1999. She played in all the Solheim Cup matches up to 2000. In 2004 she announced her retirement from the US LPGA Tour because of injury. The following year she started work as a TV commentator for NBC and the Golf Channel, notoriously describing the US team at the 2007 Solheim Cup as "choking freaking dogs". While she apologised for her poor choice of words, a reputation for plain speaking has enhanced her broadcasting career.

Pettersen, Suzann (NOR)

Born Oslo, April 7 1981
Turned professional 2000

Five times Norwegian Amateur champion, Suzann was World Amateur champion in 2000. She won the French Open in 2001 and made her Solheim Cup début in the 2002 match at Barsebäck. One of the best performers on the week and was unbeaten going into the singles. She also played in the 2003, 2005, 2007, 2009 and 2011 matches and scored her first major success when she won the McDonald's LPGA Championship in 2007 going on that year to finish second to Lorena Ochoa in the LPGA money list. She won three times in 2011, twice on the LPGA and once on the LET, to finish the season in second place on the Rolex rankings.

Prado, Catherine (née Lacoste) (FRA)

Born Paris 27 June 1945

The only amateur golfer ever to win the US Women's Open she won the title at Hot Springs, Virginia, in 1967. She was also the first non-American to take the title and the youngest. Two years later she won both the US and British Amateur titles. She was a four times winner of her own French Championship in 1967, 1969, 1970 and 1972 and won the Spanish title in 1969, 1972 and 1976. She comes from a well-known French sporting family.

Rawls, Betsy (USA)

Born Spartanburg, South Carolina, 4 May 1928
Turned professional 1951

Winner of the 1951, 1953, 1957 and 1960 US Women's Open and the US LPGA Championship in 1959 and 1969 as well as two Western Opens when the Western Open was a Major. She scored 55 victories on the LPGA Tour between 1951 and 1972. One of the best shot makers in women's golf who was noted for her game around and on the greens.

Reid MBE, Dale (SCO)

Born Ladybank, Fife, 20 March 1959
Turned professional 1979

Scored 21 wins in her professional career between 1980 and 1991 and was so successful in leading Europe's Solheim Cup side to victory against the Americans at Loch Lomond in 2000 that she was again captain in 2002 when the Americans won. She had played in the 1990, 1992, 1994 and 1996 matches Following the team's success in the 2000 Solheim Cup she received an MBE.

Robertson MBE, Belle (SCO)

Born Southend, Argyll, 11 April 1936

One of Scotland's most talented amateur golfers who was Scottish Sportswoman of the Year in 1968, 1971, 1978 and 1981. She was Woman Golfer of the Year in 1971, 1981 and 1985. A former Ladies' British Open Amateur Champion and six times Scottish Ladies' Champion, she competed in nine Curtis Cups acting as non-playing captain in 1974 and 1976.

Sander, Anne (Welts, Decker, *née* Quast) (USA)

Born Marysville, 1938

A three times winner of the US Ladies' title in 1958, 1961 and 1963, she also won the British Ladies' title in 1980. She made eight appearances in the Curtis Cup stretching from 1958 to 1990. Only Carole Semple Thompson has played more often, having played ten times.

Saunders, Vivien (ENG)

Born Sutton, Surrey, 24 November 1946
Turned professional 1969

Founder of the Women's Professional Golfers' Association (European Tour) in 1978 and chairman for the first two years. In 1969 she was the first European golfer to qualify for the LPGA Tour in America. She is keen to become a re-instated amateur again.

Segard, Mme Patrick (de St Saveur, *née* Lally Vagliano) (FRA)

Former chairperson of the Women's Committee of the World Amateur Golf Council holding the post from 1964 to 1972. A four times French champion

(1948, 50, 51 and 52) she also won the British (1950), Swiss (1949 and 1965), Luxembourg (1949), Italian (1949 and 1951) and Spanish (1951) amateur titles. She represented France from 1937 to 1939, from 1947 to 1965 and again in 1970.

Semple Thompson, Carol (USA)

Born 1950

Winner of six titles including the US Ladies' in 1973 and the British Ladies in 1974, he has played in 12 Curtis Cups between 1974 and 2002 and holed the 27-foot winning putt in the 2002 match. At 53 she is the oldest US Curtis Cup Player. She captained the side in 1998, 2006 and in 2008 when the match was played over the Old Course at St Andrews for the first time. In 2003 she was named winner of the Bob Jones award for sportsmanship and in 2005 received the PGA of America Lady of the Year trophy.

Sheehan, Patty (USA)

Born Middlebury, Vermont, 27 October 1956
Turned professional 1980

Scored 35 victories between 1981 and 1996 including six Majors – the LPGA Championship in 1983, 1984 and 1994, the US Women's Open in 1993 and 1994 and the Nabisco Championship in 1996. She also won the British Women's Open at Woburn in 1992 before it was designated a major. As an amateur she won all her four games in the 1980 Curtis Cup. She is a member of the LPGA Hall of Fame. She played in four Solheim Cup games between 1990 and 1996 and captained the side in 2002 and 2003.

Shin, Ji-Yai (KOR)

Born Chonnam, Korea, 28 April 1988
Turned professional 2006

She played 18 events on the Korean LPGA Tour in 2007 and won nine times, winning twice as much as her nearest rival with a then record total of $725,000. She was Korea's Player of the Year – a title she retained in 2008 when she became the first player to win all three events that comprise that circuit's Grand Slam. She had broken almost every record set on the Korean Tour by Se Ri Pak before the start of the 2008 season. In 2008 she won her first major – the Ricoh British Women's Open at Sunningdale – and went on to win two more times on the LPGA Tour taking the Mizuno Classic and the end-of-season ADT Championship in which she beat Karrie Webb by a shot to win US $1 million. She was the first non-member to win three times on that Tour. In addition she had three other top 10 finishes and earned US$1.77 million in prize-money. In 2008 she won 11 times – the three on the LPGA Tour, seven times in Korea and once in Japan. In 2009 she earned LPGA Rookie of the Year honours but was pipped at the post by Lorena Ochoa for the Rolex Player of the Year. By the end of 2010 she had played 60 events on the LPGA Tour and missed just one cut. She has won eight times in America and on a further 26 occasions internationally.

Annika Sörenstam (SWE)

Born Stockholm, 9 October 1970
Turned professional 1992

Winner of the US Women's Open in 1995 and 1996 she and Karrie Webb of Australia have battled for the headlines on the LPGA Tour over the past few years. A prolific winner of titles in America. She won four in a row in early summer 2000 as she and Webb battled again for the No. 1 spot in 2001. Sörenstam was the No. 1 earner in 1995, 1997 and 1998, Webb in 1996, 1999 and 2000. At the Standard Register Ping event she became the first golfer to shoot 59 on the LPGA Tour. Her second round score 59 included 13 birdies, 11 of them in her first 12 holes. Her 36-hole total of 124 beat the record set by Webb the previous season by three. Her 54-hole score of 193 matched the record set by Karrie Webb and her 72-hole total of 261 which gave her victory by three shots from Se Ri Pak matched the low total on Tour set by Se Ri Pak in 1998. Sörenstam's 27-under-par winning score was a new record for the Tour beating the 26-under-par score Webb returned in the Australian Ladies' Masters in 1999. Her sister Charlotta also plays on the LPGA and Evian Tours.

Before turning professional she finished runner-up in the 1992 US Women's Championship. Sörenstam continued on her winning way in 2002 when her victories included another major – the Kraft Nabisco Championship. By the end of August she had won six times in the US and once more in Europe. By the beginning of October she had won nine times on the 2002 LPGA Tour and collected her 40th LPGA title. Only four players have won more than 9 events in one LPGA season. By October she had won $2.5 million world wide. In 2003 she was awarded the Golf Writers award in Britain for the golfer who had done most for European golf. In 2004 she quickly passed through the 50 mark in titles won in America. Before the middle of October her tally was 54 she had passed the $2 million mark in American Tour earnings for the year. In 2004 she added another major to her list of achievements winning the McDonald's LPGA Championship. She remains the dominant force in women's professional golf. When Annika won the Mizuno Classic in Japan she became the first player for 34 years to win 10 titles in a season.

In 2003 she took up the challenge of playing on the US Men's Tour teeing up in a blaze of publicity in the Colonial event in Texas but missed the half-way cut. She won her fifth Major when she took the McDonald's LPGA Championship in June and when she won the Weetabix British Women's Open at Royal Lytham and St Annes she completed a Grand Slam of major titles. Her tally is now six Majors. Her win at Lytham was her sixth major success. By the end of August she had won 46 LPGA tournaments and was inducted into the World Golf Hall of Fame. When she won the Mizuno Classic for the third successive year she was winning her 46th LPGA title and had wrapped up the Player of the Year and top money earner award. In 2004 she quickly passed through the 50 mark in titles won and before the middle of October had passed the $2 million mark in US PGA Tour earnings for a fourth successive year. She added another major to her personal tally when she won the McDonald's LPGA Championship. 2005 was another stellar year for Annika who took her career wins on the LPGA Tour to 66 with 10 more victories from her 20 starts. She easily topped the money list with over $2 million and moved her career earnings on the US Tour to $18,332,764. During the year she also won her own event in Sweden.

Her majors total at the end of 2005 after further Grand Slam victories in the Kraft Nabisco Championship and McDonald's LPGA Championship moved to nine. Although she did not win Player of the Year honours in 2006 – that went to Mexico's Lorena Ochoa – Annika again had an excellent season, winning three times and coming second on a further five occasions. She has now won 69 times and her earnings in America have gone through $20 million. She added a further major win to her list of Grand Slam successes and with Liselotte Neumann won the World Cup of Golf in South Africa early in the year. She also hosted and then won her own event in Sweden and beat Helen Alfredsson and Karrie Webb to the first prize at the Dubai Ladies Masters in November. In 2007 her appearances were curtailed because of injury and she announced her retirement from full-time professional golf in 2008 despite having won the SBS Open in Hawaii, the Stanford International and the Michelob Ultra Open in the United States. In her last season she earned $1,617,411 taking her total on Tour since 1994 to $22,454,692. Now runs her own event in Sweden. Appointed an ambassador in the bid to have golf included in the Olympic Games, she gave birth to her first child in 2009. She announced in 2010 she was expecting her second child.

Steinhauer, Sherri (USA)

Born Madison, Wisconsin, 27 December 1962
Turned professional 1985

Winner of the Weetabix Women's British Open at Woburn in 1999 and at Royal Lytham and St Annes in 1998 and again there in 2006. Her third victory was her first major success because the British Women's Open had been awarded major status. She has also played in four Solheim Cup matches.

Stephenson, Jan (AUS)

Born Sydney, 22 December 1951
Turned professional 1973

She won three majors on the LPGA Tour – the 1981 du Maurier Classic, the 1982 LPGA Championship and the 1983 US Women's Open. She was twice Australian Ladies champion in 1973 and 1977.

Streit, Marlene Stewart (CAN)

Born Cereal, Alberta, 9 March 1934

One of Canada's most successful amateurs she won her national title ten times between 1951 and 1973. She won the 1953 British Amateur, the US Amateur in 1956 and the Australian Ladies in 1963. She was Canadian Woman Athlete of the Year in 1951, 1953, 1956, 1960 and 1963.

Stupples, Karen (ENG)

Born Dover, England, 24 June 1973

English professional who lives in Orlando but hit the headlines at Sunningdale in the summer of 2004 when she won the Weetabix British Women's Open with a 19 under par total of 269. In the final round she began by making an eagle at the first and holing her second shot for an eagle 2 at the second. She finally clinched victory with the help of three birdies in a row on the back nine. Earlier in the year she had won on the LPGA Tour which she had joined in 1999. She has played golf since she was 11. She made her début in the Solheim Cup in 2005 and in 2011 gained a point for Europe without playing in the singles after Cristie Kerr pulled out through injury.

Suggs, Louise (USA)

Born Atlanta, Georgia, 7 September 1923
Turned professional 1948

Winner of 58 titles on the LPGA Tour after a brilliant amateur career which included victories in the 1947 US Amateur and the 1948 British Amateur Championships. She won 11 Majors including the US Women's Open in 1949 and 1952 and the LPGA Championship in 1957. A founder member of the US Tour she was an inaugural honoree when the LPGA Hall of Fame was instituted in 1967. In 2006 she was

Yani Tseng (TPE)

Born Taoyuan, near Teipei, Taiwan, 1989
Turned professional 2007

With 11 victories around the world – including seven titles on the LPGA where she won nearly $3 million during 2011 – Tseng became the dominant player in women's golf. At just 22-years-old, she's won five major titles, the youngest golfer, male or female, ever to do so.

A top-ranked Taiwanese amateur, she was the Asia-Pacific Junior Champion in 2003 and 2005. In 2004 she won the USGA Women's Amateur Public Links Championship, defeating Michelle Wie in the final. After turning professional, she competed initially on the Asian Golf Tour and in Canada. She joined the LPGA in 2008 and won her first major on the circuit that summer when she outlasted Sweden's Maria Hjörth at the fourth extra hole of a play-off for the McDonald's LPGA Championship. She enjoyed an even more successful season in 2010 when she won two more majors – the Kraft Nabisco and the Ricoh Women's British Open. Her victory at Birkdale meant she became the youngest woman ever to win three major titles.

Living in a house in Florida formerly owned by Annika Sörenstam, she has been mentored by the Swede, effectively succeeding both Sörenstam and Lorena Ochoa, who shared the No 1 spot for a decade, as the game's best player. By any standard, 2011 was an extraordinary season for the Taiwanese golfer. She won all of the first four tournaments she entered around the globe: the Taifong Ladies Open on the LPGA of Taiwan Tour; the ISPS Handa Women's Australian Open and ANZ RACV Ladies Open on the Australian Ladies Professional Golf Tour and the Ladies European Tour (LET) and the Honda LPGA Thailand, the season-opener on the LPGA. Thereafter, she was runner up at the Kraft Nabisco, the first major of the season, before adding to her impressive haul of victories in the most prized events with wins at the Wegmans LPGA and the Women's British Open. At Carnoustie, she was the first champion to mount a successful defence. And on the LPGA, where she posted 14 top tens in 22 events, she was only the 17th golfer since 1950 to win six tournaments or more in a single season.

Karrie Webb (AUS)

Born Ayr, Queensland, 21 December 1974
Turned professional 1994

Blonde Australian who is rewriting the record books with her performances on the LPGA Tour. Peter Thomson, the five times Open champion considers she is the best golfer male or female there is and Greg Norman, who was her inspiration as a teenager, believes she can play at times better than Tiger Woods although Webb herself hates comparisons. She scored her first Major win in 1995 when she took the Weetabix Women's British Open – a title she won again in 1997. When she joined the LPGA Tour she won the 1999 du Maurier Classic, the 2000 Nabisco Championship and the 2000 and 2001 US Women's Open – five Majors out of eight (by the end of July 2001) – the most impressive run since Mickey Wright won five out of six in the early 1960s. In 2002 she became the first player to complete a career Grand Slam when she won her third Weetabix British Open which had become an official major on the US LPGA Tour. It was her sixth major title in four years. Her winning total at Turnberry was 15 under par 273. Enjoys a close rivalry with Annika Sörenstam. In 2005 she was inducted into the World Golf Hall of Fame. She added to her majors tally in 2006 when she beat Lorena Ochoa in a play-off for the Kraft Nabisco Championship. Later she lost a play-off to Se Ri Pak for another major – the McDonald's LPGA Championship. She is the only player to have victories in the current four majors and the du Maurier event, now discarded as a major.

awarded the Bob Jones award for outstanding sportsmanship and for being a perfect ambassador for the game. She comes from Atlanta and knew Bobby Jones when she was younger.

Thomas, Vicki (née Rawlings) (WAL)

Born Northampton, 27 October 1954

One of Wales' most accomplished players who took part in six Curtis Cup matches between 1982 and 1992. She won the Welsh Championship eight times between 1979 and 1994 as well as the British Ladies' Stroke Play in 1990.

Thompson, Alexis (USA)

Born Florida, 10 February 1995
Turned professional 2010

An outstanding amateur who won the US Junior girls in 2008, she was the youngest player at the age of 12 ever to qualify for the US Women's Open. After winning four and halving one of her matches in the Curtis Cup, she turned professional at 15 in the summer of 2010. She finished 10th at the US Women's Open and two weeks later at the Evian Masters was runner-up. After just three professional events she'd won $314,842. The LGU caused a stir when they declined to give the teenager an exemption into qualifying for the 2010 Women's British Open at Birkdale. In 2011 Alexis won the Navistar LPGA Classic in Alabama by five shots to become the youngest ever winner on the LPGA circuit. Better known as Lexi, she then became the second youngest ever winner on the LET when she won the Dubai Ladies Masters by four strokes. Aware of her exceptional talent, the LPGA changed their rules – which did not allow players to compete on Tour until they were 18 – in order that the teenager could play full time on the Tour in 2012.

Varangot, Brigitte (FRA)

Born Biarritz, 1 May 1940

Winner of the French Amateur title five times in six years from 1961 and again in 1973. Her run in the French Championship was impressive from 1960 when her finishes were 2, 1, 1, 2, 1, 1, 1, 2. She was also a triple winner of the British Championship in 1963, 1965 and 1968. One of France's most successful players she also won the Italian title in 1970.

Walker OBE, Mickey (ENG)

Born Alwoodley, Yorkshire, 17 December 1952
Turned professional 1973

Always a popular and modest competitor she followed up an excellent amateur career by doing well as a professional. Twice a Curtis Cup player she won the Ladies' British Open Amateur in 1971 and 1972, the English Ladies' in 1973 and had victories, too, in Portugal, Spain and America where she won the 1972 Trans-Mississippi title. She won six times as a professional but is perhaps best known for her stirring captaincy of the first four European Solheim Cup sides leading them to a five point success at Dalmahoy. In 1992 she galvanised her side by playing them tapes of the men's Ryder Cup triumphs. Now a club professional she also works regularly as a television commentator for Sky

Whitworth, Kathy (USA)

Born Monahans, Texas, 27 September 1939
Turned professional 1958

Won 88 titles on the LPGA Tour between 1959 and 1991 – more than any one else male or female. Her golden period was in the 1960s when she won eight events in 1965, nine in 1966, eight in 1967 and 10 in 1968. When she finished third in the 1981 US Women's Open she became the first player to top $1 million in prize money on the LPGA Tour. She was the seventh member of the LPGA Tour Hall of Fame when inducted in 1975. Began playing golf at the age of 15 and made golfing history when she teamed up with Mickey Wright to play in the previously all male Legends of Golf event. Winner of six Majors – including three LPGA Championship wins in 1967, 1971 and 1975. In addition she won two Titleholders' Championships (1966 and 1967) and the 1967 Western Open when they were Majors. Enjoyed a winning streak of 17 successive years on the LPGA Tour.

Wie, Michelle (USA)

Born Hawaii, 11 October 1989
Turned professional 2005

As an amateur she finished third in the Weetabix British Women's Open in July 2005 and turned professional in October as a 16-year-old with multi-million contract guarantees. In her first event as a professional in the Samsung Championship she finished fourth behind Annika Sörenstam but then was disqualified for a dropped ball infringement incurred in the third round – and spotted by an American journalist who did not report it until the following day. In 2006 she continued to play in a few men's events including the Omega European Masters at Crans-sur-Sierre but failed to make the cut in any. She did make the cut in all four majors in 2006. She combines her professional career with her school work in Hawaii and it is reported she hopes to go eventually to Stanford University. In 2008 she earned a card on the LPGA Tour at the Qualifying School. She was chosen as a wild card and played with distinction in the 2009 Solheim Cup side won by the Americans and later in the year won her first event

on the LPGA Tour when she took the Lorena Ochoa Mexico Classic.

Wright, Janette (née Robertson) (SCO)

Born Glasgow, 7 January 1935

Another of Scotland's most accomplished amateur players she competed four times in the Curtis Cup and was four times Scottish champion between 1959 and 1973. Formerly married to the late Innes Wright. Her daughter Pamela was Collegiate Golfer of the Year 1988 and LPGA Rookie of the Year in 1989.

Wright, Mickey (USA)

Born San Diego, California, 14 February 1935
Turned professional 1954

Her 82 victories on the LPGA Tour between 1956 and 1973 was bettered only by Kathy Whitworth who has 88 official victories. One of the greatest golfers in the history of the Tour she had a winning streak of 14 successive seasons. Winner of 13 Major titles she is the only player to date to have won three in one season. In 1961 she took the US Women's Open, the LPGA Championship and the Titleholders' Championship. That year she became only the second player to win both the US Women's Open and LPGA Championship in the same year having done so previously in 1958. Scored 79 of her victories between 1956 and 1969 when averaging almost eight wins a season. During this time she enjoyed a tremendous rivalry with Miss Whitworth.

Yokomine, Sakura (JPN)

Born Konoya Kagoshima, 13 December 1985
Turned professional 2005

Winner of 17 events on the Japan LPGA Tour. She was top earner in Japan in 2009 but took second spot in 2010 to Korean golfer Ahn Sun-Ju.

Norway's Suzann Pettersen – a born leader

Norwegian professional Suzann Pettersen had a great 2011. There were two LPGA wins and 11 top-10 finishes easing her into second place in the Rolex World Golf Ranking behind pacesetter Yani Tseng.

Suzann led the LPGA ranking in greens in regulation (75 per cent); she finished sixth in the scoring average table (70.97), and was fifth in season earnings with more than $1.3 million.

But what Pettersen may well be remembered most for in 2011was her emerging role as a general on the course at the Solheim Cup – the role Colin Montgomerie played for so long for Europe in the Ryder Cup

Pettersen showed her mettle when it mattered most, winning her crucial singles match by two holes in dramatic fashion over Michelle Wie, but also had a heavy influence on her European teammates.

Suzann can look forward to another successful season with confidence.

Famous Personalities of the Past

In making the difficult choice of the names to be included, effort has been made to acknowledge the outstanding players and personalities of each successive era from the early pioneers to the stars of recent times.

Alliss, Percy	Compston, Archie	King, Sam	Park, Mungo	Tait, Freddie
Anderson, Jamie	Cotton, Sir Henry	Kirkaldy, Andrew	Park, Willie	Taylor, JH
Anderson, Willie	Crawley, Leonard	Laidlay, John	Park, Willie Jr	Tolley, Cyril
Archer, George	Curtis, The Sisters	Leitch, Cecil	Patton, Billy Joe	Travis, Walter
Armour, Tommy	Daly, Fred	Lema, Tony	Philp, Hugh	Tumba, Sven
Auchterlonie,	Darwin, Bernard	Little, Lawson	Picard, Henry	Valentine, Jessie
Willie	Demeret, Jimmy	Locke, Bobby	Price-Fisher,	Van Donck, Flory
Balding, Al	Dobereiner, Peter	Longhurst, Henry	Elizabeth	Vardon, Harry
Ballesteros,	Duncan, George	Lunt, Michael	Ray, Ted	Vare, Glenna
Severiano	Faulkner, Max	McCormack, Mark	Rees, Dai	Von Nida, Norman
Ball, John	Ferguson, Bob	McDonald, CB	Robertson, Allan	Walker, George
Barnes, Jim	Fernie, Willie	Mackenzie, Alister	Rosburg, Bob	Ward, Charlie
Barton, Pamela	Garrett, Maureen	Mackenzie, Keith	Ryder, Samuel	Ward, Harvie
Berg, Patty	Garvey, Philomena	Massy, Arnaud	Sarazen, Gene	Wethered, Joyce
Bolt, Tommy	Goldschmid, Isa	Micklem, Gerald	Sayers, Ben	Wethered, Roger
Boros, Julis	Hagen, Walter	Middlecoff, Cary	Sewgolum,	Whitcombes, The
Bousfield, Ken	Harper, Chandler	Minoprio, Gloria	Sewunker	White, Ronnie
Bradshaw, Harry	Henning, Harold	Mitchell, Abe	Shade, Ronnie	Will, George
Braid, James	Herd, Sandy	Moody, Orville	Smith, Frances	Wilson, Enid
Brewer, Gay	Hilton, Harold	Morgan, Wanda	Smith, Horton	Wind, Herbert
Brown, Eric	Hogan, Ben	Morris, Old Tom	Smith, Macdonald	Warren
Bruen, Jimmy	Howard, Barclay	Morris, Young Tom	Snead, Sam	Wood, Craig
Camicia, Mario	Hutchinson,	Nelson, Byron	Solheim, Karsten	Wooldridge, Ian
Campbell, Dorothy	Horace	Norman, Moe	Souchak, Mike	Yates, Charlie
Carr, Joe	Jarman, Ted	Ouimet, Francis	Spearman, Marley	Zaharias, "Babe"
Coe, Charlie	Jones, Bob	Panton, John	Stewart, Payne	

Alliss, Percy (1897–1975)

Father of Peter Alliss he finished in the top six in The Open Championship seven times, including joint third at Carnoustie in 1931, two strokes behind winner Tommy Armour. Twice winner of the Match Play Championship, five times German Open champion and twice winner of the Italian Open. He was a Ryder Cup player in 1933–35–37, an international honour also gained by his son. Spent six yesrs as professional at the Wansee Club in Berlin before moving back to Britain to work at Beaconsfield, Temple Newsam and for 30 years at Ferndown in Dorset.

Anderson, Jamie (1842–1912)

Winner of three consecutive Open Championships – 1877–78–79. A native St Andrean, he once claimed to have played 90 consecutive holes on the Old Course without a bad or unintended shot. He was noted for his straight hitting and accurate putting.

Anderson, Willie (1878–1910)

Took his typically Scottish flat swing to America where he won the US Open four times in a five year period from 1901. Only Bobby Jones, Ben Hogan and Jack Nicklaus have also won the US Open four times.

Archer, George (1940–2005)

The 6ft 5in tall former cowboy won The Masters in 1969 – one of four golfers who won their first major that year. A superb putter Archer was dogged throughout his career by injury but he won 12 times on the PGA Tour and a further 19 times on the US Senior Tour now the Champions Tour. Elizabeth, one of his two daughters, made headlines when she caddied for her father and became the first woman to do so at Augusta.

Armour, Tommy   (1896–1968)

Born in Edinburgh, he played for Britain against America as an amateur and, after emigrating, for America against Britain as a professional in the fore-runners of the Walker and Ryder Cup matches. Won the US Open in 1927, the USPGA in 1930 and the 1931 Open at Carnoustie. Became an outstanding coach and wrote several bestselling instruction books. Known as "The Silver Scot".

Auchterlonie, Willie   (1872–1963)

Won The Open at Prestwick in 1893 at the age of 21 with a set of seven clubs he had made himself. Found-ed the famous family club-making business in St Andrews. He believed that golfers should master half, three-quarter and full shots with each club. Appoint-ed Honorary Professional to The R&A in 1935.

Balding, Al   (1924–2006)

A lovely swinger of the club, he was the first Canadi-an to win on the US Tour when he took the Mayfair Inn Open in Florida in 1955. In 1968, in partnership with Stan Leonard, he won the World Cup in Rome and was himself low individual scorer that year.

Ball, John   (1861–1940)

Finished fourth in The Open of 1878 at the age of 16 and became the first amateur to win the title in 1890 when The Open was played at Prestwick. He won the Amateur Championship eight times and shares with Bobby Jones the distinction of being the winner of The Open and Amateur in the same year – 1890. He grew up on the edge of the links area which became the Royal Liverpool Golf Club and the birth-place of the Amateur. He was a master at keeping the ball low in the wind, but with the same straight-faced club could cut the ball up for accurate approach shots. His run of success could have been greater but for military service in the South African campaign and the First World War.

Barnes, Jim   (1887–1966)

Raised in Cornwall before emigrating to California, where he took US citizenship, the 6ft 4ins golfer enjoyed outstanding success in the professional major championships of the early 20th century. He won The Open at Prestwick in 1925 and enjoyed a consistent record in the oldest major throughout the 1920s. He also made his mark with a string of top ten finishes in the US Open before winning America's national championship in 1921 in Maryland by nine strokes, a record which stood for nearly 80 years. And in the US PGA Championship, which was init-ially a match-play tournament, he won the first two stagings in 1916 and 1919.

Barton, Pamela   (1917–1943)

At the age of 19 she held both the British and Amer-ican Ladies Championships in 1936. She was French champion at 17, runner-up in the British in both 1934 and '35 and won the title again in 1939. A Curtis Cup team member in 1934 and '36 she was a Flight Offi-cer in the WAAF when she was killed in a plane crash at an RAF airfield in Kent.

Berg, Patty   (1915–2006)

The golf pioneer who won an LPGA Tour record 15 major titles and was one of the 13 founding members of the tour in 1950. She was the LPGA Tour's first president from 1950–52 and was the tour's money leader in 1954, '55 and '57 ending her career with 60 victories. She was a member of the LPGA Tour and World Golf Halls of Fame. She was described as a pioneer, an athlete, a mentor, a friend and an enter-tainer and had a great sense of humour.

Bolt, Tommy   (1916–2008)

The 1958 US Open champion and two-time Ryder Cup player who is remembered as much for his short temper as his short game. He had a penchant for throwing clubs insisting it was better to throw them ahead of you in order to avoid having to walk back for them! Known as "Terrible Tommy" he was a founding member of the US Champions Tour. In the 1957 Ryder Cup at Lindrick he lost a bad-tempered game to fiery Scot Eric Brown.

Boros, Julius   (1920–1994)

Became the oldest winner of a major championship when he won the USPGA in 1968 at the age of 48. He twice won the US Open, in 1952 and again 11 years later at Brookline when he was 43. In a play-off he beat Jackie Cupit by three shots and Arnold Palmer by six. He played in four Ryder Cup matches between 1959–67, winning nine of his 16 matches and losing only three.

Bousfield, Ken   (1919–2000)

Although a short hitter even by the standards of his era, he won five out of 10 matches in six Ryder Cup appearances from 1949–61. He captured the PGA Match Play Championship in 1955, one of eight tour-nament victories in Britain, and also won six Euro-pean Opens. He represented England in the World Cup at Wentworth in 1956 and Tokyo in 1957.

Bradshaw, Harry   (1913–1950)

One of Ireland's most loved golfers whose swing Bernard Darwin described as "rustic and rugged". With Christy O'Connor he won the Canada Cup (World Cup) for Ireland in Mexico in 1958 but he is also remembered for losing the 1949 Open to Bobby Locke after having hit one shot out of a bottle at the fifth on the second day. That bit of bad luck, it was later considered, cost him £10,000.

Braid, James   (1870–1950)

Together with Harry Vardon and J.H. Taylor he formed the Great Triumvirate and dominated the game for 20 years before the 1914–18 war. In a 10-year period from 1901 he became the first player in the history of the event to win The Open five times –

Severiano Ballesteros

1957–2011

Adventurous, exciting to watch and always unpredictable, the qualities which laid the foundation for the success of Severiano Ballesteros as a driven stroke-play champion were, if anything, even more formidable assets when the Spaniard conquered the arena of match-play. As well as his five major titles, the crowning achievement of a charismatic career cut short at the early age of 54, was an example he set for European golf in the Ryder Cup.

Of the many attributes Ballesteros shared with Arnold Palmer, the swashbuckling adventurer to whom he was most often compared, fearlessness was perhaps the most significant trait. His whole career was governed by passion and romanticism. And, just like Palmer in America, his blows of brilliance enlarged the audience for professional golf in Europe through TV exposure.

  While the world of golf loved Seve's ebullience, he was held in particularly high esteem in the British Isles. The galleries in the UK were smitten from the moment at Royal Birkdale in 1976 when he executed a devious chip sending it running between the bunkers on the home hole rather than taking the aerial route. It was a shot of such sublime touch and imagination, no one who saw the teenager pull it off would have been surprised when the Spaniard went to have his name inscribed on the Claret Jug three times in 1979, 1984 and 1988. All told he won 52 titles between 1976 and 1999 including two stagings of The Masters at Augusta in 1980 and 1983.

When asked to choose the greatest player he'd ever seen, Lee Trevino selected the Spaniard. "Jack Nicklaus made a plan," he said. "Tiger Woods makes a plan. Seve never made a plan. He just made things happen. He had something we didn't have."

Born in a small village near Santander in the north of Spain, Seve was surrounded by family who played the game and caddied at Pedrena. As a boy, his brother Manuel gave him the gift of a 3 iron and the youngster used the club to perfect a variety of shots on a local beach. He became a professional before celebrating his 17th birthday and two years later made his mark in The Open at Birkdale when he led for three days and finished runner-up alongside Jack Nicklaus to Johnny Miller.

Apart from his triumphs on the British linksland, Ballesteros was more at home at Augusta National than anywhere else. It's worth recalling, before chronic back trouble sapped his power, how long Seve was off the tee. The combination of distance and touch was perfect for the Masters. His performances in Georgia in 1980 and 1983 were as dazzling as anything ever produced at Augusta. The bogeys which punished Seve's wayward tendencies were exceeded by electrifying surges of birdies and eagles. When Seve was around, the game was always human, never robotic. For example, in Friday's second round of the 1980 Masters, Seve struck a hook so far left on the 17th hole that his ball finished on the seventh green. However, after taking a free drop, he launched a blind iron shot onto the correct green and recovered by holing the improbable birdie putt.

When the 23-year-old slipped into a Green Jacket, church bells in his home town of Pedrena rang out in celebration. There was more music in 1983 when he started his final round at Augusta with a devastating flurry of birdie, eagle, par, birdie – four under par for the opening four holes – which the Spaniard regarded as "the best I ever played in my life." The greatest stroke, though, was surely that 15 foot birdie putt on the 18th green at St Andrews which sealed his second Open triumph. Ballesteros calls it "El Momento" and a silhouette of his ensuing celebration is surely the defining image of his career.

In the Ryder Cup, the arrival of Ballesteros and the example he set to others changed everything. There was an intensity about Ballesteros' play which galvanised the European cause. In many respects, the story of the modern Ryder Cup can be told in two distinct phases: before and after Seve. He played eight times in the match, finishing on the winning side four times, and was a winning captain in 1997.

Problems in his lower back caused a deterioration in his game in the Nineties and the last of his 50 European Tour wins came at the Spanish Open in 1995. He was diagnosed with a brain tumour after collapsing with an epileptic fit at Madrid Airport in 2008. Caught up in the most daunting challenge of his life, Ballesteros endured four operations, six subsequent courses of chemotherapy and radio-therapy treatment with the resilience of a champion before passing away in 2010. He may have died tragically early but the passion with which he played the game ensures his memory will live for ever.

and also finished second on three occasions. In that same period he won the Match Play Championship four times and the French Open. He was a tall, powerful player who hit the ball hard but always retained an appearance of outward calm. He was one of the founder members of the Professional Golfers' Association and did much to elevate the status of the professional golfer. He was responsible for the design of many golf courses and served as professional at Walton Heath for 45 years. He was an honorary member of that club for 25 years and became one of its directors. He was also an honorary member of The R&A.

Brewer, Gay (1932–2007)
Winner of the 1967 Masters he was one of the most popular figures on the US Tour and later the Champions Tour. His love of the game, his joviality and his story-telling were all part of the legacy of the man from Lexington, Kentucky, whose loopy swing was one of the most unorthodox.

Brown, Eric (1925–1986)
Twice captained the Ryder Cup side and for many years partnered John Panton for Scotland in the World Cup. A larger-than-life personality, he was one of two Cup captains who came from the Bathgate club. The other was Bernard Gallacher, who played in the 1969 match which Brown captained.

Bruen, Jimmy (1920–1972)
Won the Irish Amateur at the age of 17 and defended the title successfully the following year. At 18 he became the youngest ever Walker Cup player at that time and in practice for the match at St Andrews in 1938 equalled the then amateur course record of 68 set by Bobby Jones.

Camicia, Mario (1941–2011)
Often referred to as Italy's "Mr Golf" Mario was a passionate lover of the game who did much to make Italians more aware of and more interested in the game. For many years he ran the Italian Open, wrote in magazines and newspapers and became the country's first television golf commentator. He was the voice of golf in Italy who enjoyed the success Costantino Rocca, the Molinari brothers and Matteo Manassero had on the international scene. Commenting on his death Franco Chimenti, President of the Italian Federation, said: "The game has lost a good friend."

Campbell, Dorothy Iona (1883–1946)
One of only two golfers to win the British, American and Canadian Ladies titles. In total she won these three major championships seven times.

Carr, Joe (1922–2004)
The first Irishman to captain the Royal and Ancient Golf Club of St Andrews, he was winner of three

British Amateur Championship titles in 1953, 1958 and 1960. He played in or captained Walker Cup sides from 1947 to 1963 making a record 11 appearances. He was the first Irishman to play in The Masters at Augusta, made 23 consecutive appearances for Ireland in the Home Internationals and was a regular winner of the West of Ireland and East of Ireland Championships. At one point in an illustrious career he held 18 different course records. An ebullient, fast-talking personality with a somewhat eccentric swing, he was one of Ireland's best known and best loved golfers. In 2007 he was inducted posthumously into the World Golf Hall of Fame in St Augustine, Florida.

Coe, Charlie (1923–2007)
Another fine American amateur golfer who finished runner-up with Arnold Palmer to Gary Player in the 1961 Masters at Augusta. Twice US Amateur champion in 1949 and 1958, he played in six Walker Cup matches and was non-playing captain in 1959. He won seven and halved two of the 13 games he played. Winner of the Bobby Jones award in 1964. Born in Oklahoma City, he never considered turning professional.

Compston, Archie (1893–1962)
Beat Walter Hagen 18 and 17 in a 72-hole challenge match at Moor Park in 1928 and tied for second place in the 1925 Open. Played in the Ryder Cup in 1927–29–31.

Cotton, Sir Henry (1907–1987)
The first player to be knighted for services to golf, he died a few days before the announcement of the award was made. He won The Open Championship three times, which included a round of 65 at Royal St George's in 1934 after which the famous Dunlop golf ball was named. His final 71 at Carnoustie to win the 1937 Championship in torrential rain gave him great satisfaction and he set another record with a 66 at Muirfield on the way to his third triumph in 1948 watched by King George VI. He won the Match Play Championship three times and was runner-up on three occasions. He also won 11 Open titles in Europe, played three times in the Ryder Cup and was non-playing captain in 1953. Sir Henry worked hard to promote the status of professional golf and also championed the cause of young golfers, becoming a founder member of the Golf Foundation. He was a highly successful teacher, author and architect, spending much time at Penina, a course he created in southern Portugal. He was an honorary member of The R&A.

Crawley, Leonard (1903–1981)
Played four times in the Walker Cup in 1932–34–38–47 and won the English Amateur in 1931. He also played first-class cricket for Worcestershire and Essex and toured the West Indies with the MCC in 1936. After the Second World War he was golf correspondent for the Daily Telegraph for 30 years.

The Curtis sisters, Harriet   (1878–1944)
               Margaret (1880–1965)
Donors of the Curtis Cup still contested biennially between the USA and GB&I. Harriet won the US Women's Amateur in 1906 and lost in the following year's final to her sister Margaret, who went on to win the championship three times.

Daly, Fred (1911–1990)

Daly won The Open at Royal Liverpool in 1947 and in four of the next five years was never out of the top four in the Championship. At Portrush, where he was born, he finished fourth to Max Faulkner in 1951, the only time The Open has been played in Northern Ireland. He was Ulster champion 11 times and three times captured the prestigious PGA Match Play Championship. He was a member of the Ryder Cup team four times, finishing on a high note at Wentworth in 1953 when he won his foursomes match in partnership with Harry Bradshaw and then beat Ted Kroll 9 and 7 in the singles.

Darwin, Bernard (1876–1961)

One of the most gifted and authoritative writers on golf, he was also an accomplished England international player for more than 20 years. While in America to report the 1922 Walker Cup match for The Times, he was called in to play and captain the side when Robert Harris became ill. A grandson of Charles Darwin, he was captain of The R&A in 1934–35. In 1937 he was awarded the CBE for services to literature. He was inducted posthumously into the World Golf Hall of Fame in 2005.

Demaret, Jimmy (1910–1983)

Three times Masters champion, coming from five strokes behind over the final six holes to beat Jim Ferrier by two in 1950, he also won six consecutive tournaments in 1940 while still performing as a night club singer. He won all six games he played in the 1947, 1949 and 1951 Ryder Cup matches.

Dey, Joseph C (Joe) (1907–1991)

A former sportswriter who covered the final leg of Bobby Jones' Grand Slam in 1930 he joined the USGA and srved as executive director from 1934 to 1968. Following his retirement he was appointed the first Commissioner of the PGA Tour – a post he held from 1969 to 1974. Dey also helped to synchronise the rules of golf around the world, instigated the PGA Tour's Players Championship and in 1975 was honorary captain of the Royal and Ancient Golf Club of St Andrews.

Dobereiner, Peter (1925–1996)

A multi-talented journalist in various fields who wrote eloquently, knowledgeably and amusingly on golf in many books, Golf Digest, and Golf World magazines and in The Observer and Guardian newspapers for whom he was correspondent for many years. Born of English-Scottish-Danish-Red Indian and German parentage he claimed he stubbornly refused all

efforts by King's College, Taunton and Lincoln College, Oxford to impart a rudimentary education so chose journalism as a profession.

Duncan, George (1884–1964)

Won The Open in 1920 by making up 13 shots on the leader over the last two rounds and came close to catching Walter Hagen for the title two years later. Renowned as one of the fastest players, his book was entitled Golf at the Gallop.

Faulkner, Max (1916–2005)

One of the game's most extrovert and colourful personalities, who won the 1951 Open Championship at Royal Portrush, the only time the event was played in Northern Ireland. He played in five Ryder Cups and was deservedly if belatedly recognised for his contribution to the game with an honour in 2001 when he was awarded the OBE. His son-in-law is Brian Barnes, another golfing extrovert.

Ferguson, Bob (1848–1915)

The Open Championship winner three times in succession between 1880–82. He then lost a 36-hole play-off for the title by one stroke to Willie Fernie in 1883. He had shown his potential when, at the age of 18, he had won a tournament at Leith Links against the game's leading professionals.

Fernie, Willie (1851–1924)

In 1882 he was second to Bob Ferguson in The Open over his home course at St Andrews. The following year he beat the same player in a 36-hole play-off for the championship over Ferguson's home links at Musselburgh.

Garrett, Maureen (née Ruttle) (1922–2011)

President of the Ladies' Golf Union from 1982 to 1985, she captained the Curtis Cup (1960) and Vagliano Trophy (1961) teams. In 1983 won the Bobby Jones award presented annually by the United States Golf Association to a person who emulates Jones' spirit, personal qualities and attitude to the game and its players.

Garvey, Philomena (1927–2009)

Born in Drogheda she was one of Ireland's most successful competitors winning the Irish Ladies title 15 times between 1946 and 1970. She played six times in the Curtis Cup between 1948 and 1960 and won the British Ladies Amateur title in 1957. In 1964 she turned professional but was later re-instated an amateur.

Goldschmid Isa (née Bevione) (1925–2002)

One of Italy's greatest amateurs, she won her national title 21 times between 1947 and 1974 and was ten times Italian Open champion between 1952 and 1969. Among her other triumphs were victories in the 1952 Spanish Ladies and the 1973 French Ladies.

Hagen, Walter   (1892–1969)

A flamboyant character who used a hired Rolls Royce as a changing room because professionals were not allowed in many clubhouses, he once gave his £50 cheque for winning The Open to his caddie. He won four consecutive USPGA Championships from 1924 when it was still decided by matchplay. He was four times a winner of The Open, in 1922–24–28–29 and captured the US Open title in 1914 and 1919. He captained and played in five Ryder Cup encounters between 1927–35, winning seven of his nine matches and losing only once. He was non-playing captain in 1937.

Harper, Chandler   (1914–2004)

Born in Portsmouth, VA, he was winner of the 1950 US PGA Championship. He won over ten tournaments and was elected to the US PGA Hall of Fame in 1969. Once shot 58 (29-29) round a 6100 yards course in Portsmouth.

Henning, Harold   (1934–2005)

One of three brothers from a well-known South African golf family he was a regular winner of golf events in his home country and Europe and had two wins on the US Tour. Played ten times for South Africa in the World Cup winning the event with Gary Player in Madrid in 1965.

Herd, Alexander 'Sandy'   (1868–1944)

When he first played in The Open at the age of 17 he possessed only four clubs. His only Championship success came in the 1902 Open at Hoylake, the first player to capture the title using the new rubber-cored ball. He won the Match Play Championship at the age of 58 and took part in his last Open at St Andrews in 1939 at the age of 71.

Hilton, Harold   (1869–1942)

Winner of the Amateur Championship four times between 1900 and 1913, he also became the first player and the only Briton to hold both the British and US Amateur titles in the same year 1911. He won The Open in 1892 at Muirfield, the first time the Championship was extended to 72 holes, and again in 1897 at Hoylake. A small but powerful player he was the first editor of Golf Monthly.

Hogan, Ben   (1912–1997)

One of only five players to have won all four major championships, his record of capturing three in the same season has been matched by Tiger Woods. He dominated the golfing scene in America after the Second World War and in 1953 won the Masters, US Open and The Open Championship. A clash of dates between The Open and USPGA Championship prevented an attempt on the Grand Slam, but his poor state of health after a near fatal car crash four years earlier would have made the matchplay format of 10 rounds in six days the USPGA an impossibility. After his car collided with a Greyhound bus in fog, it was feared that Hogan might never walk again. He had won three majors before the accident and he returned to capture six more. His only appearance in The Open was in his tremendous season of 1953 and he recorded rounds of 73-71-70-68 to win by four strokes at Carnoustie. His dramatic life story was made into a Hollywood film entitled Follow the Sun starring Glenn Ford as Hogan.

Howard, Barclay (1953 – 2008)

Leading amateur in the 1997 Open at Royal Troon he battled leukemia which had been diagnosed after he played in his second Walker Cup in 1997. When Dean Robertson won the 1999 Italian Open he dedicated his victory to Barclay as tribute to the courage and adversity he showed in attempting to beat the disease.

Hutchinson, Horace   (1859–1932)

Runner-up in the first Amateur Championship in 1885, he won the title in the next two years and reached the final again in 1903. He represented England from 1902–07. He was a prolific writer on golf and country life and became the first English captain of The R&A in 1908.

Jarman, Ted   (1907–2003)

He competed in the 1935 Ryder Cup at Ridgewood, New Jersey, and until his death in 2003 he had been the oldest living Cup golfer. When he was 76 years old and before he had to stop playing because of arthritis he shot a 75.

Jones, Bobby   (1902–1971)

Always remembered for his incredible and unrepeatable achievement in 1930 of winning The Open and Amateur Championships of Britain and America in one outstanding season – the original and unchallenged Grand Slam. At the end of that year he retired from competitive golf at the age of 28. His victories included four US Opens, five US Amateur titles, three Opens in Britain and one Amateur Championship. Although his swing was stylish and fluent, he suffered badly from nerves and was often sick and unable to eat during championships. He was also an accomplished scholar, gaining first-class honours degrees in law, English literature and mechanical engineering at three different universities. He subsequently opened a law practice in Atlanta and developed the idea of creating the Augusta National course and staging an annual invitation event which was to become known as The Masters. He was made an honorary member of the Royal and Ancient Golf Club in 1956 and two years later was given the freedom of the Burgh of St Andrews at an emotional ceremony. He died after many years of suffering from a crippling spinal disease. The tenth hole on the Old Course bears his name.

King, Sam (1911–2003)

He played Ryder Cup golf immediately before and after World War II and came third in the 1939 Open behind Dick Burton at St Andrews. In the 1947 Ryder Cup he prevented an American whitewash in the singles by beating Herman Kaiser. He was British Senior Champion in 1961 and 1962 and was often described as "the old master" – a golfer noted for his long, straight drives and superb putting.

Kirkaldy, Andrew (1860–1934)

First honorary professional appointed by The R&A, he lost a play-off for The Open Championship of 1889 to Willie Park at Musselburgh. He was second in the championship three times, a further three times finished third and twice fourth. A powerful player, he was renowned for speaking his mind.

Laidlay, John Ernest (1860–1940)

The man who first employed the overlapping grip which was later credited to Harry Vardon and universally known as the Vardon grip, Laidlay was a finalist in the Amateur Championship six times in seven years from 1888, winning the title twice at a time when John Ball, Horace Hutchinson and Harold Hilton were at their peak. He was runner-up in The Open to Willie Auchterlonie at Prestwick in 1893. Among the 130 medals he won, were the Gold Medal and Silver Cross in R&A competitions.

Leitch, Charlotte Cecilia "Cecil" (1891–1977)

Christened Charlotte Cecilia, but universally known as Cecil, her list of international victories would undoubtedly have been greater but for the blank golfing years of the first world war. She first won the British Ladies Championship in 1908 at the age of 17. In 1914 she took the English, French and British titles and successfully defended all three when competition was resumed after the war. In all she won the French Championship five times, the British four times, the English twice, the Canadian once. Her total of four victories in the British has never been beaten and has been equalled only by her great rival Joyce Wethered. The victory in Canada was by a margin of 17 and 15 in the 36-hole final.

Lema, Tony (1934–1966)

His first visit to Britain, leaving time for only 27 holes of practice around the Old Course at St Andrews, culminated in Open Championship victory in 1964 by five shots over Jack Nicklaus. He had won three tournaments in four starts in America before arriving in Scotland and gave great credit for his Open success to local caddie Tip Anderson and to the putter Arnold Palmer had loaned him for the week. He played in the Ryder Cup in 1963 and 1965 with an outstanding record. He lost only once in 11 matches, halved twice and won eight. Lema and his wife were killed when a private plane in which they were travelling to a tournament crashed in Illinois.

Little, Lawson (1910–1968)

Won the Amateur Championships of Britain and America in 1934 and successfully defended both titles the following year. He then turned his amateur form into a successful professional career, starting in 1936 with victory in the Canadian Open. He won the US Open in 1940 after a play-off against Gene Sarazen.

Locke, Bobby (1917–1987)

The son of Northern Irish emigrants to South Africa, Arthur D'Arcy Locke was playing off plus four by the age of 18 and won the South African Boys, Amateur and Open Championships. On his first visit to Britain in 1936 he was leading amateur in The Open Championship. Realising that his normal fade was leaving him well short of the leading players, he deliberately developed the hook shot to get more run on the ball. It was to become his trade-mark throughout a long career. He was encouraged to try the American tour in 1947 and won five tournaments, one by the record margin of 16 shots. More successes followed and the USPGA framed a rule which banned him from playing in their events, an action described by Gene Sarazen as "the most disgraceful action by any golf organisation". Disillusioned by the American attitude, Locke then played most of his golf in Europe, winning The Open four times. He shared a period of domination with Peter Thomson between 1949–1958 when they won the championship four times each, only Max Faulker in 1951 and Ben Hogan in 1953 breaking the sequence. In his final Open victory at St Andrews in 1957 he failed to replace his ball in the correct spot on the 18th green after moving it from fellow competitor Bruce Crampton's line. The mistake, which could have led to disqualification, was only spotted on television replays. The R&A Championship Committee rightly decided that Locke, who had won by three strokes, had gained no advantage, and allowed the result to stand. Following a career in which he won over 80 events around the world he was made an honorary member of The R&A in 1976.

Longhurst, Henry (1909–1978)

Golf captain of Cambridge University he was winner of the German Amateur title and runner-up in the French and Swiss Championships in 1936. He became the most perceptive and readable golf correspondent of his time and a television commentator who never wasted a single word. His relaxed, chatty style was based on the premise that he was explaining the scene to a friend in his favourite golf club bar. For 25 years his *Sunday Times* column ran without a break and became compulsory reading for golfers and non-golfers alike. He had a brief spell as a member of parliament and was awarded the CBE for services to golf.

Lunt, Michael (1935–2007)

The former Amateur and English Amateur champion who played most of his golf at Walton Heath died during his captaincy of the Royal and Ancient Golf

Club of St Andrews – an honour which was well-deserved for a golfer who was liked and admired as much for his work as an administrator as his prowess on the links. Son of Stanley Lunt, the 1934 English amateur champion, Michael played on four Walker Cup teams including the one that shocked the Americans by drawing at Five Farms in 1965. He was also a member of the winning Great Britain and Ireland side captained by Joe Carr in the World Amateur Team Championship for the Eisenhower Trophy a year earlier at Olgiata in Rome. After working in the family business he moved to the Slazenger company and later was secretary manager at the Royal Mid-Surrey club before he retired. He is survived by his wife Vicki and son and daughter.

McCormack, Mark (1931–2003)

The Cleveland lawyer who created a golf management empire after approaching Arnold Palmer to look after his affairs. A keen golfer himself, he became one of the most influential and powerful men in sport, managing many golfing legends including Tiger Woods. He was responsible for the development of the modern game commercially and started the World Match Play Championship at Wentworth in 1964.

McDonald, C.B. (1855–1939)

Credited with building the first 18-hole golf course in the United States and instrumental in forming the United States Golf Association. He won the first US Amateur Championship in 1895. He was elected posthumously into the World Golf Hall of Fame in 2007.

Mackenzie, Alister (1870–1934)

A family doctor and surgeon, he became involved with Harry S. Colt in the design of the Alwoodley course in Leeds, where he was a founder member and honorary secretary. He eventually abandoned his medical career and worked full time at golf course architecture. There are many outstanding examples of his work in Britain, Australia, New Zealand and America. His most famous creation, in partnership with Bobby Jones, is the Augusta National course in Georgia, home of The Masters.

Mackenzie, Keith (1921–1990)

The commanding secretary of the Royal and Ancient Golf Club of St Andrews from 1967 to 1983 who, along with Arnold Palmer, Jack Nicklaus and Gary Player ensured The Open, the oldest of the four majors, remained a truly international event. In addition to his normal club duties, he travelled extensively as an ambassador for The Open making friends with the professionals and encouraging foreign participation in the Championship.

Massy, Arnaud (1877–1958)

The first non-British player to win The Open Championship. Born in Biarritz, France, he defeated J.H. Taylor by two strokes at Hoylake in 1907. Four years later he tied for the title with Harry Vardon at Royal St George's, but in the play-off conceded at the 35th hole when he was five strokes behind. He won the French Open four times, the Spanish on three occasions and the Belgian title once.

Micklem, Gerald (1911–1988)

A pre-war Oxford Blue, he won the English Amateur Championship in 1947 and 1953 and played in the Walker Cup team four times between 1947 and 1955. He was non-playing captain in 1957 and 1959. In 1976 he set a record of 36 consecutive appearances in the President's Putter, an event that he won in 1953. In addition to his playing success he was a tireless administrator, serving as chairman of The R&A Rules, Selection and Championship Committees. He was president of the English Golf Union and the European Golf Association and captain of The R&A. In 1969 he received the Bobby Jones award for distinguished sportsmanship and services to the game. He was elected posthumously into the World Golf Hall of Fame in 2007.

Middlecoff, Cary (1921–1998)

Dentist turned golf professional, he became one of the most prolific winners on the US tour, with 37 victories that included two US Opens and a Masters victory. In the US Open of 1949 he beat Sam Snead and Clayton Heafner at Medinah, and seven years later recaptured the title by one shot ahead of Ben Hogan and Julius Boros at Oak Hill. His Masters success came in 1955 when he established a record seven-shot winning margin over Hogan.

Minoprio, Gloria (1907–1958)

Striking a telling blow for women's liberty on the links, Minopro was the first female golfer to wear trousers when competing in the 1933 English Ladies Close Championship. Her stylish navy outfit, white makeup and scarlet lipstick sparked controversy among the Ladies Golf Union which duly condemned the departure at Westward Ho! from billowing skirts. In a further break with convention, she played with only one club, a cleek, similar to a 3 iron. Her striking ensemble is on display today at the British Golf Museum in St Andrews. Outwith golf, she was a magician who performed for the maharajahs.

Mitchell, Abe (1897–1947)

Said by J.H. Taylor to be the finest player never to win an Open, he finished in the top six five times. He was more successful in the Match Play Championship, with victories in 1919, 1920 and 1929. He taught the game to St Albans seed merchant Samuel Ryder and is the figure depicted on top of the famous golf trophy.

Moody, Orville (1933–2008)

His only victory on the PGA Tour came in the 1969 US Open for which he had had to qualify. A descendent of the native American Choctaw tribe, he is best remembered, however, for popularising the long-shafted (broom handle) putter which he had first seen used by Charlie Owens, another "yips" sufferer. If Owens invented the 50in shafted putter Moody brought it to everyone's attention when he won the 1989 US Senior Open using one. Sam Torrance, Peter Senior and Bernhard Langer all started using it after golf's ruling bodies declared the putter legal.

Morgan, Wanda   (1910–1995)

Three-time English Amateur champion, in 1931–36–37, she also captured the British title in 1935 and played three times in the Curtis Cup from 1932–36.

Morris, Old Tom (1821–1908)

Apprenticed as a feathery ball maker to Allan Robertson in St Andrews at the age of 18 he was one of the finest golfers of his day when he took up the position of Keeper of the Green at Prestwick, where he laid out the original 12-hole course. He was 39 when he finished second in the first Open in 1860, but subsequently won the title four times. His success rate might have been much greater if he had been a better putter. His son once said: "He would be a much better player if the hole was a yard closer." A man of fierce conviction, he returned to St Andrews to take up the duties of looking after the Old Course at a salary of £50 per year, paid by The R&A. He came to regard the course as his own property and was once publicly reprimanded for closing it without authority because he considered it needed a rest. A testimonial in 1896 raised £1,240 pounds towards his old age from golfers around the world and when he retired in 1903 The R&A continued to pay his salary. He died after a fall on the stairs of the New Club in 1908, having outlived his wife, his daughter and his three sons.

Morris, Young Tom   (1851–1875)

Born in St Andrews, but brought up in Prestwick, where his father had moved to become Keeper of the Green, he won a tournament against leading professionals at the age of 13. He was only 17 when he succeeded his father as Open champion in 1868 and then defended the title successfully in the following two years to claim the winner's belt outright. There was no championship in 1871, but when the present silver trophy – the Claret Jug – became the prize in 1872, Young Tom's was the first name engraved thereon. His prodigious talent was best demonstrated in his third successive Open victory in 1870 when he played 36 holes at Prestwick in 149 strokes, 12 shots ahead of his nearest rival, superb scoring given the equipment and the condition of the course at that time. He married in November 1874 and was playing with his father in a money match at North Berwick the following year when a telegram from St Andrews sent them hurrying back across the Firth of Forth in a private yacht. Young Tom's wife and baby had both died in childbirth. He played golf only twice after that,

in matches that had been arranged long in advance, and fell into moods of deep depression. He died on Christmas morning of that same year from a burst artery in the lung. He was 24 years old. A public subscription paid for a memorial which still stands above his grave in the cathedral cemetery.

Nelson, Byron   (1912–2006)

John Byron Nelson left a legacy which many will aspire to emulate but which few will achieve. He joined the professional circuit in 1935 after a caddie shack apprenticeship which he shared with Ben Hogan and quickly established himself, winning the New Jersey Open in 1935 and going on to take The Masters title two years later. Between 1935 and 1946 he had 54 wins but although he won The Masters in 1937 and 1942, the US Open in 1939 and the US PGA Championship in 1940 and 1945 he didn't manage to pull off a Grand Slam having never won The Open Championship. The 1939 US Open is probably best remembered as the tournament Sam Snead threw away, history tending to overlook the achievement of Byron Nelson, the man who eventually took the title. After a three-way play-off with Craig Wood and Densmore Shute, Nelson went on to win the decisive 18 holes by three shots from Wood. America's entry into the second world war called a temporary halt to competitive golf for many. Nelson, denied the opportunity to serve his country due to a blood disorder, continued to play throughout 1943 and 1944, re-establishing his prominent position when full competition resumed in 1945, winning 18 times including 11 events in a row between March and August – a record unlikely ever to be broken. He was twice a member of US Ryder Cup teams – in 1937 and 1947 and had been picked for the postponed matches in 1939 and 1941. He returned to that competition in 1965 when he captained the victorious US team. His only win in Europe was the 1955 French Open. He was a father figure in US golf and until he retired in 2001 was one of The Masters honorary starters along with the late Gene Sarazen and Sam Snead. In company with Snead and his old sparring partner Ben Hogan, Byron Nelson was one of the sport's most revered figures and had a particularly close friendship with five times Open champion Tom Watson.

Norman, Moe   (1929–2004)

Eccentric Canadian golf star who was renowned for the accuracy of his unusual swing. Twice Canadian Amateur Champion and winner of 13 Canadian Tour titles, he was inducted into the Canadian Golf Hall of Fame in 1995. He played very quickly, seldom slowing to line up a putt. He never had a lesson. He was such a character that Wally Uihlein, president of Titleist and Footjoy, paid him $5,000 a month for the last 10 years of his life for just "being himself".

Ouimet, Francis   (1893–1967)

Regarded as the player who started the American golf boom after beating Harry Vardon and Ted Ray in a play-off for the 1913 US Open as a young amateur. Twice a winner of the US Amateur, he was a member of every Walker Cup team from 1922 to 1934 and non-playing captain from then until 1949. In 1951 he became the first non-British national to be elected captain of The R&A and was a committee member of the USPGA for many years.

Panton, John   (1926–2009)

Former honorary Professional to the Royal and Ancient Golf Club of St Andrews he was one of Scotland's best known, admired and loved profesionals who spent most of his working life at the Glenbervie Club near Stirling. A renowned iron-player he was leading British player in the 1956 Open and beat Sam Snead for the World Seniors' title in 1967 at Southport. He played in three Ryder Cup matches and was 12 times a contestant in the World Cup with the late Eric Brown as his regular partner. It was a partnership that earned considerable admiration although the two were so different in character – Panton quiet and unassuming, Brown extrovert and noisy! He won the Association of Golf Writers Trophy in 1967 for his contribution to the game and was honoured by The Queen with an MBE for his services to the game. In later years he lived with his daughter, herself a professional player of note, at Sunningdale. The ginger beer and lime drink now available in golf clubhouses was John's normal tipple and now bears his name! Over the years he took his film camera with him and left a unique library of some of the golfing greats in action.

Park, Mungo   (1839–1904)

Younger brother to Willie Park, he spent much of his early life at sea, but won The Open Championship in 1874 at the age of 35, beating Young Tom Morris into second place by two shots on his home course at Musselburgh.

Park, Willie   (1834–1903)

Winner of the first Open Championship in 1860. He won the title three more times, in 1863, 1866 and 1875, and was runner-up on four occasions. For 20 years he issued a standing challenge to play any man in the world for £100 a side. His reputation was built largely around a successful putting stroke and he always stressed the importance of never leaving putts short.

Park Jr, Willie   (1864–1925)

Son of the man who won the first Open Championship, Willie Park Jr captured the title twice – in 1887 and 1889 – and finished second to Harry Vardon in 1898. He was also an accomplished clubmaker who did much to popularise the bulger driver with its convex face. He patented the wry-neck putter in 1891. One of the first and most successful professionals to design golf courses, he was responsible for many layouts in Britain, Europe and America and also wrote two highly successful books on the game.

Patton, Billy Joe   (1922–2011)

Educated at Wake Forest, he is best remembered for holing out in one at the sixth hole en route to a closing 71 in the 1954 Masters at Augusta and failing by just one shot to play off for the Green Jacket with eventual winner Sam Snead and Ben Hogan. He played in five Walker Cups and captained the US side in 1969. In 1962 he won the USGA Bob Jones award for outstanding sportsmanship.

Philp, Hugh   (1782–1856)

One of the master craftsmen in St Andrews in the early days of the 19th century, he was renowned for his skill in creating long-nosed putters. After his death his business was continued by Robert Forgan. Philp's clubs are much prized collector's items.

Picard, Henry   (1907–1997)

Winner of The US Masters in 1938 and the 1939 USPGA Championship, where he birdied the final hole to tie with Byron Nelson and birdied the first extra hole for the title. Ill health cut short a career in which he won 27 tournaments.

Price-Fisher, Elizabeth (1923–2008)

Born in London she played in six Curtis Cup matches and, in addition to winning the 1959 British Women's Championship took titles in Denmark and Portugal, She turned professional in 1968 but was later reinstated as an amateur in 1971. For many years she worked as the ladies golf correspondent for the *Daily Telegraph* in London.

Ray, Ted   (1877–1943)

Born in Jersey, his early years in golf were in competition with Channel Islands compatriot Harry Vardon and his fellow members of the Great Triumvirate, J.H. Taylor and James Braid. His only victory in The Open came in 1912, but he was runner-up to Taylor the following year and second again, to Jim Barnes of America, in 1925 when he was 48 years of age. He claimed the US Open title in 1920 and remains one of only three British players to win The Open and the US Open on both sides of the Atlantic. The others are Harry Vardon and Tony Jacklin.

Rees, Dai   (1913–1983)

One of Britain's outstanding golfers for three decades, he played in nine Ryder Cup matches between 1937 and 1961 and was playing captain of the 1957 team which won the trophy for the first time since 1933. He was non-playing captain in 1967. He was runner-up in The Open three times and won the PGA Match Play title four times. He was made an honorary member of the Royal and Ancient Golf Club in 1976.

Robertson, Allan   (1815–1859)

So fearsome was Robertson's reputation as a player that when The R&A staged an annual competition for local professionals, he was not allowed to take part in order to give the others a chance. A famous maker of feather golf balls, he strongly resisted the advance of the more robust gutta percha. Tom Morris senior was his apprentice and they were reputed never to have lost a foursomes match in which they were partners.

Rosburg, Bob (1926–2009)

The 1959 US PGA Championship also made a name for himself as a golf commentator. After his playing days were over he was employed by Roone Arledge, the head of sport for ABC television, as golf's first on-course reporter – a job he did for 30 years. His characteristic "say-it-as-it-is" style means he will always be remembered by his response to the question regularly posed by one of his fellow commentators in the box ... when asked how the ball was lying Rossie's regular reply was "He's got no chance!"

Ryder, Samuel (1858–1936)

The prosperous seed merchant was so impressed with the friendly rivalry between British and American professionals at an unofficial match at Wentworth in 1926 that he donated the famous gold trophy for the first Ryder Cup match the following year. The trophy is still presented today for the contest between America and Europe.

Sarazen, Gene (1902–1999)

Advised to find an outdoor job to improve his health, Sarazen became a caddie and then an assistant professional. At the age of 20 he became the first player to win the US Open and PGA titles in the same year. In claiming seven major titles he added The Open at Prince's in 1932 and when he won the second Masters tournament in 1935 he became the first of only five players to date who have won all four Grand Slam trophies during their careers. He played "the shot heard around the world" on his way to his 1935 Masters victory, holing a four-wood across the lake at the 15th for an albatross (double eagle) two. At the age of 71 he played in The Open at Troon and holed-in-one at the Postage Stamp eighth. The next day he holed from a bunker for a two at the same hole. He acted as an honorary starter at the Masters, hitting his final shot only a month before his death at 97.

Sayers, Ben (1857–1924)

A twinkling, elphin figure, the diminutive Sayers played a leading part in the game for more than four decades. He represented Scotland against England from 1903 to 1913 and played in every Open from 1880 to 1923.

Sewgolum, Sewsunker "Pappa" (1930–1978)

A former caddie he played every shot unconventionally with his left hand on the club beneath his right. He first made headlines when he beat a field of white golfers in the Natal Open at the prestigious Durban Country Club. He won the Dutch Open title three

times in 1959, 1960 and 1964. The municipal course in Durban bears his name and in 2003 he received a posthumous achievement award.

Shade, Ronnie D.B.M. (1938–1984)

One of Scotland's greatest golfers whom many considered the world's top amateur in the mid 60s. After losing the 1962 Scottish Amateur Golf Championship final to Stuart Murray, he won that title five years in a row winning 43 consecutive ties before losing in the fourth round to Willie Smeaton at Muirfield in 1968. Taught by his father John, professional at the Duddingston club in Edinburgh, he was often referred to as "Right Down the Bloody Middle" because of his initials and consistent play. Shade won the Scottish and Irish Open Championships as a professional but was re-instated as an amateur before his death from cancer at the age of 47.

Smith, Frances – née Bunty Stephens (1925–1978)

Dominated post-war women's golf, winning the British Ladies Championship in 1949 and 1954, was three times a winner of the English and once the victor in the French Championship. She represented Great Britain & Ireland in six consecutive encounters from 1950, losing only three of her 11 matches, and was non-playing captain of the team in 1962 and 1972. She was awarded the OBE for her services to golf.

Smith, Horton (1908–1963)

In his first winter on the US professional circuit as a 20-year-old in 1928–29 he won eight out of nine tournaments. He was promoted to that year's Ryder Cup team and played again in 1933 and 1935 and remained unbeaten He won the first Masters in 1934 and repeated that success two year's later. He received the Ben Hogan Award for overcoming illness or injury and the Bobby Jones Award for distinguished sportsmanship in golf.

Smith, Macdonald (1890–1949)

Born into a talented Carnoustie golfing family, he was destined to become one of the finest golfers never to win The Open. He was second in 1930 and 1932, was twice third and twice fourth. His best chance came at Prestwick in 1925 when he led the field by five strokes with one round to play, but the enthusiastic hordes of Scottish supporters destroyed his concentration and he finished with an 82 for fourth place.

Snead, Sam (1912–2002)

Few would argue that "Slammin' Sam Snead" possessed the sweetest swing in the history of the game. 'He just walked up to the ball and poured honey all over it', it was said. Raised during the Depression in Hot Springs, Virginia, he also died there on May 23 2002, four days short of his 90th birthday. His seven major titles comprised three Masters, three USPGA

Championships and the 1946 Open at St Andrews, while he was runner-up four times but never won the US Open. But for the Second World War he would surely have added several more. He achieved a record 82 PGA Tour victories in America, the last of them at age 52, and was just as prolific round the world across six decades. He played in seven Ryder Cup matches, captained the 1969 United States team which tied at Royal Birkdale and after his retirement acted as honorary starter at The Masters until his death. Perhaps his greatest achievement came in the 1979 Quad Cities Open when he scored 67 and 66. He was 67 years of age at the time.

Solheim, Karsten   (1912–2000)

A golfing revolutionary who discovered the game at the age of 42 and, working in his garage, invented the Ping putter with its unique heel-toe weighting design, later adopted in his irons. A keen supporter of women's golf, he presented the Solheim Cup for a biennial competition between the American and European Ladies' Tours.

Souchak, Mike (1927 – 2008)

He won 15 times on the PGA Tour in the 1950's and 1960's, competed in the 1959 and 1961 Ryder Cups and played for 11 years on the Champions Tour before retiring. Although he never won a major title he finished 11 times in the top 10 in majors coming third twice in the US Open.

Spearman, Marley (1938 – 2011)

Superb ambassador for golf in the 1950s and 1960s whose exuberance and *joie de vivre* is legendary. Three times a Curtis Cup player she won the British Ladies in 1961 and again in 1962. She was English champion in 1964. In 1962 was awarded the Association of Golf Writers' Trophy for her services to golf.

Stewart, Payne   (1957–1999)

Four months after winning his second US Open title Payne Stewart was killed in a plane crash. Only a month earlier he had been on the winning United States Ryder Cup team. His first major victory was in the 1989 USPGA Championship and he claimed his first US Open title two years later after a play-off against Scott Simpson. In 1999 he holed an 18-foot winning putt to beat Phil Mickleson for the US title he was never able to defend. In 1985 he finished a stroke behind Sandy Lyle in The Open at Royal St George's and five years later he shared second place when Nick Faldo won the Championship at St Andrews.

Tait, Freddie   (1870–1900)

In 1890 Tait set a new record of 77 for the Old Course, lowering that to 72 only four years later. He was three times the leading amateur in The Open Championship and twice won the Amateur Championship, in 1896 and 1898. The following year he lost at the 37th hole of an historic final to John Ball at

Prestwick. He was killed while leading a charge of the Black Watch at Koodoosberg Drift in the Boer War.

Taylor, J.H.   (1871–1963)

Winner of The Open Championship five times between 1894 and 1913, Taylor was part of the Great Triumvirate with James Braid and Harry Vardon. He tied for the title with Vardon in 1896, but lost in the play-off and was runner-up another five times. He also won the French and German Opens and finished second in the US Open. A self-educated man, he was a thoughtful and compelling speaker and became the founding father of the Professional Golfers' Association. He was made an honorary member of The R&A in 1949.

Tolley, Cyril   (1896–1978)

Won the first of his two Amateur Championships in 1920 while still a student at Oxford and played in the unofficial match which preceded the Walker Cup a year later. He played in six Walker Cup encounters and was team captain in 1924. Tolley is the only amateur to have won the French Open, a title he captured in 1924 and 1928. After winning the Amateur for the second time in 1929 he was favourite to retain the title at St Andrews the following summer but was beaten by a stymie at the 19th hole in the fourth round by Bobby Jones in the American's Grand Slam year.

Travis, Walter   (1862–1925)

Born in Australia, he won the US Amateur Championship in 1900 at the age of 38, having taken up the game only four years earlier. He won again the following year and in 1903. He became the first overseas player to win the Amateur title in Britain in 1904, using a centre-shafted Schenectady putter he had just acquired. The club was banned a short time later. He was 52 years old when he last reached the semi-finals of the US Amateur in 1914.

Tumba, Sven   (1931–2011)

A legendary ice-hockey player who played 245 times for his country and a top class soccer player he turned to golf in 1970 and was responsible for popularising the game in Sweden. Having played in the Eisenhower Trophy and won the Swedish Match Play Championship he founded his own club at Ullna and later opened the first golf course in Moscow. Helped by some of the biggest world stars including Jack Nicklaus he introduced top class professional golf with his Scandinavian Enterprise Open. Later in life he organised the World Golfers' Championship, played in 40 different countries. Always enthusiastic and well-loved, Sven was truly a Swedish sporting legend to whom golf owes much.

Valentine, Jessie   (1915–2006)

A winner of titles before and after World War II, she was an impressive competitor and was one of the first ladies to make a career out of professional golf. She won the British Ladies as an amateur in 1937 and again in 1955 and 1958 and was Scottish champion in 1938 and 1939 and four times between 1951 and 1956. But for the war years it is certain she would have had more titles and victories. She played in seven Curtis Cups between 1936 and 1958 and represented Scotland in the Home Internationals on 17 occasions between 1934 and 1958.

Van Donck, Flory (1912–1992)

Although his style was unorthodox he will always be remembered as a great putter. He remains Belgium's most successful player. He won the Belgian title 16 times between 1939 and 1956 and was successful, too, often more than once in the Dutch, Italian, French, German, Swiss and Portuguese Championships. In 1963 he won seven titles in Europe. Twice runner-up in The Open in 1956 to Peter Thomson at Hoylake and in 1959 to Gary Player at Muirfield he represented 19 times in the World Cup including the 1967 competition at the age of 67.

Vardon, Harry (1870–1937)

Still the only player to have won The Open Championship six times, Vardon, who was born in Jersey, won his first title in 1896, in a 36-hole play-off against J.H. Taylor and his last in 1914, this time beating Taylor by three shots. He won the US Open in 1900 and was beaten in a play-off by Francis Ouimet in 1913. He was one of the most popular of the players at the turn of the century and did much to popularise the game in America with his whistle-stop exhibition tours. He popularised the overlapping grip which still bears his name, although it was first used by Johnny Laidlay. He was also the originator of the modern upright swing, moving away from the flat sweeping action of previous eras. After his Open victory of 1903, during which he was so ill he thought he would not be able to finish, he was diagnosed with tuberculosis. His legendary accuracy and low scoring are commemorated with the award of two Vardon Trophies – in America for the player each year with the lowest scoring average and in Europe for the golfer who tops the money list.

Vare, Glenna – née Collett (1903–1989)

Won the first of her six US Ladies Amateur titles at the age of 19 in 1922 and the last in 1935. A natural athlete, she attacked the ball with more power than was normal in the women's game. The British title eluded her, although at St Andrews in 1929 she was three-under par and five up on Joyce Wethered after 11 holes, but lost to a blistering counter-attack. She played in the first Curtis Cup match in 1932 and was a member of the team in 1936, 1938 and 1948 and was captain in 1934 and 1950.

Von Nida, Norman (1914–2007)

Generally considered the father of Australian golf, he won over 80 titles worldwide. The Australian devel-

opment Tour is named after him. Played extensively in Britain in the 1940s and 1960s. In later life he was registered bind. Generally regarded as the first golfer to make his income on Tour rather than being based at a club. In 1947 he won seven times in Europe.

Walker, George (1874–1953)

The President of the United States Golf Association who donated the trophy for the first match in 1922, at Long Island, New York, and which is still presented to the winning team in the biennial matches between the USA and Great Britain & Ireland. His grandson and great grandson, George Walker Bush and George Bush Jr have both become Presidents of the United States.

Ward, Charles Harold (1911–2001)

Charlie Ward played in three Ryder Cup matches from 1947–1951 and was twice third in The Open, behind Henry Cotton at Muirfield in 1948 and Max Faulkner at Royal Portrush in 1951.

Ward, Harvie (1926–2004)

Born in Tarboro, North Carolina, he was winner of the Amateur Championship in 1952 when he beat Frank Stranahan 6 and 5 at Prestwick, he went on to win the US title in 1955 and 1956 and the Canadian Amateur in 1964. He played in the 1953, 1955 and 1959 Walker Cup matches and won all of his six games.

Wethered, Joyce – Lady Heathcoat-Amory (1901–1997)

Entered her first English Ladies Championship in 1920 at the age of 18 and beat holder Cecil Leitch in the final. She remained unbeaten for four years, winning 33 successive matches. After they had played together at St Andrews, Bobby Jones remarked: "I have never played golf with anyone, man or woman, amateur or professional, who made me feel so utterly outclassed."

Wethered, Roger (1899–1983)

Amateur champion in 1923 and runner-up in 1928 and 1930, he played five times in the Walker Cup, acting as playing captain at Royal St George's in 1930, and represented England against Scotland every year from 1922 to 1930. In The Open Championship at St Andrews in 1921 he tied with Jock Hutchison despite incurring a penalty for treading on his own ball. Due to play in a cricket match in England the following day, he was persuaded to stay in St Andrews for the play-off, but lost by 150–159 over 36 holes.

Whitcombe, Ernest (1890–1971)
Charles (1895–1978)
Reginald (1898–1957)

The remarkable golfing brothers from Burnham, Somerset, were all selected for the Ryder Cup team of 1935. Charlie and Eddie were paired together and won the only point in the foursomes in a heavy 9–3 defeat by the American team. Reg won the gale-lashed Open at Royal St George's in 1938, with a final round of 78 on a day when the exhibition tent was blown into the sea. Ernest finished second to Walter Hagen in 1924 and Charlie was third at Muirfield in 1935.

White, Ronnie (1921–2005)
A five times Walker Cup team member between 1947 and 1953 he was one of the most impressive players in post-war amateur golf. He won six and halved one of the 10 games he played in the Walker Cup. He won the English Amateur Championship in 1949, the English Amateur Stroke-play title the following two years and was silver medallist as leading amateur in The Open Championship in 1961 played at his home club of Royal Birkdale.

Will, George (1937–2010)
George Will from Ladybank in Fife was a three-time Ryder Cup player in 1963–65 and 67. He was for many years the club professional at Sundridge Park where he was longtime coach to former Walker Cup and European Tour player Roger Chapman but was also long-time coach to the Belgian National team. An always stylish player he was a former Scottish Boys, British Youths and Army champion.

Wilson, Enid (1910–1996)
Completed a hat-trick of victories in the Ladies British Amateur Championship from 1931–33. She was twice a semi-finalist in the American Championship, won the British Girls' and English Ladies' titles and played in the inaugural Curtis Cup match, beating Helen Hicks 2 and 1 in the singles. Retiring early from competitive golf, she was never afraid to express strongly held views on the game in her role as women's golf correspondent of the *Daily Telegraph*.

Wind, Herbert Warren (1917–2005)
One of if not the most distinguished writers on golf in America, he authored 14 books on the game he loved with a passion. A long-time contributor to the *New Yorker* magazine, he is still the only writer to have received the United States Golf Association's Bobby Jones award for distinguished sportsmanship – an honour bestowed on him in 1995, the year the Association celebrated its centenary. The award was appropriate because he was a life-long admirer of Jones and was a regular at The Masters each year where he has been given the credit for naming, in 1958, the difficult stretch of holes from the 11th to the 13th as Amen Corner, arguing you said "Amen" if you negotiated them without dropping a shot.

Wood, Craig (1901–1968)
Both Masters and US Open champion in 1941, Wood finally made up for a career of near misses, having lost play-offs for all four major championships between 1933 and 1939. He was three times a member of the American Ryder Cup team.

Wooldridge, Ian (1932–2007)
One of the most respected sports writers who enjoyed nothing more than covering golf. His *Daily Mail* column was required reading for 40 years.

Yates, Charlie (1913–2005)
Great friend of the late Bobby Jones he was top amateur in the US Masters in 1934, 1939 and 1940. In 1938 came to Royal Troon and won the British Amateur title beating R. Ewing 3 and 2. For many years acted as chairman of the press committee at The Masters and staged annual parties for visiting golf writers in the Augusta Clubhouse. He was a long-time Vice President of the Association of Golf Writers.

Zaharias, Mildred "Babe" – née Didrickson (1915–1956)
As a 17-year-old, Babe, as she was universally known, broke three records in the 1932 Los Angeles Olympics – the javelin, 80 metres hurdles and high jump, but her high jump medal was denied her when judges decided her technique was illegal. Turning her attention to golf, she rapidly established herself as the most powerful woman golfer of the time and in 1945 played and made the cut in the LA Open on the men's PGA Tour. She won the final of the US Amateur by 11 and 9 in 1946, became the first American to win the British title the following year, then helped launch the women's professional tour. She won the US Women's Open in 1948, 1950 and 1954 and in 1950 won six of the nine events on the tour. In 1952 she had a major operation for cancer, but when she won her third and final Open two years later it was by the margin of 12 shots. She was voted Woman Athlete of the Year five times between 1932 and 1950 and Greatest Female Athlete of the Half-Century in 1949.

What is the answer?

Q: Is the use of a suction cup on the end of a putter grip to retrieve the ball from the hole permissible?

A: Yes. The use of a suction cup in this way is a permitted exception under Rule 4-1a.

Tumba's popularity helped grow the game in Sweden

He became the most versatile and succesful athlete ever in Sweden. Sven Tumba played ice hockey for Sweden and was voted the best player in the world after having won World and Olympic Championships. He played football for Sweden, represented Sweden in water-skiing and having won the Scandinavian Match Play Championship at Bogstad GC in Oslo was included in the national team at the Eisenhower Trophy at Puerta de Hierro in 1970.

He had an enormous energy and dealt with life as would an untamed horse. When awarded Best Ice Hockey Player on live TV he was supposed to jump onto the ice through a narrow gap to find the puck in the middle of the rink to skate towards the empty goal and to score.

Unfortunately he got too excited, slipped before reaching the ice and fell flat on his stomach, loosing his stick. However he quickly recovered, found his stick, caught hold of the puck, rushed at the goal to miss it completely.

But at the same time this sequence of event made him even more popular and it was his popularity as a man and as an athlete that boosted the growth of golf in Sweden. Sven Tumba was a man of the people and if he found golf so attractive, then so must we. He made the game visible and the media, not least television, followed his every move. He caused a stampede.

He was also full of ideas and managed to lure Arnold Palmer to Sweden for an exhibition tour, a very successful endeavour. He got Volvo, the car company, to sponsor a tournament and in addition persuaded jack Nicklaus to play. The tournament still exists although under another name.

Thanks to his contacts through ice hockey he actually got permission to build a nine-hole golf course in Moscow, officially opened by Leonid Brezhnev. With Tumba anything was possible. As a golf player he was a volcano. He loved the game. He respected it, cherished but, sadly, it cannot be played at a galloping pace. Born in 1931, much-loved Sven Tumba died last year.

Göran Zachrisson

USA retain Llandudno Cup in California

Britain and Ireland's Club professionals have still to beat the Americans on their home ground. In the 25th Ryder-Cup style match played at Corde Valle, San Martin, California, the USA ran out 17½–8½ winners for the second successive time. The Americans have now won the trophy 17 times since the match was instituted in 1973. Great Britain and Ireland have won on five occasions most recently at the K Club near Dublin in 2005. The points were shared in three matches.

Although the four balls series were halved, each side winning four points, it was in the foursomes that the Americans took control. Jim Remy, the USA captain, had told his men to concentrate on the foursomes and they responded winning six and a half of the eight points to take a commanding five point lead into the final series of singles.

It meant the GB&I side captained by Russell Weir from Dunoon faced an uphill task on the final day with the Americans requiring to win only two and a half points from the 10 games to retain the Cup, three to win the match.

The winning points came quickly. Marty Jertson had two eagles on the way to beating Craig Goodfellow 3 and 2, Danny Balin, who earlier in the competition had scored a hole-in-one, came from one down with two to play to beat Chris Gill and when Sonny Skinner halved with Stuart Little the Americans knew the Cup would be staying in the USA. Although Robert Giles and David Shacklady won and Stuart Giles secured a half-point, the Americans took the singles series 7–3.

In one of the lowest scoring singles, Ganton's Gary Brown had six birdies but lost 3 and 2 to Faber Jamerson who was out in 29 and eight under par after 13 holes. Top GB&I points scorer was David Shacklady from Mossock Hall with two and a half points out of a possible five.

Full details can be found on page 211.

The next match, in 2013, will be staged at Slaley Hall in Northumberland.

Montgomerie's goal — to become the oldest winner on Tour

Colin Montgomerie, eight times European top money earner, may not have enjoyed his most lucrative year on the course in 2011 but he remains as competitive and enthusiastic about his golf game.

Much of last year his golf fame suffered because he was involved in many off the course commitments, some with an element of danger attached to them like the five day trip he made with PGA Tour officials (and with the Ryder Cup in his luggage) to Afghanistan to entertain the troops.

"That was a reality check. The lads out there are doing a marvellous job but you do not realise just how brave and courageous they are until you actually are there talking with them, seeing them some with terrible injuries."

That trip took almost a year to organise but as far as Colin was concerned it was worth it even if at times a little scary. "When they ask you to provide your dental records that's a bit worrying and makes you realise the dangers."

When he was in Kabul — where he felt rather more anxious than when based at Camp Bastion — he did not get the chance to see the Kabul course heavily mined and littered with burned out tanks. Nobody who plays there ever looks for a ball in the rough!

At the end of the year, globetrotting golfing ambassador Montgomerie also visited China, Australia, Bahrein — where the first Volvo Champions event was played on the course Colin designed — Kuwait and Oman where there is only one course but interest in golf is steadily growing.

In 2012, however, the retiring Ryder Cup captain will be concentrating on his golf after a year in which he spent 265 days on the road. He remains enthusiastic about his ability to compete. "I have a goal and that is to become the oldest winner on the European Tour and make it back into the top 50 in the world rankings."

This year he will have much more time to practice. He admits he loves the game and still has the drive and ambition to do well. He remains competitive but if he loses that competitiveness he will not continue to play on the main Tour.

He has always said that he was not all that keen on playing the Senior Tour but will play in the Senior British Open in 2013 a few weeks after turning 50 and he would like to play in at the US Senior Open (both won last year by Bernhard Langer) as well but only if exempt.

The last two years have been manic for Montgomerie because of Ryder Cup duties but in 2012 it is his own GoBack golf that will be his main interest.

PGA captain Eddie Bullock and former captain Parnell Reilly accompanied Colin Montgomerie on his trip last year to Afghanistan. All were impressed by the professionalism of the soldiers many of whom took the opportunity to sharpen up their golf with a lesson from Monty who also took the Ryder Cup to show the troops.

PART XIV

Governance
of the Game

R&A Rules Limited

With effect from 1st January 2004, the responsibilities and authority of The Royal and Ancient Golf Club of St Andrews in making, interpreting and giving decisions on the Rules of Golf and on the Rules of Amateur Status were transferred to R&A Rules Limited.

Gender

In the Rules of Golf, the gender used in relation to any person is understood to include both genders.

Golfers with Disabilities

The R&A publication entitled "A Modification of the Rules of Golf for Golfers with Disabilities", that contains permissible modifications of the Rules of Golf to accommodate disabled golfers, is available through The R&A.

Handicaps

The Rules of Golf do not legislate for the allocation and adjustment of handicaps. Such matters are within the jurisdiction of the National Union concerned and queries should be directed accordingly.

RULES
OF GOLF

As Approved by
R&A Rules Limited
and the
United States Golf Association

32nd Edition
Effective 1 January 2012

Principle changes introduced in the 2012 Code

Definitions

Addressing the Ball

The Definition is amended so that a player has addressed the ball simply by grounding his club immediately in front of or behind the ball, regardless of whether or not he has taken his stance. Therefore, the Rules generally no longer provide for a player addressing the ball in a hazard. (See also related change to Rule 18-2b)

Rules

Rule 1-2. Exerting Influence on Movement of Ball or Altering Physical Conditions

The Rule is amended to establish more clearly that, if a player intentionally takes an action to influence the movement of a ball or to alter physical conditions affecting the playing of a hole in a way that is not permitted by the Rules, Rule 1-2 applies only when the action is not already covered in another Rule. For example, a player improving the lie of his ball is in breach of Rule 13-2 and therefore that Rule would apply, whereas a player intentionally improving the lie of a fellow-competitor's ball is not a situation covered by Rule 13-2 and, therefore, is governed by Rule 1-2.

Rule 6-3a. Time of Starting

Rule 6-3a is amended to provide that the penalty for starting late, but within five minutes of the starting time, is reduced from disqualification to loss of the first hole in match play or two strokes at the first hole in stroke play. Previously this penalty reduction could be introduced as a condition of competition.

Rule 12-1. Seeing Ball; Searching for Ball

Rule 12-1 is reformatted for clarity. In addition, it is amended to (i) permit a player to search for his ball anywhere on the course when it may be covered by sand and to clarify that there is no penalty if the ball is moved in these circumstances, and (ii) apply a penalty of one stroke under Rule 18-2a if a player moves his ball in a hazard when searching for it when it is believed to be covered by loose impediments.

Rule 13-4. Ball in Hazard; Prohibited Actions

Exception 2 to Rule 13-4 is amended to permit a player to smooth sand or soil in a hazard at any time, including before playing from that hazard, provided it is for the sole purpose of caring for the course and Rule 13-2 is not breached.

Rule 18-2b. Ball Moving After Address

A new Exception is added that exonerates the player from penalty if his ball moves after it has been addressed when it is known or virtually certain that he did not cause the ball to move. For example, if it is a gust of wind that moves the ball after it has been addressed, there is no penalty and the ball is played from its new position.

Rule 19-1. Ball in Motion Deflected or Stopped; By Outside Agency

The note is expanded to prescribe the various outcomes when a ball in motion has been deliberately deflected or stopped by an outside agency.

Rule 20-7c. Playing from Wrong Place; Stroke Play

Note 3 is amended so that if a player is to be penalised for playing from a wrong place, in most cases the penalty will be limited to two strokes, even if another Rule has been breached prior to his making the stroke.

Appendix IV

A new Appendix is added to prescribe general regulations for the design of devices and other equipment, such as tees, gloves and distance measuring devices.

Rules of Amateur Status

Definitions

Amateur Golfer

The Definition is amended to establish more clearly that an "amateur golfer", regardless of whether he plays competitively or recreationally, is one who plays golf for the challenge it presents, not as a profession and not for financial gain.

Golf Skill or Reputation

A time limit of five years is introduced for the retention of "golf reputation" after the player's golf skill has diminished.

Prize Vouchers

The Definition is expanded to allow prize vouchers to be used for the purchase of goods or services from a golf club.

Rules

Rule 1-3 Amateurism; Purpose of the Rules

Rule 1-3 is amended to re-state why there is a distinction between amateur and professional golf and why certain limits and restrictions are needed in the amateur game.

Rule 2-1 Professionalism; General

The existing Rules on professionalism are consolidated and re-formatted into new Rule 2-1.

Rule 2-2 Professionalism; Contracts and Agreements

National Golf Unions or Associations – New Rule 2-2(a) is added to allow an amateur golfer to enter into a contract and/or agreement with his national golf union or association, provided he does not obtain any financial gain, directly or indirectly, while still an amateur golfer.

Professional Agents, Sponsors and Other Third Parties – New Rule 2-2(b) is added to allow an amateur golfer, who is at least 18 years of age, to enter into a contract and/or agreement with a third party solely in relation to the golfer's future as a professional golfer, provided he does not obtain any financial gain, directly or indirectly, while still an amateur golfer.

Rule 3-2b Hole-in-One Prizes

New Rule 3-2b excludes from the general prize limit prizes (including cash prizes) awarded for achieving a hole-in-one while playing a round of golf. This exception is specific to prizes for holes-in-one (not longest drive or nearest the hole) and neither separate events nor multiple-entry events qualify.

Rule 4-3 Subsistence Expenses

New Rule added to allow an amateur golfer to receive subsistence expenses to assist with general living costs, provided the expenses are approved by and paid through the player's national golf union or association.

How to use the rule book

It is understood that not everyone who has a copy of the Rules of Golf will read it from cover to cover. Most golfers only consult the Rule book when they have a Rules issue on the course that needs to be resolved. However, to ensure that you have a basic understanding of the Rules and that you play golf in a reasonable manner, it is recommended that you at least read the Quick Guide to the Rules of Golf and the Etiquette Section contained within this publication.

In terms of ascertaining the correct answer to Rules issues that arise on the course, use of the Rule book's Index should help you to identify the relevant Rule. For example, if a player accidentally moves his ball-marker in the process of lifting his ball on the putting green, identify the key words in the question, such as "ball-marker", "lifting ball" and "putting green" and look in the Index for these headings. The relevant Rule (Rule 20-1) is found under the headings "ball-marker" and "lifted ball" and a reading of this Rule will confirm the correct answer.

In addition to identifying key words and using the Index in the Rules of Golf, the following points will assist you in using the Rule book efficiently and accurately:

Understand the Words
The Rule book is written in a very precise and deliberate fashion. You should be aware of and understand the following differences in word use:
- may   =   optional
- should   =   recommendation
- must   =   instruction (and penalty if not carried out)
- a ball   =   you may substitute another ball (e.g. Rules 26, 27 and 28)
- the ball =   you must not substitute another ball (e.g. Rules 24-2 and 25-1)

Know the Definitions
There are over fifty defined terms (e.g. abnormal ground condition, through the green, etc) and these form the foundation around which the Rules of Play are written. A good knowledge of the defined terms (which are italicised throughout the book) is very important to the correct application of the Rules.

The Facts of the Case
To answer any question on the Rules you must consider the facts of the case in some detail. You should identify:
- The form of play (e.g. match play or stroke play, single, foursome or four-ball)
- Who is involved (e.g. the player, his partner or caddie, an outside agency)
- Where the incident occurred (e.g. on the teeing ground, in a bunker or water hazard, on the putting green)
- What actually happened
- The player's intentions (e.g. what was he doing and what does he want to do)
- The timing of the incident (e.g. has the player now returned his score card, has the competi tion closed)

Refer to the Book
As stated above, reference to the Rule book Index and the relevant Rule should provide the answer to the majority of questions that can arise on the course. If in doubt, play the course as you find it and play the ball as it lies. On returning to the Clubhouse, refer the matter to the Committee and it may be that reference to the "Decisions on the Rules of Golf" will assist in resolving any queries that are not entirely clear from the Rule book itself.

Contents

Section I —
Etiquette; Behaviour on the Course

Introduction

This section provides guidelines on the manner in which the game of golf should be played. If they are followed, all players will gain maximum enjoyment from the game. The overriding principle is that consideration should be shown to others on the course at all times.

The Spirit of the Game

Golf is played, for the most part, without the supervision of a referee or umpire. The game relies on the integrity of the individual to show consideration for other players and to abide by the Rules. All players should conduct themselves in a disciplined manner, demonstrating courtesy and sportsmanship at all times, irrespective of how competitive they may be. This is the spirit of the game of golf.

Safety

Players should ensure that no one is standing close by or in a position to be hit by the club, the ball or any stones, pebbles, twigs or the like when they make a stroke or practice swing.

Players should not play until the players in front are out of range.

Players should always alert greenstaff nearby or ahead when they are about to make a stroke that might endanger them.

If a player plays a ball in a direction where there is a danger of hitting someone, he should immediately shout a warning. The traditional word of warning in such situations is "fore".

Consideration for Other Players

No Disturbance or Distraction

Players should always show consideration for other players on the course and should not disturb their play by moving, talking or making unnecessary noise.

Players should ensure that any electronic device taken onto the course does not distract other players.

On the teeing ground, a player should not tee his ball until it is his turn to play.

Players should not stand close to or directly behind the ball, or directly behind the hole, when a player is about to play.

On the Putting Green

On the putting green, players should not stand on another player's line of putt or, when he is making a stroke, cast a shadow over his line of putt.

Players should remain on or close to the putting green until all other players in the group have holed out.

Scoring

In stroke play, a player who is acting as a marker should, if necessary, on the way to the next tee, check the score with the player concerned and record it.

Pace of Play

Play at Good Pace and Keep Up

Players should play at a good pace. The Committee may establish pace of play guidelines that all players should follow.

It is a group's responsibility to keep up with the group in front. If it loses a clear hole and it is delaying the group

behind, it should invite the group behind to play through, irrespective of the number of players in that group. Where a group has not lost a clear hole, but it is apparent that the group behind can play faster, it should invite the faster moving group to play through.

Be Ready to Play

Players should be ready to play as soon as it is their turn to play. When playing on or near the putting green, they should leave their bags or carts in such a position as will enable quick movement off the green and towards the next tee. When the play of a hole has been completed, players should immediately leave the putting green.

Lost Ball

If a player believes his ball may be lost outside a water hazard or is out of bounds, to save time, he should play a provisional ball.

Players searching for a ball should signal the players in the group behind them to play through as soon as it becomes apparent that the ball will not easily be found. They should not search for five minutes before doing so. Having allowed the group behind to play through, they should not continue play until that group has passed and is out of range.

Priority on the Course

Unless otherwise determined by the Committee, priority on the course is determined by a group's pace of play. Any group playing a whole round is entitled to pass a group playing a shorter round. The term "group" includes a single player.

Care of the Course

Bunkers

Before leaving a bunker, players should carefully fill up and smooth over all holes and footprints made by them and any nearby made by others. If a rake is within reasonable proximity of the bunker, the rake should be used for this purpose.

Repair of Divots, Ball-Marks and Damage by Shoes

Players should carefully repair any divot holes made by them and any damage to the putting green made by the impact of a ball (whether or not made by the player himself). On completion of the hole by all players in the group, damage to the putting green caused by golf shoes should be repaired.

Preventing Unnecessary Damage

Players should avoid causing damage to the course by removing divots when taking practice swings or by hitting the head of a club into the ground, whether in anger or for any other reason.

Players should ensure that no damage is done to the putting green when putting down bags or the flagstick.

In order to avoid damaging the hole, players and caddies should not stand too close to the hole and should take care during the handling of the flagstick and the removal of a ball from the hole. The head of a club should not be used to remove a ball from the hole.

Players should not lean on their clubs when on the putting green, particularly when removing the ball from the hole.

The flagstick should be properly replaced in the hole before the players leave the putting green.

Local notices regulating the movement of golf carts should be strictly observed.

Conclusion; Penalties for Breach

If players follow the guidelines in this section, it will make the game more enjoyable for everyone.

If a player consistently disregards these guidelines during a round or over a period of time to the detriment of others, it is recommended that the Committee considers taking appropriate disciplinary action against the offending player. Such action may, for example, include prohibiting play for a limited time on the course or in a certain number of competitions. This is considered to be justifiable in terms of protecting the interests of the majority of golfers who wish to play in accordance with these guidelines.

In the case of a serious breach of etiquette, the Committee may disqualify a player under Rule 33-7.

Section II — Definitions

The Definitions are listed alphabetically and, in the Rules themselves, defined terms are in *italics*.

Abnormal Ground Conditions

An *"abnormal ground condition"* is any *casual water, ground under repair* or hole, cast or runway on the *course* made by a *burrowing animal*, a reptile or a bird.

Addressing the Ball

A player has *"addressed the ball"* when he has grounded his club immediately in front of or immediately behind the ball, whether or not he has taken his *stance*.

Advice

"Advice" is any counsel or suggestion that could influence a player in determining his play, the choice of a club or the method of making a *stroke*.

Information on the *Rules*, distance or matters of public information, such as the position of *hazards* or the *flagstick* on the *putting green*, is not *advice*.

Ball Deemed to Move

See *"Move or Moved"*.

Ball Holed

See *"Holed"*.

Ball Lost

See *"Lost Ball"*.

Ball in Play

A ball is *"in play"* as soon as the player has made a *stroke* on the *teeing ground*. It remains *in play* until it is *holed*, except when it is *lost, out of bounds* or lifted, or another ball has been *substituted*, whether or not the substitution is permitted; a ball so *substituted* becomes the *ball in play*.

If a ball is played from outside the *teeing ground* when the player is starting play of a hole, or when attempting to correct this mistake, the ball is not *in play* and Rule 11-4 or 11-5 applies. Otherwise, *ball in play* includes a ball played from outside the *teeing ground* when the player elects or is required to play his next *stroke* from the *teeing ground*.

Exception in match play: Ball *in play* includes a ball played by the player from outside the *teeing ground* when starting play of a hole if the *opponent* does not require the *stroke* to be cancelled in accordance with Rule 11-4a.

Best-Ball

See *"Forms of Match Play"*.

Bunker

A *"bunker"* is a *hazard* consisting of a prepared area of ground, often a hollow, from which turf or soil has been removed and replaced with sand or the like.

Grass-covered ground bordering or within a *bunker*, including a stacked turf face (whether grass-covered or earthen), is not part of the *bunker*. A wall or lip of the *bunker* not covered with grass is part of the *bunker*. The margin of a *bunker* extends vertically downwards, but not upwards.

A ball is in a *bunker* when it lies in or any part of it touches the *bunker*.

Burrowing Animal

A *"burrowing animal"* is an animal (other than a worm, insect or the like) that makes a hole for habitation or shelter, such as a rabbit, mole, groundhog, gopher or salamander.

Note: A hole made by a non-burrowing animal, such as a dog, is not an *abnormal ground condition* unless marked or declared as *ground under repair*.

Caddie

A *"caddie"* is one who assists the player in accordance with the *Rules*, which may include carrying or handling the player's clubs during play.

When one *caddie* is employed by more than one player, he is always deemed to be the *caddie* of the player sharing the *caddie* whose ball (or whose *partner's* ball) is involved, and *equipment* carried by him is deemed to be that player's *equipment*, except when the *caddie* acts upon specific directions of another player (or the *partner* of another player) sharing the *caddie*, in which case he is considered to be that other player's *caddie*.

Casual Water

"Casual water" is any temporary accumulation of water on the *course* that is not in a *water hazard* and is visible before or after the player takes his *stance*. Snow and natural ice, other than frost, are either *casual water* or *loose impediments*, at the option of the player. Manufactured ice is an *obstruction*. Dew and frost are not *casual water*.

A ball is in *casual water* when it lies in or any part of it touches the *casual water*.

Committee

The *"Committee"* is the committee in charge of the competition or, if the matter does not arise in a competition, the committee in charge of the *course*.

Competitor

A *"competitor"* is a player in a stroke play competition. A *"fellow-competitor"* is any person with whom the *competitor* plays. Neither is *partner* of the other.

In stroke play *foursome* and *four-ball* competitions, where the context so admits, the word *"competitor"* or *"fellow-competitor"* includes his *partner*.

Course
The *"course"* is the whole area within any boundaries established by the *Committee* (see Rule 33-2).

Equipment
"Equipment" is anything used, worn or carried by the player or anything carried for the player by his *partner* or either of their *caddies*, except any ball he has played at the hole being played and any small object, such as a coin or a tee, when used to mark the position of a ball or the extent of an area in which a ball is to be dropped. *Equipment* includes a golf cart, whether or not motorised.

Note 1: A ball played at the hole being played is *equipment* when it has been lifted and not put back into play.

Note 2: When a golf cart is shared by two or more players, the cart and everything in it are deemed to be the *equipment* of one of the players sharing the cart.

If the cart is being moved by one of the players (or the *partner* of one of the players) sharing it, the cart and everything in it are deemed to be that player's *equipment*. Otherwise, the cart and everything in it are deemed to be the *equipment* of the player sharing the cart whose ball (or whose *partner's* ball) is involved.

Fellow-Competitor
See *"Competitor"*.

Flagstick
The *"flagstick"* is a movable straight indicator, with or without bunting or other material attached, centred in the *hole* to show its position. It must be circular in cross-section. Padding or shock absorbent material that might unduly influence the movement of the ball is prohibited.

Forecaddie
A *"forecaddie"* is one who is employed by the *Committee* to indicate to players the position of balls during play. He is an *outside agency*.

Forms of Match Play
Single: A match in which one player plays against another player.

Threesome: A match in which one player plays against two other players, and each *side* plays one ball.

Foursome: A match in which two players play against two other players, and each *side* plays one ball.

Three-Ball: Three players play a match against one another, each playing his own ball. Each player is playing two distinct matches.

Best-Ball: A match in which one player plays against the better ball of two other players or the best ball of three other players.

Four-Ball: A match in which two players play their better ball against the better ball of two other players.

Forms of Stroke Play
Individual: A competition in which each *competitor* plays as an individual.

Foursome: A competition in which two *competitors* play as *partners* and play one ball.

Four-Ball: A competition in which two *competitors* play as *partners*, each playing his own ball. The lower score of the *partners* is the score for the hole. If one *partner* fails to complete the play of a hole, there is no penalty.

Note: For bogey, par and Stableford competitions, see Rule 32-1.

Four-Ball
See *"Forms of Match Play"* and *"Forms of Stroke Play"*.

Foursome
See *"Forms of Match Play"* and *"Forms of Stroke Play"*.

Ground Under Repair
"Ground under repair" is any part of the *course* so marked by order of the *Committee* or so declared by its authorised representative. All ground and any grass, bush, tree or other growing thing within the *ground under repair* are part of the *ground under repair*. Ground under repair includes material piled for removal and a hole made by a greenkeeper, even if not so marked. Grass cuttings and other material left on the *course* that have been abandoned and are not intended to be removed are not *ground under repair* unless so marked.

When the margin of *ground under repair* is defined by stakes, the stakes are inside the *ground under repair*, and the margin of the *ground under repair* is defined by the nearest outside points of the stakes at ground level. When both stakes and lines are used to indicate *ground under repair*, the stakes identify the *ground under repair* and the lines define the margin of the *ground under repair*. When the margin of *ground under repair* is defined by a line on the ground, the line itself is in the *ground under repair*. The margin of *ground under repair* extends vertically downwards but not upwards.

A ball is in *ground under repair* when it lies in or any part of it touches the *ground under repair*.

Stakes used to define the margin of or identify *ground under repair* are *obstructions*.

Note: The *Committee* may make a Local Rule prohibiting play from *ground under repair* or an environmentally-sensitive area defined as *ground under repair*.

Hazards
A *"hazard"* is any bunker or water hazard.

Hole
The *"hole"* must be 4¼ inches (108 mm) in diameter and at least 4 inches (101.6 mm) deep. If a lining is used, it must be sunk at least 1 inch (25.4 mm) below the *putting green* surface, unless the nature of the soil makes it impracticable to do so; its outer diameter must not exceed 4 1/4 inches (108 mm).

Holed
A ball is *"holed"* when it is at rest within the circumference of the *hole* and all of it is below the level of the lip of the *hole*.

Honour
The player who is to play first from the *teeing ground* is said to have the *"honour"*.

Lateral Water Hazard
A *"lateral water hazard"* is a water hazard or that part of a *water hazard* so situated that it is not possible, or is deemed by the *Committee* to be impracticable, to drop a ball behind the *water hazard* in accordance with Rule 26-1b. All ground and water within the margin of a *lateral water hazard* are part of the *lateral water hazard*.

When the margin of a *lateral water hazard* is defined by stakes, the stakes are inside the *lateral water hazard*, and the margin of the *hazard* is defined by the nearest outside points of the stakes at ground level. When both stakes and lines are used to indicate a *lateral water hazard*, the stakes identify the *hazard* and the lines define the *hazard* margin. When the margin of a *lateral water hazard* is defined by a line on the ground, the line itself is in the *lateral water hazard*. The margin of a *lateral water hazard* extends vertically upwards and downwards.

A ball is in a *lateral water hazard* when it lies in or any part of it touches the *lateral water hazard*.

Stakes used to define the margin of or identify a *lateral water hazard* are *obstructions*.

Note 1: That part of a *water hazard* to be played as a *lateral water hazard* must be distinctively marked. Stakes or lines used to define the margin of or identify a *lateral water hazard* must be red.

Note 2: The *Committee* may make a Local Rule prohibiting play from an environmentally-sensitive area defined as a *lateral water hazard*.

Note 3: The *Committee* may define a *lateral water hazard* as a *water hazard*.

Line of Play

The *"line of play"* is the direction that the player wishes his ball to take after a *stroke*, plus a reasonable distance on either side of the intended direction. The *line of play* extends vertically upwards from the ground, but does not extend beyond the *hole*.

Line of Putt

The *"line of putt"* is the line that the player wishes his ball to take after a *stroke* on the *putting green*. Except with respect to Rule 16-1e, the *line of putt* includes a reasonable distance on either side of the intended line. The *line of putt* does not extend beyond the *hole*.

Loose Impediments

"Loose impediments" are natural objects, including:
- stones, leaves, twigs, branches and the like,
- dung, and •
- worms, insects and the like, and the casts and heaps made by them,

provided they are not:
- fixed or growing,
- solidly embedded, or
- adhering to the ball.

Sand and loose soil are *loose impediments* on the *putting green*, but not elsewhere.

Snow and natural ice, other than frost, are either *casual water* or *loose impediments*, at the option of the player.

Dew and frost are not *loose impediments*.

Lost Ball

A ball is deemed *"lost"* if:
a.   It is not found or identified as his by the player within five minutes after the player's *side* or his or their *caddies* have begun to search for it; or
b.   The player has made a *stroke* at a *provisional ball* from the place where the original ball is likely to be or from a point nearer the *hole* than that place (see Rule 27-2b); or
c.   The player has put another *ball into play* under penalty of stroke and distance under Rule 26-1a, 27-1 or 28a; or
d.   The player has put another *ball into play* because it is known or virtually certain that the ball, which has not been found, has been *moved* by an *outside agency* (see Rule 18-1), is in an *obstruction* (see Rule 24-3), is in an *abnormal ground condition* (see Rule 25-1c) or is in a *water hazard* (see Rule 26-1b or c); or
e.   The player has made a *stroke* at a *substituted ball*.

Time spent in playing a *wrong ball* is not counted in the five-minute period allowed for search.

Marker

A *"marker"* is one who is appointed by the *Committee* to record a *competitor's* score in stroke play. He may be a *fellow-competitor*. He is not a *referee*.

Move or Moved

A ball is deemed to have *"moved"* if it leaves its position and comes to rest in any other place.

Nearest Point of Relief

The *"nearest point of relief"* is the reference point for taking relief without penalty from interference by an immovable *obstruction* (Rule 24-2), an *abnormal ground condition* (Rule 25-1) or a *wrong putting green* (Rule 25-3).

It is the point on the *course* nearest to where the ball lies:
(i)   that is not nearer the *hole*, and
(ii)   where, if the ball were so positioned, no interference by the condition from which relief is sought would exist for the *stroke* the player would have made from the original position if the condition were not there.

Note: In order to determine the *nearest point of relief* accurately, the player should use the club with which he would have made his next *stroke* if the condition were not there to simulate the *address* position, direction of play and swing for such a *stroke*.

Observer

An *"observer"* is one who is appointed by the *Committee* to assist a *referee* to decide questions of fact and to report to him any breach of a *Rule*. An *observer* should not attend the *flagstick*, stand at or mark the position of the *hole*, or lift the ball or mark its position.

Obstructions

An *"obstruction"* is anything artificial, including the artificial surfaces and sides of roads and paths and manufactured ice, except:
a.   Objects defining *out of bounds*, such as walls, fences, stakes and railings;
b.   Any part of an immovable artificial object that is *out of bounds*; and
c.   Any construction declared by the *Committee* to be an integral part of the *course*.

An *obstruction* is a movable *obstruction* if it may be moved without unreasonable effort, without unduly delaying play and without causing damage. Otherwise, it is an immovable *obstruction*.

Note: The *Committee* may make a Local Rule declaring a movable *obstruction* to be an immovable *obstruction*.

Opponent

An *"opponent"* is a member of a *side* against whom the player's *side* is competing in match play.

Out of Bounds

"Out of bounds" is beyond the boundaries of the *course* or any part of the *course* so marked by the *Committee*.

When *out of bounds* is defined by reference to stakes or a fence or as being beyond stakes or a fence, the *out of bounds* line is determined by the nearest inside points at ground level of the stakes or fence posts (excluding angled supports). When both stakes and lines are used to indicate *out of bounds*, the stakes identify *out of bounds* and the lines define *out of bounds*. When *out of bounds* is defined by a line on the ground, the line itself is *out of bounds*. The *out of bounds* line extends vertically upwards and downwards.

A ball is *out of bounds* when all of it lies *out of bounds*. A player may stand *out of bounds* to play a ball lying within bounds.

Objects defining *out of bounds* such as walls, fences, stakes and railings are not *obstructions* and are deemed to be fixed. Stakes identifying *out of bounds* are not *obstructions* and are deemed to be fixed.

Note 1: Stakes or lines used to define *out of bounds* should be white.

Note 2: A *Committee* may make a Local Rule declaring stakes identifying but not defining *out of bounds* to be *obstructions*.

Outside Agency

In match play, an *"outside agency"* is any agency other than either the player's or *opponent's side*, any *caddie* of either *side*, any ball played by either *side* at the hole being played or any *equipment* of either *side*.

In stroke play, an *outside agency* is any agency other than the *competitor's side*, any *caddie* of the *side*, any ball played by the *side* at the hole being played or any *equipment* of the *side*.

An *outside agency* includes a *referee*, a *marker*, an *observer* and a *forecaddie*. Neither wind nor water is an *outside agency*.

Partner

A *"partner"* is a player associated with another player on the same *side*. In *threesome*, *foursome*, *best-ball* or *four-ball* play, where the context so admits, the word "player" includes his *partner* or *partners*.

Penalty Stroke

A *"penalty stroke"* is one added to the score of a player or *side* under certain *Rules*. In a *threesome* or *foursome*, *penalty strokes* do not affect the order of play.

Provisional Ball

A *"provisional ball"* is a ball played under Rule 27-2 for a ball that may be *lost* outside a *water hazard* or may be *out of bounds*.

Putting Green

The *"putting green"* is all ground of the hole being played that is specially prepared for putting or otherwise defined as such by the *Committee*. A ball is on the *putting green* when any part of it touches the *putting green*.

R&A

The *"R&A"* means R&A Rules Limited.

Referee

A *"referee"* is one who is appointed by the *Committee* to decide questions of fact and apply the *Rules*. He must act on any breach of a *Rule* that he observes or is reported to him.

A *referee* should not attend the *flagstick*, stand at or mark the position of the *hole*, or lift the ball or mark its position.

Exception in match play: Unless a *referee* is assigned to accompany the players throughout a match, he has no authority to intervene in a match other than in relation to Rule 1-3, 6-7 or 33-7.

Rub of the Green

A *"rub of the green"* occurs when a ball in motion is accidentally deflected or stopped by any *outside agency* (see Rule 19-1).

Rule or Rules

The term *"Rule"* includes:

a.   The Rules of Golf and their interpretations as con tained in "Decisions on the Rules of Golf";

b.   Any Conditions of Competition established by the *Committee* under Rule 33-1 and Appendix I;

c.   Any Local Rules established by the *Committee* under Rule 33-8a and Appendix I; and

d.   The specifications on:

(i)   clubs and the ball in Appendices II and III and their interpretations as contained in "A Guide to the Rules on Clubs and Balls"; and

(ii)   devices and other equipment in Appendix IV.

Side

A *"side"* is a player, or two or more players who are *partners*. In match play, each member of the opposing *side* is an *opponent*. In stroke play, members of all *sides* are *competitors* and members of different *sides* playing together are *fellow-competitors*.

Single

See *"Forms of Match Play"* and *"Forms of Stroke Play"*.

Stance

Taking the *"stance"* consists in a player placing his feet in position for and preparatory to making a *stroke*.

Stipulated Round

The *"stipulated round"* consists of playing the holes of the *course* in their correct sequence, unless otherwise authorised by the *Committee*. The number of holes in a *stipulated* round is 18 unless a smaller number is authorised by the *Committee*. As to extension of *stipulated round* in match play, see Rule 2-3.

Stroke

A *"stroke"* is the forward movement of the club made with the intention of striking at and moving the ball, but if a player checks his downswing voluntarily before the clubhead reaches the ball he has not made a *stroke*.

Substituted Ball

A *"substituted ball"* is a ball put into play for the original ball that was either *in play*, *lost*, *out of bounds* or lifted.

Teeing Ground

The *"teeing ground"* is the starting place for the hole to be played. It is a rectangular area two club-lengths in depth, the front and the sides of which are defined by the outside limits of two tee-markers. A ball is outside the *teeing ground* when all of it lies outside the *teeing ground*.

Three-Ball

See *"Forms of Match Play"*.

Threesome

See *"Forms of Match Play"*.

Through the Green

"Through the green" is the whole area of the *course* except:

a.   The *teeing ground* and *putting green* of the hole being played; and

b.   All *hazards* on the *course*.

Water Hazard

A *"water hazard"* is any sea, lake, pond, river, ditch, surface drainage ditch or other open water course (whether or not containing water) and anything of a similar nature on the *course*. All ground and water within the margin of a *water hazard* are part of the *water hazard*.

When the margin of a *water hazard* is defined by stakes, the stakes are inside the *water hazard*, and the margin of the *hazard* is defined by the nearest outside points of the stakes at ground level. When both stakes and lines are used to indicate a *water hazard*, the stakes identify the *hazard* and the lines define the *hazard* margin. When the margin of a *water hazard* is defined by a line on the ground, the line itself is in the *water hazard*. The margin of a *water hazard* extends vertically upwards and downwards.

A ball is in a *water hazard* when it lies in or any part of it touches the *water hazard*.

Stakes used to define the margin of or identify a *water hazard* are *obstructions*.

Note 1: Stakes or lines used to define the margin of or identify a *water hazard* must be yellow.

Note 2: The *Committee* may make a Local Rule prohibiting play from an environmentally-sensitive area defined as a *water hazard*.

Wrong Ball

A *"wrong ball"* is any ball other than the player's:

* *ball in play*;
* *provisional ball*; or
* second ball played under Rule 3-3 or Rule 20-7c in stroke play;

and includes:

* another player's ball;
* an abandoned ball; and
* the player's original ball when it is no longer *in play*.

Note: Ball in play includes a ball *substituted* for the *ball in play*, whether or not the substitution is permitted.

Wrong Putting Green

A *"wrong putting green"* is any *putting green* other than that of the hole being played. Unless otherwise prescribed by the *Committee*, this term includes a practice *putting green* or pitching green on the *course*.

Section III — The Rules of Play

The Game

Rule 1 – The Game

Definitions

All defined terms are in *italics* and are listed alphabetically in the Definitions section – see pages 584–587.

1-1. General

The Game of Golf consists of playing a ball with a club from the *teeing ground* into the *hole* by a *stroke* or successive *strokes* in accordance with the *Rules*.

1-2. Exerting Influence on Movement of Ball or Altering Physical Conditions

A player must not (i) take an action with the intent to influence the movement of a *ball in play* or (ii) alter physical conditions with the intent of affecting the playing of a hole.

Exceptions: An action expressly permitted or expressly prohibited by another *Rule* is subject to that other *Rule*, not Rule 1-2.

An action taken for the sole purpose of caring for the *course* is not a breach of Rule 1-2.

*PENALTY FOR BREACH OF RULE 1-2:

Match play – Loss of hole; Stroke play – Two strokes.

In the case of a serious breach of Rule 1-2, the Committee may impose a penalty of disqualification.

Note 1: A player is deemed to have committed a serious breach of Rule 1-2 if the *Committee* considers that the action taken in breach of this Rule has allowed him or another player to gain a significant advantage or has placed another player, other than his *partner*, at a significant disadvantage.

Note 2: In stroke play, except where a serious breach resulting in disqualification is involved, a player in breach of Rule 1-2 in relation to the movement of his own ball must play the ball from where it was stopped, or, if the ball was deflected, from where it came to rest. If the movement of a player's ball has been intentionally influenced by a *fellow-competitor* or other *outside agency*, Rule 1-4 applies to the player (see Note to Rule 19-1).

1-3. Agreement to Waive Rules

Players must not agree to exclude the operation of any *Rule* or to waive any penalty incurred.

PENALTY FOR BREACH OF RULE 1-3:

Match play – Disqualification of both *sides*;

Stroke play – Disqualification of *competitors* concerned.

(Agreeing to play out of turn in stroke play – see Rule 10-2c)

1-4. Points Not Covered by Rules

If any point in dispute is not covered by the *Rules*, the decision should be made in accordance with equity.

Rule 2 – Match Play

Definitions

All defined terms are in *italics* and are listed alphabetically in the Definitions section – see pages 584–587.

2-1. General

A match consists of one *side* playing against another over a *stipulated round* unless otherwise decreed by the *Committee*.

In match play the game is played by holes.

Except as otherwise provided in the *Rules*, a hole is won by the *side* that *holes* its ball in the fewer *strokes*. In a handicap match, the lower net score wins the hole.

The state of the match is expressed by the terms: so many "holes up" or "all square", and so many "to play".

A *side* is "dormie" when it is as many holes up as there are holes remaining to be played.

2-2. Halved Hole

A hole is halved if each *side holes* out in the same number of *strokes*.

When a player has *holed* out and his *opponent* has been left with a *stroke* for the half, if the player subsequently incurs a penalty, the hole is halved.

2-3. Winner of Match

A match is won when one *side* leads by a number of holes greater than the number remaining to be played.

If there is a tie, the *Committee* may extend the *stipulated round* by as many holes as are required for a match to be won.

2-4. Concession of Match, Hole or Next Stroke

A player may concede a match at any time prior to the start or conclusion of that match.

A player may concede a hole at any time prior to the start or conclusion of that hole.

A player may concede his *opponent's* next *stroke* at any time, provided the *opponent's* ball is at rest. The *opponent* is considered to have *holed* out with his next *stroke*, and the ball may be removed by either *side*.

A concession may not be declined or withdrawn.

(Ball overhanging hole – see Rule 16-2)

2-5. Doubt as to Procedure; Disputes and Claims

In match play, if a doubt or dispute arises between the players, a player may make a claim. If no duly authorised representative of the *Committee* is available within a reasonable time, the players must continue the match without delay. The *Committee* may consider a claim only if it has been made in a timely manner and if the player making the claim has notified his *opponent* at the time (i) that he is making a claim or wants a ruling and (ii) of the facts upon which the claim or ruling is to be based. A claim is considered to have been made in a timely manner if, upon discovery of circumstances giving rise to a claim, the player makes his claim (i) before any player in the match plays from the next *teeing ground*, or (ii) in the case of the last hole of the match, before all players in the match leave the *putting green*, or (iii) when the circumstances giving rise to the claim are discovered after all the players in the match have left the *putting green* of the final hole, before the result of the match has been officially announced.

A claim relating to a prior hole in the match may only be considered by the *Committee* if it is based on facts previously unknown to the player making the claim and he had been given wrong information (Rules 6-2a or 9) by an *opponent*. Such a claim must be made in a timely manner.

Once the result of the match has been officially announced, a claim may not be considered by the *Committee*, unless it is satisfied that (i) the claim is based on facts which were previously unknown to the player making the claim at the time the result was officially announced, (ii) the player making the claim had been given wrong information by an *opponent* and (iii) the *opponent* knew he was giving wrong information. There is no time limit on considering such a claim.

Note 1: A player may disregard a breach of the *Rules* by his *opponent* provided there is no agreement by the *sides* to waive a *Rule* (Rule 1-3).

Note 2: In match play, if a player is doubtful of his rights or the correct procedure, he may not complete the play of the hole with two balls.

2-6. General Penalty

The penalty for a breach of a *Rule* in match play is loss of hole except when otherwise provided.

Rule 3 – Stroke Play

Definitions

All defined terms are in *italics* and are listed alphabetically in the Definitions section – see pages 584–587.

3-1. General; Winner

A stroke play competition consists of *competitors* completing each hole of a *stipulated round* or rounds and, for each round, returning a score card on which there is a gross score for each hole. Each *competitor* is playing against every other *competitor* in the competition.

The *competitor* who plays the *stipulated round* or rounds in the fewest *strokes* is the winner.

In a handicap competition, the *competitor* with the lowest net score for the *stipulated round* or rounds is the winner.

3-2. Failure to Hole Out

If a *competitor* fails to hole out at any hole and does not correct his mistake before he makes a *stroke* on the next *teeing ground* or, in the case of the last hole of the round, before he leaves the *putting green*, he is disqualified.

3-3. Doubt as to Procedure

a. Procedure

In stroke play, if a *competitor* is doubtful of his rights or the correct procedure during the play of a hole, he may, without penalty, complete the hole with two balls.

After the doubtful situation has arisen and before taking further action, the *competitor* must announce to his *marker* or *fellow-competitor* that he intends to play two balls and which ball he wishes to count if the *Rules* permit.

The *competitor* must report the facts of the situation to the *Committee* before returning his score card. If he fails to do so, he is disqualified.

Note: If the *competitor* takes further action before dealing with the doubtful situation, Rule 3-3 is not applicable. The score with the original ball counts or, if the original ball is not one of the balls being played, the score with the first ball put into play counts, even if the *Rules* do not allow the procedure adopted for that ball. However, the *competitor* incurs no penalty for having played a second ball, and any *penalty strokes* incurred solely by playing that ball do not count in his score.

b. Determination of Score for Hole

(i) If the ball that the *competitor* selected in advance to count has been played in accordance with the *Rules*, the score with that ball is the *competitor's* score for the hole. Otherwise, the score with the other ball counts if the *Rules* allow the procedure adopted for that ball.

(ii) If the *competitor* fails to announce in advance his decision to complete the hole with two balls, or which ball he wishes to count, the score with the original ball counts, provided it has been played in accordance with the *Rules*. If the original ball is not one of the balls being played, the first ball put into play counts, provided it has been played in accordance with the *Rules*. Otherwise, the score with the other ball counts if the *Rules* allow the procedure adopted for that ball.

Note 1: If a *competitor* plays a second ball under Rule 3-3, the *strokes* made after this Rule has been invoked with the

ball ruled not to count and *penalty strokes* incurred solely by playing that ball are disregarded.

Note 2: A second ball played under Rule 3-3 is not a *provisional ball* under Rule 27-2.

3-4. Refusal to Comply with a Rule

If a *competitor* refuses to comply with a *Rule* affecting the rights of another *competitor*, he is disqualified.

3-5. General Penalty

The penalty for a breach of a *Rule* in stroke play is two strokes except when otherwise provided.

Clubs and the Ball

The *R&A* reserves the right, at any time, to change the *Rules* relating to clubs and balls (see Appendices II and III) and make or change the interpretations relating to these *Rules*.

Rule 4 – Clubs

A player in doubt as to the conformity of a club should consult the *R&A*.

A manufacturer should submit to the *R&A* a sample of a club to be manufactured for a ruling as to whether the club conforms with the *Rules*. The sample becomes the property of the *R&A* for reference purposes. If a manufacturer fails to submit a sample or, having submitted a sample, fails to await a ruling before manufacturing and/or marketing the club, the manufacturer assumes the risk of a ruling that the club does not conform with the *Rules*.

Definitions

All defined terms are in *italics* and are listed alphabetically in the Definitions section – see pages 584–587.

4-1. Form and Make of Clubs

a. General

The player's clubs must conform with this Rule and the provisions, specifications and interpretations set forth in Appendix II.

Note: The *Committee* may require, in the conditions of a competition (Rule 33-1), that any driver the player carries must have a clubhead, identified by model and loft, that is named on the current List of Conforming Driver Heads issued by the *R&A*.

b. Wear and Alteration

A club that conforms with the *Rules* when new is deemed to conform after wear through normal use. Any part of a club that has been purposely altered is regarded as new and must, in its altered state, conform with the *Rules*.

4-2. Playing Characteristics Changed and Foreign Material

a. Playing Characteristics Changed

During a *stipulated round*, the playing characteristics of a club must not be purposely changed by adjustment or by any other means.

b. Foreign Material

Foreign material must not be applied to the club face for the purpose of influencing the movement of the ball.

> *PENALTY FOR CARRYING, BUT NOT MAKING STROKE WITH, CLUB OR CLUBS IN BREACH OF RULE 4-1 or 4-2:
>
> Match play – At the conclusion of the hole at which the breach is discovered, the state of the match is adjusted by deducting one hole for each hole at which a breach occurred; maximum deduction per round – Two holes.
>
> Stroke play – Two strokes for each hole at which any breach occurred; maximum penalty per round – Four strokes (two strokes at each of the first two holes at which any breach occurred).

Match play or stroke play – If a breach is discovered between the play of two holes, it is deemed to have been discovered during play of the next hole, and the penalty must be applied accordingly.

Bogey and par competitions – See Note 1 to Rule 32-1a.

Stableford competitions – See Note 1 to Rule 32-1b.

*Any club or clubs carried in breach of Rule 4-1 or 4-2 must be declared out of play by the player to his *opponent* in match play or his *marker* or a *fellow-competitor* in stroke play immediately upon discovery that a breach has occurred. If the player fails to do so, he is disqualified.

PENALTY FOR MAKING STROKE WITH CLUB IN
BREACH OF RULE 4-1 or 4-2:
Disqualification.

4-3. Damaged Clubs: Repair and Replacement
a. Damage in Normal Course of Play

If, during a *stipulated round*, a player's club is damaged in the normal course of play, he may:

(i)   use the club in its damaged state for the remainder of the *stipulated round*; or

(ii) without unduly delaying play, repair it or have it repaired; or

(iii) as an additional option available only if the club is unfit for play, replace the damaged club with any club. The replacement of a club must not unduly delay play (Rule 6-7) and must not be made by borrowing any club selected for play by any other person playing on the *course* or by assembling components carried by or for the player during the *stipulated round*.

PENALTY FOR BREACH OF RULE 4-3a:
See Penalty Statements for Rule 4-4a or b, and Rule 4-4c.

Note: A club is unfit for play if it is substantially damaged, e.g. the shaft is dented, significantly bent or breaks into pieces; the clubhead becomes loose, detached or significantly deformed; or the grip becomes loose. A club is not unfit for play solely because the club's lie or loft has been altered, or the clubhead is scratched.

b. Damage Other Than in Normal Course of Play

If, during a *stipulated round*, a player's club is damaged other than in the normal course of play rendering it non-conforming or changing its playing characteristics, the club must not subsequently be used or replaced during the round.

PENALTY FOR BREACH OF RULE 4-3b: Disqualification.

c. Damage Prior to Round

A player may use a club damaged prior to a round, provided the club, in its damaged state, conforms with the *Rules*.

Damage to a club that occurred prior to a round may be repaired during the round, provided the playing characteristics are not changed and play is not unduly delayed.

PENALTY FOR BREACH OF RULE 4-3c:
See Penalty Statement for Rule 4-1 or 4-2.

(Undue delay – see Rule 6-7)

4-4. Maximum of Fourteen Clubs
a. Selection and Addition of Clubs

The player must not start a *stipulated round* with more than fourteen clubs. He is limited to the clubs thus selected for that round, except that if he started with fewer than fourteen clubs, he may add any number, provided his total number does not exceed fourteen.

The addition of a club or clubs must not unduly delay play (Rule 6-7) and the player must not add or borrow any club selected for play by any other person playing on the *course* or by assembling components carried by or for the player during the *stipulated round*.

b. Partners May Share Clubs

Partners may share clubs, provided that the total number of clubs carried by the *partners* so sharing does not exceed fourteen.

PENALTY FOR BREACH OF RULE 4-4a or b,
REGARDLESS OF NUMBER OF EXCESS CLUBS
CARRIED:

Match play – At the conclusion of the hole at which the breach is discovered, the state of the match is adjusted by deducting one hole for each hole at which a breach occurred; maximum deduction per round – Two holes.

Stroke play – Two strokes for each hole at which any breach occurred; maximum penalty per round – Four strokes (two strokes at each of the first two holes at which any breach occurred).

Match play or stroke play – If a breach is discovered between the play of two holes, it is deemed to have been discovered during play of the hole just completed, and the penalty for a breach of Rule 4-4a or b does not apply to the next hole.

Bogey and par competitions – See Note 1 to Rule 32-1a.

Stableford competitions – See Note 1 to Rule 32-1b.

c. Excess Club Declared Out of Play

Any club or clubs carried or used in breach of Rule 4-3a(iii) or Rule 4-4 must be declared out of play by the player to his *opponent* in match play or his *marker* or a *fellow-competitor* in stroke play immediately upon discovery that a breach has occurred. The player must not use the club or clubs for the remainder of the *stipulated round*.

PENALTY FOR BREACH OF RULE 4-4c:
Disqualification.

Rule 5 – The Ball

A player in doubt as to the conformity of a ball should consult the *R&A*.

A manufacturer should submit to the *R&A* samples of a ball to be manufactured for a ruling as to whether the ball conforms with the *Rules*. The samples become the property of the *R&A* for reference purposes. If a manufacturer fails to submit samples or, having submitted samples, fails to await a ruling before manufacturing and/or marketing the ball, the manufacturer assumes the risk of a ruling that the ball does not conform with the *Rules*.

Definitions

All defined terms are in *italics* and are listed alphabetically in the Definitions section – see pages 584–587.

5-1. General

The ball the player plays must conform to the requirements specified in Appendix III.

Note: The *Committee* may require, in the conditions of a competition (Rule 33-1), that the ball the player plays must be named on the current List of Conforming Golf Balls issued by the *R&A*.

5-2. Foreign Material

The ball the player plays must not have foreign material applied to it for the purpose of changing its playing characteristics.

PENALTY FOR BREACH OF RULE 5-1 or 5-2:
Disqualification.

5-3. Ball Unfit for Play

A ball is unfit for play if it is visibly cut, cracked or out of shape. A ball is not unfit for play solely because mud or other materials adhere to it, its surface is scratched or scraped or its paint is damaged or discoloured.

If a player has reason to believe his ball has become unfit for play during play of the hole being played, he may lift the ball, without penalty, to determine whether it is unfit.

Before lifting the ball, the player must announce his intention to his *opponent* in match play or his *marker* or a *fellow-competitor* in stroke play and mark the position of the ball. He may then lift and examine it, provided that he gives his *opponent*, *marker* or *fellow-competitor* an opportunity to examine the ball and observe the lifting and replacement. The ball must not be cleaned when lifted under Rule 5-3.

If the player fails to comply with all or any part of this procedure, or if he lifts the ball without having reason to believe that it has become unfit for play during play of the hole being played, he incurs a penalty of one stroke.

If it is determined that the ball has become unfit for play during play of the hole being played, the player may *substitute* another ball, placing it on the spot where the original ball lay. Otherwise, the original ball must be replaced. If a player *substitutes* a ball when not permitted and makes a *stroke* at the wrongly *substituted ball*, he incurs the general penalty for a breach of Rule 5-3, but there is no additional penalty under this Rule or Rule 15-2.

If a ball breaks into pieces as a result of a *stroke*, the *stroke* is cancelled and the player must play a ball, without penalty, as nearly as possible at the spot from which the original ball was played (see Rule 20-5).

*PENALTY FOR BREACH OF RULE 5-3:
Match play – Loss of hole; Stroke play – Two strokes.

*If a player incurs the general penalty for a breach of Rule 5-3, there is no additional penalty under this Rule.

Note 1: If the *opponent*, *marker* or *fellow-competitor* wishes to dispute a claim of unfitness, he must do so before the player plays another ball.

Note 2: If the original lie of a ball to be placed or replaced has been altered, see Rule 20-3b.

(Cleaning ball lifted from putting green or under any other Rule – see Rule 21)

Player's Responsibilities

Rule 6 – The Player

Definitions
All defined terms are in *italics* and are listed alphabetically in the Definitions section – see pages 584–587

6-1. Rules
The player and his *caddie* are responsible for knowing the *Rules*. During a *stipulated round*, for any breach of a *Rule* by his *caddie*, the player incurs the applicable penalty.

a. Match Play
Before starting a match in a handicap competition, the players should determine from one another their respective handicaps. If a player begins a match having declared a handicap higher than that to which he is entitled and this affects the number of strokes given or received, he is disqualified; otherwise, the player must play off the declared handicap.

b. Stroke Play
In any round of a handicap competition, the *competitor* must ensure that his handicap is recorded on his score card before it is returned to the *Committee*. If no handicap is recorded on his score card before it is returned (Rule 6-6b), or if the recorded handicap is higher than that to which he is entitled and this affects the number of strokes received, he is disqualified from the handicap competition; otherwise, the score stands.

Note: It is the player's responsibility to know the holes at which handicap strokes are to be given or received.

6-3. Time of Starting and Groups
a. Time of Starting
The player must start at the time established by the *Committee*.

PENALTY FOR BREACH OF RULE 6-3a:
If the player arrives at his starting point, ready to play, within five minutes after his starting time, the penalty for failure to start on time is loss of the first hole in match play or two strokes at the first hole in stroke play. Otherwise, the penalty for breach of this Rule is disqualification.

Bogey and par competitions – See Note 2 to Rule 32-1a. Stableford competitions – See Note 2 to Rule 32-1b.

Exception: Where the *Committee* determines that exceptional circumstances have prevented a player from starting on time, there is no penalty.

b. Groups
In stroke play, the *competitor* must remain throughout the round in the group arranged by the *Committee*, unless the *Committee* authorises or ratifies a change.

PENALTY FOR BREACH OF RULE 6-3b:
Disqualification.
(Best-ball and four-ball play – see Rules 30-3a and 31-2)

6-4. Caddie
The player may be assisted by a *caddie*, but he is limited to only one *caddie* at any one time.

*PENALTY FOR BREACH OF RULE 6-4:
Match play – At the conclusion of the hole at which the breach is discovered, the state of the match is adjusted by deducting one hole for each hole at which a breach occurred; maximum deduction per round – Two holes.

Stroke play – Two strokes for each hole at which any breach occurred; maximum penalty per round – Four strokes (two strokes at each of the first two holes at which any breach occurred).

Match play or stroke play – If a breach is discovered between the play of two holes, it is deemed to have been discovered during play of the next hole, and the penalty must be applied accordingly.

Bogey and par competitions – See Note 1 to Rule 32-1a. Stableford competitions – See Note 1 to Rule 32-1b.

*A player having more than one *caddie* in breach of this Rule must immediately upon discovery that a breach has occurred ensure that he has no more than one *caddie* at any one time during the remainder of the *stipulated round*. Otherwise, the player is disqualified.

Note: The *Committee* may, in the conditions of a competition (Rule 33-1), prohibit the use of *caddies* or restrict a player in his choice of *caddie*.

6-5. Ball
The responsibility for playing the proper ball rests with the player. Each player should put an identification mark on his ball.

a. Recording Scores
After each hole the *marker* should check the score with the *competitor* and record it. On completion of the round the *marker* must sign the score card and hand it to the *competitor*. If more than one *marker* records the scores, each must sign for the part for which he is responsible.

b. Signing and Returning Score Card
After completion of the round, the *competitor* should check his score for each hole and settle any doubtful points with the *Committee*. He must ensure that the *marker* or *markers* have signed the score card, sign the score card himself and return it to the *Committee* as soon as possible.

PENALTY FOR BREACH OF RULE 6-6b:
Disqualification.

c. Alteration of Score Card
No alteration may be made on a score card after the *competitor* has returned it to the *Committee*.

d. Wrong Score for Hole
The *competitor* is responsible for the correctness of the score recorded for each hole on his score card. If he returns a score for any hole lower than actually taken, he is disqualified. If he returns a score for any hole higher than actually taken, the score as returned stands.

Note 1: The *Committee* is responsible for the addition of scores and application of the handicap recorded on the score card – see Rule 33-5.

Note 2: In *four-ball* stroke play, see also Rules 31-3 and 31-7a.

6-7. Undue Delay; Slow Play
The player must play without undue delay and in accordance with any pace of play guidelines that the *Committee* may establish. Between completion of a hole and playing from the next *teeing ground*, the player must not unduly delay play.

PENALTY FOR BREACH OF RULE 6-7:
Match play – Loss of hole; Stroke play – Two strokes.
Bogey and par competitions – See Note 2 to Rule 32-1a.
Stableford competitions – See Note 2 to Rule 32-1b.
For subsequent offence – Disqualification.

Note 1: If the player unduly delays play between holes, he is delaying the play of the next hole and, except for bogey, par and Stableford competitions (see Rule 32), the penalty applies to that hole.

Note 2: For the purpose of preventing slow play, the *Committee* may, in the conditions of a competition (Rule 33-1), establish pace of play guidelines including maximum periods of time allowed to complete a *stipulated round*, a hole or a *stroke*.

In match play, the *Committee* may, in such a condition, modify the penalty for a breach of this Rule as follows:
First offence – Loss of hole;
Second offence – Loss of hole;
For subsequent offence – Disqualification.

In stroke play, the *Committee* may, in such a condition, modify the penalty for a breach of this Rule as follows:
First offence – One stroke;
Second offence – Two strokes;
For subsequent offence – Disqualification.

6-8. Discontinuance of Play; Resumption of Play
a. When Permitted
The player must not discontinue play unless:
(i)   the *Committee* has suspended play;
(ii) he believes there is danger from lightning;
(iii) he is seeking a decision from the *Committee* on a doubtful or disputed point (see Rules 2-5 and 34-3); or
(iv) there is some other good reason such as sudden illness. Bad weather is not of itself a good reason for discontinuing play.

If the player discontinues play without specific permission from the *Committee*, he must report to the *Committee* as soon as practicable. If he does so and the *Committee* considers his reason satisfactory, there is no penalty. Otherwise, the player is disqualified.

Exception in match play: Players discontinuing match play by agreement are not subject to disqualification, unless by so doing the competition is delayed.

Note: Leaving the *course* does not of itself constitute discontinuance of play.

b. Procedure When Play Suspended by Committee
When play is suspended by the *Committee*, if the players in a match or group are between the play of two holes, they must not resume play until the *Committee* has ordered a resumption of play. If they have started play of a hole, they may discontinue play immediately or continue play of the hole, provided they do so without delay. If the players choose to continue play of the hole, they are permitted to discontinue play before completing it. In any case, play must be discontinued after the hole is completed.

The players must resume play when the *Committee* has ordered a resumption of play.

PENALTY FOR BREACH OF RULE 6-8b:
Disqualification.

Note: The *Committee* may provide, in the conditions of a competition (Rule 33-1), that in potentially dangerous situations play must be discontinued immediately following a suspension of play by the *Committee*. If a player fails to discontinue play immediately, he is disqualified, unless circumstances warrant waiving the penalty as provided in Rule 33-7.

c. Lifting Ball When Play Discontinued
When a player discontinues play of a hole under Rule 6-8a, he may lift his ball, without penalty, only if the *Committee* has suspended play or there is a good reason to lift it. Before lifting the ball the player must mark its position. If the player discontinues play and lifts his ball without specific permission from the *Committee*, he must, when reporting to the *Committee* (Rule 6-8a), report the lifting of the ball.

If the player lifts the ball without a good reason to do so, fails to mark the position of the ball before lifting it or fails to report the lifting of the ball, he incurs a penalty of one stroke.

d. Procedure When Play Resumed
Play must be resumed from where it was discontinued, even if resumption occurs on a subsequent day. The player must, either before or when play is resumed, proceed as follows:
(i)   if the player has lifted the ball, he must, provided he was entitled to lift it under Rule 6-8c, place the original ball or a *substituted ball* on the spot from which the original ball was lifted. Otherwise, the original ball must be replaced;
(ii) if the player has not lifted his ball, he may, provided he was entitled to lift it under Rule 6-8c, lift, clean and replace the ball, or substitute a ball, on the spot from which the original ball was lifted. Before lifting the ball he must mark its position; or
(iii) if the player's ball or ball-marker is moved (including by wind or water) while play is discontinued, a ball or ball-marker must be placed on the spot from which the original ball or ball-marker was moved.

Note: If the spot where the ball is to be placed is impossible to determine, it must be estimated and the ball placed on the estimated spot. The provisions of Rule 20-3c do not apply.

*PENALTY FOR BREACH OF RULE 6-8d:
Match play – Loss of hole; Stroke play – Two strokes.

*If a player incurs the general penalty for a breach of Rule 6-8d, there is no additional penalty under Rule 6-8c.

Rule 7 – Practice
Definitions
All defined terms are in *italics* and are listed alphabetically in the Definitions section – see pages 584–587.

7-1. Before or Between Rounds
a. Match Play
On any day of a match play competition, a player may practise on the competition *course* before a round.

b. Stroke Play
Before a round or play-off on any day of a stroke play competition, a *competitor* must not practise on the competition *course* or test the surface of any *putting green* on the *course* by rolling a ball or roughening or scraping the surface.

When two or more rounds of a stroke play competition are to be played over consecutive days, a *competitor* must not practise between those rounds on any competition *course* remaining to be played, or test the surface of any *putting green* on such *course* by rolling a ball or roughening or scraping the surface.

Exception: Practice putting or chipping on or near the first *teeing ground* or any practice area before starting a round or play-off is permitted.

PENALTY FOR BREACH OF RULE 7-1b:
Disqualification.

Note: The *Committee* may, in the conditions of a competition (Rule 33-1), prohibit practice on the competition *course* on any day of a match play competition or permit practice on the competition *course* or part of the *course* (Rule 33-2c) on any day of or between rounds of a stroke play competition.

7-2. During Round
A player must not make a practice *stroke* during play of a hole.

Between the play of two holes a player must not make a practice *stroke*, except that he may practise putting or chipping on or near:
a. the *putting green* of the hole last played,
b. any practice *putting green*, or
c. the *teeing ground* of the next hole to be played in the round, provided a practice *stroke* is not made from a *hazard* and does not unduly delay play (Rule 6-7).
Strokes made in continuing the play of a hole, the result of which has been decided, are not practice *strokes*.

Exception: When play has been suspended by the *Committee*, a player may, prior to resumption of play, practise
(a) as provided in this Rule,
(b) anywhere other than on the competition *course* and
(c) as otherwise permitted by the *Committee*.

PENALTY FOR BREACH OF RULE 7-2:
Match play – Loss of hole; Stroke play – Two strokes.
In the event of a breach between the play of two holes, the penalty applies to the next hole.

Note 1: A practice swing is not a practice *stroke* and may be taken at any place, provided the player does not breach the *Rules*.
Note 2: The *Committee* may, in the conditions of a competition (Rule 33-1), prohibit:
(a) practice on or near the *putting green* of the hole last played, and
(b) rolling a ball on the *putting green* of the hole last played.

Rule 8 – Advice; Indicating Line of Play
Definitions
All defined terms are in *italics* and are listed alphabetically in the Definitions section – see pages 584–587.

8-1. Advice
During a *stipulated round*, a player must not:
a. give *advice* to anyone in the competition playing on the *course* other than his *partner*, or
b. ask for *advice* from anyone other than his *partner* or either of their *caddies*.

8-2. Indicating Line of Play
a. Other Than on Putting Green
Except on the *putting green*, a player may have the *line of play* indicated to him by anyone, but no one may be positioned by the player on or close to the line or an extension of the line beyond the *hole* while the *stroke* is being made. Any mark placed by the player or with his knowledge to indicate the line must be removed before the *stroke* is made.

Exception: Flagstick attended or held up – see Rule 17-1.

b. On the Putting Green
When the player's ball is on the *putting green*, the player, his *partner* or either of their *caddies* may, before but not during the *stroke*, point out a line for putting, but in so doing the *putting green* must not be touched. A mark must not be placed anywhere to indicate a line for putting.

PENALTY FOR BREACH OF RULE:
Match play – Loss of hole; Stroke play – Two strokes.

Note: The *Committee* may, in the conditions of a team competition (Rule 33-1), permit each team to appoint one person who may give *advice* (including pointing out a line for putting) to members of that team. The *Committee* may establish conditions relating to the appointment and permitted conduct of that person, who must be identified to the *Committee* before giving *advice*.

Rule 9 – Information as to Strokes Taken
Definitions
All defined terms are in *italics* and are listed alphabetically in the Definitions section – see pages 584–587.

9-1. General
The number of *strokes* a player has taken includes any *penalty strokes* incurred.

9-2. Match Play
a. Information as to Strokes Taken
An *opponent* is entitled to ascertain from the player, during the play of a hole, the number of *strokes* he has taken and, after play of a hole, the number of *strokes* taken on the hole just completed.

b. Wrong Information
A player must not give wrong information to his *opponent*. If a player gives wrong information, he loses the hole.

A player is deemed to have given wrong information if he:
(i)   fails to inform his *opponent* as soon as practicable that he has incurred a penalty, unless (a) he was obviously proceeding under a *Rule* involving a penalty and this was observed by his *opponent*, or (b) he corrects the mistake before his *opponent* makes his next *stroke*; or
(ii) gives incorrect information during play of a hole regarding the number of *strokes* taken and does not correct the mistake before his *opponent* makes his next *stroke*; or
(iii) gives incorrect information regarding the number of *strokes* taken to complete a hole and this affects the *opponent's* understanding of the result of the hole, unless he corrects the mistake before any player makes a *stroke* from the next *teeing ground* or, in the case of the last hole of the match, before all players leave the *putting green*.

A player has given wrong information even if it is due to the failure to include a penalty that he did not know he had incurred. It is the player's responsibility to know the *Rules*.

9-3. Stroke Play
A *competitor* who has incurred a penalty should inform his *marker* as soon as practicable.

Order of Play

Rule 10 – Order of Play

Definitions

All defined terms are in *italics* and are listed alphabetically in the Definitions section – see pages 584–587.

10-1. Match Play

a. When Starting Play of Hole

The *side* that has the *honour* at the first *teeing ground* is determined by the order of the draw. In the absence of a draw, the *honour* should be decided by lot.

The *side* that wins a hole takes the *honour* at the next *teeing ground*. If a hole has been halved, the *side* that had the *honour* at the previous *teeing ground* retains it.

b. During Play of Hole

After both players have started play of the hole, the ball farther from the *hole* is played first. If the balls are equidistant from the *hole* or their positions relative to the *hole* are not determinable, the ball to be played first should be decided by lot.

Exception: Rule 30-3b (*best-ball* and *four-ball* match play).

Note: When it becomes known that the original ball is not to be played as it lies and the player is required to play a ball as nearly as possible at the spot from which the original ball was last played (see Rule 20-5), the order of play is determined by the spot from which the previous *stroke* was made. When a ball may be played from a spot other than where the previous *stroke* was made, the order of play is determined by the position where the original ball came to rest.

c. Playing Out of Turn

If a player plays when his *opponent* should have played, there is no penalty, but the *opponent* may immediately require the player to cancel the *stroke* so made and, in correct order, play a ball as nearly as possible at the spot from which the original ball was last played (see Rule 20-5).

10-2. Stroke Play

a. When Starting Play of Hole

The *competitor* who has the *honour* at the first *teeing ground* is determined by the order of the draw. In the absence of a draw, the *honour* should be decided by lot.

The *competitor* with the lowest score at a hole takes the *honour* at the next *teeing ground*. The *competitor* with the second lowest score goes next and so on. If two or more *competitors* have the same score at a hole, they play from the next *teeing ground* in the same order as at the previous *teeing ground*.

Exception: Rule 32-1 (handicap bogey, par and Stableford competitions).

b. During Play of Hole

After the *competitors* have started play of the hole, the ball farthest from the *hole* is played first. If two or more balls are equidistant from the *hole* or their positions relative to the *hole* are not determinable, the ball to be played first should be decided by lot.

Exceptions: Rules 22 (ball assisting or interfering with play) and 31-4 (*four-ball* stroke play).

Note: When it becomes known that the original ball is not to be played as it lies and the *competitor* is required to play a ball as nearly as possible at the spot from which the original ball was last played (see Rule 20-5), the order of play is determined by the spot from which the previous *stroke* was made. When a ball may be played from a spot other than where the previous *stroke* was made, the order of play is determined by the position where the original ball came to rest.

c. Playing Out of Turn

If a *competitor* plays out of turn, there is no penalty and the ball is played as it lies. If, however, the *Committee* determines that *competitors* have agreed to play out of turn to give one of them an advantage, they are disqualified.

(Making stroke while another ball in motion after stroke from putting green – see Rule 16-1f)

(Incorrect order of play in foursome stroke play – see Rule 29-3)

10-3. Provisional Ball or Another Ball from Teeing Ground

If a player plays a *provisional ball* or another ball from the *teeing ground*, he must do so after his *opponent* or *fellow-competitor* has made his first *stroke*. If more than one player elects to play a *provisional ball* or is required to play another ball from the *teeing ground*, the original order of play must be retained. If a player plays a *provisional ball* or another ball out of turn, Rule 10-1c or 10-2c applies.

Teeing Ground

Rule 11 – Teeing Ground

Definitions

All defined terms are in *italics* and are listed alphabetically in the Definitions section – see pages 584–587.

11-1. Teeing

When a player is putting a ball into play from the *teeing ground*, it must be played from within the *teeing ground* and from the surface of the ground or from a conforming tee (see Appendix IV) in or on the surface of the ground.

For the purposes of this Rule, the surface of the ground includes an irregularity of surface (whether or not created by the player) and sand or other natural substance (whether or not placed by the player).

If a player makes a *stroke* at a ball on a non-conforming tee, or at a ball teed in a manner not permitted by this Rule, he is disqualified.

A player may stand outside the *teeing ground* to play a ball within it.

11-2. Tee-Markers

Before a player makes his first *stroke* with any ball on the *teeing ground* of the hole being played, the tee-markers are deemed to be fixed. In these circumstances, if the player moves or allows to be moved a tee-marker for the purpose of avoiding interference with his *stance*, the area of his intended swing or his *line of play*, he incurs the penalty for a breach of Rule 13-2.

11-3. Ball Falling off Tee

If a ball, when not *in play*, falls off a tee or is knocked off a tee by the player in *addressing* it, it may be re-teed, without penalty. However, if a *stroke* is made at the ball in these circumstances, whether the ball is moving or not, the *stroke* counts, but there is no penalty.

11-4. Playing from Outside Teeing Ground

a. Match Play

If a player, when starting a hole, plays a ball from outside the *teeing ground*, there is no penalty, but the *opponent* may immediately require the player to cancel the *stroke* and play a ball from within the *teeing ground*.

b. Stroke Play

If a *competitor*, when starting a hole, plays a ball from outside the *teeing ground*, he incurs a penalty of two strokes and must then play a ball from within the *teeing ground*.

If the *competitor* makes a *stroke* from the next *teeing ground* without first correcting his mistake or, in the case of the last hole of the round, leaves the *putting green* without first declaring his intention to correct his mistake, he is disqualified.

The *stroke* from outside the *teeing ground* and any subsequent *strokes* by the *competitor* on the hole prior to his correction of the mistake do not count in his score.

11-5. Playing from Wrong Teeing Ground
The provisions of Rule 11-4 apply.

Playing the Ball

Rule 12 – Searching for and Identifying Ball

Definitions
All defined terms are in *italics* and are listed alphabetically in the Definitions section – see pages 584–587.

12-1. Seeing Ball; Searching for Ball
A player is not necessarily entitled to see his ball when making a *stroke*.

In searching for his ball anywhere on the *course*, the player may touch or bend long grass, rushes, bushes, whins, heather or the like, but only to the extent necessary to find or identify the ball, provided that this does not improve the lie of the ball, the area of his intended *stance* or swing or his *line of play*; if the ball is *moved*, Rule 18-2a applies except as provided in clauses a–d of this Rule.

In addition to the methods of searching for and identifying a ball that are otherwise permitted by the *Rules*, the player may also search for and identify a ball under Rule 12-1 as follows:

a. Searching for or Identifying Ball Covered by Sand
If the player's ball lying anywhere on the *course* is believed to be covered by sand, to the extent that he cannot find or identify it, he may, without penalty, touch or move the sand in order to find or identify the ball. If the ball is found, and identified as his, the player must re-create the lie as nearly as possible by replacing the sand. If the ball is *moved* during the touching or moving of sand while searching for or identifying the ball, there is no penalty; the ball must be replaced and the lie re-created.

In re-creating a lie under this Rule, the player is permitted to leave a small part of the ball visible.

b. Searching for or Identifying Ball Covered by Loose Impediments in Hazard
In a *hazard*, if the player's ball is believed to be covered by *loose impediments* to the extent that he cannot find or identify it, he may, without penalty, touch or move *loose impediments* in order to find or identify the ball. If the ball is found or identified as his, the player must replace the *loose impediments*. If the ball is *moved* during the touching or moving of *loose impediments* while searching for or identifying the ball, Rule 18-2a applies; if the ball is *moved* during the replacement of the *loose impediments*, there is no penalty and the ball must be replaced.

If the ball was entirely covered by *loose impediments*, the player must re-cover the ball but is permitted to leave a small part of the ball visible.

c. Searching for Ball in Water in Water Hazard
If a ball is believed to be lying in water in a *water hazard*, the player may, without penalty, probe for it with a club or otherwise. If the ball in water is accidentally *moved* while probing, there is no penalty; the ball must be replaced, unless the player elects to proceed under Rule 26-1. If the *moved* ball was not lying in water or the ball was accidentally *moved* by the player other than while probing, Rule 18-2a applies.

d. Searching for Ball Within Obstruction or Abnormal Ground Condition
If a ball lying in or on an *obstruction* or in an *abnormal ground condition* is accidentally *moved* during search, there is no penalty; the ball must be replaced unless the player elects to proceed under Rule 24-1b, 24-2b or 25-1b as applicable. If the player replaces the ball, he may still proceed under one of those Rules, if applicable.

PENALTY FOR BREACH OF RULE 12-1:
Match Play – Loss of Hole; Stroke Play – Two Strokes.

(Improving lie, area of intended *stance* or swing, or line of play – see Rule 13-2)

Rule 12-2. Lifting Ball for Identification
The responsibility for playing the proper ball rests with the player. Each player should put an identification mark on his ball.

If a player believes that a ball at rest might be his, but he cannot identify it, the player may lift the ball for identification, without penalty. The right to lift a ball for identification is in addition to the actions permitted under Rule 12-1.

Before lifting the ball, the player must announce his intention to his *opponent* in match play or his *marker* or a *fellow-competitor* in stroke play and mark the position of the ball. He may then lift the ball and identify it, provided that he gives his *opponent*, *marker* or *fellow-competitor* an opportunity to observe the lifting and replacement. The ball must not be cleaned beyond the extent necessary for identification when lifted under Rule 12-2.

If the ball is the player's ball and he fails to comply with all or any part of this procedure, or he lifts his ball in order to identify it without having good reason to do so, he incurs a penalty of one stroke. If the lifted ball is the player's ball, he must replace it. If he fails to do so, he incurs the general penalty for a breach of Rule 12-2, but there is no additional penalty under this Rule.

Note: If the original lie of a ball to be replaced has been altered, see Rule 20-3b.

*PENALTY FOR BREACH OF RULE 12-2:
Match Play – Loss of hole; Stroke Play – Two strokes.

*If a player incurs the general penalty for a breach of Rule 12-2, there is no additional penalty under this Rule.

Rule 13 – Ball Played as It Lies

Definitions
All defined terms are in *italics* and are listed alphabetically in the Definitions section – see pages 584–587.

13-1. General
The ball must be played as it lies, except as otherwise provided in the *Rules*. (Ball at rest moved – see Rule 18)

13-2. Improving Lie, Area of Intended Stance or Swing, or Line of Play
A player must not improve or allow to be improved:
- the position or lie of his ball,
- the area of his intended *stance* or swing,
- his *line of play* or a reasonable extension of that line beyond the *hole*, or
- the area in which he is to drop or place a ball,

by any of the following actions:
- pressing a club on the ground,
- moving, bending or breaking anything growing or fixed (including immovable *obstructions* and objects defining *out of bounds*),
- creating or eliminating irregularities of surface,
- removing or pressing down sand, loose soil, replaced divots or other cut turf placed in position, or
- removing dew, frost or water.

However, the player incurs no penalty if the action occurs:

- in grounding the club lightly when *addressing the ball*,
- in fairly taking his *stance*,
- in making a *stroke* or the backward movement of his club for a *stroke* and the *stroke* is made,
- in creating or eliminating irregularities of surface within the *teeing ground* or in removing dew, frost or water from the *teeing ground*, or
- on the *putting green* in removing sand and loose soil or in repairing damage (Rule 16-1).
Exception: Ball in *hazard* – see Rule 13-4.

13-3. Building Stance
A player is entitled to place his feet firmly in taking his *stance*, but he must not build a *stance*.

13-4. Ball in Hazard; Prohibited Actions
Except as provided in the *Rules*, before making a *stroke* at a ball that is in a *hazard* (whether a *bunker* or a *water hazard*) or that, having been lifted from a *hazard*, may be dropped or placed in the *hazard*, the player must not:
a.   Test the condition of the *hazard* or any similar *hazard*;
b.   Touch the ground in the *hazard* or water in the *water hazard* with his hand or a club; or
c.   Touch or move a *loose impediment* lying in or touching the *hazard*.
Exceptions:
1. Provided nothing is done that constitutes testing the condition of the *hazard* or improves the lie of the ball, there is no penalty if the player (a) touches the ground or *loose impediments* in any *hazard* or water in a *water hazard* as a result of or to prevent falling, in removing an *obstruction*, in measuring or in marking the position of, retrieving, lifting, placing or replacing a ball under any *Rule* or (b) places his clubs in a *hazard*.
2. At any time, the player may smooth sand or soil in a *hazard* provided this is for the sole purpose of caring for the *course* and nothing is done to breach Rule 13-2 with respect to his next *stroke*. If a ball played from a *hazard* is outside the *hazard* after the *stroke*, the player may smooth sand or soil in the *hazard* without restriction.
3. If the player makes a *stroke* from a *hazard* and the ball comes to rest in another *hazard*, Rule 13-4a does not apply to any subsequent actions taken in the *hazard* from which the *stroke* was made.
Note: At any time, including at *address* or in the backward movement for the *stroke*, the player may touch, with a club or otherwise, any *obstruction*, any construction declared by the *Committee* to be an integral part of the *course* or any grass, bush, tree or other growing thing.
PENALTY FOR BREACH OF RULE:
   Match play – Loss of hole; Stroke play – Two strokes.
   (Searching for ball – see Rule 12-1)
   (Relief for ball in water hazard – see Rule 26)

Rule 14 – Striking the Ball

Definitions
All defined terms are in *italics* and are listed alphabetically in the Definitions section – see pages 584–587.

14-1. Ball to be Fairly Struck At
The ball must be fairly struck at with the head of the club and must not be pushed, scraped or spooned.

14-2. Assistance
a. Physical Assistance and Protection from Elements
A player must not make a *stroke* while accepting physical assistance or protection from the elements.

b. Positioning of Caddie or Partner Behind Ball
A player must not make a *stroke* with his *caddie*, his *partner* or his *partner's caddie* positioned on or close to an extension of the *line of play* or *line of putt* behind the ball.

Exception: There is no penalty if the player's *caddie*, his *partner* or his *partner's caddie* is inadvertently located on or close to an extension of the *line of play* or *line of putt* behind the ball.
PENALTY FOR BREACH OF RULE 14-1 or 14-2:
   Match play – Loss of hole; Stroke play – Two strokes.

14-3. Artificial Devices, Unusual Equipment and Unusual Use of Equipment
The *R&A* reserves the right, at any time, to change the *Rules* relating to artificial devices, unusual *equipment* and the unusual use of *equipment*, and to make or change the interpretations relating to these *Rules*.

A player in doubt as to whether use of an item would constitute a breach of Rule 14-3 should consult the *R&A*.

A manufacturer should submit to The *R&A* a sample of an item to be manufactured for a ruling as to whether its use during a *stipulated round* would cause a player to be in breach of Rule 14-3. The sample becomes the property of The *R&A* for reference purposes. If a manufacturer fails to submit a sample or, having submitted a sample, fails to await a ruling before manufacturing and/or marketing the item, the manufacturer assumes the risk of a ruling that use of the item would be contrary to the *Rules*.

Except as provided in the *Rules*, during a *stipulated round* the player must not use any artificial device or unusual *equipment* (see Appendix IV for detailed specifications and interpretations), or use any *equipment* in an unusual manner:
a.   That might assist him in making a *stroke* or in his play; or
b.   For the purpose of gauging or measuring distance or conditions that might affect his play; or
c.   That might assist him in gripping the club, except that:
   (i)   gloves may be worn provided that they are plain gloves;
   (ii) resin, powder and drying or moisturising agents may be used; and
   (iii) a towel or handkerchief may be wrapped around the grip.
Exceptions:
1. A player is not in breach of this Rule if (a) the *equipment* or device is designed for or has the effect of alleviating a medical condition, (b) the player has a legitimate medical reason to use the *equipment* or device, and (c) the *Committee* is satisfied that its use does not give the player any undue advantage over other players.
2. A player is not in breach of this Rule if he uses *equipment* in a traditionally accepted manner.
PENALTY FOR BREACH OF RULE 14-3:
   Disqualification.

Note: The *Committee* may make a Local Rule allowing players to use devices that measure or gauge distance only.

14-4. Striking the Ball More Than Once
If a player's club strikes the ball more than once in the course of a *stroke*, the player must count the *stroke* and add a *penalty stroke*, making two *strokes* in all.

14-5. Playing Moving Ball
A player must not make a *stroke* at his ball while it is moving.
   Exceptions:
   - Ball falling off tee – Rule 11-3
   - Striking the ball more than once – Rule 14-4
   - Ball moving in water – Rule 14-6
   When the ball begins to *move* only after the player has begun the *stroke* or the backward movement of his club for the *stroke*, he incurs no penalty under this Rule for playing a moving ball, but he is not exempt from any penalty under the following Rules:

- Ball at rest *moved* by player – Rule 18-2a
- Ball at rest moving after *address* – Rule 18-2b

(Ball purposely deflected or stopped by player, partner or caddie – see Rule 1-2)

14-6. Ball Moving in Water

When a ball is moving in water in a *water hazard*, the player may, without penalty, make a *stroke*, but he must not delay making his *stroke* in order to allow the wind or current to improve the position of the ball. A ball moving in water in a *water hazard* may be lifted if the player elects to invoke Rule 26.

PENALTY FOR BREACH OF RULE 14-5 or 14-6:
Match play – Loss of hole; Stroke play – Two strokes.

Rule 15 – Substituted Ball; Wrong Ball

Definitions
All defined terms are in *italics* and are listed alphabetically in the Definitions section – see pages 584–587.

15-1. General

A player must hole out with the ball played from the *teeing ground*, unless the ball is *lost* or *out of bounds* or the player *substitutes* another ball, whether or not substitution is permitted (see Rule 15-2). If a player plays a *wrong ball*, see Rule 15-3.

15-2. Substituted Ball

A player may *substitute* a ball when proceeding under a *Rule* that permits the player to play, drop or place another ball in completing the play of a hole. The *substituted ball* becomes the *ball in play*.

If a player *substitutes* a ball when not permitted to do so under the *Rules*, that *substituted ball* is not a *wrong ball*; it becomes the *ball in play*. If the mistake is not corrected as provided in Rule 20-6 and the player makes a *stroke* at a wrongly *substituted ball*, he loses the hole in match play or incurs a penalty of two strokes in stroke play under the applicable *Rule* and, in stroke play, must play out the hole with the *substituted ball*.

Exception: If a player incurs a penalty for making a *stroke* from a wrong place, there is no additional penalty for substituting a ball when not permitted.

(Playing from wrong place – see Rule 20-7)

15-3. Wrong Ball
a. Match Play

If a player makes a *stroke* at a *wrong ball*, he loses the hole.

If the *wrong ball* belongs to another player, its owner must place a ball on the spot from which the *wrong ball* was first played.

If the player and *opponent* exchange balls during the play of a hole, the first to make a *stroke* at a *wrong ball* loses the hole; when this cannot be determined, the hole must be played out with the balls exchanged.

Exception: There is no penalty if a player makes a *stroke* at a *wrong ball* that is moving in water in a *water hazard*. Any *strokes* made at a *wrong ball* moving in water in a *water hazard* do not count in the player's score. The player must correct his mistake by playing the correct ball or by proceeding under the *Rules*.

(Placing and Replacing – see Rule 20-3)

b. Stroke Play

If a *competitor* makes a *stroke* or *strokes* at a *wrong ball*, he incurs a penalty of two strokes.

The *competitor* must correct his mistake by playing the correct ball or by proceeding under the *Rules*. If he fails to correct his mistake before making a *stroke* on the next *teeing ground* or, in the case of the last hole of the round, fails to declare his intention to correct his mistake before leaving the *putting green*, he is disqualified.

Strokes made by a *competitor* with a *wrong ball* do not count in his score. If the *wrong ball* belongs to another *competitor*, its owner must place a ball on the spot from which the *wrong ball* was first played.

Exception: There is no penalty if a *competitor* makes a *stroke* at a *wrong ball* that is moving in water in a *water hazard*. Any *strokes* made at a *wrong ball* moving in water in a *water hazard* do not count in the *competitor's* score.

(Placing and Replacing – see Rule 20-3)

The Putting Green

Rule 16 – The Putting Green
Definitions
All defined terms are in *italics* and are listed alphabetically in the Definitions section – see pages 584–587.

16-1. General
a. Touching Line of Putt

The *line of putt* must not be touched except:
(i) the player may remove *loose impediments*, provided he does not press anything down;
(ii) the player may place the club in front of the ball when *addressing* it, provided he does not press anything down;
(iii) in measuring – Rule 18-6;
(iv) in lifting or replacing the ball – Rule 16-1b;
(v) in pressing down a ball-marker;
(vi) in repairing old *hole* plugs or ball marks on the *putting green* – Rule 16-1c; and
(vii) in removing movable *obstructions* – Rule 24-1.

(Indicating line for putting on putting green – see Rule 8-2b)

b. Lifting and Cleaning Ball

A ball on the *putting green* may be lifted and, if desired, cleaned. The position of the ball must be marked before it is lifted and the ball must be replaced (see Rule 20-1). When another ball is in motion, a ball that might influence the movement of the ball in motion must not be lifted.

c. Repair of Hole Plugs, Ball Marks and Other Damage

The player may repair an old *hole* plug or damage to the *putting green* caused by the impact of a ball, whether or not the player's ball lies on the *putting green*. If a ball or ball-marker is accidentally *moved* in the process of the repair, the ball or ball-marker must be replaced. There is no penalty, provided the movement of the ball or ball-marker is directly attributable to the specific act of repairing an old *hole* plug or damage to the *putting green* caused by the impact of a ball. Otherwise, Rule 18 applies.

Any other damage to the *putting green* must not be repaired if it might assist the player in his subsequent play of the hole.

d. Testing Surface

During the *stipulated round*, a player must not test the surface of any *putting green* by rolling a ball or roughening or scraping the surface.

Exception: Between the play of two holes, a player may test the surface of any practice *putting green* and the *putting green* of the hole last played, unless the *Committee* has prohibited such action (see Note 2 to Rule 7-2).

e. Standing Astride or on Line of Putt

The player must not make a *stroke* on the *putting green* from a *stance* astride, or with either foot touching, the *line of putt* or an extension of that line behind the ball.

Exception: There is no penalty if the *stance* is inadvertently taken on or astride the *line of putt* (or an extension of that line behind the ball) or is taken to avoid standing on another player's *line of putt* or prospective *line of putt*.

f. Making Stroke While Another Ball in Motion

The player must not make a *stroke* while another ball is in motion after a *stroke* from the *putting green*, except that if a player does so, there is no penalty if it was his turn to play.

(Lifting ball assisting or interfering with play while another ball in motion – see Rule 22)

PENALTY FOR BREACH OF RULE 16-1:

Match play – Loss of hole; Stroke play – Two strokes.

(Position of caddie or partner – see Rule 14-2)
(Wrong putting green – see Rule 25-3)

16-2. Ball Overhanging Hole

When any part of the ball overhangs the lip of the *hole*, the player is allowed enough time to reach the *hole* without unreasonable delay and an additional ten seconds to determine whether the ball is at rest. If by then the ball has not fallen into the *hole*, it is deemed to be at rest. If the ball subsequently falls into the *hole*, the player is deemed to have *holed* out with his last *stroke*, and must add a *penalty stroke* to his score for the hole; otherwise, there is no penalty under this Rule.

(Undue delay – see Rule 6-7)

Rule 17 – The Flagstick

Definitions

All defined terms are in *italics* and are listed alphabetically in the Definitions section – see pages 584–587.

17-1. Flagstick Attended, Removed or Held Up

Before making a *stroke* from anywhere on the *course*, the player may have the *flagstick* attended, removed or held up to indicate the position of the *hole*.

If the *flagstick* is not attended, removed or held up before the player makes a *stroke*, it must not be attended, removed or held up during the *stroke* or while the player's ball is in motion if doing so might influence the movement of the ball.

Note 1: If the *flagstick* is in the *hole* and anyone stands near it while a *stroke* is being made, he is deemed to be attending the *flagstick*.

Note 2: If, prior to the *stroke*, the *flagstick* is attended, removed or held up by anyone with the player's knowledge and he makes no objection, the player is deemed to have authorised it.

Note 3: If anyone attends or holds up the *flagstick* while a *stroke* is being made, he is deemed to be attending the *flagstick* until the ball comes to rest.

(Moving attended, removed or held-up flagstick while ball in motion – see Rule 24-1)

17-2. Unauthorised Attendance

If an *opponent* or his *caddie* in match play or a *fellow-competitor* or his *caddie* in stroke play, without the player's authority or prior knowledge, attends, removes or holds up the *flagstick* during the *stroke* or while the ball is in motion, and the act might influence the movement of the ball, the *opponent* or *fellow-competitor* incurs the applicable penalty.

*PENALTY FOR BREACH OF RULE 17-1 or 17-2:

Match play – Loss of hole; Stroke play – Two strokes.

*In stroke play, if a breach of Rule 17-2 occurs and the *competitor's* ball subsequently strikes the *flagstick*, the person attending or holding it or anything carried by him, the *competitor* incurs no penalty. The ball is played as it lies, except that if the *stroke* was made on the *putting green*, the *stroke* is cancelled and the ball must be replaced and replayed.

17-3. Ball Striking Flagstick or Attendant

The player's ball must not strike:
a. The *flagstick* when it is attended, removed or held up;
b. The person attending or holding up the *flagstick* or anything carried by him; or

c. The *flagstick* in the *hole*, unattended, when the *stroke* has been made on the *putting green*.

Exception: When the *flagstick* is attended, removed or held up without the player's authority – see Rule 17-2.

PENALTY FOR BREACH OF RULE 17-3:

Match play – Loss of hole; Stroke play – Two strokes and the ball must be played as it lies.

17-4. Ball Resting Against Flagstick

When a player's ball rests against the *flagstick* in the *hole* and the ball is not *holed*, the player or another person authorised by him may move or remove the *flagstick*, and if the ball falls into the *hole*, the player is deemed to have *holed* out with his last *stroke*; otherwise, the ball, if *moved*, must be placed on the lip of the *hole*, without penalty.

Ball Moved, Deflected or Stopped

Rule 18 – Ball at Rest Moved

Definitions

All defined terms are in *italics* and are listed alphabetically in the Definitions section – see pages 584–587.

18-1. By Outside Agency

If a ball at rest is *moved* by an *outside agency*, there is no penalty and the ball must be replaced. Note: It is a question of fact whether a ball has been *moved* by an *outside agency*. In order to apply this Rule, it must be known or virtually certain that an *outside agency* has *moved* the ball. In the absence of such knowledge or certainty, the player must play the ball as it lies or, if the ball is not found, proceed under Rule 27-1.

(Player's ball at rest moved by another ball – see Rule 18-5)

18-2. By Player, Partner, Caddie or Equipment

a. General

Except as permitted by the *Rules*, when a player's ball is in *play*, if

(i) the player, his *partner* or either of their *caddies*:
- lifts or *moves* the ball,
- touches it purposely (except with a club in the act of *addressing* the ball), or
- causes the ball to *move*, or

(ii) the *equipment* of the player or his *partner* causes the ball to *move*,

the player incurs a penalty of one stroke.

If the ball is *moved*, it must be replaced, unless the movement of the ball occurs after the player has begun the *stroke* or the backward movement of the club for the *stroke* and the *stroke* is made.

Under the *Rules* there is no penalty if a player accidentally causes his ball to *move* in the following circumstances:
- In searching for a ball covered by sand, in the replacement of *loose impediments* moved in a *hazard* while finding or identifying a ball, in probing for a ball lying in water in a *water hazard* or in searching for a ball in an *obstruction* or an *abnormal ground condition* – Rule 12-1
- In repairing a *hole* plug or ball mark – Rule 16-1c
- In measuring – Rule 18-6
- In lifting a ball under a *Rule* – Rule 20-1
- In placing or replacing a ball under a *Rule* – Rule 20-3a
- In removing a *loose impediment* on the *putting green* – Rule 23-1
- In removing movable *obstructions* – Rule 24-1

b. Ball Moving After Address

If a player's *ball in play* moves after he has *addressed* it (other than as a result of a *stroke*), the player is deemed to have *moved* the ball and incurs a penalty of one stroke.

The ball must be replaced, unless the movement of the ball occurs after the player has begun the *stroke* or the backward movement of the club for the *stroke* and the *stroke* is made.

Exception: If it is known or virtually certain that the player did not cause his ball to *move*, Rule 18-2b does not apply.

18-3. By Opponent, Caddie or Equipment in Match Play

a. During Search

If, during search for a player's ball, an *opponent*, his *caddie* or his *equipment moves* the ball, touches it or causes it to *move*, there is no penalty. If the ball is *moved*, it must be replaced.

b. Other Than During Search

If, other than during search for a player's ball, an *opponent*, his *caddie* or his *equipment moves* the ball, touches it or purposely or causes it to *move*, except as otherwise provided in the *Rules*, the opponent incurs a penalty of one stroke. If the ball is *moved*, it must be replaced.

(Playing a wrong ball – see Rule 15-3)
(Ball moved in measuring – see Rule 18-6)

18-4. By Fellow-Competitor, Caddie or Equipment in Stroke Play

If a *fellow-competitor*, his *caddie* or his *equipment moves* the player's ball, touches it or causes it to *move*, there is no penalty. If the ball is *moved*, it must be replaced.

(Playing a wrong ball – see Rule 15-3)

18-5. By Another Ball

If a *ball in play* and at rest is *moved* by another ball in motion after a *stroke*, the *moved* ball must be replaced.

18-6. Ball Moved in Measuring

If a ball or ball-marker is *moved* in measuring while proceeding under or in determining the application of a *Rule*, the ball or ball-marker must be replaced. There is no penalty, provided the movement of the ball or ball-marker is directly attributable to the specific act of measuring. Otherwise, the provisions of Rule 18-2a, 18-3b or 18-4 apply.

*PENALTY FOR BREACH OF RULE:
Match play – Loss of hole; Stroke play – Two strokes.

*If a player who is required to replace a ball fails to do so, or if he makes a *stroke* at a ball *substituted* under Rule 18 when such *substitution* is not permitted, he incurs the general penalty for breach of Rule 18, but there is no additional penalty under this Rule.

Note 1: If a ball to be replaced under this Rule is not immediately recoverable, another ball may be *substituted*.

Note 2: If the original lie of a ball to be placed or replaced has been altered, see Rule 20-3b.

Note 3: If it is impossible to determine the spot on which a ball is to be placed or replaced, see Rule 20-3c.

Rule 19 – Ball in Motion Deflected or Stopped

Definitions

All defined terms are in *italics* and are listed alphabetically in the Definitions section – see pages 584–587.

19-1. By Outside Agency

If a player's ball in motion is accidentally deflected or stopped by any *outside agency*, it is a *rub of the green*, there is no penalty and the ball must be played as it lies, except:

a. If a player's ball in motion after a *stroke* other than on the *putting green* comes to rest in or on any moving or animate *outside agency*, the ball must *through the green* or in a *hazard* be dropped, or on the *putting green* be placed, as near as possible to the spot directly under the place where the ball came to rest in or on the *outside agency*, but not nearer the *hole*, and

b. If a player's ball in motion after a *stroke* on the *putting green* is deflected or stopped by, or comes to rest in or on, any moving or animate *outside agency*, except a worm, insect or the like, the *stroke* is cancelled. The ball must be replaced and replayed.

If the ball is not immediately recoverable, another ball may be *substituted*.

Exception: Ball striking person attending or holding up *flagstick* or anything carried by him – see Rule 17-3b.

Note: If a player's ball in motion has been deliberately deflected or stopped by an *outside agency:*

(a) after a *stroke* from anywhere other than on the *putting green*, the spot where the ball would have come to rest must be estimated. If that spot is:

   (i) *through the green* or in a *hazard*, the ball must be dropped as near as possible to that spot;

   (ii) *out of bounds*, the player must proceed under Rule 27-1; or

   (iii) on the *putting green*, the ball must be placed on that spot.

(b) after a *stroke* on the *putting green*, the *stroke* is cancelled. The ball must be replaced and replayed.

If the *outside agency* is a *fellow-competitor* or his *caddie*, Rule 1-2 applies to the *fellow-competitor*.

(Player's ball deflected or stopped by another ball – see Rule 19-5)

19-2. By Player, Partner, Caddie or Equipment

If a player's ball is accidentally deflected or stopped by himself, his *partner* or either of their *caddies* or *equipment*, the player incurs a penalty of one stroke. The ball must be played as it lies, except when it comes to rest in or on the player's, his *partner's* or either of their *caddies'* clothes or *equipment*, in which case the ball must *through the green* or in a *hazard* be dropped, or on the *putting green* be placed, as near as possible to the spot directly under the place where the ball came to rest in or on the article, but not nearer the *hole*.

Exceptions:

1. Ball striking person attending or holding up *flagstick* or anything carried by him – see Rule 17-3b.

2. Dropped ball – see Rule 20-2a.

(Ball purposely deflected or stopped by player, partner or caddie – see Rule 1-2)

19-3. By Opponent, Caddie or Equipment in Match Play

If a player's ball is accidentally deflected or stopped by an *opponent*, his *caddie* or his *equipment*, there is no penalty. The player may, before another *stroke* is made by either *side*, cancel the *stroke* and play a ball, without penalty, as nearly as possible at the spot from which the original ball was last played (Rule 20-5) or he may play the ball as it lies. However, if the player elects not to cancel the *stroke* and the ball has come to rest in or on the *opponent's* or his *caddie's* clothes or *equipment*, the ball must *through the green* or in a *hazard* be dropped, or on the *putting green* be placed, as near as possible to the spot directly under the place where the ball came to rest in or on the article, but not nearer the *hole*.

Exception: Ball striking person attending or holding up *flagstick* or anything carried by him – see Rule 17-3b.

(Ball purposely deflected or stopped by opponent or caddie – see Rule 1-2)

19-4. By Fellow-Competitor, Caddie or Equipment in Stroke Play

See Rule 19-1 regarding ball deflected by *outside agency*.

Exception: Ball striking person attending or holding up *flagstick* or anything carried by him – see Rule 17-3b.

19-5. By Another Ball
a. At Rest
If a player's ball in motion after a *stroke* is deflected or stopped by a *ball in play* and at rest, the player must play his ball as it lies. In match play, there is no penalty. In stroke play, there is no penalty, unless both balls lay on the *putting green* prior to the *stroke*, in which case the player incurs a penalty of two strokes.

b. In Motion
If a player's ball in motion after a *stroke* other than on the *putting green* is deflected or stopped by another ball in motion after a *stroke*, the player must play his ball as it lies, without penalty.

If a player's ball in motion after a *stroke* on the *putting green* is deflected or stopped by another ball in motion after a *stroke*, the player's *stroke* is cancelled. The ball must be replaced and replayed, without penalty.

Note: Nothing in this Rule overrides the provisions of Rule 10-1 (Order of Play in Match Play) or Rule 16-1f (Making Stroke While Another Ball in Motion).

PENALTY FOR BREACH OF RULE:
Match play – Loss of hole; Stroke play – Two strokes.

Relief Situations and Procedure

Rule 20 – Lifting, Dropping and Placing; Playing from Wrong Place

Definitions
All defined terms are in *italics* and are listed alphabetically in the Definitions section – see pages 584–587.

20-1. Lifting and Marking
A ball to be lifted under the *Rules* may be lifted by the player, his *partner* or another person authorised by the player. In any such case, the player is responsible for any breach of the Rules.

The position of the ball must be marked before it is lifted under a *Rule* that requires it to be replaced. If it is not marked, the player incurs a penalty of one stroke and the ball must be replaced. If it is not replaced, the player incurs the general penalty for breach of this Rule but there is no additional penalty under Rule 20-1.

If a ball or ball-marker is accidentally *moved* in the process of lifting the ball under a *Rule* or marking its position, the ball or ball-marker must be replaced. There is no penalty, provided the movement of the ball or ballmarker is directly attributable to the specific act of marking the position of or lifting the ball. Otherwise, the player incurs a penalty of one stroke under this Rule or Rule 18-2a.

Exception: If a player incurs a penalty for failing to act in accordance with Rule 5-3 or 12-2, there is no additional penalty under Rule 20-1.

Note: The position of a ball to be lifted should be marked by placing a ball-marker, a small coin or other similar object immediately behind the ball.

If the ball-marker interferes with the play, *stance* or *stroke* of another player, it should be placed one or more clubhead-lengths to one side.

20-2. Dropping and Re-Dropping
a. By Whom and How
A ball to be dropped under the Rules must be dropped by the player himself. He must stand erect, hold the ball at shoulder height and arm's length and drop it. If a ball is dropped by any other person or in any other manner and the error is not corrected as provided in Rule 20-6, the player incurs a penalty of one stroke.

If the ball, when dropped, touches any person or the *equipment* of any player before or after it strikes a part of

the *course* and before it comes to rest, the ball must be re-dropped, without penalty. There is no limit to the number of times a ball must be re-dropped in these circumstances. (Taking action to influence position or movement of ball – see Rule 1-2)

b. Where to Drop
When a ball is to be dropped as near as possible to a specific spot, it must be dropped not nearer the *hole* than the specific spot which, if it is not precisely known to the player, must be estimated.

A ball when dropped must first strike a part of the *course* where the applicable *Rule* requires it to be dropped. If it is not so dropped, Rules 20-6 and 20-7 apply.

c. When to Re-Drop
A dropped ball must be re-dropped, without penalty, if it:
(i) rolls into and comes to rest in a *hazard*;
(ii) rolls out of and comes to rest outside a *hazard*;
(iii) rolls onto and comes to rest on a *putting green*;
(iv) rolls and comes to rest *out of bounds*;
(v) rolls and comes to rest in a position where there is interference by the condition from which relief was taken under Rule 24-2b (immovable obstruction), Rule 25-1 (abnormal ground conditions), Rule 25-3 (wrong putting green) or a Local Rule (Rule 33-8a), or rolls back into the pitch-mark from which it was lifted under Rule 25-2 (embedded ball);
(vi) rolls and comes to rest more than two club-lengths from where it first struck a part of the *course*; or
(vii) rolls and comes to rest nearer the *hole* than:
  (a) its original position or estimated position (see Rule 20-2b) unless otherwise permitted by the *Rules*; or
  (b) the *nearest point of relief* or maximum available relief (Rule 24-2, 25-1 or 25-3); or
  (c) the point where the original ball last crossed the margin of the *water hazard* or *lateral water hazard* (Rule 26-1).

If the ball when re-dropped rolls into any position listed above, it must be placed as near as possible to the spot where it first struck a part of the *course* when re-dropped.

Note 1: If a ball when dropped or re-dropped comes to rest and subsequently *moves*, the ball must be played as it lies, unless the provisions of any other *Rule* apply.

Note 2: If a ball to be re-dropped or placed under this Rule is not immediately recoverable, another ball may be *substituted*.

(Use of dropping zone – see Appendix1; Part B; Section 8)

20-3. Placing and Replacing
a. By Whom and Where
A ball to be placed under the *Rules* must be placed by the player or his *partner*.

A ball to be replaced under the *Rules* must be replaced by any one of the following: (i) the person who lifted or *moved* the ball, (ii) the player, or (iii) the player's *partner*. The ball must be placed on the spot from which it was lifted or *moved*. If the ball is placed or replaced by any other person and the error is not corrected as provided in Rule 20-6, the player incurs a penalty of one stroke. In any such case, the player is responsible for any other breach of the *Rules* that occurs as a result of the placing or replacing of the ball.

If a ball or ball-marker is accidentally *moved* in the process of placing or replacing the ball, the ball or ball-marker must be replaced. There is no penalty, provided the movement of the ball or ball-marker is directly attributable to the specific act of placing or replacing the ball or removing the ball-marker. Otherwise, the player incurs a penalty of one stroke under Rule 18-2a or 20-1.

If a ball to be replaced is placed other than on the spot from which it was lifted or *moved* and the error is not corrected as provided in Rule 20-6, the player incurs the general penalty, loss of hole in match play or two strokes in stroke play, for a breach of the applicable *Rule*.

b. Lie of Ball to be Placed or Replaced Altered
If the original lie of a ball to be placed or replaced has been altered:

(i) except in a *hazard*, the ball must be placed in the nearest lie most similar to the original lie that is not more than one club-length from the original lie, not nearer the *hole* and not in a *hazard*;

(ii) in a *water hazard*, the ball must be placed in accordance with Clause (i) above, except that the ball must be placed in the *water hazard*;

(iii) in a *bunker*, the original lie must be re-created as nearly as possible and the ball must be placed in that lie.

Note: If the original lie of a ball to be placed or replaced has been altered and it is impossible to determine the spot where the ball is to be placed or replaced, Rule 20-3b applies if the original lie is known, and Rule 20-3c applies if the original lie is not known.

Exception: If the player is searching for or identifying a ball covered by sand – see Rule 12-1a.

c. Spot Not Determinable
If it is impossible to determine the spot where the ball is to be placed or replaced:

(i) *through the green*, the ball must be dropped as near as possible to the place where it lay but not in a *hazard* or on a *putting green*;

(ii) in a *hazard*, the ball must be dropped in the *hazard* as near as possible to the place where it lay;

(iii) on the *putting green*, the ball must be placed as near as possible to the place where it lay but not in a *hazard*.

Exception: When resuming play (Rule 6-8d), if the spot where the ball is to be placed is impossible to determine, it must be estimated and the ball placed on the estimated spot.

d. Ball Fails to Come to Rest on Spot
If a ball when placed fails to come to rest on the spot on which it was placed, there is no penalty and the ball must be replaced. If it still fails to come to rest on that spot:

(i) except in a *hazard*, it must be placed at the nearest spot where it can be placed at rest that is not nearer the *hole* and not in a *hazard*;

(ii) in a *hazard*, it must be placed in the *hazard* at the nearest spot where it can be placed at rest that is not nearer the *hole*. If a ball when placed comes to rest on the spot on which it is placed, and it subsequently *moves*, there is no penalty and the ball must be played as it lies, unless the provisions of any other *Rule* apply.

*PENALTY FOR BREACH OF RULE 20-1, 20-2 or 20-3:
Match play – Loss of hole; Stroke play – Two strokes.

*If a player makes a *stroke* at a ball *substituted* under one of these Rules when such substitution is not permitted, he incurs the general penalty for breach of that Rule, but there is no additional penalty under that Rule. If a player drops a ball in an improper manner and plays a wrong place or if the ball has been put into play by a person not permitted by the Rules and then played from a wrong place, see Note 3 to Rule 20-7c.

20-4. When Ball Dropped or Placed is in Play
If the player's *ball in play* has been lifted, it is again in play when dropped or placed.

A *substituted ball* becomes the *ball in play* when it has been dropped or placed.

(Ball incorrectly substituted – see Rule 15-2)

(Lifting ball incorrectly substituted, dropped or placed – see Rule 20-6)

20-5. Making Next Stroke from Where Previous Stroke Made
When a player elects or is required to make his next *stroke* from where a previous *stroke* was made, he must proceed as follows:

(a) On the Teeing Ground: The ball to be played must be played from within the *teeing ground*. It may be played from anywhere within the *teeing ground* and may be teed.

(b) Through the Green: The ball to be played must be dropped and when dropped must first strike a part of the *course through the green*.

(c) In a Hazard: The ball to be played must be dropped and when dropped must first strike a part of the *course in the hazard*.

(d) On the Putting Green: The ball to be played must be placed on the *putting green*.

PENALTY FOR BREACH OF RULE 20-5:
Match play – Loss of hole; Stroke play – Two strokes.

20-6. Lifting Ball Incorrectly Substituted, Dropped or Placed
A ball incorrectly *substituted*, dropped or placed in a wrong place or otherwise not in accordance with the *Rules* but not played may be lifted, without penalty, and the player must then proceed correctly.

20-7. Playing from Wrong Place
a. General
A player has played from a wrong place if he makes a *stroke* at his *ball in play*:

(i) on a part of the *course* where the *Rules* do not permit a *stroke* to be made or a ball to be dropped or placed; or

(ii) when the *Rules* require a dropped ball to be re-dropped or a *moved* ball to be replaced.

Note: For a ball played from outside the *teeing ground* or from a wrong *teeing ground* – see Rule 11-4.

b. Match Play
If a player makes a *stroke* from a wrong place, he loses the hole.

c. Stroke Play
If a *competitor* makes a *stroke* from a wrong place, he incurs a penalty of two strokes under the applicable *Rule*. He must play out the hole with the ball played from the wrong place, without correcting his error, provided he has not committed a serious breach (see Note 1).

If a *competitor* becomes aware that he has played from a wrong place and believes that he may have committed a serious breach, he must, before making a *stroke* on the next *teeing ground*, play out the hole with a second ball played in accordance with the *Rules*. If the hole being played is the last hole of the round, he must declare, before leaving the *putting green*, that he will play out the hole with a second ball played in accordance with the *Rules*.

If the *competitor* has played a second ball, he must report the facts to the *Committee* before returning his score card; if he fails to do so, he is disqualified. The *Committee* must determine whether the *competitor* has committed a serious breach of the applicable *Rule*. If he has, the score with the second ball counts and the competitor must add two penalty strokes to his score with that ball. If the *competitor* has committed a serious breach and has failed to correct it as outlined above, he is disqualified.

Note 1: A *competitor* is deemed to have committed a serious breach of the applicable *Rule* if the *Committee* considers he has gained a significant advantage as a result of playing from a wrong place.

Note 2: If a *competitor* plays a second ball under Rule 20-7c and it is ruled not to count, *strokes* made with that ball and *penalty strokes* incurred solely by playing that ball are disregarded. If the second ball is ruled to count, the *stroke* made from the wrong place and any *strokes* subsequently taken with the original ball including *penalty strokes* incurred solely by playing that ball are disregarded.

Note 3: If a player incurs a penalty for making a *stroke* from a wrong place, there is no additional penalty for:

(a) *substituting* a ball when not permitted;

(b) dropping a ball when the *Rules* require it to be placed, or placing a ball when the *Rules* require it to be dropped;

(c) dropping a ball in an improper manner; or

(d) a ball being put into play by a person not permitted to do so under the *Rules*.

Rule 21 – Cleaning Ball

Definitions

All defined terms are in *italics* and are listed alphabetically in the Definitions section – see pages 584–587.

A ball on the *putting green* may be cleaned when lifted under Rule 16-1b. Elsewhere, a ball may be cleaned when lifted, except when it has been lifted:

a. To determine if it is unfit for play (Rule 5-3);

b. For identification (Rule 12-2), in which case it may be cleaned only to the extent necessary for identification; or

c. Because it is assisting or interfering with play (Rule 22).

If a player cleans his ball during play of a hole except as provided in this Rule, he incurs a penalty of one stroke and the ball, if lifted, must be replaced. If a player who is required to replace a ball fails to do so, he incurs the general penalty under the applicable *Rule*, but there is no additional penalty under Rule 21.

Exception: If a player incurs a penalty for failing to act in accordance with Rule 5-3, 12-2 or 22, there is no additional penalty under Rule 21.

Rule 22 – Ball Assisting or Interfering with Play

Definitions

All defined terms are in *italics* and are listed alphabetically in the Definitions section – see pages 584–587.

22-1. Ball Assisting Play

Except when a ball is in motion, if a player considers that a ball might assist any other player, he may:

a. Lift the ball if it is his ball; or

b. Have any other ball lifted.

A ball lifted under this Rule must be replaced (see Rule 20-3). The ball must not be cleaned, unless it lies on the *putting green* (see Rule 21).

In stroke play, a player required to lift his ball may play first rather than lift the ball.

In stroke play, if the *Committee* determines that *competitors* have agreed not to lift a ball that might assist any *competitor*, they are disqualified.

Note: When another ball is in motion, a ball that might influence the movement of the ball in motion must not be lifted.

22-2. Ball Interfering with Play

Except when a ball is in motion, if a player considers that another ball might interfere with his play, he may have it lifted.

A ball lifted under this Rule must be replaced (see Rule 20-3). The ball must not be cleaned, unless it lies on the *putting green* (see Rule 21).

In stroke play, a player required to lift his ball may play first rather than lift the ball.

Note 1: Except on the *putting green*, a player may not lift his ball solely because he considers that it might interfere with the play of another player. If a player lifts his ball without being asked to do so, he incurs a penalty of one stroke for a breach of Rule 18-2a, but there is no additional penalty under Rule 22.

Note 2: When another ball is in motion, a ball that might influence the movement of the ball in motion must not be lifted.

PENALTY FOR BREACH OF RULE:

Match play – Loss of hole; Stroke play – Two strokes.

Rule 23 – Loose Impediments

Definitions

All defined terms are in *italics* and are listed alphabetically in the Definitions section – see pages 584–587.

23-1. Relief

Except when both the *loose impediment* and the ball lie in or touch the same *hazard*, any *loose impediment* may be removed without penalty.

If the ball lies anywhere other than on the *putting green* and the removal of a *loose impediment* by the player causes the ball to *move*, Rule 18-2a applies.

On the *putting green*, if the ball or ball-marker is accidentally *moved* in the process of the player removing a *loose impediment*, the ball or ball-marker must be replaced. There is no penalty, provided the movement of the ball or ball-marker is directly attributable to the removal of the *loose impediment*. Otherwise, if the player causes the ball to *move*, he incurs a penalty of one stroke under Rule 18-2a.

When a ball is in motion, a *loose impediment* that might influence the movement of the ball must not be removed.

Note: If the ball lies in a *hazard*, the player must not touch or move any *loose impediment* lying in or touching the same *hazard* – see Rule 13-4c.

PENALTY FOR BREACH OF RULE:

Match play – Loss of hole; Stroke play – Two strokes.

(Searching for ball in hazard – see Rule 12-1)

(Touching line of putt – see Rule 16-1a)

Rule 24 – Obstructions

Definitions

All defined terms are in *italics* and are listed alphabetically in the Definitions section – see pages 584–587.

24-1. Movable Obstruction

A player may take relief, without penalty, from a movable *obstruction* as follows:

a. If the ball does not lie in or on the *obstruction*, the *obstruction* may be removed. If the ball *moves*, it must be replaced, and there is no penalty, provided that the movement of the ball is directly attributable to the removal of the *obstruction*. Otherwise, Rule 18-2a applies.

b. If the ball lies in or on the *obstruction*, the ball may be lifted and the *obstruction* removed. The ball must *through the green* or in a *hazard* be dropped, or on the *putting green* be placed, as near as possible to the spot directly under the place where the ball lay in or on the *obstruction*, but not nearer the *hole*.

The ball may be cleaned when lifted under this Rule.

When a ball is in motion, an *obstruction* that might influence the movement of the ball, other than *equipment* of any player or the *flagstick* when attended, removed or held up, must not be moved.

(Exerting influence on ball – see Rule 1-2)

Note: If a ball to be dropped or placed under this Rule is not immediately recoverable, another ball may be *substituted*.

24-2. Immovable Obstruction
a. Interference
Interference by an immovable *obstruction* occurs when a ball lies in or on the *obstruction*, or when the *obstruction* interferes with the player's *stance* or the area of his intended swing. If the player's ball lies on the *putting green*, interference also occurs if an immovable *obstruction* on the *putting green* intervenes on his *line of putt*. Otherwise, intervention on the *line of play* is not, of itself, interference under this Rule.

b. Relief
Except when the ball is in a *water hazard* or a *lateral water hazard*, a player may take relief from interference by an immovable *obstruction* as follows:

(i) Through the Green: If the ball lies *through the green*, the player must lift the ball and drop it, without penalty, within one club-length of and not nearer the *hole* than the *nearest point of relief*. The *nearest point of relief* must not be in a *hazard* or on a *putting green*. When the ball is dropped within one club-length of the *nearest point of relief*, the ball must first strike a part of the *course* at a spot that avoids interference by the immovable *obstruction* and is not in a *hazard* and not on a *putting green*.

(ii) In a Bunker: If the ball is in a *bunker*, the player must lift the ball and drop it either:
   (a) Without penalty, in accordance with Clause (i) above, except that the *nearest point of relief* must be in the *bunker* and the ball must be dropped in the *bunker*; or
   (b) Under penalty of one stroke, outside the *bunker* keeping the point where the ball lay directly between the *hole* and the spot on which the ball is dropped, with no limit to how far behind the *bunker* the ball may be dropped.

(iii) On the Putting Green: If the ball lies on the *putting green*, the player must lift the ball and place it, without penalty, at the *nearest point of relief* that is not in a *hazard*. The *nearest point of relief* may be off the *putting green*.

(iv) On the Teeing Ground: If the ball lies on the *teeing ground*, the player must lift the ball and drop it, without penalty, in accordance with Clause (i) above.

The ball may be cleaned when lifted under this Rule.

(Ball rolling to a position where there is interference by the condition from which relief was taken – see Rule 20-2c(v))

Exception: A player may not take relief under this Rule if (a) interference by anything other than an immovable *obstruction* makes the *stroke* clearly impracticable or (b) interference by an immovable *obstruction* would occur only through use of a clearly unreasonable *stroke* or an unnecessarily abnormal *stance*, swing or direction of play.

Note 1: If a ball is in a *water hazard* (including a *lateral water hazard*), the player may not take relief from interference by an immovable *obstruction*. The player must play the ball as it lies or proceed under Rule 26-1.

Note 2: If a ball to be dropped or placed under this Rule is not immediately recoverable, another ball may be *substituted*.

Note 3: The *Committee* may make a Local Rule stating that the player must determine the *nearest point of relief* without crossing over, through or under the *obstruction*.

24-3. Ball in Obstruction Not Found
It is a question of fact whether a ball that has not been found after having been struck toward an *obstruction* is in the *obstruction*. In order to apply this Rule, it must be known or virtually certain that the ball is in the *obstruction*.

In the absence of such knowledge or certainty, the player must proceed under Rule 27-1.

a. Ball in Movable Obstruction Not Found
If it is known or virtually certain that a ball that has not been found is in a movable *obstruction*, the player may *substitute* another ball and take relief, without penalty, under this Rule. If he elects to do so, he must remove the *obstruction* and *through the green* drop a ball, or on the *putting green* place a ball, as near as possible to the spot directly under the place where the ball last crossed the outermost limits of the movable *obstruction*, but not nearer the *hole*.

b. Ball in Immovable Obstruction Not Found
If it is known or virtually certain that a ball that has not been found is in an immovable *obstruction*, the player may take relief under this Rule. If he elects to do so, the spot where the ball last crossed the outermost limits of the *obstruction* must be determined and, for the purpose of applying this Rule, the ball is deemed to lie at this spot and the player must proceed as follows:

(i) Through the Green: If the ball last crossed the outermost limits of the immovable *obstruction* at a spot *through the green*, the player may *substitute* another ball, without penalty, and take relief as prescribed in Rule 24-2b(i).

(ii) In a Bunker: If the ball last crossed the outermost limits of the immovable *obstruction* at a spot in a *bunker*, the player may *substitute* another ball, without penalty, and take relief as prescribed in Rule 24-2b(ii).

(iii) In a Water Hazard (including a Lateral Water Hazard): If the ball last crossed the outermost limits of the immovable *obstruction* at a spot in a *water hazard*, the player is not entitled to relief without penalty. The player must proceed under Rule 26-1.

(iv) On the Putting Green: If the ball last crossed the outermost limits of the immovable *obstruction* at a spot on the *putting green*, the player may *substitute* another ball, without penalty, and take relief as prescribed in Rule 24-2b(iii).

PENALTY FOR BREACH OF RULE:
Match play – Loss of hole; Stroke play – Two strokes.

Rule 25 – Abnormal Ground Conditions, Embedded Ball and Wrong Putting Green

Definitions
All defined terms are in *italics* and are listed alphabetically in the Definitions section – see pages 584–587.

25-1. Abnormal Ground Conditions
a. Interference
Interference by an *abnormal ground condition* occurs when a ball lies in or touches the condition or when the condition interferes with the player's *stance* or the area of his intended swing. If the player's ball lies on the *putting green*, interference also occurs if an *abnormal ground condition* on the *putting green* intervenes on his *line of putt*. Otherwise, intervention on the *line of play* is not, of itself, interference under this Rule.

Note: The *Committee* may make a Local Rule stating that interference by an *abnormal ground condition* with a player's *stance* is deemed not to be, of itself, interference under this Rule.

b. Relief
Except when the ball is in a *water hazard* or a *lateral water hazard*, a player may take relief from interference by an *abnormal ground condition* as follows:

(i) Through the Green: If the ball lies *through the green*, the player must lift the ball and drop it, without penalty, within one club-length of and not nearer the *hole* than the *nearest point of relief.* The *nearest point of relief* must not be in a *hazard* or on a *putting green.* When the ball is dropped within one club-length of the *nearest point of relief,* the ball must first strike a part of the *course* at a spot that avoids interference by the condition and is not in a *hazard* and not on a *putting green.*

(ii) In a Bunker: If the ball is in a *bunker,* the player must lift the ball and drop it either:

    (a) Without penalty, in accordance with Clause (i) above, except that the *nearest point of relief* must be in the *bunker* and the ball must be dropped in the *bunker* or, if complete relief is impossible, as near as possible to the spot where the ball lay, but not nearer the *hole,* on a part of the *course* in the *bunker* that affords maximum available relief from the condition; or

    (b) Under penalty of one stroke, outside the *bunker* keeping the point where the ball lay directly between the *hole* and the spot on which the ball is dropped, with no limit to how far behind the *bunker* the ball may be dropped.

(iii) On the Putting Green: If the ball lies on the *putting green,* the player must lift the ball and place it, without penalty, at the *nearest point of relief* that is not in a *hazard* or, if complete relief is impossible, at the nearest position to where it lay that affords maximum available relief from the condition, but not nearer the *hole* and not in a *hazard.* The *nearest point of relief* or maximum available relief may be off the *putting green.*

(iv) On the Teeing Ground: If the ball lies on the *teeing ground,* the player must lift the ball and drop it, without penalty, in accordance with Clause (i) above.

The ball may be cleaned when lifted under Rule 25-1b.

(Ball rolling to a position where there is interference by the condition from which relief was taken – see Rule 20-2c(v))

Exception: A player may not take relief under this Rule if (a) interference by anything other than an *abnormal ground condition* makes the *stroke* clearly impracticable or (b) interference by an *abnormal ground condition* would occur only through use of a clearly unreasonable *stroke* or an unnecessarily abnormal *stance,* swing or direction of play.

Note 1: If a ball is in a *water hazard* (including a *lateral water hazard*), the player is not entitled to relief, without penalty, from interference by an *abnormal ground condition.* The player must play the ball as it lies (unless prohibited by Local Rule) or proceed under Rule 26-1.

Note 2: If a ball to be dropped or placed under this Rule is not immediately recoverable, another ball may be *substituted.*

c. Ball in Abnormal Ground Condition Not Found

It is a question of fact whether a ball that has not been found after having been struck toward an *abnormal ground condition* is in such a condition. In order to apply this Rule, it must be known or virtually certain that the ball is in the *abnormal ground condition.* In the absence of such knowledge or certainty, the player must proceed under Rule 27-1.

If it is known or virtually certain that a ball that has not been found is in an *abnormal ground condition,* the player may take relief under this Rule. If he elects to do so, the spot where the ball last crossed the outermost limits of the *abnormal ground condition* must be determined and, for the purpose of applying this Rule, the ball is deemed to lie at this spot and the player must proceed as follows:

(i) Through the Green: If the ball last crossed the outermost limits of the *abnormal ground condition* at a spot *through the green,* the player may *substitute* another

ball, without penalty, and take relief as prescribed in Rule 25-1b(i).

(ii) In a Bunker: If the ball last crossed the outermost limits of the *abnormal ground condition* at a spot in a *bunker,* the player may *substitute* another ball, without penalty, and take relief as prescribed in Rule 25-1b(ii).

(iii) In a Water Hazard (including a Lateral Water Hazard): If the ball last crossed the outermost limits of the *abnormal ground condition* at a spot in a *water hazard,* the player is not entitled to relief without penalty. The player must proceed under Rule 26-1.

(iv) On the Putting Green: If the ball last crossed the outermost limits of the *abnormal ground condition* at a spot on the *putting green,* the player may *substitute* another ball, without penalty, and take relief as prescribed in Rule 25-1b(iii).

25-2. Embedded Ball

A ball embedded in its own pitch-mark in the ground in any closely-mown area *through the green* may be lifted, cleaned and dropped, without penalty, as near as possible to the spot where it lay but not nearer the *hole.* The ball when dropped must first strike a part of the *course through the green.* "Closely-mown area" means any area of the *course,* including paths through the rough, cut to fairway height or less.

25-3. Wrong Putting Green

a. Interference

Interference by a *wrong putting green* occurs when a ball is on the *wrong putting green.* Interference to a player's *stance* or the area of his intended swing is not, of itself, interference under this Rule.

b. Relief

If a player's ball lies on a *wrong putting green,* he must not play the ball as it lies. He must take relief, without penalty, as follows: The player must lift the ball and drop it within one club-length of and not nearer the *hole* than the *nearest point of relief.* The *nearest point of relief* must not be in a *hazard* or on a *putting green.* When dropping the ball within one club-length of the *nearest point of relief,* the ball must first strike a part of the *course* at a spot that avoids interference by the *wrong putting green* and is not in a *hazard* and not on a *putting green.* The ball may be cleaned when lifted under this Rule.

PENALTY FOR BREACH OF RULE:
Match play – Loss of hole; Stroke play – Two strokes.

Rule 26 – Water Hazards
(Including Lateral Water Hazards)

Definitions

All defined terms are in *italics* and are listed alphabetically in the Definitions section – see pages 584–587.

26-1. Relief for Ball in Water Hazard

It is a question of fact whether a ball that has not been found after having been struck toward a *water hazard* is in the *hazard.* In the absence of knowledge or virtual certainty that a ball struck toward a *water hazard,* but not found, is in the *hazard,* the player must proceed under Rule 27-1.

If a ball is found in a *water hazard* or if it is known or virtually certain that a ball that has not been found is in the *water hazard* (whether the ball lies in water or not), the player may under penalty of one stroke:

a. Proceed under the stroke and distance provision of Rule 27-1 by playing a ball as nearly as possible at the spot from which the original ball was last played (see Rule 20-5); or

b. Drop a ball behind the *water hazard,* keeping the point at which the original ball last crossed the margin of the *water hazard* directly between the *hole* and the spot on which the ball is dropped, with no limit to how far behind the *water hazard* the ball may be dropped; or

c. As additional options available only if the ball last crossed the margin of a *lateral water hazard*, drop a ball outside the *water hazard* within two club-lengths of and not nearer the *hole* than (i) the point where the original ball last crossed the margin of the *water hazard* or (ii) a point on the opposite margin of the *water hazard* equidistant from the *hole*.

When proceeding under this Rule, the player may lift and clean his ball or *substitute* a ball.

(Prohibited actions when ball is in a hazard – see Rule 13-4)

(Ball moving in water in a water hazard – see Rule 14-6)

26-2. Ball Played Within Water Hazard
a. Ball Comes to Rest in Same or Another Water Hazard

If a ball played from within a *water hazard* comes to rest in the same or another *water hazard* after the *stroke*, the player may:

(i) proceed under Rule 26-1a. If, after dropping in the *hazard*, the player elects not to play the dropped ball, he may:

   (a) proceed under Rule 26-1b, or if applicable Rule 26-1c, adding the additional penalty of one stroke prescribed by the Rule and using as the reference point the point where the original ball last crossed the margin of this *hazard* before it came to rest in this *hazard*; or

   (b) add an additional penalty of one stroke and play a ball as nearly as possible at the spot from which the last *stroke* from outside a *water hazard* was made (see Rule 20-5); or

(ii) proceed under Rule 26-1b, or if applicable Rule 26-1c; or

(iii) under penalty of one stroke, play a ball as nearly as possible at the spot from which the last *stroke* from outside a *water hazard* was made (see Rule 20-5).

b. Ball Lost or Unplayable Outside Hazard or Out of Bounds

If a ball played from within a *water hazard* is *lost* or deemed unplayable outside the *hazard* or is *out of bounds*, the player may, after taking a penalty of one stroke under Rule 27-1 or 28a:

(i) play a ball as nearly as possible at the spot in the *hazard* from which the original ball was last played (see Rule 20-5); or

(ii) proceed under Rule 26-1b, or if applicable Rule 26-1c, adding the additional penalty of one stroke prescribed by the Rule and using as the reference point the point where the original ball last crossed the margin of the *hazard* before it came to rest in the *hazard*; or

(iii) add an additional penalty of one stroke and play a ball as nearly as possible at the spot from which the last *stroke* from outside a *water hazard* was made (see Rule 20-5).

Note 1: When proceeding under Rule 26-2b, the player is not required to drop a ball under Rule 27-1 or 28a. If he does not drop a ball, he is not required to play it. He may alternatively proceed under Rule 26-2b(ii) or (iii).

Note 2: If a ball played from within a *water hazard* is deemed unplayable outside the *hazard*, nothing in Rule 26-2b precludes the player from proceeding under Rule 28b or c.

PENALTY FOR BREACH OF RULE:
Match play – Loss of hole; Stroke play – Two strokes.

Rule 27 – Ball Lost or Out of Bounds; Provisional Ball
Definitions
All defined terms are in *italics* and are listed alphabetically in the Definitions section – see pages 584–587.

27-1. Stroke and Distance; Ball Out of Bounds; Ball Not Found Within Five Minutes
a. Proceeding Under Stroke and Distance

At any time, a player may, under penalty of one stroke, play a ball as nearly as possible at the spot from which the original ball was last played (see Rule 20-5), i.e. proceed under penalty of stroke and distance.

Except as otherwise provided in the *Rules*, if a player makes a *stroke* at a ball from the spot at which the original ball was last played, he is deemed to have proceeded under penalty of stroke and distance.

b. Ball Out of Bounds

If a ball is *out of bounds*, the player must play a ball, under penalty of one stroke, as nearly as possible at the spot from which the original ball was last played (see Rule 20-5).

c. Ball Not Found Within Five Minutes

If a ball is *lost* as a result of not being found or identified as his by the player within five minutes after the player's *side* or his or their *caddies* have begun to search for it, the player must play a ball, under penalty of one stroke, as nearly as possible at the spot from which the original ball was last played (see Rule 20-5).

Exception: If it is known or virtually certain that the original ball, that has not been found, has been moved by an *outside agency* (Rule 18-1), is in an *obstruction* (Rule 24-3), is in an *abnormal ground condition* (Rule 25-1) or is in a *water hazard* (Rule 26-1), the player may proceed under the applicable *Rule*.

PENALTY FOR BREACH OF RULE 27-1:
Match play – Loss of hole; Stroke play – Two strokes.

27-2. Provisional Ball
a. Procedure

If a ball may be *lost* outside a *water hazard* or may be *out of bounds*, to save time the player may play another ball provisionally in accordance with Rule 27-1. The player must inform his *opponent* in match play or his *marker* or a *fellow-competitor* in stroke play that he intends to play a *provisional ball*, and he must play it before he or his *partner* goes forward to search for the original ball.

If he fails to do so and plays another ball, that ball is not a *provisional ball* and becomes the *ball in play* under penalty of stroke and distance (Rule 27-1); the original ball is *lost*.

(Order of play from teeing ground – see Rule 10-3)

Note: If a *provisional ball* played under Rule 27-2a might be *lost* outside a *water hazard* or *out of bounds*, the player may play another *provisional ball*. If another *provisional ball* is played, it bears the same relationship to the previous *provisional ball* as the first *provisional ball* bears to the original ball.

b. When Provisional Ball Becomes Ball in Play

The player may play a *provisional ball* until he reaches the place where the original ball is likely to be. If he makes a *stroke* with the *provisional ball* from the place where the original ball is likely to be or from a point nearer the *hole* than that place, the original ball is *lost* and the *provisional ball* becomes the *ball in play* under penalty of stroke and distance (Rule 27-1).

If the original ball is *lost* outside a *water hazard* or is *out of bounds*, the *provisional ball* becomes the *ball in play*, under penalty of stroke and distance (Rule 27-1).

Exception: If it is known or virtually certain that the original ball, that has not been found, has been moved by an *outside agency* (Rule 18-1), or is in an *obstruction* (Rule 24-3) or an *abnormal ground condition* (Rule 25-1c), the player may proceed under the applicable *Rule*.

c. When Provisional Ball to be Abandoned

If the original ball is neither *lost* nor *out of bounds*, the player must abandon the *provisional ball* and continue playing the original ball. If it is known or virtually certain that the original ball is in a *water hazard,* the player may proceed in accordance with Rule 26-1. In either situation, if the player makes any further *strokes* at the *provisional ball,* he is playing a *wrong ball* and the provisions of Rule 15-3 apply.

Note: If a player plays a *provisional ball* under Rule 27-2a, the *strokes* made after this Rule has been invoked with a *provisional ball* subsequently abandoned under Rule 27-2c and penalties incurred solely by playing that ball are disregarded.

Rule 28 – Ball Unplayable

Definitions

All defined terms are in *italics* and are listed alphabetically in the Definitions section – see pages 584–587.

The player may deem his ball unplayable at any place on the *course,* except when the ball is in a *water hazard.* The player is the sole judge as to whether his ball is unplayable.

If the player deems his ball to be unplayable, he must, under penalty of one stroke:

a. Proceed under the stroke and distance provision of Rule 27-1 by playing a ball as nearly as possible at the spot from which the original ball was last played (see Rule 20-5); or

b. Drop a ball behind the point where the ball lay, keeping that point directly between the *hole* and the spot on which the ball is dropped, with no limit to how far behind that point the ball may be dropped; or c. Drop a ball within two club-lengths of the spot where the ball lay, but not nearer the *hole.*

If the unplayable ball is in a *bunker,* the player may proceed under Clause a, b or c. If he elects to proceed under Clause b or c, a ball must be dropped in the *bunker.*

When proceeding under this Rule, the player may lift and clean his ball or *substitute* a ball.

PENALTY FOR BREACH OF RULE:
Match play – Loss of hole; Stroke play – Two strokes.

Other Forms of Play

Rule 29 – Threesomes and Foursomes

Definitions

All defined terms are in *italics* and are listed alphabetically in the Definitions section – see pages 584–587.

29-1. General

In a *threesome* or a *foursome,* during any *stipulated round* the *partners* must play alternately from the *teeing grounds* and alternately during the play of each hole. *Penalty strokes* do not affect the order of play.

29-2. Match Play

If a player plays when his *partner* should have played, his *side* loses the hole.

29-3. Stroke Play

If the *partners* make a *stroke* or *strokes* in incorrect order, such *stroke* or *strokes* are cancelled and the *side* incurs a penalty of two strokes. The *side* must correct the error by playing a ball in correct order as nearly as possible at the spot from which it first played in incorrect order (see Rule 20-5). If the *side* makes a *stroke* on the next *teeing ground* without first correcting the error or, in the case of the last hole of the round, leaves the *putting green* without declaring its intention to correct the error, the *side* is disqualified.

Rule 30 – Three-Ball, Best-Ball and Four-Ball Match Play

Definitions

All defined terms are in *italics* and are listed alphabetically in the Definitions section – see pages 584–587.

30-1. General

The Rules of Golf, so far as they are not at variance with the following specific Rules, apply to *three-ball, best-ball* and *four-ball* matches.

30-2. Three-Ball Match Play
a. Ball at Rest Moved or Purposely Touched by an Opponent

If an *opponent* incurs a penalty stroke under Rule 18-3b, that penalty is incurred only in the match with the player whose ball was touched or *moved.* No penalty is incurred in his match with the other player.

b. Ball Deflected or Stopped by an Opponent Accidentally

If a player's ball is accidentally deflected or stopped by an *opponent,* his *caddie* or *equipment,* there is no penalty. In his match with that *opponent* the player may, before another *stroke* is made by either *side,* cancel the *stroke* and play a ball, without penalty, as nearly as possible at the spot from which the original ball was last played (see Rule 20-5) or he may play the ball as it lies. In his match with the other *opponent,* the ball must be played as it lies.

Exception: Ball striking person attending or holding up *flagstick* or anything carried by him – see Rule 17-3b.

(Ball purposely deflected or stopped by *opponent* – see Rule 1-2)

30-3. Best-Ball and Four-Ball Match Play
a. Representation of Side

A *side* may be represented by one *partner* for all or any part of a match; all *partners* need not be present. An absent *partner* may join a match between holes, but not during play of a hole.

b. Order of Play

Balls belonging to the same *side* may be played in the order the *side* considers best.

c. Wrong Ball

If a player incurs the loss of hole penalty under Rule 15-3a for making a *stroke* at a *wrong ball,* he is disqualified for that hole, but his *partner* incurs no penalty even if the *wrong ball* belongs to him. If the *wrong ball* belongs to another player, its owner must place a ball on the spot from which the *wrong ball* was first played.

(Placing and Replacing – see Rule 20-3)

d. Penalty to Side

A *side* is penalised for a breach of any of the following by any *partner:*
- Rule 4   Clubs
- Rule 6-4   Caddie
- Any Local Rule or Condition of Competition for which the penalty is an adjustment to the state of the match.

e. Disqualification of Side

(i) A *side* is disqualified if any *partner* incurs a penalty of disqualification under any of the following:

• Rule 1-3	Agreement to Waive Rules
• Rule 4	Clubs
• Rule 5-1 or 5-2	The Ball
• Rule 6-2a	Handicap
• Rule 6-4	Caddie
• Rule 6-7	Undue Delay; Slow Play
• Rule 11-1	Teeing
• Rule 14-3	Artificial Devices, Unusual Equipment and Unusual Use of Equipment

- Rule 33-7   Disqualification Penalty Imposed by Committee

(ii) A *side* is disqualified if all *partners* incur a penalty of disqualification under any of the following:

- Rule 6-3   Time of Starting and Groups
- Rule 6-8   Discontinuance of Play

(iii) In all other cases where a breach of a *Rule* would result in disqualification, the player is disqualified for that hole only.

f. Effect of Other Penalties

If a player's breach of a *Rule* assists his *partner's* play or adversely affects an *opponent's* play, the *partner* incurs the applicable penalty in addition to any penalty incurred by the player.

In all other cases where a player incurs a penalty for breach of a *Rule*, the penalty does not apply to his *partner*. Where the penalty is stated to be loss of hole, the effect is to disqualify the player for that hole.

Rule 31 – Four-Ball Stroke Play

Definitions

All defined terms are in *italics* and are listed alphabetically in the Definitions section – see pages 584–587.

31-1. General

The Rules of Golf, so far as they are not at variance with the following specific Rules, apply to *four-ball* stroke play.

31-2. Representation of Side

A *side* may be represented by either *partner* for all or any part of a *stipulated round*; both *partners* need not be present. An absent *competitor* may join his *partner* between holes, but not during play of a hole.

31-3. Scoring

The *marker* is required to record for each hole only the gross score of whichever *partner's* score is to count. The gross scores to count must be individually identifiable; otherwise, the *side* is disqualified. Only one of the *partners* need be responsible for complying with Rule 6-6b.

(Wrong score – see Rule 31-7a)

31-4. Order of Play

Balls belonging to the same *side* may be played in the order the *side* considers best.

31-5. Wrong Ball

If a *competitor* is in breach of Rule 15-3b for making a *stroke* at a *wrong ball*, he incurs a penalty of two strokes and must correct his mistake by playing the correct ball or by proceeding under the *Rules*. His *partner* incurs no penalty, even if the *wrong ball* belongs to him.

If the *wrong ball* belongs to another *competitor*, its owner must place a ball on the spot from which the *wrong ball* was first played.

(Placing and Replacing – see Rule 20-3)

31-6 Penalty to Side

A *side* is penalised for a breach of any of the following by any *partner*:

- Rule 4   Clubs
- Rule 6-4   Caddie
- Any Local Rule or Condition of Competition for which there is a maximum penalty per round.

31-7. Disqualification Penalties

a. Breach by One Partner

A *side* is disqualified from the competition if either *partner* incurs a penalty of disqualification under any of the following:

- Rule 1-3   Agreement to Waive Rules
- Rule 3-4   Refusal to Comply with a Rule
- Rule 4   Clubs
- Rule 5-1 or 5-2   The Ball

- Rule 6-2b   Handicap
- Rule 6-4   Caddie
- Rule 6-6b   Signing and Returning Score Card
- Rule 6-6d   Wrong Score for Hole
- Rule 6-7   Undue Delay; Slow Play
- Rule 7-1   Practice Before or Between Rounds
- Rule 10-2c   Sides Agree to Play Out of Turn
- Rule 11-1   Teeing
- Rule 14-3   Artificial Devices, Unusual Equipment and Unusual Use of Equipment
- Rule 22-1   Ball Assisting Play
- Rule 31-3   Gross Scores to Count Not Individually Identifiable
- Rule 33-7   Disqualification Penalty Imposed by Committee

b. Breach by Both Partners

A *side* is disqualified from the competition:

(i) if each *partner* incurs a penalty of disqualification for a breach of Rule 6-3 (Time of Starting and Groups) or Rule 6-8 (Discontinuance of Play), or

(ii) if, at the same hole, each *partner* is in breach of a *Rule* the penalty for which is disqualification from the competition or for a hole.

c. For the Hole Only

In all other cases where a breach of a *Rule* would result in disqualification, the *competitor* is disqualified only for the hole at which the breach occurred.

31-8. Effect of Other Penalties

If a *competitor's* breach of a *Rule* assists his *partner's* play, the *partner* incurs the applicable penalty in addition to any penalty incurred by the *competitor*.

In all other cases where a *competitor* incurs a penalty for breach of a *Rule*, the penalty does not apply to his *partner*.

Rule 32 – Bogey, Par and Stableford Competitions

Definitions

All defined terms are in *italics* and are listed alphabetically in the Definitions section – see pages 584–587.

32-1. Conditions

Bogey, par and Stableford competitions are forms of stroke play in which play is against a fixed score at each hole. The *Rules* for stroke play, so far as they are not at variance with the following specific Rules, apply.

In handicap bogey, par and Stableford competitions, the *competitor* with the lowest net score at a hole takes the *honour* at the next *teeing ground*.

a. Bogey and Par Competitions

The scoring for bogey and par competitions is made as in match play.

Any hole for which a *competitor* makes no return is regarded as a loss. The winner is the *competitor* who is most successful in the aggregate of holes.

The *marker* is responsible for marking only the gross number of *strokes* for each hole where the *competitor* makes a net score equal to or less than the fixed score.

Note 1: The *competitor's* score is adjusted by deducting a hole or holes under the applicable *Rule* when a penalty other than disqualification is incurred under any of the following:

- Rule 4   Clubs
- Rule 6-4   Caddie
- Any Local Rule or Condition of Competition for which there is a maximum penalty per round.

The *competitor* is responsible for reporting the facts regarding such a breach to the *Committee* before he returns his score card so that the *Committee* may apply the penalty.

If the *competitor* fails to report his breach to the *Committee*, he is disqualified.

Note 2: If the *competitor* is in breach of Rule 6-3a (Time of Starting) but arrives at his starting point, ready to play, within five minutes after his starting time, or is in breach of Rule 6-7 (Undue Delay; Slow Play), the *Committee* will deduct one hole from the aggregate of holes. For a repeated offence under Rule 6-7, see Rule 32-2a.

b. Stableford Competitions

The scoring in Stableford competitions is made by points awarded in relation to a fixed score at each hole as follows:

Hole Played In	Points
More than one over fixed score or no score returned .	0
One over fixed score.	1
Fixed score	2
One under fixed score	3
Two under fixed score	4
Three under fixed score	5
Four under fixed score	6

The winner is the *competitor* who scores the highest number of points.

The *marker* is responsible for marking only the gross number of *strokes* at each hole where the *competitor's* net score earns one or more points.

Note 1: If a *competitor* is in breach of a *Rule* for which there is a maximum penalty per round, he must report the facts to the *Committee* before returning his score card; if he fails to do so, he is disqualified. The *Committee* will, from the total points scored for the round, deduct two points for each hole at which any breach occurred, with a maximum deduction per round of four points for each *Rule* breached.

Note 2: If the *competitor* is in breach of Rule 6-3a (Time of Starting) but arrives at his starting point, ready to play, within five minutes after his starting time, or is in breach of Rule 6-7 (Undue Delay; Slow Play), the *Committee* will deduct two points from the total points scored for the round. For a repeated offence under Rule 6-7, see Rule 32-2a.

Note 3: For the purpose of preventing slow play, the *Committee* may, in the conditions of a competition (Rule 33-1), establish pace of play guidelines, including maximum periods of time allowed to complete a *stipulated round*, a hole or a *stroke*.

The *Committee* may, in such a condition, modify the penalty for a breach of this Rule as follows: First offence – Deduction of one point from the total points scored for the round; Second offence – Deduction of a further two points from the total points scored for the round; For subsequent offence – Disqualification

32-2. Disqualification Penalties
a. From the Competition

A *competitor* is disqualified from the competition if he incurs a penalty of disqualification under any of the following:

• Rule 1-3	Agreement to Waive Rules
• Rule 3-4	Refusal to Comply with a Rule
• Rule 4	Clubs
• Rule 5-1 or 5-2	The Ball
• Rule 6-2b	Handicap
• Rule 6-3	Time of Starting and Groups
• Rule 6-4	Caddie
• Rule 6-6b	Signing and Returning Score Card
• Rule 6-6d	Wrong Score for Hole, i.e. when the recorded score is lower than actually taken, except that no penalty is incurred when a breach of this Rule does not affect the result of the hole

• Rule 6-7	Undue Delay; Slow Play
• Rule 6-8	Discontinuance of Play
• Rule 7-1	Practice Before or Between Rounds
• Rule 11-1	Teeing
• Rule 14-3	Artificial Devices, Unusual Equipment and Unusual Use of Equipment
• Rule 22-1	Ball Assisting Play
• Rule 33-7	Disqualification Penalty Imposed by Committee

b. For a Hole

In all other cases where a breach of a *Rule* would result in disqualification, the *competitor* is disqualified only for the hole at which the breach occurred.

Administration

Rule 33 – The Committee

Definitions

All defined terms are in *italics* and are listed alphabetically in the Definitions section – see pages 584–587.

33-1. Conditions; Waiving Rule

The *Committee* must establish the conditions under which a competition is to be played.

The *Committee* has no power to waive a Rule of Golf.

Certain specific *Rules* governing stroke play are so substantially different from those governing match play that combining the two forms of play is not practicable and is not permitted. The result of a match played in these circumstances is null and void and, in the stroke play competition, the *competitors* are disqualified.

In stroke play, the *Committee* may limit a *referee's* duties.

33-2. The Course
a. Defining Bounds and Margins

The *Committee* must define accurately:
(i)   the *course* and *out of bounds*,
(ii) the margins of *water hazards* and *lateral water hazards*,
(iii) *ground under repair*, and
(iv) *obstructions* and integral parts of the *course*.

b. New Holes

New *holes* should be made on the day on which a stroke play competition begins and at such other times as the *Committee* considers necessary, provided all *competitors* in a single round play with each *hole* cut in the same position.

Exception: When it is impossible for a damaged *hole* to be repaired so that it conforms with the Definition, the *Committee* may make a new *hole* in a nearby similar position.

Note: Where a single round is to be played on more than one day, the *Committee* may provide, in the conditions of a competition (Rule 33-1), that the *holes* and *teeing grounds* may be differently situated on each day of the competition, provided that, on any one day, all *competitors* play with each *hole* and each *teeing ground* in the same position.

c. Practice Ground

Where there is no practice ground available outside the area of a competition *course*, the *Committee* should establish the area on which players may practise on any day of a competition, if it is practicable to do so. On any day of a stroke play competition, the *Committee* should not normally permit practice on or to a *putting green* or from a *hazard* of the competition *course*.

d. Course Unplayable

If the *Committee* or its authorised representative considers that for any reason the *course* is not in a playable condition or that there are circumstances that render the proper playing of the game impossible, it may, in match play or stroke play, order a temporary suspension of play or, in stroke play, declare play null and void and cancel all scores for the round in question. When a round is cancelled, all penalties incurred in that round are cancelled.

(Procedure in discontinuing and resuming play – see Rule 6-8)

33-3. Times of Starting and Groups

The *Committee* must establish the times of starting and, in stroke play, arrange the groups in which *competitors* must play.

When a match play competition is played over an extended period, the *Committee* establishes the limit of time within which each round must be completed. When players are allowed to arrange the date of their match within these limits, the *Committee* should announce that the match must be played at a stated time on the last day of the period, unless the players agree to a prior date.

33-4. Handicap Stroke Table

The *Committee* must publish a table indicating the order of holes at which handicap strokes are to be given or received.

33-5. Score Card

In stroke play, the *Committee* must provide each *competitor* with a score card containing the date and the *competitor's* name or, in *foursome* or *four-ball* stroke play, the *competitors'* names.

In stroke play, the *Committee* is responsible for the addition of scores and application of the handicap recorded on the score card.

In *four-ball* stroke play, the *Committee* is responsible for recording the better-ball score for each hole and in the process applying the handicaps recorded on the score card, and adding the better-ball scores.

In bogey, par and Stableford competitions, the *Committee* is responsible for applying the handicap recorded on the score card and determining the result of each hole and the overall result or points total.

Note: The *Committee* may request that each *competitor* records the date and his name on his score card.

33-6. Decision of Ties

The *Committee* must announce the manner, day and time for the decision of a halved match or of a tie, whether played on level terms or under handicap.

A halved match must not be decided by stroke play. A tie in stroke play must not be decided by a match.

33-7. Disqualification Penalty; Committee Discretion

A penalty of disqualification may in exceptional individual cases be waived, modified or imposed if the *Committee* considers such action warranted.

Any penalty less than disqualification must not be waived or modified.

If a *Committee* considers that a player is guilty of a serious breach of etiquette, it may impose a penalty of disqualification under this Rule.

33-8. Local Rules
a. Policy

The *Committee* may establish Local Rules for local abnormal conditions if they are consistent with the policy set forth in Appendix I.

b. Waiving or Modifying a Rule

A Rule of Golf must not be waived by a Local Rule. However, if a *Committee* considers that local abnormal conditions interfere with the proper playing of the game to the extent that it is necessary to make a Local Rule that modifies the Rules of Golf, the Local Rule must be authorised by The *R&A*.

Rule 34 – Disputes and Decisions

Definitions

All defined terms are in *italics* and are listed alphabetically in the Definitions section – see pages 584–587.

34-1. Claims and Penalties
a. Match Play

If a claim is lodged with the *Committee* under Rule 2-5, a decision should be given as soon as possible so that the state of the match may, if necessary, be adjusted. If a claim is not made in accordance with Rule 2-5, it must not be considered by the *Committee*.

There is no time limit on applying the disqualification penalty for a breach of Rule 1-3.

b. Stroke Play

In stroke play, a penalty must not be rescinded, modified or imposed after the competition has closed. A competition is closed when the result has been officially announced or, in stroke play qualifying followed by match play, when the player has teed off in his first match.

Exceptions: A penalty of disqualification must be imposed after the competition has closed if a *competitor:*

(i) was in breach of Rule 1-3 (Agreement to Waive Rules); or

(ii) returned a score card on which he had recorded a handicap that, before the competition closed, he knew was higher than that to which he was entitled, and this affected the number of strokes received (Rule 6-2b); or

(iii) returned a score for any hole lower than actually taken (Rule 6-6d) for any reason other than failure to include a penalty that, before the competition closed, he did not know he had incurred; or

(iv) knew, before the competition closed, that he had been in breach of any other *Rule* for which the penalty is disqualification.

34-2. Referee's Decision

If a *referee* has been appointed by the *Committee*, his decision is final.

34-3. Committee's Decision

In the absence of a *referee*, any dispute or doubtful point on the *Rules* must be referred to the *Committee*, whose decision is final.

If the *Committee* cannot come to a decision, it may refer the dispute or doubtful point to the Rules of Golf Committee of the *R&A*, whose decision is final.

If the dispute or doubtful point has not been referred to the Rules of Golf Committee, the player or players may request that an agreed statement be referred through a duly authorised representative of the *Committee* to the Rules of Golf Committee for an opinion as to the correctness of the decision given. The reply will be sent to this authorised representative.

If play is conducted other than in accordance with the Rules of Golf, the Rules of Golf Committee will not give a decision on any question.

Appendix I - Contents

Appendix I - Local Rules; Conditions of the Competition

Definitions
All defined terms are in *italics* and are listed alphabetically in the Definitions section – see pages 584–587.

Part A - Local Rules

As provided in Rule 33-8a, the Committee may make and publish Local Rules for local abnormal conditions if they are consistent with the policy established in this Appendix. In addition, detailed information regarding acceptable and prohibited Local Rules is provided in "Decisions on the Rules of Golf" under Rule 33-8 and in "Guidance on Running a Competition".

If local abnormal conditions interfere with the proper playing of the game and the Committee considers it necessary to modify a Rule of Golf, authorisation from the *R&A* must be obtained.

1. Defining Bounds and Margins
Specifying means used to define out *of bounds, water hazards, lateral water hazards, ground under repair, obstructions* and integral parts of the course (Rule 33-2a).

2. Water Hazards
a. Lateral Water Hazards
Clarifying the status of water hazards that may be *lateral water hazards* (Rule 26).

b. Ball Played Provisionally Under Rule 26-1
Permitting play of a ball provisionally under Rule 26-1 for a ball that may be in a *water hazard* (including a *lateral water hazard*) of such character that, if the original ball is not found, it is known or virtually certain that it is in the *water hazard* and it would be impracticable to determine whether the ball is in the *hazard* or to do so would unduly delay play.

3. Areas of the Course Requiring Preservation; Environmentally-Sensitive Areas
Assisting preservation of the *course* by defining areas, including turf nurseries, young plantations and other parts of the *course* under cultivation, as *ground under repair* from which play is prohibited.

When the *Committee* is required to prohibit play from environmentally-sensitive areas that are on or adjoin the *course*, it should make a Local Rule clarifying the relief procedure.

4. Course Conditions – Mud, Extreme Wetness, Poor Conditions and Protection of Course
a. Lifting an Embedded Ball, Cleaning
Temporary conditions that might interfere with proper playing of the game, including mud and extreme wetness, warranting relief for an embedded ball anywhere *through the green* or permitting lifting, cleaning and replacing a ball anywhere *through the green* or on a closely-mown area *through the green*.

b. "Preferred Lies" and "Winter Rules"
Adverse conditions, including the poor condition of the *course* or the existence of mud, are sometimes so general, particularly during winter months, that the *Committee* may decide to grant relief by temporary Local Rule either to protect the *course* or to promote fair and pleasant play. The Local Rule should be withdrawn as soon as the conditions warrant.

5. Obstructions
a. General
Clarifying status of objects that may be *obstructions* (Rule 24).

Declaring any construction to be an integral part of the *course* and, accordingly, not an *obstruction*, e.g. built-up sides of *teeing grounds, putting greens* and *bunkers* (Rules 24 and 33-2a).

b. Stones in Bunkers
Allowing the removal of stones in *bunkers* by declaring them to be movable *obstructions* (Rule 24-1).

c. Roads and Paths

(i)   Declaring artificial surfaces and sides of roads and paths to be integral parts of the course, or

(ii) Providing relief of the type afforded under Rule 24-2b from roads and paths not having artificial surfaces and sides if they could unfairly affect play.

d. Immovable Obstructions Close to Putting Green

Providing relief from intervention by immovable *obstructions* on or within two club-lengths of the putting green when the ball lies within two clublengths of the immovable *obstruction*.

e. Protection of Young Trees

Providing relief for the protection of young trees.

f. Temporary Obstructions

Providing relief from interference by temporary obstructions (e.g. grandstands, television cables and equipment, etc).

6. Dropping Zones

Establishing special areas on which balls may or must be dropped when it is not feasible or practicable to proceed exactly in conformity with Rule 24-2b or 24-3 (Immovable Obstruction), Rule 25-1b or 25-1c (Abnormal Ground Conditions), Rule 25-3 (Wrong Putting Green), Rule 26-1 (Water Hazards and Lateral Water Hazards) or Rule 28 (Ball Unplayable).

Part B Specimen Local Rules

Within the policy established in Part A of this Appendix, the Committee may adopt a Specimen Local Rule by referring, on a score card or notice board, to the examples given below. However, Specimen Local Rules of a temporary nature should not be printed on a score card.

1. Water Hazards; Ball Played Provisionally Under Rule 26-1

If a *water hazard* (including a *lateral water hazard*) is of such size and shape and/or located in such a position that:

(i)   it would be impracticable to determine whether the ball is in the *hazard* or to do so would unduly delay play, and

(ii) if the original ball is not found, it is known or virtually certain that it is in the *water hazard*, the *Committee* may introduce a Local Rule permitting the play of a ball provisionally under Rule 26-1. The ball is played provisionally under any of the applicable options under Rule 26-1 or any applicable Local Rule. In such a case, if a ball is played provisionally and the original ball is in a *water hazard*, the player may play the original ball as it lies or continue with the ball played provisionally, but he may not proceed under Rule 26-1 with regard to the original ball.

In these circumstances, the following Local Rule is recommended:

"If there is doubt whether a ball is in or is lost in the water hazard (specify location), the player may play another ball provisionally under any of the applicable options in Rule 26-1.

If the original ball is found outside the water hazard, the player must continue play with it.

I f the original ball is found in the water hazard, the player may either play the original ball as it lies or continue with the ball played provisionally under Rule 26-1.

If the original ball is not found or identified within the five-minute search period, the player must continue with the ball played provisionally.

PENALTY FOR BREACH OF LOCAL RULE:
Match play – Loss of hole; Stroke play – Two strokes."

2. Areas of the Course Requiring Preservation; Environmentally- Sensitive Areas
a. Ground Under Repair; Play Prohibited

If the *Committee* wishes to protect any area of the *course*, it should declare it to be *ground under repair* and prohibit play from within that area. The following Local Rule is recommended:

"The _____(defined by ____) is ground under repair from which play is prohibited. If a player's ball lies in the area, or if it interferes with the player's stance or the area of his intended swing, the player must take relief under Rule 25-1.

PENALTY FOR BREACH OF LOCAL RULE:
Match play – Loss of hole; Stroke play – Two strokes."

b. Environmentally-Sensitive Areas

If an appropriate authority (i.e. a Government Agency or the like) prohibits entry into and/or play from an area on or adjoining the *course* for environmental reasons, the *Committee* should make a Local Rule clarifying the relief procedure.

The *Committee* has some discretion in terms of whether the area is defined as *ground under repair*, a *water hazard* or *out of bounds*. However, it may not simply define the area to be a *water hazard* if it does not meet the Definition of a "*Water Hazard*" and it should attempt to preserve the character of the hole.

The following Local Rule is recommended:

"I. Definition

An environmentally-sensitive area (ESA) is an area so declared by an appropriate authority, entry into and/or play from which is prohibited for environmental reasons. These areas may be defined as ground under repair, a water hazard, a lateral water hazard or out of bounds at the discretion of the Committee, provided that in the case of an ESA that has been defined as a water hazard or a lateral water hazard, the area is, by definition, a water hazard.

Note: The Committee may not declare an area to be environmentally-sensitive.

II. Ball in Environmentally-Sensitive Area
a. Ground Under Repair

If a ball is in an ESA defined as ground under repair, a ball must be dropped in accordance with Rule 25-1b.

If it is known or virtually certain that a ball that has not been found is in an ESA defined as ground under repair, the player may take relief, without penalty, as prescribed in Rule 25-1c.

b. Water Hazards and Lateral Water Hazards

If the ball is found in or if it is known or virtually certain that a ball that has not been found is in an ESA defined as a water hazard or lateral water hazard, the player must, under penalty of one stroke, proceed under Rule 26-1.

Note: If a ball, dropped in accordance with Rule 26 rolls into a position where the ESA interferes with the player's stance or the area of his intended swing, the player must take relief as provided in Clause III of this Local Rule.

c. Out of Bounds

If a ball is in an ESA defined as out of bounds, the player must play a ball, under penalty of one stroke, as nearly as possible at the spot from which the original ball was last played (see Rule 20-5).

III. Interference with Stance or Area of Intended Swing

Interference by an ESA occurs when the ESA interferes with the player's stance or the area of his intended swing. If interference exists, the player must take relief as follows:

(a) Through the Green: If the ball lies through the green, the point on the course nearest to where the ball lies must be determined that (a) is not nearer the hole, (b) avoids interference by the ESA and (c) is not in a hazard or on a putting green. The player must lift the ball and drop it, without penalty, within one club-length of the point so determined on a part of the course that fulfils (a), (b) and (c) above.

(b) In a Hazard: If the ball is in a hazard, the player must lift the ball and drop it either:

(i) Without penalty, in the hazard, as near as possible to the spot where the ball lay, but not nearer the hole, on a part of the course that provides complete relief from the ESA; or

(ii) Under penalty of one stroke, outside the hazard, keeping the point where the ball lay directly between the hole and the spot on which the ball is dropped, with no limit to how far behind the hazard the ball may be dropped. Additionally, the player may proceed under Rule 26 or 28 if applicable.

(c) On the Putting Green: If the ball lies on the putting green, the player must lift the ball and place it, without penalty, in the nearest position to where it lay that affords complete relief from the ESA, but not nearer the hole or in a hazard.

The ball may be cleaned when lifted under Clause III of this Local Rule.

Exception: A player may not take relief under Clause III of this Local Rule if (a) interference by anything other than an ESA makes the stroke clearly impracticable or (b) interference by an ESA would occur only through use of a clearly unreasonable stroke or an unnecessarily abnormal stance, swing or direction of play.

PENALTY FOR BREACH OF LOCAL RULE:
Match play – Loss of hole; Stroke play – Two strokes.

Note: In the case of a serious breach of this Local Rule, the Committee may impose a penalty of disqualification."

3. Protection of Young Trees

When it is desired to prevent damage to young trees, the following Local Rule is recommended:

"Protection of young trees identified by _____. If such a tree interferes with a player's stance or the area of his intended swing, the ball must be lifted, without penalty, and dropped in accordance with the procedure prescribed in Rule 24-2b (Immovable Obstruction). If the ball lies in a water hazard, the player must lift and drop the ball in accordance with Rule 24-2b(i), except that the nearest point of relief must be in the water hazard and the ball must be dropped in the water hazard or the player may proceed under Rule 26. The ball may be cleaned when lifted under this Local Rule.

Exception: A player may not obtain relief under this Local Rule if (a) interference by anything other than such a tree makes the stroke clearly impracticable or (b) interference by such a tree would occur only through use of a clearly unreasonable stroke or an unnecessarily abnormal stance, swing or direction of play.

PENALTY FOR BREACH OF LOCAL RULE:
Match play – Loss of hole; Stroke play – Two strokes."

4. Course Conditions – Mud, Extreme Wetness, Poor Conditions and Protection of the Course

a. Relief for Embedded Ball

Rule 25-2 provides relief, without penalty, for a ball embedded in its own pitch-mark in any closely-mown area *through the green*. On the *putting green*, a ball may be lifted and damage caused by the impact of a ball may be repaired (Rules 16-1b and c). When permission to take relief for an embedded ball anywhere *through the green* would be warranted, the following Local Rule is recommended:

"Through the green, a ball that is embedded in its own pitch-mark in the ground may be lifted, without penalty, cleaned and dropped as near as possible to where it lay but not nearer the hole. The ball when dropped must first strike a part of the course through the green.

Exceptions:
A player may not take relief under this Local Rule if the ball is embedded in sand in an area that is not closely mown.

A player may not take relief under this Local Rule if interference by anything other than the condition covered by this Local Rule makes the stroke clearly impracticable.

PENALTY FOR BREACH OF LOCAL RULE:
Match play – Loss of hole; Stroke play – Two strokes."

b. Cleaning Ball

Conditions, such as extreme wetness causing significant amounts of mud to adhere to the ball, may be such that permission to lift, clean and replace the ball would be appropriate. In these circumstances, the following Local Rule is recommended:

"(Specify area) a ball may be lifted, cleaned and replaced without penalty.

Note: The position of the ball must be marked before it is lifted under this Local Rule – see Rule 20-1.

PENALTY FOR BREACH OF LOCAL RULE:
Match play – Loss of hole; Stroke play – Two strokes."

c. "Preferred Lies" and "Winter Rules"

Ground under repair is provided for in Rule 25 and occasional local abnormal conditions that might interfere with fair play and are not widespread should be defined as *ground under repair*.

However, adverse conditions, such as heavy snows, spring thaws, prolonged rains or extreme heat can make fairways unsatisfactory and sometimes prevent use of heavy mowing equipment. When such conditions are so general throughout a *course* that the *Committee* believes "preferred lies" or "winter rules" would promote fair play or help protect the *course*, the following Local Rule is recommended:

"A ball lying on a closely-mown area through the green (or specify a more restricted area, e.g. at the 6th hole) may be lifted, without penalty, and cleaned. Before lifting the ball, the player must mark its position. Having lifted the ball, he must place it on a spot within (specify area, e.g. six inches, one club-length, etc.) of and not nearer the hole than where it originally lay, that is not in a hazard and not on a putting green.

A player may place his ball only once, and it is in play when it has been placed (Rule 20-4). If the ball fails to come to rest on the spot on which it is placed, Rule 20-3d applies. If the ball when placed comes to rest on the spot on which it is placed and it subsequently moves, there is no penalty and the ball must be played as it lies, unless the provisions of any other Rule apply.

If the player fails to mark the position of the ball before lifting it or moves the ball in any other manner, such as rolling it with a club, he incurs a penalty of one stroke.

Note: "Closely-mown area" means any area of the course, including paths through the rough, cut to fairway height or less.

*PENALTY FOR BREACH OF LOCAL RULE:
Match play – Loss of hole; Stroke play – Two strokes.

*If a player incurs the general penalty for a breach of this Local Rule, no additional penalty under the Local Rule is applied."

d. Aeration Holes

When a *course* has been aerated, a Local Rule permitting relief, without penalty, from an aeration hole may be warranted. The following Local Rule is recommended:

"Through the green, a ball that comes to rest in or on an aeration hole may be lifted, without penalty, cleaned and dropped, as near as possible to the spot where it lay but not nearer the hole. The ball when dropped must first strike a part of the course through the green.

On the putting green, a ball that comes to rest in or on an aeration hole may be placed at the nearest spot not nearer the hole that avoids the situation.

PENALTY FOR BREACH OF LOCAL RULE:
Match play – Loss of hole; Stroke play – Two strokes."

e. Seams of Cut Turf

If a Committee wishes to allow relief from seams of cut turf, but not from the cut turf itself, the following Local Rule is recommended:

"Through the green, seams of cut turf (not the turf itself) are deemed to be ground under repair. However, interference by a seam with the player's stance is deemed not to be, of itself, interference under Rule 25-1. If the ball lies in or touches the seam or the seam interferes with the area of intended swing, relief is available under Rule 25-1. All seams within the cut turf area are considered the same seam.

PENALTY FOR BREACH OF LOCAL RULE:
Match play – Loss of hole; Stroke play – Two strokes."

5. Stones in Bunkers

Stones are, by definition, loose impediments and, when a player's ball is in a hazard, a stone lying in or touching the hazard may not be touched or moved (Rule 13-4). However, stones in bunkers may represent a danger to players (a player could be injured by a stone struck by the player's club in an attempt to play the ball) and they may interfere with the proper playing of the game.

When permission to lift a stone in a bunker is warranted, the following Local Rule is recommended:

"Stones in bunkers are movable obstructions (Rule 24-1 applies)."

6. Immovable Obstructions Close to Putting Green

Rule 24-2 provides relief, without penalty, from interference by an immovable obstruction, but it also provides that, except on the putting green, intervention on the line of play is not, of itself, interference under this Rule.

However, on some courses, the aprons of the putting greens are so closely mown that players may wish to putt from just off the green. In such conditions, immovable obstructions on the apron may interfere with the proper playing of the game and the introduction of the following Local Rule providing additional relief, without penalty, from intervention by an immovable obstruction would be warranted:

"Relief from interference by an immovable obstruction may be taken under Rule 24-2.

In addition, if a ball lies through the green and an immovable obstruction on or within two club-lengths of the putting green and within two club-lengths of the ball intervenes on the line of play between the ball and the hole, the player may take relief as follows:

The ball must be lifted and dropped at the nearest point to where the ball lay that (a) is not nearer the hole, (b) avoids intervention and (c) is not in a hazard or on a putting green.

If the player's ball lies on the putting green and an immovable obstruction within two club-lengths of the putting green intervenes on his line of putt, the player may take relief as follows:

The ball must be lifted and placed at the nearest point to where the ball lay that (a) is not nearer the hole, (b) avoids intervention and (c) is not in a hazard.

The ball may be cleaned when lifted.

Exception: A player may not take relief under this Local Rule if interference by anything other than the immovable obstruction makes the stroke clearly impracticable.

PENALTY FOR BREACH OF LOCAL RULE:
Match play – Loss of hole; Stroke play – Two strokes."

Note: The Committee may restrict this Local Rule to specific holes, to balls lying only in closely-mown areas, to specific obstructions, or, in the case of obstructions that are not on the putting green, to obstructions in closely-mown areas if so desired. "Closely-mown area" means any area of the course, including paths through the rough, cut to fairway height or less.

7. Temporary Obstructions

When temporary obstructions are installed on or adjoining the course, the Committee should define the status of such obstructions as movable, immovable or temporary immovable obstructions.

a. Temporary Immovable Obstructions

If the Committee defines such obstructions as temporary immovable obstructions, the following Local Rule is recommended:

"I. Definition

A temporary immovable obstruction (TIO) is a non-permanent artificial object that is often erected in conjunction with a competition and is fixed or not readily movable.

Examples of TIOs include, but are not limited to, tents, scoreboards, grandstands, television towers and lavatories. Supporting guy wires are part of the TIO, unless the Committee declares that they are to be treated as elevated power lines or cables.

II. Interference

Interference by a TIO occurs when (a) the ball lies in front of and so close to the TIO that the TIO interferes with the player's stance or the area of his intended swing, or (b) the ball lies in, on, under or behind the TIO so that any part of the TIO intervenes directly between the player's ball and the hole and is on his line of play; interference also exists if the ball lies within one club-length of a spot equidistant from the hole where such intervention would exist.

Note: A ball is under a TIO when it is below the outermost edges of the TIO, even if these edges do not extend downwards to the ground.

III. Relief

A player may obtain relief from interference by a TIO, including a TIO that is out of bounds, as follows:

(a) Through the Green: If the ball lies through the green, the point on the course nearest to where the ball lies must be determined that (a) is not nearer the hole, (b) avoids interference as defined in Clause II and (c) is not in a hazard or on a putting green. The player must lift the ball and drop it, without penalty, within one club-length of the point so determined on a part of the course that fulfils (a), (b) and (c) above.

(b) In a Hazard: If the ball is in a hazard, the player must lift and drop the ball either:

(i) Without penalty, in accordance with Clause III(a) above, except that the nearest part of the course affording complete relief must be in the hazard and the ball must be dropped in the hazard or, if complete relief is impossible, on a part of the course within the hazard that affords maximum available relief; or

(ii) Under penalty of one stroke, outside the hazard as follows: the point on the course nearest to where the ball lies must be determined that (a) is not nearer the hole, (b) avoids interference as defined in Clause II and (c) is not in a hazard. The player must drop the ball within one club-length of the point so determined on a part of the course that fulfils (a), (b) and (c) above.

The ball may be cleaned when lifted under Clause III.

Note 1: If the ball lies in a hazard, nothing in this Local Rule precludes the player from proceeding under Rule 26 or Rule 28, if applicable.

Note 2: If a ball to be dropped under this Local Rule is not immediately recoverable, another ball may be substituted.

Note 3: A Committee may make a Local Rule (a) permitting or requiring a player to use a dropping zone when taking relief from a TIO or (b) permitting a player, as an additional relief option, to drop the ball on the opposite side of the TIO from the point established under Clause III, but otherwise in accordance with Clause III.

Exceptions: If a player's ball lies in front of or behind the TIO (not in, on or under the TIO), he may not obtain relief under Clause III if:

Interference by anything other than the TIO makes it clearly impracticable for him to make a stroke or, in the case of intervention, to make a stroke such that the ball could finish on a direct line to the hole;

Interference by the TIO would occur only through use of a clearly unreasonable *stroke* or an unnecessarily abnormal stance, swing or direction of play; or

In the case of intervention, it would be clearly impracticable to expect the player to be able to strike the ball far enough towards the hole to reach the TIO.

A player who is not entitled to relief due to these exceptions may, if the ball lies through the green or in a bunker, obtain relief as provided in Rule 24-2b, if applicable. If the ball lies in a water hazard, the player may lift and drop the ball in accordance with Rule 24-2b(i), except that the nearest point of relief must be in the water hazard and the ball must be dropped in the water hazard, or the player may proceed under Rule 26-1.

IV. Ball in TIO Not Found

If it is known or virtually certain that a ball that has not been found is in, on or under a TIO, a ball may be dropped under the provisions of Clause III or Clause V, if applicable. For the purpose of applying Clauses III and V, the ball is deemed to lie at the spot where it last crossed the outermost limits of the TIO (Rule 24-3).

V. Dropping Zones

If the player has interference from a TIO, the Committee may permit or require the use of a dropping zone. If the player uses a dropping zone in taking relief, he must drop the ball in the dropping zone nearest to where his ball originally lay or is deemed to lie under Clause IV (even though the nearest dropping zone may be nearer the hole).

Note: A Committee may make a Local Rule prohibiting the use of a dropping zone that is nearer the hole.

PENALTY FOR BREACH OF LOCAL RULE:
Match play – Loss of hole; Stroke play – Two strokes."

b. Temporary Power Lines and Cables

When temporary power lines, cables, or telephone lines are installed on the *course*, the following Local Rule is recommended:

"Temporary power lines, cables, telephone lines and mats covering or stanchions supporting them are obstructions:

1. If they are readily movable, Rule 24-1 applies.

2. If they are fixed or not readily movable, the player may, if the ball lies through the green or in a bunker, obtain relief as provided in Rule 24-2b. If the ball lies in a water hazard, the player may lift and drop the ball in accordance with Rule 24-2b(i), except that the nearest point of relief

must be in the water hazard and the ball must be dropped in the water hazard or the player may proceed under Rule 26.

3. If a ball strikes an elevated power line or cable, the stroke is cancelled and the player must play a ball as nearly as possible at the spot from which the original ball was played in accordance with Rule 20-5 (Making Next Stroke from Where Previous Stroke Made).

Note: Guy wires supporting a temporary immovable obstruction are part of the temporary immovable obstruction, unless the Committee, by Local Rule, declares that they are to be treated as elevated power lines or cables.

Exception: A stroke that results in a ball striking an elevated junction section of cable rising from the ground must not be replayed.

4. Grass-covered cable trenches are ground under repair, even if not marked, and Rule 25-1b applies.

PENALTY FOR BREACH OF LOCAL RULE:
Match play – Loss of hole; Stroke play – Two strokes."

8. Dropping Zones

If the *Committee* considers that it is not feasible or practicable to proceed in accordance with a Rule providing relief, it may establish dropping zones in which balls may or must be dropped when taking relief. Generally, such dropping zones should be provided as an additional relief option to those available under the Rule itself, rather than being mandatory.

Using the example of a dropping zone for a *water hazard*, when such a dropping zone is established, the following Local Rule is recommended:

"If a ball is in or it is known or virtually certain that a ball that has not been found is in the water hazard (specify location), the player may:

(i)   proceed under Rule 26; or

(ii) as an additional option, drop a ball, under penalty of one stroke, in the dropping zone.

PENALTY FOR BREACH OF LOCAL RULE:
Match play – Loss of hole; Stroke play – Two strokes."

Note: When using a dropping zone the following provisions apply regarding the dropping and re-dropping of the ball:

(a)   The player does not have to stand within the dropping zone when dropping the ball.

(b)   The dropped ball must first strike a part of the *course* within the dropping zone.

(c)   If the dropping zone is defined by a line, the line is within the dropping zone.

(d)   The dropped ball does not have to come to rest within the dropping zone.

(e)   The dropped ball must be re-dropped if it rolls and comes to rest in a position covered by Rule 20-2c(i-vi).

(f)   The dropped ball may roll nearer the *hole* than the spot where it first struck a part of the *course*, provided it comes to rest within two club-lengths of that spot and not into any of the positions covered by (e).

(g)   Subject to the provisions of (e) and (f), the dropped ball may roll and come to rest nearer the *hole* than:
- its original position or estimated position (see Rule 20-2b);
- the *nearest point of relief* or maximum available relief (Rule 24-2, 25-1 or 25-3); or
- the point where the original ball last crossed the margin of the *water hazard* or *lateral water hazard* (Rule 26-1).

9. Distance-Measuring Devices

If the *Committee* wishes to act in accordance with the Note under Rule 14-3, the following wording is recommended:

"(Specify as appropriate, e.g. In this competition, or For all play at this course, etc.), a player may obtain distance information by using a device that measures distance only. If, during a stipulated round, a player uses a distance-measuring device that is designed to gauge or measure other conditions that might affect his play (e.g. gradient, windspeed, temperature, etc.), the player is in breach of Rule 14-3, for which the penalty is disqualification, regardless of whether any such additional function is actually used."

Part C – Conditions of the Competition

Rule 33-1 provides, "The Committee must establish the conditions under which a competition is to be played." The conditions should include many matters such as method of entry, eligibility, number of rounds to be played, etc. which it is not appropriate to deal with in the Rules of Golf or this Appendix. Detailed information regarding these conditions is provided in "Decisions on the Rules of Golf" under Rule 33-1 and in "Guidance on Running a Competition".

However, there are a number of matters that might be covered in the Conditions of the Competition to which the Committee's attention is specifically drawn. These are:

1. Specification of Clubs and the Ball
The following conditions are recommended only for competitions involving expert players:

a. List of Conforming Driver Heads
On its website (www.randa.org) the R&A periodically issues a List of Conforming Driver Heads that lists driving clubheads that have been evaluated and found to conform with the Rules of Golf. If the Committee wishes to limit players to drivers that have a clubhead, identified by model and loft, that is on the List, the List should be made available and the following condition of competition used:

"Any driver the player carries must have a clubhead, identified by model and loft, that is named on the current List of Conforming Driver Heads issued the R&A.

Exception: A driver with a clubhead that was manufactured prior to 1999 nis exempt from this condition.

*PENALTY FOR CARRYING, BUT NOT MAKING STROKE WITH, CLUB OR CLUBS IN BREACH OF CONDITION:

Match play – At the conclusion of the hole at which the breach is discovered, the state of the match is adjusted by deducting one hole for each hole at which a breach occurred; maximum deduction per round – Two holes.
Stroke play – Two strokes for each hole at which any breach occurred; maximum penalty per round – Four strokes (two strokes at each of the first two holes at which any breach occurred).
Match play or stroke play – If a breach is discovered between the play of two holes, it is deemed to have been discovered during play of the next hole, and the penalty must be applied accordingly.
Bogey and par competitions – See Note 1 to Rule 32-1a.
Stableford competitions – See Note 1 to Rule 32-1b.

*Any club or clubs carried in breach of this condition must be declared out of play by the player to his opponent in match play or his marker or a fellow-competitor in stroke play immediately upon discovery that a breach has occurred. If the player fails to do so, he is disqualified.

PENALTY FOR MAKING STROKE WITH CLUB IN BREACH OF CONDITION:
Disqualification."

b. List of Conforming Golf Balls
On its website (www.randa.org) the R&A periodically issues a List of Conforming Golf Balls that lists balls that have been tested and found to conform with the Rules of Golf. If the Committee wishes to require players to play a model of golf ball on the List, the List should be made available and the following condition of competition used:

"The ball the player plays must be named on the current List of Conforming Golf Balls issued by the R&A.
PENALTY FOR BREACH OF CONDITION:
Disqualification."

c. One Ball Condition
If it is desired to prohibit changing brands and models of golf balls during a *stipulated round*, the following condition is recommended:
"Limitation on Balls Used During Round: (Note to Rule 5-1)

(i) "One Ball" Condition
During a stipulated round, the balls a player plays must be of the same brand and model as detailed by a single entry on the current List of Conforming Golf Balls.
Note: If a ball of a different brand and/or model is dropped or placed it may be lifted, without penalty, and the player must then proceed by dropping or placing a proper ball (Rule 20-6).

PENALTY FOR BREACH OF CONDITION:
Match play – At the conclusion of the hole at which the breach is discovered, the state of the match is adjusted by deducting one hole for each hole at which a breach occurred; maximum deduction per round – Two holes.
Stroke play – Two strokes for each hole at which any breach occurred; maximum penalty per round – Four strokes (two strokes at each of the first two holes at which any breach occurred).
Bogey and Par competitions – See Note 1 to Rule 32-1a.
Stableford competitions – See Note 1 to Rule 32-1b.

(ii) Procedure When Breach Discovered
When a player discovers that he has played a ball in breach of this condition, he must abandon that ball before playing from the next teeing ground and complete the round with a proper ball; otherwise, the player is disqualified. If discovery is made during play of a hole and the player elects to substitute a proper ball before completing that hole, the player must place a proper ball on the spot where the ball played in breach of the condition lay."

2. Caddie (Note to Rule 6-4)
Rule 6-4 permits a player to use a *caddie*, provided he has only one *caddie* at any one time. However, there may be circumstances where a *Committee* may wish to prohibit *caddies* or restrict a player in his choice of *caddie*, e.g. professional golfer, sibling, parent, another player in the competition, etc. In such cases, the following wording is recommended:

Use of Caddie Prohibited
"A player is prohibited from using a caddie during the stipulated round."

Restriction on Who May Serve as Caddie
"A player is prohibited from having _____ serve as his caddie during the stipulated round.
*PENALTY FOR BREACH OF CONDITION:
Match play – At the conclusion of the hole at which the breach is discovered, the state of the match is adjusted by deducting one hole for each hole at which a breach occurred; maximum deduction per round – Two holes.
Stroke play – Two strokes for each hole at which any breach occurred; maximum penalty per round – Four strokes (two strokes at each of the first two holes at which any breach occurred).
Match play or stroke play – If a breach is discovered between the play of two holes, it is deemed to have been discovered during play of the next hole, and the penalty must be applied accordingly.
Bogey and par competitions – See Note 1 to Rule 32-1a.
Stableford competitions – See Note 1 to Rule 32-1b.

*A player having a caddie in breach of this condition must immediately upon discovery that a breach has occurred ensure that he conforms with this condition for the remainder of the stipulated round. Otherwise, the player is disqualified."

3. Pace of Play (Note 2 to Rule 6-7)
The *Committee* may establish pace of play guidelines to help prevent slow play, in accordance with Note 2 to Rule 6-7.

4. Suspension of Play Due to a Dangerous Situation (Note to Rule 6-8b)
As there have been many deaths and injuries from lightning on golf courses, all clubs and sponsors of golf competitions are urged to take precautions for the protection of persons against lightning. Attention is called to Rules 6-8 and 33-2d. If the *Committee* desires to adopt the condition in the Note under Rule 6-8b, the following wording is recommended:

"When play is suspended by the Committee for a dangerous situation, if the players in a match or group are between the play of two holes, they must not resume play until the Committee has ordered a resumption of play. If they are in the process of playing a hole, they must discontinue play immediately and not resume play until the Committee has ordered a resumption of play. If a player fails to discontinue play immediately, he is disqualified, unless circumstances warrant waiving the penalty as provided in Rule 33-7.

The signal for suspending play due to a dangerous situation will be a prolonged note of the siren."

The following signals are generally used and it is recommended that all *Committees* do similarly:

Discontinue Play Immediately: One prolonged note of siren.

Discontinue Play: Three consecutive notes of siren, repeated.

Resume Play: Two short notes of siren, repeated.

5. Practice
a. General
The *Committee* may make regulations governing practice in accordance with the Note to Rule 7-1, Exception (c) to Rule 7-2, Note 2 to Rule 7 and Rule 33-2c.

b. Practice Between Holes (Note 2 to Rule 7)
If the *Committee* wishes to act in accordance with Note 2 to Rule 7-2, the following wording is recommended:

"Between the play of two holes, a player must not make any practice stroke on or near the putting green of the hole last played and must not test the surface of the putting green of the hole last played by rolling a ball.

PENALTY FOR BREACH OF CONDITION:
Match play – Loss of next hole.
Stroke play – Two strokes at the next hole.
Match play or stroke play – In the case of a breach at the last hole of the stipulated round, the player incurs the penalty at that hole."

6. Advice in Team Competitions (Note to Rule 8)
If the *Committee* wishes to act in accordance with the Note under Rule 8, the following wording is recommended:

"In accordance with the Note to Rule 8 of the Rules of Golf, each team may appoint one person (in addition to the persons from whom advice may be asked under that Rule) who may give advice to members of that team. Such person (if it is desired to insert any restriction on who may be nominated insert such restriction here) must be identified to the Committee before giving advice."

7. New Holes (Note to Rule 33-2b)
The *Committee* may provide, in accordance with the Note to Rule 33-2b, that the *holes* and *teeing grounds* for a single round of a competition being held on more than one day may be differently situated on each day.

8. Transportation
If it is desired to require players to walk in a competition, the following condition is recommended:

"Players must not ride on any form of transportation during a stipulated round unless authorised by the Committee.

*PENALTY FOR BREACH OF CONDITION:
Match play – At the conclusion of the hole at which the breach is discovered, the state of the match is adjusted by deducting one hole for each hole at which a breach occurred; maximum deduction per round – Two holes.
Stroke play – Two strokes for each hole at which any breach occurred; maximum penalty per round – Four strokes (two strokes at each of the first two holes at which any breach occurred).
Match play or stroke play – If a breach is discovered between the play of two holes, it is deemed to have been discovered during play of the next hole, and the penalty must be applied accordingly.
Bogey and par competitions – See Note 1 to Rule 32-1a.
Stableford competitions – See Note 1 to Rule 32-1b.

*Use of any unauthorised form of transportation must be discontinued immediately upon discovery that a breach has occurred. Otherwise, the player is disqualified."

9. Anti-Doping
The *Committee* may require, in the conditions of competition, that players comply with an anti-doping policy.

10. How to Decide Ties
In both match play and stroke play, a tie can be an acceptable result. However, when it is desired to have a sole winner, the *Committee* has the authority, under Rule 33-6, to determine how and when a tie is decided. The decision should be published in advance.

The *R&A* recommends:

Match Play
A match that ends all square should be played off hole by hole until one side wins a hole. The play-off should start on the hole where the match began. In a handicap match, handicap strokes should be allowed as in the stipulated round.

Stroke Play
(a) In the event of a tie in a scratch stroke play competition, a play-off is recommended. The play-off may be over 18 holes or a smaller number of holes as specified by the Committee. If that is not feasible or there is still a tie, a hole-by-hole play-off is recommended.
(b) In the event of a tie in a handicap stroke play competition, a play-off with handicaps is recommended. The play-off may be over 18 holes or a smaller number of holes as specified by the Committee. It is recommended that any such play-off consist of at least three holes.
   In competitions where the handicap stroke allocation table is not relevant, if the play-off is less than 18 holes, the percentage of 18 holes played should be applied to the players' handicaps to determine their play-off handicaps. Handicap stroke fractions of one half stroke or more should count as a full stroke and any lesser fraction should be disregarded.
   In competitions where the handicap stroke table is relevant, such as four-ball stroke play and bogey, par and Stableford competitions, handicap strokes should be taken as they were assigned for the competition using the players' respective stroke allocation table(s).
(c) If a play-off of any type is not feasible, matching score cards is recommended. The method of matching cards should be announced in advance and should also provide what will happen if this procedure does not produce a winner. An acceptable method of matching cards is to determine the winner on the basis of the

best score for the last nine holes. If the tying players have the same score for the last nine, determine the winner on the basis of the last six holes, last three holes and finally the 18th hole. If this method is used in a competition with a multiple tee start, it is recommended that the "last nine holes, last six holes, etc." is considered to be holes 10-18, 13-18, etc.

For competitions where the handicap stroke table is not relevant, such as individual stroke play, if the last nine, last six, last three holes scenario is used, one-half, one-third, one-sixth, etc. of the handicaps should be deducted from the score for those holes. In terms of the use of fractions in such deductions, the Committee should act in accordance with the recommendations of the relevant handicapping authority.

In competitions where the handicap stroke table is relevant, such as four-ball stroke play and bogey, par and Stableford competitions, handicap strokes should be taken as they were assigned for the competition, using the players' respective stroke allocation table(s).

11. Draw for Match Play
Although the draw for match play may be completely blind or certain players may be distributed through different quarters or eighths, the General Numerical Draw is recommended if matches are determined by a qualifying round.

General Numerical Draw
For purposes of determining places in the draw, ties in qualifying rounds other than those for the last qualifying place are decided by the order in which scores are returned, with the first score to be returned receiving the lowest available number, etc. If it is impossible to determine the order in which scores are returned, ties are determined by a blind draw.

UPPER HALF	LOWER HALF
64 QUALIFIERS	
1 vs. 64	2 vs. 63
32 vs. 33	31 vs. 34
16 vs. 49	15 vs. 50
17 vs. 48	18 vs. 47
8 vs. 57	7 vs. 58
25 vs. 40	26 vs. 39
9 vs. 56	10 vs. 55
24 vs. 41	23 vs. 42
4 vs. 61	3 vs. 62
29 vs. 36	30 vs. 35
13 vs. 52	14 vs. 51
20 vs. 45	19 vs. 46
5 vs. 60	6 vs. 59
28 vs. 37	27 vs. 38
12 vs. 53	11 vs. 54
21 vs. 44	22 vs. 43
32 QUALIFIERS	
1 vs. 32	2 vs. 31
16 vs. 17	15 vs. 18
8 vs. 25	7 vs. 26
9 vs. 24	10 vs. 23
4 vs. 29	3 vs. 30
13 vs. 20	14 vs. 19
5 vs. 28	6 vs. 27
12 vs. 21	11 vs. 22
16 QUALIFIERS	
1 vs. 16	2 vs.15
8 vs. 9	7 vs.10
4 vs. 13	3 vs.14
8 QUALIFIERS	
1 vs. 8	2 vs. 7
4 vs. 5	3 vs. 6

Appendices II, III and IV
Definitions
All defined terms are in italics and are listed alphabetically in the Definitions section – see pages 584–587.

The R&A reserves the right, at any time, to change the Rules relating to clubs, balls, devices and other equipment and make or change the interpretations relating to these Rules. For up to date information, please contact the R&A or refer to www.randa.org/equipmentrules.

Any design in a club, ball, device or other equipment that is not covered by the Rules, which is contrary to the purpose and intent of the Rules or that might significantly change the nature of the game, will be ruled on by the R&A.

The dimensions and limits contained in Appendices II, III and IV are given in the units by which conformance is determined. An equivalent imperial/metric conversion is also referenced for information, calculated using a conversion rate of 1 inch = 25.4 mm.

Appendix II – Design of Clubs

A player in doubt as to the conformity of a club should consult the R&A.

A manufacturer should submit to the R&A a sample of a club to be manufactured for a ruling as to whether the club conforms with the Rules.

The sample becomes the property of the R&A for reference purposes. If a manufacturer fails to submit a sample or, having submitted a sample, fails to await a ruling before manufacturing and/or marketing the club, the manufacturer assumes the risk of a ruling that the club does not conform with the Rules.

The following paragraphs prescribe general regulations for the design of clubs, together with specifications and interpretations. Further information relating to these regulations and their proper interpretation is provided in "A Guide to the Rules on Clubs and Balls".

Where a club, or part of a club, is required to meet a specification within the Rules, it must be designed and manufactured with the intention of meeting that specification.

1. Clubs
a. General
A club is an implement designed to be used for striking the ball and generally comes in three forms: woods, irons and putters distinguished by shape and intended use. A putter is a club with a loft not exceeding ten degrees designed primarily for use on the putting green.

The club must not be substantially different from the traditional and customary form and make. The club must be composed of a shaft and a head and it may also have material added to the shaft to enable the player to obtain a firm hold (see 3 below). All parts of the club must be fixed so that the club is one unit, and it must have no external attachments. Exceptions may be made for attachments that do not affect the performance of the club.

b. Adjustability
All clubs may incorporate features for weight adjustment. Other forms of adjustability may also be permitted upon evaluation by the R&A. The following requirements apply to all permissible methods of adjustment:

(i)   the adjustment cannot be readily made;

(ii) all adjustable parts are firmly fixed and there is no reasonable likelihood of them working loose during a round; and

(iii) all configurations of adjustment conform with the *Rules*.

During a *stipulated round*, the playing characteristics of a club must not be purposely changed by adjustment or by any other means (see Rule 4-2a).

c. Length

The overall length of the club must be at least 18 inches (0.457 m) and, except for putters, must not exceed 48 inches (1.219 m).

For woods and irons, the measurement of length is taken when the club is lying on a horizontal plane and the sole is set against a 60 degree plane as shown in Fig. I. The length is defined as the distance from the point of the intersection between the two planes to the top of the grip. For putters, the measurement of length is taken from the top of the grip along the axis of the shaft or a straight line extension of it to the sole of the club.

d. Alignment

When the club is in its normal address position the shaft must be so aligned so that:

(i) the projection of the straight part of the shaft on to the vertical plane through the toe and heel must diverge from the vertical by at least 10 degrees (see Fig. II). If the overall design of the club is such that the player can effectively use the club in a vertical or close-to-vertical position, the shaft may be required to diverge from the vertical in this plane by as much as 25 degrees;

(ii) the projection of the straight part of the shaft on to the vertical plane along the intended *line of play* must not diverge from the vertical by more than 20 degrees forwards or 10 degrees backwards (see Fig. III).

Except for putters, all of the heel portion of the club must lie within 0.625 inches (15.88 mm) of the plane containing the axis of the straight part of the shaft and the intended (horizontal) *line of play* (see Fig. IV).

2. Shaft

a. Straightness

The shaft must be straight from the top of the grip to a point not more than 5 inches (127 mm) above the sole, measured from the point where the shaft ceases to be straight along the axis of the bent part of the shaft and the neck and/or socket (see Fig. V).

b. Bending and Twisting Properties

At any point along its length, the shaft must:

(i) bend in such a way that the deflection is the same regardless of how the shaft is rotated about its longitudinal axis; and

(ii) twist the same amount in both directions.

c. Attachment to Clubhead

The shaft must be attached to the clubhead at the heel either directly or through a single plain neck and/or socket. The length from the top of the neck and/or socket to the sole of the club must not exceed 5 inches (127 mm), measured along the axis of, and following any bend in, the neck and/or socket (see Fig. VI).

Exception for Putters: The shaft or neck or socket of a putter may be fixed at any point in the head.

3. Grip (see Fig. VII)

The grip consists of material added to the shaft to enable the player to obtain a firm hold. The grip must be fixed to the shaft, must be straight and plain in form, must extend to the end of the shaft and must not be moulded for any part of the hands. If no material is added, that portion of the shaft designed to be held by the player must be considered the grip.

(i) For clubs other than putters the grip must Fig. VII be circular in cross-section, except that a Circular cross-section continuous, straight, Non-circular slightly raised rib may be incorporated along the cross-section (putters only) full length of the grip, and a slightly indented spiral is permitted on a wrapped grip or a replica of one.

(ii) A putter grip may have a non-circular cross-section, provided the cross-section has no concavity, is symmetrical and remains generally similar Waist throughout the length of (not permitted) the grip. (See Clause (v) overleaf). Bulge (not permitted)

(iii) The grip may be tapered but must not have any bulge or waist. Its cross-sectional dimensions measured in any direction must not exceed 1.75 inches (44.45 mm).

(iv) For clubs other than putters the axis of the grip must coincide with the axis of the shaft.

(v) A putter may have two grips provided each is circular in cross-section, the axis of each coincides with the axis of the shaft, and they are separated by at least 1.5 inches (38.1 mm).

4. Clubhead

a. Plain in Shape

The clubhead must be generally plain in shape. All parts must be rigid, structural in nature and functional. The clubhead or its parts must not be designed to resemble any other object. It is not practicable to define plain in shape precisely and comprehensively. However, features that are deemed to be in breach of this requirement and are therefore not permitted include, but are not limited to:

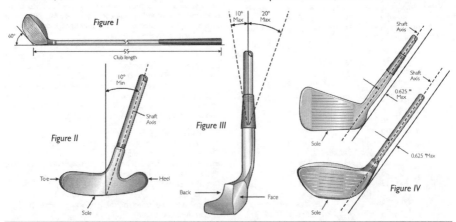

Figure I

Figure II

Figure III

Figure IV

(i) All Clubs
- holes through the ace;
- holes through the head (some exceptions may be made for putters and cavity back irons);
- features that are for the purpose of meeting dimensional specifications;
- features that extend into or ahead of the face;
- features that extend significantly above the top line of the head;
- furrows in or runners on the head that extend into the face (some exceptions may be made for putters); and
- optical or electronic devices.

(ii) Woods and Irons
- all features listed in (i) above;
- cavities in the outline of the heel and/or the toe of the head that can be viewed from above;
- severe or multiple cavities in the outline of the back of the head that can be viewed from above;
- transparent material added to the head with the intention of rendering conforming a feature that is not otherwise permitted; and
- features that extend beyond the outline of the head when viewed from above.

b. Dimensions, Volume and Moment of Inertia
(i) Woods
When the club is in a 60 degree lie angle, the dimensions of the clubhead must be such that:
- the distance from the heel to the toe of the clubhead is greater than the distance from the face to the back;
- the distance from the heel to the toe of the clubhead is not greater than 5 inches (127 mm); and
- the distance from the sole to the crown of the clubhead, including any permitted features, is not greater than 2.8 inches (71.12 mm).

These dimensions are measured on horizontal lines between vertical projections of the outermost points of:
- the heel and the toe; and
- the face and the back (see Fig. VIII, dimension A);
and on vertical lines between the horizontal projections of the outermost points of the sole and the crown (see Fig. VIII, dimension B). If the outermost point of the heel is not clearly defined, it is deemed to be 0.875 inches (22.23 mm) above the horizontal plane on which the club is lying (see Fig. VIII, dimension C).

The volume of the clubhead must not exceed 460 cubic centimetres (28.06 cubic inches), plus a tolerance of 10 cubic centimetres (0.61 cubic inches).

When the club is in a 60 degree lie angle, the moment of inertia component around the vertical axis through the clubhead's centre of gravity must not exceed 5900 g cm^2 (32.259 oz in^2), plus a test tolerance of 100 g cm^2 (0.547 oz in^2).

(ii) Irons
When the clubhead is in its normal address position, the dimensions of the head must be such that the distance from the heel to the toe is greater than the distance from the face to the back.

(iii) Putters (see Fig. IX)
When the clubhead is in its normal address position, the dimensions of the head must be such that:
- the distance from the heel to the toe is greater than the distance from the face to the back;
- the distance from the heel to the toe of the head is less than or equal to 7 inches (177.8 mm);
- the distance from the heel to the toe of the face is greater than or equal to two thirds of the distance from the face to the back of the head;
- the distance from the heel to the toe of the face is greater than or equal to half of the distance from the heel to the toe of the head; and
- the distance from the sole to the top of the head, including any permitted features, is less than or equal to 2.5 inches (63.5 mm).

For traditionally shaped heads, these dimensions will be measured on horizontal lines between vertical projections of the outermost points of:
- the heel and the toe of the head;
- the heel and the toe of the face; and
- the face and the back;
and on vertical lines between the horizontal projections of the outermost points of the sole and the top of the head.

For unusually shaped heads, the toe to heel dimension may be made at the face.

c. Spring Effect and Dynamic Properties
The design, material and/or construction of, or any treatment to, the clubhead (which includes the club face) must not:
(i) have the effect of a spring which exceeds the limit set forth in the Pendulum Test Protocol on file with the R&A; or
(ii) incorporate features or technology including, but not limited to, separate springs or spring features, that have the intent of, or the effect of, unduly influencing the clubhead's spring effect; or
(iii) unduly influence the movement of the ball.
Note: (i) above does not apply to putters.

d. Striking Faces
The clubhead must have only one striking face, except that a putter may have two such faces if their characteristics are the same, and they are opposite each other.

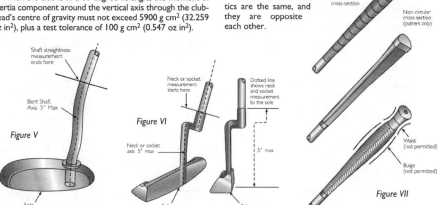

Shaft straightness measurement ends here

Bent Shaft Axis 5° Max

Figure V

Sole

Neck or socket measurement starts here

Figure VI

Neck or socket axis 5° max

Sole

Dotted line shows neck and socket measurement to the sole

5° max

Sole

Circular cross-section

Non-circular cross-section (putters only)

Waist (not permitted)

Bulge (not permitted)

Figure VII

5. Club Face
a. General
The face of the club must be hard and rigid and must not impart significantly more or less spin to the ball than a standard steel face (some exceptions may be made for putters). Except for such markings listed below, the club face must be smooth and must not have any degree of concavity.

b. Impact Area Roughness and Material
Except for markings specified in the following paragraphs, the surface roughness within the area where impact is intended (the "impact area") must not exceed that of decorative sandblasting, illustrative or of fine milling (see Fig. X).

The whole of the impact area must be of the same material (exceptions may be made for clubheads made of wood).

c. Impact Area Markings
If a club has grooves and/or punch marks in the impact area they must meet the following specifications:

(i) Grooves
- Grooves must be straight and parallel.
- Grooves must have a symmetrical cross-section and have sides which do not converge (see Fig. XI).
- *For clubs that have a loft angle greater than or equal to 25 degrees, grooves must have a plain cross-section.
- The width, spacing and cross-section of the grooves must be consistent throughout the impact area (some exceptions may be made for woods).
- The width (W) of each groove must not exceed 0.035 inches (0.9 mm), using the 30 degree method of measurement on file with the R&A.
- The depth of any punch mark must not exceed 0.040 inches (1.02 mm).
- Punch marks must not have sharp edges or raised lips.
- *For clubs that have a loft angle greater than or equal to 25 degrees, punch mark edges must be substantially in the form of a round having an effective radius which is not less than 0.010 inches (0.254 mm) when measured as shown in Figure XIII, and not greater than 0.020 inches (0.508 mm). Deviations in effective radius within 0.001 inches (0.0254 mm) are permissible.

Note 1: The groove and punch mark specifications above indicated by an asterisk (*) apply only to new models of clubs manufactured on or after 1 January 2010 and any club where the face markings have been purposely altered, for example, by re-grooving. For further information on the status of clubs available before 1 January 2010, refer to the "Equipment Search" section of www.randa.org.

Note 2: The Committee may require, in the conditions of competition, that the clubs the player carries must conform to the groove and punch mark specification above indicated by an asterisk (*). This condition is recommended only for competitions involving expert players. For further information, refer to Decision 4-1/1 in "Decisions on the Rules of Golf".

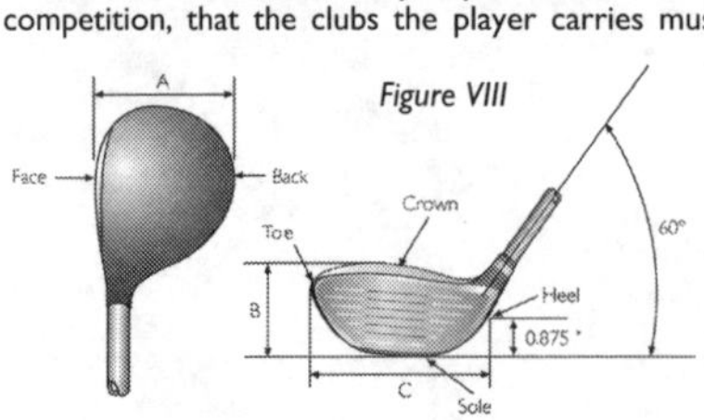

d. Decorative Markings
The centre of the impact area may be indicated by a design within the boundary of a square whose sides are 0.375 inches (9.53 mm) in length. Such a design must not unduly influence the movement of the ball. Decorative markings are permitted outside the impact area.

e. Non-Metallic Club Face Markings
The above specifications do not apply to clubheads made of wood on which the impact area of the face is of a material of hardness less than the hardness of metal and whose loft angle is 24 degrees or less, but markings which could unduly influence the movement of the ball are prohibited.

f. Putter Face Markings
Any markings on the face of a putter must not have sharp edges or raised lips. The specifications with regard to roughness, material and markings in the impact area do not apply.

Appendix III – The Ball

1. General
The ball must not be substantially different from the traditional and customary form and make. The material and construction of the ball must not be contrary to the purpose and intent of the Rules.

2. Weight
The weight of the ball must not be greater than 1.620 ounces avoirdupois (45.93 g).

3. Size
The diameter of the ball must not be less than 1.680 inches (42.67mm).

4. Spherical Symmetry
The ball must not be designed, manufactured or intentionally modified to have properties which differ from those of a spherically symmetrical ball.

5. Initial Velocity
The initial velocity of the ball must not exceed the limit specified under the conditions set forth in the Initial Velocity Standard for golf balls on file with the R&A.

6. Overall Distance Standard
The combined carry and roll of the ball, when tested on apparatus approved by the R&A, must not exceed the distance specified under the conditions set forth in the Overall Distance Standard for golf balls on file with the R&A.

Appendix IV – Devices and Other Equipment

A player in doubt as to whether use of a device or other equipment would constitute a breach of the Rules should consult the R&A.

A manufacturer should submit to the R&A a sample of a device or other equipment to be manufactured for a ruling as to whether its use during a stipulated round would cause a player to be in breach of Rule 14-3. The

Figure VIII

Face — Back

Crown

Toe

Heel

0.875"

Sole

60°

A

B

C

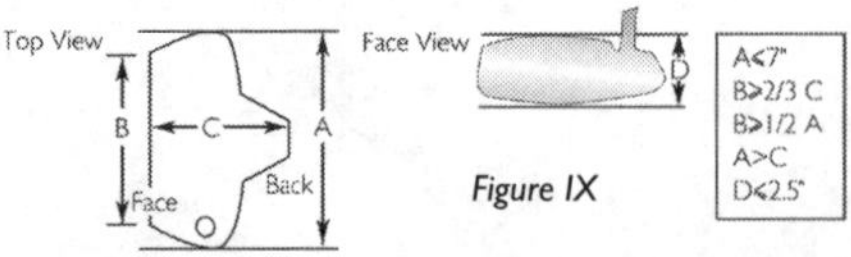

Top View

B — C — A

Face

Back

Face View

D

Figure IX

A<7"
B>2/3 C
B>1/2 A
A>C
D<2.5"

Illustrative impact area

Figure X

sample becomes the property of the *R&A* for reference purposes. If a manufacturer fails to submit a sample or, having submitted a sample, fails to await a ruling before manufacturing and/or marketing the device or other equipment, the manufacturer assumes the risk of a ruling that use of the device or other equipment would be contrary to the *Rules*.

The following paragraphs prescribe general regulations for the design of devices and other equipment, together with specifications and interpretations. They should be read in conjunction with Rule 11-1 (Teeing) and Rule 14-3 (Artificial Devices, Unusual Equipment and Unusual Use of Equipment).

1. Tees (Rule 11)

A tee is a device designed to raise the ball off the ground. A tee must not:

- be longer than 4 inches (101.6 mm);
- be designed or manufactured in such a way that it could indicate *line of play*;
- unduly influence the movement of the ball; or
- otherwise assist the player in making a *stroke* or in his play.

2. Gloves (Rule 14-3)

Gloves may be worn to assist the player in gripping the club, provided they are plain.

A "plain" glove must:

- consist of a fitted covering of the hand with a separate sheath or opening for each digit (fingers and thumb); and
- be made of smooth materials on the full palm and gripping surface of the digits.

A "plain" glove must not incorporate:

- material on the gripping surface or inside of the glove, the primary purpose of which is to provide padding or which has the effect of providing padding. Padding is defined as an area of glove material which is more than 0.025 inches (0.635 mm) thicker than the adjacent areas of the glove without the added material;

Note: Material may be added for wear resistance, moisture absorption or other functional purposes, provided it does not exceed the definition of padding (see above).

- straps to assist in preventing the club from slipping or to attach the hand to the club;
- any means of binding digits together;
- material on the glove that adheres to material on the grip;
- features, other than visual aids, designed to assist the player in placing his hands in a consistent and/or specific position on the grip;
- weight to assist the player in making a *stroke*;
- any feature that might restrict the movement of a joint; or

- any other feature that might assist the player in making a *stroke* or in his play.

3. Shoes (Rule 14-3)

Shoes that assist the player in obtaining a firm *stance* may be worn. Subject to the conditions of competition, features such as spikes on the sole are permitted, but shoes must not incorporate features:

- designed to assist the player in taking his *stance* and/or building a *stance*;
- designed to assist the player with his alignment; or
- that might otherwise assist the player in making a *stroke* or in his play.

4. Clothing (Rule 14-3)

Articles of clothing must not incorporate features:

- designed to assist the player with his alignment; or
- that might otherwise assist the player in making a *stroke* or in his play.

5. Distance-Measuring Devices (Rule 14-3)

During a *stipulated round*, the use of any distance measuring device is not permitted unless the Committee has introduced a Local Rule to that effect (see Note to Rule 14-3 and Appendix I; Part B; Section 9).

Even when the Local Rule is in effect, the device must be limited to measuring distance only. Features that would render use of the device contrary to the Local Rule include, but are not limited to:

- the gauging or measuring of slope;
- the gauging or measuring of other conditions that might affect play (e.g. wind speed or direction, or other climate-based information such as temperature, humidity, etc.);
- recommendations that might assist the player in making a *stroke* or in his play (e.g. club selection, type of shot to be played, green reading or any other advice related matter); or
- calculating the effective distance between two points based on slope or other conditions affecting shot distance.

Such non-conforming features render use of the device contrary to the *Rules*, irrespective of whether or not:

- the features can be switched off or disengaged; and
- the features are switched off or disengaged.

A multi-functional device, such as a smartphone or PDA, may be used as a distance measuring device provided it contains a distance measuring application that meets all of the above limitations (i.e. it must measure distance only). In addition, when the distance measuring application is being used, there must be no other features or applications installed on the device that, if used, would be in breach of the *Rules*, whether or not they are actually used.

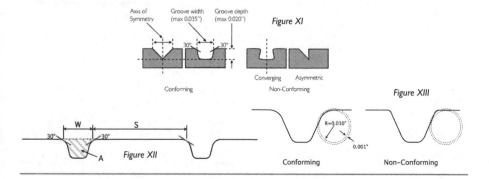

Figure XI

Figure XIII

Figure XII

Conforming · Converging / Asymmetric Non-Conforming · Conforming · Non-Conforming

RULES OF AMATEUR STATUS
As approved by R&A Rules Limited
Effective from 1st January 2012

Preamble
The *R&A* reserves the right to change the Rules of Amateur Status and to make and change the interpretations of the Rules of Amateur Status at any time. For up to date information, please contact the *R&A* or refer to www.randa.org. In the Rules of Amateur Status, the gender used in relation to any person is understood to include both genders.

Definitions
The Definitions are listed alphabetically and, in the *Rules* themselves, defined terms are in *italics*.

Amateur Golfer
An "*amateur golfer*", whether he plays competitively or recreationally, is one who plays golf for the challenge it presents, not as a profession and not for financial gain.

Committee
The "*Committee*" is the appropriate *Committee* of the *Governing Body*.

Golf Skill or Reputation
It is a matter for the *Governing Body* to decide whether a particular *amateur golfer* has *golf skill or reputation*.

Generally, an *amateur golfer* is only considered to have *golf skill* if he:
(a) has had competitive success at regional or national level or has been selected to represent his national, regional, state or county golf union or association; or
(b) competes at an elite level.

Golf reputation can only be gained through *golf skill* and such *reputation* is deemed to continue for five years after that player's *golf skill* has fallen below the standard set by the *Governing Body*.

Governing Body
The "*Governing Body*" for the administration of the Rules of Amateur Status in any country is the national golf union or association of that country.

Note: In Great Britain and Ireland, the *R&A* is the *Governing Body*.

Instruction
"*Instruction*" covers teaching the physical aspects of playing golf, i.e. the actual mechanics of swinging a golf club and hitting a golf ball.

Note: Instruction does not cover teaching the psychological aspects of the game or the etiquette or Rules of Golf.

Junior Golfer
A "*junior golfer*" is an *amateur golfer* who has not reached a specified age as determined by the *Governing Body*.

Prize Voucher
A "*prize voucher*" is a voucher, gift certificate, gift card, or the like approved by the Committee in charge of a competition for the purchase of goods or services from a professional's shop, a golf club or other retail source.

R&A
The "*R&A*" means R&A Rules Limited.

Retail Value
The "*retail value*" of a prize is the price at which the prize is generally available from a retail source at the time of the award.

Rule or Rules
The term "*Rule*" or "*Rules*" refers to the Rules of Amateur Status and their interpretations as contained in "Decisions on the Rules of Amateur Status".

Symbolic Prize
A "*symbolic prize*" is a trophy made of gold, silver, ceramic, glass or the like that is permanently and distinctively engraved.

Testimonial Award
A "*testimonial award*" is an award for notable performances or contributions to golf as distinguished from competition prizes. A *testimonial award* may not be a monetary award.

USGA
The "*USGA*" means the United States Golf Association.

Rule 1 – Amateurism
1-1. General
An amateur golfer must play the game and conduct himself in accordance with the Rules.

1-2. Amateur Status
Amateur Status is a universal condition of eligibility for playing in golf competitions as an *amateur golfer*. A person who acts contrary to the *Rules* may forfeit his amateur status and as a result will be ineligible to play in amateur competitions.

1-3. Purpose of the Rules
The purpose of the *Rules* is to maintain the distinction between amateur and professional golf and to ensure that amateur golf, which is largely self-regulating with regard to the Rules of Golf and handicapping, is free from the pressures that may follow from uncontrolled sponsorship and financial incentive.

Through appropriate limits and restrictions, the *Rules* are also intended to encourage amateur golfers to focus on the game's challenges and inherent rewards, rather than any financial gain.

1-4. Doubt as to Rules
A person who is in doubt as to whether taking a proposed course of action is permitted under the *Rules* should consult the *Governing Body*.

An organiser or sponsor of an amateur golf competition or a competition involving *amateur golfers* who is in doubt as to whether a proposal is in accordance with the *Rules* should consult the *Governing Body*.

Rule 2 – Professionalism
2-1. General
An amateur golfer must not conduct or identify himself as a professional golfer.

For the purpose of applying these *Rules*, a professional golfer is one who:
• plays the game as his profession; or
• works as a professional golfer; or
• enters a golf competition as a professional; or
• holds or retains membership of any Professional Golfers' Association (PGA); or
• holds or retains membership of a Professional Tour limited exclusively to professional golfers.

Exception: An *amateur golfer* may hold or retain a category of PGA membership, provided this category does not confer any playing rights and it is purely for administrative purposes.

Note 1: An *amateur golfer* may enquire as to his likely prospects as a professional golfer, including applying unsuccessfully for the position of a professional golfer, and he may work in a professional's shop and receive payment or compensation, provided he does not infringe the *Rules* in any other way.

Note 2: If an *amateur golfer* must compete in one or more qualifying competitions in order to be eligible for membership of a Professional Tour, he may enter and play in such qualifying competitions without forfeiting his Amateur Status, provided, in advance of play and in writing, he waives his right to any prize money in the competition.

2-2. Contracts and Agreements
(a) National Golf Unions or Associations
An *amateur golfer* may enter into a contract and/or an agreement with his national golf union or association, provided that he does not obtain payment, compensation or any financial gain, directly or indirectly, whilst still an *amateur golfer*, except as otherwise provided in the *Rules*.

(b) Professional Agents, Sponsors and Other Third Parties
An *amateur golfer* may enter into a contract and/or an agreement with a third party (including but not limited to a professional agent or a sponsor), provided:
(i) the golfer is at least 18 years of age,
(ii) the contract or agreement is solely in relation to the golfer's future as a professional golfer and does not stipulate playing in certain amateur or professional events as an *amateur golfer*, and
(iii) except as otherwise provided in the *Rules*, the *amateur golfer* does not obtain payment, compensation or any financial gain, directly or indirectly, whilst still an *amateur golfer*.

Exception: In special individual circumstances, an *amateur golfer* under the age of 18 may apply to the *Governing Body* to be allowed to enter into such a contract, provided it is of no more than 12 months duration and it is non-renewable.

Note 1: An *amateur golfer* is advised to consult the *Governing Body* prior to signing any such third party contract and/or agreement to ensure that it complies with the *Rules*.

Note 2: If an *amateur golfer* is in receipt of an educational golf scholarship (see Rule 6-5), or may apply for such a scholarship in the future, he is advised to contact the national body regulating such scholarships and/or the relevant educational institution to ensure that any third party contracts and/ or agreements are allowable under the applicable scholarship regulations.

Rule 3 – Prizes
3-1. Playing for Prize Money
An *amateur golfer* must not play golf for prize money or its equivalent in a match, competition or exhibition.

However, an *amateur golfer* may participate in a golf match, competition or exhibition where prize money or its equivalent is offered, provided that prior to participation he waives his right to accept prize money in that event.

Exception: Where prize money is offered for a hole-in-one made while playing a round of golf, an *amateur golfer* is not required to waive his right to accept that prize money prior to participation (see Rule 3-2b).

(Conduct contrary to the purpose of the Rules – see Rule 7-2)

(Policy on gambling – see Appendix)

3-2. Prize Limits
a. General
An *amateur golfer* must not accept a prize (other than a symbolic prize) or prize voucher of retail value in excess of £500 or the equivalent, or such a lesser figure as may be decided by the *Governing Body*. This limit applies to the total prizes or *prize vouchers* received by an *amateur golfer* in any one competition or series of competitions.

Exception: Hole-in-one prizes – see Rule 3-2b.

Note 1: The prize limits apply to any form of golf competition, whether on a golf course, driving range or golf simulator, including nearest the hole and longest drive competitions.

Note 2: The responsibility to prove the *retail value* of a particular prize rests with the Committee in charge of the competition.

Note 3: It is recommended that the total value of prizes in a gross competition, or each division of a handicap competition, should not exceed twice the prescribed limit in an 18-hole competition, three times in a 36-hole competition, five times in a 54-hole competition and six times in a 72-hole competition.

b. Hole-in-One Prizes
An *amateur golfer* may accept a prize in excess of the limit in Rule 3-2a, including a cash prize, for a hole-in-one made while playing a round of golf.

Note: The hole-in-one must be made during a round of golf and be incidental to that round. Separate multiple-entry contests, contests conducted other than on a golf course (e.g. on a driving range or golf simulator) and putting contests do not qualify under this provision and are subject to the restrictions and limits in Rules 3-1 and 3-2a.

3-3. Testimonial Awards
a. General
An *amateur golfer* must not accept a *testimonial award* of *retail value* in excess of the limits prescribed in Rule 3-2.

b. Multiple Awards
An *amateur golfer* may accept more than one testimonial award from different donors, even though their total retail value exceeds the prescribed limit, provided they are not presented so as to evade the limit for a single award.

Rule 4 – Expenses
4-1. General
Except as provided in the Rules, an *amateur golfer* must not accept expenses, in money or otherwise, from any source to play in a golf competition or exhibition.

4-2. Receipt of Competition Expenses
An *amateur golfer* may receive reasonable competition expenses, not exceeding the actual expenses incurred, to play in a golf competition or exhibition as prescribed in clauses a-g of this Rule.

If an *amateur golfer* is in receipt of an educational golf scholarship (see Rule 6-5), or may apply for such a scholarship in the future, he is advised to contact the national body regulating such scholarships and/or the relevant educational institution to ensure that any competition expenses are allowable under the applicable scholarship regulations.

a. Family Support
An *amateur golfer* may receive expenses from a member of his family or a legal guardian.

b. Junior Golfers
A *junior golfer* may receive expenses when competing in a competition limited exclusively to *junior golfers*.

Note: If a competition is not limited exclusively to *junior golfers*, a *junior golfer* may receive expenses when competing in that competition, as prescribed in Rule 4-2c.

c. Individual Events
An *amateur golfer* may receive expenses when competing in individual events provided he complies with the following provisions:
(i) Where the competition is to take place in the player's own country the expenses must be approved by and

paid through the player's national, regional, state or county golf union or association, or with the approval of such body, may be paid by the player's golf club.

(ii) Where the competition is to take place in another country the expenses must be approved by and paid through the player's national, regional, state or county golf union or association or, subject to the approval of the player's national union or association, paid by the body controlling golf in the territory in which he is competing.

The *Governing Body* may limit the receipt of expenses to a specific number of competitive days in any one calendar year and an *amateur golfer* must not exceed any such limit. In such a case, the expenses are deemed to include reasonable travel time and practice days in connection with the competitive days.

Exception: An *amateur golfer* must not receive expenses, directly or indirectly, from a professional agent (see Rule 2-2) or any other similar source as may be determined by the *Governing Body*.

Note: Except as provided in the *Rules*, an *amateur golfer* of *golf skill or reputation* must not promote or advertise the source of any expenses received (see Rule 6-2).

d. Team Events

An *amateur golfer*, may receive expenses when he is representing:

* his country,
* his regional, state or county golf union or association,
* his golf club,
* his business or industry, or
* a similar body

in a team competition, practice session or training camp.

Note 1: A "similar body" includes a recognised educational institution or military service.

Note 2: Unless otherwise stated, the expenses must be paid by the body that the *amateur golfer* is representing or the body controlling golf in the country in which he is competing.

e. Invitation Unrelated to Golf Skill

An *amateur golfer* who is invited for reasons unrelated to *golf skill* (e.g. a celebrity, a business associate or customer) to take part in a golf event may receive expenses.

f. Exhibitions

An *amateur golfer* who is participating in an exhibition in aid of a recognised charity may receive expenses, provided that the exhibition is not run in connection with another golfing event in which the player is competing.

g. Sponsored Handicap Competitions

An *amateur golfer* may receive expenses when competing in a sponsored handicap competition, provided the competition has been approved as follows:

(i) Where the competition is to take place in the player's own country, the annual approval of the *Governing Body* must first be obtained in advance by the sponsor; and

(ii) Where the competition is to take place in more than one country or involves golfers from another country, the annual approval of each *Governing Body* must first be obtained in advance by the sponsor. The application for this approval should be sent to the *Governing Body* in the country where the competition commences.

4-3. Subsistence Expenses

An *amateur golfer* may receive reasonable subsistence expenses, not exceeding actual expenses incurred, to assist with general living costs, provided the expenses are approved by and paid through the player's national golf union or association.

In determining whether such subsistence expenses are necessary and/ or appropriate, the national golf union or association, which has the sole discretion in the approval of such expenses, should consider, among other factors, applicable socio-economic conditions.

Exception: An *amateur golfer* must not receive subsistence expenses, directly or indirectly, from a professional agent (see Rule 2-2) or any other similar source as may be determined by the *Governing Body*.

Rule 5 – Instruction

5-1. General

Except as provided in the Rules, an *amateur golfer* must not receive payment or compensation, directly or indirectly, for giving golf *instruction*.

5-2. Where Payment Permitted
a. Schools, Colleges, Camps, etc.

An *amateur golfer* who is (i) an employee of an educational institution or system or (ii) a counsellor at a camp or other similar organised programme, may receive payment or compensation for golf instruction to students in the institution, system or camp, provided that the total time devoted to such instruction comprises less than 50 percent of the time spent in the performance of all duties as such an employee or counsellor.

b. Approved Programmes

An *amateur golfer* may receive expenses, payment or compensation for giving golf *instruction* as part of a programme that has been approved in advance by the *Governing Body*.

5-3. Instruction in Writing

An *amateur golfer* may receive payment or compensation for golf *instruction* in writing, provided his ability or reputation as a golfer was not a major factor in his employment or in the commission or sale of his work.

Rule 6 – Use of Golf Skill or Reputation

The following regulations under Rule 6 only apply to *amateur golfers* of *golf skill* or *reputation*.

6-1. General

Except as provided in the *Rules*, an *amateur golfer* of *golf skill* or *reputation* must not use that skill or reputation for any financial gain.

6-2. Promotion, Advertising and Sales

An *amateur golfer* of *golf skill* or *reputation* must not use that skill or reputation to obtain payment, compensation, personal benefit or any financial gain, directly or indirectly, for (i) promoting, advertising or selling anything, or (ii) allowing his name or likeness to be used by a third party for the promotion, advertisement or sale of anything.

Exception: An *amateur golfer* of *golf skill or reputation* may allow his name or likeness to be used to promote:

(a) his national, regional, state or county golf union or association; or

(b) a recognised charity (or similar good cause); or

(c) subject to the permission of his national golf union or association, any golf competition or other event that is considered to be in the best interests of, or would contribute to the development of, the game.

The *amateur golfer* must not obtain any payment, compensation or financial gain, directly or indirectly, for allowing his name or likeness to be used in these ways.

Note 1: An *amateur golfer* of *golf skill or reputation* may accept golf equipment from anyone dealing in such equipment provided no advertising is involved.

Note 2: Limited name and logo recognition is allowed on golf equipment and clothing. Further information relating to this Note and its proper interpretation is provided in "Decisions on the Rules of Amateur Status".

6-3. Personal Appearance

An *amateur golfer* of *golf skill* or *reputation* must not use that skill or reputation to obtain payment, compensation, personal benefit or any financial gain, directly or indirectly, for a personal appearance.

Exception: An *amateur golfer* of *golf skill* or *reputation* may receive actual expenses in connection with a personal appearance provided no golf competition or exhibition is involved.

6-4. Broadcasting and Writing

An *amateur golfer* of *golf skill* or *reputation* may receive payment, compensation, personal benefit or financial gain from broadcasting or writing provided:

(a) the broadcasting or writing is part of his primary occupation or career and golf *instruction* is not included (Rule 5); or

(b) if the broadcasting or writing is on a part-time basis, the player is actually the author of the commentary, articles or books and golf *instruction* is not included.

Note: An *amateur golfer* of *golf skill* or *reputation* must not promote or advertise anything within the commentary, article or books (see Rule 6-2).

6-5. Educational Grants, Scholarships and Bursaries

An *amateur golfer* of *golf skill* or *reputation* may accept the benefits of an educational grant, scholarship or bursary, the terms and conditions of which have been approved by the *Governing Body*.

A *Governing Body* may pre-approve the terms and conditions of educational grants, scholarships and bursaries, such as those that comply with the regulations of the National Collegiate Athletic Association (NCAA) in the United States of America, or other similar organisations governing athletes at educational institutions.

If an *amateur golfer* is in receipt of an educational golf scholarship, or may apply for such a scholarship in the future, he is advised to contact the national body regulating such scholarships and/or the relevant educational institution to ensure that any third party contracts and/or agreements (Rule 2-2b) or competition expenses (Rule 4-2) are allowable under the applicable scholarship regulations.

6-6. Membership

An *amateur golfer* of *golf skill* or *reputation* may accept an offer of membership of a Golf Club or privileges at a golf course, without full payment for the class of membership or privilege, unless such an offer is made as an inducement to play for that Club or course.

Rule 7 – Other Conduct Incompatible with Amateurism

7-1. Conduct Detrimental to Amateurism

An *amateur golfer* must not act in a manner that is detrimental to the best interests of the amateur game.

7-2. Conduct Contrary to the Purpose of the Rules

An *amateur golfer* must not take any action, including actions relating to golf gambling, that is contrary to the purpose of the *Rules*.

(Policy on gambling – see Appendix)

Rule 8 – Procedure for Enforcement of the Rules

8-1. Decision on a Breach

If a possible breach of the *Rules* by a person claiming to be an *amateur golfer* comes to the attention of the *Committee*, it is a matter for the *Committee* to decide whether a breach has occurred. Each case will be investigated to the extent deemed appropriate by the *Committee* and considered on its merits. The decision of the *Committee* is final, subject to an appeal as provided in these *Rules*.

8-2. Enforcement

Upon a decision that a person has breached the *Rules*, the *Committee* may declare the Amateur Status of the person forfeited or require the person to refrain or desist from specified actions as a condition of retaining his Amateur Status.

The *Committee* should notify the person and may notify any interested golf union or association of any action taken under Rule 8-2.

8-3. Appeals Procedure

Each *Governing Body* should establish a process or procedure through which any decision concerning enforcement of these *Rules* may be appealed by the person affected.

Rule 9 – Reinstatement of Amateur Status

9-1. General

The *Committee* has the sole authority to:

- reinstate to Amateur Status a professional golfer and/or other persons who have infringed the *Rules*,
- prescribe a waiting period necessary for reinstatement, or
- deny reinstatement, subject to an appeal as provided in the *Rules*.

9-2. Applications for Reinstatement

Each application for reinstatement will be considered on its merits, with consideration normally being given to the following principles:

a. Awaiting Reinstatement

Amateur and professional golf are two distinct forms of the game which provide different opportunities and neither benefits if the process of changing status from professional to amateur is too easy. Furthermore, there needs to be a deterrent against all breaches of the *Rules*. Therefore, an applicant for reinstatement to Amateur Status must undergo a period awaiting reinstatement as prescribed by the *Committee*.

The period awaiting reinstatement generally starts from the date of the person's last breach of the *Rules* unless the *Committee* decides that it starts from either (a) the date when the person's last breach became known to the *Committee*, or (b) such other date determined by the *Committee*.

b. Period Awaiting Reinstatement
(i) Professionalism

Generally, the period awaiting reinstatement is related to the period the person was in breach of the *Rules*. However, no applicant is normally eligible for reinstatement until he has conducted himself in accordance with the *Rules* for a period of at least one year.

It is recommended that the following guidelines on periods awaiting reinstatement be applied by the *Committee*:

Period of Breach	Period Awaiting Reinstatement:
under 5 years	1 year
5 years or more	2 years

However, the period may be extended if the applicant has played extensively for prize money, regardless of performance. In all cases, the *Committee* reserves the right to extend or to shorten the period awaiting reinstatement.

(ii) Other Breaches of the Rules

A period awaiting reinstatement of one year will normally be required. However, the period may be extended if the breach is considered serious.

c. Number of Reinstatements

A person is not normally eligible to be reinstated more than twice.

d. Players of National Prominence

A player of national prominence who has been in breach of the *Rules* for more than five years is not normally eligible for reinstatement.

e. Status While Awaiting Reinstatement

An applicant for reinstatement must comply with these *Rules*, as they apply to an *amateur golfer*, during his period awaiting reinstatement.

An applicant for reinstatement is not eligible to enter competitions as an *amateur golfer*. However, he may enter competitions and win a prize solely among members of a Club where he is a member, subject to the approval of the Club. He must not represent such a Club against other Clubs unless with the approval of the Clubs in the competition and/or the organising Committee.

An applicant for reinstatement may enter competitions that are not limited to *amateur golfers*, subject to the conditions of competition, without prejudicing his application, provided he does so as an applicant for reinstatement. He must waive his right to any prize money offered in the competition and must not accept any prize reserved for an *amateur golfer* (Rule 3-1).

9-3. Procedure for Applications

Each application for reinstatement must be submitted to the *Committee*, in accordance with such procedures as may be laid down and including such information as the *Committee* may require.

9-4. Appeals Procedure

Each *Governing Body* should establish a process or procedure through which any decision concerning reinstatement of Amateur Status may be appealed by the person affected.

Rule 10 – Committee Decision

10-1. Committee's Decision

The *Committee's* decision is final, subject to an appeal as provided in Rules 8-3 and 9-4.

10-2. Doubt as to Rules

If the *Committee* of a *Governing Body* considers the case to be doubtful or not covered by the *Rules*, it may, prior to making its decision, consult with the Amateur Status Committee of the R&A.

Appendix – Policy of Gambling

General

An "amateur golfer", whether he plays competitively or recreationally, is one who plays golf for the challenge it presents, not as a profession and not for financial gain.

Excessive financial incentive in amateur golf, which can result from some forms of gambling or wagering, could give rise to abuse of the *Rules* both in play and in manipulation

of handicaps to the detriment of the integrity of the game.

There is a distinction between playing for prize money (Rule 3-1), gambling or wagering that is contrary to the purpose of the *Rules* (Rule 7-2), and forms of gambling or wagering that do not, of themselves, breach the *Rules*. An *amateur golfer* or a Committee in charge of a competition where *amateur golfers* are competing should consult with the *Governing Body* if in any doubt as to the application of the *Rules*. In the absence of such guidance, it is recommended that no cash prizes be awarded so as to ensure that the *Rules* are upheld.

Acceptable Forms of Gambling

There is no objection to informal gambling or wagering among individual golfers or teams of golfers when it is incidental to the game. It is not practicable to define informal gambling or wagering precisely, but features that would be consistent with such gambling or wagering include:

- the players in general know each other;
- participation in the gambling or wagering is optional and is limited to the players;
- the sole source of all money won by the players is advanced by the players; and
- the amount of money involved is not generally considered to be excessive.

Therefore, informal gambling or wagering is acceptable provided the primary purpose is the playing of the game for enjoyment, not for financial gain.

Unacceptable Forms of Gambling

Other forms of gambling or wagering where there is a requirement for players to participate (e.g. compulsory sweepstakes) or that have the potential to involve considerable sums of money (e.g. calcuttas and auction sweepstakes – where players or teams are sold by auction) are not approved.

Otherwise, it is difficult to define unacceptable forms of gambling or wagering precisely, but features that would be consistent with such gambling or wagering include:

- participation in the gambling or wagering is open to non-players; and
- the amount of money involved is generally considered to be excessive.

An *amateur golfer's* participation in gambling or wagering that is not approved may be considered contrary to the purpose of the *Rules* (Rule 7-2) and may endanger his Amateur Status.

Furthermore, organised events designed or promoted to create cash prizes are not permitted. Golfers participating in such events without first irrevocably waiving their right to prize money are deemed to be playing for prize money, in breach of Rule 3-1.

Note: The Rules of Amateur Status do not apply to betting or gambling by *amateur golfers* on the results of a competition limited to or specifically organised for professional golfers.

INDEX

The Rules of Golf are here indexed according to the
pertinant rule number, definition or appendix that has gone before.

Items marked with as asterisk refer to Rules of Amateur Status

The R&A and the modern game

What is The R&A?

The R&A takes its name from The Royal and Ancient Golf Club of St Andrews, which traces its origins back over 250 years. Although the golf club still exists to meet the needs of more than 2,000 international members, The R&A has grown apart to focus on its role as golf's world governance and development body and organiser of The Open Championship.

The R&A is golf's world rules and development body and organiser of The Open Championship. It operates with the consent of 141 national and international amateur and professional organisations from almost 126 countries and on behalf of an estimated 30 million golfers in Europe, Africa, Asia Pacific and the Americas.

The R&A and the United States Golf Association have jointly issued the Rules of Golf since 1952. The USGA is the governing body for the Rules of Golf in the United States and Mexico.

By making The Open Championship one of the world's great sporting events and an outstanding commercial success, The R&A is able to invest a substantial annual surplus for the development of the game through The R&A Foundation. The Foundation is the charitable body that channels money from The Open directly into grassroots development projects around the world.

Particular emphasis is placed on the encouragement of junior golf, on the development of the game in emerging golfing nations, on coaching and the provision of more accessible courses and improved practice facilities.

The R&A also provides best practice guidance on all aspects of golf course management, to help golf grow throughout the world in a commercially and environmentally sustainable way.

Useful links

www.randa.org
www.opengolf.com
www.bestcourseforgolf.org
www.wagr.randa.org
www.theroyalandancientgolfclub.org
www.britishgolfmuseum.co.uk

The future of the game

The R&A is committed to promoting and developing golf both nationally and internationally. Two factors make this possible. One is the annual surplus from The Open Championship and the other is The R&A's position of global influence. Combined, these give scope for the worldwide advancement of golf.

A major priority for The R&A is providing funding for training and the development of the game around the world. In recent years, a determined effort has been directed towards financing development in countries where golf is a relatively new sport. Major contributions are made to women's golf and the Golf Foundation receives substantial help to assist with its work of introducing young people to the game.

The R&A is highly conscious of the need and its obligation to serve the game worldwide. Since 1997 The R&A has provided financial support towards the African VI Tournament. The South American Men's and Women's Amateur Team Championship are also supported as are the equivalent events in the Asia-Pacific region.

The R&A Foundation supports university golf throughout Great Britain and Ireland with the aim of encouraging students to remain competitive while completing their formal education.

The R&A takes a lead in and offers advice on all aspects of golf course management worldwide, with developments in greenkeeping and environmental issues foremost among its concerns. Again, it is particularly concerned with offering assistance in countries where golf is still in its infancy.

Funding the future

Most of The R&A's funding comes from The Open Championship. Worldwide television rights are an important source of income, along with spectator ticket sales, catering, merchandising, corporate hospitality and sponsorship.

The Open Championship is broadcast throughout the world. Television coverage of The Open has a global household reach of 400 million and is delivered by 46 broadcasters in 193 territories. It is the world's largest annual televised sports event alongside Wimbledon.

In recent years The R&A has been at the forefront of modern technology, extending its range of activities to Digital Media rights, whereby income is generated through the internet, and mobile communication devices. These, combined with merchandising, licensing and publishing, increase the ways in which The R&A is able to provide financial assistance for the development of golf throughout the world.

In 2004, Rolex began to sponsor the publication and distribution of the Rules of Golf book, ensuring that golfers worldwide can have a copy of the current Rules of Golf free of charge. Over 4 million copies are distributed and the book is available in over 30 different languages.

Doosan, HSBC, Mercedes, Nikon and Rolex are patrons of the Open Championship. Through their association with The Open, the Patrons provide additional income for the funding of golf development projects worldwide.

The rules of the game

In almost every country where the game is played, the rules followed are those set by The R&A. The exceptions are the USA and Mexico, where the code is set by the United States Golf Association, and Canada, which is self-governing but affiliated to The R&A. There are 141 associations and unions affiliated to The R&A.

The R&A is responsible for the Rules of Golf, the rules affecting equipment standards and the Rules of Amateur Status. The Rules of Golf Committee reviews the Rules of Golf and interprets and makes decisions on the playing Rules. The Equipment Standards Committee interprets and gives decisions on those rules that deal with the form and make of golf clubs and the specifications of the ball. The Amateur Status Committee reviews, interprets and amends the Rules of Amateur Status. All work closely with the equivalent committees of the USGA.

To meet the needs of golfers worldwide the Rules of Golf are published in over 30 languages and in audio CD format. Supplementing these are the biennial decisions on the Rules of Golf. Each volume contains over 1,100 decisions. Together, these help to ensure a consistent interpretation of the Rules throughout the world. The R&A also publish modifications of the Rules for golfers with disabilities.

The Rules Department answers thousands of queries from golf clubs, associations and professional tours on the playing Rules, the equipment Rules and on the Amateur Code.

Rules education is a priority for The R&A. Each year a Referees School is held in St Andrews, and overseas Rules Schools are held on a regular basis. Since the beginning of 2001, countries visited include

Argentina, Brazil, the Dominican Republic, Ecuador, Germany, Guatemala, Japan, Luxembourg, New Zealand, Poland, Russia, Singapore, South Africa, South Korea, Thailand and the United Arab Emirates. In 2010, schools were also held in Costa Rica, Columbia and Kenya.

R&A Championships

The R&A promotes, organises and controls a number of championships and matches at both national and international level. Of these events, the biggest and most prestigious is The Open Championship.

In 1920, The Royal and Ancient Golf Club took over the running of the Amateur and Open Championships. The Boys Amateur Championship followed in 1948 and the British Youths Open Championship in 1963. The British Mid-Amateur Championship replaced the Youths event in 1995 but was discontinued in 2007.

In 1969, the Club introduced the Seniors Open Amateur Championship for players aged 55 and over. In 1991, it became involved with and now organises The Senior Open Championship, in conjunction with the PGA European Seniors Tour. The Junior Open Championship, first played in 1994, came under The R&A umbrella in 2000.

The Walker Cup, which is the most famous of the international amateur matches, is played between teams from Great Britain & Ireland and the United States and is run jointly with the United States Golf Association.

The R&A also administers the St Andrews Trophy, inaugurated in 1956, and the Jacques Leglise Trophy, an event for boys. Both are played between teams from Great Britain & Ireland and the Continent of Europe. When these matches are played in Europe, they are organised by the European Golf Association.

The Great Britain and Ireland team selection for the Walker Cup and the St Andrews Trophy is undertaken by The R&A.

In 2004, The Royal and Ancient Golf Club transferred to The R&A the responsibilities and authority of the Club for all aspects of running championships and matches at national and international level.

Governing Organisations – Professional Golf

The Professional Golfers' Association (PGA)

The PGA was founded in 1901 and is the oldest PGA in the world. It has continued to develop steadily over the years; in the mid seventies major re-structuring of the Association took place with the development of two separate divisions. The administrative operation moved to The Belfry in 1977 to advance and develop the services available to club professionals, and shortly afterwards the Tournament Division established a new base at the Wentworth Club.

In 1984 it was decided that the interests of the members of each division would be best served by forming two separate organisations and on 1st January 1985 The Professional Golfers' Association and the European Tour became independent of each other.

The PGA's activities include training and further education of assistants and members and the organisation of tournaments at national level. National Headquarters is also the administrative base to accounts, marketing, media and the commercial activities of the Association.

There are seven regional headquarters located throughout Great Britain and Ireland and each region organises its own tournaments.

Classes of Membership

Class AA
Only Professionals who have a PGA Qualification; have been qualified for at least three years, and who have engaged in (at least) the minimum amount of proessional development are recognised as class 'AA'.

Class A
A class 'A' status designation is carried by PGA Professionals who have a PGA Qualification and who have either been qualified for less than three years, and/or who have not engaged in sufficient recognised professional devlopment at the time of the annual re-grading of PGA membership status.

Class TP1
Must be a current full member of either the European Tour, Ladies' European Tour, European Seniors' Tour or any tour belonging to the International Federation of PGA Tours subject to the relevant categories as defined by the Association at the time.

Class TP2
Must be a current full member of either the European Tour, Ladies' European Tour or European Seniors' Tour subject to the relevant categories as defined by the Association at the time.

Class TP3
Must be a member of the PGA Europro Tour finishing 1–80 in the immediately preceding year's Order of Merit.

Class TP4
Must be qualified as an active playing Member within PGA Tournaments where Tournament entry criteria so permit and be in the top 100 players in the preceding year home region Order of Merit.

Life Member
Must be a member of the Association who has been recommended by the Board of Directors to Special General Meeting of the Association for appointment as a Life Member and whose recommendation has been approved.

Honorary Member
Must be a member who in the opinion of the Executive Committee through their past or continuing membership and contribution to the Association justifies retaining full privileges of membership as an Honorary Member.

Inactive Member
Shall have been a member for a continuous period of 10 years and no longer engaged in a direct or commercial capacity in the golf industry.

Retired Member
Shall have been a member for a periods of at least 35 years and not be engaged in a direct or commercial capacity in the golf industry.

As well as the class 'A/AA' status, PGA Members are also differentiated through formal recognition of their previous exierence, further education, achievements, accreditation, etc. Once qualified, and with a minimum length of time served in the golf industry, a Member can submit an application to be awarded any one of four additional titles. They rank hierarchically from PGA Advanced Professional up to PGA Master Professional – as below:

Advanced Professional
Qualified members for a minimum of five years. Over a long period of time have demonstrated a strong desire to improve understanding and knowledge. Through attendance at courses, seminars and by taking qualifications related to golf, have

shown commitment and willingness to develop self. Written articles and/or delivered seminars. Recognised by peers as having a high level of skill and knowledge, or qualified through the PGA Advanced Diploma programme.

Fellow Professional

Qualified members for a minimum of eight years. Consistently demonstrated an ability to work at a very high level with contribution to: development of players at different levels and/or a very strong reputation as an ethical business person who has established an extensive business that has benefited the golfing community and/or a strong reputation in equipment technology and/or repairs, which has enhanced the reputations of golf professionals and/or has written articles/books and presented at conferences.

Advanced Fellow Professional

Qualified members for a minimum of ten years. Very strong national – possibly international reputation in one or more areas – coaching, course design, business, retail, equipment technology. Someone who has demonstrated strong leadership and has enhanced the world of golf and may have coached at the highest level or developed a programme method that has enabled ordinary players to play the game and/or designed a number of recognised golf courses and/or developed a strong golf business that has brought benefits to golf and golfers and/or innovative in the retail world with a strong sense of business ethics and/or designed/developed/improved some aspect of equipment (to include training aids or computer software) that has benefited a wide range of people in golf and/or a golf writer whose work has contributed strongly to the understanding and development of golf performance and/or a charity worker whose contribution has helped improve the lot of the disadvantaged through golf or in golf and/or written a number of books, articles and presented at prestigious conferences and seminars.

Master Professional

Qualified member for a minimum of fifteen years. Held in high national or international esteem. Made a significant contribution to the development of golf as a player, coach, administrator or course designer. Someone who has left their mark at conferences and/or through books, articles or videos.

Tel 01675 470333   *Fax* 01675 477888

The Professional Golfers' Associations of Europe

The PGAs of Europe is as an Association of National PGAs (31 European and 7 International) with a collective membership in excess of 21,000 golf professionals whose objective is to represent, promote and advise PGAs on a business-to-business basis. At all times striving to raise standards and opportunities in the education and employment of golf professionals while also representing member countries in dealing with influential bodies and governments regarding the promotion of the game and the interests of PGA professionals.

The PGAs of Europe guides the administration of the professional game throughout the continent and sometimes beyond in order to ensure excellence in the delivery of those services necessary to guarantee highly qualified, highly skilled PGA Professionals equipped to lead the advancement of the game around the world.

It is also a partner in the Ryder Cup with specific responsibility for the management of the Ryder Cup European Development Trust and is widely acknowledged as a lead body in the delivery of golf development expertise on a global basis through its collaboration the The R&A in implementing its Golf Development Programme.

The purpose of the PGAs of Europe is to:

(1) Unify and improve standards of education and qualification;

(2) Advise and assist golf professionals to achieve properly rewarded employment;

(3) Provide relevant playing opportunities;

(4) Be the central point of advice, information and support;

(5) Be a respected link with other golfing bodies throughout Europe and the rest of the world – all for the benefit of its members and the enhancement of the sport.

Tel 01675 477899   *Fax* 01675 4778980

European Tour

The European Tour offers Membership rights and playing opportunities for those players who have earned an Exempt Category on the Tour. To be eligible to become a Full Member of The European Tour for the first time a player must have either graduated from the European Challenge Tour by virtue of his performance in the previous season, gained one of the exemptions available at the annually competed European Tour Qualifying School or won a European Tour/Challenge Tour sanctioned event.

Full details are available from The Wentworth Headquarters:

Tel +44 1344 840400   *Fax* +44 1344 840500

Website www.europeantour.com

Ladies' European Tour

The Ladies European Tour was founded in 1978 to further the development of women's professional golf with a focus in Europe and its membership is open to all nationalities. A qualifying school is held annually and an amateur wishing to participate must have a handicap of 3 or less. Full details can be obtained from the Tour Headquarters at Buckinghamshire Golf Club.

Tel 01895 831028   *Fax* 01895 832301

Governing Organisations – Amateur Golf

Home Unions

The English Golf Union

The English Golf Union was founded in 1924 and embraces 35 County Unions with 1,949 affiliated clubs. Its objects are:

(1) To further the interests of Amateur Golf in England.

(2) To assist in maintaining a uniform system of handicapping.

(3) To arrange an English Championship; an English Strokeplay Championship; an English County Championship, International and other Matches and Competitions.

(4) To cooperate with The Royal and Ancient Golf Club of St Andrews and the Council of National Golf Unions.

(5) To cooperate with other National Golf Unions and Associations in such manner as may be decided.

Tel 01526 354500   *Fax* 01526 354020

The previously separate English Golf Union and English Women's Golf Association have merged and from January 2012 became one governing body entitled England Golf which will represent all amateur golfers in England. For further information, see pages 692 and 696.

The Scottish Golf Union

The Scottish Golf Union, the governing body for men's golf in Scotland, is dedicated to inspiring people to play golf and to developing and sustaining the game throughout the country. Its over-arching intention is to make golf available to everyone, in an environment that will actively encourage players to fulfil their potential.

Its aims are to:

• **Grow the game** – work with others to develop and grow golf in Scotland by increasing the number of people playing and enjoying golf.

• **Develop talent** – ensure that the pathways to develop young talent are in place to produce excellent golfers at all levels.

• **Support Clubs** – provide core services including handicapping, course rating, membership, marketing and advice on Governance and Legislation to support affiliated clubs.

The organisation is governed by a non executive board of directors who oversee the management of the organisation and an executive council, comprising representatives from 16 area associations, which provides the board with advice on policy matters.

Tel 01334 466477   *Fax* 01334 461361

Golfing Union of Ireland

The Golfing Union of Ireland, founded in 1891, embraces 430 Clubs. Its objects are:

(1) Securing the federation of the various Clubs.

(2) Arranging Amateur Championships, Inter-Provincial and Inter-Club Competitions, and International Matches.

(3) Securing a uniform standard of handicapping.

(4) Providing for advice and assistance, other than financial, to affiliated Clubs in all matters appertaining to Golf, and generally to promote the game in every way, in which this can be better done by the Union than by individual Clubs.

Its functions include the holding of the Open and Close Championships for Amateur Golfers and Tournaments for Team Matches.

Its organisation consists of Provincial Councils in each of the four Provinces elected by the Clubs in the Province – each province electing a limited number of delegates to the Central Council which meets annually.

Tel 00 353 1 505 4000   *Fax* 00 353 1 505 4001

The Golf Union of Wales

The Golf Union of Wales was founded in 2007 following the merger of the Welsh Golfing Union (1895) and the Welsh Ladies Golf Union (1904). The GUW, the first of the Home Unions to merge, has 158 affiliated clubs and its mission statement is:-

To encourage participation and excellence for all golfers at all levels whilst maintaining and preserving the traditions of honesty, integrity and fair play.

The GUW's key goals are:

(1) To develop a network of thriving clubs to "secure the future of Welsh Golf.

(2) To provide competition opportunities for golfers of all ages and standards.

(3) To achieve international success for Wales and its players and produce world class golfers.

The Golf Union of Wales is a limited company with a board of non-executive directors and a Council of 19 members elected by the clubs.

Tel 01633 435040   Fax 01633 693568
E-mail office@golfunionwales.org

The Council of National Golf Unions

The British Golf Unions Joint Advisory Committee, later The Council of National Golf Unions (CONGU), came into existence at a conference held in York on 14th February 1924. The conference was convened by the Royal and Ancient Golf Club of St Andrews as a means of enabling the representatives of the Golf Unions of Great Britain and Ireland to formulate a definitive system of calculating Scratch Scores and to arrive at a uniform system of handicapping based on Scratch Scores.

The Consultative Committee was appointed to receive and consider schemes for calculating and allocating the Scratch Scores and adjustments to handicaps throughout Great Britain and Ireland. The Standard Scratch Score and Handicapping Scheme was prepared by the Council in 1925 and has been in operation throughout Great Britain and Ireland since 1st March 1926.

I n 2000/2001 discussions began between CONGU and the Ladies Golf Union (LGU), who were reviewing their own system. From these discussions the Unified Handicap System (UHS) emerged. It was passed by CONGU in September 2003 and by the LGU in January 2004. The joint system for men and ladies became effective from 1st February 2004.

The Constitution of CONGU was amended in 2004 to reflect the joint system. This has been further amended in 2007/2008 to recognise the amalgamation of the Welsh Unions and will again be changed to recognise the formation of England Golf following the merger of the English Unions. The CONGU Council now consists of an independent chairperson and sixteen representatives nominated by the six Unions/Associations in Great Britain and Ireland. The six are: England Golf, Golf Union of Wales, Golfing Union of Ireland, Irish Ladies' Golf Union, Scottish Golf Union and Scottish Ladies' Golfing Association. The Royal and Ancient Golf Club of St. Andrews and The Ladies' Golf Union have one representative each on The Council.

March 2012 will see the introduction of the latest updates to the UHS, which is part of the continual process of review and improvement. CONGU have a number of sub-committees, the two most active being the Statistics and Technical Committees. These two Committees continually listen to comments and suggestions, analyse results and data, project the effect any changes would make, and make recommendations for changes to the Board, who must then give approval before they are accepted into the system. This continual process ensures that we have an
.

effective and relevant handicap system. Contact with other handicapping authorities, particularly the EGA, is maintained so that research and technical developments are shared.

Tel 0151 336 3936

Government of the Amateur and Open Golf Championships

In December 1919, on the invitation of the clubs who had hitherto controlled the Amateur and Open Golf Championships, The Royal and Ancient Golf Club took over the government of those events. These two championships are now controlled by a committee appointed by The R&A.

Tel 01334 460000   Fax 01334 460001

European Golf Association
Association Européenne de Golf

Formed at a meeting held 20 November 1937 in Luxembourg, membership is restricted to European national amateur golf associations or unions. The Association concerns itself solely with matters of an international character. The association is presently composed of 30 member countries and is governed by the following committees:

- Executive Committee
- Championship Committee
- Professional Technical Committee
- EGA Handicapping & Course Rating Committee

Prime objectives are:

(a) To encourage international development of golf, to strengthen bonds of friendship existing between it members.
(b) To encourage the formation of new golf organisations representing the golf activities of European countries.
(c) To co-ordinate the dates of the Open and Amateur championships of its members and to arrange, in conjuction with host Federations, European championships and specific matches of international character.
(d) To ratify and publish the calendar dates of the major Amateur and Professional championships and international matches in Europe.
(e) To create and maintain international relationships in the field of golf and undertake any action useful to the cause of golf on an international level.

The headquarters are situated in Epalinges, Switzerland.

Ladies' Golf Union (LGU)

Founded in 1893, the Ladies' Golf Union (LGU) is the encompassing body for ladies' amateur golf in Great Britain & Ireland. The LGU's administrative base is in St. Andrews, Fife, Scotland, while activities, championships, matches and events take place in Great Britain & Ireland and internationally.

The organisation's strategic objectives have been defined as follows:

To provide ladies and girls with opportunities to participate in the highest standard elite golf competitions;

To achieve international success for Great Britain & Ireland lady and girl golfers and teams;

To increase awareness and raise the profile of ladies' and girls' golf through the Ricoh Women's British Open and other golf events;

To provide a collective strong voice for, and represent the interests of, ladies' and girls' golf in partnership with the national organisations for ladies' golf;

To actively influence and drive equality in golf; and

To be operationally and financially sustainable.

The members of the LGU are the national governing bodies for ladies' golf in the Home Countries – the English Women's Golf Association Limited, the Irish Ladies Golf Union Limited, the Scottish Ladies Golfing Association Limited and the Golf Union of Wales Limited. Annual playing lady members of clubs affiliated to these bodies pay a small annual subscription for remittance to the LGU as a contribution to its activities.

A number of overseas unions, associations and clubs are also affiliated to the LGU.

The LGU's Executive Council is led by a Chairman, whose term of office is three years, and comprises a representative from each of the national governing bodies, two members appointed for reasons of specific skills and contributions, and a non-voting President.

Operational activities are undertaken by a wholly owned subsidiary, LGU Championships Limited (LGUCL), while the LGU holds the assets of the organisation, including property and memorabilia. The members of the Executive Council also serve as members of the Board of LGUCL. Collectively, the LGU and LGUCL are referred to as the LGU Group. The strategic direction and policies of the LGU Group are determined by the Executive Council/Board members, while responsibility for implementing these policies and strategies is vested in a team of staff, headed by the CEO.

The Annual General Meeting of the LGU is held in February, with the National Organisations being the voting members.

The LGU Group owns and runs the Ricoh Women's British Open, founded by the LGU in 1976 and one of the four Major Tournaments for professional lady golfers. LGUCL also has responsibility for running, on an annual basis:

the Ladies' British Open Amateur Championship

the Ladies' British Open Amateur Stroke Play Championship

the Girls' British Open Amateur Championship

the Senior Ladies' British Open Amateur Championship

the three sets of Home International Matches

In addition, international events involving Great Britain & Ireland teams, such as the Curtis Cup (against the USA) and Vagliano Trophy (against the Continent of Europe) are organised and controlled by LGUCL on home soil. Both at home and abroad, the LGU Group selects and prepares the teams, provides uniforms and meets the costs of participation in these matches.

The LGU acts as the co-ordinating body for the Astor Trophy (former Commonwealth Trophy) matches in whichever one of the five participating countries (GB&I, Australia, Canada, South Africa, New Zealand) it is held, four yearly, by rotation.

The LGU also maintains and regulates a number of competitions played under handicap and aimed at supporting participation in the game by club golfers. The Peugeot LGU Coronation Foursomes attracts over 35,000 participants each year, while the Breakthrough Brooch attracts over 1200 clubs and raises significant funds for the LGU's partner charity. Other handicap competitions – the Australian (Commonwealth) spoons and the Challenge Bowls are

Jill Edwards, MBE, President of the Ladies' Golf Union

delivered with the support of the National Organisations.

A Yearbook is published annually, detailing regulations and venues for forthcoming championships and matches, results of past events and other relevant useful information.

In endeavouring to advance and safeguard ladies' golf, the LGU actively maintains contact with other golfing organisations – The R&A, CONGU, the United States Golf Association, the Professional Golfers Association, the European Golf Association, the Ladies' European Tour, the European Tour and the Ladies' Professional Golf Association. The organisation is also represented on the Rolex Rankings Committee which maintains and publishes the ladies' professional rankings.

Maintaining contact with these organisations keeps the LGU at the forefront of developments and emerging issues and provides an active opportunity to influence and protect the future of the ladies' game.

Tel 01334 475811   *Fax* 01334 472818

United States Golf Association

The USGA is dedicated to promoting and conserving the best interests and true spirit of the game of golf.

Founded on December 22, 1894 by representatives of five American golf clubs, the USGA was originally charged with conducting national championships, implementing a uniform code of rules and maintaining a national system of handicapping.

Today, the USGA comprises more than 9,000 member clubs and courses and its principal functions remain largely unchanged. The USGA annually conducts the U.S. Open, U.S. Women's Open, U.S. Senior Open and 10 national amateur championships. On a biennial basis, it also conducts two state team championships and helps conduct the Walker Cup Match, Curtis Cup Match and World Amateur Team Championships. More than 35,000 players representing more than 80 countries submit entries to play in USGA championships each year.

The USGA and The R&A together govern the game worldwide, including joint administration of the Rules of Golf, Rules of Amateur status and equipment standards. The organizations also work in partnership to administer the World Amateur Golf Rankings, the world's pre-eminent amateur golf ranking system for men and women.

The USGA maintains Handicap and Course Rating and Systems used on six continents in more than 50 countries and also provides handicap computation services to more than 70 national, regional and state golf associations through the Golf Handicap and Information Network.

Additional responsibilities assumed by the association encompass turfgrass and environmental research conducted by the USGA Green Section, a global leader in the development and support of sustainable golf course management practices since 1920; and preservation and promotion of the game's rich history in the USGA Museum and Arnold Palmer Center for Golf History, which houses the world's largest and most complete golf library. Since 1965, the USGA has supported philanthropic activities dedicated to maintaining and improving the opportunities for all individuals to partake fully in the game.

Tel 001 908 234 2300   *Fax* 001 908 234 9687

Glen D Nager of Washington, DC, took over this year as the new President of the United States Golf Association. He served as general counsel to the USGA from 2006 to 2008.

Nager, a partner in the Washington, DC, office of the International law firm Jones Day, is a graduate of the University of Texas and Stanford Law School, where he was president of the Law Review. Among his clerkships was service in 1983 with Justice Sandra Day O'Connor of the US Supreme Court. He lives in the District of Columbia.

As President he will chair the Commercial, Compensation and Rules of Golf Committees and will also serve on the Equipment Standards, Joint Equipment Standards, Management and Joint Rules of Golf Committees.

Major Championship and International Conditions

UK CHAMPIONSHIPS

Men

Amateur Championship

The Championship, until 1982, was decided entirely by match play over 18 holes except for the final which was over 36 holes. Since 1983 the Championship has comprised two stroke play rounds of 18 holes each from which the leading 64 players and ties over the 36 holes qualify for the match play stages. Matches are over 18 holes except for the final which is over 36 holes. Full particulars can be obtained from the Entries Department, R&A, St Andrews, Fife KY16 9JD. Tel: 01334 460000; Fax 01334 460005; e-mail entries@randa.org

Seniors Open Amateur Championship

The Championship consists of 18 holes on each of two days, the leading 60 players and ties over the 36 holes then playing a further 18 holes the following day. Entrants must have attained the age of 55 years prior to the first day of the Championship. Full particulars can be obtained from the Entries Department, R&A, St Andrews, Fife KY16 9JD. Tel 01344 460000; fax 01334 460005; e-mail entries@randa.org

National Championships

The English, Irish, Scottish and Welsh Amateur Championships are played by holes, each match consisting of one round of 18 holes except the final which is contested over 36 holes. Only the English Golf Union hold a 36-hole qualifier for their event. Full particulars of conditions of entry and method of play can be obtained from the secretaries of the respective national Unions.

English Open Amateur Stroke Play Championship (The Brabazon)

The Championship consists of one round of 18 holes on each of two days after which the leading 60 and those tying for 60th place play a further two rounds. The remainder are eliminated.

Conditions for entry include: entrants must have a handicap not exceeding one; the maximum number of entries eligible for qualifying shall be 264 (132 to play at each of the Regional Qualifying courses. Certain players are exempt from qualifying.

Full particulars of conditions of entry and method of play can be obtained from the Secretary, English Golf Union, National Golf Centre, The Broadway, Woodhall Spa, Lincs LN10 6PU. Tel: 01526 354500; Fax: 01526 354020.

Scottish Open Amateur Stroke Play Championship

The Championship consists of one round of 18 holes on each of two days after which the leading 40 and those tying for 40th place play a further two rounds. The remainder are eliminated. Full particulars of conditions of entry and method of play can be obtained from the Events Department of the Scottish Golf Union, The Duke's, St Andrews, Fife KY16 8NX. Tel: 01334 466477; Fax: 01334 461361.

Boys

Boys Amateur Championship

The Championship, until 2009, was decided entirely by match play over 18 holes except for the final which was over 36 holes. Since 2010 the Championship has comprised two stroke play rounds of 18 holes each from which the leading 64 players and ties over the 36 holes qualify for the match play stages. Matches are over 18 holes except for the final which is over 36 holes. Full particulars can be obtained from the Entries Department, R&A, St Andrews, Fife KY16 9JD. Tel: 01334 460000; Fax 01334 460005; e-mail entries@randa.org

Ladies

Ladies' British Open Amateur Championship

The Championship consists of one 18-hole qualifying round on each of two days. The players returning the 64 lowest scores over 36 holes shall qualify for match play. Ties for the last place(s) shall be decided by card countback using the 18 hole second round score.

Ladies' British Open Amateur Stroke Play Championship

The Championship consists of 72 holes stroke play; 18 holes are played on each of two days after which the first 40 and all ties for 40th place qualify for a further 36 holes on the third day. Handicap limit is 6.4. Full details can be obtained from LGU Championships Ltd, The Scores, St Andrews, Fife KY16 9AT.

Ricoh Women's British Open Championship

The Ricoh Women's British Open is a designated major in ladies' professional golf and is the only such major played outside the USA. Owned by LGU Championships Ltd, the championship consists of 72 holes stroke play. 18 holes are played on each of four days, the field being reduced after the first 36 holes. Certain categories of players gain automatic entry to the championship because of past performance in the Ricoh Women's British Open or from current performance in the Rolex Rankings and the LET, LPGA and JLPGA money lists. Those not automatically exempt can gain entry through pre-qualifying and final qualifying competitions.

Full particulars of the above three championships can be obtained from the LTU Championships Ltd, The Scores, St Andrews, Fife KY16 9AT.

Tel: 01334 475811; Fax: 01334 472818.

National Championships

Conditions of entry and method of play for the English, Scottish, Welsh and Irish Ladies' Close Championships can be obtained from the Registered Offices of the respective associations.

Other championships organised by the respective national associations, from whom full particulars can be obtained, include English Ladies', Intermediate, English Ladies' Stroke Play, Scottish Girls' Open Amateur Stroke Play (under 21) and Welsh Ladies' Open Amateur Stroke Play.

Girls

Girls' British Open Amateur Championship

The Championship consists of two 18-hole qualifying rounds, followed by match play. The players returning the 64 lowest scores over 36 holes qualify for the match play. Ties for the last place(s) shall be decided by card countback using the 18 hole second round score.

Entrants must be under 18 years of age on the 1st January in the year of the Championship.

The Championship is open to players of the female gender who are members of a recognised golf club, who have amateur status in accordance with the current rules and who hold a CONGU exact handicap of not more than 8.4 or overseas equivalent at the date of entry.

Full particulars can be obtained from the Administrator, LGU, The Scores, St Andrews, Fife KY16 9AT. Tel: 01334 475811; Fax: 01334 472818.

National Championships

The English, Scottish, Irish and Welsh Girls' Close Championships are open to all girls of relevant nationality and appropriate age which may vary from country to country. A handicap limit may be set by some countries. Full particulars can be obtained via the secretaries of the respective associations.

EUROPEAN CHAMPIONSHIPS

Founded in 1986 by the European Golf Association, the International Amateur and Ladies Amateur Championships are held on an annual basis since 1990. These Championships consist of one round of 18 holes on each of three days after which the leading 70 and those tying for 70th place play one further round.

Full particulars of conditions of entry and method of play can be obtained from the European Golf Association.

Since 1991, the European Golf Association also holds an International Mid-Amateur Championship on an annual basis. The Championship consist of one round of 18 holes on each of two days after which the leading 90 and those tying for 90th place play one further round.

Full particulars of conditions of entry and method of play can be obtained from the European Golf Association.

Since 1996, the European Golf Association holds an International Seniors Championship for ladies and men on an annual basis.

The Championship consists of one round of 18 holes on each of two days after which there is a cut in both ladies and men categories. The competitors who pass the cut play one further round.

Additionally, a nation's cup is played within the tournament on the first two days. Teams are composed of three players. The two best gross scores out of three will count each day. The total aggregate of the four scores over two days will constitute the team's score.

Full particulars of conditions of entry and method of play can be obtained from the European Golf Association, Place de la Croix-Blanche 19, PO Box CH-1066 Epilanges, Switzerland. Tel: +41 21 784 32 32; Fax: +412 1 784 35 91.

TEAM CHAMPIONSHIPS

Men's Amateur

Walker Cup – Great Britain and Ireland v United States of America

Mr George Herbert Walker of the United States presented a Cup for international competition to be known as *The United States Golf Association International Challenge Trophy*, popularly described as *The Walker Cup*.

The Cup shall be played for by teams of amateur golfers selected from Clubs under the jurisdiction of the United States Golf Association on the one side and from England, Ireland, Scotland and Wales on the other.

The Walker Cup shall be held every two years in the United States of America and Great Britain and Ireland alternately.

The teams shall consist of not more than ten players and a captain.

The contest consists of four foursomes and eight singles matches over 18 holes on the first day and four foursomes and 10 singles on the final day.

St Andrews Trophy – Great Britain and Ireland v Continent of Europe

First staged in 1956, the St Andrews Trophy is a biennial international match played between two selected teams of amateur golfers representing Great Britain and Ireland and the Continent of Europe. Each team consists of nine players and the match is played over two consecutive days with four morning foursomes followed each afternoon by eight singles. Selection of the Great Britain and Ireland team is carried out by the R&A Selection Committee. The European Golf Association select the Continent of Europe team.

Eisenhower Trophy – Men's World Team Championship

Founded in recognition of the need for an official world amateur team championship, the first event was played at St Andrews in 1958 and the Trophy has been played for every second year in different countries around the world.

Each country enters a team of four players who play strokeplay over 72 holes, the total of the three best individual scores to be counted for each round.

European Team Championship

Founded in 1959 by the European Golf Association for competition among member countries of the Association. The Championship has recently been changed to be played on an annual basis and played in rotation round the countries, which are grouped in four geographical zones.

Each team consists of six players who play two qualifying rounds of 18 holes, the five best scores of each round constituting the team aggregate. Flights for match play are then arranged according to qualifying rankings. The match play consists of two foursomes and five singles on each of three days.

A similar championship is held in alternate years for Youths teams, under 21 years of age and every year for Boys teams, under 18 years of age.

Raymond Trophy – Home Internationals

The first official International Match recorded was in 1902 at Hoylake between England and Scotland who won 32 to 25 on a holes up basis.

In 1932 International Week was inaugurated under the auspices of the British Golf Unions' Joint Advisory Council with the full approval of the four National Golf Unions who are now responsible for running the matches. Teams of 11 players from England, Ireland, Scotland and Wales engage in matches consisting of five foursomes and ten singles over 18 holes, the foursomes being in the morning and the singles in the afternoon. Each team plays every other team.

The eligibility of players to play for their country shall be their eligibility to play in the Amateur Championship of their country.

Sir Michael Bonallack Trophy – Europe v Asia/Pacific

First staged in 1998, the Sir Michael Bonallack Trophy is a biennial international match played between two selected teams of amateur golfers representing Europe and Asia/Pacific. Each team consists of 12 players and the match is played over three days with five four balls in the morning and five foursomes in the afternoon of the first two days, followed by 12 singles on the last day. Selection of the European team is carried out by the European Golf Association. The Asia/Pacific Golf Confederation selects the Asia/Pacific team.

Men's Professional

The Ryder Cup

This is a biennial match now played between 12-man professional teams from Europe and the United States. The competition started in 1927 between teams from Great Britain and the United States. In 1926 an unofficial match took place at Wentworth Club, Surrey, England, following which Samuel Ryder, a prosperous businessman who owned the Heath and Heather Seed Company, famous for their penny packets of seeds which garden lovers adored, in St Albans, England, famously remarked: "We must do this again." Samuel Ryder donated a trophy – a golden chalice – at a cost of £250. The first official match took place in 1927 at the Worcester Country Club in Worcester, Massachusetts. The United States led 18-3 with one match tied before in 1979 players from the Continent of Europe became eligible. Between 1979 and 2010 Europe has eight victories and the United States seven with one tie. The United States will be seeking their 26th win overall and Europe their 12th when The 2012 Ryder Cup takes place at Medinah Country Club, Illinois, with the format of eight fourballs, eight foursomes and 12 singles which was introduced in 1981

The World Cup of Golf

This is an annual competition founded in 1953 as the Canada Cup – it became The World Cup of Golf in 1967 – by John Jay Hopkins, the noted Canadian industrialist. It has since the start brought together countries each represented by two man teams with the winning team having the lowest aggregate score over 72-holes. Italy became the 16th different country to win The World Cup and in 2011 they defended the 56th edition at the 25th destination to be visited – the Mission Hills Resort, Hainan Island, China – when the format comprised fourballs on the first and third days and foursomes on the second and final day with 28 teams, each one of different nationality, competing at the final stage following a series of World Qualifying Competitions.

Vivendi Seve Trophy

This is a biennial match between ten-man teams from Continental Europe and Great Britain and Ireland. Instigated by the late Seve Ballesteros in 2000 as a team competition to be contested in non-Ryder Cup years, Great Britain and Ireland gained their sixth win in seven editions when they won at Saint-Nom-la-Bretèche, Paris, France, in 2011. The match comprises of two series of five fourball matches; four greensomes; four foursomes; and ten singles on the final day.

Llandudno Trophy (PGA Cup) – Great Britain and Ireland v United States of America

The Llandudno International Trophy was first awarded to England in 1939 after winning the first Home Tournament Series against Ireland, Scotland and Wales. With the outbreak of war the series was abolished and the Trophy formed part of Percy Alliss's personal collection. After Percy's death his son Peter donated the Llandudno Trophy to be awarded to the winner of the then annual PGA Cup Match. Now it is a biennial match played since 1973 in Ryder Cup format between Great Britain and Ireland and the United States of America involving top club professionals. No prize money is awarded to the competitors who compete solely for their country. Selection of the Great Britain and Ireland team is determined following completion of the Glenmuir PGA Club Professionals Championship.

Ladies Amateur

Curtis Cup – Great Britain and Ireland v United States

For a trophy presented by the late Misses Margaret and Harriot Curtis of Boston, USA, for biennial competition between amateur teams from the United States of America and Great Britain and Ireland. The match is sponsored jointly by the United States Golf Association and the Ladies' Golf Union who may select teams of not more than eight players.

The match, held over three days, consists of three foursomes and three four-ball matches on each of the first two days and eight singles of 18 holes on the final day.

Vagliano Trophy – Great Britain and Ireland v Continent of Europe

For a trophy presented to the Comité des Dames de la Fédération Française de Golf and the Ladies' Golf Union by Monsieur AA Vagliano, originally for annual competition between teams of women amateur golfers from France and Great Britain and Ireland but, since 1959, by mutual agreement, for competition between teams from the Continent of Europe and Great Britain and Ireland.

The match is played biennially, alternately in Great Britain and Ireland and on the Continent of Europe, with teams of not more than nine players plus a non-playing captain. The match consists of four foursomes and eight singles of 18 holes on each of two days. The foursomes are played each morning.

Espirito Santo Trophy – Women's World Team Championship

Presented by Mrs Ricardo Santo of Portugal for biennial competition between teams of not more than three women amateur golfers who represent a national association affiliated to the World Amateur Golf Council. First competed for in 1964. The Championship consists of 72 holes strokeplay, 18 holes on each of four days, the two best scores in each round constituting the team aggregate.

Lady Astor Trophy – Five Nations Tournament (formerly Commonwealth Tournament)

For a trophy presented by Nancy, Viscountess Astor CH, and the Ladies' Golf Union for competition once in every four years between teams of women amateur golfers from Commonwealth countries.

The inaugural Commonwealth Tournament was played at St Andrews in 1959 between teams from Australia, Canada, New Zealand, South Africa and Great Britain and was won by the British team. The tournament is played in rotation in the competing countries, Great Britain, Australia, Canada, New Zealand and South Africa, each country being entitled to nominate six players including a playing or non-playing captain. In 2011, a Great Britain and Ireland team will compete for the first time.

Each team plays every other team and each team match consists of two foursomes and four singles over 18 holes. The foursomes are played in the morning.

European Team Championships

Founded in 1959 by the European Golf Association for competition among member countries of the Association. The Championship is held annually and played in rotation round the countries, which are grouped in four geographical zones.

Each team consists of six players who play two qualifying rounds of 18 holes, the five best scores of each round constituting the team aggregate. Flights for matchplay are then arranged according to qualifying rankings. The matchplay consists of two foursomes and five singles on each of three days.

A similar championship is held in alternate years for Lady Juniors teams, under 21 years of age and every year for Girls teams, under 18 years of age.

Home Internationals

Teams from England, Scotland, Ireland and Wales compete annually for a trophy presented to the LGU by the late Mr TH Miller. The qualifications for a player being eligible to play for her country are the same as those laid down by each country for its Close Championship.

Each team, consisting of not more than eight players, plays each other team, a draw taking place to decide the order of play between the teams. The matches consist of three foursomes and six singles, each of 18 holes.

Ladies Professional

Solheim Cup – Europe v United States

The Solheim Cup, named after Karsten Solheim who founded the sponsoring Ping company, is the women's equivalent of the Ryder Cup. In 1990 the inaugural competition between the top women professional golfers from Europe and America took place in Florida.

The matches are played biennially in alternate continents. The format is foursomes and fourball matches on the first two days, followed by singles on the third in accordance with the conditions as agreed between the Ladies European Tour and the United States LPGA Tour.

Juniors

R&A Trophy – Boys' Home Internationals

Teams comprising 11 players from England, Scotland, Ireland and Wales compete against one another over three days in a single round robin for-

mat. Each fixture comprises five morning foursomes followed by ten afternoon singles.

To be eligible for selection, players must be under the age of 18 at 00.00 hours on 1st January in the year of the matches and have eligibility to play in their national championships.

Jacques Léglise Trophy – Great Britain and Ireland v Continent of Europe

The Jacques Léglise Trophy is an annual international match played between two selected teams of amateur boy golfers representing Great Britain and Ireland and the Continent of Europe. Each team consists of nine players and the match is played over two consecutive days with four morning foursomes followed each afternoon by eight singles. Selection of the Great Britain and Ireland team is carried out by the R&A Selection Committee. The European Golf Association selects the Continent of Europe team

To be eligible for selection, players must be under the age of 18 at 00.00 hours on 1st January in the year of the matches.

Junior Ryder Cup

First staged in 1995, the Junior Ryder Cup is a biennial international match played between two selected teams of amateur golfers representing Europe and the USA, prior to the Ryder Cup. Each team consists of four girls and four boys under 16 as well as two girls and two boys under 18. The match is played over two consecutive days with six four balls on the first day and six mixed four balls on the second day.

Selection of the European team is carried out by the European Golf Association. Players and captains are then invited to watch the Ryder Cup.

Girls' Home Internationals

Teams from England, Ireland, Scotland and Wales compete annually for the Stroyan Cup. The qualifications for a player for the Girls' International Matches shall be the same as those laid down by each country for its Girls' Close Championship except that a player shall be under 18 years on the 1st January in the year of the Tournament.

Each team, consisting of not more than eight players, plays each other team, a draw taking place to decide the order of play between the teams. The matches consist of three foursomes and six singles, each of 18 holes.

The Junior Open

Run by The R&A every two years for junior golfers nominated by their various Federations. It is always held during The Open week at a venue close to the course where the Championship is being played.

PART XV

Golf History

R&A Championships and Team Events

In 2004, The Royal and Ancient Golf Club of St Andrews devolved responsibility for the running of The Open Championship and other key golfing events to The R&A. The history of championships and team events organised by The R&A and by The R&A and other golfing bodies are outlined below. Current championship and match conditions are defined elsewhere in the volume.

Championships solely under the administration of The R&A:
The Open Championship
The Amateur Championship
The Seniors Open Amateur Championship
The Boys Amateur Championship
The Junior Open Championship

Team events organised by The R&A:
The Boys Home Internationals

Team events organised by The R&A and other golfing bodies:
The Walker Cup (R&A/USGA)
The World Amateur Team Championships (R&A as part of the International Golf Federation)
The St Andrews Trophy (R&A/EGA)
The Jacques Léglise Trophy (R&A/EGA)
The Senior Open Championship

The Open Championship
The Open Championship began in 1860 at the Prestwick Golf Club and the original trophy was an ornate Challenge Belt, which was subscribed for and presented by the members of Prestwick Golf Club. What is now recognised as the first Open Championship was played on October 17, 1860 at the end of the club's autumn meeting. A total of eight players competed in three rounds of the 12 hole course. No prize money for The Open was awarded until 1863, the winner simply received the Belt for a year. In 1863 it was decided to give money prizes to those finishing second, third and fourth but the winner still only received the Belt. It was not until 1864 that the winner received £6. The average field in the 1860s was only 12 players.

The original rules of the competition stated that the Belt "becomes the property of the winner by being won three years in succession". In 1870 Tom Morris Junior won for the third year in a row and took possession of the Belt. He won £6 for his efforts out of a total prize fund of £12. No Championship was held in 1871 whilst the Prestwick Club entered into discussions with The Royal and Ancient Golf

Club and the Honourable Company of Edinburgh Golfers over the future of the event.

One of the key turning points in the history of The Open took place at the Spring Meeting of the Prestwick Club in April 1871. At that meeting it was proposed that "in contemplation of St Andrews, Musselburgh and other clubs joining in the purchase of a Belt to be played for over four or more greens, it is not expedient for the Club to provide a Belt to be played solely for at Prestwick". From that date onwards, The Open ceased to be under the sole control of the Prestwick Golf Club.

The Championship was played again under this new agreement in 1872. A new trophy, the now famous Claret Jug, was purchased for presentation to the winner. Until 1891, the host club remained responsible for all arrangements regarding the Championship, which continued to be played over 36 holes in one day.

In 1892, the Honourable Company of Edinburgh Golfers took four radical steps to transform The Open Championship. It extended play to 72 holes over two days, imposed an entrance charge for all competitors, changed the venue to a new course at Muirfield and increased the total prize fund from £28 10s to £100. These actions were all taken unilaterally by the club. The increased purse to counter a rival tournament held at Musselburgh.

A meeting was held between the three host clubs on June 9, 1893, for the purpose of "placing the competition for The Open Championship on a basis more commensurate with its importance than had hitherto existed". Three resolutions were agreed. Two English clubs, St George's, Sandwich and Royal Liverpool, would be invited to stage the Championship and join the rota, now of five clubs. Four rounds of 18 holes would be played over two days. Each of the five clubs would contribute £15 annually to the cost and the balance would come from an entry fee for all competitors. The prize money would total £100, with £30 for the winner. The date of each year's championship would be set by the host club, which would also bear any additional necessary expenses. The representatives of the five clubs became known as the Delegates of the Associated Clubs.

The increasing number of entrants caused a cut to be introduced after two rounds in 1898 and between 1904 and 1906 the Championship was played over three days. It then reverted to two days in 1907 with the introduction of qualifying rounds. The entire field had to qualify and there were no exemptions.

On January 24, 1920, the Delegates of the Associated Clubs asked The Royal and Ancient Golf Club to take over "the management of the Championship and the custody of the Challenge Cup". The new Championship Committee was responsible for running both The Open and Amateur Championships and in 1922 it was decided that The Open should only be played over links courses. The venues included in today's circuit are: Carnoustie, Muirfield, Royal Birkdale, Royal Liverpool, Royal Lytham & St Annes, Royal St George's, Royal Troon, the Old Course, St Andrews and Turnberry.

Prestwick, birth place of The Open, played host to the Championship 24 times, the last in 1925. Other courses that have been used in the past are: Musselburgh (1874, 1877, 1880, 1883, 1886, 1889); Royal Cinque Ports, Deal (1909, 1920); Princes, Sandwich (1932) and Royal Portrush (1951).

The Open was played regularly over three days starting in 1926, with a round on each of the first two days and two rounds on the final day, which from 1927 onwards was a Friday. The total prize money had reached £500 by 1939. The prize money was increased to £1000 in 1946 and reached £5000 in 1959.

As The Open went into its second century in the 1960s, it grew tremendously both as a Championship and a spectator event. In 1963, exemptions from pre-qualifying were introduced for the leading players. Play was extended to four days in 1966, with the Championship finishing with a single round on the Saturday. In 1968, a second cut after 54 holes was introduced to further reduce the field on the final day and this remained in effect until 1985. To cope with the increasing spectator numbers, facilities were much improved. Grandstands were first introduced at The Open in 1960 and they became a standard feature from 1963 onwards.

Regional qualifying had been tried as an experiment for one year in 1926, but did not become a regular feature until 1977. Some players were exempt but had to take part in final qualifying, while others were exempt from both regional and final qualifying. In 2004, International Final Qualifying was introduced, enabling players around the world to qualify on five different Continents.

Since 1980, the Championship has been scheduled to end on a Sunday instead of a Saturday. In the event of a tie for first place, play-offs took place over 36 holes up until 1963, when they were reduced to 18 holes. In 1985 a four-hole play-off, followed by sudden death, was introduced.

The Open Championship was first televised live in 1955 and was shown on the BBC. In 1958, the television coverage lasted for a total of three hours, one and a half hours on each of the final two days. In 2011, the total coverage was 3,676 hours worldwide of which 57% was live.

Admission charges to watch The Open were introduced in 1926. Paid admissions went over 50,000 for the first time in 1968 at Carnoustie and over 100,000 for the first time at St Andrews in 1978. The 200,000 attendance figure was reached for the

first time at St Andrews in 1990. A new record was set at the Home of Golf in 2000 when 238,787 watched the Millennium Open.

Growth of prize money

Year	Total Prize Money	First Prize
1861	£0	£0
1871	No Championship	
1881	£21	£8
1891	£28.50	£10
1901	£125	£50
1911	£135	£50
1921	£225	£75
1931	£500	£100
1941	No Championship	
1951	£1,700	£300
1961	£8,500	£1,400
1971	£45,000	£5,500
1981	£200,000	£25,000
1991	£900,000	£90,000
2001	£3,300,000	£600,000
2011	£5,000,000	£900,000

Harry Vardon has scored most victories in The Open Championship. He won it six times between 1896 and 1914. JH Taylor, James Braid, Peter Thomson and Tom Watson have each won The Open five times. Between 1860 and 1889, all of The Open winners were Scottish. John Ball Jr became the first Englishman and the first amateur to claim the title in 1890. Arnaud Massy from France was the first Continental winner in 1907.

Four players have completed a hat trick of Open wins: Tom Morris Jr 1868–1870; Jamie Anderson 1877–1879; Bob Ferguson 1880–1882; Peter Thomson 1954–1956.

The Open Championship has been won by an amateur player six times – John Ball in 1890, Harold Hilton in 1892 and 1897 and Bobby Jones in 1926, 1927 and 1930. Walter Hagen was the first native born American to win The Open when he triumphed in 1922. Jock Hutchison, who had won the previous year, was resident in America at the time of his victory although he was born in St Andrews.

The Amateur Championship

What became recognised as the first Amateur Championship was held at Hoylake in 1885, although earlier national amateur competitions had been played at St Andrews in 1857, 1858 and 1859. The Royal and Ancient Golf Club had considered holding a national amateur tournament in 1876 but decided not to proceed with the idea.

In December 1884, Thomas Owen Potter, the Secretary of Royal Liverpool Golf Club, proposed holding a championship for amateur players. The event was to be open to members of recognised clubs and it was hoped that it would make the game more popular and lead to improved standards of play.

A total of 44 players from 12 clubs entered the first championship. The format was matchplay, with the ruling that if two players tied they would both advance to the following round and play one another again. There were three semi-finalists: John Ball, Horace Hutchinson and Allan Macfie. After a bye to the final, Macfie beat Hutchinson 7 and 6.

Following the success of the first tournament, it was agreed that a championship open to all amateurs should be played at St Andrews, Hoylake and Prestwick in rotation.

Twenty-four golf clubs subscribed for the trophy, which was acquired in 1886. They were:

Alnmouth	Royal Aberdeen
Bruntsfield	Royal Albert (Montrose)
Dalhousie	Royal and Ancient
Formby	Royal Blackheath
Gullane	Royal Burgess
Honourable Company	Royal Liverpool
Innerleven	Royal North Devon
Kilspindie	Royal St George's
King James VI	Royal Wimbledon
North Berwick New	Tantallon
Panmure	Troon
Prestwick	West Lancashire

Representatives, known as Delegates of the Associated Clubs, were elected from these clubs to run the Championship and in 1919 they approached The Royal and Ancient Golf Club to accept future management. The Club agreed and in 1920 the Championship Committee was formed. This committee became responsible for organising the Amateur and Open and for making decisions on the conditions of play. It was not until 1922, however, that the 1885 tournament was officially recognised as the first Amateur Championship and Allan Macfie the first winner.

The venue circuit gradually increased. Sandwich was added in 1892, Muirfield in 1897 and Westward Ho! in 1912. The Championship was first played in Ireland in 1949 (Portmarnock) and Wales in 1951 (Porthcawl).

Prior to 1930, only two non-British players won the Amateur Championship title, Walter Travis, in 1904, and Jesse Sweetser, in 1926. Both hailed from the United States, the former via Australia.

The Americans began to make their presence felt more strongly in the 1930s, with four Americans winning five Amateur Championships. Bobby Jones took the title at St Andrews 1930, the year in which he achieved the Grand Slam. Lawson Little won in 1934 and 1935, Robert Sweeney in 1937 and Charles Yates in 1938.

Following a break during World War II, the Amateur Championship resumed in 1946 at Birkdale when the handicap limit was raised from one to two as an encouragement to those amateurs who had been on war service.

Attempts were made during the 1950s and 1960s to control large numbers of entries. In 1956 the field was limited to 200 so that the quarter-finals, semi-finals and the final could be played over 36 holes. This experiment lasted two years, when it was decided that only the semi-finals and final should be played over two rounds.

Regional qualifying over 36 holes was introduced in 1958 when 14 courses throughout the UK were selected. Using this method, the original entry of 500 was reduced to 200. Any player with a handicap of 5 or better could enter.

In 1961 regional qualifying was scrapped and the quarter-finals and semi-finals were played over 18 holes. Then in 1983 at Turnberry, 36 holes of strokeplay qualifying were introduced during the first two days. This format continues, with the leading 64 players and ties qualifying for the matchplay stages.

The Senior Open Championship

The Senior Open Championship has been part of the European Seniors Tour since 1987, and in 2003 was added to the Champions Tour as one of the five major world events in senior golf. The European Seniors Tour jointly administers the event alongside The R&A. Previous winners include former Open champions Gary Player, Bob Charles and Tom Watson.

The Seniors Open Amateur Championship

The Seniors Open Amateur Championship was the first tournament to be initiated by The Royal and Ancient Golf Club. Prestwick Golf Club had been responsible for starting the Open Championship, while Royal Liverpool Golf Club had introduced the Amateur Championship. Other events, such as the Boys Amateur Championship and Boys Home Internationals were introduced by private individuals and then handed over, by agreement, to The R&A.

The Seniors Open Amateur Championship made its début at Formby in 1969. It started as a means to help choose a Great Britain and Ireland team for the World Senior Amateur Team Championship which had begun in 1967 at Pinehurst, North Carolina, under the auspices of the World Amateur Golf Council.

Initially, the World Senior team event was to be played every two years, alternating with the competition for the Eisenhower Trophy, but it did not survive beyond 1969. The success of the Seniors Open Amateur Championship, however, was evident from the start and it became a popular event in its own right.

It began as a 36-hole strokeplay event, held over two days for players over the age of 55. The handicap limit was 5 and the field was restricted to 100. The winner was Reg Pattinson, who duly played his way onto the World Amateur Senior team in which he was partnered by Alan Cave, AL Bentley and AT Kyle. The short-lived World Senior event was played in 1969 over the Old Course at St Andrews and was won for the second time by the United States. Great Britain and Ireland finished third out of an entry of only 13 teams.

Before the present format was introduced, various alternatives were tried, in order to satisfy increasing entry demands. Two courses were used in 1971, allowing an entry of 250 with the handicap limit being increased to 9. In 1974, a limit of 130 was imposed. Subsidiary competitions were introduced according to age group: 55–59, 60–64 and 65 and over. A fourth age group was added in 1975 for the over 70s and the entry limit was increased to 140. The special categories changed in 1999, to one only for the 65 and over age group.

Today, the Seniors Open Amateur Championship attracts a wide international field, with 144 competitors playing two rounds and the leading 60 players and ties completing a further 18 holes.

The Boys Amateur Championship

The Boys Amateur Championship was introduced in 1921 for the under-16 age group. For the first two years it was played at Royal Ascot under the guidance of DM Mathieson and Colonel Thomas South. In 1948, Colonel South announced his intention to retire from his duties in connection with the event, declaring that "nothing would give him greater pleasure than that The Royal and Ancient Golf Club should take over the conduct of the Championship".

The venue for the first Boys Amateur Championship to be played under the administration of The Royal and Ancient Golf Club was the Old Course, St Andrews. A sub-committee ran the event until 1952 when it was finally handed over to the Championship Committee.

Since that year a prize has been presented to the best performing 16-year-old. This, the Peter Garner Bowl, commemorates the death of a competitor who was killed in a road accident while returning from the 1951 Championship.

Sir Michael Bonallack enjoyed early success in the Boys Amateur Championship. He won in 1952, and went on to win the Amateur Championship in 1961, 1965, 1968, 1969 and 1970.

Professionals who won the title earlier in their careers include Ronan Rafferty (1979), José María Olazábal (1983) and more recently Sergio García (1997).

The Junior Open Championship

Inaugurated in 1994, the Junior Open Championship came under The R&A's administrative control in 2000. All national golf unions and federations are invited to send their leading boy and girl under the age of 16 to compete in the three-day event. In previous years, only one player from each union or federation could enter. The biennial event is run on a course close to The Open Championship and in the same week so that all participants can spend time watching the world's finest players in action.

To encourage entries worldwide, there are three categories of competition defined by varying handicap limits. Gold is for those with a handicap of 3 and under, silver 4–9 and bronze 10–18.

TEAM EVENTS

The Walker Cup

The United States Golf Association International Challenge Trophy was originally intended to be presented to the winners of a contest to which all golf playing nations would be invited to compete. However, as The R&A tactfully pointed out to their counterparts in the USGA in 1921, the only two countries capable of entering a team were Great Britain and America.

By this simple process of elimination the trophy presented by USGA President George Herbert Walker became the focal point of a biennial series between the finest amateur players of the two countries. The first unofficial match was played in 1921 on the eve of the Amateur Championship at Hoylake when 19-year-old Bobby Jones helped the American team to a 9–3 victory. For the next three years the event was played annually, but settled into its biennial pattern after 1924.

It was not until 1938 at St Andrews that Great Britain and Ireland recorded a first victory. In 1965 the score was 11–11. There were 2 halved matches.

Only after the first success in America, with a 12½–11½ victory at Peachtree in Georgia in 1989, did the GB&I team finally end American domination of the matches. In the years that followed there were home wins at Porthcawl in 1995 and Nairn in 1999. The GB&I run of victories continued at Ocean Forest in 2001 and Ganton in 2003, before winning most recently at Royal Aberdeen in 2011.

The man after whom the trophy and the matches are named has another claim to a place in world history. His grandson, George Herbert Walker Bush and his great-grandson have both held office as President of the United States of America.

The Eisenhower Trophy

The United States Golf Association approached The Royal and Ancient Golf Club in 1958 with the proposal that the two bodies should sponsor a worldwide amateur golf event. The new competition would take place biennially in non-Walker Cup years, with the first being played at St Andrews in 1958. All golfing bodies that observed the Rules of Golf and Amateur Status as approved by The R&A and the USGA were invited to send one representative to a meeting in Washington at which President Dwight D Eisenhower presented a trophy to be awarded to the winning country. The committee of the event was to be known as the World Amateur Golf Council, which is now the International Golf Federation.

The key objective of the new council was "to foster friendship and sportsmanship among the peoples of the world through the conduct of an Amateur Team Championship for The Eisenhower Trophy". In a meeting with the President in the Rose Garden of the White House, Eisenhower offered his advice to the delegates: "I suggest, aside from the four hotshot golfers you bring, that you take along some high-handicap fellows and let them play at their full handicaps ...

This way golf doesn't become so important". This observation led to the creation of a "Delegates and Duffers Cup" for officials and non-playing captains.

The format decided for the Eisenhower Trophy was strokeplay. Each team consisted of four players who would play four rounds. The team score for each round was the three best individual scores. The first competition was held in St Andrews and attracted teams from 29 countries. After 72 holes of golf, the American and Australian teams were both tied on an aggregate score of 918. A play-off was held and the Australian team won by two strokes. So far this has been the only play-off in the history of the event.

Australia went on to win the trophy twice more, in 1966 and 1996. However, the USA have dominated the event, winning it 13 times in total. The Great Britain and Ireland team have won four times, in 1964, 1976, 1988 and 1998. In 2002 teams were reduced from four to three players with the best two scores counting in each round and for the first time England, Ireland, Scotland and Wales entered separate teams. In 2008, Scotland claimed its first victory in the Eisenhower Trophy at the Royal Adelaide Golf Club, Australia. Fifty years after the Australians won the first Championship at the Old Course in St Andrews, the Scots took the Trophy home from Australia. A parallel event for women, playing for the Espirito Santo Trophy, is held at the same venue prior to the Eisenhower.

The St Andrews Trophy

In November 1955 the Championship Committee of The Royal and Ancient Golf Club put forward a recommendation that "the European Golf Association should be approached with a view to arranging an international match between a Great Britain and Ireland and European side".

The GB&I team, captained by Gerald Micklem, duly triumphed by a score of 12½ to 2½ in the first match played over the West Course at Wentworth in 1956. A resounding success, it was immediately established as a biennial event in non-Walker Cup years and in 1964 the Club donated the St Andrews Trophy to be presented to the winning team.

Although Great Britain and Ireland have dominated the match, winning 23 of the 26 encounters, the Continent of Europe had a convincing victory at Villa d'Este in Italy in 1998 and suffered only a narrow 13–11 defeat at Turnberry in 2000. The Continent of Europe are the current holders of the trophy, winning in 2010 by a score of 14 to 10 at Castelconturbia, near Milan in Italy.

The Jacques Léglise Trophy

The annual boys international match involving GB&I against a team from the Continent of Europe was introduced in 1958. This event was dominated originally by the British and Irish side, which won every match through 1966 prompting the match to be discontinued because it was a one-sided affair.

The match was revived in 1977 when the Continental team won by 7 points to 6. A new trophy, donated by Jean-Louis Dupont on behalf of Golf de Chantilly in memory of Jacques Léglise, a leading French golf administrator, was presented for the first time in 1978 when the Continental team again won. Since then the Continental side has triumphed a further eight times, most recently in 2010. The 2010 match at Castelconturbia resulted in a 15½–8½ victory for the Continent of Europe. The 2008 match at Kingsbarns resulted in a 14–10 victory for GB&I. Great Britain and Ireland won the 2011 match with an impressive 14½–9½ victory over the Continent of Europe. The match was played in conjunction with the Boys Amateur Championship and Home International events until 1995. Since 1996 it has been played concurrently with the St Andrews Trophy, although the Jacques Léglise Trophy remains an annual competition.

The Boys Home Internationals

Introduced at Dunbar in 1923, the Boys Home Internationals started off as a match played between England and Scotland. It was traditionally associated with the Boys Amateur Championship, being played the day before and acting as a prelude to the main event.

The Royal and Ancient Golf Club accepted responsibility for the Boys Amateur Championship in 1949 and with it the running of the England v Scotland match. The Championship Committee originally carried out team selection. Today, representatives from the four Home Unions select the teams.

In 1972, a team match between Ireland and Wales was added to the fixture and the current format was established in 1996. The four home countries compete against one another over three consecutive days in a round robin series. Each fixture comprises five morning foursomes, followed by ten afternoon singles.

In 1997, there was a significant break with the past when, for the first time, the venue chosen for the Boys Home Internationals differed to that for the Boys Amateur Championship. This practice has remained, helping to shape the individual identity of the inter-national matches. Since 1985, the R&A Trophy has been awarded to the winning team.

Important dates in the history of St Andrews, The Open Championship and The R&A

1457	Golf is banned by King James II of Scotland; instead, archery is encouraged.
1552	Archbishop John Hamilton grants citizens rights to play games, including golf, on the links.
1744	First set of 13 rules laid out by golfers at Leith.
1754	Twenty-two noblemen and gentlemen of Fife form Society of St Andrews Golfers.
1764	A round at St Andrews changes from 22 to 18 holes and becomes the standard.
1834	King William IV confers his patronage and the Society of St Andrews Golfers becomes The Royal and Ancient Golf Club.
1854	The Royal and Ancient Clubhouse is built.
1860	First Open Championship is held at Prestwick and won by Willie Park Sr.
1870	Tom Morris Jr wins Open Belt for third time and gets to keep it.
1872	The Royal and Ancient Golf Club, Prestwick and Honourable Company of Edinburgh Golfers take over the running of The Open.
1873	First time The Open is played at St Andrews and first time the Claret Jug is presented.
1894	United States Golf Association is formed.
1897	The R&A becomes accepted authority for golf and forms the Rules of Golf Committee.
1904	Lost ball search time reduced from 10 to five minute.
1919	The R&A takes over the running of the Amateur Championship.
1920	The R&A takes responsibility for The Open Championship
1920	First R&A–USGA rules conference
1926	The Open is first played over three days.
1929	USGA legitimises larger ball (1.68in). Smaller ball (1.62in) still used elsewhere.
1929	Steel shafts are legalised.
1951	The R&A and USGA meet to unify rules.
1952	The R&A and USGA standardise rules except for ball size. Stymie is abolished.
1955	First live television coverage of The Open Championship by the BBC.
1956	First four-yearly rules revision.
1960	First grandstands erected at The Open Championship.
1963	Last 36-hole play-off for The Open Championship.
1966	First live coverage of The Open Championship in America.
1966	Open played over four days for first time at Muirfield.
1974	1.68in ball becomes compulsory in The Open Championship for first time.
1980	The Open ends on a Sunday for the first time at Muirfield.
1984	New dropping procedure at arms length from the shoulder.
1985	The R&A change play-off arrangements for The Open to four holes.
1990	The American size 1.68in ball becomes the only legal ball.
2004	The Royal and Ancient Golf Club celebrates its 250th anniversary. Responsibility for external activities, such as running The Open and administering the Rules, is devolved to a newly formed group of companies known as The R&A.
2007	Old Course first used for the Ricoh Women's British Open Championship.
2008	Curtis Cup played over the Old Course for the first time.
2010	The Open celebrates 150 years and is played at the Home of Golf for the 28th time

Interesting Facts and Unusual Incidents

Royal golf clubs

● The right to the designation *Royal* is bestowed by the favour of the Sovereign or a member of the Royal House. In most cases the title is granted along with the bestowal of royal patronage on the club. The Perth Golfing Society was the first to receive the designation *Royal*. That was accorded in June 1833. King William IV bestowed the honour on The Royal and Ancient Club in 1834. The most recent Club to be so designated is Royal Mayfair Golf & Country Club in Edmonton, Canada. The club was granted Royal status in October 2005. The next most recent was Royal Mariánské Lázně in the Czech Republic. In 2003, the club was given the Royal title as a result of its association in the early part of the 20th century with King Edward VII. A full list of Royal clubs can be found on pages 688–689.

Royal and Presidential golfers

● In the long history of the Royal and Ancient game no reigning British monarch has played in an open competition. In 1922 the Duke of Windsor, when Prince of Wales, competed in The Royal and Ancient Autumn Medal at St Andrews. He also took part in competitions at Mid-Surrey, Sunningdale, Royal St George's and in the Parliamentary Handicap. He occasionally competed in American events, sometimes partnered by a professional. On a private visit to London in 1952, he competed in the Autumn competition of Royal St George's at Sandwich, scoring 97. As Prince of Wales he played on courses all over the world and, after his abdication, as Duke of Windsor he continued to enjoy the game for many years.

● King George VI, when still Duke of York, in 1930, and the Duke of Kent, in 1937, also competed in the Autumn Meeting of The Royal and Ancient, when they had formally played themselves into the Captaincy of the Club and each returned his card in the medal round. So too did Prince Andrew, the Duke of York, when he became captain in 2003. He also played in the medal and won the mixed foursomes the following day playing with former British ladies champion Julie Otto.

● King Leopold of Belgium played in the Belgian Amateur Championship at Le Zoute, the only reigning monarch ever to have played in a national championship. The Belgian King played in many competitions subsequent to his abdication. In 1949 he reached the quarter-finals of the French Amateur Championship at St Cloud, playing as Count de Rethy.

● King Baudouin of Belgium in 1958 played in the triangular match Belgium–France–Holland and won his match against a Dutch player. He also took part in the Gleneagles Hotel tournament (playing as Mr B. de Rethy), partnered by Dai Rees in 1959.

● United States President George Bush accepted an invitation in 1990 to become an Honorary Member of The Royal and Ancient Golf Club of St Andrews. The honour recognised his long connection and that of his family with golf and The R&A. Both President Bush's father, Prescott Bush Sr, and his grandfather, George Herbert Walker – who donated the Walker Cup – were presidents of the United States Golf Association. Other Honorary Members of The R&A include Kel Nagle, Jack Nicklaus, Arnold Palmer, Gene Sarazen, Peter Thomson, Roberto de Vicenzo, Gary Player and five-times Open Championship winner Tom Watson, who was made an honorary member in 1999 on his 50th birthday.

● In September 1992, The Royal and Ancient Golf Club of St Andrews announced that His Royal Highness The Duke of York had accepted the Club's invitation of Honorary Membership. The Duke of York is the sixth member of the Royal Family to accept membership along with Their Royal Highnesses The Duke of Edinburgh and The Duke of Kent. He has since become a single handicapper, and has appeared in a number of pro-ams, partnering The Open and Masters champion Mark O'Meara to victory in the Alfred Dunhill Cup pro-am at St Andrews in 1998. His Royal Highness was Captain for 2003–2004, the year in which the Club celebrated its 250th anniversary.

First lady golfer

● Mary Queen of Scots, who was beheaded on 8th February, 1587, was probably the first lady golfer so mentioned by name. As evidence of her indifference to the fate of Darnley, her husband who was murdered at Kirk o' Field, Edinburgh, she was charged at her trial with having played at golf in the fields beside Seton a few days after his death.

Record championship victories

● In the Amateur Championship at Muirfield, 1920, Captain Carter, an Irish golfer, defeated an American entrant by 10 and 8. This is the only known instance where a player has won every hole in an Amateur Championship tie.

● In the final of the Canadian Ladies' Championship at Rivermead, Ottawa, in 1921, Cecil Leitch defeated Mollie McBride by 17 and 15. Miss Leitch lost only 1 hole in the match, the ninth. She was 14 up at the end of the first round, making only 3 holes necessary in the second. She won 18 holes out of 21 played, lost 1, and halved 2.

● In the final of the French Ladies' Open Championship at Le Touquet in 1927, Mlle de la Chaume (St Cloud) defeated Mrs Alex Johnston (Moor Park) by 15 and 14, the largest victory in a European golf championship.

● At Prestwick in 1934, W. Lawson Little of Presidio, San Francisco, defeated James Wallace, Troon Portland, by 14 and 13 in the final of the Amateur Championship, the record victory in the Championship. Wallace failed to win a single hole.

Players who have won two or more majors in the same year

(The first Masters Tournament was played in 1934)

1922	Gene Sarazen – USPGA, US Open
1924	Walter Hagen – USPGA, The Open
1926	Bobby Jones – US Open, The Open
1930	Bobby Jones – US Open, The Open (Bobby Jones also won the US Amateur and British Amateur in this year)
1932	Gene Sarazen – US Open, The Open
1941	Craig Wood – Masters, US Open
1948	Ben Hogan – USPGA, US Open
1949	Sam Snead – USPGA, Masters
1951	Ben Hogan – Masters, US Open
1953	Ben Hogan – Masters, US Open, The Open
1956	Jack Burke – USPGA, Masters
1960	Arnold Palmer – Masters, US Open
1962	Arnold Palmer – Masters, The Open
1963	Jack Nicklaus – USPGA, Masters
1966	Jack Nicklaus – Masters, The Open
1971	Lee Trevino – US Open, The Open
1972	Jack Nicklaus – Masters, US Open
1974	Gary Player – Masters, The Open
1975	Jack Nicklaus – USPGA, Masters
1977	Tom Watson – Masters, The Open
1980	Jack Nicklaus – USPGA, US Open
1982	Tom Watson – US Open, The Open
1990	Nick Faldo – Masters, The Open
1994	Nick Price – The Open, US PGA
1998	Mark O'Meara – Masters, The Open
2000	Tiger Woods* – US Open, The Open, USPGA
2008	Padraig Harrington – The Open, US PGA
2010	Yani Tseng – Women's British Open, Kraft Nabisco
2011	Yani Tseng – Women's British Open, LPGA

*Woods also won the 2001 Masters to become the first player to hold all four Majors at the same time. He was 65-under-par for the four events.

Outstanding records in championships, international matches and on the professional circuit

● The record number of victories in The Open Championship is six, held by Harry Vardon who won in 1896-98-99-1903-11-14.

● Five-time winners of the Championship are J.H. Taylor in 1894-95-1900-09-13; James Braid in 1901-05-06-08-10; Peter Thomson in 1954-55-56-58-65 and Tom Watson in 1975-77-80-82-83. Thomson's 1965 win was achieved when the Championship had become a truly international event. In 1957 he finished second behind Bobby Locke. By winning again in 1958 Thomson was prevented only by Bobby Locke from winning five consecutive Open Championships.

● Four successive victories in The Open by *Young Tom Morris* is a record so far never equalled. He won in 1868-69-70-72. (The Championship was not played in 1871.) Other four-time winners are Bobby Locke in 1949-50-52-57, Walter Hagen in 1922-24-28-29, Willie Park 1860-63-66-75, and *Old* Tom Morris 1861-62-64-67.

● Since the Championship began in 1860, players who have won three times in succession are Jamie Anderson, Bob Ferguson, and Peter Thomson.

● Robert Tyre Jones won The Open three times in 1926-27-30; the Amateur in 1930; the American Open in 1923-26-29-30; and the American Amateur in 1924-25-27-28-30. In winning the four major golf titles of the world in one year (1930) he achieved a feat unlikely ever to be equalled. Jones retired from competitive golf after winning the 1930 American Open, the last of these Championships, at the age of 28.

● Jack Nicklaus has had the most wins (six) in the US Masters Tournament, followed by Arnold Palmer with four.

● In modern times there are four championships generally regarded as standing above all others – The Open, US Open, US Masters, and USPGA. Five players have held all these titles, Gene Sarazen, Ben Hogan, Gary Player, Jack Nicklaus and Tiger Woods in that order. In 1978 Nicklaus became the first player to have held each of them at least three times. His record in these events is: The Open 1966-70-78; US Open 1962-67-72-80; US Masters 1963-65-66-72-75-86; USPGA 1963-71-73-75-80. His total of major championships is now 18. In 1998 at the age of 58, Nicklaus finished joint sixth in the Masters. By not playing in The Open Championship that year, he ended a run of 154 successive major championships for which he was eligible (stretching back to 1957).

In 1953 Ben Hogan won the Masters, US Open and The Open, but did not compete in the USPGA because of a dates clash with The Open.

In 2000 Tiger Woods won the US Open by 15 strokes (a major championship record), The Open by eight strokes, and the USPGA in the play-off. In 2001 he then added the Masters winning by two shots to become the first player to hold all four major titles at the same time. He was 65-under-par for the four events.

● In the 1996 English Amateur Championship at Hollinwell, Ian Richardson (50) and his son, Carl, of Burghley Park, Lincolnshire, both reached the semi-finals. Both lost.

● The record number of victories in the US Open is four, held by Willie Anderson, Bobby Jones, Ben Hogan and Jack Nicklaus.

● Bobby Jones (amateur), Gene Sarazen, Ben Hogan, Lee Trevino, Tom Watson and Tiger Woods are the only players to have won The Open and US Open Championships in the same year. Tony Jacklin won The Open in 1969 and the US Open in 1970 and for a few weeks was the holder of both.

● In winning the Amateur Championship in 1970 Michael Bonallack became the first player to win in three consecutive years.

● The English Amateur record number of victories is held by Michael Bonallack, who won the title five times.

● John Ball holds the record number of victories in the Amateur Championship, which he won eight times. Next comes Michael Bonallack (who was internationally known as The Duke) with five wins.

● Cecil Leitch and Joyce Wethered each won the British Ladies' title four times.

● The Scottish Amateur record was held by Ronnie Shade, who won five titles in successive years, 1963 to 1967. His long reign as Champion ended when he was beaten in the fourth round of the 1968 Championship after winning 44 consecutive matches.

● Joyce Wethered established an unbeaten record by winning the English Ladies' in five successive years from 1920 to 1924 inclusive.

● In winning the Amateur Championships of Britain and America in 1934 and 1935 Lawson Little won 31 consecutive matches. Other dual winners of these championships in the same year are R.T. Jones (1930) and Bob Dickson (1967).

● Peter Thomson's victory in the 1971 New Zealand Open Championship was his ninth in that event.

● In a four-week spell in 1971, Lee Trevino won in succession the US Open, the Canadian Open and The Open Championship.

● Michael Bonallack and Bill Hyndman were the Amateur Championship finalists in both 1969 and 1970. This was the first time the same two players reached the final in successive years.

● On the US professional circuit the greatest number of consecutive victories is 11, achieved by Byron Nelson in 1945. Nelson also holds the record for most victories in one calendar year, again in 1945 when he won a total of 18 tournaments.

● Raymond Floyd, by winning the Doral Classic in March 1992, joined Sam Snead as the only winners of US Tour events in four different decades.

● Sam Snead won tournaments in six decades. His first win was the 1936 West Virginia PGA. In 1980 he won the Golf Digest Commemorative and in 1982 the Legends of Golf with Don January.

● Neil Coles has won official Tour events in six decades. His first victory was in 1958 and he was a winner on the European Senior Tour in June 2000 when he took the Microlease Jersey Senior Open. Coles still plays well enough to beat his age. Now 67, he shot a closing 64 in the final round of the 2003

Travis Perkins Senior Open over the Edinburgh course he helped design.

● Jack Nicklaus and the late Walter Hagen have had five wins each in the USPGA Championship. All Hagen's wins were at match play; all Nicklaus's at stroke play.

● In 1953 Flory van Donck of Belgium had seven major victories in Europe, including The Open Championships of Switzerland, Italy, Holland, Germany and Belgium.

● Mrs Anne Sander won four major amateur titles each under a different name. She won the US Ladies' in 1958 as Miss Quast, in 1961 as Mrs Decker, in 1963 as Mrs Welts and the British Ladies' in 1980 as Mrs Sander.

● The highest number of appearances in the Ryder Cup matches is held by Nick Faldo who made his eleventh appearance in 1997.

● The greatest number of appearances in the Walker Cup matches is held by Irishman Joe Carr who made his tenth appearance in 1967.

● In the Curtis Cup Mary McKenna made her ninth consecutive appearance in 1986.

● Players who have represented their country in both Walker and Ryder Cup matches are: for the United States, Fred Haas, Ken Venturi, Gene Littler, Jack Nicklaus, Tommy Aaron, Mason Rudolph, Bob Murphy, Lanny Wadkins, Scott Simpson, Tom Kite, Jerry Pate, Craig Stadler, Jay Haas, Bill Rodgers, Hal Sutton, Curtis Strange, Davis Love III, Brad Faxon, Scott Hoch, Phil Mickelson, Corey Pavin, Justin Leonard, Tiger Woods, David Duval, Anthony Kim, Dustin Johnson and Rickie Fowler; and for Great Britain & Ireland, Norman Drew, Peter Townsend, Clive Clark, Peter Oosterhuis, Howard Clark, Mark James, Michael King, Gordon Brand Jr, Paul Way, Ronan Rafferty, Sandy Lyle, Philip Walton, David Gilford, Colin Montgomerie, Peter Baker, Padraig Harrington, Andrew Coltart, Oliver Wilson, Justin Rose, Luke Donald, Paul Casey, Graeme McDowell and Rory McIlroy.

Remarkable recoveries in matchplay

● There have been two remarkable recoveries in the Walker Cup Matches. In 1930 at Sandwich, J.A. Stout, Great Britain, round in 68, was 4 up at the end of the first round against Donald Moe. Stout started in the second round, 3, 3, 3, and was 7 up. He was still 7 up with 13 to play. Moe, who went round in 67, won back the 7 holes to draw level at the 17th green. At the 18th or 36th of the match, Moe, after a long drive placed his iron shot within three feet of the hole and won the match by 1 hole.

● In 1936 at Pine Valley, George Voigt and Harry Girvan for America were 7 up with 11 to play against Alec Hill and Cecil Ewing. The British pair drew level at the 17th hole, or 35th of the match, and the last hole was halved.

● In the 1965 Piccadilly Match Play Championship Gary Player beat Tony Lema after being 7 down with 17 to play.

● Bobby Cruickshank, the old Edinburgh player, had an extraordinary recovery in a 36-hole match in a USPGA Championship for he defeated Al Watrous after being 11 down with 12 to play.

● In a match at the Army GC, Aldershot, on 5th July, 1974, for the Gradoville Bowl, M.C. Smart was 8 down with 8 to play against Mike Cook. Smart succeeded in winning all the remaining holes and the 19th for victory.

● In the 1982 Suntory World Match Play Championship Sandy Lyle beat Nick Faldo after being 6 down with 18 to play.

● In the 1991 Ryder Cup at Kiawah, Colin Montgomerie, on his début, was five down to Mark Calcavecchia at the turn. The American was still four up with four to play. Although the Scot finished double bogey, par, double bogey, par, he won all the closing holes and squared the match when the American missed the hole from two feet on the last.

Oldest champions

The Open Championship: Belt Tom Morris in 1867 – 46 years 99 days. *Cup* Roberto de Vicenzo, 44 years 93 days, in 1967; Harry Vardon, 44 years 42 days, in 1914; J.H. Taylor, 42 years 97 days, in 1913; Darren Clarke, 42 years 11 months, in 2011.

Amateur Championship Hon. Michael Scot, 54, at Hoylake in 1933.

British Ladies Amateur Mrs Jessie Valentine, 43, at Hunstanton in 1958.

Scottish Amateur J.M. Cannon, 53, at Troon in 1969.

English Amateur Terry Shingler, 41 years 11 months at Walton Heath 1977; Gerald Micklem, 41 years 8 months, at Royal Birkdale 1947.

Welsh Amateur John Jermine, 56, at St David's, in 2000

US Open Hale Irwin, 45, at Medinah, Illinois, in 1990.

US Amateur Jack Westland, 47, at Seattle in 1952 (He had been defeated in the 1931 final, 21 years previously, by Francis Ouimet).

US Masters Jack Nicklaus, 46, in 1986.

European Tour Des Smyth, 48 years, 14 days, Madeira Open 1982; Neil Coles, 48 years 14 days, Sanyo Open 1982

European Senior Tour Neil Coles, 65, in 2000

USPGA Julius Boros, 48, in 1968. Lee Trevino, 44, in 1984.

USPGA Tour Sam Snead, 52, at Greensborough Open in 1965. Sam Snead, 61, equal second in Glen Campbell Open 1974.

Youngest champions

The Open Championship: Belt Tom Morris, Jr, 17 years 5 months, in 1868. *Cup* Willie Auchterlonie, 21 years 24 days, in 1893; Tom Morris, Jr, 21 years 5 months, in 1872; Severiano Ballesteros, 22 years 103 days, in 1979.

US Open Championship: In 2011 Rory McIlroy, at the age of 22, became the youngest player to win the event since Bobby Jones' victory in 1923 at the age of 21.

Amateur Championship J.C. Beharrell, 18 years 1 month, at Troon in 1956; R. Cole (RSA) 18 years 1 month, at Carnoustie in 1966.

British Ladies Amateur May Hezlett, 17, at Newcastle, Co. Down, in 1899; Michelle Walker, 18, at Alwoodley in 1971.

English Amateur Nick Faldo, 18, at Lytham St Annes in 1975; Paul Downes, 18, at Birkdale in 1978; David Gilford, 18, at Woodhall Spa in 1984; Ian Garbutt, 18, at Woodhall Spa in 1990; Mark Foster, 18, at Moortown in 1994.

English Amateur Strokeplay Ronan Rafferty, 16, at Hunstanton in 1980.

British Ladies Open Strokeplay Helen Dobson, 18, at Southerness in 1989.

British Boys Championship Mark Mouland (WAL) 15 years 120 days at Sunningdale in 1976; Pablo Martin (ESP) 15 years 120 days at Ganton 2001.

More records can be found on pages 470–482

Disqualifications

Disqualifications are now numerous, usually for some irregularity over signing a scorecard or for late arrival at the first tee. We therefore show here only incidents in major events involving famous players or players who were in a winning position or incidents which were in themselves unusual.

● J.J. McDermott, the American Open Champion 1911–12, arrived for The Open Championship at Prestwick in 1914 to discover that he had made a mistake of a week in the date the championship began. The American could not play, as the qualifying rounds were completed on the day he arrived.

● In the Amateur Championship at Sandwich in 1937, Brigadier-General Critchley, arriving at Southampton from New York on the *Queen Mary*, which had been delayed by fog, flew by specially chartered aeroplane to Sandwich. He circled over the clubhouse, so the officials knew he was nearly there, but he arrived six minutes late, and his name had been struck out. At the same championship a player, entered from Burma, who had travelled across the Pacific and the American Continent, and was also on the *Queen Mary*, travelled from Southampton by motor car and arrived four hours after his starting time to find after journeying more than halfway round the world he was struck out.

● An unprecedented disqualification was that of A. Murray in the New Zealand Open Championship, 1937. Murray, who was New Zealand Champion in 1935, was playing with J.P. Hornabrook, New Zealand Amateur Champion, and at the 8th hole in the last round, while waiting for his partner to putt, Murray dropped a ball on the edge of the green and made a practice putt along the edge. Murray returned the lowest score in the championship, but he was disqualified for taking the practice putt.

● At The Open Championship at St Andrews in 1946, John Panton, Glenbervie, in the evening practised putting on a green on the New Course, which was one of the qualifying courses. He himself reported his inadvertence to The Royal and Ancient and he was disqualified.

● At The Open Championship, Sandwich, 1949, C. Rotar, an American, qualified by four strokes to compete in the championship but he was disqualified because he had used a putter which did not conform to the accepted form and make of a golf club, the socket being bent over the centre of the club head. This is the only case where a player has been disqualified in The Open Championship for using an illegal club.

● In the 1957 American Women's Open Championship, Mrs Jackie Pung had the lowest score, 298 over four rounds, but lost the championship. The card she signed for the final round read *five* at the 4th hole instead of the correct *six*. Her total of 72 was correct but the error, under rigid rules, resulted in her disqualification. Betty Jameson, who partnered Mrs Pung and also returned a wrong score, was also disqualified.

● Mark Roe and Jesper Parnevik were disqualified in bizarre circumstances in the 2003 Open at Royal St George's, Sandwich. Roe had shot 67 to move into contention but it was discovered after they left the recorder's hut that they had not exchanged cards. Roe's figures were returned on a card with Parnevik's name on it and vice versa. The R&A have since changed the rules to allow the official scorer to erase the wrong name and put the correct one on the card ensuring a Roe–Parnevik incident can never happen again.

● Teenager Michelle Wie will not be allowed to forget her début on the LPGA Tour as a professional in the Samsung World Championship. Although she completed four rounds and finished fourth behind Annika Sörenstam, she was disqualified for taking a drop nearer to the hole in the third round. A reporter, Michael Bamberger from *Sports Illustrated*, saw the incident but did not report it to officials until the next day after he had spoken with his editor. Officials only decided to disqualify the youngster after measuring out distances at the spot where she took the drop with a yard of string.

● Kevin Stadler, son of Ryder Cup and former Masters champion Craig Stadler, was disqualified in the 2005 Funai Classic in Orlando for disclosing he had a bent shaft in his wedge. Lying 163rd in the money list and needing a good finish to keep his card, he was lying joint fifth going into the final round. He discovered the shaft of his wedge was bent on the second hole on the final day and was disqualified for playing with an illegal club – ironically, one that could never have helped him play a decent shot.

Longest match

● W.R. Chamberlain, a retired farmer, and George New, a postmaster at Chilton Foliat, on 1st August, 1922, met at Littlecote, the 9-hole course of Sir Ernest Wills, and agreed to play every Thursday afternoon over the course. This continued until New's sudden death on 13th January, 1938. An accurate record of the match was kept, giving details of each round including wind direction and playing conditions. In the elaborate system nearly two million facts were recorded. They played 814 rounds, and aggregated 86,397 strokes, of which Chamberlain took 44,008 and New 42,371. New, therefore, was 1,637 strokes up. The last round of all was halved, a suitable end to such an unusual contest.

Longest ties

● The longest known ties in 18-hole match play rounds in major events were in an early round of the News of the World Match Play Championship at Turnberry in 1960, when W.S. Collins beat W.J. Branch at the 31st hole, and in the third round of the same tournament at Walton Heath in 1961 when Harold Henning beat Peter Alliss also at the 31st hole.

● In the 1970 Scottish Amateur Championship at Balgownie, Aberdeen, E. Hammond beat J. McIvor at the 29th hole in their second round tie.

● C.A. Palmer beat Lionel Munn at the 28th hole at Sandwich in 1908. This is the record tie of the British Amateur Championship. Munn has also been engaged in two other extended ties in the Amateur Championship. At Muirfield, in 1932, in the semi-final, he was defeated by John de Forest, the ultimate winner, at the 26th hole, and at St Andrews, in 1936, in the second round he was defeated by J.L. Mitchell, again at the 26th hole.

The following examples of long ties are in a different category for they occurred in competitions, either stroke play or match play, where the conditions stipulated that in the event of a tie, a further stated number of holes had to be played – in some cases 36 holes, but mostly 18. With this method a vast number of extra holes was sometimes necessary to settle ties.

● The longest known was between two American women in a tournament at Peterson (New Jersey) when 88 extra holes were required before Mrs Edwin Labaugh emerged as winner.

● In a match on the Queensland course, Australia, in October, 1933, H.B. Bonney and Col H.C.H. Robertson versus B.J. Canniffe and Dr Wallis Hoare required to play a further four 18-hole matches after being level at the end of the original 18 holes. In the fourth replay Hoare and Caniffe won by 3 and 2 which meant that 70 extra holes had been necessary to decide the tie.

● After finishing all square in the final of the Dudley GC's foursomes competition in 1950, F.W. Mannell and A.G. Walker played a further three 18-hole replays against T. Poole and E. Jones, each time finishing all square. A further 9 holes were arranged and Mannell and Walker won by 3 and 2 making a total of 61 extra holes to decide the tie.

● R.A. Whitcombe and Mark Seymour tied for first prize in the Penfold £750 Tournament at St Annes-on-Sea, in 1934. They had to play off over 36 holes and tied again. They were then required to play another 9 holes when Whitcombe won with 34 against 36. The tournament was over 72 holes. The first tie added 36 holes and the extra 9 holes made an aggregate of 117 holes to decide the winner. This is a record in first-class British golf but in no way compares with other long ties as it involved only two replays – one of 36 holes and one of 9.

● In the American Open Championship at Toledo, Ohio, in 1931, G. Von Elm and Billy Burke tied for the title. Each returned aggregates of 292. On the first replay both finished in 149 for 36 holes but on the second replay Burke won with a score of 148 against 149. This is a record tie in a national open championship.

● Cary Middlecoff and Lloyd Mangrum were declared co-winners of the 1949 Motor City Open on the USPGA Tour after halving 11 sudden death holes.

● Australian David Graham beat American Dave Stockton at the tenth extra hole in the 1998 Royal Caribbean Classic, a record on the US Senior Tour.

● Paul Downes was beaten by Robin Davenport at the 9th extra hole in the 4th round of the 1981 English Amateur Championship, a record marathon match for the Championship.

● Severiano Ballesteros was beaten by Johnny Miller at the 9th extra hole of a sudden-death play-off at the 1982 Million Dollar Sun City Challenge.

● José Maria Olazábal beat Ronan Rafferty at the 9th extra hole to win the 1989 Dutch Open on the Kennemer Golf and Country Club course. Roger Chapman had been eliminated at the first extra hole.

Long drives

It is impossible to state with any certainty what is the longest ever drive. Many long drives have never been measured and many others have most likely never been brought to our attention. Then there are several outside factors which can produce freakishly long drives, such as a strong following wind, downhill terrain or bonehard ground. Where all three of these favourable conditions prevail outstandingly long drives can be achieved. Another consideration is that a long drive made during a tournament is a different proposition from one made for length alone, either on the practice ground, a long driving competition or in a game of no consequence. All this should be borne in mind when considering the long drives shown here.

● When professional Carl Hooper hit a wayward drive on the 3rd hole (456 yards) at the Oak Hills Country Club, San Antonio, during the 1992 Texas Open, he wrote himself into the record books but out of the tournament. The ball kept bouncing and rolling on a tarmac cart path until it was stopped by a fence – 787 yards away. It took Hooper two recovery shots with a 4-iron and then an 8-iron to return to the fairway. He eventually holed out for a double bogey six and failed to survive the half-way qualifying cut.

● Tommie Campbell of Portmarnock hit a drive of 392 yards at Dun Laoghaire GC in July 1964.

● Playing in Australia, American George Bayer is reported to have driven to within chipping distance of a 589 yards hole. "It was certainly a drive of over 500 yards", said Bayer acknowledging the strong fol-

lowing wind, sharp downslope where his ball landed and the bone-hard ground.

● In September, 1934, over the East Devon course, T.H.V. Haydon, Wimbledon, drove to the edge of the 9th green which was a hole of 465 yards, giving a drive of not less than 450 yards.

● E.C. Bliss drove 445 yards at Herne Bay in August, 1913. The drive was measured by a government surveyor who also measured the drop in height from tee to resting place of the ball at 57 feet.

Long carries

● At Sitwell Park, Rotherham, in 1935 the home professional, W. Smithson, drove a ball which carried a dyke at 380 yards from the 2nd tee.

● George Bell, of Penrith GC, New South Wales, Australia, using a number 2 wood drove across the Nepean River, a certified carry of 309 yards in a driving contest in 1964.

● After the 1986 Irish Professional Championship at Waterville, Co. Kerry, four long-hitting professionals tried for the longest-carry record over water, across a lake in the Waterville Hotel grounds. Liam Higgins, the local professional, carried 310 yards and Paul Leonard 311, beating the previous record by 2 yards.

● In the 1972 Algarve Open at Penina, Henry Cotton vouched for a carry of 305 yards over a ditch at the 18th hole by long-hitting Spanish professional Francisco Abreu. There was virtually no wind assistance.

● At the Home International matches at Portmarnock in 1949 a driving competition was held in which all the players in all four teams competed. The actual carry was measured and the longest was 280 yards by Jimmy Bruen.

● On 6th April, 1976, Tony Jacklin hit a number of balls into Vancouver harbour, Canada, from the 495-foot high roof of a new building complex. The longest carry was measured at 389 yards.

Long hitting

There have been numerous long hits, not on golf courses, where an outside agency has assisted the length of the shot. Such an example was a "drive" by Liam Higgins in 1986, on the Airport runway at Baldonal, near Dublin, of 632 yards.

● How's this for a long shot? Odd Marthinussen was holidaying in Haparanda in Sweden when he holed in one at the 14th. So what! The curious thing about this ace is that while he teed up in Sweden the green is in Finland which is in a different time zone. Registered as an ace in both countries, the time it took for the ball to go from tee to cup was estimated at 1 hour and 4 seconds ... surely the longest hole ever reported by Simon Pia in his column in *The Scotsman* newspaper.

Longest albatrosses

● The longest-known albatrosses (three under par) recorded at par 5 holes are:

● 647 yards-2nd hole at Guam Navy Club by Chief Petty Officer Kevin Murray of Chicago on 3rd January, 1982.

● 609 yards-15th hole at Mahaka Inn West Course, Hawaii, by John Eakin of California on 12th November, 1972.
● 602 yards-16th hole at Whiting Field Golf Course, Milton, Florida, by 27-year-old Bill Graham with a drive and a 3-wood, aided by a 25 mph tail wind.
● The longest-known albatrosses in open championships are: 580 yards 14th hole at Crans-sur-Sierre, by American Billy Casper in the 1971 Swiss Open; 558 yards 5th hole at Muirfield by American Johnny Miller in the 1972 Open Championship.
● In the 1994 German Amateur Championship at Wittelsbacher GC, Rohrenfield, Graham Rankin, a member of the visiting Scottish national team, had a two at the 592 yard 18th.

Eagles (multiple and consecutive)

● Wilf Jones scored three consecutive eagles at the first three holes at Moor Hall GC when playing in a competition there on August Bank Holiday Monday 1968. He scored 3, 1, 2 at holes measuring 529 yards, 176 yards and 302 yards.
● In a round of the 1980 Jubilee Cup, a mixed four-somes match play event of Colchester GC, Mrs Nora Booth and her son Brendan scored three consecutive gross eagles of 1, 3, 2 at the eighth, ninth and tenth holes.
● Three players in a four-ball match at Kington GC, Herefordshire, on 22nd July, 1948, all had eagle 2s at the 18th hole (272 yards). They were R.N. Bird, R. Morgan and V. Timson.
● Four Americans from Wisconsin on holiday at Gleneagles in 1977 scored three eagles and a birdie at the 300-yard par-4 14th hole on the King's course. The birdie was by Dr Kim Lulloff and the eagles by Dr Gordon Meiklejohn, Richard Johnson and Jack Kubitz.
● In an open competition at Glen Innes GC, Australia on 13th November, 1977, three players in a four-ball scored eagle 3s at the 9th hole (442 metres). They were Terry Marshall, Roy McHarg and Jack Rohleder.
● David McCarthy, a member of Moortown Golf Club, Leeds, had three consecutive eagles (3, 3, 2) on the 4th, 5th and 6th holes during a Pro-Am competition at Lucerne, Switzerland, on 7th August, 1992.

Speed of golf ball and club head and effect of wind and temperature

● In The Search for the Perfect Swing, a scientific study of the golf swing, a first class golfer is said to have the club head travelling at 100 mph at impact. This will cause the ball to leave the club at 135 mph. An outstandingly long hitter might manage to have the club head travelling at 130 mph which would produce a ball send-off speed of 175 mph. The resultant shot would carry 280 yards.
● According to Thomas Hardman, Wilson's director of research and development, wind will reduce or increase the flight of a golf ball by approximately 1½ yards for every mile per hour of wind. Every two degrees of temperature will make a yard difference in a ball's flight.

Most northerly course

● Although the most northerly course used to be in Iceland, Björkliden Arctic Golf Club, Sweden, 250 km north of the Arctic Circle, has taken over that role. This may soon change, however, when a course opens in Narvic, Norway, which could be a few metres further north than Björkliden.

Most southerly course

● Golf's most southerly course is Scott Base Country Club, 13° north of the South Pole. The course is run by the New Zealand Antarctic Programme and players must be kitted in full survival gear. The most difficult aspect is finding the orange golf balls which tend to get buried in the snow. Other obstacles include penguins, seals and skuas. If the ball is stolen by a skua then a penalty of one shot is incurred; but if the ball hits a skua it counts as a birdie.

"I'm sure they shouldn't have been allowed on. I don't think they're members"

Highest golf courses

● The highest golf course in the world is thought to be the Tuctu GC in Peru which is 14,335 feet above sea-level. High courses are also found in Bolivia with the La Paz GC being about 13,500 feet. In the Himalayas, near the border with Tibet, a 9-hole course at 12,800 feet has been laid out by keen golfers in the Indian Army.
● The highest course in Europe is at Sestriere in the Italian Alps, 6,500 feet above sea-level.
● The highest courses in Great Britain are West Monmouthshire in Wales at 1,513 feet, Leadhills in Scotland at 1,500 feet and Kington in England at 1,284 feet.

Longest courses

● The longest course in the world is Dub's Dread GC, Piper, Kansas, USA measuring 8,101 yards (par 78).

- The longest course for The Open Championship was 7,361 yards at Carnoustie in 1999.

Longest holes

- The longest hole in the world, as far as is known, is the 6th hole measuring 782 metres (860 yards) at Koolan Island GC, Western Australia. The par of the hole is 7. There are several holes over 700 yards throughout the world.
- The longest hole for The Open Championship is the 577 yards 6th hole at Royal Troon.

Longest tournaments

- The longest tournament held was over 144 holes in the World Open at Pinehurst, N Carolina, USA, first held in 1973. Play was over two weeks with a cut imposed at the halfway mark.
- An annual tournament, played in Germany on the longest day of the year, comprises 100 holes' medal play. Best return, in 1995, was 399 strokes.

Largest entries

- The Open – 2,500, St Andrews, 2010.
- The Amateur – 537, Muirfield, 1998.
- US Open – 9,086, Bethpage Park GC, NY, 2009.
- The largest entry for a PGA European Tour event was 398 for the 1978 Colgate PGA Championship. Since 1985, when the all-exempt ruling was introduced, all PGA tournaments have had 144 competitors, slightly more or less.
- In 1952, Bobby Locke, The Open Champion, played a round at Wentworth against any golfer in Britain. Cards costing 2s. 6d. each (12½p), were taken out by 24,000 golfers. The challenge was to beat the local par by more than Locke could beat the par at Wentworth. 1,641 competitors, including women, succeeded in *beating* the Champion and each received a certificate signed by him. As a result of this challenge the British Golf Foundation benefited to the extent of £3,026, the proceeds from the sale of cards. A similar tournament was held in the US and Canada when 87,094 golfers participated; 14,667 players bettered Ben Hogan's score under handicap. The fund benefited by $80,024.

Largest prize money

- The Machrie Tournament of 1901 was the first tournament with a first prize of £100. It was won by J.H. Taylor, then The Open Champion, who beat James Braid in the final.
- The richest events (at time of writing) are the – US Open and US PGA Championships which carry a prize-fund of $7.5 million. The bonus for victory in the Fedex Cup is $10 million. The biggest first prize is the $1,710,000 which goes to the winner of The Players' Championship on the PGA Tour in America.

Holing-in-one – odds against

- At the Wanderers Club, Johannesburg in January, 1951, forty-nine amateurs and professionals each played three balls at a hole 146 yards long. Of the 147 balls hit, the nearest was by Koos de Beer, professional at Reading Country Club, which finished 10½ inches from the hole. Harry Bradshaw, the Irish professional who was touring with the British team in South Africa, touched the pin with his second shot, but the ball rolled on and stopped 3 feet 2 inches from the cup.
- A competition on similar lines was held in 1951 in New York when 1,409 players who had done a hole-in-one held a competition over several days at short holes on three New York courses. Each player was allowed a total of five shots, giving an aggregate of 7,045 shots. No player holed-in-one, and the nearest ball finished 3½ inches from the hole.
- A further illustration of the element of luck in holing-in-one is derived from an effort by Harry Gonder, an American professional, who in 1940 stood for 16 hours 25 minutes and hit 1,817 balls trying to do a 160 yard hole-in-one. He had two official witnesses and caddies to tee and retrieve the balls and count the strokes. His 1,756th shot struck the hole but stopped an inch from the hole. This was his nearest effort.
- From this and other similar information an estimate of the odds against holing-in-one at any particular hole within the range of one shot was made at somewhere between 1,500 and 2,000 to 1 by a proficient player. Subsequently, however, statistical analysis in America has come up with the following odds: a male professional or top amateur 3,708 to 1; a female professional or top amateur 4,648 to 1; an average golfer 42,952 to 1.

Hole-in-one first recorded

- The earliest recorded hole-in-one was in 1869 at The Open Championship when Tom Morris Jr completed the 145-yard 8th hole at Prestwick in one. This was the first ace in competition for The Open Championship Challenge Belt.
- The first hole-in-one recorded with the 1.66 inch ball was in 1972 by John G. Salvesen, a member of The R&A Championship Committee. At the time this size of ball was only experimental. Salvesen used a 7-iron for his historical feat at the 11th hole on the Old Course, St Andrews.

Holing-in-one in important events

Since the day of the first known hole-in-one by Tom Morris Jr, at the 8th hole (145 yards) at Prestwick in the 1869 Open Championship, holes-in-one, even in championships, have become too numerous for each to be recorded. Only where other unusual or interesting circumstances prevailed are the instances shown here.

- All hole-in-one achievements are remarkable. Many are extraordinary. Among the more amazing was that of 2-handicap Leicestershire golfer Bob Taylor, a member of the Scraptoft Club. During the final practice day for the 1974 Eastern Counties Foursomes Championship on the Hunstanton Links, he holed his tee shot with a one-iron at the 188-yard 16th. The next day, in the first round of the competition, he repeated the feat, the only difference being that because of a change of wind he used a six-iron. When he stepped on to the 16th tee the following day his partner jokingly offered him odds of 1,000,000 to one against holing-in-one for a third successive time. Taylor again used his six-iron – and holed in one!

● 1878 – Jamie Anderson, competing in The Open Championship at Prestwick, holed in one at the 11th. In these days The Open was played over three rounds of 12 holes so his ace, the first hole-in-one in competition for the Claret Jug – came at his penultimate hole in his third round. Although it seemed then that he was winning easily, it turned out afterwards that if he had not taken this hole in one stroke he would very likely have lost. Anderson was just about to make his tee shot when Andy Stuart (winner of the first Irish Open Championship in 1892), who was acting as marker to Anderson, remarked he was standing outside the teeing ground, and that if he played the stroke from there he would be disqualified. Anderson picked up his ball and teed it in a proper place. Then he holed-in-one. He won the Championship by one stroke.

● On a Friday the 13th in 1990, Richard Allen holed-in-one at the 13th at the Barwon Heads Golf Club, Victoria, Australia, and then lost the hole. He was giving a handicap stroke to his opponent, brother-in-law Jason Ennels, who also holed-in-one.

● 1906 – R. Johnston, North Berwick, competing in The Open Championship, did the 14th hole at Muirfield in one. Johnston played with only one club throughout – an adjustable head club.

● 1959 – The first hole-in-one in the US Women's Open Championship was recorded. It was by Patty Berg on the 7th hole (170 yards) at Churchill Valley CC, Pittsburgh.

● 1962 – On 6th April, playing in the second round of the Schweppes Close Championship at Little Aston, H. Middleton of Shandon Park, Belfast, holed his tee shot at the 159-yard 5th hole, winning a prize of £1,000. Ten minutes later, playing two matches ahead of Middleton, R.A. Jowle, son of the professional, Frank Jowle, holed his tee shot at the 179-yard 9th hole. As an amateur he was rewarded by the sponsors with a £30 voucher.

● 1963 – By holing out in one stroke at the 18th hole (156 yards) at Moor Park on the first day of the Esso Golden round-robin tournament, H.R. Henning, South Africa, won the £10,000 prize offered for this feat.

● 1967 – Tony Jacklin in winning the Masters tournament at St George's, Sandwich, did the 16th hole in one. His ace has an exceptional place in the records for it was seen by millions on TV, the ball was in view in its flight till it went into the hole in his final round of 64.

● 1971 – John Hudson, 25-year-old professional at Hendon, achieved a near miracle when he holed two consecutive holes-in-one in the Martini Tournament at Norwich. They were at the 11th and 12th holes (195 yards and 311 yards respectively) in the second round.

● 1971 – In The Open Championship at Birkdale, Lionel Platts holed-in-one at the 212-yard 4th hole in the second round. This was the first instance of an Open Championship hole-in-one being recorded by television. It was incidentally Platts' seventh ace of his career.

● In the 2006 Ryder Cup at the K Club, Ireland, Paul Casey holed his 4-iron shot at the 14th to score the fifth ace in the history of the competition. The following day, at the same hole, Scott Verplank became the first American to score a Ryder Cup hole-in-one. Others who have enjoyed aces in the match include Peter Butler in 1973, Nick Faldo in 1993 and Costantino Rocca and Howard Clark in 1995 at Oak Hill.

● 1973 – In the 1973 Open Championship at Troon, two holes-in-one were recorded, both at the 8th hole, known as the Postage Stamp, in the first round. They were achieved by Gene Sarazen and amateur David Russell, who were by coincidence respectively the oldest and youngest competitors.

● Mrs Argea Tissies, whose husband Hermann took 15 at Royal Troon's Postage Stamp 8th hole in the 1950 Open, scored a hole-in-one at the 2nd hole at Punta Ala in the second round of the Italian Ladies' Senior Open of 1978. Exactly five years later on the same date, at the same time of day, in the same round of the same tournament at the same hole, she did it again with the same club.

● In less than two hours play in the second round of the 1989 US Open at Oak Hill Country Club, Rochester, New York, four competitors – Doug Weaver, Mark Wiebe, Jerry Pate and Nick Price – each holed the 167-yard 6th hole in one. The odds against four professionals achieving such a record in a field of 156 are reckoned at 332,000 to 1.

● On 20th May, 1998, British golf journalist Derek Lawrenson, an eight-handicapper, won a Lamborghini Diablo car, valued at over £180,000, by holing his three-iron tee shot to the 175-yard 15th hole at Mill Ride, Berkshire. He was taking part in a charity day and was partnering England football stars Paul Ince and Steve McManaman.

● David Toms took the lead in the 2001 USPGA Championship at Atlanta Athletic Club with a hole-in-one at the 15th hole in the third round and went on to win. Nick Faldo (4th hole) and Scott Hoch (17th hole) also had holes-in-one during the event.

● In the 2006 Ryder Cup at the K Club, Ireland, Paul Casey holed his 4-iron shot at the 14th to score the fifth ace in the history of the competition. The following day, at the same hole, Scott Verplank became the first American to score a Ryder Cup hole-in-one.

Holing-in-one – longest holes

● Bob Mitera, as a 21-year-old American student, standing 5 feet 6 inches and weighing under 12 stones, claimed the world record for the longest hole-in-one. Playing over the appropriately named Miracle Hill course at Omaha, on 7th October, 1965, Bob holed his drive at the 10th hole, 447 yards long. The ground sloped sharply downhill.

- Two longer holes-in-one have been achieved, but because they were at dog-leg holes they are not generally accepted as being the longest holes-in-one. They were 496 yards (17th hole, Teign Valley) by Shaun Lynch in July 1995 and 480 yards (5th hole, Hope CC, Arkansas) by L. Bruce on 15th November, 1962.
- In March, 1961, Lou Kretlow holed his tee shot at the 427-yard 16th hole at Lake Hefner course, Oklahoma City, USA.
- The longest known hole-in-one in Great Britain was the 393-yard 7th hole at West Lancashire GC, where in 1972 the assistant professional Peter Parkinson holed his tee shot.
- Paul Neilson, a 34-year-old golfer at South Winchester, holed in one at the club's par 4 fifth hole – 391 yards.
- Other long holes-in-one recorded in Great Britain have been 380 yards (5th hole at Tankersley Park) by David Hulley in 1961; 380 yards (12th hole at White Webbs) by Danny Dunne on 30th July, 1976; 370 yards (17th hole at Chilwell Manor, distance from the forward tee) by Ray Newton in 1977; 365 yards (10th hole at Harewood Downs) by K. Saunders in 1965; 365 yards (7th hole at Catterick Garrison GC) by Leslie Bruckner on 18th July, 1980.
- The longest-recorded hole-in-one by a woman was that accomplished in September, 1949 by Marie Robie – the 393-yard hole at Furnace Brook course, Wollaston, Mass, USA.

Holing-in-one – greatest number by one person

59–Amateur Norman Manley of Long Beach, California.
50–Mancil Davis, professional at the Trophy Club, Fort Worth, Texas.
31–British professional C.T. le Chevalier who died in 1973.
22–British amateur, Jim Hay of Kirkintilloch GC.

At One Hole
13–Joe Lucius at 15th hole of Mohawk, Ohio.
5–Left-hander, the late Fred Francis at 7th (now 16th) hole of Cardigan GC.

Holing-in-one – greatest frequency

- The record for the greatest number of holes-in-one in a calendar year is 14, claimed in 2007 by Californian Jacqueline Gagne who hit her fourteenth ace at Mission Hills in front of a television crew who had been sent to check if her claims for the previous 13 were true.
- J.O. Boydstone of California made 11 aces in 1962.
- John Putt of Frilford Heath GC had six holes-in-one in 1970, followed by three in 1971.
- Douglas Porteous, of Ruchill GC, Glasgow, achieved seven holes-in-one in the space of eight months. Four of them were scored in a five-day period from 26th to 30th September, 1974, in three consecutive rounds of golf. The first two were achieved at Ruchill GC in one round, the third there two days later, and the fourth at Clydebank and District GC after another two days.

The following May, Porteous had three holes-in-one, the first at Linn Park GC incredibly followed by two more in the one round at Clober GC.
- Mrs Kathleen Hetherington of West Essex has holed-in-one five times, four being at the 15th hole at West Essex. Four of her five aces were within seven months in 1966.
- Mrs Dorothy Hill of Dumfries and Galloway GC holed-in-one three times in 11 days in 1977.
- James C. Reid of Brodick, aged 59 and 8 handicap in 1987, achieved 14 holes-all-one, all but one on Isle of Arran courses. His success was in spite of severe physical handicaps of a stiff left knee, a damaged right ankle, two discs removed from his back and a hip replacement.
- Jean Nield, a member at Chorlton-cum-Hardy and Bramall Park, has had eleven holes-in-one and her husband Brian, who plays at Bramall Park, has had five – a husband and wife total of 16.
- Peter Gibbins holed his tee shot at the 359 yards par 4 13th hole at Hazlemere on November 2 1984 using a 3-wood that was in his bag for the first time. That spectacular ace was his third but he has had nine more since then.

Holing successive holes-in-one

- Successive holes-in-one are rare; successive par 4 holes-in-one may be classed as near miracles. N.L. Manley performed the most incredible feat in September, 1964, at Del Valle Country Club, Saugus, California, USA. The par 4 7th (330 yards) and 8th (290 yards) are both slightly downhill, dog-leg holes. Manley had aces at both, en route to a course record of 61 (par 71).
- The first recorded example in Britain of a player holing-in-one stroke at each of two successive holes was achieved on 6th February, 1964, at the Walmer and Kingsdown course, Kent. The young assistant professional at that club, Roger Game (aged 17) holed out with a 4-wood at the 244-yard 7th hole, and repeated the feat at the 256-yard 8th hole, using a 5-iron.
- The first occasion of holing-in-one at consecutive holes in a major professional event occurred when John Hudson, 25-year-old professional at Hendon, holed-in-one at the 11th and 12th holes at Norwich during the second round of the 1971 Martini tournament. Hudson used a 4-iron at the 195-yard 11th and a driver at the 311-yard downhill 12th hole.
- Assistant professional Tom Doty (23 years), playing in a friendly match on a course near Chicago in October, 1971, had a remarkable four-hole score which included two consecutive holes-in-one, sandwiched either side by an albatross and an eagle: 4th hole (500 yards)-2; 5th hole (360 yards dog-leg)-1; 6th hole (175 yards)-1; 7th hole (375 yards)-2. Thus he was 10 under par for four consecutive holes.
- At the Standard Life Loch Lomond tournament on the European Tour in July 2000 Jarmo Sandelin holed-in-one at the 17th with the final shot there in the third round and fellow Swede Mathias Gronberg

holed-in-one with the first shot there in the last round. A prize of $100,000 was only on offer in the last round.

Holing-in-one twice (or more) in the same round by the same person

What might be thought to be a very rare feat indeed – that of holing-in-one twice in the same round – has in fact happened on many occasions as the following instances show. It is, nevertheless, compared to the number of golfers in the world, still something of an outstanding achievement. The first known occasion was in 1907 when J. Ireland playing in a three-ball match at Worlington holed the 5th and 18th holes in one stroke and two years later in 1909 H.C. Josecelyne holed the 3rd (175 yards) and the 14th (115 yards) at Acton on 24th November.

● The first mention of two holes-in-one in a round by a woman was followed later by a similar feat by another lady at the same club. On 19th May, 1942, Mrs W. Driver, of Balgowlah Golf Club, New South Wales, holed out in one at the 3rd and 8th holes in the same round, while on 29th July, 1948, Mrs F. Burke at the same club holed out in one at the second and eighth holes.

● The Rev Harold Snider, aged 75, scored his first hole-in-one on 9th June, 1976 at the 8th hole of the Ironwood course, near Phoenix. By the end of his round he had scored three holes-in-one, the other two being at the 13th (110 yards) and 14th (135 yards). Ironwood is a par-3 course, giving more opportunity of scoring holes-in-one but, nevertheless, three holes-in-one in one round on any type of course is an outstanding achievement.

● When the Hawarden course in North Wales comprised only nine holes, Frank Mills in 1994 had two holes-in-one at the same hole in the same round. Each time, he hit a seven iron to the 134-yard 3rd and 12th.

● The youngest player to achieve two holes-in-one in the same round is thought to be Christopher Anthony Jones on 14 September, 1994. At the age of 14 years and 11 months he holed-in-one at the Sand Moor, Leeds, 137-yard 10th and then at the 156-yard 17th.

● The youngest woman to have performed the feat was a 17-year-old, Marjorie Merchant, playing at the Lomas Athletic GC, Argentina, at the 4th (170 yards) and 8th (130 yards) holes.

● Tony Hannam, left-handed, handicap 16 and age 71, followed a hole-in-one at the 142 yards 4th of the Bude and North Cornwall Golf Club course with another at the 143-yard 10th on Friday, 18th September, 1992.

● Brothers Eric and John Wilkinson were playing together at the Ravensworth Golf Club on Tyneside in 2001 and both holed-in-one at the 148 yards eighth. Eric (46) played first and then John to the hidden green but there is no doubting this unusual double ace. The club's vice-captain Dave Johnstone saw both balls go in! Postman Eric plays off 9. John, a county planner, has a handicap of 20. Next time they played the hole both missed the green.

● Chris Valerro, a 22-handicapper from the Liberty Lake Golf Club, Spokane, Washington, aced the 143 yards 3rd hole at his home club with a 7-iron and then the 140 yards 11th hole with his 8-iron.

● Edinburgh golfer, 25-year-old Chris Tugwell, was representing the Lothianburn club when he aced the 157-yard seventh with a nine iron and then went on to hole-in-one again at the 168-yard 12th with a five iron.

● Eugene O'Brien scored a hole-in-one double on one of Britain's most difficult courses when he aced the 13th and 16th holes at Carnoustie.

● Yusuka Miyazato, a multiple winner on the Japanese circuit, had two holes in one in the same round on the second day at the Montreux Golf Club in 2006.

● Milwaukee resident Sanjay Kuttemperoor scored two aces in 2006 at the Treetops Resort, Michigan, the first on the 150-yard fifth and the second on the 135-yard ninth.

● Some golfers go through their life without ever having a coveted hole-in-one but Alan Domingo had two within an hour in the same round at the Hawick Club in 2011. He aced the 144 yards eighth and then did the same at the 198 yards 13th.

● 75-year-old Peter Wafford, who plays off 13 at Bush Hill Park Golf Club, had a red letter day when playing in a match against Chigwell at Chigwell in 2011. Although only having recently taken up golf he had two holes in one in the same round beating estimated odds of 67 million to one against that happening.

Holes-in-one on the same day

● In July 1987, at the Skerries Club, Co Dublin, Rank Xerox sponsored two tournaments, a men's 18-hole four-ball with 134 pairs competing and a 9-hole mixed foursomes with 33 pairs. During the day each of the four par-3 holes on the course were holed-in-one: the 2nd by Noel Bollard, the 5th by Bart Reynolds, the 12th by Jackie Carr and the 15th by Gerry Ellis.

● Wendy Russell holed-in-one at the consecutive par threes in the first round of the British Senior Ladies' at Wrexham in 1989.

● Clifford Briggs, aged 65, holed-in-one at the 14th at Parkstone GC on the same day as his wife Gwen, 60, aced the 16th.

● In the final round of the 2000 Victor Chandler British Masters at Woburn Alastair Forsyth holed-in-one at the second. Playing partner Roger Chapman then holed-in-one at the eighth.

Two holes-in-one at the same hole in the same game

● *First in World:* George Stewart and Fred Spellmeyer at the 18th hole, Forest Hills, New Jersey, USA in October 1919.

● *First in Great Britain:* Miss G. Clutterbuck and Mrs H.M. Robinson at the 15th hole (120 yards), St Augustine GC, Ramsgate, on 8th May, 1925.

● *First in Denmark:* In a Club match in August 1987 at Himmerland, Steffan Jacobsen of Aalborg and Peter Forsberg of Himmerland halved the 15th hole in one shot, the first known occasion in Denmark.

● *First in Australia:* Dr & Mrs B. Rankine, playing in a mixed "Canadian foursome" event at the Osmond Club near Adelaide, South Australia in April 1987, holed-in-one in consecutive shots at the 2nd hole (162 metres), he from the men's tee with a 3-iron and his wife from the ladies' tee with a 1½ wood.

● Jack Ashton, aged 76, holed-in-one at the 8th hole of the West Kent Golf Club at Downe but only got a half. Opponent Ted Eagle, in receipt of shot, made a 2, net 1.

● Dr Martin Pucci and Trevor Ironside will never forget one round at the Macdonald Club in Ellon last year. Playing in an open competition the two golfers with Jamie Cowthorne making up the three-ball reached the tee at the 169yards short 11th. Dr Pucci, with the honour, hit a 5-iron, Mr Ironside a 6-iron at the hole where only the top of the flag is visible. Both hit good shots but when they reached the green they could spot only one ball   and that was Mr Cowthorne's. Then they realised that something amazing might have happened. When they reached the putting surface they discovered that both Dr Pucci's and Mr Ironside's balls were wedged into the hole. Both had made aces. It was Dr Pucci's sixth and Mr Ironside's second.

● Eric and John Wilkinson went out for their usual weekly game at the Ravensworth Golf Club in Wrekenton on Tyneside in 2001 and both holed in one at the 148 yards eighth. Neither Eric, a 46-year-old 9-handicapper who has been playing golf since he was 14, nor John, who has been playing golf for ten years and has a handicap of 20, saw the balls go in because the green is over a hill but club vice-captain Dave Johnston did and described the incident as "amazing". Next time the brothers played the hole both missed the green!

● Richard Evans and Mark Evans may not be related but they have one thing in common – they both holed in one at the same hole when playing in a club competition. The double ace occurred in 2003 at Glynhir Golf Club's third hole which measures 189 yards. Thirty-seven-year-old surveyor Richard, who plays off 7, hit first and made his first hole-in-one in the 15 years he has played the game. His opponent, car worker Mark whose handicap is 12, then followed him in.

● Richard Hall, who plays off 12, and high handicapper Peter McEvoy had never had a hole-in-one until one Saturday night in 2003 at Shandon Park Golf Club in Belfast. Friends since their schooldays they play a lot of golf together so there was much excitement when Hall holed his 5-iron shot for an ace at the 180 yards eighth. Then he challenged McEvoy to match it. And he did!

● Brothers Hanks and Davis Massey were playing a late afternoon practice round at TPC Sawgrass in Florida in 2008 when they came to the par 3 third. Eleven-year-old Hanks was up first and hit a 9-iron 108 yards into the hole. He and his father Scott ran up to the green in wild celebration forgetting that nine-year-old Davis had still to play. When he did he pulled out an 8-iron and also aced.

● Ross Roger and John Downie, two 13-year-olds playing in a foursomes match at the Clober Club in Milngavie near Glasgow, Scotland, made their own little bit of golfing history when they stepped on to the 15th tee and both holed out in one. Ross, teeing up first, watched his ball drop into the hole for his first ace then stepped back and saw John do the same thing.

Three holes-in-one at the same hole in the same game

● During the October monthly medal at Southport & Ainsdale Golf Club on Saturday October 18, 2003, three holes-in-one were achieved at the 153-yard 8th by Stuart Fawcett (5 handicap), Brian Verinder (17 handicap) and junior member Andrew Kent (12 handicap). The players were not playing in the same group.

Holing-in-one – youngest and oldest players

● Elsie McLean, 102, from Chico, California, holed-in-one in April 2007.

● In January 1985 Otto Bucher of Switzerland holed-in-one at the age of 99 on La Manga's 130-yard 12th hole.

● In 2005, Bim Smith, a member of Rochester & Cobham Park Golf Club, Kent, hit a hole-in-one – his fourth – three days before his 91st birthday.

● Bob Hope had a hole-in-one at Palm Springs, California, at the age of 90.

● 76-year-old lady golfer Mrs Felicity Sieghart achieved two holes-in-one when playing in a club Stableford competition at the Aldeburgh club in 2003. Mrs Sieghart aced the 134 yards eighth and the 130 yards 17th – but sadly did not win the competition.

● The youngest player ever to achieve a hole in one is now believed to be Matthew Draper, who was only five when he aced the 122-yard fourth hole at Cherwell Edge, Oxfordshire, in June 1997. He used a wood.

● Six-year-old Tommy Moore aced the 145-yard fourth hole at Woodbrier, West Virginia, in 1968. He had another at the same hole before his seventh birthday.

● Keith Long was just five when he aced on a Mississippi golf course in 1998.

● Five-year-old Eleanor Gamble became one of the youngest to have a hole in one when she made an ace at the Cambridge Lakes club in 2011.

● Alex Evans, aged eight, holed-in-one with a 4-wood at the 136-yard 4th hole at Bromborough, Merseyside, in 1994.

● Nine-year-old Kate Langley from Scotter in Lincolnshire, is believed to have became the youngest girl to score an ace. It is reported that she holed in one at the 134 yards first hole at Forest Pines Beeches in Scunthorpe after having had a lesson from local professional David Edwards. Kate was nine years and 166 days when she hit the ace – 199 days younger than Australian Kathryn Webb who had held the record previously.

● In 2007, 13-year-old Lauren Taylor from Rugby scored two aces and made history at her club. Her first ace was scored on the 145 yard 12th, where she used a seven iron for her shot over the brook whilst playing in a junior medal competition. Her second came during the second round of the 36-hole Junior Championship This time it was achieved on the 100 yard 8th (which plays much harder due to it being all up-hill), using a pitching wedge. From the tee you cannot see what is happening on the green.

Holing-in-one – miscellaneous incidents

● Chemistry student Jason Bohn, aged 19, of State College, Pennsylvania, supported a charity golf event at Tuscaloosa, Alabama, in 1992 when twelve competitors were invited to try to hole-in-one at the 135-yard second hole for a special prize covered by insurance. One attempt only was allowed. Bohn succeeded and was offered US$1m (paid at the rate of $5,000 a month for the next 20 years) at the cost of losing his amateur status. He took the money.

● The late Harry Vardon, who scored the greatest number of victories in The Open Championship, only once did a hole-in-one. That was in 1903 at Mundesley, Norfolk, where Vardon was convalescing from a long illness.

● In a guest day at Rochford Hundred, Essex, in 1994, there were holes-in-one at all the par threes. First Paul Cairns, of Langdon Hills, holed a 4-iron at the 205-yard 15th, next Paul Francis, a member of the home club, sank a 7-iron at the 156-yard seventh and finally Jim Crabb, of Three Rivers, holed a 9-iron at the 136-yard 11th.

● In April 1988, Mary Anderson, a bio-chemistry student at Trinity College, Dublin, holed-in-one at the 290-yard 6th hole at Island GC, Co Dublin.

● In April 1984 Joseph McCaffrey and his son, Gordon, each holed-in-one in the Spring Medal at the 164-yard 12th hole at Vale of Leven Club, Dunbartonshire.

● In 1977, 14-year-old Gillian Field after a series of lessons holed-in-one at the 10th hole at Moor Place GC in her first round of golf.

● When he holed-in-one at the second hole in a match against D. Graham in the 1979 Suntory World Match Play at Wentworth, Japanese professional Isao Aoki won himself a Bovis home at Gleneagles worth, inclusive of furnishings, £55,000. Brian Barnes has aced the short 10th and Thomas Bjørn won a car when he aced the short 14th in 2003.

● On the morning after being elected captain for 1973 of the Norwich GC, J.S. Murray hit his first shot as captain straight into the hole at the 169-yard 1st hole.

● At Nuneaton GC in 1999 the men's captain and the ladies' captain both holed-in-one during their captaincies.

● Using the same club and ball, 11-handicap left-hander Christopher Smyth holed-in-one at the 2nd hole (170 yards) in two consecutive medal competitions at Headfort GC, Co. Meath, in January, 1976.

● Playing over Rickmansworth course at Easter, 1960, Mrs A.E. (Paddy) Martin achieved a remarkable sequence of aces. On Good Friday she sank her tee shot at the 3rd hole (125 yards). The next day, using the same ball and the same 8-iron, at the same hole, she scored another one. And on the Monday (same ball, same club, same hole) she again holed out from the tee.

● At Barton-on-Sea in February 1989 Mrs Dorothy Huntley-Flindt, aged 91, holed-in-one at the par-3 13th. The following day Mr John Chape, a fellow member in his 80s, holed the par- 3 5th in one.

● In 1995 Roy Marsland of Ratho Park, Edinburgh, had three holes-in-one in nine days: at Prestonfield's 5th, at Ratho Park's 3rd and at Sandilands' 2nd.

● Michael Monk, age 82, a member of Tandridge Golf Club, Surrey, waited until 1992 to record his first hole-in-one. It continued a run of rare successes for his family. In the previous 12 months, Mr Monk's daughter, Elizabeth, 52, daughter-in-law, Celia, 48, and grandson, Jeremy, 16, had all holed-in-one on the same course.

● Lou Holloway, a left-hander, recorded his second hole-in-one at the Mount Derby course in New Zealand 13 years after acing the same hole while playing right-handed.

● Ryan Procop, an American schoolboy, holed-in-one at a 168-yard par 3 at Glen Eagles GC, Ohio, with a putter. He confessed that he was so disgusted with himself after a 12 on the previous hole that he just grabbed his putter and hit from the tee.

● Ernie and Shirley Marsden, of Warwick Golf Club, are believed in 1993 to have equalled the record for holes-in-one by a married couple. Each has had three, as have another English couple, Mr and Mrs B.E. Simmonds.

● Russell Pughe, a 12-handicapper from Nottinghamshire, holed-in-one twice in three days at the 274-yard par-4 18th hole at Sidmouth in Devon in 1998. The hole has a blind tee shot.

● Robert Looney aced the 170 yards 13th at the Thorny Lea Golf Club in Brockton, Massachussetts, 30 years after his father made a hole-in-one at the same hole.

● The odds on the chances of two players having a hole in one when playing together are long but it happened to former club captain Robert Smallwood, a 58-year-old retired IBM manager, and current captain Mike Wheeler, a 57-year-old retired financial consultant, when they went out for a round at Irvine Golf Club in Ayrshire in 2005. Playing in the rain, Mr Smallwood, using a driver, had his ace at the 289 yards fourth before Mr Wheeler holed in one at the 279 yards fifth.

● Texan blind golfer Charles Adams, sank his tee shot on the 102-yard 14th hole at Stone Creek Golf Club, Oregon City, Oregon, on October 4, 2006, during the US Blind Golf Association National Championship, the first hole-in-one in the 61-year history of the tournament.

● Blind golfer Sheila Drummond, a member of the US Blind Golf Association, is believed to be the only

blind woman golfer to have holed-in-one. Sheila's feat was accomplished in August 2007 at the 144-yard par-3 at Mahoning Valley CC in Lehighton, PA.
● Jim Gales, who was awarded the MBE for his services to blind golf, scored a hole in one in 2010 at Wellsgreen, Fife, while practising for the Scottish Pan-Disability Open. Other blind golfers who have scored aces include Jan Dinsdale (NIR), Joel Ludvicek (USA) and Zohar Sharon (ISR).
● Bob Taylor, a Leicestershire County player, achieved what many would consider the impossible when he holed in one at the same hole on three successive days at the Hunstanton Club. Playing in the Eastern Countries Foursomes in 1974 he aced the 188 yards 16th using first a 1-iron and then a 6-iron on the next two occasions.

Challenge matches

One of the first recorded professional challenge matches was in 1843 when Allan Robertson beat Willie Dunn in a 20-round match at St Andrews over 360 holes by 2 rounds and 1 to play. Thereafter until about 1905 many matches are recorded, some for up to £200 a side – a considerable sum for the time. The Morrises, the Dunns and the Parks were the main protagonists until Vardon, Braid and Taylor took over in the 1890s. Often matches were on a home-and-away basis over 72 holes or more, with many spectators; Vardon and Willie Park Jr attracted over 10,000 at North Berwick in 1899.

Between the wars Walter Hagen, Archie Compston, Henry Cotton and Bobby Locke all played several such matches. Compston surprisingly beat Hagen by 18 up and 17 to play at Moor Park in 1928; yet typically Hagen went on to win The Open the following week at Sandwich. Cotton played classic golf at Walton Heath in 1937 when he beat Densmore Shute for £500-a-side at Walton Heath by 6 and 5 over 72 holes.

Curious and large wagers

(See also bets recorded under Cross-Country Matches and in Challenge Matches)

● In The Royal and Ancient Golf Club minutes an entry on 3rd November, 1820 was made in the following terms:

> Sir David Moncrieffe, Bart, of Moncrieffe, backs his life against the life of John Whyte-Melville, Esq, of Strathkinnes, for a new silver club as a present to the St Andrews Golf Club, the price of the club to be paid by the survivor and the arms of the parties to be engraved on the club, and the present bet inscribed on it. No balls to be attached to it. In testimony of which this bet is subscribed by the parties thereto.

Thirteen years later, Mr Whyte-Melville, in a feeling and appropriate speech, expressed his deep regret at the lamented death of Sir David Moncrieffe, one of the most distinguished and zealous supporters of the club. Whyte-Melville, while lamenting the cause that led to it, had pleasure in fulfilling the duty imposed upon him by the bet, and accordingly delivered to the captain the silver putter. Whyte-Melville in 1883 was elected captain of the club a second time; he died in his eighty-sixth year in July, 1883, before he could take office and the captaincy remained vacant for a year. His portrait hangs in The Royal and Ancient clubhouse and is one of the finest and most distinguished pictures in the smoking room.
● In 1914 Francis Ouimet, who in the previous autumn had won the American Open Championship after a triangular tie with Harry Vardon and Ted Ray, came to Great Britain with Jerome D. Travers, the holder of the American amateur title, to compete in the British Amateur Championship at Sandwich. An American syndicate took a bet of £30,000 to £10,000 that one or other of the two United States champions would be the winner. It only took two rounds to decide the bet against the Americans. Ouimet was beaten by a then quite unknown player, H.S. Tubbs, while Travers was defeated by Charles Palmer, who was 56 years of age at the time.
● In 1907 John Ball for a wager undertook to go round Hoylake during a dense fog in under 90, in not more than two and a quarter hours and without losing a ball. Ball played with a black ball, went round in 81, and also beat the time.
● The late Ben Sayers, for a wager, played the 18 holes of the Burgess Society course scoring a four at every hole. Sayers was about to start against an American, when his opponent asked him what he could do the course in. Fours replied Sayers, meaning 72, or an average of 4s for the round. A bet was made, then the American added, Remember a three or a five is not a four. There were eight bogey 5s and two 3s on the Burgess course at the time Old Ben achieved his feat.

Feats of endurance

Although golf is not a game where endurance, in the ordinary sense in which the term is employed in sport, is required, there are several instances of feats on the links which demanded great physical exertion.

● Four British golfers, Simon Gard, Nick Harley, Patrick Maxwell and his brother Alastair Maxwell, completed 14 rounds in one day at Iceland's Akureyri Golf Club, the most northern 18-hole course in the world, during June 1991 when there was 24-hour daylight. It was claimed a record and £10,000 was raised for charity.
● In 1971 during a 24-hour period from 6 pm on 27th November until 5.15 pm on 28th November, Ian Colston completed 401 holes over the 6,061 yards Bendigo course, Victoria, Australia. Colston was a top marathon athlete but was not a golfer. However prior to his golfing marathon he took some lessons and became adept with a 6-iron, the only club he used throughout the 401 holes. The only assistance Colston had was a team of harriers to carry his 6-iron and look for his ball, and a band of motorcyclists who provided light during the night. This is, as far as is known, the greatest number of holes played in 24 hours on foot on a full-size course.
● In 1934 Col Bill Farnham played 376 holes in 24 hours 10 minutes at the Guildford Lake Course,

Guildford, Connecticut, using only a mashie and a putter.

● To raise funds for extending the Skipton GC course from 12 to 18 holes, the club professional, 24-year-old Graham Webster, played 277 holes in the hours of daylight on Monday 20th June, 1977. Playing with nothing longer than a 5-iron he averaged 81 per 18-hole round. Included in his marathon was a hole-in-one.

● Michael Moore, a 7 handicap 26-year-old member of Okehampton GC, completed on foot 15 rounds 6 holes (276 holes) there on Sunday, 25th June, 1972, in the hours of daylight. He started at 4.15 am and stopped at 9.15 pm. The distance covered was estimated at 56 miles.

● On 21st June, 1976, 5-handicapper Sandy Small played 15 rounds (270 holes) over his home course Cosby GC, length 6,128 yards, to raise money for the Society of Physically Handicapped Children. Using only a 5-iron, 9-iron and putter, Small started at 4.10 am and completed his 270th hole at 10.39 pm with the aid of car headlights. His fastest round was his first (40 minutes) and slowest his last (82 minutes). His best round of 76 was achieved in the second round.

● During the weekend of 20th–21st June, 1970, Peter Chambers of Yorkshire completed over 14 rounds of golf over the Scarborough South Cliff course. In a non-stop marathon lasting just under 24 hours, Chambers played 257 holes in 1,168 strokes, an average of 84.4 strokes per round.

● Bruce Sutherland, on the Craiglockhart Links, Edinburgh, started at 8.15 pm on 21st June, 1927, and played almost continuously until 7.30 pm on 22nd June, 1927. During the night four caddies with acetylene lamps lit the way, and lost balls were reduced to a minimum. He completed fourteen rounds. Mr Sutherland, who was a physical culture teacher, never recovered from the physical strain and died a few years later.

● Sidney Gleave, motorcycle racer, and Ernest Smith, golf professional at Davyhulme Club, Manchester, on 12th June, 1939, played five rounds of golf in five different countries – Scotland, Ireland, Isle of Man, England and Wales. Smith had to play the five rounds under 80 in one day to win the £100 wager. They travelled by plane, and the following was their programme:

Start 3.40a.m. at Prestwick St Nicholas (Scotland), finished 1 hour 35 minutes later on 70.

2nd Course – Bangor, Ireland. Started at 7.15 a.m. and took 1 hour 30 minutes to finish on 76.

3rd Course – Castletown, Isle of Man. Started 10.15 am, scored 76 in 1 hour 40 minutes.

4th Course – Blackpool, Stanley Park, England. Started at 1.30 pm and scored 72 in 1 hour 55 minutes.

5th Course – Hawarden, Wales, started at 6 pm and finished 2 hours 15 minutes later with a score of 72.

● On 19th June, 1995, Ian Botham, the former England cricketer, played four rounds of golf in Ireland, Wales, Scotland and England. His playing companions were Gary Price, the professional at Branston, and

Tony Wright, owner of Craythorne, Burton-on-Trent, where the last 18 holes were completed. The other courses were St Margaret's, Anglesey and Dumfries & Galloway. The first round began at 4.30 am and the last was completed at 8.30 pm.

● On Wednesday, 3rd July, 1974, E.S. Wilson, Whitehead, Co. Antrim and Dr G.W. Donaldson, Newry, Co. Down, played a nine-hole match in each of seven countries in the one day. The first 9 holes was at La Moye (Channel Islands) followed by Hawarden (Wales), Chester (England), Turnberry (Scotland), Castletown (Isle of Man), Dundalk (Eire) and Warrenpoint (N Ireland). They started their first round at 4.25 am and their last round at 9.25 pm. Wilson piloted his own plane throughout.

● In June 1986 to raise money for the upkeep of his medieval church, the Rector of Mark with Allerton, Somerset, the Rev Michael Pavey, played a sponsored 18 holes on 18 different courses in the Bath & Wells Diocese. With his partner, the well-known broadcaster on music, Antony Hopkins, they played the 1st at Minehead at 5.55 am and finished playing the 18th at Burnham and Berrow at 6.05 pm. They covered 240 miles in the "round" including the distances to reach the correct tee for the "next" hole on each course. Par for the "round" was 70. Together the pair raised £10,500 for the church.

● To raise funds for the Marlborough Club's centenary year (1988), Laurence Ross, the Club professional, in June 1987, played eight rounds in 12 hours. Against a par of 72, he completed the 576 holes in 3 under par, playing from back tees and walking all the way.

● As part of the 1992 Centenary Celebrations of the Royal Cinque Ports Golf Club at Deal, Kent, and to support charity, a six-handicap member, John Brazell, played all 37 royal courses in Britain and Ireland in 17 days. He won 22 matches, halved three, lost 12; hit 2,834 shots for an average score of 76.6; lost 11 balls and made 62 birdies. The aim was to raise £30,000 for Leukaemia Research and the Spastics Society.

● To raise more than £500 for the Guide Dogs for the Blind charity in the summer of 1992, Mrs Cheryle Power, a member of the Langley Park Golf Club, Beckenham, Kent, played 100 holes in a day – starting at 5 am and finishing at 8.45 pm.

● David Steele, a former European Tour player, completed 17½ rounds, 315 holes, between 6 am and 9.45 pm in 1993 at the San Roque club near Gibraltar in a total of 1,291 shots. Steele was assisted by a caddie cart and raised £15,000 for charity.

● In 2005 Bernard Wood, a member of Rossendale Golf Club, played all the 18-hole courses in Scotland – 377 in all – to raise money for the Kirsty Appeal which supports the Frances House Children's Hospice in Manchester.

Fastest rounds

● Dick Kimbrough, 41, completed a round on foot on 8th August, 1972, at North Platte CC, Nebraska (6,068 yards) in 30 minutes 10 seconds. He carried only a 3-iron.

● At Mowbray Course, Cape Town, November 1931, Len Richardson, who had represented South Africa in the Olympic Games, played a round which measured 6,248 yards in 31 minutes 22 seconds.

● The women's all-time record for the fastest round played on a course of at least 5,600 yards is held by Sue Ledger, 20, who completed the East Berks course in 38 minutes 8 seconds, beating the previous record by 17 minutes.

● In April, 1934, after attending a wedding in Bournemouth, Hants, Captain Gerald Moxom hurried to his club, West Hill in Surrey, to play in the captain's prize competition. With daylight fading and still dressed in his morning suit, he went round in 65 minutes and won the competition with a net 71 into the bargain.

● On 14th June, 1922, Jock Hutchison and Joe Kirkwood (AUS) played round the Old Course at St Andrews in 1 hour 20 minutes. Hutchison, out in 37, led by three holes at the ninth and won by 4 and 3.

● Fastest rounds can also take another form – the time taken for a ball to be propelled round 18 holes. The fastest known round of this type is 8 minutes 53.8 seconds on 25th August, 1979 by 42 members at Ridgemount CC Rochester, New York, a course measuring 6,161 yards. The Rules of Golf were observed but a ball was available on each tee; to be driven off the instant the ball had been holed at the preceding hole.

● The fastest round with the same ball took place in January 1992 at the Paradise Golf Club, Arizona. It took only 11 minutes 24 seconds; 91 golfers being positioned around the course ready to hit the ball as soon as it came to rest and then throwing the ball from green to tee.

● In 1992 John Daly and Mark Calcavecchia were both fined by the USPGA Tour for playing the final round of the Players' Championship in Florida in 123 minutes. Daly scored 80, Calcavecchia 81.

Curious scoring

● C.W. Allen of Leek Golf Club chipped-in four times in a round in which he was partnered by K. Brint against G. Davies and R. Hollins. The shortest chip was a yard, the longest 20 yards.

● Tony Blackwell, playing off a handicap of four, broke the course record at Bull Bay, Anglesey, by four strokes when he had a gross 60 (net 56) in winning the club's town trophy in 1996. The course measured 6,217 yards.

● In the third round of the 1994 Volvo PGA Championship at Wentworth, Des Smyth, of Ireland, made birdie twos at each of the four short holes, the 2nd, 5th, 10th and 14th. He also had a two at the second hole in the fourth round.

● Also at Wentworth, in the 1994 World Match Play Championship, Seve Ballesteros had seven successive twos at the short holes – and still lost his quarter-final against Ernie Els.

● R.H. Corbett, playing in the semi-final of the Tangye Cup at Mullion in 1916, did a score of 27. The remarkable part of Corbett's score was that it was made up of nine successive 3s, bogey being 5, 3, 4, 4, 5, 3, 4, 4, 3.

● At Little Chalfont in June 1985 Adrian Donkersley played six successive holes in 6, 5, 4, 3, 2, 1 from the 9th to the 14th holes against a par of 4, 4, 3, 4, 3, 3.

● On 2nd September, 1920, playing over Torphin, near Edinburgh, William Ingle did the first five holes in 1, 2, 3, 4, 5.

● In the summer of 1970, Keith McMillan, on holiday at Cullen, had a remarkable series of 1, 2, 3, 4, 5 at the 11th to 15th holes.

● Marc Osborne was only 14 years of age when he equalled the Betchworth Park amateur course record with a 66 in July, 1993. He was playing in the Mortimer Cup, a 36-hole medal competition, and had at the time a handicap of 6.8.

● Playing at Addington Palace, July, 1934, Ronald Jones, a member of Hendon Club, holed five consecutive holes in 5, 4, 3, 2, 1.

● Harry Dunderdale of Lincoln GC scored 5, 4, 3, 2, 1 in five consecutive holes during the first round of his club championship in 1978. The hole-in-one was the 7th, measuring 294 yards.

● At the Open Amateur Tournament of the Royal Ashdown Forest in 1936 Bobby Locke in his morning round had a score of 72, accomplishing every hole in 4.

● George Stewart of Cupar had a four at every hole over the Queen's course at Gleneagles despite forgetting to change into his golf shoes and therefore still wearing his street shoes.

● Henry Cotton told of one of the most extraordinary scoring feats ever. With some other professionals he was at Sestrieres in the 30s for the Italian Open Championship and Joe Ezar, a colourful character in those days on both sides of the Atlantic, accepted a wager from a club official – 1,000 lira for a 66 to break the course record; 2,000 for a 65; and 4,000 for a 64. *I'll do 64*, said Ezar, and proceeded to jot down the hole-by-hole score figures he would do next day for that total. With the exception of the ninth and tenth holes where his predicted score was 3, 4 and the actual score was 4, 3, he accomplished this amazing feat exactly as nominated.

● Nick Faldo scored par figures at all 18 holes in the final round of the 1987 Open Championship at Muirfield to win the title.

● During the Colts Championship at Knowle Golf Club, Bristol, Chris Newman (Cotswold Hills) scored eight consecutive 3s with birdies at four of the holes.

● At the Toft Hotel Golf Club captain's day event L. Heffernan had an ace, D. Patrick a 2, R. Barnett a 3 and D. Heffernan a 4 at the 240 yard par-4 ninth.

● In the European Club Championship played at the Parco de Medici Club in Rome in 1998, Belgian Dimitri van Hauwaert from Royal Antwerp had an albatross 2, Norwegian Marius Bjornstad from Oslo an eagle 3 and Scotsman Andrew Hogg from Turriff a birdie 4 at the 486 metre par-5 eighth hole.

● Earle F. Wilson from Brewerton, Alabama, has had an ace, an albatross and has fired eight birdies in a row.

High scores

● In the qualifying competition at Formby for the 1976 Open Championship, Maurice Flitcroft, a 46-year-old crane driver from Barrow-in-Furness, took 121 strokes for the first round and then withdrew saying, *I have no chance of qualifying*. Flitcroft entered as a professional but had never before played 18 holes. He had taken the game up 18 months previously but, as he was not a member of a club, had been limited to practising on a local beach. His round was made up thus: 7, 5, 6, 6, 6, 6, 12, 6, 7-61; 11, 5, 6, 8, 4, 9, 5, 7, 5-60, total 121. After his round Flitcroft said, "I've made a lot of progress in the last few months and I'm sorry I did not do better. I was trying too hard at the beginning but began to put things together at the end of the round". R&A officials, who were not amused by the bogus professional's efforts, refunded the £30 entry money to Flitcroft's two fellow-competitors. Flitcroft has since tried to qualify for The Open under assumed names: Gerard Hoppy from Switzerland and Beau Jolley (as in the wine)!

● Playing in the qualifying rounds of the 1965 Open Championship at Southport, an American self-styled professional entrant from Milwaukee, Walter Danecki, achieved the inglorious feat of scoring a total of 221 strokes for 36 holes, 81 over par. His first round over the Hillside course was 108, followed by a second round of 113. Walter, who afterwards admitted he felt *a little discouraged and sad*, declared that he entered because he was *after the money*.

● The highest individual scoring ever known in the rounds connected with The Open Championship occurred at Muirfield, 1935, when a Scottish professional started 7, 10, 5, 10, and took 65 to reach the 9th hole. Another 10 came at the 11th and the player decided to retire at the 12th hole. There he was in a bunker, and after playing four shots he had not regained the fairway.

● In 1883 in The Open Championship at Musselburgh, Willie Fernie, the winner, had a 10, the only time double figures appeared on the card of The Open Champion of the year. Fernie won after a tie with Bob Ferguson, and his score for the last hole in the tie was 2. He holed from just off the green to win by one stroke.

● In the first Open Championship at Prestwick in 1860 a competitor took 21, the highest score for one hole ever recorded in this event. The record is preserved in the archives of the Prestwick Golf Club, where the championship was founded.

● In the first round of the 1980 US Masters, Tom Weiskopf hit his ball into the water hazard in front of the par-3 12th hole five times and scored 13 for the hole.

● In the French Open at St Cloud, in 1968, Brian Barnes took 15 for the short 8th hole in the second round. After missing putts at which he hurriedly snatched while the ball was moving he penalised himself further by standing astride the line of a putt. The amazing result was that he actually took 12 strokes from about three feet from the hole. The highest scores on the European Tour were also recorded in the French Open. Philippe Porquier had a 20 at La Baule in 1978 and Ian Woosnam a 16 at La Boulie in 1986.

● US professional Dave Hill 6-putted the fifth green at Oakmont in the 1962 US Open Championship.

● Many high scores have been made at the Road Hole at St Andrews. Davie Ayton, on one occasion, was coming in a certain winner of The Open Championship when he got on the road and took 11. In 1921, at The Open Championship, one professional took 13. In 1923, competing for the Autumn Medal of The Royal and Ancient, J.B. Anderson required a five and a four to win the second award, but he took 13 at the Road Hole. Anderson was close to the green in two, was twice in the bunkers in the face of the green, and once on the road. In 1935, R.H. Oppenheimer tied for the Royal Medal (the first award) in the Autumn Meeting of The Royal and Ancient. On the play-off he was one stroke behind Captain Aitken when they stood on the 17th tee. Oppenheimer drove three balls out of bounds and eventually took 11 to the Road Hole.

● British professional Mark James scored 111 in the second round of the 1978 Italian Open. He played the closing holes with only his right hand due to an injury to his left hand.

● In the 1927 Shawnee Open, Tommy Armour took 23 strokes to the 17th hole. Armour had won the American Open Championship a week earlier. In an effort to play the hole in a particular way, Armour hooked ball after ball out of bounds and finished with a 21 on the card. There was some doubt about the accuracy of this figure and on reaching the clubhouse Armour stated that it should be 23. This is the highest score by a professional in a tournament.

Freak matches

● In 1912, the late Harry Dearth, an eminent vocalist, attired in a complete suit of heavy armour, played a match at Bushey Hall. He was beaten 2 and 1.

"I think this might be a knight to remember"

● In 1914, at the start of the First World War, J.N. Farrar, a native of Hoylake, was stationed at Royston, Herts. A bet was made of 10-1 that he would not go round Royston under 100 strokes, equipped in full infantry marching order, water bottle, full field kit and haversack. Farrar went round in 94. At the camp were several golfers, including professionals, who tried the same feat but failed.

● Captain Pennington took part in a match *from the air* against A.J. Young, the professional at Sonning. Captain Pennington, with 80 golf balls in the locker of his machine, had to find the Sonning greens by dropping the balls as he circled over the course. The balls were covered in white cloth to ensure that they did not bounce once they struck the ground. The airman completed the course in 40 minutes, taking 29 *strokes*, while Young occupied two hours for his round of 68. Captain Pennington was eventually killed in an air crash in 1933.

● In April 1924, at Littlehampton, Harry Rowntree, an amateur golfer, played the better ball of Edward Ray and George Duncan, receiving an allowance of 150 yards to use as he required during the round. Rowntree won by 6 and 5 and had used only 50 yards 2 feet of his handicap. At one hole Duncan had a two – Rowntree, who was 25 yards from the hole, took this distance from his handicap and won the hole in one. Ray (died 1945) afterwards declared that, conceding a handicap of one yard per round, he could win every championship in the world. And he might, when reckoning is taken of the number of times a putt just stops an inch or two or how much difference to a shot three inches will make for the lie of the ball, either in a bunker or on the fairway. Many single matches on the same system have been played. An 18 handicap player opposed to a scratch player should make a close match with an allowance of 50 yards.

● The first known instance of a golf match by telephone occurred in 1957, when the Cotswold Hills Golf Club, Cheltenham, England, won a golf tournament against the Cheltenham Golf Club, Melbourne, Australia, by six strokes. A large crowd assembled at the English club to wait for the 12,000 miles telephone call from Australia. The match had been played at the suggestion of a former member of the Cotswold Hills Club, Harry Davies, and was open to every member of the two clubs. The result of the match was decided on the aggregate of the eight best scores on each side and the English club won by 564 strokes to 570.

Golf matches against other sports

● H.H. Hilton and Percy Ashworth, many times racket champion, contested a driving match, the former driving a golf ball with a driver, and the latter a racket ball with a racket. Best distances: Against breeze – Golfer 182 yards; Racket player 125 yards. Down wind – Golfer 230 yards; Racket player 140 yards. Afterwards Ashworth hit a golf ball with the racket and got a greater distance than with the racket ball, but was still a long way behind the ball driven by Hilton.

● In December, 1913, F.M.A. Webster, of the London Athletic Club, and Dora Roberts, with javelins, played a match with the late Harry Vardon and Mrs Gordon Robertson, who used the regulation clubs and golf balls. The golfers conceded two-thirds in the matter of distance, and they won by 5 up and 4 to play in a contest of 18 holes. The javelin throwers had a mark of two feet square in which to *hole out* while the golfers had to get their ball into the ordinary golf hole. Mr Webster's best throw was one of 160 feet.

● In 1913, at Wellington, Shropshire, a match between a golfer and a fisherman casting a 2½ oz weight was played. The golfer, Rupert May, took 87; the fisherman J.J.D. Mackinlay, in difficulty because of his short casts, 102. His longest cast, 105 yards, was within 12 yards of the world record at the time, held by French angler, Decautelle. When within a rod's length of a hole he ran the weight to the rod end and dropped into the hole. Five times he broke his line, and was allowed another shot without penalty.

"Looks like it's fish for dinner tonight"

● In 1954, at the Southbroom Club, South Africa, a match over 9 holes was played between an archer and a fisherman against two golfers. The participants were all champions of their own sphere and consisted of Vernon Adams (archer), Dennis Burd (fisherman), Jeanette Wahl (champion of Southbroom and Port Shepstone), and Ron Burd (professional at Southbroom). The conditions were that the archer had holed out when his arrows struck a small leather bag placed on the green beside the hole and in the event of his placing his approach shot within a bow's length of the pin he was deemed to have 1-putted. The fisherman, to achieve a 1-putt, had to land his sinker within a rod's length of the pin. The two golfers were ahead for brief spells, but it was the opposition who led at the deciding 9th hole where *Robin Hood* played a perfect approach for a birdie.

● An *Across England* combined match was begun on 11th October, 1965, by four golfers and two archers from Crowborough Beacon Golf Club, Sussex, accompanied by *Penny*, a white Alsatian dog, whose duty it was to find lost balls. They teed off from Carlisle Castle via Hadrian's Wall, the Pennine Way, finally holing out in the 18th hole at Newcastle United GC in 612 teed shots. Casualties included 110 lost golf balls and 19 lost or broken arrows. The match took 5½ days, and the distance travelled was about 60 miles. The golfers were Miss P. Ward, K. Meaney, K. Ashdown and C.A. Macey; the archers were W.H. Hulme and T. Scott. The first arrow was fired from the battlements of Carlisle Castle, a distance of nearly 300 yards, by Cumberland Champion R. Willis, who also fired the second arrow right across the River Eden. R. Clough, president of Newcastle United GC, holed the last two putts. The match was in aid of *Guide Dogs for the Blind* and *Friends of Crowborough Hospital.*

● Several matches have taken place between a golfer on the one side and an archer on the other. The wielder of the bow and arrow has nearly always proved the victor. In 1953 at Kirkhill Golf Course, Lanarkshire, five archers beat six golfers by two games to one. There were two special rules for the match; when an archer's arrow landed six feet from the hole or the golfer's ball three feet from the hole, they were counted as holed. When the arrows landed in bunkers or in the rough, archers lifted their arrow and added a stroke. The sixth archer in this match called off and one archer shot two arrows from each of the 18 tees.

"This doesn't appear to be covered by the Rules"

Cross-country matches

● Taking 1 year, 114 days, Floyd Rood golfed his way from coast to coast across the United States. He took 114,737 shots including 3,511 penalty shots for the 3,397 mile course.

● Two Californian teenagers, Bob Aube (17) and Phil Marrone (18) went on a golfing safari in 1974 from San Francisco to Los Angeles, a trip of over 500 miles lasting 16 days. The first six days they played alongside motorways. Over 1,000 balls were used.

● In 1830, the Gold Medal winner of The Royal and Ancient backed himself for 10 sovereigns to drive from the 1st hole at St Andrews to the toll bar at

Cupar, distance nine miles, in 200 teed shots. He won easily.

● In 1848, two Edinburgh golfers played a match from Bruntsfield Links to the top of Arthur's Seat – an eminence overlooking the Scottish capital, 822 feet above sea level.

● On a winter's day in 1898, Freddie Tait backed himself to play a gutta ball in 40 teed shots from Royal St George's Clubhouse, Sandwich, to the Cinque Ports Club, Deal. He was to hole out by hitting any part of the Deal Clubhouse. The distance as the crow flies was three miles. The redoubtable Tait holed out with his 32nd shot, so effectively that the ball went through a window.

● In 1900 three members of the Hackensack (NJ) Club played a game of four-and-a-half hours over an extemporised course six miles long, which stretched from Hackensack to Paterson. Despite rain, cornfields, and wide streams, the three golfers – J.W. Hauleebeek, Dr E.R. Pfaare, and Eugene Crassons – completed the round, the first and the last named taking 305 strokes each, and Dr Pfaare 327 strokes. The players used only two clubs, the mashie and the cleek.

● On 3rd December, 1920, P. Rupert Phillips and W. Raymond Thomas teed up on the first tee of the Radyr Golf Club and played to the last hole at Southerndown. The distance as the crow flies was 15½ miles, but circumventing swamps, woods, and plough, they covered, approximately, 20 miles. The wager was that they would not do the hole in 1,000 strokes, but they holed out at their 608th stroke two days later. They carried large ordnance maps.

● On 12th March, 1921, A. Stanley Turner, Macclesfield, played from his house to the Cat and Fiddle Inn, five miles distance, in 64 strokes. The route was broken and hilly with a rise of nearly 1,000 feet. Turner was allowed to tee up within two club lengths after each shot and the wagering was 6-4 against his doing the distance in 170 strokes.

● In 1919, a golfer drove a ball from Piccadilly Circus and, proceeding via the Strand, Fleet Street and Ludgate Hill, *holed out* at the Royal Exchange, London. The player drove off at 8 am on a Sunday, a time when the usually thronged thoroughfares were deserted.

● On 23rd April, 1939, Richard Sutton, a London stockbroker, played from Tower Bridge, London, to White's Club, St James's Street, in 142 strokes. The bet was he would not do *the course* in under 200 shots. Sutton used a putter, crossed the Thames at Southwark Bridge, and hit the ball short distances to keep out of trouble.

● Golfers produced the most original event in Ireland's three-week national festival of An Tostal, in 1953 – a cross-country competition with an advertised £1,000,000 for the man who could hole out in one. The 150 golfers drove off from the first tee at Kildare Club to hole out eventually on the 18th green, five miles away, on the nearby Curragh course, a distance of 8,800 yards. The unusual hazards to be negotiated included the main Dublin-Cork railway line and highway, the Curragh Racecourse, hoofprints left by Irish thoroughbred racehorses out exercising on the plains from nearby stables, army tank tracks and about 150 telephone lines. The Golden Ball Trophy, which is played for annually – a standard size golf ball in gold, mounted on a black marble pillar beside the silver figure of a golfer on a green marble base, designed by Captain Maurice Cogan, Army GHQ, Dublin – was for the best gross. And it went to one of the longest hitters in international golf – Amateur Champion, Irish internationalist and British Walker Cup player Joe Carr, with the remarkable score of 52.

● In 1961, as a University Charities Week stunt, four Aberdeen University students set out to golf their way up Ben Nevis (4,406 feet). About half-way up, after losing 63 balls and expending 659 strokes, the quartet conceded victory to Britain's highest mountain.

● Among several cross-country golfing exploits, one of the most arduous was faced by Iain Williamson and Tony Kent, who teed off from Cained Point on the summit of Fairfield in the Lake District. With the hole cut in the lawn of the Bishop of Carlisle's home at Rydal Park, it measured 7,200 yards and passed through the summits of Great Rigg Mann, Heron Pike and Nab Scar, descending altogether 1,900 feet. Eight balls were lost and the two golfers holed out in a combined total of 303 strokes.

● In 2011, Trevor Sandford from Bearsted in Kent played golf on each of the 31 days of August on 31 different courses close to the 31 junctions of the M25 motorway. During Trevor's feat, in which he raised over £8,000 for Cancer Research UK, he walked 210 miles and took 2,789 strokes.

"When I asked for a driver, this isn't exactly what I had in mind"

Long-lived golfers

● James Priddy, aged 80, played in the Seniors' Open at his home club, Weston-super-Mare, Avon, on 27th June, 1990, and scored a gross 70 to beat his age by ten shots.

● The oldest golfer who ever lived is believed to have been Arthur Thompson of British Columbia, Canada. He equalled his age when 103 at Uplands GC, a course of over 6,000 yards. He died two years later.

● Nathaniel Vickers celebrated his 103rd birthday on Sunday, 9th October, 1949, and died the following day. He was the oldest member of the United States Senior Golf Association and until 1942 he competed regularly in their events and won many trophies in the various age divisions. When 100 years old, he apologised for being able to play only nine holes a day. Vickers predicted he would live until 103 and he died a few hours after he had celebrated his birthday.

● American George Miller, who died in 1979 aged 102, played regularly when 100 years old.

● In 1999 94-year-old Mr W. Seneviratne, a retired schoolmaster who lived and worked in Malaysia, was still practising every day and regularly competing in medal competitions at the Royal Colombo Golf Club which was founded in 1879.

● Bim Smith, a member of Rochester & Cobham Park Golf Club, Kent, achieved a hole-in-one three days before his 91st birthday.

● Phyllis Tidmarsh, aged 90, won a Stableford competition at Saltford Golf Club, near Bath, when she returned 42 points. Her handicap was cut from 28 to 27.

● George Swanwick, a member of Wallasey, celebrated his 90th birthday with a lunch at the club on 1st April, 1971. He played golf several times a week, carrying his own clubs, and had holed-in-one at the ages of 75 and 85. His ambition was to complete the sequence aged 95 ... but he died in 1973 aged 92.

● The 10th Earl of Wemyss played a round on his 92nd birthday, in 1910, at Craigielaw. At the age of 87 the Earl was partnered by Harry Vardon in a match at Kilspindie, the golf course on his East Lothian estate at Gosford. After playing his ball the venerable earl mounted a pony and rode to the next shot. He died on 30th June, 1914.

● F.L. Callender, aged 78, in September 1932, played nine consecutive rounds in the Jubilee Vase, St Andrews. He was defeated in the ninth, the final round, by 4 and 2. Callender's handicap was 12. This is the best known achievement of a septuagenarian in golf.

● George Evans shot a remarkable one over par 71 at Brockenhurst Manor – remarkable because Mr Evans was 87 at the time. Playing with him that day was Hampshire, Isle of Wight and Channel Islands President John Nettell and former Ferndown pro Doug Sewell. "It's good to shoot a score under your own age, but when its 16 shots better that must be a record", said Mr Nettell. Mr Evans qualified for four opens while professional at West Hill, Surrey.

● Bernard Matthews, aged 82, of Banstead Downs Club, handicap 6, holed the course in 72 gross in August 1988. A week later he holed it in 70, twelve shots below his age. He came back in 31, finishing 4, 3, 3, 2, 3, against a par of 5, 4, 3, 3, 4. Mr Matthews's eclectic score at his Club is 37, or one over 2's.

Playing in the dark

On numerous occasions it has been necessary to hold lamps, lighted candles, or torches at holes in order that players might finish a competition. Large entries, slow play, early darkness and an eclipse of the sun have all been causes of playing in darkness.

● Since 1972, the Whitburn Golf Club at South Shields, Tyne and Wear, has held an annual Summer Solstice Competition. All competitors, who draw lots for starting tees, must begin before 4.24 and 13 seconds am, the time the sun rises over the first hole on the longest day of the year.

● At The Open Championship in Musselburgh in November 1889 many players finished when the light had so far gone that the adjacent street lamps were lit. The cards were checked by candlelight. Several players who had no chance of the championship were paid small sums to withdraw in order to permit others who had a chance to finish in daylight. This was the last championship at Musselburgh.

● At the Southern Section of the PGA tournament on 25th September, 1907, at Burnham Beeches, several players concluded the round by the aid of torch lights placed near the holes.

● In the Irish Open Championship at Portmarnock in September, 1907, a tie in the third round between W.C. Pickeman and A. Jeffcott was postponed owing to darkness, at the 22nd hole. The next morning Pickeman won at the 24th.

● The qualifying round of the American Amateur Championship in 1910 could not be finished in one day, and several competitors had to stop their round on account of darkness, and complete it early in the morning of the following day.

● On 10th January, 1926, in the final of the President's Putter, at Rye, E.F. Storey and R.H. Wethered were all square at the 24th hole. It was 5 pm and so dark that, although a fair crowd was present, the balls could not be followed. The tie was abandoned and the Putter held jointly for the year. Each winner of the Putter affixes the ball he played; for 1926 there are two balls, respectively engraved with the names of the finalists.

● In the 1932 Walker Cup contest at Brooklyn, a total eclipse of the sun occurred.

● At Perth, on 14th September, 1932, a competition was in progress under good clear evening light, and a full bright moon. The moon rose at 7.10 and an hour later came under eclipse to the earth's surface. The light then became so bad that on the last three greens competitors holed out by the aid of the light from matches.

● At Carnoustie, 1932, in the competition for the *Craw's Nest Tassie* the large entry necessitated competitors being sent off in 3-ball matches. The late players had to be assisted by electric torches flashed on the greens.

● In February, 1950, Max Faulkner and his partner, R. Dolman, in a Guildford Alliance event finished their round in complete darkness. A photographer's flash bulbs were used at the last hole to direct Faulkner's approach. Several of the other competitors also finished in darkness. At the last hole they had only the light from the clubhouse to aim at and one played his approach so boldly that he put his ball through the hall doorway and almost into the dressing room.

● On the second day of the 1969 Ryder Cup contest, the last 4-ball match ended in near total darkness on the 18th green at Royal Birkdale. With the help of the clubhouse lights the two American players, Lee Trevino and Miller Barber, along with Tony Jacklin for Britain each faced putts of around five feet to win their match. All missed and their game was halved.

The occasions mentioned above all occurred in competitions where it was not intended to play in the dark. There are, however, numerous instances where players set out to play in the dark either for bets or for novelty.

● On 29th November, 1878, R.W. Brown backed himself to go round the Hoylake links in 150 strokes, starting at 11 pm. The conditions of the match were that Mr Brown was only to be penalised *loss of distance* for a lost ball, and that no one was to help him to find it. He went round in 147 strokes, and won his bet by the narrow margin of three strokes.

● In 1876 David Strath backed himself to go round St Andrews under 100, in moonlight. He took 95, and did not lose a ball.

● In September 1928, at St Andrews, the first and last holes were illuminated by lanterns, and at 11 pm four members of The Royal and Ancient set out to play a foursome over the 2 holes. Electric lights, lanterns, and rockets were used to brighten the fairway, and the headlights of motor cars parked on Links Place formed a helpful battery. The 1st hole was won in four, and each side got a five at the 18th. About 1,000 spectators followed the freak match, which was played to celebrate the appointment of Angus Hambro to the captaincy of the club.

● In 1931, Rufus Stewart, professional, Kooyonga Club, South Australia, and former Australian Open Champion, played 18 holes of exhibition golf at night without losing a single ball over the Kooyonga course, and completed the round in 77.

● At Ashley Wood Golf Club, Blandford, Dorset, a night-time golf tournament was arranged annually with up to 180 golfers taking part over four nights. Over £6000 has been raised in four years for the Muscular Dystrophy Charity.

● At Pannal, 3rd July, 1937, R.H. Locke, playing in bright moonlight, holed his tee shot at the 15th hole, distance 220 yards, the only known case of holing-in-one under such conditions.

Fatal and other accidents on the links

The history of golf is, unfortunately, marred by a great number of fatal accidents on or near the course. In the vast majority of such cases they have been caused either by careless swinging of the club or by an uncontrolled shot when the ball has struck a spectator or bystander. In addition to the fatal accidents there is an even larger number on record which have resulted in serious injury or blindness. We do not propose to list these accidents except where they have some unusual feature. We would remind all golfers of the tragic consequences which have so often been caused by momentary carelessness. The fatal accidents which follow have an unusual cause and other accidents given may have their humorous aspect.

● English tournament professional Richard Boxall was three shots off the lead in the third round of the 1991 Open Championship when he fractured his left leg driving from the 9th tee at Royal Birkdale. He was taken from the course to hospital by ambulance and was listed in the official results as "retired" which entitled him to a consolation prize of £3000.

A month later, Russell Weir of Scotland, was competing in the European Teaching Professionals' Championship near Rotterdam when he also fractured his left leg driving from the 7th tee in the first round.

● In July, 1971, Rudolph Roy, aged 43, was killed at a Montreal course; in playing out of woods, the shaft of his club snapped, rebounded off a tree and the jagged edge plunged into his body.

● Harold Wallace, aged 75, playing at Lundin Links with two friends in 1950, was crossing the railway line which separates the fifth green and sixth tee, when a light engine knocked him down and he was killed instantly.

● In the summer of 1963, Harold Kalles, of Toronto, Canada, died six days after his throat had been cut by a golf club shaft, which broke against a tree as he was trying to play out of a bunker.

● At Jacksonville, Florida, on 18th March, 1952, two women golfers were instantly killed when hit simultaneously by the whirling propeller of a navy fighter plane. They were playing together when the plane with a dead engine coming in out of control, hit them from behind.

● In May, 1993, at Ponoka Community GC, Alberta, Canada, Richard McCulough hit a poor tee shot on the 13th hole and promptly smashed his driver angrily against a golf cart. The head of the driver and six inches of shaft flew through the air, piercing McCulough's throat and severing his carotid artery. He died in hospital.

● Britain's first national open event for competitors aged over 80, at Moortown, Leeds in September, 1992, was marred when 81-year-old Frank Hart collapsed on the fourth tee and died. Play continued and Charles Mitchell, aged 80, won the Stableford competition with a gross score of 81 for 39 points.

● Playing in the 1993 Carlsburg-Tetley Cornish Festival at Tehidy Park, Ian Cornwell was struck on the leg by a wayward shot from a player two groups behind. Later, as he was leaving the 16th green, he was hit again, this time below the ear, by the same player, knocking him unconscious. This may be the first time that a player has been hit twice in the same round by the same player.

Lightning on the links

There have been a considerable number of fatal and serious accidents through players and caddies having been struck by lightning on the course. The Royal and Ancient and the USGA have, since 1952, provided for discontinuance of play during lightning storms under the Rules of Golf (Rule 37, 6) and the United States Golf Association has given the following guide for personal safety during thunderstorms:

(a) Do not go out of doors or remain out during thunderstorms unless it is necessary. Stay inside of a building where it is dry, preferably away from fireplaces, stoves, and other metal objects.

(b) If there is any choice of shelter, choose in the following order:
   1. Large metal or metal-frame buildings.
   2. Dwellings or other buildings which are protected against lightning.
   3. Large unprotected buildings.
   4. Small unprotected buildings.

(c) If remaining out of doors is unavoidable, keep away from:
   1. Small sheds and shelters if in an exposed location.
   2. Isolated trees.
   3. Wire fences.
   4. Hilltops and wide open spaces.

(d) Seek shelter in:
   1. A cave.
   2. A depression in the ground.
   3. A deep valley or canyon.
   4. The foot of a steep or overhanging cliff.
   5. Dense woods.
   6. A grove of trees.

Note – Raising golf clubs or umbrellas above the head is dangerous.

● A serious incident with lightning involving well-known golfers was at the 1975 Western Open in Chicago when Lee Trevino, Jerry Heard and Bobby Nichols were all struck and had to be taken to hospital. At the same time Tony Jacklin had a club thrown 15 feet out of his hands.

● Two well-known competitors were struck by lightning in European events in 1977. They were Mark James of Britain in the Swiss Open and Severiano Ballesteros of Spain in the Scandinavian Open. Fortunately neither appeared to be badly injured.

● Two spectators were killed by lightning in 1991: one at the US Open and the other at US PGA Championship.

Spectators interfering with balls

● Deliberate interference by spectators with balls in play during important money matches was not unknown in the old days when there was intense rivalry between the *schools* of Musselburgh, St Andrews, and North Berwick, and disputes arose in stake matches caused by the action of spectators in kicking the ball into either a favourable or an unfavourable position.

● Tom Morris, in his last match with Willie Park at Musselburgh, refused to go on because of interference by the spectators, and in the match on the same course about 40 years later, in 1895, between Willie Park Jr and J.H. Taylor, the barracking of the crowd and interference with play was so bad that when the Park-Vardon match came to be arranged in 1899, Vardon refused to accept Musselburgh as a venue.

● Even in modern times spectators have been known to interfere deliberately with players' balls, though it is usually by children. In the 1972 Penfold Tournament at Queen's Park, Bournemouth, Christy O'Connor Jr had his ball stolen by a young boy, but not being told of this at the time had to take the penalty for a lost ball. O'Connor finished in a tie for first place, but lost the play-off.

● In 1912 in the last round of the final of the Amateur Championship at Westward Ho! between Abe Mitchell and John Ball, the drive of the former to the short 14th hit an open umbrella held by a lady protecting herself from the heavy rain, and instead of landing on the green the ball was diverted into a bunker. Mitchell, who was leading at the time by 2 holes, lost the hole and Ball won the Championship at the 38th hole.

● In the match between the professionals of Great Britain and America at Southport in 1937 a dense crowd collected round the 15th green waiting for the Sarazen-Alliss match. The American's ball landed in the lap of a woman, who picked it up and threw it so close to the hole that Sarazen got a two against Alliss' three.

● In a memorable tie between Bobby Jones and Cyril Tolley in the 1930 Amateur Championship at St Andrews, Jones' approach to the 17th green struck spectators massed at the left end of the green and led to controversy as to whether it would otherwise have gone on to the famous road. Jones himself had deliberately played for that part of the green and had requested stewards to get the crowd back. Had the ball gone on to the road, the historic Jones Quadrilateral of the year – The Open and Amateur Championships of Britain and the United States – might not have gone into the records.

● In the 1983 Suntory World Match Play Championship at Wentworth Nick Faldo hit his second shot over the green at the 16th hole into a group of spectators. To everyone's astonishment and discomfiture the ball reappeared on the green about 30ft from the hole, propelled there by a thoroughly misguided and anonymous spectator. The referee ruled that Faldo should play the ball where it lay on the green. Faldo's opponent, Graham Marsh, understandably upset by the incident, took three putts against Faldo's two, thus losing a hole he might well otherwise have won. Faldo won the match 2 and 1, but lost in the final to Marsh's fellow Australian Greg Norman by 3 and 2.

Golf balls killing animals and fish, and incidents with animals

● An astounding fatality to an animal through being hit by a golf ball occurred at St Margaret's-at-Cliffe Golf Club, Kent on 13th June, 1934, when W.J. Robinson, the professional, killed a cow with his tee shot to the 18th hole. The cow was standing in the fairway about 100 yards from the tee, and the ball struck her on the back of the head. She fell like a log, but staggered to her feet and walked about 50 yards before dropping again. When the players reached her she was dead.

● J.W. Perret, of Ystrad Mynach, playing with Chas R. Halliday, of Ralston, in the qualifying rounds of the Society of One Armed Golfers' Championship over the Darley course, Troon, on 27th August, 1935, killed two gulls at successive holes with his second shots. The *deadly* shots were at the 1st and 2nd holes.

● On the first day of grouse shooting of the 1975 season (12th August), 11-year-old schoolboy Willie Fraser, of Kingussie, beat all the guns when he killed a grouse with his tee shot on the local course.

● On 10th June, 1904, while playing in the Edinburgh High Constables' Competition at Kilspindie, Captain Ferguson sent a long ball into the rough at the Target hole, and on searching for it found that it had struck and killed a young hare.

● Playing in a mixed open tournament at the Waimairi Beach Golf Club in Christchurch, New Zealand, in the summer of 1961, Mrs R.T. Challis found her ball in fairly long spongy grass where a placing rule applied. She picked up, placed the ball and played her stroke. A young hare leaped into the air and fell dead at her feet. She had placed the ball on the leveret without seeing it and without disturbing it.

● In 1906 in the Border Championship at Hawick, a gull and a weasel were killed by balls during the afternoon's play.

● A golfer at Newark, in May, 1907, drove his ball into the river. The ball struck a trout 2lb in weight and killed it.

● On 24th April, 1975, at Scunthorpe GC, Jim Tollan's drive at the 14th hole, called *The Mallard*, struck and killed a female mallard duck in flight. The duck was stuffed and is displayed in the Scunthorpe Clubhouse.

● A. Samuel, Melbourne Club, at Sandringham, was driving with an iron club from the 17th tee, when a kitten, which had been playing in the long grass, sprang suddenly at the ball. Kitten and club arrived at the objective simultaneously, with the result that the kitten took an unexpected flight through the air, landing some 20 yards away.

● As Susan Rowlands was lining up a vital putt in the closing stages of the final of the 1978 Welsh Girls' Championship at Abergele, a tiny mouse scampered up her trouser leg. After holing the putt, the mouse ran down again. Susan, who won the final, admitted that she fortunately had not known it was there.

Interference by birds and animals

● Crows, ravens, hawks and seagulls frequently carry off golf balls, sometimes dropping the ball actually on the green, and it is a common incident for a cow to swallow a golf ball. A plague of crows on the Liverpool course at Hoylake are addicted to golf balls – they stole 26 in one day – selecting only new balls.

It was suggested that members should carry shotguns as a 15th club!

● A match was approaching a hole in a rather low-lying course, when one of the players made a crisp chip from about 30 yards from the hole. The ball trickled slowly across the green and eventually disappeared into the hole. After a momentary pause, the ball was suddenly ejected on to the green, and out jumped a large frog.

● A large black crow named Jasper which frequented the Lithgow GC in New South Wales, Australia, stole 30 golf balls in the club's 1972 Easter Tournament.

● As Mrs Molly Whitaker was playing from a bunker at Beachwood course, Natal, South Africa, a large monkey leaped from a bush and clutched her round the neck. A caddie drove it off by clipping it with an iron club.

● In Massachusetts a goose, having been hit rather hard by a golf ball which then came to rest by the side of a water hazard, took revenge by waddling over to the ball and kicking it into the water.

● In the summer of 1963, S.C. King had a good drive to the 10th hole at the Guernsey Club. His partner, R.W. Clark, was in the rough, and King helped him to search. Returning to his ball, he found a cow eating it. Next day, at the same hole, the positions were reversed, and King was in the rough. Clark placed his woollen hat over his ball, remarking, *I'll make sure the cow doesn't eat mine.* On his return he found the cow thoroughly enjoying his hat; nothing was left but the pom-pom.

● On 5 August 2000 in the first round of the Royal Westmoreland Club Championship in Barbados, Kevin Edwards, a five-handicapper, hit a tee shot at the short 15th to a few feet of the hole. A monkey then ran onto the green, picked up the ball, threw it into the air a few times, then placed it in the hole before running off. Mr Edwards had to replace his ball, but was obliged afterwards to buy everyone a drink at the bar by virtue of a newly written rule.

Armless, one-armed, legless and ambidextrous players

● In September, 1933, at Burgess Golfing Society of Edinburgh, the first championship for one-armed golfers was held. There were 43 entries and 37 of the competitors had lost an arm in the 1914–18 war. Play was over two rounds and the championship was won by W.E. Thomson, Eastwood, Glasgow, with a score of 169 (82 and 87) for two rounds. The Burgess course was 6,300 yards long. Thomson drove the last green, 260 yards. The championship and an international match are played annually.

● In the Boys' Amateur Championship 1923, at Dunbar and 1949 at St Andrews, there were competitors each with one arm. The competitor in 1949, R.P. Reid, Cupar, Fife, who lost his arm working a machine in a butcher's shop, got through to the third round.

● There have been cases of persons with no arms playing golf. One, Thomas McAuliffe, who held the club between his right shoulder and cheek, once went round Buffalo CC, USA, in 108.

● Group Captain Bader, who lost both legs in a flying accident prior to the World War 1939–45, took part in golf competitions and reached a single-figure handicap in spite of his disability.

● In 1909, Scott of Silloth, and John Haskins of Hoylake, both one-armed golfers, played a home and away match for £20-a-side. Scott finished five up at Silloth. He was seven up and 14 to play at Hoylake but Haskins played so well that Scott eventually only won by 3 and 1. This was the first match between one-armed golfers. Haskins in 1919 was challenged by Mr Mycock, of Buxton, another one-armed player. The match was 36 holes, home and away. The first half was played over the Buxton and High Peak Links, and the latter half over the Liverpool Links, and resulted in a win for Haskins by 11 and 10. Later in the same year Haskins received another challenge to play against Alexander Smart of Aberdeen. The match was 18 holes over the Balgownie Course, and ended in favour of Haskins.

● In a match, November, 1926, between the Geduld and Sub Nigel Clubs – two golf clubs connected with the South African gold mines of the same names – each club had two players minus an arm. The natural consequence was that the quartet were matched. The players were – A.W.P. Charteris and E. Mitchell, Sub Nigel; and E.P. Coles and J. Kirby, Geduld. This is the first record of four one-armed players in a foursome.

● At Joliet Country Club, USA, a one-armed golfer named D.R. Anderson drove a ball 300 yards.

● Left-handedness, but playing golf right-handed, is prevalent and for a man to throw with his left hand and play golf right-handed is considered an advantage, for Bobby Jones, Jesse Sweetser, Walter Hagen, Jim Barnes, Joe Kirkwood and more recently Johnny Miller were eminent golfers who were left-handed and ambidextrous.

● In a practice round for The Open Championship in July, 1927, at St Andrews, Len Nettlefold and Joe Kirkwood changed sets of clubs at the 9th hole. Nettlefold was a left-handed golfer and Kirkwood right-handed. They played the last nine, Kirkwood with the left-handed clubs and Nettlefold with the right-handed clubs.

● The late Harry Vardon, when he was at Ganton, got tired of giving impossible odds to his members and beating them, so he collected a set of left-handed clubs, and rating himself at scratch, conceded the handicap odds to them. He won with the same monotonous regularity.

● Ernest Jones, who was professional at the Chislehurst Club, was badly wounded in the war in France in 1916 and his right leg had to be amputated below the knee. He persevered with the game, and before the end of the year he went round the Clacton course balanced on his one leg in 72. Jones later settled in the United States where he built fame and fortune as a golf teacher.

● Major Alexander McDonald Fraser of Edinburgh had the distinction of holding two handicaps simultaneously in the same club – one when he played left-handed and the other for his right-handed play. In medal competitions he had to state before teeing up which method he would use.

● Former England test cricketer Brian Close once held a handicap of 2 playing right-handed, but after retiring from cricket in 1977 decided to apply himself as a left-handed player. His left-handed handicap at the time of his retirement was 7. Close had the distinction of once beating Ted Dexter, another distinguished test cricketer and noted golfer twice in the one day, playing right-handed in the morning and left-handed in the afternoon.

Blind and blindfolded golf

● Major Towse, VC, whose eyes were shot out during the South African War, 1899, was probably the first blind man to play golf. His only stipulations when playing the game were that he should be allowed to touch the ball with his hands to ascertain its position, and that his caddie could ring a small bell to indicate the position of the hole. Major Towse, who played with considerable skill, was also an expert oarsman and bridge player. He died in 1945, aged 81.

● The United States Blind Golfers' Association in 1946 promoted an Invitational Golf Tournament for the blind at Inglewood, California, to be held annually. In 1953 there were 24 competitors, of which 11 completed the two rounds of 36 holes. The winner was Charley Boswell who lost his eyesight leading a tank unit in Germany in 1944.

● In July, 1954, at Lambton Golf and Country Club, Toronto, the first international championship for the blind was held. It resulted in a win for Joe Lazaro, of Waltham, Mass., with a score of 220 for the two rounds. He drove the 215-yard 16th hole and just missed an ace, his ball stopping 18 inches from the hole. Charley Boswell, who won the United States Blind Golfers' Association Tournament in 1953, was second. The same Charles Boswell, of Birmingham, Alabama holed the 141-yard 14th hole at the Vestavia CC in one in October, 1970.

● Another blind person to have holed-in-one was American Ben Thomas while on holiday in South Carolina in 1978.

● Rick Sorenson undertook a bet in which, playing 18 holes blindfolded at Meadowbrook Course, Minneapolis, on 25th May, 1973, he was to pay $10 for every hole over par and receive $100 for every hole in par or better. He went round in 86 losing $70 on the deal.

● Alfred Toogood played blindfolded in a match against Tindal Atkinson at Sunningdale in 1912. Toogood was beaten 8 and 7. Previously, in 1908, I. Millar, Newcastle-upon-Tyne, played a match blindfolded against A.T. Broughton, Birkdale, at Newcastle, County Down.

● Wing-Commander *Laddie* Lucas, DSO, DFC, MP, played over Sandy Lodge golf course in Hertfordshire on 7th August, 1954, completely blindfolded and had a score of 87.

Trick shots

● Joe Kirkwood, Australia, specialised in public exhibitions of trick and fancy shots. He played all kinds of strokes after nominating them, and among his ordinary strokes nothing was more impressive than those hit for low flight. He played a full drive from the face of a wrist watch, and the toe of a spectator's shoe, full strokes at a suspended ball, and played for slice and pull at will, and exhibited his ambidexterity by playing left-handed strokes with right-handed clubs. Holing six balls, stymieing, a full shot at a ball catching it as it descended, and hitting 12 full shots in rapid succession, with his face turned away from the ball, were shots among his repertoire. In playing the last named Kirkwood placed the balls in a row, about six inches apart, and moved quickly along the line. Kirkwood, who was born in Australia lived for many years in America. He died in November, 1970 aged 73.

● On 2nd April, 1894, a 3-ball match was played over Musselburgh course between Messrs Grant, Bowden, and Waggot, the clubmaker, the latter teeing on the face of a watch at each tee. He finished the round in 41 the watch being undamaged in any way.

● In a match at Esher on 23rd November, 1931, George Ashdown, the professional, played his tee shot for each of the 18 holes from a rubber tee strapped to the forehead of Miss Ena Shaw.

● E.A. Forrest, a South African professional in a music hall turn of trick golf shots, played blindfolded shots, one being from the ball teed on the chin of his recumbent partner.

● The late Paul Hahn, an American trick specialist could hit four balls with two clubs. Holding a club in each hand he hit two balls, hooking one and slicing the other with the same swing. Hahn had a repertoire of 30 trick shots. In 1955 he flew round the world, exhibiting in 14 countries and on all five continents.

Balls colliding and touching

● Competing in the 1980 Corfu International Championship, Sharon Peachey drove from one tee and her ball collided in mid-air with one from a competitor playing another hole. Her ball ended in a pond.

● Playing in the Cornish team championship in 1973 at West Cornwall GC Tom Scott-Brown, of West Cornwall GC, and Paddy Bradley, of Tehidy GC, saw their drives from the fourth and eighth tees collide in mid-air.

● During a fourball match at Guernsey Club in June, 1966, near the 13th green from the tee, two of the players, D.G. Hare and S. Machin, chipped up simultaneously; the balls collided in mid-air and Machin's ball hit the green, then the flagstick, and dropped into the hole for a birdie 2.

● In May, 1926, during the meeting of the Army Golfing Society at St Andrews, Colonel Howard and Lieutenant-Colonel Buchanan Dunlop, while playing in the foursomes against J. Rodger and J. Mackie, hit full iron shots for the seconds to the 16th green. Each thought he had to play his ball first, and hidden by a bunker the players struck their balls simultaneously. The balls, going towards the hole about 20 yards from the pin and five feet in the air, met with great force and dropped either side of the hole five yards apart.

● In 1972, before a luncheon celebrating the centenary year of the Ladies' Section of Royal Wimbledon GC, a 12-hole competition was held during which two competitors, Mrs L. Champion and Mrs A. McKendrick, driving from the eighth and ninth tees respectively, saw their balls collide in mid-air.

● In 1928, at Wentworth Falls, Australia, Dr Alcorn and E.A. Avery, of Leura Club, were playing with professional E. Barnes. The tee shots of Avery and Barnes at the 9th hole finished on opposite sides of the fairway. Both players unknowingly hit their seconds (chip shots) at the same time. Dr Alcorn, standing at the pin, suddenly saw two balls approaching the hole from different angles. They met in the air and dropped into the hole.

● At Rugby, 1931, playing in a 4-ball match, H. Fraser pulled his drive from the 10th tee in the direction of the ninth tee. Simultaneously a club member, driving from the ninth tee, pulled his drive. The tees were about 350 yards apart. The two balls collided in mid-air.

● Two golf balls, being played in opposite directions, collided in flight over Longniddry Golf Course on 27th June, 1953. Immediately after Stewart Elder, of Longniddry, had driven from the third tee, another ball, which had been pulled off line from the second fairway, which runs alongside the third, struck his ball about 20 feet above the ground. S.J. Fleming, of Tranent, who was playing with Elder, heard a loud crack and thought Elder's ball had exploded. The balls were found undamaged about 70 yards apart.

Three and two balls dislodged by one shot

● In 1934 on the short 3rd hole (now the 13th) of Olton Course, Warwickshire, J.R. Horden, a scratch golfer of the club, sent his tee shot into long wet grass a few feet over the back of the green. When he played an *explosion* shot three balls dropped on to the putting green, his own and two others.

● A.M. Chevalier, playing at Hale, Cheshire, March, 1935, drove his ball into a grass bunker, and when he reached it there was only part of it showing. He played the shot with a niblick and to his amazement not one but three balls shot into the air. They all dropped back into the bunker and came to rest within a foot of each other. Then came another surprise. One of the *finds* was of the same manufacture and bore the same number as the ball he was playing with.

● Playing to the 9th hole, at Osborne House Club, Isle of Wight, George A. Sherman lost his ball which had sunk out of sight on the sodden fairway. A few weeks later, playing from the same tee, his ball again was plugged, only the top showing. Under a local rule he lifted his ball to place it, and exactly under it lay the ball he had lost previously.

Balls in strange places

● Playing at the John O' Gaunt Club, Sutton, near Biggleswade (Beds), a member drove a ball which did not touch the ground until it reached London – over 40 miles away. The ball landed in a vegetable lorry which was passing the golf course and later fell out of a package of cabbages when they were unloaded at Covent Garden, London.

● In the English Open Amateur Stroke Play at Moortown in 1974, Nigel Denham, a Yorkshire County player, in the first round saw his overhit second shot to the 18th green bounce up some steps into the clubhouse. His ball went through an open door, ricocheted off a wall and came to rest in the men's bar, 20 feet from the windows. As the clubhouse was not out of bounds Denham decided to play the shot back to the green and opened a window 4 feet by 2 feet through which he pitched his ball to 12 feet from the flag. (Several weeks later The R&A declared that Denham should have been penalised two shots for opening the window. The clubhouse was an immovable obstruction and no part of it should have been moved.)

● In The Open Championship at Sandwich, 1949, Harry Bradshaw, Kilcroney, Dublin, at the 5th hole in his second round, drove into the rough and found his ball inside a beer bottle with the neck and shoulder broken off and four sharp points sticking up. Bradshaw, if he had treated the ball as in an unplayable lie might have been involved in a disqualification, so he decided to play it where it lay. With his blaster he smashed the bottle and sent the ball about 30 yards. The hole, a par 4, cost him 6.

● Kevin Sharman of Woodbridge GC hit a low, very straight drive at the club's 8th hole in 1979. After some minutes' searching, his ball was found embedded in a plastic sphere on top of the direction post.

● On the Dublin Course, 16th July, 1936, in the Irish Open Championship, A.D. Locke, the South African, played his tee shot at the 100-yard 12th hole, but the ball could not be found on arrival at the green. The marker removed the pin and it was discovered that the ball had been entangled in the flag. It dropped near the edge of the hole and Locke holed the short putt for a birdie two.

● While playing a round on the Geelong Golf Club Course, Australia, Easter, 1923, Captain Charteris topped his tee shot to the short 2nd hole, which lies over a creek with deep and steep clay banks. His ball came to rest on the near slope of the creek bank. He elected to play the ball as it lay, and took his niblick. After the shot, the ball was nowhere to be seen. It was found later embedded in a mass of gluey clay stuck fast to the face of the niblick. It could not be shaken off. Charteris did what was afterwards approved by The R&A, cleaned the ball and dropped it behind without penalty.

● In October, 1929, at Blackmoor Golf Club, Bordon, Hants, a player driving from the first tee holed out his ball in the chimney of a house some 120 yards distant and some 40 yards out of bounds on the right. The owner and his wife were sitting in front of the fire when they heard a rattle in the chimney and were astonished to see a golf ball drop into the fire.

● A similar incident occurred in an inter-club match between Musselburgh and Lothianburn at Prestongrange in 1938 when a member of the former team hooked his ball at the 2nd hole and gave it up for lost. To his amazement a woman emerged from one of the houses adjacent to this part of the course and handed back the ball which she said had come down the chimney and landed on a pot which was on the fire.

● In July, 1955, J. Lowrie, starter at the Eden Course, St Andrews, witnessed a freak shot. A visitor drove from the first tee just as a north-bound train was passing. He sliced the shot and the ball disappeared through an open window of a passenger compartment. Almost immediately the ball emerged again, having been thrown back on to the fairway by a man in the compartment, who waved a greeting which presumably indicated that no one was hurt.

● At Coombe Wood Golf Club, a player hit a ball towards the 16th green where it landed in the vertical exhaust of a tractor which was mowing the fairway. The greenkeeper was somewhat surprised to find a temporary loss of power in the tractor. When sufficient compression had built up in the exhaust system, the ball was forced out with tremendous velocity, hit the roof of a house nearby, bounced off and landed some three feet from the pin on the green.

● There have been many occasions when misdirected shots have finished in strange places after an unusual line of flight and bounce. At Ashford, Middlesex, John Miller, aged 69, hit his tee shot out of bounds at the 12th hole (237 yards). It struck a parked car, passed through a copse, hit more cars, jumped a canopy, flew through the clubhouse kitchen window, finishing in a cooking stock-pot, without once touching the ground. Mr Miller had previously done the hole in one on four occasions.

"Waiter. There's a golf ball in my soup"

● When carrying out an inspection of the air conditioning system at St John's Hospital, Chelmsford, in 1993, a golf ball was found in the ventilator immediately above the operating theatre. It was probably the result of a hooked drive from the first tee at Chelms-

ford Golf Club, which is close by, but the ball can only have entered the duct on a rebound through a three-inch gap under a ventilator hood and then descended through a series of sharp bends to its final resting place.

Balls Hit To and From Great Heights

● In 1798 two Edinburgh golfers undertook to drive a ball over the spire of St Giles' Cathedral, Edinburgh, for a wager. Mr Sceales, of Leith, and Mr Smellie, a printer, were each allowed six shots and succeeded in sending the balls well over the weather-cock, a height of more than 160 feet from the ground.

● Some years later Donald McLean, an Edinburgh lawyer, won a substantial bet by driving a ball over the Melville Monument in St Andrew Square, Edinburgh – height, 154 feet.

● Tom Morris in 1860, at the famous bridge of Ballochmyle, stood in the quarry beneath and, from a stick elevated horizontally, attempted to send golf balls over the bridge. He could raise them only to the pathway, 400 feet high, which was in itself a great feat with the gutta ball.

● Captain Ernest Carter, on 28th September, 1922, drove a ball from the roadway at the 1st tee on Harlech Links against the wall of Harlech Castle. The embattlements are 200 feet over the level of the roadway, and the point where the ball struck the embattlements was 180 yards from the point where the ball was teed. Captain Carter, who was laid odds of £100 to £1, used a baffy.

● In 1896 Freddie Tait, then a subaltern in the Black Watch, drove a ball from the Rookery, the highest building on Edinburgh Castle, in a match against a brother officer to hole out in the fountain in Princes Street Gardens 350 feet below and about 300 yards distant.

● Prior to the 1977 Lancôme Tournament in Paris, Arnold Palmer hit three balls from the second stage of the Eiffel Tower, over 300 feet above ground. The longest was measured at 403 yards. One ball was hooked and hit a bus but no serious damage was done as all traffic had been stopped for safety reasons.

● Long drives have been made from mountain peaks, across the gorge at Victoria Falls, from the Pyramids, high buildings in New York, and from many other similar places. As an illustration of such freakish *drives* a member of the New York Rangers' Hockey Team from the top of Mount Edith Cavell, 11,033 feet high, drove a ball which struck the Ghost Glacier 5000 feet below and bounced off the rocky ledge another 1000 feet – a total drop of 2000 yards. Later, in June, 1968, from Pikes Peak, Colorado (14,110 feet), Arthur Lynskey hit a ball which travelled 200 yards horizontally but 2 miles vertically.

Remarkable Shots

● Remarkable shots are as numerous as the grains of sand; around every 19th hole, legends are recalled of astounding shots. One shot is commemorated by a memorial tablet at the 17th hole at the Lytham and St Annes Club. It was made by Bobby Jones in the final round of The Open Championship in 1926. He was partnered by Al Watrous, another American player. They had been running neck and neck and at the end of the third round, Watrous was just leading Jones with 215 against 217. At the 16th Jones drew level then on the 17th he drove into a sandy lie in broken ground. Watrous reached the green with his second. Jones took a mashie-iron (the equivalent to a 4-iron today) and hit a magnificent shot to the green to get his 4. This remarkable recovery unnerved Watrous, who 3-putted, and Jones, getting another 4 at the last hole against 5, won his first Open Championship with 291 against Watrous' 293. The tablet is near the spot where Jones played his second shot.

● Arnold Palmer (USA), playing in the second round of the Australian Wills Masters tournament at Melbourne, in October, 1964, hooked his second shot at the 9th hole high into the fork of a gum tree. Climbing 20 feet up the tree, Palmer, with the head of his 1-iron reversed, played a hammer stroke and knocked the ball some 30 yards forward, followed by a brilliant chip to the green and a putt.

● In the foursome during the Ryder Cup at Moortown in 1929, Joe Turnesa hooked the American side's second shot at the last hole behind the marquee adjoining the clubhouse, Johnny Farrel then pitched the ball over the marquee on to the green only feet away from the pin and Turnesa holed out for a 4.

Miscellaneous Incidents and Strange Golfing Facts

● Gary Player of South Africa was honoured by his country by having his portrait on new postage stamps which were issued on 12th December, 1976. It was the first time a specific golfer had ever been depicted on any country's postage stamps. In 1981 the US Postal Service introduced stamps featuring Bobby Jones and Babe Zaharias. They are the first golfers to be thus honoured by the United States.

● Gary Harris, aged 18, became the first player to make five consecutive appearances for England in the European Boys Team Championship at Vilamoura, Portugal, in 1994.

● In February, 1971, the first ever golf shots on the moon's surface were played by Captain Alan Shepard, commander of the Apollo 14 spacecraft. Captain Shepard hit two balls with an iron head attached to a makeshift shaft. With a one-handed swing he claimed he hit the first ball 200 yards aided by the reduced force of gravity on the moon. Subsequent findings put this distance in doubt. The second was a shank. Acknowledging the occasion The R&A sent Captain Shepard the following telegram: *Warmest congratulations to all of you on your great achievement and safe return. Please refer to Rules of Golf section on etiquette, paragraph 6, quote – before leaving a bunker a player should carefully fill up all holes made by him therein, unquote.* Shepard presented the club to the USGA Museum in 1974.

● Charles (Chick) Evans competed in every US Amateur Championship held between 1907 and 1962 by which time he was 72 years old. This amounted to 50 consecutive occasions discounting the six years of the two World Wars when the championship was not held.

● In winning the 1977 US Open at Southern Hills CC, Tulsa, Oklahoma, Hubert Green had to contend with a death threat. Coming off the 14th green in the final round, he was advised by USGA officials that a phone call had been received saying that he would be killed. Green decided that play should continue and happily he went on to win, unharmed.

● It was discovered at the 1977 USPGA Championship that the clubs with which Tom Watson had won The Open Championship and the US Masters earlier in the year were illegal, having grooves which exceeded the permitted specifications. The set he used in winning the 1975 Open Championship were then flown out to him and they too were found to be illegal. No retrospective action was taken.

● Mrs Fred Daly, wife of the former Open champion, saved the clubhouse of Balmoral GC, Belfast, from destruction when three men entered the professional's shop on 5th August, 1976, and left a bag containing a bomb outside the shop beside the clubhouse when refused money. Mrs Daly carried the bag over to a hedge some distance away where the bomb exploded 15 minutes later. The only damage was broken windows. On the same day several hours afterwards, Dungannon GC in Co. Tyrone suffered extensive damage to the clubhouse from terrorist bombs. Co. Down GC, proposed venue of the 1979 home international matches suffered bomb damage in May that year and through fear for the safety of team members the 1979 matches were cancelled.

● The Army Golfing Society and St Andrews on 21st April, 1934, played a match 200-a-side, the largest golf match ever played. Play was by foursomes. The Army won 58, St Andrews 31 and 11 were halved.

● Jamie Ortiz-Patino, owner of the Valderrama Golf Club at Sotogrande, Spain, paid a record £84,000 (increased to £92,400 with ten per cent buyers premium) for a late seventeenth- or early eighteenth-century rake iron offered at auction in Musselburgh in July, 1992. The iron, which had been kept in a garden shed, was bought to be exhibited in a museum being created in Valderrama.

● In 1986 Alistair Risk and three colleagues on the 17th green at Brora, Sutherland, watched a cow giving birth to twin calves between the markers on the 18th tee, causing them to play their next tee shots from in front of the tee. Their application for a ruling from The R&A brought a Rules Committee reply that while technically a rule had been broken, their action was considered within the spirit of the game and there should be no penalty. The Secretary added that the Rules Committee hoped that mother and twins were doing well.

● In view of the increasing number of people crossing the road (known as Granny Clark's Wynd) which runs across the first and 18th fairways of the Old Course, St Andrews, as a right of way, the St Andrews Links committee decided in 1969 to control the flow by erecting traffic lights, with appropriate green for go, yellow for caution and red for stop. The lights are controlled from the starter's box on the first tee. Golfers on the first tee must wait until the lights turn to green before driving off and a notice has been erected at the Wynd warning pedestrians not to cross at yellow or stop.

● A traffic light for golfers was also installed in 1971 on one of Japan's most congested courses. After putting on the uphill 9th hole of the Fukuoka course in Southern Japan, players have to switch on a go-ahead signal for following golfers waiting to play their shots to the green.

● A 22-year-old professional at Brett Essex GC, Brentwood, David Moore, who was playing in the Mufulira Open in Zambia in 1976, was shot dead it is alleged by the man with whom he was staying for the duration of the tournament. It appeared his host then shot himself.

● Peggy Carrick and her daughter, Angela Uzielli, won the Mothers and Daughters Tournament at Royal Mid-Surrey in 1994 for the 21st time.

● Patricia Shepherd has won the ladies' club championship at Turriff GC Aberdeenshire 30 consecutive times from 1959 to 1988.

● Mrs Jackie Mercer won the South African Ladies' Championship in 1979, 31 years after her first victory in the event as Miss Jacqueline Smith.

● During The Royal and Ancient Golf Club of St Andrews' medal meeting on 25th September, 1907, a member of The Royal and Ancient drove a ball which struck the sharp point of a hatpin in the hat of a lady who was crossing the course. The ball was so firmly impaled that it remained in position. The lady was not hurt.

● John Cook, former English Amateur Champion, narrowly escaped death during an attempted coup against King Hassan of Morocco in July 1971. Cook had been playing in a tournament arranged by King Hassan, a keen golfer, and was at the King's birthday party in Rabat when rebels broke into the party demanding that the King give up his throne. Cook and many others present were taken hostage.

● When playing from the 9th tee at Lossiemouth golf course in June, 1971, Martin Robertson struck a Royal Navy jet aircraft which was coming in to land at the nearby airfield. The plane was not damaged.

● At a court in Inglewood, California, in 1978, Jim Brown was convicted of beating and choking an opponent during a dispute over where a ball should have been placed on the green.

● During the Northern Ireland troubles a home-made hand grenade was found in a bunker at Dungannon GC, Co. Tyrone, on Sunday, 12th September, 1976.

● Tiger Woods, 18, became both the youngest and the first black golfer to win the United States Amateur Championship at Sawgrass in 1994. He went on to win the title three years in a row and then won the first major championship he played as a professional, the 1997 Masters, by a record 12 strokes and with a record low aggregate of 270, 18 under par.

● To mark the centenary of the Jersey Golf Club in 1978, the Jersey Post Office issued a set of four spe-

cial stamps featuring Jersey's most famous golfer, Harry Vardon. The background of the 13p stamp was a brief biography of Vardon's career reproduced from the Golfer's Handbook.

● Forty-one-year-old John Mosley went for a round of golf at Delaware Park GC, Buffalo, New York, in July, 1972. He stepped on to the first tee and was challenged over a green fee by an official guard. A scuffle developed, a shot was fired and Mosley, a bullet in his chest, died on the way to hospital. His wife was awarded $131,250 in an action against the City of Buffalo and the guard. The guard was sentenced to 7¹/₂ years for second-degree manslaughter.

● When three competitors in a 1968 Pennsylvania pro-am event were about to drive from the 16th tee, two bandits (one with pistol) suddenly emerged from the bushes, struck one of the players and robbed them of wristwatches and $300.

● In the 1932 Walker Cup match at Brooklyn, Leonard Crawley succeeded in denting the cup. An errant iron shot to the 18th green hit the cup, which was on display outside the clubhouse.

● In Johannesburg, South Africa, three golf officials appeared in court accused of violating a 70-year-old Sunday Observance Law by staging the final round of the South African PGA championship on Sunday, 28th February, 1971. The Championship should have been completed on the Saturday but heavy rain prevented any play.

● In The Open Championship of 1876, at St Andrews, Bob Martin and David Strath tied at 176. A protest was lodged against Strath alleging he played his approach to the 17th green and struck a spectator. The Royal and Ancient ordered the replay, but Strath refused to play off the tie until a decision had been given on the protest. No decision was given and Bob Martin was declared the Champion.

● At Rose Bay, New South Wales, on 11th July, 1931, D.J. Bayly MacArthur, on stepping into a bunker, began to sink. MacArthur, who weighed 14 stone, shouted for help. He was rescued when up to the armpits. He had stepped on a patch of quicksand, aggravated by excess of moisture.

● The late Bobby Cruickshank was the victim of his own jubilation in the 1934 US Open at Merion. In the 4th round while in with a chance of winning he half-topped his second shot at the 11th hole. The ball was heading for a pond in front of the green but instead of ending up in the water it hit a rock and bounced on to the green. In his delight Cruickshank threw his club into the air only to receive a resounding blow on the head as it returned to earth.

● A dog with an infallible nose for finding lost golf balls was, in 1971, given honorary membership of the Waihi GC, Hamilton, New Zealand. The dog, called Chico, was trained to search for lost balls, to be sold back to the members, the money being put into club funds.

● By 1980 Waddy, an 11-year-old beagle belonging to Bob Inglis, the secretary of Brokenhurst Manor GC, had found over 35,000 golf balls.

● Herbert M. Hepworth, Headingley, Leeds, Lord Mayor of Leeds in 1906, scored one thousand holes in 2, a feat which took him 30 years to accomplish. It was celebrated by a dinner in 1931 at the Leeds club. The first 2 of all was scored on 12th June, 1901, at Cobble Hall Course, Leeds, and the 1,000th in 1931 at Alwoodley, Leeds. Hepworth died in November, 1942.

● Fiona MacDonald was the first female to play in the Oxford and Cambridge University match at Ganton in 1986.

● Mrs Sara Gibbon won the Farnham (Surrey) Club's Grandmother's competition 48 hours after her first grand-child was born.

● At Carnoustie in the first qualifying round for the 1952 Scottish Amateur Championship a competitor drove three balls in succession out of bounds at the 1st hole and thereupon withdrew.

● In 1993, the Clark family from Hagley GC, Worcs, set a record for the county's three major professional events. The Worcestershire Stroke Play Championship was won by Finlay Clark, the eldest son, who beat his father Iain and younger brother Cameron, who tied second. In the Match Play Iain beat his son Finlay by 2 and 1 in the final; Cameron won the play-off for third place. Then in the Worcestershire Annual Pro-Am it was Cameron's turn to win, with his brother Finlay coming second and father Iain third. To add to the achievements of the family, Cameron also won the Midland Professional Match Play Championship.

● During a Captain–Pro foursomes challenge match at Chelmsford in 1993, Club Professional Dennis Bailey, put the ball into a hole only once in all 18 holes – when he holed-in-one at the fourth.

● In 1891, a new kind of matchplay – bogey – was introduced at Great Yarmouth Golf Club where the scratch score of the course was taken and each hole given a value known as the ground score. One of the club's members was described as a "regular bogey-man", a name suggested by a music hall song that was currently popular … and the name stuck.

● Mrs C.C. Gray was Todmorden Golf Club's Ladies Champion 38 out of 42 times between 1951 and 1992, a fact recorded in the Guinness Book of Records.

● Llanymynech is a golf club situated in two countries with 15 holes in Wales and three in England. On the fourth tee, players drive from England and putt out in Wales.

● Gary Sutherland, with only his golf bag as his suitcase and using public transport, competed an unusual tribute to his late father by playing 18 rounds on 18 courses on 18 different islands in Scotland. His travels began on the 13-hole course at Port Bannatyne on Bute, took him among other islands to Orkney, Shetland, Harris, South Uist, Arran and ended at Machrie on Islay. Accompanied by his friend golf architect Brian Noble, Sutherland found the trip rekindled his own love of a game his father had enjoyed so much. … and he has recorded his adventures in a new book The Fairway Isles.

Strange local rules

● The Duke of Windsor, who played on an extraordinary variety of the world's courses, once took advantage of a local rule at Jinja in Uganda and lifted his ball from a hippo's footprint without penalty.

● At the Glen Canyon course in Arizona a local rule provides that If your ball lands within a club length of a rattlesnake you are allowed to move the ball.

● Another local rule in Uganda reads: If a ball comes to rest in dangerous proximity to a crocodile, another ball may be dropped.

"I reckon that qualifies as dangerous proximity"

● The 6th hole at Koolan Island GC, Western Australia, also serves as a local air strip and a local rule reads: Aircraft and vehicular traffic have right of way at all times.

● A local rule at the RAF Waddington GC reads: When teeing off from the 2nd, right of way must be given to taxiing aircraft.

Open Championship Timeline

1860 The first Open Championship is played at Prestwick. There are eight competitors and the trophy, an ornate red leather belt, is won by Willie Park Sr.

1863 Prize money is first awarded, but only to second, third and fourth place finishers. The winner first receives a cash prize of £6 in 1864.

1870 Tommy Morris Jr takes possession of the Challenge Belt after winning The Open for the third consecutive year.

1873 The Claret Jug is first awarded. Played at St Andrews, it is the first time the Championship is held outside Prestwick.

1890 John Ball becomes the first amateur and the first Englishman to win The Open.

1892 Play is extended to two days over 72 holes at Muirfield. Competitors are charged an entrance fee.

1898 The "cut" is introduced after 36 holes.

1907 Arnaud Massy from France is the first continental player to win The Open. Qualifying rounds are first played.

1909 The Golf Exhibition tent makes its first appearance, as a display venue for leading manufacturers.

1922 It is decided that The Open should only be played over links courses.

1925 Prestwick hosts its 24th and final Open Championship.

1926 Admission charges are introduced. Play is extended to three days.

1955 The Open is broadcast live on television by the BBC.

1960 Grandstands are introduced at the Centenary Open played in St Andrews.

1963 Exemptions from pre-qualifying are introduced for the leading players.

1966 America receives its first live Open broadcast. The Championship is played over three days.

1968 The double cut is introduced after 54 holes and remains in effect until 1985.

1970 Jack Nicklaus and Doug Sanders became the first duo to compete in an 18-hole play-off.

1973 The 1.62 inch ball is last used at The Open.

1976 Japan receives its first live Open transmission.

1977 Regional qualifying is introduced as a preliminary to Final Qualifying for most players.

1980 The Championship ends on a Sunday for the first time.

1985 The four-hole play-off, followed by sudden death, is introduced.

2000 A new record is set at the Home of Golf when 238,787 watch the Millennium Open.

2002 History is made when The Open ends for the first time in a four-way tie. In another first, the four-hole play-off results in a tie.

2004 International Final Qualifying is introduced, allowing players to qualify at five international locations.

2006 The 135th Open Championship is broadcast globally for 2,051 hours. Fifty-seven broadcasters across 162 territories show coverage of The Open to a potential household reach of 410 million.

2007 Ireland's Padraig Harrington becomes the first European to win The Open since Paul Lawrie in 1999 and only the second Irishman. Fred Daly preceded him in 1947.

2009 Tom Watson, aged 59 years, 10 months, 15 days, becomes the oldest ever runner-up. Matteo Manassero, aged 16 years and 3 months, becomes the youngest winner of the Silver Medal for the leading amateur.

2010 Golf's oldest Major celebrates its 150th anniversary as The Open is played at the Home of Golf for the 28th time.

Timeline for the Rules of Golf

The earliest known Rules of Golf were drawn up in 1744 by what was to become the Honourable Company of Edinburgh Golfers. For the next 100 years, each club could issue and revise its own code of Rules, and these were mainly based on the codes issued by The Royal and Ancient Golf Club, the Edinburgh Burgess Golfing Society or the Honourable Company. Some of the rules followed by individual clubs were identical to one of these codes, while others were worded with reference to the features of a particular course.

Starting in the second half of the 19th century, more and more clubs based their codes on those issued by The Royal and Ancient Golf Club. In 1897 its governance role was formalised with the creation of the Rules of Golf Committee.

1744 The Honourable company of Edinburgh Golfers produce a written code of rules. Known as the Thirteen Articles, Rule 1 states: "You must tee your ball within a club-length of the hole".

1754 Largely copying from the 1744 Rules, the Society of St Andrews Golfers (later to become The Royal and Ancient Golf Club) record their own Rules in the minutes.

1775 Methods of settling disputes first appear in the Honourable Company's Rules. "Any dispute arising between parties on the green shall be determined by the Captain for the time, if present, or by the latest Captain who may be on the ground".

1812 The R&A's 1754 code is revised and for the first time the Rules of Golf refer to bunkers and the putting green.

1842 The revised R&A code stipulates that "one round of the links, or 18 holes, is reckoned a match" for the first time.

1851 A revised R&A code is issued. In response to the advent of the gutta percha ball, a new rule allows that: "If a ball shall split into two or more pieces, a fresh ball shall be put down in playing for a medal".

1875 Attending the flagstick and dealing with balls resting against the flagstick appear in the Rules for the first time.

1882 The revised R&A code contains an index and a glossary of terms for the first time.

1882 The glossary of terms in the R&A code defines the size of the hole as being four inches in diameter and lined with iron.

1886 The Royal Isle of Wight Golf Club issues a version of the Rules of Golf, which defines the size of the hole as being four inches in diameter and six inches deep.

1888 Local Rules for Playing the Links at St Andrews are separated out from the main Rules of Golf for the first time by The R&A.

1891 The revised R&A code defines the hole as being four and a quarter inches in diameter and at least four inches deep. This remains the definition.

1897 The Royal and Ancient Golf Club is officially recognised as the game's governing body for the Rules of Golf.

1909 Limits on the form and make of clubs are applied for the first time.

1920 The R&A and the USGA agreed that from May 1st, 1921, "the weight of the ball should be no greater than 1.62 ounces and the size not less than 1.62 inches in diameter".

1929 Steel shafts are legalised.

1939 The maximum number of clubs that can be carried is 14.

1952 The R&A and the USGA establish a unified code of Rules.

1960 Distance measuring devices are banned.

1984 The ball is no longer dropped over the player's shoulder, but at arm's length and at shoulder height.

1988 First Joint Decisions on the Rules of Golf book published by The R&A and the USGA.

1990 The 1.68-inch ball becomes the only legal ball, marking the demise of the 1.62-inch British ball.

2002 The R&A announces its decision to limit driver 'spring-like' effect from 2008, with an elite level Condition of Competition effective 1 January 2003.

2004 Entire Rule book redrafted for clarity, adopting a more modern style. Etiquette section amended and expanded. Limits introduced on size and dimensions of wood heads and club length (excluding putters).

2010 New groove specifications introduced, effective immediately at elite level by Condition of Competition. Club level golfers exempt until at least 2024.

Royal Clubs

There are currently 63 clubs with royal titles granted by the British Royal family. In 2009, Auckland Golf Club, New Zealand, was granted Royal status by Her Majesty Queen Elizabeth II as was the Mayfair Golf Club in Edmonton, Canada, in 2005. In 2004, Wellington Golf Club received the title from HRH The Duke of York. Mariánské Lázně Golf Club was honoured in 2003. The club had strong connections with British Royalty in the past; King Edward VII holidayed there, in what is now the Czech Republic. Apart from Mariánské Lázně, the Royal Clubs are in the United Kingdom or the Commonwealth. The oldest club with Royal connections is The Royal and Ancient Golf Club of St Andrews, founded in 1754 and given Royal patronage by King William IV in 1834. Royal Perth Golf Club, which was founded in 1824, received the patronage of King William IV a year earlier, in 1833.

Club	Year Founded	Year of Royal Patronage	Royal Patron
Royal Ancient Golf Club, St Andrews	1754	1834	William IV
Royal Aberdeen	1780	1903	Edward VII (Leopold patron in 1872)
Royal Adelaide	1892	1923	George V
Royal Ascot	1887	1887	Victoria 1887; Elizabeth II 1977
Royal Ashdown Forest	1888	1893	Victoria
Royal Auckland	1894	2009	Elizabeth II
Royal Belfast	1881	1885	Edward, Prince of Wales (later Edward VII)
Royal Birkdale	1889	1951	George VI
Royal Blackheath	1766	1857	Not known
Royal Burgess	1773	1929	George V
Royal Calcutta	1829	1912	George V
Royal Canberra	1926	1933	George V
Royal Cape	1885	1910	George V
Royal Cinque Ports	1892	1910	George V
Royal Colombo	1879	1928	George V
Royal Colwood	1913	1931	George V
Royal County Down	1889	1908	Edward VII
Royal Cromer	1888	1887	Edward, Prince of Wales (later Edward VII)
Royal Dornoch	1877	1906	Edward VII
Royal Dublin	1885	1891	Victoria
Duff House Royal	1909	1925	Princess Louise, Dowager Duchess of Fife
Royal Durban	1892	1932	George V
Royal Eastbourne	1887	1887	Victoria
Royal Epping Forest	1888	1888	Victoria
Royal Fremantle	1905	1930	George V
Royal Guernsey	1890	1891	Victoria

Club	Year Founded	Year of Royal Patronage	Royal Patron
Royal Harare	1898	1929	George V
Royal Hobart	1900	1925	George V
The Royal Household	1901	1901	Edward VII
Royal Jersey	1878	1879	Victoria
Royal Johannesburg	1890	1931	George V
Royal Liverpool	1869	1871	Prince Arthur, Duke of Connaught
Royal Lytham	1886	1926	George V
Royal Malta	1888	1888	Prince Alfred, Duke of Edinburgh
Royal Mariánské Lázně	1905	2003	Elizabeth II
Royal Mayfair	1922	2005	Elizabeth II
Royal Melbourne	1891	1895	Victoria
Royal Mid Surrey	1892	1926	George V
Royal Montreal	1873	1884	Victoria
Royal Montrose	1810	1845	Prince Albert
Royal Musselburgh	1774	1876	Prince Arthur, Duke of Connaught
Royal Nairobi	1906	1935	George V
Royal North Devon	1864	1866	Edward, Prince of Wales (later Edward VII)
Royal Norwich	1893	1893	George, Duke of York (later George V)
Royal Ottawa	1891	1912	George V
Royal Perth	1824	1833	William IV
Royal Perth (Australia)	1895	1937	George VI
Royal Port Alfred	1907	1924	George V
Royal Porthcawl	1891	1909	Edward VII
Royal Portrush	1888	1892	George, Duke of York (later George V)
Royal Quebec	1874	1934	George V
Royal Queensland	1920	1921	George V
Royal Regina	1899	1999	Elizabeth II
Royal St Davids	1894	1908	Edward, Prince of Wales (later Edward VII)
Royal St George's	1887	1902	Edward VII
Royal Sydney	1893	1897	Victoria
Royal Tarlair	1926	1926	Princess Louise, Dowager Duchess of Fife
Royal Troon	1878	1978	Elizabeth II
Royal Wellington	1895	2004	Prince Andrew, Duke of York
Royal West Norfolk	1892	1892	Edward, Prince of Wales (later Edward VII)
Royal Wimbledon	1865	1882	Victoria
Royal Winchester	1888	1913	George V
Royal Worlington and Newmarket	1893	1895	Victoria

Websites

The R&A	www.randa.org
United States Golf Association	www.usga.org
English Golf Union	www.englishgolfunion.org
Golf Union of Ireland	www.gui.ie
Scottish Golf Union	www.scottishgolfunion.org
Welsh Golf Union	www.welshgolf.org
European Golf Association	www.ega-golf.ch
Ladies Golf Union (LGU)	www.lgu.org
English Ladies (ELGA)	www.englishladiesgolf.org
Irish Ladies (ILGU)	www.ilgu.ie
European Tour	www.europeantour.com
US PGA Tour	www.pgatour.com
Australasian Tour	www.pgatour.com.au
Asian Tour	www.asiantour.com
Japanese Tour	www.jgto.org
South African Sunshine Tour	www.sunshinetour.com
LPGA Tour	www.lpga.com
Ladies European Tour (LET)	www.ladieseuropeantour.com
Japanese Ladies Tour	www.lpga.or.jp (Japanese only)
Asian Ladies Tour	www.lagt.org
Australian Ladies Tour	www.alpgtour.com
South African Ladies Tour	www.wpga.co.za
Futures Tour	www.duramedfuturestour.com
The Open	www.opengolf.com
US Open	www.usopen.com
The Masters	www.masters.org
US PGA Championship	www.pga.com/pgachampionship/2010
PGA (The Belfry)	www.pga.info
PGAs of Europe	www.pgae.com
PGA of America	www.pga.com

Severiano Ballesteros	www.seveballesteros.com
Angel Cabrera	www.angelcabrera.com
Michael Campbell	www.cambogolf.com
Paul Casey	www.paul-casey.com
Darren Clarke	www.darrenclarke.com
Ernie Els	www.ernieels.com
Nick Faldo	www.nickfaldo.com
Niclas Fasth	www.niclasfasth.com
Sergio García	www.sergiogarcia.com
Retief Goosen	www.retiefgoosen.com
Padraig Harrington	www.padraigharrington.com
David Howell	www.davidhowellgolf.com
Miguel Angel Jiménez	www.mmiworldwide.com
Bernhard Langer	www.bernhardlanger.de
Thomas Levet	www.thomas-levet.com
Paul McGinley	www.paulmcginley.net
Rory McIlroy	www.rorymcilroy,com
Phil Mickelson	www.phil-mickelson.com
Colin Montgomerie	www.colinmontgomerie.com
Jack Nicklaus	www.nicklaus.com
Greg Norman	www.shark.com
Lorena Ochoa	www.lorenaochoa.com
Geoff Ogilvy	www.prosportmanagement.com
José Maria Olazábal	www.gmi.com
Arnold Palmer	www.arnoldpalmer.com
Ian Poulter	www.ianpoulter.co.uk
Eduardo Romero	www.eduardoromero.com
Justin Rose	www.justinrose.com
Adam Scott	www.adamscott.com.au
Jeev Milkha Singh	www.jeevmilkhasingh.net
Annika Sörenstam	www.annikasorenstam.com
Henrik Stenson	www.henrikstenson.com
Lee Westwood	www.westyuk.com
Tiger Woods	www.tigerwoods.com
Ian Woosnam	www.woosie.com

New role for the PGA Tour in South America

Experienced tournament organiser Jack Warfield has been given the job of running the new PGA Tour Latino America which is scheduled to start later this year. The 11-event schedule, which will be expanded in 2013 to 14 events, is a joint venture between the existing Tour de Las Americas, the PGA Tour, the South American Federations, promoters and sponsors. The new Tour will run from September to December with events being staged in Argentina, Brazil, Chile, Colombia, Mexico, Peru and Puerto Rico.

Tim Finchem, the PGA Tour commissioner, announcing the new initiative, said: "With South America hosting the Olympic Games with golf included in 2016 the time is right for this opportunity to help the further development of the game in that part of the world and to help produce the Latin American stars of the future."

It is anticipated that the new Tour will give top money earners access to the Nationwide Tour in America.

England Golf to represent all English amateurs

The previously separate English Golf Union (EGU) and English Women's Golf Association (EWGA) have merged and from January 2012 became one governing body entitled England Golf which will represent all amateur golfers in England.

The merger proposal was approved at simultaneous meetings by 86 per cent of the voting members of the EGU, meeting at its headquarters in Woodhall Spa; and by 100 per cent of the voting members of the EWGA, meeting at the National Motor Cycle Museum at Solihull. Both organisations had to approve the proposal by a majority of at least 75 per cent for it to be successful.

The decision has been hailed as a triumph for golf and a vital step forward for the game. Nigel Evans, Chairman EGU and Sylvia Perrins, Interim Chairman EWGA said: "This merger is in the best interests of golf and we are delighted that it has been given overwhelming support by our members. We look forward to a new era and to realising our vision for the future.

"England Golf will speak with one voice and send out the powerful, modern message that golf is a game for all, for men and women, boys and girls.

"A unified organisation, which promotes both the men's and women's game, will be more attractive to new golfers, will help us to grow the game, will be more appealing to commercial partners and sponsors and will mean we can be more cost effective."

The merger vote followed a long period of consultation and preparation, which began in 2009 when a steering group was formed of members of both organisations. Following lengthy discussions, and the involvement of ten working groups, the proposal was produced and ratified by the Boards of both organisations before being put to the voting members.

Amateur golf in Wales is organized by one body – the Golf Union of Wales – and there have been moves in Scotland to bring together the men's and women's organisations.

PART XVI

Directory of Golfing Organisations Worldwide

Directory of Golfing Organisations Worldwide

National Associations

The R&A
Ch Exec, Peter Dawson, Beach House, Golf Place, St Andrews, Fife KY16 9JD
Tel (01334) 460000   Fax (01334) 460001
E-mail thechiefexecutive@randa.org
Website www.randa.org

CONGU – Council of National Golf Unions
Sec, Melvyn Goddard, 1 Peerswood Court, Little Neston, Neston CH64 0US
Tel (0151) 336 3936 – office
E-mail secretary@congu.com
Website www.congu.com

Ladies European Tour
Exec Dir, A Armas, Buckinghamshire GC, Denham Court Drive, Denham UB9 5PG
Tel (01895) 831028   Fax (01895) 832301
E-mail mail@ladieseuropeantour.com
Website www.ladieseuropeantour.com

Ladies' Golf Union
Ch Exec, S Malcolm, The Scores, St Andrews, Fife KY16 9AT
Tel (01334) 475811   Fax (01334) 472818
E-mail info@lgu.org
Website www.lgu.org

The Professional Golfers' Association
Ch Exec, Sandy Jones, Centenary House, The Belfry, Sutton Coldfield B76 9PT
Tel (01675) 470333   Fax (01675) 477888
Website www.pga.info

East Region: Sec, J Smith, Bishop's Stortford GC, Dunmow Road, Bishop's Stortford, Herts CM23 5HP
Tel (01279) 652070   Fax (01279) 652732
E-mail john.smith@pga.org.uk

Midland Region: Sec, J Sewell, Forward House, 17 High Street, Henley In Arden, Warwickshire B95 5AA
Tel (01564) 330635
E-mail jon.sewell@pga.org.uk

North Region: Sec, G Maly, No 2 Cottage, Bolton GC, Lostock Park, Chorley New Rd, Bolton, Lancs BL6 4AJ
Tel (01204) 496137   Fax (01204) 847959
E-mail graham.maly@pga.org.uk

South Region: Sec, S Smith, Clandon Regis GC, Epsom Rd, West Clandon, Guildford, Surrey GU4 7TT

Tel (01483) 224200   Fax (01483) 223224
E-mail south.region@pga.org.uk

West Region: Sec, G Ross, The Lodge House, Woodbury Park Hotel, Golf and Country Club, Woodbury Castle, Woodbury, Exeter, Devon EX5 1JJ
Tel (01395) 232288
E-mail glenn.ross@ pga.org.uk

Irish Region: Sec, M McCumiskey, Dundalk GC, Blackrock, Dundalk, Co Louth, Eire
Tel +353 42 932 1193   Fax +353 42 932 1899
E-mail michael.mccumiskey@pga.org.uk

Scottish Region: Sec, M MacDougall, King's Lodge, Gleneagles, Auchterarder PH3 1NE
Tel (01764) 661840   Fax (01764) 661841
E-mail michael.macdougall@pga.org.uk

PGA European Tour
Exec Dir, G O'Grady, PGA European Tour, Wentworth Drive, Virginia Water, Surrey GU25 4LX
Tel (01344) 840400   Fax (01344) 840500
E-mail info@europeantour.com
Website www.europeantour.com

PGAs of Europe
Ch Exec, I Randell, Centenary House, The Belfry, Sutton Coldfield, B76 9PT
Tel (01675) 477899   Fax (01675) 477890
E-mail info@pgae.com   Website www.pgae.com

International Golf Federation
Exec Dir, Antony Scanlon, Maison Du Sport International, Av De Rhodanie 54, 1007 Lausanne, Switzerland
E-mail igfinfo@igfmail.org

Artisan Golfers' Association
Hon Sec, K Stevens, 48 The Avenue, Lightwater, Surrey GU18 5RG
Tel (01276) 475103
E-mail kevin@stevens85.freeserve.co.uk
Website www.agagolf.co.uk

Association of Golf Writers
A group of 30 newspapermen attending the Walker Cup match at St Andrews in 1938 founded the Association to protect the interests of golf writers. The

principal objective is to maintain a close liaison with all the governing bodies and promoters to ensure good working conditions.

Admin, Andrew Farrell, 1 Pilgrims Bungalow, Mulberry Hill, Chilham, Kent CT4 8AH
Tel/Fax (01227) 732496
E-mail enquiry@agwgolf.org
Website www.agwgolf.org

BAGCC – British Association of Golf Course Constructors

The BAGCC has a small but highly prestigious membership of constructors who have performed work to the highest standard from initial consultation to survey work and design through to the construction of a course and then its regular maintenance. Membership is granted only if the candidates satisfy the demanding criteria of experience, professionalism and workmanship set down by the Association.

Sec, Brian Pierson, 32 New Rd, Ringwood BH24 3AU
Tel (01425) 475584
E-mail brian.pierson@btopenworld,com
Website www.bagcc.org.uk

BALASA – British Amputee & Les Autres Sports Association

Golf Coordinator, Richard Saunders, 25 Kiln Lane, Manningtree, Essex CO11 1HQ
Tel (07967) 169951

British Golf Collectors' Society

Sec, A Thorpe, 22 Cherry Tree Close, Brinsley, Nottingham NG16 5BA
Tel/Fax (01773) 780420
E-mail anthonythorpe@ntlworld.com
Website www.britgolfcollectors.wyenet.co.uk

BGIA – British Golf Industry Association

Federation House, Stoneleigh Park, Warks CV8 2RF
Tel (02476) 414999 (x207)
Fax (02476) 414990
E-mail info@bgia.org.uk
Website www.bgia.org.uk

British Golf Museum

Dir, P N Lewis, Bruce Embankment, St Andrews, Fife KY16 9AB
Tel (01334) 460046   *Fax* (01334) 460064
Website www.britishgolfmuseum.co.uk

BIGGA – British & International Golf Greenkeepers Association

The British & International Golf Greenkeepers Association which has over 6,000 members, was formally created in January from an amalgamation of the British Golf Greenkeepers Association, The English and International Golf Greenkeepers Association and The Scottish and International Golf Greenkeepers Association. BIGGA is dedicated to the continuing professional development of its members and strives, by education and training, for standards of excellence in golf course management. BIGGA organise an annual education conference and Europe's largest indoor turf show

Ch Exec, J Croxton, BIGGA House, Aldwark, Alne, York Y061 1UF
Tel (01347) 833800   *Fax* (01347) 833801
E-mail info@bigga.co.uk
Website www.bigga.org.uk

BRTMA – British Rootzone & Topdressing Manufacturers Association

Federation House, Stoneleigh Park, Warks CV8 2RF
Tel (024) 7641 4999   *Fax* (024) 7641 4990
E-mail brtma@sportsandplay.com
Website www.brtma.com

BTLIA – British Turf & Landscape Irrigation Association

Sec, M Jones, 41 Pennine Way, Great Eccleston, Preston PR3 0YS
Tel/Fax (01995) 670675
E-mail ntfoundation@btconnect.com
Website www.btlia.org.uk

Club Managers Association of Europe

CEO, Jerry Kilby, Federation House, Stoneleigh Park, Warks CV8 2RF
Tel (02476) 692359   *Fax* (02476) 414990
E-mail jerry.kilby@cmaeurope.eu
Website www.cmaeurope.org

EDGA – European Disabled Golf Association

Sec/Treas, Pieter van Duyn, Wederikhof 8, NL-2215 GJ Voorhout, The Netherlands
Tel +31 252 224161   *E-mail* mail@edgagolf.com
Website www.edgagolf.com

EGIA – European Golf Industry Association

Federation House, Stoneleigh Park, Warks CV8 2RF
Tel (024) 7641 4999   *Fax* (024) 7641 4990
E-mail egia@sportsandplay.com

EIGCA – European Institute of Golf Course Architects

The EIGCA represents the vast majority of qualified and experienced golf course architects throughout Europe. Its goals are to enhance its professional status and to provide educational courses to train future architects.

Exec Off, Mrs Julia Green, Meadow View House, Tannery Lane, Bramley, Surrey GU5 0AJ
Tel/Fax (01483) 891831   *Fax* (01483) 891846
E-mail enquiries@eigca.org   *Website* www.eigca.org

Golf Club Managers' Association

Membership of the Association is approximately 2,300, consisting of managers/secretaries and owners of clubs and golfing associations situated mainly in the UK and Europe. The Association offers advice on all aspects of managing a golf club and has an extensive information library available to its members through its website.

Ch Exec, K Lloyd, 7a Beaconsfield Rd, Weston-super-Mare BS23 1YE
Tel (01934) 641166   *Fax* (01934) 644254
E-mail hq@gcma.org.uk   *Website* www.gcma.org.uk

Golf Club Stewards' Association

The Golf Club Stewards' Association was founded in 1912 to promote the interests of members and to serve as an employment agency for golf club stewards.

Sec, KG Brothwell, 11 King Charles Court, Sunderland, Tyne & Wear SR5 4PD
Tel (01915) 190137   *E-mail* k.brothwell@sky.com
Website www.club_noticeboard.co.uk

Golf Consultants Association
Federation House, Stoneleigh Park, Warks CV8 2RF
Tel (024) 7641 4999   Fax (024) 7641 4990
E-mail gca@sportsandplay.com
Website www.golfconsultants.org.uk

Golf Foundation
Ch. Exec, Michael Round, The Spinning Wheel, High St,
Hoddesdon, Herts EN11 8BP
Tel (01992) 449830   Fax (01992) 449840
E-mail info@golf-foundation.org
Website www.golf-foundation.org

Golf Society of Great Britain
Founded in 1955 by the late Sir Aynsley Bridgland of
Prince's Golf Club with the object of promoting good-
will and providing funds to further the interest of the
game in all its aspects, the Society now has about 850
members and continues its founder's aims of promoting amateur golf through the sponsorship of junior golf
tournaments and through donations to the Junior Section of the Society's participating clubs. Five to six
meetings are held each year in the UK plus Spring and
Autumn Tours abroad.

Sec, Brian Ward, Parkhouse Lodge, Mill Lane, Holmes
Chapel, Cheshire CW4 8AU
Tel (07760) 777736
E-mail secretary@golfsocietygb.com
Website www.golfsocietygb.com

Handigolf Foundation
Sec, Ray Lee, 404 Westthorne Ave, Eltham, London
SE9 5TL
Tel (0208) 850 7407
E-mail rayndpam@hotmail.com
Website www.handigolf.org

National Association of Public Golf Courses
Affiliated to the English Golf Union, the Association was
founded in 1927 by golf course architect FG Hawtree
and five times Open champion JH Taylor to provide a
relationship between public and proprietory golf clubs,
and local councils and course owners.
Hon Sec, E Mitchell, 12 Newton Close, Redditch
B98 7YR
Tel (01527) 542106
E-mail secretary@napgc.org.uk
Website www.napgc.org.uk

National Golf Clubs' Advisory Association
Founded in 1922, the Association's aims are to pro-
tect the interests of golf clubs in general; to give legal
advice and direction, under the opinion of Counsel,
on the administrative and legal responsibilities of golf
clubs;.and to provide a mediation service to members'
clubs within the UK.
Ch Exec, Michael Shaw LLM
Nat Sec, J Howe, The Threshing Barn, Homme Castle
Barns, Shelsley Walsh, Worcs WR6 6RR
Tel (01886) 812943
Fax (01886) 812935
E-mail jackie.ngaa@idealnet.co.uk
Website www.ngcaa.org.uk

One-Armed Golfers, Society of
Hon Sec, Peter Priscott, 25 Malsters Close, Mundford,
Thetford, Norfolk IP26 5HJ
Tel (01842) 878554
E-mail PeterPriscott@aol.com
Website www.onearmgolf.org

Public Schools Old Boys Golf Association
Hon Sec, P de Pinna, Bruins, Wythwood,
Haywards Heath, West Sussex RH16 4RD
Tel (01444) 454883
Email fred-.die_@tiscali.co.uk

Public Schools' Golfing Society
Hon Sec, N D Owen,1 Bruce Grove, Orpington, Kent
BR6 0HF
Tel (01689) 810225
E-mail nick.owen@ndowen.com

STRI – Sports Turf Research Institute
STRI is an independent consultancy and research
organisation specialising in golf courses. Recognised
throughout the world for its expertise in both agro-
nomic and environmental issues relating to golf, STRI
is the official adviser to The R&A's Championship
Committee for all 'Open' venues. STRI undertakes
research into turfgrass and sports surface science,
promoting innovative solutions. For golf courses, it
provides advisory and architectural services and gives
ecological advice. In addition, STRI organises training
and produces publications.
Ch Exec, Dr I G McKillop; Marketing, Carolyn
Beadsmoore, St Ives Estate, Bingley, West Yorks
BD16 1AU
Tel (01274) 565131
Fax (01274) 561891
E-mail info@stri.co.uk
Website www.stri.co.uk

Country and Regional Unions and Associations

England

England Golf
The previously separate English Golf Union (EGU) and
English Women's Golf Association (EWGA) have
merged and from January 2012 became one governing
body which will represent all amateur golfers in England.

Key points of the merger:
- The headquarters of England Golf will initially be at
  the National Golf Centre at Woodhall Spa. The
  EWGA offices in Edgbaston will continue in use until
  at least October 2012 (*see page 697).
- The counties will continue to be the voting members.
  Counties will be encouraged to merge their Unions
  and Associations, but this will not be mandatory.

- The Board of England Golf will initially include 10 stakeholder non-executive directors, six nominated by the EGU and four women nominated by the EWGA. One of these 10 will be nominated as Chairman.
- The first sole President of England Golf will be a woman. The President will be supported by the immediate Past President and the President-Elect. One of these three will always be a woman.
- Club golf will go on, from day-to-day, as it does now, but members will benefit from the positive perceptions created by the merger and by the better support available for clubs.
- All the championships and tournaments currently run by the EWGA and the EGU will continue.
- The regional and group structures of the two organisations will continue to run competitions. The decision-making role of the EWGA regional committees will end.
- Affiliation fees for men and women will be harmonised and will be equal by 1 January 2014. Women will continue to pay an additional subscription to the Ladies Golf Union.

Ch Exec, John Petrie, National Golf Centre,
The Broadway, Woodhall Spa, Lincs LN10 6PU
Tel (01526) 354500
Fax (01526) 354020
E-mail info@englishgolfunion.org
Website www.englishgolfunion.org

*English Women's Golf Association
CEO, Mr P J Robinson, 11 Highfield Rd, Edgbaston,
Birmingham B15 3EB
Tel (0121) 456 2088   *Fax* (0121) 452 5978
E-mail office@englishwomensgolf.org
Website www.englishwomensgolf.org

Midland Group: *Sec*, T G Arnold, 11 Duckworth
Rd, Corby, Northants NN17 2RZ
Tel (01536) 743829
Fax (07005) 801 042
E-mail secretary@midlandgolfunion.co.uk
Website www.midlandgolfunion.co.uk

Northern Group: *Sec*, J D Trickett, 8 Derriman
Grove, Sheffield S11 9LE
Tel/Fax (0114) 249 1625
E-mail dennistrickett@yahoo.co.uk
Website www.ncgu.co.uk

South Eastern Group: *Sec*, B J Thompson,
8 Poplar Close, Silsoe, Beds MK45 4EE
Tel (01525) 860010
E-mail secretary@southeastgolfunion.co.uk
Website www.southeastgolfunion.co.uk

South Western Group: *Sec*, T C Reynolds,
The Haven, Velator, Nr Braunton, N Devon
EX33 2DX
Tel/Fax (01271) 812228
E-mail swcga@talktalk.net

English Men's County Unions

Bedfordshire CGU
Sec, S K Goode, 54 Swasedale Rd, Luton LU3 2UD
Tel (01582) 521716
E-mail secretary@bedsgolfunion.org
Website www.bedsgolfunion.org

Berks, Bucks & Oxon UGC
Sec, P M J York, Bridge House, Station Approach,
Great Missenden HP16 9AZ
Tel (01494) 867341   *Fax* (01494) 867342
E-mail secretary@bbogolf.com
Website www.bbogolf.com

Cambridgeshire Area GU
Sec, H S V Fleming, The Old Chapel, New Path,
Fordham CB7 5JX
Tel (01638) 732028
E-mail hamishfleming@fordhamchapel.plus.com
Website www.cagu.co.uk

Cheshire UGC
Sec, S J Foster, County Office Chester GC, Curzon
Park North, Chester CH4 8AR
Tel (01244) 678004
E-mail secretary@cheshiregolf.org.uk
Website www.cheshiregolf.org.uk

Cornwall GU
Hon Sec, P F Batty, 3 Clemens Close, Newquay,
Cornwall TR7 2SG
Tel/Fax (01637) 873117
E-mail secretary@cornwallgolfunion.org.uk
Website www.cornwallgolfunion.org.uk

Cumbria UGC
Hon Sec, T F Stout, Kingston House, Moresby,
Whitehaven CA28 8UW
Tel (01946) 693036
E-mail cumbriaugcsec@yahoo.co.uk
Website www.cumbria-golf-union.org.uk

Derbyshire UGC
Hon Sec, P McGrath, 36 Ilkeston Rd, Stapleford, Notts
NG9 8JL
Tel (0115) 922 3603
E-mail secretary@dugc.co.uk
Website www.dugc.co.uk

Devon CGU
Sec, John Hirst, 20 Plymouth Rd, Tavistock PL19 8AY
Tel (01822) 610640   *Fax* (01822) 610540
E-mail info@devongolfunion.org.uk
Website www.devongolfunion.org.uk

Dorset CGU
Sec, Ian Hulse, 5 St James Rd, Ferndown, Dorset
BH22 9NY
Tel (01202) 861185   *E-mail* secretary@dcgu.org.uk
Website www.dcgu.org.uk

Durham CGU
Sec, G P Hope, 7 Merrion Close, Moorside,
Sunderland SR3 2QP
Tel/Fax (0191) 522 8605
E-mail secretary@durhamcountygolfunion.co.uk
Website www.durhamcountygolfunion.co.uk

Essex GU
Sec, A T Lockwood, 2d Maldon Rd, Witham, Essex
CM8 2AB
Tel (01376) 500998   *Fax* (01376) 500842
E-mail info@essexgolfunion.org
Website www.essexgolfunion.org

Gloucestershire GU
Sec, I Watkins, The Vyse, Olde Lane,
Toddington, Glos GL54 5DW
Tel/Fax (01242) 621476

E-mail secretary@gloucestershiregolfunion.co.uk
Website www.gloucestershiregolfunion.co.uk

Hampshire, Isle of Wight & Channel Islands GU
Sec, Barry Morgan, c/o Liphook GC, Wheatsheaf Enclosure, Liphook, Hants GU30 7EH
Tel/Fax (01428) 725580
E-mail hgu@hampshiregolf.co.uk
Website www.hampshiregolf.org.uk

Hertfordshire GU
Sec, Chris Murray, CEO, Chestfield Downs GC, Jacks Hill, Graveley, Herts SG4 7EQ
Tel (08081) 682333
E-mail secretary@hertsgolfunion.com
Website www.hertsgolfunion.com

Isle of Man GU
Hon Sec, Joe Boyd, Cheu-Ny-Hawiney, Phildraw Rd, Ballasalla, Isle of Man IM9 3EG
Tel/Fax (01624) 823098
E-mail joeboyd@manx.net
Website www.isleofmangolf.im

Kent CGU
Sec, J G Young, Littlestone GC, St Andrew's Rd, Littlestone, New Romney, Kent TN28 8RB
Tel (01797) 367725   *Fax* (01797) 367726
E-mail kcgu@kentgolf.co.uk
Website www.kentgolf.org

Lancashire UGC
Sec, A V Moss, 5 Dicconson Terrace, Lytham St Annes FY8 5JY
Tel (01253) 733323   *Fax* (01253) 795721
E-mail secretary@lancashiregolf.org
Website www.lancashiregolf.org

Leicestershire & Rutland GU
Hon Sec, B Tuttle, 63 Gwendoline Dr., Countesthorpe, Leicester LE8 5SJ
Tel (0116) 277 1900
E-mail lrgusecretary@gmail.com
Website www.lrgu.net

Lincolnshire UGC
Hon Sec, H Harrison, 27 Orchard Close, Morton, Gainsborough DN21 3BP
Tel (01427) 616904
E-mail secretary@lugc.co.uk
Website www.lugc.co.uk

Middlesex CGU
Sec, M Wilcox, Northwick Park Golf Centre, Watford Rd, Harrow HA1 3TZ
Tel (0208) 864 4744
Fax (0208) 864 4554
E-mail secretary@mcgu.co.uk
Website www.mcgu.co.uk

Norfolk CGU
Hon Sec, D Horsburgh, 5 Bishops Croft, Barningham, Bury St Edmunds IP31 1BZ
Tel (01359) 221281
E-mail dandmhorsburgh@talktalk.net
Website www.norfolkcountygolfunion.co.uk

Northamptonshire GU
Hon Sec, J Pearson, 150 Church Green Rd, Bletchley, Milton Keynes MK3 6DD
Tel (01908) 648657

E-mail secretary@northantsgolfunion.co.uk
Website www.northantsgolfunion.co.uk

Northumberland UGC
Hon Sec, W E Procter, Eastfield House, Moor Rd South, Gosforth, Newcastle upon Tyne NE3 1NP
Tel (0191) 285 4981
E-mail secretary@nugc.org.uk
Website www.nugc.org.uk

Nottinghamshire UGC
Hon Sec, C Bee, 270 Wollaton Rd, Wollaton, Nottingham NG8 1GN
Tel/Fax (0115) 928 4891
E-mail secretary@nottsgolf.com
Website www.nottsgolf.com

Shropshire & Herefordshire UGC
Hon Sec, J R Davies, 23 Poplar Crescent, Bayston Hill, Shrewsbury SY3 0QB
Tel (01743) 872655
E-mail bdavies@blueyonder.co.uk
Website www.shugc.com

Somerset GU
Hon Sec, A King, Tweedside, Goosenford, Cheddon Fitzpaine, Taunton TA2 8LJ
Tel/Fax (01823) 412510
E-mail secretary@somersetgolfunion.co.uk
Website www.somersetgolfunion.co.uk

Staffordshire UGC
Sec, M A Payne, 20 Kingsbrook Drive, Hillfield, Solihull B91 3UU
Tel (0121) 704 4779   *Fax* (0121) 711 2841
E-mail martin.payne11@btinternet.com
Website www.golfinstaffs.co.uk

Suffolk GU
Hon Sec, C A Wilderspin, 10a Chestnut Avenue, Oulton Broad, Lowestoft, Suffolk, NR32 3JA
Tel (01502) 588 028
E-mail secretary@suffolkgolfunion.co.uk
Website www.suffolkgolfunion.co.uk

Surrey CGU
Sec, J A Davies, Sutton Green GC, New Lane, Sutton Green GU4 7QF
Tel (01483) 755788   *Fax* (01483) 751771
E-mail secretary@surreygolf.org
Website www.surreygolf.org

Sussex CGU
Sec, A Vasant, J.P., Eastbourne Down GC, East Dean Rd, Eastbourne, East Sussex BN20 8ES
Tel (01323) 746677   *Fax* (01323) 746777
E-mail countyoffice@sussexgolf.org
Website www.sussexgolf.org

Warwickshire UGC
Sec, M Nixon, 93 Amis Way, Stratford upon Avon, Warks CV37 7JD
Tel/Fax (01789) 297198
E-mail matt@nixongolf.com
Website www.warksgolf.co.uk

Wiltshire CGU
Sec, D Lewis, 39 Ashley Piece, Ramsbury, SN8 2QE
E-mail secretary@wcgu.org.uk
Website www.wcgu.org.uk

Worcestershire UGC
Hon Sec, A Boyd, The Bear's Den, Upper St,
Defford, Worcester WR8 9BG
Tel (01386) 750657   Fax (01386) 750472
E-mail menssecretary
                @worcestershireamateurgolf.co.uk
Website www.worcestershireamateurgolf.co.uk

Yorkshire UGC
Hon Sec, K H Dowswell, 33 George St, Wakefield
WFI 1LX
Tel (01924) 383869   Fax (01924) 383634
E-mail yorkshiregolf@lineone.net
Website www.yorkshireunionofgolf.co.uk

English Women's County Associations

Bedfordshire LCGA
Hon Sec, Mrs Paula Foot, 34 Vicarage Road, Silsoe,
Bedford MK45 4EF
Tel (01525) 862758
E-mail paula@chilternbrands.com
Website blcga.co.uk

Berkshire LCGA
Hon Sec, Mrs Nicky Luff, 9 Elmwood, Maidenhead
Court Park, Maidenhead, Berkshire SL6 8HX
Tel (01628) 674977
E-mail nicky.luff@btinternet.com

Buckinghamshire CLGA
Hon Sec, Mrs Lynda Hilton, Peartree Cottage,
Hodgemoor View, Chalfont St Giles HP8 4LS
Tel (01494) 876303
E-mail lynda.hilton@btinternet.com
Website bclga.org.uk

Cambs & Hunts LCGA
Hon Sec, Mrs Jacquie Richardson, Peel House,
11 Doddington Rd, Benwick, March PE15 0UT
Tel (01354) 677856
E-mail j.s.richardson@btinternet.com
Website chlgaco.uk

Cheshire CLGA
Hon Sec, Mrs A McCormick, Frinton, 22 Buxton Rd
West, Disley, Stockport SK12 2LY
Tel (01663) 766807
E-mail ann.mccormick4@ntlworld.com

Cornwall LCGA
Hon Sec, Mrs Pat Crowson, 41 Old Coach Road,
Playing Place, Truro TR3 6ET
Tel (01872) 864412
E-mail pat_pmc41@yahoo.co.uk   Website clga.co.uk

Cumbria LCGA
Hon Sec, Mrs Sandra Stoker, Yew Tree Cottage, Main
Rd, Endmoor, Kendal LA8 0EU
Tel (01539) 567826
E-mail stokers1985@btinternet.com

Derbyshire LCGA
Hon Sec, Mrs Tracy Pierrepont, 22 Narnos Grove,
Nuthall, Notts NG16 1QA
Tel (0115) 975 0107
E-mail tracypierrepont@gmail.com

Devon CLGA
Hon Sec, Mrs Deborah Harris, Fairmile, 20 Church Rd,
Alphington, Exeter EX2 8SH

Tel (01392) 669504
E-mail devonladiessecretary@hotmail.com

Dorset LCGA
Hon Sec, Mrs Zoe Ashley, Honeypot Cottage, 12
Glenwood Rd, West Moors,Ferndown BH22 0EP
Tel (01202) 827722
E-mail zoe.odlcga@yahoo.co.uk

Durham CLGA
Hon Sec, Mrs Ann Corbett, 1 Corby Mews,
Ashbrooke Rd, Sunderland SR2 7HQ
Tel (0191) 522 9448
E-mail corbettann@hotmail.co.uk
Website durhamladiesgolf.org.uk

Essex LCGA
Hon Sec, Mrs Nicola Thomas, 6 Heathgate, Wickham
Bishops, CM8 3NZ
Tel (01621) 891592
E-mail ath1343349@aol.com
Website essexladiesgolf.org

Gloucestershire LCGA
Hon Sec, Mrs Gillian Merry, Myles House, Ashmead,
Cam, Dursley GL11 5EN
Tel (01453) 542569
E-mail GillianMerry@talktalk.net

Hampshire LCGA
Hon Sec, Mrs Gill Staley, Garth House, 55 Elvetham
Rd, Fleet GU51 4QP
Tel (01252) 616442
E-mail gill@staley.org.uk
Website www.hampshireladiesgolf.co.uk

Hertfordshire CLGA
Hon Sec, Mrs Linda Battye, 12 Manor Links,
Bishop's Stortford CM23 5RA
Tel (01279) 505393
E-mail lindabattye@gmail.co
Website www.hclga.co.uk

Kent CLGA
Hon Sec, Mrs Sarah Brooks, 10 Hayle Mill, Hayle Mill
Rd, Maidstone ME15 6JW
Tel (01622) 761841
E-mail pumplodge@aol.com
Website kentladiesgolf.org.uk

Lancashire LCGA
Hon Sec, Miss Elaine Clark, 3 Derwent Dr,
Littleborough, Lancs OL15 0BT
Tel (01706) 376689   E-mail lancs2009@live.co.uk

Leicestershire & Rutland LCGA
Hon Sec, Mrs Anita Higginson, The Old Rectory, Main
St, Peatling Parva, Leics LE17 5QA
Tel (01162) 478240
E-mail higginsons@talk21.com

Lincolnshire LCGA
Hon Sec, Mrs Beverley Dolman, 10 Caudebec Close,
Uppingham, Rutland LE15 9SY
Tel (01572) 821382
E-mail beverleydolman@hotmail.com

Middlesex LCGA
Hon Sec, Mrs Anne Henderson, 5 Ford End, Denham
Village, Uxbridge UB9 5AL

Tel (01895) 835154
E-mail anne@eigergroup.co.uk

Norfolk LCGA
Hon Sec, Mrs Yvette Douglas, 204 Norwich Rd,
Fakenham NR21 8LX
Tel (01328) 863296
E-mail douglas.yvette@btinternet.com

Northamptonshire LCGA
Hon Sec, Mrs Ginny Jolliffe, 20 Kingsthorpe Grove,
Northampton NN2 6NT
Tel (01604) 716023
E-mail ginnyjol@talktalk.net

Northumberland LCGA
Hon Sec, Mrs Helen Woodhouse, Coruisk, Elm Rd,
Ponteland, Newcastle upon Tyne NE20 9BS
Tel (01661) 825054
E-mail helenj.woodhouse@gmail.com
Website www.nlcga.co.uk

Nottinghamshire LCGA
Hon Sec, Mrs Bridgett A Patrick, 18 Delville Ave,
Keyworth, Nottingham NG12 5JA
Tel (0115) 937 3237
E-mail bapatrick@btinternet.com

Oxfordshire LCGA
Hon Sec, Mrs Iona Smith, Field House, Childrey,
Wantage OX12 9UT
Tel (01235) 751250
E-mail nsirsmith@btopenworld.com
Website olcga.org.uk

Shropshire LCGA
Hon Sec, Mrs Ann Holland, 2 Honeybourne Rd,
Alveley, Bridgnorth WV15 6PP

Somerset LCGA
Hon Sec, Mrs Sheena Smith, "Findlater" Long Load,
Langport, Somerset TA10 9LE
Tel (01458) 241577
E-mail sheena136@btinternet.com

Staffordshire LCGA
Hon Sec, Mrs Pam Siviter, 69 Ward St, Coseley,
W Midlands WV14 9LQ
Tel/Fax (01902) 689940
E-mail pam.siviter@blueyonder.co.uk

Suffolk LCGA
Hon Sec, Mrs Jeanette Longman, The Old School
House, Chilleford, IP12 3PS
Tel (01394) 450939
E-mail jeanette.longman@gmail.com
Website suffolkladiesgolf.org.uk

Surrey LCGA
Sec, Mrs Penelope Hall, SLGCA, c/o Sutton Green
GC, Sutton Green, Guildford GU4 7QF
Tel (01483) 751622   Fax (01483) 751771
E-mail secretary@slcga.org
Website www.slcga.org

Sussex CLGA
Hon Sec, Mrs Ann Carnegie, 7 The Wad, West
Wittering, West Sussex PO20 8AH
Tel (01243) 511307
E-mail ann@thecarnegies.net
Website sclga.com

Warwickshire LCGA
Hon Sec, Mrs Elizabeth Murdoch, Plestowes House,
Hareway Lane, Barford, Warwick CV35 8DD
Tel (01926) 624503
E-mail liz@murdochonline.co.uk
Website warksgolf.co.uk

Wiltshire LCGA
Hon Sec, Mrs Penny Telling, Swanborough Cottage,
46 Mill Lane, Poulshot, Devizes SN10 1SA
Tel (01380) 828370
E-mail pennytelling@aol.com

Worcestershire and Herefordshire CLGA
Hon Sec, Mrs Valerie Evans, 19 Dugard Way,
Droitwich Spa, Worcestershire WR9 8UX
Tel (01905) 778773
E-mail valerie.evans11@btinternet.com

Yorkshire LCGA
Hon Sec, Mrs Dawn Clegg, 10 Usher Park Rd, Haxby,
York YO32 3RY
Tel (01904) 761987
E-mail dawnhclegg@hotmail.com
Website www.ylcga.org

English County PGAs

Bedfordshire & Cambridgeshire PGA
Sec, B Wake, 6 Gazelle Close, Eaton Socon,
St Neots PE19 8QF
Tel (01480) 219760
E-mail brian.wake@btopenworld.com

Berks, Bucks & Oxon PGA
Hon Sec, Martin Morbey, Valderrama, Haywards Road,
Drayton, Oxon OX14 4LB
E-mail admin@bbopga.co.uk
Website www.bbopga.co.uk

Cheshire and North Wales PGA
Sec, G Maly, No 2 Cottage, Bolton GC, Lostock Park,
Chorley New Road, Bolton BL6 4AJ
Tel (01204) 496137   Fax (01204) 847959
E-mail graham.maly@pga.org.uk

Cornwall PGA
Sec, J Greenaway, Bowood Park GC, Camelford
PL32 9RF
Tel (01840) 213017   Fax (01840) 212622
E-mail golf@bowood-park.co.uk
Website www.bowood-park.co.uk

Derbyshire PGA
Sec, M Ronan, 31 Wilsthorpe Rd, Breaston,
DE72 3EA
Tel (01332) 874897   Mobile (07918) 621588
E-mail mikeronan@hotmail.co.uk

Devon PGA
Sec, R Goodey, 1 Brookside Cres., Exeter EX4 8NF
Tel (07967) 769485
E-mail robingoodey@blueyonder.co.uk
Website www.devonpga.co.uk

Dorset PGA
Sec, D Parsons, Bridport & West Dorset GC, Burton
Rd, Bridport, Dorset DT6 4PS
Tel (01308) 421491
E-mail bridproshop@tesco.net

Essex PGA
Sec, S Garland-Collins, 27 Willowdene Court,
Brentwood, Essex CM14 5ET
Tel/Fax (01277) 223510
E-mail essexpga@googlemail.com
Website www.essexpga.com

Gloucestershire & Somerset PGA
Sec, E Goodwin, Cirencester GC, Cheltenham Rd,
Cirencester, GL7 7BH
Tel (01285) 652465

Hampshire PGA
Sec, D L Wheeler, South Winchester GC, Pitt,
Winchester SO22 5QX
Tel (01962) 860928
E-mail hampshirepga@yahoo.co.uk
Website www.hampshire-pga.co.uk

Hertfordshire PGA
Sec, M E Plumbley, Stavonga Dell, Pasture Rd,
Letchworth SG6 3LP
Tel/Fax (01462) 670774
E-mail meplumbley@hertspga.org
Website www.hertspga.org

Kent PGA
Contact South Region PGA

Lancashire PGA
Sec, G Maly, No 2 Cottage, Bolton GC, Lostock Park,
Chorley New Road, Bolton BL6 4AJ
Tel (01204) 496137   *Fax* (01204) 847959
E-mail graham.maly@pga.org.uk

Leicestershire PGA
Sec, Jim Pochin, c/o Rothley Park GC, Westfield Lane,
Rothley, Leicerstershire LE7 7LH
Mobile (07784) 783299
E-mail james.pochin@virgin.net

Lincolnshire PGA
Sec, D Drake, 23 Manor Rd, Saxilby, Lincoln LN1 2HX
Tel (01522) 703331

Middlesex PGA
Sec, S Rist, 64 Dorchester Avenue, Palmers Green
London N13 5DX
Tel (0208) 803 9702
E-mail steve@mdxpga.co.uk
Website www.mdxpga.co.uk

Norfolk PGA
Sec, John Paling, Squirrels Reach, Folgate Lane,
Old Costessey, Norwich NR8 5EF
Tel (01603) 741301
E-mail jandjpaling@uwclub.net
Website www.club-noticeboard.co.uk

North East & North West PGA
Hon Sec, T Flowers, 10 Rosedale Rd, Belmont,
Durham DH1 2AS
Tel (0191) 383 9385
E-mail tom.flowers@fsmail.net

Northamptonshire PGA
Sec, R Lobb, 15 Manor Rd, Pitsford, Northampton
NN6 9AR
Tel (01604) 881367   *Mobile* (07968) 164151
E-mail richard.lobb@northamptonshiregolf.org.uk
Website www.northamptonshirepga.co.uk

Nottinghamshire PGA
Sec, R Carter, 3 Henley Rise, Sherwood, Nottingham
NG5 1FQ
Tel (01158) 412276
E-mail secretary@nottspga.co.uk
Website www.nottspga.co.uk

Shropshire & Hereford PGA
Sec, P Hinton, 29 Stourbridge Rd, Bridgnorth,
WV15 5AZ
Tel (01746) 762045
E-mail paulhinton@enta.net
Website www.a1golf.biz

Staffordshire PGA
Sec, R Hill, 80 Old Town Mews, Stratford upon Avon
CV37 6GR
Tel (07791) 289 941

Suffolk PGA
Sec, A E D Garnett, 9 Furness Close, Ipswich IP2 9YA
Tel (01473) 685529
E-mail tonygarnett@talktalk.net

Surrey PGA
Contact South Region PGA

Sussex PGU
Sec, C Pluck, 96 Cranston Ave, Bexhill,
East Sussex TN39 3NL
Tel/Fax (01424) 221298
E-mail sussexpgu@g.mail.com
Website www.spgu.co.uk

Warwickshire PGA
Sec, N Selwyn-Smith, 18 Cornfield Ave, Stoke Heath,
Bromsgrove B60 3QU
Tel (01527) 875 750
E-mail neilss@execgolf.co.uk

Wiltshire PGA
Sec, M Walters, Erlestoke Sands GC, Erlestoke,
Devizes SN10 5UB
Tel (01380) 831027

Worcestershire PGA
Sec, K Ball, 136 Alvechurch Rd, West Heath,
Birmingham B31 3PW
Tel (0121) 475 7400
E-mail kenball@talktalk.net

Yorkshire PGA
Sec, J Pape, 22 The Locks, Pottery Lane, Woodlesford,
Leeds LS26 8PU
Tel (0113) 282 8984

England and Wales Blind Golf
Sec, J T O'Brien, 23 Logan St, Market Harborough
LE16 9AW
Tel (01858) 465625
E-mail jim.taggartt@talktalk.net
Website www.blindgolf.co.uk

Ireland

Golfing Union of Ireland
Gen Sec, Pat Finn, National Headquarters, Carton
Demesne, Maynooth, Co. Kildare

Tel +353 1 505 4000   *Fax* +353 1 505 4001
E-mail information@gui.ie
Website www.gui.ie

Irish Men's Branches

Connacht Branch: *Gen Sec,* E Lonergan,
Breaffy Business Centre, Breaffy, Castlebar, Mayo
E-mail guibc@eircom.net

Leinster Branch: *Exec Off* T Thompson,
Carton Demesne, Maynooth, Co.Kildare
Tel +353 1 601 6842   *Fax* +353 1 601685
E-mail info@leinster.gui.ie

Munster Branch: *Exec Off,* K Walsh,
6 Townview, Mallow, Co Cork
Tel +353 22 21026   *Fax* +353 22 42373
E-mail guimb@iol.ie

Ulster Branch: *Gen Sec,* K Stevens, Unit 5,
Forestgrove Business Park, Newtownbreda Rd, Belfast
BT8 6AW
Tel (028) 9049 1891   *Fax* (028) 9049 1615
E-mail ulster.golf@btconnect.com

Irish Ladies' Golf Union
Ch Exec, Bernie Cullen, 103-105 Q House, 76 Furze
Rd, Sandyford Ind. Est., Dublin 18
Tel +353 1 293 4833
E-mail bernie@ilgu.ie   *Website* www.ilgu.ie

Irish Ladies' Districts

Eastern District: *Hon Sec,* Mrs R Hayes, 51
College Grove, Castle Knock, Dublin 15
Tel +353 1 822 6380
E-mail easterndistrict@eircom.net

Midland District: *Hon Sec,* Mrs Yvonne
MacSweeney, Old Town Lane, Castlebridge, Wexford
Tel +353 83 404 7246
E-mail midlanddistrict@gmail.com

Northern District: *Hon Sec* Mrs S Robinson, 41
Ballyreagh Rd, Portrush, Co.Antrim BT56 8LR
Tel 028 70 824253 *E-mail* dunlucevolvo@yahoo.co.uk

Southern District: *Hon Sec,* Ms E Smith, Prague,
30 Shamrock Hill, Clonmel, Co.Tipperary
Tel +353 52 89316   *E-mail* eilism1@eircom.net

Western District: *Hon Sec,* Mrs Rita Grealish,
Glenmore, Carnmore, Oranmore, Co.Galway
Tel +353 83 404 7131
E-mail ilguwest@eircom.net

Scotland

Scottish Golf Union
Ch Exec, H Grey, The Duke's, St Andrews KY16 8NX
Tel (01334) 466477   *Fax* (01334) 461361
E-mail sgu@scottishgolf.org
Website www.scottishgolf.org

Scottish Men's Associations/Unions
Angus CGA: *Sec,* W Miller, 48 Buddon Drive,
Monifieth DD5 4TJ
Tel (01382) 533728
E-mail billhmill@blueyonder.co.uk

Argyll & Bute GU: *Sec,* L. Pirie, 54 Banchory Ave,
Inchinnan, Renfrewshire PA49PZ
Tel (0141) 561 0535   *E-mail* lrpirie@aol.com
Website www.argyllandbutegolfunion.com

Ayrshire GA: *Sec,* A J Malcolm, 17 Auchincruive Av,
Prestwick KA9 2DT
Tel (01292) 477657
E-mail ayrshiregolf@fsmail.net
Website www.ayrshiregolf.blogspot.com

Borders GA: *Sec,* R G Scott, 3 Whytbank Row,
Clovenfords, Nr Galashiels TD1 3NE
Tel/Fax (01896) 850570
E-mail rscott.bga@btinternet.com
Website www.bordergolf.co.uk

Clackmannanshire CGU: *Sec,* T Johnson, 75
Dewar Ave, Kincardine on Forth FK10 4RR
Tel 01259) 731520   *Fax* (01259) 769445
E-mail thjohn01@aol.com

Dunbartonshire GU: *Sec,* A Harris, 11
Millersneuk Dr, Lenzie, Kirkintilloch, Glasgow G66 5JF
Tel (0141) 776 3535
E-mail secretary@dgu.org.uk
Website www.dgu.org.uk

Fife GA: *Sec,* J Scott, Lauriston, East Links, Leven
KY8 4JL
Tel (01333) 423798
Fax (01333) 439910
E-mail jscottfga@blueyonder.co.uk
Website www.fifegolf.org

Glasgow GU: *Sec,* R J G Jamieson, 32 Eglinton St,
Beith KA15 1AH
Tel/Fax (01505) 503000
E-mail r.jamieson-accountants@fsmail.net
Website www.glasgowgolfunion.org

Lanarkshire GA: *Sec,* T Logan, 41 Woodlands
Drive, Coatbridge ML5 1LB
Tel (01236) 428799   *E-mail* tlogan.lga@hotmail.co.uk

Lothians GA: *Sec,* A G Shaw, 34 Caroline Terrace,
Edinburgh EH12 8QX
Tel 0131 334 7291   *Fax* 0131 334 9269
E-mail AllanGShaw@hotmail.com
Website www.lothiansgolfassociation.org.uk

North District SGU: *Sec,* P L Abbott, 21 Manse Rd,
Nairn IV12 4RW
Tel (01667) 453625
E-mail p.l.a@btinternet.com
Website www.sgunorth.com

North-East District GA: *Sec,* G M Young, 24
Shore St, Cairnbulg, Fraserburgh AB43 8YL
Tel (01346) 582324
E-mail georgemyoung24@btinternet.com
Website www.sgunortheast.com

Perth & Kinross CGU: *Sec,* J J E Simpson, 11
Dunbarney Av, Bridge of Earn, Perth PH2 9BP
Tel (01738) 812588
E-mail auntyeedie@hotmail.com
Website www.perthandkinrosscountygolf.net

Renfrewshire GU: *Sec,* I Storie, 35 Balmoral Rd,
Elderslie PA5 9RA
Tel (01505) 343872

E-mail ian.storie@ntlworld.com
Website www.renfrewshiregolfunion.co.uk

South of Scotland GA: *Sec,* J Burns, Glanavon, 14 Millfield Ave, Stranraer DG9 0EG
Tel (01776) 704778   *Fax* (01776) 870445
E-mail stranraergolf@btclick.com

Stirlingshire GU: *Sec,* J Elliott, 65 Rosebank Ave, Falkirk FK1 5JR
Tel (01324) 634 118
E-mail johnelliott65@blueyonder.co.uk
Website www.stirlingshiregolfunion.co.uk

Scottish Blind Golf Society
Sec, R Clayden, 5 The Round, Dunfermline, Fife KY12 7YH
Tel (01383) 737717
Website www.scottishblindgolf.com

Scottish Midland Golfing Alliance
Sec, E Sherry, Lundin Tower, Pilmuir Rd, Lundin Links KY8 6BD

Scottish Ladies' Golfing Association
Sec, Dr S Hartley, The Den, 2 Dundee Rd, Perth PH2 7DW
Tel (01738) 442357   *Fax* (01738) 442380
E-mail secretary@slga.co.uk
Website www.slga.co.uk

Aberdeen LCGA
Hon Sec, Miss K Stalker, 2 Braemar Court, Fraserburgh AB43 9XE
Tel (01346) 513308
E-mail karen@fairways.eclipse.co.uk
Website www.alcga.co.uk

Angus LCGA
Hon Sec, Mrs M Raitt, 22 Briar Grove, Forfar DD8 1DQ
Tel (01307) 464931
E-mail the.raitts@btinternet.com

Ayrshire LCGA
Hon Sec, Fiona Collier, Monkton Hall Lodge, Southwoods, Monkton, Prestwick KA9 1UR
Tel (01292) 315982
E-mail secretary@alcga.com

Border Ladies' CGA
Hon Sec, Julie Birdsall, Highridgehall, Kelso TD5 7QD
Tel (01890) 830605
E-mail highridgehall@btinternet.com
Website www.borderladiesgolf.com

Dumfriesshire LCGA
Hon Sec, Mrs E C Scott, Treweryn, 24 Carlisle Rd, Lockerbie DG11 2DN
Tel (01576) 203507
E-mail malcolmscott228@btinternet.com

Dunbartonshire & Argyll LCGA
Hon Sec, Mrs J Shankland, 25 Thorn Dr., Bearsden, Glasgow G61 4ND
Tel (0141) 942 4696
E-mail je.shankland@btinternet.com
Website www.dalcga.ik.com

East Lothian LCGA
Hon Sec, Gill Ellis-Pow, 85 Laburnum Ave, Port Seton EH32 0UD
Tel (01875) 811527
E-mail agellis-pow@yahoo.co.uk

Fife CLGA
Hon Sec, Mrs Barbara Linton, 5 Abden Ave, Kinghorn KY3 9TQ
Tel (01592) 890140
E-mail pendantiques@btopenworld.com

Galloway CLGA
Hon Sec, Sally Huntly, Tramerry, Wigtown DG8 9JP
Tel (01988) 402309

Lanarkshire LCGA
Capt, Anne Lloyd, 9 Jardine Ter., Gartcosh, Glasgow G69 8AR
Tel (0781) 887 8187
E-mail anne.Lloyd@hotmail.co.uk
Website www.llcga.co.uk

Midlothian CLGA
Hon Sec, Mrs H Anderson, 10 Woodhall Bank, Colinton, Edinburgh EH13 0HY
Tel (0131) 477 1131
E-mail mclga66@hotmail.co.uk
Website www.mclga.co.uk

Northern Counties' LGA
Hon Sec, Mrs J Coulthard, The Larches, Skye of Curr Rd, Dulnain Bridge, Grantown-on-Spey PH26 3PA
Tel (01479) 851361
E-mail jacqui.coulthard@btinternet.com

Perth & Kinross LCGA
Hon Sec, Mrs J Milne, 91 David Douglas Ave., Scone PH2 6QG
Tel (01738) 553352
E-mail jilliancmilne@hotmail.com

Renfrewshire LCGA
Hon Sec, Mrs J Irvine, Wrayburn, Woodside Lane, Brookfield PA5 8UW
Tel (01505) 328411
E-mail jean.Irvine@sky.com   *Website* rlgca.co.uk

Stirling & Clackmannan CLGA
Hon Sec, Mrs A Hunter, 22 Muirhead Rd, Stenhousemuir, FK5 4JA
Tel (01324) 554515
E-mail annathunter@btinternet.com

Scottish Veteran Ladies' Golfing Association
Hon Sec, Mrs J C Lambert, Balcary, Barcloy Rd, Rockcliffe, Dalbeattie DG5 4QJ
Tel (01556) 630419
E-mail jeanc.lambert@btinternet.com
Website www.svlga.co.uk

Wales

Golf Union of Wales
Ch Exec, Richard Dixon, Catsash, Newport, Gwent NP18 1JQ
Tel (01633) 436040   *Fax* (01633) 693568
E-mail office@golfunionwales.org
Website www.golfunionwales.org

Welsh Men's Unions

Anglesey GU
Hon Sec, GP Jones, 20 Gwelfor Estate, Cemaes Bay,
Anglesey LL67 0NL
Tel (01407) 710755
E-mail garethgwelfor@aol.com
Website www.anglestgolfunion.co.uk

Brecon & Radnor GU
Hon Sec, Martyn Hughes, 1 Wool Row, Brecon Rd,
Builth Wells LD2 3ED
Tel (01982) 552852
E-mail martynhughes49@googlemail.com

Caernarfonshire & District GU
Hon Sec, EG Angel, 13 Glanrafon Est., Bontnewydd,
Caernarfon, Gwynedd LL55 2UW
Tel (01286) 675798
E-mail einionecdgu@talktalk.net

Denbighshire GU
Hon Sec, D Ethelston, Gwylfa, Garth Rd, Garth,
Llangollen LL20 7UR
Tel (01978) 820722   E-mail ethelgarth@aol.com
Website www.dgugolf.co.uk

Dyfed GU
WD Booth, Rhyd, Croes Y Llan, Llangoedmor,
Cardigan SA43 2LH
Tel (01239) 615334
E-mail wdjbooth@btinternet.com
Website www.dyfedgolf.co.uk

Union of Flintshire Golf Clubs
Hon Sec, Mrs G Snead, 1 Cornist Cottages, Flint
CH6 5RH
Tel (01352) 733461
E-mail gsnead@hotmail.co.uk

Glamorgan County GU
Hon Sec, P Austerberry, 10 Chestnut Tree Close,
Radyr, Cardiff CF15 8RY
Tel (02920) 419823
E-mail p.austerberry@ntlworld.com

Gwent GU
Sec, WG Harris, 4 Rolls Walk, Mount Pleasant,
Rogerstone, Gwent NP10 0AE
Tel (01633) 663750
E-mail w.graham.harris@ntlworld.com
Website www.gwentgolf.co.uk

North Wales PGA
See Cheshire & North Wales PGA, page 700

South Wales PGA
See West Region PGA, page 694

Welsh Ladies' County Associations

Caernarvonshire & Anglesey LCGA
Hon Sec, Mrs J Harvey, 10 Craig y Don, Pensarn,
Abergele LL22 7RL
Tel (01745) 827239
E-mail alecharvey32@btinternet.com

Carmarthenshire & Pembrokeshire LCGA
Hon Sec, Mrs P Taggart, Neuadd Cothi, Pontargothi,
Nantaredig, Carmarthenshire SA16 0HT
Tel (01267) 290174
E-mail pdtaggart@btconnect.com

Denbighshire & Flintshire LCGA
Hon Sec, Mrs K Harcombe, 6 Birch Drive, Gresford,
Wrexham LL12 8YZ
Tel (01978) 855933
E-mail kim.harcombe@btinternet.com

Glamorgan LCGA
Hon Sec, Mrs G J Phillips, 17 Martin Close, Heol
Gerrig, Merthyr Tydfil CF48 1TY
Tel (01685) 385245
E-mail gloheolg@aol.com
Website www.glamorganladiesgolf.co.uk

Mid Wales LCGA
Hon Sec, Mrs L Price, Coygen, Lower Chapel, Brecon,
Powys LD3 9RE
Tel (01874) 690258
E-mail coygen@btclick.com

Monmouthshire LCGA
Hon Sec, Mrs EL Davidson, Jon-Len, Goldcliff,
Newport NP18 2AU
Tel (01633) 274477
E-mail lena_mlcga@hotmail.co.uk

Europe

European Golf Association
Gen Sec, Johnny Storjohann, Place de la Croix Blanche
19, Case Postale CH-1066 Epalinges, Switzerland
Tel +41 21 785 7060   Fax +41 21 785 7069
E-mail info@ega-golf.ch
Website www.ega-golf.ch

Albanian Golf Federation
Gen Sec, Marin Harxhi, Rr.Suleyman Delvina, P.142/3
Ap.12, AL-Piranë
Tel +355 68 603 3626
E-mail info@fshgolf.org   Website www.fshgolf.org

Austrian Golf Association
Gen Sec, Robert Fiegl, Marxergasse 25, AT-1030 Wien
Tel +43 1 505 3245   Fax +43 1 505 4962
E-mail oegv@golf.at   Website www.golf.at

Royal Belgian Golf Federation
Gen Sec, Christian Moyson, Chaussée de la Hulpe 110,
BE-1000 Brussels
Tel +32 2 672 2389   Fax +32 2 675 4619
E-mail info@golfbelgium.be
Website www.golfbelgium.be

Bulgarian Golf Association
Gen Sec, Seth Underwood, 19 Oborishte Street,
BG-1504 Sofia
Tel +359 2943 0610   Fax +359 2946 3740
E-mail s.underwood@golfbg.com
Website www.golfbg.com

Croatian Golf Federation
Chair, Dino Klisovic, The Regent Esplanade Hotel,
Mihanoviceva 1, HR-10000 Zagreb
Tel +385 1 456 6050
E-mail hrvatskigolfsavez@yahoo.com
Website www.golf.hr

Cyprus Golf Federation
Gen Sec, Nick Rossides, Olympic House, Amfipoleos
21, Office B208, CY-2025 Nicosia

Tel +357 22 449874   *Fax* +357 22 449876
E-mail cgf@cgf.org.cy   *Website* www.cgf.org.cy

Czech Golf Federation
Gen Sec, Miroslav Holub, Erpet Golf Centre, Strakonickà 2860, CZ-150 00 Pragha 5-Smichov
Tel +420 296 373111   *Fax* +420 296 373201
E-mail cgf@cgf.cz   *Website* www.cgf.cz

Danish Golf Union
Gen Sec, Morten Backhausen, Idrættens Hus, Brøndby Stadion 20, DK-2605 Brøndby
Tel +45 43 262 700   *Fax* +45 43 262 701
E-mail info@dgu.org   *Website* www.dgu.org

Estonian Golf Association
Sec Gen, Rein Raudsepp, Liivalaia 9, EE-10118 Tallinn
Fax +372 6 314343
E-mail rein.r@golf.ee
Website www.golf.ee

Finnish Golf Union
Gen Sec, Petri Peltoniemi, Radiokatu 20, FI-00093 SLU
Tel +358 9 3481 2520   *Fax* +358 9 147 145
E-mail office@golf.fi   *Website* www.golf.fi

French Golf Federation
Ch Exec, Christophe Muniesa, 68 rue Anatole France, FR-92309 Levallois-Perret Cedex
Tel +33 1 41 497 700   *Fax* +33 1 41 497 701
E-mail ffgolf@ffgolf.org
Website www.ffgolf.org

German Golf Association
Exec Dir, Florian Bruhns, Kreuzberger Ring 64, Postfach 2106, DE-65011 Wiesbaden
Tel +49 611 990 200   *Fax* +49 611 990 20170
E-mail info@dgv.golf.de   *Website* www.golf.de

Hellenic Golf Federation
Gen Sec, Michael Sideris, PO Box 70003, GR-166 10 Glyfada, Athens
Tel +30 210 894 1933   *Fax* +30 210 894 5162
E-mail info@hgf.gr   *Website* www.hgf.gr

Hungarian Golf Federation
Gen Sec, Ms Lilla Ádám, Istvanmezei út 1-3, HU-1146 Budapest
Tel/Fax +36 1 460 6859
E-mail hungolf@hungolf.hu
Website: www.hungolf.hu

Golf Union of Iceland
Gen Sec, Hordur Thorsteinsson, Sport Center, Laugardal, IS-104 Reykjavik
Tel +354 514 4050   *Fax* +354 514 4051
E-mail gsi@golf.is   *Website* www.golf.is

Italian Golf Federation
Sec Gen, Stefano Manca, Viale Tiziano 74, IT-00196 Roma
Tel +39 06 323 1825   *Fax* +39 06 322 0250
E-mail fig@federgolf.it
Website www.federgolf.it

Kazakhstan Golf Federation
Gen Sec, Konstantin Lifanov, c/o Nurtau GC, Alatau Sanatorium, Karasayskiy Region, Kamenka Village, KZ-040918 Almaty obl., Rep of Kazakhstan
Tel +7 727 295 8823   *Fax* +7 727 295 8830
E-mail golfpro1@yandex.ru

Latvia Golf Federation
Gen Sec, Santa Puce, Milgrāvja Iela 16, LV-1034 Riga
Tel +371 6739 4399   *Fax* +371 6739 4034
E-mail info@golfaskola.lv   *Website* www.lgf.lv

Liechtenstein Golf Association
Pres, Carlo Rampone, Postfach 264, LI-9490 Vaduz
Tel +42 3 232 1991   *Fax* +42 3 232 1992
E-mail info@golf-verband.li
Website www.golf.li

Lithuanian Golf Federation
Pres, Rolandas Dovidaitis, Rotuses a.10, LT-44279 Kaunas
Tel +370 698 38866
E-mail info@golfofederacija.lt
Website www.golfofederacija.lt

Luxembourg Golf Federation
Sec, Roger Weber, Domaine de Belenhaff, LU-6141 Junglinster
Tel +352 26 78 2383   *Fax* +352 26 78 2393
E-mail flgsecretariat@flgolf.lu
Website www.flgolf.lu

Macedonian Golf Federation
Gen Sec, Marijan Pop-Angelov, Albert Ajnstajn 6A, MK-1000 Skopje
Tel +389 71 508222   *Fax* +389 26 134224
E-mail mkgolffederation@gmail.com

Malta Golf Association
Pres, William Beck, Aldo Moro St, MT-Marsa LQA 09, Malta
Tel +356 2122 3704   *Fax* +356 2122 7020
E-mail association@maltagolf.org
Website www.maltagolf.org

Netherlands Golf Federation
Gen Sec, Jeroen Stevens, PO Box 8585, NL-3503 RN Utrecht
Tel +31 30 242 6370   *Fax* +31 30 242 6380
E-mail golf@ngf.nl   *Website* www.ngf.nl

Norwegian Golf Federation
Gen Sec, Geir Ove Berg, NO-0840 Oslo
Tel +47 21 029 150   *Fax* +47 21 029 151
E-mail post@golfforbundet.no
Website www.golfforbundet.no

Polish Golf Union
Gen Sec, Bartlomiej Chelmecki, Lim Centre, Al.Jerozolimskie 65/79, PL-00-697 Warszawa
Tel +48 22 630 5560   *Fax* +48 22 630 5561
E-mail pzg@pzgolf.pl
Website www.pzgolf.pl

Portuguese Golf Federation
Gen Sec, Miguel Franco De Sousa, Av das Túlipas No 6, Edifico Miraflores17°, Miraflores, PT-1495-161 Algés
Tel +351 214 123 780
Fax +351 214 107 972
E-mail fpg@fpg.pt   *Website* www.fpg.pt

Romanian Golf Federation
Gen Sec, Mircea Asanache, 44 Carierei Str., Breaza, RO-105400 Prahova
Tel +40 244 343 850   *Fax* +40 244 343 525
E-mail gen.secretary@frgolf.ro
Website www.frgolf.ro

Russian Golf Association
Gen Sec, Victor Motchalov, Office 242A, 8
Luzhnetskaya nab, RU – 119992 Moskva
Tel +7 495 363 2385   *Fax* +7 495 725 4719
E-mail russgolf@mail.ru   *Website* www.rusgolf.ru

San Marino Golf Federation
Sec Gen, Dr E Casali, Via Rancagalia 30, SM-47899
Serravalle, San Marino
Tel +378 (0549) 885 600
Fax +378 (0549) 885 651
E-mail dzanotti@omniway.sm

Serbia Golf Association
Chair, Vladimir Dukanovic, Ada Ciganlija 2, RS-11000
Belgrad
Tel +381 11 333 2851   *Fax* +381 11 305 6837
E-mail office@golfas.rs
Website www.golfasocijacijasrbije.rs

Slovak Golf Association
Gen Sec, Juraj Špánik, Kukucínova, Kukucínova 26,
SK-831 02 Bratislava, Slovak Republic
Tel/Fax +421 2 4445 0727
E-mail skga@skga.sk   *Website* www.skga.sk

Slovenian Golf Association
Sec, Gorazd Kogoj, Dunajska 22, SI-1511 Ljubljana
Tel +386 1 430 3200   *Fax* +386 1 430 3201
E-mail golfzveza@golfzveza-slovenije.si
Website www.golfzveza-slovenije.si

Royal Spanish Golf Federation
Man Dir, Jorge Sagardoy Fidalgo, Arroyo del Monte 5,
ES-28035 Madrid
Tel +34 91 555 2682   *Fax* +34 91 556 3290
E-mail rfegolf@rfegolf.es
Website www.rfegolf.es

Swedish Golf Federation
Gen Sec, Gunnar Håkansson, PO Box 84,
Kevingestrand, SE-182 11 Danderyd
Tel +46 8 622 1500   *Fax* +46 8 755 8439
E-mail info@sgf.golf.se
Website www.sgf.golf.se

Swiss Golf Association
Gen Sec, Christian Bohm, Place de la Croix Blanche 19,
CH-1066 Epalinges
Tel +41 21 785 7000   *Fax* +41 21 785 7009
E-mail info@asg.ch   *Website* www.asg.ch

Turkish Golf Federation
Pres, Ahmet Agaoglu, GSGM Ulus Is Hani A Blok 2.,
Kat 205 Ulus 06050, TR-Ankara
Tel +90 312 309 3945
Fax +90 312 309 1840
E-mail info@tgf.org.tr
Website www.tgf.org.tr

Ukrainian Golf Federation
Gen Sec, Sergey Kozyrenko, 39 Pushkinskya str. Suite
28, UA-01004 Kyiv
Tel +380 672 345143
Fax +380 44 279 3763
E-mail ukrgolf@mail.ru
Website www.ukrgolf.com

Professional Associations

Austria PGA
Gen Sec, Ulrich Wolbitsch, Grabentrasse 26/1a,
AT-8010 Graz
Tel +43 316 890 503   *Fax* +43 316 890 50315
E-mail office@apga.info   *Website* www.apga.info

Belgian PGA
Off, Bernard de Bruyckere, Jozef Mertensstraat 46,
BE-1702 Groot-Bijgaarden
Tel +32 2463 1963
E-mail info@pga.be   *Website* www.pga.be

Bulgarian PGA
Gen Sec. Neil Turley, Oboriste Street 19. BG-1504
Sofia
Tel /Fax +359 2 943 0610
E-mail info@pga-bulgaria.com
Website www.pga-bulgaria.com

Croatia PGA
Off, Nikola Smoljenovic, Fancevljec Prilaz 16,
HR-10010 Zagreb
Tel +385 1 667 3308   *Fax* +385 1 660 6798
E-mail golf-pga@pga.hr   *Website* www.pga.hr

Czech Republic PGA
Gen Sec, Michael Jon, Villa Golfista, Amerika 782/1C,
CZ-353 01 Marianske Lazne
Tel +420 724 050050   *Fax* +420 354 621357
E-mail pga@pga.cz   *Website* www.pga.cz

Denmark PGA
Off, Joan Ejlertsen, Kong Christians Allé 37, DK-9000,
Aalborg
Tel +45 20 73 00 41   *Fax* +45 98 662 236
E-mail info@pga.dk   *Website* www.pga.dk

Estonia PGA
Gen Sec, Pail Pohi, Roosikrantsi 9-47, EE 10119 Tallin
Tel +372 56 492210   *Fax* +372 682 8819
E-mail juha.hamalainen@pga.ee

Finland PGA
Off, Teemu Laakso, Radiokatu 20, FI-00093 SLU
Tel +358 9 3481 2377   *Fax* +358 9 3481 2378
E-mail pgafinland@pga.fi
Website www.pga.fi

France PGA
Off, Yves Bechu, National Golf Club, 2 Avenue du
Golf, FR-78 280 Guyancourt
Tel +33 1 34 52 0846
Fax +33 1 3057 4704
E-mail y.bechu@pgafrance.org
Website www.pgafrance.org

PGA of Germany
Ch Exec, Professional Golf AG, Landsbergerstr., 290,
DE-80687 München
Tel +49 8917 95880   *Fax* +49 8917 958829
E-mail info@pga.de   *Website* www.pga.de

Greece PGA
Gen Sec, Adonis Sotiropoulos, 9 Harilaou Trikoupi
str, GR-166 75 Glyfada Athens
Tel +30 6938 261 200
Fax +30 2241 052 798
E-mail info@greekpga.com
Website www.greekpga.com

Hungary PGA
Gen Sec, Áron Makszin, 1016 Krisztina krt 71, 4/1,
Hungary
Tel +36 23 545 440   *Fax* +36 70 454 5663
E-mail makszin@yahoo.com
Website www.pgah.hu

Iceland PGA
Gen Sec, Agnar Már Jonsson, Engjavegur 6, IS-104
Reykjavik
Tel +354 514 4050   *Fax* +354 514 4051
E-mail agnarj@simnet.is   *Website* www.pga.is

Italy PGA
Gen Sec, Luca Salvetti, Via Marangoni 3, IT-20124
Milano
Tel +39 02 670 5670   *Fax* +39 02 669 3600
E-mail pgaitaly@tin.it   *Website* www.pga.it

Luxembourg PGA
Gen Sec, Julien Pailler, Luxembourg GC Belenhaff,
LU-26141 Junglinster
Tel/Fax +352 348394
E-mail leon@golfpro.lu   *Website* www.pga.lu

Malta PGA
Off, Kenneth Cachia, The Royal Malta GC, Aldo Moro
St, Marsa LQA 06
Tel +356 212 39302   *Fax* +356 212 27020
E-mail info@pgamalta.com
Website www.pgamalta.com

Netherlands PGA (Holland PGA)
Gen Sec, Frank Kirsten, Postbus 642, NL-6200 AP
Maastricht
Tel+31 30 228 7018   *Fax* +31 30 225 0261
E-mail info@pgaholland.nl
Website www.pgaholland.nl

Norway PGA
Gen Sec, Peter Söder, Spikkestadveien 83, NO-3440
Royken
Tel +47 993 44000
E-mail peter.soder@pganorway.no
Website www.pganorway.no

Poland PGA
Gen Sec, Filip Naglak, ul.Kwiatowa 16, PL-81638
Gdynia
Tel +48 58 624 7813   *Fax* +48 58 624 4309
E-mail marek.podstolski@pgapolska.com
Website www.pgapolska.com

Portugal PGA
Gen Sec, Nelson Cavalheiro, Av Das Túlipas 6-Edif.,
Miraflores 17°, Miraflores, PT-1495-161 Algés
Tel +351 214 123 780   *Fax* +351 214 107 972
E-mail nelsoncavalheiro@gmail.com
Website www.pgaportugal.pt

Russia PGA
Gen Sec, Denis Zherebko, Office 242a, Build 8,
Luzhnetskaya nab, RU-119992 Moscow
Tel +7 495 363 2385   *Fax* +7 495 725 4719
E-mail pga@russgolf.ru   *Website* www.rusga.ru

Slovakia PGA
Off, Martina Svobodova, Orenburska Str.66, SK-821
06 Bratislava
Tel +421 52 466 4332   *Fax* +421 52 466 1330

E-mail martina@golfrelax.sk
Website www.pga.sk

Slovenia PGA
Gen Sec, Bogdan Palovšnik, Dunajska cesta 22, SL-1000
Ljubljana
Tel +386 4 148 7280   *Fax* +386 1430 3201
E-mail info@pgaslo.si   *Website* www.pgaslo.si

Spain PGA
Gen Sec, Carlos Mayo, c/ Capitán Haya 22-5C,
ES-28020 Madrid
Tel +34 91 555 1393   *Fax* +34 91 597 0170
E-mail pga@pgaspain.com   *Website* www.pgaspain.com

Swedish PGA
Gen Sec, Mikael Sorling, Malmovagen 647-36,
SE-230 40 Bara
Tel +46 35 320 30   *Fax* +46 4044 7656
E-mail pga@pgasweden.com
Website www.pgasweden.com

Swiss PGA
Gen Sec, Peter Schwager, Zürcherstrasse 20, CH-9014
St Gallen
Tel +41 71 277 1717   *Fax* +41 71 277 7317
E-mail info@swisspga.ch
Website www.swisspga.ch

Turkey PGA
Gen Sec, Andrew McNabola, Doktorlar Sitesi A7
Blok Daire 6, Nato Yolu, Bosna Bulvari, Cen-
gelkoy, Istanbul
Tel +90 533 773 3019
E-mail andrewmmcnabola@gmail.com

North America: Canada and USA

Royal Canadian Golf Association
Exec Dir, Scott Simmons, Suite 1 1333 Dorval Drive,
Oakville, Ontario L6M 4X7
Tel +1 905 849 9700   *Fax* +1 905 845 7040
E-mail ssimmons@golfcanada.ca
Website www.rcga.org

Canadian Ladies' Golf Association
See Royal Canadian Golf Association

National Golf Foundation
Ch Exec, Joseph Beditz, 1150 South US Highway One,
Jupiter, Florida 33477
Tel +1 561 744 6006
Website www.ngf.org

United States Golf Association
Pres, Walter W Driver jr, Golf House, PO Box 708,
Far Hills, NJ 07931-0708
Tel +1 908 234 2300   *Fax* +1 908 234 9687
E-mail usga@usga.org   *Website* www.usga.org

Professional Associations

Canadian PGA
Ch Exec, Gary Bernard, 13450 Dublin Line RR#1,
Acton, Ontario L7J 2W7
Tel +1 519 853 5450   *Fax* +1 519 853 5449
E-mail cpga@canadianpga.org
Website www.cpga.com

Canadian Tour
Comm, Ian Mansfield, 212 King Street West, Suite 203,
Toronto, Ontario M58 1K5
Tel +1 416 204 1564   *Fax* +1 416 204 1368
Website cantour.com

Ladies' Professional Golf Association
Comm, Carolyn Vesper Bivens, 100 International Golf
Drive, Daytona Beach, Florida 32124-1092
Tel +1 386 274 6200   *Fax* +1 386 274 1099
Website www.lpga.com

PGA of America
Ch Exec, Joe Steranka, 100 Avenue of the Champions,
Palm Beach Gardens, Florida 33418
Tel +1 561 624 8400   *Fax* +1 561 624 8448
Website www.pgaonline.com

PGA Tour
Comm, Tim Finchem, PGA Tour, 112 PGA Tour
Boulevard, Ponte Vedra Beach, Florida 32082
Tel +1 904 285 3700
Fax +1 904 285 7913
Website www.pgatour.com

The Caribbean and Central America

Caribbean Golf Association
Sec, David G Bird, PO Box 31329, Grand Cayman,
KY1-1206, Cayman Islands
Tel +1 345 947 1903   *Fax* +1 345 947 3439
E-mail bird@candw.ky
Website www.cgagolfnet.com

Bahamas Golf Federation
Sec, Dudley Martinborough, PO Box SS-19092,
Nassau, Grand Bahama
Tel +1 242 394 3134
E-mail admin@bgfnet.com
Website www.bgfnet.com

Barbados Golf Association
Pres, Birchmore Griffith, PO Box 149W, Worthing,
Christ Church, Barbados BB-15000
Tel +1 246 437 2609   *Fax* +1 246 437 7792
E-mail carib@caribsurf.com
Website www.barbadosgolfassociation.com

Bermuda Golf Association
Sec, Jarryd Dillas, Victoria Place Building, 31 Victoria
Street, Hamilton, HM 10, Bermuda
Tel +1 441 295 9972   *Fax* +1 441 295 0304
E-mail bdagolf@logic.bm
Website www.bermudagolfasociation.net

Cayman Islands Golf Association
Sec, David G Bird, PO Box 31329, Grand Cayman,
KY1-1206
Tel +1 345 947 1903   *Fax* +1 345 947 3439
E-mail bird@candw.ky
Website www.ciga.ky

Costa Rica Golf Federation
Gen Man, Saadat Awan, PO Box 10969, San José 1000
Tel +506 296 5772   *Fax* +506 231 1914
E-mail info@anagolf.com
Website www.anagolf.com

Fedogolf (Dominican Republic)
Exec Dir, Carlos Lizarazo, Calle Macao No.7,
Urbanizacion Tenis Club, Arroyo Hondo, Santo
Domingo, Dominican Republic
Tel +1 809 338 1005   *Fax* +1 809 338 1008
E-mail administracion@fedogolf.org.do
Website www.golfdominicano.com

El Salvador Golf Federation
Pres, Jose Maria Duran Pacheco, Apartado Postal 165,
San Salvador, El Salvador
Tel/Fax +1 503 2264 1581
E-mail fesagolf@yahoo.com

National Golf Association of Guatemala
Exec Asst, Nancy Fuentes, 11 Avenida 14-86 zona 10,
Guatemala Cuidad 01010
Tel +502 2336 0602   *Fax* +502 2366 7848
E-mail asogolf@asogolfguatemala.org
Website www.asogolfguatemala.org

Hondureña Golf Association
Pres, Henry Kattan, Residential Piñares, Km 6.5
Paseo al Hatillo, PO Box 3555, Tegucigalpa, Honduras
Tel +504 211 9260   *Fax* +504 9992 3489
E-mail Hondurasgolf@gmail.com
Website www.hondurasgolf.org

Jamaica Golf Association
Hon Sec, Orville Marshall, Constant Spring GC,
Constant Spring, Kingston 8
Tel +1 876 755 3593   *Fax* +1 876 924 7635
E-mail jamgolf2@cwjamaica.com
Website www.jagolfassociation.com

Mexican Golf Federation
Exec Dir, Fernando Erana, Av.Insurgentes Sur 1605
10° Piso Torre Mural, Col. San Jose Insurgentes,
C.P. 03900 México, D.F.
Tel +525 1084 2176   *Fax* +525 1084 2179
E-mail direccionfmg@mexgolf.org
Website www.mexgolf.org

Nicaraguan Golf Federation
Exec Sec, J A Narvaez, Nejapa GCC, Managua
Tel +505 8850 5877   *Fax* +505 2278 0333
E-mail procalsa1@hotmail.com

OECS Golf Association
Sec, Eddie Smith, c/o PO Box 895, Basseterre, St Kitts
Tel +1 869 465 3214
E-mail beale_one@ yahoo.com

Panama Golf Association
Exec Dir, Luiz Heley Bárcenas, PO Box 8613, Panama 5
Tel +507 266 7436   *Fax* +507 220 3994
E-mail apagolf@yahoo.es

Puerto Rico Golf Association
Pres, Sidney Wolf, 264 Matadero – Suite 11, San Juan,
Puerto Rico 00920
Tel +1 787 793 3444   *Fax* +1 787 723 3138
E-mail swolf00@gmail.com
Website www.prga.org

St Maarten Golf Association
Pres, Steve Mix, PO Box 720, Philipsburg, St Maarten,
Netherlands Antilles
Tel +44 599 551 2105   *Fax* +44 599 542 1261
E-mail info@stmaartengolf.com

Trinidad & Tobago Golf Association

Pres, Robert Costelloe, c/o St Andrews GC, PO Box 3403, Moka, Maraval, Trinidad, Maraval, T&T, W.I.
Tel +1 868 629 7127
Fax +1 868 629 0411
E-mail ttga@live.com
Website www.trinidadandtobagogolfassociation.com

Turks & Caicos Golf Association

Pres, Fraser Dods, PO Box 319, Providenciales, Turks & Caicos Islands
Tel +1 649 946 4417   *Fax* +1 649 946 4437
E-mail physiologic@tciway.tc

Virgin Islands Golf Federation

Sec, Doug Menzies, PO Box 5187, Kingshill, St Croix, US Virgin Islands 00851
Tel +1 305 281 2670
E-mail dmenzies@vihealth.com

Professional Association

Jamaica PGA

Chairman, O Marshall, 9 Park Ave., Kingston 5
Tel +1 876 881 4444   *E-mail* pgajamaica@gmail.com

Mexico PGA

Off, D Ross, Nadadores 30, Col.Country Club, Mexico DF, CP 04210
Tel +52 55 5544 6644   *Fax* +52 55 5689 4254
E-mail info@pgamexico.org
Website www.pgamexico.org

South America

South American Golf Federation

Exec Sec, Rafael Enrique Otero Carrera 27 No 156-56 Of 903, Bogotá, Colombia
Tel +57 1 313 0624   *Fax* +57 1 313 0391
E-mail fedesud@cable.net.co
Website www.fedsudgolf.com

Argentine Golf Association

Exec Dir, Mark Lawrie, Av Corrientes 538-Pisos 11y12, 1043 CF, Buenos Aires
Tel +54 11 4325 1113   *Fax* +54 11 4325 8660
E-mail golf@aag.org.ar   *Website* www.aag.org.ar

Bolivian Golf Federation

Sec, Gonzalo Viladegut, Calle Cochabamba Esquina Saavedra, Edif Torre Empresarial Piso 2 Of No.4, Santa Cruz
Tel/Fax +591 339 4035
E-mail fbgolf@entelnet.bo
Website www.boliviagolf.com

Brasilian Golf Confederation

Exec Sec, M A Aguiar Giusti, Rua Paez de Araújo 29 conj 42/43, cep 04531-090, São Paulo
Tel/Fax +55 11 3168 4366
E-mail golfe@cbg.com.br   *Website* www.cbg.com.br

Chilean Golf Federation

Sec, Mauricio Hederra Pinto, Málaga 655, Las Condes, Santiago
Tel +56 2 690 8700   *Fax* +56 2 690 8720
E-mail secretaria@chilegolf.cl
Website www.chilegolf.cll

Colombian Golf Federation

Sec, Bernardo Mariño González, cra. 7#72-64 Int 26, Bogotá DC
Tel +57 1 310 7664   *Fax* +57 1 235 5091
E-mail fedegolf@federacioncolombianadegolf.com
Website www.federacioncolombianadegolf.com

Ecuador Golf Federation

Sec, Marcelo Roldós Prosser, Av Amazonas N.28-17 y Alemania, Edif.Skorpios Piso 8 of.812, Quito
Tel +593 2 2922 128   *Fax* +593 2 2442 986
E-mail fedecuat@feg.org.ec
Website www.feg.org.ec

Guyana Golf Union

Sec, c/o Demerara Bauxite Co Ltd, Mackenzie, Guyana

Paraguay Golf Association

Sec, Alejandro Rubin, Eduardo Vístor Haedo, No.407 c/ Alberdi, Edif Libra – Planta Baja, Asunción
Tel +595 21 491 217   *Fax* +595 21 447 218
E-mail secretaria@apg.org.py
Website www.apg.org.py

Peru Golf Federation

Exec Dir, Eduardo Ibarra, Calle Conde de la Monclova 315 Of 308, San Isidro, Lima
Tel +51 1 441 1500   *Fax* +51 1 441 1992
E-mail fepegolf@terra.com.pe
Website www.fpg.org.pe

Uruguay Golf Association

Hon Sec, Dr Paul Arrighi, José Ellauri 357 apto.303, Montevideo
Tel/Fax +598 2 711 5285
E-mail augolf@adinet.com.uy
Website www.aug.com.uy

Venezuela Golf Federation

Exec Dir, Julio L Torres, Edifico IASA Mezzanina Of 02, Av. Eugenio Mendoza La Castellana 1060, Municipio Chacao, Caracas 1060
Tel/Fax +58 212 265 2839
E-mail fvg@fvg.org   *Website* www.fvg.or

Professional Association

Brazil PGA

Sec, Eliecer Antolinez, Rua Francisco de Paula Brito, 317-Planalto Paulista, cep 04071 050 São Paulo-SP
Tel/Fax +55 11 2276 0745
E-mail pgabrasil@aol.com.br
Website www.pgadobrasil.com.br

Africa

African Golf Confederation

Pres, Gert Cloete, PO Box 2122, Windhoek, Namibia
Fax +264 64 405644
E-mail prado@iway.na

Algerian Golf Federation

Pres, Noureddine Djoudi, 28 rue Ahmed, Ouaked, Dely Ibrahim
Tel/Fax +213 35021
E-mail djoudimn@hotmail.com

Arab Golf Federation

Sec Gen, Adel Zarouni, PO Box 31410, Dubai, UAE
Tel +9714 295 2277   *Fax* +9714 95 2288

E-mail info@ugagolf.com
Website www.arabgolf.org

Botswana Golf Union
Exec Sec, Joseph Marudu, PO Box 1033, Gaborone
Tel +267 316 1116   *Fax* +267 391 2262
E-mail bgu@it.bw

D R of Congo Golf Federation
Pres, Alain Nitu, c/o Rainbow Connections, Carrefour
des Jeunes, 5151 Avenue Kasa-Vuba, Q/Matonge,
Commune Kalamu, Kinshasa
E-mail alainnitu@hotmail.com

Egyptian Golf Federation
Golf Man, Gerard Bent, 6 St. 301, New Maadi, Cairo
Tel +2010 005 0435
E-mail gerardbent@egyptiangolffederation.org
Website www.egyptiangolffederation.org

Gabon Golf Federation
Sec, BP 15159 Libreville
Tel +241 760 378   *Fax* +241 729 079
E-mail golfclublibreville@gmail.com

Ghana Golf Association
Hon Sec, George Lee Mensah, c/o National Sport
Council, PO Box 1272, Accra
Tel/Fax +233 21 923434   *Fax* +233 21 220953
E-mail ghanagolfass@yahoo.co.uk

Ghana Ladies Golf Union
Hon Sec, Mrs M Amu, PO Box 70, Accra

Ivory Coast (Côte d'Ivoire) Golf Federation
Sec, Bendey-Diby Valentin, O8 BP 01, Abidjan 08
Tel +225 2243 1076   *Fax* +225 2243 3772
E-mail f.golfci@aviso.ci   *Website* www.fgolfci.com

Kenya Golf Union
Hon Sec, Parshu Harini, PO Box 49609, 00100 Nairobi
Tel +254 203 76 3898   *Fax* +254 203 76 5118
E-mail kgu@iconnect.co.ke
Website www.kgu.org.ke

Kenya Ladies' Golf Union
Hon Sec, A Sangar, PO Box 1675-1, Nairobi
Tel +254 2 733 794

KwaZulu-Natal Golf Union
Sec, RT Runge, PO Box 1939, Durban 4000
Tel +27 (0)31 202 7636   *Fax* +27 (0)31 202 1022
E-mail kzngu@kzngolf.co.za

Liberia Golf Association
Pres, Dr C Nelson Oniyama, c/o Monrovia Breweries
Inc., Monrovia

Libyan Golf Federation
Gen Sec, Mustafa Ewkaiat, PO Box 3674, Tripoli
Tel +218 21 478 0510
E-mail golf_libya@hotmail.com

Malawi Golf Union
Hon Sec, James Hinde, PO Box 1198, Blantyre 8
Tel +265 1 824 108   *Fax* +265 1 824 027
E-mail medlife@malawi.net

Mauritius Golf Federation
Pres, Raj Ramlackhan, 42 Sir William Newton Street,
Port Louis
Tel +230 208 4224   *Fax* +230 483 5163
E-mail mgolffed@intnet.mu

The Royal Moroccan Golf Federation
Sec Gen, Abdelal Latif Benali, Route des Zaers, Rabat,
Dar El Salam
Tel +212 3775 5636   *Fax* +212 3775 1026
E-mail abdellatif.benali@manara.ma

Namibia Golf Federation
Treas, Hugh Mortimer, PO Box 2122, Windhoek,
Namibia
Tel +264 61 205 5223
Fax +264 61 205 5220
E-mail gm@wccgolf.com.na
Website www.wccgolf.com.na

Nigeria Golf Federation
Sec, Patrick Uwagbale, National Stadium Surulere,
PO Box 145, Lagos
Tel +234 1 545 6209
Fax +234 1 545 0530
E-mail nigeriagolffederation@yahoo.com

Nigerian Ladies Golf Union
Sec, Mrs M Edozi, c/o Benin GC, Benin City

Senegalese Golf Federation
Dep Gen Sec, Mr Moustaph Baïdy Bâ, BP 24105
Ouakam Dakar, Senegal

Sierra Leone Golf Federation
Pres, Freetown GC, PO Box 237, Lumley Beach,
Freetown
E-mail fadi@sierratel.sl

South African Golf Association
Exec Dir, BA Younge, PO Box 65303, Benmore 2010
RSA
Tel +27 11 476 1713   *Fax* +27 086 503 4653
E-mail admin@saga.co.za   *Website* www.saga.co.za

Women's Golf South Africa
Hon Sec, Mrs V Horak, PO Box 209, Randfontein
1760, RSA
Tel/Fax +27 11 416 1263
E-mail salgu@global.co.za   *Website* www.salgu.co.za

Swaziland Golf Union
Sec, AP Dunn, PO Box 1739, Mbabane, H100
Swaziland
Tel +268 404 4735   *Fax* +268 404 5401
E-mail adunn2@fnb.co.za

Tanzania Golf Union
Golf Dir, Farayi Chitengwa, c/o Gymkhana Club,
PO Box 286, Dar Es Salaam
Tel +255 222 138445   *Fax* +255 222 113583
E-mail info@tgu.or.tz   *Website* www.tgu.com

Tunisian Golf Federation
Sec Gen, Mohamed Moncef Gaida, Maison de Fédéra-
cions Sportives, 1004 Cité Olympique, Tunis
Tel +216 71 237 087   *Fax* +216 71 237 299
E-mail ftg@ftg.org.tn
Website www.ftg.org.tn

Uganda Golf Union
Hon Sec, Gadi A Musasizi, Kitante Road, PO Box 2574,
Kampala
Tel +256 712 877 036   *Fax* +256 41 304 832
E-mail gmusasizi@yahoo.com

Uganda Ladies Golf Union
Hon Sec, Mrs R Tumusiime, PO Box 624, Kampala
E-mail ugagolf@africaonline.co.ug

Zaire Golf Federation
Pres, Tshilombo Mwin Tshitol, BP 1648, Lubumbashi

Zambia Golf Union
Hon Sec, A C Mwangata, 37A Twaliilubula Ave,
Parklands, PO Box 21602, Kitwe
Tel +260 96 780 095   Fax +260 2 226 884
E-mail anthony@coppernet.zm

Zambia Ladies Golf Union
Hon Sec, Mrs H Kapya, PO Box 22151, Kitwe

Zimbabwe Golf Association
Sec, John Nixon, PO Box 3327, Harare
Tel +263 4 746 141 Fax +263 4 746 228

Professional Associations

South African PGA
Sec, Anne Du Toit, PO Box 949 Bedfordview 2008, RSA
Tel +27 11 485 1370   Fax +27 11 640 4372
E-mail admin@pgasa.com   Website www.pgasa.com

South African Women's PGA
Sec, Mrs V Harrington, PO Box 781547, Sandton 2146
Tel/Fax +27 11 477 8606

South Africa Sunshine Tour
Exec Dir, Louis Martin, 15 Postnet Suite #185,
Private Bag X15, Somerset West 7129
Tel +27 21 850 6500   Fax +27 21 852 8271

Middle East

Bahrain Golf Committee
Sec Gen, Muneer Ahmed, PO Box 38938, Riffa,
Kingdom of Bahrain
Tel +973 1777 7179   Fax +973 1776 9484
E-mail bgassoc@batelco.com.bh

Emirates Golf Association
Gen Man, Saeed Al Budoor, PO Box 31410, Dubai,
UAE
Tel +971 4 3684 988   Fax +971 4 295 2288
E-mail info@ugagolf.com   Website www.ugagolf.com

Islamic Republic of Iran Golf Federation
Sec Gen, Mohammad Reza Naddafpour, Enghelab Club,
Vali-e-asr Avenue, PO Box 15815-1881, Tehran
Tel/Fax +98 21 2201 5617
E-mail info@golfir.com   Website www.golfir.com

Israel Golf Federation
Sec, Mrs Irit Peleg, PO Box 141, IL-38900 Caesarea
Tel +972 4 610 9600   Fax +972 77 870 273
E-mail info@israelgolffed.org
Website www.israelgolffed.org

Jordan Golf Federation
Sec, Ali A Shahin, PO Box 141331, Amman 11814
Tel +962 795 525187   Fax +962 658 56913
E-mail ashahin70@yahoo.com

Kuwait Golf Federation
Pres, Saud Al Hajeri, PO Box 1192, Fintas Z-code
51013
Tel +965 390 5287

Lebanese Golf Federation
Tech Comm, Karim S Salaam, c/o GC of Lebanon,
PO Box 11-3099, Beirut
Tel 9611 861862   Fax +9611 866253
E-mail info@lebanesegolffederation.org

Qatar Golf Association
Pres, Hassan Nasser Al Noaimi, PO Box 13530, Doha
Tel 974 4483 2677   Fax +974 4483 2610
E-mail info@qga.com.qa   Website www.qga.com.qa

Saudi Arabian Golf Federation
Sec, Jun Saporsantos, PO Box 325422, Riyadh 11371,
Saudi Arabia
Tel +966 1 4090 004   Fax +966 1 4090 002
E-mail saudigolf@yahoo.com
Website www.ksagolf.com

Professional Associations

Israel PGA
Sec, R Cordoba-Core, Sokolov 10, Block B Floor 2,
Apartment 6, Hertzlya
Tel +972 4 6636 1172   Fax +972 4 6636 1173

United Arab Emirates PGA
Off, J Danby, Nad Al Sheba Golf, PO Box 52872,
Dubai
Tel +971 4 336 3666   Fax +971 4 336 1624
E-mail jdanby@dubaigolf.com

Asia

Asia-Pacific Golf Confederation
Hon Sec, Colin Phillips, Golf Australia, Level 3, 95
Coventry St, South Melbourne, Victoria-3205
Tel +613 9626 5050   Fax +613 9626 5095
E-mail apgc@golfaustralia.org.au

Bangladesh Golf Federation
Pres, General Moeen U Ahmed ndc, psc, c/o
Kurmitola GC, Dhaka Cantonment, Dhaka-1206
Tel +880 2 8752 523   Fax +880 2 8752 521
E-mail kgcdhaka@hotmail.com

Bhutan Golf Confederation
Sec Gen, Tsheringh Namgay, PO Box 939, Thimphu,
Bhutan
Tel 975 2 322 138   Fax 975 2 323 937
E-mail t_namgay@yahoo.com

Cambodian Golf Association
Sec Gen, Lt Gen Eth Sarath, 295 Eo Street Kampuchea
Krom, Sangleat Mittapheap, Khan 7 Makara, Phnom
Penh
Tel +855 1243 7888
Fax +855 2388 0045
E-mail ethsarath@hotmail.com
Website www.cambodiangolf-federation.com

China Golf Association
Sec Gen, Zhang Xiaoning, 5 Tiyuguan Rd, Beijing,
100763 China
Tel +86 10 6711 7897
Fax +86 10 6716 2993
E-mail chinagolf@263.net
Website www.golf.org.cn

Chinese Taipei Golf Association
Sec Gen, Hann-Ji Wang, 12 F-1 125 Nanjing East Rd,
Section 2, Taipei, Taiwan 104, Chinese Taipei
Tel +886 22 516 5611   Fax +886 22 516 3208
E-mail garoc.tw@msa.hinet.net
Website www.taiwangolf.org

National Golf Association of Fiji
Gen Sec, Mosese Waqavonovono, PO Box 5363,
Raiwaqa, Suva, Fiji
Tel/Fax +679 337 1191
E-mail ngaf@connect.com.fi

Guam National Golf Federation
Pres, Samuel Teker, Suite 2A 130 Aspinall Ave, Agana,
Guam 96910
Tel +1 671 653 3100   Fax +1 671 472 2601
E-mail st@tttguamlawyers.com

Hong Kong Golf Association Ltd
Ch Exec, F 1 Valentine, Rm 2003, Olympic House,
1 Stadium Path, So Kon Po, Causeway Bay,
Hong Kong
Tel +852 2504 8659   Fax +852 2845 1553
E-mail hkgolf@hkga.com   Website www.hkga.com

Indian Golf Union
Sec-Gen, W/Cdr Satish Aparajit (Retd), First Floor 24,
Adchina, New Delhi 110017
Tel +91 11 265 25772   Fax +91 11 265 25770
E-mail tigu@vsnl.net   Website www.tigu.in

Indonesian Golf Association
Sec Gen, Kusnan Ismukanto, Gd Direkso Gelora Bung
Karno 2nd Floor, Jl.Pintu Satu, Senayan Jakarta-10270
Tel +62 21 573 2811   Fax +62 21 573 1291
E-mail pgi@pgionline.org
Website www.pgionline.org

Japan Golf Association
Exec Dir, Takashi Omori, Kyobashi YS Bldg 2nd Floor,
1-12-5 Kyobashi, Chuo-Ku, Tokyo 104-0031
Tel +81 3 3566 0003   Fax +81 3 3566 0101
E-mail info@jga.or.jp   Website www.jga.or.jp

Korean Golf Association
Exec Dir, D W Kim, #513-12, Munbal-ri, Gyoha-eup,
Paju-si, Gyeonggi-do 413-832, Korea
Tel +82 31 955 2255   Fax +82 31 955 2300
E-mail kga@kgagolf.or.kr   Website www.kgagolf.or.kr

Kyrgyzstan Golf
Sec, 217 Moskovskaia Street, Leninskiy District,
Bishkek City 720010, Kyrgyz Republic
Tel +7 996 905 170   Fax +7 996 831 014
E-mail o.larina@skd.kg

Lao National Golf Federation
Sec, Sangkhom Phomphakdy, PO Box 4300, 33 Wat
Xiengnhum St, Sethathirat Rd, Vientiane, Lao PDR
Tel/Fax +856 2121 7294
E-mail sangkhom52@hotmail.com

Golf Association of Macau
Sec, Michelle Leong, Rm 15, Estrada Vitoria S/N,
Centro Desportivo, Vitoria, Macau
Tel +853 831 555   Fax +853 832 555

Malaysian Golf Association
Hon Sec, V Ravindran, 14 Jalan 4/76C, Desa Pandan,
55100 Kuala Lumpur
Tel +60 3 9283 7300   Fax +60 3 9282 9300

E-mail mga@tm.net.my
Website www.mgaonline.com.my

Mongolian Golf Association
Sec Gen, Enkh Amgalan.L., MCS Plaza, 4 Seoul St,
Ulaanbaatar – 210644, Mongolia
Tel +976 11 323 705   Fax +976 11 311 323
E-mail enkh_amgalan@mcs.mn

Golf Federation of the Union of Myanmar
Gen Sec, U Aung Hla Han, no.46 Pyay Rd, Building C 6
1 / 2 miles, Hlaing Township, Yangon
Tel +95 1 537 241   Fax +95 1 538 686
E-mail aunghhan@baganmail.net.mm

Nepal Golf Association
Sec, Tashi Ghale, GPO Box 1665 Naya, Baneshwar,
Kathmandu
Tel +977 1 447 2836   Fax +977 1 478 0191
E-mail hotel@rsingi.wlink.com.np

Pakistan Golf Federation
Pres, Lt Gen Ashfaq Parvez Kayani, Jhelum Road,
PO Box 1295, Rawalpindi
Tel +92 51 556 8177   Fax +92 51 225 5440
E-mail pakgolffed@yahoo.com

National Golf Association of the Philippines
Sec Gen, Godofredo R Balindez jr, Room 307 Building
B, Philsports Complex, Mercalo Av, Pasig City, Metro
Manila 1603 Philippines
Tel +632 517 9778   Fax +632 706 5926
E-mail ngapgolf@hotmail.com
Website www.ngapgolf.com

Singapore Golf Association
Gen Man, Col (rtd) Peter Teo, Tanglin Post Office,
PO Box 457, Singapore 912416
Tel +65 6 256 1318   Fax +65 6 256 1917
E-mail sga@pacific.net.sg
Website www.sga.org.sg

Sri Lanka Golf Union
Hon Sec, AG Punchihewa, PO Box 309, 223 Model
Farm Rd, Colombo 8, Sri Lanka
Tel +94 11 266 7771   Fax +94 11 461 6056
E-mail golfsrilanka@rcgcsl.com

Thailand Golf Association
Sec Gen, Air Mrshl Bureerat Ratanavanich, PO Box
1190, Ramkamhaeng, Bangkok 10241
Tel +66 2 369 3777   Fax +66 2 369 3776
E-mail secretary@tga.or.th   Website www.tga.or.th

Vietnam Golf Association
Sec Gen, Dr Nguyen Ngoc Chu, Suite 114 National
Convention Centre, Me Tri, Tu Liem, Hanoi
Tel/Fax +844 7833 194
E-mail chunn@hn.vnn.vn

Professional Associations

Asian PGA
Sec, Ramlan Dato Harun, 415-417 Block A Kelana
Business Centre, 97 Jalan SS 7/2 Kelana Jaya,
Selangor, Malaysia
Tel +603 7492 0099   Fax +603 7492 0098
Website www.asianpgatour.com

Asia PGA Tour
Chief Exec, Justin Strachan, 15/F, One Harbourfront, 18 Tak Fung Street, Hunghom, Kowloon, Hong Kong
Tel +852 2330 8227   *Fax* +852 2801 5743
E-mail apgatour@asiaonline.net
Website www.asianpgatour.com

PGA Republic of China
2nd Floor 196 Cheng-Teh Road, Taipei, Taiwan
Tel +886 2 8220318   *Fax* +886 2 8229684
E-mail garoc.tw@msa.hinet.net
Website www.twgolf.org

Hong Kong PGA
Sec, Mr M Lai Wai Sing, Room 702 Landmark North, Sheung Shui, NT Hong Kong
Tel +852 523 3171

Indian PGA
Sec, P K Bhattacharyya, 109A, 1513 Guman Puri Complex (First Floor), Kotia, Mubarak Pur, New Delhi – 110 003
Tel +91 11 3250 5456
Fax +91 91 11 2461 6331
E-mail pgaofindia@gmail.com

Japan Ladies PGA
7-16-3 Ginza, Nitetsu Kobiki Bldg 8F, Chuo-ku, Tokyo 104-0061
Tel +81 3 3546 7801   *Fax* +81 3 3546 7805

Japan PGA
Int Com, Seien Kobayakawa, Top Hamamatsucho Bldg, 1-5-12 Shiba.Minato-Ku, 8FL, Tokyo 105-0014
Tel +81 3 5419 2614   *Fax* +81 3 5419 2622
E-mail bp@pga.or.jp

PGA of Malaysia
Sec, Brig-Gen Mahendran, 1B Jalan Mamanda 7, Ampang Point, 6800 Selangor Darul Ehsan, Malaysia

Australasia and the Pacific

Golf Australia
Ch Exec, Stephen Pitt, Level 3,95 Coventry St, South Melbourne, Victoria-3205
Tel +613 9626 5050   *Fax* +613 9626 5095
E-mail info@golfaustralia.org.au
Website www.golfaustralia.org.au

Womens Golf Australia
See Golf Australia

Cook Islands Golf Association
Sec, Mrs Tereapii Urlich, Rarotonga GC, PO Box 151, Rarotonga, Cook Islands
Tel +682 20621   *Fax* +682 20631
E-mail toots@oyster.net.ck

National Golf Association of Fiji
Pres, I Bainimara c/o Air Terminal Services (Fiji) Ltd, PO Box 18140, Suva, Fiji Islands
Tel +679 338 5089   *Fax* +679 992 2601
E-mail ibainimara@hotmail.com

New Zealand Golf Incorporated
Ch Exec, Dean Murphy, PO Box 331768, Takapuna, New Zealand
Tel +64 9 485 3230   *Fax* +64 9 486 6745
E-mail nzgolf@nzgolf.org.nz
Website www.nzgolf.org.nz

Womens' Golf New Zealand Inc
See New Zealand Golf Incorporated

Papua New Guinea Golf Association
Pres, S Walker, PO Box 4632, Boroko, NCD
Tel +675 323 1120   *Fax* +675 323 1300
E-mail swalker@brianbell.com.pg

Papua New Guinea Ladies Golf Association
Hon Sec, Mrs L Illidge, PO Box 348, Lae MP 411

Samoa Golf Incorporated
Sec, Vincent Fepuleai, PO Box 3770, Apia, Samoa
Tel +685 24839   *Mobile* +685 7704767
E-mail golfhut@ipasifika.net

Vanuatu Golf Association
Chairman, Bernie Cain, PO Box 358, Port Vila, Vanuatu, Pacific Ocean
Tel +678 22178   *Fax* +678 25037
E-mail vilare@vanuatu.com.vu

Professional Associations

Australian PGA
Ch Exec, Max Garske, 600 Thompson Rd, Sandhurst, Victoria 3977
Tel +61 2 9439 8111   *Fax* +61 2 9439 7888
E-mail maxgpga@oze-mail.com.au
Website www.pga.org.au

Australian Ladies Professional Golf
Ch Exec, Warren Savil, PO Box 447, Mudgeeraba, Queensland 4213
Tel +61 7 5592 9343   *Fax* +61 7 5592 9344
E-mail warrens@alpg.com.au
Website www.alpg.com.au

PGA Tour Australasia
Exec Dir, Andrew Georgiou, Suite 302, 77 Berry St, North Sydney, NSW 2060
Tel +61 2 9956 0000   *Fax* +61 2 9956 0099
Website pgatour.com.au

New Zealand PGA
Exec Dir, PO Box 11-934, Wellington
Tel +64 4 4722 687   *Fax* +64 4 4722 925
E-mail postmaster@pga.org.nz
Website www.pga.org.nz

Kent benefitted £77 million from The Open

The 2011 Open Championship won by Darren Clarke at Royal St George's last July delivered a £77 million benefit to the county of Kent according to an independent economic assessment organized by The R&A.

The headline figure includes an economic impact of £24.1 million and a destination marketing benefit of £52.6 million. Within the boundaries of East Kent, comprising the districts of Canterbury, Thanet, Dover and Shepway, the economic impact was £21.2 million.

Commenting on the research findings Peter Dawson, Chief Executive of The R&A, said: "We found a worthy winner in Darren Clarke at Royal St George's and we are delighted that the Championship also delivered a significant economic impact to the local community."

Not only was there considerable economic benefit to the county but the legacy of almost 300 hours of scenic images of the Kent countryside, viewed globally on television, is sure to bring benefits to the area for years to come.

Officials from The R&A and local authority representatives have had meetings in Dover to discuss necessary transport infrastructure enhancements before The Open returns to the South East.

A total of 180,000 spectators visited The Open Championship last year and 37,000 passengers travelled to Royal St George's on the special High Speed train service from London St Pancras. Flybe bookings at Manston Kent International Airport were up 70% in July with a 40% increase in bookings on the carrier's Edinburgh service.

PART XVI

Clubs and Courses

Compiled by Paula Taylor

Club Centenaries

1911

Aberystwyth
Ardee
Beau Desert
Betchworth Park
Boyle
Breightmet
City of Derry
Cliftonville
Clonmel
Consett and District
Coombe Hill
Crewe
Croham Hurst
Davyhulme Park
Hawarden
Heworth (N. Yorkshire)
Hillside
Killin
Kintore
Luffenham Heath
Muthill
Renishaw Park
Rothley Park
St Austell
Silsden
Warren
Whickham
Whinhill
Whitstable and Seasalter
Worksop

1912

Aberlady
Aquarius
Ashton-under-Lyne
Banbridge
Bedford & County
Boldon
Branshaw
Camberley Heath
Childwall
Clontarf
Cooden Beach
Dinas Powis
Dumfries & County
Essex Golf Centres,
  Hainault Forest
Fishwick Hall
Gatley
Heaton Park Golf Centre
Heworth (Tyne & Wear)
Holyhead
Kinsale Ringenane
Maesteg
Market Rasen & District
Northenden
Port Bannatyne
Ravelston
Reddish Vale
St George's Hill
Saline
Southport Golf Links
Thetford
Upavon
Waterford
Werneth Low
Whalley
Woodcote Park

1913

The Addington
Ashton & Lea
Bargoed
Baxenden & District
Bidston
Blackmoor
Bowring
Bramley
Bull Bay
Castle
Clones
Coxmoor
Davenport
Dore & Totley
Dukinfield
Ellesmere
Ferndown
Garforth
Gathurst
Gay Hill
Hazel Grove
Highcliffe Castle
Letterkenny
Linlithgow
Lytham Green Drive
Milford Haven
Okehampton
Oxley Park
Portumna
Redditch
Royal Automobile Club
St Regulus Ladies'
Sale
Seahouses
Sitwell Park
Stocksfield
Tynemouth
Wheatley

1914

Anglesey
Apsley Guise and Woburn
  Sands
Balmoral
Blackwood
Buckingham
Burnside
Crosland Heath
Eaglescliffe
Eden Course (St Andrews)
Green Hawarth
Hockley
Nevill
Newtownstewart
Oakdale
Routenburn
Shirley Park
Sonning
Southsea
Sutton Bridge
Thirsk & Northallerton
Whitchurch (Cardiff)

Golf Clubs and Courses

How to use this section

Clubs in England, Ireland and Wales are listed in alphabetical order by country and county. Note that some clubs and courses are affiliated to a county different to that in which they are physically located. Clubs in Scotland are grouped under recognised administrative regions. The Great Britain and Ireland county index can be found on page 682.

European clubs and clubs from the rest of the world are listed alphabetically by country and grouped under regional headings. The index for Europe can be found on page 805 and the index for the rest of the world is on page 855. In most European countries, only 18 hole courses are included.

All clubs and courses are listed in the the general index at the back of the book.

With the publication of the 2010 edition, we began introducing a new international look to the *R&A Golfer's*

Handbook and to accommodate our global expansion of results and club information, we have modified entries to the Club's Directory as detailed below.

It is apparent that information previously displayed of green fees, membership, personnel, additional features, etc., can be best imparted as current data via the websites that the majority of clubs now operate. Currently, nearly 80 per cent of golf clubs operate websites, a number that is growing by around four per cent per annum.

Club details (see Key to Symbols below)
The date after the name of the club indicates the year it was founded. Courses are private unless otherwise stated. Many public courses play host to members' clubs. Information on these can be obtained from the course concerned.

We are indebted to club secretaries in the British Isles and continental Europe for the information supplied.

Key to Symbols

☎ Telephone	✍ Secretary
☐ Fax	⊕ Additional information in the absence of a website
✉ E-mail	
▤ Website	

European Dialling Codes

Austria +43	Iceland +354	Poland +48
Belgium +32	Repubic of	Portugal +351
Cyprus +357	Ireland +353	Slovenia +386
Czech Republic +420	Italy +39	Spain +34
	Latvia +371	Sweden +46
Denmark +45	Luxembourg +352	Switzerland +41
Finland +358		
France +33	Malta +356	Turkey +90
Germany +49	Netherlands +31	
Greece +30		
Hungary +36	Norway +47	

Great Britain and Ireland County Index

England

Bedfordshire

Aspley Guise & Woburn Sands (1914)
West Hill, Aspley Guise, Milton Keynes MK17 8DX
- ☎ **(01908) 583596**
- 📠 (01908) 288140
- ✉ info@aspleyguisegolfclub.co.uk
- ✍ Karen Evans (01908) 583596
- 🖥 www.aspleyguisegolfclub.co.uk

Aylesbury Vale (1991)
Proprietary
Wing, Leighton Buzzard LU7 0UJ
- ☎ **(01525) 240196**
- 📠 (01525) 240848
- ✉ info@avgc.co.uk
- ✍ C Wright (Sec/Mgr)
- 🖥 www.avgc.co.uk

Beadlow Manor Hotel G&CC (1973)
Proprietary
Beadlow, Shefford SG17 5PH
- ☎ **(01525) 860800**
- 📠 (01525) 861345
- ✉ office@beadlowmanor.co.uk
- ✍ Graham Wilson (Gen Mgr)
- 🖥 www.beadlowmanor.co.uk

The Bedford (1999)
Proprietary
Carnoustie Drive, Great Denham Golf Village, Biddenham MK40 4FF
- ☎ **(01234) 320022**
- 📠 (01234) 320023
- ✉ thebedford@btopenworld.com
- ✍ Geoff Swain
- 🖥 www.thebedfordgc.com

Bedford & County (1912)
Green Lane, Clapham, Bedford MK41 6ET
- ☎ **(01234) 352617**
- 📠 (01234) 357195
- ✉ office@bandcgc.co.uk
- ✍ R MacDonald (Gen Mgr)
- 🖥 www.bandcgc.co.uk

Bedfordshire (1891)
Spring Lane, Stagsden, Bedford MK43 8SR
- ☎ **(01234) 822555**
- 📠 (01234) 825052
- ✉ office@bedfordshiregolf.com
- ✍ Geraint Dixon (Gen Mgr)
- 🖥 www.bedfordshiregolf.com

Caddington (1985)
Proprietary
Chaul End Road, Caddington LU1 4AX
- ☎ **(01582) 415573**
- 📠 (01582) 415314
- ✉ info@caddingtongolfclub.co.uk
- ✍ D Isger
- 🖥 www.caddingtongolfclub.co.uk

Chalgrave Manor (1994)
Proprietary
Dunstable Road, Chalgrave, Toddington LU5 6JN
- ☎ **(01525) 876556**
- 📠 (01525) 876556
- ✉ steve@chalgravegolf.co.uk
- ✍ S Rumball
- 🖥 www.chalgravegolf.co.uk

Colmworth (1992)
Proprietary
New Road, Colmworth MK44 2NN
- ☎ **(01234) 378181**
- 📠 (01234) 376678
- ✉ julie@colmworthgc.fsnet.co.uk
- ✍ C Porch (01933) 412398
- 🖥 www.colmworthgolfclub.co.uk

Colworth (1985)
Colworth House, Sharnbrook, Bedford MK44 1LQ
- ☎ **(01234) 782442**
- ✉ secretary@colworthgolf.co.uk
- ✍ Dennis Stott (Sec)
- 🖥 www.colworthgolf.co.uk

Dunstable Downs (1906)
Whipsnade Road, Dunstable LU6 2NB
- ☎ **(01582) 604472**
- 📠 (01582) 478700
- ✉ dunstabledownsgc@btconnect.com
- ✍ Alan Sigee
- 🖥 www.dunstabledownsgolf.co.uk

Henlow (1985)
RAF Henlow, Henlow SG16 6DN
- ☎ **(01462) 851515 Ext 7083**
- 🖥 www.henlowgolfclub.co.uk

John O'Gaunt (1948)
Sutton Park, Sandy, Biggleswade SG19 2LY
- ☎ **(01767) 260360**
- 📠 (01767) 262834
- ✉ simon@johnogauntgolfclub.co.uk
- ✍ Simon Davis (Gen Mgr)
- 🖥 www.johnogauntgolfclub.co.uk

Leighton Buzzard (1925)
Plantation Road, Leighton Buzzard LU7 3JF
- ☎ **(01525) 244800**
- 📠 (01525) 244801
- ✉ secretary@leightonbuzzardgolf.net
- ✍ D Mutton (01525) 244800
- 🖥 www.leightonbuzzardgolf.net

Mentmore G&CC (1992)
Mentmore, Leighton Buzzard LU7 0UA
- ☎ **(01296) 662020**
- 📠 (01296) 662592
- ✉ cmoore@mentmorecountryclub.co.uk
- ✍ Clint Moore
- 🖥 www.mentmorecountryclub.co.uk

The Millbrook (1980)
Ampthill MK45 2JB
- ☎ **(01525) 840252**
- 📠 (01525) 406249
- ✉ info@themillbrook.com
- ✍ DC Cooke (01525) 840252
- 🖥 www.themillbrook.com

Mount Pleasant (1992)
Proprietary
Station Road, Lower Stondon, Henlow SG16 6JL
- ☎ **(01462) 850999**
- 📠 (01462) 850257
- ✉ tarasimkins@mountpleasantgolfclub.co.uk
- ✍ Tara Simkins (Gen Mgr)
- 🖥 www.mountpleasantgolfclub.co.uk

Mowsbury (1975)
Public
Kimbolton Road, Bedford MK41 8BJ
- ☎ **(01234) 772700**
- ✍ TW Gardner (01234) 771041

Pavenham Park (1994)
Proprietary
Pavenham, Bedford MK43 7PE
- ☎ **(01234) 822202**
- 📠 (01234) 826602
- ✉ office@pavenhampark.com
- ✍ S Pepper
- 🖥 www.pavenhampark.com

South Beds (1892)
Warden Hill Road, Luton LU2 7AE
- ☎ **(01582) 591500**
- 📠 (01582) 495381
- ✉ office@southbedsgolfclub.co.uk
- ✍ RJ Wright (01582) 591500
- 🖥 www.southbedsgolfclub.co.uk

Stockwood Park (1973)
Public
Stockwood Park, London Rd, Luton LU1 4LX
- ☎ **(01582) 413704**
- 📠 (01582) 481001
- ✉ spgc@hotmail.co.uk
- ✍ Brian E Clark (Club Admin Officer)
- 🖥 www.activeluton.co.uk

Tilsworth (1972)
Pay and play
Dunstable Rd, Tilsworth, Dunstable LU7 9PU
- ☎ **(01525) 210721/210722**
- 📠 (01525) 210465
- ✉ info@tilsworthgolf.co.uk
- ✍ N Webb
- 🖥 www.tilsworthgolf.co.uk

Wyboston Lakes (1978)
Public
Wyboston Lakes, Wyboston MK44 3AL
- ☎ **(01480) 223004**
- 📠 (01480) 407330
- ✍ DJ Little (Mgr)
- 🖥 www.wybostonlakes.co.uk

Berkshire

Bearwood Golf Club   (1986)
Mole Road, Sindlesham, Berkshire
RG11 5DB
- ☎ (0118) 976 0060
- 🖥 (0118) 977 2687
- ✉ barrytustin@btconnect.com
- ✍ BFC Tustin (Mgr)
- 🖥 www.bearwoodgolfclub.com

Bearwood Lakes   (1996)
Proprietary
Bearwood Road, Sindlesham RG41 4SJ
- ☎ (0118) 979 7900
- 🖥 (0118) 979 2911
- ✉ info@bearwoodlakes.co.uk
- ✍ Carl Rutherford (MD)
- 🖥 www.bearwoodlakes.co.uk

The Berkshire   (1928)
Swinley Road, Ascot SL5 8AY
- ☎ (01344) 621495
- 🖥 (01344) 623328
- ✉ admin@theberkshire.co.uk
- ✍ Lt Col JCF Hunt (01344) 621496
- 🖥 www.theberkshire.co.uk

Billingbear Park   (1985)
Pay and play
The Straight Mile, Wokingham RG40 5SJ
- ☎ (01344) 869259
- 🖥 (01344) 869259
- ✉ info@billingbearpark.com
- ✍ Mrs JR Blainey
- 🖥 www.billingbearpark.co.uk

Bird Hills Golf Centre   (1985)
Public
Drift Road, Hawthorn Hill, Maidenhead
SL6 3ST
- ☎ (01628) 771030
- 🖥 (01628) 631023
- ✉ info@birdhills.co.uk
- ✍ Hannah Edwards
- 🖥 www.birdhills.co.uk

Blue Mountain Golf Centre
(1993)
Pay and play
Wood Lane, Binfield RG42 4EX
- ☎ (01344) 300200
- 🖥 (01344) 360960
- ✉ bluemountain@crown-golf.co.uk
- ✍ Grant Convey (Gen Mgr)
- 🖥 www.crown-golf.co.uk

Calcot Park   (1930)
Bath Road, Calcot, Reading RG31 7RN
- ☎ (0118) 942 7124
- 🖥 (0118) 945 3373
- ✉ info@calcotpark.com
- ✍ Kim Brake
- 🖥 www.calcotpark.com

Castle Royle   (1994)
Knowl Hill, Reading RG10 9XA
- ☎ (01628) 825442

Caversham Heath   (2000)
Proprietary
Chazey Heath, Mapledurham, Reading
RG4 7UT
- ☎ (0118) 947 8600
- 🖥 (0118) 947 8700
- ✉ info@cavershamgolf.co.uk
- ✍ Michael Palk
- 🖥 www.cavershamgolf.co.uk

Datchet   (1890)
Buccleuch Road, Datchet SL3 9BP
- ☎ (01753) 543887 (Clubhouse)
- 🖥 (01753) 541872
- ✉ secretary@datchetgolfclub.co.uk
- ✍ KR Smith (01753) 543887
- 🖥 www.datchetgolfclub.co.uk

Deanwood Park   (1995)
Pay and play
Stockcross, Newbury RG20 8JP
- ☎ (01635) 48772
- 🖥 (01635) 48772
- ✉ golf@deanwoodpark.co.uk
- ✍ John Bowness
- 🖥 www.deanwoodpark.co.uk

Donnington Grove Country Club
Donnington Grove, Grove Road, Donnington
RG14 2LA
- ☎ (01635) 581000
- 🖥 (01635) 552259
- ✉ enquiries@parasampia.com
- ✍ S Greenacre (Mgr)
- 🖥 www.parasampia.com

Donnington Valley   (1985)
Proprietary
Snelsmore House, Snelsmore Common,
Newbury RG14 3BG
- ☎ (01635) 568142
- 🖥 (01635) 41889
- ✉ golf@donningtonvalley.co.uk
- ✍ Peter Smith (01635) 568144
- 🖥 www.donningtonvalleygolfclub.co.uk

Downshire   (1973)
Public
Easthampstead Park, Wokingham
RG40 3DH
- ☎ (01344) 302030
- 🖥 (01344) 301020
- ✉ downshiregc@bracknell-forest.gov.uk
- ✍ P Stanwick (Golf Mgr)
- 🖥 www.bracknell-forest.gov.uk/downshiregolf

East Berkshire   (1903)
Ravenswood Ave, Crowthorne RG45 6BD
- ☎ (01344) 772041
- 🖥 (01344) 777378
- ✉ thesecretary@eastberkshiregolfclub.com
- ✍ C Day
- 🖥 www.eastberkshiregolfclub.com

Goring & Streatley   (1895)
Rectory Road, Streatley-on-Thames
RG8 9QA
- ☎ (01491) 873229
- 🖥 (01491) 875224
- ✉ secretary@goringgolf.co.uk
- ✍ M Evans
- 🖥 www.goringgolf.co.uk

Hennerton   (1992)
Proprietary
Crazies Hill Road, Wargrave RG10 8LT
- ☎ (0118) 940 1000
- 🖥 (0118) 940 1042
- ✉ info@hennertongolfclub.co.uk
- ✍ G Johnson (0118) 940 1000
- 🖥 www.hennertongolfclub.co.uk

Hurst Ladies   (1979)
Public
c/o Dinton Pastures Country Park, Davis
Street, Hurst, Wokingham RG10 0SU
- ☎ (01189) 751693
- ✍ Mrs A Haynes
- ⊕ Mens Club have disbanded – Ladies
  continues. Course still operating
  under countryside services.

Lavender Park
Swinley Road, Ascot SL5 8BD
- ☎ (01344) 893344
- 🖥 www.lavenderparkgolf.co.uk

Maidenhead   (1896)
Shoppenhangers Road, Maidenhead
SL6 2PZ
- ☎ (01628) 624693

The Berkshire Trophy

The Berkshire Trophy, an important 72-hole Tournament in The R&A Calendar for Amateurs with a handicap of +1 or better. Hosted by the Berkshire Golf Club (founded in 1928), the Trophy was first contested in 1946. Its distinquished list of past winners includes Sir Michael Bonallack, Peter Oosterhuis, Nick Faldo, Sandy Lyle and Ross Fisher.

The Club also hosts The Lady Astor Salver for for Amateur Ladies, first contested in 1951.

☎ (01628) 780758
✉ manager@maidenheadgolf.co.uk
✍ J Pugh
▤ www.maidenheadgolf.co.uk

Mapledurham (1992)
Mapledurham, Reading RG4 7UD
☎ **(0118) 946 3353**
✉ d.reeves@clubhaus.com

Mill Ride (1990)
Mill Ride, Ascot SL5 8LT
☎ **(01344) 886777**
📠 (01344) 886820
✉ r.greenwood@mill-ride.com
✍ Robin Greenwood (Gen Mgr)
▤ www.mill-ride.com

Newbury & Crookham
(1873)
Bury's Bank Road, Greenham Common, Newbury RG19 8BZ
☎ **(01635) 40035**
✉ ed.richardson@newburygolf.co.uk
✍ E Richardson (01635) 40035
▤ www.newburygolf.co.uk

Newbury Racecourse
(1994)
The Racecourse, Newbury RG14 7NZ
☎ **(01635) 551464**
✍ N Mitchell
▤ www.nrgc.co.uk

Reading (1910)
17 Kidmore End Road, Emmer Green, Reading RG4 8SG
☎ **(0118) 947 2909**
📠 (0118) 946 4468
✉ secretary@readinggolfclub.com
✍ A Chaundy (0118) 947 2909
▤ www.readinggolfclub.com

Royal Ascot (1887)
Winkfield Road, Ascot SL5 7LJ
☎ **(01344) 625175**
📠 (01344) 872330
✉ admin@royalascotgolfclub.co.uk
✍ Mrs S Thompson (01344) 625175
▤ www.royalascotgolfclub.co.uk

The Royal Household
(1901)
Buckingham Palace, London SW1 1AA
☎ **(0207) 930 4832**
📠 (0207) 663 4083
✉ rhgc@royal.gsx.gov.uk
✍ Peter Walter (Secretary)
⊕ Members and guests only.

Sand Martins (1993)
Proprietary
Finchampstead Road, Wokingham RG40 3RQ
☎ **(0118) 979 2711**
📠 (0118) 977 0282
✉ info@sandmartins.com
✍ Mr Rob Gumbrell (Mgr) (0118) 9029967
▤ www.sandmartins.com

Sonning (1914)
Proprietary
Duffield Road, Sonning, Reading RG4 6GJ
☎ **(0118) 969 3332**
📠 (0118) 944 8409
✉ secretary@sonning-golf-club.co.uk
✍ Chris Foley
▤ www.sonning-golf-club.co.uk

Swinley Forest (1909)
Coronation Road, Ascot SL5 9LE
☎ **(01344) 620197**
📠 (01344) 874733
✉ office@swinleyfgc.co.uk
✍ Stewart Zuill (01344) 295283
⊕ 18h L6062 Par 69 SSS 70

Temple (1909)
Henley Road, Hurley, Maidenhead SL6 5LH
☎ **(01628) 824795**
📠 (01628) 828119
✉ secretary@templegolfclub.co.uk
✍ KGM Adderley (01628) 824795
▤ www.templegolfclub.co.uk

Theale Golf Club (1996)
Proprietary
North Street, Theale, Reading RG7 5EX
☎ **(01189) 305331**
✉ info@thealegolf.com
✍ M Lowe
▤ www.thealegolf.com

West Berkshire (1975)
Proprietary
Chaddleworth, Newbury RG20 7DU
☎ **(01488) 638574**
📠 (01488) 638781
✉ info@thewbgc.co.uk
✍ Mrs CM Clayton
▤ www.thewbgc.co.uk

Winter Hill (1976)
Proprietary
Grange Lane, Cookham SL6 9RP
☎ **(01628) 527613**
📠 (01628) 527479
✉ winterhilladministration@johnlewis.co.uk
✍ Clare Leech (01628) 536071
▤ www.winterhillgolfclub.net

Wokefield Park (1998)
Proprietary
Goodboys Lane, Mortimer, Reading RG7 3AH
☎ **(0118) 933 4072**
📠 (0118) 933 4031
✉ wokgolfteam@devervenues.co.uk
✍ Tim Gilpin (Mgr)
▤ www.deveregolf.co.uk

Buckinghamshire

Aylesbury Golf Centre
(1992)
Public
Hulcott Lane, Bierton HP22 5GA
☎ **(01296) 393644**
✉ kevinpartington@hotmail.co.uk

✍ K Partington (Mgr)
▤ www.aylesburygolfclub.co.uk

Aylesbury Park (1996)
Proprietary
Andrews Way, Oxford Road, Aylesbury HP17 8QQ
☎ **(01296) 399196**
✉ info@aylesburyparkgolf.com
✍ Damian Brooks
▤ www.aylesburyparkgolf.com

Beaconsfield (1902)
Seer Green, Beaconsfield HP9 2UR
☎ **(01494) 676545**
📠 (01494) 681148
✉ secretary@beaconsfieldgolfclub.co.uk
▤ www.beaconsfieldgolfclub.co.uk

Buckingham (1914)
Tingewick Road, Buckingham MK18 4AE
☎ **(01280) 815566**
📠 (01280) 821812
✉ admin@buckinghamgolfclub.co.uk
✍ P Frost
▤ www.buckinghamgolfclub.co.uk

Buckinghamshire (1992)
Proprietary
Denham Court Mansion, Denham Court Drive, Denham UB9 5PG
☎ **(01895) 835777**
📠 (01895) 835210
✉ enquiries@buckinghamshiregc.co.uk
✍ D Griffiths (01895) 836803
▤ www.buckinghamshiregc.com

Burnham Beeches (1891)
Green Lane, Burnham, Slough SL1 8EG
☎ **(01628) 661448**
📠 (01628) 668968
✉ enquiries@bbgc.co.uk
✍ P C Dawson (Mgr)
▤ www.bbgc.co.uk

Chartridge Park (1989)
Chartridge, Chesham HP5 2TF
☎ **(01494) 791772**
✉ info@cpgc.co.uk
▤ www.cpgc.co.uk

Chesham & Ley Hill (1900)
Ley Hill, Chesham HP5 1UZ
☎ **(01494) 784541**
📠 (01494) 785506
✉ secretary@cheshamgolf.co.uk
✍ James Short
▤ www.cheshamgolf.co.uk

Chiltern Forest (1979)
Aston Hill, Halton, Aylesbury HP22 5NQ
☎ **(01296) 631267**
📠 (01296) 632709
✉ generalmanager@chilternforest.co.uk
✍ Anthony Roberts (Gen Mgr) (01296) 631267
▤ www.chilternforest.co.uk

Denham (1910)
Tilehouse Lane, Denham UB9 5DE
☎ **(01895) 832022**
🖳 (01895) 835340
✍ JW Tucker
🖹 www.denhamgolfclub.co.uk

Ellesborough (1905)
Butlers Cross, Aylesbury HP17 0TZ
☎ **(01296) 622114**
🖳 (01296) 622114
🖂 office@ellesboroughgolf.co.uk
✍ Mr Andy Hayes
🖹 www.ellesboroughgolf.co.uk

Farnham Park (1974)
Public
Park Road, Stoke Poges, Slough SL2 4PJ
☎ **(01753) 643332**
🖳 (01753) 646617
🖂 farnhamparkgolf@southbucks
.gov.uk
✍ Nigel Whitton Golf Mgr
🖹 www.farnhamparkgolfcourse.co.uk

Flackwell Heath (1904)
Treadaway Road, Flackwell Heath, High
Wycombe HP10 9PE
☎ **(01628) 520929**
🖳 (01628) 530040
🖂 secretary@fhgc.co.uk
✍ P Clarke
🖹 www.fhgc.co.uk

Gerrards Cross (1921)
Chalfont Park, Gerrards Cross SL9 0QA
☎ **(01753) 883263**
🖳 (01753) 883593
🖂 secretary@gxgolf.co.uk
✍ Simon Maynard
🖹 www.gxgolf.co.uk

Harewood Downs (1907)
Cokes Lane, Chalfont St Giles HP8 4TA
☎ **(01494) 762184**
🖳 (01494) 766869
🖂 secretary@hdgc.co.uk
✍ SJ Thornton (01494) 762184
🖹 www.hdgc.co.uk

Harleyford (1996)
Harleyford Estate, Henley Road, Marlow
SL7 2SP
☎ **(01628) 816161**
🖳 (01628) 816160
🖂 info@harleyfordgolf.co.uk
✍ Trevor Collingwood 01628 816164
🖹 www.harleyfordgolf.co.uk

Hazlemere (1982)
Penn Road, Hazlemere, High Wycombe
HP15 7LR
☎ **(01494) 719300**
🖳 (01494) 713914
🖂 enquiries@hazlemeregolfclub.co.uk
✍ Chris Mahoney
🖹 www.hazlemeregolfclub.co.uk

Hedsor (2000)
Pay and play
Broad Lane, Wooburn Common, Bucks
HP10 0JW
☎ **(01628) 851285**

🖂 info@hedsorgolfcourse.co.uk
✍ Stuart Cannon
🖹 www.hedsorgolfcourse.co.uk

Huntswood (1996)
Pay and play
Taplow Common Road, Burnham SL1 8LS
☎ **(01628) 667144**
🖳 (01628) 663145
🖂 huntswoodgc@btconnect.com
✍ John Lake (01628) 667144
🖹 www.huntswoodgolf.com

Iver (1983)
Hollow Hill Lane, Iver SL0 0JJ
☎ **(01753) 655615**
🖂 ivergolf@fsmail.net
🖹 www.ivergolfcourse.co.uk

Ivinghoe (1967)
Proprietary
Wellcroft, Ivinghoe, Leighton Buzzard
LU7 9EF
☎ **(01296) 668696**
🖳 (01296) 662755
🖂 info@ivinghoegolfclub.co.uk
✍ Mrs E Culley (01296) 668696
🖹 www.ivinghoegolfclub.co.uk

Kingfisher CC (1995)
Proprietary
Buckingham Road, Deanshanger, Milton
Keynes MK19 6JY
☎ **(01908) 560354**
🖂 sales.kingfisher@btopenworld.com
🖹 www.kingfisher-uk.com

The Lambourne Club (1992)
Proprietary
Dropmore Road, Burnham SL1 8NF
☎ **(01628) 666755**
🖳 (01628) 663301
🖂 info@lambourneclub.co.uk
✍ D Hart (Gen Mgr)
🖹 www.lambourneclub.co.uk

Little Chalfont (1981)
Lodge Lane, Chalfont St Giles HP8 4AJ
☎ **(01494) 764877**

Magnolia Park
Arncott Road, Boarstall HP18 9XX
☎ **(01844) 239700**
🖳 (01844) 238991
🖂 info@magnoliapark.co.uk
✍ Debbie Ludlow
🖹 www.magnoliapark.co.uk

Oakland Park (1994)
Proprietary
Three Households, Chalfont St Giles HP8
4LW
☎ **(01494) 871277**
🖳 (01494) 874692
🖂 info@oaklandparkgolf.co.uk
✍ I Donnelly (Gen Mgr)
🖹 www.oaklandparkgolf.co.uk

Princes Risborough (1990)
Lee Road, Saunderton Lee, Princes
Risborough HP27 9NX
☎ **(01844) 346989 (Clubhouse)**

🖳 (01844) 274938
🖂 mlgolfltd@uwclub.net
✍ J Murray (Man Dir)
🖹 www.prgc.co.uk

Richings Park (1996)
Proprietary
North Park, Iver SL0 9DL
☎ **(01753) 655352**
🖳 (01753) 655409
🖂 info@richingspark.co.uk
✍ Steve Coles (01753) 655370
🖹 www.richingspark.co.uk

Silverstone (1992)
Proprietary
Silverstone Road, Stowe, Buckingham
MK18 5LH
☎ **(01280) 850005**
🖳 (01280) 850156
🖂 proshop@silverstonegolfclub
.co.uk
✍ S Barnes
🖹 www.silverstonegolfclub.co.uk

Stoke Park (1908)
Park Road, Stoke Poges SL2 4PG
☎ **(01753) 717171**
🖳 (01753) 717181
🖂 info@stokepark.com
✍ Miss Kelly Ford (01753) 717116
🖹 www.stokepark.com

Stowe (1974)
Stowe, Buckingham MK18 5EH
✍ D Procter (01280) 818024

Thorney Park (1992)
Proprietary
Thorney Mill Road, Iver SL0 9AL
☎ **(01895) 422095**
🖳 (01895) 431307
🖂 sales@thorneypark.co.uk
✍ P Gray
🖹 www.thorneypark.com

Three Locks (1992)
Great Brickhill, Milton Keynes
MK17 9BH
☎ **(01525) 270050**
🖳 (01525) 270470
🖂 info@threelocksgolfclub.co.uk
✍ P Critchley
🖹 www.threelocksgolfclub.co.uk

Wavendon Golf Centre
(1990)
Pay and play
Lower End Road, Wavendon, Milton Keynes
MK17 8DA
☎ **(01908) 281811**
🖳 (01908) 281257
🖂 wavendon@hotmail.co.uk
✍ G Iron
🖹 www.jackbarker.com

Weston Turville (1973)
Proprietary
New Road, Weston Turville, Aylesbury
HP22 5QT
☎ **(01296) 424084**
🖳 (01296) 395376

✉ enquiries@westonturvillegolfclub
.co.uk
🖉 D Allen
🖥 www.westonturvillegolfclub.co.uk

Wexham Park (1977)
Pay and play
Wexham Street, Wexham, Slough SL3 6ND
☎ **(01753) 663271**
📠 (01753) 663318
✉ info@wexhamparkgolfcourse.co.uk
🖉 J Kennedy
🖥 www.wexhamparkgolfcourse.co.uk

Whiteleaf (1907)
Whiteleaf, Princes Risborough HP27 0LY
☎ **(01844) 343097/274058**
✉ info@whiteleafgolfclub.co.uk
🖉 M Piercy (01844) 345472
🖥 www.whiteleafgolfclub.co.uk

Windmill Hill (1972)
Pay and play
Tattenhoe Lane, Bletchley MK3 7RB
☎ **(01908) 631113 (Bookings)**
✉ info@thewindmillonline.co.uk
🖉 Diana Allen (01908) 647615
🖥 www.thewindmillonline.co.uk

Woburn (1976)
Little Brickhill, Milton Keynes MK17 9LJ
☎ **(01908) 370756**
📠 (01908) 378436
✉ enquiries@woburngolf.com
🖉 Jason O'Malley (Gen Mgr)
🖥 www.discoverwoburn.co.uk

Wycombe Heights (1991)
Pay and play
Rayners Avenue, Loudwater, High Wycombe
HP10 9SZ
☎ **(01494) 816686**
📠 (01494) 816728
✉ info@wycombeheightsgc.co.uk
🖉 Steve West
🖥 www.wycombeheightsgc.co.uk

Cambridgeshire

Abbotsley (1986)
Proprietary
Potton Road, St Neots PE19 6XN
☎ **(01480) 474000**
📠 (01480) 471018
✉ sales@abbotsley.com
🖉 Helen Ladis (01480) 474000
🖥 www.abbotsley.com

Bourn (1991)
Proprietary
Toft Road, Bourn, Cambridge CB23 2TT
☎ **(01954) 718057**
📠 (01954) 718908
✉ info@bourngolfandleisure.co.uk
🖥 www.bourngolfand leisure.co.uk

Brampton Park (1991)
Buckden Road, Brampton, Huntingdon
PE28 4NF
☎ **(01480) 434700**
✉ admin@bramptonparkgc.co.uk

🖉 Lisa Charlton (Gen Mgr)
🖥 www.bramptonparkgc.co.uk

Cambridge (1995)
Station Road, Longstanton, Cambridge
CB4 5DS
☎ **(01954) 789388**
✉ klgcambridgegolf@tiscali.co.uk
🖉 K Green

Cambridge Meridian
(1944)
Proprietary
Comberton Road, Toft, Cambridge
CB23 2RY
☎ **(01223) 264700**
📠 (01223) 264701
✉ meridian@golfsocieties.com
🖉 Steve Creighton
🖥 www.golfsocieties.com

Cromwell (1986)
Pay and play
Potton Road, St Neots PE19 6XN
☎ **(01480) 408900**
📠 (01480) 471018
✉ sales@abbotsley.com
🖉 Helen Lavis (01480) 474000
🖥 www.abbotsley.com

Elton Furze (1993)
Proprietary
Bullock Road, Haddon, Peterborough
PE7 3TT
☎ **(01832) 280189**
📠 (01832) 280299
✉ helen@efgc.co.uk
🖉 Fiona Martin (Sec)
🖥 www.efgc.co.uk

Ely City (1961)
107 Cambridge Road, Ely CB7 4HX
☎ **(01353) 662751**
📠 (01353) 668636
✉ info@elygolf.co.uk
🖉 Tom Munt (Mgr)
  (01353) 662751
🖥 www.elygolf.co.uk

Girton (1936)
Dodford Lane, Girton CB3 0QE
☎ **(01223) 276169**
📠 (01223) 277150
✉ info@girtongolf.co.uk
🖉 Miss VM Webb
🖥 www.girtongolf.co.uk

The Gog Magog (1901)
Shelford Bottom, Cambridge CB22 3AB
☎ **(01223) 247626**
📠 (01223) 414990
✉ secretary@gogmagog.co.uk
🖉 Mr K Mader
🖥 www.gogmagog.co.uk

Hemingford Abbots Golf
Club (1991)
Proprietary
New Farm Lodge, Cambridge Road,
Hemingford Abbots, Cambs PE18 9HQ
☎ **(01480) 495000**
📠 (01480) 496000

🖉 RD Paton
🖥 www.astroman.co.uk

Heydon Grange G&CC
(1994)
Heydon, Royston SG8 7NS
☎ **(01763) 208988**
📠 (01763) 208926
✉ enquiries@heydongrange.co.uk
🖉 S Akhtar
🖥 www.heydongrange.co.uk

Lakeside Lodge (1992)
Public & Proprietary
Fen Road, Pidley, Huntingdon PE28 3DF
☎ **(01487) 740540**
📠 (01487) 740852
✉ info@lakeside-lodge.co.uk
🖉 Mrs J Hopkins
🖥 www.lakeside-lodge.co.uk

March (1922)
Frogs Abbey, Grange Rd, March
PE15 0YH
☎ **(01354) 652364**
✉ secretary@marchgolfclub.co.uk
🖉 M Simpson
🖥 www.marchgolfclub.co.uk

Menzies Cambridgeshire
(1974)
Proprietary
Bar Hill, Cambridge CB23 8EU
☎ **(01954) 780098**
📠 (01954) 780010
✉ cambridge.golfpro@menzieshotels
.co.uk
🖉 Tom Turner (Golf Ops Mgr)
🖥 www.menzieshotels.co.uk

New Malton (1993)
Proprietary/Members/
Malton Lane, Meldreth, Royston
SG8 6PE
☎ **(01763) 262200**
📠 (01763) 262209
✉ info@newmaltongolf.co.uk
🖉 Brian Mudge (Professional)
🖥 www.newmaltongolf.co.uk

Old Nene G&CC (1992)
Muchwood Lane, Bodsey, Ramsey
PE26 2XQ
☎ **(01487) 815622**
✉ george.stoneman@virgin.net

Orton Meadows (1987)
Public
Ham Lane, Peterborough PE2 5UU
☎ **(01733) 237478**
✉ omgc@btinternet.com
🖉 WL Stocks (01733) 237478
🖥 www.omgc.co.uk

Peterborough Milton
(1937)
Milton Ferry, Peterborough PE6 7AG
☎ **(01733) 380489**
📠 (01733) 380489
✉ admin@pmgc.org.uk
🖉 Andy Izod (01733) 380489
🖥 www.pmgc.org.uk

Ramsey   (1964)
4 Abbey Terrace, Ramsey, Huntingdon PE26 1DD
- ☎ **(01487) 812600**
- 📠 (01487) 815746
- ✉ admin@ramseyclub.co.uk
- 🖉 John Bufton
- 🖥 www.ramseyclub.co.uk

St Ives   (1923)
Needingworth Road, St Ives PE27 6NB
- ☎ **(01480) 499920 Ext 4**
- 📠 (01480) 301489
- ✉ manager@stivesgolfclub.co.uk
- 🖉 Mike Kjenstad (01480) 499920 Ext 4
- 🖥 www.stivesgolfclub.co.uk

St Neots   (1890)
Crosshall Road, St Neots PE19 7GE
- ☎ **(01480) 472363**
- 📠 (01480) 472363
- ✉ office@stneots-golfclub.co.uk
- 🖉 M.V.Truswell
- 🖥 www.stneots-golfclub.co.uk

Stilton Oaks   (1997)
Proprietary
High Street, Stilton, Cambridgeshire PE7 3RB
- ☎ **(01733) 245233**
- 🖉 Mr D Darke (Mgr)

Thorney Golf Centre   (1991)
Public
English Drove, Thorney, Peterborough PE6 0TJ
- ☎ **(01733) 270570**
- 📠 (01733) 270842
- ✉ info@thorneygolfcentre.com
- 🖉 Jane Hind
- 🖥 www.thorneygolfcentre.com

Thorpe Wood   (1975)
Pay and play
Nene Parkway, Peterborough PE3 6SE
- ☎ **(01733) 267701**
- 📠 (01733) 332774
- ✉ enquiries@thorpewoodgolfcourse .co.uk
- 🖉 R Palmer
- 🖥 www.thorpewoodgolfcourse.co.uk

Tydd St Giles Golf & Leisure Estate   (1993)
Proprietary
Kirkgate, Tydd St Giles, Cambridge PE13 5NZ
- ☎ **(01945) 871007**
- ✉ enquiries@tyddgolf.com
- 🖉 Daniel Newell
- 🖥 www.pureleisuregroup.com

Waterbeach   (1968)
Public
Waterbeach Barracks, Waterbeach, Cambridge CB5 9PA
- ☎ **(01223) 441199 (Sec)**
- 📠 (01223) 204636
- ✉ waterbeach.golfclub@btconnect .com

- 🖉 Maj (Retd) DA Hornby (Hon)
- 🖥 www.waterbeachgolfclub.co.uk

Channel Islands

Alderney
Route des Carrieres, Alderney GY9 3YD
- ☎ **(01481) 822835**

La Grande Mare   (1994)
Proprietary
Vazon Bay, Castel, Guernsey GY5 7LL
- ☎ **(01481) 253544**
- 📠 (01481) 255194
- ✉ golf@lagrandemare.com
- 🖉 N Graham (01481) 253544
- 🖥 www.lagrandemare.com

Les Mielles G&CC   (1994)
Public
St Ouens Bay, Jersey JE3 7FQ
- ☎ **(01534) 482787**
- 📠 (01534) 485414
- ✉ golf@lesmielles.co.je
- 🖉 J Le Brun (Golf Dir)
- 🖥 www.lesmielles.com

La Moye   (1902)
La Moye, St Brelade, Jersey JE3 8GQ
- ☎ **(01534) 743401**
- 📠 (01534) 747289
- ✉ secretary@lamoyegolfclub.co.uk
- 🖉 A H Mackenzie
- 🖥 www.lamoyegolfclub.co.uk

Les Ormes   (1996)
Mont à la Brune, St Brelade, Jersey JE3 8FL
- ☎ **(01534) 497000**
- 📠 (01534) 499122
- ✉ reception@lesormes.je
- 🖉 M Harris (01534) 497015
- 🖥 www.lesormes.je

Royal Guernsey   (1890)
L'Ancresse, Guernsey GY3 5BY
- ☎ **(01481) 246523**
- 📠 (01481) 243960
- ✉ bob.rggc@cwgsy.net
- 🖉 R Bushby (01481) 246523
- 🖥 www.royalguernseygolfclub.com

Royal Jersey   (1878)
Grouville, Jersey JE3 9BD
- ☎ **(01534) 854416**
- ✉ thesecretary@royaljersey.com
- 🖉 DJ Attwood
- 🖥 www.royaljersey.com

St Clements   (1925)
Public
St Clements, Jersey JE2 6QN
- ☎ **(01534) 721938**
- ✉ stclementsgolf@jerseymail.co.uk

St Pierre Park   (1986)
Rohais, St Peter Port, Guernsey GY1 1FD
- ☎ **(01481) 727039**
- 📠 (01481) 712041
- ✉ golf@stpierrepark.co.uk
- 🖉 James Child
- 🖥 www.stpierreparkgolf.co.uk

Wheatlands Golf Club   (2004)
Off Old Beaumont Hill, St Peter, Jersey JE3 7ED
- ☎ **(01534) 888877**
- 📠 (01534) 769880
- ✉ info@wheatlandsjersey.com
- 🖥 www.wheatlandsgolf.com

Cheshire

Alder Root   (1993)
Proprietary
Alder Root Lane, Winwick, Warrington WA2 8RZ
- ☎ **(01925) 291919**
- 📠 (01925) 291961
- ✉ office@alderrootgolfclub.com
- 🖉 E Lander
- 🖥 www.alderroot.com

Alderley Edge   (1907)
Brook Lane, Alderley Edge SK9 7RU
- ☎ **(01625) 586200**
- ✉ office@aegc.co.uk
- 🖉 J Dixon (01625) 583073
- 🖥 www.aegc.co.uk

Aldersey Green   (1993)
Proprietary
Aldersey, Chester CH3 9EH
- ☎ **(01829) 782157**
- ✉ bradburygolf@aol.com
- 🖥 alderseygreengolfclub.co.uk

Altrincham Municipal   (1893)
Public
Stockport Road, Timperley, Altrincham WA15 7LP
- ☎ **(0161) 928 0761**
- 🖉 C J Schofield 0161 861 0201
- 🖥 www.altrinchamgolfclub.org

Alvaston Hall   (1992)
Proprietary
Middlewich Road, Nantwich CW5 6PD
- ☎ **(01270) 628473**

Antrobus   (1993)
Proprietary
Foggs Lane, Antrobus, Northwich CW9 6JQ
- ☎ **(01925) 730890**
- 🖉 Vacant
- 🖥 www.antrobusgolfclub.co.uk

Ashton-on-Mersey   (1897)
Church Lane, Sale M33 5QQ
- ☎ **(0161) 976 4390 (Clubhouse)**
- 📠 (0161) 976 4390
- ✉ golf.aomgc@btconnect.com
- 🖉 R Coppock (0161) 976 4390
- 🖥 www.aomgc.co.uk

Astbury   (1922)
Peel Lane, Astbury, Congleton CW12 4RE
- ☎ **(01260) 272772**
- 📠 (01260) 276420
- ✉ admin@astburygolfclub.com

✍ P Bentley (01260) 272772
🖥 www.astburygolfclub.com

Birchwood (1979)
Kelvin Close, Birchwood, Warrington WA3 7PB
☎ **(01925) 818819, Pro Shop**
(01925) 225216
📠 (01925) 822403
📧 enquiries@birchwoodgolfclub
.co.uk
✍ A Harper (Facilities Mgr)
🖥 www.birchwoodgolfclub.co.uk

Bramall Park (1894)
20 Manor Road, Bramhall, Stockport SK7 3LY
☎ **(0161) 485 3119 (Clubhouse)**
📠 (0161) 485 7101
📧 secretary@bramallparkgolfclub
.co.uk
✍ DE Shardlow (Hon Sec)
(0161) 485 7101
🖥 www.bramallparkgolfclub.co.uk

Bramhall (1905)
Ladythorn Road, Bramhall, Stockport SK7 2EY
☎ **(0161) 439 6092**
📠 (0161) 439 6092
📧 office@bramhallgolfclub.com
✍ R Attwater (Hon) (0161) 439 6092
🖥 www.bramhallgolfclub.com

Carden Park Hotel Golf Resort & Spa
Chester CH3 9DQ
☎ **(01829) 731534**
📠 (01829) 731599
📧 reservations.carden@devere-hotels.com
✍ K Proctor (01829) 731000
🖥 www.cardenpark.co.uk

Cheadle (1885)
Shiers Drive, Cheadle Road, Cheadle SK8 1HW
☎ **(0161) 491 4452**
📧 cheadlegolfclub@msn.com
✍ J V Heyes
🖥 www.cheadlegolfclub.com

Chester (1901)
Curzon Park, Chester CH4 8AR
☎ **(01244) 677760**
📧 secretary@chestergolfclub.co.uk
✍ Mark J Williams (01244) 677760
🖥 www.chestergc.co.uk

Congleton (1898)
Biddulph Road, Congleton CW12 3LZ
☎ **(01260) 273540**
📠 (01260) 290902
📧 congletongolfclub@btconnect.com
✍ D Lancake
🖥 www.congletongolf.co.uk

Crewe (1911)
Fields Road, Haslington, Crewe CW1 5TB
☎ **(01270) 584227 (Steward)**
📠 (01270) 256482
📧 secretary@crewegolfclub.co.uk

✍ H Taylor (01270) 584099
🖥 www.crewegolfclub.co.uk

Davenport (1913)
Worth Hall, Middlewood Road, Poynton SK12 1TS
☎ **(01625) 876951**
📠 (01625) 877489
📧 admin@davenportgolf.co.uk
✍ JC Souter (01625) 876951
🖥 www.davenportgolf.co.uk

Delamere Forest (1910)
Station Road, Delamere, Northwich CW8 2JE
☎ **(01606) 883800**
📧 delamere@btconnect.com
info@delameregolf.co.uk
✍ M Towers (01606) 883800
🖥 www.delameregolf.co.uk

Disley (1889)
Stanley Hall Lane, Disley, Stockport SK12 2JX
☎ **(01663) 764001**
📠 (01663) 762678
📧 secretary@disleygolfclub.co.uk
✍ P Housley
🖥 www.disleygolfclub.co.uk

Dukinfield (1913)
Yew Tree Lane, Dukinfield SK16 5GF
☎ **(0161) 338 2340**
📠 (0161) 303 0205
📧 secretary@dukinfieldgolfclub
.co.uk
✍ K Marsh (0161) 338 2340
🖥 www.dukinfieldgolfclub.co.uk

Dunham Forest G&CC (1961)
Oldfield Lane, Altrincham WA14 4TY
☎ **(0161) 928 2605**
📠 (0161) 929 8975
📧 enquiries@dunhamforest.com
✍ Mrs A Woolf
🖥 www.dunhamforest.com

Eaton (1965)
Guy Lane, Waverton, Chester CH3 7PH
☎ **(01244) 335885**
📠 (01244) 335782
📧 office@eatongolfclub.co.uk
✍ K Brown
🖥 www.eatongolfclub.co.uk

Ellesmere Port (1971)
Public
Chester Road, Childer Thornton, South Wirral CH66 1QF
☎ **(0151) 339 7689**

Frodsham (1990)
Simons Lane, Frodsham WA6 6HE
☎ **(01928) 732159**
📧 office@frodshamgolf.co.uk
🖥 www.frodshamgolf.co.uk

Gatley (1912)
Waterfall Farm, Styal Road, Heald Green, Cheadle SK8 3TW
☎ **(0161) 437 2091**

📧 secretary@gatleygolfclub.com
✍ Michael J Coffey
🖥 www.gatleygolfclub.com

Gorstyhill Golf Club
Wychwood Village, Weston, Crewe, Cheshire CW2 5TD
☎ **(01270) 829166**
📧 info@gorstyhillgolf.co.uk
🖥 www.gorstyhillgolf.co.uk

Hale (1903)
Rappax Road, Hale, Altrincham WA15 0NU
☎ **(0161) 980 4225**
📧 secretary@halegolfclub.com
✍ C E J Wright
🖥 www.halegolfclub.com

Hartford Golf Club (2000)
Burrow Hill, Hartford, Cheshire CW8 3AP
☎ **(01606) 871162**
📠 (01606) 872182
📧 info@hartfordgolf.co.uk
🖥 www.hartfordgolf.co.uk

Hazel Grove (1913)
Buxton Road, Hazel Grove, Stockport SK7 6LU
☎ **(0161) 483 3978**
(Clubhouse)
📠 (0161) 483 3978
📧 secretary@hazelgrovegolfclub.com
✍ Jane Hill (0161) 483 3978 Opt 4
🖥 www.hazelgrovegolfclub.com

Heaton Moor (1892)
Mauldeth Road, Heaton Mersey, Stockport SK4 3NX
☎ **(0161) 432 2134**
📠 (0161) 432 2134
📧 heatonmoorgolfclub@yahoo.co.uk
✍ D Linsley
🖥 www.heatonmoorgolfclub.co.uk

Helsby (1901)
Tower's Lane, Helsby WA6 0JB
☎ **(01928) 722021**
📠 (01928) 726816
📧 secretary@helsbygolfclub.org
✍ C A Stubbs
🖥 www.helsbygolfclub.org

Heyrose (1989)
Proprietary
Budworth Road, Tabley, Knutsford WA16 0HZ
☎ **(01565) 733664**
📠 (01565) 734578
📧 info@heyrosegolfclub.com
✍ Mrs H Marsh
🖥 www.heyrosegolfclub.com

High Legh Park
Pay and play
Warrington Road, High Legh, Knutsford, Cheshire WA16 0WA
☎ **(01565) 830888**
📠 (01565) 830999
📧 info@highleghpark.com
✍ Martin Cooper (Course Director)
🖥 www.highleghpark.com

Houldsworth (1910)
Houldsworth Park, Houldsworth Street, Reddish, Stockport SK5 6BN
☎ **(0161) 442 1712**
📠 (0161) 947 9678
📧 houldsworthsecretary@hotmail.co.uk
✍ K Smith (Sec) (0161) 442 1712
🖥 www.houldsworthgolfclub.co.uk

Knights Grange (1983)
Public
Grange Lane, Winsford CW7 2PT
☎ **(01606) 552780**
📧 pam.littler @cheshirewestandchester.gov.uk
✍ Mrs P Littler (Mgr)

Knutsford (1891)
Mereheath Lane, Knutsford WA16 6HS
☎ **(01565) 633355**
📧 secretary@knutsfordgolf.com
✍ Neil Fergusson

Leigh (1906)
Kenyon Hall, Broseley Lane, Culcheth, Warrington WA3 4BG
☎ **(01925) 763130**
📠 (01925) 765097
📧 golf@leighgolf.fsnet.co.uk
✍ Antony O'Neill (01925) 762943
🖥 www.leighgolf.co.uk

Lymm (1907)
Whitbarrow Road, Lymm WA13 9AN
☎ **(01925) 755020**
📠 (01925) 755020
📧 lymmgolfclub@btconnect.com
✍ A Scully
🖥 www.lymm-golf-club.co.uk

Macclesfield (1889)
The Hollins, Macclesfield SK11 7EA
☎ **(01625) 423227**
📠 (01625) 260061
📧 secretary@maccgolfclub.co.uk
✍ B Littlewood
🖥 www.maccgolfclub.co.uk

Malkins Bank Golf Course (1980)
Public
Betchton Road, Malkins Bank, Sandbach CW11 4XN
☎ **(01270) 765931**
📠 (01270) 764730
📧 malkins.bank@cheshireeast.gov.uk
✍ P Dickenson (Sec) (07970) 281965
🖥 www.congleton.gov.uk

Marple (1892)
Barnsfold Road, Hawk Green, Marple, Stockport SK6 7EL
☎ **(0161) 427 2311 Ext 1**
📠 (0161) 427 2311 / (0161) 427 95
📧 secretary@marple.co.uk
✍ W Hibbert (0161) 427 2311/427 9525
🖥 www.marplegolfclub.co.uk

Mellor & Townscliffe (1894)
Tarden, Gibb Lane, Mellor, Stockport SK6 5NA
☎ **(0161) 427 9700 (Clubhouse)**
📠 (0161) 427 9700
✍ JV Dixon (0161) 427 2208
🖥 www.mellorgolf.co.uk

Mere G&CC (1934)
Chester Road, Mere, Knutsford WA16 6LJ
☎ **(01565) 830155**
📠 (01565) 830713
📧 sales@meregolf.co.uk
✍ P Whitehead
🖥 www.meregolf.co.uk

Mersey Valley (1995)
Proprietary
Warrington Road, Bold Heath, Widnes WA8 3XL
☎ **(0151) 424 6060**
📠 (0151) 257 9097
📧 chrismgerrard@yahoo.co.uk
✍ RM Bush (Man Dir)
🖥 www.merseyvalleygolfclub.com

Mobberley (1996)
Burleyhurst Lane, Mobberley, Knutsford WA16 7JZ
☎ **(01565) 880188**
📠 (01565) 880178
📧 info@mobgolfclub.co.uk
✍ Gary Donnison (Golf Director)
🖥 www.mobgolfclub.co.uk

Mollington Grange (1999)
Townfield Lane, Mollington, Chester CH1 6NJ
☎ **(01244) 851185**
📠 (01244) 851349
📧 info@mollingtongolfclub.co.uk
✍ Ray Stringer
🖥 www.mollingtongolfclub.co.uk

Mottram Hall Hotel (1991)
Proprietary
Wilmslow Road, Mottram St Andrew, Prestbury SK10 4QT
☎ **(01625) 820064**
📠 (01625) 829284
📧 mhgolf@devere-hotels.com
✍ Tim Hudspith (Head Golf & Leisure)
🖥 www.deveregolf.co.uk

Peover (1996)
Proprietary
Plumley Moor Road, Lower Peover WA16 9SE
☎ **(01565) 723337**
📠 (01565) 723311
📧 mail@peovergolfclub.co.uk
✍ PA Naylor (Man Dir)
🖥 www.peovergolfclub.co.uk

Portal G&CC (1992)
Cobblers Cross Lane, Tarporley CW6 0DJ
☎ **(01829) 733933**
📧 enquiries@portalgolf.co.uk
🖥 www.portalgolf.co.uk

Portal Premier (1990)
Forest Road, Tarporley CW6 0JA
☎ **(01829) 733884**
📧 enquiries.premier@portalgolf.co.uk
🖥 www.portalgolf.co.uk

Poulton Park (1978)
Dig Lane, Cinnamon Brow, Warrington WA2 0SH
☎ **(01925) 812034/822802**
📧 secretary@poultonparkgolfclub.co.uk
🖥 www.poultonparkgolfclub.co.uk

Prestbury (1920)
Macclesfield Road, Prestbury, Macclesfield SK10 4BJ
☎ **(01625) 828241**
📠 (01625) 828241
📧 office@prestburygolfclub.com
✍ N Young (01625) 828241
🖥 www.prestburygolfclub.com

Pryors Hayes (1993)
Proprietary
Willington Road, Oscroft, Tarvin CH3 8NL
☎ **(01829) 741250**
📠 (01829) 749077
📧 info@pryors-hayes.co.uk
✍ JM Quinn
🖥 www.pryorshayes.com

Queens Park (1985)
Public
Queens Park Drive, Crewe CW2 7SB
☎ **(01270) 662378**

Reaseheath (1987)
1 Ash Grove, Nantwich, Cheshire CW5 7DQ
☎ **(01270) 625131**
📠 (01270) 625665
📧 j.soddy@sky.com
✍ John Soddy (01270) 629869
🖥 www.reaseheath.ac.uk

Reddish Vale (1912)
Southcliffe Road, Reddish, Stockport SK5 7EE
☎ **(0161) 480 2359**
📠 (0161) 480 2359
📧 admin@rvgc.co.uk
✍ D J Sanders
🖥 www.rvgc.co.uk

Ringway (1909)
Hale Mount, Hale Road, Hale Barns, Altrincham WA15 8SW
☎ **(0161) 980 2630**
📠 (0161) 980 4414
📧 fiona@ringwaygolfclub.co.uk
✍ Ms F Cornelius
🖥 www.ringwaygolfclub.co.uk

Romiley (1897)
Goosehouse Green, Romiley, Stockport SK6 4LJ
☎ **(0161) 430 2392**
📧 office@romileygolfclub.org
✍ C D Haworth
🖥 www.romileygolfclub.org

Runcorn (1909)

Clifton Road, Runcorn WA7 4SU
- ☎ **(01928) 572093 (Members)**
- 🖳 (01928) 574214
- ✉ secretary@runcorngolfclub.co.uk
- ✍ G H Mayne (01928) 574214
- 🖥 www.runcorngolfclub.co.uk

Sale (1913)

Sale Lodge, Golf Road, Sale M33 2XU
- ☎ **(0161) 973 1638**
- 🖳 (0161) 962 4217
- ✉ mail@salegolfclub.com
- ✍ CJ Boyes (Hon Sec)
- 🖥 www.salegolfclub.com

Sandbach (1895)

*Middlewich Road, Sandbach, Cheshire
CW11 9EA*
- ☎ **(01270) 762117**
- ✉ sec@sandbachgolfclub.co.uk
- ✍ D Ludley
- 🖥 www.sandbachgolfclub.co.uk

Sandiway (1920)

Chester Road, Sandiway CW8 2DJ
- ☎ **(01606) 883247**
- 🖳 (01606) 888548
- ✉ information@sandiwaygolf.co.uk
- ✍ Yvonne Bould (01606) 880811
- 🖥 www.sandiwaygolf.co.uk

Stamford (1901)

*Oakfield House, Huddersfield Road,
Stalybridge SK15 3PY*
- ☎ **(01457) 832126**
- ✉ admin@stamfordgolfclub.co.uk
- ✍ J Kitchen
- 🖥 www.stamfordgolfclub.co.uk

Stockport (1905)

*Offerton Road, Offerton, Stockport
SK2 5HL*
- ☎ **(0161) 427 8369**
- 🖳 (0161) 427 8369
- ✉ info@stockportgolf.co.uk
- ✍ J O Bolt
- 🖥 www.stockportgolf.co.uk

Styal (1994)

Proprietary
Station Road, Styal SK9 4JN
- ☎ **(01625) 531359 (Bookings)**
- 🖳 (01625) 416373
- ✉ gtraynor@styalgolf.co.uk
- ✍ G Traynor
- 🖥 www.styalgolf.co.uk

Sutton Hall (1995)

Proprietary
*Aston Lane, Sutton Weaver, Runcorn
WA7 3ED*
- ☎ **(01928) 790747**
- 🖳 (01928) 759174
- ✉ info@suttonhallgolf.co.uk
- ✍ M Faulkner
- 🖥 www.suttonhallgolf.co.uk

The Tytherington Club
(1986)
Macclesfield SK10 2JP
- ☎ **(01625) 506000**

- 🖳 (01625) 506040
- ✉ tytherington.events
  @theclubcompany.com
- ✍ James Gathercole
- 🖥 www.theclubcompany.com

Upton-by-Chester (1934)

Upton Lane, Chester CH2 1EE
- ☎ **(01244) 381183**
- 🖳 (01244) 376955
- ✉ admin@uptongc.com
- ✍ Anne Jennings (01244) 381183
- 🖥 www.uptonbychestergolfclub.co.uk

Vale Royal Abbey (1998)

Proprietary
Whitegate, Northwich CW8 2BA
- ☎ **(01606) 301291**
- 🖳 (01606) 301784
- ✉ secretary@vra.co.uk
- ✍ Ian Embury
- 🖥 www.vra.co.uk

Vicars Cross (1939)

*Tarvin Road, Great Barrow, Chester
CH3 7HN*
- ☎ **(01244) 335174**
- 🖳 (01244) 335686
- ✉ manager@vicarscrossgolf.co.uk
- ✍ Mrs K Hunt
- 🖥 www.vicarscrossgolf.co.uk

Walton Hall (1972)

Public
*Warrington Road, Higher Walton,
Warrington WA4 5LU*
- ☎ **(01925) 266775**
- ✉ theclub@waltonhallgolfclub.co.uk
- ✍ Dave Johnson (01925) 266775
- 🖥 www.waltonhallgolfclub.co.uk

Warrington (1903)

*Hill Warren, London Road, Appleton
WA4 5HR*
- ☎ **(01925) 261775**
- 🖳 (01925) 265933
- ✉ secretary@warringtongolfclub
  .co.uk
- ✍ D S Macphee (01925) 261775
- 🖥 www.warringtongolfclub.co.uk

Werneth Low (1912)

*Werneth Low Road, Gee Cross, Hyde
SK14 3AF*
- ☎ **(0161) 368 2503**

Widnes (1924)

Highfield Road, Widnes WA8 7DT
- ☎ **(0151) 424 2995**
- 🖳 (0151) 495 2849
- ✉ office@widnesgolfclub.co.uk
- ✍ Mrs Nicola Ogburn
- 🖥 www.widnesgolfclub.co.uk

Wilmslow (1889)

*Great Warford, Mobberley, Knutsford
WA16 7AY*
- ☎ **(01565) 872148**
- 🖳 (01565) 873148
- ✉ admin@wilmslowgolfclub.co.uk
- ✍ Keith Melia (Gen Mgr)
- 🖥 www.wilmslowgolfclub.co.uk

Woodside (1999)

Proprietary
*Knutsford Road, Cranage, Holmes Chapel,
Cheshire CW4 8HJ*
- ☎ **(01477) 532388**
- 🖳 (01477) 549207
- ✉ info@woodsidegolf.co.uk
- ✍ Marie-Therese Whelan
- 🖥 www.woodsidegolf.co.uk

Cornwall

Bowood Park (1992)

*Valley Truckle, Lanteglos, Camelford
PL32 9RF*
- ☎ **(01840) 213017**
- 🖳 (01840) 212622
- ✉ info@bowood-park.co.uk
- ✍ Gerald Simmons
- 🖥 www.bowood-park.co.uk

Bude & North Cornwall
(1891)
Burn View, Bude EX23 8DA
- ☎ **(01288) 352006**
- 🖳 (01288) 356855
- ✉ secretary@budegolf.co.uk
- ✍ Mr I V Roddy (Mgr/Sec)
- 🖥 www.budegolf.co.uk

Budock Vean Hotel Golf &
Country Club (1932)
Mawnan Smith, Falmouth TR11 5LG
- ☎ **(01326) 252102**
- 🖳 (01326) 250892
- ✉ relax@budockvean.co.uk
- ✍ Keith Rashleigh (01326) 377091

Cape Cornwall G&CC
(1990)
St Just, Penzance TR19 7NL
- ☎ **(01736) 788611**
- 🖳 (01736) 788611
- ✉ golf@capecornwall.com
- ✍ Ben Ludwell (Mgr)
- 🖥 www.capecornwall.com

Carlyon Bay (1926)

Proprietary
Carlyon Bay, St Austell PL25 3RD
- ☎ **(01726) 814250**
- 🖳 (01726) 814250
- ✉ golf@carlyonbay.com
- ✍ P Martin
- 🖥 www.carlyongolf.com

China Fleet CC (1991)

Saltash PL12 6LJ
- ☎ **(01752) 848668**
- 🖳 (01752) 848456
- ✉ golf@china-fleet.co.uk
- ✍ Mrs L Goddard
- 🖥 www.china-fleet.co.uk

Falmouth (1894)

Proprietary
Swanpool Road, Falmouth TR11 5BQ
- ☎ **(01326) 311262/314296**
- 🖳 (01326) 211447

clubsec@falmouthgolfclub.com
Steve Burrows (Director)
www.falmouthgolfclub.com

Isles of Scilly (1904)
Carn Morval, St Mary's, Isles of Scilly `
TR21 0NF
☎ (01720) 422692
iosgcsec@googlemail.com
Peter Leahy (Hon Sec)
www.islesofscillygolfclub.co.uk

Killiow (1987)
Proprietary
Killiow, Kea, Truro TR3 6AG
☎ (01872) 270246
killiowsec@yahoo.co.uk

Lanhydrock Hotel & Golf Club (1991)
Proprietary
Lostwithiel Road, Bodmin PL30 5AQ
☎ (01208) 262570
(01208) 262579
info@lanhydrockhotel.com
G Bond (Dir)
www.lanhydrockhotel.com

Launceston (1927)
St Stephen, Launceston PL15 8HF
☎ (01566) 773442
(01566) 777506
secretary@launcestongolfclub
.co.uk
A Creber
www.launcestongolfclub.co.uk

Looe (1933)
Bin Down, Looe PL13 1PX
☎ (01503) 240239
(01503) 240864
enquiries@looegolfclub.co.uk
M D Joy (Hon)
www.looegolfclub.co.uk

Lostwithiel G&CC (1990)
Lower Polscoe, Lostwithiel PL22 0HQ
☎ (01208) 873550
(01208) 873479
reception@golf-hotel.co.uk
D Higman
www.golf-hotel.co.uk

Merlin (1991)
Proprietary
Mawgan Porth, Newquay TR8 4DN
☎ (01841) 540222
(01841) 541031
play@merlingolfcourse.co.uk
Mr Richard Burrough
www.merlingolfcourse.co.uk

Mullion (1895)
Cury, Helston TR12 7BP
☎ (01326) 240276
(01326) 241527
secretary@mulliongolfclub.plus
.com
R Griffiths (01326) 240685
www.mulliongolfclub.co.uk

Newquay (1890)
Tower Road, Newquay TR7 1LT
☎ (01637) 872091
(01637) 874066
newquaygolf@btconnect.com
J Gilbert (01637) 874354
www.newquaygolfclub.co.uk

Perranporth (1927)
Budnic Hill, Perranporth TR6 0AB
☎ (01872) 572454
secretary@perranporthgolfclub
.co.uk
DC Mugford
www.perranporthgolfclub.co.uk

Porthpean (1992)
Proprietary
Porthpean, St Austell PL26 6AY
☎ (01726) 64613
(01726) 64613
porthpeangolfclub@hotmail
.co.uk
Michelle Baily (Mgr)
www.porthpeangolfclub.co.uk

Praa Sands Golf and Country Club (1971)
Public
Praa Sands, Penzance TR20 9TQ
☎ (01736) 763445
(01736) 763741
praasands2@haulfryn.co.uk
Simon Spencer 01736 762201
www.praa-sands.com

Radnor (1988)
Proprietary
Radnor Road, Treleigh, Redruth, Cornwall
TR16 5EL
☎ (01209) 211059
jonradnor@btconnect.com
Jon Barber
www.radnorgolfandleisure
.co.uk

Roserrow (1996)
Proprietary
St Minver, Wadebridge PL27 6QT
☎ (01208) 863000
(01208) 863002
info@roserrow.co.uk
Hayley Lane
www.roserrow.co.uk

St Austell (1911)
Tregongeeves Lane, St Austell PL26 7DS
☎ (01726) 74756
(01726) 71978
office@staustellgolf.co.uk
P Clemo
www.staustellgolf.co.uk

St Enodoc (1890)
Rock, Wadebridge PL27 6LD
☎ (01208) 863216
(01208) 862976
enquiries@st-enodoc.co.uk
TD Clagett
www.st-enodoc.co.uk

St Kew (1993)
Proprietary
St Kew Highway, Wadebridge, Bodmin
PL30 3EF
☎ (01208) 841500
(01208) 841500
stkewgolf@btconnect.com
J Brown (Prop)

Tehidy Park (1922)
Camborne TR14 0HH
☎ (01209) 842208
(01209) 842208
secretary-
manager@tehidyparkgolfclub.co.uk
I J Veale (Sec/Mgr)
www.tehidyparkgolfclub.co.uk

Tregenna Castle Hotel (1982)
St Ives TR26 2DE
☎ (01736) 795254
hotel@tregenna-castle.co.uk
www.tregenna-castle.co.uk

Treloy (1991)
Treloy, Newquay TR8 4JN
☎ (01637) 878554
www.treloygolfclub.co.uk

Trethorne (1991)
Kennards House, Launceston PL15 8QE
☎ (01566) 86903
gen@trethornegolfclub.com
www.trethornegolfclub.com

Trevose (1924)
Constantine Bay, Padstow PL28 8JB
☎ (01841) 520208
(01841) 521057
info@trevose-gc.co.uk
P Gammon (Prop),
www.trevose-gc.co.uk

Truro (1937)
Treliske, Truro TR1 3LG
☎ (01872) 278684
(01872) 225972
trurogolfclub@tiscali.co.uk
L Booker (Sec/Mgr)
www.trurogolf.co.uk

West Cornwall (1889)
Lelant, St Ives TR26 3DZ
☎ (01736) 753401
secretary@westcornwallgolfclub
.co.uk
GM Evans
www.westcornwallgolfclub.co.uk

Whitsand Bay Hotel (1906)
Portwrinkle, Torpoint PL11 3BU
☎ (01503) 230276 (Clubhouse)
www.whitsandbayhotel.co.uk

Cumbria

Alston Moor (1906)
The Hermitage, Alston CA9 3DB
☎ (01434) 381675

✉ secretary@alstonmoorgolfclub
.org.uk
🖳 Paul Parkin (01434) 381704
🖳 www.alstonmoorgolfclub.org.uk

Appleby (1903)
Brackenber Moor, Appleby CA16 6LP
☎ **(017683) 51432**
🖳 (017683) 52773
✉ enquiries@applebygolfclub.co.uk
🖳 JMF Doig (Hon)
🖳 www.applebygolfclub.co.uk

Barrow (1922)
Rakesmoor Lane, Hawcoat, Barrow-in-
Furness LA14 4QB
☎ **(01229) 825444**
✉ barrowgolf@supanet.com
🖳 S G Warbrick (Hon)
🖳 www.barrowgolfclub.co.uk

Brampton (Talkin Tarn)
(1909)
Tarn Road, Brampton CA8 1HN
☎ **(0169) 772255**
🖳 (0169) 7741487
✉ secretary@bramptongolfclub.com
🖳 IJ Meldrum (01228) 520982
🖳 www.bramptongolfclub.com

Brayton Park (1986)
Pay and play
The Garth, Home Farm, Brayton, Aspatria
CA7 3SX
☎ **(01697) 323539**

Carlisle (1908)
Aglionby, Carlisle CA4 8AG
☎ **(01228) 513029**
🖳 (01228) 513303
✉ secretary@carlislegolfclub.org
🖳 Roger Johnson
🖳 www.carlislegolfclub.org

Carus Green (1996)
Proprietary
Burneside Road, Kendal LA9 6EB
☎ **(01539) 721097**
🖳 (01539) 721097
✉ info@carusgreen.co.uk
🖳 G Curtin or W Dand
🖳 www.carusgreen.co.uk

Casterton (1955)
Proprietary
Sedbergh Road, Casterton, Nr Kirkby
Lonsdale LA6 2LA
☎ **(015242) 71592**
✉ castertongc@hotmail.com
🖳 J & E Makinson (Props)
🖳 www.castertongolf.co.uk

Cockermouth (1896)
Embleton, Cockermouth CA13 9SG
☎ **(017687) 76223/76941**
🖳 (017687) 76941
✉ secretary@cockermouthgolf
.co.uk
🖳 RS Wimpress (01900) 825431
🖳 www.cockermouthgolf.co.uk

Dalston Hall (1990)
Pay and play
Dalston Hall, Dalston, Carlisle CA5 7JX
☎ **(01228) 710165**
🖳 (01228) 710165
✉ info@dalstonholidaypark.com
🖳 PS Holder
🖳 www.dalstonhallholidaypark.co.uk

The Dunnerholme Golf
Club (1905)
Duddon Road, Askam-in-Furness
LA16 7AW
☎ **(01229) 462675**
🖳 (01229) 462675
✉ dunnerholmegolfclub@btinternet
.com
🖳 Lynda Preston (Sec)
🖳 www.thedunnerholmegolfclub
.co.uk

Eden (1992)
Proprietary
Crosby-on-Eden, Carlisle CA6 4RA
☎ **(01228) 573003**
🖳 (01228) 818435
🖳 www.edengolf.co.uk

Furness (1872)
Central Drive, Walney Island, Barrow-in-
Furness LA14 3LN
☎ **(01229) 471232**
🖳 (01229) 475100
✉ furnessgolfclub@chessbroadband
.co.uk
🖳 Mr R S Turner (Secretary)
🖳 www.furnessgolfclub.co.uk

Grange Fell (1952)
Fell Road, Grange-over-Sands LA11 6HB
☎ **(015395) 32536**
✉ gfgc@etherway.net
🖳 JG Park (015395) 58513

Grange-over-Sands (1919)
Meathop Road, Grange-over-Sands
LA11 6QX
☎ **(015395) 33180**
🖳 (015395) 33754
✉ office@grangegolfclub.com
🖳 G Whitfield (015395) 33180
🖳 www.grangegolfclub.co.uk

Haltwhistle (1967)
Wallend Farm, Greenhead, Carlisle
CA8 7HN
☎ **(01697) 747367**
🖳 Patrick Peace (Hon Sec)
🖳 www.haltwhistlegolf.co.uk

Kendal (1891)
The Heights, Kendal LA9 4PQ
☎ **(01539) 723499 (Bookings)**
✉ secretary@kendalgolfclub.co.uk
🖳 I Clancy (01539) 733708
🖳 www.kendalgolfclub.co.uk

Keswick (1978)
Threlkeld Hall, Threlkeld, Keswick
CA12 4SX
☎ **(017687) 79324**
🖳 (017687) 79861

✉ secretary@keswickgolfclub.com
🖳 May Lloyd (017687) 79324 ext 1
🖳 www.keswickgolfclub.com

Kirkby Lonsdale (1906)
Scaleber Lane, Barbon, Kirkby Lonsdale
LA6 2LJ
☎ **(015242) 76366**
🖳 (015242) 76503
✉ info@kirkbylonsdalegolfclub.com
🖳 D Towers (015242) 76365
🖳 www.kirkbylonsdalegolfclub.com

Maryport (1905)
Bankend, Maryport CA15 6PA
☎ **(01900) 812605**
🖳 (01900) 815626
✉ maryportgolfclub.co.uk
🖳 Mrs L Hayton (01900) 815626

Penrith (1890)
Salkeld Road, Penrith CA11 8SG
☎ **(01768) 891919**
🖳 (01768) 891919
✉ secretary@penrithgolfclub.co.uk
🖳 S D Wright (01768) 891919
🖳 www.penrithgolfclub.com

Seascale (1893)
Seascale CA20 1QL
☎ **(019467) 28202/28800**
🖳 (019467) 28042
✉ seascalegolfclub@googlemail.com
🖳 JDH Stobart (019467) 28202
🖳 www.seascalegolfclub.co.uk

Sedbergh (1896)
Proprietary
Dent Road, Sedbergh LA10 5SS
☎ **(015396) 21551**
🖳 (015396) 21827
✉ info@sedberghgolfclub.com
🖳 Craig or Steve Gardner
🖳 www.sedberghgolfclub.co.uk

Silecroft (1903)
Silecroft, Millom LA18 4NX
☎ **(01229) 774250**
✉ sgcsecretary@hotmail.co.uk
🖳 K Newton (01229) 770467
🖳 www.silecroftgolfclub.co.uk

Silloth-on-Solway (1892)
Silloth, Wigton CA7 4BL
☎ **(016973) 31304**
🖳 (016973) 31782
✉ office@sillothgolfclub.co.uk
🖳 Alan Oliver
🖳 www/sillothgolfclub.co.uk

Silverdale (1906)
Red Bridge Lane, Silverdale, Carnforth
LA5 0SP
☎ **(01524) 701300**
🖳 (01524) 701986
✉ info@silverdalegolfclub.co.uk
🖳 B Hebdon (01524) 702074
🖳 www.silverdalegolfclub.co.uk

St Bees (1929)
Peckmill, Beach Road, St Bees CA27 0EJ
☎ **(01946) 820319**

lhinde21@btinternet.com
L Hinde
www.stbeesgolfclub.org.uk

Stony Holme   (1974)
Public
St Aidan's Road, Carlisle CA1 1LS
☎ **(01228) 625511**
A McConnell (01228) 625511

Ulverston   (1895)
Bardsea Park, Ulverston LA12 9QJ
☎ **(01229) 582824**
🖷 (01229) 588910
enquiries@ulverstongolf.co.uk
Mr Charles Dent
www.ulverstongolf.co.uk

Windermere   (1891)
Cleabarrow, Windermere LA23 3NB
☎ **(015394) 43123**
🖷 (015394) 46370
office@windermeregolfclub.co.uk
Carol Slater (Sec/Mgr)
www.windermeregolfclub.co.uk

Workington   (1893)
Branthwaite Road, Workington CA14 4SS
☎ **(01900) 603460**
secretary@workingtongolfclub.com
P Hoskin (Sec)
www.workingtongolfclub.com

Derbyshire

Alfreton   (1892)
Oakerthorpe, Alfreton DE55 7LH
☎ **(01773) 832070**
S Bradley (07712) 136647
www.alfretongolfclub.co.uk

Allestree Park   (1949)
Public
Allestree Hall, Allestree, Derby DE22 2EU
☎ **(01332) 550616**
mail@allestreeparkgolfclub.co.uk
C Barker
www.allestreeparkgolfclub.co.uk

Ashbourne   (1886)
Wyaston Road, Ashbourne DE6 1NB
☎ **(01335) 342078**
🖷 (01335) 347937
ashbournegc@tiscali.co.uk
Andrew Smith
www.ashbournegolfclub.co.uk

Bakewell   (1899)
Station Road, Bakewell DE4 1GB
☎ **(01629) 812307**
administrator@bakewellgolfclub
.co.uk
Mr G Holmes
www.bakewellgolfclub.co.uk

Birch Hall
Sheffield Road, Unstone S18 5DH
☎ **(01246) 291979**

Bondhay   (1991)
Bondhay Lane, Whitwell, Worksop S80 3EH
☎ **(01909) 723608**
🖷 (01909) 720226
enquiries@bondhaygolfclub.com
M Hardisty (Mgr)
www.bondhaygolfclub.com

Brailsford   (1994)
Proprietary
Pools Head Lane, Brailsford, Ashbourne
DE6 3BU
☎ **(01335) 360096**
🖷 (01335) 360077
vivian.craig@clowes-
developments.com
T Payne (tpayne@talktalk.net)
www.brailsfordgolfcourse.co.uk

Breadsall Priory Hotel
G&CC   (1976)
Moor Road, Morley, Derby DE7 6DL
☎ **(01332) 836016**
🖷 (01332) 836089
mhrs.emags.golf@marriotthotels
.com
I Knox (Dir of Golf)
www.marriottgolf.co.uk

Broughton Heath   (1988)
Proprietary
Bent Lane, Church Broughton DE65 5BA
☎ **(01283) 521235**
info@broughtonheathgc.co.uk
J Bentley (Mgr)
www.broughtonheathgc.co.uk

Burton-on-Trent   (1894)
43 Ashby Road East, Burton-on-Trent
DE15 0PS
☎ **(01283) 544551**
clubmanager
@burtonontrentgolfclub.co.uk
S A Dixon (01283) 544551
www.burtonontrentgolfclub.co.uk

Buxton & High Peak   (1887)
Townend, Buxton SK17 7EN
☎ **(01298) 26263**
🖷 (01298) 26333
sec@bhpgc.co.uk
Garry Bagguley (Sec)
www.bhpgc.co.uk

Cavendish   (1925)
Watford Road, Buxton SK17 6XF
☎ **(01298) 79708**
🖷 (01298) 79708
admin@cavendishgolfclub.com
S A Davis
www.cavendishgolfclub.com

Chapel-en-le-Frith   (1905)
The Cockyard, Manchester Road, Chapel-en-
le-Frith SK23 9UH
☎ **(01298) 812118**
🖷 (01298) 814990
info@chapelgolf.co.uk
Denise Goldfinch (01298) 813943
www.chapelgolf.co.uk

Chesterfield   (1897)
Walton, Chesterfield S42 7LA
☎ **(01246) 279256**
🖷 (01246) 276622
secretary@chesterfieldgolfclub
.co.uk
T H Glover
www.chesterfieldgolfclub.co.uk

Chevin   (1894)
Duffield, Derby DE56 4EE
☎ **(01332) 841864**
🖷 (01332) 844028
secretary@chevingolf.co.uk
M E Riley
www.chevingolf.co.uk

Derby   (1923)
Public
Wilmore Road, Sinfin, Derby DE24 9HD
☎ **(01332) 766323**
secretary@derbygolfclub.co.uk
DP Anderson
www.derbygolfclub.co.uk

Erewash Valley   (1905)
Stanton-by-Dale DE7 4QR
☎ **(0115) 932 3258**
🖷 (0115) 944 0061
secretary@erewashvalley.co.uk
Andrew Burrows
www.erewashvalley.co.uk

Glossop & District   (1894)
Sheffield Road, Glossop SK13 7PU
☎ **(01457) 865247**
   (Clubhouse)
🖷 (01457) 864003
glossopgolfclub@talktalk.net
K Harrison
www.glossopgolfclub.co.uk

Grassmoor Golf Centre
(1990)
Proprietary
North Wingfield Road, Grassmoor,
Chesterfield S42 5EA
☎ **(01246) 856044**
🖷 (01246) 853486
enquiries@grassmoorgolf.co.uk
H Hagues (Club Manager)
www.grassmoorgolf.co.uk

Horsley Lodge   (1990)
Proprietary
Smalley Mill Road, Horsley DE21 5BL
☎ **(01332) 780838**
🖷 (01332) 781118
richard@horsleylodge.co.uk
Dennis Wake (07771) 874 882
www.horsleylodge.co.uk

Kedleston Park   (1947)
Kedleston, Quarndon, Derby DE22 5JD
☎ **(01332) 840035**
🖷 (01332) 840035
secretary@kedlestonparkgolfclub
.co.uk
R Simpson (Gen Mgr)
www.kedlestonparkgolfclub.co.uk

Lafarge Golf Club (1985)
Lafarge Cement, Hope Works, Hope Valley, Derbyshire S33 6RP
- ☎ **(01433) 622315**
- ✍ DS Smith

Matlock (1906)
Chesterfield Road, Matlock Moor, Matlock DE4 5LZ
- ☎ **(01629) 582191**
- 🖷 (01629) 582135
- ✉ secretary@matlockgolfclub.co.uk
- ✍ M Wain (01629) 582191 option 4
- 🖥 www.matlockgolfclub.co.uk

Maywood (1990)
Proprietary
Rushy Lane, Risley, Derby DE72 3SW
- ☎ **(0115) 939 2306**
- ✉ maywoodgolfclub@btinternet.com
- ✍ WJ Cockeram (0115) 932 6772
- 🖥 www.maywoodgolfclub.com

Mickleover (1923)
Uttoxeter Road, Mickleover DE3 9AD
- ☎ **(01332) 516011 (Clubhouse)**
- 🖷 (01332) 516011
- ✉ secretary@mickleovergolfclub.com
- ✍ GW Finney (01332) 516011
- 🖥 www.mickleovergolfclub.com

New Mills (1907)
Shaw Marsh, New Mills, High Peak SK22 4QE
- ☎ **(01663) 743485**
- ✍ Margaret Palmer (01663) 744330 (Sec)
- 🖥 www.newmillsgolfclub.co.uk

Ormonde Fields (1926)
Nottingham Road, Codnor, Ripley DE5 9RG
- ☎ **(01773) 742987**
- 🖷 (01773) 744848
- ✉ info@ormondefieldsgolfclub.co.uk
- ✍ K Constable
- 🖥 www.ormondefieldsgolfclub.co.uk

Shirland (1977)
Proprietary
Lower Delves, Shirland DE55 6AU
- ☎ **(01773) 834935**
- ✉ geofftowle@hotmail.com

Sickleholme (1898)
Bamford, Sheffield S33 0BH
- ☎ **(01433) 651306**
- 🖷 (01433) 659498
- ✉ sickleholme.gc@btconnect.com
- ✍ PH Taylor (Mgr)
- 🖥 www.sickleholme.co.uk

Stanedge (1934)
Walton Hay Farm, Chesterfield S45 0LW
- ☎ **(01246) 566156**
- ✉ chrisshaw56@tiscali.co.uk
- ✍ Mr Chris Shaw 0776 742 6584
- 🖥 www.stanedgegolfclub.co.uk

Devon

Ashbury (1991)
Higher Maddaford, Okehampton EX20 4NL
- ☎ **(01837) 55453**
- 🖥 www.ashburyhotel.co.uk

Axe Cliff (1894)
Proprietary
Squires Lane, Axmouth, Seaton EX12 4AB
- ☎ **(01297) 21754**
- ✉ D.Quinn@axecliff.co.uk
- 🖥 www.axecliff.co.uk

Bigbury (1923)
Bigbury-on-Sea, South Devon TQ7 4BB
- ☎ **(01548) 810557**
- ✉ enquiries@bigburygolfclub.co.uk
- ✍ Nigel Blenkarne (Director of Golf)
- 🖥 www.bigburygolfclub.com

Bovey Castle (1929)
Proprietary
North Bovey, Devon TQ13 8RE
- ☎ **(01647) 445009**
- 🖷 (01647) 440961
- ✉ richard.lewis@boveycastle.com
- ✍ R Lewis
- 🖥 www.boveycastle.com

Bovey Tracey Golf Club (2005)
Pay and play
Monks Way, Bovey Tracey, Newton Abbot, Devon TQ13 9NG
- ☎ **(01626) 836464**
- ✉ bertony@btinternet.com
- ✍ D Dyer (Mgr)
- 🖥 www.wolleighgc.co.uk

Chulmleigh (1976)
Pay and play
Leigh Road, Chulmleigh EX18 7BL
- ☎ **(01769) 580519**
- 🖷 (01769) 580519
- ✉ chulmleighgolf@aol.com
- ✍ RW Dow
- 🖥 www.chulmleighgolf.co.uk

Churston (1890)
Churston, Dartmouth Road, Brixham TQ5 0LA
- ☎ **(01803) 842751**
- 🖷 (01803) 845738
- ✉ manager@churstongolf.com
- ✍ SR Bawden (01803) 842751
- 🖥 www.churstongolf.com

Dainton Park (1993)
Proprietary
Totnes Road, Ipplepen, Newton Abbot TQ12 5TN
- ☎ **(01803) 815000**
- 🖷 (01803) 815001
- ✉ info@daintonparkgolf.co.uk
- ✍ Mr Daniel Wood
- 🖥 www.daintonparkgolf.co.uk

Dartmouth G&CC (1992)
Blackawton, Nr Dartmouth, Devon TQ9 7DE
- ☎ **(01803) 712686**
- 🖷 (01803) 712628
- ✉ info@dgcc.co.uk
- ✍ J Waugh (Sec), A Chappell (Assist. Sec)
- 🖥 www.dgcc.co.uk

Dinnaton – McCaulays Health Club, Ivybridge Fitness & Golf (1989)
Ivybridge PL21 9HU
- ☎ **(01752) 892512**
- 🖷 (01752) 698334
- ✉ info@mccaulays.com
- ✍ P Hendriksen
- 🖥 www.mccaulays.com

Downes Crediton (1976)
Hookway, Crediton EX17 3PT
- ☎ **(01363) 773025**
- 🖷 (01363) 775060
- ✉ golf@downescreditongc.co.uk
- ✍ Robin Goodey (01363) 773025
- 🖥 www.downescreditongc.co.uk

East Devon (1902)
Links Road, Budleigh Salterton EX9 6DG
- ☎ **(01395) 443370**
- 🖷 (01395) 445547
- ✉ secretary@edgc.co.uk
- ✍ J Reynolds (01395) 443370
- 🖥 www.edgc.co.uk

Elfordleigh Hotel G&CC (1932)
Proprietary
Colebrook, Plympton, Plymouth PL7 5EB
- ☎ **(01752) 348425**
- 🖷 (01752) 344581
- ✉ enquiries@elfordleigh.co.uk
- ✍ Derek Mills (01752) 556205
- 🖥 www.elfordleigh.co.uk

Exeter G&CC (1895)
Countess Wear, Exeter EX2 7AE
- ☎ **(01392) 874139**
- ✉ golf@exetergcc.co.uk
- 🖥 www.exetergcc.com

Fingle Glen (1989)
Proprietary
Tedburn St Mary, Exeter EX6 6AF
- ☎ **(01647) 61817**
- 🖷 (01647) 61135
- ✉ mail@fingleglengolfhotel.co.uk
- ✍ P Miliffe
- 🖥 www.fingleglengolfhotel.co.uk

Great Torrington (1895)
The Club House, Weare Trees, Torrington EX38 7EZ
- ☎ **(01805) 622229**
- 🖷 (01805) 623878
- ✉ torringtongolfclub@btconnect.com
- ✍ Mr G S C Green
- 🖥 www.torringtongolfclub.co.uk

Hartland Forest   (1980)
Hartland Forest Golf & Leisure Parc,
Woolsery, Bideford EX39 5RA
- ☎ **(01237) 431777**
- 📠 hfgadmin@gmail.com
- 🖳 www.hartlandforestgolf.co.uk

Hele Park Golf Centre
(1993)
Proprietary
Ashburton Road, Newton Abbot TQ12 6JN
- ☎ **(01626) 336060**
- 📠 (01626) 332661
- ✉ info@heleparkgolf.co.uk
- ⚲ Wendy Stanbury
- 🖳 www.heleparkgolf.co.uk

Highbullen Hotel G&CC
(1961)
Proprietary
Chittlehamholt, Umberleigh EX37 9HD
- ☎ **(01769) 540561**
- 📠 (01769) 540492
- ✉ info@highbullen.co.uk
- ⚲ John Aryes (01769) 540664
- 🖳 www.highbullen.co.uk

Holsworthy   (1937)
Killatree, Holsworthy EX22 6LP
- ☎ **(01409) 253177**
- 📠 (01409) 255393
- ✉ info@holsworthygolfclub.co.uk
- ⚲ Mrs C F Harper
- 🖳 www.holsworthygolfclub.co.uk

Honiton   (1896)
Middlehills, Honiton EX14 9TR
- ☎ **(01404) 44422**
- ✉ secretary@honitongolfclub.fsnet
  .co.uk
- ⚲ Graham Burch (Administrator)
- 🖳 www.honitongolf club.co.uk

Hurdwick   (1990)
Tavistock Hamlets, Tavistock PL19 0LL
- ☎ **(01822) 612746**
- ✉ info@hurdwickgolf.com
- ⚲ Mr M J Wood (Mgr)
- 🖳 www.hurdwickgolf.com

Ilfracombe   (1892)
Hele Bay, Ilfracombe EX34 9RT
- ☎ **(01271) 862176**
- ✉ ilfracombegolfclub@btinternet.com
- ⚲ Mr D Cook
- 🖳 www.ilfracombegolfclub.com

Libbaton   (1988)
High Bickington, Umberleigh EX37 9BS
- ☎ **(01769) 560269**
- 📠 (01769) 560342
- ✉ gerald.herniman@tesco.net
- ⚲ Gerald Herniman
- 🖳 www.libbaton-golf-club.com

Mortehoe & Woolacombe
(1992)
Easewell, Mortehoe, Ilfracombe EX34 7EH
- ☎ **(01271) 870566**
- ⚲ M Wilkinson (01271) 870745

Okehampton   (1913)
Okehampton EX20 1EF
- ☎ **(01837) 52113**
- 📠 (01837) 53541
- ✉ secretary@okehamptongolfclub
  .co.uk
- ⚲ Beverley Lawson
- 🖳 www.okehamptongolfclub.co.uk

Padbrook Park   (1992)
Proprietary
Cullompton EX15 1RU
- ☎ **(01884) 836100**
- 📠 (01884) 836101
- ✉ info@padbrookpark.co.uk
- ⚲ Cary Rawlings (Mgr)
- ⊕ 40 Bed Hotel, 10 bay Driving
  Range.
- 🖳 www.padbrookpark.co.uk

Portmore Golf Park   (1993)
Proprietary
Landkey Road, Barnstaple EX32 9LB
- ☎ **(01271) 378378**
- ✉ contact@portmoregolf.co.uk
- ⚲ C Webber
- 🖳 www.portmoregolf.co.uk

Royal North Devon   (1864)
Golf Links Road, Westward Ho! EX39 1HD
- ☎ **(01237) 473817 (Clubhouse)**
- 📠 (01237) 423456
- ✉ info@royalnorthdevongolfclub
  .co.uk
- ⚲ M Evans (01237) 473817
- 🖳 www.royalnorthdevongolfclub
  .co.uk

Saunton   (1897)
Saunton, Braunton EX33 1LG
- ☎ **(01271) 812436**
- 📠 (01271) 814241
- ✉ gm4@sauntongolf.co.uk
- ⚲ P McMullen (Mgr)
- 🖳 www.sauntongolf.co.uk

Sidmouth   (1889)
Cotmaton Road, Sidmouth EX10 8SX
- ☎ **(01395) 513451**
- 📠 (01395) 514661
- ✉ secretary@sidmouthgolfclub.co.uk
- ⚲ JP Lee (Mgr) (01395) 513451
- 🖳 www.sidmouthgolfclub.co.uk

Sparkwell   (1993)
Pay and play
Sparkwell, Plymouth PL7 5DF
- ☎ **(01752) 837219**
- 📠 (01752) 837219
- ⚲ G Adamson

Staddon Heights   (1904)
Plymstock, Plymouth PL9 9SP
- ☎ **(01752) 402475**
- 📠 (01752) 401998
- ✉ golf@shgc.uk.net
- ⚲ TJH Aggett (01752) 402475
- 🖳 www.staddonheightsgolf.co.uk

Stover   (1930)
Bovey Road, Newton Abbot TQ12 6QQ
- ☎ **(01626) 352460**

- 📠 (01626) 330210
- ✉ info@stovergolfclub.co.uk
- ⚲ W Hendry
- 🖳 www.stovergolfclub.co.uk

Tavistock   (1890)
Down Road, Tavistock PL19 9AQ
- ☎ **(01822) 612344**
- 📠 (01822) 612344
- ✉ info@tavistockgolfclub.org.uk
- ⚲ J Coe
- 🖳 www.tavistockgolfclub.org.uk

Teign Valley   (1995)
Christow, Exeter EX6 7PA
- ☎ **(01647) 253026**
- 📠 (01647) 253026
- ✉ andy@teignvalleygolf.co.uk
- ⚲ Andy Stubbs
- 🖳 www.teignvalleygolf.co.uk

Teignmouth   (1924)
Haldon Moor, Exeter Road, Teignmouth
TQ14 9NY
- ☎ **(01626) 777070**
- 📠 (01626) 777304
- ✉ info@teignmouthgolfclub.co.uk
- ⚲ Ian Evans
- 🖳 www.teignmouthgolfclub.co.uk

Thurlestone   (1897)
Thurlestone, Kingsbridge TQ7 3NZ
- ☎ **(01548) 560405**
- 📠 (01548) 562149
- ✉ info@thurlestonegolfclub.co.uk
- ⚲ Russell Thomas (01548) 560405
- 🖳 www.thurlestonegolfclub.co.uk

Tiverton   (1932)
Post Hill, Tiverton EX16 4NE
- ☎ **(01884) 252114**
  (Clubhouse)
- ✉ tivertongolfclub@lineone.net
- ⚲ R Jessop (Gen Mgr)
- 🖳 www.tivertongolfclub.co.uk

Torquay   (1909)
Petitor Road, St Marychurch, Torquay
TQ1 4QF
- ☎ **(01803) 327471**
- 📠 (01803) 316116
- ✉ info@torquaygolfclub.co.uk
- ⚲ C M Nolan (01803) 314591
- 🖳 www.torquaygolfclub.co.uk

Warren   (1892)
Dawlish Warren EX7 0NF
- ☎ **(01626) 862255**
- ✉ assistant@dwgc.co.uk
- ⚲ Cathie Stokes
- 🖳 www.dwgc.co.uk

Waterbridge   (1992)
Pay and play
Down St Mary, Crediton EX17 5LG
- ☎ **(01363) 85111**
- ⚲ G & A Wren (Props)
- 🖳 www.waterbridgegc.co.uk

Willingcott Valley   (1996)
Willingcott, Woolacombe EX34 7HN
- ☎ **(01271) 870173**

✉ secretary.willingcottgolfclub
@virgin.net
🖥 www.willingcott.co.uk

Woodbury Park (1992)
Woodbury Castle, Woodbury EX5 1JJ
☎ (01395) 233500

Wrangaton (1895)
Golf Links Road, Wrangaton, South Brent
TQ10 9HJ
☎ (01364) 73229
📠 (01364) 73229
✉ wrangatongolf@btconnect.com
✍ R Clark (01364) 73229
🖥 www.wrangatongolfclub.co.uk

Yelverton (1904)
Golf Links Road, Yelverton PL20 6BN
☎ (01822) 852824
📠 (01822) 854869
✉ secretary@yelvertongolf.co.uk
✍ Steve West (01822) 852824
🖥 www.yelvertongolf.co.uk

Dorset

The Ashley Wood (1896)
Wimborne Road, Blandford Forum
DT11 9HN
☎ (01258) 452253
📠 (01258) 450590
✉ generalmanager
@ashleywoodgolfclub.com
✍ M Batty
🖥 www.ashleywoodgolfclub.com

Bridport & West Dorset
(1891)
The Clubhouse, Burton Road, Bridport
DT6 4PS
☎ (01308) 421095/422597
(Clubhouse)
📠 (01308) 421095
✉ secretary@bridportgolfclub.org.uk
✍ R Wilson (01308) 421095
🖥 www.bridportgolfclub.org.uk

Broadstone (Dorset)
(1898)
Wentworth Drive, Broadstone BH18 8DQ
☎ (01202) 692595
📠 (01202) 642520
✉ office@broadstonegolfclub.com
✍ David Morgan (Gen Mgr) (01202)
642521
🖥 www.broadstonegolfclub.com

Bulbury Woods (1989)
Bulbury Lane, Lytchett Minster, Poole
BH16 6EP
☎ (01929) 459574
✉ enquiries@bulbury-woods.co.uk
🖥 www.bulbury-woods.co.uk

Came Down (1896)
Higher Came, Dorchester DT2 8NR
☎ (01305) 813494
📠 (01305) 815122
✉ manager@camedowngolfclub.co.uk

✍ Matthew Staveley (Gen Mgr)
🖥 www.camedowngolfclub.co.uk

Canford Magna (1994)
Proprietary
Knighton Lane, Wimborne BH21 3AS
☎ (01202) 592552
📠 (01202) 592550
✉ admin@canfordmagnagc.co.uk
✍ S Hudson (Dir) (01202) 592505
🖥 www.canfordmagnagc.co.uk

Canford School (1987)
Canford School, Wimborne BH21 3AD
☎ (01202) 841254
📠 (01202) 881009
✉ golfclub@canford.com
✍ M Burley (Mgr) (01202) 847485
🖥 www.canford.com

Charminster (1998)
Proprietary
Wolfedale Golf Course, Charminster,
Dorchester DT2 7SG
☎ (01305) 260186

Chedington Court (1991)
South Perrott, Beaminster DT8 3HU
☎ (01935) 891413
✉ info@chedingtoncourtgolfclub.com
✍ M Bowling (Manager)
🖥 www.chedingtoncourtgolfclub.com

Christchurch (1977)
Pay and play
Riverside Avenue, Bournemouth BH7 7ES
☎ (01202) 436436 (Bookings)
📠 (01202) 436400
✉ ben.chant@playgolfworld.com
✍ Ben Chant
🖥 www.playgolfbournemouth.com

Crane Valley (1992)
Proprietary
The Clubhouse, Verwood BH31 7LH
☎ (01202) 814088
📠 (01202) 813407
✉ general@crane-valley.co.uk
✍ A Blackwell (Gen Mgr)
🖥 www.crane-valley.co.uk

The Dorset G&CC (1978)
Hyde, Bere Regis, Nr. Poole, Wareham
BH20 7NT
☎ (01929) 472244
📠 (01929) 471294
✉ admin@dorsetgolfresort.com
✍ G Packer (Mgr)
🖥 www.dorsetgolfresort.com

Dudmoor Golf Course
(1985)
Pay and play
Dudmoor Farm Road, (off Fairmile Road),
Christchurch, Dorset BH23 6AQ
☎ (01202) 473826
📠 (01202) 480207
✉ peter@dudmoorgolfcourse.co.uk
✍ Peter Hornsby
🖥 www.dudmoorfarm.co.uk

Dudsbury (1992)
Proprietary
64 Christchurch Road, Ferndown BH22 8ST
☎ (01202) 593499
📠 (01202) 594555
✉ info@dudsburygolfclub.co.uk
✍ Steve Pockneall
🖥 www.dudsburygolfclub.co.uk

Ferndown (1913)
119 Golf Links Road, Ferndown BH22 8BU
☎ (01202) 653950
📠 (01202) 653960
✉ golf@ferndowngolfclub.co.uk
✍ Séan Malherbe (Gen Mgr)
🖥 www.ferndowngolfclub.co.uk

Ferndown Forest (1993)
Forest Links Road, Ferndown BH22 9PH
☎ (01202) 876096
📠 (01202) 894095
✉ golf@ferndownforestgolf.co.uk
✍ Chris Lawford
🖥 www.ferndownforestgolf.co.uk

Folke Golf Club (1995)
Proprietary
c/o Folke Golf Centre, Alweston, Sherborne,
Dorset DT9 5HR
☎ (01963) 23330
📠 (01963) 23330
✉ info@folkegolfcentre.co.uk
✍ Steve Harris
🖥 www.folkegolfcentre.co.uk

Halstock (1988)
Pay and play
Common Lane, Halstock BA22 9SF
☎ (01935) 891689
📠 (01935) 891839
✉ halstockgolf@yahoo.com
✍ Paul Flitton
🖥 www.halstockgolfclub.co.uk

Highcliffe Castle (1913)
107 Lymington Road, Highcliffe-on-Sea,
Christchurch BH23 4LA
☎ (01425) 272210/272953
📠 (01425) 272953
✉ secretary@highcliffecastlegolfclub
.co.uk
✍ G Fisher (01425) 272210
🖥 www.highcliffecastlegolfclub.co.uk

Isle of Purbeck (1892)
Proprietary
Studland BH19 3AB
☎ (01929) 450361
📠 (01929) 450501
✉ iop@purbeckgolf.co.uk
✍ Mrs C Robinson
🖥 www.purbeckgolf.co.uk

Knighton Heath (1976)
Francis Avenue, Bournemouth BH11 8NX
☎ (01202) 572633
📠 (01202) 590774
✉ khgc@btinternet.com
✍ Mr G Davis
🖥 www.knightonheathgolfclub.co.uk

For key to symbols see page 717

Lyme Regis (1893)
Timber Hill, Lyme Regis DT7 3HQ
☎ **(01297) 442963**
✉ secretary@lymeregisgolfclub
.co.uk
🖥 www.lymeregisgolfclub.co.uk

Meyrick Park (1890)
Pay and play
Central Drive, Meyrick Park, Bournemouth
BH2 6LH
☎ **(01202) 786000**
✉ m.gracehaus.com
🖥 www.clubhaus.com

Moors Valley (1988)
Proprietary
Horton Road, Ringwood BH24 2ET
☎ **(01425) 479776**
✉ golf@moorsvalleygolf.co.uk
♠ Desmond Meharg (Mgr)
🖥 www.moors-valley.co.uk/golf

Parkstone (1909)
Links Road, Parkstone, Poole BH14 9QS
☎ **(01202) 707138**
🖳 (01202) 706027
✉ admin@parkstonegolfclub.co.uk
♠ Gary Peddie (Gen Mgr)
🖥 www.parkstonegolfclub.co.uk

Parley Court (1992)
Proprietary
Parley Green Lane, Hurn, Christchurch
BH23 6BB
☎ **(01202) 591600**
🖳 (01202) 579043
✉ info@parleygolf.co.uk
♠ Mr Adrian Perry
🖥 www.parleygolf.co.uk

Queens Park
(Bournemouth) (1905)
Public
Queens Park West Drive, Queens Park,
Bournemouth BH8 9BY
☎ **(01202) 302611 Secretary**
🖳 (01202) 302611
✉ secretary@queensparkgolfclub
.co.uk
♠ P Greenwood (01202) 302611
🖥 www.queensparkgolfclub.co.uk

Remedy Oak (2006)
Proprietary
Horton Road, Woodlands, Dorset
BH21 8ND
☎ **(01202) 812070**
🖳 (01202) 812071
✉ info@remedyoak.com
♠ Nigel Tokely
🖥 www.remedyoak.com

Sherborne (1894)
Higher Clatcombe, Sherborne DT9 4RN
☎ **(01935) 812274**
🖳 (01935) 814218
✉ secretary@sherbornegolfclub
.co.uk
♠ Geoff Scott
🖥 www.sherbornegolfclub.co.uk

Solent Meads Golf Centre
(1965)
Public
Rolls Drive, Southbourne, Bournemouth
BH6 4NA
☎ **(01202) 420795**
✉ solentmeads@yahoo.co.uk
♠ Matt Steward (01202) 420795
🖥 www.solentmeads.com

Sturminster Marshall
(1992)
Pay and play
Moor Lane, Sturminster Marshall BH21
4AH
☎ **(01258) 858444**
✉ mike@sturminstermarshallgolfclub
.co.uk
♠ Mike Dodd
🖥 www.sturminstermarshallgolfclub
.co.uk

Wareham (1908)
Sandford Road, Wareham BH20 4DH
☎ **(01929) 554147**
🖳 (01929) 557993
✉ warehamgolf@tiscali.co.uk
♠ Richard Murgatroyd
🖥 www.warehamgolfclub.com

Weymouth (1909)
Links Road, Weymouth DT4 0PF
☎ **(01305) 750331**
🖳 (01305) 788029
✉ weymouthgolfclub@googlemail
.com
♠ Julie Fairbank (Club Administrator)
🖥 www.weymouthgolfclub.co.uk

Durham

Barnard Castle (1898)
Harmire Road, Barnard Castle DL12 8QN
☎ **(01833) 638355**
🖳 (01833) 695551
♠ J A Saunders
🖥 www.barnardcastlegolfclub.org

Beamish Park (1906)
Beamish, Stanley DH9 0RH
☎ **(0191) 370 1382**
🖳 (0191) 370 2937
✉ beamishgolf@btconnect.com
♠ John Bosanko (Hon Sec) (0191)
370 1382
🖥 www.beamishgolfclub.co.uk

Billingham (1967)
Sandy Lane, Billingham TS22 5NA
☎ **(01642) 533816/554494**
🖳 (01642) 533816
✉ billinghamgc@btconnect.com
♠ Julie Lapping (Sec/Mgr) (01642)
533816
🖥 www.billinghamgolfclub.com

Bishop Auckland (1894)
High Plains, Durham Road, Bishop Auckland
DL14 8DL
☎ **(01388) 661618**

🖳 (01388) 607005
✉ enquiries@bagc.co.uk
♠ D J Perriss
🖥 www.bagc.co.uk

Blackwell Grange (1930)
Briar Close, Blackwell, Darlington
DL3 8QX
☎ **(01325) 464458**
✉ secretary@blackwellgrangegolf
.com
♠ D C Christie (Hon)
🖥 www.blackwellgrangegolf.com

Brancepeth Castle (1924)
The Clubhouse, Brancepeth Village, Durham
DH7 8EA
☎ **(0191) 378 0075**
🖳 (0191) 378 3835
✉ enquiries@brancepeth-castle-
golf.co.uk
♠ Arthur Chadwick
🖥 www.brancepeth-castle-golf
.co.uk

Castle Eden (1927)
Castle Eden, Hartlepool TS27 4SS
☎ **(01429) 836510**
✉ castleedengolfclub@hotmail.com
♠ S J Watkin (0794) 114 1057
🖥 www.castleedengolfclub.co.uk

Chester-Le-Street (1908)
Lumley Park, Chester-Le-Street DH3 4NS
☎ **(0191) 388 3218**
✉ clsgcoffice@tiscali.co.uk
♠ Bill Routledge
🖥 www.clsgolfclub.co.uk

Consett & District (1911)
Elmfield Road, Consett DH8 5NN
☎ **(01207) 502186**
(Clubhouse)
🖳 (01207) 505060
✉ consettgolfclub@btconnect.com
♠ Vincent Kelly (Sec/Treasurer)
🖥 www.consettgolfclub.com

Crook (1919)
Low Job's Hill, Crook DL15 9AA
☎ **(01388) 762429**
🖳 (01388) 762137
✉ secretary@crookgolfclub.co.uk
♠ L Shaw
🖥 www.crookgolfclub.co.uk

Darlington (1908)
Haughton Grange, Darlington DL1 3JD
☎ **(01325) 355324**
✉ office@darlington-gc.co.uk
♠ M Etherington
🖥 www.darlington-gc.co.uk

Dinsdale Spa (1910)
Neasham Road, Middleton, St George,
Darlington DL2 1DW
☎ **(01325) 332297**
🖳 (01325) 332297
✉ dinsdalespagolf@btconnect.com
♠ A Patterson
🖥 www.dinsdalespagolfclub.co.uk

Durham City (1887)
Littleburn, Langley Moor, Durham DH7 8HL
☎ **(0191) 378 0069**
🖳 (0191) 378 4265
✉ enquiries@durhamcitygolf.co.uk
🖉 David Stainsby (0191) 378 0069
🖥 www.durhamcitygolf.co.uk

Eaglescliffe (1914)
Yarm Road, Eaglescliffe, Stockton-on-Tees TS16 0DQ
☎ **(01642) 780238 (Clubhouse)**
🖳 (01642) 781128
✉ secretary@eaglescliffegolfclub.co.uk
🖉 Alan McNinch (01642) 780238
🖥 www.eaglescliffegolfclub.co.uk

Hartlepool (1906)
Hart Warren, Hartlepool TS24 9QF
☎ **(01429) 274398**
🖳 (01429) 274129
✉ hartlepoolgolf@btconnect.com
🖉 G Laidlaw (Mgr) (01429) 274398
🖥 www.hartlepoolgolfclub.co.uk

High Throston (1997)
Proprietary
Hart Lane, Hartlepool TS26 0UG
☎ **(01429) 275325**
🖉 Mrs J Sturrock

Knotty Hill Golf Centre
(1992)
Pay and play
Sedgefield, Stockton-on-Tees TS21 2BB
☎ **(01740) 620320**
🖳 (01740) 622227
✉ knottyhill@btconnect.com
🖉 D Craggs (Mgr)
🖥 www.knottyhill.com

Mount Oswald (1934)
Pay and play
South Road, Durham City DH1 3TQ
☎ **(0191) 386 7527**
🖳 (0191) 386 0975
✉ info@mountoswald.co.uk
🖉 N Galvin
🖥 www.mountoswald.co.uk

Norton (1989)
Pay and play
Junction Road, Norton, Stockton-on-Tees TS20 1SU
☎ **(01642) 676385**

Oakleaf Golf Complex (1993)
Pay and play
School Aycliffe Lane, Newton Aycliffe DL5 6QZ
☎ **(01325) 310820**
🖳 (01325) 300873
✉ info@great-aycliffe.gov.uk
🖉 A Bailey (Mgr)
🖥 www.great-aycliffe.gov.uk

Ramside (1995)
Proprietary
Ramside Hall Hotel, Carrville, Durham DH1 1TD
☎ **(0191) 386 9514**

🖳 (0191) 386 9519
✉ kevin.jackson@ramsidehallhotel.co.uk
🖉 Kevin Jackson
🖥 www.ramsidehallhotel.co.uk

Roseberry Grange (1987)
Public
Grange Villa, Chester-Le-Street DH2 3NF
☎ **(0191) 370 0660**
🖳 (0191) 370 2047
✉ chrisjones@chester-le-street.gov.uk
🖉 R McDermott (Hon)

Royal Hobson (1978)
Hobson, Burnopfield, Newcastle-upon-Tyne NE16 6BZ
☎ **(01207) 271605**
✉ secretary@hobsongolfclub.co.uk
🖉 A J Giles (01207) 270941
🖥 www.hobsongolfclub.co.uk

Seaham (1908)
Shrewsbury Street, Dawdon, Seaham SR7 7RD
☎ **(0191) 581 2354**
✉ seahamgolfclub@btconnect.com
🖉 T Johnson (0191) 581 1268
🖥 www.seahamgolfclub.co.uk

Seaton Carew (1874)
Tees Road, Hartlepool TS25 1DE
☎ **(01429) 266249**
🖳 (01429) 267952
✉ seatoncarewgolfclub@btconnect.com
🖉 Secretary (01429) 266249 Ext 2
🖥 www.seatoncarewgolfclub.co.uk

South Moor (1923)
The Middles, Craghead, Stanley DH9 6AG
☎ **(01207) 232848/283525**
🖳 (01207) 284616
✉ secretary@southmoorgc.co.uk
🖉 M Brennan (0191) 373 0391
🖥 www.southmoorgc.co.uk

Stressholme (1976)
Public
Snipe Lane, Darlington DL2 2SA
☎ **(01325) 461002**
🖳 (01325) 461002
✉ stressholme@btconnect.com
🖉 R Givens
🖥 www.darlington.gov.uk/golf

Woodham G&CC (1983)
Proprietary
Burnhill Way, Newton Aycliffe DL5 4PN
☎ **(01325) 320574**
🖳 (01325) 315254
✉ woodhamproshop@googlemail.com
🖉 Ernie Wilson (Mgr)
🖥 www.woodhamgolfandcountryclub.co.uk

The Wynyard Club (1996)
Proprietary
Wellington Drive, Wynyard Park, Billingham TS22 5QJ
☎ **(01740) 644399**

🖳 (01740) 644599
✉ chris@wynardgolfclub.co.uk
🖉 C Mounter (Golf Dir)
🖥 www.wynardgolfclub.co.uk

Essex

Abridge G&CC (1964)
Epping Lane, Stapleford Tawney RM4 1ST
☎ **(01708) 688396**
✉ info@abridgegolf.com
🖉 Manager
🖥 www.abridgegolf.com

Ballards Gore G&CC (1980)
Proprietary
Gore Road, Canewdon, Rochford SS4 2DA
☎ **(01702) 258917**
🖳 (01702) 258571
✉ secretary@ballardsgore.com
🖉 Susan May (Sec)
🖥 www.ballardsgore.com

Basildon (1967)
Pay and play
Clay Hill Lane, Sparrow's Hearne, Basildon, Essex SS16 5HL
☎ **(01268) 533297**
✉ basildongc@onetel.com
🖉 G Eaton
🖥 www.basildongolfclub.org.uk

Belfairs (1926)
Public
Eastwood Road North, Leigh-on-Sea SS9 4LR
☎ **(01702) 525345 (Starter)**

Belhus Park G&CC (1972)
Pay and play
Belhus Park, South Ockendon RM15 4QR
☎ **(01708) 854260**
🖉 D Clifford

Bentley (1972)
Ongar Road, Brentwood CM15 9SS
☎ **(01277) 373179**
🖳 (01277) 375097
✉ info@bentleygolfclub.com
🖉 Andy Hall
🖥 www.bentleygolfclub.com

Benton Hall Golf & Country Club (1993)
Proprietary
Wickham Hill, Witham CM8 3LH
☎ **(01376) 502454**
🖳 (01376) 521050
✉ bentonhall.retail@theclubcompany.com
🖉 Scott Clark
🖥 www.theclubcompany.com

Birch Grove (1970)
Layer Road, Colchester CO2 0HS
☎ **(01206) 734276**
🖳 (01206) 734276
✉ maureen@birchgrove.fsbusiness.co.uk
🖉 Mrs M Marston
🖥 www.birchgrovegolfclub.co.uk

Boyce Hill (1922)
Vicarage Hill, Benfleet SS7 1PD
☎ **(01268) 793625**
📠 (01268) 750497
✉ secretary@boycehillgolfclub.co.uk
🖊 D Kelly
💻 www.boycehillgolfclub.co.uk

Braintree (1891)
Kings Lane, Stisted, Braintree CM77 8DD
☎ **(01376) 346079**
📠 (01376) 348677
✉ manager@braintreegolfclub.co.uk
🖊 Mr N Hawkins
💻 www.braintreegolfclub.co.uk

Braxted Park (1953)
Braxted Park, Witham CM8 3EN
☎ **(01376) 572372**
📠 (01376) 572372
✉ golf@braxtedpark.com
🖊 Mrs V Keeble
💻 www.braxtedpark.com

Bunsay Downs Golf Club
(1982)
Proprietary
Little Baddow Road, Woodham Walter,
Maldon CM9 6RU
☎ **(01245) 222648/222369**
✉ info@bunsaydownsgc.co.uk
🖊 J Durham (01245) 223258
💻 www.bunsaydownsgc.co.uk

Burnham-on-Crouch (1923)
Ferry Road, Creeksea, Burnham-on-Crouch
CM0 8PQ
☎ **(01621) 782282**
📠 (01621) 784489
✉ burnhamgolf@hotmail.com
🖊 S K Golf Ltd
💻 www.burnhamgolfclub.co.uk

The Burstead (1993)
Proprietary
Tye Common Road, Little Burstead,
Billericay CM12 9SS
☎ **(01277) 631171**
📠 (01277) 632766
✉ info@thebursteadgolfclub.com
🖊 Stuart Mence (Managing Director)
💻 www.thebursteadgolfclub.com

Canons Brook (1962)
Elizabeth Way, Harlow CM19 5BE
☎ **(01279) 421482**
📠 (01279) 626393
✉ manager@canonsbrook.com
🖊 Mrs SJ Langton
💻 www.canonsbrook.com

Castle Point (1988)
Public
Waterside Farm, Somnes Avenue, Canvey
Island SS8 9FG
☎ **(01268) 510830**
🖊 Mrs B de Koster

Channels (1974)
Belsteads Farm Lane, Little Waltham,
Chelmsford CM3 3PT
☎ **(01245) 440005**

📠 (01245) 442032
✉ info@channelsgolf.co.uk
🖊 Mrs SJ Larner
💻 www.channelsgolf.co.uk

Chelmsford (1893)
Widford Road, Chelmsford CM2 9AP
☎ **(01245) 256483**
📠 (01245) 256483
✉ office@chelmsfordgc.co.uk
🖊 G Winckless (01245) 256483
💻 www.chelmsfordgc.co.uk

Chigwell (1925)
High Road, Chigwell IG7 5BH
☎ **(020) 8500 2059**
📠 (020) 8501 3410
✉ info@chigwellgolfclub.co.uk
🖊 James Fuller (Gen Mgr)
💻 www.chigwellgolfclub.co.uk

Chingford (1923)
158 Station Road, Chingford, London
E4 6AN
☎ **(0208) 529 2107**
🖊 B W Woods

Clacton-on-Sea (1892)
West Road, Clacton-on-Sea CO15 1AJ
☎ **(01255) 421919**
📠 (01255) 424602
✉ secretary@clactongolfclub.com
🖊 Brian Telford
💻 www.clactongolfclub.com

Colchester GC (1907)
21 Braiswick, Colchester CO4 5AU
☎ **(01206) 853396**
📠 (01206) 852698
✉ secretary@colchestergolfclub
.com
🖊 Julie Ruscoe
💻 www.colchestergolfclub.com

Colne Valley (1991)
Station Road, Earls Colne CO6 2LT
☎ **(01787) 224343**
📠 (01787) 224126
✉ info@colnevalleygolfclub.co.uk
🖊 T Smith (01787) 224343
💻 www.colnevalleygolfclub.co.uk

Crondon Park (1994)
Proprietary
Stock Road, Stock CM4 9DP
☎ **(01277) 841115**
📠 (01277) 841356
✉ info@crondon.com
🖊 P Cranwell
💻 www.crondon.com

Crowlands Heath Golf Club
(2000)
Pay and play
Wood Lane, Dagenham, Essex
RM8 1JX
☎ **(020) 8984 7373**
📠 (020) 8984 0505
✉ chris@chrisjenkinsgolf.com
🖊 Marcus Radmore (Mgr)
💻 www.chrisjenkinsgolf.com

Elsenham Golf and Leisure
(1997)
Proprietary
Hall Road, Elsenham, Bishop's Stortford
CM22 6DH
☎ **(01279) 812865**
✉ info@elsenhamgolfandleisure.co.uk
🖊 Martin McKenna (Gen Mgr)
💻 www.egcltd.co.uk

Epping Golf Club (1996)
Proprietary
Flux Lane, Epping, Essex CM16 7NJ
☎ **(01992) 572282**
📠 (01992) 575512
✉ info@eppinggolfcourse.org.uk
🖊 Mr Neil Sjöberg
⊕ Half mile walk from Epping Central
Line Underground Station.
💻 www.eppinggolfcourse.org.uk

Essex G&CC (1990)
Earls Colne, Colchester CO6 2NS
☎ **(01787) 224466**
✉ essex.golfops@theclubcompany
.com
💻 www.theclubcompany.com

Five Lakes Resort (1995)
Colchester Road, Tolleshunt Knights,
Maldon CM9 8HX
☎ **(01621) 868888 (Hotel)**
✉ office@fivelakes.co.uk
💻 www.fivelakes.co.uk

Forrester Park (1975)
Beckingham Road, Great Totham, Maldon
CM9 8EA
☎ **(01621) 891406**
📠 (01621) 891903
✉ housemanager@forresterparkltd
.com
🖊 T Forrester-Muir
💻 www.forresterparkltd.com

Frinton (1895)
1 The Esplanade, Frinton-on-Sea CO13 9EP
☎ **(01255) 674618**
📠 (01255) 682450
✉ enquiries@frintongolfclub.com
🖊 Malcolm Boucher
💻 www.frintongolfclub.com

Garon Park Golf Complex
(1993)
Pay and play
Eastern Avenue, Southend-on-Sea, Essex
SS9 4FA
☎ **(01702) 601701**
📠 (01702) 601033
✉ debbie@garonparkgolf.co.uk
🖊 Mrs Debbie Wright
💻 www.garonparkgolf.co.uk

Gosfield Lake (1986)
Hall Drive, Gosfield, Halstead CO9 1SE
☎ **(01787) 474747**
📠 (01787) 476044
✉ gosfieldlakegc@btconnect.com
🖊 JA O'Shea (Sec/Mgr)
💻 www.gosfield-lake-golf-club.co.uk

Hainault Golf Club (1912)
Public
Romford Road, Chigwell Row IG7 4QW
☎ **(020) 8500 2131**
(Proshop/Reception)
✍ Gary Ivory (Mgr)
🖥 www.hainaultgolfclub.co.uk

Hanover G&CC (1991)
Proprietary
Hullbridge Road, Rayleigh SS6 9QS
☎ **(01702) 232377**
✉ hanovergolf@aol.com

Hartswood (1967)
Pay and play
King George's Playing Fields, Brentwood
CM14 5AE
☎ **(01277) 214830 (Bookings)**
🖵 (01277) 218850
✍ D Bonner (01227) 218850

Harwich & Dovercourt
(1906)
Station Road, Parkeston, Harwich
CO12 4NZ
☎ **(01255) 503616**
🖵 (01255) 503323
✉ secretary
@harwichanddovercourtgolfclub
.com
✍ PJ Cole (Hon Sec)
🖥 www.harwichanddovercourtgolfclub
.com

Ilford (1907)
291 Wanstead Park Road, Ilford IG1 3TR
☎ **(020) 8554 2930**
🖵 (020) 8554 0822
✉ secretary@ilfordgolfclub.com
✍ Janice Pinner (Mgr)
🖥 www.ilfordgolfclub.com

Langdon Hills (1991)
Proprietary
Lower Dunton Road, Bulphan RM14 3TY
☎ **(01268) 548444/544300**
🖵 (01268) 490084
✉ secretary@golflangdon.co.uk
✍ K Thompson (01268) 400064
🖥 www.langdonhillsgolfclub.co.uk

Lexden Wood (1993)
Proprietary
Bakers Lane, Colchester CO3 4AU
☎ **(01206) 843333**
🖵 (01206) 854775
✉ info@lexdenwood.com
✍ K Hanvey
🖥 www.lexdenwood.com

Lords Golf & CC (Notley)
(1995)
The Green, White Notley, Witham, Essex
CM8 1RG
☎ **(01376) 329328**
🖵 (01376) 569051
✉ julia@lordsgolf&countryclub.co.uk
✍ Julia Keenes
🖥 www.lordsgolf&countryclub.co.uk

Loughton (1981)
Pay and play
Clays Lane, Debden Green, Loughton
IG10 2RZ
☎ **(020) 8502 2923**
✍ A Day

Maldon (1891)
Beeleigh Langford, Maldon CM9 4SS
☎ **(01621) 853212**
🖵 (01621) 855232
✉ maldon.golf@virgin.net
✍ Viv Locke
🖥 www.maldon-golf.co.uk

Maylands (1936)
Proprietary
Colchester Road, Harold Park, Romford
RM3 0AZ
☎ **(01708) 341777**
🖵 (01708) 343777
✉ maylands@maylandsgolf.com
✍ (01708) 341777
🖥 www.maylandsgolf.com

North Weald (1996)
Proprietary
Rayley Lane, North Weald, Epping
CM16 6AR
☎ **(01992) 522118**
✉ info@northwealdgolfclub
.co.uk
✍ T Lloyd-Skinner
🖥 www.northwealdgolfclub.co.uk

Orsett (1899)
Brentwood Road, Orsett RM16 3DS
☎ **(01375) 891352**
🖵 (01375) 892471
✉ enquiries@orsettgolfclub.co.uk
✍ GH Smith (01375) 893409
🖥 www.orsettgolfclub.co.uk

Regiment Way Golf Centre
(1995)
Pay and play
Back Lane, Little Waltham, Chelmsford
CM3 3PR
☎ **(01245) 361100**
🖵 (01245) 442032
✉ info@regimentway.co.uk
✍ D Wallbank
🖥 www.channelsgolf.co.uk

Risebridge (1972)
Pay and play
Risebridge Chase, Lower Bedfords Road,
Romford RM1 4DG
☎ **(01708) 741429**
✉ pa.jennings@btconnect.co.uk
✍ P Jennings

Rivenhall Oaks Golf Centre
(1994)
Pay and play
Forest Road, Witham, Essex CM8 2PS
☎ **(01376) 510222**
🖵 (01376) 500316
✉ info@rivenhalloaksgolf.com
✍ B Chapman
🖥 www.rivenhalloaksgolf.com

Rochford Hundred (1893)
Rochford Hall, Hall Road, Rochford
SS4 1NW
☎ **(01702) 544302**
🖵 (01702) 541343
✉ admin@rochfordhundredgolfclub
.co.uk
✍ N T Wells
🖥 www.rochfordhundredgolfclub
.co.uk

Romford (1894)
Heath Drive, Gidea Park, Romford
RM2 5QB
☎ **(01708) 740007 (Members)**
🖵 (01708) 752157
✉ info@romfordgolfclub.co.uk
✍ M R J Hall (01708) 740986
🖥 www.romfordgolfclub.com

Royal Epping Forest (1888)
Forest Approach, Station Road, Chingford,
London E4 7AZ
☎ **(020) 8529 2195**
✉ office@refgc.co.uk
✍ Mrs D Woodland (0208) 529 2195
🖥 www.refgc.co.uk

Saffron Walden (1919)
Windmill Hill, Saffron Walden CB10 1BX
☎ **(01799) 522786**
🖵 (01799) 520313
✉ office@swgc.com
✍ Mrs Stephanie Standen
🖥 www.swgc.com

South Essex G&CC
Herongate, Brentwood CM13 3LW
☎ **(01277) 811289**
🖵 (01277) 811304
✉ southessexgolf@crown-golf.co.uk
✍ P Lecras (Gen Mgr)
🖥 www.crown-golf.co.uk

St Cleres (1994)
Proprietary
St Cleres Hall, Stanford-le-Hope SS17 0LX
☎ **(01375) 361565**
🖵 (01375) 361565
✉ david.wood@foremostgolf.com
✍ D Wood (01375) 361565

Stapleford Abbotts (1989)
Proprietary
Horseman's Side, Tysea Hill, Stapleford
Abbotts RM4 1JU
☎ **(01708) 381108**
🖵 (01708) 386345
✉ staplefordabbotts@crown-golf
.co.uk
✍ C Whittaker (Gen Mgr)
🖥 www.staplefordabbotts.golf.co.uk

Stock Brook Manor (1992)
Proprietary
Queen's Park Avenue, Stock, Billericay
CM12 0SP
☎ **(01277) 658181**
🖵 (01277) 633063
✉ events@stockbrook.com
✍ C Laurence (Golf Dir)
🖥 www.stockbrook.com

The Warren   (1932)
Proprietary
Woodham Walter, Maldon CM9 6RW
☎ **(01245) 223258/223198**
🖳 (01245) 223989
📧 enquiries@warrengolfclub.co.uk
🖋 J Durham (01245) 223258
🖥 www.warrengolfclub.co.uk

Theydon Bois   (1897)
Theydon Road, Theydon Bois, Epping CM16 4EH
☎ **(01992) 813054**
🖳 (01992) 815602
📧 theydonboisgolf@btconnect.com
🖋 D Bowles (01992) 813054
🖥 www.theydongolf.co.uk

Thorndon Park   (1920)
Ingrave, Brentwood CM13 3RH
☎ **(01277) 810345**
🖳 (01277) 810645
📧 office@thorndonpark.com
🖋 Mr G Thomas (mgr)
🖥 www.thorndonparkgolfclub.com

Thorpe Hall   (1907)
Thorpe Hall Avenue, Thorpe Bay SS1 3AT
☎ **(01702) 582205/(01702) 588195 Pro Shop**
🖳 (01702) 584498
📧 sec@thorpehallgc.co.uk
🖋 Ms F Gale
🖥 www.thorpehallgc.co.uk

Three Rivers G&CC   (1973)
Stow Road, Purleigh, Chelmsford CM3 6RR
☎ **(01621) 828631**
🖳 (01621) 828060
🖋 F Teixeria (Gen Mgr)
🖥 www.threeriversclub.com

Toot Hill   (1991)
Proprietary
School Road, Toot Hill, Ongar CM5 9PU
☎ **(01277) 365747**
🖳 (01277) 364509
📧 office@toothillgolfclub.co.uk
🖋 Mrs Cameron
🖥 www.toothillgolfclub.co.uk

Top Meadow   (1986)
Fen Lane, North Ockendon RM14 3PR
☎ **(01708) 852239 (Clubhouse)**
📧 info@topmeadow.co.uk
🖋 D Stock
🖥 www.topmeadow.co.uk

Towerlands Unex   (1985)
Panfield Road, Braintree CM7 5BJ
☎ **(01376) 326802**
🖳 (01376) 552487
📧 info@towerlandspark.com
🖋 Colin Cooper
🖥 www.towerlandspark.com

Upminster   (1928)
114 Hall Lane, Upminster RM14 1AU
☎ **(01708) 222788**
🖳 (01708) 222484
📧 secretary@upminstergolfclub.co.uk

🖋 RP Winmill
🖥 www.upminstergolfclub.co.uk

Wanstead   (1893)
Overton Drive, Wanstead, London E11 2LW
☎ **(0208) 989 3938**
🖳 (020) 8532 9138
📧 wgclub@aol.com
🖋 W T Cranston
🖥 www.wansteadgolf.org.uk

Warley Park   (1975)
Magpie Lane, Little Warley, Brentwood CM13 3DX
☎ **(01277) 224891**
🖳 (01277) 200679
📧 enquiries@warleyparkgc.co.uk
🖋 N Hawkins
🖥 www.warleyparkgc.co.uk

Weald Park   (1994)
Coxtie Green Road, South Weald, Brentwood CM14 5RJ
☎ **(01277) 375101**
🖥 www.wealdparkhotel.co.uk

West Essex   (1900)
Bury Road, Sewardstonebury, Chingford, London E4 7QL
☎ **(020) 8529 7558**
🖳 (020) 8524 7870
📧 sec@westessexgolfclub.co.uk
🖋 Mrs Emma Clifford
🖥 www.westessexgolfclub.co.uk

Woodford   (1890)
2, Sunset Avenue, Woodford Green IG8 0ST
☎ **(020) 8504 0553 (Clubhouse)**
🖳 (020) 8559 0504
📧 office@woodfordgolf.co.uk
🖋 PS Willett (020) 8504 3330
🖥 www.woodfordgolf.co.uk

Woolston Manor   (1994)
Woolston Manor, Abridge Road, Chigwell, Essex IP7 6BX
☎ **(020) 8500 2549**
🖳 (020) 8501 5452
📧 bradley@woolstonmanor.co.uk
🖋 P Spargo
🖥 www.woolstonmanor.co.uk

Gloucestershire

Brickhampton Court Golf Complex   (1995)
Proprietary
Cheltenham Road East, Churchdown, Gloucestershire GL2 9QF
☎ **(01452) 859444**
🖳 (01452) 859333
📧 info@brickhampton.co.uk
🖋 Natalie Dyke
🖥 www.brickhampton.co.uk

Bristol & Clifton   (1891)
Beggar Bush Lane, Failand, Clifton, Bristol BS8 3TH
☎ **(01275) 393474/393117**

🖳 (01275) 394611
📧 office@bristolgolf.co.uk
🖋 J S Macpherson (01275) 393474
🖥 www.bristolgolf.co.uk

Broadway   (1895)
Willersey Hill, Broadway, Worcs WR12 7LG
☎ **(01386) 853683**
🖳 (01386) 858643
📧 secretary@broadwaygolfclub.co.uk
🖋 Mr V Tofts
🖥 www.broadwaygolfclub.co.uk

Canons Court   (1982)
Pay and play
Bradley Green, Wotton-under-Edge GL12 7PN
☎ **(01453) 843128**
🖋 A Bennett
🖥 www.canonscourtgolf.co.uk

Chipping Sodbury   (1905)
Trinity Lane, Chipping Sodbury, Bristol BS37 6PU
☎ **(01454) 319042 (Members)**
🖳 (01454) 320052
📧 info@chippingsodburygolfclub.co.uk
🖋 Bob Williams
🖥 www.chippingsodburygolfclub.co.uk

Cirencester   (1893)
Cheltenham Road, Bagendon, Cirencester GL7 7BH
☎ **(01285) 652465**
🖳 (01285) 650665
📧 info@cirencestergolfclub.co.uk
🖋 R Collishaw (01285) 652465
🖥 www.cirencestergolfclub.co.uk

Cleeve Hill   (1892)
Pay and play
Cleeve Hill, Cheltenham GL52 3PW
☎ **(01242) 672025**
🖳 (01242) 678444
📧 hughfitzsimons@btconnect.com
🖋 Hugh Fitzsimons (Mgr)
🖥 www.cleevehillgolfclub.co.uk

Cotswold Edge   (1980)
Upper Rushmire, Wotton-under-Edge GL12 7PT
☎ **(01453) 844167**
🖳 (01453) 845120
📧 cotswoldedge@freenetname.co.uk
🖋 NJ Newman
🖥 www.cotswoldedgegolfclub.org.uk

Cotswold Hills   (1902)
Ullenwood, Cheltenham GL53 9QT
☎ **(01242) 515264**
🖳 (01242) 515317
📧 contact.us@cotswoldhills-golfclub.com
🖋 Mrs A Hale (Club Mgr)
🖥 www.cotswoldhills-golfclub.com

Dymock Grange   (1995)
The Old Grange, Leominster Road, Dymock GL18 2AN
☎ **(01531) 890840**

Filton (1909)
Golf Course Lane, Bristol BS34 7QS
☎ (0117) 969 4169
🖥 (0117) 931 4359
📧 thesecretary@filtongolfclub.co.uk
🖊 T Atkinson (0117) 969 4169
🖥 www.filtongolfclub.co.uk

Forest Hills (1992)
Proprietary
Mile End Road, Coleford GL16 7BY
☎ (01594) 810620
🖥 (01594) 810823
🖊 D Bowen (01594) 837134
🖥 www.fweb.org.uk/forestgolf

Forest of Dean (1973)
Lords Hill, Coleford GL16 8BE
☎ (01594) 832583
🖥 (01594) 832584
📧 enquiries@bellshotel.co.uk
🖊 H Wheeler (Hon Sec)
🖥 www.bellshotel.co.uk

Gloucester Golf & Country Club (1976)
Matson Lane, Gloucester, Gloucestershire
GL4 6EA
☎ (01452) 525653
🖊 K Wood (01452) 411311 (Mgr)

Henbury (1891)
Henbury Road, Westbury-on-Trym, Bristol
BS10 7QB
☎ (0117) 950 0044
🖥 (0117) 959 1928
📧 thesecretary@henburygolfclub
.co.uk
🖊 Derek Howell (0117) 950 0044
🖥 www.henburygolfclub.co.uk

Hilton Puckrup Hall Hotel
(1992)
Puckrup, Tewkesbury GL20 6EL
☎ (01684) 296200/271591
🖥 (01684) 850788
🖊 R Lazenby
🖥 www.puckrupgolf.co.uk

The Kendleshire (1997)
Proprietary
Henfield Road, Coalpit Heath, Bristol
BS36 2TG
☎ (0117) 956 7007
🖥 (0117) 957 3433
📧 info@kendleshire.com
🖊 P Murphy
🖥 www.kendleshire.com

Knowle (1905)
Fairway, West Town Lane, Brislington,
Bristol BS4 5DF
☎ (0117) 977 0660
🖥 (0117) 972 0615
📧 admin@knowlegolfclub.co.uk
🖊 (0117) 977 0660
🖥 www.knowlegolfclub.co.uk

Lilley Brook (1922)
Cirencester Road, Charlton Kings,
Cheltenham GL53 8EG
☎ (01242) 526785

📧 caroline@lilleybrook.co.uk
🖊 C Kirby (Sec)
🖥 www.lilleybrook.co.uk

Long Ashton (1893)
Clarken Coombe, Long Ashton, Bristol
BS41 9DW
☎ (01275) 392229
🖥 (01275) 394395
📧 secretary@longashtongolfclub
.co.uk
🖊 Victoria Rose
🖥 www.longashtongolfclub.co.uk

Lydney (1909)
Naas Course, Naas Lane, Lydney
GL15 5ES
☎ (01594) 842775
🖊 J Mills (01594) 841186
🖥 www.lydneygolfclub.co.uk

Minchinhampton (1889)
Minchinhampton, Stroud GL6 9BE
☎ (01453) 832642 (Old) 833866
(New)
🖥 (01453) 837360
📧 rob@mgcnew.co.uk
🖊 R East (01453) 833866
🖥 www.minchinhamptongolfclub
.co.uk

Naunton Downs (1993)
Proprietary
Naunton, Cheltenham GL54 3AE
☎ (01451) 850090
📧 admin@nauntondowns.co.uk
🖊 Jane Ayers
🖥 www.nauntondowns.co.uk

Newent (1994)
Pay and play
Coldharbour Lane, Newent GL18 1DJ
☎ (01531) 820478
📧 newentgolf@btconnect.com
🖊 T Brown
🖥 www.newentgolf.co.uk

Painswick (1891)
Golf Course Road, Painswick, Stroud
GL6 6TL
☎ (01452) 812180
📧 secretary.painswick@virginmedia
.com
🖊 Mrs Ann Smith
🖥 www.painswickgolf.com

Rodway Hill (1991)
Pay and play
Newent Road, Highnam GL2 8DN
☎ (01452) 384222
🖥 (01452) 313814
📧 info@rodway-hill-golf-course.co.uk
🖊 A Price
🖥 www.rodway-hill-golf-course.co.uk

Sherdons Golf Centre
(1993)
Pay and play
Tredington, Tewkesbury GL20 7BP
☎ (01684) 274782
🖥 (01684) 275358
📧 info@sherdons.co.uk

🖊 R Chatham
🖥 www.sherdons.co.uk

Shirehampton Park (1904)
Park Hill, Shirehampton, Bristol BS11 0UL
☎ (0117) 982 2083
🖥 (0117) 982 5280
📧 info@shirehamptonparkgolfclub
.co.uk
🖊 Karen Rix (0117) 982 2083
🖥 www.shirehamptonparkgolfclub
.co.uk

Stinchcombe Hill (1889)
Stinchcombe Hill, Dursley GL11 6AQ
☎ (01453) 542015
📧 secretary@stinchcombehill.plus
.com
🖥 www.stinchcombehillgolfclub.com

Tewkesbury Park Hotel
(1976)
Lincoln Green Lane, Tewkesbury GL20 7DN
☎ (01684) 295405 (Hotel)
🖥 (01684) 292386
📧 golfsec.tewkesburypark
@bespokehotels.com
🖊 Club Golf Sec (01684) 272322
🖥 www.tewkesburyparkgolfclub.co.uk

Thornbury Golf Centre
(1992)
Bristol Road, Thornbury BS35 3XL
☎ (01454) 281144
🖥 (01454) 281177
📧 info@thornburygc.co.uk
🖊 M Drake (Mgr)
🖥 www.thornburygc.co.uk

Woodlands G&CC (1989)
Pay and play
Trench Lane, Almondsbury, Bristol BS32 4JZ
☎ (01454) 619319
🖥 (01454) 619397
📧 golf@woodlands-golf.com
🖊 D Knipe
🖥 www.woodlands-golf.com

Woodspring G&CC (1994)
Proprietary
Yanley Lane, Long Ashton, Bristol
BS41 9LR
☎ (01275) 394378
🖥 (01275) 394473
📧 info@woodspring-golf.com
🖊 D Knipe
🖥 www.woodspring-golf.com

Hampshire

Alresford (1890)
Cheriton Road, Tichborne Down, Alresford
SO24 0PN
☎ (01962) 733746
🖥 (01962) 736040
📧 secretary@alresfordgolf.co.uk
🖊 D Maskery
🖥 www.alresfordgolf.co.uk

Alton   (1908)
Old Odiham Road, Alton GU34 4BU
☎ **(01420) 82042**

Ampfield Par Three   (1962)
Proprietary
Winchester Road, Ampfield, Romsey SO51 9BQ
☎ **(01794) 368480**
🖾 Mark Hazell (MD) 01794 368 480
🖳 www.ampfieldgolf.com

Andover   (1907)
51 Winchester Road, Andover SP10 2EF
☎ **(01264) 323980**
🖵 (01264) 358040
🖂 secretary@andovergolfclub.co.uk
🖾 Jon Lecisie (01264) 358040
🖳 www.andovergolfclub.co.uk

Army   (1883)
Laffan's Road, Aldershot GU11 2HF
☎ **(01252) 337272**
🖵 (01252) 337562
🖂 secretary@armygolfclub.com
🖾 Jim Galley
🖳 www.armygolfclub.com

Barton-on-Sea   (1897)
Milford Road, New Milton BH25 5PP
☎ **(01425) 615308**
🖵 (01425) 621457
🖂 admin@barton-on-sea-golf.co.uk
🖾 I Prentice
🖳 www.barton-on-sea-golf.co.uk

Basingstoke   (1907)
Kempshott Park, Basingstoke RG23 7LL
☎ **(01256) 465990**
🖵 (01256) 331793
🖂 office@basingstokegolfclub.co.uk
🖾 John Hiscock
🖳 www.basingstokegolfclub.co.uk

Bishopswood   (1978)
Proprietary
Bishopswood Lane, Tadley, Basingstoke RG26 4AT
☎ **(01189) 408600**
🖂 kpickett@bishopswoodgc.co.uk
🖾 Mrs J Jackson-Smith (0118) 982 0312 (Sec)
🖳 www.bishopswoodgc.co.uk

Blackmoor   (1913)
Whitehill, Bordon GU35 9EH
☎ **(01420) 472775**
🖵 (01420) 487666
🖂 admin@blackmoorgolf.co.uk
🖾 Mrs J Dean (Admin Mgr)
🖳 www.blackmoorgolf.co.uk

Blacknest   (1993)
Blacknest GU34 4QL
☎ **(01420) 22888**
🖵 (01420) 22001
🖂 blacknestgolfclub@yahoo.com
🖾 A Corbett

Botley Park Hotel G&CC   (1989)
Winchester Road, Boorley Green, Botley SO3 2UA
☎ **(01489) 780888 Ext 451**

🖵 (01489) 789242
🖂 golf.botley@macdonald-hotels.co.uk
🖾 Dean Rossilli (Gen Mgr)
🖳 www.macdonald-hotels.co.uk

Bramshaw   (1880)
Brook, Lyndhurst SO43 7HE
☎ **(023) 8081 3433**
🖵 (023) 8081 3460
🖂 golf@bramshaw.co.uk
🖾 Ian Baker
🖳 www.bramshaw.co.uk

Brokenhurst Manor   (1915)
Sway Road, Brockenhurst SO42 7SG
☎ **(01590) 623332**
🖵 (01590) 624691
🖂 secretary@brokenhurst-manor.org.uk
🖾 Neil Hallam Jones
🖳 www.brokenhurst-manor.org.uk

Burley   (1905)
Cott Lane, Burley, Ringwood BH24 4BB
☎ **(01425) 402431**
🖵 (01425) 404168
🖂 secretary@burleygolfclub.co.uk
🖾 Mrs L J Harfield (01425) 402431
🖳 www.burleygolfclub.co.uk

Cams Hall Estate   (1993)
Proprietary
Cams Hall Estate, Fareham PO16 8UP
☎ **(01329) 827222**
🖵 (01329) 827111
🖂 camshall@crown-golf.co.uk
🖾 R Climas (Sec/Mgr)
🖳 www.camshallgolf.co.uk

Chilworth   (1989)
Main Road, Chilworth, Southampton SO16 7JP
☎ **(023) 8074 0544**

Corhampton   (1891)
Corhampton, Southampton SO32 3GZ
☎ **(01489) 877279**
🖵 (01489) 877680
🖂 secretary@corhamptongc.co.uk
🖾 Bob Ashton
🖳 www.corhamptongc.co.uk

Dibden Golf Centre
(1974)
Public
Main Road, Dibden, Southampton SO45 5TB
☎ **(023) 8020 7508**
(Bookings)
🖳 www.nfdc.gov.uk/golf

Dummer   (1992)
Proprietary
Dummer, Basingstoke RG25 2AD
☎ **(01256) 397950 (Pro Shop)**
🖵 (01256) 397889
🖂 enquiries@dummergolfclub.com
🖾 Steve Wright (Mgr) (01256) 397888
🖳 www.dummergolfclub.com

Dunwood Manor   (1969)
Danes Road, Awbridge, Romsey SO51 0GF
☎ **(01794) 340549**
🖵 (01794) 341215
🖂 admin@dunwood-golf.co.uk
🖾 Hazel Johnson/Kenny Bygate
🖳 www.dunwoodgolf.co.uk

Fleetlands   (1961)
Fareham Road, Gosport PO13 0AW
☎ **(023) 9254 4492**

Four Marks   (1994)
Headmore Lane, Four Marks, Alton GU34 3ES
☎ **(01420) 587214**
🖵 (01420) 587324
🖾 General Manager
🖳 www.fourmarksgolf.co.uk

Furzeley   (1993)
Pay and play
Furzeley Road, Denmead PO7 6TX
☎ **(023) 9223 1180**
🖵 (023) 9223 0921
🖂 furzeleygc@btinternet.com
🖾 R Brown

Gosport & Stokes Bay   (1885)
Fort Road, Haslar, Gosport PO12 2AT
☎ **(023) 925 27941**
🖵 (023) 925 27941
🖂 secretary @gosportandstokesbaygolfclub .co.uk
🖾 Clun Manager (023) 925 27941
🖳 www.gosportandstokesbaygolfclub .co.uk

The Hampshire   (1993)
Pay and play
Winchester Road, Goodworth Clatford, Andover SP11 7TB
☎ **(01264) 357555**
🖵 (01264) 356606
🖂 enquiries@thehampshiregolfclub .co.uk
🖾 J Miles
🖳 www.thehampshiregolfclub.co.uk

Hartley Wintney   (1891)
London Road, Hartley Wintney, Hook RG27 8PT
☎ **(01252) 844211**
🖵 (01252) 844211
🖂 office@hartleywintneygolfclub.com
🖾 P J Gaylor
🖳 www.hartleywintneygolfclub.com

Hayling   (1883)
Links Lane, Hayling Island PO11 0BX
☎ **(023) 9246 4446**
🖂 members@haylinggolf.co.uk
🖾 Ian Walton (023) 9246 4446
🖳 www.haylinggolf.co.uk

Hockley   (1914)
Twyford, Winchester SO21 1PL
☎ **(01962) 713165**
🖂 admin@hockleygolfclub.com
🖾 Mrs A Pfam
🖳 www.hockleygolfclub.com

Lee-on-the-Solent (1905)
Brune Lane, Lee-on-the-Solent PO13 9PB
☎ **(023) 9255 1170**
📠 (023) 9255 4233
📧 enquiries@leegolf.co.uk
✎ Rob Henderson (Mgr) (023) 9255 1170
🖥 www.leegolf.co.uk

Liphook (1922)
Liphook GU30 7EH
☎ **(01428) 723271/723785**
📠 (01428) 724853
📧 secretary@liphookgolfclub.com
✎ John Douglass
🖥 www.liphookgolfclub.com

Meon Valley Marriott Hotel & Country Club (1979)
Proprietary
Sandy Lane, Shedfield, Southampton SO32 2HQ
☎ **(01329) 833455**
📠 (01329) 834411
📧 george.mcmenemy @marriotthotels.com
✎ GF McMenemy (Golf Dir)
🖥 www.marriottgolf.co.uk

New Forest (1888)
Southampton Road, Lyndhurst SO43 7BU
☎ **(023) 8028 2752**
📠 (023) 8028 4030
📧 secretarynfgc@aol.com
✎ Derek Hurlstone/Graham Lloyd
🖥 www.newforestgolfclub.co.uk

North Hants (1904)
Minley Road, Fleet GU51 1RF
☎ **(01252) 616443**
📠 (01252) 811627
📧 secretary@northhantsgolf.co.uk
✎ C J Gotla
🖥 www.northhantsgolf.co.uk

Old Thorns (1982)
Longmoor Road, Griggs Green, Liphook GU30 7PE
☎ **(01428) 724555**
📠 (01428) 725036
📧 proshop@oldthorns.com
✎ Greg Knights
🖥 www.oldthorns.com

Otterbourne Golf Centre (1995)
Pay and play
Poles Lane, Otterbourne, Winchester SO21 2EL
☎ **(01962) 775225**
📧 info@chilworthgolfclub.com
✎ C Garner
🖥 www.chilworthgolfclub.com

Park (1995)
Pay and play
Avington, Winchester SO21 1BZ
☎ **(01962) 779945 (Clubhouse)**
📠 (01962) 779530
📧 office@avingtongolf.co.uk
✎ R Stent (Prop)
🖥 www.avingtongolf.co.uk

Paultons Golf Centre (1922)
Pay and play
Old Salisbury Road, Ower, Romsey SO51 6AN
☎ **(023) 8081 3992**
🖥 www.crown-golf.co.uk

Petersfield (1892)
Tankerdale Lane, Liss GU33 7QY
☎ **(01730) 895165**
📧 manager@petersfieldgolfclub.co.uk
✎ PD Badger
🖥 www.petersfieldgolfclub.co.uk

Petersfield Pay and Play
Pay and play
139 Sussex Road, Petersfield GU31 4LE
☎ **(01730) 267732**
✎ PD Badger

Portsmouth (1926)
Pay and play
Crookhorn Lane, Widley, Waterlooville PO7 5QL
☎ **(023) 9237 2210**
📧 portsmouthgc@btconnect.com
✎ Mr Iden Adams (Sec) (023) 9220 1827
🖥 www.portsmouthgc.com

Quindell (1997)
Skylark Meadows, Whiteley, Fareham PO15 6RS
☎ **(01329) 844441**
📠 (01329) 836736
📧 sales@quindell.com
✎ Rob Terry
🖥 www.quindell.com

Romsey (1900)
Nursling, Southampton SO16 0XW
☎ **(023) 8073 4637**
📠 (023) 8074 1036
📧 secretary@romseygolfclub.co.uk
✎ Mike Batty
🖥 www.romseygolfclub.com

Rowlands Castle (1902)
Links Lane, Rowlands Castle PO9 6AE
☎ **(023) 9241 2784**
📠 (023) 9241 3649
📧 manager@rowlandscastlegolf .co.uk
✎ KD Fisher (023) 9241 2784
🖥 www.rowlandscastlegolfclub.co.uk

Royal Winchester (1888)
Sarum Road, Winchester SO22 5QE
☎ **(01962) 852462**
📠 (01962) 865048
📧 manager@royalwinchestergolf .com
✎ A Buck
🖥 www.royalwinchestergolfclub.com

Sandford Springs (1988)
Wolverton, Tadley RG26 5RT
☎ **(01635) 296800**
📠 (01635) 296801
📧 andreww@sandfordsprings.co.uk
✎ Andrew Wild (01635) 296800
🖥 www.sandfordsprings.co.uk

Somerley Park (1995)
Somerley, Ringwood BH24 3PL
☎ **(01425) 461496**
📧 gordon@ringwood.force9.co.uk
✎ Gordon Scott
🖥 www.somerleyparkgolfclub.co.uk

South Winchester
Pitt, Winchester, Hampshire SO22 5QW
☎ **(01962) 877800**
📠 (01962) 877900
📧 winchester-sales@crown-golf.co.uk
✎ L Ross (Gen Mgr) (01962) 877800
🖥 www.crown-golf.co.uk

Southampton Municipal (1935)
Public
1 Golf Course Road, Bassett, Southampton SO16 7AY
☎ **(023) 807 60546**
📧 mick.carter7@ntlworld.com
✎ E Hemsley
🖥 www.southamptongolfclub.co.uk

Southsea (1914)
Public
The Clubhouse, Burrfields Road, Portsmouth PO3 5JJ
☎ **(023) 9266 8667**
📠 (023) 9266 8667
📧 southseagolfclub@tiscali.co.uk
✎ R Collinson (02392) 699110
🖥 www.southsea-golf.co.uk

Southwick Park (1977)
Pinsley Drive, Southwick PO17 6EL
☎ **(023) 9238 0131 Option 1**
📠 (0871) 855 6809
📧 jameslever @southwickparkgolfclub.co.uk
✎ J R Lever
🖥 www.southwickparkgolfclub .co.uk

Southwood (1977)
Public
Ively Road, Farnborough GU14 0LJ
☎ **(01252) 548700**
📠 (01252) 549091
📧 ianattoe@ddesure.co.uk
✎ Chris Hudson (01252) 665452
🖥 www.southwoodgolfclub.co.uk

Stoneham (1908)
Monks Wood Close, Bassett, Southampton SO16 3TT
☎ **(023) 8076 9272**
📠 (023) 8076 6320
📧 richard@stonehamgolfclub .org.uk
✎ R Penley-Martin (Mgr)
🖥 www.stonehamgolfclub.org.uk

Test Valley (1992)
Micheldever Road, Overton, Basingstoke RG25 3DS
☎ **(01256) 771737**
📧 info@testvalleygolf.com
🖥 www.testvalleygolf.com

Tylney Park   (1973)
Proprietary
Rotherwick, Hook RG27 9AY
☎ **(01256) 762079**
🖳 (01256) 763079
📧 contact@tylneypark.co.uk
🖊 Alasdair Hay (Mgr)
📧 www.tylneypark.co.uk

Waterlooville   (1907)
*Cherry Tree Ave, Cowplain, Waterlooville
PO8 8AP*
☎ **(023) 9226 3388**
🖳 (023) 9224 2980
📧 secretary@waterloovillegolfclub
.co.uk
🖊 J Hay
📧 www.waterloovillegolfclub.co.uk

Wellow   (1991)
Proprietary
*Ryedown Lane, East Wellow, Romsey
SO51 6BD*
☎ **(01794) 322872**
🖳 (01794) 323832
🖊 Mrs C Gurd
📧 www.wellowgolfclub.co.uk

Weybrook Park   (1971)
Rooksdown Lane, Basingstoke RG24 9NT
☎ **(01256) 320347**
🖳 (01256) 812973
📧 info@weybrookpark.co.uk
🖊 Mrs S Bowen (Sec)/Mr A Dillon
(Mgr)
📧 www.weybrookpark.co.uk

Wickham Park   (1991)
Proprietary
*Titchfield Lane, Wickham, Fareham
PO17 5PJ*
☎ **(01329) 833342**
🖳 (01329) 834798
📧 wickhampark@crown-golf.co.uk
🖊 Jonathan Tubb
📧 www.crown-golf.co.uk

Worldham   (1993)
Proprietary
Cakers Lane, Worldham, Alton GU34 3BF
☎ **(01420) 543151/544606**
🖳 (01420) 544606
📧 manager@worldhamgolfclub.co.uk
🖊 Ian Yates (01420) 544606
📧 www.worldhamgolfclub.co.uk

Herefordshire

Belmont Lodge   (1983)
Ruckhall Lane, Belmont, Hereford HR2 9SA
☎ **(01432) 352666**
🖳 (01432) 358090
📧 info@belmont-hereford.co.uk
🖊 Christopher T Smith (Gen Mgr)
📧 www.belmont-hereford.co.uk

Burghill Valley   (1991)
Proprietary
*Tillington Road, Burghill, Hereford
HR4 7RW*
☎ **(01432) 760456**

🖳 (01432) 761654
📧 admin@bvgc.co.uk
🖊 Mrs D Harrison (Office Mgr)
📧 www.bvgc.co.uk

Cadmore Lodge   (1990)
Pay and play
*Berrington Green, Tenbury Wells, Worcester
WR15 8TQ*
☎ **(01584) 810044**
🖳 (01584) 810044
📧 reception.cadmore
@cadmorelodge.com
🖊 Mike Miles
📧 www.cadmorelodge.co.uk

Hereford Golf Club   (1983)
Public
*Hereford Halo Leisure & Golf Club, Holmer
Road, Hereford HR4 9UD*
☎ **(01432) 344376**
🖳 (01432) 266281
🖊 G Morgan (Mgr)

Herefordshire   (1896)
*Raven's Causeway, Wormsley, Hereford
HR4 8LY*
☎ **(01432) 830219**
📧 herfordshire.golf@breathe.com
🖊 D Gwynne
📧 www.herefordshiregolfclub.co.uk

Kington   (1926)
Bradnor Hill, Kington HR5 3RE
☎ **(01544) 230340**
🖳 (01544) 231951
📧 info@kingtongolf.co.uk
🖊 N P Venables (01544) 388259
📧 www.kingtongolf.co.uk

Leominster   (1967)
Ford Bridge, Leominster HR6 0LE
☎ **(01568) 610055**
🖳 (01568) 610055
📧 contact@leominstergolfclub.co.uk
🖊 I T Hamilton (01568) 610055
📧 leominstergolfclub.co.uk

Ross-on-Wye   (1903)
Two Park, Gorsley, Ross-on-Wye HR9 7UT
☎ **(01989) 720267**
🖳 (01989) 720212
📧 admin@therossonwyegolfclub
.co.uk
🖊 Sarah Creighton
📧 www.therossonwyegolfclub.co.uk

Sapey   (1991)
Proprietary
Upper Sapey, Worcester WR6 6XT
☎ **(01886) 853288**
🖳 (01886) 853485
📧 anybody@sapeygolf.co.uk
🖊 Miss L Stevenson (01886) 853506
📧 www.sapeygolf.co.uk

South Herefordshire   (1992)
*Twin Lakes, Upton Bishop, Ross-on-Wye
HR9 7UA*
☎ **(01989) 780535**
🖳 (01989) 740611

📧 info@herefordshiregolf.co.uk
🖊 James Leaver
📧 www.herefordshiregolf.co.uk

Summerhill   (1994)
Proprietary
*Clifford, Nr. Hay-on-Wye, Hereford HR3
5EW*
☎ **(01497) 820451**
📧 competitions
@summerhillgolfcourse.co.uk
🖊 Michael Tom
📧 www.summerhillgolfcourse.co.uk

Hertfordshire

Aldenham G&CC   (1975)
Proprietary
*Church Lane, Aldenham, Watford WD25
8NN*
☎ **(01923) 853929**
🖳 (01923) 858472
📧 info@aldenhamgolfclub.co.uk
🖊 Mrs J Phillips
📧 www.aldenhamgolfclub.co.uk

Aldwickbury Park   (1995)
Proprietary
*Piggottshill Lane, Wheathampstead Road,
Harpenden AL5 1AB*
☎ **(01582) 760112**
🖳 (01582) 760113
📧 info@aldwickburyparkgc.co.uk
🖊 T Hall
📧 www.aldwickburyparkgolfclub
.com

Arkley   (1909)
Rowley Green Road, Barnet EN5 3HL
☎ **(020) 8449 0394**
📧 secretary@arkley.demon.co.uk
🖊 A N Welsh
📧 www.arkleygolfclub.co.uk

Ashridge   (1932)
Little Gaddesden, Berkhamsted HP4 1LY
☎ **(01442) 842244**
🖳 (01442) 843770
📧 info@ashridgegolfclub.ltd.uk
🖊 Secretary
📧 www.ashridgegolfclub.ltd.uk

Barkway Park   (1992)
Proprietary
*Nuthampstead Road, Barkway, Royston
SG8 8EN*
☎ **(01763) 849070**
📧 gc@barkwaypark.fsnet.co.uk
🖊 GS Cannon
📧 www.barkwaypark.co.uk

Batchwood Hall   (1935)
Pay and play
Batchwood Drive, St Albans AL3 5XA
☎ **(01727) 844250**
📧 batchwood@leisureconnection
.co.uk
🖊 Luke Askew
📧 www.leisureconnection.co.uk

Batchworth Park (1996)
London Road, Rickmansworth WD3 1JS
☎ **(01923) 711400**
🖥 (01923) 710200
📧 manager@crown-golf.co.uk
✍ Rob Davies
🖳 www.batchworthparkgolf.co.uk

Berkhamsted (1890)
The Common, Berkhamsted HP4 2QB
☎ **(01442) 865832**
🖥 (01442) 863730
📧 Steve@berkhamstedgc.co.uk
✍ S H Derbyshire
🖳 www.berkhamstedgolfclub.co.uk

Bishop's Stortford (1910)
Dunmow Road, Bishop's Stortford CM23 5HP
☎ **(01279) 654715**
🖥 (01279) 655215
📧 office@bsgc.co.uk
✍ Judy Barker
🖳 www.bsgc.co.uk

Boxmoor (1890)
18 Box Lane, Hemel Hempstead HP3 0DJ
☎ **(01442) 242434 (Clubhouse)**
🖳 www.boxmoorgolfclub.co.uk

Brickendon Grange (1964)
Pembridge Lane, Brickendon, Hertford SG13 8PD
☎ **(01992) 511258**
🖥 (01992) 511411
📧 play@bggc.org.uk
✍ Jane Coulcher
🖳 www.bggc.org.uk

Briggens Park (1988)
Proprietary
Briggens Park, Stanstead Road, Stanstead Abbotts SG12 8LD
☎ **(01279) 793867**
🖥 (01279) 793867
📧 briggensparkgolf@aol.com
✍ Trevor Mitchell
🖳 www.briggensparkgolfclub.co.uk

Brocket Hall (1992)
Proprietary
Welwyn AL8 7XG
☎ **(01707) 368808**
🖥 (01707) 390052
📧 louis.matamala@brocket-hall.co.uk
✍ Louis Matamala (01707) 368740
🖳 www.brocket-hall.co.uk

Brookmans Park (1930)
Brookmans Park, Hatfield AL9 7AT
☎ **(01707) 652487**
🖥 (01707) 661851
📧 info@bpgc.co.uk
✍ Una Handley
🖳 www.bpgc.co.uk

Bushey G&CC (1980)
High Street, Bushey WD23 1TT
☎ **(020) 8950 2283 Pro Shop**
   (020) 8950 2215
🖥 (020) 8386 1181
📧 info@busheycountryclub.com

✍ Mark Young
🖳 www.busheycountryclub.com

Bushey Hall (1890)
Proprietary
Bushey Hall Drive, Bushey WD23 2EP
☎ **(01923) 222253**
🖥 (01923) 229759
📧 gordon@golfclubuk.co.uk
✍ Gordon Dawson
🖳 www.busheyhallgolfclub.co.uk

Chadwell Springs GC (1974)
Pay and play
Hertford Road, Ware SG12 9LE
☎ **(01920) 462075/(01920) 451447**
📧 chadwell.golfshop@virgin.net
✍ David Smith PGA Pro/Manager
🖳 www.chadwellspringsgolfshop.co.uk

Chesfield Downs (1991)
Pay and play
Jack's Hill, Graveley, Stevenage SG4 7EQ
☎ **(08707) 460020**

Cheshunt (1976)
Public
Park Lane, Cheshunt EN7 6QD
☎ **(01992) 629777**
📧 accounts.cpgc@btconnect.com
✍ B Furne

Chorleywood (1890)
Common Road, Chorleywood WD3 5LN
☎ **(01923) 282009**
🖥 (01923) 286739
📧 secretary@chorleywoodgolfclub.co.uk
✍ RA Botham
🖳 www.chorleywoodgolfclub.co.uk

Dyrham Park CC (1963)
Galley Lane, Barnet EN5 4RA
☎ **(020) 8440 3361**
🖥 (020) 8441 9836
📧 enquiries@dyrhampark.com
✍ David Adams
🖳 www.dyrhampark.com

East Herts (1899)
Hamels Park, Buntingford SG9 9NA
☎ **(01920) 821978**
🖥 (01920) 823700
📧 gm@easthertsgolfclub.co.uk
✍ Ms A McDonald
🖳 www.easthertsgolfclub.co.uk

Great Hadham (1993)
Proprietary
Great Hadham Road, Bishop's Stortford SG10 6JE
☎ **(01279) 843558**
🖥 (01279) 842122
📧 ian@ghgcc.co.uk
✍ I Bailey
🖳 www.ghgcc.co.uk

The Grove (2003)
Pay and play
Chandler's Cross, Rickmansworth WD3 4TG
☎ **(01923) 294266**

🖥 (01923) 294268
📧 golf@thegrove.co.uk
✍ Anna Darnell (Dir of Golf)
🖳 www.thegrove.co.uk

Hadley Wood (1922)
Beech Hill, Hadley Wood, Barnet EN4 0JJ
☎ **(020) 8449 4328**
🖥 (020) 8364 8633
📧 gm@hadleywoodgc.com
✍ WM Beckett (Gen Mgr)
🖳 www.hadleywoodgc.com

Hanbury Manor G&CC (1990)
Ware SG12 0SD
☎ **(01920) 487722**
🖥 (01920) 487692
📧 mhrs.stngs.golfevents@marriotthotels.com
✍ Mike Harrison (Director of Clubs)
🖳 www.hanbury-manor.co.uk

Harpenden (1894)
Hammonds End, Harpenden AL5 2AX
☎ **(01582) 712580**
🖥 (01582) 712725
📧 office@harpendengolfclub.co.uk
✍ FLK Clapp (Gen Mgr)
🖳 www.harpendengolfclub.co.uk

Harpenden Common (1931)
East Common, Harpenden AL5 1BL
☎ **(01582) 711320**
🖥 (01582) 711321
📧 admin@hcgc.co.uk
✍ Terry Crump (01582) 711325
🖳 www.harpendencommongolfclub.co.uk

Hartsbourne G&CC (1946)
Hartsbourne Avenue, Bushey Heath WD23 1JW
☎ **(020) 8421 7272**
🖥 (020) 8950 5357
📧 ian@hartsbournecountryclub.co.uk
✍ I Thomas
🖳 www.hartsbournecountryclub.co.uk

Hatfield London CC (1976)
Bedwell Park, Essendon, Hatfield AL9 6HN
☎ **(01707) 260360**
🖥 (01707) 278475
📧 info@hatfieldlondon.co.uk
✍ H Takeda
🖳 www.hatfieldlondon.co.uk

The Hertfordshire (1995)
Proprietary
Broxbournebury Mansion, White Stubbs Lane, Broxbourne EN10 7PY
☎ **(01992) 466666**
📧 hertfordshire@americangolf.co.uk

Kingsway Golf Centre (1991)
Proprietary
Cambridge Road, Melbourn, Royston SG8 6EY
☎ **(01763) 262943**

For key to symbols see page 717

☎ (01763) 263038
✉ kingswaygolf@btconnect.com
✍ Chris Page
🖳 www.kingswaygolfcentre.co.uk

Knebworth (1908)

Deards End Lane, Knebworth SG3 6NL
☎ **(01438) 812752 (Clubhouse)**
🖥 (01438) 815216
✉ admin@knebworthgolfclub.com
✍ Steve Barrett
🖳 www.knebworthgolfclub.com

Lamerwood (1996)

Codicote Road, Wheathampstead AL4 8RH
☎ **(01582) 833013**
🖥 (01582) 832604
✉ lamerwood.cc@virgin.net
✍ R Darling (Gen Mgr)
🖳 www.lamerwood.humaxuk.com

Letchworth (1905)

Letchworth Lane, Letchworth Garden City
SG6 3NQ
☎ **(01462) 683203**
🖥 (01462) 484567
✉ secretary@letchworthgolfclub.com
✍ Mrs Niki Hunter
🖳 www.letchworthgolfclub.com

Little Hay Golf Complex (1977)

Pay and play
Box Lane, Bovingdon, Hemel Hempstead
HP3 0XT
☎ **(01442) 833798**
🖥 (01442) 831399
✉ georgereid@sportspace.co.uk
✍ George Reid (Mgr)
🖳 www.sportspace.co.uk

Manor of Groves G&CC (1991)

Proprietary
High Wych, Sawbridgeworth CM21 0JU
☎ **(01279) 600777**
🖥 (01279) 600374
✉ golfsecretary@manorofgroves
   .co.uk
✍ R Walker (01279) 603559
🖳 www.manorgolf.net

Mid Herts (1892)

Gustard Wood, Wheathampstead
AL4 8RS
☎ **(01582) 832242**
🖥 (01582) 834834
✉ secretary@mid-hertsgolfclub.co.uk
✍ Martin Bennet
🖳 www.mid-hertsgolfclub.co.uk

Mill Green (1994)

Proprietary
Gypsy Lane, Mill Green, Welwyn Garden
City AL7 4TY
☎ **(01707) 276900**
🖥 (01707) 276898
✉ millgreen@crown-golf.co.uk
✍ Tim Hudson
🖳 www.millgreengolf.co.uk

Moor Park (1923)

Rickmansworth WD3 1QN
☎ **(01923) 773146**
🖥 (01923) 777109
✉ jon.moore@moorparkgc.co.uk
✍ JM Moore (01923) 773146
🖳 www.moorparkgc.co.uk

Old Fold Manor (1910)

Old Fold Lane, Hadley Green, Barnet
EN5 4QN
☎ **(020) 8440 9185**
🖥 (020) 8441 4863
✉ manager@oldfoldmanor.co.uk
✍ B Cullen (Mgr)
🖳 www.oldfoldmanor.co.uk

Oxhey Park (1991)

Pay and play
Prestwick Road, South Oxhey, Watford
WD19 7EX
☎ **(01923) 248213/210118**
✉ oxheyparkgolf@live.com
✍ James Wright (Prop)
🖳 www.oxheyparkgolfclub.co.uk

Panshanger Golf Complex (1976)

Public
Old Herns Lane, Welwyn Garden City
AL7 2ED
☎ **(01707) 333312/333350
   (Bookings)**
🖥 (01707) 390010
✉ trish.skinner@talk21.com
✍ Trish Skinner (07982) 259475
🖳 www.finesseleisure.com

Porters Park (1899)

Shenley Hill, Radlett WD7 7AZ
☎ **(01923) 854127**
🖥 (01923) 855475
✉ enquiries@porterspark.com
✍ P Marshall
🖳 www.porterspark.com

Potters Bar (1923)

Darkes Lane, Potters Bar, Hertfordshire
EN6 1DF
☎ **(01707) 652020**
🖥 (01707) 655051
✉ louise@pottersbargolfclub.com
✍ Louise Alabaster
🖳 www.pottersbargolfclub.com

Radlett Park Golf Club (1984)

Proprietary
Watling Street, Nr. Radlett WD6 3AA
☎ **(0208) 953 6115**
🖥 (0208) 207 6390
✉ info@radlettparkgolfclub.com
✍ Marc Warwick (Mgr/Pro) (0208)
   238694
🖳 www.radlettparkgolfclub.com

Redbourn (1970)

Proprietary
Kinsbourne Green Lane, Redbourn, St
Albans AL3 7QA
☎ **(01582) 793493**
🖥 (01582) 794362

✉ info@redbourngc.co.uk
✍ T Hall (01582) 793493
🖳 www.redbourngolfclub.com

Rickmansworth (1937)

Public
Moor Lane, Rickmansworth WD3 1QL
☎ **(01923) 775278**

Royston (1892)

Baldock Road, Royston SG8 5BG
☎ **(01763) 242696**
🖥 (01763) 246910
✉ roystongolf@btconnect.com
✍ S Clark (Mgr)
🖳 www.roystongolfclub.co.uk

Sandy Lodge (1910)

Sandy Lodge Lane, Northwood, Middx HA6
2JD
☎ **(01923) 825429**
🖥 (01923) 824319
✉ clivebailey@sandylodge.co.uk
✍ C H Bailey
🖳 www.sandylodge.co.uk

Shendish Manor Hotel & Golf Course (1988)

Pay and play
Shendish Manor, London Road, Apsley
HP3 0AA
☎ **(01442) 251806**
🖥 (01442) 230683
✉ golf@shendish-manor.com
✍ Seema Patel (Mgr) (01442) 251806
🖳 www.shendish-manor.com

South Herts (1899)

Links Drive, Totteridge, London N20 8QU
☎ **(020) 8445 2035**
🖥 (020) 8445 7569
✉ secretary@southhertsgolfclub
   .co.uk
✍ John Charlton (020) 8445 2035
🖳 www.southhertsgolfclub.co.uk

Stevenage (1980)

Public
Aston Lane, Stevenage SG2 7EL
☎ **(01438) 880424**
✍ P Winston

Verulam (1905)

226 London Road, St Albans AL1 1JG
☎ **(01727) 853327**
🖥 (01727) 812201
✉ gm@verulamgolf.co.uk
✍ R Farrer
🖳 www.verulamgolf.co.uk

Welwyn Garden City (1922)

Mannicotts, High Oaks Road, Welwyn
Garden City AL8 7BP
☎ **(01707) 325243**
🖥 (01707) 393213
✉ secretary
   @welwyngardencitygolfclub.co.uk
✍ D Spring (Gen Mgr)
🖳 www.welwyngardencitygolfclub
   .co.uk

West Herts (1890)
Cassiobury Park, Watford WD3 3GG
☎ **(01923) 236484**
📠 (01923) 222300
📧 gm@westhertsgolf.demon.co.uk
✍ R M McCue
🖥 www.westhertsgolfclub.co.uk

Wheathampstead (2001)
Pay and play
Harpenden Road, Wheathampstead, St Albans AL4 8EZ
☎ **(01582) 833941**
📠 (01582) 833941
📧 nlawrencegolfacademy@hotmail
.co.uk
✍ N Lawrence
🖥 www.wheathampstead.net/
golf-course

Whipsnade Park (1974)
Studham Lane, Dagnall HP4 1RH
☎ **(01442) 842330**
📠 (01442) 842090
📧 secretary@whipsnadeparkgolf
.co.uk
✍ R Whalley
🖥 www.whipsnadeparkgolf.co.uk

Whitehill (1990)
Proprietary
Dane End, Ware SG12 0JS
☎ **(01920) 438495**
📧 whitehillgolf@btconnect.com
🖥 www.whitehillgolf.co.uk

Isle of Man

Castletown Golf Links
(1892)
Proprietary
Fort Island, Derbyhaven IM9 1UA
☎ **(01624) 822211**
📠 (01624) 829661
📧 golfaccounts@manx.net
🖥 www.golfiom.com

Douglas (1891)
Public
Pulrose Road, Douglas IM2 1AE
☎ **(01624) 675952 (Clubhouse)**
📠 (01624) 616865
📧 douglasgolfclub@manx.net
✍ Mrs E Vincent (01624) 616865
🖥 www.douglasgolfclub.com

King Edward Bay (1893)
Groudle Road, Onchan IM3 2JR
☎ **(01624) 620430/673821**

Mount Murray G&CC
(1994)
Proprietary
Santon IM4 2HT
☎ **(01624) 695308**
📠 (01624) 611116
📧 sales@mountmurray.com
✍ A Laing (Pro)
🖥 www.mountmurray.com

Peel (1895)
Rheast Lane, Peel IM5 1BG
☎ **(01624) 842227**
📠 (01624) 843456
📧 peelgc@manx.net
✍ N Richmond (01624) 843456
🖥 www.peelgolfclub.com

Port St Mary (1903)
Public
Kallow Road, Port St Mary IM9 5EJ
☎ **(01624) 834932**
📠 (01624) 837231
✍ N Swimmin (07624) 498848

Ramsey (1891)
Brookfield Avenue, Ramsey IM8 2AH
☎ **(01624) 813365/812244**
📠 (01624) 815833
📧 ramseygolfclub@manx.net
✍ Mr J M Ferrier (01624) 812244
🖥 www.ramseygolfclub.im

Rowany (1895)
Rowany Drive, Port Erin IM9 6LN
☎ **(01624) 834108**
📠 (01624) 834072
📧 rowany@iommail.net
✍ CA Corrin (Mgr)
🖥 www.rowanygolfclub.com

Isle of Wight

Cowes (1909)
Crossfield Avenue, Cowes PO31 8HN
☎ **(01983) 280135 (Steward)**
📠 (01983) 292303
📧 secretary@cowesgolfclub.co.uk
✍ C lacey (01983) 292303
🖥 www.cowesgolfclub.co.uk

Freshwater Bay (1894)
Afton Down, Freshwater, Isle of Wight PO40 9TZ
☎ **(01983) 752955**
📠 (01983) 756704
📧 secretary@freshwaterbaygolfclub
.co.uk
✍ Kevin Garrett (01983) 752955
🖥 www.freshwaterbaygolfclub.co.uk

Newport (1896)
St George's Down, Shide, Newport PO30 3BA
☎ **(01983) 525076**
📠 (01983) 526711
📧 newportgc@btconnect.com
✍ Graham Darke (Pro) (01983) 525076
🖥 www.newportgolfclub.co.uk

Osborne (1904)
Osborne House Estate, East Cowes PO32 6JX
☎ **(01983) 295421**
📠 (01983) 292781
📧 manager@osbornegolfclub.co.uk
✍ AC Waite
🖥 www.osbornegolfclub.co.uk

Ryde (1895)
Binstead Road, Ryde PO33 3NF
☎ **(01983) 614809**
📠 (01983) 567418
📧 ryde.golfclub@btconnect.com
✍ RA Dean
🖥 www.rydegolf.co.uk

Shanklin & Sandown (1900)
The Fairway, Lake, Sandown PO36 9PR
☎ **(01983) 403217**
📠 (01983) 403007
📧 club@ssgolfclub.com
✍ AC Creed
🖥 www.ssgolfclub.com

Ventnor (1892)
Steephill Down Road, Ventnor PO38 1BP
☎ **(01983) 853326/853388**
📧 secretary@ventnorgolfclub
.co.uk
🖥 www.ventnorgolfclub.co.uk

Westridge (1990)
Pay and play
Brading Road, Ryde PO33 1QS
☎ **(01983) 613131**
📠 (01983) 567017
📧 westgc@aol.com
✍ Simon Hayward
🖥 www.westridgegolfcentre.co.uk

Kent

Aquarius (1912)
Marmora Rd, Honor Oak, London SE22 0RY
☎ **(020) 8693 1626**
📧 secretary@aquariusgolfclub.co.uk
✍ J Halliday
🖥 www.aquariusgolfclub.co.uk

Ashford (1903)
Sandyhurst Lane, Ashford TN25 4NT
☎ **(01233) 622655**
📠 (01233) 627494
📧 info@ashfordgolfclub.co.uk
✍ S Naylor (01233) 622655
🖥 www.ashfordgolfclub.co.uk

Austin Lodge (1991)
Upper Auston Lodge Road, Eynsford, Swanley DA4 0HU
☎ **(01322) 863000**

Barnehurst (1903)
Public
Mayplace Road East, Bexley Heath DA7 6JU
☎ **(01322) 523746**

Bearsted (1895)
Ware Street, Bearsted, Maidstone ME14 4PQ
☎ **(01622) 738198**
📠 (01622) 735608
📧 bearstedgolfclub@tiscali.co.uk
✍ Stuart Turner (01622) 738198
🖥 www.bearstedgolfclub.co.uk

Beckenham Place Park
(1907)
Public
Beckenham Hill Road, Beckenham BR3 2BP
☎ **(020) 8650 2292**
✉ beckenhamgolf@glendale-services
.co.uk
▤ www.glendale-services.co.uk

Bexleyheath   (1909)
Mount Road, Bexleyheath DA6 8JS
☎ **(020) 8303 6951**
✉ bexleyheathgolf@aol.com
✐ Mrs J Smith

Birchwood Park   (1990)
*Birchwood Road, Wilmington, Dartford
DA2 7HJ*
☎ **(01322) 662038**
▤ www.birchwoodparkgc.co.uk

Boughton   (1993)
Pay and play
*Brickfield Lane, Boughton, Faversham
ME13 9AJ*
☎ **(01227) 752277**
🖷 (01227) 752361
✉ greg@pentlandgolf.co.uk
✐ Sue Coleman
▤ www.pentlandgolf.co.uk

Broke Hill   (1993)
Sevenoaks Road, Halstead TN14 7HR
☎ **(01959) 533225**
✉ broke-sales@crows-golf.co.uk
▤ www.brokehillgolf.co.uk

Bromley   (1948)
Pay and play
Magpie Hall Lane, Bromley BR2 8JF
☎ **(020) 8462 7014**
🖷 (020) 8462 6916
✉ bromleygolfclub.co.uk
✐ Dave Langford (01959) 573376

Broome Park   (1981)
*Broome Park Estate, Barham, Canterbury
CT4 6QX*
☎ **(01227) 830728**
🖷 (01227) 832591
✉ golf@broomepark.co.uk
✐ Mrs D Burtenshaw
▤ www.broomepark.co.uk

Canterbury   (1927)
*Scotland Hills, Littlebourne Road,
Canterbury CT1 1TW*
☎ **(01227) 453532**
🖷 (01227) 784277
✉ secretary@canterburygolfclub
.co.uk
✐ Jonathan Webb (Secretary)
▤ www.canterburygolfclub.co.uk

Chart Hills   (1993)
Proprietary
Weeks Lane, Biddenden, Ashford TN27 8JX
☎ **(01580) 292222**
🖷 (01580) 292233
✉ info@charthills.co.uk
✐ David Colyer
▤ www.charthills.co.uk

Chelsfield Lakes Golf Centre   (1992)
Pay and play
Court Road, Orpington BR6 9BX
☎ **(01689) 896266**
🖷 (01689) 824577
✉ chelsfieldlakes@crown-golf.co.uk
✐ Alex Taylor (Mgr)
▤ www.chelsfieldlakesgolf.co.uk

Cherry Lodge   (1969)
*Jail Lane, Biggin Hill, Westerham
TN16 3AX*
☎ **(01959) 572250**
✉ info@cherrylodgegc.co.uk
✐ Craig Sutherland
▤ www.cherrylodgegc.co.uk

Chestfield   (1925)
103 Chestfield Road, Whitstable CT5 3LU
☎ **(01227) 794411**
🖷 (01227) 794454
✉ generalmanager@chestfield-
golfclub.co.uk
✐ Alan Briggs
▤ www.chestfield-golfclub.co.uk

Chislehurst   (1894)
*Camden Place, Camden Park Road,
Chislehurst BR7 5HJ*
☎ **(020) 8467 6798**
🖷 (020) 8295 0874
✉ thesecretary@chislehurstgolfclub
.co.uk
✐ M Hickson (020) 8467 2782
▤ www.chislehurstgolfclub.co.uk

Cobtree Manor Park   (1984)
Public
*Chatham Road, Boxley, Maidstone
ME14 3AZ*
☎ **(01622) 753276**
✉ cobtree@mytimegolf.co.uk
✐ Steve Miller
▤ www.cobtreemanorparkgolfcourse
.co.uk

Darenth Valley   (1973)
Pay and play
*Station Road, Shoreham, Sevenoaks
TN14 7SA*
☎ **(01959) 522944 (Clubhouse)**
🖷 (01959) 525089
✉ enquiries@dvgc.co.uk
✐ Deborah Terry
▤ www.dvgc.co.uk

Dartford   (1897)
*The Clubhouse, Heath Lane (Upper),
Dartford DA1 2TN*
☎ **(01322) 223616**
🖷 (01322) 226455
✉ dartfordgolf@hotmail.com
✐ Mrs Amanda Malas (01322) 226455
▤ www.dartfordgolfclub.co.uk

Deangate Ridge Golf & Sports Complex   (1972)
Public
Duxcourt Road, Hoo, Rochester ME3 8RZ
☎ **(01634) 254481 (Gen Mgr)**
✉ leisure@medway.gov.uk

✐ Lee Mills (Gen Mgr) (01634)
254481
▤ www.deangateridge.co.uk

Eastwell Manor   (2008)
Boughton Lees, Ashford, Kent TN25 4HR
☎ **(01233) 213100**
🖷 (01233) 213105
✉ enquiries@eastwellmanor.co.uk
✐ Phil Redman (Mgr)
▤ www.eastwellmanor.co.uk

Eltham Warren   (1890)
Bexley Road, Eltham, London SE9 2PE
☎ **(0208) 850 4477**
🖷 (0208) 850 0522
✉ secretary@elthamwarren.idps
.co.uk
✐ DJ Mabbott (020) 8850 4477
▤ www.elthamwarrengolfclub.co.uk

Etchinghill   (1995)
Pay and play
*Canterbury Road, Etchinghill, Folkestone
CT18 8FA*
☎ **(01303) 863863**
🖷 (01303) 863210
✉ deb@pentlandgolf.co.uk
✐ D Francis (01303) 864576
▤ www.pentlandgolf.co.uk

Faversham   (1902)
Belmont Park, Faversham ME13 0HB
☎ **(01795) 890561**
🖷 (01795) 890760
✉ themanager@favershamgolf
.co.uk
✐ J Edgington
▤ www.favershamgolf.co.uk

Fawkham Valley   (1987)
*Gay Dawn Farm, Fawkham, Dartford
DA3 8LZ*
☎ **(01474) 707144**
✉ fvgolfcourse@googlemail.com
✐ J Marchant
▤ www.fawkhamvalleygolf.co.uk

Gillingham   (1905)
Woodlands Road, Gillingham ME7 2AP
☎ **(01634) 853017/850999**
✉ golf@gillinghamgolf.idps.co.uk
✐ Miss K Snow (01634) 853017
▤ www.gillinghamgolfclub.co.uk

Hawkhurst   (1968)
High Street, Hawkhurst TN18 4JS
☎ **(01580) 752396**
🖷 (01580) 754074
✉ hawkhurstgolfclub@tiscali
.co.uk
▤ HawkhurstGolfClub.org.uk

Hemsted Forest   (1969)
Proprietary
Golford Road, Cranbrook TN17 4AL
☎ **(01580) 712833**
🖷 (01580) 714274
✉ golf@hemstedforest.co.uk
✐ K Stevenson
▤ www.hemstedforest.co.uk

Herne Bay   (1895)
Eddington, Herne Bay CT6 7PG
☎ **(01227) 374097**
📧 sue.brown@hernebaygolfclub.co.uk
🖥 www.hernebaygolfclub.co.uk

Hever Castle   (1993)
Proprietary
Hever Road, Hever TN8 7NP
☎ **(01732) 700771**
📠 (01732) 700775
📧 mail@hever.co.uk
✍ Jon Wittenberg
🖥 www.hever.co.uk

High Elms   (1969)
Public
High Elms Road, Downe, Orpington BR6 7SZ
☎ **(01689) 858175**
📠 (01689) 856326
✍ Mrs P O'Keeffe (Hon)
🖥 www.highelmsgolfclub.com

Hilden Golf Centre
Pay and play
Rings Hill, Hildenborough, Tonbridge TN11 8LX
☎ **(01732) 833607**
📠 (01732) 834484
📧 info@hildenpark.co.uk
✍ Jan Parfett
🖥 www.hildenpark.co.uk

Hythe Imperial   (1950)
Prince's Parade, Hythe CT21 6AE
☎ **(01303) 233745**
📠 (01303) 267554 (Professional)
📧 h6862-th@accor.com
✍ Clare Gibson (01303) 233724
🖥 www.mercure-uk.com

The Kent & Surrey G&CC
(1972)
Proprietary
Crouch House Road, Edenbridge TN8 5LQ
☎ **(01732) 867381**
📠 (01732) 867167
📧 info@thekentandsurrey.com
✍ Mark Hickson
🖥 www.thekentandsurrey.com

Kent National G&CC   (1993)
Watermans Lane, Brenchley, Tonbridge TN12 6ND
☎ **(01892) 724400**
📧 info@kentnational.com
🖥 www.@kentnational.com

Kings Hill   (1996)
Proprietary
Fortune Way, Kings Hill, West Malling, Kent ME19 4GF
☎ **(01732) 875040/842121**
   (Bookings)
📠 (01732) 875019
📧 office@kingshill.co.uk
✍ Margaret Gilbert (Mgr)
🖥 www.kingshillgolf.co.uk

Knole Park   (1924)
Seal Hollow Road, Sevenoaks TN15 0HJ
☎ **(01732) 452150**
📠 (01732) 463159
📧 secretary@knoleparkgolfclub.co.uk
✍ N Statham (01732) 452150
🖥 www.knoleparkgolfclub.co.uk

Lamberhurst   (1890)
Church Road, Lamberhurst TN3 8DT
☎ **(01892) 890591**
📠 (01892) 891140
📧 secretary@lamberhurstgolfclub
   .com
✍ Mrs S Deadman (01892) 890591
🖥 www.lamberhurstgolfclub.com

Langley Park   (1910)
Barnfield Wood Road, Beckenham BR3 6SZ
☎ **(020) 8658 6849**
📠 (020) 8658 6310
📧 manager@langleyparkgolf.co.uk
✍ S Naylor (Gen Mgr)
🖥 www.langleyparkgolf.co.uk

Leeds Castle   (1928)
Pay and play
Leeds Castle, Hollingbourne, Maidstone ME17 1PL
☎ **(01622) 880467/767828**
📠 (01622) 735616
📧 stevepurves@leeds-castle.co.uk
🖥 www.leeds-castle.com

Littlestone   (1888)
St Andrews Road, Littlestone, New Romney TN28 8RB
☎ **(01797) 362310**
📠 (01797) 362740
📧 secretary@littlestonegolfclub
   .org.uk
✍ S Fullager (01797) 363355
🖥 www.littlestonegolfclub.org.uk

Littlestone Warren   (1993)
Pay and play
St Andrews Road, Littlestone, New Romney TN28 8RB
☎ **(01797) 362231**
📠 (01797) 362740
📧 secretary@littlestonegolfclub
   .org.uk
✍ S Fullager 01797 363355
🖥 www.romneywarrengolfclub.org.uk

London Beach Golf Club
(1998)
Pay and play
Ashford Road, St Michaels, Tenterden TN30 6HX
☎ **(01580) 767616**
📠 (01580) 763884
📧 enquiries@londonbeach.com
✍ P Edmonds
🖥 www.londonbeach.com

London Golf Club   (1993)
Stansted Lane, Ash, Nr Brands Hatch, Kent TN15 7EH
☎ **(01474) 879899**
📠 (01474) 879912

📧 golf@londongolf.co.uk
✍ Austen Gravestock
🖥 www.londongolf.co.uk

Lullingstone Park   (1967)
Public
Parkgate Road, Chelsfield, Orpington BR6 7PX
☎ **(01959) 533793**
✍ CJ Pocock (0208) 303 9535
🖥 www.lullingstoneparkgolfclub.com

Lydd   (1994)
Proprietary
Romney Road, Lydd, Romney Marsh TN29 9LS
☎ **(01797) 320808**
📠 (01797) 321482
📧 golf@lyddgolfclub.co.uk
✍ Carole Harradine
🖥 www.lyddgolfclub.co.uk

Mid Kent   (1908)
Singlewell Road, Gravesend DA11 7RB
☎ **(01474) 568035**
📠 (01474) 564218
📧 pamholden@mkgc.co.uk
✍ Mrs P Holden (01474) 568035
🖥 www.mkgc.co.uk

Nizels   (1992)
Nizels Lane, Hildenborough, Tonbridge TN11 8NU
☎ **(01732) 833833**
📧 nizels@theclubcompany.com
🖥 www.theclubcompany.com

North Foreland   (1903)
Convent Road, Broadstairs, Kent CT10 3PU
☎ **(01843) 862140**
📠 (01843) 862663
📧 office@northforeland.co.uk
✍ AJ Adams (01843) 862140
🖥 www.northforeland.co.uk

Oastpark   (1992)
Pay and play
Malling Road, Snodland ME6 5LG
☎ **(01634) 242661**
📠 (01634) 240744
📧 oastparkgolfclub@btconnect.com
✍ Lesley Murrock (01634) 242818

Park Wood   (1994)
Proprietary
Chestnut Avenue, Tatsfield, Westerham TN16 2EG
☎ **(01959) 577744**
📠 (01959) 577765
📧 mail@parkwoodgolf.co.uk
✍ John Barnes (Gen Mgr)
🖥 www.parkwoodgolf.co.uk

Pedham Place Golf Centre
(1996)
Proprietary
London Road, Swanley BR8 8PP
☎ **(01322) 867000**
📠 (01322) 861646
📧 info@ppgc.co.uk
✍ Tim Milford (Head Pro)
🖥 www.ppgc.co.uk

Poult Wood   (1974)
Public
Higham Lane, Tonbridge TN11 9QR
☎ (01732) 364039 (Bookings)

Prince's   (1906)
Proprietary
Sandwich Bay, Sandwich CT13 9QB
☎ (01304) 611118
🖷 (01304) 612000
✉ office@princesgolfclub.co.uk
✏ J T George (Dir) (01304) 626909
🖥 www.princesgolfclub.co.uk

Redlibbets   (1996)
Proprietary
West Yoke, Ash, Nr Sevenoaks TN15 7HT
☎ (01474) 879190
🖷 (01474) 879290
✉ info@redlibbets.com
✏ K Morris
🖥 www.redlibbets.co.uk

The Ridge   (1993)
Proprietary
Chartway Street, Sutton Valence, Maidstone
ME17 3JB
☎ (01622) 844382
✉ info@theridgegolfclub.co.uk
✏ Jemma Stoner (Gen Mngr)
🖥 www.theridgegolfclub.co.uk

Rochester & Cobham Park
(1891)
Park Pale, by Rochester ME2 3UL
☎ (01474) 823411
🖷 (01474) 824446
✉ rcpgc@talk21.com
✏ J S Aughterlony
🖥 www.rochesterandcobhamgc.co.uk

Royal Blackheath   (1608)
Court Road, Eltham, London SE9 5AF
☎ (020) 8850 1795
🖷 (020) 8859 0150
✉ info@rbgc.com
✏ G Hogg
🖥 www.royalblackheath.com

Royal Cinque Ports   (1892)
Golf Road, Deal CT14 6RF
☎ (01304) 374007 (Office)
🖷 (01304) 379530
✉ ken.hannah@royalcinqueports.com
✏ Ken Hannah (01304) 374007
🖥 www.royalcinqueports.com

Royal St George's   (1887)
Sandwich CT13 9PB
☎ (01304) 613090
🖷 (01304) 611245
✉ secretary@royalstgeorges.com
✏ Colonel T Checketts OBE
🖥 www.royalstgeorges.com

Sene Valley   (1888)
Sene, Folkestone CT18 8BL
☎ (01303) 268513
🖷 (01303) 237513
✉ senevalleygolf@btconnect.com
✏ Gordon Syers (Mgr)
🖥 www.senevalleygolfclub.co.uk

Sheerness   (1909)
Power Station Road, Sheerness ME12 3AE
☎ (01795) 662585
🖷 (01795) 668100
✉ secretary@sheernessgolfclub.co.uk
✏ D Nehra
🖥 www.sheernessgolfclub.co.uk

Shooter's Hill   (1903)
Lowood, Eaglesfield Road, London
SE18 3DA
☎ (020) 8854 6368
🖷 (020) 8854 0469
✉ john@shgc.uk.com
✏ J Clement (020) 8854 6368
🖥 www.shgc.uk.com

Shortlands   (1894)
Meadow Road, Shortlands, Bromley
BR2 0DX
☎ (020) 8460 2471
🖷 (020) 8460 8828
✉ enquiries@shortlandsgolfclub.co.uk
✏ PS May (020) 8460 8828
🖥 www.shortlandsgolfclub.co.uk

Sidcup   (1891)
Hurst Road, Sidcup DA15 9AW
☎ (020) 8300 2150
🖷 (020) 8300 2150
✉ sidcupgolfclub@googlemail.com
✏ Steve Armstrong (020) 8300 2150
🖥 www.sidcupgolfclub.co.uk

Sittingbourne & Milton Regis   (1929)
Wormdale, Newington, Sittingbourne
ME9 7PX
☎ (01795) 842261
✉ sittingbournegc@btconnect.com
✏ Charles Maxted
🖥 www.sittingbournegolfclub.com

Southern Valley   (1999)
Pay and play
Thong Lane, Gravesend, Kent DA12 4LT
☎ (01474) 568568
🖷 (01474) 360366
✉ info@southernvalley.co.uk
✏ Paul Thornberry (Managing Director)
🖥 www.southernvalley.co.uk

St Augustines   (1907)
Cottington Road, Cliffsend, Ramsgate
CT12 5JN
☎ (01843) 590333
🖷 (01843) 590444
✉ sagc@ic24.net
✏ RM Cooper
🖥 www.staugustinesgolfclub.co.uk

Staplehurst Golf Centre
Cradducks Lane, Staplehurst TN12 0DR
☎ (01580) 893362
🖥 www.staplehurstgolfcentre.co.uk

Sundridge Park   (1901)
Garden Road, Bromley BR1 3NE
☎ (020) 8460 0278
🖷 (020) 8289 3050
✉ luke@spgc.co.uk
✏ Luke Edgcumbe (020) 8460 0278
🖥 www.spgc.co.uk

Sweetwoods Park   (1994)
Proprietary
Cowden, Edenbridge TN8 7JN
☎ (01342) 850729
🖷 (01342) 850866
✉ golf@sweetwoodspark.com
🖥 www.sweetwoodspark.com

Tenterden   (1905)
Woodchurch Road, Tenterden TN30 7DR
☎ (01580) 763987
🖷 (01580) 763430
✉ enquiries@tenterdengolfclub.co.uk
✏ Mrs Teresa Cuff
🖥 www.tenterdengolfclub.co.uk

Thamesview Golf Centre
(1991)
Pay and play
Fairway Drive, Summerton Way,
Thamesmead, London SE28 8PP
☎ (020) 8310 7975
🖷 (020) 8312 0546
✉ golf@tvgc.co.uk
✏ Stephen Lee
🖥 www.tvgc.co.uk

The Halford-Hewitt Cup

The Halford Hewitt Cup was founded in 1924 as a competition for old boys of 64 English and Scottish public schools.

Described as "the greatest of all truly amateur tournaments", the cup is hosted by the Royal Cinque Ports Golf Club. In 1950, the competition became too large for a single club to host so Royal St George's Golf Club was asked to help. Since then, half the field has played its initial two rounds at Royal St George's.

Tudor Park   (1988)
Proprietary
Ashford Road, Bearsted, Maidstone
ME14 4NQ
☎ **(01622) 739412**
🖥 (01622) 735360
📧 brad.mclean1@marriotthotels.com
✍ Brad McLean
🖳 www.marriottgolf.com

Tunbridge Wells   (1889)
Langton Road, Tunbridge Wells TN4 8XH
☎ **(01892) 523034**
📧 tunbridgewelgolf@btconnect.com
✍ Peter Annington (01892) 536918
🖳 www.tunbridgewellsgolf.com

Upchurch River Valley
(1991)
Pay and play
Oak Lane, Upchurch, Sittingbourne
ME9 7AY
☎ **(01634) 360626**
🖥 (01634) 387784
📧 secretary@urvgc.co.uk
✍ Graham Driscoll (01634) 260594
🖳 www.urvgc.co.uk

Walmer & Kingsdown
(1909)
The Leas, Kingsdown, Deal CT14 8EP
☎ **(01304) 373256**
🖥 (01304) 382336
📧 info@kingsdowngolf.co.uk
✍ David Nehra
🖳 www.kingsdowngolf.co.uk

Weald of Kent   (1992)
Proprietary
Maidstone Road, Headcorn TN27 9PT
☎ **(01622) 890866**
🖥 (01622) 890070
📧 proshop@weald-of-kent.co.uk
✍ Matt Pickard (Golf Operations Mgr)
🖳 www.weald-of-kent.co.uk

West Kent   (1916)
Milking Lane, Downe, Orpington
BR6 7LD
☎ **(01689) 851323**
🖥 (01689) 858693
📧 golf@wkgc.co.uk
✍ Sean Trussell
🖳 www.wkgc.co.uk

West Malling   (1974)
Addington, Maidstone ME19 5AR
☎ **(01732) 844785**
📧 mail@westmallinggolf.com
🖳 www.westmallinggolf.com

Westerham   (1997)
Proprietary
Valence Park, Brasted Road, Westerham
TN16 1LJ
☎ **(01959) 567100**
🖥 (01959) 567101
📧 info@westerhamgc.co.uk
✍ R Sturgeon (Gen Mgr)
🖳 www.westerhamgc.co.uk

Westgate & Birchington
(1893)
176 Canterbury Road, Westgate-on-Sea
CT8 8LT
☎ **(01843) 831115/833905**
📧 wandbgc@tiscali.co.uk
✍ TJ Sharp
🖳 www.westgate-and-birchington-golfclub.co.uk

Whitstable & Seasalter
(1911)
Collingwood Road, Whitstable CT5 1EB
☎ **(01227) 272020**
🖥 (01227) 280822
📧 wandsgolfclub@talktalk.net
✍ MD Moore
🖳 www.whitstableandseasalter golfclub.co.uk

Wildernesse   (1890)
Park Lane, Seal, Kent TN15 0JE
☎ **(01732) 761199**
🖥 (01732) 763809
📧 secretary@wildernesse.co.uk
✍ Maj (Mr A Lawrence
🖳 www.wildernesse.co.uk

Woodlands Manor   (1928)
Woodlands, Tinkerpot Lane, Sevenoaks
TN15 6AB
☎ **(01959) 523806**
📧 info@woodlandsmanorgolf.co.uk
✍ CG Robins (01959) 523806
🖳 www.woodlandsmanorgolf.co.uk

Wrotham Heath   (1906)
Seven Mile Lane, Comp, Sevenoaks
TN15 8QZ
☎ **(01732) 884800**
📧 wrothamheathgolf@btconnect.com

✍ J H Hodgson
🖳 www.wrothamheathgolfclub.co.uk

Lancashire

Accrington & District   (1893)
West End, Oswaldtwistle, Accrington
BB5 4LS
☎ **(01254) 381614**
🖥 (01254) 350111
📧 info@accringtongolfclub.com
✍ S Padbury (01254) 350112
🖳 www.accringtongolfclub.com

Ashton & Lea   (1913)
Tudor Ave, Off Blackpool Rd, Lea, Preston
PR4 0XA
☎ **(01772) 735282**
🖥 (01772) 735762
📧 info@ashtonleagolfclub.co.uk
✍ S Plumb (01772) 735282
🖳 www.ashtonleagolfclub.co.uk

Ashton-in-Makerfield
(1902)
Garswood Park, Liverpool Road, Ashton-in-Makerfield, Wigan WN4 0YT
☎ **(01942) 727267**
🖥 (01942) 719330
📧 secretary@ashton-in-makerfieldgolfclub.co.uk
✍ G S Lacy
🖳 www.ashton-in-makerfieldgolfclub.co.uk

Ashton-under-Lyne   (1912)
Gorsey Way, Hurst, Ashton-under-Lyne
OL6 9HT
☎ **(0161) 330 1537**
📧 info@ashtongolfclub.co.uk
🖳 www.ashtongolfclub.co.uk

Bacup   (1910)
Maden Road, Bankside Lane, Bacup OL13 8HN
☎ **(01706) 873170**
📧 secretary_bgc@btconnect.com
✍ Mrs A Cook (01706) 874372

Baxenden & District   (1913)
Top o' th' Meadow, Baxenden, Accrington
BB5 2EA
☎ **(01254) 234555**
📧 baxgolf@hotmail.com
✍ N Turner (01706) 225423
🖳 www.baxendengolf.co.uk

The St George's Grand Challenge Cup

Inaugurated in 1888, the St George's Grand Challenge Cup is open to amateur golfers from recognised golf clubs and is presented by Royal St George's Golf Club, host to many top amateur and professional tournaments including The Open Championship, the Walker Cup, the Curtis Cup and the PGA Championship.

Sir Michael Bonallack (successful on three occasions), Jack Nicklaus and Lee Westwood are among the competition's prestigious winners.

Beacon Park G&CC   (1982)
Public
Beacon Lane, Dalton, Up Holland WN8 7RU
- ☎ **(01695) 622700**
- 🖳 info@beaconparkgolf.com
- ✍ Mark Prosser
- 🖩 www.beaconparkgolf.com

Blackburn   (1894)
Beardwood Brow, Blackburn BB2 7AX
- ☎ **(01254) 51122**
- 🖳 (01254) 665578
- 🖂 sec@blackburngolfclub.com
- ✍ N C Readett (Hon Sec)
- 🖩 www.blackburngolfclub.com

Blackpool North Shore
(1904)
Devonshire Road, Blackpool FY2 0RD
- ☎ **(01253) 352054**
- 🖳 (01253) 591240
- 🖂 office@bnsgc.com
- ✍ Mrs C L Woosnam (01253) 352054 ext 1
- 🖩 www.bnsgc.com

Blackpool Park   (1925)
Public
North Park Drive, Blackpool FY3 8LS
- ☎ **(01253) 397916**
- 🖳 (01253) 397916
- 🖂 secretary@blackpoolparkgc.co.uk
- ✍ Don McLeod
- 🖩 www.blackpoolparkgc.co.uk

Bolton   (1891)
Lostock Park, Bolton BL6 4AJ
- ☎ **(01204) 843067**
- 🖳 (01204) 843067
- 🖂 secretary@boltongolfclub.co.uk
- ✍ S Higham (01204) 843067
- 🖩 www.boltongolfclub.co.uk

Bolton Old Links   (1891)
Chorley Old Road, Montserrat, Bolton BL1 5SU
- ☎ **(01204) 842307**
- 🖳 (01204) 497549
- 🖂 mail@boltonoldlinksgolfclub.co.uk
- ✍ Mrs J Boardman (01204) 842307
- 🖩 www.boltonoldlinksgolfclub.co.uk

Bolton Open Golf Course
Pay and play
Longsight Park, Longsight Lane, Harwood BL2 4JX
- ☎ **(01204) 597659/309778**

Brackley Municipal   (1977)
Public
Bullows Road, Little Hulton, Worsley M38 9TR
- ☎ **(0161) 790 6076**

Breightmet   (1911)
Red Bridge, Ainsworth, Bolton BL2 5PA
- ☎ **(01204) 527381**
- ✍ R K Green
- 🖩 www.breightmetgolfclub.co.uk

Brookdale   (1896)
Medlock Road, Woodhouses, Failsworth M35 9WQ
- ☎ **(0161) 681 4534**
- 🖳 (0161) 688 6872
- 🖂 brookdalegolf@btconnect.com
- ✍ P Brownlow
- 🖩 www.brookdalegolf.co.uk

Burnley   (1905)
Glen View, Burnley BB11 3RW
- ☎ **(01282) 455266**
- 🖳 (01282) 451281
- 🖂 burnleygolfclub@onthegreen .co.uk
- ✍ D A Brown
- 🖩 www.burnleygolfclub.com

Bury   (1890)
Unsworth Hall, Blackford Bridge, Bury BL9 9TJ
- ☎ **(0161) 766 4897**
- 🖳 (0161) 796 3480
- 🖂 secretary@burygolfclub.com
- ✍ David Parkinson
- 🖩 www.burygolfclub.com

Castle Hawk   (1975)
Chadwick Lane, Castleton, Rochdale OL11 3BY
- ☎ **(01706) 640841**
- 🖂 teeoff@castlehawk.co.uk

Chorley   (1897)
Hall o' th' Hill, Heath Charnock, Chorley PR6 9HX
- ☎ **(01257) 480263**
- 🖳 (01257) 480722
- 🖂 secretary@chorleygolfclub .freeserve.co.uk
- ✍ Mrs A Green (01257) 480263
- 🖩 www.chorleygolfclub.co.uk

Clitheroe   (1891)
Whalley Road, Clitheroe BB7 1PP
- ☎ **(01200) 422292**
- 🖳 (01200) 422292
- 🖂 secretary@clitheroegolfclub.com
- ✍ Michael Walls
- 🖩 www.clitheroegolfclub.com

Colne   (1901)
Law Farm, Skipton Old Road, Colne BB8 7EB
- ☎ **(01282) 863391**
- 🖳 (01282) 870547
- 🖂 colnegolfclub@hotmail.co.uk
- ✍ A Turpin (Hon)
- 🖩 www.colnegolfclub.com

Crompton & Royton
(1908)
High Barn, Royton, Oldham OL2 6RW
- ☎ **(0161) 624 0986**
- 🖳 (0161) 652 4711
- 🖂 secretary @cromptonandroytongolfclub.co.uk
- ✍ J A Osbaldeston (0161) 624 0986
- 🖩 www.cromptonandroytongolfclub .co.uk

Darwen   (1893)
Winter Hill, Duddon Avenue, Darwen BB3 0LB
- ☎ **(01254) 701287**
- 🖳 (01254) 773833
- 🖂 admin@darwengolfclub.com
- ✍ J Howarth (01254) 704367
- 🖩 www.darwengolfclub.com

Dean Wood   (1922)
Lafford Lane, Up Holland, Skelmersdale WN8 0QZ
- ☎ **(01695) 622219**
- 🖳 (01695) 622245
- 🖂 ray.benton@deanwoodgolfclub .co.uk
- ✍ WR Benton
- 🖩 www.deanwoodgolfclub.co.uk

Deane   (1906)
Broadford Road, Deane, Bolton BL3 4NS
- ☎ **(01204) 61944**
- 🖳 (01204) 652047
- 🖂 secretary@deanegolfclub.com
- ✍ Frank Hodgkiss (01204) 651808
- 🖩 www.deanegolfclub.co.uk

Dunscar   (1908)
Longworth Lane, Bromley Cross, Bolton BL7 9QY
- ☎ **(01204) 303321**
- 🖳 (01204) 303321
- 🖂 dunscargolfclub@uk2.net
- ✍ Mrs A E Jennings (01204) 303321
- 🖩 www.dunscargolfclub.co.uk

Duxbury Park   (1975)
Public
Duxbury Hall Road, Duxbury Park, Chorley PR7 4AS
- ☎ **(01257) 235095**
- 🖳 (01257) 241378
- 🖂 fholding2008@hotmail.co.uk
- ✍ F Holding (01257) 262209

Fairhaven   (1895)
Oakwood Avenue, Ansdell, Lytham St Annes FY8 4JU
- ☎ **(01253) 736741**
- 🖳 (01253) 736741
- 🖂 secretary@fairhavengolfclub.co.uk
- ✍ R Thompson
- 🖩 www.fairhavengolfclub.co.uk

Fishwick Hall   (1912)
Glenluce Drive, Farringdon Park, Preston PR1 5TD
- ☎ **(01772) 798300**
- 🖳 (01772) 704600
- 🖂 fishwickhallgolfclub@supanet.com
- ✍ Secretary
- 🖩 www.fishwickhallgolfclub.co.uk

Fleetwood   (1932)
Golf House, Princes Way, Fleetwood FY7 8AF
- ☎ **(01253) 773573**
- 🖂 secretary@fleetwoodgolf.co.uk
- ✍ Ernie Langford
- 🖩 www.fleetwoodgolf.co.uk

Gathurst (1913)
Miles Lane, Shevington, Wigan WN6 8EW
- ☎ **(01257) 252861 (Clubhouse)**
- 🖵 (01257) 255953
- ✉ secretary@gathurstgolfclub.co.uk
- ✍ Mrs I Fyffe (01257) 255235
- 🌐 www.gothurstgolfclub.co.uk

Ghyll (1907)
Ghyll Brow, Skipton Row, Barnoldswick BB18 6JH
- ☎ **(01282) 842466**
- ✉ secretary@ghyllgolfclub.co.uk
- ✍ R Presland (01282) 844359
- 🌐 www.ghyllgolfclub.co.uk

Great Harwood (1896)
Harwood Bar, Whalley Road, Great Harwood BB6 7TE
- ☎ **(01254) 884391**
- ✍ J Spibey
- 🌐 www.greatharwoodgolfclub.co.uk

Green Haworth (1914)
Green Haworth, Accrington BB5 3SL
- ☎ **(01254) 237580**
- ✉ enquiries@greenhaworth.co.uk
- 🌐 www.greenhaworthgolfclub.co.uk

Greenmount (1920)
Greenmount, Bury BL8 4LH
- ☎ **(01204) 883712**
- ✉ secretary@greenmountgolfclub
.co.uk
- ✍ D Beesley
- 🌐 www.greenmountgolfclub.co.uk

Haigh Hall (1972)
Public
Haigh Hall Country Park, Haigh, Wigan WN2 1PE
- ☎ **(01942) 833337 (Clubhouse)**
- ✉ secretary@haighhall-golfclub.co.uk
- ✍ SG Eyres
- 🌐 www.haighhall-golfclub.co.uk

Hart Common (1995)
Proprietary
Westhoughton Golf Centre, Wigan Road, Westhoughton BL5 2BX
- ☎ **(01942) 813195**
- ✍ B Hill (01942) 813195

Harwood (1926)
Roading Brook Road, Bolton BL2 4JD
- ☎ **(01204) 522878**
- ✉ secretary@harwoodgolfclub.co.uk
- ✍ H Howard
- 🌐 www.harwoodgolfclub.co.uk

De Vere Herons Reach (1993)
Proprietary
East Park Drive, Blackpool FY3 8LL
- ☎ **(01253) 766156**
- 🖵 (01253) 798800
- ✉ richard.bowman@devere-hotels.com
- ✍ P Heaton
- 🌐 www.deveregolf.co.uk

Heysham (1910)
Trumacar Park, Middleton Road, Heysham, Morecambe LA3 3JH
- ☎ **(01524) 851011**
- 🖵 (01524) 853030
- ✉ secretary@heyshamgolfclub.co.uk
- ✍ Mrs G E Gardner
- 🌐 www.heyshamgolfclub.co.uk

Hindley Hall (1905)
Hall Lane, Hindley, Wigan WN2 2SQ
- ☎ **(01942) 255131**
- ✉ hindleyhallgolfclub@hotmail.co.uk
- ✍ Ian Rimmer (01942) 255131
- 🌐 www.hindleyhallgolfclub.co.uk

Horwich (1895)
Victoria Road, Horwich BL6 5PH
- ☎ **(01204) 696980**

Hurlston Hall Golf & Country Club (1994)
Proprietary
Hurlston Lane, Southport Road, Scarisbrick L40 8HB
- ☎ **(01704) 840400**
- 🖵 (01704) 841404
- ✉ info@hurlstonhall.co.uk
- ✍ Aoife O'Brien (MD)
- 🌐 www.hurlstonhall.co.uk

Ingol (1981)
Proprietary
Tanterton Hall Road, Ingol, Preston PR2 7BY
- ☎ **(01772) 734556**
- ✉ ingol@golfers.net
- 🌐 www.ingolgolfclub.co.uk

Knott End (1910)
Wyreside, Knott End-on-Sea, Poulton-le-Fylde FY6 0AA
- ☎ **(01253) 810576**
- 🖵 (01253) 813446
- ✉ louise@knottendgolfclub.com
- ✍ Louise Freeman (01253) 810576
- 🌐 www.knottendgolfclub.com

Lancaster (1889)
Ashton Hall, Ashton-with-Stodday, Lancaster LA2 0AJ
- ☎ **(01524) 751247 (Secretary)**
- ✉ secretary@lancastergc.co.uk
- ✍ G Yates (01524) 751247
- 🌐 www.lancastergc.co.uk

Lansil (1947)
Caton Road, Lancaster LA4 3PE
- ☎ **(01524) 39269**
- ✍ M Lynch (01524) 62785
- 🌐 www.lansilgolfclub.org.uk

Leyland (1924)
Wigan Road, Leyland PR25 5UD
- ☎ **(01772) 436457**
- 🖵 (01772) 435605
- ✉ manager@leylandgolfclub.co.uk
- ✍ S Drinkall
- 🌐 www.leylandgolfclub.co.uk

Lobden (1888)
Whitworth, Rochdale OL12 8XJ
- ☎ **(01706) 343228**
- 🖵 (01706) 343228
- ✉ lobdengc@hotmail.com
- ✍ B Harrison (01706) 852752

Longridge (1877)
Fell Barn, Jeffrey Hill, Longridge, Preston PR3 2TU
- ☎ **(01772) 783291**
- 🖵 (01772) 783022
- ✉ secretary@longridgegolfclub.co.uk
- ✍ D Carling
- 🌐 www.longridgegolfclub.co.uk

Lowes Park (1915)
Hilltop, Lowes Road, Bury BL9 6SU
- ☎ **(0161) 764 1231**
- ✉ lowesparkgc@btconnect.com
- ✍ Alan Taylor
- 🌐 www.lowesparkgc.co.uk

Lytham Green Drive (1913)
Ballam Road, Lytham St Annes FY8 4LE
- ☎ **(01253) 737390**
- 🖵 (01253) 731350
- ✉ secretary@lythamgreendrive.co.uk
- ✍ I Stewart (01253) 737390
- 🌐 www.lythamgreendrive.co.uk

Marland (1928)
Public
Springfield Park, Bolton Road, Rochdale OL11 4RE
- ☎ **(01706) 649801**

Marsden Park (1969)
Public
Townhouse Road, Nelson BB9 8DG
- ☎ **(01282) 661912**
- 🖵 (01282) 661384
- ✉ martin.robinson
@pendleleisuretrust.co.uk
- ✍ D Walton (01282) 835833
- 🌐 www.pendleleisuretrust.co.uk

Morecambe (1905)
Bare, Morecambe LA4 6AJ
- ☎ **(01524) 412841**
- 🖵 (01524) 400088
- ✉ secretary@morecambegolfclub
.com
- ✍ Mrs J Atkinson (01524) 412841
- 🌐 www.morecambegolfclub.com

Mossock Hall (1996)
Proprietary
Liverpool Road, Bickerstaffe L39 0EE
- ☎ **(01695) 421717**
- 🖵 (01695) 424961
- ✉ info@mossockhallgolfclub.co.uk
- ✍ Mel Brooke
- 🌐 www.mossockhallgolfclub.co.uk

Mytton Fold Hotel & Golf Complex (1994)
Proprietary
Whalley Road, Langho BB6 8AB
- ☎ **(01254) 240662 (Hotel)**
- 🖵 (01254) 248119
- ✉ golfshop@myttonfold.co.uk

✍ L Moorhouse
▤ www.myttonfold.co.uk

Nelson (1902)
Kings Causeway, Brierfield, Nelson BB9 0EU
☎ **(01282) 611834**
▢ (01282) 611834
✉ secretary@nelsongolfclub.com
✍ Richard M Lees
▤ www.nelsongolfclub.com

Oak Royal Golf & Country Club (2008)
Proprietary
Bury Lane, Withnell, Nr Chorley PR6 8SW
☎ **01254 830616**
✉ enquiries@oakroyalgolf-countryclub.co.uk
✍ Kath Downes
▤ www.oakroyalgolf-countryclub.co.uk

Oldham (1892)
Lees New Road, Oldham OL4 5PN
☎ **(0161) 624 4986**
▢ (0161) 624 4986
✉ info@oldhamgolfclub.com
✍ J Brooks

Ormskirk (1899)
Cranes Lane, Lathom, Ormskirk L40 5UJ
☎ **(01695) 572112**
▢ (01695) 572227
✉ mail@ormskirkgolfclub.com
✍ R K Oakes (01695) 572227
▤ www.ormskirkgolfclub.com

Pennington (1977)
Public/Municipal
Pennington Country Park, Leigh WN7 3PA
☎ **(01942) 741873/(01942) 682852 Shop**
✉ penningtongolfclub@blueyonder.co.uk
✍ Mr B W Lythgoe
▤ www.penningtongolfclub.co.uk

Penwortham (1908)
Blundell Lane, Penwortham, Preston PR1 0AX
☎ **(01772) 744630**
▢ (01772) 740172
✉ admin@penworthamgc.co.uk
✍ N Annandale
▤ www.penworthamgc.co.uk

Pleasington (1891)
Pleasington, Blackburn BB2 5JF
☎ **(01254) 202177**

✉ secretary-manager@pleasington-golf.co.uk
✍ C J Williams
▤ www.pleasington-golf.co.uk

Poulton-le-Fylde (1982)
Public
Myrtle Farm, Breck Road, Poulton-le-Fylde FY6 7HJ
☎ **(01253) 892444**
✉ greenwood-golf@hotmail.co.uk
✍ S Wilkinson
▤ www.poultonlefyldegolfclub.co.uk

Preston (1892)
Fulwood Hall Lane, Fulwood, Preston PR2 8DD
☎ **(01772) 700011**
▢ (01772) 794234
✉ secretary@prestongolfclub.com
✍ Mark Caunce
▤ www.prestongolfclub.com

Regent Park (Bolton) (1931)
Pay and play
Links Road, Chorley New Road, Bolton BL6 4AF
☎ **(01204) 495421**
✍ N Brazell (Professional) (01204) 495421
⊕ 18 hole Pay and Play. Food Available. Club comps on Saturdays.

Rishton (1927)
Eachill Links, Hawthorn Drive, Rishton BB1 4HG
☎ **(01254) 884442**
▢ (01254) 887701
✉ rishtongc@onetel.net
✍ Mr J Hargreaves MBE (Gen Mgr)
▤ www.rishton-golf-club.co.uk

Rochdale (1888)
Edenfield Road, Bagslate, Rochdale OL11 5YR
☎ **(01706) 643818 (Clubhouse)**
▢ (01706) 861113
✉ manager@rochdalegolfclub.co.uk
✍ P Kershaw (01706) 643818 (opt 2)
▤ www.rochdalegolfclub.co.uk

Rossendale (1903)
Ewood Lane Head, Haslingden, Rossendale BB4 6LH
☎ **(01706) 831339**
▢ (01706) 228669
✉ admin@rossendalegolfclub.net
✍ K Wilson
▤ www.rossendalegolfclub.net

Royal Lytham & St Annes (1886)
Links Gate, Lytham St Annes FY8 3LQ
☎ **(01253) 724206**
▢ (01253) 780946
✉ bookings@royallytham.org
✍ RJG Cochrane
▤ www.royallytham.org

Saddleworth (1904)
Mountain Ash, Uppermill, Oldham OL3 6LT
☎ **(01457) 873653**
▢ (01457) 820647
✉ secretary@saddleworthgolfclub.org.uk
✍ Paul Green
▤ www.saddleworthgolfclub.org.uk

Shaw Hill Hotel G&CC (1925)
Proprietary
Preston Road, Whittle-le-Woods, Chorley PR6 7PP
☎ **(01257) 269221**
▢ (01257) 261223
✉ info@shaw-hill.co.uk
✍ Lawrence Bateson (Secretary)
▤ www.shaw-hill.co.uk

St Annes Old Links (1901)
Highbury Road East, Lytham St Annes FY8 2LD
☎ **(01253) 723597**
▢ (01253) 781506
✉ secretary@stannesoldlinks.com
✍ Mrs Jane Donohoe
▤ www.stannesoldlinks.com

Standish Court (1995)
Pay and play
Rectory Lane, Standish, Wigan WN6 0XD
☎ **(01257) 425777**
▢ (01257) 425777
✉ info@standishgolf.co.uk
✍ S McGrath
▤ www.standishgolf.co.uk

Stonyhurst Park (1979)
Stonyhurst, Hurst Green, Clitheroe BB7 9QB
☎ **(01254) 826478 (not manned)**
✉ jandbaus@btinternet.com
✍ JR Austin (01254) 240314
▤ www.stonyhurstpark.co.uk

Towneley (1932)
Public
Towneley Park, Todmorden Road, Burnley BB11 3ED
☎ **(01282) 451636**

The Lytham Trophy

Founded by the Royal Lytham & St Annes Golf Club in 1965, the Lytham Trophy is a 72 hole scratch stroke play competition for amateur golfers and is classified as a Category A event by The R&A's World Amateur Golf Rankings.

Notable past winners include Sir Michael Bonallack, Peter McEvoy, Paul Broadhurst and Lloyd Saltman.

For key to symbols see page 717

✉ secretarytowneleygolfclub.co.uk
✍ Peter Witt
🖳 www.towneleygolfclub.co.uk

Tunshill (1901)
Kiln Lane, Milnrow, Rochdale OL16 3TS
☎ **(01706) 342095**
✉ secretary@tunshillgolfclub.co.uk
✍ S Reade (01706) 342095
🖳 www.tunshillgolfclub.co.uk

Turton (1908)
Wood End Farm, Hospital Road, Bromley Cross, Bolton BL7 9QD
☎ **(01204) 852235**
📠 (01204) 856921
✉ info@turtongolfclub.com
✍ John Drabble
🖳 www.turtongolfclub.com

Walmersley (1906)
Garrett's Close, Walmersley, Bury BL9 6TE
☎ **(0161) 764 1429**
📠 (0161) 764 7770
✉ walmersleygc@btconnect.com
✍ V Slater (0161) 764 7770
🖳 www.walmersleygolfclub.co.uk

Werneth (1908)
Green Lane, Garden Suburb, Oldham OL8 3AZ
☎ **(0161) 624 1190**
✉ secretary@wernethgolfclub.co.uk
✍ JH Barlow
🖳 www.wernethgolfclub.co.uk

Westhoughton (1929)
Long Island, Westhoughton, Bolton BL5 2BR
☎ **(01942) 811085**
✉ honsec.wgc@btconnect.com
✍ Dave Moores (Club Mobile 07760 754933)
🖳 www.westhoughtongolfclub.co.uk

Whalley (1912)
Long Leese Barn, Clerkhill Road, Whalley BB7 9DR
☎ **(01254) 822236**
📠 (01254) 824766
✍ P R Benson (01282) 773354
🖳 www.whalleygolfclub.co.uk

Whittaker (1906)
Littleborough OL15 0LH
☎ **(01706) 378310**
✍ Paul Jones (07930) 569260
🖳 www.secretarywgc.com

Wigan (1898)
Arley Hall, Haigh, Wigan WN1 2UH
☎ **(01257) 421360**
📠 (01257) 426500
✉ info@wigangolfclub.co.uk
✍ A Lawless (Ass Sec)
🖳 www.wigangolfclub.co.uk

Wilpshire (1890)
72 Whalley Road, Wilpshire, Blackburn BB1 9LF
☎ **(01254) 248260**
📠 (01254) 246745
✉ admin@wilpshiregolfclub.co.uk
✍ SH Tart
🖳 www.wilpshiregolfclub.co.uk

Leicestershire

Beedles Lake (1993)
170 Broome Lane, East Goscote LE7 3WQ
☎ **(0116) 260 6759/7086**
📠 (0116) 269 4127
✉ joncoleman@jelson.co.uk
✍ Jon Coleman (Mgr)
🖳 www.beedleslake.co.uk

Birstall (1900)
Station Road, Birstall, Leicester LE4 3BB
☎ **(0116) 267 4450**
✉ sue@birstallgolfclub.co.uk
✍ Mrs SE Chilton (0116) 267 4322
🖳 www.birstallgolfclub.co.uk

Breedon Priory Golf Centre (1990)
Green Lane, Wilson, Derby DE73 8LG
☎ **(01332) 863081**
✉ lee@breedonpriory.co.uk
✍ Lee Sheldon (Mgr)

Charnwood Forest (1890)
Breakback Road, Woodhouse Eaves, Loughborough LE12 8TA
☎ **(01509) 890259**
✉ secretary @charnwoodforestgolfclub.com
✍ PK Field
🖳 www.charnwoodforestgolfclub.com

Cosby (1895)
Chapel Lane, Broughton Road, Cosby, Leicester LE9 1RG
☎ **(0116) 286 4759**
📠 (0116) 286 4484
✉ secretary@cosbygolfclub.co.uk
✍ Peggy Remington (0116) 286 4759 Opt 1
🖳 www.cosbygolfclub.co.uk

Enderby (1986)
Public
Mill Lane, Enderby, Leicester LE19 4LX
☎ **(0116) 284 9388**
📠 (0116) 284 9388
🖳 www.enderbygolfshopandcourse .co.uk

Forest Hill (1991)
Proprietary
Markfield Lane, Botcheston LE9 9FH
☎ **(01455) 824800**
📠 (01455) 828522
✉ admin@foresthillgolfclub.co.uk
✍ Una Handley
🖳 www.foresthillgolfclub.co.uk

Glen Gorse (1933)
Glen Road, Oadby, Leicester LE2 4RF
☎ **(0116) 271 4159**
📠 (0116) 271 4159
✉ secretary@gggc.org
✍ Mrs J James (0116) 271 4159
🖳 www.gggc.org

Hinckley (1894)
Leicester Road, Hinckley LE10 3DR
☎ **(01455) 615124**

📠 (01455) 890841
✉ proshop@hinckleygolfclub.com
✍ R Mather (Sec) Catherine Merrie (Finance & Admin)
🖳 www.hinckleygolfclub.com

Humberstone Heights (1978)
Public
Gipsy Lane, Leicester LE5 0TB
☎ **(0116) 299 5570/1**
✉ hhgc@talktalk.net
✍ Mrs M Weston
🖳 www.humberstoneheightsgc .co.uk

Kibworth (1904)
Weir Road, Kibworth Beauchamp, Leicestershire LE8 0LP
☎ **(0116) 279 2301**
📠 (0116) 279 6434
✉ secretary@kibworthgolfclub .freeserve.co.uk
🖳 www.kibworthgolfclub.co.uk

Kilworth Springs (1993)
Proprietary
South Kilworth Road, North Kilworth, Lutterworth LE17 6HJ
☎ **(01858) 575082**
📠 (01858) 575078
✉ admin@kilworthsprings.co.uk
✍ Jeremy Wilkinson (Manager)
🖳 www.kilworthsprings.co.uk

Kirby Muxloe (1893)
Station Road, Kirby Muxloe, Leicester LE9 2EP
☎ **(0116) 239 3457**
📠 (0116) 238 8891
✉ kirbymuxloegolf@btconnect.com
✍ B N Whipham (Mgr/Professional) (0116) 239 3457
🖳 www.kirbymuxloe-golf.co.uk

Lingdale (1967)
Joe Moore's Lane, Woodhouse Eaves, Loughborough LE12 8TF
☎ **(01509) 890703**
📠 (01509) 890703
✉ secretary@lingdalegolfclub.co.uk
✍ T Walker
🖳 www.lingdalegolfclub.co.uk

Longcliffe (1906)
Snells Nook Lane, Nanpantan, Loughborough LE11 3YA
☎ **(01509) 239129**
📠 (01509) 231286
✉ secretary@longcliffegolf.co.uk
✍ Mr B Jones
🖳 www.longcliffegolf.co.uk

Lutterworth (1904)
Rugby Road, Lutterworth, Leicestershire LE17 4HN
☎ **(01455) 552532**
📠 (01455) 553586
✉ sec@lutterworthgc.co.uk
✍ J Faulks (01455) 552532
🖳 www.lutterworthgc.co.uk

Market Harborough (1898)
Great Oxendon Road, Market Harborough
LE16 8NF
☎ **(01858) 463684**
🖥 (01858) 432906
✉ proshop@mhgolf.co.uk
⌂ F J Baxter
🖥 www.mhgolf.co.uk

Melton Mowbray (1925)
Waltham Rd, Thorpe Arnold, Melton
Mowbray LE14 4SD
☎ **(01664) 562118**
🖥 (01664) 562118
✉ meltonmowbraygc@btconnect
.com
⌂ Sue Millward/Marilyn Connelly
🖥 www.mmgc.org

Oadby (1974)
Public
Leicester Road, Oadby, Leicester LE2 4AJ
☎ **(0116) 270 9052/270 0215**
✉ secretaryogc@talktalk.net
⌂ RA Primrose (0116) 270 3828
🖥 www.oadbygolfclub.co.uk

Park Hill Golf Club (1994)
Proprietary
Park Hill, Seagrave LE12 7NG
☎ **(01509) 815454**
🖥 (01509) 816062
✉ mail@parkhillgolf.co.uk
⌂ JP Hutson
🖥 www.parkhillgolf.co.uk

Rothley Park (1911)
Westfield Lane, Rothley, Leicester LE7 7LH
☎ **(0116) 230 2809**
🖥 (0116) 237 4847
✉ clubmanager@rothleypark.co.uk
⌂ Danny Spillane (Mgr) (0116) 230
2809
🖥 www.rothleypark.com

Scraptoft (1928)
Beeby Road, Scraptoft, Leicester LE7 9SJ
☎ **(0116) 241 9000**
🖥 (0116) 241 9000
✉ secretary@scraptoft-golf.co.uk
⌂ Paul Henry (0116) 241 9000
🖥 www.scraptoft-golf.co.uk

Six Hills (1986)
Pay and play
Six Hills, Melton Mowbray LE14 3PR
☎ **(01509) 881225**
🖥 (01509) 881846
⌂ Mrs J Showler

Stapleford Park (2000)
Stapleford park, Melton Mowbray LE14 2EF
☎ **(01572) 787044**
🖥 (01572) 787001
✉ clubs@stapleford.co.uk
⌂ Richard Alderson
🖥 www.staplefordpark.com

The Leicestershire (1890)
Evington Lane, Leicester LE5 6DJ
☎ **(0116) 273 8825**
🖥 (0116) 249 8799

✉ secretary
@theleicestershiregolfclub.co.uk
⌂ Tim Stephens (0116) 273 8825
🖥 www.theleicestershiregolfclub.co.uk

Ullesthorpe Court Hotel
(1976)
Proprietary
Frolesworth Road, Ullesthorpe, Lutterworth
LE17 5BZ
☎ **(01455) 209023**
🖥 (01455) 202537
✉ bookings@ullesthorpecourt.co.uk
⌂ AP Parr (ext 2446)
🖥 www.bw-ullesthorpecourt.co.uk

Western Park (1910)
Public
Scudamore Road, Leicester LE3 1UQ
☎ **(0116) 287 5211**
⌂ Paul Williams
🖥 www.westerpkgc.co.uk

Whetstone (1965)
Proprietary
Cambridge Road, Cosby, Leicester LE9 1SJ
☎ **(0116) 286 1424**
🖥 (0116) 286 1424
⌂ N Morris
🖥 www.whetstonegolfclub.co.uk

Willesley Park (1921)
Measham Road, Ashby-de-la-Zouch
LE65 2PF
☎ **(01530) 414596**
🖥 (01530) 564169
✉ info@willesleypark.com
⌂ Tina Harlow (01530) 414596
🖥 www.willesleypark.com

Lincolnshire

Ashby Decoy (1936)
Ashby Decoy, Burringham Road, Scunthorpe
DN17 2AB
☎ **(01724) 866561**
🖥 (01724) 271708
✉ info@ashbydecoygolfclub.co.uk
⌂ Mrs J Harrison (01724) 866561
🖥 www.ashbydecoy.co.uk

Belton Park (1890)
Belton Lane, Londonthorpe Road, Grantham
NG31 9SH
☎ **(01476) 567399**
🖥 (01476) 592078
✉ greatgolf@beltonpark.co.uk
⌂ S Rowley (01476) 542900
🖥 www.beltonpark.co.uk

De Vere Belton Woods
Hotel (1991)
Belton, Grantham NG32 2LN
☎ **(01476) 593200**
🖥 (01476) 574547
✉ belton.woods@devere-hotels.co.uk
⌂ A Cameron (01476) 514364
🖥 www.devere.co.uk

Blankney (1904)
Proprietary
Blankney, Lincoln LN4 3AZ
☎ **(01526) 320263**
🖥 (01526) 322521
✉ manager@blankneygolfclub
.co.uk
⌂ G Bradley (01526) 320202
🖥 www.blankneygolfclub.co.uk

Boston (1900)
Cowbridge, Horncastle Road, Boston
PE22 7EL
☎ **(01205) 350589**
🖥 (01205) 367526
✉ steveshaw@bostongc.co.uk
⌂ SP Shaw (01205) 350589
🖥 www.bostongc.co.uk

Boston West (1995)
Proprietary
Hubbert's Bridge, Boston PE20 3QX
☎ **(01205) 290670**
🖥 (01205) 290725
✉ info@bostonwestgolfclub.co.uk
⌂ MJ Couture (01205) 290670
🖥 www.bostonwestgolfclub.co.uk

Burghley Park (1890)
St Martin's, Stamford PE9 3JX
☎ **(01780) 753789**
✉ secretary@burghleyparkgolfclub
.co.uk
⌂ S Last (Sec/Mgr)
🖥 www.burghleyparkgolfclub.co.uk

Canwick Park (1893)
Canwick Park, Washingborough Road,
Lincoln LN4 1EF
☎ **(01522) 542912/522166**
✉ manager@canwickpark.org
⌂ N Porteus (01522) 542912
🖥 www.canwickpark.org

Carholme (1906)
Carholme Road, Lincoln LN1 1SE
☎ **(01522) 523725**
🖥 (01522) 533733
✉ secretary@carholmegolfclub
.co.uk
⌂ J Lammin
🖥 www.carholmegolfclub.co.uk

Cleethorpes (1894)
Kings Road, Cleethorpes DN35 0PN
☎ **(01472) 816110 option 1**
✉ secretary@cleethorpesgolfclub
.co.uk
⌂ AJ Thompson (01472) 816110
option 3
🖥 www.cleethorpesgolfclub.co.uk

Elsham (1900)
Barton Road, Elsham, Brigg DN20 0LS
☎ **(01652) 680291**
🖥 (0872) 1113238
✉ office@elshamgolfclub.co.uk
⌂ T Hartley (Mgr)
🖥 www.elshamgolfclub.co.uk

Forest Pines Hotel & Golf Resort (1996)
Proprietary
Ermine Street, Brigg DN20 0AQ
☎ **(01652) 650756 Golf Shop**
🖳 (01652) 650495
📧 forestpines@qhotels.co.uk
🖎 Andrew Cook (Director of Golf)
🖥 www.qhotels.co.uk

Gainsborough (1894)
Proprietary
Thonock, Gainsborough DN21 1PZ
☎ **(01427) 613088**
📧 info@gainsboroughgc.co.uk
🖎 S Keane (Operations Manager)
🖥 www.gainsboroughgc.co.uk

Gedney Hill (1991)
Public
West Drove, Gedney End Hill PE12 0NT
☎ **(01406) 330922**

Grange Park (1992)
Proprietary
Butterwick Road, Messingham, Scunthorpe DN17 3PP
☎ **(01724) 762945**
📧 info@grangepark.com
🖎 I Cannon (Mgr)
🖥 www.grangepark.com

Grimsby (1922)
Littlecoates Road, Grimsby DN34 4LU
☎ **(01472) 342630 (Clubhouse)**
  356981 (Pro-S
🖳 (01472) 342630
📧 secretary@grimsbygc.fsnet.co.uk
🖎 D McCully (01472) 342630
🖥 www.grimsbygolfclub.com

Holme Hall (1908)
Holme Lane, Bottesford, Scunthorpe DN16 3RF
☎ **(01724) 862078**
🖳 (01724) 862081
📧 secretary@holmehallgolf.co.uk
🖎 Gerald Pearce
🖥 www.holmehallgolf.co.uk

Horncastle (1990)
West Ashby, Horncastle LN9 5PP
☎ **(01507) 526800**
📧 info@twinlakescentre.com
🖥 www.horncastlegolfclub.com

Humberston Park
Humberston Avenue, Humberston DN36 4SJ
☎ **(01472) 210404**

Immingham (1975)
St Andrews Lane, Off Church Lane, Immingham DN40 2EU
☎ **(01469) 575298**
🖳 (01469) 577636
🖎 C Todd (Mgr)
🖥 www.immgc.com

Kenwick Park (1992)
Kenwick, Louth LN11 8NY
☎ **(01507) 605134**

🖳 (01507) 606556
📧 secretary@kenwickparkgolf.co.uk
🖎 C James (Gen Mgr)
🖥 www.kenwickparkgolf.co.uk

Kirton Holme (1992)
Proprietary
Holme Road, Kirton Holme, Boston PE20 1SY
☎ **(01205) 290669**
🖎 Mrs T Welberry
🖥 www.kirtonholmegolfcourse.com

Lincoln (1891)
Torksey, Lincoln LN1 2EG
☎ **(01427) 718721**
🖳 (01427) 718721
📧 manager@lincolngc.co.uk
🖎 Craig Innes
🖥 www.lincolngc.co.uk

Louth (1965)
Crowtree Lane, Louth LN11 9LJ
☎ **(01507) 603681**
🖳 (01507) 608501
📧 louthgolfclub@btconnect.com
🖎 Simon Moody (Gen Mgr)
🖥 www.louthgolfclub.com

Manor (Laceby) (1992)
Proprietary
Laceby Manor, Laceby, Grimsby DN37 7LD
☎ **(01472) 873468**
📧 judith@lacebymanorgolfclub.co.uk
🖎 Mrs J Mackay
🖥 www.lmgc.co.uk

Market Rasen & District (1912)
Legsby Road, Market Rasen LN8 3DZ
☎ **(01673) 842319**
🖳 (01673) 849245
📧 marketrasengolf@onetel.net
🖎 JP Smith
🖥 www.marketrasengolfclub.co.uk

Market Rasen Racecourse (1990)
Pay and play
Legsby Road, Market Rasen LN8 3EA
☎ **(01673) 843434**
🖳 (01673) 844532
📧 marketrasen
  @jockeyclubracecourses.com
🖥 www.marketrasenraces.co.uk

Martin Moor (1993)
Proprietary
Martin Road, Blankney LN4 3BE
☎ **(01526) 378243**
📧 enquiries@martinmoorgolfclub
  .co.uk
🖎 Alan Roberts/Carole Roberts
⊕ 9 hole course with 18 seperate tees. Visitors/Societies/Corporate events welcome

Millfield (1984)
Proprietary
Laughterton, Lincoln LN1 2LB
☎ **(01427) 718473**
📧 millfieldgolfclub@gmail.com

🖎 John Thomson (Sec)
🖥 www.millfieldgolfclub.co.uk

North Shore (1910)
Proprietary
North Shore Road, Skegness PE25 1DN
☎ **(01754) 763298**
🖳 (01754) 761902
📧 info@northshorehotel.co.uk
🖎 B Howard (01754) 899030
🖥 www.northshorehotel.co.uk

Pottergate (1992)
Moor Lane, Branston, Lincoln
☎ **(01522) 794867**
🖳 (01522) 794867
📧 pottergategc@hotmail.co.uk
🖎 Lee Tasker
🖥 www.pottergategolfclub.co.uk

RAF Coningsby (1972)
RAF Coningsby, Lincoln LN4 4SY
☎ **(01526) 342581 Ext 6828**
🖎 N Parsons (01526) 347946

Sandilands (1901)
Proprietary
Sandilands, Sutton-on-Sea LN12 2RJ
☎ **(01507) 441432**
🖳 (01507) 441617
📧 sandilandsgolf@googlemail.com
🖎 Simon Sherratt (Pro/Mgr)
🖥 www.sandilandsgolfclub.co.uk

Seacroft (1895)
Drummond Road, Seacroft, Skegness PE25 3AU
☎ **(01754) 763020**
🖳 (01754) 763020
📧 enquiries@seacroft-golfclub.co.uk
🖎 R England (Mgr)
🖥 www.seacroft-golfclub.co.uk

Sleaford (1905)
Willoughby Road, Greylees, Sleaford, Lincs NG34 8PL
☎ **(01529) 488273**
🖳 (0872) 110 7871
📧 manager@sleafordgolfclub.co.uk
🖎 Mr N Porteus
🖥 www.sleafordgolfclub.co.uk

South Kyme (1990)
Skinners Lane, South Kyme, Lincoln LN4 4AT
☎ **(01526) 861113**
🖳 (01526) 861080
📧 southkymegc@hotmail.com
🖎 P Chamberlain
🖥 www.skgc.co.uk

Spalding (1907)
Surfleet, Spalding PE11 4EA
☎ **(01775) 680386**
🖳 (01775) 680988
📧 secretary@spaldinggolfclub.co.uk
🖎 Mrs C J Douglas (01775) 680386
🖥 www.spaldinggolfclub.co.uk

Stoke Rochford (1924)
Great North Rd, Grantham NG33 5EW
☎ **(01476) 530275**

For key to symbols see page 717

☎ (01476) 530237
✉ secretary@stokerochfordgolfclub
.co.uk
✍ A J Wheeler
🖥 www.stokerochfordgolfclub.co.uk

Sudbrook Moor   (1991)
Public
*Charity Street, Carlton Scroop, Grantham
NG32 3AT*
☎ **(01400) 250796 all enquiries**
✍ Judith Hutton
🖥 www.sudbrookmoor.co.uk

Sutton Bridge   (1914)
*New Road, Sutton Bridge, Spalding PE12
9RQ*
☎ **(01406) 350323 (Clubhouse)**
✉ suttonbridgegc@yahoo.co.uk
✍ PL Land (01945) 410076
🖥 www.club-noticeboard.co.uk/
suttonbridge

Tetney   (1993)
Station Road, Tetney, Grimsby DN36 5HY
☎ **(01472) 211644**
☎ (01472) 211644
✍ J Abrams

Toft Hotel   (1988)
Proprietary
Toft, Bourne PE10 0JT
☎ **(01778) 590616**
🖥 www.thetofthotelgolfclub.com

Waltham Windmill   (1997)
Proprietary
Cheapside, Waltham, Grimsby DN37 0HT
☎ **(01472) 824109**
🖥 www.walthamgolf.co.uk

Welton Manor   (1995)
Proprietary
Hackthorn Road, Welton LN2 3PA
☎ **(01673) 862827**
☎ (01673) 861888
✉ info@weltonmanorgolfcentre.co.uk
✍ David Ottenell/Hayley Olliver
🖥 www.weltonmanorgolfcentre.co.uk

Woodhall Spa   (1891)
Proprietary
Woodhall Spa LN10 6PU
☎ **(01526) 352511**
☎ (01526) 351817
✉ booking@englishgolfunion.org
✍ Richard A Latham
🖥 www.woodhallspagolf.com

Woodthorpe Hall   (1986)
Woodthorpe, Alford LN13 0DD
☎ **(01507) 450000**
☎ (01507) 450000
✉ woodthorpehallgolfclub@live.co.uk
✍ Joan Smith (01507) 450000
🖥 www.woodthorpehall.co.uk

London Clubs

Aquarius *Kent*
Bush Hill Park *Middlesex*
Central London Golf Centre *Surrey*
Chingford *Essex*
Dulwich & Sydenham Hill *Surrey*
Eltham Warren *Kent*
Finchley *Middlesex*
Hampstead *Middlesex*
Hendon *Middlesex*
Highgate *Middlesex*
Leaside *Middlesex*
London Scottish *Surrey*
Mill Hill *Middlesex*
Muswell Hill *Middlesex*
North Middlesex *Middlesex*
Richmond Park *Surrey*
Roehampton Club *Surrey*
Royal Blackheath *Kent*
Royal Epping Forest *Essex*
Royal Mid-Surrey *Surrey*
Royal Wimbledon *Surrey*
Shooter's Hill *Kent*
South Herts *Hertfordshire*
Thameside Golf Centre *Kent*
Trent Park *Middlesex*
Wanstead *Essex*
West Essex *Essex*
Wimbledon Common *Surrey*
Wimbledon Park *Surrey*

Manchester

Blackley   (1907)
Victoria Avenue East, Manchester M9 7HW
☎ **(0161) 643 2980**
☎ (0161) 653 8300
✉ office@blackleygolfclub.com
✍ B Beddoes (0161) 654 7770
🖥 www.blackleygolfclub.com

Boysnope Park   (1998)
Proprietary
*Liverpool Road, Barton Moss, Eccles
M30 7RF*
☎ **(0161) 707 6125**
☎ (0161) 707 1888
✉ karensmith63@btconnect.com
✍ Jean Stringer (0161) 707 6125
🖥 www.boysnopegolfclub.co.uk

Chorlton-cum-Hardy   (1902)
*Barlow Hall, Barlow Hall Road, Manchester
M21 7JJ*
☎ **(0161) 881 3139**
☎ (0161) 881 4532
✉ chorltongolf@hotmail.com
✍ IR Booth (0161) 881 5830
🖥 www.chorltoncumhardygolfclub
.co.uk

Davyhulme Park   (1911)
*Gleneagles Road, Davyhulme, Manchester
M41 8SA*
☎ **(0161) 748 2260**
✉ davyhulmeparkgolfclub@email.com
🖥 www.davyhulmeparkgc.info

Denton   (1909)
*Manchester Road, Denton, Manchester
M34 2GG*
☎ **(0161) 336 3218**
☎ (0161) 336 4751
✉ info@dentongolfclub.com
✍ ID McIlvanney
🖥 www.dentongolfclub.com

Didsbury   (1891)
*Ford Lane, Northenden, Manchester
M22 4NQ*
☎ **(0161) 998 9278**
☎ (0161) 902 3060
✉ golf@didsburygolfclub.com
✍ John K Mort (Mgr)
🖥 www.didsburygolfclub.com

Ellesmere   (1913)
*Old Clough Lane, Worsley, Manchester
M28 7HZ*
☎ **(0161) 790 2122**
☎ (0161) 790 2122
✉ honsec@ellesmeregolfclub.co.uk
✍ A T Leaver (0161) 790 2122
🖥 www.ellesmeregolfclub.co.uk

Fairfield Golf & Sailing Club
(1892)
*Booth Road, Audenshaw, Manchester
M34 5QA*
☎ **(0161) 301 4528**
✉ manager@fairfieldgolfclub.co.uk
✍ John Paton (Mgr)
🖥 www.fairfieldgolfclub.co.uk

Flixton   (1893)
*Church Road, Flixton, Urmston, Manchester
M41 6EP*
☎ **(0161) 748 2116**
☎ (0161) 748 2116
✉ flixtongolfclub@mail.com
✍ A Braithwaite
🖥 www.flixtongolfclub.co.uk

Great Lever & Farnworth
(1901)
Plodder Lane, Farnworth, Bolton BL4 0LQ
☎ **(01204) 656493**
☎ (01204) 656137
✉ greatlever@btconnect.com
✍ MJ Ivill (01204) 656137

Heaton Park Golf Centre
(1912)
Pay and play
*Heaton Park, Middleton Road, Prestwich
M25 2SW*
☎ **(0161) 654 9899**
☎ (0161) 653 2003
✉ hpbookings@macktrading.net
✍ Brian Dique (Gen Mgr)
🖥 www.mackgolf.co.uk

New North Manchester
(1923)
*Rhodes House, Manchester Old Road,
Middleton M24 4PE*
☎ **(0161) 643 9033**
☎ (0161) 643 7775
✉ tee@nmgc.co.uk
✍ G Heaslip
🖥 www.northmanchestergolfclub
.co.uk

Northenden (1912)
Palatine Road, Manchester M22 4FR
☎ **(0161) 998 4738**
🖷 (0161) 945 5592
✉ manager@northendengolfclub.com
✍ Alison Davidson (Mgr) (0161) 998 4738
🖳 www.northendengolfclub.com

Old Manchester (1818)
Club
☎ **(0161) 766 4157**

Pike Fold (1909)
Hills Lane, Pole Lane, Unsworth, Bury BL9 8QP
☎ **(0161) 766 3561**
🖷 (0161) 351 2189
✉ secretary@pikefold.co.uk
✍ Martin Jeffs (Secretary)
🖳 www.pikefold.co.uk

Prestwich (1908)
Hilton Lane, Prestwich M25 9XB
☎ **(0161) 772 0700**
✉ prestwichgolf@btconnect.com
🖳 www.prestwichgolf.co.uk

Stand (1904)
The Dales, Ashbourne Grove, Whitefield, Manchester M45 7NL
☎ **(0161) 766 2388**
🖷 (0161) 796 3234
✉ secretary@standgolfclub.co.uk
✍ M A Cowsill (0161) 766 3197
🖳 www.standgolfclub.co.uk

Swinton Park (1906)
East Lancashire Road, Swinton, Manchester M27 5LX
☎ **(0161) 794 0861**
✉ info@spgolf.co.uk
🖳 www.spgolf.co.uk

The Manchester (1882)
Hopwood Cottage, Rochdale Road, Middleton, Manchester M24 6QP
☎ **(0161) 643 3202**
🖷 (0161) 643 3202
✉ secretary@mangc.co.uk
✍ Stephen Armstead
🖳 www.mangc.co.uk

Whitefield (1932)
Higher Lane, Whitefield, Manchester M45 7EZ
☎ **(0161) 351 2700**
🖷 (0161) 351 2712
✉ enquiries@whitefieldgolfclub.com
✍ Mrs M Rothwell
🖳 www.whitefieldgolfclub.co.uk

Withington (1892)
243 Palatine Road, West Didsbury, Manchester M20 2UE
☎ **(0161) 445 9544**
🖷 (0161) 445 5210
✉ secretary@withingtongolfclub .co.uk
✍ PJ Keane
🖳 www.withingtongolfclub.co.uk

Worsley (1894)
Stableford Avenue, Monton Green, Eccles, Manchester M30 8AP
☎ **(0161) 789 4202**
🖷 (0161) 789 3200
✉ office@worsleygolfclub.co.uk
✍ J D Clarke
🖳 www.worsleygolfclub.co.uk

Merseyside

Allerton Municipal (1934)
Public
Allerton Road, Liverpool L18 3JT
☎ **(0151) 428 1046**

Arrowe Park (1931)
Public
Arrowe Park, Woodchurch, Birkenhead CH49 5LW
☎ **(0151) 677 1527, (0151) 678 5285 clubhouse**
✉ contact@arroweparkgolfclub.co.uk
✍ P Hickey
🖳 www.arroweparkgolfclub.co.uk

Bidston (1913)
Bidston Link Road, Wallasey, Wirral CH44 2HR
☎ **(0151) 638 3412**
🖷 (0151) 638 8685
✉ info@bidstongolf.co.uk
🖳 www.bidstongolf.co.uk

Bootle (1934)
Pay and play
Dunnings Bridge Road, Litherland L30 2PP
☎ **(0151) 928 1371**
🖷 (0151) 949 1815
✉ bootlegolfcourse@btconnect.com
✍ G Howarth

Bowring (1913)
Public
Bowring Park, Roby Road, Huyton L36 4HD
☎ **(0151) 489 1901**
✉ dgwalker36@tiscali.co.uk

Brackenwood (1933)
Public
Bracken Lane, Bebington, Wirral L63 2LY
☎ **(0151) 608 3093**
✉ secretary@brackenwoodgolf.co.uk
✍ GW Brogan (0151) 339 9817
🖳 www.brackenwoodgolf.co.uk

Bromborough (1903)
Raby Hall Road, Bromborough CH63 0NW
☎ **(0151) 334 2155**
🖷 (0151) 334 7300
✉ enquiries@bromboroughgolfclub .org.uk
✍ Alisdair Mackay (0151) 334 2155
🖳 www.bromboroughgolfclub.org.uk

Caldy (1907)
Links Hey Road, Caldy, Wirral CH48 1NB
☎ **(0151) 625 5660**
🖷 (0151) 625 7394
✉ secretarycaldygc@btconnect.com

✍ Gail M Copple
🖳 www.caldygolfclub.co.uk

Childwall (1912)
Naylors Road, Gateacre, Liverpool L27 2YB
☎ **(0151) 487 0654**
🖷 (0151) 487 0654
✉ office@childwallgolfclub.co.uk
✍ Peter Bowen
🖳 www.childwallgolfclub.co.uk

Eastham Lodge (1973)
117 Ferry Road, Eastham, Wirral CH62 0AP
☎ **(0151) 327 3003 (Clubhouse)**
🖷 (0151) 327 7574
✉ easthamlodge.g.c@btinternet.com
✍ Mr Nick Sargent (Director of Golf)
🖳 www.easthamlodgegolfclub.co.uk

Formby (1884)
Golf Road, Formby, Liverpool L37 1LQ
☎ **(01704) 872164**
🖷 (01704) 833028
✉ info@formbygolfclub.co.uk
✍ M Betteridge (01704) 872164
🖳 www.formbygolfclub.co.uk

Formby Hall Golf Resort & Spa (1996)
Proprietary
Southport Old Road, Formby L37 1NN
☎ **(01704) 875699**
🖷 (01704) 832134
✉ golf@formbyhallgolfresort.co.uk
✍ Mark Williams
🖳 www.formbyhallgolfresort.co.uk

Formby Ladies' (1896)
Golf Road, Formby, Liverpool L37 1YH
☎ **(01704) 873493**
🖷 (01704) 874127
✉ secretary@formbyladiesgolfclub .co.uk
✍ Mrs CA Bromley (01704) 873493
🖳 www.formbyladiesgolfclub.co.uk

Grange Park (1891)
Prescot Road, St Helens WA10 3AD
☎ **(01744) 22980 (Members)**
🖷 (01744) 26318
✉ secretary@grangeparkgolfclub .co.uk
✍ G Brown (01744) 26318
🖳 www.grangeparkgolfclub.co.uk

Haydock Park (1877)
Golborne Park, Newton Lane, Newton-le-Willows WA12 0HX
☎ **(01925) 228525**
🖷 (01925) 224984
✉ secretary@haydockparkgc.co.uk
✍ David Hughes
🖳 www.haydockparkgc.co.uk

Hesketh (1885)
Cockle Dick's Lane, Cambridge Road, Southport PR9 9QQ
☎ **(01704) 536897**
🖷 (01704) 539250
✉ secretary@heskethgolfclub.co.uk

✍ N P Annandale (Sec) (01704)
536897 ext 1
▤ www.heskethgolfclub.co.uk

Heswall   (1902)
Cottage Lane, Gayton, Heswall CH60 8PB
☎ (0151) 342 1237
▢ (0151) 342 6140
✉ dawn@heswallgolfclub.com
✍ Graham Capewell (Manager)
▤ www.heswallgolfclub.com

Hillside   (1911)
Hastings Road, Hillside, Southport PR8 2LU
☎ (01704) 567169
▢ (01704) 563192
✉ secretary@hillside-golf-club.co.uk
✍ SH Newland (01704) 567169
▤ www.hillside-golfclub.co.uk

Houghwood   (1996)
Proprietary
Billinge Hill, Crank Road, Crank, St Helens
WA11 8RL
☎ (01744) 894754
▢ (01744) 894754
✉ office@houghwoodgolf.co.uk
✍ P Turner (Man Dir)
▤ www.houghwoodgolfclub.co.uk

Hoylake Municipal   (1933)
Public
Carr Lane, Hoylake, Wirral CH47 4BG
☎ (0151) 632 2956/4883
    (Bookings)
✍ P Davies (0151) 632 0523
▤ www.hoylakegolfclub.com

Huyton & Prescot   (1905)
Hurst Park, Huyton Lane, Huyton L36 1UA
☎ (0151) 489 3948
▢ (0151) 489 0797
✉ secretary@huytonandprescotgolf
.co.uk
✍ L Griffin(0151) 489 3948
▤ www.huytonandprescot.
myprogolfer.co.uk

Leasowe   (1891)
Leasowe Road, Moreton, Wirral CH46 3RD
☎ (0151) 677 5852
▢ (0151) 641 8519
✉ secretary@leasowegolfclub.co.uk
✍ David Knight (0151) 677 5852
▤ www.leasowegolfclub.co.uk

Lee Park   (1954)
Childwall Valley Road, Gateacre, Liverpool
L27 3YA
☎ (0151) 487 3882 (Clubhouse)
▢ (0151) 498 4666
✉ lee.park@virgin.net
✍ Steve Settle
▤ www.leepark.co.uk

Prenton   (1905)
Golf Links Road, Prenton, Birkenhead
CH42 8LW
☎ (0151) 609 3426
✉ nigel.brown@prentongolfclub.
co.uk
✍ N Brown
▤ www.prentongolfclub.co.uk

RLGC Village Play   (1895)
Club
c/o 18 Waverley Road, Hoylake, Wirral
CH47 3DD
☎ (07885) 507263
▢ (0151) 632 5156
✉ pdwbritesparks@sky.com
✍ PD Williams (0151) 632 5156

Royal Birkdale   (1889)
Waterloo Road, Birkdale, Southport
PR8 2LX
☎ (01704) 552020
▢ (01704) 552021
✉ secretary@royalbirkdale.com
✍ Mike Gilyeat (Sec)
▤ www.royalbirkdale.com

Royal Liverpool   (1869)
Meols Drive, Hoylake CH47 4AL
☎ (0151) 632 3101/3102
▢ (0151) 632 6737
✉ secretary@royal-liverpool-golf.com
✍ D R Cromie
▤ www.royal-liverpool-golf.com

Sherdley Park Municipal
(1974)
Public
Eltonhead Road, Sutton, St Helens,
Merseyside WA9 5DE
☎ (01744) 813149
▢ (01744) 817967
✉ sherdleyparkgolfcourse@sthelens
.gov.uk
✍ Ian Corice (Mgr)
▤ www.sthelens.gov.uk/goactive

Southport & Ainsdale
(1906)
Bradshaws Lane, Ainsdale, Southport PR8
3LG
☎ (01704) 578000
▢ (01704) 570896
✉ secretary@sandagolfclub.co.uk
✍ MJ Vanner
▤ www.sandagolfclub.co.uk

Southport Golf Links
(1912)
Public
Park Road West, Southport PR9 0JS
☎ (01704) 535286

Southport Old Links   (1926)
Moss Lane, Southport PR9 7QS
☎ (01704) 228207
▢ (01704) 505353
✉ secretary@solgc.freeserve.co.uk
✍ BE Kenyon
▤ www.solgc.freeserve.co.uk

Wallasey   (1891)
Bayswater Road, Wallasey CH45 8LA
☎ (0151) 691 1024
▢ (0151) 638 8988
✉ wallaseygc@aol.com
✍ JT Barraclough (0151) 691 1024
▤ www.wallaseygolfclub.com

Warren   (1911)
Public
Grove Road, Wallasey, Wirral CH45 0JA
☎ (0151) 639 8323 (Clubhouse)
▤ www.warrengc.freeserve.co.uk

West Derby   (1896)
Yew Tree Lane, Liverpool L12 9HQ
☎ (0151) 254 1034
▢ (0151) 259 0505
✉ secretary@westderbygc.co.uk
✍ AP Milne (0151) 254 1034
▤ www.westderbygc.co.uk

West Lancashire   (1873)
Hall Road West, Blundellsands, Liverpool
L23 8SZ
☎ (0151) 924 1076
▢ (0151) 931 4448
✉ sec@westlancashiregolf.co.uk
✍ S King (0151) 924 1076
▤ www.westlancashiregolf.co.uk

Wirral Ladies   (1894)
93 Bidston Road, Birkenhead, Wirral
CH43 6TS
☎ (0151) 652 1255
▢ (0151) 651 3775
✉ wirral.ladies@btconnect.com
✍ Mr P Greville
▤ www.wirral-ladies-golf-club.co.uk

Woolton   (1900)
Doe Park, Speke Road, Woolton, Liverpool
L25 7TZ
☎ (0151) 486 2298
▢ (0151) 486 1664
✉ golf@wooltongolf.co.uk
✍ Miss T Rawlinson (0151) 486 2298
opt 4
▤ www.wooltongolfclub.com

Middlesex

Airlinks   (1984)
Public
Southall Lane, Hounslow TW5 9PE
☎ (020) 8561 1418

Ashford Manor   (1898)
Fordbridge Road, Ashford TW15 3RT
☎ (01784) 424644
▢ (01784) 424649
✉ secretary@amgc.co.uk
✍ Peter Dawson (Business Manager)
▤ www.amgc.co.uk

Brent Valley   (1909)
Public
Church Road, Hanwell, London W7 3BE
☎ (020) 8567 4230 (Clubhouse)

Bush Hill Park   (1895)
Bush Hill, Winchmore Hill, London
N21 2BU
☎ (020) 8360 5738
▢ (020) 8360 5583
✉ chris@bhpgc.com
✍ M Berry
▤ www.bhpgc.com

Crews Hill (1916)
Cattlegate Road, Crews Hill, Enfield EN2 8AZ
☎ **(020) 8363 6674**
✉ manager@crewshillgolfclub.com
✍ Brian Cullen
🖥 www.crewshillgolfclub.com

David Lloyd Hampton Golf Club (1977)
Pay and play
Staines Road, Twickenham TW2 5JD
☎ **(0208) 783 1698**
📠 (0208) 783 9475
✉ golf.hampton@davidlloyd.co.uk
✍ Jamie Skinner
🖥 www.davidlloyd.co.uk

Ealing (1898)
Perivale Lane, Greenford UB6 8TS
☎ **(020) 8997 0937**
📠 (020) 8998 0756
✉ info@ealinggolfclub.co.uk
✍ David Jones
🖥 www.ealinggolfclub.co.uk

Enfield (1893)
Old Park Road South, Enfield EN2 7DA
☎ **(020) 8363 3970**
📠 (020) 8342 0381
✉ secretary@enfieldgolfclub.co.uk
✍ Darryl Canthorne
🖥 www.enfieldgolfclub.co.uk

Finchley (1929)
Nether Court, Frith Lane, London NW7 1PU
☎ **(020) 8346 2436**
📠 (020) 8343 4205
✉ secretary@finchleygolfclub.co.uk
✍ MD Gottlieb
🖥 www.finchleygolfclub.com

Fulwell (1904)
Wellington Road, Hampton Hill TW12 1JY
☎ **(020) 8977 2733**
📠 (020) 8977 7732
✉ secretary@fulwellgolfclub.co.uk
✍ Alistair Cook
🖥 www.fulwellgolfclub.co.uk

Grim's Dyke (1909)
Oxhey Lane, Hatch End, Pinner HA5 4AL
☎ **(020) 8428 4539**
📠 (020) 8421 5494
✉ secretary@grimsdyke.co.uk
✍ R Jones (020) 8428 4539
🖥 www.club-noticeboard
.co.uk/grimsdyke

Hampstead (1893)
82 Winnington Road, London N2 0TU
☎ **(020) 8455 0203**
📠 (020) 8731 6194
✉ secretary@hampsteadgolfclub
.co.uk
✍ Marie Smith
🖥 www.hampsteadgolfclub.co.uk

Harrow Hill Golf Course (1982)
Public
Kenton Road, Harrow, Middx HA1 2BW
☎ **(0208) 8643754**
✉ info@harrowgolf.co.uk
✍ S Bishop
🖥 www.harrowgolf.co.uk

Harrow School (1978)
High Street, Harrow-on-the-Hill HA1 3HP
☎ **(0208) 872 8000**
✉ hsgcsecretary@harrowschool
.org.uk
✍ V A Mrowiec (020) 8872 8290
🖥 www.harrowschoolgolfclub.co.uk

Haste Hill (1930)
Public
The Drive, Northwood HA6 1HN
☎ **(01923) 825224**
📠 (01923) 826485
✉ hastehillgc@yahoo.co.uk
✍ S Cella

Heath Park (1975)
Stockley Road, West Drayton
☎ **(01895) 444232**
📠 (01895) 444232
✉ heathparkgolf@yahoo.co.uk
✍ B Sharma (Prop)

Hendon (1903)
Ashley Walk, Devonshire Road, London NW7 1DG
☎ **(020) 8346 6023**
📠 (020) 8343 1974
✉ admin@hendongolfclub.co.uk
✍ Gabriela Segal (Sec)
🖥 www.hendongolfclub.co.uk

Highgate (1904)
Denewood Road, Highgate, London N6 4AH
☎ **(020) 8340 1906 (Clubhouse)**
📠 (020) 8348 9152
✉ admin@highgategc.co.uk
✍ N Higginson (020) 8340 3745
🖥 www.highgategc.co.uk

Horsenden Hill (1935)
Public
Woodland Rise, Greenford UB6 0RD
☎ **(020) 8902 4555**
✉ hhgchonsec@aol.com
✍ John Leach (0208) 922 3472
🖥 www.horsendenhillgolfclub.co.uk

Hounslow Heath (1979)
Public
Staines Road, Hounslow TW4 5DS
☎ **(020) 8570 5271**
📠 (020) 8570 5205
✉ golf@hhgc.uk.com
✍ J Swanson
🖥 www.hhgc.uk.com

Leaside GC (1974)
Pay and play
Lee Valley Leisure, Picketts Lock Lane, Edmonton, London N9 0AS
☎ **(020) 8803 3611**

Mill Hill (1925)
100 Barnet Way, Mill Hill, London NW7 3AL
☎ **(020) 8959 2339**
📠 (020) 8906 0731
✉ cluboffice@millhillgc.co.uk
✍ David Beal
🖥 www.millhillgc.co.uk

Muswell Hill (1893)
Rhodes Avenue, London N22 7UT
☎ **(020) 8888 1764**
📠 (020) 8889 9380
✉ manager@muswellhillgolfclub.co.uk
✍ A Hobbs (020) 8888 1764
🖥 www.muswellhillgolfclub.co.uk

North Middlesex (1905)
The Manor House, Friern Barnet Lane, Whetstone, London N20 0NL
☎ **(020) 8445 1604**
📠 (020) 8445 5023
✉ manager@northmiddlesexgc.co.uk
✍ Mr Howard Till
🖥 www.northmiddlesexgc.co.uk

Northwood (1891)
Rickmansworth Road, Northwood HA6 2QW
☎ **(01923) 821384**
📠 (01923) 840150
✉ secretary@northwoodgolf.co.uk
✍ S Proudfoot
🖥 www.northwoodgolf.co.uk

Perivale Park (1932)
Public
Stockdove Way, Argyle Road, Greenford UB6 8JT
☎ **(020) 8575 7116**
✍ J Mealyer

Pinner Hill (1927)
Southview Road, Pinner Hill HA5 3YA
☎ **(020) 8866 0963**
📠 (020) 8868 4817
✉ phgc@pinnerhillgc.com
✍ Alan Findlater (Gen Mgr)
🖥 www.pinnerhillgc.com

Ruislip (1936)
Public
Ickenham Road, Ruislip HA4 7DQ
☎ **(01895) 638835/623980**
📠 (01895) 635780
✉ ruislipgolf@btconnect.com
✍ N Jennings

Stanmore (1893)
29 Gordon Avenue, Stanmore HA7 2RL
☎ **(020) 8954 2599**
📠 (020) 8954 2599
✉ secretary@stanmoregolfclub.co.uk
✍ Allan Knott (020) 8954 2599
🖥 www.stanmoregolfclub.co.uk

Stockley Park (1993)
Pay and play
The Clubhouse, Stockley Park, Uxbridge UB11 1AQ
☎ **(020) 8813 5700/561 6339
(Bookings)**

✉ k.soper@stockleyparkgolf.com
🖥 www.stockleyparkgolf.com

Strawberry Hill   (1900)
Wellesley Road, Strawberry Hill,
Twickenham TW2 5SD
☎ **(020) 8894 0165**
📠 secretary@shgc.net
✍ Secretary (020) 8894 0165
🖥 www.shgc.net

Sudbury   (1920)
Bridgewater Road, Wembley HA0 1AL
☎ **(020) 8902 3713 (office)**
📠 (020) 8902 3713
✉ enquiries@sudburygolfclubltd.co.uk
✍ N Cropley (Gen Mgr)
🖥 www.sudburygolfclubltd.co.uk

Sunbury   (1993)
Proprietary
Charlton Lane, Shepperton TW17 8QA
☎ **(01932) 771414**
✉ sunbury@crown-golf.co.uk
🖥 www.crown-golf.co.uk

Trent Park   (1973)
Pay and play
Bramley Road, Southgate, London
N14 4UW
☎ **(020) 8367 4653**
📠 (020) 8366 4581
✉ trentpark@crown-golf.co.uk
🖥 www.trentparkgolf.co.uk

Uxbridge   (1947)
Public
The Drive, Harefield Place, Uxbridge
UB10 8AQ
☎ **(01895) 231169**
📠 (01895) 810262
✉ uxbridgegolf@btconnect.com
✍ Mrs A James (01895) 272457
🖥 www.uxbridgegolfclub.co.uk

West Middlesex   (1891)
Greenford Road, Southall UB1 3EE
☎ **(020) 8574 3450**
📠 (020) 8574 2383
✉ westmid.gc@virgin.net
✍ Miss R Khanna
🖥 www.westmiddxgolfclub.co.uk

Wyke Green   (1928)
Syon Lane, Isleworth, Osterley TW7 5PT
☎ **(020) 8560 8777**
📠 (020) 8569 8392
✉ office@wykegreengolfclub.co.uk
✍ D Pearson
🖥 www.wykegreengolfclub.co.uk

Norfolk

Barnham Broom Hotel
(1977)
Honingham Road, Barnham Broom,
Norwich NR9 4DD
☎ **(01603) 759393 (Hotel)**
📠 (01603) 758224
✉ golf@barnham-broom.co.uk

✍ M Breen (01603) 757504
🖥 www.barnham-broom.co.uk

Bawburgh   (1978)
Glen Lodge, Marlingford Road, Bawburgh,
Norwich NR9 3LU
☎ **(01603) 740404**
📠 (01603) 740403
✉ info@bawburgh.com
✍ I Ladbrooke (Gen Mgr)
🖥 www.bawburgh.com

Caldecott Hall   (1993)
Pay and play
Caldecott Hall, Beccles Road, Fritton, Great
Yarmouth NR31 9EY
☎ **(01493) 488488**
📠 (01493) 488561
✉ reception_caldecotthall@hotmail.
co.uk
✍ Jill Braybrooke
🖥 www.caldecotthall.co.uk

Costessey Park   (1983)
Costessey Park, Costessey, Norwich
NR8 5AL
☎ **(01603) 746333**
📠 (01603) 746185
✉ cpgc@ljgroup.com
✍ GC Stangoe
🖥 www.costesseypark.com

Dereham   (1934)
Quebec Road, Dereham NR19 2DS
☎ **(01362) 695900**
📠 (01362) 695904
✉ office@derehamgolfclub.com
✍ Mr Tim Evans
🖥 www.derehamgolfclub.com

Dunham   (1979)
Proprietary
Little Dunham, Swaffham PE32 2DF
☎ **(01328) 701906**
✉ info@dunhamgolfclub.com
🖥 www.dunhamgolfclub.com

De Vere Dunston Hall   (1994)
Pay and play
Ipswich Road, Dunston, Norwich NR14 8PQ
☎ **(01508) 470178**

Eagles   (1990)
Pay and play
39 School Road, Tilney All Saints, Kings
Lynn PE34 4RS
☎ **(01553) 827147**
📠 (01553) 829777
✉ shop@eagles-golf-tennis.co.uk
✍ D W Horn
🖥 www.eagles-golf-tennis.co.uk

Eaton   (1910)
Newmarket Road, Norwich NR4 6SF
☎ **(01603) 451686**
📠 (01603) 457539
✉ admin@eatongc.co.uk
✍ P Johns
🖥 www.eatongc.co.uk

Fakenham   (1973)
The Race Course, Hempton Road,
Fakenham NR21 7NY
☎ **(01328) 855678**

📠 (01328) 855678
✉ fakenhamgolf@tiscali.co.uk
✍ G Cocker (01328) 855678
🖥 www.fakenhamgolfclub.co.uk

Feltwell   (1976)
Thor Ave, Wilton Road, Feltwell, Thetford
IP26 4AY
☎ **(01842) 827644**
📠 (01842) 829065
✉ sec.feltwellgc@virgin.net
✍ Jonathan Moore
🖥 www.club-noticeboard.co.uk

Gorleston   (1906)
Warren Road, Gorleston, Gt Yarmouth
NR31 6JT
☎ **(01493) 661911**
📠 (01493) 661911
✉ manager@gorlestongolfclub.co.uk
✍ David James (01493) 661911
🖥 www.gorlestongolfclub.co.uk

Great Yarmouth & Caister
(1882)
Beach House, Caister-on-Sea, Gt Yarmouth
NR30 5TD
☎ **(01493) 728699**
📠 (01493) 728831
✉ office@caistergolf.co.uk
✍ Brian Lever
🖥 www.caistergolf.co.uk

Hunstanton   (1891)
Golf Course Road, Old Hunstanton
PE36 6JQ
☎ **(01485) 532811**
📠 (01485) 532319
✉ secretary@hunstantongolfclub.com
✍ BRB Carrick
🖥 www.hunstantongolfclub.com

King's Lynn   (1923)
Castle Rising, King's Lynn PE31 6BD
☎ **(01553) 631654**
📠 (01553) 631036
✉ secretary@kingslynngc.co.uk
✍ M Bowman
🖥 www.kingslynngc.co.uk

Links Country Park Hotel
& Golf Club   (1903)
West Runton, Cromer NR27 9QH
☎ **(01263) 838383**
📠 (01263) 838264
✉ links@mackenziehotels.com
✍ Marc Mackenzie
🖥 www.links-hotel.co.uk

Marriott Sprowston Manor
Hotel   (1980)
Wroxham Road, Sprowston, Norwich
NR7 8RP
☎ **(0870) 400 7229**
📠 (0870) 400 7329
✉ keith.grant@marriotthotels.com
✍ Keith Grant
🖥 www.marriott.co.uk/nwigs

Mattishall   (1990)
Proprietary
South Green, Mattishall, Dereham
☎ **(01362) 850464**

🏠 B Hall
🖥 www.mattishallgolfclub.co.uk

Middleton Hall (1989)
Proprietary
Middleton, King's Lynn PE32 1RY
☎ **(01553) 841800**
📧 enquiries@middletonhallgolfclub.com
🏠 M Johnson
🖥 www.middletonhallgolfclub.com

Mundesley (1901)
Links Road, Mundesley NR11 8ES
☎ **(01263) 720095**
📠 (01263) 722849
📧 manager@mundesleygolfclub.com
🏠 R Pudney
🖥 www.mundesleygolfclub.com

The Norfolk G&CC (1993)
Proprietary
Hingham Road, Reymerston, Norwich NR9 4QQ
☎ **(01362) 850297**
📧 norfolkgolfse@ukonline.co.uk
🖥 www.thenorfolk.co.uk

RAF Marham (1974)
RAF Marham, Kings Lynn PE33 9NP
☎ **(01760) 337261 ext 7262**
🖥 www.marhamgolf.co.uk

Richmond Park (1990)
Saham Road, Watton IP25 6EA
☎ **(01953) 881803**
📠 (01953) 881817
📧 info@richmondpark.co.uk
🏠 S Jessop
🖥 www.richmondpark.co.uk

Royal Cromer (1888)
Overstrand Road, Cromer NR27 0JH
☎ **(01263) 512884**
📠 (01263) 512430
📧 general.manager@royal-cromer.com
🏠 Gary Richardson
🖥 www.royalcromergolfclub.com

Royal Norwich (1893)
Drayton High Road, Hellesdon, Norwich NR6 5AH
☎ **(01603) 429928**
📠 (01603) 417945
📧 mail@royalnorwichgolf.co.uk
🏠 Phil Grice (Gen Mgr)
🖥 www.royalnorwichgolf.co.uk

Royal West Norfolk (1892)
Brancaster, King's Lynn PE31 8AX
☎ **(01485) 210087**
📠 (01485) 210087
📧 secretary@rwngc.org
🏠 Ian Symington
🖥 www.rwngc.org

Ryston Park (1932)
Ely Road, Denver, Downham Market PE38 0HH
☎ **(01366) 382133**

📠 (01366) 383834
📧 rystonparkgc@talktalkbusiness.net
🏠 WJ Flogdell
🖥 www.club-noticeboard.co.uk

Sheringham (1891)
Sheringham NR26 8HG
☎ **(01263) 823488**
📠 (01263) 826129
📧 info@sheringhamgolfclub.co.uk
🏠 T E Duke (01263) 823488
🖥 www.sheringhamgolfclub.co.uk

Swaffham (1922)
Cley Road, Swaffham PE37 8AE
☎ **(01760) 721621**
📠 (01760) 336998
📧 manager@swaffhamgc.co.uk
🖥 www.club-noticeboard.co.uk

Thetford (1912)
Brandon Road, Thetford IP24 3NE
☎ **(01842) 752258 (Clubhouse)**
📠 (01842) 766212
📧 thetfordgolfclub@btconnect.com
🏠 Mrs Diane Hopkins (01842) 752169
🖥 www.thetfordgolfclub.co.uk

Wensum Valley (1990)
Proprietary
Beech Avenue, Taverham, Norwich NR8 6HP
☎ **(01603) 261012**
📠 (01603) 261664
📧 enqs@wensumvalleyhotel.co.uk
🏠 Mrs B Hall
🖥 www.wensumvalleyhotel.co.uk

Weston Park (1993)
Proprietary
Weston Longville, Norwich NR9 5JW
☎ **(01603) 872363**
📠 (01603) 873040
📧 golf@weston-park.co.uk
🏠 C E Ashmore (Sales & Membership Mgr)
🖥 www.weston-park.co.uk

Northamptonshire

Brampton Heath (1995)
Pay and play
Sandy Lane, Church Brampton NN6 8AX
☎ **(01604) 843939**
📠 (01604) 843885
📧 info@bhgc.co.uk
🏠 Carl Sainsbury (Head Pro)
🖥 www.bhgc.co.uk

Cold Ashby (1974)
Proprietary
Stanford Road, Cold Ashby, Northampton NN6 6EP
☎ **(01604) 740548**
📠 (01604) 743025
📧 info@coldashbygolfclub.com
🏠 DA Croxton (Prop)
🖥 www.coldashbygolfclub.com

Collingtree Park Golf Course (1990)
Proprietary
Windingbrook Lane, Northampton NN4 0XN
☎ **(01604) 700000**
📠 (01604) 702600
📧 enquiries@collingtreeparkgolf.com
🏠 Kevin Whitehouse (Dir of Golf)
🖥 www.collingtreeparkgolf.com

Daventry & District (1907)
Norton Road, Daventry NN11 2LS
☎ **(01327) 702829**
📧 ddgc@hotmail.co.uk
🏠 Colin Long
🖥 www.daventrygolfclub.co.uk

Delapre (1976)
Pay and play
Eagle Drive, Nene Valley Way, Northampton NN4 7DU
☎ **(01604) 764036**
📠 (01604) 706378
📧 delapre@jbgolf.co.uk
🏠 Greg Iron (Centre Mgr) John Cuddiny (PGA Pro)
🖥 www.delapregolfcentre.co.uk

Farthingstone Hotel (1974)
Farthingstone, Towcester NN12 8HA
☎ **(01327) 361291**
📠 (01327) 361645
📧 interest@farthingstone.co.uk
🏠 C Donaldson
🖥 www.farthingstone.co.uk

Hellidon Lakes Hotel G&CC (1991)
Hellidon, Nr. Daventry, Northamptonshire NN11 6LN
☎ **(01327) 262550**
📠 (01327) 262559
🏠 MA Thomas
🖥 www.hellidon.co.uk

Kettering (1891)
Headlands, Kettering NN15 6XA
☎ **(01536) 511104**
📠 (01536) 523788
📧 secretary@kettering-golf.co.uk
🏠 JM Gilding (01536) 511104
🖥 www.kettering-golf.co.uk

Kingfisher Hotel (1995)
Proprietary
Buckingham Road, Deanshanger, Milton Keynes MK19 6JY
☎ **(01908) 560354/562332**
📧 sales.kingfisher@btopenworld.com
🖥 www.kingfisher-hotelandgolf.co.uk

Kingsthorpe (1908)
Kingsley Road, Northampton NN2 7BU
☎ **(01604) 711173**
📠 (01604) 710610
📧 secretary@kingsthorpe-golf.co.uk
🏠 DS Wade (01604) 710610
🖥 www.kingsthorpe-golf.co.uk

Northampton   (1893)
Harlestone, Northampton NN7 4EF
☎ **(01604) 845155**
🖳 (01604) 820262
📧 golf@northamptongolfclub.co.uk
🖊 B Randall (Director of Golf)
🖥 www.northamptongolfclub.co.uk

Northamptonshire County
(1909)
Church Brampton, Northampton NN6 8AZ
☎ **(01604) 843025**
🖳 (01604) 843463
📧 secretary@countygolfclub.org.uk
🖊 Peter Walsh (01604) 843025
🖥 www.countygolfclub.org.uk

Oundle   (1893)
Benefield Road, Oundle PE8 4EZ
☎ **(01832) 273267**
🖳 (01832) 273008
📧 office@oundlegolfclub.com
🖊 L Quantrill (01832) 272267
🖥 www.oundlegolfclub.com

Overstone Park   (1994)
Proprietary
Overstone Park Ltd, Billing Lane,
Northampton NN6 0A5
☎ **(01604) 647666**
🖳 (01604) 642635
📧 enquiries@overstonepark.com
🖊 Nigel Wardle (Gen Mgr)
🖥 www.overstonepark.com

Priors Hall   (1965)
Public
Stamford Road, Weldon, Corby NN17 3JH
☎ **(01536) 260756**
🖳 (01536) 260756
📧 p.ackroyd1@btinternet.com
🖊 P Ackroyd (01536) 263722

Rushden   (1919)
Kimbolton Road, Chelveston,
Wellingborough, Northamptonshire
NN9 6AN
☎ **(01933) 418511**
🖳 (01933) 418511
📧 secretary@rushdengolfclub.org
🖊 EJ Williams
🖥 www.rushdengolfclub.org

Staverton Park   (1977)
Staverton Park, Staverton, Daventry
NN11 6JT
☎ **(01327) 302000/302118**

Stoke Albany   (1995)
Proprietary
Ashley Road, Stoke Albany, Market
Harborough LE16 8PL
☎ **(01858) 535208**
🖳 (01858) 535505
📧 info@stokealbanygolfclub.co.uk
🖊 R Want
🖥 www.stokealbanygolfclub.com

Wellingborough   (1893)
Harrowden Hall, Great Harrowden,
Wellingborough NN9 5AD
☎ **(01933) 677234/673022**

🖳 (01933) 679379
📧 david.waite
    @wellingboroughgolfclub.com
🖊 David Waite (01933) 677234
🖥 www.wellingboroughgolfclub.com

Whittlebury Park G&CC
(1992)
Proprietary, Public,
Whittlebury, Towcester NN12 8WP
☎ **(01327) 850000**
🖳 (01327) 850001
📧 enquiries@whittlebury.com
🖊 Alison Trubshaw
🖥 www.whittlebury.com

Northumberland

Allendale   (1906)
High Studdon, Allenheads Road, Allendale,
Hexham NE47 9DH
☎ **(0700) 580 8246**
📧 secretary@allendale-golf.co.uk
🖊 Mrs A Woodcock (Hon)
🖥 www.allendale-golf.co.uk

Alnmouth   (1869)
Foxton Hall, Alnmouth NE66 3BE
☎ **(01665) 830231**
🖳 (01665) 830922
📧 secretary@alnmouthgolfclub.com
🖊 P Simpson
🖥 www.alnmouthgolfclub.com

Alnmouth Village   (1869)
Marine Road, Alnmouth NE66 2RZ
☎ **(01665) 830370**
📧 bobhill53@live.co.uk
🖊 R A Hill (01665) 833189
🖥 www.alnmouthvillagegolfclub.co.uk

Alnwick Castle   (1907)
Proprietary
Swansfield Park, Alnwick NE66 2AB
☎ **(01665) 602632**
📧 secretary@alnwickgolfclub.co.uk
🖊 Club Manager (01665) 602632
🖥 www.alnwickcastlegolfclub.co.uk

Arcot Hall   (1909)
Dudley, Cramlington NE23 7QP
☎ **(0191) 236 2794**
🖳 (0191) 217 0370
📧 arcothall@tiscali.co.uk
🖊 Brian Rumney (0191) 236 2794
🖥 www.arcothallgolfclub.com

Bamburgh Castle   (1904)
The Club House, 40 The Wynding,
Bamburgh NE69 7DE
☎ **(01668) 214378**
🖳 (01668) 214607
📧 sec@bamburghcastlegolfclub.co.uk
🖊 MND Robinson (01668) 214321
🖥 www.bamburghcastlegolfclub.co.uk

Bedlingtonshire   (1972)
Acorn Bank, Hartford Road, Bedlington
NE22 6AA
☎ **(01670) 822457**

🖳 (01670) 823048
📧 secretary@bedlingtongolfclub.com
🖊 J Laverick (01670) 822457
🖥 www.bedlingtongolfclub.com

The Belford   (1993)
South Road, Belford NE70 7DP
☎ **(01668) 213323**
🖳 (01668) 213282
🖊 HS Adair
🖥 www.thebelford.com

Bellingham   (1893)
Boggle Hole, Bellingham NE48 2DT
☎ **(01434) 220530/220152**
📧 admin@bellinghamgolfclub.com
🖊 Craig Wright
🖥 www.bellinghamgolfclub.com

Berwick-upon-Tweed
(Goswick)   (1890)
Goswick, Berwick-upon-Tweed TD15 2RW
☎ **(01289) 387256**
🖳 (01289) 387392
📧 goswickgc@btconnect.com
🖊 IAM Alsop
🖥 www.goswicklinksgc.co.uk

Blyth   (1905)
New Delaval, Blyth NE24 4DB
☎ **(01670) 540110**
🖳 (01670) 540134
📧 clubmanager@blythgolf.co.uk
🖊 J C Hall
🖥 www.blythgolf.co.uk

Burgham Park Golf &
Leisure Club   (1994)
Proprietary
Felton, Morpeth NE65 9QP
☎ **(01670) 787898**
🖳 (01670) 787164
📧 info@burghampark.co.uk
🖊 William Kiely
🖥 www.burghampark.co.uk

Close House Hotel & Golf
(1968)
Proprietary
Close House, Heddon-on-the-Wall,
Newcastle-upon-Tyne NE15 0HT
☎ **(01661) 852255**
🖳 (01661) 853322
📧 events@closehouse.co.uk
🖊 John Glendinning
🖥 www.closehouse.co.uk

Dunstanburgh Castle   (1900)
Embleton NE66 3XQ
☎ **(01665) 576562**
🖳 (01665) 576562
📧 enquiries@dunstanburgh.com
🖊 Irene Williams (Mgr)
🖥 www.dunstanburgh.com

Hexham   (1892)
Spital Park, Hexham NE46 3RZ
☎ **(01434) 603072**
🖳 (01434) 601865
📧 info@hexhamgolf.co.uk
🖊 Dawn Wylie (01434) 603072
🖥 www.hexhamgolf.co.uk

Leen Valley Golf Club (1994)
Pay and play
Wigwam Lane, Hucknall NG15 7TA
- ☎ **(0115) 964 2037**
- 🖷 (0115) 964 2724
- ✉ leenvalley@live.co.uk
- ✍ Robert Kerr
- 🖥 www.leenvalleygolfclub.co.uk

Linden Hall (1997)
Proprietary
Longhorsley, Morpeth NE65 8XF
- ☎ **(01670) 500011**
- 🖷 (01670) 500001
- ✉ golf@lindenhall.co.uk
- ✍ Stuart Carnie (Golf Mgr)
- 🖥 www.macdonaldhotels.co.uk/
lindenhall

Longhirst Hall Golf Course
(1997)
Longhirst Hall, Longhirst NE61 3LL
- ☎ **(01670) 791562 (Clubhouse)**
- 🖷 (01670) 791768
- ✉ enquiries@longhirstgolf.co.uk
- ✍ Graham Chambers (01670) 791562
- 🖥 www.longhirstgolf.co.uk

Magdalene Fields (1903)
Pay and play
Magdalene Fields, Berwick-upon-Tweed
TD15 1NE
- ☎ **(01289) 306130**
- 🖷 (01289) 306384
- ✉ secretary.magdalenefields
@hotmail.co.uk
- ✍ C J Reid (Sec)
- 🖥 www.magdalene-fields.co.uk

Matfen Hall Hotel (1994)
Proprietary
Matfen, Hexham NE20 0RH
- ☎ **(01661) 886400 (golf)**
- 🖷 (01661) 886055
- ✉ golf@matfenhall.com
- ✍ Peter Smith
- 🖥 www.matfenhall.com

Morpeth (1906)
The Clubhouse, Morpeth NE61 2BT
- ☎ **(01670) 504942**
- 🖷 (01670) 504918
- ✉ admin@morpethgolf.co.uk
- ✍ Terry Minett
- 🖥 www.morpethgolf.co.uk

Newbiggin (1884)
Newbiggin-by-the-Sea NE64 6DW
- ☎ **(01670) 817344 (Clubhouse)**
- ✉ info@newbiggingolfclub.co.uk
- ✍ J Oliphant (Sec)/J Young (Mgr)
- 🖥 www.newbiggingolfclub.co.uk

Percy Wood Golf &
   Country Retreat (1993)
Coast View, Swarland, Morpeth NE65 9JG
- ☎ **(01670) 787940 (Clubhouse)**
- ✉ enquiries@percywood.com
- 🖷 (01670) 787010
- 🖥 www.percywood.co.uk

Ponteland (1927)
53 Bell Villas, Ponteland, Newcastle-upon-
Tyne NE20 9BD
- ☎ **(01661) 822689**
- 🖷 (01661) 860077
- ✉ secretary@thepontelandgolfclub
.co.uk
- ✍ G Waugh
- 🖥 www.thepontelandgolfclub.co.uk

Prudhoe (1930)
Eastwood Park, Prudhoe-on-Tyne
NE42 5DX
- ☎ **(01661) 832466 ext 20**
- 🖷 (01661) 830710
- ✉ secretary@prudhoegolfclub.co.uk
- ✍ ID Pauw
- 🖥 www.prudhoegolfclub.co.uk

Rothbury (1891)
Whitton Bank Road, Rothbury, Morpeth
NE65 7RX
- ☎ **(01669) 621271 Ext 2**
- ✉ secretary@rothburygolfclub.com
- ✍ LF Brown (0191) 215 0268
- 🖥 www.rothburygolfclub.com

Seahouses (1913)
Beadnell Road, Seahouses NE68 7XT
- ☎ **(01665) 720794**
- 🖷 (01665) 721799
- ✉ secretary@seahousesgolf.co.uk
- ✍ Alan Patterson
- 🖥 www.seahousesgolf.co.uk

De Vere Slaley Hall (1988)
Slaley, Hexham NE47 0BX
- ☎ **(01434) 673154**
- ✉ slaley.hall@devere-hotels.com
- 🖥 www.devere.co.uk

Stocksfield (1913)
New Ridley, Stocksfield NE43 7RE
- ☎ **(01661) 843041**
- 🖷 (01661) 843046
- ✉ info@sgcgolf.co.uk
- ✍ B Garrow (Acting Sec)
- 🖥 www.sgcgolf.co.uk

Warkworth (1891)
The Links, Warkworth, Morpeth,
Northumberland NE65 0SW
- ☎ **(01665) 711596**
- ✍ David Arkley
- 🖥 www.warkworthgolfclub
@btconnect.com

Wooler (1975)
Dod Law, Doddington, Wooler NE71 6AL
- ☎ **(01668) 282135**
- ✍ S Lowrey (01668) 281631
- 🖥 www.woolergolf.co.uk

Nottinghamshire

Beeston Fields (1923)
Beeston, Nottingham NG9 3DD
- ☎ **(0115) 925 7062**
- 🖷 (0115) 925 4280
- ✉ info@beestonfields.co.uk

- ✍ J Lewis
- 🖥 www.beestonfields.co.uk

Brierley Forest (1993)
Main Street, Huthwaite, Sutton-in-Ashfield
NG17 2LG
- ☎ **(01623) 550761**
- 🖷 (01623) 550761
- ✍ D Crafts (01623) 514234

Bulwell Forest (1902)
Hucknall Road, Bulwell, Nottingham
NG6 9LQ
- ☎ **(0115) 976 3172 (secretary)**
- ✉ secretary@bulwellforestgolfclub
.co.uk
- ✍ R D Savage
- 🖥 www.bulwellforestgolfclub.co.uk

Chilwell Manor (1906)
Meadow Lane, Chilwell, Nottingham
NG9 5AE
- ☎ **(0115) 925 8958**
- 🖷 (0115) 922 0575
- ✉ info@chilwellmanorgolfclub.co.uk
- ✍ C Lawrence
- 🖥 www.chilwellmanorgolfclub.co.uk

College Pines (1994)
Proprietary
Worksop College Drive, Sparken Hill,
Worksop S80 3AL
- ☎ **(01909) 501431**
- 🖷 (01909) 481227
- ✉ snelljunior@btinternet.com
- ✍ C Snell (Golf Dir)
- 🖥 www.collegepinesgolfclub.co.uk

Coxmoor (1913)
Coxmoor Road, Sutton-in-Ashfield
NG17 5LF
- ☎ **(01623) 557359**
- 🖷 (01623) 557435
- ✉ secretary@coxmoorgolfclub.co.uk
- ✍ Mrs J Chambers
- 🖥 www.coxmoorgolfclub.co.uk

Edwalton (1982)
Pay and play
Wellin Lane, Edwalton, Nottingham
NG12 4AS
- ☎ **(0115) 923 4775**
- 🖷 (0115) 923 1647
- ✉ edwalton@glendale-services.co.uk
- ✍ Ms D J Kerrison
- 🖥 www.glendale-golf.com

Kilton Forest (1978)
Public
Blyth Road, Worksop S81 0TL
- ☎ **(01909) 486563**
- ✍ JA Eyre (Hon)

Mapperley (1907)
Central Avenue, Plains Road, Mapperley,
Nottingham NG3 6RH
- ☎ **(0115) 955 6672**
- 🖷 (0115) 955 6670
- ✉ secretary@mapperleygolfclub.org
- ✍ Michael Mulhern
- 🖥 www.mapperleygolfclub.org

Newark　(1901)
Coddington, Newark NG24 2QX
☎ **(01636) 626282**
🖥 (01636) 626497
📠 manager@newarkgolfclub.co.uk
✍ DA Collingwood (01636) 626282
🖥 www.newarkgolfclub.co.uk

Norwood Park Golf Centre
(1999)
Propreitary
Norwood Park, Southwell NG25 0PF
☎ **(01636) 816626**
📠 golf@norwoodpark.co.uk
✍ Paul Thornton
🖥 www.norwoodgolf.co.uk

Nottingham City　(1910)
Public
Norwich Gardens, Bulwell, Nottingham
NG6 8LF
☎ **(0115) 927 2767 (Pro Shop)**
📠 garyandkate1@talktalk.net
✍ GJ Chappell (07740) 288694
🖥 www.nottinghamcitygolfclub.co.uk

Notts　(1887)
Hollinwell, Kirkby-in-Ashfield NG17 7QR
☎ **(01623) 753225**
🖥 (01623) 753655
📠 office@nottsgolfclub.co.uk
✍ S E Lawrence
🖥 www.nottsgolfclub.co.uk

Oakmere Park　(1974)
Oaks Lane, Oxton NG25 0RH
☎ **(0115) 965 3545**
🖥 (0115) 965 5628
📠 enquiries@oakmerepark.co.uk
✍ D St-John Jones
🖥 www.oakmerepark.co.uk

Radcliffe-on-Trent　(1909)
Dewberry Lane, Cropwell Road, Radcliffe-
on-Trent NG12 2JH
☎ **(0115) 933 3000**
🖥 (0115) 911 6991
📠 bill.dunn@radcliffeontrentgc.co.uk
✍ B Dunn
🖥 www.radcliffeontrentgc.co.uk

Ramsdale Park Golf Centre
(1992)
Pay and play
Oxton Road, Calverton NG14 6NU
☎ **(0115) 965 5600**
🖥 (0115) 965 4105
📠 info@ramsdaleparkgc.co.uk
✍ N Birch (Mgr)
🖥 www.ramsdaleparkgc.co.uk

Retford　(1920)
Brecks Road, Ordsall, Retford DN22 7UA
☎ **(01777) 703733/711188**
🖥 (01777) 710412
📠 retfordgolfclub@lineone.net
✍ Lesley Redfearn & Diane Moore
🖥 www.retfordgolfclub.co.uk

Ruddington Grange　(1988)
Wilford Road, Ruddington, Nottingham
NG11 6NB
☎ **(0115) 984 6141**

🖥 (0115) 940 5165
📠 info@ruddingtongrange.co.uk
✍ P Deacon
🖥 www.ruddingtongrange.co.uk

Rufford Park G&CC　(1990)
Proprietary
Rufford Lane, Rufford, Newark NG22 9DG
☎ **(01623) 825253**
🖥 (01623) 825254
📠 enquiries@ruffordpark.co.uk
✍ Club Manager (01623) 825253
🖥 www.ruffordpark.co.uk

Rushcliffe　(1909)
Stocking Lane, East Leake, Loughborough
LE12 5RL
☎ **(01509) 852959**
🖥 (01509) 852688
📠 secretary@rushcliffegolfclub.com
✍ C Bee
🖥 www.rushcliffegolfclub.com

Serlby Park　(1906)
Serlby, Doncaster DN10 6BA
☎ **(01777) 818268**
📠 serlbysec@talktalkbusiness.net
✍ KJ Crook (01302) 742280

Sherwood Forest　(1895)
Eakring Road, Mansfield NG18 3EW
☎ **(01623) 626689/627403**
🖥 (01623) 420412
📠 info@sherwoodforestgolfclub
.co.uk
✍ Maj Gary J Mason BEM (01623)
626689
🖥 www.sherwoodforestgolfclub
.co.uk

Southwell　(1993)
Proprietary
Southwell Racecourse, Rolleston, Newark
NG25 0TS
☎ **(01636) 813706**
🖥 (01636) 812271
📠 southwellgolfclub@southwellgolf
.com
✍ P Salter (Sec) (01636) 819197
🖥 www.southwellgolfclub.com

Springwater　(1991)
Proprietary
Moor Lane, Calverton, Nottingham
NG14 6FZ
☎ **(0115) 965 4946**
🖥 (0115) 965 2344
📠 admin@springwatergolfclub
.com
✍ E Brady (0115) 952 3956
🖥 www.springwatergolfclub.com

Stanton-on-the-Wolds
(1906)
Golf Course Road, Stanton-on-the-Wolds,
Nottingham NG12 5BH
☎ **(0115) 937 4885**
🖥 (0115) 937 1652
📠 info@stantongc.co.uk
✍ MJ Price (0115) 937 1650
🖥 www.stantongolfclub.co.uk

The Nottinghamshire
G&CC　(1991)
Stragglethorpe, Nr Cotgrave Village,
Cotgrave NG12 3HB
☎ **(0115) 933 3344**
🖥 (0115) 933 4567
📠 general@thenottinghamshire.com
✍ Nick Lenty
🖥 www.thenottinghamshire.com

Trent Lock Golf Centre
(1991)
Proprietary
Lock Lane, Sawley, Long Eaton NG10 2FY
☎ **(0115) 946 4398**
🖥 (0115) 946 1183
📠 enquiries@trentlockgolf.com
✍ R Prior (F & B Mgr)
🖥 www.trentlock.co.uk

Wollaton Park　(1927)
Wollaton Park, Nottingham NG8 1BT
☎ **(0115) 978 7574**
📠 secretary@wollatonparkgolfclub
.com
✍ Avril J Jamieson
🖥 www.wollatonparkgolfclub.com

Worksop　(1911)
Windmill Lane, Worksop S80 2SQ
☎ **(01909) 477731**
🖥 (01909) 530917
📠 thesecretary@worksopgolfclub
.com
✍ G.J.Bardill (01909) 477731
🖥 www.worksopgolfclub.com

Oxfordshire

Aspect Park　(1988)
Remenham Hill, Henley-on-Thames RG9
3EH
☎ **(01491) 578306**

Badgemore Park　(1972)
Proprietary
Henley-on-Thames RG9 4NR
☎ **(01491) 637300**
🖥 (01491) 576899
📠 info@badgemorepark.com
✍ J Connell (Mgr) (01491) 637300
🖥 www.badgemorepark.com

Banbury Golf Club　(1993)
Pay and play
Aynho Road, Adderbury, Banbury
OX17 3NT
☎ **(01295) 810419**
🖥 (01295) 810056
📠 Mr M Reed
🖥 www.banburygolfclub.co.uk

Bicester Hotel Golf and Spa
(1973)
Chesterton, Bicester OX26 1TE
☎ **(01869) 241204**
📠 jamie.herbert
@bicesterhotelgolfandspa.com
✍ M Odom (01869) 241204
🖥 www.bicestergolf.co.uk

Burford (1936)
Burford OX18 4JG
- ☎ **(01993) 822583**
- 📠 (01993) 822801
- ✉ secretary@burfordgolfclub.co.uk
- ✍ RP Thompson
- 🖥 www.burfordgolfclub.co.uk

Carswell CC (1993)
Carswell, Faringdon SN7 8PU
- ☎ **(01367) 870422**
- 📠 (01367) 870592
- ✉ info@carswellgolfandcountryclub.co.uk
- ✍ G Lisi (Prop)
- 🖥 www.carswellgolfandcountryclub.co.uk

Cherwell Edge (1980)
Chacombe, Banbury OX17 2EN
- ☎ **(01295) 711591**
- ✉ enquiries@cherwelledgegolfclub.co.uk
- 🖥 www.cherwelledgegolfclub.co.uk

Chipping Norton (1890)
Southcombe, Chipping Norton OX7 5QH
- ☎ **(01608) 642383**
- 📠 (01608) 645422
- ✉ golfadmin@chippingnortongolfclub.com
- ✍ Lindsey Dray (Operations Mgr)
- 🖥 www.chippingnortongolfclub.com

Drayton Park (1992)
Pay and play
Steventon Road, Drayton, Abingdon, OX14 4la OX14 4lA
- ☎ **(01235) 550607/528989**
- 📠 (01235) 525731
- ✉ draytonpark@btclick.com
- ✍ Rob Bolton (01235) 528989
- 🖥 www.draytonparkgolfclubabingdon.co.uk

Feldon Valley (1992)
Proprietary
Sutton Lane, Lower Brailes, Banbury OX15 5BB
- ☎ **(01608) 685633**
- ✉ info@feldonvalley.co.uk
- ✍ Neil Simpson (Dir) (01608) 685633
- 🖥 www.feldonvalley.co.uk

Frilford Heath (1908)
Frilford Heath, Abingdon OX13 5NW
- ☎ **(01865) 390864**
- 📠 (01865) 390823
- ✉ generalmanager@frilfordheath.co.uk
- ✍ A B W James
- 🖥 www.frilfordheath.co.uk

Hadden Hill (1990)
Proprietary
Wallingford Road, Didcot OX11 9BJ
- ☎ **(01235) 510410**
- 📠 (01235) 511260
- ✉ info@haddenhillgolf.co.uk
- ✍ A.C.Smith
- 🖥 www.haddenhillgolf.co.uk

Henley (1907)
Harpsden, Henley-on-Thames RG9 4HG
- ☎ **(01491) 575742**
- 📠 (01491) 412179
- ✉ info@henleygc.com
- ✍ Gary Oatham (01491) 635305
- 🖥 www.henleygc.com

Hinksey Heights Golf Club (1995)
Public
South Hinksey, Oxford OX1 5AB
- ☎ **(01865) 327775**
- ✉ sec@oxford-golf.co.uk
- ✍ Jane Binning
- 🖥 www.oxford-golf.co.uk

Huntercombe (1901)
Nuffield, Henley-on-Thames RG9 5SL
- ☎ **(01491) 641207**
- 📠 (01491) 642060
- ✉ office@huntercombegolfclub.co.uk
- ✍ GNV Jenkins
- 🖥 www.huntercombegolfclub.co.uk

Kirtlington (1995)
Proprietary
Kirtlington, Oxon OX5 3JY
- ☎ **(01869) 351133**
- 📠 (01869) 331143
- ✉ info@kirtlingtongolfclub.com
- ✍ Miss P Smith (Sec/Mgr)
- 🖥 www.kirtlingtongolfclub.com

North Oxford (1907)
Banbury Road, Oxford OX2 8EZ
- ☎ **(01865) 554415**
- 📠 (01865) 554924
- ✍ R J Harris (Mgr) (01865) 554924 opt 2
- 🖥 www.nogc.co.uk

Oxford Golf Club (1875)
Hill Top Road, Oxford OX4 1PF
- ☎ **(01865) 242158**
- 📠 (01865) 250023
- ✉ sgcltd@btopenworld.com
- ✍ C G Whittle (01865) 242158
- 🖥 www.oxfordgolfclub.net

The Oxfordshire (1993)
Proprietary
Rycote Lane, Milton Common, Thame OX9 2PU
- ☎ **(01844) 278300**
- 📠 (01844) 278003
- ✉ info@theoxfordshiregolfclub.com
- ✍ Mr C Hanks
- 🖥 www.theoxfordshiregolfclub.com

RAF Benson (1975)
Royal Air Force, Benson, Wallingford OX10 6AA
- ☎ **(01491) 837766 Ext 7322**
- ✍ A Molloy (01491) 827017

Rye Hill (1992)
Proprietary
Milcombe, Banbury OX15 4RU
- ☎ **(01295) 721818**
- 📠 (01295) 720089
- ✉ info@ryehill.co.uk
- ✍ Tony Pennock
- 🖥 www.ryehill.co.uk

The Springs Hotel & Golf Club (1998)
Proprietary
Wallingford Road, North Stoke, Wallingford OX10 6BE
- ☎ **(01491) 827310**
- 📠 (01491) 827312
- ✉ proshop@thespringshotel.com
- ✍ M Ackerman (01491) 827315
- 🖥 www.thespringshotel.com

Studley Wood (1996)
Proprietary
The Straight Mile, Horton-cum-Studley, Oxford OX33 1BF
- ☎ **(01865) 351144**
- 📠 (01865) 351166
- ✉ admin@swgc.co.uk
- ✍ Ken Heathcote (01865) 351144
- 🖥 www.studleywoodgolfclub.co.uk

Tadmarton Heath (1922)
Wigginton, Banbury OX15 5HL
- ☎ **(01608) 737278**
- 📠 (01608) 730548
- ✉ secretary@tadmartongolf.com
- ✍ JR Cox (01608) 737278
- 🖥 www.tadmartongolf.com

Waterstock (1994)
Proprietary
Thame Road, Waterstock, Oxford OX33 1HT
- ☎ **(01844) 338093**
- 📠 (01844) 338036
- ✉ wgc_oxford@btinternet.com
- ✍ AJ Wyatt
- 🖥 www.waterstockgolf.co.uk

Witney Lakes (1994)
Downs Road, Witney OX29 0SY
- ☎ **(01993) 893011**
- ✉ golf@witney-lakes.co.uk
- 🖥 www.witney-lakes.co.uk

The Wychwood (1992)
Proprietary
Lyneham, Chipping Norton OX7 6QQ
- ☎ **(01993) 831841**
- 📠 (01993) 831775
- ✉ info@thewychwood.com
- ✍ Mrs S J Lakin (administrator)
- 🖥 www.thewychwood.com

Rutland

Greetham Valley (1992)
Proprietary
Greetham, Oakham LE15 7SN
- ☎ **(01780) 460444**
- 📠 (01780) 460623
- ✉ info@greethamvalley.co.uk
- ✍ RE Hinch
- 🖥 www.greethamvalley.co.uk

Luffenham Heath   (1911)
Ketton, Stamford PE9 3UU
☎ **(01780) 720205**
🖳 (01780) 722146
📧 jringleby@theluffenhamheathgc
.co.uk
✍ JR Ingleby
🖥 www.luffenhamheath.co.uk

RAF Cottesmore   (1982)
Oakham, Leicester LE15 7BL
☎ **(01572) 812241 Ext 8112**
📧 ctsdepth-
aesffs@cottesmore.raf.mod.uk

Rutland County Golf Club
(1991)
Proprietary
Pickworth, Stamford PE9 4AQ
☎ **(01780) 460239/460330**
🖳 (01780) 460437
📧 info@rutlandcountygolf.co.uk
✍ G Lowe (Golf Dir)
🖥 www.rutlandcountygolf.co.uk

Shropshire

Aqualate   (1995)
Pay and play
Stafford Road, Newport TF10 9DB
☎ **(01952) 811699**
🖳 (01952) 825343
✍ HB Dawes (Mgr) (01952) 811699
🖥 www.aqualategolf..co.uk

Arscott   (1992)
Proprietary
Arscott, Pontesbury, Shrewsbury SY5 0XP
☎ **(01743) 860114**
🖳 (01743) 860114
📧 golf@arscott.dydirect.net
✍ Sian Hinkins
🖥 www.arscottgolfclub.co.uk

Bridgnorth   (1889)
Stanley Lane, Bridgnorth WV16 4SF
☎ **(01746) 763315**
🖳 (01746) 763315
📧 secretary@bridgnorthgolfclub
.co.uk
✍ A M Jones
🖥 www.bridgnorthgolfclub.co.uk

Brow
Proprietary
Welsh Frankton, Ellesmere SY12 9HW
☎ **(01691) 622628**
📧 browgolf@btinternet.com
🖥 www.thebrowgolfclub.com

Chesterton Valley   (1993)
Proprietary
Chesterton, Worfield, Bridgnorth
WV15 5NX
☎ **(01746) 783682**
📧 cvgc@hotmail.co.uk
✍ P Hinton
🖥 www.a1golf.biz

Church Stretton   (1898)
Trevor Hill, Church Stretton SY6 6JH
☎ **(01694) 722281**
📧 secretary@churchstrettongolfclub
.co.uk
✍ J Townsend (Mgr) (07973) 762510
🖥 www.churchstrettongolfclub.co.uk

Cleobury Mortimer   (1993)
Proprietary
Wyre Common, Cleobury Mortimer
DY14 8HQ
☎ **(01299) 271112 (Clubhouse)**
🖳 (01299) 271468
📧 pro@cleoburygolfclub.com
✍ G Pain (Gen Mgr)
🖥 www.cleoburygolfclub.com

Hawkstone Park Golf Club
(1920)
Proprietary
Weston-under-Redcastle, Shrewsbury
SY4 5UY
☎ **(01939) 200365**
🖳 (01939) 200365
📧 secretary@hpgcgolf.com
✍ T Harrop
🖥 www.hpgcgolf.com

Hill Valley G&CC   (1975)
Proprietary
Terrick Road, Whitchurch SY13 4JZ
☎ **(01948) 667788**
📧 general.hillvalley@mcdonald-
hotels.co.uk
🖥 www.hillvalleygolfclub.co.uk

Horsehay Village Golf
Centre   (1999)
Pay and play
Wellington Road, Horsehay, Telford
TF4 3BT
☎ **(01952) 632070**
🖳 (01952) 632074
📧 horsehayvillagegolfcentre@telford
.gov.uk
✍ M Maddison (Mgr)
🖥 www.telford.gov.uk/golf

Lilleshall Hall   (1937)
Abbey Road, Lilleshall, Newport TF10 9AS
☎ **(01952) 604776**
🖳 (01952) 604272
📧 honsec@lhgc.entdsl.com
✍ A Marklew (01952) 604776
🖥 www.lilleshallhallgolfclub.co.uk

Llanymynech   (1933)
Pant, Oswestry SY10 8LB
☎ **(01691) 830983**
🖳 (01691) 183 9184
📧 secretary@llanymynechgolfclub
.co.uk
✍ Howard Jones
🖥 www.llanymynechgolfclub.co.uk

Ludlow   (1889)
Bromfield, Ludlow SY8 2BT
☎ **(01584) 856285**
🖳 (01584) 856366
📧 secretary@ludlowgolfclub.com
✍ R Price (01584) 856285
🖥 www.ludlowgolfclub.com

Market Drayton   (1906)
Sutton, Market Drayton TF9 2HX
☎ **(01630) 652266**
📧 market.draytongc@btconnect.com
✍ CK Stubbs
🖥 www.marketdraytongolfclub.co.uk

Mile End   (1992)
Proprietary
Mile End, Oswestry SY11 4JF
☎ **(01691) 671246**
🖳 (01691) 670580
📧 info@mileendgolfclub.co.uk
✍ R Thompson
🖥 www.mileendgolfclub.co.uk

Oswestry   (1903)
Aston Park, Queens Head, Oswestry
SY11 4JJ
☎ **(01691) 610535**
🖳 (01691) 610535
📧 secretary@oswestrygolfclub.co.uk
✍ John Evans (01691) 610535
🖥 www.oswestrygolfclub.co.uk

Patshull Park Hotel G&CC
(1980)
Pattingham WV6 7HR
☎ **(01902) 700100**
🖳 (01902) 700874
✍ John Poole
🖥 www.patshull-park.co.uk

Severn Meadows   (1990)
Proprietary
Highley, Bridgnorth WV16 6HZ
☎ **(01746) 862212**
📧 noel@severnmeadows.com
✍ Noel Woodman
🖥 www.severnmeadows.com

Shifnal   (1929)
Decker Hill, Shifnal TF11 8QL
☎ **(01952) 460330**
🖳 (01952) 460330
📧 secretary@shifnalgolf.com
✍ NR Milton (01952) 460330
🖥 www.shifnalgolf.com

Shrewsbury   (1891)
Condover, Shrewsbury SY5 7BL
☎ **(01743) 872977**
🖳 (01743) 872977
📧 info@shrewsburygolfclub.co.uk
✍ Anthony Rowe (01743) 872977
🖥 www.shrewsburygolfclub.co.uk

The Shropshire   (1992)
Muxton, Telford TF2 8PQ
☎ **(01952) 677800**
🖳 (01952) 677622
📧 sales@theshropshire.co.uk
✍ James Lever
🖥 www.theshropshire.co.uk

Telford   (1976)
Proprietary
Great Hay Drive, Sutton Heights, Telford
TF7 4DT
☎ **(01952) 429977**
🖳 (01952) 586602
📧 ibarklem@aol.com

🖂 I Lucas
🖅 www.telford-golfclub.co.uk

Worfield (1991)
Proprietary
Worfield, Bridgnorth WV15 5HE
☎ **(01746) 716541**
🖳 (01746) 716302
🖂 enquiries@worfieldgolf.co.uk
🖊 W Weaver (Gen Mgr)
🖅 www.worfieldgolf.co.uk

Wrekin (1905)
Wellington, Telford TF6 5BX
☎ **(01952) 244032**
🖳 (01952) 252906
🖂 secretary@wrekingolfclub.co.uk
🖊 B P Everitt
🖅 www.wrekingolfclub.co.uk

Somerset

Bath (1880)
Sham Castle, North Road, Bath BA2 6JG
☎ **(01225) 463834**
🖳 (01225) 331027
🖂 enquiries@bathgolfclub.org.uk
🖊 (01225) 463834
🖅 www.bathgolfclub.org.uk

Brean (1973)
Coast Road, Brean, Burnham-on-Sea TA8 2QY
☎ **(01278) 752111**
🖳 (01278) 752111
🖂 proshop@brean.com
🖊 D Haines (Director of Golf)
🖅 www.breangolfclub.co.uk

Burnham & Berrow (1890)
St Christopher's Way, Burnham-on-Sea TA8 2PE
☎ **(01278) 785760**
🖳 (01278) 795440
🖂 secretary.bbgc@btconnect.com
🖊 MA Blight (01278) 785760
🖅 www.burnhamandberrowgolfclub.co.uk

Cannington (1993)
Pay and play
Cannington Centre for Land Based Studies, Bridgwater TA5 2LS
☎ **(01278) 655050**
🖳 (01278) 655055
🖂 macrowr@bridgwater.ac.uk
🖊 R Macrow (Mgr)
🖅 www.canningtongolfcentre.co.uk

Clevedon (1891)
Castle Road, Clevedon BS21 7AA
☎ **(01275) 874057**
🖳 (01275) 341228
🖂 secretary@clevedongolfclub.co.uk
🖊 J Cunning (01275) 874057
🖅 www.clevedongolfclub.co.uk

Enmore Park (1906)
Enmore, Bridgwater TA5 2AN
☎ **(01278) 672100**
🖳 (01278) 672101

🖂 manager@enmorepark.co.uk
🖊 S.Varcoe (01278) 672100
🖅 www.enmorepark.co.uk

Entry Hill (1985)
Public
Entry Hill, Bath BA2 5NA
☎ **(01225) 834248**
🖂 entryhillgolfcourse.co.uk
🖊 J Sercombe

Farrington (1992)
Proprietary
Marsh Lane, Farrington Gurney, Bristol BS39 6TS
☎ **(01761) 451596**
🖳 (01761) 451021
🖂 info@farringtongolfclub.net
🖊 J Cowgill
🖅 www.farringtongolfclub.net

Fosseway CC (1970)
Charlton Lane, Midsomer Norton, Radstock BA3 4BD
☎ **(01761) 412214**
🖳 (01761) 418357
🖂 club@centurionhotel.co.uk
🖊 Ray D'Arcy
🖅 www.centurionhotel.co.uk

Frome (1994)
Proprietary
Critchill Manor, Frome BA11 4LJ
☎ **(01373) 453410**
🖂 secretary@fromegolfclub.co.uk
🖊 Mrs S Austin/Mrs J Vowell
🖅 www.fromegolfclub.co.uk

Isle of Wedmore (1992)
Proprietary
Lineage, Lascots Hill, Wedmore BS28 4QT
☎ **(01934) 712452**
🖂 office@wedmoregolfclub.com
🖊 AC Edwards (01934) 712222
🖅 www.wedmoregolfclub.com

Kingweston (1983)
(Sec) 12 Lowerside Road, Glastonbury, Somerset BA6 9BH
☎ **(01458) 834086**

Lansdown (1894)
Lansdown, Bath BA1 9BT
☎ **(01225) 422138**
🖳 (01225) 339252
🖂 admin@lansdowngolfclub.co.uk
🖊 Mrs E Bacon
🖅 www.lansdowngolfclub.co.uk

Long Sutton (1991)
Pay and play
Long Load, Langport TA10 9JU
☎ **(01458) 241017**
🖳 (01458) 241022
🖂 reservations@longsuttongolf.com
🖊 Gareth Harding
🖅 www.longsuttongolf.com

The Mendip (1908)
Gurney Slade, Radstock BA3 4UT
☎ **(01749) 840570**
🖳 (01749) 841439

🖂 secretary@mendipgolfclub.com
🖊 J Scott
🖅 www.mendipgolfclub.com

Mendip Spring (1992)
Proprietary
Honeyhall Lane, Congresbury BS49 5JT
☎ **(01934) 852322**
🖳 (01934) 853021
🖂 info@mendipspringgolfclub.com
🖊 A Melhuish
🖅 www.mendipspringgolfclub.com

Minehead & West Somerset (1882)
The Warren, Minehead TA24 5SJ
☎ **(01643) 702057**
🖳 (01643) 705095
🖂 secretary@mineheadgolf.co.uk
🖅 www.minehead-golf-club.co.uk

Oake Manor (1993)
Oake, Taunton TA4 1BA
☎ **(01823) 461993**
🖳 (01823) 461996
🖂 golf@oakemanor.com
🖊 R Gardner (Golf Mgr)
🖅 www.oakemanor.com

Orchardleigh Golf Club (1996)
Proprietary
Frome BA11 2PH
☎ **(01373) 454200**
🖳 (01373) 454202
🖂 info@orchardleighgolf.co.uk
🖊 Peter Holloway (Director of Golf)
🖅 www.orchardleighgolf.co.uk

Saltford (1904)
Golf Club Lane, Saltford, Bristol BS31 3AA
☎ **(01225) 873513**
🖳 (01225) 873525
🖂 secretary@saltfordgolfclub.co.uk
🖊 M Penn (01225) 873513
🖅 www.saltfordgolfclub.co.uk

Stockwood Vale (1991)
Public
Stockwood Lane, Keynsham, Bristol BS31 2ER
☎ **(0117) 986 6505**
🖳 (0117) 986 8974
🖂 stockwoodvale@aol.com
🖊 M Edenborough
🖅 www.stockwoodvale.com

Tall Pines (1990)
Proprietary
Cooks Bridle Path, Downside, Backwell, Bristol BS48 3DJ
☎ **(01275) 472076**
🖳 (01275) 474869
🖊 T Murray
🖅 www.tallpinesgolf.co.uk

Taunton & Pickeridge (1892)
Corfe, Taunton TA3 7BY
☎ **(01823) 421537**
🖳 (01823) 421742
🖂 mail@tauntongolf.co.uk

For key to symbols see page 717

⚥ S Stevenson (Golf Professional)
▤ www.tauntongolf.co.uk

Taunton Vale   (1991)
Proprietary
Creech Heathfield, Taunton TA3 5EY
☎ **(01823) 412220**
▢ (01823) 413583
✉ admin@tauntonvalegolf.co.uk
⚥ Mrs J Wyatt
▤ www.tauntonvalegolf.co.uk

Tickenham   (1994)
Proprietary
*Clevedon Road, Tickenham, Bristol
BS21 6RY*
☎ **(01275) 856626**
✉ info@tickenhamgolf.co.uk
▤ www.tickenhamgolf.co.uk

Vivary   (1928)
Public
Vivary Park, Taunton TA1 3JW
☎ **(01823) 289274 (Clubhouse)**
▢ 01823 353757
✉ vivarygolfclub2@btconnect.com
⚥ Bob Stout

Wells   (1893)
East Horrington Road, Wells BA5 3DS
☎ **(01749) 675005**
▢ (01749) 683170
✉ secretary@wellsgolfclub.co.uk
⚥ Eira Powell (01749) 675005
▤ www.wellsgolfclub.co.uk

Weston-super-Mare   (1892)
*Uphill Road North, Weston-super-Mare
BS23 4NQ*
☎ **(01934) 626968**
▢ (01934) 621360
✉ wsmgolfclub@eurotelbroadband
.com
⚥ Mrs K Drake (01934) 626968
▤ www.westonsupermaregolfclub
.com

Wheathill   (1993)
Proprietary
Wheathill, Somerton TA11 7HG
☎ **(01963) 240667**
▢ (01963) 240230
✉ wheathill@wheathill.fsnet.co.uk
⚥ A England
▤ www.wheathillgc.co.uk

Wincanton Golf Course
(1994)
Proprietary
The Racecourse, Wincanton BA9 8BJ
☎ **(01963) 435850**
▢ (01963) 34668
✉ wincanton@thejokeyclub.co.uk
⚥ Andrew England
▤ wincantonracecourse.co.uk

Windwhistle   (1932)
Cricket St Thomas, Chard TA20 4DG
☎ **(01460) 30231**
▢ (01460) 30055
✉ info@windwhistlegolfclub.co.uk
⚥ Miss Sarah Wills
▤ www.windwhistlegolfclub.co.uk

Worlebury   (1908)
*Monks Hill, Worlebury, Weston-super-Mare
BS22 9SX*
☎ **(01934) 625789**
▢ (01934) 621935
✉ secretary@worleburygc.co.uk
⚥ A S Horsburgh
▤ www.worleburygc.co.uk

Yeovil   (1907)
Sherborne Road, Yeovil BA21 5BW
☎ **(01935) 422965**
▢ (01935) 411283
✉ office@yeovilgolfclub.com
⚥ S Greatorex (01935) 422965
▤ www.yeovilgolfclub.com

Staffordshire

Alsager G&CC   (1992)
*Audley Road, Alsager, Stoke-on-Trent
ST7 2UR*
☎ **(01270) 875700**
▢ (01270) 882207
✉ offers@alsagergolfclub.com
⚥ M Davenport
▤ www.alsagergolfclub.com

Aston Wood   (1994)
Blake Street, Sutton Coldfield B74 4EU
☎ **(0121) 580 7803**
▢ (0121) 353 0354
✉ enquiries@astonwoodgolfclub
.co.uk
⚥ Simon Smith
▤ www.astonwoodgolfclub.co.uk

Barlaston   (1987)
Meaford Road, Stone ST15 8UX
☎ **(01782) 372867 (Admin)
372795 (Pro-Shop)**
▢ (01782) 373648
✉ barlaston.gc@virgin.net
⚥ C P Holloway (01782 372867)
▤ www.barlastongolfclub.co.uk

Beau Desert   (1911)
Hazel Slade, Cannock WS12 0PJ
☎ **(01543) 422626/422773**
▢ (01543) 451137
✉ enquiries@bdgc.co.uk
⚥ Stephen Mainwaring 01543)
422626
▤ www.bdgc.co.uk

Bloxwich   (1924)
136 Stafford Road, Bloxwich WS3 3PQ
☎ **(01922) 476593**
▢ (01922) 493449
✉ secretary@bloxwichgolfclub.com
⚥ RJ Wormstone
▤ www.bloxwichgolfclub.com

Branston G&CC   (1975)
*Burton Road, Branston, Burton-on-Trent
DE14 3DP*
☎ **(01283) 528320**
▢ (01283) 566984
✉ info@branstonclub.co.uk
⚥ Richard Odell (Director of Golf)
▤ www.branstonclub.co.uk

Brocton Hall   (1894)
Brocton, Stafford ST17 0TH
☎ **(01785) 661901**
▢ (01785) 661591
✉ secretary@broctonhall.com
⚥ JDS Duffy (01785) 661901
▤ www.broctonhall.com

Burslem   (1907)
*Wood Farm, High Lane, Stoke-on-Trent
ST6 7JT*
☎ **(01782) 837006**
✉ alanbgc@talktalkbusiness.net
⚥ A Porter

Calderfields   (1983)
Proprietary
Aldridge Road, Walsall WS4 2JS
☎ **(01922) 646888 (Clubhouse)**
✉ calderfields@bigfoot.com
▤ www.calderfieldsgolf.com

Cannock Park   (1993)
Public
Stafford Road, Cannock WS11 2AL
☎ **(01543) 578850**
▢ (01543) 578850
✉ seccpgc@yahoo.co.uk
⚥ CB Milne (01543) 571091
▤ www.cpgc.freeserve.co.uk

The Chase   (1991)
Proprietary
Pottal Pool Road, Penkridge ST19 5RN
☎ **(01785) 712888**
▢ (01785) 712692
✉ manager@thechasegolf.co.uk
⚥ Bryan Davies
▤ www.thechasegolf.co.uk

The Craythorne   (1974)
*Craythorne Road, Rolleston on Dove, Burton
upon Trent DE13 0AZ*
☎ **(01283) 564329**
▢ (01283) 511908
✉ admin@craythorne.co.uk
⚥ AA Wright (Man Dir/Owner)
▤ www.craythorne.co.uk

Dartmouth   (1910)
Vale Street, West Bromwich B71 4DW
☎ **(0121) 588 2131**
▢ (0121) 588 5746
⚥ CF Wade (0121) 532 4070
▤ www.dartmouthgolfclub.co.uk

Denstone College   (1991)
Denstone, Uttoxeter ST14 5HN
☎ **(01889) 590484**
▢ (01889) 590744
✉ andy.oakes@uwclub.net
⚥ Andy Oakes
▤ www.denstonecollege.org

Drayton Park   (1897)
Drayton Park, Tamworth B78 3TN
☎ **(01827) 251139**
▢ (01827) 284035
✉ admin@draytonparkgc.com
⚥ Jon Northover
▤ www.draytonparkgc.com

Druids Heath (1974)
Stonnall Road, Aldridge WS9 8JZ
☎ **(01922) 455595**
✉ admin@druidsheathgc.co.uk
✍ KI Taylor
🖥 www.druidsheathgc.co.uk

Enville (1935)
Highgate Common, Enville, Stourbridge
DY7 5BN
☎ **(01384) 872074**
🖷 (01384) 873396
✉ manager@envillegolfclub.co.uk
✍ H L Mulley (Mgr)
🖥 www.envillegolfclub.com

Great Barr (1961)
Chapel Lane, Birmingham B43 7BA
☎ **(0121) 358 4376**
🖷 (0121) 358 4376
✉ info@greatbarrgolfclub.co.uk
✍ Miss L Pollard (0121) 358 4376
🖥 www.greatbarrgolfclub.co.uk

Greenway Hall (1909)
Pay and play
Stockton Brook, Stoke-on-Trent ST9 9LJ
☎ **(01782) 503158**
🖷 (01782) 504691
✉ jackbarker_greenwayhallgolfclub
@hotmail.com
✍ J Latham (Mgr)
🖥 www.jackbarker.com

Handsworth (1895)
11 Sunningdale Close, Handsworth Wood,
Birmingham B20 1NP
☎ **(0121) 554 3387**
🖷 (0121) 554 6144
✉ info@handsworthgolfclub.net
✍ PS Hodnett (Hon)
🖥 www.handsworthgolfclub.com

Himley Hall (1980)
Pay and play
Himley Hall Park, Dudley DY3 4DF
☎ **(01902) 895207**
🖷 (01902) 895207
✉ himleygolf@hotmail.co.uk
✍ B Sparrow (01902) 894973
🖥 www.himleyhallgolfclub.com

Ingestre Park (1977)
Ingestre, Stafford ST18 0RE
☎ **(01889) 270845**
🖷 (01889) 271434
✉ manager@ingestregolf.co.uk
✍ D Warrilow (Mgr)
🖥 www.ingestregolf.com

Izaak Walton (1993)
Cold Norton, Stone ST15 0NS
☎ **(01785) 760900**
🖷 (01785) 760900 (opt 4)
✉ secretary@izaakwaltongolfclub
.co.uk
✍ Charlie Lightbown
🖥 www.izaakwaltongolfclub.co.uk

Keele Golf Centre (1973)
Pay and play
Keele Road, Newcastle-under-Lyme
ST5 5AB
☎ **(01782) 627596**

🖷 (01782) 714555
✍ L Harris (01782) 751173

Lakeside (1969)
Rugeley Power Station, Rugeley WS15 1PR
☎ **(01889) 575667**
✉ lakeside.golfclub@unicombox.co.uk
✍ TA Yates
🖥 www.lakesidegolf.co.uk

Leek (1892)
Birchall, Leek ST13 5RE
☎ **(01538) 384779**
🖷 (01538) 384779
✉ enquiries@leekgolfclub.co.uk
✍ DT Brookhouse
🖥 www.leekgolfclub.co.uk

**Lichfield Golf and Country
Club** (1991)
Proprietary
Elmhurst, Lichfield WS13 8HE
☎ **(01543) 417333**
🖷 (01543) 418098
✉ r.gee@theclubcompany.com
✍ Richard Gee
🖥 www.theclubcompany.com

Little Aston (1908)
Roman Road, Streetly, Sutton Coldfield
B74 3AN
☎ **(0121) 353 2942**
🖷 (0121) 580 8387
✉ manager@littleastongolf.co.uk
✍ Glyn Ridley (Mgr) (0121) 353 2942
🖥 www.littleastongolf.co.uk

Manor (Kingstone) (1991)
Proprietary
Leese Hill, Kingstone, Uttoxeter ST14 8QT
☎ **(01889) 563234**
🖷 (01889) 563234
✉ manorgc@btinternet.com
✍ S Foulds
🖥 www.manorgolfclub.net

Newcastle-under-Lyme
(1908)
Whitmore Road, Newcastle-under-Lyme
ST5 2QB
☎ **(01782) 617006**
🖷 (01782) 617531
✉ info@newcastlegolfclub.co.uk
✍ Joe Hyde (Acting Mgr)
🖥 www.newcastlegolfclub.co.uk

Onneley (1968)
Onneley, Crewe, Cheshire CW3 9QF
☎ **(01782) 750577**
✉ admin@onneleygolfclub.co.uk
✍ Iain Corville (Mgr) (01782) 721459
🖥 www.onneleygolf.co.uk

Oxley Park (1913)
Stafford Road, Bushbury, Wolverhampton
WV10 6DE
☎ **(01902) 773989**
🖷 (01902) 773981
✉ office@oxleyparkgolfclub.co.uk
🖥 www.oxleyparkgolfclub.co.uk

Parkhall (1989)
Public
Hulme Road, Weston Coyney, Stoke-on-
Trent ST3 5BH
☎ **(01782) 599584**
🖷 (01782) 599584
✍ M Robson

Penn (1908)
Penn Common, Wolverhampton WV4 5JN
☎ **(01902) 341142**
🖷 (01902) 620504
✉ secretary@penngolfclub.co.uk
✍ D J Tonks
🖥 www.penngolfclub.co.uk

Perton Park (1990)
Proprietary
Wrottesley Park Road, Perton,
Wolverhampton WV6 7HL
☎ **(01902) 380073**
🖷 (01902) 326219
✉ admin@pertongolfclub.co.uk
✍ Simon Edwin (Gen Mgr)
🖥 www.pertongolfclub.co.uk

Sandwell Park (1895)
Birmingham Road, West Bromwich B71 4JJ
☎ **(0121) 553 4637**
🖷 (0121) 525 1651
✉ secretary@sandwellparkgolfclub
.co.uk
🖥 www.sandwellparkgolfclub.co.uk

Sedgley (1992)
Pay and play
Sandyfields Road, Sedgley, Dudley DY3 3DL
☎ **(01902) 880503**
✉ sedgleygolfcentre@yahoo.co.uk
✍ David Cox

South Staffordshire (1892)
Danescourt Road, Tettenhall,
Wolverhampton WV6 9BQ
☎ **(01902) 751065**
🖷 (01902) 751159
✉ suelebeau@southstaffsgc.co.uk
✍ P Baker (Professional)
🖥 www.southstaffsgc.co.uk

St Thomas's Priory (1995)
Armitage Lane, Armitage, Rugeley
WS15 1ED
☎ **(01543) 492096**
✉ rohanlonpro@acl.com
🖥 www.st-thomass-golfclub.com

Stafford Castle (1906)
Proprietary
Newport Road, Stafford ST16 1BP
☎ **(01785) 223821**
🖷 (01785) 223821
✉ sharonscgc@btconnect.com
✍ Mrs S Calvert
🖥 www.staffordcastlegolfclub.com

Stone (1896)
The Fillybrooks, Stone ST15 0NB
☎ **(01785) 813103**
✍ D M Cole (01785) 817746
🖥 www.stonegolfclub.co.uk

Swindon   (1976)
Proprietary
Bridgnorth Road, Swindon, Dudley DY3 4PU
☎ **(01902) 897031**
🖳 (01902) 326219
📧 admin@swindongolfclub.co.uk
✍ Mark Allen (Mgr)
🖥 www.swindongolfclub.co.uk

Tamworth   (1976)
Public
Eagle Drive, Amington, Tamworth B77 4EG
☎ **(01827) 709303**
🖳 (01827) 709304
✍ Elaine Pugh

Three Hammers Golf Complex   (1964)
Pay and play
Old Stafford Road, Cross Green, Wolverhampton WV10 7PP
☎ **(01902) 790428**
🖳 (01902) 791777
📧 Info@3hammers.co.uk
✍ Mr Julian Chessom
🖥 www.3hammers.co.uk

Trentham   (1894)
14 Barlaston Old Road, Trentham, Stoke-on-Trent ST4 8HB
☎ **(01782) 658109**
🖳 (01782) 644024
📧 secretary@trenthamgolf.org
✍ Richard Minton (Gen Mgr)
🖥 www.trenthamgolf.org

Trentham Park   (1936)
Trentham Park, Stoke-on-Trent ST4 8AE
☎ **(01782) 642245**
🖳 (01782) 658800
📧 manager@trenthamparkgolfclub .com
✍ Gordon Martin (01782) 658800
🖥 www.trenthamparkgolfclub.com

Uttoxeter   (1970)
Wood Lane, Uttoxeter ST14 8JR
☎ **(01889) 566552**
🖳 (01889) 566552
📧 admin@uttoxetergolfclub.com
✍ Mr A McCanaless
🖥 www.uttoxetergolfclub.com

Walsall   (1907)
Broadway, Walsall WS1 3EY
☎ **(01922) 613512**
🖳 (01922) 616460
📧 secretary@walsallgolfclub.co.uk
✍ P Thompson (01922) 613512
🖥 www.walsallgolfclub.co.uk

Wergs   (1990)
Pay and play
Keepers Lane, Tettenhall WV6 8UA
☎ **(01902) 742225**
🖳 (01902) 844553
📧 wergs.golfclub@btinternet.com
✍ Tina Bennett (Mgr)
🖥 www.wergs.com

Westwood   (1923)
Newcastle Road, Wallbridge, Leek ST13 7AA
☎ **(01538) 398385**

🖳 (01538) 382485
📧 westwoodgolfclubleek@btconnect .com
✍ Mr A J Horton
🖥 www.westwoodgolfclubleek.co.uk

Whiston Hall   (1971)
Whiston, Cheadle ST10 2HZ
☎ **(01538) 266260**
📧 enq@whistonhall.com
🖥 www.whistonhall.com

Whittington Heath   (1886)
Tamworth Road, Lichfield WS14 9PW
☎ **(01543) 432317 (Admin) 432212 (Steward)**
🖳 (01543) 433962
📧 info@whittingtonheathgc.co.uk
✍ Mrs JA Burton
🖥 www.whittingtonheathgc.co.uk

Wolstanton   (1904)
Dimsdale Old Hall, Hassam Parade, Wolstanton, Newcastle ST5 9DR
☎ **(01782) 622413**
🖳 (01782) 622413
✍ Mrs VJ Keenan (01782) 622413
🖥 www.wolstantongolfclub.com

Suffolk

Aldeburgh   (1884)
Aldeburgh IP15 5PE
☎ **(01728) 452890**
🖳 (01728) 452937
📧 info@aldeburghgolfclub.co.uk
✍ G Hogg
🖥 www.aldeburghgolfclub.co.uk

Beccles   (1899)
The Common, Beccles NR34 9BX
☎ **(01502) 712244**
📧 alan@ereira.wanadoo.co.uk
✍ A Ereira (07896) 087297
🖥 www.becclesgolfclub.co.uk

Brett Vale   (1992)
Proprietary
Noakes Road, Raydon, Ipswich IP7 5LR
☎ **(01473) 310718**
📧 info@brettvalegolf.co.uk
✍ L Williams
🖥 www.brettvale.co.uk

Bungay & Waveney Valley
(1889)
Outney Common, Bungay NR35 1DS
☎ **(01986) 892337**
🖳 (01986) 892222
📧 golf@bungaygc.co.uk
✍ A Collison (Director of Golf)
🖥 www.club-noticeboard.co.uk/bungay

Bury St Edmunds   (1924)
Tut Hill, Fornham All Saints, Bury St Edmunds IP28 6LG
☎ **(01284) 755979**
🖳 (01284) 763288
📧 secretary@burygolf.co.uk

✍ M Verhelst
🖥 www.burystedmundsgolfclub .co.uk

Cretingham   (1984)
Grove Farm, Cretingham, Woodbridge IP13 7BA
☎ **(01728) 685275**
🖳 (01728) 685488
📧 cretinghamgolf@tiscali.co.uk
✍ Mrs K Jackson
🖥 www.cretinghamgolfclub.co.uk

Diss   (1903)
Stuston Common, Diss IP21 4AA
☎ **(01379) 641025**
🖳 (01379) 644586
📧 sec.dissgolf@virgin.net
✍ Thomas Bailey (01379) 641025
🖥 www.club-noticeboard.co.uk

Felixstowe Ferry   (1880)
Ferry Road, Felixstowe IP11 9RY
☎ **(01394) 286834**
🖳 (01394) 273679
📧 secretary@felixstowegolf.co.uk
✍ R Baines (01394) 286834
🖥 www.felixstowegolf.co.uk

Flempton   (1895)
Flempton, Bury St Edmunds IP28 6EQ
☎ **(01284) 728291**
📧 secretary@flempton.com
✍ MS Clark
🖥 www.flemptongolfclub.co.uk

Fynn Valley   (1991)
Proprietary
Witnesham, Ipswich IP6 9JA
☎ **(01473) 785267**
🖳 (01473) 785632
📧 enquiries@fynn-valley.co.uk
✍ AR Tyrrell (01473) 785267
🖥 www.fynn-valley.co.uk

Halesworth   (1990)
Proprietary
Bramfield Road, Halesworth IP19 9XA
☎ **(01986) 875567**
🖳 (01986) 874565
📧 info@halesworthgc.co.uk
✍ Chris Aldred (Mgr)
🖥 www.halesworthgc.co.uk

Haverhill   (1974)
Coupals Road, Haverhill CB9 7UW
☎ **(01440) 761951**
🖳 (01440) 761951
📧 HAVERHILLGOLF@coupalsroad .eclipse.co.uk
✍ Mrs L Farrant, Mrs K Wilby (Mgr)
🖥 www.club-noticeboard.co.uk

Hintlesham   (1991)
Proprietary
Hintlesham, Ipswich IP8 3JG
☎ **(01473) 652761**
🖳 (01473) 652750
📧 sales@hintleshamgolfclub.com
✍ Henry Roblin (Owner/Director)
🖥 www.hintleshamgolfclub.com

Ipswich (Purdis Heath)
(1895)
Purdis Heath, Bucklesham Road, Ipswich IP3 8UQ
☎ **(01473) 728941**
🖥 (01473) 715236
📧 neill@ipswichgolfclub.com
✍ NM Ellice (01473) 728941
🖥 www.ipswichgolfclub.com

Links (Newmarket)   (1902)
Cambridge Road, Newmarket CB8 0TG
☎ **(01638) 663000**
🖥 (01638) 661476
📧 secretary@linksgolfclub.co.uk
✍ ML Hartley
🖥 www.linksgolfclub.co.uk

Newton Green   (1907)
Newton Green, Sudbury CO10 0QN
☎ **(01787) 377217**
🖥 (01787) 377549
📧 info@newtongreengolfclub.co.uk
✍ Mrs C List
🖥 www.newtongreengolfclub.co.uk

Rookery Park   (1891)
Beccles Road, Carlton Colville, Lowestoft NR33 8HJ
☎ **(01502) 509190**
🖥 (01502) 509191
📧 office@rookeryparkgolfclub.co.uk
✍ R Pettett
🖥 www.rookeryparkgolfclub.co.uk

Royal Worlington & Newmarket   (1893)
Golf Links Road, Worlington, Bury St Edmunds IP28 8SD
☎ **(01638) 712216 (Clubhouse)**
📧 secretary@royalworlington.co.uk
✍ S Ballentine (01638) 717787
🖥 www.royalworlington.co.uk

Rushmere   (1927)
Rushmere Heath, Ipswich IP4 5QQ
☎ **(01473) 725648**
🖥 (01473) 273852
📧 rushmeregolfclub@btconnect.com
✍ RWG Tawell (01473) 725648
🖥 www.club-noticeboard.co.uk/rushmere

Seckford   (1991)
Seckford Hall Road, Great Bealings, Woodbridge IP13 6NT
☎ **(01394) 388000**
🖥 (01394) 382818
📧 secretary@seckfordgolf.co.uk
✍ G Cook
🖥 www.seckfordgolf.co.uk

Southwold   (1884)
The Common, Southwold IP18 6TB
☎ **(01502) 723234**
📧 mail@southwoldgolfclub.co.uk
✍ R Wilshaw (01502) 723248
🖥 www.southwoldgolfclub.co.uk

Stoke-by-Nayland   (1972)
Keepers Lane, Leavenheath, Colchester CO6 4PZ
☎ **(01206) 262836**

🖥 (01206) 265840
📧 golfsecretary@stokebynayland.com
✍ A Bullock (01206) 265815
🖥 www.stokebynayland.com

Stowmarket   (1902)
Lower Road, Onehouse, Stowmarket IP14 3DA
☎ **(01449) 736473**
🖥 (01449) 736826
📧 mail@stowmarketgolfclub.co.uk
✍ Alan Feltham (01449) 736473
🖥 www.club-noticeboard.co.uk/stowmarket

The Suffolk Golf & Spa Hotel   (1974)
Proprietary
Fornham St Genevieve, Bury St Edmunds IP28 6JQ
☎ **(01284) 706777**
🖥 (01284) 706721
📧 proshop.suffolkgolf@ohiml.com
✍ Stephen Hall (Director of Golf)
🖥 www.oxfordhotelsandinns.com

Thorpeness Hotel & Golf Course   (1923)
Proprietary
Thorpeness, Leiston IP16 4NH
☎ **(01728) 454926**
🖥 (01728) 453868
📧 christopher@thorpeness.co.uk
✍ Christopher Oldrey (01728) 452176
🖥 www.thorpeness.co.uk

Ufford Park Hotel Golf & Spa   (1992)
Pay and play
Yarmouth Road, Melton, Woodbridge, Suffolk IP12 1QW
☎ **(01394) 382836**
🖥 (01394) 383582
📧 golf@uffordparkco.uk
✍ Michael Halliday
🖥 www.uffordpark.co.uk

Waldringfield   (1983)
Newbourne Road, Waldringfield, Woodbridge IP12 4PT
☎ **(01473) 736768**
📧 enquiries@waldringfieldgc.co.uk
✍ Pat Whitham
🖥 www.waldringfieldgc.co.uk

Woodbridge   (1893)
Bromeswell Heath, Woodbridge IP12 2PF
☎ **(01394) 382038**
🖥 (01394) 382392
📧 info@woodbridgegolfclub.co.uk
✍ AJ Bull
🖥 www.woodbridgegolfclub.co.uk

Surrey

Abbey Moor   (1991)
Pay and play
Green Lane, Addlestone KT15 2XU
☎ **(01932) 570741/570765**

🖥 (01932) 561313
✍ Richard Payne (01932) 570741

The Addington   (1913)
Proprietary
205 Shirley Church Road, Croydon CR0 5AB
☎ **(020) 8777 1055**
🖥 (020) 8777 6661
📧 info@addingtongolf.com
✍ Oliver Peel
🖥 www.addingtongolf.com

Addington Court   (1932)
Pay and play
Featherbed Lane, Addington, Croydon CR0 9AA
☎ **(020) 8657 0281 (Bookings)**
🖥 (020) 8651 0282
📧 addington@crown-golf.co.uk
✍ B Chard (020) 657 0281
🖥 www.addingtoncourt-golfclub.co.uk

Addington Palace   (1930)
Addington Park, Gravel Hill, Addington CR0 5BB
☎ **(020) 8654 3061**
🖥 (020) 8655 3632
📧 info@addingtonpalacegolf.co.uk
✍ Roger Williams
🖥 www.addingtonpalacegolf.co.uk

Banstead Downs   (1890)
Burdon Lane, Belmont, Sutton SM2 7DD
☎ **(020) 8642 2284**
🖥 (020) 8642 5252
📧 secretary@bansteaddowns.com
✍ R D Bauser
🖥 www.bansteaddowns.com

Barrow Hills   (1970)
Longcross, Chertsey KT16 0DS
☎ **(01344) 635770**
✍ R Hammond (01483) 234807

Betchworth Park   (1911)
Reigate Road, Dorking RH4 1NZ
☎ **(01306) 882052**
📧 manager@betchworthparkgc.co.uk
✍ Richard Hall (Sec/Mgr)
🖥 www.betchworthparkgc.co.uk

Bletchingley   (1993)
Proprietary
Church Lane, Bletchingley RH1 4LP
☎ **(01883) 744666 Functions 744848 Golf**
🖥 (01883) 744284
📧 stevec1412@yahoo.co.uk
✍ Steven Cookson (Golf Operations Mgr)
🖥 www.bletchingleygolf.co.uk

Bowenhurst Golf Centre   (1994)
Mill Lane, Crondall, Farnham GU10 5RP
☎ **(01252) 851695**
🖥 (01252) 852225
✍ GL Corbey (01252) 851695

Bramley   (1913)
Bramley, Guildford GU5 0AL
☎ **(01483) 892696**
🖥 (01483) 894673
📧 secretary@bramleygolfclub.co.uk
✍ Jeremy Lucas (Club Mgr) (01483) 892696
🖳 www.bramleygolfclub.co.uk

Broadwater Park   (1989)
Pay and play
Guildford Road, Farncombe, Godalming GU7 3BU
☎ **(01483) 429955**
📧 info@broadwaterparkgolf.co.uk
✍ Kevin Milton
🖳 www.broadwaterparkgolfclub.co.uk

Burhill   (1907)
Burwood Road, Walton-on-Thames KT12 4BL
☎ **(01932) 227345**
🖥 (01932) 267159
📧 info@burhillgolf-club.co.uk
✍ D Cook (Gen Mgr)
🖳 www.burhillgolf-club.co.uk

Camberley Heath   (1912)
Golf Drive, Camberley GU15 1JG
☎ **(01276) 23258**
🖥 (01276) 692505
📧 info@camberleyheathgolfclub.co.uk
✍ Chris Donovan
🖳 www.camberleyheathgolfclub.co.uk

Central London Golf Centre   (1992)
Public
Burntwood Lane, Wandsworth, London SW17 0AT
☎ **(020) 8871 2468**
🖥 (020) 8874 7447
📧 info@clgc.co.uk
✍ Michael Anscomb (Mgr)
🖳 www.clgc.co.uk

Chessington Golf Centre   (1983)
Pay and play
Garrison Lane, Chessington KT9 2LW
☎ **(020) 8391 0948**
🖥 (020) 8397 2068
📧 info@chessingtongolf.co.uk
✍ M Bedford
🖳 www.chessingtongolf.co.uk

Chiddingfold   (1994)
Petworth Road, Chiddingfold GU8 4SL
☎ **(01428) 685888**
🖥 (01428) 685939
📧 chiddingfoldgolf@btconnect.com

Chipstead   (1906)
How Lane, Chipstead, Coulsdon CR5 3LN
☎ **(01737) 555781**
🖥 (01737) 555404
📧 office@chipsteadgolf.co.uk
✍ Gary Torbett (Director)
🖳 www.chipsteadgolf.co.uk

Chobham   (1994)
Chobham Road, Knaphill, Woking GU21 2TZ
☎ **(01276) 855584**

🖥 (01276) 855663
📧 info@chobhamgolfclub.co.uk
✍ Adrian Wratting
🖳 www.chobhamgolfclub.co.uk

Clandon Regis   (1994)
Epsom Road, West Clandon GU4 7TT
☎ **(01483) 224888**
🖥 (01483) 211781
📧 office@clandonregis-golfclub.co.uk
✍ Paul Napier (Gen Mgr)
🖳 www.clandonregis-golfclub.co.uk

Coombe Hill   (1911)
Golf Club Drive, Coombe Lane West, Kingston KT2 7DF
☎ **(0208) 336 7600**
🖥 (0208) 336 7601
📧 office@chgc.net
✍ Colin Chapman (CEO)
🖳 www.coombehillgolfclub.com

Coombe Wood   (1904)
George Road, Kingston Hill, Kingston-upon-Thames KT2 7NS
☎ **(0208) 942 0388 (Clubhouse)**
🖥 (0208) 942 5665
📧 geoff.seed@coombewoodgolf.com
✍ G Seed (0208) 942 0388
🖳 www.coombewoodgolf.com

Coulsdon Manor   (1937)
Pay and play
Coulsdon Court Road, Old Coulsdon, Croydon CR5 2LL
☎ **(020) 8660 6083**
🖥 (020) 8668 3118
📧 sales.coulsdon@ohiml.com
✍ A Oxby (020) 8668 0414
🖳 www.oxfordhotelsandinns.com

The Cranleigh   (1985)
Barhatch Lane, Cranleigh GU6 7NG
☎ **(01483) 268855**
📧 clubshop@cranleighgolfandleisure.co.uk
🖳 www.cranleighgolfandleisure.co.uk

Croham Hurst   (1911)
Croham Road, South Croydon CR2 7HJ
☎ **(020) 8657 5581**
🖥 (020) 8657 3229
📧 secretary@chgc.co.uk
✍ S Mackinson
🖳 www.chgc.co.uk

Cuddington   (1929)
Banstead Road, Banstead SM7 1RD
☎ **(020) 8393 0952**
🖥 (020) 8786 7025
📧 secretary@cuddingtongc.co/uk
✍ Mrs S Burr (020) 8393 0952
🖳 www.cuddingtongc.co.uk

Dorking   (1897)
Deepdene Avenue, Chart Park, Dorking RH5 4BX
☎ **(01306) 886917**
📧 info@dorkinggolfclub.co.uk
🖳 www.dorkinggolfclub.co.uk

Drift   (1975)
Proprietary
The Drift, East Horsley KT24 5HD
☎ **(01483) 284641**
🖥 (01483) 284642
📧 info@driftgolfclub.com
✍ Ben Beagley (GM)
🖳 www.driftgolfclub.com

Dulwich & Sydenham Hill   (1894)
Grange Lane, College Road, London SE21 7LH
☎ **(020) 8693 3961**
📧 secretary@dulwichgolf.co.uk
🖳 www.dulwichgolf.co.uk

Effingham   (1927)
Guildford Road, Effingham KT24 5PZ
☎ **(01372) 452203**
🖥 (01372) 459959
📧 secretary@effinghamgolfclub.com
✍ Steve Hoatson (Golf Mgr) (01372) 452203
🖳 www.effinghamgolfclub.com

Epsom   (1889)
Longdown Lane South, Epsom Downs, Surrey KT17 4JR
☎ **(01372) 721666**
🖥 (01372) 817183
📧 stuart@epsomgolfclub.co.uk
✍ Stuart Walker (Pro)
🖳 www.epsomgolfclub.co.uk

Farnham   (1896)
The Sands, Farnham GU10 1PX
☎ **(01252) 782109**
🖥 (01252) 781185
📧 farnhamgolfclub@tiscali.co.uk
✍ G Cowlishaw (01252) 782109
🖳 www.farnhamgolfclub.co.uk

Farnham Park   (1966)
Pay and play
Folly Hill, Farnham GU9 0AU
☎ **(01252) 715216**
📧 farnhamparkgolf@googlemail.com
✍ J Van Der Merwe
⊕ 9 hole par 3 course

Foxhills   (1975)
Stonehill Road, Ottershaw KT16 0EL
☎ **(01932) 872050**
🖥 (01932) 874762
📧 golf@foxhills.co.uk
✍ R Hyder
🖳 www.foxhills.co.uk

Gatton Manor Hotel & Golf Club   (1969)
Proprietary
Standon Lane, Ockley, Dorking, Surrey RH5 5PQ
☎ **(01306) 627555**
🖥 (01306) 627713
📧 info@gattonmanor.co.uk
✍ Patrick Kiely (owner)
🖳 www.gattonmanor.co.uk

Goal Farm Par Three (1978)
Proprietary
Gole Road, Pirbright GU24 0PZ
☎ **(01483) 473183**
🖳 (01483) 473205
✉ secretary@goalfarmgolfclub.co.uk
🖊 R Little
🖥 www.goalfarmgolfclub.co.uk

Guildford (1886)
High Path Road, Merrow, Guildford GU1 2HL
☎ **(01483) 563941**
✉ secretary@guildfordgolfclub.co.uk
🖊 M R J Couzens
🖥 www.guildfordgolfclub.co.uk

Hampton Court Palace (1895)
Hampton Wick, Kingston-upon-Thames KT1 4AD
☎ **(020) 8977 2423**
🖳 (020) 8614 4747
✉ hamptoncourtpalace@crown-golf.co.uk
🖊 Matthew Hazelden

Hankley Common (1896)
Tilford, Farnham GU10 2DD
☎ **(01252) 792493**
🖳 (01252) 795699
✉ lynne@hankley.co.uk
🖊 IM McColl (01252) 797711
🖥 www.hankley.co.uk

Hazelwood Golf Centre (1992)
Pay and play
Croysdale Avenue, Green Street, Sunbury-on-Thames TW16 6QU
☎ **(01932) 770932**
🖳 (01932) 770933
✉ hazelwoodgolf@btconnect.com
🖊 Roger Ward

Hersham Golf Club (1997)
Proprietary
Assher Road, Hersham, Surrey KT12 4RA
☎ **(01932) 267666**
🖳 (01932) 240975
✉ hvgolf@tiscali.co.uk
🖊 R Hutton (Golf Dir)
🖥 www.hershamgolfclub.co.uk

The Hindhead (1904)
Churt Road, Hindhead GU26 6HX
☎ **(01428) 604614**
🖳 (01428) 608508
✉ secretary@the-hindhead-golf-club.co.uk
🖥 www.the-hindhead-golf-club.co.uk

Hoebridge Golf Centre (1982)
Public
Old Woking Road, Old Woking GU22 8JH
☎ **(01483) 722611**
🖳 (01483) 740369
✉ info@hoebridgegc.co.uk
🖊 M O'Connell (Senior Gen Mgr)
🖥 www.hoebridgegc.co.uk

Horne Park (1994)
Proprietary
Croydon Barn Lane, Horne, South Godstone RH9 8JP
☎ **(01342) 844443**
🖳 (01342) 841828
✉ info@hornepark.co.uk
🖊 Neil Burke
🖥 www.hornepark.co.uk

Horton Park Golf Club (1987)
Pay and play
Hook Road, Epsom KT19 8QG
☎ **(020) 8393 8400 (Enquiries)**
🖳 (020) 8394 3854
✉ info@hortonparkgolf.com
🖊 Gillian Nichols
🖥 www.hortonparkgolf.com

Hurtmore (1992)
Pay and play
Hurtmore Road, Hurtmore, Surrey GU7 2RN
☎ **(01483) 426492**
🖳 (01483) 426121
✉ general@hurtmore-golf.co.uk
🖊 Maxine Burton (01483) 426492
🖥 www.hurtmore-golf.co.uk

Kingswood (1928)
Proprietary
Sandy Lane, Kingswood, Tadworth KT20 6NE
☎ **(01737) 832188**
🖳 (01737) 833920
✉ sales@kingswood-golf.co.uk
🖊 Mark Stewart (Secretary)
🖥 www.kingswood-golf.co.uk

Laleham (1903)
Proprietary
Laleham Reach, Chertsey KT16 8RP
☎ **(01932) 564211**
✉ info@laleham-golf.co.uk
🖊 Managing Director
🖥 www.laleham-golf.co.uk

Leatherhead (1903)
Proprietary
Kingston Road, Leatherhead KT22 0EE
☎ **(01372) 843966**
🖳 (01372) 842241
✉ sales@lgc-golf.co.uk
🖊 Timothy Lowe
🖥 www.lgc-golf.co.uk

Limpsfield Chart (1889)
Westerham Road, Limpsfield RH8 0SL
☎ **(01883) 723405/722106**
✉ secretary@limpsfieldchartgolf.co.uk
🖊 K Johnson
🖥 www.limpsfieldchartgolf.co.uk

Lingfield Park (1987)
Racecourse Road, Lingfield RH7 6PQ
☎ **(01342) 834602**
✉ cmorley@lingfieldpark.co.uk

London Scottish (1865)
Windmill Enclosure, Wimbledon Common, London SW19 5NQ
☎ **(020) 8788 0135**

🖳 (020) 8789 7517
✉ secretary.lsgc@btconnect.com
🖊 S Barr (020) 8789 1207
⊕ Red upper outer garment must be worn.
🖥 www.londonscottishgolfclub.co.uk

Malden (1893)
Traps Lane, New Malden KT3 4RS
☎ **(020) 8942 0654**
✉ manager@maldengolfclub.com
🖥 www.maldengolfclub.com

Merrist Wood (1997)
Coombe Lane, Worplesdon, Guildford GU3 3PE
☎ **(01483) 238890**
🖳 (01483) 238896
🖊 Martin Huckleby
🖥 www.merristwood-golfclub.co.uk

Milford (1993)
Proprietary
Station Lane, Milford GU8 5HS
☎ **(01483) 419200**
🖳 (01483) 419199
✉ milford-manager@crown-golf.co.uk
🖊 Rebecca Prout
🖥 www.milfordgolf.co.uk

Mitcham (1924)
Carshalton Road, Mitcham Junction CR4 4HN
☎ **(020) 8640 4197**
🖳 (020) 8648 4197
✉ mitchamgc@hotmail.co.uk
🖊 DJ Tilley (020) 8648 4197
🖥 www.mitchamgolfclub.co.uk

Moore Place (1926)
Public
Portsmouth Road, Esher KT10 9LN
☎ **(01372) 463533**
🖥 www.moore-place.co.uk

New Zealand (1895)
Woodham Lane, Addlestone KT15 3QD
☎ **(01932) 345049**
✉ roger.marrett@nzgc.org
🖊 RA Marrett (01932) 342891

North Downs (1899)
Northdown Road, Woldingham, Caterham CR3 7AA
☎ **(01883) 652057**
🖳 (01883) 652832
✉ secretary@northdownsgolfclub.co.uk
🖊 K R Robinson (Sec) (01883) 652057
🖥 www.northdownsgolfclub.co.uk

Oak Park (1984)
Proprietary
Heath Lane, Crondall, Farnham GU10 5PB
☎ **(01252) 850850**
🖳 (01252) 850851
✉ oakpark@crown-golf.co.uk
🖊 S Edwin
🖥 www.oakparkgolf.co.uk

Oaks Sports Centre (1973)
Public
*Woodmansterne Road, Carshalton
SM5 4AN*
☎ **(020) 8643 8363**
🖥 (020) 8661 7880
✉ info@theoaksgolf.co.uk
✍ G Edginton
🖥 www.theoaksgolf.co.uk

Pachesham Park Golf Centre (1990)
Pay and play
Oaklawn Road, Leatherhead KT22 0BP
☎ **(01372) 843453**
🖥 (01372) 841796
✉ enquiries@pacheshamgolf.co.uk
✍ P Taylor
🖥 www.pacheshamgolf.co.uk

Pine Ridge (1992)
Pay and play
*Old Bisley Road, Frimley, Camberley
GU16 9NX*
☎ **(01276) 675444**
🖥 (01276) 678837
✉ pineridge@crown-golf.co.uk
✍ Elaine Jackson (Sec/Mgr)
🖥 www.pineridgegolf.co.uk

Purley Downs (1894)
*106 Purley Downs Road, South Croydon
CR2 0RB*
☎ **(020) 8657 8347**
🖥 (020) 8651 5044
✉ info@purleydowns.co.uk
✍ Mr S Graham
🖥 www.purleydowns.co.uk

Puttenham (1894)
Puttenham, Guildford GU3 1AL
☎ **(01483) 810498**
🖥 (01483) 810988
✉ enquiries@puttenhamgolfclub
.co.uk
✍ G Simmons
🖥 www.puttenhamgolfclub.co.uk

Pyrford (1993)
Warren Lane, Pyrford GU22 8XR
☎ **(01483) 723555**
🖥 (01483) 729777
✉ pyrford@crown-golf.co.uk
✍ Andrew Lawrence
🖥 www.pyrfordgolf.co.uk

Redhill (1993)
Pay and play
Canada Avenue, Redhill RH1 5BF
☎ **(01737) 770204**
✉ info@redhillgolfcentre.co.uk
✍ S Furlonger
🖥 www.redhillgolfcentre.co.uk

Redhill & Reigate (1887)
Members Club
*Clarence Lodge, Pendleton Road, Redhill
RH1 6LB*
☎ **(01737) 240777/244433**
🖥 (01737) 242117
✉ mail@rrgc.net
✍ D Simpson (01737) 240777
🖥 www.rrgc.net

Reigate Heath (1895)
The Club House, Reigate Heath RH2 8QR
☎ **(01737) 242610**
✉ manager@reigateheathgolfclub
.co.uk
✍ Richard Arnold (01737) 242610
🖥 www.reigateheathgolfclub.co.uk

Reigate Hill
Proprietary
Gatton Bottom, Reigate RH2 0TU
☎ **(01737) 645577**
🖥 (01737) 642650
✉ proshop@reigatehillgolfclub.co.uk
✍ John Holmes
🖥 www.reigatehillgolfclub.co.uk

The Richmond (1891)
Sudbrook Park, Richmond TW10 7AS
☎ **(020) 8940 4351**
🖥 (020) 8332 7914
✉ admin@therichmondgolfclub.co.uk
✍ J Maguire (020) 8940 4351
🖥 www.therichmondgolfclub.com

Richmond Park (1923)
Public
*Roehampton Gate, Richmond Park, London
SW15 5JR*
☎ **(020) 8876 3205/1795**
✉ richmondpark@glendale-
services.co.uk
🖥 www.richmondparkgolf.co.uk

Roehampton Club (1901)
Roehampton Lane, London SW15 5LR
☎ **(020) 8480 4200**
🖥 (020) 8480 4265
✉ tristan.mcillroy@roehamptonclub
.co.uk
✍ Tristan McIllroy
🖥 www.roehamptonclub.co.uk

Rokers Golf Course (1993)
Pay and play
*Holly Lane, Aldershot Road, Guildford
GU3 3PB*
☎ **(01483) 236677**
✉ golf@rokers.co.uk
✍ C Tegg
🖥 www.rokersgolf.co.uk

Royal Automobile Club (1913)
*Woodcote Park, Wilmerhatch Lane, Epsom
KT18 7EW*
☎ **(01372) 273091**
🖥 (01372) 276117
✉ golf@royalautomobileclub.co.uk
✍ Richard Griffiths (01372) 273091
🖥 www.royalautomobileclub.co.uk

Royal Mid-Surrey (1892)
*Old Deer Park, Twickenham Road,
Richmond TW9 2SB*
☎ **(020) 8940 1894**
🖥 (020) 8939 0150
✉ secretary@rmsgc.co.uk
✍ Peter Foord
🖥 www.rmsgc.co.uk

Royal Wimbledon (1865)
*29 Camp Road, Wimbledon, London
SW19 4UW*
☎ **(020) 8946 2125**
🖥 (020) 8944 8652
✉ secretary@rwgc.co.uk
✍ R J Brewer
🖥 www.rwgc.co.uk

Rusper (1992)
Proprietary
Rusper Road, Newdigate RH5 5BX
☎ **(01293) 871871/871456**
✉ nikki@ruspergolfclub.co.uk
✍ Mr Simon Adby (Mgr)
🖥 www.ruspergolfclub.co.uk

Sandown Park Golf Centre (1960)
Public
More Lane, Esher KT10 8AN
☎ **(01372) 469260**
✍ Nick Jones & Craig Morley
(Directors)
🖥 www.sandownparkgolf.com

Selsdon Park Hotel (1929)
Proprietary
*Addington Road, Sanderstead, South
Croydon CR2 8YA*
☎ **(020) 768 3116**
🖥 (020) 8657 3401
✉ chris.baron@principal-hayley.com
✍ Mr C Baron
🖥 www.principal-hayley.com

Shirley Park (1914)
194 Addiscombe Road, Croydon CR0 7LB
☎ **(020) 8654 1143**
🖥 (020) 8654 6733
✉ secretary@shirleyparkgolfclub
.co.uk
✍ Steve Murphy
🖥 www.shirleyparkgolfclub.co.uk

Silvermere (1976)
Pay and play
Redhill Road, Cobham KT11 1EF
☎ **(01932) 584300**
🖥 (01932) 584301
✉ sales@silvermere-golf.co.uk
✍ Mrs P Devereux (01932) 584306
🖥 www.silvermere-golf.co.uk

St George's Hill (1912)
*Golf Club Road, St George's Hill, Weybridge
KT13 0NL*
☎ **(01932) 847758**
🖥 (01932) 821564
✉ admin@stgeorgeshillgolfclub.co.uk
✍ B J Hill
🖥 www.stgeorgeshillgolfclub.co.uk

Sunningdale (1900)
*Ridgemount Road, Sunningdale, Berks
SL5 9RR*
☎ **(01344) 621681**
🖥 (01344) 620154
✉ info@sunningdalegolfclub.co.uk
✍ S Toon
🖥 www.sunningdale-golfclub.co.uk

Sunningdale Ladies   (1902)
Cross Road, Sunningdale SL5 9RX
- ☎ **(01344) 620507**
- ✉ golf@sunningdaleladies.co.uk
- ✍ Simon Sheppard
- 🖥 www.sunningdaleladies.co.uk

Surbiton   (1895)
Woodstock Lane, Chessington KT9 1UG
- ☎ **(020) 8398 3101**
- 📠 (020) 8339 0992
- ✉ enqs@surbitongolfclub.com
- ✍ CJ Cornish
- 🖥 www.surbitongolfclub.com

Surrey Downs   (2001)
Proprietary
Outwood Lane, Kingswood KT20 6JS
- ☎ **(01737) 839090**
- 📠 (01737) 839080
- ✉ booking@surreydownsgc.co.uk
- ✍ P Townson
- 🖥 www.surreydownsgc.co.uk

Surrey National   (1999)
Rook Lane, Chaldon, Caterham CR3 5AA
- ☎ **(01883) 344555**
- ✉ caroline@surreynational.co.uk
- ✍ S Hodsdon (Gen Mgr)
- 🖥 www.surreynational.co.uk

Sutton Green   (1994)
New Lane, Sutton Green, Guildford GU4 7QF
- ☎ **(01483) 747898**
- 📠 (01483) 750289
- ✉ admin@suttongreengc.co.uk
- ✍ J Buchanan
- 🖥 www.suttongreengc.co.uk

The Swallow Farleigh Court   (1997)
Proprietary
Old Farleigh Road, Farleigh CR6 9PX
- ☎ **(01883) 627711**
- ✉ swallow.farleigh@swallowhotels.com
- 🖥 www.swallowhotels.com

Tandridge   (1924)
Oxted RH8 9NQ
- ☎ **(01883) 712273 (Clubhouse)**
- 📠 (01883) 730537
- ✉ secretary@tandridgegolfclub.com
- ✍ A J Tanner
- 🖥 www.tandridgegolfclub.com

Thames Ditton & Esher   (1892)
Portsmouth Road, Esher KT10 9AL
- ☎ **(020) 8398 1551**

Tyrrells Wood   (1924)
The Drive, Tyrrells Wood, Leatherhead KT22 8QP
- ☎ **(01372) 376025 (2 lines)**
- 📠 (01372) 360836
- ✉ office@tyrrellswoodgolfclub.com
- 🖥 www.tyrrellswoodgolfclub.com

Walton Heath   (1903)
Deans Lane, Walton-on-the-Hill, Tadworth KT20 7TP
- ☎ **(01737) 812060**

- 📠 (01737) 814225
- ✉ secretary@waltonheath.com
- ✍ Stuart Christie (01737) 812380
- 🖥 www.waltonheath.com

Wentworth Club   (1924)
Wentworth Drive, Virginia Water GU25 4LS
- ☎ **(01344) 842201**
- 📠 (01344) 842804
- ✍ Stuart Christie (Admin)
- 🖥 www.wentworthclub.com

West Byfleet   (1906)
Sheerwater Road, West Byfleet KT14 6AA
- ☎ **(01932) 343433**
- ✉ admin@wbgc.co.uk
- ✍ I R Attoe (Gen Mgr) (01932) 343433
- 🖥 www.wbgc.co.uk

West Hill   (1909)
Bagshot Road, Brookwood GU24 0BH
- ☎ **(01483) 474365**
- 📠 (01483) 474252
- ✉ secretary@westhill-golfclub.co.uk
- ✍ Gina Rivett
- 🖥 www.westhill-golfclub.co.uk

West Surrey   (1910)
Enton Green, Godalming GU8 5AF
- ☎ **(01483) 421275**
- 📠 (01483) 415419
- ✉ office@wsgc.co.uk
- ✍ Alister Tawse (Golf Mgr)
- 🖥 www.wsgc.co.uk

Wildwood Golf & CC   (1992)
Proprietary
Horsham Road, Alfold GU6 8JE
- ☎ **(01403) 753255**
- ✉ info@wildwoodgolf.co.uk
- 🖥 www.wildwoodgolf.co.uk

Wimbledon Common   (1908)
19 Camp Road, Wimbledon Common, London SW19 4UW
- ☎ **(020) 8946 0294 (Pro Shop)**
- 📠 (020) 8947 8697
- ✉ office@wcgc.co.uk
- ✍ Katerina Angliss (Office Mgr) (020) 8946 7571
- 🖥 www.wcgc.co.uk

Wimbledon Park   (1898)
Home Park Road, London SW19 7HR
- ☎ **(020) 8946 1250**
- 📠 (020) 8944 8688
- ✉ secretary@wpgc.co.uk
- ✍ P Shanahan
- 🖥 www.wpgc.co.uk

Windlemere   (1978)
Pay and play
Windlesham Road, West End, Woking GU24 9QL
- ☎ **(01276) 858727 or (01276) 858271**
- 📠 (01276) 858271
- ✉ mikew@windlemeregolf.co.uk
- ✍ C D Smith/M Walsh

Windlesham   (1994)
Proprietary
Grove End, Bagshot GU19 5HY
- ☎ **(01276) 452220**
- 📠 (01276) 452290
- ✉ admin@windleshamgolf.com
- ✍ Scott Patience
- 🖥 www.windleshamgolf.com

The Wisley   (1991)
Ripley, Woking GU23 6QU
- ☎ **(01483) 212110**
- 📠 (01483) 211662
- ✉ reception@thewisley.com
- ✍ Wayne Sheffield
- 🖥 www.thewisley.com

Woking   (1893)
Pond Road, Hook Heath, Woking GU22 0JZ
- ☎ **(01483) 760053**
- 📠 (01483) 772441
- ✉ info@wokinggolfclub.co.uk
- ✍ G Ritchie
- 🖥 www.wokinggolfclub.co.uk

Woldingham   (1996)
proprietary
Halliloo Valley Road, Woldingham CR3 7HA
- ☎ **(01883) 653501**
- 📠 (01883) 653502
- ✉ info@woldingham-golfclub.co.uk
- ✍ Michael Chubb
- 🖥 www.woldingham-golfclub.co.uk

Woodcote Park   (1912)
Meadow Hill, Bridle Way, Coulsdon CR5 2QQ
- ☎ **(0208) 668 2788**
- 📠 (0208) 660 0918
- ✉ info@woodcotepgc.com
- ✍ AP Dawson
- 🖥 www.woodcotepgc.com

Worplesdon   (1908)
Heath House Road, Woking GU22 0RA
- ☎ **(01483) 472277**
- 📠 (01483) 473303
- ✉ office@worplesdongc.co.uk
- ✍ CK Symington
- 🖥 www.worplesdongc.co.uk

Sussex (East)

Beauport Park Golf Course   (1973)
Pay and play
Battle Road, St Leonards-on-Sea, East Sussex TN37 7BP
- ☎ **(01424) 854245**
- 📠 (01424) 854245
- ✉ info@beauportparkgolf.co.uk
- ✍ C Giddins
- 🖥 www.beauportparkgolf.co.uk

Brighton & Hove   (1887)
Devils Dyke Road, Brighton BN1 8YJ
- ☎ **(01273) 556482**
- 📠 (01273) 554247
- ✉ phil@brightongolf.co.uk

🖎 P Bonsall (Golf Dir)
🖳 www.brightonandhovegolfclub
.co.uk

Cooden Beach   (1912)
*Cooden Sea Road, Bexhill-on-Sea
TN39 4TR*
☎ **(01424) 842040**
🖳 (01424) 842040
🖂 enquiries@coodenbeachgc.com
🖎 KP Wiley (01424) 842040
🖳 www.coodenbeachgc.com

Crowborough Beacon
(1895)
Beacon Road, Crowborough TN6 1UJ
☎ **(01892) 661511**
🖂 secretary@cbgc.co.uk
🖎 John Holmes (Mgr)
🖳 www.crowboroughbeacongolfclub
.co.uk

Dale Hill Hotel & GC   (1973)
Ticehurst, Wadhurst TN5 7DQ
☎ **(01580) 201090**
🖳 (01580) 201249
🖂 golf@dalehill.co.uk
🖎 John Tolliday (Dir of Golf)
🖳 www.dalehill.co.uk

Dewlands Manor   (1992)
Cottage Hill, Rotherfield TN6 3JN
☎ **(01892) 852266**
🖳 (01892) 853015
🖎 T Robins
⊕ 15 minute Tee Times relaxed golf.

Dyke Golf Club   (1906)
*Devil's Dyke, Devil's Dyke Road, Brighton
BN1 8YJ*
☎ **(01273) 857296**
🖳 (01273) 857078
🖂 manager@dykegolfclub.co.uk
🖎 Megan Bibby (Gen Mgr)
🖳 www.dykegolf.com

East Brighton   (1893)
Roedean Road, Brighton BN2 5RA
☎ **(01273) 604838**
🖳 (01273) 680277
🖂 office@ebgc.co.uk
🖎 G McKay
🖳 www.ebgc.co.uk

East Sussex National Golf
Resort and Spa   (1989)
Proprietary
Little Horsted, Uckfield TN22 5ES
☎ **(01825) 880088**
🖳 (01825) 880066
🖂 reception@eastsussexnational
.co.uk
🖎 DT Howe
🖳 www.eastsussexnational.co.uk

Eastbourne Downs   (1908)
East Dean Road, Eastbourne BN20 8ES
☎ **(01323) 720827**
🖂 secretary@ebdownsgolf.co.uk
🖎 Denise McDowell & Lorna Hardy
🖳 www.ebdownsgolf.co.uk

Eastbourne Golfing Park
Ltd   (1992)
Pay and play
Lottbridge Drove, Eastbourne BN23 6QJ
☎ **(01323) 520400**
🖳 (01323) 520400
🖂 egpltd@uk2.net
🖎 Maggie Garbutt
🖳 www.eastbournegolfingpark.com

Highwoods   (1925)
Ellerslie Lane, Bexhill-on-Sea TN39 4LJ
☎ **(01424) 212625**
🖳 (01424) 216866
🖂 highwoods@btconnect.com
🖎 AP Moran
🖳 www.highwoodsgolfclub.co.uk

Hollingbury Park   (1908)
Public
Ditchling Road, Brighton BN1 7HS
☎ **(01273) 552010**
🖳 www.hollingburygolfclub.co.uk

Holtye   (1893)
Holtye, Cowden, Nr Edenbridge TN8 7ED
☎ **(01342) 850635**
🖳 (01342) 851139
🖂 secretary@holtye.com
🖎 Mrs I O Martin (01342) 850635
🖳 www.holtye.com

Horam Park   (1985)
Pay and play
Chiddingly Road, Horam TN21 0JJ
☎ **(01435) 813477**
🖳 (01435) 813677
🖂 angie@horampark.com
🖎 Mrs A Briggs
🖳 www.horamparkgolfclub.co.uk

Lewes   (1896)
Chapel Hill, Lewes BN7 2BB
☎ **(01273) 473245**
🖳 (01273) 483474
🖂 secretary@lewesgolfclub.co.uk
🖎 Mr L C Dorn (01273) 483474
🖳 www.lewesgolfclub.co.uk

Mid Sussex   (1995)
Proprietary
Spatham Lane, Ditchling BN6 8XJ
☎ **(01273) 846567**
🖳 (01273) 847815
🖂 admin@midsussexgolfclub.co.uk
🖎 A McNiven (Golf Dir)
🖳 www.midsussexgolfclub.co.uk

Nevill   (1914)
*Benhall Mill Road, Tunbridge Wells
TN2 5JW*
☎ **(01892) 525818**
🖳 (01892) 517861
🖂 manager@nevillgolfclub.co.uk
🖎 FW Prescott
🖳 www.nevillgolfclub.co.uk

Peacehaven   (1895)
Proprietary
Brighton Road, Newhaven BN9 9UH
☎ **(01273) 514049**
🖂 henry@golfatpeacehaven.co.uk

🖎 Henry Hilton (01273) 514049
🖳 www.golfatpeacehaven.co.uk

Piltdown   (1904)
Piltdown, Uckfield TN22 3XB
☎ **(01825) 722033**
🖳 (01825) 724192
🖂 secretary@piltdowngolfclub.co.uk
🖎 Iain Wallace
🖳 www.piltdowngolfclub.co.uk

Royal Ashdown Forest
(1888)
*Chapel Lane, Forest Row, East Sussex
RH18 5LR*
☎ **(01342) 822018 (Old)**
🖳 (01342) 825211
🖂 office@royalashdown.co.uk
🖎 D S Holmes
🖳 www.royalashdown.co.uk

Royal Eastbourne   (1887)
Paradise Drive, Eastbourne BN20 8BP
☎ **(01323) 744045**
🖳 (01323) 744048
🖂 sec@regc.co.uk
🖎 David Lockyer (01323) 744045
🖳 www.regc.co.uk

Rye   (1894)
New Lydd Road, Camber, Rye TN31 7QS
☎ **(01797) 225241**
🖳 (01797) 225460
🖂 links@ryegolfclub.co.uk
🖎 J H Laidler (Sec)
🖳 www.ryegolfclub.co.uk

Seaford   (1887)
Firle Road, Seaford BN25 2JD
☎ **(01323) 892442**
🖳 (01323) 894113
🖂 secretary@seafordgolfclub.co.uk
🖎 LM Dennis-Smither (Gen Sec)
🖳 www.seafordgolfclub.co.uk

Seaford Head   (1887)
Public
Southdown Road, Seaford BN25 4JS
☎ **(01323) 890139**
🖳 (01323) 890139
🖂 seafordheadgolfclub.co.uk
🖎 RW Andrews (01323) 894843
🖳 www.seaheadgc@tiscali.co.uk

Sedlescombe   (1990)
Kent Street, Sedlescombe TN33 0SD
☎ **(01424) 871700**
🖂 golf@golfschool.co.uk

Wellshurst G&CC   (1992)
Proprietary
North Street, Hellingly BN27 4EE
☎ **(01435) 813636**
🖳 (01435) 812444
🖂 info@wellshurst.com
🖎 M Adams (Man Dir)
🖳 www.wellshurst.com

West Hove   (1910)
Badgers Way, Hangleton, Hove BN3 8EX
☎ **(01273) 413411 (Clubhouse)**
🖳 (01273) 439988

✉ info@westhovegolfclub.co.uk
✍ Gary Salt (Mgr) (01273) 419738
🖥 www.westhovegolfclub.info

Willingdon (1898)
Southdown Road, Eastbourne BN20 9AA
☎ **(01323) 410981**
🖥 (01323) 411510
✉ secretary@willingdongolfclub.co.uk
✍ Mrs J Packham (01323) 410981
🖥 www.willingdongolfclub.co.uk

Sussex (West)

Avisford Park (1990)
Pay and play
Yapton Lane, Walberton, Arundel
BN18 0LS
☎ **(01243) 554611**
🖥 (01243) 554958
✉ avisfordparkgolf@aol.com
✍ Sarah Chitty
🖥 www.avisfordparkgolfclub.com

Bognor Regis (1892)
Downview Road, Felpham, Bognor Regis
PO22 8JD
☎ **(01243) 821929**
🖥 (01243) 860719
✉ sec@bognorgolfclub.co.uk
🖥 www.bognorgolfclub.co.uk

Burgess Hill Golf Centre
(1995)
Pay and play
Cuckfield Road, Burgess Hill
☎ **(01444) 258585 (shop)**
🖥 (01444) 247318
✉ enquiries@burgesshillgolfcentre
.co.uk
✍ CJ Collins (Mgr)
🖥 www.burgesshillgolfcentre.co.uk

Chartham Park (1993)
Proprietary
Felcourt, East Grinstead RH19 2JT
☎ **(01342) 870340**
🖥 (01342) 870719
✉ d.hobbs@theclubcompany.com
✍ David Hobbs (PGA Pro)
🖥 www.theclubcompany.com

Chichester (1990)
Proprietary
Hunston Village, Chichester PO20 1AX
☎ **(01243) 533833**
🖥 (01243) 538989
✉ info@chichestergolf.com
✍ Helen Howard (01243) 536666
🖥 www.chichestergolf.com

Copthorne (1892)
Borers Arms Road, Copthorne RH10 3LL
☎ **(01342) 712508**
🖥 (01342) 717682
✉ info@copthornegolfclub.co.uk
✍ JP Pyne (01342) 712033
🖥 www.copthornegolfclub.co.uk

Cottesmore (1975)
Proprietary
Buchan Hill, Pease Pottage, Crawley
RH11 9AT
☎ **(01293) 528256**
🖥 (01293) 522819
✉ cottesmore@crowngolf.co.uk
✍ N Miller
🖥 www.cottesmoregolf.co.uk

Cowdray Park (1904)
Proprietary
Petworth Road, Midhurst GU29 0BB
☎ **(01730) 813599**
🖥 (01730) 815900
✉ enquiries@cowdraygolf.co.uk
✍ M Purves
🖥 www.cowdraygolf.co.uk

Effingham Park (1980)
Proprietary
West Park Road, Copthorne RH10 3EU
☎ **(01342) 716528**
✉ mark.root@mill-cop/com
🖥 www.crown-golf.co.uk

Foxbridge (1993)
Foxbridge Lane, Plaistow RH14 0LB
☎ **(01403) 753303 (Bookings)**

Golf at Goodwood (1892)
Kennel Hill, Goodwood, Chichester
PO18 0PN
☎ **(01243) 755130**
🖥 (01243) 755135
✉ golf@goodwood.com
🖥 www.goodwood.com

Ham Manor (1936)
West Drive, Angmering, Littlehampton
BN16 4JE
☎ **(01903) 783288**
🖥 (01903) 850886
✉ secretary@hammanor.co.uk
✍ Paul Bodle
🖥 www.hammanor.co.uk

Hassocks (1995)
Pay and play
London Road, Hassocks BN6 9NA
☎ **(01273) 846990**
🖥 (01273) 846070
✉ hassocksgolfclub@btconnect.com
✍ Mr H Chambers (Gen Mgr)
🖥 www.hassocksgolfclub.co.uk

Haywards Heath (1922)
High Beech Lane, Haywards Heath
RH16 1SL
☎ **(01444) 414457**
🖥 (01444) 458319
✉ info@haywardsheathgolfclub.co.uk
✍ G K Honeysett
🖥 www.haywardsheathgolfclub.co.uk

Hill Barn (1935)
Public
Hill Barn Lane, Worthing BN14 9QE
☎ **(01903) 237301**
🖥 (01903) 217613
✉ info@hillbarn.com
✍ R Haygarth (01903) 237301
🖥 www.hillbarngolf.com

Horsham (1993)
Pay and play
Worthing Road, Horsham RH13 0AX
☎ **(01403) 271525**
✉ secretary@horshamgolfandfitness
.co.uk
🖥 www.horshamgolfandfitness.co.uk

Ifield (1927)
Rusper Road, Ifield, Crawley RH11 0LN
☎ **(01293) 520222**

Lindfield (1990)
Proprietary
East Mascalls Lane, Lindfield RH16 2QN
☎ **(01444) 484467**
🖥 (01444) 482709
✉ info@thegolfcollege.com
✍ Paul Lyons
🖥 www.thegolfcollege.com

Littlehampton (1889)
170 Rope Walk, Littlehampton BN17 5DL
☎ **(01903) 717170**
🖥 (01903) 726629
✉ lgc@talk21.com
✍ S Graham
🖥 www.littlehamptongolf.co.uk

Mannings Heath (1905)
Proprietary
Fullers, Hammerpond Road, Mannings
Heath, Horsham RH13 6PG
☎ **(01403) 210228**
🖥 (01403) 270974
✉ enquiries@manningsheath.com
✍ Steve Slinger (01403) 220340
🖥 www.exclusivehotels.co.uk

Pease Pottage Golf Centre
(1986)
Horsham Road, Pease Pottage, Crawley
RH11 9AP
☎ **(01293) 521706**
🖥 (01293) 521706
✍ A Venn (01293) 521766

Petworth Downs Golf Club
(1989)
Pay and play
London Road, Petworth GU28 9LX
☎ **(01798) 344097**
✉ petworthdowns@hotmail.com
✍ Annabel Hall (0771) 156 7466
🖥 www.petworthgolf.com

Pyecombe (1894)
Clayton Hill, Pyecombe, Brighton BN45 7FF
☎ **(01273) 845372**
🖥 (01273) 843338
✉ info@pyecombegolfclub.com
✍ Alan Davey
🖥 www.pyecombegolfclub.com

Rustington (1992)
Public
Golfers Lane, Angmering BN16 4NB
☎ **(01903) 850790**
🖥 (01903) 850982
✉ info@rgcgolf.com
✍ Mr S Langmead
🖥 www.rgcgolf.com

Selsey (1908)
Golf Links Lane, Selsey PO20 9DR
☎ **(01243) 605176 (Members)**
🖳 (01243) 607101
📧 secretary@selseygolfclub.co.uk
✍ BE Rogers (01243) 608935
🖥 www.selseygolfclub.co.uk

Shillinglee Park (1980)
Pay and play
Chiddingfold, Godalming GU8 4TA
☎ **(01428) 653237**

Singing Hills (1992)
Proprietary
Muddleswood Road, Albourne, Brighton BN6 9EB
☎ **(01273) 835353**
🖳 (01273) 835444
📧 info@singinghills.co.uk
✍ Jane Covey
🖥 www.singinghills.co.uk

Slinfold Golf & Country Club (1993)
Proprietary
Stane Street, Slinfold, Horsham RH13 0RE
☎ **(01403) 791154 (Clubhouse)**
🖳 (01403) 791465
📧 info.slinfold@ccgclubs.com
✍ S Blake (Gen Mgr)
🖥 www.ccgslinford.com

Tilgate Forest (1982)
Public
Titmus Drive, Tilgate, Crawley RH10 5EU
☎ **(01293) 530103**

West Chiltington (1988)
Proprietary
Broadford Bridge Road, West Chiltington RH20 2YA
☎ **(01798) 813574**
🖳 (01798) 812631
📧 debbie@westchiltgolf.co.uk
✍ D Haines
🖥 www.westchiltgolf.co.uk

West Sussex (1931)
Golf Club Lane, Wiggonholt, Pulborough RH20 2EN
☎ **(01798) 872563**
🖳 (01798) 872033
📧 secretary@westsussexgolf.co.uk
✍ A D Stubbs
🖥 www.westsussexgolf.co.uk

Worthing (1905)
Links Road, Worthing BN14 9QZ
☎ **(01903) 260801**
🖳 (01903) 694664
📧 enquiries@worthinggolf.com
✍ John Holton
🖥 www.worthinggolf.co.uk

Tyne & Wear

Backworth (1937)
The Hall, Backworth, Shiremoor, Newcastle-upon-Tyne NE27 0AH
☎ **(0191) 268 1048**

📧 backworth.miners@virgin.net
✍ J A Wilkinson
🖥 www.backworthgolf.co.uk

Birtley (1922)
Birtley Lane, Birtley DH3 2LR
☎ **(0191) 410 2207**
🖳 (0191) 410 2207
📧 birtleygolfclub@aol.com
✍ K Self
🖥 www.birtleyportobellogolfclub .co.uk

Boldon (1912)
Dipe Lane, East Boldon, Tyne & Wear NE36 0PQ
☎ **(0191) 536 5360 (Clubhouse)**
🖳 (0191) 537 2270
📧 info@boldongolfclub.co.uk
✍ Chris Brown (0191) 536 5360
🖥 www.boldongolfclub.co.uk

City of Newcastle (1891)
Three Mile Bridge, Gosforth, Newcastle-upon-Tyne NE3 2DR
☎ **(0191) 285 1775**
🖳 (0191) 284 0700
📧 info@cityofnewcastlegolfclub.co.uk
✍ AJ Matthew (Mgr)
🖥 www.cityofnewcastlegolfclub.co.uk

Garesfield (1922)
Chopwell NE17 7AP
☎ **(01207) 561309**
🖳 (01207) 561309
📧 garesfieldgc@btconnect.com
✍ Mr Alan Hill
🖥 www.garesfieldgolfclub.co.uk

Gosforth (1906)
Broadway East, Gosforth, Newcastle upon Tyne NE3 5ER
☎ **(0191) 285 0553**
🖳 (0191) 284 6274
📧 gosforth.golf@virgin.net
✍ G Garland (0191) 285 3495
🖥 www.gosforthgolfclub.co.uk

Hetton-le-Hill
Pay and play
Elemore Golf Course, Elemore Lane DH5 0QT
☎ **(0191) 517 3061**
🖳 (0191) 517 3054
📧 elemortgolfclub@talktalkbusiness .net
✍ William Allen
🖥 www.elemort.co.uk

Heworth (1912)
Gingling Gate, Heworth, Gateshead NE10 8XY
☎ **(0191) 469 9832**
🖳 (0191) 469 9898
📧 secretary@theheworthgolfclub .co.uk
✍ G Peters
🖥 www.theheworthgolfclub.co.uk

Houghton-le-Spring (1908)
Copt Hill, Houghton-le-Spring, Tyne & Wear DH5 8LU
☎ **(0191) 584 7421 (Pro Shop)**

🖳 (0191) 584 0048
📧 houghton.golf@virgin.net
✍ Graeme Robinson (Professional)
🖥 www.houghtongolfclub.co.uk

Newcastle United (1892)
Ponteland Road, Cowgate, Newcastle-upon-Tyne NE5 3JW
☎ **(0191) 286 9998 (Clubhouse)**
🖳 (0191) 286 4323
📧 info@newcastleunitedgolfclub .co.uk
✍ P Jobe (Sec/Treasurer)
🖥 www.newcastleunitedgolfclub.co.uk

Northumberland (1898)
High Gosforth Park, Newcastle-upon-Tyne NE3 5HT
☎ **(0191) 236 2498/2009**
🖳 (0191) 236 2036
📧 sec@thengc.co.uk
✍ Jamie Forteath
🖥 www.thengc.co.uk

Parklands (1971)
Proprietary
High Gosforth Park, Newcastle-upon-Tyne NE3 5HQ
☎ **(0191) 236 3322**
📧 parklands@newcastle-racecourse.co.uk
✍ G Brown (Hon Sec)
🖥 www.parklandsgolf.co.uk

Ravensworth (1906)
Angel View, Long Bank, Gateshead NE9 7NE
☎ **(0191) 487 6014**
📧 secretary@ravensworthgolfclub .co.uk
✍ Marcus Humphrey
🖥 www.ravensworthgolfclub.co.uk

Ryton (1891)
Doctor Stanners, Clara Vale, Ryton NE40 3TD
☎ **(0191) 413 3253**
🖳 (0191) 413 1642
📧 secretary@rytongolfclub.co.uk
✍ Mr K McLeod
🖥 www.rytongolfclub.co.uk

South Shields (1893)
Cleadon Hills, South Shields NE34 8EG
☎ **(0191) 456 0475**
📧 thesecretary@south-shields-golf.freeserve.co.uk

Tynemouth (1913)
Spital Dene, Tynemouth, North Shields NE30 2ER
☎ **(0191) 257 4578**
🖳 (0191) 259 5193
📧 secretary@tynemouthgolfclub.com
✍ TJ Scott (0191) 257 3381
🖥 www.tynemouthgolfclub.com

Tyneside (1879)
Westfield Lane, Ryton NE40 3QE
☎ **(0191) 413 2742**
🖳 (0191) 413 0199
📧 secretary@tynesidegolfclub.co.uk

✍ Alastair Greenfiled
(0191) 413 2742
🖥 www.tynesidegolfclub.co.uk

Wallsend (1973)
Rheydt Avenue, Bigges Main, Wallsend
NE28 8SU
☎ **(0191) 262 1973**
✍ D Souter

Washington (1979)
Stone Cellar Road, High Usworth,
Washington NE37 1PH
☎ **(0191) 417 8346**
📧 graeme.amanda@btopenworld
.com
🖥 www.georgewashington.co.uk

Wearside (1892)
Coxgreen, Sunderland SR4 9JT
☎ **(0191) 534 2518**
🖥 (0191) 534 6186
📧 secretary@wearsidegolf.com
✍ P Hall
🖥 www.wearsidegolf.com

Westerhope (1941)
Whorlton Grange, Westerhope, Newcastle-
upon-Tyne NE5 1PP
☎ **(0191) 286 7636**
🖥 (0191) 214 6287
📧 wgc@btconnect.com
✍ D Souter (0191) 286 7636
🖥 www.westerhopegolfclub.com

Whickham (1911)
Hollinside Park, Fellside Road, Whickham,
Newcastle-upon-Tyne NE16 5BA
☎ **(0191) 488 1576 (Clubhouse)**
🖥 (0191) 488 1577
📧 enquiries@whickhamgolfclub.co.uk
✍ Mr M E Pearse
🖥 www.whickhamgolfclub.co.uk

Whitburn (1931)
Lizard Lane, South Shields NE34 7AF
☎ **(0191) 529 2177**
📧 wgcsec@hotmail.com
✍ Mr R Button (Sec) (0191) 529 2177
option 1
🖥 www.golf-whitburn.co.uk

Whitley Bay (1890)
Claremont Road, Whitley Bay NE26 3UF
☎ **(0191) 252 0180**
🖥 (0191) 297 0030
📧 whtglfclb@aol.com
✍ F Elliott (0191) 252 0180
🖥 www.whitleybaygolfclub.co.uk

Warwickshire

Ansty (1990)
Pay and play
Brinklow Road, Ansty, Coventry CV7 9JL
☎ **(024) 7662 1341/7660 2568**
🖥 (024) 7660 2568
✍ K Smith
🖥 www.anstygolfandconference.co.uk

Atherstone (1894)
The Outwoods, Coleshill Road, Atherstone
CV9 2RL
☎ **(01827) 713110**

The Belfry (1977)
Pay and play
Wishaw, Sutton Coldfield B76 9PR
☎ **(01675) 470301**
🖥 (01675) 470256
📧 enquiries@thebelfry.com
✍ Gary Silcock (Dir. of Golf)
🖥 www.thebelfry.com

Boldmere (1936)
Public
Monmouth Drive, Sutton Coldfield,
Birmingham BJ3 6JR
☎ **(0121) 354 3379**
🖥 (0121) 353 5576
📧 boldmeregolfclub@hotmail.com
✍ R Leeson
🖥 www.boldmeregolfclub.co.uk

Bramcote Waters (1995)
Pay and play
Bazzard Road, Bramcote, Nuneaton
CV11 6QJ
☎ **(01455) 220807**
📧 bwgc@hotmail.co.uk
✍ Sara Britain (01455) 220807
🖥 www.bramcotewatersgolfclub
.co.uk

City of Coventry (Brandon Wood) (1977)
Public
Brandon Lane, Coventry CV8 3GQ
☎ **(024) 7654 3141**
🖥 (024) 7654 5108
📧 brandongolf@coventrysports.uk
✍ N Orton (Mgr)
🖥 www.brandonwood.co.uk

Copsewood Grange (1924)
Allard Way, Copsewood, Coventry CV3 1JP
☎ **(024) 76448355**
✍ REC Jones (024) 7645 2973
🖥 www.copsewoodgrange.co.uk

Copt Heath (1907)
1220 Warwick Road, Knowle, Solihull
B93 9LN
☎ **(01564) 731620**
🖥 (01564) 731621
📧 golf@copt-heath.co.uk
✍ CV Hadley
🖥 www.coptheathgolf.co.uk

Coventry (1887)
St Martins Road, Finham, Coventry CV3 6RJ
☎ **(024) 7641 4152**
🖥 (024) 7669 0131
📧 secretary@coventrygolfclub.net
✍ A Smith (024) 7641 4152
🖥 www.coventrygolfclub.net

Coventry Hearsall (1894)
Beechwood Avenue, Coventry CV5 6DF
☎ **(024) 7671 3470**
🖥 (024) 7669 1534
📧 secretary@hearsallgolfclub.co.uk

✍ R Meade
🖥 www.hearsallgolfclub.co.uk

Edgbaston (1896)
Church Road, Edgbaston, Birmingham
B15 3TB
☎ **(0121) 454 1736**
🖥 (0121) 454 2395
📧 secretary@edgbastongc.co.uk
✍ AD Grint
🖥 www.edgbastongc.co.uk

Harborne (1893)
40 Tennal Road, Harborne, Birmingham
B32 2JE
☎ **(0121) 427 3058**
🖥 (0121) 427 4039
📧 adrian@harbornegolfclub.org.uk
✍ Adrian Cooper (0121) 427 3058
🖥 www.harbornegolfclub.com

Harborne Church Farm (1926)
Public
Vicarage Road, Harborne, Birmingham
B17 0SN
☎ **(0121) 427 1204**
🖥 (0121) 428 3126
🖥 www.golfbirmingham.co.uk

Hatchford Brook (1969)
Public
Coventry Road, Sheldon, Birmingham
B26 3PY
☎ **(0121) 743 9821**
🖥 (0121) 743 3420
📧 idt@hbgc.freeserve.co.uk
✍ ID Thomson (0121) 742 6643
🖥 www.golfpro-direct.co.uk/hbgc

Henley G&CC (1994)
Proprietary
Birmingham Road, Henley-in-Arden
B95 5QA
☎ **(01564) 793715**
🖥 (01564) 795754
📧 enquiries@henleygcc.co.uk
✍ G Waller (Director)
🖥 www.henleygcc.co.uk

Hilltop (1979)
Public
Park Lane, Handsworth, Birmingham
B21 8LJ
☎ **(0121) 554 4463**
✍ K Highfield (Mgr & Professional)

Ingon Manor (1993)
Ingon Lane, Snitterfield, Stratford-on-Avon
CV37 0QE
☎ **(01789) 731857**
📧 golf@ingonmanor.co.uk
✍ Richard James Hampton
🖥 www.ingonmanor.co.uk

Kenilworth (1889)
Crewe Lane, Kenilworth CV8 2EA
☎ **(01926) 854296**
🖥 (01926) 864453
📧 secretary@kenilworthgolfclub
.co.uk
✍ Rob Griffiths (01926) 858517
🖥 www.kenilworthgolfclub.co.uk

Ladbrook Park   (1908)
Poolhead Lane, Tanworth-in-Arden, Solihull
B94 5ED
☎ **(01564) 742264**
📠 (01564) 742909
📧 secretary@ladbrookparkgolf.co.uk
🖥 www.ladbrookparkgolf.co.uk

Lea Marston Hotel & Leisure Complex   (2002)
Proprietary
Haunch Lane, Lea Marston, Warwicks
B76 0BY
☎ **(01675) 470707**
📠 (01675) 470871
📧 golf.shop@leamarstonhotel.co.uk
✍ Darren Lewis (Mgr)
🖥 www.leamarstonhotel.co.uk

Leamington & County   (1907)
Golf Lane, Whitnash, Leamington Spa CV31
2QA
☎ **(01926) 425961**
📧 secretary@leamingtongolf.co.uk
✍ David M Beck
🖥 www.leamingtongolf.co.uk

Marriott Forest of Arden Hotel   (1970)
Maxstoke Lane, Meriden, Coventry CV7
7HR
☎ **(01676) 526113**
📠 (01676) 523711
📧 mhrs.cvtgs.golf@marriotthotels
.com
✍ I Burns (Golf Dir)
🖥 www.marriott.com/cvtgs

Maxstoke Park   (1898)
Castle Lane, Coleshill, Birmingham B46 2RD
☎ **(01675) 466743**
📠 (01675) 466185
📧 info@maxstokeparkgolfclub.com
🖥 www.maxstokeparkgolfclub.com

Menzies Welcombe Hotel, Spa & Golf Club
Warwick Road, Stratford-on-Avon
CV37 0NR
☎ **(01789) 413800**
📠 (01789) 262028
✍ Dan Hacker (Director)
🖥 www.welcombehotelstratford
.co.uk

Moor Hall   (1932)
Moor Hall Drive, Four Oaks, Sutton
Coldfield B75 6LN
☎ **(0121) 308 6130**
📠 (0121) 308 9560
📧 secretary@moorhallgolfclub.co.uk
✍ DJ Etheridge
🖥 www.moorhallgolfclub.co.uk

Newbold Comyn   (1973)
Public
Newbold Terrace East, Leamington Spa
CV32 4EW
☎ **(01926) 421157**
📧 ian@viscount5.freeserve.co.uk
✍ I Shepherd (07799) 248729

North Warwickshire   (1894)
Hampton Lane, Meriden, Coventry CV7 7LL
☎ **(01676) 522464 (Clubhouse)**
📠 (01676) 523004
📧 nwgcltd@btconnect.com
✍ Bob May (Hon) (01676) 522915
🖥 www.northwarwickshiregolfclubltd
.co.uk

Nuneaton   (1905)
Golf Drive, Whitestone, Nuneaton
CV11 6QF
☎ **(024) 7634 7810**
📠 (024) 7632 7563
📧 nuneatongolfclub@btconnect.com
✍ Tracey Carpenter
🖥 www.nuneatongolfclub.co.uk

Oakridge   (1993)
Proprietary
Arley Lane, Ansley Village, Nuneaton
CV10 9PH
☎ **(01676) 541389**
📠 (01676) 542709
📧 shane-lovric@golfatoakridge.com
✍ Mrs S Lovric (Admin)
🖥 www.oakridgegolfclub.co.uk

Olton   (1893)
Mirfield Road, Solihull B91 1JH
☎ **(0121) 704 1936**
📠 (0121) 711 2010
📧 secretary@oltongolfclub.co.uk
✍ R Gay (0121) 704 1936
🖥 www.oltongolfclub.co.uk

Purley Chase   (1980)
Pipers Lane, Ridge Lane, Nuneaton
CV10 0RB
☎ **(024) 7639 3118**
📠 (024) 7639 8015
📧 events@purleychase.com
✍ Linda Jackson

Pype Hayes   (1932)
Public
Eachelhurst Road, Walmley, Sutton
Coldfield, West Midlands B76 1EP
☎ **(0121) 351 1014**
📠 (0121) 313 0206
✍ C Marson

Robin Hood   (1893)
St Bernards Road, Solihull B92 7DJ
☎ **(0121) 706 0061**
📠 (0121) 700 7502
📧 manager@robinhoodgolfclub.co.uk
✍ M J Ward
🖥 www.robinhoodgolfclub.co.uk

Rugby   (1891)
Clifton Road, Rugby CV21 3RD
☎ **(01788) 544637 (Clubhouse)**
📠 (01788) 542306
📧 rugbygolfclub@tiscali.co.uk
✍ John Drake (01788) 542306
🖥 www.rugbygc.co.uk

Shirley   (1955)
Stratford Road, Monkspath, Solihull B90
4EW
☎ **(0121) 744 6001 opt 5**

📠 (0121) 746 5645
📧 enquiries@shirleygolfclub.co.uk
✍ Patricia Harris (Mgr)
🖥 www.shirleygolfclub.co.uk

Stonebridge   (1996)
Proprietary
Somers Road, Meriden CV7 7PL
☎ **(01676) 522442**
📠 (01676) 522447
📧 sales@stonebridgegolf.co.uk
✍ Mark Clarke
🖥 www.stonebridgegolf.co.uk

Stoneleigh Deer Park Golf Club   (1991)
Proprietary
The Clubhouse, Coventry Road, Stoneleigh
CV8 3DR
☎ **(024) 7663 9991**
📠 (024) 7651 1533
📧 info@stoneleighdeerparkgolfclub
.com
✍ C Reay
🖥 www.stoneleighdeerparkgolfclub
.com

Stratford Oaks   (1991)
Proprietary
Bearley Road, Snitterfield, Stratford-on-Avon
CV37 0EZ
☎ **(01789) 731980**
📠 (01789) 731981
📧 admin@stratfordoaks.co.uk
✍ ND Powell (Golf Dir)
🖥 www.stratfordoaks.co.uk

Stratford-on-Avon   (1894)
Tiddington Road, Stratford-on-Avon
CV37 7BA
☎ **(01789) 205749**
📠 (01789) 414909
📧 sec@stratford.co.uk
✍ C J Hughes (01789) 205749
🖥 www.stratfordgolf.co.uk

Sutton Coldfield   (1889)
110 Thornhill Road, Sutton Coldfield
B74 3ER
☎ **(0121) 353 9633**
📠 (0121) 353 5503
📧 admin@suttoncoldfieldgc.com
✍ I H Phillips, KM Tempest
🖥 www.suttoncoldfieldgc.com

Walmley   (1902)
Brooks Road, Wylde Green, Sutton Coldfield
B72 1HR
☎ **(0121) 373 0029**
📠 (0121) 377 7272
📧 secretary@walmleygolfclub.co.uk
✍ J C Shakespeare
🖥 www.walmleygolfclub.co.uk

Warwick   (1971)
Public & Proprietary
Warwick Racecourse, Warwick CV34 6HW
☎ **(01926) 494316**
📧 info@warwickgolfcentre.co.uk
✍ Mrs R Dunkley
🖥 www.warwickgolfcentre.co.uk

The Warwickshire (1993)
Proprietary
Leek Wootton, Warwick CV35 7QT
☎ **(01926) 409409**

West Midlands (2003)
Marsh House Farm Lane, Barston, Solihull B92 0LB
☎ **(01675) 444890**
📠 (01675) 444891
✉ mark@wmgc.co.uk
✍ Mark Harrhy (01675) 444890
🖥 www.wmgc.co.uk

Whitefields Golf Club & Draycote Hotel (1992)
Proprietary
London Road, Thurlaston, Rugby CV23 9LF
☎ **(01788) 815555**
📠 (01788) 521695
✉ mail@draycotehotel.co.uk
✍ B Coleman (01788) 815555
🖥 www.draycote-hotel.co.uk

Widney Manor (1993)
Pay and play
Saintbury Drive, Widney Manor, Solihull B91 3SZ
☎ **(0121) 704 0704**
📠 (0121) 704 7999
✍ Tim Atkinson

Windmill Village (1990)
Proprietary
Birmingham Road, Allesley, Coventry CV5 9AL
☎ **(024) 7640 4041**
📠 (024) 7640 4042
✉ leisure@windmillvillagehotel.co.uk
✍ Oliver Thomas (Mgr)
🖥 www.windmillvillagehotel.co.uk

Wishaw (1992)
Proprietary
Bulls Lane, Wishaw, Sutton Coldfield B76 9QW
☎ **(0121) 313 2110**
✉ golf@wishawgc.co.uk
✍ PH Burwell
🖥 www.wishawgc.co.uk

Wiltshire

Bowood Hotel, Spa and Golf Resort (1992)
Proprietary
Derry Hill, Calne SN11 9PQ
☎ **(01249) 822228**
📠 (01249) 822218
✉ j.hansel@bowood.org
✍ Paul McLean
🖥 www.bowood.org

Broome Manor (1976)
Public
Pipers Way, Swindon SN3 1RG
☎ **(01793) 532403**
✉ secretary@bmgc.co.uk
✍ C Beresford 01793 526544
🖥 www.bmgc.co.uk

Chippenham (1896)
Malmesbury Road, Chippenham SN15 5LT
☎ **(01249) 652040**
📠 (01249) 446681
✉ chippenhamgolf@btconnect.com
✍ Mrs P Dawson
🖥 www.chippenhamgolfclub.com

Cricklade House (1992)
Pay and play
Common Hill, Cricklade SN6 6HA
☎ **(01793) 750751**
📠 (01793) 751767
✉ reception@crickladehotel.co.uk
✍ C Withers/P Butler
🖥 www.crickladehotel.co.uk

Cumberwell Park (1994)
Proprietary
Bradford-on-Avon BA15 2PQ
☎ **(01225) 863322**
📠 (01225) 868160
✉ enquiries@cumberwellpark.com
✍ Alistair James
🖥 www.cumberwellpark.com

Defence Academy (1953)
Shrivenham, Swindon SN6 8LA
☎ **(01793) 785725**
✉ golfclub.hq@da.mod.uk
✍ A Willmett (Mgr)
🖥 www.dagc.org.uk

Erlestoke (1992)
Proprietary
Erlestoke, Devizes SN10 5UB
☎ **(01380) 831069**
✉ info@erlestokegolfclub.co.uk
✍ R Goboroonsingh
🖥 www.erlestokegolfclub.co.uk

Hamptworth G&CC (1994)
Elmtree Farmhouse, Hamptworth Road, Landford SP5 2DU
☎ **(01794) 390155**
📠 (01794) 390022
✉ info@hamptworthgolf.co.uk
✍ Janet Facer
🖥 www.hamptworthgolf.co.uk

High Post (1922)
Great Durnford, Salisbury SP4 6AT
☎ **(01722) 782356**
📠 (01722) 782674
✉ manager@highpostgolfclub.co.uk
✍ P Hickling (01722) 782356
🖥 www.highpostgolfclub.co.uk

Highworth (1990)
Public
Swindon Road, Highworth SN6 7SJ
☎ **(01793) 766014**
✍ Geoff Marsh

Kingsdown (1880)
Kingsdown, Corsham SN13 8BS
☎ **(01225) 742530**
📠 (01225) 743472
✉ kingsdowngolfclub@btconnect.com
✍ N Newman (01225) 743472
🖥 www.kingsdowngolfclub.co.uk

Manor House (1992)
Proprietary
Castle Combe SN14 7JW
☎ **(01249) 782982**
📠 (01249) 782992
✉ enquiries@manorhousegolf.co.uk
✍ Stephen Browning
🖥 www.manorhousegolfclub.co.uk

Marlborough (1888)
The Common, Marlborough SN8 1DU
☎ **(01672) 512147**
📠 (01672) 513164
✉ gm@marlboroughgolfclub.co.uk
✍ L J Trute
🖥 www.marlboroughgolfclub.co.uk

Monkton Park Par Three (1965)
Pay and play
Chippenham SN15 3PP
☎ **(01249) 653928**
🖥 www.pitchandputtgolf.com

North Wilts (1890)
Bishops' Cannings, Devizes SN10 2LP
☎ **(01380) 860257**
📠 (01380) 860877
✉ secretary@northwiltsgolf.com
✍ Mrs P Stephenson
🖥 www.northwiltsgolf.com

Oaksey Park (1991)
Pay and play
Oaksey, Malmesbury SN16 9SB
☎ **(01666) 577995**
✉ info@oakseypark.co.uk
🖥 www.oakseyparkgolf.co.uk

Ogbourne Downs (1907)
Ogbourne St George, Marlborough SN8 1TB
☎ **(01672) 841327**
✉ office@ogbournedowns.co.uk
✍ Geoff Scott (01672) 841327
🖥 www.ogbournedowns.co.uk

Rushmore (1997)
Proprietary
Tollard Royal, Salisbury SP5 5QB
☎ **(01725) 516326**
📠 (01725) 516437
✉ golfmanager@rushmoreuk.com
✍ Declan Healy (Gen Mgr) (01725) 516391
🖥 www.rushmoregolfclub.co.uk

Salisbury & South Wilts (1888)
Netherhampton, Salisbury SP2 8PR
☎ **(01722) 742645 ext.1**
📠 (01722) 742676
✉ mail@salisburygolf.co.uk
✍ Alex Taylor (Secretary)
🖥 www.salisburygolf.co.uk

Shrivenham Park (1967)
Pay and play
Pennyhooks Lane, Shrivenham, Swindon SN6 8EX
☎ **(01793) 783853**

For key to symbols see page 717

✉ info@shrivenhampark.com
✍ G Platt (01793) 783853
🖥 www.shrivenhampark.com

Tidworth Garrison (1908)
Bulford Road, Tidworth SP9 7AF
☎ (01980) 842301 (Clubhouse)
📠 (01980) 842301
✉ secretary@tidworthgolfclub.co.uk
✍ RG Moan (01980) 842301
🖥 www.tidworthgolfclub.co.uk

Upavon (1912)
Douglas Avenue, Upavon SN9 6BQ
☎ (01980) 630787/630281
✉ play@upavongolfclub.co.uk
✍ L Mitchell
🖥 www.upavongolfclub.co.uk

West Wilts (1891)
Elm Hill, Warminster BA12 0AU
☎ (01985) 213133
✉ sec@westwiltsgolfclub.co.uk
✍ GN Morgan
🖥 www.westwiltsgolfclub.co.uk

Whitley (1993)
Pay and play
Corsham Road, Whitley, Melksham SN12 8EQ
☎ (01225) 790099
✉ info@whitleygolfclub.com
✍ Tom Nicholas (01225) 790099
🖥 www.whitleygolfclub.com

The Wiltshire (1991)
Proprietary
Vastern, Wootton Bassett, Swindon SN4 7PB
☎ (01793) 849999
📠 (01793) 849988
✉ reception@the-wiltshire.co.uk
✍ Jennifer Shah (Gen Mgr)
🖥 www.the-wiltshire.co.uk

Wrag Barn G&CC (1990)
Shrivenham Road, Highworth, Swindon SN6 7QQ
☎ (01793) 861327
📠 (01793) 861325
✉ manager@wragbarn.com
✍ T Lee
🖥 www.wragbarn.com

Worcestershire

Royal Worlington & Newmarket (1985)
Dagnell End Road, Redditch B98 9BE
☎ (01638) 712216 (Clubhouse)
✉ secretary@royalworlington.co.uk
✍ S Ballentine (01638) 717787
🖥 www.royalworlington.co.uk

Bank House Hotel G&CC (1992)
Bransford, Worcester WR6 5JD
☎ (01886) 833545
📠 (01886) 833545
✉ bransfordgolfclub@brook-hotels.co.uk

✍ Matt Nixon
🖥 www.brook-hotels.co.uk

Blackwell (1893)
Blackwell, Bromsgrove, Worcestershire B60 1PY
☎ (0121) 445 1994
📠 (0121) 445 4911
✉ secretary@blackwellgolfclub.com
✍ Finlay Clark
🖥 www.blackwellgolfclub.com

Brandhall (1906)
Public
Heron Road, Oldbury, Warley B68 8AQ
☎ (0121) 552 2195
📠 (0121) 552 1758
✉ john_robinson@sandwell.gov.uk
✍ J Robinson
🖥 www.slt@sandwell.gov.uk

Bromsgrove Golf Centre (1992)
Proprietary
Stratford Road, Bromsgrove B60 1LD
☎ (01527) 575886
📠 (01527) 570964
✉ enquiries@bromsgrovegolfcentre.com
✍ P Morris (Director) P Brothwood (Sec)
🖥 www.bromsgrovegolfcentre.com

Churchill & Blakedown (1926)
Churchill Lane, Blakedown, Kidderminster DY10 3NB
☎ (01562) 700018
✉ admin@churchillblakedowngolfclub.co.uk
✍ Trevor Hare
🖥 www.churchillblakedowngolfclub.co.uk

Cocks Moor Woods (1926)
Public
Alcester Road South, King's Heath, Birmingham, West Midlands B14 6ER
☎ (0121) 464 3584
✍ P J Ellison
🖥 www.golfbirmingham.co.uk

Droitwich G&CC (1897)
Ford Lane, Droitwich WR9 0BQ
☎ (01905) 774344
📠 (01905) 796503
✍ CS Thompson
🖥 www.droitwichgolfclub.co.uk

Dudley (1893)
Turners Hill, Rowley Regis B65 9DP
☎ (01384) 233877
📠 (01384) 233877
✉ secretary@dudleygolfclub.com
✍ W B Whitcombe
🖥 www.dudleygolfclub.com

Evesham (1894)
Craycombe Links, Fladbury, Pershore WR10 2QS
☎ (01386) 860395
✉ eveshamgolf@btopenworld.com

✍ Mr Jerry Cain
🖥 www.eveshamgolfclub.co.uk

Fulford Heath (1933)
Tanners Green Lane, Wythall, Birmingham B47 6BH
☎ (01564) 822806 (Clubhouse)
📠 (01564) 822629
✉ secretary@fulfordheathgolfclub.co.uk
✍ Mrs J Morris (01564) 824758
🖥 www.fulfordheathgolfclub.co.uk

Gay Hill (1913)
Hollywood Lane, Birmingham B47 5PP
☎ (0121) 430 8544
📠 (0121) 436 7796
✉ secretary@ghgc.org.uk
✍ Mrs D L O'Reilly (0121) 430 8544
🖥 www.ghgc.org.uk

Habberley (1924)
Low Habberley, Kidderminster DY11 5RF
☎ (01562) 745756
✉ info@habberleygolfclub.co.uk
✍ DS McDermott
🖥 www.habberleygolfclub.co.uk

Hagley (1980)
Proprietary
Wassell Grove, Hagley, Stourbridge DY9 9JW
☎ (01562) 883701
📠 (01562) 887518
✉ manager@hagleygc.freeserve.co.uk
✍ GF Yardley (01562) 883701
🖥 www.hagleygolfandcountryclub.co.uk

Halesowen (1906)
The Leasowes, Halesowen B62 8QF
☎ (0121) 501 3606
✉ office@halesowengc.co.uk
✍ Mrs N Heath
🖥 www.halesowengc.co.uk

Kidderminster (1909)
Russell Road, Kidderminster DY10 3HT
☎ (01562) 822303
📠 (01562) 827866
✉ secretary@thekidderminstergolfclub.com
✍ Malcolm Pritchard (Sec)
🖥 www.thekidderminstergolfclub.com

Kings Norton (1892)
Brockhill Lane, Weatheroak, Alvechurch, Birmingham B48 7ED
☎ (01564) 826789
📠 (01564) 826955
✉ info@kingsnortongolfclub.co.uk
✍ T Webb (Mgr)
🖥 www.kingsnortongolfclub.co.uk

Little Lakes (1975)
Lye Head, Bewdley, Worcester DY12 2UZ
☎ (01299) 266385
📠 (01299) 266398
✉ info@littlelakes.co.uk
✍ J Dean (01562) 741704
🖥 www.littlelakes.co.uk

Moseley   (1892)
Springfield Road, Kings Heath, Birmingham B14 7DX
- ☎ **(0121) 444 4957**
- 📠 (0121) 441 4662
- ✉ secretary@moseleygolfclub.co.uk
- ✍ Mr M W Wake
- 🖳 www.moseleygolf.co.uk

North Worcestershire
(1907)
Frankley Beeches Road, Northfield, Birmingham B31 5LP
- ☎ **(0121) 475 1047**
- 📠 (0121) 476 8681
- ✉ secretary@nwgolfclub.com
- ✍ C Overton

Ombersley Golf Club
(1991)
Pay and play
Bishopswood Road, Ombersley, Droitwich WR9 0LE
- ☎ **(01905) 620747**
- 📠 (01905) 620047
- ✉ enquiries@ombersleygolfclub.co.uk
- ✍ G Glenister (Gen Mgr)
- 🖳 www.ombersleygolfclub.co.uk

Perdiswell Park   (1978)
Pay and play
Bilford Road, Worcester WR3 8DX
- ☎ **(01905) 754668**
- 📠 (01905) 756608
- ✉ perdiswell@leisureconnection.co.uk
- ✍ B F Hodgetts (01905) 640456
- 🖳 www.harpersfitness.co.uk

Pitcheroak   (1973)
Public
Plymouth Road, Redditch B97 4PB
- ☎ **(01527) 541054**
- ✍ R Barnett

Ravenmeadow   (1995)
Hindlip Lane, Claines, Worcester WR3 8SA
- ☎ **(01905) 757525**
- 📠 (01905) 458876
- ✍ James Leaver (Mgr) (01905) 458876
- 🖳 info@ravenmeadowgolf.co.uk

Redditch   (1913)
Lower Grinsty, Green Lane, Callow Hill, Redditch B97 5PJ
- ☎ **(01527) 543079**
- 📠 (01527) 547413
- ✉ lee@redditchgolfclub.com
- ✍ W Kerr
- 🖳 www.redditchgolfclub.com

Rose Hill   (1921)
Public
Lickey Hills, Rednal, Birmingham B45 8RR
- ☎ **(0121) 453 3159**
- 📠 (0121) 457 8779
- ✉ mark.toombs@birmingham.gov.uk
- ✍ D C Walker
- 🖳 www.rosehill-golfclub.co.uk

Stourbridge   (1892)
Worcester Lane, Pedmore, Stourbridge DY8 2RB
- ☎ **(01384) 395566**
- 📠 (01384) 444660
- ✉ secretary@stourbridgegolfclub.co.uk
- ✍ Mr M Hughes
- 🖳 www.stourbridgegolfclub.co.uk

Tolladine   (1898)
The Fairway, Tolladine Road, Worcester WR4 9BA
- ☎ **(01905) 21074 (Clubhouse)**

The Vale   (1991)
Proprietary
Hill Furze Road, Bishampton, Pershore WR10 2LZ
- ☎ **(01386) 462781 ext 229**
- 📠 (01386) 462597
- ✉ clubmanager@thevalegolf.co.uk
- ✍ Simon Williams
- 🖳 www.thevalegolf.co.uk

Warley Woods   (1921)
Pay and play
Lightwoods Hill, Warley B67 5ED
- ☎ **(0121) 429 2440**
- 📠 (0121) 420 4430
- ✉ golfshop@warleywoods.org.uk
- 🖳 www.warleywoods.org.uk

Wharton Park   (1992)
Proprietary
Longbank, Bewdley DY12 2QW
- ☎ **(01299) 405222 (restaurant)**
- 📠 (01299) 405121
- ✉ enquiries@whartonpark.co.uk
- ✍ Kevin Fincher
- 🖳 www.whartonpark.co.uk

Worcester G&CC   (1898)
Boughton Park, Worcester WR2 4EZ
- ☎ **(01905) 422555**
- 📠 (01905) 749090
- ✉ worcestergcc@btconnect.com
- ✍ PA Tredwell (01905) 422555
- 🖳 www.worcestergcc.co.uk

Worcestershire   (1879)
Wood Farm, Malvern Wells WR14 4PP
- ☎ **(01684) 575992**
- 📠 (01684) 893334
- ✉ secretary@worcsgolfclub.co.uk
- ✍ Terry Smith (Sec)
- 🖳 www.worcsgolfclub.co.uk

Wyre Forest Golf Centre
Pay and play
Zortech Avenue, Kidderminster DY11 7EX
- ☎ **(01299) 822682**
- ✉ chris@wyreforestgolf.com

Yorkshire (East)

Allerthorpe Park   (1994)
Proprietary
Allerthorpe, York YO42 4RL
- ☎ **(01759) 306686**
- 📠 (01759) 305106
- ✉ enquiries@allerthorpeparkgolfclub.com
- ✍ Alex Drinkall/Jan Drinkall
- 🖳 www.allerthorpeparkgolfclub.com

Beverley & East Riding
(1889)
The Westwood, Beverley HU17 8RG
- ☎ **(01482) 868757**
- 📠 (01482) 868757
- ✉ golf@beverleygolfclub.karoo.co.uk
- ✍ A Ashby (01482) 869519
- 🖳 www.beverleygolfclub.co.uk

Boothferry   (1982)
Proprietary
Spaldington Lane, Spaldington, Nr Howden DN14 7NG
- ☎ **(01430) 430364**
- ✉ info@boothferrygolfclub.co.uk
- ✍ Ben McAllister
- 🖳 www.boothferrygolfclub.co.uk

Bridlington   (1905)
Belvedere Road, Bridlington YO15 3NA
- ☎ **(01262) 672092/606367**
- ✉ enquiries@bridlingtongolfclub.co.uk
- ✍ ARA Howarth (01262) 606367
- 🖳 www.bridlingtongolfclub.co.uk

The Bridlington Links
(1993)
Pay and play
Flamborough Road, Marton, Bridlington YO15 1DW
- ☎ **(01262) 401584**
- 📠 (01262) 401702
- ✉ bridlingtonlinks@hotmail.co.uk
- ✍ Wayne Stephens (Sec)
- 🖳 www.bridlington-links.co.uk

Brough   (1893)
Cave Road, Brough HU15 1HB
- ☎ **(01482) 667291**
- 📠 (01482) 669873
- ✉ gt@brough-golfclub.co.uk
- ✍ G W Townhill (Professional)
- 🖳 www.brough-golfclub.co.uk

Cave Castle   (1989)
South Cave, Nr Brough HU15 2EU
- ☎ **(01430) 421286**
- 📠 (01430) 421118
- ✉ admin@cavecastlegolf.co.uk
- ✍ J Simpson (Admin)
- 🖳 www.cavecastlegolf.co.uk

Cherry Burton   (1993)
Proprietary
Leconfield Road, Cherry Burton, Beverley HU17 7RB
- ☎ **(01964) 550924**
- ✉ info@cherryburtongolf.co.uk
- ✍ John Gray 01964 550924
- 🖳 cherryburtongolf.co.uk

Cottingham   (1994)
Proprietary
Woodhill Way, Cottingham, Hull HU16 5SW
- ☎ **(01482) 846030**

(01482) 845932
✉ info@cottinghamparks.co.uk
✍ RJ Wiles (01482) 846030
▤ www.cottinghamparks.co.uk

Driffield   (1923)
Sunderlandwick, Driffield YO25 9AD
☎ **(01377) 253116**
▢ (01377) 240599
✉ info@driffieldgolfclub.co.uk
✍ Maxine Moorhouse (Assist. Sec)
▤ www.driffieldgolfclub.co.uk

Flamborough Head   (1931)
Lighthouse Road, Flamborough, Bridlington
YO15 1AR
☎ **(01262) 850333**
✉ enquiries
  @flamboroughheadgolfclub.co.uk
✍ GS Thornton (Sec)
▤ www.flamboroughheadgolfclub
  .co.uk

Ganstead Park   (1976)
Proprietary
Longdales Lane, Coniston, Hull HU11 4LB
☎ **(01482) 811280 (Steward)**
▢ (01482) 817754
✉ secretary@gansteadpark.co.uk
✍ M Milner (01482) 817754
▤ www.gansteadpark.co.uk

Hainsworth Park   (1983)
Brandesburton, Driffield YO25 8RT
☎ **(01964) 542362**
▢ (01964) 544666
✉ sec@hainsworthparkgolfclub.co.uk
✍ A Higgins, BW Atkin (Prop)
▤ www.hainsworthparkgolfclub.co.uk

Hessle   (1898)
Westfield Road, Raywell, Cottingham
HU16 5ZA
☎ **(01482) 306840**
▢ (01482) 652679
✉ secretary@hesslegolfclub.co.uk
✍ Paul Haddon
▤ www.hesslegolfclub.co.uk

Hornsea   (1898)
Rolston Road, Hornsea HU18 1XG
☎ **(01964) 532020**
▢ (01964) 532080
✉ info@hornseagolfclub.co.uk
▤ www.hornseagolfclub.co.uk

Hull   (1904)
The Hall, 27 Packman Lane, Kirk Ella, Hull
HU10 7TJ
☎ **(01482) 660970**
▢ (01482) 660978
✉ secretary@hullgolfclub1921.karoo
  .co.uk
✍ DJ Crossley
▤ www.hullgolfclub.com

KP Club   (1995)
Proprietary
Pocklington, York, East Yorkshire YO42 1UF
☎ **(01759) 303090**
✉ info@kpclub.co.uk
✍ Aaron Pheasant
▤ www.kpclub.co.uk

Springhead Park   (1930)
Public
Willerby Road, Hull HU5 5JE
☎ **(01482) 656309**
✍ P Smith

Sutton Park   (1935)
Public
Salthouse Road, Hull HU8 9HF
☎ **(01482) 374242**
▢ (01482) 701428
✍ S J Collins

Withernsea   (1909)
Egroms Lane, Withernsea HU19 2NA
☎ **(01964) 612258 (Clubhouse)**
▢ (01964) 612078
✉ info@withernseagolfclub.co.uk
✍ S Dale (Admin)
▤ www.withernseagolfclub.co.uk

Yorkshire (North)

Aldwark Manor   (1978)
Aldwark, Alne, York YO61 1UF
☎ **(01347) 838353**
▢ (01347) 833991
✍ A Grindlay (01347) 838353
▤ www.Qhotels.co.uk

Ampleforth College   (1972)
Castle Drive, Gilling East, York
YO62 4HP
☎ **(01439) 788212**
▢ (01904) 762012
✉ sec@ampleforthgolf.co.uk
✍ Dr M Wilson (01904) 768861
▤ www.ampleforthgolf.co.uk

Bedale   (1894)
Leyburn Road, Bedale DL8 1EZ
☎ **(01677) 422451**
▢ (01677) 427143
✉ office@bedalegolfclub.com
✍ Mike Mayman (01677) 422451
▤ www.bedalegolfclub.com

Bentham   (1922)
Proprietary
Robin Lane, Bentham, Lancaster LA2 7AG
☎ **(015242) 62455**
✉ golf@benthamgolfclub.co.uk
✍ C Cousins (Pro)
▤ www.benthamgolfclub.co.uk

Catterick   (1930)
Leyburn Road, Catterick Garrison DL9 3QE
☎ **(01748) 833268**
✉ secretary@catterickgolfclub.co.uk
✍ M Young
▤ www.catterickgolfclub.co.uk

Cleveland   (1887)
Majuba Road, Redcar TS10 5BJ
☎ **(01642) 471798**
▢ (01642) 487619
✉ majuba@btconnect.com
▤ www.clevelandgolfclub.co.uk

Crimple Valley   (1976)
Pay and play
Hookstone Wood Road, Harrogate
HG2 8PN
☎ **(01423) 883485**
▢ (01423) 881018
✍ Paul Johnson

Drax   (1989)
Drax, Selby YO8 8PQ
☎ **(01757) 617228**
▢ (01757) 617228
✉ draxgolfclub@btinternet.com
✍ Denise Smith
▤ www.draxgolfclub.com

Easingwold   (1930)
Stillington Road, Easingwold, York
YO61 3ET
☎ **(01347) 822474**
▢ (01347) 823948
✉ enquiries@easingwoldgolfclub
  .co.uk
✍ C H Bailey
▤ www.easingwoldgolfclub.co.uk

Filey   (1897)
West Ave, Filey YO14 9BQ
☎ **(01723) 513293**
✉ secretary@fileygolfclub.com
✍ Mrs V Gilbank
▤ www.fileygolfclub.com

Forest of Galtres   (1993)
Proprietary
Moorlands Road, Skelton, York YO32 2RF
☎ **(01904) 766198**
▢ (01904) 769400
✉ secretary@forestofgaltres.co.uk
✍ Mrs SJ Procter
▤ www.forestofgaltres.co.uk

Forest Park   (1991)
Proprietary
Stockton-on Forest, York YO32 9UW
☎ **(01904) 400425**
✉ admin@forestparkgolfclub.co.uk
✍ S Crossley (01904) 400688
▤ www.forestparkgolfclub.co.uk

Fulford (York) Golf Club
(1906)
Heslington Lane, York YO10 5DY
☎ **(01904) 413579**
▢ (01904) 416918
✉ info@fulfordgolfclub.co.uk
✍ GS Pearce
▤ www.fulfordgolfclub.co.uk

Ganton   (1891)
Station Road, Ganton, Scarborough
YO12 4PA
☎ **(01944) 710329**
▢ (01944) 710922
✉ secretary@gantongolfclub.com
✍ PE Ware
▤ www.gantongolfclub.com

Harrogate   (1892)
Forest Lane Head, Harrogate HG2 7TF
☎ **(01423) 863158 (Clubhouse)**
▢ (01423) 798310

✉ secretary@harrogate-gc.co.uk
✍ Ruth Skaife-Clarke
🖥 www.harrogate-gc.co.uk

Heworth (1911)
Muncaster House, Muncastergate, York YO31 9JY
☎ (01904) 424618
✉ golf@heworth-gc.fsnet.co.uk
🖥 www.heworthgolfclub.co.uk

Hunley Hall (1993)
Brotton, Saltburn TS12 2FT
☎ (01287) 676216
🖳 (01287) 678250
✉ enquiries@hhgc.co.uk
✍ G Briffa (01287) 676216
🖥 www.hhgc.co.uk

Kirkbymoorside (1951)
Manor Vale, Kirkbymoorside, York YO62 6EG
☎ (01751) 431525
🖳 (01751) 433190
✉ enqs@kirkbymoorsidegolf.co.uk
✍ Mrs R Rivis
🖥 www.kirkbymoorsidegolf.co.uk

Knaresborough (1920)
Boroughbridge Road, Knaresborough HG5 0QQ
☎ (01423) 862690
🖳 (01423) 869345
✉ secretary@kgc.uk.com
✍ M Taylor
🖥 www.knaresboroughgolfclub
.co.uk

Malton & Norton (1910)
Welham Park, Welham Road, Norton, Malton YO17 9QE
☎ (01653) 697912
🖳 (01653) 697844
✉ maltonandnorton@btconnect.com
✍ Mr N J Redman
🖥 www.maltonandnortongolfclub
.co.uk

Masham (1895)
Burnholme, Swinton Road, Masham, Ripon HG4 4NS
☎ (01765) 688054
✉ info@mashamgolfclub.co.
✍ S Blades
🖥 www.mashamgolfclub.co.

Middlesbrough (1908)
Brass Castle Lane, Marton, Middlesbrough TS8 9EE
☎ (01642) 311515
🖳 (01642) 319607
✉ enquiries@middlesbroughgolfclub
.co.uk
✍ Ian Jackson (Mgr/Sec)
🖥 www.middlesbroughgolfclub.co.uk

Middlesbrough Municipal (1977)
Public
Ladgate Lane, Middlesbrough TS5 7YZ
☎ (01642) 315533
🖳 (01642) 300726

✉ maurice_gormley@middlesbrough
.gov.uk
✍ M Gormley (Mgr)
🖥 www.middlesbroughcouncil.gov.uk

Oakdale (1914)
Oakdale, Oakdale Glen, Harrogate HG1 2LN
☎ (01423) 567162
🖳 (01423) 536030
✉ manager@oakdalegolfclub.co.uk
✍ MJ Cross
🖥 www.oakdalegolfclub.co.uk

The Oaks (1996)
Proprietary
Aughton Common, Aughton, York YO42 4PW
☎ (01757) 288001 (Clubhouse)
✉ sheila@theoaksgolfclub.co.uk
🖥 www.theoaksgolfclub.co.uk

Pannal (1906)
Follifoot Road, Pannal, Harrogate HG3 1ES
☎ (01423) 872628
🖳 (01423) 870043
✉ secretary@pannalgolfclub.co.uk
✍ NG Douglas
🖥 www.pannalgolfclub.co.uk

Pike Hills (1904)
Tadcaster Road, Askham Bryan, York YO23 3UW
☎ (01904) 700797
🖳 (01904) 700797
✉ secretary@pikehillsgolfclub.co.uk
✍ David Winterburn (01904) 700797
🖥 www.pikehillsgolfclub.co.uk

Richmond (1892)
Bend Hagg, Richmond DL10 5EX
☎ (01748) 825319
🖳 (01748) 821709
✉ secretary@richmondyorksgolfclub
.co.uk
✍ AE Lancaster (01748) 823231
🖥 www.richmondyorksgolfclub.co.uk

Ripon City Golf Club (1907)
Palace Road, Ripon HG4 3HH
☎ (01765) 603640
🖳 (01765) 692880
✉ secretary@riponcitygolfclub.com
✍ MJ Doig MBE
🖥 www.riponcitygolfclub.co.uk

Romanby Golf and Country Club (1993)
Pay and play
Yafforth Road, Northallerton DL7 0PE
☎ (01609) 778855
✉ info@romanby.com
🖥 www.romanby.com

Rudding Park (1995)
Pay and play
Rudding Park, Harrogate HG3 1JH
☎ (01423) 872100
✉ sales@ruddingpark.com
🖥 www.ruddingpark.com

Saltburn (1894)
Hob Hill, Saltburn-by-the-Sea TS12 1NJ
☎ (01287) 622812
🖳 (01287) 625988
✉ secretary@saltburngolf.co.uk
✍ Mrs J Annis
🖥 www.saltburngolf.co.uk

Sandburn Hall (2005)
Proprietary
Scotchman Lane, Flaxton, York YO60 7RB
☎ (01904) 469922
🖳 (01904) 469923
✉ alistair@sandburnhall.co.uk
✍ Alistair Nicol (Golf Mgr)
🖥 www.sandburnhall.co.uk

Scarborough North Cliff (1909)
North Cliff Avenue, Burniston Road, Scarborough YO12 6PP
☎ (01723) 355397
🖳 (01723) 362134
✉ info@northcliffgolfclub.co.uk
✍ Mr J Barnfather
🖥 www.northcliffgolfclub.co.uk

Scarborough South Cliff (1902)
Deepdale Avenue, Scarborough YO11 2UE
☎ (01723) 360522
🖳 (01723) 360523
✉ clubsecretary@southcliffgolfclub
.com
✍ D Roberts
🖥 www.southcliffgolfclub.com

Scarthingwell (1993)
Scarthingwell, Tadcaster LS24 9DG
☎ (01937) 557878
🖳 (01937) 557909
✉ ben.burlingham
@scarthingwellgolfcourse.co.uk
✍ Ben Burlingham
🖥 www.scarthingwellgolfcourse.co.uk

Selby (1907)
Mill Lane, Brayton, Selby YO8 9LD
☎ (01757) 228622
🖳 (01757) 228622
✉ secretary@selbygolfclub.co.uk
✍ Sally Mihale
🖥 www.selbygolfclub.co.uk

Settle (1895)
Giggleswick, Settle BD24 0DH
☎ (01729) 825288
✉ info@settlegolfclub.co.uk
✍ Alan Wright (07801) 550 358
🖥 www.settlegolfclub.co.uk

Skipton (1893)
Short Lee Lane, Skipton BD23 3LF
☎ (01756) 793257 Pro (01756) 795657 Office
✉ enquiries@skiptongolfclub.co.uk
✍ Beverley Keyworth
🖥 www.skiptongolfclub.co.uk

Teesside (1900)
Acklam Road, Thornaby TS17 7JS
☎ (01642) 676249

For key to symbols see page 717

☐ (01642) 676252
✉ teessidegolfclub@btconnect.com
✍ M Fleming (01642) 616516
▤ www.teessidegolfclub.co.uk

Thirsk & Northallerton
(1914)
Thornton-le-Street, Thirsk YO7 4AB
☎ **(01845) 525115**
☐ (01845) 525119
✉ secretary@tngc.co.uk
✍ Secretary (01845) 525115 ext 1
▤ www.tngc.co.uk

Whitby   (1892)
Sandsend Road, Low Straggleton, Whitby YO21 3SR
☎ **(01947) 600660**
☐ (01947) 600660
✉ office@whitbygolfclub.co.uk
✍ T Mason
▤ www.whitbygolfclub.co.uk

Wilton   (1952)
Wilton, Redcar, Cleveland TS10 4QY
☎ **(01642) 465265**
✉ secretary@wiltongolfclub.co.uk
✍ C Harvey (01642) 465265
▤ www.wiltongolfclub.co.uk

York   (1890)
Lords Moor Lane, Strensall, York YO32 5XF
☎ **(01904) 491840**
☐ (01904) 491852
✉ secretary@yorkgolfclub.co.uk
✍ MJ Wells
▤ www.yorkgolfclub.co.uk

Yorkshire (South)

Abbeydale   (1895)
Twentywell Rise, Twentywell Lane, Dore, Sheffield S17 4QA
☎ **(0114) 236 0763**
☐ (0114) 236 0762
✉ abbeygolf@btconnect.com
✍ Mrs JL Wing (Office Mgr)
▤ www.abbeydalegolfclub.co.uk

Barnsley   (1925)
Public
Wakefield Road, Staincross, Barnsley S75 6JZ
☎ **(01226) 382856**
✉ barnsleygolfclub@btconnect.com
✍ Trevor Jones
▤ www.barnsleygolfclub.co.uk

Bawtry   (1974)
Cross Lane, Austerfield, Doncaster DN10 6RF
☎ **(01302) 711409**
☐ (01302) 711445
✉ enquiries@bawtrygolfclub.co.uk
▤ www.bawtrygolfclub.co.uk

Beauchief   (1925)
Public
Abbey Lane, Beauchief, Sheffield S8 0DB
☎ **(0114) 236 7274**

✉ e-mail@beauchiefgolfclub.co.uk
✍ Mrs B Fryer
▤ www.beauchiefgolfclub.co.uk

Birley Wood   (1974)
Public
Birley Lane, Sheffield S12 3BP
☎ **(0114) 264 7262**
✉ birleysec@hotmail.com
▤ www.birleywood.free-online.co.uk

Concord Park   (1952)
Pay and play
Shiregreen Lane, Sheffield S5 6AE
☎ **(0114) 257 7378**
✉ concordparkgc@tiscali.co.uk

Crookhill Park   (1974)
Public
Carr Lane, Conisborough, Doncaster DN12 2AH
☎ **(01709) 862979**
✉ secretary@crookhillpark.co.uk
✍ A Goddard (Sec)
▤ www.crookhillpark.co.uk

Doncaster   (1894)
Bawtry Road, Bessacarr, Doncaster DN4 7PD
☎ **(01302) 865632**
☐ (01302) 865994
✉ doncastergolf@aol.com
✍ Malcolm Macphee
▤ www.doncastergolfclub.co.uk

Doncaster Town Moor
(1895)
Bawtry Road, Belle Vue, Doncaster DN4 5HU
☎ **(01302) 533167**
☐ (01302) 533448
✉ dtmgc@btconnect.com
✍ Mike Pears
▤ www.doncastertownmoorgolfclub .co.uk

Dore & Totley   (1913)
Bradway Road, Bradway, Sheffield S17 4QR
☎ **(0114) 236 0492**
☐ (0114) 235 3436
✉ dore.totley@btconnect.com
✍ Mrs SD Haslehurst (0114) 236 9872
▤ www.doreandtotleygolfclub.co.uk

Grange Park   (1972)
Pay and play
Upper Wortley Road, Kimberworth, Rotherham S61 2SJ
☎ **(01709) 558884**

Hallamshire   (1897)
Sandygate, Sheffield S10 4LA
☎ **(0114) 230 2153**
☐ (0114) 230 5413
✉ secretary@hallamshiregolfclub.com
✍ R Hill (0114) 230 2153
▤ www.hallamshiregolfclub.co.uk

Hallowes   (1892)
Dronfield, Sheffield S18 1UR
☎ **(01246) 413734**

☐ (01246) 413753
✉ secretary@hallowesgolfclub.org
✍ N Ogden
▤ www.hallowesgolfclub.org

Hickleton   (1909)
Hickleton, Doncaster DN5 7BE
☎ **(01709) 896081**
✉ info@hickletongolfclub.co.uk
✍ Susan Leach (Sec)
▤ www.hickletongolfclub.co.uk

Hillsborough   (1920)
Worrall Road, Sheffield S6 4BE
☎ **(0114) 234 9151 (Secretary)**
☐ (0114) 229 4105
✉ admin@hillsboroughgolfclub.co.uk
✍ Lewis Horsman (0114) 234 9151
▤ www.hillsboroughgolfclub.co.uk

Lees Hall   (1907)
Hemsworth Road, Norton, Sheffield S8 8LL
☎ **(0114) 255 4402**
✉ secretary@leeshallgolfclub.co.uk
▤ www.leeshallgolfclub.co.uk

Lindrick   (1891)
Lindrick Common, Worksop, Notts S81 8BH
☎ **(01909) 475282**
☐ (01909) 488685
✉ briannoble@lindrickgolfclub.co.uk
✍ Mr Brian Noble (01909) 475282
▤ www.lindrickgolfclub.co.uk

Owston Hall (the Robin Hood golf course)   (1996)
Proprietary
Owston Hall, Owston, Doncaster DN6 9JF
☎ **(01302) 722800**
☐ (01302) 728885
✉ proshop@owstonhall.com
✍ Gerry Briggs
▤ www.owstonhall.com

Owston Park   (1988)
Public
Owston Lane, Owston, Carcroft DN6 8EF
☎ **(01302) 330821**
✉ michael.parker@foremostgolf.com
✍ MT Parker
▤ www.owstonparkgolfcourse.co.uk

Phoenix   (1932)
Pavilion Lane, Brinsworth, Rotherham S60 5PA
☎ **(01709) 363788**
☐ (01709) 363788
✉ secretary@phoenixgolfclub.co.uk
✍ I Gregory (01709) 363788
▤ www.phoenixgolfclub.co.uk

Renishaw Park   (1911)
Golf House, Mill Lane, Renishaw, Sheffield S21 3UZ
☎ **(01246) 432044**
☐ (01246) 432116
✉ secretary@renishawparkgolf .co.uk
✍ Mark Nelson
▤ www.renishawparkgolf.co.uk

Rother Valley Golf Centre
(1997)
Proprietary
Mansfield Road, Wales Bar, Sheffield S26 5PQ
- ☎ **(0114) 247 3000**
- 🖥 (0114) 247 6000
- ✉ info@rothervalleygolfcentre.co.uk
- ✍ Mr R Hanson
- 🖥 www.rothervalleygolfcentre.co.uk

Rotherham   (1902)
Thrybergh Park, Rotherham S65 4NU
- ☎ **(01709) 850466**
- 🖥 (01709) 859517
- ✉ manager@rotherhamgolfclub.com
- 🖥 www.rotherhamgolfclub.com

Roundwood   (1976)
Green Lane, Rawmarsh, Rotherham S62 6LA
- ☎ **(01709) 826061**
- 🖥 (01709) 523478
- ✉ golf.secretary@roundwoodgolfclub.co.uk
- ✍ G Billups (01709) 525208
- 🖥 www.roundwoodgolfclub.co.uk

Sandhill   (1993)
Proprietary
Little Houghton, Barnsley S72 0HW
- ☎ **(01226) 753444**
- 🖥 (01226) 753444
- ✉ steven.gavin409@googlemail.com
- ✍ S Gavin (01226) 780025
- 🖥 www.sandhillgolfclub.co.uk

Sheffield Transport
(1923)
Meadow Head, Sheffield S8 7RE
- ☎ **(0114) 237 3216**

Silkstone   (1893)
Field Head, Elmhirst Lane, Silkstone, Barnsley S75 4LD
- ☎ **(01226) 790328**
- 🖥 (01226) 794902
- ✉ silkstonegolf@hotmail.co.uk
- ✍ Alan Cook
- 🖥 www.silkstone-golf-club.co.uk

Sitwell Park   (1913)
Shrogs Wood Road, Rotherham S60 4BY
- ☎ **(01709) 541046**
- 🖥 (01709) 703637
- ✉ secretary@sitwellgolf.co.uk
- ✍ S G Bell
- 🖥 www.sitwellgolf.co.uk

Stocksbridge & District
(1924)
Royd Lane, Deepcar, Sheffield S36 2RZ
- ☎ **(0114) 288 7479/288 2003**
- 🖥 (0114) 283 1460
- ✉ stocksbridgegolf@live.co.uk
- ✍ Mrs A Methley (0114) 288 2003
- 🖥 www.stocksbridgeanddistrict golfclub.com

Styrrup Hall   (2000)
Proprietary
Main Street, Styrrup, Doncaster DN11 8NB
- ☎ **(01302) 751112 (Golf) 759933 (Clubhouse)**
- 🖥 (01302) 750622
- ✉ office@styrrupgolf.co.uk
- ✍ Dianne Stokoe (Sec/Mgr)
- 🖥 www.styrrupgolf.co.uk

Tankersley Park   (1907)
Park Lane, High Green, Sheffield S35 4LG
- ☎ **(0114) 246 8247**
- 🖥 (0114) 245 7818
- ✉ secretary@tpgc.freeserve.co.uk
- ✍ A Brownhill (0114) 246 8247
- 🖥 www.tankersleyparkgolfclub.org.uk

Thorne   (1980)
Pay and play
Kirton Lane, Thorne, Doncaster DN8 5RJ
- ☎ **(01405) 815173 (bookings 01405 812084)**
- 🖥 (01405) 741899
- ✉ carolinehighfield@live.co.uk
- ✍ E Highfield (Golf Shop)
- 🖥 www.thornegolf.co.uk

Tinsley Park   (1920)
Public
High Hazels Park, Darnall, Sheffield S9 4PE
- ☎ **(0114) 244 8974**
- ✍ Wayne Yellott (Professional)
- 🖥 www.tinsleyparkgolfcourse.co.uk

Wath   (1904)
Abdy Rawmarsh, Rotherham S62 7SJ
- ☎ **(01709) 878609**
- 🖥 (01709) 877097
- ✉ golf@wathgolfclub.co.uk
- ✍ M Godfrey (01709) 878609 ext 1
- 🖥 www.wathgolfclub.co.uk

Wheatley   (1914)
Armthorpe Road, Doncaster DN2 5QB
- ☎ **(01302) 831655**
- 🖥 (01302) 812736
- ✉ secretary@wheatleygolfclub.co.uk
- ✍ Ken Gosden
- 🖥 www.wheatleygolfclub.co.uk

Wortley   (1894)
Hermit Hill Lane, Wortley, Sheffield S35 7DF
- ☎ **(0114) 288 8469**
- 🖥 (0114) 288 8488
- ✉ wortley.golfclub@btconnect.com
- ✍ Roy Cooke
- 🖥 www.wortleygolfclub.co.uk

Yorkshire (West)

The Alwoodley   (1907)
Wigton Lane, Alwoodley, Leeds LS17 8SA
- ☎ **(0113) 268 1680**
- ✉ alwoodley@btconnect.com
- ✍ Mrs J Slater
- 🖥 www.alwoodley.co.uk

Bagden Hall Hotel   (1993)
Wakefield Road, Scissett HD8 9LE
- ☎ **(01484) 865330**

Baildon   (1896)
Moorgate, Baildon, Shipley BD17 5PP
- ☎ **(01274) 584266**
- ✉ secretary@baildongolfclub.com
- ✍ J A Cooley (01274) 584266
- 🖥 www.baildongolfclub.com

Ben Rhydding   (1947)
High Wood, Ben Rhydding, Ilkley LS9 8SB
- ☎ **(01943) 608759**
- ✉ secretary@benrhyddinggc.freeserve.co.uk
- ✍ J D B Watts
- 🖥 www.benrhyddinggolfclub.com

Bingley St Ives   (1931)
St Ives Estate, Bingley BD16 1AT
- ☎ **(01274) 562436**
- 🖥 (01274) 511788
- ✉ secretary@bingleystivesgc.co.uk
- ✍ RA Adams
- 🖥 www.bingleystivesgc.co.uk

Bracken Ghyll   (1993)
Skipton Road, Addingham, Ilkley LS29 0SL
- ☎ **(01943) 831207**
- 🖥 (01943) 839453
- ✉ office@brackenghyll.co.uk
- ✍ Geoff Cooke OBE
- 🖥 www.brackenghyll.co.uk

The Bradford Golf Club
(1891)
Hawksworth Lane, Guiseley, Leeds LS20 8NP
- ☎ **(01943) 875570**
- ✉ secretary@bradfordgolfclub.co.uk
- ✍ James Washington
- 🖥 www.bradfordgolfclub.co.uk

Bradford Moor   (1906)
Scarr Hall, Pollard Lane, Bradford BD2 4RW
- ☎ **(01274) 771716**
- ✉ bfdmoorgc@hotmail.co.uk
- ✍ C P Bedford (01274) 771693
- 🖥 www.bradfordmoorgolfclub.co.uk

Bradley Park   (1978)
Public
Bradley Road, Huddersfield HD2 1PZ
- ☎ **(01484) 223772**
- 🖥 (01484) 451613
- ✉ parnellreilly@pgabroadband.com
- ✍ Derek M Broadbent
- 🖥 www.bradleyparkgolfclub.com

Branshaw   (1912)
Branshaw Moor, Oakworth, Keighley BD22 7ES
- ☎ **(01535) 643235**
- 🖥 (01535) 643235
- ✉ enquiries@branshawgolfclub.co.uk
- ✍ Simon Jowitt
- 🖥 www.branshawgolfclub.co.uk

Calverley   (1980)
Woodhall Lane, Pudsey LS28 5QY
- ☎ **(0113) 256 9244**
- 📠 (0113) 256 4362
- 📧 calverleygolf@btconnect.com
- ✎ N Wendel-Jones (Mgr)

Castlefields   (1903)
Rastrick Common, Brighouse HD6 3HL
- 📧 secretary@castlefieldsgolfclub
  .co.uk
- ✎ David Bartliff
- 📱 www.castlefieldsgolfclub.co.uk

City Golf Course   (1997)
Pay and play
*Red Cote Lane, Kirkstall Road, Leeds
LS4 2AW*
- ☎ **(0113) 263 3030**
- 📠 (0113) 263 3044
- ✎ P Cole (Mgr)

City of Wakefield   (1936)
Public
*Lupset Park, Horbury Road, Wakefield
WF2 8QS*
- ☎ **(01924) 367442**

Clayton   (1906)
*Thornton View Road, Clayton, Bradford
BD14 6JX*
- ☎ **(01274) 880047**
- 📧 tking@otto-uk.com
- 📱 www.claytongolfclub.co.uk

Cleckheaton & District
    (1900)
*483 Bradford Road, Cleckheaton
BD19 6BU*
- ☎ **(01274) 851266 (Secretary)**
- 📠 (01274) 871382
- 📧 info@cleckheatongolfclub.co.uk
- ✎ Dick Guiver
- 📱 www.cleckheatongolfclub.fsnet.com

Cookridge Hall   (1997)
Proprietary
*Cookridge Lane, Cookridge, Leeds
LS16 7NL*
- ☎ **(0113) 230 0641**
- 📠 (0113) 203 0198
- 📧 info@cookridgehall.co.uk
- ✎ Gary Day
- 📱 www.cookridgehall.co.uk

Crosland Heath   (1914)
*Felks Stile Road, Crosland Heath,
Huddersfield HD4 7AF*
- ☎ **(01484) 653216**
- 📠 (01484) 461079
- 📧 golf@croslandheath.co.uk
- ✎ S Robinson
- 📱 www.croslandheath.co.uk

Crow Nest Park   (1995)
*Coach Road, Hove Edge, Brighouse
HD6 2LN*
- ☎ **(01484) 401121**
- 📧 info@crownestgolf.co.uk
- ✎ L Holmes
- 📱 www.crownestgolf.co.uk

De Vere Oulton Park Golf
    Club   (1990)
Public
*Rothwell Lane, Oulton, Leeds, West
Yorkshire LS26 8HN*
- ☎ **(0113) 282 3152**
- 📠 (0113) 282 6290
- ✎ A Cooper (Mgr)

Dewsbury District   (1891)
*The Pinnacle, Sands Lane, Mirfield
WF14 8HJ*
- ☎ **(01924) 492399**
- 📠 (01924) 491928
- 📧 info@dewsburygolf.co.uk
- ✎ A M Thorpe
- 📱 www.dewsburygolf.co.uk

East Bierley   (1928)
*South View Road, Bierley, Bradford
BD4 6PP*
- ☎ **(01274) 681023**
- 📧 rjwelch@talktalk.net
- ✎ RJ Welch (01274) 683666

Elland   (1910)
*Hammerstone Leach Lane, Hullen Edge,
Elland HX5 0TA*
- ☎ **(01422) 372505**
- 📧 ellandgolfclub@ellandgolfclub
  .plus.com
- ✎ PA Green (01422) 251431
- 📱 www.ellandgolfclub.plus.com

Fardew   (1993)
Pay and play
*Nursery Farm, Carr Lane, East Morton,
Keighley BD20 5RY*
- ☎ **(01274) 561229**
- 📧 davidheaton@btconnect.com
- ✎ A Stevens
- 📱 www.fardewgolfclub.co.uk

Ferrybridge   (2002)
*PO Box 39, Stranglands Lane, Knottingley
WF11 8SQ*
- ☎ **(01977) 884165**
- 📠 (01977) 884001
- 📧 Trevor.Ellis@Scottish-southern
- ✎ TD Ellis

Fulneck   (1892)
Fulneck, Pudsey LS28 8NT
- ☎ **(0113) 256 5191**
- 📧 fulneckgolf@aol.com
- ✎ Mr S Tempest (Hon Sec)
- 📱 www.fulneckgolfclub.co.uk

Garforth   (1913)
Long Lane, Garforth, Leeds LS25 2DS
- ☎ **(0113) 286 3308**
- 📠 (0113) 286 3308
- 📧 garforthgcltd@lineone.net
- ✎ D R Carlisle
- 📱 www.garforthgolfclub.co.uk

Gotts Park   (1933)
Public
*Armley Ridge Road, Armley, Leeds
LS12 2QX*
- ☎ **(0113) 234 2019**
- ✎ M Gill (0113) 256 2994

Halifax   (1895)
Union Lane, Ogden, Halifax HX2 8XR
- ☎ **(01422) 244171**
- 📠 (01422) 241459
- 📧 halifax.golfclub@virgin.net
- 📱 www.halifaxgolfclub.co.uk

Halifax Bradley Hall   (1907)
Holywell Green, Halifax HX4 9AN
- ☎ **(01422) 374108**
- 📧 bhgc@gotadsl.co.uk
- ✎ Mrs J Teale
- 📱 www.bradleyhallgolf.co.uk

Halifax West End   (1906)
*Paddock Lane, Highroad Well, Halifax
HX2 0NT*
- ☎ **(01422) 341878**
- 📠 (01422) 410540
- 📧 westendgc@btinternet.com
- ✎ S J Boustead (01422) 341878
- 📱 www.westendgc.co.uk

Hanging Heaton   (1922)
*Whitecross Road, Bennett Lane, Dewsbury
WF12 7DT*
- ☎ **(01924) 461606**
- 📠 (01924) 430100
- 📧 derek.atkinson@hhgc.org
- ✎ Derek Atkinson (01924) 430100
- 📱 www.hangingheatongolfclub.co.uk

Headingley   (1892)
Back Church Lane, Adel, Leeds LS16 8DW
- ☎ **(0113) 267 9573 (Clubhouse)**
- 📠 (0113) 281 7334
- 📧 manager@headingleygolfclub.co.uk
- ✎ Mr J L Hall
- 📱 www.headingleygolfclub.co.uk

Headley   (1907)
*Headley Lane, Thornton, Bradford
BD13 3LX*
- ☎ **(01274) 833481**
- 📠 (01274) 833481
- 📧 admin@headleygolfclub.co.uk
- ✎ D Britton
- 📱 www.headleygolfclub.co.uk

Hebden Bridge   (1930)
*Great Mount, Wadsworth, Hebden Bridge
HX7 8PH*
- ☎ **(01422) 842896**
- 📧 hbgc@btconnect.com
- ✎ Stepney Calvert (01422) 842896
- 📱 www.hebdenbridgegolfclub.co.uk

Horsforth   (1906)
*Layton Rise, Layton Road, Horsforth, Leeds
LS18 5EX*
- ☎ **(0113) 258 6819**
- 📠 (0113) 258 9336
- 📧 secretary@horsforthgolfclub.co.uk
- ✎ Mrs LA Harrison-Elrick
- 📱 www.horsforthgolfclub.co.uk

Howley Hall   (1900)
Scotchman Lane, Morley, Leeds LS27 0NX
- ☎ **(01924) 350100**
- 📠 (01924) 350104
- 📧 office@howleyhall.co.uk
- ✎ D Jones (01924) 350100
- 📱 www.howleyhall.co.uk

Huddersfield (1891)

Fixby Hall, Lightridge Road, Huddersfield
HD2 2EP
- ☎ **(01484) 426203**
- ☐ (01484) 424623
- ✉ secretary@huddersfield-golf.co.uk
- ✍ S.A.Jones
- 🖥 www.huddersfield-golf.co.uk

Ilkley (1890)

Myddleton, Ilkley LS29 0BE
- ☎ **(01943) 607277**
- ☐ (01943) 816130
- ✉ honsec@ilkleygolfclub.co.uk
- ✍ Office (01943) 600214
- 🖥 www.ilkleygolfclub.co.uk

Keighley (1904)

Howden Park, Utley, Keighley BD20 6DH
- ☎ **(01535) 604778**
- ☐ (01535) 604778
- ✉ manager@keighleygolfclub.com
- ✍ G Cameron Dawson
- 🖥 www.keighleygolfclub.com

Leeds (1896)

Elmete Lane, Roundhay, Leeds LS8 2LJ
- ☎ **(0113) 265 8775**
- ☐ (0113) 232 3369
- ✉ secretary@leedsgolfclub.com
- ✍ P Mawman (0113) 265 9203
- 🖥 www.leedsgolfclub.co.uk

Leeds Golf Centre (1994)

Proprietary
Wike Ridge Lane, Shadwell, Leeds
LS17 9JW
- ☎ **(0113) 288 6000**
- ☐ (0113) 288 6185
- ✉ info@leedsgolfcentre.com
- ✍ A Herridge (Director of Golf)
- 🖥 www.leedsgolfcentre.com

Lightcliffe (1907)

Knowle Top Road, Lightcliffe HX3 8SW
- ☎ **(01422) 202459**
- ✍ RP Crampton (01484) 384672

Lofthouse Hill

Leeds Road, Lofthouse Hill, Wakefield
WF3 3LR
- ☎ **(01924) 823703**
- ☐ (01924) 823703
- ✍ P Moon
- 🖥 www.lofthousehillgolfclub.co.uk

Longley Park (1910)

Maple Street, Huddersfield HD5 9AX
- ☎ **(01484) 426932**
- ☐ (01484) 515280
- ✉ longleyparkgolfclub@12freeukisp
.co.uk
- ✍ J Ambler (01484) 431885

Low Laithes (1925)

Park Mill Lane, Flushdyke, Ossett WF5 9AP
- ☎ **(01924) 266067**
- ☐ (01924) 266266
- ✉ info@lowlaithesgolfclub.co.uk
- ✍ P Browning (Sec/Mgr)
- 🖥 www.lowlaithesgolfclub.co.uk

The Manor

Proprietary
Bradford Road, Drighlington, Bradford
BD11 1AB
- ☎ **(01132) 852644**
- ☐ (01332) 879961
- ✉ themanorgolfclub@hotmail.co.uk
- ✍ G Thompson (Sec/Mgr)
- 🖥 www.themanorgolfclub.co.uk

Marriott Hollins Hall Hotel (1999)

Hollins Hill, Baildon, Shipley BD17 7QW
- ☎ **(01274) 534212**
- ☐ (01274) 534220
- ✉ mhrs.lbags.golf@marriotthotels
.com
- ✍ Stuart Carnie (01274) 534250
- 🖥 www.hollinshallgolf.com

Marsden (1921)

Hemplow, Marsden, Huddersfield
HD7 6NN
- ☎ **(01484) 844253**
- ✉ secretary@marsdengolf.co.uk
- ✍ R O'Brien
- 🖥 www.marsdengolf.co.uk

Meltham (1908)

Thick Hollins Hall, Meltham, Huddersfield
HD9 4DQ
- ☎ **(01484) 850227**
- ✉ admin@meltham-golf.co.uk
- ✍ J R Dixon (Hon)
- 🖥 www.meltham-golf.co.uk

Mid Yorkshire (1993)

Proprietary
Havercroft Lane, Darrington, Pontefract
WF8 3BP
- ☎ **(01977) 704522**
- ☐ (01977) 600823
- ✉ admin@midyorkshiregolfclub.com
- ✍ Robert Pointon
- 🖥 www.midyorkshiregolfclub.com

Middleton Park (1933)

Public
Ring Road, Beeston Park, Middleton
LS10 3TN
- ☎ **(0113) 270 0449**
- ✉ secretary@middletonparkgolfclub
.co.uk
- 🖥 www.middletonparkgolfclub.co.uk

Moor Allerton (1923)

Coal Road, Wike, Leeds LS17 9NH
- ☎ **(0113) 266 1154**
- ☐ (0113) 268 0059
- ✉ info@magc.co.uk
- ✍ RM Crann (Mgr)
- 🖥 www.magc.co.uk

Moortown (1909)

Harrogate Road, Leeds LS17 7DB
- ☎ **(0113) 268 6521**
- ☐ (0113) 268 0986
- ✉ secretary@moortown-gc.co.uk
- ✍ Mr Peter Rishworth
- 🖥 www.moortown-gc.co.uk

Normanton (1903)

Hatfeild Hall, Aberford Road, Stanley,
Wakefield WF3 4JP
- ☎ **(01924) 377943**
- ☐ (01924) 200777
- ✉ office@normantongolf.co.uk
- ✍ Lynne Pickles
- 🖥 www.normantongolf.co.uk

Northcliffe (1921)

High Bank Lane, Shipley, Bradford
BD18 4LJ
- ☎ **(01274) 584085**
- ☐ (01274) 584148
- ✉ northcliffegc@hotmail.co.uk
- ✍ C Malloy (01274) 596731
- 🖥 www.northcliffegc.org.uk

Otley (1906)

West Busk Lane, Otley LS21 3NG
- ☎ **(01943) 465329**
- ☐ (01943) 850387
- ✉ office@otleygolfclub.co.uk
- ✍ PJ Clarke Ext 1
- 🖥 www.otleygolfclub.co.uk

Outlane (1906)

Slack Lane, off New Hey Road, Outlane,
Huddersfield HD3 3FQ
- ☎ **(01422) 374762**
- ☐ (01422) 311789
- ✉ secretary@outlanegolfclub.ltd.uk
- ✍ P Turner
- 🖥 www.outlanegolfclub.ltd.uk

Pontefract & District (1904)

Park Lane, Pontefract WF8 4QS
- ☎ **(01977) 792241**
- ☐ (01977) 792241
- ✉ manager@pdgc.co.uk
- ✍ J Heald (Mgr) (01977) 792241
- 🖥 www.pdgc.co.uk

Queensbury (1923)

Brighouse Road, Queensbury, Bradford
BD13 1QF
- ☎ **(01274) 882155**
- ☐ (01274) 882155
- ✉ queensburygolf@talktalk.net
- ✍ MH Heptinstall
- 🖥 www.queensburygc.co.uk

Rawdon (1896)

Buckstone Drive, Micklefield Lane, Rawdon
LS19 6BD
- ☎ **(0113) 250 6040**
- ✉ info@rgltc.co.uk
- ✍ Phil Denison
- 🖥 www.rgltc.co.uk

Riddlesden (1927)

Howden Rough, Riddlesden, Keighley
BD20 5QN
- ☎ **(01535) 602148**
- ✍ S Morton (01535) 602148

Roundhay (1923)

Public
Park Lane, Leeds LS8 2EJ
- ☎ **(0113) 266 2695**
- ✉ geoff.hodgson@sky.com
- ✍ G M Hodgson (Hon Sec)
- 🖥 www.roundhaygc.com

Ryburn (1910)
Norland, Sowerby Bridge, Halifax HX6 3QP
☎ **(01422) 831355**
✉ secretary@ryburngolfclub.co.uk
✍ Raymond Attiwell (07904) 834320
▤ www.ryburngolfclub.co.uk

Sand Moor (1926)
Alwoodley Lane, Leeds LS17 7DJ
☎ **(0113) 268 5180**
📠 (0113) 266 1105
✉ info@sandmoorgolf.co.uk
✍ Jackie Hogan (0113) 268 5180
▤ www.sandmoorgolf.co.uk

Scarcroft (1937)
Syke Lane, Leeds LS14 3BQ
☎ **(0113) 289 2311**
📠 (0113) 289 3835
✉ secretary@scarcroftgolfclub.co.uk
✍ R A Simpson (Sec/Mgr)
▤ www.scarcroftgolfclub.co.uk

Shipley (1896)
Beckfoot Lane, Cottingley Bridge, Bingley BD16 1LX
☎ **(01274) 568652**
📠 (01274) 567739
✉ office@shipleygc.co.uk
✍ Mrs MJ Simpson (01274) 568652
▤ www.shipleygolfclub.com

Silsden (1911)
Brunthwaite Lane, Brunthwaite, Silsden BD20 0ND
☎ **(01535) 652998**
✉ info@silsdengolfclub.co.uk
✍ M Twigg
▤ www.silsdengolfclub.co.uk

South Bradford (1906)
Pearson Road, Odsal, Bradford BD6 1BH
☎ **(01274) 679195**
✉ secsouthbradford@btconnect.com
✍ B Broadbent (01274) 679195
▤ www.southbradfordgolfclub.co.uk

South Leeds (1906)
Gipsy Lane, Ring Road, Beeston, Leeds LS11 5TU
☎ **(0113) 277 1676**

📠 (0113) 277 1676
✉ south-leeds@btconnect.com
✍ B Clayton (0113) 277 1676
▤ www.southleedsgolfclub.co.uk

Temple Newsam (1923)
Public
Temple Newsam Road, Halton, Leeds LS15 0LN
☎ **(0113) 264 5624**
✉ secretary@tngc.co.uk
✍ Mrs Christine P Wood
▤ www.tngolfclub.co.uk

Todmorden (1894)
Rive Rocks, Cross Stone, Todmorden OL14 8RD
☎ **(01706) 812986**
✉ secretarytodgolfclub@msn.com
✍ Peter H Eastwood
▤ www.todmordengolfclub.co.uk

Wakefield (1891)
28 Woodthorpe Lane, Sandal, Wakefield WF2 6JH
☎ **(01924) 258778**
📠 (01924) 242752
✉ wakefieldgolfclub
@woodthorpelane.freeserve.co.uk
✍ Elizabeth Newton
(01924) 258778
▤ www.wakefieldgolfclub.co.uk

Waterton Park (1995)
The Balk, Walton, Wakefield WF2 6QL
☎ **(01924) 259525**
📠 (01924) 256969
✉ wparkgolfclub@btconnect.com
✍ M Pearson (01924) 255557

West Bradford (1900)
Chellow Grange Road, Haworth Road, Bradford BD9 6NP
☎ **(01274) 542767**
📠 (01274) 482079
✉ secretary@westbradfordgolfclub.co.uk
✍ B K Sutcliffe (Hon Sec)
(01274) 542767
▤ www.westbradfordgolfclub.co.uk

Wetherby (1910)
Linton Lane, Linton, Wetherby LS22 4JF
☎ **(01937) 580089**
📠 (01937) 581915
✉ manager@wetherbygolfclub.co.uk
✍ Darren Tear
▤ www.wetherbygolfclub.co.uk

Whitwood (1987)
Public
Altofts Lane, Whitwood, Castleford WF10 5PZ
☎ **(01977) 512835**

Willow Valley Golf (1993)
Pay and play
Clifton, Brighouse HD6 4JB
☎ **(01274) 878624**
✉ sales@wvgc.co.uk
✍ H Newton
▤ www.wvgc.co.uk

Woodhall Hills (1905)
Woodhall Road, Calverley, Pudsey LS28 5UN
☎ **(0113) 256 4771 (Clubhouse)**
📠 (0113) 255 4594
✉ woodhallgolf@btconnect.com
✍ J Hayes (0113) 255 4594
▤ www.woodhallhillsgolfclub.com

Woodsome Hall (1922)
Woodsome Hall, Fenay Bridge, Huddersfield HD8 0LQ
☎ **(01484) 602971**
📠 (01484) 608260
✍ TJ Mee (01484) 602739
(Gen Mgr)
▤ www.woodsomehall.co.uk

Woolley Park (1995)
Proprietary
New Road, Woolley, Wakefield WF4 2JS
☎ **(01226) 380144 (Bookings)**
📠 (01226) 390295
✉ woolleyparkgolf@yahoo.co.uk
✍ RP Stoffel (01226) 382209
▤ www.woolleyparkgolfclub.co.uk

For key to symbols see page 717

Who is known as "The Black Knight"?
The answer can be found on page 905

Ireland

Co Antrim

Antrim (1997)
Public
Allen Park Golf Centre, 45 Castle Road,
Antrim BT41 4NA
- ☎ (028) 9442 9001
- ✉ allenpark@antrim.gov.uk
- ✍ Marie Agnew (Mgr)
- 🖥 www.antrim.gov.uk

Ballycastle (1890)
Cushendall Road, Ballycastle BT64 6QP
- ☎ (028) 2076 2536
- 🖵 (028) 2076 9909
- ✉ info@ballycastlegolfclub.com
- ✍ Mr D Douglas (Hon Sec)
- 🖥 www.ballycastlegolfclub.com

Ballyclare (1923)
25 Springvale Road, Ballyclare BT39 9JW
- ☎ (028) 9334 2352 (Clubhouse)
- ✉ info@ballyclaregolfclub.net
- 🖥 www.ballyclaregolfclub.net

Ballymena (1903)
128 Raceview Road, Ballymena BT42 4HY
- ☎ (028) 2586 1207/1487
- 🖵 (028) 2586 1487
- ✉ admin@ballymenagolfclub.com
- ✍ Ken Herbison (Hon Sec)

Bentra
Public
Slaughterford Road, Whitehead BT38 9TG
- ☎ (028) 9335 8000
- 🖵 (028) 9336 6676
- ✉ greenspace@carrickfergus.org
- ✍ S Daye (028) 9335 8039
- 🖥 www.bentragolf.co.uk

Burnfield House
10 Cullyburn Road, Newtownabbey
BT36 5BN
- ☎ (028) 9083 8737
- ✉ michaelhj@ntlworld.com
- 🖥 www.burnfieldhousegolfclub.co.uk

Bushfoot (1890)
50 Bushfoot Road, Portballintrae BT57 8RR
- ☎ (028) 2073 1317
- 🖵 (028) 2073 1852
- ✉ bushfootgolfclub@btconnect.com
- ✍ T McFaull (Hon Sec)
- 🖥 www.bushfootgolfclub.co.uk

Cairndhu (1928)
192 Coast Road, Ballygally, Larne
BT40 2QG
- ☎ (028) 2858 3324
- 🖵 (028) 2858 3324
- ✉ cairndhugc@btconnect.com
- ✍ N McKinstry (Sec/Mgr) (028) 2858 3324
- 🖥 www.cairndhugolfclub.co.uk

Carrickfergus (1926)
35 North Road, Carrickfergus BT38 8LP
- ☎ (028) 9336 3713
- 🖵 (028) 9336 3023
- ✉ carrickfergusgc@btconnect.com
- ✍ I McLean (Hon Sec)
- 🖥 www.carrickfergusgolfclub.com

Cushendall (1937)
21 Shore Road, Cushendall BT44 0NG
- ☎ (028) 2177 1318
- 🖵 (028) 2177 1318
- ✉ cushendallgc@btconnect.com
- ✍ S McLaughlin (028) 2175 8366

Down Royal (1990)
Proprietary
6 Dungarton Road, Maze, Lisburn
BT27 5RT
- ☎ (028) 9262 1339
- 🖵 (028) 9262 1339
- ✉ info@downroyalgolf.com
- ✍ Bill McCappin (Mgr)
- 🖥 www.downroyalgolf.com

Galgorm Castle (1997)
Proprietary
200 Galgorm Road, Ballymena BT42 1HL
- ☎ (028) 256 46161
- 🖵 (028) 256 51151
- ✉ golf@galgormcastle.com
- ✍ G Henry (Gen Mgr)
- 🖥 www.galgormcastle.com

Gracehill (1995)
Proprietary
141 Ballinlea Road, Stranocum, Ballymoney
BT53 8PX
- ☎ (028) 2075 1209
- 🖵 (028) 2075 1074
- ✉ info@gracehillgolfclub.co.uk
- ✍ M McClure (Mgr)
- 🖥 www.gracehillgolfclub.co.uk

Greenacres (1996)
153 Ballyrobert Road, Ballyclare BT39 9RT
- ☎ (028) 933 54111
- 🖥 www.greenacresgolfclub.co.uk

Greenisland (1894)
156 Upper Road, Greenisland,
Carrickfergus BT38 8RW
- ☎ (028) 9086 2236
- ✉ greenisland.golf@btconnect.com
- ✍ FF Trotter (Hon)
- 🖥 www.greenislandgolfclub.co.uk

Hilton Templepatrick (1999)
Proprietary
Castle Upton Estate, Paradise Walk,
Templepatrick BT39 0DD
- ☎ (028) 9443 5542
- 🖵 (028) 9443 5511
- ✉ eamonn.logue@hilton.com
- ✍ Eamonn Logue (Golf Ops Mgr)
- 🖥 www.hiltontemplepatrickgolf.com

Larne (1894)
54 Ferris Bay Road, Islandmagee, Larne
BT40 3RJ
- ☎ (028) 9338 2228
- 🖵 (028) 9338 2088
- ✉ info@larnegolfclub.co.uk
- ✍ RI Johnston

Lisburn (1891)
68 Eglantine Road, Lisburn BT27 5RQ
- ☎ (028) 9267 7216
- 🖵 (028) 9260 3608
- ✉ info@lisburngolfclub.com
- ✍ John McKeown (Gen Mgr)
- 🖥 www.lisburngolfclub.com

Mallusk (1992)
Antrim Road, Glengormley, Newtownabbey
BT36 4RF
- ☎ (028) 9084 3799

Massereene (1895)
51 Lough Road, Antrim BT41 4DQ
- ☎ (028) 9442 8096 (office)
- ✉ info@massereene.com
- 🖥 www.massereene.com

Rathmore
Bushmills Road, Portrush BT56 8JG
- ☎ (028) 7082 2996
- 🖵 (028) 7082 2996
- ✉ rathmoregolfclubvalley@msn.com
- ✍ W McIntyre (Club Admin.)
- 🖥 www.rathmoregolfclub.com

Royal Portrush (1888)
Dunluce Road, Portrush BT56 8JQ
- ☎ (028) 7082 2311
- 🖵 (028) 7082 3139
- ✉ info@royalportrushgolfclub.com
- ✍ Miss W Erskine
- 🖥 www.royalportrushgolfclub.com

Whitehead (1904)
McCrae's Brae, Whitehead, Carrickfergus
BT38 9NZ
- ☎ (028) 9337 0820
- 🖵 (028) 9337 0825
- ✉ robin@whiteheadgc.fsnet.co.uk
- ✍ RA Patrick (Hon)
- 🖥 www.whiteheadgolfclub.com

Co Armagh

Ashfield (1990)
Freeduff, Cullyhanna, Newry BT35 0JJ
- ☎ (028) 3086 8180

Cloverhill (1999)
Proprietary
Lough Road, Mullaghbawn BT35 9XP
- ☎ (028) 3088 9374
- ✉ info@cloverhillgc.com/pilky-03@hotmail.com
- ✍ Colin Pilkington
- 🖥 www.cloverhillgolfclub.co.uk

County Armagh   (1893)

7 Newry Road, Armagh BT60 1EN
- ☎ **(028) 37 525861/(028) 37 525864 (Pro Sh**
- ✆ (028) 3752 8768
- 📧 lynne@golfarmagh.co.uk
- ✍ Mrs Lynne Fleming (028) 3752 5861
- 🖥 www.golfarmagh.co.uk

Edenmore G&CC   (1992)

Edenmore House, 70 Drumnabreeze Road, Magheralin, Craigavon BT67 0RH
- ☎ **(028) 9261 9241**
- ✆ (028) 9261 3310
- 📧 info@edenmore.com
- ✍ K Logan (Sec/Mgr)
- 🖥 www.edenmore.com

Loughgall Country Park & Golf Course

11-14 Main Street, Loughgall
- ☎ **(028) 3889 2900**
- 📧 g.ferson@btinternet.com
- 🖥 www.armagh.gov.uk

Lurgan   (1893)

The Demesne, Windsor Avenue, Lurgan BT67 9BN
- ☎ **(028) 3832 2087 (Clubhouse)**
- ✆ (028) 3831 6166
- 📧 lurgangolfclub@btconnect.com
- ✍ Muriel Sharpe
- 🖥 www.lurgangolfclub.com

Portadown   (1902)

192 Gilford Road, Portadown BT63 5LF
- ☎ **(028) 383 55356**
- ✆ (028) 383 91394
- 📧 info@portadowngolfclub.co.uk
- ✍ Barbara Currie (Sec/Mgr)
- 🖥 www.portadowngolfclub.co.uk

Silverwood   (1983)

Turmoyra Lane, Silverwood, Lurgan BT66 6NG
- ☎ **(028) 3832 5380**
- ✆ (028) 3834 7272
- 📧 silverwoodgolfclub@myrainbow.com
- ✍ S Ashe
- 🖥 www.silverwoodgolfclub.com

Tandragee   (1922)

Markethill Road, Tandragee BT62 2ER
- ☎ **(028) 3884 1272 (Clubhouse)**
- ✆ (028) 3884 0664
- 📧 office@tandragee.co.uk
- ✍ A Hewitt (028) 3884 1272
- 🖥 www.tandragee.co.uk

Belfast

Ballyearl Golf Centre

Public
585 Doagh Road, Newtownabbey BT36 5RZ
- ☎ **(028) 9084 8287**
- ✆ (028) 9084 4896
- 📧 sbartley@newtownabbey.gov.uk
- 🖥 wwwnewtownabbey.gov.uk

Balmoral   (1914)

518 Lisburn Road, Belfast BT9 6GX
- ☎ **(028) 9038 1514**
- 📧 admin@balmoralgolf.com
- 🖥 www.balmoralgolf.com

Belvoir Park   (1927)

73 Church Road, Newtownbreda, Belfast BT8 7AN
- ☎ **(028) 9049 1693**
- ✆ (028) 9064 6113
- 📧 info@belvoirparkgolfclub.com
- ✍ Ann Vaughan (028) 9049 1693
- 🖥 www.belvoirparkgolfclub.com

Castlereagh Hills Golf Course   (2005)

Pay and play
73 Upper Braniel Road, Belfast BT5 7TX
- ☎ **(028) 9044 8477**
- ✆ (028) 9044 9646
- 📧 golfclub@castlereagh.gov.uk
- ✍ Lea Booth
- 🖥 www.castlereaghhills.com

Dunmurry   (1905)

91 Dunmurry Lane, Dunmurry, Belfast BT17 9JS
- ☎ **(028) 9061 0834**
- ✆ (028) 9060 2540
- 📧 dunmurrygc@hotmail.com
- ✍ T Cassidy (Golf Mgr)
- 🖥 www.dunmurrygolfclub.co.uk

Fortwilliam   (1891)

8A Downview Avenue, Belfast B15 4EZ
- ☎ **(028) 9037 0770**
- ✆ (028) 9078 1891
- 📧 administrator@fortwilliam.co.uk
- ✍ Pat Toal CB (Hon Sec)
- 🖥 www.fortwilliam.co.uk

The Knock Club   (1895)

Summerfield, Dundonald, Belfast BT16 2QX
- ☎ **(028) 9048 3251**
- ✆ (028) 9048 7277
- 📧 knockgolfclub@btconnect.com
- ✍ Anne Armstrong
- 🖥 www.knockgolfclub.co.uk

Malone   (1895)

240 Upper Malone Road, Dunmurry, Belfast BT17 9LB
- ☎ **(028) 9061 2758**
- ✆ (028) 9043 1394
- 📧 manager@malonegolfclub.co.uk
- ✍ Peter Kelly (028) 9061 2758
- 🖥 www.malonegolfclub.co.uk

Ormeau   (1893)

50 Park Road, Belfast BT7 2FX
- ☎ **(028) 9064 1069 (Members)**

Shandon Park   (1926)

73 Shandon Park, Belfast BT5 6NY
- ☎ **(028) 9080 5030**
- ✆ (028) 9080 5999
- 📧 shandonpark@btconnect.com
- ✍ GA Bailie (Gen Mgr)
- 🖥 www.shandonpark.com

Co Carlow

Borris   (1907)

Deerpark, Borris
- ☎ **(059) 977 3310 (office)**
- ✆ (059) 977 3750
- 📧 borrisgolfclub@eircom.net
- ✍ Shena Walsh (059) 977 3310

Carlow   (1899)

Deer Park, Dublin Road, Carlow
- ☎ **(059) 913 1695**
- ✆ (059) 914 0065
- 📧 carlowgolfclub@eircom.net
- ✍ D MacSweeney (Gen Mgr)
- 🖥 www.carlowgolfclub.com

Mount Wolseley   (1996)

Tullow
- ☎ **(059) 915 1674**
- ✆ (059) 915 2123
- 📧 golf@mountwolseley.ie
- ✍ John Lawler (Director of Golf)
- 🖥 www.mountwolseley.ie

Co Cavan

Belturbet   (1950)

Erne Hill, Belturbet
- ☎ **(049) 952 2287**

Blacklion   (1962)

Toam, Blacklion, via Sligo
- ☎ **(071) 985 3024**
- ✆ (071) 985 3024
- ✍ P Gallery (Hon)
- 🖥 www.blackliongolf.eu

Cabra Castle   (1978)

Kingscourt
- ☎ **(042) 966 7030**
- ✆ (042) 966 7039
- 📧 kevcarry@gmail.com
- ✍ Kevin Carry (087) 655 7538

County Cavan   (1894)

Arnmore House, Drumelis, Cavan
- ☎ **(049) 433 1541**
- ✆ (049) 433 1541
- 📧 info@cavangolf.ie
- ✍ James Fraker
- 🖥 www.cavangolf.ie

Slieve Russell G&CC   (1994)

Ballyconnell
- ☎ **(049) 952 6458**
- ✆ (049) 952 6640
- 📧 slieve-russell@quinn-hotels.com
- ✍ (049) 952 5091
- 🖥 www.slieverussell.ie

Virginia   (1945)

Park Hotel, Virginia
- ☎ **(049) 854 8066**
- ✍ P Gill (087) 681 3387

Co Clare

Clonlara   (1993)

Clonlara
- ☎ **(061) 354141**

✉ clonlaragolfclub@eircom.net
✍ Tom Carroll

Doonbeg (2002)
Doonbeg, Co Clare
☎ **(065) 905 5600**
✉ reservations@doonbeggolfclub
.com
🖥 www.doonbeggolfclub.com

Dromoland Castle (1964)
Newmarket-on-Fergus
☎ **353 (61) 368444**
✉ golf@dromoland.ie
🖥 www.dromoland.ie

East Clare (1992)
Bodyke
☎ **(061) 921322**

Ennis (1907)
Drumbiggle, Ennis
☎ **(065) 682 4074**
✉ info@ennisgolfclub.com
🖥 www.ennisgolfclub.com

Kilkee (1896)
East End, Kilkee
☎ **(065) 905 6048**
📠 (065) 905 6977
✉ kilkeegolfclub@eircom.net
✍ Jim Leyden (Sec/Mgr)
🖥 www.kilkeegolfclub.ie

Kilrush (1934)
Parknamoney, Kilrush
☎ **(065) 905 1138**
✉ info@kilrushgolfclub.com
🖥 www.kilrushgolfclub.com

Lahinch (1892)
Lahinch
☎ **(065) 708 1003**
📠 (065) 708 1592
✉ info@lahinchgolf.com
✍ Paddy Keane (Gen Mgr)
🖥 www.lahinchgolf.com

Shannon (1966)
Shannon
☎ **(061) 471849**
📠 (061) 471507
✉ info@shannongolfclub.ie
✍ M Corry (061) 471849
🖥 www.shannongolfclub.ie

Spanish Point (1915)
Spanish Point, Miltown Malbay
☎ **(065) 708 4219**
🖥 www.spanish-point.com

Woodstock (1993)
Shanaway Road, Ennis
☎ **(065) 682 9463**
📠 (065) 682 0304
✉ proshopwoodstock@eircom
.net
✍ Avril Guerin (Sec/Mgr)
🖥 www.woodstockgolfclub.com

Co Cork

Bandon (1909)
Castlebernard, Bandon
☎ **(023) 88 41111**
📠 (023) 88 20819
✉ enquiries@bandongolfclub.com
✍ Kay Walsh
🖥 www.bandongolfclub.com

Bantry Bay (1975)
Donemark, Bantry, West Cork
☎ **(027) 50579/53773**
📠 (027) 53790
✉ info@bantrygolf.com
✍ Steve Cameron (Mgr) (027) 50579
🖥 www.bantrygolf.com

Berehaven (1902)
Millcove, Castletownbere
☎ **(027) 70700**
📠 (027) 71957
✉ info@berehavengolf.com
✍ B Twomey (Hon)
🖥 www.berehavengolf.com

Charleville (1909)
Charleville
☎ **(063) 81257**
📠 (063) 81274
✉ info@charlevillegolf.com
✍ P Nagle (Sec/Mgr)
🖥 www.charlevillegolf.com

Cobh (1987)
Ballywilliam, Cobh
☎ **(021) 812399**

Coosheen (1989)
Coosheen, Schull
☎ **(028) 28182**

Cork (1888)
Little Island, Cork
☎ **(021) 435 3451/3037**
📠 (021) 435 3410
✉ info@corkgolfclub.ie
✍ M Sands (021) 435 3451
🖥 www.corkgolfclub.ie

Doneraile (1927)
Doneraile
☎ **(022) 24137**
✉ info@donerailegolfclub.com
🖥 www.donerailegolfclub.com

Douglas (1909)
Douglas, Cork
☎ **(021) 489 1086**
📠 (021) 436 7200
✉ admin@douglasgolfclub.ie
✍ Ronan Burke (Mgr)
🖥 www.douglasgolfclub.ie

Dunmore Golf Club (1967)
Muckross, Clonakilty
☎ **023 8834644**
✉ dunmoregolfclub@gmail.com
✍ Liam Santry
🖥 www.dunmoregolfclub.ie

East Cork (1971)
Gortacrue, Midleton
☎ **(021) 463 1687**
📠 (021) 461 3695
✉ eastcorkgolfclub@eircom.net
✍ M Moloney (Sec/Mgr)
🖥 www.eastcorkgolfclub.com

Fermoy (1892)
Corrin, Fermoy
☎ **(025) 32694**
📠 (025) 33072
✉ fermoygolfclub@eircom.net
✍ K Murphy
🖥 www.fermoygolfclub.ie

Fernhill (1994)
Carrigaline
☎ **(021) 437 2226**
✉ fernhill@iol.ie
🖥 www.fernhillgolfhotel.com

Fota Island Resort (1993)
Proprietary
Fota Island, Cork
☎ **(021) 488 3700**
📠 (021) 488 3713
✉ reservations@fotaisland.ie
✍ Jonathon Woods
🖥 www.fotaisland.ie

Frankfield (1984)
Frankfield, Douglas
☎ **(0214) 363124/3611299**
📠 (01214) 366205
✉ frankfieldhouse@gmail.com
✍ James St Leger
🖥 www.frankfieldhouse.com

Glengarriff (1935)
Glengarriff
☎ **(027) 63150**
📠 (027) 63575
✉ glengarriff@gmail.com
✍ N Deasy (Hon)
🖥 www.glengarriffgolfclub.com

Harbour Point (1991)
Proprietary
Clash Road, Little Island
☎ **(021) 435 3094**
✉ hpoint@iol.ie
🖥 www.harbourpointgolfclub.com

Kanturk (1971)
Fairyhill, Kanturk
☎ **(029) 50534**

Kinsale Farrangalway (1993)
Farrangalway, Kinsale
☎ **(021) 477 4722**
✉ office@kinsalegolf.com
🖥 www.kinsalegolf.com

Kinsale Ringenane (1912)
Ringenane, Belgooly, Kinsale
☎ **(021) 477 2197**

Lee Valley G&CC (1993)
Clashanure, Ovens, Cork
☎ **(021) 733 1721**
✉ reservations@leevalleygcc.ie
🖥 www.leevalleygcc.ie

Macroom (1924)
Lackaduve, Macroom
☎ **(026) 41072**
🖴 (026) 41391
📧 mcroomgc@lol.ie
✍ C O'Sullivan (Mgr)
🖥 www.macroomgolfclub.com

Mahon (1980)
Clover Hill, Blackrock, Cork
☎ **(021) 429 2543**
🖴 (021) 429 2604
📧 mahon@golfnet.ie
✍ M Groeger (086) 813 5769
🖥 www.mahongolfclub.com

Mallow (1948)
Ballyellis, Mallow
☎ **(022) 21145**
🖴 (022) 42501
📧 mallowgolfclubmanager@eircom
.net
✍ D Curtin (Sec/Mgr)
🖥 www.mallowgolfclub.net

Mitchelstown (1910)
Gurrane, Mitchelstown
☎ **(025) 24072**
🖴 (025) 86631
📧 info@mitchelstown-golf.com
✍ Dan Kelleher
🖥 www.mitchelstown-golf.com

Monkstown (1908)
Parkgarriffe, Monkstown
☎ **(021) 484 1376**
🖴 (021) 484 1722
📧 office@monkstowngolfclub.com
✍ H Madden (Sec/Mgr)
🖥 www.monkstowngolfclub.com

Muskerry (1907)
Carrigrohane, Co. Cork
☎ **(021) 438 5297**
🖴 (021) 451 6860
📧 muskgc@eircom.net
✍ H Gallagher
🖥 www.muskerrygolfclub.ie

Old Head Golf Links (1997)
Kinsale
☎ **(021) 477 8444**
🖴 (021) 477 8022
📧 info@oldhead.com
✍ Danny Brassil (Dir of Golf)
🖥 www.oldhead.com

Raffeen Creek (1989)
Ringaskiddy
☎ **(021) 437 8430**

Skibbereen (1904)
Licknavar, Skibbereen
☎ **(028) 21227**
🖴 (028) 22994
📧 info@skibbgolf.com
✍ Club Aministrator
🖥 www.skibbgolf.com

Youghal (1898)
Knockaverry, Youghal
☎ **(024) 92787/92861**
🖴 (024) 92641
📧 youghalgolfclub@eircom.net
✍ Margaret O'Sullivan
🖥 www.youghalgolfclub.ie

Co Donegal

Ballybofey & Stranorlar
(1957)
The Glebe, Stranorlar
☎ **(074) 913 1093**
🖴 (074) 913 0158
📧 info@ballybofeyandstranorlar
golfclub.com
✍ Cathal Patton (074) 913 1093
🖥 www.ballybofeyandstranorlar
golfclub.com

Ballyliffin (1947)
Ballyliffin, Inishowen
☎ **(07493) 76119**
🖴 (07493) 76672
📧 info@ballyliffingolfclub.com
✍ John Farren (Gen Mgr)
🖥 www.ballyliffingolfclub.com

Buncrana (1951)
Public
Buncrana
☎ **(07493) 62279**
📧 buncranagc@eircom.net
✍ F McGrory (Hon) (07493) 62279
🖥 www.buncranagolfclub.com

Bundoran (1894)
Bundoran
☎ **(07198) 41302**
🖴 (07198) 42014
📧 bundorangolfclub@eircom.net
✍ Noreen Allen (Sec/Mgr)
🖥 www.bundorangolfclub.com

Cruit Island (1985)
Kincasslagh, Dunglow
☎ **(074) 954 3296**
🖥 www.homepage.eirecom.net/
~cruitisland

Donegal (1959)
Murvagh, Laghey
☎ **(074) 973 4054**
🖴 (074) 973 4377
📧 info@donegalgolfclub.ie
✍ Grainne Dorrian
🖥 www.donegalgolfclub.ie

Dunfanaghy (1906)
Kill, Dunfanaghy, Letterkenny
☎ **(074) 913 6335**
📧 dunfanaghygolf@eircom.net
🖥 www.dunfanaghygolfclub.com

Greencastle (1892)
Greencastle
☎ **(074) 93 81013**
🖴 (074) 93 81015
📧 b_mc_caul@yahoo.com
✍ Billy McCaul
🖥 www.greencastlegc.com

Gweedore (1926)
Pay and play
Magheragallon, Derrybeg, Letterkenny
☎ **(07495) 31140**
📧 eugenemccafferty@hotmail.com
✍ Eugene McCafferty
🖥 www.gweedoregolfclub.com

Letterkenny (1913)
Barnhill, Letterkenny
☎ **(+353) 7491 21150**
🖴 (+353) 7491 21175
📧 info@letterkennygolfclub.com
✍ Cynthia Fuery (Hon Sec) (+353)
7491 21150
🖥 www.letterkennygolfclub.com

Narin & Portnoo (1930)
Narin, Portnoo
☎ **(074) 954 5107**
📧 narinportnoo@eircom.net
🖥 www.narinportnoogolfclub.ie

North West (1891)
Lisfannon, Buncrana
☎ **(074) 936 0127**
🖴 (074) 936 3284
📧 secretary@northwestgolfclub.com
✍ Eddie Curran (086) 604 7299
🖥 www.northwestgolfclub.com

Otway (1893)
Saltpans, Rathmullan, Letterkenny
☎ **(074) 915 1665**
📧 tolandkevin@eircom.net
✍ Kevin Toland

Portsalon (1891)
Portsalon, Fanad
☎ **(074) 915 9459**
🖴 (074) 915 9919
📧 portsalongolfclub@eircom.net
✍ P Doherty
🖥 www.portsalongolfclub.com

Redcastle (1983)
Redcastle, Moville
☎ **(074) 938 5555**
🖴 (074) 938 2214
✍ M Wilson

Rosapenna (1894)
Downings, Rosapenna
☎ **(074) 55301**
🖴 (074) 55128
📧 rosapenna@eircom.net
✍ Frank Casey
🖥 www.rosapenna.ie

St Patricks Courses (1994)
Carrigart
☎ **(074) 55114**

Co Down

Ardglass (1896)
Castle Place, Ardglass BT30 7PP
☎ **(028) 4484 1219**
🖴 (028) 4484 1841
📧 info@ardglassgolfclub.com
✍ Mrs D Turley
🖥 www.ardglassgolfclub.com

Ardminnan (1995)
Pay and play
15 Ardminnan Road, Portaferry BT22 1QJ
- ☎ **(028) 4277 1321**
- 📠 (028) 4277 1321
- ✉ lesliejardine104@yahoo.co.uk
- ✍ L Jardine

Banbridge (1912)
116 Huntly Road, Banbridge BT32 3UR
- ☎ **(028) 4066 2211 (office)**
- 📠 (028) 4066 9400
- ✉ info@banbridgegolfclub.com
- ✍ Mrs Sandra Duprey (Club Mgr)
- 🖥 www.banbridgegolfclub.com

Bangor (1903)
Broadway, Bangor BT20 4RH
- ☎ **(028) 9127 0922**
- ✉ office@bangorgolfclubni.co.uk
- ✍ Mr Stephen Bell
- 🖥 www.bangorgolfclubni.co.uk

Blackwood (1995)
150 Crawfordsburn Road, Bangor
BT19 1GB
- ☎ **(028) 9185 2706**
- 📠 (028) 9185 3785
- ✉ blackwoodgc@btconnect.com
- ✍ Chris Widdowson
- 🖥 www.blackwoodgc@btopenworld
.com

Bright Castle (1970)
14 Coniamstown Road, Bright, Downpatrick
BT30 8LU
- ☎ **(028) 4484 1319**

Carnalea (1927)
Station Road, Bangor BT19 1EZ
- ☎ **(028) 9127 0368**
- 📠 (028) 9127 3989
- ✉ nicola@carnaleagolfclub.com
- ✍ Nicola Greene (028) 9127 0368
- 🖥 www.carnaleagolfclub.com

Clandeboye (1933)
Conlig, Newtownards BT23 7PN
- ☎ **(028) 9127 1767 (office)**
- 📠 (028) 9147 3711
- ✉ cgc-ni.@btconnect.com
- ✍ Gary Steele (Gen Mgr)
- 🖥 www.cgc-ni.com

Crossgar (1993)
231 Derryboye Road, Crossgar BT30 9DL
- ☎ **(028) 4483 1523**

Donaghadee (1899)
84 Warren Road, Donaghadee BT21 0PQ
- ☎ **(028) 9188 3624**
- 📠 (028) 9188 8891
- ✉ office@donaghadeegolfclub.net
- ✍ Jim Cullen
- 🖥 www.donaghadeegolfclub.com

Downpatrick (1930)
Saul Road, Downpatrick BT30 6PA
- ☎ **(028) 4461 5947**
- ✉ office@downpatrickgolf.org.uk
- ✍ Elaine Carson (028) 4461 5947
- 🖥 www.downpatrickgolf.org.uk

Helen's Bay (1896)
Golf Road, Helen's Bay, Bangor BT19 1TL
- ☎ **(028) 9185 2815 (office)**
- 📠 (028) 9185 2660
- ✉ mail@helensbaygc.com
- ✍ John McCullough (Sec)
- 🖥 www.helensbaygc.com

Holywood (1904)
Nuns Walk, Demesne Road, Holywood
BT18 9LE
- ☎ **(028) 9042 2138**
- 📠 (028) 9042 5040
- ✉ mail@holywoodgolfclub.co.uk
- ✍ Paul Gray (Gen Mgr)
- 🖥 www.holywoodgolfclub.co.uk

Kilkeel (1948)
Mourne Park, Kilkeel BT34 4LB
- ☎ **(028) 4176 2296/5095**
- 📠 (028) 4176 5579
- ✉ info@kilkeelgolfclub.org
- ✍ SC McBride (Hon)
- 🖥 www.kilkeelgolfclub.org

Kirkistown Castle (1902)
142 Main Road, Cloughey, Newtownards
BT22 1JA
- ☎ **(028) 4277 1233**
- 📠 (028) 4277 1699
- ✉ kirkistown@supanet.com
- ✍ R Coulter (028) 4277 1233
- 🖥 www.linksgolfkirkistown.com

Mahee Island (1929)
Comber, 14 Mahee Island, Newtownlands
BT23 6ET
- ☎ **(028) 9754 1234**
- ✉ adrian.ross@ntlworld.com
- 🖥 www.maheeislandgolfclub.com

Mount Ober G&CC (1985)
Ballymaconaghy Road, Knockbracken,
Belfast BT8 6SB
- ☎ **(028) 9079 2108 (Bookings)**
- 📠 (028) 9070 5862
- ✉ info@mountober.com
- ✍ E Williams (Sec/Mgr)
- 🖥 www.mountober.com

Mourne (1946)
Club
36 Golf Links Road, Newcastle BT33 0AN
- ☎ **(028) 4372 3218/3889**
- 📠 (028) 4372 2575
- ✉ info@mournegolfclub.co.uk
- ✍ P Keown (Hon)
- 🖥 www.mournegolfclub.co.uk

Ringdufferin G&CC (1993)
Ringdufferin Road, Toye, Downpatrick
BT30 9PH
- ☎ **(028) 4482 8812**
- ✉ willismarshall@utvinternet.com

Rockmount (1995)
Proprietary
28 Drumalig Road, Carryduff, Belfast
BT8 8EQ
- ☎ **(028) 9081 2279**
- 📠 (028) 9081 5851
- ✉ d.patterson@btconnect.com
- ✍ D Patterson (Mgr)
- 🖥 www.rockmountgolfclub.com

Royal Belfast (1881)
Holywood, Craigavad BT18 0BP
- ☎ **(028) 9042 8165**
- 📠 (028) 9042 1404
- ✉ admin@royalbelfast.com
- ✍ Mrs SH Morrison
- 🖥 www.royalbelfast.com

Royal County Down (1889)
Newcastle BT33 0AN
- ☎ **(028) 4372 3314**
- 📠 (028) 4372 6281
- ✉ golf@royalcountydown.org
- ✍ David Wilson
- 🖥 www.royalcountydown.org

Scrabo (1907)
233 Scrabo Road, Newtownards BT23 4SL
- ☎ **(028) 9181 2355**
- 📠 (028) 9182 2919
- ✉ admin.scrabogc@btconnect.com
- 🖥 www.scrabo-golf-club.org

The Spa (1907)
Grove Road, Ballynahinch BT24 8PN
- ☎ **(028) 9756 2365**
- 📠 (028) 9756 4158
- ✉ spagolfclub@btconnect.com
- ✍ TG Magee
- 🖥 www.spagolfclub.net

Temple (1994)
60 Church Road, Boardmills, Lisburn
BT27 6UP
- ☎ **(028) 9263 9213**
- 📠 (028) 9263 8637
- ✉ info@templegolf.com
- ✍ B McConnell (Mgr)
- 🖥 www.templegolf.com

Warrenpoint (1893)
Lower Dromore Rd, Warrenpoint
BT34 3LN
- ☎ **(028) 4175 2219 (Clubhouse)**
- 📠 (028) 4175 2918
- ✉ office@warrenpointgolf.com
- ✍ D Moan (028) 4175 3695 (Office)
- 🖥 www.warrenpointgolf.com

Co Dublin

Balbriggan (1945)
Blackhall, Balbriggan
- ☎ **(01) 841 2229**
- 📠 (01) 841 3927
- ✉ balbriggangolfclub@eircom.net
- ✍ Brian Finn (Hon Sec)
- 🖥 www.balbriggangolfclub.com

Balcarrick Golf Club (1972)
Corballis, Donabate
- ☎ **(01) 843 6957**
- 📠 (01) 843 6228
- ✉ balcarr@iol.ie
- 🖥 www.balcarrickgolfclub.com

Beaverstown   (1985)
Beaverstown, Donabate
☎ **(01) 843 6439/6721**
🖳 (01) 843 5059
📧 office@beaverstown.com
✍ Gillian Harris (Administrator)
🖳 www.beaverstown.com

Beech Park   (1983)
Johnstown, Rathcoole
☎ **(01) 458 0522**
🖳 (01) 458 8365
📧 info@beechpark.ie
✍ Mr K M Young (Gen Mgr)
🖳 www.beechpark.ie

Coldwinters   (1994)
Newtown House, St Margaret's
☎ **(01) 864 0324**

Corrstown Golf Club   (1993)
Corrstown, Killsallaghan
☎ **(01) 864 0533**
🖳 (01) 864 0537
📧 info@corrstowngolfclub.com
✍ M Jeanes
🖳 www.corrstowngolfclub.com

Donabate   (1925)
Balcarrick, Donabate
☎ **(01) 843 6346**
📧 info@donabategolfclub.com
🖳 www.donabategolfclub.com

Dublin Mountain   (1993)
Gortlum, Brittas
☎ **(01) 458 2622**
🖳 (01) 458 2048
📧 dmgc.ie
✍ F Carolan
🖳 www.dublinmountaingolf.com

Dun Laoghaire   (1910)
Eglinton Park, Tivoli Road, Dun Laoghaire
☎ **(01) 280 3916**
🖳 www.dunlaoghairegolfclub.ie

Forrest Little   (1940)
Forrest Little, Cloghran, Swords
☎ **(01) 840 1763**
🖳 (01) 840 1000
📧 margaret@forrestlittle.ie
✍ Kevin McIntyre
🖳 www.forrestlittle.com

Glencullen
Glencullen, Co Dublin
☎ **(01) 295 2895**
🖳 www.glencullengc.ie

Hermitage   (1905)
Lucan
☎ **(01) 626 5396**
🖳 (01) 623 8881
📧 hermitagegolf@eircom.net
✍ Eddie Farrell
🖳 www.hermitagegolf.ie

Citywest   (1998)
City West Hotel, Saggert
☎ **(01) 401 0878**
🖳 (01) 458 8756

✍ Tony Shine
🖳 www.citywesthotel.com

Hollywood Lakes   (1992)
Ballyboughal, Co Dublin
☎ **(01) 843 3406/7**
🖳 (01) 843 3002
📧 hollywoodlakesgc@eircom.net
✍ Seamus Kelly (Gen Mgr)
🖳 www.hollywoodlakesgolfclub.com

The Island Golf Club   (1890)
Corballis, Donabate
☎ **+353 1843 6205**
🖳 +353 1843 6860
📧 info@theislandgolfclub.com
✍ Louise McAlley (01) 843 6205
🖳 www.theislandgolfclub.com

Killiney   (1903)
Ballinclea Road, Killiney
☎ **(01) 285 2823**
🖳 (01) 285 2861
📧 killineygolfclub@eircom.net
✍ MF Walsh CCM
🖳 www.killineygolfclub.ie

Kilternan   (1987)
Kilternan
☎ **(01) 295 5559**
📧 kgc@kilternan-hotel.ie

Lucan   (1897)
Celbridge Road, Lucan
☎ **(01) 628 0246**
🖳 (01) 628 2929
📧 admin@lucangolf.ie
✍ Francis Duffy (Sec/Mgr)
🖳 www.lucangolfclub.ie

Luttrellstown Castle G&CC   (1993)
Porterstown Road, Castleknock, Dublin 15
☎ **(353) 1 860 9600**
🖳 (353) 1 860 9601
📧 info@luttrellstown.ie
✍ Colm Haunon
🖳 www.luttrellstowncastleresort.com

Malahide   (1892)
Beechwood, The Grange, Malahide
☎ **(01) 846 1611**
🖳 (01) 846 1270
📧 manager@malahidegolfclub.ie
✍ Mark Gannon (Gen Mgr)
🖳 www.malahidegolfclub.ie

Milltown   (1907)
Lower Churchtown Road, Milltown, Dublin 14
☎ **(01) 497 6090**
🖳 (01) 497 6008
📧 info@milltowngolfclub.ie
✍ J Burns (Gen Mgr)
🖳 www.milltowngolfclub.ie

Portmarnock   (1894)
Portmarnock
☎ **(01) 846 2968 (Clubhouse)**
🖳 (01) 846 2601
✍ JJ Quigley (01) 846 2968 (Gen Mgr)
🖳 www.portmarnockgolfclub.ie

Portmarnock Hotel & Golf Links   (1995)
Proprietary
Strand Road, Portmarnock
☎ **(01) 846 1800**
🖳 (01) 846 2442
📧 golfres@portmarnock.com
✍ Moira Cassidy (Golf Dir)
🖳 www.portmarnock.com

Rush   (1943)
Rush
☎ **(01) 843 8177**
🖳 (01) 843 8177
📧 info@rushgolfclub.com
✍ Noeline Quirke (Sec/Mgr)
🖳 www.rushgolfclub.com

Silloge Park Golf Club   (2010)
Old Ballymun Road, Swords
☎ **(01) 842 9956**
📧 info@sillogeparkgolfclub.com
✍ Damien Connolly
🖳 www.sillogeparkgolfclub.com

Skerries   (1905)
Hacketstown, Skerries
☎ **(01) 849 1567 (Clubhouse)**
🖳 (01) 849 1591
📧 admin@skerriesgolfclub.ie
✍ I Fraher (01) 849 1567
🖳 www.skerriesgolfclub.ie

Slade Valley   (1970)
Lynch Park, Brittas
☎ **(01) 458 2183**
🖳 (01) 458 2784
📧 info@sladevalleygolfclub.ie
✍ D Clancy
🖳 www.sladevalleygolfclub.ie

The South County Golf Club   (2002)
Lisheen Road, Brittas, Co Dublin
☎ **(01) 458 2965**
🖳 (01) 458 2842
📧 info@southcountygolf.ie
✍ Michael Diskin (Gen Mgr)
🖳 www.southcountygolf.com

St Margaret's G&CC   (1992)
St Margaret's, Dublin
☎ **(01) 864 0400**
🖳 (01) 864 0408
📧 reservations@stmargaretsgolf.com
✍ Gary Kearney (Gen Mgr)
🖳 www.stmargaretsgolf.com

Swords   (1996)
Balheary Avenue, Swords
☎ **(01) 840 9819/890 1030**
🖳 (01) 840 9819
📧 info@swordsopengolfcourse.com
✍ O McGuinness (Mgr)
🖳 www.swordsopengolfcourse.com

Turvey   (1994)
Turvey Avenue, Donabate
☎ **(01) 843 5169**
🖳 (01) 843 5179

✉ turveygc@eircom.net
✍ Aoife Griffin
▤ www.turveygolfclub.com

Westmanstown (1988)
Clonsilla, Dublin 15
☎ **(01) 820 5817**
📠 (01) 820 5858
✉ info@westmanstowngolfclub.ie
✍ Edward Doyle (Director of Golf)
▤ www.westmanstowngolfclub.ie

Woodbrook (1926)
Dublin Road, Bray
☎ **(01) 282 4799**
✉ golf@woodbrook.ie
✍ Jim Melody (Gen Mgr)
▤ www.woodbrook.ie

Dublin City

Carrickmines (1900)
Golf Lane, Carrickmines, Dublin 18
☎ **(01) 295 5972**
📠 (01) 214 9674
✉ carrickminesgolf@eircom.net
✍ B Levis 00353 871682150 (Mobile)

Castle (1913)
Woodside Drive, Rathfarnham, Dublin 14
☎ **(01) 490 4207**
📠 (01) 492 0264
✉ info@castlegc.ie
✍ John McCormack (Gen Mgr)
▤ www.castlegc.ie

Clontarf (1912)
Donnycarney House, Malahide Road,
Dublin 3
☎ **(01) 833 1892**
📠 (01) 833 1933
✉ info@clontarfgolfclub.ie
✍ A Cahill (Mgr)
▤ www.clontarfgolfclub.ie

Deer Park (1974)
Deer Park Hotel, Howth
☎ **(01) 832 6039**

Edmondstown (1944)
Rathfarnham, Dublin 16
☎ **(01) 493 2461**
📠 (01) 493 3152
✉ info@edmondstowngolfclub.ie
✍ SS Davies (01) 493 1082
▤ www.edmondstowngolfclub.ie

Elm Park (1925)
Nutley House, Donnybrook, Dublin 4
☎ **(01) 269 3438/269 3014**
📠 (01) 269 4505
✉ office@elmparkgolfclub.ie
✍ A McCormack (01) 269 3438
▤ www.elmparkgolfclub.ie

Grange (1910)
Whitechurch Road, Rathfarnham, Dublin 14
☎ **(01) 493 2889**
📠 (01) 493 9490
✉ administration@grangegolfclub.ie
✍ Billy Meehan (Gen Mgr)
▤ www.grangegolfclub.ie

Hazel Grove (1988)
Mount Seskin Road, Jobstown, Dublin 24
☎ **(01) 452 0911**

Howth (1916)
Carrickbrack Road, Sutton, Dublin 13
☎ **(01) 832 3055**
📠 (01) 832 1793
✉ gm@howthgolfclub.ie
✍ Darragh Tighe MPGA (01) 832
3055
▤ www.howthgolfclub.ie

Kilmashogue (1994)
St Columba's College, Whitechurch, Dublin
16
☎ **(087) 274 9844**

Newlands (1910)
Newlands Cross, Dublin 22
☎ **(01) 459 3157**
📠 (01) 459 3498
✉ info@newlandsgolf.com
✍ Gay Nolan (Gen Mgr)
▤ www.newlandsgolf.com

Rathfarnham (1899)
Newtown, Dublin 16
☎ **(01) 493 1201/493 1561**
📠 (01) 493 1561
✉ info@rathfarnhamgolfclub.ie
✍ John Lawler (01) 493 1201
▤ www.rathfarnhamgolfclub.ie

Royal Dublin (1885)
North Bull Island Nature Reserve,
Dollymount, Dublin 3
☎ **(01) 833 6346**
📠 (01) 833 6504
✉ info@theroyaldublingolfclub
.com
✍ Dermot Sherlock (Hon Sec) (01)
833 6346
▤ www.theroyaldublingolfclub.com

St Anne's (1921)
North Bull Nature Reserve, Dollymount,
Dublin 5
☎ **(01) 833 6471**
📠 (01) 833 4618
✉ info@stanneslinksgolf.com
✍ Ted Power
▤ www.stanneslinksgolf.com

Stackstown (1975)
Kellystown Road, Rathfarnham,
Dublin 16
☎ **(01) 494 1993**
📠 (01) 493 3934
✉ info@stackstowngolfclub.ie
✍ Raymond Murphy (Gen Mgr)
▤ www.stackstowngolfclub.com

Sutton (1890)
Cush Point, Sutton, Dublin 13
☎ **(01) 832 3013**
📠 (01) 832 1603
✉ info@suttongolfclub.org
✍ E O'Brien (Hon Sec)
▤ www.suttongolfclub.org

Co Fermanagh

Castle Hume (1991)
Belleek Road, Enniskillen BT93 7ED
☎ **(028) 6632 7077**
📠 (028) 6632 7076
✉ info@castlehumegolf.com
✍ Patrick Duffy (Admin)
▤ www.castlehumegolf.com

Enniskillen (1896)
Castlecoole, Enniskillen BT74 6HZ
☎ **(028) 6632 5250**
📠 (028) 6632 5250
✉ enniskillengolfclub@mail.com
✍ Darryl Robinson
(Club Steward)
▤ www.enniskillengolfclub.com

Co Galway

Ardacong
Milltown Road, Tuam, Co Galway
☎ **(093) 25525**

Athenry (1902)
Palmerstown, Oranmore
☎ **(091) 794466**
📠 (091) 794971
✉ athenrygc@eircom.net
▤ www.athenrygolfclub.net

Ballinasloe (1894)
Rosgloss, Ballinasloe
☎ **(0905) 42126**

Bearna (1996)
Corboley, Bearna
☎ **(091) 592677**
📠 (091) 592674
✉ info@bearnagolfclub.com
✍ Pat Donnellan
▤ www.bearnagolfclub.com

Connemara (1973)
Public
Ballyconneely, Clifden
☎ **(095) 23502/23602**
📠 (095) 23662
✉ info@connemaragolflinks.net
✍ K Burke (Sec/Mgr)
▤ www.connemaragolflinks.com

Connemara Isles
Annaghvane, Lettermore, Connemara
☎ **(091) 572498**

Curra West (1996)
Curra, Kylebrack, Loughrea
☎ **(091) 45121**

Galway (1895)
Blackrock, Salthill, Galway
☎ **(091) 522033**
📠 (091) 529783
✉ info@galwaygolf.com
✍ P Fahy
▤ www.galwaygolf.com

Galway Bay Golf Resort

(1993)
Renville, Oranmore
☎ +353 (91) 790711/2
🖹 www.galwaybaygolfresort.com

Glenlo Abbey

Glenlo Abbey Hotel, Bushy Park, Galway
☎ (091) 519698
🖹 www.glenlo.com

Gort   (1924)

Castlequarter, Gort
☎ (091) 632244
📠 (091) 632387
✉ info@gortgolf.com
✍ J Skehill (Hon)
🖹 www.gortgolf.com

Loughrea   (1924)

Graigue, Loughrea
☎ (091) 841049
✉ loughreagolfclub@eircom.net

Mountbellew   (1929)

Shankill, Mountbellew, Ballinasloe
☎ (090) 967 9259
✉ mountbellewgc@eircom.net
✍ Padraic Costello
🖹 www.mountbellewgolfclub.com

Oughterard   (1973)

Gortreevagh, Oughterard
☎ (091) 552131
📠 (091) 552733
✉ oughterardgc@eircom.net
✍ Richard McNamarg
🖹 www.oughterardgolfclub.com

Portumna   (1913)

Ennis Road, Portumna
☎ (090) 97 41059
📠 (090) 97 41798
✉ portumnagc@eircom.net
✍ Michael Ryan (Secretary)
🖹 www.portumnagolfclub.ie

Tuam   (1904)

Barnacurragh, Tuam
☎ (093) 28993
📠 (093) 26003
✉ tuamgolfclub@eircom.net
✍ Mary Burns (Sec/Mgr)
🖹 www.tuamgolfclub.com

Co Kerry

Ardfert   (1993)

Sackville, Ardfert, Tralee
☎ (066) 713 4744

Ballybeggan Park

Ballybeggan, Tralee, Co Kerry
☎ (066) 712 6188

Ballybunion Golf Club

(1893)
Sandhill Road, Ballybunion, Ireland
☎ +353 (68) 27146
📠 +353 (68) 27387

✉ info@ballybuniongolfclub.ie
✍ Vari McGreevy
🖹 www.ballybuniongolfclub.ie

Ballyheigue Castle   (1995)

Ballyheigue, Tralee
☎ (066) 713 3555
📠 (066) 713 3934
✍ J Casey (Sec/Mgr)
🖹 www.ballyheiguecastlegolfclub.com

Beaufort   (1994)

Churchtown, Beaufort, Killarney
☎ (064) 44440
📠 (064) 44752
✉ beaufortgc@eircom.net
✍ C Kelly
🖹 www.beaufortgolfclub.com

Castlegregory   (1989)

Stradbally, Castlegregory
☎ (066) 713 9444
📠 (066) 713 9958
✉ info@castlegregorygolflinks.com
✍ M Keane (Hon Sec)
🖹 www.castlegregorygolfclub.com

Ceann Sibeal   (1924)

Ballyferriter
☎ (066) 915 6255/6408
📠 (066) 915 6409
✉ dinglegc@iol.ie
✍ S Fahy (Mgr)
🖹 www.dinglelinks.com

Dooks   (1889)

Glenbeigh
☎ (066) 976 8205
📠 (066) 976 8476
✉ office@dooks.com
✍ Brian Hurley
🖹 www.dooks.com

Kenmare   (1903)

Kenmare
☎ (064) 6641291
📠 (064) 6642061
✉ info@kenmaregolfclub.com
✍ John Sullivan
🖹 www.kenmaregolfclub.com

Kerries   (1995)

Tralee
☎ (066) 712 2112

Killarney   (1893)

Mahoney's Point, Killarney
☎ (064) 31034
📠 (064) 33065
✉ reservations@killarney-golf.com
✍ Maurice O'Meara (Gen Mgr)
🖹 www.killarney-golf.com

Killorglin   (1992)

Stealroe, Killorglin
☎ (669) 761 979
📠 (669) 761 437
✉ kilgolf@iol.ie
✍ B Dodd
🖹 www.killorglingolf.ie

Parknasilla   (1974)

Parknasilla, Sneem
☎ (064) 66 45145
📠 (064) 66 45323
✉ parknasillagolfclub@eircom.net
✍ M Walsh (Mgr)

Ring of Kerry G&CC   (1998)

Proprietary
Templenoe, Killarney
☎ (064) 66 42000
📠 (064) 66 42533
✉ james@ringofkerrygolf.com
✍ James Mitchell (Gen Mgr)
🖹 www.ringofkerrygolf.com

Tralee   (1896)

West Barrow, Ardfert
☎ (066) 713 6379
✉ info@traleegolfclub.com
🖹 www.traleegolfclub.com

Waterville Golf Links

(1889)
Waterville Golf Links, Ring of Kerry,
Waterville
☎ +353-66-947 4102
📠 +353-66-947 4482
✉ wvgolf@iol.ie
✍ Noel Cronin (Sec/Mgr)
🖹 www.watervillegolflinks.ie

Co Kildare

Athy   (1906)

Geraldine, Athy
☎ (059) 863 1729
📠 (059) 863 4710
✉ info@athygolfclub.com
✍ Kathleen Gray (Sec/Administrator)
🖹 www.athygolfclub.com

Bodenstown   (1972)

Bodenstown, Sallins
☎ (045) 897096
📠 (045) 898126
✉ bodenstown@eircom.net
✍ Tom Keightley (0872 264133
🖹 www.bodenstown.com

Carton House   (2002)

Carton House, Maynooth
☎ +353 (0)1 505 2000
📠 +353 (0)1 651 7703
✉ reservations@cartonhouse.com
✍ Francis Howley (Director of Golf)
🖹 www.cartonhouse.com

Castlewarden G&CC   (1989)

Straffan
☎ (01) 458 9254
📠 (01) 458 8972
✉ info@castlewardengolfclub.ie
✍ Andy Callanan
🖹 www.castlewardengolfclub.ie

Celbridge Elm Hall

Elmhall, Celbridge, Co Kildare
☎ (01) 628 8208

Cill Dara (1920)
Little Curragh, Kildare Town
☎ **(045) 521295**

Craddockstown (1991)
Blessington Road, Naas
☎ **(045) 897610**
✉ enquiries@craddockstown.com
🖳 www.craddockstown.com

The Curragh (1883)
Curragh
☎ **(045) 441238/441714**
🖳 (045) 442476
✉ curraghgolf@eircom.net
✍ Ann Culliton (045) 441714
🖳 www.curraghgolf-club.com

Highfield Golf & Country Club (1992)
Proprietary
Carbury, Co. Kildare
☎ **(046) 973 1021**
🖳 (046) 973 1021
✉ highfieldgolf@eircom.net
✍ Philomena Duggan (Sec/Mgr)
🖳 www.highfield-golf.ie

The K Club (1991)
Straffan
☎ **(01) 601 7300**
🖳 (01) 601 7399
✉ golf@kclub.ie
✍ B Donald (Golf Dir)
   01601 7302
🖳 www.kclub.ie

Kilkea Castle (1995)
Castledermot
☎ **(059) 914 5555**
✉ kilkeagolfclub@eircom.net
🖳 www.kilkeacastlehotelgolf.com

Killeen (1986)
Killeenbeg, Kill
☎ **(045) 866003**
🖳 (045) 875881
✉ admin@killeengc.ie
✍ M Kelly
🖳 www.killeengolf.com

Knockanally (1985)
Donadea, Naas, North Kildare
☎ **(045) 869322**
✉ golf@knockanally.com
✍ Helen Melady
🖳 www.knockanally.com

Naas (1896)
Kerdiffstown, Naas
☎ **(045) 874644**
🖳 (045) 896109
✉ info@naasgolfclub.com
✍ Denis Mahon (Mgr)
🖳 www.naasgolfclub.com

Newbridge (1997)
Tankardsgarden, Newbridge
☎ **(045) 486110**

Co Kilkenny

Callan (1929)
Geraldine, Callan
☎ **(056) 7725136**
🖳 (056) 7755155
✉ info@callangolfclub.com/
   manager@callangolfclub.com
✍ Deirdre Power (Sec/Mgr)
   (056) 77 25136
🖳 www.callangolfclub.com

Castlecomer (1935)
Dromgoole, Castlecomer
☎ **(056) 4441139**
🖳 (056) 4441139
✉ castlecomergolf@eircom.net
✍ M Dooley (Hon)
🖳 www.castlecomergolfclub.com

Kilkenny (1896)
Glendine, Kilkenny
☎ **(056) 776 5400**
🖳 (056) 772 3593
✉ enquiries@kilkennygolfclub.com
✍ Sean Boland (056) 776 5400
🖳 www.kilkennygolfclub.com

Mount Juliet (1991)
Thomastown
☎ **(056) 777 3071**
🖳 (056) 777 3078
✉ golfinfo@mountjuliet.ie
✍ William Kirby
🖳 www.mountjuliet.com

Co Laois

Abbeyleix (1895)
Rathmoyle, Abbeyleix
☎ **(057) 8731450**
✉ info@abbeyleixgolfclub.ie
✍ Gery O'Hara (Hon Sec)
🖳 www.abbeyleixgolfclub.ie

The Heath (1930)
The Heath, Portlaoise
☎ **(057) 864 6533**
🖳 (057) 864 6735
✉ info@theheathgc.ie
✍ Christy Crawford (Hon)
🖳 www.theheathgc.ie

The Heritage Golf & Spa Resort (2004)
Proprietary
The Heritage Golf & Spa Resort, Killenard
☎ **(057) 864 2321**
🖳 (057) 864 2392
✉ info@theheritage.com
✍ Niall Carroll (Golf Ops Mgr)
🖳 www.theheritage.com

Mountrath (1929)
Knockanina, Mountrath
☎ **(0502) 32558/32643**
✉ mountrathgc@eircom.net
🖳 www.mountrathgolfclub.ie

Portarlington (1908)
Garryhinch, Portarlington
☎ **(057) 862 23115**
🖳 (057) 862 23044
✉ portarlingtongc@eircom.net
✍ Jerry Savage
🖳 www.portarlingtongolf.com

Rathdowney (1930)
Coulnaboul West, Rathdowney
☎ **(0505) 46170**
🖳 (0505) 46065
✉ rathdowneygolf@eircom.net
✍ Martin O'Brian (Hon) (0505) 46338
🖳 www.rathdowneygolfclub.com

Co Leitrim

Ballinamore (1941)
Creevy, Ballinamore
☎ **(078) 964 4346**
✍ G Mahon (078) 964 4031,

Co Limerick

Abbeyfeale (1993)
Dromtrasna, Collins Abbeyfeale
☎ **(068) 32033**
✉ abbeyfealegolf@eircim.net
🖳 www.abbeyfealegolfclub.com

Adare Manor (1900)
Adare
☎ **(061) 396204**
🖳 (061) 396800
✉ info@adaremanorgolfclub.com
✍ Dr Milo Spillane
🖳 www.adaremanorgolfclub.com

Castletroy (1937)
Golf Links Road, Castleroy, Co. Limerick
☎ **(061) 335753 (club)**
🖳 (061) 335373
✉ golf@castletroygolfclub.ie
✍ Patrick Keane (Gen Mgr)
🖳 www.castletroygolfclub.ie

Limerick (1891)
Ballyclough, Limerick
☎ **(061) 414083**
🖳 (061) 319219
✉ information@limerickgolfclub.ie
✍ P Murray (Gen Mgr) (061) 415146
🖳 www.limerickgolfclub.ie

Limerick County G&CC (1994)
Ballyneety, Co. Limerick
☎ **(061) 351881**
🖳 (061) 351384
✉ info@limerickcounty.com
🖳 www.limerickcounty.com

Newcastle West (1938)
Rathgonan, Ardagh, Co. Limerick
☎ **(069) 76500**
🖳 (069) 76511
✉ info@newcastlewestgolf.com
✍ John Whelan (Sec/Mgr)
🖳 www.newcastlewestgolf

Rathbane   (1998)
Public
Rathbane, Crossagalla, Limerick
- ☎ **(061) 313655**
- 📠 (061) 313655
- ✍ John O'Sullivan

Co Londonderry

Benone Par Three
53 Benone Avenue, Benone, Limavady
BT49 0LQ
- ☎ **(028) 7775 0555**
- ✍ MI Clark

Brown Trout   (1984)
209 Agivey Road, Aghadowey, Coleraine
BT51 4AD
- ☎ **(028) 7086 8209**
- 📠 (028) 7086 8878
- ✉ bill@browntroutinn.com
- ✍ B O'Hara (Sec/Mgr)
- 🖳 www.browntroutinn.com

Castlerock   (1901)
65 Circular Road, Castlerock BT51 4TJ
- ☎ **(028) 7084 8314**
- 📠 (028) 7084 9440
- ✉ info@castlerockgc.co.uk
- ✍ M Steen (Sec/Mgr)
- 🖳 www.castlerockgc.co.uk

City of Derry   (1911)
49 Victoria Road, Londonderry BT47 2PU
- ☎ **(028) 7134 6369**
- 📠 (028) 7131 0008
- ✉ info@cityofderrygolfclub.com
- ✍ Tony McCann
- 🖳 www.cityofderrygolfclub.com

Foyle   (1994)
Proprietary
12 Alder Road, Londonderry BT48 8DB
- ☎ **(028) 7135 2222**
- 📠 (028) 7135 3967
- ✉ mail@foylegolf.club24.co.uk
- ✍ Rob Gallagher (028) 71 352222
- 🖳 www.foylegolfcentre.co.uk

Kilrea   (1919)
47a Lisnagrot Road, Kilrea BT51 5SF
- ☎ **(028) 295 40044**
- ✉ kilreagc@hotmail.co.uk
- ✍ M R Dean (028) 295 40044
- 🖳 www.kilreagolfclub.co.uk

Moyola Park   (1976)
15 Curran Road, Castledawson,
Magherafelt BT45 8DG
- ☎ **(028) 7946 8468**
- 📠 (028) 7946 8626
- ✉ moyolapark@btconnect.com
- ✍ S McKenna (Hon)
- 🖳 www.moyolapark.com

Portstewart   (1894)
117 Strand Road, Portstewart BT55 7PG
- ☎ **(028) 7083 2015**
- 📠 (028) 7083 4097
- ✉ info@portstewartgc.co.uk
- ✍ M Moss BA (028) 7083 3839
- 🖳 www.portstewartgc.co.uk

Roe Park   (1993)
Public/Hotel
Roe Park Golf Club, Radisson Blu Roe Park
Resort, Roe Park, Limavady BT49 9LB
- ☎ **(028) 7776 0105**
- 📠 (028) 777 22313
- ✉ roeparkgolf.limavady@RadissonBlu
  .com
- ✍ Terry Kelly (028) 777 60105
- 🖳 www.radissonroepark.com

Traad Ponds
Shore Road, Magherafelt BT45 6LR
- ☎ **(028) 7941 8865**

Co Longford

County Longford   (1894)
Glack, Dublin Road, Longford
- ☎ **(043) 334 6310**
- 📠 (043) 334 7082
- ✉ colonggolf@eircom.net
- ✍ Ms Pauline Corry
- 🖳 www.countylongfordgolfclub.com

Co Louth

Ardee   (1911)
Townparks, Ardee
- ☎ **(041) 685 3227**
- 📠 (041) 685 6137
- ✉ ardeegolfclub@eircom.net
- ✍ Noel Malone (Sec)
- 🖳 www.ardeegolfclub.com

Carnbeg   (1996)
Carnbeg, Dundalk, Co Louth
- ☎ **(042) 933 2518**
- ✉ carnbeggolfcourse@eircom.net
- 🖳 www.dundalk.parkinn.ie

County Louth   (1892)
Baltray, Drogheda
- ☎ **(041) 988 1530**
- 📠 (041) 988 1531
- ✉ reservations@countylouthgolfclub
  .com
- ✍ M Delany
- 🖳 www.countylouthgolfclub.com

Dundalk   (1904)
Blackrock, Dundalk
- ☎ **(042) 932 1731**
- 📠 (042) 932 2022
- ✉ manager@dundalkgolfclub.ie
- ✍ R Woods (Sec/Mgr)
- 🖳 www.dundalkgolfclub.ie

Greenore   (1896)
Greenore
- ☎ **(042) 937 3212/3678**
- 📠 (042) 937 3678
- ✉ greenoregolfclub@eircom.net
- ✍ Linda Clarke
- 🖳 www.greenoregolfclub.com

Killinbeg   (1991)
Killin Park, Dundalk
- ☎ **(042) 933 9303**

Seapoint   (1993)
Termonfeckin, Drogheda
- ☎ **(041) 982 2333**
- 📠 (041) 982 2331
- ✉ golflinks@seapoint.ie
- 🖳 www.seapointgolflinks.ie

Townley Hall   (1994)
Tullyallen, Drogheda
- ☎ **(041) 984 2229**
- ✉ townleyhall@oceanfree.net

Co Mayo

Achill   (1951)
Keel, Achill
- ☎ **(098) 43456**
- 📠 (098) 43456
- ✉ achillislandgolfclub@gmail.com
- ✍ Hugo Boyle (087) 798 1225
- 🖳 www.achillgolf.com

Ashford Castle
Cong
- ☎ **(092) 46003**

Ballina   (1910)
Mossgrove, Shanaghy, Ballina
- ☎ **(096) 21050**
- ✉ ballinagc@eircom.net
- 🖳 www.ballina-golf.com

Ballinrobe   (1895)
Cloonacastle, Ballinrobe, Co Mayo
- ☎ **(094) 954 1118**
- 📠 (094) 954 1889
- ✉ info@ballinrobegolfclub.com
- ✍ John G Burke
- 🖳 www.ballinrobegolfclub.com

Ballyhaunis   (1929)
Coolnaha, Ballyhaunis
- ☎ **(0907) 30014**

Belmullet   (1925)
Carne, Belmullet
- ☎ **(00353) 97 82292**
- ✉ sefirot-liam@hotmail.com
- ✍ Liam Power (Hon Sec)
- 🖳 www.belmulletgolfclub.ie

Castlebar   (1910)
Hawthorn Avenue, Rocklands,
Castlebar
- ☎ **(094) 21649**
- 📠 (094) 26088
- ✉ info@castlebargolfclub.ie
- ✍ Bernie Murray
- 🖳 www.castlebar.ie/golf

Claremorris   (1917)
Pay and play
Castlemacgarrett, Claremorris
- ☎ **(094) 937 1527**
- 📠 (094) 937 2919
- ✉ info@claremorrisgolfclub.com
- ✍ N McCarthy (Hon)
- 🖳 www.claremorrisgolfclub.com

Mulranny (1968)
Mulranny, Westport
☎ **(098) 36262**

Swinford (1922)
Brabazon Park, Swinford
☎ **(+353) 94 925 1378**

Westport (1908)
Carrowholly, Westport
☎ **(098) 28262**
🖥 (098) 24648
📧 info@westportgolfclub.com
✍ Sean Durkan
🖥 www.westportgolfclub.com

Co Meath

Ashbourne (1991)
Archerstown, Ashbourne, Co.Meath
☎ **(01) 835 2005**
🖥 (01) 835 9261
📧 info@ashbournegolfclub.ie
✍ Paul Wisniewski
🖥 www.ashbournegolfclub.ie

Black Bush (1987)
Thomastown, Dunshaughlin
☎ **(01) 825 0021**
🖥 (01) 825 0400
📧 info@blackbushgolfclub.ie
✍ Kate O'Rourke (Admin)
(01) 825 0021
🖥 www.blackbushgolfclub.ie

County Meath (1898)
Newtownmoynagh, Trim
☎ **(046) 9431463**
🖥 www.trimgolf.net

Glebe
Kildalkey Road, Trim, Meath
☎ **(00353) 4694 31926**
📧 glebegc@eircom.net
🖥 www.glebegolfclub.com

Gormanston College
(1961)
Franciscan College, Gormanston
☎ **(01) 841 2203**
🖥 (01) 841 2685
✍ Br Laurence Brady
🖥 www.gormanstoncollege.ie

Headfort (1928)
Kells
☎ **(046) 924 0146**
🖥 (046) 924 9282
📧 hgcadmin@eircom.net
✍ Nora Murphy (Admin)
🖥 www.headfortgolfclub.ie

Kilcock (1985)
Gallow, Kilcock
☎ **(01) 628 7592**
📧 info@kilcockgolfclub.ie
🖥 www.kilcockgolfclub.ie

Laytown & Bettystown
(1909)
Bettystown, Co. Meath
☎ **(041) 982 7170**
🖥 (041) 982 8506
📧 links@landb.ie
✍ Helen Finnegan
🖥 www.landb.ie

Moor Park (1993)
Moortown, Navan
☎ **(046) 27661**

Navan (1996)
Public
Proudstown, Navan, Co Meath
☎ **(046) 907 2888**
🖥 (046) 907 6722
📧 info@navangolfclub.ie
✍ Sheila Slattery
🖥 www.navangolfclub.ie

Royal Tara (1906)
Bellinter, Navan
☎ **(046) 902 5508/902 5584**
🖥 (046) 902 6684
📧 info@royaltaragolfclub.com
✍ John McGarth (Hon)
🖥 www.royaltaragolfclub.com

Summerhill
Agher, Rathmoylan, Co Meath
☎ **(046) 955 7857**

Co Monaghan

Castleblayney Golf Club,
Concrawood (1985)
Onomy, Castleblayney
☎ **(042) 974 9485**
🖥 (042) 975 4576
📧 info@concrawood.ie
✍ Adrian Kelly
🖥 www.concrawood.ie

Clones (1913)
Hilton Demesne, Clones
☎ **(047) 56017**
🖥 (047) 56017
📧 clonesgolfclub@eircom.net
✍ Paul Fitzpatrick (087) 766 1778
🖥 www.clonesgolfclub.com

Nuremore Hotel & CC
(1964)
Nuremore Hotel, Carrickmacross
☎ **(042) 966 1438**
🖥 (042) 966 1853
📧 info@nuremore.com
✍ Maurice Cassidy (Director)
🖥 www.nuremore.com

Rossmore (1916)
Rossmore Park, Cootehill Road, Monaghan
☎ **(047) 81316**
🖥 (047) 71227
📧 rossmoregolfclub@eircom.net
✍ J McKenna (Hon)
🖥 www.rossmoregolfclub.com

Co Offaly

Birr (1893)
The Glenns, Birr
☎ **(057) 91 20082**
🖥 (057) 91 22155
📧 birrgolfclub@eircom.net
✍ Tony Hogan (Hon)
🖥 www.birrgolfclub.ie

Castle Barna (1992)
Castlebarnagh, Daingean, Offaly
☎ **(057) 935 3384**
🖥 (057) 935 3077
📧 info@castlebarna.ie
✍ E Mangan
🖥 www.castlebarna.ie

Edenderry (1910)
Kishawanny, Edenderry
☎ **(046) 973 1072**
📧 enquiries@edenderrygolfclub.com
🖥 www.edenderrygolfclub.com

Esker Hills G&CC (1996)
Proprietary
Tullamore, Co Offaly
☎ **(057) 93 55999**
🖥 (057) 93 55021
📧 info@eskerhillsgolf.com
✍ C Guinan
🖥 www.eskerhillsgolf.com

Tullamore (1896)
Brookfield, Tullamore
☎ **(057) 93 21439**
🖥 (057) 83 41806
📧 tullamoregolfclub@eircom.net
✍ H Egan (057) 93 21439
🖥 www.tullamoregolfclub.ie

Co Roscommon

Athlone (1892)
Hodson Bay, Athlone
☎ **(090) 649 2073/649 2235**
🖥 (090) 649 4080
📧 athlonegolfclub@eircom.net
✍ I Dockery
🖥 www.athlonegolfclub.ie

Ballaghaderreen (1936)
Aughalustia, Ballaghaderreen
☎ **(094) 986 0295**
📧 info@ballaghaderreengolfclub.com
✍ Hon Secretary
🖥 www.ballaghaderreengolfclub.com

Boyle (1911)
Knockadoo, Brusna, Boyle
☎ **(071) 966 2594**
✍ J Mooney (Hon) (087) 776 0161

Castlerea (1905)
Clonallis, Castlerea
☎ **(0871) 278066**
📧 castlereagolf@oceanfree.net
✍ Cathering O'Loughlin
🖥 www.castlereagolfclub.com

Roscommon (1904)
Mote Park, Roscommon
☎ **(09066) 26382**
📠 (09066) 26043
📧 rosgolf@eircom.net
✍ M Dolan (087) 225 4695

Strokestown (1995)
Strokestown, Co Roscommon
☎ **(07196) 33660**
📧 strokestowngolfclub@gmail.com
✍ L Glover (Hon)
🖥 www.strokestowngolfclub.com

Co Sligo

Ballymote (1943)
Ballinascarrow, Ballymote
☎ **(071) 918 3504**
📠 (071) 918 3504
📧 ballymotegolfclub@gmail.ie
✍ J O'Connor
🖥 www.ballymotegolfclub.com

County Sligo (1894)
Rosses Point
☎ **(071) 9177134/9177186**
📠 (071) 9177460
📧 teresa@countysligogolfclub.ie
✍ David O'Donovan
🖥 www.countysligogolfclub.ie

Enniscrone (1931)
Ballina Road, Enniscrone
☎ **(096) 36297**
📠 (096) 36657
📧 enniscronegolf@eircom.net
✍ Pat Sweeney (Sec/Mgr)
🖥 www.enniscronegolf.com

Strandhill (1932)
Strandhill
☎ **(00353) 71 91 68188**
📧 strandhillgc@eircom.net
🖥 www.strandhillgc.com

Tubbercurry (1990)
Ballymote Road, Tubbercurry
☎ **(071) 918 5849 (Societies)**
(086) 8306174
📧 contact@tubbercurrygolfclub.com
✍ Billy Kilgannon (071) 918 6124
🖥 www.tubbercurrygolfclub.com

Co Tipperary

Ballykisteen Hotel & Golf Resort (1994)
Proprietary
Ballykisteen, Limerick Junction
☎ **(+353) 062 33333 (hotel)**
📠 (+353) 062 31555
📧 golf.ballykisteen@ballykisteenhotel.com
✍ Mike Keegan (+353 087 667 9495)
🖥 www.ballykisteenhotel.com

Cahir Park (1967)
Kilcommon, Cahir, Co Tipperary
☎ **(052) 7441474**
📠 (052) 7442717
📧 cahirgolfclub@hotmail.com
✍ Paul Adamson (Club Sec)
🖥 www.cahirgolfclub.com

Carrick-on-Suir (1939)
Garravoone, Carrick-on-Suir, County Tipperary
☎ **(051) 640047**
📠 (051) 640558
📧 info@carrickgolfclub.com
✍ Michael Kelly (Hon Sec)
🖥 www.carrickgolfclub.com

Clonmel (1911)
Lyreanearla, Mountain Road, Clonmel
☎ **(052) 61 24050**
📠 (052) 61 83349
📧 cgc@indigo.ie
✍ A Myles-Keating (052) 6124050 (Ext 20)
🖥 www.clonmelgolfclub.com

Dundrum Golf & Leisure Resort (1993)
Dundrum, Cashel
☎ **(062) 71717**
📧 golfshop@dundrumhouse.ie
✍ William Crowe (Mgr) (062) 71717
🖥 www.dundrumhousehotel.com

Nenagh (1929)
Beechwood, Nenagh
☎ **(067) 31476**
📠 (067) 34808
📧 nenaghgolfclub@eircom.net
✍ Paddy Heffernan
🖥 www.nenaghgolfclub.com

Roscrea (1892)
Derryvale, Roscrea
☎ **00353 (0) 505 21130**
📠 00353 (0) 505 23410
📧 info@roscreagolfclub.ie
✍ Marie Kennedy
🖥 www.roscreagolfclub.ie

Slievenamon (1999)
Proprietary
Clonacody, Lisronagh, Co Tipperary
☎ **(052) 61 32213**
📠 (052) 61 30875
📧 info@slievnamongolfclub.com
✍ B Kenny (052) 61 32213
🖥 www.slievnamongolfclub.com

Templemore (1970)
Manna South, Templemore
☎ **(0504) 32923/31400**
📧 johnkm@tinet.ie
✍ John Hackett

Thurles (1909)
Turtulla, Thurles
☎ **(0504) 21983**
📠 (0504) 90806
📧 office@thurlesgolfclub.com
✍ Tom Ryan (Hon Sec)
🖥 www.thurlesgolfclub.com

Tipperary (1896)
Rathanny, Tipperary
☎ **(062) 51119**
📧 tipperarygolfclub@eircom.net
✍ Michael Tobin (Sec/Mgr)
🖥 www.tipperarygolfclub.com

Co Tyrone

Auchnacloy (1995)
Pay and play
99 Tullyvar Road, Auchnacloy
☎ **(028) 8255 7050**
📧 Sidney.houston@yahoo.co.uk
✍ S Houston

Benburb Valley
Maydown Road, Benburb BT71 7LJ
☎ **(028) 3754 9868**

Dungannon (1890)
34 Springfield Lane, Mullaghmore, Dungannon BT70 1QX
☎ **(028) 8772 2098**
📠 (028) 8772 7338
📧 dungannongolfclub2009@hotmail.co.uk
✍ ST Hughes
🖥 www.dungannongolfclub.com

Fintona (1904)
Eccleville Desmesne, 1 Kiln Street, Fintona BT78 2BJ
☎ **(028) 8284 1480**
📧 fintonagolfclub@btconnect.com

Killymoon (1889)
200 Killymoon Road, Cookstown BT80 8TW
☎ **(028) 8676 3762**
📠 (028) 8676 3762
📧 killymoongolf@btconnect.com
✍ N Weir
🖥 www.killymoongolfclub.com

Newtownstewart (1914)
38 Golf Course Road, Newtownstewart BT78 4HU
☎ **(028) 8166 1466**
📠 (028) 8166 2506
📧 newtown.stewart@lineone.net
✍ Lorraine Donnell (Administrator)
🖥 www.newtownstewartgolfclub.com

Omagh (1910)
83A Dublin Road, Omagh BT78 1HQ
☎ **(028) 8224 3160/1442**

Strabane (1908)
Ballycolman, Strabane BT82 9PH
☎ **(028) 7138 2271/2007**
📠 (028) 7188 6514
📧 strabanegc@btconnect.com
✍ Claire Keys
🖥 www.strabanegolfclub.co.uk

Co Waterford

Dungarvan (1924)
Knocknagranagh, Dungarvan
☎ **(058) 43310/41605**
📠 (058) 44113
📧 dungarvangc@eircom.net
✍ Irene Lynch (Mgr)
🖥 www.dungarvangolfclub.com

Dunmore East (1993)
Proprietary
Dunmore East
☎ **(051) 383151**
📠 (051) 383151
📧 info@dunmoreeastgolfclub.ie
✍ Alan Skehan
🖥 www.dunmoreeastgolfclub.ie

Faithlegg (1993)
Faithlegg House, Faithlegg
☎ **(051) 380587/380592**
📠 (051) 382010
📧 golf@fhh.ie
✍ Ryan Hunt (051) 380588
🖥 www.faithlegg.com

Gold Coast (1993)
Ballinacourty, Dungarvan
☎ **(058) 42249/44055**
📠 (058) 43378
📧 info@goldcoastgolfclub.com
✍ Mark Lenihan/Brendan O'Brien
(058) 44055
🖥 www.goldcoastgolfclub.com

Lismore (1965)
Ballyin, Lismore
☎ **(058) 54026**
📠 (058) 53338
📧 lismoregolfclub@eircom.net
✍ W Henry
🖥 www.lismoregolf.org

Tramore (1894)
Newtown, Tramore
☎ **(051) 386170/381247**
📠 (051) 390961
📧 info@tramoregolfclub.com
✍ Don Buckley (Gen Mgr)
🖥 www.tramoregolfclub.com

Waterford (1912)
Newrath, Waterford
☎ **+353 (0) 51 876748**
📠 +353 (0) 51 853405
📧 info@waterfordgolfclub.com
✍ Damien Maquire (Sec/Mgr)
🖥 www.waterfordgolfclub.com

Waterford Castle (1991)
Proprietary
The Island, Ballinakill, Waterford
☎ **(051) 871633**
📧 golf@waterfordcastle.com
🖥 www.waterfordcastle.com

West Waterford G&CC
(1993)
Dungarvan
☎ **(058) 43216/41475**
📠 (058) 44343
📧 info@westwaterfordgolf.com
✍ A Spratt (Director)
🖥 www.westwaterfordgolf.com

Co Westmeath

Ballinlough Castle
Clonmellon, Co Westmeath
☎ **(044) 64544**

Delvin Castle (1992)
Clonyn, Delvin
☎ **(044) 96 64315**
📧 info@delvincastlegolf.com
✍ F Dillon
🖥 www.delvincastlegolf.com

**Glasson Country House
Hotel and Golf Club** (1993)
Glasson, Athlone
☎ **00353 (0) 90 6485120**
📠 (00353 0) 90 6485444
📧 info@glassongolf.ie
✍ Gareth Jones
🖥 www.glassongolfhotel.ie

Moate (1900)
Aghanargit, Moate
☎ **(090) 648 1271**
📠 (090) 648 2645
📧 moategolfclub@eircom.net
✍ A O'Brien
🖥 www.moategolfclub.ie

Mount Temple G&CC
(1991)
Proprietary
Mount Temple, Moate
☎ **(090) 648 1841**
📧 mounttemple@eircom.net
✍ M Dolan
🖥 www.mounttemplegolfclub.com

Mullingar (1894)
Belvedere, Mullingar
☎ **(0 0353 44) 934 8366**
📧 mullingargolfclub@hotmail.com
🖥 www.mullingargolfclub.com

Co Wexford

Courtown (1936)
Kiltennel, Gorey
☎ **(053) 942 5166**
📠 (053) 942 5553
📧 info@courtowngolfclub.com
✍ S O'Hara
🖥 www.courtowngolfclub.com

Enniscorthy (1906)
Knockmarshall, Enniscorthy
☎ **(053) 92 33191**
📠 (053) 92 37637
📧 honsec@enniscorthygc.ie
✍ John Cullen
🖥 www.enniscorthygc.ie

New Ross (1905)
Tinneranny, New Ross
☎ **(051) 421433**
📠 (051) 420098
📧 newrossgolf@eircom.net
✍ Kathleen Daly (Sec/Mgr) (051)
421433
🖥 www.newrossgolfclub.net

Rosslare (1905)
Rosslare Strand, Rosslare
☎ **(053) 913 2203 (office)**
📠 (053) 913 2263
📧 office@rosslaregolf.com
✍ Frank Codd (Hon Sec)
🖥 www.rosslaregolf.com

St Helen's Bay (1993)
Proprietary
St Helen's, Kilrane, Rosslare Harbour
☎ **(053) 91 33234**
📧 info@sthelensbay.com
🖥 www.sthelensbay.com

Tara Glen (1984)
Ballymoney, Gorey, Co Wexford
☎ **(053) 942 5413**
📠 (053) 942 5612
📧 taraglenplc@eircom.net
✍ Marion Siggins
🖥 www.tataglen.ie

Wexford (1960)
Mulgannon, Wexford
☎ **(05391) 42238**
📠 (05391) 42243
📧 info@wexfordgolfclub.ie
✍ Roy Doyle (Hon Sec)
🖥 www.wexfordgolfclub.ie

Co Wicklow

Arklow (1927)
Abbeylands, Arklow
☎ **(0402) 32492**
📠 (0402) 91604
📧 arklowgolflinks@eircom.net
✍ D Canavan (Hon Sec)/D Roche
(Mgr)
🖥 www.arklowgolfclublinks.com

Baltinglass (1928)
Baltinglass
☎ **(059) 648 1350**
📧 baltinglassgolfclub@eircom.net
🖥 www.baltinglassgolfclub.ie

Blainroe (1978)
Blainroe
☎ **(0404) 68168**
📠 (0404) 69369
📧 info@blainroe.com
✍ Patrick Bradshaw
🖥 www.blainroe.com

Boystown
Baltyboys, Blessington, Co Wicklow
☎ **(045) 867146**

Bray   (1897)
Greystones Road, Bray
☎ **(01) 276 3200**
✉ info@braygolfclub.com
🖳 www.braygolfclub.com

Charlesland   (1992)
Greystones
☎ **(01) 287 4350**
🖳 (01) 287 0078
✉ teetimes@charlesland.com
🖉 Gerry O'Brien (Mgr)
🖳 www.charlesland.com

Delganey   (1908)
Delgany
☎ **(01) 287 4536**
🖳 (01) 287 3977
✉ delganygolf@eircom.net
🖉 Peter Ribeiro (Gen Mgr)
🖳 www.delganygolfclub.com

Djouce   (1995)
Roundwood
☎ **(01) 281 8585**
✉ djoucegolfclub@gmail.com
🖉 D McGillycuddy (Mgr)
🖳 www.djoucegolfclub.com

Druid's Glen   (1995)
Newtownmountkennedy
☎ **(01) 287 3600**
🖳 (01) 287 3699
✉ info@druidsglen.ie
🖉 D Flinn (Gen Mgr)
🖳 www.druidsglen.ie

Druid's Heath   (2003)
Newtownmountkennedy
☎ **(01) 287 3600**
🖳 (01) 287 3699
✉ info@druidsglen.ie
🖉 D Flinn (Gen Mgr)
🖳 www.druidsglen.ie

The European Club   (1989)
Brittas Bay, Wicklow
☎ **(0404) 47415**
🖳 (0404) 47449
✉ info@theeuropeanclub.com

🖉 P Ruddy
🖳 www.theeuropeanclub.com

Glen of the Downs   (1998)
Coolnaskeagh, Delgany, Co Wicklow
☎ **(01) 287 6240**
🖳 (01) 287 0063
✉ info@glenofthedowns.com
🖉 Derek Murphy
🖳 www.glenofthedowns.com

Glenmalure   (1991)
Greenane, Rathdrum
☎ **(0404) 46679**
✉ info@glenmaluregolf.ie
🖉 Tina O'Shaughnessy (Hon Sec)
🖳 www.glenmaluregolf.com

Greystones   (1895)
Greystones
☎ **(01) 287 4136**
🖳 (01) 287 3749
✉ secretary@greystonesgc.com
🖉 Angus Murray (Mgr)
🖳 www.greystonesgc.com

Kilcoole   (1992)
Kilcoole
☎ **(01) 287 2066**
✉ adminkg@eircom.net
🖳 www.kilkoolegolfclub.com

Old Conna   (1987)
Ferndale Road, Bray
☎ **(01) 282 6055**
🖳 (01) 282 5611
✉ info@oldconna.com
🖉 Tom Sheridan (Gen Mgr)
🖳 www.oldconna.com

Powerscourt (East)
   (1996)
Powerscourt Estate, Enniskerry
☎ **(01) 204 6033**
🖳 (01) 276 1303
🖉 B Gibbons (Mgr)
🖳 www.powerscourt.ie

Powerscourt (West)   (2003)
Powerscourt Estate, Enniskerry
☎ **(01) 204 6033**
🖳 (01) 276 1303
🖉 B Gibbons (Mgr)
🖳 www.powerscourt.ie

Rathsallagh   (1993)
Proprietary
Dunlavin
☎ **(045) 403316**
🖳 (045) 403295
✉ info@rathsallagh.com/golf
   @rathsallagh.com
🖉 J O'Flynn (045) 403316
🖳 www.rathsallagh.com

Roundwood   (1995)
Ballinahinch, Newtownmountkennedy
☎ **(01) 281 8488**
✉ rwood@indigo.ie
🖳 www.roundwoodgolf.com

Tulfarris   (1987)
Blessington Lakes, Blessington
☎ **(045) 867644**
🖳 (045) 867601
✉ golf@tulfarris.com
🖉 A Williams (Mgr)

Vartry Lakes   (1997)
Proprietary
Roundwood
☎ **(01) 281 7006**
🖳 www.wicklow.ie

Wicklow   (1904)
Dunbur Road, Wicklow
☎ **(0404) 67379**
🖳 (0404(64756
✉ info@wicklowgolfclub.ie
🖉 J Kelly
🖳 www.wicklowgolfclub.ie

Woodenbridge   (1884)
Vale of Avoca, Arklow
☎ **(0402) 35202**
🖳 (0402) 35754
✉ reception@woodenbridge.ie
🖉 Gerry Coloman
🖳 www.woodenbridgegolfclub.com

For key to symbols and European dialling codes see page 717

Who is known as "Buffalo Bill"?

The answer can be found on page 905

Scotland

Aberdeenshire

Aboyne (1883)
Formaston Park, Aboyne AB34 5HP
- ☎ (013398) 86328
- 🖳 (013398) 87078
- ✉ aboynegolfclub@btconnect.com
- ✍ Mrs M Ferries (013398) 87078
- 🖥 www.aboynegolfclub.co.uk

Aboyne Loch Golf Centre (2000)
Pay and play
Aboyne Loch, Aboyne AB34 5BR
- ☎ (013398) 86444
- ✉ info@thelodgeontheloch.com
- 🖥 www.thelodgeontheloch.com

Alford (1982)
Montgarrie Road, Alford AB33 8AE
- ☎ (019755) 62178
- 🖳 (019755) 64910
- ✉ info@alford-golf-club.co.uk
- ✍ Mrs Julie Alexander
- 🖥 www.alford-golf-club.co.uk

Auchenblae Golf Course (1894)
Pay and play
Auchenblae, Laurencekirk AB30 1TX
- ☎ (01561) 320002 (Group Bookings)
- ✍ J Thomson (01561) 320245
- 🖥 www.auchenblaegolfcourse.co.uk

Ballater (1892)
Victoria Road, Ballater AB35 5LX
- ☎ (013397) 55567
- ✉ sec@ballatergolfclub.co.uk
- ✍ Colin Smith
- 🖥 www.ballatergolfclub.co.uk

Ballindalloch Castle (2003)
Pay and play
Lagmore, Ballindalloch, Banffshire AB37 9AA
- ☎ (01807) 500305
- ✉ golf@ballindallochcastle.co.uk
- 🖥 www.ballindallochcastle.co.uk

Banchory (1904)
Kinneskie Road, Banchory AB31 5TA
- ☎ (01330) 822365
- 🖳 (01330) 822491
- ✉ bgc.secretary@btconnect.com
- ✍ Mrs A Smart
- 🖥 www.banchorygolfclub.co.uk

Braemar (1902)
Cluniebank Road, Braemar AB35 5XX
- ☎ (013397) 41618
- ✉ info@braemargolfclub.co.uk
- ✍ C McIntosh (013397) 41618
- 🖥 www.braemargolfclub.co.uk

Craibstone (1999)
Public
Craibstone Estate, Bucksburn, Aberdeen AB29 9YA
- ☎ (01224) 716777
- ✉ craibstonegolf@sac.co.uk

Cruden Bay (1899)
Aulton Road, Cruden Bay, Peterhead AB42 0NN
- ☎ (01779) 812285
- 🖳 (01779) 812945
- ✉ robbie@crudenbaygolfclub.co.uk
- ✍ Mr R G Stewart (PGA Director of Golf)
- 🖥 www.crudenbaygolfclub.co.uk

Cullen (1879)
The Links, Cullen, Buckie AB56 4WB
- ☎ (01542) 840685
- ✉ cullengolfclub@btinternet.com
- ✍ Mrs H Bavidge
- 🖥 www.cullengolfclub.co.uk

Duff House Royal Golf Club (1910)
The Barnyards, Banff AB45 3SX
- ☎ (01261) 812062
- 🖳 (01261) 812224
- ✉ info@duffhouseroyal.com
- ✍ James Cameron
- 🖥 www.duffhouseroyal.com

Fraserburgh (1777)
Philorth Links, Fraserburgh AB43 8TL
- ☎ (01346) 516616
- ✉ secretary@fraserburghgolfclub.org
- ✍ Lorraine Duncan
- 🖥 www.fraserburghgolfclub.org

Huntly (1892)
Cooper Park, Huntly AB54 4SH
- ☎ (01466) 792643
- 🖳 (01466) 792643
- ✉ huntlygc@btconnect.com
- ✍ A Donald (01466) 792643
- 🖥 www.huntlygc.com

Inchmarlo (1995)
Proprietary
Glassel Road, Banchory AB31 4BQ
- ☎ (01330) 826424
- 🖳 (01330) 826425
- ✉ secretary@inchmarlo.com
- ✍ Andrew Shinie (01330) 826427
- 🖥 www.inchmarlogolf.com

Insch (1906)
Golf Terrace, Insch AB52 6JY
- ☎ (01464) 820363
- ✉ administrator@inschgolfclub.co.uk
- ✍ Sarah Ellis (Administrator)
- 🖥 www.inschgolfclub.co.uk

Inverallochy
Public
Whitelink, Inverallochy, Fraserburgh AB43 8XY
- ☎ (01346) 582000

- 🖳 (01346) 582000
- ✉ inverallochygolf@btconnect.com
- ✍ GM Young
- 🖥 www.inverallochygolfclub.com

Inverurie (1923)
Davah Wood, Inverurie AB51 5JB
- ☎ (01467) 624080
- 🖳 (01467) 672869
- ✉ administrator@inveruriegc.co.uk
- ✍ Alan Donald (01467) 624080
- 🖥 www.inveruriegc.co.uk

Keith (1963)
Mar Court, Fife Keith, Keith AB55 5GF
- ☎ (01542) 882469
- ✉ secretary@keithgolfclub.co.uk
- ✍ Diane Morrison
- 🖥 www.keithgolfclub.co.uk

Kemnay (1908)
Monymusk Road, Kemnay AB51 5RA
- ☎ (01467) 642225
- 🖳 (01467) 643561
- ✉ administrator@kemnaygolfclub.co.uk
- ✍ F Webster (Secretary)
- 🖥 www.kemnaygolfclub.co.uk

Kintore (1911)
Balbithan Road, Kintore AB51 0UR
- ☎ (01467) 632631
- 🖳 (01467) 632995
- ✉ kintoregolfclub@lineone.net
- ✍ C Lindsay
- 🖥 www.kintoregolfclub.net

Longside (1973)
West End, Longside, Peterhead AB42 4XJ
- ☎ (01779) 821558
- ✉ info@longsidegolf.wanadoo.co.uk
- ✍ J Taylor (01779) 821558
- 🖥 www.longsidegolfclub.co.uk

Lumphanan (1924)
Owned privately
Main Road, Lumphanan, Banchory AB31 4PY
- ☎ (01339) 883480
- ✉ info@lumphanangolfclub.co.uk
- ✍ Y Taite (Sec) (01339) 883696
- 🖥 www.lumphanangolfclub.co.uk

McDonald (1927)
Hospital Road, Ellon AB41 9AW
- ☎ (01358) 720576
- 🖳 (01358) 720001
- ✉ mcdonald.golf@virgin.net
- ✍ G Ironside
- 🖥 www.ellongolfclub.co.uk

Meldrum House (1998)
Meldrum House Estate, Oldmeldrum AB51 0AE
- ☎ (01651) 873553
- ✉ info@meldrumhousegolfclub.co.uk
- 🖥 www.meldrumhousegolfclub.co.uk

Newburgh-on-Ythan
(1888)
Beach Road, Newburgh, Aberdeenshire
AB41 6BY
- ☎ **(01358) 789058**
- 🖷 (01358) 788104
- 🖂 secretary@newburghgolfclub.co.uk
- ✍ Administrator: (01358) 789084
- 🖳 www.newburghgolfclub.co.uk

Newmachar   (1989)
Swailend, Newmachar, Aberdeen
AB21 7UU
- ☎ **(01651) 863002**
- 🖷 (01651) 863055
- 🖂 info@newmachargolfclub.co.uk
- ✍ Alasdair MacGregor
- 🖳 www.newmachargolfclub.co.uk

Oldmeldrum   (1885)
Kirk Brae, Oldmeldrum AB51 0DJ
- ☎ **(01651) 872648/873555**
- 🖷 (01651) 872896
- 🖂 admin@oldmeldrumgolf.co.uk
- ✍ Hamish Dingwall (Administrator)
- 🖳 www.oldmeldrumgolf.co.uk

Peterhead   (1841)
Craigewan Links, Peterhead AB42 1LT
- ☎ **(01779) 472149/480725**
- 🖷 (01779) 480725
- 🖂 phdgc@freenetname.co.uk
- ✍ D.G.Wood
- 🖳 www.peterheadgolfclub.co.uk

Rosehearty   (1874)
c/o Mason's Arms Hotel, Rosehearty,
Fraserburgh AB43 7JJ
- ☎ **(01346) 571250 (Capt)**
- 🖂 scotthornal@cbtinternet.com

Rothes   (1990)
Proprietary
Blackhall, Rothes, Aberlour AB38 7AN
- ☎ **(01340) 831443**
- 🖷 (01340) 831443
- 🖂 rothesgolfclub@tiscali.co.uk
- ✍ Kenneth MacPhee (01340) 831676
- 🖳 www.rothesgolfclub.co.uk

Royal Tarlair   (1926)
Buchan Street, Macduff AB44 1TA
- ☎ **(01261) 832897**
- 🖷 (01261) 833455
- 🖂 info@royaltarlair.co.uk
- ✍ Mrs Muriel McMurray
- 🖳 www.royaltarlair.co.uk

Stonehaven   (1888)
Cowie, Stonehaven AB39 3RH
- ☎ **(01569) 762124**
- 🖷 (01569) 765973
- 🖂 info@stonehavengolfclub.com
- ✍ Mrs M H Duncan
- 🖳 www.stonehavengolfclub.com

Strathlene   (1877)
Portessie, Buckie AB56 4DJ
- ☎ **(01542) 831798**
- 🖂 strathlenegc@gmail.com
- ✍ David Lyun
- 🖳 www.strathlenegolfclub.co.uk

Tarland   (1908)
Aberdeen Road, Tarland AB34 4TB
- ☎ **(013398) 81000**
- 🖷 (013398) 81000
- 🖂 secretary@tarlandgolfclub.co.uk
- ✍ Mrs C Foreman (admin) (019756) 51484
- 🖳 www.tarlandgolfclub.co.uk

Torphins   (1896)
Bog Road, Torphins AB31 4JU
- ☎ **(013398) 82115**
- 🖂 stuartmacgregor5@btinternet.com
- ✍ S MacGregor (013398) 82402
- 🖳 www.torphinsgolfclub.com

Turriff   (1896)
Rosehall, Turriff AB53 4HD
- ☎ **(01888) 562982 Pro Shop**
  (01888) 563025
- 🖷 (01888) 568050
- 🖂 secretary@turriffgolf.sol.co.uk
- ✍ M Smart
- 🖳 www.turriffgolfclub.com

Aberdeen Clubs

Bon Accord   (1872)
Club
19 Golf Road, Aberdeen AB24 5QB
- ☎ **(01224) 633464**

Caledonian   (1899)
Club
20 Golf Road, Aberdeen AB2 1QB
- ☎ **(01224) 632443**

Northern   (1897)
Public
22 Golf Road, Aberdeen AB24 5QB
- ☎ **(01224) 636440**
- 🖷 (01224) 622679
- 🖂 ngcgolf@hotmail.com
- ✍ D Johnstone
- 🖳 www.northerngolfclub.co.uk

Aberdeen Courses

Auchmill   (1975)
Bonnyview Road, West Heatheryfold,
Aberdeen AB16 7FQ
- ☎ **(01224) 715214**
- 🖷 (01224) 715226
- 🖂 auchmill.golf@btconnect.com
- ✍ Yvonne Sangster (01224) 715214
- 🖳 www.auchmill.co.uk

Balnagask   (1955)
Public
St Fitticks Road, Aberdeen
- ☎ **(01224) 871286**
- 🖷 (01224) 873418
- 🖂 nicebay@btconnect.com
- ✍ W Gordon

Deeside   (1903)
Golf Road, Bieldside, Aberdeen AB15 9DL
- ☎ **(01224) 869457**
- 🖷 (01224) 861800
- 🖂 admin@deesidegolfclub.com

- ✍ Ms D Pern (01224) 869457
- 🖳 www.deesidegolfclub.com

Fyvie   (2003)
Pay and play
Fyvie, Turriff, Aberdeenshire AB53 8QR
- ☎ **(01651) 891166**
- 🖷 (01651) 891166
- 🖂 info@fyviegolfcourse.co.uk
- ✍ Alexander Rankin
- 🖳 www.fyviegolfcourse.co.uk

Murcar Links   (1909)
Bridge of Don, Aberdeen AB23 8BD
- ☎ **(01224) 704354**
- 🖷 (01224) 704354
- 🖂 golf@murcarlinks.com
- ✍ Carol O'Neill
- 🖳 www.murcarlinks.com

Peterculter   (1989)
Proprietary
Oldtown, Burnside Road, Peterculter
AB14 0LN
- ☎ **(01224) 735245**
- 🖷 (01224) 735580
- 🖂 info@petercultergolfclub.co.uk
- ✍ D Vannet
- 🖳 www.petercultergolfclub.co.uk

Portlethen   (1983)
Badentoy Road, Portlethen, Aberdeen
AB12 4YA
- ☎ **(01224) 781090**
- 🖷 (01224) 783383
- 🖂 admin@portlethengolfclub.com
- 🖳 www.portlethengolfclub.com

Royal Aberdeen   (1780)
Links Road, Bridge of Don, Aberdeen
AB23 8AT
- ☎ **(01224) 702571**
- 🖷 (01224) 826591
- 🖂 admin@royalaberdeengolf.com
- ✍ Ronnie Macaskill (Dir. of Golf)
- 🖳 www.royalaberdeengolf.com

Westhill   (1977)
Westhill Heights, Westhill AB32 6RY
- ☎ **(01224) 742567**
- 🖷 (01224) 749124
- 🖂 westhillgolf@btconnect.com
- ✍ George Bruce (Admin)
- 🖳 www.westhillgolfclub.co.uk

Angus

Arbroath Artisan   (1903)
Public
Elliot, Arbroath DD11 2PE
- ☎ **(01241) 872069**
- 🖷 (01241) 875837
- 🖂 captain@arbroathartisangolfclub .co.uk
- ✍ J R Tollerton
- 🖳 www.arbroathartisangolfclub.co.uk

Ballumbie Castle   (2000)
3 Old Quarry Road, Dundee DD4 0SY
- ☎ **(01382) 770028**
- 🖷 (01382) 730008
- 🖂 ballumbie2000@yahoo.com

　Stephen Harrod
📧 www.ballumbiecastlegolfclub.com

Brechin (1893)
Trinity, Brechin DD9 7PD
☎ **(01356) 625270
(bookings/pro)**
📠 (01356) 625270
📧 brechingolfclub@tiscali.com
　 S Rennie (Manager)
📧 www.brechingolfclub.co.uk

Caird Park (1926)
Public
Mains Loan, Caird Park, Dundee DD4 9BX
☎ **(01382) 453606/461460**
📠 (01382) 461460
📧 cp.golf.club@btconnect.com
　 G Martin (07961) 159636

Camperdown (1960)
Public
Camperdown Park, Dundee DD2 4TF
☎ **(01382) 623398**

Downfield (1932)
Turnberry Ave, Dundee DD2 3QP
☎ **(01382) 825595**
📠 (01382) 813111
📧 downfieldgc@aol.com
　 Mrs M Campbell
📧 www.downfieldgolf.co.uk

Edzell (1895)
High St, Edzell DD9 7TF
☎ **(01356) 647283**
📠 (01356) 648094
📧 secretary@edzellgolfclub.com
　 IG Farquhar (01356) 647283
📧 www.edzellgolfclub.com

Forfar (1871)
Cunninghill, Arbroath Road, Forfar DD8 2RL
☎ **(01307) 463773/462120**
📠 (01307) 468495
📧 info@forfargolfclub.com
　 S Wilson
📧 www.forfargolfclub.com

Kirriemuir (1884)
Northmuir, Kirriemuir DD8 4LN
☎ **(01575) 573317**
📠 (01575) 574608
📧 enquiries@kirriemuirgolfclub.co.uk
　 C Gowrie
📧 www.kirriemuirgolfclub.co.uk

Monifieth Golf Links
Medal Starter's Box, Princes Street,
Monifieth DD5 4AW
☎ **(01382) 532767 (Bookings)**
📠 (01382) 535816
📧 secretary@monifiethlinks.com
　 J Brodie (Managing Sec),
📧 www.monifiethgolf.co.uk

Montrose Golf Links (1562)
Public
Traill Drive, Montrose DD10 8SW
☎ **(01674) 672932**
📠 (01674) 671800
📧 secretary@montroselinks.co.uk

　 Miss Claire Penman
📧 www.montroselinks.co.uk

Montrose Caledonia (1896)
Club
Dorward Road, Montrose DD10 8SW
☎ **(01674) 672313**

Panmure (1845)
Barry, Carnoustie DD7 7RT
☎ **(01241) 855120**
📠 (01241) 859737
📧 secretary@panmuregolfclub.co.uk
　 Charles JR Philip
📧 www.panmuregolfclub.co.uk

Royal Montrose (1810)
Club
Traill Drive, Montrose DD10 8SW
☎ **(01674) 672376**
📧 secretary@royalmontrosegolf.com
　 Ian Mitchell (07792) 626931
📧 www.royalmontrosegolf.com

Carnoustie Clubs

Carnoustie Caledonia
(1887)
Club
Links Parade, Carnoustie DD7 7JF
☎ **(01241) 852115**
　 R Reyner
📧 www.carnoustiecaledonia.co.uk

Carnoustie Ladies (1873)
Club
12 Links Parade, Carnoustie DD7 7JF
☎ **(01241) 855252**

Carnoustie Mercantile
(1896)
Club
Links Parade, Carnoustie DD7 7JE

The Carnoustie Golf Club
(1842)
Club
3 Links Parade, Carnoustie DD7 7JF
☎ **(01241) 852480**
📧 admin@carnoustiegolfclub.com
　 AJR Mackenzie
📧 www.carnoustiegolfclub.com

Carnoustie Courses

Buddon Links (1981)
Public
20 Links Parade, Carnoustie DD7 7JF
☎ **(01241) 802270**
📠 (01241) 802271
📧 golf@carnoustiegolflinks.co.uk
　 G Duncan
📧 www.carnoustiegolflinks.co.uk

Burnside (1914)
Public
20 Links Parade, Carnoustie DD7 7JF
☎ **(01241) 802270**
📠 (01241) 802271

📧 golf@carnoustiegolflinks.co.uk
　 G Duncan
📧 www.carnoustiegolflinks.co.uk

Carnoustie Championship
(1842)
Public
20 Links Parade, Carnoustie DD7 7JF
☎ **(01241) 802270**
📠 (01241) 802271
📧 golf@carnoustiegolflinks.co.uk
　 G Duncan
📧 www.carnoustiegolflinks.co.uk

Argyll & Bute

Blairmore & Strone (1896)
High Road, Strone, Dunoon PA23 8TH
☎ **(01369) 840676**
📧 thompsongg@talk21.com
　 Graham Thompson (01369)
840208
📧 www.blairmoregc.co.uk

Bute (1888)
32 Marine Place, Ardbeg, Rothesay, Isle of
Bute PA20 0LF
☎ **(01700) 503091**
📧 administrator@butegolfclub.com
　 F Robinson (01700) 503091
📧 www.butegolfclub.com

Carradale (1906)
Carradale, Campbeltown PA28 6QT
☎ **(01583) 431788**
📧 margaretrichardson1977@live
.co.uk
　 Margaret Richardson (Sec)
📧 www.carradalegolf.com

Colonsay
Owned privately
Isle of Colonsay PA61 7YR
☎ **(01951) 200290**

Cowal (1891)
Ardenslate Road, Dunoon PA23 8LT
☎ **(01369) 705673**
📠 (01369) 705673
📧 secretary@cowalgolfclub.com
　 A Douglas (01369) 705673
📧 www.cowalgolfclub.com

Craignure (1895)
Scallastle, Craignure, Isle of Mull PA65 6BA
☎ **(01688) 302517**
📧 pvnbook2@aol.com

Dalmally (1986)
Old Saw Mill, Dalmally PA33 1AE
☎ **(01838) 200619**
📧 dalmallygolfclub@btinternet.com
　 S Tollan (01631) 710401
📧 www.dalmallygolfclub.co.uk

Dunaverty (1889)
Southend, Campbeltown PA28 6RW
☎ **(01586) 830677**
📠 (01586) 830677
📧 dunavertygc@aol.com
　 Bill Brannigan
📧 www.dunavertygolfclub.com

Gigha　(1992)
Pay and play
Isle of Gigha, Kintyre PA41 7AA
☎ **(01583) 505242**
✉ johngigha@hotmail.co.uk
✍ J Bannatyne
🖳 www.gigha.org

Glencruitten　(1908)
Glencruitten Road, Oban PA34 4PU
☎ **(01631) 562868**
✉ enquiries@obangolf.com
✍ AG Brown (01631) 564604
🖳 www.obangolf.com

Helensburgh　(1893)
25 East Abercromby Street, Helensburgh G84 9HZ
☎ **(01436) 674173**
📠 (01436) 671170
✉ secretary@helensburghgolfclub .co.uk
✍ Martyn Lawrie (Gen Mgr) (01436) 674173
🖳 www.helensburghgolfclub.co.uk

Innellan　(1891)
Knockamillie Road, Innellan, Dunoon
☎ **(01369) 830242**
✉ innellangolfclub@btconnect.com
✍ R Milliken (01369) 830415

Inveraray　(1893)
North Cromalt, Inveraray, Argyll
☎ **(01499) 600286**
✍ D MacNeill

Islay　(1891)
25 Charlotte St, Port Ellen, Isle of Islay PA42 7DF
☎ **(01496) 300094**
🖳 www.islay.golf.btinternet.co.uk

Isle of Seil　(1996)
Pay and play
Balvicar, Isle of Seil PA34 4TF
☎ **(01852) 300548**
✉ geolladam@yahoo.co.uk
✍ G Adam

Kyles of Bute　(1906)
The Moss, Kames, Tighnabruaich PA21 2AB
✍ Dr J Thomson 01700 811 603
🖳 www.kylesofbutegolfclub.co.uk

Lochgilphead　(1963)
Blarbuie Road, Lochgilphead PA31 8LE
☎ **(01546) 602340**
✍ Bill Dick
🖳 www.lochgilphead-golf.com

Lochgoilhead　(1994)
Public
Drimsynie Estate, Lochgoilhead PA24 8AD
☎ **(01301) 703247**
📠 (01301) 703538
✉ info@argyllholidays.com
✍ Colin Park
🖳 www.argyllholidays.com

Machrihanish　(1876)
Machrihanish, Campbeltown PA28 6PT
☎ **(01586) 810213**
📠 (01586) 810221
✉ secretary@machgolf.com
✍ Mrs A Anderson
🖳 www.machgolf.com

Millport　(1888)
Millport, Isle of Cumbrae KA28 0HB
☎ **(01475) 530311**
📠 (01475) 530306
✉ secretary@millportgolfclub.co.uk
✍ William Reid (01475) 530306
🖳 www.millportgolfclub.co.uk

Port Bannatyne　(1912)
Bannatyne Mains Road, Port Bannatyne, Isle of Bute PA20 0PH
☎ **(01700) 504544**
✍ R Jardine (01700) 500195
🖳 www.portbannatynegolf.co.uk

Rothesay　(1892)
Canada Hill, Rothesay, Isle of Bute PA20 9HN
☎ **(01700) 503554**
✉ rothesaygolfclub@bt.com
✍ Joan Torrence
🖳 www.rothesaygolfclub.com

Tarbert　(1910)
Kilberry Road, Tarbert PA29 6XX
☎ **(01880) 820565**
✍ P Cupples (01546) 606896

Taynuilt　(1987)
Golf Club House, Taynuilt, Argyll PA35 1JH
☎ **(01866) 822429**
📠 (01866) 822255 (phone first)
✉ secretary@taynuiltgolfclub.co.uk
✍ J J Church (01631) 770 633
🖳 www.taynuiltgolfclub.co.uk

Tobermory　(1896)
Erray Road, Tobermory, Isle of Mull PA75 6PS
☎ **(01688) 302387**
✉ secretary@tobermorygolfclub .com
🖳 www.tobermorygolfclub.com

Ayrshire

Annanhill　(1957)
Public
Irvine Road, Kilmarnock KA1 2RT
☎ **(01563) 521512 (Starter)**
✉ annanhillgolfclub@btconnect.com
✍ T Denham (01563) 521644/525557
🖳 www.annanhillgc.co.uk

Ardeer　(1880)
Greenhead Avenue, Stevenston KA20 4LB
☎ **(01294) 464542**
📠 (01294) 464542
✉ info@ardeergolfclub.co.uk
✍ John Boyle (01294) 464542
🖳 www.ardeergolfclub.co.uk

Ballochmyle　(1937)
Ballochmyle, Mauchline KA5 6LE
☎ **(01290) 550469**
✉ ballochmylegolf@btconnect.com
✍ J Davidson
🖳 www.ballochmylegolfclub.co.uk

Beith　(1896)
Threepwood Road, Beith KA15 2JR
☎ **(01505) 503166**
(Clubhouse)
✍ Joe McSorley (Captain)
🖳 www.beithgolfclub.co.uk

Brodick　(1897)
Brodick, Isle of Arran KA27 8DL
☎ **(01770) 302349**
📠 (01770) 302349
✉ enquiries@brodickgolf.com
✍ Ann Hart (Sec)
🖳 www.brodickgolfclub.com

Brunston Castle　(1992)
Golf Course Road, Dailly, Girvan KA26 9GD
☎ **(01465) 811471**
📠 (01465) 811545
✉ golf@brunstoncastle.co.uk
✍ M Edens
🖳 www.brunstoncastle.co.uk

Caprington　(1958)
Public
Ayr Road, Kilmarnock KA1 4UW
☎ **(01563) 53702 (Club)**
✉ caprington.golf@btconnect.com
✍ Michael McDonnell
　Mob 0791 564 8834

Corrie　(1892)
Corrie, Sannox, Isle of Arran KA27 8JD
☎ **(01770) 810223/810606**
✍ George E Welford (01770) 600403
🖳 www.corriegolf.com

Dalmilling　(1961)
Public
Westwood Avenue, Ayr KA8 0QY
☎ **(01292) 263893**

Doon Valley　(1927)
1 Hillside, Patna, Ayr KA6 7JT
☎ **(01292) 531607**
📠 (01292) 532489
✍ H Johnstone

Dundonald Links　(2003)
Pay and play
Ayr Road, Irvine KA11 5BF
☎ **(01294) 314000**
📠 (01294) 314001
✉ reservations@dundonaldlinks.com
✍ Guy Redford
🖳 www.dundonaldlinks.com

Girvan　(1860)
Public
Golf Course Road, Girvan KA26 9HW
☎ **(01465) 714272/714346**
(Starter)
📠 (01465) 714346
✍ WB Tait

Glasgow GC Gailes Links
(1892)
Gailes, Irvine KA11 5AE
☎ (01294) 311258
🖳 (01294) 279366
✉ secretary@glasgow-golf.com
✍ AG McMillan (0141) 942 2011
📧 www.glasgowgolfclub.com

Irvine (1887)
Bogside, Irvine KA8 8SN
☎ (01294) 275979
🖳 (01294) 278209
✉ secretary@theirvinegolfclub.co.uk
✍ W McMahon

Irvine Ravenspark (1907)
Public
Kidsneuk Lane, Irvine KA12 8SR
☎ (01294) 271293
✉ secretary@irgc.co.uk
✍ T McFarlane (01294) 213537
📧 www.irgc.co.uk

Kilbirnie Place (1925)
Largs Road, Kilbirnie KA25 7AT
☎ (01505) 683398
🖳 01505 684444
✉ kilbirnie.golfclub@tiscali.co.uk
✍ Mr J Melvin
📧 www.kilbirnieplacegolfclub.webs
.com

Kilmarnock (Barassie)
(1887)
29 Hillhouse Road, Barassie, Troon
KA10 6SY
☎ (01292) 313920/311077
🖳 (01292) 318300
✉ golf@kbgc.co.uk
✍ D Wilson (01292) 313920
📧 www.kbgc.co.uk

Lamlash (1889)
Lamlash, Isle of Arran KA27 8JU
☎ (01770) 600296
(Clubhouse)
✉ lamlashgolfclub@btconnect.com
✍ D Bilsland
📧 www.lamlashgolfclub.co.uk

Largs (1891)
Irvine Road, Largs KA30 8EU
☎ (01475) 673594 (Secretary's office)
🖳 (01475) 673594
✉ secretary@largsgolfclub.co.uk
✍ Barry Streets
📧 www.largsgolfclub.co.uk

Lochranza Golf Course
(1899)
Pay and play
Lochranza, Isle of Arran KA27 8HL
☎ (0177083) 0273
✉ office@lochgolf.demon.co.uk
✍ N Wells
📧 www.lochranzagolf.com

Loudoun Gowf (1908)
Galston KA4 8PA
☎ (01563) 821993
🖳 (01563) 820011
✉ secy@loudoungowfclub.co.uk
✍ WB Buchanan (01563) 821993
📧 www.loudoungowfclub.co.uk

Machrie Bay (1900)
Pay and play
Machrie Bay, Brodick, Isle of Arran
KA27 8DZ
☎ (01770) 840310
✉ machriebayclubsec@googlemail
.com
✍ E Ross
📧 www.machriebay.com

Muirkirk (1991)
Pay and play
c/o 65 Main Street, Muirkirk KA18 3QR
☎ (01290) 660184 (night)
✍ R Bradford

New Cumnock (1902)
Lochill, Cumnock Road, New Cumnock
KA18 4BQ
☎ (01290) 332761
✍ J McGinn

Prestwick (1851)
2 Links Road, Prestwick KA9 1QG
☎ (01292) 477404
🖳 (01292) 477255
✉ bookings@prestwickgc.co.uk

✍ K W Goodwin
📧 www.prestwickgc.co.uk

Prestwick St Cuthbert
(1899)
East Road, Prestwick KA9 2SX
☎ (01292) 477101
🖳 (01292) 671730
✉ secretary@stcuthbert.co.uk
✍ Jim Jess
📧 www.stcuthbert.co.uk

Prestwick St Nicholas
(1851)
Grangemuir Road, Prestwick KA9 1SN
☎ (01292) 477608
🖳 (01292) 473900
✉ secretary@prestwickstnicholas
.com
✍ Tom Hepburn
📧 www.prestwickstnicholas.com

Routenburn (1914)
Routenburn Road, Largs KA30 8QS
☎ (01475) 686475 –
steward/Clubhouse
✍ RB Connal (01475) 672757

Royal Troon (1878)
Craigend Road, Troon KA10 6EP
☎ (01292) 311555
🖳 (01292) 318204
✉ admin@royaltroon.com
✍ D L K Brown (Sec) (01292) 310060
📧 www.royaltroon.com

Seafield (1930)
Public
Belleisle Park, Doonfoot Road, Ayr
KA7 4DU
☎ (01292) 441258
✉ info@ayrseafieldgolfclub.co.uk
📧 www.ayrseafieldgolfclub.co.uk

Shiskine (1896)
Shiskine, Blackwaterfoot, Isle of Arran
KA27 8HA
☎ (01770) 860226
🖳 (01770) 860205
✉ info@shiskinegolf.com
✍ Pietre Johnston
📧 www.shiskinegolf.com

The Edward Trophy

The Edward family, well-known Glasgow jewellers, presented the trophy in 1892 for all amateurs whose handicaps did not exceed three and who were members of any club in membership with the Scottish Golf Union in the counties of Lanark, Ayrshire, Dunbarton. Stirling, Renfrew, Argyll, Bute and Glasgow. The event was, therefore, originally created as a competition for West of Scotland golfers.

Until 1927 it was played over 36 holes at various venues but the Edward family asked Glasgow Golf Club if they would consider playing it annually on the club's course at Gailes in Ayrshire. The club agreed and so the event has been played at Gailes every year since.

William Tulloch's feat of winning the trophy five times in the 1920s and 30s has not been equalled. In 2008, it became an SGU Order of Merit event over 72 holes.

For key to symbols see page 717

Skelmorlie   (1891)
Skelmorlie PA17 5ES
☎ **(01475) 520152**
✉ sec@skelmorliegolf.co.uk
✍ Mrs Shelagh Travers (Hon)
🖳 www.skelmorliegolf.co.uk

Troon Municipal
Public
Harling Drive, Troon KA10 6NF
☎ **(01292) 312464**

Troon Portland   (1894)
Club
1 Crosbie Road, Troon KA10
☎ **(01292) 313488**

Troon St Meddans   (1909)
Club
Harling Drive, Troon KA10 6NF
✉ secretary
   @troonstmeddansgolfclub.com
✍ Jim Pennington (01563) 851339

Turnberry Hotel   (1906)
Turnberry KA26 9LT
☎ **(01655) 331000**
🖳 (01655) 331069
✉ turnberry.reservations@westin
   .com
✍ Richard Hall (Head golf Proff)
🖳 www.westin.com/turnberry

West Kilbride   (1893)
*Fullerton Drive, Seamill, West Kilbride
KA23 9HT*
☎ **(01294) 823911**
🖳 (01294) 829573
✉ golf@westkilbridegolfclub.com
✍ J W Campbell
🖳 www.westkilbridegolfclub.com

Western Gailes   (1897)
Gailes, Irvine KA11 5AE
☎ **(01294) 311649**
🖳 (01294) 312312
✉ enquiries@westerngailes.com
✍ Jerry Kessell
🖳 www.westerngailes.com

Whiting Bay   (1895)
*Golf Course Road, Whiting Bay, Isle of
Arran KA27 8QT*
☎ **(01770) 700487**
✉ info@whitingbaygolf.com
✍ Mr Richard Fletcher (01770) 700
   487
🖳 www.whitingbaygolf.com

Borders

Duns   (1894)
Hardens Road, Duns TD11 3NR
☎ **(01361) 882194**
✉ secretary@dunsgolfclub.com
✍ G Clark (01361) 883599
🖳 www.dunsgolfclub.com

Eyemouth   (1894)
Gunsgreen House, Eyemouth TD14 5DX
☎ **(018907) 50551 (Clubhouse)**

Galashiels   (1884)
*Ladhope Recreation Ground, Galashiels
TD1 2NJ*
☎ **(01896) 753724**
✉ secretary@galashiels-golfclub.co.uk
✍ R Gass (01896) 755307
🖳 www.galashiels-golfclub.co.uk

Hawick   (1877)
Vertish Hill, Hawick TD9 0NY
☎ **(01450) 372293**
🖳 (01450) 372293
✉ thesecretary@hawickgolfclub.com
✍ J Reilly
🖳 www.hawickgolfclub.com

The Hirsel   (1948)
Kelso Road, Coldstream TD12 4NJ
☎ **(01890) 882678**
🖳 (01890) 882233
✉ bookings@hirselgc.co.uk
✍ Mr Allan Rodger
🖳 www.hirselgc.co.uk

Jedburgh   (1892)
Dunion Road, Jedburgh TD8 6TA
☎ **(01835) 863587**
✉ info@jedburghgolfclub.co.uk
✍ R Nagle (01835) 866271
🖳 www.jedburghgolfclub.co.uk

Kelso   (1887)
Golf Course Road, Kelso TD5 7SL
☎ **(01573) 223009**
🖳 (01573) 228490
✉ secretary@kelsogolfclub.com
✍ DR Jack
🖳 www.kelsogolfclub.com

Langholm   (1892)
Langholm DG13 0JR
☎ **(07724) 875151**
✉ golf@langholmgolfclub.co.uk
✍ Pauline Irving
🖳 www.langholmgolfclub.co.uk

Lauder   (1896)
Pay and play
Galashiels Road, Lauder TD2 6RS
☎ **(01578) 722526**
🖳 (01578) 722526
✉ secretary@laudergolfclub.co.uk
✍ R Towers (01578) 722240
🖳 www.laudergolfclub.co.uk

Melrose   (1880)
Dingleton Road, Melrose TD6 9HS
☎ **(01896) 822855**
🖳 (01896) 822855
✉ melrosegolfclub@tiscali.co.uk
✍ LM Wallace (01835) 823553
🖳 www.melrosegolfclub.co.uk

Minto   (1928)
Denholm, Hawick TD9 8SH
☎ **(01450) 870220**
🖳 (01450) 870126
✉ mintogolfclub@btconnect.com
✍ J Simpson
🖳 www.mintogolf.co.uk

Newcastleton   (1894)
Pay and play
Holm Hill, Newcastleton TD9 0QD
☎ **(013873) 75608**
✍ GA Wilson

Peebles   (1892)
Kirkland Street, Peebles EH45 8EU
☎ **(01721) 720197**
✉ secretary@peeblesgolfclub.com
✍ William Baird (Administrator)
🖳 www.peeblesgolfclub.com

The Roxburghe Hotel & Golf Course   (1997)
Proprietary
Heiton, Kelso TD5 8JZ
☎ **(01573) 450333**
🖳 (01573) 450611
✉ golf@roxburghe.net
✍ Craig Montgomerie (Director of
   Golf)
🖳 www.roxburghegolfclub.co.uk

Selkirk   (1883)
The Hill, Selkirk TD7 4NW
☎ **(01750) 20621**
✉ secretary@selkirkgolfclub.co.uk
✍ A Robertson (01750) 20519 (pm)
🖳 www.selkirkgolfclub.co.uk

St Boswells   (1899)
Braeheads, St Boswells, Melrose TD6 0DE
☎ **(01835) 823527**
✉ secretary@stboswellsgolfclub.co.uk
✍ Sue Brooks (Secretary)
🖳 www.stboswellsgolfclub.co.uk

Torwoodlee   (1895)
*Edinburgh Road, Galashiels, Torwoodlee
TD1 2NE*
☎ **(01896) 752260**
🖳 (01896) 752306
✉ torwoodleegolfclub@btconnect
   .com
✍ L Moffat (Administrator)
🖳 www.torwoodleegolfclub.org.uk

Woll Golf Course   (1993)
Proprietary
*New Woll Estate, Ashkirk, Selkirkshire
TD7 4PE*
☎ **(01750) 32711**
✉ wollgolf@tiscali.co.uk
✍ Nicholas Brown (01750) 32711
🖳 www.wollgolf.co.uk

West Linton   (1890)
Medwyn Road, West Linton EH46 7HN
☎ **(01968) 660970**
🖳 (01968) 660622
✉ secretarywlgc@btinternet.com
✍ John Johnson (01968) 661121
🖳 www.wlgc.co.uk

Clackmannanshire

Alloa   (1891)
Schawpark, Sauchie, Alloa FK10 3AX
☎ **(01259) 722745**
🖳 (01259) 218796

✉ secretary@alloagolfclub.co.uk
✍ Secretary
🖥 www.alloagolfclub.co.uk

Alva
Beauclerc Street, Alva FK12 5LH
☎ (01259) 760431

Braehead (1891)
Cambus, Alloa FK10 2NT
☎ (01259) 725766
🖷 (01259) 214070
✉ enquiries@braeheadgolfclub.co.uk
✍ Ronald Murray
🖥 www.braeheadgolfclub.com

Dollar (1890)
Brewlands House, Dollar FK14 7EA
☎ (01259) 742400
🖷 (01259) 743497
✉ info@dollargolfclub.com
✍ W D Carln
🖥 www.dollargolfclub.com

Tillicoultry (1899)
Alva Road, Tillicoultry FK13 6BL
☎ (01259) 750124
🖷 (01259) 750124
✉ tillygolf@btconnect.com
✍ M Todd
🖥 www.tillygc.co.uk

Tulliallan (1902)
Kincardine, Alloa FK10 4BB
☎ (01259) 730396
🖷 (01259) 731395
✉ tulliallangolf@btconnect.com
✍ Amanda Maley
🖥 www.tulliallangolf.co.uk

Dumfries & Galloway

Brighouse Bay (1999)
Pay and play
Borgue, Kirkcudbright DG6 4TS
☎ (01557) 870509
✉ admin@brighousebaygolfclub.co.uk
🖥 www.brighousebay-golfclub.co.uk

Castle Douglas (1905)
Abercromby Road, Castle Douglas DG7 1BA
☎ (01556) 502801
✉ cdgolfclub@aol.com
✍ J Duguid (01556) 503527
🖥 www.cdgolf.co.uk

Colvend (1905)
Sandyhills, Dalbeattie DG5 4PY
☎ (01556) 630398
🖷 (01556) 630495
✉ secretary@colvendgolfclub.co.uk
✍ R N Bailey
🖥 www.colvendgolfclub.co.uk

Crichton Golf Club (1884)
Public/Private
Bankend Road, Dumfries DG1 4TH
☎ (01387) 264946
✉ crichtongolf@hotmail.co.uk
✍ Lee Sterritt (Match Sec)
🖥 www.crichtongolf.limewebs.com

Dalbeattie (1894)
Maxwell Park, Dalbeattie DG5 4JR
☎ (01556) 611421
✉ jbhenderson45@gmail.com
✍ J B Henderson
🖥 www.dalbeattiegc.co.uk

Dumfries & County (1912)
Nunfield, Edinburgh Road, Dumfries DG1 1JX
☎ (01387) 253585
🖷 (01387) 253585
✉ admin@thecounty.co.uk
✍ BRM Duguid (01387) 253585
🖥 www.thecounty.org.uk

Dumfries & Galloway (1880)
2 Laurieston Avenue, Maxwelltown, Dumfries DG2 7NY
☎ (01387) 253582
🖷 (01387) 263848
✉ info@dandggolfclub.co.uk
✍ Joe Fergusson (Professional) (01387) 256902
🖥 www.dandggolfclub.co.uk

Dumriesshire Golf Academy – Pines Golf Club (1998)
Pay and play
Lockerbie Road, Dumfries DG1 3PF
☎ (01387) 247444
✉ info@dumfriesshiregolfcentre.com
✍ B McLeod
🖥 www.dumfriesgolf.com

Gatehouse (1921)
Lauriston Road, Gatehouse of Fleet, Castle Douglas DG7 2BE
☎ (01557) 814766 (Clubhouse – unmanned)
✉ info@gatehousegolfclub.com
✍ M Ashmore (01559) 814884
🖥 www.gatehousegolfclub.com

Hoddom Castle (1973)
Pay and play
Hoddom Bridge, Ecclefechan DG11 1AS
☎ (01576) 300251
✉ hoddomcastle@aol.com
🖥 www.hoddomcastle.co.uk

Kirkcudbright (1893)
Stirling Crescent, Kirkcudbright DG6 4EZ
☎ (01557) 330314
🖷 (01557) 330314
✉ kbtgolfclub@lineone.net
✍ N Little (Manager)
🖥 www.kirkcudbrightgolf.co.uk

Lochmaben (1926)
Castlehill Gate, Lochmaben DG11 1NT
☎ (01387) 810552
✉ enquiries@lochmabengolf.co.uk
✍ JM Dickie (Sec)
🖥 www.lochmabengolf.co.uk

Lockerbie (1889)
Corrie Road, Lockerbie DG11 2ND
☎ (01576) 203363
🖷 (01576) 203363

✉ enquiries@lockerbiegolf
✍ Gillian Shanks
🖥 www.lockerbiegolf.co.uk

Moffat (1884)
Coatshill, Moffat DG10 9SB
☎ (01683) 220020
✉ bookings@moffatgolfclub.co.uk
✍ Club Mgr (01683) 220020
🖥 www.moffatgolfclub.co.uk

New Galloway (1902)
New Galloway, Dumfries DG7 3RN
☎ (01644) 420737
✉ brown@nggc.co.uk
✍ Ian Brown
🖥 www.nggc.co.uk

Newton Stewart (1981)
Kirroughtree Avenue, Minnigaff, Newton Stewart DG8 6PF
☎ (01671) 402172
✉ enquiries@newtonstewartgolfclub.com
✍ Mrs L Hamilton
🖥 www.newtonstewartgolfclub.com

Portpatrick (1903)
Golf Course Road, Portpatrick DG9 8TB
☎ (01776) 810273
🖷 (01776) 810811
✉ enquiries@portpatrickgolfclub.com
✍ Manager
🖥 www.portpatrickgolfclub.com

Powfoot (1903)
Cummertrees, Annan DG12 5QE
☎ (01461) 204100
🖷 (01461) 204111
✉ info@powfootgolfclub.com
✍ SR Gardner (Mgr)
🖥 www.powfootgolfclub.com

Sanquhar (1894)
Blackaddie Road, Sanquhar, Dumfries DG4 6JZ
☎ (01659) 50577
✉ tich@rossirene.fsnet.co.uk
✍ Ian Macfarlane
🖥 www.scottishgolf.com

Southerness (1947)
Southerness, Dumfries DG2 8AZ
☎ (01387) 880677
🖷 (01387) 880471
✉ admin@southernessgc.sol.co.uk
✍ P F K Scott
🖥 www.southernessgolfclub.com

St Medan (1904)
Monreith, Newton Stewart DG8 8NJ
☎ (01988) 700358
✉ mail@stmedangolfclub.co.uk
✍ William G McKeand (01988) 700804
🖥 www.stmedangolfclub.co.uk

Stranraer (1905)
Creachmore, Leswalt, Stranraer DG9 0LF
☎ (01776) 870245
🖷 (01776) 870445
✉ stranraergolf@btclick.com

✍ J Burns
▤ www.stranraergolfclub.net

Thornhill (1893)
Blacknest, Thornhill DG3 5DW
☎ **(01848) 330546 (clubhouse)**
✉ info@thornhillgolfclub.co.uk
✍ A Hillier (Co-ordinator)
▤ www.thornhillgolfclub.co.uk

Wigtown & Bladnoch (1960)
Lightlands Terrace, Wigtown DG8 9DY
☎ **(01988) 403354**
✍ IM Thin

Wigtownshire County (1894)
Mains of Park, Glenluce, Newton Stewart
DG8 0NN
☎ **(01581) 300420**
📠 (01581) 300420
✉ enquiries
@wigtownshirecountygolfclub.com
▤ www.wigtownshirecountygolfclub
.com

Dunbartonshire

Balmore (1894)
Balmore, Torrance G64 4AW
☎ **(01360) 620284**
📠 (01360) 622742
✉ balmoregolf@btconnect.com
✍ Karen Dyer (01360) 620284
▤ www.balmoregolfclub.co.uk

Bearsden (1891)
Thorn Road, Bearsden, Glasgow G61 4BP
☎ **(0141) 586 5300**
📠 (0141) 586 5300
✉ secretary@bearsdengolfclub.com
✍ Alan Harris
▤ www.bearsdengolfclub.com

Cardross (1895)
Main Road, Cardross, Dumbarton G82 5LB
☎ **(01389) 841213 (Clubhouse)**
📠 (01389) 842162
✉ golf@cardross.com
✍ G A Mill (01389) 841754
▤ www.cardross.com

Clober (1951)
Craigton Road, Milngavie, Glasgow
G62 7HP
☎ **(0141) 956 1685**
✉ clobergolfclub@gmail.com
✍ Gary McFarlane
▤ www.clobergolfclub.co.uk

Clydebank & District
(1905)
Hardgate, Clydebank G81 5QY
☎ **(01389) 383831**
📠 (01389) 383831
✉ admin@clydebankanddistrict
golfclub.co.uk
✍ Miss M Higgins (01389) 383831
▤ www.clydebankanddistrictgolfclub
.co.uk

Clydebank Overtoun (1927)
Public
Overtoun Road, Dalmuir, Clydebank
G81 3RE
☎ **(0141) 952 2070 (Clubhouse)**

Dougalston (1977)
Strathblane Road, Milngavie, Glasgow
G62 8HJ
☎ **(0141) 955 2400**
📠 (0141) 955 2406
✉ secretary.esportadougalstongc
@hotmail.co.uk
✍ Mr S Gilbey
▤ www.esporta.com

Douglas Park (1897)
Hillfoot, Bearsden, Glasgow G61 2TJ
☎ **(0141) 942 2220 (Clubhouse)**
📠 (0141) 942 0985
✉ secretary@douglasparkgolfclub
.co.uk
✍ Christine Scott (0141) 942 0985
▤ www.douglasparkgolfclub.co.uk

Dullatur (1896)
1a Glendouglas Drive, Craigmarloch,
Cumbernauld G68 0DW
☎ **(01236) 723230**
📠 (01236) 727271
✉ secretary@dullaturgolf.com
✍ John Bryceland B.E.M (01236)
723230
▤ www.dullaturgolf.com

Dumbarton (1888)
Broadmeadow, Dumbarton G82 2BQ
☎ **(01389) 765995**
✉ secretary@dumbartongolfclub
.co.uk
✍ M Buchanan
▤ www.dumbartongolfclub.co.uk

Hayston (1926)
Campsie Road, Kirkintilloch, Glasgow
G66 1RN
☎ **(0141) 775 0723**
📠 (0141) 776 9030
✉ secretary@haystongolf.com
✍ Jim Smart
▤ www.haystongolf.com

Hilton Park (1927)
Auldmarroch Estate, Stockiemuir Road,
Milngavie G62 7HB
☎ **(0141) 956 4657**
📠 (0141) 956 1215
✉ office@hiltonpark.co.uk
✍ Mr Gordon Simpson (0141) 956
4657
▤ www.hiltonpark.co.uk

Kirkintilloch (1895)
Todhill, Campsie Road, Kirkintilloch
G66 1RN
☎ **(0141) 776 1256**
📠 (0141) 775 2424
✉ secretary@kirkintillochgolfclub
.co.uk
✍ T Cummings (0141) 775 2387
▤ www.kirkintillochgolfclub.co.uk

Lenzie (1889)
19 Crosshill Road, Lenzie G66 5DA
☎ **(0141) 776 1535**
📠 (0141) 777 7748
✉ club-secretary@ntlbusiness.com
✍ Roy McKee (0141) 776 1535
▤ www.lenziegolfclub.co.uk

Loch Lomond (1994)
Rossdhu House, Luss G83 8NT
☎ **(01436) 655555**
📠 (01436) 655500
✉ info@lochlomond.com
✍ Bill Donald (Gen Mgr)
▤ www.lochlomond.com

Milngavie (1895)
Laighpark, Milngavie, Glasgow G62 8EP
☎ **(0141) 956 1619**
📠 (0141) 956 4252
✉ secretary@milngaviegolfclub.co.uk
✍ S Woods
▤ www.milngaviegolfclub.com

Palacerigg (1975)
Public
Palacerigg Country Park, Cumbernauld
G67 3HU
☎ **(01236) 734969**
📠 (01236) 721461
✉ palacerigg-golfclub@lineone.net
✍ P O'Hara
▤ www.palacerigg.co.uk

Ross Priory (1978)
Proprietary
Ross Loan, Gartocharn, Alexandria
G83 8NL
☎ **(01389) 830398**
📠 (01389) 830357
✉ ross.priory@strath.ac.uk
✍ R Cook 0141 548 2960
▤ www.strath.ac.uk/rosspriory/golf

Vale of Leven (1907)
Northfield Road, Bonhill, Alexandria
G83 9ET
☎ **(01389) 752351**
📠 (01389) 758866
✉ rbarclay@volgc.org
✍ R Barclay
▤ www.volgc.org

Westerwood Hotel G&CC
(1989)
Pay and play
St Andrews Drive, Cumbernauld G68 0EW
☎ **(01236) 725281**
📠 (01236) 738478
✉ westerwoodgolf@qhotels.co.uk
✍ Vincent Brown
▤ www.qhotels.co.uk

Windyhill (1908)
Windyhill, Bearsden G61 4QQ
☎ **(0141) 942 2349**
📠 (0141) 942 5874
✉ secretary@windyhill.co.uk
✍ JM Young
▤ www.windyhillgolfclub.co.uk

Fife

Aberdour (1896)
Seaside Place, Aberdour KY3 0TX
☎ (01383) 860080
🖷 (01383) 860050
✉ manager@aberdourgolfclub.co.uk
✍ Jane Cuthill
🖳 www.aberdourgolfclub.co.uk

Anstruther (1890)
Marsfield Shore Road, Anstruther KY10 3DZ
☎ (01333) 310956
🖷 (01333) 310956
✉ captain@anstruther.co.uk
✍ M MacDonald
🖳 www.anstruthergolf.co.uk

Auchterderran (1904)
Public
Woodend Road, Cardenden KY5 0NH
☎ (01592) 721579

Balbirnie Park (1983)
Balbirnie Park, Markinch, Fife KY7 6NR
☎ (01592) 612095
🖷 (01592) 612383
✉ administrator@balbirniegolf.com
✍ J Donnelly (Club Administrator)
🖳 www.balbirniegolf.com

Ballingry (1981)
Pay and play
Lochore Meadows Country Park, Crosshill, Lochgelly KY5 8BA
☎ (01592) 860086
✉ terryir@hotmail.co.uk
✍ Terry Ironside

Burntisland (1797)
Club
51 Craigkennochie Terrace, Burntisland KY3 9EN
☎ (01592) 872728
✉ bigmac@waitrose.com
✍ AD McPherson
🖳 www.burntislandgolfclub.co.uk

Burntisland Golf House Club (1898)
Dodhead, Kircaldy Road, Burntisland KY3 9LQ
☎ (01592) 874093
✉ info@burntislandgolfhouseclub.co.uk
✍ Administration (01592) 874093 Ext 4
🖳 www.burntislandgolfhouseclub.co.uk

Canmore (1897)
Venturefair Avenue, Dunfermline KY12 0PE
☎ (01383) 724969
✉ canmoregolfclub@btconnect.com
✍ D Maccallum (Sec)
🖳 www.canmoregolfclub.co.uk

Charleton (1994)
Proprietary
Charleton, Colinsburgh KY9 1HG
☎ (01333) 340505
🖷 (01333) 340583
✉ clubhouse@charleton.co.uk
✍ Laura Paterson
🖳 www.charleton.co.uk

Cowdenbeath (1991)
Public
Seco Place, Cowdenbeath KY4 8PD
☎ (01383) 511918
✉ mail@cowdenbeath-golfclub.com
✍ Secretary
🖳 www.cowdenbeath-golfclub.com

Crail Golfing Society (1786)
Balcomie Clubhouse, Fifeness, Crail KY10 3XN
☎ (01333) 450686
🖷 (01333) 450416
✉ info@crailgolfingsociety.co.uk
✍ D Roy (01333) 450686
🖳 www.crailgolfingsociety.co.uk

Cupar (1855)
Hilltarvit, Cupar KY15 5JT
☎ (01334) 653549
🖷 (01334) 653549
✉ cupargc@fsmail.net
✍ James Elder
🖳 www.cupargolfclub.co.uk

Drumoig (1996)
Drumoig Hotel, Drumoig, Leuchars, St Andrews, Fife KY16 0BE
☎ (01382) 541898
🖷 (01382) 541898
✉ drumoiggolf@btconnect.com
✍ Gordon Taylor
🖳 www.drumoigleisure.com

Dunfermline (1887)
Pitfirrane, Crossford, Dunfermline KY12 8QW
☎ (01383) 723534
✉ secretary@dunfermlinegolfclub.com
✍ R De Rose
🖳 www.dunfermlinegolfclub.com

Dunnikier Park (1963)
Public
Dunnikier Way, Kirkcaldy KY1 3LP
☎ (01592) 261599
✉ dunnikierparkgolfclub@btinternet.com
✍ G Macdonald
🖳 www.dunnikierparkgolfclub.com

Earlsferry Thistle (1875)
Club
Melon Park, Elie KY9 1AS
✍ J Peters (01333) 424315

Elmwood Golf Course (1997)
Pay and play
Stratheden, Nr Cupar KY15 5RS
☎ (01334) 658780
🖷 (01334) 658781
✉ clubhouse@elmwood.co.uk/ s.sulaiman@elmwood.ac.uk
✍ Sharif Sulaiman (Golf Admin) (01334) 658780
🖳 www.elmwoodgc.co.uk

Falkland (1976)
The Myre, Falkland KY15 7AA
☎ (01337) 857404
✉ falklandgolfclub@gmail.com
✍ Mrs H Brough
🖳 www.falklandgolfclub.com

Glenrothes (1958)
Public
Golf Course Road, Glenrothes KY6 2LA
☎ (01592) 754561/758686
🖷 (01592) 754561
✉ secretary@glenrothesgolf.org.uk
✍ Miss C Dawson
🖳 www.glenrothesgolf.org.uk

Golf House Club (1875)
Elie, Leven KY9 1AS
☎ (01333) 330301
🖷 (01333) 330895
✉ secretary@golfhouseclub.org
✍ G Scott (01333) 330301
🖳 www.golfhouseclub.org

Kinghorn (1887)
Public
Burntisland Road, Kinghorn KY3 9RS
☎ (01592) 890345
✉ kgclub@tiscali.co.uk
✍ Gordon Tulloch (01592) 891008
🖳 www.kinghorngolfclub.co.uk

Kinghorn Ladies (1894)
Club
Golf Clubhouse, Burntisland Road, Kinghorn KY3 9RS
☎ (01592) 890345
✉ kgclub@tiscali.co.uk
🖳 www.kinghorngolfclub.co.uk

Kingsbarns Golf Links (2000)
Pay and play
Kingsbarns, Fife KY16 8QD
☎ (01334) 460860
🖷 (01334) 460877
✉ info@kingsbarns.com
✍ Alan Hogg (Chief Executive)
🖳 www.kingsbarns.com

Kirkcaldy (1904)
Balwearie Road, Kirkcaldy KY2 5LT
☎ (01592) 205240
✉ enquiries@kirkcaldygolfclub.co.uk
✍ M Langstaff
🖳 www.kirkcaldygolfclub.co.uk

Ladybank (1879)
Annsmuir, Ladybank, Fife KY15 7RA
☎ (01337) 830814
🖷 (01337) 831505
✉ info@ladybankgolf.co.uk
✍ FH McCluskey
🖳 www.ladybankgolf.co.uk

Leslie (1898)
Balsillie Laws, Leslie, Glenrothes KY6 3EZ
☎ (01592) 620040
✉ gordon.lewis1@sky.com
✍ G Lewis

Leven Golfing Society
(1820)
Club
Links Road, Leven KY8 4HS
☎ **(01333) 426096/424229**
🖷 (01333) 424229
📧 secretary@levengolfingsociety
.co.uk
♙ Verne Greger
🖥 www.levengolfingsociety.co.uk

Leven Links   (1846)
The Promenade, Leven KY8 4HS
☎ **(01333) 421390 (Starter)**
🖷 (01333) 428859
📧 secretary@leven-links.com
♙ (01333) 428859 (Links Committee)
🖥 www.leven-links.com

Leven Thistle   (1867)
Club
Balfour Street, Leven KY8 4JF
☎ **(01333) 426333**
🖷 (01333) 439910
📧 secretary@leventhistlegolf.org.uk
♙ Ian Winn (01333) 426333
🖥 www.leventhistlegolf.org.uk

Lundin   (1868)
Golf Road, Lundin Links KY8 6BA
☎ **(01333) 320202**
🖷 (01333) 329743
📧 secretary@lundingolfclub.co.uk
♙ AJ McDonald
🖥 www.lundingolfclub.co.uk

Lundin Ladies   (1891)
Woodielea Road, Lundin Links KY8 6AR
☎ **(01333) 320832 (Office)**
📧 llgolfclub@tiscali.co.uk
♙ Moraig Orton (Captain)
🖥 www.lundinladiesgolfclub.co.uk

Methil   (1892)
Club
Links House, Links Road, Leven KY8 4HS
☎ **(01333) 425535**
🖷 (01333) 425187
📧 andrew.traill@btconnect.com
♙ ATJ Traill

Pitreavie   (1922)
Queensferry Road, Dunfermline KY11 8PR
☎ **(01383) 722591**
🖷 (01383) 722592
📧 secretary@pitreaviegolfclub.co.uk
♙ Malcom A Brown
🖥 www.pitreaviegolfclub.co.uk

Saline   (1912)
Kinneddar Hill, Saline KY12 9LT
☎ **(01383) 852591**
🖷 (01383) 852591
📧 salinegolfclub@btconnect.com
♙ D Hatton
🖥 www.saline-golf-club.co.uk

Scoonie   (1951)
Public
North Links, Leven KY8 4SP
☎ **(01333) 307007**
🖷 (01333) 307008

📧 manager@scooniegolfclub.com
♙ Mr J Divers
🖥 www.scooniegolfclub.com

Scotscraig   (1817)
Golf Road, Tayport DD6 9DZ
☎ **(01382) 552515**
🖷 (01382) 553130
📧 scotscraig@scotscraiggolfclub.com
♙ BD Liddle
🖥 www.scotscraiggolfclub.com

St Michaels   (1903)
Gallow Hill, Leuchars KY16 0DX
☎ **(01334) 839365 (Clubhouse)**
🖷 (01334) 838789
📧 stmichaelsgc@btclick.com
♙ D S Landsburgh (01334) 838666
🖥 www.stmichaelsgolfclub.co.uk

Thornton   (1921)
Station Road, Thornton KY1 4DW
☎ **(01592) 771173 (Starter)**
🖷 (01592) 774955
📧 thorntongolf@btconnect.com
♙ WD Rae (01592) 771111
🖥 www.thorntongolfclub.co.uk

St Andrews Clubs

The Royal and Ancient Golf Club of St Andrews   (1754)
Club
St Andrews KY16 9JD
☎ **(01334) 460000**

The Standard Life Amateur Champion Gold Medal

It was on July 11th 1870 that the Captain and Council of Innerleven Golf Club, the forerunner to Leven Golfing Society, were notified by their Secretary that the Standard Assurance Company (now Standard Life plc) had presented a Gold Medal for annual competition and Thursday 4th August had been fixed for the event.

The inaugural competition was won by James Elder of Leven Golf Club with a single round score of 85. The competition was, "open to members of Innerleven, Leven and Lundin Golf Clubs and the members of such other clubs as the Captain and Council of Innerleven shall approve, but makers of clubs or balls, or professionals, may not compete".

The competition, hosted annually by Leven Golfing Society and Standard Life plc, continued over 18 holes until 1966 when a 36 holes event was introduced and three years later it moved to the current 72 hole format over two days.

From that historic date, Standard Life has each year presented a gold medallion to the winner and, in more recent times, silver and bronze medallions to the second and third.

Over the decades the tournament, which is played in early August over the classic Leven Links, has grown in stature and is now considered one of the most prestigious competitions in Scottish Golf.

One of the great winners from the past was former Walker Cup player Eric McCruvie who won the medal on no fewer than seven occasions between 1927 and 1950, whilst previous winners who have subsequently gone on to successful professional careers include Pierre Ulrich Johansson, Andrew Coltart and Lee Westwood.

While winning the medal remains a much sought-after prize, each year, every entrant who takes the tee can proudly claim to have played in the world's oldest open amateur stroke-play competition at the eleventh oldest club.

For key to symbols see page 717

🖳 (01334) 460001
📧 thesecretary@randagc.org
✍ P Dawson
🖥 www.theroyalandancientgolfclub
.org

St Andrews Thistle Golf Club (1817)
Club
c/o Links House, 13 The Links, S Andrews,
Fife KY16 9JB
☎ **(01334) 477377**
📧 thistle-secretary@tiscali.co.uk
✍ Andy Christie

St Regulus Ladies' (1913)
Club
9 Pilmour Links, St Andrews KY16 9JG
☎ **(01334) 477797**
🖳 (01334) 477797
📧 admin@st-regulus-lgc.co.uk
✍ Honorary Secretary
🖥 www.st-regulus-lgc.co.uk

The St Rule Club (1898)
Club
12 The Links, St Andrews KY16 9JB
☎ **(01334) 472988**
🖳 (01334) 472988
📧 admin@thestruleclub.co.uk
✍ Mr Neil Doctor

The New Golf Club (1902)
3-5 Gibson Place, St Andrews KY16 9JE
☎ **(01334) 473426**
🖳 (01334) 477570
📧 admin@newgolfclubstandrews
.co.uk
✍ The Secretary
🖥 www.newgolfclubstandrews.co.uk

The St Andrews (1843)
Links House, 13 The Links, St Andrews
KY16 9JB
☎ **(01334) 479799**
🖳 (01334) 479577
📧 sec@thestandrewsgolfclub.co.uk
✍ T Gallacher (01334) 479799
🖥 www.thestandrewsgolfclub.co.uk

St Andrews Courses

Balgove Course (1993)
Public
St Andrews Links, Pilmour House, St
Andrews KY16 9SF
☎ **(01334) 466666**
🖳 (01334) 479555
📧 reservations@standrews.org.uk
✍ Euan Loudon (Chief Executive)
🖥 www.standrews.org.uk

The Castle Course (2008)
Public
St Andrews Links, Pilmour House, St
Andrews KY16 9SF
☎ **(01334) 466666**
🖳 (01334) 479555
📧 reservations@standrews.org.uk
✍ Euan Loudon (Chief Executive)
🖥 www.standrews.org.uk

Duke's (1995)
Craigtoun, St Andrews KY16 8NS
☎ **(01334) 470214**
🖳 (01334) 479456
📧 reservations@oldcoursehotel
.co.uk
✍ David Scott (Mgr) (01334) 470214
🖥 www.playthedukes.com

Eden Course (1914)
Public
St Andrews Links, Pilmour House, St
Andrews KY16 9SF
☎ **(01334) 466666**
🖳 (01334) 479555
📧 reservations@standrews.org.uk
✍ Euan Loudon (Chief Executive)
🖥 www.standrews.org.uk

Jubilee Course (1897)
Public
St Andrews Links, Pilmour House, St
Andrews KY16 9SF
☎ **(01334) 466666**
🖳 (01334) 479555
📧 reservations@standrews.org.uk
✍ Euan Loudon (Chief Executive)
🖥 www.standrews.org.uk

New Course (1895)
Public
St Andrews Links, Pilmour House, St
Andrews KY16 9SF
☎ **(01334) 466666**
🖳 (01334) 479555
📧 reservations@standrews.org.uk
✍ Euan Loudon (Chief Executive)
🖥 www.standrews.org.uk

Old Course (c1400)
Public
St Andrews Links, Pilmour House, St
Andrews KY16 9SF
☎ **(01334) 466666**
🖳 (01334) 479555
📧 reservations@standrews.org.uk
✍ Euan Loudon (Chief Executive)
🖥 www.standrews.org.uk

Strathtyrum Course (1993)
Public
St Andrews Links, Pilmour House, St
Andrews KY16 9SF
☎ **(01334) 466666**
🖳 (01334) 479555
📧 reservations@standrews.org.uk
✍ Euan Loudon (Chief Executive)
🖥 www.standrews.org.uk

Glasgow

Alexandra Park (1880)
Public
Alexandra Park, Dennistoun, Glasgow
G31 8SE
☎ **(0141) 276 0600**
✍ F Derwin

Bishopbriggs (1906)
Brackenbrae Road, Bishopbriggs, Glasgow
G64 2DX
☎ **(0141) 772 1810**
📧 thesecretarybgc@yahoo.co.uk
🖥 www.thebishopbriggsgolfclub.com

Cathcart Castle (1895)
Mearns Road, Clarkston G76 7YL
☎ **(0141) 638 9449**
📧 secretary@cathcartcastle.com
🖥 www.cathcartcastle.com

The Tennant Cup

The Tennant Cup, presented by Glasgow Golf Club Captain Sir Charles Tennant in 1880, is the oldest golfing trophy in the world for open competition among amateur golfers under medal conditions.

Originally played over two 10-hole rounds at Alexandra Park, it became an 18-hole competition when the course was extended in 1885.

In 1893, the event was transferred to the club's Gailes course and was played there before moving to Killermont in 1906.

In 1927, the competition was extended to two rounds over Killermont and that event was won by William Tulloch of Cathkin Braes, who had been the last player to win in over 18 holes.

In 1976, it was extended to 72 holes with two rounds at Gailes on the Saturday and two at Killermont the following day. That has been the format ever since.

For key to symbols see page 717

Cawder   (1933)
Cadder Road, Bishopbriggs, Glasgow
G64 3QD
- ☎ **(0141) 761 1281**
- 📠 (0141) 761 1285
- ✉ secretary@cawdergolfclub.com
- 🏌 Fraser Gemmell (0141) 761 1281
- 📖 www.cawdergolfclub.com

Cowglen   (1906)
301 Barrhead Road, Glasgow G43 1EU
- ☎ **(0141) 632 7463**
- 📠 (0141) 632 7463
- ✉ secretary@cowglengolfclub.co.uk
- 🏌 Mrs Anne Burnside
- 📖 www.cowglengolfclub.co.uk

Glasgow   (1787)
Killermont, Bearsden, Glasgow G61 2TW
- ☎ **(0141) 942 1713**
- 📠 (0141) 942 0770
- ✉ secretary@glasgowgolfclub.com
- 🏌 A G McMillan (0141) 942 2011
- 📖 www.glasgowgolfclub.com

Haggs Castle   (1910)
70 Dumbreck Road, Dumbreck, Glasgow
G41 4SN
- ☎ **(0141) 427 0480**
- 📠 (0141) 427 1157
- ✉ secretary@haggscastlegolfclub.com
- 🏌 A Williams (0141) 427 1157
- 📖 www.haggscastlegolfclub.com

Knightswood   (1929)
Public
Knightswood Park, Lincoln Avenue, Glasgow
G13 3DN
- ☎ **(0141) 959 6358**

Lethamhill   (1933)
Public
Cumbernauld Road, Glasgow G33 1AH
- ☎ **(0141) 770 6220**

Linn Park   (1924)
Public
Simshill Road, Glasgow G44 5TA
- ☎ **(0141) 633 0377**

Pollok   (1892)
90 Barrhead Road, Glasgow G43 1BG
- ☎ **(0141) 632 1080**
- ✉ secretary@pollokgolf.com
- 📖 www.pollokgolf.com

Ralston   (1904)
Strathmore Avenue, Ralston, Paisley PA1 3DT
- ☎ **(0141) 882 1349**
- 📠 (0141) 883 9837
- ✉ thesecretary@ralstongolf.co.uk
- 🏌 B W Hanson
- 📖 www.ralstongolfclub.com

Rouken Glen   (1922)
Pay and play
Stewarton Road, Thornliebank, Glasgow
G46 7UZ
- ☎ **(0141) 638 7044**
- 📠 (0141) 638 6115
- ✉ deaconsbank@ngclubs.co.uk
- 🏌 S Armstrong

Sandyhills   (1905)
223 Sandyhills Road, Glasgow G32 9NA
- ☎ **(0141) 778 1179**
- ✉ admin@sandyhillsgolfclub.co.uk
- 🏌 J Thomson
- 📖 www.sandyhillsgolfclub.co.uk

Williamwood   (1906)
Clarkston Road, Netherlee, Glasgow
G44 3YR
- ☎ **(0141) 637 1783**
- 📠 (0141) 571 0166
- ✉ secretary@williamwoodgc.co.uk
- 🏌 LW Conn (0141) 629 1981
- 📖 www.williamwoodgc.co.uk

Highland

Caithness & Sutherland

Bonar Bridge/Ardgay
(1904)
Migdale Road, Bonar-Bridge, Sutherland
IV24 3EJ
- ☎ **(01863) 766199 (Clubhouse)**
- ✉ nielsenhunter@btinternet.com
- 🏌 Jeani Hunter (01863) 766 199
- 📖 www.bbagc.co.uk

Brora   (1891)
Golf Road, Brora KW9 6QS
- ☎ **(01408) 621417**
- 📠 (01408) 622157
- ✉ secretary@broragolf.co.uk
- 🏌 AJA Gill
- 📖 www.broragolf.co.uk

The Carnegie Club   (1995)
Skibo Castle, Dornoch, Sutherland IV25
3RQ
- ☎ **(01862) 881 260**
- 📠 (01862) 881 260
- ✉ sharon.stewart@carnegieclubs
  .co.uk
- 🏌 Sharon Stewart
- 📖 www.carnegieclubs.com

Durness   (1988)
Pay and play
Balnakeil, Durness IV27 4PN
- ☎ **(01971) 511364**
- 📠 (01971) 511321
- ✉ lucy@durnessgolfclub.org
- 🏌 Mrs L Mackay (01971) 511364
- 📖 www.durnessgolfclub.org

Golspie   (1889)
Visitors welcome
Ferry Road, Golspie KW10 6ST
- ☎ **(01408) 633266**
- ✉ info@golspie-golf-club.co.uk
- 🏌 RI Beaton (Hon) (01408 633927)
- 📖 www.golspie-golf-club.co.uk

Helmsdale   (1895)
Strath Road, Helmsdale KW8 6JL
- ☎ **(01431) 821063**
- 🏌 R Sutherland
- 📖 www.helmsdale.org

Lybster   (1926)
Main Street, Lybster KW1 6BL
- ☎ **(01593) 721316**
- 🏌 AG Calder (01593) 721316
- 📖 www.lybstergolfclub.co.uk

Reay   (1893)
Reay, Thurso, Caithness KW14 7RE
- ☎ **(01847) 811288**
- ✉ info@reaygolfclub.co.uk
- 🏌 W McIntosh
- 📖 www.reaygolfclub.co.uk

Royal Dornoch   (1877)
Golf Road, Dornoch IV25 3LW
- ☎ **(01862) 810219**
- 📠 (01862) 810792
- ✉ bookings@royaldornoch.com
- 🏌 Neil Hampton (Gen Mgr)
- 📖 www.royaldornoch.com

Thurso   (1893)
Pay and play
Newlands of Geise, Thurso KW14 7XD
- ☎ **(01847) 893807**
- 📠 (01847) 892575
- ✉ info@thursogolfclub.co.uk
- 🏌 RM Black
- 📖 www.thursogolfclub.co.uk

Ullapool   (1998)
Pay and play
North Road, Ullapool IV26 2TH
- ☎ **(01854) 613323**
- ✉ mail@ullapoolgolfclub.co.uk
- 🏌 A Paterson
- 📖 www.ullapoolgolfclub.co.uk

Wick   (1870)
Reiss, Wick KW1 5LJ
- ☎ **(01955) 602726**
- ✉ wickgolfclub@hotmail.com
- 🏌 S Busby (01955) 603874
- 📖 www.wickgolfclub.com

Inverness

Abernethy   (1893)
Nethy Bridge PH25 3EB
- ☎ **(01479) 821305**
- ✉ info@abernethygolfclub.com
- 🏌 Mr M Wright (Captain)
- 📖 www.abernethygolfclub.com

Aigas   (1993)
Proprietary
mains of Aigas, Beauly, Inverness IV4 7AD
- ☎ **(01463) 782942**
- ✉ info@aigas-holidays.co.uk
- 📖 www.aigas-holidays.co.uk

Alness   (1904)
Ardross Rd, Alness, Ross-shire IV17 0QA
- ☎ **(01349) 883877**
- ✉ info@alnessgolfclub.co.uk
- 🏌 Mr Richard Green
- 📖 www.alnessgolfclub.co.uk

Boat-of-Garten   (1898)
Boat-of-Garten PH24 3BQ
- ☎ **(01479) 831282**

☐ (01479) 831523
✉ office@boatgolf.com
✍ W.N McConachie
(clubsec@boatgolf.com)
▤ www.boatgolf.com

Carrbridge (1980)

Inverness Road, Carrbridge PH23 3AU
☎ **(01479) 841623 (Clubhouse)**
✉ secretary@carrbridgegolf.co.uk
✍ The Secretary
▤ www.carrbridgegolf.co.uk

Fort Augustus (1904)

Pay and play
Markethill, Fort Augustus PH32 4DS
☎ **(01320) 366660**
✉ fortaugustusgc@aol.com
✍ K Callow
▤ www.fortaugustusgc.webeden
.co.uk

Fort William (1974)

North Road, Fort William PH33 6SN
☎ **(01397) 704464**
✉ fwgolf41@msn.com
✍ Ian Robertson
▤ www.fortwilliamgolf.co.uk

Fortrose & Rosemarkie

(1888)
Ness Road East, Fortrose IV10 8SE
☎ **(01381) 620529/620733**
☐ (01381) 621328
✉ secretary@fortrosegolfclub.co.uk
✍ M MacDonald
▤ www.fortrosegolfclub.co.uk

Grantown-on-Spey (1890)

Golf Course Road, Grantown-on-Spey
PH26 3HY
☎ **(01479) 872079**
☐ (01479) 873725
✉ secretary
@grantownonspeygolfclub.co.uk
✍ PR Mackay
▤ www.grantownonspeygolfclub
.co.uk

Invergordon (1893)

King George Street, Invergordon IV18 0BD
☎ **(01349) 852715**
✉ invergordongolf@tiscali.co.uk
✍ David Jamieson
▤ www.invergordongolf.co.uk

Inverness (1883)

Culcabock Road, Inverness IV2 3XQ
☎ **(01463) 239882**
☐ (01463) 240616
✉ manager@invernessgolfclub.co.uk
✍ E Forbes
▤ www.invernessgolfclub.co.uk

Kingussie (1891)

Pay and play
Gynack Road, Kingussie PH21 1LR
☎ **(01540) 661600 (Office)**
☐ (01540) 662066
✉ sec@kingussie-golf.co.uk
✍ Ian Chadburn
▤ www.kingussie-golf.co.uk

Loch Ness (1996)

Proprietary
Fairways, Castle Heather, Inverness IV2 6AA
☎ **(01463) 713335**
☐ (01463) 712695
✉ info@golflochness.com
✍ Secretary (01463) 713335
▤ www.golflochness.com

Muir of Ord (1875)

Great North Road, Muir of Ord IV6 7SX
☎ **(01463) 870825**
✉ muir.golf@btconnect.com
✍ Mr A Pollock (Sec)
▤ www.muirofordgolfclub.co.uk

Nairn (1887)

Seabank Road, Nairn IV12 4HB
☎ **(01667) 453208**
☐ (01667) 456328
✉ bookings@nairngolfclub.co.uk
✍ Yvonne Forgan (Mgr)
▤ www.nairngolfclub.co.uk

Nairn Dunbar (1899)

Lochloy Road, Nairn IV12 5AE
☎ **(01667) 452741**
☐ (01667) 456897
✉ secretary@nairndunbar.com
✍ J Gibson
▤ www.nairndunbar.com

Newtonmore (1893)

Owned privately
Golf Course Road, Newtonmore PH20 1AT
☎ **(01540) 673878**
✉ secretary@newtonmoregolf.com
✍ Heather Bruce (Office Mgr)
▤ www.newtonmoregolf.com

Strathpeffer Spa (1888)

Golf Course Road, Strathpeffer IV14 9AS
☎ **(01997) 421219**
☐ (01997) 421011
✉ mail@strathpeffergolfclub.co.uk
✍ Mrs Margaret Spark
▤ www.strathpeffergolf.co.uk

Tain (1890)

Chapel Road, Tain IV19 1JE
☎ **(01862) 892314**
☐ (01862) 892099
✉ info@tain-golfclub.co.uk
✍ Secretary
▤ www.tain-golfclub.co.uk

Tarbat (1909)

Pay and play
Portmahomack, Tain IV20 1YB
☎ **(01862) 871278**

Torvean (1962)

Public
Glenurquhart Road, Inverness IV3 8JN
☎ **(01463) 225651**
☐ (01463) 711417
✉ admin@torveangolfclub.co.uk
✍ John Robertson (Administrator)
▤ www.torveangolfclub.co.uk

Orkney & Shetland

Orkney (1889)

Grainbank, Kirkwall, Orkney KW15 1RD
☎ **(01856) 872457**
☐ (01856) 872457
✍ Gary Farqumar
▤ www.orkneygolfclub.co.uk

Sanday (1977)

Pay and play
Sanday, Orkney KW17 2BW
☎ **(01857) 600341**
☐ (01857) 600341
✉ nearhouse@triscom.co.uk
✍ R Thorne
⊕ Day Fee £5, Associate Membership
(no further fees) £20

Shetland (1891)

Dale, Gott, Shetland ZE2 9SB
☎ **(01595) 840369**
☐ (01595) 840369
✉ info@shetlandgolfclub.co.uk
✍ S Lamb
▤ www.shetlandgolfclub.co.uk

Stromness (1890)

Stromness, Orkney KW16 3DU
☎ **(01856) 850772**
✍ Colin McLeod
▤ www.stromnessgc.co.uk

Whalsay (1976)

Public
Skaw Taing, Whalsay, Shetland ZE2 9AL
☎ **(01806) 566450/566481**
✉ alan.solvei@lineone.net
✍ HA Sandison, C Hutchison
▤ www.whalsaygolfclub.com

West Coast

Askernish (1891)

Pay and play
Lochboisdale, Askernish, South Uist HS81
5ST
☎ **(01878) 710312**
✉ rthomp4521@btinternet.com
✍ A MacIntyre
▤ www.askernishgolfclub.com

Gairloch (1898)

Gairloch, Ross-Shire IV21 2BE
☎ **(01445) 712407**
✉ gairlochgolfclub@hotmail.co.uk
✍ J Powell
▤ www.gairlochgolfclub.co.uk

Isle of Harris (1975)

Pay and play
Scarista, Isle of Harris HS3 3HX
☎ **(01859) 550226**
☐ (01859) 550226
✉ harrisgolf@ic24.net
✍ R A MacDonald
▤ www.harrisgolf.com

Isle of Skye (1964)

Sconser, Isle of Skye IV48 8TD
☎ **(01478) 650414**

For key to symbols see page 717

Lochcarron   (1908)
Lochcarron, Strathcarron IV54 8YS
- ✉ secretary@lochcarrongolf.co.uk
- 🖎 Gerald Arscott (015995) 77219
- 🗐 www.lochcarrongolf.co.uk

Skeabost   (1982)
Skeabost Bridge, Isle of Skye IV51 9NP
- ☎ **(01470) 532202**

Stornoway   (1890)
Lady Lever Park, Stornoway, Isle of Lewis HS2 0XP
- ☎ **(01851) 702240**
- ✉ admin@stornowaygolfclub.co.uk
- 🖎 KW Galloway (01851) 702533
- 🗐 www.stornowaygolfclub.co.uk

Traigh   (1947)
Arisaig, Inverness-shire PH39 4NT
- ☎ **(01687) 450337**
- 🖎 R Burt (01687) 462 512
- 🗐 www.traighgolf.co.uk

Lanarkshire

Airdrie   (1877)
Rochsoles, Airdrie ML6 0PQ
- ☎ **(01236) 762195**
- 🖳 (01236) 760584
- ✉ airdrie.golfclub@btconnect.com
- 🖎 R M Marshall

Bellshill   (1905)
Community Road, Orbiston, Bellshill ML4 2RZ
- ☎ **(01698) 745124**
- 🖳 (01698) 292576
- ✉ info@bellshillgolfclub.com
- 🖎 Tony Deerin (Secretary)
- 🗐 www.bellshillgolfclub.com

Biggar   (1895)
Public
The Park, Broughton Road, Biggar ML12 6HA
- ☎ **(01899) 220618 (Clubhouse)**
- ✉ frazer@shaungabbit.fsnet.co.uk
- 🖎 F F H Andrews (Sec) (01899) 220624

Blairbeth   (1910)
Burnside, Rutherglen, Glasgow G73 4SF
- ☎ **(0141) 634 3355 (Clubhouse)**
- 🖳 (0141) 634 3355
- ✉ secretary@blairbethgolfclub.co.uk
- 🖎 (0141) 634 3325
- 🗐 www.blairbethgolfclub.co.uk

Bothwell Castle   (1922)
Uddington Road, Bothwell, Glasgow G71 8TD
- ☎ **(01698) 801971**
- 🖳 (01698) 801971
- ✉ secretary@bcgolf.co.uk
- 🖎 Jim Callaghan CCM (01698) 801971
- 🗐 www.bcgolf.co.uk

Calderbraes   (1891)
57 Roundknowe Road, Uddingston G71 7TS
- ☎ **(01698) 813425**
- ✉ calderbraesgolfclub@tiscali.co.uk
- 🖎 S McGuigan (0141) 573 2497
- 🗐 www.calderbraesgolfclub.com

Cambuslang   (1892)
30 Westburn Drive, Cambuslang G72 7NA
- ☎ **(0141) 641 3130**
- 🖳 (0141) 641 3130
- ✉ cambuslanggolfclub@tiscali.co.uk
- 🖎 RM Dunlop
- 🗐 www.cambuslandgolf.org

Carluke   (1894)
Hallcraig, Mauldslie Road, Carluke ML8 5HG
- ☎ **(01555) 770574/771070**
- 🖳 (01555) 770574
- ✉ carlukegolfsecy@tiscali.co.uk
- 🖎 G White (01555) 770574
- 🗐 www.carlukegolfclub.com

Carnwath   (1907)
1 Main Street, Carnwath ML11 8JX
- ☎ **(01555) 840251**
- 🖳 (01555) 841070
- ✉ carnwathgc@hotmail.co.uk
- 🖎 Mrs L Jardine
- 🗐 www.carnwathgc.co.uk

Cathkin Braes   (1888)
Cathkin Road, Rutherglen, Glasgow G73 4SE
- ☎ **(0141) 634 6605**
- ✉ secretary@cathkinbraesgolfclub .co.uk
- 🖎 DE Moir
- 🗐 www.cathkinbraesgolfclub.co.uk

Coatbridge Municipal   (1971)
Public
Townhead Road, Coatbridge ML52 2HX
- ☎ **(01236) 28975**

Colville Park   (1923)
Jerviston Estate, Motherwell ML1 4UG
- ☎ **(01698) 263017**
- 🗐 www.colvillepark.co.uk

Crow Wood   (1925)
Cumbernauld Road, Muirhead, Glasgow G69 9JF
- ☎ **(0141) 799 1943**
- 🖳 (0141) 779 4873
- ✉ secretary@crowwood-golfclub.co.uk
- 🖎 Margaret Laughrey (0141) 779 4954
- 🗐 www.crowwood-golfclub.co.uk

Dalziel Park   (1997)
100 Hagen Drive, Motherwell ML1 5RZ
- ☎ **(01698) 862862**

Douglas Water   (1922)
Rigside, Lanark ML11 9NB
- ☎ **(01555) 880361**
- 🖳 (01555) 880361
- 🖎 S Hogg
- 🗐 www.douglaswatergolf.co.uk

Drumpellier   (1894)
Drumpellier Ave, Coatbridge ML5 1RX
- ☎ **(01236) 424139**
- 🖳 (01236) 428723
- ✉ administrator@drumpelliergolfclub .com
- 🖎 JM Craig
- ⊕ Visitors; Weekdays only Round £35.00 / Day £50.00

East Kilbride   (1900)
Chapelside Road, Nerston, East Kilbride G74 4PH
- ☎ **(01355) 581804 (Clubhouse)**
- 🖳 (01355) 581807
- ✉ secretary@ekgolfclub.co.uk
- 🖎 Fraser Gow (01355) 581800
- 🗐 www.ekgolfclub.co.uk

Easter Moffat   (1922)
Mansion House, Plains, Airdrie ML6 8NP
- ☎ **(01236) 842878**
- ✉ secretary@emgc.co.uk

Hamilton Golf Club   (1892)
Riccarton, Ferniegair, Hamilton ML3 7UE
- ☎ **(01698) 282872**
- 🖳 (01698) 204650
- ✉ secretary@hamiltongolfclub.co.uk
- 🖎 G B Mackenzie (Mgr)
- 🗐 www.hamiltongolfclub.co.uk

Hollandbush   (1954)
Public
Acretophead, Lesmahagow, Coalburn ML11 0JS
- ☎ **(01555) 893484**
- ✉ mail@hollandbushgolfclub.co.uk
- 🖎 J Hamilton (Secretary)
- 🗐 www.hollandbushgolfclub.co.uk

Kirkhill   (1910)
Greenlees Road, Cambuslang, Glasgow G72 8YN
- ☎ **(0141) 641 3083 (Clubhouse)**
- 🖳 (0141) 641 8499
- ✉ secretary@kirkhillgolfclub.org.uk
- 🖎 C Downes (0141) 641 8499
- 🗐 www.kirkhillgolfclub.org.uk

Lanark   (1851)
The Moor, Lanark ML11 7RX
- ☎ **(01555) 663219**
- 🖳 (01555) 663219
- ✉ lanarkgolfclub@supanet.com
- 🖎 GH Cuthill
- 🗐 www.lanarkgolfclub.co.uk

Langlands   (1985)
Public
Langlands Road, East Kilbride G75 0QQ
- ☎ **(01355) 248173**

Larkhall   (1909)
Public
Burnhead Road, Larkhall, Glasgow
- ☎ **(01698) 881113**
- 🖎 M Mallinson

Leadhills   (1895)
1 New Row, Wanlockhead, Leadhills, Nr Biggar ML12 6UJ
- ☎ **(01659) 74272**

✉ jack@gsx-r750cc.fsnet.co.uk
✍ Jack Arrigoni
🖥 See Golf Central

Mount Ellen   (1904)
Iochend Road, Gartcosh, Glasgow G69 9EY
☎ **(01236) 872277**
🖷 (01236) 872249
✉ secretary@mountellengolfclub
.co.uk
✍ Robert Watt
🖥 www.mountellengolfclub.co.uk

Mouse Valley   (1993)
East End, Cleghorn, Lanark ML11 8NR
☎ **(01555) 870015**
🖷 (01555) 870022
✉ info@kames-golf-club.com
🖥 www.kames-golf-club.com

Shotts   (1895)
Blairhead, Benhar Road, Shotts ML7 5BJ
☎ **(01501) 820431**
🖷 (01501) 825868
✉ info@shottsgolfclub.co.uk
✍ GT Stoddart (01501) 825868
🖥 www.shottsgolfclub.co.uk

Strathaven   (1908)
Glasgow Road, Strathaven ML10 6NL
☎ **(01357) 520421**
🖷 (01357) 520539
✉ info@strathavengc.com
✍ IF Neil
🖥 www.strathavengc.com

Strathclyde Park   (1936)
Public
Mote Hill, Hamilton ML3 6BY
☎ **(01698) 429350**
✍ K Will
⊕ 24 bay driving range. Large Practice
area. Large Putting Green.

Torrance House   (1969)
Public
Strathaven Road, East Kilbride, Glasgow
G75 0QZ
☎ **(01355) 248638**
✉ secretary@torrancehousegc.co.uk
✍ Margaret D McKerlie
(01355) 249720

Wishaw   (1897)
55 Cleland Road, Wishaw ML2 7PH
☎ **(01698) 372869 (Clubhouse)**
🖷 (01698) 356930
✉ jwdouglas@btconnect.com
✍ JW Douglas (01698) 357480
⊕ WD-U until 4.00pm NA-Sat U-Sun

Lothians

East Lothian

Aberlady   (1912)
Club
Aberlady EH32 0RB
✉ ithomps3@aol.com

Archerfield Links   (2004)
Dirleton, East Lothian EH39 5HU
☎ **(01620) 897050**
🖷 (08700) 515487
✉ mail@archerfieldgolfclub.com
✍ Stuart Bayne (Dir of Golf)
🖥 www.archerfieldgolfclub.com

Bass Rock   (1873)
Club
43a High Street, North Berwick EH39 4HH
☎ **(01620) 894071**
✉ bassrockgolfclub@hotmail.com
✍ J Bullough (01620) 894071

Castle Park   (1994)
Pay and play
Gifford, Haddington EH41 4PL
☎ **(01620) 810733**
✉ castleparkgolf@hotmail.com
✍ JT Wilson (01620) 810733
🖥 www.castleparkgolfclub.co.uk

Dirleton Castle   (1854)
Club
15 The Pines, Gullane EH31 2DT
☎ **(01620) 843591**
✍ J Taylor
🖥 www.dirletoncastlegolfclub.org.uk

Dunbar   (1856)
East Links, Dunbar EH42 1LL
☎ **(01368) 862317**
🖷 (01368) 865202
✉ secretary@dunbargolfclub.com
✍ John I Archibald (Club Mgr)
🖥 www.dunbargolfclub.com

Gifford   (1904)
Edinburgh Road, Gifford EH41 4JE
☎ **(01620) 810591 (Starter)**
🖷 (01620) 810267
✉ secretary@giffordgolfclub.com
✍ Robert Stewart (01620) 810267
🖥 www.giffordgolfclub.com

Glen (North Berwick)   (1906)
East Links, Tantallon Terrace, North
Berwick EH39 4LE
☎ **(01620) 892726**
🖷 (01620) 895447
✉ secretary@glengolfclub.co.uk
✍ Rita Wilson (Office Mgr)
🖥 www.glengolfclub.co.uk

Gullane   (1882)
West Links Road, Gullane, East Lothian
EH31 2BB
☎ **(01620) 842255**
🖷 (01620) 842327
✉ secretary@gullanegolfclub.com
✍ S Anthony
🖥 www.gullanegolfclub.com

Haddington   (1865)
Amisfield Park, Haddington EH41 4PT
☎ **(01620) 823627**
🖷 (01620) 826580
✉ info@haddingtongolf.co.uk
✍ A Murdie (office Administrator)
🖥 www.haddingtongolf.co.uk

The Honourable Company of Edinburgh Golfers   (1744)
Duncur Road, Muirfield, Gullane EH31 2EG
☎ **(01620) 842123**
🖷 (01620) 842977
✉ hceg@muirfield.org.uk
✍ ANG Brown
🖥 www.muirfield.org.uk

Kilspindie   (1867)
Aberlady EH32 0QD
☎ **(01875) 870358**
✉ kilspindie@btconnect.com
✍ PB Casely
🖥 www.kilspindlegolfclub.com

Longniddry   (1921)
Links Road, Longniddry EH32 0NL
☎ **(01875) 852141**
🖷 (01875) 853371
✉ secretary@longniddrygolfclub
.co.uk
✍ RMS Gunning
🖥 www.longniddrygolfclub.co.uk

Luffness New   (1894)
Aberlady EH32 0QA
☎ **(01620) 843114**
🖷 (01620) 842933
✉ secretary@luffnessnew.com
✍ Gp Capt AG Yeates (01620)
843336
🖥 www.luffnessgolf.com

Musselburgh   (1938)
Monktonhall, Musselburgh EH21 6SA
☎ **(0131) 665 2005**
🖷 (0131) 665 4435
✉ secretary@themusselburghgolfclub
.com
✍ P Millar
🖥 www.themusselburghgolfclub
.com

Musselburgh Old Course   (1982)
Public
10 Balcarres Road, Musselburgh EH21 7SD
☎ **(0131) 665 6981**
🖷 (0131) 653 1770
✉ oldcourseclub@unicombox.com
✍ K Bentley (Sec) (0131) 665 6981
🖥 www.mocgc.com

North Berwick   (1832)
West Links, Beach Road, North Berwick
EH39 4BB
☎ **(01620) 895040**
🖷 (01620) 893274
✉ secretary@northberwickgolfclub
.com
✍ Christopher Spencer (01620)
895040
🖥 www.northberwickgolfclub.com

Royal Musselburgh   (1774)
Prestongrange House, Prestonpans
EH32 9RP
☎ **(01875) 810276 (advance
bookings) opt 3**

(01875) 810276
royalmusselburgh@btinternet.com
Mr D Thomson
www.royalmusselburgh.co.uk

Tantallon   (1853)
Club
32 Westgate, North Berwick EH39 4AH
☎ **(01620) 892114**
(01620) 894399
secretary@tantallongolfclub.co.uk
I F Doig
www.north-berwick.co.uk/tantallon

Thorntree Golf Club   (1856)
Club
Prestongrange House, Prestonpans EH32 9RP
☎ **(0131) 552 3559**
Arthur Reid

Whitekirk   (1995)
Pay and play
Whitekirk, North Berwick EH39 5PR
☎ **(01620) 870300**
(01620) 870330
countryclub@whitekirk.com
D Brodie
www.whitekirk.com

Winterfield   (1935)
Public
St Margarets, North Road, Dunbar EH42 1AU
☎ **(01368) 862280**
kevinphillips@tiscali.co.uk

Midlothian

Baberton   (1893)
50 Baberton Avenue, Juniper Green, Edinburgh EH14 5DU
☎ **(0131) 453 4911**
(0131) 453 4678
manager@baberton.co.uk
K A Nicholson (0131) 453 4911
www.baberton.co.uk

Braid Hills   (1893)
Public
Braid Hills Road, Edinburgh EH10 6JY
☎ **(0131) 447 6666 (Starter)**

Braids United   (1897)
Club
22 Braid Hills Approach, Edinburgh EH10 6JY
☎ **(07541) 136133**
golf@braids-united.co.uk
WJ Mitchell (0131) 476 2238
www.braids-united.co.uk

Broomieknowe   (1905)
36 Golf Course Road, Bonnyrigg EH19 2HZ
☎ **(0131) 663 9317**
(0131) 663 2152
administrator@broomieknowe.com
R H Beattie
www.broomieknowe.com

Bruntsfield Links Golfing Society   (1761)
The Clubhouse, 32 Barnton Avenue, Edinburgh EH4 6JH
☎ **(0131) 336 1479**
(0131) 336 5538
secretary@bruntsfield.sol.co.uk
Cdr DM Sandford
www.bruntsfieldlinks.co.uk

Carrick Knowe   (1930)
Public
Glendevon Park, Edinburgh EH12 5VZ
☎ **(0131) 337 1096 (Starter)**

Craigmillar Park   (1895)
1 Observatory Road, Edinburgh EH9 3HG
☎ **(0131) 667 2837**
(0131) 662 8091
secretary@craigmillarpark.co.uk
Mrs D Nichol (0131) 667 0047
www.craigmillarpark.co.uk

Duddingston   (1895)
Duddingston Road West, Edinburgh EH15 3QD
☎ **(0131) 661 7688**
(0131) 652 6057
secretary@duddingstongolf.co.uk
Duncan Ireland
www.duddingstongolfclub.co.uk

Glencorse   (1890)
Milton Bridge, Penicuik EH26 0RD
☎ **(01968) 677177**
(01968) 674399
secretary@glencorsegolfclub.com
W Oliver (01968) 677189
www.glencorsegolfclub.com

Gogarburn   (1975)
Members and Visitors
Hanley Lodge, Newbridge, Midlothian EH28 8NN
☎ **(0131) 333 4718**
secretary@gogarburngc.co.uk
Sandra Raine (0131) 333 3496
www.gogarburngc.com

Kings Acre   (1997)
Proprietary
Lasswade EH18 1AU
☎ **(0131) 663 3456**
(0131) 663 7076
info@kings-acregolf.com
Alan Murdoch (Dir of Golf)
www.kings-acregolf.com

Kingsknowe   (1907)
326 Lanark Road, Edinburgh EH14 2JD
☎ **(0131) 441 1144**
(0131) 441 2079
clubmanager@kingsknowe.com
Richard J McLuckie (0131) 441 1145
www.kingsknowe.com

Liberton   (1920)
Kingston Grange, 297 Gilmerton Road, Edinburgh EH16 5UJ
☎ **(0131) 664 3009**
info@libertongc.co.uk

John Masterton
www.libertongc.co.uk

Lothianburn   (1893)
106a Biggar Road, Edinburgh EH10 7DU
☎ **(0131) 445 5067**
info@lothianburngc.co.uk
(0131) 445 5067
www.lothianburngc.co.uk

Marriott Dalmahoy Hotel & CC
Dalmahoy, Kirknewton EH27 8EB
☎ **(0131) 335 8010**
(0131) 335 3577
Neal Graham (Golf Dir),

Melville Golf Centre   (1995)
Pay and play
Lasswade, Edinburgh EH18 1AN
☎ **(0131) 663 8038 (range, shop, tuition)**
(0131) 654 0814
golf@melvillegolf.co.uk
Mr & Mrs MacFarlane (Props)
www.melvillegolf.co.uk

Merchants of Edinburgh   (1907)
10 Craighill Gardens, Morningside, Edinburgh EH10 5PY
☎ **(0131) 447 1219**
(0131) 446 9833
admin@merchantsgolf.com
J Leslie
www.merchantsgolf.com

Mortonhall   (1892)
231 Braid Road, Edinburgh EH10 6PB
☎ **(0131) 447 6974**
(0131) 447 8712
clubhouse@mortonhallgc.co.uk
Ms BM Giefer
www.mortonhallgc.co.uk

Murrayfield   (1896)
43 Murrayfield Road, Edinburgh EH12 6EU
☎ **(0131) 337 3478**
(0131) 313 0721
john@murrayfieldgolfclub.co.uk
Mr J A Fraser (0131) 337 3478
www.murrayfieldgolfclub.co.uk

Newbattle   (1896)
Abbey Road, Eskbank, Dalkeith EH22 3AD
☎ **(0131) 663 2123**
(0131) 654 1810
mail@newbattlegolfclub.com
HG Stanners (0131) 663 1819
www.newbattlegolfclub.com

Prestonfield   (1920)
6 Priestfield Road North, Edinburgh EH16 5HS
☎ **(0131) 667 9665**
(0131) 777 2727
generalmanager@prestonfieldgolf.com
Carol King (Sec)
www.prestonfieldgolf.com

Ratho Park (1928)
Ratho, Edinburgh EH28 8NX
☎ **(0131) 335 0068**
🖳 (0131) 333 1752
✉ secretary@rathoparkgolfclub.co.uk
✍ CR Innes (0131) 335 0068
🖥 www.rathoparkgolfclub.co.uk

Ravelston (1912)
24 Ravelston Dykes Road, Edinburgh EH4 3NZ
☎ **(0131) 315 2486**
🖳 (0131) 315 2486
✉ ravelstongc@hotmail.com
✍ Jim Lowrie
🖥 www.ravelstongolfclub.com

Royal Burgess Golfing Society of Edinburgh
(1735)
181 Whitehouse Road, Barnton, Edinburgh EH4 6BU
☎ **(0131) 339 2075**
🖳 (0131) 339 3712
✉ generalmanager@royalburgess
.co.uk
✍ G Callander (0131) 339 2075
🖥 www.royalburgess.co.uk

Silverknowes (1947)
Public
Silverknowes Parkway, Edinburgh EH4 5ET
☎ **(0131) 336 3843 (Starter)**

Swanston New Golf Course
(1927)
111 Swanston Road, Fairmilehead, Edinburgh EH10 7DS
☎ **(0131) 445 2239**
🖳 (0131) 445 5720
✉ golf@swanston.co.uk
✍ Colin McClung
🖥 www.swanstongolf.co.uk

Torphin Hill (1895)
37-39 Torphin Road, Edinburgh EH13 0PG
☎ **(0131) 441 1100**
🖳 (0131) 441 7166
✉ torphinhillgc@unicombox.com
✍ Secretary
🖥 www.torphinhill.com

Turnhouse (1897)
154 Turnhouse Road, Corstorphine, Edinburgh EH12 0AD
☎ **(0131) 339 1014**
🖳 (0131) 339 5141
✉ secretary@turnhousegc.com
✍ Lindsay Gordon (Secretary)
🖥 www.turnhousegc.com

West Lothian

Bathgate (1892)
Edinburgh Road, Bathgate EH48 1BA
☎ **(01506) 630505**
🖳 (01506) 636775
✉ bathgate.golfclub@lineone.net
✍ G Flannigan (01506) 630505
🖥 www.bathgategolfclub.com

Bridgend & District (1994)
Willowdean, Bridgend, Linlithgow EH49 6NW
☎ **(01506) 834140**
🖳 (01506) 834706
✍ George Green
🖥 www.bridgendgolfclub.com

Deer Park G&CC (1978)
Golf Course Road, Knightsridge, Livingston EH54 8AB
☎ **(01506) 446699**
🖳 (01506) 435608
✉ jdouglas@muir-group.co.uk
✍ John Douglas (Gen Mgr)
🖥 www.deer-park.co.uk

Dundas Parks (1957)
South Queensferry EH30 9SS
☎ **(0131)331 4252**
✉ cmkwood@btinternet.com
✍ Mrs C Wood (07747) 854802
🖥 www.dundasparks.co.uk

Greenburn (1953)
6 Greenburn Road, Fauldhouse EH47 9HJ
☎ **(01501) 770292**
🖳 (01501) 772615
✉ administrator@greenburngolfclub.co.uk
✍ Thomas Hamill
🖥 www.greenburngolfclub.co.uk

Harburn (1932)
West Calder EH55 8RS
☎ **(01506) 871131**
🖳 (01506) 870286
✉ info@harburngolfclub.co.uk
✍ H Warnock (01506) 871131
🖥 www.harburngolfclub.co.uk

Linlithgow (1913)
Braehead, Linlithgow EH49 6QF
☎ **(01506) 842585**
🖳 (01506) 842764
✉ linlithgowgolf@talk21.com
✍ TI Adams
🖥 www.linlithgowgolf.co.uk

Niddry Castle (1983)
Castle Road, Winchburgh EH52 2RQ
☎ **(01506) 891097**
✉ secretary@niddrycastlegc.co.uk
✍ B Brooks
🖥 www.niddrycastlegc.co.uk

Oatridge (2000)
Pay and play
Ecclesmachen, Broxburn, West Lothian EH52 6NH
☎ **(01506) 859636**
✉ oatridge@btconnect.com
✍ Jim Thomson
🖥 www.oatridge.ac.uk

Polkemmet (1981)
Public
Whitburn, Bathgate EH47 0AD
☎ **(01501) 743905**
🖳 (01501) 744780
✉ polkemmet@westlothian.gov.uk

✍ Stuart Mungall (01501) 743905
🖥 www.beecraigs.com

Pumpherston (1895)
Drumshoreland Road, Pumpherston EH53 0LH
☎ **(01506) 432869/433336**
🖳 (01506) 438250
✉ sheena.corner@tiscali.co.uk
✍ James Taylor (01506) 433336
🖥 www.pumpherstongolfclub.co.uk

Rutherford Castle (1998)
Proprietary
West Linton EH46 7AS
☎ **(01968) 661233**
🖳 (01968) 661233
✉ clubhouse@rutherfordcastle.org.uk
✍ Derek Mitchell (Mgr)
🖥 www.rutherfordcastlegc.org.uk

Uphall (1895)
Houston Mains, Uphall EH52 6JT
☎ **(01506) 856404**
🖳 (01506) 855358
✉ uphallgolfclub@btconnect.com
✍ Gordon Law (Club Administrator Mgr)
🖥 www.uphallgolfclub.com

West Lothian (1892)
Airngath Hill, Bo'ness EH49 7RH
☎ **(01506) 826030**
🖳 (01506) 826030
✉ manager@westlothiangc.com
✍ Alan E Gibson (01506) 826030
🖥 www.westlothiangc.com

Moray

Buckpool (1933)
Barhill Road, Buckie AB56 1DU
☎ **(01542) 832236**
🖳 (01542) 832236
✉ golf@buckpoolgolf.com
✍ Mrs I Coull
🖥 www.buckpoolgolf.com

Dufftown (1896)
Tomintoul Road, Dufftown AB55 4BS
☎ **(01340) 820325**
🖳 (01340) 820325
✉ admin@dufftowngolfclub.com
✍ IR Montgomery
🖥 www.dufftowngolfclub.com

Elgin (1906)
Hardhillock, Birnie Road, Elgin IV30 8SX
☎ **(01343) 542338**
🖳 (01343) 542341
✉ secretary@elgingolfclub.com
✍ YM Forgan
🖥 www.elgingolfclub.com

Forres (1889)
Muiryshade, Forres IV36 2RD
☎ **(01309) 672949**
🖳 (01309) 672261
✉ forresgolfclub@tiscali.co.uk
✍ David Mackintosh
🖥 www.forresgolfclub.co.uk

Garmouth & Kingston (1932)
Spey Street, Garmouth, Fochabers
IV32 7NJ
☎ **(01343) 870388**
🖳 (01343) 870388
📧 garmouthgolfclub@aol.com
✍ Mrs I Fraser
🖥 www.garmouthkingstongolfclub
.com

Hopeman (1909)
Hopeman, Moray IV30 5YA
☎ **(01343) 830578**
🖳 (01343) 830152
📧 hopemangc@aol.com
✍ J Fraser (01343) 835068
🖥 www.hopemangc.co.uk

Moray (1889)
Stotfield Road, Lossiemouth IV31 6QS
☎ **(01343) 812018**
🖳 (01343) 815102
📧 secretary@moraygolf.co.uk
✍ SM Crane
🖥 www.moraygolf.co.uk

Spey Bay (1904)
Proprietary
The Links, Spey Bay, Fochabers IV32 7PJ
☎ **(01343) 820424**
📧 info@speybay.co
✍ Mr Iain Ednie
🖥 www.speybay.co

Perth & Kinross

Aberfeldy (1895)
Taybridge Road, Aberfeldy PH15 2BH
☎ **(01887) 820535**
🖳 (01887) 820535
📧 feldyde@tiscali.co.uk
✍ Jim Adams
🖥 www.aberfeldygolfclub.co.uk

Alyth (1894)
Pitcrocknie, Alyth PH11 8HF
☎ **(01828) 632268**
🖳 (01828) 633491
📧 enquiries@alythgolfclub.co.uk
✍ J Docherty
🖥 www.alythgolfclub.co.uk

Auchterarder (1892)
Orchil Road, Auchterarder PH3 1LS
☎ **(01764) 662804**
🖳 (01764) 664423
📧 secretary@auchterardergolf
.co.uk
✍ D.D.Smith
🖥 www.auchterardergolf.co.uk

Bishopshire (1903)
Pay and play
Kinnesswood, Woodmarch, Kinross
KY13 9HX
📧 ian-davidson@tiscali.co.uk
✍ Ian Davidson (01592) 773224

Blair Atholl (1896)
Invertilt Road, Blair Atholl PH18 5TG
☎ **(01796) 481407**
✍ T Boon 01796 481611

Blairgowrie (1889)
Rosemount, Blairgowrie PH10 6LG
☎ **(01250) 872622**
🖳 (01250) 875451
📧 office@theblairgowriegolfclub.co.uk
✍ Douglas Cleeton (Managing
  Secretary)
🖥 www.theblairgowriegolfclub.co.uk

Callander (1890)
Aveland Road, Callander FK17 8EN
☎ **(01877) 330090**
🖳 (01877) 330062
📧 callandergolf@btconnect.com
✍ Miss E Macdonald
🖥 www.callandergolfclub.co.uk

Comrie (1891)
Laggan Braes, Comrie PH6 2LR
☎ **(01764) 670055**
📧 enquiries@comriegolf.co.uk
✍ Manager
🖥 www.comriegolf.co.uk

Craigie Hill (1909)
Cherrybank, Perth PH2 0NE
☎ **(01738) 622644**
🖳 (01738) 620829
📧 admin@craigiehill.co.uk
✍ Administration (01738) 620829
🖥 www.craigiehill.co.uk

Crieff (1891)
Perth Road, Crieff PH7 3LR
☎ **(01764) 652909 (Bookings)**
🖳 (01764) 653803
📧 secretary@crieffgolf.co.uk
✍ David S Ramsay (01764) 652397
🖥 www.crieffgolf.co.uk

Dalmunzie (1948)
Glenshee, Blairgowrie PH10 7QE
☎ **(01250) 885226**
📧 enquiries@dalmunziecottages.com
✍ S Winton (Mgr)
🖥 www.dalmunziecottages.com

Dunkeld & Birnam (1892)
Fungarth, Dunkeld PH8 0ES
☎ **(01350) 727524**
🖳 (01350) 728660
📧 secretary-dunkeld@tiscali.co.uk
✍ Jane Burnett
🖥 www.dunkeldandbirnamgolfclub
.co.uk

Dunning (1953)
Rollo Park, Dunning PH2 0QX
☎ **(01764) 684747**
📧 secretary@dunninggolfclub.co.uk
✍ Neil C Morton (01738) 626701
🖥 www.dunninggolfclub.co.uk

Foulford Inn (1995)
Pay and play
Crieff PH7 3LN
☎ **(01764) 652407**

🖳 (01764) 652407
📧 foulford@btconnect.com
✍ M Beaumont
🖥 www.foulfordinn.co.uk

The Gleneagles Hotel (1924)
Auchterarder PH3 1NF
☎ **(01764) 662231**
🖳 (01764) 662134
📧 resort.sales@gleneagles.com
✍ Bernard Murphy (Hotel)
🖥 www.gleneagles.com

Glenisla (1998)
Proprietary
Pitcrocknie Farm, Alyth PH11 8JJ
☎ **(01828) 632445**
🖥 www.golf-glenisla.co.uk

Killin (1911)
Killin FK21 8TX
☎ **(01567) 820312**
🖳 (01567) 820312
📧 info@killingolfclub.co.uk
🖥 www.killingolfclub.co.uk

King James VI (1858)
Moncreiffe Island, Perth PH2 8NR
☎ **(01738) 632460**
📧 mansec@kingjamesvi.com
✍ M Brown
🖥 www.kingjamesvi.com

Kinross Golf Courses (1900)
c/o The Green Hotel, 2 The Muirs, Kinross
KY13 8AS
☎ **(01577) 863407**
📧 bookings@golfkinross.com
🖥 www.golfkinross.com

Mains of Taymouth Golf Club (1992)
Pay and play
Mains of Taymouth, Kenmore, Aberfeldy
PH15 2HN
☎ **(01887) 830226**
🖳 (01887) 830775
📧 info@taymouth.co.uk
✍ R Menzies (Mgr)
🖥 www.kenmoregolfcourse.co.uk

Milnathort (1910)
South Street, Milnathort, Kinross KY13 9XA
☎ **(01577) 864069**
📧 milnathort.gc@btconnect.com
✍ K Dziennik (Admin. Mgr)

Muckhart (1908)
Drumburn Road, Muckhart, Dollar
FK14 7JH
☎ **(01259) 781423**
📧 enquiries@muckhartgolf.com
✍ A Houston
🖥 www.muckhartgolf.com

Murrayshall (1981)
Murrayshall, New Scone, Perth PH2 7PH
☎ **(01738) 554804**
🖳 (01738) 552595
📧 info@murrayshall.co.uk
✍ M Lloyd (Mgr)
🖥 www.murrayshall.co.uk

Muthill (1911)
Peat Road, Muthill PH5 2DA
☎ **(01764) 681523**
🖥 (01764) 681557
📧 muthillgolfclub@btconnect.com
✍ Nan Shaw
🖳 www.muthillgolfclub.co.uk

North Inch (1892)
Public
c/o Perth & Kinross Council, The
Environment Services, Pullar House, 35
Kinnoull St, Perth PH1 5GD
☎ **(01738) 636481 (Starter)**
🖥 (01738) 476410
📧 northinchgolf@pkc.gov.uk
✍ Alison White
🖳 www.pkc.gov.uk/northinchgolf

Pitlochry (1909)
Proprietary
Golf Course Road, Pitlochry PH16 5QY
☎ **(01796) 472792 (Bookings)**
🖥 (01796) 473947 (bookings)
📧 pro@pitlochrygolf.co.uk
✍ Mark Pirie (01796) 472792
🖳 www.pitlochrygolf.co.uk

Royal Perth Golfing Society
(1824)
Club
1/2 Atholl Crescent, Perth PH1 5NG
☎ **(01738) 622265**
📧 secretary@royal-perth-golfing-society.org.uk
✍ DP McDonald (Gen Sec) (01738) 622265,
🖳 www.royal-perth-golfing-society.org.uk

St Fillans (1903)
South Loch Earn Rd, St Fillans PH6 2NJ
☎ **(01764) 685312**
🖥 01764 685312
📧 stfillansgc@aol.com
✍ G Hibbert (01764) 685312
🖳 www.st-fillans-golf.com

Strathmore Golf Centre
(1995)
Proprietary
Leroch, Alyth, Blairgowrie PH11 8NZ
☎ **(01828) 633322**
🖥 (01828) 633533
📧 enquiries@strathmoregolf.com
✍ David Norman
🖳 www.strathmoregolf.com

Strathtay (1909)
Donfield, Strathtay, Pitlochry PH9 0PG
☎ **(01887) 840493**
✍ James Wilson
🖳 www.strathtaygolfclub.com

Taymouth Castle (1923)
Kenmore, Aberfeldy PH15 2NT
☎ **(01887) 830234**
🖥 (01887) 830234
📧 secretary@taymouthcastlegolfclub.com
✍ W R McGregor (Sec)
🖳 www.taymouthcastlegolfclub.com

Whitemoss (1994)
Whitemoss Road, Dunning, Perth PH2 0QX
☎ **(01738) 730300**
🖥 (01738) 730490
📧 info@whitemossgolf.com
✍ A Nicolson
🖳 www.whitemossgolf.com

Renfrewshire

Barshaw (1927)
Public
Barshaw Park, Glasgow Road, Paisley, PA2
☎ **(0141) 889 2908**

Bonnyton (1957)
Eaglesham, Glasgow G76 0QA
☎ **(01355) 303030**
🖥 (01355) 303151
📧 secretarybgc@btconnect.com
✍ M Crichton
🖳 www.bonnytongolfclub.com

Caldwell (1903)
Caldwell, Uplawmoor G78 4AU
☎ **(01505) 850329**
🖥 (01505) 850604
📧 Secretary@caldwellgolfclub.co.uk
✍ K Morrison (01505) 850366
🖳 www.caldwellgolfclub.co.uk

Cochrane Castle (1895)
Scott Avenue, Craigston, Johnstone PA5 0HF
☎ **(01505) 320146**
🖥 (01505) 325338
📧 secretary@cochranecastle.com
✍ Mrs PIJ Quin
🖳 www.cochranecastle.com

East Renfrewshire (1922)
Pilmuir, Newton Mearns G77 6RT
☎ **(01355) 500256**
🖥 (01355) 500323
📧 secretary@eastrengolfclub.co.uk
✍ G J Tennant (01355) 500256
🖳 www.eastrengolfclub.co.uk

Eastwood (1893)
Muirshield, Loganswell, Newton Mearns,
Glasgow G77 6RX
☎ **(01355) 500285**
🖥 (01355) 500333
📧 eastwoodgolfclub@btconnect.com
✍ I Brown (01355) 500280
🖳 www.eastwoodgolfclub.co.uk

Elderslie (1908)
63 Main Road, Elderslie PA5 9AZ
☎ **(01505) 323956**
🖥 (01505) 340346
📧 eldersliegolfclub@btconnect.com
✍ Mrs A Anderson
🖳 www.eldersliegolfclub.com

Erskine (1904)
Golf Road, Bishopton PA7 5PH
☎ **(01505) 862302**
🖥 (01505) 862898
📧 secretary@erskinegolfclub.wanadoo.co.uk
✍ DF McKellar
🖳 www.erskinegolfclublimited.co.uk

Fereneze (1904)
Fereneze Avenue, Barrhead G78 1HJ
☎ **(0141) 881 1519**
🖥 (0141) 881 7149
📧 ferenezegc@lineone.net
✍ G McCreadie (0141) 881 7149
🖳 www.ferenezegolfclub.co.uk

Gleddoch (1974)
Langbank PA14 6YE
☎ **(01475) 540711**

Gourock (1896)
Cowal View, Gourock PA19 1HD
☎ **(01475) 631001**
📧 secretary@gourockgolfclub.com
✍ Margaret Paterson
🖳 www.gourockgolfclub.com

Greenock (1890)
Forsyth Street, Greenock PA16 8RE
☎ **(01475) 720793**
📧 secretary@greenockgolfclub.co.uk
✍ Mrs Heather Sinclair (01475) 791912
🖳 www.greenockgolfclub.co.uk

Kilmacolm (1891)
Porterfield Road, Kilmacolm PA13 4PD
☎ **(01505) 872139**
🖥 (01505) 874007
📧 secretary@kilmacolmgolfclub.com
✍ VR Weldin
🖳 www.kilmacolmgolfclub.com

Lochwinnoch (1897)
Burnfoot Road, Lochwinnoch PA12 4AN
☎ **(01505) 842153**
🖥 (01505) 843668
📧 admin@lochwinnochgolf.co.uk
✍ RJG Jamieson
🖳 www.lochwinnochgolf.co.uk

Old Course Ranfurly Golf
Club (1905)
Ranfurly Place, Bridge of Weir PA11 3DE
☎ **(01505) 613612**
(Clubhouse)
🖥 (01505) 613214
📧 secretary@oldranfurly.com
✍ J M R Doyle (01505) 613214
🖳 www.oldranfurly.com

Paisley (1895)
Braehead Road, Paisley PA2 8TZ
☎ **(0141) 884 2292**
(Clubhouse)
📧 paisleygolfclub@btconnect.com
✍ John Devenny (Sec/Mgr)
(0141) 884 3903
🖳 www.paisleygolfclub.com

Port Glasgow (1895)
Devol Road, Port Glasgow PA14 5XE
☎ **(01475) 704181**
🖥 01475 700334
📧 secretary@portglasgowgolfclub.com
✍ James Downie
🖳 www.portglasgowgolfclub.com

Ranfurly Castle   (1889)

Golf Road, Bridge of Weir PA11 3HN
☎ **(01505) 612609**
🖥 (01505) 610406
📧 secranfur@aol.com
✍ J King
🖥 www.ranfurlycastlegolfclub.co.uk

Renfrew   (1894)

Blythswood Estate, Inchinnan Road, Renfrew PA4 9EG
☎ **(0141) 886 6692**
🖥 (0141) 886 1808
📧 andy.mclaughlin@renfrewgolfclub.net
✍ Andy McLaughlin
🖥 www.renfrewgolfclub.net

Whitecraigs   (1905)

72 Ayr Road, Giffnock, Glasgow G46 6SW
☎ **(0141) 639 4530**
🖥 (0141) 616 3648
📧 whitecraigsgc@btconnect.com
✍ I M Brown
🖥 www.whitecraigsgolfclub.com

Stirlingshire

Aberfoyle   (1890)

Braeval, Aberfoyle FK8 3UY
☎ **(01877) 382493**
📧 secretary@aberfoylegolf.co.uk
✍ EJ Barnard (Sec) (01360) 550847
🖥 www.aberfoylegolf.com

Balfron   (1992)

Kepculloch Road, Balfron G63 0QP
☎ **(0781) 482 7620**
📧 brian.a.davidson23@btinternet.com
✍ Brian Davidson (01360) 550613
🖥 www.balfrongolfsociety.org.uk

Bonnybridge   (1925)

Larbert Road, Bonnybridge, Falkirk FK4 1NY
☎ **(01324) 812822/812323**

🖥 (01324) 812323
📧 bgcl@hotmail.co.uk
✍ Alexander Nolton (01324) 812323

Bridge of Allan   (1895)

Sunnylaw, Bridge of Allan, Stirling
☎ **(01786) 832332**
📧 secretary@bofagc.com
✍ David Smeaton
🖥 www.bofagc.com

Buchanan Castle   (1936)

Proprietary
Drymen G63 0HY
☎ **(01360) 660307**
📧 info@buchanancastlegolfclub.co.uk
✍ Ms JA Dawson
🖥 www.buchanancastlegolfclub.com

Campsie   (1897)

Crow Road, Lennoxtown, Glasgow G66 7HX
☎ **(01360) 310244**
📧 campsiegolfclub@aol.com
✍ K Stoddart (Administrator)
🖥 www.campsiegolfclub.org.uk

Dunblane New   (1923)

Perth Road, Dunblane FK15 0LJ
☎ **(01786) 821527**
🖥 (01786) 825066
📧 secretary@dngc.co.uk
✍ RD Morrison
🖥 www.dngc.co.uk

Falkirk   (1922)

Stirling Road, Camelon, Falkirk FK2 7YP
☎ **(01324) 611061/612219**
🖥 (01324) 639573
📧 secretary@falkirkgolfclub.co.uk
✍ Aileen Jenkins
🖥 www.falkirkgolfclub.co.uk

Falkirk Tryst   (1885)

86 Burnhead Road, Larbert FK5 4BD
☎ **(01324) 562415**
🖥 (01324) 562054
📧 secretary@falkirktrystgolfclub.com

✍ RC Chalmers (01324) 562054
🖥 www.falkirktrystgolfclub.com

Glenbervie   (1932)

Stirling Road, Larbert FK5 4SJ
☎ **(01324) 562605**
🖥 (01324) 551054
📧 secretary@glenberviegolfclub.com
✍ IR Webster CA
🖥 www.glenberviegolfclub.com

Grangemouth   (1973)

Public
Polmonthill, Polmont FK2 0YA
☎ **(01324) 711500**
📧 grangemouthgolfclub@btopenword.com
✍ Jim McNairney

Kilsyth Lennox   (1905)

Tak-Ma-Doon Road, Kilsyth G65 0RS
☎ **(01236) 824115 (Bookings)**
🖥 (01236) 823089
📧 admin@kilsythlennox.com
✍ L Reeds (01236) 824115
🖥 www.kilsythlennox.com

Polmont   (1901)

Manuel Rigg, Maddiston, Falkirk FK2 0LS
☎ **(01324) 711277 (Clubhouse)**
🖥 (01324) 712504
📧 polmontgolfclub@btconnect.com
✍ Mrs M Fellows (01324) 711277

Stirling   (1869)

Queen's Road, Stirling FK8 3AA
☎ **(01786) 464098**
🖥 (01786) 460090
📧 enquiries@stirlinggolfclub.tv
✍ AMS Rankin (01786) 464098 Option 2
🖥 www.stirlinggolfclub.com

Strathendrick   (1901)

Glasgow Road, Drymen G63 0AA
☎ **(01360) 660695**
✍ M Quyn (01360) 660733
🖥 www.strathendrickgolfclub.co.uk

Kingsbarns is Scottish Course of the Year again

Kingsbarns Golf Links was voted the Golf Course of the Year for the fourth time at the 2011 Golf Tourism Scotland Gold Standard Award – the industry's Oscars.

The course earned the award ahead of the Old and New Courses at St Andrews, Carnoustie and the Ailsa course at Turnberry Hotel among others.

Kingsbarns has consistently performed well in international rankings. In *Golfweek* it gained No 1 spot for a modern course (built after 1960) in Great Britain and Ireland.

For key to symbols see page 717

Wales

Cardiganshire

Aberystwyth (1911)
Brynymor Road, Aberystwyth SY23 2HY
☎ **(01970) 615104**
📠 aberystwythgolf@talk21.com
🖎 Emlyn Thomas
🖳 www.aberystwythgolfclub.com

Borth & Ynyslas (1885)
Borth, Ceredigion SY24 5JS
☎ **(01970) 871202**
📠 (01970) 871202
🖎 secretary@borthgolf.co.uk
🖎 Owen Lawrence
🖳 www.borthgolf.co.uk

Cardigan (1895)
Gwbert-on-Sea, Cardigan SA43 1PR
☎ **(01239) 621775**
📠 (01239) 621775
🖎 cgc@btconnect.com
🖎 Clive Day (Sec) (01239) 621775
🖳 www.cardigangolf.co.uk

Cilgwyn (1905)
Llangybi, Lampeter SA48 8NN
☎ **(01570) 493286**
🖎 J M Jones
🖳 www.cilgwyngolf.co.uk

Penrhos G&CC (1991)
Llanrhystud, Ceredigion SY23 5AY
☎ **(01974) 202999**
📠 (01974) 202100
🖎 info@penrhosgolf.co.uk
🖎 R Rees-Evans
🖳 www.penrhosgolf.co.uk

Carmarthenshire

Ashburnham (1894)
Cliffe Terrace, Burry Port SA16 0HN
☎ **(01554) 832269**
📠 (01554) 836974
🖎 golf@ashburnhamgolfclub.co.uk
🖎 Mr Huw Morgan
🖳 www.ashburnhamgolfclub.co.uk

Carmarthen (1907)
Blaenycoed Road, Carmarthen SA33 6EH
☎ **(01267) 281588**
📠 (01267) 281493
🖎 carmarthengolfclub@btinternet
.com
🖎 Shan Lewis
🖳 www.carmarthengolf.com

Derllys Court (1993)
Proprietary
Derllys Court, Llysonnen Road, Carmarthen
SA33 5DT
☎ **(01267) 211575**
📠 (01267) 211575
🖎 derllys@hotmail.com
🖎 R Walters
🖳 www.derllyscourtgolfclub.com

Garnant Park (1997)
Garnant, Ammanford SA18 1NP
☎ **(01269) 823365**
📠 (01269) 823365
🖎 garnantgolf@carmarthenshire
.gov.uk
🖎 Vince Mosson
🖳 www.parcgarnantgolf.co.uk

Glyn Abbey (1992)
Proprietary
Trimsaran SA17 4LB
☎ **(01554) 810278**
📠 (01554) 810889
🖎 course-enquiries@glynabbey.co.uk
🖎 Martin Lane (Mgr)
🖳 www.glynabbey.co.uk

Glynhir (1909)
Glynhir Road, Llandybie, Ammanford
SA18 2TF
☎ **(01269) 851365**
📠 (01269) 851365
🖎 glynhirgolfclub@tiscali.co.uk
🖎 Mr Roburt Edwards
🖳 www.glynhirgolfclub.co.uk

Saron Golf Course (1990)
Pay and play
Penwern, Saron, Llandysul SA44 4EL
☎ **(01559) 370705**
📠 (01559) 370705
🖎 Mr C Searle
⊕ Answer telephone 24hrs

Conwy

Abergele (1910)
Tan-y-Gopa Road, Abergele LL22 8DS
☎ **(01745) 824034**
📠 (01745) 824772
🖎 secretary@abergelegolfclub.co.uk
🖎 CP Langdon
🖳 www.abergelegolfclub.co.uk

Betws-y-Coed (1977)
Clubhouse, Betws-y-Coed LL24 0AL
☎ **(01690) 710556**
🖎 info@golf-betws-ycoed.co.uk/
betwsycoedgclub
@btinternet.com
🖎 Adam Brown
🖳 www.golf-betws-y-coed.co.uk

Conwy (Caernarvonshire)
(1890)
Beacons Way, Morfa, Conwy LL32 8ER
☎ **(01492) 592423**
📠 (01492) 593363
🖎 secretary@conwygolfclub.com
🖎 Chris Chance (01492) 592423
🖳 www.conwygolfclub.com

Llandudno (Maesdu) (1915)
Hospital Road, Llandudno LL30 1HU
☎ **(01492) 876450**

📠 (01492) 876450
🖎 secretary@maesdugolfclub.co.uk
🖎 G Dean
🖳 www.maesdugolfclub.co.uk

Llanfairfechan (1971)
Llannerch Road, Llanfairfechan LL33 0EB
☎ **(01248) 680144**
🖎 K V Williams

North Wales (Llandudno)
(1894)
72 Bryniau Road, West Shore, Llandudno
LL30 2DZ
☎ **(01492) 875325**
📠 (01492) 872420
🖎 enquiries@northwalesgolfclub
.co.uk
🖎 Nick Kitchen (01492) 875325
🖳 www.northwalesgolfclub.co.uk

Old Colwyn (1907)
Woodland Avenue, Old Colwyn LL29 9NL
☎ **(01492) 515581**
🖎 colwyngolfclub@tiscali.co.uk
🖎 Mike Eccles (07760) 119445
🖳 www.oldcolwyngolfclub.co.uk

Penmaenmawr (1910)
Conway Old Road, Penmaenmawr
LL34 6RD
☎ **(01492) 623330**
📠 (01492) 622105
🖎 clubhouse@pengolf.co.uk
🖎 Mrs AH greenwood
🖳 www.pengolf.co.uk

Rhos-on-Sea (1899)
Penrhyn Bay, Llandudno LL30 3PU
☎ **(01492) 549641**
📠 (01492) 549100
🖎 rhosonseagolfclub@btinternet
.com
🖎 G Simmonds & I Taylor
🖳 www.rhosgolf.co.uk

Denbighshire

Bryn Morfydd Hotel
(1982)
Llanrhaeadr, Denbigh LL16 4NP
☎ **(01745) 890280**
📠 (01745) 890488
🖎 brynmorfydd@live.co.uk
🖎 BW Astle (07752) 527257
🖳 www.bryn-morfydd.co.uk

Denbigh (1908)
Henllan Road, Denbigh LL16 5AA
☎ **(01745) 816669**
📠 (01745) 814888
🖎 denbighgolfclub@aol.com
🖎 JR Williams (01745) 816669
🖳 www.denbighgolfclub.co.uk

Kinmel Park   (1989)
Pay and play
Bodelwyddan LL18 5SR
☎ **(01745) 833548**
✉ info@kinmelgolf.co.uk
🖎 Mrs Fetherstonhaugh
🖥 www.kinmelgolf.co.uk

Prestatyn   (1905)
Marine Road East, Prestatyn LL19 7HS
☎ **(01745) 854320**
🖴 (01745) 834320
✉ enquiries@prestatyngolfclub.co.uk
🖥 www.prestatyngolfclub.co.uk

Rhuddlan   (1930)
Meliden Road, Rhuddlan LL18 6LB
☎ **(01745) 590217**
🖴 (01745) 590472
✉ secretary@rhuddlangolfclub.co.uk
🖎 Mr J M Wood
🖥 www.rhuddlangolfclub.co.uk

Rhyl   (1890)
Coast Road, Rhyl LL18 3RE
☎ **(01745) 353171**
🖴 (01745) 353171
✉ rhylgolfclub@btconnect.com
🖎 Gill Davies
🖥 www.rhylgolfclub.co.uk

Ruthin-Pwllglas   (1920)
Pwllglas, Ruthin LL15 2PE
☎ **(01824) 702296**
✉ neillroberts@aol.com
🖎 Neil L Roberts 01824 704651
🖥 www.ruthinpwllglasgc.co.uk

St Melyd   (1922)
The Paddock, Meliden Road, Prestatyn
LL19 8NB
☎ **(01745) 854405**
🖴 (01745) 856908
✉ enquiries@stmelydgolfltd.co.uk
🖎 Janette Williams
🖥 www.stmelydgolf.co.uk

Vale of Llangollen   (1908)
Holyhead Road, Llangollen LL20 7PR
☎ **(01978) 860906**
✉ secretary@vlgc.co.uk
🖥 www.vlgc.co.uk

Flintshire

Caerwys   (1989)
Pay and play
Caerwys, Mold CH7 5AQ
☎ **(01352) 721222**

Hawarden   (1911)
Groomsdale Lane, Hawarden, Deeside
CH5 3EH
☎ **(01244) 531447**
🖴 (01244) 536901
✉ secretary@hawardengolfclub
.co.uk
🖎 A Rowland
🖥 www.hawardengolfclub.co.uk

Holywell   (1906)
Brynford, Holywell CH8 8LQ
☎ **(01352) 710040 opt 2**
✉ secretary@holywellgolf.co.uk
🖎 Matt Parsley
🖥 www.holywellgolf.co.uk

Kinsale   (1996)
Pay and play
Llanerchymor, Holywell CH8 9DX
☎ **(01745) 561080**
🖎 S Leverett
🖥 www.kinsalegolf.wordpress.com

Mold   (1909)
Cilcain Road, Pantymwyn, Mold CH7 5EH
☎ (01352) 740318/741513
🖴 (01352) 741517
✉ info@moldgolfclub.co.uk
🖎 C Mills (01352) 741513
🖥 www.moldgolfclub.co.uk

Northop Country Park
(1994)
Northop, Chester CH7 6WA
☎ **(01352) 840440**
🖴 (01352) 840445
✉ john@northoppark.co.uk
🖎 John Nolan (01352) 840440 press 1
🖥 www.northoppark.co.uk

Old Padeswood   (1978)
Proprietary
Station Road, Padeswood, Mold CH7 4JL
☎ **(01244) 547401 Ext 2
(Clubhouse)**
🖴 (01244) 545082
✉ sec@oldpadeswoodgolfclub.co.uk
🖎 Robert Jones (01244) 550414
🖥 www.oldpadeswoodgolfclub.co.uk

Padeswood & Buckley   (1933)
The Caia, Station Lane, Padeswood, Mold
CH7 4JD
☎ **(01244) 550537**
🖴 (01244) 541600
✉ admin@padeswoodgolf.plus.com
🖎 Mrs S A Davies
🖥 www.padeswoodgolfclub.com

Pennant Park   (1998)
Proprietary
Whitford, Holywell CH8 9AE
☎ **(01745) 563000**
🖥 www.pennant-park.co.uk

Gwynedd

Aberdovey   (1892)
Aberdovey LL35 0RT
☎ **(01654) 767493**
🖴 (01654) 767027
✉ sec@aberdoveygolf.co.uk
🖎 Gareth Pritchard (Mgr)
🖥 www.aberdoveygolf.co.uk

Abersoch   (1907)
Golf Road, Abersoch LL53 7EY
☎ **(01758) 712636**
✉ admin@abersochgolf.co.uk
🖥 www.abersochgolf.co.uk

Bala   (1973)
Penlan, Bala LL23 7YD
☎ **(01678) 520359**
🖴 (01678) 521361
✉ balagolf@btconnect.com
🖎 G Rhys Jones
🖥 www.golffbala.co.uk

Dolgellau   (1910)
Proprietary
Hengwrt Estate, Pencefn Road, Dolgellau
LL40 2ES
☎ **(01341) 422603**
✉ info@dolgellaugolfclub.com
🖎 M White
🖥 www.dolgellaugolfclub.com

Ffestiniog   (1893)
Y Cefn, Ffestiniog
☎ **(01766) 762637 (Clubhouse)**
✉ info@ffestinioggolf.org
🖎 G Hughes (01766) 590617
🖥 www.ffestinioggolf.org

Nefyn & District   (1907)
Morfa Nefyn, Pwllheli LL53 6DA
☎ **(01758) 720966 (Clubhouse)**
🖴 (01758) 720476
✉ secretary@nefyn-golf-club.com
🖎 S Dennis (01758) 720966
🖥 www.nefyn-golf-club.com

Porthmadog   (1905)
Morfa Bychan, Porthmadog LL49 9UU
☎ **(01766) 514124**
🖴 (01766) 514124
✉ secretary@porthmadog-golf-
club.co.uk
🖎 GT Jones (Mgr)
🖥 www.porthmadog-golf-club.co.uk

Pwllheli   (1900)
Golf Road, Pwllheli LL53 5PS
☎ **(01758) 701644**
🖴 (01758) 701644
✉ admin@pwllheligolfclub.co.uk
🖎 Dennis Moore (Gen Mgr)
🖥 www.pwllheligolfclub.co.uk

Royal St David's   (1894)
Harlech LL46 2UB
☎ **(01766) 780203**
🖴 (0844) 811 1484
✉ secretary@royalstdavids.co.uk
🖎 T Davies (01766) 780361
🖥 www.royalstdavids.co.uk

Royal Town of Caernarfon
(1909)
Aberforeshore, LLanfaglan, Caernarfon LL54
5RP
☎ **(01286) 673783**
🖴 (01286) 673783
✉ secretary@caernarfongolfclub
.co.uk
🖎 EG Angel
🖥 www.caernarfongolfclub.co.uk

St Deniol   (1906)
Penybryn, Bangor LL57 1PX
☎ **(01248) 353098**
🖴 (01248) 370792

✉ secretary@st-deiniol.co.uk
✍ RD Thomas MBE (01248) 353098
▤ www.st-deiniol.co.uk

Isle of Anglesey

Anglesey (1914)
Station Road, Rhosneigr LL64 5QX
☎ **(01407) 811127**
✉ info@theangleseygolfclub.com
✍ M Tommis (01407) 811127
▤ www.angleseygolfclub.co.uk

Baron Hill (1895)
Beaumaris LL58 8YW
☎ **(01248) 810231**
▯ (01248) 810231
✉ golf@baronhill.co.uk
✍ A Pleming
▤ www.baronhill.co.uk

Bull Bay (1913)
Bull Bay Road, Amlwch LL68 9RY
☎ **(01407) 830960**
▯ (01407) 832612
✉ info@bullbaygc.co.uk
✍ John Burns
▤ www.bullbaygc.co.uk

Henllys Hall (1996)
Llanfaes, Beaumaris LL58 8HU
☎ **(01248) 811717**
▯ (01248) 811511
✉ hg@hpb.co.uk
✍ Peter Maton
▤ www.henllysgolfclub.co.uk

Holyhead (1912)
Trearddur Bay, Anglesey LL65 2YL
☎ **(01407) 763279/762119**
▯ (01407) 763279
✉ holyheadgolfclub@tiscali.co.uk
✍ S Elliott (01407) 763279
▤ www.holyheadgolfclub.co.uk

Llangefni (1983)
Public
Llangefni LL77 8YQ
☎ **(01248) 722193**

RAF Valley
Anglesey LL65 3NY
☎ **(01407) 762241**
✉ constables@constables.wanadoo
.com
▤ www.rafvalleygolfclub.co.uk

Storws Wen (1996)
Proprietary
Brynteg, Benllech LL78 8JY
☎ **(01248) 852673**
✉ storws.wen.golf@hotmail.co.uk
✍ E Rowlands (Gen Mgr)
▤ www.storwswen.org

Mid Glamorgan

Aberdare (1921)
Proprietary
Abernant, Aberdare CF44 0RY
☎ **(01685) 871188 (Clubhouse)**

✉ aberdaregolfclub@hotmail.co.uk
✍ Rhys James (Pro & Club Mgr)
▤ www.aberdaregolfclub.com

Bargoed (1913)
Heolddu, Bargoed CF81 9GF
☎ **(01443) 830143**
▯ (01443) 830608
✍ Mrs Denise Richards (01443)
830608

Bryn Meadows Golf Hotel
(1973)
Maes-y-Cwmmer, Ystrad Mynach, Nr
Caerphilly CF82 7SN
☎ **(01495) 225590/224103**
▯ (01495) 228272
✉ reception@brynmeadows.co.uk
✍ S Mayo
▤ www.brynmeadows.co.uk

Caerphilly (1905)
Pencapel, Mountain Road, Caerphilly
CF83 1HJ
☎ **(029) 2086 3441**
▯ (029) 2086 3441
✉ secretary&caerphillygolfclub.com
✍ Roger Chaffey (029) 2086 3441
▤ www.caerphillygolfclub.com

Coed-y-Mwstwr (1994)
Coychurch, Bridgend CF35 6AF
☎ **(01656) 864934**
▯ (01656) 864934
✉ secretary@www.coed-y-mwstwr
.co.uk
✍ Gareth Summerton
▤ www.coed-y-mwstwr.co.uk

Creigiau (1921)
Creigiau, Cardiff CF15 9NN
☎ **(029) 2089 0263**
▯ (029) 2089 0706
✉ creigiaugolfclub@btconnect.com
✍ Gareth Morgan
▤ www.creigiaugolfclub.co.uk

Grove (1996)
Proprietary
South Cornelly, Bridgend CF33 4RP
☎ **(01656) 788771**
▯ (01656) 788414
✉ enquiries@grovegolf.com
✍ M Thomas
▤ www.grovegolf.com

Llantrisant & Pontyclun
(1927)
Ely Valley Road, Talbot Green, Llantrisant
CF72 8AL
☎ **(01443) 224601**
▯ (01443) 224601
✉ llantrisantgolf@btconnect.com
✍ Andrew Bowen (Professional)
▤ www.llantrisantgolfclub.co.uk

Maesteg (1912)
Mount Pleasant, Neath Road, Maesteg
CF34 9PR
☎ **(01656) 734106**
▯ (01656) 731822

✉ manager@maesteg-golf.co.uk
✍ Mr Mark Wilson (Gen Mgr)
▤ www.maesteg-golf.co.uk

Merthyr Tydfil (1909)
Cloth Hall Lane, Cefn Coed, Merthyr Tydfil
CF48 2NU
☎ **(01685) 373131**
✍ K Anderson
▤ www.merthyrtydfilgolfclub.co.uk

Mountain Ash (1907)
Cefnpennar, Mountain Ash CF45 4DT
☎ **(01443) 479459 (office)**
▯ (01443) 479628
✉ sec@mountainashgc.co.uk
✍ (01443) 479459 ext 1
▤ www.mountainashgc.co.uk

Mountain Lakes (1988)
Heol Penbryn, Blaengwynlais, Caerphilly
CF83 1NG
☎ **(029) 2086 1128**

Pontypridd (1905)
Ty Gwyn Road, Pontypridd CF37 4DJ
☎ **(01443) 409904**
▯ (01443) 491622
✉ rebekah.craven
@pontypriddgolfclub.co.uk
✍ Rebekah Craven (01443) 409904
▤ www.pontypriddgolfclub.co.uk

Pyle & Kenfig (1922)
Waun-y-Mer, Kenfig, Bridgend CF33 4PU
☎ **(01656) 783093**
▯ (01656) 772822
✉ secretary@pandkgolfclub.co.uk
✍ Mrs Bev Cronin (01656) 771613
▤ www.pandkgolfclub.co.uk

Rhondda (1910)
Penrhys, Ferndale, Rhondda CF43 3PW
☎ **(01443) 441384**
▯ (01443) 441384
✉ manager@rhonddagolf.co.uk
✍ Ian Ellis (01443) 441384
▤ www.rhonddagolf.co.uk

Ridgeway (1997)
Proprietary
Caerphilly Mountain, Caerphilly CF83 1LY
☎ **(029) 2088 2255**
✉ petethepro@tiscali.co.uk
✍ Hilary Mears
▤ www.ridgeway-golf.co.uk

Royal Porthcawl (1891)
Rest Bay, Porthcawl CF36 3UW
☎ **(01656) 782251**
▯ (01656) 771687
✉ office@royalporthcawl.com
✍ MK Bond
▤ www.royalporthcawl.com

Southerndown (1905)
Ogmore-by-Sea, Bridgend CF32 0QP
☎ **(01656) 880476**
▯ (01656) 880317
✉ admin@southerndowngolfclub.com
✍ AJ Hughes (01656) 881111
▤ www.southerndowngolfclub.com

Whitehall   (1922)
The Pavilion, Nelson, Treharris CF46 6ST
☎ **(01443) 740245**
✉ m.wilde001@tiscali.co.uk
✍ PM Wilde
🖥 www.whitehallgolfclub1922.co.uk

Monmouthshire

Alice Springs   (1989)
Proprietary
Kemeys Commander, Usk NP15 1PP
☎ **(01873) 880914**
🖨 (01873) 881381
✉ golf@alicespringsgolfclub.co.uk
🖥 www.alicespringsgolfclub.co.uk

Blackwood   (1914)
Cwmgelli, Blackwood NP12 1BR
☎ **(01495) 223152**
✉ blackwoodgolfclub@btconnect.com
✍ Mr John Bills
🖥 www.blackwoodgolfclub.org.uk

The Celtic Manor Resort
(1995)
Proprietary
Coldra Woods, The Usk Valley, NP18 1HQ
☎ **(01633) 413000**
🖨 (01633) 410309
✉ postbox@celtic-manor.com
✍ Matthew Lewis (Director of Golf)
🖥 www.celtic-manor.com

Dewstow   (1988)
Proprietary
Caerwent, Monmouthshire NP26 5AH
☎ **(01291) 430444**
🖨 (01291) 425816
✉ info@dewstow.com
✍ D Bradbury
🖥 www.dewstow.com

Greenmeadow G&CC   (1979)
Treherbert Road, Croesyceiliog, Cwmbran NP44 2BZ
☎ **(01633) 869321**
🖨 (01633) 868430
✉ info@greenmeadowgolf.com
✍ PJ Richardson (01633) 869321
🖥 www.greenmeadowgolf.com

Llanwern   (1928)
Tennyson Avenue, Llanwern, Newport NP18 2DY
☎ **(01633) 412029**
🖨 (01633) 412260
✉ llanwerngolfclub@btconnect.com
✍ Mrs A Webber
🖥 www.llanwerngolfclub.co.uk

Marriott St Pierre Hotel & CC   (1962)
St Pierre Park, Chepstow NP16 6YA
☎ **(01291) 625261**
🖨 (01291) 629975
✉ chepstow@btconnect.com
✍ Mr Arnie Pidgeon (01291) 635218

Monmouth   (1896)
Leasbrook Lane, Monmouth NP25 3SN
☎ **(01600) 712212**
🖨 (01600) 772399
✉ sec@monmouthgolfclub.co.uk
✍ P Tully (01600) 712212
🖥 www.monmouthgolfclub.co.uk

Monmouthshire   (1892)
Llanfoist, Abergavenny NP7 9HE
☎ **(01873) 852606**
🖨 (01873) 850470
✉ monmouthshiregc@btconnect.com
✍ C Sobik (Gen Mgr)
🖥 www.monmouthshiregolfclub.co.uk

Newport   (1903)
Great Oak, Rogerstone, Newport NP10 9FX
☎ **(01633) 892643**
🖨 (01633) 896676
✉ newportgolfclub@btconnect.com
✍ R Thomas (01633) 892643
🖥 www.newportgolfclub.org.uk

Oakdale   (1990)
Pay and play
Llwynon Lane, Oakdale NP12 0NF
☎ **(01495) 220044**
✍ M Lewis (Dir)
⊕ 18 bay floodlit golf practice range. Snooker, Pool, Darts, Licensed Bar. PGA Professional Mathew Griffiths

Pontnewydd   (1875)
Maesgwyn Farm, Upper Cwmbran, Cwmbran, Torfaen NP44 1AB
☎ **(01633) 482170**

🖨 (01633) 484447
✉ ctphillips@virgin.net
✍ CT Phillips (01633) 484447
🖥 www.pontnewyddgolf.uk

Pontypool   (1903)
Lasgarn Lane, Trevethin, Pontypool NP4 8TR
☎ **(01495) 763655**
🖨 (01495) 755564
✉ pontypoolgolf@btconnect.com
✍ L Dodd
🖥 www.pontypoolgolf.co.uk

Raglan Parc   (1994)
Parc Lodge, Raglan NP5 2ER
☎ **(01291) 690077**
✉ golf@raglanparc.co.uk
🖥 www.raglanparc.co.uk

The Rolls of Monmouth
(1982)
The Hendre, Monmouth NP25 5HG
☎ **(01600) 715353**
🖨 (01600) 713115
✉ sandra@therollsgolfclub.co.uk
✍ Mrs SJ Orton
🖥 www.therollsgolfclub.co.uk

Shirenewton   (1995)
Shirenewton, Chepstow NP16 6RL
☎ **(01291) 641642**

Tredegar & Rhymney   (1921)
Tredegar, Rhymney NP22 5HA
☎ **(01685) 840743**
✉ tandrgc@googlemail.com
✍ Will Price (07761) 005184
🖥 www.tandrgc.co.uk

Tredegar Park   (1923)
Parc-y-Brain Road, Rogerstone, Newport NP10 9TG
☎ **(01633) 895219**
🖨 (01633) 897152
✉ secretary@tredegarparkgolfclub.co.uk
✍ S Salway (01633) 894433
🖥 www.tredegarparkgolfclub.co.uk

Wernddu Golf Centre   (1992)
Proprietary
Old Ross Road, Abergavenny NP7 8NG
☎ **(01873) 856223**

The Duncan Putter

The Duncan Putter was started in 1959 by ex-Walker Cup Captain Tony Duncan in memory of his father, John Duncan – one of the founders of Southerndown Golf Club where the tournament is staged evey April.

A 72-hole scratch competiton, it was originally an invitation event designd to give young Welsh golfers the opportunity to compete against top English amateurs. It is now a Welsh Order of Merit open-entry event which attracts aspiring young golfers from all parts of the UK and occasionally from Europe.

Former winners include Peter McEvoy, Gary Wolstenholme and Nigel Edwards.

📞 (01873) 852177
📧 info@wernddu-golf-club.co.uk
✍ S Cole (Sec)
📄 www.wernddu-golf-club.co.uk

West Monmouthshire
(1906)
Golf Road, Pond Road, Nantyglo, Ebbw Vale NP23 4QT
📞 **(01495) 310233**
📧 care@westmongolfclub.co.uk
✍ L B Matthews (01495) 310233
📄 www.westmongolfclub.co.uk

Woodlake Park (1993)
Proprietary
Glascoed, Usk NP4 0TE
📞 **(01291) 673933**
📱 (01291) 673811
📧 golf@woodlake.co.uk
✍ MJ Wood
📄 www.woodlake.co.uk

Pembrokeshire

Haverfordwest (1904)
Arnolds Down, Haverfordwest SA61 2XQ
📞 **(01437) 763565**
📱 (01437) 764143
📧 haverfordwestgc@btconnect.com
✍ M Foley (01437) 764523
📄 www.haverfordwestgolfclub.co.uk

Milford Haven (1913)
Hubberston, Milford Haven SA72 3RX
📞 **(01646) 697762**
📱 (01646) 697870
📧 milfordgolfclub@aol.com
✍ W S Brown
📄 www.mhgc.co.uk

Newport Links (1925)
Newport SA42 0NR
📞 **(01239) 820244**
📱 (01239) 821338
📧 info@newportlinks.co.uk
✍ Mrs A Payne (Mgr)
📄 www.newportlinks.co.uk

Priskilly Forest (1992)
Castle Morris, Haverfordwest SA62 5EH
📞 **(01348) 840276**
📱 (01348) 840276
📧 jevans@priskilly-forest.co.uk
✍ P Evans
📄 www.priskilly-forest.co.uk

South Pembrokeshire
(1970)
Military Road, Pembroke Dock SA72 6SE
📞 **(01646) 621453**
📧 spgc06@tiscali.co.uk
✍ P Fisher (01646) 621453
📄 www.southpembsgolf.co.uk

St Davids City (1903)
Whitesands Bay, St Davids SA62 6PT
📞 **(01437) 721751 (Clubhouse)**
📧 ronaldjgriffiths@btinternet.com
✍ J Griffiths (01437) 721073
📄 www.stdavidscitygolfclub.com

Tenby (1888)
The Burrows, Tenby SA70 7NP
📞 **(01834) 842978**
📱 (01834) 845603
📧 info@tenbygolf.co.uk
✍ DJ Hancock (01834) 842978
📄 www.tenbygolf.co.uk

Trefloyne (1996)
Proprietary
Trefloyne Park, Penally, Tenby SA70 7RG
📞 **(01834) 842165**
📱 (01834) 844288
📧 sarah@trefloyne.com
✍ Sarah Knight
📄 www.trefloyne.com

Powys

Brecon (1902)
Newton Park, Llanfaes, Brecon LD3 8PA
📞 **(01874) 622004**
📧 info@brecongolfclub.co.uk
✍ I Chambers (01874) 611545
📄 www.brecongolfclub.co.uk

Builth Wells (1923)
Golf Links Road, Builth Wells LD2 3NF
📞 **(01982) 553296**
📧 info@builthwellsgolf.co.uk
✍ S Edwards (Professional) (01982) 551155
📄 www.builthwellsgolf.co.uk

Cradoc (1967)
Penoyre Park, Cradoc, Brecon LD3 9LP
📞 **(01874) 623658**
📱 (01874) 611711
📧 secretary@cradoc.co.uk
✍ Robert Southcott (01874) 623658
📄 www.cradoc.co.uk

Knighton (1906)
Ffrydd Wood, Knighton LD7 1DL
📞 **(01547) 528646**
✍ DB Williams (Hon)
📄 www.knightongolfclub.co.uk

Llandrindod Wells (1905)
The Clubhouse, Llandrindod Wells LD1 5NY
📞 **(01597) 823873**
📱 (01597) 828881
📧 secretary@lwgc.co.uk
✍ Mrs Terry Evans (01597) 823873
📄 www.lwgc.co.uk

Machynlleth (1904)
Felingerrig, Machynlleth SY20 8UH
📞 **(01654) 702000**
📧 machgolf2@tiscali.co.uk
✍ John Lewis (Secretary)
📄 www.machynllethgolf.co.uk

Mid-Wales Golf Centre
(1992)
Maesmawr Golf Club, Caersws, Nr Newtown SY17 5SB
📞 **(01686) 688303**
📱 (01686) 688303
✍ Mrs Penny Dewinton Davies

Rhosgoch (1984)
Rhosgoch, Builth Wells LD2 3JY
📞 **(01497) 851251**
📧 rhosgochgolf@yahoo.co.uk
✍ C Dance (Sec) N Lloyd (Mgr)
📄 www.rhosgoch-golf.co.uk

St Giles Newtown (1895)
Pool Road, Newtown SY16 3AJ
📞 **(01686) 625844**
📧 stgilesgolf@gmail.com
✍ Wyn Evans (07739 884198)
📄 www.stgilesgolf.co.uk

St Idloes (1906)
Penrhallt, Llanidloes SY18 6LG
📞 **(01686) 412559**
📧 st.idloesgolfclub@btconnect.com
✍ Mr E Parry (Sec)
📄 www.stidloesgolfclub.co.uk

Welsh Border Golf Complex (1991)
Pay and Play – Proprietary
Bulthy Farm, Bulthy, Middletown SY21 8ER
📞 **(01743) 884247**
📧 info@welshbordergolf.com
✍ K Farr (07966) 530042
📄 www.welshbordergolf.com

Welshpool (1907)
Golfa Hill, Welshpool SY21 9AQ
📞 **(01938) 850249**
📧 secretary@welshpoolgolfclub.co.uk
✍ Siân Whiteoak
📄 www.welshpoolgolfclub.co.uk

South Glamorgan

Brynhill (1921)
Port Road, Barry CF62 8PN
📞 **(01446) 720277**
📱 (01446) 740422
📧 postbox@brynhillgolfclub.co.uk
✍ Louise Edwards (01446) 720277
📄 www.brynhillgolfclub.co.uk

Cardiff (1921)
Sherborne Avenue, Cyncoed, Cardiff CF23 6SJ
📞 **(02920) 754772**
📱 (02920) 680011
📧 cardiff.golfclub@virgin.net
✍ Mrs K Newling (029) 2075 3320
📄 www.cardiffgolfclub.co.uk

Cottrell Park Golf Resort
(1996)
Proprietary
St Nicholas, Cardiff CF5 6SJ
📞 **(01446) 781781**
📱 (01446) 781187
📧 admin@cottrellpark.com
✍ Mr Derek Smith
📄 www.cottrellpark.com

Dinas Powis (1912)
Old Highwalls, Dinas Powis CF64 4AJ
📞 **(029) 2051 2727**
📱 (029) 2051 2727
📧 dinaspowisgolfclub@yahoo.co.uk

Sally Phelps
www.dpgc.co.uk

Glamorganshire (1890)
Lavernock Road, Penarth CF64 5UP
☎ (029) 2070 1185
▢ (029) 2071 3333
✉ glamgolf@btconnect.com
✍ BM Williams (029) 2070 1185
▤ www.glamorganshiregolfclub.co.uk

Llanishen (1905)
Heol Hir, Cardiff CF14 9UD
☎ (029) 207 55078
✉ secretary.llanishengc@virgin.net
✍ Colin Duffield (029) 207 55078
▤ www.llanishengc.co.uk

Peterstone Lakes (1990)
Proprietary
Peterstone, Wentloog, Cardiff CF3 2TN
☎ (01633) 680009
▢ (01633) 680563
✉ peterstone_lakes@yahoo.com
✍ P Millar
▤ www.peterstonelakes.com

Radyr (1902)
Drysgol Road, Radyr, Cardiff CF15 8BS
☎ (029) 2084 2408
▢ (029) 2084 3914
✉ manager@radyrgolf.co.uk
✍ Manager
▤ www.radyrgolf.co.uk

RAF St Athan (1977)
Clive Road, St Athan CF62 4JD
☎ (01446) 751043
▢ (01446) 751862
✉ rafstathan@golfclub.fsbusiness
.co.uk
✍ A McKinotry (01446) 751043
▤ www.rafstathangc.co.uk

St Andrews Major (1993)
Proprietary
Coldbrook Road East, Cadoxton, Barry
CF6 3BB
☎ (01446) 722227
▢ (01446) 748953
✉ info@standrewsmajorgolfclub
.com
✍ A Edmunds
▤ www.standrewsmajorgolfclub
.com

St Mellons (1937)
St Mellons, Cardiff CF3 2XS
☎ (01633) 680408
▢ (01633) 681219
✉ stmellons@golf2003.fsnet.co.uk
✍ R Haggerty (01633) 680408
▤ www.stmellonsgolfclub.co.uk

Vale Hotel Golf & Spa Resort (1994)
Hensol Park, Hensol CF7 8JY
☎ (01443) 665899
✉ golf@vale-hotel.com
▤ www.vale-hotel.com

Wenvoe Castle (1936)
Wenvoe, Cardiff CF5 6BE
☎ (029) 205 94371
✉ wenvoe-castlegc@virgin.net

Whitchurch (Cardiff) (1914)
Pantmawr Road, Whitchurch, Cardiff
CF14 7TD
☎ (029) 2062 0985
▢ (029) 2052 9860
✉ secretary
@whitchurchcardiffgolfclub.com
✍ G Perrott
▤ www.whitchurchcardiffgolfclub.com

West Glamorgan

Allt-y-Graban (1993)
Allt-y-Graban Road, Pontlliw, Swansea
SA4 1DT
☎ (01792) 885757

Clyne (1920)
120 Owls Lodge Lane, Mayals, Swansea
SA3 5DP
☎ (01792) 401989
▢ (01792) 401078
✉ clynegolfclub@supanet.com
✍ DR Thomas (Mgr)
▤ www.clynegolfclub.com

Fairwood Park (1969)
Proprietary
Blackhills Lane, Fairwood, Swansea SA2 7JN
☎ (01792) 297849
▢ (01792) 297849
✉ info@fairwoodpark.com
✍ E Golbas (Mgr)
▤ www.fairwoodpark.com

Glynneath (1931)
Penygraig, Pontneathvaughan, Glynneath
SA11 5UH
☎ (01639) 720452
▢ (01639) 720452
✉ enquiries@glynneathgolfclub.co.uk
✍ Shane McMenamin
▤ www.glynneathgolfclub.co.uk

Gower
Cefn Goleu, Three Crosses, Gowerton,
Swansea SA4 3HS
☎ (01792) 872480
✉ adrian.richards@btconnect.com
▤ www.gowergolf.co.uk

Lakeside (1992)
Water Street, Margam, Port Talbot
SA13 2PA
☎ (01639) 899959
▤ www.lakesidegolf.co.uk

Langland Bay (1904)
Langland Bay Road, Langland, Swansea
SA3 4QR
☎ (01792) 361721
▢ (01792) 361082
✉ info@langlandbaygolfclub.com
✍ Mr A Minty (Director)
▤ www.langlandbaygolfclub.com

Morriston (1920)
160 Clasemont Road, Morriston, Swansea
SA6 6AJ
☎ (01792) 796528
▢ (01792) 796528
✉ morristongolf@btconnect.com
✍ Robert Howells (01792) 796528
▤ www.morristongolfclub.co.uk

Neath (1934)
Cadoxton, Neath SA10 8AH
☎ (01639) 632759
▢ (01639) 639955
✉ info@neathgolfclub.co.uk
✍ D M Gee
▤ www.neathgolfclub.co.uk

Palleg & Swansea Valley Golf Course (1930)
Proprietary
Palleg Road, Lower Cwmtwrch, Swansea
Valley SA9 2QQ
☎ (01639) 842193
▢ (01639) 845661
✉ gc.gcgs@btinternet.com
✍ Graham Coombe (PGA Pro/
Director)
▤ www.palleg-golf.com

Pennard (1896)
2 Southgate Road, Southgate, Swansea
SA3 2BT
☎ (01792) 233131
▢ (01792) 235125
✉ sec@pennardgolfclub.com
✍ Mrs S Crowley (01792) 235120
▤ www.pennardgolfclub.com

Pontardawe (1924)
Cefn Llan, Pontardawe, Swansea SA8 4SH
☎ (01792) 863118
▢ (01792) 830041
✉ enquiries@pontardawegolfclub
.co.uk
✍ R W Grove (Hon)
▤ www.pontardawegolfclub.co.uk

Swansea Bay (1892)
Proprietary
Jersey Marine, Neath SA10 6JP
☎ (01792) 812198
✉ swanseabaygolfclub@hotmail.co.uk
✍ Mrs J Richardson (01792) 812198

Tawe Vale (1965)
Clydach, Swansea SA6 5QR
☎ (01792) 841257
✉ secretarytawevalegolfclub
@btconnect.com
✍ DE Jones (01792) 842929
▤ www.tawevalegolfclub.co.uk

Wrexham

Chirk (1990)
Proprietary
Chirk, Wrexham LL14 5AD
☎ (01691) 774407
✉ enquiries@chirkgolfclub.co.uk
✍ Trudi Maddison (Manager)
▤ www.chirkgolfclub.co.uk

Clays Golf Centre   (1992)
Proprietary
Bryn Estyn Road, Wrexham LL13 9UB
☎ **(01978) 661406**
🖳 (01978) 661406
🖂 sales@claysgolf.co.uk
✍ Steve Williams
🖳 www.claysgolf.co.uk

Moss Valley   (1990)
Moss Road, Wrexham LL11 6HA
☎ **(01978) 720518**
🖳 (01978) 720518
🖂 info@mossvalleygolf.co.uk
✍ John Nolan (07588) 104761
🖳 www.mossvalleygolf.co.uk

Plassey Oaks Golf Complex
(1992)
Eyton, Wrexham LL13 0SP
☎ **(01978) 780020**
🖳 (01978) 781397
🖂 hjones@plasseygolf.com
✍ OJ Jones (01978) 780020
🖳 www.plasseygolf.com

Wrexham   (1906)
Holt Road, Wrexham LL13 9SB
☎ **(01978) 364268**
🖳 (01978) 362168
🖂 info@wrexhamgolfclub.co.uk
✍ R West (01978) 364268
🖳 www.wrexhamgolfclub.co.uk

For key to symbols see page 717

In Wales Pugh is as much a role model as Tiger

Rhys Pugh, the Pontypridd teenager who scored three points out of three in the Walker Cup last year, is as much a role model for young golfers in Wales as Tiger Woods according to the Rhondda Club's David Pocock who received the Golf Union of Wales 2011 PGA Club Professional of the Year award.

Pocock, who has only been in the job 18 months, has already made a massive impact providing coaching at 30 schools and for more than 100 juniors at his club.

"The work Golf Development Wales do makes it very, very easy," he said. "They are there for advice, funding and support. Zoe Thacker, the golf development officer in South Wales, has been brilliant for our golf club. We now have the biggest junior academy in Wales.

"Rhys, the youngest member of the Walker Cup side at Royal Aberdeen, has become a role model for these kids, as many of them have heard of him as they have of Tiger Woods."

Pugh, who was named Welsh Amateur of the Year, is now studying on a golf scholarship at Tennessee in America, but was delighted to receive the award on his return to Wales. "It is a great honour to receive this recognition, it has been a good year for me with the highlight being the Walker Cup," he said. "It was great to play in and do well."

His singles wins in the Cup match were over World No 3 Patrick Rodgers and US Amateur champion Kelly Kraft. In the foursomes, playing with Scotland's James Byrne, he beat World No 1 Patrick Catlay and Chris Williams.

Golf volunteers and professionals in Pontypridd and the Rhondda picked up four out of six 2011 Golf Union of Wales awards.

In addition to Pugh and Pocock, Pontypridd junior organiser Ian Pickering was the Volunteer of the Year, while Pontypridd's Jamie Donaldson was the Welsh Tour Pro of the Year. Carmarthen were the Club of the Year, with North Wales' golfer Amy Boulden sharing the Welsh amateur award with Pugh.

Donaldson ended the season in the top 40 in Europe and has set his sights on challenging for a Ryder Cup place this year.

"I would love to get into the Ryder Cup team. I know that will be difficult as I am outside the world's top 50, but it is possible and I will certainly do my best to try and make it happen."

Pickering was delighted to receive recognition on behalf of the team at Pontypridd golf club who have transformed the fortunes of the junior section.

"It is a great honour to get an award like this and I was delighted to collect it on behalf of the team at Pontypridd," said Pickering, who is also heavily involved with Glamorgan County with both boys and girls.

"You do not do this sort of thing for recognition, to be honest just seeing the faces of the kids is all the reward you need. We have come a long way in a short time and a lot of people have put in the effort to get us there, but it is really nice to come to be recognised by the Golf Union of Wales."

Carmarthen earned the Club of the Year award for a remarkable turnaround in their fortunes. In the last three years they have increased membership by more than 100 as they have taken advantage of Golf Union of Wales and Ryder Cup Wales schemes, spending money in the right areas.

Continent of Europe –
Country and Region Index

Austria

St Lorenzen (1990)
8642 St Lorenzen, Gassing 22
☎ **(03864) 3961**
📠 (03864) 3961-2
📧 gclorenzen@golf.at
✍ Peter Redl
🖥 www.gclorenzen.at

Innsbruck & Tirol

Achensee (1934)
Golf und Landclub Achensee, 6213 Pertisau/Tirol
☎ **(05243) 5377**
📧 golfclub-achensee@tirol.com
🖥 www.golfclub-achensee.com

Innsbruck-Igls (1935)
Oberdorf 11, 6074 Rinn
☎ **(05223) 78177**
📠 (05223) 78177-77
📧 office@golfclub-innsbruck-igls.at
🖥 www.golfclub-innsbruck-igls.at

Kaiserwinkl GC Kössen (1988)
6345 Kössen, Mühlau 1
☎ **(05375) 2122**
📠 (05375) 2122-13
📧 club@golf-koessen.at
✍ Stefan Emberger
🖥 www.golf-koessen.at

Golfclub Kitzbühel (1955)
Ried Kaps 3, 6370 Kitzbühel
☎ **(05356) 63007 Members**
📠 (05356) 630077
📧 gckitzbuehel@golf.at
✍ Werner Gandler
🖥 www.golfclub-kitzbuehel.at

Kitzbühel-Schwarzsee (1988)
6370 Kitzbühel, Golfweg Schwarzsee 35
☎ **(05356) 66660 70**
📠 (05356) 66660 71

Seefeld-Wildmoos (1969)
6100 Seefeld, Postfach 22
☎ **(0699) 1-606606-0**
📠 (0699) 4-606606-3
📧 info@seefeldgolf.com
✍ Mr Werner Seelos
🖥 www.seefeldgolf.com

Klagenfurt & South

Bad Kleinkirchheim-Reichenau (1977)
9564 Padergassen, Plass 19
☎ **(04275) 594**

Golfpark Klopeinersee-Sudkarnten (1988)
9122 St Kanzian, Grabelsdorf 94
☎ **(04239) 3800-0**
📠 (04239) 3800-18
📧 office@golfklopein.at
🖥 www.golfklopein.at

Kärntner GC Dellach (1927)
Golfstrasse 3, 9082 Maria Wörth, Golfstr 3
☎ **(04273) 2515**
📠 (04273) 2515-20
📧 office@kgcdellach.at
✍ Ronald Krach (Mgr)
🖥 www.kgcdellach.at

Golfclub Klagenfurt-Seltenheim (1996)
Seltenheimerstr. 137, A-9061 Wolfnitz
☎ **0043 463 40223**
📧 office@gcseltenheim.at
🖥 www.gcseltenheim.at

Golfclub Millstatter See
Am Golfplatz 1, 9872 Millstatt
☎ **+43 (0)4762 82542**
📧 gcmillstatt@golf.at
🖥 www.golf-millstatt.at

Moosburg-Pörtschach (1986)
9062 Moosburg, Golfstr 2
☎ **(04272) 83486**
📠 (04272) 834 8620
📧 moosburg@golfktn.at
✍ Tanja Starzacher
🖥 www.golfmoosburg.at

Wörthersee-Velden (1988)
9231 Köstenberg, Golfweg 41
☎ **(04274) 7045**
📠 (04274) 7087-15
📧 golf-velden@golfktn.at
✍ Map. Roland Sint (Mgr)
🖥 www.golfvelden.at

Linz & North

Amstetten-Ferschnitz (1972)
3325 Ferschnitz, Gut Edla 18
☎ **(07473) 8293**
📧 office@golfclub-amstetten.at
🖥 www.golfclub-amstetten.at

Böhmerwald GC Ulrichsberg (1990)
4161 Ulrichsberg, Seitelschlag 50
☎ **(07288) 8200**
📧 office@boehmerwaldgolf.at
🖥 www.boehmerwaldgolf.at

Celtic Golf Course – Schärding (1994)
Maad 2, 4775 Taufkirchen/Pram
☎ **(0043) 7719 8110**
📧 office@gcschaerding.at
🖥 www.gcschaerding.at

Golfresort Haugschlag (1987)
3874 Haugschlag 160
☎ **(02865) 8441**
📠 (02865) 8441-522
📧 info@golfresort.at
🖥 www.golfresort.at

Herzog Tassilo (1991)
Blankenbergerstr 30, 4540 Bad Hall
☎ **(07258) 5480**
📠 (07258) 29858
📧 golfherzogtassilo@golf.at
🖥 www.golfherzogtassilo.at

Golf Resort Kremstal (1989)
Am Golfplatz 1, 4531 Kematen/Krems
☎ **0043 (0)7228 7644**
📠 0043 (0)7228 7644 7
📧 info@golfresort-kremstal.at
✍ Günter Obermayr
🖥 www.golfresort-kremstal.at
www.golfvillage.at

Linz-St Florian (1960)
4490 St Florian, Tillysburg 28
☎ **(07223) 828730**
📧 gclinz@golf.at
🖥 www.gclinz.at

Linzer Golf Club Luftenberg (1990)
4222 Luftenberg, Am Luftenberg 1a
☎ **(07237) 3893**
📠 (07237) 3893-40
📧 gclinz-luftenberg@golf.at
🖥 www.gclinz-luftenberg.at

Maria Theresia (1989)
Letten 5, 4680 Haag am Hausruck
☎ **(07732) 3944**
🖥 www.members.eunet.at/ gcmariatheresia

Ottenstein (1988)
3532 Niedergrünbach 60
☎ **(02826) 7476**
📠 (02826) 7476-4
📧 info@golfclub-ottenstein.at
🖥 www.golfclub-ottenstein.at

St Oswald-Freistadt (1988)
Am Golfplatz 1, 4271 St Oswald
☎ **(07945) 7938**
📠 (07945) 79384

St Pölten Schloss Goldegg (1989)
3100 St Pölten Schloss Goldegg
☎ **(02741) 7360/7060**

Union Golfclub Schloss Ernegg (1973)
3261 Steinakirchen, Ernegg 4
☎ **+43 (0) 7488) 76770**
📠 +43 (0) 7488) 71171
📧 gcernegg@golf.at
✍ Kristel Josel (Mgr)
🖥 www.ernegg.at

For key to symbols and European dialling codes see page 717

Traunsee Kircham
4656 Kircham, Kampesberg 38
☎ **(07619) 2576**

Weitra (1989)
3970 Weitra, Hausschachen
☎ **(02856) 2058**
✉ gcweitra@golf.at
🖥 www.gcweitra.at

Wels (1981)
4616 Weisskirchen, Golfplatzstrasse 2
☎ **(07243) 56038**
✉ gcwels@golf.at
🖥 www.golfclub-wels.at

Salzburg Region

Bad Gastein (1960)
5640 Bad Gastein, Golfstrasse 6
☎ **0043 (6434) 2775**
🖳 0043 (6434) 2775-4
✉ info@golfclub-gastein.com
🖉 Verena Kuhlank
🖥 www.golfclub-gastein.com

GC Sonnberg (1993)
5241 Höhnart, Strass 1
☎ **0043 (7743) 20066**
🖳 0043 (7743) 20077
✉ golf@gcsonnberg.at
🖉 E Reinhard (Mgr)
🖥 www.gcsonnberg.at

Goldegg
5622 Goldegg, Maierhof 4
☎ **(06415) 8585**
🖳 (06415) 8585-4
✉ info@golfclub-goldegg.com
🖥 www.golfclub-goldegg.com

Gut Altentann (1989)
Hof 54, 5302 Henndorf am Wallersee
☎ **(06214) 6026-0**
🖳 (06214) 6105-81
✉ office@gutaltentann.com
🖉 Catarina Hofmann
🖥 www.gutaltentann.com

Gut Brandlhof G&CC
(1983)
5760 Saalfelden am Steinernen Meer, Hohlwegen 4
☎ **(06582) 7800-555**

Lungau (1991)
5582 St Michael, Feldnergasse 165
☎ **(06477) 7448**
🖳 (06477) 7448-4
✉ gclungau@golf.at
🖥 www.golfclub-lungau.at

Am Mondsee (1986)
St Lorenz 400, 5310 Mondsee
☎ **(06232) 3835-0**
🖳 (06232) 3835-83
✉ gcmondsee@golf.at
🖥 www.golfclubmondsee.at

Radstadt Tauerngolf (1991)
Römerstrasse 18, 5550 Radstadt
☎ **(06452) 5111**
🖳 (06452) 5111/15
✉ info@radstadtgolf.at
🖥 www.radstadtgolf.at

G&CC Salzburg-Klessheim
(1955)
Klessheim 21, 5071 Wals
☎ **(0662) 850851**
🖳 (0662) 857925
✉ office@gccsalzburg.at
🖥 www.golfclub-klessheim.com

Salzburg Romantikourse Schloss Fuschl (1865)
5322 Hof/Salzburg
☎ **(06229) 2390**
🖳 (06229) 2390
✉ fuschl@golfclub-salzburg.at
🖥 www.golfclub-salzburg.at

Salzkammergut (1933)
Wirling 36, 5351 Aigen-Voglhub, Bad Ischl
☎ **(06132) 26340**
🖳 (06132) 26708
✉ office@salzkammergut-golf.at
🖉 Cornelia Kogler
🖥 www.salzkammergut-golf.at

Urslautal (1991)
Schinking 81, 5760 Saalfelden
☎ **(06584) 2000**
🖳 (06584) 7475-10
✉ info@golf-urslautal.at
🖥 www.golf-urslautal.at

Zell am See-Kaprun (1983)
Golfstrasse 25, A-5700 Zell am See
☎ **+43 6542 56161**
🖳 +43 6542 56161-16
✉ geringer@golf-zellamsee.at
🖥 www.golf-zellamsee.at

Steiermark

Bad Gleichenberg (1984)
Am Hoffeld 3, 8344 Bad Gleichenberg
☎ **(03159) 3717**
✉ gcgleichenberg@golf.at
🖥 www.golf-badgleichenberg.at

Dachstein Tauern (1990)
8967 Haus/Ennstal, Oberhaus 59
☎ **(03686) 2630**
🖳 (03686) 2630-15
✉ gccschladming@golf.at
🖥 www.schladming-golf.at

Ennstal-Weissenbach G&LC
(1977)
Austria 8940 Liezen, Postfach 193
☎ **(03612) 24821**
🖳 (03612) 24821-4
✉ glcennstal@golf.at
🖉 Thomas Aigner
🖥 www.glcennstal.at

Graz (1989)
8051 Graz-Thal, Windhof 137
☎ **(0316) 572867**

Gut Murstätten (1989)
8403 Lebring, Oedt 14
☎ **(03182) 3555**
✉ gcmurstaetten@golf.at
🖥 www.gcmurstaetten.at

Maria Lankowitz (1992)
Puchbacher Str 109, 8591 Maria Lankowitz
☎ **(03144) 6970**

Murhof (1963)
8130 Frohnleiten, Adriach 53
☎ **(03126) 3010-40**
🖳 (03126) 3000-28
✉ gcmurhof@golf.at
🖥 www.murhof.at

Murtal (1995)
Frauenbachstr 51, 8724 Spielberg
☎ **(03512) 75213**
🖳 (03512) 75213
✉ gcmurtal@golf.at
🖥 www.gcmurtal.at

Reiting G&CC (1990)
8772 Traboch, Schulweg 7
☎ **(0663) 833308/ (03847) 5008**

St Lorenzen (1990)
8642 St Lorenzen, Gassing 22
☎ **(03864) 3961**
🖳 (03864) 3961-2
✉ gclorenzen@golf.at
🖥 www.gclorenzen.at

Schloss Frauenthal (1988)
8530 Deutschlandsberg, Ulrichsberg 7
☎ **(03462) 5717**
✉ office@gcfrauenthal.at
🖥 www.gcfrauenthal.at

Golf & Country Club Schloss Pichlarn (1972)
8952 Irdning/Ennstal, Zur Linde 1
☎ **+43 3682-24440-540**
🖳 +43 3682-24440-580
✉ golf@pichlarn.at
🖥 www.pichlarn.at

TGC Fuerstenfeld (1984)
8282 Loipersdorf, Gillersdorf 50
☎ **(03382) 8533**
🖳 (03382) 8533-33
✉ office@thermergolf.at
🖥 www.thermergolf.at

Vienna & East

Adamstal (1994)
Gaupmannsgraben 21, 3172 Ramsal
☎ **(02764) 3500**
🖥 www.adamstal.at

For key to symbols and European dialling codes see page 717

Bad Tatzmannsdorf Reiters G&CC   (1991)
Am Golfplatz 2, 7431 Bad Tatzmannsdorf
- ☎ **(0043) 3353 8282-0**
- 📠 (0043) 3353 8282-1735
- 📧 golfclub@burgenlandresort.at
- 🖥 www.reitersburgenlandresort.at

Brunn G&CC   (1988)
2345 Brunn/Gebirge, Rennweg 50
- ☎ **(02236) 33711**
- 📠 (02236) 33863
- 📧 club@gccbrunn.at
- 🖥 www.gccbrunn.at

Colony Club Gutenhof
(1988)
2325 Himberg, Gutenhof
- ☎ **(02235) 87055-0**
- 📠 (02235) 87055-14
- 📧 club@colonygolf.com
- ✍ Magira-Xenia Glatz
- 🖥 www.colonygolf.com

Eldorado Bucklige Welt
(1990)
Golfplatz 1, 2871 Zöbern
- ☎ **(02642) 8451**
- 🖥 www.golf1.at

Enzesfeld   (1970)
2551 Enzesfeld
- ☎ **(02256) 81272**
- 📠 (02256) 81272-4
- 📧 office@gcenzesfeld.at
- 🖥 www.gcenzesfeld.at

Föhrenwald   (1968)
2700 Wiener Neustadt, Postfach 105
- ☎ **(02622) 29171**
- 📠 (02622) 29171-4
- 📧 office@gcf.at
- ✍ Zelester Elgar (Mgr)
- 🖥 www.gcf.at

Fontana   (1996)
Fontana Allee 1, 2522 Oberwaltersdorf
- ☎ **(02253) 6062202**
- 📠 (02253) 6062200
- 📧 gcfontana@fontana.at
- 🖥 www.fontana.at

Hainburg/Donau   (1977)
2410 Hainburg, Auf der Heide 762
- ☎ **(02165) 62628**
- 📠 (02165) 626283
- 📧 gchainburg@golf.at
- ✍ Dietmar Haderer (Mgr)
- 🖥 www.golfclub-hainburg.at

Lengenfeld   (1995)
Am Golfplatz 1, 3552 Lengenfeld
- ☎ **(02719) 8710**

Neusiedlersee-Donnerskirchen   (1988)
7082 Donnerskirchen
- ☎ **(02683) 8171**

Schloss Ebreichsdorf   (1988)
2483 Ebreichsdorf, Schlossallee 1
- ☎ **(02254)73888**
- 📠 (02254) 73888-13
- 📧 office@gcebreichsdorf.at
- 🖥 www.gcebreichsdorf.at

Schloss Schönborn   (1987)
2013 Schönborn 4
- ☎ **(02267) 2863/2879**
- 📧 golfclub@gcschoenborn.com
- 🖥 www.gcschoenborn.com

Schönfeld   (1989)
A-2291 Schönfeld, Am Golfplatz 1
- ☎ **+43 (02213) 2063**
- 📧 gcschoenfeld@golf.at
- 🖥 www.golf.at/clubdetail.asp?clubnr=315

Semmering   (1926)
2680 Semmering
- ☎ **(02664) 8154**

Golfclub Spillern   (1993)
Wiesenerstrasse 100, A-2104 Spillern
- ☎ **+43 (0)22 668 1211**
- 📠 +43 (0)22 668 121120
- 📧 gcspillern.at
- ✍ J Culen
- 🖥 www.gcspillern.at

Thayatal Drosendorf   (1994)
Autendorf 18, 2095 Drosendorf
- ☎ **(02915) 62625**

Wien   (1901)
1020 Wien, Freudenau 65a
- ☎ **(01) 728 9564 (Clubhouse)**
- 📠 (01) 728 9564-20
- 📧 gcwien@golf.at
- 🖥 www.gcwien.at

Wien-Süssenbrunn   (1995)
Weingartenallee 22, 1220 Wien
- ☎ **+43 (01) 256 8282**
- 📠 +43 (01) 246 8282 -44
- 📧 golf@sportparkwien.at
- ✍ Michel Prassé
- 🖥 www.gcwien-sb.at

Wienerwald   (1981)
1130 Wien, Altgasse 27
- ☎ **(0222) 877 3111 (Sec)**

Vorarlberg

Bludenz-Braz   (1996)
Oberradin 60, 6751 Braz bei Bludenz
- ☎ **(05552) 33503**
- 📠 (05552) 33503-3
- 📧 gcbraz@golf.at
- 🖥 www.gc-bludenz-braz.at

Bregenzerwald   (1997)
Unterlitten 3a, 6943 Riefensberg
- ☎ **(05513) 8400**
- 📠 (05513) 8400-4
- 📧 office@golf-bregenzerwald.com
- 🖥 www.golf-bregenzerwald.com

Montafon   (1992)
6774 Tschagguns, Zelfenstrasse 110
- ☎ **(05556) 77011**
- 📧 info@golfclub-montafon.at
- 🖥 www.golfclub-montafon.at

Belgium

Antwerp Region

Bossenstein   (1989)
Moor 16, Bossenstein Kasteel, 2520 Broechem
- ☎ **(03) 485 64 46**
- 📧 bossenstein.shop@skynet.be

Cleydael G&CC   (1988)
Groenenhoek 7-9, 2630 Aartselaar
- ☎ **(03) 870 56 80**
- 📠 (03) 887 14 75
- 📧 info@cleydael.be
- ✍ Maryse Bal (Gen Sec)
- 🖥 www.cleydael.be

Kempense   (1986)
Kiezelweg 78, 2400 Mol-Rauw
- ☎ **00 32 (0)14 81 46 41 (Clubhouse)**
- 📧 kempense@pandora.be
- 🖥 www.golf.be/kempense

Lilse Golf & Country   (1907)
Haarlebeek 3, 2275 Lille
- ☎ **(014) 55 19 30**
- 📠 (014) 55 19 31
- 📧 info@lilsegolfcountry.be
- ✍ Vink Nienue
- 🖥 www.lilsegolfcountry.be

Golf Club Nuclea Mol   (1984)
Goorstraat, 2400 Mol
- ☎ **+32 14 37 0915**
- 📧 andre.verbruggen2@telenet.be
- ✍ André Verbruggen
- 🖥 www.golfclubnucleamol.be

Rinkven G&CC   (1980)
Sint Jobsteenweg 120, 2970 Schilde
- ☎ **(03) 380 12 80**
- 📠 (03) 384 29 33
- 📧 info@rinkven.be
- 🖥 www.rinkven.be

Royal Antwerp   (1888)
Georges Capiaulei 2, 2950 Kapellen
- ☎ **(03) 666 84 56**
- 📠 (03) 666 44 37
- 📧 info@ragc.be
- ✍ Jean-Noel Raymakers (Mgr)
- 🖥 www.ragc.be

Steenhoven   (1985)
Steenhoven 89, 2400 Postel-Mol
- ☎ **(014) 37 36 61**
- 📠 (014) 37 36 62
- 📧 info@steenhoven.be
- ✍ Luc Hannes (Mgr/Sec)
- 🖥 www.steenhoven.be

Ternesse G&CC   (1976)
Uilenbaan 15, 2160 Wommelgem
- ☎ **(03) 355 14 30**
- ✉ info@ternessegolf.be
- 🖥 www.ternessegolf.be

Ardennes & South

Andenne   (1988)
Ferme du Moulin 52, Stud, 5300 Andenne
- ☎ **(085) 84 34 04**
- 📠 (085) 84 34 04
- ✉ jojadin@hotmail.com
- ✍ Josiane Colson
- 🖥 www.golfclubandenne.be

Château Royal d'Ardenne
Tour Léopold, Ardenne 6, 5560 Houyet
- ☎ **(082) 66 62 28**

Falnuée   (1987)
Rue E Pirson 55, 5032 Mazy
- ☎ **(081) 63 30 90**
- 📠 (081) 63 21 41
- ✉ info@falnuee.be
- ✍ Eric Jottrand/Anne Sophie Jottrand
- 🖥 www.falnuee.be

Five Nations C C   (1990)
*Ferme du Grand Scley, 5372 Méan
(Havelange)*
- ☎ **(086) 32 32 32**

Mont Garni Golf Club   (1990)
Rue du Mont Garni, 3 7331 Saint Ghislain
- ☎ **+32 65.52.94.10**
- 📠 +32 65 62 34 10
- ✉ secretariat@golfmontgarni.be
- ✍ Marie van der Schueren/Jodi De Frenne
- 🖥 www.golfmontgarni.be

Rougemont   (1987)
Chemin du Beau Vallon 45, 5170 Profondeville
- ☎ **(081) 412131**
- 📠 (081) 412142
- ✉ rougemont@skynet.be
- 🖥 www.golfderougemont.be

Royal GC du Hainaut   (1933)
Rue de la Verrerie 2, 7050 Erbisoeul
- ☎ **(065) 22 96 10 (Clubhouse)**
- 📠 (065) 22 02 09
- ✉ info@golfhainaut.be
- 🖥 www.golfhainaut.be

Brussels & Brabant

Bercuit   (1965)
Les Gottes 3, 1390 Grez-Doiceau
- ☎ **(010) 84 15 01**
- 📠 (010) 84 55 95
- ✉ info@golfdubercuit.be
- 🖥 www.golfdubercuit.be

Brabantse Golf   (1982)
Steenwagenstraat 11, 1820 Melsbroek
- ☎ **(02) 751 82 05**
- 📠 (02) 751 84 25
- ✉ secretariaat@brabantsegolf.be
- ✍ Marleen Van Hoof (Secretary)
- 🖥 www.brabantsegolf.be

La Bruyère   (1988)
Rue Jumerée 1, 1495 Sart-Dames-Avelines
- ☎ **(071) 87 72 67**
- ✉ info@golflabruyere.be
- 🖥 www.golflabruyere.be

Golf du Château de la Bawette   (1988)
Chaussée du Chateau de la Bawette 5, 1300 Wavre
- ☎ **(010) 22 33 32**
- 📠 (010) 22 90 04
- ✉ info@labawette.com
- 🖥 www.golflabawette.com

Château de la Tournette
Chemin de Baudemont 21, 1400 Nivelles
- ☎ **(067) 89 42 66**
- 📠 (067) 21 95 17
- ✉ info@tournette.com
- 🖥 www.tournette.com

L'Empereur   (1989)
Rue Emile François No.31, 1474 Ways (Genappe)
- ☎ **(067) 77 15 71**
- 📠 (067) 77 18 33
- ✉ info@golfempereur.com
- ✍ Capart
- 🖥 www.golfempereur.com

Hulencourt   (1989)
Bruyère d'Hulencourt 15, 1472 Vieux Genappe
- ☎ **(067) 79 40 40**
- ✉ info@golfhulencourt.be
- 🖥 www.golfhulencourt.be

Kampenhout   (1989)
Wildersedreef 56, 1910 Kampenhout
- ☎ **(016) 65 12 16**
- 📠 (016) 65 16 80
- ✉ golfclubkampenhout@skynet.be
- 🖥 www.golfclubkampenhout.be

Keerbergen   (1968)
Vlieghavelaan 50, 3140 Keerbergen
- ☎ **(015) 22 68 78**
- 📠 (015) 23 57 37
- ✉ keerbergen.golfclub@skynet.be
- 🖥 www.golfkeerbergen.be

Louvain-la-Neuve   (1989)
Rue A Hardy 68, 1348 Louvain-la-Neuve
- ☎ **(010) 45 05 15**
- 📠 (010) 45 44 17
- ✉ info@golflln.com
- 🖥 www.golflln.com

Overijse   (1986)
Gemslaan 55, 3090 Overijse
- ☎ **(02) 687 50 30**
- ✉ ogc@golf-overijse.be
- 🖥 www.overijsegolfclub.be

Pierpont   (1992)
1 Grand Pierpont, 6210 Frasnes-lez-Gosselies
- ☎ **(071) 8808 30**

Rigenée   (1981)
Rue de Châtelet 62, 1495 Villers-la-Ville
- ☎ **(071) 87 77 65**
- ✉ golf@rigenee.be
- 🖥 www.rigenee.be

Royal Amicale Anderlecht   (1987)
Rue Schollestraat 1, 1070 Brussels
- ☎ **(02) 521 16 87**
- 📠 (02) 521 51 56
- ✉ info@golf-anderlecht.com
- 🖥 www.golf-anderlecht.com

Royal Golf Club de Belgique   (1906)
Château de Ravenstein, 3080 Tervuren
- ☎ **+32 (0) 2 767 58 01**
- 📠 +32 (0) 2 767 28 41
- ✉ info@rgcb.be
- ✍ Jos Vankriekelsienne (Dir)
- 🖥 www.rgcb.be

Royal Waterloo Golf Club   (1923)
Vieux Chemin de Wavre 50, 1380 Lasne
- ☎ **(00) 322 633 1850**
- 📠 (00) 322 633 2866
- ✉ infos@golfwaterloo.be
- ✍ Henri Bailly
- 🖥 www.rwgc.be

Sept Fontaines   (1987)
1021, Chaussée d'Alsemberg, 1420 Braine L'Alleud
- ☎ **(02) 353 02 46/353 03 46**
- 📠 (02) 354 68 75
- ✉ info@golf7fontaines.be
- ✍ Manuel Weymeersch
- 🖥 www.golf7fontaines.be

Winge G&CC   (1988)
Leuvensesteenweg 252, 3390 Sint Joris Winge
- ☎ **(016) 63 40 53**
- 📠 (016) 63 21 40
- ✉ winge@golf.be
- 🖥 www.golf.be/winge

East

Avernas   (199)
Route de Grand Hallet 19A, 4280 Hannut
- ☎ **(019) 51 30 66**
- 📠 (019) 51 53 43
- ✉ info@golfavernas.be
- 🖥 www.golfavernas.be

Durbuy   (1991)
Route d'Oppagne 34, 6940 Barvaux-su-Ourthe
- ☎ **(086) 21 44 54**

Flanders Nippon Hasselt
(1988)
Vissenbroekstraat 15, 3500 Hasselt
- ☎ (011) 26 34 82
- ✉ flanders.nippon.golf@pandora.be
- 🖃 www.flandersnippongolf.be

Henri-Chapelle (1988)
Rue du Vivier 3, B-4841 Henri-Chapelle
- ☎ (087) 88 19 91
- 🖥 (087) 88 36 55
- ✉ info@golfhenrichapelle.be
- 🖃 www.golfhenrichapelle.be

International Gomze Golf Club (1986)
Sur Counachamps 8, 4140 Gomze Andoumont
- ☎ (04) 360 92 07
- 🖥 (04) 360 92 06
- ✉ gomzegolf@skynet.be
- ✍ Michele Quentainmount
- 🖃 www.gomze.be

Limburg G&CC (1966)
Golfstraat 1, 3530 Houthalen
- ☎ (089) 38 35 43
- 🖥 (089) 84 12 08
- ✉ limburggolf@telenet.be
- ✍ Jan Hendrikx
- 🖃 www.lgcc.be

Royal GC du Sart Tilman (1939)
Route du Condroz 541, 4031 Liège
- ☎ (041) 336 20 21
- ✉ secretariat|@rgcst.be
- 🖃 www.rgcst.be

Royal Golf des Fagnes (1930)
1 Ave de l'Hippodrome, 4900 Spa
- ☎ (087) 79 30 30
- 🖥 (087) 79 30 39
- ✉ info@golfdespa.be
- 🖃 www.golfdespa.be

Spiegelven GC Genk (1988)
Wiemesmeerstraat 109, 3600 Genk
- ☎ (0032) 893 59616
- 🖥 (0032) 893 64184
- ✉ info@spiegelven.be
- 🖃 www.spiegelven.be

West & Oost Vlaanderen

Damme G&CC (1987)
Doornstraat 16, 8340 Damme-Sijsele
- ☎ (050) 35 35 72
- 🖥 (050) 35 89 25
- ✉ info@dammegolf.be
- ✍ Chris Morton
- 🖃 www.dammegolf.be

Oudenaarde G&CC (1975)
Kasteel Petegem, Kortrykstraat 52, 9790 Wortegem-Petegem
- ☎ (055) 33 41 61
- 🖥 (055) 31 98 49

- ✉ oudenaarde@golf.be
- 🖃 www.golfoudenaarde.be

De Palingsbeek (1991)
Eekhofstraat 14, 8902 Hollebeke-Ieper
- ☎ (057) 20 04 36
- 🖥 (057) 21 89 58
- ✉ golfpalingsbeek@skynet.be
- ✍ Ian Connerty
- 🖃 www.golfpalingbeek.be

Royal Latem (1909)
9830 St Martens-Latem
- ☎ +32 9 282 54 11
- 🖥 +32 9 282 90 19
- ✉ secretary@latemgolf.be
- ✍ Ph Buysse
- 🖃 www.latemgolf.be

Royal Ostend (1903)
Koninklijke Baan 2, 8420 De Haan
- ☎ (059) 23 32 83
- 🖃 www.golfoostende.be

Royal Zoute (1899)
Caddiespad 14, 8300 Knokke-le-Zoute
- ☎ (050) 60 16 17 (Clubhouse)
- 🖥 (050) 62 30 29
- ✉ golf@zoute.be
- ✍ (050) 60 12 27
- 🖃 www.zoute.be

Waregem (1988)
Bergstraat 41, 8790 Waregem
- ☎ (056) 60 88 08
- ✉ waregem@golf.be
- 🖃 www.golf.be/waregem

Cyprus

Aphrodite Hills GC (2002)
3 Aphrodite Avenue, Aphrodite Hills, Kouklia, 8509 Paphos
- ☎ 00357 2682 8200
- 🖥 00357 2695 6706
- ✉ golfreservations@aphroditehills.com
- ✍ Nuno T Bastos
- 🖃 www.aphroditehills.com

Minthis Hills GC (1994)
P O Box 62085, 8060 Paphos
- ☎ 00357 2664 2774/5
- 🖥 00357 2664 2776
- ✉ golfers2@cytanet.com.cy
- ✍ Mr Stelios Patsalides
- 🖃 www.cyprusgolf.com

Vikla G&CC (1992)
Vikla Village, Kellaki, Limassol
- ☎ 00 357 99 674 218
- 🖥 00 357 25 760 750
- ✉ viklagolf@cytanet.com.cy
  info@vikla-golf.com
- 🖃 www.vikla-golf.com

Paphos (2004)
Box 484 Kamares Club, PO Box 60156, 8101 Paphos
- ☎ 00357 269 11415

- ✉ heatherharper@cytanet.com.cy
- ✍ Mr Ian Harper

Czech Republic

Karlovy Vary (1904)
Prazska 125, PO Box 67, 360 01 Karlovy Vary
- ☎ (017) 333 1001-2

Lísnice (1928)
252 10 Mnísek pod Brdy
- ☎ (0318) 599 151
- 🖃 www.gkl.cz

Royal Golf Club Mariánské Lázne (1905)
PO Box 47, 353 01 Mariánské Lázne
- ☎ +420 354 604300
- 🖥 +420 354 625195
- ✉ office@golfml.cz
- ✍ Cerna Jana/Nechanicky Oldrich
- 🖃 www.golfml.cz

Park Golf Club Mittal Ostrava (1968)
Dolni 412, 747 15 Silherovice
- ☎ (+420) 595 054 144
- 🖥 (+420) 595 054 144
- ✉ golf@golf-ostrava.cz
- ✍ Ing. Paval Pniak
- 🖃 www.golf-ostrava.cz

Podebrady (1964)
Na Zalesi 530, 29080 Podebrady
- ☎ (0324) 610928
- 🖃 www.golfpodebrady.cz

Semily (1970)
Bavlnarska 521, 513 01 Semily
- ☎ (0431) 622443/624428
- 🖃 www.semily.cz

Denmark

Bornholm Island

Bornholm (1972)
Plantagevej 3B, 3700 Rønne
- ☎ 56 95 68 54
- ✉ info@bornholmsgolfklub.dk
- 🖃 www.bornholmsgolfklub.dk

Nexø
Dueodde Golfbane, Strandmarksvejen 14, 3730 Nexø
- ☎ 56 48 89 87
- 🖥 56 48 89 69
- ✉ ngk@dueodde-golf.dk
- 🖃 www.dueodde-golf.dk

Nordbornholm-Rø   (1987)
Spellingevej 3, Rø, 3760 Gudhjem
☎ 56 48 40 50
✉ mail@roegolfbane.dk
🖳 www.roegolfbane.dk

Funen

Faaborg   (1989)
Dalkildegards Allee 1, 5600 Faaborg
☎ 62 61 77 43

Lillebaelt   (1990)
O.Hougvej 130, 5500 Middelfart
☎ 64 41 80 11
📠 64 41 14 11
✉ gkl@post10.tele.dk
🖳 www.gkl.dk

Odense   (1927)
Hestehaven 200, 5220 Odense SØ
☎ 65 95 90 00
✉ sekretariatet@odensegolfklub.dk
🏌 Hans Henrik Burkal
🖳 www.odensegolfklub.dk

Proark Golf Odense Eventyr   (1993)
Falen 227, 5250 Odense SV
☎ 7021 1900
📠 6562 2021
✉ pgoe@proarkgolf.dk
🏌 Ulla Vahl-Møller (Golf Mgr)
🖳 www.proarkgolf.dk

SCT. Knuds Golfklub (1954)
Slipshavnsvej 16, 5800 Nyborg
☎ 65 31 12 12
📠 65 30 28 04
✉ mail@sct-knuds.dk
🏌 Margit Madsen
🖳 www.sct-knuds.dk

Svendborg   (1970)
Tordensgaardevej 5, Sørup, 5700 Svendborg
☎ 62 22 40 77
📠 62 20 29 77
✉ info@svendborg-golf.dk
🖳 www.svendborg-golf.dk

Vestfyns   (1974)
Rønnemosegård, Krengerupvej 27, 5620 Glamsbjerg
☎ 63 72 19 20
✉ vestfyn@golfonline.dk
🖳 www.vestfynsgolfklub.dk

Jutland

Aarhus   (1931)
Ny Moesgaardvej 50, 8270 Hojbjerg
☎ 86 27 63 22
📠 86 27 63 21
✉ aarhusgolf@mail.dk
🖳 www.aarhusgolf.dk

Blokhus Golf Klub   (1993)
Hunetorpvej 115, Box 37, 9492 Blokhus
☎ 98 20 95 00
📠 98 20 95 01
✉ info@blokhusgolfklub.dk
🖳 www.blokhusgolf.dk

Breinholtgård   (1992)
Koksspangvej 17-19, 6710 Esbjerg V
☎ 75 11 57 00
📠 75 11 55 12
✉ bgk@tiscali.dk
🖳 www.bggc.dk

Brønderslev Golfklub (1971)
Golfvejen 83, 9700 Brønderslev
☎ 98 82 32 81
✉ info@broenderslevgolfklub.dk
🏌 Ulla Gade
🖳 www.broenderslevgolfklub.dk

Brundtlandbanen   (2000)
Brundtland Allé 1-3, 6520 Toftlund
☎ 73 83 16 00
✉ info@brundtland.dk
🖳 www.brundtland.dk

Dejbjerg   (1966)
Letagervej 1, Dejbjerg, 6900 Skjern
☎ 97 35 00 09
📠 96 80 11 18
✉ kontor@dejbjerggk.dk
🏌 Hanne Häggavist
🖳 www.dejbjerggk.dk

Ebeltoft   (1966)
Galgebakken 14, 8400 Ebeltoft
☎ 87 59 6000
✉ post@ebeltoft-golfclub.dk

Esbjerg   (1921)
Sønderhedevej 11, Marbaek, 6710 Esbjerg
☎ 75 26 92 19
📠 75 26 94 19
✉ kontor@egk.dk
🖳 www.egk.dk

Fanø Golf Links   (1901)
Golfvejen 5, 6720 Fanø
☎ 76 66 00 77
📠 76 66 00 44
✉ golf@fanoe-golf-links.dk
🖳 www.fanoe-golf-links.dk

Grenaa   (1981)
Vestermarken 1, DK-8500 Grenaa
☎ +45 863 27929
📠 +45 863 09654
✉ info@grenaagolfklub.dk
🖳 www.grenaagolfklub.dk

Gyttegård   (1974)
Billundvej 43, 7250 Hejnsvig
☎ +45 75 33 63 82
✉ info@gyttegaardgolfklub.dk
🖳 www.gyttegaardgolfklub.dk

Haderslev   (1971)
Viggo Carstensvej 7, 6100 Haderslev
☎ 74 52 83 01

Han Herreds
Starkaervej 20, 9690 Fjerritslev
☎ 98 21 26 66 / 98 21 26 78

Henne   (1989)
Hennebysvej 30, 6854 Henne
☎ 75 25 56 10
✉ post@hennegolfklub.dk
🏌 Beverley Elston
🖳 www.hennegolfklub.dk

Herning   (1964)
Golfvej 2, 7400 Herning
☎ 97 21 00 33
✉ info@herninggolfklub.dk
🖳 www.herninggolfklub.dk

Himmerland G&CC   (1979)
Centervej 1, Gatten, 9640 Farsö
☎ 96 49 61 00
✉ hgcc@himmerlandgolf.dk
🖳 www.himmerlandgolf.dk

Hirtshals   (1990)
Kjulvej 10, PO Box 51, 9850 Hirtshals
☎ 98 94 94 08

Hjarbaek Fjord   (1992)
Lynderup, 8832 Skals
☎ 86 69 62 88
📠 86696268
✉ pghf@proarkgolf.dk
🖳 www.proarkgolf.dk

Hjorring   (1985)
Vinstrupvej 30, 9800 Hjorring
☎ 98 91 18 28
📠 98 90 31 00
✉ info@hjoerringgolf.dk
🖳 www.hjoerringgolf.dk

Holmsland Klit
Klevevej 19, Søndervig, 6950 Ringkøbing
☎ 97 33 88 00
🖳 www.holmslandklitgolf.dk

Holstebro Golf Klub   (1970)
Råsted, 7570 Vemb
☎ 97 48 51 55
✉ post@holstebro-golfklub.dk
🏌 Kjeld Rasmussen
🖳 www.holstebro-golfklub.dk

Horsens   (1972)
Silkeborgvej 44, 8700 Horsens
☎ 75 61 51 51
🖳 www.horsensgolf.dk

Hvide Klit   (1972)
Hvideklitvej 28, 9982 Aalbaek
☎ 98 48 90 21
📠 98 48 91 12
✉ info@hvideklit.dk
🖳 www.hvideklit.dk

Juelsminde   (1973)
Bobroholtvej 11a, 7130 Juelsminde
☎ 75 69 34 92
📠 75 69 46 11
✉ golf@juelsmindegolf.dk
🖳 www.juelsmindegolf.dk

Kaj Lykke (1988)
Kirkebrovej 5, 6740 Bramming
☎ **00 45 - 75 10 22 46**
📠 00 45 - 75 10 26 68
📧 post@kajlykkegolfklub.dk
✍ Mrs Susanne Noergaard (Sec)
🖥 www.kajlykkegolfklub.dk

Kalo (1992)
Aarhusvej 32, 8410 Rønde
☎ **86 37 36 00**
📠 86 37 36 46

Kolding (1933)
Egtved Alle 10, 6000 Kolding
☎ **75 52 37 93**
📠 75 52 42 42
📧 kgc@koldinggolfclub.dk
✍ Ronny Kert (Mgr)
🖥 www.koldinggolfclub.dk

Lemvig (1986)
Søgårdevejen 6, 7620 Lemvig
☎ **97 81 09 20**
📧 lemviggolfklub@lemviggolfklub.dk
🖥 www.lemviggolfklub.dk

Løkken (1990)
Vrenstedvej 226, PO Box 43, 9480 Løkken
☎ **98 99 26 57**
📠 98 99 26 58
📧 info@loekken-golfklub.dk
🖥 www.loekken-golfklub.dk

Nordvestjysk (1971)
Nystrupvej 19, 7700 Thisted
☎ **97 97 41 41**

Odder (1990)
Akjaervej 200, Postbox 46, 8300 Odder
☎ **86 54 54 51**
📠 86 54 54 58
📧 oddergolf@oddergolf.dk
✍ Karen Frederiksen
🖥 www.oddergolf.dk

Ornehoj Golfklub
Lundegard 70, 9260 Gistrup-Aalborg
☎ **98 31 43 44**
📧 golfklubben@mail.dk
🖥 www.ornehojgolfklub.dk

Randers (1958)
Himmelbovej 22, Fladbro, 8900 Randers
☎ **86 42 88 69**
📧 postmaster@randersgolf.dk
🖥 www.randersgolf.dk

Ribe (1979)
Rønnehave, Snepsgårdevej 14, 6760 Ribe
☎ **30 73 65 18**

Rold Skov (1991)
Golfvej 1, 9520 Skørping
☎ **96 82 8300**
📠 96 82 8309
📧 info@roldskovgolf.dk
🖥 www.roldskovgolf.dk

Royal Oak (1992)
Golfvej, Jels, 6630 Rødding
☎ **74 55 32 94**
📧 golf@royal-oak.dk
🖥 www.royal-oak.dk

Silkeborg (1966)
Sensommervej 15C, 8600 Silkeborg
☎ **86 85 33 99**
📠 86 85 35 22
📧 kontor@silkeborggolf.dk
✍ Mads Rügholm (Mgr)
🖥 www.silkeborggolf.dk

Sønderjyllands (1968)
Uge Hedegård, 6360 Tinglev
☎ **74 68 75 25**
📧 sonderjylland@mail.dk
🖥 www.sdj-golfklub.dk

Varde (1991)
Gellerupvej 111b, 6800 Varde
☎ **+45 75 22 49 44**
📧 vardegolfklub@sport.dk
🖥 www.vardegolfklub.dk

Vejle (1970)
Faellessletgard, Ibaekvej, 7100 Vejle
☎ **75 85 81 85**
📠 75 85 83 01
📧 info@vgc.dk
🖥 www.vgc.dk

Viborg (1973)
Spangsbjerg Alle 50, Overlund, 8800 Viborg
☎ **86 67 30 10**
📧 mail@viborggolfklub.dk
🖥 www.viborggolfklub.dk

Zealand

Asserbo Golf Club (1946)
Bødkergaardsvej 9, 3300 Frederiksvaerk
☎ **47 72 14 90**
📠 47 72 14 26
📧 agc@agc.dk
✍ Arne Larsen
🖥 www.agc.dk

Copenhagen (1898)
Dyrehaven 2, 2800 Kgs. Lyngby
☎ **39 63 04 83**
📧 info@kgkgolf.dk
✍ S Pedersen (Mgr)
🖥 www.kgkgolf.dk

Dragør Golfklub (1991)
Kalvebodvej 100, 2791 Dragør
☎ **32 53 89 75**
📠 32 53 88 09
📧 post@dragor-golf.dk
🖥 www.dragor-golf.dk

Falster (1994)
Virketvej 44, 4863 Eskilstrup, Falster Island
☎ **54 43 81 43**
📠 54 43 81 23
📧 info@falster-golfklub.dk
✍ Knud Erik Melgaard
🖥 www.falster-golfklub.dk

Frederikssund (1974)
Egelundsgården, Skovnaesvej 9, 3630 Jaegerspris
☎ **+45 47 31 08 77**
📠 +45 47 31 21 77
📧 fgk@fgkgolf.dk
✍ Jorgen Bundgaard
🖥 www.frederikssundgolfklub.dk

Furesø (1974)
Hestkøbgård, Hestkøb Vaenge 4, 3460 Birkerød
☎ **+45 45 81 74 44**
📧 info@fggolf.dk
✍ Lars Lindegren
🖥 www.fggolf.dk

Gilleleje (1970)
Ferlevej 52, 3250 Gilleleje
☎ **49 71 80 56**
📠 49 71 80 86
📧 info@gillelejegolfklub.dk
🖥 www.gillelejegolfklub.dk

Hedeland (1980)
Staerkendevej 232A, 2640 Hedehusene
☎ **46 13 61 88**
📠 46 13 62 78
📧 klub@hedeland-golf.dk
🖥 www.hedeland-golf.dk

Helsingør
GL Hellebaekvej, 3000 Helsingør
☎ **49 21 29 70**

Hillerød (1966)
Nysøgårdsvej 9, Ny Hammersholt, 3400 Hillerød
☎ **48 26 50 46/48 25 40 30 (Pro)**
📠 48 25 29 87
📧 klubben@hillerodgolf.dk
🖥 www.hillerodgolf.dk

Hjortespring Golfklub (1980)
Klausdalsbrovej 602, 2750 Ballerup
☎ **44 68 90 09**
📠 44 68 90 04
📧 post@hjgk.dk
✍ Jens Åge Dalby
🖥 www.hjgk.dk

Holbaek (1964)
Dragerupvej 50, 4300 Holbaek
☎ **59 43 45 79**
📠 59 43 51 61
📧 info@holbakgolfklub.dk
✍ Jorgen Buur (Mgr)
🖥 www.holbakgolfklub.dk

Køge Golf Klub (1970)
Gl.Hastrupvej12, 4600 Køge
☎ **+45 56 65 10 00**
📠 +45 56 65 13 45
📧 admin@kogegolf.dk
✍ Helge Caspersen
🖥 www.kogegolf.dk

Kokkedal (1971)
Kokkedal Alle 9, 2970 Horsholm
☎ **45 76 99 59**
📠 45 76 99 03

✉ kg@kokkedalgolf.dk
✍ Ken Lauritsen (Golf Mgr)
🖥 www.kokkedalgolf.dk

Korsør Golf Club (1964)
Ornumuey 8, Postbox 53, 4220 Korsør
☎ 58 37 18 36
📠 58 37 18 39
✉ golf@korsoergolf.dk
✍ Kevin O'Donoghue
🖥 www.korsoergolf.dk

Mølleåens (1970)
Stenbaekgård, Rosenlundvej 3, 3540 Lynge
☎ 48 18 86 31/48 18 86 36
(Pro)

Odsherred (1967)
Stårupvej 2, 4573 Hojby
☎ 59 30 20 76
✉ sek@odsherredgolf.dk
🖥 www.odsherredgolf.dk

Roskilde (1973)
Gedevad, Kongemarken 34, 4000 Roskilde
☎ 46 37 01 81

Rungsted (1937)
Vestre Stationsvej 16, 2960 Rungsted Kyst
☎ 45 86 34 44
✉ info@rungstedgolfklub.dk
🖥 www.rungstedgolfklub.dk

Simon's (1993)
Nybovej 5, 3490 Kvistgaard
☎ +45 49 19 14 78
📠 49 19 14 70
✉ info@simonsgolf.dk
🖥 www.simonsgolf.dk

Skjoldenaesholm (1992)
Skjoldenaesvej 101, 4174 Jystrup
☎ +45 57 53 88 10
✉ pgs@proarkgolf.dk
🖥 www.proarkgolf.dk

Søllerød (1972)
Brillerne 9, 2840 Holte
☎ 45 80 17 84
📠 45 80 70 08
✉ info@sollerodgolf.dk
✍ Helle Hessellund
🖥 www.sollerodgolf.dk

Sorø (1979)
Suserupvej 7a, 4180 Sorø
☎ 57 84 93 95
🖥 www.soroegolf.dk

Sydsjaellands (1974)
Borupgården, Mogenstrup, 4700 Naestved
☎ (+45) 55 76 15 55
✉ sydsjaelland@golfonline.dk
🖥 www.sydsjaellandsgolfklub.dk

Vaerloese Golfklub (1993)
Christianshoejvej 22, 3500 Vaerloese
☎ (+45) 4447 2124
📠 (+45) 4447 2128
✉ mail@vaerloese-golfklub.dk
✍ Tine Lunding (Sec)
🖥 www.vaerloese-golfklub.dk

Finland

Central

Etelä-Pohjanmaan (1986)
P O Box 136, 60101 Seinäjoki
☎ (06) 423 4545
🖥 www.ruuhikoskigolf.fi

Karelia Golf (1987)
Vaskiportintie, 80780 Kontioniemi
☎ (013) 732411

Kokkolan (1957)
P O Box 164, 67101 Kokkola
☎ (06) 823 8600
✉ toimisto@kokkolangolf.fi
🖥 www.kokkolangolf.fi

Laukaan Peurunkagolf
(1989)
Valkolantie 68, 41530 Laukaa
☎ (014) 3377 300
🖥 www.golfpiste.com/lpg

Tarina Golf (1988)
Golftie 135, 71800 Siilinjärvi
☎ (017) 462 5299
✉ toimisto@tarinagolf.fi
🖥 www.tarinagolf.fi

Vaasan Golf (1969)
Golfkenttätie 61, 65380 Vaasa
☎ (06) 356 9989
📠 (06) 356 9091
✉ toimisto@vaasangolf.fi
✍ Mr Petri Jolkkonen (Mgr)
🖥 www.vaasangolf.fi

Helsinki & South

Aura Golf (1958)
Ruissalon Puistotie 536, 20100 Turku
☎ (02) 258 9201/9221
📠 (02) 258 9121
✉ office@auragolf.fi
🖥 www.auragolf.fi

Espoo Ringside Golf
(1990)
Nurmikartanontie 5, 02920 Espoo
☎ (09) 849 4940
📠 (09) 853 7132
✉ caddie@ringsidegolf.fi
✍ Ari Vepsä
🖥 www.ringsidegolf.fi

Espoon Golfseura (1982)
Mynttiläntie 1, 02780 Espoo
☎ (09) 8190 3444
🖥 www.espoongolfseura.fi

Harjattula G&CC (1989)
Harjattulantie 84, 20960 Turku
☎ (02) 276 2180
🖥 www.harjattula.fi

Helsingin Golfklubi (1932)
Talin Kartano, 00350 Helsinki
☎ +358 9 225 23710
📠 +358 9 225 23737
✉ toimisto@helsingingolfklubi.fi
✍ Elkka Ulander
🖥 www.helsingingolfklubi.fi

Hyvinkään (1989)
Golftie 63, 05880 Hyvinkää
☎ (019) 456 2400
✉ caddiemaster@hyvigolf.fi
🖥 www.hyvigolf.fi

Keimola Golf (1988)
Kirkantie 32, 01750 Vantaa
☎ (09) 276 6650

Kurk Golf (1985)
02550 Evitskog
☎ (09) 819 0480
✉ kurk@kurkgolf.fi
🖥 www.kurkgolf.fi

Master Golf (1988)
Bodomin kuja 7, 02940 Espoo
☎ (09) 849 2300
📠 (09) 849 23011
🖥 www.mastergolf.fi

Meri-Teijo (1990)
Mathildedalin Kartano, 25660 Mathildedal
☎ (02) 736 3955

Messilä (1988)
Messiläntie 240, 15980 Messilä
☎ (03) 884040

Nevas Golf (1988)
01150 Söderkulla
☎ (010) 400 6400
✉ ng@nevasgolf.fi
🖥 www.nevasgolf.fi

Nordcenter G&CC (1988)
10410 Aminnefors
☎ (019) 2766850
🖥 www.nordcenter.com

Nurmijärven (1990)
Ratasillantie 70, 05100 Röykkä
☎ (09) 276 6230
✉ caddiemaster@nurmijarvi-golf.fi
🖥 www.nurmijarvi-golf.fi

Peuramaa Golf (1991)
Peuramaantie 152, 02400 Kirkkonummi
☎ (09) 295 588
✉ office@peuramaagolf.com
🖥 www.peuramaagolf.com

Pickala Golf (1986)
Golfkuja 5, 02580 Siuntio
☎ (09) 221 9080
📠 (09) 221 90899
✉ toimisto@pickalagolf.fi
🖥 www.pickalagolf.fi

Ruukkigolf (1986)
PL 9, 10420 Skuru
☎ (019) 245 4485

✉ toimisto@ruukkigolf.fi
🖥 www.ruukkigolf.fi

Sarfvik   (1984)
P O Box 27, 02321 Espoo
☎ **(09) 221 9000**
✉ sarfvik@golfsarfvik.fi

Sea Golf Rönnäs   (1989)
Kabbölentie 319, 07750 Isnäs
☎ **+358 (0) 19 634 434**
✉ toimisto@seagolf.fi
🖥 www.seagolf.fi

St Laurence Golf   (1989)
Kaivurinkatu 133, 08200 Lohja
☎ **+358 (0)19 357 821**
✉ caddie.master@stlaurencegolf.fi
🖥 www.stlaurencegolf.fi

Suur-Helsingin Golf   (1965)
Rinnekodintie 29, 02980 Espoo
☎ **+358 9 4399 7110**
📠 +358 9 437121
✉ toimisto@shg.fi
🖥 www.shg.fi

Golf Talma   (1989)
Nygårdintie 115-6, 04240 Talma
☎ **(09) 274 6540**
📠 (09) 274 65432
✉ golftalma@golftalma.fi
✍ Olli-Pekka Nissinen (Mgr)
🖥 www.golftalma.fi

Tuusula   (1983)
Kirkkotie 51, 04301 Tuusula
☎ **(042) 410241**
🖥 www.golfpiste.com/tgk

Virvik Golf   (1981)
Virvik, 06100 Porvoo
☎ **(915) 579292**

North

Green Zone Golf   (1987)
Näräntie, 95400 Tornio
☎ **(016) 431711**

Katinkulta   (1990)
88610 Vuokatti
☎ **(08) 669 7488**
✉ golf.katinkulta@sok-fi
🖥 www.katinkultagolf.fi

Oulu   (1964)
Sankivaaran Golfkeskus, 90650 Oulu
☎ **(08) 531 5222**
📠 (08) 531 5129
✉ caddiemaster@oulugolf.fi
🖥 www.oulugolf.fi

South East

Imatran Golf   (1986)
Golftie 11, 55800 Imatra
☎ **(05) 473 4954**

Kartano Golf   (1988)
P O Box 60, 79601 Joroinen
☎ **(017) 572257**

Kerigolf   (1990)
Kerimaantie 65, 58200 Kerimäki
☎ **(015) 252600**
✉ clubhouse@kerigolf.fi
🖥 www.kerigolf.fi

Koski Golf   (1987)
Eerolanväylä 126, 45700 Kuusankoski
☎ **+358 207 129 820**
📠 +358 207 129 829
✉ toimisto@koskigolf.fi
🖥 www.koskigolf.fi

Kymen Golf   (1964)
Mussalo Golfcourse, 48310 Kotka
☎ **(05) 210 3700**
🖥 www.kymengolf.fi

Lahden Golf   (1959)
Takkulantie, 15230 Lahti
☎ **(03) 784 1311**

Porrassalmi   (1989)
Annila, 50100 Mikkeli
☎ **(015) 335518/335446**

Vierumäki Golf   (1988)
Kaskelantie 10, 19120 Vierumäki
☎ **+358 (0) 40 837 6149**
📠 +358 (0) 3 8424 7015
✉ jan.ruoho@vierumaki.fi
✍ Jan Ruoho (Dir)
🖥 www.vierumakigolf.fi

South West

Porin Golfkerho   (1939)
P O Box 25, 28601 Pori
☎ **(02) 630 3888**
✉ toimisto@kalafornia.com
🖥 www.kalafornia.com

River Golf   (1988)
Taivalkunta, 37120 Nokia
☎ **(03) 340 0234**

Salo Golf   (1988)
Anistenkatu 1, 24100 Salo
☎ **(02) 721 7300**
📠 (02) 721 7310
✉ caddiemaster@salogolf.fi
✍ Mr Mika Havulinna
🖥 www.salogolf.fi

Tammer Golf   (1965)
Toimelankatu 4, 33560 Tampere
☎ **(03) 261 3316**

Tawast Golf   (1987)
Tawastintie 48, 13270 Hämeenlinna
☎ **(03) 630 610**
📠 (03) 630 6120
✉ tawast@tawastgolf.fi
🖥 www.tawastgolf.fi

Vammala   (1991)
38100 Karkku
☎ **(03) 513 4070**

Wiurila G&CC   (1990)
Viurilantie 126, 24910 Halikko
☎ **+35 8272 78100**
📠 +35 8272 78107
✉ toimisto@wgcc.fi
🖥 www.wgcc.fi

Yyteri Golf   (1988)
Karhuluodontie 85, 28840 Pori
☎ **(02) 638 0380**
🖥 www.yyterilinks.com

France

Bordeaux & South West

Albret   (1986)
Le Pusocq, 47230 Barbaste
☎ **05 53 65 53 69**

Arcachon   (1955)
Golf International d'Arcachon, 35 Bd
d'Arcachon, 33260 La Teste De Buch
☎ **05 56 54 44 00**
📠 05 56 66 86 32
✉ golfarcachon@free.fz

Arcangues   (1991)
64200 Arcangues
☎ **05 59 43 10 56**
📠 05 59 43 12 60
✉ golf.arcangues@wanadoo.fz
🖥 www.golfdarcangues.com

Biarritz   (1888)
Ave Edith Cavell, 64200 Biarritz
☎ **05 59 03 71 80**
✉ info@golfbiarritz.com
🖥 www.golf-biarritz.com

Biscarrosse   (1989)
Avenue du Golf, F-40600 Biscarrosse
☎ **05 58 09 84 93**
📠 05 58 09 84 50
✉ golfdebiscarrosse@wanadoo.fr
🖥 www.biscarrossegolf.com

Blue Green-Artiguelouve
(1986)
Domaine St Michel, Pau-Artiguelouve,
64230 Artiguelouve
☎ **05 59 83 09 29**

Blue Green-Seignosse   (1989)
Avenue du Belvédère, 40510 Seignosse
☎ **05 58 41 68 30**
✉ golfseignosse@wanadoo.fr
🖥 www.golfseignosse.com

Bordeaux-Cameyrac   (1972)
33450 St Sulpice-et-Cameyrac
☎ **(+33) (0)5 56 72 96 79**

✉ contact@golf-bordeaux-
cameyrac.com
🖥 www.golf-bordeaux-cameyrac.com

Bordeaux-Lac (1976)
Public
Avenue de Pernon, 33300 Bordeaux
☎ 05 56 50 92 72
✉ golf.bordeaux@wanadoo.fr
🖥 www.golfbordeauxlac.com

Bordelais (1900)
*Domaine de Kater, Allee F Arago, 33200
Bordeaux-Caudéran*
☎ 05 56 28 56 04
📠 05 56 28 59 71
✉ golfbordelais@wanadoo.fr
✍ Franck Koenig
🖥 www.golf-bordelais.fr

Casteljaloux (1989)
*Route de Mont de Marsan, 47700
Casteljaloux*
☎ 05 53 93 51 60
✉ golfdecasteljaloux@tiscali.fr
🖥 www.golf-casteljaloux.com

Chantaco (1928)
Route d'Ascain, 64500 St Jean-de-Luz
☎ 05 59 26 14 22/05 59 26 19
22
📠 05 59 26 48 37
✉ contact@chantaco.com
🖥 www.golfdechantaco.com

Château des Vigiers G&CC
(1992)
24240 Monestier
☎ 05 53 61 50 33
📠 05 53 61 50 31
✉ golf@vigiers.com
✍ Matthew Storm
🖥 www.vigiers.com

Chiberta (1926)
Boulevard des Plages, 64600 Anglet
☎ 05 59 63 83 20

Domaine de la Marterie
(1987)
St Felix de Reillac, 24260 Le Bugue
☎ 05 53 05 61 00
🖥 www.marterie.fr

Graves et Sauternais (1989)
St Pardon de Conques, 33210 Langon
☎ 05 56 62 25 43
📠 05 56 76 83 72
✉ golf.langon@laposte.net

Gujan (1990)
Route de Souguinet, 33470 Gujan Mestras
☎ 05 57 52 73 73

Hossegor (1930)
333 Avu du Golf, 40150 Hossegor
☎ 05 58 43 56 99
📠 05 58 43 98 52
✉ golf.hossegor@wanadoo.fr
✍ Christophe Raillard
🖥 www.golfhossegor.com

Lacanau Golf & Hotel
(1980)
*Domaine de l'Ardilouse, 33680 Lacanau-
Océan*
☎ (+33) 556 039292
✉ info@golf-hotel-lacanau.fr
🖥 www.golf-hotel-lacanau.fr

Makila
Route de Cambo, 64200 Bassussarry
☎ 05 59 58 42 42

Médoc
*Chemin de Courmateau, Louens, 33290 Le
Pian Médoc*
☎ 05 56 70 11 90

Moliets (1989)
Public
Rue Mathieu Desbieys, 40660 Moliets
☎ 05 58 48 54 65
📠 05 58 48 54 88
✉ resa@golfmoliets.com
✍ Breton
🖥 www.golfmoliets.com

Pau (1856)
Rue du Golf, 64140 Billère
☎ +33 (05) 5913 1856
✉ pau.golfclub@wanadoo.fr
🖥 www.paugolfclub.com

Pessac (1989)
Rue de la Princesse, 33600 Pessac
☎ 05 57 26 03 33

Stade Montois (1993)
Pessourdat, 40090 Saint Avit
☎ 05 58 75 63 05

Villeneuve sur Lot G&CC
(1987)
*'La Menuisière', 47290 Castelnaud de
Gratecambe*
☎ 05 53 01 60 19
📠 05 53 01 78 99
✉ info@vsgolf.com
✍ Jenny Lyon
🖥 www.vsgolf.com

Brittany

Ajoncs d'Or (1976)
*Kergrain Lantic, 22410 Saint-Quay
Portrieux*
☎ 02 96 71 90 74
✉ golfdesajoncsdor@wanadoo.fr

Baden
Kernic, 56870 Baden
☎ 02 97 57 18 96

Belle Ile en Mer (1987)
Les Poulins, 56360 Belle-Ile-en-Mer
☎ 02 97 31 64 65

Brest Les Abers (1990)
Kerhoaden, 29810 Plouarzel
☎ 02 98 89 68 33

✉ golf@abersgolf.com
🖥 www.abersgolf.com

Brest-Iroise (1976)
*Parc de Lann-Rohou, Saint-Urbain, 29800
Landerneau*
☎ 02 98 85 16 17
📠 02 98 85 19 39
✉ golfhotel@brest-iroise.com
🖥 www.brest-iroise.com

Dinard (1887)
*53 Boulevard de la Houle, 35800 St-Briac-
sur-Mer*
☎ 02 99 88 32 07
📠 02 99 88 04 53
✉ dinardgolf@dinardgolf.com
✍ Jean-Guillaurne Legros
🖥 www.dinardgolf.com

La Freslonnière (1989)
Le Bois Briand, 35650 Le Rheu
☎ 02 99 14 84 09
📠 02 99 14 94 98
✉ lafreslo@wanadoo.fr
🖥 www.lafreslonniere.com

L'Odet (1986)
Clohars-Fouesnant, 29950 Benodet
☎ 02 98 54 87 88
📠 02 98 54 61 40
✉ odet@bluegreen.com
✍ Jean-Luc Leroux
🖥 www.bluegreen.com

Les Ormes (1988)
*Château des Ormes, Epiniac, 35120 Dol-
de-Bretagne*
☎ 02 99 73 54 44

Pléneuf-Val André
*Rue de la Plage des Vallées, 22370 Pléneuf-
Val André*
☎ 02 96 63 01 12

Ploemeur Océan Formule
Golf (1990)
Kerham Saint-Jude, 56270 Ploemeur
☎ 02 97 32 81 82
🖥 www.formule-golf.com

Quimper-Cornouaille (1959)
*Manoir du Mesmeur, 29940 La Forêt-
Fouesnant*
☎ 02 98 56 97 09
📠 02 98 56 86 81
✉ golf-de-cornouaille@wanadoo.fr
🖥 www.golfdecornouaille.com

Rennes (1957)
*Le Temple du Cerisier, 35136 St-Jacques-
de-la-Lande*
☎ 02 99 30 18 18
✉ directeur.rennes@formulegolf.com

Rhuys-Kerver (1988)
Public
*Formule Golf, Domaine de Kerver, 56730
St-Gildas-de-Rhuys*
☎ 02 97 45 30 09
📠 02 97 45 36 58
✉ golf.rhuys@formule-golf.com
🖥 www.formule-golf.com

Les Rochers (1989)
Route d'Argentré du Plessis 3, 35500 Vitré
☎ 02 99 96 52 52

Sables-d'Or-les-Pins (1925)
22240 Fréhel
☎ 02 96 41 42 57

St Laurent (1975)
Ploemel, 56400 Auray
☎ 02 97 56 85 18
✉ golf.stlaurent@formule-golf.com
🖥 www.formule-golf.com

St Malo Hotel G&CC (1986)
Le Tronchet, 35540 Miniac-Morvan
☎ 02 99 58 96 69
✉ saintmalogolf@st-malo.com
🖥 www.saintmalogolf.com

St Samson (1965)
Route de Kérénoc, 22560 Pleumeur-Bodou
☎ 02 96 23 87 34

St Cast Pen Guen (1926)
22380 Saint-Cast-le-Guildo
☎ 02 96 41 91 20
🖶 02 96 41 77 62
✉ golf.stcast@wanadoo.fr
✍ Jean Marie Vilpasteur
🖥 www.golf-st-cast.com

Val Queven (1990)
Public
Kerruisseau, 56530 Queven
☎ 02 97 05 17 96
🖥 www.formule-golf.com

Burgundy & Auvergne

Aubazine (1977)
Public
19190 Aubazine
☎ 03 55 27 25 66

Beaune-Levernois (1990)
21200 Levernois
☎ 03 80 24 10 29
🖶 03 80 24 03 78
✉ golfdebeaune@wanadoo.fr
🖥 www.golfbeaune.free.fr

Chalon-sur-Saône (1976)
Parc de Saint Nicolas, 71380 Chatenoy-en-Bresse
☎ 03 85 93 49 65
✉ contact@golfchalon.com
🖥 www.golf_chalon_sur_saone.com

Chambon-sur-Lignon (1986)
Riondet, La Pierre de la Lune, 43400 Le Chambon-sur-Lignon
☎ 04 71 59 28 10
🖥 www.golf-chambon.com

Château d'Avoise (1992)
9 Rue de Mâcon, 71210 Montchanin
☎ 03 85 78 19 19

Château de Chailly (1990)
Chailly-sur-Armançon, 21320 Pouilly-en-Auxois
☎ 03 80 90 30 40
🖶 03 80 90 30 05
✉ reservation@chailly.com
🖥 www.chailly.com

Domaine de Roncemay (1989)
89110 Aillant-sur-Tholon
☎ 03 86 73 50 50
🖶 03 86 73 69 46
✉ info@roncemay.com
✍ Franzoise Couilloud
🖥 www.roncemay.com

Jacques Laffite Dijon-Bourgogne (1972)
Bois des Norges, 21490 Norges-la-Ville
☎ 03 80 35 71 10
🖶 03 80 35 79 27
✉ contacts@golfdijonbourgogne.com
🖥 www.golfdijonbourgogne.com

Limoges-St Lazare (1976)
Public
Avenue du Golf, 87000 Limoges
☎ 05 55 28 30 02

Mâcon La Salle (1989)
La Salle-Mâcon Nord, 71260 La Salle
☎ 03 85 36 09 71
🖶 03 85 36 06 70
✉ golf.maconlasalle@wanadoo.fr
🖥 www.golfmacon.com

Le Nivernais
Public
Le Bardonnay, 58470 Magny Cours
☎ 03 58 18 30

La Porcelaine
Célicroux, 87350 Panazol
☎ 05 55 31 10 69
✉ golf@golf.porcelaine.com
🖥 www.golf-porcelaine.com

St Junien (1997)
Les Jouberties, 87200 Saint Junien
☎ 05 55 02 96 96
✉ info@golfdesaintjunien.com
🖥 www.golfdesaintjunien.com

Sporting Club de Vichy (1907)
Allée Baugnies, 03700 Bellerive/Allier
☎ 04 70 32 39 11

Val de Cher (1975)
03190 Nassigny
☎ 04 70 06 71 15
🖶 04 70 06 70 00
✉ golfvaldecher@free.fr
🖥 http://golfclub.valdecher.free.fr

Les Volcans (1984)
La Bruyère des Moines, 63870 Orcines
☎ 04 73 62 15 51
🖶 04 73 62 26 52
✉ golfdesvolcans@nat.fr

✍ Gabriel Martin
🖥 www.golfdesvolcans.com

Centre

Les Aisses (1992)
RN20 Sud, 45240 La Ferté St Aubin
☎ 02 38 64 80 87
✉ golfdesaisses@wanadoo.fr
🖥 www.aissesgolf.com

Ardrée (1988)
37360 St Antoine-du-Rocher
☎ 02 47 56 77 38
✉ tours.ardree@bluegreen.com
🖥 www.bluegreen.com/tours
www.golf-ardree.com

Aymerich Golf 'Les Dryades' (1987)
36160 Pouligny-Notre-Dame
☎ 02 54 06 60 67
🖶 02 54 30 10 24
✉ aymerichgolf.lesdryades@orange.fr

Les Bordes (1987)
41220 Saint Laurent-Nouan
☎ 02 54 87 72 13
🖶 02 54 87 78 61
✉ reception@lesbordes.com
✍ Mark Vickery (Managing Director)
🖥 www.lesbordes.com

Château de Cheverny (1989)
La Rousselière, 41700 Cheverny
☎ 02 54 79 24 70
🖶 02 54 79 25 52
✉ contact@golf-cheverny.com
🖥 www.golf-cheverny.com

Château de Maintenon (1989)
Route de Gallardon, 28130 Maintenon
☎ 02 37 27 18 09

Château des Sept Tours (1989)
Le Vivier des Landes, 37330 Courcelles de Touraine
☎ 02 47 24 69 75

Cognac (1987)
Saint-Brice, 16100 Cognac
☎ 05 45 32 18 17

Le Connétable (1987)
Parc Thermal, 86270 La Roche Posay
☎ 05 49 86 25 10

Domaine de Vaugouard (1987)
Chemin des Bois, Fontenay-sur-Loing, 45210 Ferrières
☎ 02 38 89 79 00

Haut-Poitou (1987)
86130 Saint-Cyr
☎ 05 49 62 53 62
🖶 05 49 88 77 14

✉ contact@golfduhautpoitou.com
🖥 www.golfduhautpoitou.com

Loudun-Roiffe (1985)
Domaine St Hilaire, 86120 Roiffe
☎ 05 49 98 78 06
🖥 www.golf-loudun.com

Marcilly (1986)
Domaine de la Plaine, 45240 Marcilly-en-Villette
☎ 02 38 76 11 73
🖳 02 38 76 18 73
✉ golf@marcilly.com
🖎 Emilie/Sophie
🖥 www.marcilly.com

Niort (1984)
Chemin du Grand Ormeau, 79000 Niort Romagne
☎ 05 49 09 01 41
🖳 05 49 73 41 53
✉ contact@golfclubniort.fr
🖎 Eric Fleury
🖥 www.golfclubniort.fr

Orléans Donnery
Château de la Touche, 45450 Donnery
☎ 02 38 59 25 15

Golf du Perche (1987)
La Vallée des Aulnes, 28400 Souancé au Perche
☎ 02 37 29 17 33
✉ golfduperche@wanadoo.fr
🖥 www.golfduperche.fr

Petit Chêne (1987)
Le Petit Chêne, 79310 Mazières-en-Gâtine
☎ 05 49 63 20 95

La Picardière
Chemin de la Picardière, 18100 Vierzon
☎ 02 48 75 21 43

Poitiers
635 route de Beauvoir, 86550 Mignaloux Beauvoir
☎ 05 49 55 10 50
🖳 05 49 62 26 70
✉ golf-poitiers@monalisahotels.com

Poitou (1991)
Domaine des Forges, 79340 Menigoute
☎ 0549 69 91 77
✉ info@golfdesforges.com
🖥 www.golfdesforges.com

La Prée-La Rochelle (1988)
La Richardière, 17137 Marsilly
☎ 05 46 01 24 42
✉ golflarochelle@wanadoo.fr
🖥 www.golflarochelle.com

Royan (1977)
Maine-Gaudin, 17420 Saint-Palais
☎ 05 46 23 16 24
✉ golfderoyan@wanadoo.fr
🖥 www.golfderoyan.com

Saintonge (1953)
Fontcouverte, 17100 Saintes
☎ 05 46 74 27 61

Sancerrois (1989)
St Thibault, 18300 Sancerre
☎ 02 48 54 11 22
🖳 02 48 54 28 03
✉ golf.sancerre@wanadoo.fr
🖎 D Gaucher
🖥 www.golf-sancerre.com

Touraine (1971)
Château de la Touche, 37510 Ballan-Miré
☎ 02 47 53 20 28

Val de l'Indre (1989)
Villedieu-sur-Indre, 36320 Tregonce
☎ 02 54 26 59 44

Channel Coast & North

Abbeville (1989)
Route du Val, 80132 Grand-Laviers
☎ 03 22 24 98 58
🖳 03 22 24 98 58
✉ abbeville.golfclub@wanadoo.fr
🖥 www.golf.abbeville.com

L'Ailette (1985)
02860 Cerny en Laonnais
☎ 03 23 24 83 99
🖳 03 23 24 84 66
✉ golfdelailette@wanadoo.fr
🖎 Philippe Courtin (Dir)
🖥 www.ailette.org

Amiens (1925)
80115 Querrieu
☎ 03 22 93 04 26
✉ golfamiens@aol.com
🖥 www.golfamiens.fr

Apremont Golf Country Club (1992)
60300 Apremont
☎ 03 44 25 61 11
🖳 03 44 25 11 72
✉ apremont@club-albatros.com
🖎 E Jacob
🖥 www.apremont-golf.com

Arras (1989)
Rue Briquet Taillandier, 62223 Anzin-St-Aubin
☎ 03 21 50 24 24
✉ golf@golf-arras.com
🖥 www.golf-arras.com

Belle Dune
Promenade de Marquenterre, 80790 Fort-Mahon-Plage
☎ 03 22 23 45 50

Bois de Ruminghem (1991)
1613 Rue St Antoine, 62370 Ruminghem
☎ 03 21 35 31 37
✉ info@golfdubois.com
🖎 Mr Boris Janjic/Mrs Els Verheyen
🖥 www.golfdubois.com

Bondues (1968)
Château de la Vigne, 5910 Bondues
☎ 03 20 23 20 62
🖳 03 20 23 24 11
✉ contact@golfdebondues.com
🖥 www.golfdebondues.com

Champagne (1986)
02130 Villers-Agron
☎ 03 23 71 62 08
✉ golf.de.champagne@wanadoo.fr
🖥 www.golf-de-champagne.com

Chantilly (1909)
Allée de la Ménagerie, 60500 Chantilly
☎ 03 44 57 04 43
🖳 03 44 57 26 54
✉ contact@golfdechantilly.com
🖎 Remy Dorbeau
🖥 www.golfdechantilly.com

Chaumont-en-Vexin (1968)
Château de Bertichère, 60240 Chaumont-en-Vexin
☎ 03 44 49 00 81
🖳 03 44 49 32 71
✉ golfdechaumont@golf-paris.net
🖥 www.golf-paris.net

Club du Lys – Chantilly (1929)
Rond-Point du Grand Cerf, 60260 Lamorlaye
☎ 03 44 21 26 00
🖳 03 44 21 35 52
✉ clubdulys@wanadoo.fr
🖎 Christophe Rondelé
🖥 www.club-lys-chantilly.com

Compiègne (1896)
Avenue Royale, 60200 Compiègne
☎ 03 44 38 48 00
🖳 03 44 40 23 59
✉ directeur-golfcompiegne@orange.fr
🖎 Stephane Banteilla (Director)
🖥 www.golf-compiegne.com

Deauville l'Amiraute (1992)
CD 278, Tourgéville, 14800 Deauville
☎ 02 31 14 42 00
🖥 www.amiraute-resort.com

Domaine du Tilleul (1984)
Landouzy-la-Ville, 02140 Vervins
☎ 03 23 98 48 00

Dunkerque (1991)
Public
Fort Vallières, Coudekerque-Village, 59380 Coudekerque
☎ 03 28 61 07 43
✉ golf@golf-dk.com
🖥 www.golf-dk.com

Golf de Raray (1987)
4 Rue Nicolas de Lancy, 60810 Raray
☎ 03 44 54 70 61
🖳 03 44 54 74 97
✉ golfpari@wanadoo.fr
🖥 www.golfraray.com

Golf Dolce Chantilly (1991)
Route d'Apremont, 60500 Vineuil St-Firmin
☎ 03 44 58 47 74
🖥 03 44 58 50 28
📧 golf.chantilly@dolce.com
✍ Pierre Jacob (Mgr)
📋 www.dolce.com

Hardelot Dunes Course
(1991)
Ave du Golf, 62152 Hardelot
☎ 03 21 83 73 10
🖥 03 21 83 24 33
📧 hardelot@opengolfclub.com
✍ Ken Strachan (Mgr)
📋 www.hardelot-golf.com

Hardelot Pins Course (1931)
Ave du Golf, 62152 Hardelot
☎ 03 21 83 73 10
🖥 03 21 83 24 33
📧 hardelot@opengolfclub.com
✍ Ken Strachan (Mgr)
📋 www.hardelot-golf.com

Morfontaine (1913)
60128 Mortefontaine
☎ 03 44 54 68 27
🖥 03 44 54 60 57
📧 morfontaine@wanadoo.fr
✍ Jean-Maurice Dulout
📋 www.golfdemorfontaine.fr

Mormal (1991)
Bois St Pierre, 59144 Preux-au-Sart
☎ 03 27 63 07 00
🖥 03 27 39 93 62
📧 info@golf-mormal.com
📋 www.golf-mormal.com

Nampont-St-Martin (1978)
Maison Forte, 80120 Nampont-St-Martin
☎ 03 22 29 92 90/03 22 29 89 87
🖥 03 22 29 97 54
📧 golfdenampont@wanadoo.fr
📋 www.golfdenampont.com

Rebetz (1988)
Route de Noailles, 60240 Chaumont-en-Vexin
☎ 03 44 49 15 54
📋 www.rebetz.com

Saint-Omer
Chemin des Bois, Acquin-Westbécourt, 62380 Lumbres
☎ 03 21 38 59 90

Le Sart (1910)
5 Rue Jean-Jaurès, 59650 Villeneuve D'Ascq
☎ 03 20 72 02 51
🖥 03 20 98 73 28
📧 contact@golfdusart.com
📋 www.golfdusart.com

Thumeries (1935)
Bois Lenglart, 59239 Thumeries
☎ 03 20 86 58 98
🖥 03 20 86 52 66
📧 golfdethumeries@free.fr

✍ Fransoise Dumoulin
📋 www.golfdethumeries.com

Le Touquet 'La Forêt'
(1904)
Ave du Golf, BP 41, 62520 Le Touquet
☎ 03 21 06 28 00
🖥 03 21 06 28 01
📧 letouquet@opengolfclub.com
✍ Gilles Grattepanche
📋 www.opengolfclub.com

Le Touquet 'La Mer' (1931)
Ave du Golf, BP 41, 62520 Le Touquet
☎ 03 21 06 28 00
🖥 03 21 06 28 01
📧 letouquet@opengolfclub.com
✍ Gilles Grattepanche
📋 www.opengolfclub.com

Le Touquet 'Le Manoir'
(1994)
Ave du Golf, BP 41, 62520 Le Touquet
☎ 03 21 06 28 00
🖥 03 21 06 28 01
📧 letouquet@opengolfclub.com
✍ Gilles Grattepanche
📋 www.opengolfclub.com

Val Secret (1984)
Brasles, 02400 Château Thierry
☎ 03 23 83 07 25
📧 accueil@golfvalsecret.com
📋 www.golfvalsecret.com

Vert Parc (1991)
3 Route d'Ecuelles, 59480 Illies
☎ 03 20 29 37 87
🖥 03 20 49 76 39
📧 golfduvertparc@sfr.fr
📋 www.golflevertparc.com

Wimereux (1901)
Avenue F. Mitterrand, 62930 Wimereux
☎ 03 21 32 43 20
📧 accueil@golf-wimereux.com
📋 www.golf-wimereux.com

Corsica

Sperone (1990)
Domaine de Sperone, 20169 Bonifacio
☎ 04 95 73 17 13
📧 golf@sperone.com
📋 www.sperone.com

Ile de France

Ableiges (1989)
95450 Ableiges
☎ 01 30 27 97 00
🖥 01 30 27 97 10
📧 golf@ableigesgolf.com
📋 www.ableiges-golf.com

Bellefontaine (1987)
95270 Bellefontaine
☎ 01 34 71 05 02
🖥 01 34 71 90 90

📧 golf-bellefontaine@wanadoo.fr
📋 www.golfdebellefontaine.com

Bussy-St-Georges (1988)
Promenade des Golfeurs, 77600 Bussy-St-Georges
☎ 01 64 66 00 00

Cély (1990)
Le Château, Route de Saint-Germain, 77930 Cély-en-Bière
☎ 01 64 38 03 07
📋 www.celygolf.com

Cergy Pontoise (1988)
2 Allee de l'Obstacle d'Eau, 95490 Vaureal
☎ 01 34 21 03 48

Chevannes-Mennecy (1994)
91750 Chevannes
☎ 01 64 99 88 74
📧 legolfchevannes@wanadoo.fr

Clement Ader (1990)
Domaine Château Pereire, 77220 Gretz
☎ 01 64 07 34 10
📧 golfclementader@voila.fr
📋 www.golfclementader.com

Coudray (1960)
Ave du Coudray, 91830 Le Coudray-Montceaux
☎ 01 64 93 81 76
🖥 01 64 93 99 95
📧 golf.du.coudray@wanadoo.fr
📋 www.golfcoudray.org

Courson Monteloup (1991)
91680 Bruyères-le-Chatel
☎ 01 64 58 80 80
📋 www.golf-stadefrancais.com

Crécy-la-Chapelle (1987)
Domaine de la Brie, Route de Guérard, F 77580 Crécy-la-Chapelle
☎ 01 64 75 34 44
🖥 01 64 75 34 45
📧 info@domainedelabrie.com
📋 www.crecygolfclub.com

Disneyland Golf (1992)
1 Allee de la Mare Houleuse, 77700 Magny-le-Hongre
☎ 01 60 45 68 90
📧 dlp.nwy.golf@disney.com
📋 www.disneylandparis.com

Domaine de Belesbat
(1989)
Courdimanche-sur-Essonne, 91820 Boutigny-sur-Essonne
☎ 01 69 23 19 10
📋 www.belesbat.com

Domont-Montmorency
Route de Montmorency, 95330 Domont
☎ 01 39 91 07 50

Étiolles Colonial CC (1990)
Vieux Chemin de Paris, 91450 Étiolles
☎ 01 69 89 59 59

✉ golf@etiollescolonial.com
🖥 www.etiollescolonial.com

Fontainebleau   (1909)
Route d'Orleans, 77300 Fontainebleau
☎ 01 64 22 22 95
🖷 01 64 22 63 76
✉ golf.fontainebleau@orange.fr
✍ Christian Mascher (Mgr)
🖥 www.golfdefontainebleau.org

Fontenailles   (1991)
Domaine de Bois Boudran, 77370 Fontenailles
☎ 01 64 60 51 00

Forges-les-Bains   (1989)
Rue du Général Leclerc, 91470 Forges-les-Bains
☎ 01 64 91 48 18
🖷 01 64 91 40 52
✉ golf.forges-les-bains@wanadoo.fr
🖥 www.golf-forgeslesbains.com

Greenparc   (1993)
Route de Villepech, 91280 St Pierre-du-Perray
☎ 01 60 75 40 60

L'Isle Adam   (1995)
1 Chemin des Vanneaux, 95290 L'Isle Adam
☎ 01 34 08 11 11

Marivaux   (1992)
Bois de Marivaux, 91640 Janvry
☎ 01 64 90 85 85
🖷 01 64 90 82 22
✉ contact@golfmarivaux.com
🖥 www.golfmarivaux.com

Meaux-Boutigny   (1985)
Rue de Barrois, 77470 Boutigny
☎ 01 60 25 63 98

Mont Griffon   (1990)
RD 909, 95270 Luzarches
☎ 01 34 68 10 10
✉ golf@golfmontgriffon.com
🖥 www.golfmontgriffon.com

Montereau La Forteresse   (1989)
Domaine de la Forteresse, 77940 Thoury-Ferrottes
☎ (+33) 01 60 96 95 10
🖷 (+33) 01 60 96 01 41
✉ contact@golf-forteresse.com
✍ Aurelie Maloubier
🖥 www.golf-forteresse.com

Ormesson   (1969)
Chemin du Belvedère, 94490 Ormesson-sur-Marne
☎ 01 45 76 20 71

Ozoir-la-Ferrière   (1926)
Château des Agneaux, 77330 Ozoir-la-Ferrière
☎ 01 60 02 60 79

Paris International   (1991)
18 Route du Golf, 95560 Baillet-en-France
☎ 01 34 69 90 00

St Germain-les-Corbeil
6 Ave du Golf, 91250 St Germain-les-Corbeil
☎ 01 60 75 81 54

Seraincourt   (1964)
Gaillonnet-Seraincourt, 95450 Vigny
☎ 01 34 75 47 28

Villarceaux   (1971)
Château du Couvent, 95710 Chaussy
☎ 01 34 67 73 83
🖷 01 34 67 72 66
✉ villarceaux@wanadoo.fr
🖥 www.villarceaux.com

Villeray   (1974)
Public
Melun-Sénart, St Pierre du Perray, 91100 Corbeil
☎ 01 60 75 17 47

Languedoc-Roussillon

Cap d'Agde   (1989)
Public
4 Ave des Alizés, 34300 Cap d'Agde
☎ 04 67 26 54 40
✉ golf@ville-agde.fr
🖥 www.ville-agde.fr

Carcassonne   (1988)
Route de Ste-Hilaire, 11000 Carcassonne
☎ 06 13 20 85 43

Coulondres   (1984)
72 Rue des Erables, 34980 Saint-Gely-du-Fesc
☎ 04 67 84 13 75
🖥 www.coulondres.com

Domaine de Falgos   (1992)
BP 9, 66260 St Laurent-de-Cerdans
☎ 04 68 39 51 42
🖷 04 68 39 52 30
✉ contact@falgos.com
🖥 www.falgos.com

Fontcaude   (1991)
Route de Lodève, Domaine de Fontcaude, 34990 Juvignac
☎ 04 67 45 90 10
🖷 04 67 45 90 20
✉ golf@golfhotelmontpellier.com
🖥 www.golfhotelmontpellier.com

La Grande-Motte   (1987)
Clubhouse du Golf, 34280 La Grande-Motte
☎ 04 67 56 05 00

Montpellier Massane   (1988)
Domaine de Massane, 34670 Baillargues
☎ 04 67 87 87 87

Nîmes Campagne   (1968)
1360 chemin du Mas de Campagne, 30900 Nîmes
☎ 04 66 70 17 37

☎ 04 66 70 03 14
✉ resa@golfnimescampagne.fr
✍ Ruven Estelle
🖥 www.golfnimescampagne.fr

Nîmes-Vacquerolles   (1990)
1075 chemin du golf, 30900 Nîmes
☎ 04 66 23 33 33
🖷 04 66 23 94 94
✉ vacquerolles.opengolfclub @wanadoo.fr
🖥 www.golf-nimes.com

Saint Cyprien Golf Resort   (1976)
Le Mas D'Huston, 66750 St Cyprien Plage
☎ 04 68 37 63 63
🖷 04 68 37 64 64
✉ golf@saintcyprien-golfresort.com
🖥 www.saintcyprien-golfresort.com

St Thomas   (1992)
Route de Bessan, 34500 Béziers
☎ 04 67 39 03 09
✉ info@golfsaintthomas.com
🖥 www.golfsaintthomas.com

Loire Valley

Avrillé   (1988)
Château de la Perrière, 49240 Avrillé
☎ 02 41 69 22 50
🖷 02 41 34 44 60
✉ avrille@bluegreen.com
✍ J Goudard (Dir)
🖥 www.bluegreen.com

Baugé-Pontigné   (1994)
Public
Route de Tours, 49150 Baugé
☎ 02 41 89 01 27
🖷 02 41 89 05 50
✉ golf.bauge@wanadoo.fr
🖥 www.golf-bauge.fr

La Bretesche   (1967)
Domaine de la Bretesche, 44780 Missillac
☎ 02 51 76 86 86

Carquefou   (1991)
Boulevard de l'Epinay, 44470 Carquefou
☎ 02 40 52 73 74

Cholet   (1989)
Allée du Chêne Landry, 49300 Cholet
☎ 02 41 71 05 01

La Domangère
La Roche-sur-Yon, Route de la Rochelle, 85310 Nesmy
☎ 02 51 07 65 90
🖥 www.golf-domangere.com

Fontenelles
Public
Saint-Gilles-Croix-de-Vie, 85220 Aiguillon-sur-Vie
☎ 02 51 54 13 94

Golf D'Anjou (1990)
Route de Cheffes, 49330 Champigné
- ☎ 02 41 42 01 01
- 🖨 02 41 42 04 37
- ✉ accueil@anjougolf.com
- ✍ Sean Adamson
- 🖥 www.anjougolf.com

Ile d'Or (1988)
BP 90410, 49270 La Varenne
- ☎ 02 40 98 58 00
- ✉ nantesiledor@wanadoo.fr

International Barriere-La Baule (1976)
44117 Saint-André-des Eaux
- ☎ 02 40 60 46 18
- 🖨 02 40 60 41 41
- ✉ golfinterlabaule@lucienbarriere.com
- ✍ Nathalie Primas
- 🖥 www.lucienbarriere.com

Laval-Changé (1972)
La Chabossiere, 53000 Changé-les-Laval
- ☎ 02 43 53 16 03
- 🖨 02 43 49 35 15
- ✉ laval53.golf@sfr.fr
- 🖥 www.laval53-golf.com

Le Mansgolfier (1990)
Rue du Golf, 72190 Sargé les Le Mans
- ☎ 02 43 76 25 07
- ✉ lemansgolfier@wanadoo.fr

Le Mans Mulsanne (1961)
Route de Tours, 72230 Mulsanne
- ☎ 02 43 42 00 36

Le Mansgolfier Golf Club (1990)
Rue du Golf, 72190 Sarge les Le Mans
- ☎ 02 43 76 25 07
- 🖨 02 43 76 45 25
- ✉ lemansgolfier@wanadoo.fr
- 🖥 www.lemansgolfier.com

Nantes (1967)
44360 Vigneux de Bretagne
- ☎ 02 40 63 25 82
- ✉ golfclubnantes@aol.com
- 🖥 www.golfclubnantes.com

Nantes Erdre (1990)
Chemin du Bout des Landes, 44300 Nantes
- ☎ 02 40 59 21 21
- 🖨 02 40 94 14 32
- ✉ golf.nanteserdre@nge-nantes.fr
- 🖥 www.nge.fr

Les Olonnes
Gazé, 85340 Olonne-sur-Mer
- ☎ 02 51 33 16 16

Pornic (1912)
49 Boulevard de l'Océan, Sainte-Marie/Mer, 44210 Pornic
- ☎ 02 40 82 06 69

Port Bourgenay (1990)
Avenue de la Mine, Port Bourgenay, 85440 Talmont-St-Hilaire
- ☎ 02 51 23 35 45

Sablé-Solesmes (1991)
Domaine de l'Outinière, Route de Pincé, 72300 Sablé-sur-Sarthe
- ☎ 02 43 95 28 78
- 🖨 02 43 92 39 05
- ✉ golf-sable-solesmes@wanadoo.fr
- ✍ Yves Pironneau
- 🖥 www.golf-sable-solesmes.com

St Jean-de-Monts (1988)
Ave des Pays de la Loire, 85160 Saint Jean-de-Monts
- ☎ 02 51 58 82 73

Savenay (1990)
44260 Savenay
- ☎ 02 40 56 88 05

Normandy

Bellême-St-Martin (1988)
Les Sablons, 61130 Bellême
- ☎ 02 33 73 00 07

Cabourg-Le Home (1907)
38 Av Président Réné Coty, Le Home Varaville, 14390 Cabourg
- ☎ 02 31 91 25 56
- ✉ golf-cabourg-le-home@worldonline.fr

Caen (1990)
Le Vallon, 14112 Bieville-Beuville
- ☎ 02 31 94 72 09

Champ de Bataille (1988)
Château du Champ de Bataille, 27110 Le Neubourg
- ☎ 02 32 35 03 72
- ✉ info@champdebataille.com
- 🖥 www.champdebataille.com

Clécy (1988)
Manoir de Cantelou, 14570 Clécy
- ☎ 02 31 69 72 72
- ✉ golf-de-clecy@golf-de-clecy.com
- 🖥 www.golf-de-clecy.com

Coutainville (1925)
Ave du Golf, 50230 Agon-Coutainville
- ☎ 02 33 47 03 31

Deauville St Gatien (1987)
14130 St Gatien-des-Bois
- ☎ 02 31 65 19 99
- ✉ contact@golfdeauville.com
- 🖥 www.golfdeauville.com

Dieppe-Pourville (1897)
51 Route de Pourville, 76200 Dieppe
- ☎ 02 35 84 25 05
- ✉ golf-de-dieppe@wanadoo.fr
- 🖥 www.golf-dieppe.com

Étretat (1908)
BP No 7, Route du Havre, 76790 Étretat
- ☎ 02 35 27 04 89

Forêt Verte
Bosc Guerard, 76710 Montville
- ☎ 02 35 33 62 94

Golf barrière de Deauville (1929)
14 Saint Arnoult, 14800 Deauville
- ☎ 02 31 14 24 24
- ✉ golfdeauville@lucienbarriere.com
- 🖥 www.lucienbarriere.com

Golf de Jumièges (1991)
Jumièges, 76480 Duclair
- ☎ 02 35 05 32 97
- ✉ jumieges.golf@ucpa.asso.fr

Granville (1912)
Bréville, 50290 Bréhal
- ☎ 02 33 50 23 06
- 🖨 02 33 61 91 87
- ✉ contact@golfdegranville.com
- 🖥 www.golfdegranville.com

Le Havre (1933)
Hameau Saint-Supplix, 76930 Octeville-sur-Mer
- ☎ 02 35 46 36 50
- 🖨 02 35 46 32 66
- ✉ contact@golfduhavre.com
- ✍ Christian Coty (President)
- 🖥 www.golfduhavre.com

Houlgate (1981)
Route de Gonneville, 14510 Houlgate
- ☎ 02 31 24 80 49

Omaha Beach (1986)
Ferme St Sauveur, 14520 Port-en-Bessin
- ☎ 02 31 22 12 12
- 🖨 02 31 22 12 13
- ✉ omaha.beach@wanadoo.fr
- 🖥 www.omahabeachgolfclub.com

Rouen-Mont St Aignan (1911)
Rue Francis Poulenc, 76130 Mont St Aignan
- ☎ 02 35 76 38 65

Golf-hotel St Saëns (1987)
Domaine du Vaudichon, 76680 St Saëns
- ☎ 02 35 34 25 24
- ✉ golf@golfdesaintsaens.com
- 🖥 www.golfdesaintsaens.com

Golf barrière de St Julien (1987)
St Julien-sur-Calonne, 14130 Pont-l'Évêque
- ☎ 02 31 64 30 30
- ✉ golfsaintjulien@lucienbarriere.com
- 🖥 www.lucienbarriere.com

Le Vaudreuil (1962)
27100 Le Vaudreuil
- ☎ 02 32 59 02 60

North East

Ammerschwihr (1990)
Allée du golf, 68770 Ammerschwihr
- ☎ +33 3 89 47 17 30
- 🖨 +33 3 89 47 17 77
- ✉ golf-mail@golf-ammerschwihr.com
- 🖥 www.golf-ammerschwihr.com

Bâle G&CC   (1926)
Rue de Wentzwiller, 68220 Hagenthal-le-Bas
- ☎ +33 (0)3 89 68 50 91
- ⌨ +33 (0)3 89 68 55 66
- ✉ info@gccbasel.ch
- 🖥 www.gccbasel.ch

Besançon   (1968)
La Chevillote, 25620 Mamirolle
- ☎ 03 81 55 73 54
- 🖥 www.golfbesancon.com

Bitche   (1988)
Rue des Prés, 57230 Bitche
- ☎ 03 87 96 15 30

Château de Bournel   (1990)
25680 Cubry
- ☎ 03 81 86 00 10
- ✉ info@bournel.com
- 🖥 www.bournel.com

Combles-en-Barrois   (1948)
14 Rue Basse, 55000 Combles-en-Barrois
- ☎ 03 29 45 16 03

Épinal   (1985)
Public
Rue du Merle-Blanc, 88001 Épinal
- ☎ 03 29 34 65 97

Golf de Faulquemont-Pontpierre   (1993)
Avenue Jean Monnett, 57380 Faulquemont
- ☎ 03 87 81 30 52
- ✉ golf.faulquemont@wanadoo.fr
- 🖥 www.golf-faulquemont.com

Golf Hotel Club de la Forêt d'Orient   (1990)
Route de Geraudot, 10220 Rouilly Sacey
- ☎ 03 25 43 80 80
- ⌨ 03 25 41 57 58
- ✉ contact@hotel-foret-orient.com
- 🖥 www.hotel-foret-orient.com

Gardengolf Metz
3 Rue Félix Savart, 57070 Metz Technopole 2000
- ☎ 03 87 78 71 04
- ✉ contact@gardengolfmetz.com
- 🖥 www.gardengolfmetz.com

Grande Romanie   (1988)
La Grande Romanie, 51460 Courtisols
- ☎ 03 26 66 65 97
- ⌨ 03 26 66 65 97
- ✉ contact@par72.net
- 🖥 wwwpar72.net

La Grange aux Ormes   (1990)
La Grange aux Ormes, 57155 Marly
- ☎ 03 87 63 10 62
- ⌨ 03 87 55 01 77
- ✉ info@grange-aux-ormes.com
- ✍ Pierre Bogenez
- 🖥 www.grange-aux-ormes.com

Kempferhof   (1988)
Golf-Hôtel-Restaurant, 67115 Plobsheim
- ☎ 0033 (0) 3 88 98 72 72
- ⌨ 0033 (0) 3 88 98 74 76
- ✉ info@golf-kempferhof.com
- 🖥 www.golf-kempferhof.com

La Largue G&CC   (1988)
25 Rue du Golf, 68580 Mooslargue
- ☎ 03 89 07 67 67
- ✉ lalargue@golf-lalargue.com
- 🖥 www.golf-lalargue.com

Les Rousses   (1986)
1305 Route du Noirmont, 39220 Les Rousses
- ☎ 03 84 60 06 25

Metz-Cherisey   (1963)
Château de Cherisey, 57420 Cherisey
- ☎ 03 87 52 70 18

Nancy-Aingeray   (1962)
Aingeray, 54460 Liverdun
- ☎ 03 83 24 53 87

Nancy-Pulnoy   (1993)
10 Rue du Golf, 54425 Pulnoy
- ☎ 03 83 18 10 18

Reims-Champagne   (1928)
Château des Dames de France, 51390 Gueux
- ☎ 03 26 05 46 10

Golf du Rhin   (1969)
Ile du Rhin, F-68490 Chalampé
- ☎ +33 3 89 83 28 32
- ⌨ +33 3 89 83 28 42
- ✉ golfdurhin@wanadoo.fr
- ✍ Mr Michel Zimmerlin
- 🖥 www.golfdurhin.com

Rougemont-le-Château   (1990)
Route de Masevaux, 90110 Rougemont-le-Château
- ☎ 03 84 23 74 74
- ⌨ 03 84 23 03 15
- ✉ golf.rougemont@wanadoo.fr
- ✍ Lionel Burnet
- 🖥 www.golf.rougemont.com

Strasbourg   (1934)
Route du Rhin, 67400 Illkirch
- ☎ 03 88 66 17 22
- ⌨ 03 88 65 05 67
- ✉ golf.strasbourg@wanadoo.fr
- 🖥 www.golf-strasbourg.com

Domaine du Val de Sorne   (1989)
Domaine de Val de Sorne, 39570 Vernantois
- ☎ 03 84 43 04 80
- ⌨ 03 84 47 31 21
- ✉ info@valdesorne.com
- 🖥 www.valdesorne.com

La Wantzenau   (1991)
C D 302, 67610 La Wantzenau
- ☎ 03 88 96 37 73

Paris Region

Béthemont-Chisan CC   (1989)
12 Rue du Parc de Béthemont, 78300 Poissy
- ☎ 01 39 75 51 13

La Boulie
La Boulie, 78000 Versailles
- ☎ 01 39 50 59 41

Feucherolles   (1992)
78810 Feucherolles
- ☎ 01 30 54 94 94
- ⌨ 01 30 54 92 37
- ✉ cchateaugolf@aol.com
- 🖥 www.golf-de-feucherolles.com

Fourqueux   (1963)
Rue Saint Nom 36, 78112 Fourqueux
- ☎ 01 34 51 41 47

Golf National   (1990)
2 Avenue du Golf, 78280 Guyancourt
- ☎ 01 30 43 36 00
- ✉ gn@golf-national.com
- 🖥 www.golf-national.com

Isabella   (1969)
RN12, Sainte-Appoline, 78370 Plaisir
- ☎ 01 30 54 10 62
- ✉ info@golfisabella.com
- 🖥 www.golfisabella.com

Joyenval   (1992)
Chemin de la Tuilerie, 78240 Chambourcy
- ☎ 01 39 22 27 50
- ⌨ 01 39 79 12 90
- ✉ joyenval@golfdejoyenval.com
- 🖥 www.joyenval.fr

Rochefort   (1964)
78730 Rochefort-en-Yvelines
- ☎ 01 30 41 31 81

St Cloud   (1911)
60 Rue du 19 Janvier, Garches 92380
- ☎ 01 47 01 01 85

St Germain   (1922)
Route de Poissy, 78100 St Germain-en-Laye
- ☎ 01 39 10 30 30
- ✉ info@golfsaintgermain.org
- 🖥 www.golfsaintgermain.org

St Quentin-en-Yvelines
Public
RD 912, 78190 Trappes
- ☎ 01 30 50 86 40

St Nom-La-Bretêche   (1959)
Hameau Tuilerie-Bignon, 78860 St Nom-La-Bretèche
- ☎ 01 30 80 04 40

La Vaucouleurs (1987)
Rue de l'Eglise, 78910 Civry-la-Forêt
- ☎ 01 34 87 62 29
- 🖥 01 34 87 70 09
- ✉ vaucouleurs@vaucouleurs.fr
- ✍ J Pelard
- 🖥 www.vaucouleurs.fr

Les Yvelines (1989)
Château de la Couharde, 78940 La-Queue-les-Yvelines
- ☎ 01 34 86 48 89
- 🖥 01 34 86 50 31
- ✉ lesyvelines@opengolfclub.com
- 🖥 www.opengolfclub.com

Provence & Côte d'Azur

Aix Marseille (1935)
13290 Les Milles
- ☎ 04 42 24 40 41/04 42 24 23 01
- ✉ golfaixmarseille@aol.com

Barbaroux (1989)
Route de Cabasse, 83170 Brignoles
- ☎ 04 94 69 63 63
- 🖥 04 94 59 00 93
- ✉ contact@barbaroux.com
- 🖥 www.barbaroux.com

Les Baux de Provence (1989)
Domaine de Manville, 13520 Les Baux-de-Provence
- ☎ 04 90 54 40 20
- ✉ golfbauxdeprovence@wanadoo.fr
- 🖥 www.golfbauxdeprovence.com

Beauvallon-Grimaud
Boulevard des Collines, 83120 Sainte-Maxime
- ☎ 04 94 96 16 98

Biot (1930)
La Bastide du Roy, 06410 Biot
- ☎ 04 93 65 08 48

Cannes Mandelieu (1891)
Route de Golf, 06210 Mandelieu
- ☎ 04 92 97 32 00
- 🖥 04 93 49 92 90

Cannes Mandelieu Riviera (1990)
Avenue des Amazones, 06210 Mandelieu
- ☎ 04 92 97 49 49

Cannes Mougins (1923)
175 Avenue du Golf, 06250 Mougins
- ☎ 04 93 75 79 13
- 🖥 04 93 75 27 60
- ✉ golf-cannes-mougins@wanadoo.fr
- ✍ Monsieur Bernard Biard
- 🖥 www.golf-cannes-mougins.com

Châteaublanc
Les Plans, 84310 Morières-les-Avignon
- ☎ 04 90 33 39 08
- ✉ info@golfchateaublanc.com
- 🖥 www.golfchateaublanc.com

Digne-les-Bains (1990)
Public
57 Route du Chaffaut, 0400 Digne-les-Bains
- ☎ 04 92 30 58 00
- 🖥 04 92 30 58 13
- ✉ contact@golfdignelalavande.com
- 🖥 www.golfdignelalavande.com

Estérel Latitudes (1989)
Ave du Golf, 83700 St Raphaël
- ☎ 04 94 52 68 30

Frégate (1992)
Dolce Frégate Provence, RD 559, 83270 St Cyr-sur-Mer
- ☎ 04 94 29 38 00
- 🖥 04 94 29 96 94
- ✉ golf-fregate@dolce.com
- 🖥 www.golfdolcefregate.com

Gap-Bayard (1988)
Centre d'Oxygénation, 05000 Gap
- ☎ 04 92 50 16 83
- 🖥 04 92 50 17 05
- ✉ gap-bayard@wanadoo.fr
- ✍ Rostaing
- 🖥 www.gap-bayard.com

Golf Claux-Amic (1992)
1 Route des Trois Ponts, 06130 Grasse
- ☎ 04 93 60 55 44
- ✉ info@claux-amic.com
- 🖥 www.chateau-taulane.com

Golf de Roquebrune (1989)
Golf de Roquebrune, CD7, 83520 Roquebrune-sur-Argens
- ☎ 04 94 19 60 35
- ✉ contact@golfderoquebrune.com
- ✍ Mathieu Sevestre (Mgr)
- 🖥 www.golfderoquebrune.com

Grand Avignon (1989)
Les Chênes Verts, 84270 Vedene - Avignon
- ☎ 04 90 31 49 94
- 🖥 04 90 31 01 21
- ✉ info@golfgrandavignon.com
- 🖥 www.golfgrandavignon.com

La Grande Bastide (1990)
Chemin des Picholines 761, 06740 Châteauneuf de Grasse
- ☎ 04 93 77 70 08
- 🖥 04 93 77 72 36
- ✉ grandebastide@opengolfclub.com
- ✍ Alexis Davet (Mgr)
- 🖥 www.opengolfclub.com

Luberon (1986)
La Grande Gardette, 04860 Pierrevert
- ☎ 04 92 72 17 19
- 🖥 04 92 72 59 12
- ✉ info@golf-du-luberon.com
- ✍ Philippe Berrut
- 🖥 www.golf-du-luberon.com

Marseille La Salette (1988)
65 Impasse des Vaudrans, 13011 La Valentine Marseille
- ☎ 04 91 27 12 16
- ☎ 04 91 27 21 33
- ✉ lasalette@opengolfclub.com
- 🖥 www.opengolfclub.com

Miramas (1993)
Mas de Combe, 13140 Miramas
- ☎ 04 90 58 56 55

Monte Carlo (1910)
Route du Mont-Agel, 06320 La Turbie
- ☎ 04 92 41 50 70
- 🖥 04 93 41 09 55
- ✉ monte-carlo-golf-club@wanadoo.fr

Opio-Valbonne (1966)
Route de Roquefort-les-Pins, 06650 Opio
- ☎ 04 93 12 00 08
- 🖥 www.opengolfclub.com

Pont Royal (1992)
Pont Royal, 13370 Mallemort
- ☎ 04 90 57 40 79

Royal Mougins (1993)
424 Avenue du Roi, 06250 Mougins
- ☎ 04 92 92 49 69 (reception)
- ✉ contact@royalmougins.fr
- 🖥 www.royalmougins.fr

Saint Donat G&CC (1993)
270 Route de Cannes, 06130 Grasse
- ☎ +33 493 097660
- 🖥 +33 493 097663
- ✉ info@golfsaintdonat.com
- ✍ Gaelle Secretary
- 🖥 www.golfsaintdonat.com

Les Domaines de Saint Endréol Golf & Spa Resort (1992)
Route de Bagnols-en-Fôret, 83 920 La Motte-en-Provence
- ☎ 04 94 51 89 89
- 🖥 04 94 51 89 90
- ✉ accueil.golf@st-endreol.com
- 🖥 www.st-endreol.com

Sainte Victoire (1985)
Domaine de Château L'Arc, 13710 Fuveau
- ☎ 0442 298343
- 🖥 0442 534268
- ✉ saintevictoiregolfclub@wanadoo.fr
- 🖥 www.saintevictoiregolfclub.com

La Sainte-Baume (1988)
Golf Hotel, Domaine de Châteauneuf, 83860 Nans-les-Pins
- ☎ 04 94 78 60 12
- 🖥 04 94 78 63 52
- ✉ saintebaume@opengolfclub.com
- ✍ Marie-Pierre Picard
- 🖥 www.opengolfclub.com

Sainte-Maxime
Route de Débarquement, 83120 Sainte-Maxime
- ☎ 04 94 55 02 02

Servanes (1989)
Domaine de Servanes, 13890 Mouriès
- ☎ 04 90 47 59 95

✉ servanes@opengolfclub.com
🖥 www.opengolfclub.com

Taulane
Domaine du Château de Taulane, RN 85, 83840 La Martre
☎ 04 93 60 31 30
✉ resagolf@chateau-taulane.com
🖥 www.chateau-de-taulane.com

Valcros   (1964)
Domaine de Valcros, 83250 La Londe-les-Maures
☎ 04 94 66 81 02
📠 04 94 66 90 48
✉ golfdevalcros@wanadoo.fr

Valescure   (1895)
BP 451, 83704 St-Raphaël Cedex
☎ 04 94 82 40 46

Rhone-Alps

Aix-les-Bains   (1904)
Avenue du Golf, 73100 Aix-les-Bains
☎ 04 79 61 23 35
📠 04 79 34 06 01
✉ info@golf-aixlesbains.com
✍ Gerard Bourge
🖥 www.golf-aixlesbains.com

Albon   (1989)
Domaine de Senaud, Albon, 26140 St Rambert d'Albon
☎ 04 75 03 03 90
✉ golf.albon@wanadoo.fr
🖥 www.golf-albon.com

Annecy   (1953)
Echarvines, 74290 Talloires
☎ (0033)4 50 60 12 89
📠 (0033)4 50 60 08 80
✉ accueil@golf-lacannecy.com
✍ Emmanuelle Kipper (Mgr)
🖥 www.golf-lacannecy.com

Annonay-Gourdan   (1988)
Domaine de Gourdan, 07430 Saint Clair
☎ 04 75 67 03 84

Les Arcs
B P 18, 73706 Les Arcs Cedex
☎ 04 79 07 43 95

Bossey G&CC   (1985)
Château de Crevin, 74160 Bossey
☎ 04 50 43 95 50
✉ accueilgolf@golfbossey.com
🖥 www.golfbossey.com

La Bresse
Domaine de Mary, 01400 Condessiat
☎ 04 74 51 42 09

Chamonix   (1934)
35 Route du Golf, 74400 Chamonix
☎ +33 4 50 53 06 28
📠 +33 4 50 53 38 69
✉ info@golfdechamonix.com
🖥 www.golfdechamonix.com

Le Clou   (1985)
01330 Villars-les-Dombes
☎ 04 74 98 19 65
✉ golfduclou.fr@freesbee.fr
🖥 www.golfduclou.fr

Divonne   (1931)
Ave des Thermes, 01220 Divonne-les-Bains
☎ 04 50 40 34 11
📠 04 50 40 34 25
✉ golf@domaine-de-divonne.com
🖥 www.domaine-de-divonne.com

Esery   (1990)
Esery, 74930 Reignier
☎ 00334 50 36 58 70
📠 00334 50 36 57 62
✉ info@golf-club-esery.com
✍ Emmanuel Ballongue
🖥 www.golf-club-esery.com

Evian Masters   (1904)
Rive Sud du lac de Genève, 74500 Évian
☎ 04 50 26 85 00
📠 04 50 75 65 54
✉ golf@evianroyalresort.com
🖥 www.evianroyalresort.com

Giez   (1991)
Lac d'Annecy, 74210 Giez
☎ 04 50 44 48 41
📠 04 50 32 55 93
✉ as.golfdegiez@wanadoo.fr
🖥 www.golfdegiez.fr

Le Gouverneur
Château du Breuil, 01390 Monthieux
☎ 04 72 26 40 34
✉ golfgouverneur@worldonline.fr
🖥 www.golfgouverneur.fr

Grenoble-Bresson   (1990)
Route de Montavie, 38320 Eybens
☎ 04 76 73 65 00

Grenoble-Charmeil
(1988)
38210 St Quentin-sur-Isère
☎ 04 76 93 67 28
✉ info@golfhotelgrenoble.com
🖥 www.golfhotelgrenoble.com

Grenoble-Uriage   (1921)
Les Alberges, 38410 Uriage
☎ 04 76 89 03 47
✉ golfuriage@wanadoo.fr
🖥 www.golfuriage.com

Golf Club de Lyon   (1921)
38280 Villette-d'Anthon
☎ 04 78 31 11 33
📠 04 72 02 48 27
✉ info@golfclubdelyon.com
✍ F Barba
🖥 www.golfclubdelyon.com

Lyon-Verger   (1977)
69360 Saint-Symphorien D'Ozon
☎ 04 78 02 84 20

Maison Blanche G&CC
(1991)
01170 Echenevex
☎ 04 50 42 44 42

Méribel   (1966)
BP 54, 73550 Méribel
☎ 04 79 00 52 67
✉ info@golf-meribel.com
🖥 www.golf-meribel.com

Mionnay La Dombes
(1986)
Chemin de Beau-Logis, 01390 Mionnay
☎ 04 78 91 84 84

Mont-d'Arbois   (1964)
74120 Megève
☎ 04 50 21 29 79

Pierre Carée   (1984)
74300 Flaine
☎ 04 50 90 85 44

St Etienne   (1989)
62 Rue St Simon, 42000 St Etienne
☎ 04 77 32 14 63

Salvagny   (1987)
100 Rue des Granges, 69890 La Tour de Salvagny
☎ 04 78 48 83 60
✉ accueil@golf-salvagny.com
🖥 www.golf-salvagny.com

La Sorelle   (1991)
Domaine de Gravagnieux, 01320 Villette-sur-Ain
☎ 04 74 35 47 27

Tignes   (1968)
Val Claret, 73320 Tignes
☎ 04 79 06 37 42 (Summer)
📠 04 79 00 53 17
✉ golf.tignes@compagniedesalpes.fr
✍ Fred Scuiller (Mgr)
🖥 www.tignes.net

Valdaine   (1989)
Domaine de la Valdaine, Montboucher/Jabron, 26740 Montelimar-Montboucher
☎ 04 75 00 71 33
🖥 www.domainedelavaldaine.com

Valence St Didier   (1983)
26300 St Didier de Charpey
☎ 04 75 59 67 01

Toulouse & Pyrenees

Albi Lasbordes   (1989)
Château de Lasbordes, 81000 Albi
☎ 05 63 54 98 07
📠 05 63 54 98 06
✉ contact@golfalbi.com
🖥 www.golfalbi.com

Ariège (1986)
Unjat, 09240 La Bastide-de-Serou
☎ 05 61 64 56 78

Auch Embats (1970)
Route de Montesquiou, 32000 Auch
☎ 05 62 61 10 11/06 81 18 41
43
📠 05 62 611057
🖳 www.golf-auch-embats.com

**Golf County Club de
Bigorre** (1992)
65200 Pouzac, Bagnères de Bigorre
☎ (33) (0) 5 62 91 06 20
📠 (33) (0) 5 62 91 38 00
✉ contact@golf-bigorre.fr
🖳 www.golf-bigorre.fr

Étangs de Fiac (1987)
Brazis, 81500 Fiac
☎ 05 63 70 64 70
✉ golf.fiac-sw@wanadoo.fr
🖳 www.etangsdefiac.com

Florentin-Gaillac (1990)
Le Bosc, Florentin, 81150 Marssac-sur-Tarn
☎ 05 63 55 20 50

Golf de tarbes (1987)
1 Rue du Bois, 65310 Laloubère
☎ 05 62 45 14 50
✉ golf.des.tumulus@wanadoo.fr
🖳 www.perso.wanadoo.fr/tumulus

Guinlet (1986)
32800 Eauze
☎ 05 62 09 80 84
🖳 www.guinlet.fr

Lannemezan (1962)
*250 Rue uu Dr Vererschlag, 65300
Lannemezan*
☎ 0562 98 01 01
📠 0562 98 52 32
✉ golflannemezan@wanadoo.fr
✍ Valerie Lasserre (Assistant Mgr)
🖳 www.golflannemezan.com

Lourdes (1988)
Chemin du Lac, 65100 Lourdes
☎ 05 62 42 02 06
📠 05 62 42 02 06
✉ golf.lourdes@wanadoo.fr

Mazamet-La Barouge
(1956)
81660 Pont de l'Arn
☎ 05 63 61 08 00/05 63 67 06
72
✉ golf.labarouge@wanadoo.fr
🖳 www.golf-mazamet.net

Toulouse (1951)
31320 Vieille-Toulouse
☎ 05 61 73 45 48

Toulouse-Palmola (1974)
Route d'Albi, 31660 Buzet-sur-Tarn
☎ 05 61 84 20 50
✉ golf.palmola@wanadoo.fr

Toulouse-Teoula (1991)
*71 Avenue des Landes, 31830 Plaisance du
Touch*
☎ 05 61 91 98 80
📠 05 61 91 49 66
✉ contact@golftoulouseteoula.com
🖳 www.golftoulouseteoula.com

Germany

Berlin & East

Balmer See (1995)
Drewinscher Weg 1, 17429 Benz/Otbalm
☎ (038379) 28199
📠 (038379) 28200
✉ info@golfhotel-usedom.de
🖳 www.golfhotel-usedom.de

**Golf- und Land-Club
Berlin-Wannsee e.V.** (1895)
Golfweg 22, 14109 Berlin
☎ (030) 806 7060
📠 (030) 806 706-10
✉ info@wannsee.de
🖳 www.wannsee.de

**Berliner G&CC Motzener
See** (1991)
*Am Golfplatz 5, 15749 Mittenwalde OT
Motzen*
☎ (033769) 50130
✉ info@golfclubmotzen.de
🖳 www.golfclubmotzen.de

GC Dresden Elbflorenz
(1992)
*Ferdinand von Schillstr 4a, 01728
Possendorf*
☎ (035206) 2430
📠 (035206) 24317
✉ info@golfclub-dresden.de
✍ Alfred Hagh
🖳 www.golfclub-dresden.de

Potsdamer GC (1990)
*Zachower Strasse, 14669 Ketzin OT
Tremmen*
☎ (033233) 7050
📠 (033233) 70519
✉
clubsekretariat@potsdamergolfclub
.de
🖳 www.pgc.de

Schloss Meisdorf (1996)
Petersberger Trift 33, 06463 Meisdorf
☎ (034743) 98450

**Golfclub Schloss
Wilkendorf** (1991)
*Am Weiher 1, 15345 Altlandsberg-
Wilkendorf*
☎ (0049) 3341 330960
📠 (0049) 3341 330961
✉ service@golfclub-schloss-
wilkendorf.de

🖳 www.golfclub-schloss-
wilkendorf.de

**Golf-und Country Club
Seddiner See** (1994)
Zum Weiher 44, 14552 Michendorf
☎ (033205) 7320
📠 (036) 308140
✉ info@gccseddinersee.de
✍ Mr Horst Schubert (Mgr)
🖳 www.gccseddinersee.de

Seddiner See (1993)
Zum Weiher 44, 14552 Wildenbruch
☎ (033205) 7320
📠 (033205) 73229
✉ info@gccseddiner-see.de
🖳 www.gccseddiner-see.de

Golfresort Semlin am See
(1992)
Ferchesarerstrasse 8b, 14712 Semlin
☎ (03385) 554410
📠 (03385) 554400
✉ golf@golfresort-semlin.de
🖳 www.golfresort-semlin.de

**Sporting Club Berlin
Schwantzelsee e.V** (1992)
Parkallee 3, 15526 Bad Sarrow
☎ (033631) 63300
📠 (033631) 63310
✉ info@sporting-club-berlin.de
🖳 www.sporting-club-berlin.com

Bremen & North West

Bremer Schweiz e.v. (1991)
Wölpscherstr 4, 28779 Bremen
☎ (0421) 609 5331
📠 (0421) 609 5333
✉ info@golfclub-bremerschweiz.de
🖳 www.golfclub-bremerschweiz.de

Herzogstadt Celle (1985)
Beukenbusch 1, D 29229 Celle
☎ (05086) 395
📠 (05086) 8288
✉ golfclub-celle@t-online.de
✍ Godlind Reif/Michael Olville
⊕ English Speaking
🖳 www.golf-celle.de

Küsten GC Hohe Klint
(1978)
Hohe Klint, 27478 Cuxhaven
☎ (04723) 2737
🖳 www.golf-cuxhaven.de

Münster-Wilkinghege (1963)
Steinfurter Str 448, 48159 Münster
☎ (0251) 214090
📠 (0251) 214 0940
✉ kontakt@golfclub-wilkinghege.de
🖳 www.golfclub-wilkinghege.de

Oldenburgischer (1964)
Wemkenstr. 13, 26180 Rastede
☎ (04402) 7240

📟 (04402) 70417
🖂 info@oldenburgischer-golfclub.de
🖳 www.oldenburgischer-golfclub.de

Ostfriesland (1980)
Fliederstrasse 5, 26639 Wiesmoor
☎ **(04944) 6440**
📟 (04944) 6441
🖂 golf@golfclubostfriesland.de
✍ Stephan Hueller
🖳 www.golfclub-ostfriesland.de

Soltau (1982)
Hof Loh, 29614 Soltau
☎ **(05191) 967 63 33**
📟 (05191) 967 63 34
🖂 info@golf-soltau.de
✍ Bernd Ingendahl
🖳 www.golf-soltau.de

Syke (1989)
Schultenweg 1, 28857 Syke-Okel
☎ **(04242) 8230**

Tietlingen (1979)
29683 Fallingbostel
☎ **(05162) 3889**
🖂 info@golfclub-tietlingen.de
🖳 www.golfclub-tietlingen.de

Verden (1988)
Holtumer Str 24, 27283 Verden
☎ **(04230) 1470**

Worpswede (1974)
Giehlermühlen, 27729 Vollersode
☎ **(04763) 7313**

Club Zur Vahr (1905)
Bgm-Spitta-Allee 34, 28329 Bremen
☎ **Bremen (0421) 204480**
🖂 info@club-zur-vahr-bremen.de
🖳 www.club-zur-vahr-bremen.de

Central North

Dillenburg
Auf dem Altscheid, 35687 Dillenburg
☎ **(02771) 5001**
📟 (02771) 5002
🖂 info@gc-dillenburg.de
🖳 www.gc-dillenburg.de

Fulda Rhoen (1971)
Am Golfplatz, 36145 Hofbieber
☎ **(06657) 1334**
📟 (06657) 914809
🖂 info@golfclub-fulda.de
✍ Nick Staples
🖳 www.golfclub-fulda.de

Hofgut Praforst (1992)
Dr-Detlev-Rudelsdorff-Allee 3, 36088 Hünfeld
☎ **(06652) 9970**
🖂 info@praforst.de
🖳 www.praforst.de

Kassel-Wilhelmshöhe
(1958)
Ehlenerstr 21, 34131 Kassel
☎ **(0561) 33509**
📟 (0561) 37729
🖂 mail@golfclub-kassel.de
🖳 www.golfclub-kassel.de

Kurhessischer GC Oberaula
(1987)
Am Golfplatz, 36278 Oberaula
☎ **(06628) 91540**
🖂 info@golfclub-oberaula.de
🖳 www.golf-oberaula.de

Licher Golf Club (1992)
35423 Lich, Golfplatz Kolnhausen
☎ **(06404) 91071**
📟 (06404) 91072
🖂 info@licher-golf-club.de
🖳 www.licher-golf-club.de

Schloss Braunfels (1970)
Homburger Hof, 35619 Braunfels
☎ **(06442) 4530**
📟 (06442) 6683
🖂 info@golfclub-braunfels.de
✍ Gregor Sommer
🖳 www.golfclub-braunfels.de

Schloss Sickendorf (1990)
Schloss Sickendorf, 36341 Lauterbach
☎ **(06641) 96130**
🖂 info@gc-lauterbach.de
🖳 www.gc-lauterbach.de

Winnerod (1999)
Parkstr 22, 35447 Reiskirchen
☎ **(06408) 9513-0**
📟 (06408) 9513-13
🖂 info@golfpark.de
✍ Michael Sonnenstatter (Mgr)
🖳 www.golfpark.de

Zierenberg Gut Escheberg
(1995)
Gut Escheberg, 34289 Zierenberg
☎ **(05606) 2608**
🖳 www.golfclub-escheberg.de

Central South

Bad Kissingen (1910)
Euerdorferstr 11, 97688 Bad Kissingen
☎ **(0971) 3608**

Bad Vilbeler Golfclub Lindenhof e.V. (1994)
61118 Bad Vilbel-Dortelweil
☎ **+49 (0)6101 5245200**
📟 +49 (0)6101 5245202
🖂 info@bvgc.de
🖳 www.bvgc.de

Golfclub Eschenrod e.V.
(1996)
Postfach 1227, Lindenstr. 46, 63679 Schotten
☎ **(06044) 8401**

📟 (06044) 951159
🖂 br.golf@t-online.de
🖳 www.eschenrod.de

Frankfurter Golf Club
(1913)
Golfstrasse 41, 60528 Frankfurt/Main
☎ **(069) 666 2318 0**
📟 (069) 666 2318 20
🖂 info@fgc.de
✍ Mrs Sanja Bradley
🖳 www.fgc.de

Hanau-Wilhelmsbad (1958)
Franz-Ludwig-von-Cancrin-Weg 1a, 63454 Hanau
☎ **(06181) 1 80 19 0**
📟 (06181) 1 80 19 10

Hof Trages
Hofgut Trages, 63579 Freigericht
☎ **(06055) 91380**
🖳 www.hoftrages.de

Homburger (1899)
Saalburgchaussee 2, 61350 Bad Homburg
☎ **(06172) 306808**

Idstein (2001)
Am Nassen Berg, 65510 Idstein
☎ **(06126) 9322-13**
🖳 www.golfpark-idstein.de

Idstein-Wörsdorf (1989)
Gut Henriettenthal, 65510 Idstein
☎ **(06126) 9322-0**
🖳 www.golfpark-idstein.de

Kitzingen (1980)
Zufahrt über Steigweg, 97318 Kitzingen
☎ **(09321) 4956**
📟 (09321) 21936
🖂 golfkitzingen@aol.com
🖳 www.golfclub-kitzingen.de

Kronberg G&LC (1954)
Schloss Friedrichshof, Hainstr 25, 61476 Kronberg/Taunus
☎ **(06173) 1426**
📟 (06173) 5953
🖳 www.gc-kronberg.de

Main-Spessart (1990)
Postfach 1204, 97821 Marktheidenfeld-Eichenfürst
☎ **(09391) 8435**
🖂 info@main-spessart-golf.de
🖳 www.main-spessart-golf.de

Main-Taunus (1979)
Lange Seegewann 2, 65205 Wiesbaden
☎ **(06122) 588680 (Sec)**
📟 (06122) 936099
🖂 clubinfo@golf-club-maintaunus.de
✍ Markus Erdmann
🖳 www.golfclub-maintaunus.de

Mannheim-Viernheim
(1930)
Alte Mannheimer Str 3, 68519 Viernheim
☎ **(06204) 6070-0**

□ (06204) 607044
✉ info@gcmv.de
🖳 www.gcmv.de

Maria Bildhausen (1992)
Rindhof 1, 97702 Münnerstadt
☎ (09766) 1601
□ (09766) 1602
✉ info@maria-bildhausen.de
🖳 www.maria-bildhausen.de

Neuhof
Hofgut Neuhof, 63303 Dreieich
☎ (06102) 327927/327010
□ (06102) 327012
✉ info@golfclubneuhof.de
🖳 www.golfclubneuhof.de

Rhein Main (1977)
Steubenstrasse 9, 65189 Wiesbaden
☎ (0611) 373014

Rheinblick
Weisser Weg, 65201 Wiesbaden-Frauenstein
☎ (0611) 420675

Rheintal (1971)
An der Bundesstrr 291, 68723 Oftersheim
☎ (06202) 56390

St. Leon-Rot Betriebsgesellschaft mbH & Co.KG (1996)
Opelstrasse 30, 68789 St. Leon-Rot
☎ +49 62 27 86 08- 0
□ +49 62 27 86 08-88
✉ info@gc-slr.de
🖳 www.gc-slr.de

Spessart (1972)
Golfplatz Alsberg, 63628 Bad Soden-Salmünster
☎ (06056) 91580
□ (06056) 915820
🖳 www.gc-spessart.com

Taunus Weilrod (1979)
Merzhäuser Strasse, 61276 Weilrod-Altweilnau
☎ (06083) 95050
✉ golfclub-taunus-weilrod.de
🖳 www.golfclub@taunus-weilrod.de

Wiesbadener Golf Club e.v. (1893)
Chausseehaus 17, 65199 Wiesbaden
☎ (0611) 460238
□ (0611) 463251
✉ info@wiesbadener-golfclub.de
🖳 www.wiesbadener-golfclub.de

Golf- und Landclub Wiesloch (1983)
Hohenhardter Hof, 69168 Wiesloch-Baiertal
☎ (06222) 78811-0
□ (06222) 78811-11
✉ info@golfclub-wiesloch.de
🖳 www.golfclub-wiesloch.de

Hamburg & North

Altenhof (1971)
Eckernförde, 24340 Altenhof
☎ (04351) 41227

An der Pinnau e.V. (1982)
Pinneberger strasse 81a, 25451 Quickborn-Renzel
☎ (04106) 81800
□ (04106) 82003
✉ info@pinnau.de
✍ Christoph Lampe
🖳 www.pinnau.de

Behinderten Golf Club Deutschland e.V. (1994)
Hauptstrausse 3 c, 37434 Bodensee
☎ +49 (0) 55079799108
□ +49 (0) 5507 979144
✉ rollydrive@aol.com
🖳 www.bgc-golf.de

Brodauer Mühle (1986)
Baumallee 14, 23730 Gut Beusloe
☎ (04561) 8140
✉ gc-brodauermuehle@t-online.de
🖳 www.gc-brodauermuehle.de

Buchholz-Nordheide (1982)
An der Rehm 25, 21244 Bucholz
☎ (04181) 36200
□ (04181) 97294
✉ gc-buchholz@t-online.de
🖳 www.golfclub-buchholz.de

Buxtehude (1982)
Zum Lehmfeld 1, 21614 Buxtehude
☎ (04161) 81333
✉ post@golfclubbuxtehude.de
🖳 www.golfclubbuxtehude.de

Deinster Mühle (1994)
Im Mühlenfeld 30, 21717 Deinste
☎ (04149) 925112
✉ golfpark@allesistgdn.de
🖳 www.allesistgdn.de

Föhr (1925)
25938 Nieblum
☎ (04681) 580455
□ (04681) 580456
✉ info@golfclubfohr.de
🖳 www.golfclubfohr.de

Gut Apeldör (1996)
Apeldör 2, 25779 Hennstedt
☎ (04836) 9960-0
□ (04836) 9960-33
✉ info@apeldoer.de
✍ Karsten Voss
🖳 www.apeldoer.de

Gut Grambek (1981)
Schlosstr 21, 23883 Grambek
☎ (04542) 841474
□ (04542) 841476
✉ info@gcgrambek.de
🖳 www.gcgrambek.de

Gut Kaden (1984)
Kadenerstrasse 9, 25486 Alveslohe
☎ (04193) 9929-0

Gut Uhlenhorst (1989)
24229 Daenischenhagen, Mühlenstrasse 37
☎ (04349) 91700
□ (04349) 919400
✉ E-mail:golf@gut-uhlenhorst.de
🖳 www.gut-uhlenhorst.de

Gut Waldhof (1969)
Am Waldhof, 24629 Kisdorferwohld
☎ (04194) 99740
🖳 www.gut-waldhof.de

Gut Waldshagen (1996)
24306 Gut Waldshagen
☎ (04522) 766766
□ (04522) 766767
✉ info@gut-golf.de
🖳 www.gut-golf.de

Hamburger Golf-Club Falkenstein (1906)
In de Bargen 59, 22587 Hamburg
☎ (040) 812177
□ (040) 817315
✉ info@golfclub-falkenstein.de
✍ Berthold Apel
🖳 www.golfclub-falkenstein.de

Hamburg Ahrensburg (1964)
Am Haidschlag 39-45, 22926 Ahrensburg
☎ (04102) 51309

Hamburg Hittfeld (1957)
Am Golfplatz 24, 21218 Seevetal
☎ (04105) 2331

Hamburg Holm (1993)
Haverkamp 1, 25488 Holm
☎ (04103) 91330
□ (04103) 913313
✉ info@hchh.de
🖳 www.gchh.de

Hamburg Walddörfer (1960)
Schevenbarg, 22949 Ammersbek
☎ (040) 605 1337
□ (040) 605 4879
✉ info@gchw.de
🖳 www.gchw.de

Golfclub Hohen Wieschendorf e.V. (1992)
Am Golfplatz 1, 23968 Hohen Wieschendorf
☎ (0049) 384 28660
□ (0049) 384 286666
✉ info@howido.de
🖳 www.howido.de

Hoisdorf (1977)
Hof Bornbek/Hoisdorf, 22952 Lütjensee
☎ (04107) 7831
□ (04107) 9934
✉ info@gc-hoisdorf.com
🖳 www.gc-hoisdorf.com

Jersbek   (1986)
*GolfClub Jersbek e.V., Oberteicher Weg,
22941 Jersbek*
☎ **(04532) 20950**
📠 (04532) 24779
📧 mail@golfclub-jersbek.de
🖥 www.golfclub-jersbek.de

Kieler GC Havighorst
(1988)
Havighorster Weg 20, 24211 Havighorst
☎ **(04302) 965980**
📧 golfclub.havighorst@t-online.de

**Lübeck-Travemünder Golf
Klub e.V**   (1921)
*Kowitzberg 41, 23570 Lübeck-
Travemünde*
☎ **(04502) 74018**
📠 (04502) 72184
📧 info@ltgk.de
🖥 www.ltgk.de

**Mittelholsteinischer
Aukrug**   (1969)
Zum Glasberg 9, 24613 Aukrug-Bargfeld
☎ **(04873) 595**

Peiner Hof
Peiner Hag, 25497 Prisdorf
☎ **(04101) 73790**
🖥 www.peinerhof.de

Am Sachsenwald   (1985)
Am Riesenbett, 21521 Dassendorf
☎ **(04104) 6120**
📧 gc-sachsenwald@t-online.de
🖥 www.gc-sachsenwald.de

**Golf Club Schloss
Breitenburg e.v**
25524 Breitenburg
☎ **(04828) 8188**
📠 (04828) 8100
📧 golfclubschlossbreitenburg@t-
online.de
🖉 Elke Gräfin zu Rantzau
🖥 www.golfclubschlossbreitenberg.de

Schloss Lüdersburg
(1985)
*Lüdersburger Strasse 21, 21379
Lüdersburg*
☎ **(04139) 6970-0**
📧 info@luedersburg.de
🖥 www.luedersburg.de

St Dionys   (1972)
Widukindweg, 21357 St Dionys
☎ **(04133) 213311**
📠 (04133) 213313
📧 info@golfclub-st-dionys.de
🖥 www.golfclub-st-dionys.de

GC Sylt e.V.   (1982)
Norderrung 5, 25996 Wenningstedt
☎ **(04651) 99598-0**
📧 golfclubsylt@t-online.de
🖥 www.golfclubsylt.de

**Golfanlage Seeschlösschen
Timmendorfer Strand**
(1973)
*Am Golfplatz 3, 23669 Timmendorfer
Strand*
☎ **(04503) 704400**
📠 (04503) 704400-14
📧 info@gc-timmendorf.de
🖉 Mrs Birgit Krause (Club Mgr)
🖥 www.gc-timmendorf.de

G&CC Treudelberg   (1990)
Lemsahler Landstr 45, 22397 Hamburg
☎ **(040) 608 228877**
📠 (040) 608 228879
📧 golf@treudelberg.com
🖥 www.treudelberg.com

**Wentorf-Reinbeker Golf-
Club e.V.**   (1901)
Golfstrasse 2, 21465 Wentorf
☎ **(040) 72 97 80 68**
📠 (040) 72 97 80 67
📧 sekretariat@wrgc.de
🖥 www.wrgc.de

Hanover &
Weserbergland

Bad Salzuflen G&LC   (1956)
Schwaghof 4, 32108 Bad Salzuflen
☎ **(05222) 10773**

**British Army Golf Club
(Sennelager)**   (1963)
Bad Lippspringe, BFPO 16
☎ **(05252) 53794**
📠 (05252) 53811
📧 manager@sennelagergolfclub.de
🖥 www.sennelagergolfclub.de

Burgdorf   (1969)
Waldstr 27, 31303 Burgdorf-Ehlershausen
☎ **(05085) 7628**
📠 (05085) 6617
📧 info@burgdorfergolfclub.de
🖥 www.burgdorfergolfclub.de

Gifhorn   (1982)
Wilscher Weg 69, 38518 Gifhorn
☎ **(05371) 16737**

Gütersloh Garrison   (1963)
Princess Royal Barracks, BFPO 47
☎ **(05241) 236938**
📧 timothyholt14@hotmail.com

Hamelner Golfclub e.V.
(1985)
Schwöbber 8, 31855 Aerzen
☎ **(05154) 987 0**
📧 info@hamelner-golfclub.de
🖥 www.hamelner-golfclub.de

Hannover   (1923)
Am Blauen See 120, 30823 Garbsen
☎ **(05137) 73068**
📠 (05137) 75851

📧 info@golfclub-hannover.de
🖥 www.golfclub-hannover.de

Hardenberg   (1969)
Gut Levershausen, 37154 Northeim
☎ **(05551) 908380**
📠 (05551) 9083820
📧 info@gchardenberg.de
🖥 www.gchardenberg.de

Isernhagen   (1983)
Auf Gut Lohne 22, 30916 Isernhagen
☎ **(05139) 893185**
🖥 www.golfclub-isernhagen.de

GC Langenhagen e.v.   (1989)
Hainhaus 22, D-30855 Langenhagen
☎ **(0511) 736832**
📠 (0511) 726 1990
📧 golfclub-langenhagen@t-online.de
🖥 www.golfclub-langenhagen.de

Lippischer Golfclub e.V.
(1980)
Huxoll 14, 32825 Blomberg-Cappel
☎ **(05236) 459**
📠 (05236) 8102
📧 sekretariat@lippischergolfclub.de
🖥 www.lippischergolfclub.de

Marienfeld   (1986)
Remse 27, 33428 Marienfeld
☎ **(05247) 8880**
📠 (05247) 80386
📧 info@gc-marienfeld.de
🖉 John Pollitt (Mgr)
🖥 www.gc-marienfeld.de

Paderborner Land   (1983)
Wilseder Weg 25, 33102 Paderborn
☎ **(05251) 4377**

Ravensberger Land
Sudstrasse 96, 32130 Enger-Pödinghausen
☎ **(09224) 79751**
📠 (09224) 699446
📧 golfclub-ravensberger-land
@teleos-web.de
🖥 www.golfclub-ravensberger-land.de

Senne GC Gut Welschof
(1992)
*Augustdorferstr 72, 33758 Schloss Holte-
Stukenbrock*
☎ **(05207) 920936**
📧 info@senne_golfclub.de
🖥 www.senne_golfclub.de

Sieben-Berge Rheden
(1965)
Schloss Str 1a, 31039 Rheden
☎ **(05182) 52336**
📠 (05182) 923350
📧 info@gc7berge.de
🖥 www.gc7berge.de

Weserbergland   (1982)
Weissenfelder Mühle, 37647 Polle
☎ **(05535) 8842**

Westfälischer Gütersloh
Gütersloher Str 127, 33397 Rietberg
☎ **(05244) 2340/10528**
✉ golf-club@golf-gt.de
🖥 www.golf-gt.de

Widukind-Land (1985)
Auf dem Stickdorn 63, 32584 Löhne
☎ **(05228) 7050**

Munich & South Bavaria

Allgäuer G&LC (1984)
Hofgut Boschach, 87724 Ottobeuren
☎ **(08332) 9251-0**
📠 (08332) 5161
✉ info@aglc.de
🖥 www.aglc.de

Altötting-Burghausen
(1986)
Piesing 4, 84533 Haiming
☎ **(08678) 986903**
📠 (08678) 986905
✉ office@gc-altoetting-burghausen.de
🖋 Johann Brehm (President)
🖥 www.gc-altoetting-burghausen.de

Augsburg (1959)
Engelshofer Str 2, 86399 Bobingen-Burgwalden
☎ **(08234) 5621**
🖥 www.golfclub-augsburg.de

Bad Tölz (1973)
83646 Wackersberg
☎ **(08041) 9994**

Beuerberg (1982)
Gut Sterz, 82547 Beuerberg
☎ **(08179) 671 or 782**
✉ beurberg@golf.de
🖥 www.gc-beurberg.de

Chieming (1982)
Kötzing 1, D-83339 Chieming
☎ **(08669) 87330**
✉ info@golfchieming.de
🖥 www.golfchieming.de

Donauwörth (1995)
Lederstatt 1, 86609 Donauwörth
☎ **(0906) 4044**
📠 (0906) 999 8164
✉ info@gc-donauwoerth.de
🖋 Claudia Slimpfie-Taslican
🖥 www.gc-donauwoerth.de

Ebersberg (1988)
Postfach 1351, 85554 Ebersberg
☎ **(08094) 8106**
📠 (08094) 8386
✉ info@gc-ebersberg.de
🖋 Stefan Schreyer (Mgr)
🖥 www.gc-ebersberg.de

Erding-Grünbach (1973)
Am Kellerberg, 85461 Grünbach
☎ **(08122) 49650**
📠 (08122) 49684

Eschenried (1983)
Kurfürstenweg 10, 85232 Eschenried
☎ **(08131) 56740**
📠 (08131) 567418
✉ info@golf-eschenried.de
🖥 www.gc-eschenried.de

Feldafing (1926)
Tutzinger Str 15, 82340 Feldafing
☎ **(08157) 9334-0**
📠 (08157) 9334-99
✉ info@golfclub-Feldafing.de
🖥 www.golfclub-Feldafing.de

Garmisch-Partenkirchen
(1928)
Gut Buchwies, 82496 Oberau
☎ **(08824) 8344**
✉ golfclubGAP@onlinehome.de
🖥 www.golfclub-garmisch-partenkirchen.de

Gut Ludwigsberg (1989)
Augsburgerstr 51, 86842 Turkheim
☎ **(08245) 3322**

Gut Rieden
Gut Rieden, 82319 Starnberg
☎ **(08151) 90770**

Hohenpähl (1988)
82396 Pähl
☎ **(08808) 9202-0**
📠 (08808) 9202-22
✉ info@gchp.de
🖋 Claus Ammer
🖥 www.gchp.de

Holledau
Weihern 3, 84104 Rudelzhausen
☎ **(08756) 96010**

Höslwang im Chiemgau
(1975)
Kronberg 3, 83129 Höslwang
☎ **(08075) 714**
✉ info@golfclub-hoeslwang.de
🖥 www.golfclub-hoeslwang.de

Iffeldorf (1989)
Gut Rettenberg, 82393 Iffeldorf
☎ **0049 (8856) 92550**
📠 0049 (8856) 925559
✉ sekretariat@golf-iffeldorf.de
🖋 Uwe Hinz
🖥 www.golf-iffeldorf.de

Landshut (1989)
Oberlippach 2, 84095 Furth-Landshut
☎ **(08704) 8378**
📠 (08704) 8379
✉ gc.landshut@t-online.de
🖥 www.golf-landshut.de

Mangfalltal G&LC
Oed 1, 83620 Feldkirchen-Westerham
☎ **(08063) 6300**
🖥 www.glcm.de

Margarethenhof (1982)
Gut Steinberg, 83666
Waakirchen/Marienstein
☎ **(08022) 7506-0**

✉ info@margarethenhof.com
🖥 www.margarethenhof.com

Memmingen Gut
Westerhart (1994)
Westerhart 1b, 87740 Buxheim
☎ **(08331) 71016**
📠 (08331) 71018
✉ gc-memmingen@t-online.de
🖥 www.golfclub-memmingen.de

Golfclub München
Eichenried (1989)
Münchner Strasse 57, 85452 Eichenried
☎ **(08123) 93080**
📠 (08123) 930893
✉ info@gc-eichenried.de
🖥 www.gc-eichenried.de

München West-
Odelzhausen (1988)
Gut Todtenried, 85235 Odelzhausen
☎ **(08134) 1618**

München-Riedhof e.V.
(1991)
82544 Egling-Riedhof, Riedhof 16
☎ **(08171) 21950**
✉ info@riedhof.de
🖥 www.riedhof.de

Münchener (1910)
Tölzerstrasse 95, 82064 Strasslach
☎ **(08170) 450**

Olching (1980)
Feursstrasse 89, 82140 Olching
☎ **(08142) 48290**
✉ sportbuero@golfclub-olching.de
🖥 www.golfclub-olching.de

Pfaffing Wasserburger
Golfclub Pfaffing München-Ost e.V, wsw
Golf AG, Köckmühle 132, 83539 Pfaffing
☎ **(08076) 91650**
✉ info@golfclub-pfaffing.de
🖥 www.golfclub-pfaffing.de

Reit im Winkl-Kössen
(1986)
Postfach 1101, 83237 Reit im Winkl
☎ **(08640) 798250**

Rottaler G&CC (1972)
Am Fischgartl 2, 84332 Hebertsfelden
☎ **(08561) 5969**
📠 (08561) 2646
✉ info@rottaler-gc.de
🖥 www.rottaler-gc.de

Rottbach (1997)
Weiherhaus 5, 82216 Rottbach
☎ **(08135) 93290**
✉ info@rottbach.de
🖥 www.golfanlage-rottbach.de

Schloss Maxlrain
Freiung 14, 83104 Maxlrain-Tuntenhausen
☎ **(08061) 1403**
📠 (08061) 30146

✉ info@golfclub-maxlrain.de
🖥 www.golfclub-maxlrain.de

Sonnenalp Oberallgäu
(1976)
Hotel Sonnenalp, 87527 Ofterschwang
☎ **(08321) 272181/(08326) 3859410**
☐ (08326) 3859412
✉ info@golfresort-sonnenalp.de
🖥 www.golfresort-sonnenalp.de

Starnberg   (1986)
Uneringerstr, 82319 Starnberg
☎ **(08151) 12157**
☐ (08151) 29115
✉ club@gcstarnberg.de
🖥 www.gcstarnberg.de

Tegernseer GC Bad Wiessee   (1958)
Rohbognerhof, 83707 Bad Wiessee
☎ **(08022) 8769**
☐ (08022) 82747
✉ info@tegernseer-golf-club.de
✍ Eva Meisinger
🖥 www.tegernseer-golf-club.de

Tutzing   (1983)
82327 Tutzing-Deixlfurt
☎ **(08158) 3600**

Waldegg-Wiggensbach
(1988)
Hof Waldegg, 87487 Wiggensbach
☎ **(08370) 93073**
☐ (08370) 93074
✉ info@golf-wiggensbach.com
🖥 www.golf-wiggensbach.com

Wittelsbacher GC Rohrenfeld-Neuburg
(1988)
Rohrenfeld, 86633 Neuburg/Donau
☎ **(08431) 90859-0**
☐ (08431) 90859-99
✉ info@wbgc.de
✍ Frank Thonig (Gen Mgr)
🖥 www.wbgc.de

Wörthsee   (1982)
Gut Schluifeld, 82237 Wörthsee
☎ **(08153) 93477-0**
☐ (08153) 93477-40
✉ info@golfclub-woerthsee.de
✍ Andrè Mosig
🖥 www.golfclub-woerthsee.de

Nuremberg & North Bavaria

Abenberg   (1988)
Am Golfplatz 19, 91183 Abenberg
☎ **(09178) 98960**

Bad Windsheim   (1992)
Otmar-Schaller-Alleen, 91438 Bad Windsheim
☎ **(09841) 5027**

☐ (09841) 3448
✉ gcbadwindsheim@t-online.de
🖥 www.golf-bw.de

Bamberg   (1973)
Postfach 1525, 96006 Bamberg
☎ **(09547) 7109**
✉ leimershof@golfclubbamberg.de
🖥 www.golfclubbamberg.de

Donau GC Passau-Rassbach
(1986)
Rassbach 8, 94136 Thyrnau-Passau
☎ **(08501) 91313**
☐ (08501) 91314
✉ info@golf-passau.de
✍ Anetseder Leonhard
🖥 www.golf-passau.de

Fränkische Schweiz   (1974)
Kanndorf 8, 91316 Ebermannstadt
☎ **(09194) 4827**
☐ (09194) 5410
✉ fraenkischeschweiz@t-online.de
🖥 www.gc-fs.de

Golf Club Fürth e.V.   (1951)
Am Golfplatz 10, 90768 Fürth
☎ **(0911) 757522**
✉ info@golfclub-fuerth.de
🖥 www.golfclub-fuerth.de

Gäuboden   (1992)
Gut Fruhstorf, 94330 Aiterhofen
☎ **(09421) 72804**

Golf Resort Bad Griesbach
(1989)
Holzhäuser 8, 94086 Bad Griesbach
☎ **(08532) 790-0**
☐ (08532) 790-45
✉ golfresort@hartl.de
🖥 www.hartl.de

Hof   (1985)
Postfach 1324, 95012 Hof
☎ **(09281) 470155**

Lauterhofen   (1987)
Ruppertslohe 18, 92283 Lauterhofen
☎ **(09186) 1574**

Lichtenau-Weickershof
(1980)
Weickershof 1, 91586 Lichtenau
☎ **(09827) 92040**

Oberfranken Thurnau
(1965)
Postfach 1349, 95304 Kulmbach
☎ **(09228) 319**

Oberpfälzer Wald G&LC
(1977)
Ödengrub, 92431 Kemnath bei Fuhrn
☎ **(09439) 466**

Oberzwieselau   (1990)
94227 Lindberg
☎ **(01049) 9922/2367**
🖥 www.golfpark-oberzwieselau.de

Regensburg   (1966)
93093 Jagdschloss Thiergarten
☎ **(09403) 505**
☐ (09403) 4391
✉ sekretariat@golfclub-regensburg.de
✍ Christian Frük
🖥 www.golfclub-regensburg.de

Am Reichswald   (1960)
Schiestlstr 100, 90427 Nürnberg
☎ **(0911) 305730**
☐ (0911) 301200
✉ info@golfclub-nuernberg.de
✍ Kornelia Knoblich/Petra Ketzmer
🖥 www.golfclub-nurnburg.de

Sagmühle   (1984)
Golfplatz Sagmühle 1, 94086 Bad Griesbach
☎ **(08532) 2038**

Schloss Fahrenbach   (1993)
95709 Tröstau
☎ **(09232) 882-256**
🖥 www.golfhotel-fahrenbach.de

Schloss Reichmannsdorf
(1991)
Schlosshof 4, 96132 Schlüsselfeld
☎ **(09546) 9215-10**
☐ (09546) 9215-20
✉ info@golfanlage-reichmannsdorf.de
✍ Franz von Schrottenberg
🖥 www.golfanlage-reichmannsdorf.de

Schlossberg   (1985)
Grünbach 8, 94419 Reisbach
☎ **(08734) 7035**

Schwanhof   (1994)
Klaus Conrad Allee 1, 92706 Luhe-Wildenau
☎ **(09607) 92020**

Die Wutzschleife   (1997)
Hillstett 40, 92444 Rötz
☎ **(09976) 184460**
☐ (09976) 18180
✉ info@golfanlage-wutzschleife.de
🖥 www.golfanlage-wutzschleife.de

Rhineland North

Golf und Landclub Ahaus
(1987)
Schmäinghook 36, 48683 Ahaus-Alstätte
☎ **(02567) 405**
☐ (02567) 3524
✉ info@glc-ahaus.de
🖥 www.glc-ahaus.de

Alten Fliess   (1995)
Am Alten Fliess 66, 50129 Bergheim
☎ **(02238) 94410**

Artland   (1988)
Westerholte 23, 49577 Ankum
☎ **(05466) 301**
✉ info@artlandgolf.de
🖥 www.artlandgolf.de

Bergisch-Land (1928)
Siebeneickerst 386, 42111 Wuppertal
- ☎ **(02053) 7177**
- 📠 (02053) 7303
- ✉ info@golfclub-bergischland.de
- 👤 Philipp Pfannkuche
- 🖥 www.golfclub-bergischland.de

Bochum (1982)
Im Mailand 127, 44797 Bochum
- ☎ **(0234) 799832**

Dortmund (1956)
Reichmarkstr 12, 44265 Dortmund
- ☎ **(0231) 774133/774609**

Düsseldorfer GC (1961)
Rommeljansweg 12, D-40882 Ratingen
- ☎ **0049 (0) 2102 81092**
- 📠 0049 (0) 2102 81782
- ✉ info@duesseldorfer-golf-club.de
- 👤 Henrike Kleyoldt
- 🖥 www.duesseldorfer-golf-club.de

Elfrather Mühle (1991)
An der Elfrather Mühle 145, 47802 Krefeld
- ☎ **(02151) 4969-0**
- 📠 (02151) 477459
- ✉ info@gcem.de
- 🖥 www.gcem.de

Erftaue (1991)
Zur Mühlenerft 1, 41517 Grevenbroich
- ☎ **(02181) 280637**
- ✉ gc.erftaue@t-online.de
- 🖥 www.golf-erftaue.de

Essener Golfclub Haus Oefte (1959)
Laupendahler Landstr, 45219 Essen-Kettwig
- ☎ **(02054) 83911**
- 📠 (02054) 83850
- ✉ info@golfclub-oefte.de
- 👤 Heidrùn Vodnik (Sec)
- 🖥 www.golfclub-oefte.de

Euregio Bad Bentheim (1987)
Postbox 1205, Am Hauptelick 8, 48443 Bad Bentheim
- ☎ **(05922) 7776-0**
- 🖥 www.golfclub-euregio.de

Grevenmühle Ratingen (1988)
Grevenmühle, 40882 Ratingen-Homberg
- ☎ **(02102) 9595-0**

Haus Bey (1992)
An Haus Bey 16, 41334 Nettetal
- ☎ **(02153) 9197-0**
- 📠 (02153) 919750
- ✉ golf@hausbey.de
- 👤 Elmar Claus
- 🖥 www.hausbey.de

Haus Kambach (1989)
Kambachstrasse 9-13, 52249 Eschweiler-Kinzweiler
- ☎ **(02403) 50890**

- 📠 (02403) 21270
- ✉ info@golf-kambach.de
- 🖥 www.golf-kambach.de

Hubbelrath (1961)
Bergische Landstr 700, 40629 Düsseldorf
- ☎ **(02104) 72178**
- 📠 (02104) 75685
- ✉ info@gc-hubbelrath.de
- 🖥 www.gc-hubbelrath.de

Hummelbachaue Neuss (1987)
Norfer Kirchstrasse, 41469 Neuss
- ☎ **(02137) 91910**

Issum-Niederrhein (1973)
Pauenweg 68, 47661 Issum 1
- ☎ **(02835) 92310**
- 📠 (02835) 9231-20
- 🖥 www.gc-issum.de

Golf- and Land-Club Köln e.V. (1906)
Golfplatz 2, 51429 Bergisch Gladbach
- ☎ **0049 (0) 2204-9276-0**
- 📠 0049 (0) 2204-9276-15
- ✉ info@glckoeln.de
- 👤 Achim Lehmstardt (Gen Mgr)
- 🖥 www.glckoeln.de

Kosaido International (1989)
Am Schmidtberg 11, 40629 Düsseldorf
- ☎ **(02104) 77060**
- 📠 (02104) 770611
- ✉ info@kosaido.de
- 🖥 www.kosaido.de

Krefeld (1930)
Eltweg 2, 47809 Krefeld
- ☎ **(02151) 156030**
- 📠 (02151) 15603 222
- ✉ kgc@krefelder-gc.de
- 👤 Ula Weinforth
- 🖥 www.krefelder-gc.de

Mühlenhof G&CC (1990)
Greilack 29, 47546 Kalkar
- ☎ **0049 (2824) 924092**
- 📠 0049 (2824) 924093
- ✉ awilmsen@muehlenhof.net
- 👤 Annette Wilmsen
- 🖥 www.muehlenhof.net

Nordkirchen (1974)
Am Golfplatz 6, 59394 Nordkirchen
- ☎ **(02596) 9191**
- 🖥 www.glc-nordkirchen.de

Op de Niep (1995)
Bergschenweg 71, 47506 Neukirchen-Vluyn
- ☎ **(02845) 28051**

Osnabrück (1955)
Am Golfplatz 3, 49143 Bissendorf
- ☎ **(05402) 5636**
- ✉ info@ogc.de
- 🖥 www.ogc.de

Rheine/Mesum (1998)
Wörstr 201, 48432 Rheine
- ☎ **(05975) 9490**
- ✉ info@golfclub-rheine.de
- 🖥 www.golfclub-rheine.de

Rittergut Birkhof (1996)
Rittergut Birkhof, 41352 Korschenbroich
- ☎ **(02131) 510660**

St Barbara's Royal Dortmund (1969)
Hesslingweg, 44309 Dortmund
- ☎ **(0231) 202551**

Schloss Georghausen (1962)
Georghausen 8, 51789 Lindlar-Hommerich
- ☎ **(02207) 4938**
- ✉ gcschlossgeorghausengolf.de
- 🖥 www.golfclub-schloss-georghausen.de

Schloss Haag (1996)
Bartelter Weg 8, 47608 Geldern
- ☎ **(02831) 94777**

Schloss Myllendonk (1965)
Myllendonkerstr 113, 41352 Korschenbroich 1
- ☎ **(02161) 641049**
- 📠 (02161) 648806
- ✉ info@gcsm.de
- 👤 Peter Géronne
- 🖥 www.gcsm.de

Golfclub Schloss Westerholt e.V. (1993)
Schloss Strasse 1, 45701 Herten-Westerholt
- ☎ **(0209) 165840**
- 📠 (0209) 165415
- ✉ info@gc-westerholt.de
- 🖥 www.gc-westerholt.de

Golf- und Landclub Schmitzhof (1975)
Arsbeckerstr 160, 41844 Wegberg
- ☎ **(02436) 39090**
- 📠 (02436) 390915
- ✉ info@golfclubschmitzhof.de
- 🖥 www.golfclubschmitzhof.de

Siegen-Olpe (1966)
Am Golfplatz, 57482 Wenden
- ☎ **(02762) 9762-0**
- 📠 (02762) 9762-12
- ✉ info@gcso.de
- 👤 Stefan Eisenschmitt
- 🖥 www.gcso.de

Golfclub Siegerland e.V. (1993)
Berghäuser Weg, 57223 Kreuztal-Mittelhees
- ☎ **(02732) 59470**
- 📠 (02732) 594724
- ✉ info@golfclub-siegerland.de
- 👤 Ursula Kaidel
- 🖥 www.golfclub-siegerland.de

Teutoburger Wald   (1990)
Postfach 1250, 33777 Halle/Westfalen
☎ +49 5201 6279
📠 +49 5201 6222
📧 info@gctw-halle.de
🖥 www.gctw.de

Unna-Fröndenberg   (1985)
Schwarzer Weg 1, 58730 Fröndenberg
☎ (02373) 70068
📠 (02373) 70069
📧 info@gcuf.de
✍ Mariya Mikli
🖥 www.gcuf.de

Vechta-Welpe   (1989)
Welpe 2, 49377 Vechta
☎ (04441) 5539/82168
📠 (04441) 852480
📧 info@golfclub-vechta.de
✍ Maria Kortenbusch
🖥 www.golfclub-vechta.de

Velbert – Gut Kuhlendahl
Kuhlendahler Str 283, 42553 Velbert
☎ (02053) 923290
📧 golfclub-velbert@t-online.de
🖥 www.gcvelbert.de

**Golf & Country Club
Velderhof**   (1997)
Velderhof, 50259 Pulheim
☎ (02238) 923940
📠 (02238) 9239440
📧 info@velderhof.de
✍ Eva Harzheim
🖥 www.velderhof.de

**Vestischer GC
Recklinghausen**   (1974)
Bockholterstr 475, 45659 Recklinghausen
☎ (02361) 93420
📧 vest.golfclub@t-online.de
🖥 www.gc-recklinghausen.de

Wasserburg Anholt   (1972)
Schloss 3, 46419 Isselburg Anholt
☎ (02874) 915120
📧 sekretariat@golfclub-anholt.de
🖥 www.golfclub-anholt.de

Golfclub Weselerwald
(1988)
Steenbecksweg 12, 46514 Schermbeck
☎ (02856) 91370
📠 (02856) 913715
📧 info@gcww.de
✍ John Emery
🖥 www.gcww.de

West Rhine   (1956)
Javelin Barracks, BFPO 35
☎ +49 2163 974463
📠 +49 2163 80049
📧 secretary@westrhinegc.co.uk
✍ David W Hampson
🖥 www.westrhinegc.co.uk

Westerwald   (1979)
Steinebacherstr, 57629 Dreifelden
☎ (02666) 8220

📧 gcwesterwald@t-online.de
🖥 ww.gc-westerwald.de

Rhineland South

Bad Neuenahr G&LC   (1979)
Remagener Weg, 53474 Bad Neuenahr-Ahrweiler
☎ (02641) 950950

Golf-Resort Bitburger Land
(1995)
Zur Weilersheck 1, 54636 Wissmannsdorf
☎ (06527) 9272-0
📠 (06527) 9272-30
📧 info@bitgolf.de
🖥 www.bitgolf.de

**Bonn-Godesberg in
Wachtberg**   (1960)
Landgrabenweg, 53343 Wachtberg-Niederbachen
☎ (0228) 344003

Burg Overbach   (1984)
Postfach 1213, 53799 Much
☎ (02245) 5550
📠 (02245) 8247
📧 widl@golfclub-burg-overbach.de
✍ Günter Widl
🖥 www.golfclub-burg-overbach.de

Burg Zievel   (1994)
Burg Zievel, 53894 Mechernich
☎ (02256) 1651

Eifel   (1977)
Kölner Str, 54576 Hillesheim
☎ (06593) 1241

Gut Heckenhof   (1993)
53783 Eitorf
☎ (02243) 9232-0
📧 info@gut-heckenhof.de
🖥 www.gut-heckenhof.de

Internationaler GC Bonn
(1992)
Gut Grossenbusch, 53757 St Augustin
☎ (02241) 39880
📧 info@gcbonn.de
🖥 www.golf-course-bonn.de

Jakobsberg   (1990)
Im Tal der Loreley, 56154 Boppard
☎ (06742) 808491
📧 golf@jakobsberg.de
🖥 www.jakobsberg.de

Kyllburger Waldeifel
Lietzenhof, 54597 Burbach
☎ (06553) 961039
🖥 www.golf-lietzenhof.de

Mittelrheinischer Bad Ems
(1938)
Denzerheide, 56130 Bad Ems
☎ (02603) 6541
📧 info@mgcbadems.de
🖥 ww3w.mgcbadems.de

Nahetal   (1971)
Drei Buchen, 55583 Bad Münster am Stein
☎ (06708) 2145
🖥 www.golfclub-nahetal.de

Stromberg-Schindeldorf
(1987)
Park Village Golfanlagen, Buchenring 6, 55442 Stromberg
☎ (06724) 93080

Trier   (1977)
54340 Ensch-Birkenheck
☎ (06507) 993255
📧 info@golf-club-trier-de
🖥 www.golf-club-trier.de

Waldbrunnen   (1983)
Brunnenstr 11, 53578 Windhagen
☎ (02645) 8041
📠 (02645) 8042
📧 info@golfclub-waldbrunnen.de
✍ Mrs B Thomas
🖥 www.golfclub-waldbrunnen.de

Wiesensee   (1992)
Am Wiesensee, 56459 Westerburg-Stahlhofen
☎ (02663) 991192
📧 golfclub.wiesensee@lindner.de
🖥 www.golfclub-wiesensee.de

Saar-Pfalz

Pfalz Neustadt   (1971)
Im Lochbusch, 67435 Neustadt-Geinsheim
☎ (06327) 97420
📧 gc-pfalz@t-online.de
🖥 www.gc-pfalz.de

Saarbrücken   (1961)
Oberlimbergerweg, 66798 Wallerfangen-Gisingen
☎ (06837) 91800/1584
🖥 www.golfclub-saarbruecken.de

Websweiler Hof   (1991)
Websweiler Hof, 66424 Homburg/Saar
☎ (06841) 7777-60
🖥 www.golf-saar.de

Westpfalz Schwarzbachtal
(1988)
66509 Rieschweiler
☎ (06336) 6442
📠 (06336) 6408
📧 egw@golf.de
🖥 www.gcwestpfalz.de

Woodlawn Golf Course
6792 Ramstein Flugplatz
☎ (06371) 476240
📠 (06371) 42158
✍ R Nichols (Gen Mgr)
🖥 www.ramsteingolf.com

Stuttgart & South West

Bad Liebenzell
Golfplatz 1-9, 75378 Bad Liebenzell
☎ **(07052) 9325-0**
🖶 (07052) 9325-25
✉ info@gcbl.de
🖥 www.gcbl.de

Bad Rappenau (1989)
Ehrenbergstrasse 25a, 74906 Bad Rappenau
☎ **(07264) 3666**

Bad Salgau (1995)
Koppelweg 103, 88348 Bad Salgau
☎ **(07581) 527459**
✉ info@gc-bs.de
🖥 www.gc-bs.de

Baden Hills Golf & Curling Club e.v. (1982)
Cabot Trail G208, 77836 Rheinmünster
☎ **(07229) 185100**
🖶 (07229) 1851011
✉ baden-hills@t-online.de
🖥 www.baden-hills.de

Baden-Baden (1901)
Fremersbergstr 127, 76530 Baden-Baden
☎ **(07221) 23579**
🖶 (07221) 3025659
✉ info@golfclub-baden-baden.de
🖉 Gerhard Kaufmann (Mgr)
🖥 www.golfclub-baden-baden.de

GC Bodensee Weissenberg eV (1986)
Lampertsweiler 51, D-88138 Weissensberg
☎ **+41 (8389) 89190**
✉ info@gcbw.de
🖥 www.gcbw.de

Freiburg (1970)
Krüttweg 1, 79199 Kirchzarten
☎ **(07661) 9847-0**
🖶 (07661) 984747
✉ fgc@freiburger-golfclub.de
🖉 Andrea Bührer
🖥 www.freiburger-golfclub.de

Fürstlicher Golfclub Waldsee (1998)
Hopfenweiler, 88339 Bad Waldsee
☎ **(07524) 4017 200**
🖶 (07524) 4017 100
✉ club@waldsee-golf.de
🖥 www.waldsee-golf.de

Hechingen Hohenzollern (1955)
Postfach 1124, 72379 Hechingen
☎ **(07471) 6478**
✉ info@golfclub-hechingen.de
🖥 www.golfclub-hechingen.de

Heidelberg-Lobenfeld (1968)
Biddersbacherhof, 74931 Lobbach-Lobenfeld
☎ **(06226) 952110**

🖶 (06226) 952111
✉ golf@gchl.de
🖥 www.gchl.de

Heilbronn-Hohenlohe (1964)
Hofgasse, 74639 Zweiflingen-Friedrichsruhe
☎ **(07941) 920810**
🖥 www.friedrichsruhe.de

Hetzenhof
Hetzenhof 7, 73547 Lorch
☎ **(07172) 9180-0**
✉ info@golfclub-hetzenhof.de
🖥 www.golfclub-hetzenhof.de

Hohenstaufen (1959)
Unter den Ramsberg, 73072 Donzdorf-Reichenbach
☎ **(07162) 27171**
✉ gc-hohenstaufen@online.de
🖥 www.gc-hohenstaufen.de

Kaiserhöhe (1995)
Im Laber 4a, 74747 Ravenstein
☎ **(06297) 399**
🖶 (06297) 599
✉ info@golfclub-kaiserhoehe.de
🖉 Martin Arzberger
🖥 www.gc-kaiserhoehe.de

Golf-Club Konstanz e.V. (1965)
Hofgut Kargegg 1, D-78476 Allensbach-Langenrain
☎ **+49 (0) 75 33 93 03 - 0**
✉ info@golfclubkonstanz.de
🖥 www.golfclubkonstanz.de

Lindau-Bad Schachen (1954)
Am Schönbühl 5, 88131 Lindau
☎ **(08382) 96170**
✉ info@gc-lindau-bad-schachen.de
🖥 www.gc-lindau-bad-schachen.de

Markgräflerland Kandern (1984)
Feuerbacher Str 35, 79400 Kandern
☎ **(07626) 97799-0**
🖶 (07626) 97799-22
✉ info@gc-mk.com
🖥 www.golfclub-markgraeferland.com

Neckartal (1974)
Aldinger Str. 975, 70806 Kornwestheim
☎ **(07141) 871319**
🖶 (07141) 81716
✉ info@gc-neckartal.de
🖥 www.gc-neckartal.de

Nippenburg (1993)
Nippenburg 21, 71701 Schwieberdingen
☎ **(07150) 39530**

Obere Alp (1989)
Am Golfplatz 1-3, 79780 Stühlingen
☎ **(07703) 9203-0**
🖶 (07703) 9203-18
✉ secretariat@golf-oberealp.de
🖥 www.golf-oberealp.de

Oberschwaben-Bad Waldsee (1968)
Hopfenweiler 2d, 88339 Bad Waldsee
☎ **(07524) 5900**

Oeschberghof L & GC (1976)
Golfplatz 1, 78166 Donaueschingen
☎ **(0771) 84525**

Land-und Golfclub Oschberghof (1976)
Golfplatz 1, 78166 Donaueschingen
☎ **(0771) 84525**
🖶 (0771) 84540
✉ golf@oeschberghof.com
🖥 www.oeschberghof.com

Owingen-Überlingen e.V - Hofgut Lugenhof (1989)
Alte Owinger Str 93, 88696 Owingen
☎ **(07551) 83040**
🖶 (07551) 830422
✉ welcome@golfclub-owingen.de
🖥 www.golfclub-owingen.de

Pforzheim Karlshäuser Hof (1987)
Karlshäuser Weg, 75248 Ölbronn-Dürrn
☎ **(07237) 9100**
🖶 (07237) 5161
✉ info@gc-pf.de
🖉 Andreas List (CM)
🖥 www.gc-pf.de

Reischenhof (1987)
Industriestrasse 12, 88489 Wain
☎ **(07353) 1732**
🖥 www.golf.de/gc-reischenhof

Reutlingen-Sonnenbühl (1987)
Im Zerg, 72820 Sonnenbühl
☎ **(07128) 92660**

Rhein Badenweiler (1971)
79401 Badenweiler
☎ **(07632) 7970**

Rickenbach (1979)
Hennematt 20, 79736 Rickenbach
☎ **(07765) 777**
🖶 (07765) 544
✉ info@golfclub-rickenbach.de
🖥 www.golfclub-rickenbach.de

Schloss Klingenburg e.v. (1978)
Schloss Klingenburg, 89343 Jettingen-Scheppach
☎ **(08225) 3030**
🖶 (08225) 30350
✉ info@golf-klingenburg.de
🖥 www.golf-klingenburg.de

Schloss Langenstein (1991)
Schloss Langenstein, 78359 Orsingen-Nenzingen
☎ **(07774) 50651**

✉ golf-sekretariat@schloss-langenstein.com
▤ www.schloss-langenstein.com

Schloss Liebenstein (1982)
Postfach 27, 74380 Neckarwestheim
☎ (07133) 9878-0
📠 (07133) 9878-18
✉ info@gc-sl.de
🖎 Rüdiger Schmid
▤ www.golfclubliebenstein.de

Schloss Weitenburg (1984)
Sommerhalde 11, 72181 Starzach-Sulzau
☎ (07472) 15050
📠 (07472) 15051
✉ info@gcsw.de
▤ www.gcsw.de

Sinsheim-Buchenauerhof
(1993)
Buchenauerhof 4, 74889 Sinsheim
☎ (07265) 7258
✉ mail@ golfclubsinsheim.de
▤ www.golfclubsinsheim.de

Steisslingen (1991)
Brunnenstr 4b, 78256 Steisslingen-Wiechs
☎ (07738) 7196
📠 (07738) 923297
✉ info@golfclub-steisslingen.de
🖎 Peter Ridley
▤ www.golfclub-steisslingen.de

Stuttgarter Golf-Club
Solitude (1927)
Schlossfeld, 71297 Mönsheim
☎ (07044) 911 0410
📠 (07044) 911 0420
✉ info@golfclub-stuttgart.com
🖎 Birgif Geise
▤ www.golfclub-stuttgart.com

Ulm e.V. (1963)
Wochenauer Hof 2, 89186 Illerrieden
☎ (07306) 929500
✉ GolfClubUlm@t-online.de
▤ www.GolfClubUlm.de

Greece

Afandou (1973)
Afandou, Rhodes
☎ (0241) 51255

Corfu (1972)
PO Box 71, Ropa Valley, 49100 Corfu
☎ (26610) 94220
✉ cfugolf@hol.gr
▤ www.corfugolfclub.com

Glyfada Golf Club of
Athens (1966)
PO Box 70116, 166-10 Glyfada, Athens
☎ +30 210 894 6459
📠 +30 210 894 6834
✉ ggca@otenet.gr
🖎 Nicole Kavadias
▤ www.ggca.gr

Hungary

Birdland G&CC (1991)
Thermal krt.10, 9740 Bükfürdö
☎ (+36) 94 358060
✉ info@birdland.hu
▤ www.birdland.hu

Budapest G&CC
Golf u.1, 2024 Kisoroszi
☎ (1) 36 26 392 465

European Lakes G&CC
(1994)
Kossuth u.3, 7232 Hencse
☎ (82) 481245
📠 (82) 481248
✉ info@europeanlakes.com
🖎 Medea Zag
⊕ Soft spikes only - No metal spikes
▤ www.europeanlakes.com

Old Lake (1998)
PO Box 127, 2890 Tata-Remeteségpuszta
☎ (34) 587620
📠 (34) 587623
✉ club@oldlakegolf.com
🖎 Dr Ba'bos Réka (Club Director)
▤ www.oldlakegolf.com

Pannonia G&CC (1996)
Alcsútdoboz, 8087 Mariavölgy
☎ 0036 (22) 594200
📠 0036 (22) 594205
✉ info@golfclub.hu
▤ www.golfclub.hu

St Lorence G&CC
Pellérdi ut 55, 7634 Pécs
☎ (72) 252844/252142

Iceland

Akureyri (1935)
PO Box 317, 602 Akureyri
☎ +354 4622974
✉ gagolf@gagolf.is
🖎 Halla Sif Svavarsdóttir
▤ www.gagolf.is

Borgarness (1973)
Hamar, 310 Borgarnes
☎ (345) 437 1663
✉ hamar@gbborgarnes.net
▤ www.golf.is/gb
    www.gbborgarnes.net

Golfklubbur Sudurnesja
(1964)
PO Box 112, 232 Keflavik
☎ (421) 4100
✉ gs@gs.is
🖎 Gunnar Johannsson
▤ www.gs.is

Húsavík (1967)
PO Box 23, Kötlum, 640 Húsavik
☎ (464) 1000
✉ palmi.palmason@tmd.is

Isafjardar (1978)
PO Box 367, 400 Isafjördur
☎ (456) 5081
✉ gi@snerpa.is

Jökull (1973)
Postholf 67, 355 Olafsvík
☎ (436) 1666

Keilir (1967)
Box 148, 222 Hafnarfjördur
☎ (565) 3360
✉ keilir@ishoff.is
▤ www.keilir.is

Kopavogs og Gardabaejar
(1994)
Postholf 214, 212 Gardabaer
☎ (+354) 565 7373
✉ gkg@gkg.is
▤ www.gkg.is

Leynir (1965)
PO Box 9, Akranes
☎ (00354) 431 2771
✉ leynir@simnet.is
▤ www.golf.is/gl   www.leynir.is

Ness-Nesklúbburinn (1964)
PO Box 66, 172 Seltjarnarnes
☎ (561) 1930
✉ nk@centrum.is
▤ www.golf.is/nk

Oddafellowa (1990)
Urridavatnsdölum, 210 Gardabaer
☎ (565) 9094
▤ www.oddur.is

Olafsfjardar (1968)
Skeggjabrekku, 625 Olafsfjördur
☎ (466) 2611

Reykjavíkur (1934)
Grafarholt, 112 Reykjavík
☎ +354 (585) 0200/0210
✉ gr@grgolf.is
▤ www.grgolf.is

Saudárkróks (1970)
Hlidarendi, Postholf 56, 550 Saudárkrókur
☎ (453) 5075

Vestmannaeyja (1938)
Postholf 168, 902 Vestmannaeyar
☎ (481) 2363

Italy

Como/Milan/Bergamo

Ambrosiano (1994)
Cascina Bertacca, 20080 Bubbiano-Milan
☎ (0290) 840820
✉ info@golfclubambrosiano.com
▤ www.golfclubambrosiano.com

Barlassina CC (1956)
Via Privata Golf 42, 20030 Birago di Camnago (MI)
☎ **(0362) 560621/2**
✉ bccgolf@libero.it

Bergamo L'Albenza (1961)
Via Longoni 12, 24030 Almenno S. Bartolomeo (BG)
☎ **(035) 640028**
🖷 (035) 643066
✉ secreteria@golfbergamo.it
✍ Achille Ridamouti (Sec)
🖥 www.golfbergamo.it

Bogogno (1996)
Via Sant'Isidoro 1, 28010 Bogogno
☎ **(0322) 863794**
✉ info@circologolfbogogno.com
🖥 www.circolo9golfbogogno.com

Golf Brianza Country Club (1996)
Cascina Cazzu, 4, 20040 Usmate Velate (Mi)
☎ **(039) 682 9089/079**
🖷 (039) 682 9059
✉ brianzagolf@tin.it
✍ Francesco Alajmo (Mgr)
🖥 www.brianzagolf.it

Carimate (1962)
Via Airoldi 2, 22060 Carimate (CO)
☎ **(031) 790226**
🖷 (031) 791927
✉ info@golfcarimate.it
✍ Giuseppe Nava
🖥 www.golfcarimate.it

Castelconturbia (1984)
Via Suno, 28010 Agrate Conturbia
☎ **(0322) 832093**
✉ castelconturbia@tin.it
🖥 www.golfclubcastelconturbia.it

Castello di Tolcinasco (1993)
20090 Pieve Emanuele (MI)
☎ **(02) 9042 8035**
🖷 (02) 9078 9051
✉ golf@golftolcinasco.it
🖥 www.golftolcinasco.it

Franciacorta (1986)
Via Provinciale 34b, 25040 Nigoline di Corte Franca, (Brescia)
☎ **(030) 984167**
✉ franciacortagolfclub@libero.it

Menaggio & Cadenabbia (1907)
Via Golf 12, 22010 Grandola E Uniti
☎ **(0344) 32103**
✉ segretaria@golfclubmenaggio.it
🖥 www.menaggio.it

Milano (1928)
20.900 Parco di Monza (MI)
☎ **(039) 303081/2/3**

🖷 (039) 304427
✉ info@golfclubmilano.com
✍ Arnaldo Cocuzza (Mgr)
🖥 www.golfclubmilano.it

Molinetto CC (1982)
SS Padana Superiore 11, 20063 Cernusco S/N (MI)
☎ **(02) 9210 5128/9210 5983**

Monticello (1975)
Via Volta 63, 22070 Cassina Rizzardi (Como)
☎ **(031) 928055**
✉ monticello@tin.it
🖥 www.golfmonticello.it

La Pinetina Golf Club (1971)
Via al Golf 4, 22070 Appiano Gentile (CO)
☎ **(031) 933202**
🖷 (031) 890342
✉ info@golfpinetina.it
✍ Simone Laureti (Club Mgr)
🖥 www.golfpinetina.it

Le Robinie (1992)
Via per Busto Arsizio 9, 21058 Solbiate Olona (VA)
☎ **(039) 331 329260**
🖷 (039) 331 329266
✉ info@lerobinie.com
🖥 www.lerobinie.com

La Rossera (1970)
Via Montebello 4, 24060 Chiuduno
☎ **(035) 838600**
✉ golfrossera@libero.it

Le Rovedine (1978)
Via Karl Marx, 20090 Noverasco di Opera (Mi)
☎ **(02) 5760 6420**
✉ info@rovedine.com
🖥 www.rovedone.com

Varese (1934)
Via Vittorio Veneto 59, 21020 Luvinate (VA)
☎ **(0332) 229302/821293**
🖷 (0332) 811293
✉ info@golfclubvarese.it
✍ Carlo Giraldi
🖥 www.golfclubvarese.it

Vigevano (1974)
Via Chitola 49, 27029 Vigevano (PV)
☎ **(0381) 346628/346077**
✉ golfvigevano@yahoo.it

Villa D'Este (1926)
Via Cantù 13, 22030 Montorfano (CO)
☎ **(031) 200200**
🖷 (031) 200786
✉ info@golfvilladeste.com
✍ Andrea Contigiani
🖥 www.golfvilladeste.com

Zoate
20067 Zoate di Tribiano (MI)
☎ **(02) 9063 2183/9063 1861**

Elba

Acquabona (1971)
57037 Portoferraio, Isola di Elba (LI)
☎ **(0565) 940066**

Emilia Romagna

Adriatic GC Cervia (1985)
Via Jelenia Gora No 6, 48016 Cervia-Milano Marittima
☎ **(0544) 992786**

Bologna (1959)
Via Sabattini 69, 40050 Monte San Pietro (BO)
☎ **(051) 969100**

Croara Country Club (1976)
Loc. Croara Nuova 23010 Gazzola (PC)
☎ **(0523) 977105**
✉ info@croaracountryclub.com
🖥 www.croaracountryclub.com

Matilde di Canossa (1987)
Via Casinazzo 1, 42100 San Bartolomeo, Reggio Emilia
☎ **(0522) 371295**
✉ golfcanossa@libero.it
🖥 www.tiscali.it/golfcanossa

Modena G&CC (1987)
Via Castelnuovo Rangone 4, 41050 Colombaro di Formigine (MO)
☎ **(059) 553482**
🖷 (059) 553696
✉ segretaria@modenagolf.it
✍ Davide Colombarini
🖥 www.modenagolf.it

Riolo Golf La Torre (1992)
Via Limisano 10, Riolo Terme (RA)
☎ **(0546) 74035**
🖷 (0546) 74076
✉ info@golflatorre.it
✍ Lamberto Di Giacinto
🖥 www.golflatorre.it

La Rocca (1985)
Via Campi 8, 43038 Sala Baganza (PR)
☎ **(0521) 834037**
🖥 www.officeitalia.it/golflarocca

Gulf of Genoa

Garlenda (1965)
Via Golf 7, 17033 Garlenda
☎ **(0182) 580012**
🖷 (0182) 580561
✉ info@garlendagolf.it
✍ Claudio Rota
🖥 www.garlendagolf.it

Marigola (1975)
Via Biaggini 5, 19032 Lerici (SP)
☎ **(0187) 970193**
✉ info@golfmarigola.it
🖥 www.golfmarigola.it

Pineta di Arenzano   (1959)
Piazza del Golf 3, 16011 Arenzano (GE)
☎ (010) 911 1817

Rapallo   (1930)
Via Mameli 377, 16035 Rapallo (GE)
☎ (0185) 261777

Sanremo-Circolo Golf degli Ulivi   (1932)
Via Campo Golf 59, 18038 Sanremo
☎ (0184) 557093
✉ info@golfsanremo.com
▤ www.golfsanremo.com

Versilia   (1990)
Via Sipe 100, 55045 Pietrasanta (LU)
☎ (0584) 88 15 74

Lake Garda & Dolomites

Asiago   (1967)
Via Meltar 2, 36012 Asiago (VI)
☎ (0424) 462721
▤ www.golfasiago.it

Bogliaco   (1912)
Via Golf 21, 25088 Toscolano-Maderno
☎ (0365) 643006
🖳 (0365) 643006
✉ golfbogliaco@tin.it
▤ www.bogliaco.com

Ca' degli Ulivi   (1988)
Via Ghiandare 2, 37010 Marciaga di Costermano (VR)
☎ (045) 627 9030
✉ info@golfcadegliulivi.it
▤ www.golfcadegliulivi.it

Campo Carlo Magno   (1922)
Golf Hotel, 38084 Madonna di Campiglio (TN)
☎ (0465) 440622

Folgaria   (1987)
Loc Costa di Folgaria, 38064 Folgaria (TN)
☎ (0464) 720480

Gardagolf CC   (1985)
Via Angelo Omodeo 2, 25080 Soiano Del Lago (BS)
☎ (0365) 674707 (Sec)
🖳 (0365) 674788
✉ info@gardagolf.it
▤ www.gardagolf.it

Karersee-Carezza
Loc Carezza 171, 39056 Welschofen-Nova Levante
☎ (0471) 612200

Petersberg   (1987)
Unterwinkel 5, 39050 Petersberg (BZ)
☎ +39 0471 615122
🖳 +39 0471 615229
✉ info@golfclubpetersberg.it
✍ Hans-Peter Thaler
▤ www.golfclubpetersberg.it

Ponte di Legno   (1980)
Corso Milano 36, 25056 Ponte di Legno (BS)
☎ (0364) 900306

Verona   (1963)
Ca' del Sale 15, 37066 Sommacampagna
☎ (045) 510060
🖳 (045) 510242
✉ golfverona@libero.it
▤ www.golfclubverona.com

Naples & South

Riva Dei Tessali   (1971)
74011 Castellaneta
☎ (099) 843 9251

San Michele
Loc Bosco 8/9, 87022 Cetraro (CS)
☎ (0982) 91012
✉ sanmichele@sanmichele.it
▤ www.sanmichele.it

Rome & Centre

Country Club Castelgandolfo   (1987)
Via Santo Spirito 13, 00040 Castelgandolfo
☎ (06) 931 2301
🖳 (06) 931 2244
✉ info@golfclubcastelgandolfo.it
▤ www.countryclubcastelgandolfo.it

Fioranello
CP 96, 00134 Roma (RM)
☎ (06) 713 8080 - 213
✉ info@fioranellogolf.it
▤ www.fioranellogolf.com

Marco Simone   (1989)
Via di Marco Simone, 00012 Guidonia (RM)
☎ (0774) 366469

Marediroma
Via Enna 30, 00040 Ardea (RM)
☎ (06) 913 3250
✉ info@golfmarediroma.it
▤ www.golfmarediroma.it

Nettuno
Via della Campana 18, 00048 Nettuno (RM)
☎ (06) 981 9419

Oasi Golf Club   (1988)
Via Cogna 5, 04011 Aprilia (Roma)
☎ 0039-06-92746252/9268120
🖳 0039-06-9268502
✉ info@oasigolf.it
✍ Marina Lanza (President)
▤ www.oasigolf.it

Olgiata   (1961)
Largo Olgiata 15, 00123 Roma
☎ (06) 308 89141
✉ secretaria@olgiatagolfclub.it
▤ www.olgiatagolfclub.it

Parco de' Medici   (1989)
Viale Salvatore Rebecchini, 00148 Roma
☎ (06) 655 3477
✉ info@sheratongolf.it
▤ www.sheraton.com/golfrome
   www.golfclubparcodemedici.com

Pescara   (1992)
Contrado Cerreto 58, 66010 Miglianico (CH)
☎ (0871) 959566

Le Querce
San Martino, 01015 Sutri (VT)
☎ (0761) 600789
✉ info@golfclublequerce.it
▤ www.golfclublequerce.it

Roma   (1903)
Via Appia Nuova 716A, 00178 Roma
☎ (06) 780 3407

Tarquinia
Loc Pian di Spille, Via degli Alina 271, 01016 Marina Velca/Tarquinia (VT)
☎ (0766) 812109

Sardinia

Is Molas   (1975)
CP 49, 09010 Pula
☎ (070) 924 1013/4
🖳 (070) 924 2121
✉ ismolasgolf@ismolas.it
▤ www.ismolas.it

Pevero GC Costa Smeralda   (1972)
Cala di Volpe, 07021 Porto Cervo (SS)
☎ +39 0789 958000
🖳 +39 0789 96572
✉ pevero@starwoodhotels.cpm
✍ Richard Cau (Sec)
▤ www.golfclubpevero.com

Sicily

Il Picciolo   (1988)
Strada Statale 120 km 200, 95012 Castiglione di Sicilia, (CT)-ITALIA
☎ +39 (0942) 986252
🖳 +39 (0942) 986138
✉ segreteria@ilpicciologolf.com
✍ Alfredo Petralia
▤ www.ilpicciologolf.com

Turin & Piemonte

Alpino Di Stresa   (1924)
Viale Golf Panorama 48, 28839 Vezzo (VB)
☎ (0323) 20642
🖳 (0323) 208900
✉ info@golfalpino.it
✍ Alessandro Aina
▤ www.golfalpino.it

Biella Le Betulle (1958)
Valcarozza, 13887 Magnano (BI)
☎ **(015) 679151**
🖥 (015) 679276
📧 info@golfclubbiella.it
✍ Riccardo Valzorio (Sec)
🖳 www.golfclubbiella.it

Golf Club del Cervino
(1955)
11021 Breuil- Cervinia (AO)
☎ **+39 0166 949131**
📧 info@golfcervino.com
🖳 www.golfcervino.com

Cherasco CC (1982)
Via Fraschetta 8, 12062 Cherasco (CN)
☎ **(0172) 489772/488489**
🖥 (0172) 488320
📧 info@golfcherasco.com
✍ Corrado Graglia (Dir)
🖳 www.golfcherasco.com

Claviere (1923)
Strada Nazionale 45, 10050 Claviere (TO)
☎ **(0122) 878917**

Courmayeur
11013 Courmayeur (AO)
☎ **(0165) 89103**

Cuneo (1990)
Via degli Angeli 3, 12012 Mellana-Bóves
(CN)
☎ **(0171) 387041**

Le Fronde (1973)
Via Sant-Agostino 68, 10051 Avigliana (TO)
☎ **(011) 932 8053/0540**

I Girasoli (1991)
Via Pralormo 315, 10022 Carmagnola (TO)
☎ **(011) 979 5088**
🖥 (011) 979 5228
📧 info@girasoligolf.it
✍ Renzo Dutto
🖳 www.girasoligolf.it

Iles Borromees (1987)
Loc Motta Rossa, 28833 Brovello
Carpugnino (VB)
☎ **(0323) 929285**
🖥 (0323) 929190
📧 info@golfdesiles.it
✍ Marco Garbaccio
🖳 www.golfdesiles.it

Golf dei Laghi (1993)
Via Trevisani 6, 21028 Travedona Monate
(VA)
☎ **(0332) 978101**

Margara (1975)
Via Tenuta Margara 7, 15043 Fubine (AL)
☎ **(0131) 778555**
🖥 (0131) 778772
📧 margara@golfmargara.com
✍ Gian Marco Griffi
🖳 www.golfmargara.it

La Margherita
Strada Pralormo 29, Carmagnola (TO)
☎ **(011) 979 5113**
📧 golf.lamargherita@libero.it
🖳 www.golfclubmargherita.com

La Serra (1970)
Via Astigliano 42, 15048 Valenza (AL)
☎ **(0131) 954778**
📧 golfclublaserra@tin.it

Sestrieres (1932)
Piazza Agnelli 4, 10058 Sestrieres (TO)
☎ **(0122) 755170/76243**

Stupinigi (1972)
Corso Unione Sovietica 506, 10135 Torino
☎ **(011) 347 2640**

Torino (1924)
Via Agnelli 40, 10070 Fiano Torinese
☎ **+39 (011) 923 5440/923 5670**
🖥 +39 (011) 923 5886
📧 info@circologolftorino.it
✍ Mr Mauro Stroppiana
🖳 www.circologolftorino.it

Vinovo (1986)
Via Stupinigi 182, 10048 Vinovo (TO)
☎ **(011) 965 3880**

Tuscany & Umbria

Casentino (1985)
6 Via Fronzola, 52014 Poppi (Arezzo)
☎ **(0575) 529810**
🖥 (0575) 520167
📧 info@golfclubcasentino.it
✍ Luca Alterini
🖳 www.golfclubcasentino.it

Circolo Golf Ugolino (1933)
Strada Chiantigiana 3, 50015 Grassina
☎ **(055) 230 1009/1085**
🖥 (055) 230 1141
📧 info@golfugolino.it

Conero GC Sirolo (1987)
Via Betellico 6, 60020 Sirolo (AN)
☎ **(071) 736 0613**

Cosmopolitan G&CC (1992)
Viale Pisorno 60, 56018 Tirrenia
☎ **(050) 33633**
🖥 (050) 384707
📧 info@cosmopolitangolf.it
🖳 www.cosmopolitangolf.it

Lamborghini-Panicale (1992)
Loc Soderi 1, 06064 Panicale (PG)
☎ **(075) 837582**
🖥 (075) 837582
📧 info@lamborghini.191.it
✍ Zeke Martinez
🖳 www.lamborghinionline.it

Montecatini (1985)
Via Dei Brogi 1652, Loc Pievaccia, 51015
Monsummano Terme (Pistoia)
☎ **(0572) 62218**

🖥 (0572) 617435
📧 golf_.montecatini@virgiuo.it
✍ Giannini Maria Stella
🖳 www.montecatinigolf.com

Le Pavoniere (1986)
Via Traversa Il Crocifisso, 59100 Prato
☎ **(0574) 620855**

Golf Club Perugia (1959)
06132-Loc S.Sabina (PG)
☎ **(075) 517 2204**
🖥 (075) 517 2370
📧 info@golfclubperugia.it
✍ Matteo Bragone (Mgr)
🖳 www.golfclubperugia.it

Poggio dei Medici (1995)
Via San Gavino, 27 - Loc. Cignano, I-50038
Scarperia, (Florence)
☎ **(+39) 055 84350**
🖥 (+39) 055 843439
📧 info@golfpoggiodeimedici.com
✍ Cristiano Bevilacqua (Mgr)
🖳 www.golfpoggiodeimedici.com

Punta Ala (1964)
Via del Golf 1, 58040 Punta Ala (GR)
☎ **(0564) 922121/922719**
🖳 www.puntaAla.net/golf

Tirrenia (1968)
Viale San Guido, 56018 Tirrenia (PI)
☎ **(050) 37518**

Venice & North East

Albarella Golf Club
Isola di Albarella, 45010 Rosolina (RO)
☎ **(0426) 330124**
🖥 (0426) 330830
✍ Gabriele Marangon

Cansiglio (1956)
CP 152, 31029 Vittorio Veneto
☎ **(0438) 585398**
🖥 (0438) 585398
📧 golfcansiglio@tin.it
🖳 www.golfclubcansiglio.it

Colli Berici (1986)
Strada Monti Comunali, 36040 Brendola
(VI)
☎ **(0444) 601780**

Frassanelle (1990)
Via Rialto, 5/A - 35030 Rovolon (PD)
☎ **(049) 991 0722**
📧 info@golffrassanelle.it
🖳 www.golffrassanelle.it

Lignano
Via Bonifica 3, 33054 Lignano Sabbiadoro
(UD)
☎ **(0431) 428025**
🖳 www.golflignano.it

La Montecchia (1989)
Via Montecchia 12, 35030 Selvazzano
(PD)
☎ **(049) 805 5550**

☎ (049) 805 5737
✉ info@golfmontecchia.it
🖥 www.golfmontecchia.it

Padova   (1964)
35050 Valsanzibio di Galzigano Terme (PD)
☎ **(049) 913 0078**
✉ info@golfpadova.it
🖥 www.golfpadova.it

San Floriano-Gorizia
(1987)
Castello di San Floriano, 34070 San Floriano del Collio (GO)
☎ **(0481) 884252/884234**

Trieste   (1954)
Via Padriciano 80, 34012 Trieste
☎ **(040) 226159/226270**

Udine   (1971)
Via dei Faggi 1, Località Villaverde, 33034 Fagagna (UD)
☎ **(0432) 800418**
📠 (0432) 801312
✉ info@golfudine.com
🖥 www.golfudine.com

Venezia   (1928)
Strada Vecchia 1, 30126 Alberoni (Venezia)
☎ **(041) 731333**
📠 (041) 731339
✉ info@circologolfvenezia.it
🖥 www.circologolfvenezia.it

Villa Condulmer   (1960)
Via della Croce 3, 31020 Zerman di Mogliano Veneto - Tv
☎ **(041) 457062**
📠 (041) 457202
✉ info@golfvillacondulmer.com
🖥 www.golfvillacondulmer.com

Latvia

Ozo Golf Club   (2002)
Milgravju iela 16, Riga, LV-1034
☎ **+371 6739 4399**
📠 +371 6739 4034
✉ ozogolf@apollo.lv
🖥 www.ozogolf.lv

Saliena   (2006)
Egluciems, Babites pagasts, Rigas rajons LV-2107
☎ **+371 6716 0300**
📠 +371 6714 6322
✉ golf@saliena.com
🖥 www.saliena.com

Viesturi Golf Club   (1998)
Viesturi-1, Jaunmārupe, Mārupes pagasts, LV-2166
☎ **+371 2921 9699**
📠 +371 6747 0030
✉ sandra@golfsviesturi.lv
🖥 www.golfsviesturi.lv

Luxembourg

Christnach   (1993)
Am Lahr, 7641 Christnach
☎ **87 83 83**
📠 87 95 64
✉ gcc@gns.lu
👤 Claus Uwe Leske (Mgr)
🖥 www.golfclubchristnach.lu

Clervaux   (1992)
Mecherwee, 9748 Eselborn
☎ **92 93 95**
📠 92 94 51
✉ gcclerv@pt.lu
🖥 www.golfclervaux.lu

Gaichel
Rue de Eischen, 8469 Gaichel
☎ **39 71 08**
✉ infogolf@golfgaichel.com
🖥 www.golfgaichel.com

Golf de Luxembourg   (1993)
Domaine de Belenhaff, L-6141 Junglinster
☎ **(00252) 78 00 68-1**
📠 (00352) 78 71 28
✉ info@golfdeluxembourg.lu
🖥 www.golfdeluxembourg.lu

Grand-Ducal de Luxembourg   (1936)
1 Route de Trèves, 2633 Senningerberg
☎ **34 00 90-1**
📠 34 83 91
✉ gcgd@pt.lu
👤 Mr Philippe Dewolf
🖥 www.gcgd.lu

Kikuoka Country Club   (1991)
Scheierhaff, L-5412 Canach
☎ **+352 35 61 35**
📠 +352 35 74 50
✉ playgolf@kikuoka.lu
🖥 www.kikuoka.lu

Malta

Royal Malta   (1888)
Aldo Moro Street, Marsa MRS 9064
☎ **(356) 21 22 70 19**
📠 (356) 21 22 70 20
✉ sales@royalmaltagolfclub.com
🖥 www.royalmaltagolfclub.com

Netherlands

Amsterdam & Noord Holland

Amsterdam Old Course
(1990)
Zwarte Laantje 4, 1099 CE Amsterdam
☎ **(020) 663 1766**

📠 (020) 663 4621
✉ info@amsterdamoldcourse.nl
👤 Mr B Flik
🖥 www.amsterdamoldcourse.nl

Amsterdamse   (1934)
Bauduinlaan 35, 1047 HK Amsterdam
☎ **(020) 497 7866**
📠 (020) 497 5966
✉ agc1934@wxs.nl
🖥 www.amsterdamsegolfclub.nl

BurgGolf Purmerend   (1989)
Westerweg 60, 1445 AD Purmerend
☎ **(+31) 299 689160**
✉ purmerend@burggolf.nl
🖥 www.burggolf.nl

Haarlemmermeersche Golf Club   (1986)
Spieringweg 745, 2142 ED Cruquius
☎ **(023) 558 9000**
📠 (023) 558 9009
✉ info@haarlemmermeerschegolfclub.nl
🖥 www.haarlemmermeerschegolfclub.nl

Heemskerkse   (1998)
Communicatieweg 18, 1967 PR Heemskerk
☎ **(0251) 250088**
📠 (0251) 241627
✉ manager@heemskerksegolfclub.nl
🖥 www.heemskerksegolfclub.nl

Kennemer G&CC   (1910)
Kennemerweg 78, 2042 XT Zandvoort
☎ **+31 (0)23 571 2836/8456**
📠 +31 (0)23 571 9520
✉ info@kennemergolf.nl
👤 Mr J Gelderman
🖥 www.kennemergolf.nl

De Noordhollandse
(1982)
Sluispolderweg 6, 1817 BM Alkmaar
☎ **(072) 515 6807**
📠 (072) 520 9918
✉ secretariaat @denoordhollandsegolfclub.nl
👤 Anita Von Schie (Club Mgr)
🖥 www.denoordhollandsegolfclub.nl

Olympus   (1976)
Abcouderstraatweg 46, 1105 AA Amsterdam Zuid-Oost
☎ **(0294) 281241**
🖥 www.olympusgolf.nl

Spaarnwoude   (1977)
Het Hoge Land 5, 1981 LT Velsen-Zuid
☎ **(023) 538 2708 (club)**
🖥 www.gcspaarnwoude.nl

Waterlandse   (1990)
Buikslotermeerdijk 141, 1027 AC Amsterdam
☎ **(020) 636 1040**
✉ info@golfbaanamsterdam.nl
🖥 www.golfbaanamsterdam.nl

Zaanse (1988)
Zuiderweg 68, 1456 NH Wijdewormer
☎ (0299) 438199
🖳 (0299) 474416
🖂 secretariaat@zaansegolfclub.com
🖥 www.zaansegolfclub.com

Breda & South West

Brugse Vaart (1993)
Brugse Vaart 10, 4501 NE Oostburg
☎ (0117) 453410
🖳 (0117) 455511
🖂 info@golfoostburg.com
🖥 www.golfoostburg.com

Domburgsche (1914)
Schelpweg 26, 4357 BP Domburg
☎ (0118) 586106
🖳 (0118) 586109
🖂 secretariaat@domburgschegolfclub
.nl
🖥 www.domburgschegolfclub.nl

Efteling Golf Park (1995)
Postbus 18, 5170 AA Kaatsheuvel, Holland
☎ +31 (0) 416 288 499
🖂 golfpark@efteling.com
🖥 www.efteling.nl

Grevelingenhout (1988)
Oudendijk 3, 4311 NA Bruinisse
☎ (0111) 482650
🖳 (0111) 481566

Oosterhoutse (1985)
Dukaatstraat 21, 4903 RN Oosterhout
☎ (0162) 458759
🖳 (0162) 433285
🖂 info@ogcgolf.nl
🖥 www.ogcgolf.nl

Princenbosch (1991)
Bavelseweg 153, 5126 PX Molenschot
☎ (0161) 431811
🖳 (0161) 434254
🖂 golfclub@princenbosch.nl
✍ Mr R C J Beenackers
🖥 www.princenbosch.nl

Toxandria (1928)
Veenstraat 89, 5124 NC Molenschot
☎ (0161) 411200
🖳 (0161) 411715
🖂 bestuur@toxandria.nl
🖥 www.toxandria.nl

De Woeste Kop (1986)
Justaasweg 4, 4571 NB Axel
☎ (0115) 564467
🖂 dewoestekop@planet.nl
🖥 www.dewoestekop.nl

Wouwse Plantage (1981)
Zoomvlietweg 66, 4624 RP Bergen op Zoom
☎ (0165) 377100
🖳 (0165) 377101
🖂 secretariaat@golfwouwseplantage
.nl

✍ R W Van de Pol
🖥 www.golfwouwseplantage.nl

East Central

Breuninkhof
Bussloselaan 6, 7383 RP Bussloo
☎ (0571) 261955
🖂 carla@unigolf.ni

Edese (1978)
Papendallaan 22, 6816 VD Arnhem
☎ (026) 482 1985
🖳 (026) 482 1348
🖂 info@edesegolf.nl
🖥 www.edesegolf.nl

De Graafschap (1987)
Sluitdijk 4, 7241 RR Lochem
☎ (0573) 254323
🖳 (0573) 258450
🖂 info@lochemsegolfclub.nl
✍ P Grootoonk
🖥 www.lochemsegolfclub.nl

Hattemse G&CC (1930)
Veenwal 11, 8051 AS Hattem
☎ (038) 444 1909
🖂 secretariaat@golfclub-hattem.nl
🖥 www.golfclub-hattem.nl

Keppelse (1926)
Oude Zutphenseweg 15, 6997 CH Hoog-Keppel
☎ (0314) 301416
🖂 dekeppelse@planet.nl
🖥 www.keppelse.com

De Koepel (1983)
Postbox 88, 7640 AB Wierden
☎ (0546) 576150/574070
🖳 (0546) 578109
🖂 info@golfclubdekoepel.nl
🖥 www.golfclubdekoepel.nl

Golfbaan Het Rijk van Nunspeet (1987)
Public
Plesmanlaan 30, 8072 PT Nunspeet
☎ (0341) 255255
🖂 info@golfbaanhetrijkvannunspeet
.nl
🖥 www.golfenophetrijk.nl

Rosendaelsche (1895)
Apeldoornseweg 450, 6816 SN Arnhem
☎ (026) 442 1438
🖂 info@rosendaelsche.nl
🖥 www.rosendaelsche.nl

Sallandsche De Hoek (1934)
Golfweg 2, 7431 PR Diepenveen
☎ (0570) 593269
🖳 (0570) 590102
🖂 secretariaat@sallandsche.nl
✍ Mrs J Visschers
🖥 www.sallandsche.nl

Golfbaan Het Rijk van Sybrook (1992)
Veendijk 100, 7525 PZ Enschede
☎ (0541) 530331
🖂 info@golfbaanhetrijkvansybrook.nl
🖥 www.golfengohetrijk.nl

Twentsche (1926)
Almelosestraat 17, 7495 TG Ambt Delden
☎ (074) 384 1167
🖳 (074) 384 1067
🖂 info@twentschegolfclub.nl
🖥 www.twentschegolfclub.nl

Veluwse (1957)
Nr 57, 7346 AC Hoog Soeren
☎ (055) 519 1275
🖳 (055) 519 1126
🖂 secretariaat@veluwsegolfclub.nl
🖥 www.veluwsegolfclub.nl

Welderen (1994)
POB 114, 6660AC Elst
☎ (0481) 376591
🖳 (0481) 377055
🖂 golfclub@welderen.nl
✍ E Kleyngeld (Sec)
🖥 www.golfclubwelderen.nl

Eindhoven & South East

Best G&CC (1988)
Golflaan 1, 5683 RZ Best
☎ (0499) 391443
🖂 vereniging@bestgolf.nl
🖥 www.bestgolf.nl

BurgGolf Gendersteyn Veldhoven (1994)
Locht 140, 5504 RP Veldhoven
☎ (040) 253 4444
🖂 gendersteyn@burggolf.nl
🖥 www.burggolf.nl

Golfclub BurgGolf Wijchen (1985)
Public
Weg Door de Berendonck 40, 6603 LP Wijchen
☎ (024) 642 0039
🖂 wijchen@burggolf.nl
🖥 www.burggolf.nl

Crossmoor G&CC (1986)
Laurabosweg 8, 6006 VR Weert
☎ (0495) 518438
🖂 crossmoor@planel.nl
🖥 www.crossmoor.nl

De Dommel (1928)
Zegenwerp 12, 5271 NC St Michielsgestel
☎ (073) 551 9168
🖳 (073) 551 9441
🖂 info@gcdedommel.nl
🖥 www.gcdedommel.nl

Eindhovensche Golf (1930)
Eindhovenseweg 300, 5553 VB Valkenswaard
☎ (040) 201 4816

☎ (040) 207 6177
✉ egolf@iae.nl
🖳 www.eindhovenschegolf.nl

Geijsteren G&CC   (1974)
Het Spekt 2, 5862 AZ Geijsteren
☎ **(0478) 531809/532592**
🖳 (0478) 532963
✉ gc.geijsteren@planet.nl
🖳 www.golfclubgeijsteren.nl

Havelte   (1986)
Kolonieweg 2, 7970 AA Havelte
☎ **(0521) 342200**
✉ info@golfclubhavelte.nl
🖳 www.golfclubhavelte.nl

Haviksoord   (1976)
Maarheezerweg Nrd 11, 5595 XG Leende (NB)
☎ **(040) 206 1818**
🖳 (040) 206 2761
✉ info@haviksoord.nl
🖳 www.haviksoord.nl

Herkenbosch   (1991)
Stationsweg 100, 6075 CD Herkenbosch
☎ **(0475) 529529**
🖳 (0475) 533580
✉ herkenbosch@burggolf.nl
🖳 www.gccherkenbosch.nl

Het Rijk van Nijmegen
(1985)
Postweg 17, 6561 KJ Groesbeek
☎ **(024) 397 6644**
✉ info@golfbaanhetrijkvannijmegen
.nl
🖳 www.golfenophetrijk.nl

De Peelse Golf   (1991)
Maasduinenweg 1, 5977 NP Evertsoord-Sevenum
☎ **(077) 467 8030**
🖳 (077) 467 8031
✉ info@depeelsegolf.nl
🖳 www.depeelsegolf.nl

De Schoot   (1973)
Schootsedijk 18, 5491 TD Sint Oedenrode
☎ **(04134) 73011**
🖳 (04134) 71358
✉ info@golfbaandeschoot.nl
🖳 www.golfbaandeschoot.nl

Tongelreep G&CC   (1984)
Charles Roelslaan 15, 5644 HX Eindhoven
☎ **(040) 252 0962**
🖳 (040) 293 2238
✉ gcc@golfdetongelreep.nl
✍ H C Smits (Sec)
🖳 www.golfdetongelreep.nl

Welschap   (1993)
Welschapsedijk 164, 5657 BB Eindhoven
☎ **(040) 251 5797**
✉ secretariaat@golfclubwelschap.nl
🖳 www.golfclubwelschap.nl

Limburg Province

Brunssummerheide   (1985)
Rimburgerweg 50, Brunssum
☎ **(045) 527 0968**
🖳 (045) 527 3939
✉ secr@golfbrunssummerheide.nl
🖳 www.golfbrunssummerheide.nl

Hoenshuis G&CC   (1987)
Hoensweg 17, 6367 GN Voerendaal
☎ **+31 (0) 45 575 33 00**
🖳 +31 (0) 45 575 09 00
✉ info@hoenshuis.nl
🖳 www.hoenshuisgolf.nl

De Zuid Limburgse G&CC
(1956)
Aubelsweg 1, 6281 NC Gulpen-Wittem, (GPS: Landsrade 1, 6271 NZ Gulpen-Wittem)
☎ **(043) 455 1397/1254**
🖳 (043) 455 1576
✉ secretariaat@zlgolf.nl
🖳 www.zlgolf.nl

North

BurgGolf St Nicobasga
(1990)
Legemeersterweg 16-18, 8527 DS Legemeer
☎ **(0513) 499466**
✉ st.nicobasga@burggolf.nl
🖳 www.burggolf.nl

Gelpenberg   (1970)
Gebbeveenweg 1, 7854 TD Aalden
☎ **(0591) 371929**
✉ info@dgcdegelpenberg/nl
🖳 www.dgcdegelpenberg.nl

Holthuizen   (1985)
Oosteinde 7a, 9301 ZP Roden
☎ **(050) 501 5103**
✉ golfclub.holthuizen@planet.nl
🖳 www.gc-holthuizen.nl

Lauswolt G&CC   (1964)
Van Harinxmaweg 8A, PO Box 36, 9244 ZN Beetsterzwaag
☎ **(0512) 383590**
✉ algemeen@golfclublauswolt.nl
🖳 www.golfclublauswolt.nl

Noord-Nederlandse G&CC
(1950)
Pollselaan 5, 9756 CJ Glimmen
☎ **(050) 406 2004**
🖳 (050) 406 1922
✉ secretariaat@nngcc.nl
✍ The Secretary
🖳 www.nngcc.nl

De Semslanden   (1986)
Nieuwe Dijk 1, 9514 BX Gasselternijveen
☎ **(0599) 564661/565531**
✉ semslanden@planet.nl
🖳 www.golfclubdesemslanden.nl

Rotterdam & The Hague

Broekpolder   (1981)
Watersportweg 100, 3138 HD Vlaardingen
☎ **(010) 249 5566**
✉ secretariaat@golfclubbroekpolder
.nl
🖳 www.golfclubbroekpolder.nl

Golf & Country Club Capelle a/d IJssel   (1977)
Gravenweg 311, 2905 LB Capelle a/d IJssel
☎ **(010) 442 2485**
🖳 (010) 284 0606
✉ info@golfclubcapelle.nl
🖳 www.golfclubcapelle.nl

Cromstrijen   (1989)
Veerweg 26, 3281 LX Numansdorp
☎ **(0186) 654455**
🖳 (0186) 654681
✉ info@golfclubcromstrijen.nl
🖳 www.golfclubcromstrijen.nl

De Hooge Bergsche   (1989)
Rottebandreef 40, 2661 JK Bergschenhoek
☎ **(010) 522 0052/522 0703**
🖳 (08) 422 32305
✉ secretariaat@hoogebergsche.nl
🖳 www.hoogebergsche.nl

Koninklijke Haagsche G&CC   (1893)
Groot Haesebroekeseweg 22, 2243 EC Wassenaar
☎ **(070) 517 9607**
🖳 (070) 514 0171
✉ secretariaat@khgcc.nl
✍ H P Wirth (Mgr)
🖳 www.khgcc.nl

Kralingen
Kralingseweg 200, 3062 CG Rotterdam
☎ **(010) 452 2283**
✉ secretaris@gckralingen.nl
🖳 www.gckralingen.nl

Leidschendamse Leeuwenbergh   (1988)
Elzenlaan 31, 2495 AZ Den Haag
☎ **(070) 395 4556**
🖳 (070) 399 8615
✉ secretariaat@leeuwenbergh.nl
🖳 www.leeuwenbergh.nl

De Merwelanden   (1985)
Public
Golfbaan Crayestein, Baanhoekweg 50, 3313 LP Dordrecht
☎ **(078) 621 1221**

Noordwijkse Golf Club
(1915)
Randweg 25, PO Box 70, 2200 AB Noordwijk
☎ **(0252) 373761**
🖳 (0252) 370044
✉ info@noordwijksegolfclub.nl

✍ N H Smittenaar
🖳 www.noordwijksegolfclub.nl

Oude Maas (1975)
(Rhoon Golfcenter), Veerweg 2a, 3161 EX Rhoon
☎ **(010) 501 5135**
📠 golfcluboudemaas@kebelfoon.nl
🖳 www.golfcluboudemaas.nl

Rijswijkse (1987)
Delftweg 59, 2289 AL Rijswijk
☎ **(070) 395 4864**
🖳 (070) 399 5040
📠 secretariaat@rijswijksegolf.nl
🖳 www.rijswijksegolf.nl

Wassenaarse Golfclub Rozenstein (1984)
Dr Mansveltkade 15, 2242 TZ Wassenaar
☎ **+31 (070) 511 7846**
📠 secretariaat@rozenstein.nl
🖳 www.rozenstein.nl

Westerpark Zoetermeer (1985)
Heuvelweg 3, 2716 DZ Zoetermeer, Ogoo-Burg Golf
☎ **(0900) 28744653**
🖳 (079) 3203132
📠 zoetermeer@burggolf.nl
✍ Mr V Slooten
🖳 www.burggolf.nl

Zeegersloot (1984)
Kromme Aarweg 5, PO Box 190, 2400 AD Alphen a/d Rijn
☎ **(0172) 474567**
🖳 (0172) 494660
📠 secretariaat@zeegersloot.nl
🖳 www.zeegersloot.nl

Utrecht & Hilversum

Almeerderhout (1986)
Watersnipweg 19-21, 1341 AA Almere
☎ **(036) 521 9160**
🖳 (036) 521 9131
📠 secretariaat@almeerderhout.nl
🖳 www.almeerderhout.nl

Anderstein (1986)
Woudenbergseweg 13a, 3953 ME Maarsbergen
☎ **(0343) 431330**
🖳 (0343) 432062
📠 info@golfclubanderstein.nl
🖳 www.golfclubanderstein.nl

De Batouwe (1990)
Oost Kanaalweg 1, 4011 LA Zoelen
☎ **(0344) 624370**
🖳 (0344) 613096
📠 secretariaat@debatouwe.nl
✍ Mrs ER de Regt-uan Dijk
🖳 www.debatouwe.nl

Flevoland (1979)
Parlaan 2A, 8241 BG Lelystad
☎ **(0320) 230077**

🖳 (0320) 230932
📠 info@golfflevo.nl
🖳 www.golfflevo.nl

De Haar (1974)
PO Box 104, Parkweg 5, 3450 AC Vleuten
☎ **(030) 677 2860**
🖳 (030) 677 3903
📠 gcdehaar@xs4all.nl
🖳 www.gcdehaar.nl

Hilversumsche Golf Club (1910)
Soestdijkerstraatweg 172, 1213 XJ Hilversum
☎ **(035) 683 8859**
📠 info@hilversumschegolfclub.nl
✍ Mrs M G Van Den Hengel-Smink
🖳 www.hilversumschegolfclub.nl

De Hoge Kleij (1985)
Loes van Overeemlaan 16, 3832 RZ Leusden
☎ **(033) 461 6944**
🖳 (033) 465 2921
📠 secretariaat@hogekleij.nl
🖳 www.hogekleij.nl

Nieuwegeinse (1985)
Postbus 486, 3437 AL Nieuwegein
☎ **(030) 604 2192**

Utrechtse Golf Club 'De Pan' (1894)
Amersfoortseweg 1, 3735 LJ Bosch en Duin
☎ **(030) 696 9120**
🖳 (030) 696 3769
📠 secretariaat@ugcdepan.nl
🖳 www.ugcdepan.nl

Zeewolde (1984)
Golflaan 1, 3896 LL Zeewolde
☎ **(036) 522 2103**
🖳 (036) 522 4100
📠 secretariaat@golfclub-zeewolde.nl
✍ B Beekmans (Mgr)
🖳 www.golfclub-zeewolde.nl

Norway

Arendal og Omegn (1986)
Nes Verk, 4900 Tvedestrand
☎ **37 19 90 30**
📠 post@arendalgk.no
🖳 www.arendalgk.no

Baerum GK (1972)
Hellerudveien 26, 1350 Lommedalen
☎ **67 87 67 00**
🖳 67 87 67 20
📠 bmgk@bmgk.no
✍ Brede Kristoffersen
🖳 www.bmgk.no

Bergen Golf Clubb (1937)
Ervikveien 120, 5106 Øvre Ervik
☎ **55 19 91 80**
🖳 55 19 91 81

📠 info@bgk.no
🖳 www.bgk.no

Borre (1991)
Semb Hovedgaard, 3186 Horten
☎ **416 27000**
🖳 33 07 15 16
📠 borregb@online.no
✍ Thomas Pedersen
🖳 www.borregolf.no

Borregaard (1927)
PO Box 348, 1702 Sarpsborg
☎ **69 12 15 00**
📠 borregaardgk@golf.no
🖳 www.borregaardgk.no

Drøbak (1988)
Belsjøveien 50, 1440 Drøbak
☎ **+47 64 98 96 50**
📠 dgkodrobakgolf.no
🖳 www.drobakgolf.no

Elverum (1980)
PO Box 71, 2401 Elverum
☎ **62 41 35 88**
📠 post@elverumgolf.no
🖳 www.elverumgolf.no

Grenland (1976)
Luksefjellvn 578, 3721 Skien
☎ **35 50 62 70**
🖳 35 59 06 10
📠 post@grenlandgolf.no
🖳 www.grenlandgolf.no

Groruddalen (1988)
Postboks 37, Stovner, 0913 Oslo
☎ **22 79 05 60**
📠 post@grorudgk.no
🖳 www.grorudgk.no

Hemsedal (1994)
3560 Hemsedal
☎ **32 06 23 77**

Kjekstad (1976)
PO Box 201, 3440 Royken
☎ **31 29 79 90**

Kristiansand (2003)
PO Box 6090 Søm, 4691 Kristiansand
☎ **38 14 85 60**
🖳 38 04 34 15
📠 post@kristiansandgk.no
🖳 www.kristiansandgk.no

Larvik (1989)
Fritzøe Gård, 3267 Larvik
☎ **33 140 140**
🖳 33 14 01 49
📠 klubben@larvikgolf.no
✍ Horten Ertsas
🖳 www.larvikgolf.no

Narvik (1992)
8523 Elvegard
☎ **76 95 12 01**
📠 post@narvikgolf.no
🖳 www.narvikgolf.no

Nes   (1988)
Rommen Golfpark, 2160 Vormsund
☎ 63 91 20 30
✉ bente@nesgolfklubb.no
🖥 www.nesgolfklubb.no

Onsøy   (1987)
Golfveien, 1626 Manstad
☎ +47 69 33 91 50

Oppdal   (1987)
PO Box 19, 7340 Oppdal
☎ 72 42 25 10

Oppegård   (1985)
Kongeveien 198, 1415 Oppegård
☎ 66 81 59 90
📠 66 81 59 91
✉ leder@opgk.no
🖥 www.opgk.no

Oslo   (1924)
Bogstad, 0757 Oslo
☎ 22 51 05 60
📠 22 51 05 61
✉ post@oslogk.no
🖉 Niels Vik
🖥 www.oslogk.no

Ostmarka   (1989)
Postboks 63, 1914 Ytre Enebakk
☎ 64 92 38 40

Oustoen CC   (1965)
PO Box 100, 1330 Fornebu
☎ 67 83 23 80/22 56 33 54
✉ occ@occ.no
🖥 www.occ.no

Skjeberg   (1986)
PO Box 528, 1701 Sarpsborg
☎ 69 16 63 10

Sorknes   (1990)
PB 100, 2451 Rena
☎ 45 20 86 00
✉ post@sorknesgk.no
🖥 www.sorknesgk.no

Stavanger   (1956)
Longebakke 45, 4042 Hafrsfjord
☎ 519 39100
📠 519 39110
✉ steinar@sgk.no
🖥 www.sgk.no

Trondheim   (1950)
PO Box 169, 7401 Trondheim
☎ 73 53 18 85
🖥 www.golfklubben.no

Tyrifjord   (1982)
Sturoya, 3531 Krokleiva
☎ 32 16 13 60
📠 32 16 13 40
🖥 www.tyrifjord-golfklubb.no

Vestfold   (1958)
PO Box 64, 3108 Vear
☎ 33 36 25 00
📠 33 36 25 01

✉ vgk@vestfoldgolfklubb.no
🖉 Knut Gran
🖥 www.vgk.no

Poland

Amber Baltic   (1993)
Baltycka Street 13, 72-514 Kolczewo
☎ (091) 32 65 110/120
✉ abgc@abgc.pol.pl
🖥 www.abgc.pl

Portugal

Algarve

**Clube de Golfe de Vale do
Lobo**   (1968)
Vale Do Lobo, 8135-864 Vale do Lobo
☎ +351 289 353 465
✉ golf@vdl.pt
🖥 www.valedolobo.com

Floresta Parque   (1987)
Vale do Poço, Budens, 8650 Vila do Bispo
☎ (282) 690 054
📠 (282) 695 157
✉ alan.hodsongolf@vigiasa.com
🖉 Alan Hodson

Oceânico Pinhal   (1976)
*Apartado 970, 8126-912 Vilamoura,
Algarve*
☎ (0289) 310390
📠 (0289) 310393
✉ bookings@oceanicogolf.com
🖥 www.oceanicogolf.com

Oceânico Academy Course
(2008)
*Apartado 970, 8126-912 Vilamoura,
Algarve*
☎ 00 351 282 320 800
📠 00 351 282 313 760
✉ bookings@oceanicogolf.com
🖥 www.oceanicogolf.com

Oceânico Faldo Course
(2008)
*Apartado 970, 8126-912 Vilamoura,
Algarve*
☎ 00 351 282 320 800
📠 00 351 282 313 760
✉ bookings@oceanicogolf.com
🖥 www.oceanicogolf.com

Oceânico Laguna   (1990)
*Apartado 970, 8126-912 Vilamoura,
Algarve*
☎ (0289) 310180
📠 (0289) 310183
✉ bookings@oceanicogolf.com
🖥 www.oceanicogolf.com

Oceânico Millennium   (2000)
*Apartado 970, 8126-912 Vilamoura,
Algarve*
☎ (0289) 310188
📠 (0289) 310183
✉ bookings@oceanicogolf.com
🖥 www.oceanicogolf.com

Oceânico O'Connor Jnr
(2008)
*Apartado 970, 8126-912 Vilamoura,
Algarve*
☎ 00 351 282 320 800
📠 00 351 282 313 760
✉ bookings@oceanicogolf.com
🖥 www.oceanicogolf.com

Oceânico Old Course   (1969)
*Apartado 970, 8126-912 Vilamoura,
Algarve*
☎ (289) 310341
📠 (289) 310321
✉ bookings@oceanicogolf.com
🖥 www.oceanicogolf.com

Oceânico Victoria   (2004)
*Apartado 970, 8126-912 Vilamoura,
Algarve*
☎ 00 351 289 320 100
📠 00 351 289 320 104
✉ bookings@oceanicogolf.com
🖥 www.oceanicogolf.com

Palmares   (1975)
Apartado 74, Meia Praia, 8601 901 Lagos
☎ +351 282 790500
📠 +351 282 290509
✉ golf@palmaresgolf.com
🖥 www.palmaresgolf.com

Penina   (1966)
PO Box 146, Penina, 8501-952 Portimào
☎ (351) 282 420223
📠 (351) 282 420252
✉ golf.penina@lemeridien.com
🖥 www.lemeridien.com/peninagolf

Pestana   (1991)
Apartado 1011, 8400-908 Carvoeiro Lga
☎ (0282) 340900
✉ info@pestanagolf.com
🖥 www.pestanagolf.com

Pestana Alto Golf   (1991)
Quinta do Alto do Poço, 8501 906 Alvor
☎ (00351) 282 460870
📠 (00351) 282 460879
✉ info@pestanagolf.com
🖥 www.pestanagolf.com

Pine Cliffs G&CC   (1991)
*Praia da Falesia, PO Box 644, 8200-909
Albufeira*
☎ (+351) 289 500100
✉ sheraton.algarve@starwoodhotels
.com

Pinheiros Altos   (1992)
Quinta do Lago, 8135 Almancil
☎ (0289) 359910
📠 (0289) 394392
✉ golf@pinheirosaltos.pt

🖉 Christophe Rindlisbacher
📧 www.pinheirosaltos.pt

Quinta do Lago (1974)
Quinta Do Lago, 8135-024 Almancil
☎ (+351) 289 390 700
📠 (+351) 289 394 013
📧 geral@quintadolagogolf.com
🖉 Patrick Murphy
📧 www.quintadolagogolf.com

Salgados
Apartado 2362, Vale do Rabelho, 8200
917 Albufeira
☎ (0289) 583030

San Lorenzo (1888)
Quinta do Lago, 8135 Almancil
☎ +351 289 396 522
📠 +351 289 396 908
📧 sanlorenzo@jjwhotels.com
🖉 António Rosa Santos (Mgr)
📧 www.sanlorenzogolfcourse.com

Vale de Milho (1990)
Apartado 1273, Praia do Carvoeiro, 8401-
911 Carvoeiro Lga
☎ (282) 358502
📠 (282) 358497
📧 reservas@valedemilhogolf.com
🖉 M Stilwell (Director)
📧 www.valedemilhogolf.com

Clube de Golfe de Vale do Lobo (1968)
Vale Do Lobo, 8135-864 Vale do Lobo
☎ +351 289 353 465
📠 +351 289 353 003
📧 golf@vdl.pt
🖉 Hernani Estevão (Golf Mgr)
📧 www.valedolobo.com

Vila Sol Spa & Golf Resort (1991)
Alto do Semino, Morgadinhos, Vilamoura,
8125-307-Quarteira
☎ (+351) 289 300505
📧 golfreservation@vilasol.pt
📧 www.vilasol.pt

Batalha Golf Course (1996)
Rua do Bom Jesus, Aflitos, 9545-234 Fenais
da Luz (Açores)
☎ +351 296 498 599/560
📠 +351 296 498 612
📧 info@azoresgolfislands.com
🖉 Pilar Melo Antunes
📧 www.azoresgolfislands.com

Furnas Golf Course (1936)
Achada das Furnas, 9675 Furnas
☎ (+351) 296 498 559/560
📠 (+351) 296 498 612
📧 info@azoresgolfislands.com
🖉 Pilar Melo Antunes
📧 www.azoresgolfislands.com

Terceira Island (1954)
Caixa Postal 15, 9760 909 Praia da
Victória (Açores)
☎ (0295) 902444

Aroeira (1972)
Herdade da Aroeira, 2820-567 Charneca
da Caparica
☎ +351 (212) 979 110/1
📧 golf.reservas@aroeira.com
📧 www.aroeira.com

Belas Clube de Campo (1998)
Alameda do Aqueduto, Escritórios Belas
Clube de Campo, 2605-193 Belas
☎ (00351) 21 962 6640
📠 (00351) 21 962 6641
📧 golfe@planbelas.pt
🖉 Salvador Leite de Castro (Sec)
📧 www.belasclubedecampo.pt

Estoril (1936)
Avenida da República, 2765-273 Estoril
☎ (351) 21466 0367
📠 (351) 21468 2796
📧 reserva@golfestoril.com
📧 www.palacioestorilhotel.com

Estoril-Sol Golf Academy (1976)
Quinta do Outeira, Linhó, 2710 Sintra
☎ (01) 923 2461

Lisbon Sports Club (1922)
Casal da Carregueira, 2605-213 Belas
☎ (21) 431 0077
📧 geral@lisbonclub.com
📧 www.lisbonclub.com

Marvão (1998)
Quinta do Prado, São Salvador da
Aramenha, 7330-328 Marvão
☎ (245) 993 755

Golf do Montado (1992)
Urbanização do Golf Montando, Lte no.1 -
Algeruz, 2950-051 Palmela
☎ (265) 708150
📧 geral@golfdomontando.com.pt
📧 www.golfmontando.com.pt

Penha Longa (1992)
Estrada da Lagoa Azul, Linhó, 2714-511
Sintra
☎ (021) 924 9011
📧 reservas.golf@penhalonga.com
📧 www.penhalonga.com

Quinta da Beloura (1994)
Estrada de Albarraque, 2710 692 Sintra
☎ (021) 910 6350
📧 beloura.golfe@pestana.com
📧 www.pestanagolf.com

Quinta da Marinha Oitavos Golfe (2001)
Quinta da Marinha, Casa da Quinta No25,
2750-715 Cascais
☎ 351 21 486 06 00
📧 oitavosgolfe@quinta-da-marinha.pt
📧 www.quintadamarinha-oitavosgolfe.pt

Quinta do Perú Golf & Country Club (1994)
Alameda da Serra 2, 2975-666 Quinta do
Conde
☎ (021) 213 4320
📠 (021) 213 4321
📧 pedro@golfquintadoperu.com
🖉 Pedro De Mello Breyner (Club Mgr)
📧 www.golfquintadoperu.com

Tróia Golf Championship Course (1980)
Tróia, 7570-789 Carvalhal
☎ (+351) 265 494 112
📠 (+351) 265) 494 315
📧 troiagolf@sonae.pt
📧 www.troiagolf.com

Vimeiro
Praia do Porto Novo, Vimeiro, 2560 Torres
Vedras
☎ (061) 984157

Madeira (1991)
Sto Antonio da Serra, 9200 Machico,
Madeira
☎ (091) 552345/552356

Palheiro (1993)
Rua do Balancal No.29, 9060-414 Funchal,
Madeira
☎ (00351) 291 790 120
📧 reservations.golf@palheiroestate.com
📧 www.palheiroestate.com

Amarante (1997)
Quinta da Deveza, Fregim, 4600-593
Amarante
☎ +351 255 44 60 60
📧 sgagolfeamarante@oninet.pt
📧 www.amarantegolfclube.com

Golden Eagle (1994)
E.N. 1, Km 63/64, Asseicera, 2040-481 Rio
Maior
☎ +351 243 940040
📠 +351 243 940049
📧 reservations@goldeneagle.pt
🖉 David Ashington
📧 www.goldeneagle.pt

Miramar (1932)
*Av Sacadura Cabral, Miramar, 4405-013
Arcozelo V.N.Gaia*
☎ **(022) 762 2067**
🖳 (022) 762 7859
📧 cgm@cgm.pt
🖉 President Alvaro Teles De Meneses
🖹 www.cgm.pt

Montebelo
Farminhão, 3510 Viseu
☎ **(032) 856464**

Oporto Golf Club (1890)
Sisto-Paramos, 4500 Espinho
☎ **(022) 734 2008**
🖳 (022) 734 6895
📧 oportogolfclub@oninet.pt
🖹 www.oportogolfclub.com

Ponte de Lima
*Quinta de Pias, Fornelos, 4490 Ponte de
Lima*
☎ **(058) 43414**

Praia d'el Rey G&CC (1997)
Vale de Janelas, Apartado 2, 2510 Obidos
☎ **(+351) 262 905005**
📧 golf@praia-del-rey.com
🖹 www.praia-del-rey.com

Golfe Quinta da Barca
(1997)
Barca do Lago, 4740-476 Esposende
☎ **(+351) 2539 66723**
📧 lcatarino@quintabarca.com
🖹 www.quintabarca.com

Vidago Palace Golf Course
(1936)
*Parque de Vidago, Apartado 16, 5425-307
Vidago*
☎ **00351 276 990 980**
🖳 00351 276 990 912
📧 golf@vidagopalace.com
🖉 Santiago Villar (Asst Mgr)
🖹 www.vidagopalace.com

Slovenia

Bled G&CC (1937)
Public
Kidriceva 10 c, 4260 Bled
☎ **+386 (0)4 537 77711**
📧 info@golf.bled.si
🖹 www.golf.bled.si

Castle Mokrice (1992)
*Terme Catez, Topliska Cesta 35, 8250
Brezice*
☎ **(00386) 7 457 4260**
🖳 (00386) 7 495 7007
📧 golf@terme-catez.si
🖉 Aleš Stopar
🖹 www.terme-catez.si

Lipica (1989)
Lipica 5, 66210 Sezana
☎ **+386 (0)5 734 6373**

🖳 +386 (0)5 739 1725
📧 golf@lipica.org
🖹 www.lipica.org

Spain

Alicante & Murcia

Alicante (1998)
*Av. Locutor Vicente Hipolito 37, Playa San
Juan, 03540 Alicante*
☎ **(96) 515 37 94/515 20 43**
🖳 (96) 516 37 07
📧 clubgolf@alicantegolf.com
🖉 Angel LLopes Molina (Mgr)
🖹 www.alicantegolf.org

Altorreal (1994)
*Urb Altorreal, 30500 Molina de Segura
(Murcia)*
☎ **(968) 64 81 44**

Bonalba (1993)
*Partida de Bonalba, 03110 Mutxamiel
(Alicante)*
☎ **(96) 595 5955**
📧 golfbonalba@golfbonalba.com
🖹 www.golfbonalba.com

Don Cayo (1974)
*Apartado 341, 03599 Altea La Vieja
(Alicante)*
☎ **(96) 584 80 46**
🖳 (96) 584 65 19
📧 info@golfdoncayo.com
🖉 Alexis Garca-Valdes (Mgr)
🖹 www.golfdoncayo.com

Ifach (1974)
*Crta Moraira-Calpe Km 3, Apdo 28, 03720
Benisa (Alicante)*
☎ **(96) 649 71 14**
🖳 (96) 649 9908
📧 golfifach@gmail.com
🖉 Gonzalo Gonzalez
⊕ 9 holes, 3 Par 4's - Par 60

Jávea (1981)
Apartado 148, 03730 Jávea, (Alicante)
☎ **(96) 579 25 84**

La Manga (1971)
Los Belones, 30385 Cartagena (Murcia)
☎ **(968) 175000 ext 1360**
🖳 (968) 175058
📧 golf@lamangaclub.es
🖹 www.lamangaclub.com

La Marquesa (1989)
*Ciudad Quesada II, 03170 Rojales,
(Alicante)*
☎ **(+34) 96 671 42 58**
🖳 (+34) 96 671 42 67
📧 info@lamarquesagolf.es
🖹 www.lamarquesagolf.es

Las Ramblas (1991)
*Crta Alicante-Cartagena Km48, 03189 Urb
Villamartin, Orihuela (Alicante)*
☎ **(96) 677 4728**
🖳 (96) 677 4733
📧 golflasramblas@grupoquara.com
🖹 www.grupoquara.com

Real Campoamor (1989)
*Crta Cartagena-Alicante Km48, Apdo 17,
03189 Orihuela-Costa (Alicante)*
☎ **(96) 532 13 66**
🖳 (96) 532 05 06
📧 golf@lomasdecampoamor.es
🖉 Elena Gonzalez
🖹 www.lomasdecampoamor.com

La Sella Golf (1991)
*Ctra La Xara-Jesús Pobre, 03749 Jesús
Pobre (Alicante)*
☎ **(96) 645 42 52/645 41 10**
🖳 (96) 645 42 01
📧 info@lasellagolf.com
🖹 www.lasellagolfresort.com

Villamartin (1972)
*Crta Alicante-Cartagena Km50, 03189 Urb
Villamartin, Orihuela (Alicante)*
☎ **(96) 676 51 27/676 51 60**
🖳 (96) 676 51 70
📧 golfvillamartin@grupoquara.com
🖹 www.grupoquara.com

Almería

Almerimar (1976)
Urb Almerimar, 04700 El Ejido (Almería)
☎ **(950) 48 02 34**

**El Cortijo Grande Golf
Resort** (1976)
*Apdo 2, Cortijo Grande, 04639 Turre
(Almería)*
☎ **(950) 479176**
📧 golf@cortijogrande.net
🖹 www.cortijogrande.net

La Envia (1993)
Apdo 51, 04720 Aguadulce (Almería)
☎ **(950) 55 96 41**

Playa Serena (1979)
*Paseo del golf No.8, 04740 Roquetas de
Mar (Almería)*
☎ **+34 (950) 33 30 55**
🖳 +34 (950) 33 30 55
📧 info@golfplayaserena.com
🖹 www.golfplayaserena.com

Badajoz & West

Guadiana (1992)
*Crta Madrid-Lisboa Km 393, Apdo 171,
06080 Badajoz*
☎ **(924) 44 81 88**

Norba (1988)
Apdo 880, 10080 Cáceres
☎ **(927) 23 14 41**

Salamanca (1988)
*Monte de Zarapicos, 37170 Zarapicos
(Salamanca)*
- ☎ **(923) 32 91 00**
- ☐ (923) 32 91 05
- ✉ club@salamancagolf.com
- 🖳 www.salamancagolf.com

Balearic Islands

Canyamel
*Urb Canyamel, Crta de Cuevas, 07580
Capdepera, (Mallorca)*
- ☎ **(971) 56 44 57**

Capdepera (1989)
Apdo 6, 07580 Capdepera, Mallorca
- ☎ **(971) 56 58 75/56 58 57**

Ibiza (1990)
Apdo 1270, 07840 Santa Eulalia, (Ibiza)
- ☎ **(971) 19 61 18**

Mallorca Marriott Golf Son Antem (1993)
*Carretera Ma 19, Salida 20-07620
Llucmajor, Mallorca*
- ☎ **(+34) 971 12 92 00**
- ☐ (+34) 971 12 92 01
- ✉ mhrs.pmigs.golf.reservation
  @marriott.com
- ✍ Bernat Hobera (Pres)
- 🖳 www.sonantemgolf.com

Pollensa (1986)
*Ctra Palma-Pollensa Km 49.3, 07460
Pollensa, (Mallorca)*
- ☎ **(0034) 971 533216**
- ☐ (0034) 971 533265
- ✉ rec@golfpollensa.com
- ✍ Cesar Riera
- 🖳 www.golfpollensa.com

Poniente (1978)
Costa de Calvia, 07181 Calvia (Mallorca)
- ☎ **(971) 13 01 48**
- ☐ (971) 13 01 76
- ✉ golf@ponientegolf.com
- ✍ Mr Jose Jimenez (Mgr)
- 🖳 www.ponientegolf.com

Pula Golf (1995)
*Ctra. Son Servera-Capdepera, E-07550 Son
Servera-Mallorca*
- ☎ **(971) 81 70 34**
- ☐ (971) 81 70 35
- ✉ reservas@pulagolf.com
- ✍ Rahel Wanke
- 🖳 www.pulagolf.com

Real Golf Bendinat
(1986)
C. Campoamor, 07181 Calviá, (Mallorca)
- ☎ **(971) 40 52 00**
- ☐ (971) 70 07 86
- ✉ golfbendinat@terra.es
- ✍ Alison Bradshaw
- 🖳 www.realgolfbendinat.com

Santa Ponsa (1976)
Santa Ponsa, 07180 Calvia (Mallorca)
- ☎ **(971) 69 02 11**
- ✉ golf1@habitatgolf.es
- 🖳 www.habitatgolf.es

Golf Son Parc Menorca
(1977)
*Urb. Son Parc s/n, ES Mercadal-Menorca,
Baleares*
- ☎ **+34 (971)-188875/359059**
- ✉ info@golfsonparc.com
- 🖳 www.golfsonparc.com

Son Servera (1967)
*Costa de Los Pinos, 07759 Son Servera,
(Mallorca)*
- ☎ **(971) 84 00 96**

Son Vida (1964)
Urb Son Vida, 07013 Palma (Mallorca)
- ☎ **(971) 79 12 10**

Vall d'Or Golf (1985)
Apdo 23, 07660 Cala D'Or, (Mallorca)
- ☎ **(971) 83 70 68/83 70 01**
- ☐ (971) 83 72 99
- ✉ valldorgolf@valldorgolf.com
- ✍ Julia Jana Litten (Sec)/Israel
  Rodrigues Rojas (Mgr)
- 🖳 www.valldorgolf.com

Barcelona & Cataluña

Aro-Mas Nou (1990)
Apdo 429, 17250 Playa de Aro
- ☎ **(972) 82 69 00**

Bonmont Terres Noves
(1990)
*Urb Terres Noves, 43300 Montroig
(Tarragona)*
- ☎ **(977) 81 81 40**
- 🖳 www.bonmont.com

Caldes Internacional (1992)
*Apdo 200, 08140 Caldes de Montbui
(Barcelona)*
- ☎ **(93) 865 38 28**

Club de Golf Costa Dorada Tarragona (1983)
Apartado 600, 43080 Tarragona
- ☎ **(977) 65 3361/(977) 65 3605**
- ☐ (977) 65 3028
- ✉ club@golfcostadoratarragona
  .com
- 🖳 www.golfcostadoradatarragona
  .com

Costa Brava (1962)
*La Masia, 17246 Sta Cristina d'Aro
(Girona)*
- ☎ **(972) 83 71 50**
- ☐ (972) 83 72 72
- ✉ info@golfcostabrava.com
- ✍ Ma Victoria Figueras Garcia
- 🖳 www.golfcostabrava.com

Empordà Golf Resort (1990)
*Crta Torroella de Montgri, 17257 Gualta
(Gerona)*
- ☎ **(972) 76 04 50/76 01 36**
- ☐ (972) 75 71 00
- ✉ info@empordagolf.com
- ✍ Anna Gurana
- 🖳 www.empordagolf.com

Fontanals de Cerdanya
(1994)
*Fontanals de Cerdanya, 17538 Soriguerola
(Girona)*
- ☎ **(972) 14 43 74**

Golf Girona (1992)
*Urbanització Golf Girona s/n, 17481 Sant
Julia de Ramis, (Girona)*
- ☎ **(972) 17 16 41**
- ✉ golfgirona@golfgirona.com
- 🖳 www.golfgirona.com

Llavaneras (1945)
*Cami del Golf 45-51, 08392 San Andreu de
Llavaneras, (Barcelona)*
- ☎ **(93) 792 60 50**
- ☐ (93) 795 25 58
- ✉ lucas.bueno@golfllavaneras.com
- ✍ Mr Lucas Bueno (Gen Mgr)
- 🖳 www.golfllavaneras.com

Masia Bach (1990)
*Ctra Martorell-Capellades, 08635 Sant
Esteve Sesrovires*
- ☎ **(93) 772 8800**

Osona Montanya (1988)
*Masia L'Estanyol, 08553 El Brull
(Barcelona)*
- ☎ **(93) 884 01 70**

Peralada Golf (1993)
La Garriga, 17491 Peralada, Girona
- ☎ **+34 972 538 287**
- ☐ +34 972 538 236
- ✉ casa.club@golfperalada.com
- ✍ Nuria Bech Diumenge (Mgr)
- 🖳 www.golfperalada.com

Golf Platja de Pals (1966)
Pay and play
Ctra. Golf, Num. 64, Pals - Girona 17256
- ☎ **(+34) 972 66 77 39**
- ☐ (+34) 972 63 67 99
- ✉ recep@golfplatjadepals.com
- ✍ Alexandra Reig (Mgr)
- 🖳 www.golfplatjadepals.com

Reus Aigüesverds (1989)
*Crta de Cambrils, Mas Guardià, E-43206
Reus-Tarragona*
- ☎ **(977) 75 27 25**
- ☐ (977) 12 03 91
- ✉ info@golfreusaiguesverds.com
- ✍ J Mourges (Mgr)
- 🖳 www.golfreusaiguesverds.com

Terramar (1922)
Apdo 6, 08870 Sitges
- ☎ **(93) 894 05 80/894 20 43**
- ✉ reservas@golfterramar.com
- 🖳 www.golfterramar.com

Torremirona   (1994)
Ctra N-260 Km 46, 17744 Navata
(Girona)
☎ **(+34) 972 55 37 37**
✉ golf@torremirona.com
🖥 www.torremirona.com

Burgos & North

Castillo de Gorraiz   (1993)
Urb Castillo de Gorraiz, 31620 Valle de
Egues (Navarra)
☎ **(948) 33 70 73**
✉ administracion@golfgorraiz.com
🖥 www.golfgorraiz.com

Izki Golf   (1992)
C/Arriba, S/N, 01119 Urturi (Alava)
☎ **(945) 378262**
📠 (945) 378266
✉ izkigolf@izkigolf.com
📠 (945) 378262
🖥 www.izkigolf.com

Larrabea   (1989)
Crta de Landa, 01170 Legutiano, (Alava)
☎ **(945) 46 58 44/46 58 41**

Lerma   (1991)
Ctra Madrid-Burgos Km195, 09340 Lerma
(Burgos)
☎ **(947) 17 12 14/17 12 16**
✉ golflerma@csa.es

La Llorea   (1994)
Crta Nacional 632, Km 62, 33394
Gijön/Xixón
☎ **(985) 10 30**
📠 (985) 36 47 26
✉ administraciongolf.pdm@gijon.es
🖥 www.golflallorea.com

Real Golf Castiello   (1958)
Apdo Correos 161, 33200 Gijón
☎ **(985) 36 63 13**
✉ administracion@castiello.com
🖥 www.castiello.com

Real Golf Pedreña   (1928)
Apartado 233, Santander
☎ **(942) 50 00 01/50 02 66**

Real San Sebastián   (1910)
PO Box 6, Fuenterrabia, (Guipúzcoa)
☎ **(943) 61 68 45**
📠 (943) 61 14 91
✉ rgcss@golfsansebastian.com
📠 Bertol Oria
🖥 www.golfsansebastian.com

Real Golf Club De Zarauz
    (1916)
Lauaxeta, 7, Zarauz, (Guipúzcoa)
☎ **(943) 83 01 45**
📠 (943) 13 15 68
✉ info@golfzarauz.com
📠 Beatriz Aseguinolaza
🖥 www.golfzarauz.com

Ulzama   (1965)
31779 Guerendiain (Navarra)
☎ **(948) 30 51 62**

Canary Islands

Amarilla   (1988)
Urb Amarilla Golf, San Miguel de Abona,
38630 Santa Cruz de Tenerife
☎ **(922) 73 03 19**

Costa Teguise   (1978)
Avenida del Golf s/n, 35508 Costa Teguise
☎ **(928) 59 05 12**
📠 (928) 59 23 37
✉ info@lanzarote-
golf.com/info@lanzarote-golf.e
🖥 www.lanzarote-golf.com

Maspalomas   (1968)
Av de Neckerman, Maspalomas, 35100
Gran Canaria
☎ **(928) 76 25 81/76 73 43**
🖥 www.maspalomasgolf.net

Real Club de Golf de
    Tenerife   (1932)
Campo de Golf No.1 38350, Tacoronte,
Tenerife
☎ **(922) 63 66 07**
📠 (922) 63 64 80
✉ info@rcgt.es
📠 Vidal Carralero Ceva (Mgr)
🖥 www.rcgt.es

Real Golf Las Palmas   (1891)
PO Box 93, 35380 Santa Brigida, Gran
Canaria
☎ **(928) 35 10 50/35 01 04**
✉ rcglp@realclubdegolfdelaspalmas
.com
🖥 www.realclubdegolfdelaspalmas
.com

Golf del Sur   (1987)
San Miguel de Abona, 38620 Tenerife
(Canarias)
☎ **(922) 73 81 70**
📠 (922) 78 82 72
✉ golfdelsur@aymesichgolf.com
🖥 www.golfdelsur.es

Córdoba

Club de Campo de Córdoba
    (1976)
Apartado 436, 14080 Córdoba
☎ **(957) 35 02 08**
✉ administracion@golfcordoba.com
🖥 www.golfcordoba.com

Pozoblanco   (1982)
Ctra. La Canaleja Km. 3, 14400
Pozoblanco, Córdoba
☎ **(957) 33 91 71**

Galicia

Aero Club de Santiago
    (1976)
General Pardiñas 34, Santiago de
Compostela (La Coruña)
☎ **(981) 59 24 00**
✉ reception@aerosantiago.es
🖥 www.aerosantiago.es

Aero Club de Vigo   (1951)
Reconquista 7, 36201 Vigo
☎ **(986) 48 66 45/48 75 09**

La Toja   (1970)
Isla de La Toja, El Grove, Pontevedra
☎ **(986) 73 01 58/73 08 18**

Ria de Vigo   (1993)
San Lorenzo-Domaio, 36957 Moaña
(Pontevedra)
☎ **(986) 32 70 51**
✉ info@riadevigogolf.com
🖥 www.riadevigogolf.com

Granada

Granada
Avda de los Corsarios, 18110 Las Gabias
(Granada)
☎ **(958) 58 44 36**

Madrid Region

Barberán   (1967)
Apartado 150.239, Cuatro Vientos, 28080
Madrid
☎ **(91) 509 00 59/509 11 40**

La Dehesa   (1991)
Avda. de la Universidad, 10, 28691
Villanueva La Cañada
☎ **(91) 815 70 22**
✉ dehesa-direccion
@infonegocio.com

Herreria   (1966)
PO Box 28200, San Lorenzo del Escorial,
(Madrid)
☎ **(91) 890 51 11**
✉ lsveiro@golflaherreria.com
🖥 www.golflaherreria.com

Jarama R.A.C.E.   (1967)
Urb Ciudalcampo, 28707 San Sebastian de
los Reyes, (Madrid)
☎ **(91) 657 00 11**
✉ golf@race.es
🖥 www.race.es

Lomas-Bosque   (1973)
Urb El Bosque, 28670 Villaviciosa de Odón,
(Madrid)
☎ **(91) 616 75 00**

La Moraleja   (1976)
La Moraleja, Alcobendas (Madrid)
☎ **(91) 650 07 00**

info@golflamoraleja.com
www.golflamoraleja.com

Olivar de la Hinojosa
(1995)
Avda de Dublin, Campo de las Naciones,
28042 Madrid
☎ (91) 721 18 89

Puerta de Hierro   (1895)
Avda de Miraflores, Ciudad Puerta de
Hierro, 28035 Madrid
☎ (91) 316 1745
▯ (91) 373 8111
✉ lmalonso@rcphierro.com

Los Retamares   (1991)
Crta Algete-Alalpardo Km 2300, 28130
Valdeolmos (Madrid)
☎ (91) 620 25 40

Somosaguas   (1971)
Avda de la Cabaña, 28223 Pozuelo de
Alarcón, (Madrid)
☎ (91) 352 16 47

Valdeláguila   (1975)
Apdo 9, Alcalá de Henares, (Madrid)
☎ (91) 885 96 59

Villa de Madrid CC   (1932)
Crta Castilla, 28040 Madrid
☎ (0034) 91 550 2010
✉ deportes@clubvillademadrid.com
www.clubvillademadrid.com

Malaga Region

Alhaurín   (1994)
Crta A-387 Km 3.4, Alhaurín el Grande-
Mijas
☎ +34 95 25 95 970
▯ +34 95 25 94 586
✉ reservasgolf@alhauringolf.com
www.alhauringolf.com

Añoreta   (1989)
Avenida del Golf, 29730 Rincón de la
Victoria, (Málaga)
☎ (952) 40 40 00

La Cala Resort   (1991)
La Cala de Mijas, 29649 Mijas-Costa
(Málaga)
☎ (952) 66 90 00
✉ golf@lacala.com
www.lacala.com

Guadalhorce   (1988)
Crtra de Cártama Km7, Apartado 48,
29590 Campanillas (Málaga)
☎ (952) 17 93 78

Lauro   (1992)
Los Caracolillos, 29130 Alhaurín de la
Torre, (Málaga)
☎ (95) 241 2767/296 3091
✉ info@laurogolf.com
www.laurogolf.com

Málaga Club de Campo
(1925)
Parador de Golf, Apdo 324, 29080 Málaga
☎ (952) 38 12 55

Mijas Golf International
(1976)
Apartado 145, Fuengirola, Málaga
☎ (952) 47 68 43
✉ info@ mijasgolf.org
www.mijasgolf.org

Miraflores   (1989)
Urb Riviera del Sol, 29647 Mijas-Costa
☎ +34 (952) 93 19 60

Torrequebrada   (1976)
Public
Apdo 120, Crta de Cadiz Km 220, 29630
Benalmadena
☎ (95) 244 27 42
✉ bookings@golftorrequebrada.com
www.golftorrequebrada.com

Marbella & Estepona

Alcaidesa Links   (1992)
CN-340 Km124.6, 11315 La Linea (Cádiz)
☎ (956) 79 10 40

Aloha   (1975)
Nueva Andalucía, 29660 Marbella
☎ (952) 81 37 50/90 70 85/86
✉ office@clubdegolfaloha.com
www.clubdegolfaloha.com

Los Arqueros Golf &
Country Club SA   (1991)
Crta de Ronda Km44.5, 29679 Benahavis
(Málaga)
☎ +34 952 784712
▯ +34 952 786707
✉ admin.losarquerosgolf
@es.taylorwimpey.com
✐ Lidia Martin
www.losarquerosgolf.com

Atalaya G&CC   (1968)
Crta Benahavis 7, 29688 Málaga
☎ (952) 88 28 12

Las Brisas   (1968)
Apdo 147, 29660 Nueva Andalucia,
(Málaga)
☎ (952) 81 08 75/81 30 21
✉ info@lasbrisasgolf.com
www.lasbrisasgolf.com

La Cañada   (1982)
Ctra Guadiaro Km 1, 11311 Guadiaro
(Cádiz)
☎ (956) 79 41 00

Estepona   (1989)
Arroyo Vaquero, Apartado 532, 29680
Estepona (Málaga)
☎ (+34) 95 293 7605
✉ information@esteponagolf.com
www.esteponagolf.com

Guadalmina   (1959)
Guadalmina Alta, San Pedro de Alcántara,
29678 Marbella (Málaga)
☎ (952) 88 65 22

Marbella   (1994)
CN 340 Km 188, 29600 Marbella
(Málaga)
☎ (952) 83 05 00

Monte Mayor   (1989)
PO Box 962, 29679 Benahavis (Málaga)
☎ (+34) 95 293 7111
✉ reservations@montemayorgolf
.com
www.montemayorgolf.com

Los Naranjos   (1977)
Apdo 64, 29660 Nueva Andalucía,
Marbella
☎ (952) 81 52 06/81 24 28

El Paraiso   (1973)
Ctra Cádiz-Màlaga Km 167, 29680
Estepona (Málaga)
☎ (95) 288 38 35
▯ (95) 288 58 27
✉ info@elparaisogolfclub.com
www.elparaisogolfclub.com

La Quinta G&CC   (1989)
Urb. La Quinta, Nueva Andalucía 29660,
(Marbella-Málaga)
☎ +34 (952) 76 23 90
✉ reservas@laquintagolf.com
www.laquintagolf.com

Santa María G&CC   (1991)
Urb. Elviria, Crta N340 Km 192, 29604
Marbella (Málaga)
☎ (952) 83 10 36
▯ (952) 83 47 97
✉ caddymaster@santamariagolfclub
.com
✐ Rosa Olmo
www.santamariagolfclub.com

Sotogrande   (1964)
Paseo del Parque, s/n, 11310 Sotogrande,
Cádiz
☎ +34 956 785014
✉ info@golfsotogrande.com
www.golfsotogrande.com

The San Roque Club   (1990)
CN 340 Km 127, San Roque, 11360 Cádiz
☎ (956) 61 30 30
▯ (956) 61 30 12
✉ info@sanroqueclub.com
✐ Guillermo Navarro
www.sanroqueclub.com

Valderrama   (1985)
Avenida de los Cortjos S/N, 11310
Sotogrande (Cadiz)
☎ (956) 79 12 00
▯ (956) 79 60 28
✉ greenfees@valderrama.com
✐ Derek Brown
www.valderrama.com

La Zagaleta (1994)
Crta San Pedro-Ronda Km 9, 29679
Benahavis
☎ (95) 285 54 53

Seville & Gulf of Cádiz

Costa Ballena (1997)
Crta Sta Maria-Chipiona, 11520 Rota
☎ (956) 84 70 70

Isla Canela (1993)
Crta de la Playa, 21400 Ayamonte (Huelva)
☎ (959) 47 72 63
✉ golf@islacanela.es
🖳 www.islacanela.es

Islantilla (1993)
Paseo Barranco Del Moro, S/N, 21410 Isla
Cristina (Huelva)
☎ (959) 48 60 39/48 60 49
📞 (959) 48 61 04
✉ reservasgolf@islantillagolfresort
.com
🖳 www.istantillagolfresort.com

Montecastillo (1992)
Carretera de Arcos, 11406 Jérez
☎ (956) 15 12 00
✉ commercial@montecastillo.com
🖳 www.montecastillo.com

Montenmedio G&CC (1996)
N-340 KM 42,5, 11150 Vejer-Barbate
(Cádiz)
☎ (956) 45 50 04
📞 (956) 45 12 95
✉ info@montenmedio.es
✍ Migual Marin (Mgr)
🖳 www.monteenmedio.es

Novo Sancti Petri (1990)
Urb. Novo Sancti Petri, Playa de la Barrosa,
11139 Chiclana de la Frontera
☎ 0034 (956) 49 40 05
📞 0034 (956) 49 43 50
✉ sales@golf-novosancti.es
✍ Mrs Claudia Kühleitner (Sales &
Marketing Mgr)
🖳 www.golf-novosancti.es

Pineda De Sevilla (1939)
Apartado 1049, 41080 Sevilla
☎ (954) 61 14 00

Real Sevilla (1992)
Autovía Sevilla-Utrera, 41089 Montequinto
(Sevilla)
☎ (954) 12 43 01
🖳 www.sevillagolf.com

Vista Hermosa (1975)
Apartado 77, Urb Vista Hermosa, 11500
Puerto de Santa María, Cádiz
☎ (956) 87 56 05

Zaudin
Crta Tomares-Mairena, 41940 Tomares
(Sevilla)
☎ (954) 15 41 59

Valencia & Castellón

Escorpión (1975)
Apartado Correos 1, Betera (Valencia)
☎ (96) 160 12 11
📞 (96) 169 01 87
✉ escorpion@clubescorpion.com
🖳 www.clubescorpion.com

Real Club De Golf Manises
(1954)
C/ Maestrat, 1, 46940 Manises (Valencia)
☎ +34 96 153 40 69
📞 +34 96 152 38 04
✉ info@clubgolfmanises.es
✍ D. Juan Jose Penalba Belda (Mgr)
🖳 www.realclubgolfmanises.es

Mediterraneo CC (1978)
Urb La Coma, 12190 Borriol, (Castellón)
☎ (964) 32 1653 (bookings)
✉ club@ccmediterraneo.com
🖳 www.ccmediterraneo.com

Oliva Nova (1995)
46780 Oliva (Valencia)
☎ (096) 285 76 66
✉ golf@chg.es
🖳 www.olivanovagolf.com

Panorámica (1995)
Urb Panorámica, 12320 San Jorge
(Castellón)
☎ (964) 49 30 72

El Saler (1968)
Avd. de los pinares 151, 46012 El Saler
(Valencia)
☎ (96) 161 0384
✉ saler.golf@parador.es
🖳 www.parador.es

Valladolid

Entrepinos (1990)
Avda del Golf 2, Urb Entrepinos, 47130
Simancas (Valladolid)
☎ (983) 59 05 11/59 05 61
📞 (983) 59 07 65
✉ golfentrepinos@golfentrepinos
.com
✍ Angel Santiago Calleja (Mgr)
🖳 www.golfentrepinos.com

Zaragoza

Club de Golf La Penaza
(1973)
Apartado 3039, Zaragoza
☎ (976) 34 28 00/34 22 48
📞 (976) 34 28 00
✉ administracion@golflapenaza.com
✍ Pablo Menendez
🖳 www.golflapenaza.com

Sweden

East Central

Ängsö (1979)
Box 1007, 72126 Västerås
☎ (0171) 441012
✉ kansli@angsogolf.org
🖳 www.angsogolf.org

Arboga
PO Box 263, 732 25 Arboga
☎ (0589) 70100
✉ arbogagk@arbogagk.nu
🖳 www.arbogagk.nu

Askersund (1980)
Kärravägen 30, 696 75 Ammeberg
☎ (0583) 34943
📞 (0583) 34945
✉ info@askersundsgk.golf.se
🖳 www.golf.se/askersundsgk

Burvik (1990)
Burvik, 740 12 Knutby
☎ (0174) 43060
📞 (0174) 43062
✉ info:burvik.se
🖳 www.burvik.se

Edenhof (1991)
740 22 Bälinge
☎ (018) 334185
✉ info@edenhof.se

Enköping (1970)
Box 2006, 745 02 Enköping
☎ (0171) 20830
📞 (0171) 20823
✉ info@enkopinggolf.se
🖳 www.enkopinggolf.se

Eskilstuna (1951)
Strängnäsvägen, 633 49 Eskilstuna
☎ (016) 142629
✉ info@eskilstunagk.se
🖳 www.eskilstunagk.se

Fagersta (1970)
Box 2051, 737 02 Fagersta
☎ (0223) 54060

Frösåker Golf & Country
Club (1989)
Frösåker Gård, Box 17015, 720 17
Västerås
☎ (021) 25401
📞 (021) 25485
✉ fgcc@telia.com
🖳 www.fgcc.se

Fullerö (1988)
Jotsberga, 725 91 Västerås
☎ (021) 50262
📞 (021) 50431
✉ info@fullerogk.se
🖳 www.fullerogk.se

Gripsholm (1991)
Box 133, 647 23 Mariefred
☎ (0159) 350050
🖳 www.golf.se/gripsholmsgk

Grönlund (1989)
PO Box 38, 740 10 Almunge
☎ (0174) 20670
📞 (0174) 20455
📧 info@gronlundgk.se
🖳 www.gronlundgk.se

Gustavsvik (1988)
Box 22033, 702 02 Örebro
☎ (019) 244486
📧 info@gvgk.se
🖳 www.gvgk.se

Katrineholm (1959)
Jättorp, 641 93 Katrineholm
☎ (0150) 39270
📞 (0150) 39011
📧 info@katrineholmsgk.golf.se
✍ Olof Pettersson (Mgr)
🖳 www.katrineholmsgolf.nu

Köping (1963)
Box 278, 731 26 Köping
☎ (0221) 81090
📞 (0221) 81277
📧 info@kopingsgk.golf.sc
🖳 www.kopingsgk.nu

Kumla (1987)
Box 46, 692 21 Kumla
☎ (019) 577370

Linde (1984)
Dalkarlshyttan, 711 31 Lindesberg
☎ (0581) 87050
📞 (0581) 87059
📧 info@lindegk.com
🖳 www.lindegk.com

Mosjö (1989)
Mosjö Gård, 705 94 Örebrö
☎ (019) 225780

Nora (1988)
Box 108, 713 23 Nora
☎ (0587) 311660

Nyköpings (1951)
ÁRILLA, 611 92 Nyköping
☎ (0155) 216617
📞 (0155) 97185
📧 info@nykopingsgk.se
✍ Gary Cosford
🖳 www.nykopingsgk.se

Örebro (1939)
Lanna, 719 93 Vintrosa
☎ (019) 164070
🖳 www.golf.se/golfklubbar/
orebrogk

Roslagen
Box 110, 761 22 Norrtälje
☎ (0176) 237194

Sala (1970)
Norby Fallet 100, 733 92 Sala
☎ (0224) 53077/53055/53064
📞 (0224) 53143
📧 info@salagk.nu
✍ Hans Eljansbo
🖳 www.salagk.nu

Sigtunabygden (1961)
Box 89, 193 22 Sigtuna
☎ (08) 592 54012
📞 (08) 592 54167
📧 info@sigtunagk.com
🖳 www.sigtunagk.com

Skepptuna
Skepptuna, 195 93 Märsta
☎ (08) 512 93069
🖳 www.skepptunagk.nu

Södertälje (1952)
Box 9074, 151 09 Södertälje
☎ (08) 550 91995

Strängnäs (1968)
Kilenlundavägen 3, 645 47 Strängnäs
☎ (0152) 14731
📞 (0152) 14716
📧 info@strangnasgk.se
🖳 www.strangnasgk.se

Torshälla (1960)
Box 128, 64422 Torshälla
☎ (016) 358722
📞 (016) 357491
📧 kansli@torshallagk.se
🖳 www.torshallagk.com

Tortuna
Nicktuna, Tortuna, 725 96 Västerås
☎ (021) 65300
📧 kansli@tortunagk.com

Trosa (1972)
Box 80, 619 22 Trosa
☎ (0156) 22458

Upsala (1937)
Håmö Gård, Läby, 755 92 Uppsala
☎ (018) 460120
📞 (018) 461205
📧 info@upsalagk.se
🖳 www.upsalagk.se

Vassunda (1989)
Smedby Gård, 741 91 Knivsta
☎ +46 (0) 185 72040
📧 info@vassundagk.se
🖳 www.vassundagk.se

Västerås (1931)
Bjärby, 724 81 Västerås
☎ (021) 357543
📧 info@vasterasgk.se
🖳 www.vasterasgk.se

Far North

Boden (1946)
Tallkronsvägen 2, 961 51 Boden
☎ (0921) 69140

Funäsdalsfjällen (1972)
Golfbanevägen 8, 840 96 Ljusnedal
☎ (0684) 668241
📧 kansli@ffjgk.nu
🖳 www.ffjgk.nu

Gällivare-Malmberget
(1973)
Box 35, 983 21 Malmberget
☎ (0970) 20770
📧 gmgk@telia.com
🖳 www.gmgk.se

Haparanda (1989)
Mattila 140, 953 35 Haparanda
☎ (0922) 10660

Härnösand (1957)
Box 52, 871 22 Härnösand
☎ (0611) 67000
🖳 www.harnosand.gk.just.nu

Kalix (1990)
Nyborgsvägen 175, 95251 Kalix
☎ (0923) 15945/15935
📞 (0923) 77735
📧 info@kalixgolfklubb.se
🖳 www.kalixgolfklubb.se

Luleå (1955)
Golfbaneväg 80, 975 96 Luleå
☎ (0920) 256300
📞 (0920) 256362
📧 kansli@luleagolf.se
🖳 www.luleagolf.se

Norrmjöle (1992)
905 82 Umeå
☎ (090) 81581
📞 (090) 81565
📧 kansli@norrmjole-golf.se
🖳 www.norrmjole-golf.se

Örnsköldsviks GK Puttom
(1967)
Ovansjö 232, 891 95 Arnäsvall
☎ (0660) 254001
📧 kansli@puttom.se
🖳 www.puttom.se

Östersund-Frösö (1947)
Kungsgården 205, 832 96 Frösön
☎ (063) 576030
🖳 www.ofg.nu

Piteå (1960)
Nötöv 119, 941 41 Piteå
☎ (0911) 14990

Skellefteå (1967)
Rönnbäcken, 931 92 Skellefteå
☎ (0910) 779333
📧 info@skelleftegolf.nu
🖳 www.skelleftegolf.nu

Sollefteå (1970)
Box 213, 881 25 Sollefteå
☎ (0620) 21477/12670

Sundsvall   (1952)
Golfvägen 5, 86234 Kvissleby
☎ **+46 60 515175**
✉ info@sundsvallgk.golf.se
🖳 www.sundsvallgk.com

Timrå
Golfbanevägen 2, 860 32 Fagervik
☎ **(060) 570153**
✉ info@timragk.golf.se
🖳 www.timragk.se

Umeå   (1954)
Enkan Ramborgs väg 10, 913 35 Holmsund
☎ **(090) 58580/58585**
📠 (090) 58589
✉ info@umgk.se
🖳 www.umgk.se

Gothenburg

Albatross   (1973)
Lillhagsvägen, 422 50 Hisings-Backa
☎ **(031) 551901/550500**

Chalmers
Härrydavägen 50, 438 91 Landvetter
☎ **+46 (0) 31 91 84 30**
✉ info@chgk.se
🖳 www.chgk.se

Delsjö   (1962)
Kallebäck, 412 76 Göteborg
☎ **(031) 406959**
🖳 www.degk.se

Forsgårdens   (1982)
Gamla Forsv 1, 434 47 Kungsbacka
☎ **(0300) 566350**
📠 (0300) 566351
✉ kansli@forsgarden.se
🖳 www.forsgarden.se

Göteborg   (1902)
Box 2056, 436 02 Hovås
☎ **(031) 282444**

Gullbringa G&CC   (1968)
Kulperödsvägen 6, 442 95 Hålta
☎ **(0303) 227161**
📠 (0303) 227778
✉ kansli@gullbringagolf.se
🔏 A Joelsson-Soetting
🖳 www.gullbringagolf.se

Kungälv-Kode GK   (1990)
Ö Knaverstad 140, 442 97 Kode
☎ **+46 303 513 00**
📠 +46 303 502 05
✉ info@kkgk.se
🔏 Pär Svensson
🖳 www.kkgk.se

Kungsbacka   (1971)
Hamravägen 15, 429 44 Särö
☎ **(031) 938180**
📠 (031) 938170
✉ info@kungsbackagk.se
🔏 Andri Reumert
🖳 www.kungsbackagk.se

Lysegården   (1966)
Box 532, 442 15 Kungälv
☎ **(0303) 223426**
✉ info@lysegarden.sgk.golf.se
🖳 www.lysegarden.sgk.se

Mölndals   (1979)
Hällesåkersvägen 14, 437 91 Lindome
☎ **(031) 993030**
📠 (031) 994901
✉ molndalsgk@telia.com
🔏 Lars-Erik Hagbert
🖳 www.molndalsgk.se

Öijared   (1958)
Pl 1082, 448 92 Floda
☎ **(0302) 37300**
📠 (0302) 37306
✉ reception@oigk.se
🔏 Pia Orrgren (Man Dir)
🖳 www.oigk.se

Partille   (1986)
Golfrundan 5, 433 51 Öjersjö
☎ **+46 31 987043**
📠 +46 31 987757
✉ info@partillegk.se
🔏 Patrik Skoog
🖳 www.partillegk.se

Sjögärde
43963 Frillesås
☎ **+46 (0) 340 657865**
📠 +46 (0) 340 657861
✉ info@sjogarde.se
🖳 www.sjogarde.se

Stenungsund   (1993)
Lundby Pl 7480, 444 93 Spekeröd
☎ **(0303) 778470**
🖳 www.stenungsundgk.se

Stora Lundby   (1983)
Valters Väg 2, 443 71 Grabo
☎ **(0302) 44200**
🖳 www.storalundbygk.o.se

Malmö & South Coast

Abbekas   (1989)
Kroppsmarksvagen, 274 56 Abbekas
☎ **(0411) 533233**
✉ info@abbekasgk.golf.se
🖳 www.abbekasgk.se

Barsebäck G&CC   (1969)
246 55 Löddeköpinge
☎ **(046) 776230**
📠 (046) 772630
✉ bgcc@barseback-golf.se
🖳 www.barsebackresort.se

Bokskogen   (1963)
Torupsvägen 408-140, 230 40 Bara
☎ **(040) 406900**

Falsterbo   (1909)
Fyrvägen 34, 239 40 Falsterbo
☎ **+46 (0)40 470078/475078**
📠 +46 (0)40 472722

✉ info@falsterbogk..se
🖳 www.falsterbogk.com

Flommens   (1935)
239 40 Falsterbo
☎ **(040) 475016**
✉ info@flommensgk.se
🖳 www.flommensgk.se

Kävlinge   (1989)
Box 138, 244 22 Kävlinge
☎ **(046) 736270**
📠 (046) 728486
✉ info@kavlingegk.golf.se
🖳 www.kavlingegk.com

Ljunghusen   (1932)
Kinellsvag, Ljunghusen, 236 42 Höllviken
☎ **(040) 458000**
📠 (040) 454265
✉ info@ljgk.se
🔏 Stig Persson
🖳 www.ljgk.se

Lunds Akademiska   (1936)
Kungsmarken, 225 92 Lund
☎ **(046) 99005**
📠 (046) 99146
✉ info@lagk.se
🖳 www.lagk.se

Malmö Burlöv   (1981)
Segesvängen, 212 27 Malmö
☎ **(040) 292535/292536**
✉ malmoburlovgk@telia.com
🖳 www.malmoburlovgk.com

Örestads GK   (1986)
Golfvägen, Habo Ljung, 234 22 Lomma
☎ **(040) 410580**
📠 (040) 416320
✉ info@orestadsgk.com
🔏 Niklas Karlsson
🖳 www.orestadsgk.com

Österlen   (1945)
Djupadal, 272 95 Simrishamn
☎ **(0414) 412550**
📠 (0414) 412551
✉ info@osterlensgk.com
🔏 Stefan Minell
🖳 www.osterlensgk.com

Romeleåsen   (1969)
Kvarnbrodda 1191, 247 96 Veberöd
☎ **+46 46 820 12**
📠 +46 46 821 13
✉ info@ragk.se
🔏 Stellan Ragnar
🖳 www.ragk.se

Söderslätts   (1993)
Ellaboda, Grievievägen 260-10, 235 94 Vellinge
☎ **(040) 429680**
✉ info@soderslattsgK.golf.se
🖳 www.4.golf.se/soderslattsgk

Tegelberga   (1988)
Alstad Pl 140, 231 96 Trelleborg
☎ **(040) 485690**
🖳 www.golf.se/tegelbergagk

Tomelilla (1987)
Ullstorp, 273 94 Tomelilla
☎ **(0417) 19430**
📠 (0417) 13657
✉ info@tomelillagolfklub.com
🖥 www.tomelillagolfklubb.com

Trelleborg Golf Club (1963)
Maglarp, Pl 431, 231 93 Trelleborg
☎ **(0410) 330460**
📠 (0410) 330281
✉ kansli@trelleborgsgk.se
✍ Helen Nilsson
🖥 www.trelleborgsgk.se

Vellinge (1991)
Toftadals Gård, 235 41 Vellinge
☎ **(040) 443255**
📠 (040) 443179
✉ info@vellingegk.golf.se
🖥 www.vellingegk.se

Ystad (1930)
Långrevsvägen, 270 22 Köpingebro
☎ **(0411) 550350**
✉ info@ystadgk.com
🖥 www.ystadgk.se

North

Alvkarleby
Västanåvägen 5, 814 94 Alvkarleby
☎ **(026) 72757**
📠 (026) 82307
✉ info@alvkarlebygk.se
🖥 www.alvkarlebygk.com

Avesta (1963)
Friluftsvägen 10, 774 61 Avesta
☎ **(0226) 55913/10866/12766**
📠 (0226) 12578
✉ info@avestagk.se
🖥 www.avestagk.se

Bollnäs (1963)
Norrfly 1634, 823 91 Kilafors
☎ **(0278) 650540**
📠 (0278) 651220
✉ info@bollnasgk.com
🖥 www.bollnasgk.com

Dalsjö (1989)
Dalsjö 3, 781 94 Borlänge
☎ **(0243) 220080**
✉ info@dalsjogolf.se
🖥 www.dalsjogolf.se

Falun-Borlänge (1956)
Storgarden 10, 791 93 Falun
☎ **(023) 31015**
🖥 www.fbgu.se

Gävle (1949)
Bönavägen 23, 805 95 Gävle
☎ **(026) 120333/120338**

Hagge (1963)
Hagge, 771 90 Ludvika
☎ **(0240) 28087/28513**

Hofors (1965)
Box 117, 813 22 Hofors
☎ **(0290) 85125**

Högbo (1962)
Daniel Tilas Väg 4, 811 92 Sandviken
☎ **(026) 215015**
✉ info@hogbogk.golf.se
🖥 www.golf.se/hogbogk/

Hudiksvall (1964)
Tjuvskär, 824 01 Hudiksvall
☎ **+46 (0) 650 542080**

Leksand (1977)
Box 25, 793 21 Leksand
☎ **(0247) 14640**

Ljusdal (1973)
Svinhammarsv.2, 82735 Ljusdal
☎ **(0651) 16883**
📠 (0651) 16883
✉ kansli@golfiljusdal.nu
🖥 www.golfiljusdal.nu

Mora (1980)
Box 264, 792 24 Mora
☎ **(0250) 592990**
✉ info@moragk.se
🖥 www.moragk.se

Rättvik (1954)
Box 29, 795 21 Rättvik
☎ **(0248) 51030**
📠 (0248) 12081

Sälenfjallens (1991)
Box 20, 780 67 Sälen
☎ **(0280) 20670**
✉ info@salenfjallensgk.se
🖥 www.salenfjallensgk.se

Säter (1984)
Box 89, 783 22 Säter
☎ **(0225) 50030**

Snöå Golfklubb (1990)
Snöå Bruk, S-780 51 Dala-Järna
☎ **+46 281 24072**
📠 +46 281 24009
✉ snoa.gk@telia.com
✍ Kjell Redhe
🖥 www.snoagk.se

Söderhamns GK (1961)
835 Sofieholm, 826 91 Söderhamn
☎ **+46 270 281 300**
📠 +46 270 281 003
✉ info@soderhamnsgk.com
✍ Hans Wirtavuori
🖥 www.soderhamnsgk.com

Sollerö (1991)
Levsnäs, 79290 Sollerön
☎ **(0250) 22236**

Skane & South

Allerum (1992)
Tursköpsvägen 154, 260 35 Ödåkra
☎ **(042) 93051**

📠 (042) 93045
✉ info@allerumgk.nu
🖥 www.allerum.nu

Ängelholm (1973)
Box 1117, 262 22 Ängelholm
☎ **(0431) 430260/431460**
🖥 www.golf.se/golfklubbar/
angelholmsgk

Araslöv
Starvägen 1, 291 75 Färlöv
☎ **(044) 71600**

Båstad (1929)
Box 1037, 269 21 Båstad
☎ **(0431) 78370**
📠 (0431) 73331
✉ info@ bgk.se
🖥 www.bgk.se

Bedinge (1931)
Golfbanevägen, 231 76 Beddingestrand
☎ **(0410) 25514**

Bjäre
Salomonhög 3086, 269 93 Båstad
☎ **(0431) 361053**

Bosjökloster (1974)
243 95 Höör
☎ **(0413) 25858**

Carlskrona (1949)
PO Almö, 370 24 Nättraby
☎ **(0457) 35123**
🖥 www.carlskronagk.com

Degeberga-Widtsköfle
*Segholmsu.126, Box 71, 297 21
Degeberga*
☎ **(044) 355035**
✉ dwgk@telia.com
🖥 www.dwgolfklubb.com

Eslöv (1966)
Box 150, 241 22 Eslöv
☎ **(0413) 18610**
📠 (0413) 18613
✉ info@eslovsgk.golf.se
🖥 www.eslovsgk.se

Hässleholm (1978)
Skyrup, 282 95 Tyringe
☎ **(0451) 53111**

Helsingborg (1924)
260 40 Viken
☎ **(042) 236147**
✉ office@helsingborgsgk.com
🖥 www.helsingborgsgk.com

Karlshamn (1962)
Box 188, 374 23 Karlshamn
☎ **(0454) 50085**
📠 (0454) 50160
✉ info@karlshamnsgk.com
✍ Eva Tigerman
🖥 www.karlshamnsgk.com

Kristianstad GK   (1924)
Box 41, 296 21 Åhus
☎ **(044) 247656**
📠 (044) 247635
📧 info@kristianstadsgk.com
♿ Mats Welff
🖳 www.kristianstadsgk.com

Landskrona   (1960)
Erikstorp, 261 61 Landskrona
☎ **(0418) 446260**
📠 (0418) 446262
📧 info@landskronagk.se
🖳 www.landskronagk.se

Mölle   (1943)
260 42 Mölle
☎ **(042) 347520**
📠 (042) 347523
📧 info@mollegk.se
🖳 www.mollegk.se

Örkelljunga   (1989)
Rya 472, 286 91 Örkelljunga
☎ **(0435) 53690/53640**
📠 (0435) 53670
📧 info@orkelljungagk.com
🖳 www.orkelljungagk.com

Östra Göinge   (1981)
Riksvägen 12, 289 21 Knislinge
☎ **(044) 60060**
📧 info@ostragoinge.golf.se
🖳 www.golf.se/ostragoingegk

Perstorp   (1963)
Gustavsborg 501, 284 91 Perstorp
☎ +46 (0) 435 35411
📠 +46 (0) 435 35959
📧 kansli@ppgk.nu
🖳 www.ppgk.nu

Ronneby   (1963)
Box 26, 372 21 Ronneby
☎ **(0457) 10315**
🖳 www.golf.se/ronnebygk

Rya   (1934)
PL 5500, 255 92 Helsingborg
☎ **(042) 220182**
📧 kansli@rya.nu
🖳 www.rya.nu

St Arild   (1987)
Golfvagen 48, 260 41 Nyhamnsläge
☎ **(042) 346860**
📠 (042) 346042
📧 kansliet@starild.se
🖳 www.starild.se

Skepparslov   (1984)
Sätesvägen 14, 291 92 Kristianstad
☎ **(044) 229508**
📧 kansli@skepparslovgk.se
🖳 www.skepparslovsgk.se

Söderåsen   (1966)
Box 41, 260 50 Billesholm
☎ **(042) 73337**
📠 (042) 73963
📧 info@soderasensgk.golf.se
🖳 www.soderasensgk.se

Sölvesborg
Box 204, 294 25 Sölvesborg
☎ **(0456) 70650**
📧 info@solvesborggk.se
🖳 www.solvesborggk.se

Svalöv   (1989)
Månstorp Pl 1365, 268 90 Svalöv
☎ **(0418) 662462**
📠 (0418) 663284
📧 svagk@telia.com
🖳 www.svagk.se

Torekov   (1924)
Råledsv 31, 260 93 Torekov
☎ **(0431) 449840**
📧 info@togk.se
🖳 www.togk.se

Trummenas   (1989)
373 02 Ramdala
☎ +46 (0) 455 360507
📠 +46 (0) 455 360571
📧 trummenas.gk@telia.com
🖳 www.trummenasgk.se

Vasatorp   (1973)
P O Box 130 35, S-250 13 Helsingborg
☎ +46 42 23 50 58
📠 +46 42 23 51 35
📧 info@vasatorpsgk.se
🖳 www.vasatorpsgk.se

South East

Älmhult   (1975)
Pl 1215, 343 90 Älmhult
☎ **(0476) 14135**

Åtvidaberg   (1954)
Västantorp, 597 41 Åtvidaberg
☎ **(0120) 35425**

Ekerum Golf Resort   (1990)
387 92 Borgholm, Öland
☎ **(0485) 80000**
📠 (0485) 80010
📧 info@ekerum.com
🖳 www.ekerum.com

Eksjö   (1938)
Skedhult, 575 96 Eksjö
☎ **(0381) 13525**
📧 kansli@eksjogk.nu
♿ Peter Börjesson
🖳 www.eksjogk.nu

Emmaboda   (1976)
Kyrkogatan, 360 60 Vissefjärda
☎ **(0471) 20505/20540**
📠 (0471) 20440
📧 info@emmabodagk.golf.se
🖳 www.golf.se/golfklubbar/
   emmabodagk

Finspångs   (1965)
Viberga Gård, 612 92 Finspång
☎ **(0122) 13940**
📠 (0122) 18888
📧 info@finspangsgk.golf.se
🖳 www.finspangsgk.se

Gotska   (1986)
Annelund, 62141 Visby, Gotland
☎ **(0498) 215545**
📠 (0498) 256332
📧 info@gotskagk.golf.se
🖳 www.gotskagk.se

Grönhögen   (1996)
PL 1270, 380 65 Öland
☎ **(0485) 665995**
🖳 www.gronhogen.se

Gumbalde
Box 35, 620 13 Ståga, Gotland
☎ **(0498) 482880**

Hooks
560 13 Hok
☎ **(0393) 21420**
🖳 www.hooksgk.com

Jönköpings GK   (1936)
Kättilstorp, 556 27 Jönköping
☎ **(036) 76567**
📠 (036) 76511
📧 info@jonkopingsgk.se
🖳 www.jonkopingsgk.se

Kalmar   (1947)
Box 278, 391 23 Kalmar
☎ **(0480) 472111**
📠 (0480) 472314
📧 reception@kalmar-gk.se
♿ Jimmy Grön
🖳 www.kalmargk.se

Lagan   (1966)
Box 63, 340 14 Lagan
☎ **(0372) 30450/35460**
📠 (0372) 35307
📧 info@lagansgk.se
🖳 www.lagansgk.se

Landeryds GK   (1987)
Bogestad Gård, 585 93 Linköping
☎ **(+46) 133 62200**
📠 (+46) 133 62208
📧 bjorn.sturehed@landerydsgolf.se
♿ Björn Sturehed
🖳 www.landerydsgolf.se

Lidhems   (1988)
360 14 Väckelsång
☎ **(0470) 33660**
🖳 www.golf.se/lidhemsgk

Linköping   (1945)
Universitets vägen 8, 583 30 Linköping
☎ **(013) 262990**
📠 (013) 140769
📧 lggolf@telia.com
♿ Kent Andersson
🖳 www.linkopingsgk.se

Mjölby   (1986)
Blixberg, Miskarp, 595 92 Mjölby
☎ **(0142) 12570**
📠 (0142) 16553
📧 kansli@mjolbygk.se
🖳 www.mjolbygk.se

Motala (1956)
PO Box 264, 591 23 Motala
☎ **(0141) 50840**
📠 (0141) 208990
📧 info@motalagk.golf.se
🖥 www.motalagk.se

Nässjö (1988)
Box 5, 571 21 Nässjö
☎ **(0380) 10022**

Norrköping (1928)
Alsatersvagen 40, 605 97 Norrköping
☎ **(011) 158240**
📠 (011) 158249
📧 info@ngk.nu
✍ Morgan Allard
🖥 www.ngk.nu

Oskarshamn (1972)
Box 148, 572 23 Oskarshamn
☎ **(0491) 94033**

Skinnarebo (1990)
Skinnarebo, 555 93 Jönköping
☎ **(036) 69075**
📠 (036) 362975
📧 info@skinnarebogcc.golf.se
🖥 www.skinnarebo.se

Söderköping (1983)
Hylinge, 605 96 Norrköping
☎ **(011) 70579**

Tobo (1971)
Fredensborg 133, 598 91 Vimmerby
☎ **(0492) 30346**
📧 info@tobogk.com
🖥 www.tobogk.com

Tranås (1952)
Norrc byvagen 8, Norrabyvagen 8, 57343 Tranas
☎ **(0140) 311661**
📠 (0140) 16161
📧 info@tranasgk.se
🖥 www.tranasgk.se

Vadstena (1957)
Hagalund, Box 122, 592 23 Vadstena
☎ **(0143) 12440**
📠 (0143) 12709
📧 kansli@vadstenagk.nu
🖥 www.vadstenagk.nu

Värnamo (1962)
Näsbyholm 5, 331 96 VÄRNAMO
☎ **(0370) 23991**
📠 (0370) 23992
📧 info@varnamogk.se
✍ Pia Berglund
🖥 www.varnamogk.se

Västervik (1959)
Box 62, Ekhagen, 593 22 Västervik
☎ **(0490) 32420**

Växjö (1959)
Box 227, 351 05 Växjö
☎ **(0470) 21515**
🖥 www.vaxjogk.com

Vetlanda (1983)
Box 249, 574 23 Vetlanda
☎ **(0383) 18310**

Visby Golf Club (1958)
Västergarn Kronholmen 415, 622 30 Gotlands Tofta
☎ **+46 498 200930**
📠 +46 498 200932
📧 info@visbygk.com
✍ Matz Bengtsson (Gen Mgr)
🖥 www.visbygk.com

Vreta Kloster
Box 144, 590 70 Ljungsbro
☎ **(013) 169700**
📧 info@vkgk.se
🖥 www.vkgk.se

South West

Alingsås (1985)
Hjälmared 4050, 441 95 Alingsås
☎ **(0322) 52421**

Bäckavattnet (1977)
Marbäck, 305 94 Halmstad
☎ **(035) 162040**
🖥 www.backavattnetsgk.com

Billingens GK (1949)
St Kulhult, 540 17 Lerdala
☎ **+46 511 80291**
📧 info@billingensgk.se
✍ Anders Karisson
🖥 www.billingensgk.se

Borås (1933)
Östra Vik, Kråkered, 504 95 Borås
☎ **(033) 250250**

Ekarnas (1970)
Balders Väg 12, 467 31 Grästorp
☎ **(0514) 12061**
📧 info@ekarnasgk.golf.se
🖥 www.golf.se//ekarnasgk

Falkenberg (1949)
Golfvägen, 311 72 Falkenberg
☎ **(0346) 50287**
📠 (0346) 50997
📧 info@falkenberggk.golf.se
✍ Lars Andersson (Sec)
🖥 www.falkenbergsgolfklubb.se

Falköping (1965)
Box 99, 521 02 Falköping
☎ **(0515) 31270**
📠 (0515) 31389
📧 info@falkopingsgk.com
✍ Peter Fritzson
🖥 www.falkopingsgk.com

Halmstad (1930)
302 73 Halmstad
☎ **+46 35 176800/176801**
📠 +46 35 176820
📧 info@hgk.se
🖥 www.hgk.se

Haverdals (1988)
Slingervägen 35, 30570 Haverdal
☎ **(035) 144990**
📠 (035) 53890
📧 info@haverdalsgk.golf.se
✍ Ann Jacobsson
🖥 www.haverdalsgk.com

Hökensås (1962)
PO Box 116, 544 22 Hjo
☎ **(0503) 16059**

Holms (1990)
Nannarp, 305 92 Halmstad
☎ **(035) 38189**
📧 info@holmsgk.golf.se
🖥 www.holmsgk.com

Hulta (1972)
Box 54, 517 22 Bollebygd
☎ **(033) 204340**
📠 (033) 204345
📧 info@hultagk.se
✍ David Kirkham
🖥 www.hultagk.se

Knistad G&CC
541 92 Skövde
☎ **(0500) 463170**

Laholm (1964)
Vallen 15, 31298 Vaxtorp
☎ **+46 430 30601**
📠 +46 430 30891
📧 info@laholmgk.com
🖥 www.laholmgk.com

Lidköping (1967)
Box 2029, 531 02 Lidköping
☎ **(0510) 546144**
🖥 www.lidkopingsgk.se

Mariestads Golf Course (1975)
Gummerstadsvägen 45, 542 94 Mariestad
☎ **(0501) 17383**
📠 (0501) 78117
📧 info@mariestadsgk.se
🖥 www.mariestadsgk.se

Marks (1962)
Brättingstorpsvägen 28, 511 58 Kinna
☎ **(0320) 14220**
📧 info@marksgk.se
🖥 www.marksgk.se

Onsjö (1974)
Box 6331 A, 462 42 Vänersborg
☎ **(0521) 68870**
📠 (0521) 17106
🖥 www.onsjogk.com

Ringenäs (1987)
Strandlida, 305 91 Halmstad
☎ **(035) 161590**
📧 ringenas.golf@telia.com
🖥 www.ringenasgolfbana.com

Skogaby (1988)
312 93 Laholm
☎ **(0430) 60190**

(0430) 60225
✉ skogaby.gk@telia.com
🖥 www.skogabygk.se

Sotenas Golfklubb   (1988)
Pl Onna, 450 46 Hunnebostrand
☎ **(0523) 52302**
🖥 www.sotenasgolf.com

Töreboda   (1965)
Box 18, 545 21 Töreboda
☎ **(0506) 12305**

Trollhättan   (1963)
Stora Ekeskogen, 466 91 Sollebrunn
☎ **(0520) 441000**

Ulricehamn   (1947)
523 33 Ulricehamn
☎ **(0321) 27950**
✉ info@ulricehamngk.golf.se
🖥 www.golf.se/ulricehamngk

Vara-Bjertorp   (1987)
Bjertorp, 535 91 Kvänum
☎ **+46 (512) 20261**
📠 +46 (512) 20259
✉ info@vara-bjertorpgk.se
📇 Mr Christian Tiden
🖥 www.vara-bjertorpgk.se

Varberg   (1950)
432 77 Tvååker
☎ **+46 340 480380**
📠 +46 340 44135
✉ info@varbergsgk.se
🖥 www.varbergsgk.se

Vinberg   (1992)
Sannagård, 311 95 Falkenberg
☎ **(0346) 19020**
📠 (0346) 19042
✉ info@vinbergsgolfklubb.se
🖥 www.vinhergsgolfklubb.se

Stockholm

Ågesta   (1958)
123 52 Farsta
☎ **(08) 447 3330**

Botkyrka
Malmbro Gård, 147 91 Grödinge
☎ **(08) 530 29650**
✉ info@botkyrkagk.golf.se
🖥 www.golf.se/botkyrkagk

Bro-Bålsta   (1978)
Jurstagarosvagen 2, 197 91 Bro
☎ **(08) 582 41310**
📠 (08) 582 40006
✉ info@bbgk@telia.com
🖥 www.brobalstagk.se

Djursholm   (1931)
Hagbardsvägen 1, 182 63 Djursholm
☎ **(08) 5449 6451**
📠 (08) 5449 6456
✉ info@dgk.nu
🖥 www.dgk.nu (Swedish only)

Fågelbro G&CC   (1991)
Fågelbro Säteri, 139 60 Värmdö
☎ **+46 (08) 571 41800**
📠 +46 (08) 571 40671
✉ kansli@fagelbrogolf.se
📇 Anders Green
🖥 www.fagelbrogolf.se

Haninge   (1983)
Årsta Slott, 136 91 Haninge
☎ **(08) 500 32850**
✉ info@haninggk.golf.se
🖥 www.haningegk.se

Huvudstadens
Lindö Park, 186 92 Vallentuna
☎ **(08) 511 70055**
(Bookings)
✉ info@huvudstadensgolf.se
🖥 www.huvudstadensgolf.se

Ingarö   (1962)
Fågelviksvägen 1, 134 64 Ingarö
☎ **(08) 556 50200**
✉ info@igk.se
🖥 www.igk.se

Kungsängen   (1992)
Box 133, 196 21 Kungsängen
☎ **(08) 584 50730**
✉ info@kungsangenc.se
🖥 www.kungsangengc.se

Lidingö   (1933)
Box 1035, 181 21 Lidingö
☎ **(08) 731 7900**
✉ kansli@lidingogk.se
🖥 www.lidingogk.se

Lindö   (1978)
186 92 Vallentuna
☎ **(08) 514 30990**

Nya Johannesberg G&CC
(1990)
762 95 Rimbo
☎ **(08) 514 50000**
🖥 www.golf.se/golfklubbar/
johannesberggcc

Nynäshamn   (1977)
Korunda 40, 148 91 Osmo
☎ **(08) 524 30590/524 30599**
📠 (08) 524 30598
✉ kansli@nynashamnsgk.se
🖥 www.nynashamnsgk.a.se

Österakers
Hagby 1, 184 92 Akersberga
☎ **(08) 540 85165**
✉ kansli@ostgk.se
🖥 www.ostgk.se   www.hagbygolf.se

Österhaninge   (1992)
Husby V.11, 136 91 Haninge
☎ **(08) 500 32285**
✉ info@osterhaningegk.golf.se
🖥 www.osterhaningegk.se

Royal Drottningholm Golf Club   (1958)
Lovö Kyrkallé 1, 178 93 Drottningholm
☎ **(08) 759 0085**
📠 (08) 759 0851
✉ info@kdrgk.se
📇 Stefan Andorff
🖥 www.kdrgk.se

Saltsjöbaden   (1929)
Box 51, 133 21 Saltsjöbaden
☎ **+46 (0)8 717 0125**
📠 +46 (0)8 717 9713
✉ klubb@saltsjobadengk.se
🖥 www.saltsjobadengk.se

Sollentuna   (1967)
Skillingegården, 192 77 Sollentuna
☎ **(08) 594 70995**
✉ intendent@sollentunagk.se
🖥 www.sollentunagk.se

Stockholm   (1904)
Kevingestrand 20, 182 57 Danderyd
☎ **(08) 544 90710**

Täby   (1968)
Skålhamra Gård, 187 70 Täby
☎ **(08) 510 23261**

Ullna   (1981)
Roslagsvagen 36, 184 94 Åkersberga
☎ **(08) 514 41230**
✉ ullna@ullnagolf.se
🖥 www.ullnagolf.se

Ulriksdal   (1965)
Box 8088, 170 08 Solna
☎ **(08) 855393**
✉ info@ulriksdalsgk.se
🖥 www.ulriksdalsgk.se

Vallentuna   (1989)
Box 266, 186 24 Vallentuna
☎ **(08) 514 30560/1**
🖥 www.vallentunagk.nu

Viksjö   (1969)
Fjällens Gård, 175 45 Järfälla
☎ **(08) 580 31300/31310**
🖥 www.golf.se/viksjogk

Wäsby
Box 2017, 194 02 Upplands Väsby
☎ **(08) 514 103 50**

Wermdö G&CC   (1966)
Torpa, 139 40 Värmdö
☎ **(08) 574 60700**
📠 (08) 574 60729
✉ wgcc@telia.com
🖥 www.wgcc.se

West Central

Arvika   (1974)
Box 197, 671 25 Arvika
☎ **(0570) 54133**
🖥 www.arvikagk.nu

Billerud (1961)
Valnäs, 660 40 Segmon
☎ **(0555) 91313**
📞 (0555) 91306
📧 kansli@billerudsgk.se
🖥 www.billerudsgk.se

Eda (1992)
Noresund, 670 40 Åmotfors
☎ **(0571) 34101**
🖥 www.edagk.com

Färgelanda (1987)
Box 23, Dagsholm 1, 458 21 Färgelanda
☎ **(0528) 20385**
📧 info@fargelandagk.golf.se
🖥 www.fargelandagk.se

Fjällbacka (1965)
450 71 Fjällbacka
☎ **(0525) 31150**

Forsbacka (1969)
Box 137, 662 23 Åmål
☎ **(0532) 61690**
📧 info@forsbackagk.golf.se
🖥 www.golf.se/golfklubbar/forsbackagk/

Hammarö (1991)
Barrstigen 103, 663 91 Hammarö
☎ **(054) 522650**
📞 (054) 521863
📧 info@hammarogk.se
🖥 www.hammarogk.se

Karlskoga (1975)
Bricketorp 647, 691 94 Karlskoga
☎ **(0586) 728190**

Karlstad (1957)
Höja 510, 655 92 Karlstad
☎ **(054) 866353**
📞 (054) 866478
📧 info@karlstadgk.se
🖥 www.karlstadgk.se

Kristinehamn (1974)
Box 337, 681 26 Kristinehamn
☎ **(0550) 82310**
📧 kristinehamnsgk@telia.com
🖥 www.golf.se/golfklubbar/kristinehamnsgk

Lyckorna (1967)
Box 66, 459 22 Ljungskile
☎ **(0522) 20176**

Orust (1981)
Morlanda 135, 474 93 Ellös
☎ **+46 304 53170**
📞 +46 304 53174
📧 orustgk@telia.com
🖥 www.orustgk.se

Saxå (1964)
Saxån, 682 92 Filipstad
☎ **(0590) 24070**

Skaftö (1963)
Stockeviksvägen 2, 450 34 Fiskebäckskil
☎ **+0046 (523) 23211**
📧 kansliet@skaftogk.se
🖥 www.skaftogk.se

Strömstad (1967)
Golfbanevägen, 452 90 Strömstad 1
☎ **(0526) 61788**
🖥 www.golf.se/stromstadgk

Sunne (1970)
Box 108, 686 23 Sunne
☎ **(0565) 14100/14210**
📞 (0565) 14855
📧 info@sunnegk.se
🖥 www.sunnegk.se

Torreby (1961)
Torreby Slott, 455 93 Munkedal
☎ **(0524) 21365/21109**

Uddeholm (1965)
Risäter 20, 683 93 Råda
☎ **(0563) 60564**
📞 (0563) 60017
📧 uddeholmsgk@telia.com
🖥 www.uddeholmsgk.com

Switzerland

Bern

Golf & Country Club Blumisberg (1959)
3184 Wünnewil
☎ **(026) 496 34 38**
📞 (026) 496 35 23
📧 secretariat@blumisberg.ch
👤 Heinz Reber (Club Mgr)
🖥 www.blumisberg.ch

Les Bois (1988)
Case Postale 26, 2336 Les Bois
☎ **(032) 961 10 03**

Neuchâtel (1925)
Hameau de Voëns, 2072 Saint-Blaise
☎ **(032) 753 55 50**
📞 (032) 753 29 40
📧 secretariat@golfdeneuchatel.ch
👤 Sabine Manrau
🖥 www.golfdeneuchatel.ch

Payerne (1996)
Public
Domaine des Invuardes, 1530 Payerne
☎ **(026) 662 4220**
📧 golf.payerne@vtx.ch
🖥 www.golfpayerne.ch

Wallenried (1994)
Chemin du Golf 18, 1784 Wallenried
☎ **(026) 684 84 80**
📞 (026) 684 84 90
📧 info@golf-wallenried.ch
👤 Mario Roltaris
🖥 www.golf-wallenried.ch

Wylihof (1994)
4542 Luterbach
☎ **(032) 682 28 28**
📧 wylihof@golfclub.ch
🖥 www.golfclub.ch

Bernese Oberland

Interlaken-Unterseen (1964)
Postfach 110, 3800 Interlaken
☎ **(033) 823 60 16**
📞 (033) 823 42 03
📧 info@interlakengolf.ch
👤 Mr Martin Gadient
🖥 www.interlakengolf.ch

Riederalp (1987)
3987 Riederalp
☎ **+41 (0) 27 927 29 32**
📞 +41 (0) 27 927 29 23
📧 info@golfclub-riederalp.ch
👤 Willy Kummer
🖥 www.golfclub-riederalp.ch

Lake Geneva & South West

Bonmont (1983)
Château de Bonmont, 1275 Chéserex
☎ **(022) 369 99 00**
📧 golfhotel@bonmont.com
🖥 www.bonmont.com

Les Coullaux (1989)
1846 Chessel
☎ **(024) 481 22 46**
📞 (024) 481 66 46
📧 d.berruex@bluewiu.ch

Crans-sur-Sierre (1906)
Rue du Prado 20 – 3963 Crans-Montana
☎ **(027) 485 97 97**
📞 (026) 485 97 97
📧 info@golfcrans.ch
🖥 www.golfcrans.ch

Domaine Impérial (1987)
Villa Prangins, 1196 Gland
☎ **+41 22 999 06 00**
📞 +41 22 999 06 06
📧 info@golfdomaineimperial.com
🖥 www.golfdomaineimperial.com

Geneva (1921)
70 Route de la Capite, 1223 Cologny
☎ **(+41) 22 707 48 00**
📞 (+41) 22 707 48 20
📧 secretariat@golfgeneve.ch
👤 François Lautens

Lausanne (1921)
Route du Golf 3, 1000 Lausanne 25
☎ **(021) 784 84 84**
📞 (021) 784 84 80
📧 info@golflausanne.ch
👤 Pierre Rindlisbacher
🖥 www.golflausanne.ch

Montreux   (1900)
54 Route d'Evian, 1860 Aigle
☎ **(024) 466 46 16**
📠 (024) 466 60 47
📧 secretariat@gcmontreux.ch
🖥 www.swissgolfnetwork.ch

Sion   (2002)
Rte Vissigen 150, 1950 Sion
☎ **(+41) (0) 027 203 79 00**
📧 info@golfclubsion.ch
🖥 www.golfclubsion.ch

Verbier   (1970)
1936 Verbier
☎ **(027) 771 53 14**
📧 golf.club@verbier.ch
🖥 www.verbiergolf.com

Villars   (1922)
CP 118, 1884 Villars
☎ **(024) 495 42 14**
📧 info@golf-villars.ch
🖥 www.golf-villars.ch

Lugano & Ticino

Lugano   (1923)
6983 Magliaso
☎ **(091) 606 15 57**
📠 (091) 606 65 58
📧 info@golflugano.ch
✍ Massimo Casartelli (Mgr)
🖥 www.golflugano.ch

Patriziale Ascona   (1928)
Via al Lido 81, 6612 Ascona
☎ **(+41) 091 785 1177**
📠 (+41) 091 785 1179
📧 info@golfascona.ch
✍ Celeste Taiana (Mgr)
🖥 www.golfascona.ch

St Moritz & Engadine

Golf Club Arosa   (1944)
Postfach 95, 7050 Arosa
☎ **(081) 377 42 42**
📠 (081) 377 46 77
📧 info@golfarosa.ch
✍ Christian Danuser
🖥 www.golfarosa.ch

Bad Ragaz   (1957)
Hans Albrecht Strasse, 7310 Bad Ragaz
☎ **(081) 303 37 17**
📧 golfclub@resortragaz.ch
🖥 www.resortragaz.ch

Davos   (1929)
Postfach, 7260 Davos Dorf
☎ **(081) 46 56 34**
📠 (081) 46 25 55
📧 info@golfdavos.cl
🖥 www.golfdavos.cl

Engadin   (1893)
7503 Samedan
☎ **(081) 851 04 66**

📧 samedan@engadin-golf.ch
🖥 www.engadin-golf.ch

Lenzerheide   (1950)
7078 Lenzerheide
☎ **(081) 385 13 13**
📠 (081) 385 13 19
📧 info@golf-lenzerheide.ch
🖥 www.golf-lenzerheide.ch

Vulpera   (1923)
7552 Vulpera Spa
☎ **(081) 864 96 88**
📠 (081) 864 96 89
📧 info@vulperagolf.ch
✍ Markus Vesti
🖥 www.swissgolfnetwork.ch-9holes-
vulpera

Zürich & North

Breitenloo   (1964)
Golfstrasse 16, 8309 Oberwil b.
Nürensdorf
☎ **+41 (0) 44 836 40 80**
📠 +41 (0) 44 837 10 85
📧 sekretariat@golfbreitenloo.ch

Bürgenstock Golf Club
(1928)
6363 Oboürgen
☎ **(041) 610 2434**
📠 (041) 612 9901
📧 info@golfclub-buergenstock.ch
🖥 www.buergenstock.ch

Dolder   (1907)
Kurhausstrasse 66, 8032 Zürich
☎ **(01) 261 50 45**

Entfelden   (1988)
Muhenstrasse 52, 5036 Oberentfelden
☎ **(062) 723 89 84**

Erlen   (1994)
Schlossgut Eppishausen, Schlossstr 7, 8586
Erlen
☎ **(071) 648 29 30**
📠 (071) 648 29 40
📧 info@erlengolf.ch
✍ Christian Heller
🖥 www.erlengolf.ch

Hittnau-Zürich G&CC
(1964)
8335 Hittnau
☎ **(+41) 950 24 42**
📠 (+41) 951 01 66
📧 info@gcch.ch
🖥 www.gcch.ch

Küssnacht   (1994)
Sekretariat/Grossarni, 6403 Küssnacht am
Rigi
☎ **(041) 854 4020**
📠 (041) 854 4027
📧 gck@golfkuessnacht.ch
🖥 www.golfkuessnacht.ch

Golf Kyburg   (2004)
CH-8310 Kemptthal, Zürich
☎ **+41 52 355 06 06**
📠 +41 52 355 06 16
📧 info@golf-kyburg.ch
🖥 www.golf-kyburg.ch

Lucerne   (1903)
Dietschiberg, 6006 Luzern
☎ **(041) 420 97 87**
📠 (041) 420 82 48
📧 info@golfclubluzern.ch
🖥 www.golfclublucerne.ch

Ostschweizerischer Golf
Club   (1948)
Club
9246 Niederbüren
☎ **(071) 422 18 56**
📠 (071) 422 18 25
📧 osgc@bluewin.ch
🖥 www.osgc.ch

Schinznach-Bad   (1929)
5116 Schinznach-Bad
☎ **(056) 443 12 26**
📠 (056) 443 34 83
📧 golfclub.schinznach@bluewin.ch
🖥 www.swissgolfnetwork.ch

Schönenberg G&CC   (1967)
8824 Schönenberg
☎ **(044) 788 90 40**
📠 (044) 788 90 45
📧 info@golf-schoenenberg.ch
✍ Peter Aeschbach
🖥 www.golf-schoenenberg.ch

Golf Sempachersee   (1996)
CH-6024 Hildisrieden, Lucerne
☎ **+41 41 462 71 71**
📠 +41 41 462 71 72
📧 info@golf-sempachersee.ch
🖥 www.golf-sempachersee.ch

Zürich-Zumikon   (1929)
Weid 9, 8126 Zumikon
☎ **(0041) 43 288 1088**
📠 (0041) 43 288 1078
📧 gccz.zumikon@ggaweb.ch
✍ C R Vane Percy
🖥 www.swissgolfnetwork.ch

Turkey

Gloria Golf
Acisu Mevkii PK27 Belek, Serik, Antalya
☎ **(242) 715 15 20**

Kemer G&CC
Goturk Koyu Mevkii Kemerburgaz, Eyup,
Istanbul
☎ **(212) 239 70 10**

Klassis G&CC
Silivri, Istanbul
☎ **(212) 748 46 00**

National Golf Club, Antalya
(1994)
Belek Turizm Merkezi, 07500 Serik, Antalya
☎ **(242) 725 46 20**
📠 (242) 725 46 23
✉ info@nationalturkey.com
🖥 www.nationalturkey.com

Robinson Golf Club Nobilis
(1998)
Acisu Mevkii, Belek, 07500 Serik/Antalya, Antalya
☎ **(+90) 242 7100362**
📠 (+90) 242 7100391
✉ golf.nobilis@robinson.de
🖥 www.robinson.de

Tat Golf International
Belek International Golf, Kum Tepesi Belek, 07500 Serik, Antalya
☎ **(242) 725 53 03**

For key to symbols and international dialling codes see page 717

Italy's "Mr Golf" Mario Camicia dies at 70

Mario Camicia, the man regarded by many as 'Mr Golf' in Italy, died in 2011. He was 70.

Tournament Director of the Italian Open for many years, Milan-born Camicia was Italy's first recognised golf commentator on television. He gave his authoritative views on the game to viewers for 20 years, helping grow not only the understanding of the game but also the interest in it in his home country.

His passion for golf came through in his commentary, never more so than when Costantino Rocca holed his famous putt from the Valley of Sin on the 18th green at St Andrews in 1995 to force a play-off with John Daly for The Open Championship – a play-off Rocca lost.

Camicia was co-founder of the magazine *Golf Italiano* and was also involved with *il Grande Golf* and *Golf e Turismo* where he was still Editorial Director. He also collaborated with *Gazzetta dello Sport* and *il Giornale* and was a consultant for *Golf Style*.

Leading the tributes to Camicia'sgolfing influence.European Tour Chief Executive George O'Grady said: "Mario epitomised everything that was special about Italian golf. He was a fervent supporter, a tireless administrator and a great and passionate television commentator. He was, quite simply, unique."

Rocca's prominence in the 1990's, which included three Ryder Cup appearances, thrilled Camicia greatly as did the emergence in recent years of Edoardo and Francesco Molinari – who made the Cup team in 2010 – and Matteo Manassero, The Sir Henry Cotton Rookie of the Year in the same season.

Rocca said "I have lost a great friend and Italian golf has lost a great person. He gave a lot to this sport but his voice will always be in our hearts. Ciao Mario."

Edoardo Molinari said: "Mario was one of the most influential people in golf in Italy. When I watched golf on TV as a young kid he was the only commentator and I can still remember vividly his voice, his great sense of humour and his ability to keep you glued to the screen.

"I also remember the enthusiasm he showed when both Francesco and I made The Ryder Cup team – when I met him in Crans the day after Monty had announced the team, he hugged me like I was one of his own kids and he was the happiest man you can ever imagine."

Matteo Manassero said: "Mario had a passion for golf that was clear to everybody that knew him, both personally and through his work on television. He played an important role in bringing golf into our homes. It was a privilege to work with him on Tour and in the studio. Our sport will miss him and his spirit will surely live on here in Italy and throughout The European Tour."

Franco Chimenti, President of the Italian Golf Federation, said: "Mario was the voice of Italian golf. The game has lost a great supporter and we have lost a great friend. For me, personally, his death represents an irrepressible pain."

Rest of the World – Region and Country Index

Golf is a global game and more and more golfers are travelling further and further on holiday and often to countries less well known as golfing destinations so, from the 2009 edition *The R&A Golfer's Handbook* has added as an additional service information on clubs from around the world to its existing directory of clubs in Great Britain, Ireland and Continental Europe. The selection is by no means comprehensive but the intention to continue to improve this section continues with many new entries including seven new countries. Those clubs listed have been chosen at random from various sources.

A truly world-wide sport

If anyone remains in any doubt that golf is truly a world-wide sport they should consider the following, proof that the human spirit and a passion for the game will prevail under the most daunting of conditions.

Highest golf course – La Paz Golf Club in Bolivia stands at 10,650 feet above sea level at its highest point. One of the greatest hazards is oxygen deficiency with the compensation that a ball will fly further and faster in the thin mountain air.

Most remote golf course – Royal Thimpu Golf Club in Bhutan, a county so remote that is has only recently seen the arrival of television and the motor vehicle, lies in the heart of the Himalayas surrounded by some of the world's highest mountains.

Most southerly golf course – Ushuaia Golf Club in Argentina sits at the southern tip of the South American continent close to windy Cape Horn.

Most northerly golf course – North Cape Golf Club in Norway lies within the Arctic Circle offering a 24-hour golfing day for several months of the year.

North America

Canada

Alberta

Banff Springs
📧 www.banffspringsgolfclub.com

Jasper Park Lodge (1925)
📧 www.fairmontgolf.com

Kananaskis (1983)
📧 www.kananaskisgolf.com

Stewart Creek (2001)
📧 www.tsmv.ca

Wolf Creek (1984)
📧 www.wolfcreekgolf.com

Atlantic Canada

Crowbush Cove (2000)
📧 www.golflinkspei.com

Dundarave (1999)
📧 www.golflinkspei.com

Fox Harb'r Resort (2001)
📧 www.foxharbr.com

Highlands Links (1939)
📧 www.highlandslinksgolf.com

Humber Valley (2006)
📧 www.humbervalley.com

British Columbia

Bear Mountain (2005)
📧 www.bearmountain.ca

Chateau Whistler (1993)
📧 www.fairmont.com/whistler

Grey Wolf (1999)
📧 www.greywolfgolf.com

Predator Ridge
📧 predatorridge.com

Tobiano (2007)
📧 www.tobianogolf.com

Ontario

Deerhurst Highlands (1990)
📧 www.deerhurstresort.com

Eagles Nest (2004)
📧 www.eaglesnestgolf.com

Muskoka Bay
📧 www.muskokabayclub.com

Rocky Crest (2000)
📧 www.clublink.ca

Taboo Resort (2002)
📧 www.tabooresort.com

Saskatchewan and Manitoba

Cooke Municipal (1909)
📧 www.cookegolf.com

Dakota Dunes (2004)
📧 www.dakotadunes.ca

Falcon Lake
📧 www.falconlakegolfcourse.com

Granite Hills
📧 www.granitehills.ca

Waskesiu
📧 www.golfsask.com/waskesiu.htm

Quebec

Le Château Montebello
✉ chateaumontebello@fairmont.com

Le Diable (1998)
📧 www.golflediamant.com

Le Geant at Mont Tremblant (1995)
📧 www.tremblant.ca

Le Maitre de Mont-Tremblant (2001)
📧 www.clublink.ca

Le Manoir Richelieu
📧 www.fairmont.com/richelieu/Recreation/Golf

USA

Alabama

Kiva Dunes
📧 www.kivadunes.com

Arizona

The Boulders Resort
📧 www.theboulders.com

Camelback Inn
📧 www.camelbackinn.com

Fairmont Scottsdale
📧 www.fairmont.com

Four Seasons Scottsdale
📧 www.fourseasons.com

Loews Ventana Canyon Resort
📧 www.loewshotels.com

The Phonician
📧 www.thephoenician.com

The Lodge at Ventana Canyon
📧 www.thelodgeatventanacanyon.com

Stone Canyon
📧 www.stonecanyon.com

Westin Kierland Resort & Spa
📧 www.kierlandresort.com

California

The Breakers
📧 www.thebreakers.com

Cordevalle
📧 www.cordevalle.com

Four Seasons Aviara
📧 www.fourseasons.com

Pebble Beach
📧 www.pebblebeach.com

Las Quinta Resort
📧 www.laquintaresort.com

The Resort at Pelican Hill
📧 www.pelicanhill.com

The Ritz-Carlton, Half Moon Bay
📧 www.ritzcarlton.com

Torrey Pines
📧 www.lodgetorreypines.com

Westin Mission Hills
📧 www.westin.com

Colorado

The Broadmoor
🖹 www.broadmoor.com

The Lodge & Spa at Cordillera
🖹 www.cordilleralodge.com

Florida

Bay Hill Club & Lodge
🖹 www.bayhill.com

Boca Raton
🖹 www.bocaresort.com

Grand Cypress Resort
🖹 www.grandcypress.com

Grande Lakes Orlando
🖹 www.grandelakes.com

PGA Village
🖹 www.pgavillage.com

The Ritz-Carlton, Naples
🖹 www.ritzcarlton.com

Sandestin Resort
🖹 www.sandestin.com

Sawgrass Marriott
🖹 www.sawgrassmarriott.com

Walt Disney World Resort
🖹 www.disneyworld.com

Georgia

The Ritz-Carlton Lodge
🖹 www.ritzcarltonlodge.com

Sea Island
🖹 www.seaisland.com

Hawaii

The Fairmont Orchid
🖹 www.fairmont.com

Four Seasons (Hualalai, Lanai and Maui)
🖹 www.fourseasons.com

Grand Hyatt Kauai
🖹 www.grandhyattkauai.com

Grand Wailea
🖹 www.grandwailea.com

Kauai Marriott
🖹 www.kauaimarriott.com

Mauna Kea Beach Hotel
🖹 www.princeresortshawaii.com

Mauna Lani Bay Hotel
🖹 www.maunalani.com

The Ritz-Carlton, Kapalua
🖹 www.ritzcarlton.com

Turtle Bay
🖹 www.turtlebayresort.com

Idaho

Coeur d'Alene
🖹 www.cdaresort.com

Sun Valley
🖹 www.sunvalley.com

Indiana

French Lick Resort
🖹 www.frenchlick.com

Michigan

The Inn at Bay Harbor
🖹 www.innatbayharbor.com

Grand Traverse Resort
🖹 www.grandtraverseresort.com

Minnesota

Giant's Ridge
🖹 www.giantsridge.com

Grand View Lodge
🖹 www.grandviewlodge.com

Nevada

Wynn Las Vegas
🖹 www.wynnlasvegas.com

New York State

Turning Stone
🖹 www.turningstone.com

North Carolina

Pinehurst
🖹 www.pinehurst.com

Pine Needles and Mid Pines
🖹 www.pineneedles-midpines.com

Oregon

Bandon Dunes
🖹 www.bandondunesgolf.com

Sunriver Resort
🖹 www.sunriver-resort.com

Pennsylvania

Hershey Resorts
🖹 www.hersheypa.com

Nemacolin Woodlands Resort
🖹 www.nemacolin.com

South Carolina

Kiawah Island
🖹 www.kiawahresort.com

Sea Pines Resort
🖹 www.seapines.com

Texas

Barton Creek
🖹 www.bartoncreek.com

Weston La Cantera Resort
🖹 www.westinlacantera.com

The Woodlands Resort
🖹 www.woodlandsresort.com

Vermont

The Equinox
🖹 www.equinoxresort.com

Virginia

The Homestead
🖹 www.thehomestead.com

Kingsmill Resort
🖹 www.kingsmill.com

Williamsburg Inn
🖹 www.colonialwilliamsburgresort.com

Washington

Resort Seniahmoo
🖹 www.semiahmoo.com

West Virginia

The Greenbrier
🖹 www.greenbrier.com

Wisconsin

The American Club
🖹 www.destinationkohler.com

The Caribbean and Central America

Antigua

Cedar Valley GC
PO Box 198, Cedar Valley, St. John's, Antigua
☎ +1 268 462 0161
✉ cedarvalleyg@candw.ag
🖥 www.cedarvalleygolf.ag

Jolly Harbour GC
PO Box 1793, St. John's, Antigua
☎ +1 268 462 7771
✉ golf@jollyharbourantigua.com
🖥 www.jollyharbourantigua.com /golf.html

Aruba

Aruba GC
Golfweg z/n, PO Box 2280 San Nicolas, Aruba
☎ +1 297 842 006
✉ arubagolfclub@yahoo.com
🖥 www.golfclubaruba.com

Tierra del Sol Resort, Spa & CC
PO Box 1257, Malmokweg z/n, Aruba
☎ +1 297 60 978
✉ tdsteetime@setarnet.aw
🖥 www.tierradelsol.com

Bahamas

One & Only Atlantis
☎ +1242 888 877 7525
🖥 www.oneandonlyresorts.com

Treasure Cay
🖥 www.treasurecay.com

Barbados

Barbados GC
Barbados Golf Club
☎ +1 246 428 8463
✉ teetime@barbadosgolfclub.com
🖥 www.barbadosgolfclub.com

Sandy Lane GC
Sandy Lane Hotel, St. James
☎ +1 246 432 2829
✉ mail@sandylane.com
🖥 www.sandylane.com/golf

Bermuda

Belmont Hills G&CC
97 Middle Road, Warwick Parish, WK 09
☎ +1 441 236 6400
✉ golf@belmonthills.com
🖥 www.belmonthills.com

St George's GC
1 Park Road, St George's Parish, GE 03
☎ +1 441 234 8067
✉ sggc@bermudagolf.bm
🖥 www.stgeorgesgolf.bm

Cayman Islands

Hyatt Britannia Golf Course
PO Box 1588 George Town, Grand Cayman
☎ +1 345 949 8020
🖥 grandcayman.hyatt.com

The Links at SafeHaven
PO Box 1311 George Town, Grand Cayman
☎ +1 345 949 5988
🖥 www.safehaven.ky/links.htm

Cuba

El Varadero GC
Villa Xanadú, Dupont de Nemours, Cuba
☎ +53 45 668482
✉ info@varaderogolfclub.com
🖥 www.varaderogolfclub.com

Dominican Republic

Casa de Campo: Teeth of the Dog; The Links and Dye Fore
La Romana Province, PO Box 140, La Romana
☎ +1809 523 3333
✉ reserva@ccampo.com.do
🖥 www.casadecampo.com.do

Playa Grande Golf Course
Km 9 Carretera Rio San Juan-Cabrera, Maria Trinidad Sanchez Province, North Coast
☎ +1809 582 0860
✉ info@playagrande.com
🖥 www.playagrande.com

Grenada

Grenada G&CC
St. George, Grenada
☎ +1 473 444 4128
✉ grenadagolfclub@spiceisle.com
🖥 www.grenadagolfclub.com

Jamaica

Ironshore G&CC
🖥 www.superclubs.com

Caymanas G&CC
Caymanas Golf & Country Club
☎ +1 876 922 3388
✉ play@caymanasgolfclub.com
🖥 www.caymanasgolfclub.com

Martinique

Golf de la Martinique
97229 Les Trois-Ilets
☎ +33 5 96 68 32 81
✉ info@golfmartinique.com
🖥 www.golfmartinique.com

Mexico

Baja California

Bajamar GC
4364 Bonita Road #299 Bonita, CA 91902-1421 Ensenada, Baja California
✉ www.bajamar.com
🖥 info@bajamar.com

Centre

Club Campestre de Aguascalientes
A.C.Vista Hermosa s/n, Fracc. Campestre 20100, Aguascalientes, Ags.
☎ +52 449 914 1001
🖥 www.campestreags.com

Central Pacific Coast

Tamarindo Golf Course
k.m. 7.5 Carretera Barra de Navidad, Puerto Vallarta, Cihuatlan, Jalisco MX 48970
☎ +52 315 351 5032
🖥 www.ycwtamarindo.com

Hope you miss your plane

The Pete Dye-designed Casa De Campo in the Dominican Republic has two holes where players must hit their tee shots over the runway of an airport.

North

El Cid G&CC
Av. Camaron Sabalo s/n, P.O. Box 813,
Mazatlan, Sinaloa, Mexico 82110
☎ +52 669 913 3333
✉ reserve@elcid.com.mx
🖥 www.elcid.com

South

Club de Golf Acapulco
Av. Costera Miguel Aleman s/n Fracc. Club
Deportivo, Acapulco
☎ +52 744 484
✉ gclubgolf@prodigy.net.mx

Puerto Rico

Dorado Beach Resort & Club
100 Dorado Beach Drive, Suite 1, Dorado,
Puerto Rico 00646
☎ +1 787 796 1234
✉ jcolon@kempersports.com
🖥 www.doradobeachclubs.com

Palmas del Mar CC
PO Box 2020 , Humacao, Puerto Rico
00792
☎ +1 787 285 2221
🖥 www.palmascountryclub.com

St Kitts and Nevis

Royal St Kitts GC
PO Box 858 Basseterre, St. Kitts, WI
☎ +1 869 466 2700
✉ info@royalstkittsgolfclub.com
🖥 www.royalstkittsgolfclub.com

St Lucia

St Lucia G&CC
Cap Estates, PO Box 328, Gros Islet, WI
☎ +1 758 450 8522
✉ golf@candw.lc
🖥 www.stluciagolf.com

St Maarten

Mullet Bay Resort
☎ +1 599 545 3069

St Vincent

Trump International GC
Charles Town, Canouan Island, St. Vincent
& The Grenadines, WI
☎ +1 784 458 8000
✉ canouan@raffles.com

Trinidad and Tobago

Mount Irvine Bay Hotel and GC
PO Box 222 Scarborough, Tobago, WI
☎ +54 11 4468 1737
✉ mtirvine@tstt.net.tt
🖥 www.mtirvine.com/golf/golf.asp

Turks and Caicos

The Provo G&CC
PO Box 662, Providenciales, Turks & Caicos
Islands, WI
☎ +1 649 946 5991
✉ provogolf@tciway.tc
🖥 www.provogolfclub.com

US Virgin Islands

Buccaneer Hotel Golf Course
The Buccaneer, St Croix, US Virgin Islands
☎ +1 340 712 2144
🖥 www.thebuccaneer.com/golf.htm

South America

Argentina

Buenos Aires

Buenos Aires GC
Mayor Irusta 3777, (1661) Bella Vista,
Buenos Aires
☎ +54 11 4468 1737
✉ info@bagolf.com.ar
🖥 www.bagolf.com.ar

The Jockey Club
Av. Marquez 1702, San Isidro, Buenos Aires
☎ +54 4743 1001
✉ adm.golf@jockeyclub.org.ar

Marayuí CC
Chapadmalal, Buenos Aires Province, Costa
Atlantica
☎ +54 0223 460 5163
🖥 www.marayui.com

Olivos GC
Ruta Panamericana Ramal Pilar Km 32, Ing.
Pablo.Nogués, CP 1613, Buenos Aires
☎ +54 11 4463 1076
✉ secretaria@olivosgolf.com.ar

Sierra de la Ventana GC
Avda. del Golf 300 - Bo. Parque Golf , C.C.
Nº 33 (8168) - Sierra de la Ventana
☎ +54 0291 491 5113
✉ golfsventana@infovia.com.ar

Córdoba

Ascochinga GC
Sierras Chicas, Córdoba
☎ +54 3525 492015
🖥 www.ascochingagolf.com.ar

La Cumbre GC
Belgrano 1095, 5178 La Cumbre, Córdoba,
Sierras
☎ +54 03548 452283
✉ lacumbregolf@arnet.com.ar
🖥 www.lacumbregolf.com.ar

Jockey Club de Córdoba
Ave. Valparaíso Km. 3 1/2, Córdoba
☎ +54 03543 464 2283
✉ golf@jockeyclubcordoba.com.ar
🖥 www.jockeyclubcordoba.com.ar

Mendoza Club de Campo
Elpidio González y Tuyutí s/n 5503
Guaymallén, Mendoza
☎ +54 0261 431 5967
✉ ccampomza@nysnet.com.ar
🖥 www.clubdecampomendoza.net.ar

El Potrerillo de Larreta Resort & CC
Road to Los Paredones Km 3 -CC195-
(5186), Alta Gracia, Córdoba
☎ +54 03547 423804 425987
✉ golf@potrerillodelarreta.com
🖥 www.potrerillodelarreta.com

Cuyo

La Rioja GC
Buenos Aires 148, La Rioja, Cuyo
☎ +54 43822 426142

Amancay GC
Av. Roque Saenz Peña 8116 (Este), Alto de
Sierra, San Juan
☎ +54 0264 425 3313
🖥 www.jockeyclubvt.com.ar

San Luis GC

C.C.280, 5700 San Luis
☎ +54 02652 490013

Norte

La Esperanza GC

Salta 140, 4500 San Pedro, Jujuy
☎ +54 03884 420000

Salta Polo Club

Av. Bolivia 2800, 4400 Salta, Prov. de Salta
☎ +54 0387 439 2001
🖥 www.saltagolfclub.com.ar

Santiago del Estero GC

*Nuñez del Prado s/n (C.C. 162), 4200
Santiago del Estero*
☎ +54 0385 434 0186

Jockey Club de Tucumán

*Av.Solano Vera, Km.2 , CP 4107 Yerba
Buena, Tucumán*
☎ +54 0381 425 1038
📧 golfalpasumaj@jockeyclubtucuman
.com
🖥 www.jockeyclubtucuman.com

Parques Nacionales

Golf Club Corrientes

*Camino a Santa Ana KM. 1500, 3400
Corrientes, Litoral*
☎ +54 03783 424372

Tacurú Social Club

Ruta 12 km 7,5. Posadas, Misiones
☎ +54 03752 480524

Jockey Club de Venado Tuerto

*Castelli 657 Golf: Ruta 8 Km 372 , 2600
Venado Tuerto, Santa Fe*
☎ +54 03462 421043
🖥 www.jockeyclubvt.com.ar

Rosario GC

*Morrison 9900, 2000 Rosario, Santa Fe
Province, Litoral*
☎ +54 0341 451 3438
🖥 www.rosariogolfclub.com

Patagonia

Chapelco Golf and Resort

*Route 234, Loma Atravesada de Taylor,
San Martín de los Andes, Neuquén,
Patagonia*
☎ +54 2972 421785
📧 reservasgolf@chapelcogolf.com
🖥 www.chapelcogolf.com

Ruca Kuyen Golf & Resort

*Cruz del Sur 203, B° Las Balsas, Ruca
Kuyen, Neuquén*
☎ +54 2944 495099
📧 info@rucakuyen.com.ar
🖥 www.rucakuyen.com.ar

Llao-Llao Hotel and Resort

*Av. Ezequiel Bustillo km. 25, Bariloche, Río
Negro Province, Patagonia*
☎ +54 02944 448530
🖥 www.llaollao.com

Ushuaia GC

*Ruta 3 Camino a Lapataia, Tierra del
Fuego, Patagonia*
☎ +54 2901 432946

Brazil

Rio de Janiero

Búzios Golf Club & Resort

📧 buziosgolf@mar.com.br

Gavea Golf & Country Club

🖥 www.gaveagolf.com.br

Hotel do Frade and Golf Resort

🖥 www.hoteldofrade.com.br

Itanhangá Golf Club

🖥 www.itanhanga.com.br

São Paulo

Damha Golf Club

🖥 www.damha.com.br

Guarapiranga G&CC

🖥 www.guarapirangagolfe.com.br

Lago Azul GC

🖥 www.lagc.com.br

Quinta da Baroneza Golfe Clube

🖥 www.qbgc.com.br

São Fernando Golf Club

🖥 www.saofernando.com.br

Terras da São José – Itú

🖥 www.tsjgolfeclube.com.br

Vista Verde GC

🖥 www.vvgc.com.br

Paraná (Curitiba City)

Alphaville Graciosa Clube

🖥 www.clubealphaville.com.br

Rio Grande do Sul

Porto Alegre Country Club

🖥 www.pacc.com.br

Bahia

Commandatuba Ocean Course

🖥 www.transamerica.com.br

Costa de Sauipe Golf Links

🖥 www.costadosauipe.com.br

Iberostar Praia do Forte Golf Club

🖥 www.praiadofortegolfclub.com.br

Terravista Golf Course

🖥 www.terravistagolf.com.br

Chile

Club de Golf Los Leones

Pte. Riesco 3700, Las Condes, Santiago
☎ +56 562 719 3200
📧 clubgolf@entelchile.net
🖥 www.golflosleones.cl

Costa Rica

La Iguana Golf Course

Playa Herradura, Puntalenas, Costa Rica
☎ +506 2630 9028
📧 maria.cano@marriott.com
🖥 www.golflaiguana.com

Ecuador

Quito Tenis y Golf Club

*Urb. El Condado Av. A N73-154 y calle
B (Entrada de Socios), Quito 17012411*
☎ +593 0224 91420
📧 golf@qtgc.com
🖥 www.qtgc.com

French Guyana

Golf de l'Anse

*Centre de Loisirs du Centre Spatial,
97310 Guyane*
☎ +33 5 94 32 63 02
📧 golf-anse@wanadoo.fr

Paraquay

Carlos Franco Country GC
Arroyos y Esteros
☎ +595 16 252123
✉ secretaria@carlosfrancogolf.com
🖳 www.carlosfrancogolf.com

Paraná CC
Supercarretera a Itaipu, Hernandarias
☎ +595 61 570181
✉ secretaria@carlosfrancogolf.com
🖳 www.carlosfrancogolf.com

Hotel Resort & Casino Yacht y Golf Club Paraguay
Av. del Yacht 11, Lambaré
☎ +595 21 906 121
🖳 www.hotelyacht.com.py

Peru

Amazon Golf Course
#185 Malecon Maldonado, City of Iquitos, North East Peru
☎ +51 965 943267
✉ michaelcollis@amazongolfcourse.com
🖳 www.amazongolfcourse.com

Lima GC
Av. Camino Real 770, San Isidro, Lima 27
☎ +51 442 6006
✉ gerencia@limagolfclub.org.pe
🖳 www.limagolfclub.org.pe

Los Andes GC
Carretera Central Km. 23, Hacienda Huampani, Chosica District, Lima
☎ +51 497 1066
✉ administracion@losandesgolfclub.org
🖳 www.losandesgolfclub.org

Los Inkas GC
Av. El Golf Los Inkas s/n, Monterrico, Surco District, City of Lima
☎ +51 317 7770
✉ email@golflosinkas.com
🖳 www.losinkasgolfclub.com

Uruguay

Club del Lago Golf
Ruta 93 Km 116.500, (Departamento de Maldonado), Punta del Este
☎ +598 42 578423
✉ info@lagogolf.com
🖳 www.lagogolf.com

Fray Bentos GC
Barrio Anglo, Fray Bentos , Ciudad de Fray Bentos, Rio Negro
☎ +598 56 22427

Sheraton Colonia Golf & Spa Resort
Continuación de la Rambla de Las Américas S/N,Colonia Del Sacramento 70000
☎ +598 52 29000
✉ colonia.golf@arnet.com.ar

Venezuela

Cardon GC
Av. 1, Urb. Zarabón, Comunida Cardon, Punto Fijo, Edo. Falcón
☎ +58 0269 2483739
✉ cardongolfclub@hotmail.com

La Cumaca GC
Sector La Cumaca, Carretera vía Pozo, Urb. Villas San Diego, Country Clu, San Diego, Edo. Carabobo
☎ +58 241 8910077
✉ info@golfclublacumaca.com
🖳 www.golfclublacumaca.com

Junko GC
Urbanización Junko Country Club, Calle El Empalme, Kilómetro 19 Carretera El Junquito, Estado Vargas
☎ +58 212 412 1254
✉ junkogc@cantv.net
🖳 www.junkogolf.com

San Luis CC
Carretera vieja Tocuyito, antes de la Hacienda San Luis, Valencia, Edo. Carabobo
☎ +58 0241 824 7878
✉ info@sanluiscc.com
🖳 www.sanluiscc.com

Africa

Algeria

Algiers GC
Rue Ahmed Ouaked Dely-Ibrahim 16000
☎ +213 757 90

Botswana

Phakalane Golf Estate
Golf Drive, Phakalane, Gaborone
☎ +267 360 4000
🖳 http://golfestate.phakalane.com

Cameroon

Likomba GC
Tiko, South West Province Cameroon
☎ +237 3335 1173
🖳 www.golflikomba.com

Egypt

Cairo

Dreamland Golf and Tennis Resort
6th of October City Road, Dreamland City, Cairo
☎ +20 11 400 577
✉ pyramidsgolf@hilton.com

The Pyramids G&CC
Soleimania Golf Resort, Kilo 55 Cairo-Alexandria Desert Road 600955
☎ +20 49 600 953
✉ amers@gega.net

Alexandria

Sporting Club Golf Course Alexandria
☎ +20 3543 3627

Hurghada

Cascades Golf Resort & CC
48 km Safaga Road, Soma Bay, Red Sea
☎ +20 65 354 2333
✉ major@thecascades.com
🖳 www.residencedescascades.com

The Links at Stella di Mare
Km 46, Suez–Hurgada Road, Ain Al Sokhna
☎ +20 212 4586
✉ golf@stelladimare.com
🖳 www.stelladimare.com

Sharm el Sheikh

Jolie Ville Golf & Resort
Um Marikha Bay 46619, Sharm el Sheikh, South Sinai
☎ +20 2 269 01465
✉ monika.elbadramany@jolieville-hotels.com
🖥 www.jolieville-golf.com

Luxor

Royal Valley Golf Course
29, El Rahala El Boghdady St., Golf Area, Heliopolis, Cairo
☎ +20 2 418 5234
✉ marketing@royalvalley.com

Sinai Peninsular

Taba Heights Golf Resort
☎ +20 69 358 0073
✉ info@tabaheights.com
🖥 www.tabaheights.com

Ghana

Achimota GC
PO Box AH8, Achimota. Accra
☎ +233 21 400220
🖥 www.achimotagolf.com

Kenya

Great Rift Valley Lodge & Golf Resort
North Lake Road, Rift Valley
☎ +254 27 123129
🖥 www.heritage-eastafrica.com

Karen CC
Karen Rd, Nairobi, Kenya, PO Box 24817, Karen
☎ +254 2 882801
✉ golf@leisurelodgeresort.com
🖥 www.westerncapehotelandspa.co.za

Kitale GC
PO Box 30, Kitale
☎ +254 32 531338

Leisure Lodge Beach & Golf Resort
PO Box 84383, Mombasa
☎ +254 40 320 3624
✉ dippd@wchs.co.za
🖥 www.leisurelodgeresort.com

Limuru CC
PO Box 10, Limuru
☎ +254 667 3189

Mombasa GC
PO Box 90164, Mombasa
☎ +254 1 22853

Muthaiga GC
PO Box 41651, Nairobi,
☎ +254 2 762414
🖥 www.muthaigagolfclub.com

Nakuru GC
PO Box 652, Nakuru
☎ +254 37 40391

Nyali G&CC
Mombasa North Coast, PO Box 95678, Mombasa
☎ +254 11 47 1589

Royal Nairobi GC
P O Box 40221, Nairobi
☎ +254 2 725769

Sigona GC
PO Box 40221, Kikuya
☎ +254 154 32144
🖥 www.sigonagolf.com

Windsor G&CC
Ridgeways Road, PO Box 45587, Nairobi
☎ +254 020 862300
✉ reservations@windsor.co.ke
🖥 www.windsorgolfresort.com

Madagascar

Golf Club d'Antsirabe
Ivohitra Golf Course , BP 142 Antsirabe
☎ +261 020 44 94 387
✉ contact@golfantsirabe.com
🖥 www.golfantsirabe.com

Mauritius

Belle Mare Plage GC (The Legend, Lemuria Championship Golf Course and The Links)
Poste de Flacq
☎ +230 402 2735
✉ info@bellemareplagehotel.com
🖥 www.bellemareplagehotel.com/golf

Paradis Hotel & GC
Le Morne Peninsula
☎ +230 401 5050
🖥 www.paradis-hotel.com

Tamarina Golf Estate and Beach Club
Tamarin Bay
☎ +230 401 300
🖥 www.tamarina.mu

Le Touessrok
Trou d'Eau
☎ +230 402 7400
🖥 www.letouessrokresort.com

Morocco

Agadir

Agadir Royal GC
Km12, Route Ait Melloul, Agadir
☎ +212 4824 8551
✉ royalgolfagadir@multimania.com

Golf Club Med les Dunes
Chemin Oued Souss, Agadir
☎ +212 4883 4690

Benslimane

Ben Slimane Royal Golf
Avenue des F.A.R. BP 83 Ben Slimane, Morocco
☎ +212 332 8793

Casablanca

Anfa Royal GC
Hippodrome d'Anfa, Casablanca
☎ +212 0522 351026

Settat University Royal GC
Km 2, Route de Casablanca, BP 575 Settat, Morocco
☎ +212 2340 0755

El Jadida

El Jadida Royal Golf & Spa
Route de Casablanca km7, B.P 116 24000 El Jadida
☎ +212 523 37910
✉ H2960@accor.com
🖥 www.accorhotels.com

Fez

Fez Royal GC
Km 15, Route d'Imouzzer, Fez
☎ +212 5566 5210

Meknès

Meknès Royal GC
Jnan Al Bahraouia, Ville Ancienne, Meknès
☎ +212 5553 0753
✉ rgm@royalgolfmeknes.com
🖥 www.royalgolfmeknes.com

Rabat

Dar Es-Salam Royal Golf
KM 9, avenue Mohammed VI / route des Zaers Souissi, Rabat
☎ +212 3775 5864
✉ golfdaressalam@menara.ma
🖥 www.royalgolfdaressalam.com

Namibia

Windhoek G&CC
Western Bypass, Windhoek
☎ +264 61 205 5223
🖥 www.wccgolf.com.na

Nigeria

Ikoyi Club
6 Ikoyi Club 1938 Road, Ikoyi. PO Box 239, Lagos
☎ +234 269 5133
✉ info@ikoyiclub-1938.org
🖳 www.ikoyiclub-1938.org

Le Méridien Ibom Hotel & Golf Resort
Nwaniba Road, PMB 1200, Uyo, Akwa Ibom State
☎ +234 808 052 7411
✉ reservations.ibom@lemeridien.com
🖳 www.lemeridienibom.com

MicCom Golf Hotels and Resort
Ibokun Road, Ada, Osun Estate
☎ +234 1497 5445
🖳 www.gmiccomgolfhotels.com

Réunion

Golf du Bassin Bleu
75 rue Mahatma Gandhi-Villéle, 97435 Saint Gilles les Hauts
☎ +33 262 70 30 00
🖳 www.bassinbleu.fr

Senegal

Le Golf du Méridien-Président
Les Almadies, BP 8181 Dakar
☎ +221 33 869 69 69
✉ resa.meridien@orange.sn

Golf de Saly
BP 145, Nagaparou
☎ +221 33957 2488
🖳 www.golfsaly.com

Seychelles

Lemuria Resort Golf Course
Anse Kerlan, Ile de Praslin
☎ +248 281 281
✉ golf@lemuriaresort.com
🖳 www.lemuriaresort.com

South Africa

Eastern Cape

East London
22 Gleneagles Road, Bunkers Hill, East London
☎ +27 43 735 1356
🖳 www.elgc.co.za

Humewood GC
Marine Drive, Summerstrand, Port Elizabeth 6013
☎ +27 41 583 2137
✉ info@humewoodgolf.co.za
🖳 www.humewoodgolf.co.za

St Francis Bay GC
Lyme Road South, PO Box 3, St Francis Bay 6312
☎ +27 42 294 0467
✉ info@stfrancisclub.co.za
🖳 www.stfrancisgolf.co.za

Gauteng

Blair Atholl
Centurion, Gauteng 2068
☎ +27 11 996 6300
🖳 www.blairatholl.co.za

Blue Valley
54 Buely Avenue, Centurion
☎ +27 11 318 3410
🖳 www.bluevalley.co.za

Bryanston
63 Bryanston Drive, Byranston 2021
☎ +27 11 706 1361
🖳 www.bryanstoncc.co.za

Centurion
Centurion Drive, John Vorster Avenue, Centurion
☎ +27 12 665 0279
🖳 www.centurioncountryclub.co.za

Dainfern
633 Gateside Avenue, Fourways 2021
☎ +27 11 875 0421
🖳 www.dainfern.co.za

Glendower GC
Marais Road, Edenvale, Johannesburg 1610
☎ +27 11 453 1013
✉ glengolf@mweb.co.za
🖳 www.lglendower.co.za

Hodderfontein
Golf Course Drive, Hodderfontein, Johannesburg
☎ +27 11 608 2033
🖳 www.mgclub.co.za

Houghton GC
2nd Ave, PO Box 87240, Houghton 2041
☎ +27 11 728 7337
✉ hgcm@houghton.co.za
🖳 www.houghton.co.za

Johannesberg (Woodmead)
Lincoln Street, Woodmead, Johannesberg 2128
☎ +27 11 202 1600
🖳 www.ccj.co.za

Kyalami CC
Maple Road, Sunninghill 2157
☎ +27 11 702 1610
🖳 www.kyalamicountryclub.co.za

Maccauvlei
Old Sasolburg Road, Vereeniging
☎ +27 16 421 3196

Parkview
Emmarentia Avenue, Parkview 2122
☎ +27 11 646 5725
🖳 www.parkviewgolf.co.za

Pretoria
241 Sydney Avenue, Waterkloof 0181
☎ +27 12 400 6241
🖳 www.ptacc.co.za

Randpark (Randpark & Windsor Park)
Setperk Street, Randpark, Randburg 2194, Johannesberg
☎ +27 11 476 1691
🖳 www.randpark.co.za

Roodepoort
Hole In One Avenue, Ruimsig, Roodeport
☎ +27 11 958 1905
🖳 www.roodepoortcc.co.za

Royal Johannesberg (East & West)
1 Fairway Avenue, Linksfield North, Johannesberg 2119
☎ +27 11 640 3021
🖳 www.royaljk.za.com

Silver Lakes
263 La Quinta Street, Silver Lakes, Pretoria
☎ +27 12 809 2110
🖳 www.silverlakes.co.za

Wanderers
PO Box 55005, Northlands, Johannesburg 2116
☎ +27 11 447 3311
🖳 www.wanderersgolfclub.com

KwaZulu-Natal

Champagne Sports
Winterton 3340
☎ +27 36 468 8000
🖳 www.champagnesportsresort.com

Durban CC
PO Box 1504, Durban, 4000
☎ +27 31 313 1777
✉ mail@dcclub.co.za
🖳 www.dcclub.co.za

Mount Edgecombe CC
PO Box 1800, Mount Edgecombe 4300
☎ +27 31 595330
✉ reception@mountecc.co.za
🖳 www.mountedgecombe.com

Prince's Grant Golf Estate
Babu Bodasingh Ave, PO Box 4038, KwaDukuza/Stanger 4450
☎ +27 32 482 0041
✉ pglodge@saol.com

San Lameer
Main Road, Lower South Coast, Southbroom 4277
☎ +27 39 315 5141
🖥 www.sanlameer.co.za

Selborne CC
Old Main Road, PO Box 2, Pennington 4185
☎ +27 39 688 1891
✉ golfbookings@selborne.com
🖥 www.selborne.com

Southbroom GC
301 Captain Smith Rd, PO Box 24, Southbroom 4277
☎ +27 39 316 6051
✉ info@southbroomgolfclub.co.za
🖥 www.southbroomgolfclub.co.za

Umdoni Park
Minerva Road, Pennington 4184
☎ +27 39 975 1615
🖥 www.umdonipark.com

Zimbali
Umhali 4390
☎ +27 32 538 1041
🖥 www.zimbali.co.za

Mpumalanga

Leopard Creek CC
PO Box 385, Malelane 1320
☎ +27 13 790 3322
🖥 www.leopardcreek.co.za

Limpopo

Elements
5 Autumn Street, Rivonia 2128
☎ +27 14 736 6910
🖥 www.elementspgr.co.za

Hans Merensky Estate
PO Box 4, Phalaborwa 1390
☎ +27 15 781 5309
✉ gitw@hansmerensky.com

Legend
Entabeni Safari Conservatory, Sterkrivier
☎ +27 32 538 1205
🖥 www.legend-resort.com

Zebula
Bela Bela 0840
☎ +27 14 734 7702
🖥 www.zebula.co.za

North West

Gary Player CC
PO Box 6, Sun City 0316
☎ +27 14 557 1245/6
✉ kpayet@sunint.co.za
🖥 www.sun-international.com

Lost City GC
PO Box 5, Sun City 0316
☎ +27 14 557 3700
✉ kpayet@sunint.co.za
🖥 www.sun-international.com

Pecanwood CC
PO Box 638, Broederstroom 0240
☎ +27 21 7821118
✉ craig@pecanwood.biz

Northern Cape

Sishen
Kathu 8446, Northern Cape
☎ +27 53 723 1501
🖥 www.sishengolfclub.co.za

Western Cape

Arabella GC
PO Box 788, Kleinmond, 7195
☎ +27 28 284 9383
✉ dippd@wchs.co.za
🖥 www.westerncapehotelandspa.co.za

Atlantic Beach
1 Fairway Drive, Melkbossstrand 7441
☎ +27 21 553 2223
🖥 www.atlanticbeachgolfclub.co.za

Clovelly CC
PO Box 22119, Fish Hoek 7974
☎ +27 21 782 1118
✉ bookings@clovelly.co.za
🖥 www.clovelly.co.za

Devondale Golf Estate
Bottelary Road, Koelenhof, Stellenbosch 7605
☎ +21 865 2080
✉ info@devonvale.co.za
🖥 www.devondale.co.za

Durbanville GC
Sportsway, Durbanville 7550
☎ +27 21 975 4834
✉ manager@durbanvillegc.co.za
🖥 www.durbanvillegolfclub.co.za

Erinvale Golf & Country Club Estate
Lourensford Road, PO Box 6188, Somerset West 7129
☎ +27 21 847 1906
✉ pro-shop@erinvale.com
🖥 www.erinvalegolfclub.com

Fancourt (The Links, Montagu and Outeniqua)
Montagu Street, Blanco, PO Box 2266, George 6530
☎ +27 44 804 0030
✉ golf@fancourt.co.za
🖥 www.fancourt.co.za

George GC
PO Box 81, George, 6530
☎ +27 44 873 6116
✉ info@georgegolfclub.co.za
🖥 www.georgegolfclub.co.za

Goose Valley GC
PO Box 1320 Plettenberg Bay 6600
☎ +27 44 533 5082
✉ bookings@goosevalleygolfclub.com
🖥 www.goosevalleygolfclub.com

Hermanus GC
Main Road, PO Box 313, Hermanus 7200
☎ +27 28 312 1954
✉ bookings@hgc.co.za
🖥 www.hgc.co.za

Metropolitan GC
Fritz Sonnenberg Rd, Mouille Point, Cape Town 8001
☎ +27 21 434 9582
✉ golfmix@mweb.co.za

Mossel Bay
17th Avenue, Mossel Bay 6500
☎ +27 44 691 2379
🖥 www.mosselbaygolfclub.co.za

Mowbray GC
Raapenberg Rd, Mowbray, Cape Town 7450
☎ +27 21 685 3018
✉ info@mowbraygolfclub.co.za
🖥 www.mowbraygolfclub.co.za

Oubaii
Herold's Bay, Western Cape
☎ +27 44 851 0131
🖥 www.oubaai.co.za

Paarl GC
Wemmershoek Rd, Paarl 7646
☎ +27 21 863 1140
✉ bookings@paarlgolfclub.co.za
🖥 www.paarlgolfclub.co.za

Pearl Valley Golf Estate
PO Box 1, Paarl 7646
☎ +27 867 8000
✉ golf@pearlvalley.co.za
🖥 www.pearlvalleygolfestates.com

Pezula
Lagoonview Drive, East Head, Knysna 6570
☎ +27 44 302 5332
🖥 www.pezula.com

Pinnacle Point
1 Pinnacle Point Road, Mossel Bay 6506
☎ +27 44 693 3438
🖥 www.pinnaclepoint.co.za

Plettenberg Bay
Plesang Valley Road, Plettenberg Bay 6600
☎ +27 44 533 2132
🖥 www.plettgolf.co.za

Rondebosch GC
3 Klipfontein Road, PO Box 495, Rondebosch, Cape Town 7700
☎ +27 21 689 4176
✉ info@rgc.co.za

Royal Cape GC
174 Ottery Road, PO Box 186, Ottery 7808, Wynberg, 7800
☎ +27 21 797 5246
✉ manager@royalcapegolf.co.za
🖥 www.royalcapegolf.co.za

Simola
1 Old Cape Road, Knysna 6570
☎ +267 360 4000
🖵 www.simolaestate.co.za

Steenberg
Tokal Road, Tokal 7495
☎ +27 21 713 2233
🖵 www.steenberggolfclub.co.za

Stellenbosch GC
PO Box 1, Paarl 7646
☎ +27 21 867 8000
🖂 golf@pearlvalley.co.za
🖵 www.pearlvalleygolfestates.com

Westlake GC
Westlake Ave, Lakeside 7945
☎ +27 21 788 2530
🖂 info@westlakegolfclub.co.za
🖵 www.westlakegolfclub.co.za

De Zalze Winelands Golf Estate
PO Box 12706, Die Boord, Stellenbosch 7613
☎ +27 21 880 7300
🖂 info@dezalzegolf.com
🖵 www.dezalzegolf.com

Swaziland

Royal Swazi Spa CC
Main Road, Mbabane
☎ +268 416 5000
🖵 www.suninternation.com/
Destinations/Resorts/Golf/Pages/
Golf.aspx

Tunisia

Djerba

Djerba GC
Zone Touristique BP360, 4116 Midoun
☎ +216 75 745 055
🖂 contact@djerbagolf.com
🖵 www.djerbagolf.com

Hammamet

Golf Citrus (Le Fôret and Les Oliviers)
Hammamet BP 132, 8050 Hammamet
☎ +216 72 226 500
🖂 golf.citrus@planet.tn
🖵 www.golfcitrus.com

Yasmine Golf Course
BP 61, 8050 Hammamet
☎ +216 72 227 001
🖂 info@golfyasmine.com
🖵 www.golfyasmine.com

Monastir

Flamingo Golf Course
Route de Ouardanine, BP 40, Monastir Gare, 5079 Monastir
☎ +216 73 500 283
🖂 booking@golfflamingo.com
🖵 www.golfflamingo.com

Palm Links Golf Course
B.P: 216 Monastir République, 5060 Tunisie
☎ +216 73 521 910
🖂 info@golf-palmlinks.com
🖵 www.golf-palmlinks.com

Port el Kantaoui

El Kantaoui Golf (Sea and Panorama)
Station Touristique, 4089 El Kantaoui BP 32 Port el Kantaoui
☎ +216 73 348 756
🖵 www.kantaouigolfcourse.com.tn

The Résidence Golf Course
Boite Postale 697, 2070 La Marsa, Les Côtes de Carthage
☎ +216 71910 101
🖂 info@theresidence.com
🖵 www.theresidence.com

Tabarka

Tabarka Golf Course
Rte Touristique El Morjènel, 8110 Tabarka
☎ +216 78 670 028
🖂 info@tabarkagolf.com
🖵 www.tabarkagolf.com

Tozeur

Oasis Golf Tozeur
Société Golf Oasis BP 48, Poste Elchorfa, 2243 Tozeur
☎ +216 76 471 194
🖂 reservation.golf@tozeuroasisgolf .com
🖵 www.tozeuroasisgolf.com

Tunis/Carthage

Golf de Carthage
Choutrana II, 2036 Soukra
☎ +216 71 765 700
🖂 reservationgc@planet.tn
🖵 www.golfcarthage.com

Uganda

Entebbe Golf Club
P.O.Box 107, Entebbe
☎ +261 020 44 94 387

Uganda GC
Kitante Road. Kampala, Uganda
☎ +261 236848

Zambia

Chainama Hills
P.O Box 31385 Lusaka
☎ +260 211 250916
🖂 dngambi@yahoo.com

Livingstone GC
Victoria Falls, Southern Province
☎ +260 321 323052
🖂 info@livingstonegolf.com
🖵 www.livingstonegolf.com

Mufulira GC
PO Box 40141 / 40700, Mufulira, Copperbelt Province
☎ +260 212 411131
🖂 mufuliraclub@ovation.co.za
🖵 www.mufulira.co.za

Ndola GC
PO Box 71564, Ndola
☎ +26 005 588 6678
🖵 www.ndolagolfclub.com

Zimbabwe

Chapman GC
Samora Machel, Avenue East, Harare
☎ +263 4 747 328
🖵 www.chapmangolfclub.co.zw

Middle East

Bahrain

Awali GC
PO Box 25413, Awali, Kingdom of Bahrain
☎ +973 1775 6770
✉ secretary@awaligolfclub.com
▤ www.awaligolfclub.com
⊕ 18 hole sand course

Bahrain GC
✉ salem_1956@hotmail.com
⊕ 18 hole sand course

The Royal GC
PO Box 39117, Riffa, Kingdom of Bahrain
☎ +973 1775 0777
✉ info@theroyalgolfclub.com
▤ www.theroyalgolfclub.com

Israel

Caesarea G&CC
PO Box 4858, Caesarea 30889
☎ +972 463 61173

Gaash CC
▤ www.gaashgolfclub.co.il

Kuwait

Sahara G&CC
PO Box 29930 Safat 13160
☎ +965 4769408
✉ info@saharakuwait.com
▤ www.saharakuwait.com
⊕ Fully illuminated for night time golf

Oman

Muscat G&CC
PO Box 3358, CPO, Postal Code 111,
Sultanate of Oman
☎ +968 24 510065
✉ info@muscatgolf.com
▤ www.muscatgolf.com

The Wave GC
Madinat Al Sultan Qaboos, PO Box 87, PC
118, Sultanate of Oman
☎ +968 245 34444
✉ customerservice@thewavemuscat
.com
▤ thewavemuscat.com

Qatar

Doha GC
PO Box 13530, Doha, State of Qatar
✉ info@dohagolfclub.com

Mesaieed GC
Umm Said, Mesaieed, State of Qatar
☎ +974 476 0874
✉ mgc_golf@yahoo.co.uk

Dukhan GC
PO Box 49776, Dubai, State of Qatar
✉ qatargasgolfopen@qatargas.com.qa

Saudi Arabia

Arizona Golf Resort
PO Box 8080, Riyadh 11482
☎ +966 1 248 4444
✉ management@agr.com.sa
▤ www.agr.com.sa

United Arab Emirates

Abu Dhabi Golf & Equestrian Club
PO Box 33303
☎ +971 244 59600

Abu Dhabi GC
PO Box 51234
▤ www.adgolfclub.com

Al Badia GC
PO Box 49776, Dubai
☎ +971 460 10101

Al Ghazal GC
PO Box 3167
☎ +971 257 58040
⊕ Sand course

Al Hamra GC
PO Box 6617, Ras Al Khaimah
▤ www.alhamragolf.com

Arabian Ranches GC
PO Box 36700, Dubai
▤ www.arabianranchesgolfdubai.com

Dubai Creek Golf & Yacht Club
PO Box 6302, Dubai
▤ www.dubaigolf.com

Emirates GC
PO Box 24040, Dubai
▤ www.dubaigolf.com

Jebel Ali Golf Resort & Spa
PO Box 9255, Dubai
▤ www.jebelalo-international.com

Jumeirah Golf Estates
PO Box 262080, Dubai
▤ www.jumeirahgolfestates.com

Palm Sports Resort
PO Box 1671, Al Ain
▤ www.palmsportsresort.com

Sharjah Golf & Shooting Club
PO Box 6, Sharjah
▤ www.golfandshootingshj.com

Sharjah Wanderers GC
PO Box 1767, Sharjah
▤ www.sharjahgolf.com
⊕ 9 holes sand, 9 holes grass

The Els Club
PO Box 111123, Dubai
▤ www.elsclubdubai.com

The Montgomerie Dubai
PO Box 36700, Dubai
▤ www.themontgomerie.com

Tower Links GC
PO Box 30888, Ras Al Khaimah
☎ +971 722 79939

Asia

Bangladesh

Army GC
Dhaka Cantonment
☎ 0181 921 2211 (mobile)

Bhatiary G&CC
*C/o 24 Infantry Division, Chittagong
Cantonment*
☎ +880 031 278 7423
✉ bhatiarygolf@yahoo.com

BOF GC
*Bangladesh Ordnance Factories, Gazipur
Cantonment, Gazipur*
☎ +880 920 4613

Bogra GC
C/o 11 Infantry Division, Bogra Cantonment
☎ +880 051 82080

Dhaka Club Limited
Ramna, Dhaka-100
☎ +880 861 9180
✉ dcl@bdonline.com

Jessore G&CC
*C/o Headquarters 55 Infantry Division
(Ordnance Br), Jessore Cantonment, Jessore*
☎ +880 0421 68675
✉ +880 0421 67450

Kurmitola GC
Dhaka Cantonment, Dhaka 1206
☎ +880 875 2520
✉ kgcdhaka@hotmail.com

Mainamati G&CC
*C/o 33 Infantry Division, Comilla
Cantonment, Comilla*
☎ +880 081 76381
✉ mgcc18@yahoo.com

Rangpur GC
*C/o66 Infantry Division, Rangpur
Cantonment*
☎ +880 673000

Savar GC
*9 Infantry Division, Savar Cantonment,
Savar 01714171790 (XO)*
☎ +880 779 1839

Shaheen G&CC
*BAF Base Zahurul Haque, Patanga,
Chattigong*
☎ +880 031-250 2033
✉ sgccpbaf@gmail.com

Bhutan

Royal Bhutan GC
Chhopel Lam, Thimphu
☎ +925 232 5429

Brunei

Pantai Mentiri GC
*Km 15½ Jalan Kota Batu, Brunei
Darussalam*
☎ +673-279102
✉ infodesk@pantaimentirigolfclub
.com
🖥 www.pantaimentirigolfclub.com

Royal Brunei G&CC
*Jerudong Park, Jerudong BG3122, Brunei
Darussalam*
☎ +673 261 1582

China

Anhui

Huangshan Pine G&CC
*No. 78, Longjing, Jichang Da Av., Tunxi
District, Huangshan City, Anhui*
☎ +86 559 256 8399
✉ pine@chinahsgolf.com
🖥 www.chinahsgolf.com

Beijing

Beijing CBD International
*No.99, Gaobeidian RD, Chaoyang District,
Beijing 100023*
☎ +86 10 673 84801
✉ hongshuasale@h-cgolf.com
🖥 www.h-cgolf.com

Beijing Taiwei GC
*Xiangtang New Culture Town, Cuicun
County, Chanping District, Beijing 102212*
☎ +86 10 6072 5599
🖥 www.taiweigolf.com

Chongqing

**Chongqing International
GC**
*Huaxi Town, Banan District, Chongqing
400055*
☎ +86 23 6255 4816
✉ chongqinggolf@sina.com.cn

Fujian

Orient (Xiamen) G&CC
*Haicang Investment & Development Zone
Xiamen, Fujian Province 528234*
☎ +86 592 653 1317
✉ xiamen@orientgolf.com

Quanzhou GC
*Zimao Town, Jinjiang, Fujian Province
362213*
☎ +86 595 595 1988
✉ golf@publ.qz.fj.cn
🖥 www.qzgolf.com

Trans Strait GC
*New Village, Wenwusha Town, Changle,
Fuzhou, Fujian Province, China 350207*
☎ +86 591 2878 9567
✉ tsgolfc@pub6.fz.fj.cn

Guangdong

Dongguan Hill View GC
*Ying Bin Da Dao, Dong Cheng District,
Dongguan, Guangdong*
☎ +86 769 222 09980
✉ hillview@tom.com
🖥 www.hillview-golf.com

Nanhai Peach Garden GC
*Peach Garden, Songgang, Nanhai District,
Foshan City, Guangdong Province 528234*
☎ +86 757 852 31888
🖥 www.peachgardengolf.com

Zhuhai Golden Gulf GC
*Jinwan Road, Golden Coast, Jinwan District,
Zhuhai, Guangdong 519041*
☎ +86 756 761 4000
✉ goldengolf@zhggg.com
🖥 www.zhggg.com

Guangxi

Gentle Uptown GC
*Nanwu Road, Naning, Guangxi Province
530024*
☎ +86 771 580 5501
✉ shichangbu@gentlegolf.com
🖥 www.gentlegolf.com

Li River G&CC
*Foreign Marina, Overseas Chinese Tourism
District, Guilin, Guangxi Province 541008*
☎ +86 773 390 9080
✉ golf@chin-taiwan.com
🖥 www.royal.fide.com

Need a little help?

Dotted around the Royal Bhutan Golf Club at Thimphu are several chortens – small stone structures with religious artifacts inside that are receptacles for offerings. One wonders how many players struggling to make par have made donations.

Guizhou

Guiyang GC
Sanyuan, Zha Zuo Town Guiyang, Guizhou Province 550201
☎ +86 851 235 1888
📧 gygolfclub@163.com
🖥 www.guiyanggolf.com

Heilongjiang

Heilongjiang Harbin Baiyun GC
Harbin, Heilongjiang Province
☎ +86 451 600 5242

Hainan

Haikou Meishi Mayflower International GC
88 West Binhai Road, Haikou City, Hainan Province 570311
☎ +86 898 6871 8888
📧 websitesales@meishigolf.com
🖥 www.meishigolf.com

Kangle Garden Spa & GC
Xinglong Town, Wanning, Hainan Province 571533
☎ +86 898 6256 8888
📧 golfclub@kangleresort.com
🖥 www.kangleresort.com

Yalong Bay GC
No.168 Qiong Dong Road, Dongshan Town, Qiongshan, Hainan Province 572016
☎ +86 898 8856 5888
📧 welcome@yalongbaygolfclub.com
🖥 www.yalongbaygolfclub.com

Hebei

Grandeur South G&CC
No.1 Yongle Road, ZhuoZhou, Hebei Province 072750
☎ +86 10 8120 2880
📧 members@gsgcc.com
🖥 www.gsgcc.com

Xin'ao Group Elephant Hotel
Jinyuan Road, Economic & Technological Development Zone, Langfang City, Hebei Province 065001
☎ +86 316 606 1188
📧 pyn-golf@163.com

Henan

Synear International GC
No.86, South Bank of The Yellow River, Zhengzhou City, Henan Province 450004
☎ +86 371 636 26699
🖥 www.syneargolf.com

Hubei

Orient (Wuhan) Golf Country Club
Xingxing, Jiangti Hanyang District Wuhan, Hubei Province 430051
☎ +86 27 8461 2270
📧 wuhan@orientgolf.com
🖥 www.orientgolf.com

Hunan

Changsha Qingzhuhu International GC
Qingzhuhu, Kaifu District, Changsha City, Hunan Province 410152
☎ +86 731 678 3999
📧 golf@hunangolf.com.cn
🖥 www.hunangolf.com.cn

Hunan Dragon Lake International GC
Guan Yin Yan Reservoir, Wangcheng District, Changsha, Hunan Province 410217
☎ +86 731 838 8277
📧 longhu.hn@2118.com.cn
🖥 www.dragonlakegolf.com

Jiangsu

Gingko Lake International GC
No.1, Gingko Lake, GuLi Town, Jiangning District, Nanjing, Jiangsu Province 211164
☎ +86 25 8613 9988
📧 gingkolake@gingkolake.com
🖥 www.gingkolake.com

Nanjing Harvard GC
No. 176 Zhen Zhu Road, Pukhou District, Nanjing City, Jiangsu Province 210031
☎ +86 25 5885 3333
📧 welcome@harvardgolf.com
🖥 www.harvardgolf.com

Shanghai West Country GC
128 Huanzhen W. Road, Zhouzhuang, Kunshan, Jiangsu 215325
☎ +86 512 5720 3888
📧 golf@shanghaiwest.com
🖥 www.shanghaiwest.com

Jiangxi

Nanchang Mingya G&CC
No. 601, South Lushan Dadao, Nanchang City, Jiangxi.Province 330013
☎ +86 791 382 1600
📧 info@mingya.cn
🖥 www.mingya.cn/golf

Jilin

Changchun Jingyetan GC
Ingyuetan National Forest Park, Changchun, Jilin Province 130117
☎ +86 431 528 3815
📧 jingyuetangolf@163.com

Liaoning

Dalian Golden Pebble Beach GC
Dalian Jinshi Tan State Tourist & Vacational Zone, Liaoning 116650
☎ +86 411 8791 2343
📧 jinqiu@dalianjinshigolf.com
🖥 www.dalianjinshigolf.com

Dandong Wulong International GC
Lishugou Village, Loufang Town, Zhen An District, Dandong, Liaoning 118000
☎ +86 415 417 1857
📧 golf@wl-golf.com
🖥 www.wl-golf.com

Shanghai

Grand Shanghai International G&CC
Yang-Cheng Lake Tour & Holiday Zone, Ba Cheng Town, Kunshan Jiangsu Province 215347
☎ +86 512 5789 1999
📧 uugsighr@public1.sz.js.cn
🖥 www.grandshanghaigolfresort.com

Orient (Shanghai) G&CC
High-Technology Garden, Songjiang District, Shanghai 201600
☎ +86 21 5785 4698
📧 shanghai@orientgolf.com

Shanghai Links GC
No. 1600 Ling Bai Road, Pu Dong New District, Shanghai 201201
☎ +86 21 5897 5899
🖥 www.thelinks.com.cn

Shandong

Guoke International GC
Economic Development Area in Qihe, Shandong Province 528234
☎ +86 534 8550 0299
🖥 www.gk-golf.com

Nanshan International GC
Nanshan Tourist Zone, Dongjiang Town, Longkou, Shandong Province 265718
☎ +86 535 861 6818
📧 service@nanshangolf.com
🖥 www.nanshangolf.com

Shaanxi

Xi'an Yajian International GC
Cao-Tang Tourist & Holiday Resort, Hu County, Xi'an, Shaanxi 710304
☎ +86 29 8495 1236
📧 rivergolf@163.com

Shenzhen

Shenzhen Airport Golf Resort
Near to Bao An Airport, Shenzhen 518128
☎ +86 755 2777 9991
✉ airportgolf@sohu.com

Shenzhen GC
Shen Nan Road, Fu Tian Qu, Shenzen, Guangdong 518034
☎ +86 755 330 8888

Shenzhen Tycoon GC
Jiu Wei, Xi Xiang Town, Boan District, Shenzhen, Guangdong 518126
☎ +86 755 2748 3999
✉ member@hkcts.com
🖳 www.tycoongolf.com

Sichuan

Sichuan International GC
Mu Ma Shan Development Zone, Shuangliu Country, Chengdu, Sichuan 610026
☎ +86 28 8578 5010
✉ sigc@sigc.com
🖳 www.sigc.com

Tianjin

Tianjin Fortune Lake GC
Tuanbo Town, Jinghai County, Tianjin 300193
☎ +86 22 6850 5299
✉ tj_golf@eyou.com

Tianjin Warner International GC
N°1 Nanhai Road, Teda, Tianjin 300457
☎ +86 22 2532 6009
✉ warner@warner-golf.com
🖳 www.warnergolfclub.com

Xinjiang

Xinjiang Urumqi Xuelianshan GC
West Hot Spring Road, Shui Mo Gou District, Urumqi, Xinjiang Province 830017
☎ +86 991 487 3888
🖳 www.j-golf.com

Yunnan

Kunming Country GC
14km Anshi Highway, Kunming, Yunnan Province 650601
☎ +86 871 742 6666
✉ fhy@public.km.yn.cn

Lijiang Ancient Town International GC
Huangshan Town, Yulong, Lijiang City, Yunnan Province 674100
☎ +86 888 662 2700
✉ Lg3102331@vip.km169.net

Zhejiang

Huangzhou West Lake International CC
No.200 Zhijiang Road, Zhejiang Province 310024
☎ +86 571 8732 1700
✉ golf@westlakegolf.com
🖳 www.westlakegolf.com

Orient (Wenzhou) Golf CC
Yangyi West Suburbia Forest Park, Lucheng District, Wenzhou, Zhejiang Province 325000
☎ +86 577 8881 7718
✉ wenzhou@orientgolf.com
🖳 www.orientgolf.com

Chinese Taipei

Chang Hua GC
101 Lane 2, Ta Pu Road, Changhua City, Taiwan
☎ +886 4 7135799

Lily G&CC
55 Hu Tu Tuan, Kuan Hsi, Hsinchu County, Taiwan
☎ +886 3 5875111

National Garden GC
1-1 Shihjhen Village, Yuanli Township, Miaoli County, Taiwan
☎ +886 37 741166

North Bay G&CC
5 Tsau Pu Wei, Tsau-Li Village, Shimen Township, Taipei County, Taiwan
☎ +886 2 26382930

Sunrise G&CC
256 Yang Sheng Road, Yang Mei, Taoyuan County, Taiwan
☎ +886 3 4780099

Taichung G&CC
46 Tungshan Road, Hengshan Village, Taya, Taichung County, Taiwan
☎ +886 4 25665130~2

Taipei GC
34-1, Chihtuchi, Kengtsu-Tsun, Luchu-Hsiang, Taoyuan County, Taiwan
☎ +886 3 3241311-5

Ta Shee G&CC
168 Jih Hsin Road, Ta Hsi Township, Taoyuan County, Taiwan
☎ +886 3 3875699

Wu Fong G&CC
668 Feng-Ku Road, Feng-ku Village, Wu Feng, Taichung County, Taiwan
☎ +886 4 23301199

Hong Kong

Clear Water Bay G&CC
☎ +852 2719 1595

Discovery Bay GC
☎ +852 2987 7273

Hong Kong GC, Deep Water Bay
☎ +852 2812 7070

Hong Kong GC, Fanling
☎ +852 2670 1211

The Jockey Club
☎ +852 2791 3388

Shek O CC
☎ +852 2809 4458

Sky City Eagles GC
☎ +852 3760 6688

India

Agra GC
Tay Road, Agra 282001 UP
☎ +91 5622 226015

Bangalore GC
2 Stanley Road, High Grounds, Bangalore 560001
☎ +91 80 228 1876
✉ bgc1876@bgl.vsnl.net.in

Bombay Presidency GC
Dr Choitram Gidwani Road, Chembur, Mumbai 400074
☎ +91 22 550 5874

Chandigarh GC
Sector 6, Chandigarh
☎ +91 17 274 0350
✉ cgc@chai91.net

Cosmopolitan GC
18 Golf Club Road, Tollygunge, Calcutta 700033 West Bengal
☎ +91 33 473 1352

Delhi GC
Dr Zakhir Hussain Marg, New Delhi 10003
☎ +91 11 243 6278
✉ delhigolf@aibn.on.ca

DLF Club
DLF City, Gurgaon, Haryana
✉ karan@dlfmail.com

Eagleton GC
30th KM Bangalore-Mysore Highway, Bangalore
✉ eagleton@bgol.vsnl.net.in

Gaekwad Baroda GC
Lukshimi Villas Estate Baroda, Gujarat 390001
☎ +91 26 524 33599

Madras Gymkhana GC
Golf Annexe 334 Mount Road, Nandanam, Chennai 600035
☎ +91 44 56881

Motacamuna Gymkhana CC
Finger Post PO, The Nilgirls, Tamilnadu 643006
☎ +91 42 324 42254

Poona GC
Airport Road, Yerawada Pune 411006
☎ +91 20 266 94131

Royal Calcutta
18 Golf Club Road, Tollygunge, Calcutta 700033 West Bengal
☎ +91 33 473 1352

Tollegunge GC
120 Deshapran Sasmal Road, Calcutta
☎ +91 33 473 4539

Indonesia

Bukit Darmo Golf
Blok G-2, Jl Bukit Darmo, Surabaya 60226
☎ +62-31-7325555
🖥 www.bukitdarmogolf.com

Nirwana Bali GC
Jl. Raya Tanah Lot Kediri, Tabanan 82171, Bali
☎ +62 361 815 960
🖥 www.nirwanabaligolf.com

Satelindo Padang Golf
Bukit Sentul, Bogor 16810, West Java
☎ +62 21 879 60266
✉ marketing@golfsatelindo.com
🖥 www.golfsatelindo.co.id

Japan

Abiko CC
1110 Okahotto, Abiko-shi, Chiba Pref. 270-1137
☎ +81 (0) 4 7182 0111
🖥 www.abikogc.com

Aichi CC
20-1 Yamanonaka, Itaka-cho, Takabari, Meito-ku, Nagoya-shi, Aichi Pref. 465-0067
☎ +81 (0) 52 701 1161
🖥 www.aichicc.jp/top.htm

Hirono GC
7-3 Hirono Shijimi-cho, Miki-Shi, Hyogo Pref. 673-0541
☎ +81 (0) 794 85 0123

Hodogaya CC
1324 Kamikawaicho, Asahi-ku, Yokohama-shi, Kanagawa Pref. 241-0802
☎ +81(0) 45 921 0115
🖥 www.hodogaya-country-club.jp/

Ibaraki CC
25 Nakahozumi, Ibaraki-shi, Osaka Pref. 567-0034
☎ +81 (0) 72 625 1661
🖥 www.ibarakicc.or.jp/

Kasumigaseki CC
3398 Kasahata, Kawagoe-shi, Saitama Pref. 350-1175
☎ +81 (0) 49 231 2181
🖥 www.kasumigasekicc.or.jp/

Kawana (Fuji)
1459 Kawana, Ito City, Shizuoka, Chubu, Honshu
☎ +81 557 45 1111
🖥 www.princehotels.co.jp/kawana/

Kobe GC
Ichigaya Rokkosancho, Nadaku Kobe-shi, Hyogo Pref. 657-0101
☎ +81 (0) 78 891 0364

Koga GC
1310-1 Shishi-bu, Koga-shi, Fukuoka Pref. 811-3105
☎ +81 (0) 92 943 2261
🖥 www.kogagc.co.jp/english/index.html

Nagoya GC
35-1 Dondoro, Wago, Togo-cho, Aichi-gun, Aichi Pref. 470-0153
☎ +81 (0) 52 801 1111
🖥 www.nagoyagolfclub-wago.gr.jp/

Naruo GC
1-4 Kanagadani Nishiuneno, Kawanishi-shi, Hyogo Pref. 666-0155
☎ +81 (0) 72 794 1011
🖥 www.naruogc.or.jp/

Sagami CC
4018 Shimotsuruma, Yamato-shi, Kanagawa Pref. 242-0001
☎ +81 (0) 46 274 3130
🖥 www.h3.dion.ne.jp/~sagamicc/

Takanodai CC
1501 Yokodo-cho, Hanamigawa-ku, Chiba-shi, Chiba Pref. 262-0001
☎ +81 (0) 47 484 3151
🖥 www.takanodaicc.or.jp/

Tokyo GC
1984 Kashiwabara, Sayama-shi, Saitama Pref. 350-1335
☎ +81 (0) 4 2953 9111

Korea

Chungcheong

Cheonan Sangnok Resort Golf Course
669-1 Jangsan-ri, Susin-myeon, Cheonan-si, Chungcheongnam-do
☎ +82 41 529 9075

Gangwong

Alps Golf Course
107 Heul-ri, Ganseong-eup, Goseong-gun, Gangwon-do
☎ +82 33 681 5030
🖥 www.alpsresort.co.kr

Gyeonggi

Sky 72 GC
2029-1 Woonseo-Dong, Joong-Gu, Incheon
☎ +82 32 743 9108
🖥 www.sky72.com/en/index.jsp

Songchoo CC
San 23-1, BeeAhm-Lee, KwangJuk-Myon, YangJu-si, Gyeonggi-Do
☎ +82 31 871 9410
🖥 www.songchoo.co.kr/e-htm

Taeyoung CC
San38 Jukrung-ri Wonsam-myun Yong-in-shi, Kyuongki-do
☎ +82 31 334 5051
🖥 www.ty-cc.com/english/introd.jsp

Gyeongsang

Bomun CC
180-7 Mulcheon-ri, Cheonbuk-myeon, Gyeongju-si, Gyeongsangbuk-do
☎ +82 54 745 1680 2

Gageun GC
111-1 Ma-dong, Gyeongju-si, Gyeongsangbuk-do
☎ +82 54 740 5161

Mauna Ocean Golf
Shindaeri San 140-1 Yangnammyon Gyeongjusi, Gyeongsangbuk-do
☎ +82 54 77 0900

Jeju

Chungmun Beach GC
3125-1, Saekal-dong, Sogwipo, Cheju-Do
☎ +82 64 735 7241

Nine Bridge Golf Course
Kwangbyong-ri, Anduk-myon, South Jeju-gun, Jeju Island
☎ +82 64 793 9999
🖥 www.ninebridge.co.kr

Jeolla

Club 900
San 15-1, Ssangok-ri, Dogok-myeon, Hwasun-gun, Jeollanam-do
☎ +82 61 371 0900

Pusan

Dong Nae CC
San 128, Son-dong, Dongnae-gu, Pusan
☎ +82 51 513 0101

Seoul

Namsungdae GC
419 Jangji-dong, Songpa-gu, Seoul
☎ +82 02 403 0071

Santisuk Lang Xang GC
Km14 Thadeua Road, Ban Nahai,
Vientiane, Laos
☎ +856 21 812 071

Macau G&CC
☎ +853 871188

Labuan

Labuan GC
PO Box 276, 87008 Labuan, Labuan
☎ +60 87 412 810

Sabah

Borneo G&CC
Km 69, Papar-Beaufort Highway, 89700
Bongawan, Sabah
☎ +60 87 861 888
✉ reservation.bgcc@vhmis.com

Karambunai Resorts GC
PO Box 270, Menggatal, 88450 Kota
Kinabalu, Sabah
☎ +60 88 411 215
✉ salesmgrkrgc@borneo-resort.com
🖥 www.borneo-resort.com

Shan-Shui Golf & Country Resort
PO Box 973, Mile 9, Jalan Apas, Tawau,
91008 Tawau, Sabah
☎ +60 89 916 888
✉ ssgolfcc@tm.net.my

Sutera Harbour G&CC
1 Sutera Harbour Boulevard, 88100 Kota
Kinabalu, Sabah
☎ +60 88 318 888
✉ sutera@suteraharbour.com.my
🖥 www.suteraharbour.com.my

Sarawak

Damai G&CC
Jalan Santubong, PO Box 203, 93862
Kuching, Sarawak
☎ +60 82 846 088
✉ dgcc@po.jaring.my
🖥 www.damaigolf.com

Hornbill Golf & Jungle Club
Jalan Borneo Heights, Borneo Highlands
Resort, 94200 Padawan, Sarawak
☎ +60 82 790 800
✉ enquiry@hornbillgolf.com
🖥 www.hornbillgolf.com

Johor

Bukit Banang G&CC
No. 1, Persiaran Gemilang, Bandar Banang
Jaya, 83000 Batu Pahat, Johor
☎ +60 7 428 6001
✉ bbgcc@po.jaring.my
🖥 www.berjayaclubs.com/banang
/index.cfm

Daiman 18 Johor Bahru
No.18 Jalan Pesona, Taman Johor Jaya,
81100 Johor Bahru, Joho
☎ +60 7 353 3100
✉ daiman18@daiman.com.my
🖥 www.daiman.com.my

Desaru G&CC
PO Box 26, Bandar Penawa,
81900 Kota Tinggi, Johor
☎ +60 7 8222 333
✉ golf@desaruresort.com
🖥 www.desaruresort.com

Palm Resort G&CC
Jalan Persiaran Golf, Off Jalan Jumbo,
81250 Senai, Johor
☎ +60 7 5996 222
✉ marcomm@palmresort.com
🖥 www.palm-resort.com

Palm Villa Golf & Country Resort
PTD 44500, Jalan Pindah Utama, Bandar
Putra, PO Box 69, 81000 Kulai, Johor
☎ +60 7 599 9099
✉ Honorius@IOI.po.my

Ponderosa G&CC
10-C Jalan Bumi Hijau 3, Taman Molek,
81100 Johor Bahru, Johor
☎ +60 7 354 9999
✉ pgcc@tm.net.my
🖥 www.ponderosagolf.com

Royal Johor CC
3211 Jalan Larkin, 80200 Johor Bharu,
Johor
☎ +60 7 2224 2098
✉ rjcc@tm.net.my
🖥 www.royaljohorcountryclub.com

Sebana Cove
LB 505 Kota Tinggi PO, 81900 Kota Tinggi,
Johor
☎ +60 7 826 6688
✉ sebanacove@pacific.net.sg
🖥 www.sebanacove.com

Starhill G&CC
6.5 Km Jalan Maju Jaya, Kempas Lama,
Skudai, 81300 Johor Baru, Johor
☎ +60 7 5566 325
🖥 www.starhillgolf.com.my

Tanjong Puteri G&CC
Ptd 101446, Mukim Plentong, 81700 Pasir
Gudang, Johor
☎ +60 7 2711 888
✉ tpgolf@tm.net.my

Kedah

Black Forest G&CC
Zon Bebas Cukai, 06050 Bukit Kayu
Hitam, Kedah
☎ +60 4 9222 790
✉ blackforest@sriwani.com.my
🖥 www.blackforest.com.my

Cinta Sayang G&CC
Jalan Persiaran Cinta Sayang, 0800 Sungai
Petani, Kedah
☎ +60 4 4414 666
✉ cintasayang@cinta-sayang.com.my
🖥 www.cintasayangresort.com/
cs_golf.html

Datai Bay GC
Jalan Teluk Datai, PO Box 6, Kuah, 07000
Pulau Langkawi, Kedah
☎ +60 4 9592 700
🖥 www.dataigolf.com

Gunung Raya Golf Resort
alan Air Hangat, Kisap, Kuah, 07000 Pulau
Langkawi, Kedah
☎ +60 4 9668 148
✉ reservation@golfgr.com.my
🖥 www.golfgr.com.my

Sungai Petani Club
23-C Jalan Sungai Layar, 08000 Sungai
Petani, Kedah
☎ +60 4 422 4894
✉ info@slgcc.com.my
🖥 www.slgcc.com.my/intro.php

Kelantan

Kelantan G&CC
5488 Jalan Hospital, 15200 Kota Bahru,
Kelantan
☎ +60 9 7482 102

Kuala Lumpur

Bukit Jalil Golf & Country Resort
Jalan 3/155B, 57000 Bukit Jalil, Kuala
Lumpur
☎ +60 3 8994 1600
✉ bgrb@bukitjalil.com.my
🖥 www.berjayaclubs.com/jalil

Golf Club Perkhidmatan Awam
Bukit Kiara, Off Jalan Damansara, 60000
Kuala Lumpur
☎ +60 3 7957 1958
✉ gmkgpa@kgpagolf.com
🖥 www.kgpagolf.com

Kuala Lumpur G&CC

10, Jalan 1/70D, Off Jalan Bukit Kiara,
60000 Kuala Lumpur
☎ +60 3 2093 1111
✉ klgcc@simedarby.com
🖥 www.klgcc.com

Melaka

A'Famosa Golf Resort

Jalan Kemus, Simpang 4
78000 Alor Gajah, Melaka
☎ +60 6 5520 888
✉ enquiries@afamosa.com
🖥 www.afamosa.com

Pandanusa GC

PT.30, Pulau Besar, Mukim Pernu,Melaka
Tengah Melaka
☎ +60 6 281 5015
🖥 www.members.tripodasia
.com.my/pulaubesar

Negeri Sembilan

Nilai Springs G&CC

PT 4770, Bandar Baru Nilai, PO Box 50,
71801 Nilai, Negeri Sembilan
☎ +60 6 8508 888
✉ nsgcc@pd.jaring.my
🖥 www.nilaispringsgcc.com.my/golfing

Port Dickson G&CC

Batu 5 1/2, Jalan Pantai, 71050 Port
Dickson, Negeri Sembilan
☎ +60 6 647 3586
✉ pdgcc@po.jaring.my
🖥 www.pdgolf.com.my

Royal Palm Springs GC

Bt.13 Km.21 Jalan Pantai, Mukim Pasir
Panjang, Negeri Sembilan
☎ +60 6 661 9599
✉ palmspringsresortcity
@tancoresorts.com
🖥 www.palmspringsresortcity.com
/rpsgc/index

Pahang

Astana G&CC

Sungai Lembing, Bandar Indera Mahkota,
25200 Kuantan, Pahang
☎ +60 9 5735 135
✉ astana@tm.net.my
🖥 www.astanagolf@150m.com

Pantai Lagenda G&CC

Lot 877, Kampung Kuala Pahang, 26660
Pekan, Pahang
☎ +60 9 4251 658
✉ pigolf@tm.net.my

Penang

Bukit Jambul G&CC

No.2 Jalan Bukit Jambul, 11900 Bayan
Lepas
☎ +60 4 644 2255
✉ bcc@po.jaring.my
🖥 www.bjcc.com.my

Bukit Jawi Golf Resort

No.691 Main Road, Sg. Bakap, S.P.S.,
14200 Penang
☎ +60 4 5820 759
🖥 www.bukitjawi.com.my

Penang Golf Resort

Lot 1687 Jalan Bertam, Seberang Perai,
Utara
13200 Kepala Batas, Penang
☎ +60 4 5782 022
🖥 www.penanggolfresort.com.my

Perak

Clearwater Sanctuary Golf Resort

Lot 6019 Jalan Changkat Larang, 31000
Batu Gajah, Perak
☎ +60 5 3667 433
✉ cesgolf@po.jaring.my
🖥 www.cwsgolf.com.my

Damai Laut G&CC

Hala Damai 2, Jalan Damai Laut , Off Jalan
Teluk Senanging
32200 Lumut, Perak
☎ +60 5 6183 333
✉ resvns_dlgcc@swissgarden.com
🖥 www.swissgarden.com/hotels/sgrdl

Meru Valley G&CC

Jalan Bukit Meru, Off Jalan Jelapang,
30020 Ipoh, Perak
☎ +60 5 5293 300
✉ info@meruvalley.com.my
🖥 www.meruvalley.com.my

Selangor

Bangi Golf Resort

No.1 Persiaran Bandar, Bandar Baru Bangi
43650 Selangor
☎ +60 3 8925 3728
✉ bgr@po.jaring.my

Golf Club Sultan Abdul Aziz Shah

No.1 Rumah Kelab 13/6, 40100 Shah
Alam, Selangor
☎ +60 3 5519 1512
✉ cecy@kgsaas.com.my
🖥 www.kgaas.com.my

Kelab Golf Seri Selangor

Persiaran Damansara Indah, Off Prsn
Tropicana, Kota Damansara, 47410
Petaling Jaya, Selango
☎ +60 3 7806 1111
✉ mktg@seriselangor.com
🖥 seriselangor.com.my

Kota Permai G&CC

No.1 Jalan 31/100A, Kota Kemuning
Section 31, 40460 Shah Alam, Selangor
Darul Ehsan
☎ +60 3 5122 3700
✉ kpgcc@kotapermai.com.my
🖥 www.kotapermai.com.my

Palm Garden GC

IOI Resort, 62502 Putrajaya, Selangor
☎ +60 3 8948 7160
✉ pggc@tm.net.my
🖥 www.palmgarden.net.my

Rahman Putra GC

Jalan BRP 2/1, Bukit Rahman Putra, 47000
Sungai Buloh, Selangor
☎ +60 3 6156 6870
✉ krpm@streamyx.com
🖥 www.krpm.com.my

Terengganu

Awana Kijal Golf, Beach & Spa Resort

Km.28, Jalan Kemaman-Dungun, 24100
Kijal, Kemaman Terengganu
☎ +60 9 8641 188
✉ awanakij@tm.net.my
🖥 www.awana.com.my

Tasik Kenyir Golf Resort

Kg. Sg., Gawi, Mukim Telemong, 2300 Hulu
Tereggganu Terengganu
☎ +60 9 666 8888
✉ resort@lakekenyir.com
🖥 www.lakekenyir.com

Maldives

Kuredu Island Resort

Faadhipolhu,, Lhaviyani Atoll
☎ +960 230337
✉ info@kuredu.com
🖥 www.kuredu.com

Myanmar

Aye Thar Yar Golf Course

Aye Thar Yar,Taunggyi, Shanstate
☎ +95 81 24245
✉ ayetharyargolfresort@mptmail
.net.mm
🖥 www.ayetharyargolfresort.com

Bagan Golf Course

Nyaung Oo Township, Mandalay Division
☎ +95 2 67247
✉ bagangolfresort@mptmail.net.mm

Nepal

Le Méridien Gokarna Forest Golf Resort & Spa

Rajnikunj Gokarna, Thali, PO Box 20498,
Kathhmandu
☎ +977 1 445 1212
✉ golf@lemeridien-kathmandu.com
🖥 www.gokarna.com

Royal Nepal GC
Tilganga, Kathmandu
☎ +977 1 449 4247
✉ rngc@mail.com.np

Pakistan

Arabian Sea CC
Bin Qasim, Karachi
☎ +92 21 475 0408
✉ info@asccl.com
▤ www.asccl.com

Royal Palm G&CC
▤ www.royalpalm.com

Philippines

Fairways and Bluewater Resort
Newcoast, Balabag, Boracay Island, Province of Aklan
☎ +63 36 288 5587
✉ info@fairwaysbluewater.com
▤ www.FairwaysBluewater.com

Eagle Ridge G&CC
Barangay Javalera, Gen. Trias, Cavite
☎ +63 46 419 2841
▤ www.eagle-ridge.com.ph

Singapore

Raffles GC
Raffles Country Club, 450 Jalan Ahmad Ibrahim, Singapore 639932
☎ +65 6861 7649
✉ jacqueline@rcc.org.sg
▤ www.rcc.org.sg

Singapore Island CC
Thomson Road, PO Box 50, Singapore 915702
☎ +65 645 92222
✉ enquiry@sicc.org.sg
▤ www.sicc.org.sg

Sri Lanka

Victoria Golf & Country Resort
PO Box 7, Rajawela
☎ +94 812 376 376
✉ enquiries@victoriagolf.lk
▤ www.srilankagolf.com

Waters Edge GC
316 Ethul Kotte Road, Battaramulla
☎ +94 112 863863
✉ we@watersedge.lk
▤ www.watersedge.lk

Thailand

Central Region

Green Valley CC
92 Moo 3, Bang Na-Trat Road Km.15, Bang Chalong, Bang Phli, Samut Prakan 10540
☎ +66 2312 5883
✉ info@greenvalleybangkok.com
▤ www.greenvalleybangkok.com

Lam Luk Ka CC
29 Moo 7 Lamsai Lam Luk Ka Khlong 11, Patum Thani 12150
☎ +66 2995 2300
✉ info@lamlukkagolf.net
▤ www.lamlukkagolf.net

Royal Bangkok Sport Club
1 Henri Dunant Street, Bangkok 10330
☎ +66 66 2255 1420
▤ www.rbsc.org

Eastern Region

Eastern Star Country Club & Resort
241/5 Moo 3, Pala Ban Chang District, Rayong 21130
☎ +66 3863 0410
✉ info@easternstargolf.net
▤ www.easternstargolf.net

Laem Chabang International CC
106/8 Moo 4, Ban Bung, Sri Racha, Chon Buri 20230
☎ +66 3837 2273
▤ reservation@laemchabanggolf.com
▤ www.laemchabanggolf.com

Soi Dao Highland Golf Club & Resort
153/1 Moo 2, Thap Sai, Pong Nam Ron District, Chanthaburi 22140
☎ +66 3932 0174
▤ booking@soidaohighland.com
▤ www.soidaohighland.com

Northern Region

Chiangmai Green Valley CC
183/2 Chotana Road, Mae Sa, Mae Rim, Chiang Mai 50180
☎ +66 5329 8249
✉ info@cm_golf.com
▤ www.cm_golf.com

Gassan Khuntan Golf & Resort
222 Moo3 Thapladuk, Mae Tha, Lamphun, Thailand 51140
☎ +66 53 507006
✉ info@gassangolf.com
▤ www.gassangolf.com

Santiburi CC
12 Moo 3, Hua Doi-Sob Pau Road, Wiang Chai District, Chiang Rai 57210
☎ +66 5366 2821
✉ cr_golfreservation@santiburi.com
▤ santiburi.com
   /SantiburiGolfChiangRai

North Eastern Region

Forest Hills CC
195 Moo 3, Mittraphap Road, Muak Lek District, Saraburi 18180
☎ +66 3634 1911
✉ mail@sirjamesresort.com
▤ www.sirjamesresort.com

Mission Hills Golf Club Khao Yai
151 Moo 5,Thumbol Mhoosee, Pakchong, Nakornratchasima 30130
☎ +66 4429 7258
✉ missionhills_khaoyai@yahoo.com
▤ www.golfmissionhills.com/miskao
   .html

Suwan G&CC
15/3 Moo 2, Sisatong, A. Nakornchaisri, Nakornpathom 73120
☎ +66 343 39333
✉ reservation@suwangolf.com
▤ www.suwangolf.com

Southern Region

Loch Palm GC
38 Moo 5 Vichit Songkram Road, Kathu, Phuket 83120
☎ +66 7632 1929
✉ info@lochpalm.com
▤ www.lochpalm.com

Phuket CC
80/1 Vichit Songkram Road, Katu, Phuket 83120
☎ +66 7632 1038
✉ info@phuketcountryclub.com
▤ www.phuketcountryclub.com

Santiburi Samui CC
12/15 Moo 4, Bandonsai, Tambol Maenam, Amphur Ko Samui, Surat Thani 84330
☎ +66 7742 5031
✉ infosb@santiburi.com
▤ www.santiburi.com

Western Region

Best Ocean GC
4/5 Moo 7 Rama2 Road, Khokkham, Samutsakorn 74000
☎ +66 34 451143
▤ www.bestoceangolf.com

Mission Hills GC
27/7 Moo 7, Pang Thru, Tha Muang, Kanchanaburi 71110Tengah Melaka
☎ +66 3464 4147
✉ hills@ksc.th.com
▤ golfmissionhills.com/miskan.html

Sawang Resort GC
99 Moo 2, Sapang, Khao Yoi District,
Petchaburi 76140
☎ +66 3256 2555
✉ info@sawangresortgolf.com
🖥 www.sawangresortgolf.com

Vietnam

King's Island GC
Dong Mo, Son Tay Town, Ha Tay Province
☎ +84 34 686555
✉ kings_island@fpt.vn
🖥 www.kingsislandgolf.com

Ocean Dunes GC
1 Ton Duc Thang, Phan Thiet
☎ +84 62 823366
✉ odgc@vietnamgolfresorts.com
🖥 www.vietnamgolfresorts.com
/index.php?id=7

Tam Dao Golf & Resort
Hop Chau Commune, Tam Dao District,
Vinh Phuc Province
☎ +84 211 896554
✉ marketing@tamdaogolf.com
🖥 www.tamdaogolf.com

Australasia and the Pacific

Australia

Australian Capital Territory

Royal Canberra
Bentham St, Yarralumla, ACT 2600
☎ +61 (02) 6282 7000
✉ admin@royalcanberra.com.au

Yowani Country Club
Northbourne Ave, Lyneham, ACT 2602
☎ +61 (02)6241 2303
✉ golf@yowani.com.au

New South Wales

The Australian
53 Bannerman Crescent, Rosebery, NSW
2018
☎ +61 (02) 9663 2273

Barham
Moulamein Road, Barham, NSW 2732
☎ +61 (03) 5453 2971
✉ Barham.services.club@clubarham
.com.au

Howlong
Golf Club Drive, Howlong, NSW 2643
☎ +61 (02) 6026 5822
✉ enquiries@howlonggolf.com.au

Kooindah Waters
Kooindah Boulevard, Wyong, NSW 2259
☎ +61 (02) 4351 0700
✉ info@kooindahwatersgolf.com.au

The Lakes
Corner King St. & Vernon Ave, Eastlakes,
NSW 2018
☎ +61 (02) 9669 1311

New South Wales
Henry Head, Botany Bay National Park,
La Perouse
☎ + 61 (02) 9661 4455
✉ admin@nswgolfclub.com.au

Royal Sydney
Kent Road, Rose Bay, NSW 2029
☎ +61 (02) 8362 7000
✉ reception@rsgc.com.au

Twin Creeks
Twin Creeks Drive, Luddenham, NSW 2745
☎ +61 (02) 9670 8877
✉ karinad@twincreeks.com.au

The Vintage
Vintage Drive, Rothbury, NSW 2320
☎ +61 (02) 4998 6789
✉ golf@thevintage.com.au

Yarrawonga
Gulai Road, Mulwala, NSW 2647
☎ +61 (03) 5744 3983
✉ stayandplay@yarragolf.com.au

Northern Territory

Alice Springs
Cromwell Drive, Alice Springs, NT 870
☎ +61 (08) 8952 1921
✉ admin@asgc.com.au

Darwin
Links Road, North Lakes, NT 812
☎ +61 (08) 8927 1322

Palmerston
Dwyer Circuit & University Avenue, Driver,
NT 831
☎ +61 (08) 8932 1324

Queensland

Brisbane
Tennyson Memorial Avenue,
Yeerongpilly, QLD 4105
☎ +61 (07) 3848 1008
✉ mail@brisbanegolfclub.com.au

Brookwater
1 Tournament Drive, Brookwater, QLD
4300
☎ +61 (07) 3814 5500
✉ golfshop@brookwatergolf.com

The Colonial
Paradise Springs Avenue, Robina, QLD
4226
☎ +61 (07) 5553 7008
✉ info@playmoregolf.com.au

Glades
Glades Drive, Robina, QLD 4226
☎ +61 (07) 5569 1900
✉ enquiries@theglades.com.au

Indooroopilly
Meiers Road, Indooroopilly, QLD 4068
☎ + 61 (07) 3721 2122
✉ admin@indooroopillygolf.com.au

Some like it hot

Few people would dispute the claim by the Alice Springs Golf Club in Australia's Northern Territory to be the hottest course on earth. The temperature there can rise to a staggering 122 deg. F (50 deg. C).

For key to symbols see page 717

Links Hope Island
Hope Island Road, Hope Island, QLD 4212
☎ + 61 (07) 5530 9030
✉ golf@linkshopeisland.com.au

Noosa Springs
Links Drive, Noosa Heads, QLD 4567
☎ + 61 (07) 5440 3333
✉ info@noosasprings.com.au

Robina Woods
Ron Penhaligon Way, Robina, QLD 4226
☎ + 61 (07) 5553 7520
✉ info@playmoregolf.com.au

Royal Queensland
Curtin Avenue West, Eagle Farm,
Brisbane, QLD 4009
☎ +61 (07) 3268 1127
✉ info@rqgolf.com.au

South Australia

Echunga
Cnr Hahndorf and Dolman Road, Echunga,
SA 5153
☎ +61 (08) 8388 8038
✉ info@echungagolf.com.au

Grange
White Sands Drive Seaton, South Australia
☎ +61 (08) 8355 7100
✉ info@grangegolf.com.au

Kooyonga
May Terrace, Lockleys, South Australia
☎ +61 (08) 8352 5444
✉ administrator@kooyongagolf.com.au

Mount Lofty
35 Golf Links Road, Stirling, SA 5152
☎ +61 (08) 8339 1805
✉ admin@mountloftygolfclub.com.au

Royal Adelaide
328 Tapleys Hill Road, Seaton, SA 5023
☎ +61 (08) 8356 5511
✉ ragc@royaladelaidegolf.com.au

Tea Tree Gully
Hamilton Road, Fairview Park, SA 5126
☎ +61 (08) 8251 1465
✉ ttggc@internode.net.au

Tasmania

Barnbougle Dunes
426 Waterhouse Road, Bridport, Tasmania
7262
☎ +61 (03) 363 560 094
▤ www.barnbougledunes.com

Royal Hobart
81 Seven Mile Beach Road, Seven Mile
Beach, Hobart, Tasmania 7170
☎ +61 (03) 6248 6161
✉ admin@rhgc.com.au

Victoria

Barwon Heads
Golf Links Road, Barwon Heads, VIC 3227
☎ +61 (03) 5255 6275
✉ golf@bhgc.com.au

Clifton Springs
92-94 Clearwater Drive, Clifton Springs, VIC
3222
☎ +61 (03) 5253 1488
✉ csclubhouse@iprimus.com.au

The Dunes
335 Browns Road, Rye, VIC 3941
☎ +61 (03) 5985 1334
✉ golf@thedunes.com.au

Growling Frog
1910 Donnybrook Road, Yan Yean, VIC
3755
☎ +61 (03) 9716 3477
✉ info@growlingfroggolfcourse.com.au

Huntingdale
Windsor Avenue, South Oakleigh, VIC 3167
☎ +61 (03) 9579 4622
✉ manager@huntingdalegolf.com.au

Kingston Heath
Kingston Rd, Heatherton, Melbourne, VIC
3202
☎ +61 (03) 8558 2700
✉ info@kingstonheath.com.au

Ocean Grove
Guthridge Street, Ocean Grove, VIC 3226
☎ +61 (03) 5256 2795
✉ info@oceangrovegc.com.au

Metropolitan
Golf Road, Oakleigh South, VIC 3167
☎ +61 (03) 9579 3122
✉ admin@metropolitangolf.com.au

Mornington
Tallis Drive, Mornington, VIC 3931
☎ +61 (03) 5975 2784
✉ manager@ morningtongolf.com.au

Royal Melbourne
Cheltenham Road, Black Rock, VIC 3193
☎ +61 (03) 9598 6755
✉ rmgc@royalmelbourne.com.au

Settlers Run
1 Settlers Run, Cranbourne South, VIC
3977
☎ +61 (03) 9785 6072
✉ info@settlersrun.com.au

Victoria
Park Road, Cheltenham, VIC 3192
☎ +61 (03) 9584 1733
✉ info@victoriagolf.com.au

Yarra Yarra
567 Warrigal Road East, Bentleigh East,
VIC 3165
☎ +61 (03) 9575 0595
✉ reception@yarrayarra.com.au

Western Australia

Joondalup
Country Club Bouvelard, Connolly, WA
6027
☎ +61 (08) 9400 8811
✉ proshop@joondalupresort.com.au

Kennedy Bay
Port Kennedy Drive, Port Kennedy, WA
6172
☎ +61 (08) 9524 5991
✉ info@kennedybay.com.au

Lake Karrinyup
North Beach Road, Karrinyup WA 6018
☎ +61 (08) 9422 8222
✉ info@lkcc.com.au

Mount Lawley
Walter Road, Inglewood, WA 6052
☎ +61 (08) 9271 9622
✉ admin@mlgc.org

The Vines Resort and Country Club
Verdellho Drive, The Vines, Perth, WA 6069
☎ +61 (08) 9297 3000
▤ www.vines.com.au

Cook Islands

Rarotonga Golf Club
Rarotonga, Cook Islands
☎ +682 20621

Fiji

Fiji Golf Club
Suva Area, Viti Levu
☎ +679 382872

Pacific Harbour
Suva Area, Viti Levu
📠 +679 450262

Guam

Guam International CC
495 Battulo Street, Dededo, Guam 96912
☎ +1 671 632 4422
✉ gicclub@netpci.com
▤ www.giccguam.com

New Zealand

Cape Kidnappers
☎ +64 (06) 875 1900
▤ www.capekidnappers.com

Gisborne
☎ +64 (06) 867 9849
🖹 www.gisborne.nzgolf.net

Gulf Harbour
☎ +64 (09) 424 0971
🖹 www.gulfharbour.nzgolf.net

The Hills
🖹 www.thehills.co.nz

Jack's Point
🖹 www.jackspoint.com

Kauri Cliffs
🖹 www.kauricliffs.com

Lake View
☎ +64 (07) 357 2343
🖹 www.lakeview.nzgolf.net

Lakes Resort Pauanui
☎ +64 (07) 864 9999
🖹 www.lakesresort.com

North Otoga
☎ +64 (03) 434 6169
🖹 www.northotago.nzgolf.net

Palmerston North
☎ +64 (06) 351 0700
🖹 www.pngolf.co.nz

Queens Park
☎ +64 (03) 218 8371
🖹 www.queenspark.nzgolf.net

Sherwood Park
☎ +64 (09) 434 6900
🖹 www.sherwoodpark.nzgolf.net

Waitangi
☎ +64 (09) 402 7713
📧 waitangigolf@xtra.co.nz

Papua New Guinea

Port Moresby GC
PO Box 17 Port Moresby
☎ +675 325 5367

Samoa

Penina Golf Course
77 Faleolo Strip, Mulifanua
📧 golfpenina@samoa.ws
🖹 www.peninaresortandgolfclub.com

Tonga

Tonga GC
PO Box 2568, Nuku'alofa
☎ +676 24949

Vanuatu

Port Vila G&CC
Mele, Vanuatu, South Pacific
☎ +678 22564
📧 pvgcc@vanuatu.com.vu

White Sands
PO Box 906, Port Vila, Vanuatu, South Pacific
☎ +678 22090
📧 whitesan@vanuatu.com.vu

For key to symbols see page 717

Nicknames

The Boss of the Moss – Loren Roberts.
See Who's Who in Golf, page 536

The von – Norman von Nida.
See Famous Personalities of the Past, page 573

The Wild Thing – John Daly. See Who's Who in Golf, page 508

Spaceman – Jesper Parnevik was given this name by his fellow PGA pros apparently because used to eat volcanic dust to cleanse his system.
See Who's Who in Golf, page 532

Walrus – Craig Stadler. See Who's Who in Golf, page 538

Boom Boom – Fred Couples – a reference to his impressive power off the tee.
See Who's Who in Golf, page 508

Slow Motion – Don January possessed a playing style that was always slow and smooth.
See Who's Who in Golf, page 519

The Hawk – Ben Hogan. This nickname was probably awarded for his stare and the stony silence he adopted when playing.
See Famous Personalities of the Past, page 566

The Black Knight – Gary Player invariably wore black, apparently to help him absorb the sun's energy.
See Who's Who in Golf, page 534

Buffalo Bill – Billy Casper ate buffalo meat and organic vegetables in a lifelong battle to control his weight.
See Who's Who in Golf, page 506

Japanese couple have aces seconds apart

A Japanese couple playing golf in Brazil had holes in one within seconds of each other last year. Sixty-year-old Takashi Sasaki made his ace with a 7-iron on the 166-yard fourth hole at Terras de São José Golf Club.

His wife Marli was on the women's tee and hit her ace from about 115 yards but didn't see the ball go in the hole.

Witness Valdemar Iwamoto said that "all of a sudden, we see her ball bouncing into the hole, we couldn't believe it." Neither had made a hole-in-one before.

Hollis earns her place in the World Golf Hall of Fame

Four-time LPGA major winner Hollis Stacy will be enshrined this year in the World Golf Hall of Fame as part of its Class of 2012. Stacy was selected in the Veterans Category.

"On behalf of the LPGA, I would like to congratulate Hollis on this well-deserved honour," said Michael Whan, the LPGA Tour Commissioner. "Hollis was always known as an extremely competitive player with an impeccable short game and one of the most creative golf minds of her time.

"More importantly, she will long be remembered as a truly nice person with a passion for golf and life. She is an ambassador for women's golf and we could not be more proud of her."

Stacy's career was defined by her successes in USGA events. She charged onto the golf scene by winning consecutive US Girls' Junior Championship titles from 1969–71 and remains the only player ever to win that event three times.

As a professional, she won US Women's Open championships in 1977, 1978 and 1984. Her fourth major came in 1983, when she won the Peter Jackson Classic (later named the du Maurier Classic).

During her 26-year LPGA career, Stacy scored 18 victories. In one stretch from 1977 to 1983, she registered 82 top-10 finishes.

"I totally did not expect this," Stacy said. "I'm just overwhelmed. I am humbled and so excited. It's such a great honour to be in the same group with friends like JoAnne Carner, Nancy Lopez, Patty Sheehan, Betsy King and Mickey Wright."

Eight architectural firms bid to design Olympic course

The eight finalists hoping to design the golf course for the 2016 Olympics in Rio de Janeiro have been determined.

The winning participants will design the executive project for the Olympic venue to welcome golf's return to the Olympic Games program in 2016, after 112 years of absence.

These are the contest finalists in alphabetical order:

Gary Player Design
Greg Norman Golf Course Design
Hanse Golf Design
Hawtree Ltd.
Nicklaus Design
Renaissance Golf
Robert Trent Jones II
Thomson-Perrett Golf Course Architects

The course will be built in Rio de Janeiro, more than likely in the Barra da Tijuca neighbourhood, which will hold most of the Olympic venues.

Applicants had to show prior course design experience, and have an office established in Rio. The winner will be paid $300,000 for the design.

The Olympic organizing committee has said the course should leave a legacy to the city, and serve in youth sports education and events after the games.

Index

J

K

After nearly 60 years the Irish Open heads north again

The Irish Open this year will be staged in Northern Ireland for the first time in nearly 60 years and for only the tenth time in the event's history. The move is hardly surprising.

Following the major successes of Ulstermen Graeme McDowell and Rory McIlroy in the US Open and Darren Clarke's victory at Royal St George's last year in The Open, the European Tour will take the event to Royal Portrush from June 28 to July 1.

Previous winners of the title when played at Royal Portrush were Charlie Ward in 1930, Bert Gadd in 1937 and Harry Bradshaw in 1947. Eric Brown won the title the last time it was played in Ulster at Belvoir Park in 1953 two years after The Open was won by Max Faulkner at Royal Portrush.

Darren Clarke said: "It is fantastic news that an event of the calibre of the Irish Open is coming to Portrush – a world class event on a world class golf course. I know every inch of this course and can vouch for its quality".

George O'Grady, Chief Executive of The European Tour, said: "I applaud the Northern Ireland Executive and the Irish Government for their vision in taking the Irish Open to Royal Portrush a mere three weeks prior to The Open Championship".

From the Editor

The 2012 edition of *The R&A Golfer's Handbook* depends totally on the dedicated work of the team who help compile the information. For many years, Alan and Heather Elliott have looked after the results and addresses sections. Their enthusiasm is legendary as they gather in the statistics. I owe them a debt of gratitude as I do to our typographer and printer Mick Card, the dynamo whose expertise and patience is to be commended. He always seems to achieve the impossible against the severest of deadlines.

His daughter Paula Taylor, who is also involved, has diligently looked after the clubs section now for several years while Mike Aitken, an award-winning writer formerly of *The Scotsman*, has given invaluable help on the editorial front. David Moir gave considerable advice and assistance with the expanded World Rankings section and I must not forget the sterling work put in on my behalf by Vicky Lamb of The R&A.

My thanks, too, to all my colleagues who contributed articles for the 2012 edition and to Jill Sheldon of the Phil Sheldon Library and Dave Cannon of Getty Images for the illustrations.

The book – a golfing institution first published in 1899 and sponsored now by The R&A – is published by Pan Macmillan whose Kate Hewson was the latest in a long line of managing editors who have come and gone over the years. My thanks to her and to everyone else who indirectly helped make possible this latest, more international edition.

Renton Laidlaw, Editor
December 2011